Sports Collectors Digest — Voice for the Hobby

Standard Catalog of®
SPORTS
MEMORABILIA

EDITED BY BERT LEHMAN

3RD EDITION

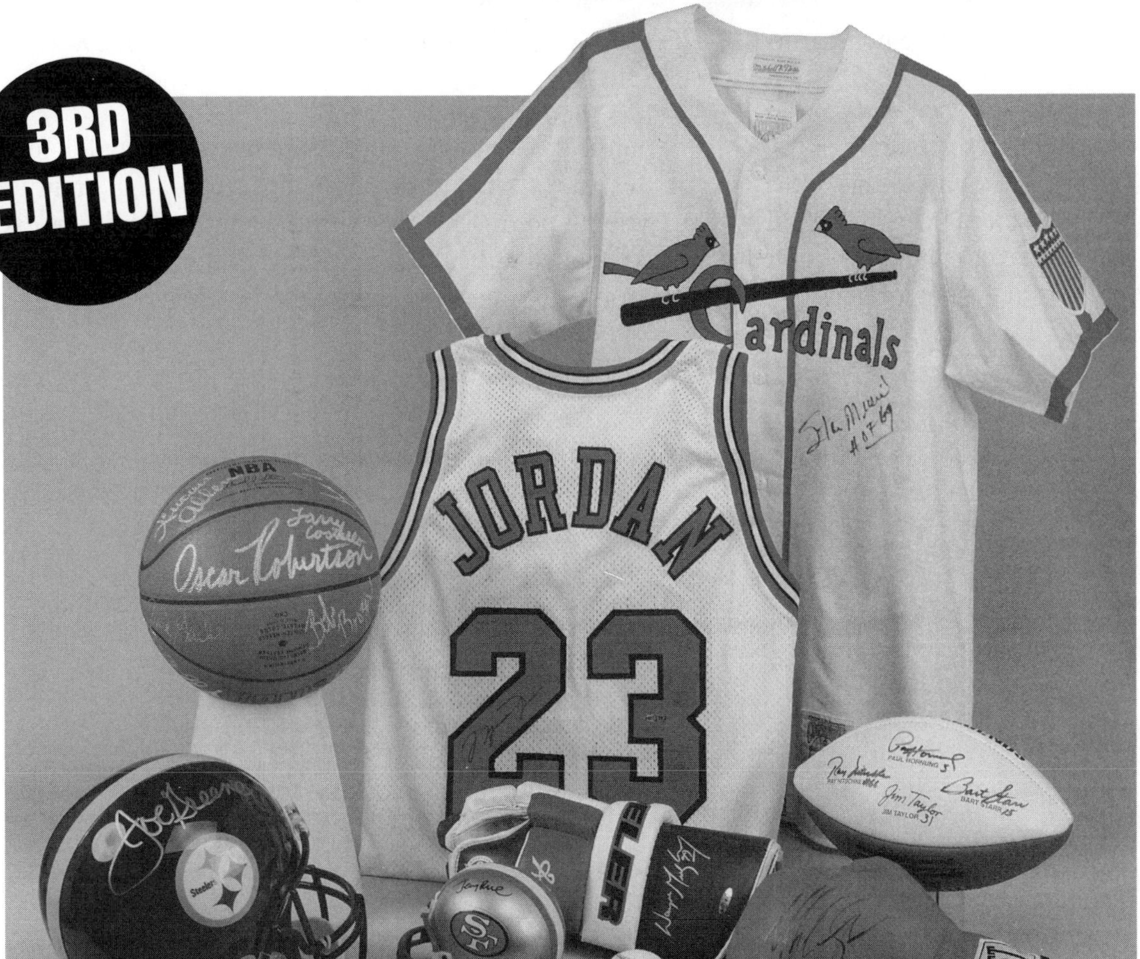

©2003 Krause Publications

Published by

krause publications
An F+W Publications Company

700 East State Street • Iola, WI 54990-0001
715-445-2214 • 888-457-2873
www.krause.com

Our toll-free number to place an order or obtain a free catalog is 800-258-0929.

Library of Congress Catalog Number: 99-63751

ISBN: 0-87349-686-8

Edited by Bert Lehman
Designed by Stacy Bloch

Printed in United States of America

Table of Contents

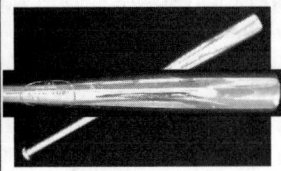

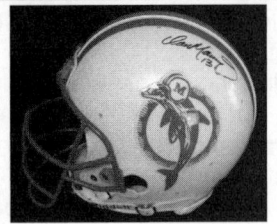

Introduction

Putting together a sports memorabilia book is no easy task. With the fact that sports memorabilia is such a broad topic, there are many decisions to be made as to what to include in the book and what not to include. Even though it is a challenging task, it is not an impossible task. With this book, the third edition of the Standard Catalog of Sports Memorabilia, we completely updated the pricing from the previous edition. We have also added 24 pages of pricing, which makes this edition the most comprehensive memorabilia book available. Some of the new items to look for include:

• Additional pricing added to the the Baseball Hall of Fame section. In this book, for some of the old-time ball players, pricing for signed typed letters, signed handwritten letters and signed checks have been added.

• Pricing for Negro League baseball players was also added to this third edition.

• Complete pricing with images for Starting Lineups, Mattel basketball figures and McFarlane Sports Picks is included. Also included in this chapter is comprehensive pricing/checklisting of vintage and new bobble heads.

• In addition to updating the pricing for the books that were listed in the previous edition, there have been pages of new book listings added to the pricing checklist for this edition.

• Fans of the square circle are not left out in the cold with this memorabilia book. Complete pricing will be included for both new and vintage wrestling cards. In addition to wrestling card pricing, complete pricing and checklisting for wrestling figures have also found its way into this book.

• For those of you who are not too concerned about the values of autographs, but are looking for information on how to start forming an autograph collection, autograph columnists Ryan Semanko and Bryan Petrulis chime in with some helpful advice. They provide helpful hints on the best ways to obtain autographs in person and through the mail. In addition, Semanko gives his opinion on the best and worst autograph signers.

— Bert Lehman

Acknowledgments

It can be argued that a book is only as good as those people who contributed to it. The list of contributors for the third edition of the *Standard Catalog of Sports Memorabilia* runs long, with more than 25 industry experts taking on the challenge, many of them contributing in more than one area.

Those who contributed, and the areas they contributed to, include:

Mike Breeden (autographs)
Robert D. Crestohl (sports publications)
Lou Criscione (sports figurines)
Michael Dachs (cereal boxes)
Dave Dame (Perez-Steele)
Paul Ferrante (stadium memorabilia)
Chuck Greenwood (team signed items, Coke bottle caps)
Murray Greig (boxing and hockey Hall of Fame autographs)
Scott Harpt (game-used bats)
Rick Haskins (pennants)
John Hickey (autographs, baseball comic books)
Jeff Hill (sports posters)
Steve Hoeker (wrestling figures)
Tom Hultman (sports beer cans)
Art Jaffe (game-used bats)
Kevin Johnson (tickets, baseball yearbooks, sports publications)

Ron Keurajian (autographs)
Rocky Landsverk (fake autographs)
Robert R. Lindley (college and NBA basketball programs)
Lou Manfra (boxing posters)
Richard Miller (books)
Bob Pace (boxing posters and programs)
R. Plapinger (books)
Bryan Petrulis (autographs)
Joe Phillips (store model gloves and store model bats)
Bruce Remick (sports beer cans)
Rick Romito (sports figurines, plates, mini-stadiums)
Ryan Semanko (autographs)
Jonathan Singer (ABA memorabilia)
John Taube (game-used bats)
Jack Torsiello (press pins)
Dennis Tuttle (ABA memorabilia)
Larry K. Wellman (tickets)
Jim Yackel (game-used equipment)
John Zaso (Z-Silk Cachets)

Chapter 1

AUTOGRAPHS

The most common memorabilia that is autographed includes balls, bats, helmets, sticks, pucks, index cards, photographs and postcards, Hall of Fame plaques and postcards, equipment (shoes, skates, helmets, jerseys, trunks), programs and books, letters and documents, bank checks, and cut signatures, which have been taken from another piece of writing, such as a manuscript, letter or check.

Autographs can be obtained several ways—writing to the player, waiting at his hotel, or attending an autograph show. The most personable, and perhaps memorable, experience would be acquiring the autograph from the player at the stadium or arena. But get there early, before practice; once a player is into his game routine he doesn't want to be distracted. Give yourself an edge over fans who are rude and obnoxious with their requests by being polite and calling the athlete by "Mr." or "Miss." Have a pen ready and keep your request simple and fast also helps.

Another alternative is at a sports card show. Show promoters often impose time/quota limitations, so if you know a player is going to be signing at a show, it's wise to get tickets in advance and get there early.

Dealers and show promoters often hold private signings with the players during which the player fills the mail-order requests sent to the dealer. Non-flat items that are signed sometimes require an extra fee. These private signings are usually advertised in hobby publications. Authenticity is generally guaranteed, and most dealers also have a return policy.

Direct requests can be sent to the player via the mail in care of his team's address, which is the best way, or his home, but the results can be unpredictable, due to the amount of mail the players receive. Some players also believe mail sent to their homes is an invasion of their privacy, so your request might go unheeded.

When dealing through the mail, send less valuable items; you don't want the post office to lose or damage them. Always include a self-addressed stamped envelope or package with the required postage for its return. A courteous, creative, brief request, which distinguishes and sets off your letter from the others, will yield better results.

Specify if the item is to be personalized or dated, and don't ask the player to sign more than two items. Perhaps you can include an extra for the player to keep, but players are becoming wary of those who request several autographs, perhaps to be sold at a later date. Thus, sometimes the player, in return for his autograph, might ask for a donation to his favorite charity.

Auctions are another source for autographed material. These events, whether by telephone, Internet, or live, often offer quality

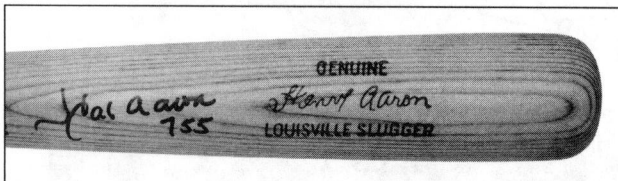

material. Items may also turn up at antique shops and flea markets, but questions regarding authenticity, value, condition and scarcity may occur if the seller has limited knowledge of the item.

Prices for autographed materials are set by the principles of supply and demand, based on regional interest, scarcity, condition (not faded, dirty, shellacked, smudged, scuffed, ripped), player popularity, and significance of the event commemorated. Factors for autographed basketballs and footballs also include the signature form (style, placement, nickname), type of ball and writing medium used.

Individually signed balls usually have the autograph on the sweet spot—the shortest distance between two seams. Team balls, those which should include the signatures of all the key players, starters and bench players, generally reserve the sweet spot for the manager's signature.

The more complete the ball is with key players, the more valuable it is. It's also easier to pinpoint the year being represented. But having other signatures, such as those of umpires and broadcasters, detracts from the value.

Some items have just select players who have signed it. These group-signed items can commemorate a particular accomplishment or event.

When examining an item for authenticity, consider the writing medium used. Was the player alive when the ink, such as in a felt-tip pen or ballpoint pen, was available? Ballpoints became prominent in the 1940s, felt tips in the 1960s and Sharpies in the 1970s. However, whatever medium is used, don't retrace the signature.

Signatures can vary, based on the writing tool, item being signed, person's age, popularity, health and mood, time spent during a signing session, and circumstances when it was signed. Learn the player's signature evolution. Slant, size, characters, flamboyancy, legibility and capitalization may all change during a player's career and after.

Forgeries can sometimes be detected by uncommon breaks, peculiarities in pressure and movement in strokes, and changes in thickness in the letters.

Facsimile signatures also exist; they are exact reproductions that are printed or screened on the item, often through computer-based technology. Rubber stamps and ghost writers have also been used by players to sign their mail.

Beginning collectors should become familiar with collector terminology in their area of interest. Utilize the knowledge of skilled, reputable, experienced dealers and maintain good rapport with them. They can be future sources in helping you build a collection.

Collections can be stored in a file cabinet or display case, with background information on the event and purchase also included. The best conditions for display cases are when effective, indirect lighting is used, so as to not damage or fade the item. The ideal temperature and humidity conditions are 65 to 70 degrees and 50 percent humidity. More valuable items can be kept in safe-deposit boxes.

It's wise to periodically check your collection for signs of deterioration, but avoid excessive handling. Restoration is best left to a professional conservator who has done that type of work before.

OFFICIAL BASEBALLS

The following is a sampling of collectible baseballs and their market value without boxes.

National League Balls

Year	President	Value
1885-1902	Nicholas Young	$1,200
1903-1909	Harry Pulliam	$950
1909-1910	John Heydler	$1,200
1910-1913	Thomas Lynch	$750
1913-1918	John Tener	$700
1918-1934	John Heydler	$900
1934-1951	Ford Frick (1930s)	$330
1934-1951	Ford Frick (1940s)	$225
1951-1969	Warren Giles (1950s)	$250
	(1960s)	$175
1970-1986	Charles Feeney (1970s)	$60
	(1980s)	$50
1986-1989	Bart Giamatti	$20
1989-1994	Bill White	$15
1994-present	Leonard Coleman	$8

American League Balls

Year	President	Value
1901-1927	Ban Johnson (1900s)	$975
1901-1927	Ban Johnson (1910s)	$825
	(1920s)	$800
1927-1931	Ernest Barnard	$800
1931-1959	William Harridge (1930s)	$500
	(1940s)	$225
	(1950s)	$300
1959-1973	Joe Cronin (1960s)	$200
	(1970s)	$175
1974-1984	Lee MacPhail (1970s)	$175
	(1980s)	$75

Year	President	Value
1984-1994	Bobby Brown	$15
1994-present	Gene Budig	$8

World Series Balls

Year	Commissioner	Value
1978-1983	Bowie Kuhn	$20 each
1978-1983	Bowie Kuhn (Haiti)	$45 each
1984-1988	Peter Ueberroth	$20 each
	Ueberroth (Haiti)	$40 each
1989	Bart Giamatti	$20
	Giamatti (Haiti)	$35
1990-1992	Fay Vincent	$20 each
	Vincent (Haiti)	$25
1992	Without Vincent signature	$35
1993-1995	No commissioner	$20
1996	With Bud Selig signature	$150
1996	Without Selig signature	$18
1997-1998	Bud Selig	$18

Commemorative Balls

Year	Event	Value
1991	Comiskey Park Inaugural Season	$15
1994	Jacobs Field Inaugural Season	$15
1995	Cal Ripken Jr.	$15
1996	La Premiera Series	$35
1996	Mickey Mantle Day	$20
1997	Jackie Robinson (AL and NL)	$18
1997	Cleveland Indians All-Star season	$20

Post-Season Balls

Year	Description	Value
1996-1998	Gene Budig (AL Championship)	$15 each
1996-1998	Leonard Coleman (NL Championship)	$15 each
1996-1998	Gene Budig (AL Division Series)	$14 each
1996-1998	Leonard Coleman (NL Division Series)	$15 each

Major League Baseball Presidents

The following list will help date baseballs:

National League

Morgan Bulkeley	1876
William Hulbert	1877-1882
Arthur Soden	1882
Abraham Mills	1883-1884
Nicholas Young	1885-1902
Harry Pulliam	1903-1909
John Heydler	1909
Thomas Lynch	1910-1913
John Ener	1913-1918
John Heydler	1918-1934
Ford Frick	1934-1951
Warren Giles	1951-1969
Charles Feeney	1970-1986
A. Bartlett Giamatti	1986-1989
William White	1989-1994
Leonard Coleman	1994-present

American League

Bancroft Johnson	1901-1927
Ernest Barnard	1927-1931
William Harridge	1931-1959
Joseph Cronin	1959-1973
Lee MacPhail	1974-1984
Bobby Brown	1984-1994
Gene Budig	1994-present

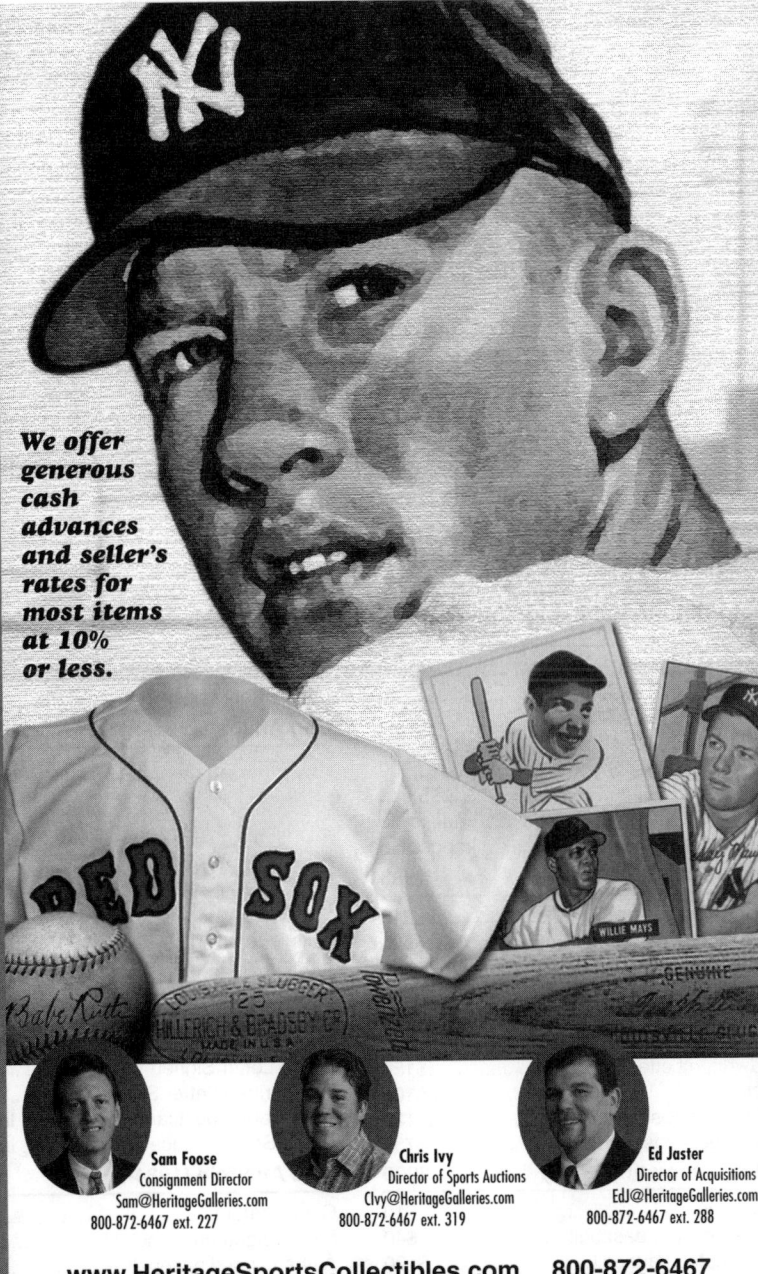

BASEBALL HALL OF FAME AUTOGRAPHS

Any baseball autograph collection worth its salt includes players who have reached the Hall of Fame. Why? Because those players represent the best of the best: the most successful and usually the most popular players to ever play the game.

When it comes to the signatures of Hall of Famers, some are naturally harder to find than others. The toughest ones are from those players who passed away in the late 19th or first part of the 20th century. That would include Cap Anson, Jake Beckley, Dan Brouthers and Alexander Cartwright—baseball figures whose autographs are virtually impossible to find on anything but a cut or a 3x5 card. Collectors pay a steep premium for these autographs, but their addition will enhance any collection.

At the other end of the spectrum is the group of living Hall of Famers who appear frequently on the autograph show circuit. In fact, some of these players earn far more money signing at shows than they did swinging a bat or pitching a ball. Keep an eye on autograph show schedules published in hobby magazines and newspapers and you'll see such names as Ernie Banks, Bob Feller, Harmon Killebrew and Brooks Robinson turning up. It's worth your while to snag signatures of these stars, if you haven't already done so. Even Hall of Famers' autographs can be affordable, especially when you compare them to the prices current stars charge.

If a player—even a Hall of Famer—is especially active on the show circuit, his autograph value will tend to stay at moderate levels. To the uninitiated, it might seem odd that the value of a baseball signed by the game's all-time home run king, Hank Aaron, is in the $60-$75 range when you might have to pay more for Derek Jeter's autograph. Similarly, a ball autographed by one of baseball's all-time best catchers, Johnny Bench, is valued at $40-$50, while a Mike Piazza-signed baseball is in the $100 range. In those examples, The Big Apple is one factor; Jeter and Piazza play in the media mecca of New York. But the big reason for the difference in the values we've cited is that Aaron and Bench were fairly active throughout the 1990s as autograph show guests (and still make appearances), while Jeter and Piazza appearances are rare—and probably will be as long as they're active players.

Many collectors try the autograph-by-mail approach with Hall of Fame players. (The institution's address: National Baseball Hall of Fame and Museum, 25 Main St., P.O. Box 590, Cooperstown, N.Y. 13326.) The success rate for certain players is good, especially if you donate money to their charities. Other players simply don't sign through the mail, period. If you do choose to send something through the mail, A) make sure it's not a valuable item that you can't replace, and B) be patient. Some players will eventually respond, but may take months to do so.

Looking ahead, remember that it helps to anticipate which players are destined for the Hall of Fame in coming years. Around the time a player is inducted, the demand for his signature rises—and so does his autograph's value. Consider the example of George Brett from the class of '99: A baseball signed by Brett was worth $35-$40 before his election to the Hall was announced. After his induction, the price rose to $60, and is now $85.

Another factor that affects the value of Hall of Famer autographs, unfortunately, is a player's death. The great Willie Stargell, for example, passed away on April 9, 2001. Afterward, collectors understandably wanted mementos related to the longtime Pittsburgh Pirate slugger, but were faced with paying a higher price than they would have paid several years ago. Patience in such cases will benefit the collector: Eventually, values of a deceased player's autograph will peak and then often drop slightly in value before stabilizing.

The following section provides current Hall of Famers' autograph values.

Hall of Fame Autographs

(with year inducted into Hall of Fame appearing above pricing columns)

Hank Aaron (1934-)   1982

Mounted Memories Photo

Cut signature	$15
Single-signature ball	$95
Authenticated baseball	$250
Single-signature bat	$175
Authenticated bat	$550
3x5 index card	$30
Photograph/baseball card	$50
Authenticated photo	$200
HOF plaque postcard	$50
Perez-Steele postcards	$30

Grover Cleveland Alexander (1887-1950)   1938

Cut signature	$450
Single-signature baseball	$6,000

Single-signature bat	Unknown
3x5 index card	$700
Photograph/baseball card	$2,500
Typed Letter Signed	$1,500
Handwritten Letter Signed	$3,500
Check	$5,000
HOF plaque postcard	Impossible
Perez-Steele postcards	Impossible

Walter Alston (1911-1984)   1983

Cut signature	$10
Single-signature baseball	$500
Single-signature bat	Unknown
3x5 index card	$50
Photograph/baseball card	$150
Typed Letter Signed	$50
Handwritten Letter Signed	$150
Check	$100
HOF plaque postcard	$125
Perez-Steele postcards	$750

Sparky Anderson (1934-)   2000

Cut signature	$10
Single-signature baseball	$40
Authenticated baseball	$120
Single-signature bat	$85
3x5 index card	$15
Photograph/baseball card	$20
Authenticated photograph	$75

HOF plaque postcard	$25
Perez-Steele postcards	$25

Cap Anson (1852-1922)   1939

Cut signature	$1,250
Single-signature baseball	Unknown
Single-signature bat	Unknown
3x5 index card	$2,000
Photograph/baseball card	Unknown
Typed Letter Signed	$2,000
Handwritten Letter Signed	$3,500
HOF plaque postcard	Impossible
Perez-Steele postcards	Impossible

Luis Aparicio (1934-)   1984

Cut signature	$8
Single-signature baseball	$40
Authenticated baseball	$85
Single-signature bat	$100
3x5 index card	$10
Photograph/baseball card	$20
Authenticated photograph	$40

Price Your Collection With Confidence

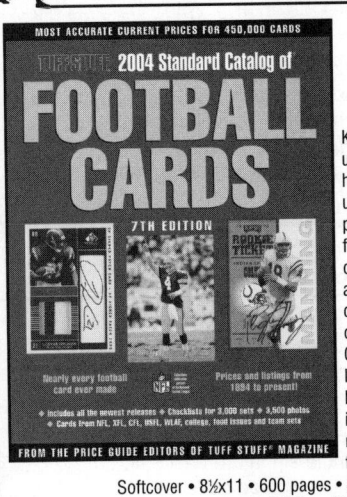

Tuff Stuff® 2004 Standard Catalog of® Football Cards
7th Edition
From the Price Guide Editors of *Tuff Stuff®* magazine
Keep up with the trends of the unpredictable sports collectibles hobby. Score unbeatable deals using the most comprehensive pricing guide for football cards from *Tuff Stuff®*, the pricing leader of sports cards and collectibles and Krause Publications, the official collectibles publication partner of the National Football League. Complete coverage ensures cataloging of nearly every known football card since 1894 and continuing into 2003, from all the top card manufacturers. You'll get values for more than 440,000 cards.

Softcover • 8½x11 • 600 pages • 3,200+ b&w photos
Item# SCFC7 • $24.99

Tuff Stuff® 2003 Standard Catalog of® Basketball Cards
6th Edition
From the Price Guide Editors of *Tuff Stuff®* magazine
Let the price guide editors of *Tuff Stuff®* provide values for your entire basketball card collection. More than 155,000 cards are covered in this price guide, which lists all known cards printed since 1948. Cards from the NBA, WNBA, and CBA, as well as college, high school, and Olympic athletes are listed from all popular card manufacturers including Fleer, Topps, Upper Deck, Pacific, Press Pass, SAGE, and Star Co. Pricing is also given for Starting Lineups, McFarlane, and other collectible figurines.

Softcover • 8½x11 • 384 pages • 2,000+ b&w photos
Item# SCBC6 • $21.95

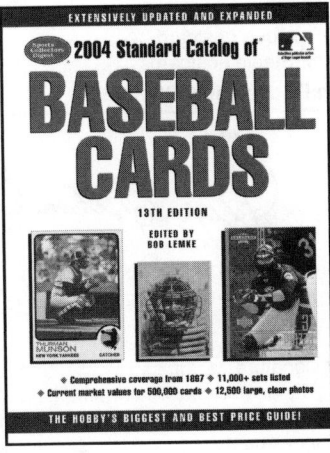

2004 Standard Catalog of® Baseball Cards
13th Edition
edited by Bob Lemke
Compete in today's increasingly complex market with the biggest and best reference catalog in the hobby as it continues to grow. You need an up-to-date price guide just to stay on top of the hobby! The 2004 edition, containing a record 1,728 large-format pages, is filled with pictures, facts and-most importantly-accurate market valuations for more than half a million baseball cards and related collectibles and collectible sets from 1869-2003.

Softcover • 8¼x10⅞
1,728 pages
12,000+ b&w photos
Item# SB13 • $39.99

2003 Baseball Card Price Guide
17th Edition
From the Price Guide Editors of *Sports Collectors Digest*
Introducing the most practical, accurate, and comprehensive price guide for all modern issues from 1981 to 2003 from the price guide editors of *Sports Collectors Digest*. This seventeenth edition covers more than 275,000 baseball cards and inserts, as well as assorted memorabilia including autographs, game-used jerseys, bat inserts, and much more! Includes wax box and pack pricing for each product and a tutorial explaining hobby terms.

Softcover • 6x9 • 1,152 pages
2,000 b&w photos
Item# BP17 • $17.99

The Encyclopedia of Professional Wrestling
100 Years of History, Headlines and Hitmakers, 2nd Edition
by Kristian Pope & Ray Whebbe Jr.
If you enjoy the thrill of professional wrestling, you'll love the updated biographies of more than 500 professional wrestlers, tons of insider information, and more than 1,000 new photos. Each bio features ring name, aliases, career highlights, and best matches. Find out who the first professional wrestler is, how the Rock came to be, about the inter-gender champion Andy Kaufman, and how Muhammed Ali took Japanese wrestling by storm.

Softcover • 8¼x10⅞
256 pages
500 b&w photos • 500+ color photos
Item# EPWRE2 • $24.99

Antique Golf Collectibles
A Price and Reference Guide
2nd Edition
by Chuck Furjanic
Everything you need to know about golf and golf collectibles is in this photo-packed, information-filled book. Updated with hundreds of additional items and new chapters on golf bags and tips on buying and selling golf collectibles. Includes thousands of listings, including three different value grades and historical backgrounds on products and manufacturers.

Softcover • 8½x11
408 pages
500 b&w photos
50 color photos
Item# GOLF3 • $29.95

To order call **800-258-0929** Offer SPB3

 Krause Publications, Offer SPB3
P.O. Box 5009, Iola WI 54945-5009
www.krausebooks.com

Please add $4.00 for the first book and $2.25 each additional for shipping & handling to U.S. addresses. Non-U.S. addresses please add $20.95 for the first book and $5.95 each additional.

Residents of CA, IA, IL, KS, NJ, PA, SD, TN, WI please add appropriate sales tax.

HOF plaque postcard $20
Perez-Steele postcards $20

Luke Appling (1907-1991)　　　1964

Cut signature $5
Single-signature baseball $100
Single-signature bat $200
3x5 index card $10
Photograph/baseball card $35
Typed Letter Signed $25
Handwritten Letter Signed...................$75
HOF plaque postcard $15
Perez-Steele postcards $40

Richie Ashburn (1927-1997)　　　1995

Cut signature $8
Single-signature baseball $75
Single-signature bat $125
3x5 index card $15
Photograph/baseball card $30
HOF plaque postcard $75
Perez-Steele postcards $100

Earl Averill (1902-1983)　　　1975

Cut signature $10
Single-signature baseball $500
Single-signature bat ....Unknown
3x5 index card $40
Photograph/baseball card $75
Typed Letter Signed $50
Handwritten Letter Signed.................$125
HOF plaque postcard $30
Perez-Steele postcards $450

Frank "Home Run" Baker (1886-1963)　　　1955

Cut signature $175
Single-signature baseball $2,500
Single-signature bat ....Unknown
3x5 index card $300
Photograph/baseball card $700
Typed Letter Signed $450
Handwritten Letter Signed.................$850
Check $800
HOF plaque postcard ....Impossible
Perez-Steele postcards ....Impossible

Dave Bancroft (1891-1972)　　　1971

Cut signature $50
Single-signature baseball $2,000
Single-signature bat ....Unknown
3x5 index card $100
Photograph/baseball card $325
Typed Letter Signed $150
Handwritten Letter Signed.................$400
HOF plaque postcard $600
Perez-Steele postcards ....Impossible

Ernie Banks (1931-)　　　1977

Mounted Memories Photo

Cut signature $10
Single-signature baseball $60
Authenticated baseball $160
Single-signature bat $135

3x5 index card $15
Photograph/baseball card $35
HOF plaque postcard $25
Perez-Steele postcards $30

Al Barlick (1915-1995)　　　1989

Cut signature $5
Single-signature baseball $50
Single-signature bat $125
3x5 index card $10
Photograph/baseball card $25
Typed Letter Signed $25
Handwritten Letter Signed...................$75
Check $20
HOF plaque postcard $20
Perez-Steele postcards $20

Edward Barrow (1868-1953)　　　1953

Cut signature $75
Single-signature baseball $4,000
Single-signature bat ....Unknown
3x5 index card $160
Photograph/baseball card $1,000
Typed Letter Signed $225
Handwritten Letter Signed.................$500
Check $75
HOF plaque postcard ....Impossible
Perez-Steele postcards ....Impossible

Jake Beckley (1867-1918)　　　1971

Cut signature .... $5,000-$10,000
Single-signature baseball ....Unknown
3x5 index card ....Unknown
Photograph/baseball card ....Unknown
HOF plaque postcard ....Impossible
Perez-Steele postcards ....Impossible

Cool Papa Bell (1903-1991)　　　1974

Note: Increase 25% for pre-stroke signature
Cut signature $20
Single-signature baseball $250
Single-signature bat $600
3x5 index card $35
Photograph/baseball card $100
HOF plaque postcard $100
Perez-Steele postcards $70

Johnny Bench (1947-)　　　1989

Steiner Sports Photo

Cut signature $10
Single-signature baseball $50
Authenticated baseball $120
Single-signature bat $170
3x5 index card $20
Photograph/baseball card $35
Authenticated photograph $80
HOF plaque postcard $40
Perez-Steele postcards $35

Chief Bender (1883-1954)　　　1953

Cut signature $175
Single-signature baseball $2,500

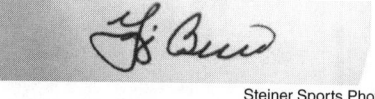

Single-signature bat ....Unknown
3x5 index card $250
Photograph/baseball card $700
Typed Letter Signed $400
Handwritten Letter Signed.................$900
Check $700
HOF plaque postcard ....Impossible
Perez-Steele postcards ....Impossible

Yogi Berra (1925-)　　　1972

Steiner Sports Photo

Cut signature $8
Single-signature baseball $50
Authenticated baseball $175
Single-signature bat $175
3x5 index card $15
Photograph/baseball card $35
HOF plaque postcard $25
Perez-Steele postcards $30

Jim Bottomley (1900-1959)　　　1974

Cut signature $225
Single-signature baseball $3,500
Single-signature bat ....Unknown
3x5 index card $300
Photograph/baseball card $800
Typed Letter Signed $550
Handwritten Letter Signed.................$900
Check $1,250
HOF plaque postcard ....Impossible
Perez-Steele postcards ....Impossible

Lou Boudreau (1917-2001)　　　1970

Cut signature $5
Single-signature baseball $50
Single-signature bat $125
3x5 index card $10
Photograph/baseball card $25
Typed Letter Signed $25
Handwritten Letter Signed...................$75
HOF plaque postcard $10
Perez-Steele postcards $25

Roger Bresnahan (1879-1944)　　　1945

Cut signature $600
Single-signature baseball $7,000
Single-signature bat ....Unknown
3x5 index card $650
Photograph/baseball card $3,000
Typed Letter Signed $1,200

Handwritten Letter Signed....................$3,500
HOF plaque postcard ....Impossible
Perez-Steele postcards ....Impossible

George Brett (1953-)   1999

Cut signature..$10
Single-signature baseball.......................$85
Authenticated baseball..........................$190
Single-signature bat $150
3x5 index card.......................................$20
Photograph/baseball card $60
HOF plaque postcard $60
Perez-Steele postcards $75

Lou Brock (1939-)   1985

Mounted Memories Photo

Cut signature..$8
Single-signature baseball...........................$40
Authenticated baseball.............................$150
Single-signature bat $125
3x5 index card.......................................$10
Photograph/baseball card $20
Authenticated photograph $90
HOF plaque postcard $35
Perez-Steele postcards $20

Dan Brouthers (1858-1932)   1945

Cut signature........................ $5,000-$10,000
Single-signature baseball ....Unknown
Single-signature bat ....Unknown
3x5 index card..................................Unknown
Photograph/baseball card ....Unknown
HOF plaque postcard ....Impossible
Perez-Steele postcards ....Impossible

Mordecai Brown (1876-1948)   1949

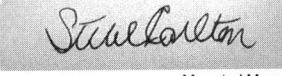

Cut signature......................................$600
Single-signature baseball....................$7,000
Single-signature bat ....Unknown
3x5 index card.....................................$500
Photograph/baseball card $3,000
Typed Letter Signed $1,200
Handwritten Letter Signed....................$3,500
HOF plaque postcard ....Impossible
Perez-Steele postcards ....Impossible

Morgan Bulkeley (1837-1922)   1937

Cut signature......................................$750
Single-signature baseball ....Unknown
Single-signature bat ....Unknown
3x5 index card...................................$1,200
Photograph/baseball card ....Unknown
Typed Letter Signed $1,500
Handwritten Letter Signed....................$3,000
Check $1,500
HOF plaque postcard ....Impossible
Perez-Steele postcards ....Impossible

Jim Bunning (1931-)   1996

Cut signature..$8
Single-signature baseball...........................$40
Single-signature bat $100
3x5 index card..$8
Photograph/baseball card $25
HOF plaque postcard $35

Perez-Steele postcards $25

Jesse Burkett (1868-1953)   1946

Cut signature......................................$900
Single-signature baseball...............Unknown
Single-signature bat ....Unknown
3x5 index card.....................................$700
Photograph/baseball card ....Unknown
Typed Letter Signed $2,000
Handwritten Letter Signed....................$4,000
HOF plaque postcard .... Impossible
Perez-Steele postcards .... Impossible

Roy Campanella (1921-1993)   1969

Cut signature......................................$250
Single-signature baseball....................$2,500
Single-signature bat ....Unknown
3x5 index card.....................................$500
Photograph/baseball card $700
Typed Letter Signed $500
Handwritten Letter Signed.....................$800
HOF plaque postcard $250
Perez-Steele postcards $175

Rod Carew (1945-)   1991

Steiner Sports Photo

Cut signature..$8
Single-signature baseball..........................$50
Authenticated baseball............................$150
Single-signature bat $150
3x5 index card.......................................$12
Photograph/baseball card $35
Authenticated photo $100
HOF plaque postcard $50
Perez-Steele postcards $40

Max Carey (1890-1976)   1961

Cut signature.. $15
Single-signature baseball.......................$800
Single-signature bat ....Unknown
3x5 index card.......................................$40
Photograph/baseball card $150
Typed Letter Signed $50
Handwritten Letter Signed.....................$175
Check $35
HOF plaque postcard $95
Perez-Steele postcards .... Impossible

Steve Carlton (1944-)   1994

Mounted Memories Photo

Cut signature..$8
Single-signature baseball..........................$40
Authenticated Baseball............................$100
Single-signature bat $100
3x5 index card.......................................$10
Photograph/baseball card $25
Authenticated photograph $70
HOF plaque postcard $35
Perez-Steele postcards $30

Gary Carter (1954-)   2003

Cut signature..$5
Single-signature baseball..........................$50
Authenticated baseball............................$140
Single-signature bat $100

3x5 index card..$5
Photograph/baseball card $20

Alexander Cartwright (1820-1892)   1938

Cut signature......................................$750
Single-signature baseball...............Unknown
Single-signature bat ....Unknown
3x5 index card...................................$1,200
Photograph/baseball card ....Unknown
Typed Letter Signed $1,500
Handwritten Letter Signed....................$4,000
Check $2,000
HOF plaque postcard .... Impossible
Perez-Steele postcards .... Impossible

Orlando Cepeda (1937-)   1999

Mounted Memories Photo

Cut signature..$5
Single-signature baseball..........................$40
Authenticated baseball............................$100
Single-signature bat $100
Authenticated bat $250
3x5 index card..$8
Photograph/baseball card $20
Authenbticated photograph $50
HOF plaque postcard $30
Perez-Steele postcards $30

Henry Chadwick (1824-1908)   1938

Cut signature....................................$2,500
Single-signature baseball...............Unknown
Single-signature bat ....Unknown
Photograph/baseball card ....Unknown
Typed Letter Signed $5,000
HOF plaque postcard .... Impossible
Perez-Steele postcards .... Impossible

Frank Chance (1877-1924)   1946

Cut signature....................................$2,500
Single-signature baseball ....Unknown
Single-signature bat ....Unknown
Photograph/baseball card ....Unknown
Typed Letter Signed $5,500
HOF plaque postcard .... Impossible
Perez-Steele postcards .... Impossible

Happy Chandler (1898-1991)   1982

Cut signature..$5
Single-signature baseball..........................$75
Single-signature bat $300
3x5 index card.......................................$15
Photograph/baseball card $40
Typed Letter Signed $25
Handwritten Letter Signed.......................$75
Check $50
HOF plaque postcard $20
Perez-Steele postcards $40

Oscar Charleston (1896-1954)   1976

Cut signature....................................$1,200
Single-signature baseball....................$7,000
Single-signature bat ....Unknown
3x5 index card...................................$3,000
Photograph/baseball card $3,000
HOF plaque postcard .... Impossible
Perez-Steele postcards .... Impossible

Jack Chesbro (1874-1931)   1946

Cut signature....................................$4,000

Single-signature baseball ....Unknown
Single-signature bat ....Unknown
Photograph/baseball card ....Unknown
Typed Letter Signed $8,000
Check $15,000
HOF plaque postcard ....Impossible
Perez-Steele postcards ....Impossible

Nestor Chylak (1922-1982) 1999

Cut signature $125
Single-signature baseball $1,500
Single-signature bat ....Unknown
Photograph/baseball card $425
Typed Letter Signed $250
Handwritten Letter Signed...................$500
HOF plaque postcard ....Impossible
Perez-Steele postcards ....Impossible

Fred Clarke (1872-1960) 1945

Cut signature $150
Single-signature baseball $2,750
Single-signature bat ....Unknown
3x5 index card $300
Photograph/baseball card $550
Typed Letter Signed $350
Handwritten Letter Signed...................$700
HOF plaque postcard ....Impossible
Perez-Steele postcards ....Impossible

John Clarkson (1861-1909) 1963

Cut signature $2,500
Single-signature baseball ....Unknown
Single-signature bat ....Unknown
Photograph/baseball card ....Unknown
HOF plaque postcard ....Impossible
Perez-Steele postcards ....Impossible

Roberto Clemente (1934-1972) 1973

Cut signature $300
Single-signature baseball $2,500
Single-signature bat ....Unknown
3x5 index card $375
Photograph/baseball card $750
Typed Letter Signed $650
Handwritten Letter Signed...................$1,500
Check $600
HOF plaque postcard ....Impossible
Perez-Steele postcards ....Impossible

Ty Cobb (1886-1961) 1936

Cut signature $500
Single-signature baseball $5,500
Single-signature bat ....Unknown
3x5 index card $700
Photograph/baseball card $2,500
Typed Letter Signed $1,250
Handwritten Letter Signed...................$2,500
Check $750
HOF plaque postcard ....Impossible
Perez-Steele postcards ....Impossible

Mickey Cochrane (1903-1962) 1947

Cut signature $125
Single-signature baseball $1,500
Single-signature bat ....Unknown
3x5 index card $250
Photograph/baseball card $550
Typed Letter Signed $300
Handwritten Letter Signed...................$600
Check $150
HOF plaque postcard .... Impossible
Perez-Steele postcards .... Impossible

Eddie Collins (1887-1951) 1939

Cut signature $250
Single-signature baseball $5,500
Single-signature bat ....Unknown
Photograph/baseball card $1,000
Typed Letter Signed $400
Handwritten Letter Signed...................$1,000
Check $1,500
HOF plaque postcard .... Impossible
Perez-Steele postcards .... Impossible

Jimmy Collins (1870-1943) 1945

Cut signature $2,500
Single-signature baseball ....Unknown
Single-signature bat ....Unknown
Photograph/baseball card ....Unknown
Typed Letter Signed $5,000
HOF plaque postcard .... Impossible
Perez-Steele postcards .... Impossible

Earle Combs (1899-1976) 1970

Cut signature $25
Single-signature baseball $1,000
Single-signature bat ....Unknown
3x5 index card $150
Photograph/baseball card $200
Typed Letter Signed $75
Handwritten Letter Signed...................$275
Check $75
HOF plaque postcard $250
Perez-Steele postcards .... Impossible

Charles Comiskey (1859-1931) 1939

Cut signature $450
Single-signature baseball $5,500
Single-signature bat ....Unknown
3x5 index card $500
Photograph/baseball card $3,500
Typed Letter Signed $750
Handwritten Letter Signed...................$2,500
HOF plaque postcard .... Impossible
Perez-Steele postcards .... Impossible

Jocko Conlan (1899-1989) 1974

Cut signature $10
Single-signature baseball $200
Single-signature bat $250
3x5 index card $20
Photograph/baseball card $60
Typed Letter Signed $40
Handwritten Letter Signed...................$100
HOF plaque postcard $20
Perez-Steele postcards $60

Thomas Connolly (1870-1961) 1953

Cut signature $350
Single-signature baseball $4,500
Single-signature bat ....Unknown
3x5 index card $400
Photograph/baseball card $1,500
Typed Letter Signed $600
Handwritten Letter Signed...................$1,500
HOF plaque postcard .... Impossible
Perez-Steele postcards .... Impossible

Roger Connor (1857-1931) 1976

Cut signature .... $5,000-$10,000
Single-signature baseball ....Unknown
Single-signature bat ....Unknown
Photograph/baseball card ....Unknown
HOF plaque postcard .... Impossible
Perez-Steele postcards .... Impossible

Stan Coveleski (1889-1984) 1969

Cut signature $10
Single-signature baseball $400
Single-signature bat ....Unknown
3x5 index card $25
Photograph/baseball card $100
Typed Letter Signed $50
Handwritten Letter Signed...................$150
HOF plaque postcard $30
Perez-Steele postcards $300

Sam Crawford (1880-1968) 1957

Cut signature $100
Single-signature baseball $3,500
Single-signature bat ....Unknown
3x5 index card $250
Photograph/baseball card $1,000
Typed Letter Signed $275
Handwritten Letter Signed...................$375
HOF plaque postcard $400
Perez-Steele postcards .... Impossible

Joe Cronin (1906-1984) 1956

Cut signature $15
Single-signature baseball $450
Single-signature bat ....Unknown
3x5 index card $30
Photograph/baseball card $100
Typed Letter Signed $50
Handwritten Letter Signed...................$150
Check $150
HOF plaque postcard $50
Perez-Steele postcards $700

Candy Cummings (1848-1924) 1939

Cut signature .... $10,000-$20,000

Single-signature baseball ....Unknown
Single-signature bat ....Unknown
Photograph/baseball card ....Unknown
HOF plaque postcard ....Impossible
Perez-Steele postcards ....Impossible

Ki Ki Cuyler (1899-1950)   1968

Cut signature $200
Single-signature baseball $3,500
Single-signature bat ....Unknown
3x5 index card $250
Photograph/baseball card $700
Typed Letter Signed $500
Handwritten Letter Signed.....................$850
Check $4,000
HOF plaque postcard ....Impossible
Perez-Steele postcards ....Impossible

Ray Dandridge (1913-1994)   1987

Cut signature $20
Single-signature baseball $75
Single-signature bat $175
3x5 index card $30
Photograph/baseball card $50
HOF plaque postcard $20
Perez-Steele postcards $20

George Davis (1870-1940)   1998

Cut signature .... $7,500-$15,000
Single-signature baseball ....Unknown
Single-signature bat ....Unknown
3x5 index card ....Unknown
Photograph/baseball card ....Unknown
HOF plaque postcard ....Impossible
Perez-Steele postcards ....Impossible

Leon Day (1916-1995)   1995

Cut signature $25
Single-signature baseball $200
Single-signature bat $300
3x5 index card $35
Photograph/baseball card $75
HOF plaque postcard ....Impossible
Perez-Steele postcards ....Impossible

Dizzy Dean (1911-1974)   1953

Cut signature $75
Single-signature baseball $1,250
Single-signature bat ....Unknown
3x5 index card $100
Photograph/baseball card $350
Typed Letter Signed $200
Handwritten Letter Signed.....................$400
HOF plaque postcard $135
Perez-Steele postcards ....Impossible

Ed Delahanty (1867-1903)   1945

Cut signature .... $10,000-$20,000
Single-signature baseball ....Unknown
Single-signature bat ....Unknown
Photograph/baseball card ....Unknown
HOF plaque postcard ....Impossible
Perez-Steele postcards ....Impossible

Bill Dickey (1907-1993)   1954

Cut signature $10
Single-signature baseball $250

Single-signature bat $500
3x5 index card $20
Photograph/baseball card $50
Typed Letter Signed $50
Handwritten Letter Signed.....................$175
Check $100
HOF plaque postcard $50
Perez-Steele postcards $80

Martin DiHigo (1905-1971)   1977

Cut signature $650
Single-signature baseball $4,000
Single-signature bat ....Unknown
3x5 index card $800
Photograph/baseball card $3,000
HOF plaque postcard .... Impossible
Perez-Steele postcards .... Impossible

Joe DiMaggio (1914-1999)   1955

Cut signature $50
Single-signature baseball $300
Single-signature bat $1,800
3x5 index card $150
Photograph/baseball card $200
Typed Letter Signed $150
Handwritten Letter Signed.....................$500
Check $350
HOF plaque postcard $150
Perez-Steele postcards $350

Larry Doby (1924-2003)   1998

Steiner Sports Photo

Cut signature $8
Single-signature baseball $40
Single-signature bat $75
3x5 Index card $10
Photograph/baseball card $25
Authenticated photograph $100
HOF plaque postcard $25
Perez-Steele postcards $25

Bobby Doerr (1918-)   1986

Cut signature $5
Single-signature baseball $30
Single-signature bat $85
3x5 index card $8
Photograph/baseball card $12
HOF plaque postcard $10
Perez-Steele postcards $15

Don Drysdale (1936-1993)   1984

Cut signature $20
Single-signature baseball $175
Single-signature bat $200
3x5 index card $30
Photograph/baseball card $60
HOF plaque postcard $35
Perez-Steele postcards $35

Hugh Duffy (1866-1954)   1945

Cut signature $275
Single-signature baseball $5,000
Single-signature bat ....Unknown

3x5 index card $500
Photograph/baseball card $1,000
Typed Letter Signed $550
Handwritten Letter Signed..................$1,500
HOF plaque postcard .... Impossible
Perez-Steele postcards .... Impossible

Leo Durocher (1905-1991)   1994

Cut signature $10
Single-signature baseball $175
Single-signature bat $400
3x5 index card $30
Photograph/baseball card $60
Typed Letter Signed $45
Handwritten Letter Signed.....................$125
Check $400
HOF plaque postcard .... Impossible
Perez-Steele postcards .... Impossible

Billy Evans (1864-1956)   1973

Cut signature $100
Single-signature baseball $3,500
Single-signature bat ....Unknown
3x5 index card $200
Photograph/baseball card $500
Typed Letter Signed $200
Handwritten Letter Signed.....................$450
HOF plaque postcard .... Impossible
Perez-Steele postcards .... Impossible

Johnny Evers (1881-1947)   1946

Cut signature $450
Single-signature baseball $6,000
Single-signature bat ....Unknown
3x5 index card $500
Photograph/baseball card $2,750
Typed Letter Signed $1,000
Handwritten Letter Signed..................$3,000
Check $2,500
HOF plaque postcard .... Impossible
Perez-Steele postcards .... Impossible

Buck Ewing (1859-1906)   1939

Cut signature .... $10,000-$20,000
Single-signature baseball ....Unknown
Single-signature bat ....Unknown
Photograph/baseball card ....Unknown
HOF plaque postcard .... Impossible
Perez-Steele postcards .... Impossible

Red Faber (1888-1976)   1964

Cut signature $25
Single-signature baseball $700
Single-signature bat ....Unknown
3x5 index card $35
Photograph/baseball card $200

Typed Letter Signed $75
Handwritten Letter Signed.......................$225
HOF plaque postcard $150
Perez-Steele postcards ....Impossible

Bob Feller (1918-)   **1962**

Steiner Sports Photo

Cut signature $8
Single-signature baseball $35
Authenticated baseball $80
Single-signature bat $75
3x5 index card $8
Photograph/baseball card $15
Authenticated photograph $40
HOF plaque postcard $15
Perez-Steele postcards $20

Rick Ferrell (1905-1995)   **1984**

Cut signature $5
Single-signature baseball $45
Single-signature bat $150
3x5 index card $10
Photograph/baseball card $20
Typed Letter Signed $30
Handwritten Letter Signed...........................$75
Check $30
HOF plaque postcard $25
Perez-Steele postcards $30

Rollie Fingers (1946-)   **1992**

Mounted Memories Photo

Cut signature $5
Single-signature baseball $35
Authenticated baseball $60
Single-signature bat $75
3x5 index card $5
Photograph/baseball card $20
HOF plaque postcard $15
Perez-Steele postcards $20

Carlton Fisk (1947-)   **2000**

Steiner Sports Photo

Cut signature $10
Single-signature baseball $60
Authenticated baseball $150
Single-signature bat $125
3x5 index card $15
Photograph/baseball card $40
HOF plaque postcard $50
Perez-Steele postcards $50

Elmer Flick (1876-1971)   **1963**

Cut signature $40
Single-signature baseball $2,500
Single-signature bat ....Unknown
3x5 index card $75
Photograph baseball card $300

Typed Letter Signed $150
Handwritten Letter Signed.......................$350
HOF plaque postcard $550
Perez-Steele postcards .... Impossible

Whitey Ford (1926-)   **1974**

Mounted Memories Photo

Cut signature $10
Single-signature baseball $50
Authenticated baseball $150
Single-signature bat $100
3x5 index card $15
Photograph/baseball card $50
HOF plaque postcard $20
Perez-Steele postcards $35

Bill Foster (1904-1978)   **1996**

Cut signature $2,500
Single-signature baseball ....Unknown
Single-signature bat ....Unknown
3x5 index card $3,000
Photograph/baseball card ....Unknown
HOF plaque postcard .... Impossible
Perez-Steele postcards .... Impossible

Rube Foster (1878-1930)   **1981**

Cut signature $2,000
Single-signature baseball $13,000
Single-signature bat ....Unknown
3x5 index card $3,800
Photograph/baseball card $6,000
HOF plaque postcard .... Impossible
Perez-Steele postcards .... Impossible

Nellie Fox (1927-1975)   **1997**

Cut signature $125
Single-signature baseball $1,250
Single-signature bat ....Unknown
3x5 index card $250
Photograph/baseball card $300
Typed Letter Signed $250
Handwritten Letter Signed.......................$400
Check $250
HOF plaque postcard .... Impossible
Perez-Steele postcard .... Impossible

Jimmie Foxx (1907-1967)   **1951**

Cut signature $300
Single-signature baseball $2,500
Single-signature bat ....Unknown
3x5 index card $350
Photograph/baseball card $800
Typed Letter Signed $600
Handwritten Letter Signed....................$1,000
HOF plaque postcard $3,000
Perez-Steele postcards .... Impossible

Ford Frick (1894-1978)   **1970**

Cut signature $20
Single-signature baseball $750
Single-signature bat ....Unknown
3x5 index card $50
Photograph/baseball card $175
Typed Letter Signed $75

Handwritten Letter Signed.......................$200
Check $100
HOF plaque postcard $200
Perez-Steele postcards .... Impossible

Frankie Frisch (1898-1973)   **1947**

Cut signature $25
Single-signature baseball $1,000
Single-signature bat ....Unknown
3x5 index card $75
Photograph/baseball card $250
Typed Letter Signed $100
Handwritten Letter Signed.......................$300
Check $150
HOF plaque postcard $200
Perez-Steele postcards .... Impossible

Pud Galvin (1855-1902)   **1965**

Cut signature .... $7,500-$15,000
Single-signature baseball ....Unknown
Single-signature bat ....Unknown
Photograph/baseball card ....Unknown
HOF plaque postcard .... Impossible
Perez-Steele postcards .... Impossible

Lou Gehrig (1903-1941)   **1939**

Cut signature $1,000
Single-signature baseball $6,500
Single-signature bat ....Unknown
3x5 index card $1,250
Photograph/baseball card $5,000
Typed Letter Signed $2,500
Handwritten Letter Signed....................$7,500
Check $5,000
HOF plaque postcard .... Impossible
Perez-Steele postcards .... Impossible

Charlie Gehringer (1903-1993)   **1949**

Cut signature $5
Single-signature baseball $100
Single-signature bat $400
3x5 index card $20
Photograph/baseball card $35
Typed Letter Signed $50
Handwritten Letter Signed.......................$150
Check $500
HOF plaque postcard $35
Perez-Steele postcards $70

Bob Gibson (1935-)   **1981**

Tri-Star Productions Photo

Cut signature $8
Single-signature baseball $45
Authenticated baseball $140
Single-signature bat $100
3x5 index card $10
Photograph/baseball card $75
Authenticated photograph $90
HOF plaque postcard $20
Perez-Steele postcards $20

Josh Gibson (1911-1947)   1972

Cut signature $700
Single-signature baseball $6,500
Single-signature bat ....Unknown
3x5 index card $1,000
Photograph/baseball card $2,000
HOF plaque postcard ....Impossible
Perez-Steele postcards ....Impossible

Warren Giles (1896-1979)   1979

Cut signature $20
Single-signature baseball $1,000
Single-signature bat ....Unknown
3x5 index card $50
Photograph/baseball card $150
Typed Letter Signed $50
Handwritten Letter Signed....................$150
HOF plaque postcard ....Impossible
Perez-Steele postcards ....Impossible

Lefty Gomez (1908-1989)   1972

Cut signature $25
Single-signature baseball $225
Single-signature bat $400
3x5 index card $40
Photograph/baseball card $50
Typed Letter Signed $75
Handwritten Letter Signed....................$175
HOF plaque postcard $35
Perez-Steele postcards $80

Goose Goslin (1900-1971)   1968

Cut signature $60
Single-signature baseball $3,500
Single-signature bat ....Unknown
3x5 index card $100
Photograph/baseball card $350
Typed Letter Signed $225
Handwritten Letter Signed....................$450
HOF plaque postcard $3,000
Perez-Steele postcards ....Impossible

Hank Greenberg (1911-1986)   1956

Cut signature $25
Single-signature baseball $600
Single-signature bat ....Unknown
3x5 index card $45
Photograph/baseball card $125
Typed Letter Signed $100
Handwritten Letter Signed....................$300
HOF plaque postcard $90
Perez-Steele postcards $325

Clark Griffith (1869-1955)   1946

Cut signature $100
Single-signature baseball $2,500
Single-signature bat ....Unknown
3x5 index card $150
Photograph/baseball card $550
Typed Letter Signed $225
Handwritten Letter Signed....................$600
Check $450
HOF plaque postcard ....Impossible
Perez-Steele postcards ....Impossible

Burleigh Grimes (1893-1985)   1964

Cut signature $15
Single-signature baseball $250
Single-signature bat ....Unknown
3x5 index card $30
Photograph/baseball card $50
Typed Letter Signed $50
Handwritten Letter Signed....................$150
Check $75
HOF plaque postcard $30
Perez-Steele postcards $160

Lefty Grove (1900-1975)   1947

Cut signature $30
Single-signature baseball $1,500
Single-signature bat ....Unknown
3x5 index card $100
Photograph/baseball card $225
Typed Letter Signed $150
Handwritten Letter Signed....................$300
Check $100
HOF plaque postcard $175
Perez-Steele postcards .... Impossible

Chick Hafey (1903-1973)   1971

Chick Hafey

Cut signature $35
Single-signature baseball $1,750
Single-signature bat ....Unknown
3x5 index card $75
Photograph/baseball card $250
Typed Letter Signed $125
Handwritten Letter Signed....................$400
HOF plaque postcard $600
Perez-Steele postcards .... Impossible

Jesse Haines (1893-1978)   1970

Cut signature $15
Single-signature baseball $750
Single-signature bat ....Unknown
3x5 index card $40
Photograph/baseball card $75
Typed Letter Signed $45
Handwritten Letter Signed....................$100
Check $25
HOF plaque postcard $150
Perez-Steele postcards .... Impossible

Billy Hamilton (1866-1940)   1961

Cut signature $1,500
Single-signature baseball ....Unknown
Single-signature bat ....Unknown
Photograph/baseball card ....Unknown
Typed Letter Signed $4,000
HOF plaque postcard .... Impossible
Perez-Steele postcards .... Impossible

Ned Hanlon (1857-1937)   1996

Cut signature 1,500
Single-signature baseball ....Unknown
Single-signature bat ....Unknown
Photograph/baseball card ....Unknown
Typed Letter Signed $3,000
HOF plaque postcard .... Impossible
Perez-Steele postcards .... Impossible

Will Harridge (1883-1971)   1972

Cut signature $50
Single-signature baseball $1,500
Single-signature bat ....Unknown
3x5 index card $125
Photograph/baseball card $250
Typed Letter Signed $100
Handwritten Letter Signed....................$275
HOF plaque postcard .... Impossible
Perez-Steele postcards .... Impossible

Bucky Harris (1896-1977)   1975

Cut signature $40
Single-signature baseball $1,000
Single-signature bat ....Unknown
3x5 index card $60
Photograph/baseball card $150

Typed Letter Signed $125
Handwritten Letter Signed....................$250
HOF plaque postcard $350
Perez-Steele postcards .... Impossible

Gabby Hartnett (1900-1972)   1955

Cut signature $50
Single-signature baseball $800
Single-signature bat ....Unknown
3x5 index card $75
Photograph/baseball card $200
Typed Letter Signed $125
Handwritten Letter Signed....................$300
Check $75
HOF plaque postcard $325
Perez-Steele postcards .... Impossible

Harry Heilmann (1894-1951)   1952

Harry Heilmann

Cut signature $350
Single-signature baseball $5,000
Single-signature bat ....Unknown
3x5 index card $375
Photograph/baseball card $2,000
Typed Letter Signed $750
Handwritten Letter Signed.................$2,500
Check $1,500
HOF plaque postcard .... Impossible
Perez-Steele postcards .... Impossible

Billy Herman (1909-1992)   1975

Cut signature $5
Single-signature baseball $50
Single-signature bat $175
3x5 index card $12
Photograph/baseball card $25
Typed Letter Signed $25
Handwritten Letter Signed......................$60
Check $25
HOF plaque postcard $15
Perez-Steele postcards $20

Harry Hooper (1887-1974)   1971

Harry Hooper

Cut signature $25
Single-signature baseball $750
Single-signature bat ....Unknown
3x5 index card $45
Photograph/baseball card $175
Typed Letter Signed $75
Handwritten Letter Signed....................$200
Check $50
HOF plaque postcard $275
Perez-Steele postcards .... Impossible

Rogers Hornsby (1896-1963)   1942

*Rogers Hornsby
1959*

Cut signature $275
Single-signature baseball $2,750

Single-signature bat ....Unknown
3x5 index card $375
Photograph/baseball card $750
Typed Letter Signed $500
Handwritten Letter Signed............$1,250
HOF plaque postcard ....Impossible
Perez-Steele postcards ....Impossible

Waite Hoyt (1899-1984) 1969

Cut signature $5
Single-signature baseball $250
Single-signature bat ....Unknown
3x5 index card $15
Photograph/baseball card $45
Typed Letter Signed $30
Handwritten Letter Signed.....................$100
Check $25
HOF plaque postcard $75
Perez-Steele postcards $450

Cal Hubbard (1900-1977) 1976

Cut signature $50
Single-signature baseball $1,250
Single-signature bat ....Unknown
3x5 index card $80
Photograph/baseball card $250
Typed Letter Signed $100
Handwritten Letter Signed.....................$300
Check $100
HOF plaque postcard $500
Perez-Steele postcards ....Impossible

Carl Hubbell (1903-1988) 1947

Cut signature $15
Single-signature baseball $250
Single-signature bat ....Unknown
3x5 index card $25
Photograph/baseball card $60
Typed Letter Signed $50
Handwritten Letter Signed.....................$125
Check $100
HOF plaque postcard $50
Perez-Steele postcards $80

Miller Huggins (1879-1929) 1964

Cut signature $1,250
Single-signature baseball ....Unknown
Single-signature bat ....Unknown
Photograph/baseball card ....Unknown
Typed Letter Signed $2,500
Handwritten Letter Signed..................$5,500
HOF plaque postcard ....Impossible
Perez-Steele postcards ....Impossible

William Hulbert (1832-1882) 1995

Cut signature - letter...........................$1,750
Single-signature baseball ....Unknown
Single-signature bat ....Unknown
3x5 index card ....Unknown
Photograph/baseball card ....Unknown
Typed Letter Signed $3,500
HOF plaque postcard ....Impossible
Perez-Steele postcards ....Impossible

Catfish Hunter (1946-1999) 1987

Cut signature $8
Single-signature baseball $100
3x5 index card $10
Photograph/baseball card $35
HOF plaque postcard $20
Perez-Steele postcards $30

Monte Irvin (1919-) 1973

Cut signature $8
Single-signature baseball $35
Authenticated baseball $70
Single-signature bat $85
3x5 index card $10
Photograph/baseball card $10
HOF plaque postcard $10
Perez-Steele postcards $20

Reggie Jackson (1946-) 1993

Cut signature $10
Single-signature baseball $70
Authenticated baseball $160
Single-signature bat $225
3x5 index card $20
Photograph/baseball card $50
Authenticated photograph $100
HOF plaque postcard $60
Perez-Steele postcards $60

Travis Jackson (1903-1987) 1982

Cut signature $15
Single-signature baseball $375
3x5 index card $25
Photograph/baseball card $50
Typed Letter Signed $50
Handwritten Letter Signed.....................$125
HOF plaque postcard $40
Perez-Steele postcards $80

Fergie Jenkins (1943-) 1991

Cut signature $8
Single-signature baseball $30
Authenticated baseball $100
Single-signature bat $75
3x5 index card $10
Photograph/baseball card $15
HOF plaque postcard $15
Perez-Steele postcards $15

Hugh Jennings (1869-1928) 1945

Cut signature $2,500
Single-signature baseball ....Unknown
Single-signature bat ....Unknown
Photograph/baseball card ....Unknown
Typed Letter Signed $5,500
HOF plaque postcard ....Impossible
Perez-Steele postcards ....Impossible

Ban Johnson (1864-1931) 1937

Cut signature $250
Single-signature baseball ....Unknown
Single-signature bat ....Unknown
3x5 index card $300
Photograph/baseball card ....Unknown
Typed Letter Signed $500
Handwritten Letter Signed..................$3,500
Check $1,000
HOF plaque postcard ....Impossible
Perez-Steele postcards ....Impossible

Judy Johnson (1900-1989) 1975

Cut signature $10
Single-signature baseball $200
Single-signature bat ....Unknown
3x5 index card $15
Photograph/baseball card $95
HOF plaque postcard $50
Perez-Steele postcards $60

Walter Johnson (1887-1946) 1936

Cut signature $500
Single-signature baseball $3,500
Single-signature bat ....Unknown
3x5 index card $750
Photograph/baseball card $2,000
Typed Letter Signed $1,000
Handwritten Letter Signed..................$2,000
Check $650
HOF plaque postcard ....Unknown
Perez-Steele postcards ....Impossible

Addie Joss (1880-1911) 1978

Cut signature ....$10,000-$20,000
Single-signature baseball ....Unknown
Single-signature bat ....Unknown
Photograph/baseball card ....Unknown
HOF plaque postcard ....Impossible
Perez-Steele postcards ....Impossible

Al Kaline (1934-) 1980

Mounted Memories Photo

Cut signature $8
Single-signature baseball $40
Authenticated baseball $125
Single-signature bat $100
3x5 index card $8
Photograph/baseball card $25
HOF plaque postcard $15
Perez-Steele postcards $25

Tim Keefe (1857-1933) 1964

Cut signature ....$10,000-$20,000
Single-signature baseball ....Unknown
Single-signature bat ....Unknown
Photograph/baseball card ....Unknown
HOF plaque postcard ....Impossible
Perez-Steele postcards ....Impossible

Wee Willie Keeler (1872-1923) 1939

Cut signature $2,500
Single-signature baseball ....Unknown
Single-signature bat ....Unknown
Photograph/baseball card ....Unknown
Typed Letter Signed $5,500
HOF plaque postcard ....Impossible
Perez-Steele postcards ....Impossible

George Kell (1922-) 1983

Cut signature $8
Single-signature baseball $30
Authenticated baseball $80
Single-signature bat $75
3x5 index card $8
Photograph/baseball card $15
Authenticated photograph $30
HOF plaque postcard $8
Perez-Steele postcards $15

Joe Kelley (1871-1943) 1971

Cut signature $1,000
Single-signature baseball ....Unknown
Single-signature bat ....Unknown
Photograph/baseball card ....Unknown
Typed Letter Signed $2,000
Handwritten Letter Signed..................$5,000
HOF plaque postcard ....Impossible
Perez-Steele postcards ....Impossible

George Kelly (1895-1984) 1973

Cut signature $15
Single-signature baseball $375
Single-signature bat ....Unknown
3x5 index card $20

Photograph/baseball card $50
Typed Letter Signed $50
Handwritten Letter Signed.....................$100
Check $20
HOF plaque postcard $35
Perez-Steele postcards $325

Mike "King" Kelly (1857-1894) 1945

Cut signature .... $10,000-$20,000
Single-signature baseball ....Unknown
Single-signature bat ....Unknown
Photograph/baseball card ....Unknown
HOF plaque postcard ....Impossible
Perez-Steele postcards ....Impossible

Harmon Killebrew (1936-) 1984

Cut signature $5
Single-signature baseball $40
Authenticated baseball $120
Single-signature bat $135
3x5 index card $10
Photograph/baseball card $30
HOF plaque postcard $30
Perez-Steele postcards $30

Ralph Kiner (1922-) 1975

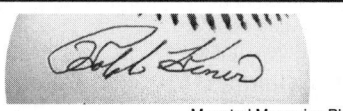

Mounted Memories Photo

Cut signature $8
Single-signature baseball $35
Authenticated baseball $80
Single-signature bat $85
3x5 index card $8
Photograph/baseball card $20
HOF plaque postcard $20
Perez-Steele postcards $25

Chuck Klein (1904-1958) 1980

Cut signature $275
Single-signature baseball $4,500
Single-signature bat ....Unknown
3x5 index card $300
Photograph/baseball card $1,000
Typed Letter Signed $500
Handwritten Letter Signed..................$1,200
HOF plaque postcard ....Impossible
Perez-Steele postcards ....Impossible

Bill Klem (1874-1951) 1953

Cut signature $250
Single-signature baseball $3,000
Single-signature bat ....Unknown
3x5 index card $600
Photograph/baseball card $800
Typed Letter Signed $550
Handwritten Letter Signed..................$1,000

HOF plaque postcard ....Impossible
Perez-Steele postcards .... Impossible

Sandy Koufax (1935-) 1972

Cut signature $10
Single-signature baseball $175
Authenticated baseball $500
Single-signature bat $225
3x5 index card $30
Photograph/baseball card $100
HOF plaque postcard $65
Perez-Steele postcards $50

Nap Lajoie (1875-1959) 1937

Cut signature $275
Single-signature baseball $4,000
Single-signature bat ....Unknown
3x5 index card $350
Photograph/baseball card $1,500
Typed Letter Signed $600
Handwritten Letter Signed..................$1,750
HOF plaque postcard .... Impossible
Perez-Steele postcards .... Impossible

Kenesaw Landis (1866-1944) 1944

Cut signature $125
Single-signature baseball $3,500
Single-signature bat ....Unknown
3x5 index card $600
Photograph/baseball card $1,000
Typed Letter Signed $250
Handwritten Letter Signed.....................$500
HOF plaque postcard .... Impossible
Perez-Steele postcards .... Impossible

Tommy Lasorda (1927-) 1997

Cut signature $10
Single-signature baseball $60
Single-signature bat $125
3x5 index card $10
Photograph/baseball card $35
HOF plaque postcard $50
Perez-Steele postcards $50

Tony Lazzeri (1903-1946) 1991

Cut signature $350
Single-signature baseball $5,000
Single-signature bat ....Unknown
3x5 index card $450
Photograph/baseball card $1,250
Typed Letter Signed $750
Handwritten Letter Signed..................$2,500
HOF plaque postcard .... Impossible
Perez-Steele postcards .... Impossible

Bob Lemon (1920-2000) 1976

Cut signature $8

Single-signature baseball $50
Single-signature bat $100
3x5 index card $8
Photograph/baseball card $25
HOF plaque postcard $10
Perez-Steele postcards $25

Buck Leonard (1907-1997) 1972

Note: Increase 50% for pre-stroke signature
Cut signature $8
Single-signature baseball $70
Single-signature bat $125
3x5 index card $10
Photograph/baseball card $35
HOF plaque postcard $35
Perez-Steele postcards $30

Freddie Lindstrom (1905-1981) 1976

Cut signature $20
Single-signature baseball $650
Single-signature bat ....Unknown
3x5 index card $30
Photograph/baseball card $100
Typed Letter Signed $60
Handwritten Letter Signed.....................$150
HOF plaque postcard $75
Perez-Steele postcards .... Impossible

John "Pop" Lloyd (1884-1965) 1977

Cut signature $1,000
Single-signature baseball $7,000
Single-signature bat ....Unknown
3x5 index card $1,200
Photograph/baseball card $3,000
HOF plaque postcard .... Impossible
Perez-Steele postcards .... Impossible

Ernie Lombardi (1908-1977) 1986

Cut signature $25
Single-signature baseball $1,500
Single-signature bat ....Unknown
3x5 index card $75
Photograph/baseball card $200
Typed Letter Signed $100
Handwritten Letter Signed.....................$250
HOF plaque postcard .... Impossible
Perez-Steele postcards .... Impossible

Al Lopez (1908-) 1977

Cut signature $15
Single-signature baseball $100
Single-signature bat $150
3x5 index card $20
Photograph/baseball card $60
HOF plaque postcard $45
Perez-Steele postcards $75

Ted Lyons (1900-1986) 1955

Cut signature $10
Single-signature baseball $275
Single-signature bat ....Unknown
3x5 index card $30
Photograph/baseball card $50
Typed Letter Signed $50
Handwritten Letter Signed.....................$100
Check $50
HOF plaque postcard $45
Perez-Steele postcards $225

Connie Mack (1862-1956) 1937

Cut signature $100

Single-signature baseball $1,250
Single-signature bat ....Unknown
3x5 index card $250
Photograph/baseball card $350
Typed Letter Signed $200
Handwritten Letter Signed....................$350
HOF plaque postcard ....Impossible
Perez-Steele postcards ....Impossible

Larry MacPhail (1890-1975)   1978

Cut signature $125
Single-signature baseball $1,500
Single-signature bat ....Unknown
3x5 index card $175
Photograph/baseball card $400
Typed Letter Signed $225
Handwritten Letter Signed....................$400
Check $100
HOF plaque postcard ....Impossible
Perez-Steele postcards ....Impossible

Lee MacPhail (1917-)   1998

Cut signature $10
Single-signature baseball $75
Single-signature bat $125
3x5 index card $15
Photograph...$30
HOF plaque postcard $35
Perez-Steele postcard $50

Mickey Mantle (1931-1995)   1974

Cut signature $75
Single-signature baseball $350
Single-signature bat $1,500
3x5 index card $125
Photograph/baseball card $150
HOF plaque postcard $250
Perez-Steele postcards $200

Heinie Manush (1901-1971)   1964

Cut signature $35
Single-signature baseball $2,500
Single-signature bat ....Unknown
3x5 index card $75
Photograph/baseball card $200
Typed Letter Signed $100
Handwritten Letter Signed....................$225
Check $60
HOF plaque postcard $350
Perez-Steele postcards ....Impossible

Rabbit Maranville (1891-1954)   1954

Cut signature $250
Single-signature baseball $3,500
Single-signature bat ....Unknown
3x5 index card $300
Photograph/baseball card $1,000
Typed Letter Signed $600

Handwritten Letter Signed....................$1,250
HOF plaque postcard ....Impossible
Perez-Steele postcards ....Impossible

Juan Marichal (1937-)   1983

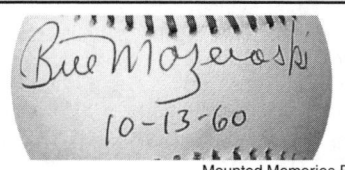
Mounted Memories Photo

Cut signature $8
Single-signature baseball $35
Authenticated baseball $70
Single-signature bat $85
3x5 index card $10
Photograph/baseball card $20
HOF plaque postcard $15
Perez-Steele postcards $20

Rube Marquard (1889-1980)   1971

Cut signature $15
Single-signature baseball $600
Single-signature bat ....Unknown
3x5 index card $20
Photograph/baseball card $150
Typed Letter Signed $75
Handwritten Letter Signed....................$200
HOF plaque postcard $45
Perez-Steele postcards ....Impossible

Eddie Mathews (1931-2001)   1978

Cut signature $10
Single-signature baseball $75
Single-signature bat $125
3x5 index card $15
Photograph/baseball card $30
HOF plaque postcard $20
Perez-Steele postcards $20

Christy Mathewson (1880-1925)   1936

Cut signature $2,000
Single-signature baseball ....Unknown
Single-signature bat ....Unknown
3x5 index card $2,500
Photograph/baseball card $7,500
Typed Letter Signed $4,000
Handwritten Letter Signed.................$10,000
Check $6,000
HOF plaque postcard ....Impossible
Perez-Steele postcards ....Impossible

Willie Mays (1931-)   1979

Mounted Memories Photo

Cut signature $15
Single-signature baseball $85
Authenticated baseball $230
Single-signature bat $200
Authenticated bat $350
3x5 index card $25
Photograph/baseball card $50
Authenticated photograph $180
HOF plaque postcard $45
Perez-Steele postcards $50

Bill Mazeroski (1936-)   2001

Mounted Memories Photo

Cut signature $8
Single-signature baseball $40
Single-signature bat $85
3x5 index card $10
Photograph/baseball card $25
Authenticated photograph $50
HOF plaque postcard $30
Perez-Steele postcards $35

Joe McCarthy (1887-1978)   1957

Cut signature $20
Single-signature baseball $700
Single-signature bat ....Unknown
3x5 index card $40
Photograph/baseball card $125
Typed Letter Signed $50
Handwritten Letter Signed....................$200
HOF plaque postcard $100
Perez-Steele postcards ....Impossible

Tom McCarthy (1864-1922)   1946

Cut signature $2,000
Single-signature baseball ....Unknown
3x5 index card $2,500
Photograph/baseball card ....Unknown
Typed Letter Signed $5,000
HOF plaque postcard ....Impossible
Perez-Steele postcards ....Impossible

Willie McCovey (1938-)   1986

Mounted Memories Photo

Cut signature $8
Single-signature baseball $50
Authenticated baseball $130
Single-signature bat $150
3x5 index card $12
Photograph/baseball card $35
HOF plaque postcard $25
Perez-Steele postcards $25

Joe McGinnity (1871-1929)   1946

Cut signature $3,000
Single-signature baseball ....Unknown
Single-signature bat ....Unknown
Photograph/baseball card ....Unknown
Typed Letter Signed $6,000
HOF plaque postcard ....Impossible
Perez-Steele postcards ....Impossible

Bill McGowan (1871-1954)   1992

Cut signature $200
Single-signature baseball ....Unknown
Single-signature bat ....Unknown
3x5 index card $400
Photograph/baseball card $750
Typed Letter Signed $350
Handwritten Letter Signed....................$800
HOF plaque postcard ....Impossible
Perez-Steele postcards ....Impossible

John McGraw (1873-1934)   1937

Cut signature $700

John J. McGraw [signature]

Single-signature baseball $6,500
Single-signature bat ....Unknown
3x5 index card $750
Photograph/baseball card $3,000
Typed Letter Signed $1,500
Handwritten Letter Signed....................$3,000
HOF plaque postcard ....Impossible
Perez-Steele postcards ....Impossible

Bill McKechnie (1886-1965)   **1962**

Bill McKechnie [signature]

Cut signature.......................................$75
Single-signature baseball $2,000
Single-signature bat ....Unknown
3x5 index card $150
Photograph/baseball card $300
Typed Letter Signed $125
Handwritten Letter Signed......................$300
HOF plaque postcard ....Impossible
Perez-Steele postcards ....Impossible

Bid McPhee (1859-1943)   **2000**

Cut signature .... $5,000-$10,000
Single-signature baseball ....Unknown
3x5 index card ....Unknown
Photograph/baseball card ....Unknown
HOF plaque postcard ....Impossible
Perez-Steele postcards ....Impossible

**Joe "Ducky" Medwick
(1911-1975)**   **1968**

Joe Medwick [signature]

Cut signature.......................................$30
Single-signature baseball $750
3x5 index card $45
Photograph/baseball card $150
Typed Letter Signed $80
Handwritten Letter Signed.....................$200
HOF plaque postcard $125
Perez-Steele postcards ....Impossible

Johnny Mize (1913-1993)   **1981**

Cut signature.......................................$10
Single-signature baseball $125
Single-signature bat $175
3x5 index card $15
Photograph/baseball card $40
Typed Letter Signed $40
Handwritten Letter Signed.......................$75
HOF plaque postcard $20
Perez-Steele postcards $40

Joe Morgan (1943-)   **1990**

Cut signature...$8
Single-signature baseball $35
Authenticated baseball $100
Single-signature bat $100
Authenticated bat $400
3x5 index card $10
Photograph/baseball card $20
Authenticated photograph $100
HOF plaque postcard $20
Perez-Steele postcards $20

Eddie Murray (1956-)   **2003**

Cut signature...$5
Single-signature baseball $100
Authenticated baseball $240
Single-signature bat $150
3x5 index card $10
Photograph/baseball card $75

Stan Musial (1920-)   **1969**

Mounted Memories Photo

Cut signature.......................................$12
Single-signature baseball $60
Authenticated baseball $150
Single-signature bat $150
3x5 index card $20
Photograph/baseball card $40
Authenticated photograph $100
HOF plaque postcard $30
Perez-Steele postcards $80

Hal Newhouser (1921-1998)   **1992**

Cut signature...$5
Single-signature baseball $75
Single-signature bat $100
3x5 index card $10
Photograph/baseball card $30
Typed Letter Signed $40
Handwritten Letter Signed.......................$60
Check $50
HOF plaque postcard $20
Perez-Steele postcards $20

Kid Nichols (1869-1953)   **1949**

Cut signature.....................................$400
Single-signature baseball $5,000
Single-signature bat ....Unknown
3x5 index card $500
Photograph/baseball card $2,500
Typed Letter Signed $750
Handwritten Letter Signed...................$2,500
HOF plaque postcard .... Impossible
Perez-Steele postcards .... Impossible

Phil Niekro (1939-)   **1997**

Cut signature...$8
Single-signature baseball $40
Authenticated baseball $70
Single-signature bat $85
3x5 index card $10
Photograph/baseball card $25
HOF plaque postcard $40
Perez-Steele postcards $40

James O'Rourke (1852-1919)   **1945**

Cut signature........................ $5,000-$10,000
Single-signature baseball ....Unknown
Single-signature bat ....Unknown
Photograph/baseball card ....Unknown
HOF plaque postcard .... Impossible
Perez-Steele postcards .... Impossible

Mel Ott (1909-1958)   **1951**

Mel Ott [signature]

Cut signature.....................................$300

Single-signature baseball $4,500
Single-signature bat ....Unknown
3x5 index card $500
Photograph/baseball card $1,000
Typed Letter Signed $750
Handwritten Letter Signed...................$1,250
Check $2,000
HOF plaque postcard .... Impossible
Perez-Steele postcards .... Impossible

Satchel Paige (1906-1982)   **1971**

Cut signature.....................................$100
Single-signature baseball $1,200
Single-signature bat ....Unknown
3x5 index card $125
Photograph/baseball card $250
HOF plaque postcard $275
Perez-Steele postcards $3,500

Jim Palmer (1945-)   **1990**

[signature]
Mounted Memories Photo

Cut signature.......................................$10
Single-signature baseball $40
Authenticated baseball $125
Single-signature bat $105
3x5 index card $15
Photograph/baseball card $25
Authenticated photograph $40
HOF plaque postcard $30
Perez-Steele postcards $25

Herb Pennock (1894-1948)   **1948**

Cut signature.....................................$275
Single-signature baseball $5,500
Single-signature bat ....Unknown
3x5 index card $300
Photograph/baseball card $1,250
Typed Letter Signed $600
Handwritten Letter Signed...................$1,500
Check $700
HOF plaque postcard .... Impossible
Perez-Steele postcards .... Impossible

Tony Perez (1942-)   **2000**

Cut signature...$8
Single-signature baseball $35
Authenticated baseball $100
Single-signature bat $85
Authenticated bat $300
3x5 index card $10
Photograph/baseball card $20
HOF plaque postcard $25
Perez-Steele postcards $30

Gaylord Perry (1938-)   **1991**

Cut signature...$8
Single-signature baseball $30
Authenticated baseball $80
Single-signature bat $75
3x5 index card $8
Photograph/baseball card $15
Authenticated photograph $60
HOF plaque postcard $12
Perez-Steele postcards $15

Ed Plank (1875-1926)   **1946**

Cut signature...................................$2,500
Single-signature baseball ....Unknown
Single-signature bat ....Unknown
Photograph/baseball card ....Unknown
Typed Letter Signed $5,500
HOF plaque postcard .... Impossible
Perez-Steele postcards .... Impossible

Kirby Puckett (1960-)   2001

Cut signature $10
Single-signature baseball $80
Authenticated baseball $210
Single-signature bat $150
3x5 index card $20
Photograph/baseball card $50
HOF plaque postcard $60
Perez-Steele postcards $60

Charles Radbourne (1854-1897)   1939

Cut signature .... $10,000-$20,000
Single-signature baseball ....Unknown
Single-signature bat ....Unknown
Photograph/baseball card ....Unknown
HOF plaque postcard ....Impossible
Perez-Steele postcards ....Impossible

Pee Wee Reese (1918-1999)   1984

Cut signature $10
Single-signature baseball $100
Single-signature bat $175
3x5 index card $15
Photograph/baseball card $60
HOF plaque postcard $50
Perez-Steele postcards $60

Sam Rice (1890-1974)   1963

Cut signature $35
Single-signature baseball $1,500
Single-signature bat ....Unknown
3x5 index card $90
Photograph/baseball card $225
Typed Letter Signed $100
Handwritten Letter Signed...............$250
HOF plaque postcard $175
Perez-Steele postcards ....Impossible

Branch Rickey (1881-1965)   1967

Cut signature $125
Single-signature baseball $2,500
Single-signature bat ....Unknown
3x5 index card $300
Typed Letter Signed $225
Handwritten Letter Signed...............$400
Photograph/baseball card $400
HOF plaque postcard ....Impossible
Perez-Steele postcards ....Impossible

Eppa Rixey (1891-1963)   1963

Cut signature $125
Single-signature baseball $3,500
Single-signature bat ....Unknown
3x5 index card $200
Photograph/baseball card $750
Typed Letter Signed $300
Handwritten Letter Signed...............$750
Check $150
HOF plaque postcard ....Impossible
Perez-Steele postcards ....Impossible

Phil Rizzuto (1917-)   1994

Cut signature $8
Single-signature baseball $40
Authenticated baseball $130

Mounted Memories Photo

Single-signature bat $100
Authenticated bat $300
3x5 index card $10
Photograph/baseball card $30
Authenticated photograph $80
HOF plaque postcard $35
Perez-Steele postcards $30

Robin Roberts (1926-)   1976

Cut signature $8
Single-signature baseball $30
Authenticated baseball $90
Single-signature bat $75
3x5 index card $8
Photograph/baseball card $15
Authenticated photograph $40
HOF plaque postcard $10
Perez-Steele postcards $20

Brooks Robinson (1937-)   1983

Cut signature $8
Single-signature baseball $35
Authenticated baseball $120
Single-signature bat $100
Authenticated bat $350
3x5 index card $10
Photograph/baseball card $20
HOF plaque postcard $10
Perez-Steele postcards $20

Frank Robinson (1935-)   1982

Cut signature $8
Single-signature baseball $45
Authenticated baseball $110
Single-signature bat $165
3x5 index card $10
Photograph/baseball card $30
HOF plaque postcard $20
Perez-Steele postcards $25

Jackie Robinson (1919-1972)   1962

Cut signature $225
Single-signature baseball $2,250
Single-signature bat ....Unknown
3x5 index card $400
Photograph/baseball card $700
Typed Letter Signed $500
Handwritten Letter Signed...............$800
Check $250
HOF plaque postcard $700
Perez-Steele postcards ....Impossible

Wilbert Robinson (1863-1934)   1945

Cut signature $750
Single-signature baseball $8,000
Single-signature bat ....Unknown
3x5 index card $800
Photograph/baseball card $2,500
Typed Letter Signed $1,500
Handwritten Letter Signed...............$3,500
HOF plaque postcard ....Impossible
Perez-Steele postcards ....Impossible

Joe "Bullet" Rogan (1889-1967)   1998

Cut signature $2,500
Single-signature baseball $7,500
Single-signature bat ....Unknown
3x5 index card $2,500
Photograph ....Unknown

HOF plaque postcard ....Impossible
Perez-Steele postcards ....Impossible

Edd Roush (1893-1988)   1962

Cut signature $10
Single-signature baseball $300
Single-signature bat ....Unknown
3x5 index card $15
Photograph/baseball card $50
Typed Letter Signed $50
Handwritten Letter Signed...............$150
Check $35
HOF plaque postcard $35
Perez-Steele postcards $65

Red Ruffing (1904-1986)   1967

Cut signature $20
Single-signature baseball $400
Single-signature bat ....Unknown
3x5 index card $45
Photograph/baseball card $125
Typed Letter Signed $75
Handwritten Letter Signed...............$225
Check $150
HOF plaque postcard $150
Perez-Steele postcards $425

Amos Rusie (1871-1942)   1977

Cut signature $1,500
Single-signature baseball ....Unknown
Single-signature bat ....Unknown
Photograph/baseball card ....Unknown
Typed Letter Signed $4,000
HOF plaque postcard ....Impossible
Perez-Steele postcards ....Impossible

Babe Ruth (1895-1948)   1936

Cut signature $1,000
Single-signature baseball $6,000
3x5 index card $1,500
Photograph/baseball card $3,500
Typed Letter Signed $3,500
Handwritten Letter Signed...............$8,000
Check $1,750
HOF plaque postcard ....Impossible
Perez-Steele postcards ....Impossible

Nolan Ryan (1947-)   1999

Tri-Star Productions Photo

Cut signature $10
Single-signature baseball $90
Authenticated baseball $210
Single-signature bat $150
3x5 index card $15
Photograph/baseball card $50
Authenticated photo $100
HOF plaque postcard $75
Perez-Steele postcards $75

Ray Schalk (1892-1970) — 1955

Cut signature	$40
Single-signature baseball	$1,500
Single-signature bat	Unknown
3x5 index card	$100
Photograph/baseball card	$275
Typed Letter Signed	$125
Handwritten Letter Signed	$300
HOF plaque postcard	$300
Perez-Steele postcards	Impossible

Mike Schmidt (1949-) — 1995

Steiner Sports Photo

Item	Price
Cut signature	$10
Single-signature baseball	$70
Authenticated baseball	$180
Single-signature bat	$160
3x5 index card	$15
Photograph/baseball card	$60
Authenticated photograph	$140
HOF plaque postcard	$60
Perez-Steele postcards	$60

Al "Red" Schoendienst (1923-) — 1989

Cut signature	$8
Single-signature baseball	$40
Authenticated baseball	$70
Single-signature bat	$85
3x5 index card	$8
Photograph/baseball card	$20
HOF plaque postcard	$15
Perez-Steele postcards	$20

Tom Seaver (1944-) — 1992

Mounted Memories Photo

Item	Price
Cut signature	$10
Single-signature baseball	$50
Authenticated baseball	$120
Single-signature bat	$125
3x5 index card	$15
Photograph/baseball card	$35
Authenticated photograph	$100
HOF plaque postcard	$45
Perez-Steele postcards	$40

Frank Selee (1859-1909) — 1999

Cut signature	$10,000-$20,000
Single-signature baseball	Unknown
Single-signature bat	Unknown
3x5 index card	$600
Photograph/baseball card	Unknown
HOF plaque postcard	Impossible
Perez-Steele postcards	Impossible

Joe Sewell (1898-1990) — 1977

Cut signature	$5
Single-signature baseball	$100
Single-signature bat	$200
3x5 index card	$8
Photograph/baseball card	$40
Typed Letter Signed	$40
Handwritten Letter Signed	$75
Check	$25
HOF plaque postcard	$15
Perez-Steele postcards	$50

Al Simmons (1902-1956) — 1953

Cut signature	$150
Single-signature baseball	$3,000
Single-signature bat	Unknown
3x5 index card	$325
Photograph/baseball card	$700
Typed Letter Signed	$425
Handwritten Letter Signed	$750
Check	$400
HOF plaque postcard	Impossible
Perez-Steele postcards	Impossible

George Sisler (1893-1973) — 1939

Cut signature	$25
Single-signature baseball	$1,750
Single-signature bat	Unknown
3x5 index card	$90
Photograph/baseball card	$300
Typed Letter Signed	$125
Handwritten Letter Signed	$450
Check	$300
HOF plaque postcard	$175
Perez-Steele postcards	Impossible

Enos Slaughter (1916-2002) — 1985

Mounted Memories Photo

Item	Price
Cut signature	$8
Single-signature baseball	$40
Single-signature bat	$85
3x5 index card	$8
Photograph/baseball card	$20
Authenticated photograph	$60
HOF plaque postcard	$10
Perez-Steele postcards	$20

Hilton Smith (1907-1983) — 2001

Cut signature	$400
Single-signature baseball	Unknown
Single-signature bat	Unknown
3x5 index card	$800
Photograph/baseball card	Unknown
HOF plaque postcard	Impossible
Perez-Steele postcards	Impossible

Ozzie Smith (1954-) — 2002

Steiner Sports Photo

Item	Price
Cut signature	$5
Single-signature baseball	$55
Authenticated baseball	$150
Single-signature bat	Unknown
Authenticated bat	$360
Photograph/baseball card	$35
Authenticated photograph	$130
HOF plaque postcard	$50

Duke Snider (1926-) — 1980

Cut signature	$8
Single-signature baseball	$50
Authenticated baseball	$150
Single-signature bat	$125
3x5 index card	$12
Photograph/baseball card	$25
Authenticated photograph	$80
HOF plaque postcard	$18
Perez-Steele postcards	$25

Warren Spahn (1921-2003) — 1973

Mounted Memories Photo

Item	Price
Cut signature	$8
Single-signature baseball	$40
Authenticated baseball	$80
Single-signature bat	$85
3x5 index card	$10
Photograph/baseball card	$25
Authenticated Photo	$60
HOF plaque postcard	$10
Perez-Steele postcards	$25

Al Spalding (1850-1915) — 1939

Cut signature	$750
Single-signature baseball	Unknown
Single-signature bat	Unknown
3x5 index card	$1,750
Photograph/baseball card	Unknown
Typed Letter Signed	$1,500
Handwritten Letter Signed	$4,000
HOF plaque postcard	Impossible
Perez-Steele postcards	Impossible

Tris Speaker (1888-1958) — 1937

Cut signature	$300
Single-signature baseball	$3,500
Single-signature bat	Unknown
3x5 index card	$400
Photograph/baseball card	$1,250
Typed Letter Signed	$750
Handwritten Letter Signed	$1,500
HOF plaque postcard	Impossible
Perez-Steele postcards	Impossible

Willie Stargell (1940-2001) — 1988

Mounted Memories Photo

Item	Price
Cut signature	$15
Single-signature baseball	$75
Single-signature bat	$120
3x5 index card	$20
Photograph/baseball card	$30
HOF plaque postcard	$28
Perez-Steele postcards	$30

Turkey Stearnes (1901-1979) — 2000

Cut signature	$500

Single-signature baseball ....Unknown
3x5 index card $1,200
Photograph/baseball card ....Unknown
HOF plaque postcard ....Impossible
Perez-Steele postcards ....Impossible

Casey Stengel (1890-1975)   1966

Cut signature $35
Single-signature baseball $750
Single-signature bat ....Unknown
3x5 index card $80
Photograph/baseball card $250
Typed Letter Signed $125
Handwritten Letter Signed.....................$300
Check $150
HOF plaque postcard $175
Perez-Steele postcards ....Impossible

Don Sutton (1945-)   1998

Cut signature $8
Single-signature baseball $40
Authenticated baseball $115
Single-signature bat $80
3x5 index card $10
Photograph/baseball card $30

Bill Terry (1898-1989)   1954

Cut signature $10
Single-signature baseball $275
Single-signature bat $500
3x5 index card $25
Photograph/baseball card $40
Typed Letter Signed $50
Handwritten Letter Signed.......................$100
Check $30
HOF plaque postcard $45
Perez-Steele postcards $80

Sam Thompson (1860-1922)   1974

Cut signature .... $7,500-$15,000
Single-signature baseball ....Unknown
Single-signature bat ....Unknown
Photograph/baseball card ....Unknown
HOF plaque postcard ....Impossible
Perez-Steele postcards ....Impossible

Joe Tinker (1880-1948)   1946

Cut signature $700
Single-signature baseball $6,500
Single-signature bat ....Unknown
3x5 index card $800
Photograph/baseball card $4,000
Typed Letter Signed $1,500
Handwritten Letter Signed.................$4,000
HOF plaque postcard ....Impossible
Perez-Steele postcards ....Impossible

Pie Traynor (1899-1972)   1948

Cut signature $75
Single-signature baseball $1,250

Single-signature bat ....Unknown
3x5 index card $175
Photograph/baseball card $275
Typed Letter Signed $200
Handwritten Letter Signed.....................$400
Check $375
HOF plaque postcard $500
Perez-Steele postcards .... Impossible

Dazzy Vance (1891-1961)   1955

Cut signature $150
Single-signature baseball $2,750
Single-signature bat ....Unknown
3x5 index card $300
Photograph/baseball card $550
Typed Letter Signed $375
Handwritten Letter Signed.....................$600
Check $1,000
HOF plaque postcard .... Impossible
Perez-Steele postcards .... Impossible

Arky Vaughan (1912-1952)   1985

Cut signature $250
Single-signature baseball $3,000
Single-signature bat ....Unknown
3x5 index card $300
Photograph/baseball card $750
Typed Letter Signed $500
Handwritten Letter Signed.....................$1,000
HOF plaque postcard .... Impossible
Perez-Steele postcards .... Impossible

Bill Veeck (1914-1986)   1991

Cut signature $50
Single-signature baseball $750
Single-signature bat ....Unknown
3x5 index card $150
Photograph/baseball card $250
Typed Letter Signed $100
Handwritten Letter Signed.....................$275
HOF plaque postcard .... Impossible
Perez-Steele postcards .... Impossible

Rube Waddell (1876-1914)   1946

Cut signature .... $10,000-$20,000
Single-signature baseball ....Unknown
Single-signature bat ....Unknown
Photograph/baseball card ....Unknown
HOF plaque postcard .... Impossible
Perez-Steele postcards .... Impossible

Honus Wagner (1874-1955)   1936

Cut signature $350
Single-signature baseball $5,000
Single-signature bat ....Unknown
3x5 index card $400

Photograph/baseball card $1,500
Typed Letter Signed $1,250
Handwritten Letter Signed.................$2,750
Check $800
HOF plaque postcard .... Impossible
Perez-Steele postcards .... Impossible

Bobby Wallace (1873-1960)   1953

Cut signature $250
Single-signature baseball $4,000
Single-signature bat ....Unknown
3x5 index card $300
Photograph/baseball card $1,000
Typed Letter Signed $500
Handwritten Letter Signed...................$1,000
HOF plaque postcard .... Impossible
Perez-Steele postcards .... Impossible

Ed Walsh (1881-1959)   1946

Cut signature $175
Single-signature baseball $3,250
3x5 index card $275
Photograph/baseball card $750
Typed Letter Signed $450
Handwritten Letter Signed.....................$900
HOF plaque postcard .... Impossible
Perez-Steele postcards .... Impossible

Lloyd Waner (1906-1982)   1967

Cut signature $10
Single-signature baseball $450
Single-signature bat ....Unknown
3x5 index card $20
Photograph/baseball card $75
Typed Letter Signed $50
Handwritten Letter Signed.....................$100
Check $50
HOF plaque postcard $30
Perez-Steele postcards $3,500

Paul Waner (1903-1965)   1952

Cut signature $125
Single-signature baseball $2,000
Single-signature bat ....Unknown
3x5 index card $300
Photograph/baseball card $500
Typed Letter Signed $300
Handwritten Letter Signed.....................$600
HOF plaque postcard .... Impossible
Perez-Steele postcards .... Impossible

Monte Ward (1860-1925)   1964

Cut signature $3,000
Single-signature baseball ....Unknown
Single-signature bat ....Unknown
Photograph/baseball card ....Unknown
HOF plaque postcard .... Impossible
Perez-Steele postcards .... Impossible

Earl Weaver (1930-)   1996

Cut signature $8
Single-signature baseball $35
Authenticated baseball $85
Single-signature bat $75
3x5 index card $8
Photograph/baseball card $20
HOF plaque/postcard $30
Perez-Steele postcards $30

George Weiss (1895-1972)   1971

Cut signature $50
Single-signature baseball $2,000
Single-signature bat ....Unknown
3x5 index card $150
Photograph/baseball card $400
Typed Letter Signed $125
Handwritten Letter Signed.....................$400
Check $400
HOF plaque postcard ....Unknown
Perez-Steele postcards ....Impossible

Mickey Welch (1859-1941)   1973

Cut signature $2,500
Single-signature baseball ....Unknown
Single-signature bat ....Unknown
3x5 index card $2,750
Photograph/baseball card ....Unknown
HOF plaque postcard ....Impossible
Perez-Steele postcards ....Impossible

Willie Wells (1905-1989)   1997

Cut signature $350
Single-signature baseball $1,500
Single-signature bat ....Unknown
3x5 index card $500
Photograph/baseball card $600
HOF plaque postcard ....Impossible
Perez-Steele postcards ....Impossible

Zack Wheat (1888-1972)   1959

Cut signature $30
Single-signature baseball $1,000
Single-signature bat ....Unknown
3x5 index card $80
Photograph/baseball card $225
Typed Letter Signed $125
Handwritten Letter Signed.....................$350
Check $100
HOF plaque postcard $350
Perez-Steele postcards ....Impossible

Hoyt Wilhelm (1923-2002)   1985

Cut signature $8
Single-signature baseball $40
Single-signature bat $75
3x5 index card $8
Photograph/baseball card $20
HOF plaque postcard $15
Perez-Steele postcards $20

Billy Williams (1938-)   1987

Cut signature $8
Single-signature baseball $40
Authenticated ball $80
Single-signature bat $85
3x5 index card $8
Photograph/baseball card $20
HOF plaque postcard $12
Perez-Steele postcards $15

Smokey Joe Williams (1885-1951)   1999

Cut signature $2,000

Single-signature baseball ....Unknown
Single-signature bat ....Unknown
3x5 index card $3,000
Photograph/baseball card ....Unknown
HOF plaque postcard ....Impossible
Perez-Steele postcards ....Impossible

Ted Williams (1918-2002)   1966

Cut signature $40
Single-signature baseball $350
Authenticated baseball $1,300
Single-signature bat $1,000
Authenticated bat $2,500
3x5 index card $100
Photograph/baseball card $150
HOF plaque postcard $250
Perez-Steele postcards $300

Vic Willis (1876-1947)   1995

Cut signature $1,500
Single-signature baseball ....Unknown
Single-signature bat ....Unknown
Photograph/baseball card ....Unknown
HOF plaque postcard ....Impossible
Perez-Steele postcards ....Impossible

Hack Wilson (1900-1948)   1979

Cut signature $550
Single-signature baseball $6,000
Single-signature bat ....Unknown
3x5 index card $600
Photograph/baseball card $2,750
Typed Letter Signed $1,250
Handwritten Letter Signed..................$3,500
Check $2,000
HOF plaque postcard ....Impossible
Perez-Steele postcards ....Impossible

Dave Winfield (1951-)   2001

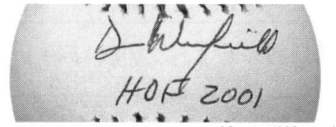

Mounted Memories Photo

Cut signature $10
Single-signature baseball $60
Authenticated baseball $150
Single-signature bat $200
Authenticated bat $400
3x5 index card $10
Photograph/baseball card $35
Authenticated photograph $130
HOF plaque postcard $60
Perez-Steele postcards $60

George Wright (1847-1937)   1937

Cut signature $800
Single-signature baseball ....Unknown
Single-signature bat ....Unknown
3x5 index card $1,200
Photograph/baseball card ....Unknown
Typed Letter Signed $2,500
HOF plaque postcard ....Impossible
Perez-Steele postcards ....Impossible

Harry Wright (1835-1895)   1953

Cut signature $2,500
Single-signature baseball ....Unknown
Single-signature bat ....Unknown
Photograph/baseball card ....Unknown
Typed Letter Signed $5,500
HOF plaque postcard ....Impossible

Perez-Steele postcards ....Impossible

Early Wynn (1920-1999)   1972

Cut signature $8
Single-signature baseball $75
Single-signature bat $100
3x5 index card $12
Photograph/baseball card $35
HOF plaque postcard $25
Perez-Steele postcards $25

Carl Yastrzemski (1939-)   1989

Cut signature $10
Single-signature baseball $75
Authenticated baseball $210
Single-signature bat $150
3x5 index card $15
Photograph/baseball card $40
HOF plaque postcard $45
Perez-Steele postcards $35

Tom Yawkey (1903-1976)   1980

Cut signature $125
Single-signature baseball $2,000
Single-signature bat ....Unknown
3x5 index card $300
Photograph/baseball card $500
Typed Letter Signed $250
Handwritten Letter Signed.....................$500
HOF plaque postcard ....Impossible
Perez-Steele postcards ....Impossible

Cy Young (1867-1955)   1937

Cut signature $300
Single-signature baseball $3,500
Single-signature bat ....Unknown
3x5 index card $350
Photograph/baseball card $1,500
Typed Letter Signed $750
Handwritten Letter Signed..................$2,500
HOF plaque postcard ....Impossible
Perez-Steele postcards ....Impossible

Ross Youngs (1897-1927)   1972

Cut signature $1,500
Single-signature baseball ....Unknown
Single-signature bat ....Unknown
Photograph/baseball card ....Unknown
Typed Letter Signed $3,500
HOF plaque postcard ....Impossible
Perez-Steele postcards ....Impossible

Robin Yount (1955-)   1999

Cut signature $8
Single-signature baseball $75
Authenticated baseball $150
Single-signature bat $125
3x5 index card $12
Photograph/baseball card $40
HOF plaque postcard $60
Perez-Steele postcards $60

ACTIVE BASEBALL PLAYER AUTOGRAPHS

In the years following our national pastime's World Series-stopping strike of 1994 and early 1995, Major League Baseball embarked on a mission to win back its fans. One of the methods, in theory, was for players to be more accommodating to autograph requests. Not surprisingly, many players carried out the mission and continue to do so. (Cal Ripken Jr., for example, has always been a model for other players in the area of fan interaction; he built his reputation in large part by signing for as many fans as he possibly could before or after a game.) Other players, though, try to avoid autograph requests.

Ultimately, though, the demand for autographs outweighs the time a star player can devote to signing. Derek Jeter, Mike Piazza and Alex Rodriguez couldn't possibly fulfill every request for an autograph; if they sign for 50 people during batting practice before a game, there may be hundreds of others who get "shut out." Some players hesitate to sign even one autograph because it opens a veritable floodgate of other requests. Unlike Hall of Famers and retired players—who may go months at a time without mention in the media—today's stars are in the news practically every day during the season. Many of them are so recognizable that they get autograph requests whenever they're in a public place. Unfortunately for collectors, these heavy everyday demands on players make their autographs difficult to obtain.

But none of this means that autograph collectors should stop asking today's players to sign a ball or photo or card. Persistence is the key to this hobby. With some players, you may actually have to wait until they retire (that's persistence). Retired players, as we know, have the time to make several autograph show appearances a year—appearances that can supplement their income. (On the other hand, today's stars may never need any extra income.)

So where can you get autographs from active players? The best time remains at spring training. Teams work out from mid-February through late March in either Florida or Arizona, and the atmosphere is much more relaxed than during the season, so players are generally more willing to sign.

Spring training is also the best time to snag autographs of up-and-coming players who may become less and less accessible as their stars rise. Mark Prior of the Chicago Cubs, Dontrelle Willis of the Florida Marlins and, of course, former Japanese home run champion Hideki Matsui of the New York Yankees will get much more swamped with autograph requests in coming years than what they experienced in their first spring training camps.

If you can't make it to Florida or Arizona in February or March, the end of the winter is a good time to start mailing requests to players in care of their respective teams' spring training headquarters. (Such publications as *USA Today's Baseball Weekly* list spring training addresses during the off-season.) You'll find the response rate for mail-order requests is better during spring training than it is during the season.

The most obvious place to try for in-person autographs of current players is at the ballpark during the regular season. But the competition from other fans and collectors can be fierce, even if you take the steps outlined in "Collecting Strategy." If you want a little less competition, keep an eye on events calendars in your local newspapers. An athlete's occasional speaking engagement, promotional appearance, seminar or charity dinner can provide autograph opportunities that don't necessarily draw a crowd.

Active Players' Autographs

Jeff Abbott

Ball	$25
Photo	$12
3x5 Index Card	$3
Bat	$40

Bobby Abreu

Ball	$35
Authenticated Ball	$80
Photo	$20
3x5 Index Card	$5
Bat	$50

Juan Acevedo

Ball	$25
Photo	$12
3x5 Index Card	$3
Bat	$40

Antonio Alfonseca

Ball	$25
Authenticated Ball	$110
Photo	$12
Authenticated Photo	$80
3x5 Index Card	$3
Bat	$40

Edgardo Alfonzo

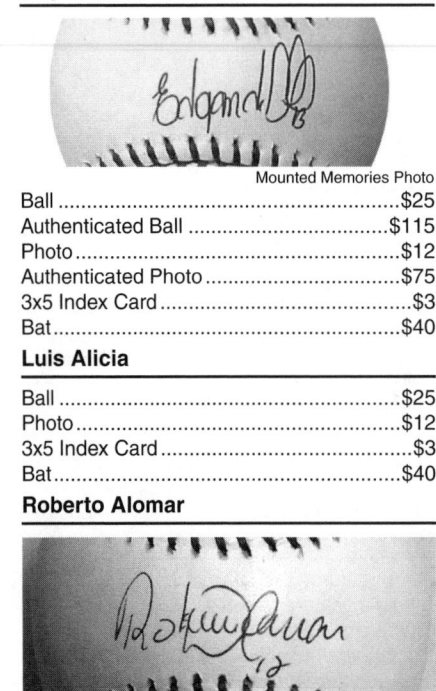

Mounted Memories Photo

Ball	$25
Authenticated Ball	$115
Photo	$12
Authenticated Photo	$75
3x5 Index Card	$3
Bat	$40

Luis Alicia

Ball	$25
Photo	$12
3x5 Index Card	$3
Bat	$40

Roberto Alomar

Steiner Sports Photo

Ball	$40

Authenticated Ball	$180
Photo	$25
3x5 Index Card	$5
Bat	$60

Sandy Alomar Jr.

Ball	$30
Photo	$15
3x5 Index Card	$5
Bat	$40

Moises Alou

Ball	$35
Photo	$20
3x5 Index Card	$5
Bat	$60

Wilson Alvarez

Ball	$25
Photo	$15
3x5 Index Card	$3
Bat	$40

Brady Anderson

Ball	$35
Photo	$20
3x5 Index Card	$5
Bat	$50

Brian Anderson

Ball	$25
Photo	$12

3x5 Index Card $3
Bat $40

Garret Anderson

Ball $30
Authenticated Ball $110
Photo $15
3x5 Index Card $3
Bat $50

Rich Ankiel

Ball $25
Photo $12
3x5 Index Card $5
Bat $40

Kevin Appier

Ball $30
Photo $15
3x5 Index Card $3
Bat $50

Tony Armas Jr.

Ball $25
Authenticated Ball $60
Photo $15
3x5 Index Card $3
Bat $40

Andy Ashby

Ball $25
Photo $12
3x5 Index Card $3
Bat $40

Pedro Astacio

Ball $25
Photo $12
3x5 Index Card $3
Bat $40

Rich Aurilia

Ball $25
Photo $10
Authenticated Photo $40
3x5 Index Card $3
Bat $40

Brad Ausmus

Ball $25
Photo $10
3x5 Index Card $3
Bat $40

Carlos Baerga

Ball $25
Photo $10
3x5 Index Card $3
Bat $40

Jeff Bagwell

Tri-Star Productions Photo

Ball $40
Authenticated Ball $195
Photo $30
Authenticated Photo $70
3x5 Index Card $10
Bat $100
Authenticated Bat $330

Rocco Baldelli

Ball $35

Photo $20
3x5 Index Card $5
Bat $50

James Baldwin

Ball $30
Photo $15
3x5 Index Card $3
Bat $50

Michael Barrett

Ball $25
Photo $10
3x5 Index Card $3
Bat $40

Tony Batista

Ball $30
Photo $15
3x5 Index Card $3
Bat $50

Danny Bautista

Ball $25
Photo $10
3x5 Index Card $3
Bat $40

Rod Beck

Ball $30
Photo $15
3x5 Index Card $5
Bat $50

Josh Beckett

Ball $25
Authenticated Ball $100
Photo $15
3x5 Index Card $3
Bat $40

David Bell

Ball $30
Photo $15
3x5 Index Card $3
Bat $50

Jay Bell

Ball $30
Photo $15
3x5 Index Card $3
Bat $40

Mark Bellhorn

Ball $30
Photo $15
3x5 Index Card $3
Bat $40

Ronnie Belliard

Ball $25
Photo $10
3x5 Index Card $3
Bat $40

Carlos Beltran

Ball $25
Authenticated Ball $60
Photo $10
3x5 Index Card $3
Bat $40

Adrian Beltre

Ball $25
Photo $10
Authenticated Photo $25

3x5 Index Card $3
Bat $40

Armando Benitez

Ball $35
Photo $20
3x5 Index Card $3
Bat $50

Mike Benjamin

Ball $25
Photo $10
3x5 Index Card $3
Bat $40

Kris Benson

Ball $25
Photo $10
3x5 Index Card $3
Bat $40

Jason Bere

Ball $30
Photo $15
3x5 Index Card $3
Bat $40

Lance Berkman

Tri-Star Productions Photo

Ball $40
Authenticated Ball $120
Photo $25
Authenticated Photo $50
3x5 Index Card $5
Bat $60
Authenticated Bat $320

Craig Biggio

Tri-Star Productions Photo

Ball $40
Authenticated Ball $125
Photo $25
Authenticated Photo $60
3x5 Index Card $5
Bat $60

Hank Blalock

Ball $30
Authenticated Ball $70
Photo $20
3x5 Index Card $3
Bat $50

Geoff Blum

Ball $25
Photo $10
3x5 Index Card $3
Bat $40

Barry Bonds

Ball $175
Authenticated Ball $300
Photo $100
Authenticated Photo $200
3x5 Index Card $25
Bat $500
Authenticated Bat $700

Aaron Boone

Ball $30
Photo $15
3x5 Index Card $3
Bat $50

Bret Boone

Ball $35
Photo $20
3x5 Index Card $5
Bat $60

Pedro Borbon

Ball $25
Photo $10
3x5 Index Card $3
Bat $40

Mike Bordick

Ball $30
Authenticated Ball $75
Photo $15
3x5 Index Card $3
Bat $50

Joe Borowski

Ball $25
Photo $15
3x5 Index Card $3
Bat $40

Ricky Bottalico

Ball $25
Photo $10
3x5 Index Card $3
Bat $40

Jeff Brantley

Ball $25
Photo $10
3x5 Index Card $3
Bat $40

Milton Bradley

Ball $30
Photo $20
3x5 Index Card $3
Bat $50

Darren Bragg

Ball $25
Photo $10
3x5 Index Card $3
Bat $40

Russ Branyan

Ball $25
Photo $10
3x5 Index Card $3
Bat $40

Doug Brocail

Ball $25
Photo $10
3x5 Index Card $3
Bat $40

Dee Brown

Ball $25

Photo $10
3x5 Index Card $3
Bat $40

Kevin Brown

Ball $50
Photo $35
3x5 Index Card $10
Bat $75

Mark Buehrle

Mounted Memories Photo

Ball $30
Photo $15
Authenticated Photo $35
3x5 Index Card $3
Bat $50

Dave Burba

Ball $25
Photo $10
3x5 Index Card $3
Bat $40

John Burkett

Ball $30
Photo $15
3x5 Index Card $3
Bat $40

Ellis Burks

Ball $35
Photo $20
3x5 Index Card $5
Bat $60

A. J. Burnett

Ball $25
Authenticated Ball $80
Photo $12
3x5 Index Card $3
Bat $40

Jeromy Burnitz

Ball $30
Authenticated Ball $80
Photo $15
3x5 Index Card $3
Bat $40

Pat Burrell

Ball $35
Authenticated Ball $100
Photo $20
3x5 Index Card $5
Bat $50

Sean Burroughs

Ball $30
Photo $15
3x5 Index Card $3
Bat $50

Paul Byrd

Ball $25
Photo $15
3x5 Index Card $3
Bat $40

Eric Byrnes

Ball $30
Photo $15
3x5 Index Card $3
Bat $40

Miguel Cairo

Ball $25
Photo $10
3x5 Index Card $3
Bat $40

Mike Cameron

Ball $30
Photo $15
3x5 Index Card $3
Bat $40

Chris Carpenter

Ball $25
Photo $10
3x5 Index Card $3
Bat $40

Mike Caruso

Ball $25
Photo $10
3x5 Index Card $3
Bat $40

Sean Casey

Ball $35
Authenticated Ball $80
Photo $20
Authenticated Photo $35
3x5 Index Card $5
Bat $60
Authenticated Bat $75

Vinny Castilla

Mounted Memories Photo

Ball $30
Photo $15
3x5 Index Card $5
Bat $50

Roger Cedeno

Ball $25
Photo $15
3x5 Index Card $3
Bat $40

Shawn Chacon

Ball $30
Photo $15
3x5 Index Card $3
Bat $50

Eric Chavez

Ball $25
Authenticated Ball $50
Photo $10
Authenticated Photo $35
3x5 Index Card $3
Bat $40

Jeff Cirillo

Ball $25
Authenticated Ball $60
Photo $12

Steiner Sports Photo

Authenticated Photo $40
3x5 Index Card $3
Bat $40

Tony Clark

Ball $30
Authenticated Ball $80
Photo $15
3x5 Index Card $3
Bat $50
Authenticated Bat $100

Royce Clayton

Ball $25
Photo $10
3x5 Index Card $3
Bat $40

Roger Clemens

Tri-Star Productions Photo

Ball $125
Authenticated Ball $400
Photo $75
Authenticated Photo $125
3x5 Index Card $20
Bat $250

Matt Clement

Ball $30
Photo $15
3x5 Index Card $3
Bat $40

Bartolo Colon

Ball $30
Photo $15
3x5 Index Card $5
Bat $50

Jeff Conine

Mounted Memories Photo

Ball $30
Photo $15
3x5 Index Card $3
Bat $50

Ron Coomer

Ball $25
Photo $10
3x5 Index Card $3
Bat $40

Marty Cordova

Ball $25
Authenticated Ball $70
Photo $12
Authenticated Photo $40

Steiner Sports Photo

3x5 Index Card $3
Bat $40

Rheal Cormier

Ball $25
Photo $12
3x5 Index Card $3
Bat $40

Craig Counsell

Ball $25
Photo $10
3x5 Index Card $3
Bat $40

Deivi Cruz

Ball $25
Photo $12
3x5 Index Card $3
Bat $40

Jose Cruz Jr.

Ball $35
Authenticated Ball $75
Photo $20
3x5 Index Card $5
Bat $60
Authenticated Bat $75

Omar Daal

Ball $35
Photo $20
3x5 Index Card $3
Bat $50

Johnny Damon

Ball $30
Authenticated Ball $40
Photo $15
Authenticated Photo $20
3x5 Index Card $5
Bat $50

Brian Daubach

Ball $25
Photo $10
3x5 Index Card $3
Bat $40

Carlos Delgado

Ball $40
Authenticated Ball $160
Photo $30
Authenticated Photo $35
3x5 Index Card $5
Bat $75

Ryan Dempster

Ball $25
Authenticated Ball $75
Photo $10
3x5 Index Card $3
Bat $40

Delino DeShields

Ball $25
Photo $10

3x5 Index Card $3
Bat $40

Mike DiFelice

Ball $25
Photo $10
3x5 Index Card $3
Bat $40

Darren Dreifort

Ball $25
Photo $15
3x5 Index Card $3
Bat $40

J. D. Drew

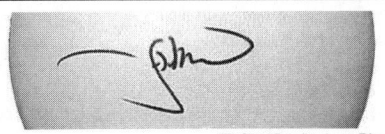
Tri-Star Productions Photo

Ball $40
Authenticated Ball $100
Photo $25
Authenticated Photo $60
3x5 Index Card $10
Bat $75
Authenticated Bat $100

Adam Dunn

Mounted Memories Photo

Ball $40
Authenticated Ball $115
Photo $25
Authenticated Photo $40
3x5 Index Card $10
Bat $75

Shawon Dunston

Ball $25
Photo $15
3x5 Index Card $3
Bat $40

Erubiel Durazo

Ball $30
Photo $20
3x5 Index Card $3
Bat $50

Ray Durham

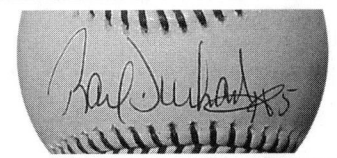
Mounted Memories Photo

Ball $25
Authenticated Ball $50
Photo $12
3x5 Index Card $3
Bat $40

Jermaine Dye

Ball $30
Authenticated Ball $80
Photo $15
3x5 Index Card $3
Bat $40

Damion Easley

Ball	$25
Photo	$10
3x5 Index Card	$3
Bat	$40

David Eckstein

Ball	$25
Photo	$10
3x5 Index Card	$3
Bat	$40

Jim Edmonds

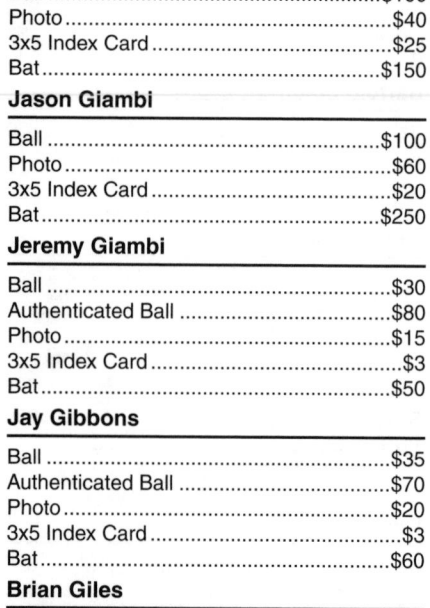

Tri-Star Productions Photo

Ball	$40
Photo	$25
3x5 Index Card	$5
Bat	$60

Scott Elarton

Ball	$25
Photo	$10
3x5 Index Card	$3
Bat	$40

Alan Embree

Ball	$25
Photo	$10
3x5 Index Card	$3
Bat	$40

Juan Encarnacion

Ball	$25
Photo	$10
3x5 Index Card	$3
Bat	$40

Scott Erickson

Ball	$30
Photo	$20
3x5 Index Card	$3
Bat	$50

Darin Erstad

Ball	$25
Photo	$10
3x5 Index Card	$3
Bat	$40

Shawn Estes

Ball	$25
Photo	$10
3x5 Index Card	$3
Bat	$40

Carl Everett

Ball	$30
Photo	$15
3x5 Index Card	$3
Bat	$40

Jorge Fabregas

Ball	$25
Photo	$10
3x5 Index Card	$3
Bat	$40

Jeff Fassero

Ball	$25
Photo	$10

3x5 Index Card	$3
Bat	$40

Carlos Febles

Ball	$25
Photo	$10
3x5 Index Card	$3
Bat	$40

Mike Fetters

Ball	$25
Photo	$10
3x5 Index Card	$3
Bat	$40

Robert Fick

Ball	$25
Authenticated Ball	$60
Photo	$10
3x5 Index Card	$3
Bat	$40

Steve Finley

Ball	$25
Photo	$12
3x5 Index Card	$3
Bat	$40

John Flaherty

Ball	$25
Photo	$10
3x5 Index Card	$3
Bat	$40

Darrin Fletcher

Ball	$25
Photo	$10
3x5 Index Card	$3
Bat	$40

Cliff Floyd

Ball	$30
Authenticated Ball	$70
Photo	$15
3x5 Index Card	$3
Bat	$40

Andy Fox

Ball	$25
Photo	$10
3x5 Index Card	$3
Bat	$40

John Franco

Ball	$35
Authenticated Ball	$110
Photo	$20
3x5 Index Card	$3
Bat	$50

Julio Franco

Ball	$30
Photo	$15
3x5 Index Card	$3
Bat	$50

Matt Franco

Ball	$25
Photo	$10
3x5 Index Card	$3
Bat	$40

Travis Fryman

Ball	$25
Photo	$10
3x5 Index Card	$3
Bat	$40

Brad Fullmer

Ball	$25
Photo	$10
3x5 Index Card	$3
Bat	$40

Rafael Furcal

Ball	$35
Photo	$20
3x5 Index Card	$3
Bat	$50

Andres Galarraga

Ball	$35
Photo	$20
3x5 Index Card	$3
Bat	$50

Eric Gagne

Ball	$40
Photo	$25
3x5 Index Card	$5
Bat	$60

Ron Gant

Ball	$30
Photo	$15
3x5 Index Card	$3
Bat	$50

Freddy Garcia

Ball	$35
Photo	$20
3x5 Index Card	$5
Bat	$50

Nomar Garciaparra

Ball	$100
Photo	$40
3x5 Index Card	$25
Bat	$150

Jason Giambi

Ball	$100
Photo	$60
3x5 Index Card	$20
Bat	$250

Jeremy Giambi

Ball	$30
Authenticated Ball	$80
Photo	$15
3x5 Index Card	$3
Bat	$50

Jay Gibbons

Ball	$35
Authenticated Ball	$70
Photo	$20
3x5 Index Card	$3
Bat	$60

Brian Giles

Steiner Sports Photo

Ball	$30

Authenticated Ball $80
Photo $20
Authenticated Photo $65
3x5 Index Card $3
Bat $50

Marcus Giles

Ball $25
Photo $10
3x5 Index Card $3
Bat $40

Joe Girardi

Ball $35
Authenticated Ball $50
Photo $20
3x5 Index Card $5
Bat $50

Doug Glanville

Ball $25
Photo $10
3x5 Index Card $3
Bat $40

Troy Glaus

Ball $40
Authenticated Ball $190
Photo $30
3x5 Index Card $7
Bat $75

Tom Glavine

Mounted Memories Photo

Ball $50
Authenticated Ball $150
Photo $35
Authenticated Photo $100
3x5 Index Card $10
Bat $75

Alex Gonzalez

Ball $30
Authenticated Ball $140
Photo $15
Authenticated Photo $110
3x5 Index Card $3
Bat $40
Authenticated Bat $200

Juan Gonzalez

Ball $45
Authenticated Ball $115
Photo $30
Authenticated Photo $65
3x5 Index Card $5
Bat $60

Luis Gonzalez

Steiner Sports Photo

Ball $30
Authenticated Ball $140
Photo $15
3x5 Index Card $3
Bat $50
Authenticated Bat $125

Tom Gordon

Ball $25
Photo $10
3x5 Index Card $3
Bat $40

Mark Grace

Ball $35
Photo $20
3x5 Index Card $5
Bat $50

Tony Graffanino

Ball $25
Photo $10
3x5 Index Card $3
Bat $40

Danny Graves

Ball $25
Photo $10
3x5 Index Card $3
Bat $40

Shawn Green

Ball $50
Photo $35
3x5 Index Card $10
Bat $75

Rusty Greer

Ball $25
Photo $12
3x5 Index Card $3
Bat $40

Ben Grieve

Ball $30
Photo $15
3x5 Index Card $5
Bat $50
Authenticated Bat $75

Ken Griffey Jr.

Steiner Sports Photo

Ball $75
Authenticated Ball $200
Photo $50
Authenticated Photo $120
3x5 Index Card $20
Bat $150
Authenticated Bat $350

Jason Grimsley

Ball $25
Photo $10
3x5 Index Card $3
Bat $40

Mark Grudzielanek

Ball $25
Photo $10
3x5 Index Card $3
Bat $40

Marquis Grissom

Ball $25
Photo $10
3x5 Index Card $3
Bat $40

Vladimir Guerrero

Mounted Memories Photo

Ball $75
Authenticated Ball $180
Photo $40
Authenticated Photo $105
3x5 Index Card $10
Bat $150
Authenticated Bat $350

Wilton Guerrero

Ball $25
Photo $10
3x5 Index Card $3
Bat $40

Jose Guillen

Ball $25
Photo $10
3x5 Index Card $3
Bat $40

Mark Guthrie

Ball $25
Photo $15
3x5 Index Card $3
Bat $40

Ricky Gutierrez

Ball $25
Photo $10
3x5 Index Card $3
Bat $40

Cristian Guzman

Ball $25
Photo $10
3x5 Index Card $3
Bat $40

Jerry Hairston Jr.

Ball $30
Authenticated Ball $45
Photo $15
3x5 Index Card $3
Bat $50

Roy Halladay

Ball $35
Photo $20
3x5 Index Card $3
Bat $50

Joey Hamilton

Ball $25
Photo $10
3x5 Index Card $3
Bat $40

Mike Hampton

Mounted Memories Photo

Ball $40
Authenticated Ball $140
Photo $25
Authenticated Photo $80

3x5 Index Card $5
Bat $60

Pete Harnisch

Ball $25
Photo $10
3x5 Index Card $3
Bat $40

Shigetoshi Hasegawa

Ball $30
Photo $15
3x5 Index Card $3
Bat $40

Todd Helton

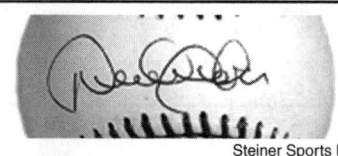
Mounted Memories Photo

Ball $60
Authenticated Ball $140
Photo $40
Authenticated Photo $75
3x5 Index Card $5
Bat $80

Rick Helling

Ball $30
Authenticated Ball $50
Photo $15
3x5 Index Card $3
Bat $40

Wes Helms

Ball $25
Photo $10
3x5 Index Card $3
Bat $40

Rickey Henderson

Mounted Memories Photo

Ball $80
Authenticated Ball $200
Photo $50
3x5 Index Card $20
Bat $150

Pat Hentgen

Ball $35
Photo $20
3x5 Index Card $5
Bat $50

Jose Hernandez

Ball $25
Photo $15
3x5 Index Card $3
Bat $40

Livan Hernandez

Ball $35
Photo $20
3x5 Index Card $3
Bat $50

Orlando Hernandez

Ball $40
Authenticated Ball $200

Photo $25
Authenticated Photo $120
3x5 Index Card $5
Bat $60

Richard Hidalgo

Ball $35
Photo $20
3x5 Index Card $5
Bat $50

Bobby Higginson

Ball $25
Authenticated Ball $80
Photo $12
3x5 Index Card $3
Bat $40

Shea Hillenbrand

Mounted Memories Photo

Ball $35
Authenticated Ball $80
Photo $20
3x5 Index Card $3
Bat $50
Authenticated Bat $80

A.J. Hinch

Ball $25
Authenticated Ball $40
Photo $10
3x5 Index Card $3
Bat $40

Eric Hinske

Ball $30
Authenticated Ball $80
Photo $20
3x5 Index Card $3
Bat $50

Sterling Hitchcock

Ball $25
Photo $15
3x5 Index Card $3
Bat $40

Trevor Hoffman

Ball $40
Photo $25
3x5 Index Card $3
Bat $60

Todd Hollandsworth

Ball $25
Photo $10
3x5 Index Card $3
Bat $40

Aubrey Huff

Ball $30
Photo $15
3x5 Index Card $3
Bat $45

Todd Hundley

Ball $25
Photo $10
3x5 Index Card $3
Bat $40

Brian Hunter

Ball $25
Photo $10
3x5 Index Card $3
Bat $40

Torii Hunter

Ball $40
Authenticated Ball $100
Photo $30
Authenticated Photo $60
3x5 Index Card $5
Bat $60

Adam Hyzdu

Ball $25
Photo $10
3x5 Index Card $3
Bat $40

Hideki Irabu

Ball $25
Photo $10
3x5 Index Card $3
Bat $40

Kazuhisa Ishii

Ball $40
Authenticated Ball $230
Photo $25
3x5 Index Card $3
Bat $60

Jason Isringhausen

Ball $25
Photo $10
3x5 Index Card $3
Bat $40

Mike Jackson

Ball $25
Photo $10
3x5 Index Card $3
Bat $40

Geoff Jenkins

Ball $35
Photo $20
3x5 Index Card $3
Bat $50

Jason Jennings

Ball $25
Photo $10
3x5 Index Card $3
Bat $40

Derek Jeter

Steiner Sports Photo

Ball $175
Authenticated Ball $450
Photo $100
Authenticated Photo $300
3x5 Index Card $25
Bat $250
Authenticated Bat $700

Jose Jimenez

Ball $25
Photo $10

3x5 Index Card $3
Bat $40

Charles Johnson

Ball $30
Photo $15
3x5 Index Card $3
Bat $50

Nick Johnson

Ball $35
Authenticated Ball $80
Photo $20
3x5 Index Card $3
Bat $50

Randy Johnson

Steiner Sports Photo

Ball $125
Authenticated Ball $275
Photo $75
Authenticated Photo $249
3x5 Index Card $15
Bat $175

Andruw Jones

Steiner Sports Photo

Ball $35
Authenticated Ball $120
Photo $25
3x5 Index Card $5
Bat $50
Authenticated Bat $130

Chipper Jones

Ball $50
Authenticated Ball $170
Photo $35
Authenticated Photo $80
3x5 Index Card $5
Bat $80
Authenticated Bat $150

Jacque Jones

Ball $30
Photo $15
3x5 Index Card $3
Bat $50

Brian Jordan

Mounted Memories Photo

Ball $35

Authenticated Ball $55
Photo $20
Authenticated Photo $40
3x5 Index Card $3
Bat $50

Gabe Kapler

Ball $25
Photo $10
Autenticated Photo $30
3x5 Index Card $3
Bat $40

Eric Karros

Ball $30
Photo $20
3x5 Index Card $3
Bat $50

Austin Kearns

Ball $35
Authenticated Ball $90
Photo $25
3x5 Index Card $3
Bat $50

Jason Kendall

Ball $35
Photo $20
3x5 Index Card $3
Bat $50

Adam Kennedy

Ball $30
Photo $15
3x5 Index Card $3
Bat $40

Jeff Kent

Ball $45
Authenticated Ball $120
Photo $30
3x5 Index Card $5
Bat $60

Byung-Hyun Kim

Ball $25
Photo $10
3x5 Index Card $3
Bat $40

Ryan Klesko

Ball $35
Photo $20
3x5 Index Card $3
Bat $50
Authenticated Bat $80

Chuck Knoblauch

Ball $35
Photo $20
3x5 Index Card $3
Bat $50

Billy Koch

Ball $25
Photo $10
3x5 Index Card $3
Bat $40

Paul Konerko

Ball $30
Photo $20
3x5 Index Card $3
Bat $50

Corey Koskie

Ball $25
Photo $10
3x5 Index Card $3
Bat $40

Chad Kreuter

Ball $25
Photo $10
3x5 Index Card $3
Bat $40

Barry Larkin

Ball $35
Authenticated Ball $115
Photo $25
3x5 Index Card $5
Bat $60

Matt Lawton

Ball $25
Photo $10
3x5 Index Card $3
Bat $40

Ricky Ledee

Ball $25
Photo $12
Authenticated Photo $50
3x5 Index Card $3
Bat $40

Carlos Lee

Ball $25
Authenticated Ball $30
Photo $10
3x5 Index Card $3
Bat $40

Derek Lee

Ball $25
Photo $10
3x5 Index Card $3
Bat $40

Travis Lee

Ball $30
Photo $20
3x5 Index Card $3
Bat $50

Al Leiter

Steiner Sports Photo

Ball $30
Authenticated Ball $100
Photo $20
3x5 Index Card $3
Bat $50

Darren Lewis

Ball $25
Photo $10
3x5 Index Card $3
Bat $40

Cory Lidle

Ball $25
Photo $15
3x5 Index Card $3
Bat $40

Mike Lieberthal

Ball	$30
Photo	$20
3x5 Index Card	$3
Bat	$40

Kerry Lightenberg

Ball	$25
Photo	$10
Authenticated Photo	$30
3x5 Index Card	$3
Bat	$40

Jose Lima

Ball	$25
Photo	$10
3x5 Index Card	$3
Bat	$40

Graeme Lloyd

Ball	$25
Photo	$10
3x5 Index Card	$3
Bat	$40

Keith Lockhart

Ball	$25
Photo	$10
3x5 Index Card	$3
Bat	$40

Esteban Loaiza

Ball	$30
Photo	$20
3x5 Index Card	$3
Bat	$40

Paul Lo Duca

Ball	$35
Photo	$25
3x5 Index Card	$3
Bat	$50

Kenny Lofton

Ball	$35
Photo	$20
3x5 Index Card	$5
Bat	$60

Rich Loiselle

Ball	$25
Photo	$10
3x5 Index Card	$3
Bat	$40

Terrance Long

Ball	$25
Authenticcated Ball	$60
Photo	$10
Authenticated Photo	$25
3x5 Index Card	$3
Bat	$40

Javy Lopez

Ball	$40
Photo	$30
Authenticated Ball	$40
3x5 Index Card	$5
Bat	$75

Mark Loretta

Ball	$25
Photo	$10
3x5 Index Card	$3
Bat	$40

Derek Lowe

Ball	$35
Photo	$25
3x5 Index Card	$3
Bat	$50

Mike Lowell

Ball	$30
Photo	$20
3x5 Index Card	$3
Bat	$50

John Mabry

Ball	$25
Photo	$10
3x5 Index Card	$3
Bat	$40

Greg Maddux

Ball	$75
Authenticated Ball	$210
Photo	$50
Authenticated Photo	$140
3x5 Index Card	$15
Bat	$125

Eli Marrero

Ball	$25
Authenticated Ball	$60
Photo	$10
3x5 Index Card	$3
Bat	$40

Edgar Martinez

Ball	$40
Authenticated Ball	$110
Photo	$30
3x5 Index Card	$5
Bat	$75

Pedro Martinez

Ball	$125
Authenticated Ball	$350
Photo	$50
3x5 Index Card	$20
Bat	$200

Tino Martinez

Steiner Sports Photo

Ball	$40
Authenticated Ball	$200
Photo	$30
3x5 Index Card	$5
Bat	$75

Hideki Matsui

Ball	$100
Authenticated Ball	$650
Photo	$60
3x5 Index Card	$15
Bat	$150
Authenticated Bat	$850

Gary Matthews Jr.

Ball	$25
Photo	$10
3x5 Index Card	$3
Bat	$40

Brent Mayne

Ball	$25
Photo	$10
3x5 Index Card	$3
Bat	$40

Joe Mays

Ball	$25
Authenticated Ball	$70
Photo	$10
3x5 Index Card	$3
Bat	$40

Dave McCarty

Ball	$25
Photo	$10
3x5 Index Card	$3
Bat	$40

Quinton McCracken

Ball	$25
Photo	$10
3x5 Index Card	$3
Bat	$40

Fred McGriff

Ball	$40
Photo	$30
3x5 Index Card	$10
Bat	$75

Mark McLemore

Ball	$25
Photo	$10
3x5 Index Card	$3
Bat	$40

Pat Meares

Ball	$25
Photo	$10
3x5 Index Card	$3
Bat	$40

Gil Meche

Ball	$25
Photo	$10
3x5 Index Card	$3
Bat	$40

Ramiro Mendoza

Ball	$40
Authenticated Ball	$60
Photo	$30
3x5 Index Card	$5
Bat	$60

Orlando Merced

Ball	$25
Photo	$10
3x5 Index Card	$3
Bat	$40

Jose Mesa

Ball	$25
Photo	$15
3x5 Index Card	$3
Bat	$40

Doug Mientkiewicz

Ball	$25
Photo	$15
3x5 Index Card	$3
Bat	$40

Kevin Millar

Ball	$25

Authenticated Ball $60
Photo $12
3x5 Index Card $3
Bat $40

Kevin Millwood

Ball $25
Authenticated Ball $50
Photo $15
3x5 Index Card $3
Bat $40

Eric Milton

Ball $25
Authenticated Ball $70
Photo $12
3x5 Index Card $3
Bat $40

Raul Mondesi

Ball $35
Authenticated Ball $110
Photo $25
Authenticated Photo $75
3x5 Index Card $5
Bat $50

Melvin Mora

Ball $25
Photo $15
Authenticated Photo $30
3x5 Index Card $3
Bat $40

Matt Morris

Ball $25
Authenticated Ball $70
Photo $10
3x5 Index Card $3
Bat $40

Jamie Moyer

Ball $30
Photo $20
3x5 Index Card $3
Bat $50

Bill Mueller

Ball $25
Photo $10
3x5 Index Card $3
Bat $40

Mark Mulder

Ball $35
Photo $25
3x5 Index Card $3
Bat $50

Terry Mulholland

Ball $25
Photo $10
3x5 Index Card $3
Bat $40

Mike Mussina

Ball $75
Authenticated Ball $210
Photo $40

Authenticated Photo $150
3x5 Index Card $5
Bat $100

Charles Nagy

Ball $25
Photo $15
3x5 Index Card $3
Bat $40

Denny Neagle

Ball $25
Photo $15
3x5 Index Card $3
Bat $40

Jeff Nelson

Ball $25
Photo $15
3x5 Index Card $3
Bat $40

Robb Nen

Ball $25
Photo $10
3x5 Index Card $3
Bat $40

Phil Nevin

Ball $25
Photo $10
3x5 Index Card $3
Bat $40

Trot Nixon

Ball $30
Photo $20
3x5 Index Card $3
Bat $50

Hideo Nomo

Ball $45
Photo $35
3x5 Index Card $5
Bat $60

Troy O'Leary

Ball $30
Photo $20
3x5 Index Card $3
Bat $50

John Olerud

Ball $30
Photo $20
3x5 Index Card $3
Bat $50

Magglio Ordonez

Ball $25
Authenticated Ball $100
Photo $15
Authenticated Photo $50
3x5 Index Card $3
Bat $40

Rey Ordonez

Ball $25
Photo $10
Authenticated Photo $60
3x5 Index Card $3
Bat $40

Jesse Orosco

Ball $30
Photo $20

3x5 Index Card $3
Bat $40

David Ortiz

Ball $25
Photo $10
3x5 Index Card $3
Bat $40

Jose Ortiz

Ball $25
Authenticated Ball $45
Photo $10
3x5 Index Card $3
Bat $40

Roy Oswalt

Tri-Star Productions Photo

Ball $35
Photo $25
Authenticated Photo $40
3x5 Index Card $3
Bat $50

Rafael Palmeiro

Ball $60
Authenticated Ball $150
Photo $40
Authenticated Photo $140
3x5 Index Card $10
Bat $100
Authenticated Bat $350

Dean Palmer

Ball $25
Photo $15
3x5 Index Card $3
Bat $40

Chan Ho Park

Ball $35
Photo $25
3x5 Index Card $5
Bat $50

Corey Patterson

Ball $25
Photo $15
3x5 Index Card $3
Bat $40

Troy Percival

Ball $25
Photo $10
3x5 Index Card $3
Bat $40

Andy Pettitte

Steiner Sports Photo

Ball $50
Authenticated Ball $180
Photo $75

Authenticated Photo $150
3x5 Index Card $15
Bat $100

Mike Piazza

Ball $100
Photo $75
3x5 Index Card $20
Bat $150

Juan Pierre

Ball $25
Authenticated Ball $60
Photo $10
3x5 Index Card $3
Bat $40

Sidney Ponson

Ball $25
Photo $15
3x5 Index Card $3
Bat $40

Jorge Posada

Ball $40
Authenticated Ball $170
Photo $30
3x5 Index Card $5
Bat $60

Mark Prior

Ball $60
Authenticated Ball $130
Photo $40
3x5 Index Card $10
Bat $80

Albert Pujols

Tri-Star Productions Photo

Ball $50
Authenticated Ball $180
Photo $40
Authenticated Photo $120
3x5 Index Card $10
Bat $75

Mark Quinn

Ball $25
Photo $10
3x5 Index Card $3
Bat $40

Brad Radke

Ball $25
Photo $15
3x5 Index Card $3
Bat $40

Aramis Ramirez

Ball $25
Photo $10
3x5 Index Card $3
Bat $40

Manny Ramirez

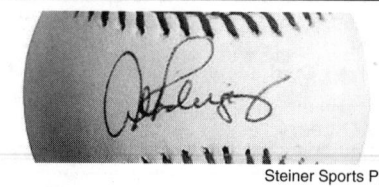

Mounted Memories Photo

Ball $80
Authenticated Ball $140
Photo $50
Authenticated Photo $65
3x5 Index Card $5
Bat $150

Pokey Reese

Ball $25
Photo $10
3x5 Index Card $3
Bat $40

Edgar Renteria

Ball $30
Photo $20
3x5 Index Card $3
Bat $40

Mariano Rivera

Steiner Sports Photo

Ball $75
Authenticated Ball $250
Photo $50
Authenticated Photo $180
3x5 Index Card $5
Bat $100

John Rocker

Ball $25
Photo $15
3x5 Index Card $3
Bat $40

Alex Rodriguez

Steiner Sports Photo

Ball $100
Authenticated Ball $170
Photo $75
Authenticated Photo $95
3x5 Index Card $20
Bat $200
Authenticated Bat $350

Ivan Rodriguez

Ball $40
Authenticated Ball $150
Photo $30
Authenticated Photo $80
3x5 Index Card $10
Bat $100

Kenny Rogers

Ball $25
Photo $15
3x5 Index Card $3
Bat $40

Scott Rolen

Ball $35
Photo $25
3x5 Index Card $5
Bat $50

Jimmy Rollins

Ball $25
Authenticated Ball $50
Photo $15
3x5 Index Card $3
Bat $40

C.C. Sabathia

Ball $30
Photo $20
3x5 Index Card $3
Bat $50

Tim Salmon

Ball $30
Photo $20
3x5 Index Card $5
Bat $50

Rey Sanchez

Ball $25
Photo $10
3x5 Index Card $3
Bat $40

Jared Sandberg

Ball $25
Photo $15
3x5 Index Card $3
Bat $40

Reggie Sanders

Ball $25
Photo $12
3x5 Index Card $3
Bat $40

Benito Santiago

Mounted Memories Photo

Ball $25
Photo $15
3x5 Index Card $3
Bat $40

Kazuhiro Sasaki

Ball $30
Photo $20
3x5 Index Card $3
Bat $50

Curt Schilling

Ball $90
Authenticated Ball $135
Photo $50
Authenticated Photo $180
3x5 Index Card $10
Bat $125

Jason Schmidt

Ball $30
Photo $20
3x5 Index Card $3
Bat $40

David Segui

Ball $25
Photo $15
3x5 Index Card $3
Bat $40

Aaron Sele

Ball $25

Photo $15
3x5 Index Card $3
Bat $40

Richie Sexson

Ball $35
Authenticated Ball $80
Photo $25
3x5 Index Card $3
Bat $60

Ben Sheets

Steiner Sports Photo

Ball $35
Authenticated Ball $60
Photo $25
Authenticated Photo $85
3x5 Index Card $5
Bat $50

Gary Sheffield

Mounted Memories Photo

Ball $60
Authenticated Ball $150
Photo $40
3x5 Index Card $10
Bat $90
Authenticated Bat $600

Tsuyoshi Shinjo

Ball $25
Photo $10
3x5 Index Card $3
Bat $40

Ruben Sierra

Ball $30
Photo $15
3x5 Index Card $5
Bat $50

Randall Simon

Ball $25
Photo $10
3x5 Index Card $3
Bat $40

Heathcliff Slocumb

Ball $25
Photo $10
3x5 Index Card $3
Bat $40

Bud Smith

Ball $25
Authenticated Ball $70
Photo $10
3x5 Index Card $3
Bat $40

John Smoltz

Mounted Memories Photo

Ball $65
Authenticated Ball $150
Photo $40
Authenticated Photo $65
3x5 Index Card $10
Bat $90

J.T. Snow

Ball $25
Photo $10
3x5 Index Card $3
Bat $40

Alfonso Soriano

Steiner Sports Photo

Ball $50
Photo $40
3x5 Index Card $5
Bat $75

Sammy Sosa

Mounted Memories Photo

Ball $175
Authenticated Ball $550
Photo $75
Authenticated Photo $250
3x5 Index Card $25
Bat $250
Authenticated Bat $300

Shane Spencer

Ball $30
Authenticated Ball $70
Photo $20
Authenticated Photo $50
3x5 Index Card $3
Bat $40

Matt Stairs

Ball $30
Authenticated Ball $60
Photo $20
3x5 Index Card $3
Bat $50

Mike Stanton

Ball $30
Photo $20
3x5 Index Card $3
Bat $40

Garrett Stephenson

Ball $25
Photo $10
3x5 Index Card $3
Bat $40

Shannon Stewart

Ball $35
Authenticated Ball $75
Photo $25
3x5 Index Card $5
Bat $50

B. J. Surhoff

Ball $30
Photo $15

3x5 Index Card $3
Bat $40

Ichiro Suzuki

Ball $150
Authenticated Ball $400
Photo $75
3x5 Index Card $25
Bat $200

Mike Sweeney

Ball $35
Photo $25
3x5 Index Card $5
Bat $60

Kevin Tapani

Ball $25
Photo $10
3x5 Index Card $3
Bat $40

Fernando Tatis

Ball $25
Photo $10
3x5 Index Card $3
Bat $40

Eddie Taubensee

Ball $25
Photo $10
3x5 Index Card $3
Bat $40

Miguel Tejada

Ball $50
Photo $35
Authenticated Photo $60
3x5 Index Card $5
Bat $75

Frank E. Thomas

Mounted Memories Photo

Ball $40
Authenticated Ball $75
Photo $30
3x5 Index Card $10
Bat $75

Jim Thome

Ball $40
Authenticated Ball $45
Photo $30
3x5 Index Card $5
Bat $75

Michael Tucker

Ball $25
Photo $15
3x5 Index Card $3
Bat $40

Ugueth Urbina

Ball $25
Photo $15
3x5 Index Card $3
Bat $40

John Valentin

Ball $25
Photo $15
3x5 Index Card $3
Bat $40

Jose Valentin

Ball	$25
Photo	$12
3x5 Index Card	$3
Bat	$40

Jason Varitek

Ball	$30
Photo	$20
3x5 Index Card	$3
Bat	$40

Greg Vaughn

Ball	$30
Photo	$20
3x5 Index Card	$5
Bat	$50

Mo Vaughn

Ball	$35
Authenticated Ball	$90
Photo	$25
Authenticated Photo	$120
3x5 Index Card	$5
Bat	$60

Robin Ventura

Steiner Sports Photo

Ball	$40
Authenticated Ball	$110
Photo	$30
Authenticated Photo	$90
3x5 Index Card	$5
Bat	$60

Jose Vidro

Ball	$35
Authenticated Ball	$75
Photo	$25
3x5 Index Card	$5
Bat	$50

Fernando Vina

Ball	$25
Photo	$10
3x5 Index Card	$3
Bat	$40

Omar Vizquel

Steiner Sports Photo

Ball	$40
Authenticated Ball	$90
Photo	$30
3x5 Index Card	$5
Bat	$60

Billy Wagner

Ball	$35
Photo	$25
3x5 Index Card	$5
Bat	$60

Tim Wakefield

Ball	$25
Photo	$15
3x5 Index Card	$3
Bat	$40

Matt Walbeck

Ball	$25
Photo	$12
3x5 Index Card	$3
Bat	$40

Larry Walker

Ball	$50
Photo	$35
3x5 Index Card	$5
Bat	$75

Todd Walker

Ball	$25
Photo	$10
3x5 Index Card	$3
Bat	$40

Jarrod Washburn

Ball	$35
Photo	$25
3x5 Index Card	$3
Bat	$50

Jeff Weaver

Ball	$30
Photo	$20
3x5 Index Card	$3
Bat	$50

David Wells

Ball	$50
Authenticated Ball	$200
Photo	$40
3x5 Index Card	$10
Bat	$75

Vernon Wells

Ball	$35
Authenticated Ball	$60
Photo	$25
3x5 Index Card	$3
Bat	$50

Rondell White

Ball	$25
Photo	$15
3x5 Index Card	$3
Bat	$40

Bernie Williams

Ball	$80
Authenticated Ball	$250
Photo	$70
3x5 Index Card	$15
Bat	$150
Authenticated Bat	$600

Woody Williams

Ball	$40
Photo	$30
3x5 Index Card	$3
Bat	$60

Scott Williamson

Ball	$30
Photo	$20
3x5 Index Card	$3
Bat	$40

Dontrelle Willis

Ball	$40
Authenticated Ball	$60

Photo ... $25

Authenticated Photo	$35
3x5 Index Card	$5
Bat	$60

Dan Wilson

Ball	$25
Photo	$10
3x5 Index Card	$3
Bat	$40

Preston Wilson

Ball	$25
Photo	$15
3x5 Index Card	$3
Bat	$40

Randy Winn

Ball	$30
Photo	$20
3x5 Index Card	$3
Bat	$40

Randy Wolf

Ball	$30
Photo	$20
3x5 Index Card	$3
Bat	$40

Kerry Wood

Ball	$60
Authenticated Ball	$120
Photo	$40
Authenticated Photo	$90
3x5 Index Card	$10
Bat	$90

Jaret Wright

Ball	$25
Photo	$10
3x5 Index Card	$3
Bat	$40

Dmitri Young

Ball	$25
Authenticated Ball	$60
Photo	$15
3x5 Index Card	$3
Bat	$40

Kevin Young

Ball	$25
Photo	$15
3x5 Index Card	$3
Bat	$40

Carlos Zambrano

Ball	$30
Photo	$20
3x5 Index Card	$3
Bat	$50

Todd Zeile

Ball	$30
Authenticated Ball	$80
Photo	$20
Authenticated Photo	$55
3x5 Index Card	$3
Bat	$50
Authenticated Bat	$180

Barry Zito

Ball	$50
Photo	$35
3x5 Index Card	$5
Bat	$70

RETIRED BASEBALL PLAYERS AUTOGRAPHS

This section is devoted mainly—but not exclusively—to prominent former baseball players whose credentials were solid, but not quite enough to merit Hall of Fame induction. That means you'll find current autograph values for hundreds of players who put up impressive stats during their careers and became fan favorites in the process. There are:

• sluggers like Dave Kingman (442 career home runs), Graig Nettles (389 HRs), Frank "Hondo" Howard (382 HRs) and Dick Allen (351 HRs).

• popular, productive Yankees stars like Nettles, Roger Maris (275 HRs), Bobby Murcer (252 HRs), Thurman Munson (.292 career average) and Don Mattingly (.307, 222 HRs), who played for the Bronx Bombers for all or much of their careers.

• fathers of famous sons—baseball-playing dads who were pretty talented in their own right: Ken Griffey Jr.'s father Ken Sr. (.296 career average) and Barry Bonds' father Bobby (332 HRs, 461 steals).

• such personalities as Joe Garagiola and Bob Uecker, who followed unspectacular playing careers (Garagiola: .257 batting average; Uecker: .200) with long stints as popular announcers.

The section also includes would-be Hall of Famers like Tony Oliva and Tony Conigliaro, who suffered serious injuries that curtailed their playing days.

But the most prominent names in this section are two "should-be" Hall of Famers (at least in the minds of their supporters): Joe Jackson and Pete Rose. These two legends are connected in baseball lore, unfortunately, through their alleged ties to gambling and subsequent ban from the game. In terms of autographs, though, they reflect the extremes of the marketplace.

Rose, one of baseball's most active signers, has been extremely visible on the show circuit. In recent years, his autograph prices have been stable at around $50 for a signed baseball and $40 for a signed photo. On the surface, he's undervalued (considering that he was a popular player and manager, is baseball's all-time hits leader, and is always controversial). But the healthy supply of Rose signatures keeps the price affordable.

"Shoeless" Joe Jackson's autograph, on the other hand, is one of the scarcest in baseball history. Because he was unable to read and write, he didn't sign many autographs. Thus, serious collectors have to pay a small fortune to get one when it surfaces. How rare is Shoeless Joe's autograph? The Web site BlackBetsy.com wrote in December 2000, "We are aware of about 30 verified and authenticated Joe Jackson autographs and we are aware of about 10 to 20 more that are Joe Jackson-signed items…but that have not been verified or authenticated." As a result, Jackson's signature on photos, balls or cuts can cost tens of thousands of dollars.

Finally, this section is home to a handful of retired players who might be destined for the Hall of Fame but who—at this writing—haven't yet been voted in.

In some cases (Paul Molitor and Wade Boggs), it's simply a matter of time. In other cases (Jim Rice and Bruce Sutter), it's not so automatic.

Boggs' 3,010 hits in 18 seasons for the Red Sox, Yankees and Devil Rays all but ensures his spot in the Hall of Fame. Boggs retired after the 1999 season and is eligible for induction in 2005.

Rice and Sutter, on the other hand, are on the bubble. Rice blasted 382 HRs and had a .298 average in 16 seasons. And Bruce Sutter posted 300 saves and a 2.83 ERA in 12 seasons. To earn HOF induction, a player needs to be named on at least 75 percent of the ballots cast by the Baseball Writers' Association of America (BBWAA).

Retired Players Autographs
*Indicates player is deceased

Tommie Aaron *

Ball	$250
Photo	$100
3x5 Index Card	$40
Bat	$400

Cal Abrams *

Ball	$50
Photo	$25
3x5 Index Card	$10
Bat	$100

Joe Adcock *

Ball	$150
Photo	$40
3x5 Index Card	$20
Bat	$300

Tommie Agee *

Ball	$40
Photo	$20
3x5 Index Card	$4
Bat	$75

Harry Agganis *

Ball	$500
Photo	$300
3x5 Index Card	$125
Bat	Unknown

Willie Aikens

Ball	$25
Photo	$10
3x5 Index Card	$3
Bat	$40

Danny Ainge

Ball	$40
Photo	$25
3x5 Index Card	$10
Bat	$75

Dick Allen

Mounted Memories Photo

Ball	$45
Authenticated Ball	$100
Photo	$30
3x5 Index Card	$10
Bat	$75

Gene Alley

Ball	$25
Photo	$15
3x5 Index Card	$3
Bat	$40

Bob Allison*

Ball	$100
Photo	$40
3x5 Index Card	$20
Bat	$200

Sandy Alomar Sr.

Ball	$25
Photo	$15
3x5 Index Card	$5
Bat	$40

Felipe Alou

Ball	$35
Photo	$20
3x5 Index Card	$10
Bat	$50

Jesus Alou

Ball	$25
Photo	$15
3x5 Index Card	$5
Bat	$40

Matty Alou

Ball $25
Photo $15
3x5 Index Card $5
Bat $40

Sandy Amoros *

Ball $225
Photo $75
3x5 Index Card $25
Bat $400

Joaquin Andujar

Ball $30
Photo $20
3x5 Index Card $8
Bat $50

Johnny Antonelli

Ball $30
Photo $15
3x5 Index Card $5
Bat $40

Tony Armas Sr.

Ball $30
Photo $20
3x5 Index Card $3
Bat $50

Bobby Avila

Ball $25
Photo $15
3x5 Index Card $3
Bat $40

Ed Bailey

Ball $20
Photo $10
3x5 Index Card $3
Bat $40

Harold Baines

Ball $35
Authenticated Ball $60
Photo $25
3x5 Index Card $5
Bat $50

Dusty Baker

Ball $40
Authenticated Ball $70
Photo $25
3x5 Index Card $5
Bat $65

Steve Balboni

Ball $25
Photo $12
3x5 Index Card $3
Bat $40

George Bamberger

Ball $30
Photo $12
3x5 Index Card $3
Bat $40

Sal Bando

Ball $20
Photo $12
3x5 Index Card $5
Bat $40

Floyd Bannister

Ball $25

Photo $12
3x5 Index Card $3
Bat $40

Steve Barber

Ball $25
Photo $12
3x5 Index Card $5
Bat $40

Jesse Barfield

Ball $25
Photo $15
3x5 Index Card $3
Bat $40

Len Barker

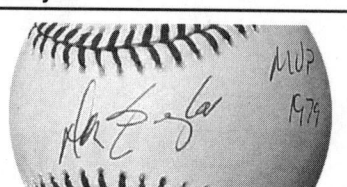

Ball $25
Authenticated Ball $50
Photo $12
3x5 Index Card $3
Bat $40

Rex Barney *

Ball $75
Photo $40
3x5 Index Card $15
Bat $100

Kevin Bass

Ball $25
Photo $10
3x5 Index Card $3
Bat $40

Earl Battey *

Ball $25
Photo $10
3x5 Index Card $3
Bat $40

Hank Bauer

Mounted Memories Photo

Ball $30
Authenticated Ball $50
Photo $15
3x5 Index Card $5
Bat $40

Don Baylor

Mounted Memories Photo

Ball $35
Authenticated Ball $75
Photo $25
3x5 Index Card $5
Bat $60

Steve Bedrosian

Ball $25
Photo $12
3x5 Index Card $5
Bat $40

Mark Belanger *

Ball $75
Photo $40
3x5 Index Card $10
Bat $125

Bo Belinsky*

Ball $75
Photo $40
3x5 Index Card $15
Bat $150

Buddy Bell

Ball $25
Authenticated Ball $40
Photo $12
3x5 Index Card $3
Bat $40

Derek Bell

Ball $25
Authenticated Ball $40
Photo $15
Authenticated Photo $30
3x5 Index Card $3
Bat $40

George Bell

Ball $35
Photo $20
3x5 Index Card $5
Bat $50

Gus Bell *

Ball $100
Photo $35
Authenticated Photo $45
3x5 Index Card $10
Bat $150

Albert Belle

Ball $40
Photo $25
Authenticated Photo $70
3x5 Index Card $5
Bat $75

Andy Benes

Ball $30
Photo $15
3x5 Index Card $5
Bat $50

Moe Berg *

Ball $1,000
Photo $400
3x5 Index Card $125
Bat ....Unknown

Jim Bibby

Ball $25
Photo $12
Authenticated Photo $30
3x5 Index Card $5
Bat $40

Dante Bichette

Ball $30
Photo $20

Mounted Memories Photo

3x5 Index Card	$5
Bat	$40

Bud Black

Ball	$25
Photo	$15
3x5 Index Card	$3
Bat	$40

Joe Black*

Ball	$50
Photo	$25
3x5 Index Card	$10
Bat	$100

Ewell Blackwell *

Ball	$80
Photo	$35
3x5 Index Card	$15
Bat	$125

Paul Blair

Ball	$25
Photo	$10
3x5 Index Card	$5
Bat	$40

Johnny Blanchard

Ball	$25
Photo	$12
3x5 Index Card	$5
Bat	$40

Steve Blass

Ball	$25
Photo	$12
3x5 Index Card	$5
Bat	$40

Jeff Blauser

Ball	$25
Photo	$12
3x5 Index Card	$5
Bat	$40

Curt Blefary*

Ball	$60
Photo	$25
3x5 Index Card	$10
Bat	$85

Ron Blomberg

Ball	$25
Photo	$12
3x5 Index Card	$5
Bat	$40

Vida Blue

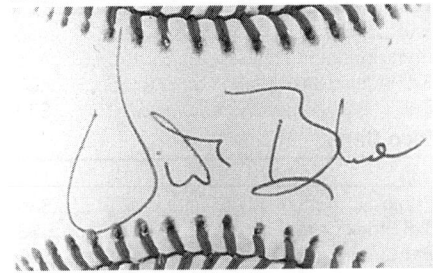

Ball	$35
Photo	$20
3x5 Index Card	$7
Bat	$50

Bert Blyleven

Ball	$35
Photo	$20
3x5 Index Card	$5
Bat	$50

Mike Boddicker

Ball	$30
Photo	$15
3x5 Index Card	$5
Bat	$40

Wade Boggs

Mounted Memories Photo

Ball	$65
Authenticated Ball	$190
Photo	$45
Authenticated Photo	$85
3x5 Index Card	$10
Bat	$125

Frank Bolling

Ball	$25
Photo	$12
3x5 Index Card	$5
Bat	$40

Milt Bolling

Ball	$25
Photo	$12
3x5 Index Card	$5
Bat	$40

Bobby Bonds*

Ball	$50
Authenticated Ball	$100
Photo	$25
3x5 Index Card	$10
Bat	$100

Bobby Bonilla

Ball	$30
Authenticated Ball	$75
Photo	$20
3x5 Index Card	$5
Bat	$50

Bob Boone

Ball	$30
Photo	$20
3x5 Index Card	$5
Bat	$40

Ray Boone

Ball	$25
Photo	$12
3x5 Index Card	$5
Bat	$40

Frenchy Bordagaray *

Ball	$75
Photo	$30
3x5 Index Card	$10
Bat	$100

Pat Borders

Ball	$25
Authenticated Ball	$80
Photo	$15
3x5 Index Card	$5
Bat	$40

Lyman Bostock Jr. *

Ball	$750
Photo	$300
3x5 Index Card	$75
Bat	Unknown

Jim Bouton

Ball	$30
Photo	$15
3x5 Index Card	$5
Bat	$40

Larry Bowa

Ball	$30
Photo	$20
3x5 Index Card	$5
Bat	$40

Clete Boyer

Ball	$30
Photo	$12
Authenticated Photo	$15
3x5 Index Card	$5
Bat	$40

Ken Boyer *

Ball	$600
Photo	$275
3x5 Index Card	$100

Bobby Bragan

Ball	$25
Photo	$12
3x5 Index Card	$5
Bat	$40

Ralph Branca

Ball	$35
Photo	$15
3x5 Index Card	$5
Bat	$50

Bob Brenly

Ball	$30
Photo	$15
3x5 Index Card	$5
Bat	$40

Rocky Bridges

Ball	$25
Photo	$12
3x5 Index Card	$5
Bat	$40

Nellie Briles

Ball	$25
Photo	$10
3x5 Index Card	$3
Bat	$40

Greg Brock

Ball	$25
Photo	$12
3x5 Index Card	$3
Bat	$40

Ernie Broglio

Ball	$30
Photo	$15

3x5 Index Card $5
Bat $40

Hubie Brooks

Ball $25
Photo $12
3x5 Index Card $5
Bat $40

Scott Brosius

Ball $40
Photo $25
3x5 Index Card $5
Bat $60

Dr. Bobby Brown

Ball $40
Photo $25
3x5 Index Card $10
Bat $60

Gates Brown

Ball $25
Photo $12
3x5 Index Card $3
Bat $40

Tom Browning

Ball $25
Authenticated Ball $50
Photo $12
3x5 Index Card $3
Bat $40

Tom Brunansky

Ball $25
Photo $10
3x5 Index Card $3
Bat $40

Billy Bruton *

Ball $75
Photo $30
3x5 Index Card $10
Bat $100

Bill Buckner

Ball $35
Photo $25
3x5 Index Card $5
Bat $50

Don Buford

Ball $25
Photo $12
3x5 Index Card $3
Bat $40

Bob Buhl *

Ball $40
Photo $20
3x5 Index Card $5
Bat $60

Jay Buhner

Ball $35
Photo $25
3x5 Index Card $5
Bat $50

Al Bumbry

Ball $25
Photo $12
3x5 Index Card $5
Bat $40

Lew Burdette

Ball $30
Photo $15
3x5 Index Card $5
Bat $50

Smoky Burgess *

Ball $75
Photo $30
3x5 Index Card $10
Bat $100

Glenn Burke *

Ball $125
Photo $60
3x5 Index Card $25
Bat .... Unknown

Jeff Burroughs

Ball $25
Photo $12
3x5 Index Card $5
Bat $40

Rick Burleson

Ball $25
Photo $12
3x5 Index Card $3
Bat $40

Brett Butler

Ball $30
Photo $15
3x5 Index Card $5
Bat $40

Tommy Byrne

Ball $35
Photo $15
3x5 Index Card $5
Bat $50

Enos Cabell

Ball $25
Photo $12
3x5 Index Card $3
Bat $40

Mike Caldwell

Ball $25
Photo $12
3x5 Index Card $3
Bat $40

Johnny Callison

Ball $25
Photo $12
3x5 Index Card $3
Bat $40

Dolph Camilli *

Ball $75
Photo $30
3x5 Index Card $8
Bat $100

Ken Caminiti

Ball $35
Photo $20
3x5 Index Card $3
Bat $50

Bert Campaneris

Ball $25
Photo $12
3x5 Index Card $3
Bat $40

Dave Campbell

Ball $25
Photo $12
3x5 Index Card $3
Bat $40

John Candelaria

Ball $25
Authenticated Ball $50
Photo $12
3x5 Index Card $3
Bat $40

Tom Candiotti

Ball $30
Photo $15
3x5 Index Card $3
Bat $40

Jose Canseco

Mounted Memories Photo

Ball $35
Authenicated Ball $90
Photo $20
3x5 Index Card $8
Bat $60

Bernie Carbo

Ball $25
Photo $12
3x5 Index Card $3
Bat $40

Jose Cardenal

Ball $25
Photo $12
3x5 Index Card $3
Bat $40

Andy Carey

Ball $25
Photo $12
3x5 Index Card $3
Bat $40

Chico Carrasquel

Ball $25
Photo $12
3x5 Index Card $3
Bat $40

Joe Carter

Ball $35
Photo $20
3x5 Index Card $3
Bat $50

Rico Carty

Ball $30
Photo $20
3x5 Index Card $3
Bat $40

Dave Cash

Ball	$25
Photo	$12
3x5 Index Card	$3
Bat	$40

Norm Cash *

Ball	$500
Photo	$250
3x5 Index Card	$75
Bat	$750

John Castino

Ball	$25
Photo	$12
3x5 Index Card	$3
Bat	$40

Bill Caudill

Ball	$25
Photo	$12
3x5 Index Card	$3
Bat	$40

Phil Cavarretta

Ball	$40
Photo	$20
3x5 Index Card	$5
Bat	$50

Cesar Cedeno

Ball	$30
Photo	$15
3x5 Index Card	$3
Bat	$50

Rick Cerone

Ball	$25
Photo	$12
3x5 Index Card	$3
Bat	$40

Bob Cerv

Ball	$30
Photo	$15
3x5 Index Card	$3
Bat	$40

Ron Cey

Mounted Memories Photo

Ball	$25
Authenticated Ball	$70
Photo	$12
3x5 Index Card	$3
Bat	$40

Chris Chambliss

Ball	$30
Authenticated Ball	$70
Photo	$20
Authenticated Photo	$50
3x5 Index Card	$3
Bat	$50

Dean Chance

Ball	$35
Photo	$20
3x5 Index Card	$7
Bat	$50

Spud Chandler *

Ball	$100
Photo	$40
3x5 Index Card	$10
Bat	$125

Harry Chappas

Mounted Memories Photo

Ball	$30
Photo	$20
3x5 Index Card	$5
Bat	$50

Joe Charboneau

Ball	$25
Photo	$12
3x5 Index Card	$3
Bat	$40

Norm Charlton

Ball	$25
Photo	$12
3x5 Index Card	$5
Bat	$40

Tom Cheney *

Ball	$50
Photo	$20
3x5 Index Card	$8
Bat	$75

Eddie Cicotte *

Ball	$2,000
Photo	$800
3x5 Index Card	$400
Bat	Unknown

Jack Clark

Ball	$35
Photo	$25
3x5 Index Card	$7
Bat	$50

Will Clark

Ball	$40
Photo	$30
3x5 Index Card	$10
Bat	$60

Donn Clendenon

Ball	$25
Authenticated Ball	$70
Photo	$12
3x5 Index Card	$3
Bat	$40

Tony Cloninger

Ball	$25
Photo	$12
3x5 Index Card	$3
Bat	$40

Jim Coates

Ball	$25
Photo	$12

3x5 Index Card	$3
Bat	$40

Rocky Colavito

Ball	$50
Authenticated Ball	$70
Photo	$35
Authenticated Photo	$45
3x5 Index Card	$10
Bat	$150

Nate Colbert

Ball	$25
Photo	$12
3x5 Index Card	$3
Bat	$40

Jerry Coleman

Ball	$30
Authenticated Ball	$80
Photo	$12
3x5 Index Card	$3
Bat	$40

Vince Coleman

Ball	$35
Photo	$20
3x5 Index Card	$3
Bat	$50

Joe Collins *

Ball	$150
Photo	$40
3x5 Index Card	$10
Bat	$175

Dave Concepcion

Mounted Memories Photo

Ball	$35
Authenticated Ball	$50
Photo	$20
3x5 Index Card	$5
Bat	$50

David Cone

Ball	$40
Authenticated Ball	$200
Photo	$30
Authenticated Photo	$220
3x5 Index Card	$5
Bat	$50

Tony Conigliaro *

Ball	$750
Photo	$350
3x5 Index Card	$100
Bat	Unknown

Gene Conley

Ball	$30
Photo	$20
3x5 Index Card	$8
Bat	$50

Chuck Connors *

Ball	$175
Photo	$60
3x5 Index Card	$25
Bat	$250

Cecil Cooper

Ball	$35
Photo	$25
3x5 Index Card	$5
Bat	$50

Walker Cooper *

Ball	$150
Photo	$50
3x5 Index Card	$10
Bat	$200

Wes Covington

Ball	$40
Photo	$25
3x5 Index Card	$10
Bat	$50

Al Cowens *

Ball	$60
Photo	$25
3x5 Index Card	$10
Bat	$80

Billy Cox *

Ball	$500
Photo	$125
3x5 Index Card	$50
Bat	Unknown

Bobby Cox

Ball	$35
Photo	$20
3x5 Index Card	$5
Bat	$40

Roger Craig

Ball	$25
Photo	$12
3x5 Index Card	$3
Bat	$40

Roger "Doc" Cramer *

Ball	$250
Photo	$50
3x5 Index Card	$20
Bat	Unknown

Del Crandall

Ball	$35
Photo	$20
3x5 Index Card	$5
Bat	$50

Tim Crews *

Ball	$150
Photo	$50
3x5 Index Card	$20
Bat	$200

Warren Cromartie

Ball	$25
Photo	$12
3x5 Index Card	$3
Bat	$40

Jose Cruz Sr.

Ball	$30
Photo	$15
3x5 Index Card	$3
Bat	$40

Frank Crosetti *

Ball	$60
Photo	$30
3x5 Index Card	$10
Bat	$100

Terry Crowley

Ball	$25
Photo	$12
3x5 Index Card	$3
Bat	$40

Mike Cuellar

Ball	$25
Photo	$15
3x5 Index Card	$3
Bat	$40

Mike Curtis

Ball	$25
Authenticated Ball	$70
Photo	$12
3x5 Index Card	$5
Bat	$40

Babe Dahlgren *

Ball	$150
Photo	$50
3x5 Index Card	$20
Bat	$200

Alvin Dark

Ball	$30
Photo	$15
3x5 Index Card	$3
Bat	$40

Ron Darling

Ball	$30
Photo	$18
3x5 Index Card	$3
Bat	$40

Danny Darwin

Ball	$25
Photo	$12
3x5 Index Card	$3
Bat	$40

Darren Daulton

Ball	$30
Authenticated Ball	$75
Photo	$15
3x5 Index Card	$3
Bat	$50

Alvin Davis

Ball	$25
Photo	$12
3x5 Index Card	$3
Bat	$40

Chili Davis

Ball	$25
Photo	$12
3x5 Index Card	$3
Bat	$40

Eric Davis

Ball	$30
Photo	$20
3x5 Index Card	$3
Bat	$50

Glenn Davis

Ball	$25
Photo	$12
3x5 Index Card	$3
Bat	$40

Mark Davis

Ball	$25

Photo	$12
3x5 Index Card	$3
Bat	$40

Ron Davis

Ball	$25
Photo	$12
3x5 Index Card	$3
Bat	$40

Storm Davis

Ball	$25
Photo	$12
3x5 Index Card	$3
Bat	$40

Tommy Davis

Ball	$25
Photo	$12
3x5 Index Card	$3
Bat	$40

Willie Davis

Ball	$25
Photo	$12
3x5 Index Card	$3
Bat	$40

Andre Dawson

Mounted Memories Photo

Ball	$35
Authenticated Ball	$120
Photo	$25
Authenticated Photo	$35
3x5 Index Card	$8
Bat	$50

Paul "Daffy" Dean *

Ball	$250
Photo	$100
3x5 Index Card	$40
Bat	Unknown

Dave DeBusschere *

Ball	$60
Photo	$40
3x5 Index Card	$10
Bat	$75

Doug DeCinces

Ball	$25
Photo	$12
3x5 Index Card	$3
Bat	$40

Rick Dempsey

Ball	$25
Photo	$12
3x5 Index Card	$3
Bat	$40

John Denny

Ball	$25
Photo	$12
3x5 Index Card	$3
Bat	$40

Bucky Dent

Mounted Memories Photo

Ball	$35
Authenticated Ball	$60
Photo	$20
Authenticated Photo	$30
3x5 Index Card	$5
Bat	$50

Bob Dernier

Ball	$25
Photo	$12
3x5 Index Card	$3
Bat	$40

Bo Diaz *

Ball	$75
Photo	$40
3x5 Index Card	$10
Bat	$100

Rob Dibble

Ball	$25
Photo	$12
3x5 Index Card	$3
Bat	$40

Larry Dierker

Ball	$25
Photo	$12
3x5 Index Card	$3
Bat	$40

Dom DiMaggio

Ball	$50
Photo	$30
3x5 Index Card	$10
Bat	$75

Vince DiMaggio *

Ball	$300
Photo	$100
3x5 Index Card	$25
Bat	Unknown

Al Downing

Ball	$25
Photo	$12
3x5 Index Card	$3
Bat	$40

Brian Downing

Ball	$25
Photo	$12
3x5 Index Card	$3
Bat	$40

Doug Drabek

Ball	$25
Photo	$12

3x5 Index Card	$3
Bat	$40

Dave Dravecky

Ball	$25
Photo	$12
3x5 Index Card	$3
Bat	$40

Chuck Dressen *

Ball	$600
Photo	$250
3x5 Index Card	$75
Bat	Unknown

Walt Dropo

Ball	$30
Photo	$12
3x5 Index Card	$3
Bat	$40

Dave Duncan

Ball	$25
Photo	$12
3x5 Index Card	$3
Bat	$40

Ryne Duren

Ball	$25
Photo	$12
3x5 Index Card	$3
Bat	$40

Leon Durham

Ball	$25
Photo	$12
3x5 Index Card	$3
Bat	$40

Duffy Dyer

Ball	$25
Photo	$12
3x5 Index Card	$3
Bat	$40

Len Dykstra

Ball	$35
Photo	$20
3x5 Index Card	$3
Bat	$50

Luke Easter *

Ball	$300
Photo	$150
3x5 Index Card	$50
Bat	Unknown

Dennis Eckersley

Ball	$40
Authenticated Ball	$100
Photo	$25
3x5 Index Card	$10
Bat	$60

Bob Elliot *

Ball	Unknown
Photo	$300
3x5 Index Card	$100
Bat	Unknown

Dock Ellis

Ball	$25
Authenticated Ball	$50
Photo	$12
Authenticated Photo	$20
3x5 Index Card	$3
Bat	$40

Woody English *

Ball	$75
Photo	$35
3x5 Index Card	$10
Bat	$100

Del Ennis *

Ball	$100
Photo	$40
3x5 Index Card	$10
Bat	$150

Carl Erskine

Ball	$30
Photo	$15
Authenticated Photo	$15
3x5 Index Card	$3
Bat	$40

Andy Etchebarren

Ball	$25
Photo	$12
3x5 Index Card	$3
Bat	$40

Darrell Evans

Ball	$25
Photo	$12
3x5 Index Card	$3
Bat	$40

Dwight Evans

Ball	$35
Photo	$25
3x5 Index Card	$3
Bat	$50

Hoot Evers *

Ball	$175
Photo	$50
3x5 Index Card	$15
Bat	$225

Elroy Face

Ball	$25
Photo	$12
3x5 Index Card	$3
Bat	$40

Ferris Fain *

Ball	$50
Photo	$25
3x5 Index Card	$10
Bat	$75

Dick Farrell *

Ball	$500
Photo	$200
3x5 Index Card	$50
Bat	Unknown

Joe Ferguson

Ball	$25
Photo	$12
3x5 Index Card	$3
Bat	$40

Sid Fernandez

Ball	$25
Photo	$12
3x5 Index Card	$3
Bat	$40

Tony Fernandez

Ball	$25
Photo	$12

3x5 Index Card $3
Bat $40

Wes Ferrell *

Ball $350
Photo $150
3x5 Index Card $35
Bat ....Unknown

Boo Ferriss

Ball $25
Photo $12
3x5 Index Card $3
Bat $40

Cecil Fielder

Ball $35
Photo $20
3x5 Index Card $5
Bat $50

Mark Fidrych

Ball $30
Photo $15
3x5 Index Card $5
Bat $40

Ed Figueroa

Ball $25
Photo $12
3x5 Index Card $3
Bat $40

Chuck Finley

Ball $30
Photo $15
3x5 Index Card $3
Bat $40

Bill Fischer

Ball $25
Photo $12
3x5 Index Card $3
Bat $40

Mike Flanagan

Ball $30
Photo $20
3x5 Index Card $3
Bat $40

Curt Flood *

Ball $350
Photo $150
3x5 Index Card $50
Bat $450

Tim Foli

Ball $25
Photo $12
3x5 Index Card $3
Bat $40

Bob Forsch

Ball $25
Photo $12
3x5 Index Card $3
Bat $40

Ken Forsch

Ball $25
Photo $12
3x5 Index Card $3
Bat $40

George Foster

Ball $25
Photo $12
Authenticated Photo $30
3x5 Index Card $3
Bat $50

Bill Freehan

Ball $25
Photo $12
3x5 Index Card $3
Bat $40

Jim Fregosi

Ball $25
Photo $12
3x5 Index Card $3
Bat $40

Bob Friend

Ball $20
Photo $15
3x5 Index Card $5

Carl Furillo *

Ball $400
Photo $150
3x5 Index Card $75
Bat ....Unknown

Gary Gaetti

Ball $30
Photo $15
3x5 Index Card $3
Bat $40

Greg Gagne

Ball $25
Photo $12
3x5 Index Card $3
Bat $40

Chick Gandil *

Ball $1,500
Photo $500
3x5 Index Card $250
Bat ....Unknown

Oscar Gamble

Ball $25
Photo $12
3x5 Index Card $3
Bat $40

Jim Gantner

Ball $25
Photo $12
3x5 Index Card $3
Bat $40

Joe Garagiola

Ball $50
Photo $30
3x5 Index Card $10
Bat $75

Mike Garcia *

Ball $350
Photo $150
3x5 Index Card $40
Bat ....Unknown

Phil Garner

Ball $25
Photo $12
3x5 Index Card $3
Bat $40

Ralph Garr

Ball $25
Photo $12
3x5 Index Card $3
Bat $40

Ned Garver

Ball $22
Photo $15
3x5 Index Card $5

Steve Garvey

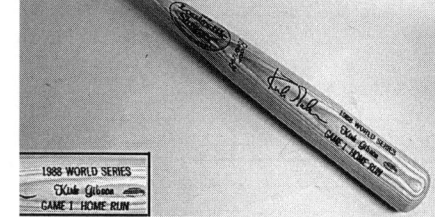

Mounted Memories Photo

Ball $35
Authenticated Ball $65
Photo $20
Authenticated Photo $35
3x5 Index Card $8
Bat $50

Cito Gaston

Ball $25
Photo $12
3x5 Index Card $3
Bat $40

Jim Gentile

Ball $25
Photo $12
3x5 Index Card $3
Bat $40

Cesar Geronimo

Ball $30
Photo $12
3x5 Index Card $5
Bat $40

Kirk Gibson

Ball $40
Photo $30
3x5 Index Card $10
Bat $60

Jim Gilliam *

Ball $400
Photo $200
3x5 Index Card $75
Bat ....Unknown

Al Gionfriddo *

Ball $40
Photo $20
3x5 Index Card $10
Bat $75

Dan Gladden

Ball $25
Photo $12
3x5 Index Card $3
Bat $40

Dwight Gooden

Mounted Memories Photo

Ball $35
Authenticated Ball $115
Photo $25
3x5 Index Card $10
Bat $50

Joe Gordon *

Ball $600
Photo $200
3x5 Index Card $75
Bat ....Unknown

Sid Gordon *

Ball $300
Photo $150
3x5 Index Card $60
Bat ....Unknown

Goose Gossage

Ball $30
Authenticated Ball $60
Photo $20
Authenticated Photo $45
3x5 Index Card $8
Bat $40

Jim "Mudcat" Grant

Ball $25
Photo $15
3x5 Index Card $3
Bat $40

Pete Gray *

Ball $60
Photo $30
3x5 Index Card $15
Bat $100

Mike Greenwell

Ball $25
Photo $12
3x5 Index Card $3
Bat $40

Bobby Grich

Ball $30
Photo $20
3x5 Index Card $3
Bat $40

Ken Griffey Sr.

Ball $35
Authenticated Ball $70
Photo $20
3x5 Index Card $5
Bat $50

Charlie Grimm *

Ball $400
Photo $200
3x5 Index Card $75
Bat ....Unknown

Dick Groat

Ball $35
Photo $25
3x5 Index Card $5
Bat $50

Jerry Grote

Ball $25
Photo $12
3x5 Index Card $3
Bat $40

Kelly Gruber

Ball $25
Photo $12
3x5 Index Card $3
Bat $40

Pedro Guerrero

Ball $30
Photo $20
3x5 Index Card $5
Bat $40

Ron Guidry

Ball $40
Authenticated Ball $70
Photo $30
Authenticated Photo $50
3x5 Index Card $10
Bat $50

Ozzie Guillen

Ball $25
Photo $12
3x5 Index Card $3
Bat $40

Don Gullett

Ball $25
Photo $12
3x5 Index Card $3
Bat $40

Randy Gumpert

Ball $25
Photo $12
3x5 Index Card $3
Bat $40

Tony Gwynn

Ball $75

Authenticated Ball $170
Photo $60
Authenticated Photo $100
3x5 Index Card $20
Bat $125
Authenticated Bat $400

Harvey Haddix *

Ball $150
Photo $50
3x5 Index Card $15
Bat $200

Atlee Hammaker

Ball $25
Photo $12
3x5 Index Card $3
Bat $40

Fred Haney *

Ball $400
Photo $200
3x5 Index Card $50
Bat ....Unknown

Ron Hansen

Ball $25
Photo $12
3x5 Index Card $3
Bat $40

Mel Harder*

Ball $40
Photo $20
3x5 Index Card $8
Bat $75

Mike Hargrove

Ball $30
Photo $20
3x5 Index Card $3
Bat $40

Tommy Harper

Ball $25
Photo $12
3x5 Index Card $3
Bat $40

Toby Harrah

Ball $25
Photo $12
3x5 Index Card $3
Bat $40

Bud Harrelson

Ball $25
Photo $15
3x5 Index Card $3
Bat $40

Ken Harrelson

Ball $40
Photo $30
3x5 Index Card $5
Bat $50

Mickey Hatcher

Ball $25

Photo $12
3x5 Index Card $3
Bat $40

Von Hayes

Ball $25
Photo $12
3x5 Index Card $3
Bat $40

Richie Hebner

Ball $35
Photo $25
3x5 Index Card $5
Bat $40

Jim Hegan *

Ball $150
Photo $50
3x5 Index Card $20
Bat ....Unknown

Dave Henderson

Ball $25
Photo $12
3x5 Index Card $3
Bat $40

George Hendrick

Ball $25
Photo $12
3x5 Index Card $3
Bat $40

Ellie Hendricks

Ball $25
Photo $12
3x5 Index Card $3
Bat $40

Tom Henke

Ball $25
Photo $12
3x5 Index Card $3
Bat $40

Tommy Henrich

Ball $40
Photo $30
3x5 Index Card $10
Bat $65

Keith Hernandez

Mounted Memories Photo

Ball $40
Authenticated Ball $90
Photo $30
3x5 Index Card $8
Bat $60

Willie Hernandez

Ball $25
Photo $12
3x5 Index Card $3
Bat $40

Orel Hershiser

Ball $40

Steiner Sports Photo

Authenticated Ball $100
Photo $30
Authenticated Photo $80
3x5 Index Card $10
Bat $60

Whitey Herzog

Ball $30
Photo $20
3x5 Index Card $5
Bat $40

Larry Hisle

Ball $25
Photo $12
3x5 Index Card $3
Bat $40

Butch Hobson

Ball $25
Photo $12
3x5 Index Card $3
Bat $40

Gil Hodges *

Ball $1,700
Photo $600
3x5 Index Card $250

Tommy Holmes

Ball $25
Photo $12
3x5 Index Card $3
Bat $40

Burt Hooten

Ball $25
Photo $12
3x5 Index Card $3
Bat $40

Bob Horner

Ball $25
Photo $12
3x5 Index Card $3
Bat $40

Willie Horton

Ball $25
Photo $12
3x5 Index Card $3
Bat $40

Charlie Hough

Ball $25
Photo $12
3x5 Index Card $3
Bat $40

Ralph Houk

Ball $35
Photo $25
3x5 Index Card $5
Bat $50

Elston Howard *

Ball $500
Photo $250
3x5 Index Card $100
Bat ....Unknown

Frank Howard

Mounted Memories Photo

Ball $30
Photo $20
3x5 Index Card $8
Bat $50

Art Howe

Ball $25
Photo $12
3x5 Index Card $3
Bat $40

Steve Howe

Ball $25
Photo $12
3x5 Index Card $3
Bat $40

Dick Howser

Ball $150
Photo $50
3x5 Index Card $25
Bat $200

Lamarr Hoyt

Ball $25
Photo $12
3x5 Index Card $3
Bat $40

Al Hrabosky

Ball $25
Photo $12
3x5 Index Card $3
Bat $40

Kent Hrbek

Ball $30
Photo $20
3x5 Index Card $3
Bat $40

Randy Hundley

Ball $25
Photo $12
3x5 Index Card $3
Bat $40

Ron Hunt

Ball $25
Photo $12
3x5 Index Card $3
Bat $40

Clint Hurdle

Ball $25
Photo $12
3x5 Index Card $3
Bat $40

Bruce Hurst

Ball $25
Photo $12
3x5 Index Card $3
Bat $40

Fred Hutchinson *

Ball $500
Photo $250
3x5 Index Card $100
Bat ....Unknown

Pete Incaviglia

Ball $25
Photo $15
3x5 Index Card $3
Bat $40

Bo Jackson

Tri-Star Productions Photo

Ball $50
Authenticated Ball $125
Photo $40
3x5 Index Card $15
Bat $75

Joe Jackson *

Ball .... $25,000-$30,000
Photo .... $10,000-$15,000
3x5 Index Card .... $8,000-$12,000

Vic Janowicz

Ball $75
Photo $50
3x5 Index Card $20
Bat $150

Joey Jay

Ball $25
Photo $12
3x5 Index Card $3
Bat $40

Gregg Jefferies

Ball $25
Photo $12
3x5 Index Card $3
Bat $40

Jackie Jensen *

Ball $500
Photo $250
3x5 Index Card $50
Bat ....Unknown

Sam Jethroe *

Ball $40
Photo $25
3x5 Index Card $10
Bat $60

Tommy John

Ball $30

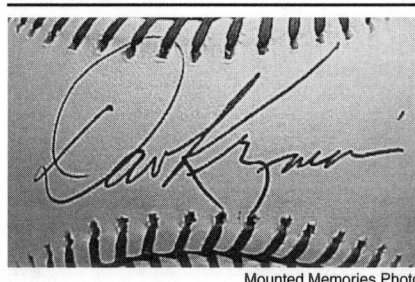
Mounted Memories Photo

Authenticated Ball $40
Photo $20
Authenticated Photo $30
3x5 Index Card $5
Bat $40

Davey Johnson

Ball $30
Authenticated Ball $50
Photo $20
3x5 Index Card $5
Bat $40

Alex Johnson

Ball $25
Photo $12
3x5 Index Card $3
Bat $40

Howard Johnson

Ball $25
Photo $12
3x5 Index Card $3
Bat $40

Jay Johnstone

Ball $25
Photo $12
3x5 Index Card $3
Bat $40

Cleon Jones

Ball $25
Photo $12
Authenticated Photo $40
3x5 Index Card $3
Bat $40

Eddie Joost

Ball $25
Photo $12
3x5 Index Card $3
Bat $40

Wally Joyner

Ball $30
Photo $20
3x5 Index Card $3
Bat $40

David Justice

Ball $50
Authenticated Ball $90
Photo $35
Authenticated Photo $130
3x5 Index Card $8
Bat $75
Authenticated Bat $600

Jim Kaat

Ball $35
Authenticated Ball $100
Photo $25
3x5 Index Card $5
Bat $50

Steve Kemp

Ball $25

Photo $12
3x5 Index Card $3
Bat $40

Don Kessinger

Ball $25
Photo $12
3x5 Index Card $3
Bat $40

Jimmy Key

Ball $30
Authenticated Ball $70
Photo $20
Authenticated Photo $60
3x5 Index Card $3
Bat $40

Darryl Kile *

Ball $75
Photo $40
3x5 Index Card $10
Bat $100

Jeff King

Ball $25
Photo $12
3x5 Index Card $3
Bat $40

Brian Kingman

Ball $25
Photo $12
3x5 Index Card $3
Bat $40

Dave Kingman

Mounted Memories Photo

Ball $35
Photo $25
3x5 Index Card $3
Bat $50

Ron Kittle

Ball $25
Photo $12
3x5 Index Card $3
Bat $40

Ted Kluszewski *

Ball $300
Photo $100
3x5 Index Card $35
Bat $500

Ray Knight

Ball $25
Authenticated Ball $70
Photo $12

3x5 Index Card $3
Bat $40

Mark Koenig *

Ball $75
Photo $35
3x5 Index Card $10
Bat $100

Jim Konstanty

Ball $400
Photo $150
3x5 Index Card $50
Bat ....Unknown

Jerry Koosman

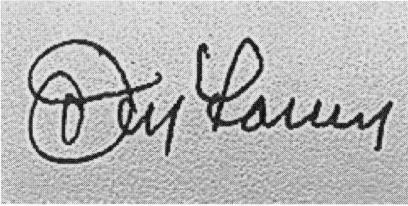

Mounted Memories Photo

Ball $30
Authenticated Ball $70
Photo $20
3x5 Index Card $3
Bat $40

Ed Kranepool

Ball $25
Photo $12
Authenticated Photo $30
3x5 Index Card $3
Bat $40

John Kruk

Ball $25
Photo $15
3x5 Index Card $3
Bat $40

Tony Kubek

Ball $100
Photo $75
3x5 Index Card $20
Bat $125

Harvey Kuenn *

Ball $350
Photo $100
3x5 Index Card $40
Bat ....Unknown

Bill Kunkel

Ball $175
Photo $60
3x5 Index Card $25
Bat $250

Clem Labine

Ball $30
Photo $20
3x5 Index Card $3
Bat $40

Mark Langston

Ball $25
Photo $12
3x5 Index Card $3
Bat $40

Carney Lansford

Ball $25

Photo $12
3x5 Index Card $3
Bat $40

Don Larsen

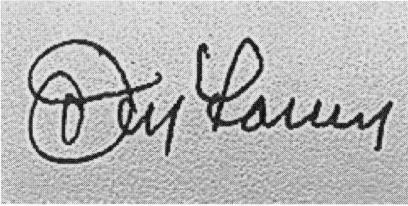

Mounted Memories Photo

Ball $35
Authenticated Ball $100
Photo $20
Authenticated Photo $50
3x5 Index Card $8
Bat $50

Tony LaRussa

Ball $40
Photo $30
3x5 Index Card $8
Bat $50

Frank Lary

Ball $25
Photo $12
3x5 Index Card $3
Bat $40

Charlie Lau

Ball $150
Photo $50
3x5 Index Card $25
Bat $200

Cookie Lavagetto

Ball $150
Photo $75
3x5 Index Card $25
Bat $200

Vern Law

Ball $25
Photo $12
3x5 Index Card $3
Bat $40

Bill Lee

Ball $25
Photo $12
3x5 Index Card $3
Bat $40

Ron LeFlore

Ball $25
Photo $12
3x5 Index Card $3
Bat $40

Mark Lemke

Ball $25
Photo $12
3x5 Index Card $3
Bat $40

Jim Lemon

Ball $25
Photo $12
3x5 Index Card $3
Bat $40

Phil Linz

Ball $25
Photo $15
3x5 Index Card $5

Pat Listach

Ball $25
Photo $12
3x5 Index Card $3
Bat $40

Billy Loes

Ball $35
Photo $25
3x5 Index Card $5
Bat $50

Johnny Logan

Ball $25
Photo $12
3x5 Index Card $3
Bat $40

Mickey Lolich

Ball $25
Photo $12
3x5 Index Card $3
Bat $40

Sherm Lollar *

Ball $200
Photo $100
3x5 Index Card $30
Bat ....Unknown

Vic Lombardi*

Ball $75
Photo $35
3x5 Index Card $10
Bat $100

Jim Lonborg

Ball $25
Photo $12
3x5 Index Card $3
Bat $40

Dale Long *

Ball $150
Photo $60
3x5 Index Card $20
Bat $200

Ed Lopat *

Ball $200
Photo $75
3x5 Index Card $25
Bat $300

Davey Lopes

Ball $25
Photo $12
3x5 Index Card $3
Bat $40

Greg Luzinski

Ball $25
Photo $15
Authenticated Photo $30
3x5 Index Card $3
Bat $40

Sparky Lyle

Ball $25
Authenticated Ball $50
Photo $12

Steiner Sport Photo

3x5 Index Card $3
Bat $40

Fred Lynn

Mounted Memories Photo

Ball $35
Authenticated Ball $55
Photo $20
3x5 Index Card $5
Bat $50

Garry Maddox

Ball $25
Photo $12
3x5 Index Card $3
Bat $40

Bill Madlock

Mounted Memories Photo

Ball $35
Authenticated Ball $50
Photo $25
3x5 Index Card $5
Bat $50

Sal Maglie *

Ball $250
Photo $100
3x5 Index Card $25
Bat $400

Frank Malzone

Ball $25
Photo $12
3x5 Index Card $3
Bat $40

Marty Marion

Ball $35
Photo $20
3x5 Index Card $5
Bat $50

Roger Maris *

Ball $2,000
Photo $700
3x5 Index Card $400
Bat $2,500

Mike A. Marshall

Ball $25

Photo $12
3x5 Index Card $3
Bat $40

Mike G. Marshall

Ball $350
Photo $200
3x5 Index Card $50
Bat $400

Billy Martin *

Ball $250
Photo $125
3x5 Index Card $50
Bat $350

Dennis Martinez

Ball $35
Photo $25
3x5 Index Card $5
Bat $50

Ramon Martinez

Ball $25
Photo $12
3x5 Index Card $3
Bat $40

Tippy Martinez

Ball $25
Photo $12
3x5 Index Card $3
Bat $40

John Matlack

Ball $25
Photo $12
3x5 Index Card $3
Bat $40

Gary Matthews

Ball $25
Photo $12
3x5 Index Card $3
Bat $40

Don Mattingly

Mounted Memories Photo

Ball $60
Authenticated Ball $180
Photo $45
Authenticated Photo $65
3x5 Index Card $20
Bat $100
Authenticated Bat $650

Gene Mauch

Ball $35
Photo $25
3x5 Index Card $5
Bat $50

Lee May

Ball $25
Photo $12

3x5 Index Card $3
Bat $40

John Mayberry

Ball $25
Photo $12
3x5 Index Card $3
Bat $40

Lee Maye*

Ball $40
Photo $25
3x5 Index Card $10
Bat $60

Lee Mazzilli

Ball $25
Photo $12
3x5 Index Card $3
Bat $40

Bake McBride

Ball $25
Photo $12
3x5 Index Card $3
Bat $40

Tim McCarver

Ball $40
Photo $30
3x5 Index Card $8
Bat $60

Mike McCormick

Ball $30
Photo $20
3x5 Index Card $5
Bat $40

Mickey McDermott

Ball $25
Photo $12
3x5 Index Card $5
Bat $40

Ben McDonald

Ball $25
Photo $12
3x5 Index Card $3
Bat $40

Gil McDougald

Ball $35
Photo $25
3x5 Index Card $5
Bat $50

Jack McDowell

Ball $25
Photo $12
3x5 Index Card $3
Bat $40

Sam McDowell

Ball $25
Photo $12
3x5 Index Card $3
Bat $40

Willie McGee

Ball $35
Photo $25
3x5 Index Card $3
Bat $50

Scott McGregor

Ball $25

Photo $12
3x5 Index Card $3
Bat $40

Tug McGraw

Ball $35
Authenticated Ball $50
Photo $25
3x5 Index Card $7
Bat $50

Mark McGwire

Ball $500
Authenticated Ball $900
Photo $200
3x5 Index Card $50
Bat $700

Denny McLain

Ball $35
Photo $25
3x5 Index Card $7
Bat $50

Roy McMillan *

Ball $75
Photo $40
3x5 Index Card $10
Bat $100

Dave McNally *

Ball $50
Photo $25
3x5 Index Card $10
Bat $75

Brian McRae

Ball $25
Photo $12
3x5 Index Card $3
Bat $40

Hal McRae

Ball $30
Photo $20
3x5 Index Card $5
Bat $50

Kevin McReynolds

Ball $25
Photo $12
3x5 Index Card $3
Bat $40

Bill Melton

Ball $25
Photo $15
3x5 Index Card $3
Bat $40

Andy Messersmith

Ball $25
Photo $12
3x5 Index Card $3
Bat $40

Butch Metzger

Ball $25
Photo $12
3x5 Index Card $3
Bat $40

Gene Michael

Ball $25
Photo $12
3x5 Index Card $3
Bat $40

John Milner *

Ball $50
Photo $30
3x5 Index Card $8
Bat $75

Minnie Minoso

Mounted Memories Photo

Ball $35
Authenticated Ball $45
Photo $25
3x5 Index Card $10
Bat $50

Kevin Mitchell

Ball $30
Photo $20
Authenticated Ball $30
3x5 Index Card $3
Bat $50

"Vinegar Bend" Mizell *

Ball $75
Photo $35
3x5 Index Card $10
Bat $100

Paul Molitor

Ball $75
Authenticated Ball $200
Photo $50
3x5 Index Card $15
Bat $100

Rick Monday

Ball $25
Photo $12
3x5 Index Card $3
Bat $40

Don Money

Ball $25
Photo $12
3x5 Index Card $3
Bat $40

Wally Moon

Ball $25
Photo $12
3x5 Index Card $3
Bat $40

Terry Moore *

Ball $75
Photo $30
3x5 Index Card $10
Bat $125

Mickey Morandini

Ball $25
Photo $12
3x5 Index Card $3
Bat $40

Omar Moreno

Ball $25
Photo $12
3x5 Index Card $3
Bat $40

Jack Morris

Ball $35
Authenticated Ball $60
Photo $25
3x5 Index Card $5
Bat $50

Omar Moreno

Ball $25
Photo $15
3x5 Index Card $5

Manny Mota

Ball $30
Photo $20
3x5 Index Card $3
Bat $40

Van Lingle Mungo *

Ball $150
Photo $50
3x5 Index Card $20
Bat $200

Thurman Munson *

Ball $2,000
Photo $750
3x5 Index Card $350
Bat ....Unknown

Bobby Murcer

Mounted Memories Photo

Ball $30
Authenticated Ball $100
Photo $20
3x5 Index Card $5
Bat $40

Dale Murphy

Mounted Memories Photo

Ball $50
Authenticated Ball $110
Photo $40
Authenticated Photo $60
3x5 Index Card $10
Bat $75

Danny Murtaugh *

Ball $400
Photo $175
3x5 Index Card $50
Bat ....Unknown

Charlie Neal *

Ball $75
Photo $30
3x5 Index Card $10
Bat $100

Graig Nettles

Mounted Memories Photo

Ball $30
Authenticated Ball $60
Photo $20
Authenticated Photo $35
3x5 Index Card $5
Bat $50

Don Newcombe

Ball $35
Authenticated Ball $65
Photo $20
3x5 Index Card $8
Bat $50

Bobo Newsom *

Ball $500
Photo $250
3x5 Index Card $75
Bat ....Unknown

Joe Niekro

Ball $30
Photo $20
3x5 Index Card $5
Bat $50

Otis Nixon

Ball $25
Photo $12
3x5 Index Card $3
Bat $40

Jim Northrup

Ball $25
Photo $12
3x5 Index Card $3
Bat $40

Joe Nuxhall

Ball $25
Photo $12
3x5 Index Card $3
Bat $40

Lefty O'Doul *

Ball $700
Photo $300
3x5 Index Card $75
Bat ....Unknown

Paul O'Neill

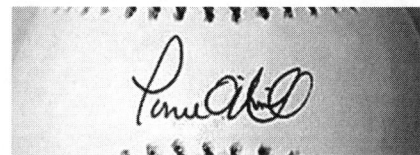

Ball $40
Authenticated Ball $190
Photo $30
Authenticated Photo $140
3x5 Index Card $5
Bat $60

Johnny Oates

Ball $25
Photo $12
3x5 Index Card $3
Bat $40

Blue Moon Odom

Ball $25
Photo $12
3x5 Index Card $3
Bat $40

Ken Oberkfell

Ball $25
Photo $12
3x5 Index Card $3
Bat $40

Ben Oglivie

Ball $30
Photo $15
3x5 Index Card $3
Bat $40

Steve Olin *

Ball $150
Photo $75
3x5 Index Card $20
Bat $200

Jose Oliva *

Ball $75
Photo $40
3x5 Index Card $15
Bat $100

Tony Oliva

Ball $30
Photo $15
3x5 Index Card $5
Bat $50

Al Oliver

Mounted Memories Photo

Ball $30
Authenticated Ball $55
Photo $20
Authenticated Photo $25
3x5 Index Card $5
Bat $50

Claude Osteen

Ball $25
Photo $12
3x5 Index Card $3
Bat $40

Amos Otis

Ball $25
Photo $12
3x5 Index Card $3
Bat $40

Ed Ott

Ball $25
Photo $12
3x5 Index Card $3
Bat $40

Mickey Owen

Ball $35
Photo $20
3x5 Index Card $5
Bat $50

Andy Pafko

Ball $25
Authenticated Ball $50
Photo $12
Authenticated Photo $40
3x5 Index Card $3
Bat $40

Mike Pagliarulo

Ball $25
Photo $12
3x5 Index Card $3
Bat $40

Dave Parker

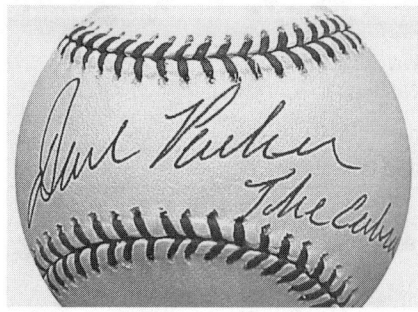

Mounted Memories Photo

Ball $35
Authenticated Ball $85
Photo $25
3x5 Index Card $8
Bat $50

Wes Parker

Ball $25
Photo $12
3x5 Index Card $3
Bat $40

Mel Parnell

Ball $25
Photo $12

3x5 Index Card $3
Bat $40

Lance Parrish

Ball $30
Authenticated Ball $80
Photo $15
3x5 Index Card $3
Bat $40

Camilo Pascual

Ball $40
Photo $30
3x5 Index Card $8
Bat $50

Freddie Patek

Ball $25
Photo $12
3x5 Index Card $3
Bat $40

Albie Pearson

Ball $25
Photo $12
3x5 Index Card $3
Bat $40

Tony Pena

Ball $30
Photo $15
3x5 Index Card $5
Bat $40

Terry Pendleton

Mounted Memories Photo

Ball $30
Photo $15
3x5 Index Card $3
Bat $40

Joe Pepitone

Mounted Memories Photo

Ball $30
Authenticated Ball $50
Photo $15
Authenticated Photo $25
3x5 Index Card $3
Bat $40

Jim Perry

Ball $25
Photo $12
3x5 Index Card $3
Bat $40

Johnny Pesky

Ball $30
Photo $15
3x5 Index Card $3
Bat $40

Rico Petrocelli

Ball $25
Photo $12
3x5 Index Card $3
Bat $40

Tony Phillips

Ball $25
Photo $10
3x5 Index Card $3
Bat $40

Billy Pierce

Ball $25
Photo $12
3x5 Index Card $3
Bat $40

Jimmy Piersall

Ball $30
Photo $15
3x5 Index Card $3
Bat $40

Lou Piniella

Ball $35
Authenticated Ball $80
Photo $25
Authenticated Photo $90
3x5 Index Card $7
Bat $50

Vada Pinson *

Ball $200
Photo $75
3x5 Index Card $25
Bat $300

Juan Pizarro

Ball $35
Photo $20
3x5 Index Card $7
Bat $50

Johnny Podres

Ball $25
Authenticated Ball $60
Photo $12
3x5 Index Card $3
Bat $40

Darrell Porter *

Ball $60
Photo $40
3x5 Index Card $10
Bat $80

Boog Powell

Ball $35

Photo $20
3x5 Index Card $8
Bat $50

Vic Power

Ball $25
Photo $12
3x5 Index Card $3
Bat $40

Dan Quisenberry *

Ball $75
Photo $40
3x5 Index Card $10
Bat $100

Tim Raines

Ball $30
Authenticated Ball $100
Photo $15
3x5 Index Card $5
Bat $40

Pedro Ramos

Ball $25
Photo $12
3x5 Index Card $3
Bat $40

Willie Randolph

Ball $35
Photo $25
3x5 Index Card $5
Bat $50

Vic Raschi *

Ball $250
Photo $125
3x5 Index Card $25
Bat $300

Jeff Reardon

Ball $25
Photo $12
3x5 Index Card $3
Bat $40

Ron Reed

Ball $25
Photo $10
3x5 Index Card $3
Bat $40

Jimmie Reese *

Ball $100
Photo $40
3x5 Index Card $15
Bat $150

Pete Reiser *

Ball $250
Photo $100
3x5 Index Card $25
Bat $350

Rick Reuschel

Ball $25
Photo $12
3x5 Index Card $3
Bat $40

Jerry Reuss

Ball $25
Photo $10
3x5 Index Card $3
Bat $40

Allie Reynolds *

Ball	$200
Photo	$60
3x5 Index Card	$20
Bat	$250

Harold Reynolds

Ball	$25
Photo	$12
3x5 Index Card	$3
Bat	$40

Rick Rhoden

Ball	$25
Photo	$12
3x5 Index Card	$3
Bat	$40

Dusty Rhodes

Ball	$25
Photo	$12
3x5 Index Card	$3
Bat	$40

Jim Rice

Ball	$35
Authenticated Ball	$60
Photo	$25
3x5 Index Card	$8
Bat	$50

J.R. Richard

Mounted Memories Photo

Ball	$25
Photo	$12
Authenticated Photo	$20
3x5 Index Card	$3
Bat	$40

Paul Richards *

Ball	$200
Photo	$60
3x5 Index Card	$20
Bat	Unknown

Bobby Richardson

Ball	$35
Authenticated Ball	$50
Photo	$20
3x5 Index Card	$5
Bat	$50

Dave Righetti

Ball	$25
Photo	$12
3x5 Index Card	$3
Bat	$40

Bill Rigney *

Ball	$50
Photo	$30
3x5 Index Card	$10
Bat	$75

Billy Ripken

Ball	$25
Photo	$12

3x5 Index Card	$3
Bat	$40

Cal Ripken Jr.

Tri-Star Productions Photo

Ball	$125
Authenticated Ball	$300
Photo	$50
Authenticated Photo	$125
3x5 Index Card	$25
Bat	$200
Authenticated Bat	$750

Cal Ripken Sr.

Ball	$75
Photo	$35
3x5 Index Card	$15
Bat	$100

Mickey Rivers

Ball	$25
Photo	$12
3x5 Index Card	$3
Bat	$40

Eddie Robinson

Ball	$25
Photo	$12
3x5 Index Card	$3
Bat	$40

Preacher Roe

Ball	$30
Photo	$20
3x5 Index Card	$5
Bat	$40

Bob "Buck" Rodgers

Ball	$25
Photo	$12
3x5 Index Card	$3
Bat	$40

Aurelio Rodriguez *

Ball	$50
Photo	$25
3x5 Index Card	$8
Bat	$75

Steve Rogers

Ball	$25
Photo	$12
3x5 Index Card	$3
Bat	$40

Cookie Rojas

Ball	$25
Photo	$12
3x5 Index Card	$3
Bat	$40

Red Rolfe*

Ball	$500
Photo	$200
3x5 Index Card	$50
Bat	Unknown

Pete Rose

Ball	$50
Authenticated Ball	$110

3x5 Index Card	$3
Bat	$40

Mounted Memories Photo

Photo	$40
Authenticated Photo	$90
3x5 Index Card	$20
Bat	$125
Authenticated Bat	$325

John Roseboro *

Ball	$50
Photo	$30
3x5 Index Card	$5
Bat	$75

Al Rosen

Ball	$35
Authenticated Ball	$70
Photo	$25
3x5 Index Card	$10
Bat	$60

Joe Rudi

Ball	$25
Photo	$12
3x5 Index Card	$3
Bat	$40

Pete Runnels *

Ball	$100
Photo	$50
3x5 Index Card	$10
Bat	$150

Bill Russell

Ball	$25
Photo	$12
3x5 Index Card	$3
Bat	$40

Bret Saberhagen

Ball	$30
Authenticated Ball	$45
Photo	$15
3x5 Index Card	$3
Bat	$40

Chris Sabo

Ball	$25
Photo	$12
3x5 Index Card	$3
Bat	$40

Johnny Sain

Ball	$25
Photo	$12
3x5 Index Card	$3
Bat	$40

Juan Samuel

Ball	$25
Photo	$12
3x5 Index Card	$3
Bat	$40

Ryne Sandberg

Tri-Star Productions Photo

Ball	$50
Authenticated Ball	$150
Photo	$40
Authenticated Photo	$90
3x5 Index Card	$15
Bat	$75
Authenticated Bat	$280

Deion Sanders

Ball	$50
Photo	$40
3x5 Index Card	$10
Bat	$75

Manny Sanguillen

Ball	$25
Photo	$12
3x5 Index Card	$3
Bat	$40

Ron Santo

Ball	$35
Photo	$20
3x5 Index Card	$5
Bat	$50

Hank Sauer *

Ball	$75
Photo	$35
3x5 Index Card	$10
Bat	$100

Steve Sax

Ball	$25
Photo	$12
3x5 Index Card	$3
Bat	$40

Mike Scioscia

Ball	$25
Photo	$12
3x5 Index Card	$3
Bat	$40

Herb Score

Ball	$25
Authenticated Ball	$45
Photo	$12
3x5 Index Card	$3
Bat	$40

George Scott

Ball	$30
Photo	$20
3x5 Index Card	$3
Bat	$40

Mike Scott

Ball	$25
Photo	$12
3x5 Index Card	$3
Bat	$40

Kevin Seitzer

Ball	$25
Photo	$12

3x5 Index Card	$3
Bat	$40

Bobby Shantz

Ball	$30
Photo	$15
3x5 Index Card	$5
Bat	$40

Larry Sherry

Ball	$25
Photo	$12
3x5 Index Card	$3
Bat	$40

Chris Short *

Ball	$200
Photo	$100
3x5 Index Card	$35
Bat	$300

Eric Show *

Ball	$100
Photo	$50
3x5 Index Card	$20
Bat	$150

Roy Sievers

Ball	$25
Photo	$12
Authenticated Photo	$20
3x5 Index Card	$3
Bat	$40

Ted Simmons

Ball	$30
Photo	$15
3x5 Index Card	$3
Bat	$40

Harry "Suitcase" Simpson *

Ball	$350
Photo	$175
3x5 Index Card	$50
Bat	Unknown

Ken Singleton

Ball	$25
Photo	$12
3x5 Index Card	$3
Bat	$40

Dick Sisler *

Ball	$50
Photo	$25
3x5 Index Card	$8
Bat	$75

Sibby Sisti

Ball	$25
Photo	$12
3x5 Index Card	$3
Bat	$40

Bill "Moose" Skowron

Ball	$30
Authenticated Ball	$50
Photo	$15
3x5 Index Card	$3
Bat	$40

Roy Smalley Jr.

Ball	$25
Photo	$12

3x5 Index Card	$3
Bat	$40

Roy Smalley Sr.

Ball	$25
Photo	$12
3x5 Index Card	$3
Bat	$40

John Smiley

Ball	$25
Photo	$12
3x5 Index Card	$3
Bat	$40

Lee Smith

Ball	$35
Authenticated Ball	$50
Photo	$25
3x5 Index Card	$5
Bat	$50

Lonnie Smith

Ball	$25
Photo	$12
3x5 Index Card	$3
Bat	$40

Reggie Smith

Ball	$25
Photo	$12
3x5 Index Card	$3
Bat	$40

Luis Sojo

Ball	$25
Authenticated Ball	$50
Photo	$12
3x5 Index Card	$3
Bat	$40

Mario Soto

Ball	$25
Photo	$12
3x5 Index Card	$3
Bat	$40

Billy Southworth*

Ball	$400
Photo	$250
3x5 Index Card	$100
Bat	Unknown

Jim Spencer *

Ball	$50
Photo	$30
3x5 Index Card	$8
Bat	$75

Eddie Stanky *

Ball	$100
Photo	$50
3x5 Index Card	$15
Bat	$150

Bob Stanley

Ball	$25
Photo	$12
3x5 Index Card	$3
Bat	$40

Fred Stanley

Ball	$25
Photo	$12
3x5 Index Card	$3
Bat	$40

Rusty Staub

Mounted Memories Photo

Ball	$35
Authenticated Ball	$50
Photo	$25
Authenticated Photo	$30
3x5 Index Card	$8
Bat	$50

Terry Steinbach

Ball	$25
Photo	$12
3x5 Index Card	$3
Bat	$40

Vern Stephens*

Ball	$500
Photo	$300
3x5 Index Card	$100
Bat	Unknown

Dave Stewart

Ball	$25
Authenticated Ball	$70
Photo	$12
3x5 Index Card	$3
Bat	$40

Dave Stieb

Ball	$25
Photo	$12
3x5 Index Card	$3
Bat	$40

Steve Stone

Ball	$35
Photo	$25
3x5 Index Card	$5
Bat	$50

Mel Stottlemyre

Ball	$30
Authenticated Ball	$50
Photo	$20
3x5 Index Card	$3
Bat	$40

Todd Stottlemyre

Ball	$30
Authenticated Ball	$45
Photo	$20
3x5 Index Card	$3
Bat	$40

Monty Stratton *

Ball	$350
Photo	$150
3x5 Index Card	$50
Bat	Unknown

Darryl Strawberry

Ball	$35
Authenticated Ball	$70
Photo	$25
Authenticated Photo	$70
3x5 Index Card	$10
Bat	$50

Clyde Sukeforth *

Ball	$50
Photo	$30
3x5 Index Card	$8
Bat	$75

Rev. Billy Sunday *

Ball	$2,500
Photo	$1,000
3x5 Index Card	$400
Bat	Unknown

Rick Sutcliffe

Ball	$25
Photo	$12
3x5 Index Card	$3
Bat	$40

Bruce Sutter

Mounted Memories Photo

Ball	$35
Authenticated Ball	$80
Photo	$25
3x5 Index Card	$5
Bat	$50

Ron Swoboda

Ball	$25
Photo	$12
3x5 Index Card	$3
Bat	$40

Frank Tanana

Ball	$25
Authenticated Ball	$50
Photo	$12
Authenticated Photo	$20
3x5 Index Card	$3
Bat	$40

Chuck Tanner

Ball	$25
Photo	$12
3x5 Index Card	$3
Bat	$40

Danny Tartabull

Ball	$25

Photo	$12
3x5 Index Card	$3
Bat	$40

Birdie Tebbetts *

Ball	$125
Photo	$50
3x5 Index Card	$20
Bat	$150

Kent Tekulve

Ball	$25
Photo	$15
3x5 Index Card	$3
Bat	$40

Johnny Temple *

Ball	$75
Photo	$40
3x5 Index Card	$10
Bat	$125

Garry Templeton

Ball	$25
Photo	$15
3x5 Index Card	$3
Bat	$40

Gene Tenace

Ball	$25
Photo	$15
3x5 Index Card	$3
Bat	$40

Ralph Terry

Ball	$35
Photo	$20
3x5 Index Card	$3
Bat	$50

Wayne Terwilliger

Ball	$25
Photo	$15
3x5 Index Card	$3
Bat	$40

Mickey Tettleton

Ball	$25
Photo	$15
3x5 Index Card	$3
Bat	$40

Bobby Thigpen

Ball	$25
Photo	$15
3x5 Index Card	$3
Bat	$40

Frank J. Thomas

Ball	$25
Photo	$15
3x5 Index Card	$3
Bat	$40

Gorman Thomas

Mounted Memories Photo

Ball	$25
Authenticated Ball	$50

Photo $15
3x5 Index Card $3
Bat $40

Danny Thompson *

Ball $250
Photo $100
3x5 Index Card $20
Bat $300

Bobby Thomson

Ball $35
Authenticated Ball $60
Photo $20
3x5 Index Card $10
Bat $50
Authenticated Bat $200

Andre Thornton

Ball $25
Photo $15
3x5 Index Card $3
Bat $40

Marv Throneberry *

Ball $100
Photo $35
3x5 Index Card $15
Bat $150

Luis Tiant

Ball $25
Photo $15
3x5 Index Card $3
Bat $40

Frank Torre

Ball $25
Photo $15
3x5 Index Card $3
Bat $40

Joe Torre

Ball $75
Authenticated Ball $210
Photo $50
Authenticated Photo $180
3x5 Index Card $20
Bat $100

Alan Trammell

Mounted Memories Photo

Ball $30
Authenticated Ball $90
Photo $20
Authenticated Photo $40
3x5 Index Card $3
Bat $40

Tom Tresh

Ball $25
Authenticated Ball $45
Photo $15
3x5 Index Card $3
Bat $40

Manny Trillo

Ball $25

Photo $15
3x5 Index Card $3
Bat $40

Virgil Trucks

Ball $25
Photo $15
3x5 Index Card $3
Bat $40

Bob Turley

Ball $30
Photo $15
3x5 Index Card $3
Bat $50

Bob Uecker

Ball $50
Photo $35
3x5 Index Card $10
Bat $75

Bobby Valentine

Mounted Memories Photo

Ball $25
Authenticated Ball $85
Photo $15
Authenticated Photo $30
3x5 Index Card $3
Bat $40

Fernando Valenzuela

Ball $40
Photo $30
3x5 Index Card $10
Bat $75

Elmer Valo *

Ball $60
Photo $35
3x5 Index Card $8
Bat $80

Johnny VanderMeer *

Ball $50
Photo $30
3x5 Index Card $10
Bat $75

Andy Van Slyke

Ball $25
Photo $15
Authenticated Photo $25
3x5 Index Card $3
Bat $40

Mickey Vernon

Ball $25
Photo $15
3x5 Index Card $3
Bat $40

Zoilo Versalles

Ball $175
Photo $100
3x5 Index Card $25
Bat $250

Frank Viola

Ball $25
Photo $15
3x5 Index Card $3
Bat $40

Bill Virdon

Ball $25
Photo $15
3x5 Index Card $3
Bat $40

Pete Vuckovich

Ball $40
Photo $30
3x5 Index Card $10
Bat $60

Dixie Walker *

Ball $300
Photo $150
3x5 Index Card $35
Bat $500

Harry Walker *

Ball $75
Photo $30
3x5 Index Card $10
Bat $100

Rube Walker *

Ball $200
Photo $50
3x5 Index Card $20
Bat $300

Bucky Walters *

Ball $125
Photo $50
3x5 Index Card $15
Bat $200

Jerome Walton

Ball $25
Photo $15
3x5 Index Card $3
Bat $40

Bill Wambsganss*

Ball $300
Photo $150
3x5 Index Card $50
Bat ....Unknown

Claudell Washington

Ball $25
Photo $15
3x5 Index Card $3
Bat $40

Bob Watson

Ball $25
Photo $15
3x5 Index Card $3
Bat $40

Walt Weiss

Ball $25
Photo $15
3x5 Index Card $3
Bat $40

Bob Welch

Ball $25
Photo $15
3x5 Index Card $3
Bat $40

Vic Wertz *

Ball $300
Photo $125
3x5 Index Card $40
Bat $500

Wes Westrum *

Ball $50
Photo $25
3x5 Index Card $8
Bat $75

John Wetteland

Ball $25
Photo $15
Authenticated Photo $100
3x5 Index Card $3
Bat $40

Lou Whitaker

Ball $30
Photo $15
3x5 Index Card $3
Bat $40

Bill White

Ball $25
Photo $15
3x5 Index Card $3
Bat $40

Frank White

Ball $25
Photo $15
3x5 Index Card $3
Bat $40

Roy White

Ball $25
Photo $15
3x5 Index Card $3
Bat $40

Alan Wiggins *

Ball $100
Photo $50
3x5 Index Card $25
Bat $150

Dick Williams

Ball $30
Photo $25
3x5 Index Card $5
Bat $40

Earl Williams

Ball $25
Photo $15
Authenticated Photo $20
3x5 Index Card $3
Bat $40

Ken Williams *

Ball $500
Photo $300
3x5 Index Card $75
Bat ....Unknown

Matt Williams

Ball $35
Photo $25
3x5 Index Card $5
Bat $50
Authenticated Bat $150

Mitch Williams

Ball $25
Photo $15
3x5 Index Card $3
Bat $40

Maury Wills

Ball $35
Authenticated Ball $50
Photo $25
3x5 Index Card $5
Bat $50

Don Wilson *

Ball $400
Photo $200
3x5 Index Card $100
Bat ....Unknown

Mookie Wilson

Ball $25
Authenticated Ball $70
Photo $15
3x5 Index Card $3
Bat $40

Willie Wilson

Ball $25
Photo $15
3x5 Index Card $3
Bat $40

Smoky Joe Wood *

Ball $250
Photo $125
3x5 Index Card $50
Bat ....Unknown

Wilbur Wood

Ball $25
Photo $15

3x5 Index Card $3
Bat $40

Gene Woodling *

Ball $50
Photo $30
3x5 Index Card $8
Bat $75

Jimmy Wynn

Ball $25
Photo $15
3x5 Index Card $3
Bat $40

Steve Yeager

Ball $25
Photo $15
3x5 Index Card $3
Bat $40

Rudy York *

Ball $400
Photo $200
3x5 Index Card $75
Bat ....Unknown

Eddie Yost

Ball $25
Photo $15
3x5 Index Card $3
Bat $40

Don Zimmer

Mounted Memories Photo

Ball $35
Authenticated Ball $60
Photo $25
Authenticated Photo $50
3x5 Index Card $5
Bat $50

NEGRO LEAGUE PLAYER AUTOGRAPHS

*Indicates Player Is Deceased

Newt Allen *

Photo	$250-$300
Ball	$500-$750
Cut signature or 3x5 index card	$100-$125

Tom Alston *

Photo	$30-$35
Ball	$50
Cut signature or 3x5 index card	$10-$12

George Altman

Photo	$20-$25
Ball	$30
Cut signature or 3x5 index card	$6-$8

Russell Awkard

Photo	$20-$25
Ball	$30
Cut signature or 3x5 index card	$6

Gene Baker *

Photo	$25
Ball	$30
Cut signature or 3x5 index card	$7-$8

Dan Bankhead *

Photo	$100-$150
Ball	$250-$350
Cut signature or 3x5 index card	$35-$50

Sam Bankhead *

Photo	$200-$250
Ball	$300-$500
Cut signature or 3x5 index card	$50-$75

David Barnhill *

Photo	$200-$300
Ball	$500-$750
Cut signature or 3x5 index card	$75-$100

Frank Barnes

Photo	$20-$25
Ball	$25-$30
Cut signature or 3x5 index card	$6-$8

Gene Benson

Photo	$20-$25
Ball	$30
Cut signature or 3x5 index card	$5-$6

Bill "Fireball" Beverly *

Photo	$25-$30
Ball	$35
Cut signature or 3x5 index card	$8-$10

Dennis Biddle

Photo	$20
Ball	$25
Cut signature or 3x5 index card	$5

Charlie Biot *

Photo	$20-$25
Ball	$25-$30
Cut signature or 3x5 index card	$6-$8

Joe Black

Photo	$15
Ball	$25
Cut signature or 3x5 index card	$6-$8

Lyman Bostock Sr.

Photo	$20-$25

Ball	$30
Cut signature or 3x5 index card	$6

Chet Brewer *

Photo	$100-$150
Ball	$200-$300
Cut signature or 3x5 index card	$40

Ray Brown *

Photo	$100-$150
Ball	$200-$300
Cut signature or 3x5 index card	$40

Bill Byrd *

Photo (scarce)	$1,000
Ball (scarce)	$2,000
Cut signature or 3x5 index card (scarce)	$500

Bill "Ready" Cash

Photo	$25-$30
Ball	$30-$35
Cut signature or 3x5 index card	$6-$8

Bus Clarkson *

Photo	$200
Ball	$300
Cut signature or 3x5 index card	$75

Sam Crawford *

Photo	$300-$500
Ball	$750-$1,000
Cut signature or 3x5 index card	$100-$150

George Crowe

Photo	$20-$25
Ball	$25-$30
Cut signature or 3x5 index card	$6-$7

Jimmie Crutchfield *

Photo	$50-$75
Ball	$100-$125
Cut signature or 3x5 index card	$12-$15

Piper Davis *

Photo	$35-$40
Ball	$40-$50
Cut signature or 3x5 index card	$9-$10

Lou Dials *

Photo	$35-$50
Ball	$75-$100
Cut signature or 3x5 index card	$10-$15

Mahlon Duckett

Photo	$10-$15
Ball	$30
Cut signature or 3x5 index card	$7-$9

Luke Easter *

Photo	$50-$75
Ball	$200-$300
Cut signature or 3x5 index card	$30-$40

Howard Easterling *

Photo (scarce)	$200
Ball (scarce)	$300
Cut signature or 3x5 index card (scarce)	$100

Wilmer Fields

Photo	$10-$15

Ball	$25
Cut signature or 3x5 index card	$8

Josh Gibson Jr.

Photo	$10-$15
Ball	$25
Cut signature or 3x5 index card	$8

George Giles *

Photo	$100-$150
Ball	$200-$300
Cut signature or 3x5 index card	$20-$30

Willie Grace

Photo	$25-$30
Ball	$30
Cut signature or 3x5 index card	$8-$10

Nap Gulley *

Photo	$25-$30
Ball	$50-$75
Cut signature or 3x5 index card	$5-$7

Sam Hairston *

Photo	$20
Ball	$25
Cut signature or 3x5 index card	$5-$7

Jehosie Heard

Photo	$25
Ball	$30
Cut signature or 3x5 index card	$6-$8

Arthur "Rats" Henderson *

Photo	$300-$400
Ball	$500-$600
Cut signature or 3x5 index card	$75

Bill Holland *

Photo	$35-$40
Ball	$40-$50
Cut signature or 3x5 index card	$10-$12

Cowan "Bubba" Hyde *

Photo	$20-$25
Ball	$25-$30
Cut signature or 3x5 index card	$5-$7

Connie Johnson

Photo	$20-$25
Ball	$30
Cut signature or 3x5 index card	$7-$8

Don Johnson

Photo	$25
Ball	$30
Cut signature or 3x5 index card	$6-$8

Josh Johnson

Photo	$25
Ball	$30
Cut signature or 3x5 index card	$6-$8

Clinton "Casey" Jones

Photo	$25-$30
Ball	$30-$35
Cut signature or 3x5 index card	$9-$12

Brooks Lawrence *

Photo	$25
Ball	$30
Cut signature or 3x5 index card	$7-$9

Rufus Lewis *

Photo .... $20-$25
Ball $30
Cut signature or 3x5 index card $7

Lester Lockett

Photo $20
Ball $30
Cut signature or 3x5 index card .... $7-$9

Biz Mackey *

Photo (scarce) $2,000
Ball (scarce) $3,000
Cut signature or 3x5 index card
    (scarce) $1,000

Dave Malarcher *

Photo .... $300-$500
Ball .... $750-$1,000
Cut signature or 3x5 index card .... $100-$150

Max Manning *

Photo $20
Ball $25
Cut signature or 3x5 index card $5

Luis Marquez *

Photo .... $50-$75
Ball .... $75-$100
Cut signature or 3x5 index card .... $15-$20

Verdell "Lefty" Mathis *

Photo .... $20-$25
Ball .... $30-$40
Cut signature or 3x5 index card .... $7-$8

Webster McDonald *

Photo (scarce) $200
Ball (scarce) $300
Cut signature or 3x5 index card
    (scarce) .... $75-$100

Charlie Neal *

Photo .... $25-$30
Ball $40
Cut signature or 3x5 index card .... $8-$10

Ray Noble *

Photo .... $25-$30
Ball .... $35-$40
Cut signature or 3x5 index card .... $8-$10

Buck O'Neil

Photo .... $25-$30
Ball $35
Cut signature or 3x5 index card .... $6-$8

William Warren Peace

Photo .... $20-$25
Ball .... $25-$30
Cut signature or 3x5 index card .... $7-$8

Jim Pendleton *

Photo .... $25-$30
Ball .... $30-$35
Cut signature or 3x5 index card .... $6-$8

Art "Superman" Pennington

Photo $25
Ball $30
Cut signature or 3x5 index card .... $6-$8

Willie Pope

Photo .... $20-$25
Ball .... $25-$30
Cut signature or 3x5 index card .... $5-$7

Dave Pope *

Photo $25
Ball $50
Cut signature or 3x5 index card $15

Ted "Double Duty" Radcliffe

Photo .... $20-$25
Ball $40
Cut signature or 3x5 index card .... $6-$8

Dick "Cannonball" Redding *

Photo (scarce) $2,000
Ball (scarce) $3,000
Cut signature or 3x5 index card
    (scarce) $1,000

Bobby Robinson

Photo .... $15-$20
Ball .... $35-$40
Cut signature or 3x5 index card $10

George Shively *

Photo (scarce) $200
Ball (scarce) $300
Cut signature or 3x5 index card
    (scarce) $100

Hilton Smith *

Photo .... $75-$100
Ball .... $100-$150
Cut signature or 3x5 index card .... $25-$30

Paul "Jack" Stevens *

Photo (scarce) $300
Ball (scarce) $500
Cut signature or 3x5 index card
    (scarce) .... $75-$100

Toni Stone *

Photo .... $50-$75
Ball $100
Cut signature or 3x5 index card $20

Alfred "Slick" Surratt

Photo $20
Ball $25

Cut signature or 3x5 index card .... $5-$7

Mule Suttles *

Photo (scarce) $1,500
Ball (scarce) $2,000
Cut signature or 3x5 index card
    (scarce) $750

Hank Thompson *

Photo .... $75-$90
Ball $100
Cut signature or 3x5 index card .... $15-$20

Bob Thurman *

Photo $25
Ball $30
Cut signature or 3x5 index card .... $6-$8

Luis Tiant Sr. *

Photo .... $75-$100
Ball .... $125-$175
Cut signature or 3x5 index card .... $25-$40

Quincy Trouppe *

Photo .... $125-$175
Ball .... $250-$300
Cut signature or 3x5 index card .... $25-$40

Armando Vasquez

Photo .... $15-$20
Ball .... $25-$30
Cut signature or 3x5 index card $12

Artie Wilson

Photo $25
Ball $30
Cut signature or 3x5 index card .... $6-$8

Earl Wilson Sr. *

Photo $25
Ball $30
Cut signature or 3x5 index card .... $7-$8

Jud Wilson *

Photo (scarce) $2,000
Ball (scarce) $3,000
Cut signature or 3x5 index card
    (scarce) $1,000

Wild Bill Wright *

Photo .... $100-$150
Ball .... $125-$175
Cut signature or 3x5 index card .... $35-$50

AUTOGRAPHED TEAM BASEBALLS

Key signatures follow each team name

1920 Boston (AL) - Barrow, Hendryx, Hooper, Pennock, Hoyt .... $800-$1,250

1920 Boston (NL) - Maranville, Powell, Mann .... $600-$900

1920 Brooklyn - Robinson, Konetchy, Myers, Wheat, Grimes, Marquard .... $1,200-$1,750

1920 Chicago (AL) - Collins, Risberg, Weaver, Leibold, Felsch, Jackson, Schalk, Faber, Williams, Kerr, Cicotte... $ uncertain

1920 Chicago (NL) - Hollocher, Flack, Robertson, Alexander.. $900-$1,400

1920 Cincinnati - Daubert, Roush.......................... $450-$700

1920 Cleveland - Wambsganss, Chapman, Gardner, Smith, Speaker, Jamieson, O'Neill, Sewell, Coveleski....$1,300-$2,000

1920 Detroit - Jennings, Heilmann, Cobb, Veach ...$1,700-$2,500

1920 New York (AL) - Huggins, Pratt, Ruth, Mays, Shawkey .... $2,200-$3,400

1920 New York (NL) - McGraw, Kelly, Bancroft, Frisch, Youngs, Toney, Nehf, Barnes.. $1,700-$2,750

1920 Philadelphia (AL) - Mack.. $600-$850

1920 Philadelphia (NL) - Stengel, Williams, Meusel, Wheat, Rixey .... $800-$1,300

1920 Pittsburgh - Carey, McKechnie, Traynor, Cooper .... $675-$1,000

1920 St. Louis (AL) - Sisler, Tobin, Jacobson, Williams, Shocker.. $425-$675

1920 St. Louis (NL) - Rickey, Fournier, Hornsby, Stock, Doak, Haines .... $1,150-$1,750

1920 Washington - Griffith, Judge, Harris, Rice, Milan, Johnson.. $1,300-$2,000

1921 Boston (AL) - Duffy, McInnis, Pratt, Leibold, Menosky, Jones, Pennock .... $550-$875

1921 Boston (NL) - Barbare, Boeckel, Southworth, Powell, Cruise, Oeschger.. $400-$600

1921 Brooklyn - Robinson, Schmandt, Johnston, Griffith, Wheat, Grimes.. $800-$1,200

1921 Chicago (AL) - Sheely, Collins, Hooper, Strunk, Schalk, Faber .... $725-$1,100

1921 Chicago (NL) - Evers, Grimes, Flack, Maisel, Barber, Alexander.. $1,200-$1,800

1921 Cincinnati - Daubert, Groh, Bressler, Roush, Duncan, Rixey, Marquard.. $550-$825

1921 Cleveland - Speaker, Sewell, Gardner, Jamieson, O'Neill, Coveleski .... $725-$1,200

1921 Detroit - Cobb, Blue, Heilmann, Veach, Bassler, Jones .... $800-$1,200

1921 New York (AL) - Huggins, Ward, Baker, Meusel, Ruth, Mays, Hoyt.. $3,000-$6,000

1921 New York (NL) - McGraw, Kelly, Bancroft, Frisch, Youngs, Meusel, Snyder, Stengel, Nehf.. $2,000-$3,000

1921 Philadelphia (AL) - Mack, Witt, T. Walker........ $500-$775

1921 Philadelphia (NL) - Konetchy, Williams, Meusel, Bruggy, Stengel .... $400-$600

1921 Pittsburgh - Cutshaw, Maranville, Carey, Bigbee, Traynor, Cuyler, Cooper.. $800-$1,200

1921 St. Louis (AL) - Sisler, Tobin, Jacobson, Williams, Severeid, Shocker.. $425-$625

1921 St. Louis (NL) - Rickey, Fournier, Hornsby, Stock, Smith, Mann, McHenry, Clemons, Dillhoefer, Haines, Doak .... $1,075-$1,600

1921 Washington - Judge, Harris, Shanks, Rice, Gharrity, Goslin, Johnson.. $1,000-$1,500

1922 Boston (AL) - Duffy, Burns, Pratt, Harris, Pennock.. $500-$750

1922 Boston (NL) - Marquard .... $400-$575

1922 Brooklyn - Johnston, Robinson, Myers, Wheat, DeBerry, Ruether, Vance, Grimes, T. Griffith .... $1,000-$1,500

1922 Chicago (AL) - Sheely, Collins, Hooper, Mostil, Schalk, Evers, Faber .... $1,200-$1,750

1922 Chicago (NL) - Grimes, Hollocher, Friberg, Miller, O'Farrell, Hartnett, Alexander .... $800-$1,200

1922 Cincinnati - Daubert, Pinelli, Harper, Duncan, Hargrave, Roush, Rixey .... $450-$700

1922 Cleveland - Speaker, McGinnis, Sewell, Uhle, Jamieson, O'Neill, Coveleski.. $675-$1,000

1922 Detroit - Cobb, Blue, Rigney, Heilmann, Veach, Bassler.. $800-$1,200

1922 New York (AL) - Pipp, Meusel, Ruth, Schang, Baker, Bush, Shawkey, Hoyt, Huggins .... $2,000-$3,000

1922 New York (NL) - McGraw, Kelly, Frisch, Bancroft, Youngs, Stengel, Meusel, Snyder, Jackson, Nehf .... $2,000-$3,000

1922 Philadelphia (AL) - Mack, Hauser, Galloway, Rommel, Miller .... $500-$750

1922 Philadelphia (NL) - Walker, Williams, Lee, Henline .... $325-$500

1922 Pittsburgh - McKechnie, Tierney, Carey, Maranville, Traynor, Russell, Bigbee, Gooch, Cuyler, Cooper .... $1,100-$1,600

1922 St. Louis (AL) - Sisler, McManus, Tobin, Jacobson, Williams, Severeid, Shocker .... $400-$650

1922 St. Louis (NL) - Rickey, Hornsby, Toporcer, Stock, Smith, Schultz, Bottomley, Haines .... $1,350-$2,000

1922 Washington - Harris, Rice, Goslin, Johnson $900-$1,400

1923 Boston (AL) - Burns, Flagstead, Harris, Ehmke, Chance .... $900-$1,400

1923 Boston (NL) - McInnis, Southworth, Powell, Marquard .... $375-$550

1923 Brooklyn - Robinson, Fournier, Johnston, Wheat, Grimes, Vance .... $1,100-$1,600

1923 Chicago (AL) - Collins, Hooper, Falk, Schalk, Faber, Lyons .... $750-$1,200

1923 Chicago (NL) - Grimes, Friberg, Statz, Miller, O'Farrell, Hartnett, Alexander, Aldridge.................. $800-$1,000

1923 Cincinnati - Roush, Duncan, Hargrave, Luque, Rixey.. $400-$600

1923 Cleveland - Speaker, Sewell, Summa, Jamieson, Uhle, Coveleski .... $800-$1,200

1923 Detroit - Cobb, Rigney, Heilmann, Manush, Daus .... $900-$1,500

1923 New York (AL) - Huggins, Pipp, Ruth, Witt, Meusel, Gehrig, Pennock, Hoyt.. $2,500-$3,750

1923 New York (NL) - McGraw, Kelly, Frisch, Bancroft, Youngs, Jackson, Stengel, Terry, Wilson, Ryan........... $2,100-$3,150

1923 Philadelphia (AL) - Mack, Hauser .... $475-$700

1923 Philadelphia (NL) - Holke, Tierney, Mokan, Henline .... $300-$450

1923 Pittsburgh - McKechnie, Grimm, Maranville, Traynor, Barnhart, Carey, Cuyler, Morrison .... $1,000-$1,500

1923 St. Louis (AL) - McManus, Tobin, Jacobson, Williams, Severeid, Shocker.. $350-$525

1923 St. Louis (NL) - Rickey, Bottomley, Hornsby, Myers, Smith, Haines .... $1,200-$1,800

1923 Washington - Judge, Harris, Rice, Leibold, Goslin, Ruel, Johnson.. $900-$1,400

1924 Boston (AL) - Harris, Boone, Flagstead, Ruffing .... $350-$525

1924 Boston (NL) - Stengel, Bancroft, Marquard ....$700-$900

1924 Brooklyn - Robinson, Fournier, High, Brown, Wheat, Grimes, Vance .... $1,000-$1,500

1924 Chicago (AL) - Evers, Sheely, Collins, Hooper, Mostil, Falk, Schalk, Thurston, Lyons, Faber.............. $1,300-$1,800

1924 Chicago (NL) - Grantham, Heathcote, Hartnett, Alexander.. $725-$1,200

1924 Cincinnati- Critz, Pinelli, Walker, Roush, Mays, Rixey .... $400-$600

1924 Cleveland - Speaker, Burns, Sewell, Jamieson, Myatt, Shaute, Coveleski .... $800-$1,000

1924 Detroit - Cobb, Blue, Pratt, Heilmann, Manush, Bassler, Gehringer .... $1,000-$1,550

1924 New York (AL) - Huggins, Dugan, Ruth, Meusel, Combs, Gehrig, Pennock, Hoyt........................... $3,000-$4,500

1924 New York (NL) - McGraw, Kelly, Frisch, Jackson, Youngs, Wilson, Snyder, Terry, Lindstrom, Bentley ...... $1,900-$2,900

1924 Philadelphia (AL) - Miller, Simmons, Lamar. $600-$1,000

1924 Philadelphia (NL) - Holke, Wrightstone, Williams .... $300-$450

1924 Pittsburgh - McKechnie, Maranville, Traynor, Carey, Cuyler, Cooper................................... $800-$1,225

1924 St. Louis (AL) - Sisler, McManus, Robertson, Jacobson, Williams, Severeid .... $400-$600

1924 St. Louis (NL) - Rickey, Bottomley, Hornsby, Blades, Hafey .... $1,300-$1,800

1924 Washington - Harris, Judge, Rice, Goslin, Johnson .... $1,000-$1,500

1925 Boston (AL) - Prothro, Boone, Carlyle, Ruffing....$300-$500

1925 Boston (NL) - Bancroft, Burrus, Welsh, Felix, Stengel, Marquard .... $600-$900

1925 Brooklyn - Robinson, Fournier, Stock, Cox, Brown, Wheat, Taylor, Vance, Grimes .... $900-$1,500

1925 Chicago (AL) - Collins, Sheely, Hooper, Falk, Schalk, Lyons, Faber, Bender............................ $900-$1,500

1925 Chicago (NL) - Maranville, Grimm, Freigau, Jahn, Hartnett, Alexander.................................. $800-$1,200

1925 Cincinnati - Walker, Roush, Hargrave, Rixey .. $350-$575

1925 Cleveland - Speaker, Burns, Sewell, McNulty, Buckeye .... $550-$925

1925 Detroit - Cobb, Blue, Heilmann, Wingo, Manush, Gehringer.. $900-$1,300

1925 New York (AL) - Huggins, Gehrig, Ruth, Hoyt, Pennock, Durocher.................................... $2,750-$4,175

1925 New York (NL) - McGraw, Terry, Kelly, Jackson, Lindstrom, Youngs, Meusel, Frisch, Wilson .... $1,800-$2,700

1925 Philadelphia (AL) - Mack, Hale, Miller, Simmons, Lamar, Cochrane, Foxx, Rommel, Grove.................... $1,400-$2,100

1925 Philadelphia (NL) - Hawks, Williams, Harper .. $300-$475

1925 Pittsburgh - McKechnie, Grantham, Wright, Traynor, Cuyler, Carey, Barnhart, Smith, Meadows......... $800-$1,200

1925 St. Louis (AL) - Sisler, Rice, Jacobson, Williams .... $375-$600

1925 St. Louis (NL) - Rickey, Bottomley, Hornsby, Hafey, Mueller, Blades, Haines .... $1,300-$2,000

1925 Washington - Harris, Judge, Rice, Goslin, Johnson, Coveleski .... $1,000-$1,500

1926 Boston (AL) - Jacobson, Ruffing .... $300-$475

1926 Boston (NL) - Bancroft, J. Smith, Brown .... $325-$525

1926 Brooklyn - Robinson, Herman, Wheat, Maranville, Carey, Grimes, Vance .... $1,200-$1,800

1926 Chicago - McCarthy, Adams, Wilson, Stephenson, Hartnett, Alexander................................... $900-$1,400

1926 Chicago (AL) - Collins, Barrett, Mostil, Falk, Schalk, Lyons, Faber .... $600-$900

1926 Cincinnati - Walker, Roush, Donahue, Rixey .. $325-$575

1926 Cincinnati - Speaker, Burns, J. Sewell, Summa, Uhle .... $600-$900

1926 Detroit - Cobb, Gehringer, Heilmann, Manush, Fothergill.. $800-$1,200

1926 New York (AL) - Huggins, Gehrig, Lazzeri, Ruth, Combs, Meusel, Pennock, Hoyt..................... $3,500-$5,000

1926 New York (NL) - McGraw, Kelly, Frisch, Jackson, Lindstrom, Youngs, Terry, Ott.................. $1,800-$2,750

1926 Philadelphia (AL) - Mack, French, Simmons, Cochrane, Foxx .... $1,300-$2,100

1926 Philadelphia (NL) - Williams, Leach, Mokan, Wilson .... $250-$400

1926 Pittsburgh - McKechnie, Grantham, Wright, Traynor, Waner, Carey, Cuyler, Smith, Cronin, Kremer, Meadows .... $800-$1,200

1926 St. Louis (AL) - Sisler, Miller, Rice, Shang ...... $350-$500

1926 St. Louis (NL) - Hornsby, Bottomley, Bell, Southworth, Douthit, Blades, Hafey, Rhem, Haines, Alexander... $1,600-$2,300

1926 Washington - Harris, Myer, Rice, McNeely, Goslin, Johnson, Coveleski.................................... $800-$1,200

1927 Boston (AL) - Tobin, Ruffing .... $300-$450

1927 Boston (NL) - Bancroft, High, Richbourg, Brown .... $300-$450

1927 Brooklyn - Robinson, Carey, Vance .... $800-$1,200

1927 Chicago (AL) - Schalk, Clancy, Metzler, Falk, Lyons, Faber .... $350-$550

1927 Chicago (NL) - McCarthy, Grimm, Webb, Wilson, Stephenson, Hartnett, Root................................ $500-$800

1927 Cincinnati - Hargrave, Kelly, Rixey .... $300-$450

1927 Cleveland - Burns, Fonseca, J. Sewell, Jamieson, Miller .... $300-$450

1927 Detroit - Gehringer, Heilmann, Manush, Fothergill, Collins .... $375-$625

1927 New York (AL) - Gehrig, Lazzeri, Ruth, Combs, Meusel, Hoyt, Moore, Pennock .... $8,000-$16,000

1927 New York (NL) - McGraw, Terry, Hornsby, Jackson, Lindstrom, Harper, Roush, Grimes .... $1,800-$2,700

1927 Philadelphia (AL) - Mack, Dykes, Hale, Cobb, Simmons, French, Cochrane, Collins, Wheat, Foxx, Grove .... $2,200-$3,300

1927 Philadelphia (NL) - Wrightstone, Thompson, Leach .... $275-$400

1927 Pittsburgh - Harris, Grantham, Traynor, P. Waner, L. Waner, Barnhart, Cuyler, Groh, Cronin, Kremer............. $1,000-$1,200

1927 St. Louis (AL) - Sisler, Miller, Williams, Schang .. $400-$650

1927 St. Louis (NL) - Bottomley, Frisch, Maranville, Haines, Alexander... $1,200-$1,750

1927 Washington - Harris, Judge, Rice, Speaker, Goslin, Ruel, Lisenbee, Hadley, Johnson, Coveleski .... $1,200-$1,800

1928 Boston (AL) - Myer, Williams, Ruffing.............. $300-$475

1928 Boston (NL) - Hornsby, Sisler, Richbourg..... $800-$1,200

1928 Brooklyn - Robinson, Bissonette, Bancroft, Hendrick, Herman, Carey, Lopez, Vance....................... $1,000-$1,400

1928 Chicago (AL) - Schalk, Kamm, Metzler, Lyons, Walsh, Faber .... $500-$775

1928 Chicago (NL) - McCarthy, Cuyler, Wilson, Stephenson, Hartnett... $450-$725

1928 Cincinnati - Kelly, Allen, Rixey........................ $300-$425

1928 Cleveland - Fonseca, Sewell, Hodapp, Jamieson .... $300-$425

1928 Detroit - Gehringer, Heilmann, Rice .... $325-$500

1928 New York (AL) - Huggins, Gehrig, Lazzeri, Koenig, Ruth, Combs, Dickey, Pipgras, Hoyt, Pennock, Coveleski .... $3,500-$5,000

1928 New York (NL) - McGraw, Terry, Jackson, Lindstrom, Ott, Welsh, O'Doul, Hogan, Roush, Benton, Fitzsimmons, Hubbell .... $1,300-$1,750

1928 Philadelphia (AL) - Mack, Bishop, Hale, Cobb, Miller, Simmons, Cochrane, Foxx, Speaker, Collins, Grove, Quinn .... $2,000-$3,000

1928 Philadelphia (NL) - Whitney, Klein, Leach....... $300-$500
1928 Pittsburgh - Grantham, Wright, Traynor, P. Waner, L. Waner, Brickell, Grimes .... $500-$750
1928 St. Louis (AL) - Manush, Crowder .... $300-$450
1928 St. Louis (NL) - McKechnie, Bottomley, Frisch, Maranville, Hafey, Haines, Alexander................................. $1,200-$1,800
1928 Washington - Harris, Judge, Reeves, Rice, Barnes, Goslin, Cronin, Sisler, Jones .... $500-$750
1929 Boston (AL) - Rothrock, Ruffing .... $250-$350
1929 Boston (NL) - Sisler, Maranville, Richbourg, Clark, Evers..................................... $700-$1,200
1929 Brooklyn - Robinson, Bancroft, Gilbert, Herman, Frederick, Bressler, Carey, Vance .... $850-$1,300
1929 Chicago (AL) - Shires, Reynolds, Lyons, Faber...$275-$450
1929 Chicago (NL) - McCarthy, Hornsby, Cuyler, Wilson, Hartnett, Malone .... $800-$1,200
1929 Cincinnati - Kelly, Dressen, Swanson, Gooch, Rixey... $275-$425
1929 Cleveland - Fonseca, Hodapp, Sewell, Falk, Averill, Sewell, Ferrell .... $300-$500
1929 Detroit - Harris, Alexander, Gehringer, Heilmann, Rice, Johnson .... $300-$500
1929 New York (AL) - Huggins, Gehrig, Lazzeri, Ruth, Combs, Dickey, Wells, Hoyt, Pennock....................... $2,800-$4,250
1929 New York (NL) - McGraw, Terry, Jackson, Lindstrom, Ott, Roush, Hubbell .... $1,000-$1,600
1929 Philadelphia (AL) - Mack, Foxx, Miller, Haas, Simmons, Cochrane, Cronin, Collins, Earnshaw, Grove .... $800-$1,200
1929 Philadelphia (NL) - Hurst, Thompson, Thevenow, Whitney, Klein, Sothern, O'Doul.......................... $300-$450
1929 Pittsburgh - Grantham, Bartell, Traynor, P. Waner, L. Waner, Comorosky, Grimes .... $500-$800
1929 St. Louis (AL) - Kress, Schulte, Manush, Ferrell .$325-$550
1929 St. Louis (NL) - McKechnie, Bottomley, Frisch, Orsatti, Douthit, Hafey, Wilson, Johnson, Haines, Alexander................................ $900-$1,400
1929 Washington - Johnson, Judge, Myer, Cronin, Rice, Goslin .... $1,300-$1,850
1930 Boston (AL) - Webb, Ruffing.......................... $225-$350
1930 Boston (NL) - McKechnie, Sisler, Maranville, Grimes .... $450-$750
1930 Brooklyn - Robinson, Bissonette, Wright, Herman, Frederick, Lopez, Vance .... $650-$1,200
1930 Chicago (AL) - Watwood, Jolley, Reynolds, Lyons, Appling, Faber .... $250-$400
1930 Chicago (NL) - McCarthy, Grimm, Cuyler, Wilson, Hartnett, Hornsby, Kelly .... $900-$1,450
1930 Cincinnati - Durocher, Cuccinello, Heilmann, Walker, Kelly, Rixey............................... $900-$1,450
1930 Cleveland - Morgan, Hodapp, J. Sewell, Porter, Averill, Jamieson, L. Sewell, Ferrell........................... $300-$475
1930 Detroit - Harris, Alexander, Gehringer, McManus, Stone, Hoyt, Greenberg .... $300-$475
1930 New York (AL) - Gehrig, Lazzeri, Chapman, Ruth, Hoyt, Combs, Ruffing, Gomez, Pennock, Dickey ..... $2,500-$3,750
1930 New York (NL) - McGraw, Terry, Jackson, Lindstrom, Ott, Leach, Hogan, Bancroft, Roush, Hubbell .... $1,200-$1,800
1930 Philadelphia (AL) - Mack, Foxx, Dykes, Miller, Simmons, Cochrane, Collins, Grove .... $700-$1,000
1930 Philadelphia (NL) - Hurst, Whitney, O'Doul, Davis, Alexander, Klein............................... $500-$700
1930 Pittsburgh - Grantham, Bartell, Traynor, P. Waner, L. Waner, Comorosky .... $450-$700
1930 St. Louis (AL) - Kress, Goslin, Ferrell, Manush ...$375-$575
1930 St. Louis (NL) - Street, Bottomley, Frisch, Gelbert, Adams, Watkins, Douthit, Hafey, Wilson, Grimes, Haines, Dean .... $700-$1,000

1930 Washington - Johnson, Judge, Myer, Cronin, Rice, Manush, Goslin, Marberry .... $1,500-$2,250
1931 Boston (AL) - Webb.. $200-$300
1931 Boston (NL) - Maranville, Schulmerich, Berger, McKechnie .... $300-$500
1931 Brooklyn - O'Doul, Lopez, Lombardi, Vance, Robinson .... $800-$1,200
1931 Chicago (AL) - Blue, Appling, Faber, Lyons..... $250-$375
1931 Chicago (NL) - Grimm, Hornsby, English, Cuyler, Wilson, Taylor, Hartnett, Herman.......................... $750-$1,200
1931 Cincinnati - Hendrick, Cuccinello, Stripp, Roush, Heilmann, Rixey .... $325-$500
1931 Cleveland - Morgan, Porter, Averill .... $250-$375
1931 Detroit - Alexander, Gehringer, Rogell, Stone, Hoyt, Harris .... $300-$500
1931 New York (AL) - Gehrig, Lazzeri, Sewell, Ruth, Combs, Chapman, Dickey, Ruffing, Gomez, Pennock, McCarthy .... $3,000-$4,500
1931 New York (NL) - Terry, Jackson, Lindstrom, Ott, Leach, Hogan, Walker, Hubbell, McGraw..... $1,000-$1,500
1931 Philadelphia (AL) - Mack, Foxx, Simmons, Cochrane, Grove, Earnshaw, Hoyt...................... $700-$1,000
1931 Philadelphia (NL) - Hurst, Mallon, Arlett, Klein, Davis .... $300-$450
1931 Pittsburgh - Grantham, Traynor, P. Waner, L. Waner .... $425-$700
1931 St. Louis (AL) - Melillo, Kress, Schulte, Goslin, Ferrell .... $300-$450
1931 St. Louis (NL) - Bottomley, Frisch, Hafey, Hallahan, Grimes, Haines........................... $550-$900
1931 Washington - Cronin, Rice, West, Manush, Crowder, Marberry, Johnson.................................. $1,200-$1,800
1932 Boston (AL) - Alexander, Jolley, Morris .... $225-$350
1932 Boston (NL) - Maranville, Berger, Worthington, McKechnie .... $300-$450
1932 Brooklyn - Kelly, Wright, Stripp, Wilson, Taylor, O'Doul, Lopez, Clark, Vance, Hoyt, Carey...................... $600-$950
1932 Chicago (AL) - Appling, Lyons, Faber............. $325-$500
1932 Chicago (NL) - Grimm, Herman, Cuyler, Moore, Stephenson, Hartnett, Hornsby, Warneke, Grimes... $700-$1,000
1932 Cincinnati - Hendrick, Durocher, Herman, Lombardi, Hafey, Heilmann, Frey........................... $450-$750
1932 Cleveland - Cissell, Porter, Averill, Vosmik ...... $250-$375
1932 Detroit - Gehringer, Walker, Harris .... $300-$500
1932 New York (AL) - Gehrig, Lazzeri, Sewell, Ruth, Combs, Dickey, Ruffing, Gomez, Allen, Pennock, McCarthy .... $1,750-$4,000
1932 New York (NL) - Terry, Ott, Lindstrom, McGraw, Hogan, Jackson, Jo-Jo Moore, Hoyt, Hubbell .... $900-$1,325
1932 Philadelphia (AL) - Cramer, Haas, Simmons, Cochrane, Grove, Mack.................................... $500-$750
1932 Philadelphia (NL) - Hurst, Bartell, Klein, Davis, Lee, Davis .... $300-$425
1932 Pittsburgh - Vaughn, Traynor, P. Waner, L. Waner .... $525-$750
1932 St. Louis (AL) - Burns, Scharien, Goslin, Ferrell .... $300-$450
1932 St. Louis (NL) - Watkins, Martin, Orsatti, Frisch, Bottomley, Medwick, Dean, Haines.............................. $500-$700
1932 Washington - Cronin, Reynolds, Manush, Rice, Crowder, Johnson .... $1,200-$1,800
1933 Boston (AL) - Hodapp, Johnson, Ferrell .... $250-$375
1933 Boston (NL) - Maranville, Moore, Cantwell, McKechnie .... $300-$450
1933 Brooklyn - Wright, Frederick, Wilson, Lopez, Mungo, Carey .... $700-$1,000
1933 Chicago (AL) - Appling, Swanson, Simmons, Lyons, Faber .... $375-$575

1933 Chicago (NL) - Grimm, Stephenson, Hartnett, Cuyler, Bush, Grimes, Billy Herman .... $400-$600
1933 Cincinnati - Bottomley, Hafey, Lombardi, Durocher, Rixey .... $400-$600
1933 Cleveland - Averill, Johnson .... $800-$1,200
1933 Detroit - Greenberg, Gehringer, Harris .... $375-$600
1933 New York (AL) - Gehrig, Lazzeri, Sewell, Ruth, Combs, Chapman, Dickey, Gomez, Allen, Ruffing, Pennock, McCarthy .... $2,800-$4,200
1933 New York (NL) - Terry, Ott, Jackson, Hubbell....$750-$1,000
1933 Philadelphia (AL) - Foxx, Higgins, Cochrane, Grove, Mack .... $400-$600
1933 Philadelphia (NL) - Klein, Fullis, Schulmerich, Davis.. $300-$450
1933 Pittsburgh - Piet, Vaughan, Traynor, Waner, Lindstrom, Waner, Hoyt .... $575-$900
1933 St. Louis (AL) - West, Ferrell, Hornsby........... $450-$675
1933 St. Louis (NL) - Collins, Frisch, Durocher, Martin, Medwick, Hornsby, Haines, Dean, Vance, Grimes .$900-$1,500
1933 Washington - Kuhel, Myer, Cronin, Goslin, Manush, Rice, Crowder, Whitehill.................................... $475-$725
1934 Boston (AL) - Harris, Reynolds, Johnson, R. Ferrell, W. Ferrell, Grove, Pennock .... $375-$525
1934 Boston (NL) - McKechnie, Jordan, Maranville, Frankhouse .... $325-$450
1934 Brooklyn - Stengel, Leslie, Stripp, Boyle, Koenecke, Lopez, Mungo .... $250-$500
1934 Chicago (AL) - Appling, Simmons, Conlan ...... $400-$575
1934 Chicago (NL) - Grimm, Billy Herman, Hack, Cuyler, Klein, Hartnett .... $325-$600
1934 Cincinnati - Bottomley, Hafey, Lombardi .... $300-$525
1934 Cleveland - Johnson, Trosky, Hale, Knickerbocker, Averill, Vosmik, Harder .... $775-$1,250
1934 Detroit - Cochrane, Greenberg, Gehringer, Fox, Goslin, Rowe, Bridges .... $525-$800
1934 New York (AL) - McCarthy, Gomez, Lazzeri, Dickey, Gehrig, Ruffing, Grimes, Ruth, Combs........... $2,600-$3,900
1934 New York (NL) - Terry, Jackson, Ott, Hubbell... $400-$575
1934 Philadelphia (AL) - Mack, Foxx, Higgins, Cramer, Johnson .... $300-$500
1934 Philadelphia (NL) - Chiozza, Bartell, J. Moore, Allen, Todd .... $200-$300
1934 Pittsburgh - Traynor, Vaughan, P. Waner, L. Waner, Lindstrom, Hoyt, Grimes .... $550-$875
1934 St. Louis (AL) - Hornsby, West, Hemsley .... $400-$675
1934 St. Louis (NL) - Frisch, Collins, Durocher, Martin, Orsatti, Medwick, Davis, Dean, Haines, Grimes, Vance.... $575-$900
1934 Washington - Cronin, Manush...................... $275-$450
1935 Boston (AL) - Cronin, Cooke, R. Johnson, R. Ferrell, W. Ferrell, Grove .... $300-$500
1935 Boston (NL) - McKechnie, Lee, Ruth, Maranville .... $1,000-$1,500
1935 Brooklyn - Stengel, Leslie, Stripp, Lopez .... $300-$475
1935 Chicago (AL) - Appling, Simmons, Conlan, Lyons, Stratton .... $375-$575
1935 Chicago (NL) - Grimm, Herman, Lee, Klein, Demaree, Galan, Hartnett, Cuyler, Lindstrom, Hack .... $500-$750
1935 Cincinnati - Bottomley, Herman, Lombardi, Cuyler, Hafey, Derringer.. $350-$575
1935 Cleveland - Johnson, Averill .... $700-$1,200
1935 Detroit - Cochrane, Greenberg, Gehringer, Goslin .... $500-$750
1935 New York (AL) - McCarthy, Gehrig, Lazzeri, Dickey, Combs, Ruffing, Gomez .... $1,300-$2,000
1935 New York (NL) - Terry, Jackson, Ott, Leiber, Hubbell... $475-$800
1935 Philadelphia (AL) - Mack, Foxx, Moses, Cramer $300-$450

1935 Philadelphia (NL) - Moore, Allen .... $500-$1,000
1935 Pittsburgh - Traynor, Vaughan, P. Waner, L. Waner, Hoyt .... $500-$700
1935 St. Louis (AL) - Hornsby, West, Solters, Andrews $450-$675
1935 St. Louis (NL) - Frisch, Collins, Durocher, Martin, Medwick, Haines, P. Dean, D. Dean .... $350-$575
1935 Washington - Harris, Myer, Travis, Powell, Manush, Bolton .... $250-$375
1936 Boston (AL) - Cronin, Foxx, R. Ferrell, Hanush, Grove .... $400-$600
1936 Boston (NL) - McKechnie, Jordan, Cuccinello, Lopez .... $250-$350
1936 Brooklyn - Stengel, Hassett, Stripp, Bordagaray, Lindstrom .... $275-$425
1936 Chicago (AL) - Appling, Lyons, Stratton .... $250-$400
1936 Chicago (NL) - Grimm, Herman, Demaree, Hartnett, Klein, French .... $300-$450
1936 Cincinnati - Scarsella, Cuyler, Lombardi, Hafey . $275-$450
1936 Cleveland - Trosky, Hale, Weatherly, Averill, Sullivan, Allen .... $200-$325
1936 Detroit - Cochrane, Gehringer, Simmons, Goslin, Greenberg .... $400-$575
1936 New York (AL) - McCarthy, Gehrig, Lazzeri, DiMaggio, Dickey, Ruffing, Gomez .... $1,150-$1,750
1936 New York (NL) - Terry, Jackson, Ott, Moore, Mancuso, Hubbell .... $450-$700
1936 Philadelphia (AL) - Mack, Finney, Moses........ $250-$375
1936 Philadelphia (NL) - Camilli, Klein, Moore .... $200-$300
1936 Pittsburgh - Traynor, Suhr, Vaughan, P. Waner, L. Waner, Hoyt .... $425-$700
1936 St. Louis (AL) - Hornsby, Bottomley, Clift, Bell $450-$725
1936 St. Louis (NL) - Frisch, Mize, Durocher, Martin, Alston, Dean, Haines .... $425-$675
1936 Washington - Harris, Travis, Chapman, Stone ... $200-$350
1937 Boston (AL) - Foxx, Cronin, Higgins, Chapman, Cramer, Doerr, Ferrell, Grove .... $450-$550
1937 Boston (NL) - Lopez, McKechnie .... $200-$350
1937 Brooklyn - Hassett, Manush, Phelps, Hoyt, Grimes .... $350-$500
1937 Chicago (AL) - Appling, Stratton, Lyons .... $250-$425
1937 Chicago (NL) - Herman, Demaree, Hartnett, Carleton, Grimm .... $275-$400
1937 Cincinnati - Wallace, Hafey, Cuyler, Lombardi $350-$500
1937 Cleveland - Campbell, Sotters, Pytlak, Feller, Averill .... $225-$375
1937 Detroit - Greenberg, Gehringer, Goslin, Cochrane .... $400-$700
1937 New York (AL) - Gehrig, Lazzeri, DiMaggio, Dickey, Gomez, Ruffing, McCarthy .... $1,450-$2,500
1937 New York (NL) - Bartell, Ott, Ripple, Moore, Hubbell, Melton, Terry... $400-$600
1937 Philadelphia (AL) - Moses, Johnson, Mack..... $225-$375
1937 Philadelphia (NL) - Camilli, Whitney, Klein...... $200-$300
1937 Pittsburgh - Vaughan, Waner, Waner, Todd, Traynor, Hoyt .... $425-$650
1937 St. Louis (AL) - Clift, Bell, West, Vosmik, Hornsby, Bottomley... $425-$650
1937 St. Louis (NL) - Mize, Durocher, Padgett, Medwick, Martin, Frisch, Dean, Haines .... $375-$600
1937 Washington (AL) - Travis, Lewis, Stone, Almada, Simmons, R. Ferrell, Harris .... $300-$425
1938 Boston (AL) - Foxx, Doerr, Cronin, Higgins, Chapman, Cramer, Vosmik, Grove.. $550-$900
1938 Boston (NL) - Stengel, Lopez, MacFayden ..... $350-$575
1938 Brooklyn - Grimes, Durocher, Phelps, Cuyler, Manush, Hoyt .... $2,000-$2,750

1941 Cleveland Indians

1944 Cleveland Indians

1947 Chicago Cubs

1938 Chicago (AL) - Hayes, Appling, Steinbacher, Walker, Stratton .... $250-$450

1938 Chicago (NL) - Herman, Hack, Reynolds, Hartnett, Garbark, Lee, Grimm, Dean, Lazzeri .... $800-$1000

1938 Cincinnati - McKechnie, McCormick, Berger, Lombardi, Derringer, Vander Meer .... $250-$400

1938 Cleveland - Trosky, Averill, Heath, Pytlak, Boudreau, Feller .... $250-$400

1938 Detroit - Cochrane, Greenberg, Gehringer, Walker, Bridges .... $400-$700

1938 New York (AL) - McCarthy, Gehrig, DiMaggio, Dickey, Ruffing, Gomez .... $900-$1,200

1938 New York (NL) - Terry, Ott, Moore, Danning, Hubbell .... $350-$550

1938 Philadelphia (AL) - Mack, Moses, Johnson ..... $400-$600

1938 Philadelphia (NL) - Weintraub .... $250-$325

1938 Pittsburgh - Traynor, Vaughan, P. Waner, L. Waner, Rizzo, Manush, Brown .... $700-$1,000

1938 St. Louis (AL) - McQuinn, Kress, Almada .... $200-$300

1938 St. Louis (NL) - Frisch, Mize, Slaughter, Medwick, Martin .... $400-$650

1938 Washington - Harris, Myer, Travis, Case, Simmons, Ferrell, Goslin, Ferrell .... $300-$475

1939 Boston (AL) - Cronin, Foxx, Doerr, Williams, Cramer, Grove .... $450-$650

1939 Boston (NL) - Stengel, Hassett, Cuccinello, Lopez, Simmons .... $300-$450

1939 Brooklyn - Durocher, Lazzeri .... $250-$450

1939 Chicago (AL) - Kuhel, Appling, McNair, Lyons ..... $200-$350

1939 Chicago (NL) - Hartnett, Herman, Leiber, Galan, Hartnett, Dean .... $275-$400

1939 Cincinnati - McKechnie, McCormick, Goodman, Lombardi, Simmons, Walters, Derringer .... $325-$500

1939 Cleveland - Trosky, Hale, Keltner, Boudreau, Feller .... $225-$350

1939 Detroit - Greenberg, Gehringer, McCosky, Averill, Bridges .... $300-$500

1939 New York (AL) - McCarthy, Rolfe, Keller, DiMaggio, Selkirk, Dickey, Ruffing, Gehring, Gomez .... $750-$1,400

1939 New York (NL) - Terry, Bonura, Ott, Demaree, Danning, Lazzeri, Hubbell .... $325-$550

1939 Philadelphia (AL) - Mack, Moses, Johnson, Collins .... $300-$400

1939 Philadelphia (NL) - Suhr, Arnovich, Davis .... $175-$275

1939 Pittsburgh - Traynor, Fletcher, Vaughan, P. Waner, L. Waner, Manush .... $500-$1,000

1939 St. Louis (AL) - McQuinn, Laabs .... $200-$300

1939 St. Louis (NL) - Mize, Slaughter, Medwick, P. Martin .... $375-$550

1939 Washington - Harris, Vernon, Lewis, Case, Wright, Ferrell, Leonard .... $200-$300

1940 Boston (AL) - Cronin, Foxx, Doerr, Williams, Wilson, Grove .... $600-$1,000

1940 Boston (NL) - Stengel, Rowell, Cooney, Lopez ... $500-$750

1940 Brooklyn - Durocher, Reese, Medwick .... $450-$800

1940 Chicago (AL) - Appling, Wright, Solters, Lyons $200-$300

1940 Chicago (NL) - Hartnett, Herman, Dean .... $200-$300

1940 Cincinnati - McKechnie, F. McCormick, Lombardi .... $350-$550

1940 Cleveland - Boudreau, Weatherly, Feller, Smith ... $200-$300

1940 Detroit - York, Gehringer, McCosky, Greenberg, Newsom .... $500-$750

1940 New York (AL) - McCarthy, DiMaggio, Dickey, Ruffing, Gomez .... $450-$700

1940 New York (NL) - Terry, Ott, Demaree, Danning, Hubbell .... $400-$600

1940 Philadelphia (AL) - Mack, Moses, Hayes, Simmons .... $400-$750

1940 Philadelphia (NL) - .... $250-$400

1940 Pittsburgh - Frisch, Vaughan, P. Waner, L. Waner, Lopez .... $500-$1,000

1940 St. Louis (AL) - Judnich, Radcliff .... $175-$275

1940 St. Louis (NL) - Mize, Slaughter, P. Martin, Medwick .... $325-$475

1940 Washington - Harris, Lewis, Ferrell, Vernon .... $200-$325

1941 Boston (AL) - Cronin, Foxx, Doerr, DiMaggio, Williams, Grove .... $500-$675

1941 Boston (NL) - Cooney, Waner, Stengel .... $300-$400

1941 Brooklyn - Durocher, Camilli, Herman, Reese, Medwick, Waner .... $750-$1,250

1941 Chicago (AL) - Appling, Lyons .... $225-$350

1941 Chicago (NL) - Hack, Herman, Dean .... $175-$300

1941 Cincinnati - McKechnie, Lombardi, Waner ...... $400-$600

1941 Cleveland - Boudreau, Heath, Lemon, Feller .. $200-$400

1941 Detroit - Gehringer, McCosky, Radcliff, Greenberg, Benton .... $450-$700

1941 New York (AL) - McCarthy, Rizzuto, DiMaggio, Dickey, Gomez, Ruffing .... $800-$1,200

1941 New York (NL) - Terry, Bartell, Ott, Hubbell ..... $525-$600

1941 Philadelphia (AL) - Mack, Siebert, Moses, Chapman, Collins, Simmons .... $325-$500

1941 Philadelphia (NL) - Litwhiler, Etten .... $400-$500

1941 Pittsburgh - Frisch, Vaughan, Lopez, Waner .. $700-$800

1941 St. Louis (AL) - Ferrell .... $200-$325

1941 St. Louis (NL) - Mize, Brown, Slaughter, Hopp, Musial .... $300-$450

1941 Washington - Harris, Vernon, Travis, Ferrell, Wynn .... $225-$350

1942 Boston (AL) - Cronin, Doerr, Williams, Foxx.... $400-$575
1942 Boston (NL) - Stengel, Lombardi, Sain, Spahn..$800-$1,000
1942 Brooklyn - Durocher, Herman, Reese, Vaughan, Reiser, Medwick, Wyatt, French........................$400-$600
1942 Chicago (AL) - Appling, Lyons ....$250-$350
1942 Chicago (NL) - Cavarretta, Hack, Novikoff, Foxx ....$250-$400
1942 Cincinnati - McKechnie, Vander Meer............$200-$325
1942 Cleveland - Boudreau..................................$200-$300
1942 Detroit - Gehringer, Trucks, Newhouser...........$300-$400
1942 New York (AL) - McCarthy, Gordon, Rizzuto, DiMaggio, Dickey, Ruffing, Gomez ....$600-$900
1942 New York (NL) - Ott, Mize, Hubbell..................$500-$800
1942 Philadelphia (AL) - Mack, Collins ....$300-$450
1942 Philadelphia (NL) - Waner..............................$500-$750
1942 Pittsburgh - Frisch, Lopez ....$700-$900
1942 St. Louis (AL) - Ferrell ....$200-$375
1942 St. Louis (NL) - Slaughter, Musial, W. Cooper, M. Cooper, Beazley...$750-$1,000
1942 Washington - Harris, Vernon, Wynn...............$200-$300
1943 Boston (AL) - Cronin, Doerr..........................$300-$550
1943 Boston (NL) - Stengel, McCarthy ....$250-$325
1943 Brooklyn - Durocher, Herman, Vaughan, Bordagaray, Walker, Olmo, Waner, Hodges, Medwick, Wyatt........$350-$700
1943 Chicago (AL) - Appling, Grove........................$200-$350
1943 Chicago (NL) - Cavarretta, Nicholson, Goodman ....$250-$400
1943 Cincinnati - McKechnie, McCormick, VanderMeer ....$200-$350
1943 Cleveland - Boudreau, Smith.........................$200-$275
1943 Detroit - Cramer, Wakefield, Trout, Trucks ....$200-$300
1943 New York (AL) - McCarthy, Dickey, Chandler...$1,200-$1,500
1943 New York (NL) - Ott, Witek, Medwick, Lombardi, Adams ....$325-$500
1943 Philadelphia (AL) - Mack, Kell ....$200-$350
1943 Philadelphia (NL) - Rowe, Barrett ....$400-$600
1943 Pittsburgh - Frisch, Elliott, Lopez, Sewell........$225-$350
1943 St. Louis (AL) - Ferrell, Dean..........................$200-$350
1943 St. Louis (NL) - Musial, W. Cooper..................$350-$475
1943 Washington - Vernon, Wynn, Gomez.............$200-$300
1944 Boston (AL) - Cronin, Doerr, Fox, Johnson, Hughson ....$225-$350
1944 Boston (NL) - Holmes..................................$200-$300
1944 Brooklyn - Durocher, Walker, Galan, P. Waner, L. Waner, Vaughan..$250-$500
1944 Chicago (AL) - Schalk.................................$200-$325
1944 Chicago (NL) - Grimm, Cavarretta, Dallessandro, Foxx ....$175-$325
1944 Cincinnati - McKechnie, McCormick, Tiptop, Walters ....$200-$325
1944 Cleveland - Boudreau..................................$275-$450
1944 Detroit - Wakefield, Newhouser ....$225-$375
1944 New York (AL) - McCarthy, Lindell, Martin, Waner ....$250-$425
1944 New York (NL) - Ott, Weintraub, Medwick, Lombardi, Voiselle ....$400-$600
1944 Philadelphia (AL) - Mack, Simmons................$250-$400
1944 Philadelphia (NL) ....$300-$500
1944 Pittsburgh - Russell, Lopez, Sewell, Frisch.....$300-$400
1944 St. Louis (AL) - Kreevich, Potter ....$300-$500
1944 St. Louis (NL) - Marion, Musial, Hopp, W. Cooper, Martin, M. Cooper ....$400-$500
1944 Washington - Spence, Ferrell, Wynn...............$200-$300
1945 Boston (AL) - Cronin....................................$200-$300
1945 Boston (NL) - Holmes..................................$175-$250
1945 Brooklyn - Durocher, Galan, Walker, Rosen, Olmo ....$200-$350

1945 Chicago (AL) - Appling ....$175-$300
1945 Chicago (NL) - Grimm, Cavarretta, Johnson, Hack, Wyse ....$350-$500
1945 Cincinnati - McKechnie ....$225-$325
1945 Cleveland - Boudreau, Feller........................$275-$350
1945 Detroit (AL) - Greenberg, Newhouser.............$325-$450
1945 New York (AL) - McCarthy, Waner, Ruffing......$200-$325
1945 New York (NL) - Ott, Lombardi, Mungo ....$300-$650
1945 Philadelphia (AL) - Mack, Kell.......................$225-$350
1945 Philadelphia (NL) - Wasdell, Foxx...................$700-$900
1945 Pittsburgh - Frisch, Lopez, Waner ....$600-$800
1945 St. Louis (AL) - Muncrief ....$600-$800
1945 St. Louis (NL) - Kurowski, Schoendienst, Barrett, Burkhart, Brecheen ....$200-$350
1945 Washington - Lewis, Ferrell, Wolff.................$200-$300
1946 Boston (AL) - Cronin, Doerr, Pesky, DiMaggio, Williams, Ferriss...$300-$450
1946 Boston (NL) - Holmes, Herman, Sain, Spahn . $200-$350
1946 Brooklyn - Durocher, Reese, Medwick, Higbe $350-$500
1946 Chicago (AL) - Lyons, Appling, Caldwell ....$250-$350
1946 Chicago (NL) - Grimm, Waitkus.....................$175-$275
1946 Cincinnati - McKechnie, Walters ....$200-$300
1946 Cleveland - Boudreau, Edwards, Lemon, Feller..$250-$350
1946 Detroit - Kell, Newhouser................................$225-$350
1946 New York (AL) - McCarthy, Rizzuto, DiMaggio, Dickey, Berra, Ruffing, Chandler............................$550-$1,000
1946 New York (NL) - Ott, Mize, Lombardi ....$500-$650
1946 Philadelphia (AL) - Mack, Valo, McCosky, Kell $300-$400
1946 Philadelphia (NL) - Ennis, Rowe ....$200-$300
1946 Pittsburgh - Frisch, Kiner, Lopez....................$800-$950
1946 St. Louis (AL) - Stephens ....$200-$300
1946 St. Louis (NL) - Musial, Schoendienst, Kurowski, Slaughter, Walker, Garagiola, Pollet ....$400-$600
1946 Washington - Vernon, Grace, Leonard, Wynn $200-$300
1947 Boston (AL) - Cronin, Doerr, Pesky, Williams, Dobson ....$250-$400
1947 Boston (NL) - Elliott, Holmes, Spahn, Sain .....$200-$325
1947 Brooklyn - Robinson, Reese, Vaughan, Snider, Hodges, Branca, Hatten ....$900-$1,100
1947 Chicago (AL) - Lyons, Appling, Wright ....$200-$300
1947 Chicago (NL) - Grimm, Pafko, Cavarretta........$200-$300
1947 Cincinnati - Galan, Kluszewski, Blackwell.......$200-$300
1947 Cleveland - Boudreau, Mitchell, Feller, Lemon $250-$350
1947 Detroit - Kell, Newhouser, Trucks....................$250-$350
1947 New York (AL) - McQuinn, Rizzuto, DiMaggio, Berra, Reynolds, Shea ....$1,000-$1,250
1947 New York (NL) - Ott, Mize, Cooper, Jansen.....$350-$600
1947 Philadelphia (AL) - Mack, Valo, Fox, Marchildon..$225-$350
1947 Philadelphia (NL) - Walker, Leonard, Rowe.... $250-$400
1947 Pittsburgh - Herman, Greenberg, Kiner..........$200-$300
1947 St. Louis (AL) - Dean, V. Stephens ....$225-$350
1947 St. Louis (NL) - Musial, Schoendienst, Garagiola, Medwick, Munger.......................................$275-$400
1947 Washington - Vernon, Wynn ....$200-$300
1948 Boston (AL) - McCarthy, Doerr, Pesky, Williams ....$250-$375
1948 Boston (NL) - Dark, Sain, Spahn, Holmes, Southworth ....$500-$600
1948 Brooklyn - Durocher, Hodges, Robinson, Reese, Furillo, Campanella, Roe, Vaughan, Snider, Branca, Erskine ....$600-$900
1948 Chicago (AL) - Lyons, Appling.......................$200-$300
1948 Chicago (NL) - Grimm ....$200-$300
1948 Cincinnati- Kluszewski ....$200-$300
1948 Cleveland - Boudreau, Mitchell, Bearden, Lemon, Feller, Paige...$400-$575

1955 Boston Red Sox

1960 Chicago White Sox

1961 Detroit Tigers

1948 Detroit - Kell, Cramer, Newhouser, Trucks....... $250-$350

1948 New York (AL) - Rizzuto, DiMaggio, Berra, Raschi.... $1,250

1948 New York (NL) - Ott, Durocher, Mize .... $400-$600

1948 Philadelphia (AL) - Mack, Fox .... $225-$350

1948 Philadelphia (NL) - Sisler, Ashburn, Leonard, Rowe,
Roberts .... $300-$450

1948 Pittsburgh - Kiner, Murtaugh, Sewell .... $275-$375

1948 St. Louis (AL) - Zanilla, Sanford .... $200-$400

1948 St. Louis (NL) - Schoendienst, Slaughter, Musial,
Garagiola, Medwick .... $275-$400

1948 Washington - Vernon, Wynn .... $225-$325

1949 Boston (AL) - McCarthy, Doerr, Williams,
Parnell... $200-$325

1949 Boston (NL) - Spahn, Sain .... $275-$350

1949 Brooklyn - Hodges, Robinson, Reese, Furillo, Roe,
Newcombe, Campanella, Snider, Connors.......... $700-$900

1949 Chicago (AL) - Appling .... $200-$300

1949 Chicago (NL) - Grimm, Frisch, Burgess .... $250-$350

1949 Cincinnati - Kluszewski .... $200-$275

1949 Cleveland - Boudreau, Vernon, Mitchell, Lemon, Feller,
Wynn... $225-$300

1949 Detroit - Kell, Wertz, Evers, Trucks .... $200-$300

1949 New York (AL) - Stengel, Rizzuto, Berra, DiMaggio, Mize,
Raschi, Reynolds............................. $1,200-$1,500

1949 New York (NL) - Durocher, Mize, Marshall, Thomson,
Irvin.. $275-$550

1949 Philadelphia (AL) - Mack, Fox .... $225-$325

1949 Philadelphia (NL) - Sisler, Meyer, Roberts...... $300-$500

1949 Pittsburgh - Hopp, Kiner................................ $300-$500

1949 St. Louis (AL) - Dillinger, Sievers.................... $200-$300

1949 St. Louis (NL) - Schoendienst, Musial, Slaughter,
Garagiola, Pollet .... $225-$350

1949 Washington - E. Robinson, Yost..................... $200-$300

1950 Boston (AL) - McCarthy, Dropo, Doerr, Pesky,
Williams .... $250-$350

1950 Boston (NL) - Jethroe, Spahn, Sain .... $200-$300

1950 Brooklyn - Hodges, Robinson, Reese, Furillo, Roe,
Campanella, Newcombe, Snider .... $600-$900

1950 Chicago (AL) - Fox, Appling........................... $200-$300

1950 Chicago (NL) - Frisch, Pafko .... $200-$300

1950 Cincinnati - Kluszewski, Adcock..................... $200-$300

1950 Cleveland - Boudreau, Rosen, Doby, Mitchell, Lemon,
Wynn, Feller... $250-$350

1950 Detroit - Kell, Wertz, Groth, Evers .... $300-$400

1950 New York (AL) - Stengel, Martin, Rizzuto, Bauer,
DiMaggio, Woodling, Berra, Mize, Ford .... $675-$1,000

1950 New York (NL) - Dark, Irvin, Jansen, Maglie.... $300-$450

1950 Philadelphia (AL) - Mack, Dillinger, Lehner..... $300-$400

1950 Philadelphia (NL) - Ennis, Ashburn, Roberts, Simmons,
Konstanty... $300-$450

1950 Pittsburgh - Hopp, Kiner.. $350

1950 St. Louis (AL) - Garver, Siever .... $200-$275

1950 St. Louis (NL) - Musial, Schoendienst,
Garagiola .... $225-$325

1950 Washington - Vernon .... $200-$275

1951 Boston (AL) - Doerr, Pesky, Boudreau .... $200-$300

1951 Boston (NL) - Spahn, Sain .... $200-$250

1951 Brooklyn - Hodges, Robinson, Reese, Snider,
Campanella, Roe, Newcombe .... $575-$675

1951 Chicago (AL) - Fox, Minoso .... $200-$300

1951 Chicago (NL) - Frisch, Connors, Burgess........ $225-$325

1951 Cincinnati - Kluszewski, Adcock .... $175-$275

1951 Cleveland - Lopez, Avila, Feller, Wynn, Lemon... $225-$325

1951 Detroit - Kell, Trucks.................................... $250-$400

1951 New York (AL) - Stengel, Mize, Rizzuto, Brown, DiMaggio,
Mantle, McDougald, Berra, Martin................. $2,500-$4,500

1951 New York (NL) - Durocher, Dark, Mays, Irvin,
Maglie.. $1,000-$1,150

1951 Philadelphia (AL) - Fain, Shantz .... $200-$400

1951 Philadelphia (NL) - Ashburn, Roberts............. $175-$275

1951 Pittsburgh - Kiner, Garagiola........................ $275-$375

1951 St. Louis (AL) - Paige, Gaedel........................ $400-$600

1951 St. Louis (NL) - Schoendienst, Slaughter, Musial,
Garagiola .... $225-$325

1951 Washington - Vernon .... $100-$225

1952 Boston (AL) - Boudreau, Goodman, Kell,
Williams .... $175-$275

1952 Boston (NL) - Grimm, Mathews, Spahn .... $250-$325

1952 Brooklyn - Hodges, Robinson, Reese, Furillo, Snider,
Campanella, Black, Erskine...................... $500-$750

1952 Chicago (AL) - Fox, Minoso .... $200-$300

1952 Chicago (NL) - Fondy, Baumholtz, Sauer,
Hacker .... $175-$275

1952 Cincinnati - Hornsby, Kluszewski, Adcock ...... $275-$400

1952 Cleveland - Avila, Rosen, Mitchell, Wynn, Garcia, Lemon,
Feller.. $300-$500

1952 Detroit - Kell, Kuenn.................................... $200-$300

1952 New York (AL) - Stengel, Martin, Reynolds, Mantle, Berra,
Raschi, Woodling, Brown, Mize, Rizzuto .... $650-$800

1952 New York (NL) - Durocher, Dark, Irvin, Maglie,
Wilhelm.. $300-$425

1952 Philadelphia (AL) - Fain, Shantz .... $200-$300

1952 Philadelphia (NL) - Ashburn, Roberts............. $200-$300

1952 Pittsburgh - Groat, Kiner, Garagiola............... $200-$300

1952 St. Louis (AL) - Hornsby, Paige .... $350-$500

1952 St. Louis (NL) - Schoendienst, Slaughter,
Musial .... $275-$400

1952 Washington - Vernon .... $175-$250

1953 Boston - Boudreau, Goodman, Kell, Williams,
Parnell .... $400-$550

1953 Brooklyn - Hodges, Meyer, Reese, Furillo, Snider, Robinson, Campanella, Erskine, Gilliam .... $700-$1,000
1953 Chicago (AL) - Fox, Minoso, Trucks .... $225-$350
1953 Chicago (NL) - Fondy, Baumholtz, Kiner, Garagiola, Banks .... $200-$300
1953 Cincinnati - Hornsby, Kluszewski, Bell .... $275-$400
1953 Cleveland - Lopez, Rosen, Westlake, Mitchell, Lemon, Wynn, Feller .... $225-$300
1953 Detroit - Kuenn, Boone, Kaline .... $200-$275
1953 Milwaukee - Grimm, Adcock, Mathews, Spahn, Burdette .... $300-$375
1953 New York (AL) - Stengel, Martin, Rizzuto, Mantle, Berra, Mize, Ford .... $750-$1,200
1953 New York (NL) - Durocher, Dark, Mueller, Thomson, Irvin .... $275-$450
1953 Philadelphia (AL) - Philley .... $200-$300
1953 Philadelphia (NL) - Ashburn, Roberts .... $175-$275
1953 Pittsburgh - Kiner, Garagiola .... $200-$300
1953 St. Louis (AL) - Marion, Paige, Wertz .... $175-$250
1953 St. Louis (NL) - Schoendienst, Slaughter, Musial, Haddix, Staley .... $225-$275
1953 Washington - Vernon, Busby, Porterfield .... $175-$250
1954 Baltimore - Larsen, Turley .... $150-$225
1954 Boston - Boudreau, Jensen, Williams .... $400-$500
1954 Brooklyn - Alston, Hodges, Gilliam, Reese, Furillo, Lasorda, Robinson, Campanella, Erskine, Newcombe, Snider .... $1,200-$1,400
1954 Chicago (AL) - Fox, Kell, Trucks, Minoso .... $200-$325
1954 Chicago (NL) - Banks, Kiner, Garagiola .... $300-$500
1954 Cincinnati - Kluszewski, Temple .... $175-$275
1954 Cleveland - Lopez, Avila, Lemon, Wynn, Feller...$300-$450
1954 Detroit - Kuenn, Kaline .... $350-$425
1954 Milwaukee - Grimm, Adcock, Mathews, Aaron, Spahn, Burdette .... $275-$400
1954 New York (AL) - Stengel, Rizzuto, Mantle, Berra, Slaughter, Grim, Ford .... $500-$900
1954 New York (NL) - Durocher, Mays, Irvin, Antonelli, Maglie, Wilhelm .... $1,200-$1,500
1954 Philadelphia (NL) - Ashburn, Burgess, Roberts...$250-$350
1954 Philadelphia (AL) - Finigan .... $175-$250
1954 Pittsburgh - Gordon .... $150-$250
1954 St. Louis - Schoendienst, Musial, Moon .... $200-$300
1954 Washington - Vernon, Killebrew .... $150-$225
1955 Baltimore - Robinson .... $225-$325
1955 Boston - Goodman, Jensen, Piersall, Williams....$500-$600
1955 Brooklyn - Hodges, Gilliam, Reese, Labine, Furillo, Snider, Campanella, Newcombe, Robinson, Erskine, Koufax .... $2,500-$4,000
1955 Chicago (AL) - Fox, Kell, Donovan, Trucks ...... $200-$300
1955 Chicago (NL) - Banks .... $175-$250
1955 Cincinnati - Kluszewski, Burgess .... $200-$300
1955 Cleveland - Lopez, Smith, Kiner, Colavito, Lemon, Wynn, Score, Feller .... $375-$525
1955 Detroit - Kuenn, Kaline, Bunning .... $200-$275
1955 Kansas City - Boudreau, Slaughter .... $200-$275
1955 Milwaukee - Mathews, Aaron, Adcock, Spahn, Burdette .... $250-$400
1955 New York (AL) - Stengel, Mantle, Slaughter, Howard, Martin, Berra, Rizzuto, Ford, Larsen .... $500-$900
1955 New York (NL) - Durocher, Mays, Irvin, Antonelli .... $275-$475
1955 Philadelphia - Ashburn, Roberts .... $175-$250
1955 Pittsburgh - Groat, Clemente, Friend .... $500-$800
1955 St. Louis - Musial, Schoendienst, Boyer, Virdon, Haddix .... $200-$300
1955 Washington - Vernon, Killebrew .... $150-$225
1956 Baltimore - Kell, Gastall, Robinson .... $175-$250

1956 Boston - Vernon, Jensen, Williams .... $300-$400
1956 Brooklyn - Hodges, Gilliam, Reese, Furillo, Snider, Campanella, Koufax, Newcombe, Erskine, Drysdale, Robinson .... $700-$900
1956 Chicago (AL) - Fox, Aparicio, Kell................ $200-$300
1956 Chicago (NL) - Banks, Irvin .... $200-$275
1956 Cincinnati - Kluszewski, Robinson .... $225-$325
1956 Cleveland - Lopez, Colavito, Lemon, Wynn, Score, Feller .... $500-$550
1956 Detroit - Kuenn, Kaline, Bunning .... $200-$300
1956 Kansas City - Boudreau, Slaughter, Lasorda....... $200-$300
1956 Milwaukee - Grimm, Adcock, Mathews, Aaron, Spahn, Burdette .... $275-$425
1956 New York (AL) - Stengel, Martin, Mantle, Howard, Rizzuto, Slaughter, Berra, Bauer, Ford .... $650-$1,000
1956 New York (NL) - White, Schoendienst, Mays, Antonelli .... $275-$475
1956 Philadelphia - Ashburn, Roberts .... $150-$225
1956 Pittsburgh - Mazeroski, Groat, Clemente, Virdon .... $900-$1,000
1956 St. Louis - Musial, Boyer, Schoendienst, Pettee ...$175-$300
1956 Washington - Killebrew .... $150-$225
1957 Baltimore - Kell, Robinson .... $200-$300
1957 Boston - Jensen, Williams, Vernon................ $200-$275
1957 Brooklyn - Hodges, Gilliam, Reese, Furillo, Snider, Campanella, Koufax, Drysdale .... $1,000-$1,300
1957 Chicago (AL) - Lopez, Fox, Aparicio................ $200-$300
1957 Chicago (NL) - Banks .... $175-$250
1957 Cincinnati - Robinson, Kluszewski .... $250-$375
1957 Cleveland - Colavito, Maris, Wynn, Wilhelm.... $450-$600
1957 Detroit - Kuenn, Kaline, Bunning .... $180-$270
1957 Kansas City - Martin .... $175-$275
1957 Milwaukee - Schoendienst, Mathews, Aaron, Adcock, Spahn .... $1,000-$1,500
1957 New York (AL) - Stengel, Slaughter, Berra, Howard, Sturdivant, Ford .... $700-$900
1957 New York (NL) - Mays, Schoendienst, McCormick, White .... $250-$350
1957 Philadelphia - Ashburn, Sanford, Roberts ...... $275-$375
1957 Pittsburgh - Mazeroski, Groat, Clemente, Friend .... $900-$1,000
1957 St. Louis - Musial, Boyer, Wilhelm .... $200-$300
1957 Washington - Killebrew .... $150-$225
1958 Baltimore - Robinson, Wilhelm .... $150-$225
1958 Boston - Runnels, Williams .... $275-$500
1958 Chicago (AL) - Fox, Aparicio, Cash, Wynn ...... $200-$300
1958 Chicago (NL) - Banks .... $175-$250
1958 Cincinnati - Robinson, Pinson .... $150-$300
1958 Cleveland - Vernon, Colavito, Maris, Wilhelm, Lemon .... $200-$300
1958 Detroit - Martin, Kaline, Kuenn, Bunning .... $200-$300
1958 Kansas City - Maris .... $400-$550
1958 Los Angeles - Alston, Hodges, Furillo, Snider, Reese, Drysdale, Koufax, Howard .... $350-$600
1958 Milwaukee - Schoendienst, Mathews, Aaron, Spahn, Burdette .... $525-$800
1958 New York - Kubek, Mantle, Berra, Howard, Slaughter, Turley, Ford, Larsen .... $1,100-$1,350
1958 Philadelphia - Ashburn, Roberts .... $200-$350
1958 Pittsburgh - Kluszewski, Mazeroski, Groat, Clemente, Friend .... $575-$850
1958 San Francisco - Cepeda, Mays, White, McCormick .... $450-$600
1958 St. Louis - Musial, Boyer .... $175-$250
1958 Washington - Pearson, Killebrew .... $150-$225
1959 Baltimore - Robinson, Wilhelm................ $175-$250
1959 Boston - Runnels, Williams .... $150-$250

1959 Chicago (AL) - Lopez, Fox, Aparicio, Cash, Kluszewski, Wynn .... $350-$525
1959 Chicago (NL) - Banks, Williams .... $175-$250
1959 Cincinnati - Robinson, Pinson .... $300-$500
1959 Cleveland - Martin, Colavito, Perry, Score ...... $175-$250
1959 Detroit - Kaline, Bunning $250
1959 Kansas City - Maris .... $200-$400
1959 Los Angeles - Alston, Hodges, Gilliam, Snider, Koufax, Furillo, Drysdale, Howard, Wills .... $800-$1,000
1959 Milwaukee - Adcock, Mathews, Aaron, Vernon, Slaughter, Schoendienst, Spahn .... $500-$600
1959 New York - Stengel, Kubek, Mantle, Berra, Howard, Slaughter, Ford, Larsen .... $450-$600
1959 Philadelphia - Sparky Anderson, Ashburn, Roberts .... $300-$400
1959 Pittsburgh - Stuart, Mazeroski, Groat, Clemente, Kluszewski, Friend .... $600-$800
1959 San Francisco - Cepeda, Mays, McCovey, McCormick .... $250-$375
1959 St. Louis - Musial, Boyer, White, McDaniel, Gibson .... $175-$250
1959 Washington - Killebrew, Allison, Kaat .... $150-$225
1960 Baltimore - Hansen, Robinson, Wilhelm .... $175-$250
1960 Boston - Runnels, Williams .... $375-$500
1960 Chicago (AL) - Lopez, Fox, Aparicio, Kluszewski, Wynn, Score .... $300-$500
1960 Chicago (NL) - Grimm, Boudreau, Banks, Santo, Ashburn, Williams .... $175-$250
1960 Cincinnati - Robinson, Martin, Pinson .... $250-$350
1960 Cleveland - Aspromonte, Kuenn, Piersall, Perry .... $250-$325
1960 Detroit - Cash, Colavito, Kaline, Bunning .... $250-$350
1960 Kansas City - Bauer, Herzog, Throneberry ..... $150-$225
1960 Los Angeles - Alston, Wills, Howard, Davis, Snider, Hodges, Davis, Koufax, Drysdale, Gilliam .... $425-$500
1960 Milwaukee - Adcock, Mathews, Aaron, Schoendienst, Spahn, Burdette, Torre .... $300-$400
1960 New York - Stengel, Kubek, Maris, Mantle, Howard, Berra, Ford .... $500-$750
1960 Philadelphia - Callison, Roberts .... $100-$150
1960 Pittsburgh - Stuart, Mazeroski, Clemente, Law, Vernon .... $800-$1,200
1960 San Francisco - McCovey, Mays, Cepeda, McCormick, Marichal .... $250-$375
1960 St. Louis - White, Boyer, Musial, McCarver, Gibson .... $250-$350
1960 Washington - Killebrew, Versalles, Kaat .... $175-$275
1961 Baltimore - Robinson, Powell, Wilhelm .... $150-$225
1961 Boston - Jensen, Yastrzemski .... $175-$250
1961 Chicago (AL) - Lopez, Fox, Aparicio, Pierce, Wynn .... $175-$250
1961 Chicago (NL) - Banks, Santo, Ashburn, Hubbs, Brock, Williams .... $175-$275
1961 Cincinnati - Robinson, Pinson, Jay .... $325-$500
1961 Cleveland - Piersall, McDowell .... $125-$175
1961 Detroit - Cash, Kaline, Colavito, Bunning, Freehan .... $250-$350
1961 Kansas City - Howser, Throneberry .... $75-$250
1961 Los Angeles (AL) - Kluszewsky, Wagner .... $200-$300
1961 Los Angeles (NL) - Alston, Wills, T. Davis, W. Davis, Howard, Snider, Drysdale, Koufax .... $275-$400
1961 Milwaukee - Adcock, Mathews, Aaron, Torre, Spahn, Martin .... $175-$275
1961 Minnesota - Lavagetto, Killebrew, Martin, Versalles, Kaat .... $200-$300
1961 New York - Kubek, Maris, Mantle, Berra, Howard, Tresh, Ford .... $1,400-$1,800

1969 Atlanta Braves

1961 Philadelphia - Callisom, Roberts .... $100-$150
1961 Pittsburgh - Stuart, Mazeroski, Clemente, Clendenon, Friend .... $550-$850
1961 San Francisco - McCovey, Mays, Cepeda, Marichal, McCormick .... $250-$350
1961 St. Louis - White, Boyer, Musial, Schoendienst, McCarver, Gibson .... $275-$350
1961 Washington - Vernon .... $150-$225
1962 Baltimore - Robinson, Powell, Roberts, Wilhelm .... $175-$250
1962 Boston - Yastrzemski .... $175-$250
1962 Chicago (AL) - Lopez, Fox, Wynn, Peters, DeBusschere .... $200-$400
1962 Chicago (NL) - Banks, Hubbs, Santo, Brock, Williams .... $172-$275
1962 Cincinnati - Robinson, Pinson .... $250-$450
1962 Cleveland - McDowell .... $125-$200
1962 Detroit - Cash, Kaline, Colavito, Bunning .... $125-$200
1962 Houston - Aspromonte .... $300-$425
1962 Kansas City - Howser, Segui .... $100-$175
1962 Los Angeles (AL) - Lee Thomas, Fregosi .... $150-$225
1962 Los Angeles (NL) - Alston, Gilliam, Wills, Howard, W. Davis, T. Davis, Snider, Drysdale, Koufax .... $400-$800
1962 Milwaukee - Adcock, Mathews, Aaron, Uecker, Spahn .... $300-$400
1962 Minnesota - Versalles, Killebrew, Oliva, Kaat .. $175-$275
1962 New York (AL) - Tresh, Maris, Mantle, Howard, Berra, Kubek, Terry, Ford .... $550-$800
1962 New York (NL) - Stengel, Hodges, Kranepool . $300-$450
1962 Philadelphia - Callison, Maheffey .... $100-$150
1962 Pittsburgh - Mazeroski, Groat, Clemente, Clendenon, Stargell .... $500-$750
1962 San Francisco - Cepeda, Mays, McCovey, Marichal, McCormick, Perry .... $400-$600
1962 St. Louis - White, Boyer, Musial, Schoendienst, Gibson .... $275-$350
1962 Washington - Vernon .... $150-$275
1963 Baltimore - Aparicio, Robinson, Powell, Roberts .... $200-$250
1963 Boston - Yastrzemski .... $150-$250
1963 Chicago (AL) - Lopez, Fox, Peters, Wilhelm, DeBusschere .... $175-$250
1963 Chicago (NL) - Banks, Hubbs, Santo, Brock, Williams .... $175-$250
1963 Cincinnati - Rose, Harper, Pinson, Robinson . $200-$275
1963 Cleveland - Adcock, McDowell, John .... $100-$150
1963 Detroit - Cash, Kaline, Colavito, Lolich, McLain... $125-$200
1963 Houston - Staub, Aspromonte, Morgan, Umbricht .... $175-$250
1963 Kansas City - Harrelson, Segui .... $150-$225

1963 Los Angeles (AL) - Fregosi, Chance .... $100-$150
1963 Los Angeles (NL) - Alston, Gilliam, Wills, Howard, W. Davis, T. Davis, Koufax, Drysdale .... $450-$650
1963 Milwaukee - Mathews, Aaron, Torre, Uecker, Spahn .... $150-$225
1963 Minnesota - Versalles, Killebrew, Oliva, Kaat .. $175-$275
1963 New York (AL) - Maris, Howard, Mantle, Berra, Ford .... $450-$650
1963 New York (NL) - Stengel, Snider, Kranepool, Hodges .... $275-$400
1963 Philadelphia - Allen .... $100-$150
1963 Pittsburgh - Clendenon, Mazeroski, Clemente, Stargell, Mota .... $450-$800
1963 San Francisco - Cepeda, Mays, McCovey, Marichal, Larsen, Perry .... $225-$450
1963 St. Louis - Groat, Boyer, McCarver, Musial, Gibson .... $300-$550
1963 Washington - Vernon, Hodges .... $100-$150
1964 Baltimore - Aparicio, Robinson, Powell, Piniella, Roberts .... $200-$275
1964 Boston - Herman, Yastrzemski .... $200-$300
1964 Chicago (AL) - Lopez, Wilhelm .... $100-$150
1964 Chicago (NL) - Banks, Santo, Williams, Brock, Kessinger .... $150-$225
1964 Cincinnati - Rose, Robinson, Pinson, Perez ... $175-$250
1964 Cleveland - McDowell, Tiant, John .... $100-$150
1964 Detroit - Cash, Kaline, Freehan, Lolich, McLain .. $150-$200
1964 Houston - Fox, Aspromonte, Staub, Morgan ... $200-$300
1964 Kansas City - Colavito, Campaneris, Odom .... $150-$250
1964 Los Angeles (AL) - Adcock, Fregosi, Chance ... $75-$100
1964 Los Angeles (NL) - Alston, Wills, Howard, W. Davis, T. Davis, Koufax, Drysdale .... $250-$400
1964 Milwaukee - Mathews, Aaron, Carty, Torre, Spahn, Niekro .... $300-$400
1964 Minnesota - Versalles, Oliva, Killebrew, Kaat .. $200-$250
1964 New York (AL) - Berra, Maris, Mantle, Howard, Ford, Stottlemyre .... $350-$500
1964 New York (NL) - Stengel, Kranepool .... $350-$500
1964 Philadelphia - Allen, Bunning .... $100-$135
1964 Pittsburgh - Clendenon, Mazeroski, Clemente, Mota .... $450-$650
1964 San Francisco - Cepeda, Mays, McCovey, Snider, Marichal, Perry, Larsen .... $200-$300
1964 St. Louis - White, Boyer, Brock, McCarver, Uecker, Gibson .... $375-$550
1964 Washington - Hodges .... $225-$350
1965 Baltimore - Powell, Aparicio, Robinson, Blefary, Palmer, Roberts .... $200-$300
1965 Boston - Herman, Yastrzemski .... $200-$275
1965 California - Fregosi .... $115-$200
1965 Chicago (AL) - Lopez, John, Wilhelm .... $125-$175
1965 Chicago (NL) - Banks, Santo, Williams............ $100-$150
1965 Cincinnati - Rose, Robinson, Pinson, Perez ... $200-$400
1965 Cleveland - Colavito, McDowell, Tiant .... $125-$325
1965 Detroit - Cash, Kaline, Freehan, McLain, Lolich .. $150-$200
1965 Houston - Morgan, Staub, Fox, Roberts .... $150-$225
1965 Kansas City - Campaneris, Hunter, Paige, Odom .... $200-$400
1965 Los Angeles - Alston, Lefebvre, Wills, W. Davis, Koufax, Drysdale .... $350-$550
1965 Milwaukee - Mathews, Aaron, Torre, Niekro .... $250-$350
1965 Minnesota - Versalles, Oliva, Killebrew, Kaat .. $325-$575
1965 New York (AL) - Mantle, Howard, Maris, Murcer, Stottlemyre, Ford .... $400-$575
1965 New York (NL) - Stengel, Kranepool, Swoboda, Berra, Spahn .... $300-$375
1965 Philadelphia - Allen, Bunning, Jenkins............ $150-$250

1965 Pittsburgh - Mazeroski, Clemente, Stargell .. $1,300-$1,400
1965 San Francisco - McCovey, Mays, Cepeda, Marichal, Perry, Spahn .... $200-$350
1965 St. Louis - Schoendienst, White, Boyer, Brock, McCarver, Uecker, Gibson, Carlton................................ $300-$350
1965 Washington - Hodges, Howard, McCormick ... $150-$225
1966 Atlanta - Mathews, Aaron, Torre, Niekro.......... $325-$400
1966 Baltimore - Aparicio, B. Robinson, F. Robinson, Palmer .... $250-$450
1966 Boston - Herman, Yastrzemski, Lonborg......... $200-$300
1966 California - Fregosi..................................... $80-$120
1966 Chicago (AL) - Agee, John, Wilhelm .... $150-$250
1966 Chicago (NL) - Banks, Santo, Jenkins, Roberts.. $125-$200
1966 Cincinnati - Perez, Rose, Helms, Harper, Pinson... $125-$175
1966 Cleveland - Colavito, Tiant, McDowell .... $100-$175
1966 Detroit - Cash, Kaline, Freehan, McLain, Lolich.. $125-$200
1966 Houston - Morgan, Staub, Roberts .... $100-$150
1966 Kansas City - Campaneris, Hunter, Odom...... $100-$150
1966 Los Angeles - Wills, W. Davis, T. Davis, Koufax, Drysdale, Sutton .... $175-$400
1966 Minnesota - Killebrew, Oliva, Kaat.................. $150-$225
1966 New York (AL) - Maris, Mantle, Howard, Stottlemyre, Ford .... $400-$600
1966 New York (NL) - Kranepool, Boyer, Swoboda, Ryan .... $175-$250
1966 Philadelphia - White, Allen, Uecker, Bunning, Jenkins .... $100-$150
1966 Pittsburgh - Clendenon, Mazeroski, Clemente, Stargell, Mota.. $800-$1,200
1966 San Francisco - McCovey, Mays, Cepeda, Marichal, Perry .... $175-$250
1966 St. Louis - Schoendienst, Cepeda, Brock, McCarver, Gibson, Carlton.. $250-$400
1966 Washington - Hodges, Howard .... $125-$200
1967 Atlanta - Aaron, Carty, Uecker, Niekro............. $150-$225
1967 Baltimore (AL) - Powell, Aparicio, B. Robinson, F. Robinson, Palmer..................................... $200-$300
1967 Boston (AL) - Yastrzemski, Howard, Lonborg, Lyle .... $600-$1,200
1967 California (AL) - Fregosi .... $75-$125
1967 Chicago (AL) - Colavito, Boyer, John, Wilhelm $100-$175
1967 Chicago (NL) - Durocher, Banks, Santo, Williams, Jenkins .... $125-$175
1967 Cincinnati - Pinson, Rose, Bench .... $150-$225
1967 Cleveland (AL) - Adcock, McDowell, Tiant ...... $100-$150
1967 Detroit (AL) - Cash, Kaline, Freehan, Mathews, McLain, Lolich .... $150-$225
1967 Houston - Mathews, Morgan, Staub............... $100-$150
1967 Kansas City (AL) - Appling, Jackson, Hunter, Odom... $150-$225
1967 Los Angeles - Alston, Davis, Drysdale, Sutton $200-$275
1967 Minnesota (AL) - Killebrew, Carew, Oliva, Kaat . $275-$375
1967 New York (AL) - Mantle, Howard, Stottlemyre, Ford .... $350-$450
1967 New York (NL) - Kranepool, Harrelson, Swoboda, Seaver, Koosman .... $325-$475
1967 Philadelphia - White, Allen, Uecker, Groat, Bunning .... $100-$150
1967 Pittsburgh - Mazeroski, Wills, Clemente, Stargell .... $400-$600
1967 San Francisco (NL) - McCovey, Mays, McCormick, Perry, Marichal.. $175-$250
1967 St. Louis - Schoendienst, Cepeda, Maris, Brock, McCarver, Carlton, Gibson .... $550-$750
1967 Washington (AL) - Hodges, Howard .... $175-$250
1968 Atlanta - Aaron, Torre, Niekro .... $200-$300

1968 Baltimore - Weaver, Powell, B. Robinson, F. Robinson...$150-$250
1968 Boston - Yastrzemski, Howard, Lyle...............$150-$200
1968 California - Fregosi....................................$100-$125
1968 Chicago (AL) - Lopez, Aparicio, John..............$100-$150
1968 Chicago (NL) - Durocher, Banks, Santo, Williams, Jenkins...$125-$200
1968 Cincinnati - Perez, Rose, Pinson, Bench........$175-$250
1968 Cleveland - Tiant, McDowell..........................$100-$150
1968 Detroit - Cash, Freehan, Kaline, McLain, Lolich, Mathews...$375-$600
1968 Houston - Staub, Morgan.............................$100-$150
1968 Los Angeles - Alston, Davis, Drysdale, Sutton...$125-$200
1968 Minnesota - Carew, Oliva, Killebrew, Kaat.......$175-$250
1968 New York (AL) - Mantle, Bahnsen...................$200-$300
1968 New York (NL) - Hodges, Kranepool, Harrelson, Swoboda, Koosman, Seaver, Ryan....................$500-$800
1968 Oakland - Bando, Jackson, Odom, Hunter, Fingers...$200-$300
1968 Philadelphia - White, Allen..........................$75-$125
1968 Pittsburgh - Mazeroski, Wills, Clemente, Stargell, Oliver, Bunning...$450-$650
1968 San Francisco - McCovey, Bonds, Mays, Marichal, Perry, McCormick.......................................$175-$250
1968 St. Louis - Schoendienst, Cepeda, Maris, Brock, Simmons, Gibson, Carlton, McCarver.................$450-$600
1968 Washington - Howard...................................$100-$150
1969 Atlanta - Cepeda, Aaron, Evans, Niekro, Wilhelm...$200-$300
1969 Baltimore - Weaver, Powell, B. Robinson, F. Robinson, Cueller, Palmer......................................$150-$275
1969 Boston - Yastrzemski, Lyle............................$300-$400
1969 California - Fregosi, Wilhelm........................$75-$125
1969 Chicago (AL) - Lopez, Aparicio, John..............$150-$200
1969 Chicago (NL) - Durocher, Banks, Santo, Williams, Jenkins...$125-$200
1969 Cincinnati - Perez, Rose, Bench....................$175-$250
1969 Cleveland - McDowell, Tiant.........................$75-$125
1969 Detroit - Cash, Kaline, Freehan, McLain, Lolich...$125-$175
1969 Houston - Morgan......................................$75-$125
1969 Kansas City - Piniella................................$250-$375
1969 Los Angeles - Alston, Sizemore, Wills, Davis, Drysdale, Bunning, Buckner, Garvey............................$175-$250
1969 Minnesota - Carew, Killebrew, Oliva, Nettles, Kaat...$275-$375
1969 Montreal - Staub.....................................$275-$450
1969 New York (AL) - Murcer, Munson, Stottlemyre.....$200-$275
1969 New York (NL) - Harrelson, Swoboda, Seaver, Koosman, Ryan..$750-$2,000
1969 Oakland - Bando, Jackson, Odom, Hunter, Fingers, Blue...$250-$325
1969 Philadelphia - Allen..................................$100-$150
1969 Pittsburgh - Oliver, Mazeroski, Clemente, Stargell, Bunning...$325-$575
1969 San Diego - Colbert, Gaston, J. Niekro..........$200-$300
1969 San Francisco - McCovey, Bonds, Mays, Marichal, Perry...$125-$250
1969 Seattle - T. Davis, Harper, Segui..................$400-$600
1969 St. Louis - Pinson, Torre, Simmons, Gibson, Carlton, Schoendienst, Brock, McCarver.......................$125-$225
1969 Washington - Williams, Howard......................$150-$200
1970 Atlanta - Cepeda, Aaron, Evans, Niekro, Wilhelm...$125-$200
1970 Baltimore - Weaver, Powell, B. Robinson, F. Robinson, Palmer...$325-$400
1970 Boston - Yastrzemski, Lyle............................$125-$175
1970 California - Fregosi....................................$75-$125

1970 Chicago (AL) - Aparicio, John.........................$150-$200
1970 Chicago (NL) - Durocher, Banks, Santo, Williams, Jenkins, Wilhelm...$150-$225
1970 Cincinnati - Anderson, Concepcion, Perez, Rose, Bench...$225-$300
1970 Cleveland - Nettles, Pinson, McDowell...........$125-$150
1970 Detroit - Cash, Kaline, Freehan, Lolich...........$100-$150
1970 Houston - Morgan......................................$75-$125
1970 Kansas City - Lemon, Piniella.......................$125-$175
1970 Los Angeles - Alston, Wills, Garvey, Buckner, Sutton...$175-$250
1970 Milwaukee - Harper....................................$100-$175
1970 Minnesota - Killebrew, Oliva, Carew, Perry, Kaat, Tiant...$200-$400
1970 Montreal - Staub, Morton.............................$100-$150
1970 New York (AL) - Murcer, Munson, Stottlemyre.$275-$375
1970 New York (NL) - Hodges, Koosman, Harrelson, Swoboda, Kranepool, Seaver, Ryan, Clendenon.................$275-$400
1970 Oakland - Bando, Jackson, Hunter, Fingers....$150-$250
1970 Philadelphia - Bowa, McCarver, Bunning, Luzinski...$100-$150
1970 Pittsburgh - Mazeroski, Clemente, Stargell, Oliver...$600-$800
1970 San Diego - Colbert, Gaston.........................$100-$150
1970 San Francisco - McCovey, Bonds, Mays, Foster, Perry, Marichal...$175-$275
1970 St. Louis - Allen, Torre, Brock, Simmons, Gibson, Carlton...$150-$200
1970 Washington - Williams, Howard......................$150-$200
1971 Atlanta - Aaron, Evans, Williams, Cepeda, Niekro, Wilhelm...$125-$200
1971 Baltimore - Weaver, Powell, B. Robinson, F. Robinson, Palmer...$250-$300
1971 Boston - Aparicio, Fisk, Lyle, Tiant..................$125-$175
1971 California - Fregosi....................................$100-$125
1971 Chicago (AL) - John....................................$100-$125
1971 Chicago (NL) - Santo, Williams, Banks, Jenkins...$100-$150
1971 Cincinnati - Concepcion, Perez, Rose, Foster, Bench...$175-$250
1971 Cleveland - Chambliss, Nettles, Pinson, McDowell...$100-$125
1971 Detroit - Martin, Cash, Kaline, Freehan, Lolich....$150-$200
1971 Houston - Morgan......................................$75-$125
1971 Kansas City - Lemon, Piniella.......................$75-$125
1971 Los Angeles - Alston, Wills, Garvey, Buckner, Sutton, Wilhelm...$175-$250
1971 Milwaukee - Harper....................................$75-$100
1971 Minnesota - Killebrew, Carew, Oliva, Blyleven, Kaat...$100-$150
1971 Montreal - Staub.......................................$75-$100
1971 New York (AL) - Murcer, Munson, Stottlemyre....$250-$450
1971 New York (NL) - Hodges, Kranepool, Harrelson, Seaver, Ryan, Koosman.......................................$250-$375
1971 Oakland - Bando, Jackson, Hunter, Blue, Fingers...$200-$275
1971 Philadelphia - Bowa, McCarver, Luzinski, Bunning...$100-$150
1971 Pittsburgh - Clemente, Oliver, Stargell, Mazeroski...$500-$700
1971 San Diego - Colbert, Gaston.........................$100-$150
1971 San Francisco - McCovey, Bonds, Mays, Kingman, Foster, Marichal, Perry.......................................$175-$300
1971 St. Louis - Schoendienst, Torre, Brock, Simmons, Carlton, Gibson...$150-$250
1971 Washington - Williams, Harrah, Howard, McLain...$200-$250

1972 Atlanta - Mathews, Aaron, Evans, Cepeda, Niekro .... $125-$200
1972 Baltimore - Weaver, Powell, Robinson .... $150-$175
1972 Boston - Aparicio, Yastrzemski, Fisk, Tiant ..... $150-$200
1972 California - Pinson, Ryan .... $100-$150
1972 Chicago (AL) - Allen, Gossage .... $275-$300
1972 Chicago (NL) - Durocher, Santo, Williams, Jenkins .... $100-$150
1972 Cincinnati - Anderson, Perez, Morgan, Concepcion, Rose, Bench, Foster .... $275-$375
1972 Cleveland - Nettles, Bell, Perry .... $100-$125
1972 Detroit - Cash, Northrup, Freehan, Kaline, Lolich .... $150-$225
1972 Houston - Durocher .... $100-$150
1972 Kansas City - Piniella .... $175-$200
1972 Los Angeles - Alston, Garvey, Robinson, Davis, Sutton, John, Wilhelm .... $175-$250
1972 Milwaukee - Scott .... $75-$110
1972 Minnesota - Killebrew, Carew, Oliva, Blyleven, Kaat .... $125-$175
1972 Montreal - Singleton, McCarver .... $100-$150
1972 New York (AL) - Murcer, Munson, Stottlemyre.....$200-$275
1972 New York (NL) - Hodges, Berra, Staub, Kranepool, Harrelson, Mays, Seaver, Matlack, Koosman .... $200-$300
1972 Oakland - Bando, Jackson, Cepeda, Hunter, Fingers, Blue .... $350-$400
1972 Philadelphia - Bowa, Luzinski, McCarver, Boone, Schmidt, Carlton .... $125-$175
1972 Pittsburgh - Stargell, Clemente, Oliver, Mazeroski .... $500-$725
1972 San Diego - Colbert, Gaston .... $75-$100
1972 San Francisco - McCovey, Bonds, Mays, Marichal .... $200-$300
1972 St. Louis - Schoendienst, Torre, Brock, Simmons, Gibson .... $150-$200
1972 Texas - Williams, Howard, Harrah.................... $150-$210
1973 Atlanta - Mathews, Aaron, P. Niekro, J. Niekro $125-$200
1973 Baltimore - Weaver, Powell, Robinson, Bumbry, Palmer .... $175-$250
1973 Boston - Yastrzemski, Aparicio, Fisk, Cepeda, Evans, Tiant... $100-$175
1973 California - Pinson, Robinson, Ryan .... $75-$150
1973 Chicago (AL) - Kaat, Gossage.......................... $75-$125
1973 Chicago (NL) - Kessinger, Williams, Jenkins..... $75-$100
1973 Cincinnati - Anderson, Perez, Concepcion, Rose, Bench, Foster.................................. $225-$350
1973 Cleveland - Perry .... $85-$125
1973 Detroit - Martin, Cash, Northrup, Freehan, Kaline, Lolich, Perry .... $150-$180
1973 Houston - Richard, Durocher.......................... $200-$225
1973 Kansas City - Piniella, Brett............................ $175-$300
1973 Los Angeles - Alston, Buckner, Cey, Davis, Garvey, Sutton, John .... $125-$200
1973 Milwaukee - Thomas .... $80-$120
1973 Minnesota - Carew, Oliva, Killebrew, Kaat, Blyleven .... $100-$150
1973 Montreal - Singleton .... $80-$100
1973 New York (AL) - Nettles, Murcer, Munson, Stottlemyre, McDowell, Lyle .... $200-$235
1973 New York (NL) - Berra, Harrelson, Staub, Jones, Kranepool, Seaver, Koosman .... $275-$425
1973 Oakland - Bando, Jackson, Hunter, Blue, Fingers.. $275-$425
1973 Philadelphia - Bowa, Schmidt, Luzinski, Boone, Carlton .... $125-$175
1973 Pittsburgh - Oliver, Stargell, Parker.................. $125-$175
1973 San Diego - Winfield...................................... $100-$125

1973 San Francisco - McCovey, Bonds, Matthews, Marichal .... $100-$150
1973 St. Louis - Schoendienst, Torre, Brock, Simmons, McCarver, Gibson .... $100-$150
1973 Texas - Martin, Harrah, Burroughs, Madlock ..... $65-$125
1974 Atlanta - Mathews, Evans, Aaron, P. Niekro .... $150-$200
1974 Baltimore - Weaver, Powell, Robinson, Palmer .. $200-$300
1974 Boston - Yastrzemski, Evans, Fisk, Cooper, Rice, Lynn, McCarver, Marichal .... $150-$225
1974 California - Robinson, Ryan .... $100-$150
1974 Chicago (AL) - Allen, Kaat, Gossage .... $75-$125
1974 Chicago (NL) - Kessinger, Madlock .... $75-$100
1974 Cincinnati - Anderson, Perez, Morgan, Concepcion, Foster, Rose, Bench .... $225-$350
1974 Cleveland - G. Perry, J. Perry .... $100-$150
1974 Detroit - Freehan, Horton, Kaline, Lolich .... $150-$200
1974 Houston - Wilson, Richard .... $75-$100
1974 Kansas City - Brett, Pinson .... $100-$150
1974 Los Angeles - Alston, Garvey, Cey, Buckner, Sutton, Marshall, John .... $150-$225
1974 Milwaukee - Yount .... $150-$200
1974 Minnesota - Carew, Oliva, Killebrew, Blyleven. $125-$150
1974 Montreal - Singleton, Davis, Carter .... $75-$100
1974 New York (AL) - Nettles, Murcer, Munson, Lyle, McDowell .... $175-$250
1974 New York (NL) - Harrelson, Staub, Jones, Kranepool, Koosman, Seaver .... $135-$200
1974 Oakland - Bando, Jackson, Hunter, Blue, Fingers.. $250-$375
1974 Philadelphia - Bowa, Schmidt, Luzinski, Boone . $100-$150
1974 Pittsburgh - Oliver, Stargell, Parker, Tekulve... $150-$200
1974 San Diego - McCovey, Winfield .... $75-$125
1974 San Francisco - Kingman, Bonds .... $50-$100
1974 St. Louis - Torre, McBride, Brock, Simmons, McCarver, Gibson .... $125-$175
1974 Texas - Martin, Hargrove, Harrah, Burroughs, Jenkins .... $100-$145
1975 Atlanta - Evans, Niekro.................................. $100-$150
1975 Baltimore - Weaver, Robinson, Palmer .... $150-$250
1975 Boston - Yastrzemski, Evans, Lynn, Rice, Fisk, Cooper, Conigliaro, Tiant........................... $375-$550
1975 California - Ryan .... $200-$275
1975 Chicago (AL) - Kaat, Gossage .... $75-$100
1975 Chicago (NL) - Madlock.................................. $75-$125
1975 Cincinnati - Anderson, Perez, Morgan, Concepcion, Rose, Foster, Bench .... $350-$400
1975 Cleveland - Robinson .... $150-$225
1975 Detroit - Freehan, Horton, Lolich .... $75-$115
1975 Houston - Richard .... $65-$95
1975 Kansas City - Brett, Killebrew.......................... $150-$200
1975 Los Angeles - Alston, Garvey, Cey, Buckner, Sutton, John .... $125-$175
1975 Milwaukee - Yount, Aaron .... $200-$275
1975 Minnesota - Carew, Bostock, Oliva, Blyleven .. $200-$300
1975 Montreal - Carter .... $75-$125
1975 New York (AL) - Martin, Nettles, Bonds, Munson, Piniella, Hunter, Lyle, Guidry .... $250-$450
1975 New York (NL) - Kranepool, Staub, Kingman, Grote, Seaver, Koosman....................................... $115-$125
1975 Oakland - Bando, Jackson, Williams, Blue, Fingers, Odom .... $250-$350
1975 Philadelphia - Allen, Schmidt, Luzinski, Boone, McCarver, Carlton.. $100-$150
1975 Pittsburgh - Stargell, Parker, Oliver, Candelaria, Tekulve .... $175-$225
1975 San Diego - McCovey, Winfield .... $85-$125
1975 San Francisco - Murcer, Clark .... $45-$100

1975 St. Louis - Schoendienst, Brock, Simmons, Hernandez, Gibson .... $100-$150
1975 Texas - Martin, Harrah, Jenkins, Perry............. $100-$200
1976 Atlanta - Murphy, Niekro .... $75-$100
1976 Baltimore - Weaver, Jackson, Robinson, Palmer .... $150-$200
1976 Boston - Yastrzemski, Evans, Lynn, Rice, Fisk, Cooper, Tiant, Jenkins .... $175-$300
1976 California - Ryan .... $125-$175
1976 Chicago (AL) - Gossage .... $60-$90
1976 Chicago (NL) - Madlock .... $60-$90
1976 Cincinnati - Anderson, Perez, Morgan, Concepcion, Rose, Griffey, Foster, Bench, Zachry .... $400-$600
1976 Cleveland - Robinson, Powell, Bell .... $75-$125
1976 Detroit - Staub, Freehan, Horton, Fidrych .... $100-$125
1976 Houston - Richard .... $60-$90
1976 Kansas City - Brett .... $125-$200
1976 Los Angeles - Alston, Garvey, Cey, Buckner, Sutton, John .... $100-$150
1976 Milwaukee - Yount, Aaron, Frisella .... $100-$150
1976 Minnesota - Carew, Bostock, Oliva, Blyleven .... $75-$125
1976 Montreal - Carter, Dawson .... $75-$125
1976 New York (AL) - Martin, Nettles, Munson, Hunter, Lyle .... $150-$300
1976 New York (NL) - Kranepool, Harrelson, Kingman, Torre, Koosman, Seaver, Lolich .... $150-$200
1976 Oakland - Williams, Blue, Fingers .... $100-$125
1976 Philadelphia - Allen, Bowa, Schmidt, Luzinski, Boone, McCarver, Carlton, Kaat .... $125-$200
1976 Pittsburgh - Stargell, Parker, Oliver, Candelaria, Tekulve .... $150-$175
1976 San Diego - Winfield, McCovey, Jones, Metzger .... $100-$125
1976 San Francisco - Evans, Murcer, Clark .... $75-$100
1976 St. Louis - Schoendienst, Hernandez, Brock, Simmons .... $125-$200
1976 Texas - Harrah, Thompson, Perry, Blyleven .... $75-$100
1977 Atlanta - Niekro... $60-$90
1977 Baltimore - Weaver, Murray, Robinson, Palmer...$100-$150
1977 Boston - Evans, Lynn, Yastrzemski, Fisk, Rice, Tiant, Jenkins .... $125-$175
1977 California - Grich, Bonds, Ryan...................... $100-$150
1977 Chicago (AL) - B. Lemon .... $60-$90
1977 Chicago (NL) - Buckner, Trillo, Murcer, R. Reuschel .... $60-$75
1977 Cincinnati - Anderson, Morgan, Concepcion, Rose, Griffey, Foster, Bench, Seaver .... $275-$300
1977 Cleveland - Robinson, Bell, Eckersley............. $125-$175
1977 Detroit - Staub, Trammell, Whitaker, Morris ..... $100-$150
1977 Houston - Richard .... $60-$90
1977 Kansas City - Brett .... $150-$200
1977 Los Angeles - Lasorda, Garvey, Cey, Mota, John, Sutton .... $175-$250
1977 Milwaukee - Cooper, Yount........................... $75-$125
1977 Minnesota - Carew, Bostock........................... $85-$100
1977 Montreal - Perez, Dawson, Carter .... $80-$120
1977 New York (AL) - Martin, Nettles, Jackson, Munson, Piniella, Guidry, Lyle, Hunter............................. $350-$450
1977 New York (NL) - Harrelson, Kranepool, Kingman, Grote, Koosman, Seaver .... $100-$150
1977 Oakland - Allen, Armas, Blue .... $60-$90
1977 Philadelphia - Bowa, Schmidt, Luzinski, Boone, McCarver, Carlton, Kaat .... $125-$175
1977 Pittsburgh - Stargell, Parker, Oliver, Gossage, Tekulve .... $125-$200
1977 San Diego - Winfield, Kingman, Fingers.......... $100-$150
1977 San Francisco - McCovey, Madlock, Clark...... $100-$150

1977 Seattle - R. Jones, Segui .... $125-$175
1977 St. Louis - Hernandez, Brock, Simmons .... $80-$120
1977 Texas - Perry, Blyleven.................................. $50-$100
1977 Toronto - Rader, Fairly.................................. $150-$200
1978 Atlanta - Murphy, Horner, Niekro .... $75-$100
1978 Baltimore - Weaver, Murray, Palmer................ $125-$175
1978 Boston - Evans, Lynn, Yastrzemski, Fisk, Rice, Eckersley .... $100-$150
1978 California - Bostock, Ryan.............................. $80-$120
1978 Chicago (AL) - Bob Lemon............................ $60-$90
1978 Chicago (NL) - Murcer, Kingman....................... $60-$90
1978 Cincinnati - Anderson, Morgan, Concepcion, Rose, Foster, Bench, Seaver .... $150-$200
1978 Cleveland - Bell .... $85-$100
1978 Detroit - Whitaker, Trammell, Staub, Morris ..... $100-$150
1978 Houston - Richard .... $60-$90
1978 Kansas City - Brett .... $120-$180
1978 Los Angeles - Lasorda, Garvey, Cey, Guerrero, John, Sutton .... $150-$225
1978 Milwaukee - Molitor, Yount............................ $80-$120
1978 Minnesota - Carew .... $70-$125
1978 Montreal - Perez, Dawson, Carter .... $80-$120
1978 New York (AL) - Martin, Jackson, Lyle, Munson, Guidry, Hunter, Gossage, Lemon, Piniella .... $275-$400
1978 New York (NL) - Kranepool, Koosman............... $75-$100
1978 Oakland - Armas, Carty................................. $60-$90
1978 Philadelphia - Schmidt, Luzinski, Boone, Carlton, Kaat .... $125-$175
1978 Pittsburgh - Stargell, Parker, Blyleven, Candelaria, Tekulve .... $125-$175
1978 San Diego - Smith, Winfield, Perry, Fingers .... $125-$175
1978 San Francisco - McCovey, Clark, Blue............ $100-$150
1978 Seattle - R. Jones, B. Robertson .... $60-$90
1978 St. Louis - Boyer, Hernandez, Brock, Simmons.. $130-$160
1978 Texas - Harrah, Oliver, Jenkins .... $75-$100
1978 Toronto - Carty, Mayberry .... $65-$150
1979 Atlanta - Murphy, Horner, Niekro .... $75-$125
1979 Baltimore - Weaver, Murray, Flanagan, Palmer .. $175-$250
1979 Boston - Lynn, Rice, Fisk, Yastrzemski, Eckersley .... $125-$175
1979 California - Carew, Lansford, Baylor, Ryan ..... $125-$175
1979 Chicago (AL) - Ortz .... $75-$100
1979 Chicago (NL) - Buckner, Kingman, Sutter .... $60-$90
1979 Cincinnati - Morgan, Concepcion, Griffey, Foster, Bench, Seaver .... $125-$175
1979 Cleveland - Harrah .... $60-$90
1979 Detroit - Anderson, Whitaker, Trammell, Staub, Morris.. $200-$250
1979 Houston - Richard .... $75-$100
1979 Kansas City - Brett, Quisenberry .... $100-$150
1979 Los Angeles - Lasorda, Garvey, Cey, Guerrero, Sutcliffe, Sutton .... $100-$150
1979 Milwaukee - Molitor, Yount............................. $150-$200
1979 Minnesota - Castino, Koosman .... $75-$90
1979 Montreal - Perez, Dawson, Carter, Staub, Raines .... $100-$150
1979 New York (AL) - Martin, Nettles, Jackson, Munson, Murcer, John, Guidry, Tiant, Gossage, Kaat, Hunter.............. $175-$250
1979 New York (NL) - Kranepool .... $85-$100
1979 Oakland - Armas, Henderson .... $75-$90
1979 Philadelphia - Rose, Trillo, Bowa, Schmidt, Luzinski, Boone, Carlton, Kaat .... $150-$200
1979 Pittsburgh - Stargell, Madlock, Parker, Candelaria, Blyleven, Tekulve .... $275-$375
1979 San Diego - Smith, Winfield, Perry, Fingers, Lolich .... $125-$175
1979 San Francisco - McCovey, Clark, Madlock, Blue $125-$150

1979 Seattle - Bochte, W. Horton .... $60-$90

1979 St. Louis - Boyer, Hernandez, Brock, Simmons ..$125-$175

1979 Texas - Bell, Oliver, Jenkins, Lyle...................... $65-$95

1979 Toronto - Griffin, Stieb .... $60-$90

1980 Atlanta - Horner, Murphy, Niekro .... $90-$125

1980 Baltimore - Weaver, Murray, Stone, Palmer .... $150-$225

1980 Boston - Perez, Evans, Lynn, Rice, Fisk, Yastrzemski,
Eckersley .... $125-$200

1980 California - Carew, Lansford........................... $75-$100

1980 Chicago (AL) - Baines .... $60-$90

1980 Chicago (NL) - Buckner, Kingman .... $60-$90

1980 Cincinnati - Concepcion, Griffey, Foster, Bench,
Seaver .... $75-$100

1980 Cleveland - Harrah, Charboneau........................ $45-$75

1980 Detroit - Anderson, Whitaker, Trammell, Gibson,
Morris .... $100-$150

1980 Houston - Morgan, Ryan .... $125-$175

1980 Kansas City - Brett, Quisenberry .... $175-$250

1980 Los Angeles - Lasorda, Garvey, Guerrero, Welch, Sutton,
Howe, Valenzuela .... $100-$150

1980 Milwaukee - Molitor, Yount............................. $80-$120

1980 Minnesota - Koosman .... $60-$85

1980 Montreal - Dawson, Carter, Raines .... $100-$150

1980 New York (AL) - Nettles, Jackson, Piniella, Murcer,
Guidry, Tiant, Gossage, John, Perry, Kaat........... $200-$250

1980 New York (NL) - Wilson.................................. $75-$100

1980 Oakland - Martin, Henderson .... $140-$210

1980 Philadelphia - Rose, Bowa, Schmidt, Luzinski, Boone,
Carlton, Lyle.. $275-$350

1980 Pittsburgh - Stargell, Madlock, Parker, Candelaria,
Tekulve, Blyleven .... $150-$175

1980 San Diego - Smith, Winfield, Fingers................ $80-$120

1980 San Francisco - Clark, McCovey, Blue.............. $75-$120

1980 Seattle - Bochte, W. Horton .... $60-$90

1980 St. Louis - Schoendienst, Hernandez, Simmons,
Kaat .... $80-$120

1980 Texas - Bell, Oliver, Staub, Jenkins, Perry, Lyle . $75-$100

1980 Toronto - Stieb... $60-$90

1981 Atlanta - Murphy, Butler, Perry, Niekro............. $100-$150

1981 Baltimore - Weaver, Murray, C. Ripken Jr.,
Palmer .... $100-$150

1981 Boston - Lansford, Rice, Yastrzemski,
Eckersley .... $175-$200

1981 California - Carew, Lynn .... $60-$90

1981 Chicago (AL) - Baines, Fisk, Luzinski, Hoyt....... $75-$100

1981 Chicago (NL) - Buckner .... $60-$90

1981 Cincinnati - Concepcion, Griffey, Foster, Bench,
Seaver .... $80-$120

1981 Cleveland - Harrah, Blyleven .... $60-$90

1981 Detroit - Anderson, Whitaker, Trammell, Gibson,
Morris .... $100-$125

1981 Houston - Ryan, Sutton .... $100-$125

1981 Kansas City - Brett, Quisenberry .... $75-$100

1981 Los Angeles - Garvey, Cey, Guerrero, Sax, Valenzuela,
Stewart .... $275-$350

1981 Milwaukee - Yount, Molitor, Fingers................. $100-$150

1981 Minnesota - Koosman, Ward .... $60-$90

1981 Montreal - Dawson, Raines, Carter .... $150-$175

1981 New York - Kingman, Staub .... $100-$125

1981 New York (AL) - Nettles, Jackson, Winfield, Murcer,
Piniella, Guidry, John, Gossage........................... $200-$250

1981 Oakland - Martin, Henderson .... $125-$200

1981 Philadelphia - Rose, Bowa, Schmidt, Boone, Sandberg,
Carlton, Lyle.. $100-$150

1981 Pittsburgh - Parker, Stargell, Madlock.............. $75-$125

1981 San Diego - Smith, Kennedy .... $60-$95

1981 San Francisco - Morgan, Clark, Blue................ $65-$95

1981 Seattle - Henderson..................................... $50-$85

1981 St. Louis - Hernandez, Kaat........................... $100-$135

1981 Texas - Bell, Oliver, Jenkins .... $65-$95

1981 Toronto - Bell, Barfield, Stieb......................... $60-$100

1982 Atlanta - Murphy, Butler, Niekro .... $90-$150

1982 Baltimore - Weaver, Murray, Ripken, Palmer... $100-$150

1982 Boston - Lansford, Rice, Yastrzemski, Boggs, Perez,
Eckersley .... $150-$250

1982 California - Carew, Jackson, Lynn, Boone, John,
Tiant.. $125-$200

1982 Chicago (AL) - Baines, Fisk, Luzinski, Hoyt, Lyle.. $75-$125

1982 Chicago (NL) - Buckner, Sandberg, Jenkins,
Hernandez.. $80-$120

1982 Cincinnati - Concepcion, Bench, Seaver .... $150-$200

1982 Cleveland - Harrah, Blyleven .... $60-$90

1982 Detroit - Anderson, Whitaker, Trammell, Gibson,
Johnson, Morris .... $100-$150

1982 Houston - Ryan, Sutton................................. $75-$125

1982 Kansas City - Brett, Quisenberry .... $75-$100

1982 Los Angeles - Garvey, Sax, Guerrero, Valenzuela,
Stewart... $100-$150

1982 Milwaukee - Yount, Molitor, Vuckovich, Fingers,
Sutton .... $250-$350

1982 Minnesota- Hrbek, Brunansky, Viola .... $60-$90

1982 Montreal - Oliver, Dawson, Raines, Carter,
Reardon.. $100-$125

1982 New York (AL) - Lemon, Nettles, Winfield, Piniella,
Murcer, Mattingly, John, Guidry, Gossage .... $125-$175

1982 New York (NL) - Kingman, Foster .... $80-$120

1982 Oakland - Martin, Henderson .... $150-$180

1982 Philadelphia - Rose, Schmidt, Carlton, Lyle.... $150-$175

1982 Pittsburgh - Madlock, Parker, Stargell, Candelaria,
Tekulve... $200

1982 San Diego - Kennedy, Gwynn.......................... $80-$120

1982 San Francisco - Robinson, Morgan, Clark,
Leonard .... $60-$90

1982 Seattle - Perry .... $60-$90

1982 St. Louis - Hernandez, Smith, McGee............. $275-$350

1982 Texas - Bell .... $60-$90

1982 Toronto - Barfield, Stieb................................ $60-$90

1983 Atlanta - Murphy, Butler, Niekro...................... $60-$90

1983 Baltimore - Murray, Ripken, Palmer................ $450-$500

1983 Boston - Boggs, Rice, Yastrzemski, Eckersley.... $150-$200

1983 California - Carew, Lynn, Boone, Jackson, John .. $80-$120

1983 Chicago (AL) - Baines, Kittle, Fisk, Hoyt.......... $150-$180

1983 Chicago (NL) - Buckner, Sandberg, Jenkins,
Hernandez.. $100-$150

1983 Cincinnati - Concepcion, Bench...................... $75-$100

1983 Cleveland - Franco, Harrah, Blyleven .... $60-$90

1983 Detroit - Anderson, Whitaker, Trammell, Johnson,
Morris.. $125-$150

1983 Houston - Ryan .... $125-$150

1983 Kansas City - Brett, Quisenberry, Perry .... $80-$120

1983 Los Angeles - Sax, Guerrero, Valenzuela, Welch,
Stewart, Hershiser... $125-$175

1983 Milwaukee - Yount, Molitor, Simmons, Fingers,
Kuenn.. $100-$200

1983 Minnesota - Hrbek, Brunansky, Viola .... $60-$90

1983 Montreal - Oliver, Dawson, Raines, Carter .... $75-$100

1983 New York (AL) - Martin, Nettles, Winfield, Piniella, Murcer,
Guidry, Gossage .... $200-$300

1983 New York (NL) - Strawberry, Foster, Staub, Kingman,
Seaver .... $100-$150

1983 Oakland - Lansford, Henderson .... $75-$85

1983 Philadelphia - Rose, Morgan, Schmidt, Perez, Denny,
Hernandez... $175-$250

1983 Pittsburgh - Madlock, Parker, Candelaria, Tekulve .. $100

1983 San Diego - Garvey, Gwynn .... $100-$150
1983 San Francisco - Robinson.......................... $60-$90
1983 Seattle - Perry .... $60-$90
1983 St. Louis - Smith, McGee, Hernandez........... $100-$125
1983 Texas - Bell, Stewart .... $60-$90
1983 Toronto - Bell, Fernandez, Stieb .... $60-$90
1984 Atlanta - Murphy .... $60-$90
1984 Baltimore - Murray, Ripken, Palmer.............. $175-$225
1984 Boston - Buckner, Boggs, Rice, Clemens .... $85-$110
1984 California - Carew, Lynn, Boone, Jackson, John...$80-$120
1984 Chicago (AL) - Baines, Fisk, Seaver.............. $75-$90
1984 Chicago (NL) - Sandberg, Sutcliffe, Eckersley.....$175-$275
1984 Cincinnati - Rose, Concepcion, Parker, Perez, Davis .... $125-$150
1984 Cleveland - Franco, Blyleven $125
1984 Detroit - Anderson, Whitaker, Trammell, Johnson, Gibson, Morris, Hernandez.......................... $350-$500
1984 Houston - Davis, Ryan.............................. $65-$100
1984 Kansas City - Brett, Saberhagen.................. $100-$150
1984 Los Angeles - Sax, Guerrero, Valenzuela, Hershiser .... $125-$150
1984 Milwaukee - Yount, Sutton .... $100-$125
1984 Minnesota - Hrbek, Puckett, Viola .... $85-$150
1984 Montreal - Dawson, Raines, Carter, Rose....... $100-$150
1984 New York (AL) - Berra, Mattingly, Winfield, Piniella, Niekro, Guidry.......................... $125-$175
1984 New York (NL) - Hernandez, Strawberry, Foster, Gooden.. $125-$150
1984 Oakland - Morgan, Lansford, Henderson .... $85-$100
1984 Philadelphia - Schmidt, Carlton .... $100-$150
1984 Pittsburgh - Madlock, Candelaria, Tekulve......... $65-$90
1984 San Diego - Garvey, Nettles, Gwynn, Gossage...$175-$250
1984 San Francisco - Oliver, Leonard, Clark............. $75-$90
1984 Seattle - Davis, Tartabull, Langston .... $60-$90
1984 St. Louis - O. Smith, McGee........................ $125-$150
1984 Texas - Stewart .... $60-$90
1984 Toronto - Bell, Fernandez, Stieb.................. $100-$125
1985 Atlanta - Murphy .... $60-$90
1985 Baltimore - Weaver, Murray, Ripken, Lynn .... $50-$85
1985 Boston - Boggs, Rice, Clemens .... $60-$90
1985 California - Carew, Jackson, Boone, Sutton, John.. $80-$120
1985 Chicago (AL) - Guillen, Baines, Fisk, Seaver .... $75-$100
1985 Chicago (NL) - Sandberg, Eckersley .... $60-$90
1985 Cincinnati - Rose, Concepcion, Parker, Perez, Davis.. $75-$125
1985 Cleveland - Franco, Carter, Blyleven .... $50-$85
1985 Detroit - Anderson, Whitaker, Trammell, Gibson, Morris.. $75-$125
1985 Houston - Davis, Ryan.............................. $75-$100
1985 Kansas City - Brett, Saberhagen .... $300-$400
1985 Los Angeles - Sax, Oliver, Hershiser, Valenzuela.. $60-$150
1985 Milwaukee - Yount, Fingers .... $60-$90
1985 Minnesota - Hrbek, Puckett, Viola, Blyleven...... $75-$100
1985 Montreal - Dawson, Raines .... $45-$75
1985 New York (AL) - Berra, Martin, Mattingly, Winfield, Henderson, Guidry, Niekro .... $125-$175
1985 New York (NL) - Hernandez, Johnson, Strawberry, Foster, Carter, Gooden.......................... $200-$300
1985 Oakland - Lansford, Kingman, Sutton................. $60-$90
1985 Philadelphia - Schmidt, Carlton .... $75-$100
1985 Pittsburgh - Madlock .... $60-$90
1985 San Diego - Garvey, Nettles, Gwynn, Gossage.....$75-$100
1985 San Francisco - Leonard............................ $60-$90
1985 Seattle - Tartabull, Langston .... $60-$90
1985 St. Louis - Clark, McGee, Coleman................ $175-$250

1985 Texas - Harrah .... $70-$95
1985 Toronto - Fernandez, Bell, Fielder, Stieb......... $100-$150
1986 Atlanta - Murphy .... $50-$80
1986 Baltimore - Weaver, Murray, Ripken, Lynn .... $75-$100
1986 Boston - Boggs, Rice, Clemens, Seaver .... $200-$400
1986 California - Joyner, Boone, Jackson, Sutton .... $60-$90
1986 Chicago (AL) - Baines, Fisk, Carlton, Seaver.... $75-$100
1986 Chicago (NL) - Sandberg, Palmeiro, Eckersley... $175-$200
1986 Cincinnati - Parker, Davis, Concepcion, Perez, Rose.. $60-$90
1986 Cleveland - Franco, Carter, Niekro .... $60-$75
1986 Detroit - Anderson, Whitaker, Trammell, Gibson, Morris.. $100-$125
1986 Houston - Davis, Scott, Ryan .... $75-$100
1986 Kansas City - Howser, Brett, Jackson, Saberhagen.. $60-$90
1986 Los Angeles - Guerrero, Valenzuela, Hershiser... $75-$100
1986 Milwaukee - Yount, Molitor......................... $50-$75
1986 Minnesota - Hrbek, Puckett, Blyleven, Viola...... $80-$120
1986 Montreal - Dawson, Raines .... $50-$75
1986 New York (AL) - Mattingly, Winfield, Henderson, Guidry, John.. $125-$200
1986 New York (NL) - Hernandez, Strawberry, Carter, Mitchell, Foster, Gooden.. $350-$525
1986 Oakland - Canseco, McGwire, Stewart........... $100-$125
1986 Philadelphia - Schmidt, Carlton .... $75-$100
1986 Pittsburgh - Bonds, Bonilla .... $50-$75
1986 San Diego - Garvey, Gwynn, Gossage .... $60-$75
1986 San Francisco - Clark, Carlton..................... $50-$75
1986 Seattle - Tartabull, Langston .... $60-$75
1986 St. Louis - Smith, McGee .... $75-$100
1986 Texas - Sierra....................................... $60-$75
1986 Toronto - Fernandez, Bell, Stieb.................. $60-$75
1987 Atlanta - Murphy, Niekro .... $50-$75
1987 Baltimore - Murray, Ripken, Lynn .... $60-$85
1987 Boston - Boggs, Rice, Clemens .... $75-$100
1987 California - Joyner, Boone, Buckner, Sutton........ $65-$80
1987 Chicago (AL) - Fisk, Baines .... $75-$115
1987 Chicago (NL) - Sandberg, Dawson, Palmeiro...... $50-$75
1987 Cincinnati - Rose, Parker, Davis, Concepcion .. $75-$100
1987 Cleveland - Carter, Franco, Niekro, Carlton....... $75-$100
1987 Detroit - Anderson, Whitaker, Trammell, Gibson, Morris.. $175-$200
1987 Houston - Davis, Ryan .... $100-$165
1987 Kansas City - Brett, Tartabull, Jackson, Saberhagen.. $85-$100
1987 Los Angeles - Lasorda, Sax, Guerrero, Hershiser, Valenzuela.. $80-$120
1987 Milwaukee - Molitor, Yount......................... $45-$90
1987 Minnesota - Hrbek, Puckett, Viola, Blyleven, Carlton.. $300-$400
1987 Montreal - Raines .... $75-$100
1987 New York (AL) - Mattingly, Henderson, Winfield, John, Guidry.. $100-$150
1987 New York (NL) - Hernandez, Johnson, Strawberry, Carter, Gooden.. $150-$175
1987 Oakland - McGwire, Canseco, Jackson, Stewart, Eckersley.. $100-$150
1987 Philadelphia - Schmidt .... $50-$75
1987 Pittsburgh - Bonilla, Van Slyke, Bonds............. $75-$100
1987 San Diego - Gwynn, Garvey, Gossage .... $50-$75
1987 San Francisco - Clark, Mitchell, Williams........ $100-$150
1987 Seattle - Langston, Reynolds...................... $75-$100
1987 St. Louis - Smith, McGee .... $175-$225
1987 Texas - Sierra...................................... $60-$90
1987 Toronto - Fernandez, Bell, McGriff, Stieb, Niekro.. $75-$100
1988 Atlanta - Murphy .... $50-$80

1988 Baltimore - Robinson, Murray, Ripken, Lynn ..... $75-$100
1988 Boston - Boggs, Rice, Clemens .... $175-$200
1988 California - Joyner, Boone, Buckner .... $60-$75
1988 Chicago (AL) - Fisk, Baines .... $65-$75
1988 Chicago (NL) - Grace, Sandberg, Dawson, Palmeiro,
  Gossage .... $50-$80
1988 Cincinnati - Sabo .... $75-$100
1988 Cleveland - Franco, Carter .... $50-$75
1988 Detroit - Whitaker, Trammell, Lynn, Morris .... $85-$100
1988 Houston - Davis, Ryan .... $75-$125
1988 Kansas City - Brett, Tartabull, Jackson, Buckner,
  Saberhagen .... $100-$125
1988 Los Angeles - Sax, Gibson, Hershiser,
  Valenzuela .... $200-$300
1988 Milwaukee - Yount, Molitor .... $50-$75
1988 Minnesota - Hrbek, Puckett, Viola, Blyleven,
  Carlton .... $60-$85
1988 Montreal - Raines .... $50-$75
1988 New York (AL) - Martin, Mattingly, Winfield, Henderson,
  John, Guidry .... $150-$200
1988 New York (NL) - Hernandez, Johnson, Strawberry, Carter,
  Gooden .... $75-$150
1988 Oakland - McGwire, Lansford, Canseco, Parker, Stewart,
  Welch, Eckersley .... $200-$250
1988 Philadelphia - Schmidt .... $75-$100
1988 Pittsburgh - Bonilla, Van Slyke, Bonds, Drabek .. $50-$75
1988 San Diego - Gwynn $175
1988 San Francisco - Clark, Mitchell, Williams .... $60-$85
1988 Seattle - Langston .... $50-$75
1988 St. Louis - Smith, McGee, Guerrero .... $45-$70
1988 Texas - Sierra .... $50-$75
1988 Toronto - McGriff, Fernandez, Bell, Stieb .... $60-$85
1989 Atlanta - Murphy .... $100-$150
1989 Baltimore - Robinson, Ripken .... $75-$125
1989 Boston - Boggs, Clemens .... $75-$100
1989 California - Joyner, Blyleven .... $50-$75
1989 Chicago (AL) - Fisk, Baines .... $50-$75
1989 Chicago (NL) - Grace, Sandberg, Dawson ...... $150-$225
1989 Cincinnati - Davis, Perez, Larkin $175
1989 Cleveland - Carter .... $100-$125
1989 Detroit - Anderson, Trammell, Lynn, Morris .... $50-$75
1989 Houston - Davis .... $40-$60
1989 Kansas City - Brett, Jackson, Boone, Tartabull,
  Saberhagen .... $100-$150
1989 Los Angeles - Lasorda, Murray, Randolph, Gibson,
  Hershiser, Valenzuela $250
1989 Milwaukee - Yount, Molitor $150
1989 Minnesota - Hrbek, Puckett, Viola .... $50-$85
1989 Montreal - Raines .... $75-$100
1989 New York (AL) - Mattingly, Sax, Winfield,
  Gossage .... $100-$125
1989 New York (NL) - Johnson, Strawberry, Hernandez, Carter,
  Gooden .... $75-$145
1989 Oakland - LaRussa, McGwire, Canseco, D. Henderson,
  R. Henderson, Parker, Stewart, Eckersley $700
1989 Philadelphia - Dykstra, Schmidt $150
1989 Pittsburgh - Bonilla, Van Slyke, Bonds .... $75-$100
1989 San Diego - Clark, Gwynn .... $50-$85
1989 San Francisco - Clark, Williams, Mitchell,
  Gossage .... $350-$400
1989 Seattle - Griffey Jr. .... $175-$250
1989 St. Louis - Guerrero, Smith, McGee .... $85-$125
1989 Texas - Palmeiro, Franco, Sierra, Baines, Ryan $175
1989 Toronto - McGriff, Fernandez, Stieb .... $100-$150
1990 Atlanta - Justice, Murphy .... $100-$175
1990 Baltimore - F. Robinson, C. Ripken Jr. .... $75-$100
1990 Boston - Boggs, Clemens .... $100-$150

1990 California - Joyner, Winfield, Blyleven .... $75-$100
1990 Chicago (AL) - Fisk .... $50-$85
1990 Chicago (NL) - Dawson, Grace, Sandberg $275
1990 Cincinnati - Larkin, Davis, Piniella .... $225-$300
1990 Cleveland - Hernandez .... $40-$60
1990 Detroit - Anderson, Fielder, Morris, Trammell,
  Whitaker .... $75-$100
1990 Houston - Davis, Biggio, Scott $120
1990 Kansas City - Brett, Tartabull, Jackson,
  Saberhagen .... $75-$125
1990 Los Angeles - Lasorda, Murray, Gibson,
  Valenzuela .... $85-$125
1990 Milwaukee - Yount, Molitor, Parker .... $50-$75
1990 Minnesota - Hrbek, Puckett .... $50-$85
1990 Montreal - Raines .... $50-$85
1990 New York (AL) - Mattingly .... $125-$175
1990 New York (NL) - Strawberry, Johnson, Viola,
  Gooden .... $150-$200
1990 Oakland - McGwire, Randolph, Canseco, R. Henderson,
  D. Henderson, Baines, McGee, Welch, Stewart,
  Eckersley .... $150-$200
1990 Philadelphia - Dykstra, Murphy .... $40-$60
1990 Pittsburgh - Bonds, Bonilla, Van Slyke, Drabek $200
1990 San Diego - Gwynn, Carter, Clark .... $50-$75
1990 San Francisco - Clark, Mitchell, Williams .... $75-$100
1990 Seattle - Ken Griffey Jr., Ken Griffey Sr. .... $75-$100
1990 St. Louis - Guerrero, Smith, McGee .... $50-$85
1990 Texas - Palmeiro, Franco, Sierra, Ryan .... $85-$100
1990 Toronto - McGriff, Stieb, Fernandez $150
1991 Atlanta - Glavine, Pendleton .... $150-$200
1991 Baltimore - F. Robinson, Ripken .... $65-$100
1991 Boston - Boggs, Clemens .... $80-$100
1991 California - Joyner, Winfield .... $45-$65
1991 Chicago (AL) - Fisk, Thomas .... $85-$150
1991 Chicago (NL) - Sandberg, Dawson $275
1991 Cincinnati - Larkin, Davis, Piniella .... $65-$85
1991 Cleveland - Swindell .... $45-$75
1991 Detroit - Anderson, Whitaker, Trammell, Fielder $75-$100
1991 Houston - Bagwell, Harnisch .... $50-$75
1991 Kansas City - Brett, Saberhagen, Tartabull .... $85-$100
1991 Los Angeles - Lasorda, Murray, Strawberry .... $65-$90
1991 Milwaukee - Yount, Molitor .... $85-$100
1991 Minnesota - Knoblauch, Morris, Puckett, Hrbek .. $150-$225
1991 Montreal - Calderon .... $30-$50
1991 New York (AL) - Mattingly .... $75-$125
1991 New York (NL) - Johnson, Gooden, Viola .... $60-$90
1991 Oakland - R. Henderson, Stewart, Eckersley,
  Canseco $450
1991 Philadelphia - Dykstra, Murphy .... $50-$85
1991 Pittsburgh - Bonds, Bonilla .... $100-$150
1991 San Diego - Gwynn, McGriff, Fernandez .... $50-$80
1991 San Francisco - Mitchell, Clark .... $40-$60
1991 Seattle - Griffey Jr., Griffey Sr. $175
1991 St. Louis - O. Smith, L. Smith .... $45-$60
1991 Texas - Franco, Ryan, Sierra, Palmeiro .... $60-$85
1991 Toronto - Carter, Alomar, Stieb .... $80-$125
1992 Atlanta - Pendleton, Justice, Glavine $325
1992 Baltimore - Devereaux, Ripken, Mussina $115
1992 Boston - Boggs, Clemens $100
1992 California - Langston $75
1992 Chicago (AL) - Thomas, McDowell $85
1992 Chicago (NL) - Maddux, Grace, Dawson, Sandberg $125
1992 Cincinnati - Larkin, Rijo $85
1992 Cleveland - Baerga, Belle, Nagy $100
1992 Detroit - Fryman, Whitaker, Trammell, Fielder $85
1992 Houston - Biggio, Bagwell $40
1992 Kansas City - Brett, Jefferies, Joyner $85

1992 Los Angeles - Karros, Butler $80
1992 Milwaukee - Listach, Yount, Eldred, Molitor $120
1992 Minnesota - Puckett, Knoblauch $85
1992 Montreal - Grissom, Walker, Martinez $50
1992 New York (AL) - Mattingly $90
1992 New York (NL) - Murray, Bonilla, Cone $85
1992 Oakland - Eckersley, McGwire, Henderson, Canseco.. $150
1992 Philadelphia - Hollins, Dykstra, Kruk, Schilling,
Daulton $100
1992 Pittsburgh - Bonds, Van Slyke, Drabek $125
1992 San Diego - Gwynn, Sheffield, McGriff $85
1992 San Francisco - Clark, Williams $110
1992 Seattle - Griffey Jr., Martinez $115
1992 St. Louis - O. Smith, L. Smith, Lankford $60
1992 Texas - Sierra, Gonzalez $125
1992 Toronto - Alomar, Carter, Winfield, Morris $200
1993 Atlanta - Maddux, McGriff $250
1993 Baltimore - Ripken, Mussina .... $200-$250
1993 Boston - Dawson, Clemens, Vaughn .... $150-$200
1993 California - Salmon, Langston $75
1993 Chicago (AL) - Thomas, McDowell $175
1993 Chicago (NL) - Sandberg, Grace $85
1993 Cincinnati - Larkin, Rijo $45
1993 Cleveland - Baerga, Belle, Nagy $125
1993 Colorado - Galarraga, Hayes $150
1993 Detroit - Whitaker, Trammell, Fielder $200
1993 Florida - Harvey, Weiss, Destrade $350
1993 Houston - Swindell, Drabek, Bagwell $40
1993 Kansas City - Brett, Cone $110
1993 Los Angeles - Piazza, Karros $150
1993 Milwaukee - Listach, Hamilton, Vaughn, Yount $50
1993 Minnesota - Puckett, Winfield $100
1993 Montreal - D. Martinez, Grissom, Walker $50
1993 New York (AL) - Boggs, Mattingly $115
1993 New York (NL) - Bonilla, Murray, Gooden $75
1993 Oakland - Sierra, McGwire, Eckersley $75
1993 Philadelphia - Schilling, Dykstra, Kruk, Daulton $300
1993 Pittsburgh - Van Slyke, Bell $95
1993 San Diego - Gwynn, Sheffield $80
1993 San Francisco - Bonds, Clark $200
1993 Seattle - Griffey Jr., R. Johnson $85
1993 St. Louis - O. Smith, Lankford $50
1993 Texas - Ryan, Gonzalez, Canseco $125
1993 Toronto - Alomar, Molitor, Carter, Olerud, Stewart .. $200
1994 Atlanta - Maddux, McGriff $275
1994 Baltimore - Ripken, Mussina $125
1994 Boston - Greenwell, Clemens, Vaughn $125
1994 California - Salmon, Langston, Edmonds, Jackson.. $200
1994 Chicago (AL) - Thomas, McDowell, Ventura $125
1994 Chicago (NL) - Sandberg, Grace $95
1994 Cincinnati - Larkin $65
1994 Cleveland - Baerga, Belle, Lofton, Martinez, Nagy... $175
1994 Colorado - Galarraga, Hayes $150
1994 Detroit - Whitaker, Trammell, Fielder, Anderson $95
1994 Florida - Sheffield, Harvey $75
1994 Houston - Drabek, Bagwell $50
1994 Kansas City - Appier, Cone $95
1994 Los Angeles - Piazza, Karros $150
1994 Milwaukee - Eldred, Vaughn $85
1994 Minnesota - Puckett, Winfield, Knoblauch $200
1994 Montreal - D. Martinez, Grissom, Walker $60
1994 New York (AL) - Boggs, Mattingly, Key, Abbott $125
1994 New York (NL) - Bonilla $75
1994 Oakland - Sierra, McGwire, Eckersley $110
1994 Philadelphia - Dykstra, Kruk, Daulton $250
1994 Pittsburgh - Van Slyke, Bell $85
1994 San Diego - Gwynn $80

1994 San Francisco - Bonds, Clark $150
1994 Seattle - Griffey Jr., R. Johnson, Piniella $85
1994 St. Louis - O. Smith, Lankford $65
1994 Texas - Ryan, Gonzalez, Canseco $125
1994 Toronto - Alomar, Molitor, Carter, Olerud, Stewart ... $200
1995 Atlanta - Smoltz, Glavine $250
1995 Baltimore - Ripken, Mussina $125
1995 Boston - Canseco $110
1995 California - D. Easley, C. Davis $125
1995 Chicago (AL) - Thomas, Ventura, Guillen $110
1995 Chicago (NL) - Sosa, Sandberg $145
1995 Cincinnati - Larkin $150
1995 Cleveland - Thome, A. Belle $250
1995 Colorado - Bichette, Castilla, Galarraga, Walker,
Burks $135
1995 Detroit - Fielder, Fryman, Trammell $100
1995 Florida - Sheffield, W. Fraser $175
1995 Houston - Bagwell, D. Bell $125
1995 Kansas City - Hamelin, Gaetti, Cone, Gagne $90
1995 Los Angeles - Piazza, Nomo $125
1995 Milwaukee - Garner, Seitzer, Cirillo $75
1995 Minnesota - Knoblauch, Puckett $90
1995 Montreal - P. Martinez, M. Alou, Grissom $110
1995 New York (AL) - O'Neill, Boggs $125
1995 New York (NL) - Saberhagen $95
1995 Oakland - McGwire $75
1995 Philadelphia - Dykstra, Daulton, Morandini, Schilling.....$95
1995 Pittsburgh - King $100
1995 San Diego - Gwynn, Caminiti, Finley $90
1995 San Francisco - Bonds $140
1995 Seattle - Griffey, Buhner $150
1995 St. Louis - O. Smith, Gilkey $125
1995 Texas - Gonzalez, Rodriguez $125
1995 Toronto - R. Alomar, Molitor, J. Carter $100
1996 Atlanta - Maddux, Glavine, Justice, Grissom $175
1996 Baltimore - Ripken, R. Alomar, Mussina $100
1996 Boston - Vaughn, Clemens $110
1996 California - Salmon $90
1996 Chicago (AL) - Thomas, Ventura, Guillen $100
1996 Chicago (NL) - Sosa, Grace $110
1996 Cincinnati - Larkin, Boone $90
1996 Cleveland - Thome, Lofton, Nagy $175
1996 Colorado - Bichette, Castilla, Walker, Galarraga,
Burks $145
1996 Detroit - Clark $80
1996 Florida - Sheffield, K. Brown, C. Johnson,
A. Leiter .... $180-$200
1996 Houston - Bagwell, Biggio $100
1996 Kansas City -.. $80
1996 Los Angeles - Piazza, Mondesi, Nomo, Karros $110
1996 Milwaukee - G. Vaughn $90
1996 Minnesota - Molitor, Knoblauch $90
1996 Montreal - P. Martinez, M. Alou, Grudzielanek $75
1996 New York (AL) - Jeter, T. Martinez, Torre, Williams,
O'Neill $325
1996 New York (NL) - Hundley, Gilkey, J. Kent $175
1996 Oakland - McGwire $120
1996 Philadelphia - Dykstra, Schilling $90
1996 Pittsburgh - Kendall $80
1996 San Diego - Gwynn, R. Henderson $100
1996 San Francisco - Bonds, Baker $250
1996 Seattle - Griffey, Buhner, Rodriguez $120
1996 St. Louis - O. Smith, Gaetti, LaRussa $175
1996 Texas - Gonzalez, Clark $90
1996 Toronto - J. Guzman, Olerud, Hentgen $80
1997 Anaheim - Edmonds, Salmon $100
1997 Atlanta - C. Jones, Maddux, Glavine, Lofton, Smoltz..$150

1997 Baltimore - C. Ripken, Mussina $110
1997 Boston - Vaughn, Garciaparra $100
1997 Chicago (AL) - Thomas, Belle $110
1997 Chicago (NL) - Sosa, Grace $120
1997 Cincinnati - Larkin, Tomko, Stynes $100
1997 Cleveland - Thome, Justice, M. Williams $175
1997 Colorado - Bichette, Castilla, Galarraga, Walker $140
1997 Detroit - Easley, Clark, Higginson $75
1997 Florida - M. Alou, K. Brown, Sheffield, Bonilla, Leyland $155
1997 Houston - Bagwell, Biggio, Kile $145
1997 Kansas City - Damon, Bell $125
1997 Los Angeles - Piazza, Mondesi, Nomo $110
1997 Milwaukee - Garner, Cirillo $90
1997 Minnesota - Molitor, Knoblauch $90
1997 Montreal - Guerrero, P. Martinez, F. Alou $150
1997 New York (AL) - Jeter, Williams, Torre, O'Neill $600
1997 New York (NL) - Hundley, Franco $150
1997 Oakland - Canseco $100
1997 Philadelphia - Rolen, Jefferies $135
1997 Pittsburgh - Kendall $125
1997 San Diego - Gwynn, Caminiti .... $150-$200
1997 San Francisco - Bonds, Baker $250
1997 Seattle - A. Rodriguez, Griffey $125
1997 St. Louis - McGwire, Gant $150
1997 Texas - Gonzalez, Rodriguez $100
1997 Toronto - Clemens, Delgado $100
1998 Anaheim - Edmonds, Salmon $110
1998 Arizona - Lee, Bell, M. Williams, Showalter $245
1998 Atlanta - Glavine, Maddux, C. Jones, Galarraga $295
1998 Baltimore - Ripken, Mussina $120
1998 Boston - Vaughn, Garciaparra, P. Martinez $110
1998 Chicago (AL) - Thomas, Belle $100
1998 Chicago (NL) - Sosa, Wood $375
1998 Cincinnati - Larkin, Tomko, Greene .... $125-$150
1998 Cleveland - Thome, Justice, Lofton $210
1998 Colorado - Bichette, Castilla, Walker $190
1998 Detroit - Clark, Higginson, Easley, Cruz $130
1998 Florida - Renteria, Hernandez, Leyland $80
1998 Houston - Bagwell, Biggio, R. Johnson, M. Alou $180
1998 Kansas City - Palmer $90
1998 Los Angeles - Sheffield, Mondesi $110
1998 Milwaukee - Cirillo, Vina, Jenkins $90
1998 Minnesota - Molitor $100
1998 Montreal - Guerrero, F. Alou $90
1998 New York (AL) - Jeter, Wells, Williams, Brosius, Torre $900
1998 New York (NL) - Piazza, Nomo, Franco $225
1998 Oakland - Grieve, Henderson $120
1998 Philadelphia - Rolen, Schilling $110
1998 Pittsburgh - Kendall, Guillen $125
1998 San Diego - K. Brown, Gwynn, Caminiti, Hoffman, Vaughn $225
1998 San Francisco - Bonds, Baker $250
1998 Seattle - Griffey, A. Rodriguez $160
1998 St. Louis - McGwire, Drew, LaRussa $250
1998 Tampa Bay - McGriff, Boggs $275
1998 Texas - Gonzalez, Rodriguez $100
1998 Toronto - Clemens, Canseco $140
1999 Anaheim - Edmonds, Salmon, Vaughn $110
1999 Arizona - M. Williams, Showalter, R. Johnson $245
1999 Atlanta - Glavine, Maddux, C. Jones, Smoltz $295
1999 Baltimore - C. Ripken, Mussina, Belle $120
1999 Boston - Garciaparra, P. Martinez $110
1999 Chicago (AL) - Thomas, Durham $100
1999 Chicago (NL) - Sosa, Grace $200
1999 Cincinnati - Larkin, Tomko, Greene, Vaughn $200

1999 Cleveland - Thome, Justice, Lofton $190
1999 Colorado - Bichette, Castilla, Walker $180
1999 Detroit - Clark, Higginson, Easley, Cruz $135
1999 Florida - Hernandez, Floyd $80
1999 Houston - Bagwell, Biggio, M. Alou $180
1999 Kansas City - Beltran, Dye $90
1999 Los Angeles - K. Brown, Sheffield, Mondesi $110
1999 Milwaukee - Cirillo, Vina, Nomo, Jenkins $90
1999 Minnesota - Radke, Walker $100
1999 Montreal - Guerrero, F. Alou $90
1999 New York (AL) - Jeter, Clemens, Williams, Brosius, Torre $900
1999 New York (NL) - Piazza, Franco $140
1999 Oakland - Grieve, Giambi $110
1999 Philadelphia - Rolen, Schilling $110
1999 Pittsburgh - Kendall, Guillen $125
1999 San Diego - Gwynn, Caminiti, Hoffman $225
1999 San Francisco - Bonds, Baker, Kent $250
1999 Seattle - Griffey, A. Rodriguez, Buhner $130
1999 St. Louis - McGwire, Drew, Tatis, Renteria $240
1999 Tampa Bay - McGriff, Boggs, Canseco $275
1999 Texas - Gonzalez, Rodriguez $110
1999 Toronto - Wells, Delgado $90
2000 Anaheim - Salmon, Vaughn $110
2000 Arizona - M. Williams, R. Johnson $245
2000 Atlanta - Glavine, Maddux, C. Jones, Smoltz $295
2000 Baltimore - Ripken, Mussina, Belle $120
2000 Boston - Garciaparra, P. Martinez $110
2000 Chicago (AL) - Thomas, Durham $100
2000 Chicago (NL) - Sosa, Grace $200
2000 Cincinnati - Griffey, Casey $125
2000 Cleveland - Thome, Lofton $190
2000 Colorado - Cirillo, Walker $180
2000 Detroit - Clark, Higginson, Easley, Cruz $135
2000 Florida - Floyd, Lee $80
2000 Houston - Bagwell, Biggio, M. Alou $180
2000 Kansas City - Beltran, Dye $90
2000 Los Angeles - K. Brown, Sheffield $110
2000 Milwaukee - Burnitz, Jenkins $90
2000 Minnesota - Lawton, Radke $100
2000 Montreal - Guerrero, F. Alou $90
2000 New York (AL) - Jeter, Clemens, Williams, Brosius, Torre $320
2000 New York (NL) - Piazza, Franco $140
2000 Oakland - Grieve, Giambi $110
2000 Philadelphia - Rolen, Lieberthal $110
2000 Pittsburgh - Kendall, Giles $125
2000 San Diego - Gwynn, Hoffman $225
2000 San Francisco - Bonds, Baker, Kent $275
2000 Seattle - A. Rodriguez, Buhner $130
2000 St. Louis - McGwire, Drew, Tatis, Renteria $240
2000 Tampa Bay - McGriff, Williams $275
2000 Texas - Martinez, Rodriguez $110
2000 Toronto - Wells, Delgado $90
2001 Anaheim - Anderson, Salmon $110
2001 Arizona - M. Williams, R. Johnson $245
2001 Atlanta - Glavine, Maddux, C. Jones, Smoltz $295
2001 Baltimore - Ripken, Hairston $120
2001 Boston - Garciaparra, P. Martinez $110
2001 Chicago (AL) - Thomas, Durham $100
2001 Chicago (NL) - Sosa, Wood $200
2001 Cincinnati - Griffey, Casey $125
2001 Cleveland - Thome, Lofton $200
2001 Colorado - Helton, Walker $180
2001 Detroit - Clark, Higginson, Easley, Cruz $135
2001 Florida - Floyd, Johnson $80
2001 Houston - Bagwell, Biggio, M. Alou $180

2001 Kansas City - Beltran, Dye $90
2001 Los Angeles - K. Brown, Sheffield $110
2001 Milwaukee - Burnitz, Jenkins, Sexson $90
2001 Minnesota - Radke, Lawton...................................... $100
2001 Montreal - Guerrero, F. Alou $90
2001 New York (AL) - Jeter, Clemens, Williams, Brosius, Torre.. $320
2001 New York (NL) - Piazza, Franco................................ $140
2001 Oakland - Giambi, Hudson $110
2001 Philadelphia - Rolen, Lee, Burrell, Abreu................. $250
2001 Pittsburgh - Kendall, Giles $125
2001 San Diego - Gwynn, Hoffman $225
2001 San Francisco - Bonds, Baker, Kent $450
2001 Seattle - Martinez, Cameron, Suzuki $130
2001 St. Louis - McGwire, Drew, Renteria $240
2001 Tampa Bay - McGriff, Grieve $275
2001 Texas - A. Rodriguez, I. Rodriguez $110
2001 Toronto - Fullmer, Delgado $90
2002 Anaheim - G. Anderson, Salmon, Erstad, Glaus...... $175
2002 Arizona - R. Johnson, Schilling, L. Gonzalez $150
2002 Atlanta - C. Jones, A. Jones, Maddux, Glavine, Smoltz.. $120
2002 Baltimore - Julio, R. Lopez, T. Batista $100
2002 Boston - Garciaparra, P. Martinez $125
2002 Chicago (AL) - F. Thomas, Ordonez, Konerko.......... $100

2002 Chicago (NL) - Sosa, Wood, Alou $120
2002 Cincinnati - Griffey, Casey, Larkin, Dunn................. $100
2002 Cleveland - Sabathia, Thome, Vizquel $100
2002 Colorado - Walker, Helton $100
2002 Detroit - Higginson, D. Young $100
2002 Florida - Lowell, Burnett, Castillo.............................. $90
2002 Houston - Bagwell, Biggio, Oswalt $125
2002 Kansas City - Beltran, Sweeney, Ibanez $100
2002 Los Angeles - K. Brown, Green $100
2002 Milwaukee - Sexson, Jenkins, Sheets $90
2002 Minnesota - T. Hunter, Radke.................................. $100
2002 Montreal - V. Guerrero, Vidro, Vazquez $75
2002 New York (AL) - Jeter, Clemens, Mussina, Giambi, Williams $150
2002 New York (NL) - Piazza, Alomar $120
2002 Oakland - Hudson, Zito, Mulder............................... $110
2002 Philadelphia - Abreu, Burrell $100
2002 Pittsburgh - Kendall, Giles $100
2002 San Diego - Hoffman, Klesko $100
2002 San Francisco - Bonds, Kent, Baker $200
2002 Seattle - Martinez, Garcia, Ichiro $150
2002 St. Louis - Drew, Renteria, Morris $140
2002 Tampa Bay - Grieve, Winn.. $75
2002 Texas - A. Rodriguez, I. Rodriguez $150
2002 Toronto - Delgado, Halladay, Hinske $100

WORLD SERIES BASEBALLS

Prices are listed for both the winning and losing teams for each year the World Series has been played since 1920. (The scarcity of multi-signed items from before 1920 makes pricing highly speculative.) The price assumes that the ball contains the signatures of the majority of the players on the team, including all of the key players listed.

Year	W/L	Team	Key Signatures	NM Price
1920	Winner	Cleveland Indians	Bagby, Caldwell, Chapman, Coveleski, Gardner, Jamieson, O'Neill, J. Sewell, Smith, Speaker, Wambsganss	$2,000
	Loser	Brooklyn Dodgers	Grimes, Konetchy, Marquard, Myers, Pfeffer, W. Robinson, Wheat	$1,500
1921	Winner	New York Giants	Bancroft, Barnes, Burns, Frisch, Kelly, McGraw, Meusel, Nehf, Smith, Snyder, Toney, Youngs	$2,500
	Loser	New York Yankees	Baker, Hoyt, Huggins, Mays, Meusel, Pipp, Ruth, Shawkey, Ward	$3,500
1922	Winner	New York Giants	Bancroft, Barnes, Frisch, Kelly, McGraw, Meusel, Nehf, Stengel, Snyder, Youngs	$2,500
	Loser	New York Yankees	Baker, Bush, Hoyt, Huggins, Meusel, Pipp, Ruth, Schang, Shawkey	$2,800
1923	Winner	New York Yankees	Bush, Gehrig, Hoyt, Huggins, Jones, Meusel, Pennock, Pipp, Ruth, Ward, Witt	$3,000
	Loser	New York Giants	Bancroft, Frisch, Jackson, Kelly, McGraw, Meusel, Ryan, Stengel, Youngs	$2,500
1924	Winner	Washington Senators	Goslin, Harris, Johnson, Judge, Rice, Zachery	$1,800
	Loser	New York Giants	Barnes, Frisch, Gowdy, Jackson, Kelly, McGraw, Meusel, Snyder, Terry Wilson, Youngs	$2,200
1925	Winner	Pittsburgh Pirates	Barnhart, Carey, Cuyler, Grantham, McKechnie, Meadows, Smith, Traynor, Wright	$1,000
	Loser	Washington Senators	Coveleski, Goslin, Harris, Johnson, Judge, Rice	$1,500
1926	Winner	St. Louis Cardinals	Alexander, Bell, Blades, Bottomley, Douthit, Hafey, Haines, Hornsby, Rhem, Southworth	$1,800
	Loser	New York Yankees	Combs, Hoyt, Huggins, Gehrig, Lazzeri, Meusel, Pennock, Ruth	$4,000
1927	Winner	New York Yankees	Combs, Hoyt, Huggins, Gehrig, Lazzeri, Meusel, Moore, Pennock, Ruth	$20,000-$60,000
	Loser	Pittsburgh Pirates	Barnhart, Cronin, Cuyler, Grantham, Groh, Harris, Hill, Kremer, Traynor, L. Waner, P. Waner	$900
1928	Winner	New York Yankees	Combs, Durocher, Gehrig, Hoyt, Huggins, Lazzeri, Meusel, Pipgras, Pennock, Ruth	$10,000
	Loser	St. Louis Cardinals	Alexander, Bottomley, Frisch, Hafey, Haines, Maranville, McKechnie	$1,250-$2,000
1929	Winner	Philadelphia Athletics	Cochrane, Collins, Cronin, Earnshaw, Foxx, Grove, Haas, Mack, Miller, Simmons	$1,000
	Loser	Chicago Cubs	Cuyler, Hartnett, Hornsby, Malone, McCarthy, Root, Wilson	$1,000
1930	Winner	Philadelphia Athletics	Cochrane, Collins, Dykes, Foxx, Grove, Mack, Miller, Simmons	$800-$1,000
	Loser	St. Louis Cardinals	Adams, Bottomley, Douthit, Frisch, Gelbert, Grimes, Hafey, Haines, Street, Watkins, Wilson	$800-$1,000
1931	Winner	St. Louis Cardinals	Cochrane, Earnshaw, Foxx, Grove, Hoyt, Mack, Simmons	$900-$1,000
	Loser	Philadelphia Athletics	Mack, Foxx, Simmons, Cochrane, Grove, Earnshaw, Hoyt	$1,000-$1,500
1932	Winner	New York Yankees	Allen, Combs, Dickey, Gehrig, Gomez, Lazzeri, McCarthy, Ruffing, Ruth, Sewell	$4,000
	Loser	Chicago Cubs	Bush, Cuyler, Grimes, Grimm, Hartnett, Herman, Hornsby, Moore, Stephenson, Warneke	$900
1933	Winner	New York Giants	Hubbell, Jackson, Ott, Schumacher, Terry, Vergez	$800-$1,000
	Loser	Washington Senators	Cronin, Crowder, Goslin, Kuhel, Manush, Myer, Whitehill	$650-$800

1926 St. Louis Cardinals

1931 Philadelphia Athletics

1936 New York Yankees

1952 New York Yankees

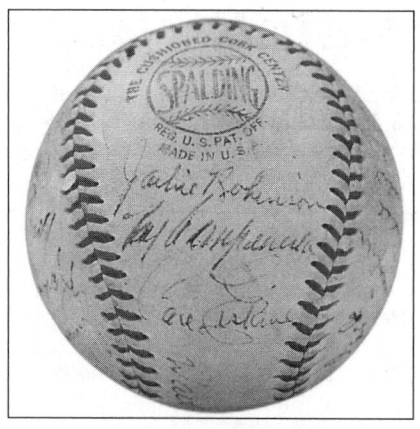

1955 Brooklyn Dodgers

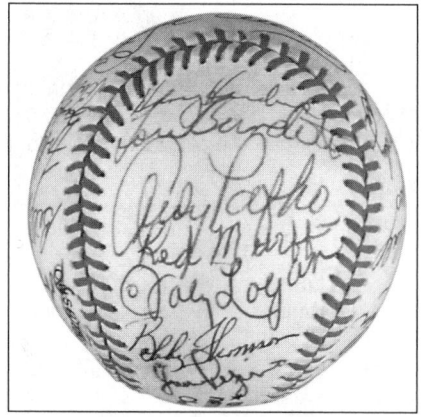

1957 Milwaukee Braves

Year	W/L	Team	Key Signatures	NM Price
1934	Winner	St. Louis Cardinals	Collins, D. Dean, P. Dean, Durocher, Frisch, Haines, Martin, Medwick....	$800-$1,000
	Loser	Detroit Tigers	Bridges, Cochrane, Gehringer, Goslin, Greenberg, Rowe	$850
1935	Winner	Detroit Tigers	Bridges, Cochrane, Gehringer, Goslin, Greenberg, Rowe	$700
	Loser	Chicago Cubs	Cuyler, Demaree, Galan, Grimm, Hack, Hartnett, Herman, Klein, Lee, Lindstrom, Warneke..	$700
1936	Winner	New York Yankees	Dickey, DiMaggio, Gehrig, Gomez, Lazzeri, McCarthy, Pearson, Ruffing....	$1,700-$2,000
	Loser	New York Giants	Hubbell, Jackson, Leiber, Mancuso, Moore, Ott, Terry..........................	$700-$1,900
1937	Winner	New York Yankees	Dickey, DiMaggio, Gehrig, Gomez, Lazzeri, McCarthy, Ruffing	$2,000-$7,000
	Loser	New York Giants	Bartell, Hubbell, Leiber, Melton, Moore, Ott, Ripple, Terry	$600-$700
1938	Winner	New York Yankees	Dickey, DiMaggio, Gehrig, Gomez, McCarthy, Ruffing	$1,200-$1,500
	Loser	Chicago Cubs	Bryant, Dean, Garbark, Grimm, Hack, Hartnett, Herman, Lazzeri, Lee, Reynolds	$750-$900
1939	Winner	New York Yankees	Dickey, DiMaggio, Gomez, Keller, McCarthy, Rolfe, Ruffing, Selkirk	$1,500
	Loser	Cincinnati Reds	Derringer, Goodman, Lombardi, McCormick, Walters	$400
1940	Winner	Cincinnati Reds	Derringer, Lombardi, McCormick, Ripple, Walters, Werber......................	$450
	Loser	Detroit Tigers	Averill, Gehringer, Greenberg, McCosky, Newsom, Rowe, York	$500-$600
1941	Winner	New York Yankees	Dickey, DiMaggio, Gomez, McCarthy, Rizzuto, Ruffing.........................	$1,000
	Loser	Brooklyn Dodgers	Camilli, Durocher, Herman, Higbe, Medwick, Reese, Reiser, Wyatt	$600-$900
1942	Winner	St. Louis Cardinals	Slaughter, Musial, W. Cooper, M. Cooper, Beazley...........................	$750-$900
	Loser	New York Yankees	Dickey, DiMaggio, Gomez, Gordon, McCarthy, Rizzuto, Ruffing	$800-$1,000
1943	Winner	New York Yankees	Chandler, Dickey, Johnson, Keller, McCarthy, Russo........................	$750-$1,200
	Loser	St. Louis Cardinals	M. Cooper, W. Cooper, Lanier, Musial...	$450
1944	Winner	St. Louis Cardinals	M. Cooper, W. Cooper, Hopp, Marion, Musial...................................	$450
	Loser	St. Louis Browns	Kreevich, Kramer, McQuinn, Potter, Stephens	$350-$600
1945	Winner	Detroit Tigers	Cramer, Greenberg, Newhouser, Trout, York	$350-$400
	Loser	Chicago Cubs	Cavarretta, Grimm, Hack, Johnson, Nicholson, Pafko, Wyse	$350-$400
1946	Winner	St. Louis Cardinals	Garagiola, Kurowski, Musial, Pollet, Schoendienst, Slaughter, Walker	$600-$700
	Loser	Boston Red Sox	Cronin, DiMaggio, Doerr, Ferriss, Hughson, Pesky, Williams.....................	$450-$700
1947	Winner	New York Yankees	Berra, DiMaggio, Henrich, McQuinn, Reynolds, Rizzuto, Shea	$1,000-$1,200
	Loser	Brooklyn Dodgers	Branca, Furillo, Hatten, Hodges, Reese, Robinson, Snider, Stankey, Vaughan.......	$1,000
1948	Winner	Cleveland Indians	Bearden, Boudreau, Feller, Gordon, Keltner, Lemon, Mitchell, Paige	$500
	Loser	Boston Braves	Dark, B. Elliott, Heath, Holmes, Sain, Spahn, Stankey	$500
1949	Winner	New York Yankees	Bauer, Berra, DiMaggio, Henrich, Raschi, Rizzuto, Reynolds, Stengel	$1,200-$1,500
	Loser	Brooklyn Dodgers	Branca, Campanella, Connors, Furillo, Hodges, Newcombe, Reese, Robinson, Snider..	$800-$1,000
1950	Winner	New York Yankees	Bauer, Berra, DiMaggio, Ford, Henrich, Mize, Raschi, Rizzuto, Stengel..	$800-$1,000
	Loser	Philadelphia Phillies	Ashburn, Ennis, Hammer, Konstanty, Roberts, Simmons	$400
1951	Winner	New York Yankees	Bauer, Berra, DiMaggio, Jensen, Mantle, McDougald, Mize, Raschi, Rizzuto, Stengel..	$4,000
	Loser	New York Giants	Dark, Durocher, Irvin, Jansen, Maglie, Mays, Thomson..........................	$750-$1,000
1952	Winner	New York Yankees	Bauer, Berra, Mantle, Martin, Mize, Raschi, Reynolds, Rizzuto, Stengel	$800-$1,000
	Loser	Brooklyn Dodgers	Avila, Easter, Doby, Feller, Garcia, Lemon, Mitchell, Rosen, Wynn	$900-$1,200
1953	Winner	New York Yankees	Bauer, Berra, Ford, Mantle, Martin, Mize, Raschi, Rizzuto, Stengel	$1,000
	Loser	Brooklyn Dodgers	Doby, Feller, Garcia, Lopez, Lemon, Mitchell, Rosen, Westlake, Wynn	$900
1954	Winner	New York Giants	Antonelli, Dark, Durocher, Irvin, Mueller, Mays, Wilhelm	$1,000-$1,500
	Loser	Cleveland Indians	Avila, Doby, Feller, Garcia, Lemon, Lopez, Rosen, Wynn	$450
1955	Winner	Brooklyn Dodgers	Alston, Campanella, Erskine, Furillo, Gilliam, Hodges, Koufax, Newcombe, Podres, Reese, Snider, Robinson, Zimmer	$3,000

1963 New York Yankees

1968 St. Louis Cardinals

1969 New York Mets

Year	W/L	Team	Key Signatures	NM Price
	Loser	New York Yankees	Bauer, Berra, Ford, Howard, Larsen, Mantle, Stengel	$900-$1,200
1956	Winner	New York Yankees	Bauer, Berra, Ford, Howard, Larsen, Mantle, Martin, Skowron, Stengel.....	$1,000-$1,200
	Loser	Brooklyn Dodgers	Alston, Campanella, Drysdale, Erskine, Furillo, Gilliam, Hodges, Koufax, Newcombe, Reese, Robinson, Snider	$900
1957	Winner	Milwaukee Braves	Aaron, Adcock, Burdette, Mathews, Schoendienst, Spahn	$1,200
	Loser	New York Yankees	Bauer, Berra, Ford, Howard, Larsen, Kubek, Mantle, Skowron, Stengel, Sturdivant	$1,000
1958	Winner	New York Yankees	Berra, Ford, Howard, Kubek, Larsen, Mantle, Stengel, Turley	$1,000-$1,200
	Loser	Milwaukee Braves	Aaron, Adcock, Burdette, Mathews, Schoendienst, Spahn	$700
1959	Winner	Los Angeles Dodgers	Alston, Drysdale, Gilliam, Hodges, Howard, Koufax, Snider, Wills, Zimmer	$700-$900
	Loser	Chicago White Sox	Aparicio, Cash, Fox, Kluszewski, Lopez, Shaw, Wynn	$500-$750
1960	Winner	Pittsburgh Pirates	Clemente, Friend, Groat, Law, Mazeroski, Stuart, Vernon	$1,500-$2,000
	Loser	New York Yankees	Berra, Ford, Howard, Kubek, Mantle, Maris, Skowron, Stengel	$700
1961	Winner	New York Yankees	Berra, Ford, Howard, Kubek, Mantle, Maris	$1,800-$2,000
	Loser	Cincinnati Reds	Coleman, Freese, Jay, O'Toole, Pinson, Robinson	$600-$1,200
1962	Winner	New York Yankees	Berra, Ford, Howard, Kubek, Mantle, Maris, Terry, Tresh	$750
	Loser	San Francisco Giants	Cepeda, Marichal, Mays, McCormick, McCovey	$500
1963	Winner	Los Angeles Dodgers	Alston, T. Davis, W. Davis, Drysdale, Gilliam, Koufax, Wills	$550
	Loser	New York Yankees	Berra, Ford, Howard, Kubek, Mantle, Maris, Terry, Tresh	$700
1964	Winner	St. Louis Cardinals	Boyer, Brock, Flood, Gibson, Groat, McCarver, White	$500
	Loser	New York Yankees	Berra, Ford, Howard, Kubek, Mantle, Maris, Stottlemyre, Tresh	$500-$700
1965	Winner	Los Angeles Dodgers	Alston, W. Davis, Drysdale, Gilliam, Lefebvre, Koufax, Wills	$400-$500
	Loser	Minnesota Twins	Grant, Kaat, Killebrew, Oliva, Versalles	$350
1966	Winner	Baltimore Orioles	Aparicio, Blair, Blefary, Johnson, McNally, Palmer, Powell, B. Robinson, F. Robinson	$350-$450
	Loser	Los Angeles Dodgers	Alston, T. Davis, W. Davis, Drysdale, Koufax, Sutton, Wills	$350
1967	Winner	St. Louis Cardinals	Brock, Carlton, Cepeda, Flood, Gibson, Maris, McCarver, Schoendienst ..	$400-$600
	Loser	Boston Red Sox	Conigliaro, Lonborg, Lyle, Petrocelli, Scott, Williams, Yastrzemski	$800
1968	Winner	Detroit Tigers	Cash, Freehan, Kaline, Lolich, McLain	$500
	Loser	St. Louis Cardinals	Brock, Carlton, Cepeda, Flood, Gibson, Maris, McCarver, Schoendienst ..	$350-$450
1969	Winner	New York Mets	Agee, Hodges, Koosman, Kranepool, Ryan, Seaver, Swoboda	$2,000-$2,500
	Loser	Baltimore Orioles	Blair, Cuellar, McNally, B. Robinson, F. Robinson, Palmer, Powell, Weaver	$300-$500
1970	Winner	Baltimore Orioles	Blair, Cueller, McNally, B. Robinson, F. Robinson, Palmer, Powell, Weaver	$325
	Loser	Cincinnati Reds	Anderson, Bench, Carbo, Concepcion, May, McRae, Perez, Rose	$300-$600
1971	Winner	Pittsburgh Pirates	Blass, Clemente, Mazeroski, Oliver, Sanguillen, Stargell	$800
	Loser	Baltimore Orioles	Cueller, Dobson, McNally, B. Robinson, F. Robinson, Palmer, Powell, Weaver ...	$300
1972	Winner	Oakland Athletics	Bando, Blue, Campaneris, Fingers, Hunter, Jackson, Williams	$200-$400
	Loser	Cincinnati Reds	Anderson, Bench, Concepcion, Foster, McRae, Morgan, Perez, Rose	$400
1973	Winner	Oakland Athletics	Bando, Blue, Campaneris, Fingers, Hunter, Jackson, Williams	$300-$450
	Loser	New York Mets	Berra, Koosman, Kranepool, Mays, Milner, Seaver, Staub	$300-$400
1974	Winner	Oakland Athletics	Bando, Blue, Campaneris, Fingers, Hunter, Jackson, Williams	$450-$1,000
	Loser	Los Angeles Dodgers	Alston, Buckner, Cey, Garvey, John, Lopes, Russell, Sutton, Wynn	$300
1975	Winner	Cincinnati Reds	Anderson, Bench, Concepcion, Foster, Griffey, Morgan, Perez, Rose	$570
	Loser	Boston Red Sox	Carbo, Cooper, Evans, Fisk, Lee, Lynn, Petrocelli, Rice, Tiant, Wise, Yastrzemski	$400-$600
1976	Winner	Cincinnati Reds	Anderson, Bench, Concepcion, Foster, Griffey, Morgan, Perez, Rose, Zachary	$500
	Loser	New York Yankees	Chambliss, Hunter, Lyle, Martin, Munson, Nettles, Randolph	$300-$800

1972 Oakland A's

1974 Los Angeles Dodgers

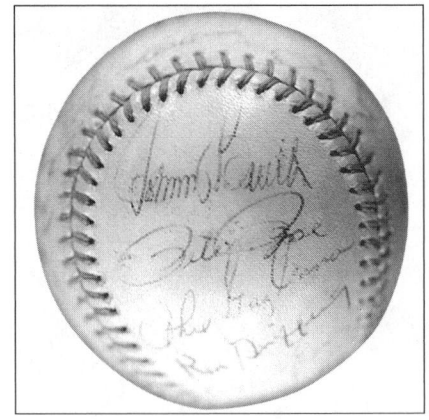
1975 Cincinnati Reds

Year	W/L	Team	Key Signatures	NM Price
1977	Winner	New York Yankees	Guidry, Hunter, Jackson, Lyle, Martin, Munson, Nettles, Piniella	$500-$800
	Loser	Los Angeles Dodgers	Baker, Cey, Garvey, John, Lasorda, Lopes, Russell, Smith, Sutton	$300
1978	Winner	New York Yankees	Gossage, Guidry, Hunter, Jackson, Lyle, Martin, Munson, Piniella	$400-$700
	Loser	Los Angeles Dodgers	Baker, Cey, Garvey, John, Lasorda, Lopes, Russell, Smith, Sutton	$250
1979	Winner	Pittsburgh Pirates	Blyleven, Candelaria, Madlock, Parker, Stargell, Tekulve	$300
	Loser	Baltimore Orioles	Flanagan, D. Martinez, Murray, Palmer, Singleton, Weaver	$200
1980	Winner	Philadelphia Phillies	Boone, Bowa, Carlton, Luzinski, Rose, Schmidt, Trillo	$300-$600
	Loser	Kansas City Royals	Brett, Leonard, McRae, Otis, Porter, Quisenberry, White, Wilson	$250-$700
1981	Winner	Los Angeles Dodgers	Baker, Cey, Garvey, Guerrero, Lasorda, Lopes, Russell, Sax, Valenzuela	$325
	Loser	New York Yankees	Gossage, Guidry, Jackson, John, Murcer, Nettles, Piniella, Winfield	$400
1982	Winner	St. Louis Cardinals	Andujar, Hernandez, Kaat, McGee, O. Smith, Sutter	$350
	Loser	Milwaukee Brewers	Caldwell, Cooper, Fingers, Molitor, Oglivie, Thomas, Vuckovich, Yount	$350
1983	Winner	Baltimore Orioles	Altobelli, Boddicker, D. Martinez, Murray, Palmer, C. Ripken Jr.	$450
	Loser	Philadelphia Phillies	Carlton, Denny, Morgan, Perez, Rose, Schmidt	$250
1984	Winner	Detroit Tigers	Anderson, Gibson, Evans, Hernandez, Johnson, Morris, Parrish, Trammell, Whitaker	$500
	Loser	San Diego Padres	Garvey, Gossage, Gwynn, Nettles	$250
1985	Winner	Kansas City Royals	Brett, Howser, McRae, Saberhagen, Quisenberry, White, Wilson	$400-$900
	Loser	St. Louis Cardinals	Clark, Coleman, McGee, O. Smith, Tudor	$250
1986	Winner	New York Mets	Carter, Dykstra, Gooden, Hernandez, D. Johnson, Mitchell, Strawberry, Wilson	$400-$900
	Loser	Boston Red Sox	Baylor, Boggs, Boyd, Buckner, Clemens, Evans, D. Henderson, Hurst, Rice, Seaver	$300
1987	Winner	Minnesota Twins	Blyleven, Brunansky, Gaetti, Hrbek, Kelly, J. Niekro, Puckett, Reardon, Viola	$400
	Loser	St. Louis Cardinals	Clark, Coleman, McGee, O. Smith, Tudor	$200
1988	Winner	Los Angeles Dodgers	Gibson, Guerrero, Hershiser, Lasorda, Sax, Valenzuela	$250
	Loser	Oakland Athletics	Canseco, Eckersley, LaRussa, McGwire, Steinbach, Stewart, Weiss	$225
1989	Winner	Oakland Athletics	Canseco, Eckersley, R. Henderson, LaRussa, McGwire, Steinbach, Stewart, Weiss	$300
	Loser	San Francisco Giants	Butler, Clark, Mitchell, Williams	$225
1990	Winner	Cincinnati Reds	Davis, Dibble, Larkin, Morris, Myers, O'Neill, Piniella, Rijo, Sabo	$300
	Loser	Oakland Athletics	Canseco, Eckersley, R. Henderson, LaRussa, McGwire, Stewart, Welch	$225
1991	Winner	Minnesota Twins	Aguilera, Davis, Erickson, Hrbek, Kelly, Knoblauch, Morris, Puckett, Tapani	$400
	Loser	Atlanta Braves	Avery, Blauser, Cox, Gant, Glavine, Justice, Pendleton, Smoltz, Wohlers	$250
1992	Winner	Toronto Blue Jays	Alomar, Borders, Carter, Cone, Gaston, Key, Morris, Olerud, Stieb, Stottlemyre, Winfield, White	$400
	Loser	Atlanta Braves	Avery, Cox, Gant, Glavine, Justice, Pendleton, Reardon, Sanders, Smoltz	$300
1993	Winner	Toronto Blue Jays	Alomar, Carter, Gaston, Henderson, Hentgen, Key, Molitor, Morris, Olerud, Stottlemyre, Stewart, White	$400
	Loser	Philadelphia Phillies	Daulton, Dykstra, Green, Hollins, Kruk, Schilling, Williams	$250
1994			No World Series	
1995	Winner	Atlanta Braves	Avery, Cox, Glavine, Grissom, C. Jones, Justice, Klesko, Lopez, Maddux, McGriff, Smoltz, Wohlers	$400
	Loser	Cleveland Indians	Alomar, Baerga, Belle, Hershiser, Lofton, D. Martinez, Mesa, Murray, Nagy, Ramirez, Thome	$350
1996	Winner	New York Yankees	Boggs, Cone, Jeter, T. Martinez, Pettitte, Rivera, Torre, Wetteland, Williams	$600
	Loser	Atlanta Braves	Cox, Glavine, C. Jones, Justice, Klesko, Lopez, Maddux, McGriff, Smoltz, Wohlers	$300

1981 New York Yankees

1986 New York Mets

1991 Cincinnati Reds

Year	W/L	Team	Key Signatures	NM Price
1997	Winner	Florida Marlins	Bonilla, Brown, Fernandez, Hernandez, Johnson, Leyland, Nen, Renteria, Sheffield	$500
	Loser	Cleveland Indians	Alomar, Grissom, Hershiser, Ramirez, Thome, Vizquel	$300
1998	Winner	New York Yankees	Brosius, Jeter, Knoblauch, Wells, Williams	$500-$600
	Loser	San Diego Padres	Gwynn, Vaughn	$300
1999	Winner	New York Yankees	Jeter, Hernandez, Leyritz, T. Martinez, Rivera, Williams	$1,300-$1,500
	Loser	Atlanta Braves	Glavine, C. Jones, A. Jones, Maddux	$200
2000	Winner	New York Yankees	Brosius, Jeter, Justice, T. Martinez, Rivera, Williams	$1,500-$2,000
	Loser	New York Mets	Hampton, Payton, Piazza, Ventura	$300
2001	Winner	Arizona Diamondbacks	M. Williams, R. Johnson, Schilling	$245
	Loser	New York Yankees	Jeter, Clemens, Williams, Torre	$320
2002	Winner	Anaheim Angels	G. Anderson, Salmon, Erstad, Glaus	$175
	Loser	San Francisco Giants	Bonds, Kent, Baker	$200

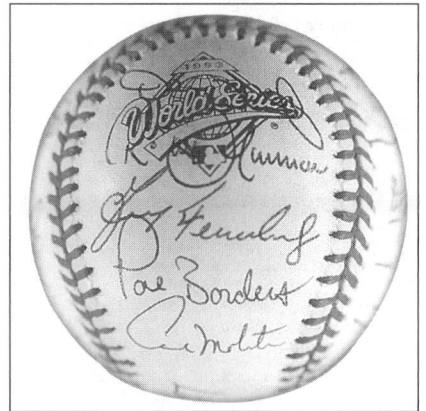

1993 Toronto Blue Jays

1995 Cleveland Indians

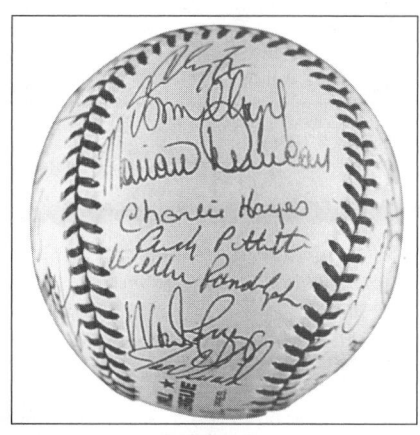

1996 New York Yankees

BASKETBALL AUTOGRAPHS
HALL OF FAMERS

Kareem Abdul-Jabbar (1947-) 1995

Mounted Memories Photo

Basketball.....................................$125-$150
Cut signature..$15
3x5 index card.......................................$25
8x10 photograph $50

Signed as Lew Alcindor

Basketball............................$1,000-$1,200
3x5 index card......................................$250
8x10 photograph $500

Forrest "Phog" Allen (1885-1974) 1959

Basketball..Unknown
Cut signature.......................................$200
3x5 index card......................................$300
8x10 photograph ....Unknown

Tiny Archibald (1948-) 1991

Basketball...$75
Cut signature..$5
3x5 index card.......................................$10
8x10 photograph $20

Paul Arizin (1928-) 1978

Basketball..$60-$85
Cut signature..$5
3x5 index card...$8
8x10 photograph $20

Red Auerbach (1917-) 1969

Basketball...$150
Cut signature..$15
3x5 index card.......................................$25
8x10 photograph $50

Thomas Barlow (1896-1983) 1981

Basketball..Unknown
Cut signature..$40
3x5 index card.................................$40-$60
8x10 photograph ....$125-$200

Leon Barmore (1944-) 2003

Basketball...$60
Cut signature..$5
3x5 signature...$7
8x10 photograph $15

Rick Barry (1944-) 1987

Basketball..$75-$100
Cut signature..$5

Mounted Memories Photo

3x5 index card.......................................$10
8x10 photograph $25

Elgin Baylor (1934-) 1977

Basketball...$100
Cut signature..$5
3x5 index card.......................................$10
8x10 photograph $30

John Beckman (1895-1968) 1973

Basketball..Unknown
Cut signature..$75
3x5 index card.................................$75-$100
8x10 photograph ....Unknown

Clair Bee (1896-1983) 1968

Basketball..Unknown
Cut signature..$50
3x5 index card.......................................$75
8x10 photograph ....Unknown

Walt Bellamy (1939-) 1993

Basketball...$75
Cut signature..$5
3x5 index card.......................................$10
8x10 photograph $20

Sergei Belov (1944-) 1992

Basketball..$75-$100
Cut signature..$10
3x5 index card.......................................$15
8x10 photograph $30

Danny Biasone (1909-1992) 2000

Basketball..Unknown
Cut signature..$25
3x5 index card.......................................$40
8x10 photograph $100

Dave Bing (1943-) 1990

Basketball...$75
Cut signature..$5
3x5 index card.......................................$10
8x10 photograph $20

Larry Bird (1956-) 1998

Mounted Memories Photo

Basketball.....................................$150-$200
Authenticated basketball $500
Cut Signature..$25
3x5 index card.......................................$35
8x10 photograph $60

Carol Blazejowski (1956-) 1994

Basketball..$60-$85
Cut signature..$3
3x5 index card...$5
8x10 photograph $15

Ernest Blood (1872-1955) 1960

Basketball..Unknown
Cut signature.......................................$250
3x5 index card......................................$300
8x10 photograph ....Unknown

Bennie Borgmann (1899-1978) 1961

Basketball..Unknown
Cut signature..$40
3x5 index card.......................................$60
8x10 photograph ....Unknown

Bill Bradley (1943-) 1983

Basketball...$125
Cut signature..$10
3x5 index card.......................................$20
8x10 photograph ....$35-$50

Joseph Brennan (1900-1989) 1975

Basketball..Unknown
Cut signature..$15
3x5 index card.................................$20-$75
8x10 photograph ....$100-$350

Larry Brown (1940-) 2002

Basketball...$80
Cut signature..$5
3x5 signature...$7
8x10 photograph $25

Lou Carnesseca (1925-) 1992

Basketball...$75
Cut signature..$5
3x5 index card.......................................$10
8x10 photograph $20

Pete Carril (1930-) 1997

Basketball..Unknown
Cut signature..$5

3x5 index card $10
8x10 photograph $20

Alfred Cervi (1917-)   **1985**

Basketball $75
Cut signature $5
3x5 index card $10
8x10 photograph $20

Wilt Chamberlain (1936-1999)   **1979**

Mounted Memories Photo

Basketball $350
Cut signature $50
3x5 index card .... $50-$75
8x10 photograph .... $150-$175

John Chaney (1932-)   **2001**

Basketball $75
Cut signature $5
3x5 index card $10
8x10 photograph $25

Jody Conradt (1941-)   **1998**

Basketball $75
Cut signature $5
3x5 index card $7
8x10 photograph $15

Charles Cooper (1907-1980)   **1977**

Basketball .... Unknown
Cut signature $20
3x5 index card $30
8x10 photograph $75

Kresimir Cosic (1948-1995)   **1996**

Basketball $85
Cut signature $5
3x5 index card $10
8x10 photograph $20

Bob Cousy (1928-)   **1971**

Basketball .... $100-$125
Cut signature $10
3x5 index card $20
8x10 photograph $40

Dave Cowens (1948-)   **1991**

Basketball $100
Cut signature $5
3x5 index card $10
8x10 photograph $30

Joan Crawford (1937-)   **1997**

Basketball $100
Cut signature $5
3x5 index card $10
8x10 photograph $25

Denny Crum (1937-)   **1994**

Basketball $75
Cut signature $5

3x5 index card $10
8x10 photograph $20

Billy Cunningham (1943-)   **1986**

Basketball $85
Cut signature $10
3x5 index card $15
8x10 photograph $25

Denise Curry (1959-)   **1997**

Basketball $85
Cut signature $5
3x5 index card $10
8x10 photograph $20

Chuck Daly (1930-)   **1994**

Basketball $75
Cut signature $5
3x5 index card $7
8x10 photograph $20

Robert Davies (1920-1990)   **1970**

Basketball .... Unknown
Cut signature $20
3x5 index card .... $25-$50
8x10 photograph .... $100-$250

Everett Dean (1898-1993)   **1966**

Basketball .... Unknown
Cut signature $50
3x5 index card $100
8x10 photograph $350

Forrest DeBernardi (1899-1970)   **1961**

Basketball .... Unknown
Cut signature $75
3x5 index card .... $50-$100
8x10 photograph .... Unknown

Dave DeBusschere (1940-2003)   **1983**

Mounted Memories Photo

Basketball .... $150-$200
Cut signature $10
3x5 index card $20
8x10 photograph $50

Henry Dehnert (1898-1979)   **1969**

Basketball .... Unknown
Cut signature $40
3x5 index card .... $60-$125
8x10 photograph .... Unknown

Antonio Diaz-Miguel (1933-2000)   **1997**

Basketball $150
Cut signature $10
3x5 index card $20
8x10 photograph $50

Anne Donovan (1961-)   **1995**

Basketball $75
Cut signature $5
3x5 index card $8
8x10 photograph $20

Robert Douglas (1882-1979)   **1972**

Basketball .... Unknown
Cut signature $75
3x5 index card $125
8x10 photograph .... Unknown

Wayne Embry (1937-)   **1999**

Basketball $75
Cut signature $5
3x5 index card $10
8x10 photograph $20

Paul Endacott (1902-1977)   **1972**

Basketball .... Unknown
Cut signature $50
3x5 index card $75
8x10 photograph .... $200-$250

Alex English (1954-)   **1997**

Basketball $100
Cut signature $5
3x5 index card $10
8x10 photo $25

Julius Erving (1950-)   **1993**

Steiner Sports Photo

Basketball .... $125-$175
Authenticated basketball $300
Cut signature $20
3x5 index card $30
8x10 photograph $50

Bud Foster (1906-1996)   **1964**

Basketball $200
Cut signature $20
3x5 index card $30
8x10 photograph .... $60-$100

Walt Frazier (1945-)   **1987**

Steiner Sports Photo

Basketball $100
Authenticated basketball $150
Cut signature $5
3x5 index card $10
8x10 photograph $30
Authenticated 8x10 photograph $40

Max "Marty" Friedman (1889-1986) **1972**

Basketball .... Unknown
Cut signature $20
3x5 index card $40
8x10 photograph $75

Joe Fulks (1921-1976)   **1978**

Basketball .... Unknown
Cut signature $40
3x5 index card .... $60-$100
8x10 photograph .... $200-$350

Clarence Gaines (1923-)   **1982**

Basketball $75
Cut signature $5
3x5 index card $10
8x10 photograph $20

Laddie Gale (1917-1996)   **1977**

Basketball......................................Unknown
Cut signature.......................................$15
3x5 index card.....................................$25
8x10 photograph..................................$50

Harry Gallatin (1927-)   **1991**

Basketball...$75
Cut signature...$5
3x5 index card.....................................$10
8x10 photograph..................................$20

Jack Gardner (1910-2000)   **1984**

Basketball......................................Unknown
Cut signature.......................................$15
3x5 index card.....................................$25
8x10 photograph................................$100

William "Pop" Gates (1917-1999)   **1989**

Basketball.............................$125-$150
Cut signature.......................................$10
3x5 index card.....................................$20
8x10 photograph .... $35-$50

George Gervin (1952-)   **1996**

Basketball...$100
Cut signature...$5
3x5 index card.....................................$10
8x10 photograph..................................$25

Tom Gola (1933-)   **1976**

Basketball...$75
Cut signature...$5
3x5 index card.......................................$8
8x10 photograph..................................$20

Alexsandr Gomelsky (1928-)   **1995**

Basketball...$125
Cut signature.......................................$15
3x5 index card.....................................$20
8x10 photograph..................................$35

Gail Goodrich (1943-)   **1996**

Basketball...$100
Cut signature...$5
3x5 index card.....................................$10
8x10 photograph..................................$30

Edward Gottlieb (1898-1979)   **1972**

Basketball......................................Unknown
Cut signature.......................................$30
3x5 index card.............................$50-$75
8x10 photograph ....Unknown

Hal Greer (1936-)   **1982**

Basketball...$75
Cut signature...$5
3x5 index card.......................................$8
8x10 photograph..................................$20

Robert Gruenig (1913-1958)   **1963**

Basketball......................................Unknown
Cut signature.....................................$200
3x5 index card...................................$250
8x10 photograph ....Unknown

Cliff Hagan (1931-)   **1978**

Basketball...........................$75-$100
Cut signature...$5
3x5 index card.......................................$8
8x10 photograph..................................$20

Alex Hannum (1923-2002)   **1998**

Basketball...$100
Cut signature...$5
3x5 index card.....................................$10
8x10 photograph..................................$30

Victor Hanson (1903-1982)   **1960**

Basketball......................................Unknown
Cut signature.......................................$50
3x5 index card.....................................$75
8x10 photograph ....Unknown

Lusia Harris-Stewart (1955-)   **1992**

Basketball...$60
Cut signature...$5
3x5 index card.......................................$8
8x10 photograph..................................$15

Les Harrison (1904-1997)   **1980**

Basketball......................................Unknown
Cut signature.......................................$10
3x5 index card.....................................$15
8x10 photograph..................................$40

Marv Harshman (1917-)   **1985**

Basketball...$60
Cut signature...$5
3x5 index card.......................................$8
8x10 photograph..................................$15

Don Haskins (1930-)   **1997**

Basketball...$75
Cut signature...$5
3x5 index card.......................................$8
8x10 photograph..................................$20

John Havlicek (1940-)   **1984**

Basketball...$125
Cut signature.......................................$10
3x5 index card.....................................$15
8x10 photograph..................................$40

Connie Hawkins (1942-)   **1992**

Basketball...$75
Cut signature...$5
3x5 index card.....................................$10
8x10 photograph..................................$25

Elvin Hayes (1945-)   **1990**

Basketball...$100
Cut signature...$5
3x5 index card.....................................$10
8x10 photograph..................................$25

Marques Haynes (1926-)   **1998**

Basketball...$75
Cut signature...$5
3x5 index card.....................................$10
8x10 photograph..................................$20

Chick Hearn (1917-2002)   **2003**

Basketball...$175
Cut signature.......................................$20
3x5 signature.....................................$25
8x10 photograph..................................$50

Tommy Heinsohn (1934-)   **1986**

Basketball...$100
Cut signature...$5
3x5 index card.....................................$10
8x10 photograph..................................$30

Edgar Hickey (1902-1980)   **1979**

Basketball......................................Unknown
Cut signature.......................................$50
3x5 index card.....................................$75
8x10 photograph ....Unknown

Paul Hinkle (1899-1992)   **1965**

Basketball......................................Unknown
Cut signature.......................................$25
3x5 index card.....................................$40
8x10 photograph................................$125

Howard Hobson (1903-1991)   **1965**

Basketball......................................Unknown
Cut signature.......................................$50
3x5 index card.....................................$75
8x10 photograph ....Unknown

Nat Holman (1896-1995)   **1964**

Basketball...$225
Cut signature.......................................$25
3x5 index card.....................................$35
8x10 photograph................................$100

Red Holzman (1920-1998)   **1986**

Basketball...$200
Cut signature.......................................$10
3x5 index card.....................................$20
8x10 photograph..................................$60

Robert Houbregs (1932-)   **1987**

Basketball...$75
Cut signature...$5
3x5 index card.......................................$8
8x10 photograph..................................$15

Bailey Howell (1937-)   **1997**

Basketball...$75
Cut signature...$5
3x5 index card.......................................$8
8x10 photo..$15

Chuck Hyatt (1908-1978)   **1959**

Basketball......................................Unknown
Cut signature.......................................$50
3x5 index card.....................................$75
8x10 photograph ....Unknown

Henry Iba (1904-1993)   **1969**

Basketball...$300
Cut signature.......................................$20
3x5 index card.....................................$35
8x10 photograph .... $50-$125

Edward "Ned" Irish (1905-1982)   **1964**

Basketball......................................Unknown
Cut signature.......................................$20
3x5 index card.......................$40-$100
8x10 photograph ....Unknown

Dan Issel (1948-)   **1993**

Basketball...$100
Cut signature...$5
3x5 index card.....................................$10
8x10 photograph..................................$25

Buddy Jeannette (1917-1998)   **1994**

Buddy Jeannette HOF

Basketball...$150
Cut signature.......................................$10
3x5 index card.....................................$15
8x10 photograph..................................$40

Magic Johnson (1959-)   **2002**

Mounted Memories Photo

Basketball........................ $175-$250
Cut signature.......................................$25

3x5 signature..............................$40
8x10 photograph $60

William Johnson (1911-1980)   1977

Basketball...........................Unknown
Cut signature.............................$30
3x5 index card $40
8x10 photograph ....Unknown

Neil Johnston (1929-1978)   1990

Basketball...........................Unknown
Cut signature.............................40
3x5 index card $50
8x10 photograph ....Unknown

K.C. Jones (1932-)   1989

Basketball...............................$100
Cut signature...............................$5
3x5 index card $10
8x10 photograph $25

Sam Jones (1933-)   1984

Basketball...............................$100
Cut signature...............................$5
3x5 index card $10
8x10 photograph $25

Bobby Knight (1931-)   1991

Basketball...............................$100
Cut signature.............................$10
3x5 index card $15
8x10 photograph $30

Edward Krause (1913-1942)   1976

Basketball...........................Unknown
Cut signature...........................$300
3x5 index card $400
8x10 photograph ....Unknown

Mike Krzyzewski (1947-)   2001

Basketball...............................$100
Cut signature...............................$5
3x5 index card $15
8x10 photograph $30

John Kundla (1916-)   1995

Basketball.................................$60
Cut signature...............................$5
3x5 index card $8
8x10 photograph $15

Bob Kurland (1924-)   1961

Basketball.................................$75
Cut signature...............................$5
3x5 index card $8
8x10 photograph $20

Bob Lanier (1948-)   1992

Basketball.................................$80
Cut signature...............................$8
3x5 index card $8
8x10 photograph $25

Joe Lapchick (1900-1970)   1966

Basketball...........................Unknown
Cut signature.............................$75
3x5 index card $100
8x10 photograph ....Unknown

Meadowlark Lemon (1932-)   2003

Basketball...............................$100
Cut signature.............................$10
3x5 signature.............................$15
8x10 photograph $30

Nancy Lieberman-Cline (1958-)   1996

Basketball.................................$75

Cut signature...............................$5
3x5 index card $8
8x10 photograph $15

Earl Lloyd (1928-)   2003

Basketball................... $75-$100
Cut signature...............................$5
3x5 index card $7
8x10 photograph ....$15-$40

Clyde Lovellette (1929-)   1988

Basketball.................................$75
Cut signature...............................$5
3x5 index card $8
8x10 photograph $15

Jerry Lucas (1940-)   1980

Basketball...............................$100
Cut signature...............................$5
3x5 index card $10
8x10 photograph $25

Angelo Luisetti (1916-2002)   1959

Basketball................... $75-$250
Cut signature...............................$5
3x5 index card .... $10-$30
8x10 photograph .... $20-$100

Ed Macauley (1928-)   1960

Basketball.................................$80
Cut signature...............................$5
3x5 index card $8
8x10 photograph $20

Moses Malone (1955-)   2001

Basketball................. $85-$125
Cut signature.............................$10
3x5 index card $15
8x10 photograph .... $20-$35
Authenticated 8x10 photograph $40

Pete Maravich (1947-1988)   1987

Full Name
Basketball............................. $1,000-$2,500
Cut signature...........................$300
3x5 index card $350
8x10 photograph .... $600-$1,500
"Pistol Pete" Only
Basketball............................. $700-$1,200
Cut signature...........................$200
3x5 index card .... $200-$250
8x10 photograph .... $400-$500

Slater Martin (1925-)   1982

Basketball.................................$75
Cut signature...............................$5
3x5 index card $8
8x10 photograph $15

Bob McAdoo (1961-)   2000

Basketball................... $75-$100
Cut signature...............................$5
3x5 index card $8
8x10 photograph $20

Branch McCracken (1908-1970)   1960

Basketball...........................Unknown
Cut signature.............................$50
3x5 index card $75
8x10 photograph ....Unknown

Jack McCracken (1911-1958)   1962

Basketball...........................Unknown
Cut signature...........................$250
3x5 index card $300
8x10 photograph ....Unknown

Bobby McDermott (1914-1963)   1988

Basketball...........................Unknown
Cut signature...........................$150
3x5 index card $200
8x10 photograph ....Unknown

Al McGuire (1928-2001)   1992

Basketball...............................$175
Cut signature.............................$10
3x5 index card $20
8x10 photograph $50

Dick McGuire (1926-)   1993

Basketball.................................$75
Cut signature...............................$5
3x5 index card $8
8x10 photograph $20

Frank McGuire (1916-1994)   1977

Basketball...............................$300
Cut signature.............................$35
3x5 index card .... $25-$50
8x10 photograph .... $50-$125

Kevin McHale (1957-)   1999

Basketball................... $100-$125
Cut signature.............................$10
3x5 index card $15
8x10 photograph $35

John McLendon (1915-1999)   1979

Basketball...............................$125
Cut signature...............................$5
3x5 index card $10
8x10 photograph $30

Walter Meanwell (1884-1953)   1959

Basketball...........................Unknown
Cut signature...........................$300
3x5 index card $350
8x10 photograph ....Unknown

Dino Meneghin (1950-)   2003

Basketball...............................$100
Cut signature.............................$10
3x5 signature.............................$15
8x10 photograph $30

Ray Meyer (1913-)   1979

Basketball.................................$80
Cut signature...............................$5
3x5 index card $10
8x10 photograph $25

Ann Meyers (1955-)   1993

Basketball.................................$75
Cut signature...............................$5
3x5 index card $8
8x10 photograph $15

George Mikan (1924-)   1959

Basketball................... $125-$150
Cut signature.............................$20
3x5 index card $25
8x10 photograph $50

Vern Mikkelsen (1928-)   1995

Basketball.................................$80
Cut signature...............................$5
3x5 index card $10
8x10 photograph $20

Cheryl Miller (1964-)   1995

Basketball.................................$80
Cut signature...............................$5
3x5 index card $8
8x10 photograph $20

Ralph Miller (1919-2001)　　　**1988**

Basketball...Unknown
Cut signature...$5
3x5 index card..$10
8x10 photograph......................................$25

William Mokray (1907-1974)　　　**1965**

Basketball...Unknown
Cut signature...$75
3x5 index card..$100
8x10 photograph...............................Unknown

Earl Monroe (1944-)　　　**1990**

Steiner Sports Photo

Basketball.................................. $75-$125
Cut signature...$5
3x5 index card..$10
8x10 photograph......................................$20

Billie Moore (1943-)　　　**1999**

Basketball...$60
Cut signature...$5
3x5 index card..$7
8x10 photograph......................................$15

Calvin Murphy (1948-)　　　**1993**

Basketball...$75
Cut signature...$5
3x5 index card..$8
8x10 photograph......................................$20

Charles Murphy (1907-1992)　　　**1960**

Basketball...$250
Cut signature...$15
3x5 index card..$25
8x10 photograph......................................$50

James Naismith (1861-1939)　　　**1959**

Basketball...Unknown
Cut signature...$500
3x5 index card................... $700-$2,500
8x10 photograph...............................Unknown

Pete Newell (1915-)　　　**1979**

Basketball...Unknown
Cut signature...$10
3x5 index card..$15
8x10 photograph......................................$30

C. M. Newton (1930-)　　　**2000**

Basketball...$60
Cut signature...$5
3x5 index card..$8
8x10 photograph......................................$15

Aleksandar Nikolic (1924-2000)　　　**1998**

Basketball...$250
Cut signature...$20
3x5 index card..$25
8x10 photograph....................................$100

Larry O'Brien (1917-1990)　　　**1991**

Basketball...$400

Cut signature...$35
3x5 index card.................................$50-$75
8x10 photograph....................................$150

Lute Olsen (1934-)　　　**2002**

Basketball...$75
Cut signature...$5
3x5 index card..$7
8x10 photograph......................................$20

Harlan Page (1887-1965)　　　**1962**

Basketball...Unknown
Cut signature...$100
3x5 index card.............................$50-$125
8x10 photograph...............................Unknown

Robert Parish (1953-)　　　**2003**

Basketball...$80
Cut signature...$5
3x5 index card..$10
8x10 photograph......................................$25

Drazen Petrovic (1964-93)　　　**2002**

Basketball.............................. $350-$400
Cut signature...$40
3x5 signature..................................$25-$60
8x10 photograph.....................$100-$200

Bob Pettit (1932-)　　　**1971**

Basketball...$100
Cut signature...$5
3x5 index card..$10
8x10 photograph......................................$25

Andy Phillip (1922-2001)　　　**1961**

Basketball.............................. $125-$150
Cut signature...$5
3x5 index card..$10
8x10 photograph............................ $30-$50

Maurice Podoloff (1890-1985)　　　**1974**

Basketball...Unknown
Cut signature...$25
3x5 index card.............................$40-$125
8x10 photograph...............................Unknown

Jim Pollard (1922-1993)　　　**1978**

Basketball...$250
Cut signature...$10
3x5 index card..$15
8x10 photograph......................................$75

Jack Ramsay (1925-)　　　**1992**

Basketball...$80
Cut signature...$5
3x5 index card..$20
8x10 photograph......................................$20

Frank Ramsey (1931-)　　　**1982**

Basketball...$75
Cut signature...$5
3x5 index card..$10
8x10 photograph......................................$15

Willis Reed (1942-)　　　**1982**

Basketball...$100
Cut signature...$8
3x5 index card..$12
8x10 photograph......................................$30
Authenticated 8x10 photograph..............$90

Arnie Risen (1924-)　　　**1998**

Basketball...$75
Cut signature...$5
3x5 index card..$10
8x10 photograph......................................$20

Oscar Robertson (1938-)　　　**1980**

Mounted Memories Photo

Full Name
Basketball...$125
Cut signature...$20
3x5 index card..$25
8x10 photograph......................................$50
"Big O" Only
Basketball...$80
Cut signature...$8
3x5 index card..$12
8x10 photograph......................................$30

John Roosma (1900-1983)　　　**1961**

Basketball...Unknown
Cut signature...$25
3x5 index card.............................$35-$100
8x10 photograph...............................Unknown

Adolph Rupp (1901-1977)　　　**1969**

Basketball...$700
Cut signature...$75
3x5 index card..$100
8x10 photograph.....................$300-$350

Bill Russell (1934-)　　　**1975**

Tri-Star Productions Photo

Basketball...$350
Authenticated basketball.......................$800
Cut signature...$50
3x5 index card..$60
8x10 photograph.....................$100-$150

John Russell (1902-1973)　　　**1964**

Basketball...Unknown
Cut signature...$50
3x5 index card..$60
8x10 photograph...............................Unknown

Abe Saperstein (1901-1966)　　　**1971**

Basketball...Unknown
Cut signature.............................$75-$150
3x5 index card.............................$100-$200
8x10 photograph.....................$350-$500

Dolph Schayes (1928-)　　　**1973**

Basketball...$75
Cut signature...$5
3x5 index card..$10
8x10 photograph......................................$20

Ernest Schmidt (1911-1986)　　　**1974**

Basketball...Unknown
Cut signature...$25
3x5 index card.............................$40-$100
8x10 photograph...............................Unknown

John Schommer (1884-1960)　　　**1959**

Basketball...Unknown

Cut signature $125
3x5 index card $150
8x10 photograph ....Unknown
Barney Sedran (1891-1964)   1962

Basketball ....Unknown
Cut signature $125
3x5 index card $150
8x10 photograph ....Unknown
Uljana Semjonova (?-)   1993

Basketball ....Unknown
Cut signature $15
3x5 index card $35
8x10 photograph ....Unknown
Bill Sharman (1926-)   1976

Basketball $75
Cut signature $5
3x5 index card $7
8x10 photograph $20
Dean Smith (1931-)   1983

Basketball $125
Cut signature $20
3x5 index card $25
8x10 photograph $40
Amos Alonzo Stagg (1862-1965)   1959

Basketball ....Unknown
Cut signature $300
3x5 index card $400
8x10 photograph ....Unknown
Christian Steinmetz (1887-1963)   1961

Basketball ....Unknown
Cut signature $150
3x5 index card $200
8x10 photograph ....Unknown
Earl Strom (1927-1994)   1995

Basketball $250
Cut signature $25
3x5 index card $40
8x10 photograph $100
Pat Summitt (1952-)   2000

Basketball $80
Cut signature $5
3x5 index card $10
8x10 photograph $25
Chuck Taylor (1901-1969)   1969

Basketball ....Unknown
Cut signature $100
3x5 index card $150
8x10 photograph ....Unknown
Isiah Thomas (1961-)   2000

Mounted Memories Photo

Basketball $125
Cut signature $10
3x5 index card $15
8x10 photograph $30
David Thompson (1954-)   1996

Basketball $80
Cut signature $5

3x5 index card $10
8x10 photograph $25
John Thompson (1906-1990)   1962

Basketball $300
Cut signature $25
3x5 index card ....$35-$75
8x10 photograph ....$100-$200
John R. Thompson (1941-)   1999

Basketball $80
Cut signature $5
3x5 index card $10
8x10 photograph $25
Nate Thurmond (1941-)   1985

Basketball $75
Cut signature $5
3x5 index card $10
8x10 photograph $20
Arthur Trester (1878-1944)   1961

Basketball ....Unknown
Cut signature $400
3x5 index card $500
8x10 photograph ....Unknown
Jack Twyman (1934-)   1983

Basketball $80
Cut signature $5
3x5 index card $10
8x10 photograph $15
Wes Unseld (1946-)   1988

Basketball $80
Cut signature $5
3x5 index card $10
8x10 photograph $25
Robert Vandivier (1903-1993)   1975

Basketball $250
Cut signature $25
3x5 index card $35
8x10 photograph $60
Edward Wachter (1883-1966)   1961

Basketball ....Unknown
Cut signature $75
3x5 index card $100
8x10 photograph ....Unknown
Margaret Wade (1912-1995)   1985

Basketball $250
Cut signature $15
3x5 index card $25
8x10 photograph $75
Bill Walton (1952-)   1993

Mounted Memories Photo

Basketball $100
Authenticated basketball $100
Cut signature $10
3x5 index card $15
8x10 photograph $30

David Walsh (1889-1975)   1961

Basketball ....Unknown
Cut signature $50
3x5 index card $75
8x10 photograph ....Unknown
Robert Wanzer (1921-)   1987

Basketball $75
Cut signature $5
3x5 index card $8
8x10 photograph $15
Stanley Watts (1911-2000)   1986

Basketball $125
Cut signature $10
3x5 index card $15
8x10 photograph $25
Clifford Wells (1896-1977)   1972

Basketball ....Unknown
Cut signature $50
3x5 index card $75
8x10 photograph ....Unknown
Jerry West (1938-)   1980

Basketball $150
Cut signature $10
3x5 index card $20
8x10 photograph $40
Nera White (1935-)   1992

Basketball ....Unknown
Cut signature $10
3x5 index card $15
8x10 photograph $25
Lenny Wilkens (1937-)   1989 and 1998

Basketball $100
Cut signature $8
3x5 index card $12
8x10 photograph $25
John Wooden (1910-)   1960, 1973

Basketball $125
Cut signature $10
3x5 index card $15
8x10 photograph $30
Morgan Wootten (1931-)   2000

Basketball $75
Cut signature $5
3x5 index card $8
8x10 photograph $15
James Worthy (1961-)   2003

Basketball $100
Cut signature $5
3x5 signature $10
8x10 photograph $30
Authenticated 8x10 photograph $40
George Yardley (1928-)   1996

Basketball $75
Cut signature $5
3x5 signature $10
8x10 photograph $20
Kay Yow (1942-)   2002

Basketball $60
Cut signature $5
3x5 signature $7
8x10 photograph $15
Fred Zollner (1901-1982)   1999

Basketball ....Unknown
Cut signature $35
3x5 signature ....$50-$75
8x10 photograph ....Unknown

BASKETBALL AUTOGRAPHS

INACTIVE PLAYERS

NOTE: PRICING IS FOR NBA INDOOR/OUTDOOR BASKETBALLS
*Indicates Player Is Deceased

Player	8x10 photo	Auth. photo	Ball	Auth. ball
Zaid Abdul-Aziz	$8		$40	
M. Abdul-Rauf	$12		$50	
Alvan Adams	$10		$50	
Michael Adams	$10		$50	
Rick Adelman	$15		$60	
Mark Aguirre	$15		$60	
Danny Ainge	$25		$75	
Cory Alexander	$8		$40	
Steve Alford	$8		$40	
Lucius Allen	$8		$40	
Cadillac Anderson	$8		$40	
B.J. Armstrong	$15	$25	$50	
Al Attles	$12		$50	
Dennis Awtrey	$8		$40	
James Bailey	$8		$40	
Thurl Bailey	$10		$40	
Greg Ballard	$8		$40	
Gene Banks	$10		$40	
Mike Bantom	$8		$40	

Tri-Star Productions Photo

Player	8x10 photo	Auth. photo	Ball	Auth. ball
Charles Barkley	$40		$100	$320
Jim Barnes *	$20		$75	
Marvin Barnes	$8		$40	
Jim Barnett	$8		$40	
Dick Barnett	$20		$60	
John Battle	$8		$40	
Butch Beard	$8		$40	
Ralph Beard	$8		$40	
Zelmo Beaty *	$40		$125	
Byron Beck	$8		$40	
William Bedford	$8		$40	
Benoit Benjamin	$12		$50	
Kent Benson	$10		$40	
Al Bianchi	$8		$40	
Len Bias *	$400		$750	
Henry Bibby	$12		$50	
Otis Birdsong	$10		$50	
Uwe Blab	$12		$50	
Rolando Blackman	$15		$60	
John Block	$8		$40	
Tom Boerwinkle	$10		$50	
Muggsy Bogues	$15		$60	
Manute Bol	$15		$60	
Ron Boone	$12		$50	
Bob Boozer	$12		$50	
Sam Bowie	$15		$60	
Dudley Bradley	$8		$40	
Carl Braun	$20		$60	

Player	8x10 photo	Auth. photo	Ball	Auth. ball
Randy Breuer	$10		$40	
Jim Brewer	$8		$40	
Ron Brewer	$8		$40	
Frank Brickowski	$8		$40	
Junior Bridgeman	$12		$50	
Bill Bridges	$8		$40	
Allan Bristow	$8		$40	
Michael Brooks	$8		$40	
Fred Brown	$10		$50	
Roger Brown *	$40		$100	
Joe Bryant	$15		$50	
Quinn Buckner	$10		$40	
Tom Burleson	$15		$50	
Michael Cage	$12		$50	
Joe Caldwell	$10		$40	
Corky Calhoun	$8		$40	
Mack Calvin	$8		$40	
Rick Carlisle	$10		$40	
Antoine Carr	$10		$40	
Austin Carr	$15		$50	
Kenny Carr	$8		$40	
M.L. Carr	$15		$50	
Joe Barry Carroll	$10		$40	
Fred Carter	$10		$40	
Bill Cartwright	$20		$60	
Harvey Catchings	$10		$40	
Terry Catledge	$8		$40	
Duane Causwell	$8		$40	
Cedric Ceballos	$15		$50	
Tom Chambers	$15		$50	
Don Chaney	$8		$40	
Rex Chapman	$12		$50	
Len Chappell	$8		$40	
Maurice Cheeks	$15		$50	
Phil Chenier	$12		$50	
Pete Chilcutt	$8		$40	
Jim Chones	$10		$50	
Archie Clark	$15		$50	
Jim Cleamons	$8		$40	
John Clemens	$8		$40	
Sweetwater Clifton	$50		$150	
Doug Collins	$20		$60	
Gene Conley	$20		$60	
Chuck Connors	$60		$200	
Michael Cooper	$15		$50	
Wayne Cooper	$8		$40	
Dave Corzine	$8		$40	
Larry Costello *	$25		$100	
Mel Counts	$8		$40	
Charlie Criss	$8		$40	
Pat Cummings	$8		$40	
Terry Cummings	$15		$60	
Earl Cureton	$8		$40	
Quintin Dailey	$8		$40	
Louie Dampier	$15		$50	
Bob Dandridge	$15		$50	
Mel Daniels	$18		$60	

Player	8x10 photo	Auth. photo	Ball	Auth. ball
Adrian Dantley	$18		$60	
Brad Daugherty	$15		$60	
Brad Davis	$8		$40	
Mark Davis	$8		$40	
Walter Davis	$5		$50	

Mounted Memories Photo

Player	8x10 photo	Auth. photo	Ball	Auth. ball
Darryl Dawkins	$20	$25	$75	
Johnny Dawkins	$10		$40	
Todd Day	$8		$40	
Bison Dele *	$30		$100	
Connie Dierking	$15		$50	
Coby Dietrick	$8		$40	
Ernie DiGregorio	$15		$60	
Terry Dischinger	$8		$40	
James Donaldson	$10		$60	
Sherman Douglas	$8		$40	
John Drew	$10		$40	
Larry Drew	$8		$40	
Clyde Drexler	$35		$85	
Kevin Duckworth	$8		$40	
Joe Dumars	$15		$60	
Mike Dunleavy	$15		$50	
T.R. Dunn	$8		$40	
Jim Eakins	$8		$40	
Mark Eaton	$15		$50	
Blue Edwards	$8		$40	
James Edwards	$10		$40	
Craig Ehlo	$10		$40	
Mario Elie	$10		$40	
Sean Elliott	$15		$50	
Dale Ellis	$10		$40	
Leroy Ellis	$8		$40	
Pervis Ellison	$12		$50	
Len Elmore	$10		$40	
Keith Erickson	$8		$40	
Mike Evans	$8		$40	

Player	8x10 photo	Auth. photo	Ball	Auth. ball
Patrick Ewing	$75		$200	
Mike Farmer	$8		$40	
Duane Ferrell	$8		$40	
Bob Ferry	$8		$40	
Hank Finkel	$8		$40	
Jerry Fleishman	$8		$40	
Vern Fleming	$10		$40	
Eric "Sleepy" Floyd	$12		$50	
Chris Ford	$12		$50	
Phil Ford	$15		$50	
Fred Foster *	$25		$100	

Player	8x10 photo	Auth. photo	Ball	Auth. ball
James Fox	$8		$40	
World B. Free	$15		$60	
Donnie Freeman	$8		$40	
Bill Gabor	$15		$50	
Mike Gale	$8		$40	
Dave Gambee	$8		$40	
Kevin Gamble	$8		$40	
Kenny Gattison	$10		$40	
Jack George *	$25		$100	
Gus Gerard	$8		$40	
John Gianelli	$8		$40	
Armen Gilliam	$12		$50	
Herm Gilliam	$8		$40	
Artis Gilmore	$20		$75	
Mike Glenn	$8		$40	
Mike Gminski	$12		$40	
Gerald Govan	$8		$40	
Joe Graboski *	$25		$100	
Bud Grant	$30		$85	
Harvey Grant	$12		$40	
A.C. Green	$20		$60	
Johnny Green	$8		$40	
Rickey Green	$8		$40	
Sihugo Green *	$100		$400	
David Greenwood	$8		$40	
Kevin Grevey	$10		$40	
Darrell Griffith	$8		$40	
Dick Groat	$25		$75	
Ernie Grunfeld	$15		$50	
Richie Guerin	$20		$60	
Matt Guokas	$10		$40	
Happy Hairston *	$50		$125	
Tommy Hammonds	$8		$40	
Bill Hanzlik	$8		$40	
Derek Harper	$12		$50	
Ron Harper	$20		$60	
Clem Haskins	$8		$40	
Steve Hawes	$8		$40	
Hersey Hawkins	$10		$40	
Tom Hawkins	$8		$40	
Spencer Haywood	$20		$60	
Walt Hazzard	$15		$50	
Garfield Heard	$10		$40	
Gerald Henderson	$10		$40	
Fred Hetzel	$8		$40	
Art Heyman	$10		$45	
Rod Higgins	$8		$40	
Armond Hill	$8		$40	
Darnell Hillman	$15		$50	
Roy Hinson	$8		$40	
Craig Hodges	$8		$40	
Lionel Hollins	$12		$50	
Tito Horford	$8		$40	
Jeff Hornacek	$12		$50	
Phil Hubbard	$8		$40	
Lou Hudson	$18		$50	
Rod Hundley	$15		$50	
Bobby Hurley	$15		$50	
Marc Iavaroni	$8		$40	
Darrall Imhoff	$8		$40	
George Irvine	$8		$40	
Lucious Jackson	$8		$40	
Phil Jackson	$50		$175	
Clem Johnson	$8		$40	

Player	8x10 photo	Auth. photo	Ball	Auth. ball

Tri-Star Productions Photo

Player	8x10 photo	Auth. photo	Ball	Auth. ball
Dennis Johnson	$15	$30	$50	
Eddie Johnson	$8	$20	$40	
George L. Johnson	$8		$40	
George T. Johnson	$8		$40	
Gus Johnson *	$75		$350	

Steiner Productions Photo

Player	8x10 photo	Auth. photo	Ball	Auth. ball
Larry Johnson	$20	$40	$90	
Marques Johnson	$15		$50	
Mickey Johnson	$8		$40	
Ollie Johnson	$8		$40	
Steve Johnson	$8		$40	
Vinnie Johnson	$12		$40	
Bobby Jones	$15		$50	
Caldwell Jones	$18		$60	
Steve Jones	$8		$40	
Wali Jones	$8		$40	

Mounted Memories Photo

Player	8x10 photo	Auth. photo	Ball	Auth. ball
Michael Jordan	$150	$550	$500	$1,500
George Karl	$15		$50	
Rich Kelley	$8		$40	
Clark Kellogg	$10		$40	
Larry Kenon	$8		$40	
Johnny Kerr	$10		$40	
Jerome Kersey	$12		$50	
Toby Kimball	$8		$40	

Player	8x10 photo	Auth. photo	Ball	Auth. ball
Bo Kimble	$12		$50	
Albert King	$15		$50	
Bernard King	$25		$75	
Jim King	$8		$40	
Stacey King	$10		$40	
Greg Kite	$10		$40	
Joe Kleine	$15		$40	
Billy Knight	$12		$40	
Don Kojis	$8		$40	
Jon Koncak	$12		$40	
Jim Krebs *	$200		$500	
Larry Krystkowiak	$8		$40	
Steve Kuberski	$8		$40	
Kevin Kunnert	$8		$40	
Mitch Kupchak	$15		$50	
Sam Lacey	$13		$75	
Bill Laimbeer	$20		$60	
Jeff Lamp	$10		$40	
Andrew Lang	$8		$40	
Antonio Lang	$8		$40	
Tony Lavelli *	$35		$100	
Allen Leavell	$8		$40	
Jeff Lebo	$8		$40	
Clyde Lee	$8		$40	
George Lee	$8		$40	
Keith Lee	$8		$40	
Ronnie Lee	$8		$40	
Tim Legler	$10		$40	
Bob Leonard	$18		$50	

Mounted Memories Photo

Player	8x10 photo	Auth. photo	Ball	Auth. ball
Fat Lever	$12		$50	
Cliff Levingston	$12		$40	
Fred Lewis *	$40		$100	
Reggie Lewis *	$75		$350	
Alton Lister	$10		$40	
Brad Lohaus	$8		$40	
Luc Longley	$15		$50	
Jim Loscutoff	$15		$50	
Kevin Loughery	$8		$40	
Bob Love	$12		$50	
Sidney Lowe	$10		$40	
John Lucas	$15		$60	
Maurice Lucas	$15		$60	
Don Maclean	$8		$40	
Mark Macon	$10		$40	
Kyle Macy	$8		$40	
Rick Mahorn	$10		$40	
Dan Majerle	$15		$50	
Jeff Malone	$12		$50	
Ed Manning	$8		$40	
Sarunas Marciulionis	$15		$50	

Player	8x10 photo	Auth. photo	Ball	Auth. ball
Jack Marin	$10		$50	
Cedric Maxwell	$15	$40	$60	
Vernon Maxwell	$10		$40	
Don May	$8		$40	
Scott May	$15		$50	
John McCarthy	$8		$40	
Rodney McCray	$12		$40	
Xavier McDaniel	$20		$60	
George McGinnis	$15		$50	
Jon McGlocklin	$15		$50	
Kevin McKenna	$8		$40	
Stan McKenzie	$8		$40	
"Bones" McKinney *	$35		$150	
William McKinney	$8		$40	
McCoy McLemore	$8		$40	
Nate McMillan	$10		$40	
Tom McMillen	$20		$60	
Jim McMillian	$8		$40	
Mark McNamara	$8		$40	
Bill Melchionni	$8		$40	
John Mengelt	$8		$40	
Joe Meriweather	$8		$40	
Oliver Miller	$8		$40	
Terry Mills	$8		$40	
Harold Miner	$15		$50	
Steve Mix	$10		$40	
Doug Moe	$12		$40	
Paul Mokeski	$8		$40	
Sidney Moncrief	$15		$50	
John Moore	$8		$40	
Rick Mount	$12		$40	
Chris Mullin	$20		$60	
Jeff Mullins	$15		$50	
Gheorghe Muresan	$20		$60	
Larry Nance	$15		$60	
Swen Nater	$10		$40	
Calvin Natt	$8		$40	
Lloyd Neal	$8		$40	
Don Nelson	$15		$50	
Chuck Nevitt	$10		$40	
Mike Newlin	$8		$40	
Kurt Nimphius	$8		$40	
Norm Nixon	$12		$50	
Ken Norman	$8		$40	
Willie Norwood	$8		$40	
Ed O'Bannon	$8		$40	
Mike O'Koren	$10		$40	
Hakeem Olajuwon	$40		$150	
Mark Olberding	$8		$40	
Jawann Oldham	$8		$40	
Louis Orr	$8		$40	
Billy Owens	$8		$40	
Tom Owens	$8		$40	
Togo Palazzi	$8		$40	
Billy Paultz	$10		$40	
Jim Paxson	$10		$40	
John Paxson	$15		$50	
John Pelkington	$8		$40	
Will Perdue	$15		$50	
Sam Perkins	$30		$60	
Curtis Perry	$8		$40	
Chuck Person	$10		$40	
Bobby Phills *	$40		$150	
Ricky Pierce	$8		$40	
Ed Pinckney	$12		$40	

Player	8x10 photo	Auth. photo	Ball	Auth. ball
Olden Polynice	$12		$40	
Ben Poquette	$8		$40	
Howard Porter	$8		$40	
Kevin Porter	$8		$40	
Cincy Powell	$10		$40	
Paul Pressey	$8		$40	
Mark Price	$15		$50	
Dino Radja	$15		$50	
Kurt Rambis	$15		$50	
Clifford Ray	$8		$40	
Khalid Reeves	$8		$40	
J.R. Reid	$12		$50	
Robert Reid	$12		$50	
Kevin Restani	$8		$40	
Clint Richardson	$8		$40	
M. Ray Richardson	$10		$40	
Pooh Richardson	$12		$40	
Pat Riley	$40		$80	
Mike Riordan	$8		$40	
Doc Rivers	$15		$50	
Fred Roberts	$8		$40	
Alvin Robertson	$12		$50	
Rick Robey	$8		$40	
Cliff Robinson	$10		$40	
David Robinson	$40		$125	
Flynn Robinson	$8		$40	
Rumeal Robinson	$10		$40	
Truck Robinson	$12		$40	
Dave Robisch	$8		$40	
Red Rocha	$12		$50	
John Roche	$8		$40	
Dennis Rodman	$30	$90	$80	$200
Tree Rollins	$15		$50	
Dan Roundfield	$10		$40	
Curtis Rowe	$8		$40	
Clifford Rozier	$8		$40	
Jeff Ruland	$12		$50	
Campy Russell	$15		$50	
Cazzie Russell	$20		$75	
Arvydas Sabonis	$15		$50	
John Salley	$15		$50	
Ralph Sampson	$20		$75	
Satch Sanders	$15		$50	
Woody Sauldsberry	$10		$40	
Danny Schayes	$10		$40	
Duane Schintzius	$10		$40	
Dale Schlueter	$8		$40	
Detlef Schrempf	$12		$50	
Alvin Scott	$8		$40	
Byron Scott	$15		$50	
Charlie Scott	$20		$60	
Dennis Scott	$15		$50	
Malik Sealy *	$40		$150	
Ken Sears	$10		$40	
Rony Seikaly	$15		$50	
Charles Shackleford	$10		$40	
Lonnie Shelton	$8		$40	
Purvis Short	$8		$40	
Gene Shue	$12		$40	
John Shumate	$8		$40	
Jerry Sichting	$10		$40	
Jack Sikma	$15		$50	
James Silas	$15		$50	
Paul Silas	$20		$60	
Lionel Simmons	$8		$40	

Player	8x10 photo	Auth. photo	Ball	Auth. ball
Ralph Simpson	$8		$40	
Scott Skiles	$15		$50	
Jerry Sloan	$25		$60	
Bingo Smith	$8		$40	
Kenny Smith	$12		$50	
Randy Smith	$12		$40	
Rik Smits	$15		$50	
Dick Snyder	$8		$40	
Ricky Sobers	$8		$40	
Rory Sparrow	$12		$40	
Dave Stallworth	$8		$40	
Steve Stipanovich	$8		$40	
John Stockton	$50		$150	
Jon Sunvold	$8		$40	
Roy Tarpley	$10		$40	
Brian Taylor	$8		$40	
Tom Thacker	$8		$40	
Reggie Theus	$15		$50	
LaSalle Thompson	$8		$40	
Mychal Thompson	$10		$40	
Rod Thorn	$8		$40	
Otis Thorpe	$15		$50	
Sedale Threatt	$12		$40	
Wayman Tisdale	$12		$40	
Rudy Tomjanovich	$20		$60	
Andrew Toney	$12		$40	
Kelly Tripucka	$12		$40	
Trent Tucker	$10		$40	
Mel Turpin	$8		$40	
Dave Twardzik	$8		$40	
Darnell Valentine	$10		$40	
Dick Van Arsdale	$10		$40	
Tom Van Arsdale	$10		$40	
Jan Van Breda Kolff	$10		$40	
Norm Van Lier	$12		$40	
Kiki Vandeweghe	$15		$50	
Loy Vaught	$15		$50	
Danny Vranes	$8		$40	
Neal Walk	$8		$40	
Chet Walker	$15		$50	
Foots Walker	$8		$40	
Kenny Walker	$10		$40	
Wally Walker	$8		$40	
Rex Walters	$8		$40	
Kermit Washington	$10		$40	
Slick Watts	$15		$50	
Spud Webb	$20		$60	
Marvin Webster	$8		$40	
Scott Wedman	$8		$40	
Robert Weiss	$8		$40	
Bill Wennington	$12		$40	
Walt Wesley	$8		$40	
Mark West	$10		$40	
Paul Westphal	$15		$50	
Jo Jo White	$20	$40	$60	
Sidney Wicks	$12		$50	
Jamaal Wilkes	$20		$50	
Dominique Wilkins	$35		$125	
Gerald Wilkins	$12		$40	
Chuck Williams	$8		$40	
Buck Williams	$12		$40	
Gus Williams	$12		$40	
Herb Williams	$10		$40	
Hot Rod Williams	$8		$40	
Jayson Williams	$18		$50	
David Wingate	$8		$40	
Brian Winters	$8		$40	
Willie Wise	$15		$50	
Joe Wolf	$8		$40	
Al Wood	$8		$40	
Haywoode Workman	$8		$40	
Orlando Woolridge	$15		$50	

ACTIVE PLAYERS

Player	8x10 photo	Auth. photo	Ball	Auth. ball
S. Abdur-Rahim	$20		$50	
Courtney Alexander	$10		$40	
Ray Allen	$25		$80	
Derek Anderson	$15		$40	
Kenny Anderson	$20		$50	
Nick Anderson	$15		$50	
Greg Anthony	$15		$50	
Gilbert Arenas	$15		$50	
Darrell Armstrong	$15		$50	
Ron Artest	$20		$60	
Stacey Augmon	$15		$50	
Isaac Austin	$15		$50	
William Avery	$20		$50	
Jennifer Azzi	$15		$60	
Vin Baker	$30		$80	
Dana Barros	$15		$50	
Brent Barry	$15		$50	
Jon Barry	$15		$50	
Tony Battie	$15		$50	
Shane Battier	$25		$60	
Travis Best	$15		$50	
Mike Bibby	$30		$75	
Chauncy Billups	$15		$50	
Mookie Blaylock	$20		$50	
Carlos Boozer	$20		$50	
Shawn Bradley	$15		$50	
Elton Brand	$30	$75	$60	
Terrell Brandon	$20		$50	
Dee Brown	$15		$50	
Kwame Brown	$15		$50	

Player	8x10 photo	Auth. photo	Ball	Auth. ball
Kobe Bryant	$75	$220	$150	$500
Jud Buechler	$10		$40	
Caron Butler	$15		$50	
Jason Caffey	$10		$40	

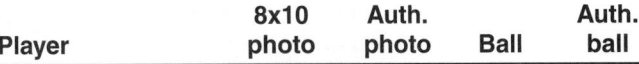

Player	8x10 photo	Auth. photo	Ball	Auth. ball

Mounted Memories Photo

Player	8x10 photo	Auth. photo	Ball	Auth. ball
Marcus Camby	$25		$60	$130
Elden Campbell	$15		$50	

Mounted Memories Photo

Player	8x10 photo	Auth. photo	Ball	Auth. ball
Vince Carter	$50	$140	$150	$350
Sam Cassell	$20		$60	
Calbert Cheaney	$15		$50	
Chris Childs	$15		$50	
Doug Christie	$15		$50	

Mounted Memories Photo

Player	8x10 photo	Auth. photo	Ball	Auth. ball
Keon Clark	$15	$30	$50	
Mateen Cleaves	$15		$50	
Derrick Coleman	$15		$90	
Bimbo Coles	$15		$50	
Austin Croshere	$15		$50	
Del Curry	$12		$40	

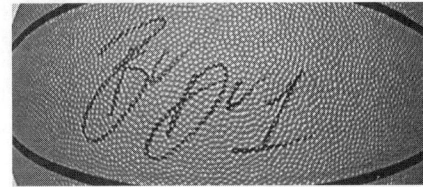

Steiner Sports Photo

Player	8x10 photo	Auth. photo	Ball	Auth. ball
Baron Davis	$15		$50	

Player	8x10 photo	Auth. photo	Ball	Auth. ball
Dale Davis	$15		$50	
Hubert Davis	$15		$50	
Tony Delk	$15		$50	
Vinny Del Negro	$15		$50	
Vlade Divac	$20		$60	
Juan Dixon	$25		$60	
Chris Dudley	$15		$50	

Player	8x10 photo	Auth. photo	Ball	Auth. ball
Tim Duncan	$50		$150	
Mike Dunleavy	$20		$50	
Laphonso Ellis	$15		$50	
Melvin Ely	$10		$40	
Danny Ferry	$15		$50	
Michael Finley	$20		$60	
Danny Fortson	$20		$60	
Rick Fox	$25		$60	
Steve Francis	$30	$100	$75	$330
Kevin Garnett	$50		$150	$350
Chris Gatling	$15		$50	
Matt Geiger	$15		$50	
Kendall Gill	$15		$50	
Drew Gooden	$15		$50	
Brian Grant	$15		$50	
Horace Grant	$20		$60	
Tom Gugliotta	$20		$60	
A.J. Guyton	$20		$50	
Marcus Haislip	$15		$50	
Richard Hamilton	$20		$60	
Anfernee Hardaway	$25	$45	$75	
Tim Hardaway	$20	$45	$60	
Matt Harpring	$15		$50	
Al Harrington	$15		$50	
Othella Harrington	$15		$50	
Nene Hilario	$15		$50	
Grant Hill	$40		$100	
Tyrone Hill	$15		$50	
C. Holdsclaw	$30		$75	
Robert Horry	$20	$50	$60	
Alan Houston	$15		$50	
Juwan Howard	$25		$60	
Larry Hughes	$15		$50	
Zydrunas Ilgauskas	$15		$50	
Allen Iverson	$50	$90	$160	
Jimmy Jackson	$15		$50	
Mark Jackson	$15		$50	
LeBron James	$50		$175	$650
Antawn Jamison	$15		$50	
Richard Jefferson	$50		$130	
Jared Jeffries	$15		$50	
Avery Johnson	$15		$50	
Ervin Johnson	$15	$100	$50	$550
Eddie Jones	$20		$50	
Popeye Jones	$15		$50	
Shawn Kemp	$25		$60	

Player	8x10 photo	Auth. photo	Ball	Auth. ball
Steve Kerr	$15		$50	

Steiner Sports Photo

Player	8x10 photo	Auth. photo	Ball	Auth. ball
Jason Kidd	$40	$110	$80	$250
Kerry Kittles	$15		$50	
Brevin Knight	$12	$30	$75	
Travis Knight	$15		$50	
Toni Kukoc	$20		$50	
Christian Laettner	$25		$60	
Raef LaFrentz	$15		$50	
Trajan Langdon	$15	$20	$50	
Lisa Leslie	$15		$50	
Rebecca Lobo	$20		$50	
Felipe Lopez	$15		$50	
George Lynch	$15		$50	
Corey Maggette	$15		$50	

Steiner Sports Photo

Player	8x10 photo	Auth. photo	Ball	Auth. ball
Karl Malone	$40	$130	$100	$250
Danny Manning	$25		$75	
Stephon Marbury	$25		$80	
Donyell Marshall	$20		$60	
Jamal Mashburn	$25		$70	
Anthony Mason	$15		$50	
Walter McCarty	$15		$50	
Nikki McCray	$15		$50	

Mounted Memories Photo

Player	8x10 photo	Auth. photo	Ball	Auth. ball
Antonio McDyess	$20	$40	$60	$145
Tracy McGrady	$50	$200	$100	$350
Aaron McKie	$15		$50	
Ron Mercer	$15		$50	

Player	8x10 photo	Auth. photo	Ball	Auth. ball
Darius Miles	$15		$50	

Steiner Sports Photo

Player	8x10 photo	Auth. photo	Ball	Auth. ball
Reggie Miller	$40	$100	$200	

Mounted Memories Photo

Player	8x10 photo	Auth. photo	Ball	Auth. ball
Yao Ming	$40		$100	$250
Eric Montross	$15		$50	
Hanno Mottola	$15		$50	
Alonzo Mourning	$30	$60	$80	$190
Dikembe Mutombo	$20		$75	
Johnny Newman	$12		$50	
Dirk Nowitzki	$30		$80	
Charles Oakley	$15		$50	
Lamar Odom	$15		$50	
Michael Olowokandi	$25		$75	

Steiner Sports Photo

Player	8x10 photo	Auth. photo	Ball	Auth. ball
Jermaine O'Neal	$25	$50	$60	$155

Steiner Sports Photo

Player	8x10 photo	Auth. photo	Ball	Auth. ball
Shaquille O'Neal	$75	$225	$175	$475
Greg Ostertag	$15		$50	
Bo Outlaw	$15		$50	

Player	8x10 photo	Auth. photo	Ball	Auth. ball
Tony Parker	$25		$60	
Cherokee Parks	$15		$50	
Gary Payton	$25		$75	
Anthony Peeler	$15		$50	
Ticha Penicheiro	$20		$50	
Wesley Person	$15		$50	

Steiner Sports Photo

Player	8x10 photo	Auth. photo	Ball	Auth. ball
Paul Pierce	$30	$80	$75	$140
Scottie Pippen	$50		$125	
Terry Porter	$15		$50	
Tayshaun Prince	$15		$50	
Theo Ratliff	$15		$50	
Glen Rice	$20		$60	
Quentin Richardson	$15		$50	
Mitch Richmond	$20		$60	
Isaiah Rider	$15		$50	
Cliff Robinson	$15		$50	

Steiner Sports Photo

Player	8x10 photo	Auth. photo	Ball	Auth. ball
Glenn Robinson	$15		$50	
Rodney Rodgers	$15		$50	
Jalen Rose	$20		$60	
Kareem Rush	$15		$50	
Byron Russell	$15		$50	
Brian Shaw	$15		$50	
Joe Smith	$20		$50	
Steve Smith	$15		$50	
Latrell Sprewell	$30		$75	
Jerry Stackhouse	$35		$75	
Dawn Staley	$25		$60	
John Starks	$15	$30	$50	$100
Damon Stoudamire	$20		$60	
Amare Stoudemire	$35		$75	
Rod Strickland	$20		$50	
Bob Sura	$15		$50	
Sheryl Swoopes	$15		$50	
Wally Szczerbiak	$20	$45	$60	
Jason Terry	$15		$50	
Kenny Thomas	$15		$50	
Kurt Thomas	$15		$50	
Tim Thomas	$15		$50	
Otis Thorpe	$20		$60	
Robert Traylor	$20		$60	
Nikoloz Tskitishvili	$15		$50	

Player	8x10 photo	Auth. photo	Ball	Auth. ball

Mounted Memories Photo

Player	8x10 photo	Auth. photo	Ball	Auth. ball
Nick Van Exel	$25	$40	$60	$145

Mounted Memories Photo

Keith Van Horn	$30		$75	
Jacque Vaughn	$20		$60	
Antoine Walker	$20		$100	
Samaki Walker	$20		$60	
Ben Wallace	$25		$60	
John Wallace	$15		$50	
Rasheed Wallace	$30		$75	
Zhi Zhi Wang	$15		$50	

Steiner Sports Photo

Charlie Ward	$18	$80	$75	
C. Weatherspoon	$15		$50	
Chris Webber	$40		$80	
Bonzi Wells	$20		$60	
Jason Williams	$30		$75	
Jay Williams	$30		$75	
Scott Williams	$15		$50	
Walt Williams	$15		$50	
Corliss Williamson	$15		$50	
Kevin Willis	$15		$50	
Vincent Yarbrough	$15		$50	

FOOTBALL AUTOGRAPHS
PRO FOOTBALL HALL OF FAMERS

Herb Adderley (1939-)   **1980**

Football..$85
Helmet..$180
Mini-Helmet...$40
Cut signature...$5
Goal Line Art..$15
8x10 photograph...................................$15

George Allen (1918-1990)   **2002**

Football.................................$300-$800
Helmet...Unknown
Mini-Helmet..............................Unknown
Cut signature.........................$75-$250
Goal Line Art.............................Unknown
8x10 photograph...................$150-$500

Marcus Allen (1960-)   **2003**

Mounted Memories Photo

Football..$125
Helmet..$250
Mini-Helmet...$75
Cut signature.......................................$10
Goal Line Art.................................$35-$80
8x10 photograph...................................$40

Lance Alworth (1940-)   **1978**

Football..$125
Helmet..$225
Mini-Helmet...$75
Cut signature.......................................$10
Goal Line Art..$45
8x10 photograph...................................$30

Doug Atkins (1930-)   **1982**

Football..$85
Helmet..$180
Mini-Helmet...$40
Cut signature...$6
Goal Line Art..$15
8x10 photograph...................................$20

Morris "Red" Badgro (1902-1998)   **1981**

Football.................................$100-$135
Helmet..$190
Mini-Helmet...$70
Cut signature...$5
Goal Line Art..$25
8x10 photograph...................................$40

Lem Barney (1945-)   **1992**

Football..$85
Helmet..$180
Mini-Helmet...$40
Cut signature...$5
Goal Line Art..$15
8x10 photograph...................................$15

Cliff Battles (1910-1981)   **1968**

Football..Unknown
Helmet..Unknown
Mini-Helmet...................................Unknown

Cut signature.......................................$75
Goal Line Art........................... Impossible
8x10 photograph.....................$200-$250

Sammy Baugh (1914-)   **1963**

Football..$150
Helmet..$250
Mini-Helmet...$85
Cut signature.......................................$10
Goal Line Art..$50
8x10 photograph...................................$35

Chuck Bednarik (1925-)   **1967**

Football.............................. $75-$100
Helmet............................... $180-$200
Mini-Helmet...$40
Cut signature...$5
Goal Line Art..$15
8x10 photograph...................................$20

Bert Bell (1895-1959)   **1963**

Football..Unknown
Helmet..Unknown
Mini-Helmet...................................Unknown
Cut signature......................................$125
Goal Line Art........................... Impossible
8x10 photograph..................................$400

Bobby Bell (1940-)   **1983**

Football..$85
Helmet..$180
Mini-Helmet...$40
Cut signature...$5
Goal Line Art..$15
8x10 photograph...................................$18

Raymond Berry (1933-)   **1973**

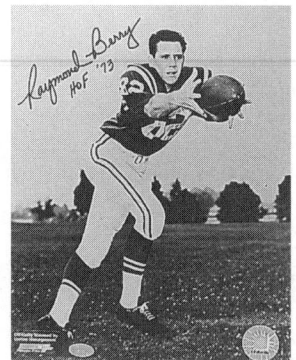

Mounted Memories Photo

Football..$85
Helmet..$180
Mini-Helmet...$40
Cut signature...$5
Goal Line Art..$20
8x10 photograph...................................$18

Elvin Bethea (1946-)   **2003**

Football..$85
Helmet............................... $180-$200
Mini-Helmet...$45
Cut signature...$5
Goal Line Art..$25
8x10 photograph...................................$25

Charles Bidwill (1895-1947)   **1967**

Football..Unknown
Helmet..Unknown
Mini-Helmet...................................Unknown
Cut signature.........................$500-$700
Goal Line Art........................... Impossible
8x10 photograph...........................Unknown

Fred Biletnikoff (1943-)   **1988**

Mounted Memories Photo

Football.................................$75-$110
Helmet............................... $180-$200
Mini-Helmet...$50
Cut signature.......................................$10
Goal Line Art..$25
8x10 photograph...................................$25

George Blanda (1927-)   **1981**

Mounted Memories Photo

Football.................................$75-$125
Helmet............................... $180-$225
Mini-Helmet...............................$60-$95
Cut signature.......................................$10
Goal Line Art...........................$25-$50
8x10 photograph.....................$25-$40

Mel Blount (1948-)   **1989**

Football..$85
Helmet..$200
Mini-Helmet...$50
Cut signature...$5

Mounted Memories Photo

Goal Line Art $25
8x10 photograph $20
Terry Bradshaw (1948-)   **1989**

Steiner Sports Photo

Football.. $125-$200
Authenticated Football............................$275
Helmet... $250-$300
Authenticated Helmet $600
Mini-Helmet .... $75-$125
Authenticated Mini-Helmet $300
Cut signature $10
Goal Line Art .... $50-$75
8x10 photograph $60
Authenticated 8x10 photograph $180
Jim Brown (1936-)   **1971**

Mounted Memories Photo

Football... $150-$300
Helmet... $250-$300
Mini-Helmet .... $100-$125
Cut signature $10
Goal Line Art $70
8x10 photograph $80
Paul Brown (1908-1991)   **1967**

Football... $300-$350
Helmet...Unknown
Mini-Helmet ....Unknown
Cut signature $25
Goal Line Art .... $100-$150
8x10 photograph $75

Roosevelt Brown (1932-)   **1975**

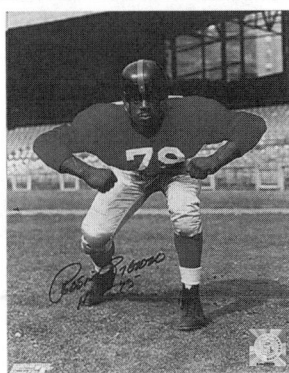

Mounted Memories Photo

Football..$85
Helmet..$180
Mini-Helmet $40
Cut signature $10
Goal Line Art $15
8x10 photograph $15
Willie Brown (1940-)   **1984**

Football..$85
Helmet..$180
Mini-Helmet $40
Cut signature $6
Goal Line Art $20
8x10 photograph $15
Buck Buchanan (1940-1992)   **1990**

Football.. $200-$250
Helmet...Unknown
Mini-Helmet ....Unknown
Cut signature $20
Goal Line Art $75
8x10 photograph $60
Nick Buoniconti (1940-)   **2001**

Football.. $75-$110
Helmet... $180-$225
Mini-Helmet $60
Cut signature $5
Goal Line Art $40
8x10 photograph $25
Dick Butkus (1942-)   **1979**

Mounted Memories Photo

Football.. $125-$150
Helmet... $225-$250
Mini-Helmet .... $50-$75
Cut signature $10
Goal Line Art $40
8x10 photograph $30
Earl Campbell (1955-)   **1991**

Football.. $100-$125
Authenticated football............................$240
Helmet... $200-$225
Mini-Helmet $60
Cut signature $10
Goal Line Art $35

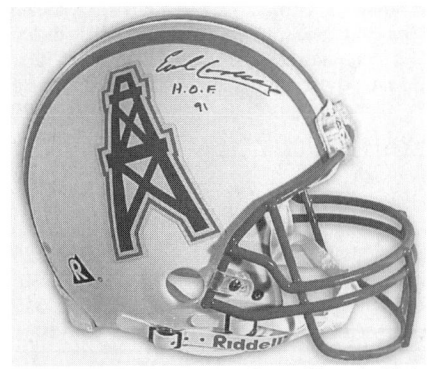

Mounted Memories Photo

8x10 photograph $30
Authenticated 8x10 photograph $85
Tony Canadeo (1919-)   **1974**

Football..$85
Helmet..$180
Mini-Helmet $50
Cut signature $4
Goal Line Art $20
8x10 photograph $20
Joe Carr (1880-1939)   **1963**

Football...Unknown
Helmet...Unknown
Mini-Helmet ....Unknown
Cut signature ....Unknown
Goal Line Art .... Impossible
8x10 photograph .... $750-$1,000
Dave Casper (1951-)   **2002**

Football..$85
Helmet... $180-$200
Mini-Helmet $50
Cut signature $5
Goal Line Art $35
8x10 photograph $20
Guy Chamberlin (1894-1967)   **1965**

Football...Unknown
Helmet...Unknown
Mini-Helmet ....Unknown
Cut signature .... $200-$600
Goal Line Art .... Impossible
8x10 photograph ....Unknown
Jack Christiansen (1928-1986)   **1970**

Football...Unknown
Helmet...Unknown
Mini-Helmet ....Unknown
Cut signature .... $40-$100
Goal Line Art .... Impossible
8x10 photograph .... $250-$350
Dutch Clark (1906-1978)   **1963**

Football...Unknown
Helmet...Unknown
Mini-Helmet ....Unknown
Cut signature .... $50-$100
Goal Line Art .... Impossible
8x10 photograph .... $300-$400
George Connor (1925-)   **1975**

Football..$85
Helmet..$180
Mini-Helmet $50
Cut signature $6
Goal Line Art $25
8x10 photograph $20
Jimmy Conzelman (1898-1970)   **1964**

Football...Unknown

Helmet ....Unknown
Mini-Helmet ....Unknown
Cut signature ....$150-$200
Goal Line Art ....Impossible
8x10 photograph $500
Lou Creekmur (1927-)   **1996**

Football...$80
Helmet..$180
Mini-Helmet $40
Cut signature $5
Goal Line Art $15
8x10 photograph $10
Larry Csonka (1946-)   **1987**

Mounted Memories Photo

Football............................... $85-$150
Helmet .... $200-$225
Mini-Helmet .... $60-$75
Cut signature $6
Goal Line Art $40
8x10 photograph $40
Al Davis (1929-)   **1992**

Football...$300
Helmet .... $350-$500
Mini-Helmet .... $150-$250
Cut signature $50
Goal Line Art .... $150-$200
8x10 photograph $150
Willie Davis (1934-)   **1981**

Football............................... $75-$85
Helmet .... $180-$200
Mini-Helmet $50
Cut signature $7
Goal Line Art $20
8x10 photograph $20
Len Dawson (1935-)   **1987**

Mounted Memories Photo

Football............................... $75-$125
Helmet .... $180-$200
Mini-Helmet $50
Cut signature $8
Goal Line Art $25
8x10 photograph $25
Joe DeLamielleure (1951-)   **2003**

Football............................... $75-$85
Helmet .... $180-$200

Mini-Helmet $45
Cut signature $5
Goal Line Art $30
8x10 photograph $25
Eric Dickerson (1960-)   **1999**

Mounted Memories Photo

Football...$90
Helmet .... $200-$275
Mini-Helmet $60
Authenticated Mini-Helmet $140
Cut signature $5
Goal Line Art $35
8x10 photograph $25
Dan Dierdorf (1949-)   **1996**

Football...$90
Helmet 180
Mini-Helmet $60
Cut signature $5
Goal Line Art $30
8x10 photograph $20
Mike Ditka (1939-)   **1988**

Mounted Memories Photo

Football...$125
Helmet..$225
Mini-Helmet .... $50-$75
Cut signature $10
Goal Line Art $30
8x10 photograph $30
Art Donovan (1925-)   **1968**

Mounted Memories Photo

Football...$85
Helmet..$200
Mini-Helmet $40
Cut signature $7
Goal Line Art $20
8x10 photograph $20
Tony Dorsett (1954-)   **1994**

Football............................... $85-$100
Authenticated Football...........................$125
Helmet .... $200-$225
Mini-Helmet $60
Cut signature $3
Goal Line Art $40
8x10 photograph $30
Authenticated 8x10 photograph $50
Paddy Driscoll (1896-1968)   **1965**

Football...Unknown
Helmet...Unknown
Mini-Helmet ....Unknown
Cut signature .... $200-$250
Goal Line Art .... Impossible
8x10 photograph ....Unknown
Bill Dudley (1921-)   **1966**

Football...$75
Helmet..$170
Mini-Helmet $40
Cut signature $6
Goal Line Art $20
8x10 photograph $20
Turk Edwards (1907-1973)   **1969**

Football...Unknown
Helmet...Unknown
Mini-Helmet ....Unknown
Cut signature .... $100-$400
Goal Line Art .... Impossible
8x10 photograph .... $400-$1,000
Weeb Ewbank (1907-1998)   **1978**

Football...$125
Helmet .... $200-$250
Mini-Helmet $75
Cut signature $5
Goal Line Art $40
8x10 photograph $30
Tom Fears (1923-2000)   **1970**

Football............................... $75-$125
Helmet..$180
Mini-Helmet $60
Cut signature $10
Goal Line Art $25
8x10 photograph $45
Jim Finks (1904-1994)   **1995**

Football............................... $300-$500
Helmet...Unknown
Mini-Helmet ....Unknown
Cut signature .... $75-$200
Goal Line Art .... Impossible
8x10 photograph .... $200-$300
Ray Flaherty (1904-1994)   **1976**

Football............................... $75-$200
Helmet...Unknown
Mini-Helmet ....Unknown
Cut signature $10
Goal Line Art .... $20-$40
8x10 photograph .... $25-$75
Len Ford (1926-1972)   **1976**

Football...Unknown
Helmet...Unknown

Mini-Helmet ....Unknown
Cut signature $400
Goal Line Art ....Impossible
8x10 photograph ....Unknown

Dan Fortmann (1916-1995)   **1965**

Football ....Unknown
Helmet ....Unknown
Mini-Helmet ....Unknown
Cut signature $25
Goal Line Art ....Impossible
8x10 photograph .... $125-$150

Dan Fouts (1951-)   **1993**

Football $150
Helmet $225
Mini-Helmet $60
Cut signature $5
Goal Line Art $35
8x10 photograph $30

Frank Gatski (1922-)   **1985**

Football $85
Helmet $180
Mini-Helmet $40
Cut signature $3
Goal Line Art $15
8x10 photograph $20

Bill George (1930-1982)   **1974**

Football ....Unknown
Helmet ....Unknown
Mini-Helmet ....Unknown
Cut signature .... $75-$200
Goal Line Art ....Impossible
8x10 photograph .... $300-$600

Joe Gibbs (1940-)   **1996**

Football .... $125-$150
Helmet ....$225-$250
Mini-Helmet $75
Cut signature $6
Goal Line Art $40
8x10 photograph .... $30-$60

Frank Gifford (1930-)   **1977**

Mounted Memories Photo

Football .... $125-$170
Authenticated Football $215
Helmet $235
Authenticated Helmet $375
Mini-Helmet $85
Cut signature $15
Goal Line Art $60
8x10 photograph $45

Sid Gillman (1911-2003)   **1983**

Football .... $75-$100
Helmet $180
Mini-Helmet $50

Cut signature $5
Goal Line Art $30
8x10 photograph $20

Otto Graham (1921-)   **1965**

Tri-Star Productions Photo

Football $125
Helmet .... $225-$250
Mini-Helmet $60
Cut signature $3
Goal Line Art $40
8x10 photograph .... $20-$40

Red Grange (1903-1991)   **1963**

Football .... $500-$600
Helmet ....Unknown
Mini-Helmet ....Unknown
Cut signature $50
Goal Line Art .... $150-$195
8x10 photograph .... $150-$200

Bud Grant (1927-)   **1994**

Football .... $75-$125
Helmet .... $180-$200
Mini-Helmet $60
Cut signature $3
Goal Line Art $35
8x10 photograph $25

Joe Greene (1946-)   **1987**

Football .... $85-$125
Helmet $200
Mini-Helmet $50
Cut signature $3
Goal Line Art $30
8x10 photograph $25

Forrest Gregg (1933-)   **1977**

Mounted Memories Photo

Football .... $75-$100
Helmet .... $180-$200
Mini-Helmet $50
Cut signature $9
Goal Line Art $35
8x10 photograph $25

Bob Griese (1945-)   **1990**

Mounted Memories Photo

Football $125
Helmet $220
Mini-Helmet $60
Cut signature $7
Goal Line Art $35
8x10 photograph $25

Lou Groza (1924-2000)   **1974**

Football .... $75-$100
Helmet .... $180-$210
Mini-Helmet $50
Cut signature $6
Goal Line Art $35
8x10 photograph $25

Joe Guyon (1892-1971)   **1966**

Football ....Unknown
Helmet ....Unknown
Mini-Helmet ....Unknown
Cut signature .... $150-$400
Goal Line Art ....Impossible
8x10 photograph .... $400-$1,000

George Halas (1895-1983)   **1963**

Football ....Unknown
Helmet ....Unknown
Mini-Helmet ....Unknown
Cut signature .... $50-$75
Goal Line Art ....Impossible
8x10 photograph .... $200-$300

Jack Ham (1948-)   **1988**

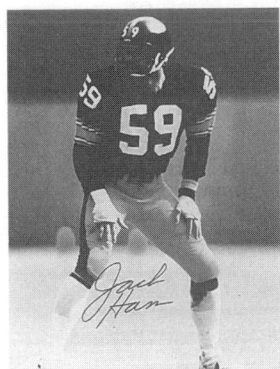

Mounted Memories Photo

Football .... $75-$100
Helmet $200
Authenticated Helmet $400
Mini-Helmet $45
Cut signature $3
Goal Line Art $25
8x10 photograph $20

Dan Hampton (1957-)   **2002**

Football $85
Helmet $190
Mini-Helmet $50

Cut signature $5
Goal Line Art $30
8x10 photograph $20

John Hannah (1951-)   1991

Football.....................................$75-$100
Helmet ....$180-$225
Mini-Helmet $60
Cut signature $6
Goal Line Art $35
8x10 photograph $30

Franco Harris (1950-)   1990

Mounted Memories Photo

Football...................................$100-$150
Authenticated Football.........................$200
Helmet ....$225-$300
Authenticated Helmet $375
Mini-Helmet .... $60-$90
Cut signature $10
Goal Line Art $60
8x10 photograph $40
Authenticated 8x10 photograph $110

Mike Haynes (1953-)   1997

Football...$75
Helmet $180
Mini-Helmet $40
Cut signature $7
Goal Line Art $30
8x10 photograph $18

Ed Healey (1894-1978)   1964

Football.....................................Unknown
Helmet ....Unknown
Mini-Helmet ....Unknown
Cut signature $60
Goal Line Art ....Impossible
8x10 photograph .... $150-$250

Mel Hein (1909-1992)   1963

Football.....................................Unknown
Helmet ....Unknown
Mini-Helmet ....Unknown
Cut signature $20
Goal Line Art ....Impossible
8x10 photograph ....$50-$100

Ted Hendricks (1947-)   1990

Football...$85
Helmet $180
Mini-Helmet $40
Cut signature $10
Goal Line Art $20
8x10 photograph $25

Pete Henry (1897-1952)   1963

Football.....................................Unknown
Helmet ....Unknown
Mini-Helmet ....Unknown
Cut signature $300

Goal Line Art ....Impossible
8x10 photograph $600

Arnie Herber (1910-1969)   1966

Football.....................................Unknown
Helmet ....Unknown
Mini-Helmet ....Unknown
Cut signature ....$250-$400
Goal Line Art ....Impossible
8x10 photograph ....Unknown

Bill Hewitt (1909-1947)   1971

Football.....................................Unknown
Helmet ....Unknown
Mini-Helmet ....Unknown
Cut signature ....$400-$750
Goal Line Art ....Impossible
8x10 photograph ....Unknown

Clarke Hinkle (1909-1988)   1964

Football.....................................Unknown
Helmet ....Unknown
Mini-Helmet ....Unknown
Cut signature .... $25-$75
Goal Line Art ....Impossible
8x10 photograph ....$200-$350

Elroy Hirsch (1923-)   1968

Football............................... $85-$125
Helmet ....$200-$225
Mini-Helmet $50
Cut signature $5
Goal Line Art $15
8x10 photograph $20

Paul Hornung (1935-)   1986

Steiner Sports Photo

Football.......................................$85-$125
Helmet ....$200-$225
Authenticated Helmet $275
Mini-Helmet $50
Cut signature $5
Goal Line Art $25
8x10 photograph $20
Authenticated 8x10 photograph $25

Ken Houston (1944-)   1986

Football...$85
Helmet $180
Mini-Helmet $40
Cut signature $4
Goal Line Art $20
8x10 photograph $15

Cal Hubbard (1900-1977)   1963

Football.....................................Unknown
Helmet ....Unknown
Mini-Helmet ....Unknown
Cut signature $65
Goal Line Art ....Impossible
8x10 photograph .... $250-$400

Sam Huff (1934-)   1982

Mounted Memories Photo

Football....................................$85-$100
Helmet $200
Mini-Helmet $50
Cut signature $3
Goal Line Art $30
8x10 photograph $30

Lamar Hunt (1932-)   1972

Football....................................$85-$150
Helmet ....$200-$250
Mini-Helmet ....$60-$100
Cut signature $8
Goal Line Art .... $25-$60
8x10 photograph $40

Don Hutson (1913-1997)   1963

Football................................. $200-$250
Helmet $300
Mini-Helmet ....$125-$175
Cut signature $15
Goal Line Art .... $60-$125
8x10 photograph .... $75-$100

Jimmy Johnson (1938-)   1994

Football.................................. $75-$100
Helmet $180
Mini-Helmet $40
Cut signature $3
Goal Line Art $25
8x10 photograph $20

John Henry Johnson (1929-)   1987

Football...$85
Helmet ....$180-$200
Mini-Helmet $40
Cut signature $7
Goal Line Art $20
8x10 photograph $15

Charlie Joiner (1947-)   1996

Football...$85
Helmet $180
Mini-Helmet $40
Cut signature $5
Goal Line Art $15
8x10 photograph $18

Deacon Jones (1938-)   1980

Football.................................. $75-$100
Helmet ....$180-$200
Mini-Helmet $45
Cut signature $6
Goal Line Art $20
8x10 photograph $15

Stan Jones (1931-)   1991

Football...$85
Helmet $180

Mini-Helmet $40
Cut signature $3
Goal Line Art $20
8x10 photograph $15

Henry Jordan (1935-1976)   **1995**

Football..............................Unknown
Helmet...............................Unknown
Mini-Helmet ....Unknown
Cut signature $200
Goal Line Art ....Impossible
8x10 photograph ....Unknown

Sonny Jurgensen (1934-)   **1983**

Mounted Memories Photo

Football........................... $85-$125
Helmet............................. $200-$235
Mini-Helmet $60
Cut signature $5
Goal Line Art $35
8x10 photograph $40

Jim Kelly (1960-)   **2002**

Mounted Memories Photo

Football........................... $100-$135
Helmet.....................................$225
Mini-Helmet $90
Cut signature $10
Goal Line Art $65
8x10 photograph $40

Leroy Kelly (1942-)   **1994**

Football.....................................$85
Helmet.....................................$200
Mini-Helmet $40
Cut signature $3
Goal Line Art $15
8x10 photograph $15

Walt Kiesling (1903-1962)   **1966**

Football..............................Unknown
Helmet...............................Unknown
Mini-Helmet ....Unknown
Cut signature .... $200-$700
Goal Line Art ....Impossible
8x10 photograph .... $500-$1,500

Frank "Bruiser" Kinard (1914-1985)   **1971**

Football..............................Unknown

Helmet...............................Unknown
Mini-Helmet ....Unknown
Cut signature .... $50-$150
Goal Line Art ....Impossible
8x10 photograph .... $250-$600

Paul Krause (1942-)   **1998**

Football.....................................$85
Helmet............................. $180-$200
Mini-Helmet $50
Cut signature $3
Goal Line Art $25
8x10 photograph $15

Curly Lambeau (1898-1965)   **1963**

Football..............................Unknown
Helmet...............................Unknown
Mini-Helmet ....Unknown
Cut signature .... $500-$750
Goal Line Art ....Impossible
8x10 photograph ....Unknown

Jack Lambert (1952-)   **1990**

Football........................... $100-$150
Helmet............................. $225-$250
Mini-Helmet $75
Cut signature $5
Goal Line Art $40
8x10 photograph $30

Tom Landry (1924-2000)   **1990**

Football........................... $200-$250
Helmet.....................................$350
Mini-Helmet $125
Cut signature $15
Goal Line Art .... $75-$125
8x10 photograph .... $50-$85

Dick Lane (1928-2002)   **1974**

Football...................................$100
Helmet............................. $200-$225
Mini-Helmet $60
Cut signature $5
Goal Line Art $25
8x10 photograph $20

Jim Langer (1948-)   **1987**

Mounted Memories Photo

Football.....................................$85
Helmet.....................................$180
Mini-Helmet $40
Cut signature $8
Goal Line Art $20
8x10 photograph $15

Willie Lanier (1945-)   **1986**

Football.....................................$85
Helmet.....................................$180
Mini-Helmet $40
Cut signature $3
Goal Line Art $20
8x10 photograph $15

Steve Largent (1954-)   **1995**

Mounted Memories Photo

Football.................................. $85-$125
Helmet................................. $200-$225
Authenticated Helmet $400
Mini-Helmet .... $50-$75
Cut signature $8
Goal Line Art $45
8x10 photograph $35

Yale Lary (1930-)   **1979**

Football.....................................$85
Helmet.....................................$180
Mini-Helmet $40
Cut signature $3
Goal Line Art $15
8x10 photograph $15

Dante Lavelli (1923-)   **1975**

Football.....................................$85
Helmet.....................................$180
Mini-Helmet $40
Cut signature $3
Goal Line Art $15
8x10 photograph $15

Bobby Layne (1926-1986)   **1967**

Football........................... $500-$750
Helmet...............................Unknown
Mini-Helmet ....Unknown
Cut signature $50
Goal Line Art ....Impossible
8x10 photograph .... $175-$225

Tuffy Leemans (1912-1979)   **1978**

Football..............................Unknown
Helmet...............................Unknown
Mini-Helmet ....Unknown
Cut signature .... $100-$150
Goal Line Art ....Impossible
8x10 photograph .... $250-$600

Marv Levy (1928-)   **2001**

Football........................... $75-$100
Helmet............................. $180-$200
Mini-Helmet $50
Cut signature $6
Goal Line Art $30
8x10 photograph $25

Bob Lilly (1939-)   **1980**

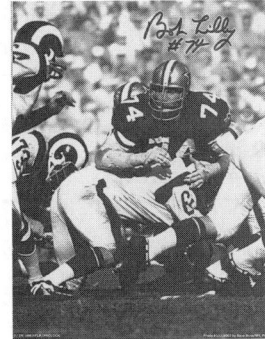

Mounted Memories Photo

Football..$85-$100
Helmet...$200
Mini-Helmet...$45
Cut signature..$3
Goal Line Art...$20
8x10 photograph.......................................$15

Larry Little (1945-) — 1993

Football..$85
Helmet...$180
Mini-Helmet...$40
Cut signature..$5
Goal Line Art...$15
8x10 photograph.......................................$15

James Lofton (1956-) — 2003

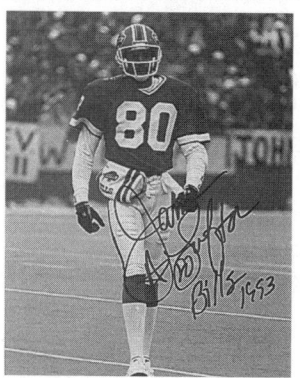

Mounted Memories Photo

Football..$85
Helmet...$200
Mini-Helmet...$50
Cut signature..$5
Goal Line Art...$35
8x10 photograph.......................................$25

Vince Lombardi (1913-1970) — 1971

Football..Unknown
Helmet...Unknown
Mini-Helmet.....................................Unknown
Cut signature.................................$125-$200
Goal Line Art.................................Impossible
8x10 photograph........................$500-$750

Howie Long (1960-) — 2000

Mounted Memories Photo

Football..$85-$150
Helmet...$200-$250
Mini-Helmet..................................$50-$85
Cut signature..$10
Goal Line Art...............................$20-$60
8x10 photograph.......................$25-$40

Ronnie Lott (1959-) — 2000

Football.......................................$100-$125
Helmet...$170-$250
Mini-Helmet...$75
Cut signature..$6
Goal Line Art...$50
8x10 photograph.......................................$40

Sid Luckman (1916-1998) — 1965

Football.......................................$125-$150
Helmet...$250-$275
Mini-Helmet..................................$85-$100
Cut signature..$15
Goal Line Art...$40
8x10 photograph.......................................$75

Link Lyman (1898-1972) — 1964

Football..Unknown
Helmet...Unknown
Mini-Helmet.....................................Unknown
Cut signature.................................$125-$250
Goal Line Art.................................Impossible
8x10 photograph........................$400-$750

Tom Mack (1943-) — 1999

Football..$85
Helmet...$150
Mini-Helmet...$40
Cut signature..$4
Goal Line Art...$25
8x10 photograph.......................................$15

John Mackey (1941-) — 1992

Football..$85
Helmet...$180
Mini-Helmet...$40
Cut signature..$3
Goal Line Art...$20
8x10 photograph.......................................$15

Tim Mara (1887-1959) — 1963

Football..Unknown
Helmet...Unknown
Mini-Helmet.....................................Unknown
Cut signature.................................$500-$600
Goal Line Art.................................Impossible
8x10 photograph..........................Unknown

Wellington Mara (1916-) — 1997

Football...$75-$100
Helmet...$180-$225
Mini-Helmet...$50
Cut signature..$5
Goal Line Art...$20
8x10 photograph.......................................$20

Gino Marchetti (1927-) — 1972

Mounted Memories Photo

Football..$85
Helmet...$180
Mini-Helmet...$40
Cut signature..$3
Goal Line Art...$20
8x10 photograph.......................................$15

George P. Marshall (1887-1969) — 1963

Football..Unknown
Helmet...Unknown

Mini-Helmet.....................................Unknown
Cut signature.................................$400-$600
Goal Line Art.................................Impossible
8x10 photograph..........................Unknown

Ollie Matson (1930-) — 1972

Football..$100
Helmet...$200
Mini-Helmet...$50
Cut signature..$5
Goal Line Art...$30
8x10 photograph.......................................$25

Don Maynard (1935-) — 1987

Mounted Memories Photo

Football..$100
Helmet...$200
Mini-Helmet...$45
Cut signature..$7
Goal Line Art...$25
8x10 photograph.......................................$15

George McAfee (1918-) — 1966

Football..$85
Helmet...$180
Mini-Helmet...$45
Cut signature..$7
Goal Line Art...$20
8x10 photograph.......................................$15

Mike McCormack (1930-) — 1984

Football..$85
Helmet...$180
Mini-Helmet...$40
Cut signature..$5
Goal Line Art...$15
8x10 photograph.......................................$15

Tommy McDonald (1934-) — 1998

Football..$85
Helmet...$180
Mini-Helmet...$40
Cut signature..$6
Goal Line Art...$20
8x10 photograph.......................................$15

Hugh McElhenny (1928-) — 1970

Football...$75-$100
Helmet...$180-$200
Mini-Helmet...$40
Cut signature..$5
Goal Line Art...$25
8x10 photograph.......................................$20

John McNally (1903-1985) — 1963

Football..Unknown
Helmet...Unknown
Mini-Helmet.....................................Unknown
Cut signature.................................$100-$400
Goal Line Art.................................Impossible
8x10 photograph..........................Unknown

Mike Michalske (1903-1983) — 1964

Football..Unknown
Helmet...Unknown

Mini-Helmet ....Unknown
Cut signature ....$50-$75
Goal Line Art ....Impossible
8x10 photograph $250

Wayne Millner (1913-1976)　　　**1968**

Football ....Unknown
Helmet ....Unknown
Mini-Helmet ....Unknown
Cut signature ....$75-$150
Goal Line Art ....Impossible
8x10 photograph ....$300-$400

Bobby Mitchell (1935-)　　　**1983**

Football $85
Helmet $180
Mini-Helmet $50
Cut signature $3
Goal Line Art $25
8x10 photograph $20

Ron Mix (1938-)　　　**1979**

Football $85
Helmet $180
Mini-Helmet $40
Cut signature $6
Goal Line Art $20
8x10 photograph $15

Joe Montana (1956-)　　　**2000**

Mounted Memories Photo

Football ....$175-$200
Authenticated Football $400
Helmet ....$275-$300
Authenticated Helmet $550
Mini-Helmet ....$100-$125
Authenticated Mini-Helmet $300
Cut signature $20
Goal Line Art $85
8x10 photograph ....$50-$75
Authenticated 8x10 Photo $90

Lenny Moore (1933-)　　　**1975**

Football $85
Helmet $180
Mini-Helmet $40
Cut signature $7
Goal Line Art $20
8x10 photograph $15

Marion Motley (1920-1999)　　　**1968**

Football ....$100-$125
Helmet $225
Mini-Helmet ....$60-$75
Cut signature $5
Goal Line Art $40
8x10 photograph $30

Mike Munchak (1960-)　　　**2001**

Football $85
Helmet $180
Mini-Helmet $50
Cut signature $6
Goal Line Art $30
8x10 photograph $25

Anthony Munoz (1958-)　　　**1998**

Football $85
Helmet ....$180-$250
Mini-Helmet $50
Cut signature $3
Goal Line Art $20
8x10 ....$20

George Musso (1910-2000)　　　**1982**

Football ....$85-$100
Helmet ....$180-$200
Mini-Helmet $60
Cut signature $5
Goal Line Art $25
8x10 photograph ....$30-$50

Bronko Nagurski (1908-1990)　　　**1963**

Football ....$400-$600
Helmet ....Unknown
Mini-Helmet ....Unknown
Cut signature $50
Goal Line Art ....Impossible
8x10 photograph $150

Joe Namath (1943-)　　　**1985**

Mounted Memories Photo

Football ....$150-$225
Authenticated Football $550
Helmet ....$300-$400
Authenticated Helmet $600
Mini-Helmet ....$100-$150
Cut signature $20
Goal Line Art $75
8x10 photograph $60
Authenticated 8x10 photograph $230

Earle "Greasy" Neale (1891-1973)　　　**1969**

Football ....Unknown
Helmet ....Unknown
Mini-Helmet ....Unknown
Cut signature ....$100-$250
Goal Line Art ....Impossible
8x10 photograph ....Unknown

Ernie Nevers (1903-1976)　　　**1963**

Football ....Unknown
Helmet ....Unknown
Mini-Helmet ....Unknown
Cut signature $65
Goal Line Art ....Impossible
8x10 photograph ....$250-$350

Ozzie Newsome (1956-)　　　**1999**

Football $85
Helmet ....$200-$250
Mini-Helmet $50
Cut signature $5
Goal Line Art $20
8x10 photograph $20

Ray Nitschke (1936-1998)　　　**1978**

Football ....$150-$175
Helmet $300

Mini-Helmet ....$100-$125
Cut signature $10
Goal Line Art $60
8x10 photograph $40

Chuck Noll (1932-)　　　**1993**

Football $100
Helmet $180
Mini-Helmet $50
Cut signature $3
Goal Line Art $20
8x10 photograph $15

Leo Nomellini (1924-2000)　　　**1969**

Football $100
Helmet $180
Mini-Helmet $60
Cut signature $10
Goal Line Art $25
8x10 photograph $25

Merlin Olsen (1940-)　　　**1982**

Football ....$85-$125
Helmet $200
Mini-Helmet $60
Cut signature $7
Goal Line Art $40
8x10 photograph $30

Jim Otto (1938-)　　　**1980**

Mounted Memories Photo

Football $85
Helmet $180
Mini-Helmet $45
Cut signature $6
Goal Line Art $20
8x10 photograph $20

Steve Owen (1898-1964)　　　**1966**

Football ....Unknown
Helmet ....Unknown
Mini-Helmet ....Unknown
Cut signature ....$350-$600
Goal Line Art ....Impossible
8x10 photograph ....Unknown

Alan Page (1945-)　　　**1988**

Football ....$75-$100
Helmet ....$180-$200
Mini-Helmet $50
Cut signature $3
Goal Line Art $25
8x10 photograph $20

Ace Parker (1912-)　　　**1972**

Football $85
Helmet $180
Mini-Helmet $40
Cut signature $3
Goal Line Art $20
8x10 photograph $15

Jim Parker (1934-) — 1973

Football	$85
Helmet	$180
Mini-Helmet	$40
Cut signature	$3
Goal Line Art	$20
8x10 photograph	$15

Walter Payton (1954-1999) — 1993

Football	$250-$300
Helmet	$350-$400
Mini-Helmet	$175-$200
Cut signature	$30-$50
Goal Line Art	$125-$150
8x10 photograph	$75-$150
Authenticated 8x10 photograph	$200

Joe Perry (1927-) — 1969

Football	$100
Helmet	$200
Mini-Helmet	$40
Cut signature	$8
Goal Line Art	$25
8x10 photograph	$20

Pete Pihos (1923-) — 1970

Football	$85
Helmet	$180
Mini-Helmet	$40
Cut signature	$3
Goal Line Art	$20
8x10 photograph	$15

Hugh Ray (1884-1956) — 1966

Football	Unknown
Helmet	Unknown
Mini-Helmet	Unknown
Cut signature	$750-$1,000
Goal Line Art	Impossible
8x10 photograph	Unknown

Dan Reeves (1912-1971) — 1967

Football	Unknown
Helmet	Unknown
Mini-Helmet	Unknown
Cut signature	$500-$750
Goal Line Art	Impossible
8x10 photograph	Unknown

Mel Renfro (1941-) — 1996

Football	$85
Helmet	$180
Mini-Helmet	$40
Cut signature	$5
Goal Line Art	$20
8x10 photograph	$15

John Riggins (1949-) — 1992

Steiner Sports Photo

Football	$225-$300
Authenticated Football	$500
Helmet	$325-$400
Authenticated Helmet	$700
Mini-Helmet	$125-$175

Authenticated Mini-Helmet	$350
Cut signature	$20-$40
Goal Line Art	$150
8x10 photograph	$100

Jim Ringo (1931-) — 1981

Football	$85
Helmet	$180
Mini-Helmet	$40
Cut signature	$5
Goal Line Art	$20
8x10 photograph	$15

Andy Robustelli (1925-) — 1971

Football	$75-$100
Helmet	$200
Mini-Helmet	$50
Cut signature	$3
Goal Line Art	$20
8x10 photograph	$20

Art Rooney (1901-1988) — 1964

Football	Unknown
Helmet	Unknown
Mini-Helmet	Unknown
Cut signature	$50
Goal Line Art	Impossible
8x10 photograph	$100-$225

Dan Rooney (1932-) — 2000

Football	$75-$100
Helmet	$180-$200
Mini-Helmet	$40-$75
Cut signature	$5
Goal Line Art	$30
8x10 photograph	$25

Pete Rozelle (1926-1996) — 1985

Football	$250-$300
Helmet	Unknown
Mini-Helmet	$150-$200
Cut signature	$20-$75
Goal Line Art	$75-$150
8x10 photograph	$75-$150

Bob St. Clair (1931-) — 1990

Football	$75-$100
Helmet	$180
Mini-Helmet	$50
Cut signature	$6
Goal Line Art	$30
8x10 photograph	$20

Gale Sayers (1943-) — 1977

Mounted Memories Photo

Football	$125
Authenticated Football	$230
Helmet	$200-$250
Mini-Helmet	$50
Authenticated Mini-Helmet	$120
Cut signature	$7
Goal Line Art	$30
8x10 photograph	$25

Joe Schmidt (1932-) — 1973

Football	$85
Helmet	$180
Mini-Helmet	$40
Cut signature	$3
Goal Line Art	$20
8x10 photograph	$15

Tex Schramm (1920-) — 1991

Mounted Memories Photo

Football	$85
Helmet	$180
Mini-Helmet	$40
Cut signature	$6
Goal Line Art	$20
8x10 photograph	$15

Lee Roy Selmon (1954-) — 1995

Football	$85
Helmet	$180
Mini-Helmet	$50
Cut signature	$3
Goal Line Art	$20
8x10 photograph	$20

Billy Shaw (1938-) — 1999

Football	$85
Helmet	$175
Mini-Helmet	$40
Cut signature	$3
Goal Line Art	$20
8x10 photograph	$15

Art Shell (1946-) — 1989

Football	$100
Helmet	$180
Mini-Helmet	$60
Cut signature	$4
Goal Line Art	$35
8x10 photograph	$25

Don Shula (1930-) — 1997

Mounted Memories Photo

Football	$150
Helmet	$250
Mini-Helmet	$85
Cut signature	$15
Goal Line Art	$60
8x10 photograph	$40

O.J. Simpson (1947-) — 1985

Football	$125-$150

Helmet..............................$225-$275
Mini-Helmet.................................$75
Cut signature..............................$25
Goal Line Art.........................$35-$60
8x10 photograph..........................$45
Mike Singletary (1958-)   **1998**

Mounted Memories Photo

Football.....................................$100
Helmet.................................$200-$275
Mini-Helmet.................................$50
Cut signature................................$7
Goal Line Art................................$30
8x10 photograph..........................$20
Jackie Slater (1955-)   **2001**

Football..$85
Helmet...$180
Mini-Helmet.................................$50
Cut signature................................$3
Goal Line Art................................$40
8x10 photograph..........................$25
Jackie Smith (1940-)   **1994**

Football..$85
Helmet...$180
Mini-Helmet.................................$40
Cut signature................................$3
Goal Line Art................................$20
8x10 photograph..........................$15
John Stallworth (1952-)   **2002**

Football.....................................$100
Helmet...$200
Mini-Helmet.................................$60
Cut signature................................$8
Goal Line Art................................$40
8x10 photograph..........................$30
Bart Starr (1934-)   **1977**

Football.....................................$150
Authenticated Football..................$300
Helmet...$250
Mini-Helmet...............................$100
Cut signature..............................$20
Goal Line Art................................$60

Mounted Memories Photo

8x10 photograph..........................$50
Authenticated 8x10 photograph.............$150
Roger Staubach (1942-)   **1985**

Mounted Memories Photo

Football..................................$150-$200
Authenticated Football..................$300
Helmet.................................$275-$300
Mini-Helmet.........................$85-$125
Cut signature..............................$20
Goal Line Art................................$75
8x10 photograph..........................$75
Ernie Stautner (1925-)   **1969**

Football..$85
Helmet...$180
Mini-Helmet.................................$40
Cut signature................................$4
Goal Line Art................................$20
8x10 photograph..........................$15
Jan Stenerud (1942-)   **1991**

Football..$85
Helmet...$195
Mini-Helmet.................................$50
Cut signature................................$5
Goal Line Art................................$15
8x10 photograph..........................$15
Dwight Stephenson (1957-)   **1998**

Football..$85
Helmet...$190
Mini-Helmet.................................$45
Cut signature................................$3
Goal Line Art................................$20
8x10 photograph..........................$15
Hank Stram (1923-)   **2003**

Football.....................................$100
Helmet...$200
Mini-Helmet.................................$50
Cut signature................................$5
Goal Line Art................................$30
8x10 photograph..........................$25
Ken Strong (1906-1979)   **1967**

Football...................................Unknown
Helmet....................................Unknown
Mini-Helmet............................Unknown
Cut signature..............................$50
Goal Line Art.......................Impossible
8x10 photograph...............$200-$250

Joe Stydahar (1912-1977)   **1967**

Football...................................Unknown
Helmet....................................Unknown
Mini-Helmet............................Unknown
Cut signature.........................$50-$100
Goal Line Art.......................Impossible
8x10 photograph..................$275-$400
Lynn Swann (1952-)   **2001**

Mounted Memories Photo

Football..................................$150-$200
Helmet.................................$275-$300
Mini-Helmet.......................$100-$150
Cut signature..............................$20
Goal Line Art.......................$75-$150
8x10 photograph..........................$50
Fran Tarkenton (1940-)   **1986**

Football..................................$100-$150
Helmet.................................$235-$250
Mini-Helmet.................................$75
Cut signature..............................$10
Goal Line Art.......................$25-$60
8x10 photograph..........................$40
Charley Taylor (1941-)   **1984**

Football..$85
Helmet...$195
Mini-Helmet.................................$40
Cut signature................................$4
Goal Line Art................................$20
8x10 photograph..........................$15
Jim Taylor (1935-)   **1976**

Football..................................$85-$125
Helmet.................................$200-$225
Mini-Helmet.........................$50-$75
Cut signature................................$5
Goal Line Art.......................$20-$60
8x10 photograph..........................$25
Lawrence Taylor (1959-)   **1999**

Football.....................................$125
Authenticated Football..................$300
Helmet...$210
Authenticated Helmet..................$550
Mini-Helmet.................................$70
Authenticated Mini-Helmet..........$175
Cut signature................................$8
Goal Line Art................................$40
8x10 photograph..........................$30
Authenticated 8x10 photograph.............$110
Jim Thorpe (1888-1953)   **1963**

Football...................................Unknown
Helmet....................................Unknown
Mini-Helmet............................Unknown
Cut signature.....................$700-$1,200
Goal Line Art.......................Impossible
8x10 photograph............$1,500-$3,500

Y.A. Tittle (1926-)   **1971**

Football $100
Helmet $225
Mini-Helmet $50
Cut signature $4
Goal Line Art $25
8x10 photograph $25
Authenticated 8x10 photograph $40

George Trafton (1896-1971)   **1964**

Football ....Unknown
Helmet ....Unknown
Mini-Helmet ....Unknown
Cut signature ....$75-$150
Goal Line Art ....Impossible
8x10 photograph ....Unknown

Charley Trippi (1922-)   **1968**

Football $85
Helmet $175
Mini-Helmet $45
Cut signature $3
Goal Line Art $15
8x10 photograph $15

Emlen Tunnell (1925-1975)   **1967**

Football ....Unknown
Helmet ....Unknown
Mini-Helmet ....Unknown
Cut signature ....$50-$100
Goal Line Art ....Impossible
8x10 photograph ....$200-$400

Clyde "Bulldog" Turner (1919-1998)   **1966**

Football $150
Helmet $250
Mini-Helmet ....$100-$150
Cut signature $10
Goal Line Art $40
8x10 photograph $50

Johnny Unitas (1933-2002)   **1979**

Mounted Memories Photo

Football ....$175-$200
Authenticated Football $550
Helmet ....$250-$350
Authenticated Helmet $1,200
Mini-Helmet $125
Cut signature $20
Goal Line Art $75
8x10 photograph $50

Gene Upshaw (1945-)   **1987**

Football $85
Helmet $200
Mini-Helmet $50
Cut signature $7
Goal Line Art $25
8x10 photograph $20

Norm Van Brocklin (1926-1983)   **1971**

Football ....Unknown

Helmet ....Unknown
Mini-Helmet ....Unknown
Cut signature ....$60-$150
Goal Line Art ....Impossible
8x10 photograph ....$225-$400

Steve Van Buren (1920-)   **1965**

Football $85
Helmet $175
Mini-Helmet $45
Cut signature $3
Goal Line Art $20
8x10 photograph $15

Doak Walker (1927-1998)   **1986**

Football $200
Helmet ....$225-$300
Mini-Helmet ....$100-$125
Cut signature $20
Goal Line Art $60
8x10 photograph $50

Bill Walsh (1931-)   **1993**

Football $125
Helmet ....$200-$250
Mini-Helmet $80
Cut signature $10
Goal Line Art $50
8x10 photograph $35

Paul Warfield (1942-)   **1983**

Football ....$85-$100
Helmet ....$175-$200
Mini-Helmet $50
Cut signature $3
Goal Line Art $20
8x10 photograph $20

Bob Waterfield (1920-1983)   **1965**

Football ....Unknown
Helmet ....Unknown
Mini-Helmet ....Unknown
Cut signature $75
Goal Line Art ....Impossible
8x10 photograph ....$225-$250

Mike Webster (1952-2002)   **1997**

Football $125
Helmet $225
Mini-Helmet $75
Cut signature $8
Goal Line Art $50
8x10 photograph $30

Arnie Weinmeister (1923-2000)   **1984**

Football $100
Helmet $200
Mini-Helmet $60
Cut signature $5
Goal Line Art $25
8x10 photograph $35

Randy White (1953-)   **1994**

Mounted Memories Photo

Football ....$85-$100

Helmet ....$175-$200
Mini-Helmet $50
Cut signature $4
Goal Line Art $25
8x10 photograph $20

Dave Wilcox (1942-)   **2000**

Football $85
Helmet $175
Mini-Helmet $40
Cut signature $6
Goal Line Art $20
8x10 photograph $15

Bill Willis (1921-)   **1977**

Football $85
Helmet $175
Mini-Helmet $50
Cut signature $6
Goal Line Art $25
8x10 photograph $20

Larry Wilson (1938-)   **1978**

Football $85
Helmet $175
Mini-Helmet $40
Cut signature $3
Goal Line Art $25
8x10 photograph $15

Kellen Winslow (1957-)   **1995**

Football $100
Helmet $200
Mini-Helmet $50
Cut signature $3
Goal Line Art $25
8x10 photograph $15

Alex Wojciechowicz (1915-1992)   **1968**

Football ....$175-$225
Helmet ....Unknown
Mini-Helmet ....Unknown
Cut signature $10
Goal Line Art ....$450-$800
8x10 photograph $75

Willie Wood (1936-)   **1989**

Football $85
Helmet $175
Mini-Helmet $40
Cut signature $3
Goal Line Art $20
8x10 photograph $15

Rony Yary (1946-)   **2001**

Football $85
Helmet $200
Mini-Helmet $50
Cut signature $6
Goal Line Art $25
8x10 photograph $20

Jack Youngblood (1950-)   **2001**

Football $100
Helmet $200
Mini-Helmet $50
Cut signature $6
Goal Line Art $30
8x10 photograph $20

FOOTBALL AUTOGRAPHS

INACTIVE PLAYERS
* Indicates Player Is Deceased

Player	Signed 8x10 Photo	Authenticated Photo	Signed Mini-Helmet	Authenticated Mini	Signed Football	Authenticated Football	Signed Helmet	Authenticated Helmet
Karim Abdul-Jabbar	$12		$35		$85		$190	
Dan Abramowicz	$10		$35		$85		$190	
Mike Adamle	$10		$35		$85		$190	
Julius Adams	$10		$35		$85		$190	
Sam Adams	$10		$35		$85		$190	
Troy Aikman	$60	$100	$125	$160	$160	$325	$275	$500
Frankie Albert *	$15		$50		$125		$225	
Lionel Aldridge *	$40		$125		$150		$275	
Terry Allen	$20		$40		$100		$200	
Jeff Alm *	$40		*		$150		$300	
Lyle Alzado *	$100		*		$300		$500	
Alan Ameche *	$100		*		$350		$500	
Dick Anderson	$15		$45		$90		$200	
Donny Anderson	$12		$40		$85		$200	
"Flipper" Anderson	$10		$35		$85		$190	
Jamal Anderson	$25		$50		$100		$200	
Ken Anderson	$25		$50		$110		$210	
Neal Anderson	$10		$35		$85		$190	
Ottis Anderson	$15		$50		$100		$200	
William Andrews	$10		$35		$85		$190	
Fred Arbanas	$10		$35		$85		$190	
Bruce Armstrong	$15		$40		$85		$190	
Otis Armstrong	$10		$35		$85		$190	
Jon Arnett	$10		$35		$85		$190	
Steve Atwater	$10	$35	$35		$85		$190	
Coy Bacon	$10		$35		$85		$190	
Chris Bahr	$10		$35		$85		$190	
Matt Bahr	$10		$35		$85		$190	
Bubba Baker	$10		$35		$85		$190	
Terry Baker	$30		$50		$125		$225	
Jim Bakken	$10		$35		$85		$190	
Pete Banaszak	$10		$35		$85		$190	
Carl Banks	$12		$40		$90		$190	
Tom Banks	$10		$35		$85		$190	
Steve Bartkowski	$15		$45		$90		$200	
Mike Bass	$12		$40		$90		$190	
Bill Bates	$15		$40		$85		$190	
Maxie Baughan	$10		$35		$85		$190	
Mark Bavaro	$10		$35		$85		$190	
Bubba Bean	$10		$35		$85		$190	
Gary Beban	$20		$50		$100		$200	
Don Beebe	$10		$35		$85		$190	
Ricky Bell *	$125		*		$300		$500	
Joe Bellino	$15		$45		$100		$210	
Rolf Benirschke	$10		$35		$85		$190	
Cornelius Bennett	$12		$40		$85		$190	
Edgar Bennett	$12		$40		$85		$190	
Bill Bergey	$10		$35		$85		$190	
Rod Bernstine	$10		$35		$85		$190	
Angelo Bertelli *	$50		$150		$200		$375	
Jay Berwanger *	$25		$75		$150		$275	
Verlon Biggs	$10		$35		$85		$190	
Todd Blackledge	$10		$35		$85		$190	
Glenn Blackwood	$10		$35		$85		$190	
Lyle Blackwood	$10		$35		$85		$190	
Doc Blanchard	$20		$50		$110		$225	
Bennie Blades	$10		$35		$85		$190	
Brian Blades	$10		$35		$85		$190	
Matt Blair	$10		$35		$85		$190	
Rocky Bleier	$20		$50		$100		$215	
Steve Bono	$15		$45		$90		$190	
Emerson Boozer	$10		$35		$85		$190	
Jeff Bostic	$10		$35		$85		$190	
Brian Bosworth	$15		$45		$90		$200	
Ken Bowman	$10		$35		$85		$190	
Mike Bragg	$10		$35		$85		$190	
Cliff Branch	$15		$45		$95		$200	
Zeke Bratkowski	$10		$35		$85		$190	
Jim Braxton *	$80		*		$200		$350	
Jim Breech	$10		$35		$85		$190	
Louis Breeden	$10		$35		$85		$190	
John Brockington	$15		$45		$90		$200	
John Brodie	$40		$75		$150		$300	
Robert Brooks	$20		$45		$100		$200	
Tom Brookshier	$10		$35		$85		$190	
Bob Brown * (GB)	$40		*		$150		$275	
Dave Brown	$10		$35		$85		$190	
Jerome Brown *	$75		*		*		*	
Larry Brown (Wash.)	$15		$40		$90		$200	
Larry Brown (Dal.)	$15		$40		$90		$200	
Roger Brown	$10		$35		$85		$190	
Timmy Brown	$10		$35		$85		$190	
Ross Browner	$10		$35		$85		$190	
Bobby Bryant	$12		$40		$85		$190	

Mounted Memories Photo

Troy Aikman

Mounted Memories Photo

Ottis Anderson

Mounted Memories Photo

Steve Atwater

Player	Signed 8x10 Photo	Authenticated Photo	Signed Mini-Helmet	Authenticated Mini	Signed Football	Authenticated Football	Signed Helmet	Authenticated Helmet
Kelvin Bryant	$15		$40		$90		$200	
Willie Buchanon	$10		$35		$85		$190	
Doug Buffone	$10		$35		$85		$190	
Norm Bulaich	$10		$35		$85		$190	
Ronnie Bull	$10		$35		$85		$190	
Ken Burrough	$10		$35		$85		$190	
Jim Burt	$12		$35		$85		$190	
Dexter Bussey	$10		$35		$85		$190	
Jerry Butler	$10		$35		$85		$190	
Kevin Butler	$10		$35		$85		$190	
Leroy Butler	$12		$35		$85		$190	
Marion Butts	$10		$35		$85		$190	
Dave Butz	$15		$40		$90		$200	
Keith Byars	$15		$45		$90		$200	
Earnest Byner	$15		$40		$90		$200	
Dennis Byrd	$10		$35		$85		$190	
Lee Roy Caffey *	$50		*		$150		$250	
J.V. Cain *	$150		*		*		*	
Billy Cannon	$20		$50		$100		$210	
Gino Cappelletti	$10		$35		$85		$190	
John Cappelletti	$20		$50		$100		$210	
Harold Carmichael	$15		$40		$90		$190	
Mark Carrier	$10		$35		$85		$190	
Rae Carruth	$10		$35		$85		$190	
Harry Carson	$15		$40		$90		$200	
Anthony Carter	$10		$35		$85		$190	
Cris Carter	$30		$60		$110	$190	$210	
Howard Cassady	$20		$50		$100		$210	
Chuck Cecil	$10		$35		$85		$190	
Wally Chambers	$10		$35		$85		$190	
Bob Chandler *	$35		$100		$150		$250	
Don Chandler	$15		$40		$90		$190	
Wes Chandler	$12		$35		$85		$190	
Raymond Chester	$12		$35		$85		$190	
Mark Chmura	$20		$45		$90		$200	
Todd Christensen	$15		$45		$100		$200	
Boobie Clark *	$50		*		$150		$275	
Dwight Clark	$20	$50	$50		$100		$225	
Gary Clark	$15		$45		$90		$200	
Mark Clayton	$15		$45		$90		$200	
Ben Coates	$15		$40		$90		$190	
Don Cockroft	$10		$35		$85		$190	
Monte Coleman	$10		$35		$85		$190	
Cris Collinsworth	$15		$45		$90		$200	
Neil Colzie *	$30		$75		$125		$225	
Bobby Joe Conrad	$10		$35		$85		$190	
Earl Cooper	$10		$35		$85		$190	
Doug Cosbie	$12		$40		$85		$190	
Bruce Coslet	$10		$35		$85		$190	
Jimbo Covert	$10		$35		$85		$190	
Al Cowlings	$10		$35		$85		$190	
Fred Cox	$10		$35		$85		$190	
Roger Craig	$15		$40	$50	$90		$200	
Joe Cribbs	$10		$35		$85		$190	
Nolan Cromwell	$10		$35		$85		$190	
Irv Cross	$10		$35		$85		$190	
Randy Cross	$15		$40		$90		$200	
John David Crow	$20		$50		$100		$210	
Curley Culp	$10		$35		$85		$190	
Bennie Cunningham	$12		$40		$85		$190	

Mounted Memories Photo

Player	Signed 8x10 Photo	Authenticated Photo	Signed Mini-Helmet	Authenticated Mini	Signed Football	Authenticated Football	Signed Helmet	Authenticated Helmet
Randall Cunningham	$20		$50	$190	$90	$270	$200	$450
Sam Cunningham	$15		$40		$85		$190	
Gary Cuozzo	$15		$40		$85		$190	
Isaac Curtis	$15	$20	$40		$85		$190	
Mike Curtis	$12		$35		$85		$190	
Carroll Dale	$15		$45		$90		$200	
Dave Dalby *	$40		$75		$150		$250	
Gary Danielson	$10		$35		$85		$190	
Ben Davidson	$10		$35		$85		$190	
Clarence Davis	$12		$40		$85		$190	
Ernie Davis *	$800		*		*		*	
Glenn Davis	$20		$50		$100		$210	
Terrell Davis	$40	$75	$75		$125	$200	$225	$500
Willie Davis (K.C.)	$10		$35		$85		$190	
Pete Dawkins	$25		$60		$110		$225	
Fred Dean (S.D.)	$10		$35		$85		$190	
Steve DeBerg	$20		$50		$100		$200	
Al Del Greco	$15		$40		$85		$190	
Jack Del Rio	$10		$35		$85		$190	
Joe Delaney *	$150		*		*		*	
Tom Dempsey	$20		$50		$100		$200	
Richard Dent	$20		$50		$100		$200	
Lynn Dickey	$10		$35		$85		$190	
Hanford Dixon	$10	$20	$35		$85		$190	
Conrad Dobler	$20		$45		$90		$200	
Bobby Douglass	$15	$20	$40		$85		$190	
Boyd Dowler	$15		$45		$90		$200	
Fred Dryer	$35		$60		$115		$215	
A.J. Duhe	$10		$35		$85		$190	
Mark Duper	$15		$40		$90		$200	
Billy Joe DuPree	$12		$40		$85		$190	

Mounted Memories Photo
Steve Bono

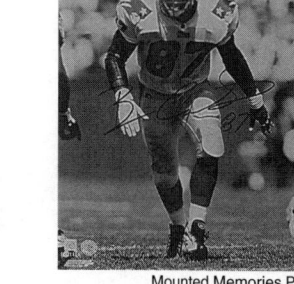
Mounted Memories Photo
Ben Coates

Player	Signed 8x10 Photo	Authenticated Photo	Signed Mini-Helmet	Authenticated Mini	Signed Football	Authenticated Football	Signed Helmet	Authenticated Helmet
John Dutton	$10		$35		$85		$190	
Kenny Easley	$10		$35		$85		$190	
Tony Eason	$10		$35		$85		$190	
Herman Edwards	$20		$50		$100		$200	
Henry Ellard	$15		$40		$85		$190	
Carl Eller	$15		$45		$90		$200	
Jumbo Elliott	$10		$35		$85		$190	
John Elway	$60		$150		$175	$350	$250	$550
Steve Emtman	$10		$35		$85		$190	
Curtis Enis	$10		$35		$85		$190	
Craig Erickson	$10		$35		$85		$190	
Boomer Esiason	$25		$50		$100	$330	$210	$650
Vince Evans	$12		$40		$85		$190	
Jim Everett	$15		$45		$90		$200	
Mel Farr	$12		$35		$85		$190	
Gary Fencik	$12		$35		$85		$190	
Joe Ferguson	$15		$40		$85		$190	
Manny Fernandez	$15		$35		$85		$190	
Vince Ferragamo	$10		$35		$85		$190	
Pat Fischer	$12		$40		$85		$190	
Marv Fleming	$15		$40		$85		$190	
Tom Flores	$15		$45		$90		$200	
Chuck Foreman	$15		$40		$90		$200	
Barry Foster	$15		$40		$85		$190	
Bill Fralic	$10		$35		$85		$190	
Russ Francis	$15		$45		$90		$200	
Wallace Francis	$10		$35		$85		$190	
Clint Frank *	$125		*		$250		*	
Tony Franklin	$10		$35		$85		$190	
Tucker Fredrickson	$10		$35		$85		$190	
Frenchy Fuqua	$15		$40		$85		$190	
John Friesz	$10		$35		$85		$190	
Irving Fryar	$15		$40		$85		$190	
William Fuller	$10		$35		$85		$190	
Steve Furness *	$40		$85		$150		$240	
Roman Gabriel	$20		$50		$100		$200	
Tony Galbreath	$10		$35		$85		$190	
Alvin Garrett	$10		$35		$85		$190	
Mike Garrett	$20		$50		$100		$210	
Gary Garrison	$10		$35		$85		$190	
Walt Garrison	$20		$45		$90		$200	
Mark Gastineau	$15	$20	$45		$90		$200	
Willie Gault	$12		$35		$85		$190	
Roy Gerela	$15		$40		$85		$190	
Cookie Gilchrist	$10		$35		$85		$190	
Joe Gilliam *	$50		$100		$175		$275	
Pete Gogolak	$12		$35		$85		$190	
Bob Golic	$10		$35		$85		$190	
Mike Golic	$10		$35		$85		$190	
Jim Grabowski	$15		$40		$90		$190	
Randy Gradishar	$15		$40		$90		$190	
Larry Grantham	$10		$35		$85		$190	
Leon Gray *	$35		$75		$125		$225	
Mel Gray Jr.	$12		$35		$85		$190	
Mel Gray Sr.	$10		$35		$85		$190	
Elvis Grbac	$15		$45		$90		$190	
Darrell Green	$25		$50		$100		$200	
Eric Green	$15		$40		$85		$190	
Roy Green	$10		$35		$85		$190	
Kevin Greene	$20		$50		$100		$210	

Player	Signed 8x10 Photo	Authenticated Photo	Signed Mini-Helmet	Authenticated Mini	Signed Football	Authenticated Football	Signed Helmet	Authenticated Helmet
L.C. Greenwood	$25		$50		$100		$210	
Rosey Grier	$20	$30	$45		$100		$200	
Archie Griffin	$20		$50		$100		$210	
Russ Grimm	$12		$35		$85		$190	
Steve Grogan	$15		$40		$85		$190	
Ralph Guglielmi	$15		$40		$85		$190	
Ray Guy	$15		$45		$90		$200	
Pat Haden	$15		$40		$90		$190	
John Hadl	$15		$40		$90		$190	

Mounted Memories Photo

Player	Signed 8x10 Photo	Authenticated Photo	Signed Mini-Helmet	Authenticated Mini	Signed Football	Authenticated Football	Signed Helmet	Authenticated Helmet
Charles Haley	$20		$45		$100		$200	
Rodney Hampton	$10		$35		$85		$190	
Chris Hanburger	$12		$40		$85		$190	
Terry Hanratty	$15		$40		$85		$190	
Jim Harbaugh	$20		$45		$90		$190	
Ronnie Harmon	$10		$35		$85		$190	
Tom Harmon *	$150		*		$300		*	
Alvin Harper	$12		$35		$85		$190	
Cliff Harris	$12		$40		$85		$190	
James Harris	$10		$35		$85		$190	
Jim Hart	$12		$40		$85		$190	
Leon Hart *	$40		$75		$125		$275	
Ken Harvey	$10		$35		$85		$190	
Len Hauss	$10		$35		$85		$190	
Alex Hawkins	$10		$35		$85		$190	
Bob Hayes *	$30	$80	$75		$125		$250	
Lester Hayes	$15		$45		$90		$200	
Abner Haynes	$10		$35		$85		$190	
Bobby Hebert	$10		$35		$85		$190	
Hollywood Henderson	$12		$40		$85		$190	
Charley Hennigan	$10		$35		$85		$190	
Efren Herrera	$10		$35		$85		$190	

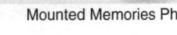

Mounted Memories Photo

John Elway

Mounted Memories Photo

Jim Everett

Player	Signed 8x10 Photo	Authenticated Photo	Signed Mini-Helmet	Authenticated Mini	Signed Football	Authenticated Football	Signed Helmet	Authenticated Helmet
Craig Heyward	$12		$35		$85		$190	
Wally Hilgenberg	$10		$35		$85		$190	
Calvin Hill	$40		$75		$125		$250	
Greg Hill	$10		$35		$85		$190	
Winston Hill	$15		$40		$85		$190	
Leroy Hoard	$12		$40		$85		$190	
Merril Hoge	$12		$40		$85		$190	
Ernie Holmes	$20		$45		$90		$200	
E.J. Holub	$10		$35		$85		$190	
Les Horvath *	$100		*		$300		*	
Jeff Hostetler	$20		$45		$90		$200	
Chuck Howley	$20		$45		$90		$200	
John Huarte	$35		$75		$115		$225	
Marv Hubbard	$15		$40		$85		$190	
Kent Hull	$10		$35		$85		$190	
Claude Humphrey	$12		$40		$85		$190	
Stan Humphries	$15		$40		$85		$190	
Michael Irvin	$35	$45	$60	$65	$110		$225	
Bo Jackson	$40	$75	$150	$125	$250		$250	$550
Harold Jackson	$10		$35		$85		$190	
Keith Jackson	$12		$40		$85		$190	
Rich "Tombstone" Jackson	$10		$35		$85		$190	
Rickey Jackson	$10		$35		$85		$190	
Tom Jackson	$20		$50		$100		$200	
Joe Jacoby	$15		$45		$90		$200	
Craig James	$15		$45		$85		$190	
Ron Jaworski	$20		$50		$100		$200	
John Jefferson	$15		$40		$85		$190	
Roy Jefferson	$10		$35		$85		$190	
Haywood Jeffires	$10		$35		$85		$190	
Alfred Jenkins	$10		$35		$85		$190	
Dave Jennings	$10		$35		$85		$190	
Jim Jensen	$10		$35		$85		$190	
Bob Jeter	$12		$40		$85		$190	
Billy "Wh. Shoes" Johnson	$15		$45		$90		$190	
Butch Johnson	$10		$35		$85		$190	
Charley Johnson	$15		$40		$85		$190	
Jimmy Johnson (Coach)	$35		$60		$110		$225	
Norm Johnson	$10		$35		$85		$190	
Pepper Johnson	$10		$35		$85		$190	
Pete Johnson	$10	$40	$35		$85		$190	
Ron Johnson	$10		$35		$85		$190	
Daryl Johnston	$20		$50		$90		$200	
Bert Jones	$20		$50		$90		$200	
Brent Jones	$15		$45		$85		$190	
Ed "Too Tall" Jones	$20		$50		$90		$200	
June Jones	$10		$35		$85		$190	
Lee Roy Jordan	$15		$40		$85		$190	
Seth Joyner	$10		$35		$85		$190	
Charlie Justice	$20		$50		$100		$210	
Danny Kanell	$15		$40		$85		$190	
Alex Karras	$25		$50		$100		$210	
Joe Kapp	$20		$45		$90		$190	
Napoleon Kaufman	$10		$35		$85		$190	
Dick Kazmaier	$20		$50		$100		$210	
Louie Kelcher	$10		$35		$85		$190	
Larry Kelley *	$40		$100		$150		$250	
Jack Kemp	$35		$75		$125		$250	
Cortez Kennedy	$15		$40		$85		$190	
Jim Kiick	$15		$45		$90		$200	
Billy Kilmer	$15		$45		$90		$200	
Nile Kinnick *	$1,500		*		*		*	
Joe Klecko	$15		$45		$85		$190	
David Klingler	$10		$35		$85		$190	
Chuck Knox	$12		$40		$85		$190	
Bernie Kosar	$20		$50		$100		$210	
Jerry Kramer	$20		$50		$100		$210	
Tommy Kramer	$10		$35		$85		$190	
Dave Krieg	$15		$40		$85		$190	
Tim Krumrie	$10		$35		$85		$190	
Bob Kuechenberg	$15		$40		$85		$190	
Ernie Ladd	$20		$50		$85		$190	
Daryle Lamonica	$20		$50		$90		$200	
Greg Landry	$12		$40		$85		$190	
Fred Lane *	$40		$100		$150		$225	
MacArthur Lane	$10		$35		$85		$190	
Gary Larsen	$12		$40		$85		$190	
Johnny Lattner	$15		$45		$100		$200	
Joe Lavender	$15		$40		$90		$190	
Pat Leahy	$10		$35		$85		$190	
Ryan Leaf	$12		$40	$50	$85		$190	
Eddie Lebaron	$15		$45		$90		$200	
Dick LeBeau	$10		$35		$85		$190	
D.D. Lewis	$12		$35		$85		$190	
Louis Lipps	$15		$40		$85		$190	
Big Daddy Lipscomb *	$400		*		*		*	
Floyd Little	$15		$45		$90		$190	
Greg Lloyd	$15		$45		$90		$190	
Spider Lockhart *	$60		*		*		*	
Chip Lohmiller	$12		$40		$85		$190	
Neil Lomax	$15		$40		$85		$190	
Joe Don Looney *	$100		*		*		*	
Derek Loville	$10		$35		$85		$190	
Nick Lowery	$15		$40		$85		$190	
Johnny Lujack	$20		$50		$100		$210	
Lamar Lundy	$12	$30	$40		$85		$190	
Bill Maas	$10		$35		$85		$190	

Mounted Memories Photo

Michael Irvin

Mounted Memories Photo

Ron Jaworski

Player	Signed 8x10 Photo	Authenticated Photo	Signed Mini-Helmet	Authenticated Mini	Signed Football	Authenticated Football	Signed Helmet	Authenticated Helmet
John Madden	$25		$60		$110		$225	
Paul Maguire	$12		$40		$85		$190	
Don Majkowski	$10		$35		$85		$190	
Mark Malone	$15		$40		$85		$190	
Dexter Manley	$15		$45		$90		$190	
Charles Mann	$12		$40		$85		$190	
Archie Manning	$20		$50		$100		$200	
Ray Mansfield *	$75		$150		$200		$300	
Chester Marcol	$10		$35		$85		$190	
Ed Marinaro	$20		$50		$100		$210	
Dan Marino	$75	$100	$150	$170	$200	$400	$275	$700
Jim Marshall	$15	$40	$45		$90	$150	$200	
Leonard Marshall	$15	$40	$45		$90	$150	$200	
Wilber Marshall	$12		$40		$85		$190	
Harvey Martin *	$35		$75		$150		$250	
Rod Martin	$10		$35		$85		$190	
Bob Matheson *	$100		*		*		*	
Tom Matte	$12		$40		$85		$190	
Bruce Matthews	$15		$40		$85		$190	
Clay Matthews	$12		$40		$85		$190	
John Matuszak *	$150		*		$300		$500	
Larry McCarren	$10		$35		$85		$190	
Don McCauley	$10		$35		$85		$190	
Lawrence McCutcheon	$10		$35		$85		$190	
Randall McDaniel	$10		$35		$85		$190	
Wahoo McDaniel *	$25		$75		$125		$225	
Ron McDole	$12		$35		$85		$190	
Max McGee	$20		$50		$115		$210	
Reggie McKenzie	$15		$45		$85		$190	
Harold McLinton *	$100		*		*		*	
Jim McMahon	$25	$70	$60		$110		$215	
Steve McMichael	$15		$40		$85		$190	
Freeman McNeil	$10		$35		$85		$190	
Karl Mecklenberg	$15		$40		$85		$190	
Natrone Means	$15		$40		$85		$190	
Dave Meggett	$10		$35		$85		$190	
Don Meredith	$40		$100		$150		$250	
Eric Metcalf	$10		$35		$85		$190	
Terry Metcalf	$10		$35		$85		$190	
Matt Millen	$15		$40		$85		$190	
Chris Miller	$10		$35		$85		$190	
Sam Mills	$15		$40		$85		$190	
Lydell Mitchell	$12		$40		$85		$190	

Player	Signed 8x10 Photo	Authenticated Photo	Signed Mini-Helmet	Authenticated Mini	Signed Football	Authenticated Football	Signed Helmet	Authenticated Helmet
Art Monk	$30		$50		$100		$210	
Wilbert Montgomery	$10		$35		$85		$190	
Warren Moon	$25	$35	$50		$100		$210	
Herman Moore	$20		$50		$100		$200	
Nat Moore	$12		$40		$85		$190	
Wayne Moore *	$100		*		*		*	
Stanley Morgan	$10		$35		$85		$190	
Earl Morrall	$15		$40		$90		$190	
Bam Morris	$12		$40		$85		$190	
Joe Morris	$12		$40		$85		$190	
Mercury Morris	$20		$45		$90		$190	
Craig Morton	$20		$45		$90		$190	
Mark Moseley	$15		$45		$85		$190	
Haven Moses	$10		$35		$85		$190	
Chuck Muncie	$15		$45		$85		$190	
Bill Munson *	$40		$75		$125		$225	
Eddie Murray	$10		$35		$85		$190	
Browning Nagle	$10		$35		$85		$190	
Jim Nance *	$100		*		$300		*	
Renaldo Nehemiah	$12		$40		$85		$190	
Steve Nelson	$10		$35		$85		$190	
Robert Newhouse	$15		$40		$85		$190	
Nate Newton	$15		$40		$85		$190	
Hardy Nickerson	$12		$40		$85		$190	
Tommy Nobis	$15		$45		$90		$200	
Jay Novacek	$15		$45		$85		$190	
Davey O'Brien *	$400		*		*		*	
Ken O'Brien	$10		$35		$85		$190	
Christian Okoye	$15		$40		$85		$190	
Leslie O'Neal	$12		$40		$85		$190	
Dave Osborn	$10		$35		$85		$190	
Jim Otis	$12		$40		$85		$190	
Steve Owens	$12		$40		$85		$190	
Bernie Parmalee	$10		$35		$85		$190	
Lemar Parrish	$12		$35		$85		$190	
Dan Pastorini	$15		$45		$90		$190	
Drew Pearson	$15		$35		$85		$190	
Preston Pearson	$15		$45		$85		$190	
Erric Pegram	$10		$35		$85		$190	
William Perry	$15	$40	$45		$90		$190	
Lawrence Phillips	$10		$35		$85		$190	
Mike Phipps	$10	$20	$35		$85		$190	
Brian Piccolo *	$400		*		$700		*	
Carl Pickens	$15		$40		$90		$190	

Mounted Memories Photo

Daryl Johnston

Mounted Memories Photo

Jim Kiick

Mounted Memories Photo

Bernie Kosar

Mounted Memories Photo

Bob Kuechenberg

Player	Signed 8x10 Photo	Authenticated Photo	Signed Mini-Helmet	Authenticated Mini	Signed Football	Authenticated Football	Signed Helmet	Authenticated Helmet
Elijah Pitts *	$50		$125		$200		$300	
Milt Plum	$15		$40		$85		$190	

Tri-Star Productions Photo

Player	Signed 8x10 Photo	Authenticated Photo	Signed Mini-Helmet	Authenticated Mini	Signed Football	Authenticated Football	Signed Helmet	Authenticated Helmet
Jim Plunkett	$25		$60		$110		$210	
Ed Podolak	$10		$35		$85		$190	
Greg Pruitt	$15		$40		$85		$190	
Mike Pruitt	$10	$15	$35		$85		$190	
Jethro Pugh	$10		$35		$85		$190	
Sonny Randle	$12		$40		$85		$190	
Ahmad Rashad	$30		$35		$85		$190	
Tom Rathman	$13		$75		$110		$210	
Andre Reed	$20		$50		$100		$210	
Frank Reich	$15		$40		$85		$190	
Lance Rentzel	$10		$35		$85		$190	
Jack "Hacksaw" Reynolds	$10		$35		$85		$190	
Ray Rhodes	$15		$40		$85		$190	
Gerald Riggs	$10		$35		$85		$190	
Ken Riley	$10		$35		$85		$190	
Andre Rison	$15		$40		$85		$190	
Isiah Robertson	$10		$35		$85		$190	
Dave Robinson	$10		$35		$85		$190	
Eugene Robinson	$15		$40		$85		$190	
Johnny Robinson	$10		$35		$85		$190	
Reggie Roby	$15		$40		$85		$190	
Johnny Rodgers	$20		$45		$90		$200	
George Rogers	$15		$45		$90		$200	
Kyle Rote *	$25		$75		$115		$215	
Tobin Rote *	$35		$100		$150		$250	
Mike Rozier	$20	$30	$45		$90		$200	
Reggie Rucker	$10		$35		$85		$190	
Leonard Russell	$10		$35		$85		$190	
Andy Russell	$15		$40		$85		$190	
Frank Ryan	$25		$50		$90		$200	
Mark Rypien	$20		$45		$90		$200	
Rashaan Salaam	$20		$45		$90		$200	

Mounted Memories Photo

Player	Signed 8x10 Photo	Authenticated Photo	Signed Mini-Helmet	Authenticated Mini	Signed Football	Authenticated Football	Signed Helmet	Authenticated Helmet
Barry Sanders	$60	$175	$125	$200	$175	$450	$275	$650
Charlie Sanders	$10		$35		$85		$190	
Deion Sanders	$35		$75	$200	$125	$400	$250	$500
Ron Saul	$10		$35		$85		$190	
Jake Scott	$50		$80		$125		$275	
Art Schlichter	$10		$35		$85		$190	
Marty Schottenheimer	$15		$45		$90		$190	
Jay Schroeder	$10		$35		$85		$190	
Rafael Septien	$10		$35		$85		$190	
Ronnie Shanklin *	$30		$60		$100		$210	
Sterling Sharpe	$25		$60		$100		$215	
Donnie Shell	$20		$50		$100		$200	
Del Shofner	$10		$35		$85		$190	
Heath Shuler	$12		$40		$85		$190	
Mike Siani	$10		$35		$85		$190	
Jeff Siemon	$10		$35		$85		$190	
Clyde Simmons	$10		$35		$85		$190	
Phil Simms	$30		$60		$100		$215	
Billy Sims	$15	$30	$40		$90		$200	
Frank Sinkwich *	$200		*		*		*	
Tony Siragusa	$15		$45		$90		$190	
Brian Sipe	$15		$50		$90		$190	
Otis Sistrunk	$12		$40		$85		$190	
Bob Skoronski	$10		$35		$85		$190	
Bruce Smith * (Heisman)	$1,000		*		*		*	
Bubba Smith	$20		$50		$90		$200	
Irv Smith	$10		$35		$85		$190	
Jerry Smith *	$100		*		$300		*	
Neil Smith	$15		$40		$90		$190	
Robert Smith	$20		$50		$100		$200	
Sherman Smith	$10		$35		$85		$190	
Timmy Smith	$15		$45		$90		$190	
Norm Snead	$15		$40		$85		$190	
Matt Snell	$15		$45		$85		$190	
Jack Snow	$15		$40		$85		$190	
Freddie Solomon	$15		$40		$85		$190	
Chris Spielman	$10		$35		$85		$190	
Steve Spurrier	$35		$60		$110		$22	
Ken Stabler	$30	$40	$50		$100	$270	215	
Darryl Stingley	$150		*		*		*	
Korey Stringer *	$40		$100		$125		$225	
Don Strock	$15		$40		$85		$190	
Pat Sullivan	$15		$40		$90		$190	
Tom Sullivan *	$30		$60		$100		$200	

Mounted Memories Photo

Jim McMahon

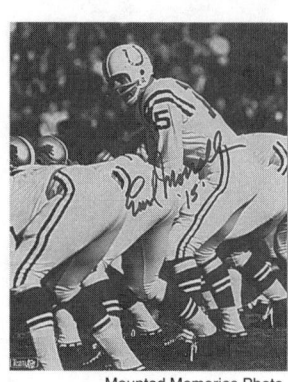

Mounted Memories Photo

Earl Morrall

Player	Signed 8x10 Photo	Authenticated Photo	Signed Mini-Helmet	Authenticated Mini	Signed Football	Authenticated Football	Signed Helmet	Authenticated Helmet
Pat Summerall	$15		$50		$100		$200	
Pat Swilling	$10		$35		$85		$190	
Diron Talbert	$15		$40		$85		$190	
Darryl Talley	$15		$40		$85		$190	
Steve Tasker	$15		$40		$85		$190	
Jack Tatum	$15		$45		$85		$190	
John Taylor	$10		$35		$85		$190	
Lionel Taylor	$10		$35		$85		$190	
Otis Taylor	$12		$40		$85		$190	

Tri-Star Productions Photo

Player	Signed 8x10 Photo	Authenticated Photo	Signed Mini-Helmet	Authenticated Mini	Signed Football	Authenticated Football	Signed Helmet	Authenticated Helmet
Joe Theismann	$30		$60		$100	$240	$225	
Yancey Thigpen	$10		$35		$85		$190	
Derrick Thomas *	$40		$100		$175		$300	
Duane Thomas	$30		$60		$100		$200	
Emmitt Thomas	$10		$35		$85		$190	
Thurman Thomas	$35		$60		$115		$215	
Fuzzy Thurston	$15		$45		$90		$200	
Mick Tingelhoff	$10		$35		$85		$190	
Richard Todd	$15		$40		$85		$190	
Al Toon	$12		$40		$85		$190	
Gino Toretta	$15		$40		$90		$200	
Bob Trumpy	$12		$40		$85		$190	
Bob Tucker	$10		$35		$85		$190	
Eric Turner *	$35		$60		$100		$200	
Jim Turner	$10		$35		$85		$190	
Wendall Tyler	$10		$35		$85		$190	
Rick Upchurch	$10		$35		$85		$190	
Mark Van Eeghen	$15		$45		$85		$190	
Jeff Van Note	$10		$35		$85		$190	
Brad Van Pelt	$10		$35		$85		$190	
Tommy Vardell	$10		$35		$85		$190	
Randy Vataha	$10		$35		$85		$190	
Billy Vessels *	$40		$100		$150		$225	
Phil Villapiano	$10		$35		$85		$190	
Bill Wade	$10		$35		$85		$190	

Player	Signed 8x10 Photo	Authenticated Photo	Signed Mini-Helmet	Authenticated Mini	Signed Football	Authenticated Football	Signed Helmet	Authenticated Helmet
Herschel Walker	$25		$50		$100		$200	
Wesley Walker	$10		$35		$85		$190	
Everson Walls	$10		$35		$85		$190	
Steve Walsh	$10		$35		$85		$190	
Charlie Ward	$40		$100		$150		$250	
Andre Ware	$15		$40		$90		$200	
Chris Warren	$12		$40		$85		$190	
Curt Warner	$10		$35		$85		$19	
Gene Washington (49ers)	$15		$40		$90		$200	
Joe Washington	$15		$40		$85		$190	
Ted Washington	$15		$40		$85		$190	
Charlie Waters	$15		$40		$85		$190	
Ricky Watters	$15		$40		$85		$190	
Alex Webster	$10		$35		$85		$190	
Roger Wehrli	$10		$35		$85		$190	
Ray Wersching	$10		$35		$85		$190	
Charles White	$15		$45		$90		$200	
Danny White	$20		$50		$100		$200	
Dwight White	$20		$50		$100		$200	
Reggie White	$35		$60		$125		$250	
Ed White	$10		$35		$85		$190	
Ken Willard	$10		$35		$85		$190	
Delvin Williams	$10		$35		$85		$190	
Doug Williams	$25		$45		$100		$200	
Sherman Williams	$10		$35		$85		$190	
Fred "Hammer" Williamson	$15		$45		$90		$190	
Marc Wilson	$10		$35		$85		$190	
Wade Wilson	$10		$35		$85		$190	
Sammy Winder	$10		$35		$85		$190	
David Woodley *	$25		$50		$100		$200	
Ickey Woods	$10		$35		$85		$190	

Tri-Star Productions Photo

Player	Signed 8x10 Photo	Authenticated Photo	Signed Mini-Helmet	Authenticated Mini	Signed Football	Authenticated Football	Signed Helmet	Authenticated Helmet
Garo Yepremian	$15		$45		$90		$200	
Steve Young	$60	$95	$125		$175	$350	$275	
Jim Youngblood	$10		$35		$85		$190	
Paul "Tank" Younger *	$20		$60		$125		$225	
Jim Zorn	$15		$40		$90		$190	

Mounted Memories Photo

ACTIVE PLAYERS

Player	Signed 8x10 Photo	Authenticated Photo	Signed Mini-Helmet	Authenticated Mini	Signed Football	Authenticated Football	Signed Helmet	Authenticated Helmet
David Akers	$15		$35		$85		$190	
Shaun Alexander	$20		$40		$85		$190	
Mike Alstott	$40		$60	$80	$110	$200	$215	$350
Morten Andersen	$25		$50		$100		$200	
Gary Anderson (k)	$20		$45		$90		$200	
Mike Anderson	$15		$40	$90	$85		$190	
Jessie Armstead	$12		$35		$85		$190	
Lavar Arrington	$35		$50		$110		$225	
Champ Bailey	$25		$45	$75	$90		$190	
Tony Banks	$12		$35		$85		$190	
Ronde Barber	$20		$45		$90		$190	
Tiki Barber	$20	$90	$50	$150	$90	$250	$190	$500
Kevan Barlow	$20		$45		$90		$190	
Charlie Batch	$12		$35		$85		$190	
Michael Bennett	$12		$35		$85		$190	
Jerome Bettis	$25	$75	$50		$100	$300	$210	
Steve Beuerlein	$15		$45		$85		$190	
Tim Biakabutuka	$12		$35		$85		$190	
Jeff Blake	$15		$40		$85		$190	
Drew Bledsoe	$40	$45	$70	$100	$125	$200	$225	$500
Dre Bly	$15		$40		$85		$190	
Kyle Boller	$12		$35		$85		$190	
Marty Booker	$20		$45		$85		$190	
Tony Boselli	$25		$50		$90		$200	
David Boston	$20		$45	$60	$85		$190	
Peter Boulware	$20		$45		$85		$190	
Kyle Brady	$20		$45		$85		$190	
Tom Brady	$40	$125	$85		$125	$305	$225	$400
Drew Brees	$25		$60	$90	$115		$200	
Aaron Brooks	$20		$45	$80	$85		$190	
Derrick Brooks	$25		$50		$100		$200	
Tim Brown	$40	$55	$85	$90	$125		$225	
Troy Brown	$20	$60	$50		$85		$190	
Isaac Bruce	$35		$60	$75	$100		$200	
Mark Brunell	$30	$75	$50	$150	$100	$175	$200	$550
Marc Bulger	$20		$45		$85		$190	
Plaxico Burress	$15		$40	$70	$85		$190	
Trung Canidate	$12		$35		$85		$190	
David Carr	$35	$150	$60	$200	$100	$350	$200	

Player	Signed 8x10 Photo	Authenticated Photo	Signed Mini-Helmet	Authenticated Mini	Signed Football	Authenticated Football	Signed Helmet	Authenticated Helmet
Quincy Carter	$12		$35		$85		$190	
Larry Centers	$12		$35		$85		$190	
Chris Chambers	$15		$40		$85		$190	
Wayne Chrebet	$20	$60	$45		$90	$250	$190	$450
Laveranues Coles	$20		$45		$90		$190	
Kerry Collins	$30		$60		$100		$200	
Curtis Conway	$12		$35		$85		$190	
Tim Couch	$30	$150	$50		$100	$180	$200	$500
Bryan Cox	$15		$40		$85		$190	
Zack Crockett	$12		$35		$85		$190	
Eric Crouch	$20	$50	$45		$100		$200	
Germane Crowell	$12		$35		$85		$190	
Daunte Culpepper	$35	$90	$60	$100	$110	$200	$225	$580
Stephen Davis	$20	$60	$45	$75	$90		$190	
Ron Dayne	$25	$75	$50	$250	$100		$200	$550
Koy Detmer	$12		$35		$85		$190	
Ty Detmer	$25		$50		$100		$200	
Trent Dilfer	$20		$45		$90		$190	
Corey Dillon	$25		$50		$100		$190	
Santana Dotson	$12		$35		$85		$190	
Hugh Douglas	$12		$35		$85		$190	
Donald Driver	$15		$45		$85		$190	
Warrick Dunn	$30		$60		$100		$210	
Kevin Dyson	$12		$35	$50	$85		$190	
Jason Elam	$15		$40		$85		$190	
Bert Emanuel	$12		$35		$85		$190	
Kevin Faulk	$20		$45		$85		$190	
Marshall Faulk	$50		$100		$150		$250	
Brett Favre	$60	$95	$100	$220	$150	$250	$250	$600
Jay Fiedler	$25		$50		$100		$190	
Doug Flutie	$35	$90	$75	$100	$125	$290	$225	
Bubba Franks	$12		$35		$85		$190	
Antonio Freeman	$12	$30	$35		$85		$190	
Chris Fuamatu-Ma'afala	$12		$35		$85		$190	
Orande Gadsden	$12		$35		$85		$190	
Joey Galloway	$20		$45		$85		$190	
Rich Gannon	$40	$120	$75	$180	$125	$250	$225	$600
Jeff Garcia	$30	$75	$60		$100		$200	
Charlie Garner	$20		$50		$100		$190	

Steiner Sports Photo

Tiki Barber

Mounted Memories Photo

Drew Brees

Mounted Memories Photo

Isaac Bruce

Tri-Star Productions Photo

David Carr

Player	Signed 8x10 Photo	Authenticated Photo	Signed Mini-Helmet	Authenticated Mini	Signed Football	Authenticated Football	Signed Helmet	Authenticated Helmet
Olandis Gary	$12		$35		$85		$190	
Eddie George	$30		$60	$180	$215	$200		
Jeff George	$15		$40		$85		$190	
Terry Glenn	$12		$35		$85		$190	
Tony Gonzalez	$25		$50		$100		$190	
Martin Gramatica	$15		$40		$85		$190	
Ahman Green	$20	$55	$50		$100	$225	$190	
Jacquez Green	$12		$35		$85		$190	
Trent Green	$25		$50		$100		$190	
William Green	$12		$35		$85		$190	
Brian Griese	$25		$50		$100	$150	$190	
Rex Grossman	$15		$40		$85		$190	
Joey Harrington	$20		$50		$100		$190	
Marvin Harrison	$35	$45	$60		$115		$200	
Matt Hasselbeck	$20		$50		$100		$200	
Garrison Hearst	$20		$50		$100		$190	
Travis Henry	$25		$50		$100		$190	
Ike Hilliard	$12		$35		$85		$190	
Kelly Holcombe	$20		$45		$90		$190	
Priest Holmes	$35	$100	$65	$125	$100		$200	$475
Torry Holt	$15		$40	$75	$85		$190	
Joe Horn	$12		$35		$85		$190	
Desmond Howard	$15	$45	$60		$100		$190	
Qadry Ismail	$12		$35		$85		$190	
Rocket Ismail	$15		$35		$85		$190	
Dexter Jackson	$20		$40		$100		$200	
Edgerrin James	$40		$75		$125	$350	$225	$600
Sebastian Janikowski	$25		$50		$100		$200	
Brad Johnson	$40		$75		$125	$175	$225	
Chad Johnson	$12		$35		$85		$190	
Keyshawn Johnson	$40	$50	$75	$100	$125	$200	$225	$325
Rob Johnson	$12		$35		$85		$190	
Joe Jurevicius	$25		$50		$100		$200	
Jevon Kearse	$30		$50		$100		$200	
Jon Kitna	$15		$40		$85		$190	
Ty Law	$12		$35		$85		$190	
Byron Leftwich	$25		$50		$100		$200	
Dorsey Levens	$15	$40	$40		$85		$190	
Chad Lewis	$12		$35		$85		$190	
Jamal Lewis	$15		$40		$85		$190	
Jermaine Lewis	$15		$40		$85		$190	

Player	Signed 8x10 Photo	Authenticated Photo	Signed Mini-Helmet	Authenticated Mini	Signed Football	Authenticated Football	Signed Helmet	Authenticated Helmet
Ray Lewis	$35	$45	$60		$100	$240	$200	
Tommy Maddox	$25		$50	$90	$100		$200	
Peyton Manning	$40	$100	$85	$160	$150	$260	$235	$410
Curtis Martin	$25	$60	$50		$100	$200	$210	
Derek Mason	$12		$35	$55	$85		$190	
Terrance Mathis	$12		$35		$85		$190	
Deuce McAllister	$20	$80	$45	$75	$90		$190	
Ed McCaffrey	$20	$45	$45		$90		$190	
Keenan McCardell	$15		$40		$85		$190	
Willis McGahee	$30		$50		$100		$200	
Willie McGinest	$12		$35		$85		$190	
Donovan McNabb	$50		$100	$300	$150	$400	$250	$600
Steve McNair	$35		$60		$125		$225	
Cade McNown	$12	$40	$35		$85	$100	$190	
Jim Miller	$15		$40		$85		$190	
Rick Mirer	$15		$40		$85		$190	
Quincy Morgan	$12		$35		$85		$190	
Sylvester Morris	$15		$40		$75	$120	$200	$150
Randy Moss	$40		$100	$150	$125	$200	$225	$550
Santana Moss	$15		$40		$85		$190	
Eric Moulds	$15	$30	$40	$65	$85		$190	
Muhsin Muhammad	$12		$35		$85		$190	
Terrence Newman	$20		$40		$100		$190	
Neil O'Donnell	$20		$45		$90		$190	
Terrell Owens	$35		$60		$110	$250	$210	$550
Orlando Pace	$20		$45		$90		$190	
Carson Palmer	$40		$75		$125		$225	
Bill Parcells	$25		$50		$100		$225	
Rodney Peete	$12		$35		$85		$190	
Chad Pennington	$40	$110	$75	$200	$125	$400	$225	$650
Julius Peppers	$25		$50		$100		$200	
Todd Pinkston	$12		$35		$85		$190	
Michael Pittman	$20		$50		$90		$190	
Jake Plummer	$25	$50	$50	$80	$100		$200	
Clinton Portis	$30		$60	$75	$100		$200	
Jerry Porter	$25		$45		$90		$190	
Peerless Price	$15		$40		$85		$190	
John Randle	$15		$40		$85		$190	
Antwaan Randle-El	$25		$50		$90		$190	
Chris Redman	$15		$45		$90		$190	
Jake Reed	$12		$35		$85		$190	
Jerry Rice	$75	$140	$125	$170	$175	$230	$350	$600
Simeon Rice	$30		$50		$100		$200	
Andre Rison	$15		$40		$85		$190	
Willie Roaf	$15		$40		$85		$190	
Koren Robinson	$12		$35		$85		$190	
Bill Romanowski	$15		$40		$85	$215	$190	
Chris Samuels	$15		$40		$85		$190	
Warren Sapp	$40	$95	$75		$125		$225	
Darnay Scott	$12		$35		$85		$190	
Bill Schroeder	$12		$35		$85		$190	
Junior Seau	$25		$60		$100		$200	
Jason Sehorn	$20	$50	$50		$90		$190	
Shannon Sharpe	$30		$60		$100		$200	
Darren Sharper	$12		$40		$85		$190	
Jamie Sharper	$12		$40		$85		$190	
Jeremy Shockey	$40		$60	$150	$100	$300	$210	
Antowain Smith	$12	$20	$35		$85	$150	$190	

Marvin Harrison

Mounted Memories Photo

Clinton Portis

Mounted Memories Photo

Player	Signed 8x10 Photo	Authenticated Photo	Signed Mini-Helmet	Authenticated Mini	Signed Football	Authenticated Football	Signed Helmet	Authenticated Helmet
Bruce Smith	$35		$60		$100		$200	
Emmitt Smith	$75	$150			$200	$650	$350	$900
Jimmy Smith	$15		$40		$85		$190	

Mounted Memories Photo

Player	Signed 8x10 Photo	Authenticated Photo	Signed Mini-Helmet	Authenticated Mini	Signed Football	Authenticated Football	Signed Helmet	Authenticated Helmet
Rod Smith	$15		$40		$85		$190	
Duce Staley	$15		$40		$85		$190	
Donte Stallworth	$15		$40		$85		$190	
James Stewart	$15		$40		$85		$190	
Kordell Stewart	$30	$55	$50		$100		$200	
J.J. Stokes	$15		$35		$85		$190	
Michael Strahan	$25		$50		$100		$190	
Tai Streets	$12		$35		$85		$190	
Dana Stubblefield	$15		$45		$85		$190	

Mounted Memories Photo

Player	Signed 8x10 Photo	Authenticated Photo	Signed Mini-Helmet	Authenticated Mini	Signed Football	Authenticated Football	Signed Helmet	Authenticated Helmet
Fred Taylor	$20	$45	$50	$75	$85	$150	$190	$275
Jason Taylor	$25		$50		$90		$190	
Vinny Testaverde	$25	$100	$60	$125	$100	$150	$200	$300
Anthony Thomas	$25	$65	$50	$70	$90		$190	
Zach Thomas	$25		$50		$85		$190	

Tri-Star Productions Photo

Player	Signed 8x10 Photo	Authenticated Photo	Signed Mini-Helmet	Authenticated Mini	Signed Football	Authenticated Football	Signed Helmet	Authenticated Helmet
LaDainian Tomlinson	$25	$70	$60	$75	$100		$200	

Player	Signed 8x10 Photo	Authenticated Photo	Signed Mini-Helmet	Authenticated Mini	Signed Football	Authenticated Football	Signed Helmet	Authenticated Helmet
Amani Toomer	$20		$50		$90		$190	

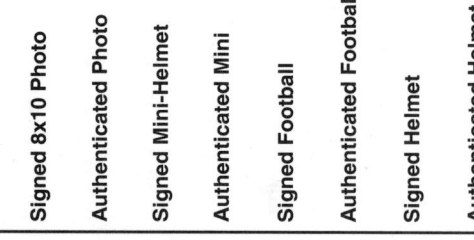

Mounted Memories Photo

Player	Signed 8x10 Photo	Authenticated Photo	Signed Mini-Helmet	Authenticated Mini	Signed Football	Authenticated Football	Signed Helmet	Authenticated Helmet
Brian Urlacher	$35	$130	$60	$180	$100	$250	$200	$475
Michael Vick	$60		$100	$120	$150	$200	$250	
Adam Vinatieri	$15	$40	$40		$85		$190	
Wesley Walls	$20		$45		$90		$190	
Hines Ward	$20		$45		$85		$190	

Mounted Memories Photo

Player	Signed 8x10 Photo	Authenticated Photo	Signed Mini-Helmet	Authenticated Mini	Signed Football	Authenticated Football	Signed Helmet	Authenticated Helmet
Kurt Warner	$50	$200	$85	$300	$125	$450	$225	$700
Peter Warrick	$20		$45	$149	$90	$250	$190	$450
Chris Weinke	$20		$45		$90	$200	$200	
Michael Westbrook	$15		$40		$85		$190	
Tyrone Wheatley	$15		$40		$85		$190	
Dan Wilkinson	$15		$40		$85		$190	
Aeneas Williams	$15		$40		$85		$190	

Mounted Memories Photo

Player	Signed 8x10 Photo	Authenticated Photo	Signed Mini-Helmet	Authenticated Mini	Signed Football	Authenticated Football	Signed Helmet	Authenticated Helmet
Ricky Williams	$40	$140	$75		$125	$350	$225	$600
Charles Woodson	$30		$60	$75	$100	$195	$200	
Rod Woodson	$25		$50		$100		$200	
Danny Wuerffel	$20		$50		$100		$200	
Frank Wycheck	$15		$40		$85		$190	
Amos Zereoue	$15		$40		$85		$190	

TEAM-SIGNED HELMETS

Team-signed full-sized football helmets are popular among collectors, both for their nostalgic feel and the display potential that they possess. Signatures of head coach, quarterback, and Hall of Famers are expected to be on the helmet. The death(s) of key members of the team also affects prices. There should be a minimum of 20 signatures on a team-signed helmet. Team-signed helmets are a popular collectible, but most have come into existence only since the late 1970s. That's because game helmets were not easily available and sporting goods manufacturers didn't make replica equipment products like they do today.

Helmets can better display team autographs because of the equipment's size. But collectors should be careful when choosing a pen for obtaining signatures. White or light helmets are far more attractive—and safe—by using a blue Sharpie. Dark helmets require a gold or silver metallic pen. However, the tips of the metallic pens are more prone to breaking and dripping ink on the helmet. So be careful!

For the most part, team-signed helmets are worth about $250 to $400, depending on whether the helmet is a replica or team-issued, and the team number of HOFers on the squad. For example, the 2000 Washington Redskins were an 8-8 team, but their signed helmet is worth $495 if the piece includes future HOFers Darrell Green, Bruce Smith and one of the hobby's most difficult autographs, Deion Sanders.

Also: note that official game helmets are heavier, sturdier and much more expensive than replicas, which have an amazing likeness except they cost around $150.

For the most part, mini-helmets are about $50 to $75 less than full-sized helmets. But since the mini-helmets are smaller, they can't contain as many signatures.

Team-signed helmets of Super Bowl champions hold a high premium among collectors. Here are some recent values of helmets:

Year	Team	Value	Year	Team	Value	Year	Team	Value
1963	Chicago Bears	$3,600	1975	Pittsburgh Steelers	$1,000		Cincinnati Bengals	$400
	New York Giants	$4,500		Dallas Cowboys	$600	1989	San Francisco 49ers	$1,000
1964	Cleveland Browns	$2,700	1976	Oakland Raiders	$1,200		Denver Broncos	$600
	Baltimore Colts	$1,200		Minnesota Vikings	$400	1990	New York Giants	$800
1965	Green Bay Packers	$3,600	1977	Dallas Cowboys	$1,000		Buffalo Bills	$500
	Cleveland Browns	$1,500		Denver Broncos	$500	1991	Washington Redskins	$800
1966	Green Bay Packers	$4,500	1978	Pittsburgh Steelers	$1,000		Buffalo Bills	$500
	Dallas Cowboys	$2,200		Dallas Cowboys	$600	1992	Dallas Cowboys	$800
	Kansas City Chiefs	$2,200	1979	Pittsburgh Steelers	$1,100		Buffalo Bills	$500
1967	Green Bay Packers	$2,500		Los Angeles Rams	$600	1993	Dallas Cowboys	$800
	Dallas Cowboys	$1,200	1980	Oakland Raiders	$1,000		Buffalo Bills	$500
1968	Baltimore Colts	$1,500		Philadelphia Eagles	$600	1994	San Francisco 49ers	$800
	Cleveland Browns	$750	1981	San Francisco 49ers	$1,200		San Diego Chargers	$400
	New York Jets	$3,000		Cincinnati Bengals	$400	1995	Dallas Cowboys	$800
1969	Minnesota Vikings	$1,000	1982	Washington Redskins	$1,000		Pittsburgh Steelers	$400
	Cleveland Browns	$450		Miami Dolphins	$600	1996	Green Bay Packers	$900
	Kansas City Chiefs	$2,400	1983	Los Angeles Raiders	$1,000		New England Patriots	$400
1970	Baltimore Colts	$1,500		Washington Redskins	$600	1997	Denver Broncos	$1,200
	Dallas Cowboys	$750	1984	San Francisco 49ers	$1,000		Green Bay Packers	$550
1971	Dallas Cowboys	$1,500		Miami Dolphins	$700	1998	Denver Broncos	$1,000
	Miami Dolphins	$600	1985	Chicago Bears	$2,700		Atlanta Falcons	$300
1972	Miami Dolphins	$1,800		New England Patriots	$600	1999	St. Louis Rams	$600
	Washington Redskins	$500	1986	New York Giants	$1,000		Tennessee Titans	$300
1973	Miami Dolphins	$1,250		Denver Broncos	$600	2000	Baltimore Ravens	$600
	Minnesota Vikings	$400	1987	Washington Redskins	$1,000		New York Giants	$350
1974	Pittsburgh Steelers	$1,200		Denver Broncos	$600			
	Minnesota Vikings	$400	1988	San Francisco 49ers	$1,000			

TEAM-SIGNED FOOTBALLS

Team-signed footballs are increasing in popularity as more and more collectors strive to collect autographed footballs from their favorite teams. Signatures of head coach, quarterback, and Hall of Famers are expected to be on the ball. The death(s) of key members of the team also affects prices.

Year	Team	Value	Year	Team	Value	Year	Team	Value
1963	Chicago Bears	$1,200	1965	Green Bay Packers	$1,200	1967	Green Bay Packers	$850
	San Diego Chargers	Uncertain		Buffalo Bills	$800		Oakland Raiders	$600
	New York Giants	$1,500		Cleveland Browns	$500		Dallas Cowboys	$400
	Boston Patriots	Uncertain		San Diego Chargers	Uncertain		Houston Oilers	$300
1964	Cleveland Browns	$900	1966	Green Bay Packers	$1,500	1968	Baltimore Colts	$600
	Buffalo Bills	$800		Kansas City Chiefs	$800		New York Jets	$1,200
	Baltimore Colts	$400		Dallas Cowboys	$750		Cleveland Browns	$300
	San Diego Chargers	Uncertain		Buffalo Bills	$500		Oakland Raiders	Uncertain

1969	Minnesota Vikings	$350
	Kansas City Chiefs	$800
	Cleveland Browns	$150
	Oakland Raiders	Uncertain
1970	Baltimore Colts	$550
	Dallas Cowboys	$250
1971	Dallas Cowboys	$500
	Miami Dolphins	$200
1972	Miami Dolphins	$600
	Washington Redskins	$250
1973	Miami Dolphins	$500
	Minnesota Vikings	$200
1974	Pittsburgh Steelers	$600
	Minnesota Vikings	$200
1975	Pittsburgh Steelers	$500
	Dallas Cowboys	$300
1976	Oakland Raiders	$600
	Minnesota Vikings	$250
1977	Dallas Cowboys	$500
	Denver Broncos	$250
1978	Pittsburgh Steelers	$500
	Dallas Cowboys	$300
1979	Pittsburgh Steelers	$550
	Los Angeles Rams	$300
1980	Oakland Raiders	$500
	Philadelphia Eagles	$300
1981	San Francisco Forty Niners	$600
	Cincinnati Bengals	$200
1982	Washington Redskins	$500
	Miami Dolphins	$300
1983	Los Angeles Raiders	$500
	Washington Redskins	$300
1984	San Francisco Forty Niners	$500
	Miami Dolphins	$350
1985	Chicago Bears	$900
	New England Patriots	$300
1986	New York Giants	$500
	Denver Broncos	$300
1987	Washington Redskins	$500
	Denver Broncos	$300
1988	San Francisco Forty Niners	$500
	Cincinnati Bengals	$200
1989	San Francisco Forty Niners	$500
	Denver Broncos	$300
1990	New York Giants	$450
	Buffalo Bills	$250
1991	Washington Redskins	$400
	Buffalo Bills	$250
1992	Dallas Cowboys	$400
	Buffalo Bills	$250
1993	Dallas Cowboys	$400
	Buffalo Bills	$250
1994	San Francisco Forty Niners	$400
	San Diego Chargers	$250
1995	Dallas Cowboys	$400
	Pittsburgh Steelers	$200
1996	Green Bay Packers	$500
	New England Patriots	$200
1997	Denver Broncos	$500
	Green Bay Packers	$275
1998	Denver Broncos	$475
	Atlanta Falcons	$150
1999	St. Louis Rams	$300
	Tennessee Titans	$150
2000	Baltimore Ravens	$300
	New York Giants	$175

HOCKEY HALL OF FAMERS AUTOGRAPHS

Note: There are no known examples of autographed pucks or 8x10 photographs by many of the early Hall of Fame players. Signatures of many are rare or nonexistent, noted by the designation "Never seen."

Sid Abel (1918-2000)   1969

Puck $60
Cut signature $20
8x10 photograph $50

Jack Adams (1895-1968)   1959

Cut signature $250

Keith Allen (1923-)   1992

Puck $20
Cut signature $7
8x10 photograph $25

Syl Apps (1915-1998)   1961

Cut signature $75
8x10 photograph $200

Al Arbour (1932-)   1996

Puck $25
Cut signature $10
8x10 photograph $25

George Armstrong (1930-)   1975

Puck $50
Cut signature $35
8x10 photograph $40

Ace Bailey (1903-1992)   1975

Puck $200
Cut signature $40
8x10 photograph $150

Don Bain (1874-1962)   1945

Cut signature .... Never seen

Hobey Baker (1892-1918)   1945

Cut signature .... Three in existence

Mounted Memories Photo

Bill Barber (1952-)   1990

Puck $25
Cut signature $7
8x10 photograph $25

Marty Barry (1905-1969)   1965

Cut signature $100
8x10 photograph $125

Andy Bathgate (1932-)   1978

Puck $50
Cut signature $10
8x10 photograph $40

Bobby Bauer (1915-1964)   1996

Cut signature $250

Jean Beliveau (1931-)   1972

Mounted Memories Photo

Puck $60
Cut signature $15
8x10 photograph $50
Authenticated 8x10 photograph $60

Clint Benedict (1894-1976)   1965

Cut signature $200

Doug Bentley (1916-1972)   1964

Cut signature $150
8x10 photograph $200

Max Bentley (1920-1984)   1966

Cut signature $200
8x10 photograph $200

Toe Blake (1912-1995)   1966

Cut signature $75
8x10 photograph $150

Leo Boivin (1932-)   **1986**

Puck $35
Cut signature $15
8x10 photograph $20

Dickie Boon (1878-1961)   **1952**

Cut signature $400

Mike Bossy (1957-)   **1991**

Puck $40
Authenticated puck.....................$50
Cut signature $10
8x10 photograph $25
Authenticated 8x10 photograph $40

Butch Bouchard (1920-)   **1966**

Puck $25
Cut signature $10
8x10 photograph $30

Frank Boucher (1901-1977)   **1958**

Cut signature $125

George Boucher (1896-1960)   **1960**

Puck $300
Cut signature $300

John Bower (1924-)   **1976**

Puck $50
Cut signature $10
8x10 photograph $40

Dubbie Bowie (1880-1959)   **1945**

Cut signature .... Never seen

Scotty Bowman (1933-)   **1991**

Puck $45
Cut signature $15
8x10 photograph $35

Frank Brimsek (1915-1999)   **1966**

Puck $150
Cut signature $40
8x10 photograph $100

Punch Broadbent (1892-1971)   **1962**

Cut signature $150
8x10 photograph $200

Turk Broda (1914-1972)   **1967**

Cut signature $200
8x10 photograph $500

John Bucyk (1935-)   **1981**

Puck $30
Cut signature $10
8x10 photograph $25

Billy Burch (1900-1950)   **1974**

Cut signature .... Never seen

Harry Cameron (1890-1953)   **1962**

Cut signature .... Never seen

Gerry Cheevers (1940-)   **1985**

Puck $40
Cut signature $7
8x10 photograph $30

King Clancy (1903-1986)   **1958**

Cut signature $100
8x10 photograph $200

Dit Clapper (1907-1978)   **1947**

Cut signature $100
8x10 photograph $125

Bobby Clarke (1949-)   **1987**

Puck $50
Cut signature $15
8x10 photograph $40

Sprague Cleghorn (1890-1956)   **1958**

Cut signature $400

Neil Colville (1914-1987)   **1967**

Cut signature $75
8x10 photograph $125

Charlie Conacher (1909-1967)   **1961**

Cut signature $300
8x10 photograph $500

Lionel Conacher (1900-1954)   **1994**

Cut signature $400

Alex Connell (1902-1958)   **1958**

Cut signature $40

Bill Cook (1896-1986)   **1952**

Cut signature $100
8x10 Photograph $200

Bun Cook (1903-1988)   **1995**

Cut signature $100

Art Coulter (1909-2000)   **1974**

Puck $150
Cut signature $50
8x10 photograph $150

Yvan Cournoyer (1943-)   **1982**

Puck $60
Cut signature $7
8x10 photograph $50

Bill Cowley (1912-1994)   **1968**

Cut signature $60
8x10 photograph $150

Rusty Crawford (1885-1971)   **1962**

Cut signature $200

Jack Darragh (1890-1924)   **1962**

Cut signature .... Never seen

Scotty Davidson (1890-1915)   **1950**

Cut signature .... Never seen

Hap Day (1901-1990)   **1961**

Cut signature $100
8x10 photograph $200

Alex Delvecchio (1931-)   **1977**

Puck $40
Cut signature $7
8x10 photograph $30

Cy Denneny (1897-1970)   **1959**

Cut signature $250

Marcel Dionne (1951-)   **1992**

Puck $50
Cut signature $15
8x10 photograph $35

Gordie Drillon (1914-1986)   **1975**

Cut signature $75

Graham Drinkwater (1875-1946)   **1950**

Cut signature .... Never seen

Ken Dryden (1947-)   **1983**

Puck $200
Cut signature $50
8x10 photograph $175

Woody Dumart (1916-)   **1992**

Puck $50
Cut signature $10
8x10 photograph $40

Thomas Dunderdale (1887-1960)   **1974**

Cut signature .... Never seen

Bill Durnan (1916-1972)   **1964**

Cut signature $400

Red Dutton (1898-1987)   **1958**

Cut signature $75
8x10 photograph $100

Babe Dye (1898-1962)   **1970**

Cut signature $200

Phil Esposito (1942-)   **1984**

Puck $75
Cut signature $15
8x10 photograph $50

Tony Esposito (1943-)   **1988**

Puck $50
Cut signature $10
8x10 photograph $40

Arthur Farrel (1877-1909)   **1965**

Cut signature .... Never seen

Bernie Federko (1956-)   **2002**

Cut signature $10
8x10 photograph $25

Viacheslav Fetisov (1958-)   **2001**

Puck $30
Cut signature $15
8x10 photograph $25

Fern Flaman (1927-)   **1990**

Puck $25
Cut signature $7
8x10 photograph $25

Frank Foyston (1891-1966)   1958

Cut signature $300

Emile Francis (1926-)   1982

Puck $50
Cut signature $10
8x10 photograph $35

Frank Frederickson (1895-1979)   1958

Cut signature $100
8x10 photograph $150

Grant Fuhr (1962-)   2003

Puck $30
Cut signature $15
8x10 photograph $30

Bill Gadsby (1927-)   1970

Puck $30
Cut signature $7
8x10 photograph $25

Bob Gainey (1953-)   1992

Puck $40
Cut signature $10
8x10 photograph $35

Chuck Gardiner (1904-1934)   1945

Cut signature .... Never seen

Herb Gardiner (1891-1972)   1958

Cut signature $200

Jimmy Gardner (1881-1940)   1962

Cut signature .... Never seen

Mike Gartner (1959-)   2001

Puck $35
Cut signature $15
8x10 photograph $25

Bernie "Boom Boom" Geoffrion (1931-)   1972

Tri-Star Production Photo

Puck $50
Cut signature $10
8x10 photograph $35
Authenticated 8x10 photograph $40

Eddie Gerard (1890-1937)   1945

Cut signature .... Never seen

Eddie Giacomin (1939-)   1987

Puck $25
Authenticated puck $30
Cut signature $10
8x10 photograph $25
Authenticated 8x10 photograph $30

Rod Gilbert (1941-)   1982

Puck $40
Cut signature $12
8x10 photograph $30

Clark Gillies (1954-)   2002

Puck $25
Cut signature $10
8x10 photograph $25

Billy Gilmour (1885-1959)   1962

Cut signature .... Never seen

Moose Goheen (1894-1979)   1952

Cut signature $150

Ebbie Goodfellow (1909-1985)   1963

Cut signature $75
8x10 photograph $125

Michel Goulet (1960-)   1998

Puck $35
Cut signature $10
8x10 photograph $25

Mike Grant (1874-1955)   1950

Cut signature .... Never seen

Wilf Green (1896-1960)   1962

Cut signature .... Never seen

Wayne Gretzky (1961-)   1999

Puck $175
Cut signature $75
8x10 photograph $150

Si Griffis (1883-1950)   1950

Cut signature .... Never seen

George Hainsworth (1895-1950)   1961

Cut signature $400

Glenn Hall (1931-)   1975

Mounted Memories Photo

Puck $60
Cut signature $10
8x10 photograph $50

Joe Hall (1882-1919)   1961

Cut signature .... Never seen

Doug Harvey (1924-1989)   1973

Cut signature $200
8x10 photograph $400

Dale Hawerchuk (1963-)   2001

Puck $30
Cut signature $10
8x10 photograph $20

George Hay (1898-1975)   1958

Cut signature $100

Riley Hern (1880-1929)   1962

Cut signature .... Never seen

Bryan Hextall (1913-1984)   1969

Cut signature $75
8x10 photograph $100

Hap Holmes (1889-1940)   1972

Cut signature .... Never seen

Tom Hooper (1883-1960)   1962

Cut signature .... Never seen

Red Horner (1909-)   1965

Puck $100
Cut signature $40
8x10 photograph $75

Tim Horton (1930-1974)   1977

Puck $400
Cut signature $200
8x10 photograph $300

Gordie Howe (1928-)   1972

Mounted Memories Photo

Puck $150
Authenticated puck $155
Cut signature $40
8x10 photograph $125
Authenticated 8x10 photograph $130

Sydney Howe (1911-1976)   1965

Cut signature $100

Harry Howell (1932-)   1979

Puck $25
Cut signature $7
8x10 photograph $25

Bobby Hull (1939-)   1983

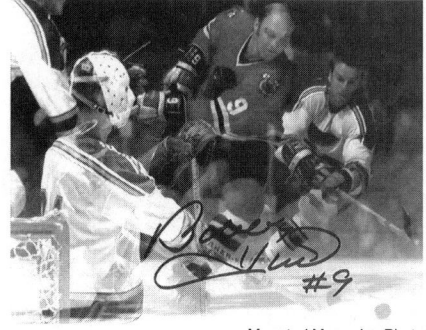

Mounted Memories Photo

Puck $75
Authenticated puck $120
Cut signature $20
8x10 photograph $60
Authenticated 8x10 photograph $80

J.B. Hutton (1877-1962)   **1962**

Cut signature .... Never seen

Harry Hyland (1889-1969)   **1962**

Hockey card .... Unlikely
Cut signature $200

Dick Irvin (1892-1957)   **1958**

Cut signature $350

Busher Jackson (1911-1966)   **1971**

Cut signature $200

Ching Johnson (1898-1979)   **1958**

Cut signature $75
8x10 photograph $100

Ernie Johnson (1886-1963)   **1952**

Cut signature .... Never seen

Tom Johnson (1928-)   **1970**

Puck $30
Cut signature $10
8x10 photograph $25

Aurel Joliat (1901-1986)   **1947**

Cut signature $150
8x10 photograph $300

Duke Keats (1895-1972)   **1958**

Cut signature $200

Red Kelly (1927-)   **1969**

Puck $25
Cut signature $7
8x10 photograph $25

Teeder Kennedy (1925-)   **1966**

Puck $30
Cut signature $10
8x10 photograph $25

Dave Keon (1940-)   **1986**

Puck $30
Cut signature $10
8x10 photograph $25

Jari Kurri (1960-)   **2001**

Puck $45
Cut signature $10
8x10 photograph $30

Elmer Lach (1918-)   **1966**

Puck $50
Cut signature $15
8x10 photograph $40

Guy Lafleur (1951)   **1988**

Puck $60
Cut signature $15
8x10 photograph $50

Pat LaFontaine (1965-)   **2003**

Puck $30
Cut signature $15
8x10 photograph $30

Newsy Lalonde (1887-1971)   **1950**

Cut signature $300

Rod Langway (1957-)   **2002**

Puck $25

Cut signature $10
8x10 photograph $25

Jacques Laperriere (1941-)   **1987**

Puck $30
Cut signature $7
8x10 photograph $25

Guy Lapointe (1948-)   **1993**

Puck $25
Cut signature $10
8x10 photograph $25

Edgar Laprade (1919-)   **1993**

Puck $25
Cut signature $10
8x10 photograph $25

Jack Laviolette (1879-1960)   **1962**

Cut signature $200

Hugh Lehman (1885-1961)   **1958**

Cut signature .... Never seen

Jacques Lemaire (1945-)   **1984**

Puck $30
Cut signature $10
8x10 photograph $20

Mario Lemieux (1965-)   **1997**

Puck $225
Cut signature $60
8x10 photograph $150

Percy LeSueur (1881-1962)   **1961**

Cut signature .... Never seen

Herb Lewis (1907-1991)   **1989**

Cut signature $75

Ted Lindsay (1925-)   **1966**

Puck $50
Cut signature $15
8x10 photograph $40

Harry Lumley (1926-1998)   **1980**

Puck $100
Cut signature $20
8x10 photograph $75

Mickey MacKay (1894-1940)   **1952**

Cut signature .... Never seen

Frank Mahovlich (1938-)   **1981**

Puck $50
Cut signature $10
8x10 photograph $30
Authenticated 8x10 photograph $40

Joe Malone (1890-1969)   **1950**

Cut signature $250

Sylvio Mantha (1902-1974)   **1960**

Cut signature $150

Jack Marshall (1877-1965)   **1965**

Cut signature .... Never seen

Fred Maxwell (1890-1975)   **1962**

Cut signature $250

Lanny McDonald (1953-)   **1992**

Puck $30
Cut signature $7

Mounted Memories Photo

8x10 photograph $15

Frank McGee (? -1916)   **1945**

Cut signature .... Never seen

Billy McGimsie (1880-1968)   **1962**

Cut signature .... Never seen

George McNamara (1886-1952)   **1958**

Hockey card .... Unlikely
Cut signature .... Never seen

Howie Meeker (1924-)   **1999**

Puck $25
Cut signature $7
8x10 photograph $15

Stan Mikita (1940-)   **1983**

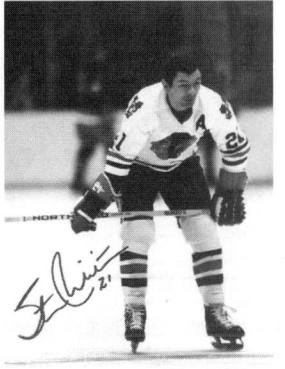

Mounted Memories Photo

Puck $40
Authenticated puck $70
Cut signature $10
8x10 photograph $30
Authenticated 8x10 photograph $60

Dickie Moore (1931-)   **1974**

Puck $40
Cut signature $10
8x10 photograph $25

Paddy Moran (1877-1966)   **1958**

Cut signature .... Never seen

Howie Morenz (1902-1937)   **1945**

Cut signature $700
8x10 photograph $1,500

Bill Mosienko (1921-1994)   **1965**

Puck $350
Cut signature $70
8x10 photograph $250

Joe Mullen (1957-)   **2000**

Puck $30
Cut signature $10
8x10 photograph $30

Frank Nighbor (1893-1966)   **1947**

Cut signature $250

Reg Noble (1895-1962)   **1962**

Cut signature .... Never seen

Buddy O'Connor (1916-1977)   **1988**

Cut signature $150

Harry Oliver (1898-1985)   **1967**

Cut signature $100
8x10 photograph $150

Bert Olmstead (1926-)   **1985**

Puck $40
Cut signature $15
8x10 photograph $35

Bobby Orr (1948-)   **1979**

Steiner Sports Photo

Puck $150
Cut signature $60
8x10 photograph $125

Bernie Parent (1945-)   **1984**

Puck $40
Cut signature $10
8x10 photograph $30

Brad Park (1948-)   **1988**

Puck $30
Cut signature $10
8x10 photograph $25

Lester Patrick (1883-1960)   **1947**

Cut signature $300
8x10 photograph $500

Lynn Patrick (1912-1980)   **1980**

Cut signature $125

Gil Perreault (1950-)   **1990**

Puck $30
1973-74 Topps card $10
Cut signature $10
8x10 photograph $25

Tommy Phillips (1880-1923)   **1945**

Cut signature .... Never seen

Pierre Pilote (1931-)   **1975**

Puck $25
Cut signature $7
8x10 photograph $15

Didier Pitre (1883-1934)   **1962**

Cut signature .... Never seen

Jacques Plante (1929-1986)   **1978**

Cut signature $250
8x10 photograph $500

Bud Poile (1924-)   **1990**

Puck $20
Cut signature $7
8x10 photograph $15

Sam Pollock (1925-)   **1978**

Puck $60
Cut signature $7
8x10 photograph $40

Denis Potvin (1953-)   **1991**

Puck $40
Authenticated puck $50
Cut signature $10
8x10 photograph $25
Authenticated 8x10 photograph $40

Babe Pratt (1916-1988)   **1966**

Cut signature $75

Joe Primeau (1906-1989)   **1963**

Cut signature $125

Marcel Pronovost (1930-)   **1978**

Puck $20
Cut signature $10
8x10 photograph $15

Bob Pulford (1936-)   **1991**

Puck $20
Cut signature $7
8x10 photograph $15

Harvey Pulford (1875-1940)   **1945**

Cut signature .... Never seen

Bill Quackenbush (1922-1999)   **1976**

Puck $150
Cut signature $45
8x10 photograph $150

Frank Rankin (1889-1932)   **1961**

Cut signature .... Never seen

Jean Ratelle (1940-)   **1985**

Puck $40
Cut signature $12
8x10 photograph $30

Chuck Rayner (1920-)   **1973**

Puck $75
Cut signature $15
8x10 photograph $40

Ken Reardon (1921-)   **1966**

Puck $30
Cut signature $7
8x10 photograph $30

Henri Richard (1936-)   **1979**

Tri-Star Productions Photo

Puck $50
Cut signature $10
8x10 photograph $30
Authenticated 8x10 photograph $40

Maurice Richard (1921-2000)   **1961**

Puck $100
Cut signature $50
8x10 photograph $125

George Richardson (1887-1916)   **1950**

Cut signature .... Never seen

Gordie Roberts (1891-1966)   **1971**

Cut signature .... Never seen

Larry Robinson (1951-)   **1995**

Puck $40
Cut signature $10
8x10 photograph $25

Art Ross (1886-1964)   **1945**

Cut signature $400

Blair Russel (1880-1961)   **1965**

Cut signature .... Never seen

Ernie Russell (1883-1963)   **1965**

Cut signature .... Never seen

Jack Ruttan (1889-1973)   **1962**

Cut signature $250

Borje Salming (1951-)   **1996**

Puck $30
Cut signature $7
8x10 photograph $20

Dennis Savard (1961-)   **2000**

Puck $30
Cut signature $8
8x10 photograph $20

Serge Savard (1946-)   **1986**

Puck $30
Cut signature $10
8x10 photograph $25

Terry Sawchuck (1929-1970)   **1971**

Cut signature $250
8x10 photograph $750

Fred Scanlan (? - ?)   **1965**

Cut signature .... Never seen

Milt Schmidt (1918-)   **1961**

Puck $30
Cut signature $10
8x10 photograph $25

Sweeney Schriner (1911-1990)   **1962**

Cut signature $125

Earl Seibert (1911-1990)   **1963**

Cut signature $100

Oliver Seibert (1881-1944)   **1961**

Cut signature .... Never seen

Eddie Shore (1902-1985)   **1947**

Cut signature $250
8x10 photograph $350

Steve Shutt (1952-)   **1993**

Puck $30
Cut signature $10
8x10 photograph $25

Babe Siebert (1904-1939)   **1964**

Cut signature $400

Joe Simpson (1893-1973)   **1962**

Cut signature $300

Darryl Sittler (1950)   **1989**

Puck $30
Cut signature $10
8x10 photograph $20

Alfred Smith (1873-1953)   **1962**

Cut signature .... Never seen

Billy Smith (1950-)   **1993**

Puck $30
Authenticated puck $40
Cut signature $10
8x10 photograph $25
Authenticated 8x10 photograph $40

Clint Smith (1913-)   **1991**

Puck $60
Cut signature $10
8x10 photograph $40

Hooley Smith (1903-1963)   **1972**

Cut signature .... Never seen

Tommy Smith (1885-1966)   **1973**

Cut signature .... Never seen

Allan Stanley (1926-)   **1981**

Puck $25
Cut signature $7
8x10 photograph $15

Barney Stanley (1893-1971)   **1962**

Cut signature $200

Peter Stastny (1956-)   **1998**

Puck $30
Cut signature $10
8x10 photograph $20

Jack Stewart (1917-1983)   **1964**

Cut signature $100

Nels Stewart (1902-1957)   **1962**

Cut signature $350

Red Storey (1918-)   **1967**

Puck $30
Cut signature $7
8x10 photograph $20

Bruce Stuart (1882-1961)   **1961**

Cut signature .... Never seen

Cyclone Taylor (1883-1979)   **1947**

Cut signature $400

Tiny Thompson (1905-1981)   **1959**

Cut signature $125
8x10 photograph $200

Vladislav Tretiak (1952-)   **1989**

Puck $35
Cut signature $10
8x10 photograph $30

Harry Trihey (1877-1942)   **1950**

Cut signature .... Never seen

Bryan Trottier (1956-)   **1997**

Mounted Memories Photo

Puck $35
Authenticated puck $60
Cut signature $8

8x10 phoptograph $25
Authenticated 8x10 photograph $60

Norm Ullman (1935-)   **1982**

Puck $25
Cut signature $7
8x10 photograph $15

Georges Vezina (1887-1926)   **1945**

Cut signature $600

Jack Walker (1888-1950)   **1960**

Hockey card.. Unlikely
Cut signature .... Never seen

Marty Walsh (1883-1915)   **1962**

Cut signature .... Never seen

Harry E. Watson (1898-1957)   **1962**

Cut signature .... Never seen

Harry P. Watson (1923-)   **1994**

Puck $30
Cut signature $7
8x10 photograph $20

Cooney Weiland (1904-1985)   **1971**

Cut signature $125

Harry Westwick (1876-1957)   **1962**

Cut signature .... Never seen

Fred Whitcroft (1882-1931)   **1962**

Cut signature .... Never seen

Gordon Wilson (1895-1970)   **1962**

Cut signature $300

Gump Worsley (1929-)   **1980**

Puck $40
Cut signature $10
8x10 photograph $30

Roy Worters (1900-1957)   **1969**

Cut signature $350

RETIRED HOCKEY PLAYER AUTOGRAPHS

Player	Puck	Auth. Puck	Photo	Auth. Photo
Glenn Anderson	$20		$15	
Murray Bannerman	$20			
Bobby Baun	$20		$12	

Mounted Memories Photo

Player	Puck	Auth. Puck	Photo	Auth. Photo
Ray Bourque	$60	$150	$50	$150
Neal Broten	$20		$10	
Herb Carnegie	$15		$12	
Wayne Cashman	$20		$10	
Dino Ciccarelli	$20		$10	
Wendel Clark	$20		$10	
Bill Clement	$15		$10	
Paul Coffey	$30		$20	
Roger Crozier *	$250		$150	
Alexandre Daigle	$10		$5	
Dick Duff	$15		$10	
Don Edwards	$15		$10	
Ron Ellis	$15		$10	
Mike Eruzionne	$20		$10	
Doug Favell	$15		$10	
Bernie Federko	$15		$10	
John Ferguson	$15		$10	
Lou Fontinato	$15		$10	

Mounted Memories Photo

Player	Puck	Auth. Puck	Photo	Auth. Photo
Grant Fuhr	$20		$15	
Gilles Gilbert	$15	$30	$10	$30
Clark Gillies	$15		$10	
Bill Goldsworthy *	$60		$50	
Butch Goring	$15		$10	
Phil Goyette	$10		$10	

Player	Puck	Auth. Puck	Photo	Auth. Photo
Vic Hadfield	$15		$10	
Billy Harris	$15		$10	
Glenn Healy	$20		$10	
Camille Henry	$15		$10	
Jim Henry	$40		$20	
Ron Hextall	$20		$10	
Larry Hillman	$10		$10	
Ken Hodge	$15		$10	
Marty Howe	$15		$10	
Mark Howe	$30		$20	
Kelly Hrudey	$20		$10	
Dennis Hull	$20		$10	
Larry Jeffrey	$10		$10	
Pat LaFontaine	$15		$10	
Al Lafrate	$10		$10	
Reggie Leach	$15		$10	
Normand Leveille	$10		$10	
Ken Linseman	$10		$10	
Rick MacLeish	$15		$10	
Keith Magnuson	$15		$10	
Pete Mahovlich	$15		$10	
Chico Maki	$10		$10	
Rick Martin	$15		$10	
John McKenzie	$30		$15	
Rick Middleton	$20		$15	
Andy Moog	$25		$15	
Cam Neely	$40		$25	
Bob Nevin	$10		$10	
Bernie Nicholls	$15		$10	
Bobby Nystrom	$30		$40	
Willie O'Ree	$15		$10	
Terry O'Reilly	$15		$10	
Mike Palmateer	$15		$10	
Jim Pappin	$10		$10	
Dean Prentice	$10		$10	

Mounted Memories Photo

Player	Puck	Auth. Puck	Photo	Auth. Photo
Brian Propp	$15		$10	
Rob Ramage	$10		$10	
Bill Ranford	$15		$10	
Glenn Resch	$25		$10	

Player	Puck	Auth. Puck	Photo	Auth. Photo
Manon Rheaume	$10		$10	
Derek Sanderson	$25		$15	
Dave Schultz	$25		$15	
Eddie Shack	$20		$15	
Charlie Simmer	$10		$10	
Ron Stewart	$10		$10	
Jean-Guy Talbot	$10		$10	
Dave Taylor	$10		$10	
Mario Tremblay	$10		$10	
Garry Unger	$10		$10	
Rogie Vachon	$25		$15	
Rick Vaive	$15		$15	
John Vanbiesbrouck	$15	$80	$10	$80
Mike Walton	$10		$10	
Kenny Wharram	$15		$10	
Tiger Williams	$20		$15	

ACTIVE HOCKEY PLAYER AUTOGRAPHS

Player	Puck	Auth. Puck	Photo	Auth. Photo
David Aebischer	$20		$10	
Jason Allison	$20		$15	
Tony Amonte	$25		$20	
Dave Andreychuk	$20		$15	
Tom Barrasso	$35		$30	

Steiner Sports Photo

Player	Puck	Auth. Puck	Photo	Auth. Photo
Ed Belfour	$40		$35	$100
Todd Bertuzzi	$25		$20	
Dan Blackburn	$20		$15	
Rob Blake	$30		$25	
Peter Bondra	$25		$20	
P. Bouchard	$20		$15	
Brian Boucher	$20		$15	
Jay Bouwmeester	$20		$15	
Martin Brodeur	$100	$130	$75	$125

Player	Puck	Auth. Puck	Photo	Auth. Photo
Pavel Bure	$40	$90	$30	$90
Valeri Bure	$15		$10	
Sean Burke	$25		$20	
Guy Carbonneau	$10		$15	
Roman Cechmanek	$15		$15	
Chris Chelios	$35	$80	$30	$110
Stanislov Chistov	$20		$15	
Dan Cloutier	$20		$15	
Mike Comrie	$35		$35	
Shayne Corson	$20		$15	
Russ Courtnall	$15		$10	
Byron Dafoe	$20		$15	
V. Damphousse	$20		$15	
Pavel Datsyuk	$25		$25	
Pavol Demitra	$20		$15	
Marc Denis	$20		$15	
Tie Domi	$20		$15	
Chris Drury	$20		$15	
Mike Dunham	$20		$15	
Patrik Elias	$20		$15	$50
Sergei Fedorov	$60	$150	$50	$150
Manny Fernandez			$25	

Player	Puck	Auth. Puck	Photo	Auth. Photo
Theo Fleury	$25		$15	
Peter Forsberg	$75		$60	
Ron Francis	$25	$90	$20	$50
Alexander Frolov	$25		$20	
Marian Gaborik	$40		$35	
Simon Gagne	$20		$15	
J.-Sebastien Giguere	$30		$30	
Doug Gilmour	$25		$20	
Scott Gomez	$20		$15	
Bill Guerin	$20		$20	

Mounted Memories Photo

Player	Puck	Auth. Puck	Photo	Auth. Photo
Dominik Hasek	$25	$100	$20	$90
Derian Hatcher	$30		$25	
Martin Havlat	$20		$15	
Dany Heatley	$60		$30	
Johan Hedberg	$20		$15	
Milan Hejduk	$25		$20	
Bobby Holik	$25		$20	
Marian Hossa	$25		$20	
Brett Hull	$75	$110	$60	$100
Jarome Iginla	$40		$30	
Jaromir Jagr	$65		$50	
Paul Kariya	$50		$40	
Nikolai Khabibulin			$25	
Saku Koivu	$25		$20	
Olaf Kolzig	$25		$15	
Alexei Kovalev	$20		$15	
Curtis Joseph	$25		$30	
Igor Larionov	$25		$20	
Vincent Lecavalier	$25		$20	
John LeClair	$25		$20	
Brian Leetch	$40	$90	$30	$90
Manny Legace	$25		$20	
Claude Lemieux	$20		$15	
Mario Lemieux	$175	$230	$175	$250
Nicklas Lidstrom	$50		$25	
Eric Lindros	$30	$90	$20	$90
Roberto Luongo	$20		$15	
Al MacInnis	$40		$30	
Patrick Marleau	$20		$15	
Mark Messier	$75	$150	$60	$150
Mike Modano	$35	$80	$25	$70
Alexander Mogilny	$20		$15	
Brenden Morrow	$20		$15	
Joe Mullen	$20		$15	

Player	Puck	Auth. Puck	Photo	Auth. Photo
Kirk Muller	$20		$15	
Larry Murphy	$20		$15	
Evgeni Nabokov	$30		$20	
Rick Nash	$30		$20	
Markus Naslund	$40		$35	
Scott Niedermayer	$25		$15	
Joe Nieuwendyk	$30		$25	
Owen Nolan	$25		$15	
Adam Oates	$25		$15	
Mattias Ohlund	$20		$10	
Chris Osgood	$20		$15	
Ziggy Palffy	$25		$20	
Jay Pandolfo			$30	
Mike Peca	$20	$60	$15	
Felix Potvin	$20		$15	
Keith Primeau	$20		$15	
Bob Probert	$15		$10	
Chris Pronger	$35		$25	
Mark Recchi	$20		$15	
Mike Richter	$35	$90	$25	$90
Gary Roberts	$20		$15	
Luc Robitaille	$20		$15	
Jeremy Roenick	$20		$15	
Dwayne Roloson	$20		$15	
Patrick Roy	$150		$130	

Mounted Memories Photo

Player	Puck	Auth. Puck	Photo	Auth. Photo
Joe Sakic	$75		$65	
Sergei Samsonov	$30		$20	
Teemu Selanne	$40		$35	
Brendan Shanahan	$40		$35	
Jason Spezza	$30		$25	
Scott Stevens	$40		$35	$90
Martin Straka	$20		$15	
Mats Sundin	$25		$20	
Gary Suter	$15		$10	
Petr Sykora	$20		$15	$50
Alex Tanguay	$25		$20	$50
Jose Theodore	$40		$30	$35
Joe Thornton	$40		$35	
Keith Tkachuk	$40		$30	
Rick Tocchet	$15		$10	
Marty Turco	$35		$25	
Pierre Turgeon	$15		$10	
Pat Verbeek	$15		$10	
Mike Vernon	$40		$30	
Kevin Weekes	$20		$15	
Doug Weight	$15		$15	
Alexei Yashin	$20		$15	
Steve Yzerman	$75	$150	$60	$150
Henrik Zetterberg	$30		$25	

BOXING AUTOGRAPHS

Charles Adkins

Cut Signature	$10
Photo	$25
Glove	$45

Virgil Akins

Cut Signature	$15
Photo	$35
Glove	$125

Muhammad Ali

Steiner Sports Photo

Cut Signature	$50
Photo	$150-$225
Glove	$200-$250
Religious Pamphlet	$75
(as Cassius Clay)	
Cut Signature	$175-$300
Photo	$400-$500
Glove	$(varies)

Lou Ambers *

Cut Signature	$20
Photo	$40
Glove	$150

Fred Apostoli *

Cut Signature	$35
Photo	$100
Glove	$350

Art Aragon

Cut Signature	$10
Photo	$20
Glove	$50

Alexis Arguello

Cut Signature	$10
Photo	$30
Glove	$75

Henry Armstrong *

Cut Signature	$100
Photo	$200
Glove	$900

Abe Attell *

Cut Signature	$75
Photo	$200
Glove	$750

Buddy Baer *

Cut Signature	$25
Photo	$50
Glove	$150

Max Baer *

Cut Signature	$150
Photo	$350

Glove	$1,500

Carmen Basilio

Cut Signature	$15
Photo	$30
Glove	$75

Nino Benvenuti

Cut Signature	$15
Photo	$65
Glove	$200

Kid Berg *

Cut Signature	$25
Photo	$60
Glove	$275

Paul Berlenbach *

Cut Signature	$30
Photo	$60
Glove	$300

Melio Bettina *

Cut Signature	$15
Photo	$35
Glove	$100

Riddick Bowe

Cut Signature	$10
Photo	$25
Glove	$75

James J. Braddock *

Cut Signature	$100
Photo	$300
Glove	$1,500

Mark Breland

Cut Signature	$10
Photo	$20
Glove	$75

Teddy Brenner

Cut Signature	$5
Photo	$20
Glove	$40

Joe Brown

Cut Signature	$10
Photo	$15
Glove	$60

Frank Bruno

Cut Signature	$5
Photo	$10
Glove	$40

Ken Buchanan

Cut Signature	$10
Photo	$25
Glove	$60

Tommy Burns *

Cut Signature	$300
Photo	$800
Glove	$3,000

Mushy Callahan

Cut Signature	$15
Photo	$30
Glove	$100

Hector Camacho

Cut Signature	$10
Photo	$20
Glove	$65

Tony Canzoneri *

Cut Signature	$60
Photo	$150
Glove	$600

Michael Carbajal

Cut Signature	$10
Photo	$15
Glove	$60

Primo Carnera *

Cut Signature	$250
Photo	$500
Glove	$2,400

Georges Carpentier *

Cut Signature	$150
Photo	$250
Glove	$1,100

Jimmy Carter *

Cut Signature	$15
Photo	$40
Glove	$100

Rubin "Hurricane" Carter

Cut Signature	$10
Photo	$25
Glove	$75

Rocky Castellani

Cut Signature	$10
Photo	$15
Glove	$75

Marcel Cerdan *

Cut Signature	$350
Photo	$900
Glove	$3,500

Bobby Chacon

Cut Signature	$10
Photo	$25
Glove	$100

Jeff Chandler

Cut Signature	$5
Photo	$10
Glove	$40

Ezzard Charles *

Cut Signature	$125
Photo	$275
Glove	$1,100

Julio Cesar Chavez

Cut Signature	$15
Photo	$40
Glove	$150

George Chuvalo

Cut Signature	$15
Photo	$30
Glove	$75

Gil Clancy

Cut Signature	$5
Photo	$10
Glove	$40

Randal "Tex" Cobb

Cut Signature $10
Photo $15
Glove $50

Gerrie Coetzee

Cut Signature $10
Photo $15
Glove $50

Curtis Cokes

Cut Signature $10
Photo $15
Glove $50

Billy Conn *

Cut Signature $35
Photo $75
Glove $300

Gerry Cooney

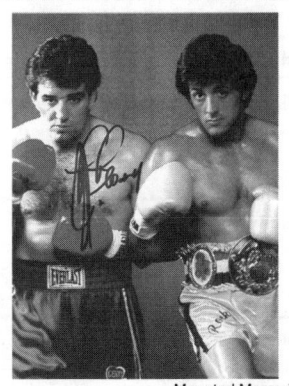

Mounted Memories Photo

Cut Signature $10
Photo $15
Glove $50

James J. Corbett *

Cut Signature $550
Photo $1,000
Glove $4,000

Johnny Coulon *

Cut Signature $60
Photo $125
Glove $500

Bobby Czyz

Cut Signature $10
Photo $15
Glove $50

Chuck Davey

Cut Signature $4
Photo $8
Glove $35

Oscar De La Hoya

Cut Signature $20
Photo $40
Glove $150

Paddy DeMarco

Cut Signature $6
Photo $15
Glove $50

Tony DeMarco

Cut Signature $6
Photo $15
Glove $50

Jack Dempsey

Cut Signature $100
Photo $225
Glove $800

Michael Dokes

Cut Signature $10
Photo $15
Glove $40

Angelo Dundee

Cut Signature $15
Photo $20
Glove $60

Chris Dundee

Cut Signature $15
Photo $40
Glove $100

Johnny Dundee *

Cut Signature $60
Photo $125
Glove $500

Don Dunphy

Cut Signature $10
Photo $20
Glove $50

Roberto Duran

Cut Signature $20
Photo $45
Glove $175

Flash Elorde

Cut Signature $25
Photo $55
Glove $250

Jimmy Ellis

Cut Signature $10
Photo $15
Glove $50

Alfredo Escalera

Cut Signature $8
Photo $15
Glove $60

Johnny Famechon

Cut Signature $8
Photo $15
Glove $60

Tommy Farr

Cut Signature $25
Photo $60
Glove $250

Jeff Fenech

Cut Signature $8
Photo $15
Glove $60

Jackie Fields

Cut Signature $10
Photo $20
Glove $60

Bob Fitzsimmons *

Cut Signature $2,500
Photo $7,500
Glove $16,000

Nat Fleischer

Cut Signature $15
Photo $30
Glove $120

George Foreman

Mounted Memories Photo

Cut Signature $25
Photo $50
Glove $125

Bob Foster

Cut Signature $10
Photo $15
Glove $75

Joe Frazier

Mounted Memories Photo

Cut Signature $15
Photo $30
Glove $100

Gene Fullmer

Cut Signature $10
Photo $20
Glove $75

Charlie Fusari

Cut Signature $5
Photo $10
Glove $40

Eddie Futch

Cut Signature $15
Photo $20
Glove $75

Tony Galento

Cut Signature $60
Photo $100
Glove $425

Ceferino Garcia

Cut Signature $10
Photo $15
Glove $50

Kid Gavilan

Cut Signature $25
Photo $50
Glove $175

Joey Giambra

Cut Signature	$10
Photo	$15
Glove	$40

Joey Giardello

Cut Signature	$10
Photo	$20
Glove	$75

Abe Goldstein *

Cut Signature	$45
Photo	$90
Glove	$390

Wilfredo Gomez

Cut Signature	$10
Photo	$20
Glove	$75

Rocky Graziano *

Cut Signature	$35
Photo	$65
Glove	$275

Emile Griffith

Cut Signature	$10
Photo	$15
Glove	$50

Marvin Hagler

Cut Signature	$20
Photo	$50
Glove	$150

Marvin Hart *

Cut Signature	$1,000
Photo	$2,500
Glove	$9,000

Thomas Hearns

Cut Signature	$15
Photo	$35
Glove	$125

Larry Holmes

Cut Signature	$20
Photo	$40
Glove	$100

Evander Holyfield

Cut Signature	$25
Photo	$40
Glove	$100

Al Hostak

Cut Signature	$15
Photo	$30
Glove	$125

Beau Jack *

Cut Signature	$15
Photo	$40
Glove	$90

James J. Jeffries *

Cut Signature	$450
Photo	$900
Glove	$3,750

Lew Jenkins

Cut Signature	$10
Photo	$15
Glove	$60

Eder Jofre

Cut Signature	$10

Photo	$25
Glove	$80

Ingemar Johansson

Cut Signature	$15
Photo	$30
Glove	$125

Harold Johnson

Cut Signature	$10
Photo	$15
Glove	$50

Jack Johnson *

Cut Signature	$1,000
Photo	$2,000
Glove	$7,500

Ralph Jones

Cut Signature	$10
Photo	$20
Glove	$75

Roy Jones

Cut Signature	$15
Photo	$40
Glove	$125

Jack Kearns

Cut Signature	$30
Photo	$60
Glove	$250

Don King

Mounted Memories Photo

Cut Signature	$10
Photo	$20
Glove	$50

Fidel LaBarba

Cut Signature	$10
Photo	$20
Glove	$75

Jake LaMotta

Cut Signature	$15
Photo	$30
Glove	$100

Roland Lastarza

Cut Signature	$10
Photo	$15
Glove	$50

Benny Leonard *

Cut Signature	$60
Photo	$150
Glove	$550

Sugar Ray Leonard

Cut Signature	$20
Photo	$35

Mounted Memories Photo

Glove	$125

Gus Lesnevich

Cut Signature	$25
Photo	$50
Glove	$215

John Henry Lewis *

Cut Signature	$65
Photo	$160
Glove	$725

Lennox Lewis

Cut Signature	$25
Photo	$50
Glove	$175

Sonny Liston *

Cut Signature	$350
Photo	$1,000
Glove	$4,000

Danny Lopez

Cut Signature	$5
Photo	$10
Glove	$40

Tommy Loughran *

Cut Signature	$35
Photo	$80
Glove	$375

Joe Louis *

Cut Signature	$200
Photo	$375
Glove	$1,700

Ray Mancini

Cut Signature	$10
Photo	$30
Glove	$100

Sammy Mandell

Cut Signature	$10
Photo	$20
Glove	$85

Rocky Marciano *

Cut Signature	$350
Photo	$900
Glove	$2,250

Buster Mathis Sr.*

Cut Signature	$15
Photo	$35
Glove	$100

Joey Maxim

Cut Signature	$10
Photo	$20
Glove	$75

Jimmy McLarnin

Cut Signature	$30
Photo	$90
Glove	$150

Ray Mercer

Cut Signature	$10
Photo	$20
Glove	$50

Freddie Mills

Cut Signature	$20
Photo	$50
Glove	$215

Charles Mitchell

Cut Signature	$20
Photo	$50
Glove	$215

Carlos Monzon *

Cut Signature	$50
Photo	$125
Glove	$325

Archie Moore *

Cut Signature	$15
Photo	$40
Glove	$125

Michael Moorer

Cut Signature	$10
Photo	$20
Glove	$60

Tommy Morrison

Mounted Memories Photo

Cut Signature	$10
Photo	$25
Glove	$50

Eddie M. Muhammad

Cut Signature	$5
Photo	$15
Glove	$55

Matthew S. Muhammad

Cut Signature	$5
Photo	$15
Glove	$55

Jose Napoles

Cut Signature	$15
Photo	$30
Glove	$90

Battling Nelson *

Cut Signature	$125
Photo	$250
Glove	$900

Terry Norris

Cut Signature	$7

Photo	$15
Glove	$60

Ken Norton

Cut Signature	$10
Photo	$25
Glove	$75

Lou Nova

Cut Signature	$5
Photo	$10
Glove	$45

Ruben Olivares

Cut Signature	$10
Photo	$20
Glove	$60

Carl Olson

Cut Signature	$7
Photo	$15
Glove	$60

Carlos Ortiz

Cut Signature	$10
Photo	$20
Glove	$75

Carlos Palmino

Cut Signature	$5
Photo	$10
Glove	$45

Bob Montgomery

Cut Signature	$6
Photo	$13
Glove	$55

Billy Papke *

Cut Signature	$300
Photo	$600
Glove	$2,250

Willie Pastrano

Cut Signature	$10
Photo	$15
Glove	$50

Floyd Patterson

Cut Signature	$10
Photo	$30
Glove	$100

Eusebio Pedroza

Cut Signature	$5
Photo	$10
Glove	$40

Willie Pep

Cut Signature	$10
Photo	$30
Glove	$75

Aaron Pryor

Cut Signature	$5
Photo	$15
Glove	$55

Dwight Qawi

Cut Signature	$5
Photo	$10
Glove	$40

Jerry Quarry *

Cut Signature	$20
Photo	$40
Glove	$100

Sugar Ramos

Cut Signature	$10
Photo	$25
Glove	$90

Tex Rickard *

Cut Signature	$170
Photo	$360
Glove	$1,600

Eddie Risko

Cut Signature	$10
Photo	$25
Glove	$85

Willie Ritchie *

Cut Signature	$20
Photo	$40
Glove	$170

Sugar Ray Robinson *

Cut Signature	$75-$100
Photo	$250
Glove	$1,000

Louis Rodriguez

Cut Signature	$10
Photo	$25
Glove	$100

Edwin Rosario

Cut Signature	$10
Photo	$20
Glove	$60

Maxie Rosenbloom *

Cut Signature	$40
Photo	$80
Glove	$350

Barney Ross *

Cut Signature	$40
Photo	$100
Glove	$350

Sandy Saddler

Cut Signature	$10
Photo	$35
Glove	$80

Johnny Saxton

Cut Signature	$10
Photo	$25
Glove	$100

Max Schmeling

Cut Signature	$20
Photo	$50
Glove	$250

Marty Servo

Cut Signature	$5
Photo	$10
Glove	$40

Jack Sharkey *

Cut Signature	$100
Photo	$200
Glove	$750

Earnie Shavers

Cut Signature	$10
Photo	$25
Glove	$60

Leon Spinks

Cut Signature	$10

Mounted Memories Photo

Photo $20
Glove $75

Michael Spinks

Cut Signature $15
Photo $30
Glove $100

John L. Sullivan *

Cut Signature $650
Photo $1,100
Glove $4,800

John Tate

Cut Signature $10
Photo $20
Glove $70

Ernie Terrell

Cut Signature $10
Photo $20
Glove $70

Pinklon Thomas

Cut Signature $10
Photo $20
Glove $70

Dick Tiger *

Cut Signature $75
Photo $200
Glove $900

Gene Tunney *

Cut Signature $100
Photo $200
Glove $900

Randy Turpin *

Cut Signature $125
Photo $200
Glove $900

Mike Tyson

Mounted Memories Photo

Cut Signature $40
Photo $100
Glove $175

Jersey Joe Walcott *

Cut Signature $35
Photo $125
Glove $325

Mickey Walker *

Cut Signature $75
Photo $200
Glove $800

Mike Weaver

Cut Signature $10

Photo $15
Glove $50

Sweet Pea Whitaker

Cut Signature $10
Photo $15
Glove $50

Jess Willard *

Cut Signature $250
Photo $600
Glove $2,400

Cleveland Williams

Cut Signature $10
Photo $20
Glove $60

Ike Williams *

Cut Signature $15
Photo $30
Glove $150

Tony Zale *

Cut Signature $15
Photo $25
Glove $90

Alfonso Zamora

Cut Signature $10
Photo $15
Glove $75

GOLF AUTOGRAPHS

*INDICATES PLAYER IS DECEASED

Tommy Aaron
Photo	$20
Ball	$25

Amy Alcott
Photo	$25
Ball	$25

Tommy Armour
Photo	$1,250
Ball	Unknown
Signature	$375
Typed Letter Signed	$750
Handwritten Letter Signed	$1,250

George Archer
Photo	$20
Ball	$25

Paul Azinger
Photo	$20
Ball	$25

Seve Ballesteros
Photo	$25
Ball	$30

Butch Baird
Photo	$15
Ball	$20

Miller Barber
Photo	$25
Ball	$25

Andy Bean
Photo	$25
Ball	$25

Chip Beck
Photo	$20
Ball	$20

Patti Berg
Photo	$30
Ball	$30

Tommy Bolt

Photo	$20
Ball	$20
Signature	$5
Typed Letter Signed	$25
Handwritten Letter Signed	$40

Julius Boros *

Photo	$125
Ball	$225
Signature	$35
Typed Letter Signed	$75
Handwritten Letter Signed	$150

Jack Burke

Photo	$20
Ball	$25
Signature	$5
Typed Letter Signed	$25
Handwritten Letter Signed	$50

Gay Brewer *
Photo	$15-$25
Ball	$20-$30

Walt Burkemo
Photo	Unknown
Ball	Unknown
Signature	$125
Typed Letter Signed	$250
Handwritten Letter Signed	Unknown

Billy Casper
Photo	$30
Ball	$35

Jim Colbert
Photo	$15
Ball	$20

Harry Cooper

Photo	$75
Ball	$100
Signature	$15
Typed Letter Signed	$50
Handwritten Letter Signed	$100

Henry Cotton

Photo	$450
Ball	Unknown
Signature	$150
Typed Letter Signed	$350
Handwritten Letter Signed	$500

Fred Couples
Photo	$40
Ball	$40

Tom Creavy

Photo	Unknown
Ball	Unknown
Signature	$300
Typed Letter Signed	Unknown
Handwritten Letter Signed	Unknown

Ben Crenshaw
Photo	$30
Ball	$30

Fred Daly

Photo	Unknown
Ball	Unknown
Signature	$100
Typed Letter Signed	$225

John Daly
Photo	$30
Ball	$30

Jimmy Demaret

Photo	$500
Ball	Unknown
Signature	$175
Typed Letter Signed	$400
Handwritten Letter Signed	$650

Leo Diegal

Photo	$350
Ball	Unknown
Signature	$125
Typed Letter Signed	$250
Handwritten Letter Signed	$400

David Duval
Photo	$40
Ball	$50

Olin Dutra
Photo	$300
Ball	Unknown
Signature	$100

(signature)

Typed Letter Signed	$225
Handwritten Letter Signed	$350

Lee Elder

Photo	$15
Ball	$20

Steve Elkington

Photo	$15
Ball	$20

Ernie Els

Photo	$30
Ball	$30

Chick Evans

(signature) Chick Evans

Photo	$600
Ball	Unknown
Signature	$225
Typed Letter Signed	$425
Handwritten Letter Signed	$650

Nick Faldo

Photo	$30
Ball	$40

Johnny Farrell

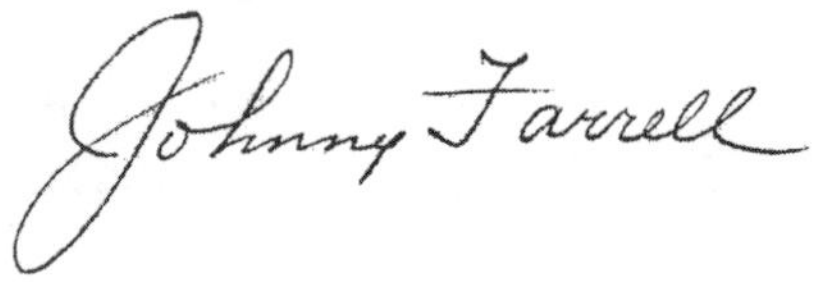

(signature) Johnny Farrell

Photo	$250
Ball	Unknown
Signature	$75
Typed Letter Signed	$150
Handwritten Letter Signed	$275

Maxie Faulkner

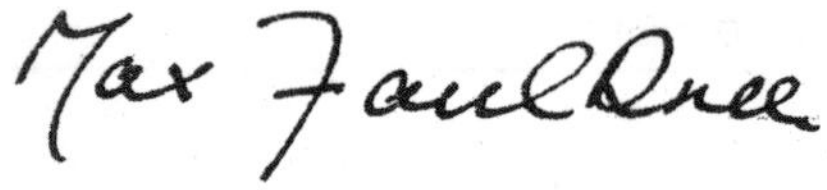

(signature) Max Faulkner

Photo	$50
Ball	$50
Signature	$20
Typed Letter Signed	$50
Handwritten Letter Signed	$100

Jim Ferrier

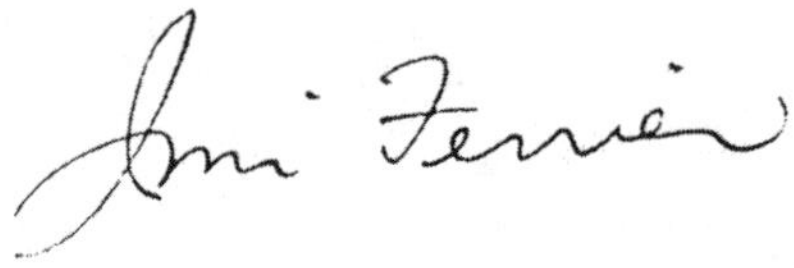

(signature) Jim Ferrier

Photo	$125
Ball	Unknown
Signature	$50
Typed Letter Signed	$100
Handwritten Letter Signed	$150

Dan Finsterwald

Photo	$20

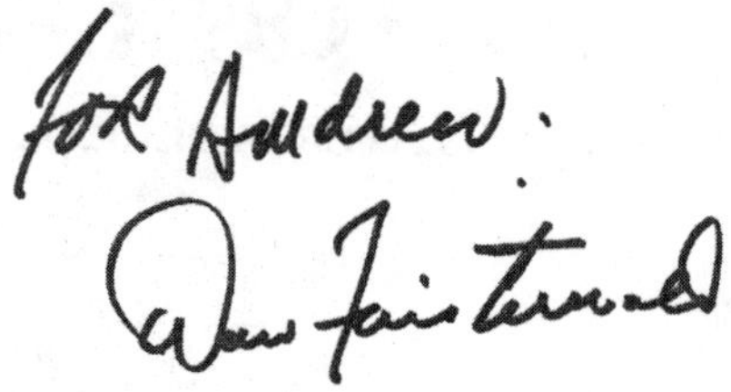

(signature) for Andrew; Dan Finsterwald

Ball	$20
Signature	$5
Typed Letter Signed	$25
Handwritten Letter Signed	$50

Jack Fleck

(signature) Jack Fleck

Photo	$25
Ball	$30
Signature	$10
Typed Letter Signed	$30
Handwritten Letter Signed	$75

Ray Floyd

Photo	$30
Ball	$30

Doug Ford

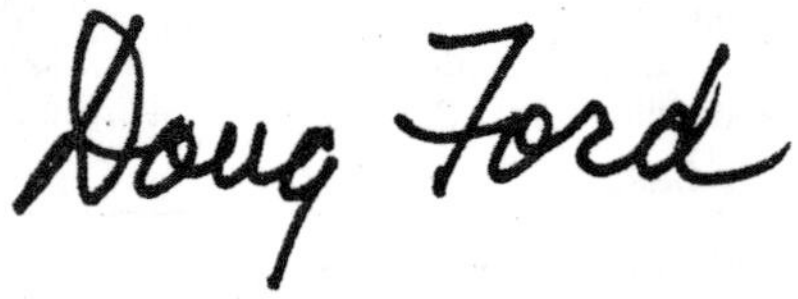

(signature) Doug Ford

Photo	$20
Ball	$20
Signature	$5
Typed Letter Signed	$25
Handwritten Letter Signed	$50

Sergio Garcia

Photo	$40
Ball	$45

Victor Ghezzi

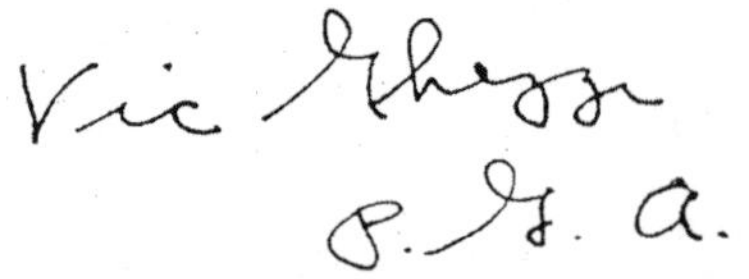

(signature) Vic Ghezzi P. G. A.

Photo	$225
Ball	Unknown
Signature	$75
Typed Letter Signed	$150
Handwritten Letter Signed	$250

Hubert Green

Photo	$25
Ball	$25

Ralph Guldahl

Photo	$1,000
Ball	Unknown
Signature	$300
Typed Letter Signed	$600
Handwritten Letter Signed	$1,000

Walter Hagen

Photo	$450

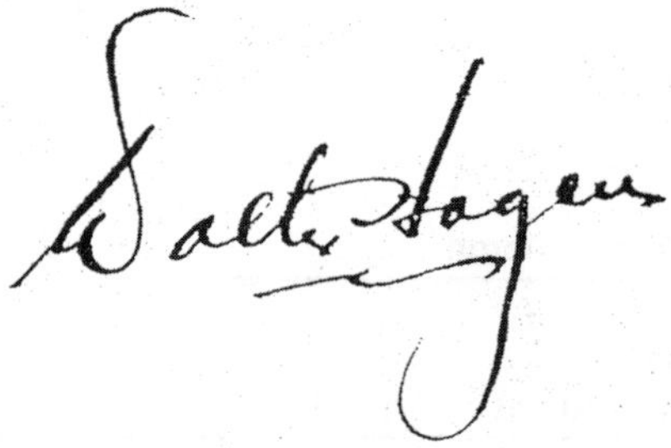

(signature) Walter Hagen

Ball	Unknown
Signature	$150
Typed Letter Signed	$350
Handwritten Letter Signed	$500

Chick Harbert

(signature) Chick Harbert

Photo	$75
Ball	$275
Signature	$20
Typed Letter Signed	$75
Handwritten Letter Signed	$100

Chandler J. Harper

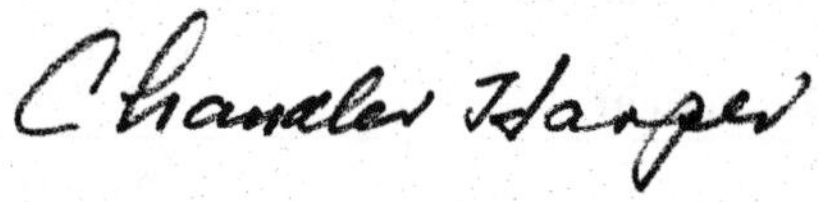

(signature) Chandler Harper

Photo	$25
Ball	$35
Signature	$10
Typed Letter Signed	$25
Handwritten Letter Signed	$60

Jay Hebert

Photo	$15
Ball	$20

Lionel Hebert

(signature) Lionel Hebert

Photo	$65
Ball	$150
Signature	$30
Typed Letter Signed	$65
Handwritten Letter Signed	$125

Ben Hogan *

(signature) Ben Hogan

Photo	$200
Ball	$300
Signature	$80
Typed Letter Signed	$175
Handwritten Letter Signed	$400

Julie Inkster

Photo	$20
Ball	$20

Hale Irwin

Photo	$20
Ball	$25

Lee Janzen

Mounted Memories Photo

Photo	$25
Ball	$25

Tony Jacklin

Photo	$15
Ball	$20

Don January

Photo	$25
Ball	$30

Bobby Jones *

Vintage
Photo	$7,500
Ball	Unknown
Signature	$1,500
Typed Letter Signed	$3,500
Handwritten Letter Signed	$6,000

Modern
Photo	$2,500
Ball	Unknown
Signature	$700
Typed Letter Signed	$1,250

Herman Keiser

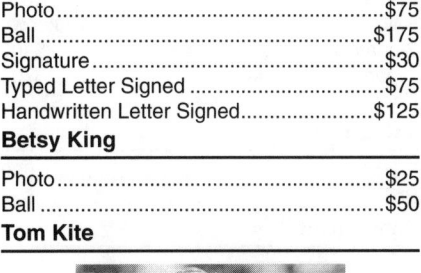

Photo	$75
Ball	$175
Signature	$30
Typed Letter Signed	$75
Handwritten Letter Signed	$125

Betsy King

Photo	$25
Ball	$50

Tom Kite

Mounted Memories Photo

Photo	$20
Ball	$25

Ted Kroll

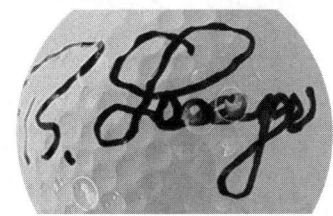

Photo	$30
Ball	$100
Signature	$15
Typed Letter Signed	$30
Handwritten Letter Signed	$60

Bernhard Langer

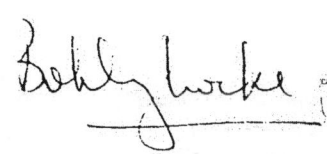

Mounted Memories Photo

Photo	$30
Ball	$30

Tom Lehman

Photo	$25
Ball	$25

Justin Leonard

Photo	$30
Ball	$30

Gene Littler

Photo	$25
Ball	$30

Bob Locke

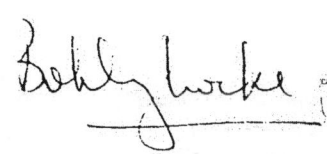

Photo	$400
Ball	Unknown
Signature	$175
Typed Letter Signed	$375
Handwritten Letter Signed	$500

Nancy Lopez

Photo	$25
Ball	$35

Davis Love III

Photo	$35
Ball	$35

Lloyd Mangrum

Photo	$325
Ball	Unknown
Signature	$100

Casey Martin

Typed Letter Signed	$225
Handwritten Letter Signed	$400

Photo	$15
Ball	$20

Fred McLeod

Photo	Unknown
Ball	Unknown
Signature	$200
Typed Letter Signed	$400
Handwritten Letter Signed	Unknown

Phil Mickelson

Photo	$30
Ball	$30

Doc Middlecoff

Photo	$125
Ball	$175
Signature	$30
Typed Letter Signed	$100
Handwritten Letter Signed	$250

Johnny Miller

Photo	$20
Ball	$25

Larry Mize

Photo	$15
Ball	$20

Colin Montgomerie

Photo	$25
Ball	$25

Orville Moody

Photo	$15
Ball	$20

Alex Morrison

Photo	Unknown
Ball	Unknown
Signature	$20
Typed Letter Signed	$40
Handwritten Letter Signed	$60

Bob Murphy

Photo	$20
Ball	$25

Kel Nagle

Photo	$40
Ball	$40
Signature	$20
Typed Letter Signed	$50
Handwritten Letter Signed	$100

Byron Nelson

Photo	$25
Ball	$40
Signature	$10
Typed Letter Signed	$40

Byron Nelson [signature]

Handwritten Letter Signed......................$125

Larry Nelson

Photo $25
Ball $25

Jack Nicklaus

Photo $100
Ball $150

Greg Norman

Photo $50
Ball $80

Mark O'Meara

Photo $35
Ball $35

Francis Ouimet

Photo $1,250
Ball ....Unknown
Signature.....................................$350
Typed Letter Signed $600
Handwritten Letter Signed...................$1,250

Alfred Padgham

[signature: A. H. Padgham]

Photo ....Unknown
Ball ....Unknown
Signature.....................................$275
Typed Letter Signed ....Unknown
Handwritten Letter Signed...............Unknown

Se Ri Pak

Photo $35
Ball $35

Arnold Palmer

Photo $80
Ball $100

Sam Parks

Photo $175
Ball $250
Signature.....................................$75
Typed Letter Signed $125
Handwritten Letter Signed.....................$250

Jesper Parnevik

Mounted Memories Photo

Photo $15
Ball $20

Steve Pate

Photo $15
Ball $20

Corey Pavin

Photo $30
Ball $35

Henry Picard

[signature: Picard]

Photo $225
Ball $350
Signature.....................................$75
Typed Letter Signed $175
Handwritten Letter Signed.....................$400

Gary Player

Photo $35
Ball $40

Nick Price

Photo $30
Ball $30

Betsy Rawls

Photo $40
Ball $60

Johnny Revolta

[signature: Johnny Revolta]

Photo $150
Ball ....Unknown
Signature.....................................$75
Typed Letter Signed $150
Handwritten Letter Signed.....................$300

Chi Chi Rodriguez

Photo $25
Ball $30

Bobby Rosburg

Photo $20
Ball $20
Signature.....................................$5
Typed Letter Signed $25
Handwritten Letter Signed.....................$50

Paul Runyan

[signature: Paul Runyan]

Photo $75
Ball $125
Signature.....................................$25
Typed Letter Signed $60
Handwritten Letter Signed.....................$100

Gene Sarazen *

Photo $75
Ball $125

Gene Sarazen [signature]

Signature.....................................$25
Typed Letter Signed $75
Handwritten Letter Signed.....................$200

Denny Shute

[signature: Denny Shute]

Photo $375
Ball ....Unknown
Signature.....................................$125
Typed Letter Signed $250
Handwritten Letter Signed.....................$400

Scott Simpson

Photo $20
Ball $25

Charles Sifford

Photo $25
Ball $30

Vijay Singh

[signature: Vijay Singh]

Photo $30
Ball $35

Horton Smith

[signature: Horton Smith]

Photo $1,000
Ball ....Unknown
Signature.....................................$400
Typed Letter Signed $700
Handwritten Letter Signed.....................$1,250

J.C. Snead

Photo $20
Ball $25

Sam Snead

[signature: Sam Snead]

Photo $100
Ball $100
Signature.....................................$20
Typed Letter Signed $75
Handwritten Letter Signed.....................$250

Annika Sorenstam

Photo $50
Ball $60

Craig Stadler

Mounted Memories Photo

Photo $30
Ball $35

Payne Stewart *

Photo $75
Ball $125

Frank Stranahan

Frank R Stranahan

Photo $50
Ball $50
Signature $25
Typed Letter Signed $75
Handwritten Letter Signed....................$100

Dave Stockton

Photo $20
Ball $25

Curtis Strange

Photo $30
Ball $35

Hal Sutton

Photo $25
Ball $30

Peter Thomson

Photo $40
Ball $45
Signature $15
Typed Letter Signed $40
Handwritten Letter Signed......................$75

Robert Toski

Bob Toski

Photo $25
Ball $30
Signature $10
Typed Letter Signed $25
Handwritten Letter Signed......................$50

Jerome Travers

Photo ....Unknown
Ball ....Unknown
Signature $150
Typed Letter Signed $275
Handwritten Letter Signed...............Unknown

Lee Trevino

Photo $35
Ball $35

Willie Turnesa

Willie Turnesa

Photo $75
Ball $150
Signature $25
Typed Letter Signed $75
Handwritten Letter Signed....................$125

Sam Urzetta

Sam Urzetta

Photo $30
Ball $40
Signature $10
Typed Letter Signed $30
Handwritten Letter Signed......................$65

Harry Vardon

Photo ....Unknown
Ball ....Unknown
Signature $750
Typed Letter Signed $1,250
Handwritten Letter Signed.................$3,000

Ken Venturi

Photo $25
Ball $30

Lanny Wadkins

Photo $25
Ball $25

Art Wall

A. D. Wall

Photo $40
Ball $100
Signature $15
Typed Letter Signed $45
Handwritten Letter Signed......................$75

Harvie Ward

E Harvie Ward

Photo $35
Ball $35
Signature $15
Typed Letter Signed $40
Handwritten Letter Signed......................$65

Tom Watson

Photo $35
Ball $40

Tom Weiskopf

Photo $20
Ball $25

Lee Westwood

Photo $15
Ball $20

Oscar Willing

Oscar F. Willing

Photo $200
Ball ....Unknown
Signature $75
Typed Letter Signed $100
Handwritten Letter Signed....................$200

Craig Wood

Photo ....Unknown
Ball ....Unknown
Signature $600
Typed Letter Signed ....Unknown
Handwritten Letter Signed...............Unknown

Tiger Woods

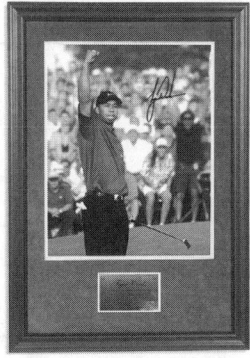

Photo.. $150-$175
Framed Photo (UDA) $1,400
Ball .... $450-$500
Pin Flag (UDA) $800

Charlie Yates

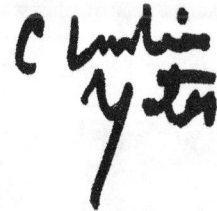

Photo...$100
Ball $125
Signature $50
Typed Letter Signed $100
Handwritten Letter Signed....................$150

Babe Didrikson Zaharias *

Photo.. $150-$200
Ball ....Unknown

Larry Ziegler

Photo $15
Ball $20

Fuzzy Zoeller

Photo $35
Ball $40

TENNIS AUTOGRAPHS

*Indicates Player Is Deceased

Andre Agassi

Photo	$60
Ball	$75
3x5 index card	$15

Arthur Ashe*

Photo	$125-$200
Ball	$200-$250
3x5 index card	$20-$30

Boris Becker

Photo	$25
Ball	$30
3x5 index card	$6

Jonas Bjorkman

Photo	$15
Ball	$20
3x5 index card	$5

Bjorn Borg

Mounted Memories Photo

Photo	$40
Ball	$45
3x5 index card	$6

Sergi Bruguera

Photo	$15
Ball	$20
3x5 index card	$5

Jennifer Capriati

Photo	$30
Ball	$35
3x5 index card	$6

Michael Chang

Photo	$30
Ball	$50
3x5 index card	$6

Amanda Coetzer

Photo	$15
Ball	$20
3x5 index card	$5

Jimmy Connors

Photo	$40
Ball	$60
3x5 index card	$7

Jim Courier

Photo	$25
Ball	$30
3x5 index card	$7

Margaret Court Smith

Photo	$20
Ball	$25
3x5 index card	$6

Lindsay Davenport

Photo	$30
Ball	$35
3x5 index card	$7

Stefan Edberg

Photo	$25
Ball	$30
3x5 index card	$7

Chris Evert

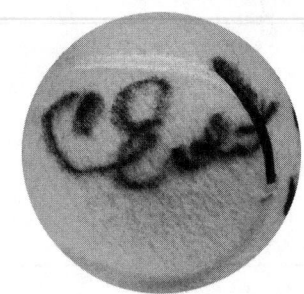

Mounted Memories Photo

Photo	$35
Ball	$50
3x5 index card	$10

Mary Joe Fernandez

Photo	$15
Ball	$20
3x5 index card	$5

Vitas Gerulaitis*

Photo	$75-$100
Ball	$90-$125
3x5 index card	$15-$25

Pancho Gonzalez *

Photo	$60
Ball	$80

3x5 index card	$20-$30

Steffi Graf

Photo	$35
Ball	$45
3x5 index card	$8

Martina Hingis

Photo	$40
Ball	$50
3x5 index card	$10

Goran Ivanisevic

Photo	$25
Ball	$30
3x5 index card	$7

Yevgeny Kafelnikov

Photo	$15
Ball	$20
3x5 index card	$5

Billie Jean King

Photo	$25
Ball	$50
3x5 index card	$6

Petr Korda

Photo	$20
Ball	$25
3x5 index card	$6

Anna Kournikova

Photo	$60
Ball	$80
3x5 index card	$15

Richard Krajicek

Photo	$15
Ball	$20
3x5 index card	$5

Rod Laver

Photo	$20
Ball	$25
3x5 index card	$6

Ivan Lendl

Photo	$30
Ball	$50
3x5 index card	$6

Todd Martin

Photo	$20
Ball	$25
3x5 index card	$5

Conchita Martinez

Photo	$15
Ball	$20
3x5 index card	$5

John McEnroe

Photo	$50
Ball	$75
3x5 index card	$15

Thomas Muster

Photo	$20
Ball	$25
3x5 index card	$6

Ilie Nastase

Photo	$35
Ball	$40
3x5 index card	$10-$12

Martina Navratilova

Photo	$30
Ball	$40
3x5 index card	$8

John Newcombe

Photo	$20
Ball	$25
3x5 index card	$6

Jana Novotna

Photo	$15
Ball	$20
3x5 index card	$5

Mary Pierce

Photo	$20
Ball	$25
3x5 index card	$6

Patrick Rafter

Photo	$15
Ball	$20
3x5 index card	$5

Bobby Riggs*

Photo	$40-$50
Ball	$60-$75
3x5 index card	$10-$20

Carlos Rios

Photo	$20
Ball	$25
3x5 index card	$6

Gabriela Sabatini

Photo	$20
Ball	$25
3x5 index card	$6

Pete Sampras

Photo	$55
Ball	$70
3x5 index card	$10

Vicario A. Sanchez

Photo	$15
Ball	$20
3x5 index card	$5

Monica Seles

Photo	$35
Ball	$50
3x5 index card	$6

Pam Shriver

Photo	$15
Ball	$20
3x5 index card	$5

Michael Stich

Photo	$15
Ball	$20
3x5 index card	$5

Bill Tilden*

Photo	$250
Ball	$300
3x5 index card	$90-$100

Malivai Washington

Photo	$20
Ball	$25
3x5 index card	$6

Mats Wilander

Photo	$20
Ball	$25
3x5 index card	$6

Venus Williams

Photo	$60
Ball	$75
3x5 index card	$15

Serena Williams

Photo	$60
Ball	$75
3x5 index card	$15

Helen Wills-Moody

Photo	$20
Ball	$25
3x5 index card	$6

AUTO RACER AUTOGRAPHS

Active and Retired
*Indicates Deceased

J.C. Agajanian *

Cut signature..$25
8x10 photo $45

Bobby Allison

Mounted Memories Photo

Cut signature..$8
8x10 photo $20

Davey Allison *

Cut signature..$40
8x10 photo $100

Donnie Allison

Cut signature..$5
8x10 photo $12

Joe Amato

Cut signature..$5
8x10 photo $10

John Andretti

Cut signature..$5
8x10 photo $20

Mario Andretti

Cut signature..$15
8x10 photo $35

Michael Andretti

Cut signature..$5
8x10 photo $25

Casey Atwood

Cut signature..$5
8x10 photo $20

Buddy Baker

Cut signature..$10
8x10 photo $20

Cannonball Baker *

Cut signature..$30
8x10 photo $65

Henry Banks

Cut signature..$6
8x10 photo $20

Kenny Brack

Cut signature..$5
8x10 photo $15

Johnny Benson

Cut signature..$5
8x10 photo $20

Joe Bessey

Cut signature..$5
8x10 photo $15

Gary Bettenhausen

Cut signature..$5
8x10 photo $20

Tony Bettenhausen *

Cut signature..$12
8x10 photo $25

Greg Biffle

Cut signature..$5
8x10 photo $20

Dave Blaney

Cut signature..$5
8x10 photo $15

Mike Bliss

Cut signature..$4
8x10 photo $8

Brett Bodine

Cut signature..$5
8x10 photo $15

Geoff Bodine

Cut signature..$7
8x10 photo $20

Todd Bodine

Cut signature..$5
8x10 photo $15

Neil Bonnett *

Cut signature..$30
8x10 photo $75

Craig Breedlove

Cut signature..$5
8x10 photo $25

Jeff Burton

Cut signature..$7
8x10 photo $25

Ward Burton

Cut signature..$7
8x10 photo $20

Kurt Busch

Cut signature..$8
8x10 photo $35

Pancho Carter

Cut signature..$5
8x10 photo $17

Helio Castroneves

Cut signature..$5
8x10 photo $20

Eddie Cheever

Cut signature..$5
8x10 photo $18

Kevin Cogan

Cut signature..$5

8x10 photo $15

Stacy Compton

Cut signature..$4
8x10 photo $10

Earl Cooper *

Cut signature..$45
8x10 photo $95

Derrick Cope

Cut signature..$5
8x10 photo $12

Ricky Craven

Cut signature..$5
8x10 photo $20

Wally Dallenbach

Cut signature..$5
8 x10 photo $15

Mark Donahue *

Cut signature..$55
8x10 photo $110

Mike Dunn

Cut signature..$4
8x10 photo $8

Dale Earnhardt *

Cut signature..$40
8x10 photo $125

Dale Earnhardt Jr.

Cut signature..$15
8x10 photo $50

Bill Elliott

Cut signature..$10
8x10 photo $30

Teo Fabi

Cut signature..$5
8x10 photo $10

Tim Fedewa

Cut signature..$5
8x10 photo $15

Adrian Fernandez

Cut signature..$5
8x10 photo $20

Gil de Ferran

Cut signature..$5
8x10 photo $20

Harvey Firestone Jr. *

Cut signature	$125
8x10 photo	$300

Christian Fittipaldi

Cut signature	$5
8x10 photo	$10

Emerson Fittipaldi

Cut signature	$10
8x10 photo	$25

A.J. Foyt

Cut signature	$12
8x10 photo	$30

Larry Foyt

Cut signature	$4
8x10 photo	$10

Dario Francitti

Cut signature	$5
8x10 photo	$22

Jeff Fuller

Cut signature	$5
8x10 photo	$15

Harry Gant

Mounted Memories Photo

Cut signature	$8
8x10 photo	$20

Don Garlits

Cut signature	$5
8x10 photo	$15

Scott Goodyear

Cut signature	$5
8x10 photo	$20

Jeff Gordon

Cut signature	$20
8x10 photo	$40

Robby Gordon

Cut signature	$5
8x10 photo	$15

David Green

Cut signature	$5
8x10 photo	$15

Jeff Green

Cut signature	$5
8x10 photo	$15

Steve Grissom

Cut signature	$5
8x10 photo	$8

Roberto Guerrero

Cut signature	$5
8x10 photo	$20

Dan Gurney

Cut signature	$8
8x10 photo	$20

Janet Guthrie

Cut signature	$5
8x10 photo	$10

Dean Hall

Cut signature	$5
8x10 photo	$8

Bobby Hamilton

Cut signature	$5
8x10 photo	$20

Kevin Harvick

Cut signature	$10
8x10 photo	$25

Jimmy Hensley

Cut signature	$5
8x10 photo	$15

Damon Hill

Cut signature	$5
8x10 photo	$22

Graham Hill *

Cut signature	$45
8x10 photo	$90

Phil Hill

Cut signature	$5
8x10 photo	$15

Ron Hornaday

Cut signature	$4
8x10 photo	$12

Sam Hornish Jr.

Cut signature	$5
8x10 photo	$25

Ernie Irvan

Cut signature	$10
8x10 photo	$30

Kenny Irwin *

Cut signature	$25
8x10 photo	$50

Dale Jarrett

Cut signature	$10
8x10 photo	$30

Jason Jarrett

Cut signature	$5
8x10 photo	$15

Ned Jarrett

Cut signature	$5
8x10 photo	$15

Gordon Johncock

Cut signature	$10
8x10 photo	$25

Jimmie Johnson

Cut signature	$12
8x10 photo	$35

Junior Johnson

Cut signature	$8
8x10 photo	$25

Parnelli Jones

Cut signature	$10
8x10 photo	$25

Matt Kenseth

Cut signature	$12
8x10 photo	$35

Steve Kinser

Cut signature	$4
8x10 photo	$8

Steve Knapp

Cut signature	$5
8x10 photo	$25

Alan Kulwicki *

Cut signature	$50
8x10 photo	$100

Bobby Labonte

Cut signature	$10
8x10 photo	$30

Terry Labonte

Cut signature	$10
8x10 photo	$25

Randy LaJoie

Cut signature	$5
8x10 photo	$15

Buddy Lazier

Cut signature	$5
8x10 photo	$10

Joe Leonard

Cut signature	$5
8x10 photo	$10

Kevin Lepage

Cut signature	$5
8x10 photo	$10

Chad Little

Cut signature	$5
8x10 photo	$15

Arie Luyendyk

Cut signature	$8
8x10 photo	$20

Jimmy Makar

Cut signature	$5
8x10 photo	$15

Nigel Mansell

Cut signature	$10
8x10 photo	$25

Dave Marcis

Cut signature	$5
8x10 photo	$15

Sterling Marlin

Cut signature	$7
8x10 photo	$30

Mark Martin

Cut signature	$12
8x10 photo	$35

Rick Mast

Cut signature	$4
8x10 photo	$8

Jeremy Mayfield

Cut signature	$5
8x10 photo	$20

Rex Mays *

Cut signature	$140
8x10 photo	$275

Roger McCluskey

Cut signature	$8
8x10 photo	$18

Mike McLaughlin

Cut signature	$5
8x10 photo	$10

Jamie McMurray

Cut signature	$5
8x10 photo	$20

Casey Mears

Cut signature	$5
8x10 photo	$15

Rick Mears

Cut signature	$10
8x10 photo	$25

Juan Montoya

Cut signature	$15
8x10 photo	$25

Ralph Moody Jr.

Cut signature	$8
8x10 photo	$15

Rob Moroso *

Cut signature	$25
8x10 photo	$50

Sterling Moss

Cut signature	$10
8x10 photo	$25

Ted Musgrave

Cut signature	$5
8x10 photo	$20

Jerry Nadeau

Cut signature	$5
8x10 photo	$15

Joe Nemechek

Cut signature	$5
8x10 photo	$15

Ryan Newman

Cut signature	$10
8x10 photo	$30

Barney Oldfield *

Cut signature	$165
8x10 photo	$350

Danny Ongais

Cut signature	$5
8x10 photo	$10

Steve Park

Cut signature	$5
8x10 photo	$20

Todd Parrot

Cut signature	$5
8x10 photo	$15

Benny Parsons

Cut signature	$5
8x10 photo	$15

Johnny Parsons *

Cut signature	$22
8x10 photo	$45

Phil Parsons

Cut signature	$10
8x10 photo	$25

David Pearson

Cut signature	$10
8x10 photo	$20

Roger Penske

Cut signature	$20
8x10 photo	$25

Andy Petree

Cut signature	$8
8x10 photo	$15

Adam Petty *

Cut signature	$50
8x10 photo	$100

Kyle Petty

Cut signature	$10
8x10 photo	$25

Lee Petty*

Cut signature	$20
8x10 photo	$50

Richard Petty

Cut signature	$20
8x10 photo	$40

Alain Prost

Cut signature	$5
8x10 photo	$15

Scott Pruett

Cut signature	$5
8x10 photo	$8

Bobby Rahal

Cut signature	$10
8x10 photo	$25

Peter Revson *

Cut signature	$45
8x10 photo	$90

Eddie Rickenbacker *

Cut signature	$125
8x10 photo	$300

Tim Richmond *

Cut signature	$50
8x10 photo	$100

Floyd Roberts *

Cut signature	$55
8x10 photo	$140

Kenny Roberts

Cut signature	$5
8x10 photo	$10

Shawna Robinson

Cut signature	$5
8x10 photo	$15

Ricky Rudd

Cut signature	$10
8x10 photo	$30

Johnny Rutherford

Cut signature	$10
8x10 photo	$25

Elliot Sadler

Cut signature	$5
8x10 photo	$20

Elton Sawyer

Cut signature	$10
8x10 photo	$15

Ken Schrader

Cut signature	$5
8x10 photo	$20

Michael Schumacher

Cut signature	$30
8x10	$75

Scott Sharp

Cut signature	$5
8x10 photo	$15

Carroll Shelby

Cut signature	$10
8x10 photo	$20

Morgan Shepherd

Cut signature	$5
8x10 photo	$15

Mike Skinner

Cut signature	$5
8x10 photo	$20

Tom Sneva

Cut signature	$10
8x10 photo	$20

Lake Speed

Cut signature	$4
8x10 photo	$8

Jimmy Spencer

Cut signature	$5
8x10 photo	$20

Lyn St. James

Cut signature	$6
8x10 photo	$12

Jackie Stewart

Cut signature	$12
8x10 photo	$25

Tony Stewart

Cut signature	$15
8x10 photo	$40

Hut Stricklin

Cut signature	$5
8x10 photo	$17

Danny Sullivan

Cut signature	$10
8x10 photo	$24

Mickey Thompson *

Cut signature	$55
8x10 photo	$110

Paul Tracy

Cut signature	$8
8x10 photo	$25

Dick Trickle

Cut signature	$5
8x10 photo	$20

Al Unser

Cut signature	$10
8x10 photo	$25

Al Unser Jr.

Cut signature	$10
8x10 photo	$25

Bobby Unser

Cut signature $5
8x10 photo $20

Jimmy Vasser

Cut signature $5
8x10 photo $20

Jacques Villeneuve

Cut signature $10
8x10 photo $20

Kenny Wallace

Cut signature $5
8x10 photo $15

Mike Wallace

Cut signature $5
8x10 photo $15

Rusty Wallace

Cut signature $15
8x10 photo $30

Darrell Waltrip

Cut signature $10
8x10 photo $30

Michael Waltrip

Cut signature $5
8x10 photo $25

Roger Ward

Cut signature $20
8x10 photo $50

A.J. Watson

Cut signature $5
8x10 photo $10

Gary Wood *

Cut signature $25
8x10 photo $50

Cale Yarborough

Cut signature $8
8x10 photo $20

Lee Roy Yarbrough

Cut signature $8
8x10 photo $16

Smokey Yunnick

Cut signature $5
8x10 photo $10

WRESTLING AUTOGRAPHS

*Indicates Deceased

Adrian Adonis *

Cut signature $10
Photo $25

Captain Lou Albano

Mounted Memories Photo

Cut signature $6
Photo $12

Arn Anderson

Cut signature $12
Photo $30

Andre The Giant *

Cut signature $45
Photo $120

Kurt Angle

Cut signature $10
Photo $30

Tony Atlas

Cut signature $5
Photo $12

"Stone Cold" Steve Austin

Steiner Sports Photo

Cut signature $10
Photo $45

Bob Backlund

Cut signature $8
Photo $20

Buff Bagwell

Cut signature $8
Photo $20

Paul Bearer

Cut signature $5
Photo $10

Brutus Beefcake

Cut signature $8
Photo $15

Chris Benoit

Cut signature $8
Photo $20

Big Show

Cut signature $8
Photo $25

Bam Bam Bigelow

Cut signature $7
Photo $15

Eric Bischoff

Cut signature $8
Photo $20

Steve Blackman

Cut signature $5
Photo $12

Jerry Blackwell

Cut signature $6
Photo $15

Tully Blanchard

Cut signature $6
Photo $15

Nick Bockwinkel

Cut signature $8
Photo $25

Booker T.

Cut signature $8
Photo $30

Boss Man

Cut signature $6
Photo $15

Bradshaw

Cut signature $5
Photo $15

D 'Lo Brown

Cut signature $6
Photo $15

King Kong Bundy

Cut signature $6
Photo $15

Jumpin' Jim Brunsell

Cut signature $4
Photo $10

Christian

Cut signature $5
Photo $15

Brian Christopher

Cut signature $8

Photo..$20

The Crusher
Cut signature....................................$12
Photo..$25

Chyna
Cut signature......................................$8
Photo..$20

Debra
Cut signature....................................$10
Photo..$20

Ted Dibiase
Cut signature......................................$6
Photo..$15

Dick the Bruiser *
Cut signature....................................$15
Photo..$40

Disco Inferno
Cut signature......................................$6
Photo..$15

Tommy Dreamer
Cut signature......................................$5
Photo..$15

Droz
Cut signature......................................$5
Photo..$12

Bubba Ray Dudley
Cut signature......................................$6
Photo..$20

D-Von Dudley
Cut signature......................................$6
Photo..$20

Spike Dudley
Cut signature......................................$5
Photo..$12

Hacksaw Jim Duggan
Cut signature......................................$5
Photo..$12

Edge
Cut signature......................................$6
Photo..$20

Miss Elizabeth *

Tri-Star Productions Photo

Cut signature....................................$10
Photo..$25

Ric Flair
Cut signature....................................$12
Photo..$35

MANKIND
with Socko

Mounted Memories Photo

Mick Foley
(Mankind/Dude Love/Cactus Jack)
Cut signature....................................$10
Photo..$25

Terry Funk
Cut signature......................................$6
Photo..$20

Greg Gagne
Cut signature......................................$6
Photo..$12

Verne Gagne
Cut signature....................................$10
Photo..$25

Gangrel
Cut signature......................................$5
Photo..$10

Gorgeous George
Cut signature....................................$25
Photo..$60

The Godfather
Cut signature......................................$6
Photo..$15

Bill Goldberg
Cut signature....................................$12
Photo..$40

Goldust
Cut signature......................................$6
Photo..$25

Chavo Guerrero
Cut signature......................................$5
Photo..$15

Eddie Guerrero
Cut signature......................................$8
Photo..$20

Bart Gunn
Cut signature......................................$5
Photo..$10

B. A. Billy Gunn
Cut signature......................................$8
Photo..$20

Scott Hall
Cut signature....................................$12
Photo..$35

Hardcore Holly
Cut signature......................................$5
Photo..$12

Jeff Hardy
Cut signature......................................$5
Photo..$20

Matt Hardy
Cut signature......................................$5
Photo..$20

Bret Hart
Cut signature....................................$10
Photo..$35

Jimmy Hart
Cut signature......................................$6
Photo..$15

Owen Hart *
Cut signature....................................$20
Photo..$50

Curt Hennig *
Cut signature....................................$10
Photo..$25

Larry "The Axe" Hennig
Cut signature......................................$6
Photo..$15

Bobby Heenan
Cut signature......................................$8
Photo..$20

Mark Henry
Cut signature......................................$6
Photo..$15

Hunter Hearst Hemsley (Triple H)
Cut signature....................................$12
Photo..$35

Hulk Hogan
Cut signature....................................$15
Photo..$40

Molly Holly
Cut signature......................................$5
Photo..$10

The Hurricane
Cut signature......................................$5
Photo..$15

Iron Sheik
Cut signature......................................$8
Photo..$25

Ivory
Cut signature......................................$5
Photo..$15

Jacqueline
Cut signature......................................$5
Photo..$15

"Road Dog" Jesse James
Cut signature......................................$8
Photo..$20

Jeff Jarrett
Cut signature......................................$8
Photo..$20

Jazz
Cut signature......................................$5
Photo..$15

Chris Jericho
Cut signature......................................$8
Photo..$25

Kamala

Cut signature $12
Photo $30

Kane

Mounted Memories Photo

Cut signature $10
Photo $20

Stacy Keibler

Cut signature $10
Photo $25

Billy Kidman

Cut signature $5
Photo $25

Konnan

Cut signature $6
Photo $15

Killer Kowalski

Mounted Memories Photo

Cut signature $5
Photo $15

Kurrgan

Cut signature $5
Photo $10

Jerry "The King" Lawler

Cut signature $8
Photo $20

Brock Lesnar

Cut signature $10
Photo $25

Lita

Cut signature $10
Photo $25

Lex Luger

Cut signature $10
Photo $25

Rocky Maivia (The Rock)

Cut signature $15
Photo $45

Dean Malenko

Cut signature $8
Photo $20

Dawn Marie

Cut signature $8
Photo $20

Maven

Cut signature $5
Photo $15

Stephanie McMahon

Cut signature $10
Photo $25

Vince McMahon

Cut signature $10
Photo $30

Marc Mero

Cut signature $6
Photo $15

Shawn Michaels

Cut signature $12
Photo $35

Midian

Cut signature $5
Photo $12

Gorilla Monsoon *

Cut signature $15
Photo $40

Rey Mysterio Jr.

Cut signature $7
Photo $25

Kevin Nash

Mounted Memories Photo

Cut signature $15
Photo $40

Mean Gene Okerlund

Cut signature $4
Photo $10

Randy Orton

Cut signature $8
Photo $18

Diamond Dallas Page

Cut signature $12
Photo $35

Kimberly Page

Cut signature $8
Photo $20

Ken Patera

Cut signature $8
Photo $20

"Rowdy" Roddy Piper

Cut signature $10
Photo $35

"Leaping Lanny" Poffo

Cut signature $7
Photo $15

Ivan Putski

Cut signature $8
Photo $20

Raven

Cut signature $8
Photo $20

Harley Race

Cut signature $10
Photo $25

Baron Von Raschke

Cut signature $10
Photo $25

Stevie Ray

Cut signature $8
Photo $15

William Regal

Cut signature $8
Photo $18

Dustin Rhodes

Cut signature $7
Photo $18

Dusty Rhodes

Cut signature $8
Photo $20

Rhyno

Cut signature $5
Photo $15

Steven Richards

Cut signature $5
Photo $15

Rikishi

Cut signature $8
Photo $20

Billy Robinson

Cut signature $15
Photo $40

Jake "The Snake" Roberts

Cut signature $8
Photo $20

Jim Ross

Cut signature $5
Photo $12

Ravashing Rick Rude *

Cut signature $20
Photo $60

Terri Runnels

Cut signature $6
Photo $20

Sable (Rena Mero)

Mounted Memories Photo

Cut signature $15
Photo $35

Bruno Sammartino

Mounted Memories Photo

Cut signature $10
Photo $20

Tito Santana

Cut signature $6
Photo $15

Saturn

Cut signature $5
Photo $10

Randy "Macho Man" Savage

Cut signature $14
Photo $35

Scotty 2 Hotty

Cut signature $8
Photo $20

Ken Shamrock

Cut signature $10
Photo $30

Papa Shango

Cut signature $6
Photo $20

Tiger Ali Singh

Cut signature $6
Photo $15

Sergeant Slaughter

Cut signature $10
Photo $25

Al Snow

Mounted Memories Photo

Cut signature $6
Photo $15

Jimmy "Superfly" Snuka

Cut signature $8
Photo $20

George "The Animal" Steele

Cut signature $6
Photo $15

Rick Steiner

Cut signature $8
Photo $20

Scott Steiner

Cut signature $8
Photo $20

Sting

Cut signature $12
Photo $35

Lance Storm

Cut signature $8
Photo $18

Trish Stratus

Cut signature $10
Photo $30

Big John Studd *

Cut signature $20
Photo $50

Sunny

Cut signature $8
Photo $20

Tajiri

Cut signature $5
Photo $12

Tazz

Cut signature $8
Photo $20

Test

Cut signature $6
Photo $15

Lou Thesz

Cut signature $8
Photo $25

The Undertaker

Cut signature $10
Photo $30

Ultimate Warrior

Cut signature $10
Photo $35

Rob Van Dam

Cut signature $8
Photo $18

Torrie Wilson

Tri-Star Productions Photo

Cut signature $10
Photo $25

Greg "The Hammer" Valentine

Cut signature $6
Photo $15

Val Venis

Cut signature $8
Photo $20

Jesse Ventura

Cut signature $25
Photo $50

Victoria

Cut signature $5
Photo $15

Kerry Von Erich *

Cut signature $10
Photo $25

Baron Von Raschke

Cut signature $10
Photo $25

Paul Wight

Cut signature $8
Photo $20

X-Pac

Cut signature $8
Photo $15

Yokozuna *

Cut signature $12
Photo $35

Larry Zbyszko

Cut signature $9
Photo $25

Chapter 2

EQUIPMENT

Until the early 1980s, most professional sports teams didn't make uniforms available to fans. But some jerseys made it into circulation through charity auctions or the occasional lucky fan who, being in the right place at the right time, actually had one tossed to him by the athlete as he left the field.

Changes in the pro teams' elitist mindset occurred in 1978, when the Philadelphia Phillies sold an entire lot of 1977 game-used jerseys to a New Jersey dealer, who then advertised them in hobby papers. Many teams have since continued this practice of bulk sales to dealers, selling all of the items at a set price, per shirt. This eliminates requiring team employees to individually price the items.

Shirts bought in bulk from the teams generally make their way to buyers at card shows, through mail-order catalogs, and in advertisements in hobby publications. Because the initial seller was the team itself, the authenticity of these jerseys is virtually uncontested, as proved by the Washington Redskins, who sold nearly 10 years worth of practice and game jerseys and sideline jackets in the summer of 2001 at their team store.

Game-used jerseys have an interesting history. Today we're seeing high interest and high dollars being paid for 19th-century baseball uniforms. Collectors have also gravitated to more limited items, such as jerseys from failed leagues, such as the American Basketball Association and United States Football League. Because these leagues were not around very long, there are fewer jerseys. And many Hall of Famers played in these leagues.

ABA jerseys can draw anywhere from a few thousand to more than $10,000 for a game-used jersey. That is due in great part to the scarcity of the materials. Many teams simply tossed away or gave away the team jerseys when the team or league folded. The Pittsburgh Condors actually gave their equipment to a prison and a boys' and girls' club.

Game-used equipment collectors consider a truly authentic item as one having been issued by the team, whose logo or name appears on the jersey. It must have discernibly been worn by the player in question. It doesn't have to be falling apart, but it shouldn't be fresh off the rack, either; it should show evidence of laundering.

Jerseys have become such a high-ticket item that it has become confusing to know what is, and isn't, a game-used item. Consider the plight of a University of Tennessee fan who bought a jersey for $1,200 that was authenticated to be a Heath Shuler gamer. When the collector approached Shuler for autographing the piece, Shuler was nice enough to point out that he not only owned each of his Tennessee game jerseys, but the model the collector had bought was by the wrong manufacturer, and had the wrong striping and tagging. Shuler then helped the collector by writing a note of these inaccuracies on letterhead so the collector could get his money returned.

So be careful! Two points to consider in establishing authenticity include wear and tagging. A jersey used for an entire season should show some signs of wear. The collar and perhaps the arm-pits should indicate sweat, or laundering out of that perspiration. Letters and numbers on the jersey should feature an even degree of wear; the edges of the characters may be a bit frayed, the letters and numbers may be loose in one or several locations, and the numbers or scripting may be wrinkled or shrunken a wee bit.

Several types of tags exist, in various colors, designs and locations.

Year tags depict the year of issuance for a jersey. Most often, these embroideries are done on a piece of fabric that is then affixed to the jersey.

Strip tags are either embroidered or printed (screened). They are shaped in strip fashion, having an accentuated rectangular shape with a line of information running horizontally on an even plane.

Flag tags are any tags attached to the jersey on only one edge, normally underneath an adjoining, larger tag (such as a manufacturer's label). Sometimes it may be attached underneath a jersey seam or to the jersey.

Name tags identify the name of the player who was originally issued the jersey. With only rare exceptions, name tags have only a player's last name. They are generally embroidered, and affixed to a strip-style tag that is sewn into the jersey. Name tags come in two varieties, based on their location on the jersey. Tags affixed to the inside back of the shirt collar are classified as "name in collar" tags, usually referred to on sale lists and in inventories as "NIC." Or, the tag may be included in the shirt's tail, with the corresponding notation being "NIT," for "name in tail." Variations of "NIT" include "NOT" (name on tail) and "NIF" or "NOF" (name in/on flap). Extra length tags indicate extra inches added into a jersey's sizing, usually done for taller players.

If questions arise concerning a jersey's authenticity, seek a second opinion. Most dealers will not object to this practice, but the time needed for an outside appraisal should be agreed upon beforehand, and stressed to the third party whose opinions are being sought.

Many forged jerseys, normally baseball knits, are subject to "simulated" wear, such as a uniform forger using sandpaper, a sharp instrument, or other foreign object to abrade and damage portions of the jersey. This gives it the appearance of moderate to extreme game usage.

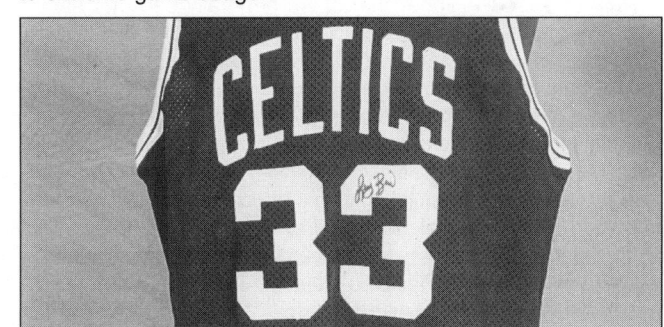

Jersey tags may be clandestinely doctored by removing legitimate tags from a lesser-valued authentic jersey and placing them into a phony item capable of being passed off as a high-ticket item. Doctoring is defined as taking an authentic jersey of a common player and changing tagging, numbering, or other factors pertinent to the jersey, to upgrade the identity of the player.

Restoration, however, involves attempting to bring jerseys (especially flannels) back to their original appearance as close as possible. Where restorations differ from doctoring and gain acceptability in the majority of hobby quarters is that, first, no attempt is made to change or upgrade the identity of the professional athlete.

Legitimate restorations never attempt to restructure or refurbish tags, because too much potential for having a restoration slip into the dark side of the realm (doctoring) exists. Tagging is generally what is used to establish just who wore an item in the first place, and how to go about arranging the restoration process - what year and player were involved - so that the proper script or insignia or numbers can be used. A legitimate restoration tries to put things back the way they originally were, not embellish identities or years of usage to make an item more attractive or saleable.

Restorations are generally accepted by hobbyists if four conditions are met:

1.) The restoration is true and accurate to the original identity of the jersey's wearer, with no illicit attempts to upgrade that wearer's identity.

2.) The restoration should try to match as closely as possible the original appearance of the item being restored.

3.) Potential buyers or traders should know in advance about any restorations.

4.) Restorations should have a slight markdown in price, depending on how many were done and the degree of quality of them.

In most instances, teams issue two of each jersey style to players under their employment. Three sets of attire is not uncommon, but this practice of three homes/three roads is not as common. In rare instances, set 4 and even set 5 shirts have surfaced. Apart from that, extra shirts tend to appear only when replacements are needed for damaged or stolen uniforms.

In the 1980s, especially, some stars have had several jerseys issued to them to be donated to fund-raisers and charity auctions, to be given to friends, or for team employees to perhaps barter with collectors. Thus, some star jerseys from the last several years may exist in more common than twos or threes for a given style, and some may only evidence minor wear.

The jersey market has a wide variety of dollar amounts assigned to its items. Certain commons of less popular teams and styles can be had for well under $200, while some totally original, authentic flannels have commanded five-figure sums in highly publicized auctions. Factors which may cause a notable markup in a jersey from the lower end of the scale include:

Scarcity—Supply/demand considerations affect the price guide scale in the equipment market. The highest dollars come with teams whose jerseys are not only scarce, but also sought by a wide range of collectors. Hall of Famers from more than 25 years ago often draw the highest prices.

New releases—Higher prices are generally seen for styles that have recently been introduced and whose numbers within the hobby are restricted due to limited time for release, until greater quantities appear.

Sleeve adornments—Although a regularly-issued logo patch will only minimally increase a shirt's price, a commemorative, memorial, or other specially-issued patch often creates a notable price increase. High popularity: Some teams' prices, even though their attire is readily available, are driven up due to long-standing fan following or current popularity due to recent on-field success.

Striking styles—Other times, a style, be it rare, common or in-between, hits a chord with collectors and finds a niche as a high-priced item, due to demand for the style itself.

These are some of the terminology and acronyms used by uniform collectors:

Airknit—Similar to mesh, but with a shinier finish and extremely small holes. Also called micromesh, this has been used in varying degrees since the mid-1980s by the NHL, NBA and NFL.

Arched lettering—Lettering that forms an arc shape on the front or back of a jersey. Examples include the names on the back on the Utah Jazz (and many other) NBA jerseys.

Charity jersey—This is a non game-worn jersey, either team/game-issued or specially ordered, made specifically for fund-raising activities, such as a charity auction. Since they are specially ordered, slight differences may exist between these jerseys and those actually used by team members.

Commemorative patch—Sleeve or jersey body insignia worn for a limited time to note a historical moment in the team or city's history. It can be done for sports-related history (1994 NFL 75th Anniversary patch), general history or specific events.

Crest—The large patch that is found on the front of an NHL jersey. Examples include the Blackhawks Indian head crest, the Blues song note crest and the "B" crest on Bruins attire.

Doctored—Illegitimate, unethical restoration, i.e., taking a B.J. Armstrong Chicago Bulls jersey and trying to pass it off as a Michael Jordan jersey.

Dual autographed—Refers to an equipment item that, used in pairs, is autographed on both items. Most commonly refers to NBA game sneakers and other sports footwear, but can also apply to hockey gloves.

Dual tagging—Denotes jerseys with a manufacturer/size tag and also a second tag, often with "exclusive" specifics. Most often associated with the NBA, and to a lesser degree, the NFL.

Exclusive tag—A tag placed by a manufacturer of a game-issued item that declares the item to be made "exclusively" for the team or league.

Extra length not tagged but evident—Authentication tags describe a jersey with obvious extra length sized into the jersey body, but with no specific tagging included to indicate the existence or amount of extra length. This is common with pre-1986 NBA attire, and often found on pro football jerseys, too.

Fishnet mesh—A mesh jersey with very large holes in the jersey body, but not in the shoulders or sleeves. These are limited to use in the NFL and college football.

Flag tag—A small square tag that is fastened underneath a larger tag on the left-hand side so that it resembles a little flag. Used most frequently by Rawlings, but other manufacturers have used them, too.

Game-issue—Refers to a jersey that was made for a player, but for some reason was not actually used. This could occur when a jersey was made for a player, who was later traded, or when an excessive amount of jerseys were made for a player. Also referred to as "team issue."

Game-used—Describes a uniform that is used by a player for actual game action. The term "game-worn" is identical in meaning.

Inspirational patch—Logo worn in tribute to a living person affiliated with the team, for either honor or support in difficulty. An example would be the patches worn by the Baltimore Orioles for Cal Ripken's final game.

Jerry West logo—NBA league logo, added to game jerseys in 1986-87, also worn in large patch form on many warm-up tops and shooting shirts a few years beforehand. The logo features a player, dribbling a basketball, modeled after a photo of the Lakers legend.

Memorial band—Similar in purpose to a memorial patch, but reflected by a black mourning band on the sleeve or, in the NBA, on the shoulder strap (1993-94 Bulls band for James Jordan, father of Michael Jordan).

Memorial patch—This sleeve or body insignia is issued in honor of a deceased person, such as a player, manager or team-related employee.

Mesh—A jersey with a consistent pattern of small holes in the body and sleeves, used extensively in the NFL and NBA and frequently in the NHL. Baseball jerseys issued prior to the early 1970s were flannels (flannel, wool and cotton mixes). Since then, Major League Baseball teams have worn knit jerseys.

Nameplate—A piece of fabric usually arched—but sometimes bar-shaped, depending on the team—upon which name letters are attached. This allows for an easier means of removing NOBs by the team; the equipment manager merely needs to remove the entire nameplate, rather than individual letters attached directly to the jersey.

NIC—Name in collar. A tag that features a player's name is found in the back of the collar inside the jersey neck.

NIF/NOF—Name in/on flap.

NIT/NOT—Name in/on tail. Name tag is affixed to shirt tail.

NIW—Name in waist. Describes a name tag affixed in the waistband of pants.

NNOB—Abbreviation for "no name on back," it applies to a jersey issued without ever having a name on the back, as opposed to one which has had the NOB removed (NOBR). For example, the Chicago Cubs and New York Yankees do not have their names on the back of home jerseys.

NOB—Name on back. Every NFL, NHL and NBA team uses this jersey feature.

NOBR—Name on back removed. Teams, especially in baseball, often send jerseys down to a minor league affiliate, having removed the former player's name from the back first. In most cases, however, the names have been stripped off the back. NOBR jerseys generally sell for half or less of what an original NOB does.

Number change—A time- and cost saving-procedure used by teams for a player who has just joined the team. He's given a jersey issued to or worn by a departed player, but the numbers have been changed to reflect the new player's identity. It can often apply to a NOB, too. Legitimate number and/or name changed jerseys generally sell for between 1/2 to 3/4 the value of an unaltered jersey, depending on the obviousness of the changes.

Official supplier—Since the mid-1980s, each major league has had an official supplier, a designated manufacturer to outfit the league's member teams with uniform attire (jerseys and pants/trunks). Official suppliers can use the company's logo or insignia on attire, other suppliers can not. Check with an established equipment dealer or the team itself for its official licensee of equipment for a particular year.

Practice jerseys (non-baseball)—Refers to jerseys worn by NFL, NHL and NBA players for practices and workouts away and apart from those prior to scheduled league games. They are usually done in team colors and logos, but are generally inferior in quality of appearance to the team's game attire. For example, they are usually without NOBs, have screened on numbers and logos instead of sewn on ones, or are mesh instead of knit.

Pre-game jersey—Applies to knit NBA warmup togs, shooting shirts and baseball warmup pullovers. They are often worn by players on the bench, too.

Provenance—A term often seen in auction catalogs, this refers to the source, usually outside the hobby, from which a choice piece was obtained. This could include an equipment manager, locker room attendant, or relatives of the player.

Restored—Some collectors will research the identity of the jersey's original wearer and/or the team it was issued for and restore the logos, letters and numbers back to their original appearance, or as close as possible. This is an accepted practice, provided the changes are accurate (keeping the player and team identity the same as originally made) and advance notice is given that the jersey has been restored.

Salesman's sample—A special jersey made by a manufacturer to show to team representatives to preview style or aesthetic changes, or to provide a prototype for what a finished product would look like if the team and manufacturer agree to do business. They often bear the uniform of a star or retired great player from the team it was made for, but are only occasionally tagged. Many of these originally legitimate jerseys are doctored by unscrupulous types to attempt to reflect game-used status.

Set number—A tagging element that indicates what specific jersey is in the group a player is issued for a given year. Traditionally, teams used to receive two home and two road jerseys. But today, teams may issue more, most notably the NBA. In recent years, the NHL has occasionally used set number tags; the NFL and NBA have rarely used them.

Simulated wear—Wear added artificially to a brand new, non game-used jersey in an attempt to give it a game-used look. This could include smudging dirt or grass on it, ripping it, sandpapering the logos or hacking up trim.

Strip tag—Multi-item tag that depicts at least two pieces of tagged information, such as "Jackson 78 1" (name, year, set) or "23 84 2 42" (uniform number, year, set, size).

Sweater—A term used largely by Canadian fans and collectors to describe hockey jerseys, i.e. "hockey sweaters."

Tags—Labels, either embroidered or screened, which are added to a jersey or pants, but are not found on non game-issued items. Tags could indicate a manufacturer, but also indicate numeric or name information, such as years, set numbers, inventory numbers, sizes, uniform numbers or player names.

Tags washed out—Legitimate depreciation that results from repeated washing. It can take the form of either a sewn-in tag made out of a weak fabric (such as felt) disintegrating from excess washings or a printed tag having the print fade to the point of being unreadable. A jersey with tags washed out should display consistency of wear - a shirt with a felt NIC tag reduced to almost nothing should not display crisp, bright numbers or logos.

Tearaway—A flimsy knit jersey used in the NFL in the 1960s and 1970s, designed to tear off the body of a player when an opposing player attempted to tackle or grab him. The NFL eventually outlawed this type of jersey.

Trim—Stripes which encircle the edge or tip of a jersey sleeve or collar.

Untagged—Describes a jersey with no tags other than a manufacturer's label. This is a common occurrence for NBA jerseys before 1987, NFL jerseys before 1990 and up to the current time for NHL jerseys.

Vertical arch—A lettering style, usually related to NOBs, where the tops and bottoms of letters are arched, rather than the arrangement of the letters themselves. Most commonly used on NOBs of jerseys issued by Wilson, although other companies have used them, too. Examples include 1979-86 Chicago Cubs baseball road jersey NOBs.

GAME-USED BASEBALL JERSEYS

"NIC" - Name in collar.   "NOB" - Name on back.

Hank Aaron: 1967 Atlanta Braves home $16,995
Jim Abbott: 1999 Milwaukee Brewers home.................... $395
Rick Aguilera: 1988 Minnesota Twins road....................... $495
Sparky Anderson: 1974 Cincinnati Reds home,
NOB, signed $1,000
Sparky Anderson: 1994 Detroit Tigers road.................... $850
Cap Anson: 1898 New York Giants road, NIT $100,000
Luis Aparicio: 1968 Chicago White Sox home, with pants,
NOB, signed $5,500
Luke Appling: 1971 Chicago White Sox road, NIC, coaching
jersey $3,750
Ernie Banks: 1968 Cubs home jersey, game-used........ $2,500
Harold Baines: 1992 Oakland A's home $275
Sal Bando: 1968 Oakland A's away $700
Don Baylor: 1979 California Angels home $995
Don Baylor: 1994 Colorado Rockies road......................... $450
Derek Bell: 1997 Houston Astros road $400
George Bell: 1985 Toronto Blue Jays road....................... $495
Albert Belle: 1997 Chicago White Sox jersey, home,
NOB $1,595
Johnny Bench: 1976 Cincinnati Reds road $2,495
Johnny Bench: 1981 Cincinnati Reds jersey, signed..... $2,500
Andy Benes: San Diego Padres road, 1993 All-Star Game...$950
Dante Bichette: 1998 Colorado Rockies home................. $650
Bert Blyleven: 1987 Minnesota Twins home..................... $545
Vida Blue: 1986 San Francisco Giants road, game worn,
NOB restored... $275
Wade Boggs: 1991 Boston Red Sox away, game worn..... $1,795
Wade Boggs: 1994 New York Yankees home, game
worn $1,450
Barry Bonds: 1989 Pittsburgh Pirates road, game worn,
NOB $3,000
Barry Bonds: 1998 San Francisco Giants home, game
worn $2,195
Bobby Bonds: 1981 Chicago Cubs home, game worn..... $400
Bobby Bonilla: 1989 Pittsburgh Pirates road, game worn,
NOB $375
Josh Booty: circa 1996-98 Florida Marlins home, game
worn $255
Larry Bowa: 1977 Philadelphia Phillies home, game worn $275
Dennis "Oil Can" Boyd: 1987 Boston Red Sox,
game worn $195
George Brett: 1984 Kansas City Royals road, game worn,
NOB $3,000
George Brett: 1991 Kansas City Royals road, game worn $2,500

George Brett: Kansas City Royals blue warm-up jersey ... $200
Brett Butler: 1986 Cleveland Indians road, game worn,
NOB..$275
Roy Campanella: 1950 Brooklyn Dodgers home, game worn,
NIT $16,000
Jose Canseco: 1991 Oakland A's road, game worn, with
pants, NOB $900
Jose Canseco: 1998 Toronto Blue Jays road, game worn....$600
Rod Carew: 1980 California Angels home, game worn.. $1,095
Steve Carlton: 1969 St. Louis Cardinals road, signed ... $1,495
Joe Carter: 1994 Toronto Blue Jays home, signed $995
Rico Carty: 1968 Atlanta Braves home $1,375
Dave Cash: 1978 Montreal Expos home, NOB $175
Ron Cey: 1987 Oakland A's road, signed.......................... $395
Will Clark: 1987 San Francisco Giants home, game
worn.. $1,050
Roger Clemens: 1987 Boston Red Sox road, with pants...$1,800
Roberto Clemente: 1957 Pittsburgh Pirates road,
restored $15,000
Ty Cobb: 1925 Detroit Tigers home, NIC $110,000
Cecil Cooper: 1975 Boston Red Sox home $350
Eric Davis: 1985 Cincinnati Reds home, NOB, signed $575
Willie Davis: 1963 Los Angeles Dodgers home, NIT $1,395
Andre Dawson: 1988 Chicago Cubs home........................ $695
Rick Dempsey: 1974 New York Yankees road $425
Paul Derringer: 1944 Chicago Cubs home flannel $2,795
Delino DeShields: 1994 Los Angeles Dodgers road $450
Joe DiMaggio: 1947 New York Yankees road $34,100
Al Downing: 1974 Los Angeles Dodgers home $800
Don Drysdale: 1959 Los Angeles Dodgers home,
signed $14,500
Shawon Dunston: 1988 Chicago Cubs home, game worn,
signed $195
Darrell Evans: 1971 Atlanta Braves home, game worn,
NOB.. $900
Chico Fernandez: 1962 Detroit Tigers home................. $2,000
Tony Fernandez: 1989 Toronto Blue Jays blue, game worn ..$500
Tony Fernandez: 1991 San Diego Padres road, game
worn.. $325
Tony Fernandez: 2001 Toronto Blue Jays blue/alternate, game
worn, NOB $900
Cecil Fielder: 1994 Detroit Tigers road, game worn $895
Steve Finley: 1996 San Diego Padres spring training top, game
worn $145
Carlton Fisk: 1990 Chicago White Sox road, game worn $895
John Flaherty: circa 1999-2000 Tampa Bay Devil Rays road,
game worn, NOB $330

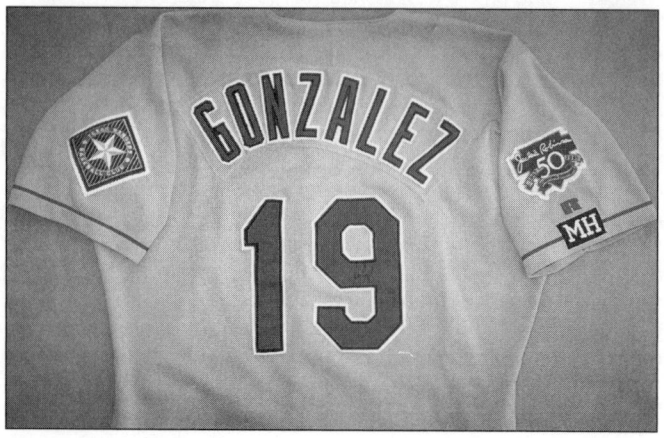

Cliff Floyd: 2001 Florida Marlins home, game worn, NOB ... $500

Andres Galarraga: 1994 Colorado Rockies home, game worn $1,150

Ron Gant: 1989 Atlanta Braves home, game worn, signed .. $895

Steve Garvey: 1981 Los Angeles Dodgers home, game worn, NOB, signed $1,195

Jim Gentile: 1965 Houston Astros home, game worn.... $1,500

Dan Gladden: 1989 Minnesota Twins home, game worn.. $295

Fred Gladding: 1965 Detroit Tigers home, game worn.. $1,250

Tom Glavine: 1994 Atlanta Braves road, game worn........ $695

Juan Gonzalez: 1993 Texas Rangers home, game worn, NOB $1,200

Juan Gonzalez: 1997 Texas Rangers road, game worn, NOB $950

Rich Gossage: 1988 Chicago Cubs road, game worn...... $350

Mark Grace: 1988 Chicago Cubs home, game worn $550

Mike Greenwell: 1989 Boston Red Sox road, game worn ... $475

Ken Griffey Jr.: 1989 Seattle Mariners road $2,495

Ken Griffey Sr.: 1981 Cincinnati Reds road, game worn .. $500

Marquis Grissom: 1993 Montreal Expos home $395

Ron Guidry: 1988 New York Yankees road, game worn ... $995

Tony Gwynn: 1989 San Diego Padres road..................... $900

Mike Hampton: 1996 Houston Astros home $500

Tommy Harper: Seattle Pilots road jersey, restored....... $1,200

Charlie Hayes: 1994 Colorado Rockies home $395

Todd Helton: 2002 Colorado Rockies purple/alternate, game worn, NOB $1,600

Rickey Henderson: 1991 Oakland A's home, NOB, signed $1,495

Orel Hershiser: 1987 Los Angeles Dodgers road............. $595

Jose Hernandez: 2003 Colorado Rockies gray/pinstriped, game worn, NOB $200

Jose Hernandez: 2003 Colorado Rockies white/pinstriped, game worn, NOB $200

Keith Hernandez: 1988 New York Mets road, NOB, signed ..$600

Teddy Higuera: 1992 Milwaukee Brewers road $240

Al Hollingsworth: 1939 Philadelphia Phillies road......... $8,470

Bob Horner: 1982 Atlanta Braves road $350

Kent Hrbek: 1992 Minnesota Twins home....................... $695

Catfish Hunter: 1971 Oakland A's road NOB $2,250

Clint Hurdle: 2003 Colorado Rockies purple/alternate, game worn, NOB $200

Bo Jackson: 1987 Kansas City Royals home $650

Reggie Jackson: 1968 Oakland A's road vest $12,995

Reggie Jackson: 1983 California Angels home, NOB, with pants.. $5,000

Gregg Jefferies: 1990 New York Mets home, NOB $450

Jose Jimenez: 2003 Colorado Rockies gray/pinstriped, game worn, NOB $200

Davey Johnson: 1967 Baltimore Orioles home, NIT $1,250

Randy Johnson: 1994 Seattle Mariners home, game worn.. $1,000

Andruw Jones: 1998 Atlanta Braves home $1,250

Chipper Jones: 1997 Atlanta Braves home $1,695

Wally Joyner: 1987 California Angels road, NOB, signed.....$295

Wally Joyner: 1996 San Diego Padres spring training top, game worn, ... $145

David Justice: 1992 Atlanta Braves home, NOB, signed...$1,150

Al Kaline: 1974 Detroit Tigers road, game worn $1,695

Eric Karros: 1994 Los Angeles Dodgers road $850

Harmon Killebrew: 1961 Minnesota Twins home, NIC .. $7,000

Dave Kingman: 1986 Oakland A's gold, game worn, NOB...$325

Ryan Klesko: 1998 Atlanta Braves home, ... $695

Ted Kluszewski: 1964 Cincinnati Reds home $1,800

Chuck Knoblauch: 1993 Minnesota Twins home $495

Sandy Koufax: 1961 Los Angeles Dodgers home, NIT....$19,950

Barry Larkin: 1993 Cincinnati Reds home, NOB, signed......$695

Tony LaRussa: 1992 Oakland A's home.......................... $375

Ron LeFlore: 1980 Montreal Expos away, NOB.............. $250

Chet Lemon: 1982 Detroit Tigers home........................... $325

Kenny Lofton: 1994 Cleveland Indians road.................... $795

Earle Mack: 1950 Philadelphia Phillies road $8,470

Mickey Mantle: 1981 New York Yankees home (spring training coach)... $7,700

Greg Maddux: 1994 Atlanta Braves road....................... $1,795

Juan Marichal: 1966 San Francisco Giants home, NIC, signed $5,500

Roger Maris: 1960 New York Yankees home, NIC....... $25,000

Dennis Martinez: 1988 Montreal Expos road, game worn ...$250

Eddie Mathews: 1966 Atlanta Braves road, signed $12,500

Don Mattingly: 1993 New York Yankees home $1,495

Willie McCovey: 1972 San Francisco Giants road, game worn, with pants, NIC $11,500

Jack McDowell: 1995 New York Yankees road, Mantle armband $795

Mark McGwire: 1987 Oakland A's home........................ $2,950

Hal McRae: 1986 Kansas City Royals away, NOB $275

Andy Messersmith: 1970 California Angels $550

Kevin Mitchell: 1988 San Francisco Giants, signed $250

Paul Molitor: 1988 Milwaukee Brewers road.................. $1,095

Bill Monbouquette: 1961 Boston Red Sox road.............. $750

Raul Mondesi: 1994 Los Angeles Dodgers home, game worn.. $1,250

Joe Morgan: 1968 Houston Astros road $5,500

Jack Morris: 1983 Detroit Tigers road, NOB.................... $850

Rance Mulliniks: 1982 Kansas City Royals road.............. $190

Dale Murphy: 1981 Atlanta Braves road, signed.............. $650

Eddie Murray: 1994 Cleveland Indians road.................... $795

Eddie Murray: 1995 Cleveland Indians World Series jersey $2,495

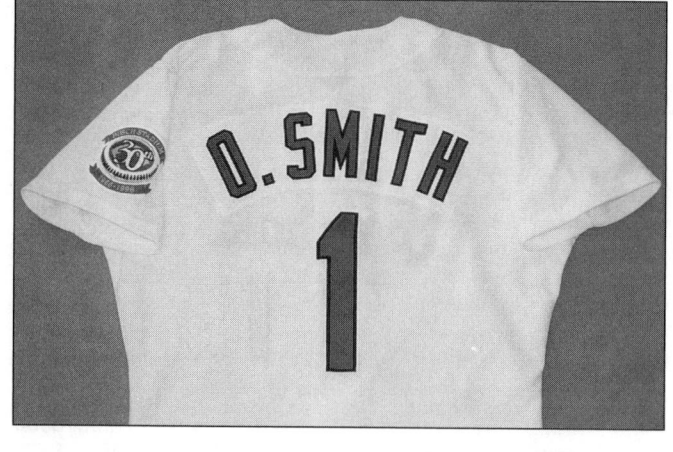

Stan Musial: 1960 St. Louis Cardinals road $13,500
Phil Niekro: 1979 Atlanta Braves road $895
Hideo Nomo: 1998 New York Mets road $650
Blue Moon Odom: 1968 Oakland A's green vest, game
    worn $450
Mel Ott: 1947 New York Giants road, game worn, NIC..... $45,000
Jim Palmer: 1970 Baltimore Orioles road, game worn,
    signed $3,500
Jim Palmer: 1981 Baltimore Orioles road $4,730
Rafael Palmeiro: 1990 Texas Rangers road, NOB, signed .. $650
Chan Ho Park: 1997 Los Angeles Dodgers home $795
Dave Parker: 1984 Cincinnati Reds home $395
Terry Pendleton: 1988 St. Louis Cardinals, NOB $575
Mike Piazza: 1994 Los Angeles Dodgers road............... $1,495
Boog Powell: 1972 Baltimore Orioles home $2,750
Kirby Puckett: 1985 Minnesota Twins road, NOB......... $2,195
Kirby Puckett: 1993 Minnesota Twins home................... $995
Tim Raines: 1987 Montreal Expos road, NOB, signed...... $595
Manny Ramirez: 1994 Cleveland Indians road $495
Allie Reynolds: 1951 New York Yankees home $5,000
Jim Rice: 1975 Boston Red Sox road $1,495
Cal Ripken Jr.: 1994 Baltimore Orioles road.................. $2,995
Bip Roberts: 1991 San Diego Padres road...................... $350
Robin Roberts: 1964 Baltimore Orioles home, signed .. $4,495
Brooks Robinson: 1957 Baltimore Orioles road, signed .. $5,000
Frank Robinson: 1973 California Angels home............. $1,695
Ivan Rodriguez: 1995 Texas Rangers home, All-Star patch. $595
Pete Rose: 1974 Cincinnati Reds home, game worn,
    NOB... $3,500
Pete Rose: Cincinnati Reds red warm-up jersey, #14 .... $250
Pete Rose: Philadelphia Phillies #14 pre-game jersey,
    signed $895
Pete Rose: 1980 Philadelphia Phillies, game worn $1,400
Babe Ruth: 1938 Brooklyn Dodgers road, game worn, with
    pants, NIC.. $110,000
Nolan Ryan: 1987 Houston Astros home, NOB $4,000
Nolan Ryan: 1990 Texas Rangers road, with pants $2,750
Bret Saberhagen: 1993 New York Mets road, signed....... $600
Tim Salmon: 1992 California Angels road, NOB............ $1,395
Ryne Sandberg: 1988 Chicago Cubs home $1,350
Deion Sanders: 1992 Atlanta Braves road.................... $800
Benito Santiago: 1998 Toronto Blue Jays road, game worn,
    NOB.. $400
Mike Schmidt: 1989 Philadelphia Phillies home $2,495
Mike Scott: 1980 New York Mets road, game worn, NOB $250
Tom Seaver: 1983 New York Mets road, game worn $3,295
Gary Sheffield: 1998 Los Angeles Dodgers home $950
Al Simmons: 1943 Boston Red Sox road, NIC $12,500
John Smiley: 1990 Pittsburgh Pirates home.................... $175
Ozzie Smith: 1996 St. Louis Cardinals home................. $1,350

Duke Snider: 1962 Los Angeles Dodgers road, NIT,
    signed $11,000
Willie Stargell: 1970 Pittsburgh Pirates home, signed... $4,495
Willie Stargell: 1982 Pittsburgh Pirates black $4,150
Terry Steinbach: 1992 Oakland A's road, NOB $350
Casey Stengel: 1962 New York Mets road, with pants.....$14,750
Rennie Stennett: 1978 Pittsburgh Pirates home.............. $350
Dave Stewart: 1983 Los Angeles Dodgers home, NOB.... $495
Darryl Strawberry: 1988 New York Mets road, signed $350
Rick Sutcliffe: 1994 St. Louis Cardinals road, NOB $395
Bruce Sutter: 1985 Atlanta Braves road $350
Don Sutton: 1974 Los Angeles Dodgers home, NOB,
    signed $1,495
Don Sutton: 1986 California Angels road, NOB............. $1,025
Danny Tartabull: 1993 New York Yankees home $695
Frank Thomas: 1995 Chicago White Sox home $2,500
Alan Trammell: 1994 Detroit Tigers home $895
Mo Vaughn: 1997 Boston Red Sox home $895
David Wells: 1999 Toronto Blue Jays home, game worn .. $850
Robin Ventura: 1994 Chicago White Sox road $695
Frank Viola: 1988 Minnesota Twins road, signed $495
Larry Walker: 2003 Colorado Rockies purple/alternate,
    game worn, NOB $700
Devon White: 1989 California Angels home, signed......... $600
Frank White: 1988 Kansas City Royals road, NOB........... $350
Hoyt Wilhelm: 1970 Atlanta Braves home, signed......... $3,350
Matt Williams: 1988 San Francisco Giants road $950
Ted Williams: 1960 Boston Red Sox home................. $60,000
Dave Winfield: 1993 Minnesota Twins home $1,200
Carl Yastrzemski: 1978 Boston Red Sox home, signed $1,795
Robin Yount: 1993 Milwaukee Brewers home $1,195

COLLECTING BATS

Game-Used Bat Collecting Gets Better With Age

By Scott Harpt

Unlike many other collecting areas, accumulating and authenticating game-used bats is not a harrowing experience if you know what you're doing. Collectors have recognized problems with graded cards in recent years, while autograph seekers have seen their share of crisis. Game-used bats though are tough to duplicate, and the knowledge base has increased to such a degree that collectors can set aside their doubts and just have fun.

Due to several years of collecting and researching by specialists in the field, collecting game-used baseball bats has now become infinitely more enjoyable, not to mention possible, for the collector. The work of these experts has allowed for growth in the hobby in several ways.

1). It has furnished the most basic collector with the ability to determine a bat's age and authenticity to a high degree of certainty.

2). It has given collectors a way to estimate current values of bats.

3). It has given collectors several options for where to obtain bats in any price range.

4). It has provided the hobby with a handful of experts who field questions and authenticate memorabilia.

In the game-used bat world, the quickest way to get to the point of enjoyment is to have a working knowledge of dating and labeling. It's exciting to look at a bat and definitively say "the code on the knob of this Adirondack tells me that it was used in 1985," or "that Louisville Slugger is a store model bat. I know because it says 'Flame Tempered' instead of 'Powerized' on the center brand." Knowing the basics does not make the average collector an automatic expert, but it does allow for quick identification of major era changes. Enter your new world with confidence.

Scott Harpt Photos

Center brand of Louisville Slugger 1980-83 labeling period. This marks the first period without the words Hillerich and Bradsby in the center brand. This label is easy to spot because it is so large (4 1/2 inches). By the next label change in 1983-85, the label became just 3 1/2 inches across.

Dating and Labeling

Bats made from 1910 (when player's names on bats became the norm) to the present, can be authenticated and dated by experts with relative ease. Without difficulty, today's collector can distinguish between a game-used and a store model bat, and even show clearly when and by whom the bat was used.

According to *MastroNet Reference* and *Price Guide for Collecting Game-Used Baseball Bats* by Dave Bushing and Dan Knoll (2001), "The narrow bat dating, along with known records, bat dimensions, and special game markings help us determine, with 100 percent certainty, whether a bat is indeed a professional model game bat made for a player as opposed to one crafted for the store trade. This degree of certainty has led to an increased collector confidence and an unparalleled interest in collecting game-used bats."

The Louisville Slugger company (known as Hillerich & Bradsby prior to 1980), has changed its labeling more than 25 times since 1910. An understanding of when these changes took place gives the collector the ability to estimate during which labeling period a bat was used. For example, until the 1973-1975 labeling period, model numbers were placed on the knob (butt end) of a Louisville Slugger. Beginning in 1976 the company moved the model number to the barrel of the bat, above the player's name. Thus, a game-used Louisville Slugger with model numbers on the knob was definitely made before 1976. If factory numbers appear on the knob of a Louisville Slugger more modern than 1976, the bat is clearly a store model example.

The Adirondack/Rawlings company, another major producer of bats used by major league ball players, has also made several (approximately 12) changes in their labeling since 1946. Beginning in the 1946-1950 labeling period, the word "Adirondack" was labeled in block print in the center brand (the labeling area in the middle of the bat). This remained true until 1961 when the word was changed to script writing. By 1983 the center brand changed to "Rawlings," and evolved into simply "R" in 1998. Adirondack added a code to the knob of its bats in 1980 making it even easier to determine, not only the labeling period, but the actual year a particular bat was made. Located directly below the model number is a one (in the 1980's) or two digit (beginning in 1989) code. For example, the single digit "2" indicates the bat was made in 1982. The code "95" signifies 1995.

Another interesting aspect of the Adirondack is the "Pro Ring" which encircles their blonde-colored bats below the center brand. The color of the ring corresponds with the primary color of the team for which an athlete played. When examining a bat used by someone who played for more than one team, the "Pro Ring" allows the collector to determine for which team the

Example of a Louisville Slugger store model center brand. Notice the words "lame Tempered" in place of "Powerized."

athlete was playing when using this particular bat. For example, a Ted Simmons bat with a red ring was used when he played with the Cardinals. An otherwise similar bat with a blue ring was issued to Simmons as a Milwaukee Brewer.

Other bat companies such as Spalding, Worth, Hoosier, Cooper, Glomar and SAM have made, and/or continue to make, bats used by major league baseball players. The research on these is much less available; however with a factual background or other specific information, these bats can be authenticated as well.

It is important to note that the information included above is an incomplete guide to dating and labeling game-used baseball bats. There are many obvious and subtle ways for making informed determinations. Included here are just a few. For a complete reference one should hunt down one of the following manuals:

MastroNet Reference and Price Guide for Collecting Game-Used Baseball Bats by Bushing and Knoll (2001) or *BATS: Professional Hillerich & Bradsby and Adirondack,* 1950-1994 by Vince Malta, Ronald Fox, Bill Riddell, and Michael Specht (1995)

With knowledge of dating and labeling now in hand, it is important to understand how these labels, along with other variables, affect the monetary value of game-used bats.

Bat Values Rationale

In a 2002 MastroNet Inc. auction, a 1948 Ted Williams bat realized a price of $50,556. This is a special bat, and the price it fetched says great things for the hobby. It does not, however offer an encompassing view into the world of game-used bat prices.

Bat values are affected by many variables. As in card collecting, player popularity and scarcity of the collectible are important, but there is much more to it than that. Unlike a card, a bat does not gain value by being in "mint" condition. In fact, many collectors prefer a bat that is cracked, shows ball marks, cleat marks, rack marks, pine tar, dead wood, tape on the handle or a uniform number written on the knob in marker. These are all clear signs of "good" game use.

The monetary value of a bat can be positively affected by many special factors. A bat with excellent provenance (factual history) authenticated by a respected expert will gain value. Bats used in World Series or All-Star games have extraordinary value; as do bats used to do exceptional things. For example, the bat Wade Boggs used during the 1990 season will not be valued as highly as the one he used to crack his 3,000th hit.

The 1948 Ted Williams bat mentioned above is among the elite. This bat was vault marked. In other words, after the 1948 season, Williams returned this bat to the Louisville Slugger factory to be used as a prototype for every game-used bat he ordered for the next two years. The vault marks are brands on the knob and barrel made by the bat manufacturer for future reference. This unbelievable provenance makes this bat sell for over $50,000 while a "normal" 1948 Williams will sell in the $15,000 range.

Acquisition

So now, informed on dating and labeling as well as factors that influence value, collectors may still be faced with a problem. Where do you find the bat you're looking for?

Many major league clubs have begun using the sale of cracked game-used bats through their clubhouse stores and Web sites as a way to raise money for charity. Online auctions through companies such as Grey Flannel Collectibles (higher end/vintage), SportsCards Plus, MastroNet Inc. (higher end/vintage) and eBay (common regional players to Hall of Famers) offer gamers to the highest bidder. A simple Internet search will yield several companies with game-used bats for sale. J.T. Sports and Left Field Collectibles are just two examples of quality companies selling game-used bats on the Internet. Many advertisers in trade magazines like *Tuff Stuff* and *Sports Collectors Digest* offer game-used bats for sale as well. And finally, dealers at shows across the country are starting to offer game-used bats at their tables.

The Experts

As the game-used bat hobby grows, so will grow the number of "experts" with bats to sell and authentication services to offer. The following is a "short list" of gentlemen who have worked tirelessly for several years to advance the hobby. They have earned the right to be called respected authorities in the field.

Dave Bushing authenticates bats for MastroNet Inc. Dave has published several books, including *MastroNet Reference and Price Guide for Collecting Game-Used Baseball Bats (2001)* which contains an extensive authentication guide with hundreds of photos (co-written with uniform expert Dan Knoll). Bushing is the repository of the Louisville Slugger archives and has all records for every bat ever made for any player of note. Bushing and Knoll also authenticate bats for SCD Authentic. To learn more about SCD Authentic check out www.scdauthentic.com

Vince Malta and John Taube collectively authenticate game-used bats for PSA/DNA and Grey Flannel Collectibles.

Vince wrote BATS: *Professional Hillerich & Bradsby and Adirondack,* 1950-1994 (1995) which was long considered the quintessential reference in the hobby. To learn more about Vince Malta or John Taube check out www.psadna.com

John is the owner of J.T. Sports which sells quality game-used bats. To learn more about J.T. Sports check out www.gameused-bats.com.

Zane Burns has been a respected buyer and seller of game-used baseball bats for several years. Zane can be reached via e-mail at zanebats@comcast.net.

Please note that there are many people selling bats today, that are completely trustworthy, who don't show up on this list. Hopefully though; the knowledge you'll gain won't allow you to be taken advantage of anyway. And after all of this, if you still feel like you don't know what you're doing; read a little more because the more you learn the more enjoyable this hobby becomes. Be patient, game-used bat collecting gets better with age.

Adirondack knob pre-1980 showing only the model number. In 1980, a code was added to the knob signifying year.

BASEBALL BATS

There are basically four categories of baseball bats that collectors pursue. They are:

1) Authentic cracked or uncracked game-used bat. The player has actually used the bat in a game; it shows wear and tear from use, including scuffs, dents, tape, filing of the handle, uniform numbers on the handles, use of pine tar, hollowed ends and cracks. The value of a bat decreases according to the size of the crack.

This bat is made to a player's specifications, with his name and signature on it, or it could be a bat ordered by the team, with the team name branded into it. Pitchers and coaches generally use these bats. Coaches' bats may carry the player's name, but are not necessarily made according to the specifics he used as an active player.

2) Authentic bats, made to the players' specifications, but which have not been used in a game. It's possible the player didn't even own the bat, which could have been ordered by the team for promotions or giveaways, or made for other businesses for resale. These bats are often used for autographing.

3) Retail or store model bats, which are purchased in sporting goods stores. They are not made according to the player's specifications, but often carry his name as an endorsement. Vintage model bats of stars before the 1950s generally sell well. Naive collectors can end up purchasing these bats for $100 to $200, thinking they are game-used bats when they aren't.

Store models can be distinguished from game-used bats because the knobs carry inch markings, a single-digit number or both initials of the player whose name is on the barrel. Also, if the bat number in the brand oval is followed by any letters, probably player initials, it's likely the bat is a store model.

4) Commemoratives: These bats are made to recognize a particular person, place or event in baseball history, such as a World Series or Hall of Fame induction. These customized bats, generally more desirable than store models, are often created for display purposes and are suitable for autographing, which makes them more valuable. Black Sharpie pens work best.

Many collectors have their commemorative bats signed by the players involved.

Here are some general guidelines for bat collectors:

Baseball's rules limit the length of bats to 42 inches long. Generally, bats weigh between 30-50 ounces.

These are the most common bat brands used by major leaguers:

1) Hillerich & Bradsby: This company has undergone several name modifications from 1884 until 1979, when its bats became more commonly known as Louisville Sluggers, H&B's most popular style. Since 1945, H&B has labeled bats with player initials and a model number on the knob, which is an identifying number for each individual style. In 1976, those numbers were moved to the barrel of the bat. If the player is contracted by the manufacturer, his name is burned into the bat barrel in autograph form. If he isn't, his name is in block letters.

Hillerich & Bradsby adopted the slogan "Powerized" in 1932 and began putting model numbers—which have one letter and at least one number—on the knob in 1944. Those numbers were removed beginning in 1976 and then placed on the barrel. The H&B logo was dropped in 1979, with Louisville Slugger becoming the brand label.

2) A.G. Spalding & Bros. bats, used primarily before the turn of the century.

3) A.J. Reach bats, which were prominent at the beginning of the century.

4) Rawlings, which labels its bats as Adirondacks. They feature a single-colored ring around the neck and a diamond-shaped trademark.

5) Worth, which entered the market in the 1970s and offers its Tennessee Thumper bats.

6) Cooper bats, produced in Canada since 1986.

7) Mizuno bats, made in Japan.

It is very difficult to verify a bat was actually used by a player in a major league game. (Was it scuffed at a softball game last week? Did the player himself use it, or did one of his teammates? Was it used only in batting practice? Often, players themselves cannot remember which stick they used.)

If you invest in one of these bats, deal only with a dealer who is an expert in the area and insist on written documentation. Reliable dealers usually get these items from unimpeachable sources—the player's attorney or agent, a family member, the clubhouse attendant or a batboy.

GAME-USED BATS

The following bat pricing is primarily comprised of the work of bat expert Art Jaffe of Left Field Collectibles. Because pricing for unique items can be very difficult to assess, keep in mind that this pricing is a general guideline – bats' values can change significantly based on condition, provenance and the game in which they were used. **Bold**=Hall of Famers, *italic*=current players, plain=retired players.

Hank Aaron: Hillerich & Bradsby, 1950s $7,500
Aaron: Adirondack, early 1970s $3,500
Bobby Abreu $275
Joe Adcock: H&B, 1965-71 .... $450
Edgardo Alfonso $225
Dick Allen: H&B, 1973-75 .... $1,000
Bob Allison: H&B, 1960s $395
Roberto Alomar: Louisville Slugger, 1990 .... $425
Alomar: Adirondack, 1999 .... $350
Sandy Alomar Jr.: Rose, 1994-95 .... $150
Matty Alou: H&B, 1965-72 .... $295
Moises Alou $200
Brady Anderson: Louisville Slugger $95
Garret Anderson $200

Luis Aparicio: H&B, 1960s $1,100
Aparicio: mid-career $750
Tony Armas: Louisville, 1984-85 .... $100
Richie Ashburn: mid-career $3,000
Carlos Baerga: Adirondack, 1995, signed $275
Jeff Bagwell $850
Harold Baines $300
Dusty Baker: Louisville Slugger, 1975-79 .... $150
Steve Balboni: Louisville, 1984-85 .... $100
Sal Bando: H&B, 1965-72 .... $175
Ernie Banks: mid-career $3,500
Don Baylor: Louisville Slugger, 1977-79 .... $200
Albert Belle: Louisville Slugger, 1995 .... $300
Carlos Beltran $200
Adrian Beltre $200

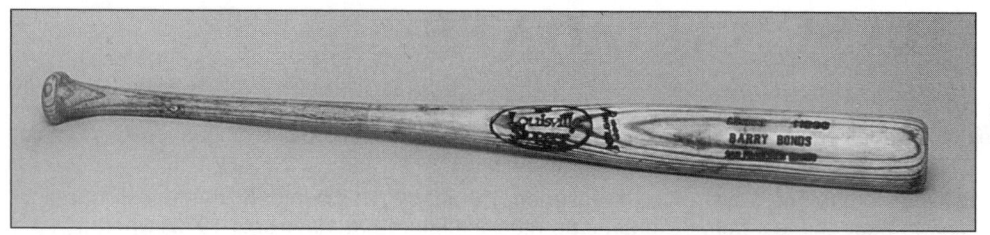

A game-used Barry Bonds personal Louisville Slugger model bat.

Johnny Bench: Adirondack, 1960s, signed $1,200
Bench: mid-career $800
Lance Berkman $600
Yogi Berra: mid-career $3,500
Dante Bichette: Louisville Slugger, 1988 .... $195
Bichette: Adirondack, 1999 .... $125
Craig Biggio: Louisville, 1993-94, signed $350
Jeff Blauser: Louisville Slugger, 1995 .... $100
Wade Boggs: H&B, 1977-79 (minors) $1,795
Wade Boggs: Louisville Slugger, 1982 .... $1,295
Wade Boggs: Louisville Slugger, 1994 .... $550
Barry Bonds: Louisville, 1993-95, signed $1,500
Bobby Bonilla: Louisville Slugger, 1986-89 .... $130
Bob Boone: Louisville, 1984-85, signed $265
Bret Boone $200
Lyman Bostock: Louisville Slugger, 1977-79 .... $350
Clete Boyer: H&B, 1965-72 .... $400
Ken Boyer: Adirondack, 1959 All-Star Game $1,495
George Brett: Louisvillle, early 1980s $1,150
Lou Brock: H&B, 1967 All-Star, signed $1,595
Lou Brock: H&B, 1973-75 .... $850
Gates Brown: H&B, 1965-72 .... $295
Kevin Brown $250
Bill Buckner: Louisville Slugger, 1973-75 .... $350
Jay Buhner: Adirondack, 1994 .... $150
Ellis Burks: Louisville Slugger, 1995 .... $85
Jeromy Burnitz: Louisville Slugger, 1997 .... $150
Pat Burrell $600
Jeff Burroughs: Worth, 1987 .... $80
Brett Butler $250
Ken Caminiti: Adirondack, 1995 .... $125
Roy Campanella: mid-career $6,500
Jose Canseco: Adirondack, 1991, signed $450
Canseco: Cooper, 1995 .... $295
Leo Cardenas: H&B, 1973-75, signed $125
Rod Carew: H&B, 1965-72, signed $1,150
Rod Carew: Louisville, 1977-79, signed $750
Rod Carew: Adirondack, 1980, signed $650
Steve Carlton: Louisville Slugger, mid-'80s $750
Gary Carter: H&B, 1973-75 .... $1,100
Gary Carter: Adirondack, mid-1980s $650
Joe Carter: Louisville Slugger, 1982-83 .... $395
Joe Carter: Louisville, 1995 .... $195
Rico Carty: H&B, 1965-72, signed $225
Sean Casey $350
Vinny Castilla: Adirondack, 1999 .... $150
Cesar Cedeno: H&B, 1970-71, signed $140
Orlando Cepeda: mid-career $800
Ron Cey: Louisville Slugger, 1975-79 .... $150
Jack Clark: Louisville Slugger, 1984-85 .... $125
Will Clark: Adirondack, 1991, signed $450
Will Clark: Louisville Slugger, ... $275
Roger Clemens $2,250
Roberto Clemente: H&B, late 1960s $7,000
Ty Cobb: mid-career $35,000
Rocky Colavito: H&B, 1965-68 .... $895

Dave Concepcion: Louisville, 1984-85, signed $250
David Cone $250
Cecil Cooper: Louisville Slugger, 1980 .... $150
Al Cowens: H&B, 1977-79 .... $40
Joe Cronin: mid-career $2,000
Johnny Damon $200
Vic Davalillo: Louisville Slugger, 1977-79 .... $150
Alvin Davis: Louisville Slugger, 1986-89 .... $50
Chili Davis: Adirondack, 1996 .... $100
Eric Davis: Louisville Slugger, 1999 .... $175
Tommy Davis: H & B, 1961-64 .... $450
Willie Davis: H&B, 1973-75 .... $350
Andre Dawson: Louisville, early 1980s $500
Doug DeCinces: Adirondack, 1987 .... $100
Carlos Delgado $500
Bill Dickey: mid-career $6,500
Joe DiMaggio: H&B, 1930s $16,500
Joe DiMaggio: H&B, 1945-51 .... $9,995
Bobby Doerr: H&B, 1949-59 .... $1,200
J.D. Drew $400
Adam Dunn $450
Shawon Dunston: Worth, 1988-89 .... $70
Jermaine Dye $200
Len Dykstra: Louisville, 1986-89 .... $150
Damion Easley: Louisville, 1998, cracked $95
Jim Edmonds $250
Jim Eisenreich: Louisville, 1995 .... $95
Mike Epstein: H&B, 1973-75 .... $200
Darin Erstad $350
Darrell Evans: Worth, 1988 .... $200
Dwight Evans: H&B, 1977-79, signed $395
Dwight Evans: Louisville Slugger, 1984-85 .... $2,000
Hoot Evers: Adirondack, 1952-57 .... $295
Tony Fernandez: Adirondack, 1991 .... $125
Cecil Fielder: Cooper, 1994 .... $250
Steve Finley: Cooper, 1993 .... $100
Carlton Fisk: Worth, 1970s, signed $750
Carlton Fisk: H&B, 1977-79 .... $1,295
George Foster: Louisville Slugger, 1977-79 .... $200
Nellie Fox: Louisville Slugger $1,250
Jimmie Foxx: mid-career $15,000
Bill Freehan: H&B, 1973-75 .... $495
Jim Fregosi: H&B, 1965-71, signed $225
Rafael Furcal $250
Andres Galarraga $250
Ron Gant: Adirondack, 1992 NLCS $350
Jim Gantner: Louisville Slugger, 1991-94 .... $80
Nomar Garciaparra: Louisville, 1999, signed $1,350
Steve Garvey: Adirondack, late 1970s $325
Steve Garvey: Louisville, 1985 All-Star Game $595
Cito Gaston: Adirondack, 1970s $175
Lou Gehrig: H&B, 1925 .... $30,000
Cesar Geronimo: H&B, 1977-79 .... $295
Jason Giambi $750
Bob Gibson: H&B, 1965-72 .... $2,200
Brian Giles $250

Dan Gladden: Worth, 1988	$150
Troy Glaus	$650
Juan Gonzalez: Adirondack, 1995	$400
Luis Gonzalez	$500
Dwight Gooden: Adirondack, 1984, signed	$195
Mark Grace: Adirondack, 1993	$350
Grace: Adirondack, 1995	$350
Hank Greenberg: mid-career	$9,000
Sean Green	$650
Mike Greenwell: Louisville Slugger, 1995	$100
Bobby Grich: Adirondack, 1981	$200
Tom Grieve: H&B, 1965-72	$110
Ken Griffey Jr.: Louisville, 1991-95, signed	$1,000
Ken Griffey Sr.: Louisville, 1973-75	$450
Ken Griffey Sr.: Louisville Slugger, 1990	$250
Marquis Grissom: Adirondack, 1993	$100
Dick Groat: H&B, 1965-72	$595
Pedro Guerrero: Louisville Slugger, 1983-85	$150
Vladimir Guerrero	$750
Ozzie Guillen: Worth, 1995	$120
Tony Gwynn: Louisville, 1998	$895
Tony Gwynn: Adirondack, 1992 All-Star	$1,200
Von Hayes: Louisville Slugger, 1986-89	$100
Todd Helton	$450
Rickey Henderson: Louisville, 1993 W.Series	$995
Henderson: Louisville Slugger, 1995	$400
George Hendrick: Louisville Slugger, 1984-85	$100
Tommy Henrich: H&B, 1940s	$1,395
Keith Hernandez: Louisville, 1980s	$225
Babe Herman: H&B, 1930s	$950
Billy Herman: mid-career	$2,500
Orel Hershiser: Louisville Slugger, 1984-85	$200
Richard Hidalgo	$200
Butch Hobson: H&B, 1977-79	$125
Gil Hodges: Louisville Slugger, 1953	$2,500
Gil Hodges: Louisville, 1953 WS	$3,500-$4,000
Chris Hoiles: Adirondack, 1994	$80
Rogers Hornsby: mid-career	$17,000
Elston Howard: H&B, pre-1964	$1,395
Frank Howard: H&B, 1965-72, signed	$595
Todd Hundley: Lousiville Slugger, 1995	$85
Torii Hunter	$375
Bo Jackson: Louisville Slugger, 1991-93	$295
Joe Jackson: H&B, 1921-30	$25,000
Reggie Jackson: Louisville, 1968-72	$2,400
Reggie Jackson: H&B, 1968-71, signed	$1,795
Reggie Jackson: Adirondack, 1971-79	$695
Reggie Jackson: Adirondack, 1985	$550
Derek Jeter	$2,000
Alex Johnson: H&B, 1973-75, signed	$295
Cliff Johnson: Louisville, early 1980s	$95
Davey Johnson: H&B, cracked 1970s, signed	$185
Howard Johnson: Adirondack, 1988	$95
Randy Johnson	$1,200
Andruw Jones	$500
Felix Jose: Louisville Slugger, 1986-89	$60
Von Joshua: H&B, 1977-79	$75
Wally Joyner: Louisville Slugger, 1991-94	$135
Dave Justice: Louisville Slugger, 1995	$275
Al Kaline: H&B, 1965-72, signed	$1,500
Kaline: H&B, late 1970s	$750
Gabe Kapler	$250
Ron Karkovice: Louisville Slugger	$70
Eric Karros	$250
George Kell: mid-career	$1,200
Jason Kendall	$250

Jeff Kent	$350
Don Kessinger: Louisville Slugger, 1973-75	$125
Harmon Killebrew: mid-career	$3,500
Killebrew: Louisville, 1971	$2,000
Ralph Kiner: mid-career	$900
Dave Kingman: Louisville, signed, '84-85	$350
Ryan Klesko	$200
Ted Kluszewski: H&B, 1958	$995
Ray Knight: H&B, 1977-79	$150
Chuck Knoblauch: Louisville Slugger, 1991-93	$175
Paul Konerko	$375
Corey Koskie	$250
John Kruk: Louisville Slugger, 1993	$175
Tony Kubek: H&B, 1965-72	$895
Harvey Kuenn: H&B, 1965-72	$695
Lee Lacy: Adirondack, 1971-79	$100
Carney Lansford: H&B, 1977-79	$125
Barry Larkin	$250
Carlos Lee	$200
Ron LeFlore: Louisville Slugger, 1977-79	$95
Chet Lemon: Louisville Slugger, 1990	$85
Paul LoDuca	$350
Davey Lopes: Adirondack, 1981	$200
Al Lopez: mid-career	$2,750
Javy Lopez	$200
John Lowenstein: H&B, 1980s	$125
Greg Luzinski: Adirondack, 1971-79	$225
Fred Lynn: Adirondack, 1990	$200
Bill Madlock: Louisville Slugger, 1984-85	$250
Greg Maddux: Louisville, 1995, signed	$1,295
Mickey Mantle: mid-career	$18,500
Marty Marion: H&B, 1940s, signed	$850
Roger Maris: H&B, 1960s	$6,500
Roger Maris: H&B, 1961	$6,500
Edgar Martinez	$350
Pedro Martinez	$1,200
Tino Martinez	$400
Eddie Mathews: H&B, 1968, signed	$3,000
Don Mattingly: Worth, 1980s	$650
Mattingly: Worth, 1994	$550
Willie Mays: H&B, 1965-72	$6,500
Mays: H&B, early 1970s	$4,000
Bill Mazeroski: Adirondack, 1960 All-Star	$4,000
Mazeroski: mid-career	$2,000
Tim McCarver: H&B, 1976	$450
Willie McCovey: Louisville, '65-71, signed	$1,495
McCovey: Louisville Slugger, 1974-75	$1,195
Fred McGriff: Louisville Slugger, 1986-89	$350
Mark McGwire: Adirondack, 1992	$1,500
McGwire: Adirondack, 1991 All-Star, signed	$3,500
Hal McRae: H&B, 1973-75	$300
Hal McRae: Louisville Slugger, 1977-79	$150
Kevin McReynolds: Adirondack, 1988	$95
Minnie Minoso: H&B, 1960 All-Star Game	$1,495
Kevin Mitchell: Mizuno, 1994	$100
Johnny Mize: mid-career	$3,000
Paul Molitor: H&B, 1977-79	$795
Molitor	$450
Rick Monday: H&B, 1965-71, signed	$175
Raul Mondesi	$200
Joe Morgan: Louisville Slugger, 1977-79	$650
Manny Mota: H&B, 1965-72	$295
Thurman Munson: H&B, 1977-79	$2,000
Bobby Murcer: H&B, 1973-75	$350
Eddie Murray: H&B, 1977-79, signed	$1,295
Murray: Louisville, 1988, signed	$595

Stan Musial: H&B, pre-1964 .... $5,500
Musial: mid-career $6,000
Tim Naehring: Louisville Slugger, 1995 .... $90
Graig Nettles: Louisville Slugger, 1984-85 .... $350
Otis Nixon: Cooper, 1995 .... $80
Matt Nokes: Louisville Slugger, 1984-85 .... $80
Hideo Nomo $650
Ben Oglivie: Louisville Slugger, 1980-83 .... $100
John Olerud $350
Tony Oliva: H&B, early 1970s $550
Al Oliver: Louisville Slugger, 1965-72 .... $200
Magglio Ordonez $300
Jorge Orta: Louisville Slugger, 1977-79 .... $80
Paul O'Neill: Louisville Slugger, ... $350
Mel Ott: mid-career $20,000
Rafael Palmeiro: Louisville Slugger, 1986 .... $750
Palmeiro $500
Dave Parker: Louisville, 1980-83 .... $250
Lance Parrish: Worth, 1980s $150
Dan Pasqua: Louisville Slugger, 1994 .... $70
Tony Pena: Louisville Slugger, 1986-89 .... $125
Terry Pendleton: Louisville, 1985 WS, signed $595
Tony Perez: Adirondack, late 1960s $850
Perez: Louisville, 1986-89, signed $550
Mike Piazza $1,000
Jim Piersall: H&B, 1950s $995
Vada Pinson: H&B, 1973-75 .... $350
Kirby Puckett: 1991 Adirondack, ALCS $1,000
Puckett: 1994 Louisville Slugger $600
Albert Pujols $850
Tim Raines: Louisville, early 1980s, signed $250
Tim Raines: Louisville, 1982 All-Star, signed $495
Manny Ramirez $600
Willie Randolph: Louisville, 1980s $250
Jody Reed: Louisville Slugger, 1995 .... $95
Pee Wee Reese: H&B, 1949-59 .... $3,500
Rich Reese: H&B, 1965-72 .... $85
Harold Reynolds: Louisville Slugger, 1984-85 .... $100
Jim Rice: Louisville Slugger, 1984-85 .... $350
Jose Rijo: Louisville Slugger, 1994 .... $125
Cal Ripken Jr.: Louisville Slugger, 1980-83 .... $2,500
Phil Rizzuto: mid-career $3,000
Brooks Robinson: H&B, 1972-75, signed $1,250
Frank Robinson: H&B, 1965-71 .... $2,000
Jackie Robinson: Louisville Slugger $25,000
Alex Rodriguez $950
Ivan Rodriguez $450
Pete Rose: H&B, 1965-72, signed $2,000
Rose: H&B, 1972-75, signed $1,595
Rose: Mizuno, 1980-83, signed $1,250
Joe Rudi: H&B, 1973-75 .... $150
Babe Ruth: H&B $25,000
Ruth: H&B, 1920s $25,000
Nolan Ryan: Louisville, 1983-85, signed $2,495
Tim Salmon $300
Ryne Sandberg: Adirondack, 1988 .... $475
Manny Sanguillen: H&B, 1965-72, signed $195
Benito Santiago: Worth, 1995 .... $100
Curt Schilling $1,100
Mike Schmidt: Louisville, 1974-75 .... $1,700
Schmidt: Adirondack, 1980s $900
Red Schoendienst: Adirondack, 1950s $895
George Scott: Louisville Slugger, 1973-75 .... $150
Tom Seaver: H&B, 1972-75, signed $1,495

Seaver: H&B, 1977-79 .... $1,625
Kevin Seitzer: Louisville Slugger, 1986-89 .... $80
Richie Sexson $250
Gary Sheffield $250
Ruben Sierra: Louisville, 1991-92, signed $125
Sierra: Adirondack, 1991 All-Star Game $245
Ted Simmons: Louisville Slugger, 1984-85 .... $150
Moose Skowron: H&B, 1950s $995
Enos Slaughter: mid-career $1,350
Roy Smalley: Louisville Slugger, 1965-72 .... $100
Ozzie Smith: H&B, 1977-79, signed $1,000
Duke Snider: mid-career $4,000
Cory Snyder: Louisville Slugger, signed $95
Alfonso Soriano $1,250
Sammy Sosa $950
Mario Soto: Louisville Slugger, 1984-85 .... $80
Willie Stargell: H&B, 1964 All-Star, signed $2,495
Stargell: H&B, late 1970s $750
Terry Steinbach: Adirondack, 1994 .... $100
Rennie Stennett: Louisville Slugger, 1975-79 .... $100
Shannon Stewart $200
B.J. Surhoff: Adirondack, 1995 .... $90
Mike Sweeney $350
Ichiro Suzuki $3,000
Danny Tartabull: Worth, 1992 .... $90
Frank Thomas $375
Gorman Thomas: Adirondack, 1981 .... $90
Jim Thome $375
Luis Tiant: H&B, 1965-72, signed $695
Miguel Tejada $550
Alan Trammell: Worth, early 1980s, signed $395
Trammell: Louisville, 1980-83, signed $395
Andy Van Slyke: Louisville, 1995 .... $275
Greg Vaughn: Adirondack, 1991 .... $125
Mo Vaughn: Louisville Slugger, 1995 .... $350
Otto Velez: H&B, 1976, cracked $90
Robin Ventura: Louisville Slugger, 1993 .... $175
Larry Walker $350
Bob Watson: Adirondack, 1971-79 .... $150
Walt Weiss: Louisville Slugger, 1995 .... $85
Weiss: Worth, 1989 ALCS $235
Bill White: H&B, 1950s $895
Devon White: Louisville Slugger, 1990 .... $100
Frank White: Adirondack, 1971-79 .... $90
Roy White: H&B, 1979 .... $175
Ernie Whitt: Louisville Slugger, 1990 .... $60
Bernie Williams $650
Billy Williams: mid-career $1,000
Dick Williams: H&B, 1950s $450
Matt Williams: Cooper, 1994 .... $295
Ted Williams: mid-career $12,500
Preston Wilson $200
Dave Winfield: H&B, 1973-75, signed $1,295
Winfield: Cooper, 1994 .... $350
Winfield: Adirondack, 1979 All-Star $1,850
Kerry Wood $350
Jimmy Wynn: H&B, 1976 .... $180
Carl Yastrzemski: H&B, 1960-64 .... $1,695
Yastrzemski: H&B, 1965-72 .... $995
Yastrzemski: Louisville, early 1980s $575
Robin Yount: H&B, 1973-75 .... $1,995
Yount: Louisville Slugger, 1984-85 .... $550
Richie Zisk: Adirondack, 1981 .... $60

The following bat pricing and information is comprised of the work of John Taube of J.T. Sports. Because pricing for unique items can be very difficult to assess, keep in mind that this pricing is a general guideline – bats' values can change significantly based on condition, provenance and the game in which they were used.

HALL OF FAMERS

Hank Aaron $4,500
    (1950's examples are very tough)
    (a 1957 All-Star example sold for $21,300)
Luis Aparicio $1,200
Luke Appling $5,000
Richie Ashburn $5,000
Earl Averill $3,500
Frank Baker $7,500
Dave Bancroft $3,250
Ernie Banks $3,750
    (a 1950's gamer sold for $6,270)
Johnny Bench $1,400
Yogi Berra $4,500
    (pre-1960 examples sell for a premium)
Jim Bottomley $3,250
Lou Boudreau $2,500
Roger Bresnahan $6,500
George Brett $1,500
    (Heavily pine tarred examples sell for a premium)
    (a 1977 All-Star bat sold for $5,604)
Lou Brock $2,200
    (a rookie example sold for $9,390)
Roy Campanella $7,500
    (Campy bats are very tough)
    (a 1950's example sold for $14,547)
Rod Carew $600
Max Carey $3,250
Gary Carter $450
Orlando Cepeda $1,100
Frank Chance $9,000
Oscar Charleston $10,500
Fred Clarke $5,000
Bob Clemente $6,500
    (grooving of barrel is sought after)
    (a signed 1965-'68 example sold for $18,953)
Ty Cobb $40,000
    (early examples are very scarce)
    (high-end examples sell for $55,000-$80,000)
    (one side written bat sold for $100,000)
Mickey Cochrane $5,500
Eddie Collins $7,500
    (a 1917-1921 example sold for $18,725)
Earle Combs $6,500
Stan Coveleski $6,000
Sam Crawford $4,500
Joe Cronin $1,200
Kiki Cuyler $2,000
Ray Dandridge $3,500
Bill Dickey $7,000
Joe DiMaggio $20,000
Larry Doby $2,500
Bobby Doerr $700
Leo Durocher $8,200
    (only one known/this is the auction price)
John Evers $7,500

Rick Ferrell $1,500
Carlton Fisk $450
Nellie Fox $1,500
Elmer Flick $750
Jimmie Foxx (1940's) $18,000
    (a vault marked example sold for $31,189)
    (a 1920's example sold for $39,648)
Frankie Frisch $3,000
Lou Gehrig $37,500
    (side written examples have sold for $75,000 and up)
    (one side written rookie bat (1923) sold for $125,000)
Charlie Gehringer $5,500
Goose Goslin $4,000
Hank Greenberg $7,500
    (Side written gamers have sold for $12,000 and up)
Chuck Hafey $2,500
Bucky Harris $1,500
Gabby Hartnett $5,000
Harry Heilmann $2,500
Billy Herman $2,000
Harry Hooper $5,500
Rogers Hornsby $17,500
    (high-end examples have sold for $25,000 and up)
    (a 1920's example sold for $29,078)
Monte Irvin $6,500
    (only a few are known to exist)
Reggie Jackson $750
    (Yankee era bats and early examples sell for a premium)
Travis Jackson $4,000
Al Kaline $1,500
George Kell $1,100
George Kelly $1,500
Harmon Killebrew $3,000
    (pre-1960 examples are very tough)
Ralph Kiner $1,200
Chuck Klein $3,000
    (a 1934-43 example sold for $12,501)
Nap Lajoie $12,500
Tony Lazzeri $8,500
    (a 1926-30 example sold for $10,330)
Fred Lindstrom $3,500
    (a 1933-34 example sold for $6,167)
John "Pop" Lloyd $6,000
Ernie Lombardi $3,000
Al Lopez $2,500
Ted Lyons $4,000
Mickey Mantle $17,500
    (high-end examples sell for a major premium)
    (a 1955 World Series bat sold for $51,518)
    (a 1950's signed bat sold for $43,244)
    (a 1955 All-Star Bat sold for $39,710)
Heinie Manush $2,750

Rabbit Maranville $3,000
Ed Mathews $3,500
    (pre-1960 bats are very desirable)
    (a 1961 HR bat sold for $13,559)
    (a 1965 HR bat sold for $17,603)
Willie Mays $7,500
    (early Mays bats sell for a premium)
    (a 1961-64 example sold for $18,725)
Bill Mazeroski $1,750
    (a 1966 example sold for $3,868)
    (1965-68 example sold for $2,922)
Willie McCovey $1,500
    (a rookie-era bat sold for $6,270)
Joe Medwick $5,000
Johnny Mize $2,500
Joe Morgan $850
    (early examples sell for a premium)
Eddie Murray $650
    (a rookie-era bat sold for $2,789)
Stan Musial $5,000
    (pre-1960 examples are very desirable)
    (His 1955 All-Star HR bat sold in excess of $20,000)
Mel Ott $25,000
    (a 1933 example sold for $30,925)
    (a side written example sold for $54,004)
Tony Perez $750
Kirby Puckett $525
Hal "ee Wee" Reese $3,250
    (a rookie-era example sold for $6,412)
    (a 1955 World Series bat sold for $8,733)
Sam Rice $5,000
Phil Rizzuto $8,500
Brooks Robinson $1,750
    (early examples sell for a premium)
Frank Robinson $2,500
    (a pre-1960 example sold for $10,000)
Jackie Robinson $20,000
    (top notch examples sell for $30,000 and up)
    (a 1956 example sold for $43,613)
Edd Roush $1,500
Babe Ruth $35,000
    (high-end and early examples sell for $50,000 and up)
    (a 1924 Signed/HR bat sold for $225,000)
    (1929 side written/HR notch bat sold for $320,000)
    (the earliest known signed bat (1916-1920) sold for $150,000)
Ray Schalk $4,000
Mike Schmidt $1,200
    (home run bats sell in the $3,500-$6,000 range)
    (a 1970's example sold for $1,760)
Red Schoendienst $700
Joe Sewell $4,000
    (a 1923-25 example sold for $5,244)

Al Simmons $2,500
  (a 1940 side written and vault
  marked for $9,000+)
George Sisler.............................. $2,500
  (one example sold for $5,244)
Enos Slaughter $1,200
Ozzie Smith $500
Duke Snider................................ $3,750
  (pre-1960 examples are very desirable)
  (look for evidence of handle tape)
Tris Speaker................................ $8,500
Willie Stargell $1,200
Casey Stengel $4,250
Bill Terry.................................... $2,500
  (one example sold for $6,345)
Joe Tinker................................... $7,500
Pie Traynor $3,500
Arky Vaughan $3,500
Honus Wagner........................... $75,000
Bobby Wallace............................ $5,000
Lloyd Waner................................ $5,000
Paul Waner................................. $3,000
  (early examples may sell for $10,000)
Zack Wheat $4,500
Billy Williams............................... $800
Ted Williams............................... $12,500
  (high-end examples sell for $20,000
  and up)
  (a 1948 vault marked bat sold for
  $58,139)
  (a 1955 All-Star/signed bat sold for
  $29,786)
Hack Wilson................................ $5,000
  (a 1932 example sold for $21,300)
Dave Winfield $550
  (Yankee era bats sell for a premium)
Carl Yastrzemski.......................... $1,100
Ross Youngs............................... $3,500
Robin Yount $650

Vintage Stars

Richie Allen................................ $1,000
Sandy Amoros $750
Hank Bauer $600
Benny Bengough $2,500
Moe Berg $5,000
Bobby Bonds $250
Ken Boyer $600
Lew Burdette $400
Chico Carrasquel.......................... $1,000
Norm Cash $950
Ray Chapman............................... $4,500
Hal Chase................................... $5,000
Rocky Colavito............................. $900
Dave Conception $200
Tony Conigliaro $1,100
Chuck Connors $2,000
Frank Crosetti $1,500
Alvin Dark $300
Tommy Davis................................ $275
Dom DiMaggio.............................. $1,200
Vince DiMaggio $1,500
Chuck Dressen.............................. $400
Joe Dugan $1,200
Del Ennis $400
Darrell Evans $200
Dwight Evans............................... $225

Curt Flood.................................... $450
George Foster $175
Bill Freehan $400
Carl Furillo $2,000
Chick Gandil $6,500
Steve Garvey $225
Kirk Gibson $275
Jim Gilliam $1,400
Joe Gordon $1,500
Dick Groat................................... $600
Heinie Groh $1,000
Tommy Henrich $1,100
Babe Herman $750
Gil Hodges $3,000
Elston Howard $1,100
Frank Howard $500
Joe Jackson
  Playing Days $100,000
  Post-Ban Signature.............. $20,000
  Post-Ban Block $10,000
  (Black Betsy sold for $577,610)
  (a side written example sold for
  $206,529)
  (a 1922-25 barnstorming example sold
  for $43,679)
Jackie Jensen............................... $400
Ken Keltner $1,000
Dave Kingman $450
Ted Kluszewski $525
Mark Koenig $2,500
Tony Kubek $1,200
Harvey Kuenn............................... $450
Davey Lopes $150
Greg Luzinski $250
Fred Lynn.................................... $250
Bill Madlock $175
Marty Marion $600
Roger Maris $5,000
  (a 1961-64 example sold for $14,087)
  (a 1962-All-Star bat sold for $10,928)
Billy Martin $2,500
Pepper Martin $1,500
Tim McCarver $300
Bob Meusel $3,000
Minnie Minoso $650
Thurman Munson $2,750
Graig Nettles $225
Tony Oliva $875
Al Oliver $250
Dave Parker $250
Joe Pepitone $600
Johnny Pesky $225
Jim Piersall $400
Lou Pinella $300
Vada Pinson $350
Wally Pipp $2,000
Boog Powell $550
Pete Reiser $550
Bobby Richardson $2,500
Swede Risberg $6,000
Pete Rose $2,200
  (a 1977 All-Star bat sold for $6,393)
  (a 1969-72 example sold for $3,780)
  (Rose bats have a wide range in price)
Al Rosen $600
Ron Santo $1,250

Ted Simmons................................ $250
Dick Sisler $400
Bill Skowron $600
  (a 1950-60 example sold for $1,071)
Rusty Staub................................. $275
Vern Stephens $300
Riggs Stephenson $1,000
Dick Stuart.................................. $500
Bobby Thomson $900
Joe Torre $750
Alan Trammell $350
Mickey Vernon $400
Bill Wambsganss $4,000
Buck Weaver $6,000
Vic Wertz $550
Lou Whitaker $250
Bill White $400
Maury Wills $750
Gus Zernial.................................. $350

Modern Stars

Edgardo Alfonzo $200
Roberto Alomar $350
Moises Alou $200
Garret Anderson $400
Jeff Bagwell $650
Harold Baines $250
Albert Belle $250
Lance Berkman $550
Craig Biggio $325
Wade Boggs $550
  (Yankee bats sell for 750)
Barry Bonds.................................. $2,500
  (2001 examples selling for $5,000
  and up)
  (2001 HR bats sell between $12,000-
  $20,000)
Pat Burrell................................... $600
Jose Canseco................................ $250
Joe Carter $175
Sean Casey $400
Will Clark $175
Andre Dawson $350
Carlos Delgado $550
J.D. Drew $400
Adam Dunn.................................. $400
Jim Edmonds................................ $450
Cecil Fielder $150
Andres Galarraga $200
Nomar Garciaparra......................... $1,450
Jason Giambi (A's) $400
Jason Giambi (NY) $1,250
Troy Glaus $550
Juan Gonzalez $325
Luis Gonzalez $350
Mark Grace.................................. $275
Ken Griffey Jr................................ $1,100
Shawn Green $550
Vladimir Guerrero $550
Tony Gwynn.................................. $575
Todd Helton.................................. $400
Rickey Henderson $450
Bo Jackson $200
Derek Jeter $2,750
Andruw Jones................................ $425
  (Home Run Bats - $675+)
Chipper Jones $575

Austin Kearns $450	Dale Murphy $350	Ryne Sandberg $450
Jeff Kent $300	Phil Nevin $150	Gary Sheffield............................... $200
Ryan Klesko $150	John Olerud................................. $225	Alfonso Soriano $1,900
Paul Konerko $350	Paul O'Neil $600	Sammy Sosa $1,200
Barry Larkin $200	Magglio Ordonez $350	(Autographed $1,500+, home run bats
Carlos Lee $150	Rafael Palmeiro $450	$3,000+)
Kenny Lofton $200	Mike Piazza $900	Darryl Strawberry $225
Edgar Martinez $450	(Mizuno's in high-demand)	Mike Sweeney $400
Tino Martinez................................ $350	Jorge Posada $375	Miguel Tejada $400
(Yankee bats sell for a premium)	Tim Raines $150	Frank Thomas $350
Don Mattingly................................ $950	Manny Ramirez $450	Jim Thome.................................. $425
(autographed bats $1,200-$1,500)	Jim Rice $400	Larry Walker $250
Fred McGriff................................. $350	Cal Ripkin $1,850	Bernie Williams............................ $550
Mark McGwire (A's) $1,500	(a 1982 rookie bat sold for $3,215)	Matt Williams $200
Mark McGwire (Cards) $2,500	Alex Rodriguez $750	Greg Vaughn $175
(signed Mac gamers sell for a major	Ivan Rodriguez $425	Mo Vaughn $225
premium)	Scott Rolen $600	
Paul Molitor.................................. $650	Tim Salmon $150	

STORE MODEL BATS

Prices are for bats in Near Mint condition.

Hank Aaron: Hillerich & Bradsby $75	Harry Davis.. $500
Joe Adcock: Adirondack $60	Bill Dickey: Hillerich & Bradsby $300
Dick Allen: Adirondack.. $45	Dom DiMaggio: Hillerich & Bradsby $110
Felipe Alou: Hillerich & Bradsby/Adirondack $30	Joe DiMaggio: Hillerich & Bradsby $600
Richie Ashburn: Hillerich & Bradsby $110	Larry Doby: Adirondack $110
Earl Averill: Spalding/Adirondack $300	Bobby Doerr: Hillerich & Bradsby $200
Frank Baker: Hillerich & Bradsby $500	Johnny Evers: Spalding $500
Dave Bancroft: Spalding $300	Carlton Fisk: Adirondack $50
Ernie Banks: Hillerich & Bradsby $75	Curt Flood: Hillerich & Bradsby $110
Hank Bauer: Adirondack/Hillerich & Bradsby $75	Nelson Fox: Hillerich & Bradsby $75
Gus Bell: Hillerich & Bradsby $60	Jimmie Foxx: Hillerich & Bradsby $200
Johnny Bench: Hillerich & Bradsby $60	Jim Fregosi: Hillerich & Bradsby $60
Yogi Berra: Hillerich & Bradsby $75	Joe Garagiola: Adirondack $90
Bobby Bonds: Hillerich & Bradsby $40	Steve Garvey: Hillerich & Bradsby $30
Ray Boone: Adirondack $60	Lou Gehrig: Hillerich & Bradsby $600
Jim Bottomley: Hillerich & Bradsby $300	Charlie Gehringer: Hillerich & Bradsby/Spalding............... $300
Lou Boudreau: Hillerich & Bradsby $300	Dick Groat: Hillerich & Bradsby $75
Ken Boyer: Hillerich & Bradsby $75	Joe Gordon: Louisville Slugger $100
Roger Bresnahan: Spalding $300	Goose Goslin: Hillerich & Bradsby $300
George Brett $30	Hank Gowdy: Hillerich & Bradsby $120
Lou Brock: Hillerich & Bradsby $120	Hank Greenberg: Hillerich & Bradsby........................ $500
Jeff Burroughs: Hillerich & Bradsby $30	Chick Hafey: Hillerich & Bradsby $300
Johnny Callison: Hillerich & Bradsby $45	Ken Harrelson: Louisville Slugger $55
Roy Campanella: Hillerich & Bradsby $300	"Bucky" Harris: Hillerich & Bradsby $200
Bert Campaneris: Hillerich & Bradsby $30	Gabby Hartnett: Spalding $300
Rod Carew: Hillerich & Bradsby $60	Harry Heilmann: Hillerich & Bradsby $200
Gary Carter: $30	Babe Herman: Hillerich & Bradsby $300
Orlando Cepeda: Hillerich & Bradsby $60	Gil Hodges: Adirondack $60
Bob Cerv: Hillerich & Bradsby $75	Rogers Hornsby: Hillerich & Bradsby $300
Frank Chance: Spalding $1,000	Frank Howard: Hillerich & Bradsby $75
Fred Clarke: Spalding $4,000	Miller Huggins: Spalding $300
Roberto Clemente: Sears $85	Monte Irvin: Hillerich & Bradsby $120
Roberto Clemente: Hillerich & Bradsby $75	Joe Jackson: Hillerich & Bradsby $3,000
Ty Cobb: Spalding $3,000	Reggie Jackson: Hillerich & Bradsby $60
Ty Cobb: Hllerich & Bradsby $600	Travis Jackson: Hillerich & Bradsby $300
Mickey Cochrane: Hillerich & Bradsby $500	Cleon Jones: Adirondack $25
Rocky Colavito: Hillerich & Bradsby $60	Al Kaline: Hillerich & Bradsby $60
Eddie Collins: Hillerich & Bradsby $300	George Kell: Hillerich & Bradsby $60
Sam Crawford: Spalding $300	George Kelly: Hillerich & Bradsby $300
Joe Cronin: Hillerich & Bradsby $200	Harmon Killebrew: Hillerich & Bradsby...................... $60
Kiki Cuyler: Hillerich & Bradsby $300	Ralph Kiner: Hillerich & Bradsby $60
	Chuck Klein: Hillerich & Bradsby $300
	Ted Kluszewski: Hillerich & Bradsby........................ $60

Tony Kubek: Adirondack $60
Harvey Kuenn: Hillerich & Bradsby $30
Nap Lajoie: Hillerich & Bradsby $2,500
Ernie Lombardi: Hillerich & Bradsby $300
Bob Lemon: Hillerich & Bradsby $120
Fred Lynn: Hillerich & Bradsby $30
Bill Madlock: Hillerich & Bradsby $30
Mickey Mantle: Hillerich & Bradsby $120
Heinie Manush: Spalding $300
Roger Maris: Hillerich & Bradsby $75
Rabbit Marranville: Hillerich & Bradsby $300
Eddie Mathews: Hillerich & Bradsby $110
Don Mattingly $30
Willie Mays: Adirondack/Hillerich & Bradsby $120
Bill Mazeroski $60
Dick McAuliffe: Hillerich & Bradsby $60
Tim McCarver: Hillerich & Bradsby $30
Willie McCovey: Adirondack/Hillerich & Bradsby $60
Joe Medwick: Hillerich & Bradsby $300
Felix Milan: Adirondack $25
Johnny Mize: Hillerich & Bradsby $200
Joe Morgan: Hillerich & Bradsby $60
Bobby Murcer: Hillerich & Bradsby $60
Eddie Murray $60
Stan Musial: Hillerich & Bradsby/Adirondack $300
Tony Oliva: Hillerich & Bradsby $60
Mel Ott: Hillerich & Bradsby $300
Tony Perez: Hillerich & Bradsby $75
John Pesky: Hillerich & Bradsby $60
Vada Pinson: Adirondack $50
Boog Powell: Hillerich & Bradsby $30
Kirby Puckett $30
Pee Wee Reese: Hillerich & Bradsby $300
Brooks Robinson: Hillerich & Bradsby $75

Frank Robinson: Hillerich & Bradsby $75
Jackie Robinson: Hillerich & Bradsby $110
Pete Rose: Hillerich & Bradsby $60
Edd Rousch: Hillerich & Bradsby $200
Babe Ruth: Hillerich & Bradsby $500
Ron Santo: Adirondack/ Hillerich & Bradsby $75
Ray Schalk: Spalding $600
Mike Schmidt $30
Red Schoendienst: Hillerich & Bradsby $75
Moose Skowron: Hillerich & Bradsby $75
Al Simmons: Hillerich & Bradsby $300
George Sisler: Hillerich & Bradsby/Spalding $200
Enos Slaughter: Hillerich & Bradsby $75
Ozzie Smith $30
Duke Snider: Hillerich & Bradsby $110
Tris Speaker: Hillerich & Bradsby $500
Willie Stargell: Hillerich & Bradsby $60
Rusty Staub: Hillerich & Bradsby $60
Vern Stephens: MacGregor Gold Smith $100
Bill Terry: Hillerich & Bradsby $300
Joe Torre: Adirondack/Hillerich & Bradsby $60
Pie Traynor: Spalding $300
Arky Vaughan: Hillerich & Bradsby $300
Honus Wagner: Hillerich & Bradsby $1,800
Lloyd Waner: Hillerich & Bradsby $300
Paul Waner: Hillerich & Bradsby/ Spalding $200
Vic Wertz: Adirondack $60
Billy Williams: Hillerich & Bradsby $60
Ted Williams: Hillerich & Bradsby $300
Maury Wills: Hillerich & Bradsby $60
Dave Winfield $30
Carl Yastrzemski: Hillerich & Bradsby $60
Heinie Zimmerman: Spalding $300

WORLD SERIES BLACK BATS

World Series Black Bats, created by Hillerich and Bradsby, are given to participating players and dignitaries from teams in the Series. They have facsimile signatures of the entire team in gold on a dark black ebony bat.

1934 Detroit Tigers .... $4,000-$5,000
1935 Detroit Tigers .... $1,750-$2,500
1936 New York Yankees .... $2,000-$2,750
1936 New York Giants .... $1,750-$2,250
1937 New York Yankees .... $1,750-$2,250
1937 New York Giants .... $1,250-$1,750
1938 New York Yankees .... $1,200-$1,500
1938 Chicago Cubs .... $1,750-$2,500
1939 New York Yankees .... $800-$1,250
1939 Cincinnati Reds .... $800-$1,000
1940 Cincinnati Reds .... $800-$1,250
1940 Detroit Tigers .... $1,000-$1,500
1941 New York Yankees .... $800-$1,200
1941 Brooklyn Dodgers .... $1,200-$1,500
1942 New York Yankees .... $1,000-$1,250
1942 St. Louis Cardinals .... $750-$1,000
1943 St. Louis Cardinals .... $750-$1,000
1943 New York Yankees .... $750-$1,000
1944 St. Louis Cardinals .... $1,000-$1,200
1944 St. Louis Browns .... $1,000-$1,200
1945 Detroit Tigers .... $1,250-$1,500
1945 Chicago Cubs .... $1,500-$1,750
1946 St. Louis Cardinals .... $1,000-$1,250
1946 Boston Red Sox .... $1,250-$1,500

1947 New York Yankees .... $750-$1,000
1947 Brooklyn Dodgers .... $750-$1,000
1948 Cleveland Indians .... $1,000-$1,250
1948 Boston Braves .... $700-$900
1949 New York Yankees .... $850-$1,150
1949 Brooklyn Dodgers .... $850-$1,150
1950 New York Yankees .... $650-$850
1950 Philadelphia Phillies .... $1,250-$1,500
1951 New York Yankees .... $1,250-$1,500
1951 New York Giants .... $750-$1,000
1952 New York Yankees .... $500-$750
1952 Brooklyn Dodgers .... $600-$800
1953 New York Yankees .... $500-$750
1953 Brooklyn Dodgers .... $650-$850
1954 New York Giants .... $600-$800
1954 Cleveland Indians .... $600-$800
1955 Brooklyn Dodgers .... $1,750-$2,500
1955 New York Yankees .... $600-$800
1956 New York Yankees .... $1,000-$1,250
1956 Brooklyn Dodgers .... $700-$850
1957 Milwaukee Braves .... $750-$950
1957 New York Yankees .... $650-$850
1958 Milwaukee Braves .... $400-$550
1958 New York Yankees .... $700-$850

1959 Los Angeles Dodgers	$750-$950
1959 Chicago White Sox	$800-$1,000
1960 New York Yankees	$575-$775
1960 Pittsburgh Pirates	$775-$1,100
1961 New York Yankees	$1,250-$1,775
1961 Cincinnati Reds	$450-$550
1962 New York Yankees	$675-$800
1962 San Francisco Giants	$475-$650
1963 Los Angeles Dodgers	$600-$725
1963 New York Yankees	$475-$595
1964 St. Louis Cardinals	$475-$595
1964 New York Yankees	$475-$595
1965 Los Angeles Dodgers	$350-$450
1965 Minnesota Twins	$350-$500
1966 Baltimore Orioles	$450-$550
1966 Los Angeles Dodgers	$450-$550
1967 Boston Red Sox	$500-$700
1967 St. Louis Cardinals	$450-$550
1968 Detroit Tigers	$650-$750
1968 St. Louis Cardinals	$450-$550
1969 Baltimore Orioles	$250-$350
1969 New York Mets	$800-$1,000
1970 Baltimore Orioles	$300-$400
1970 Cincinnati Reds	$200-$300
1971 Pittsburgh Pirates	$450-$550
1971 Baltimore Orioles	$250-$350
1972 Oakland A's	$200-$300
1972 Cincinnati Reds	$200-$300
1973 Oakland A's	$200-$300
1973 New York Mets	$375-$475
1974 Oakland A's	$200-$300
1974 Los Angeles Dodgers	$200-$300
1975 Cincinnati Reds	$350-$450
1975 Boston Red Sox	$300-$400
1976 Cincinnati Reds	$325-$425
1976 New York Yankees	$275-$350
1977 Los Angeles Dodgers	$200-$300
1977 New York Yankees	$450-$550
1978 Los Angeles Dodgers	$200-$300
1978 New York Yankees	$450-$550
1979 Baltimore Orioles	$200-$300
1979 Pittsburgh Pirates	$250-$350
1980 Kansas City Royals	$200-$300
1980 Philadelphia Phillies	$275-$375
1981 Los Angeles Dodgers	$275-$375
1981 New York Yankees	$250-$325
1982 St. Louis Cardinals	$275-$375
1982 Milwaukee Brewers	$250-$325
1983 Baltimore Orioles	$425-$525
1983 Philadelphia Phillies	$250-$350
1984 Detroit Tigers	$350-$450
1984 San Diego Padres	$225-$325
1985 St. Louis Cardinals	$200-$250
1985 Kansas City Royals	$225-$325
1986 New York Mets	$450-$600
1986 Boston Red Sox	$250-$300
1987 Minnesota Twins	$275-$375
1987 St. Louis Cardinals	$200-$250
1988 Los Angeles Dodgers	$250-$325
1988 Oakland A's	$150-$200
1989 San Francisco Giants	$175-$225
1989 Oakland A's	$175-$225
1990 Oakland A's	$175-$225
1990 Cincinnati Reds	$225-$300
1991 Minnesota Twins	$1,600-$2,000
1991 Atlanta Braves	$675-$775
1992 Toronto Blue Jays	$450-$550
1992 Atlanta Braves	$450-$550
1993 Toronto Blue Jays	$550-$750
1993 Philadelphia Phillies	$850-$1,000
1995 Atlanta Braves	$1,000-$1,200
1995 Cleveland Indians	$1,000-$1,200
1996 New York Yankees	$2,500-$2,750
1996 Atlanta Braves	$550-$750
1997 Florida Marlins	$550-$750
1997 Cleveland Indians	$1,000-$1,200
1998 New York Yankees	$2,750-$3,250
1998 San Diego Padres	$450-$550

COOPERSTOWN BAT CO. COMMEMORATIVE BATS

Cooperstown Bat Co., Cooperstown, N.Y., has produced several limited-edition bats to commemorate several players, stadiums and teams.

Cooperstown Bat Co.'s 10 Stadium Series bats include: 1) Fenway Park, 1986; 2) Wrigley Field, 1986; 3) Ebbets Field, 1987; 4) Polo Grounds, 1987; 5) Yankee Stadium, 1987; 6) Forbes Field, 1988; 7) Shibe Park, 1988; 8) Briggs/Tiger Stadium, 1989; 9) Sportsman's Park, 1989; and 10) Comiskey Park, 1990.

Cooperstown Bat Co's. annual Famous Players Series began in 1988. The bats were limited to 1,000 and were autographed. The limited edition series came to a close at 10 bats, with Johnny Bench, in 1997. The series includes these players: Pee Wee Reese, 1988; Ted Williams, 1989; Yogi Berra, 1990; Ernie Banks, 1991; Carl Yastrzemski, 1992; Stan Musial, 1993; Duke Snider, 1994; Frank Robinson, 1995; Mike Schmidt, 1996; and Johnny Bench, 1997. In 1999, Cooperstown Bat Co. introduced Famous Player Series 2. Only one player was included in this series, that being George Brett. There were 1,000 bats produced, which Brett autographed.

A Famous Pitchers Series was later added. Nolan Ryan was the first pitcher included in this series, followed by Sandy Koufax. There were 1,000 bats produced for each player, with each bat autographed.

Cooperstown Bat Co. was commissioned by the National Baseball Hall of Fame to produce a limited edition of 500 sets of five bats and a display rack for the inaugural Class of 1936—Ty Cobb, Walter Johnson, Christy Mathewson, Babe Ruth and Honus Wagner.

Cooperstown Bat Co., also in cooperation with the National Baseball Hall of Fame, produced a line of Official HOF bats featuring the living legends of the game. Each bat was made of Northern White Ash and featured the player's name engraved on the barrel. The National Baseball Hall of Fame logo was also included, along with the player's induction year and career highlights. The first run included Ernie Banks, Yogi Berra, Reggie Jackson, Fergie Jenkins, Harmon Killebrew, Stan Musial, Phil Rizzuto, Brooks Robinson, Mike Schmidt and Robin Yount. Players included in later releases included Rollie Fingers, Bob Gibson, Gaylord Perry, Warren Spahn, Early Wynn, Richie Ashburn, Bobby Doerr, Ralph Kiner, Eddie Mathews, Enos Slaughter, Will Stargell, Bob Feller, Whitey Ford, Al Kaline, George Kell and Joe Morgan.

The company also makes bats for autographing. A Cooperstown Bat Co. 1989 Cooperstown Hall of Fame autograph model bat, signed by 18 greats (including Stan Musial, Tom Seaver, Bob Gibson, Steve Carlton, Luis Aparicio, Willie Stargell and Enos Slaughter), was offered in an auction for a minimum bid of $350.

Another Cooperstown Bat Co. Hall of Fame autograph model bat, signed by 24 Hall of Famers (including Stan Musial, Ted Williams, Mike Schmidt, Willie Mays, Hank Aaron, Pete Rose, Johnny Bench, Lefty Gomez, Jocko Conlan, Happy Chandler, Duke Snider, Willie McCovey, Ernie Banks and Lou Brock), was offered in an auction for a minimum bid of $900.

Cooperstown Bat Co.'s Vintage Club Series includes bats for the Brooklyn Dodgers, 1990; Boston Braves, 1991; and Milwaukee Braves, 1992. A Brooklyn Dodgers bat, signed by 34 Dodger greats (including Sandy Koufax, Andy Pafko, Duke Snider, Carl Abrams, Ralph Branca, Don Drysdale, Billy Herman, Mickey Owen and Chuck Connor) was offered in an auction for a minimum bid of $250.

Cooperstown Bat Co. also creates bats for team autograph collectors. The 1992 Major League Team Series had bats for seven teams—California Angels, Chicago White Sox, Cincinnati Reds, Detroit Tigers, Pittsburgh Pirates, San Francisco Giants and Toronto Blue Jays.

The 1991 Major League Team Series featured six teams—Chicago Cubs, Kansas City Royals, Los Angeles Dodgers, Oakland Athletics, Philadelphia Phillies and St. Louis Cardinals.

The 1990 Major League Team Series included four teams—Baltimore Orioles, Boston Red Sox, New York Mets and New York Yankees.

Cooperstown Bat Co. has also created three Doubleday Field Bats—in 1983, 1985 and 1989. The 1983 bat is red and brown. Twenty have a plain red band at the throat of the bat; the remaining 124 have a red ring with a brown center stripe. The 1985 version was also red and brown and featured an enlarged drawing of the stadium compared to the first bat. The company has not limited production on these bats, and estimates about 1,900 have been made. About 900 of these were made before 1988 and have the red and brown stripe. Those made after 1988 have a red and brown band reading "Stadium Series."

A limited edition of 1,000 bats were issued in 1989 in red and blue to commemorate the 150th anniversary of baseball in America. The text was changed to reflect the history of the stadium, beginning with the Phinney Lot in 1839 and ending with the 1939 All-Star Game for the dedication of the Hall of Fame. The company did not number the bats in this series, so there is not an edition number stamped into the knob of the bat. There are All-Star game bats available for 1994 (Pittsburgh), 1995 (Arlington), 1996 (Philadelphia), 1997 (Cleveland), 1998 (Denver), 1999 (Boston), 2000 (Atlanta), 2001 (Seattle) and 2003 (Chicago).

Bats have also been created to commemorate the Negro League teams; the 1993 and 1994 All-Star Games; the opening of Camden Yards in Baltimore and Jacobs Field in Cleveland; Cal Ripken's consecutive games played streak; Roberto Clemente; Rusty Staub; Ralph Kiner; Ted Williams Museum; Fenway Park, the 1998 Arizona Diamondbacks, the 1998 Tampa Bay Devil Rays and the Cincinnati Reds' Big Red Machine.

World Champs bats have also been produced by Cooperstown Bat Co. This series started in 1995 with an Atlanta Braves bat. Bats were then made for the Yankees championships in 1996, 1998 and 1999, as well as for the Florida Marlins in 1997. Each bat in the series was limited to 1,000 each year.

STORE-BOUGHT GLOVES

Some of the most popular and reasonable collectibles are baseball gloves. What makes a glove collectible? Is it the maker or the style of glove? Is it the player's name who appears embossed on it or is it the condition? The answer: all of these factors.

A store-bought glove is just that: an over-the-counter purchase. Those which bear a facsimile autograph of a player are called autograph models.

The most important factor in determining the value of a glove is the player's name that appears somewhere on the face of the glove. The more significant the name, the higher the price, given that all other variants are the same.

The second-most important consideration when determining glove value is its condition. Even a relatively common player may be worth hundreds of dollars if in near mint to mint condition. This is especially true with older gloves, because it is much harder to find a near mint to mint common player from the 1920s or '30s than it is to find a similar condition glove from the 1960s or '70s.

Two very important factors in determining value—supply and demand, or the relative scarcity of some gloves versus the seemingly endless supply of others.

Rarely, if ever, is a post period glove of any player worth the same amount as one manufactured while the player was still on the diamond. So, too, are earlier model gloves of certain players.

It is generally accepted that fielder's gloves with unlaced fingers are considered prewar (WWII) models or styles, while gloves with the fingers laced are considered postwar models or styles. Various companies produced laced and unlaced gloves prior to and after World War II, but the terms prewar and postwar are used to determine the relative era of a fielder's glove using the criteria of whether or not the glove fingers are laced.

Another important value factor has to do with which hand the glove fits on. This is the area that seems to cause the most confusion, even among advanced collectors. The factories, and hence the sporting good stores, used to designate a glove either right hand or left hand by determining which hand the glove actually fit, indicating right hand for a left-handed thrower. As a result, one might find the letters RH somewhere on the box label.

The reason for this is that most collectors are right handed and they want to put the glove on and feel comfortable, so they will buy a nice right-handed model of a left-handed player for nearly the same price, yet they refuse to pay anywhere near the same price for a left-handed glove of a right-handed player.

Often, gloves were sold along with individual boxes and with hang tags that were used to price and/or describe the features of the glove. Having them with the glove adds to the overall value of the glove. Prewar hang tags add $50 while a player photo can add $50-$200, depending on the player. Postwar tags add $25, and can add $25-$100, depending on the player.

Hang tags are fairly rare because the majority of people bought the gloves to use, not as a collectible.

Plain boxes, those without pictures on them, in good condition (intact, some corners may be split, light scuffing, small surface tears, slight soiling) can add 20-50 percent in value. Postwar plain boxes add 20 percent, 1930-'45 add 30 percent, 1920-'30 add 40 percent and pre-1920 boxes add 50 percent.

Picture boxes (those with a photo or illustration of the player either posed or in action) in good condition can add two to six times to the price of the glove. Prewar boxes of Hall of Famers add four to six times the price, postwar boxes Hall of Famers add two to four times the value, while postwar boxes of non-Hall of Famers adds no more than two times the value.

Fair/Poor — Gloves in this condition are generally not collectible and often are only good for parts. Irrepairable tears, holes, severe magic marker, dry rot, water damage, and any other major problem.

Good — A glove that has been used considerably. Most of the stamping will be gone or barely visible. Leather very chaffed, thinned in spots, no form left, may still be serviceable, but only collectible if an extremely rare model, usually used as a filler until a better similar type is available.

Very Good — Well used, but most stamping visible, no form but intact, cloth label gone or worn out, piping frayed and worn.

Excellent—Well used, but cared for. Stamping visible. Dark with age but nice patina. Cloth label intact, minor piping wear. Some form left.

Excellent/Mint — The most confusing grade. Much stronger than an excellent glove but not near mint. It is an excellent glove with certain strong characteristics of a higher grade glove, i.e. super strong, bright signature, perfect cloth label, no oil stains, perfect insides, etc.

Near Mint — A glove that has seen almost no use. Still stiff in form, all stamping strong, most original silver or black ink still within stamping. Perfect insides, perfect cloth patch, has caught but a few balls. Some otherwise mint gloves may not have been used but have significant enough blemishes such as staining, cracking from dryness, scratches from some handling, to drop it into this category.

Mint — New, never played with regardless of age. A mint glove may show some shelf wear due to years, for example minute piping wear, oxidation around brass grommets, stiff due to no use, slight fading of original color, all of that must be minute and from storage, not from use.

Prices are for USA-made gloves, full size.

PREWAR GLOVES (HALL OF FAME)

Player	Value	Player	Value	Player	Value
Grover Alexander	$250-$500	Mickey Cochrane	$250-$500	Bob Feller	$50-$150
Luke Appling	$50-$150	Eddie Collins	$250-$500	Rick Ferrell	$250-$500
Earl Averill	$75-$200	Jimmy Collins	$400-$850	Elmer Flick	$400-$850
Frank Baker	$500-$1,200	Earle Combs	$250-$500	Jimmie Foxx	$250-$500
Dave Bancroft	$400-$850	Stan Coveleski	$400-$850	Frankie Frisch	$125-$375
Chief Bender	$500-$1,200	Sam Crawford	$500-$1,200	Lou Gehrig	$1,000-$7,500
Jim Bottomley	$250-$500	Joe Cronin	$50-$150	Charlie Gehringer	$125-$375
Roger Bresnahan	$500-$1,200	Kiki Cuyler	$125-$375	Lefty Gomez	$125-$375
Mordecai Brown	$500-$1,200	Dizzy Dean	$500-$1,200	Goose Goslin	$75-$200
Max Carey	$250-$500	Bill Dickey	$50-$150	Hank Greenberg	$125-$375
Frank Chance	$500-$1,200	Joe DiMaggio	$250-$500	Burleigh Grimes	$400-$850
Jack Chesbro	$500-$1,200	Bobby Doerr	$50-$150		
Fred Clarke	$500-$1,200	Johnny Evers	$500-$1,200		
Ty Cobb	$1,500-$3,000	Red Faber	$400-$850		

Player	Value
Lefty Grove	$125-$375
Chick Hafey	$250-$500
Jesse Haines	$250-$500
Bucky Harris	$750-$200
Gabby Hartnett	$125-$375
Harry Heilmann	$250-$500
Billy Herman	$50-$150
Harry Hooper	$500-$1,200
Rogers Hornsby	$200-$400
Waite Hoyt	$400-$850
Carl Hubbell	$250-$500
Joe Jackson	$850-$1,500
Travis Jackson	$125-$375
Walter Johnson	$250-$500
George Kelly	$250-$500
Chuck Klein	$125-$375
Nap Lajoie	$850-$1,500
Tony Lazzeri	$250-$500
Freddie Lindstrom	$250-$500
Ernie Lombardi	$75-$200
Al Lopez	$50-$150
Ted Lyons	$75-$200
Heinie Manush	$75-$200
Rube Marquard	$500-$1,200
Rabbit Maranville	$250-$500
Christy Mathewson	$1,000-$2,000
Joe McGinnity	$500-$1,200
Ducky Medwick	$50-$150
Johnny Mize	$50-$150
Mel Ott	$75-$200
Herb Pennock	$250-$500
Eddie Plank	$500-$1,200
Pee Wee Reese	$50-$150
Sam Rice	$250-$500
Eppa Rixey	$250-$500
Edd Roush	$250-$500
Red Ruffing	$125-$375
Babe Ruth	$1,000-$6,000
Ray Schalk	$125-$375
Joe Sewell	$250-$500
Al Simmons	$125-$375
George Sisler	$125-$375
Tris Speaker	$750-$1,500
Bill Terry	$250-$500
Joe Tinker	$500-$1,200
Pie Traynor	$125-$375
Dazzy Vance	$125-$375
Arky Vaughan	$250-$500
Rube Waddell	$500-$1,200
Honus Wagner	$1,000-$2,500
Bobby Wallace	$500-$1,200
Ed Walsh	$500-$1,200
Lloyd Waner	$125-$375
Paul Waner	$250-$500
Zack Wheat	$500-$1,200
Ted Williams	$125-$375
Hack Wilson	$250-$500
Cy Young	$250-$500
Ross Youngs	$400-$850

Postwar gloves (Hall of Famers)

Player	Value
Hank Aaron	$50-$200
Luis Aparicio	$30-$85
Richie Ashburn	$30-$60
Ernie Banks	$50-$125
Johnny Bench	$30-$85
Yogi Berra	$50-$125
Lou Boudreau	$30-$85
Lou Brock	$65-$175
Roy Campanella	$50-$125
Steve Carlton	$35-$75
Rod Carew	$25-$75
Orlando Cepeda	$35-$75
Roberto Clemente	$30-$85
Steve Carlton	$50-$125
Joe DiMaggio	$150-$375
Larry Doby	$75-$200
Don Drysdale	$40-$95
Bob Feller	$40-$95
Rollie Fingers	$30-$75
Whitey Ford	$40-$95
Nelson Fox	$40-$85
Bob Gibson	$40-$95
Lefty Gomez	$40-$95
Catfish Hunter	$40-$95
Monte Irvin	$65-$175
Reggie Jackson	$30-$85
Fergie Jenkins	$40-$95
Al Kaline	$30-$50
George Kell	$30-$85
Harmon Killebrew	$40-$95
Ralph Kiner	$30-$85
Sandy Koufax	$85-$200
Bob Lemon	$30-$85
Mickey Mantle	$75-$400
Juan Marichal	$40-$95
Eddie Mathews	$50-$125
Willie Mays	$125-$350
Willie McCovey	$65-$175
Joe Morgan	$40-$95
Stan Musial	$50-$200
Hal Newhouser	$50-$125
Jim Palmer	$40-$95
Gaylord Perry	$30-$75
Pee Wee Reese	$30-$85
Phil Rizzuto	$25-$50
Robin Roberts	$30-$85
Brooks Robinson	$30-$85
Frank Robinson	$40-$95
Red Schoendienst	$30-$85
Tom Seaver	$40-$95
Enos Slaughter	$30-$85
Duke Snider	$50-$150
Warren Spahn	$50-$150
Willie Stargell	$40-$95
Hoyt Wilhelm	$85-$200
Billy Williams	$40-$95
Ted Williams	$75-$250
Early Wynn	$30-$85
Carl Yastrzemski	$30-$85

Pre-war gloves

Player	Value
Babe Adams	$100-$250
Jimmy Archer	$150-$375
Jimmy Austin	$150-$375
Jim Bagby	$75-$200
Dick Bartell	$50-$175
Moe Berg	$500-$1,200
Wally Berger	$50-$175
Zeke Bonura	$75-$200
Rube Bressler	$225-$500
Tommy Bridges	$100-$250
Mace Brown	$50-$175
Guy Bush	$75-$200
Joe Bush	$150-$375
Dolf Camilli	$100-$250
Tex Carleton	$75-$200
George Case	$150-$375
Ray Chapman	$400-$850
Hal Chase	$1,000-$2,000
Eddie Cicotte	$500-$1,200
Harlond Clift	$100-$250
Rip Collins	$35-$125
Mort Cooper	$75-$200
Walker Cooper	$75-$200
Harry Craft	$50-$175
Doc Cramer	$75-$200
Frank Crosetti	$75-$200
General Crowder	$150-$375
Harry Danning	$50-$175
Jake Daubert	$225-$500
Harry Davis	$225-$500
Paul (Daffy) Dean	$75-$200
Paul Derringer	$75-$200
Vince DiMaggio	$35-$125
Bill Doak	$75-$200
Larry Doyle	$225-$500
Joe Dugan	$225-$500
Leo Durocher	$50-$175
Jimmy Dykes	$150-$375
George Earnshaw	$100-$250
Bibb Falk	$150-$375
Hap Felsch	$500-$1,200
Wes Ferrell	$150-$375
Fred Fitzsimmons	$150-$375
Ira Flagstead	$150-$375
Jack Fournier	$150-$375
Larry French	$50-$125
Denny Galehouse	$100-$250
Chick Gandil	$500-$1,200
Wally Gerber	$150-$375
George Gibson	$50-$175
Ival Goodman	$35-$125
Hank Gowdy	$35-$125
Pete Gray	$225-$500
Heinie Groh	$225-$500
Mule Haas	$50-$175
Stan Hack	$35-$125
Bump Hadley	$100-$250
Sammy Hale	$150-$375
Mel Harder	$150-$375
Bubbles Hargrave	$100-$250
Rollie Hemsley	$35-$125
Tommy Henrich	$50-$175
Babe Herman	$100-$250
Pinky Higgins	$35-$125
Sam Jones	$150-$375
Joe Judge	$150-$375
Willie Kamm	$150-$375
Charlie Keller	$250-$500
Ken Keltner	$75-$200
Dickie Kerr	$225-$500
Mark Koenig	$225-$500

Player	Value
Joe Kuehl	$100-$250
Whitey Kurowski	$50-$175
Tommy Leach	$225-$500
Dutch Leonard	$225-$500
Duffy Lewis	$225-$500
Hans Lobert	$100-$250
Dolf Luque	$100-$250
Gus Mancuso	$50-$175
Firpo Marberry	$225-$500
Pepper Martin	$150-$375
Carl Mays	$225-$500
Snuffy J. McInnis	$225-$500
Chief Meyers	$400-$850
Bing Miller	$150-$375
Terry Moore	$35-$125
Wally Moses	$50-$175
Johnny Mostil	$50-$175
Bob Muesel	$225-$500
Irish Muesel	$150-$375
Van Lingle Mungo	$100-$250
Buddy Myer	$75-$200
Swish Nickelson	$50-$175
Lefty O'Doul	$75-$200
Bob O'Farrell	$75-$200
Mickey Owen	$35-$125
Monte Pearson	$35-$125
Roger Peckinpaugh	$225-$500
Wally Pipp	$100-$250
Swede Risberg	$500-$1,200
Red Rolfe	$100-$250
Eddie Rommel	$75-$200
Charlie Root	$100-$250
Schoolboy Rowe	$50-$175
Muddy Ruel	$225-$500
Dutch Ruether	$225-$500
Wally Schang	$225-$500
Urban Schocker	$400-$850
Wildfire Schulte	$225-$500
Hal Schumacher	$150-$375
George Selkirk	$50-$175
Luke Sewell	$100-$250
Elmer Smith	$150-$375
Fred Snodgrass	$225-$500
Billy Southworth	$150-$375
Jake Stahl	$225-$500
Riggs Stephenson	$150-$375
Jake Tobin	$150-$375
Specs Toporcer	$150-$375
Hal Trosky	$75-$200
Dizzy Trout	$75-$200
George Uhle	$150-$375
Johnny VanderMeer	$75-$200
Jim (Hippo)Vaughn	$400-$850
Bobby Veach	$150-$375
Dixie Walker	$35-$125
Harry Walker	$50-$175
Bucky Walters	$50-$175
Bill Wambsganss	$400-$850
Lon Warneke	$50-$175
Buck Weaver	$500-$1,200
Earl Whitehill	$150-$375
Claude Williams	$500-$1,200
Cy Williams	$150-$375
Ken Williams	$75-$200
Vic Willis	$150-$375

Player	Value
Jimmie Wilson	$100-$250
Joe Wood	$400-$850
Rudy York	$35-$125
Heinie Zimmerman	$225-$500

Post-war gloves

Player	Value
Cal Abrams	$45-$95
Bobby Adams	$30-$60
Joe Adcock	$45-$95
Tommy Agee	$35-$75
Harry Agganis	$55-$100
Richie Allen	$35-$75
Gene Alley	$35-$75
Bob Allison	$25-$50
Felipe Alou	$25-$50
Matty Alou	$25-$50
Sandy Amoros	$45-$95
Sparky Anderson	$45-$95
Johnny Antonelli	$30-$60
Bobby Avila	$35-$75
Ed Bailey	$35-$75
Steve Barber	$35-$75
Rex Barney	$35-$75
Earl Battey	$30-$60
Hank Bauer	$45-$95
Frank Baumholtz	$35-$75
Glenn Beckert	$25-$50
Gus Bell	$25-$50
Floyd Bevins	$35-$75
Vern Bickford	$35-$75
Ewell Blackwell	$45-$95
Paul Blair	$30-$60
Don Blasingame	$30-$60
Curt Blefary	$30-$60
Frank Bolling	$30-$60
Milt Bolling	$35-$75
Ray Boone	$35-$75
Steve Boros	$30-$60
Jim Bouton	$40-$85
Clete Boyer	$35-$75
Ken Boyer	$45-$95
Bobby Bragan	$35-$75
Ralph Branca	$45-$95
Jackie Brandt	$30-$60
Al Brazle	$35-$75
Harry Brecheen	$35-$75
Ernie Broglio	$25-$50
Jim Brosnan	$30-$60
Bobby Brown	$35-$75
Bill Bruton	$35-$75
Bob Buhl	$30-$60
Jim Bunning	$35-$75
Lew Burdette	$35-$75
Smoky Burgess	$35-$75
Jim Busby	$30-$60
John Callison	$30-$60
Andy Carey	$30-$60
Chico Carrasquel	$30-$60
Hugh Casey	$35-$75
Norm Cash	$30-$60
Phil Cavaretta	$35-$75
Bob Cerv	$25-$50
Gino Cimoli	$35-$75
Rocky Colavito	$50-$95

Player	Value
Jerry Coleman	$35-$75
Joe Collins	$30-$60
Tony Conigliaro	$35-$75
Gene Conley	$55-$100
Chuck Connors	$100-$300
Walker Cooper	$75-$200
Clint Courtney	$30-$60
Wes Covington	$35-$75
Billy Cox	$35-$75
Roger Craig	$30-$60
Del Crandall	$35-$75
Ray Culp	$35-$75
Joe Cunningham	$30-$60
Al Dark	$30-$60
Jim Davenport	$25-$50
Tommy Davis	$30-$60
Willie Davis	$30-$60
Murry Dickson	$35-$75
Bob Dillinger	$55-$100
Dom DiMaggio	$55-$100
Dick Donovan	$30-$160
Walt Dropo	$30-$60
Ryne Duren	$25-$50
John Edwards	$25-$50
Bob Elliott	$350$75
Dick Ellsworth	$30-$60
Del Ennis	$30-$60
Mike Epstein	$30-$60
Carl Erskine	$55-$100
Hoot Evers	$30-$60
Elroy Face	$35-$75
Ferris Fain	$30-$60
Curt Flood	$40-$85
Dee Fondy	$25-$50
Ray Fosse	$35-$75
Tito Francona	$25-$50
Bill Freehan	$40-$85
Gene Freese	$35-$75
Jim Fregosi	$30-$60
Bob Friend	$35-$75
Carl Furillo	$40-$85
Joe Garagiola	$55-$100
Ned Garver	$30-$60
Jim Gentile	$30-$60
Jim Gilliam	$75-$200
Billy Goodman	$30-$60
Joe Gordon	$25-$50
Sid Gordon	$35-$75
Bob Grim	$45-$60
Dick Groat	$35-$75
Johnny Groth	$30-$60
Frankie Gustine	$25-$50
Harvey Haddix	$45-$95
Ron Hansen	$25-$50
Ken Harrelson	$35-$75
Jim Ray Hart	$35-$75
Jim Hegan	$30-$60
Solly Hemus	$30-$60
Tommy Henrich	$40-$85
Whitey Herzog	$75-$200
Don Hoak	$35-$75
Gil Hodges	$40-$85
Billy Hoeft	$35-$75
Tommy Holmes	$40-$85
Johnny Hopp	$35-$75

Player	Value	Player	Value	Player	Value
Ralph Houk	$35-$75	Jim Maloney	$35-$75	Wally Post	$300-$60
Elston Howard	$40-$85	Frank Malzone	$35-$75	Boog Powell	$30-$60
Frank Howard	$40-$85	Felix Mantilla	$35-$75	Vic Power	$30 -$60
Dixie Howell	$45-$95	Marty Marion	$35-$75	Jerry Priddy	$30-$60
Ken Hubbs	$35-$75	Roger Maris	$55-$100	Bob Purkey	$30-$60
Joe Jackson	$200-$500	Willard Marshall	$25-$50	Pete Reiser	$30-$60
Larry Jackson	$25-$50	Billy Martin	$35-$75	Rip Repulski	$30-$60
Larry Jansen	$35-$75	Dal Maxvill	$30-$60	Allie Reynolds	$75-$200
Joey Jay	$25-$50	Charlie Maxwell	$25-$50	Dusty Rhodes	$40-$85
Jackie Jenson	$30-$60	Bill Mazeroski	$45-$95	Del Rice	$30-$60
Sam Jethroe	$40-$85	Tim McCarver	$40-$85	Bobby Richardson	$40-$85
Dave Johnson	$35-$75	Mike F. McCormick	$35-$75	Jim Rivera	$35-$75
Sam Jones	$35-$75	Mike McCormick	$40-$85	Eddie Robinson	$40-$85
Willie Jones	$40-$85	Barney McCosky	$40-$85	Preacher Roe	$40-$85
Jim Kaat	$40-$85	Clyde McCullough	$25-$50	Ed Roebuck	$35-$75
Buddy Kerr	$25-$50	Mickey McDermott	$45-$95	John Romano	$35-$75
Don Kessinger	$30-$60	Gil McDougald	$30-$60	Buddy Rosar	$30-$75
Ron Kline	$35-$75	Sam McDowell	$35-$75	Pete Rose	$40-$85
Johnny Klippstein	$35-$75	Denny McLain	$45-$95	John Roseboro	$35-$75
Ted Kluszewski	$40-$85	Roy McMillan	$30-$60	Al Rosen	$40-$85
Bobby Knoop	$35-$75	George McQuinn	$55-$100	Schoolboy Rowe	$40-$85
Dave Koslo	$35-$75	Russ Meyer	$25-$50	Pete Runnels	$25-$50
Tony Kubek	$45-$95	Felix Millan	$35-$75	Bob Rush	$30-$60
Johnny Kucks	$25-$50	Eddie Miller	$30-$60	John Rutherford	$25-$50
Harvey Kuenn	$30-$60	Stu Miller	$40-$85	Johnny Sain	$40-$85
Whitey Kurowski	$35-$75	Bob Milliken	$45-$95	Jack Sanford	$35-$75
Clem Labine	$45-$95	Minnie Minoso	$65-$125	Ron Santo	$30-$60
Jim Landis	$30-$60	Dale Mitchell	$45-$95	Hank Sauer	$25-$50
Max Lanier	$45-$95	Wilmer Mizell	$45-$95	Johnny Schmitz	$25-$50
Don Larsen	$40-$85	Wally Moon	$35-$75	Dick Schofield	$30-$60
Frank Lary	$30-$60	Terry Moore	$40-$85	Herb Score	$45-$95
Vern Law	$35-$75	Walt Moryn	$30-$60	George Scott	$25-$50
Brooks Lawrence	$30-$60	Don Mossi	$30-$60	Andy Seminick	$25-$50
Frank Leja	$25-$50	Don Mueller	$30-$60	Mike Shannon	$25-$50
Jim Lemon	$25-$50	Ray Narleski	$35-$75	Bobby Shantz	$25-$50
Buddy Lewis	$30-$60	Charlie Neal	$35-$75	Larry Sherry	$25-$50
Whitey Lockman	$35-$75	Don Newcombe	$65-$125	Norm Sherry	$30-$60
Billy Loes	$45-$95	Bobo Newsom	$45-$95	George Shuba	$45-$95
Johnny Logan	$35-$75	Bill Nicholson	$40-$85	Norm Siebern	$30-$60
Mickey Lolich	$35-$75	Phil Niekro	$45-$95	Roy Sievers	$25-$50
Sherm Lollar	$35-$75	Bob Nieman	$35-$75	Curt Simmons	$30-$60
Dale Long	$35-$75	Irv Noren	$30-$60	Dick Sisler	$30-$60
Eddie Lopat	$35-$75	Joe Nuxall	$35-$75	Bob Skinner	$30-$60
Stan Lopata	$30-$60	Tony Oliva	$35-$75	Moose Skowron	$30-$60
Hector Lopez	$35-$75	Claude Osteen	$35-$75	Roy Smalley	$30-$60
Peanuts Lowrey	$30-$60	Amos Otis	$30-$60	Al Smith	$30-$60
Jerry Lynch	$25-$50	Jim O'Toole	$30-$60	Karl Spooner	$45-$95
Sal Maglie	$35-$75	Andy Pafko	$30-$60	Eddie Stanky	$35-$75
		Joe Page	$45-$95	Mickey Stanley	$30-$60
		Milt Pappas	$35-$75	Rusty Staub	$25-$50
		Wes Parker	$30-$60	Vern Stephens	$30-$60
		Mel Parnell	$45-$95	Snuffy Stirnweiss	$30-$60
		Camilo Pascual	$35-$75	Dick Stuart	$40-$85
		Albie Pearson	$30-$60	Haywood Sullivan	$25-$50
		Joe Pepitone	$35-$75	Chuck Tanner	$35-$75
		Ron Perranoski	$25-$50	Birdie Tebbetts	$40-$85
		Tony Perez	$30-$60	Johnny Temple	$25-$50
		John Pesky	$30-$60	Ralph Terry	$30-$60
		Gary Peters	$35-$75	Frank Thomas	$25-$50
		Dave Philley	$30-$60	Hank Thompson	$25-$50
		Billy Pierce	$30-$60	Bobby Thomson	$30-$60
		Jimmy Piersall	$35-$75	Luis Tiant	$35-$75
		Vada Pinson	$30-$60	Earl Torgeson	$30-$60
		Johnny Podres	$30-$60	Frank Torre	$30-$60
		Howie Pollet	$40-$85	Joe Torre	$30-$60

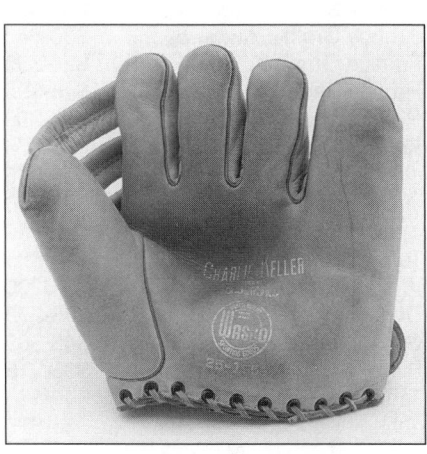

Player	Value
Tom Tresh	$35-$75
Gus Triandos	$35-$75
Virgil Trucks	$35-$75
Bob Turley	$40-$85
Bill Tuttle	$25-$50
Bob Uecker	$75-$200
Elmer Valo	$30-$60
Emil Verban	$35-$75
Mickey Vernon	$35-$75
Zoilo Versalles	$35-$75
Bill Virdon	$30-$60
Eddie Waitkus	$30-$60
Dick Wakefield	$30-$60
Rube Walker	$40-$85
Vic Wertz	$75-$200
Wes Westrum	$40-$85
Bill White	$35-$75
Dave Williams	$35-$75
Dick Williams	$35-$75
Maury Wills	$35-$75
Earl Wilson	$25-$50
Gene Wooding	$40-$85
Eddie Yost	$35-$75
Babe Young	$35-$75
Al Zarilla	$30-$60
Gus Zernial	$35-$75
Don Zimmer	$30-$60

Additional player model gloves

Richie Allen: Spalding model $65
Bobby Allison: 1960s Sonnett model $125
Luke Appling: Wilson model $85
Richie Ashburn: MacGregor model ..$45
Sal Bando: Spalding model $65
Hank Bauer: 1950s Hurricane model, signed $85
Gus Bell: 1950s MacGregor model, signed $75
Buddy Bell: Wilson model $45
Johnny Bench: 1970s Rawlings catcher's mitt, signed $150
Yogi Berra: 1950s Reach catcher's mitt, signed $50
Paul Blair: Montgomery Ward model .$65
Wade Boggs: Rawlings model $55
Bobby Bonilla: Rawlings model $35
Ken Boyer: Rawlings, three-finger... $55
George Brett: 1970s Wilson model, signed $175
Lou Brock: Franklin model $75
Roy Campanella: 1950s Wilson catcher's mitt........................... $135
Rod Carew: MacGregor model........ $65
Steve Carlton: 1970s Rawlings model, right-handed, signed.................... $85
Joe Carter: Wilson model............... $45
Norm Cash: Wilson first baseman's model.. $95
Cesar Cedeno: Rawlings model...... $45
Ron Cey: MacGregor model $45
Jack Clark: Spalding model............. $65
Roger Clemens: Wilson model $65
Roberto Clemente: 1950s Franklin model.. $150
Roberto Clemente: J.C. Higgins model.. $145
Tony Conigliaro: 1970s Hurricane model.. $110

Player	Value
Alvin Dark: 1950s Spalding model .. $60
Bill Dickey: 1940s MacGregor Goldsmith catcher's mitt $125
Joe DiMaggio: 1950s Spalding model, signed $895
Don Drysdale: 1960s Spalding model, signed $450
Dwight Evans: 1980s Wilson black model, signed $85
Hoot Evers: Hutch model $95
Bob Feller: J.C. Higgins model........ $50
Ron Fairly: Spalding six-finger model $85
Carlton Fisk: 1970s Wilson catchers mitt $85
Whitey Ford: Spalding model $70
George Foster: 1970s MacGregor model, signed $40
Nellie Fox: Wilson model fielder's glove $140
Steve Garvey: Rawlings first baseman's model $65
Bob Gibson: 1970s Rawlings model, signed $100
Kirk Gibson: Wilson model $65
Pedro Guerrero: Wilson model $35
Bucky Harris: 1920s Spalding model $150
Hurricane Hazle: 1950s Rawlings model $80
Mike Hegan: Spalding first baseman's model $65
Larry Hisle: Wilson model $45
Willie Horton: Wilson model $45
Gil Hodges: Denkert first baseman's model $75
Ken Hunt: Spalding model.............. $45
Catfish Hunter: 1970s Wilson model $40
Reggie Jackson: Rawlings model... $45
Tommy John: Wilson model, signed $65
Harmon Killebrew: 1960s Wilson model $65
Sandy Koufax: 1950s Denkert model $350
Harvey Kuenn: 1950s Wilson model $125
Ron LeFlore: Wilson model............ $45
Bob Lemon: 1950s Hurricane model $50
Johnny Logan: TruPlay model $35
Ernie Lombardi: Goldsmith catcher's model $125
Greg Luzinski: MacGregor model... $45
Fred Lynn: Wilson model $75
Billy Martin: 1950s Wilson model . $100
Don Mattingly: Franklin first baseman's model $95
John Mayberry: 1970s MacGregor first basemans mitt $35
Willie Mays: MacGregor model $75
Bill Mazeroski: 1950s MacGregor model.. $50
Willie McGee: MacGregor model $45
Johnny Mize: Wilson first baseman's model.. $95
Rick Monday: Spalding model $55
Joe Morgan: 1970s MacGregor model, signed $60
Don Mossi: Nokona model $45

Player	Value
Stan Musial: 1960s Hawthorne model, signed $140
Stan Musial: Rawlings model $85
Graig Nettles: Louisville Slugger model $40
Amos Otis: Rawlings model $55
Andy Pafko: J.C. Higgins model...... $60
Dave Parker: Rawlings model $55
Wes Parker: MacGregor model $30
Joe Pepitone: Trio-Hollander model.. $165
Gaylord Perry: 1960s Wilson model, signed $90
Rico Petrocelli: Spalding model...... $55
Jimmy Piersall: 1950s Wilson model $60
Lou Piniella: Spalding model $75
Vic Power: Franklin model.............. $50
Willie Randolph: MacGregor model..$45
Del Rice: 1960s black Denkert catcher's mitt, 1960s $100
Jim Rice: 1970s Wilson model $40
Cal Ripken Jr.: Rawlings model $65
Phil Rizzuto: Reach model............ $145
Brooks Robinson: Rawlings model $45
Frank Robinson: MacGregor model .$45
Red Ruffing: 1930s J.C. Higgins model.. $275
Babe Ruth: 1930s Spalding catcher's mitt $800
Ryne Sandberg: Rawlings model.... $65
Ron Santo: 1960s Wilson model, signed $75
Ray Schalk: 1920s Wilson model.. $195
Mike Schmidt: Franklin model......... $45
Tom Seaver: 1970s MacGregor model, signed $100
Luke Sewell: 1930s Wilson catcher's mitt... $125
Moose Skowron: 1950s Denkert model.. $45
Enos Slaughter: 1950s J.C. Higgins model, signed $125
Ozzie Smith: 1970s Rawlings model, signed $125
Roy Smalley Sr.: Rawlings model ... $50
Duke Snider: Rawlings model, unused $250
Snuffy Stirnweiss: Spalding split-finger model.. $350
Mel Stottlemyre: Spalding model.... $30
Bruce Sutter: Wilson model $55
Bill Terry: Ken-Wel fielder's glove.. $350
Manny Trillo: Wilson model............ $55
Johnny VanderMeer: Goldsmith fielder's glove.............................. $295
Bill Virdon: 1950s Denkert model ... $65
Frank White: Rawlings model $45
Ted Williams: Sears model $65
Ted Williams: Hutch model $200
Dave Winfield: Rawlings model $45
Carl Yastrzemski: 1970s Spalding, signed twice.............................. $125
Pep Young: 1940s Hutch model $75
Robin Yount: 1970s Rawlings model.. $150
Richie Zisk: Wilson model.............. $55

GAME-USED FOOTBALL JERSEYS

Troy Aikman: 1994 Dallas Cowboys throwback, NOB, game worn.. $4,000

Marcus Allen: mid-1980s Los Angeles Raiders white, NOB, game worn.. $1,150

Marcus Allen: Kansas City Chiefs red, game worn........ $1,495

Lance Allworth: San Diego Chargers blue, game worn $2,750

Ken Anderson: Cincinnati Bengals home, game worn $795

Sammy Baugh: 1951 maroon, game-worn, torn with crotch strap $18,000

Greg Bell: 1988 Los Angeles Rams Russell, game worn $300

Cornelius Bennett: 1993 Buffalo Bills, game worn $395

Jerome Bettis: 1993 Los Angeles Rams white, with pants, game worn $1,300

Jerome Bettis: 1994 Pro Bowl jersey, game worn, autographed.. $1,295

Steve Beuerlein: 1995 Jacksonville Jaguars teal, game worn $750

Fred Biletnikoff: early-1970s Oakland Raiders black home, NOB, game worn $1,850

George Blanda: 1974 Oakland Raiders home, NOB, game worn $2,500

Drew Bledsoe: 1994 New England Patriots home blue, game worn $2,000

Steve Bono: 1992 San Francisco 49ers red, autographed, game worn $295

Brian Bosworth: 1989 Seattle Seahawks white, NOB, team issued but not game used.............................. $195

Tony Brackens: 1996 Jacksonville Jaguars white, game worn $500

Terry Bradshaw: mid-1970s AFC Pro Bowl jersey, game worn $4,550

Terry Bradshaw: 1970s Pittsburgh Steelers home, game worn $4,250

Cliff Branch: late-1970s Oakland Raiders, white, game worn, autographed.. $595

Drew Brees: 2002 San Diego Chargers, game worn, autographed.. $2,500

John Brodie: 1970s San Francisco 49ers road, NOB, game worn $1,750

Jim Brown: Cleveland Browns home, game worn........ $13,950

Jerome Brown: Philadelphia Eagles, white, NOB, game worn $1,295

Tim Brown: 1994 Los Angeles Raiders home, game worn $1,100

Willie Brown: 1970s Oakland Raiders home, game worn, autographed.. $1,500

Mark Brunell: 1997 Jacksonville Jaguars teal, game worn, autographed.. $2,150

Dick Butkus: Chicago Bears home, game worn $3,950

Leroy Butler: 1993 Green Bay Packers white, game worn, autographed.. $495

Marion Butts: San Diego Chargers white mesh, #35 ..$345-$395

Earl Campbell: late-1970s Houston Oilers home, game worn $3,295

Mark Carrier: 1997 Carolina Panthers, NOB, game worn......$200

Anthony Carter: 1995 Detroit Lions white, NOB, game worn $850

Cris Carter: 1988 Philadelphia Eagles white mesh, game worn, autographed.. $1,295

Chris Chandler: 2001 Atlanta Falcons black, NOB, game worn $800

Dwight Clark: 1990s San Francisco 49ers red, game worn... $900

Kerry Collins: 1997 Carolina Panthers white, NOB, game worn... $550

Cris Collinsworth: 1980s Cincinnati Bengals black mesh, game worn... $575

Roger Craig: 1980s San Francisco 49ers home, game worn... $595

Joe Cribbs: 1980s San Francisco 49ers red, NOB, game worn... $325

Randy Cross: mid-1980s San Francisco 49ers white, NOB, game worn... $550

Germane Crowell: 1997 Detroit Lions white, NOB, game worn... $300

Larry Csonka: mid-1970s Miami Dolphins white, game worn, autographed $2,995

Curley Culp: 1979-80 Houston Oilers home, game worn . $400

Randall Cunningham: 1992 Philadelphia Eagles home, game worn, autographed.................................. $1,000

Gary Danielson: 1970s Detroit Lions white mesh, game worn... $450

Terrell Davis: 1998 Denver Broncos home, game worn $1,750

Willie Davis: 1992-93 Kansas City Chiefs white, game worn... $450

Eric Dickerson: Los Angeles Rams white, NOB, team issued but not game used.................................... $495

Eric Dickerson: 1985 Los Angeles Rams blue, game worn...$1,500

Eric Dickerson: early-1990s Atlanta Falcons black, game worn... $1,200

Curtis Dickey: mid-1980s Baltimore Colts white, game worn...$475

Lynn Dickey: 1980s Green Bay Packers white, game worn...$495

Trent Dilfer: 1998 Tampa Bay Buccaneers white, NOB, game worn... $550

Corey Dillon: 2002 Cincinnati Bengals black, NOB, game worn... $1,550

Mike Ditka: early-1970s Dallas Cowboys road, game worn...$4,000

Tony Dorsett: late-1970s Dallas Cowboys home, game worn... $3,000

Tony Dorsett: 1988 Denver Broncos home, game worn $2,400

Kenny Easley: 1986 Seattle Seahawks home, game worn ..$400

Henry Ellard: 1988 Los Angeles Rams home, game worn autographed $275

John Elway: 1990s Denver Broncos home, game worn.....$3,995

Boomer Esiason: late-1980s Cincinnati Bengals black, game worn... $650

Marshall Faulk: 1994 Indianapolis Colts home, game worn.. $2,995

Brett Favre: 1993 Green Bay Packers home green, game worn.. $4,000

Brett Favre: 1994 Green Bay Packer throwback, 75th anniversary patch, game worn..................................$4,750

Tom Fears: mid-1950s Los Angeles Rams gold, NNOB, game worn, autographed... $3,500

William Floyd: 1994 San Francisco 49ers throwback, game worn.. $650

Barry Foster: Pittsburgh Steelers black, 60-year patch, game worn.. $595

Dan Fouts: late-1970s San Diego Chargers home, game worn.. $2,500

Bill Fralic: Atlanta Falcons red, NOB, game worn............. $450

Irving Fryar: 1993 Miami Dolphins complete home uniform, game worn.. $750

Roman Gabriel: late-1960s Los Angeles Rams home, game worn.. $1,195

Jason Garrett: 1995 Dallas Cowboys white, NOB, game worn.. $175

Mark Gastineau: mid-1980s New York Jets green, game worn.. $850

Frank Gatski: 1957 Detriot Lions home, game worn $1,200

Mel Gray: 1970s St. Louis Cardinals road, NOB, game worn.. $350

Kevin Greene: late-1980s Los Angeles Rams white, NOB, game worn.. $450

Lou Groza: 1950s Cleveland Browns home, game worn.... $4,995

Paul Gruber: 1998 Tampa Bay Buccaneers white, NOB, game worn.. $250

Ray Guy: 1980s Oakland Raiders home, game worn $795

Jack Ham: early-1970s Pro Bowl jersey, game worn $1,395

Dan Hampton: 1990 NFC Pro Bowl jersey, blue, game worn.. $795

Jim Hart: 1970s St. Louis Cardinals home, game worn...... $1,200

Jim Hart: 1970s St. Louis Cardinals road, NOB, game worn.. $1,200

Bob Hayes: mid-1970s Dallas Cowboys blue, game worn ...$1,395

Ted Hendricks: late-1970s Oakland Raiders white, game worn, autographed.. $1,200

Jeff Hostetler: 1994 Los Angeles Raiders black, game worn, autographed.. $795

Desmond Howard: 1992 Washington Redskins home white, game worn.. $400

Desmond Howard: 1995 Jacksonville Jaguars white, game worn.. $1,000

Michael Husted: 1998 Tampa Bay Buccaneers red, NOB, game worn.. $125

Leroy Irvin: mid-1980s Los Angeles Rams blue, NOB, game worn, autographed.. $350

Michael Irvin: 1994 Pro Bowl jersey, game worn, autographed.. $1,495

Michael Irvin: 1994 Dallas Cowboys throwback, NOB, game worn.. $1,750

Qadry Ismail: 1993 Minnesota Vikings purple, game worn, autographed.. $395

Raghib "Rocket" Ismail: 1994 Los Angeles Raiders black, game worn, autographed.. $695

Bo Jackson: 1990 Los Angeles Raiders black, game worn.. $2,950

Dexter Jackson: Tampa Bay Buccaneers white, NOB, game worn.. $300

Harold Jackson: 1970s Los Angeles Rams road, NOB, game worn.. $450

Ron Jaworski: 1987-88 Miami Dolphins white, NOB, game worn.. $375

Jim Jensen: 1980s Miami Dolphins aqua mesh, game worn.. $225

Billy "White Shoes" Johnson: early-1980s Houston Oilers blue mesh, game worn.. $795

Swede Johnson: 1934 St. Louis Gunners, game worn......$5,500

Daryl Johnston: 1994 Dallas Cowboys throwback jersey, game worn.. $595

Brent Jones: 1992 San Francisco 49ers red jersey, worn in NFC Championship game $895

Deacon Jones: late-1960s Los Angeles Rams home, game worn.. $1,200

Freddie Jones: 1997 San Diego Chargers blue, game worn.. $300

Sonny Jurgensen: 1970s Washington Redskins home, game worn.. $3,700

Jim Kelly: 1994 Buffalo Bills blue, game worn, autographed.. $1,495

Jim Kelly: 1990 Buffalo Bills road, NOB, game worn, autographed.. $1,495

Terry Kirby: 1993 Miami Dolphins white, game worn, autographed.. $395

Bernie Kosar: 1993 Cleveland Browns road, game worn . $900

Paul Krause: 1970s Minnesota Vikings white, game worn $950

David Krieg: 1991 Seattle Seahawks blue, game worn, autographed.. $700

Willie Lanier: 1970s Kansas City Chiefs home, NOB, game worn.. $1,800

Steve Largent: 1987 Seattle Seahawks home, game worn.. $3,195

Steve Largent: 1989 Seattle Seahawks white, game worn.. $3,195

D.D. Lewis: 1970s Dallas Cowboys home, game worn $750

Bob Lilly: early-1970s Dallas Cowboys blue, game worn....$2,400

James Lofton: early-1980s Green Bay Packers home, game worn.. $900

Howie Long: 1991 Los Angeles Raiders black, game worn.. $1,500

Ronnie Lott: 1992 Los Angeles Raiders home, NOB, game worn.. $1,495

Ronnie Lott: 1993 New York Jets road, NOB, game worn, autographed $1,200

Dan Marino: mid-1980s Miami Dolphins road, game worn.. $5,000

Dan Marino: 1985 Pro Bowl white, game worn $4,500

Dan Marino: 1993 Miami Dolphins aqua, NOB, game worn, autographed.. $4,995

Harvey Martin: 1980s Pro Bowl jersey, NOB, game worn......$950

Kelvin Martin: circa 1991-1992 Dallas Cowboys white, game worn.. $175

Tony Mayberry: 1998 Tampa Bay Buccaneers red, NOB, game worn.. $125

Tony Mayberry: 1998 Tampa Bay Buccaneers white, NOB, game worn.. $125

Chester McGlockton: 1993 Los Angeles Raiders, NOB, game worn.. $650

Guy McIntyre: 1996 Philadelphia Eagles green, game worn.. $100

Dave Meggett: 1980s New York Giants blue, game worn, autographed $495

Eric Metcalf: 1994 Cleveland Browns white, game worn, autographed $395

Anthony Miller: 1993 Pro Bowl jersey, with pants, game worn.. $600

Chris Miller: 1994 Los Angeles Rams blue, game worn... $250

Jamir Miller: 2001 Cleveland Browns white, NOB, game worn.. $650

Art Monk: 1993 Washington Redskins road, NOB, game worn $1,200

Joe Montana: 1989 San Francisco 49ers home, game worn, autographed.. $10,000

Joe Montana: early-1990s San Francisco 49ers scarlet, NOB, game worn, autographed.......................... $10,000

Joe Montana: 1993 Kansas City Chiefs road, game worn ...$3,995

Joe Morris: late-1980s New York Giants white, game worn ..$500

Mike Munchak: mid-1980s Houston Oilers home, game worn $695

Chuck Muncie: late-1970s New Orleans Saints white, game worn $395

Joe Namath: 1972 New York Jets home, game worn, autographed.. $12,500

Joe Namath: New York Jets practice jersey, autographed .. $2,500

Ozzie Newsome: mid-1980s Cleveland Browns home, game worn $1,295

Ray Nitschke: 1960s Green Bay Packers home, game worn $4,000

Jay Novacek: 1986 St. Louis Cardinals maroon, game worn $350

Jay Novacek: 1994 Dallas Cowboys throwback, NOB, game worn $1,000

Christian Okoye: 1992 Kansas City Chiefs home, game worn, autographed.. $495

Merlin Olsen: 1975 Los Angeles Rams home, game worn, autographed.. $1,750

Leslie O'Neal: early-1990s San Diego Chargers blue, game worn $495

Jim Otto: 1970s Oakland Raiders home, game worn, autographed... $1,450

Walter Payton: 1977 Chicago Bears home, game worn ... $15,000

Walter Payton: 1985 Chicago Bears home, game worn, autographed.. $12,500

Rodney Peete: 1990s Detroit Lions blue mesh, game worn, autographed $350

Brian Piccolo: late-1960s Chicago Bears home, game worn $17,950

Jim Plunkett: mid-1980s Oakland Raiders black, game worn $995

Ahmad Rashad: late-1970s Minnesota Vikings white, game worn $1,100

Tom Rathman: late-1980s San Francisco 49ers red, game worn, autographed............................. $395

Andre Reed: 1990s Buffalo Bills road, NOB, game worn........$575

Andre Reed: 1993 Buffalo Bills home, game worn............ $575

Jerry Rice: 1994 San Francisco 49ers red, game worn...... $5,995

Jerry Rice: 1994 San Francisco 49ers white, game worn... $5,995

Jerry Rice: 1994 Pro Bowl jersey, blue, NOB, game worn....$6,500

John Riggins: late-1970s Washington Redskins home, game worn $3,200

Dwayne Rudd: 2002 Cleveland Browns brown, NOB, game worn.. $235

Dwayne Rudd: 2002 Cleveland Browns white, NOB, game worn.. $235

Mark Rypien: 1991 Washington Redskins home, game worn, autographed.. $695

Barry Sanders: 1990s Detroit Lions blue, game worn ... $3,495

Deion Sanders: 1992 Atlanta Falcons home, game worn, autographed.. $1,500

Deion Sanders: 1994 San Francisco 49ers throwback home, game worn $1,900

Gale Sayers: Chicago Bears home, game worn $6,950

Junior Seau: 1994 San Diego Chargers home, game worn $2,000

Sterling Sharpe: 1993 Green Bay Packers white, game worn, autographed.. $895

Sterling Sharpe: 1994 Green Bay Packers green, NOB, game worn $1,500

Phil Simms: 1989 New York Giants home blue, game worn $3,000

O.J. Simpson: 1979 San Francisco 49ers red, game worn $8,995

Jackie Slater: early-1990s Los Angeles Rams home, game worn $595

Bruce Smith: 1993 Buffalo Bills home, NOB, game worn $950

Emmitt Smith: 1994 Dallas Cowboys throwback, NOB, game worn $6,000

Emmitt Smith: 1994 Dallas Cowboys home white, game worn $6,000

Jimmy Smith: 2001 Jacksonville Jaguars teal, game worn $1,000

John Stallworth: 1987 Pittsburgh Steelers home, NOB, game worn $1,000

Bart Starr: Green Bay Packers home, game worn, autographed $5,500

Roger Staubach: 1969 Dallas Cowboys road, game worn $6,950

Lynn Swann: mid-1970s Pittsburgh Steelers home, game worn $2,350

Lynn Swann: mid-1970s AFC Pro Bowl, game worn $1,800

Pat Swilling: 1994 Detroit Lions blue mesh, throwback, game worn $650

Fran Tarkenton: 1969-70 New York Giants road, game worn $5,000

Fran Tarkenton: Minnesota Vikings home, game worn.......$3,795

Aaron Taylor: 1998 San Diego Chargers white, game worn $350

Charley Taylor: 1977 Washington Redskins red, game worn $1,700

John Taylor: 1994 San Francisco 49ers throwback, game worn $850

John Taylor: 1994 San Francisco 49ers red or white, game worn $595

Lawrence Taylor: 1992 New York Giants white, game worn, autographed $3,995

Vinny Testaverde: 1990s Tampa Bay Buccaneers home, game worn $800

Derrick Thomas: 1989 Kansas City Chiefs white, game worn $1,295

Thurman Thomas: 1994 Buffalo Bills blue, game worn.... $750

Tony Tolbert: 1999 Dallas Cowboys white, game worn.......$1,295

Wendell Tyler: 1970s Los Angeles Rams home, NOB, game worn $450

Gene Upshaw: 1970s Pro Bowl, NOB, game worn $695

Norm Van Brocklin: mid-1950s Los Angeles Rams gold, NNOB, game used.. $3,495

Herschel Walker: mid-1980s New Jersey Generals, game worn $1,895

Herschel Walker: 1989 Minnesota Vikings white, game worn $775

Herschel Walker: late-1980s Dallas Cowboys home, game worn $1,000

Peter Warrick: 2002 Cincinnati Bengals white, NOB, game worn $1,050

Bob Waterfield: 1950s Los Angeles Rams home, game worn $7,500

Ricky Watters: 1994 San Francisco 49ers red or white, game worn, autographed................................. $595

Mike Webster: 1992 Kansas City Chiefs road, game worn....$350

Danny White: mid-1980s Dallas Cowboys white, game worn $795

Jamel White: 2002 Cleveland Browns brown, NOB, game worn $300

Jamel White: 2002 Cleveland Brown white, NOB, game worn.. $300

Reggie White: 1990s Green Bay Packers white, game worn.. $1,750

Gabe Wilkins: 1995 Green Bay Packers green, NOB, game worn... $300

Kevin Williams: 1995 Dallas Cowboys white, NOB, game worn... $175

Rod Woodson: early-1990s Pittsburgh Steelers black, game worn... $750

Steve Young: 1994 San Francisco 49ers red and white, game worn.. $2,495

Jack Youngblood: early-1980s Los Angeles Rams, game worn, autographed.. $2,350

GAME-USED BASKETBALL JERSEYS

Kareem Abdul-Jabbar: early-1980s Los Angeles Lakers home, game worn.. $3,450

Kareem Abdul-Jabbar: 1988 Los Angeles Lakers road, NOB, game worn... $2,500

Danny Ainge: 1989-90 Sacramento Kings home, game worn, autographed.. $650

Ray Allen: 2000-2001 Milwaukee Bucks game worn, autographed.. $1,100

Charles Barkley: 1992-93 Phoenix Suns playoffs home, game worn... $2,795

Charles Barkley: 1993-94 Phoenix Suns purple, NOB, game worn... $2,295-$2,750

Elgin Baylor: 1970 Los Angeles Lakers home knit, NOB, game worn.. $13,500

Mike Bibby: 2000-2001 Vancouver Grizzlies game worn, autographed.. $1,250

Larry Bird: 1987-88 Boston Celtics road green, game worn... $6,500-$8,900

Larry Bird: 1991-92 Boston Celtics road, NOB, game worn.. $4,995-$7,500

Muggsy Bogues: 1993-94 Charlotte Hornets road, game worn... $450

Manute Bol: 1992-93 Philadelphia 76ers road, game worn... $300

Ron Boone: 1975 ABA West All-Star, NOB, game worn $4,150

Shawn Bradley: 1993-94 Philadelphia 76ers home, game worn... $1,000

Elton Brand: 1999-2000 Chicago Bulls game worn, autographed.. $1,750

Elton Brand: 2000-2001 Chicago Bulls game worn, autographed.. $1,250

Kobe Bryant: 1997-98 Los Angeles Lakers road, game worn, autographed.. $5,500

Vince Carter: 1998-99 Toronto Raptors game worn, autographed.. $3,250

Vince Carter: 1999-2000 Toronto Raptors game worn, autographed.. $2,750

Vince Carter: 2000-2001 Toronto Raptors game worn, autographed.. $2,750

Wilt Chamberlain: 1963-64 Philadelphia 76ers home, game worn... $29,500

Maurice Cheeks: 1988-89 Philadelphia 76ers road, with pants, game worn.. $500

Chamique Holdsclaw: 2000 Washington Mystics game worn, autographed.. $675

Cynthia Coope: 1999-2001 Houston Comets game worn, signed... $800

Louis Dampier: 1970s Kentucky Colonels ABA, NOB, game worn... $2,500

Vlade Divac: 1992-93 Los Angeles Lakers home, NOB, game worn... $700

Clyde Drexler: 1993-94 Portland Trailblazers black, game worn... $1,250

Joe Dumars: 1990-91 Detroit Pistons home, game worn....... $525

Tim Duncan: 1997-98 San Antonio Spurs game worn, autographed.. $3,750

Tim Duncan: 1998-99 San Antonio Spurs game worn, autographed.. $3,250

Tim Duncan: 1999-2000 San Antonio Spurs game worn, autographed.. $3,000

Tim Duncan: 2000-2001 San Antonio Spurs game worn, autographed.. $2,900
Lakers home, NOB, game worn.......................... $295

Sean Elliott: 1991-92 San Antonio Spurs home, game worn... $700

Alex English: 1989-90 Denver Nuggets home, game worn...$750

Julius Erving: 1978-79 Philadelphia 76ers blue road, NOB, game worn... $3,100

Patrick Ewing: 1985-86 New York Knicks road, game worn... $2,495

Patrick Ewing: 1985-86 New York Knicks home, game worn... $1,850

Patrick Ewing: 1987-88 New York Knicks home, game worn... $1,500

Patrick Ewing: 1992-93 New York Knicks home, NOB, autographed, game worn.. $1,000

Patrick Ewing: 200-2001 Seattle Sonics autographed, game worn... $875

Walt Frazier: 1970s New York Knicks road, with shorts, NOB, game worn... $3,500

Walt Frazier: 1969 New York Knicks orange shooting shirt, NOB, game worn.. $5,000

Kendall Gill: 1990-91 Charlotte Hornets road, game worn $950

Artis Gilmore: mid-1980s Chicago Bulls home, game worn... $750

Mike Gminski: 1989-90 Philadelphia 76ers road, with pants, game worn... $300

Horace Grant: 1994-95 Orlando Magic black road, game worn... $1,200

A.C. Green: 1990-91 Los Angeles Lakers road, game worn... $475

A.C. Green: 1993-94 Phoenix Suns road, game worn $500

Hal Greer: 1964 All-Star East, game worn $1,750

Tom Gugliotta: 1994-95 Washington Bullets road, game worn... $450

Cliff Hagan: 1961 All-Star West, game worn................. $2,950

Anfernee Hardaway: 1993-94 Orlando Magic road, game worn... $2,500

Anfernee Hardaway: 1993-94 Orlando Magic home, game worn... $2,500

Anfernee Hardaway: 1994-95 Orlando Magic road, game worn... $1,195

Tim Hardaway: 1994-95 Golden State Warriors white mesh, game worn... $450

Ron Harper: 1993-94 Los Angeles Clippers road, NOB, game worn... $395

Ron Harper: 1990-91 Los Angeles Clippers road, NOB, game worn.. $495

Hersey Hawkins: 1991-92 Philadelphia 76ers red, game worn, autographed.. $600

Tom Heinsohn: 1957 All-Star East with shorts, game worn.. $3,750-$5,550

Grant Hill: 1994-95 Detroit Pistons white home mesh, game worn... $2,700

Grant Hill: 1994-95 Detroit Pistons road blue, game worn... $2,700

Grant Hill: 2000-2001 Orlando Magic game worn autographed... $2,000

Chamique Holdsclaw: 1998-99 University of Tennessee game worn, autographed... $900

Chamique Holdsclaw: 2000 Washington Mystics game worn, autographed... $675

Jeff Hornacek: 1992-93 Philadelphia 76ers road, game worn... $375

Jeff Hornacek: 1992-93 Philadelphia 76ers home, NOB, game worn... $550

Juwan Howard: 1994-95 Washington Bullets road, game worn... $750

Bobby Hurley: 1993-94 Sacramento Kings road, game worn, autographed.. $550

Marc Iavaroni: 1987-88 Utah Jazz road, game worn $190

Allen Iverson: 1996-97 Philadelphia 76ers game worn, autographed.. $3,750

Allen Iverson: 1997-99 Philadelphia 76ers game worn, autographed.. $2,500

Allen Iverson: 2000-2001 Philadelphia 76ers game worn, autographed.. $4,850

Jimmy Jackson: 1994-95 Dallas Mavericks white mesh, game worn... $1,400

Mark Jackson: 1992-93 Los Angeles Clippers road, game worn... $300

Kevin Johnson: 1989-90 Phoenix Suns road, game worn, autographed.. $1,195

Kevin Johnson: 1993-94 Phoenix Suns purple, game worn... $700

Larry Johnson: 1991-92 Charlotte Hornets road teal jersey and shorts, game worn $1,495

Larry Johnson: 1992-93 Charlotte Hornets road, NOB, game worn... $1,250

Magic Johnson: 1990-91 Los Angeles Lakers road, NOB, game worn... $3,950

Magic Johnson: 1990 Los Angeles Lakers gold, game worn... $3,000

Sam Jones: 1964 All-Star East, NOB, game worn......... $4,500

Michael Jordan: 1987-88 Chicago Bulls home white, game worn... $17,750

Michael Jordan: 1992-93 Chicago Bulls white, game worn... $11,500

Michael Jordan: 1992 NBA All-Star game jersey, game worn... $22,100

Shawn Kemp: 1991-92 Seattle Supersonics road, NOB, game worn... $1,600

Shawn Kemp: 1993 All-Star game jersey, game worn... $1,100

Steve Kerr: 1992-93 Orlando Magic road, game worn...... $185

Jason Kidd: 1994-95 Dallas Mavericks white home mesh, game worn... $1,500

Toni Kukoc: 1997-98 Chicago Bulls home white, game worn... $1,295

Bill Laimbeer: 1991-92 Detroit Pistons home, game worn.....$450

Bob Lanier: 1970s Detroit Pistons home, game worn, autographed.. $4,750

Bob Lanier: 1970s Detroit Pistons road, game worn, autographed.. $3,000

Meadowlark Lemon: 1970s Harlem Globetrotters, with shorts, NOB, game worn... $4700

Lisa Lesley: 2001 Los Angeles Sparks game worn, autographed... $550

Reggie Lewis: 1992-93 Boston Celtics road, NOB, game worn... $1,200

Rebecca Lobo: 1999-2001 New York Liberty game worn, autographed... $725

Corey Maggette: 1999-2000 Orlando Magic game worn, autographed.. $1,100

Karl Malone: 1990-91 Utah Jazz home, game worn, autographed.. $3,750

Karl Malone: 1994-95 Utah Jazz purple, NOB, game worn... $2,750

Moses Malone: 1993-94 Philadelphia 76ers road, game worn... $750

Moses Malone: 1993 Philadelphia 76ers home, game worn... $1,250

Danny Manning: 1993-94 Los Angeles Clippers home, NOB... $750

Jamal Mashburn: 1994 Dallas Mavericks home white, game worn... $1,000

George McGinnis: 1977 All-Star game, NOB, game worn...$775

Tracy McGrady: 1997-98 Toronto Raptors game worn, autographed.. $3,350

Tracy McGrady: 1998-2000 Toronto Raptors game worn, autographed... $1,150-$1,500

Tracy McGrady: 2000-2001 Orlando Magic game worn, autographed.. $1,750

Kevin McHale: 1991-92 Boston Celtics road, game worn...$1,000

Reggie Miller: 1994-95 Indiana Pacers road, NOB, game worn... $1,295

Terry Mills: 1991-92 Detroit Pistons home, NOB, game worn... $350

Earl Monroe: 1976 New York Knicks home, NOB, game worn... $3,000

Alonzo Mourning: 1992-93 Charlotte Hornets home, NOB, game worn... $2,750

Alonzo Mourning: 1993-94 Charlotte Hornets road, with trunks, game worn, autographed............................. $3,200

Alonzo Mourning: 2000-2001 Miami Heat game worn, autographed.. $2,400

Chris Mullin: 1992 Olympic uniform with shorts, NOB, game worn, autographed... $3,500

Chris Mullin: 1992-93 Golden State Warriors road, game worn... $800

Dikembe Mutombo: 1992-93 Denver Nuggets blue, game worn... $1,450

Pete Myers: 1993-94 Chicago Bulls red, game worn $500

Norm Nixon: early-1980s Los Angeles Lakers home, game worn... $650

Charles Oakley: 1994-95 New York Knicks away, game worn, autographed $800

Hakeem Olajuwon: 1988-89 Houston Rockets home, game worn... $2,295

Hakeem Olajuwon: 1997-98 Houston Rockets home, game worn... $1,895

Shaquille O'Neal: 1992-93 Orlando Magic road, NOB, game worn... $5,500

Shaquille O'Neal: 1993-94 Orlando Magic home, game worn... $3,995

Shaquille O'Neal: 1998-99 Los Angeles Lakers road, game worn... $3,500

Billy Owens: 1994-95 Miami Heat home, game worn....... $495

Robert Parish: 1990-91 Boston Celtics home, game worn... $1,000

Anthony Peeler: 1992-93 Los Angeles Lakers home, game worn... $750

Drazen Petrovic: 1990-91 New Jersey Nets home, game worn... $650

Scottie Pippen: 1992-93 Chicago Bulls white, game worn... $2,250

Scottie Pippen: 1994 All-Star game jersey, blue, game worn... $4,500

Kevin Porter: 1980-81 Washington Bullets home, game worn... $325

Mark Price: 1992 Cleveland Cavaliers home, NOB, game worn... $650

Mark Price: 1994-95 Cleveland Cavaliers black road, game worn... $895

Kurt Rambis: 1993-94 Los Angeles Lakers home, game worn... $385

Big Country Reeves: 2000-2001 Vancouver Grizzlies game worn, autographed.. $1,000

Glen Rice: 1993-94 Miami Heat home, game worn.......... $950

Glen Rice: 1990-91 Miami Heat road, game worn $675

Pooh Richardson: 1993 Los Angeles Clippers white, game worn... $450

Mitch Richmond: 1992-93 Sacramento Kings home, autographed, game worn $425

J.R. Rider: 1993-94 Minnesota Timberwolves road, game worn, autographed.. $1,700

Fred Roberts: 1986-87 Boston Celtics home, knit, game worn... $350

David Robinson: 1993 NBA All-Star game, game worn $2,450

David Robinson: 1990-91 San Antonio Spurs road, game worn, autographed.. $2,295

Dennis Rodman: 1992-93 Detroit Pistons home, game worn... $995

Dennis Rodman: 1994-95 Chicago Bulls home, game worn... $1,750

Byron Scott: 1990-91 Los Angeles Lakers road, game worn, autographed.. $500

Rony Seikaly: 1990-91 Miami Heat road, game worn....... $295

Rik Smits: 1990-91 Indiana Pacers home, autographed, game worn... $600

Rory Sparrow: 1986-87 New York Knicks blue, NOB, game worn... $200

Latrell Sprewell: 1994-95 Golden State Warriors home mesh, game worn... $1,100

John Stockton: 1987-88 Utah Jazz home, game worn.......$1,795

John Stockton: 1997-98 Utah Jazz road, game worn ... $1,250

John Stockton: 1993-94 NBA All-Star jersey, game worn... $2,795

Sheryl Swoopes: 2000-2001 Houston Comets game worn, autographed $595

Isiah Thomas: 1984 All-Star East, NOB, game worn, autographed $1,750

Isiah Thomas: 1991-92 Detroit Pistons home, game worn $750

Sedale Threatt: 1990-91 Los Angeles Lakers home, game worn... $295

Trent Tucker: early-1980s New York Knicks road, game worn... $225

Loy Vaught: 1990-91 Los Angeles Clippers road, game worn, NOB... $250

Rasheed Wallace: 2000-2001 Portland Trailblazers game worn, autographed.. $695

Bill Walton: 1986-87 Boston Celtics home, NOB, game worn, autographed $2,250

Clarence Weatherspoon: 1992-93 Philadelphia 76ers home, NOB, game worn... $650

Spud Webb: 1993-94 Sacramento Kings blue, NOB, game worn... $450

Chris Webber: 1993 Golden State Warriors home, game worn... $2,500

Chris Webber: 1994-95 Washington Bullets home, game worn... $1,450

Doug West: Minnesota Timberwolves road, with trunks, game worn... $750

Jerry West: 1973 Los Angeles Lakers road, NOB, game worn... $4,000

Jerome Whitehead: late 1970s San Diego Clippers home, NOB, game worn... $300

Jamaal Wilkes: late 1970s Los Angeles Lakers road, NOB, game worn... $750

Dominique Wilkins: 1993-94 Los Angeles Clippers home, NOB, game worn... $1,000

Buck Williams: 1984-85 New Jersey Nets road, game worn... $450

Jason Williams: 1998-1999 Sacramento Kings game worn, autographed $750

Orlando Woolridge: 1993-94 Philadelphia 76ers road, game worn... $195

James Worthy: 1993-94 Los Angeles Lakers gold home, game worn... $895

GAME-USED HOCKEY JERSEYS

Syl Apps: early-1980s Los Angeles Kings gold mesh, NOB, game worn... $395

Brent Ashton: Winnipeg Jets blue mesh, NOB, game worn... $450

Tom Barrasso: 1990-91 Pittsburgh Penguins home, game worn... $950

Brian Bellows: 1990-91 Minnesota North Stars green knit, game worn... $600

Ric Bennett: 1991-92 New York Rangers blue mesh, game worn... $350

Rob Blake: 1990-91 Los Angeles Kings road, game worn, NOB... $895

Doug Bodger: 1990-91 Buffalo Sabres road, with 20th anniversary patch, NOB, game worn............................. $550

Ray Bourque: 1991-92 All-Star white knit, throwback, game worn, autographed.. $1,400

Aaron Broten: New Jersey Devils red mesh, game worn...$295

Mike Bullard: Pittsburgh Penguins black mesh, NOB, game worn... $225

Ted Bulley: late-1970s Chicago Blackhawks home, game worn, NOB... $450

Pavel Bure: 1994-95 Vancouver Canucks playoffs road jersey, game worn, autographed... $3,000

Pavel Bure: CCCP Red Russian Army lightweight jersey, game worn $1,750

Billy Carroll: 1984-85 New York Islanders white mesh, game worn $400

Gerry Cheevers: late-1970s Boston Bruins white mesh, game worn $2,500

Alain Chevrier: New Jersey Devils road knit NOB, game worn $350

Paul Coffey: 1993 All-Star game, game worn, autographed $1,995

Ed Courtenay: San Jose Sharks 1992-93 white knit, game worn $500

Russ Courtnall: Minnesota North Stars 1991-92, game worn $595

Russ Courtnall: 1993-94 Dallas Stars black knit, game worn $650

Murray Craven: Philadelphia Flyers, orange knit, game worn $275

Glen Currie: Washington Capitals white knit, NOB, game worn $275

Ken Daneyko: 1980s New Jersey Devils red knit, game worn $425

Kevin Dineen: 1992-93 Philadelphia Flyers road, NOB, game worn $550

Marcel Dionne: 1983-84 Los Angeles Kings home, NOB, game worn $2,000

Pat Flatley: 1984 New York Islanders blue mesh, game worn $650

Theo Fleury: 1990-91 Calgary Flames playoff jersey, game worn $850

Grant Fuhr: 1993-94 Buffalo Sabres blue, game worn... $2,000

Grant Fuhr: 1991-92 Toronto Maple Leafs home, game worn $2,695

Greg Gilbert: 1980s New York Islanders blue knit, game worn $400

Curt Giles: Minnesota North Stars white mesh, NOB, game worn $225

Doug Gilmour: 1990-91 Calgary Flames playoff jersey, game worn $750

Dirk Graham: 1991-92 Chicago Blackhawks road, Captain "C" patch, NOB, game worn $800

Tony Granato: 1988-89 New York Rangers home, NOB, game worn $1,450

Tony Granato: 1990 Los Angeles Kings playoff jersey, game worn $450

Adam Graves: 1991-92 New York Rangers blue, game worn $1,750

Rick Green: 1989 Montreal Canadiens playoff red, game worn $550

Wayne Gretzky: Los Angeles Kings mid-1980s home, game worn $7,900

Wayne Gretzky: Los Angeles Kings 1988-89 white, game worn, autographed.. $6,500

Dominik Hasek: 1992-93 Buffalo Sabres blue and white, game worn $2,300

Derian Hatcher: 1993-94 Dallas Stars black knit, game worn $650

Tim Higgins: New Jersey Devils red, white and green jersey, NOB, game worn $175

Gordie Howe: 1947-48 Detroit Red Wings, game worn.... $37,500

Gordie Howe: 1970 Detroit Red Wings, game worn, autographed.. $12,000

Gordie Howe: 1978-79 New England Whalers home, game worn $10,000

Kelly Hrudey: 1980s New York Islanders blue knit, game worn $475

Brett Hull: 1989-90 St. Louis Blues white knit, game worn.. $1,700

Al Iafrate: 1993-94 Washington Capitals red, knit, game worn $850

Jaromir Jagr: 1992-93 Pittsburgh Penguins white knit, game worn $2,750

Al Jensen: early-1980s Washington Capitals home jersey, NOB, game worn $175

Alexei Kasatonov: CCCP Russian red mesh, NOB, game worn $450

Steve Kasper: early-1980s Los Angeles Kings white, NOB, game worn $350

Derek King: 1990-91 New York Islanders home, NOB, game worn $650

Petr Klima: Detroit Red Wings white knit, 60-year patch, game worn $1,000

Vladimir Konstantinov: CCCP Russian lightweight orange, game worn $695

Uwe Krupp: Buffalo Sabres 1986-87 blue knit, game worn....$295

Jari Kurri: 1992-93 Los Angeles Kings road, game worn....$2,200

Guy Lafleur: 1975-76 Montreal Canadiens red, NOB, game worn $7,500

Pat LaFontaine: 1980s New York Islanders white or blue, game worn $2,000

Rod Langway: late-1980s Washington Capitals home, Captain "C" patch, NOB, game worn $500

Steve Larmer: 1980s Chicago Blackhawks white knit, game worn $950

Kevin LaVallee: St. Louis Blues white knit, NOB, game worn $250

Brian Leetch: 1993-94 New York Rangers home, game worn $2,250

Claude Lemieux: 1991-92 New Jersey Devils red, NOB, game worn $500

Mario Lemieux: 1990 Pittsburgh Penguins home knit, game worn $10,000

Mario Lemieux: 1990 All-Star game jersey, Wales white, game worn $10,000

Mario Lemieux: 1992 All-Star game jersey, game worn......$3,500

Dave Lewis: early-1980s Los Angeles Kings gold mesh, with Captain "C" patch, NOB, game worn $325

Trevor Linden: 1990s Vancouver Canucks home jersey, Captain "C" patch, game worn............................ $750

Brett Lindros: 1994-95 New York Islanders blue, game worn $1,500

Morris Lukowich: Winnipeg Jets 1984-85 blue mesh, game worn $350

Al MacInnis: 1990-91 Calgary Flames playoff jersey, game worn $895

Al MacInnis: 1992-93 Calgary Flames white knit, game worn $775

Frank Mahovlich: 1957 Toronto rookie jersey, game worn...$5,000

Dave Manson: 1994-95 Winnipeg Jets blue knit, game worn $850

Brad Maxwell: Winnipeg Jets blue knit, NOB, game worn.....$225

Mike McEwen: 1983-84 New York Islanders white mesh, game worn $325

Kirk McLean: 1992-93 Vancouver Canucks white, 100-year Stanley Cup patch, game worn.................................. $1,250

Basil McRae: 1992-93 Tampa Bay Lightning white knit, game worn... $450

Marty McSorley: 1990 Los Angeles Kings playoff jersey, game worn... $650

Wayne Merrick: 1983-84 New York Islanders blue mesh, game worn... $375

Mark Messier: 1991-92 New York Rangers home white, game worn... $3,500

Mark Messier: 1993-94 New York Rangers playoff jersey, game worn... $4,200

Mike Milbury: 1970s Boston Bruins white mesh, game worn... $525

Mike Modano: 1991-92 Minnesota North Stars white knit, game worn... $875

Mike Modano: 1992-93 All-Star game, black knit, game worn... $1,450

Andy Moog: 1993-94 Dallas Stars black, game worn $1,000

Andy Moog: mid-1980s Edmonton Oilers white mesh, game worn... $1,750

Ken Morrow: 1980s New York Islanders blue knit, game worn... $575

Kirk Muller: late-1980s New Jersey Devils home, game worn... $900

Larry Murphy: 1991-92 Pittsburgh Penguins home, NOB, game worn.. $1,195

Cam Neely: 1992-93 Boston Bruins black knit, Stanley Cup patch, game worn... $1,095

Joe Nieuwendyk: 1991-92 Calgary Flames home, Captain "C" patch, NOB, game worn................................... $625

Adam Oates: 1990s St. Louis Blues white, NOB, game worn... $1,200

Adam Oates: 1991-92 Boston Bruins black, 75-year NHL patch, game worn... $1,000

Joel Otto: 1990 Calgary Flames playoff, autographed, game used.. $595

Peter Peeters: 1978-79 Philadelphia Flyers white mesh, game used.. $550

Michel Petit: 1985-86 Vancouver Canucks gold knit, game worn... $350

Denis Potvin: 1980s New York Islanders blue, Captain "C" patch, game worn.. $3,000

Pat Price: late-1970s New York Islanders white mesh, game worn... $650

Rob Ramage: Calgary Flames away, red, game worn, autographed, with 1988 Olympic patch $375

Mark Recchi: 1992-93 Philadelphia Flyers white knit, game worn... $450

Joe Reekie: 1992-93 Tampa Bay Lightning home, with Stanley Cup patch, NOB, game worn........................... $750

Chico Resch: New Jersey Devils white mesh, game worn.....$525

Maurice "Rocket" Richard: mid-1950s Montreal Canadiens, game worn.. $9,000

Mike Richter: 1993-94 New York Rangers away, with All-Star patch, game worn.. $2,500

Larry Robinson: 1989 Montreal Canadiens playoff jersey, red, game worn.. $2,500

Larry Robinson: 1990-91 Los Angeles Kings home, game worn, autographed... $1,250

Luc Robitaille: 1990-91 Los Angeles Kings home, NOB, game worn, autographed.. $1,100

Jeremy Roenick: 1992-93 Chicago Blackhawks playoff jersey, game worn... $2,750

Jeremy Roenick: Team USA Canada Cup jersey, game worn... $1,800

Patrick Roy: 1991 All-Star game jersey, game worn $2,000

Joe Sakic: late-1980s Quebec Nordiques home, with Captain "C" patch, game worn.................................... $1,750

Joe Sakic: 1991-92 All-Star game jersey, game worn, autographed $1,650

Borje Salming: 1984 Toronto Maple Leafs blue, game worn... $900

Thomas Sandstrom: 1990 Los Angeles Kings playoff, game worn... $450

Gary Sargent: early-1980s Los Angeles Kings purple mesh, NOB, game worn.. $325

Teemu Selanne: 1992-93 Winnipeg Jets blue knit, game worn... $2,395

Brendan Shanahan: 1991-92 St. Louis Blues, white, 25th anniversary team patch, game worn $1,950

Steve Shutt: 1972-73 Montreal Canadiens red knit, NNOB, game worn.. $2,500

Charlie Simmer: mid-1980s Los Angeles Kings road purple, NOB, game worn.. $750

Darryl Sittler: mid-1970s Toronto Maple Leafs home, game worn... $1,200

Darryl Sittler: 1981-82 Philadelphia Flyers orange mesh, game worn... $950

Brian Skrudland: 1991-92 Montreal Canadiens red knit, game worn... $475

Doug Smith: early-1980s Los Angeles gold mesh, NOB, game worn... $295

Tommy Soderstrom: 1994-95 New York Islanders blue knit, game worn... $750

Peter Stastny: 1987-88 Quebec Nordiques road, Captain "C" patch, NOB, game worn................................... $2,000

Scott Stevens: 1992-93 New Jersey Devils home, with Stanley Cup and Captain "C" patches, game worn $1,200

Mats Sundin: 1992-93 Quebec Nordiques blue knit, game worn... $950

Gary Suter: 1980s Calgary Flames red knit, game worn .. $395

Gary Suter: 1990-91 Calgary Flames playoff jersey, game worn... $550

Brent Sutter: 1984-85 New York Islanders white mesh, game worn... $575

Bob Sweeney: Boston Bruins home white, NOB, game worn... $250

Dave Taylor: 1989-90 Los Angeles Kings home, with Captain "C" patch, NOB, game worn $1,000

Steve Thomas: 1980s Chicago Blackhawks red, game worn, autographed $650

Kevin Todd: 1993-94 Chicago Blackhawks throwbacks, NOB, game worn... $600

Darren Turcotte: 1989-90 New York Rangers road, game worn... $850

Mike Vernon: 1990-91 Calgary Flames playoff jersey, game worn... $695

Mike Vernon: late-1980s Calgary Flames red knit, game worn... $550

Darcy Wakaluk: 1993-94 Dallas Stars black knit, game worn... $750

Doug Weight: 1991-92 New York Rangers blue mesh, game worn... $750

Doug Wilson: 1985-86 Chicago Blackhawks home, NOB, game worn... $1,000

Steve Yzerman: 1991-92 All-Star game red knit, throwback style, game worn $1,895

Steve Yzerman: 1991-92 Detroit Red Wings home, game worn... $1,850

Rob Zamuner: 1991-92 New York Rangers blue mesh, game worn... $495

Saluting
The Red, White And Blue

The Colorful ABA Balls Are Most Treasured Game-Issued Items In Sports Memorabilia Hobby

By Dennis Tuttle

The great George Mikan had an ingenious vision, which was a fairly curious venture considering he was so near-sighted that objects were even further away than they seemingly appeared.

As the first commissioner of the newly formed American Basketball Association in 1967, Mikan, the Hall of Famer and pro basketball's first superstar, invented the forever famous red, white and blue basketball. It turned out to be a landmark perception for the league, basketball history and sports memorabilia.

"Being called the American Basketball Association, having the red, white, and blue ball wasn't bad," Mikan said. "But I also put that in because many of the arenas had very poor lighting and if you were sitting up high you couldn't see the brown ball that well. The red, white and blue ball was more viewable and it was really mesmerizing to watch it spin. The kids loved it and the ladies loved it and we couldn't keep enough in stock. We sold them by the thousands."

In fact, they sold 30 million during the ABA's life span, which lasted nine troubled seasons until the league folded in 1976. Today, official ABA basketballs are by far the most treasured game-issued ball of any sport in any era. Depending on condition, historical significance and/or autographs, the balls sell for anywhere from $800 to $9,500, with typical prices in the $1,200 to $2,200 range.

Where ABA game balls were once a scarce item, there have been about a dozen listed on eBay recently. Numerous others have popped up in large national auctions.

"People are just bringing them out of the woodwork because they're now worth something," said Roy "Pinky" Gardner, who was the equipment manager and trainer for seven years with the Kentucky Colonels.

A first-year official leather ball containing Mikan's facsimile signature still in the original plastic wrap and box recently sold at auction for $5,500. A ball in perfect condition with commissioner Dave DeBusschere's facsimile signature went for $3,300.

The original boxes that the balls were shipped in have a big value, depending on the box's condition. If the ball is still in the plastic, the price escalates by leaps.

Part of the recent fascination is due to the popular Nike commercials about the ABA. Another reason is that the balls are just way too cool.

"A lot of people out there don't realize how valuable they are," said ABA collector and historian Jonathan Singer, who believes there are far more balls in collections than the market realizes. Former players, team executives and normal fans like Tom Griffin of Southern California simply don't want to part with the keepsakes.

Like so many of us who grew up with the funkadelic ABA in the early 1970s, Griffin became enthralled by the basketball. He was a fan of the Indiana Pacers and forward Roger Brown, who developed a move in which he spun the ball in his hands just long enough to draw the stare of the defender before blowing past him to the basket.

Now, the 46-year-old Griffin has an amazing collection that includes team- and single-signed official ABA basketballs, and one each of the six balls that contain a facsimile commissioner's signature. Five of the six commissioners have signed their ball for Griffin. The only one missing is the late Jack Dolph.

"The NBA had the brown ball, but with the ABA ball it was always nice to see the rotation of the colors," he said. "I think every kid wanted one. We'd go out and shoot them in the driveway or at the gym and scuff them up. No one ever thought of saving them."

When the ABA folded with the Pacers, Denver Nuggets, San Antonio Spurs and New York (now New Jersey) Nets merging with the NBA, many of the official leather game balls were given to youth centers, prisons or simply handed out to fans. Most have become lost to time and the elements. Gardner said each team kept about 20 balls a year in stock, 12 for warmups off the shooting rack and another eight in storage.

But Rawlings, the manufacturer, had a huge supply. There were several versions of the ball sold through retail that often confuse dealers and collectors today.

There was a rubber indoor/outdoor ball that had the official ABA logo (about $20 at the time) but did not contain the commissioner's facsimile signature. The official game ball was leather, shiny, slippery and had the commissioner's name (around $45). Most clubs stamped their team name on balls used in games or practices. And there was a rubber souvenir or giveaway ball (about $8) that was of inferior quality and commonly labeled "Official Size and Weight," which the other balls did not contain.

"There's a big difference in availability and value of the game-used balls compared to the official leather game balls," said Arthur Hundhausen, a Denver lawyer, ABA collector and creator of the award-winning Web site site, www.remembertheaba.com.

"The real game-used balls usually have the team stamp," he said. "I've only seen a few of these because they have been taken home and used out on the driveway court. They're usually

This is an official ABA game ball with a Mike Storen facsimile signature. In many cases the white panels yellow, which drives down the value.

This gorgeous Dave Debusscherre signature ball is one of the most prized and plentiful of all ABA balls

pretty scruffy looking. But you could buy the official leather ball in retail stores. I'm not sure people appreciate the difference."

The interest and price escalation of the balls is such that die-hard ABA collectors like Singer cannot believe what he's seeing. As recently as 1994, Tuff Stuff valued an official ABA leather ball in excellent condition at $300.

"When I bought an ABA ball in the 1980s, I thought I'd be getting ripped off if I paid more than $200," Singer said. "Today, I couldn't touch that same ball for $2,000. That makes it tough on the collector who doesn't have unlimited finances."

Singer is among several ABA memorabilia experts who believe there are many red, white and blue basketballs that will surface over a short time.

"There are still a lot of the balls in a closet, still wrapped up in the original box," he adds. "When I got my first ball, 20 years ago, I thought it was a real find. But these are not as rare as you might think."

Nor as profitable. Amazingly, considering Mikan was a corporate expert and lawyer, the ball was never patented. Mikan and the league never reaped the millions in licensing fees rightfully due them. When the ABA and NBA merged, the NBA stalwarts killed the signature red, white and blue ball.

Then, at the 2001 All-Star Game FanFest in Washington, D.C., souvenir stands were stacked with red, white and blue basketballs with the NBA All-Star Game logo stamped on the white. The hypocrisy didn't go unnoticed. When told of this, Mikan said, "That irks me, too."

"You've got your purists who would never agree with me, and I can see Red Auerbach pitching a fit at the idea," Singer adds, "but why can't the NBA use the red, white and blue ball? The WNBA is using that orange-and-white ball. They're missing out on a big marketing adventure with the old ABA ball."

Official ABA Balls Priced As High As $2,200

The red, white and blue basketball of the old American Basketball Association has several variations that collectors should know about. Prices are subject to condition of the ball.

Rawlings' store model ball: A rubber-coated indoor/outdoor ball sold at sporting goods and department stores. The ball has the official ABA logo, but does not have the commissioner's stamp. Generally found in worse condition because it was made to be played with. Price: $100-$200.

Souvenir ball: Given away or sold at games, these are commonly confused with official game balls because they often had a commissioner's signature. But the ball is rubber without a bladder, of far inferior quality and usually stamped with "Official Size and Weight," which the official game ball does not. Price: $75-$150.

George Mikan signature official game ball: The gem of ABA basketballs. Many have yellowing in the white and this affects price. The paint on the early balls from the inaugural season of 1967 is really slippery. Price: $1,800-$2,200; in box and plastic, $3,800.

Jack Dolph signature official game ball: Another fairly difficult ball to find because the ball's popularity was just beginning to take off and production runs were much smaller. Price: $1,450-$2,000.

Bob Carlson signature official game ball: The rarest ball. Carlson was commish only one year, but collectors like the bigger-name commissioners. Price: $1,250-$1,750.

Mike Storen signature official game ball: The league's best commissioner who spearheaded most of the league's creativity in marketing and merchandise. Father of NBC sportscaster Hannah Storm. Price: $1,500-$2,100.

Ted Munchak signature official game ball: A fairly difficult ball to find, but also the commissioner with the least appeal. The ball collectors can usually find for the best bargain. Price: $1,250-$1,950.

Dave DeBusschere signature official game ball: The most common ball because retail interest drove up the quantity made. But DeBusschere's popularity as a former New York Knick has made this piece a part of his collectibility and drives the value. Price: $1,600-$2,100; in box, $2,800.

– Jonathan Singer

The ABA souvenir balls, commonly confused with official game balls, were given away and sold at games.

STADIUM MEMORABILIA

Of the many types of collectibles in the hobby, stadium memorabilia, or "stadia" as it is called by ballpark enthusiasts, is among the most historic, if not the most nostalgic. Who can forget their first trip to the ballpark? And, although stadia may be the hardest type of memorabilia to acquire and display, steeply escalating prices in the past few years reflect a desire of many collectors to place an item from a favorite ballpark — a seat, a sign, or even a turnstile — in a prominent place among their baseball memorabilia. These items are eye-catching and at the same time functional. One can, after all, sit in a ballpark seat.

Such fixtures weren't always desirable. In the 1930's-1960's, when many of the first wave of steel and concrete parks were demolished, teams had a hard time even giving them away. There was scant interest, for example, when such hallowed ballparks as Ebbets Field and the Polo Grounds were razed, and virtually none when Baker Bowl, League Park and Braves Field went under (leading, of course, to the astronomical prices of items from those long-forgotten fields).

Those fixtures (especially the seats) that did survive the scrap heap were relocated to facilities such as racetracks, fairgrounds, or minor league ballparks where they would be reused until they simply fell apart. Indeed, one of the key aspects of collecting "stadia" is the detective work that must be done to unearth these finds. In the past few years hordes of seats have been located in such nondescript locations as churches, sleep away camps, and even prisons.

Of course, with the 1970's began, haltingly, the era of modern stadia collecting. The Yankees led the way in 1974 during the remodeling of their legendary cathedral. A huge sale was held, and besides direct sales to the public right out of the stadium parking lot, seats (thousands of them) were sold, for only a few bucks, through a Winston cigarette promotion. This was followed by Comiskey Park in 1991, Arlington Stadium, Memorial Stadium in Baltimore, County Stadium in Milwaukee, Three Rivers and Riverfront (Cinergy), and the Vet in Philadelphia. With each stadium sale more and more fixtures have been made available to collectors, down to hot dog bun-warmers, trash cans, and even urinals. And so, while a Yankee Stadium wooden seat could be had for $10 in 1974, today its value is more than $1,000, and even plastic seats from the circular, multi-purpose monstrocities of the 1970's are commanding a few hundred dollars apiece. Signs, both metal and plastic, banners, and other items can reach dizzying heights as well.

Pricing these items, even the seats, which are the most plentiful, is difficult. The value is dictated by a few factors: scarcity, condition, the status of the stadium as an historic venue, or the region in which the item is being sold. A Forbes Field seat, for example, might sell for more in the Western Pennsylvania region than in Atlanta. Of course, some ballparks such as Ebbets Field transcend geographic boundaries.

The prices estimated here are arrived at from studying auction results, Internet Web sites of dealers (they are now more plentiful as opposed to only one or two a few years ago) and the opinions of collectors, some of whom have amassed as many as 50 different seats from varying eras. We will assume these seats are unrestored and in at least EX condition; restoration can lower the value of a seat, although there are some collectors who don't mind (or even prefer) the more uniform look of a restored seat.

We will differentiate between figural and non-figural seats, where applicable, and break the seats into categories according to time periods, the early seats being made of cast iron and wood by such makers as American Seating and Heywood — Wakefield, the later ones in plastic or aluminum by different manufacturers. We will not, however, differentiate between floor mounts and riser mounts (some parks featured both styles, some only one) and between the sometimes double-digit amount of styles employed over the life span of the more venerable parks, such as Old Comiskey. And, should one park suddenly make seats available due to a closing or renovation, the price will fluctuate as wildly as before and after the demolition of Cleveland Stadium in the 1990's.

Seats

Original 16 Teams' Parks

These are the classic parks, some of which predate the turn of the last century. A few parks such as Shibe (later known as Connie Mack) and Sportsman's housed two clubs, and three are left: Yankee Stadium, Fenway and Wrigley, although they have undergone renovations of varying scope. Only Fenway still features wooden seats - thousands of them. Though the New York triumvirate far outdistances the others for collectors, there are classic seats sprinkled throughout this list. The most rare, by far, are Baker Bowl, League Park and Braves Field, whose demolitions met with indifference, but whose seats are among the most attractive, especially the figurals.

Listed According to Opening Date

Ballparks	First Used	Team(s)	Wood Figural	Wood Non-Figural	Plastic
Sportsman's Park	1875	Cardinals (NL) Browns (AL)	N/A	$500	N/A
Baker Bowl	1887	Phillies (NL)	$5,000	$3,500	N/A
Shibe Park	1909	Athletics (AL) Phillies (NL)	$700	$400	N/A
Forbes Field	1909	Pirates (NL)	$1,500	$1,000	N/A
Comiskey Park	1910	White Sox (AL)	$1,000	$500	$300
League Park	1910	Indians (AL)	$5,000	$3,500	N/A
Griffith Stadium	1911	Senators (AL)	N/A	$500	N/A
Polo Grounds	1911	Giants (NL)	$3,000	$1,500	N/A
Crosley Field	1912	Reds (NL)	$2,000	$600	N/A

Crosley Field figural

Ebbets Field

Polo Grounds figural

Shibe Park figural (ribbon-end)

Listed According to Opening Date

Ballparks	First Used	Team(s)	Wood Figural	Wood Non-Figural	Plastic
Tiger Stadium	1912	Tigers (AL)	$1,000	$500	N/A
Fenway Park	1912	Red Sox (AL)	N/A	$2,800	$1,200
Ebbets Field	1913	Dodgers (NL)	N/A	$2,800	N/A
Wrigley Field	1914	Cubs (NL)	N/A	$850	$500
Braves Field	1915	Braves (NL)	$5,000	$2,500	N/A
Yankee Stadium	1923	Yankees (AL)	N/A	$2,000	$1,000
Cleveland Stadium	1932	Indians (AL)	N/A	$500	$300

Expansion/Relocation Era Parks

This group is a hodgepodge of the old (County Stadium, which was recently torn down), the new (Fulton County, which was a quasi-doughnut) and the temporary (Seals Stadium). Most notable here is Dodger Stadium, the standard bearer for westward expansion, which replaced some wooden seats within the past few years. Five of these parks held formal sales for the public.

Alphabetically Listed

Ballparks	First Used	Team(s)	Wood Figural	Wood Non-Figural	Plastic
Anaheim Stadium	1966	Angels (AL)	N/A	N/A	$300
Arlington Stadium	1972	Rangers (AL)	N/A	N/A	$200
County Stadium	1953	Braves (NL) Brewers (AL-NL)	N/A	$400	$200
Dodger Stadium	1962	Dodgers (NL)	N/A	$750	N/A
Fulton County Stadium	1966	Braves (NL)	N/A	$400	$275
Memorial Stadium	1954	Orioles (AL)	N/A	$300	N/A

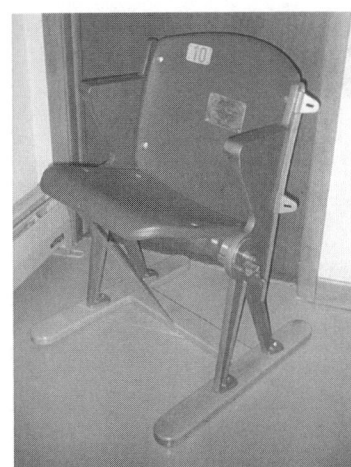

Arlington Stadium

Milwaukee County Stadium

Memorial Stadium

Ballparks	First Used	Team(s)	Wood Figural	Wood Non-Figural	Plastic
Metropolitan Stadium	1961	Twins (AL)	N/A	$400	$225
Municipal Stadium	1955	Athletics (AL)	N/A	$900	N/A
Seals Stadium	1958	Giants (NL)	N/A	$600	N/A

Bowls/Domes Era

This group is exclusively plastic. Three of the parks still exist but have been renovated. Three Rivers held an extensive auction before its demolition. The Kingdome also sold seats before it was fittingly imploded.

Ballparks	First Used	Team(s)	Wood Figural	Wood Non-Figural	Plastic
Busch Stadium	1966	Cardinals (NL)	N/A	N/A	$300
Kingdome	1977	Mariners (AL)	N/A	N/A	$250
Riverfront Stadium	1970	Reds (NL)	N/A	N/A	$250
Royals Stadium	1973	Royals (AL)	N/A	N/A	$300
Three Rivers Stadium	1970	Pirates (NL)	N/A	N/A	$400
Veterans Stadium	1971	Phillies (NL)	N/A	N/A	$400

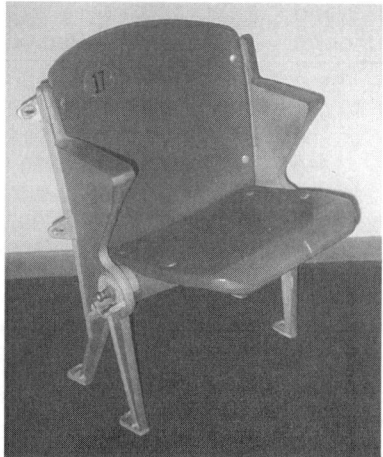

Veterans Stadium

Three Rivers Stadium (double)

Signs

There are three types of signs. First are the older, wooden type which were hand painted. Then there are those fashioned from metal alloys and from plastic. The most desirable are the wooden ones, obviously, but there are other factors that influence value. Condition is one. Another is whether the sign can be attributed to a specific team through words or a logo. Signs have been hot items at recent ballpark demolition auctions and make for terrific display items. Prices can vary from $50-$200 for a simple plastic section marker to $1,000 or more for hand-painted examples of pre-1970 or the enameled beauties that came from Yankee Stadium's renovation in the 1970s.

Memorial Stadium metal sign

Cleveland Stadium wooden sign, 1950s

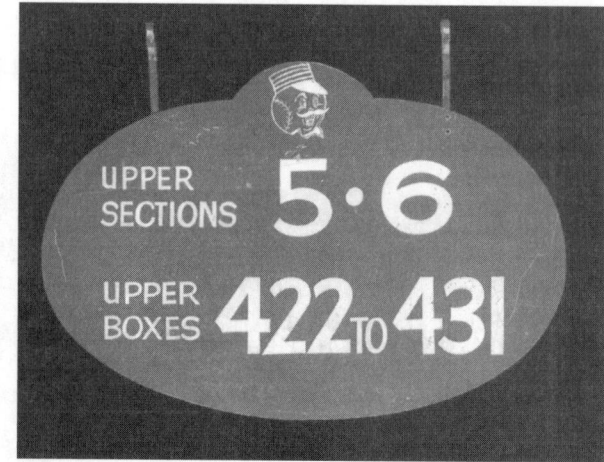

Crosley Field metal sign.

Turnstiles

These fixtures are among the most alluring for collectors. Imagine the millions of people who passed through them, the anticipation of the game as the machine clicked and whirred! These devices fall into two basic categories. First is the older, rotary style found in the older parks. They are big, bulky and beautiful. Next is the style still used today in many parks: the side-winding model.

You can expect to pay upwards of $4,000 for a Forbes Field or Shibe turnstile, providing it is not repainted and is complete, meaning that the brass cap that houses the counting mechanism is intact (many were removed for scrap). A "side winder" will run from $500-$1,000, depending on the park and the vintage. No matter what style, these are awesome stadium relics.

Polo Grounds rotating turnstile

Shibe Park rotating turnstile, 1909

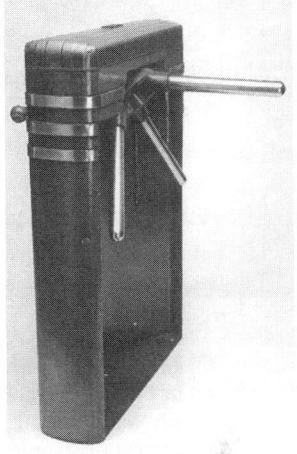

Wrigley Field sidewinding turnstile

Usher/Vendor/Police Items

It is somewhat ironic that those old-time ballpark employees with the most menial jobs sported some of the most desirable collectibles. Usher's hats and uniforms (primarily the jackets, especially those bearing a team logo) are highly desirable. The older the park, the better. A 1940s hat from Tiger Stadium could hit $500. A full uniform from Ebbets Field would be considered priceless. And what of those who served us hotdogs or ice-cold drinks? Their coolers or shirts can range from a couple hundred dollars on up. A "Yankee Stadium Police" badge will set you back at least $200, with a hat well above that.

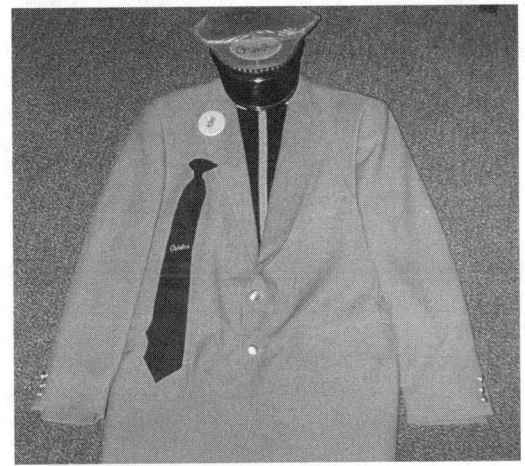

Memorial Stadium full usher's uniform

Other Fixtures

If one attends a ballpark demolition auction today they will be amazed at what people will purchase, sometimes for great sums of money. Flagpoles, bullpen phones, wall padding, ticket boxes and player lockers make interesting conversation pieces. Even restroom fixtures have popped up in collectors' homes! Probably the two most popular items from this area are banners/flags that adorned the stadium roofs, and scoreboard numerals from the older parks. Flags, many of them made of canvas and sporting the names of MLB cities, range from $250 to $500, depending on the park and the era from which they come. Banners used for World Series or All-Star games can run a few thousand dollars. Scoreboard numerals or letters can range from $250 to $1,000 as well. With the truly oddball items, it comes down to what a collector will pay—whether it be a garbage can, piece of synthetic turf, brick or cornerstone.

Chapter 3

FIGURES, PLATES

Baseball Banks

Figural banks for the most part have not yet become a mainstream collectible. That does not mean that they are not highly sought after or valuable. As collectors become more familiar with them, it is almost a certainty that they will become as desirable as other figural items. Some have mascot heads that compare favorably with the bobbing head series of the '60s. Others have team logos or player facsimile autographs. There are even a few that were made in the images of specific players. They are colorful and display beautifully. For these reasons, figural banks will almost assuredly pay "big dividends" in the future.

A number of companies emanating out of the Ohio area produced porcelain mascot banks relating to Major League teams. They were manufactured during the late '40s through the early '50s. Stanford Pottery was one of the leaders, issuing razor banks of the Cleveland Indians, Boston Braves, Pittsburgh Pirates, Brooklyn Dodgers, Detroit Tigers and various Minor League teams. They stand about 8 inches tall and glisten with color. The Gibbs-Connor Company made similar-looking banks of the Cleveland Indians using their familiar mascot "Chief Wahoo" as the model. Moyer made a generic baseball player reminiscent of the Stanford pottery line. Mint examples from these three companies can fetch very high prices.

There were also a series of glass banks in the shape of a baseball that were a give-away by Mobil Oil in the '30s and '40s. The company logo and a team logo were painted on separate panels of the ball. Known examples include the Cleveland Indians, Detroit Tigers, St. Louis Cardinals, Pittsburgh Pirates, Cincinnati Reds and the New York Yankees. Local banks used a plastic baseball with facsimile autographs of home-town team members to advertise their bank. There were probably issues

New York Yankees bank

for most of the Major League teams, with the Braves, Yankees and Dodgers being the more commonly found.

A Jackie Robinson brass bust bank was sold at souvenir stands in the late '40s and early '50s. There was also a tin litho Robinson bank that could be purchased through comic book offers. A Ted Williams bank is also known to exist. There is also a Ty Cobb look-alike cast iron bank from the early '20s.

Of all the figural baseball items, banks are probably the least known and the hardest to catalog. The banks mentioned above are only a handful of a growing list of these fabulous display pieces. With the advent of the Internet, never before seen banks are constantly "popping up" for sale. They will surely pique your interest.

Prices are based on Mint examples.

"Chief Wahoo" bank

Porcelain Banks

Stanford Pottery (also known as "Gold Tooth" banks)

Boston Braves	$450
Boston Braves w/headdress (only one known example)	$4,000
Brooklyn Dodgers	$1,500
Cleveland Indians	$300
Detroit Tigers (with mascot tiger head)	$3,000
Detroit Tigers (human head)	$2,000
Philadelphia A's (elephant)	$4,000
Pittsburgh Pirates	$600
Minor League Teams	$300

Gibbs-Connor

Cleveland Indians (leaning on baseball)	$475
Cleveland Indians (standing on base)	$550

Moyer

Generic player	$150

Glass Ball Banks

Cincinnati Reds $100
Cleveland Indians $75
Detroit Tigers...$75
Pittsburgh Pirates $75
Pittsburgh Pirates (with Ralph Kiner facsimile autograph) $125
St. Louis Cardinals $200
New York Yankees (with Lou Gehrig & Bill Dickey facsimile
    autographs)..$350

Plastic Ball Banks

Brooklyn Dodgers (all years) ....$125-$200
Milwaukee Braves ....$75-$100
New York Yankees..$125-$200
New York Giants ....$100-$150
L.A. Dodgers ....$75-$100
All other teams ....$50-$75

Miscellaneous

Ty Cobb (cast iron) ....$250-$400
Jackie Robinson - bust ....$750-$1,000
    (beware, a reproduction of this bank was issued in the '80s)
Jackie Robinson - tin litho ....$150-$200
Generic tin litho baseball banks ....$25-$75
Plastic Bank with Major League team bats (wooden bats)..............$150
Plastic bank with Major League team bats (plastic bats) ....$50-$75

Porcelain Football Banks

Moyer

1940s College Football (All Teams)....................$100-$200

Mass Illion

Tiger (mascot head) $500

Quinco

1960s College Football (mascots).....................$150-$250

Banks portraying Braves, Pirates and Indians

Jackie Robinson banks

1960s College Football (Boy Face).. $75-$100

BOBBING HEAD DOLLS

Bobbing head sports dolls (a.k.a. nodders) have become some of the hottest pieces of memorabilia over the last 10 years. Once considered a low-end collectible, bobbing head dolls are now featured in some of the largest auction houses in the hobby. Their colorful nature and smallish size make them a perfect display piece that logistically can fit into almost any collection.

The first series of bobbing head dolls first hit the scene around 1960. The early dolls were made of papier-mache and were made of this composition until the early 1970s. There are a number of different series (usually based on base color) for each of the four main North American sports (baseball, football, hockey and basketball). These early dolls are the most collectible by advanced collectors, but subsequent series made of ceramic and plastic compositions are quickly gaining in popularity. Values for bobbing head dolls, like any other area of memorabilia, are based largely on availability and condition. Gem Mint dolls will often sell for prices well above the book value.

The following price list is based on dolls that are in Mint or Near Mint (very minor flaws) condition. Excellent condition dolls usually sell for about 60% of mint prices. Dolls of poorer grades generally sell for a fraction of these prices. It must be pointed out, that because of their fragility and tendency to chip and crack, it has become a common practice to repair these dolls. Although they look great, repainted or repaired dolls generally drop in value and are not desirable by advanced collectors.

BASEBALL BOBBING HEAD DOLLS

1960-1961 Square Colored Base

This is the first ever series of baseball bobbing head dolls. Not all the major league franchises were included in this series and only two of the teams had mascot heads making this set a little less desirable than future series. The base colors are different for each franchise. The set also includes several minor league teams.

Team	Base Color	Head Style	Mint	Near Mint
Baltimore Orioles	Green	Mascot	$275	$225

Team	Base Color	Head Style	Mint	Near Mint
Boston Red Sox	Green	Boy	$400	$325
Chicago Cubs	Blue	Boy	$450	$400
Cincinnati Reds	Red	Boy	$500	$450
Los Angeles Angels	Blue	Boy	$150	$125
Los Angeles Dodgers	Orange (wood)	Boy	$400	$350
Minnesota Twins	Blue	Boy	$125	$100
New York Mets	Blue	Boy	$250	$200

Roberto Clemente

Chicago Cubs mascot

Cleveland Indians mascot

Kansas City mascot

Team	Base Color	Head Style	Mint	Near Mint
New York Yankees	Orange	Boy	$225	$200
Pittsburgh Pirates	Gold	Mascot	$225	$200
San Francisco Giants	Orange	Boy	$200	$175
Washington Senators	Blue	Boy	$1,500	$1,200
Portland Beavers*	Blue	Boy	$225	$200
Seattle Rainers*	Red	Boy	$450	$400
Tacoma Giants*	Orange	Boy	$275	$250

*indicates Minor League franchise

1961-1963 White Base

This is the first complete series of Major League baseball dolls. Issued during the same period were four actual player dolls of Mickey Mantle, Roger Maris, Willie Mays and Roberto Clemente. The white base series is generally considered the most desirable of the early dolls.

Team	Head Style	Mint	Near Mint
Anaheim Angels (label over base decal)	Boy	$300	$275
Baltimore Orioles	Mascot	$500	$450
Boston Red Sox	Boy	$300	$250
Chicago Cubs	Mascot	$500	$450
Chicago White Sox	Boy	$325	$275
Cincinnati Reds	Mascot	$550	$475
Cleveland Indians	Mascot	$700	$650
Detroit Tigers	Mascot	$425	$375
Houston Colt 45's (cowboy hat)	Boy	$375	$325
Houston Colt 45's (blue uniform w/cowboy hat)	Boy	$1,400	$1,000
Los Angeles Angels	Boy	$175	$150
Los Angeles Dodgers (embossed chest)	Boy	$175	$150
Los Angeles Dodgers (decal on chest)	Boy	$200	$175
Kansas City Athletics	Boy	$325	$300
Milwaukee Braves	Mascot	$450	$400
Minnesota Twins	Boy	$325	$300
New York Mets	Boy	$375	$350
New York Yankees	Boy	$350	$325
Philadelphia Phillies	Boy	$300	$275
Pittsburgh Pirates	Mascot	$750	$675
St. Louis Cardinals	Mascot	$80	$725
San Francisco Giants (embossed chest)	Boy	$350	$325

Team	Head Style	Mint	Near Mint
San Francisco Giants (decal on chest)	Boy	$375	$350
Washington Senators	Boy	$400	$375

INDIVIDUAL PLAYERS

Team	Mint	Near Mint
Roberto Clemente	$3,000	$2,500
Mickey Mantle	$850	$775
Mickey Mantle (Round base)	$950	$875
Roger Maris	$550	$475
Willie Mays (Dark Face)	$550	$475
Willie Mays (Light Face-Oriental features)	$500	$450
Willie Mays (with Gold base)	$1,500	$1,250

Note: Boxes for the White base series sometimes showed a drawing of the actual doll on the label. These boxes can add $75-$100 to the value of the doll. Boxes for Mantle and Maris also have their likenesses and can increase the value as much as $200.

1961-1962 Miniature Series

This series of dolls measures approximately 4.5 inches tall as opposed to the standard 6.5 inch doll. They were equipped with a magnet on the bottom of the base (presumably for mounting on the dashboards of cars). They all have white round bases (the Indians and Tigers dolls came with either white or green bases). There were miniatures for both Mickey Mantle and Roger Maris.

Team	Head Style	Mint	Near Mint
Anaheim Angels (label over base decal)	Boy	$500	$450
Baltimore Orioles	Mascot	$700	$650
Baltimore Orioles	Boy	$1,000	$900
Boston Red Sox	Boy	$500	$450
Chicago Cubs	Mascot	$650	$600
Chicago White Sox	Boy	$350	$300
Cincinnati Reds	Mascot	$650	$600
Cleveland Indians	Mascot	$700	$650
Cleveland Indians (Green base)	Mascot	$600	$550
Detroit Tigers	Mascot	$600	$550
Detroit Tigers (Green base)	Mascot	$500	$450
Houston Colt 45's (cowboy hat)	Boy	$375	$325
Houston Astros (mid 1960s issue)	Boy	$400	$350
Los Angeles Angels	Boy	$175	$150

Team	Head Style	Mint	Near Mint
Los Angeles Dodgers	Boy	$175	$150
Kansas City Athletics	Boy	$350	$325
Milwaukee Braves	Mascot	$750	$675
Minnesota Twins	Boy	$350	$325
Minneapolis Twins	Boy	$700	$650
New York Mets	Boy	$600	$575
New York Yankees	Boy	$300	$275
Philadelphia Phillies	Boy	$300	$275
Pittsburgh Pirates	Mascot	$750	$675
St. Louis Cardinals	Mascot	$900	$825
San Francisco Giants	Boy	$450	$375
Washington Senators	Boy	$400	$375

INDIVIDUAL PLAYERS

Team	Mint	Near Mint
Mickey Mantle	$2,000	$1,750
Roger Maris	$750	$675

Note: There are several styles of "boy" heads used in this series. Although some are more popular, the values are usually not affected by the style. Boxes add about $25 for team dolls and $150-$200 for both Mantle and Maris dolls.

1963-1965 Green Base

This is one of the most colorful of all the series and features the full complement of Major League teams. Although dated 1962 on the bottom of the base, these dolls were most likely first sold during the 1963 baseball season.

Team	Head Style	Mint	Near Mint
Anaheim Angels (label over base decal)	Boy	$325	$300
Baltimore Orioles	Mascot	$300	$275
Boston Red Sox (red hat)	Boy	$150	$125
Boston Red Sox (blue hat)	Boy	$350	$300
Chicago Cubs	Mascot	$550	$500
Chicago White Sox	Boy	$150	$125
Cincinnati Reds	Mascot	$200	$175
Cleveland Indians	Mascot	$450	$400
Detroit Tigers	Mascot	$225	$200
Houston Colt 45's (cowboy hat w/pistols)	Boy	$475	$425
Los Angeles	Boy	$150	$125
Los Angeles Dodgers	Boy	$150	$125
Kansas City Athletics (light blue hat)	Boy	$350	$325

Team	Head Style	Mint	Near Mint
Kansas City Athletics (dark blue hat)	Boy	$650	$600
Milwaukee Braves	Mascot	$450	$400
Minnesota Twins	Boy	$175	$150
New York Mets	Boy	$150	$125
New York Yankees	Boy	$250	$225
Philadelphia Phillies	Boy	$150	$125
Pittsburgh Pirates	Mascot	$275	$250
St. Louis Cardinals	Mascot	$250	$225
San Francisco Giants	Boy	$175	$150
Washington Senators	Boy	$375	$325

Note: Do not be fooled by ceramic green base dolls with a similar look. Ceramic dolls were issued in the 1970s and 1980s. Their values are much lower.

1963-1965 Black Face Dolls

These dolls have the same body and base type as the Green base dolls. There are two variations of faces (serious and happy) and all represent Afro-American players. Not all the teams were included. Although they were not terribly popular in the 1960s, they are the most desirable series for collectors today. There are no mascot dolls in the series.

Team	Head Style	Mint	Near Mint
Baltimore Orioles	Boy	$1,200	$1,000
Boston Red Sox	Boy	$2,000	$1,500
Chicago Cubs	Boy	$1,200	$1,000
Chicago White Sox	Boy	$1,200	$1,000
Cincinnati Reds	Boy	$1,500	$1,250
Cleveland Indians	Boy	$2,500	$2,000
Detroit Tigers	Boy	$1,750	$1,500
Houston Colt 45's	Boy	$10,000	$8,000
Los Angeles Angels	Boy	$1,750	$1,500
Los Angeles Dodgers	Boy	$1,500	$1,250
Milwaukee Braves	Boy	$2,000	$1,750
New York Mets	Boy	$1,750	$1,500
New York Yankees	Boy	$3,000	$2,500
St. Louis Cardinals	Boy	$1,500	$1,250
Washington Senators	Boy	$1,000	$850

Pittsburgh Pirates

Baltimore Orioles mascot

Roger Maris

Atlanta Braves & Baltimore Colts

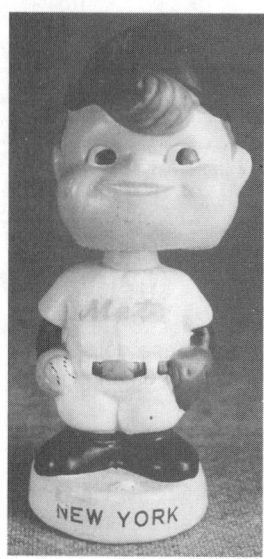
New York Mets

Mickey Mantle

Philadelphia Phillies

Roger Maris

Detroit Tigers "Green" baseball mascot

1966-1971 Gold Base

This set includes some new expansion teams and cities with new franchises.

Team	Head Style	Mint	Near Mint
Atlanta Braves	Mascot	$175	$150
Baltimore Orioles	Mascot	$200	$175
Boston Red Sox	Boy	$275	$250
California Angels	Boy	$150	$125
Chicago Cubs	Mascot	$275	$225
Chicago White Sox	Boy	$125	$100
Cincinnati Reds	Mascot	$200	$175
Cleveland Indians	Mascot	$375	$325
Detroit Tigers	Mascot	$200	$175
Houston Astros	Boy	$125	$100
Houston Astros (red hat/shooting star decal)	Boy	$750	$675
Los Angeles Dodgers	Boy	$125	$100
Kansas City Athletics (green & gold uniform)	Boy	$600	$525
Kansas City Royals	Boy	$125	$100
Milwauke Brewers	Boy	$100	$85
Minnesota Twins	Boy	$175	$150
Montreal Expos	Boy	$100	$85
New York Mets	Boy	$125	$100
New York Mets (Mr. Met)	Mascot	$400	$325
New York Yankees	Boy	$200	$175
Oakland Athletics (yellow uniform)	Boy	$75	$60
Oakland Athletics (white uniform)	Boy	$225	$200
Philadelphia Phillies	Boy	$150	$125
Pittsburgh Pirates	Mascot	$225	$200
St. Louis Cardinals	Mascot	$200	$175
San Diego Padres	Boy	$175	$150
San Francisco Giants	Boy	$150	$125
Seattle Pilots	Boy	$500	$450
Texas Rangers (cowboy hat)	Boy	$200	$175
Washington Senators	Boy	$400	$350

1970-1972 Wedge Base

This series has only nine Major League teams represented and one minor league franchise. It is not extremely popular among advanced collectors. There are no mascot heads in this series. There are several different color bases.

Team	Head Style	Mint	Near Mint
Boston Red Sox	Boy	$350	$300
California Angels	Boy	$125	$100
Chicago Cubs	Boy	$250	$225
Houston Astros (blue hat)	Boy	$200	$175
Houston Astros (orange hat)	Boy	$175	$150
Kansas City Royals	Boy	$225	$200
Minnesota Twins	Boy	$150	$125
St. Louis Cardinals	Boy	$250	$225
San Francisco Giants	Boy	$400	$350
Denver Bears*	Boy	$700	$650

*Minor League Franchise

1960s Los Angeles Dodgers Weirdo's

This series was produced in the mid 1960s. Although not much is known about them, it is one of the hottest of all the bobbing head series in the last few years. They are very comical and each one has a personality of its own. They came with funny expressions either on a hang tag or on a base decal. There are only seven different dolls known in the series with some being made as black faces, too. Dolls with original hang tags command a premium price. Prices range from $750 to several thousand dollars.

FOOTBALL BOBBING HEAD DOLLS

1961-1963 NFL Square, Wood & NFL Embossed

Team	Mint	Near Mint	Black Player Mint
Baltimore Colts	$100	$85	$450
Chicago Bears	$125	$100	$600
Cleveland Browns	$225	$200	$900
Dallas Cowboys	$400	$350	$1,000
Detroit Lions	$100	$85	$600
Green Bay Packers	$225	$200	$900
Los Angeles Rams (blue jersey)	$100	$85	$750
Los Angeles Rams (gold jersey)	$450	$400	none
Minnesota Vikings	$225	$200	none
New York Giants	$150	$125	$500
Philadelphia Eagles	$150	$125	$400
Pittsburgh Steelers	$225	$200	$900
St. Louis Cardinals	$100	$85	$650
San Francisco Forty-Niners	$100	$85	$900
Washington Redskins	$250	$225	$1,500

1960-1961 NFL Promo Dolls

These massive 13.5" tall dolls were used to promote the NFL Square base dolls of the early 1960s. They have the same style head, but do not have bases. Not all the teams are known to exist, but many of the original promos were painted over with the Eagles colors. They were not sold to the general public, but were given to stores as point of sale displays. They are extremely hard to find and even harder to find in good condition.

Team	Near Mint
Baltimore Colts	$3,000
Chicago Bears	$3,000
Cleveland Browns	$7,500
Dallas Cowboys	$5,000
Detroit Lions	$3,000
Green Bay Packers	$3,500
Los Angeles Rams	$3,000
Minnesota Vikings	none
New York Giants	$5,000
Philadelphia Eagles (winged helmet)	$5,000
Philadelphia Eagles (repaint)	$2,500
Pittsburgh Steelers	$5,000
St. Louis Cardinals	$3,500
San Francisco Forty-Niners	$2,500
Washington Redskins	$7,500

Wahington Redskins

1962-1964 NFL Kissing Pairs

Incredibly popular series of dolls that feature a football player for each NFL team and a majorette with team colors. There is a simulated kissing action produced by magnets. Two of the teams were represented with mascots (Browns and Steelers). There were also two AFL teams — the Boston Patriots and the Buffalo Bills.

Team	Mint	Near Mint
Baltimore Colts	$600	$450
Chicago Bears	$450	$350
Cleveland Browns	$1,500	$1,200
Dallas Cowboys	$350	$275
Detroit Lions	$600	$450
Green Bay Packers	$450	$350
Los Angeles Rams	$400	$325
Minnesota Vikings	$450	$350
New York Giants	$600	$450
Philadelphia Eagles	$450	$350
Pittsburgh Steelers	$1,000	$800
St. Louis Cardinals	$450	$350
San Francisco Forty-Niners	$450	$350
Washington Redskins	$1,500	$1,200
Boston Patriots - AFL	$450	$350
Buffalo Bills - AFL	$450	$350

1961-1962 AFL Round Base

There were only eight teams issued in this original series of the AFL. They all have the "toes-up" feature. It is one of the most highly sought after sets.

Team	Mint	Near Mint
Boston Patriots	$600	$500
Buffalo Bills	$600	$500
Dallas Texans	$900	$750
Denver Broncos	$900	$750
Houston Oilers	$900	$750
New York Titans	$1,500	$1,200
Oakland Raiders	$900	$750
San Diego Chargers	$600	$500

1961-1966 NFL "Toes-Up"

Incredible series with four different styles. There were also black faced dolls made with the "Toes-Up" feature. Prices reflect the average of the four types.

Team	Mint	Near Mint	Black Face Mint	Black Face NM
Atlanta Falcons	$400	$325	none	none
Baltimore Colts	$450	$375	$1,500	$1,250
Chicago Bears	$400	$325	$550	$475
Cleveland Browns	$550	$475	$1,250	$1,000
Dallas Cowboys	$450	$375	$1,750	$1,500
Detroit Lions	$400	$325	$1,000	$850
Green Bay Packers	$375	$300	$1,000	$850
Los Angeles Rams	$375	$300	$750	$600
Minnesota Vikings	$375	$300	$900	$750
New York Giants	$400	$325	$600	$500
Philadelphia Eagles	$375	$300	$600	$500
Pittsburgh Steelers	$375	$300	$900	$750
St. Louis Cardinals	$375	$300	none	none
San Francisco Forty-Niners	$400	$325	$900	$750
Washington Redskins	$600	$500	$2,500	$2,000

1963-1964 NFL Square Gold Base

Many collectors confuse this series with the earlier NFL square bases series. The helmet and face designs are totally different. These dolls have face masks and larger sized heads. Not all the NFL teams were represented.

Team	Mint	Near Mint
Baltimore Colts	$475	$375
Chicago Bears	$275	$250
Detroit Lions	$600	$500
Minnesota Vikings	$475	$375
New York Giants	$475	$375
St. Louis Cardinals	$475	$375
Washington Redskins	$400	$325

1965-1966 AFL Ear Pad Series

This series has a "funky" helmet design that looks like space helmets. The series is highly collectible. Only AFL teams were made with the exception of the extremely rare Washington Redskins of the NFL.

Team	Mint	Near Mint
Boston Patriots	$400	$350
Buffalo Bills	$400	$350
Denver Broncos	$1,500	$1,250
Kansas City Chiefs	$400	$350
Houston Oilers	$600	$500
Miami Dolphins	$600	$450
New York Jets	$900	$750
Oakland Raiders	$600	$500
San Diego Chargers	$500	$450
Washington Redskins	$1,500	$1,250

1965-1967 NFL Round Gold Base

Do not confuse these dolls with the more common Merger series dolls of the late 1960s. Although both have gold bases, the face and helmet design on these two series are totally different. This doll is slightly shorter than the Merger series and has a more mature face.

Team	Mint	Near Mint
Atlanta Falcons	$110	$90
Baltimore Colts	$175	$150
Chicago Bears	$175	$150
Cleveland Browns	$300	$250
Dallas Cowboys	$275	$225
Detroit Lions	$150	$125
Green Bay Packers	$225	$200
Los Angeles Rams	none	none
Minnesota Vikings	$225	$200
New Orleans Saints	$110	$90
New York Giants	$200	$175
Philadelphia Eagles	$150	$125
Pittsburgh Steelers	$225	$200
St. Louis Cardinals	$250	$225
San Francisco Forty-Niners	none	none
Washington Redskins	$300	$250

1965-1967 NFL Realistic Face

Same basic body type as the 1965 NFL Round Gold base, but this doll features an adult face.

Team	Mint	Near Mint
Atlanta Falcons	$150	$125
Baltimore Colts	$750	$600

Team	Mint	Near Mint
Chicago Bears	$225	$200
Cleveland Browns	$450	$400
Dallas Cowboys	$900	$750
Detroit Lions	$400	$350
Green Bay Packers	$300	$250
Los Angeles Rams	none	none
Minnesota Vikings	$600	$475
New Orleans Saints	$125	$100
New York Giants	none	none
Philadelphia Eagles	$300	$250
Pittsburgh Steelers	none	none
St. Louis Cardinals	$200	$175
San Francisco Forty-Niners	none	none
Washington Redskins	$1,250	$1,000

1968-1970 NFL/AFL Merger Series

These dolls signified the merger of the NFL and AFL. All dolls have NFL decals between their feet (identical dolls were also made with AFL stickers and will increase the value by 25-percent).

Team	Mint	Near Mint
Atlanta Falcons	$110	$90
Baltimore Colts	$175	$150
Boston Patriots	$175	$150
Buffalo Bills	$200	$175
Chicago Bears	$150	$125
Cincinnati Bengals	$110	$90
Cleveland Browns	$225	$200
Dallas Cowboys	$275	$225
Detroit Lions	$85	$70
Green Bay Packers	$225	$200
Houston Oilers	$100	$85
Kansas City Chiefs	$100	$85
Los Angeles Rams	$125	$100
Miami Dolphins	$225	$200
Minnesota Vikings	$225	$200
New Orleans Saints	$100	$85
New York Giants	$125	$100
New York Jets	$150	$125
Philadelphia Eagles	$150	$125
Pittsburgh Steelers	$225	$200
St. Louis Cardinals	$85	$70
San Diego Chargers	$150	$125
San Francisco Forty-Niners	$200	$175
Washington Redskins (5 helmet designs)	$325	$275

San Diego Charges & Oakland Raiders

HOCKEY BOBBING HEAD DOLLS

1961-1963 NHL Square Base & High Skates

In the early 1960s the NHL had only six teams. There were two separate series of nodders issued for these six teams — the regular square base and what is known as the "high skate" because of the taller nature of the blades of the skates. There is also a difference in the facial and head features on these dolls. Each of these series also came in a smaller mini variation.

Team	NHL Square: Mint	Near Mint	Mini: Mint	Near Mint
Boston Bruins	$600	$500	$75	$60
Chicago Black Hawks	$300	$225	$75	$60
Detroit Red Wings	$300	$225	$60	$50
Montreal Canadiens	$150	$125	$50	$40
New York Rangers	$225	$175	$1,500	$1,250*
Toronto Maple Leafs	$225	$175	$60	$50

*Beware as over the last several years there have been a number of Toronto Maple Leafs Minis painted over to look like the New York Rangers doll.

Team	NHL High Skate: Mint	Near Mint	Mini: Mint	Near Mint
Boston Bruins	$600	$500	$500	$425
Chicago Black Hawks	$450	$375	$450	$375

Team	NHL High Skate: Mint	Near Mint	Mini: Mint	Near Mint
Detroit Red Wings	$450	$375	$450	$375
Montreal Canadiens	$325	$275	$500	$425
New York Rangers	$450	$375	$450	$375
Toronto Maple Leafs	$450	$375	$450	$375

1967-1968 NHL Gold Base

These fabulous looking dolls were issued just shortly after the NHL expansion of 1967. The faces have a more realistic look of an adult player. Not all of the 12 teams were made.

Team	Mint	Near Mint
Boston Bruins	$750	$650
Chicago Black Hawks	$450	$375
Detroit Red Wings	$450	$375
Los Angeles Kings	$600	$500
Montreal Canadiens	$600	$500
New York Rangers	$750	$650
St. Louis Blues	$600	$500
(2 uniform colors)		
Toronto Maple Leafs	$750	$600

BASKETBALL BOBBING HEAD DOLLS

The NBA did not merchandise the bobbing head dolls as heavily as the other major North American professional sports. There were only a few teams that issued nodders during the 1960s.

Team	Base Color	Mint	Near Mint
1962 Harlem Globetrotters	Blue	$500	$425
1962 Harlem Globetrotters	Green	$400	$325
1962 Los Angeles Lakers	Green	$500	$425
1967 Los Angeles Lakers	Gold	$100	$75
1967 Los Angeles Lakers (black player)	Gold	$400	$325
1962 New York Knicks	Orange	$500	$425
1967 San Diego Rockets	Gold	$300	$250

New York Knicks Bobbing Heads

RECENT BOBBING HEAD PRICING

BASEBALL

1989 NODDERS

Player	MT
Ty Cobb	70
Lou Gehrig	80
Shoeless Joe Jackson	80
Babe Ruth	80
Honus Wagner	70

1999 MLB TEAM GIVEAWAYS

Player	MT
Willie Mays, S.F. (20,000)	200

2000 MLB TEAM GIVEAWAYS

Player	MT
Cal Ripken, Balt. Majestic	50
Florida Marlins Bobble Head Doll	35
Harmon Killebrew, Minn.	230
Kent Hrbek, Minn.	175
Tony Oliva, Minn.	75
Kirby Puckett, Minn.	200

Tom Seaver, Mets	90
Bill Mazeroski, Pitts.	60
Rafael Palmeiro, Tex.	50

2001 MLB ALL-STAR

Player	MT
Note: Comes with serial-numbered certificate	
All-Star American (25,000)	35
All-Star National (25,000)	35
Derek Jeter (2,001)	65
Randy Johnson (2,001)	40
Chipper Jones (2,001)	35
Edgar Martinez (2,001)	55
Mike Piazza (2,001)	55
Lou Piniella (2,001)	45
Cal Ripken (2,001)	55
Alex Rodriguez (2,001)	45
Kazuhiro Sasaki (wht or blue jrsy) (2,001)	50
Sammy Sosa (2,001)	40
Ichiro Suzuki (wht or blue jrsy) (5,000)	75
Joe Torre (2,001)	50
Bobby Valentine (2,001)	40

2001 MLB TEAM GIVEAWAYS

Player	MT
Roberto Alomar, Clev.	25
Brady Anderson (12,500), Balt.	60
Garret Anderson (20,000), Ana.	40
Jeff Bagwell (10,000), Hou.	45
Craig Biggio (10,000), Hou.	50
Dave Burba (10,000), Clev.	35
Bartolo Colon, Clev.	30
Larry Dieker (10,000), Hou.	55
Travis Fryman, Clev.	20
Florida Marlins mascot	30
Kirk Gibson, LA	20
Luis Gonzalez (15,000), Ariz.	40
Mark Grace (15,000), Ariz.	60
Danny Graves (10,000), Cin.	35
Pete Harnisch (10,000), Cin.	60
Richard Hidalgo (10,000), Hou.	35
Geoff Jenkins (10,000), Mil.	40
Chipper Jones, Atl.	40
Andruw Jones, Atl.	40

Barry Larkin (10,000), Cin.	60
Tommy Lasorda (30,000), LA	60
Kenny Lofton, Clev.	25
Fred McGriff, Atl.	40
Magglio Ordonez (10,000), WSox	50
Tim Salmon (20,000), Ana.	40
Sammy Sosa (10,000), Cubs	80
Frank Thomas (10,000), WSox	60
Jim Thome, Clev.	50
Bob Uecker (10,000), Mil.	25
Fernando Valenzuela, LA	20
Omar Vizquel, Clev.	45
Matt Williams (15,000), Ariz.	40
Tony Womack (15,000), Ariz.	50
Robin Yount (10,000), Mil.	35

*Note: The pricing for the three Milwaukee bobble heads above is for dolls with Piggly Wiggly bases, which were distributed at the park. Also available are Pepsi dolls, which are priced at $10 apiece.

Bert Blyleven (10,000), Minn.	100

Rod Carew (10,000), Minn.	75
Dave Winfield (10,000), Minn.	75
Kirby Puckett (15,000), Minn.	100
Mookie Wilson, Mets	65
Andy Pettitte (15,000), NYY	65
Derek Jeter (15,000), NYY	55
Tino Martinez (15,000), NYY	45
Jason Giambi (15,000), Oak.	75
Miguel Tejada, Oak	65
Larry Bowa, Phil.	25
Pat Burrell, Phil.	40
Roberto Clemente, Pitt.	100
Jim Edmonds, St. L.	20
San Diego Padres Friar	20
Willie McCovey, S.F.	65
Ichiro Suzuki (20,000), Sea.	150
Kazuhiro Sasaki (20,000), Sea.	125
Tampa Bay Raymond mascot (7,500)	35
Nolan Ryan (25,000), Tex.	75
Ivan Rodriguez (25,000), Tex.	30
Carlos Delgado (15,000), Tor	65

2001 MINOR LEAGUE TEAM GIVEAWAYS

Player	MT
Steve Balboni-Columbus (3,000)	10
Jay Buhner-Columbus (3,000)	20
Pat Burrell-Reading	20
Pat Burrell-Scranton	20
Hopalong Cassady-Columbus (3,000)	20
Jason Giambi-Modesto	25
Vladimir Guerrero-Harrisburg	25
Derek Jeter-Columbus (3,000)	35
John Kruk-Reading	20
Don Mattingly-Columbus (3,000)	45
Mark McGwire-Peoria	30
Mark McGwire-Potomac (1,000)	50
Mark McGwire-Tacoma	25
Andy Pettitte-Columbus (3,000)	25
Jorge Posada-Columbus (3,000)	30
Dave Righetti-Columbus (3,000)	20
Cal Ripken-Charlotte	40
Cal Ripken-Rochester (1,000)	60
Alex Rodriguez-Oklahoma	25
Scott Rolen-Reading	20
Mariano Rivera-Columbus (3,000)	30
Nolan Ryan-Round Rock	35
J.T. Snow-Columbus (3,000)	20
Bernie Williams-Columbus (3,000)	30
Maury Wills-Fargo-Moorehead (signed)	45

2002 ALEXANDER GLOBAL HOF

Player	MT
Aaron, Hank-1957 Braves	25
Banks, Ernie-Cubs, white/home	25
Berra, Yogi-NY Yankees	25
Gibson, Josh-Homestead Grays	25
Kell, George-Detroit Tigers	20
Kiner, Ralph-Pittsburgh Pirates	20
Smith, Ozzie-St. Louis Cardinals	20
Smith, Ozzie-San Diego Padres	20
Snider, Duke-LA Dodgers, old grey jersey	20
Weaver, Earl-Baltimore Orioles	20
Winfield, David-Totonto Blue Jays, home/wht	20
Yount, Robin-Milwaukee Brewers 1982 unif.	20

2002 MLB ALL-STAR

Note: Sold exclusively at FanFest in Milwaukee.

Player	MT
Hank Aaron, in Milw. Braves cap (2,004)	35
Barry Bonds (2,004)	35
Donald Duck (600 NL, 408 AL issued)	35
Jason Giambi (2,004)	35
Goofy (600 NL, 408 AL issued)	35
Derek Jeter (2,004)	35
Randy Johnson (2,004)	35
Mickey Mouse (600 NL, 408 AL issued)	35
Mike Piazza (2,004)	35
Ozzie Smith, HOF induction (2,004)	35
Sammy Sosa (2,004)	35
Ichiro Suzuki (2,004)	35

2002 MLB TEAM GIVEAWAYS

Player	MT
Hank Aaron, Mil.	45
Robbie Alomar, Mets	20
Matt Anderson, Det.	20
Rich Aurilia, SF.	25
Baltimore Fun Bird mascot (10,000)	20
Josh Beckett, Fla. (15,000)	15
Carlos Beltran (25,000), KC	30
Johnny Bench, Cin.	75
Lance Berkman, Hou.	23
Pat Borders (15,000), Tor.	25
Bob Brenly, Ariz.	40
Gary Carter, Mon. (5,000)	35
Orlando Cepeda, SF.	45
Rod Carew (10,000), Ana.	40
Joe Carter (15,000), Tor.	25
Eric Chavez, Oak.	35
Roger Clemens, NYY	50
Clev. Slider "Bobble Belly" mascot	20
Colo. "Dinger" mascot	25
Eric Davis, Cin.	40
Andre Dawson, Mon. (5,000)	30
Einar Diaz, Clev.	20
Brian Downing (10,000), Ana	25
Paul Lo Duca, LA	25
Adam Dunn, Cin.	25
Jermaine Dye, Oak	25
Kyle Farnsworth (Road Alternate), Cubs	20
Steve Finley, Ariz.	25
Carlton Fisk, White Sox (10,000)	35
Rafael Furcal, Atl	30
Nomar Garciaparra, Bos.	20
Jay Gibbons, Balt.	35
Brian Giles, Pitt.	25
Tom Glavine, Atl	40
Juan Gonzalez (25,000), Tex.	30
Luis Gonzalez, Ariz.	45
Shawn Green, LA	30
Bobby Grich (10,000), Ana.	25
Vladimir Guerrero, Mon. (5,000)	35
Cristian Guzman (10,000), Minn.	50
Jerry Hairston, Balt.	25
Todd Helton, Colo.	30
Tim Hudson, Oak.	35
Catfish Hunter, Oak.	40
Randy Johnson, Ariz.	35
K.C. Sluggerrr mascot (10,000)	25
Jim Kaat (10,000), Minn.	70
Tom Kelly (10,000), Minn.	30
Jason Kendall, Pitt.	25
Al Leiter, Mets.	20
Javy Lopez, Atl	30
Greg Maddux, Atl	30
Joe Mays (10,000), Minn, mini-bobble	30
Doug Mientkiewicz (10,000), Minn	95
Eric Milton (10,000), Minn.	25
Minnie Minoso, White Sox	18
Hideo Nomo, LA	20
Maggio Ordonez, White Sox	25
Chan Ho Park (25,000), Tex.	15
Phil. Phanatic Bobbing Belly	25
Pitt. Parrot mascot Bobble Belly	35
Mike Piazza, Mets	35
Jorge Posada, NYY	25
Albert Pujols, St. L	35
Tim Raines, Mon. (5,000)	50
Pokey Reese, Pitt. (36,000)	25
Alex Rodriguez (25,000), Tex.	30
Jimmy Rollins, Phil.	30
C.C. Sabathia, Clev.	20
Chris Sabo, Cin.	35
Ryne Sandberg (Home), Cubs.	60
Curt Schilling, Ariz.	30
Richie Sexson, Mil.	25
Ben Sheets, Mil.	25
Gary Sheffield, Atl	40
John Smoltz, Atl.	40
Sammy Sosa (Road), Cubs.	35
Willie Stargell, Pitt.	50
Rusty Staub, Mon. (5,000)	50
Ichiro Suzuki MVP, Sea.	75
Jim Thome, Clev.	20
Chuck Thompson (talking), Balt. (25,000)	35
Jason Tyner, T. Bay	15
Fernando Vina, St. L	40
Larry Walker, Colo.	35
Bob Wickman, Clev.	20
Bernie Williams, NYY	25
Dave Winfield (15,000), Tor.	75

2002 MINOR LEAGUE TEAM GIVEAWAYS

Team-Player	MT
Appleton Foxes-Alex Rodriguez, (1,000)	25
Fargo-Moorehead-Roger Maris, (1,000)	55
Columbus -Jorge Posada, (3,000)	15
Lowell Spinners-Carlton Fisk, (3,000)	35
Modesto A's-Mark McGwire, (1,000)	50
Modesto A's-Tim Hudson, (1,000)	40
Modesto A's-Reggie Jackson	25
Modesto A's-Jose Canseco	30
Mod. A's-Rick'y Henderson, (sea. tix holders)	30
Peoria Chiefs-Pete Vonachen	12
Peoria Chiefs-Greg Maddux	40
Peoria Chiefs-Mark Grace	30
Peoria Chiefs-Joe Girardi	20
Peoria Chiefs-Albert Pujols	25
Peoria Chiefs-Rally Redbird	30
Reading Phillies-Marlon Byrd	15
Reading Phillies-Larry Bowa	25
Reading Phillies-Jimmy Rollins	25
Phillies mascot-Screwball, Reading	15
San Antonio Missions-Mike Piazza	30
San Antonio Missions-Pedro Martinez	20
Sarasota Sox-Nomar Garciaparra, (1,000)	25
Tacoma Rainiers-Willie McCovey, (500)	50
Tacoma-A-Rod, home (1,000, season tix)	25
Tacoma-A-Rod, away (1,000, season tix)	25
Tacoma Rainiers-Jason Giambi (500)	15
Tacoma Rainiers-Juan Marichal, (500)	15

2002 MLB THE ROAD TO THE SHOW

Note: Each of the bobbers pictures a MLB player in his minor-league uniform. Individual bobbers sold through MLB.com. The entire set was sold via MinorLeagueBaseball.com. Fans who purchased the entire set received free bonus bobbles of Ichiro Suzuki and Albert Pujols.

Player	MT
Entire Set (16)	350
Bonds, Barry, Prince Will. Pirates, yellow	25
Clemens, Roger, Pawt. Red Sox, white	25
Garciaparra, Nomar, Trenton Thunder, white	25
Giambi, Jason, Tacoma Tigers, white	25
Griffey, Ken Jr., San Bernardino Spirit, wht.	25
Jeter, Derek, Tampa Yankees, white	25
Johnson, Randy, Jamestown Expos, white	25
Jones, Chipper, Macon Braves, white	25
Martinez, Pedro, Great Falls Dodgers, white	25
McGwire, Mark, Huntsville Stars, white	25
Piazza, Mike, Salem Dodgers, white	25
Pujols, Albert, St. L. Cardinals, white	25
Ramirez, Manny, Burlington Indians, white	25
Rodriguez, Alex, Appleton Foxes, white	25
Sosa, Sammy, Tulsa Drillers, white	25
Suzuki, Ichiro, Seattle Mariners, white	25

2002 MCDONALD'S/CARDINALS

Note: Set comes with a ball and stand.

Year & Player	MT
'02 J.D. Drew	30
'02 Fernando Vina	30
'02 Jim Edmonds	30
'02 Albert Pujols	30

2002 MCDONALD'S/TWINS

Note: Produced by Bobble Dreams USA, the 4-inch mini bobbles were available for purchase at Minneapolis-area McDonald's.

Player	MT
Corey Koskie	10
Torri Hunger	10

2002 NCAA TEAM GIVEAWAYS

Mascot	MT
'02 Goldie Gopher mascot, U. of Min.	15

2003 MISCELLANEOUS

Player	MT
Harvey Haddix (1,000 produced, sold by the Springfield/Clark County (Ohio) Baseball Hall of Fame as a fund-raiser)	$25

2003 MLB TEAM GIVEAWAYS

Player	MT
Rally Monkey Bobble Belly, Ana	30
Rick Dempsey, talking (25,000), Balt.	25
Paul Konerko (10,000), ChiSox	20
Ellis Burks, Clev.	15
Omar Vizquel, with sound, Clev.	20
C.C. Sabathia/Josh Bard dual, Clev	25
Alan Trammell (10,000), Det.	30
Mike Sweeney (20,000), KC	20
Eddie Guardado (10,000), Minn.	30
Torii Hunter (10,000), Minn	45
Corey Koskie (10,000), Minn	55
Paul O'Neill (18,000), NYY	22
Jason Giambi (18,000), NYY	30
Hideki Matsui (18,000), NYY	60
Miguel Tejada (15,000), Oak.	25
Barry Zito (15,000), Oak	25
Mak Mulder (15,000), Oak	33
Stomper the mascot, Oak (Kid's Club promo)	15
Lou Piniella (7,500), T.B.	20
Alex Rodriguez (25,000), Tex.	25
Rafael Palmeiro (25,000), Tex.	20
Eric Hinske (25,000), Tor.	20
Paul Molitor (25,000), Tor	30
Baxter mascot (15,000), Ariz.	35
Junior Spivey (15,000), Ariz.	35
Bobby Cox (12,000), Atl	20
Phil Niekro (12,000), Atl	25
Dale Murphy (12,000), Atl	20
Warren Spahn (12,000), Atl.	30
Marty and Joe dual (20,000), Cin	25
Austin Kearns (20,000), Cin	25
Gapper (10,000), Cin	20
Ryan Dempster (10,000), Fla.	25
Charlie Hough (10,000), Fla.	20
Jeff Conine (10,000), Fla	20
Luis Castillo (10,000), Fla.	25
10th Anniversary bobble (10,000), Fla	20
Eric Gagne, LA.	25
Brian Jordan, LA.	20
Brat mini (10,000), Milw	10
Polish Sausage mini, Milw	10
Jeffrey Hammonds (10,000), Milw.	15
Paul Molitor, Milw (white pinstripe)	25
Paul Molitor, Milw (blue, 4,000)	50
Paul Molitor, Milw (autographed, 100)	75
Italian mini (10,000), Milw	10
Frank Robinson (5,000), Mon	15
Pedro Martinez (5,000), Mon	25
Tim Wallach (5,000), Mon	20
Youppi mascot (5,000), Mon	25
Dennis Martinez (5,000), Mon	25
Mo Vaughn, Mets	25
John Franco (12,000), Mets	30
Tom Glavine (12,000), Mets	25
Bob Murphy/Ralph Kiner dual, Mets	30
1980 World Champion bobber, Phil	25
Manny Sanguillen, Pitt	25
Sanguillen signed randomly seeded	50
Bob Prince talking, Pitt	75
Jack Wilson, Pitt	20
Charlie Brown, Pitt	30
Scott Rolen (30,000), St. L.	40
Edgar Renteria (30,000), St. L.	35
Dave Winfield, S.D.	20
Randy Jones, S.D.	15
Juan Marichal (20,000), S.F.	40

ALEXANDER GLOBAL BOBBLE DOBBLES

Player	MT
Ace Toronto mascot - white jersey	20
Alomar, Roberto-Cle. blue uni. #12	20
Alomar, Roberto-Cle. road gray #12	20
Alomar, R.-NYM alt home blk	20
Alou, Moises-Cubs	20
Anderson, Sparky-Det home wht #10	20
Banks, Ernie (1,101) D&J Collectibles	15
Berkman, Lance-Hou. wht w/pinstripes	20
Bernie Brewer mascot Mil. blu/wht uni	20
Biggio, Craig, Hou. away gray	20
Bonds, Barry, S.F. 2001 home wht .	20
Bonds, Barry, S.F. alt home blk	20
Bonds, Barry, S.F. 2002 home wht	20
Bonds, Barry, 1986 Pitt.	20
Boone, Aaron, Cin. home wht.	20
Boone, Bret, Sea. wht.	20
Brenly, Bob, Ariz. home wht.	20
Brown, Kevin, L.A. home wht.	20
Buhner, Jay-Sea. Marin. home wht.	20
Burroughs, Sean-Rancho Cuca. (1,200)	15
Cameron, Mike-Sea. wht.	20
Campanella, Roy-Brklyn Dodg. home	20
Carter, Joe-Tor. home wht	20
Chavez, Eric-Oak. home wht	20
Cirillo, Jeff-Sea. home wht.	20
Clark, Tony-Det. Home wht	20
Clemens, Roger-NYY home wht	20
Clemens, Roger-NYY Road gray	20
Clemens, Roger-New Brit. Rockcats gry	20
Clemens, Roger-Columbus Clippers (3,000)	25
Clemente, Roberto-Pitts. home	30
Clemente, Roberto (1,001) D&J Collectibles	20
Clutch-Ana. mascot home wht	20
Cobb, Ty-Det. home wht classic	20
Conine, Jeff-DiMaggio Child. Hospit.	35
Counsell, Craig-Ariz. home wht	20
Counsell, Craig-Ariz. road gry	20
Damon, Johnny-Bos. home wht	20
Delgado, Carlos-Tor. home wht	20
Diamond-Tor. mascot wht	20
Dinger-Colo. mascot home wht.	20
Display Box Gonzalez Inner Carton (WS)	20
Display box Johnson Inner Carton (WS)	20

Display box Schilling Inner Carton (WS)	20
Dunn, Adam-Cinc. home wht.	20
Edmonds, Jim-St.L home wht	20
Farnsworth, Kyle Chic. Cubs alt Blue	20
Feller, Bob-Cleve. home wht	20
Feller, Bob-Cleve. Old Time	20
Fingers, Rollie-Oak.,1960s-70s	20
Finley, Steve-Ariz. home wht	20
Finley, Steve-Ariz. road gray	20
Floyd, Cliff-Fla. home wht #30	20
Fredbird-St.L mascot-wht jrsy	20
Freehan, Bill-Det. home	20
Garcia, Freddy-Sea. home wht	20
Garciaparra, N.-Bos. home wht	20
Garvey, Steve-LA 1970s	20
Garvey, Steve-S.D. 1980s	20
Gehrig, Lou-NYY Home wht Classic	20
Gehringer, Charlie-Det. old	20
Generic Baseball Boy Plain wht	20
Giambi, Jason-NYY 2002 wht	20
Gibson, Bob-St.L home wht	20
Giles, Brian-Pitt. wht	20
Glaus, Troy-Ana. wht	20
Gonzalez, Juan-Cleve. wht	20
Gonzalez, Juan-Cleve. gray #22	20
Gonzalez, Luis-Ariz. home wht	20
Gonzalez, Luis-Ariz. road gry	20
Grace, Mark-Ariz. wht #17	20
Grace, Mark-Ariz. road gray	20
Green, Shawn-LA. home wht	20
Griffey, Ken Jr.-Cinci. 2001 Home	20
Gwynn, Tony-SD wht	20
Hasegawa, Shigetoshi-Sea. home	20
Helton, Todd-Col. home	20
Higginson, Bobby-Det. 2001 home	20
Hoffman, Trevor-SD wht	20
Homer-Atl. mascot wht jrsy	20
Horton, Willie-Det. road gry #23	20
Hudson, Tim-Oak. wht	20
Ishii, Kazuhisa-LA wht	20
Jackson "Shoeless" Joe-W Sox home	20
Jenkins, Ferguson-Cubs '60s	20
Jeter, Derek-NYY 2001 home	20
Johnson, Chas.-Fla. home wht	20
Johnson, Nick-Columbus Clippers promo	20
Johnson, Randy-Ariz. 2001 home	20
Johnson, Randy-Ariz. road gray	20
Johnson, Randy-88 Indianapolis Indians	20
Jones, Andruw-Durham Bulls promo	25
Jones, Chipper-Macon Braves	25
Josh Gibson-Homestead Grays	20
Junction Jack-mascot Houston Astros	20
Kaline, Al-Det. home wht	20
Karros, Eric-LA Road gray	20
Kent, Jeff-SF Alt home blk jrsy	20
Killebrew, Harmon-(172) '65 Minn.	20
Komiyama, Satoru-NYM wht	20
Konerko, Paul-White Sox Road gray	20
Lasorda, Tommy-LA	20
Leiter, Al-NYM Alt home blk	20
Lo Duca, Paul-LA home wht	20
Lofton, Kenny-Clev. wht.	20
Maddux, Greg-Atl. home #31	20
Mariner Moose-Sea. alt home blu jrsy	20
Mariner Moose-Sea. wht jersey	20
Martinez, Edgar-Sea. wht.	20
Martinez, Pedro Boston Red Sox home	20
Martinez, Pedro-Great Falls Dod. promo	15
Martinez, Tino-NYY home wht.	20
Martinez, Tino-St. L Card 2002 wht home	20
Master Carton-Luis Gonzalez (WS)	20
Master Carton-Randy Johnson (WS)	20
Master Carton-Curt Schilling (WS)	20
Mattingly, Don-NYY home wht.	20
Mattingly, Don-Nashville Sounds promo	45
Mazeroski, Bill-Pitt Pirates-wht (past)	20
Mazeroski, Bil-Pitt Pirates-old wht	20
McGwire, Mark-St. L home wht	30
Morgan, Joe-Dur. Bulls pin uni promo	20
Morris, Matt-St. L white	20
Morris, Matt-Ark. Travelers white (1,000)	15
Mr. Met-NYM mascot home wht jrsy	20
Mr. Met-NYM mascot alt home blk jrsy	20
Mulder, Mark-Oak. white jersey	20
Munson, Thurman-NYY home wht	20
Musial, Stan-St. L Card 1942/1944	20
Mussina, Mike-NYY home wht.	20
Nevin, Phil-SD home wht	20
Nixon, Trot-Bos. home wht	20
Nomo, Hideo-LA home wht	20
Olerud, John-Sea. home #5	20
Ordonez, Magglio-WSox road gry	20
Paige, Satchell-Cleve	20
Palmeiro, Rafael-Tex. away gray	20
Parrish, Lance-Det. home	20
Paws-Det. mascot wht	20
Pettitte, Andy-NYY Grey road	20
Pettitte, Andy, NYY home white	20
Pettitte, Andy-3,600 w/o sponsor home	20
Philly Phanatic-Phil. mascot wht	20
Piazza, Mike-NYM 2001 away gray	20
Piazza, Mike-NYM 2001 home wht	20
Piazza, Mike-NYM alt home blk	20
Piazza, Mike-Norfolk Tides promo	30
Piniella, Lou-Sea. blue jacket	20
Pirate Parrot-Pitt mascot blk jersey	20
Posada, Jorge-NYY home wht.	20
Pujols, Albert-St. L home wht	20
QuackerJack-(1500) Long Island Ducks	20
Rally-Atlanta Braves mascot blue jrsy	20
Ramirez, Manny-Bos. home #24	20
Ripken, Cal Jr.-(retir) Balt. home wht	20
Rivera, Mariano-NYY home wht	20
Robinson, Brooks-Balt. wht	20
Rocky-N Brit Rockcats mascot wht/glass	20
Rodriguez, Alex-Tex Ran 2001 Home	20
Rodriguez, Ivan-Tex. 2001 home wht	20
Rolen, Scott-Phila. wht.	20
Rolen, Scott-SWB Red Barons promo	30
Rollins, Jimmy-Red Barons promo	20
Rollins, Jimmy-Reading Phillies promo	20
Rowdie-Indianapolis Indians mascot	20
Rowdy-Okl Redhawks mascot home wht	20
Ruth, Babe-NYY home wht classic	20
Ryan, Nolan-Tex. home wht #34	20
Ryan, Nolan-Hou. rainbow	20
Sasaki, Kazuhiro-Sea. road gray	20
Sasaki, Kazuhiro-Sea. home wht	20
Schilling, Curt-Ariz. World Series logo, wht	20
Schilling, Curt-Red Barons home promo	20
Schilling, Curt-Ariz. road gray	20
Schmidt, Mike-Phil. road gry #20	30
Scoop-Ana. mascot home wht	20
Sexson, Richie-Mil. home wht	20
Sheets, Ben-Indianapolis Indians	20
Shinjo, Tsuyoshi-NYM alt home blk	20
Shinjo, Tsuyoshi-SF. home wht #5	20
Slider-Cleveland Indians mascot wht	20
Smith, Bud-Mem. Redbirds wht promo	25
Soriano, Alfonso, NY Yankees	20
Sosa, Sammy-Cubs 200 SportsFest	20
Sosa, Sammy-Cubs Blue jersey	20
Sosa, Sammy-Cubs home wht	20
Stargell, Willie-Pitt. yellow/blk helmet	20
Stengel Casey-NYY home wht classic	20
Stomper-Oakl. mascot wht	20
Suzuki, Ichiro-Sea. home wht	20
Suzuki, Ichiroi-Sea. green batting practice	20
Suzuki, Ichiro-Sea. gray #51	20
Suzuki, Ichiro-Sea. blue jacket	20
Suzuki, Ichiro-Sea. alternate blue	20
Swinging Friar-SD mascot brn robe	20
Taguchi, So-St. L home wht	20
Tejada, Miguel-Oak. home wht	20
The Bird-Balt. mascot blk outfit	20
Thomas, Frank-W Sox #35 home	20
Thomas, Frank-W Sox #35 road	20
Thome, Jim-Clev. navy	20
Thome, Jim-Clev. wht	20
Thome, Jim-Clev. road gry #25	20
Torre, Joe-NYY Home wht	20
Trammell, Alan-Det. home	20
Valentine, Bobby-NYM 2001 Home	20
Vaughn, Mo-NYM alternate home	20
Ventura, Robin-NYM away gry	20
Vina, Fernando-St. L home #4	20
Vizquel, Omar-Clev. nvy blu #13	20
Vizquel, Omar-Clev. wht #13	20
Vizquel, Omar-Clev. Road gry #13	20
Vyborny, David-Blue Jackets home #9	20
Walker, Larry-Col. home	20
Wally-Boston Red Sox mascot wht	20
Wells, David-NYY home wht	20
Williams, Bernie-NYY Home	20
Williams, Matt-Ariz. home wht	20
Williams, Matt-Ariz. road gray	20
Williams, Mitch-Atlantic City Surf promo	20
Womack, Tony-Ariz. home wht	20
Womack, Tony-Ariz. road gray	20
Wood, Kerry-Cubs home wht	20
Yastrzemski, Carl-Bos, Dick Gordon (1,967)	48
Young, Cy-Bos home wht classic	50
Zimmer, Don-NYY dark blue MGR jacket	20
Zito, Barry-Oak. home wht	20

2002 ALEXANDER GLOBAL MINI MASCOT SERIES

Player	MT
Baxter, Ariz.	7
Bear, Minn	7
Dinger, Colo	7
FredBird, St. L.	7
Mariner Moose, Sea.	7
Mr. Met, Mets	7
Philly Phanatic, Phil	7
Slider, Clev.	7
Stomper, Oak.	7
Wally, Bos	7

2003 ALEXANDER GLOBAL ACTION POSE RETAIL

Player	MT
Lance Berkman, Hou	20
Barry Bonds, SF	20
Eric Chavez, Oak	20
Roger Clemens, NYY (promo)	20
Johnny Damon, Bos	20
Nomar Garciaparra, Bos	20
Jason Giambi, NYY	20
Brian Giles, Pitt	20
Troy Glaus, Ana.	20
Shawn Green, LA	20
Shea Hillenbrand, Bos	20
Eric Hinske, Tor.	20
Torii Hunter, Minn	20
Reggie Jackson, NYY	20
Derek Jeter, NYY	20
Randy Johnson, Ariz.	20
Ralph Kiner, Pitt	20
Derek Lowe, Bos.	20
Pedro Martinez, Bos	20
Tino Martinez, St. L.	20
Hideki Matsui, NYY	20
Mike Piazza, NYM	20
Mike Prior, Cubs	20
Pokey Reese, Pitt	20
Alex Rodriguez, Tex	20
Scott Rolen, St. L.	20
Tim Salmon, Ana	20
Mike Schmidt, Phil (promo)	20
Tom Seaver, NYM (promo)	20
Alfonso Soriano, NYY	20
Sammy Sosa, Cubs	20
Ichiro Suzuki, Sea.	20
Miguel Tejada, Oak	20
Jim Thome, Phil.	20
Jason Varitek, Bos	20
Tim Wakefield, Bos	20
Bernie Williams, NYY	20
Kerry Wood, Cubs	20

2003 ALEXANDER GLOBAL COOPERSTOWN

Player	MT
Ernie Banks	20
Ty Cobb	20
Lou Gehrig	20
Reggie Jackson	20
Stan Musial	20
Babe Ruth	20
Nolan Ryan	20
Cy Young	20

2003 ALEXANDER GLOBAL SUPERHEROES

Player	MT
Lance Berkman, Hou	15
Nomar Garciaparra, Bos	15
Jason Giambi, NYY	15
Jay Gibbons, Balt	15
Brian Giles, Pitt	15
Tom Glavine, NYM	15
Torii Hunter, Minn	15
Derek Jeter, NYY	15
Randy Johnson, Ariz.	15
Andruw Jones, Atl	15
Chipper Jones, Atl.	15
Pedro Martinez, Bos	15
Hideki Matsui, NYY	15
Mike Piazza, NYM	15
John Smoltz, Atl	15
Sammy Sosa, Cubs	15
Ichiro Suzuki, Sea	15
Jim Thome, Phil.	15

2003 BIG LEAGUE CHALLENGE MINI

Note: The first 6,000 fans in attendance at the Feb. 8, 2003, event received a mini bobbing head.

Player	MT
Lance Berkman	10
Brian Giles	10
Troy Glaus	10
Shawn Green	10
Rafael Palmeiro	10
Alex Rodriguez	10
Alfonso Soriano	10
Jim Thome	10

BOBBLEDREAMS

Player	MT
Rose, Pete Special (4,192)	35
Rose, Pete 2nd (10,000)	25
Pete Rose Philadelphia	25
Pete Rose Montreal	30

2003 CHICAGO WHITE SOX ALL-STARS

Note: This set was produced by Forever Collectibles and distributed through Sports Line

Player	MT
Billy Koch	30
Mark Buehrle	30
Magglio Ordonez	30
Paul Konerko	30
Bartolo Colon	30

DANBURY MINT

Player	MT
'02 Ken Griffey, Jr.	65
'02 Derek Jeter	65
02 Pedro Martinez	65
'02 Mark McGwire	65
'02 Sammy Sosa	65

DONRUSS CLASS OF '01 BOBBING HEADS

Player	MT
Bagwell, Jeff (2,000)	20
Bonds, Barry (2,000)	30
Clemens, Roger (2,000)	25
Garciaparra, Nomar (2,000)	20
Griffey, Ken (2,000)	25
Gwynn, Tony (2,000)	25
Jeter, Derek (2,000)	25
Jones, Chipper (2,000)	20
Martinez, Pedro (2,000)	20
McGwire, Mark (2,000)	30
Nomo, Hideo (2,000)	20
Piazza, Mike (2,000)	25
Pujols, Albert Road (1,000)	45
Pujols, Albert Home (2,000)	30
Ramirez, Manny (2,000)	20
Ripken, Cal (2,000)	25
Rodriguez, Alex (2,000)	20
Sasaki, Kazuhiro (2,000)	20
Shingo, Tsuyoshi (2,000)	20
Sosa, Sammy (2,000)	25
Suzuki, Ichiro Road (1,000)	50
Suzuki, Ichiro Home (2,000)	30

FOREVER COLLECTIBLES

Year & Player	MT
'02 Abreu, Bobby, Phil	25
'02 All-Star Brew Meister	25
'02 Alomar, Roberto, Mets	25
'02 Alomar, Roberto, Mets	25
'02 Alfonzo, Edgardo, Mets.	25
'03 Alfonzo, Edgardo, Mets	25
'03 Anderson, Brian, Clev	25
'02 Anderson, Sparky, Det.	25
'03 Ashburn, Richie, Phil	25
'02 Aurilia, Rich, S.F. (home)	25
'03 Aurila, Rich, SF	25
'02 Bagwell, Jeff, Hou. (home)	25
'03 Bagwell, Jeff, Hou	25
'03 Baker, Dusty, Cubs	25
'02 Banks, Ernie, Cubs (home)	25
'03 Bautista, Tony, Balt	25
'03 Beltran, Carlos, KC	25
'02 Bench, Johnny, Cin. (home)	25
'03 Benson, Kris, Pitt.	25
'02 Berkman, Lance, Hou.	25
'03 Berkman, Lance, Hou	25
'02 Berra, Yogi, Yankees (home)	25
'02 Biggio, Craig, Hou.	25
'02 Biggio, Craig, Hou	25
'02 Billy the Marlin, Fla. (home)	25
'02 Bonds, Barry, S.F. (home)	30
'03 Bonds, Barry, 5X MVP Champ	25
'03 Bonds, Barry, 2002 MVP	25
'03 Bonds, Barry, S.F.	25
'02 Boone, Bret, Sea. (home)	25
'02 Boone, Bret, Sea. (alternate)	25

'03 Boone, Bret, Sea ... 25
'02 "Brat" Sausage (Brewers All-Star) ... 25
'02 Brenly, Bob, Ariz. (wht pin/prpl cap) ... 25
'02 Brenly, Bob, Ariz. (prpl jrsy/prpl cap) ... 25
'02 Brett, George, KC (powder blue) ... 25
'02 Brett, George, KC (home) ... 25
'02 Brock, Lou, St. L. ... 25
'03 Buehrle, Mark ... 25
'03 Burnett, A.J., Fla ... 25
'02 Burrell, Pat, Phil. ... 25
'03 Burrell, Pat, Phil ... 25
'03 Byrd, Paul, ... 25
'02 Cameron, Mike, Seat. (home) ... 25
'02 Cameron, Mike, Seat. (alternate) ... 25
'03 Cameron, Mike, Seat. ... 25
'03 Carew, Rod, Minn ... 25
'03 Carter, Gary Met/Expos ... 25
'02 Casey, Sean, Cin. (home pin vest) ... 25
'03 Casey, Sean, Cin ... 25
'03 Castillo, Luis, Fla. ... 25
'03 Cepeda, Orlando, S.F. ... 25
'03 Chavez, Eric, Oak. ... 25
'02 Clemens, Roger, NYY (home) ... 25
'03 Clemens, Roger, NYY ... 25
'02 Clemente, Roberto, Pitt. (home) ... 35
'03 Clemente, Roberto, Pitt (Stats) ... 35
'03 Colon, Bartolo, ChiSox ... 25
'03 Contreras, Jose, NYY ... 25
'03 Cordova, Marty ... 25
'02 Counsell, Craig, Ariz. (wht pin/prpl cap) ... 25
'02 Counsell, Craig, Ariz. (blk jrsy/cap) ... 25
'02 Delgado, Carlos, Tor. ... 25
'03 DiMaggio, Joe (Home) ... 35
'03 DiMaggio, Joe (Road) ... 35
'03 DiMaggio, Joe (Stat) ... 35
'02 Drew, J.D., St. L. (away) ... 25
'03 Drew, J.D., St. L. ... 25
'02 Dunn, Adam, Cin. (home pin vest) ... 25
'03 Dunn, Adam, Cin. ... 25
'02 Dye, Jermaine, Oak. ... 25
'03 Dye, Jermaine, Oak ... 25
'03 Edmonds, Jim, St. L ... 25
'03 Erstad, Darin, Ana ... 25
'02 Feller, Bob (home), Clev. ... 25
'02 Fingers, Rollie, Oak. ... 25
'02 Fisk, Carlton, Boston (home) ... 25
'02 Ford, Whitey, NYY ... 25
'03 Gagne, Eric, LA ... 25
'03 Gagne, Eric, LA ... 25
'03 Garcia, Freddy, Sea ... 25
'03 Garcia, Karim, Clev ... 25
'02 Garciaparra, Nomar, Bos. (home) ... 25
'03 Garciaparra, Nomar, Bos ... 25
'03 Gehrig, Lou, NYY ... 25
'02 Giambi, Jason, NYY (home) ... 25
'02 Giambi, Jason, NYY (away) ... 25
'03 Giambi, Jason, NYY ... 25
'03 Gibbons, Jay ,Balt ... 25
'03 Gibson, Bob, St. L. ... 25
'02 Giles, Brian, Pitt. (home) ... 25
'03 Giles, Brian, Pitt ... 25
'03 Glaus, Troy, Ana. ... 25
'03 Glavine, Tom, Mets ... 25
'03 Gonzalez, Juan ... 25
'02 Gonzalez, Luiz, Ariz. (prpl jrsy/cap) ... 25
'02 Gonzalez, Luiz, Ariz. (wht pin/prpl cap) 25
'03 Gonzalez, Luiz, Ariz ... 25
'02 Grace, Mark, Ariz. (wht pin/prpl cap) ... 25
'02 Grace, Mark, Ariz. (prpl jrsy/cap) ... 25
'02 Green, Shawn, LA ... 25
'03 Green, Shawn, LA ... 25
'02 Griffey Jr. Ken, Cin. (home pin vest) ... 25
'02 Griffey/Thomas (2,500) ... 50
'03 Griffey, Ken Jr. ... 25
'03 Guerrero, Vladimir, Mon. ... 25
'02 Helton, Todd, Col. (home) ... 25
'03 Helton, Todd, Col ... 25
'02 Higginson, Bobby, Det. (home) ... 25
'03 Higginson, Bobby, Det. ... 25
'03 Hillenbrand, Shea, Bos, ... 25
'03 Hoffman, Trevor, S.D. ... 25
'02 Hudson, Tim, Oak ... 25
'02 Hudson, Tim, Oak ... 25
'03 Hunter, Catfish, NYY ... 25
'03 Hunter, Torri, Min ... 25
'03 Ibanez, Raul, KC ... 25
'02 Ichiro, Suzuki, Sea. (MVP-White) ... 25
'02 Ichiro, Suzuki, Sea. (ROY-Gray) ... 25
'02 Ichiro, Suzuki, Sea. (Alternate) ... 25
'02 Ichiro, Suzuki, Sea. (home) ... 25
'03 Ichiro, Suzuki, Sea ... 25
'02 Ishii, Kazuhisa, LA (home) ... 25
'02 Ishii, Kazuhisa, LA (away) ... 25
'03 Ishii, Kazuhisa, LA ... 25

'03 Isringhausen, Jason ... 25
'02 Jackson, Reggie, NYY ... 25
'03 Jenkins, Fergie, Cubs ... 25
'02 Jenkins, Geoff, Mil ... 25
'02 Jenkins, Geoff, Mil ... 25
'03 Jennings, Jason, Col ... 25
'02 Jeter, Derek, NYY (home) ... 25
'02 Jeter, Derek, NYY (away) ... 25
'03 Jeter, Derek, NYY ... 25
'02 Johnson, Randy, Ariz. (wht home pin) ... 25
'02 Johnson Randy, Ariz. (blk jrsy/cap) ... 25
'02 Johnson Randy, Ari.
(gray slvls pin/cap) ... 25
'03 Johnson, Randy, Ariz ... 25
'03 Jones, Andruw, Atl. ... 25
'03 Jones, Chipper, Atl ... 25
'02 Jones, Chipper, Atl. (road) ... 25
'02 Jones, Chipper, Atl. (home) ... 25
'02 Kaline, Al, Det. (home) ... 25
'03 Kearns, Austin, Cin. ... 25
'02 Kendall, Jason, Pit. (home) ... 25
'03 Kendall, Jason, Pit. ... 25
'03 Killebrew, Harmon, Minn. ... 25
'03 Kim, Sun Woo, Bos., ... 25
'03 Klesko, Ryan, S.D. ... 25
'02 Knoblauch, Chuck, KC ... 25
'02 Konerko, Paul, CWS ... 25
'03 Konerko, Paul, CWS ... 25
'03 Koskie, Corey, Min. ... 25
'03 Kotsay, Mark, SD ... 25
'02 Larkin, Barry, Cin. (home pin vest) ... 25
'03 Larkin, Barry, Cin. ... 25
'02 Lasorda, Tommy, LA ... 25
'03 Lawrence, Brian, S.D. ... 25
'02 Lawton, Matt, Cle. (home) ... 25
'03 Lawton, Matt, Cle ... 25
'03 Leiter, Al, NYM ... 25
'02 Lo Duca, Paul, L.A. ... 25
'03 Lo Duca, Paul, LA ... 25
'02 Lofton, Kenny, White Sox ... 25
'03 Lopez, Rodrigo, Balt ... 25
'03 Lowe, Derek, Bos ... 25
'03 Lowell, Mike, Fla. ... 25
'03 Maddux, Greg, Atl ... 25
'03 Mantle, Mickey, NYY, Stat ... 35
'03 Mantle, Mickey, NYY, 3X MVP ... 35
'03 Marichal, Juan, S.F. ... 25
'02 Martinez, Edgar, Sea. (alternate) ... 25
'03 Martinez, Edgar, Sea ... 25
'02 Martinez, Pedro, Bos. (home) ... 25
'03 Martinez, Pedro, Bos ... 25
'02 Martinez, Tino, St. L. (away) ... 25
'03 Martinez, Tino, St. L. ... 25
'02 Mathews, Eddie, Mil. Braves ... 25
'03 Matsui, Hideki, NYY ... 25
'02 Mattingly, Don, NYY ... 25
'03 McCovey, Willie, S.F. ... 25
'03 McGriff, Fred, Cubs ... 25
'03 Mientkiewicz, Doug, Minn. ... 25
'03 Mondesi, Raul, NYY, ... 20
'02 Morgan, Joe (home), Cin. ... 25
'03 Morris, Matt, St. L ... 25
'03 Mulder, Mark, Oak ... 25
'02 Musial, Stan, St. L. ... 35
'03 Mussina, Mike, NYY ... 25
'03 Nen, Robb, S.F., ... 25
'02 Nomo, Hideo, LA ... 25
'03 Nomo, Hideo, LA ... 25
'02 Ordonez, Magglio, CWS ... 25
'03 Ordonez, Magglio, CWS ... 25
'03 Oswalt, Roy, Hou. ... 25
'03 Palmeiro, Rafael, Tex. ... 25
'03 Pena, Carlos ... 25
'03 Perry, Gaylord, S.F. ... 25
'02 Pettitte, Andy, NYY (home) ... 25
'03 Pettitte, Andy, NYY ... 25
'02 Piazza, Mike (away), Mets ... 25
'02 Piazza, Mike (home), Mets ... 25
'02 Piazza, Mike, Mets ... 25
'03 Pierzynski, A.J., Min. ... 25
'03 Pineiro, Joel, Sea ... 20
'02 Posada, Jorge, NYY (home) ... 25
'03 Posada, Jorge, NYY ... 25
'03 Prior, Mark, Cubs, ... 25
'02 Pujols, Albert, St. L. (home) ... 25
'02 Pujols, Albert, St. L. (away) ... 25
'03 Pujols, Albert, St. L ... 25
'03 Radke, Brad, Min ... 25
'02 Ramirez, Manny, Bos. (home) ... 25
'03 Redman, Mark, Det. ... 20
'02 Ripken, Cal, Balt. ... 25
'03 Rivera, Mariano ... 25
'02 Rizzuto, Phil, NYY ... 25
'03 Robinson, Brooks, Balt ... 25

'02 Rodriguez, Alex, Tex. (home) ... 25
'03 Rodriguez, Alex, Tex ... 25
'02 Rolen, Scott, Phil. ... 25
'02 Rolen, Scott, Phil ... 25
'03 Rollins, Jimmy, Phil ... 25
'03 Ruth, Babe, NYY ... 25
'02 Ryan, Nolan, Astros (home) ... 30
'02 Ryan, Nolan, Rangers (home) ... 30
'03 Ryan, Nolan, Calif. ... 25
'03 Ryan, Nolan, Mets ... 25
'03 Sabathia, C.C. ... 25
'02 Sasaki, Kazuhiro, Sea. (Alternate) ... 25
'03 Sasaki, Kazuhiro, Seat ... 25
'02 Schilling, Curt, Ariz. (gray pin/blk cap) ... 25
'02 Schilling, Curt, Ariz. (wht pin/prpl cap) ... 25
'02 Schilling, Curt, Ariz. (blk jrsy/cap) ... 25
'03 Schilling, Curt, Ariz ... 25
'03 Schmidt, Jason, SF ... 25
'02 Schmidt, Mike, Phi. (home) ... 35
'02 Seaver, Tom, Mets (home) ... 25
'03 Sheets, Ben, Mil ... 25
'02 Sheffield, Gary, Atl (home) ... 25
'03 Sheffield, Gary, Atl ... 25
'02 Shinjo, Tsuyoshi, S.F. (home) ... 25
'03 Shinjo, Tsuyoshi, NYM ... 25
'03 Smoltz, John, Atl ... 25
'03 Soriano, Alfonso, NYY, ... 25
'02 Sosa, Sammy, Cubs (home) ... 25
'03 Sosa, Sammy, Cubs ... 25
'03 Spahn, Warren, Milw. ... 25
'03 Spivey, Junior, Ariz ... 25
'02 Stargell, Willie, Pitt. (home) ... 25
'03 Sweeney, Mark, KC ... 25
'03 Tejada, Miguel, 2002 AL MVP ... 25
'03 Tejada, Miguel, Oak ... 25
'03 Thomas, Frank, CWS ... 25
'02 Thome, Jim, Cle. (home) ... 25
'02 Thome, Jim, Cle. (road) ... 25
'03 Thome, Jim, Phil ... 25
'03 Torre, Joe, NYY ... 25
'02 Vaughn, Mo, Mets ... 25
'03 Vaughn, Mo, Mets ... 25
'02 Vizquel, Omar, Cle. (road) ... 25
'02 Vizquel, Omar, Cle. (home) ... 25
'03 Vizquel, Omar, Cle ... 25
'03 Wagner, Billy, Hou ... 25
'02 Walker, Larry, Colo. (home) ... 25
'03 Walker, Larry, Colo ... 25
'03 Washburn, Jarrod, Ana ... 25
'03 Weaver, Jeff, NYY, ... 25
'03 Weaver, Jeff, NYY ... 25
'02 Wells, David, NYY (home) ... 25
'03 Wells, David, NYY ... 25
'02 Williams, Bernie, NYY (home) ... 25
'03 Williams, Bernie, NYY ... 25
'03 Williams, Mike, Pitt. ... 20
'03 Williams, Ted, Bos., Stat ... 35
'03 Williams, Ted, Bos., 2X MVP ... 35
'03 Wilson, Preston, Fla. ... 25
'03 Wood, Kerry, Cubs ... 25
'03 Yount, Robin, Milw. ... 25
'03 Zito, Barry, Oak ... 25

2002 FOREVER COLLECTIBLES WORLD SERIES

Player	MT
Garret Anderson	25
Darin Erstad	25
Troy Glaus	25
Adam Kennedy	25
Troy Percival	25
Francisco Rodriguez	25
Tim Salmon	25
Jarrod Washburn	25
Five-player Mini-Set	30

2003 FOREVER COLLECTIBLES ALL-STARS

Player	MT
Barry Bonds	25
Nomar Garciaparra	25
Ichiro	25
Derek Jeter	25
Chipper Jones	25
Mike Piazza	25
Albert Pujols	25
Alex Rodriguez	25
Alfonso Soriano	25
Sammy Sosa	25

2003 FOREVER COLLECTIBLES MLB SUPERHEROES

Player	MT
Lance Berkman	20
Barry Bonds	20
Eric Chavez	20
Adam Dunn	20
Jim Edmonds	20
Nomar Garciaparra	20
Jason Giambi	20
Troy Glaus	20
Luis Gonzalez	20
Ken Griffey Jr.	20
Vladimir Guerrero	20
Trevor Hoffman	20
Torii Hunter	20
Kazuhisa Ishii	20
Derek Jeter	20
Randy Johnson	20
Chipper Jones	20
Ryan Klesko	20
Pedro Martinez	20
Hideki Matsui	20
Ichiro Suzuki	20
Derek Jeter	20
Chipper Jones	20
Kazuhisa Ishii	20
Albert Pujols	20
Alex Rodriguez	20
Alfonso Soriano	20
Sammy Sosa	20
Omar Vizquel	20

2003 FOREVER COLLECTIBLES GOLD GLOVE LEADERS

Player	MT
Roberto Alomar, Cle.	35
Johnny Bench, Cinci	35
Roberto Clemente, Pitt.	35
Ken Griffey Jr., Sea.	35
Keith Hernandez, Mets	35
Jim Kaat, Minn.	35
Brooks Robinson, Balt	35
Ozzie Smith, St. L	35

2003 FOREVER COLLECTIBLES GOLD GLOVE SERIES

Player	MT
Brad Ausmus, Hou	30
Barry Bonds, SF	30
Bret Boone, Sea	30
Eric Chavez, Oak	30
Jim Edmonds, St. L	30
Darin Erstad, Ana	30
Bob Gibson, St. L	30
Torii Hunger, Min	30
Ichiro Suzuki, Sea	30
Andruw Jones, Atl	30
Greg Maddux, Atl.	30
Don Mattingly, NYY	30
Mark McGwire, Oak	30
B. Molina, Ana	30
John Olerud, Sea	30
Edgar Renteria, St. L	30
Alex Rodriguez, Tex	30
K. Rogers, Tex	30
Scott Rolen, St. L	30
Fernando Vina, St. L	30
Omar Vizquel, Cle.	30
Larry Walker, Coco	30

2002 FOREVER COLLECTIBLES MINI

Year & Player	MT
'02 Alomar, Robert, Mets, home alt.	15
'02 Bagwell, Jeff, Hou. home	15
'02 Banks, Ernie, Cubs	15
'02 Berra, Yogi, NYY	15
'02 Bonds, Barry, SF, home	15
'02 Cameron, Mike, Sea. home	15
'02 Clemens, Roger, NYY, home	15
'02 Clemente, Roberto, Pitt.	15
'02 Dunn, Adam, Cin., home	15
'02 Fisk, Carlton, Bos.	15
'02 Garciaparra, Nomar, Bos., home	15
'02 Giambi, Jason, NYY home	15
'02 Giles, Brian, Pitt., home	15
'02 Ishii, Kazuhisa, LA, home	15
'02 Jeter, Derek, NYY, home	15
'02 Jeter, Derek, NYY, away	15
'02 Johnson, Randy, Ariz., home	15
'02 Jones, Chipper, Atl., home	15
'02 Konerko, Paul, White Sox, home	15
'02 Mattingly, Don, NYY	15
'02 Piazza, Mike, Mets, road	15
'02 Pujols, Albert, St. L, home	15
'02 Ripken, Cal, Balt.	15
'02 Rizzuto, Phil, NYY	15
'02 Ryan, Nolan, Hou.	15
'02 Ryan, Nolan, Tex.	15
'02 Schmidt, Mike, Phil.	15

Player	MT
'02 Sexson, Richie, Mil.	15
'02 Sosa, Sammy, Cubs, home	15
'02 Thome, Jim, Clev., home	15
'02 Vaughn, Mo, Mets, home	15
'02 Vizquel, Omar, Clev. home	15
'02 Wells, David, NYY, home	15
'02 Williams, Bernie, NYY, home	15

2003 FOREVER COLLECTIBLES MINI

Player	MT
Alfonso, E., S.F.	15
Anderson, Garret, Ana	15
Bagwell, Jeff, Hou	15
Baker, Dusty, Cubs	15
Bell, D., Phil.	15
Berkman, Lance, Hou	15
Berra, Yogi, NYY	15
Biggio, Craig, Hou	15
Bonds, Barry, SF	15
Casey, Sean, Cin	15
Clemens, Roger, NYY	15
Clemente, Roberto, Pitt	15
Drew, J.D. St. L	15
Dunn, Adam, Cin.	15
Durham, Ray, S.F.	15
Edmonds, Jim, St. L	15
Erstad, Darin, Ana	15
Ford, Whitey, NYY	15
Gagne, Eric, LA	15
Garcia, K., Seat.	15
Garciaparra, Nomar	15
Giambi, Jason	15
Giles, Brian	15
Glaus, Troy, Ana	15
Glavine, Tom, Mets	15
Gonzalez, Luis, Ariz.	15
Green, Shawn, LA	15
Griffey, Ken, Jr., Cin.	15
Hampton, Mike, Atl	15
Hillenbrand, Shea, Bos	15
Hunter, Torii, Min.	15
Ichiro, Suzuki, Seat.	15
Ishii, Kazuhisa, Sea.	15
Jackson, Reggie, NYY	15
Jeter, Derek, NYY	15
Jones, Andruw, Atl	15
Jones, Chipper, Atl	15
Kendall, Jason, Pitt.	15
Kent, Jeff, S.F.	15
Larkin, Barry, Cin.	15
Leiter, Al	15
LoDuca, Paul, LA	15
Mantle, Mickey, NYY	15
Martinez, Pedro, Bos	15
Matsui, Hideki.	15
Millwood, Kevin, Phil.	15
Milton, E., Minn	15
Mussina, Mike, NYY	15
Nen, Robb., S.F.	15
Nomo, Hideo, LA	15
Pettitte, Andy, NYY	15
Piazza, Mike, Mets	15
Pierzynski, A., Minn	15
Posada, Jorge, NYY	15
Prior, Mark, Cubs	15
Pujols, Albert, St. L	15
Radke, Brad, Minn.	15
Ramirez, Manny, Bos	15
Rivera, Mariano, NYY	15
Rizzuto, Phil, NYY	15
Rodriguez, Alex, Tex.	15
Rolen, Scott, St. L	15
Rollins, J., Phil	15
Sabathia, C.C., Cle	15
Sasaki, K., Sea.	15
Sexson, Richie, Mil.	15
Smoltz, John, Atla	15
Soriano, Alfonso, NYY	15
Sosa, Sammy, Cubs	15
Tejada, Miguel, Oak.	15
Thome, Jim, Phil	15
Torre, Joe, NYY	15
Vaughn, Mo, Mets	15
Ventura, Robin, NYY	15
Vizquel, Omar, Clev	15
Washburn, Jarrod, Ana	15
Wells, David, NYY	15
Williams, Bernie, NYY	15
Williams, Ted, Bos.	15
Wood, Kerry, Cubs	15

GIANTS/CARL'S JR.

Player	MT
'01 Dusty Baker	30

Player	MT
'01 Barry Bonds	70
'01 Jeff Kent	30
'01 J.T. Snow	30
'02 Tsuyoshi Shinjo	10
'02 Rich Aurilia	20
'02 Robb Nen	10
'02 Barry Bonds	30

NCAA TEAM GIVEAWAYS

Player	MT
'02 Tony Gywnn, S. Diego St. (10,000)	15

MEMORY COMPANY

Year & Player	MT
'02 Bonds, Barry (3,500)	60
'02 Garciaparra, Nomar (3,500)	45
'02 Griffey, Ken (3,500)	45
'02 Jeter, Derek (3,500)	60
'02 Jones, Chipper (3,500)	45
'02 McGwire Mark (3,500)	45
'02 Piazza, Mike (3,500)	45
'02 Rodriguez, Alex (3,500)	45
'02 Sosa, Sammy (3,500)	45
'02 Suzuki, Ichiro (3,500)	45

PRO TEAM GENERIC BOBBERS

Team	MT
'01 Anaheim Angels	30
'01 Atlanta Braves	30
'01 Arizona Diamondbacks	30
'01 Baltimore Orioles	30
'01 Boston Red Sox	30
'01 Chicago Cubs	30
'01 Chicago White Sox	30
'01 Cincinnati Reds	30
'01 Cleveland Indians	30
'01 Colorado Rockies	30
'01 Detroit Tigers	30
'01 Florida Marlins	30
'01 Houston Astros	30
'01 Kansas City Royals	30
'01 Los Angeles Dodgers	30
'01 Milwaukee Brewers	30
'01 Minnesota Twins	30
'01 New York Mets	30
'01 New York Yankees	30
'01 Oakland Athletics	30
'01 Philadelphia Phillies	30
'01 Pittsburgh Pirates	30
'01 San Diego Padres	30
'01 San Francisco Giants	30
'01 St. Louis Cardinals	30
'01 Seattle Mariners	30
'01 Tampa Bay Devil Rays	30
'01 Texas Rangers	30
'02 Anaheim Angels	30
'02 Atlanta Braves	30
'02 Arizona Diamondbacks	30
'02 Baltimore Orioles	30
'02 Boston Red Sox	30
'02 Chicago Cubs	30
'02 Chicago White Sox	30
'02 Cincinnati Reds	30
'02 Cleveland Indians	30
'02 Colorado Rockies	30
'02 Detroit Tigers	30
'02 Florida Marlins	30
'02 Houston Astros	30
'02 Kansas City Royals	30
'02 Los Angeles Dodgers	30
'02 Milwaukee Brewers	30
'02 Minnesota Twins	30
'02 New York Mets	30
'02 New York Yankees	30
'02 Oakland Athletics	30
'02 Philadelphia Phillies	30
'02 Pittsburgh Pirates	30
'02 San Diego Padres	30
'02 St. Louis Cardinals	30
'02 Seattle Mariners	30
'02 Tampa Bay Devil Rays	30
'02 Texas Rangers	30

2003 MEMORY CO. PLAYERS

Player	MT
Barry Bonds, SF	55
Roger Clemens, NYY	55
Jason Giambi, NYY	55
Todd Helton, Colo.	55
Ichiro, Sea.	55
Derek Jeter, NYY	55
Randy Johnson, Ariz.	55
Pedro Martinez, Bos.	55
Albert Pujols, StL	55
Curt Schilling, Ariz	55

2002 POST CEREAL 3-INCH TALL

Player	MT
Jeff Bagwell	5
Jason Giambi	5
Luis Gonzalez	5
Chipper Jones	5
Pedro Martinez	5
Mike Piazza	5
Alex Rodriguez	5
Sammy Sosa	5
Ichiro Suzuki	5
Bernie Williams	5
American League	5
National League	5

2003 POST CEREAL MINI

Player	MT
Jason Giambi	5
Troy Glaus	5
Ken Griffey Jr.	3
Torii Hunter	3
Mike Piazza	3
Alex Rodriguez	6
Curt Schilling	3
John Smoltz	2
Sammy Sosa	5
Ichiro Suzuki	5

SAM PLAYERS

Note: Gold base SAM bobbing heads were scheduled to be signed by the player but were not. These were released without a signature. Also, there were two models or versions of the 1997 gray uniform Ken Griffey Jr. issued with differences in color shade and with different model numbers as reflected on the certificates enclosed with the bobbing heads. Model number 2400-G was a 500-issue size edition with a darker brown bat and somewhat lighter skin tone than model number 2400-GA with an edition size of 1,000.

Player	MT
Aaron, Hank 500 HR	100
Alomar, Roberto	50
Aparicio, Luis	90
Banks, Ernie	90
Banks, Ernie #4 (Error)	150
Banks, Ernie 500 HR	90
Bench, Johnny	175
Berra, Yogi	60
Berra, Yogi Autographed	150
Brett, George Blue	100
Brett, George White	75
Carew, Rod	100
Carlton, Steve	150
Carter, Gary	125
Clemens, Roger	125
Clemente, Roberto	250
Cobb. Ty	90
Drew, J.D.	50
Drysdale, Don	60
Fingers, Rollie A's	125
Fingers, Rollie Brewers	75
Ford, Whitey	60
Ford, Whitey Autographed	150
Garciaparra, Nomar	60
Gehrig, Lou	100
Gibson, Bob	125
Gonzalez, Juan	50
Griffey, Ken White	60
Griffey, Ken Aqua	80
Griffey, Ken Gray, model #2400-GA (1,000)	90
Griffey, Ken Reds Cap B.	75
Griffey, Ken Autographed	375
Gwynn, Tony P/S	75
Gwynn, Tony Blue	95
Jackson, Martinez	150
Jackson, Reggie	125
Jackson, Reggie 500 HR	90
Jeter, Derek PS	85
Jeter, Derek Grey	75
Jeter, Derek Autographed	200
Jones, Chipper	50
Jordan, Michael Barons	90
Mantle, Mickey PS	125
Mantle, Mickey Grey	75
Maris, Roger PS	100
Maris, Roger Grey	60
Mays, Willie	100
Mays, Willie 500 HR	90
McCovey, Willie	60
McCovey, Willie 500 HR	90
McGwire, Mark White	80
McGwire, Mark Red	60

Player	MT
McGwire, Mark Grey	60
Morgan, Joe	125
Murray, Eddie	175
Murray, Eddie 500 HR	90
Musial, Stan	60
Nomo, Hideo	50
Paige, Satchel	150
Palmer, Jim	100
Perry, Gaylord	40
Perez, Tony	80
Piazza, Mike	75
Puckett, Kirby	200
Ripken, Cal White	75
Ripken, Cal Black	75
Ripken, Cal Gray	75
Ripken, Cal Signed	325
Rizzuto, Phil	80
Robinson, Brooks	100
Robinson, Frank	60
Robinson, Frank 500 HR	90
Robinson, Jackie	80
Rodriguez, Alex	50
Rodriguez, Ivan	50
Rose, Pete	250
Ruth, Babe	100
Ryan, Nolan Regular	80
Ryan, Nolan Angels	80
Ryan, Nolan Astros	80
Ryan, Nolan Mets	80
Ryan, Nolan Rangers	80
Schmidt, Mike	90
Schmidt, Mike 500 HR	90
Seaver, Tom	60
Seaver, Tom Autographed	250
Sosa, Sammy Blue	60
Sosa, Sammy Pin Stripe	60
Thomas, Frank	60
Thomas, Frank Pinstripe	400
Snider, Duke	200
Stargell, Willie Yellow	125
Stargell, Willie Black	100
Thome, Jim	50
Vaughn, Mo	50
Vaughn, Mo Signed	150
Walker, Larry	50
Williams, Ted	200
Williams, Ted 500 HR	125
Yastrzemski, Carl	350

SAM MASCOTS

Team	MT
Atlanta Braves	50
Baltimore Orioles	50
Chicago Cubs	50
Cincinnati Reds	50
Clev Indians	50
Detroit Tigers	50
Pittsburgh Pirates	50
St. Louis Cardinals	50

SAM TEAMS

Note: In 1999, SAM produced a series of 30 MLB baseball team dolls in 1999 which featured multi-racial heads (either white, black face or brown faces). Only one type head was manufactured for each team (for example: the Pirates feature a black-faced player, the Cubs a white-faced player and the Mets a brown-faced player).

Team	MT
Anaheim Angels (1,000)	50
Arizona Diamondbacks (1,000)	50
Atlanta Braves (1,000)	50
Baltimore Orioles (1,000)	50
Boston Red Sox (1,000)	50
Chicago Cubs (1,000)	50
Chicago White Sox (1,000)	50
Cincinnati Reds (1,000)	50
Cleveland Indians (1,000)	50
Colorado Rockies (1,000)	50
Detroit Tigers (1,000)	50
Florida Marlins (1,000)	50
Houston Astros (1,000)	50
Kansas City Royals (1,000)	50
Los Angeles Dodgers (1,000)	50
Milwaukee Brewers (1,000)	50
Minnesota Twins (1,000)	50
Montreal Expos (1,000)	50
New York Mets (1,000)	50
New York Yankees (1,000)	50
Oakland Athletics (1,000)	50
Philadelphia Phillies (1,000)	50
Pittsburgh Pirates (1,000)	50
St. Louis Cardinals (1,000)	50

Jason Williams (4,000), Mem.	80
Crunch the mascot (4,000), Minn.	15
Kevin Garnett (6,000), Minn., white	35
Kevin Garnett, Minn, blue	35
Kevin McHale (4,000), Minn., blue sweat.	30
Wally Szczerbiak (4,000), Minn., blue.	40
Jason Kidd, NJ	45
Jason Kidd, NJ, signed, season tix holders	75
Keith Van Horn,NJ	20
Allan Houston, NY.	25
Darrell Armstrong (5,000), Orl.	20
Patrick Ewing (5,000), Orl.	55
Grant Hill (5,000), Orl.	40
Tracy McGrady (5,000), Orl.	65
Mike Miller (5,000), Orl.	15
Moses Malone (5,000), Phi.	40
Dikembe Mutombo (5,000), Phi.	50
Stephon Marbury (8,000), Pho.	20
Dan Majerle (8,000), Pho.	25
Arvydas Sabonis, Port.	20
Antonio Daniels (3,000), S.A.	15
Tim Duncan (3,000), S.A.	100
Rashard Lewis, Sea.	15
Desmond Mason, Sea.	40
Nate McMillan, Sea.	20
Gary Payton, Sea. white (10,000).	35
Marshall mascot, Utah	15
Karl Malone, Utah	45
Jerry Sloan, Utah	20
Kwame Brown, Wash.	15

2002 WNBA TEAM GIVEAWAYS

Player	MT
Richie Adubato, N.Y. coach	25
Van Chancellor, Hou. coach	45
Becky Hammon, N.Y.	50
Teresa Weatherspoon, N.Y.	50

2002-03 NBA TEAM GIVEAWAYS

Player	MT
NBA On TNT set (5,000), Atlanta Ernie Johnson, Charles Barkley and Kenny Smith (5,000 fans received entire set)	35
Glenn Robinson, Atl. (5,000)	10
Red Auerbach, Bos. (10,000)	30
Jalen Rose, Chi	25
Johnny "Red" Kerr, Chi	15
Joe Tait bobble belly, Cle.	15
Mark Cuban, Dal. (5,000)	10
Richard Hamilton, Det (10,000)	15
Richard Hamilton, Det (10,000), talking	20
Jon Barry, Det (10,000)	25
Jerry Stackhouse, Det (10,000)	20
Ben Wallace, Det. (10,000) Big Hair, road	20
Ben Wallace, Det (10,000), talking	30
Zeljko Rebraca, Det. (10,000)	15
Chauncey Billups, Det (10,000)	10
Corliss Williamson, Det (10,000)	15
Alvin Attles, G.S (5,000)	25
Rick Barry , G.S. (5,000)	15
Nate Thurmond, G.S. (5,000)	20
Chris Mullin, G.S. (5,000)	25
Antawn Jamison, G.S. (5,000)	25
Thunder mascot, G.S. (mini-ticket plans)	30
Yao Ming, Hou.	35
Calvin Murphy, Hou.	35
Elgin Baylor, LAC (5,000)	25
Stromile Swift, Mem	20
Ray Allen, Mil. (5,000)	25
Bango mascot, Mil (5,000)	40
Rasho Nesterovic, Minn.	20
Flip Saunders, Minn	35
Joe Smith, Minn.	25
Walt "Clyde" Frazier, NY	35
Doc Rivers, Orl. (5,000)	15
Tracy McGrady, Orl. (5,000)	35
Julius Erving Bobblehead, Orl (5,000)	50
Dan Majerle, Phoe (7,000)	35
Connie Hawkins, Phoe (7,000)	30
Amare Stoudemire, Phoe (7,000)	35
Malik Rose, SA (3,000)	40
Tim Duncan, SA (3,000)	45
Tony Parker, SA (3,000)	40
Ray Allen, Sea. (10,000)	30
Kevin Calabro, Sea, Talking (10,000)	35
Gary Payton, Sea, Talking (10,000)	25
Brent Barry, Sea Talking (10,000)	20
John Stockton, Utah	20
Andrei Kirilenko , Utah	15
Bear mascot, Utah	15
Jared Jeffries, Wash.	15

ALEXANDER GLOBAL BOBBLE DOBBLES

Player	MT
Blue Devil-Duke mascot	20

Daniels, Antonio-S.A. white promo	75
Daniels, Antonio-S.A. road jsy promo	60
Garnett, Kevin-Minn. blue uni promo	30
Garnett, Kevin-Minn. black uni promo	30
Gorilla, Phoe. Suns mascot promo	35
Lewis, Rashard-Seattle Sonics away	20
Lewis, Rashard-Sea Sonics away green	20
Marion, Shawn-Phoe. (8,000) promo	35
Marshall, Donyell-Utah pur. (1,500) pro	20
Marshall, Donyell-Utah wht (1,500) pro	20
Mashburn, Jamal-Char. (1,000) promo	55
Mason, Desmond-Seattle Sonics away	20
Mason, Desmond-Sea Sonics away green	20
McMillan, Nate-Sea Sonics 1975-95 wht	20
McMillian, Nate-Sea Sonics old Sonics	20
Payton, Gary-Seattle Sonics away	20
Payton, Gary-Sea Sonics 1975-95 away grn	20
Raptor-Toronto mascot home wht	20
Russell, Bryon-Utah white promo	30
Szczerbiak, Wally-Minn., white. promo	20

2002 CARL'S JR SACRAMENTO KINGS

Player	MT
Doug Christie	20
Peja Stojakovic	40
Mike Bibby	35
Vlade Divac	25
Scot Pollard	20

2003 CARL'S JR SACRAMENTO KINGS

Player	MT
Bobby Jackson	15
Keon Clark	15
Gerald Wallace	15
Scot Pollard	20
Hedo Turkoglu	15

FOREVER COLLECTIBLES 2002-03 NBA CURRENT PLAYERS

Player	MT
Shareef Abdur-Rahim, Atl	25
Ray Allen, Milw.	25
Vin Baker, Bos.	25
Mike Bibby, Sac	25
Elton Brand, LAC	25
Kobe Bryant, LAL	30
Caron Butler, Mia	25
Marcus Camby, Den.	25
Vince Carter, Tor.	25
Baron Davis, NO.	25
Juan Dixon, Wash	25
Tim Duncan, S.A.	25
Michael Finley, Dal	25
Derek Fisher, LAL	25
Rick Fox, LAL	25
Steve Francis, Hou	25
Kevin Garnett, Minn.	25
Pau Gasol, Mem.	25
Brian Grant, Mia	25
Robert Horry, LAL	25
Allen Iverson, Phi	25
Bobby Jackson, Sac	25
Antawn Jamison, Golden St.	25
Eddie Jones, Mia	25
Jason Kidd, NJ	25
Stephon Marbury, Phoe	25
Shawn Marion, Phoe	25
Jamal Mashburn, NO	25
Kenyon Martin, NJ	25
Antonio McDyess, NYK	25
Tracy McGrady, Orl	25
Darius Miles, Clev.	25
Andre Miller, LAC	25
Reggie Miller, Ind	25
Yao Ming, Hou	25
Steve Nash, Dal	25
Dirk Nowitzki, Dal.	25
Lamar Odom, LAC	25
Jermaine O'Neal, Ind.	25
Shaquille O'Neal, LAL	30
Gary Payton, Sea	25
Paul Pierce, Bos	25
Quentin Richardson, LAC	25
David Robinson, SA	25
Glenn Robinson, Atl	25
Kareem Rush, LAL	25
Jerry Stackhouse, Det.	25
Jason Terry, Atl.	25
Antoine Walker, Bos	25
Dajuan Wagner, Clev	25
Ben Wallace, Det	25

Rasheed Wallace, Port.	25
Chris Webber, Sac	25
Jay Williams, Chi.	25

CURRENT PLAYERS - MINI

Player	MT
Ron Artest	15
Tony Battie	15
Mike Bibby	15
Kwame Brown	15
Kobe Bryant	15
Vince Carter	15
Tony Delk	15
Vlade Divac	15
Juan Dixon	15
Tim Duncan	15
Michael Finley	15
Kevin Garnett	15
Larry Hughes	15
Allen Iverson	15
Jason Kidd	15
Raef LaFrentz	15
Todd MacCulloch	15
Aaron McKie	15
Tracy McGrady	15
Brad Miller	15
Reggie Miller	15
Steve Nash	15
Dirk Nowitzki	15
Jermaine O'Neal	15
Shaquille O'Neal	15
Paul Pierce	15
Jerry Stackhouse	15
Predrag Stojakovic	15
Keith VanHorne	15
Antoine Walker	15
Ben Wallace	15
Chris Webber	15

2003 ALL-STARS

Player	MT
Kobe Bryant	25
Tim Duncan	25
Kevin Garnett	25
Allen Iverson	25
Jason Kidd	25
Tracy McGrady	25
Yao Ming	25
Steve Nash	25
Shaquille O'Neal	25
Paul Pierce	25
Jerry Stackhouse	25

2002-03 RETIRED PLAYERS

Player	MT
Rick Barry	25
Elgin Baylor	25
Larry Bird (1984 championship), home	25
Larry Bird, stat	25
Bob Cousy	25
Darryl Dawkins	25
Dave DeBusschere	25
Patrick Ewing	25
Walt Frazier	25
George Gervin	25
John Havlicek	25
Bob Lanier	25
Moses Malone	25
Kevin McHale	25
Earl Monroe	25
Robert Parrish	25
Willis Reed	25
Oscar Robertson	25
David Thompson	25
Wes Unseld	25
Jerry West	25
Bill Walton	25

RETIRED PLAYERS - MINI

Player	MT
Elgin Baylor	15
Joe Dumars	15
Darryl Dawkins	15
Patrick Ewing	15
Walt Frazier	15
Earl Monroe	15
Robert Parrish	15
Isiah Thomas	15
Jerry West	15

2002 WNBA

Player	MT
Sue Bird	25
Lisa Leslie	25
Sheryl Swoopes	25
Teresa Weatherspoon	25

2003 COLLEGE COACHES

Coach	MT
Jim Boeheim, Syracuse	25
Jim Calhoun, UCONN	25
John Chaney, Temple	25
Bob Huggins, Cinci	25
Tom Izzo, Mich. St.	25
Rick Majerus, Utah	25
Jim O'Brien, Ohio State	25
Lute Olson, Ariz.	25
Gary Williams, Maryland	25

2003 COLLEGE COACHES MINI-BOBBLE

Coach	MT
Jim Boeheim, Syracuse	15
Jim Calhoun, UCONN	15
John Chaney, Temple	15
Bob Huggins, Cinci	15
Tom Izzo, Mich. St.	15
Rick Majerus, Utah	15
Jim O'Brien, Ohio State	15
Lute Olson, Ariz.	15
Gary Williams, Maryland	15

2003-04 NBA AWARDS

Note: 2,003 of each produced

Player	MT
Wallace B	25
Stoudemire A	25
Duncan T.	25

2003-04 NBA DRAFT PICKS

Note: 504 of each produced

Player	MT
James L.	35
Milicic F.	25
Wade D.	25
Hinrich K.	25
Sweetney M.	25
Anthony C.	30
Ford T.J.	25

2003 TEAM USA

Note: 2,003 of each produced

Player	MT
Malone K.	25
O'Neal J.	25
Bryant K.	25
Iverson A.	25
Bibby M.	25
Duncan T.	25
McGrady T.	25
Kidd J.	25
Allen R.	25
Brand E.	25
Jefferson R.	25
Collison N.	25
Malone K. , Stat	25
O'Neal J., Stat	25
Bryant K., Stat	25
Iverson A., Stat.	25
Bibby M., Stat	25
Duncan T., Stat	25
McGrady T., Stat	25
Kidd J., Stat	25
Allen R., Stat	25
Brand E., Stat	25
Jefferson R., Stat.	25
Collison N., Stat.	25
Bird L., Road	25
Bird L., Road	25
Bird L., Stat 1984 Home	25
Bird L. Indiana State Uniform	25

2003-04 NBA WORLD CHAMPIONS 8-INCH

Note: 5,000 of each produced

Player	MT
Duncan T	25
Robinson D.	25
Parker T.	25
Jackson S.	25
Ginobili E.	25
Coach Popovich	25

2003-04 NBA WORLD CHAMPIONS 10-INCH

Note: 5,000 of each produced

Player	MT
Duncan T.	30
Robinson D.	30
Parker T.	30
Jackson S.	30
Ginobili E.	30
Coach Popovich	30

2002 HARLEM GLOBETROTTERS

Player	MT
Hubert "Geese" Ausbie (1,000)	25
Sweet Lou Dunbar (1,000)	25
Marques Haynes (1,000)	25
Curly "Boo" Johnson (1,000)	25
Curly Neal (1,000)	25
Reece "Goose" Tatum (1,000)	25

LITTLE DRIBBLERS

Team	MT
Baltimore Bullets	300
Chicago Bulls	150
Detroit Pistons	130
Milwaukee Bucks	80
New York Knicks	30
Philadelphia 76ers	100

MCDONALD'S/PHILLY

Year & Player	MT
'01 Allen Iverson (white)	30
'01 Allen Iverson (blue)	30
'01 Allen Iverson (black)	30

MEMORY COMPANY

Year & Team	MT
'02 Atlanta Hawks	30
'02 Boston Celtics	30
'02 Charlotte Hornets	30
'02 Chicago Bulls	30
'02 Cleveland Cavaliers	30
'02 Dallas Mavericks	30
'02 Denver Nuggets	30
'02 Detroit Pistons	30
'02 Golden State Warriors	30
'02 Houston Rockets	30
'02 Indiana Packers	30
'02 Los Angeles Clippers	30
'02 Los Angeles Lakers	30
'02 Miami Heat	30
'02 Memphis Grizzlies	30
'02 Milwaukee Bucks	30
'02 Minnesota Timberwolves	30
'02 New Jersey Nets	30
'02 New York Knicks	30
'02 Orlando Magic	30
'02 Philadelphia 76ers	30
'02 Phoenix Suns	30
'02 Portland Trailblazers	30
'02 San Antonio Spurs	30
'02 Sacramento Kings	30
'02 Seattle Supersonics	30
'02 Utah Jazz	30
'02 Washington Wizards	30

NCAA TEAM GIVEAWAYS

Year & Player	MT
'01 Melvin Watkins, Texas A&M (1,500)	30
'02 Billy Donovan (5,000), Fla.	25

OIL CAN HENRY'S/PORTLAND TRAIL BLAZERS

Note: Available with purchase of premium oil change.

Years & Player	MT
'00-'01 Arvydas Sabonis	15
'02-'03 Bill Walton (7,632)	20

SAM BOBBING HEADS

Player	MT
Bird, Larry White	100
Bird, Larry Green	100
Harlem Globetrotters (1,500)	40
Jordan, Michael Red	150
Jordan, Michael White	125
Robinson, David White	100
Robinson, David Black	100
Rodman, Dennis Red	40
Rodman, Dennis Green	40

UPPER DECK PLAYMAKERS

Year & Player	MT
'00 Larry Bird	20
'00 Kobe Bryant	25
'00 Vince Carter	25
'00 Allen Iverson	30
'00 Allen Iverson, With Tattoos	35
'00 Shaquille O'Neal	25
'00 Shaq O'Neal, With Tattoos	30
'01 Kobe Bryant, Back to Back	20
'01 Kobe Bryant, Warm Up Uniform	15
'01 Vince Carter, Warm up Uniform	15
'01 Baron Davis	20
'01 Tim Duncan, Warm Up Uniform	15
'01 Allen Iverson, Warm Up Uniform	15

Player	MT
'01 Jason Kidd,	15
'01 Karl Malone	15
'01 Dirk Nowitzki	15
'01 Lamar Odom	15
'01 Shaq O'Neal, Warm Up Uniform	15
'01 Shaq O'Neal, Back to Back	20
'01 Byron Russell,	15
'01 Latrell Sprewell,	15
'01 John Stockton, Warm Up Uniform	15
'01 Predrag Stojakovic	15
'02 Shaquille O'Neal	10
'02 Shaquille O'Neal, Minneapolis Lakers	15
'02 Allen Iverson	10
'02 Vince Carter	10
'02 Tim Duncan	10
'02 Jason Kidd	10
'02 Paul Pierce	10
'02 Steve Francis	10
'02 Darius Miles	10
'02 Dirk Nowitzki	10
'02 Jay Williams	10
'02 Mike Bibby	10
'02 Kobe Bryant, Minneapolis Lakers	15
'02 Tony Parker	15

2001-02 UPPER DECK PLAYMAKERS CARD SET UNSIGNED

Note: These were inserted one per box. There are home and road jersey versions, with the home version having a production quantity of 100.

Player	MT
Kwame Brown, road	25
Kwame Brown, home	40
Kobe Bryant, road	40
Kobe Bryant, home	55
Tyson Chandler, road	25
Tyson Chandler, home	40
Eddy Curry, road	20
Eddy Curry, home	35
Julius Erving, road	45
Julius Erving, home	60
Kevin Garnett, road	30
Kevin Garnett, home	45
Eddie Griffin, road	25
Eddie Griffin, home	40
Allen Iverson, road	30
Allen Iverson, home	45
Joe Johnson, road	20
Joe Johnson, home	35
Kenyon Martin, road	20
Kenyon Martin, home	35
Tracy McGrady, road	30
Tracy McGrady, home	45
Jason Richardson, road	40
Jason Richardson, home	55
Latrell Sprewell, road	25
Latrell Sprewell, home	40

2001-02 UPPER DECK PLAYMAKERS CARD SET SIGNED

Note: These were inserted 1:14. Home jersey versions were shortprinted (production runs listed in parentheses).

Player	MT
Kwame Brown, road	40
Kobe Bryant, road	250
Tyson Chandler, road	40
Eddy Curry, road	40
Julius Erving, road (33)	250
Kevin Garnett, road	150
Eddie Griffin, road	40
Joe Johnson, road	40
Kenyon Martin, road	75
Jason Richardson, road	90

2002-03 UPPER DECK NBA PLAYMAKERS

Notes: Inserts: 1:12 Road uniform player spinning basketball. 1:240 Road uniform with actual NBA game-used floor as base; Players with game-used floor base include; Kobe Bryant, Shaq O'Neal, Allen Iverson, Tim Duncan, Jason Kidd, Chris Webber, Kevin Garnett

Player	MT
Bryant, Kobe	15
O'Neal, Shaq	15
Iverson, Allen	15
Carter, Vince	15
Duncan, Tim	15
Kidd, Jason	15
McGrady, Tracy	15
Nowitzki, Dirk	15
Pierce, Paul	15

Player	MT
Webber, Chris	15
Garnett, Kevin	15
Francis, Steve	15
Miles, Darius	15
Bibby, Mike	15
Williams, Jay	15
Ming, Yao	15

FOOTBALL

'01 BOBBING HEADS

Player	MT
Michael Vick	25
Cleveland Browns "Dawgs"Taco Bell issue	
Chomps	5
C.B.	5
Trapper	5
T.D.	5
Crusher	5

2002 ALEXANDER GLOBAL HOF BOBBLE DOBBLES

Player	MT
George Allen (2,002)	25
Dave Casper (2,002)	25
Dan Hampton (2,002)	25
Jim Kelly (5,012)	25
John Stallworth (3,082)	25

ALEXANDER GLOBAL BOBBLE DOBBLES

Player	MT
Aikman, Troy-Dallas	20
Champ, Bailey-Washington	20
Barber, Tiki-N.Y.	20
Bell, Kendrell-Pittsburgh	20
Bennett,Michael-Minnesota	20
Bettis, Jerome-Pittsburgh Home #36	35
Bettis, Jerome-Pittsburgh	35
Bledsoe, Drew-Bills	20
Bledsoe, Drew-New England	20
Brady, Tom-New England	20
Brady, Tom-New Eng. Home/Super Bowl	20
Brown, Courtney-Cleveland	20
Brown, Tim-Oakland	20
Brown, Troy-New England	20
Bruce, Isaac-St. Louis	20
Brunell, Mark-Jacksonville	20
Burress, Plaxico-Pittsburgh	25
Carter, Cris-Minnesota	20
Chambers, Chris-Miami	30
Chrebet, Wayne-New York	20
Collins, Kerry-New York	20
Couch, Tim-Cleveland	20
Culpepper, Daunte-Minnesota home #11	20
Culpepper, Daunte-Minnesota	20
Davis, Stephen-Washington	20
Davis, Terrell-Denver	20
Dillon, Corey-Cincinnati	20
Elway, John-Denver blue	20
Farr, Mel-Detroit	20
Faulk, Marshall St. Louis home	20
Faulk, Marshall-St. Louis home/grn base	20
Faulk, Marshall-St. Louis blue unif.	20
Favre, Brett-Green Bay grn jrsy/grn base	25
Favre, Brett-Green Bay grn jrsy/blue base	25
Favre, Brett Green Bay	25
Fiedler, Jay-Miami	30
Flutie, Doug-Buffalo	20
Fuamatu-Ma'afala Chris-Pittsburg	20
Gannon, Rich-Oakland	20
Gannon, Rich AFC Pro Bowl	20
Garcia, Jeff-San Francisco	20
Garcia, Jeff NFC Pro Bowl	20
Generic AFC Pro Bowl red uni/blk guy	20
Generic AFC Pro Bowl red uni/wht guy	20
Generic NFC Pro Bowl blue uni/blk guy	20
Generic NFC Pro Bowl blue uni/wht guy	20
George, Eddie-Tennessee	20
Gildon, Jason-Pittsburgh	25
Grbac, Elvis-Baltimore	20
Green, Darrell-Washington	20
Green, Trent-Kansas City	20
Green, William-Cleveland	20
Griese, Brian-Denver	20
Harrison, Marvin-Indianapolis	20
Henry, Anthony-Cleveland	20
James, Edgerrin-Indianapolis blue uni	20
James, E.-Indianapolis blue uni/grn base	20
Johnson, Brad-Tampa	20
Johnson, Kevin-Cleveland	20
Johnson, Keyshawn-Tampa	20
Johnson, Rob-Buffalo	20
Kearse, Jevon-Tennessee	20
Kosar, Bernie-Cleveland	20

	MT
Lewis, Ray-Baltimore	35
Manning, Peyton-Indianapolis #18	20
Manning, Peyton-Indianapolis green base	20
Mare, Olindo-Miami	30
Marino, Dan-Miami green jersey	25
Marino, Dan-Miami #13wht/teal pants	25
Marino, Dan-Miami QB club logo	25
Martin, Curtis-New York Jets #28	20
Martin, Curtis-New York Jets	20
McCaffrey, Ed-Denver home	20
McCaffrey, Ed-Generic orange/wht	20
McCaffrey, Ed-Generic - Wht blk pants	20
McNabb, Donovan-Philadelphia green	20
McNabb, Donovan-Phil home sign series	20
McNabb, Donovan-Phil green base	20
McNabb, Donovan (1,200) D&J Collect.	15
McNair, Steve-Tennessee	20
Miller, Jamir-Cleveland	20
Moss, Randy-Minnesota home	20
Moss, Randy-Minnesota	20
Owens, Terrell-San Francisco home	20
Sapp, Warren-Tampa home	20
Sapp, Warren-Tampa home wht	20
Schmidt, Joe-Detroit	20
Seau, Junior-San Diego	20
Smith, Emmitt-Dallas home	25
Smith, Emmitt-Dallas green base	25
Smith, Emmitt-Dallas	25
Stewart, Kordell-Pittsburgh	20
Taylor, Jason-Miami	30
Testaverde, Vinny-New York Jets	20
Thomas, Anthony-Chicago	20
Thomas, Zach-Miami	20
Tomlinson, LaDainian-San Diego home	20
Tomlinson, LaDainian-San Diego	20
Toro-Houston Texans mascot	20
Univ of Hawaii	20
Urlacher, B.-Chi. blue Cadillac promo	75
Urlacher, Brian-Chi. blue, w/o sponsor	35
Vick, Michael-Atlanta blk jrsy	20
Vick, Michael-Atlanta	20
Vinatieri, Adam-New England	20
Ward, Hines-Pittsburgh	25
Warner, Kurt-St. Louis home	20
Warner, Kurt-NFC Pro Bowl	20
Warner, Kurt-St. Louis	20
Warren, Gerard-Cleveland	20
Williams, Ricky-New Orleans #34	20
Williams, Ricky-New Orleans	20
Young, Steve-San Francisco	20
Young, Steve-SF red/QB club logo	20
Zereoue, Amos-Pittsburgh	20

2002 ARIZONA RATTLERS DANNY WHITE

Note: These three dolls were a giveaway at the June 16, 2002, Arizona Rattlers' game in the Arena League. One bobble head was given per ticket.

Player	MT
Danny White (Arizona State jersey)	35
Danny White (Dallas Cowboys jersey)	35
Danny White (Rattlers coach)	35

BOBBLE DREAMS

Year & Player	MT
'01 Marino, Dan (10,000)	25
'01 Montana, Joe (10,000)	25
'01 Unitas, Johnny (10,000)	25
'02 Montana, Joe (1,977) D&J, Notre Dame	25
'02 Payton, Walter (2,400 blue) D&J	20
'02 Payton, Walter (1,000 white) D&J	20
'02 Thomas, Anthony, McDonald's	25
'02 Urlacher, Brian, McDonald's	25
'02 Marino, Dan Records	25
'02 Shula, Don	25
'02 Montana, Joe Records	25
'02 Elway, John	25

COWBOYS/PEPSI GENESCO

Player	MT
'01 Tony Dorsett	15
'01 Daryl Johnston	15
'01 Ed "Too Tall" Jones	15
'01 Bob Lilly	15
'01 Jay Novacek	15
'01 Randy White	15

COWBOYS/GENESCO TICKET PREMIUM

Genesco produced an Emmitt Smith bobbing head doll as a premium for fans who bought tickets to the Oct. 28, 2001 Cowboys game vs. Arizona.

Player	MT
'01 Emmitt Smith	25

FOREVER COLLECTIBLES

2002 COACHES

Coach	MT
Dave McGinnis, Ariz.	25
Dan Reeves, Atl.	25
Gregg Williams, Buff.	25
Dick Jauron, Chi.	25
Dick LeBeau, Cin.	25
Dave Campo, Dall.	25
Mike Shanahan, Den.	25
Mike Sherman, G.B.	25
Dom Capers, Hou.	25
Tom Coughlin, Jax.	25
Dick Vermeil, K.C.	25
Dave Wannstedt, Mia	25
Bill Belichick, N.E.	25
Jim Haslett, N.O.	25
Jim Fassel, NYG	25
Herman Edwards, NYJ	25
Bill Callhan, Oak.	25
Andy Reid, Phil.	25
Bill Cowher, Pitt.	25
Marty Schottenheimer, S.D.	25
Steve Mariucci, S.F.	25
Mike Holmgren, Sea.	25
Mike Martz, St. L.	25
Jon Gruden, T.B.	25
Jeff Fisher, Tenn.	25

2002 MASCOTS

Players	MT
Big Red the Bird, Ariz.	25
Freddie Falcon, Atl	25
Edgar, Allen and Poe, Balt	25
Sir Purr the Panter, Car.	25
Who Dey, Cinc.	25
The Dawg Pound, Clev.	25
Rowdy, Dal	25
Miles, Den.	25
Roary the Lion, Det.	25
Toro the Bull, Hou.	25
Spike and Spirit, Ind.	25
Jaxon De Ville, Jax.	25
K.C. Wolf, K.C.	25
T.D. the Dolphin, Mia.	25
Vikadontis Rex, Minn	25
Pat, N.E.	25
Mambo, N.O.	25
Swoop the Eagle, Phil.	25
The Terrible Fan, Pitt	25
Sourdough Sam, S.F.	25
Blitz, Sea.	25
Captain Fear the Buccaneer, T.B.	25
T-Rac the Racoon, Tenn.	25

2002 PLAYERS

Players	MT
David Boston, Ariz.	25
Jake Plummer, Ariz.	25
Michael Vick, Atl.	25
Warrick Dunn, Atl	25
Ray Lewis, Balt.	25
Drew Bledsoe, Buff.	25
Eric Moulds, Buff.	25
Julius Peppers, Car.	25
Chris Weinke, Car.	25
Dan Morgan, Car.	25
Wesley Walls, Car.	25
Muhsin Muhammad, Car.	25
Steve Smith, Car.	25
DeShaun Foster, Car.	25
John Kasay, Car.	25
Todd Steussie, Car.	25
Anthony Thomas, Chi.	25
Brian Urlacher, Chi.	25
Corey Dillon, Cin.	25
Courtney Brown, Clev.	25
Tim Couch, Clev.	25
Emmitt Smith, Dal.	25
Brian Griese, Den.	25
Ed McCaffrey, Den.	25
Shannon Sharpe, Den.	25
Rod Smith, Den.	25
Joey Harrington, Det.	25
Brett Favre, G.B.	25
Ahman Green, G.B.	25
David Carr, Hou.	25
Tony Boselli, Hou.	25
Jamie Sharper, Hou.	25
Houston Texans (for ticket holders)	25
Houston Texans (home uniform)	25
Houston Texans (away uniform)	25
Houston Texans (alternate uniform)	25

Players	MT
Houston Texans (inaugural logo, female)	25
Houston Texans (split face male)	25
Houston Texans (first game, opening day)	25
Edgerrin James, Ind.	25
Peyton Manning, Ind.	25
Mark Brunell, Jax.	25
Tony Gonzalez, K.C.	25
Priest Holmes, K.C.	25
Zach Thomas, Mia.	25
Ricky Williams, Mia.	25
Daunte Culpepper, Minn.	25
Randy Moss, Minn.	25
Tom Brady, N.E.	25
Troy Brown, N.E.	25
Ty Law, N.E.	25
Aaron Brooks, N.O.	25
Tiki Barber, NYG	25
Kerry Collins, NYG	25
Jason Sehorn, NYG	25
Michael Strahan, NYG	25
Wayne Chrebet, NYJ	25
Curtis Martin, NYJ	25
Tim Brown, Oak.	25
Jerry Rice, Oak.	25
Charles Woodson, Oak.	25
Donovan McNabb, Phi.	25
Kendrell Bell, Pitt	25
Jerome Bettis, Pitt.	25
Tommy Maddux, Pitt.	25
Hines Ward, Pitt.	25
Doug Flutie, S.D.	25
Junior Seau, S.D.	25
LaDainian Tomlinson, S.D.	25
Jeff Garcia, S.F.	25
Terrell Owens, S.F.	25
Shaun Alexander, Sea.	25
Marshall Faulk, St. L.	25
Kurt Warner, St. L.	25
Keyshawn Johnson, T.B.	25
Warren Sapp, T.B.	25
Eddie George, Tenn.	25
Jevon Kearse, Tenn.	25
Steve McNair, Tenn.	25
Champ Bailey, Wash.	25
Stephen Davis, Wash.	25
Darrell Green, Wash.	25

2002 SUPER BOWL MVP SERIES

Players (5,000 of each)	MT
Bart Starr, G.B. Super Bowl I	30
Len Dawson, K.C. Super Bowl IV	30
Larry Csonka, Mia., Super Bowl VIII	30
Marcus Allen, Raiders, Super Bowl XVIII	30
Jerry Rice, S.F., SB XXIII	30
Troy Aikman, Dal, Super Bowl XXVII	30
Steve Young, S.F., Super Bowl XXIX	30
John Elway, Den, SB XXXIII	30

2003 COLLEGE COACHES/PLAYERS

Subject	MT
Joe Paterno	25
John Capelleti	25

2003 OHIO STATE NATIONAL CHAMPS

Subject	MT
Mike Doss, crystal ball (5,000)	25
Matt Wilhelm, crystal ball (5,000)	25
Coach Jim Tressel, crystal ball (5,000)	25
Mascot, crystal ball (5,000)	25
Mike Doss, gold ball (5,000)	25
Matt Wilhelm, gold ball (5,000)	25
Coach Jim Tressel, cap, gold ball (5,000)	25
Mascot, cap (5,000)	25

2003 OHIO STATE NATIONAL CHAMPS MINI 3-INCH

Subject	MT
Mike Doss	15
Matt Wilhelm	15
Coach Jim Tressel	15
Mascot	15

2003 SUPER BOWL XXXVII TAMPA BAY CHAMPIONS

Player	MT
Mike Alstott	25
Ronde Barber	25
Derrick Brooks	25
Martin Gramatica	25
Jon Gruden	25
Dexter Jackson	25
Brad Johnson	25
Keyshawn Johnson	25
Joe Jurevicius	25

Player	MT
John Lynch	25
Keenan McCardell	25
Michael Pittman	25
Simeon Rice	25
Warren Sapp	25

2003 SUPER BOWL XXXVII TAMPA BAY CHAMPIONS RING BASE

Player	MT
Ronde Barber	25
Derrick Brooks	25
Martin Gramatica	25
Dexter Jackson	25
Brad Johnson	25
Keyshawn Johnson	25
Joe Jurevicius	25
Keenan McCardell	25
Michael Pittman	25
Warren Sapp	25

2003 SUPER BOWL XXXVII TAMPA BAY CHAMPIONS CAP AND TEE

Player	MT
Mike Alstott	30
Ronde Barber	30
Derrick Brooks	30
Jon Gruden	30
Brad Johnson	30
Joe Jurevicius	30
John Lynch	30
Simeon Rice	30
Warren Sapp	30

2003 SUPER BOWL XXXVII TAMPA BAY CHAMPIONS – MINI

Subject	MT
Mike Alstott	8
Ronde Barber	8
Derrick Brooks	8
Jon Gruden	8
Dexter Jackson	8
Joe Jurevicius	8
Brad Johnson	8
Keyshawn Johnson	8
John Lynch	8
Keenan McCardell	8
Michael Pittman	8
Simeon Rice	8
Warren Sapp	8
Dwight Smith	8

2003 PRO BOWL

Player	MT
Generic Pro Bowl	20
Drew Bledsoe	25
Brett Favre	25
Rich Gannon	25
Ahman Green	25
Priest Holmes	25
Terrell Owens	25
Jerry Rice	25
Warren Sapp	25
Jeremy Shockey	25
Brian Urlacher	25
Michael Vick	25
Hines Ward	25
Ricky Williams	25

2003 THROWBACK UNIFORMS

Player (5,000 of each)	MT
Champ Bailey	25
Joey Calloway	25
Joey Harrington	25
Randy Moss	25
LaDainian Tomlinson	25

2003 ALTERNATE UNIFORMS

Player (5,000 of each)	MT
Jerome Bettis	25
Tom Brady	25
Mark Brunell	25
David Carr	25
Tim Couch	25
Deuce McAllister	25
Donovan McNabb	25
Steve McNair	25
Julius Peppers	25
Clinton Portis	25
Michael Vick	25
Ricky Williams	25

2003 DRAFT DAY

Player (504 of each)	MT
Rogers, C.	25
Johnson A.	25

	MT
Newman T.	25
Sullivan J.	25
Leftwich B.	25
Gross J.	25
Williams K.	25
Suggs T.	25
Trufant M.	25
Haynes M.	25
McDougle J.	25
Grossman R.	25
McGahee W.	25
Johnson L.	25
Bailey B.	25
Doss M.	25
Peterson K.	25
Askew B.J.	25
Grant W.C.	25
Ragone D.	25
Simms C.	25
Pinner A.	25
Wilhelm M.	25
Suggs L.	25
Henson D.	25
Dorsey K.	25

2003 GAME-LOOK

Players (5,000 of each)	MT
Smith E.	20
Vick M.	20
Finneran B.	20
Dunn W.	20
Price P.	20
Lewis R.	20
Lewis J.	20
Heap T.	20
Bledsoe D.	20
Moulds E.	20
Henry T.	20
Spikes T.	20
Peppers J.	20
Walls W.	20
Davis S.	20
Morgan D.	20
Stewart K.	20
Thomas A.	20
Booker MN.	20
Brown M.	20
Urlacher B.	20
Palmer C. Game Worn	20
Dillon C.	20
Warrick P.	20
Couch T.	20
Johnson K.	20
Green W.	20
Northcutt D.	20
Galloway J.	20
Williams R.	20
Bryant A.	20
Plummer J.	20
Griese B.	20
Portis C.	20
Smith R.	20
McCaffrey B.	20
Sharpe S.	20
Elam J.	20
Rogers C., Game Worn	20
Harrington J.	20
Schroeder B.	20
Green A.	20
Sharper D	20
Bgaja-Biamila K	20
Driver D.	20
McKenzie M.	20
Favre B.	20
Johnson A. Game Worn	20
Carr D.	20
Boselli T.	20
Glann A.	20
Manning P.	20
James E.	20
Harrison M.	20
Leftwich B, Game Worn	20
Douglas H.	20
Brunell M.	20
Taylor F.	20
Gonzalez T.	20
Holmes P.	20
Green T.	20
Kennison E.	20
Williams R.	20
Thomas Z.	20
Seau J.	20
Fiedler J.	20
Taylor J.	20

Madison S. 20
Chambers C. 20
Gadsen O. 20
Williams R., Game Worn 20
Culpepper D. 20
Moss R. 20
Bennet N. 20
Brady T. 20
Brown T. 20
Law T. 20
Vinatieri A. 20
Smith A. 20
Faulk K. 20
Milloy L. 20
Brooks A. 20
McAllister D. 20
Barber T. 20
Collins K. 20
Shockey J, Game Worn White 20
Strahan M. 20
Toomer, A. 20
Barrow M 20
Martin C 20
Chrebet W. 20
Pennington C. 20
Moss S. 20
Lewis M. 20
Robertson D., Game worn 20
Abraham J., Game Worn 20
Rice J. 20
Gannon R. 20
Garner C. 20
Romanowski B. 20
Woodson R. 20
Porter J. 20
Rice J., Game Worn 20
McNabb D., Game Worn White 20
Freeman A. 20
Staley D. 20
Thrash J. 20
Vincent T. 20
Taylor B. 20
Dawkins B. 20
McNabb D., Game Worn 20
Bettis J. 20
Bell K. 20
Burress P. 20
Maddox T. 20
Randle El A. 20
Ward H. 20
Zereque A. 20
Gildon J. 20
Porter J. 20
Boston D. 20
Tomlinson L. 20
Brees D. 20
Owens T. 20
Garcia J. 20
Hearst G. 20
Barlow K. 20
Alexander S. 20
Hasselbeck M. 20
Faulk M. 20
Warner K. 20
Holt T. 20
Bruce I. 20
Johnson K. 20
Sapp W. 20
Alsott M. 20
Rice S. 20
Johnson B. 20
Brooks D. 20
Lynch J. 20
Barber R. 20
Jurevicius J. 20
Pittman M. 20
George E. 20
Kearse J. 20
McNair S. 20
Wychek F. 20
Bailey C. 20
Candidate T. 20
Ramsey P. 20
Coles L. 20
Trotter J. 20

2003 LEAGUE LEADERS

Players (504 of each)	MT
Derrick Brooks	30
Kerry Collins	30
Rich Gannon	30
Marvin Harrison	30
Priest Holmes	30
Deuce McAllister	30

Randy Moss 30
Julius Peppers 30
Clinton Portis 30
Simeon Rice 30
Jason Taylor 30
Ricky Williams 30

2003 HALL OF FAME SERIES BUST

Note: These feature the inductees in a suit with their bust.

Players (504 of each)	MT
Marcus Allen	30
Elvin Bethea	30
Joe DeLamielleure	30
James Lofton	30
Hank Stram	30

2003 HALL OF FAME SERIES WITHOUT BUST

Players (5,000 of each)	MT
Allen M.	25
Delamielleure J.	25
Staubach R.	25
White R.	25
Lombardi V.	25
Lofton J.,	25
Starr, B.	25
Bethea E.	25
Dawson L.	25
Csonka L.	25
Lambert J.	25
Allen M.	25

2003 18-INCH BOBBLES

Players (100 of each)	MT
Drew Bledsoe	130
Tom Brady	130
Joey Harrington	130
Tommy Maddox	130
Donovan McNabb	130
Steve McNair	130
Randy Moss	130
Terrell Owens	130
Chris Palmer	130
Chad Pennington	130
Warren Sapp	130
Jeremy Shockey	130
Brian Urlacher	130
Michael Vick	130
Ricky Williams	130

2003 MASCOT

Mascots (2,003 of each)	MT
Arizona Cardinals	20
Atlanta Falcons	20
Baltimore Ravens, Allen Mascot	20
Baltimore Ravens, Edgar Mascot	20
Baltimore Ravens, Poe Mascot	20
Buffalo Bills	20
Carolina Panthers	20
Chicago Bears Cincinnati Bengals	20
Cleveland Browns	20
Dallas Cowboys	20
Denver Broncos	20
Detroit Lions	20
Green Bay Packers	20
Houston Texans	20
Indianapolis Colts	20
Jacksonville Jaguars	20
Kansas City Chiefs	20
Miami Dolphins	20
Minnesota Vikings	20
New England Patriots	20
New Orleans Saints	20
New York Giants	20
New York Jets	20
Oakland Raiders	20
Philadelphia Eagles	20
Pittsburgh Steelers	20
San Diego Chargers	20
San Francisco 49ers	20
Seattle Seahawks	20
St. Louis Rams	20
Tampa Bay Buccaneers	20
Tennessee Titans	20
Washington Redskins	20

2003 MINI PACKS

Note: All four sold in one package.

Players (1,003 of each)	MT
Starr, Aikman, Young, Allen	20
Dawson, Czonka, Elway, Rice	20

2003 MINI INDIVIDUAL

Players	MT
Vick M.	5

Price P. 5
Dunn W. 5
Finneran B. 5
Lewis R. 5
Redman C. 5
Heap T. 5
Lewis J. 5
Bledsoe D. 5
Moulds E. 5
Spikes T. 5
Henry T. 5
Peppers J. 5
Morgan M. 5
Minter M. 5
Jenkins K. 5
Urlacher B. 5
Thomas A. 5
Booker M. 5
Stewart K. 5
Dillon C. 5
Kitna J. 5
Warrick P. 5
Coach Lewis 5
Couch T. 5
Brown C. 5
Coach Davis 5
Morgan Q. 5
Coach Parcells 5
Galloway J. 5
Williams R. 5
Hutchinson C. 5
Smith E. 5
Plummer J. 5
Portis C. 5
Smith R. 5
McCaffrey E. 5
Harrington J. 5
Porcher R. 5
Bly D. 5
Coach Mariucci S. 5
Vavre D. 5
Green A. 5
Driver D. 5
Gbaja-Biamila K. 5
Carr D. 5
Boselli T. 5
Manning P. 5
James E. 5
Harrison M. 5
Coach Dungy 5
Brunnell, M. 5
Smith J. 5
Taylor F. 5
Douglas H. 5
Gonzalez T. 5
Holmes P. 5
Green T. 5
Kennison E. 5
Williams R. 5
Thomas Z. 5
Coach Wannstedt 5
Taylor J. 5
Culpepper D. 5
Moss R 5
Bennet M. 5
Hovan C. 5
Brady T. 5
Law T. 5
Vinatieri A. 5
Brown T. 5
Brooks A. 5
McAllister D. 5
Knight S. 5
Barrow M. 5
Shockey J. 5
Strahan M. 5
Martin C. 5
Chrebet W. 5
Coach Edwards H. 5
Pennington C. 5
Porter J. 5
Rice J. 5
Brown T. 5
Gannon R. 5
McNabb D. 5
Simon C. 5
Staley D. 5
Coach Reid 5
Randle J. 5
Burress, P. 5
Maddox T. 5
Ward H. 5
Bell K. 5
Gilden J. 5

Porter, J. 5
Coach Cowher 5
Seau J. 5
Tomlinson L. 5
Brees D. 5
Boston D. 5
Owens T. 5
Garcia J. 5
Hearst G. 5
Barlow K. 5
Alexander S. 5
Hasselbeck M. 5
Randle J. 5
Springs S. 5
Faulk M. 5
Warner K 5
Bruce I. 5
Holt T. 5
Johnson K. 5
Sapp W. 5
Alstott M. 5
Coach Gruden 5
George E. 5
Kearse J. 5
McNair S. 5
Mason D 5
Bailey C. 5
Candidate T. 5
Coles L. 5
Ramsey P. 5

2003 MINI COACHES

Coaches	MT
McGinnis D.	5
Reeves D.	5
Billick B.	5
Williams G.	5
Fox J.	5
Jauron D.	5
Lewis M.	5
Davis B.	5
Parcels B.	5
Shanahan M.	5
Mariucci S.	5
Sherman M.	5
Capers D.	5
Dungy T.	5
Del Rio J.	5
Vermeil D.	5
Wannstedt D.	5
Tice M.	5
Haslett J.	5
Fassel J.	5
Edwards H.	5
Callahan B.	5
Reid A.	5
Cower B.	5
Schottenheimer M.	5
Erickson D.	5
Holmgren M.	5
Martz M.	5
Gruden J.	5
Fisher J.	5
Spurrier S.	5

2003 MINI INDIVIDUAL

Mascots	MT
Arizona Cardinals	5
Atlanta Falcons	5
Baltimore Ravens	5
Buffalo Bills	5
Carolina Panthers	5
Chicago Bears	5
Cincinnati Bengals	5
Cleveland Browns	5
Dallas Cowboys	5
Denver Broncos	5
Detroit Lions	5
Green Bay Packers	5
Houston Texans	5
Indianapolis Colts	5
Jacksonville Jaguars	5
Kansas City Chiefs	5
Miami Dolphins	5
Minnesota Vikings	5
New England Patriots	5
New Orleans Saints	5
New York Giants	5
New York Jets	5
Oakland Raiders	5
Philadelphia Eagles	5
Pittsburgh Steelers	5
San Diego Chargers	5
San Francisco 49ers	5
Seattle Seahawks	5

St Louis Rams	5
Tampa Bay Buccaneers	5
Tennessee Titans	5
Washington Redskins	5

2003 SANTA

Players (5,000 of each)	MT
Arizona Cardinals	20
Atlanta Falcons	20
Baltimore Ravens	20
Buffalo Bills	20
Carolina Panthers	20
Chicago Bears	20
Cincinnati Bengals	20
Cleveland Browns	20
Dallas Cowboys	20
Denver Broncos	20
Detroit Lions	20
Green Bay Packers	20
Houston Texans	20
Indianapolis Colts	20
Jacksonville Jaguars	20
Kansas City Chiefs	20
Miami Dolphins	20
Minnesota Vikings	20
New England Patriots	20
New Orleans Saints	20
New York Giants	20
New York Jets	20
Oakland Raiders	20
Philadelphia Eagles	20
Pittsburgh Steelers	20
San Diego Chargers	20
San Francisco 49ers	20
Seattle Seahawks	20
St. Louis Rams	20
Tampa Bay Buccaneers	20
Tennessee Titans	20
Washington Redskins	20

MCDONALD'S/PHILLY

Player	MT
'01 Donovan McNabb (home)	25
'01 Donovan McNabb (away)	25

2002 MBNA CREDIT CARD PROMOS

Player	MT
Booker, Marty	20
Carr, David	25
Harris, Franco	35
McNair, Steve	20
Miami Dolphins Mascot	20
Plummer, Jake	20
Porcher, Robert	20
Smith, Jimmy	20
Turley, Kyle	20
Webb, Richmond	20

MEMORY COMPANY

Year & Team	MT
'02 Arizona Cardinals	30
'02 Atlanta Falcons	30
'02 Baltimore Ravens	30
'02 Buffalo Bills	30
'02 Carolina Panthers	30
'02 Chicago Bears	30
'02 Cincinnati Bengals	30
'02 Cleveland Browns	30
'02 Dallas Cowboys	30
'02 Denver Broncos	30
'02 Detroit Tigers	30
'02 Green Bay Packers	30
'02 Houston Texans	30
'02 Indianapolis Colts	30
'02 Jacksonville Jaguars	30
'02 Kansas City Chiefs	30
'02 Miami Dolphins	30
'02 Minnesota Vikings	30
'02 New England Patriots	30
'02 New Orleans Saints	30
'02 New York Giants	30
'02 New York Jets	30
'02 Oakland Raiders	30
'02 Philadelphia Eagles	30
'02 Pittsburgh Steelers	30
'02 San Diego Chargers	30
'02 San Francisco 49ers	30
'02 St. Louis Rams	30
'02 Seattle Seahawks	30
'02 Tampa Bay Buccaneers	30
'02 Tennessee Titans	30
'02 Washington Redskins	30

MERGER SERIES GOLD ROUND BASES
MODERN NFL DECALS

Team	MT
Atlanta Falcons	90
Baltimore Colts	130
Buffalo Bills	175
Chicago Bears	90
Cincinnati Bengals	70
Cleveland Browns	150
Dallas Cowboys	160
Denver Broncos	150
Detroit Lions	60
Green Bay Packers	190
Houston Oilers	70
Kansas City Chiefs	70
Los Angeles Rams	90
Miami Dolphins	175
Minnesota Vikings	185
New England Patriots	110
New Orleans Saints	80
New York Giants	80
New York Jets	125
Oakland Raiders	100
Philadelphia Eagles	125
Pittsburgh Steelers	170
St. Louis Cardinals	70
San Diego Chargers	90
San Francisco 49ers	175
Washington Redskins	200

NCAA TEAM GIVEAWAYS

Year & Subject	MT
'01 Donatos promo - Woody Hayes	25
'01 Purdue -(1,500, free w/ 20 purc.)	20
'01 Mich.-Bo Schembechler (7,500),	25

ODM BOSLEY BOBBERS

Player	MT
'02 Knute Rockne	20
'02 Vince Lombardi	20

2002 PACIFIC HEADS UP

Team	MT
Michael Vick	35
Anthony Thomas	35
Emmitt Smith	50
Brett Favre	50
David Carr	65
Ricky Williams	40
Daunte Culpepper	35
Randy Moss	40
Tom Brady	50
Jerry Rice	50
Marshall Faulk	35
Kurt Warner	40
LaDainian Tomlinson	40

2002 PACIFIC HEADS UPDATE

Note: 1,000 dolls of each player produced.

Team	MT
Drew Bledsoe	30
William Green	25
Joey Harrington	40
Eddie George	25
Ahman Green	30
Peyton Manning	30
T.J. Duckett	30

PEPSI ESPN NCAA FB SPORTSCASTERS

Note: These were available via mail-in offer on Pepsi 12-packs.

Year & Sportscaster	MT
'01 Lee Corso	8
'01 Chris Fowler	8
'01 Kirk Herbstreit	8

SAM PLAYER

Player	MT
Troy Aikman, Blue	100
Terry Bradshaw	250
John Elway	250
Marshall Faulk	75
Brett Favre, Green	125
Brett Favre, White	75
Jim Kelly	75
Ronnie Lott, 49ers	75
Ronnie Lott, Jets	35
Dan Marino, White	125
Dan Marino, Blue	75
Rick Mirer	20
Art Monk	150
Joe Montana, 49ers-Red	100
Joe Montana, KC	100
Joe Montana, White	75
Jerry Rice, Red	125

Jerry Rice, White	75
Barry Sanders, Blue	100
Barry Sanders, White	75
Sayers/Piccolo Set	125
Emmitt Smith, White	75
Emmitt Smith, Blue	100
Roger Staubach	100
Lawrence Taylor	75
Steve Young	75

1995 SAM TEAM

Team	MT
Atlanta Falcons	50
Arizona Cardinals	50
Baltimore Ravens	50
Buffalo Bills	50
Carolina Panthers	50
Chicago Bears	50
Cincinnati Bengals	50
Dallas Cowboys	100
Denver Broncos	100
Detroit Lions	50
Green Bay Packers	100
Indianapolis Colts	50
Jacksonville Jaguars	50
Kansas City Chiefs	60
Miami Dolphins	60
Minnesota Vikings	50
New England Patriots	60
New York Giants	80
New York Jets	50
New Orleans Saints	50
Oakland Raiders	65
Philadelphia Eagles	60
Pittsburgh Steelers	75
St. Louis Rams	50
San Diego Chargers	50
San Francisco 49ers	100
Seattle Seahawks	50
Tampa Bay Buccaneers	60
Tennessee Oilers	50
Washington Redskins	75

SPORTSFEST 2002

Player	MT
Dick Butkus (2,500)	20
Mike Ditka (2,500)	20

SUPER BOWL XXXVI

Player	MT
Marshall Faulk (500)	35
Mardi Gras Jester (giveaway with Visa)	10

TRI-STAR PRODUCTIONS

Player	MT
'02 Jerry Rice	30

TWINS ENTERPRISE

Team	MT
Baltimore Ravens	15
Buffalo Bills	15
Cincinnati Bengals	15
Cleveland Browns	15
Denver Broncos	15
Indianapolis Colts	15
Jacksonville Jaguars	15
Kansas City Chiefs	15
Miami Dolphins	15
New England Patriots	15
New York Jets	15
Oakland Raiders	15
Pittsburgh Steelers	15
San Diego Chargers	15
Seattle Seahawks	15
Tennessee Titans	15
Arizona Cardinals	15
Atlanta Falcons	15
Carolina Panthers	15
Chicago Bears	15
Dallas Cowboys	15
Detroit Lions	15
Green Bay Packers	15
Minnesota Vikings	15
New Orleans Saints	15
New York Giants	15
Philadelphia Eagles	15
St. Louis Rams	15
San Francisco 49ers	15
Tampa Bay Buccaneers	15
Washington Redskins	15
Super Bowl XXXIV	15

UPPER DECK PLAYMAKERS

Year & Player	MT
'99 Terrell Davis	20
'99 Doug Flutie	25

'99 Peyton Manning	20
'99 Dan Marino	30
'99 Joe Montana	25
'99 Ricky Williams	20
'00 Daunte Culpepper	20
'00 Randy Moss	20
'01 Daunte Culpepper	15
'01 Marshall Faulk	15
'01 Eddie George	15
'01 Tony Gonzalez	20
'01 Trent Green	15
'01 Edgerrin James	15
'01 Peyton Manning	15
'01 Randy Moss	15
'01 Kurt Warner	15
'02 Shaun Alexander	15
'02 Jerome Bettis	15
'02 Drew Bledsoe (Bills)	15
'02 Tom Brady	15
'02 David Carr	15
'02 Tim Couch	15
'02 Marshall Faulk	15
'02 Brett Favre	15
'02 Ahman Green	15
'02 Brian Griese	15
'02 Joey Harrington	15
'02 Keyshawn Johnson	15
'02 Peyton Manning	15
'02 Donovan McNabb	15
'02 J erry Rice	15
'02 Emmitt Smith	15
'02 Anthony Thomas	15
'02 LadDainian Tomlinson	15
'02 Brian Urlacher	15
'02 Michael Vick	15
'02 Kurt Warner	15
'02 Ricky Williams	15

UPPER DECK PLAYMAKERS
SPECIAL EDITIONS

Year & Player	MT
'01 R. Moss, Rookie of the Year	20

HOCKEY

ALEXANDER GLOBAL BOBBLE DOBBLES

Note: Due to incomplete information, some 2001-02 NHL stadium giveaways are listed in this section as promos.

Player	MT
Amonte, Tony-Chic. home wht	20
Amonte, Tony-Team USA Men's	20
Bondra, Peter-Wash. away blk	20
Brewer, Eric-Team Canada wht	20
Brodeur, Martin-N.J. red	20
Brodeur, Martin-Team Canada wht	20
Bure, Pavel-Fla. red	20
Bye, Karyn-Team USA Women's	20
Chelios, Chris-Team USA Men's	20
Chelios, Chris-Det. wht	20
Dafoe, Byron-Bos. blk	20
Datsyuk, Pavel-Det. wht	20
Deadmarsh, A.-LA wht	20
Domi, Tie-Tor. home wht	20
Draper, Kris-Det. wht	20
Drury, Chris-Team USA Men's	20
Fedorov, Sergei-Det. home	20
Fedorov, Sergei-Det. away red	20
Fernandez, Manny-Minn. wht	20
Fleury, Theo-Team Canada wht	20
Foote, Adam-Team Canada wht	20
Forsberg, Peter-Colo. away	20
Gaborik, Marian-Minn. away green	20
Gadsby, Bill-Det. "Howe"	20
Gagne, Simon-Team Canada wht	20
Granato, Cammi-Team USA Women's	20
Gretzky, Wayne-Team Canada w/suit	20
Guerin, Bill-Bos. wht	20
Hasek, Dominik-Det. away	20
Hasek, Dominik-Det. home wht	20
Hedberg, Johan-Pitt. home wht	20
Hendrickson, Darby-Minn. away grn	20
Hull, Brett-Team USA Men's	20
Hull, Brett-Det. home wht	20
Hull, Brett-Det. away red	20
Iginla, Jarome-Cal.	20
Iginla, Jarome-Team Canada wht	20
Ingraham, Ca-Idaho Steelheads home	20
Jagr, Jaromir-Wash. wht	20
Jagr, Jaromir-Wash. away blk	20
Joseph, Curtis-Tor. wht	20
Joseph, Curtis-Team Canada wht	20
Jovanovski, Ed-Team Canada wht	20
Kariya, Paul-Ana. wht	20

Kariya, Paul-Team Canada wht	20
Kasparaitis, Darius-Pitt. home	20
King, Katie-Team USA Women's	20
Kolzig, Olaf-Wash. away blk	20
Kolzig, Olaf-Wash. white uni promo	30
Kuba, Filip-Minn. wht	20
LeClair, John-Philadelphia Flyers home	20
LeClair, John-Team USA Men's	20
LeClair, John-Phila. Phantoms promo	30
Leetch, Brian NY Rangers blue	20
Leetch, Brian-Team USA Men's	20
Lemieux, Mario-Pitt. Home	25
Lemieux, Mario-Team Canada wht	25
Lidstrom, Nicklas-Det., away red	20
Lindros, Eric-NY Rangers wht	20
Lindsay, Bill-Fla. home (5,000) promo	25
Lindsay, Ted-Det. "Howe" home	20
Luongo, Roberto-Fla Panthers home wht	20
MacInnis, Al-St. L Blues home wht #2	20
MacInnis, Al-Team Canada wht	20
Maltby, Kirk-Det. wht	20
McCarty, Darren-Det. wht	20
Messier, Mark-NY Rangers wht	20
Messier, Mark-Rang blu/Liberty logo	20
Mikita, Stan-Chi. "tommy hawk"	20
Mleczko, A.J.-Team USA Women's	20
Modano, Mike-Dal. home wht	20
Modano, Mike-Team USA Men's	20
Mogilny, Alexander-Tor. home	20
Moog, Andy-Ft. Worth Brahmas (3,000)	25
Niedermayer, Scott-Team Canada wht	20
Niedermayer, Scott-NJ home wht	20
Niedermayer, Scott-Team Canada wht	20
Nieuwendyk, Joe-Dal. Stars home	20
Nieuwendyk, Joe-Team Canada wht	20
Nolan, Owen-SJ Sharks home	20
Nystrom, Bob-8,000 w/sponsor home	20
Peca, Michael-Team Canada wht	20
Peca, Michael-NYI blue (1,000) w/o logo	20
Peca, Michael-NYI white (8,000) w/spon	25
Perreault, Yanic-Mont. wht	20
Pronger, Chris-St.Louis wht	20
Pronger, Chris-Team Canada wht	20
Quinn, Pat-Team Canada gray/suit	20
Ray, Rob-Buff. home wht	20
Recchi, Mark-Phil. home wht	20
Richards, Brad-(5000) T.B. wht promo	20
Richter, Mike-NY Rangers blue	20
Robitaille, Luc-Det. (1,000) away red	20
Roenick, Jeremy-Phil. home	20
Roenick, Jeremy-Phil. Phantoms (4,500)	45
Roest, Stacy-Minn. wht	20
Roloson, Dwayne-Minn. home wht	20
Roy, Patrick-Colo. wht	20
Roy, Patrick-Team Canada wht	20
Sakic, Joe-Colo. away	20
Sakic, Joe-Colo. wht	20
Sakic, Joe-Team Canada wht	20
Shanahan, Brendan-Det. away red	20
Shanahan, Brendan-Team Canada wht	20
Shanahan, Brendan-Det. white	20
Smyth, Ryan-Team Canada wht	20
Stevens, Scott-New Jersey Devils wht	20
Stevens, Scott-Team Canada wht	20
Sundin, Mats	20
Theodore, Jose-Team Canada wht	20
Thornton, Joe-Boston Bruins away blk	20
Tkachuk, Keith-St.L wht	20
Tugnutt, Ron-Columb. home	20
Vyborny, David-Columb. home	20
Weight, Doug-St. L wht	20
Young, Scott-St. L wht	20
Yzerman, Steve Det. away red	20
Yzerman, Steve-Team Canada wht	20
Yzerman, Steve-Det. home	20

2002-03 BE A PLAYER ALL-STAR EDITION

Player	MT
Martin Brodeur (1,530 produced)	30
Pavel Bure (2,010)	30
Peter Forsberg (2,031)	30
Jaromir Jagr (2,068)	30
Curtis Joseph (1,031)	30
Mario Lemieux (1,066)	30
Patrick Roy (1,033)	30
Joe Sakic (1,519)	30
José Théodore (1,560)	30
Steve Yzerman (2,019)	30

BOBBLE DREAMS

Player	MT
Bourque, Ray (7,777)	25

FOREVER COLLECTIBLES

Year & Player	MT
'03 Alfredsson, Daniel	25
'02 Allison, Jason (action)	25
'03 Allison, Jason	25
'02 Amonte, Tony (action)	25
'03 Amonte, Tony	25
'02 Barnes, Stu (action)	25
'02 Barnes, Stu	25
'03 Barnes, Stu	25
'02 Belfour, Ed (action)	25
'03 Belfour, Ed	25
'02 Bertuzzi, Todd (action)	25
'03 Bertuzzi, Todd	25
'02 Briere, Daniel (action)	25
'02 Biron, Martin (action)	25
'02 Blake, Rob (action)	25
'02 Blake, Rob #4 (away)	25
'03 Blake, Rob	25
'02 Bondra, Peter (action)	25
'02 Bondra, Peter (away)	25
'02 Brind'Amour, Rod	25
'02 Brodeur, Martin (action)	25
'02 Brodeur, Martin (away)	25
'03 Brunette, Andre	25
'02 Bure, Pavel (action)	25
'03 Bure, Pavel	25
'02 Burke, Sean (action)	25
'02 Carter, Anson (action)	25
'02 Cechmanek, Roman (action)	25
'03 Cechmanek, Roman	25
'02 Chelios, Chris (action)	25
'02 Cole, Erik (action)	25
'02 DaFoe, Byron (action)	25
'02 Datsyuk, Pavel (action)	25
'03 Datsyuk, Pavel	25
'02 Deadmarsh, Adam	25
'02 Deadmarsh, Adam (action)	25
'03 Deadmarsh, Adam	25
'02 Domi, Tie (action)	25
'02 Draper, Kris (action)	25
'03 Draper, Kris	25
'02 Drury, Chris (away)	25
'02 Drury, Chris (action)	25
'03 Drury, Chris	25
'02 Dunham, Mike (action)	25
'03 Dunham, Mike	25
'03 Dunham, Mike (alternate jersey)	25
'02 Fedorov, Sergei (action)	25
'02 Federov, S. #91 (away)	25
'02 Fernandez, Manny (action)	25
'03 Fernandez, Manny	25
'02 Fischer, Jiri (action)	25
'03 Fischer, Jiri	25
'02 Foote, Adam (action)	25
'02 Foote, A. #52 (away)	25
'02 Forsberg, Peter (action)	25
'02 Forsberg, Peter #21 (away)	25
'02 Francis, Ron	25
'03 Francis, Ron	25
'02 Gaborik, Marian (action)	25
'03 Gaborik, Marian	25
'02 Guerin, Bill (action)	25
'03 Guerin, Bill	25
'02 Hasek, D. #39 (away)	25
'02 Hasek, D. #39 (home)	25
'02 Hasek, D. #39 (Stanley Cup)	25
'02 Heatley, Dany (action)	25
'02 Hedberg, Johan (action)	25
'02 Hedberg, Johan (away)	25
'03 Hedberg, Johan	25
'02 Hendrickson, Darby (action)	25
'03 Hendrickson, Darby	25
'02 Holik, Bobby (action)	25
'02 Holmstrom, Tomas (action)	25
'02 Hull, Brett (action)	25
'02 Hull, B. #17 (away)	25
'02 Hull, B. #17 (home)	25
'02 Iginla, Jarome	25
'02 Irbe, Arturs	25
'02 Jager, Jaromir (action)	25
'02 Jagr, Jaromir #68 (away)	25
'03 Johnson, Brent	25
'02 Joseph, Curtis	25
'02 Joseph, Curtis (action)	25
'03 Joseph, Curtis	25
'03 Jovanovski, Ed	25
'02 Kariya, Paul	25
'03 Kariya, Paul	25
'02 Kasparaitis, Darius (action)	25
'03 Khabibulin, Nikolai	25
'03 Klesla, Rostislav	25
'02 Khabibulin, Nikolai (action)	25
'02 Kolzig, Olaf (action)	25
'02 Kolzig, Olaf (away)	25
'02 Kovalchuk, Ilya (action)	25
'02 Kovalev, Alexei (action)	25
'03 Kovalev, Alexei	25
'02 Lacavalier, Vincent (action)	25
'02 Lalime, Patrick (action)	25
'03 Lalime, Patrick	25
'02 Larionov, Igor (action)	25
'03 Larionov, Igor	25
'02 Leclair, John (action)	25
'02 Leetch, Brian (away)	25
'03 Leetch, Brian	25
'03 Legace, Manny	25
'03 Lemieux, Mario, S. Cup Champ, 10"	40
'03 Lemieux, Mario, S. Cup Champ, 8"	25
'02 Lidstrom, Nicklas (action)	25
'02 Lidstrom, N. #5 (away)	25
'02 Lindros, Eric (action)	25
'02 Luongo, Roberto (action)	25
'03 Luongo, Roberto	25
'02 Maltby, Kirk (action)	25
'03 Maltby, Kirk	25
'02 McCarty, Darren (action)	25
'03 McGinnis, Al	25
'02 Messier, Mark (away)	25
'02 Modano, Mike (action)	25
'02 Modano, M. #9 (away)	25
'02 Mogilny, Alexander (action)	25
'03 Mogilny, Alexander	25
'02 Nabokov, Evgeni (action)	25
'03 Nash, Rick	25
'02 Naslund, Markus (action)	25
'02 Nolan, Owen (action)	25
'03 Nolan, Owen	25
'02 Numminen, Teppo (action)	25
'02 Osgood, Chris (action)	25
'02 Osgood, Chris #35 (away)	25
'02 Palffy, Zigmund (action)	25
'02 Peca, Michael (action)	25
'02 Peca, Michael (away)	25
'02 Potvin, Felix (action)	25
'03 Potvin, Felix	25
'02 Pronger, Chris (away)	25
'03 Pronger, Chris	25
'03 Redden, Wade	25
'02 Richter, Mike (away)	25
'03 Richter, Mike	25
'02 Robitaille, Luc (action)	25
'02 Robitaille, L. #20 (away)	25
'03 Robitaille, Luc	25
'02 Roenick, Jeremy (action)	25
'02 Roenick, Jeremy (away)	25
'03 Roenick, Jeremy	25
'02 Roy, Patrick (action)	25
'02 Roy, P. #33 (away)	25
'02 Roy, P. (Stanley Cup)	25
'03 Roy, Patrick	25
'02 Sakic, Joe (action)	25
'02 Sakic, J. #19 (away)	25
'02 Sakic, J. (Stanley Cup)	25
'02 Salo, Tommy (action)	25
'03 Salo, Tommy	25
'02 Schneider, Mathieu (action)	25
'03 Selanne, Teemu	25
'02 Shanahan, Brendan (action)	25
'02 Shanahan, B. #14 (away)	25
'02 Shanahan, B. #14 (home)	25
'03 Smyth, Ryan	25
'02 Stevens, Scott (action)	25
'03 Stevens, Scott	25
'02 Sundin, Mats (action)	25
'02 Sundin, Mats.	25
"03 Sundin, Mats	25
'02 Theodore, Jose (action)	25
'02 Thibault, Jocelyn (action)	25
'02 Thornton, Joe (action)	25
'03 Tkachuck, Keith	25
'02 Turco, Marty (action)	25
'02 Yashin, Alexei (action)	25
'02 Yzerman, Steve (action)	25
'02 Yzerman, S. #19 (away)	25
'02 Yzerman, S. #19 (home)	25
'02 Yzerman, S. (Stanley Cup)	25
'03 Yzerman, Steve	25
'03 Zetterberg, Henrik	25

2002 PLAYERS - MINI

Player	MT
Brodeur, M., N.J.	15
Bure, P., NYR	15
Deadmarsh, A., L.A.	15
Fedorov, S., Det.	15
Hasek, D. (away), Det.	15
Hasek, D. (home), Det.	15
Hedberg, J., Pitt.	15
Hull, Brett (away), Det.	15
Hull, Brett (home), Det.	15
Jagr, J., Wash.	15
Joseph, C., Tor.	15
LeClair, J., Phil.	15
Lidstrom, N., Det.	15
Modano, M., Dall.	15
Peca, M., NYI	15
Roenick, J., Phil.	15
Roy, P., Colo.	15
Sakic, J., Colo.	15
Shanahan, B. (away), Det.	15
Shanahan, B. (home), Det.	15
Thornton, J., Bos.	15
Yzerman, S. (away), Det.	15
Yzerman, S. (home), Det.	15

2003 PLAYERS - MINI

Player	MT
Allison, J, LA	15
Blake, R., Colo	15
Brodeur, M., NJ	15
Bure, Pavel, NYR	15
Cechmanek, R.	15
Datsyuk, P, Det.	15
Daze, E., Chi	15
Deadmarsh, Adam, LA	15
Dupuis, P., Minn	15
Elisa, P., NJ	15
Fedorov, Sergei, Det	15
Fernandez, Manny, Minn	15
Fleury, T., Chi	15
Forsberg, P., Colo	15
Gaborik, M,Minn	15
Gagne, S., Phil	15
Hedberg, J., Pitt	15
Holik, B., NYR	15
Hrdina, J., Pitt	15
Hull, Brett, Det.	15
Johnson, B., St. L	15
Jonsson, K., NYY	15
Joseph, Curtis, Det.	15
Kovalev, A., Pitt	15
Lagenbrunner, Jamie	15
LeClair, J., Phil	15
Lemieux, Mario, S. Cup Champ	15
Lidstrom, N., Det	15
Lindross, Eric, NYR	15
Morozov, A., Pitt	15
Osgood, C. NYI	15
Palffy, Ziggy, LA	15
Parrish, M., NYI	15
Peca, Michael, NYI	15
Potvin, Felix, LA	15
Pronger, C., St. L	15
Richter, Mike, NYR	15
Robitaille, Luc, Det	15
Roenick, Jeremy, Phil	15
Ronning, C., Minn	15
Roy, Patrick, Colo	15
Sakic, Joe, Colo	15
Shanahan, B., Det	15
Sparky the NJ Devils mascot	15
Stevens, S, NJ	15
Thibault, J., Chi	15
Tkachuk, K., St. L	15
Weight, Doug, St. L	15
Yashin, A.	15
Yzerman, Steve, Det.	15
Zhamnov, A., Chi	15

2003 ALL-STAR GAME

Player	MT
Generic All-Star Game bobber	20
Brodeur, M.	25
Fedorov, S.	25
Lidstrom, N.	25
Roy, Patrick	25
Selanne, T.	25
Thornton, J.	25
Yashin, A.	25

2003 LEAGUE LEADERS

Player	MT
Thornton J	30
Brodeur M.	30
Lidstrom N	30
Naslund M.	30
Jackman, Barrett	30
Lehtinen J.	30
Yzerman S	30

2003 MASCOTS

Mascot (2,003 of each)

	MT
Anaheim Mighty Ducks, Wild Wing	20
Atlanta Thrashers, Thrash	20
Boston Bruins, Blades	20
Buffalo Sabres, Sabretooth	20
Calgary Flames, Harvey The Hound	20
Carolina Hurricanes, Stormy	20
Chicago Blackhawks, Tommy Hawk	20
Columbus Blue Jackets, Stinger	20
Colorado Avalanche, Howler	20
Detroit Red Wings, Rally Al	20
Florida Panthers, Stanley C. Panther	20
Nashville Predators, Gnash	20
New Jersey Devils, Devil	20
New York Islanders, Sparky	20
Ottawa Senators, Spartacat	20
Pittsburgh Penguins, Iceburgh	20
San Jose Sharks, Sharkie	20
Tampa Bay Lightning, Thunderbug	20
Toronto Maple Leafs, Carlton Polar Bear	20
Vancouver Canucks, Splash the Whale	20
Washington Capitals, Slapshot the Eagle	20

2003 SANTA

Player (5,000 of each)

	MT
Boston Bruins	20
Chicago Blackhawks	20
Colorado Avalanche	20
Dallas Stars	20
Detroit Red Wings	20
Edmonton Oilers	20
Minnesota Wild	20
Montreal Canadiens	20
New Jersey Devils	20
New York Islanders	20
New York Rangers	20
Ottawa Senators	20
Philadelphia Flyers	20
Pittsburgh Penguins	20
St Louis Blues	20
Toronto Maple Leafs	20
Vancouver Canucks	20

2003 STANLEY CUP CHAMPS 8-INCH

Player (5,000 of each)

	MT
Brodeur M., 2003 Champ	25
Elias P., 2003 Champ	25
Madden J., 2003 Champ	25
Stevens S., 2003 Champ	25
Gomez S., 2003 Champ	25
Langenbrunner J., 2003 Champ	25
Niedermayer S., 2003 Champ	25
Daneyko S., 2003 Champ	25
Brodeur M. 2003 Cap & T	25
Wlias P, 2003 Cap & T	25
Madden J., 2003 Cap & T	25
Steven S., 2003 Cap & T	25
Gomez S., 2003 Cap & T	25
Langenbrunner J. 2003 Cap & T	25
Niedermayer S., 2003 Cap & T	25
Daneyko K, 2003 Cap & T	25

2003 STANLEY CUP CHAMPS 10-INCH

Player (5,000 made of each)

	MT
Brodeur M., 2003 Champ	30
Elias P., 2003 Champ	30
Madden J., 2003 Champ	30
Stevens S., 2003 Champ	30
Gomez S., 2003 Champ	30
Langenbrunner J., 2003 Champ	30
Niedermayer S., 2003 Champ	30
Daneyko K., 2003 Champ	30

2003 VINTAGE COLLECTION

Player

	MT
Bobby Orr	20
Phil Esposito	20
Bobby Hull	20
Gordie Howe	20
Marcel Dionne	20
Maurice Richard	20
Mike Bossy	20
Guy LaFleur	20
John Davidson	20
Bobby Clarke	20
Johnny Bower	20
Rod Langway	20

2003-04 PLAYERS

Player (5,000 of each)

	MT
Kariya P.	20
Giguere J.S.	20
Heatley D.	20
Kovalchuk I.	20

Murray G.	20
Samsonov S.	20
Thornton J.	20
Biron M.	20
Briere D.	20
Drury C.	20
Iginla J.	20
Brind'Amour R.	20
Franics R.	20
Daze E.	20
Thibault J.	20
Zhamnov A.	20
Blake R.	20
Foot A.	20
Forsberg P.	20
Hejduk M.	20
Sakic J.	20
Kleslar R.	20
Nash R.	20
Guerin B.	20
Modano M.	20
Turco M.	20
Chelios C.	20
Datesyuk P.	20
Draper K.	20
Fedorov S.	20
Fisher J.	20
Homstrom T.	20
Hull B.	20
Joseph C.	20
Legace M.	20
Lidstrom N.	20
Maltby K.	20
McCarty D.	20
Schneider	20
Shanahan B.	20
Syzerman S.	20
Zettreberg H.	20
Comrie M.	20
Salo T.	20
Smyth R.	20
Laraque G.	20
Jokinen O.	20
Luongo R.	20
Allison J.	20
Deadmarsh A.	20
Frolov A.	20
Cechmanek R.	20
Dupuis P.	20
Fernandez M.	20
Gaborik M.	20
Koivu S	20
Theodore J.	20
Brodeur M.	20
Elias P.	20
Stevens S.	20
Dipietro R.	20
Peca M.	20
Yashin A.	20
Bure P.	20
Dunham M.	20
Holik B.	20
Kovalev A.	20
Leetch B.	20
Lindrose E.	20
Lundmark J.	20
Alfredsson D.	20
Havlat M.	20
Hossa M.	20
Lalime P.	20
Redden W.	20
Spezza J.	20
Amonte T.	20
Gagne S.	20
Leclair J.	20
Roenick J.	20
Williams J.	20
Caron S.	20
Straka M.	20
Marleu P.	20
Nabokov E.	20
Ricci M.	20
Selannie T.	20
Demitra P.	20
Macinnis A.	20
Osgood J.	20
Pronger C.	20
Tkachuk K.	20
Weight D.	20
Khabibulin N.	20
LeCavalier V.	20
St Louis M.	20
Antropov N.	20

Belfour E.	20
Domi T.	20
Mogilny A.	20
Nolan O.	20
Roberts G.	20
Sundin M.	20
Tucker D.	20
Bertuzzi T.	20
Cloutier D.	20
Jovanovski D.	20
Linden T.	20
Morrison B.	20
Naslund M.	20
Bondra P.	20
Gonchar S.	20
Jagr J.	20
Kolzig O.	20

MEMORY COMPANY

Year & Team	MT
'01 Anaheim Mighty Ducks	30
'01 Atlanta Thrashers	30
'01 Boston Bruins	30
'01 Chicago Blackhawks	30
'01 Columbus Blue Jackets	30
'01 Detriot Red Wings	30
'01 Florida Panthers	30
'01 Nashville Predators	30
'01 New Jersey Devils	30
'01 New York Rangers	30
'01 Phoenix Coyotes	30
'01 Tampa Bay Lightning	30
'01 Washington Capitals	30
'02 Anaheim Mighty Ducks	30
'02 Atlanta Thrashers	30
'02 Boston Bruins	30
'02 Buffalo Sabres	30
'02 Carolina Hurricanes	30
'02 Chicago Blackhawks	30
'02 Colorado Avalanche	30
'02 Columbus Blue Jackets	30
'02 Dallas Stars	30
'02 Detriot Red Wings	30
'02 Florida Panthers	30
'02 Los Angeles Kings	30
'02 Minnesota Wild	30
'02 Nashville Predators	30
'02 New York Islanders	30
'02 Phoenix Coyotes	30
'02 Philadelphia Flyers	30
'02 Pittsburgh Penguins	30
'02 San Jose Sharks	30
'02 St. Louis Blues	30
'02 Tampa Bay Lightning	30
'02 Washington Capitals	30

MINOR LEAGUE TEAM GIVEAWAYS

Year & Player	MT
'02 Fred Glover (3,000), Clev. AHL	20
'02 Mark Woolf (5,000), S.D. WCHL	10

2000-01 NHL TEAM GIVEAWAYS

Player	MT
Guy Hebert (5,000), Ana.	20
Paul Kariya (5,000), Ana.	30
Teemu Selanne (5,000), Ana.	30
Dominik Hasek, Buff.	30
Tomi Kallio (5,000), Atl.	45
Sergie Fedorov, Det.	25
Brendan Shanahan, Det.	25
Steve Yzerman, Det.	35
Scott Stevens, N.J.	75
Mario Lemieux (15,000), Pit	50
Nikolai Khabibulin (5,000), T.B.	40
Chris Simon, Wash	25

2001-02 NHL TEAM GIVEAWAYS

Note: Due to incomplete information, some 2001-02 NHL stadium giveaways are listed in the Alexander Global section as promos.

Player	MT
Ray Ferraro (5,000), Atl.	30
Tomi Kallio (5,000), Atl.	70
Patrik Stefan (5,000), Atl.	25
Thrash mascot (5,000), Atl.	25
Olympic bobble (5,000), Atl.	15
Dany Heatley (5,000), Atl.	45
Ilya Kovalchuk (5,000), Atl.	50
Tommy Hawk mascot (10,000), Chi.	15
Blackhawk (5,000), Chi.	15
Chris Drury (5,000), Colo.	15
Geoff Sanderson, Colum.	30
Tyler Wright, Colum.	40
Ron Tugnutt, Colum.	40

Ray Whitney, Colum.	30
Nicklas Lidstrom, Det.	20
Pavel Bure, Fla.	20
Valeri Bure, Fla.	20
Roberto Luongo, Fla.	20
Bill Lindsay, Fla.	20
L.A. Kings Olympic (10,000)	15
Mike Dunham, Nash. (10,000)	10
Ken Morrow, NYI (8,000)	25
Mark Messier, NYR	40
Marian Hossa, Otta.	25
Wade Redden, Otta.	25
Patrick Lalime, Otta.	25
Daniel Alfredsson, Otta.	25
Lemieux, Mario, Pitt	30
Al MacInnis (5,000), St. L.	50
Tyson Nash (5,000), St. L.	50
Chris Pronger (5,000), St. L	20
Vincent Lecavalier,T.B. (5,000)	25
Markus Naslund,Van.	30
Todd Bertuzzi, Van.	40
Chris Simon, Wash.	20

2002-03 NHL TEAM GIVEAWAYS

Player	MT
Dany Heatley, Atl.	30
Ilya Kovalchuk, Atl.	40
Jeff Odgers, Atl.	25
Martin Brodeur, NJ	30
Devils Mascot , NJ	25
Chris Osgood, NYI	30
Alexei Yashin, NYI	20
Sparky, NYI	25
Clark Gillies, NYI	15
Mark Parrish, NYI	20
Peter Laviolette, NYI	25
Shawn Bates, NYI	20
Roman Hamrlik, NYI	25
Bobby Holik, NYR	40
Zdeno Chara, Ott.	30
Martin Havlat, Ott.	20
Mike Fisher, Ott.	20
Spartacat, Ott.	15
Todd White, Ott.	20
Matt Cooke, Van.	20
Todd Bertuzzi, Van.	15
Markus Naslund, Van.	15

2001-02 PACIFIC HEADS UP

Player	MT
Martin Brodeur	90
Mike Cramer (Pacific owner)	60
Dominik Hasek	50
Johan Hedberg	65
Jaromir Jagr	80
Curtis Joseph	80
Paul Kariya	50
Mario Lemieux	150
Mark Messier	50
Patrick Roy	100
Joe Sakic	50
Steve Yzerman	100

2002-03 PACIFIC HEADS UP

Note: Found one per hobby box. Retail boxes feature redemption card found 1:97 packs. Bobbles numbered to 1,000.

Player	MT
Jason Allison	40
Pavel Bure	50
Mike Comrie	45
Peter Forsberg	45
Jarome Iginla	40
Saku Koivu	50
Ilya Kovalchuk	40
Brendan Shanahan	35
Joe Thornton	35
Eric Lindros	40
Evgeni Nabokov	50
Mats Sundin	45
Jose Theodore	70
Alexei Yashin	35

RED WINGS/LITTLE CAESERS

Year & Player	MT
'01 Kris Draper	10
'01 Kirk Maltby	10
'01 Darren McCarty	15

SAM PLAYERS

Player	MT
Gretzky, Wayne (500)	600
Howe, Gordie	75
Hull, Bobby	150
Leetch, Brian	75
Lemieux, Mario, black	400

Lemieux, Mario, white	100
Messier, Mark, blue	40
Messier, Mark, white (500)	150

UPPER DECK PLAYMAKERS

Year & Player	MT
'02 Brendl, Pavel	15
'02 Brodeur, Martin	15
'02 Bure, Pavel	15
'02 Hasek, Dominek	15
'02 Hejduk, Milan	15
'02 Jagr, Jamir	15
'02 Joseph, Curtis	15
'02 Kovalchuk, Ilya	15
'02 Lindros, Eric	15
'02 Modano, Mike	15
'02 Roy, Patrick	15
'02 Sakic, Joe	15
'02 Weight, Doug	15
'02 Yzerman, Steve	15

2001-02 UPPER DECK PLAYMAKERS CARD SET UNSIGNED

Note: These were inserted one per box. There are home and road jersey versions, with the home version being short-printed.

Player	MT
Martin Brodeur, road	15
Martin Brodeur, home	30
Pavel Bure, road	12
Pavel Bure, home	30
Dominik Hasek, road	20
Dominik Hasek, home	40
Jaromir Jagr, road	15
Jaromir Jagr, home	30
Curtis Joseph, road	10
Curtis Joseph, home	25
Ilya Kovalchuck, road	18
Ilya Kovalchuck, home	35
Joe Sakic, road	12
Joe Sakic, home	30
Eric Lindros, road	15
Eric Lindros, home	30
Mike Modano, road	10
Mike Modano, home	25
Patrick Roy, road	20
Patrick Roy, home	40
Doug Weight, road	10
Doug Weight, home	25
Steve Yzerman, road	20
Steve Yzerman, home	40

2001-02 UPPER DECK PLAYMAKERS CARD SET SIGNED

Note: These were inserted 1:case. Home jersey versions were shortprinted (production runs listed in parentheses).

Player	MT
Pavel Bure, road	40
Pavel Bure, home (10)	100
Martin Brodeur, road	40
Martin Brodeur, home (30)	100
Curtis Joseph, road	40
Curtis Joseph, home (31)	100
Ilya Kovalchuk, road	75
Ilya Kovalchuk, home (17)	100
Doug Weight, road	40
Doug Weight, home (39)	100
Steve Yzerman, road	90
Steve Yzerman, home (19)	200

2002-03 NHL PLAYMAKERS

Player	
Iginla, Jarome	15
Thornton, Joe	15
Koivu, Saku	15
Kariya, Paul	15
Forsberg, Peter	15
Comrie, Mike	15
Bertuzzi, Todd	15
Bure, Pavel	15
Sakic, Joe	15
Jagr, Jaromir	15
Lindros, Eric	15
Joseph, Curtis	15
Roy, Patrick	15
Brodeur, Martin	15

RACING

ALEXANDER GLOBAL PROMOTIONS NASCAR

Year & Driver	MT
'02 Casey Atwood	20
'02 Jeff Burton	20
'02 Bill Elliott	20
'02 Jeff Gordon	20
'02 Robbie Gordon	20
'02 Jeff Green	20
'02 Kevin Harvick	20
'02 Bobby Labonte	20
'02 Sterling Marlin	20
'02 Mark Martin	20
'02 Jeremy Mayfield	20
'02 Ryan Newman	20
'02 Jimmy Spencer	20
'02 Tony Stewart	20
'02 Rusty Wallace Mills Uniform	20
'02 Rusty Wallace Child Friend's Uniform	20

ALEXANDER GLOBAL PROMOTIONS NHRA

Year & Driver	MT
'02 Joe Amato	20
'02 Whit Bazemore	20
'02 Kenny Bernstein	20
'02 Tony Schumacher	20

2002 COCA-COLA, ARBY'S

Note: The bobbing head dolls were available at Arby's in 13 different states in a promotion. They are sold for $3.99 with the purchase of any Arby's Combo Meal. Each six-inch doll is hand-painted with each driver sitting in a Coca-Cola Racing Family stock car, wearing their racing suit and sunglasses, while holding a Coca-Cola.

Year & Driver	MT
'02 Dale Jarrett	10
'02 Bobby Labonte	10
'02 Ricky Rudd	10
'02 Tony Stewart	10

2002 FIRESTONE INDY 500

Note: Firestone Tires produced the bobble, which was given to those associated with the manufacturer, plus the first 1,000 fans who showed up at the Firestone garage on the race preview days.

Subject	MT
Firehawk	10

FOREVER COLLECTIBLES

Year & Driver	MT
'02 Atwood, Casey, Muppet	25
'02 Benson, Johnny	25
'02 Benson, Johnny, Muppet	25
'03 Benson, Johnny	25
'03 Benson, Johnny, stat	25
'03 Biffle, Greg	25
'03 Biffle, Greg, stat	25
'02 Burton, Jeff.	25
'03 Burton, Jeff	25
'03 Burton, Jeff, stat	25
'03 Busch, Kurt	25
'03 Busch, Kurt, stat	25
'02 Daytona Race Fan	20
'02 Elliott, Bill, Muppet	25
'03 Elliott, Bill	25
'03 Elliott, Bill, stat	25
'02 Gordon, Jeff Dupont	25
'02 Gordon, Jeff #24	25
'02 Gordon, Jeff, Looney Tunes	25
'02 Gordon, Jeff, Pepsi suit	25
'02 Gordon, Jeff, 3-time Brickyard champ	25
'02 Gordon, Jeff, 2001 points champ	25
'03 Gordon, Jeff (driver's suit)	25
'03 Gordon, Jeff, Stat bobble	25
'02 Gordon, Robby	25
'02 Green, Jeff, Looney Tunes	25
'02 Hamilton, Bobby	25
'02 Harvick, Kevin, Looney Tunes	25
'02 Harvick, Kevin #29 ROY 2001	25
'02 Harvick, Kevin #29	25
'02 Jarrett, Dale #88	25
'02 Jarrett, Dale, Muppet	25
'03 Jarrett, Dale	25
'03 Jarrett, Dale, stat	25
'02 Johnson, Jimmie	25
'03 Johnson, Jimmie	25
'03 Johnson, Jimmie, stat	25
'02 Kenseth, Matt	25
'03 Kenseth, Matt	25
'03 Kenseth, Matt, stat	25
'02 Labonte, Bobby #18	25
'02 Labonte, Bobby, Muppet	25
'03 Labonte, Bobby	25
'03 Labonte, Bobby, stat	25
'03 Labonte, Terry	25
'03 Labonte, Terry, stat	25
'02 Marlin, Sterling	25
'03 Marlin, Sterling	25
'03 Marlin, Sterling, stat	25
'02 Martin, Mark #6	25
'03 Martin, Mark	25
'03 Martin, Mark, stat	25
'02 Mayfield, Jeremy, Muppet	25
'03 Nadeau, J	25
'03 Nadeau, J., stat	25
'02 Nemechek, Joe, Looney Tunes	25
'03 Nemechek, Joe	25
'03 Nemechek, Joe, stat	25
'03 Newman, Ryan (driver's suit)	25
'03 Newman, Ryan, Rookie of Year	28
'03 Newman, Ryan, Stat bobble	25
'02 Rudd, Ricky #28	25
'02 Rudd, Ricky, Muppet	25
'03 Rudd, Ricky	25
'03 Rudd, Ricky, stat	25
'03 Sadler, Elliott	25
'03 Sadler, Elliott, stat	25
'02 Schrader, Ken #36	25
'02 Skinner, Mike	25
'02 Spencer, Jimmy, Muppet	25
'02 Stewart, Tony #20	25
'03 Stewart, Tony (driver's suit)	25
'03 Stewart, Tony, Points champ	30
'03 Stewart, Tony, Stat bobble	25
'03 Wallace, Rusty	25
'03 Wallace, Rusty, stat	25

2002 FOREVER COLLECTIBLES MINI

Driver	MT
Benson, Johnny.	10
Burton, Jeff	10
Gordon, Jeff	10
Gordon, Jeff, 3-time Brickyard champ	10
Gordon, Jeff, Pepsi suit	10
Harvick, Kevin	10
Jarrett, Dale	10
Kenseth, Matt	10
Labonte, Bobby	10
Marlin, Sterling	10
Martin, Mark	10
Rudd, Ricky	10
Schrader, Ken	10
Stewart, Tony	10
Trickle, Dick	10
Wallace, Rusty	10

2003 FOREVER COLLECTIBLES MINI

Driver	MT
Benson, Johnny	10
Burton, Jeff	10
Busch, Kurt	10
Elliott, Bill	10
Gordon, Jeff	10
Jarrett, Dale	10
Johnson, Jimmy	10
Kenseth, Matt	10
Labonte, Bobby	10
Labonte, Terry	10
Marlin, Sterling	10
Martin, Mark	10
Nadeau, Jerry	10
Newman, Ryan	10
Rudd, Ricky	10
Sadler, Elliott	10
Stewart, Tony	10
Wallace, Rusty	10

2002 INDIANAPOLIS 500 4-TIME CHAMPS

Note: Each of the bobbles fit together at the base to form a set. Bobbers in conjunction with Pepsi and Marsh Stores. Marsh Stores gave them away free with the purchase of two cases of Pepsi products. The bobbles were also available at the Indy Motor Speedway on three days.

Driver	MT
A.J. Foyt (5,000)	20
Rick Mears (5,000)	20
Al Unser (5,000)	20

SAM

Driver	MT
Earnhardt, Dale	125
Elliott, Bill	50

MISCELLANEOUS

ALEXANDER GLOBAL BOBBLE DOBBLES

Subject	MT
Ali, Muhammad (2,100)	150
Berman, Chris, ESPN.	60
Gammons, Peter, ESPN	55
Mayne, Kenny, ESPN	60
Patrick, Dan, ESPN	60
Scott, Stuart, ESPN	50
Vitale, Dick, ESPN	25
Austin, Steve (Stone Cold) WWF.	20
The Rock WWF.	20
The Undertaker WWF.	20
Triple H (HHH) WWF.	20

HORSE RACING

Figure	MT
Pat Day (Churchill Downs)	25
Chris McCarron (Hollywood Park)	35
Laffitt Pincay (Hollywood Park)	40

KEY ENTERPRISES WRESTLING

Subject	MT
Hollywood Hogan	15
Sting	10
Diamond Dallas	10
Goldberg	15

MISCELLANEOUS BOXING

Note: These bobbers were given away at a Brockton (Mass.) Rox minor-league baseball game June 9, 2003. The dolls were given to the first 1,000 fans through the gate. An additional 500 dolls were available for sale to benefit a scholarship fund.

Subject	MT
Marvin Hagler	10

2002 NIKE TIGER WOODS

Note: One of the three bobbers was offered as a gift with the purchase of a dozen Nike golf balls. Each has a green base, with Woods' name printed in black on the front of the base

Player	MT
Tiger Woods (white shirt, followthrough)	15
Tiger Woods (black cap, club behind neck)	15
Tiger Woods (blue shirt, club under arm)	15

ODM BOSLEY BOBBERS

Player	MT
'02 Joe Louis	20

2002 UPPER DECK PLAYMAKERS GOLF

Player	MT
Tiger Woods, 1997 Masters	15
Tiger Woods, 1999 PGA	15
Tiger Woods, 2000 British Open Champ	10
Tiger Woods, 2000 U.S. Open Champ	10
Tiger Woods, 2000 PGA Champ	10
Tiger Woods, 2001 Masters Champ	10
Tiger Woods, 2002 Kit Young Conf.	20
Tiger Woods, 2002 Masters	15
Tiger Woods, 2002 US Open	15

2002 SOCCER

Player	MT
Jeff Agoos, San Jose, MLS (10,000)	15
Mamadou Diallo, T.Bay, MLS (5,000)	15
Landon Donovan, U.S. Soccer Foundation	10
Darryl Doran, World Indoor Soccer, St. L.	10

Danbury Mint Sports

Danbury Mint is one of the leading sports porcelain collectible companies in the country. They began producing sports collectibles in 1998 and have created one of the most prolific lines of sports collectibles ever. They have a wide assortment of figurines, plates, stadiums, gold cards, Christmas Sculptures, Die-Cast Team Cars and many other items.

Danbury Mint is unique in how they sell their products. Danbury products are only available through direct mail order and not available in stores or from authorized dealers.

Danbury Mint figurines average 7 to 9 inches in height. They are made of a blend of cold-cast porcelain and resin. Each figurine comes with a hardwood base complete with a reproduction of the signature on the base. Danbury uses some of the best sculptors in the country including those that have previously worked for Gartlan, Salvino and the Art of Sport.

Danbury Mint figurines are not limited in any way. Danbury Mint has an assortment of figurines available. Most players are made individually, however they have produced championship team figurine sets and greatest moment sculptures complete with a replica newspaper on the figure to explain the event.

Team Figurines

Player	Mint
1927 New York Yankees	$210
1955 Brookyn Dodgers	$210
1961 New York Yankees	$210
1964-1965 Boston Celtics	$210
1966 Green Bay Packers	$210
1969 New York Mets	$210
1970 Baltimore Orioles	$210
1972 Miami Dolphins	$210
1972-1973 New York Knicks	$210
1975 Cincinnati Reds	$210
1977 Dallas Cowboys	$210
1998 Denver Broncos	$210
1999 New York Yankees	$210
Pittsburgh Steeler Steel Curtain (Joe Greene, Ernie Holmes, L.C. Greenwood and Dwight White)	$165
Pittsburgh Steeler Famous Linebacker Trio (Jack Ham, Jack Lambert and Andy Russell)	$125
Washington Redskins Linemen (Famous Hogs)	$165

Baseball players

Player	Mint
Hank Aaron	$65
Edgardo Alfonso	$65
Jeff Bagwell	$65
Ernie Banks	$65
Johnny Bench	$65
Barry Bonds	$65

Player	Mint
George Brett	$65
Lou Brock	$65
Rod Carew	$65
Roger Clemens	$65
Roberto Clemente	$65
Ty Cobb	$65
Joe DiMaggio	$65
Don Drysdale	$65
Bob Feller	$65
Rollie Fingers	$65
Carlton Fisk (1975 WS Game 6 Home Run)	$150
Nomar Garciaparra	$65
Lou Gehrig	$65
Jason Giambi	$65
Kirk Gibson (1988 WS Game 1 Home Run)	$150
Ken Griffey Jr.	$65
Tony Gwynn	$65
Reggie Jackson	$65
Derek Jeter	$65
Randy Johnson	$65
Al Kaline	$65
Jeff Kent	$65
Don Larsen (Perfect Game)	$150
Al Leiter	$65
Greg Maddux	$65
Cal Ripken Jr.	$65
Mickey Mantle	$65
Pedro Martinez	$65
Don Mattingly	$65
Willie Mays (The Catch)	$150
Bill Mazeroski (1960 World Series Home Run)	$145

Alex Rodriguez　　　**Barry Sanders**

Joe DiMaggio　　　**Derek Jeter**

1927 Yankees

1977 Dallas Cowboys

Mark McGwire

Joe Montana

Nolan Ryan

Shaquille O'Neal

Tony Gwynn

Michael Jordan

Reggie Jackson

The Rock

Warren Sapp

Player	Mint
Mark McGwire and Sammy Sosa	$145
Mark McGwire	$65
Joe Morgan	$65
Thurman Munson	$65
Stan Musial	$65
Paul O'Neill	$65
Mike Piazza	$65
Manny Ramirez	$65
Mariano Rivera	$65
Brooks Robinson	$65
Jackie Robinson	$65
Alex Rodriguez	$65
Pudge Rodriguez	$65
Babe Ruth	$65
Nolan Ryan	$65
Tom Seaver	$65
Mike Schmidt	$65
Ozzie Smith	$65
Sammy Sosa	$65
Willie Stargell	$65
Bobby Thompson's Shot Heard Around The World	$145
Omar Vizquel	$65
Larry Walker	$65
Bernie Williams	$65
Ted Williams	$65
Carl Yastrzemski	$65

Basketball

Player	Mint
Larry Bird	$65
Julius Erving	$65
Walt Frazier	$65
Grant Hill	$65
Michael Jordan (4 career figurines)	$210
Michael Jordan (3 different uniforms)	$145
Allen Iverson	$65
Magic Johnson	$65

Player	Mint
Shaquille O'Neal	$65
Isiah Thomas	$65

Football

Player	Mint
Troy Aikman	$65
Jerome Bettis	$65
Jim Brown	$65
Tim Brown	$65
Cris Carter	$65
Wayne Chrebet	$65
Tim Couch	$65
Daunte Culpepper	$65
Terrell Davis	$65
Len Dawson	$65
John Elway	$65
Marshall Faulk	$65
Brett Favre	$65
Rich Gannon	$65
Eddie George	$65
Darrell Green	$65
Mean Joe Greene	$65
Brian Griese	$65
Sonny Jurgensen	$65
Jim Kelly	$65
Jack Lambert	$65
Peyton Manning	$65
Dan Marino	$65
Donovan McNabb	$65
Joe Montana	$65
Randy Moss	$65
Ray Nitschke	$65
Walter Payton	$65
Jerry Rice	$65
Barry Sanders	$65
Warren Sapp	$65
Gale Sayers	$65
Emmitt Smith	$65
Bart Starr	$65
Roger Staubach	$65

Player	Mint
Lawrence Taylor	$65
Derrick Thomas	$65
Brian Urlacher	$65
Kurt Warner	$65

Player	Mint
Charles Woodson	$65
Steve Young	$65

Hockey

Player	Mint
Mario Lemieux (3 figure set)	$145

Golf

Player	Mint
Arnold Palmer	$50
Lining It Up Patterson	$45

Wrestling

Player	Mint
The Rock	$70

Gartlan USA

Gartlan USA was founded by Bob Gartlan in 1985. Gartlan is generally credited with starting the modern era of sports figurines. His Pete Rose figurine was the first ceramic type (platinum) sports figurine of its kind. This Gartlan Rose figurine also added a new dimension to figurine collecting. Each figurine came with a Rose autograph affixed to the figurine, thus combining autograph collecting with figurine collecting.

The Gartlan USA figurines came in two sizes, a larger 7 to 9 inch size and an exact replica in a 4 to 5 inch size. They were made of cold-cast resin. The larger figurines were almost always autographed. Edition sizes were usually tied to a famous milestone in the player's career like Pete Rose's 4,192nd record breaking hit or the year in which they were produced (Rod Carew, 1,991 were to be made in 1991). The smaller figurine edition sizes were in the 5,000 to 10,000 range and were exact duplicates of their larger counterparts. This set was comprised of 35 regular miniatures and 8 club miniatures made specially for those Gartlan collectors who joined Gartlan's collector's club. Note: (It is important to understand that edition sizes were those that were planned but not actually made. In many cases, very few figurines were produced in relation to their planned edition sizes.)

For some players, Gartlan issued Artist Proofs. These edition runs were very small-100 to 300. The player was usually done in the opposite jersey color of the regular edition and Gartlan himself signed many of these.

Gartlan's timing was perfect as in the late 1980s and early '90s autograph prices were still reasonable enabling the figurines to come out with reasonable price points usually in the $200 to $300 range. The Gartlan figurine series lasted approximately ten years until 1995.

Today, the Gartlan sports figurine line remains highly desirable with collectors and demands top dollar. No figurine line has ever appreciated as much as the Gartlan figures.

	Quantity	Price	Issue Mint
Hank Aaron			
Signed	1,982	$149.95	$350
Mini	10,000	$39.95	$40
Comm.	755	$275	$450
Club	—	$79	$125
Luis Aparicio			
Signed	1,984	$120	$150
Mini	10,000	$39.95	$40
Al Barlick			
Signed	1,989	$124.95	$150
"Cool Papa" Bell			
Signed	1,499	$124.95	$250
Johnny Bench			
Signed	1,989	$150	$300
Mini	10,000	$39.95	$40
AP	250	$150	$500
Yogi Berra			
Signed	2,150	$225	$250
Mini	10,000	$39.95	$40
AP	250	$350	$350

	Quantity	Price	Issue Mint
George Brett			
Signed	2,250	$199.95	$250
Mini	10,000	$39.95	$40
Club	—	$79.95	$125
Rod Carew			
Signed	1,991	$124.95	$250
Mini	10,000	$39.95	$40
Inc. Mini	125	$99.95	$200
Steve Carlton			
Signed	3,290	$175	$200
Mini	10,000	$39.95	$40
AP	300	$350	$425
Ray Dandridge			
Signed	1,987	$124.95	$150
Joe DiMaggio			
Signed	2,214	$275	$900
Signed Pin	325	$695	$1,800
AP	12	$695	$7,000
Carlton Fisk			
Signed	1,972	$149.95	$200
Mini	10,000	$39.95	$40
AP	300	$350	$350
Whitey Ford			
Signed	2,360	$124.95	$175
Mini	10,000	$39.95	$40
AP	250	$350	$350
Ken Griffey, Jr.			
Signed	1,989	$199.95	$250
Mini	10,000	$39.95	$40
Monte Irvin			
Signed	1,973	$99.95	$100
Mini	10,000	$39.95	$40
Ralph Kiner			
Signed	1,975	$99.95	$150
Mini	10,000	$39.95	$40
Buck Leonard			
Signed	1,972	$124.95	$175
Eddie Mathews			
Signed	1,978	$149.95	$275
Mini	10,000	$39.95	$40
Stan Musial			
Signed	1,969	$199.95	$300
Mini	10,000	$39.95	$40
AP	300	$299.95	$300
Pewter	500	$850	$850
Pete Rose			
Platinum	4,192	$125	$800
Mini	10,000	$79.95	$75

Steve Carlton

Stan Musial

Ted Williams

Carl Yastrzemski & Johnny Bench

	Quantity	Price	Issue Mint
Mike Schmidt			
Signed	1,987	$150	$500
Mini	10,000	39.95	$40
AP	20	$275	$1,500
Club	—	$79	$125
Tom Seaver			
Signed	1,992	$125	$400
Mini	10,000	$39.95	$40
Warren Spahn			
Signed	1,973	$124.95	$350
Darryl Strawberry			
Signed	2,500	$99.95	$100
Mini	10,000	$39.95	$30
Frank Thomas			
Signed	1,994	$199.95	$400
Mini	10,000	$39.95	$40
Ted Williams			
Signed	2,654	$295	$750
Mini	10,000	$39.95	$50
AP	250	$650	$825
Carl Yastrzemski			
Signed	1,989	$150	$300
Mini	10,000	$79	$80
AP	250	$150	$450

Basketball

	Quantity	Price	Issue Mint
Kareem Abdul-Jabbar			
Signed	1,989	$175	$375
Mini	10,000	$75	$100
AP	100	$200	$500
Comm	33	$275	$4,000
Club Mini	—	$75	$150
Bob Cousy			
Signed	950	$149.95	$200
Mini	5,000	$39.95	$40
Magic Johnson			
Photo Etched	1,737	$125	$300
Comm	32	$275	$6,000
AP	250	$175	$2,500
Shaquille O'Neal			
Signed	1,992	$225	$500
Mini	10,000	$39.95	$40
Club Mini	—	$39.95	$50
Isiah Thomas			
Signed	1,990	$225	$225
Mini	10,000	$79	$80
John Wooden			
Signed	1,975	$100	$150
Mini	10,000	$39.95	$40
AP	250	$350	$350

Football

	Quantity	Price	Issue Mint
Troy Aikman			
Signed	1,993	$199.95	$400
Mini	10,000	$39.95	$60
Joe Montana			
Signed	2,250	$325	$425
Mini	10,000	$39.95	$40
AP	250	$500	$750
Club Mini	—	$79	$175

Hockey

	Quantity	Price	Issue Mint
Wayne Gretzky			
Signed	1,851	$250	$500
Mini	10,000	$39.95	$70
AP	300	$695	$1,400
Club Mini	—	$75	$250
Gordie Howe			
Signed	2,358	$150	$250
Mini	10,000	$39.95	$40
Bobby Hull			
Signed	1,983	$149.95	$250
Mini	10,000	$39.95	$50
AP	300	$350	$350
Brett Hull			
Signed	1,986	$149.95	$250
Mini	10,000	$39.95	$50
AP	300	$350	$350

Golf

	Quantity	Price	Issue Mint
Sam Snead			
Signed	950	$149.95	$220
Mini	5,000	$39.95	$40

Figure skating

	Quantity	Price	Issue Mint
Kristi Yamaguchi			
Signed	950	$149.95	$150
Unsigned	5,000		$50
Mini			$20
Ceramic card			$14

HALL OF FAME BUSTS

The Baseball Hall of Fame in Cooperstown, N.Y., opened its doors for the first time in 1936. The initial inductees included Ty Cobb, Babe Ruth, Honus Wagner, Christy Mathewson, and Walter Johnson. To honor these great players, busts were sculpted with their respective likenesses. On the pedestal was a plaque with each player's career highlights. The tradition continues today.

In 1963, the Hall of Fame commissioned a Long Island company (Sports Hall of Fame Inc.), to make miniature replicas of 20 of the existing Hall of Fame busts. They were to be sold at souvenir stands at Cooperstown and at Major League parks.

They were made of plastic and stand about 6 inches tall. They came in a display window box with a listing of all the players in the series on the back. There were two separate series of 10, with the second series being slightly more rare than the first.

Collectors have found a new interest in them over the past several years. Because of their common size, they display beautifully with both Hartland statues and bobbing heads. Except for the Foxx and Greenberg statues, the set is relatively easy and inexpensive to complete. It is certainly one of the most underrated and undervalued series in the hobby today.

Player	Series	Mint in Sealed Box	Mint No Box
Ty Cobb	1	$250	$100
Mickey Cochrane	2	$250	$150
Joe Cronin	2	$350	$200
Bill Dickey	1	$125	$75
Joe DiMaggio	1	$200	$125
Bob Feller	2	$200	$150
Jimmie Foxx	2	$450	$275
Lou Gehrig	1	$175	$100
Hank Greenberg	2	$450	$300
Rogers Hornsby	1	$175	$100
Walter Johnson	1	$175	$100
Christy Mathewson	1	$175	$100

Player	Series	Mint in Sealed Box	Mint, No Box
John McGraw	2	$350	$200
Jackie Robinson	2	$350	$200
Babe Ruth	1	$175	$100
George Sisler	2	$350	$200
Tris Speaker	2	$225	$150
Pie Traynor	1	$175	$100
Honus Wagner	1	$225	$100
Paul Waner	2	$300	$150

Note: All of the boxes are identical. Statues that have yellowed or discolored are at least one-half the Mint price.

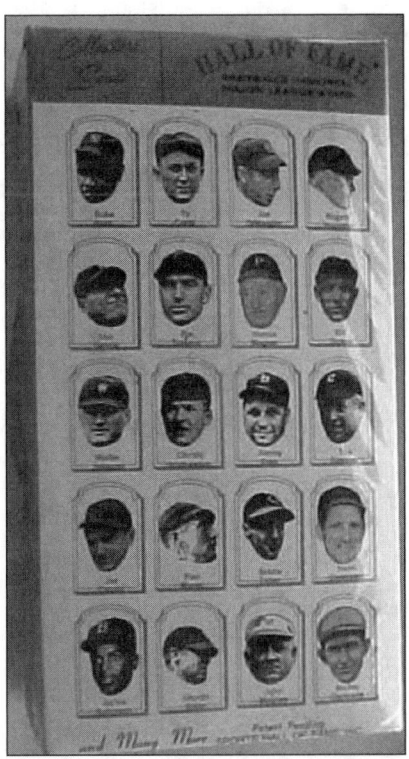

Hall of Fame series

Christy Mathewson

Ty Cobb

HARTLAND STATUES

Hartland Statues are some of the pieces of sports memorabilia most recognized by the "Baby Boomer" generation today. Most collectors from the ages of 45 to 55 remember having them or wanting them as children. The superior workmanship and attention to detail have brought in new generations of collectors of these plastic masterpieces.

Hartland Plastics of Hartland, Wis., started producing a series of western, baseball and football statues in the mid- to late '50s. The baseball line was first introduced in 1958 with three home state players, Hank Aaron, Warren Spahn and Eddie Mathews of the then Milwaukee Braves. At the end of their run in 1962, an additional 15 players would be added to the series. Of the 18 player statues issued, all but one (Babe Ruth) were current players. Amazingly, all but three of these players would eventually be inducted into the Hall of Fame.

Hartland took great pride in depicting each player with incredible facial likenesses, physical attributes, and stances. Willie Mays was portrayed making his famous "basket catch," Mickey Mantle's forearms are bulging and Nellie Fox even has his trademark "chaw of tobacco" in his cheek. They all came in one of two styles of boxes and included neck tags, brochures and removable bats (for those shown batting). The statues have a realism that is unmatched by recent issues. In the early '90s, reissues and a new line were introduced with the Hartland name, but the consensus is that although they are well made, they don't match up to the "Original 18."

In 2001, Hartland Collectibles, the modern descendant of the company that virtually created the modern collectible sports figurine more than 40 years ago, returned, hoping the current popularity of retro sports collectibles will carry over to its own baseball figurines.

The company will release enhanced versions of Hartland's original baseball-player statues. New Hartlands of such baseball greats as Mickey Mantle, Babe Ruth, Rocky Colavito and Hank Aaron will carry a $39 suggested retail price and have the same poses as the original statues but will have slight variations, such as Colavito as a member of the Indians or players wearing their road uniforms instead of the original white jerseys. The first two players released in the new version are Yogi Berra and Stan Musial.

Hartland CEO Ken Movold was able to secure licensing from MLB Properties and the Cooperstown Collection for the updated figures and hopes both the collectors who grew up with Hartland's as well as the fans of modern figurines will be interested in buying these statues. "The appeal of Hartland figurines is they had a unique way of sculpting," Movold said. "It really has that retro look. Hartland is one of the hobby's icon names." Hartland is also resurrecting its line of western horse-and-rider figurines and Movold said he would like to expand into the football market as well.

The usual factors are used in pricing original Hartlands. Condition, completeness, and scarcity are the main determinates of obtaining value. Early runs of the Hartland baseball players used a plastic that in time had a tendency to yellow. A white statue will command a far greater price than one that is off-white or yellowed. The quantities of each player made range from an estimated high of 150,000 for Spahn, Mathews, Mantle, and Ruth to as low as 5,000 to 10,000 for Rocky Colavito and Dick Groat. Groat is by far the scarcest and most sought after of the series.

Boxes and neck tags can sometimes be worth as much as the actual statue. The same factors determine the value on the newer issues, although they are almost always found in their original boxes.

The following prices are based on Mint-condition statues. Excellent to near mint statues are usually 75 percent of the mint value.

1958-1962: THE "ORIGINAL 18"
(plus batboy & minor leaguer)

Player	Pose	Statue	Box	Tag
Hank Aaron	Batting	$325	$150	$150
Luis Aparicio	Fielding	$350	$150	$175
Ernie Banks	Batting	$325	$150	$175
Yogi Berra	Fielding (w/mask)	$250	$100	$125
Rocky Colavito	Batting	$1,000	$750	$750
Don Drysdale	Pitching (w/rubber)	$425	$200	$200
Nellie Fox	Fielding	$250	$100	$150
Dick Groat	Batting	$1,800	$1,000	$1,000
Harmon Killebrew	Batting	$750	$250	$250
Mickey Mantle	Batting	$400	$150	$150
Roger Maris	Batting	$450	$150	none*
Eddie Mathews	Fielding	$250	$100	$100
Willie Mays	Fielding	$250	$100	$100
Stan Musial	Batting	$250	$100	$100
Babe Ruth	Pointing	$300	$100	$100
Duke Snider	Batting	$450	$200	$200
Warren Spahn	Pitching	$250	$100	$100
Ted Williams	Batting	$350	$200	$200
Batboy (Little Leaguer)		$200		
Minor Leaguer	Batting	$150		

Notes: There is no known Roger Maris tag. Both Maris and Killebrew came with home plates that have a tendency to warp. Batters came with one of two sizes of bats. The batboy was originally issued as the Little Leaguer but was changed because of licensing rights. It came on a card under a plastic bubble. Most cards found have "Little League" cut off the top. Beware of reproduction tags.

In 1990 the above statues were reissued as 25th anniversary statues. They are heavier and not as well painted. All will be labeled "25th Anniversary." Their values range from $50-$75 with their boxes. There are five different styles of boxes.

Safe At Second

Bat Boy

Hank Aaron

L.A. Rams

Yogi Berra

Babe Ruth

Ernie Banks

25th ANNIVERSARY LATE 1980s-EARLY 1990s HARTLAND STATUES

Hartland made a comeback in the 1980s with an anniversary set. These 25th Anniversary Hartlands are exact replicas of the originals. They have the words 25th Anniversary on the player's belt buckle or shoulder. It is sometimes hard to see.

Hartland has been bought and sold many times and its history of litigation and shenanigans would take more room to describe than what we have here. It is sufficient to say that the Hartlands produced in the early 90s were known as the Dallas Hartlands and the Hartlands produced from 1993 to 1995 by Stevens Manufacturing (a toy company) were known as the Missouri Hartlands. These were produced in such small numbers that their prices are often higher than the original Hartlands from the 1960s.

Today, Hartland is once again creating figures. There is a 3rd Anniversary set in the making. While the players are the same as the originals, they are made with a different twist, such as in a different uniform or with a different team that they played for. Ozzie Smith is the new player honored with a Hartland to date.

(all prices include the box)

Team	Mint
Hank Aaron	$95
Luis Aparicio	$75
Ernie Banks	$75
Yogi Berra	$80
Rocky Colavito	$65
Don Drysdale	$60
Nellie Fox	$60
Dick Groat	$100
Harmon Killebrew	$70
Mickey Mantle	$125
Roger Maris	$90
Eddie Mathews	$75
Willie Mays	$85
Stan Musial	$70
Babe Ruth	$100
Duke Snider	$65
Warren Spahn	$65
Ted Williams	$125
Batboy	$100

DALLAS HARTLAND STATUES - Early 1990s
(all prices include the box)

Team	Pose	Mint
Roberto Clemente	Batting	$100
Ty Cobb	Sliding	$900
Dizzy Dean	Pitching	$150
Bob Feller	Pitching	$2,000
Whitey Ford	Pitching	$75
Lou Gehrig	Batting	$200

Team	Pose	Mint
Umpire		$75
"The Confrontation"	Arguing at Home	$2,000

Notes: There are two box styles for the Clemente and Ford statues. The green box (Dallas) is more desirable. A complete "The Confrontation" is very scarce. The Umpire was sent out separately without the "arguing manager." Dizzy Dean has a tendency to discolor even if it has never been removed from the box.

MISSOURI HARTLAND STATUES - 1993-1994
(all prices include the box)

Team	Pose	Mint
Roberto Clemente	Batting	$150
Whitey Ford	Pitching	$95
Nolan Ryan (home)	Pitching	$125
Nolan Ryan (away)	Pitching	$125
Honus Wagner	Batting	$175
Carl Yastrzemski	Batting	$450
Cy Young	Pitching	$175
"Safe at Second"	Sliding/Tagging	$125

NEW HARTLAND STATUES
(all prices include the box)

Team	Mint
Ernie Banks	$40
Yogi Berra	$40
Mickey Mantle	$40
Stan Musial	$40
Ozzie Smith	$40
Warren Spahn	$40

1959-63 Football

Team	Lineman	Running Back
Baltimore Colts	$275	$275
Chicago Bears	$250	$275
Cleveland Browns	$350	$350
Dallas Cowboys	$700	$800
Detroit Lions	$300	$300
Green Bay Packers	$300	$300
Los Angeles Rams	$300	$250
Minnesota Vikings	$300	$250
New York Giants	$300	$300
Philadelphia Eagles	$250	$250
Pittsburgh Steelers	$400	$400
San Francisco 49ers	$400	$400
St. Louis Cardinals	$350	$350
Washington Redskins	$1,000	$1,000
LSU	$3,000	$3,500
Jon Arnett (Rams)		$350
Johnny Unitas (Colts)		$550

Headliners

For a brief five year period, Headliners challenged Kenner Starting Lineups for collecting supremacy in the sports figural hobby. The Headliner product was first introduced by a small company called Corinthian Marketing in 1996 with the release of a NFL Football Series. They were later bought out by the toy company Equity.

Headliners were made of polyutherane (hard plastic). The players had oversized heads and smaller bodies. Headliners were basically made in two sizes, a smaller 3 inches to 3 and ½ inch series, and a larger six-inch series. The latter series is referred to as XLs. The figures were sold in blister packs like SLUs. The SRP was about $4 for the small and $10 for the large. The smaller size was the base line or featured product and produced in much greater number than the XLs.

Baseball was made for four years (1997-2000), football was made for three years (1996-1998), hockey was made for three years (1996-1998) and basketball for two years (1997-1998). Values are shown for unopened blister packs.

BASEBALL

The most prolific of the four sports, MLB Headliners were made from 1997 to 1999. A last series was made in 2000 of XL Headliners but no smaller ones were made except for a rare and limited edition of 5,000 of Ken Griffey, Jr. in his Reds uniform.

1997 Baseball

Complete Set (33)	$180
Common player	$5
Roberto Alomar	$5
Albert Belle	$5
Wade Boggs	$5
Barry Bonds	$10
Ken Caminiti	$5
Jose Caneco (A's)	$5
Jose Canseco (Red Sox)	$20
Lenny Dykstra	$5
Andres Galarraga	$5
Ken Griffey Jr.	$10
Tony Gwynn	$6
Orel Hershiser	$5
Randy Johnson	$6
Chipper Jones	$10
David Justice	$5
Eric Karros	$5
Barry Larkin	$5
Kenny Lofton (Indians)	$5
Kenny Lofton (Braves)	$5
Fred McGriff	$5
Mark McGwire	$15
Paul Molitor	$5
Raul Mondesi	$5
Hideo Nomo	$6
Paul O'Neill	$5
Mike Piazza	$6
Cal Ripken Jr.	$15
Ivan Rodriguez	$5
Ryne Sandberg	$5
Gary Sheffield	$5
Frank Thomas	$40
Mo Vaughn	$5
Matt Williams	$5

1998 Headliners Baseball

Complete Set (41)	$200
Common piece	$6
Roberto Alomar	$6
Wade Boggs	$6
Barry Bonds	$10
Jay Buhner	$6
Ken Caminiti	$6
Roger Clemens	$10
Dennis Eckersley	$6
Jim Edmonds	$6
Juan Gonzalez	$8
Ken Griffey Jr.	$10
Tony Gwynn	$6
Orel Hershiser (Giants)	$6
Orel Hershiser (Indians)	$6
Derek Jeter	$8
Charles Johnson	$6

Randy Johnson	$6
Chipper Jones	$8
David Justice	$6
Eric Karros	$6
Barry Larkin	$6
Kenny Lofton (Braves)	$6
Kenny Lofton (Indians)	$6
Fred McGriff	$6
Raul Mondesi	$6
Hideo Nomo	$6
Paul O'Neill	$6
Rey Ordonez	$6
Chan Ho Park	$6
Mike Piazza	$7
Cal Ripken Jr.	$8
Alex Rodriguez	$10
Ivan Rodriguez	$6
Tim Salmon	$6
Deion Sanders	$6
Gary Sheffield	$6
Sammy Sosa	$15
Jim Thome	$6
Frank Thomas	$7
Bernie Williams	$7
Matt Williams (Diamondbacks)	$6
Matt Williams (Indians)	$6

1998 Headliners Baseball XL

Complete Set (12)	$200
Common piece	$12
Set price doesn't include blue versions	
Barry Bonds	$20
Andres Galarraga	$10
Ken Griffey Jr. (Blue)	$25
Ken Griffey Jr. (White)	$25

Derek Jeter	$20
Chipper Jones	$20
David Justice	$10
Mark McGwire (Blue)	$40
Mark McGwire (White)	$50
Hideo Nomo	$10
Mike Piazza	$20
Cal Ripken Jr.	$20
Alex Rodriguez	$20
Frank Thomas	$10

1998 MLB "Over the Fences" 3-Packs

McGwire/Griffey/Thomas	$40
Sam's Exclusive 2-Packs Bonds/McGwire	$40
Griffey/Ripken	$30

1998 MLB XL Home Run 2-Packs

McGwire/Griffey	$40
1998 MLB Cy Young Winners David Cone, Greg Maddux and Roger Clemens	$30

1999 - 3" Figures

Brady Anderson	$5
Jeff Bagwell	$6
Jim Edmonds	$5
Andres Galarraga	$5
Mark Grace	$4
Edgar Martinez	$5
Blue Base	$10
Mark McGwire	$10
Tim Salmon	$5
Red Base	$10
Sammy Sosa	$8
Larry Walker	$4
Green Base	$10

1999 MLB XL

Roger Clemens	$15
Roger Clemens (Yankees Special)	$25
Nomar Garciaparra	$20
Nomar Garciaparra (CVS Excl.)	$45
Juan Gonzalez	$15
Green Base	$20
Ken Griffey Jr.	$20
Tony Gwynn	$15
Red Base	$20
Mark McGwire	$30
Mark McGwire (CVS Excl.)	$50
Chan Ho Park	$12
Ivan Rodriguez	$10
Sammy Sosa	$25
Sammy Sosa (CVS Excl.)	$40
David Wells	$15
Blue Base	$20
Matt Williams	$10
Kerry Wood	$15

1999 SUPER XL

Mark McGwire	$25
Sammy Sosa	$25

1999 MLB XL 2-Packs

McGwire/Sosa	$40

2000 MLB XL

Shawn Green	$10
Ken Griffey Jr. (Limited to 5,000)	$25
Derek Jeter	$20
Pedro Martinez	$10
Mark McGwire	$25
Cal Ripken Jr.	$20
Sammy Sosa	$20

2000 Regular

Ken Griffey Jr.	$10

BASKETBALL

NBA Headliners were made for only two years due to Mattel taking over the rights for all NBA figures. The regular players were featured in 1996 and 1997. The 1996 Luc Longley is extremely rare and sought after by collectors. Dennis Rodman comes in four different hair color variations.

While there were no NBA XLs made (see college set), Equity did make some NBA Four Packs featuring top guards in one, top forwards in another and top centers in a third.

1996-97 Headliners Basketball

The inaugural Headliners basketball set contains four different hair color variations for the Dennis Rodman figurine — green, red, yellow and orange. The figures were sold in single packs, four-packs and 10-packs.

Complete Set (26): $150
Set includes Rodman Yellow
Special packs not included in set price
Charles Barkley $5
Shawn Bradley $5
Patrick Ewing.......................... $5
Horace Grant........................... $5
Anfernee Hardaway................ $8
Grant Hill $5
Juwan Howard $6
Larry Johnson $5
Shawn Kemp............................ $6
Luc Longley $20
Karl Malone $6
Jamal Mashburn $5
Antonio McDyess $5
Reggie Miller $5
Alonzo Mourning $5
Dikembe Mutombo $5
Hakeem Olajuwon $5
Scottie Pippen $10

Mitch Richmond...................... $5
Clifford Robinson $5
David Robinson $5
Glenn Robinson...................... $5
Dennis Rodman (Green) $15
Dennis Rodman (Orange) $12
Dennis Rodman (Red).......... $10
Dennis Rodman (Yellow) $10
Jerry Stackhouse.................... $6
John Starks $5
Damon Stoudamire................. $5
Centers 5-Pack (Ewing, Mourning, Mutumbo, Olajuwon)..................... $20
Forwards 4-Pack (Barkley, Kemp, Malone, Rodman) $20
Guards 4-Pack (Hardaway, Miller, Starks, Stoudamire). $20

1997-98 Headliners Basketball

Basketball
Complete Set (36): $160
Special Packs not included in Set Price
Charles Barkley $5
Muggsy Bogues $5
Cedric Ceballos $5
Clyde Drexler.......................... $6
Patrick Ewing.......................... $5
Kevin Garnett......................... $10
Horace Grant $5
Anfernee Hardaway $6

Grant Hill................................. $5
Allen Iverson $10
Larry Johnson $5
Shawn Kemp........................... $5
Jason Kidd $10
Toni Kukoc $10
Karl Malone $5
Jamal Mashburn $5
Reggie Miller $5
Alonzo Mourning $5
Dikembe Mutombo $5
Hakeem Olajuwon $5
Scottie Pippen $10
Bryant Reeves $5
Mitch Richmond $5
Clifford Robinson $5
David Robinson $5
Glenn Robinson $5
Dennis Rodman $8
Detlef Schrempf $5
Joe Smith................................ $5
Rik Smits................................. $5
Latrell Sprewell $5
Jerry Stackhouse.................... $5
John Stockton $8
Damon Stoudamire................. $5
Nick Van Exel $5
Chris Webber.......................... $7
Centers 4-Pack (Ewing, Olajuwon, Reeves, Smits) ..$20
Forwards 4-Pack (Barkley, Grant, Hill, Pippen)...................... $10
Future 4-Pack (Garnett, Iverson, Smith, Stoudmire) $20

Guards 4-Pack (Drexler, Miller, Sprewell, Van Exel) $20

Heroes of the Hardwood XL

Vince Carter.......................... $10
Shaquille O'Neal $12
Shaq O'Neal (LSU) $18
Michael Olawokandi $15
Scottie Pippen (Cent. Ark.) ...$15
Robert Traylor (Mich.)............$10

FOOTBALL

The NFL Headliners may have been the most popular of the four sports. They only came in the smaller size except for a college series in 1998 called Heroes of the Gridiron XL. This series of eight featured NFL stars in their college uniforms.

Besides the individual player packages featured each year from 1996 to 1998, Headliners did some really great multi-pack theme sets. One of the toughest to find and most popular was the Dallas Cowboy 10-pack. It featured 10 Cowboys and today goes for a premium.

Other NFL Series' produced by Headliners included a 1997 NFL "Throwback" Collection featuring players in old time uniforms, 1998 NFL in the Trenches Collection featuring players with their team helmets and 1998 NFL Sideline Quarterbacks (complete with baseball caps).

1996 Headliners Football

The 40-piece inaugural Headliners football set features top players such as Troy Aikman, Brett Favre, Emmitt Smith and Dan Marino. Figurines were sold in single blister packs.

Complete Set (40): $250
Special pack not included in set price
Troy Aikman $10
Marcus Allen $5
Drew Bledsoe $7
Tim Brown $5
Cris Carter.............................. $8
Kerry Collins........................... $8
John Elway $10
Marshall Faulk $5
Brett Favre $12

Jeff George............................. $5
Kevin Greene.......................... $5
Charles Haley $5
Jim Harbaugh $5
Jeff Hostetler $5
Stan Humphries...................... $5
Daryl Johnson $5
Jim Kelly $5
Leon Lett................................. $5
Greg Lloyd $5
Dan Marino $15
Steve McNair $6
Natrone Means $5
Rick Mirer $5
Nate Newton $5
Jay Novacek $5
Neil O'Donnell......................... $5
Jerry Rice $10
Rashaan Salaam $5
Barry Sanders $10
Deion Sanders........................ $6
Junior Seau $5

Heath Shuler........................... $5
Bruce Smith $5
Emmitt Smith $5
Kordell Stewart........................ $6
Ricky Watters $5
Reggie White $5
Kevin Williams $5
Darren Woodson...................... $5
Steve Young $8
QB's 4-Pack(Aikman, Favre, Marino, Young) $20

1997 Headliners Football

Complete Set (40):............. $220
Special packs not Included In set price
Troy Aikman $6
Marcus Allen $8
Bill Bates $5
Jerome Bettis $8
Drew Bledsoe $6
Robert Brooks $6

Tim Brown $5
Isaac Bruce $5
Mark Brunell............................ $8
Cris Carter............................. $10
Mark Chmura $6
Kerry Collins $5
Brett Favre............................. $10
Gus Frerotte $5
Eddie George $5
Jeff George $5
Kevin Greene $5
Jim Harbaugh $5
Jeff Hostetler $5
Michael Irvin $6
Keyshawn Johnson $6
Greg Lloyd............................... $5
Dan Marino (Away)................. $10
Dan Marino (Home) $10
Curtis Martin $10
Steve McNair $8
Natrone Means $5
Ken Norton Jr. $5

Jerry Rice $10
Rashaan Salaam $5
Deion Sanders $8
Junior Seau $5
Bruce Smith $5
Emmitt Smith $7
Kordell Stewart $10
Vinny Testaverde $5
Ricky Watters $5
Reggie White $5
Steve Young $5
AFC QB 4-Pack (Bledsoe, Elway, Harbaugh, Marino) $20
NVC QB 4-Pack (Aikman, Collins, Favre, Young) 20
RB's 4-Pack (Allen, Faulk, Salaam, Smith) $20
WR's 4-Pack (Carter, Johnson, Rice Sanders) $20
Heroes/Gridiron Set (Collins, Greene Sanders, White) .. $$20

1997 Throwback Collection

Marcus Allen $10
Drew Bledsoe $10
John Elway $35
Brett Favre $35
Rashaan Salaam $4
Barry Sanders $35
Junior Seau $6
Heath Shuler $5
Emmitt Smith $25
Vinny Testaverde $8
Rickey Watters $8
Reggie White $20

1997 Heroes of the Gridiron

Kerry Collins $4
Kevin Greene $4
Deion Sanders $15
Reggie White $12

1998 Headliners Football

Complete Set (45): $240
Common Figurine $5
Karim Abdul-Jabbar................ $5
Mike Alstott $5
Jerome Bettis $9
Tim Biakabutuka.................... $5
Jeff Blake......................... $5

Gilbert Brown......................... $5
Isaac Bruce $5
Mark Brunell $5
Ki-Jana Carter $5
Curtis Conway $5
Terrell Davis $7
Trent Dilfer $5
Warrick Dunn $6
John Elway $10
Steve Everitt $5
Brett Favre $10
Joey Galloway $5
Eddie George $8
Tony Gonzalez $5
Terry Glenn........................... $5
Elvis Grbac $5
Darrell Green $5
Marvin Harrison $5
Craig Heyward $5

Michael Irvin $5
Brad Johnson $5
Keyshawn Johnson.................. $6
Eddie Kennison $5
Ryan Leaf $5
Peyton Manning $10
Dan Marino $7
Curtis Martin..................... $6
Steve McNair $5
Scott Mitchell $5
Warren Moon $5
Herman Moore $5
Ken Norton Jr. $5
Jonathan Ogden $5
Orlando Pace...................... $5

John Randle.........................$5
Barry Sanders $8
Junior Seau $5
Shannon Sharpe $6
Antowain Smith $5
Neil Smith $5
Eric Swann $5
Derrick Thomas $5

1998 Heroes of the Gridiron

Terrell Davis $10
Natrone Means $5
Herman Moore $6
Derrick Thomas $6

1998 Heroes of the Gridiron XL

Terrell Davis (GA.)...............$20
Warrick Dunn (FSU)..............$15
Curtis Enis (Penn St.)..........$15
Elvis Grbac (Mich.) $10
Curtis Martin (Pitt.)...........$15
Herman Moore (UVA) $10
Deion Sanders (FSU) $15
Charles Woodson (Mich.) $18

1998 NFL in the Trenches

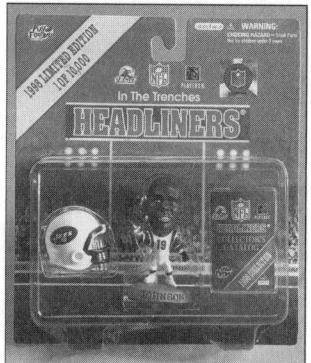

Karim Abdul-Jabbar $8
Isaac Bruce..........................$8
Mark Chmura $8
Brett Favre $20
Joey Galloway $10
Terry Glenn $10
Michael Irvin $10
Keyshawn Johnson $10

Herman Moore $10
Barry Sanders $20
Shannon Sharpe $12
Neil Smith $8

NFL Sideline Quarterbacks

Jeff Blake $6
Drew Bledsoe $8
Mark Brunell $10
Trent Dilfer $8
John Elway $22
Brett Favre..........................$20
Elvis Grbac $6
Brad Johnson $12
Dan Marino $20
Steve McNair $8
Scott Mitchell $6
Warren Moon $10

1999 NFL 2-Packs Future SB

Quarterbacks
Leaf/Marino $20

1999 NFL 2-Packs Present SB

Quarterbacks
Elway/Favre..........................$45

HOCKEY

NHL Headliners were made from 1996 to 1998. The first year they did not have a license from the NHL so the players were featured in team colors but without logos. The Headliners had NHLPA across them.

The rarest NHL Headliner may be an exclusive figure of Eric Lindros made for Hastings Hall of Fame. Some other exclusives that are hard to find are NHL Headliners that were produced for *White's Guide to Collecting Figures.* These players included Wayne Gretzky, Mario Lemieux, Jamir Jagr, Eric Lindros and Patrick Roy.

While no XL's were made in hockey except for a 1998 NHLPA series, another popular series was called NHL In The Crease. This was a series of only goalies and came with their custom made masks.

1996 Headliners Hockey

Complete Set (21):.............$130
Set Doesn't Include White's Pieces
Ray Bourque..........................$5
Pavel Bure $5
Chris Chelios $5
Sergei Fedorov $6
Wayne Gretzky $12
Wayne Gretzky (White's) $14
Jaromir Jagr $8
Jaromir Jagr (White's) $10

Jari Kurri...........................$5
Brian Leetch.........................$5
Claude Lemieux $5
Mario Lemieux $8
Mario Lemieux (White's) $14
Eric Lindros $8
Eric Lindros (White's).............$8
Mark Messier $7
Jeremy Roenick $5
Jeremy Roenick (White's) $14
Patrick Roy $12
Patrick Roy (White's)............$10
Joe Sakic $5

Teemu Salanne $6
Brendan Shanahan $5
Mats Sundin $5
Keith Tkachuk....................... $5
John Vanbiesbrouck $8

1997 Headliners Hockey

Complete Set (30) $175
Martin Brodeur $10
Pavel Bure $5
Chris Chelios........................ $5
Paul Coffey $8

Sergei Fedorov $6
Peter Forsberg....................... $8
Grant Fuhr $10
Wayne Gretzky $10
Brett Hull $8
Jaromir Jagr......................... $8
Paul Kariya $8
Jari Kurri $5
Pat LaFontaine $6
Brian Leetch $5
Claude Lemieux $5
Mario Lemieux $10
Eric Lindros $8

Mark Messier	$6
Felix Potvin	$6
Mike Richter	$6
Jeremy Roenick	$5
Patrick Roy	$8
Joe Sakic	$5
Teemu Selanne	$6
Brendan Shanahan	$5
Mats Sundin	$5
Keith Tkachuk	$5
Pierre Turgeon	$6
John Vanbiesbrouck	$8
Steve Yzerman	$6

1997/98 Headliners Hockey in the Crease

Complete Set (5)	$50
Common Player	$12
Martin Brodeur	$12
Grant Fuhr	$12
Mike Richter	$12
Patrick Roy	$12
John Vanbiesbrouck	$12

1998/99 NHL In the Crease

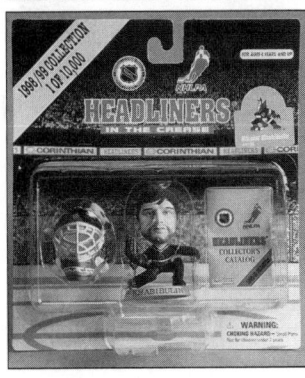

Chris Chelios	$10
Brett Hull	$10
Jaromir Jagr	$15
Paul Kariya	$15
Eric Lindros	$10
Mike Richter	$12
Patrick Roy	$20
John Vanbiesbrouck	$10

1998-99 Hockey

Jason Arnott	$5
Ed Belfour	$7
Rob Blake	$4

Ed Belfour	$10
Jeff Hackett	$8
Guy Herbert	$8
Curtis Joseph	$10
Nikolai Khabibulin	$8
Olaf Kolzig	$12
Felix Potvin	$10
Garth Snow	$8

1998 NHLPA XL

Chris Chelios	$10
Brett Hull	$10

Dino Ciccarelli	$4
Theo Fluery	$5
Grant Fuhr	$5
Doug Gilmour	$5
Chris Gratton	$4
Wayne Gretzky	$10
Jeff Hackett	$7
Guy Hebert	$5
Paul Kariya	$6
John LeClair	$6
Eric Lindros	$8
Eric Lindros (Hasting's Excl.)	$12
Mike Modano	$6
Adam Oates	$5
Zigmund Palffy	$6
Felix Potvin	$7
Joe Sakic	$4
Teemu Selanne	$5
Chris Simon	$5
Joe Thornton	$6
Steve Yzerman	$6

Silver Editions Created by EDI

1998 Barry Sanders (Ltd. 2,053)	$40
1998 Brett Favre (Ltd. 3,867)	$35
1998 Kevin Garnett (Ltd. 1,518)	$32
1999 Patrick Roy (Ltd. 913)	$30

2000 XL Century Legends

Vince Lombardi	$20
Jesse Owens	$20
Arnold Palmer	$20
Babe Ruth	$20

Romito Enterprises

Rick Romito founded Romito, Inc., in 1995. Previously to that time, Romito was very familiar with the figurine industry buying large quantities of leftover inventory from Gartlan, Sports Impressions and Salvino. Romito Baseball figurines are done in much smaller edition sizes than other companies. Edition sizes range from 100 to 1,000. Height ranges anywhere from 7 to 14 inches.

Since 1995, the Romito line has concentrated on Hall of Fame Players and near Hall of Fame Players. Romito figurines

can be divided into 5 categories, Hall of Fame, 3,000 Hit Club, 500 HR Club, New York Yankees and Unsung Heroes of Baseball. Each player features a distinctive base design, gold medallion sealed on the bottom of the base detailing player career achievements, its own serial number, and an individually numbered certificate.

Player	Edition Size	Value
Yogi Berra Autographed	100	$250
Yogi Berra	500	$120
Yogi Berra AP Autographed	25	$400
Roberto Clemente at Forbes	1,000	$170
Roberto Clemente at Forbes AP	25	$340
Roberto Clemente at 3,000	1,000	$150
Roberto Clemente at 3,000	25	$300
Bob Feller Autographed	400	$200
Bob Feller	100	$170
Bob Feller AP Autographed	25	$340
Rollie Fingers Autographed	400	$200
Rollie Fingers	100	$170
Rollie Fingers AP Autographed	25	$340
Jimmie Foxx	534	$120
Jimmie Foxx AP	25	$240

Player	Edition Size	Value
Lou Gehrig	400	$170
Lou Gehrig HOF Edition	100	$170
Lou Gehrig AP	25	$340
Catfish Hunter	400	$170
Catfish Hunter HOF Edition	100	$170
Walter Johnson	500	$170
Walter Johnson AP	25	$340
Al Kaline Autographed	400	$200
Al Kaline	100	$170
Al Kaline AP Autographed	25	$340
Don Mattingly Autographed	500	$200
Don Mattingly AP Autographed	25	$400
Bill Mazeroski Autographed	500	$200
Bill Mazeroski AP Autographed	25	$300
Thurman Munson	500	$170

Babe Ruth

Lou Gehrig

Rollie Fingers

Bob Feller

Player	Edition Size	Value
Thurman Munson AP	25	$340
Stan Musial Autographed	100	$400
Stan Musial	500	$120
Stan Musial AP Autographed	25	$600
Jackie Robinson	1,000	$170
Jackie Robinson AP	25	$340
Babe Ruth	714	$120
Babe Ruth AP	25	$240

Player	Edition Size	Value
Ron Santo Autographed	500	$120
Ron Santo AP Autographed	25	$240
Mike Schmidt Autographed	100	$400
Mike Schmidt	548	$120
Mike Schmidt AP Autographed	25	$600
Willie Stargell Autographed	400	$200
Willie Stargell	100	$170
Willie Stargell AP Autographed	25	$340

STARTING LINEUP FIGURES

In 1986, Pat McInally, a Harvard graduate and 10-year veteran of the Cincinnati Bengals, was in the process of moving his family from Cincinnati to the West Coast. Preparations included selling his condominium, and the prospective buyer was a newly hired Kenner executive.

McInally was the author of a syndicated newspaper column called "Pat Answers For Kids." The Kenner executive was in the business of developing toys for those very readers. It was suggested that McInally come up with some ideas for Kenner.

A field trip to a toy store provided some inspiration. McInally and his wife journeyed across the Ohio River to wander the aisles of one of the major toy store chains. What they found in abundant quantity were "heroes" based upon fictional characters. The question that occurred to them both was, why not make toys of real world heroes such as sports stars?

Nothing further happened until McInally moved to California, but Kenner kept in touch. Finally, arrangements were made for him to return to Cincinnati and make a presentation of his idea to the company.

On his way to the meeting, he made a brief detour to a local store to pick up a pack of baseball cards to supplement his presentation. Grabbing one of Kenner's current action figures, McInally had the "total" package for his proposal. The reaction was overwhelming. Two hours of discussion ended with only one potential snag: How to get the licensing rights? McInally thought he could help with that, as well.

On the following Monday, a trip to New York to obtain licensing rights with the major sports leagues took place. McInally proved to be the key to success there as well. At NFL Properties, they met with John Flood. Flood had been a fullback at Harvard during McInally's tenure there. After a bit of reminiscing about college, the attendees sat down and negotiated an arrangement. The next stop was MLB Properties. Once again, McInally's college and professional background proved to be a key element in getting the ball rolling. The MLB

Properties' legal counsel was Ed Durso, a former running back for the Bengals. Rick White, head of the division, was an alumnus of Chapman College in McInally's California neighborhood. The next morning, they visited the NBA's offices. The merit of the proposal and the prospect of a line featuring the full gamut of major league sports was impossible to reject. By the end of that week, commitments were in hand and Starting Lineup figurines soon became a reality.

Starting Lineups were owned and produced by Hasbro Toy Co. Hasbro obtained Tonka (which owned Kenner) in May 1990. The product development responsibility did not change, however. The Kenner logo appeared on the product through 1997 and was changed to the Hasbro logo in 1998. Prior to Tonka owning Kenner, Kenner had been a part of Kenner Parker Toys. And prior to that, it was a part of the General Mills group.

In January of 2001, Hasbro announced that it was discontinuing its entire line of figurines following the release of its 2001 baseball product lines.

All values listed are for Mint figures still in the packaging. The package must have four perfect corners and the blister bubble cannot be creased, dented, or damaged in any way.

1988 Baseball

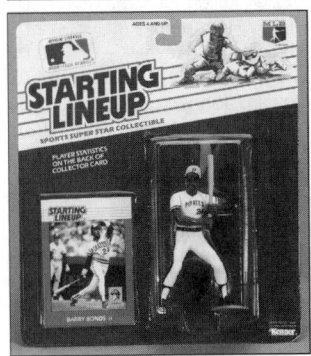

5-player stand w/box	60.00
5-player stand w/o box	40.00
Blue Collr's Showcase	50.00
All-Star Baseball	40.00
Alan Ashby	25.00
Harold Baines	15.00
Kevin Bass	12.00
Steve Bedrosian	15.00
Buddy Bell	25.00
George Bell	15.00
Mike Boddicker	30.00
Wade Boggs	35.00
Barry Bonds	130.00
Bobby Bonilla	20.00
Sid Bream	15.00
George Brett	80.00
Chris Brown	10.00
Tom Brunansky	22.00
Ellis Burks	40.00
Jose Canseco	30.00
Gary Carter	25.00
Joe Carter	30.00
Jack Clark	17.00
Will Clark	25.00
Roger Clemens	70.00
Vince Coleman	12.00
Kal Daniels	12.00
Alvin Davis	12.00
Eric Davis	10.00
Glenn Davis	12.00
Jody Davis	30.00
Andre Dawson	25.00
Rob Deer	16.00
Brian Downing	12.00
Mike Dunne	12.00
Shawon Dunston	15.00
Leon Durham	14.00
Lenny Dykstra	17.00
Dwight Evans	20.00
Carlton Fisk	65.00
John Franco	16.00
Julio Franco	18.00
Gary Gaetti	15.00
Dwight Gooden	12.00
Ken Griffey Sr.	25.00
Pedro Guerrero	10.00
Ozzie Guillen	20.00
Tony Gwynn	90.00
Mel Hall	12.00
Billy Hatcher	14.00

Von Hayes	15.00
Rickey Henderson	30.00
Keith Hernandez	15.00
Willie Hernandez	14.00
Tom Herr	25.00
Ted Higuera	15.00
Charlie Hough	25.00
Kent Hrbek	15.00
Pete Incaviglia	18.00
Howard Johnson	14.00
Wally Joyner	12.00
Terry Kennedy	28.00
John Kruk	20.00
Mark Langston	25.00
Carney Lansford	20.00
Jeffrey Leonard	15.00
Fred Lynn	27.00
Candy Maldonado	10.00
Mike Marshall	14.00
Don Mattingly	25.00
Willie McGee	35.00
Mark McGwire	150.00
Kevin McReynolds	10.00
Paul Molitor	55.00
Donnie Moore	25.00
Jack Morris	24.00
Dale Murphy	17.00
Eddie Murray	60.00
Matt Nokes	10.00
Pete O'Brien	12.00
Ken Oberkfell	15.00
Dave Parker	25.00
Larry Parrish	15.00
Ken Phelps	15.00
Jim Presley	15.00
Kirby Puckett	65.00
Dan Quisenberry	30.00
Tim Raines	30.00
Willie Randolph	25.00
Shane Rawley	12.00
Jeff Reardon	40.00
Gary Redus	12.00
Rick Reuschel	12.00
Jim Rice	24.00
Dave Righetti	15.00
Cal Ripken Jr.	250.00
Pete Rose	80.00
Nolan Ryan	225.00
Bret Saberhagen	20.00
Juan Samuel	10.00
Ryne Sandberg	70.00
Benito Santiago	22.00
Steve Sax	13.00
Mike Schmidt	55.00
Mike Scott	10.00
Kevin Seitzer	14.00
Ruben Sierra	30.00
Ozzie Smith	75.00
Zane Smith	15.00
Cory Snyder	12.00
Darryl Strawberry	10.00
Franklin Stubbs	15.00
B.J. Surhoff	35.00
Rick Sutcliffe	20.00
Pat Tabler	18.00
Danny Tartabull	17.00
Alan Trammell	22.00
Fernando Valenzuela	12.00
Andy Van Slyke	22.00
Frank Viola	18.00
Ozzie Virgil	12.00
Greg Walker	15.00
Lou Whitaker	24.00
Devon White	30.00

Dave Winfield	55.00
Mike Witt	12.00
Todd Worrell	18.00
Robin Yount	70.00

1988 Canadian

George Bell	35.00
George Brett	75.00
Wade Boggs	50.00
Gary Carter	35.00
Roger Clemens	125.00
Andre Dawson	35.00
Rickey Henderson	50.00
Don Mattingly	50.00
Tim Raines	35.00
Darryl Strawberry	35.00
Dave Winfield	80.00

1989 Baseball

Roberto Alomar	275.00
Brady Anderson	120.00
Harold Baines	25.00
Marty Barrett	20.00
Kevin Bass	15.00
Steve Bedrosian	12.00
George Bell	12.00
Damon Berryhill	25.00
Wade Boggs	30.00
Barry Bonds	125.00
Bobby Bonilla	16.00
Phil Bradley	35.00
Glenn Braggs	40.00
Mickey Brantley	60.00
George Brett	70.00
Tom Brookens	35.00
Tom Brunansky	20.00
Steve Buechele	50.00
Ellis Burks	20.00
Brett Butler	20.00
Ivan Calderon	35.00
Jose Canseco	25.00
Gary Carter	20.00
Joe Carter	25.00
Will Clark	18.00
Roger Clemens	55.00
Vince Coleman	10.00
David Cone	40.00
Kal Daniels	12.00
Alvin Davis	20.00
Chili Davis	100.00
Eric Davis	10.00
Glenn Davis	15.00
Mark Davis	40.00
Andre Dawson	20.00
Rob Deer	45.00
Bo Diaz	30.00
Billy Doran	35.00
Doug Drabek	30.00
Shawon Dunston	20.00
Lenny Dykstra	25.00
Dennis Eckersley	75.00

Kevin Elster	12.00
Scott Fletcher	130.00
John Franco	12.00
Gary Gaetti	15.00
Ron Gant	100.00
Kirk Gibson	17.00
Dan Gladden	25.00
Dwight Gooden	10.00
Mark Grace	40.00
Mike Greenwell	10.00
Mark Gubicza	10.00
Pedro Guerrero	10.00
Ozzie Guillen	35.00
Tony Gwynn	350.00
Albert Hall	60.00
Mel Hall	40.00
Billy Hatcher	15.00
Von Hayes	12.00
Rickey Henderson	20.00
Mike Henneman	20.00
Keith Hernandez	12.00
Orel Hershiser	35.00
Ted Higuera	55.00
Jack Howell	100.00
Kent Hrbek	25.00
Pete Incaviglia	40.00
Bo Jackson	25.00
Danny Jackson	30.00
Brook Jacoby	25.00
Chris James	12.00
Dion James	55.00
Gregg Jefferies	25.00
Doug Jones	25.00
Wally Joyner	14.00
John Kruk	50.00
Mark Langston	25.00
Carney Lansford	20.00
Barry Larkin	65.00
Tim Laudner	75.00
Mike LaValliere	40.00
Al Leiter	45.00
Chet Lemon	18.00
Jose Lind	45.00
Greg Maddux	275.00
Candy Maldonado	12.00
Mike Marshall	45.00
Don Mattingly	25.00
Willie McGee	25.00
Mark McGwire	65.00
Kevin McReynolds	15.00
Kevin Mitchell	20.00
Paul Molitor	35.00
Jack Morris	20.00
Dale Murphy	25.00
Randy Myers	20.00
Matt Nokes	15.00
Mike Pagliarulo	18.00
Dave Parker	25.00
Dan Pasqua	25.00
Tony Pena	35.00
Terry Pendleton	30.00
Melido Perez	32.00
Gerald Perry	35.00
Dan Plesac	50.00
Kirby Puckett	45.00
Rey Quinones	65.00
Tim Raines	11.00
Johnny Ray	100.00
Jeff Reardon	50.00
Harold Reynolds	50.00
Jim Rice	20.00
Dave Righetti	16.00
Cal Ripken Jr.	325.00
Jeff Russell	75.00

Bret Saberhagen 16.00
Chris Sabo 20.00
Luis Salazar 25.00
Juan Samuel 10.00
Ryne Sandberg 35.00
Benito Santiago 30.00
Mike Schmidt 50.00
Dick Schofield 100.00
Mike Scioscia 150.00
Mike Scott 10.00
Kevin Seitzer 12.00
Larry Sheets 25.00
John Shelby 50.00
Ruben Sierra 32.00
Don Slaught 25.00
Dave Smith 10.00
Lee Smith 55.00
Ozzie Smith 70.00
Zane Smith 55.00
Cory Snyder 17.00
Pete Stanicek 40.00
Terry Steinbach 20.00
Dave Stewart 25.00
Kurt Stillwell 15.00
Darryl Strawberry 10.00
B.J. Surhoff 110.00
Rick Sutcliffe 16.00
Bruce Sutter 100.00
Greg Swindell 25.00
Pat Tabler 13.00
Danny Tartabull 12.00
Bobby Thigpen 45.00
Milt Thompson 30.00
Robby Thompson 15.00
Alan Trammell 18.00
Jeff Treadway 35.00
Jose Uribe 15.00
Fernando Valenzuela 35.00
Andy Van Slyke 25.00
Frank Viola 12.00
Bob Walk 35.00
Greg Walker 25.00
Walt Weis 20.00
Bob Welch 22.00
Lou Whitaker 25.00
Devon White 120.00
Dave Winfield 35.00
Mike Witt 120.00
Todd Worrell 14.00
Marvell Wynne 30.00
Gerald Young 22.00
Robin Yount 70.00

1989 Canadian
George Bell 35.00
Wade Boggs 50.00
Jose Canseco 45.00
Gary Carter 35.00
Roger Clemens 200.00
Eric Davis 35.00
Andre Dawson 35.00
Gary Gaetti 35.00
Kirk Gibson 40.00
Dwight Gooden 35.00
Mike Greenwell 35.00
Rickey Henderson 45.00
Wally Joyner 35.00
Don Mattingly 50.00
Mark McGwire 300.00
Tim Raines 35.00
Cal Ripken Jr. 1000.00
Chris Sabo 35.00
Mike Schmidt 100.00
Mike Scott 35.00
Ozzie Smith 100.00

Darryl Strawberry 35.00
Alan Trammell 35.00
Fernando Valenzuela 35.00

1989 Baseball Greats
Ernie Banks, Billy Williams.... 40.00
Johnny Bench, Pete Rose.... 60.00
Don Drysdale,
  Reggie Jackson 60.00
Mickey Mantle,
  Joe DiMaggio 90.00
Eddie Mathews, Hank Aaron 50.00
Willie Mays, Willie McCovey . 45.00
Stan Musial, Bob Gibson 50.00
Babe Ruth , Lou Gehrig
  (white/gray) 55.00
  (white/white) 70.00
  (gray/white) 45.00
Stargell, Clemente 60.00
Carl Yastrzemski,
  Hank Aaron 90.00

1990 Baseball

Allan Anderson 10.00
Wally Backman 55.00
Jeff Ballard 20.00
Jesse Barfield 15.00
Steve Bedrosian 10.00
Todd Benzinger 45.00
Damon Berryhill 40.00
Wade Boggs 20.00
Barry Bonds 95.00
Bobby Bonilla 25.00
Chris Bosio 15.00
Ellis Burks 30.00
Jose Canseco 20.00
Will Clark (Batting) 10.00
Will Clark (Power) 17.00
Roger Clemens 40.00
Vince Coleman 10.00
Ron Darling 22.00
Eric Davis 12.00
Andre Dawson 18.00
Rob Dibble 25.00
Lenny Dykstra 25.00
Dennis Eckersley 40.00
Nick Esasky 40.00
Gary Gaetti 20.00
Andres Galarraga 25.00
Kirk Gibson 10.00
Dwight Gooden 10.00
Mark Grace (Batting) 18.00
Mark Grace (Power) 22.00
Mike Greenwell 10.00
Ken Griffey Jr. (R, Sliding) 75.00
Pedro Guerrero 15.00
Von Hayes 10.00
Dave Henderson 13.00
Rickey Henderson 18.00
Tom Herr 22.00

Orel Hershiser 20.00
Kent Hrbek 10.00
Bo Jackson 10.00
Gregg Jefferies 15.00
Howard Johnson 10.00
Rickey Jordan 12.00
Roberto Kelly 15.00
Barry Larkin 40.00
Greg Maddux 350.00
Joe Magrane 30.00
Don Mattingly
  (Bat in hand) 20.00
  (Power) 24.00
Fred McGriff 40.00
Mark McGwire 70.00
Kevin McReynolds 10.00
Kevin Mitchell 12.00
Paul Molitor 30.00
Eddie Murray 125.00
Matt Nokes 15.00
Paul O'Neill 70.00
Jose Oquendo 65.00
Gary Pettis 70.00
Kirby Puckett 40.00
Willie Randolph 25.00
Jody Reed 20.00
Rick Reuschel 10.00
Dave Righetti 15.00
Cal Ripken Jr. 170.00
Nolan Ryan 60.00
Chris Sabo 12.00
Juan Samuel 12.00
Ryne Sandberg 30.00
Steve Sax 10.00
Mike Scott 12.00
Gary Sheffield 35.00
John Smiley 17.00
Ozzie Smith 40.00
Dave Stewart 15.00
Darryl Strawberry (Batting) ... 10.00
  (Fielding) 10.00
Rick Sutcliffe 14.00
Mickey Tettleton 65.00
Alan Trammell 20.00
Andy Van Slyke 25.00
Frank Viola 12.00
Jerome Walton 10.00
Lou Whitaker 15.00
Mitch Williams 20.00
Dave Winfield 45.00
Robin Yount 65.00

1990 Extended
Jim Abbott 12.00
Sandy Alomar Jr. 17.00
Jose Canseco 20.00
Joe Carter 25.00
Ken Griffey Jr. (Jump) 70.00
Bo Jackson 10.00
Nolan Ryan 45.00
Ben McDonald 12.00
Jerome Walton 10.00

1991 Baseball
Jim Abbott 10.00
Sandy Alomar Jr. 16.00
Jack Armstrong 12.00
Barry Bonds 45.00
Bobby Bonilla 14.00
Tom Browning 18.00
Jose Canseco 15.00
Will Clark 16.00
Eric Davis 8.00
Andre Dawson 10.00
Delino DeShields 8.00

Doug Drabek 14.00
Shawon Dunston 12.00
Lenny Dykstra 14.00
Cecil Fielder 10.00
John Franco 10.00
Dwight Gooden 9.00
Mark Grace 15.00
Ken Griffey Jr. (Batting) 30.00
Kelly Gruber 12.00
Ozzie Guillen 12.00
Rickey Henderson 12.00
Bo Jackson (Royals) 10.00
Gregg Jefferies 13.00
Howard Johnson 10.00
Roberto Kelly 10.00
Barry Larkin 18.00
Kevin Maas 9.00
Dave Magadan 9.00
Ramon Martinez 15.00
Don Mattingly 18.00
Ben McDonald 10.00
Mark McGwire 50.00
Kevin Mitchell 10.00
Kirby Puckett 25.00
Nolan Ryan 40.00
Chris Sabo 8.00
Ryne Sandberg 30.00
Benito Santiago 12.00
Steve Sax 10.00
Dave Stewart 13.00
Darryl Strawberry (Mets) 10.00
Alan Trammell 20.00
Frank Viola 10.00
Matt Williams 20.00
Todd Zeile 10.00

1991 Extended
George Bell 10.00
Vince Coleman 10.00
Glenn Davis 10.00
Ken Griffey Jr. (Running) 35.00
Ken Griffey Sr. 20.00
Bo Jackson (White Sox) 15.00
David Justice 30.00
Tim Raines 13.00
Nolan Ryan 40.00
Darryl Strawberry (Dodgers) 10.00

1991 Headline Baseball
Jose Canseco 20.00
Will Clark 15.00
Ken Griffey Jr. 40.00
Rickey Henderson 45.00
Bo Jackson 12.00
Don Mattingly 50.00
Nolan Ryan 60.00

1992 Baseball
Roberto Alomar 15.00
George Bell 10.00
Albert Belle 15.00
Craig Biggio 25.00
Barry Bonds 30.00
Ivan Calderon 8.00
Jose Canseco 15.00
Will Clark 15.00
Roger Clemens 35.00
Rob Dibble 10.00
Scott Erickson 8.00
Cecil Fielder 8.00
Chuck Finley 12.00
Tom Glavine 35.00
Juan Gonzalez 35.00
Ken Griffey Jr.
  (Bat in hand) 35.00
  (Swing) 40.00

Tony Gwynn...................... 40.00
Dave Henderson 7.00
Rickey Henderson 15.00
Bo Jackson (Running) 9.00
Bo Jackson (Bat in hand) .. 10.00
Howard Johnson 10.00
Felix Jose............................ 7.00
David Justice 10.00
Kevin Maas......................... 8.00
Ramon Martinez 8.00
Fred McGriff 16.00
Brian McRae 9.00
Cal Ripken Jr. 70.00
Nolan Ryan........................ 35.00
Chris Sabo 8.00
Ryne Sandberg 18.00
Ruben Sierra 14.00
Darryl Strawberry 10.00
Frank Thomas (Fielding).. 25.00
Matt Williams.................... 10.00

1992 Extended
Steve Avery...................... 12.00
Bobby Bonilla 10.00
Eric Davis 8.00
Kirby Puckett 18.00
Bret Saberhagen 8.00
Tom Seaver 24.00
Danny Tartabull 10.00
Frank Thomas (Batting)..... 30.00
Todd Van Poppel................ 8.00

1992 Headline Baseball
George Brett....................... 40.00
Cecil Fielder 15.00
Ken Griffey Jr.................... 40.00
Rickey Henderson 20.00
Bo Jackson........................ 10.00
Nolan Ryan........................ 50.00
Ryne Sandberg 35.00

1993 Baseball

Roberto Alomar................. 12.00
Carlos Baerga................... 10.00
Jeff Bagwell...................... 45.00
Barry Bonds (Pirates)........ 30.00
Kevin Brown..................... 17.00
Jose Canseco 16.00
Will Clark 8.00
Roger Clemens 28.00
David Cone....................... 10.00
Travis Fryman................... 10.00
Tom Glavine 25.00
Juan Gonzalez 25.00
Ken Griffey Jr.................... 35.00
Marquis Grissom............... 12.00
Juan Guzman..................... 8.00
Eric Karros....................... 10.00
Roberto Kelly 6.00
John Kruk 10.00
Ray Lankford 12.00
Barry Larkin 15.00
Shane Mack........................ 6.00
Jack McDowell................... 9.00
Fred McGriff 15.00
Mark McGwire 40.00
Mike Mussina 35.00
Dean Palmer 10.00
Terry Pendleton 6.00
Kirby Puckett 15.00
Cal Ripken Jr. 40.00
Bip Roberts........................ 9.00
Nolan Ryan (Regular)........ 40.00
Ryne Sandberg 15.00
Gary Sheffield 12.00
John Smoltz...................... 32.00

Frank Thomas.................... 12.00
Andy Van Slyke 10.00
Robin Ventura 15.00
Larry Walker..................... 15.00

1993 Extended

Barry Bonds (Giants)......... 40.00
Carlton Fisk 20.00
Bo Jackson 10.00
Greg Maddux...................... 75.00
David Neid........................ 10.00
Nolan Ryan (Retire)........... 95.00
Benito Santiago 10.00

1993 Headline Baseball
Jim Abbott.......................... 14.00
Roberto Alomar 18.00
Tom Glavine...................... 23.00
Mark McGwire 40.00
Cal Ripken Jr. 55.00
Nolan Ryan........................ 50.00
Deion Sanders 20.00
Frank Thomas.................... 20.00

1993 Stadium Stars
Roger Clemens.................. 40.00
Cecil Fielder...................... 15.00
Ken Griffey Jr. 35.00
Nolan Ryan........................ 55.00
Ryne Sandberg.................. 30.00
Frank Thomas.................... 30.00

1994 Baseball

Kevin Appier 10.00
Steve Avery........................ 8.00
Carlos Baerga 8.00
Jeff Bagwell 17.00
Derek Bell........................ 10.00
Jay Bell 14.00
Albert Belle 8.00
Wade Boggs 8.00
Barry Bonds 14.00
John Burkett 16.00
Joe Carter........................... 7.00
Roger Clemens 20.00
David Cone 12.00
Chad Curtis 10.00
Darren Daulton................. 12.00
Delino DeShields 8.00
Alex Fernandez.................. 7.00
Cecil Fielder...................... 8.00
Andres Galarraga 8.00
Mark Grace......................... 8.00
Tommy Greene.................... 8.00
Ken Griffey Jr. 25.00
Brian Harper 8.00
Brian Harvey...................... 8.00
Charlie Hayes 8.00
Chris Hoiles....................... 8.00
Dave Hollins..................... 10.00
Gregg Jefferies 7.00
Randy Johnson.................. 50.00
David Justice 10.00

Eric Karros 8.00
Jimmy Key........................15.00
Darryl Kile.......................30.00
Chuck Knoblauch 10.00
Mark Langston 8.00
Don Mattingly....................10.00
Orlando Merced 8.00
Paul Molitor......................10.00
Mike Mussina....................12.00
John Olerud......................20.00
Tony Phillips......................7.00
Mike Piazza......................50.00
Jose Rijo.........................15.00
Cal Ripken Jr. 45.00
Ivan Rodriguez 25.00
Tim Salmon 20.00
Ryne Sandberg..................15.00
Curt Schilling 35.00
Gary Sheffield (Regular)....10.00
J.T. Snow.........................12.00
Frank Thomas....................15.00
Robby Thompson.................7.00
Greg Vaughn......................7.00
Mo Vaughn.......................15.00
Robin Ventura....................10.00
Matt Williams....................10.00
Dave Winfield....................10.00

1994 Extended
Steve Carlton (HOF).........18.00
Will Clark..........................10.00
Lenny Dykstra 15.00
Juan Gonzalez...................20.00
Kenny Lofton....................35.00
Fred McGriff 15.00
Rafael Palmeiro................25.00
Gary Sheffield (Power).......10.00

1994 Stadium Stars
Barry Bonds 45.00
Will Clark...........................15.00
Dennis Eckersley 18.00
Tom Glavine 20.00
Juan Gonzalez 20.00
Bo Jackson 45.00
Kirby Puckett 25.00
Deion Sanders 35.00

1994 Cooperstown
Ty Cobb.............................14.00
Lou Gehrig.........................14.00
Reggie Jackson 30.00
Willie Mays........................20.00
Jackie Robinson (with #42)...14.00
Jackie Robinson (with #44) .350.00
Babe Ruth..........................20.00
Honus Wagner 30.00
Cy Young 14.00

1995 Baseball

Jim Abbott...........................8.00
Moises Alou......................25.00
Carlos Baerga......................8.00
Jeff Bagwell 14.00
Albert Belle 8.00
Geronimo Berroa 10.00
Dante Bichette..................10.00
Barry Bonds 20.00
Jay Buhner.......................10.00
Jose Canseco (Rangers) ...10.00
Chuck Carr 7.00
Joe Carter............................8.00
Andujar Cedeno................10.00
Will Clark.............................8.00
Roger Clemens 20.00
Jeff Conine......................10.00
Scott Cooper......................7.00

Darren Daulton...................10.00
Carlos Delgado.................30.00
Cecil Fielder 8.00
Cliff Floyd........................17.00
Julio Franco.........................8.00
Juan Gonzalez 10.00
Ken Griffey Jr.....................30.00
Tony Gwynn 20.00
Bob Hamelin......................8.00
Jeffrey Hammonds............7.00
Randy Johnson 25.00
Jeff Kent..........................30.00
Jeff King..........................10.00
Ryan Klesko.....................25.00
Chuck Knoblauch 10.00
John Kruk 10.00
Ray Lankford 8.00
Barry Larkin 12.00
Javier Lopez.....................25.00
Al Martin..........................10.00
Brian McRae 8.00
Paul Molitor 8.00
Raul Mondesi...................20.00
Mike Mussina 10.00
Troy Neel 10.00
Dave Nilsson....................10.00
John Olerud 8.00
Paul O'Neill 10.00
Mike Piazza (Throwing)...35.00
Kirby Puckett 10.00
Cal Ripken Jr. (Regular)...35.00
Tim Salmon 10.00
Deion Sanders 15.00
Reggie Sanders 15.00
Sammy Sosa.....................70.00
Mickey Tettleton................15.00
Frank Thomas 12.00
Andy Van Slyke 10.00
Mo Vaughn 10.00
Rick Wilkins.....................10.00
Matt Williams......................7.00

1995 Extended

Jose Canseco (Red Sox) ...10.00
Rusty Greer 12.00
Kenny Lofton 35.00
Tom Pagnozzi...................10.00
Mike Piazza (Batting) 25.00
Manny Ramirez.................30.00
Cal Ripken Jr. (Streak).......70.00
Alex Rodriguez.................90.00
Mike Schmidt (HOF)..........15.00

1995 Stadium Stars
Darren Daulton...................20.00
Lenny Dykstra 20.00
Ken Griffey Jr.....................30.00
Randy Johnson 60.00
David Justice 20.00
Greg Maddux 55.00
Mark McGwire 55.00
Frank Thomas 20.00
Mo Vaughn 20.00

1995 Cooperstown

Rod Carew 12.00
Dizzy Dean 10.00
Don Drysdale 10.00
Bob Feller 10.00
Whitey Ford 10.00
Bob Gibson 10.00
Harmon Killebrew 18.00
Eddie Mathews.................. 25.00
Satchel Paige 10.00
Babe Ruth 15.00

1996 Baseball

Roberto Alomar 10.00
Jeff Bagwell (white bat) 15.00
Jeff Bagwell (black bat) 10.00
Albert Belle.......................... 8.00
Craig Biggio....................... 10.00
Barry Bonds 15.00
Ricky Bones...................... 8.00
Rico Brogna...................... 7.00
Ken Caminiti 10.00
Vinny Castilla 10.00
Will Clark 8.00
David Cone.......................... 8.00
Wil Cordero 7.00
Marty Cordova 15.00
Shawon Dunston 10.00
Lenny Dykstra 8.00
Jim Edmonds................... 25.00
Jim Eisenreich.................. 8.00
Gary Gaetti......................... 8.00
Ron Gant............................. 8.00
Ken Griffey Jr. (Regular) 20.00
Marquis Grissom 12.00
Ozzie Guillen 8.00
Brian Hunter 10.00
Derek Jeter...................... 50.00
Charles Johnson 15.00
Chipper Jones 110.00
Greg Maddux 35.00
Jeff Manto 10.00
Edgar Martinez 25.00
Fred McGriff 8.00
Mark McGwire 35.00
Raul Mondesi 8.00
Eddie Murray 15.00
Hideo Nomo (white) 20.00
       (gray) 20.00
Paul O'Neill........................ 12.00
Mike Piazza 18.00
Kirby Puckett 20.00
Cal Ripken Jr. (Diving)........ 35.00
       (Sliding) 35.00
(Diving w/sliding card) 32.00
(Sliding w/diving card) 32.00
Ivan Rodriguez 10.00
Deion Sanders 15.00
Ozzie Smith 22.00

Sammy Sosa 35.00
Terry Steinbach 8.00
Frank Thomas 12.00
Jim Thome....................... 30.00
Ryan Thompson 8.00
John Valentin 10.00
Mo Vaughn 8.00
Larry Walker 15.00
Rondell White.................. 15.00
Matt Williams 8.00

1996 Extended

Moises Alou 15.00
Garrett Anderson............. 45.00
Carlos Baerga 10.00
Dante Bichette 10.00
Joe Carter.......................... 10.00
Jeff Conine 8.00
Chad Curtis 8.00
Ken Griffey Jr. 35.00
Juan Gonzalez 18.00
David Justice 15.00
Eric Karros......................... 10.00
Barry Larkin 15.00
Don Mattingly..................... 18.00
Hal Morris........................ 12.00
Denny Neagle.................. 10.00
Rafael Palmeiro 15.00

1996 Stadium Stars

Albert Belle 15.00
Jay Buhner......................... 15.00
Jose Canseco..................... 15.00
Darren Daulton 15.00
Mark Grace......................... 15.00
Chuck Knoblauch 15.00
Javy Lopez 25.00
Mike Piazza 40.00
Cal Ripken Jr. 60.00
Robin Ventura 15.00
Matt Williams 15.00

1996 Cooperstown

Hank Aaron........................ 20.00
Grover Alexander............... 10.00
Richie Ashburn (Clover) 20.00
Rod Carew ('96 National) .. 25.00
Steve Carlton ('96 Fanfest). 20.00
Roberto Clemente 20.00
Jimmy Foxx........................ 15.00
Hank Greenberg 10.00
Rogers Hornsby................. 12.00
Harmon Killebrew (TS) 25.00
Joe Morgan 15.00
Mel Ott 10.00
Robin Roberts 15.00
Jackie Robinson 18.00

1996 Cooperstown 12" Figures

Ty Cobb 15.00
Lou Gehrig......................... 15.00
Babe Ruth Red Sox
   (Kay-Bee)........................ 25.00
Babe Ruth Yankees 20.00
Honus Wagner (Toys R Us) . 15.00
Cy Young 15.00

1997 Baseball

Roberto Alomar 12.00
Brady Anderson 10.00
Jeff Bagwell 10.00
Derek Bell 8.00
Albert Belle 10.00
Dante Bichette 10.00
Barry Bonds 15.00
Scott Brosius 10.00
Ellis Burks 10.00
Roger Clemens 15.00

Johnny Damon................. 17.00
Steve Finley 14.00
Tom Glavine 18.00
Rusty Greer 8.00
Ken Griffey Jr. 20.00
Todd Hundley 8.00
Jason Isringhausen......... 12.00
John Jaha 7.00
Randy Johnson 20.00
Chipper Jones 35.00
Brian Jordan................... 18.00
Wally Joyner 8.00
Jason Kendall 20.00
Ryan Klesko 15.00
Javier Lopez 14.00
Tino Martinez.................. 17.00
Brian McRae 8.00
Jose Mesa....................... 10.00
Paul Molitor 10.00
Raul Mondesi 10.00
Hideo Nomo 12.00
Rey Ordonez 10.00
Chan Ho Park 15.00
Mike Piazza 12.00
Manny Ramirez 18.00
Cal Ripken Jr. 16.00
Alex Rodriguez 23.00
Henry Rodriguez 12.00
Ivan Rodriguez 12.00
Ryne Sandberg 10.00
Reggie Sanders 8.00
John Smoltz 18.00
J.T. Snow 12.00
Frank Thomas 12.00
Ismael Valdes 15.00
Devon White 10.00
Bernie Williams 30.00
Matt Williams 10.00

1997 Extended

Albert Belle 8.00
Ricky Bottalico.................. 7.00
Ken Caminiti......................... 7.00
Tony Clark....................... 10.00
Roger Clemens 20.00
Dennis Eckersley 12.00
Derek Jeter 25.00
Andruw Jones 35.00
Mark McGwire 28.00
Mike Mussina 10.00
Andy Pettitte................... 18.00
Alex Rodriguez 20.00
Deion Sanders 10.00
Matt Williams 10.00

1997 Classic Doubles

Hank Aaron,
   Jackie Robinson 15.00
Ken Griffey Jr.,
   Ken Griffey Sr. 30.00
Barry Bonds, Bobby Bonds... 40.00
Greg Maddux, Cy Young.... 50.00
Randy Johnson,
   Nolan Ryan 35.00
Frank Thomas, Babe Ruth ... 20.00
Ripken Jr.,
   Brooks Robinson.............. 30.00
J. Robinson, L. Doby
   (Fanfest) 35.00
Hideo Nomo, Don Drysdale.. 15.00
Mark McGwire,
   Roger Maris 40.00
Mickey Mantle,
   Roger Maris 30.00

1997 Freeze Frame

Dante Bichette 15.00
Juan Gonzalez 15.00
Ken Griffey Jr. 30.00
Chipper Jones 25.00
Mike Piazza 20.00
Frank Thomas 20.00

1997 Stadium Stars

Hank Aaron 20.00
Ferguson Jenkins............... 15.00
Al Kaline 23.00
Mickey Mantle 35.00
Babe Ruth 25.00
Mike Schmidt...................... 20.00
Carl Yastrzemski 20.00

1997 12" Figures

Ken Griffey Jr. 35.00
Greg Maddux 25.00
Mike Piazza........................ 25.00
Cal Ripken Jr. 35.00

1997 Cooperstown

Johnny Bench 15.00
Rollie Fingers 12.00
Josh Gibson 15.00
Walter Johnson 12.00
Dottie Kamenshek 10.00
Mickey Mantle 20.00
Brooks Robinson................ 15.00
Jackie Robinson (Dodgers).. 75.00
Duke Snider 10.00
Hoyt Wilhelm 12.00
Carl Yastrzemski 10.00

1998 Baseball

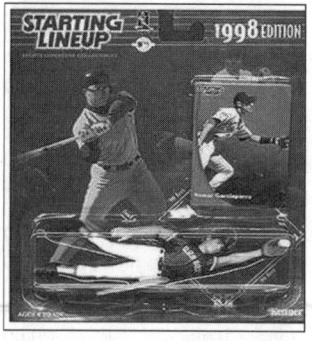

Albert Belle.......................... 8.00
Craig Biggio 10.00
Barry Bonds 17.00
Kevin Brown 10.00
Jose Canseco..................... 12.00
Will Clark 8.00
Darin Erstad.................... 24.00
Andres Galarraga 8.00
Nomar Garciaparra.......... 25.00
Tom Glavine 15.00
Juan Gonzalez 10.00
Mark Grace 10.00
Mark Grace (Cubs) 25.00
Ken Griffey Jr..................... 20.00
Mark Grudzielanek.......... 10.00
Tony Gwynn 12.00
Bobby Higginson 8.00
Glenallen Hill 8.00
Derek Jeter 20.00
Chipper Jones 25.00
David Justice 10.00
Chuck Knoblauch 10.00
Ray Lankford 8.00
Barry Larkin........................ 10.00
Mickey Morandini............. 8.00
Marc Newfield................... 8.00

Hideo Nomo 10.00
Rafael Palmeiro 10.00
Mike Piazza 15.00
Cal Ripken Jr. 15.00
Mariano Rivera 25.00
Alex Rodriguez 15.00
Deion Sanders 12.00
Gary Sheffield 12.00
Sammy Sosa (Cubs) 85.00
Ed Sprague 10.00
Frank Thomas 12.00
Jim Thome 12.00
Mo Vaughn 10.00
Larry Walker 12.00
Bernie Williams 12.00

1998 Extended

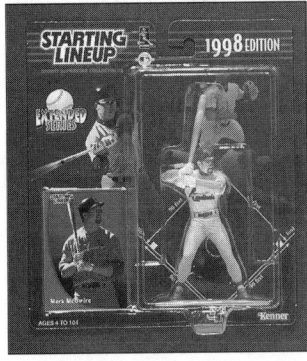

Sandy Alomar..................... 8.00
Moises Alou...................... 15.00
Jay Bell........................... 10.00
Jim Edmonds 12.00
Ken Griffey Jr..................... 18.00
Hideki Irabu...................... 7.00
Greg Maddux 20.00
Fred McGriff 10.00
Mark McGwire (Extended) 60.00
   (Home run) 28.00
Dean Palmer 8.00
Scott Rolen 35.00
Sammy Sosa (Extended) .. 65.00
   (Home run) 40.00
Larry Walker 12.00
Tony Womack................... 25.00

1998 Classic Doubles

Ken Griffey Jr.,
   Alex Rodriguez 30.00
Rey Ordonez, Derek Jeter. 20.00
Albert Belle, Frank Thomas..15.00
Ivan Rodriguez,
   Mike Piazza 24.00
Jose Canseco,
   Mark McGwire 30.00
Babe Ruth, Roger Maris.... 25.00
Nolan Ryan,
   Walter Johnson.............. 25.00
"Catfish" Hunter, R. Jackson.20.00
Yogi Berra, Thurman
   Munson 20.00
Johnny Bench, Joe Morgan .20.00
Mark McGwire,
   Sammy Sosa 45.00

1998 Freeze Frame

Jeff Bagwell 25.00
Barry Bonds 30.00
Derek Jeter....................... 25.00
Greg Maddux 25.00
Cal Ripken Jr. 30.00
Alex Rodriguez 28.00

1998 Stadium Stars

Albert Belle 15.00

Ken Griffey Jr. 24.00
Mike Piazza 25.00
Cal Ripken Jr. 24.00
Ivan Rodriguez 23.00
John Smoltz 25.00
Bernie Williams.............. 25.00
Ted Williams (Hills/Brad.)... 35.00

1998 12" Figures

Derek Jeter 30.00
Chipper Jones 25.00
Hideo Nomo 15.00
Alex Rodriguez 30.00

1998 Cooperstown

Yogi Berra 8.00
Lou Brock 15.00
Roy Campanella 10.00
Roberto Clemente 20.00
Buck Leonard 8.00
Phil Niekro 8.00
Jim Palmer 10.00
Frank Robinson 12.00
Tom Seaver 8.00
Warren Spahn 15.00
Tris Speaker 20.00

1999 Baseball

Edgardo Alfonzo............. 20.00
Wilson Alvarez................ 10.00
Jeff Bagwell 10.00
David Cone 10.00
Jose Cruz Jr. 12.00
Darin Erstad 15.00
Vinny Castilla 12.00
Tony Clark 10.00
Roger Clemens 16.00
Nomar Garciaparra
   (Regular) 15.00
   (Fanfest) 18.00
Juan Gonzalez 10.00
Ken Griffey Jr. 15.00
Vladimir Guerrero 65.00
Jose Guillen 10.00
Tony Gwynn 15.00
Livan Hernandez........... 12.00
Derek Jeter 15.00
Randy Johnson................ 18.00
Chipper Jones 15.00
Travis Lee 12.00
Kenny Lofton................... 10.00
Pedro J. Martinez........... 30.00
Tino Martinez.................. 12.00
Mark McGwire (Regular) ... 20.00
   (Wal-Mart, red hat).......... 30.00
   (Wal-Mart, blue hat)......... 40.00
Denny Neagle 10.00
Chan Ho Park 12.00
Mike Piazza 20.00
Brad Radke.................... 18.00
Manny Ramirez 15.00

Edgar Renteria 17.00
Cal Ripken Jr. 15.00
Scott Rolen 15.00
Alex Rodriguez 12.00
Ivan Rodriguez 10.00
Sammy Sosa (Regular) 20.00
   (Wal-Mart) 20.00
Omar Vizquel.................22.00
Larry Walker 14.00
Kerry Wood....................25.00

1999 Extended

Kevin Brown 10.00
Sean Casey....................22.00
J.D. Drew.......................30.00
Nomar Garciaparra 12.00
Ben Grieve 10.00
Greg Maddux 15.00
Mo Vaughn 10.00
David Wells 15.00
Bernie Williams 10.00
Jaret Wright.....................8.00

1999 Classic Doubles

Sandy Alomar 15.00
Darin Erstad......................20.00
Nomar Garciaparra 30.00
Ken Griffey Jr. 30.00
Derek Jeter 30.00
Javier Lopez 20.00
Greg Maddux 25.00
Mark McGwire....................35.00
Mark McGwire, Roger Maris.35.00
Raul Mondesi 15.00
Alex Rodriguez 30.00
Sammy Sosa, Roger Maris...35.00

1999 Cooperstown

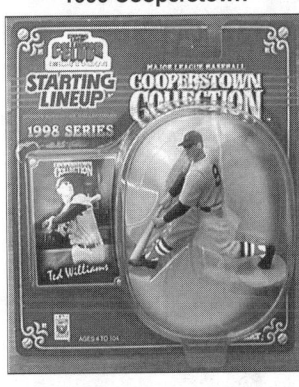

George Brett 16.00
Pepper Davis 10.00
Bob Gibson 10.00
Juan Marichal 10.00
Nolan Ryan 20.00
Earl Weaver 10.00
Ted Williams......................22.00

1999 One-On-One

Sandy Alomar,
   Ken Griffey Jr..................25.00
Jason Kendall,
   Rey Ordonez 20.00
N. Garciaparra, J. Edmonds..22.00
Chipper Jones,
   Larry Walker...................20.00
Cal Ripken Jr.,
   Kenny Lofton 20.00

1999 Sport Star

Mark McGwire...................30.00
Sammy Sosa 25.00

1999 Stadium Stars

Roger Clemens 20.00
Nomar Garciaparra 25.00
Derek Jeter 25.00

Chipper Jones...................22.00
Kenny Lofton 20.00
Mark McGwire (Regular)....35.00
   (Wal-Mart) 25.00
Alex Rodriguez...................25.00
Sammy Sosa (Wal-Mart)...25.00

1999 12" Figures

Roger Clemens 25.00
Nomar Garciaparra 25.00
Ken Griffey Jr....................25.00
Tony Gwynn 25.00
Mark McGwire 40.00
Sammy Sosa 25.00

2000 Baseball

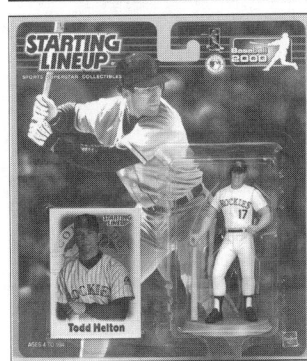

Roberto Alomar...................8.00
Barry Bonds 18.00
Bret Boone......................20.00
Jose Canseco 10.00
Roger Clemens 15.00
J.D. Drew 15.00
Nomar Garciaparra 10.00
Troy Glaus......................25.00
Shawn Green 28.00
Ken Griffey Jr....................15.00
Vladimir Guerrero...............20.00
Todd Helton 20.00
Orlando Hernandez..........12.00
Trevor Hoffman...............12.00
Derek Jeter 15.00
Randy Johnson 12.00
Chipper Jones (Fanfest)......20.00
Barry Larkin.......................8.00
Greg Maddux 10.00
Pedro J. Martinez...............22.00
Mark McGwire
   (Regular with shin guard) .. 20.00
   (Regular w/o shin guard) ... 15.00
   (500 HR Wal-Mart Excl.).... 15.00
Kevin Millwood (Fanfest) 15.00
Mike Piazza.......................12.00
Shane Reynolds 12.00
Cal Ripken Jr.....................10.00
Curt Schilling 15.00
Aaron Sele 15.00
Sammy Sosa 15.00
Matt Stairs......................10.00
Robin Ventura 15.00
Bernie Williams 10.00

2000 Extended

Roger Cedeno 10.00
Ken Griffey Jr.....................18.00
Tony Gwynn 15.00
Mike Hampton 15.00
Chipper Jones 12.00
Kevin Millwood.................15.00
Cal Ripken Jr. 15.00
Alex Rodriguez 12.00
Scott Williamson 10.00

2000 All-Century

Hank Aaron	10.00
Johnny Bench	10.00
Lou Gehrig	10.00
Mickey Mantle	15.00
Christy Mathewson	28.00
Jackie Robinson	10.00
Babe Ruth	12.00
Mike Schmidt	10.00
Honus Wagner	25.00
Cy Young	8.00

2000 Classic Doubles

Derek Jeter, Mike Piazza	30.00
Roger Clemens, C. Schilling	27.00
Jim Thome, Sean Casey	20.00
Pedro Martinez, John Smoltz	25.00
Cal Ripken Jr., Chipper Jones	20.00

2000 Baseball Elite

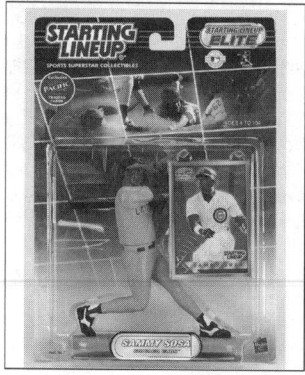

Ken Griffey Jr.	20.00
Derek Jeter	22.00
Greg Maddux	15.00
Mark McGwire	18.00
Mike Piazza	18.00
Sammy Sosa	18.00

2001 Baseball

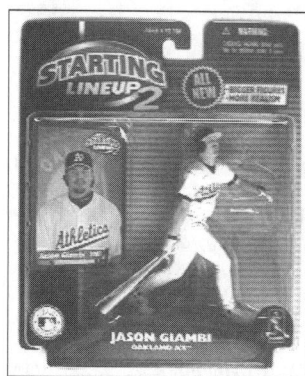

Rick Ankiel	10.00
Barry Bonds	35.00
Pat Burrell	22.00
Rafael Furcal	25.00
Nomar Garciaparra	15.00
Jason Giambi	35.00
Shawn Green	15.00
Ken Griffey Jr.	15.00
Vladimir Guerrero	15.00
Todd Helton	17.00
Derek Jeter	18.00
Randy Johnson	15.00
Chipper Jones	15.00
David Justice (Toys R Us)	20.00
Pedro J. Martinez	20.00
Mark McGwire	20.00
Magglio Ordonez	18.00
Mike Piazza	20.00
Pokey Reese	10.00
Cal Ripken Jr.	15.00
Ivan Rodriguez	10.00
Sammy Sosa	15.00
Jim Thome (Toys R Us)	22.00

2001 Insert Figures

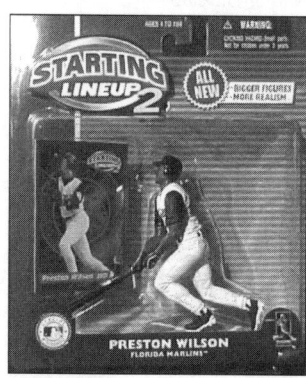

Bobby Abreu	40.00
Brian Giles	45.00
Andruw Jones	35.00
Preston Wilson	37.00

2001 Extended

Jeff Bagwell	10.00
Jim Edmonds	12.00
Tom Glavine	8.00
Jorge Posada	20.00
Alex Rodriguez (Rangers)	18.00
Frank Thomas	8.00

2001 Classic Doubles

Derek Jeter, Omar Vizquel	25.00
Ken Griffey Jr., Andruw Jones	18.00
Mark McGwire, Todd Helton	20.00
Tim Hudson, Greg Maddux	25.00
Sammy Sosa, V. Guerrero	25.00

2001 Cooperstown

Reggie Jackson	15.00
Willie McCovey	12.00
Brooks Robinson	12.00
Nolan Ryan	20.00
Tom Seaver	15.00
Willie Stargell	18.00
Robin Yount	20.00

2001 Wal-Mart Exclusives

Jermaine Dye	25.00
Andres Galarraga	12.00
Ken Griffey Jr.	12.00
Derek Jeter	35.00
Pedro Martinez	25.00
Mark McGwire	15.00
Gary Sheffield	15.00

1988 Basketball

5-player stand w/box:	60.00
5-player stand w/o box:	40.00
Kareem Abdul-Jabbar	55.00
Michael Adams	55.00
Mark Aguirre	100.00
Danny Ainge	80.00
Thurl Bailey	275.00
Charles Barkley	75.00
Walter Berry	45.00
Larry Bird	80.00
Rolando Blackman	100.00
Michael Cage	45.00
Joe Barry Carroll	50.00
Tom Chambers	45.00
Maurice Cheeks	55.00
Michael Cooper	75.00
Terry Cummings	60.00
Adrian Dantley	105.00
Brad Daugherty	50.00
Johnny Dawkins	50.00
Clyde Drexler	100.00
Mark Eaton	325.00
Dale Ellis	55.00
Alex English	75.00
Patrick Ewing	45.00
Eric "Sleepy" Floyd	65.00
Winston Garland	50.00
Armon Gilliam	45.00
Mike Gminski	50.00
David Greenwood	55.00
Derek Harper	80.00
Ron Harper	55.00
Rod Higgins	60.00
Dennis Hopson	55.00
Jeff Hornacek	60.00
Mark Jackson	45.00
Dennis Johnson	80.00
Eddie Johnson	40.00
Magic Johnson	70.00
Steve Johnson	55.00
Vinnie Johnson	150.00
Michael Jordan	115.00

Bernard King	45.00
Bill Laimbeer	135.00
Lafayette Lever	55.00
Jeff Malone	40.00
Karl Malone	800.00
Moses Malone	120.00
Danny Manning	40.00
Rodney McCray	100.00
Xavier McDaniel	55.00
Kevin McHale	55.00
Derrick McKey	50.00
Reggie Miller	250.00
Sidney Moncrief	65.00
Chris Mullin	50.00
Hakeem Olajuwon	65.00
Robert Parish	65.00
John Paxson	75.00
Sam Perkins	125.00
Chuck Person	75.00
Scottie Pippen	125.00
Terry Porter	55.00
Paul Pressey	60.00
Mark Price	125.00
Doc Rivers	60.00
Alvin Robertson	60.00
Cliff Robinson	40.00
Ralph Sampson	55.00
Danny Schayes	80.00
Jack Sikma	75.00
Kenny Smith	65.00
Steve Stipanovich	75.00
John Stockton	550.00
Isiah Thomas	55.00
LaSalle Thompson	55.00
Otis Thorpe	60.00
Wayman Tisdale	60.00
Kiki Vandeweghe	60.00
Spud Webb	45.00
Dominique Wilkins	50.00
Gerald Wilkins	40.00
Buck Williams	40.00
John Williams	50.00
Reggie Williams	55.00
Kevin Willis	55.00
James Worthy	65.00

1989 Basketball

Rex Chapman	30.00
Dell Curry	30.00
Ron Harper	30.00
Larry Nance	35.00
Kelly Tripucka	25.00

1990 Basketball

Charles Barkley	70.00
Larry Bird	80.00
Tom Chambers	15.00
Clyde Drexler	40.00
Joe Dumars	27.00
Patrick Ewing	25.00
Magic Johnson	40.00
Michael Jordan	100.00
Karl Malone	65.00
Chris Mullin	20.00
David Robinson	50.00
Byron Scott	55.00
John Stockton	60.00
Isiah Thomas	30.00
Spud Webb	17.00
Dominique Wilkins	30.00
James Worthy	18.00

1990 SLAM DUNK Red Box

Larry Bird	200.00
Patrick Ewing	100.00

Magic Johnson 150.00
Michael Jordan 300.00
Isiah Thomas 80.00
Dominique Wilkins 80.00

1990 SLAM DUNK White Box
Larry Bird 100.00
Patrick Ewing 60.00
Magic Johnson 100.00
Michael Jordan 200.00
Isiah Thomas 60.00
Dominique Wilkins 50.00

1991 Basketball

Charles Barkley 80.00
Larry Bird 70.00
Derrick Coleman 23.00
Clyde Drexler 30.00
Joe Dumars 14.00
Patrick Ewing 25.00
Kevin Johnson 25.00
Magic Johnson 30.00
Michael Jordan (Jumping) ..110.00
(Regular) 110.00
Reggie Lewis 25.00
David Robinson 15.00
Dennis Rodman 50.00
Isiah Thomas 18.00
Spud Webb 17.00
Dominique Wilkins 25.00

1992 Basketball

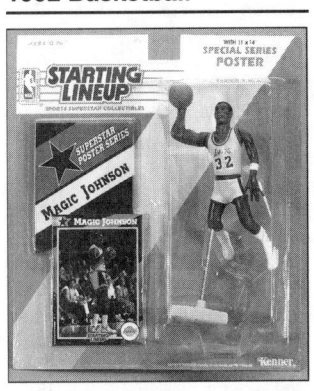

Charles Barkley 45.00
Larry Bird 60.00
Manute Bol 10.00
Dee Brown 12.00
Derrick Coleman 10.00
Vlade Divac 20.00
Clyde Drexler 25.00
Joe Dumars 12.00
Patrick Ewing 20.00
Tim Hardaway 18.00
Kevin Johnson 12.00
Larry Johnson 30.00
Magic Johnson (purple) 60.00
(yellow) 250.00
Michael Jordan (regular) 140.00
(warm up) 150.00
Dan Majerle 15.00
Karl Malone 25.00
Reggie Miller 40.00
Chris Mullin 20.00
Dikembe Mutombo 18.00
Hakeem Olajuwon 30.00
John Paxson 20.00
Scottie Pippen 30.00
Mark Price 15.00
David Robinson (regular) .. 18.00
(warm-up) 24.00
Dennis Rodman 40.00

John Stockton 30.00
Isiah Thomas 15.00

1992 Headline Basketball
Charles Barkley 85.00
Larry Bird 90.00
Patrick Ewing 45.00
Magic Johnson 75.00
Michael Jordan 150.00
Dikembe Mutombo 25.00
Scottie Pippen 50.00
David Robinson 40.00

1993 Basketball

Kenny Anderson 15.00
Stacey Augmon 12.00
Charles Barkley 27.00
Brad Daugherty 12.00
Todd Day 10.00
Clyde Drexler 20.00
Sean Elliott 18.00
Patrick Ewing 20.00
Horace Grant 25.00
Tom Gugliotta 25.00
Tim Hardaway 20.00
Larry Johnson 15.00
Michael Jordan 200.00
Shawn Kemp 15.00
Christian Laettner 20.00
Dan Majerle 10.00
Karl Malone 20.00
Alonzo Mourning 30.00
Dikembe Mutombo 15.00
Shaquille O'Neal 70.00
Scottie Pippen 30.00
Terry Porter 15.00
Mark Price 12.00
Glen Rice 20.00
Mitch Richmon 25.00
David Robinson 24.00
Detlef Schrempf 12.00
John Stockton 20.00
Dominique Wilkins 12.00

1994 Basketball

B.J. Armstrong 10.00
Stacey Augmon 10.00
Charles Barkley 20.00
Shawn Bradley 12.00
Calbert Cheaney 12.00
Derrick Coleman 10.00
Sean Elliott 10.00
LaPhonso Ellis 12.00
Patrick Ewing 12.00
Anfernee Hardaway 30.00
Jim Jackson 17.00
Larry Johnson 10.00
Shawn Kemp 10.00
Karl Malone 15.00
Jamal Mashburn 25.00

Harold Miner 12.00
Alonzo Mourning 15.00
Chris Mullin 12.00
Hakeem Olajuwon 15.00
Shaquille O'Neal 30.00
Scottie Pippen 25.00
David Robinson 18.00
Dennis Rodman (white) 50.00
(red) 100.00
Latrell Sprewell 25.00
Chris Webber 30.00
Dominique Wilkins 10.00

1995 Basketball

Charles Barkley 15.00
Tyrone Bogues 14.00
Patrick Ewing 15.00
Horace Grant
(blue goggles) 10.00
(black goggles) 20.00
Anfernee Hardaway 15.00
Grant Hill (regular) 18.00
(Kmart) 18.00
Jeff Hornacek 8.00
Jimmy Jackson 10.00
Shawn Kemp 10.00
Jason Kidd 50.00
Toni Kukoc 15.00
Dan Majerle 8.00
Karl Malone 16.00
Reggie Miller 18.00
Eric Montross 7.00
Alonzo Mourning 12.00
Hakeem Olajuwon 12.00
Shaquille O'Neal 30.00
Robert Pack 12.00
Scottie Pippen 25.00
Mark Price 10.00
Cliff Robinson 17.00
David Robinson 15.00
Glenn Robinson 25.00
Steve Smith 16.00
Latrell Sprewell 15.00
John Starks 10.00
Nick Van Exel 25.00
Clarence Weatherspoon 7.00
Chris Webber 20.00
Dominique Wilkins 10.00

1996 Basketball

Vin Baker 15.00
Charles Barkley 15.00
Clyde Drexler 16.00
Sean Elliott 8.00
Patrick Ewing 10.00
Kevin Garnett 45.00
Anfernee Hardaway 10.00
Grant Hill (dribbling) 15.00
(Pistons) 20.00

Tyrone Hill 15.00
Juwan Howard 18.00
Larry Johnson 10.00
Eddie Jones 30.00
Jason Kidd 20.00
Karl Malone 15.00
Jamal Mashburn 12.00
Antonio McDyess 18.00
Reggie Miller 12.00
Alonzo Mourning 10.00
Hakeem Olajuwon 15.00
Shaquille O'Neal 20.00
Gary Payton 40.00
Scottie Pippen 15.00
Dino Radja 10.00
Bryant Reeves 10.00
Pooh Richardson 10.00
Mitch Richmond 12.00
Cliff Robinson 10.00
David Robinson 14.00
Glenn Robinson 14.00
Dennis Rodman
(green hair) 30.00
(orange hair) 30.00
(yellow hair) 30.00
Joe Smith 16.00
Rik Smits 10.00
Jerry Stackhouse 30.00
Damon Stoudamire 17.00

1996 Extended

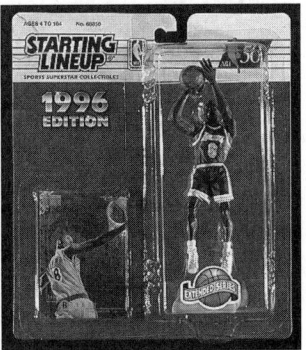

Charles Barkley 16.00
Kobe Bryant 100.00
Grant Hill 18.00
Allen Iverson 65.00
Larry Johnson 12.00
Dikembe Mutombo 14.00
Shaquille O'Neal 30.00
Damon Stoudamire 14.00

1996 Far East Basketball
Charles Barkley 18.00
Sean Elliott 10.00
Penny Hardaway 25.00
Grant Hill 15.00
Larry Johnson 10.00
Magic Johnson 250.00
Eddie Jones 30.00
Reggie Miller 12.00
Hakeem Olajuwon 15.00
Shaquille O'Neal 25.00
Scottie Pippen 12.00
Dennis Rodman
(green hair) 40.00
(orange hair) 40.00
(yellow hair) 40.00

1997 Basketball

Shareef Abdur-Rahim 20.00
Ray Allen (SLU card) 30.00
(Upper Deck card) 25.00

Kenny Anderson 10.00
Vin Baker 10.00
Charles Barkley 10.00
Terrell Brandon 15.00
Marcus Camby 15.00
Vlade Divac 10.00
Patrick Ewing 10.00
Michael Finley 30.00
Kevin Garnett (SLU card) .. 18.00
(Upper Deck card) 18.00
Horace Grant 10.00
Tim Hardaway 12.00
Grant Hill 12.00
Allan Houston 17.00
Juwan Howard 10.00
Allen Iverson (SLU card) ... 30.00
(Upper Deck card) 25.00
Mark Jackson 10.00
Shawn Kemp 10.00
Jason Kidd 15.00
Kerry Kittles 18.00
Stephon Marbury
(SLU card) 25.00
(Upper Deck card) 25.00
Reggie Miller 14.00
Alonzo Mourning 10.00
Hakeem Olajuwon 10.00
Shaquille O'Neal 15.00
Gary Payton (SLU card) 10.00
(Upper Deck card) 12.00
Scottie Pippen (SLU card) 12.00
(Upper Deck card) 15.00
Mitch Richmond 10.00
David Robinson 15.00
Dennis Rodman 20.00
Steve Smith 10.00
Latrell Sprewell 12.00
John Stockton (SLU card) 10.00
(Upper Deck card) 12.00
Damon Stoudamire
(SLU card) 10.00
(Upper Deck card) 12.00
Nick Van Exel 12.00
Loy Vaught 10.00
Antoine Walker 35.00
Chris Webber 15.00

1997 Extended

Clyde Drexler 12.00
Tim Duncan 70.00
Anfernee Hardaway 12.00
Eddie Jones 18.00
Luc Longley 10.00
Anthony Mason 12.00
Antonio McDyess 10.00
Keith Van Horn 20.00

1997 Backboard Kings
Charles Barkley 23.00
Grant Hill 23.00
Karl Malone 20.00
Shaquille O'Neal 28.00

Scottie Pippen 24.00
Damon Stoudamire 20.00

1997 Classic Doubles
Larry Bird, Kevin McHale ... 33.00
Wilt Chamberlain,
Bill Russell 33.00
Patrick Ewing, Willis Reed . 20.00
Grant Hill, Joe Dumars 25.00
Karl Malone, John Stockton .. 28.00
Hakeem Olajuwon,
Bill Russell 20.00
S. O'Neal, K. Abdul-Jabbar .. 34.00

1997 14" Figures
Charles Barkley 30.00
Grant Hill 28.00
Shawn Kemp 18.00
Shaquille O'Neal 35.00
Dennis Rodman 40.00

1998 Basketball

Vin Baker 8.00
Terrell Brandon 8.00
Kobe Bryant 30.00
Patrick Ewing 10.00
Kevin Garnett 18.00
Grant Hill 10.00
Allen Iverson 20.00
Magic Johnson 17.00
Shawn Kemp 8.00
Jason Kidd 14.00
Karl Malone 12.00
Stephon Marbury 15.00
Alonzo Mourning 10.00
Shaquille O'Neal 20.00
Dennis Rodman 12.00
Rik Smits 8.00

1998 12" Figures
Tim Duncan 35.00
Kevin Garnett 25.00
Juwan Howard 15.00
Allen Iverson 30.00
Glen Rice 15.00

1998 Collegiate Basketball
Kareem Abdul-Jabbar 10.00
Larry Bird 15.00
Patrick Ewing 10.00
Juwan Howard 10.00
Allen Iverson 25.00
Magic Johnson 12.00
Jason Kidd 100.00
Bill Russell 10.00
Sheryl Swoopes 12.00

2000 Basketball NCAA March Madness

David Robinson 10.00
Jerry Stackhouse 8.00
Sheryl Swoopes 8.00
Isiah Thomas 8.00
Bill Walton 8.00
James Worthy 8.00

1988 Football

5-player stand w/box: 60.00
5-player stand w/o box: 40.00
Blue Collr's Showcase: 60.00
Marcus Allen 75.00
Neal Anderson 35.00
Chip Banks 100.00
Mark Bavaro 50.00
Cornelius Bennett 140.00
Albert Bentley 100.00
Duane Bickett 120.00

Todd Blackledge 75.00
Brian Bosworth 42.00
Brian Brennan 65.00
Bill Brooks 110.00
James Brooks 65.00
Eddie Brown 60.00
Joey Browner 100.00
Aundray Bruce 55.00
Chris Burkett 110.00
Keith Byars 50.00
Scott Campbell 125.00
Carlos Carson 100.00
Harry Carson 60.00
Anthony Carter 85.00
Gerald Carter 50.00
Michael Carter 75.00
Tony Casillas 75.00
Jeff Chadwick 70.00
Deron Cherry 100.00
Ray Childress 100.00
Todd Christiansen 110.00
Gary Clark 80.00
Mark Clayton 100.00
Cris Collinsworth 100.00
Doug Cosbie 130.00
Roger Craig 40.00
Randall Cunningham 75.00
Jeff Davis 45.00
Ken Davis 130.00
Richard Dent 50.00
Eric Dickerson 50.00
Floyd Dixon 70.00
Tony Dorsett 280.00
Mark Duper 90.00
Tony Eason 100.00
Carl Ekern 90.00
Henry Ellard 60.00
John Elway 175.00
Phillip Epps 120.00
Boomer Esiason 75.00
Jim Everett 50.00
Brent Fullwood 110.00
Mark Gastineau 45.00
Willie Gault 110.00
Bob Golic 100.00
Jerry Gray 75.00
Darrell Green 375.00
Jacob Green 110.00
Roy Green 90.00
Steve Grogan 100.00
Ronnie Harmon 160.00
Bobby Hebert 150.00
Alonzo Highsmith 40.00
Drew Hill 40.00
Earnest Jackson 85.00
Rickey Jackson 125.00
Vance Johnson 50.00
Ed Jones 140.00
James Jones 50.00

Rod Jones 55.00
Rulon Jones 75.00
Steve Jordan 225.00
E.J. Junior 125.00
Jim Kelly 190.00
Bill Kenney 80.00
Bernie Kosar 45.00
Tommy Kramer 120.00
Dave Krieg 180.00
Tim Krumrie 140.00
Mark Lee 150.00
Ronnie Lippett 50.00
Louis Lipps 110.00
Neil Lomax 110.00
Chuck Long 60.00
Howie Long 130.00
Ronnie Lott 110.00
Kevin Mack 40.00
Mark Malone 175.00
Dexter Manley 50.00
Dan Marino 180.00
Eric Martin 55.00
Rueben Mayes 50.00
Jim McMahon 45.00
Freeman McNeil 40.00
Karl Mecklenburg 55.00
Mike Merriweather 175.00
Stump Mitchell 75.00
Art Monk 225.00
Joe Montana 200.00
Warren Moon 90.00
Stanley Morgan 50.00
Joe Morris 50.00
Darrin Nelson 125.00
Ozzie Newsome 110.00
Ken O'Brien 40.00
John Offerdahl 110.00
Christian Okoye 55.00
Mike Quick 45.00
Jerry Rice 300.00
Gerald Riggs 40.00
Reggie Rogers 50.00
Mike Rozier 40.00
Jay Schroeder 100.00
Mickey Shuler 45.00
Phil Simms 45.00
Mike Singletary 55.00
Billy Ray Smith 195.00
Bruce Smith 170.00
J.T. Smith 120.00
Troy Stradford 100.00
Lawrence Taylor 60.00
Vinny Testaverde 70.00
Andre Tippett 50.00
Anthony Toney 45.00
Al Toon 40.00
Jack Trudeau 120.00
Herschel Walker 55.00
Curt Warner 55.00
Dave Waymer 100.00
Charles White 60.00
Danny White 110.00
Randy White 225.00
Reggie White 120.00
James Wilder 50.00
Doug Williams 55.00
Marc Wilson 340.00
Sammy Winder 50.00
Kellen Winslow 375.00
Rod Woodson 400.00
Randy Wright 200.00

1989 Football

Marcus Allen 50.00

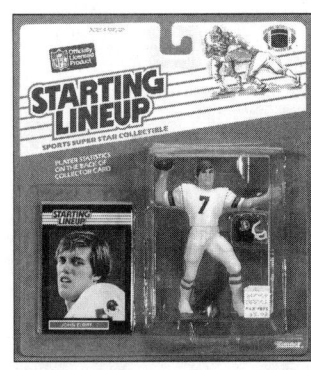

Neal Anderson 30.00
Carl Banks 100.00
Bill Bates 350.00
Mark Bavaro 45.00
Cornelius Bennett............. 50.00
Duane Bickett 130.00
Bennie Blades 120.00
Bubby Brister 60.00
Bill Brooks 90.00
James Brooks.................. 40.00
Eddie Brown..................... 50.00
Jerome Brown 275.00
Tim Brown.................... 110.00
Joey Browner 100.00
Kelvin Bryant 50.00
Jim Burt......................... 150.00
Keith Byars 175.00
Dave Cadigan................ 300.00
Anthony Carter 40.00
Michael Carter.................. 50.00
Chris Chandler 85.00
Gary Clark 45.00
Shane Conlan 90.00
Jimbo Covert 280.00
Roger Craig 30.00
Randall Cunningham......... 50.00
Richard Dent 35.00
Hanford Dixon............... 100.00
Chris Doleman.............. 120.00
Tony Dorsett (HOF) 100.00
Dave Duerson 70.00
John Elway 180.00
Boomer Esiason................ 50.00
Jim Everett 30.00
Thomas Everett 180.00
Sean Farrell................... 180.00
Bill Fralic 250.00
Irving Fryar 140.00
David Fulcher................ 100.00
Ernest Givins 65.00
Alex Gordon.................. 135.00
Charles Haley................ 200.00
Bobby Hebert 50.00
Johnny Hector 100.00
Drew Hill 30.00
Dalton Hilliard................ 40.00
Bryan Hinkle 300.00
Michael Irvin 140.00
Keith Jackson 60.00
Gary James..................... 50.00
Sean Jones 100.00
Jim Kelly 160.00
Joe Kelly........................ 75.00
Bernie Kosar 30.00
Tim Krumrie..................... 100.00
Louis Lipps 165.00
Eugene Lockhart........... 175.00
James Lofton 110.00
Neil Lomax 40.00

Chuck Long 30.00
Howie Long..................... 110.00
Ronnie Lott 100.00
Kevin Mack 35.00
Pete Mandley.................. 35.00
Dexter Manley................... 30.00
Charles Mann.................. 60.00
Lionel Manuel................. 35.00
Dan Marino 180.00
Leonard Marshall........... 120.00
Eric Martin 50.00
Rueben Mayes.................. 50.00
Vann McElroy................. 75.00
Dennis McKinnon 100.00
Jim McMahon 35.00
Steve McMichael............ 200.00
Eric McMillan.................. 90.00
Freeman McNeil 30.00
Keith Millard.................. 100.00
Chris Miller 60.00
Frank Minnifield 110.00
Art Monk 85.00
Joe Montana 110.00
Warren Moon 75.00
Joe Morris 45.00
Anthony Munoz.............. 280.00
Ricky Nattiel 45.00
Darrin Nelson 85.00
Danny Noonan 175.00
Ken O'Brien (err. spelling) ..100.00
  (correct spelling) 30.00
Steve Pelleur................. 100.00
Mike Quick....................... 30.00
Andre Reed 110.00
Jerry Rice 75.00
Mike Rozier 45.00
Jay Schroeder 40.00
John Settle.................... 75.00
Mickey Shuler 110.00
Phil Simms 30.00
Mike Singletary 40.00
Webster Slaughter.......... 50.00
Bruce Smith 150.00
Chris Spielman 185.00
John Stephens................ 35.00
Kelly Stouffe................... 40.00
Pat Swilling 65.00
Lawrence Taylor............... 55.00
Vinny Testaverde 55.00
Thurman Thomas 120.00
Andre Tippett 40.00
Anthony Toney 110.00
Al Toon 30.00
Garin Veris.................... 275.00
Herschel Walker 35.00
Curt Warner 35.00
Reggie White 60.00
Doug Williams 50.00
John Williams 80.00
Wade Wilson.................. 90.00
Mickey Woods................ 35.00
Rod Woodson 350.00
Steve Young 340.00

1989 Helmet Collection
AFC Offense Helmet 100.00
AFC Defense Helmet....... 100.00
NFC Offense Helmet 100.00
NFC Defense Helmet 100.00

1990 Football
Troy Aikman................... 60.00
Neal Anderson (blue '90) ... 20.00
  (white '89) 20.00
Mark Bavaro 60.00

Steve Beuerlein.............. 55.00
Bubby Brister 105.00
James Brooks 30.00
Tim Brown........................ 90.00
Cris Carter 175.00
Roger Craig (red '90) 25.00
  (white '89) 50.00
R. Cunningham (green '90)...30.00
  (white '89) 60.00
Hart Lee Dykes.............. 55.00
John Elway (orange '90) 85.00
  (white '89) 85.00
Boomer Esiason (black '89) ..20.00
  (white '90).......................... 20.00
Jim Everett 15.00
Simon Fletcher.............. 150.00
Doug Flutie 125.00
Dennis Gentry 45.00
Dan Hampton 100.00
Jim Harbaugh................. 65.00
Rodney Holman 50.00
Bobby Humphrey............ 25.00
Michael Irvin 80.00
Bo Jackson..................... 16.00
Keith Jackson 40.00
Vance Johnson 140.00
Jim Kelly.......................... 35.00
Bernie Kosar (brown '90) ...75.00
  (white '89) 20.00
Louis Lipps 150.00
Don Majkowski............... 20.00
Charles Mann 50.00
Lionel Manuel 20.00
Dan Marino 125.00
Tim McGee.................... 22.00
Dave Meggett 20.00
Mike Merriweather 75.00
Eric Metcalf................... 25.00
Keith Millard 40.00
Joe Montana (red '90)....... 75.00
  (white '89) 80.00
Warren Moon 35.00
Christian Okoye 15.00
Tom Rathman................. 50.00
Andre Reed...................... 30.00
Gerald Riggs 18.00
Mark Rypien 22.00
Barry Sanders 100.00
Deion Sanders............... 40.00
Ricky Sanders 15.00
Clyde Simmons.............. 70.00
Phil Simms....................... 15.00
Mike Singletary (blue '90)...30.00
  (white '89) 35.00
Webster Slaughter 55.00
Bruce Smith 80.00
John Stephens 30.00
John Taylor.................... 30.00
Thurman Thomas 40.00
Mike Tomczak................ 20.00
Greg Townsend.............. 60.00
Odessa Turner................ 25.00
Herschel Walker 20.00
Steve Walsh................... 60.00
Reggie White (green '90)...40.00
  (white '89) 30.00
Wade Wilson.................... 75.00
Ickey Woods 20.00
Donnell Woolford............ 60.00
Tim Worley 90.00
Felix Wright.................. 125.00

1991 Football
Troy Aikman 70.00

Flipper Anderson 15.00
Neal Anderson 15.00
James Brooks 15.00
Eddie Brown 15.00
Mark Carrier....................15.00
Boomer Esiason.................15.00
James Francis..................22.00
Jeff George 15.00
Rodney Hampton.............15.00
Jim Harbaugh....................25.00
Jeff Hostetler..................25.00
Bobby Humphrey 14.00
Don Majkowski...................15.00
Dan Marino 100.00
Dave Meggett....................10.00
Joe Montana 40.00
Warren Moon 24.00
Christian Okoye 10.00
Jerry Rice 50.00
Andre Rison 20.00
Barry Sanders 65.00
Phil Simms 15.00
Emmitt Smith..................165.00
Thurman Thomas................24.00
Herschel Walker 15.00

1991 Headline Football
John Elway 120.00
Boomer Esiason.................18.00
Dan Marino 120.00
Joe Montana 55.00
Jerry Rice..........................75.00
Barry Sanders 60.00

1992 Football
Troy Aikman 40.00
Earnest Byner..................12.00
Randall Cunningham 12.00
Rodney Hampton 15.00
Bobby Hebert 15.00
Jeff Hostetler 15.00
Michael Irvin 20.00
Bo Jackson 15.00
Haywood Jeffires 12.00
Seth Joyner.....................15.00
Jim Kelly 15.00
Ronnie Lott 40.00
Dan Marino 100.00
Joe Montana 40.00
Warren Moon 20.00
Rob Moore.......................12.00
Jerry Rice 35.00
Andre Rison 15.00
Mark Rypien 10.00
Barry Sanders 50.00
Deion Sanders 20.00
Emmitt Smith.....................75.00
Pat Swilling........................12.00
Derrick Thomas...............45.00
Thurman Thomas 15.00
Steve Young 55.00

1992 Headline Football
Joe Montana 25.00
Warren Moon 18.00
Mark Rypien 12.00
Barry Sanders 50.00
Emmitt Smith.....................70.00
Thurman Thomas................20.00

1993 Football
Troy Aikman 30.00
Cornelius Bennett 10.00
Randall Cunningham 15.00
Chris Doleman 20.00
John Elway.........................80.00

Barry Foster 12.00
Michael Irvin 15.00
Rickey Jackson................... 8.00
Cortez Kennedy 10.00
David Klingler 10.00
Chip Lohmiller 15.00
Russell Maryland............. 12.00
Anthony Miller 15.00
Chris Miller 7.00
Joe Montana 50.00
Warren Moon (white)......... 14.00
   (blue) 25.00
Andre Reed 12.00
Barry Sanders 35.00
Deion Sanders 15.00
Junior Seau 22.00
Sterling Sharpe............... 35.00
Emmitt Smith 25.00
Neil Smith....................... 10.00
Pete Stoyanovich............. 15.00
Ricky Watters................... 15.00
Rod Woodson.................... 25.00
Steve Young 25.00

1994 Football

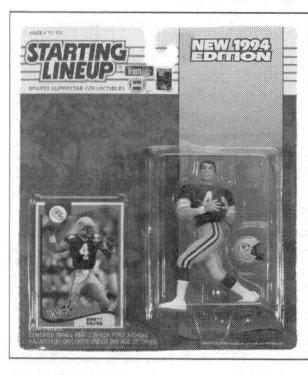

Troy Aikman....................... 20.00
Jerome Bettis.................... 25.00
Drew Bledsoe.................... 60.00
Randall Cunningham........ 12.00
Boomer Esiason 10.00
Brett Favre 120.00
Barry Foster 8.00
Rodney Hampton 10.00
Ronnie Harmon 8.00
Garrison Hearst 17.00
Raghib Ismail 17.00
Brent Jones 10.00
Cortez Kennedy 10.00
Nick Lowery 15.00
Dan Marino....................... 40.00
Eric Metcalf 10.00
Rick Mirer........................ 10.00
Joe Montana 30.00
Ken Norton....................... 35.00
Jerry Rice 20.00
Andre Rison 10.00
Barry Sanders 25.00
Deion Sanders 10.00
Junior Seau 12.00
Phil Simms 10.00
Emmitt Smith 35.00
Lawrence Taylor 15.00
Chris Warren.................... 12.00
Lorenzo White 10.00
Reggie White 20.00
Rod Woodson.................... 18.00
Steve Young 20.00

1995 Football

Troy Aikman....................... 20.00

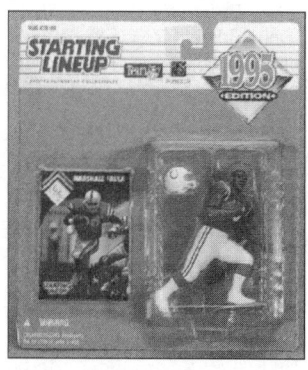

Jerome Bettis.................... 20.00
Drew Bledsoe 23.00
Steve Christie................... 8.00
Ben Coates....................... 15.00
Randall Cunningham 10.00
Willie Davis...................... 10.00
Jim Everett........................ 10.00
Marshall Faulk.................. 40.00
Brett Favre 40.00
Irving Fryar 15.00
Jeff George 10.00
Stan Humphries............... 12.00
Michael Irvin 18.00
Johnny Johnson............... 10.00
Seth Joyner 10.00
Greg Lloyd 22.00
Dan Marino 30.00
Terry McDaniel................. 10.00
Natrone Means................. 15.00
Scott Mitchell 7.00
Joe Montana...................... 40.00
Warren Moon 12.00
Hardy Nickerson 14.00
Michael Dean Perry 12.00
Jerry Rice 16.00
Barry Sanders 25.00
Deion Sanders.................. 12.00
Shannon Sharpe.............. 20.00
Emmitt Smith 30.00
Dan Wilkinson.................. 10.00
Steve Young...................... 15.00
Chris Zorich 15.00

1996 Football

Troy Aikman (regular) 20.00
   (Albertson's)................... 25.00
   (Blue sleeves w/stars)... 180.00
Terry Allen....................... 15.00
Steve Beuerlein 20.00
Jeff Blake......................... 15.00
Drew Bledsoe 15.00
Steve Bono....................... 10.00
Kyle Brady........................ 12.00
Robert Brooks................. 15.00

Dave Brown 10.00
Isaac Bruce....................... 25.00
Mark Brunell.................... 25.00
Mark Carrier...................... 7.00
Cris Carter 20.00
Kerry Collins 20.00
John Elway........................ 30.00
Marshall Faulk................... 20.00
Brett Favre (Shopko)......... 35.00
Joey Galloway.................. 20.00
Kevin Greene.................. 15.00
Dan Marino 35.00
Steve McNair.................... 25.00
Eric Metcalf 10.00
Jay Novacek 15.00
Bryce Paup 15.00
Carl Pickens 10.00
Frank Reich 20.00
Errict Rhett...................... 10.00
Jerry Rice 15.00
Rashaan Salaam 8.00
Barry Sanders................... 25.00
Deion Sanders 10.00
Junior Seau....................... 10.00
Emmitt Smith 35.00
Chris Spielman 15.00
Kordell Stewart............... 35.00
Ricky Watters................... 15.00
Reggie White 15.00
Harvey Williams 12.00
Steve Young...................... 15.00

1997 Football

Karim Abdul-Jabbar 10.00
Troy Aikman 12.00
Jamal Anderson............... 12.00
Jerome Bettis 12.00
Jeff Blake 10.00
Drew Bledsoe 15.00
Terry Bradshaw (Hill's) 20.00
Mark Brunell 12.00
Dale Carter....................... 8.00
Larry Centers 12.00
Mark Chmura 8.00
Kerry Collins 10.00
Brian Cox......................... 14.00
Terrell Davis
   (w/mustache) 50.00
Quinn Early 10.00
John Elway........................ 20.00
Brett Favre 20.00
Eddie George 30.00
Jeff George 10.00
Elvis Grbac...................... 15.00
Kevin Greene 10.00
Jim Harbaugh 7.00
Marvin Harrison 35.00
Brad Johnson................... 30.00
Keyshawn Johnson 25.00
Daryl Johnson................. 10.00
Dan Marino 15.00
Curtis Martin 35.00
Tony Martin...................... 10.00
Herman Moore................. 18.00
Jerry Rice 10.00
William Roaf..................... 15.00
Deion Sanders 10.00
Junior Seau (Super Bowl) ..25.00
Bruce Smith 10.00
Emmitt Smith (Regular) 15.00
   (Albertson's) 20.00
Phil Sparks...................... 10.00
Kordell Stewart.................. 15.00
Vinny Testaverde 10.00

Eric Turner....................... 10.00
Chris Warren 10.00
Ricky Watters 10.00
Michael Westbrook........... 16.00
Reggie White 10.00
Steve Young 20.00

1997 Classic Doubles

Barry Sanders,
   Walter Payton 100.00
D. Clark, Joe Montana 25.00
Jerry Rice, Joe Montana 35.00
Dan Marino, Bob Griese.....28.00
Brett Favre, Bart Starr 30.00
Troy Aikman,
   Roger Staubach 35.00
T. Brown, Fred Biletnikoff ...35.00
Emmitt Smith, Tony Dorsett.. 40.00

1997 Gridiron Greats

Brett Favre........................ 30.00
Kevin Green 15.00
Dan Marino 30.00
Joe Montana 30.00
Jerry Rice 35.00
Deion Sanders 18.00
Emmitt Smith..................... 35.00
Thurman Thomas 15.00
Ricky Watters 15.00

1997 Heisman

Tony Dorsett...................... 15.00
Doug Flutie........................ 15.00
Eddie George..................... 20.00
Archie Griffin 10.00
Bo Jackson........................ 12.00
Steve Owens 12.00
Johnny Rodgers 10.00
Barry Sanders 20.00
Danny Wuerffel................. 15.00

1998 Football

Troy Aikman 12.00
Terry Allen........................ 10.00
Jerome Bettis 15.00
Drew Bledsoe..................... 10.00
Tony Boselli..................... 15.00
Derrick Brooks................. 30.00
Mark Brunell...................... 12.00
Kerry Collins 12.00
Terrell Davis 18.00
Trent Dilfer...................... 18.00
Corey Dillon..................... 22.00
John Elway........................ 16.00
Brett Favre........................ 14.00
Antonio Freeman 15.00
Gus Frerotte..................... 12.00
Joey Galloway 14.00
Eddie George..................... 16.00
Terry Glenn...................... 12.00
E. Grbac (correct jersey #) ...50.00
   (incorrect jersey number)... 10.00

Raymont Harris	10.00	
Bobby Hoying	10.00	
Carnell Lake	25.00	
Lamar Lathon	10.00	
Dan Marino (Regular)	15.00	
(Super Bowl)	20.00	
Randall McDaniel	22.00	
Chester McGlockton	20.00	
Scott Mitchell	7.00	
Adrian Murrell	15.00	
Nate Newton	15.00	
Jonathan Ogden	25.00	
Orlando Pace	25.00	
Carl Pickens	12.00	
Jerry Rice	12.00	
Simeon Rice	18.00	
Barry Sanders (Meijers)	25.00	
Deion Sanders	12.00	
Antowain Smith	20.00	
Emmitt Smith	10.00	
Kordell Stewart (Hills)	20.00	
Dana Stubblefield	15.00	
Vinny Testaverde	10.00	
Tyrone Wheatley	18.00	
Reggie White	10.00	
Steve Young	12.00	

1998 Extended
Mike Alstott	25.00
Terrell Davis	18.00
Jim Harbaugh	10.00
Ryan Leaf	8.00
Peyton Manning	45.00
Curtis Martin	20.00
Steve McNair	20.00
Deion Sanders	15.00
Shannon Sharpe	16.00
Charles Woodson	22.00

1998 Classic Doubles
Jerry Rice, Steve Young	25.00
John Elway, Dan Marino	35.00
Junior Seau, Dick Butkus	15.00
Terry Allen, Eric Garrett	15.00
Troy Aikman, Emmitt Smith	30.00
Y.A. Tittle, Sam Huff	15.00
Joe Namath, Don Maynard	20.00
Deion Sanders, Herb Adderley	15.00

1998 QB Club
Drew Bledsoe	15.00
John Elway	25.00
Jim Harbaugh	15.00
Dan Marino	30.00
Emmitt Smith	30.00
Steve Young	25.00

1998 Hall of Fame
Dick Butkus	12.00
Larry Csonka	14.00
Joe Greene	15.00
Deacon Jones	12.00
Bob Lilly	12.00
Vince Lombardi	20.00
Ray Nitschke	25.00
Gale Sayers	12.00
Bart Starr	15.00
Y.A. Tittle	10.00
Gene Upshaw	12.00

1998 12" Figures
Troy Aikman (Serv. Mer.)	30.00
Drew Bledsoe	23.00
John Elway	30.00
Brett Favre	30.00
Dan Marino	30.00
Jerry Rice	30.00
Kordell Stewart (Hills)	25.00

1998 Gridiron Greats
Troy Aikman	20.00
Drew Bledsoe	20.00
Mark Brunell	20.00
John Elway	28.00
Barry Sanders	30.00
Junior Seau	20.00
Bart Starr (Shopko)	25.00
Steve Young	20.00

1998 Heisman
Marcus Allen	10.00
Earl Campbell	15.00
John Cappelletti	10.00
Glenn Davis	8.00
Paul Hornung	17.00
Desmond Howard	8.00
Rashaan Salaam	8.00
Roger Staubach	12.00
Herschel Walker	15.00
Charles Woodson	17.00

1999 Football

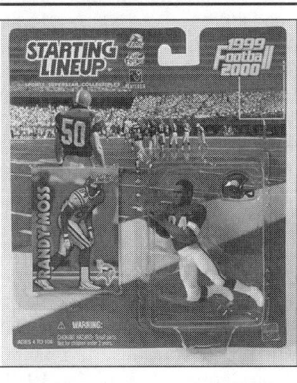

Troy Aikman	10.00
Drew Bledsoe	10.00
Mark Brunell	12.00
Chris Chandler	12.00
Wayne Chrebet	20.00
Randall Cunningham	12.00
Terrell Davis	15.00
Dermontti Dawson	27.00
Corey Dillon	10.00
Warrick Dunn	20.00
John Elway	12.00
Curtis Enis	8.00
Brett Favre	10.00
Doug Flutie	12.00
Eddie George (Oilers)	15.00
(Titans)	20.00
Napoleon Kaufman	12.00
Jim Kelly (Ames)	18.00
Ryan Leaf	8.00
Dorsey Levens	10.00
Peyton Manning	18.00
Dan Marino	12.00
Curtis Martin	12.00
Randy Moss	25.00
Jake Plummer	20.00
Jerry Rice	10.00
Andre Rison	10.00
Barry Sanders (Regular)	12.00
(Meijers)	16.00
Warren Sapp	30.00
Emmitt Smith	10.00
Jimmy Smith	24.00
Neil Smith	10.00
Robert Smith	22.00
Roger Staubach (Albertson's)	20.00
Kordell Stewart	10.00

Eric Swann	12.00
Zach Thomas	55.00
Ricky Watters	10.00
Steve Young	10.00

1999 Extended
Jamal Anderson	12.00
Charlie Batch	10.00
Tim Couch	25.00
Ed McCaffery	15.00
Donovan McNabb	35.00
John Randle	15.00
Fred Taylor	18.00
Ricky Williams	30.00

1999 Classic Doubles

Mike Alstott, Warrick Dunn	15.00
Elden Campbell, Eddie George	18.00
Cris Carter, Randy Moss	30.00
John Elway, Terrell Davis	20.00
Franco Harris, Jerome Bettis	18.00
Jack Lambert, Jack Ham	20.00
A. Manning, P. Manning	30.00
A. Munoz, B. Esiason	15.00
Ken Stabler, Dave Casper	22.00
J. Unitas, Raymond Berry	20.00

1999 QB Club
Troy Aikman	18.00
Terrell Davis	20.00
Brett Favre	20.00
Jake Plummer	18.00
Kordell Stewart	18.00

1999 Gridiron Greats
Dick Butkus	18.00
Terrell Davis	20.00
Warrick Dunn	12.00
Eddie George	20.00
Dan Marino	20.00
Curtis Martin	20.00
Barry Sanders	18.00
Kordell Stewart	15.00

1999 Heroes of the Gridiron
Charlie Batch	10.00
Mark Brunell	8.00
Ernie Davis	8.00
Warrick Dunn	8.00
Curtis Martin	15.00
Randy Moss	20.00
Jim Plunkett	10.00
Charlie Ward	8.00
Ricky Williams	25.00

1999 12" Figures
Terrell Davis	25.00
Brett Favre	25.00
Barry Sanders	30.00
Kordell Stewart	25.00
Steve Young	25.00

2000 Football

Troy Aikman	8.00

Mike Alstott	10.00
Jesse Armstead	20.00
Champ Bailey	18.00
Drew Bledsoe	10.00
Tony Brackens	12.00
Mark Brunell	8.00
Tim Couch (Regular)	12.00
(Ames Exclusive)	15.00
Daunte Culpepper	80.00
Stephen Davis	15.00
Terrell Davis	10.00
John Elway	12.00
Brett Favre	12.00
Doug Flutie	12.00
Antonio Freeman	10.00
Tony Gonzalez	18.00
Brian Griese	22.00
Torry Holt	20.00
Edgerrin James	22.00
Brad Johnson	10.00
K.. Johnson (NY Jets uniform)	12.00
(TB Buccaneers uniform)	20.00
Shaun King	18.00
Jon Kitna	15.00
Peyton Manning	14.00
Dan Marino	40.00
Steve McNair	12.00
Joe Montana	15.00
Randy Moss	15.00
Ozzie Newsome	15.00
Jim Otto	35.00
Terrell Owens	25.00
Jake Plummer	10.00
Takeo Spikes	12.00
Fred Taylor	10.00
Vinny Testaverde	10.00
Kurt Warner (old uniform)	25.00
(new uniform)	25.00
(Wal-Mart Exclusive)	25.00
Ricky Williams (old uniform)	18.00
(uniform variation)	20.00

2000 Extended
Shaun Alexander	20.00
Isaac Bruce	12.00
Cris Carter	10.00
Ron Dayne	15.00
Marvin Harrison	18.00
Jevon Kearse	18.00
Jason Sehorn	18.00
Shawn Springs	12.00
Peter Warrick (white uniform)	15.00
(black uniform)	15.00

2000 Classic Doubles
Troy Aikman, Jim Kelly	18.00
Terrell Davis, John Anderson	15.00
John Elway, Brett Favre	20.00
Brett Favre, Drew Bledsoe	18.00

Eddie George,
   Marshall Faulk 25.00
Joe Montana, Dan Marino . 35.00
Phil Simms, John Elway 18.00
P. Manning college/pro
   (Wilk's) 20.00

2000 Football Elite
Terrell Davis 10.00
Brett Favre 15.00
Peyton Manning 20.00
Joe Montana 25.00
Randy Moss 20.00
Emmitt Smith 25.00

2000 Football Hobby Set

Troy Aikman 8.00
Terrell Davis 9.00
Marshall Faulk 25.00
Peyton Manning 14.00
Randy Moss 14.00
Jake Plummer 8.00
Akili Smith 10.00
Ricky Williams 15.00
Darren Woodson 25.00

1993 Hockey

Ed Belfour 100.00
Ray Bourque 40.00
Grant Fuhr 120.00
Brett Hull 14.00
Jaromir Jagr 35.00
Pat LaFontaine 60.00
Mario Lemieux 40.00
Eric Lindros 30.00
Mark Messier 35.00
Jeremy Roenick 25.00
Patrick Roy 110.00
Steve Yzerman 30.00

1993 Canadian
Ed Belfour 60.00
Ray Bourque 20.00
Brett Hull 10.00
Jaromir Jagr 25.00
Pat LaFontaine 40.00
Mario Lemieux 20.00
Eric Lindros 30.00
Mark Messier 25.00
Jeremy Roenick 20.00
Patrick Roy 50.00
Steve Yzerman 20.00

1994 Hockey

Tom Barasso 30.00
Ray Bourque 30.00
Pavel Bure 30.00
Sergei Fedorov 22.00
Doug Gilmour 15.00
Brett Hull 12.00
Arturs Irbe 25.00
Jaromir Jagr (brown hair) .. 25.00
   (black hair) 25.00

Pat LaFontaine 16.00
Brian Leetch 20.00
Mario Lemieux 25.00
Eric Lindros 25.00
Mark Messier 50.00
Alexander Mogilny 12.00
Adam Oates 18.00
Mike Richter 25.00
Luc Robitaille 25.00
Jeremy Roenick 28.00
Teemu Selanne 22.00
Steve Yzerman 15.00

1994 Canadian
Pavel Bure 18.00
Sergei Fedorov 18.00
Grant Fuhr 75.00
Doug Gilmour 15.00
Brian Leetch 15.00
Mario Lemieux 20.00
Eric Lindros 20.00
Alexander Mogilny 12.00
Adam Oates 15.00
Mike Richter 30.00
Luc Robitaille 25.00
Teemu Selanne 20.00
Steve Yzerman 16.00

1995 Hockey

Rob Blake 14.00
Martin Brodeur 45.00
Pavel Bure 25.00
Chris Chelios 17.00
Bob Corkum 10.00
Sergei Fedorov 10.00
Theoren Fleury 20.00
Adam Graves 10.00
Dominik Hasek 50.00
Brett Hull 12.00
Mike Modano 20.00
Kirk Mueller 10.00
Cam Neely 10.00
Sandis Ozolinsh 15.00
Felix Potvin 25.00
Luc Robitaille 10.00
Brendan Shanahan 20.00
Scott Stevens 17.00
Pierre Turgeon 12.00

1995 Canadian
Tom Barasso 25.00
Rob Blake 10.00
Martin Brodeur 33.00
Chris Chelios 15.00
Theoren Fleury 15.00
Adam Graves 12.00
Dominik Hasek 50.00
Arturs Irbe 35.00
Mike Modano 15.00
Cam Neely 10.00
Felix Potvin 25.00
Brendan Shanahan 15.00
Scott Stevens 12.00

1996 Hockey

Tom Barasso (Hill's) 20.00
Brian Bradley 10.00
Jim Carey 15.00
Paul Coffey 12.00
Sergei Fedorov 10.00
Ron Francis 18.00
Dominik Hasek 40.00
Paul Kariya 22.00
Pat LaFontaine (Hill's) 15.00
John LeClair 18.00
Brian Leetch 12.00

Eric Lindros 15.00
Al MacInnis 15.00
Scott Mellanby 10.00
Mark Messier 15.00
Mike Modano 10.00
Adam Oates 15.00
Mikael Renberg 12.00
Stephane Richer 10.00
Jeremy Roenick 10.00
Patrick Roy (w/beard) 35.00
   (w/o beard) 60.00
Joe Sakic 30.00
Brendan Shanahan 30.00
Mats Sundin 22.00

1996 Canadian
Brian Bradley 10.00
Jim Carey 25.00
Sergei Fedorov 10.00
Ron Francis 12.00
Paul Kariya 22.00
John LeClair 15.00
Brian Leetch 12.00
Eric Lindros 15.00
Al MacInnis 12.00
Scott Mellanby 10.00
Mark Messier 12.00
Mikael Renberg 15.00
Patrick Roy 45.00
Joe Sakic 22.00
Mats Sundin 14.00

1997 Hockey

Daniel Alfredsson 10.00
Jason Arnott 10.00
Peter Bondra 17.00
Martin Brodeur 20.00
Chris Chelios 10.00
Paul Coffey (Boscov's) 15.00
Peter Forsberg 25.00
Wayne Gretzky 25.00
Ron Hextall 20.00
Jaromir Jagr 10.00
Patrick Lalime (R, Hill's) 22.00
Eric Lindros 10.00
Mark Messier 10.00
Chris Osgood 22.00
Sandis Ozolinsh 10.00
Zigmund Palffy 18.00
Darren Puppa 15.00
Mark Recchi 14.00
Teemu Selanne 10.00
Keith Tkachuk 15.00
John Vanbiesbrouck 20.00

1997 Canadian
Daniel Alfredson 12.00
Jason Arnott 12.00
Peter Bondra 12.00
Martin Brodeur 20.00
Chris Chelios 10.00
Peter Forsberg 20.00
Wayne Gretzky 25.00
Ron Hextall 20.00
Jaromir Jagr 10.00
Mario Lemieux (Wal-Mart) ... 30.00
Eric Lindros 10.00
Mark Messier 10.00
Chris Osgood 20.00
Sandis Ozolinsh 10.00
Zigmund Palffy 18.00
Darren Puppa 15.00
Mark Recchi 10.00
Teemu Selanne 10.00
Keith Tkachuk 15.00
John Vanbiesbrouck 20.00

1997 One-On-One
W. Gretzky, Dominik Hasek .. 70.00
Paul Kariya, Eric Lindros 25.00
Owen Nolan, Chris Osgood . 25.00
J. Roenick, Steve Yzerman 25.00
Patrick Roy, Jaromir Jagr ... 35.00
Joe Sakic, Mike Richter 25.00
Mats Sundin, Ray Bourque .. 20.00

1997 One-On-One Canadian
W. Gretzky, Dominik Hasek .. 70.00
Paul Kariya, Eric Lindros 35.00
Owen Nolan, Chris Osgood . 35.00
J. Roenick, Steve Yzerman .. 25.00
Patrick Roy, Jaromir Jagr ... 35.00
Joe Sakic, Mike Richter 30.00
Mats Sundin, Ray Bourque 25.00

1998 Hockey

Tony Amonte 18.00
Ed Belfour 15.00
Bryan Berard 15.00
Martin Brodeur 18.00
Jim Campbell 10.00
Vincent Damphousse 10.00
Wayne Gretzky (Regular) ... 18.00
(Stanley Cup) 35.00
Dominik Hasek 16.00
Jaromir Jagr 14.00
Paul Kariya 14.00
Brian Leetch 10.00
Eric Lindros 12.00
Kirk McLean 18.00
Mark Messier 12.00
Rob Neidermayer 12.00
Chris Osgood 16.00
Felix Potvin 12.00
Jeremy Roenick 12.00
Patrick Roy 15.00
Joe Sakic 20.00
Joe Thornton 25.00
Alexi Yashin 17.00
Steve Yzerman 14.00

1998 Extended
Peter Bondra 10.00
Theo Fleury 12.00
Grant Fuhr 16.00
Doug Gilmour 12.00
Nicolai Khabibulin 17.00
Olaf Kolzig 15.00
Trevor Kidd 16.00
Darren Puppa 15.00
Brendan Shanahan 14.00
John Vanbiesbrouck 12.00

1998 Classic Doubles
Wayne Gretzky,
   Mark Messier 30.00
Jaromir Jagr, Tom Barasso ... 24.00
Patrick Roy, John LeClair ... 24.00
Sergei Fedorov,
   Mike Vernon 20.00
Martin Brodeur,
   Kevin Stevens 24.00
Bobby Clarke,
   Dave Schultz 20.00

1998 One-On-One
Mike Modano, Mike Vernon .. 30.00
Keith Tkachuk, John LeClair . 20.00
B. Shanahan, Jeff Hackett 20.00
Wayne Gretzky, Pavel Bure . 25.00
Mark Messier,
   Sandis Ozolinsh 25.00
Eric Lindros, Andrew Moog ... 30.00

1998 12" Figures
Wayne Gretzky 40.00

Mario Lemieux................... 35.00
Bobby Orr......................... 23.00

1999 Hockey

Mike Dunham.................... 15.00
Peter Forsberg.................... 10.00
Wayne Gretzky.................. 12.00
Jeff Hackett...................... 12.00
Dominik Hasek................... 15.00
Jaromir Jagr...................... 12.00
Curtis Joseph 20.00
Paul Kariya....................... 12.00
Nicolai Khabibulin............ 12.00
Olaf Kolzig....................... 12.00
Nicklas Lidstrom 25.00
Eric Lindros 10.00
Mike Modano..................... 10.00
Keith Primeau 20.00
Chris Pronger 17.00
Sergei Samsonov 20.00
Steve Yzerman 12.00

1999 Classic Doubles
Grant Fuhr, Wayne Gretzky..25.00
Mark Messier, Mike Richter...20.00
Joe Sakic, Patrick Roy....... 20.00
Steve Yzerman,
   Chris Osgood.................. 20.00

1999 One-On-One
Brett Hull, Wayne Gretzky . 25.00
Curtis Joseph,
   Chris Chelios 20.00
Steve Yzerman,
   Chris Osgood................. 20.00

1999 12" Figures
Wayne Gretzky (Regular) .. 35.00
Wayne Gretzky (KayBee) .. 30.00
Dominik Hasek 35.00
Jaromir Jagr 25.00
Mark Messier..................... 20.00
Chris Osgood 20.00
Patrick Roy 30.00

2000 Hockey

Ed Belfour.......................... 20.00
R. Bourque (Avalanche uni.). 20.00
(Bruins uniform) 15.00
Rod Brind'Amour 15.00
Anson Carter 12.00
Joseph Curtis 10.00
Adam Deadmarsh............ 15.00
Stephane Fiset................. 12.00
Wayne Gretzky (Wal-Mart) 22.00
Mike Grier........................ 15.00
Derian Hatcher 10.00
Guy Hebert...................... 12.00
Arturs Irbe 12.00
Jaromir Jagr...................... 12.00
Saku Koivu...................... 17.00
Vincent Lecavalier 15.00

Claude Lemieux................ 12.00
Adam Oates....................... 10.00
Keith Primeau 10.00
Damian Rhodes 12.00
Joe Sakic.......................... 12.00
Niklas Sundstrom............ 12.00
Ron Tugnutt
   (Penguins uni.)............ 15.00
(Blue Jackets uniform) 35.00
John Vanbiesbrouck 10.00
Steve Yzerman 12.00

2000 Classic Doubles

Peter Forsberg,
   Sergei Fedorov 15.00
Jaromir Jagr, Pavel Bure.... 20.00
Paul Kariya, Miroslav Satan. 15.00
Olaf Kolzig, Patrick Roy 18.00

Convention / Show Figures

1995 Conventions
Joe Montana (Cin.) 30.00
(Del. w/sticker) 30.00
(Del. w/o sticker) 30.00
(Cal.) 30.00
(NJ) 30.00

1996 Conventions
Cal Ripken Jr. (Cincinnati) . 30.00
(Dallas) 30.00
(Santa Clara) 30.00
(New Jersey)..................... 30.00

1997 Conventions
Johnny Bench (Cincinnati) ... 10.00
Larry Johnson (NJ) 10.00
Jason Kidd (Anaheim) 35.00
Christian Laettner (Atlanta) .. 15.00
Pat McInally (Anaheim) 10.00
(Atlanta) 10.00
(Cincinnati) 10.00
(New Jersey)................... 10.00
Shaquille O'Neal (Anaheim) .20.00
Glen Rice (Atlanta) 15.00
Jerry Stackhouse (NJ) 15.00

1998 Conventions
Brett Favre (Cincinnati) 30.00
Jerry Rice (Anaheim)
   regular............................. 30.00
(Anaheim) variation 100.00
Dan Marino (NJ) 25.00

1999 Conventions
John Elway (Anaheim)
   regular............................. 25.00
(Anaheim) variation 100.00
Wayne Gretzky (NJ)
   regular............................. 25.00
(NJ) variation 125.00
Barry Sanders (Cinc)
   regular............................. 25.00
(Cincinnati) variation 100.00

2000 Conventions
Mark McGwire (Cinc.)
   regular.............................. 20.00
(Cincinnati) variation 100.00
Derek Jeter (NJ) regular 20.00
(NJ) variation 140.00

Kenner Club
Shaquille O'Neal (SD)........ 75.00
Reggie Jackson (Std. Star)...30.00
Joe Namath 40.00
Willie Mays (Std. Star) 30.00
John Vanbiesbrouck........... 25.00
Nolan Ryan
   (Freeze Frame)............. 100.00
Brett Hull, Bobby Hull......... 15.00
USA Basketball Set (3) 25.00
O'Neal/Chamberlain/
   Jabbar 35.00
Nolan Ryan (Suns) 20.00
Dan Marino, Junior Seau ... 35.00
Cade McNown 12.00
Joe Montana
   (Freeze Frame)............... 60.00
Ted Williams...................... 25.00
Wayne Gretzky
   (Freeze Frame)............... 65.00
Larry Bird
   (Backboard King) 30.00
Mario Lemieux................... 30.00
AFC Offensive Helmet Set. 30.00

One-On-One
C. Barkley, D. Wilkins 150.00
Jose Canseco,
   Alan Trammell 45.00
Carter, Davis 45.00
John Elway, Howie Long..200.00
Patrick Ewing,
   Kevin McHale 125.00
Magic Johnson, Larry Bird. 275.00
Michael Jordan, I. Thomas 275.00
Don Mattingly, Wade Boggs .70.00
J. McMahon, Chris Doleman 65.00
O'Brien, Taylor 65.00
R. Sandberg, Coleman 50.00
Mike Singletary, Mike Quick..70.00
Walker, Manley 80.00

Team Lineups

1990 Award Winners........... 50.00
1991 Award Winners........... 65.00
Boston Red Sox 80.00
Chicago Cubs 80.00
Detroit Tigers 75.00
N.Y. Mets 70.00
N.Y. Yankees.................... 140.00
Oakland A's....................... 140.00
St. Louis Cardinals............. 75.00
MLB Team of the 90's 60.00
'92 USA Olympic
   Basketball..................... 100.00

'96 Basketball (1 of 2) 20.00
'96 Basketball (2 of 2) 20.00

1989 Legends

Terry Bradshaw 75.00
Wilt Chamberlain................65.00
Mike Ditka 65.00
Julius Erving......................65.00
Joe Greene 75.00
John Havlicek....................70.00
Oscar Robertson................55.00
Gale Sayers (mustache) 50.00
(no mustache) 50.00
Johnny Unitas (high tops) ..75.00
(low tops)........................75.00

1995 Legends
Kareem Abdul-Jabbar 12.00
Terry Bradshaw 25.00
Wilt Chamberlain................12.00
Gordie Howe 10.00
Bobby Hull.........................20.00
Joe Louis...........................12.00
Rocky Marciano
   (brown hair) 200.00
(black hair)......................15.00
Arnold Palmer 8.00
Walter Payton
   (black shoes) 75.00
(white w/black tips) 85.00

1995 Canadian
Kareem Abdul-Jabbar 15.00
Wilt Chamberlain................15.00
Gordie Howe 15.00
Bobby Hull.........................15.00
Joe Louis...........................24.00
Rocky Marciano 24.00
Arnold Palmer 15.00

1996 Legends
Nadia Comaneci 5.00
Florence Griffith-Joyner........5.00
Bruce Jenner.......................5.00
Michael Johnson 8.00
Jackie Joyner-Kersee...........5.00
Olga Korbut.........................5.00
Dan O'Brien 5.00
Jesse Owens 5.00
Jim Thorpe..........................8.00

1996 Canadian
Jean Beliveau.....................15.00
Phil Esposito 15.00
Tony Esposito.....................20.00
Gordie Howe 15.00
Bobby Hull.........................15.00
Maurice Richard.................15.00

1997 Kenner 12" Specials
T. Aikman (JC Penney),
   E. Smith (JC Penney) 75.00

Dale Earnhardt (Wal-Mart) ...60.00
J. Gordon (Hill's) 50.00
Mickey Mantle (FAO's) 60.00
Joe Montana (Target) 40.00
Bobby Orr (Kay-Bee) 20.00
J. Robinson (Target) 35.00

1997 Legends

Len Dawson 12.00
Tony Esposito 15.00
Walt Frazier 10.00
Michael Johnson 10.00
Sugar Ray Leonard 15.00
Maurice Richard 10.00
Sam Snead 10.00
Joe Theismann................. 15.00
Bill Walton 14.00

1997 Canadian

Jean Beliveau................... 15.00
Mike Bossy 15.00
Marcel Dionne 15.00
Phil Esposito 15.00
Glenn Hall 25.00
Bernie Parent 25.00

1998 Kenner 12" Specials

Troy Aikman (Serv. Mer.) ... 30.00
M. Ali (Hasbro online)........ 20.00
 (Toys R Us)....................... 30.00
M. Ali (Sam's Club), Joe Frazier
 (Sam's Club) 40.00
Dale Earnhardt (Sam),
Dale Earnhardt Jr. (Sam) .. 75.00
Joe Namath (Sam's Club),
Johnny Unitas (Sam's Club) . 60.00

Arnold Palmer (Target) 30.00
Nolan Ryan (Wal-Mart) 30.00
Kordell Stewart (Hills) 25.00

1998 Legends

Muhammad Ali.................. 15.00
Larry Bird......................... 18.00
Bonnie Blair 10.00
Mike Bossy 10.00
Bobby Clarke (Boscov) 10.00
Marcel Dionne 10.00
Mike Eruzione 15.00
Bob Griese 22.00
Glenn Hall 10.00
Eric Heiden 10.00
Dan Jansen 12.00
Mario Lemieux.................. 12.00
Tommy Moe 20.00
Joe Montana..................... 20.00
Joe Namath 15.00
Pele 7.00

1999 Kenner Specials

Muhammad Ali
 (Young 12", Online) 25.00
 (Regular, Online)............. 15.00
Dan Fouts 20.00
Magic Johnson 25.00
Johnny Unitas................... 15.00

2000 Wheaties Series I

John Elway 25.00
Brett Favre 20.00
Jerry Rice 25.00
Steve Young..................... 17.00

2000 Wheaties Series II

Dan Marino 35.00

Jackie Robinson................ 15.00
Babe Ruth......................... 15.00
Nolan Ryan 30.00

1997 Racing Winning Circle

Ward Burton....................... 8.00
Dale Earnhardt ....
 (w/Burger King logo) 30.00
 (w/o Burger King logo) 30.00
John Force 10.00
Jeff Gordon (w/Pepsi logo) ...15.00
 (w/o Pepsi logo)................ 15.00
Dale Jarrett 10.00
Bobby Labonte (blond)....... 10.00
 (black) 10.00
Darrell Waltrip 10.00

1997 Racing Winner Circle Canadian

Ward Burton....................... 15.00
Dale Earnhardt.................. 20.00
Jeff Gordon 20.00
Dale Jarrett 15.00
Bobby Labonte.................. 15.00
Darrell Waltrip 15.00

1998 Racing Winner Circle Champ. Legacy

Dale Earnhardt ('80 champ) . 25.00
Dale Earnhardt ('86 champ) . 30.00
Dale Earnhardt ('93 champ) . 25.00
Dale Earnhardt ('94 champ) . 25.00
Dale Earnhardt
 ('98 Daytona)................... 40.00
Jeff Gordon ('95 champ) 20.00
Jeff Gordon ('97 champ) 20.00
Rusty Wallace ('89 champ)...20.00

1998 Racing Winning Circle

Ward Burton....................... 10.00
Dale Earnhardt
 ('97 uniform) 18.00
 ('98 uniform) 18.00
John Force (regular)........... 10.00
 (Elvis) 10.00
Jeff Gordon (regular)........... 12.00
 (Jurassic Park)................. 12.00
Kenny Irwin...................... 8.00
Dale Jarrett........................ 12.00
Bobby Labonte (regular) 10.00
 (Sm. Soldiers)................. 10.00
Mike Skinner.................... 8.00
Kenny Wallace................. 8.00
Rusty Wallace (regular) ...12.00
 (Elvis).............................. 12.00

1999 Racing Winning Circle

Dale Earnhardt
 (Coca-Cola) 18.00
 (GM Goodwrench)........... 18.00
D. Earnhardt Jr.
 (Coca-Cola) 20.00
 (AC Delco) 20.00
Jeff Gordon (Pepsi) 12.00
 (Dupont) 12.00
 (Wal-Mart) 12.00
 (Boscov) 20.00
Dale Jarrett........................ 12.00
Bobby Labonte 8.00

1999 Winning Circle 12" Figures

Dale Earnhardt................... 40.00
Jeff Gordon 35.00
Rusty Wallace 30.00

2000 Racing Winner Circle

Dale Earnhardt................... 25.00
Jeff Gordon 10.00
Dale Jarrett........................ 8.00
Tony Stewart 20.00

McFarlane Sports Picks

It was in January of 2001 that Hasbro discontinued the Starting Lineup product line, and the future for sports figure collectors looked bleak. Things changed dramatically, though, the second half of 2001 and the beginning of 2002, with McFarlane Toys stepping in to fill the void in the sports figure market.

Collectors didn't quite know what to expect from McFarlane, but it didn't take long for collectors to fall in love with McFarlane's Sports Picks. Even now, the variation/chase figures from these releases draw lots of attention from collectors. Once collectors figured out which figures were the variations, an all out blitz began in which collectors began chasing down those figures.

The biggest news of the year, though, was when McFarlane Toys announced at the 2002 Toy Fair in February that it had secured the MLB and MLBPA licenses to produce baseball figures with official logos. The baseball license was the last of the four major sports in which McFarlane secured licensing. When the

announcement was finally made at Toy Fair, it wasn't a complete surprise, as checklists were leaked out by a variety of sources weeks prior to Toy Fair, and collectors knew it was just a matter of time before the announcement would be made. Three series of McFarlane's Sports Picks baseball figures were announced to be released in 2002, with each series containing eight figures.

Then, in 2003, McFarlane Toys joined with Action Performance to form Action McFarlane, with the sole purpose of manufacturing officially licensed figures of NASCAR drivers. The drivers scheduled to appear in the first series included Dale Earnhardt Sr., Dale Earnhardt Jr., Jeff Gordon, Ryan Newman, Tony Stewart and Rusty Wallace. That series was scheduled to be released in late 2003.

All values listed are for Mint figures still in the packaging. The package must have four perfect corners and the blister bubble cannot be creased, dented, or damaged in any way.

2000-01 Baseball Series 1

Barry Bonds 20.00
Chipper Jones 10.00
Mark McGwire 20.00
Manny Ramirez 10.00
Alex Rodriguez 10.00
Sammy Sosa 15.00

2000 Baseball Sportspicks

Babbage Exclusive
Mark McGwire, Manny Ramirez 15.00

2002 Baseball Series 1

Shawn Green (white jsy, no emblem).....10.00
   (white jsy, Dodgers emblem) 15.00
   (blue jsy, no emblem)...........................20.00
   (blue jsy, Dodgers emblem) 25.00
Randy Johnson (black jersey) 10.00
   (purple jersey)....................................20.00
Pedro Martinez (white jersey)...............12.00
   (gray jersey) 20.00
Mike Piazza (black jersey)....................12.00
   (black jersey, Mizuno bat) 18.00
   (white jersey) 20.00
   (white jersey, Mizuno bat) 25.00
Albert Pujols (gray jsy, right pose).....12.00
   (gray jersey, left pose).......................15.00
   (white jersey, right pose) 30.00
   (white jersey, left pose) 35.00
Ivan Rodriguez (gray jersey) 10.00
   (blue jersey) 20.00
Sammy Sosa (blue jsy, no patch) 12.00
   (blue jsy, National emblem) 15.00
   (gray jersey, no patch) 22.00
   (gray jsy, National emblem) 25.00
Ichiro Suzuki
   (white, Seattle jsy) 18.00
   (white Mariners jsy, 51 on bat)..........18.00
   (white Mariners jsy, Mizuno bat).......20.00
   (gray Mariners jsy, 51 on bat) 25.00
   (gray Mariners jsy, Mizuno bat)............35.00

2002 Baseball Series 2

Barry Bonds (black jersey) 15.00
   (white jersey) 40.00
Roger Clemens (gray jersey)..................15.00
N. Garciaparra (white jersey) 12.00
   (gray jersey) 22.00
Ken Griffey Jr. (Reds jersey) 15.00
Derek Jeter (white jersey) 18.00
Greg Maddux (white jersey) 12.00
   (gray jersey) 20.00
Manny Ramirez (gray jersey) 12.00
   (white jersey) 22.00

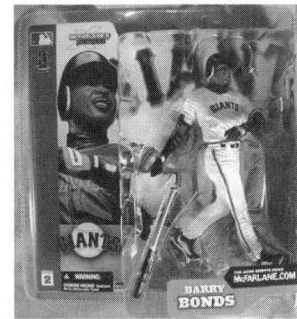

Alex Rodriguez (white jersey)................12.00
   (blue jersey) 25.00
Kerry Wood (gray jersey) 10.00
2002 BLC Chase Figures
Barry Bonds 25.00
Shawn Green 20.00
Mike Piazza 20.00

2002 Baseball Series 3

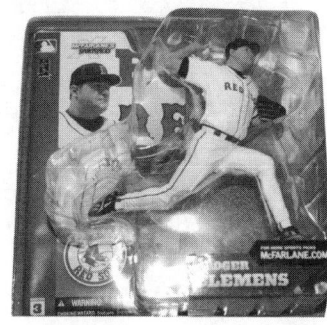

Barrett's Toy Chest

Roberto Alomar (gray jersey) 10.00
   (white jersey) 20.00
Adam Dunn (gray jersey)....................15.00
Jason Giambi (gray jersey)....................15.00
Juan Gonzalez (blue jersey)...................10.00
   (white jersey) 20.00
Vladimir Guerrero (gray jersey) 12.00
   (blue jersey) 25.00
Chipper Jones (gray jersey) 12.00
   (white jersey) 25.00
   (BLC jersey)...20.00
Roy Oswalt (white pants).....................12.00
   (gray pants)...25.00
Curt Schilling (white jersey) 12.00
   (gray jersey) 20.00
Sammy Sosa (BLC jersey) 22.00
Roger Clemens (Red Sox) 100.00
Ken Griffey Jr. (Mariners) 80.00

2003 Baseball Series 4

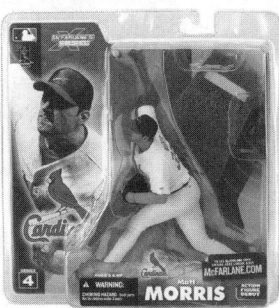

Lance Berkman (white jersey).............12.00
   (red jersey) 22.00
Trevor Hoffman (dark jersey) 10.00
   (gray jersey) 20.00

Eric Hinske (white jersey)..................25.00
   (gray jersey)..12.00
Matt Morris (white jersey)..................10.00
   (gray jersey) 20.00
Ichiro Suzuki (blue jersey) 12.00
   (gray jersey) 20.00
Larry Walker (purple jersey) 10.00

2003 Baseball Series 5

Barry Bonds (white jersey) 15.00
   (gray jersey) 30.00
   (Pirates jersey).....................................60.00
Pat Burrell (gray jersey) 15.00
Eric Gagne (white jersey 15.00
   (gray jersey) 25.00
Jason Giambi
   (New York pinstripes jersey) 15.00
   (Oakland jersey)...................................35.00
Trevor Hoffman (Camo jersey) 30.00
Torii Hunter (gray pants)....................15.00
   (white pants) 25.00
Derek Jeter (gray jersey) 15.00
Jason Kendall (white jersey)..................20.00
   (gray jersey) 30.00
Derek Lowe (gray jsy/pants)...............12.00
   (red jersey/white pants) 22.00
Greg Maddux (Cubs jersey) 45.00
Curt Schilling (Phillies jersey)................35.00
Alfonso Soriano (gray jersey) 18.00
Ichiro Suzuki (white jersey) 20.00
Miguel Tejada
   (green jersey, white pants)...................15.00
   (gray jersey) 25.00

2003 Baseball Series 6

Roger Clemens (Blue Jays jrsy) 40.00
Jim Edmonds (white jersey) 12.00
   (gray jersey) 22.00
Luis Gonzalez (white jersey) 12.00
   (black jersey) 22.00
Kazuhisu Ishii (white jersey) 10.00
   (gray jersey) 20.00
Jorge Posada (gray jersey)....................15.00
Alex Rodriguez (Mariners jrsy) 35.00
Sammy Sosa (gray jersey) 15.00
   (white/pinstripe jersey).........................30.00

Mike Sweeney (blue jersey).................12.00
  (white jersey) 22.00
Jim Thome (Phillies jersey) 12.00
  (Indians jersey) 40.00

2002 Basketball Series 1

Barrett's Toy Chest Photo

Kobe Bryant (yellow jersey)...................20.00
  (purple jersey)..80.00
Vince Carter (white jersey)....................15.00
  (purple jersey)..25.00
Tim Duncan (black jersey).....................20.00
  (white jersey) 50.00
Kevin Garnett (white jersey) 12.00
  (blue jersey)...38.00
Allen Iverson (wht jsy, clsed mouth) 15.00
  (white jersey, open mouth).....................25.00
  (black jersey, closed mouth) 55.00
  (black jersey, open mouth).....................80.00
Jason Kidd (blue jersey).......................12.00
  (white jersey) 30.00

2002 Basketball Series 2

Ray Allen (white jersey)..........................10.00
  (purple jersey)..18.00
Elton Brand (red jersey).......................12.00
  (white jersey) 23.00
Kwame Brown (blue jersey).................12.00
  (white jersey) 30.00
Steve Francis (white jersey)...................15.00
  (blue jersey)...28.00
Antawn Jamison (white jrsy)...................12.00
  (blue jersey)...25.00
Tracy McGrady (white jersey).............18.00
  (blue jersey)...40.00
Dirk Nowitzki (blue jersey)...................15.00
  (white jersey) 40.00
Shaquille O'Neal (yellow jrsy)................15.00
  (purple jersey)..35.00
John Stockton (white jersey) 12.00
  (purple jersey)..25.00

2002 Basketball Series 3

Mike Bibby (white jersey)........................12.00
  (purple jersey)..28.00
Kobe Bryant
  (purple jersey, long hair) 20.00

  (purple jersey, short hair).....................40.00
  (yellow jersey, long hair) 60.00
  (yellow jersey, short hair) 50.00
Baron Davis (white jersey)..................12.00
  (teal jersey) 25.00
Pau Gasol (black jersey)......................15.00
  (white jersey) 35.00
Juwan Howard (dark jersey)....................10.00
  (white jersey) 22.00
Eddie Jones (red jersey) 12.00
  (white jersey) 22.00
Paul Pierce (green jersey)...................15.00
  (white jersey) 35.00
Latrell Sprewell (white jersey) 12.00
  (blue jersey)...23.00
Rasheed Wallace (black jsy)...............12.00
  (white jersey) 25.00

2003 Basketball Series 4

Jermaine O'Neal (yellow jrsy...............18.00
  (white jersey) 50.00
Jalen Rose (red jersey)........................12.00
  (white jersey) 30.00
Amare Staudemire (white jsy).............15.00
  (purple jersey)..35.00
Dajuan Wagner (red jersey).................15.00
  (white jersey) 40.00

2001 Football Series 1

Barrett's Toy Chest Photo

Eddie George (blue, dirty fig) 40.00
  (blue, clean figure) 40.00
  (white, dirty figure) 65.00

  (white, clean figure) 100.00
  (w/o helmet, dirty figure)......................140.00
  (w/o helmet, clean figure) 175.00
Edgerrin James(white, dirty fig).............25.00
  (white, clean figure) 30.00
  (blue, dirty figure)................................50.00
  (blue, clean figure) 150.00
  (w/o helmet, dirty figure)......................120.00
  (w/o helmet, clean figure) 160.00
Randy Moss (purple, clean R. Moss fig) ...30.00
  (purple, clean, Moss figure) 35.00
  (white, clean R. Moss fig).......................80.00
  (white, clean Moss figure) 200.00
  (w/o helmet, clean R. Moss fig)............200.00
  (w/o helmet, clean_Moss fig) 300.00
Warren Sapp (red, dirty fig) 40.00
  (red, clean figure) 40.00
  (white, dirty figure) 75.00
  (white, clean figure) 175.00
  (w/o helmet, dirty figure)......................150.00
  (w/o helmet, clean figure) 175.00
Emmitt Smith (white, dirty, Smith) 75.00
  (wht, clean E. Smith figure)..................110.00
  (blue, clean E. Smith fig)......................650.00
  (blue, dirty, Smith figure).....................200.00
  (blue, no stars, dirty, Smith fig) 275.00
  (w/o helmet, dirty, Smith fig) 400.00
  (w/o helmet, clean, E. Smith fig)........800.00
Kurt Warner (white, dirty fig) 30.00
  (white, clean figure) 30.00
  (blue, dirty figure)................................60.00
  (blue, clean figure) 150.00
  (w/o helmet, dirty figure)......................125.00
  (w/o helmet, clean figure) 160.00

2001 Football Series 2

Barrett's Toy Chest Photo

Mark Brunell (blue, dirty fig) 15.00
  (blue, clean figure) 15.00
  (white, dirty figure) 50.00
  (white, clean figure) 50.00
  (w/o helmet, dirty figure)......................110.00
  (w/o helmet, clean figure) 110.00
Wayne Chrebet (white, dirty fig) 25.00
  (white, clean figure) 40.00
  (green, dirty figure) 65.00
  (green, clean figure) 70.00
  (w/o helmet, dirty figure)......................125.00
  (w/o helmet, clean figure) 130.00
Duante Culpepper (white, dirty fig).........25.00
  (white, clean figure) 25.00
  (purple, dirty figure) 75.00
  (purple, clean figure)............................90.00
  (w/o helmet, dirty figure)......................130.00
  (w/o helmet, clean figure) 130.00
Marshall Faulk (blue, dirty fig) 55.00
  (blue, clean figure) 55.00
  (white, dirty figure) 100.00
  (white, clean figure) 150.00
  (w/o helmet, dirty figure)......................200.00
  (w/o helmet, clean figure) 200.00

Marvin Harrison (blue, dirty fig) 20.00
   (blue, clean figure) 20.00
   (white, dirty figure) 55.00
   (white, clean figure) 55.00
   (w/o helmet, dirty figure) 125.00
   (w/o helmet, clean figure) 125.00
Brian Urlacher (blk, dirty fig) 90.00
   (black, clean figure) 100.00
   (white, dirty figure) 300.00
   (white, clean figure) 350.00
   (w/o helmet, dirty figure) 425.00
   (w/o helmet, clean figure) 425.00

2002 Football Series 3

Michael Bennett 28.00
James Jackson (3-bar facemask) 10.00
   (4-bar facemask) 15.00
LaDainian Tomlinson 30.00
Chris Weinke (lrg pants logo) 10.00
   (small logo on pants) 10.00

2002 Football Series 4

Barrett's Toy Chest Photo

Brett Favre (green jersey) 15.00
   (white jersey/white sleeves) 95.00
   (white jersey/green sleeves) 45.00
Peyton Manning (white jersey) 12.00
   (blue jersey) 25.00
Curtis Martin (green jersey) 12.00
   (white jersey) 35.00
D. McNabb (green jersey) 12.00
   (white jersey) 40.00
Terrell Owens (red jersey) 20.00
   (white jersey) 50.00
Jason Sehorn (white jsy, blue socks) 12.00
   (white jersey, red socks 12.00
   (blue jersey, blue socks.........................30.00
Michael Vick (white jersey) 50.00
   (black jersey) 160.00
R. Williams (Dolphins jersey) 35.00
   (Saints jersey).......................................75.00
   (Saints jrsy, Miami socks) 300.00

2002 Football Series 5

Barrett's Toy Chest Photo

Jerome Bettis (black jersey) 18.00
   (white jersey) 35.00

Tom Brady (white jersey) 18.00
   (blue jersey) 70.00
   (blue jersey, snow) 225.00
Stephen Davis (white jersey) 12.00
   (70th Anniversary jersey) 75.00
Jeff Garcia
   (white jsy/no stripe shoes) 15.00
   (whte jsy/ed stripe shoes) 25.00
   (red jrsy, no stripes shoes) 40.00
   (red jsy, red stripes shoes) 60.00
Tony Gonzalez (red jersey) 15.00
   (white jersey) 45.00
Ray Lewis (white jersey) 50.00
   (purple jersey) 140.00
Jerry Rice (Raiders jersey) 25.00
   (49'ers jersey) 160.00
A. Thomas (black jersey, blue mp) 15.00
   (blk jrsy/whte mouthpiece) 20.00
   (white jersey) 35.00

2000-01 NHLPA Hockey Series 1

Tony Amonte 10.00
Ray Bourque 10.00
Curtis Joseph 12.00
Paul Kariya 10.00
Patrick Roy 15.00
Steve Yzerman 20.00

2000-01 NHLPA Hockey Series 2

Brian Boucher 12.00
Pavel Bure 10.00
Dominik Hasek 15.00
Jaromir Jagr 15.00
Eric Lindros 10.00
Mark Messier...10.00

2001 Hockey Series 1

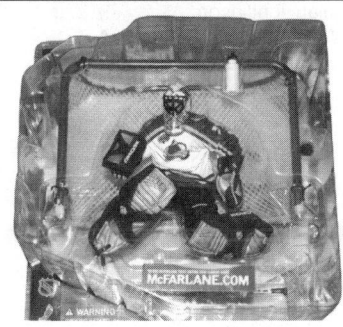

Barrett's Toy Chest Photo

Ed Belfour (no logo bottle) 30.00
   (w/logo on water bottle) 50.00
Martin Brodeur (no logo bttle) 65.00
   (w/logo on water bottle) 90.00
Peter Forsberg.......................................40.00
John Leclair..20.00
Mats Sundin 28.00
Jose Theodore (no logo bttle) 60.00
   (w/logo on water bottle) 80.00

2001 NHLPA Repainted Figures

T. Amonte (Chicago Home) 330.00
Ray Bourque (Col. Away) 90.00
Ray Bourque (Bost. Away) 425.00
Curtis Joseph (Tor. Away) 125.00
Paul Kariya (Anah. Home)....................300.00
Patrick Roy (Col. Home)........................180.00
   (logo on water bottle) 275.00
Steve Yzerman (Det. Away) 90.00
   (Detroit Home) 375.00

2001 Hockey Series 2

Dominik Hasek (white jersey) 45.00
   (red jersey) 115.00

Brett Hull (white jersey) 18.00
   (red jersey) 50.00

Jaromir Jagr (white jersey) 15.00
   (dark jersey)..30.00
Mario Lemieux (black jersey) 15.00
   (black jersey, logo stick) 25.00
   (white jersey) 30.00
   (white jersey, logo stick) 35.00
Eric Lindros (white jersey) 12.00
   (blue jersey) 30.00
Evgeni Nabokov (dark jersey) 45.00
   (white jersey) 70.00
Chris Pronger (white jersey) 12.00
   (blue jersey) 30.00
Tommy Salo (blue jersey) 12.00
   (white jersey) 55.00
Joe Thornton (white jersey) 50.00
   (black jersey) 20.00

2002 Hockey Series 3

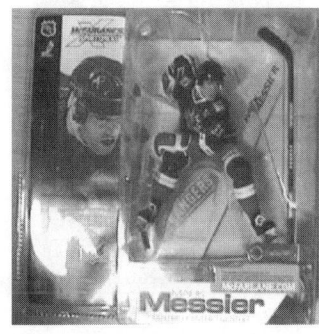

Pavel Bure (white jersey).........................12.00
   (blue jersey) 23.00
Olaf Kolzig (dark jersey) 12.00
   (white jersey) 30.00
M. Messier (light blue jersey) 15.00
   (Liberty jersey).....................................40.00
Mike Modano (green jersey) 12.00
   (white jersey) 35.00
A. Mogilny (white jersey) 15.00
   (blue jersey) 25.00
Chris Osgood (white jersey) 15.00
   (blue jersey) 28.00
Joe Sakic (blue jersey) 12.00
   (white jersey) 35.00
Scott Stevens (red jersey) 12.00
   (white jersey) 30.00
Roman Turek (white jersey) 12.00
   (black jersey) 30.00

2003 Hockey Series 4

Ron Francis (Red jersey).........................12.00
   (white jersey) 25.00
Jarome Iginla (white jersey) 12.00
   (black jersey) 28.00
Ilya Kovalchuk
   (black jsy, Thrashers logo) 15.00

(black jsy, Atlanta helmet) 15.00
   (white jsy, Thrashers logo) 50.00
   (white jsy, Atlanta helmet) 50.00
Mike Richter (white jersey) 15.00
   (blue jersey) 25.00
Jeremy Roenick
   (white jsy, Philly logo) 12.00
   (white jsy, Flyers logo) 12.00
   (black jsy, Philly logo) 30.00
   (black jsy, Flyers logo) 30.00
Tommy Salo (3rd jersey) 35.00
Brendan Shanahan (wht jrsy) 12.00
   (red jersey) 28.00
Ryan Smyth (white jersey) 12.00
   (blue jersey) 28.00
Jocelyn Thibault (white jrsy) 15.00
   (red jersey) 35.00

2003 Hockey Series 5

Dan Cloutier **(blue jersey)** 15.00
   (white jersey) 28.00
Tie Domi (white jersey) 12.00
   (blue jersey) 20.00
Marian Hossa (white jersey) 12.00
   (red jersey) 22.00
Saku Koivu (red jersey) 15.00
Mark Messier (blue Oilers jrsy) 18.00
   (white Oilers jersey) 50.00
Patrick Roy (white Canadiens jsy) 35.00
   (red Canadiens jersey) 100.00
Joe Sakic (blue jersey) 15.00
   (white jersey) 25.00

2002 McFarlane Exclusives

Team Canada Boxed Sets
   (Exclusive to Wal-Mart Can.)
Chris Pronger, Curtis Joseph,
   Steve Yzerman, Mario Lemieux 75.00
Eric Lindros, Martin Brodeur, Joe Sakic,
   Paul Kariya 75.00
Collectors Club BLC Exclusives
Nomar Garciaparra 20.00
Jason Giambi 25.00
NHL Hitz Exclusive
Chris Pronger 20.00
Limited 2-Pack Boxed Set
   (Toys R Us Canada Exclusives)
Joe Thornton, Jose Theodore 35.00
Saku Koivu, Tommy Salo 40.00
Maple Leafs 3-Pack Boxed Set
Sundin, Mogilny, Belfour 40.00

2003 McFarlane Exclusives

2003 Super Bowl Exclusives
Junior Seau 100.00
Ladainian Tomlinson 100.00
Red Wings 3-Pack Boxed Set
Hull, Joseph, Yzerman 35.00

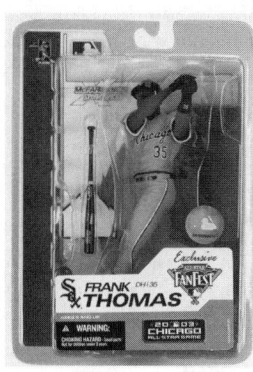

2003 MLB FanFest Exclusives
Sammy Sosa 35.00
Frank Thomas 35.00

2003 National Exclusives
Tiki Barber 40.00
Kenyon Martin 30.00
2003 Football HOF Exclusives
William Green 35.00

Mattel

All values listed are for Mint figures still in the packaging. The package must have four perfect corners and the blister bubble cannot be creased, dented, or damaged in any way.

Convention / Show Pieces

Glen Rice National Conv. 20.00
Kobe Bryant 2000 NBA AS 70.00
Vince Carter 2000 NBA AS 90.00
Steve Francis 2000 NBA AS 50.00

1998-99 Basketball Superstars

Ray Allen 16.00
Vin Baker 8.00
Charles Barkley 10.00
Kobe Bryant 22.00
Tim Duncan 30.00
Kevin Garnett 12.00
Anfernee Hardaway 10.00
Grant Hill 10.00
Allen Iverson 18.00

Michael Jordan (#1) 36.00
Michael Jordan (#2) 36.00
Jason Kidd 10.00
Reggie Miller 10.00
Alonzo Mourning 10.00
Dikembe Mutombo 10.00
Scottie Pippen 10.00
Glen Rice 10.00
Dennis Rodman 12.00
John Stockton 10.00
Keith Van Horn 12.00
Antoine Walker 12.00

1999 Basketball One-On-One

Kobe Bryant, Grant Hill 10.00
A. Hardaway, T. Hardaway 10.00
Michael Jordan, D. Robinson 14.00
Jason Kidd, John Stockton 12.00
Reggie Miller, Glen Rice 10.00
Dennis Rodman, Karl Malone 10.00

1999-00 Basketball Superstars

Vin Baker 8.00

Mike Bibby 20.00
Larry Bird 25.00
Shawn Bradley 8.00
Kobe Bryant 20.00
Vince Carter 35.00
Tim Duncan 18.00
Anfernee Hardaway 10.00
Tim Hardaway 10.00
Grant Hill 10.00
Juwan Howard 10.00

Allen Iverson..18.00
Antawn Jamison 22.00
Shawn Kemp 10.00
Raef LaFrentz...15.00
Reggie Miller 10.00
Shaquille O'Neal 20.00
Scottie Pippen 10.00
Glen Rice 8.00
Antoine Walker 10.00
Jayson Williams.......................................8.00

1999-00 College & Pro Series

Vince Carter 30.00
Glen Rice 10.00
Keith Van Horn 10.00
Antoine Walker 15.00

1999-00 NBA Maximum Air

Jordan Silv. Edition 3.5"...........................20.00
Jordan Collee POY..................................30.00
Jordan NBA ROY 30.00
Jordan Playoff Sensation 20.00
Jordan Champ '91 ....20.00
Jordan Champ '92 ....20.00
Jordan Champ '93 ....20.00
Jordan AS MVP '88 ....20.00
Jordan AS MVP '96 ....20.00
Jordan AS MVP '98 ....20.00

1999-00 NBA 13" Figures

Kobe Bryant...30.00
Tim Duncan 25.00

Grant Hill 18.00
Scottie Pippen 18.00

2000 Olympic Figures

Ray Allen 14.00
Vin Baker 8.00
Vince Carter 25.00
Tim Duncan 20.00
Kevin Garnett 18.00
Tim Hardaway 10.00
Grant Hill 10.00
Allan Houston..12.00
Jason Kidd...20.00
Alonzo Mourning 18.00
Gary Payton 15.00
Steve Smith 10.00
Team Set (Target Exclusive)...................45.00
   Carter/Kidd/Houston/Duncan/Garnett

MISCELLANEOUS FIGURES

Bobbing heads, Hartland Statues, and Hall of Fame busts all were done in a series that makes them easy to catalog. There are quite a number of baseball figurines that do not fall into a specific category, but are highly collectible nonetheless.

Babe Ruth was and still is one of the most marketed athletes of all-time. There have been a number of statues, dolls, busts and other figurines made with his likeness. Shortly following his death in 1948, a mantle clock with his bust was produced. It has two baseballs on either side of it (one celebrates his 714 career homers, the other his 60 home run season). More recent Ruth memorabilia includes a '60s chalkware statue and an '80s doll by Effenbee. No matter what the vintage, "The Babe" sells.

Ruth is not the only baseball player to be immortalized with a figurine. Chalkware statues of Ty Cobb, Nap Lajoie and Shoeless Joe Jackson are some of the most sought-after pieces of memorabilia. Busts of Ted Williams and Roberto Clemente adorn many

display cases. Jackie Robinson's image appears on a candy container and a cane top. Mickey Mantle's likeness is featured on a '60s hand-held game. The list goes on and on from the early days of "America's National Pastime" right up to the present day.

But collecting figurines is not just confined to famous ball-players or teams. There are a number of generic pieces that are also loved by collectors. Comical plaster baseball figures made by L.L. Rittgers complement any display. There are also ash-trays, salt and pepper shakers, trophies, decanters and book-ends that can spruce up your collection. Because of our fascination with the game, so many different and unique base-ball items have been produced. Just when you think you've seen it all, something else is sure to pop up.

The following price guide is just a sampling of figurines available. Use your instincts when buying figures and make sure to have fun with the hobby.

Babe Ruth Clock $2,500
Babe Ruth Chalkware Statue ('60s)................................. $150
Babe Ruth Effenbee Doll $150
Rittgers Baseball Statues (umpire, batter & pitcher) $300
Rittgers Baseball Statues (batter & catcher) $600
Ty Cobb Chalkware Statue (circa 1910).......................... $3,000
Joe Jackson Chalkware Statue (circa 1910) $3,000
Nap Lajoie Chalkware Statue (circa 1910)....................... $3,000
St. Louis Cardinals Mascot ashtray ('50s)....................... $250

Detroit Tigers Mascot ashtray ('40s)............................... $350
Pittsburgh Pirates Mascot ashtray ('40s) $350
Jackie Robinson candy container $300
Jackie Robinson cane top.. $150
Blatz Beer display $350
Brooks Robinson decanter $250
Chicago Cubs decanter $300
Baseball salt and pepper shakers............................ $50-$100 a pair

MICROSTARS

MicroStars was a short-lived venture, lasting little more than two years before going out of business. The company hit the market with a 14-figure baseball set in 1995. The set of 2-inch figures included some of the biggest stars in the game, and the unique

packaging allowed collectors to remove and later replace the figures without damaging the box. The baseball set was MicroStars' last, and today it draws little interest from collectors.

1995 Baseball

Complete Set (14): $45
Jeff Bagwell $3
Albert Belle $4
Barry Bonds $4
Will Clark $3
Roger Clemens $3
Lenny Dykstra $3

Ken Griffey Jr. $6
Jimmy Key $3
Paul Molitor.. $3
Mike Piazza $5
Kirby Puckett $4
Cal Ripken Jr. $6
Deion Sanders $4
Frank Thomas.. $6

AURORA

1965 Aurora
Great Moments in Sport
Plastic Model Kits

Aurora Plastics Corp. of West Hempstead, N.Y., was born in the late 1940s but came into production around 1952. It was founded by Abe Shikes, who started the company in an attempt to answer a demand for a better plastic hanger. Nabisco purchased the Aurora company in 1977 and quickly shut it down. Today some model molds from Aurora still exist and are being re-released under a different name on the box but with most of the original artwork. Aurora kits came unassembled as action figures that portray a famous event or accomplishment (such as Willie Mays making his famous catch off the bat of Vic Wertz in the 1954 World Series, Jimmy Brown getting his 10,000th career rushing yard and Babe Ruth's 60th home run in 1927). These models were very basic with 15 to 30 parts. The most difficult task a modeler had to do was paint the figures prior to assembly.

Original packages contained booklets with text that was written by the editors of Sport magazine.

A small plaque was intended to be placed in front of each model.

Prices are for unassembled kits with original boxes in excellent-mint condition.

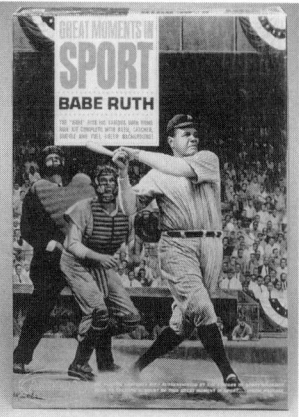 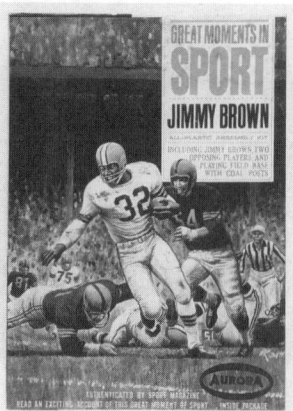

Jimmy Brown...$100-$150
Jack Dempsey/Louis Firpo ....$60-$85

Willie Mays..$150-$200
Babe Ruth..$250-$300
Johnny Unitas ....$100-$150
Jerry West... $35-$40

1965 BIG LEAGUE STARS STATUES

While the plastic statues in this set are virtually identical to the set issued in 1955 by Dairy Queen, the packaging of Big League Stars statues on a card with all the usual elements of a baseball card makes them more collectible. The DQ versions of the statues are white, while the Big League versions are bronze colored. The statues measure about 3 inches tall and were sold in a 4 x 5-inch cardboard and plastic blister pack for about 19 cents. Complete league sets were also sold in a large package. The singles package features the player's name in a large banner near the top with his team printed below and line drawings of ballplayers in action around the statue. Backs have a player portrait photo with facsimile autograph, position, team, previous year and career stats and a career summary. A perforated tab at bottom can be pulled out to make a stand for the display. Most packages are found with the hole at top punched out to allow for hanging on a hook. Values listed here are for complete statue/package combinations. Statues alone sell for $25-$50 for non-Hall of Famers; up to $800 for Mantle. Packages without the statue should be priced about one-third the values quoted here.

	NM	EX	VG
Complete Set (18):	$2500	$1250	$750
Common Player:	$60	$30	$18
(1) John Antonelli	$60	$30	$18
(2) Bob Avila	$60	$30	$18
(3) Yogi Berra	$185	$92	$55
(4) Roy Campanella	$200	$100	$60
(5) Larry Doby	$90	$45	$27
(6) Del Ennis	$60	$30	$18
(7) Jim Gilliam	$65	$32	$19
(8) Gil Hodges	$125	$62	$37
(9) Harvey Kuenn	$60	$30	$18
(10) Bob Lemon	$75	$37	$22
(11) Mickey Mantle	$800	$400	$240
(12) Eddie Mathews	$125	$62	$37
(13) Minnie Minoso	$65	$32	$19
(14) Stan Musial	$250	$125	$75
(15) Pee Wee Reese	$150	$75	$45
(16) Al Rosen	$60	$30	$18
(17) Duke Snider	$195	$97	$58
(18) Mickey Vernon	$60	$30	$18

1968 TOPPS PLAKS

Among the scarcest of Topps test issues of the late 1960s, "All Star" Baseball Plaks were plastic busts of two dozen stars of the era that came packaged like model airplane parts. The busts, which had to be snapped off a sprue, could be inserted into a base that carried the player's name. Packed with the plastic plaks was one of two checklist cards that featured six color photos per side. The 2 1/8" x 4" checklist cards, popular with superstar collectors, are considerably easier to find today than the actual plaks.

Complete set with the two checklist cards ($400 each) $4,500
1. Max Alvis..$40
2. Frank Howard $60

3. Dean Chance..$40
4. Catfish Hunter...$90
5. Jim Fregosi...$40
6. Al Kaline...$120
7. Harmon Killebrew $100
8. Gary Peters $40
9. Jim Lonborg...$40
10. Frank Robinson..$120
11. Mickey Mantle..$1,500
12. Carl Yastrzemski..$125
13. Hank Aaron...$250
14. Roberto Clemente $300
15. Richie Allen...$60

16. Tommy Davis $40
17. Orlando Cepeda $80
18. Don Drysdale..$120
19. Willie Mays...$250
20. Rusty Staub $60
21. Tim McCarver $60
22. Pete Rose $250
23. Ron Santo $60
24. Jim Wynn $40

COSTELLO COLLECTIBLES

Vince Costello, former linebacker for the Cleveland Browns, jumped into the figurine market with a series of football players in 1998. It was only natural that he did some of his Hall of Fame teammates. Hall of Fame Cleveland Browns produced were Lou Groza, Marion Motley, Otto Graham and Jim Brown.

Other players produced include Anthony Munoz, Len Dawson and Walter Payton.

Costello's figurines series include a colorful box and bases that feature the National Football Hall of Fame Building. Costello's valiant attempts at an old time figurine series seem to have stalled as there has not been a great demand for old time football stars which is a shame. It is a decent series.

Player	Edition	Price
Jim Brown Autographed	1,000	$200
Jim Brown	5,000	$75
Lenny Dawson Autographed	1,000	$180
Lenny Dawson	5,000	$75
Otto Graham Autographed	1,000	$180
Otto Graham	5,000	$75
Lou Groza Autographed	1,000	$180
Lou Groza	5,000	$75
Marion Motley Autographed	1,000	$180
Marion Motley	5,000	$75
Anthony Munoz Autographed	1,000	$180
Anthony Munoz	5,000	$75
Walter Payton	5,000	$75

Note: Very few of the edition sizes were ever made.

ART OF SPORT

PLAYER	SPORT	PRICE	EDITION SIZE
Ken Griffey, Jr. (Signed)	BASEBALL	$395.00	500
Ken Griffey, Jr. (Not signed)	BASEBALL	$225.00	1,500
Cal Ripken, Jr. (Signed)	BASEBALL	$395.00	500
Cal Ripken, Jr. (Not signed)	BASEBALL	$200.00	4,515
Troy Aikman (Signed)	FOOTBALL	$500.00	1,500
Troy Aikman (Not signed)	FOOTBALL	$225.00	500
John Elway (Signed)	FOOTBALL	$500.00	500
John Elway (Not Signed)	FOOTBALL	$225.00	700
Brett Favre (Signed)	FOOTBALL	$500.00	500
Brett Favre (Not Signed)	FOOTBALL	$225.00	1,500
Joe Greene (Signed)	FOOTBALL	$250.00	500
Jack Lambert (Signed)	FOOTBALL	$350.00	500
Dan Marino (Signed)	FOOTBALL	$500.00	500
Dan Marino (Not Signed)	FOOTBALL	$225.00	1,500
Walter Payton (Signed)	FOOTBALL	$900.00	250
Walter Payton (Not Signed)	FOOTBALL	$400.00	250
Jerry Rice (Signed)	FOOTBALL	$480.00	500
Jerry Rice (Not Signed)	FOOTBALL	$225.00	700
Barry Sanders (Signed)	FOOTBALL	$495.00	100
Barry Sanders (Not Signed)	FOOTBALL	$225.00	700
Emmitt Smith (Signed)	FOOTBALL	$500.00	500
Emmitt Smith (Not Signed)	FOOTBALL	$225.00	1,500
Seve Ballesteros	GOLF	$195.00	2,500
Sir Henry Cotton	GOLF	$195.00	2,500
Laura Davies	GOLF	$75.00	2,500
Nick Faldo	GOLF	$195.00	2,500
Walter Hagen	GOLF	$195.00	2,500
Ben Hogan	GOLF	$195.00	2,500
Bobby Jones	GOLF	$195.00	2,500
Sandy Lyle	GOLF	$195.00	2,500
Tom Morris	GOLF	$195.00	2,500
Jack Nicklaus	GOLF	$195.00	2,500
Jack Nicklaus British Open	GOLF	$500.00	500
Greg Norman	GOLF	$195.00	2,500
Arnold Palmer	GOLF	$195.00	2,500
Gary Player	GOLF	$195.00	2,500
Gene Sarazen	GOLF	$195.00	2,500
Harry Vardon	GOLF	$195.00	2,500
Tom Watson	GOLF	$195.00	2,500
Tiger Woods Black	GOLF	$195.00	2,500
Tiger Woods Red	GOLF	$195.00	2,500
Tiger Woods Trophy	GOLF	$300.00	500
Muhammed Ali Regular	BOXING	$195.00	2,500
Muhammed Ali Bronze	BOXING	$195.00	2,500

Cal Ripken Jr.

PLAYER	SPORT	PRICE	EDITION SIZE
Nigel Benn	BOXING	$195.00	2,500
Frank Bruno	BOXING	$195.00	2,500
Butterbean	BOXING	$195.00	2,500
Roberto Duran	BOXING	$195.00	2,500
Joe Frazier	BOXING	$195.00	2,500
Joe Frazier (Signed)	BOXING	$195.00	2,500
Foreman, George	BOXING	$195.00	2,500
Marvin Hagler	BOXING	$195.00	2,500
Naseem Hamed	BOXING	$195.00	2,500
Thomas Hearns	BOXING	$195.00	2,500
Larry Holmes	BOXING	$195.00	2,500
Evander Holyfield	BOXING	$195.00	2,500
Jake LaMotta (Signed)	BOXING	$195.00	2,500
Sugar Ray Leonard	BOXING	$195.00	2,500
Lennox Lewis	BOXING	$195.00	2,500
Lennox Lewis	BOXING	$195.00	2,500
Rocky Marciano	BOXING	$195.00	2,500

PLAYER	SPORT	PRICE	EDITION SIZE
Sugar Ray Robinson	BOXING	$195.00	2,500
Mike Tyson #1	BOXING	$195.00	2,500
Mike Tyson #2	BOXING	$195.00	2,500
Muhammed Ali FF	BOXING	$195.00	Open-Ended
Jack Dempsey FF	BOXING	$195.00	Open-Ended
Jack Johnson FF	BOXING	$195.00	Open-Ended
Joe Louis FF	BOXING	$195.00	Open-Ended
Rocky Marciano FF	BOXING	$195.00	Open-Ended
John Sullivan FF	BOXING	$195.00	Open-Ended
Mike Tyson FF	BOXING	$195.00	Open-Ended
Ali vs. Liston 2 Piece	BOXING	$500.00	500
Ali vs. Foreman 2 Piece	BOXING	$400.00	500
Dempsey vs. Tunney 2 Pc.	BOXING	$600.00	500
Dale Earnhardt Regular	NASCAR	$195.00	2,500
Dale Earnhardt Bronze	NASCAR	$195.00	2,500

HALLMARK

Hallmark, famous for its greeting cards, ornaments and stores throughout the country, jumped into the figural market place in 1994 with the debut of its Baseball Heroes Series. The first player created appropriately was Babe Ruth. Other series that followed were At the Ballpark, Football Legends, Hoop Stars, Hockey Greats and Stock Car Champions. There is also a list of a few sports stars that are not part of the aforementioned series.

What is nice about the Hallmark Series of sports figures is that they only do one or two players from each sport per year, not saturating the market. This makes it easy for the collector to add and build their collection. The ornaments stand about 5 inches tall and the SRP when they are introduced is approximately $15.95.

Baseball Heroes series:

1994 - Babe Ruth $60
1995 - Lou Gehrig $50
1996 - Satchel Paige $25
1997 - Jackie Robinson $25

At The Ballpark series:

1996 - Nolan Ryan $50
1997 - Hank Aaron $25
1998 - Cal Ripken Jr. $25
1999 - Ken Griffey Jr. $20
2000 - Mark McGwire $20
2001 - Sammy Sosa $20
2002 - Derek Jeter $20
2003 - Jason Giambi $20

Football Legends series:

1995 - Joe Montana $45
1996 - Troy Aikman $25
1997 - Joe Namath $25
1998 - Emmitt Smith $25
1999 - Dan Marino $30

2000 - John Elway $25
2001 - Brett Favre $20
2002 - Kurt Warner $20
2003 - Jerry Rice (S.F. 49ers) $25

Hoop Stars series:

1995 - Shaquille O'Neal $45
1996 - Larry Bird $35
1997 - Magic Johnson $30
1998 - Grant Hill $20
1999 - Scott Pippen $25
2000 - Karl Malone $25
2001 - Tim Duncan $25
2002 - Kevin Garnett $20
2003 - Kobe Bryant $20

Hockey Greats series:

1997 - Wayne Gretzky $45
1998 - Mario Lemieux $35
1999 - Gordie Howe $25
2000 - Eric Lindros $20
2001 - Jaromir Jagr $20

Stock Car Championship series:

1997 - Jeff Gordon $35
1998 - Richard Petty $35
1999 - Bill Elliott..$25

The following is a list of ornaments that were produced but were not part of a series:

1998 - Joe Montana (Notre Dame) $35
1999 - Muhammad Ali $35
2000 - Kristi Yamaguchi $25
2000 - Dale Earnhardt $35
2000 - Arnold Palmer $30
2001 - Steve Young (S.F. 49ers) $25
2001 - Peggy Fleming $25
2001 - Mickey Mantle (N. Y. Yankees) $45
2001 - Dale Jarrett.....................................$20
2002 - George Brett....................................$25
2003 - Jerry Rice (Oak. Raiders) $20
2003 - Ted Williams (Bos. Red Sox)........$25
2003 - Jimmie Johnson $25

PRO SPORT CREATIONS

Figures from Prosport Creations look similar to figures from Sports Impressions. Unfortunately, most of the pieces don't look like the players they represent. Consequently, the line never caught on with collectors, and the company disappeared from the hobby in the early '90s. (AP=Artist's Proof)

	HEIGHT	QUANTITY	MINT
Richie Ashburn			
Auto	9"	1,990	$50
AP	9"	1,990	$100
Mini	5"	3,000	$40
Rod Carew			
Auto	9"	555	$75
AP	9"	555	$100
Bill Dickey			
Facsimile	9"	1,155	$50
AP	9"	1,155	$100
Mini	5"	3,000	$40

	HEIGHT	QUANTITY	MINT
Whitey Ford			
Auto	9"	2,072	$75
AP	9"	2,072	$100
Mini	5"	3,000	$40
Steve Garvey			
Auto	9"	232	$100
AP	9"	232	$150
Bob Gibson			
Auto	9"	1,910	$70
AP	9"	1,910	$100
Mini	5"	3,000	$40

	HEIGHT	QUANTITY	MINT
Tony Gwynn			
Auto	9"	793	$125
AP	9"	793	$150
Ferguson Jenkins			
Auto	9"	490	$75
Auto AP	9"	490	$100
Harmon Killebrew			
Auto	9"	297	$200
Auto. AP	9"	297	$250
Eddie Mathews			
Auto	9"	300	$125
Auto. AP	9"	300	$150
Jim Palmer			
Auto	9"	1,499	$80
Auto. AP	9"	1,499	$150
Mini	5"	3,000	$40
Brooks Robinson			
Auto	9"	800	$125
Auto. AP	9"	800	$150

	HEIGHT	QUANTITY	MINT
Ozzie Smith			
Auto	9"	600	$175
Auto. AP	9"	600	$225
Willie Stargell			
Auto	9"	800	$100
Auto. AP	9"	800	$150

SALVINO, INC.

Salvino, Inc. has the distinct honor of being the longest running sports figurine manufacturer in the United States. Since brothers Rick and Wayne founded Salvino, Inc. in 1988, they have produced the greatest athletes of the 20th century. From Ruth to Ali to Jordan, they have become one of the industry's leaders in higher-end porcelain resin figurine production.

In their first ten years, they concentrated on smaller autographed editions. Since the price of autographs has skyrocketed, Salvino, Inc. in the last five years has turned its production to unsigned limited editions. They have created a very popular 7 Inch Prestige Series and 10 Inch Heroes of the Diamond.

SALVINO SIGNED FIGURINES	SPORT	PRICING	EDITION SIZE
Muhammed Ali (Black)	BOXING	$500.00	3,500
Muhammed Ali (White)	BOXING	$250.00	400
Elgin Baylor (Home Yellow)	BASKETBALL	$250.00	700
Elgin Baylor (Special Purple)	BASKETBALL	$400.00	300
Larry Bird (Jump Shot Home)	BASKETBALL	$400.00	1,000
Larry Bird (Jump Shot Away)	BASKETBALL	$400.00	1,000
Larry Bird (Special Dribbling)	BASKETBALL	$500.00	500
Larry Bird (Collegiate)	BASKETBALL	$500.00	1,000
Larry Bird (Crouch Shot Home)	BASKETBALL	$400.00	1,000
Larry Bird (Crouch Shot Away)	BASKETBALL	$400.00	1,000
Bjorn Borg	TENNIS	$500.00	750
Terry Bradshaw (Home Black)	FOOTBALL	$500.00	1,000
Terry Bradshaw (Away White)	FOOTBALL	$500.00	1,000
Jim Brown (Regular)	FOOTBALL	$250.00	1,000
Jim Brown (Special Brown)	FOOTBALL	$500.00	300
Roy Campenalla (Special)	BASEBALL	$500.00	200
Roy Campenalla (Regular)	BASEBALL	$400.00	2,500
Don Drysdale	BASEBALL	$250.00	2,500
A.J. Foyt	RACING	$250.00	750
Wayne Gretzky (Dealer Sp.)	HOCKEY	$900.00	368
Wayne Gretzky (Black)	HOCKEY	$500.00	950
Wayne Gretzky (White)	HOCKEY	$500.00	950
Ken Griffey (Home White)	BASEBALL	$400.00	200
Ken Griffey (Away Gray)	BASEBALL	$400.00	1,000
Ken Griffey (Reds P/S)	BASEBALL	$600.00	550
Rickey Henderson (Sliding)	BASEBALL	$350.00	1,000
Rickey Henderson (Leading Off)	BASEBALL	$500.00	550
Rickey Henderson (Special)	BASEBALL	$500.00	500
Paul Hornung (Home Green)	FOOTBALL	$300.00	500
Paul Hornung (Away White)	FOOTBALL	$300.00	500
Reggie Jackson	BASEBALL	$300.00	1,000
Magic Johnson (Home Gold)	BASKETBALL	$400.00	1,000
Magic Johnson (Away Purple)	BASKETBALL	$400.00	1,000
Magic Johnson (Collegiate)	BASKETBALL	$500.00	1,000
Michael Jordan (Dealer Sp.)	BASKETBALL	$2,000.00	368
Harmon Killebrew	BASEBALL	$300.00	1,000
Sandy Koufax (First)	BASEBALL	$300.00	2,500
Sandy Koufax (Leg Slant)	BASEBALL	$400.00	1,000

SALVINO SIGNED FIGURINES	SPORT	PRICING	EDITION SIZE
Sandy Koufax (Dealer Sp.)	BASEBALL	$900.00	368
Mario Lemieux (White Slapshot)	HOCKEY	$500.00	1,000
Mario Lemieux (Black Slapshot)	HOCKEY	$500.00	1,000
Mario Lemieux (White Skating)	HOCKEY	$500.00	750
Mario Lemieux (Black Skating)	HOCKEY	$500.00	750
Mario Lemieux (Dealer Sp.)	HOCKEY	$900.00	368
Eric Lindros (Red)	HOCKEY	$300.00	750
Eric Lindros (White)	HOCKEY	$300.00	750
Mickey Mantle (Batting)	BASEBALL	$1,000.00	682
Mickey Mantle (Fielding)	BASEBALL	$1,000.00	682
Mickey Mantle (Dealer Sp. #6)	BASEBALL	$1,500.00	368
Mickey Mantle (Dealer Sp. #7)	BASEBALL	$1,500.00	368
Mickey Mantle (RH Pinstripe)	BASEBALL	$1,000.00	900
Mickey Mantle (RH Gray)	BASEBALL	$1,000.00	900
Willie Mays (New York)	BASEBALL	$400.00	1,000
Willie Mays (San Francisco)	BASEBALL	$400.00	1,000
Willie Mays (Dealer Sp. Field)	BASEBALL	$900.00	368
Willie McCovey	BASEBALL	$500.00	200
Joe Montana (Away White)	FOOTBALL	$300.00	2,500
Joe Montana (Home Red)	FOOTBALL	$500.00	500
Joe Montana (Home Red)	FOOTBALL	$400.00	1,000
Joe Montana (Away White)	FOOTBALL	$400.00	1,000

SALVINO SIGNED FIGURINES	SPORT	PRICING	EDITION SIZE
Joe Montana (Home Kansas City)	FOOTBALL	$400.00	500
Joe Montana (Home Collegiate)	FOOTBALL	$500.00	500
Joe Montana (Away Collegiate)	FOOTBALL	$500.00	500
Eddie Murray	BASEBALL	$500.00	200
Joe Namath (Away White)	FOOTBALL	$200.00	2,500
Joe Namath (Home Green)	FOOTBALL	$400.00	500
Joe Namath (Helmet On White)	FOOTBALL	$400.00	1,000
Joe Namath (Dealer Sp.)	FOOTBALL	$950.00	368
Richard Petty (Regular)	RACING	$250.00	750
Richard Petty (Special)	RACING	$350.00	300
Brooks Robinson	BASEBALL	$300.00	1,000
Gale Sayers (Away White)	FOOTBALL	$300.00	1,000
Gale Sayers (Home Blue)	FOOTBALL	$300.00	1,000
O.J. Simpson (Home)	FOOTBALL	$400.00	1,000
O.J. Simpson (Away)	FOOTBALL	$400.00	1,000
O.J. Simpson (Collegiate Home)	FOOTBALL	$500.00	1,000
O.J. Simpson (Collegiate Away)	FOOTBALL	$500.00	1,000
Duke Snider	BASEBALL	$300.00	1,000
Bart Starr (Away White)	FOOTBALL	$300.00	500
Bart Starr (Home Green)	FOOTBALL	$300.00	500
Jim Taylor (Away White)	FOOTBALL	$300.00	500
Jim Taylor (Home Green)	FOOTBALL	$300.00	500
Darrell Waltrip	RACING	$250.00	750
Jerry West (Regular Gold)	BASKETBALL	$300.00	1,000
Jerry West (Special Purple)	BASKETBALL	$450.00	300

UNSIGNED

Michael Jordan (Away Red)	BASKETBALL	$250.00	2,500
Michael Jordan (Home White)	BASKETBALL	$250.00	2,500
Mario Lemieux	HOCKEY	$200.00	2,500
Mickey Mantle	BASEBALL	$200.00	2,500

UNSIGNED 10 INCH BASEBALL SERIES

Ernie Banks	BASEBALL	$190.00	2,500
Ty Cobb	BASEBALL	$190.00	2,500
Joe DiMaggio	BASEBALL	$100.00	2,500
Lou Gehrig	BASEBALL	$190.00	2,500
Ken Griffey	BASEBALL	$190.00	2,500
Derek Jeter	BASEBALL	$190.00	2,500
Willie McCovey	BASEBALL	$190.00	2,500
Eddie Murray	BASEBALL	$190.00	2,500
Babe Ruth	BASEBALL	$190.00	2,500

UNSIGNED 8 INCH BASEBALL SERIES

Ken Griffey	BASEBALL	$150.00	
Mark McGwire (Regular)	BASEBALL	$150.00	
Mark McGwire (Punch)	BASEBALL	$75.00	
Cal Ripken	BASEBALL	$150.00	
Sammy Sosa (Punch)	BASEBALL	$75.00	

UNSIGNED 7 INCH PRESTIGE BASEBALL SERIES

Jeff Bagwell	BASEBALL	$50.00	10,000
Albert Belle (Indians)	BASEBALL	$50.00	10,000
Albert Belle (White Sox)	BASEBALL	$50.00	10,000
Barry Bonds	BASEBALL	$50.00	10,000
Roger Clemens	BASEBALL	$50.00	10,000
Roberto Clemente	BASEBALL	$50.00	10,000
Ty Cobb	BASEBALL	$50.00	10,000
Jim Edmonds (Angels)	BASEBALL	$50.00	10,000
Jim Edmonds (Cardinals)	BASEBALL	$50.00	10,000
Nomar Garciaparra	BASEBALL	$50.00	10,000
Ken Griffey (Mariners)	BASEBALL	$50.00	10,000
Ken Griffey (Reds)	BASEBALL	$50.00	10,000
Tony Gwynn	BASEBALL	$50.00	10,000

Mickey Mantle

Roy Campanella

UNSIGNED FIGURINES	SPORT	PRICING	EDITION SIZE
UNSIGNED 7 INCH PRESTIGE BASEBALL SERIES			
Derek Jeter	BASEBALL	$50.00	10,000
Randy Johnson	BASEBALL	$50.00	10,000
Chipper Jones	BASEBALL	$50.00	10,000
Greg Maddux	BASEBALL	$50.00	10,000
Billy Martin	BASEBALL	$50.00	10,000
Pedro Martinez	BASEBALL	$50.00	10,000
Mickey Mantle (P/S)	BASEBALL	$50.00	10,000
Mickey Mantle (Gray)	BASEBALL	$50.00	10,000
Mickey Mantle/Roger Maris (Double)	BASEBALL	$50.00	10,000
Roger Maris (P/S)	BASEBALL	$50.00	10,000
Roger Maris (Gray)	BASEBALL	$50.00	10,000
Mark McGwire (Old Swing)	BASEBALL	$50.00	10,000
Mark McGwire (New Swing)	BASEBALL	$50.00	10,000
Hideo Nomo (Dodgers)	BASEBALL	$50.00	10,000
Hideo Nomo (Mets)	BASEBALL	$50.00	10,000
Mike Piazza (Dodgers)	BASEBALL	$50.00	10,000
Mike Piazza (Mets)	BASEBALL	$50.00	10,000
Cal Ripken	BASEBALL	$50.00	10,000
Alex Rodriguez (Mariners Bat)	BASEBALL	$50.00	10,000
Alex Rodriguez (Mariners Field)	BASEBALL	$50.00	10,000
Alex Rodriguez (Rangers)	BASEBALL	$50.00	10,000
Ivan Rodriguez	BASEBALL	$50.00	10,000
Scott Rolen	BASEBALL	$50.00	10,000
Babe Ruth	BASEBALL	$50.00	10,000
Babe Ruth/Lou Gehrig (2 Piece)	BASEBALL	$50.00	10,000
Sammy Sosa	BASEBALL	$50.00	10,000
Ichiro Suzuki	BASEBALL	$50.00	10,000
Frank Thomas	BASEBALL	$50.00	10,000
Larry Walker	BASEBALL	$50.00	10,000
Bernie Williams	BASEBALL	$50.00	10,000
UNSIGNED 7 INCH PRESTIGE FOOTBALL SERIES			
Troy Aikman	FOOTBALL	$50.00	10,000
John Elway	FOOTBALL	$50.00	10,000
Dan Marino	FOOTBALL	$50.00	10,000
UNSIGNED 7 INCH PRESTIGE BASKETBALL SERIES			
Kobe Bryant	BASKETBALL	$50.00	10,000
Allen Iverson	BASKETBALL	$50.00	10,000
Jason Kidd	BASKETBALL	$50.00	10,000
Shaq O'Neal	BASKETBALL	$50.00	10,000
OTHER UNSIGNED 7 INCH SALVINO FIGURES			
Mario Lemieux (Shooting)	HOCKEY	$50.00	2,500
Mario Lemieux (Skating)	HOCKEY	$50.00	2,500
Richard Petty	RACING	$50.00	2,500

SPORTS IMPRESSIONS

Sports Impressions was founded by Joe Timmerman in 1987. Based on strong friendships with Mickey Mantle and Don Mattingly, Timmerman decided to create a figurine line. These two great Yankees became good will ambassadors and the cornerstone of the Sports Impressions Line.

Sports Impressions generally were of three sizes; 5 inch, 7 inch and 10 inch. The original prices of the 5 inch series generally ran $25 to $50, the 7 inch figurines anywhere from $75 to $125 and the 10 inch figurines around the $200. price point.

Edition sizes were as high as 2,500 to 5,000 and as low as 500 to 1,500. If there was a particular important statistical number tied to a player's career, that would be used as the edition size. It is important for collectors to realize that Sports Impressions often did not make the entire run depending on how the figurines sold.

The early Sports Impressions were made of ceramic and the likeness to the players were often not the best. Later, they switched to the more popular cold-cast resin figurines and created some of the nicest ever made.

In the early 90s, Sports Impressions was sold to Enesco, manufacturer of the popular Precious Moments figures and other porcelain collectibles. Enesco began making more limited editions and included autographs on some editions. The line was discontinued around 1996. The remaining figurines were blown out and the prices came down initially. Since Sports Impressions have been gone a few years now, there is some renewed interest and prices have bounced back a bit.

PLAYER	SIZE/ DESCRIPTION	EDITION	PRICE
Hank Aaron	5 Inch Mini		$50.00
Hank Aaron	7 Inch 500 HR Club	5,755	$125.00
Hank Aaron	8 Inch Autographed	975	$250.00
Roberto Alomar	8 Inch Autographed	975	$150.00
Ernie Banks	5 Inch Mini		$50.00
Ernie Banks	7 Inch 500 HR Club	5,512	$100.00
Johnny Bench	6 Inch	2,950	$50.00
Johnnyy Bench	8 Inch	975	$200.00
Wade Boggs	7 Inch	2,500	$75.00
Barry Bonds	8 Inch Autographed	975	$400.00
Ralph Branca	8 Inch Autographed	1,951	$100.00
Jose Canseco	10 Inch	1,990	$85.00
Jose Canseco	7 Inch	2,500	$85.00
Jose Canseco	5 Inch Swinging Mini	2,950	$50.00
Jose Canseco	5 Inch Batting Mini		$50.00
Rod Carew	7 Inch	3,053	$75.00
Steve Carlton	9 Inch	500	$125.00
Gary Carter	7 Inch	5,009	$75.00
Will Clark	10 Inch	1,990	$125.00
Will Clark	7 Inch	1,990	$75.00
Will Clark	5 Inch Mini		$50.00
Roger Clemens	6 Inch	2,950	$60.00
Roger Clemens	8 Inch Autographed	975	$300.00
Roberto Clemente	7 Inch	5,000	$150.00
Roberto Clemente	5 Inch Mini		$75.00
Ty Cobb	7 Inch	5,000	$100.00
Eric Davis	7 Inch	1,990	$50.00
Eric Davis	5 Inch Mini		$40.00
Andre Dawson	7 Inch	2,500	$50.00
Lenny Dykstra	7 Inch	1,990	$75.00
Lenny Dykstra	5 Inch Mini		$50.00
Bob Feller	7 Inch	2,500	$100.00
Jimmie Foxx	7 Inch 500 HR Club	1,008	$300.00
Steve Garvey	7 Inch	2,599	$100.00
Steve Garvey	5 Inch Mini		$50.00
Lou Gehrig	7 Inch	5,000	$100.00
Kirk Gibson	7 Inch	2,500	$50.00
Tom Glavine	8 Inch Autographed	975	$250.00
Dwight Gooden	10 Inch	1,990	$90.00
Dwight Gooden	7 Inch	5,016	$50.00
Dwight Gooden	5 Inch Mini	2,950	$35.00
Mike Greenwell	7 Inch	2,500	$50.00
Mike Greenwell	5 Inch Mini	2,950	$35.00
Ken Griffey	7 Inch	1,990	$100.00
Ken Griffey	5 Inch Mini	2,950	$60.00
Tony Gwynn	7 Inch	2,500	$50.00
Tony Gwynn	5 Inch Mini		$50.00
Rickey Henderson	8 Inch	939	$125.00
Rickey Henderson	8 Inch Artist Proof	94	$250.00

PLAYER	SIZE/ DESCRIPTION	EDITION	PRICE
Keith Hernandez	7 Inch	2,500	$50.00
Orel Hershiser	7 Inch	5,055	$50.00
Bo Jackson	10 Inch	2,950	$100.00
Bo Jackson	7 Inch	2,950	$50.00
Bo Jackson	7 Inch Artist Proof		$100.00
Bo Jackson	5 Inch Mini		$40.00
Reggie Jackson	9 Inch Yankees	1,969	$100.00
Reggie Jackson	8 Inch Autographed	975	$250.00
Reggie Jackson	7 Inch Yankees	2,500	$75.00
Reggie Jackson	7 Inch 500 HR Club	5,563	$150.00
Reggie Jackson	7 Inch Angels	2,500	$75.00
Reggie Jackson	5 Inch Mini		$50.00
Greg Jeffries	7 Inch	5,009	$40.00
Howard Johnson	7 Inch	5,020	$40.00
Howard Johnson	5 Inch Mini		$25.00
David Justice	8 Inch Autographed	975	$125.00
Al Kaline	7 Inch	2,500	$75.00
Harmon Killebrew	7 Inch 500 HR Club	5,573	$225.00
Mark Langston	7 Inch	1,990	$35.00
Mickey Mantle	15 Inch Doll	1,956	$125.00
Mickey Mantle	15 Inch Doll AP	195	$250.00
Mickey Mantle	10 Inch Supersize	1,968	$200.00
Mickey Mantle	8 Inch Autographed	975	$750.00
Mickey Mantle	8 Inch	7,500	$195.00
Mickey Mantle	8 Inch Switch-Hitter Auto.	975	$1,250.00
Mickey Mantle	8 Inch Switch-Hitter	2,401	$250.00
Mickey Mantle	7 Inch 500 HR Club	5,536	$200.00
Mickey Mantle	7 Inch Autographed A.P.	106	$850.00
Mickey Mantle	7 Inch	2,500	$125.00
Mickey Mantle	6 Inch	2,950	$75.00
Mickey Mantle	5 Inch Mini		$60.00
Mickey Mantle	5 Inch Club		$95.00
Eddie Mathews	7 Inch 500 HR Club	5,512	$150.00
Don Mattingly	15 Inch Doll	1,990	$125.00
Don Mattingly	15 Inch Doll AP	199	$225.00
Don Mattingly	10 Inch	1,990	$125.00
Don Mattingly	8 Inch Autographed	975	$200.00
Don Mattingly	8 Inch Batting & Fielding		$150.00
Don Mattingly	7 Inch Franklin Glove	2,500	$250.00
Don Mattingly	7 Inch Franklin Glove Error	500	$400.00
Don Mattingly	6 Inch	2,950	$80.00
Don Mattingly	5 Inch Mini Fielding	2,950	$65.00
Don Mattingly	5 Inch Mini Batting		$65.00
Willie Mays	7 Inch 500 HR Club	5,660	$125.00
Willie Mays	7 Inch Famous Catch Fielding	5,000	$100.00
Willie Mays	5 Inch Mini		$50.00
Willie McCovey	7 Inch 500 HR Club	5,521	$300.00
Mark McGwire	10 Inch	1,990	$250.00
Mark McGwire	7 Inch	2,500	$125.00

Babe Ruth

Julius Erving

Lou Gehrig

Lawrence Taylor

PLAYER	SIZE/DESCRIPTION	EDITION	PRICE
Mark McGwire	5 Inch Mini		$75.00
Kevin McReynolds	7 Inch	5,022	$45.00
Kevin Mitchell	7 Inch	1,990	$45.00
Kevin Mitchell	5 Inch Mini		$30.00
Paul Molitor	7 Inch	2,500	$100.00
Joe Morgan	7 Inch	1,990	$100.00
Joe Morgan	5 Inch Mini		$50.00
Thurman Munson	10 Inch	995	$200.00
Thurman Munson	7 Inch	5,000	$95.00
Thurman Munson	5 Inch Mini		$50.00
Mel Ott	7 Inch 500 HR Club	1,008	
Mike Piazza	8 Inch Autographed	975	$250.00
Kirby Puckett	7 Inch	1,990	$100.00
Kirby Puckett	5 Inch Mini		$50.00
Cal Ripken	7 Inch	1,990	$125.00
Cal Ripken	5 Inch Mini		$75.00
Brooks Robinson	7 Inch	2,848	$100.00
Brooks Robinson	5 Inch		$50.00
Frank Robinson	7 Inch 500 HR Club	5,586	$150.00
Jackie Robinson	7 Inch	5,042	$80.00
Jackie Robinson	5 Inch Mini		$50.00
Babe Ruth	7 Inch 500 HR Club	5,714	$150.00
Babe Ruth	7 Inch	5,000	$90.00
Babe Ruth	5 Inch Club		$50.00
Nolan Ryan	15 Inch Doll	1,992	$125.00
Nolan Ryan	15 Inch Doll AP	199	$250.00
Nolan Ryan	10 Inch	1,990	$175.00
Nolan Ryan	9 Inch 5,000K Rangers	5,000	$125.00
Nolan Ryan	8 Inch Pitching Autographed	975	$250.00
Nolan Ryan	8 Inch Pitching		$125.00
Nolan Ryan	8 Inch Farewell Pose Auto.	975	$250.00
Nolan Ryan	8 Inch Farewell Pose	7,500	$125.00
Nolan Ryan	8 Inch No-Hitter Autographed	975	$250.00
Nolan Ryan	8 Inch No-Hitter		$125.00
Nolan Ryan	7 Inch Artist Proof	500	$195.00
Nolan Ryan	7 Inch 5,000K Mets	500	$300.00
Nolan Ryan	7 Inch 5,000K Rangers	500	$300.00
Nolan Ryan	7 Inch 5,000K Angels	500	$300.00
Nolan Ryan	7 Inch 5,000K Astros	500	$300.00
Nolan Ryan	5 Inch Mini	2,950	$50.00
Nolan Ryan	5 Inch Mini		$40.00
Nolan Ryan	5 Inch Mini With Plate Mets	3,000	$100.00
Nolan Ryan	5 Inch Mini With Plate Rangers	3,000	$100.00
Nolan Ryan	5 Inch Mini With Plate Angels	3,000	$100.00
Nolan Ryan	5 Inch Mini With Plate Astros	3,000	$100.00
Ryne Sandberg	8 Inch Autographed	975	$250.00
Ryne Sandberg	7 Inch	3,033	$80.00
Mike Schmidt	8 Inch Autographed	975	$300.00
Mike Schmidt	8 Inch	7,500	$125.00
Mike Schmidt	7 Inch 500 HR Club	5,548	$150.00
Tom Seaver	10 Inch	500	$150.00
Tom Seaver	7 Inch	3,033	$75.00
Tom Seaver	5 Inch Mini		$40.00
Duke Snider	7 Inch	2,500	$75.00
Duke Snider	5 Inch Mini		$40.00
Darryl Strawberry	7 Inch	5,018	$50.00

PLAYER	SIZE/DESCRIPTION	EDITION	PRICE
Darryl Strawberry	5 Inch Mini		$40.00
Bobby Thompson	7 Inch	1,951	$75.00
Alan Tramell	7 Inch	2,500	$60.00
Alan Tramell	5 Inch Mini	2,950	$35.00
Andy Van Slyke	7 Inch	2,500	$50.00
Robin Ventura	8 Inch Autographed	975	$125.00
Frank Viola	7 Inch	2,500	$40.00
Honus Wagner	7 Inch	5,000	$100.00
Ted Williams	10 Inch Supersize		$150.00
Ted Williams	7 Inch 500 HR Club	5,521	$150.00
Ted Williams	7 Inch	2,500	$125.00
Ted Williams	5 Inch		$75.00
David Winfield	7 Inch	2,500	$75.00
Cy Young	7 Inch	5,000	$85.00

BASKETBALL

PLAYER	SIZE/DESCRIPTION	EDITION	PRICE
Charles Barkley	10 Inch	2,500	$100.00
Larry Bird	8 Inch	2,500	$100.00
Larry Bird	8 Inch Autographed	975	$250.00
Julius Erving	9 Inch Autograhed	975	$250.00
Julius Erving	6 Inch	3,950	$100.00
Oscar Robertson	9 Inch Autograhed	975	$150.00
Oscar Robertson	6 Inch	3,950	$75.00
Shawn Kemp	10 Inch	2,500	$50.00
Alonzo Mourning	10 Inch	2,500	$75.00
Hakeem Olajuwon	10 Inch	2,500	$100.00
Scottie Pippen	10 Inch	2,500	$125.00
Chris Webber	10 Inch	2,500	$75.00

FOOTBALL

PLAYER	SIZE/DESCRIPTION	EDITION	PRICE
Troy Aikman	9 Inch	995	$150.00
Troy Aikman	6 Inch		$75.00
Randy Cunningham	9 Inch/Home	995	$100.00
Randy Cunningham	9 Inch/Away	995	$100.00
Randy Cunningham	6 Inch/Home		$60.00
Randy Cunningham	6 Inch/Away		$60.00
John Elway	9 Inch/Home	995	$150.00
John Elway	9 Inch/Away	995	$150.00
John Elway	6 Inch/Home		$75.00
John Elway	6 Inch/Away		$75.00
Boomer Esiason	9 Inch/Home	995	$100.00
Boomer Esiason	9 Inch/Away	995	$100.00
Boomer Esiason	6 Inch/Home		$60.00
Boomer Esiason	6 Inch/Away		$60.00
Jim Everett	6 Inch		$50.00
Bob Griese	8 Inch Autographed	975	$150.00
Bob Griese	6 Inch	3,950	$50.00
Jim Harbaugh	6 Inch		$40.00
Jim Kelly	9 Inch	995	$125.00
Jim Kelly	6 Inch		$75.00
Bernie Kosar	6 Inch		$40.00
Vince Lombardi	7 Inch	3,926	$125.00
Dan Marino	9 Inch/Home	995	$150.00
Dan Marino	9 Inch/Home AP	99	$350.00
Dan Marino	9 Inch/Away	995	$150.00
Dan Marino	9 Inch/Away AP	99	$350.00
Dan Marino	6 Inch/Home		$75.00
Dan Marino	6 Inch/Away		$75.00
Joe Montana	9 inch Autographed	975	$250.00
Joe Montana	9 Inch/Home	995	$150.00
Joe Montana	9 Inch/Away	995	$150.00
Joe Montana	6 Inch/Home		$75.00
Joe Montana	6 Inch/Away		$75.00
Warren Moon	6 Inch		$50.00
Christian Okoye	6 Inch		$50.00
Walter Payton	8 Inch Autographed	975	$900.00
Walter Payton	6 Inch	3,950	$100.00
Walter Payton	6 Inch Club		$125.00
Jerry Rice	9 Inch/Home	995	$200.00
Jerry Rice	9 Inch/Away	995	$200.00
Jerry Rice	6 Inch/Home		$100.00
Jerry Rice	6 Inch/Away		$100.00
Mark Rypien	6 Inch		$50.00

PLAYER	SIZE/DESCRIPTION	EDITION	PRICE
Gale Sayers	8 Inch Autographed	975	$225.00
Gale Sayers	6 Inch	3,950	$75.00
Emmitt Smith	6 Inch		$125.00
Kenny Stabler	8 Inch Autographed	975	$250.00
Kenny Stabler	6 Inch	3,950	$60.00
Lawrence Taylor	9 Inch/Home	995	$125.00
Lawrence Taylor	9 Inch/Away	995	$125.00
Lawrence Taylor	6 Inch/Home		$75.00
Lawrence Taylor	6 Inch/Away		$75.00
Thurman Thomas	6 Inch		$75.00
Johnny Unitas	8 Inch Autographed	975	$350.00
Johnny Unitas	6 Inch		$75.00
Steve Young	6 Inch		$50.00

GOLF

PLAYER	SIZE/DESCRIPTION	EDITION	PRICE
Arnie Palmer	9 Inch Autographed	975	$200.00
Arnie Palmer	6 Inch		$75.00

PLAYER	SIZE/DESCRIPTION	EDITION	PRICE
Gary Player	9 Inch Autographed	975	$150.00
Gary Player	6 Inch		$50.00

HOCKEY

PLAYER	SIZE/DESCRIPTION	EDITION	PRICE
Rod Gilbert	8 Inch Autographed	975	$100.00
Rod Gilbert	6 Inch	3,950	$40.00
Bobby Hull	8 Inch Autographed	975	$175.00
Bobby Hull	6 Inch	3,950	$50.00

RACING NASCAR

PLAYER	SIZE/DESCRIPTION	EDITION	PRICE
Geoff Bodine	8 Inch Autographed	975	$75.00
Bill Elliott	8 Inch Autographed	975	$150.00
Jeff Gordon	8 Inch Autographed	975	$250.00
Dale Jarrett	8 Inch Autographed	975	$150.00
Kyle Petty	8 Inch Autographed	975	$150.00
Rusty Wallace	8 Inch Autographed	975	$150.00
Darrell Waltrip	8 Inch Autographed	975	$150.00

SOUTHLAND PLASTICS AND ART CASTINGS

Southland Plastics was founded by partners Joe Sterkx, Jr. and Dr. Ray Maiwurm in 1998. The partnership was short lived and Southland Plastics only lasted 3 years. Their goal was to create a product line in the mold of Hartland. They had originally hoped to acquire Hartland but their attempts failed. Sterkx later formed a group that was successful in obtaining Hartland.

In the short period it produced figurines, Southland did outstanding work. They started by producing plastic figures very similar to Hartland. They even added a limited edition autograph series to the plastic figures. Only 5 players were ever produced.

In addition to their plastic figures, Southland created cast bronze statues on walnut bases. These statues were very limited 100 to 200 and were very pricey with an SRP of $995. The work again was fabulous.

SOUTHLAND PLASTICS	EDITION SIZE	PRICE
Ken Griffey Autographed	1,000	$200
Ken Griffey	10,000	$80
Tony Gwynn Autographed	1,000	$200
Tony Gwynn	10,000	$80
Greg Maddux Autographed	1,000	$200
Greg Maddux	10,000	$80
Nolan Ryan Autographed	1,000	$200
Shoeless Joe Jackson	10,000	$80

Southland Bronze		
Roberto Clemente	200	$995
Ty Cobb	200	$995
Ken Griffey	100	$995
Tony Gwynn	100	$995
Shoeless Joe Jackson	200	$995
Walter Johnson	100	$995
Greg Maddux	100	$995
Mickey Mantle	200	$995
Christy Mathewson	100	$995
Nolan Ryan	100	$995

Nolan Ryan

Babe Ruth	200	$995
Honus Wagner	100	$995
Babe Ruth & Lou Gehrig	200	$1,795
Babe Ruth & Lou Gehrig AP	25	$3,000

*Note: Very few of these were actually made. Edition sizes were very small.

OTHER STATUES

KAIL STATUES

In the early 1960s, Fred Kail produced a series of sports statues and banks that are some of the hottest figural items in the hobby today. They are made of a porcelain-like composition. The series included all of the then 14 NFL franchises and many college and even high school teams. NFL Kails range in price from $150 for the smaller variations up to $750 for the larger statues. The Washington Redskins and Dallas Cowboys are the rarest. College football statues and banks generally sell for about $100. There was also some major league baseball teams made with known teams being the New York Yankees, Baltimore Orioles and the Philadelphia Phillies. They are extremely rare. Baseball Kails prices can range from $500-$2,500 depending on the size and team.

RITTGERS STATUES

L.L. Rittgers issued a series of comical sport and non-sport statues from the late 1930s to the mid 1950s. They are most commonly identified with their ogre-like eyes. They are made of a chalkware composition. All are dated and engraved with the company letters. Prices below are for near mint examples with no repairs.

Baseball Trio	$300
Baseball Batter and Catcher	$850
Baseball Plaque	$1,500
Basketball Trio	$2,500
Bowling Duo	$300
Boxing Trio	$250
Boxing Trio with blonde boxer	$550

Football Duo $400
Wrestling Trio $250
Gorgeous George Wrestlers $1,200
Golfer & Caddie $1,000
Exercise Girl $1,000

The following is the complete list of Robert Gould statues. Prices for loose statues run from $50 for common players up to $350 for Hall of Fame players.

ROBERT GOULD
1. Willie Mays
2. Gus Zernial
3. Red Schoendienst
4. Chico Carrasquel
5. Jim Hegan
6. Curt Simmons
7. Bob Porterfield
8. Jim Busby
9. Don Mueller
10. Ted Kluszewski
11. Ray Boone
12. Smoky Burgess
13. Bob Rush
14. Early Wynn
15. Bill Bruton
16. Gus Bell
17. Jim Finigan
18. Granny Hammer
19. Hank Thompson
20. Joe Coleman
21. Don Newcombe
22. Richie Allen
23. Bobby Thomson
24. Sid Gordon
25. Gerry Coleman
26. Ernie Banks
27. Billy Pierce
28. Mel Parnell

PLATES

While limited-edition baseball plates are a relatively new hobby niche, the art of plate collecting has been around for more than a century. The first collectible plates—featuring Christmas themes and other popular subjects—were produced in Germany in the late 1800s. J. Roderick MacArthur brought the hobby to America in 1973 when he formed the Bradford Exchange. But plate collecting didn't cross over into the baseball world until the early 1980s.

In 1983, Hackett American began producing the first baseball-themed plates and several other manufacturers soon jumped on board. By the end of the decade, Gartlan USA and Sports Impressions had released numerous editions, and the Bradford Exchange entered the hobby in 1992.

If you're interested in collecting baseball plates, the usual caveats apply. Expect to pay a premium for Mint pieces in the original box, and an even bigger premium if the plate is extremely rare (check the edition size). Pay close attention to "autographed" editions. While several manufacturers—including Hackett and Sports Impressions—have produced autographed plates, many of the specimens on the market feature facsimile or "baked-in" signatures. The genuine autographs are usually signed in gold pen, and should be easily distinguishable by sight.

Since plates tend to take up a lot of room, you'll also want to give thought to display—especially if you don't have much shelf space. While most plates come with individual plastic or wooden stands, there are plenty of other options on the market, including plate frames (in all shapes and sizes), plate rails (featuring grooves that hold multiple plates securely), and shadow boxes.

BRADFORD EXCHANGE

J. Roderick MacArthur introduced collectible plates to the United States when he formed the Bradford Exchange to help collectors all over the world buy and trade collectible plates. Today, Bradford Exchange manufactures and distributes a wide variety of plates. Although most of its releases feature stars from the entertainment field, it has issued several sports plates with a number of themes.

Bradford Exchange

Ken Griffey Jr. Collection:
Most Valuable Player $30
A.L. Home Run Leader $30
M.L. RBI Leader $30
All-Star Home Run Champ $30
Welcome to the National League $35

Mark McGwire Collection
Record Breaker 9-8-98 .... $45
Record 70 HRs $45
50-50-50 Game $40
70! $40
Record Tying 61st HR $40
Full Speed to 40 .... $40
Historic 60th HR $40
The Triumph of 70 (4-plate set) $160

Mark McGwire 70th HR

Polo Grounds

Cal Ripken Jr. Collection
3,000th Hit $45
From Rookie to Legend (3-plate set) $120

Jackie Robinson Collection
Breaking Barriers $50
Player of the Year $50

Mickey Mantle Collection
500th Home Run $50
1956 World Series $60
1961 Home Run Chase $75
Bronx Bomber $50
The Oklahoma Kid $60
Triple Crown Season $45

Legends of Baseball
Babe Ruth: The Called Shot $35
Lou Gehrig: The Luckiest Man $35
Ty Cobb: The Georgia Peach .... $35-$45
Cy Young: The Perfect Game .... $35-$45
Rogers Hornsby: The .424 Season .... $30-$40
Honus Wagner: The Flying Dutchman .... $30-$40
Jimmie Foxx: The Beast .... $30-$40
Walter Johnson: The Shutout .... $30-$40
Tris Speaker: The Gray Eagle $30
Christy Mathewson: 1905 World Series .... $30-$40
Mel Ott: Master Melvin .... $30-$40
Lefty Grove: His Greatest Season .... $30-$40
Shoeless Joe Jackson .... $35-$50
Pie Traynor: Pittsburgh Champ .... $30-$40
Mickey Cochrane: Black Mike $30
Grover Alexander .... $30-$40

Take Me Out to the Ball Game
Wrigley Field, the Friendly Confines $60
Yankee Stadium, the House That Ruth Built $75
Fenway Park, Home of the Green Monster .... $25-$35
Briggs Stadium, Home of the Tigers .... $25-$35
Comiskey Park, Home of the White Sox $60
Cleveland Stadium, Home of the Indians $60
Memorial Stadium, Home of the Orioles $75
County Stadium, Home of the Champs $35
Ebbets Field, Home of the Dodgers $60
Shibe Park $50
Forbes Field $60
Polo Grounds $60

Lost Ballparks
Ebbets Field $100
Forbes Field $75
Polo Grounds $75
Shibe Field $75

Great Moments in Baseball
Joe DiMaggio: The Streak $75
Stan Musial: 5-Homer Double-Header .... $45-$55
Bobby Thomson: The Shot Heard 'Round the World ... $25-$35
Bill Mazeroski: Winning Home Run $50
Don Larsen: Perfect World Series Game .... $25-$33
Jackie Robinson: Saved Pennant $50
Satchel Paige: Greatest Games $40
Billy Martin: The Rescue Catch .... $25-$35
Dizzy Dean: World Series Shutout .... $25-$35
Carl Hubbell: The 1934 All-State $35
Ralph Kiner: The Home Run $50
Enos Slaughter: The Mad Dash .... $25-$35

Superstars of Baseball
Willie Mays $35
Carl Yastrzemski .... $70-$100
Frank Robinson .... $45-$65
Bob Gibson .... $45-$60
Harmon Killebrew $35
Don Drysdale .... $55-$80

Immortals of the Diamond
The Sultan of Swat, Babe Ruth $50
The Pride of the Yankees, Lou Gehrig $50
The Georgia Peach, Ty Cobb $60
The Winningest Pitcher, Cy Young $60

Baseball's Diamond Moments
Ted Williams: Last Time at Bat $50

Babe Ruth Centennial
The 60th Homer $40

Baseball Record Breakers
Yogi Berra $40
Lou Gehrig $40
Mike Schmidt $40
Cal Ripken Jr. $40

Bradford other sports
Basketball
Michael Jordan Series
Michael Jordan: 25,000 Points (rectangular) $35
Michael Jordan: 5-time NBA MVP $35
Michael Jordan: Breaking the Records $60
Taking It Personally $38
72 Wins $35
Heart of a Champion $35
6-Time NBA Finals $38
6-Time NBA Champion $35
Eastern Conference plate $38
4th NBA Title plate $38
Leader of the League $38
Last Shot plate $35
Career Stats mini ball $30
Sweep plate $38
In the Zone plate $38
In Command plate $40
Bulls in 5 plate $38
Above All, a Champion plate $35
Above the Rest 5-plate Panorama $200

Fishing
Rapid Strike plate $40
Sudden Strike plate $40

Football
Troy Aikman Series Series
Super Bowl XXVII Champion $35
The Huddle $30
Collector plate $30

John Elway Series
Super Bowl Champion $30
Super Bowl XXXIII MVP $35
Against All Odds $35
1998 AFC Champions $35
Bound for Glory $30
Collector's plate (orange uniform) $30
Triumph in Kansas City $30
Winning Edge $30

Brett Favre Series
Leader of the Pack $30
3 Degrees to Victory $30
Titletown $30
Pack Is Back $30
Touchdown $30
Collector plate $30

Dan Marino Series
Dan Marino 51,636 and Counting (rectangular) $35
61,361 Yards Gold $50
61,361 Yards collector $50
Collector plate $30
369 TDs plate $35
13 400-Yard Games $35
52 300-Yard Games $35

Drew Bledsoe collector plate $30
Mark Brunell collector plate $30
Joe Montana Super Bowl XXIII $30
Jerry Rice collecto rplate $30
Barry Sanders collector plate $30
Emmitt Smith Super Bowl XXX $30
Kordell Stewart collector plate $30

Hockey
Wayne Gretzky 802nd Goal plate $35

GARTLAN

Gartlan USA was based in Huntington Beach, Calif., and produced limited-edition ceramic and porcelain sports collectibles, including signed plates and ceramic plaques and cards. Plates range in size from 10 1/4" diameter to 8 1/2" to 3 1/4" mini plates. Artist's proofs are signed by the artist and player. Gartlan also offered a few plates directly through its club. Only collectors who were enrolled in the club received offers for the special plates, and Gartlan produced only enough product to cover the orders it received. These club-only plates can be very difficult to find on the secondary market.

This list of players includes the number made and price. Artist's proofs are signed by the artist and player.

Luis Aparicio signed 10 1/4" plate, 1,984: $150
Luis Aparicio 10 1/4" proof plate, 250: $100
Luis Aparicio 8 1/2" plate, 10,000: ....$30-$40
Luis Aparicio 3 1/4" plate, open: ....$10-$20
Al Barlick 3 1/4" plate, open: $20
Al Barlick Club plate, club only: $110
Johnny Bench signed 10 1/4" plate, 1,989: $325
Johnny Bench 3 1/4" plate, open: $35
Johnny Bench proof plate, 100: $395
Yogi Berra Signed 10 1/4" plate, 2,150: $200
Yogi Berra proof plate, 250: $175
Yogi Berra 8 1/2" plate, 10,000: $40
Yogi Berra 3 1/4" plate, open: $20
George Brett signed 10 1/4" plate, 2,000: $375
George Brett proof plate, 24: $750
George Brett 3 1/4" plate, open: $20
George Brett tankard, open: $30
Rod Carew signed 10 1/4" plate, 950: $175
Rod Carew 8 1/2" plate, 10,000: $40
Rod Carew 3 1/4" plate, open: $20
Carlton Fisk signed 10 1/4" plate, 950: $175
Carlton Fisk proof plate, 300: $175
Carlton Fisk 8 1/2" plate, 10,000: $40
Carlton Fisk 3 1/4" plate, open: $20
Carlton Fisk ceramic card, open: $18
Whitey Ford signed 10 1/4" plate, 2,360: $50
Whitey Ford proof plate, 250: $175
Whitey Ford 8 1/2" plate, 10,000: $25
Whitey Ford 3 1/4" plate, open: $15
Ken Griffey Jr. signed 10 1/4" plate, 1,989: $300
Ken Griffey Jr. 8 1/2" plate, 10,000: $40
Ken Griffey Jr. 3 1/4" plate, open: $20
Ken Griffey Jr. Club plate, club only: $75
Ken Griffey Jr. ceramic card, open: $12
Reggie Jackson 3 1/4" plate, open: $20
Reggie Jackson artist's proof plate, 44: $450
Pete Rose signed 10 1/4" platinum plate, 4,192: $625
Pete Rose 3 1/4" platinum plate, open: $20
Pete Rose signed 10 1/4" Diamond plate, 950: $450
Pete Rose 3 1/4" Diamond plate, open: $20
Pete Rose Club plate, club only: $150
Pete Rose 10 1/4" Farewell plate, 50: $550
Pete Rose tankard, open: $30
Mike Schmidt signed 10 1/4" plate, 1,987: $400
Mike Schmidt proof plate, 56: $600
Mike Schmidt 3 1/4" plate, open: $25
Tom Seaver signed 10 1/4" plate, 1,992: $300

Tom Seaver 8 1/2" plate, 10,000: $40
Tom Seaver 3 1/4" plate, open: $20
Tom Seaver ceramic card, open: $18
Darryl Strawberry 10 1/4" plate, 1,979: $125
Darryl Strawberry 8 1/2" plate, 10,000: $40
Darryl Strawberry 3 1/4" plate, open: $20
Frank Thomas 10 1/4" plate, 1,994: $150
Frank Thomas 8 1/2" plate, 10,000: $35
Frank Thomas 3 1/4" plate, open: $25
Frank Thomas ceramic card, open: $12
Carl Yastrzemski 10 1/4" plate, 950: $100
Carl Yastrzemski 8 1/2" plate, 10,000: $225
Carl Yastrzemski 3 1/4" plate, open: $40
Carl Yastrzemski ceramic card, open: $20

Gartlan other sports

Football
Troy Aikman 10 1/4" signed plate $125
Troy Aikman ceramic three-card set $50
Joe Montana 10 1/4" signed plate $150, artist's proof $300
Joe Montana 8 1/2" plate $150
Joe Montana mini plate $15
Roger Staubach 10 1/4" plate $100
Roger Staubach mini plate $10
Roger Staubach ceramic plaque $85
Roger Staubach ceramic card $12
Roger Staubach collector mug $30

Basketball
Kareem Abdul-Jabbar 10 1/4" signed plate $275
Kareem Abdul-Jabbar mini plate $15
Kareem Abdul-Jabbar signed watch $50
Kareem Abdul-Jabbar/Julius Erving signed watch $90
Bob Cousy 10 1/4" signed plate $100
Magic Johnson 10 1/4" signed plate $375
Magic Johnson mini plate $15
Shaquille O'Neal 10 1/4" signed plate $125
Shaquille O'Neal ceramic five-card set, signed, artist's proof .... $80, unsigned $80
Shaquille O'Neal Gartlan USA Club kit, 8 1/2" plate and club figurine $70
John Wooden 10 1/4" signed plate $60
John Wooden 8 1/2" unsigned plate $25
John Wooden mini plate $10
John Wooden five-piece set, includes two with autographs $425

Hockey
Wayne Gretzky signed plate $150
artist's proof $275
Wayne Gretzky/Gordie Howe signed 10¼-inch plate $225
artist's proof $300
Gordie Howe signed 10 1/4"-inch plate $125
Gordie Howe signed 8 1/2"-inch plate $45
Gordie Howe signed 3 1/4"-inch plate $25
Bobby Hull signed mini plate $28
Bobby and Brett Hull signed 10 1/4"-inch plate $300
Bobby and Brett Hull signed 8 1/2"-inch plate $45
Bobby and Brett Hull signed 3 1/4"-inch plate $20
Lanny McDonald signed plate, artist's proof $200
Lanny McDonald signed plate $125
Lanny McDonald mini plate $25
Darryl Sittler signed plate, artist's proof $200
Darryl Sittler hand-signed plate $125
Darryl Sittler mini plate $25

Mike Schmidt

Gordie Howe

HACKETT AMERICAN PLATES

Hackett American issued a handful of 8 1/2-inch full-color baseball plates during the mid-1980s. The plates, other than the Babe Ruth, Ty Cobb and Dwight Gooden issues, were all hand-signed by the player depicted. Hackett issued two different Reggie Jackson plates. The scarcity of these plates has made them some of the more desired and valuable sports plates in the hobby.

Hank Aaron signed	$250
Steve Carlton signed	$150
Gary Carter signed	$175
Roger Clemens signed	$300
Whitey Ford signed	$100
Steve Garvey signed	$50
Dwight Gooden, unsigned	$35
Reggie Jackson, Paluso	$300
Reggie Jackson, Alexander	$125
Wally Joyner signed	$295
Harmon Killebrew signed	$250
Sandy Koufax signed	$300
Eddie Mathews signed	$300
Willie Mays signed	$300
Pete Rose	$45
Babe Ruth unsigned	$100
Nolan Ryan signed	$700
Tom Seaver signed	$250

Henry Aaron   **Reggie Jackson**

Tom Seaver 300	$250
Don Sutton signed	$250

SPORTS IMPRESSIONS

Sports Impressions offered a wide variety of players on plates, as well as its line of figures. Most players have plates in three variations. Mini plates generally sell for $20. Regular-size (10 1/4") plates generally range from $75 to $150 and had production runs from 2,000 to 10,000. The Gold Edition is the most limited of all of the plates, with production runs of no more than 2,500. A Mickey Mantle gold plate sells for up to $200. The company also produced several player mugs.

Hank Aaron Gold Edition	$125
Wade Boggs 10 1/4" Red Sox plate, 2,000	$50
Wade Boggs 10 1/4" Red Sox gold plate, 1,000	$125
Wade Boggs mini Red Sox plate	$24
Jose Canseco 10 1/4" A's plate, 10,000	$50
Jose Canseco 10 1/4" A's gold plate, 2,500	$100
Jose Canseco mini A's plate	$24
Gary Carter 10 1/4" Mets plate, 2,000	$50
Gary Carter 10 1/4" Mets gold plate, 1,000	$100
Gary Carter mini Mets plate	$15
Will Clark 10 1/4" Giants plate, 10,000	$65
Will Clark 10 1/4" Giants gold plate, 2,500	$50
Will Clark mini Giants plate	$15
Roberto Clemente 10 1/4" Pirates plate,10,000	$125
Roberto Clemente mini Pirates plate	$50
Ty Cobb 10 1/4" Tigers plate, 10,000	$60
Ty Cobb mini Tigers plate	$20
Andre Dawson 10 1/4" Cubs plate, 10,000	$50
Andre Dawson 10 1/4" Cubs gold plate, 1,000	$100
Andre Dawson mini Cubs plate	$20
Lenny Dykstra 10 1/4" Phillies plate, 10,000	$50
Lenny Dykstra 10 1/4" Phillies gold plate, 1,000	$100
Lenny Dykstra mini Phillies plate	$20
Bob Feller 10 1/4" Indians plate, 10,000	$50
Bob Feller 10 1/4" Indians gold plate, 2,500	$100
Bob Feller mini Indians plate	$15
Lou Gehrig 10 1/4" Yankees plate, 10,000	$100

Lou Gehrig mini Yankees plate	$20
Kirk Gibson 10 1/4" Dodgers plate, 10,000	$30
Kirk Gibson 10 1/4" Dodgers gold plate, 2,500	$50
Kirk Gibson mini Dodgers plate	$12
Dwight Gooden 10 1/4" Mets gold plate, 3,500	$100
Dwight Gooden mini Mets plate	$25
Team Griffey 10 1/4" gold plate, Ken Sr. and Ken Jr., 1,991	$125
Team Griffey mini plate, Ken Sr. and Ken Jr.	$25
Tony Gwynn 7" Padres figurine, 2,500	$75-$125
Rickey Henderson 10 1/4" A's gold plate, 1,990	$125
Rickey Henderson mini A's plate	$24
Keith Hernandez 10 1/4" Mets plate, 2,000	$50
Keith Hernandez 10 1/4" Mets gold plate, 1,000	$100
Keith Hernandez mini Mets plate	$20
Orel Hershiser 10 1/4" Dodgers plate, 10,000	$35
Orel Hershiser 10 1/4" Dodgers gold plate, 2,500	$100
Orel Hershiser mini Dodgers plate	$15
Gregg Jefferies 10 1/4" Mets gold plate, 3,500	$125
Gregg Jefferies mini Mets plate	$20
Al Kaline 10 1/4" Tigers plate, 10,000	$60
Al Kaline 10 1/4" Tigers gold plate, 1,000	$125
Al Kaline mini Tigers plate	$20
Mickey Mantle mini Yankees plate, Switch Hitter	$20
Mickey Mantle 12 Yankees collectoval, The Life of a Legend, 1,968	$195
Mickey Mantle 10 1/4" Yankees gold plate, Mickey 7, 1,500	$100
Mickey Mantle 8 1/2" Yankees plate, The Golden Years, 5,000	$175
Mickey Mantle mini Yankees plate, The Golden Years	$20

Dwight Gooden

Mark McGwire

Darryl Strawberry

Mickey Mantle/Don Mattingly mini plate, Yankee Tradition $150
Don Mattingly 10 1/4" Yankees plate, Player of the Year, 5,000 ....$60
Don Mattingly 10 1/4" Yankees gold plate, Player of the Year, 2,500....$125
Don Mattingly mini Yankees plate, Player of the Year $24
Don Mattingly 10 1/4" Yankees plate, Yankee Pride $150
Don Mattingly mini Yankees plate, Yankee Pride $24
Don Mattingly 10 1/4" Yankees gold plate, #23, 1,991 ....$175
Don Mattingly mini Yankees plate, #23.......................................$20
Willie Mays 8 1/2" Giants plate, The Golden Years, 5,000 ....$125
Willie Mays mini Giants plate, The Golden Years..........................$20
Willie Mays 10 1/4" Giants gold plate, Famous Catch, 2,500.........$150
Willie Mays mini Giants plate, Famous Catch $24
Mark McGwire 10 1/4" A's gold plate, 2,500 ....$200
Mark McGwire mini A's plate..$20
Paul Molitor 10 1/4" Brewers plate, 10,000 ....$50
Paul Molitor 10 1/4" Brewers gold plate, 1,000...............................$125
Paul Molitor mini Brewers plate $20
Joe Morgan 10 1/4" Reds gold plate, 1,990 ....$150
Joe Morgan mini Reds plate $20
Thurman Munson 10 1/4" Yankees plate, 10,000.........................$50
Thurman Munson mini Yankees plate $20
Stan Musial 10 1/4" Cardinals gold plate, 1,963 ....$150
Stan Musial mini Cardinals plate $20
Brooks Robinson 10 1/4" Orioles gold plate, 1,000.......................$50
Brooks Robinson mini Orioles plate $24
Jackie Robinson 10 1/4" Dodgers gold plate, 1,956......................$150
Jackie Robinson mini Dodgers plate $24
Babe Ruth 10 1/4" Yankees plate, 10,000....................................$175
Babe Ruth mini Yankees plate $24
Nolan Ryan 10 1/4" Rangers gold plate, 5,000 Ks, 5,000 ....$175
Nolan Ryan mini Rangers plate, 5,000 Ks $20
Nolan Ryan 10 1/4" Rangers gold plate, 300 Wins, 1,990 ....$150
Nolan Ryan mini Rangers plate, 300 Wins....................................$24
Tom Seaver 10 1/4" Mets gold plate, 3,311.................................$175
Tom Seaver mini Mets plate $24
Duke Snider 10 1/4" Dodgers gold plate, Boys of Summer,1,500...$125
Duke Snider 10 1/4" Dodgers plate, Boys of Summer, 5,000...........$50
Duke Snider mini Dodgers plate, Boys of Summer $20
Duke Snider 8 1/2" Dodgers plate, 5,000, The Golden Years $125
Duke Snider mini Dodgers plate, The Golden Years.......................$24
Darryl Strawberry 10 1/4" Mets gold plate, 3,500..........................$75
Alan Trammell 10 1/4" Tigers plate, 10,000..................................$50

Ted Williams

Alan Trammell 10 1/4" Tigers gold plate, 1,000 ....$100
Alan Trammell mini Tigers plate...$50
Frank Viola 10 1/4" Twins gold plate, 2,500 ....$100-$125
Frank Viola mini Twins plate..$20
Honus Wagner 10 1/4" Pirates plate, 10,000..............................$75
Honus Wagner mini Pirates plate $20
Ted Williams 10 1/4" Red Sox gold plate, 1,960 ....$150
Ted Williams mini Red Sox plate..$24
Carl Yastrzemski 10 1/4" Red Sox plate, 1,500 ....$50
Carl Yastrzemski 10 1/4" Red Sox gold plate, 1,500.....................$100
Carl Yastrzemski mini Red Sox plate..$24
Cy Young 10 1/4" Indians plate, 10,000 ....$75
Cy Young mini Indians plate...$20

Theme Plates

THEME	SIZE	QUANTITY	PRICE
Boggs/Williams/Yastrzemski "Fenway Tradition"			
	12"	1,000	$200
Mantle/Mays/Snider "The Golden Years"			
	12"	1,000	$200
Mantle/Mays/Snider "Greatest Centerfielders"			
	Gold Edition	3,500	$150
	Mini Plate	—	$20
Mantle/Mays/Snider	10G"	3,500	$75
	Gold Edition	1,500	$150
	Mini Plate	—	$20
Robinson/Williams/Mantle/Yastrzemski "Living Triple Crown"			
	Gold Edition	1,000	$150
	10G"	10,000	$65
	Mini Plate	—	$20
Ryan/Carlton/Seaver "Kings of Ks"			
	12"	1,990	$195
Brooklyn Dodgers "Dem Bums"			
	10G"	1,000	$50
	Mini Plate	—	$20
Yankees "Living Triple Crown"			
	Mini Plate	—	$20
	10G"	—	$50
	Gold Edition	—	$150
"Yankees Tradition"	Mini Plate	—	$20
	10G"	10,000	$65
Brooklyn Dodgers "Wait till next Year"			
	10G"	5,000	$75
	Mini Plate	—	$20
Yankee Stadium	10H"	5,000	$75
	Mini Plate	—	$20

Football

Troy Aikman

Troy Aikman 10 1/4" gold plate $75
Troy Aikman 8 1/2" platinum plate..$35
Troy Aikman mini bronze plate...$15
Randall Cunningham 10 1/4" gold plate $75
Randall Cunningham 8 1/2" platinum plate....................................$35
Randall Cunningham mini bronze plate $15
John Elway 10 1/4" gold plate $75
John Elway 8 1/2" platinum plate..$35
John Elway mini bronze plate...$15
Boomer Esiason 10 1/4" gold plate...$65
Boomer Esiason 8 1/2" platinum plate $35
Boomer Esiason mini bronze plate..$15

Jim Everet 10 1/4" gold plate $75
Jim Everett 8 1/2" platinum plate.................................$35
Jim Everett mini bronze plate $15
Bob Griese 81¼4" platinum plate $35
Jim Harbaugh 10 1/4" gold plate $50
Jim Harbaugh 8 1/2" platinum plate $35
Jim Harbaugh mini bronze plate $15
Jim Kelly mini figurine $40
Jim Kelly 10 1/4" plate $75
Jim Kelly 8 1/2" platinum plate $35
Jim Kelly mini bronze plate $15
Bernie Kosar 10 1/4" gold plate $75
Bernie Kosar 8 1/2" platinum plate $35
Bernie Kosar mini bronze plate $15

Vince Lombardi

Vince Lombardi 8 1/2" plate $75
Vince Lombardi mini bronze plate $20
Vince Lombardi 8 1/2" platinum plate $50
Dan Marino 10 1/4" gold plate $75
Dan Marino 8 1/2" platinum plate $35
Dan Marino mini bronze plate $15
Art Monk 8 1/2" platinum plate $35
Joe Montana 10 1/4" plate $100
Joe Montana 8 1/2" platinum plate.................................$60
Joe Montana mini bronze plate $20
Warren Moon mini figurine $40
Warren Moon 10 1/4" gold plate....................................$75
Warren Moon 8 1/2" platinum plate $35
Warren Moon mini bronze plate $15
Christian Okoye 10 1/4" gold plate $50
Christian Okoye 8 1/2" platinum plate $35
Christian Okoye mini bronze plate $15
Walter Payton 10 1/4" gold plate $100
Walter Payton 8 1/2" platinum plate $50
Walter Payton mini bronze plate....................................$15
Jerry Rice 10 1/4" gold plate $75
Jerry Rice 8 1/2" platinum plate $35
Jerry Rice mini bronze plate $15
Mark Rypien 10 1/4" gold plate $75
Mark Rypien 8 1/2" platinum plate $35
Mark Rypien mini bronze plate $15
Barry Sanders 10 1/4" gold plate $100
Barry Sanders 8 1/2" platinum plate...............................$50
Barry Sanders mini bronze plate....................................$15

Steve Young

Deion Sanders 8 1/2" platinum plate $35
Emmitt Smith 8 1/2" platinum plate $75
Ken Stabler 8 1/2" platinum plate $35
Lawrence Taylor 10 1/4" gold plate $75
Lawrence Taylor 8 1/2" platinum plate $35
Lawrence Taylor mini bronze plate $15
Thurman Thomas 10 1/4" gold plate $75
Thurman Thomas 8 1/2" platinum plate...........................$35
Thurman Thomas mini bronze plate $15
Johnny Unitas 10 1/4" gold plate $75
Johnny Unitas 8 1/2" platinum plate $35
Johnny Unitas mini bronze plate $15
Steve Young 8 1/2" platinum plate $35

Basketball

Chicago Bulls 1993 Champions 10 1/4" plate....................$125
Chicago Bulls 1993 Champions 8 1/2" plate $40
Chicago Bulls 1993 Champions mini plate $15
1992 Olympic Dream Team 10 1/4" gold edition plate, 12"
    gold signatures $200
1992 Olympic Dream Team mug of 10 ....$10
Kenny Anderson 10 1/4" gold plate.................................$50
Kenny Anderson mini plate $15
Charles Barkley 10 1/4" plate $150
Charles Barkley 8 1/2" platinum plate $35
Charles Barkley mini plate $15
Charles Barkley Dream Team collector mug $10
Larry Bird 10 1/4" gold plate ....$100-$200
Larry Bird 8 1/2" platinum plate, two types $35
Larry Bird mini plate, three types $15
Larry Bird collector mug $10
Derrick Coleman mini plate $15
Brad Daugherty mini plate $15
Clyde Drexler 10 1/4" gold plate $75
Clyde Drexler 8 1/2" platinum plate $35
Clyde Drexler mini plate, two types................................$15
Clyde Drexler collector mug $10
Joe Dumars mini plate $15
Julius Erving 8 1/2" platinum plate $35
Patrick Ewing 10 1/4" gold plate $125
Patrick Ewing 8 1/2" platinum plate $35
Patrick Ewing mini plate $15
Tim Hardaway mini plate $15
Kevin Johnson 10 1/4" gold plate...................................$75
Kevin Johnson 8 1/2" platinum plate $35
Kevin Johnson mini plate $15
Magic Johnson 10 1/4" gold plate ....$150-$225
Magic Johnson 8 1/2" platinum plate, two types................$60
Magic Johnson mini plate, three types $150
Magic Johnson collector mug $10

Michael Jordan plate and mug

Michael Jordan 10 1/4" ....$150-$225
Michael Jordan 8 1/2" platinum plate, two types..............$60
Michael Jordan mini bronze plate, two types $25
Shawn Kemp mini plate $15
Bernard King 10 1/4" gold plate......................................$75
Bernard King mini plate $15
Christian Laettner mini plate $15
Reggie Lewis mini plate $15
Dan Majerle 10 1/4" gold plate $75

Dan Majerle 8 1/2" platinum plate	$35		Mark Price 10 1/4" gold plate	$75
Karl Malone 10 1/4" gold plate	$75		Mark Price mini plate	$15
Karl Malone 8 1/2" platinum plate	$35		Mitch Richmond mini plate	$15
Karl Malone mini plate	$15		Oscar Robertson 10 1/4" gold plate	$75
Danny Manning mini plate	$15		Oscar Robertson mini plate	$15
Kevin McHale 10 1/4" gold plate	$125		David Robinson 10 1/4" gold plate	$75
Kevin McHale mini plate	$15		David Robinson 8 1/2" platinum plate	$35
Reggie Miller 10 1/4" gold plate	$75		David Robinson mini plate, two types	$15
Reggie Miller mini plate	$15		Rony Seikaly 10 1/4" gold plate	$125
Chris Mullin 10 1/4" gold plate	$75		Rony Seikaly mini plate	$15
Chris Mullin 8 1/2" platinum plate	$35		Scott Skiles 10 1/4" gold plate	$75
Chris Mullin mini, two styles	$15		Scott Skiles mini plate	$15
Hakeem Olajuwon 10 1/4" gold plate	$75		John Starks 10 1/4" gold plate	$75
Hakeem Olajuwon mini plate	$15		Isiah Thomas 10 1/4" gold plate	$125
Shaquille O'Neal 10 1/4" gold plate	$125		Isiah Thomas 8 1/2" platinum plate	$35
Shaquille O'Neal mini plate	$15		Isiah Thomas mini plate	$15
Shaquille O'Neal collector mug	$10		Dominique Wilkins 10 1/4" gold plate	$125
John Paxson mini plate	$15		Dominique Wilkins 8 1/2" platinum plate	$50
Scottie Pippen 10 1/4" gold plate	$75		Dominique Wilkins mini plate	$15
Scottie Pippen mini plate	$15		James Worthy 10 1/4" gold plate	$150
Terry Porter mini plate	$15		James Worthy mini plate	$15

MINIATURE STADIUMS
Bridgeport Collectibles

Bridgeport Marketing of Cedarhurst, N.Y., produces miniature stadiums of cold-cast porcelain. They are hand-painted and available in a variety of sizes.

Candlestick Park - San Francisco	$50		Pro Player Stadium - Miami	$50
Lambeau Field - Green Bay	$55		Three Rivers Stadium - Pittsburgh	$55
Mile High Stadium - Denver	$55			

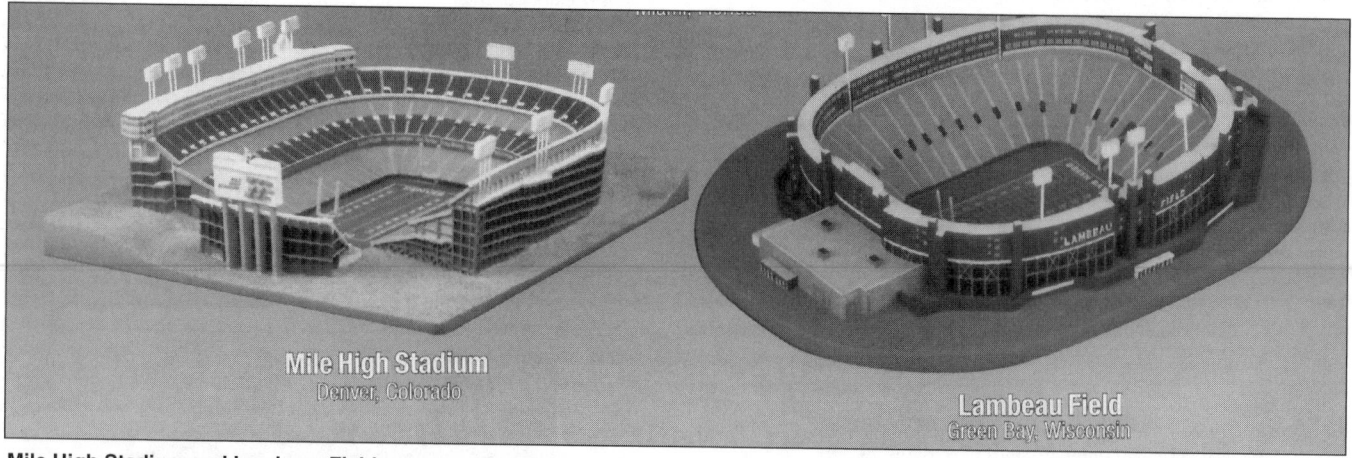

Mile High Stadium and Lambeau Field

Sport Collectors Guild Stadium Replicas

Sport Collectors Guild of Phoenix, Ariz., has produced stadium replicas from ground stone mixed with pine tar resin and secret ingredients since 1995. The patented process allows for original designs with extreme detail. Three series of stadiums are produced, including Silver Series (miniature, measuring approximately 3 x 3 x 2, not numbered), Gold Series (approximately 5 x 5 x 2, individually numbered to 4,750) and Platinum Series (approximately 11 x 10 x 3, individually numbered to 4,750). Visit the company's Web site at www.replicastadiums.com.

Gold Series

Alamodome	$50		Atlanta's Fulton County	$50
Alltel, Florida	$50		The Ballpark at Arlington	$50
America West (basketball)	$50		Bank One, Arizona	$50
America West (hockey)	$50		Boston Garden (basketball)	$50
Anaheim Stadium	$50		Boston Garden (hockey)	$50
Arlington Ballpark	$50		Bradley Center, Milwaukee	$50
Arrowhead Stadium	$50		Braves Field	$50
Astrodome (baseball)	$50		Browns Stadium	$50
Astrodome (football)	$50		Busch Stadium	$50
			Camden Yards w/warehouse	$60

Candlestick Park (baseball)..$50
Candlestick Park (football)...$50
Charlotte Coliseum...$50
Chicago Stadium (basketball)...$50
Chicago Stadium (hockey)...$50
Cinergy Field (baseball)...$50
Cinergy Field (football)..$50
Cleveland Municipal Stadium (baseball) $50
Cleveland Municipal Stadium (football) $50
Comerica Park, Detroit..$50
Comiskey Park $50
Conseco, Indianapolis $50

Coors Field

Coors Field $50

County Stadium

County Stadium, Milwaukee $50
Crosley Field $50

Dodgers Stadium

Dodger Stadium (baseball) $50
Ebbets Field $50
Ericsson Stadium $50
Fedex Field, Maryland...$50
Fenway Park..$50
First Union, Philadelphia (basketball)....................................$50
First Union, Philadelphia (hockey)...$50
Fleet Center (basketball) $50
Fleet Center (hockey)..$50
Forbes Field $50

Foxboro...$50
Georgia Dome $50
Giants Stadium (New York Giants) $50
Giants Stadium (New York Jets) $50
Great Western Forum (basketball)...$50
Great Western Forum (hockey)..$50
Griffith Stadium...$40
Gund Arena, Cleveland..$50
Heinz Field, Pittsburgh..$50
Invesco, Denver $50
Jacobs Field..$50
Joe Louis Arena $50
Kauffman Stadium, Kansas City $50
Kingdome (baseball) $50
Kingdome (football) $50
Lambeau Field $50
League Park $50
Los Angeles Memorial Coliseum (baseball) $50
Los Angeles Sports Arena (basketball) $50
Madison Square Garden (basketball) $50
Madison Square Garden (hockey) $50
Maple Leaf Garden $50
Market Square, Indiana $50
McNichols, Denver (basketball)...$50
McNichols, Denver (hockey)..$50
Mellon Arena, Pittsburgh...$50
Metrodome (baseball)..$50
Metrodome (football) $50
Metropolitan Stadium $50
Miami Arena..$50
Mile High $50
Miller Park, Milwaukee $50
Minute Maid, Houston $50
Network Associates Coliseum (baseball) $50
Nework Associates Coliseum (football) $50
New Ravens Stadium $50
Old Arlington $50
Old Colts Stadium...$50
Old Commiskey...$50
Old Memorial Stadium $50
Old Ravens Stadium $50
Old Wrigley $50
Old Yankee Stadium $50
Olympia...$50
Olympic Stadium..$50
Orlando Arena $50
Pac Bell...$50
Palace, Detroit $50
Paul Brown Stadium $50
PNC Park, Pittsburgh...$50
Polo Grounds $50
Pro Player, Florida (baseball)..$50
Pro Player, Florida (football) $50
Qualcomm, San Diego (baseball)..$50
Qualcomm, San Diego (football)..$50
Ralph Wilson, Buffalo...$50
Raymond James, Tampa $50
RCA Dome...$50
RFK Stadium $50
Riverfront Stadium $50
Rose Garden, Portland $50
Safeco Field, Seattle...$50
Savvis Center $50
Seahawkds Stadium $50
Seal Stadium $50
Shea Stadium $50
Shibe Park $50
Skydome..$50
Soldier Field..$50
Spectrum (basketball) $50
Spectrum (hockey)...$50
Sportsman Park...$50
Staples Arena (basketball)...$50
Staples Arena (hockey)..$50

Summit $50
Superdome.. $50
Tampa Stadium $50
Target Center $50
Texas Stadium $50
The Arena $50
The Coliseum, Tennessee................................. $50
Three Rivers Stadium (baseball) $50
Three Rivers Stadium (football) $50
Tiger Stadium $50
Transworld Dome, St. Louis $50
Turner Field $50
United Center (basketball)................................. $50
United Center (hockey) $50
U.S. Air Arena, Washington D.C. (basketball) ... $50
U.S. Air Arena, Washington D.C. (hockey) $50
Veterans Stadium (baseball) $50
Veterans Stadium (football) $50

Wrigley Field

Wrigley Field $50
Yankee Stadium $50

Silver Series (Mini stadiums)
Alltel, Florida $15
Anaheim Stadium $15
Arrowhead Stadium $15
Astrodome $15
Atlanta's Fulton County $15
Bank One, Arizona $15
Boston Garden (basketball)............................... $15
Boston Garden (football) $15
Browns Stadium $15
Busch Stadium $15
Camden Yards $15
Cinergy Field (football) $15
Cleveland Municipal Stadium (football) $15
Coors Field $15
County Stadium $15
Dodger Stadium (baseball) $15
Ebbetts Field $15
Fedex Field, Maryland....................................... $15
Fenway Park.. $15
Foxboro $15
Georgia Dome $15
Giants Stadium (New York Giants).................... $15
Giants Stadium (New York Jets) $15
Heinz Field, Pittsburgh $15
Invesco, Denver $15
Jacobs Field $15
Kauffman Stadium, Kansas City $15
Lambeau Field $15
Madison Square Garden (basketball)................. $15
Madison Square Garden (hockey) $15
Maple Leaf Garden $15
Mellon Arena (Pittsburgh)................................. $15
Mile High $15
Minute Maid, Houston $15
Network Associated Coliseum (baseball) $15
Network Associated Coliseum (football)............ $15

New Ravens Stadium $15
Old Comiskey Park $15
Old Wrigley $15
Old Yankee Stadium $15
Pac Bell.. $15
Paul Brown Stadium $15
PNC Park $15
Polo Grounds $15
Pro Player (baseball) $15
Pro Player (football) $15
Qualcomm, San Diego (baseball)...................... $15
Qualcomm, San Diego (football) $15
Ralph Wilson, Buffalo.. $15
Raymond James, Tampa $15
RFK Stadium $15
Soldier Field.. $15
Shea Stadium $15
Shibe Park $15
Texas Stadium $15
The Coliseum, Tennessee $15
Three Rivers (football) $15
Tiger Stadium $15
Turner Field $15
Veterans Stadium (football) $15
Wrigley Field $15
Yankee Stadium $15

Platinum Series
Camden Yards $75
County Stadium, Milwaukee $75
Fenway Park.. $75
Giants Stadium (New York Giants) $75
Giants Stadium (New York Jets) $75
Jacobs Field.. $75
Kauffman Stadium, Kansas City $75
Lambeau Field $75
Old Yankee Stadium $75
Pac Bell.. $75
PNC Park, Pittsburgh $75
Pro Player, Florida (football) $75
Safeco Field $75
Soldier Field $75
Texas Stadium $75
The Coliseum, Tennessee $75
Three Rivers (football) $75
Tiger Stadium $75
Wrigley Field $75

Collegiate Gold Series
Alabama Crimson Tide $50
ASU Sun Devils $50
Florida State Seminoles.................................... $50
Florida Gators $50
Georgia Tech Yellow Jackets $50
Georgia Bulldogs $50
Iowa Hawkeyes $50
Kansas Jayhawks $50
Michigan State Spartans $50
Michigan Wolverines $50
Notre Dame Fighting Irish.................................. $50
Purdue Boilermakers $50
Duke Blue Devils... $50
Nebraska Cornhuskers $50
Ohio State Buckeyes $50
Oklahoma Sooners $50
Penn State Nittany Lions $50
South Carolina Gamecocks $50
Tennessee Volunteers....................................... $50
Texas A&M Aggies $50
Wisconsin Badgers $50

Collegiate Silver Series (Mini stadiums)
Alabama Crimson Tide $15
Georgia Bulldogs $15
Notre Dame Fighting Irish $15
Nebraska Cornhuskers $15

Oklahoma Sooners $15	
Tennessee Volunteers $15	
Texas A&M Aggies $15	
Texas Longhorns $15	

Collegiate Platinum Series

Alabama Crimson Tide $75	
Auburn Tigers $75	
Boston College Golden Eagles $75	
Florida State Seminoles $75	
Florida Gators $75	
Georgia Bulldogs $75	
Illinois Fighting Illini $75	
Indiana Hoosiers $75	
Kentucky Wildcats $75	
LSU Tigers $75	
Maryland Terrapins $75	
Miami Hurricanes $75	
Michigan Wolverines $75	
Notre Dame Fighting Irish $75	
Purdue Boilermakers.................................$75	

Cincinnati Bearcats....................................$75	
Clemson Tigers...$75	
Duke Blue Devils.......................................$75	
Mississippi Rebels $75	
Missouri Tigers $75	
North Carolina State Wolfpack $75	
Nebraska Cornhuskers $75	
New Mexico Lobos....................................$75	
Ohio State Buckeyes $75	
Oklahoma State Cowboys $75	
Oklahoma Sooners $75	
Penn State Nittany Lions $75	
Pittsburgh Panthers $75	
South Carolina Gamecocks $75	
Tennessee Volunteers................................$75	
Texas A&M Aggies $75	
Texas Tech Red Raiders $75	
Texas Longhorns $75	
Washington State Cougars $75	

Danbury Mint Stadium Replicas

Hand-painted sculptures of college and pro stadiums and arenas have precise detail right down to scoreboards, stadium quirks and sometimes mascots. Most are around 7-by-6 inches in size and sit on a wooden base.

TEAM - STADIUM	PRICE
Alabama Crimson Tide - Bryant-Denny Stadium $75	
Anaheim Angels - Anaheim Stadium $60	
Arizona Diamondbacks - Bank One Ballpark $60	
Arizona State Sun Devils - Sun Devil Stadium $75	
Arizona Wildcats - Arizona Stadium $75	
Arkansas Razorbacks - Razorback Stadium $75	
Army Black Knights - Michie Stadium $75	
Atlanta Braves - Atlanta Fulton County Stadium $60	
Atlanta Braves - Turner Field... $60	
Atlanta Falcons - The Georgia Dome......................................$60	
Auburn Tigers - Jordan-Hare Stadium $75	
Baltimore Orioles - Baltimore Memorial Stadium $60	

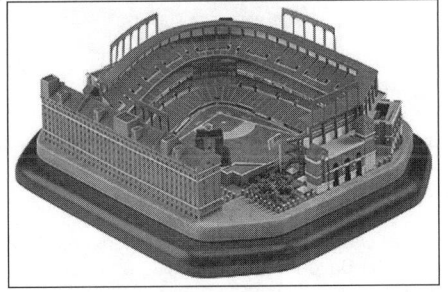

Camden Yards

Baltimore Orioles - Camden Yards.....................................$60	
Baltimore Ravens - PSINet Stadium $60	
Boston Braves - Braves Field $60	
Boston Bruins - Boston Garden $60	
Boston Celtics - Boston Garden $60	
Boston College Eagles - Alumni Stadium $75	
Boston Red Sox - Fenway Park..$60	

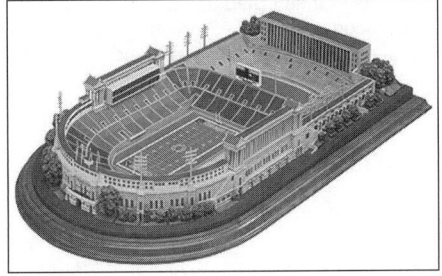

Soldier Field

Brooklyn Dodgers - Ebbets Field....................................$60	
California Golden Bears - Memorial Stadium $75	
Carolina Panthers - Ericsson Stadium...............................$60	
Charlotte Hornets - Charlotte Coliseum............................$60	
Chicago Bears - Soldier Field $60	
Chicago Bears - Soldier Field (Deluxe Version)............................$125	
Chicago Blackhawks - Chicago Stadium $60	
Chicago Bulls - Chicago Stadium $75	
Chicago Cubs - Wrigley Field $60	
Chicago White Sox - Comiskey Park $60	
Cincinnati Reds - Cinergy Field $60	
Clemson Tigers - Memorial Stadium $75	
Cleveland Browns - Browns Stadium $60	
Cleveland Browns - Municipal Stadium $60	
Cleveland Indians - Cleveland Municipal Stadium $60	
Cleveland Indians - Jacobs Field $60	
Colorado Buffaloes - Folsom Stadium $75	
Colorado Rockies - Coors Field..$60	
Dallas Cowboys - Texas Stadium $60	

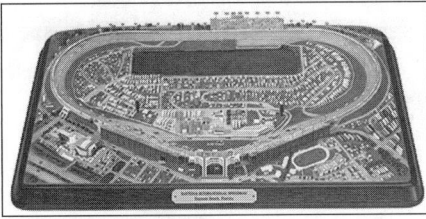

Daytona Speedway

Daytona International Speedway......................................$80	
Denver Broncos - Mile High Stadium...............................$60	
Detroit Lions - The Pontiac Silverdome $60	
Detroit Pistons - The Palace of Auburn Hills....................$60	
Detroit Tigers - Comerica Park $60	
Detroit Tigers - Tiger Stadium..$60	
Duke Blue Devils - Cameron Indoor Stadium $60	
Florida Gators - Ben Hill Griffin Stadium..........................$75	
Florida Gators Stephen C. O'Connell Center $75	
Florida State Seminoles - Doak S. Campbell Stadium $75	
Georgia Bulldogs - Sanford Stadium $75	
Georgia Tech Yellow Jackets - Bobby Dodd Stadium $75	
Green Bay Packers - Lambeau Field................................$60	
Houston Astros - Enron Field...$60	
Houston Astros - The Astrodome $60	
Indiana Hoosiers - Assembly Hall....................................$75	
Indiana Hoosiers - Memorial Stadium...............................$75	
Indianapolis Colts - RCA Dome $60	

Iowa Hawkeyes - Kinnick Stadium..$75
Jacksonville Jaguars - Alltel Stadium $60
Kansas City Chiefs - Arrowhead Stadium $60
Kansas Jayhawks - Allen Fieldhouse $60
Kansas State Wildcats - KSU Stadium $75
Kentucky - Rupp Arena $75
Kentucky Wildcats - Commonwealth Stadium...........................$60
Los Angeles Dodgers - Dodger Stadium $60
Los Angeles Lakers - The Great Western Forum.......................$60
LSU Tigers - Tiger Stadium $75
Marshall Univ. Thundering Herd - Marshall University Stadium $75
Maryland Terrapins - Byrd Stadium $75
Miami Dolphins - Pro Player Stadium......................................$60

Orange Bowl

Miami Hurricanes - The Orange Bowl $60
Michigan State Spartans - Spartan Stadium.......................$75
Michigan State Spartans - The Breslin Center....................$60
Michigan Wolverines - Crisler Arena $75
Michigan Wolverines - Michigan Stadium $75
Milwaukee Brewers - County Stadium $60
Minnesota Golden Gophers - Hubert H. Humphrey Metrodome $60
Minnesota Vikings - Hubert H. Humphrey Metrodome.............$60
Mississippi Rebels - Vaught-Hemingway Stadium $75
Missouri Tigers - Missouri Memorial Stadium $75
Montana Grizzlies - Washington Grizzly Stadium $75
Nebraska Cornhuskers - Memorial Stadium $75
New Mexico Lobos - University Stadium $75

Giants Stadium

New York Giants - Giants Stadium.....................................$60
New York Giants - The Polo Grounds $60
New York Knicks - Madison Square Garden $75
New York Mets - Shea Stadium...$60
New York Yankees - Yankee Stadium $60
North Carolina - Dean E. Smith Center $75
North Carolina State - Entertainment and Sports Arena..................$75
North Carolina State Wolfpack - Carter-Finley Stadium....................$75
North Carolina Tar Heels - Kenan Memorial Stadium $75
Northwestern Wildcats - Ryan Field....................................$75

Notre Dame Fighting Irish - Notre Dame Stadium $75
Ohio State Buckeyes - Ohio Stadium $75
Ohio State Buckeyes - The Jerome Schottenstein Center..............$75
Oklahoma Sooners - Memorial Stadium $75
Oklahoma State Cowboys - Lewis Field $75
Penn State Nittany Lions - Beaver Stadium $75
Philadelphia Eagles - Veterans Stadium $60
Philadelphia Flyers - First Union Center $75
Philadelphia Phillies - Shibe Park $60
Pittsburgh Panthers - Pitt Stadium $75
Pittsburgh Penguins - Mellon Arena $75
Pittsburgh Pirates - Forbes Field $60
Pittsburgh Pirates - Three Rivers Stadium $60
Pittsburgh Steelers - Three Rivers Stadium Franco Harris Signed $100
Pittsburgh Steelers - Three Rivers Stadium.....................$60
Purdue Boilermakers - Ross-Ade Stadium $75
San Diego Padres - Qualcomm Stadium $60
San Francisco 49ers - Candlestick Park $60
San Francisco Giants - Candlestick Park..........................$60
San Francisco Giants - Pacific Bell Park...........................$60
Seattle Mariners - Safeco Field $60
Seattle Mariners - The Kingdome $60
Seattle Seahawks - The Kingdome $60
South Carolina Gamecocks - Williams-Brice Stadium $75
St. Louis Cardinals - Busch Stadium $60
St. Louis Cardinals - Sportsman's Park $60
Stanford Cardinal - Stanford Stadium $75
Syracuse Orangemen - The Carrier Dome..........................$60
Talladega Superspeedway...$80

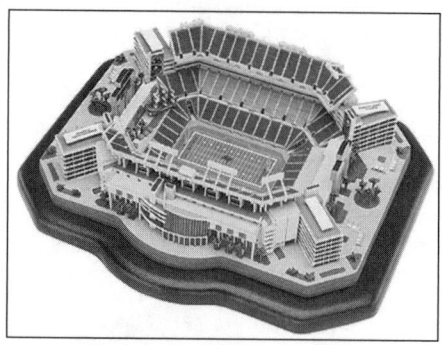

Raymond James - Tampa

Tampa Bay Buccaneers - Raymond James Stadium $75
Tampa Bay Devil Rays - Tropicana Field $60
Tennessee Volunteers - Neyland Stadium Replica $75
Texas A&M Aggies - Kyle Field $75
Texas Longhorns - Darrell K Royal Texas Memorial Stadium..........$75
Texas Rangers - The Ballpark at Arlington $60
Texas Tech Red Raiders - Jones Stadium $75
Toronto Blue Jays - SkyDome.......................................$60
UCLA - Rose Bowl..$75
UCLA Bruins - Pauley Pavilion.......................................$75
UConn Huskies - Harry A. Gampel Pavilion $75
USC - Los Angeles Memorial Coliseum $60
Virginia Cavaliers - Scott Stadium $75
Virginia Tech Hokies - Lane Stadium..............................$75
Washington Huskies - Husky Stadium............................$75
Washington Redskins - RFK Stadium.............................$60
Washington Senators - Griffith Stadium $60
Washington State Cougars - Martin Stadium $75
West Virginia Mountaineers - Mountaineer Field...............$75
Wisconsin Badgers - Camp Randall Stadium...................$75

Chapter 4

TEAM PUBLICATIONS

Yearbooks/Media Guides

Although some exist prior to World War II, it wasn't until the 1960s that what we now consider as yearbooks and media guides were produced by professional teams on a regular basis. The main problem in creating a yearbook checklist is that there is not a general consensus as to whether a certain publication should be considered a yearbook, roster sheet, media guide or something else. Many teams have labeled their publications with a variety of other names such as magazines, roster books, photo albums and sketchbooks.

To be classified as a yearbook, generally a publication must at the very least have photographs of every player on the roster, plus biographies and player statistics. If, however, a publication has photos, stats and biographies, but is labeled as a media guide, scorecard or program, then it's obviously something other than a yearbook.

The history of this category of collectible is quite intriguing—and voluminous. While many baseball, football and college teams provided roster sheets in the 1920s, the first "media guide" was produced by the Chicago Cubs as a roster sheet booklet in 1927. The Chicago Bears were the first NFL team to have a full-fledged guide, in 1934.

Just after World War II, virtually all professional sports teams had media guides and yearbooks of some sort.

Most yearbooks from the 1960s to present offer collectors an affordable alternative for under $100. Those from the 1940s and 1950s bring the top dollars, depending on scarcity and age, while those that are autographed are even more valuable.

Media guides are given to radio, television and newspaper reporters who cover teams throughout the season. They are

designed to provide the reporters with almost every imaginable kind of biographical and statistical tidbits to liven up a broadcast or story. Team histories have also been included, contributing to the guides' increase in page size over the years.

Guides are generally available only from the reporters, who sell or give them to memorabilia dealers, or from the teams. In recent years, teams have given them to season-ticket holders or sold them at the stadiums, by mail or during year-end promotional sales.

BASEBALL MEDIA GUIDES

In the 1920s, baseball journalists began using roster sheets and/or booklets—"publications" that were, essentially, the first media guides. Teams issued them to writers to provide player information for use in newspaper reports or radio broadcasts. These original guides provided little more than a complete roster and some player biographies and statistics, and were available only to ballpark insiders. It wasn't until much later that the guides were sold to the public.

Over the years, the original booklets evolved into 4x9-inch books with several hundred pages full of stats, including information about team executives, players, Minor League affiliates, prospects, team history, and spring training and post-season results. There's so much information that the guides have become popular with collectors and the general public.

Today, media guides are readily available to the public and give fans a chance to get to know their favorite team. Guides from the past 10 years can usually be found for the cover price or slightly more. Guides from the first half of the century—before the advent of mass production and distribution—are of course harder to find and more expensive. Collectors should also look out for media guides from a team's first season, from the first year in a new city or new ballpark, or with star players on the cover.

The list below includes original roster sheets, roster booklets, and media guides in Excellent condition.

Los Angeles Angels

1961 Player emerging from baseball........$75
1962 Baby with Angels logo $75
1963 Angels logo, Rigney, Haney.............$75
1964 Angels in action................................$75
1965 Dean Chance, Cy Young Award.......$40

California Angels

1966 Anaheim Stadium............................$75
1967 League logos and Anaheim $40
1968 Anaheim Stadium and logo $30
1969 New-look A.L. West.........................$30
1970 Press box and player............... $12-$15
1971 Four Angels in California .... $12-$15
1972 Del Rice................................... $10-$12
1973 Nolan Ryan.....................................$20
1974 Anaheim Stadium............................$10
1975 Dick Williams $10
1976 Angels baseball cards $10
1977 Frank Tanana $12
1978 Tanana, Ryan, Rudi..........................$15
1979 Anaheim Stadium..................... $10-$12
1980 Don Baylor.......................................$7
1981 Angels equipment $6
1982 Angels logo $7
1983 Angels in action, R. Jackson $8
1984 Angels celebrating, R. Jackson $7
1985 25th Anniversary logo $6
1986 DeCinces, Schofield, Downing $6
1987 Donnie Moore....................................$6
1988 Wally Joyner, Brian Downing...........$10
1989 All-Star Game logo $10
1990 Angels stars, Joyner, Finley $10
1991 Pitcher in action...............................$10
1992 Bryan Harvey $10
1993 Old Angels uniforms $10
1994 Tim Salmon $7
1995 Anaheim Stadium...............................$5
1996 Anderson, Edmonds, Salmon.............$5

Anaheim Angels

1997 New Anaheim Angels logo $5
1998 Edison Int'l. Field of Anaheim.............$5
1999 Gene Autry $5
2000 Players in celebration of 40th season....$5
2001 Darin Erstad, Troy Glaus $5
2002 Angels Jerseys $5
2003 World Series Trophy $10

Houston Colt .45s

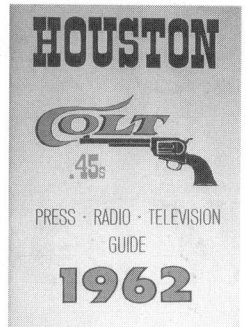

1962 .45s logo......................................$150
1963 .45s logo......................................$100
1964 Player art.....................................$100

Houston Astros

1965 New logo $75
1966 Catcher's mask...............................$75
1967 Astroturf $50
1968 Astrodome art.................................$40
1969 Baseball anniversary.......................$30
1970 Team roster $20
1971 Locker room scene..........................$20
1972 Ball, bat as pool cue $20
1973 Zodiac signs $15
1974 Big orange......................................$10
1975 Equipment .... $8-$10
1976 Bicentennial logo .... $8-$10
1977 Player art.................................... $6-$7
1978 Art... $6-$7
1979 Art... $6-$7
1980 Baseball scene $6
1981 Team logo...$6
1982 20th Anniversary in Houston .... $5-$6
1983 Nolan Ryan................................. $5-$6
1984 Equipment .... $5-$6
1985 Jersey.. $4-$6
1986 Memorabilia.....................................$10
1987 Mike Scott, Hal Lanier $10
1988 Bill Doran $10
1989 Glenn Davis $10
1990 Team logo..$10
1991 Helmet, bat, ball...............................$10
1992 Craig Biggio, Pete Harnisch $10
1993 Luis Gonzalez, Jeff Bagwell $10
1994 Cap...$9
1995 Jeff Bagwell......................................$9
1996 Craig Biggio......................................$9
1997 Bell, Biggio, Bagwell.........................$9
1998 Biggio, Bagwell, Hampton
    celebrating $10

1999 35 Great Years patch.......................$10
2000 Bagwell, Biggio at Enron Field $6
2001 Bagwell, Hidalgo................................$6
2002 Berkman, Wagner, Williams...............$5
2003 Oswalt, Miller, Ausmus $7

Philadelphia Athletics

1928 Roster sheet................................. $125
1929 Roster sheet................................. $125
1930 Roster sheet (elephant).......... $75-$100
1931 Roster sheet (elephant).......... $75-$100
1932 Roster booklet (elephant) $125
1933 Roster booklet (elephant) $100
1934 Roster booklet (elephant) $100
1935 Roster booklet (elephant) $100
1936 Team mascot (elephant)........... $55-$75
1937 Team mascot (elephant)........... $50-$75
1938 Team mascot (elephant) .... $50-$75
1939 A's and elephant...................... $50-$75
1940 Pennant and elephant .... $45-$75
1941 A's and baseball .... $45-$75
1942 .... $40-$45
1943 Team mascot with flag............. $40-$60
1944 Team mascot with flag............. $40-$60
1945 .... $40-$60
1946 Connie Mack .... $45-$60
1947 .... $35-$60
1948 Baseball and elephant............. $35-$60
1949 .... $60-$100
1950 Connie Mack .... $60-$100
1951 .... $60-$100
1952 Team mascot (elephant)......... $60-$100
1953 .... $60-$100
1954 Eddie Joost............................. $60-$100

Kansas City Athletics

1955 K.C. Municipal Stadium $75
1956 Elephant logo $75
1957 Elephant logo $75
1958 Elephant logo $75
1959 A's baseball $75
1960 Baseball and A's hat........................$75
1961 K.C. Municipal Stadium $75
1962 ....$75
1963 Player sliding, baseball....................$75
1964 1964 and A's logo.............................$75
1965 1965 and A's logo.............................$30
1966 1966 and A's logo.............................$30
1967 1967 and A's logo.............................$30

Oakland Athletics

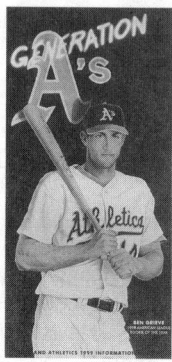 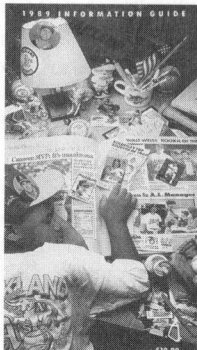

1968 Oakland Stadium, ball, logo $25
1969 Bando, Campaneris, Hunter............$20
1970 Player at bat $20

1971 A's logo and 1971............................$15
1972 A's logo and 1972............................$15
1973 A's logo and 1973............................$15
1974 A's logo and 1974............................$15
1975 A's logo and 1975............................$15
1976 A's logo and 1976...................... $8-$10
1977 A's logo and 1977...................... $7-$10
1978 A's logo and 1978...................... $7-$10
1979 A's logo and 1979...................... $6-$10
1980 A's logo and 1980..............................$6
1981 Billy Ball baseball .... $6-$7
1982 Running spikes.................................$6
1983 A's jukebox $6
1984 Oakland sportswriters $6
1985 Athletics memorabilia $6
1986 Dwayne Murphy $10
1987 All-time Athletics team....................$10
1988 Batter hitting..................................$10
1989 Canseco/Eckersley/Weiss $10
1990 World Series trophy.........................$10
1991 Team memorabilia $10
1992 25th anniversary, A's greats $10
1993 Dennis Eckersley............................$10
1994 Players $7
1995 A's logo..$7
1996 Baseballs spelling out "A's" $7
1997 Mark McGwire swinging $9
1998 Action at second base........................$7
1999 Ben Grieve artwork $7
2000 Century of A's Baseball logo $7
2001 Ja. Giambi, Chavez, Tejada...............$7
2002 Hudson, Mulder, Zito $7
2003 Zito, Tejada, Chavez..........................$9

Toronto Blue Jays

1977 Toronto Exhibition Stadium...............$45
1978 Blue Jays pitcher............................$15
1979 Blue Jays in action $15
1980 Alfredo Griffin $10
1981 Blue Jays equipment $10
1982 Blue Jays in action, Bobby Cox $10
1983 Blue Jays equipment and hat $10
1984 Blue Jays in action $10

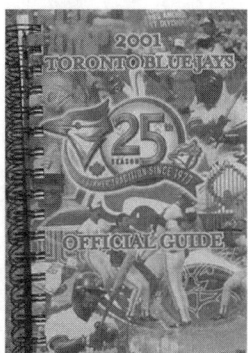

1985 Blue Jays logo $10
1986 Blue Jays 10th anniversary $10

1987 Bell, Barfield, Fernandez.................$10
1988 George Bell $10
1989 Blue Jays stars, McGriff $12
1990 Blue Jays, McGriff, Gruber $12
1991 Dave Stieb.......................................$10
1992 Roberto Alomar................................$12
1993 World Series trophy $10
1994 World Championship rings $7
1995 Blue Jays logo $7
1996 Joe Carter, Blue Jays logo $7
1997 Pat Henten holding Cy Young Award..$7
1998 Roger Clemens $7
1999 Carlos Delgado $7
2000 Shannon Stewart...............................$7
2001 25th Anniversary logo $7
2002 Three Blue Jays players $5
2003 Eric Hinske $7

Boston Braves

1927 Roster sheet $125
1928 Roster sheet..................................$100
1929 Roster sheet..................................$100
1930 Roster sheet..................................$100
1931 Roster booklet, Indian head $100
1932 Roster booklet, Indian head $100
1933 Roster booklet, Indian head $100
1934 Roster booklet, Indian head $100
1935 Roster booklet, Indian head $100
1936 Roster booklet $75
1937 Roster booklet $75
1938 Roster booklet, Bees Baseball $75
1939 Roster booklet $75
1940 Roster booklet, Casey Stengel.........$75
1941 Roster booklet, Casey Stengel.........$60
1942 Roster booklet, Indian head ..... $45-$60
1943 Roster booklet, Indian head ..... $40-$60
1944 Booklet, bat, flag, airplane........ $40-$60
1945 Roster booklet, Indian Head....... $40-$60
1946 Booklet, Billy Southworth .... $40-$60
1947 Booklet, Billy Southworth .... $60-$100
1948 Roster booklet, Bob Elliott...... $60-$100
1949 Booklet, Billy Southworth .... $50-$100
1950 Roster booklet, Braves Logo...... $50-$100
1951 Roster booklet .... $50-$100
1952 Booklet, baseball, Indian head... $50-$100

Milwaukee Braves

1953 State of Florida.............................$125
1954 Plaque honoring "the people of
  Wisconsin"..$125
1955 ....$125
1956 ....$125
1957 ....$100
1958 ....$100
1959 ....$100
1960 Pennant and Indian head $75
1961 Pennant and Indian head $75
1962 Pennant and Indian head $75
1963 Pennant and Indian head $75
1964 Aaron, Alou, Mathews, Spahn..........$75
1965 Felipe Alou, Bobby Bragan..............$75

Atlanta Braves

1966 Player hitting...................................$40
1967 Felipe Alou $40
1968 Hands gripping bat $30
1969 Players in action $30
1970 Hank Aaron $20
1971 Foot sliding into base $20
1972 Players in action .... $12-$15
1973 Players in action .... $12-$15
1974 Players in action $10
1975 Knit baseballs $10
1976 Dave Bristol .... $8-$10

1977 Braves hat .... $8-$10
1978 Atlanta-Fulton Co. Stadium $10
1979 Phil Niekro, All-Stars .... $10-$12
1980 Baseball and stadium $8
1981 Bob Horner, Dale Murphy............. $6-$8
1982 Joe Torre $6
1983 Bedrosian, Murphy, Niekro, Torre .....$6-$7
1984 Braves logo.......................................$6
1985 Dale Murphy, Bruce Sutter .... $6-$7
1986 Bobby Cox, Chuck Tanner..................$6
1987 Braves uniform .... $5-$6
1988 Dale Murphy......................................$8
1989 Gant, Glavine, Perry, Smith,
  Thomas...$10
1990 25th anniversary logo $10
1991 Ron Gant, Dave Justice $10
1992 Greg Olson, John Smoltz $10
1993 N.L. Champions................................$10
1994 Maddux, McGriff, Glavine, Justice......$7
1995 30th Season in Atlanta $7
1996 World Series Trophy $7
1997 Maddux, Smoltz, Glavine jerseys $6
1998 Bobby Cox $5
1999 Hank Aaron, Home Run #715 ....$6
2000 ....$6
2001 World Series logos, Fulton County
  Stadium, Turner Field $6
2002 Braves Logo $6
2003 Cox, Schuerholz $6

Seattle Pilots

1969 Pilots logo........................... $100-$125
1970 Pilots logo.....................................$100

Milwaukee Brewers

1971 Newspaper clipping .... $30-$40
1972 State of Wisconsin............................$10
1973 Del Crandall, George Scott $12
1974 Team mascot $10
1975 Team mascot............................. $8-$10
1976 Baseball glove .... $8-$10
1977 Robin Yount $15
1978 Larry Hisle $10
1979 George Bamberger...........................$10

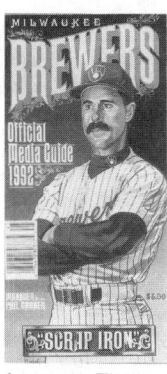

1980 Cooper, Lezcano, Thomas $6
1981 Cooper, Oglivie, Yount.................. $6-$8
1982 Rollie Fingers .... $7-$8
1983 Kuenn, Vuckovich, Yount .... $6-$8
1984 County Stadium................................$6
1985 Brewers uniform #85 ....$6
1986 Brewers pitcher in action $6
1987 Ted Higuera $6
1988 Player running $6
1989 20th anniversary logo $10
1990 Player running $10
1991 Team logo.......................................$10
1992 Phil Garner.....................................$10
1993 Pat Listach......................................$10
1994 New uniforms, 25th anniv. logo $7
1995 Bob Uecker with huge bat $8
1996 Outline of new Miller Park $6
1997 Jose Valentine $6
1998 Brewers logo $6
1999 County Stadium...............................$10
2000 Baseballs & Glove $10
2001 Miller Park Roof...............................$10
2002 Sexson, Sheets $6
2003 Melvin, Yost, Payne Jr. $8

St. Louis Cardinals

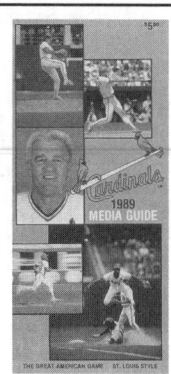

1926 Roster sheet..................................$200
1927 Roster sheet..................................$125
1928 Roster sheet..................................$125
1929 Roster sheet..................................$100
1930 Logo and 1930, sheet $115
1931 Roster sheet..................................$115
1932 Logo and 1932, booklet..................$125
1933 Logo and 1933, booklet..................$125
1934 Logo and 1934, booklet..................$115
1935 Logo and 1935, booklet..................$100
1936 Logo and 1936, booklet....................$75
1937 Logo and 1937, booklet........... $50-$75
1938 Roster booklet .... $50-$75
1939 Name and year, booklet .... $50-$75
1940 Logo and 1940, booklet........... $45-$75
1941 Logo and 1941, booklet........... $45-$60
1942 Logo, Statue of Liberty .... $45-$65
1943 Flag and logo, booklet .... $40-$70
1944 Victory V and logo, booklet....... $40-$70

1945 Logo and 1945, booklet............ $40-$60
1946 Roster booklet .... $35-$70
1947 Team logo, booklet .... $35-$60
1948 Logo and baseball, booklet ...... $35-$60
1949 Logo and baseball, booklet ...... $30-$60
1950 Baseball and players $150
1951 25th anniv. of World Champs $125
1952 Team logo.....................................$125
1953 It's the Cardinals............................$125
1954 Team logo.....................................$125
1955 Team logo.....................................$125
1956 Team logo.....................................$100
1957 Team logo.....................................$100
1958 Team mascot...................................$75
1959 Stan Musial $100
1960 Team mascot...................................$75
1961 Broglio, McDaniel, Sadecki, Simmons....
    $75
1962 Stan Musial $75
1963 Player in action................................$60
1964 Boyer, Groat, Javier, White...............$60
1965 Team logo..$60
1966 Busch Stadium, team logo $60
1967 Busch Stadium $60
1968 World Series trophy $45
1969 Bob Gibson $45
1970 Joe Torre $20
1971 Bob Gibson, Joe Torre $25
1972 Red Schoendienst, Joe Torre $20
1973 Brock, Gibson, Simmons, Torre........$20
1974 Cardinals uniform and hat .... $10-$15
1975 Lou Brock and team logo .... $10-$15
1976 Busch Stadium .... $10-$15
1977 Lou Brock, Vern Rapp .... $6-$7
1978 Cardinals equipment .... $6-$7
1979 St. Louis Arch.....................................$6
1980 Keith Hernandez...................... $6-$8
1981 Whitey Herzog........................... $6-$8
1982 Whitey Herzog..........................$7
1983 World Series celebration $7
1984 Player running .... $5-$6
1985 Busch Stadium, St. Louis Arch........$10
1986 Coleman, Herzog, McGee...............$10
1987 Whitey Herzog, former managers $10
1988 N.L. Champions celebrate...............$10
1989 Action photos, Whitey Herzog..........$10
1990 Team logo............................$8
1991 Joe Torre $10
1992 Todd Zeile.....................................$10
1993 Team logo.....................................$10
1994 Bats, home plate $7
1995 Cardinals Mascot $6
1996 Tony La Russa................................$6
1997 Busch Stadium $6
1998 Mark McGwire $10
1999 Photo of McGwire hitting 62nd HR ...$10
2000 Backs of Jerseys Stars, Hintten,
    Tatis, Lankford, Venis, Vina,
    McGwire, Kyle, Veres.........................$10
2001 Edmonds, Kyle, Ankiel, Matheny,
    Renteria, Vina.................................$10
2002 Pujols, O. Smith................................$10
2003 Pujols, Edmonds, Morris, Renteria...$10

Chicago Cubs

1927 The year, booklet............................$175
1928 The year, booklet............................$150
1929 The year, booklet............................$150
1930 The year, booklet............................$100
1931 Rogers Hornsby, booklet $100
1932 Rogers Hornsby, booklet $125
1933 Team mascot, booklet $100
1934 Team mascot, booklet $100
1935 Team mascot, booklet $115

1936 Team mascot, booklet $75
1937 Team mascot throwing, booklet........$75
1938 Team mascot hitting, booklet............$85
1939 Mascot with pennant, booklet $65
1940 Roster booklet $65
1941 Jimmy Wilson, booklet.....................$65
1942 Roster booklet $65
1943 Roster booklet $65
1944 Roster booklet $65
1945 Roster booklet $75
1946 Charlie Grimm, booklet $65
1947 Team mascot, booklet $65
1948 Roster booklet $100
1949 Roster booklet $100
1950 Roster booklet $100
1951 Roster booklet $100
1952 ....$100
1953 ....$100
1954 ....$75
1955 ....$75
1956 ....$75
1957 ....$75
1958 Team logo.......................................$75
1959 Team logo.......................................$75
1960 Team logo.......................................$50
1961 Team logo.......................................$50
1962 Team logo.......................................$50
1963 Team logo.......................................$50
1964 Team logo.......................................$50
1965 Team logo.......................................$50
1966 Team logo.......................................$30
1967 Team logo.......................................$30
1968 Team logo.......................................$30
1969 Team logo.......................................$30
1970 Team logo................................ $15-$20
1971 Team logo................................ $15-$20
1972 Team logo.......................................$15
1973 Team logo................................ $10-$15
1974 Team logo.......................................$10
1975 Team logo................................. $8-$10
1976 Team logo................................. $8-$10
1977 Team logo................................. $7-$10
1978 Team logo................................. $7-$10
1979 Team logo................................. $6-$10
1980 Team logo................................... $6-$7
1981 Team logo................................... $6-$7
1982 Team logo................................... $5-$7
1983 Wrigley Field, celebration .... $5-$7
1984 Autographed baseballs.......................$6
1985 Frey, Green, Sandberg, Sutcliffe $10
1986 Cubs second baseman (Sandberg)..$12
1987 Billy Williams $10
1988 Andre Dawson $10
1989 Wrigley Field...................................$10
1990 Wrigley Field...................................$10
1991 Ryne Sandberg $12
1992 Wrigley Field...................................$10
1993 Wrigley Field...................................$10
1994 Grace, Sandberg, Sosa.....................$7

1995 Collage $5
1996 Brian McRae $5
1997 Sammy Sosa $6
1998 Ball exploding through stat sheet $6
1999 Sammy Sosa, Kerry Wood $6
2000 Sosa, Banks, Grace, Wilson $6
2001 Nine Topps baseball cards used in
    promotion $6
2002 Sammy Sosa, Kerry Wood $6
2003 Ernie Banks, Sammy Sosa $8

Tampa Bay Devil Rays

1997 Montage of eight photos, including
    countdown billboard, construction of
    stadium $10
1998 Inaugural season artwork, Ray chasing
    an AL ball $8
1999 Original art including Musial, Arrojo,
    Raymond $8
2000 "Hitshow" with Canseco, Vaughn,
    McGriff, Castilla $7
2001 New uniforms, hats on the field $7
2002 ....$5
2003 Lou Pinella $7

Arizona Diamondbacks

1998 Mountain background, jersey No. 98 ..$8
1999 Interior of Bank One Ballpark $7
2000 Collage of 8 uniformed personnel $10
2001 Randy Johnson $10
2002 World Series Trophy $10
2003 Randy Johnson $8

Brooklyn Dodgers

1927 Roster sheet $125
1928 Name and 1928, booklet $150
1929 Name and 1929, booklet $100
1930 Name and 1930, booklet $100
1931 Name and 1931, booklet $100
1932 Name and 1932, booklet $100
1933 Logo and 1933, booklet $100
1934 Logo and 1934, booklet $100
1935 Logo and 1935, booklet $100
1936 Logo and 1936, booklet .... $55-$75
1937 Logo and 1937, booklet .... $55-$75
1938 Logo and 1938, booklet .... $50-$75
1939 100th anniversary logo .... $50-$75
1940 50th anniversary in Brooklyn .... $45-$75
1941 Team airplane $85
1942 V logo .... $45-$65
1943 Roster booklet .... $40-$65
1944 Roster booklet .... $40-$65
1945 Roster booklet .... $40-$65
1946 Roster booklet .... $35-$65
1947 Roster booklet .... $35-$70
1948 Roster booklet .... $35-$65
1949 Roster booklet $150
1950 The Bum $125
1951 The Bum $125

1952 ....$125
1953 The Bum $125
1954 ....$125
1955 Walter Alston $125
1956 Walter Alston $100
1957 Walter Alston $100

Los Angeles Dodgers

1958 Walter Alston $75
1959 L.A. Coliseum $75
1960 Dodger Stadium drawing $30
1961 Dodger Stadium $30
1962 Cartoon and airplane $50
1963 T. Davis, Drysdale, Koufax, Wills $50
1964 Players celebrating $40
1965 Championship pennants $40
1966 Mascot climbing mountains $40
1967 Mascot juggling crowns $40
1968 Walter Alston $30
1969 100th anniversary $30
1970 W. Davis, Osteen, Singer, Sizemore ...$30
1971 Dodgers in action $20
1972 Dodgers in action $20
1973 Dodgers in action $10
1974 Dodgers in action $10
1975 Steve Garvey $12
1976 Buckner, Cey, Garvey, Lopes,
    Sutton $14
1977 Tom Lasorda .... $9-$12
1978 Baker, Cey, Garvey, Smith .... $9-$14
1979 Dodger Stadium $6
1980 Team logo $6
1981 1980 highlights $7
1982 World Series trophy, Howe, Yeager $8
1983 Sax, Guerrero, Valenzuela $8
1984 Fireworks over Dodger Stadium ... $5-$6
1985 Bill Russell .... $6-$7
1986 Player swinging bat .... $4-$6
1987 Dodger Stadium $10
1988 Baseballs $10
1989 World Series trophy $10
1990 100th anniversary caps and pins $10
1991 Name and 1991 ....$10
1992 Team stadium $10
1993 Eric Karros $10
1994 Mike Piazza, Enz Karros $7
1995 Dodger Stadium $6
1996 Karros, Piazza, Mondesi, Nomo $6
1997 Rookies of the Year $6
1998 40th year anniversary logo $6
1999 Manager Davey Johnson, GM Kevin
    Malone $6
2000 Collection of Dodgers baseball
    memorabilia $6
2001 Baseball with ghosted small pictures .$5
2002 Dodger Stadium Anniversary $5
2003 Eric Gagne $8

Montreal Expos

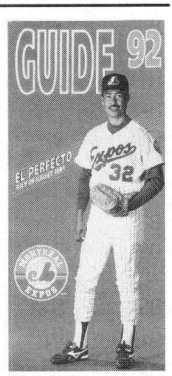

1969 Team logo $75
1970 Jarry Park $40
1971 Baseball $20
1972 Action photos, Jarry Park $20
1973 Montreal photos .... $10-$12
1974 Gene Mauch $10
1975 Players in action .... $8-$10
1976 Players in action .... $8-$10
1977 Cash, McEnaney, Perez, D. Williams $6
1978 Gary Carter, Andre Dawson $10
1979 Team logo $6
1980 Locker with uniform $6
1981 Pennant $6
1982 Players in action $6
1983 Hands holding a bat $6
1984 Team hats $6
1985 Olympic Stadium with dome $6
1986 Baseball and team logo $6
1987 Olympic Stadium with dome $10
1988 20th anniversary bat $10
1989 Hands giving hi-five $10
1990 Team logo $10
1991 Team logo $10
1992 Dennis Martinez $10
1993 25th anniversary $10
1994 New Expos logo $7
1995 Felipe Alou $5
1996 Autographed ball $5
1997 Baseball scene $5
1998 30 years anniversary logo $6
1999 Vladimir Guerrero $6
2000 Vladimir Guerrero $6
2001 Expos logo $6
2002 Player Collage $6
2003 Gary Carter $6

New York Giants

1927 Name and 1927, booklet $150
1928 Name and 1928, booklet $100
1929 Name and 1929, booklet $100
1930 Name and 1930, booklet $100
1931 Name and 1931, booklet $100
1932 Name and 1932, booklet $100
1933 Name and 1933, booklet $125
1934 Name and 1934, booklet .... $60-$100
1935 Name and 1935, booklet .... $60-$100
1936 Name and 1936 .... $55-$85
1937 Name and 1937 .... $55-$85
1938 Name and 1938 .... $50-$75
1939 New York World's Fair .... $50-$75
1940 Name and 1940 .... $45-$75
1941 Name and 1941 .... $45-$60
1942 Name and 1942 .... $45-$60
1943 Name and 1943 .... $40-$60
1944 Name and 1944 .... $40-$60
1945 Name and 1945 .... $40-$60
1946 Name and 1946 ....$150
1947 Baseball with 1947 ....$150

1948 Baseball with 1948 ....$150
1949 Baseball with 1949 ....$150
1950 Polo Grounds $125
1951 Team logo.....................................$125
1952 Leo Durocher, a Giant $125
1953 Polo Grounds $125
1954 Team logo.....................................$125
1955 The Giant $125
1956 Team hat $125
1957 Team hat $125

San Francisco Giants

1958 Candlestick Park drawing $150
1959 Players in action $100
1960 Team logo.......................................$80
1961 Giants in action $80
1962 Players in action $70
1963 Candlestick Park $70
1964 Candlestick Park $70
1965 Candlestick Park $70
1966 Baseball and team logo..................$65
1967 Team logo.......................................$45
1968 Team logo.......................................$45
1969 Team logo.......................................$45
1970 Willie Mays, Willie McCovey $25
1971 Year of the Fox $20
1972 Best in the West $20
1973 Candlestick Park $15
1974 Matthews, Bryant, Bonds $15
1975 Team logo.......................................$15
1976 Team logo................................. $8-$10
1977 Joe Altobelli, John Montefusco .. $7-$10
1978 Players in action $6
1979 Blue, Clark, Giants management $6
1980 On deck circle with team logo $6
1981 Golden Gate Bridge $6
1982 25th anniversary in city $6
1983 Team logo...$6
1984 Team logo...$6
1985 Team logo...$6
1986 Team logo...$6
1987 Team logo...$6
1988 Team logo.......................................$10
1989 Team logo.......................................$10
1990 Team logo.......................................$10
1991 Team logo.......................................$10
1992 Team uniform..................................$10
1993 Team logo.......................................$10
1994 Dusty Baker......................................$7
1995 B. Bonds, M. Williams $6
1996 B. Bonds, M. Williams $6
1997 40 years in San Francisco $6
1998 J. T. Snow, B. Mueller, B. Johnson $6
1999 "Tell it Goodbye (Candlestick)............$6
2000 Pacific Bell Park................................$6
2001 Bonds, Kent, Nen, Snow, Baker $6
2002 Barry Bonds $6
2003 Felipe Alou $6

Cleveland Indians

1927 Roster sheet...................................$125
1928 Roster sheet...................................$100
1929 Roster sheet...................................$100
1930 Roster sheet...................................$100
1931 Roster sheet...................................$100
1932 Roster booklet.................................$100
1933 Roster booklet.................................$100
1934 Roster booklet.................................$100
1935 Roster booklet.................................$100
1936 Chief and 1936, booklet .... $55-$75
1937 Chief and 1937, booklet .... $50-$75
1938 Chief and 1938, booklet .... $50-$75
1939 Chief and 1939, booklet .... $50-$75
1940 Chief and 1940, booklet .... $50-$75

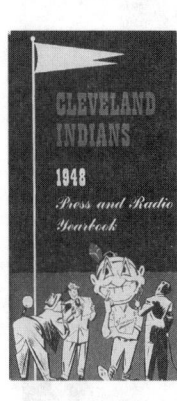

1941 Chief and 1941, booklet .... $50-$60
1942 Lou Boudreau, booklet .... $55-$60
1943 Lou Boudreau, booklet .... $50-$60
1944 Mascot and year, booklet .... $40-$60
1945 Mascot and year, booklet .... $40-$60
1946 Lou Boudreau, booklet .... $45-$60
1947 Team mascot, booklet .... $35-$60
1948 Team mascot with media...... $100-$150
1949 Team mascot...................................$100
1950 Team mascot at bat.........................$100
1951 Team mascot...................................$100
1952 Garcia, Wynn, Lemon, Feller..........$100
1953 Press box and media.......................$100
1954 Al Rosen...$100
1955 Mascot..$100
1956 Mascot..$100
1957 Kirby Farrell......................................$75
1958 Bobby Bragan, Frank Lane..............$75
1959 Rocky Colavito..................................$75
1960 Tito Francona....................................$75
1961 Jim Perry $75
1962 Team mascot.....................................$75
1963 Team uniform #20.............................$75
1964 Team mascot.....................................$75
1965 Team mascot.....................................$35
1966 Baseball with feather.........................$35
1967 Cleveland Stadium.............................$30
1968 Autographed baseball $30
1969 100th anniversary, mascot $30
1970 Team mascot.....................................$20
1971 Team hat, feather $20
1972 Players in action $20
1973 Team logo..$10
1974 Team logo..$10
1975 Frank Robinson .... $8-$10
1976 Baseball with feather .... $8-$10
1977 Player hitting .... $6-$7
1978 Baseball, logo, glove .... $6-$7
1979 Team logo .... $6-$7
1980 Fireworks over stadium .... $6-$7
1981 Team logo .... $6-$7
1982 Cleveland Stadium .... $5-$7
1983 Team logo .... $5-$7
1984 Team memorabilia .... $5-$6
1985 Bert Blyleven, Andre Thornton $7
1986 Past team uniforms .... $4-$6
1987 Joe Carter $7
1988 Indians uniform #88.............................$6
1989 Candiotti, Farrell, Jones, Swindell $10
1990 90 Years of Cleveland baseball $10
1991 Jacoby, Jones, Alomar $10
1992 60 years at Cleveland Stadium.........$10
1993 Memorabilia collage $10
1994 A. Belle, C. Baerga, K. Lofton $7
1995 Jacobs Field at night $7
1996 Player celebration $7
1997 Cleveland city outline $7
1998 Player celebration collage $7
1999 M. Hargrove, Thome, others..............$6

2000 Team Logo & Two Cleveland Players....$6
2001 Player collage, 100th anniversary
    logo..$6
2002 Vizquel, Thome, Diaz, Colon.............$6
2003 Team Logo.......................................$10

Seattle Mariners

1977 Kingdome $30
1978 Baseball with team logo $10
1979 Kingdome $10
1980 Mariners equipment $6
1981 Maury Wills $7
1982 Team logo..$6
1983 Gaylord Perry, team equipment..........$8
1984 Team logo..$6
1985 Beattie, Davis, Henderson, Langston....$7
1986 Team memorabilia $6
1987 Team logo..$6
1988 Team bat...$10
1989 Kingdome, baseball, logo $10
1990 A.L. baseballs, team logo $10
1991 Highlights..$10
1992 Team logo..$10
1993 Team logo, Kingdome........................$10
1994 Mariners cap $7
1995 Mariners logo $5
1996 A.L. West Championship.....................$6
1997 Griffey Jr., A. Rodriguiz $7
1998 Griffey Jr. holding trophy.....................$7
1999 Logo, grass background $7
2000 Game at Safeco Field $6
2001 ALCS game, plus 2001 All-Star logo .$5
2002 Lou Pinella..$5
2003 Edgar Martinez....................................$5

Florida Marlins

1993 Logo, player..$20
1994 Mascot..$10
1995 Team logo..$15
1996 Mascot..$10
1997 Logo $10
1998 Players celebrating, trophy $5
1999 Alex Fernandez, others $5
2000 Preston Wilson $5
2001 Team picture..$5

2002 Team Memorabilia Collage................$5
2003 10th Anniversary Logo $5

New York Mets

1962 First year $500
1963 Mr. Met, Stadium $150
1964 Shea Stadium.................................$100
1965 Mr. Met $100
1966 Mass media $100
1967 Donald Grant, George Weiss $100
1968 Gil Hodges, crowd shot $100
1969 Gil Hodges $100
1970 World Series ticket, action photos $75
1971 Scoreboard.......................................$50
1972 Tom Seaver $50
1973 Yogi Berra and pennant....................$50
1974 N.L. Champs flag $50
1975 Mets general managers....................$20
1976 Joe Frazier $20
1977 Mets uniform #77 ....$20
1978 Team logo, hat, glove $20
1979 Willie Mays $15
1980 Team logo...$15
1981 New York City, baseball $15
1982 George Bamberger locker $15
1983 Tom Seaver, others $15
1984 Davey Johnson.................................$15
1985 Tom Seaver, Mets stars $15
1986 R. Craig, Gooden, Shea Stadium.....$15
1987 World Series ring..............................$15
1988 Shea 25th anniversary $15
1989 Frank Cashen, Howard Johnson $15
1990 Howard Johnson $15
1991 Bud Harrelson $15
1992 Bonilla, Murray, Saberhagen,
    Torborg $15
1993 Team uniform No. 93 ....$15
1994 Dwight Gooden $7
1995 Shea Stadium....................................$7
1996 Organization of the Year Trophy $6
1997 Hundley, Franco, Gilkey $6
1998 Valentine, Ordonez, others................$6
1999 Piazza, Henderson, Ventura, others...$6
2000 Celebratory photo of 1999 Playoffs $5
2001 National League Championship Trophy,
    four pennants...$5

2002 40th Anniversary Logo $5
2003 Art Howe and Collage of photos $8

St. Louis Browns

1927 Name and 1927, booklet $150
1928 Name and 1928, booklet $125
1929 Roster booklet $125
1930 Roster booklet $125
1931 Sportsmans Park, booklet $125
1932 Sportsmans Park, booklet ...... $70-$100
1933 Sportsmans Park, booklet ...... $70-$100
1934 Roster booklet .... $65-$100
1935 Roster booklet .... $65-$100
1936 Rogers Hornsby, booklet .... $75-$80
1937 Team logo, booklet .... $60-$75
1938 Roster booklet .... $60-$75
1939 Roster booklet .... $60-$75
1940 Fred Haney, booklet, ... $55-$75
1941 Statue and 1941, booklet .... $55-$60
1942 Roster booklet .... $55-$60
1943 Team logo, booklet .... $50-$60
1944 Roster booklet .... $70-$150
1945 ....$150
1946 Team logo, booklet $150
1947 Baseball, logo..................................$150
1948 Meet the Brownies...........................$150
1949 ....$150
1950 Team logo..$150
1951 Team logo..$150
1952 Team mascot....................................$150
1953 Team mascot....................................$150

Baltimore Orioles

1954 Team mascot...................................$125
1955 Team mascot...................................$100
1956 Team mascot...................................$100
1957 Team mascot...................................$100
1958 Team mascot...................................$100
1959 Team mascot...................................$100
1960 Team mascot.....................................$75
1961 Team mascot.....................................$75
1962 Team mascot.....................................$75
1963 Team mascot.....................................$75
1964 Team mascot.....................................$75
1965 Hank Bauer $40
1966 Team mascot.....................................$40
1967 Dave McNally, Brooks Robinson $50
1968 Memorial Stadium $40
1969 View from press box $30
1970 Orioles dugout...................................$25
1971 World Series celebration $20
1972 Team mascot with pennants.............$15
1973 Player face drawing $10
1974 Orioles award winners.......................$10
1975 Players in action $10
1976 Team logo..$10
1977 Palmer, L. May, Belanger $15
1978 Earl Weaver............................. $10-$12
1979 25th anniversary hats........................$10

1980 Players celebrating.............................$6
1981 Orioles locker room $6
1982 Team logo and mascot........................$6
1983 Frank and Brooks Robinson $8
1984 World Series celebration $6
1985 Bumbry, Palmer, Singleton $7
1986 Eddie Murray, Cal Ripken $8
1987 Cal Ripken Sr. $6
1988 Team logo...$10
1989 New team uniforms $10
1990 1989 highlights $10
1991 Team stadium drawing $10
1992 Team stadium $10
1993 Team stadium $10
1994 150 Years of Baseball.........................$7
1995 Cal Ripken Jr. $20
1996 Davey Johnson $5
1997 Cartoon $5
1998 R. Miller, E. Weaver, others................$5
1999 Camden Yards....................................$10
2000 Collage of Players $10
2001 A Trophy $10
2002 Team Mascot Cartoon $5
2003 Eddie Murray $10

San Diego Padres

1969 Preston Gomez, stadium...................$75
1970 Jack Murphy Stadium $15
1971 Jack Murphy Stadium $15
1972 Padres vs. Dodgers, July 3, 1971.....$15
1973 Nate Colbert $15
1974 Player hitting $10
1975 Players in action $8
1976 Randy Jones $8
1977 Randy Jones, Butch Metzger $7
1978 Batter, pitcher in action......................$6
1979 Roger Craig, Padres stars..................$6
1980 Jerry Coleman, Dave Winfield............$8
1981 Frank Howard, stadium $7
1982 Dick Williams $6
1983 Padres memorabilia $6
1984 Team logo, Ray Kroc memorabilia....$10
1985 N.L. Champions trophy......................$10
1986 Team logo...$10

1987 Larry Bowa $10
1988 Tony Gwynn, Benito Santiago $10
1989 Team logo, stadium $10
1990 Players in action $10
1991 Padres uniform, ball, glove $10
1992 All-Star Game $10
1993 Gary Sheffield, Fred McGriff $10
1994 San Diego $7
1995 Gwynn, Caminiti, Finley.....................$7
1996 Tony Gwynn.......................................$7
1997 Pitchers $7
1998 Padre players in the community $10
1999 ....$7
2000 Four dressed as Cowboys..................$7
2001 Six Padres players.............................$7
2002 Phil Nevin, Ryan Klesko $7
2003 Padre Memorabilia Collage $7

Philadelphia Phillies

1927 Roster sheet...................................$125
1928 Roster sheet...................................$100
1929 Roster sheet...................................$100
1930 Team logo, sheet .... $75-$100
1931 Roster sheet.......................... $70-$100
1932 Team logo, booklet .... $65-$125
1933 Phillies golden anniversary .... $60-$100
1934 Team logo, booklet .... $60-$100
1935 Team logo, booklet .... $55-$100
1936 Team logo, booklet .... $55-$75
1937 Team logo, booklet .... $50-$75
1938 Roster booklet .... $50-$75
1939 Roster booklet .... $50-$75
1940 Roster booklet .... $45-$75
1941 Player hitting, booklet .... $45-$60
1942 Soldier with crossed bats .... $45-$60
1943 Roster booklet .... $40-$60
1944 Roster booklet .... $40-$60
1945 Roster booklet .... $40-$60
1946 Logo, Shibe Park, booklet .... $35-$60
1947 Logo, Shibe Park, booklet .... $35-$60
1948 Logo, Shibe Park, booklet .... $35-$60
1949 Roster booklet .... $30-$70
1950 ....$150
1951 .... $30-$50
1952 Shibe Park................................ $25-$50
1953 Player hitting............................ $25-$50
1954 Robin Roberts .... $35-$50
1955 Get Set To Go In '55................. $20-$50
1956 Crowd photo .... $20-$40
1957 Crowd photo .... $20-$40
1958 Crowd photo .... $20-$40
1959 Team logo.................................. $20-$40
1960 Team logo.................................. $20-$40
1961 Team logo.................................. $15-$40
1962 .... $15-$20
1963 .... $15-$20
1964 Team hat $150
1965 Team hat $100
1966 Team hat $100

1967 Team hat...$75
1968 Team hat...$75
1969 Team hat...$50
1970 Phillies P $50
1971 Frank Luchessi $35
1972 Team logo..$35
1973 Steve Carlton, Cy Young Award $25
1974 Players in action $20
1975 Players in action $20
1976 Players in action $15
1977 Division champs pennant $15
1978 Fireworks over stadium $15
1979 Team logo..$15
1980 Team logo, baseball $10
1981 World Series trophy.........................$10
1982 Basket of baseballs $10
1983 100th anniversary logo....................$10
1984 N.L. Championship trophy...............$10
1985 Hands holding bat $10
1986 Home plate with team logo..............$10
1987 Mike Schmidt, trophies....................$15
1988 Steve Bedrosian, Mike Schmidt.......$15
1989 Nick Leyva, Lee Thomas $15
1990 Ashburn, Carlton, Roberts, Schmidt.$15
1991 Catchers mask, baseball..................$15
1992 Memorabilia collage $15
1993 Phillies league leaders $15
1994 Jim Fregosi $7
1995 Silver anniversary of stadium logo $6
1996 All-Star Game logo $6
1997 Terry Francona $5
1998 Scott Rolen, Curt Schilling $5
1999 Curt Schilling, Scott Rolen—"Leather
       and Ace" $5
2000 Lieberthal, Glanville, Abreu $5
2001 Larry Bowa $5
2002 Five Split Photos of Players...............$5
2003 Veterans Stadium $10

Pittsburgh Pirates

1927 Roster sheet...................................$175
1928 Roster sheet...................................$100
1929 Roster sheet...................................$125
1930 Pirate and 1930, sheet $100
1931 Pirate and 1931, sheet $100
1932 Pirate and 1932, booklet $125
1933 Pirate and 1933, booklet .... $60-$100
1934 Pirate and 1934, booklet .... $60-$100
1935 Pirate and 1935, booklet .... $55-$100
1936 Pirate and 1936 .... $55-$75
1937 Pirate and 1937 .... $50-$75
1938 Pirate and 1938 .... $50-$75
1939 100th anniversary, Pirate......... $50-$75
1940 Pirate and 1940 .... $45-$75
1941 Pirate and 1941 .... $45-$60
1942 Pirate, Remember Pearl Harbor$45-$60
1943 Pirate, Buy War Bonds, Stamps$40-$60
1944 Pirate and 1944 .... $40-$60
1945 Pirate and 1945 .... $40-$60

1946 Pirate, Buy Victory Bonds .... $35-$60
1947 Billy Herman........................... $40-$60
1948 William Meyer........................... $40-$60
1949 40th anniversary........................ $30-$60
1950 Baseballs.............................. $30-$50
1951 Logo and 1951 ....$125
1952 Baseball and 1952.......................$125
1953 Fred Haney.................................$125
1954 Honus Wagner statue..................$125
1955 Baseball diamond and 1955........$125
1956 Pirate cartoon............................$125
1957 Pirate cartoon............................$100
1958 Danny Murtaugh........................$100
1959 Pirate cartoon............................$100
1960 Pirate cartoon..............................$75
1961 Pirate cartoon..............................$75
1962 Pitcher $75
1963 Baseballs......................................$75
1964 Logo and 1964 ....$60
1965 Harry Walker $60
1966 Pirate cartoon..............................$60
1967 Pirate cartoon..............................$45
1968 Larry Shepard and coaches $45
1969 100th anniversary, Forbes $30
1970 Three River Stadium model.............$30
1971 Danny Murtaugh.............................$25
1972 World Series celebration $25
1973 Clemente memorial $35
1974 Three Rivers Stadium......................$10
1975 Championship Stars, logo $10
1976 Rennie Stennett.............................$10
1977 Players in action $6
1978 Three Pirates $6
1979 Team uniform.................................$10
1980 Willie Stargell..................................$9
1981 Team logo.......................................$6
1982 Team hat...$6
1983 Team logo..$6
1984 Bill Madlock.....................................$6
1985 Tony Pena..$6
1986 Three Rivers Stadium......................$10
1987 100th anniversary logo $10
1988 Pirates memorabilia.........................$10
1989 Bonilla, LaValliere, Van Slyke $10
1990 Bonds, Bonilla, Drabek, Van Slyke ...$10
1991 N.L. Champions, logo......................$10
1992 Doug Drabek, Don Slaught $10
1993 Jim Leyland $10
1994 Three Rivers Stadium...................... $7
1995 Artwork of pirates $5
1996 Cap.. $5
1997 Uniforms, caps, logos...................... $5
1998 Previous Pirates media guides..........$5
1999 Three bats $10
2000 30 Years of Three Rivers Stadium....$10
2001 PNC Park & Lloyd McClendon $10
2002 Statue in front of PNC Park...............$7
2003 100 Year History Collage...................$7

Texas Rangers

1972 Team logo.......................................$30
1973 Burke, Herzog, Short.......................$20
1974 Billy Martin......................................$15
1975 Hargrove, Jenkins, Martin $15
1976 Toby Harrah, old-timers $6
1977 Team equipment, hat........................$6
1978 Billy Hunter......................................$6
1979 Baseball and 1979............................$6
1980 Rangers catcher...............................$6
1981 Fireworks over scoreboard.................$6
1982 Baseball with logo $6
1983 Baseball glove...................................$6
1984 Buddy Bell, others $6
1985 Team hat...$6

1986 Arlington Stadium $6
1987 Bobby Valentine $10
1988 Team logo and baseball $10
1989 Rangers uniforms............................$10
1990 Home plate with team logo..............$10
1991 Nolan Ryan......................................$15
1992 Julio Franco.....................................$10
1993 Arlington Stadium............................$10
1994 Jersey $7
1995 Ballpark at Arlington $5
1996 Ballpark at Arlington $5
1997 Juan Gonzalez $6
1998 Ivan Rodriguez $6
1999 Ivan Rodriguez $10
2000 Ivan Rodriguez $10
2001 I. Rodriguez, A. Rodriguez,
    R. Palmeiro $10
2002 Ernie Banks, Alex Rodriguez $5
2003 Rafael Palmeiro, Alex Rodriguez........$5

Cincinnati Reds

1927 Roster sheet..................................$125
1928 Roster sheet..................................$100
1929 Roster sheet..................................$100
1930 Team logo, sheet .... $65-$100
1931 Team logo, sheet .... $60-$100
1932 Team logo, booklet .... $60-$100
1933 Roster booklet .... $60-$100
1934 Cincinnati Reds, booklet........ $55-$100
1935 Team logo, booklet .... $55-$100
1936 Team logo, booklet .... $55-$75
1937 Team logo, booklet .... $50-$75
1938 Bill McKechnie, booklet .... $50-$75
1939 1869 Reds.............................. $50-$85
1940 Team logo............................... $45-$85
1941 Baseball, champions pennant $125
1942 Team logo, eagle $125
1943 Team logo, eagle $125
1944 Team logo, hitter.............................$125
1945 Baseball, eagle...............................$125
1946 Catcher and batter $125
1947 Baseball and eagle.........................$125
1948 Team logo, batter............................$125
1949 City, team logo................................$125
1950 Cartoon sportswriter.......................$100
1951 75th anniversary logo.....................$100
1952 Team logo, eagle $100
1953 ....$100
1954 ....$100
1955 Team mascot..................................$100
1956 Birdie Tebbetts...............................$100
1957 Schedule $100
1958 Team mascot batting $100
1959 Mayo Smith $100
1960 Fred Hutchinson $75
1961 Fred Hutchinson, Bill DeWitt $75
1962 Team mascot $75
1963 Team mascot....................................$75
1964 Team mascot....................................$75

1965 Team mascot $75
1966 Team mascot $75
1967 ....$75
1968 ....$40
1969 100th anniversary logo.....................$40
1970 N.L. hats...$30
1971 ....$30
1972 Baseball field....................................$20
1973 Sparky Anderson...............................$20
1974 Jack Billingham, Don Gullett $15
1975 Johnny Bench...................................$15
1976 Joe Morgan, MVP Trophy.................$20
1977 Johnny Bench...................................$20
1978 George Foster $15
1979 John McNamara.................................$15
1980 Riverfront Stadium..............................$8
1981 Players in action.................................$8
1982 Team uniform.....................................$8
1983 Russ Nixon $8
1984 Team logo...$8
1985 Riverfront Stadium..............................$8
1986 Pete Rose...$10
1987 N.L. logos $8
1988 All-Star Game logo.............................$8
1989 Autographed bats $8
1990 Lou Piniella..$10
1991 World Series trophy..........................$10
1992 Equipment $10
1993 Reds locker $10
1994 Team logo..$7
1995 Riverfront Stadium..............................$5
1996 Knight, Morris, Boone.........................$5
1997 Larkin, Sanders, Boone.....................$5
1998 Reds logo on uniform, cap $5
1999 "Cincinnati" on uniform $10
2000 Player Collage $10
2001 Jerseys...$10
2002 History of Riverfront Stadium $8
2003 Inaugural Season at Great American
    Ballpark...$10

Boston Red Sox

1927 Roster sheet...................................$125
1928 Roster sheet...................................$100
1929 Roster sheet...................................$100
1930 Roster sheet...................................$100
1931 Roster sheet...................................$100
1932 Roster sheet...................................$100
1933 Roster sheet...................................$100
1934 Roster booklet $150
1935 Roster booklet $100
1936 Roster booklet $75
1937 Roster booklet $75
1938 Roster booklet $75
1939 Jimmie Foxx, booklet................ $65-$70
1940 Team logo, booklet .... $45-$65
1941 Fenway Park, booklet .... $45-$60
1942 Baseball bats &1942, booklet... $45-$60
1943 Tufts College batting cage .... $40-$60

1944 Roster booklet .... $40-$60
1945 Name and 1945, booklet .... $40-$60
1946 Player in action....................... $35-$70
1947 World Series pennant, booklet .....$35-$60
1948 Joe McCarthy, booklet.............. $45-$60
1949 Roster booklet .... $30-$60
1950 Team mascot .... $30-$50
1951 Old-timer, current player $125
1952 Fenway Park.......................................$125
1953 Team logo...$125
1954 Team logo...$125
1955 Team logo...$125
1956 Name and 1956..................................$125
1957 Player in action $125
1958 Red Sox media $100
1959 Player in mirror $100
1960 Player on horse...................................$100
1961 Baseball glove, ball..............................$100
1962 Carl Yastrzemski, others....................$125
1963 Johnny Pesky $75
1964 Team logo..$75
1965 Team logo..$75
1966 Showerhead, team logo $40
1967 Team logo..$40
1968 A.L. Championship pennant.............$40
1969 100th anniversary................................$40
1970 Fenway Park..$20
1971 Red Sox stars......................................$20
1972 Cheering fan..$10
1973 Player in action....................................$10
1974 Darrell Johnson....................................$10
1975 Fenway Park..$10
1976 A.L. Championship pennant.............$10
1977 Don Zimmer..$10
1978 Carl Yastrzemski, Jim Rice...............$15
1979 Jim Rice..$12
1980 Carl Yastrzemski.................................$12
1981 Ralph Houk...$6
1982 Ralph Houk and players $6
1983 Dwight Evans, Bob Stanley $6
1984 Wade Boggs, Jim Rice $8
1985 Tony Armas $6
1986 Boggs, Boyd, Buckner, Gedman $8
1987 Roger Clemens, John McNamara $6
1988 Dwight Evans, Roger Clemens $8
1989 Joe Morgan $10
1990 Fenway Park..$10
1991 Ellis Burks, Tony Pena $10
1992 Roger Clemens, Butch Hobson........$10
1993 Red Sox baseball $10
1994 Mo Vaughn $7
1995 Team logos $5
1996 Mo Vaughn $5
1997 Mo Vaughn $5
1998 Nomar Garciaparra...............................$6
1999 Garciaparra, Martinez, Gordon $6
2000 Pedro Martinez, Jimmy Williams $5
2001 Garciaparra, P. Martinez, C. Young,
    J. Collins..$5
2002 Old-Time photo of Red Sox players &
    Fenway Park...$5
2003 1903 World Champions Boston
    Americans..$25

Colorado Rockies

1993 Silhouette $20
1994 Coors Field..$10
1995 Coors Field..$15
1996 Coors Field..$6
1997 Baseball scenes....................................$6
1998 All-Star Game logo, stars $6
1999 Coors Field, baseballs..........................$6
2000 Coors Field photo $6
2001 Bat, glove, baseball $6

2002 Player Collage $5
2003 Coors Field and Fireworks $7

Kansas City Royals

1969 Team logo..$60
1970 Player hitting......................................$20
1971 Team bat rack.....................................$20
1972 Royals Stadium $15
1973 Players in action $15
1974 Royals Stadium $15
1975 Player hitting......................................$15
1976 Whitey Herzog.....................................$10
1977 Players in action $6
1978 Players hitting, pitching $6
1979 1976-1978 A.L. West Champions $6
1980 Team logo, scoreboard.........................$6
1981 Players in action, logo $6
1982 Team logo, pitcher $6
1983 Statue of hitter $6
1984 George Brett and fans $8
1985 Scoreboard (A.L. West Champions)...$6
1986 World Series trophy...............................$6
1987 Players in action $6
1988 Fireworks over scoreboard.................$10
1989 Team equipment................................$10
1990 Players in action $10
1991 George Brett..$12
1992 Equipment...$10
1993 25th anniversary.................................$10
1994 Appier, Montgomery, Gagne...............$7
1995 Magazine covers $7
1996 Player photo collage $6
1997 25th Anniv. of Kaufman Stadium........$6
1998 Royals logo on wood background $6
1999 George Brett, Baseball HOF $7
2000 Art: player collage...............................$6
2001 Tucker, Sweeney, Pena $6
2002 Kaufmann Stadium 30 Year
     Anniversary...$7
2003 Mike Sweeney $7

Washington Senators

1928 Roster sheet.....................................$125
1929 Roster sheet.....................................$100

1930 Roster sheet.....................................$100
1931 Roster sheet.....................................$100
1932 Roster booklet..................................$100
1933 Roster booklet..................................$100
1933 Capitol and 1933, booklet ......$80-$115
1934 Capitol and 1934, booklet .....$80-$100
1935 Capitol and 1935, booklet .....$75-$100
1936 Capitol and 1936 ....$75
1937 Capitol and 1937 ....$75
1938 Capitol and 1938 ....$70-$75
1939 Capitol and 1939 ....$70-$75
1940 Capitol and 1940 ....$70-$75
1941 Capitol and 1941 ....$60-$65
1942 Capitol and 1942 ....$60-$65
1943 Capitol and 1943 ....$60-$65
1944 Capitol and 1944 ....$60
1945 Capitol and 1945 ....$60
1946 Capitol and 1946 ....$60
1947 Capitol and 1947 ....$55-$60
1948 Capitol and 1948 ....$55-$60
1949 Capitol and 1949 ....$55-$60
1950 Capitol and 1950 ....$50
1951 Capitol and 1951 ....$50
1952 Capitol and 1952 ....$50
1953 Capitol, bat, baseball................$45-$50
1954 Capitol, bat, baseball................$45-$50
1955 Capitol, bat, baseball................$45-$50
1956 Sportswriter $40
1957 Team mascot pitching.......................$40
1958 Golden anniversary of BBWAA $40
1959 Mascot blowing out candles .....$35-$40
1960 Home run celebration.......................$75

Becomes Minnesota Twins

1961 Doherty, Quesada, Vernon...............$75
1962 Stadium and team logo $75
1963 Stadium and team logo $75
1964 Stadium and team logo $60
1965 Stadium and team logo $35
1966 Stadium and team logo $25
1967 Pitcher and baseball.........................$25
1968 Batter and baseball $25
1969 Frank Howard $25
1970 Bob Short, Ted Williams $25
1971 Stadium and team logo $25

Detroit Tigers

1927 Roster sheet....................................$125
1928 Roster sheet....................................$100
1929 Roster sheet....................................$100
1930 Roster sheet....................................$100
1931 Roster booklet $100
1932 Roster booklet $100
1933 Tiger head and 1933, booklet $60-$100
1934 Tiger head and 1934, booklet $55-$110
1935 Tiger head and 1935, booklet $55-$115
1936 Tiger head and 1936 ....$55-$75
1937 ....$50-$75
1938 Tiger head and 1938 ....$50-$75
1939 Tiger head and 1939 ....$50-$75

1940 ....$45-$85
1941 Briggs Stadium ....$45-$60
1942 Flag over Briggs Stadium ....$45-$60
1943 Tiger head and 1943 ....$40-$60
1944 Tiger head and 1944 ....$40-$60
1945 Tiger head and 1945 ....$40-$70
1946 Tiger head and 1946 ....$35-$60
1947 Tiger head and 1947 ....$35-$60
1948 Tiger head and 1948 ....$150
1949 Tiger head and 1949 ....$150
1950 Tiger head and 1950 ....$150
1951 Tiger head and 1951 ....$150
1952 Tiger head and 1952 ....$150
1953 Tiger head and 1953 ....$150
1954 Tiger head and 1954 ....$100
1955 Tiger head and 1955 ....$100
1956 Ray Boone, Al Kaline $100
1957 Frank Lary $100
1958 Jim Bunning.....................................$100
1959 Tiger head and 1959 ....$100
1960 Tiger head and 1960 ....$75
1961 Tiger Stadium $75
1962 Players and team logo......................$75
1963 Team logo...$75
1964 Team logo...$50
1965 Team logo...$40
1966 Team mascot and 1966 ....$40
1967 Team mascot and 1967 ....$40
1968 Team mascot and 1968 ....$40
1969 Team mascot $30
1970 Team mascot fielding........................$20
1971 Team mascot throwing......................$15
1972 Team mascot fielding........................$10
1973 Team mascot fielding........................$10
1974 Team mascot sliding.........................$10
1975 Team mascot in field.........................$10
1976 Team mascot pitching.......................$10
1977 Team mascot catching......................$10
1978 Team mascot hitting $10
1979 Team logo and 1979 ....$10
1980 Team mascot in action......................$6
1981 Tiger jumping.......................................$6
1982 Team logo..$6
1983 Greenberg and Gehringer uniforms ...$6
1984 Team mascot boxing $6
1985 World Series trophy, logo $6
1986 Team mascot in stadium.....................$6
1987 Baseball and Tiger $6
1988 ....$6
1989 The Press Guide and logo................$10
1990 Uniform D $10
1991 And Once Again $10
1992 Alan Trammell, Lou Whitaker $10
1993 Tiger greats $10
1994 Team logo..$9
1995 Baseballs...$8
1996 Buddy Bell $8
1997 Stripes...$8
1998 J. Thompson, B. Higginson, T. Clark ..$8
1999 Tiger Stadium at night $10
2000 Comerica Park inaugural
     celebration $10
2001 Comerica Park at night......................$10
2002 Ernie Harwell.......................................$6
2003 Alan Trammell.......................................$6

Minnesota Twins

1961 Metropolitan Stadium drawing........$150
1962 Metropolitan Stadium $75
1963 Player hitting......................................$75
1964 Baseball and 1964............................$75
1965 All-Star Game hosts $40
1966 Player fielding $40
1967 Twins uniform $30

2002 Collage of Photos $6
2003 Players celebrating a victory $6

New York Yankees

1968 Pitcher throwing.................................$30
1969 Metropolitan Stadium $25
1970 Rod Carew, Twins stars....................$25
1971 Jim Perry $25
1972 Minnesota media $25
1973 Rod Carew $25
1974 Baseballs...$10
1975 Rod Carew, Ty Cobb $15
1976 R. Carew, H. Killebrew, others..........$15
1977 Old press guide covers.....................$10
1978 Rod Carew $10
1979 Metropolitan Stadium $6
1980 Twins baseball cards $6
1981 Twins bats, hats, uniforms $6
1982 Metrodome $6
1983 Kent Hrbek $7
1984 Twins uniforms....................................$6
1985 All-Star Game logo $6
1986 25th anniversary logo $6
1987 Gary Gaetti, Kirby Puckett..................$8
1988 World Series trophy...........................$10
1989 Kirby Puckett, Frank Viola $10
1990 Carew, Oliva, Puckett $10
1991 Drawings of Carew, Killebrew............$10
1992 Celebration, World Series trophy $10
1993 Kirby Puckett $10
1994 Autographs $7
1995 Bat, glove, uniform $6
1996 Rookies of the Year $5
1997 Team logo..$5
1998 Paul Molitor $5
1999 Collage of T. Kelly, M. Lawton,
    R. Coomer, T. Walker..............................$10
2000 Photos of All-time Twins, 40th
    Anniversary..$10
2001 Carew, Killebrew, Puckett $10
2002 Torrii Hunter, Doug Mientkiewicz,
    Gold Glove...$5
2003 2002 Organization of the Year...........$5

Chicago White Sox

1927 Roster sheet....................................$125
1928 Roster sheet....................................$100
1929 Roster sheet....................................$100
1930 Roster sheet....................................$100
1931 Roster sheet....................................$100
1932 Roster sheet....................................$100
1933 Name and 1933, sheet.......... $60-$100
1934 Name and 1934, booklet .... $55-$100
1935 Name and 1935, booklet .... $55-$100
1936 Name and 1936, booklet .... $55-$75
1937 Name and 1937, booklet .... $50-$75
1938 Name and 1938, booklet .... $50-$75
1939 Name and 1939, booklet .... $50-$75
1940 Name and 1940, booklet .... $45-$75
1941 Ted Lyons, booklet.................... $50-$60
1942 Jimmy Dykes, booklet .... $45-$60
1943 Buy More War Bonds, booklet.. $40-$60

1944 Back the attack, booklet .... $40-$60
1945 Roster booklet .... $40-$60
1946 Name and 1946, booklet .... $35-$60
1947 Ted Lyons, booklet.........................$100
1948 Team mascot and 1948, booklet $100
1949 Team logo and 1949, booklet $100
1950 Luke Appling $100
1951 Paul Richards $100
1952 Carrasquel, Fox, Minoso, Rogovin .$100
1953 Player in action $100
1954 Team mascot $100
1955 Team mascot $100
1956 Team mascot $100
1957 Team mascot $90
1958 Team mascot $90
1959 Team mascot $90
1960 Team mascot $75
1961 Name and 1961................................$75
1962 Player in action................................$75
1963 Player in action................................$75
1964 Player in action................................$75
1965 Pitcher throwing................................$40
1966 Batter hitting $30
1967 Player in action................................$25
1968 Hitter up to bat.................................$25
1969 Batter hitting $25
1970 Fielder in action $10
1971 Chuck Tanner $10
1972 Player in action................................$10
1973 Allen, Tanner, Wood $10
1974 Team logo $10
1975 A.L. 75th anniversary $6
1976 Team logo $6
1977 Team logo $6
1978 Team logo, hitter.................................$6
1979 Don Kessinger $6
1980 Fans in crowd $6
1981 Pitcher in action.................................$6
1982 Team logo $6
1983 Sportswriter equipment $6
1984 Scoreboard, A.L. West Champs.........$6
1985 Comiskey Park $6
1986 Aparicio, Appling, Guillen $7
1987 New White Sox uniform #87 ....$6
1988 Player in action..................................$6
1989 Former White Sox stars.....................$6
1990 Comiskey Park 80 years...................$10
1991 Catchers mask, uniform, bat $10
1992 Team logo $10
1993 Team logo $10
1994 Lamont, Thomas, McDowell...............$7
1995 Comiskey Park $6
1996 Thomas, Guillen, Fernandez..............$6
1997 Frank Thomas hitting..........................$6
1998 Jerry Manuel $6
1999 Players including Frank Thomas $6
2000 Players including Ray Durham $6
2001 Players including Magglio Ordonez....$6

1927 Roster sheet........................ $150-$175
1928 Roster sheet................................$150
1929 Roster sheet................................$150
1930 Roster sheet................................$150
1931 Roster sheet................................$150
1932 Roster booklet $200
1933 Roster booklet $100
1934 Roster booklet $100
1935 Roster booklet $100
1936 Joe McCarthy, booklet ... $70-$100
1937 Joe McCarthy, booklet ... $65-$100
1938 Joe McCarthy, booklet ... $65-$100
1939 Joe McCarthy, booklet ... $65-$100
1940 Joe McCarthy, booklet ..... $60-$75
1941 Joe McCarthy, booklet ..... $60-$65
1942 Joe McCarthy .... $60-$65
1943 .... $45-$65
1944 .... $45-$60
1945 Victory V and 1945.................... $40-$60
1946 Team logo and 1946................ $40-$60
1947 Team logo and 1947................ $35-$65
1948 Team logo and 1948................ $35-$60
1949 Team logo and 1949................ $30-$65
1950 Team logo and 1950....................$150
1951 Team logo and 1951....................$150
1952 Team logo and 1952....................$150
1953 Team logo and 1953....................$150
1954 Team logo and 1954....................$150
1955 Team logo and 1955....................$150
1956 Team logo and 1956....................$150
1957 Team logo and 1957....................$150
1958 Team logo and 1958....................$150
1959 Team logo and 1959....................$150
1960 Yankee Stadium $100
1961 Team logo and 1961....................$100
1962 Team logo and 1962....................$100
1963 Team logo and 1963....................$100
1964 Yogi Berra and logo $75
1965 Team logo....................................$40
1966 Yankee Stadium and logo.................$40
1967 Team logo and hitter........................$40
1968 Yankee Stadium $40
1969 Yankee glove and hat $40
1970 Mel Stottlemyre $25
1971 Logo and players in action $20
1972 Bobby Murcer, Roy White................$20
1973 Yankee Stadium $20
1974 Whitey Ford, Mickey Mantle $25
1975 Bobby Bonds, Catfish Hunter $20
1976 Yankee Stadium $20
1977 Chris Chambliss, Thurman Munson .$25
1978 Reggie Jackson, Babe Ruth.............$25
1979 Goose Gossage, Thurman Munson .$20
1980 Dick Howser, Gene Michael $15

1981 Team logo...$20
1982 Team logo...$5
1983 Billy Martin with umpire $8
1984 Righetti, Yankee no-hitters $6
1985 Don Mattingly $7
1986 Guidry, Henderson, Mattingly, Niekro $7
1987 Lou Piniella and team.......................$15
1988 Team logo...$15
1989 Dallas Green $15

1990 Baseball bat and ball.......................$15
1991 Maas, Mattingly, Meulens, Sax.........$15
1992 A tradition of great moments $15
1993 Collage $10
1994 Players $10
1995 Babe Ruth's 100th birthday $12
1996 Memorabilia.......................................$10
1997 Players $10
1998 Yankee Stadium at 75 years............$13

1999 3 Players raising their hands after
    winning the championship $10
2000 Collage: Yankees Legends...............$10
2001 World Series celebration $10
2002 100 Seasons $10
2003 Collage of Autographed Baseballs ...$10

BASEBALL YEARBOOKS

With more pictures and general content than media guides, year-books appeal to the casual baseball fan. In addition to player biographies similar to those found in media guides, yearbooks often include lengthy team histories.

Yearbooks haven't proven to be as popular as media guides with fans or collectors, which may be why several teams didn't produce them in the 1980s and 1990s. The prices below are for specimens in excellent condition. Yearbooks from 1994 to the present typically sell for their cover price—around $5.

Los Angeles Angels

1961 ....None issued
1962 Angels baby with cake....................$125
1963 Rocket, Chavez Ravine .... $35-$50
1964 Angels in action........................ $25-$35
1965 Angels in action........................ $25-$35

California Angels

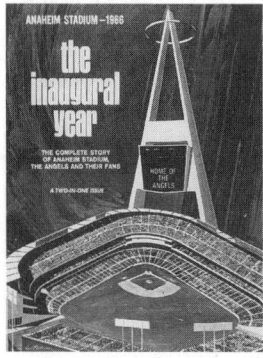

1966 Anaheim Stadium..................... $50-$65
1967 All About the Angels, with logo. $12-$15
1968-1982 .... None issued
1983 Lynn/Carew, Jackson, others ..... $8-$12
1984 Anaheim Stadium .... $5-$10
1985 25th Anniversary, Angel greats .. $7-$10
1986-1991 ....None issued
1992 Abbott, Langston, Harvey, Finley......$12
1993 Nolan Ryan.......................................$12
1994 Tim Salmon $8
1995-1997 ....None issued

Anaheim Angels

1988-1999 ....None issued
2000 Collage of current, former players $8
2001 Troy Percival, Adam Kennedy.............$6
2002 Three different versions of the team
    uniform...$6
2003 Ten Angels players with manager Mike
    Scioscia $10

Houston Colt .45s

1962 Baseball, pistol, Texas map............$150
1963 ....None issued
1964 Colt .45s logo $125

Houston Astros

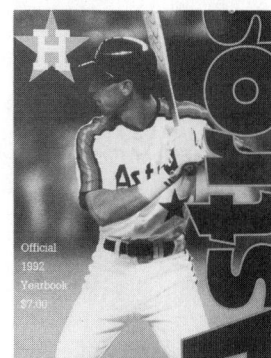

1965 Inside the Astrodome $100
1966 Astrodome $75
1967 .... None issued
1968 .... $45
1969-1971 .... None issued
1972 .... $25
1973-1976 .... None issued

1977 Photo album $20
1978 Photo album $20
1979 Photo album $20
1980-1981 .... None issued
1982 Nolan Ryan............................ $12-$15
1983-1991 .... None issued
1992 Luis Gonzalez..................................$12
1993 Photo album $12
1994 New logo, Bagwell, others $10
1995-2002 ....None issued
2003 Jeff Bagwell $10

Philadelphia Athletics

1949 Connie Mack .... $60-$125
1950 Connie Mack Golden Jubiliee. $60-$125
1951 Team mascot (elephant)......... $60-$125
1952 Team mascot (elephant)......... $60-$125
1953 Elephant pitching baseball $20
1954 Play at first base.............................$75

Kansas City Athletics

1955 A's batter ripping through
    map.................................... $100-$150
1956 Elephant mascot.................. $100-$150
1957 Kansas City Municipal
    Stadium .... $100-$150
1958 Play at first.....................................$125
1959 Kansas City Municipal Stadium......$125
1960 Baseball wearing Athletics hat $125
1961 Pitcher and baseball.......................$125
1962 A's players in action........................$125
1963 Play at home plate.................... $25-$40
1964 Player making a catch .... $25-$40
1965 A's donkey, Finley flag .... $25-$45
1966 ....$65
1967 Athletics pitcher...............................$40

Oakland Athletics

1968 Oakland Coliseum .... $75-$95
1969 Connie Mack .... $25-$35
1970 Monday, Odom, Jackson, others $25
1971 Sal Bando, Bert Campaneris.... $15-$25
1972 Dick Williams, Vida Blue........... $15-$22
1973 Rudi, Fingers, Williams, Hunter........$20
1974 One More in '74, two trophies .. $15-$20
1975 Keep it Alive in '75 ....$20
1976 Bicentennial celebration $15
1977 A's logo, arch of baseballs........... $7-$9
1978 .... None issued
1979 The Swingin A's, with logo................$20
1980-1981 .... None issued
1982 Billy Ball baseball .... $5-$10
1983 A's baseball card collage.................$15
1984-1999 .... None issued
2000 100th Anniversary of Athletcis
   baseball $10
2001 Jason Giambi $10

Toronto Blue Jays

1977 The First Year, fans .... $15-$20
1978 ....None issued
1979 Rico Carty $9
1980 Rico Carty, Roy Howell.....................$15
1981 Ernie Whitt, Jim Clancy $15
1982 Martinez, Moseby, Whitt...................$15
1983 Blue Jays baseball $15
1984 Exhibition Stadium $15
1985 Logo and year $15
1986 American League baseball, bat.......$15
1987 Barfield, Clancy, Whitt $15
1988 Blue Jay player batting $15
1989 Fred McGriff $15
1990 George Bell $15
1991 Player drawing..................................$15
1992 Roberto Alomar $15
1993 Trophy...$15
1994 Carter, Molitor, White, others...........$12
1995 Logo and baseball............................$10
1996 20th Anniv. All-Time greats $10
1997 Roger Clemens $10
1998 Roger Clemens, Carlos Delgado $10
1999 Shawn Green $10
2000 Shannon Stewart..............................$10
2001 Blue Jays players from the past $10
2002 Stewart, Delgado, Cruz $10
2003 Eric Hinske $10

Boston Braves

1946 Billy Southworth $300
1947 Billy Southworth .... $150-$165
1948-1949 .... None issued
1950 Smiling Brave $150
1951 Baseball diamond and ball $125
1952 Braves players talking $125

Milwaukee Braves

1953 Runner sliding into home ..... $150-$175

1954 To the People of Milwaukee.... $75-$100
1955 Fans and stadium.................... $50-$60
1956 Cartoon of Braves fans......... $100-$125
1957 Braves logo in crystal ball..... $100-$125
1958 Brave raising World Series
   pennant...................................... $100-$125
1959 Brave in hot-air balloon .... $65-$70
1960 Brave with two baseball bats............$60
1961 Braves player, other N.L. players.... $40-
   $65
1962 Braves logo .... $45-$60
1963 Braves player, other N.L. players......$40
1964 Aaron, Mathews, Torre, Spahn . $40-$60
1965 Bobby Bragan, Felipe Alou..............$40

Atlanta Braves

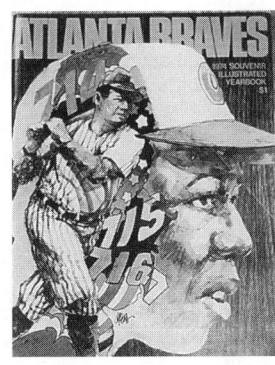

1966 Aaron, Mathews, others .... $25-$50
1967 Play at home plate.................... $10-$30
1968 Play at second base .... $10-$25
1969 Braves infielder........................ $15-$25
1970 Braves in action.................................$20
1971 Hank Aaron, Babe Ruth .... $7-$9
1972 Five Braves................................. $5-$9
1973 Braves pitcher $20
1974 Hank Aaron, Babe Ruth $20
1975 Four Braves $15
1976 Niekro, Cepeda, Aaron, others.........$15
1977 Former Braves, Hank Aaron.............$10
1978 Spahn, Niekro, Burdette $10
1979 Garber stops Roses streak ..... $12-$15
1980 Bob Horner, Bobby Cox....................$15
1981 D. Murphy, B. Horner, others $15
1982 Spahn, Horner, Aaron, others .. $12-$15
1983 Phil Niekro in an Uncle Sam outfit....$10
1984 Horner, Murphy, Aaron $10
1985 Aaron, Murphy, 20th Anniversary $10
1986 Dale Murphy, Chuck Tanner $12
1987 Dale Murphy $12
1988 Braves Illustrated..............................$10
1989 ....None issued
1990 25 years in Atlanta...........................$12
1991 ....None issued
1992 N.L. Champions $12
1993 .... None issued
1994 B. Cox, G. Maddux, others $7
1995-1997 .... None Issued
1998 Collage of players.............................$10
1999 ....$7
2000 Art...$7
2001 Braves logo $7
2002 Animation of Maddux, C. Jones,
   Sheffield, Furcal..................................$7
2003 Season Logo $7

Seattle Pilots

1969 Pilot logos, 10 pictures $150

Milwaukee Brewers

1970 Brewers hitter .... $50-$75
1971-1978 .... None issued
1979 Larry Hisle .... $5-$9
1980 Gorman Thomas .... $5-$9
1981 Molitor, Fingers, Yount, others...... $5-$9
1982 Crowd celebrating $12
1983 Robin Yount and fans $10
1984 County Stadium........................... $5-$9
1985 George Bamberger and fans........ $5-$9
1986 Brewers locker room..................... $5-$9
1987 Brewers baseball cards .... $5-$9
1988 Paul Molitor hologram.......................$10

1989 Brewer greats, Hank Aaron $12
1990 Brewers logo, Milwaukee skyline......$10
1991 Paul Molitor $12
1992 Molitor, Yount, Gantner.....................$12
1993 .... None issued
1994 New Brewer uniforms $7
1995 ....None issued
1996 John Jaha...$8
1997-2000 ....None issued
2001 Making of Miller Park.........................$8
2002 Past All-Star Games...........................$8
2003 Miller Park $7

St. Louis Cardinals

1951 Cardinal in bottom right $250
1952 Cardinal and soldier $125
1953 Stan Musial .... $125-$175
1954 Red Schoendienst...........................$100
1955 Cardinal pitcher gets the sign...........$85
1956 Cardinal pitcher gets the sign...........$85
1957 Cardinal circles the bases .... $50-$75
1958 Cardinal circles the bases .... $50-$75
1959 Stan Musial $55
1960 Cardinal catches a ball $40
1961 Curt Simmons, Ray Sadecki, others.... $40
1962 Stan Musial and his milestones ....$40-$60
1963 Musial slides into second .... $35-$50
1964 Groat, Boyer, Javier, White....... $50-$75
1965 Bob Gibson $35
1966 New Busch Stadium photo $65
1967 World Champs........................ $50-$75
1968 Busch Stadium $50
1969 Brock, Flood, Gibson, others............$30
1970 Five Cardinal drawings .... $12-$15
1971 Brock, Torre, Gibson, others..... $12-$15
1972 Cardinals fielder $25
1973 Cardinals batter........................ $15-$20
1974 Simmons, Torre $15
1975 Brock, Gibson, others.......................$20
1976 Centennial yearbook $20
1977 Lou Brock, Ty Cobb .... $12-$15
1978 .... None issued
1979 St. Louis city skyline........................$12
1980 Simmons, Hernandez.......................$10
1981-1987 .... None issued
1988 Wraparound team photo...................$12
1989 Coleman, Worrell....................... $7-$12
1990 Herzog, Busch Stadium....................$10
1991 Lee Smith $12
1992 Moore, Slaughter, Musial, Guerrero,
   Lankford, Jose $10
1993 Ozzie Smith.....................................$12
1995 K. Hill, S. Cooper, D. Jackson,
   T. Henke $10
1996-98 ....None issued

1999 Mark McGwire $10
2000 10 Greatest Moments.......................$10
2001 Baseball card collage $7

2002 Hall of Famer Ozzie Smith $8
2003 Bobble Head Dolls............................$7

Chicago Cubs

1934 Wraparound batting scene ... $200-$275
1939 Players records $200
1941 Players history, record book . $175-$250
1942 Roster, record book............. $150-$200
1948 Logo and blue 1948............. $100-$150
1949 Logo and blue 1949............... $75-$100
1950 Hat and red 1950 .... $65-$95
1951 Ball in center of red glove........ $65-$95
1952 Logo, year in red and blue....... $65-$95
1953 Cubs logo .... $65-$95
1954 Name and year......................... $65-$95
1955 Name and year......................... $65-$95
1956 Name and year .... $75-$125
1957 Head with Cubs hat.......................$125
1958-1984 .... None issued
1985 Wrigley photo .... $5-$8
1986 70th Anniversary, Ryne Sandberg $5-$7
1987 Billy Williams, Ryne Sandberg ..... $7-$8
1988 Andre Dawson.............................. $7-$9
1989 Wrigley Field Diamond Anniv. $12

1990 Photo of six bats...............................$12
1991 Ryne Sandberg $12
1992 Scoreboard, celebration $12
1993 Mark Grace $12
1994 Moments from 1984 season............$10
1995 Wrigley Field....................................$10
1996-98 ....None issued
1999 Cubs Quarterly covers: Sammy Sosa,
   others; Mark Grace; Sosa; Sosa $5
2000 Cubs Quarterly covers: Don Baylor;
   Mark Grace; Kerry Wood; Sammy Sosa...$5
2001 Kerry Wood, Sammy Sosa, others $5
2002 Sosa, Scoreboard, Flag, Marquee Sign,
   Jerseys, K. Wood.................................$7
2003 Sammy Sosa and Ernie Banks $7

Tampa Bay Devil Rays

1998 ....None issued
1999 Celebration at home plate $10
2000 Fred McGriff....................................$10
2001 Player collage $5

2002 Joe Kennedy $5

Arizona Diamondbacks

1998 Two hardbound books $10
1999-2001 .... None Issued
2002 Celebrating World Series Victory $10
2003 Collage of various players $8

Brooklyn Dodgers

1947 League Champs............................$150
1948 .... None issued
1949 League Champs............................$250
1950 Artwork of a fielder .... $175-$200
1951 Bum picking daisy petals...............$150
1952 The Bum holding a sign..................$150
1953 The Bum holding a bat $150
1954 The Bum with saw, hammer $150
1955 The Bum reaching for a star...........$300
1956 The Bum holding #6 ....$150
1957 The Bum holding pennants $175

Los Angeles Dodgers

1958 Autographed team baseball..... $150-$175
1959 Play at second base .... $75-$135
1960 Dodger stadium drawing $50
1961 Artwork of Dodger Stadium.............$50
1962 Map of area around Stadium.... $15-$20
1963 Maury Wills.....................................$50
1964 World Champions banner.................$30
1965 Dodger Stadium $35
1966 Walter Alston .... $20-$25
1967 Dodger juggling crowns........... $10-$20
1968 Drysdale, Koufax, others .... $10-$20
1969 Baseball's centennial logo .... $10-$20
1970 Dodgers and Mets mascots...... $10-$20
1971 10th Anniversary of stadium..... $10-$20
1972 Dodger Stadium .... $10-$20
1973 Willie Davis, Walter Alston....... $15-$25
1974 Jimmy Wynn .... $10-$20
1975 Steve Garvey, N.L. Champions $12-$18
1976 Davey Lopes............................ $12-$18
1977 20th Anniversary, players $10
1978 Lasorda, Garvey, Cey, others ... $12-$15
1979 Tommy Lasorda.......................... $10-$12

1980 Dodger baseball cards $10
1981 Dusty Baker, Steve Garvey ...... $10-$12
1982 World Series trophy ....$8-$12
1983 25th Anniversary in Los Angeles......$10
1984 A Winning Tradition, Lasorda ..... $7-$10
1985 Russell, Valenzuela, Garvey ...... $9-$10
1986 Guerrero, Hershiser, Marshall .... $7-$10
1987 24 previous Los Angeles
    yearbooks .... $7-$10
1988 Blueprint for Success .... $8-$9
1989 World Series trophy .... $6-$10
1990 Dodger greats painting .... $6-$10
1991 Dodgers Field of Dreams .... $5-$7
1992 Dodger greats .... $5-$7
1993 Hershiser, Lasorda collage.................$8
1994 Team photo, uniform background $8
1995 Dodger rookies of the year $8
1996 Nomo, Piazza, Mondesi, Karros $8
1997 Jackie Robinson patch, photo $10
1998 Art collage of 40 year anniversary... $10
1999 Drysdale, Campanella Dodger "Hero"
    patches $10
2000 Stadium scenes with 2000 spelled out $10
2001 Reprinted covers of yearbooks from
    1941-2000 ....$10
2002 Picture of the Dodger Stadium in 1962
    and 2002...$10
2003 Shawn Green $8

Montreal Expos

1969 Larry Jaster $50-75
1970 Expos equipment and fan........ $25-$35
1971 Fan with Expos pennant........... $25-$35
1972 Four different covers, each....... $25-$35
1973-81 .... None issued
1982 Expos celebration, All-Star logo $10
1983 Dawson, Carter, Oliver, others ... $7-$12
1984 Raines, Rose, Dawson, others... $8-$12
1985 Wallach, Raines, Dawson, others.....$10
1986 Baseball in hand................................$8
1987-91 .... None issued
1992 Gary Carter $10
1993-1998 ....None issued
1999 Vladimir Guerrero $6
2000 Vladimir Guerrero $6
2001 Vladimir Guerrero, Fernando Tatis,
    others...$6
2002 History Montage with black and white
    photos...$6
2003 Gary Carter, Jose Vidro, Valdimir
    Guerrero $6

New York Giants

1947 First Year .... $150-$200
1948-1950 .... None issued
1951 Logo, art of leaping player.............$125
1952 Durocher and Giant.......................$100
1953 Polo Grounds photo $100
1954 Giant cutting a 1951 book $150

1955 Giant holding other mascots $125
1956 Giants cap $100
1957 Photo of play at second $125

San Francisco Giants

1958 Giant with a load of books..............$250
1959 Photo of a play at third .... $75-$100
1960 Al Dark, play at first $50
1961 Giants hat...$50
1962 N.L. Champs $50
1963 Trolley car w, Giants pennant ... $30-$40
1964 Child looking at Candlestick $30
1965 Painting of a play at second $30
1966 W. Mays with S.F. baseball .... $30-$50
1967 Willie Mays, Juan Marichal...............$40
1968 Willie Mays $25
1969 Mays, Bonds, McCovey $30
1970 Photos of Mays, McCovey .... $20-$25
1971 Willie McCovey .... $15-$20
1972 Willie Mays sliding into third ..... $10-$15
1973 Marichal, Bonds, Speier .... $10-$15
1974 Young Giants '74 ....$10
1975 Gary Matthews, Mike Caldwell $12
1976 Giants memorabilia $15
1977-1979 .... None issued
1980 Giant batter $9
1981 Frank Robinson $10
1982 Silver Anniversary yearbook....... $8-$10
1983 Frank Robinson .... $7-$9
1984 Giants All-Star memorabilia......... $7-$9
1985 Horizontal A History of... .... $5-$7
1986-1991 .... None issued
1992 Will Clark $12
1993 .... None issued
1994 Willie Mays $10
1995 Matt Williams, Barry Bonds $10
1996 Mays, Bonds, McCovey, Marichal, Perry,
    Beck...$10
1997 .... None issued
1998 Brian Johnson $9
2000 Pacific Bell Park................................$5
2001 Past Giants Players $8
2002 Barry Bonds and Five other Giants
    Players...$8
2003 Felipe Alou and Barry Bonds $8

Cleveland Indians

1948 World Champs..................... $100-$150
1949 Logo wearing crown .... $60-$95
1950 Fans entering stadium.............. $50-$85
1951 50th Anniversary with logo ..... $75-$125
1952 Chain with Indians logo .... $60-$95
1953 Umpire yelling Play ball .... $65-$95
1954 Lemon, Wynn, Doby, Rosen...........$100
1955 Indian wearing crown .... $75-$100
1956 Indian mascot $85
1957 Indian mascot .... $75-$125
1958 Herb Score $250
1959 Indians logo .... $125-$175
1960 Jim Perry, Indians pitcher $100
1961 Sketch book....................................$100
1962 Team photo.......................................$75
1963 Sketch book....................................$100
1964 Indian sliding into home...................$75
1965 Past and present uniforms $65
1966 Sam McDowell .... $50-$65
1967 Picture set .... $50-$65
1968 Baseball and year.................... $25-$40
1969 Runner sliding into base...................$20
1970 Sam McDowell $25
1971 Indians in action $15
1972 Indians in action .... $7-$9
1973 Jim Perry, others...............................$15
1974-1983 .... None issued
1984 Franco, Sutcliffe, others................ $5-$6
1985-1988 .... None issued
1989 Autographed team ball $10
1990 90th Anniversary in Cleveland..........$10
1991 Score, Alomar, Chambliss $10
1992 Alomar, Hargrove $12
1993 .... None issued
1994 Hardcover, Jacobs Field $15
1995 Jacobs Field, Belle, Baerga, others..$10
1996 A. L. Championship artwork $10
1997 All-Star logo, Cleveland skyline $10
1998 Championship celebration................$10
1999 Manny Ramirez, Mike Hargrove,
    others..$9
2000 ....$7
2001 100th Anniversary logo $7
2002 Colon, Diaz, Thome, Vizquel..............$7
2003 .... None Issued

Seattle Mariners

1978-1984 .... None issued
1985 Davis, Beattie, Langston $10
1986-1993 .... None issued
1994 Griffey, Martinez, others $5
1995-1998 .... None issued
1999 K. Griffey Jr., A. Rodriguez.................$9
2000 Alex Rodriguez at Safeco Field $9
2001 Ichiro Suzuki....................................$10
2002 Boone, Garcia, E. Martinez, Cameron,
    Ichiro...$10

2003 Edgar Martinez $8

Florida Marlins

1993 Marlins hitter, pitcher, catcher $10
1994 B. Harvey, R. Lachemann, others.......$8
1995-1996 ....None issued
1997 Gary Sheffield, Jeff Conine, others $7
1998 World Series ring.............................$7
1999 Alex Fernandez, Old-Time players $6
2000 Team photo collage $6
2001 Team photo collage $6
2002 Collage of Marlins Memorabilia..........$6
2003 10th Anniversary Logo $6

New York Mets

1962 First year .... $300-$350
1963 Mr. Met leaning on bat.......... $125-$150
1964 Cartoon .... $75-$100
1965 Cartoon, Shea Stadium............ $50-$60
1966 "Go-Go-Go" Mets banner $50
1967 Cartoon .... $50-$75
1968 Gil Hodges $45
1969 Koosman, Grote, Seaver ...... $100-$125
1970 Film strips, World Series celebration$35
1971 Play at the plate........................ $35-$50
1972 Harrelson, McGraw, Seaver $15
1973 All-Star gallery w, Mays, Seaver,
    others .... $15-$35
1974 N.L. Champions pennant $15
1975 Tom Seaver .... $15-$25
1976 Mr. Met .... $15-$20
1977 Jerry Koosman .... $10-$15
1978 Play at home plate..................... $6-$10
1979 Mets logo.................................. $10-$15
1980 Mazzilli with fan, others $30
1981 Joe Torre, All-Time Mets $15
1982 George Foster, George
    Bamberger.................................... $12-$15
1983 Foster, M. Wilson, Seaver $20
1984 Orosco, Hernandez, Strawberry$15-$20
1985 Hernandez, Gooden, D. Johnson.....$15
1986 25th Anniversary logo $20
1987 World Champions logo .... $10-$15
1988 Strawberry, Gooden, Johnson,
    others..$15

1989 Strawberry, Gooden, Carter, others .$15
1990 Mets starting pitchers $15
1991 Shea Stadium..................................$10
1992 Bonilla, Saberhagen, Murray, Torborg.$15
1993 30 years at Shea $15
1994 25th Anniv. of 1969 Championship...$10
1995 Logo on bats $10
1996 Todd Hundley, Everett, others $10
1997 Motion card of Hundley swing $10
1998 Player celebration photo..................$10
1999 Al Leiter, Mike Piazza, Rey Ordonez,
    Rickey Henderson $10
2000 Edgardo Alfonzo, Al Leiter,
    Mike Piazza, others $10
2001 Mike Piazza, Armando Benitez, Edgardo
    Alfonzo, Al Leiter photo collage..............$10
2002 Collage featuring Stengel, Koosman,
    Seaver, Knight, Valentine, Franco, Piazza,
    McGraw $10
2003 Collage featuring Howe, Glavine, Leiter,
    Stanton, Piazza, Vaughn, Alomar, Floyd $10

St. Louis Browns

1944 ....$275
1945 ....$250
1946 ....$250
1947 ....$225
1948 ....$200
1949 ....$200
1950 Browns sketchbook $200
1951 Browns logo..................................$200
1952 Logo on Browns sketchbook $300
1953 ....$150

Baltimore Orioles

1954 Orioles mascot in spotlight $250
1955 Oriole mascot batting $150
1956 Oriole mascot on deck....................$125
1957 Oriole mascot pitching....................$125
1958 Oriole mascot riding a rocket..........$125
1959 Oriole mascot with report ..... $100-$125
1960 Oriole mascot sitting on eggs.........$100
1961 Oriole mascot hitting opponent $75
1962 Jim Gentile $75
1963 Brooks Robinson $75
1964 Orioles catcher $75
1965 B. Robinson, Bauer, Bunker $75
1966 Robinsons, Blefary, Powell $50
1967 Frank Robinson and fans $50
1968 Brooks and Frank Robinson $25
1969 Dave McNally $25
1970 Boog Powell............................. $20-$35
1971 B. Robinson, Palmer, others..... $15-$25
1972 Palmer, McNally, Cuellar $15
1973 Orioles player .... $12-$15
1974 Orioles jukebox .... $10-$12
1975-1979 .... None issued
1980 Orioles mascot .... $10-$12
1981 Orioles players .... $8-$10
1982 Frank Robinson, Earl Weaver..........$15

1983 Brooks Robinson .... $9-$10
1984 30th Anniversary in Baltimore .. $10-$12
1985 .... None issued
1986 Robinsons, Ripken Jr., Murray $10
1987-1992 .... None issued
1993 Camden Yards................................$10
1994 40th Anniversary Issue....................$10
1995-1997 ....None issued
1998 Cal Ripken Jr., Brady Anderson $8
1999-2003 ....None issued

San Diego Padres

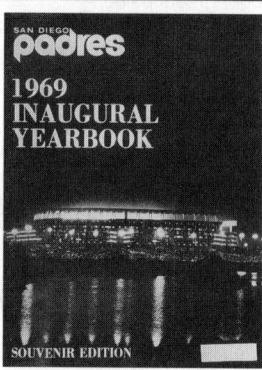

1969 Jack Murphy Stadium......................$75
1970-1978 .... None issued
1979 Dave Winfield .... $5-$6
1980 Dave Winfield .... $6-$7
1981 .... None issued
1982 Dick Williams .... $7-$12
1983 Dick Williams, Steve Garvey...... $7-$12
1984 Templeton, Williams, Garvey $12
1985 Padres hat, N.L. Championship ring $12
1986 Padres memorabilia $10
1987-1991 .... None issued
1992 Fernandez, Gwynn, Santiago...........$10
1993 25th Anniversary $10
1994-1998 ....None issued
1999 Yearbook, Media guide....................$10
2000 B. Boone, Klesko, Al Martin, Gwynn...$8
2001 Tony Gwynn.....................................$8
2002 Trevor Hoffman $8
2003 B. Lawrence, O. Perez, A. Eaton,
    J. Peavy $8

Philadelphia Phillies

1949 Batting scene....................... $175-$250
1950 Phillie and sheet music..................$150
1951 Six player drawings $400
1952 Color stadium photo .... $100-$125
1953 Phillie batter.......................... $35-$75
1954 Smiling Phillie (head only).............$100
1955 Phillie pitcher......................... $75-$100
1956 Robin Roberts, Richie Ashburn......$150
1957 Ball wearing a Phillies hat ...... $50-$100
1958 Hat on pinstriped background .. $75-$80
1959 Five balls, one with a logo .... $50-$75

1960 New faces of 1960, 11 photos..........$75
1961 First edition.....................................$150
1961 Second edition $150
1962 Four balls and logo .... $60-$75
1963 Bat, ball and logo $75
1964 First or second edition $75
1964 Third edition, Bunning, others $75
1965 Richie Allen, Jim Bunning $45
1966 Stadium photo $45
1967 Child eating a hot dog $45
1968 Phillie ballplayers..................... $35-$45
1969 Connie Mack Stadium .... $35-$45
1970 Veterans Stadium in tree bark .. $20-$40
1971 Veterans Stadium drawing...............$45
1972 Stadium, fans and players $30
1973 12 drawings, with Carlton $45
1974 12 drawings, with Carlton, Bowa $20
1975 Schmidt, Carlton...................... $20-$30
1976 Drawings with Schmidt, Carlton $12-$15
1977 Larry Bowa .... $12-$15
1978 Schmidt, Carlton, photos.............. $7-$9
1979 Schmidt, Rose, Carlton .... $7-$9
1980 Schmidt, Rose, Carlton $30
1981 World Series ring photo...................$30
1982 Schmidt, Rose, Carlton $30
1983 Centennial celebration.............. $9-$12
1984 Schmidt, Carlton, 20 others.......... $6-$7
1985 Schmidt, Carlton, Samuel, Hayes .. $7-$10
1986 Mike Schmidt at bat.................. $10-$12
1987 Schmidt, Samuel, others $10
1988 Veterans Stadium photo $10
1989 Jordan, V. Hayes, Schmidt $10
1990 Photo of John Kruk's equipment $10
1991 Veterans Stadium $10
1992 Kruk, Dykstra, Daulton, others $10
1993 Kruk, Dykstra, Daulton, others $10
1994 1993 N.L. Championship ring..............$8
1995 L. Dykstra, D. Hollins, others $8
1996 Montage of action photos $8
1997 Curt Schilling $8
1998 S. Rolen, C. Jefferies, others..............$7
1999 C. Schilling, S. Rolen, others..............$7
2000 Phillies 2000 logo $7
2001 Robert Person, Larry Bowa, Doug
    Glanville, others..$7
2002 Rollins, Abreu, J. Mesa, Lieberthal,
    others..$7
2003 Past and Present Phillies Players.......$7

Pittsburgh Pirates

1951 Forbes Field photo $250
1952 Pirate with sword and pistol............$125
1953 Buc youngster in sailboat $100
1954 Honus Wagner statue........... $100-$175
1955 Pirate batter—It's a hit! $100
1956 Pirate swinging at 1956 ball $100
1957 Pirate winding up.................... $85-$100
1958 Pirate head between two bats $65
1959 Pirate with Pa Pitt $50
1960 Pirate in sailboat..............................$95
1961 Pirate on a treasure chest $35
1962 Ball wearing bandana and cap . $35-$50
1963 Pirate batter.............................. $35-$50
1964 Pirate sliding into third $15
1965 Mgr. Harry Walker and coaches $25
1966 Wraparound Forbes Field photo.......$25
1967 Clemente, Mazeroski, others............$25
1968 Clemente, Stargell, others................$25
1969 Wraparound Forbes Field photo.......$25
1970 Three Rivers Stadium.......................$75
1971 Three Rivers Stadium.......................$75
1972 Clemente, Stargell, others................$20
1973 Clemente, Stargell, others................$20
1974 Stargell, Parker, others....................$12

PIRATES 1953 50¢

1975 Historical photos........................... $5-$6
1976 Yosemite Sam cartoon .... $5-$6
1977 Pirate baseball cards..................... $6-$7
1978 Tanner, Candelaria, others .... $5-$6
1979 Dave Parker.....................................$20
1980 The Family of Stars .... $5-$6
1981 Lacy, Rhoden, Madlock, others $10
1982 Stargell, Madlock, others.................$10
1983 Chuck Tanner ....$6-$7
1984 Madlock, Pena, Ray, others.......... $5-$6
1985 Painting of Mazs '60 homer......... $5-$9
1986 Leland, Pena, Ray, M. Brown ..... $7-$12
1987 Centennial yearbook .... $7-$12
1988 Bonds, Bonilla, Van Slyke, others.. $7-$12
1989 Photo of official N.L. balls........... $7-$12
1990 Van Slyke bat, Leyland uniform........$10
1991 Pirates greats $10
1992 Locker room, uniforms.....................$10
1993 Jay Bell $10
1994 Jim Leyland, Orlando Merced, others $9
1995 25th anniversary of stadium $9
1996-99 ....None issued
2000 Three Rivers Stadium and Past
    Players..$7
2002 "Pirates"...$7
2003 Giles, M. Williams, P. Reese,
    A. Ramirez...$7

Texas Rangers

TEXAS RANGERS OFFICIAL 1992 YEARBOOK

1972-1975 .... None issued
1976 Rangers cowgirl on horse $40
1977 Autographed Rangers ball.......... $7-$15
1978 Squared photo collage $12
1979 Jenkins, Oliver, others .... $5-$9
1980 Arlington Stadium.............................$15
1981 Rangers hitter............................... $5-$9
1982 Rangers baseball .... $10-$12
1983 .... None issued
1984 George Wright........................... $10-$12
1985 Pete O'Brien equipment $10
1986-1987 .... None issued
1988 Ruben Sierra $10
1989 .... None issued
1990 Rangers helmet rack .... $6-$8
1991 20 Years in Texas $10

1992 Nolan Ryan...............................$12
1993 Arlington Stadium tribute $10
1994 Ballpark at Arlington $8
1995 Will Clark artwork $8
1996 Nolan Ryan.......................................$10
1997 25th Anniv. logo, Gonzalez, others.....$8
1998 J. Gonzalez, I Rodriguez $8
1999 Nolan Ryan...$8
2000 Ivan Rodriguez and Rafael Palmeiro..$8
2001 Palmeiro, A. Rodriguez, I. Rodriguez,
    Caminiti...$8
2002 I. Rodriguez, Gonzalez, A. Rodriguez,
    Palmeiro & former players $8
2003 Rafael Palmeiro....................................$8

Washington Nationals, Senators

The Senators 1963 YEARBOOK

1947 "Photo Book", W. Johnson.... $250-$400
1948 .... None issued
1949 .... $150-$350
1950 .... $125-$300
1951 .... None issued
1952 Nationals batter $100
1953 Capitol building and baseball $25
1954 Bob Porterfield, Mickey Vernon $75
1955 National with four bats $75
1956 Clark C. Griffith memorial..............$100
1957 Senators pitcher .... $75-$100
1958 Roy Sievers $100
1959 100 Years of Baseball art $50
1960 Harmon Killebrew $65
1961 A Team is Born .... $100-$150
1962 Washington Stadium $75
1963 Red cover with dedication .... $30-$45
1964 Off the Floor in '64.........................$15
1965 Frank Howard signing autograph $25
1966 Senators in action............................$20
1967 Capitol and Washington
    Monument.......................................$25-$30
1968 Pitcher delivering...................... $15-$20
1969 Ted Williams .... $20-$30
1970-1971 .... None issued
Becomes Texas Rangers

Cincinnati Reds

1948 Ewell Blackwell, Ray Lamanno.......$150
1949 Bucky Walters, Harry Gumbert.......$200
1950 .... None issued
1951 75th Anniversary of N.L........ $100-$125
1952 Crosley Field .... $100-$125
1953 Reds mascot leaning on bat............$75
1954 Reds mascot swinging bat $75
1955 Reds mascot rising on bat...............$75
1956 Reds mascot swinging bat $75
1957 Reds mascot in space ship ...... $60-$75
1958 Reds mascot in orbit................. $40-$50
1959 VanderMeer, Lombardi, others $50
1960 Reds mascot, Goodman, Rixey........$30
1961 Reds mascot running after ball $95
1962 Reds mascot raising pennant...........$40

1963 Reds mascot yelling Charge $65
1964 Reds mascot in action.............$30-$40
1965 Reds mascot making catch ......$30-$40
1966 Reds mascot reaching for ball........$30
1967 Reds mascot, Crosley Field $30
1968 Autographed team baseball .....$15-$25
1969 Perez, Rose, Bench, others......$15-$25
1970 Johnny Bench.................................$25
1971 Rose, Bench, Anderson, others $15
1972 Bench, Perez, other film strips $15
1973 Morgan, Bench, others $10
1974 Pete Rose sliding into home............$20
1975 Joe Morgan....................................$30
1976 Morgan, Rose, Perez........................$10
1977 Morgan, Bench, Foster, others $12
1978 Pete Rose......................................$10
1979 Bench, Perez, Griffey, Foster...........$10
1980 Reds equipment $8
1981 Riverfront Stadium and baseball $8
1982 Binoculars on stadium seat $8
1983 Reds player signing autographs $8
1984 Bats and baseball equipment $8
1985 Pete Rose, Ty Cobb.................... $8-$10
1986 .... None issued
1987 Rose, Parker, E. Davis, others $12
1988 All-Star Game logo $10
1989 Baseball with Reds logo $10
1990 Red player with fans $10
1991 World Series trophy..........................$10
1992 Equipment collage............................$10
1993 Barry Larkin's jersey $10
1994 Reds pinstriped cap $8
1995 Big Red Machine commemorative $8
1996 Marge Schott and Schottzie $7
1997 Jeff Brantley, Barry Larkin $8
1998 ....None issued
1999 Reds logo $8
2000 Glove with Commemorative Patch. $8
2001 Ken Griffey Jr.....................................$8
2002 Cinergy Field in background,
    M. Brennamen, Joe Nuxhall $8
2003 "Spirit of Baseball" Relief found at Great
    American Ballpark $7

Boston Red Sox

1951 Fenway Park...................................$250
1952 Red Sox sliding into home..............$150
1953-1954 ....None issued
1955 Red Sox fielder.................... $115-$125
1956 Red Sox owners $75
1957 Fenway Park...................... $75-$125
1958 Red Sox signing autograph $65
1959 Red Sox pitcher................................$65
1960 Gary Geiger......................................$65
1961 Red Sox batter.................................$65
1962 Carl Yastrzemski..............................$65
1963 Johnny Pesky, Play at third base......$50
1964 Fenway Park at night.........................$50
1965 Dick Radatz............................. $40-$45
1966 Fenway Park........................... $35-$45
1967 Scott, T. Conigliaro,
    Yastrzemski.................................. $65-$75
1968 Yastrzemski, Lonborg, D. Williams ...$40
1969 Fenway Park....................................$40
1970 Lyle, Petrocelli, Yastrzemski $40
1971 Scott, Yastrzemski, Petrocelli ... $12-$15
1972 Carl Yastrzemski and fans .... $7-$12
1973 Carlton Fisk and fans $25
1974 C. Fisk with T. Munson $10
1975 Foxx, Williams, Yastrzemski, Fisk.....$40
1976 Fred Lynn $10
1977 Carl Yastrzemski...................... $10-$15
1978 Jim Rice, Carl Yastrzemski....... $12-$15
1979 Jim Rice $10

1980 Fred Lynn $8
1981 Rice, Yastrzemski, Eckersley............$10
1982 Yastrzemski, Evans, Rice, Lansford.....$10
1983 Carl Yastrzemski...............................$10
1984 Jim Rice $7
1985 Tony Armas $6
1986 Wade Boggs......................................$15
1987 R. Clemens and Fenway Park ...... $7-$9
1988 Wade Boggs, Roger Clemens ...... $7-$9
1989 Dwight Evans $10
1990 Mike Greenwell, Ellis Burks..............$10
1991 Pena, Clemens, Burks......................$10
1992 Clemens, Reardon, Viola $12
1993 Roger Clemens $10
1994-1998 ....cover
1999 Nomar Garciaparra, Pedro Martinez,
    others $9
2000 Pedro Martinez and Nomar
    Garciaparra..$9
2001 100th Anniversary Logo with past and
    present players $10
2002 Pedro Martinez, Nomar Garciaparra,
    others $9
2003 16 different players $8

Colorado Rockies

1993 Hologram of Rockies emblem $10
1994-2003 ....None issued

Kansas City Royals

1969 Pitcher inside large R $65
1970 Piniella, Otis, others $10
1971 Piniella, Otis, others $10
1972 Catcher's mitt with face $10
1973 Mayberry, Splittorff, others...............$10
1974 Otis, Mayberry, Splittorff $10
1975 Killebrew, McRae, Mayberry.............$15
1976-77 .... None issued
1978 Fans, Royals pitcher.........................$12
1979 American League players..................$12
1981 Photo of A.L. Champions $12
1982 Royals action photos........................$12
1983 Bronze Royals statue .... $7-$10
1984 Royals jacket and equipment ..... $7-$10
1985 Division championship
    celebration .... $10-$12
1986 Hand wearing World Series ring.... $5-$10
1987 Royals championship pennants ... $5-$8
1988 Fireworks over Royals Stadium........$10
1989 Royals' player locker.........................$10
1990 Royals in action $10
1991 Scoreboard replay $10
1992 Newspaper format $10
1993 Memorabilia collage $10
1994 Caricatures of players $9
1995 Organization of year trophy $7
1996 Players celebrating $7
1997 25th anniv. of Kauffman Stadium $7
1998 Autographed baseballs.......................$6
1999 George Brett in tuxedo $7

2001 Mike Sweeney and Jermaine Dye......$7
2002 Collage of Royals Players $7
2003 Mike Sweeney, Tony Pena.................$7

Detroit Tigers

1934 Batter and Mascot head $1,000
1935-1938 ....None issued
1939 "100 Years of Detroit baseball" $750
1940-1954 ....None issued
1955 Catcher Drawing..............................$300
1956 .... None issued
1957 Tiger sliding into home .... $150-$175
1958 Tiger Hall of Famers, with Cobb $150
1959 Tiger batting and logo......................$150
1960 Tiger Stadium $100
1961 Tiger head and five baseballs.....$50-$100
1962 Tiger head and nine players ....$75-$100
1963 Tiger head $100
1964 Tiger head $65
1965 Bill Freehan $65
1966 Willie Horton $65
1967 Denny McLain $45
1968 Al Kaline .... $40-$60
1969 World Series trophy..........................$45
1970 Tiger hat, bats, baseballs $25
1971 Martin, Kaline, Horton $25
1972 Mickey Lolich $15
1973 Tiger infielder in action $15
1974 Tiger sliding into home $15
1975 Ron LeFlore.............................. $12-$15
1976 75th Anniversary $15
1977 Fidrych, Staub, LeFlore .... $10-$12
1978 .... $8-$12
1979 A. Trammell, L. Whitaker .... $8-$12
1980 Trammell, Whitaker, Morris, others.. $8-$15
1981 Trammell, Whitaker, Morris, others. $7-$15
1982 Clubhouse photo with Gibson $12
1983 H. Greenberg, C. Gehringer $8
1984 Morris, Whitaker, Trammell, others $10-$12
1985 World Championship trophy $8
1986 Sparky Anderson.............................$10
1987 Tiger on top of baseball......................$8
1988 Tiger face, Eye of the Tiger $8
1989 Intend-a-Pennant..............................$10
1990 Roaring into the '90s Tiger $8
1991 Whitaker, Trammell, Fielder, others ..$12

1992 Anderson, Stengel............................$10
1993-2001 .... None issued
2002 Ernie Harwell.................................$8

Minnesota Twins

1961 Twins batters .... $125-$175
1962 Metropolitan Stadium $100
1963 Harmon Killebrew.................... $75-$100
1964 Gloved hand and baseball...............$50
1965 Autographed Twins ball .... $40-$60
1966 Tony Oliva, A.L. Champions $45
1967 Killebrew, Kaat, Oliva .... $25-$35
1968 Jim Kaat, Harmon Killebrew..... $15-$25
1969 Killebrew, Carew, Oliva, others.........$20
1970 Rod Carew $20
1971 Carew, Killebrew, Oliva, others.........$20
1972 Tony Oliva, Harmon Killebrew $15
1973 Frank Quilici $15
1974 Rod Carew .... $20-$25
1975 Rod Carew $15
1976 Rod Carew $25
1977 Past Twins yearbooks.......................$10
1978 Rod Carew $12
1979 Twins batting helmet......................$10
1980 Twins baseball cards $10
1981 20th Anniversary, Rod Carew..... $8-$12
1982 Metrodome $8
1983-1984 .... None issued
1985 Yearbook, scorecard................... $6-$10
1986 25th Anniversary celebration...... $7-$10
1987 Twins uniforms...............................$10
1988 World Champions celebration .... $8-$10
1989 Viola, Puckett, Gaetti, Reardon $10
1990 Carew, Puckett, Oliva $10
1991 Uniform collage .... $5-$7
1992 World Series trophy..........................$10
1993 .... None issued
1994 Twins greats, Killebrew, others $9
1996 Puckett, Molitor, others.......................$7
1997 ....None issued
1998 Molitor, Steinbach, others..................$9
1999 Matt Lawton, Ron Coomer, others......$8
2000 40th Anniversary Collage $8
2001 Kirby Puckett $8
2002 Team Collage Action Shots $8
2003 Team Collage $8

Chicago White Sox

1951 ....$250
1952 White Sox and year $150
1953 Comiskey Park $125
1954 White Sox batter.............................$100
1955 White Sox batter..............................$75
1956 White Sox sliding into home $75
1957 White Sox fielder .... $70-$75
1958 White Sox batter........................ $60-$65
1959 White Sox mascot with hat $125
1960 White Sox fielding..................... $50-$65
1961 White Sox pitching...........................$50
1962 White Sox batting $35

1963 White Sox fielding..................... $15-$25
1964 Fireworks at Comiskey Park..... $30-$40
1965 White Sox uniform #80 .... $25-$35
1966 White Sox batter swinging $35
1967 White Sox in action...........................$20
1968 White Sox batter at plate $20
1969 Tommy John $20
1970 White Sox in action...........................$40
1971-1981 .... None issued
1982 LaRussa, Luzinski, Fisk $10
1983 All-Star Game with Fisk, others........$10
1984 Hoyt, LaRussa, Kittle, Luzinski........$10
1985 .... None issued
1986 Walker, Guillen, J. Davis, Baines......$12
1987 .... None issued
1988 White Sox memorabilia $10
1989 .... None issued
1990 Comiskey Park .... $5-$6
1991 Comiskey Park $5
1992 Good Guys Wear Black.....................$7
1993 Cooperstown Collection $7
1994 Frank Thomas $8
1995 1917 Championship team $8
1996 F. Thomas, R. Ventura, others............$8
1997 F. Thomas, A. Belle $8
1998 Belle, Thomas, Manuel, others...........$7
1999 Five Players......................................$7
2000 Collage of approximately 150 White Sox
    baseball photos $7
2001 Collage of Four Player's Faces and the
    Manager's Face $7
2002 Ballpark Picture $7
2003 Player's Hands Slapping High-Fives ..$7

New York Yankees

1950 Yankees emblem, pennants $350
1951 Balls on shelf......................... $200-$275
1952 Yankee Stadium, action .... $165-$210
1953 Yankees infielder $160
1954 Yankee with World Series bats.......$160
1955 Yankees player drawing..................$275
1956 Yankee sliding into home................$275
1957 Bobby Richardson $275
1958 Yankee Stadium $160
1959 Yankee Stadium .... $140-$160
1960 Yankee Stadium, players ...... $110-$140
1961 Yankee Stadium sketch $160
1962 Yankee Stadium sketch $80
1963 Yankee holding three bats $70
1964 Yogi Berra, Ralph Houk $70
1965 Yankee Player..................................$70
1966 Two autographed balls $55
1967 Mickey Mantle drawing $55
1968 Mantle, Stottlemyre, others $30
1969 Mantle, Stottlemyre, others $55
1970 Murcer, Stottlemyre, others $80
1971 Murcer, White, others $12
1972 Murcer, White, Stottlemyre $25
1973 Ruth, DiMaggio, Mantle, Gehrig.......$25
1974 B. Murcer, T. Munson $25

1975 25th Annual w, past yearbooks $18
1976 Yankees Stadium.............................$30
1977 Chris Chambliss $15
1978 World Series trophy $18
1979 World Series celebration .... $12-$18
1980 Yankee Stadium $10
1981 Yankees Big Apple $18
1982 Winfield, Guidry, Gossage, others....$10
1983 Billy Martin.......................................$8
1984 Yankee greats..................................$18
1985 Maris, Mantle, Ruth, Gehrig $10

1986 Yankees MVPs $7
1987 Gehrig, Mattingly, Mantle.................$12
1988 Mattingly, Clark, Randolph .... $12-$18
1989 Yankees memorabilia $12
1990 Don Mattingly $15
1991 Pitcher vs. batter $12
1992 Don Mattingly $15
1993 Team photo.....................................$12
1994 Yankee greats..................................$15
1995 Babe Ruth $15
1996 Mickey Mantle.................................$15
1997 Championship ring $15
1998 Yankee Stadium at 75 years.............$15
1999 Players celebrating $12
2000 Derek Jeter, the "Century's team" $10
2001 World Series trophy.........................$10
2002 Past & Present Yankees Players $18
2003 100th Anniversary Logo $22

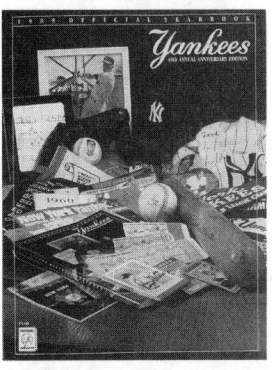

BASKETBALL MEDIA GUIDES

Atlanta Hawks

1968-69 Team mascot...............................$75
1969-70 Lou Hudson...............................$25
1970-71 Atlanta skyline, team art.............$20
1971-72 Richie Guerin, Hawks bench.......$20
1972-73 Team logo.................................$20
1973-74 Overhead shot of Omni court......$20
1974-75 Lou Hudson...............................$20
1975-76 Tom Van Ardsdale......................$20
1976-77 John Drew.................................$15
1977-78 Team logo, artwork.....................$15
1978-79 Team logo, newspaper clips........$15
1979-80 H. Brown, J. Drew, A. Hill..............$8
1980-81 Dan Roundfield vs. Abdul-Jabbar.....$8
1981-82 Action artwork...............................$8
1982-83 Dan Roundfield.............................$8
1983-84 Action artwork...............................$8
1984-85 Dominique Wilkins.........................$8
1985-86 Dominique Wilkins.........................$8
1986-87 Dominique Wilkins.........................$8
1987-88 Dominique Wilkins.........................$8
1988-89 Dominique Wilkins.........................$7
1989-90 M. Malone, D. Rivers, D. Wilkins ...$6
1990-91 "Let's Run One".............................$5
1991-92 Bob Weiss....................................$5
1992-93 Dominique Wilkins, Doc Rivers......$5
1993-94 "Atlanta Hawks Media Guide".......$5
1994-95 L. Wilkins, Red Auerbach..............$8
1995-96 Lenny Wilkins................................$6
1996-97 D. Mutombo...................................$6
1997-98 D. Mutombo, C. Laettner, others ...$6
1998-99 D. Mutombo, others........................$6
1999-00 Six players...................................$10
2000-01 Coach Lon Krueger......................$10
2001-02 Team Logo.....................................$6
2002-03 J. Terry, G. Robinson, Abdur-Rahim,
  Ratliff..$6

Boston Celtics

1951-52 Folder report with plain brown
  cover..$125-$150
1952-53 ....$25-$40
1953-54 ....$25-$40
1954-55 Player photos ....$50-$75
1955-56 Bob Cousy ....$55-$80
1956-57 Player photos ....$50-$75
1957-58 Player photos ....$45-$70
1958-59 Frank Ramsey.....................$40-$65
1959-60 Gene Conley ....$35-$50
1960-61 Boston Garden....................$30-$45
1961-62 Red Auerbach, five starters. $40-$60
1962-63 Bob Cousy ....$40-$60
1963-64 Tom Heinsohn ....$35-$50
1964-65 Boston Garden ....$15-$25
1965-66 ....$20-$30
1966-67 Bill Russell ....$25-$45
1967-68 John Havlicek......................$45-$60
1968-69 Red Auerbach, Bill Russell..........$60
1969-70 Team mascot...............................$45
1970-71 D. Cowens, D. Nelson, J. J. White,
  others..$45
1971-72 D. Cowens, J. Havlicek, J. J. White $45
1972-73 Dave Cowens, John Havlicek......$45
1973-74 Dave Cowens, John Havlicek,
  Jo Jo White...$35
1974-75 John Havlicek, Paul Silas............$30
1975-76 Dave Cowens, John Havlicek......$30
1976-77 Championship trophy $25
1977-78 John Havlicek...............................$20
1978-79 Dave Cowens...............................$20
1979-80 Larry Bird, M.L. Carr $20
1980-81 R. Auerbach, L. Bird, B. Fitch......$15
1981-82 Championship banner, trophy $15
1982-83 Team art, Larry Bird $15
1983-84 Celtics vs. Atlanta Hawks............$15
1984-85 Championship trophy $15
1985-86 Larry Bird $20
1986-87 Larry Bird photos........................$15
1987-88 Larry Bird, four other starters......$15
1988-89 Historical team photos $15
1989-90 Red Auerbach $15
1990-91 Team artwork $15
1991-92 McHale, Bird, Parrish, C. Ford $10
1992-93 Cartoon figures of Bird, others....$10
1993-94 Cartoon mascot, crowd photo.....$10
1994-95 Cartoon mascot, parquet floor $10
1995-96 Fleet Center $8
1996-97 Photos of Celtics greats $8
1997-98 R. Pitino, R. Auerbach...................$8
1998-99 Rick Pitino $8
1999-00 V. Potapenko, A. Walker $10
2000-01 Paul Pierce...................................$10
2001-02 Pierce, A. Walker...........................$8
2002-03 Pierce, A. Walker...........................$8

Chicago Bulls

1966-67 Team logo.................................$50
1967-68 Team logo.................................$45
1968-69 Team logo.................................$35
1969-70 Team logo.................................$25
1970-71 Team logo.................................$20
1971-72 Team logo.................................$20
1972-73 Chet Walker..............................$20
1973-74 Chet Walker..............................$20
1974-75 Team logo, action photos $20
1975-76 Team logo, Jerry Sloan $15
1976-77 Team artwork.............................$15
1977-78 Action photos $15
1978-79 Artis Gilmore $15

1979-80 Artis Gilmore, Jerry Sloan..........$10
1980-81 Reggie Theus.............................$10
1981-82 A. Gilmore, D. Greenwood $10
1982-83 Rod Thorn, Paul Westhead........$10
1983-84 Kevin Loughery $10
1984-85 M. Jordan, O. Woolridge $10
1985-86 S. Albeck, M. Jordan,
  O. Woolridge $35
1986-87 Michael Jordan............................$35
1987-88 Michael Jordan, action photos,
  All-Star Game logo $35
1988-89 B. Cartwright, H. Grant, M. Jordan. $25
1989-90 Bulls comics................................$15
1990-91 25th Anniversary artwork $15
1991-92...$15
1992-93 Bulls back-to-back.......................$15
1993-94 Players entrance to stadium........$12
1994-95 Aerial photo of United Center......$12
1995-96 30th Anniversary logo $10
1996-97 NBA 50th anniversary $15
1997-98 Hand with five rings....................$10
1998-99 Championship trophy $6
1999-00 Basketball....................................$10
2000-01 Elton Brand $10
2002-03 NBA Championship Trophy puzzle .. $7

Cleveland Cavaliers

1970-71 Team logo, year..........................$50
1971-72 Team logo, year..........................$25
1972-73 Team logo, year..........................$25
1973-74 Cavalier artwork $15
1974-75 Team logo, artwork......................$15
1975-76 Cleveland Coliseum $10
1976-77 Team photo $10
1977-78 Team logo, mascot $10
1978-79 C'mon Cavaliers..........................$10
1979-80 A New Era...Cavaliers II $10
1980-81 Team action photos $10
1981-82 Mike Mitchell artwork $10
1982-83 Ron Brewer, city skyline $10
1983-84 New team logo $6
1984-85 15th season Cavs basketball cards...$6
1985-86 Team artwork $6
1986-87 Lenny Wilkens $8
1987-88 B. Daugherty, R. Harper, Hot Rod
  Williams $8
1988-89 Cavaliers vs. Chicago Bulls...........$8
1989-90 20th season, L. Wilkens, action
  photos...$8
1990-91 Team uniform, action photos.........$8
1991-92 Cavs tickets $8
1992-93 Players celebrating........................$8
1993-94 Tickets, The Coliseum...................$8
1994-95 Gund Arena...................................$7
1995-96 Interior photo of Gund Arena $7

1996-97 All-Star action photos $7
1997-98 Shawn Kemp................................$7
1998-99 B. Knight, C. Henderson, others ...$7
1999-00 Price, Carr, Nance, Kemp,
   Dougherty......................................$10
2000-01 Player dribbling basketball $10
2001-02 Andre Miller................................$6
2002-03 R. Davis, D. Miles.......................$6

Dallas Mavericks

1980-81 Dallas Mavericks uniform $15
1981-82 Dallas Reunion Arena $8
1982-83 Dick Motta $8
1983-84 Mark Aguirre $8
1984-85 Rolando Blackman $8
1985-86 Mavericks in action artwork.........$10
1986-87 Derek Harper $10
1987-88 J. Donaldson, J. MacLeod, team
   logo...$10
1988-89 Roy Tarpley..............................$10
1989-90 Brad Davis, 10th Anniversary......$10
1990-91 R. Blackman, D. Harper, F. Lever ...$10
1991-92 D. Harper, R. Blackmon $8
1992-93 Doug Smith $8
1993-94 Jim Jackson $8
1994-95 J. Kidd, J. Mashburn, J. Jackson...$8
1995-96 J. Kidd, J. Mashburn, J. Jackson...$8
1996-97 D. Harper, J. Kidd, others $8
1997-98 Michael Finley $8
1998-99 Michael Finley $8
1999-00 Michael Finley $8
2000-01 Michael Finley $8
2001-02 Nowitzki, Nash $8
2002-03 Nowitzki, Nash, Finley, LaFrentz ...$8

Denver Nuggets

Denver Rockets
1968-69 ....$45
1969-70 Nuggets artwork...........................$35
1970-71 ....$35
1971-72 Ralph Simpson............................$35
1972-73 Alex Hannum...............................$35
1973-74 Team photo $35
Denver Nuggets
1974-75 L. Brown, M. Calvin, C. Scheer ...$20

1975-76 D. Issel, D. Moe, C. Scheer,
   D. Thompson $20
1976-77 Nuggets in action artwork $20
1977-78 Team logo, year...........................$15
1978-79 Team mascot................................$15
1979-80 David Thompson $8
1980-81 Dan Issel $8
1981-82 A. English, D. Issel, D. Thompson .$8
1982-83 Team logo.....................................$8
1983-84 10th Anniversary photos $6
1984-85 Nuggest in action artwork $6
1985-86 Alex English, Calvin Natt..............$8
1986-87 Alex English, team logo.................$8
1987-88 A. English, F. Lever, C. Natt..........$8
1988-89 A. English, F. Lever, D. Moe $8
1989-90 Alex English, city skyline $8
1990-91 Bernie Bickerstaff, Carl Scheer $8
1991-92 NBA Basketball in gift box.............$5
1992-93 Dan Issel $5
1993-94 Nuggets logo $8
1994-95 Get in the Game............................$8
1995-96 Bernie Bickerstaff $6
1996-97 LaPhonso Ellis, Bryant Stith..........$6
1997-98 Bill Hanzlik...................................$6
1998-99 Denver greats, D. Thompson, etc..$7
2001-02 Player Photo Collage $7
2002-03 City of Denver $7

Detroit Pistons

1958-59 ....$100-$125
1960-61 ....$60-$75
1961-62 ....$50-$60
1962-63 ....$50-$60
1963-64 ....$45-$55
1964-65 ....$45-$55
1965-66 ....$45-$55
1967-68 ....$65
1969-70 Happy Hairston $40
1970-71 ....$30
1971-72 ....$25
1972-73 Earl Lloyd $20
1973-74 ....$20
1974-75 Team logo $15
1975-76 Pistons in action artwork, logo $10
1976-77 L. Douglas, E. Money, K. Porter,
   C. Rowe..$10
1977-78 Pistons in action artwork..............$10
1978-79 Pistons in action artwork..............$10
1979-80 Silverdome, team logo $10
1980-81 Player completing tip in $10
1981-82 Kent Benson, Isiah Thomas $10
1982-83 ....$8
1983-84 Isiah Thomas, Kelly Tripucka.........$8
1984-85 Isiah Thomas $8
1985-86 Bill Laimbeer, Isiah Thomas..........$8
1986-87 Isiah Thomas $8
1987-88 Adrian Dantley...............................$8
1988-89 The Palace $8
1989-90 Championship celebration.............$6
1990-91 J. Dumars, I. Thomas, trophies $6

1991-92 J. Dumars, I. Thomas...................$6
1992-93 Chuck Daly....................................$8
1993-94 Basketball with blue seams..........$8
1994-95 B. Laimbeer, J. Dumars, T. Mills,
   I. Thomas..$8
1995-96 Joe Dumars illustration..................$8
1996-97 Grant Hill $8
1997-98 J. Dumars, G. Hill $8
1998-99 Hourglass with "bad boys" and
   current players....................................$8
1999-00 Grant Hill $10
2000-01 Jerry Stackhouse $10
2001-02 Stackhouse, B. Wallace, others.....$7
2002-03 Basketball Floor $7

Golden State Warriors

San Francisco Warriors
1962-63 ....$50
1963-64 ....$25
1964-65 ....$20
1965-66 ....$75
1966-67 ....$35
1967-68 ....$50
1968-69 Team logo....................................$40
1969-70 Nate Thurmond $40
1970-71 Nate Thurmond $30
Golden State Warriors
1971-72 Al Attles $20
1972-73 Nate Thurmond $15
1973-74 Nate Thurmond $15
1974-75 Warriors artwork...........................$15
1975-76 NBA Championship trophy...........$15
1976-77 Al Attles $15
1977-78 Warriors in action artwork $15
1978-79 Warriors in action $10
1979-80 Team logos....................................$8
1980-81 Team logo......................................$8
1981-82 Al Attles $8
1982-83 Basketball......................................$8
1983-84 Still the Best Game in Town $8
1984-85 Warriors in action artwork $8
1985-86 Sleepy Floyd, C. Mullin, P. Short ..$8
1986-87 The New Warriors $8
1987-88 Larry Smith.....................................$8
1988-89 Ralph Sampson...............................$8
1989-90 Chris Mullin $8
1990-91 Warriors in action artwork $8
1991-92 Action artwork $5
1992-93 Notebooks, calculator....................$5
1993-94 Card game with player cards.........$5
1994-95 Cartoon of players using elevator..$8
1995-96 Artwork of jerseys on wash line $6
1996-97 50th anniv. art of Warriors greats ..$6
1997-98 P. J. Carlisimo, lightning bolt.........$6
1998-99 Photo of warmup jersey $12
1999-00 Team photo $12
2000-01 Antawn Jamison, Larry Hughes ..$12
2001-02 Antawn Jamison $6
2002-03 Past & Present Players $6

Houston Rockets

San Diego Rockets
1967-68 Team logo, basketball..................$35
1968-69 Team logo $35
1969-70 Elvin Hayes $25
1970-71 Elvin Hayes $20

Houston Rockets
1971-72 Rockets in action artwork............$20
1972-73 Rockets in action artwork............$20
1973-74 M. Newlin, R. Tomjanovich..........$10
1974-75 Rudy Tomjanovich......................$10
1975-76 Mike Newlin................................$10
1976-77 Calvin Murphy, Tom Nissalke $10
1977-78 John Lucas, R. Tomjanovich $10
1978-79 R. Barry, M. Malone,
  R. Tomjanovich $10
1979-80 Moses Malone............................$10
1980-81 Rockets in action artwork............$10
1981-82 Moses Malone............................$10
1982-83 Elvin Hayes $10
1983-84 Ralph Sampson $10
1984-85 B. Fitch, H. Olajuwon, R. Sampson.$10
1985-86 R. McCray, H. Olajuwon,
  R. Sampson.....................................$10
1986-87 H. Olajuwon, R. Reid, R. Sampson $10
1987-88 Hakeem Olajuwon.......................$10
1988-89 D. Chaney, R. Tomjanovich $10
1989-90 E. Floyd, H. Olajuwon, O. Thorpe...$10
1990-91 20th Anniversary logo $10
1991-92 Rockets on a basketball $8
1992-93 Rockets on a basketball $8
1993-94 Rockets memorabilia...................$10
1994-95 ....$8
1994-95 Players, fans celebrating $8
1995-96 H. Olajuwon, C. Drexler.................$8
1996-97 Olajuwon, Drexler, Barkley............$8
1997-98 Olajuwon, Drexler, Barkley............$8
1998-99 Hakeem Olajuwon photos $8
2000-01 S. Francis, Olajuwon $8
2001-02 C. Mobley, S. Francis..................$8
2002-03 Mobley, Yao Ming, S. Francis $10

Indiana Pacers

1968-69 Mel Daniels $30
1969-70 Mel Daniels $25
1970-71 Roger Brown $20
1971-72 Bob Leonard cartoon $20
1972-73 M. Daniels, B. Leonard,
  G. McGinnis.....................................$20
1973-74 Three ABA trophies.....................$20
1974-75 Market Square Arena $15
1975-76 Team logo...................................$10
1976-77 Billy Knight $10
1977-78 Bob Leonard, team logo..............$10
1978-79 Market Square Arena $10
1979-80 Team logo.....................................$8
1980-81 Year of Excitement $8
1981-82 Jack McKinney $8
1982-83 Herb Williams $8
1983-84 Indianapolis artwork......................$8
1984-85 Pacer Pride" basketball $8
1985-86 Uniform, ball, sneaker artwork $8
1986-87 Herb Williams $8
1987-88 Jack Ramsey, player artwork $8
1988-89 Steve Stipanovich...........................$8
1989-90 Reggie Miller $8
1990-91 Pacers in action artwork................$8
1991-92 D. Schrempf, R. Miller, C. Person..$8
1992-93 D. Davis, R. Smits, R. Miller $8
1993-94 Larry Brown $8
1994-95 Larry Brown, Reggie Miller............$8
1995-96 Rik Smits $7
1996-97 Dale Davis, Antonio Davis.............$7
1997-98 Larry Bird "Back Home Again" $8
1998-99 L. Bird, R. Miller, others................$8
2001-02 Reggie Miller $7
2002-03 Jermaine O'Neal, others $7

Los Angeles Clippers

Buffalo Braves
1970-71 Team logo....................................$20
1971-72 Team logo....................................$20
1972-73 Elmore Smith vs. W. Chamberlain.. $20
1973-74 Team action photo.......................$20
1974-75 Buffalo Braves vs. K. C. Kings.....$20
1975-76 Braves in action...........................$15
1976-77 Team action photos......................$15
1977-78 Buffalo skyline.............................$15

San Diego Clippers
1978-79 Randy Smith $10
1979-80 Bill Walton $8
1980-81 Paul Silas $8
1981-82 Freeman Williams $8
1982-83 Tom Chambers..............................$8
1983-84 Terry Cummings.............................$8
1988-89 Team logo....................................$20
1989-90 Rory Sparrow with a fan...............$12
1990-91 House with basketball in driveway..$12
1991-92 Clippers on blue background $10
1992-93 Newspaper clippings $10
1993-94 10 year anniversary logo..............$8
1994-95 Diagram of basketball court $8

1995-96 Bill Fitch, player huddle $7
1996-97 Clippers logo $7
1997-98 Coach's clipboard.........................$7
1998-99 Montage of player photos.............$6
1999-00 M. Olowakandi, M. Taylor $8
2000-01 Building, Lamar Odom $8
2001-02 Miles, Odom, Brand $8
2002-03 Team Collage $8

Los Angeles Lakers

1960-61 Name, year artwork.......... $75-$125
1966-67 Team logo....................................$50
1967-68 Team logo, year...........................$45
1968-69 Elgin Baylor, Wilt Chamberlain....$45
1969-70 ....$35
1970-71 ....$35
1971-72 ....$35
1972-73 Championship trophy $30
1973-74 Gail Goodrich $30
1974-75 Gail Goodrich $30
1975-76 Kareem Abdul-Jabbar $25
1976-77 Jerry West $20
1977-78 Laker cheerleader in uniform #1 ....$20
1978-79 Kareem Abdul-Jabbar $20
1979-80 K. Abdul-Jabbar, M. Johnson $20
1980-81 K. Abdul-Jabbar, M. Johnson $20
1981-82 The Forum, artwork....................$12
1982-83 K. Abdul-Jabbar, M. Johnson,
  N. Nixon..$12
1983-84 The Forum...................................$12
1984-85 Kareem Abdul-Jabbar $12
1985-86 K. Abdul-Jabbar, championship
  trophy..$12
1986-87 Chick Hearn $12
1987-88 K. Abdul-Jabbar, M. Johnson,
  J. Worthy, trophy $12
1988-89 K. Abdul-Jabbar uniform, locker ..$12
1989-90 Magic Johnson.............................$12
1990-91 M. Johnson, S. Perkins, J. Worthy.. $12
1991-92 M. Johnson, J. Worthy $10
1992-93 Magic Johnson photos $10
1993-94 Caricatures of J. West, others.....$10
1994-95 Magic Johnson, others................$10
1995-96 D. Harris, N. Van Exel, others........$8
1996-97 S. O'Neal with jerseys $9
1997-98 S. O'Neal, N. Van Exel, E. Jones ..$8
1998-99 Shaq dunking $7
1999-00 Sketch of Phil Jackson $10
2000-01 Shaq O'Neal, Kobe Bryant..........$10
2001-02 Back 2 Back Champions $10
2002-03 Chick Hearn $10

Miami Heat

1993-94 Art of generic player.....................$9
1994-95 Art of three generic players...........$8
1995-96 P. Riley, P.J. Brown, H. Miner,
  G. Rice...$8
1996-97 P. Riley, A. Mourning, others $7
1997-98 A. Mourning, J. Mashburn, others .$7

1998-99 P. Riley, A. Mourning, T. Hardaway ...$7
1999-00 New arena, Alonzo Mourning......$10
2000-01 Seven players.............................$10
2001-02 American Flag...........................$7
2002-03 15 Year Anniversary $7

Milwaukee Bucks

1968-69 Bucks vs. Royals, W. Embry $30
1969-70 Team logo $25
1970-71 Kareem Abdul-Jabbar $25
1971-72 Kareem Abdul-Jabbar $25
1972-73 Kareem Abdul-Jabbar $25
1973-74 Lucius Allen................................$20
1974-75 K. Abdul-Jabbar, city skyline $20
1975-76 Bucks vs. Chicago Bulls action ...$15
1976-77 Gary Brokaw $15
1977-78 Brian Winters $15
1978-79 Marques Johnson artwork..........$15
1979-80 Five starters artwork $8
1980-81 Team artwork $8
1981-82 Sidney Moncrief $8
1982-83 Bucks artwork $8
1983-84 M. Johnson, S. Moncrief, D. Nelson .$6
1984-85 Sidney Moncrief $6
1985-86 Paul Pressey $8
1986-87 Sidney Moncrief, city skyline $8
1987-88 20th anniversary artwork $8
1988-89 Bucks vs. Houston Rockets...........$8
1989-90 Del Harris $8
1990-91 Action photos $8
1991-92 D. Harris, seven players $8
1992-93 M. Dunleavy, M. Malone................$8
1993-94 T. Day, B. Edwards, F. Brickowski..$8
1994-95 G. Robinson, V. Baker hologram
    inset $8
1995-96 V. Baker, G. Robinson $8
1996-97 G. Robinson, Vin Baker $8
1997-98 Art of Bucks all-time greats $8
1998-99 George Karl...................................$8
1999-00 George Karl, six players..............$10
2000-01 G. Robinson, R. Allen, others $10
2001-02 Cassell, Allen, G. Robinson,
    Thomas...$8
2002-03 Bucks Jerseys $8

Minnesota Timberwolves

1989-90 Team logo....................................$12
1990-91 Timberwolves basketball.............$12
1991-92 Ball going through a hoop $10
1992-93 Closeup of a Wolf's head $10
1993-94 Wolf howling at moon $8
1994-95 Wolf on basketball court................$8
1995-96 Trees with wolf in background $7
1996-97 Kevin Garnett $7
1997-98 K. Garnett, T. Gugliotta, S. Marbury ..$7
1998-99 Team logo on white background ...$7
1999-00 Kevin Garnett $10
2000-01 K. Garnett, T. Brandon $10
2001-02 Garnett, Szczerbiak, Brandon.......$8

New Jersey Nets

New York Nets
1968-69 Nets in action .... $15-$25
1969-70 .... $10-$20
1970-71 Nets player in action............. $7-$10
1971-72 Rick Barry, others .... $8-$12
1972-73 Eastern Div. Playoff Champions..$30
1973-74 Julius Erving................................$30
1974-75 Dave DeBusschere, Rowe $20
1975-76 Julius Erving................................$20
1976-77 Julius Erving................................$15

New Jersey Nets
1977-78 State of New Jersey, artwork $15
1978-79 Jordan, B. King, J. Williamson $15
1979-80 The Excitement is Building..........$10
1980-81 Up & Coming...............................$10
1981-82 A New Era logo $10
1982-83 Darryl Dawkins, Mike Gminski $6
1983-84 Nets in action artwork $6
1984-85 Darryl Dawkins.............................$6
1985-86 Buck Williams..............................$10
1986-87 Mike Gminski...............................$10
1987-88 M. Gminski, B. Williams,
    O. Woolridge...$10
1988-89 Donaldson, Reed, B. Williams.....$10
1989-90 Roy Hinson.................................$10
1990-91 Nets in action artwork $8
1991-92 D. Coleman, M. Blaylock, others ...$8
1992-93 Chuck Daly $8
1993-94 Derrick Coleman $8
1994-95 Kenny Anderson...........................$8
1995-96 A. Gilliam, P.J. Brown $7
1996-97 J. Calipari, S. Bradley, others $7
1997-98 S. Cassell, C. Gatling, others $7
1998-99 Road jersey No. 98......................$7
1999-00 S. Marbury, K. Van Horn $10
2000-01 K. Van Horn, Coach Scott $10
2001-02 Nets Jersey $8
2002-03 J. Kidd holding Trophy $8

New Orleans Hornets

Charlotte Hornets
1988-89 David Stern, G. Shinn, Hornets
    uniform..$25
1989-90 NBA attendance, championship
    banner..$10
1990-91 Gene Little photos $8
1991-92 Larry Johnson $5
1992-93 Larry Johnson photos $5
1993-94 Alonzo Mourning $5
1994-95 Muggsey Bogues, Del Curry $8
1995-96 L. Johnson, A. Mourning $6
1996-97 Dave Cowans $6
1997-98 A. Mason, G. Rice, D. Cowans......$6
1998-99 Hornets starting five $6
1999-00 Designed image $10
2000-01 Coach, six players $10
2001-02 B. Davis, Mashburn $5

New Orleans Hornets
2002-03 B. Davis, Mashburn $8

New York Knicks

1956-57 ....$95
1957-58 ....$95
1958-59 ....$75
1959-60 ....$75
1960-61 ....$75
1961-62 ....$75
1962-63 ....$65
1963-64 ....$65
1964-65 ....$35
1965-66 ....$35
1966-67 Cartoon player...............................$35
1967-68 ....$45
1968-69 ....$45
1969-70 D. DeBusschere, W. Reed...........$45
1970-71 ....$40
1971-72 Reed, DeBusschere, Frazier $25
1972-73 ....$25
1973-74 Championship trophy $30
1974-75 Bill Bradley uniform $20
1975-76 ....$15
1976-77 Earl Monroe $15
1977-78 Willis Reed $15
1978-79 Earl Monroe, Marvin Webster $10
1979-80 Bill Cartwright................................$10
1980-81 B. Cartwright, R. Holzman,
    J. Richardson..$10
1981-82 City skyline $10
1982-83 Hubie Brown $10
1983-84 Knicks in action $10
1984-85 Action artwork $10
1985-86 B. Cartwright, P. Ewing, B. King ..$10
1986-87 Uniforms, locker $10
1987-88 Al Bianchi, Rick Pitino $10
1988-89 P. Ewing, M. Jackson, C. Oakley.... $10
1989-90 P. Ewing, M. Jackson, S. Jackson..$10
1990-91 Patrick Ewing art $10
1991-92 P. Riley, R. Holtzman $8
1992-93 Logo, newspaper headlines $8
1993-94 Patrick Ewing $8
1994-95 Ewing, Oakley, Starks $9
1995-96 Don Nelson, P. Ewing, others........$7
1996-97 Golden Anniversary logo...............$7
1997-98 Knicks all-time greats $7

1998-99 Red Holtzman $7
1999-00 Designed photo $7
2000-01 Artwork of New York......................$7
2001-02 Madison Square Garden..............$7
2002-03 New York City Street $7

Orlando Magic

1989-90 Magic artwork...............................$20
1990-91 Matt Goukas................................$15
1991-92 S. Skiles, D. Scott, N. Anderson..$10
1992-93 Shaquille O'Neal $10
1993-94 Shaquille O'Neal dunking............$10
1994-95 H. Grant, A. Hardaway, S. O'Neal,
  D. Scott, N. Anderson $10
1995-96 B. Hill, Hardaway, Shaq, others.....$9
1996-97 Hill, Hardaway, Anderson, Grant ...$9
1997-98 C. Daly, A. Hardaway, J. Erving.....$9
1998-99 10th anniversary logo, Rich Devos,
  Pat Williams, others $8
2001-02 Player's Headshots $7

Philadelphia 76ers

1966-67 ....$45
1967-68 W. Chamberlain, B. Cunningham...$45
1968-69 Hal Greer $45
1969-70 Billy Cunningham, Hal Greer $35
1970-71 Team pictures artwork.................$20
1971-72 Team mascot...............................$20
1972-73 J. Block, B. Bridges, F. Carter $20
1973-74 Gene Shue....................................$20
1974-75 Billy Cunningham, Gene Shue....$15
1975-76 H. Catchings, B. Cunningham,
  G. McGinnis..$15
1976-77 Doug Collins, George McGinnis..$15
1977-78 Julius Erving.................................$15
1978-79 D. Collins, J. Erving, B. Jones $15
1979-80 Julius Erving.................................$15
1980-81 76ers basketball...........................$15
1981-82 Julius Erving, trophies $15
1982-83 Julius Erving.................................$15
1983-84 Julius Erving, Moses Malone $10
1984-85 Julius Erving.................................$10
1985-86 Moses Malone..............................$10
1986-87 Charles Barkley............................$10
1987-88 M. Cheeks, 25th Anniversary $10
1988-89 C. Barkley, M. Cheeks.................$10
1989-90 Charles Barkley............................$10
1990-91 Charles Barkley............................$10
1991-92 Jim Lynam, C. Barkley, H. Hawkins $10
1992-93 Hersey Hawkins $10
1993-94 ....$10
1994-95 76er greats, J. Erving, etc. $10
1995-96 Huge basketball, "It's Real" $8
1996-97 A. Iverson, Stackhouse, others $8
1997-98 Larry Brown...................................$7
1998-99 76er greats, A. Iverson, T. Ratliff...$7
1999-00 A. Iverson, J. Jones, M. Geiger ...$10
2000-01 A. Iverson, G. Lynch, others........$10
2001-02 Basketball Trophy $7

Phoenix Suns

1968-69 Team logo, year $35
1969-70 Team logo, year...........................$35
1970-71 Team logo, year...........................$20
1971-72 Connie Hawkins $20
1972-73 Suns in action $20
1973-74 Charlie Scott, Neil Walk $15
1974-75 Team logo, year $15
1975-76 Team logo, year............................$15
1976-77 Alvan Adams $10
1977-78 Paul Westphal $10
1978-79 W. Davis, R. Lee, P. Westphal $10
1979-80 John MacLeod $10
1980-81 Alvan Adams $8
1981-82 Computer graphics picture $8
1982-83 Basketball......................................$6
1983-84 Larry Nance $6
1984-85 Walter Davis $6
1985-86 Catch our Fire, team logo..............$8
1986-87 Suns artwork................................$10
1987-88 Suns basketball...........................$10
1988-89 T. Chambers, J. Hornacek, others..$10
1989-90 T. Chambers, C. Fitzsimmons,
  K. Johnson...$10
1990-91 Suns basketball...........................$10
1991-92 ....$10
1992-93 25th Anniversary, action photos ..$10
1993-94 C. Barkley, downtown Phoenix $10
1994-95 "Playing with Fire" $10
1995-96 ....$8
1996-97 A. C. Green, M. Finley, others $8
1997-98 ....$8
1998-99 Outstretched arms at tipoff............$8
1999-00 ....$8
2000-01 J. Kidd, A. Hardaway, S. Skiles $8
2001-02 Collage of Suns Players $8
2002-03 Basketball in player's hand............$8

Portland Trailblazers

1970-71 Rick Adelman $25
1971-72 Geoff Petrie $25
1972-73 Sidney Wicks................................$20
1973-74 Jack McCloskey $20

1974-75 Bill Walton $20
1975-76 Lenny Steele $15
1976-77 Bill Walton $15
1977-78 Bill Walton, NBA Champs $15
1978-79 Maurice Lucas..............................$10
1979-80 Jack Ramsey, Bill Walton $10
1980-81 Billy Bates $10
1981-82 Jim Paxson $10
1982-83 Mychal Thompson $10
1983-84 Calvin Natt....................................$10
1984-85 Sam Bowie, Kiki Vandeweghe.....$10
1985-86 Clyde Drexler $10
1986-87 Kiki Vandeweghe..........................$10
1987-88 Steve Johnson...............................$10
1988-89 Kevin Duckworth $10
1989-90 Rick Adelman, 20th anniversary $10
1990-91 Western Conference Champs.....$10
1991-92 Clyde Drexler $8
1992-93 C. Drexler, others $8
1993-94 Harry Glickman $8
1994-95 Trailblazers memorabilia...............$8
1995-96 Rose Garden Arena $6
1996-97 Arvydas Sabonis $6
1997-98 Kelvin Cato $6
1998-99 Caracatures of R. Wallace, others ... $6
2001-02 Maurice Cheeks $6

Sacramento Kings

Cincinnati Royals

1957-58 World wearing a Royals crown ..$100
1958-59 Basketball wearing Royals crown $100
1959-60 Basketball wearing Royals crown$75
1960-61 Team mascot cartoon.....................$75
1961-62 Team mascot, snake charmer.....$75
1962-63 Team mascot, with briefcase.......$75
1963-64 ....$75
1964-65 ....$75
1965-66 ....$75
1966-67 ....$75
1967-68 Ed Tucker art................................$75
1968-69 O. Robertson, W. Chamberlain ...$75
1969-70 Bob Cousy....................................$75
1970-71 N. Archibald, T. Van Ardsdale,
  N. Van Lier...$25
1971-72 Royals patch $25

Kansas City-Omaha Kings

1972-73 Team logo.....................................$35
1973-74 Nate Archibald, Bob Cousy $25
1974-75 Phil Johnson, artwork.................$20

Kansas City Kings

1975-76 Nate Archibald, Phil Johnson $15
1976-77 Five starters $15
1977-78 L. Allen, O. Birdsong, T. Burleson ..$10
1978-79 Team logo.....................................$10
1979-80 Team logo, player $8
1980-81 Scott Wedman, Reggie King $8
1981-82 Phil Ford..$8
1982-83 Axelson, Fitzsimmons, scoreboard..$6
1983-84 Team logo......................................$6

1984-85 Team photo $6

Sacramento Kings

1985-86 Team logo $6
1986-87 Kings fans in crowd $8
1987-88 We"re Building Together................$8
1988-89 Kenny Smith $8
1989-90 D. Ainge, R. McCray, W. Tisdale ...$8
1990-91 A. Bonner, L. Simmons, others $8
1991-92 W. Tisdale, dance team.................$8
1992-93 Spud Webb, Mitch Richmond........$8
1993-94 Basketball background, players $8
1994-95 Mitch Richmond $8
1995-96 Gary St. Jean, players..................$7
1996-97 Mitch Richmond $7
1997-98 Eddie Jordan $7
1998-99 Rick Adelman, player photos........$7
1999-00 Chris Webber $7
2001-02 Chris Webber $7
2002-03 Coach Adelman & five players $7

San Antonio Spurs

1973-74 Hemisfair Arena $20
1974-75 Team logo $15
1975-76 G. Gervin, J. Silas, others $15
1976-77 James Silas $10
1977-78 George Gervin $10
1978-79 Billy Paultz..................................$10
1979-80 Team logo $10
1980-81 Stan Albeck...................................$8
1981-82 George Gervin, Bruise Brothers....$8
1982-83 G. Gervin, A. Gilmore, M. Mitchell $6
1983-84 Artis Gilmore $6
1984-85 Cotton Fitzsimmons $6
1985-86 Mike Mitchell $8
1986-87 Alvin Robertson..............................$8
1987-88 Johnny Moore, Alvin Robertson....$8
1988-89 Larry Brown...................................$8
1989-90 T. Cummings, S. Elliott,
    D. Robinson $10
1990-91 David Robinson.............................$8
1991-92 David Robinson.............................$8
1992-93 20th Anniversary flag $8
1993-94 Alamodome....................................$8
1994-95 B. Hill, D. Robinson, others $8
1995-96 David Robinson.............................$7
1996-97 D. Robinson dunking $7
1997-98 T. Duncan, D. Robinson, G. Gervin ..$7
1998-99 T. Duncan, D. Robinson, A. Johnson.$7
1999-00 Tim Duncan, David Robinson $7
2000-01 Tim Duncan, David Robinson $7
2001-02 Tim Duncan...................................$7
2002-03 SBC Center...................................$7

Seattle Supersonics

1967-68 Team name, year $35
1968-69 B. Rule, T. Meschery, R. Thorn ...$30
1969-70 Lenny Wilkens...............................$25
1970-71 Basketball, year............................$20
1971-72 Sonics in action............................$20

1972-73 Spencer Haywood......................$20
1973-74 City skyline.................................$15
1974-75 F. Brown, B. Russell, S. Watts.....$15
1975-76 Photo montage...........................$10
1976-77 Sonics basketball $10
1977-78 Great Stuff! $10
1978-79 John Johnson, Jack Sikma $10
1979-80 Dennis Johnson $8
1980-81 Lonnie Shelton $8
1981-82 Jack Sikma $8
1982-83 Gus Williams $6
1983-84 Fred Brown $6
1984-85 Team logo......................................$6
1985-86 Sonics artwork $10
1986-87 T. Chambers, X. McDaniel $10
1987-88 Bernie Bickerstaff $10
1988-89 Sonics equipment, locker $10
1989-90 Derrick McKey $7
1990-91 K. C. Jones....................................$7
1991-92 25th Anniv. logo, Sonics greats ...$7
1992-93 Basketball......................................$7
1993-94 Shawn Kemp, Gary Payton $6
1994-95 Shawn Kemp $6
1995-96 Team logo......................................$6
1996-97 Gary Payton $6
1997-98 Gary Payton $6
1998-99 Logo, artwork $6
1999-00 Gary Payton, Vin Baker...............$10
2000-01 G. Payton, V. Baker, R. Lewis......$10
2001-02 Coach Nate McMillan $8
2002-03 Coach Nate McMillan $7

Toronto Raptors

1995-96 Raptors logo..................................$8
1996-97 Collage, Damon Stoudamire $7
1997-98 D. Stoudamire, M. Camby, others.....$7
1998-99 Player, crystal ball, new arena $7
1999-00 V. Carter, T. McGrady, C. Oakley....$10
2000-01 Vince Carter.................................$10
2002-03 Puzzle Pieces Photos $7

Utah Jazz

New Orleans Jazz

1974-75 New Orleans scene, logo...........$20
1975-76 ....$20
1976-77 Pete Maravich $15
1977-78 ....$10
1978-79 P. Maravich, L. Robinson.............$10

Utah Jazz

1979-80 Salt Palace $8
1980-81 Adrian Dantley, Tom Nissalke........$8
1981-82 Adrian Dantley................................$8
1982-83 A. Dantley, D. Griffith, F. Layden....$8
1983-84 Mark Eaton, Rickey Green $6
1984-85 A Winning Combination $6
1985-86 T. Bailey, K. Malone, J. Stockton.....$10
1986-87 Mark Eaton...................................$10
1987-88 T. Bailey, M. Eaton, K. Malone $10
1988-89 Karl Malone, 10th Anniversary $10

1989-90 Team logo....................................$10
1990-91 Jerry Sloan photos $10
1991-92 Player and arena caricatures $8
1992-93 Jazz memorabilia $8
1993-94 Basketball and logo......................$8
1994-95 Basketball going through hoop......$8
1995-96 Player's arm, "I Love Basketball"...$7
1996-97 Logo, "I Love Basketball".............$7
1997-98 J. Stockton, K. Malone, J. Hornacek .$7
1998-99 Jazz logo, Silver Anniversary logo.....$7
1999-00 Basketball and logo......................$7
2000-01 Jazz logo, slogan..........................$7
2001-02 John Stockton $7
2002-03 Fans and Players $10

Vancouver Grizzlies

1995-96 Shadow figure, basketball court ...$8
1996-97 G. Anthony, B. Reeves $7
1997-98 B. Reeves, R. Rogers, others........$7
1998-99 B. Reeves, Abdur-Rahim, M. Smith..$7
1999-00 B. Hill, Abdur-Rahim, M. Bibby......$7
2000-01 Abdur-Rahim, B. Reeves, others...$7
2002-03 P. Gasol, S. Battier, Jerry West ...$10

Washington Wizards

Baltimore Bullets

1964-65 Gus Johnson $40
1965-66 Media equipment.........................$35
1966-67 Media equipment.........................$35
1967-68 20th Anniversary of basketball in
    Baltimore $35
1968-69 Bullets in action $35
1969-70 E. Monroe, G. Shue, W. Unseld ..$30
1970-71 Wes Unseld.................................$30
1971-72 Team artwork $20
1972-73 Bullets in action $20

Capital Bullets

1973-74 K.C. Jones, five starters $20

Washington Bullets

1974-75 Elvin Hayes $15
1975-76 P. Chenier, E. Hayes, W. Unseld $15
1976-77 Dick Motta $10
1977-78 E. Hayes, M. Kupchak, W. Unseld,
    others $10
1978-79 The Fat Lady Sang, NBA Champs $10
1979-80 Championship trophy $8
1980-81 E. Hayes, K. Porter, G. Shue,
    W. Unseld $8
1981-82 Action photos $8
1982-83 G. Ballard, J. Lucas, J. Ruland......$8
1983-84 Rick Mahorn, Jeff Ruland..............$8
1984-85 G. Ballard, R. Mahorn, J. Ruland ..$8
1985-86 Action artwork $8
1986-87 Moses Malone..............................$8
1987-88 M. Malone, Washington Monument. $8
1988-89 Wes Unseld...................................$8
1989-90 T. Hammonds, B. King, W. Unseld... $8
1990-91 T. Hammonds, B. King, W. Unseld... $8
1991-92 Bernard King $8

1992-93 Harvey Grant, Purvis Ellison $8
1993-94 Puzzle w/ R. Chapman, others $8
1994-95 Illustration of uniforms $8
1995-96 Montage of players........................$7
1996-97 Montage of players........................$7
Washington Wizards
1997-98 MCI Center and game ticket $7
1998-99 Mitch Richmond $7
1999-00 M. Richmond, others....................$10
2000-01 M. Richmond, M. Jordan, others $10
2001-02 Jordan, Hamilton, K. Brown,
   C. Alexander....................................$7
2002-03 Pride, Courage, Committment,
   Passion...$10

American Basketball Association Media Guides

ABA media guides have long been popular and, usually, resonably priced keepsakes. The advent of online auctions has opened a whole new world of product, so most media guides after the first season of 1967-'68 range from $5 to $25. With a few exceptions, after the first season every team produced a standard-sized guide that fit into a binder.

1967-68 Anaheim Amigos (orange cover)...$100
1967-68 Denver Rockets..........................$50
1967-68 Minnesota Muskies $45
1967-68 New Orleans Buccaneers $50
1967-68 Dallas Chaparrals.......................$55
1967-68 Oakland Oaks $55
1970-71 Pittsburgh Condors
   (Brisker cover) $35
1975-76 Spirits of St. Louis (Barnes cover).. $25
1972-73 Virginia Squires (Dr. J cover) $45
1973-74 New York Nets (Dr. J cover) $25

FOOTBALL MEDIA GUIDES

Arizona Cardinals

Chicago Cardinals
1947 Team logo and 1947........................$50
1948 Team logo and 1948........................$50
1949 Team logo and 1949........................$50
1950 Team logo and 1950........................$40
1951 Team logo and 1951........................$40
1952 Team logo and 1952........................$40
1953 Team logo and 1953........................$40
1954 Team logo and 1954........................$40
1955 Team logo and 1955........................$40
1956 Team logo and 1956........................$40
1957 Team logo and 1957........................$40
1958 Team logo and 1958........................$40
1959 Team logo and 1959........................$40
St. Louis Cardinals
1960 Team mascot and 1960 ....$27
1961 Team mascot and 1961 ....$27
1962 Team mascot and 1962 ....$27
1963 Charley Johnson, Wally Lemm........$27
1964 Bobby Joe Conrad $27
1965 Jim Bakken $27
1966 Busch Stadium $27
1967 Larry Wilson $27
1968 Jim Hart, Johnny Roland.................$27
1969 Dave Williams.................................$27
1970 Cardinals in action..........................$13
1971 Team helmets..................................$13
1972 Team helmet, St. Louis Arch $13
1973 Jim Bakken......................................$15
1974 Busch Stadium $13
1975 D. Coryell, J. Hart, T. Metcalf...........$13
1976 Jim Hart...$15
1977 Cardinals vs. Dallas Cowboys.........$13
1978 St. Louis Cardinals greats $13
1979 Cardinals in action..........................$13
1980 Cardinals in action............................$6
1981 Cardinals in action............................$6
1982 Stump Mitchell..................................$6
1983 Team helmets $6

1984 25th Anniversary in St. Louis $6
1985 Team mascot, St. Louis Arch..............$6
1986 Gene Stallings $6
1987 Cardinals uniform #87 ....$6
Phoenix Cardinals
1988 N. Lomax, V. Sikahema, L. Sharpe,
   others..$6
1989 Cardinals in the desert $6
1990 Cardinals defense $6
1991Timm Rosenbach, Ken Harvey $6
1992 Greg Davis, Rich Camarillo $6
1993 Eric Swann, others $6
Arizona Cardinals
1994 Art of Buddy Ryan $6
1995 Eric Hill, fireworks.............................$6
1996 V. Tobin, A. Williams, R. Moore $6
1997 Lomas Brown $6
1998 Collage of Cardinals history $6
1999 Several players..................................$8
2000 David Boston $8
2001 Head Coach Dave McGinnis $8
2002 Player Snapshots $6

Atlanta Falcons

1966 Randy Johnson $27
1967 Team helmet.....................................$27
1968 R. Johnson, B. Lothridge, T. Nobis,
   others..$27
1969 Four Falcons linemen $27
1970 Falcons in action $19
1971 Falcon in action $16
1972 Bob Berry $16
1973 Team logos $16
1974 Bob Lee, offensive line $13
1975 Marion Campbell $13
1976 Jim Mitchell $13
1977 Steve Bartkowski $13
1978 The new training complex..................$13
1979 Falcons defensive line $12
1980 Falcons in action $10
1981 Falcons offensive...............................$9
1982 Three Falcons in action $9
1983 Team helmet, city skyline $9
1984 W. Andrews, B. Curry, B. Johnson......$9
1985 S. Bailey, R. Bryan, G. Riggs..............$9
1986 Team helmet and falcon $6
1987 Falcons media equipment $6
1988 Putting it all Together.........................$6
1989 Chris Miller $6
1990 25th Anniversary logo $6
1991 Falcons helmet..................................$6
1992 Georgia Dome...................................$6
1993 Falcon..$6
1994 Falcon..$5
1995 Football cards of eight players............$5

1996 Jessie Tuggle....................................$5
1997 Dan Reeves $5
1998 Falcons helmet $6
1999 NFC Championship Trophy $6
2000 Georgia Dome & Players....................$6
2001 Pregame Tailgate Party $6
2002 Helmet...$6

Baltimore Ravens

1996 Painting of bird $7
1997 Logo, Memorial Stadium $6
1998 Logo, artwork of new stadium $6
1999 Pro Bowl players...............................$10
2000 Brian Billick......................................$10
2001 Super Bowl trophy $10
2002 Brian Billick & Ozzie Newsome $6

Buffalo Bills

1960 Team logo and 1960........................$27
1961 Team mascot and 1961 ....$27
1962 Team mascot and 1962 ....$27
1963 Team mascot and 1963 ....$27
1964 Team logo and 1964.........................$27
1965 Team logo and 1965 ....$27
1966 Team picture.....................................$27
1967 Bills in action $27
1968 Bills in action $27
1969 John Rauch $27
1970 O.J. Simpson $30
1971 Dennis Shaw $16
1972 Dennis Shaw, O.J. Simpson $20
1973 Bills Stadium.....................................$16
1974 O.J. Simpson $20
1975 Tony Greene $13
1976 Team helmet......................................$13
1977 Team logo..$13
1978 Chuck Knox $13
1979 20th Anniversary photos $13
1980 J. Butler, J. Ferguson, J. Haslett........$9
1981 Joe Cribbs, Eastern Division
   Championship celebration $9

1982 Team helmet $9
1983 Buffalo $9
1984 25th Anniversary logo $9
1985 Past and present team helmets..........$9
1986 Scott Norwood $6
1987 Team helmet $6
1988 C. Bennett, J. Kelly, B. Smith, others ..$7
1989 Scott Norwood, others......................$6
1990 Team helmet and uniform..................$6
1991 Bills helmet......................................$6
1992 M. Levy, T. Thomas, J. Kelly $6
1993 Bills helmet......................................$6
1994 35 year logo.....................................$6
1995 J. Kelly, others $6
1996 Marv Levy...$6
1997 Thurman Thomas $6
1998 Bills lineman $6
1999 B. Smith, T. Washington, others. $10
2000 A. Winfield, E. Moulds, others $10
2001 E. Moulds, S. Cowart, R. Brown.......$10
2002 Drew Bledsoe $6

Carolina Panthers

1995 Inaugural painting of #95..................$8
1996 Artwork of panther sculpture $6
1997 Artwork of Sam Mills $6
1998 Panther logo on raised format $6
1999 Black with Panther............................$7
2000 Black with Panther............................$7
2001 Black with Panther............................$7
2002 Panther Drawing...............................$6

Chicago Bears

1934 Name and 1934................................$70
1935 Beattie Feathers $70
1936 Jack Manders $70
1937 ....$70
1938 ....$70
1939 ....$70
1940 ....$50
1941 Bears in action $50
1942 Bears in action $50
1943 Bears in action $50
1944 George Wilson $50
1945 Team picture....................................$50
1946 Name and 1946................................$50
1947 Bear sprawled over football $50
1948 Team mascot $50
1949 Team mascot $50
1950 Team mascot $40
1951 Team mascot $40
1952 Team mascot $40
1953 Team mascot $40
1954 Name and 1954................................$40
1955 Bears in action $40
1956 Bears in action $40
1957 Bears in action $40
1958 Team mascot $40
1959 Team picture....................................$40

1960 Team mascot $27
1961 Team mascot $27
1962 Bears in action $27
1963 Team mascot and 1963 ....$27
1964 World Champions banner.................$27
1965 Bears in action $27
1966 Bears action photos $27
1967 Bears in action $27
1968 Team helmet and 1968....................$27
1969 Golden Anniversary helmets $27
1970 Helmet and 1970 ....$13
1971 Helmet and 1971 ....$13
1972 Helmet and 1972 ....$13
1973 Abe Gibron $13
1974 Helmet and 1974 ....$13
1975 Doug Buffone $13
1976 Helmet and 1976 ....$13
1977 Jack Pardee $13
1978 Team logo and 1978.........................$13
1979 Bears in action $13
1980 George Halas $7
1981 Home of the Bears $7
1982 Mike Ditka $7
1983 Mike Ditka, George Halas $7
1984 Walter Payton $9
1985 Bears in action $7
1986 Bears in action $7
1987 R. Grange, B. Nagurski, W. Payton,
   G. Sayers $7
1988 Team helmet $7
1989 Bears equipment $6
1990 Team helmet.....................................$6
1991 B. George, D. Butkus, M. Singletary...$6
1992 Nine photos of Mike Ditka $6
1993 M. McCaskey, D. Wannstedt...............$6
1994 Memorabilia $6
1995 Helmet, hands holding up sign $6
1996 Bears defense in action $6
1997 Halas Hall, R. Harris, R. Salaam $6
1998 Curtis Conway $6
1999 Photo of Soldier Field........................$8
2000 Team photo.......................................$8
2001 Bear head...$8
2002 Players Huddled $6

Cincinnati Bengals

1968 Paul Brown $27
1969 Riverfront Stadium...........................$27
1970 Date Book and Media Guide, 1970 ..$13
1971 Date Book and Media Guide, 1971 ..$13
1972 Date Book and Media Guide, 1972 ..$13
1973 Date Book and Media Guide, 1973 ..$13
1974 Artwork of player over stadium $13
1975 Bengals in action $13
1976 Ken Anderson...................................$15
1977 Riverfront Stadium...........................$13
1978 Riverfront Stadium...........................$13
1979 Team helmets $13
1980 Tiger, Bengals in action $7

1981 New uniform $7
1982 K. Anderson, B. Bush, D. Lapham,
   Tiger $7
1983 Team helmet $7
1984 Ken Anderson....................................$7
1985 Cris Collinsworth $7
1986 Boomer Esiason................................$7
1987 J. Brooks, E. Brown, B. Esiason,
   others $7
1988 Tiger $6
1989 Tiger $6
1990 Tiger $6
1991 Drawing of Tiger $6
1992 Tiger artwork, 25th Anniversary $6
1993 Bengal Tiger $6
1994 Bengals helmet..................................$6
1995 Orange and black swirl $6
1996 J . Blake, C. Pickens high fiving $6
1997 Tiger $6
1998 Tiger $6
1999 Cincinnati skyline...............................$8
2000 Sketch of Paul Brown Stadium $8
2001 Photo of Paul Brown Stadium.............$8
2002 Tiger Drawing.....................................$6

Cleveland Browns

1949 Team mascot $50
1950 Cleveland Stadium and crowd..........$50
1951 Name and 1951................................$50
1952 Paul Brown $50
1953 Cartoon Brown $45
1954 Media equipment..............................$45
1955 Cartoon reporter...............................$45
1956 Cartoon reporter...............................$45
1957 Coach and player $40
1958 Browns in action $40
1959 Browns in action $40
1960 Team mascot and helmet $27
1961 Team mascot and helmet $27
1962 Jim Brown...$30
1963 Jim Brown...$30
1964 Jim Brown...$30
1965 Team helmet......................................$27
1966 Action pictures..................................$27
1967 Leroy Kelly $27
1968 Team helmet.....................................$27
1969 Team helmet.....................................$27
1970 Team helmet.....................................$13
1971 Team helmet.....................................$13
1972 Team helmet.....................................$13
1973 Team helmet.....................................$13
1974 Team helmet.....................................$13
1975 Team helmet.....................................$13
1976 Team helmet.....................................$13
1977 Team helmet.....................................$13
1978 Team helmet.....................................$13
1979 Browns in action $13
1980 Sam Rutigliano $6
1981 Brian Sipe...$7

1982 Team helmet and Cleveland $6
1983 Browns defense in action $6
1984 Ozzie Newsome $8
1985 C. Matthews, M. Schottenheimer $6
1986 Earnest Byner, Kevin Mack $6
1987 Bernie Kosar $6
1988 Earnest Byner, Bernie Kosar $6
1989 Bernie Kosar $6
1990 R. Langhorne, W. Slaughter $6
1991 Fireworks exploding over goalpost $6
1992 Player's arm and helmet $6
1993 Entrance to training facility $6
1994 75th NFL logo on pigskin $6
1995 "Browns" on white background $6
1996-1998 No Team
1999 Players, owners, head coach $15
2000 Logo $10
2001 Coach Davis, T. Couch, others $10
2002 Municipal Stadium, Browns Stadium, &
    Helmet $6

Dallas Cowboys

1960 Team mascot $27
1961 L.G. Dupre $27
1962 Players in uniforms 19, 62 .... $27
1963 Bill Howton $27
1964 Team helmet $27
1965 Bob Lilly $27
1966 Bob Hayes $27
1967 Don Meredith $27
1968 Don Perkins $27
1969 Tom Landry $27
1970 Calvin Hill $17
1971 Texas Stadium $13
1972 T. Landry, Murchison, T. Schram,
    trophy $13
1973 Mel Renfro $13
1974 Cornell Green $13
1975 Roger Staubach $15
1976 Cliff Harris $13
1977 Drew Pearson $13
1978 H. Martin, R. White, two trophies $13
1979 20th Anniversary $13
1980 Tony Dorsett $10
1981 Randy White $9
1982 Tom Landry $8
1983 Texas Stadium, Cowboys star $7
1984 25th Anniversary logo $7
1985 Randy White $7
1986 Tony Dorsett, Tom Landry $7
1987 Tony Dorsett, Herschel Walker $6
1988 Cowboys star $6
1989 Jimmy Johnson, Jimmy Jones $6
1990 Eugene Lockhart $6
1991 Troy Aikman $6
1992 Emmitt Smith $6
1993 J. Johnson, Aikman, J. Jones,
    K. Norton $6
1994 Four Super Bowl trophies $6
1995 Troy Aikman $6
1996 Five Super Bowl rings $6
1997 Darren Woodson $6
1998 Cowboys helmet $6
1999 40th anniversary logo $10
2000 Troy Aikman, Emmitt Smith $10
2001 Blue cover, silver star $10
2002 Silver Stars on Blue Background $6

Denver Broncos

1960 .... None issued
1961 Empty Denver Bears stadium $27
1962 Cartoon quarterback throwing $27
1963 Team mascot $27
1964 Lionel Taylor $27
1965 Team mascot $27

1966 Lionel Taylor $27
1967 Lou Saban $27
1968 Team helmet $27
1969 Team mascot $27
1970 Mike Haffner $13
1971 R. Jackson, F. Little, L. Saban $15
1972 Floyd Little, John Ralston $15
1973 Offensive huddle $15
1974 Team helmet, huddle $13
1975 Otis Armstrong $13
1976 Riley Odoms $15
1977 Orange Crush defense $13
1978 Mile High Stadium $13
1979 Team helmet $13
1980 Team helmet $7
1981 Broncos uniform #81 .... $7
1982 Dan Reeves $7
1983 Broncos in action $7
1984 John Elway $8
1985 Bronco silhouette $7
1986 Broncos in action $6
1987 John Elway $7
1988 Karl Mecklenburg $6
1989 Football stitching $6
1990 Team headquarters $6
1991 Defense on line of scrimmage $6
1992 Torso of player No. 92 .... $6
1993 John Elway $6
1994 35th Anniversary art $6
1995 Mike Shanahan $6
1996 Elway, Zimmerman celebrating $6
1997 Broncos new logo $6
1998 Elway lifting Lombardi trophy $6
1999 Tony Carter $20
2000 Mile High Stadium $20
2001 Invesco Field, Broncos logo $20
2002 Bronco Statue $6

Detroit Lions

1946 Team mascot $50
1947 Name and 1947 .... $50
1948 Bo McMillin $50
1949 a: Lions mascot (40 pgs.) $50
    b: Bo McMillin (20 pgs.) $40
1950 Name and 1950 .... $40
1951 a: Doak Walker (48 pgs.) $40
    b: Lions mascot (48 pgs.) $40
1952 Name and 1952 .... $40
1953 Mascot, World Champions pennant $40
1954 Mascot, World Champions pennant $40
1955 Mascot, W. Division Champs banner .. $40
1956 Briggs Stadium $40
1957 Lions in action $40
1958 Team picture $40
1959 Name and 1959 .... $40
1960 Lions in action $27
1961 Jim Gibbons $27
1962 Briggs Stadium $27
1963 Lions mascot $27

1964 Player in action $27
1965 Team helmet $27
1966 Players with uniform #s 19, 66 .... $27
1967 Team logo $27
1968 Lions in action $27
1969 Lions in action $27
1970 Lions in action $13
1971 Team helmet $13
1972 Team logo $13
1973 Team logo $13
1974 Team logo $13
1975 Lions in action $13
1976 Team helmet $13
1977 Lions in action $13
1978 Lions in action $13
1979 Monte Clark, Gary Danielson $10
1980 Lions in action $10
1981 Billy Sims $10
1982 Lions in action $6
1983 50th Anniversary logo $6
1984 Team helmet $6
1985 James Jones $6
1986 Ford, Rogers, Thomas, helmet $6
1987 Lion $6
1988 Lion $6
1989 Wayne Fontes $6
1990 J. Ball, E. Murray, B. Sanders,
    C. Spielman $7
1991 Barry Sanders $6
1992 Barry Sanders $6
1993 Lions memorabilia $6
1994 C. Spielman, J. Hanson, B. Sanders .. $6
1995 Barry Sanders $6
1996 Six player photos $6
1997 B. Sanders, H. Moore $6
1998 Actual wild lion. $6
1999 Players tackling opponent $10
2000 Pro Bowlers inc. Sloan, Porcher $10
2001 Matt Millen, Marty Mornhinweg $10
2002 Ford Field $6

Green Bay Packers

1947 C. Lambeau, championship teams ... $50
1948 Curly Lambeau $50
1949 Home of the Packers $50
1950 Name and 1950 .... $40
1951 State of Wisconsin $40
1952 State of Wisconsin $40
1953 Name and 1953 .... $40
1954 Name and 1954 .... $40
1955 State of Wisconsin $40
1956 State of Wisconsin $40
1957 Green Bay Stadium $40
1958 Green Bay Stadium $40
1959 Vince Lombardi and Stadium $45
1960 Packers in action $27
1961 West Division Champs 1960 .... $27
1962 Football in hand $27
1963 World Champions $27

1964 Team logo..$27
1965 Jim Taylor $30
1966 Bart Starr...$27
1967 Elijah Pitts $27
1968 Willie Davis.......................................$30
1969 Donny Anderson..............................$25
1970 Packers in action $20
1971 Packers training...............................$20
1972 John Brockington.............................$25
1973 Packers defense..............................$20
1974 John Brockington.............................$25
1975 Bart Starr...$17
1976 Dave Hanner, Bart Starr..................$17
1977 Lynn Dickey $13
1978 Packers entering the field................$13
1979 Bart Starr, Vince Lombardi..............$15
1980 Packers celebrating $6
1981 Mike Douglass..................................$6
1982 Jan Stenerud....................................$8
1983 Larry McCarren.................................$6
1984 Forrest Gregg $6
1985 Lynn Dickey $7
1986 Packers defense vs. Dolphins $6
1987 Mark Lee $6
1988 Lindy Infante....................................$6
1989 Lindy Infante....................................$6
1990 Tim Harris..$6
1991 Sterling Sharpe $6
1992 Mike Holmgren.................................$6
1993 Brett Favre.......................................$6
1994 LeRoy Butler.....................................$6
1995 Ken Ruettgers...................................$6
1996 Reggie White....................................$7
1997 Three Lombardi Trophies $7
1998 Brett Favre.......................................$7
1999 Ray Rhodes & Ron Wolf....................$6
2000 Mike Sherman..................................$6
2001 Team Huddled Prior to Kickoff...........$6
2002 Brett Favre.......................................$6

Houston Texans

2002 Logo $10

Indianapolis Colts

Baltimore Colts
1950 Team logo..$40
1951 ....$40
1952 ....$40
1953 Team mascot....................................$40
1954 Team mascot....................................$40
1955 Team mascot....................................$40
1956 Team mascot....................................$40
1957 Team logo...$40
1958 Memorial Stadium $40
1959 Team logo...$40
1960 World Champions pennants.............$27
1961 Team helmet, logo...........................$27
1962 Team helmet, logo............................$27
1963 Colts in action..................................$27

1964 Offensive huddle $27
1965 Colts offense $27
1966 Colts cheerleaders $27
1967 Kickoff formation..............................$27
1968 Johnny Unitas..................................$35
1969 Colts sideline...................................$27
1970 Colts offense $13
1971 Super Bowl Trophy $13
1972 The Baltimore Colts..........................$13
1973 Ted Hendricks..................................$15
1974 Colt in action $13
1975 Lydell Mitchell...................................$13
1976 Bert Jones..$13
1977 Bert Jones..$13
1978 Bert Jones, Colts in action $13
1979 Team helmet.....................................$13
1980 Team helmet.......................................$8
1981 Team helmet.......................................$8
1982 Championship pennants $8
1983 Mike Pagel..$8
Indianapolis Colts
1984 Colts in action....................................$6
1985 Team helmet, Hoosierdome $6
1986 Team helmet, NFL flag $6
1987 Team helmet.......................................$6
1988 Team helmet.......................................$6
1989 Team helmet.......................................$6
1990 Team helmet.......................................$6
1991 Aerial photo of RCA Dome..................$6
1992 Ted Marchibroda................................$6
1993 10th Anniversary logo $6
1994 Colts logo on splashy background......$6
1995 Colts helmet inside Indiana map $5
1996 Colts helmet $5
1997 Robert Irsay, individual action photos.$5
1998 Indiana outline over cityscape $5
2000 P. Manning, J. Mora, others................$6
2001 P. Manning, J. Mora, others................$6
2002 Vanderjagt, M. Pollard,
   M. Washington.....................................$6

Jacksonville Jaguars

1995 Jaguar $6
1996 M. Brunell, Jaguars $6
1997 Tom Coughlin $6
1998 Helmet, Jaguar silhouette..................$8
1999 T. Boselli, M. Brunell, F. Taylor..........$10
2000 Helmet and Jaguar $10
2001 J. Smith, K. McCardell......................$10
2002 Logo $6

Kansas City Chiefs

1960 ....$27
1961 Little cowboy shooting $27
1962 ....None issued
1963 L. Dawson, C. McClinton, H. Stram..$30
1964 Curtis McClinton.............................$27
1965 L. Dawson, J. Mays, H. Stram $30
1966 Chiefs in action...............................$27

1967 L. Hunt, H. Stram, AFL Trophy $27
1968 Chiefs in action................................$27
1969 Willie Lanier.....................................$30
1970 Hank Stram, Chiefs celebrating........$13
1971 Ed Podolak.......................................$13
1972 Arrowhead Stadium..........................$13
1973 L. Dawson, O. Taylor, H. Stram $15
1974 Chiefs in action................................$13
1975 Team helmet......................................$13
1976 Helmet, action photos.......................$13
1977 Mike Livingston, Paul Wiggin............$13
1978 Team helmet and football $13
1979 Chiefs on offense $13
1980 Marv Levy, Chiefs in action $6
1981 Gary Barbaro, Art Still, J.T. Smith......$6
1982 Joe Delaney, Jack Rudnay $6
1983 Carlos Carson, John Mackovic...........$6
1984 25th Anniversary logo $6
1985 John Mackovic, team helmet..............$6
1986 Stephone Paige $6
1987 L. Burruss, D. Cherry, A. Lewis, K. Ross.$6
1988 A. Lewis, N. Lowery, P. Palmer...........$6
1989 C. Peterson, Marty Schottenheimer ...$6
1990 Center gripping the ball $6
1991 Player photo from waist down $6
1992 Arm raising Chiefs helmet $6
1993 Football bursting through paper $6
1994 Stone arrowheads $6
1995 Stadium photo from end zone $6
1996 Players at line of scrimmage $6
1997 Fans with arms raised $6
1998 Player's back wearing Chiefs jacket ...$6
1999 40th Anniversary Logo $6
2000 D. Thomas Silhouette over Stadium ...$6
2001 Carl Peterson, Dick Vermeil...............$6
2002 40 Seasons in Kansas City $6

Miami Dolphins

1966 George Wilson...................................$27
1967 Dolphins helmet................................$27
1968 Orange Bowl.....................................$27
1969 J. Clancy, B. Griese, K. Noonan $27
1970 Team logo and 1970.........................$13
1971 B. Griese, D. Shula, P. Warfield, others.$15

1972 Garo Yepremian $13
1973 Super Bowl trophy $13
1974 Helmet and Super Bowl trophies......$13
1975 Bob Griese, Don Shula $15
1976 B. Kuechenberg, J. Langer, B. Malone. $13
1977 Bob Griese $15
1978 Nat Moore $13
1979 Delvin Williams $13
1980 Vern DenHerder $6
1981 David Woodley $6
1982 Tony Nathan $6
1983 Andra Franklin $6
1984 Dan Marino $10
1985 Clayton, Duper, Marino....................$8
1986 Joe Robbie, Dwight Stephenson $6
1987 Don Shula $6
1988 Dan Marino $8
1989 Team logo....................................$6
1990 25th Anniversary logo $6
1991 John Offerdahl...............................$6
1992 Mark Clayton, Mark Duper $6
1993 D. Shula, D. Marino, others $6
1994 Don Shula celebrating $6
1995 Dan Marino, Bryan Cox $6
1996 Dan Marino, Jimmy Johnson.............$6
1997 J. Johnson, D. Marino, others............$6
1998 J. Johnson, D. Marino, others............$6
1999 Collage of players...........................$10
2000 Dave Wannstedt, several players $10
2001 Winning TD vs. Colts.......................$10
2002 Zach Thomas, Brock Marion $6

Minnesota Vikings

1961 Team logo......................................$27
1962 Team logo......................................$27
1963 Team logo......................................$27
1964 Team logo......................................$27
1965 Team logo......................................$27
1966 Fran Tarkenton $30
1967 Vikings in action $27
1968 Joe Kapp.......................................$27
1969 Bud Grant......................................$27
1970 Fred Cox..$13
1971 Jim Marshall $15
1972 Alan Page......................................$15
1973 Fan in Viking costume $13
1974 Players during National Anthem.......$13
1975 Fans cheering.................................$13
1976 Fran Tarkenton $15
1977 Team logo......................................$13
1978 Chuck Foreman...............................$13
1979 Ahmad Rashad $15
1980 Vikings new offices, stadium $6
1981 T. Kramer, A. Rashad, S. White........$8
1982 Vikings in action $6
1983 M. Blair, Johnson, D. Martin,
   S. Studwell....................................$6
1984 Les Steckel....................................$6
1985 25th Anniversary logo $6

1986 Jerry Burns....................................$6
1987 Tommy Kramer, others $6
1988 J. Browner, C. Doleman, K. Millard,
   others..$6
1989 Tim Irwin, others..............................$6
1990 30th Anniversary logo $6
1991 Photo of HHH Dome and Skyline.......$6
1992 D. Green, R. McDaniel, others $6
1993 Team action photo $6
1994 Cris Carter.....................................$6
1995 Warren Moon...................................$6
1996 R. McDaniel being congratulated $6
1997 Warren Moon...................................$6
1998 Cris Carter, Jake Reed $6
1999 Randall Cunningham.........................$8
2000 40th Anniversary logo $8
2001 Viking head with NFL logo $8
2002 Helmet, Jersey and Logo $6

New England Patriots

Boston Patriots
1960 ....None issued
1961 ....None issued
1962 ....None issued
1963 Cartoon Patriot, reporters $27
1964 Patriots helmet $27
1965 Gino Cappelletti, Babe April $30
1966 Nick Buoniconti...............................$30
1967 Jim Nance $27
1968 Team logo......................................$27
1969 Clive Rush.....................................$27
1970 Patriots action photos......................$13

New England Patriots
1971 Foxboro Stadium $13
1972 J. Adams, J. Plunkett, R. Vataha $13
1973 Patriots coaching staff......................$13
1974 Patriots action photos......................$13
1975 Patriots fans $13
1976 Patriots of 76 ....$13
1977 Chuck Fairbanks..............................$13
1978 Patriot Superhero cartoon $13
1979 Patriots in action $13
1980 Stanley Morgan $10
1981 Ron Erhardt, action photos $6
1982 Ron Meyer......................................$6
1983 Boston sites...................................$6
1984 Steve Grogan $6
1985 Patriots helmet $6
1986 Andre Tippett..................................$6
1987 Stanley Morgan $6
1988 Raymond Clayborn $6
1989 Patriots in action $6
1990 Rod Rust $6
1991 Helmet $6
1992 Patriots logo $6
1993 Helmet $6
1994 Patriots greats, S. Grogan, others......$6
1995 D. Bledsoe, B. Coates, B. Armstrong $6
1996 B. Coates, C. Martin, B. Armstrong $6

1997 AFC Championship Trophy $6
1998 Patriots' 1997 Pro Bowl Players $6
1999 Bledsoe, B. Coates, T. Law $10
2000 Jerseys $10
2001 Mike Hartsell, Jim Finn $10
2002 Super Bowl Trophy & CMG Field........$6

New Orleans Saints

1967 Player in action $27
1968 Band playing in the stadium $27
1969 Saints defense................................$27
1970 Dan Abramowicz $13
1971 Tom Dempsey 63-yard field goal......$15
1972 J. Kupp, A. Manning, J. Strong........$13
1973 Bob Pollard....................................$13
1974 Saints defense................................$13
1975 Saints in action $13
1976 Hank Stram $13
1977 C. Muncie, H. Stram, Superdome....$13
1978 Superdome.....................................$13
1979 Joe Federspiel, Dick Nolan $13
1980 Saints helmet, uniform......................$6
1981 Archie Manning, Bum Phillips.............$7
1982 George Rogers.................................$6
1983 Team logo......................................$6
1984 Bum Phillips....................................$6
1985 Team helmet and Louisiana $6
1986 Team logo, helmet, uniform $6
1987 R. Jackson, R. Mayes, J. Mora.........$6
1988 Team helmet...................................$6
1989 Team helmet...................................$6
1990 Dalton Hilliard.................................$6
1991 25th anniversary logo $6
1992 Superdome crowd $6
1993 J. Mora, helmet, referee, musician $6
1994 Art of QB, Mardi Gras joker $6
1995 Saints player artwork........................$6
1996 Saints 30 seasons logo $6
1997 M. Ditka, W. Roaf, W. Martin $6
1998 M. Ditka, W. Roaf, W. Martin $6
1999 Saints emblem.................................$12
2000 Saints emblem.................................$12
2001 Saints emblem.................................$12
2002 Logo and Defensive Line..................$6

New York Giants

1945 Ward Cuff $50
1946 Giants in action...............................$50
1947 Giants in action...............................$50
1948 Team logo......................................$50
1949 1925 Giants....................................$50
1950 Polo Grounds $40
1951 Polo Grounds $40
1952 Radio microphone $40
1953 Steve Owens, others $40
1954 Team logo......................................$40
1955 Team logo......................................$40
1956 Team logo......................................$40
1957 Team logo......................................$40

1958 Team logo...$40
1959 Team logo...$40
1960 Team logo and 1960......................$27
1961 Team logo and 1961......................$27
1962 Team logo and 1962......................$27
1963 Team logo and 1963......................$27
1964 Team logo and 1964......................$27
1965 Team logo and 1965......................$27
1966 Team mascot and 1966..................$27
1967 Team helmet and 1967...................$27
1968 Team helmet and 1968...................$27
1969 Team helmet and 1969...................$27
1970 Team helmet and 1970...................$13
1971 Team helmet and 1971...................$13
1972 Team helmet and 1972...................$13
1973 Team helmet and 1973...................$13
1974 Team logo...$13
1975 Team helmet.....................................$13
1976 Giants Stadium construction $13
1977 Giants Stadium opening day $13
1978 Giants offensive line $13
1979 Harry Carson....................................$13
1980 H. Carson, P. Simms, L. Taylor.........$15
1981 Phil Simms, offensive line..................$6
1982 Harry Carson, Lawrence Taylor..........$8
1983 H. Carson, P. Simms, L. Taylor, others...$8
1984 Giants greats $6
1985 H. Carson, P. Simms, L. Taylor, others..$8
1986 H. Carson, P. Simms, L. Taylor, others..$8
1987 Phil Simms, Super Bowl tickets $6
1988 G. Banks, L. Marshall, L. Taylor $7
1989 Giants Stadium, previous homesites..$6
1990 M. Bavarro, P. Simms, L. Taylor..........$6
1991 Team helmet w, two SB trophies $6
1992 Team helmet on footballs $6
1993 Giants logo on red border $6
1994 Giants 70th Anniversary logo $6
1995 20 years at Giants Stadium $6
1996 Line of scrimmage faded out..............$6
1997 Giants helmet $6
1998 New York Giants on blue background....$6
2000 Helmet, Football and Jersey...............$6
2002 Michael Strahan $6

New York Jets

Media Guide

1960 ....None issued
1961 ....None issued
1962 ....None issued
1963 Artwork of player #37 ....$27
1964 Team logo and 1964......................$27
1965 Team logo and 1965......................$27
1966 Team logo and 1966......................$27
1967 Team logo and 1967......................$27
1968 Team logo and 1967......................$27
1969 Team logo and 1969......................$27
1970 Team logo and 1970......................$13
1971 Team logo and 1971......................$13
1972 Team logo and 1972......................$13
1973 Team logo and 1973......................$13

1974 Team logo and 1974.......................$13
1975 Team logo and 1975.......................$13
1976 Team logo and 1976.......................$13
1977 Team logo and 1977.......................$13
1978 Team helmet and logo $13
1979 Jets defensive line $13
1980 M. Powell, R. Todd, Statue of Liberty.....$6
1981 Bruce Harper, Marvin Powell..............$6
1982 Mark Gastineau, others.....................$6
1983 Freeman McNeil, others $6
1984 25th Anniversary logo $6
1985 M. Gastineau, F. McNeil, J. Namath ...$8
1986 M. Gastineau, J. Klecko, F. McNeil $6
1987 D. Maynard, M. Shuler, A. Toon..........$6
1988 Al Toon $6
1989 E. McMillan, M. Shuler, A. Toon $6
1990 Bruce Coslet, Dick Steinberg $6
1991 Bandaged arm holding helmet $6
1992 Art of jets flying over stadium $6
1993 Jets helmet, 25th Anniv. logo $6
1994 Helmet and NFL 75th Anniv. logo.......$6
1995 New York Jets repeated across cover ...$6
1996 Helmet, stars in background...............$6
1997 Photo of stadium at Meadowlands $6
1998 Jets original logo $6
1999 New York skyline $8
2000 Several players.................................$8
2001 Player faded into background.............$8
2002 Players Huddled $6

Oakland Raiders

Oakland Raiders

1960 ....None issued
1961 Team mascot $27
1962 ....None issued
1963 Bo Roberson $27
1964 Raiders helmet $27
1965 Oakland-Alameda Co. Stadium........$27
1966 Raiders helmet $27
1967 Player in action $27
1968 AFL Champions ring $27
1969 Dan Birdwell $27
1970 Raiders offensive huddle................. $19
1971 Raiders offense, Daryle Lamonica ...$16
1972 Team logo and 1972.........................$13
1973 Raiders in action $13
1974 Pre-game huddle..............................$13
1975 Raiders action photos $13
1976 Raider player on the sidelines $13
1977 Super Bowl XI ring $13
1978 Dave Casper in action $13
1979 20th Anniversary memorabilia..........$13
1980 Raiders third decade $10
1981 Super Bowl XV ring $7

Los Angeles Raiders

1982 Raider player on the sidelines $6
1983 Raiders in action $6
1984 Super Bowl XVIII ring $6
1985 Helmet, three Super Bowl trophies.....$6

1986 Team logo...$6
1987 Matt Millen $6
1988 Van McElroy $6
1989 Team helmet......................................$6
1990 Team helmet......................................$6
1991 Raiders offense $6
1992 Black background, logo $6
1993 Logo on back of generic player $6
1994 Helmet, 3 trophies, 35th Anniv. $6

Oakland Raiders

1995 Metallic background, logo....................$6
1996 Super Bowl trophies, helmet $6
1997 Super Bowl rings $6
1998 "Team of Decades" in silver $6
1999 3 Lombardi Trophies, logo $10
2000 3 Lombardi Trophies, helmet $10
2001 3 Lombardi Trophies, logo $10
2002 3 Lombardi Trophies, Helmet, Logo ...$6

Philadelphia Eagles

1947 Season schedule...............................$50
1948 Photo of 1947 team..........................$50
1949 Earle Neale $50
1950 Steve Van Buren................................$40
1951 Eagle $40
1952 Eagles in action $40
1953 Jim Trimble $40
1954 Eagle $40
1955 Eagle $40
1956 Hugh Devore $40
1957 25th Anniversary eagle $40
1958 L. Buck Shaw $40
1959 Eagle, Franklin Field..........................$40
1960 Franklin Field.....................................$27
1961 Eagle wearing a crown $27
1962 Baby eagle hatching from ball $27
1963 Eagle and goalposts..........................$27
1964 Franklin Field.....................................$27
1965 Norm Snead in action........................$27
1966 Tim Brown $27
1967 Harold Wells $27
1968 Norm Snead, offensive line $27
1969 Apollo XI logo $27
1970 Zodiac symbols $13
1971 Eagles history....................................$13
1972 Eddie Khayat $13
1973 Bradley, R. Gabriel, McCormack $13
1974 H. Carmichael, R. Gabriel, others $13
1975 Eagles in action $13
1976 Dick Vermiel $13
1977 Dick Vermiel, action photos $13
1978 Harold Carmichael $13
1979 H. Carmichael, W. Montqomery $13
1980 Dick Vermiel and coaches $6
1981 Team helmet......................................$6
1982 50th Anniversary logo $6
1983 Marion Campbell $6
1984 Mike Quick...$6
1985 Norman Braman $6

1986 Buddy Ryan....................................$6
1987 Reggie White..................................$8
1988 Mike Quick....................................$6
1989 Randall Cunningham......................$7
1990 R. Cunningham, offensive huddle $7
1991 Rich Kotite....................................$6
1992 Eagles defense, Jerome Brown $6
1993 Eagles helmet $6
1994 Jeffrey Lurie $6
1995 Jeffrey Lurie, Ray Rhodes.................$6
1996 Eagles helmet $6
1997 Eagles helmet $6
1998 Closeup of Eagles logo on jersey.......$6
1999 Logo with Helmet $7
2000 Helmet and Football $7
2001 Practice Facility Art........................$7
2002 Logo $6

Pittsburgh Steelers

1947 Name and 1947..............................$50
1948 Cartoon reporters...........................$50
1949 Cartoon reporters...........................$50
1950 Cartoon reporters...........................$40
1951 John P. Michelosen.........................$40
1952 Cartoon steelworker $40
1953 Steeler kicker................................$40
1954 City of Pittsburgh $40
1955 Steelers in action..........................$40
1956 Steelers in action..........................$40
1957 Brovelli, Elbert Nickel $40
1958 Steelers in action..........................$40
1959 Team mascot and logo $40
1960 Steelers in action..........................$27
1961 Team helmet.................................$27
1962 Steelers uniform $27
1963 Steelers helmet and 1963 ....$27
1964 Steelers helmet and 1964 ....$27
1965 City of Pittsburgh $27
1966 City of Pittsburgh $27
1967 Steelers in action..........................$27
1968 Team helmet.................................$27
1969 Three Rivers Stadium.....................$27
1970 Steelers in action..........................$13
1971 Black and yellow stripes $13
1972 Team helmet.................................$13
1973 Joe Greene $15
1974 Team helmet.................................$13
1975 T. Bradshaw, R. Bleier, F. Harris.......$15
1976 Team helmet.................................$13
1977 Team helmet.................................$13
1978 Team helmet.................................$13
1979 Team helmet.................................$13
1980 Steelers 1980 football.....................$6
1981 Football..$6
1982 50th Anniversary logo $6
1983 Team helmet.................................$6
1984 Franco Harris................................$8
1985 Team helmet.................................$6
1986 Team helmet.................................$6

1987 Team helmet.................................$6
1988 Chuck Noll...................................$6
1989 Team helmet, Pittsburgh.................$6
1990 Steelers '90 logo $6
1991 Helmet, stadium in background $6
1992 60 seasons anniversary logo $6
1993 Steelers logo on helmet $6
1994 Helmet..$6
1995 Logo and 1995 ....$6
1996 Logo and 1996 ....$6
1997 Helmets $6
1998 Logo and 1998 ....$6
1999 Steelers logo $8
2000 Three Rivers Stadium.....................$8
2001 New stadium.................................$8
2002 70th Anniversary Logo $6

San Diego Chargers

Los Angeles Chargers
1960 Team logo and 1960.......................$27
San Diego Chargers
1961 Team logo and 1961.......................$27
1962 Team logo and 1962.......................$27
1963 Team logo and 1963.......................$27
1964 Team logo and 1964.......................$27
1965 Team mascot and 1965...................$27
1966 Chargers in action.........................$27
1967 Jack Murphy Stadium......................$27
1968 Chargers in action.........................$27
1969 John Hadl, offensive line $27
1970 Lance Alworth $15
1971 Chargers in action.........................$13
1972 John Hadl.....................................$13
1973 Dennis Partee $13
1974 New Chargers uniform $13
1975 Don Woods...................................$13
1976 Dan Fouts.....................................$13
1977 Dan Fouts.....................................$13
1978 Joe Washington.............................$13
1979 Chargers in action.........................$13
1980 Chargers in action.........................$6
1981 Greg McCrary, Cliff McGee $6
1982 Team airplanes $6
1983 Team helmet.................................$6
1984 25th Anniversary logo $6
1985 Dan Fouts, Charlie Joiner...................$8
1986 Lionel James, others celebrating........$6
1987 Team helmet.................................$6
1988 Team logo.....................................$6
1989 Chargers in action.........................$6
1990 A. Miller, L. O'Neal, L. Williams $6
1991 Chargers logo $6
1992 Nate Lewis....................................$6
1993 Snapshots of crowd........................$6
1994 Junior Seau, fans $6
1995 AFC Championship ring, David Griggs.$6
1996 Rodney Culver...............................$6
1997 T. Martin, J. Seau, K. Gilbride, others $6
1998 R. Leaf, P. Tagliabue, J. Seau, others.$6

1999 Snapshots $6
2001 Football and Lightning Bolts $6
2002 Schottenheimer, Seau, Tomlinson,
    Conway, others $6

San Francisco 49ers

1950 Three cartoon reporters $40
1951 Team mascot.................................$40
1952 Three team mascots........................$40
1953 Team mascot.................................$40
1954 Team mascot.................................$40
1955 Action shot and team mascot..........$40
1956 Team mascot.................................$40
1957 Three team mascots........................$40
1958 Prospector firing revolvers...............$40
1959 Team mascot.................................$40
1960 Red Hickey $27
1961 Team mascot.................................$27
1962 Team mascot.................................$27
1963 Team mascot.................................$27
1964 Team mascot.................................$27
1965 Team mascot.................................$27
1966 Team mascot.................................$27
1967 49ers in action..............................$27
1968 Player on the sideline $27
1969 John Brodie, Gary Lewis $27
1970 Frankie Albert, John Brodie..............$13
1971 Candlestick Park $13
1972 Team helmet, Candlestick Park.........$13
1973 Dick Nolan....................................$13
1974 Team helmet, Golden Gate Bridge ...$13
1975 Footballs, team helmet $13
1976 Monte Clark...................................$13
1977 E. DeBartolo, K. Meyer, J. Thomas ..$13
1978 Golden Gate Bridge $13
1979 O.J. Simpson $20
1980 John Ayers, Paul Hofer......................$6
1981 Joe Montana, Fred Solomon $8
1982 The Catch, Super Bowl trophy $6
1983 Ronnie Lott....................................$6
1984 Hand holding helmet $6
1985 Randy Cross, Wendell Tyler $6
1986 40th Anniversary logo $6
1987 Joe Montana...................................$8
1988 Tom Rathman $6
1989 Joe Montana, Jerry Rice $8
1990 Roger Craig $6
1991 Jerry Rice......................................$6
1992 Joe Montana...................................$6
1993 Steve Young $6
1994 Jerry Rice......................................$5
1995 Super Bowl trophies and ring $5
1996 50th anniversary, memorabilia collage....$5
1997 Steve Mariucci................................$5
1998 B. Young, M. Hanks, T. McDonald,
    K. Norton $5
1999 S. Young, J. Rice, G. Hearst.............$6
2000 Bryant Young..................................$6
2001 Ray Brown......................................$6
2002 Garrison Hearst..............................$6

Seattle Seahawks

1976 Team helmet...................................$15
1977 S. Niehaus, J. Patera, J. Zorn...........$13
1978 Sherman Smith $13
1979 Steve Largent, Jim Zorn $13
1980 Jack Patera....................................$6
1981 Steve Largent, seahawk $8
1982 Steve Largent..................................$8
1983 Chuck Knox, Kingdome $6
1984 Chuck Knox....................................$6
1985 Players entering the field...................$6
1986 Steve Largent in action......................$8
1987 Referee signaling a TD......................$6

1988 Ron Heller, Johnny Holloway..............$6
1989 D. Krieg, S. Largent, J. L. Williams.....$6
1990 Uniform #90, equipment....................$6
1991Seahawks helmet..............................$6
1992 Tom Flores.....................................$6
1993 Cortez Kennedy...............................$6
1994 Eugene Robinson..............................$6
1995 D. Erickson, C. Warren, B. Blades......$6
1996 C. KennedyC. Warren, T. Wooden......$6
1997 C. Kennedy, M. Sinclair.....................$6
1998 W. Moon, M. Sinclair, W.Williams.......$6
1999 Coach Mike Holmgren.....................$12
2000 25th Anniversary jersey...................$12
2001 Seahawks football helmet...............$12
2002 Seahawks Stadium............................$6

St. Louis Rams

Los Angeles Rams

1945 Bob Waterfield................................$50
1946 Bob Waterfield in punting pose........$50
1947 Bob Waterfield................................$50
1948 Goat mascot...................................$50
1949 Team logo and 1949.........................$50
1950 Team logo and 1950.........................$40
1951 Team logo and 1951.........................$40
1952 Team logo and 1952.........................$40
1953 Team logo and 1953.........................$40
1954 Team logo and 1954.........................$40
1955 Team logo and 1955.........................$40
1956 Team logo and 1956.........................$40
1957 Team logo and 1957.........................$40
1958 Team logo and 1958.........................$40
1959 Team logo and 1959.........................$40
1960 Team logo and 1960.........................$27
1961 Team logo and 1961.........................$27
1962 Team logo and 1962.........................$27
1963 Team logo and 1963.........................$27
1964 Team logo and 1964.........................$27
1965 Team logo and 1965.........................$27
1966 Team logo and 1966.........................$27
1967 Team logo and 1967.........................$27
1968 Team logo and 1968.........................$27
1969 Team logo and 1969.........................$27
1970 Team logo and 1970.........................$13

1971 Team logo and 1971.........................$13
1972 Team logo and 1972.........................$13
1973 Rams in action...............................$13
1974 Team helmet...................................$13
1975 Team helmet...................................$13
1976 Team helmet...................................$13
1977 Team helmet...................................$13
1978 Old and new helmets........................$13
1979 Carroll Rosenbloom.........................$13
1980 Rams in action...............................$13
1981 Ram wearing uniform No. 81...........$13
1982 Los Angeles sites.............................$7
1983 Team helmet....................................$6
1984 Players entering field.......................$6
1985 40th Anniversary logo.......................$6
1986 Eric Dickerson.................................$7
1987 Three legs......................................$6
1988 Rams in action................................$6
1989 Team helmet, equipment....................$6
1990 Ram wearing uniform No. 90.............$6
1991 Ram wearing uniform No. 91.............$6
1992 Coach with yell horns and players......$6
1993 Players showing biceps.....................$6
1994 Group clasping hands.......................$6
Become St. Louis Rams
1995 Newspaper heralds return to NFL......$6
1996 Rams goat inside helmets..................$6
1997 Dick Vermeil with players...................$6
1998 Isaac Bruce....................................$6
1999 Quarterback Drawing.......................$6
2000 Super Bowl Trophy Artwork...............$8
2001 Marshall Faulk, Isaac Bruce..............$8
2002 Rams Drawing.................................$6

Tampa Bay Buccaneers

1976 Team helmets.................................$15
1977 Dave Pear, Lee Roy Selmon............$15
1978 John McKay...................................$13
1979 Team helmet, John McKay...............$13
1980 Jimmy Giles, fans celebrating.............$6
1981 John McKay.....................................$6
1982 Hugh Culverhouse, John McKay........$6
1983 Buccaneers in action.........................$6
1984 H. Green, J. McKay, L.R. Selmon.......$8
1985 Leeman Bennett, James Wilder.........$6
1986 Buccaneers in action.........................$6
1987 Ray Perkins.....................................$6
1988 Ray Perkins, Vinny Testaverde...........$6
1989 Buccaneers in action.........................$6
1990 Mark Carrier.....................................$6
1991 Richard Williamson............................$6
1992 Sam Wyche......................................$6
1993 Two players celebrating.....................$6
1994 John McKay, Sam Wyche...................$6
1995 LeRoy Selmon, H. Nickerson.............$6
1996 Tony Dungy, players celebrating.........$6
1997 Helmet on black background..............$6
1998 Raymond James Stadium...................$6
1999 Logo and Stadium Drawing................$6
2000 Logo..$6
2002 Logo on Football................................$6

Tennessee Titans

Houston Oilers

1960..................................None issued
1961 Team mascot.....................................$27
1962 Ed Husmann, Ivy, Al Jamison...........$27
1963 Oilers in action................................$27
1964 Sammy Baugh, Oilers in action........$27
1965 Team helmets...................................$27
1966 O. Burrell, W.K. Hicks, B. Talamini....$27
1967 Logo...$27
1968 Astrodome.......................................$27
1969 Astrodome.......................................$27

1970 Oilers artwork.................................$16
1971 Oilers sculpture...............................$16
1972 Team helmet....................................$16
1973 Team helmet....................................$16
1974 Sid Gillman, Oilers in action.............$15
1975 Oilers in action...............................$13
1976 Cheering fans..................................$13
1977 Team logo.......................................$13
1978 Oilers in action...............................$13
1979 20th Anniversary, Oilers in action.....$10
1980 Bum Phillips.....................................$10
1981 Oiler in action...................................$6
1982 Team helmets...................................$6
1983 Team helmet.....................................$6
1984 Silver Annniversary logo,. montage....$6
1985 W. Moon, M. Munchak, D. Steinkuhler..$8
1986 Artwork of group of players...............$6
1987 R. Childress, E. Givins, J. Grimsley,
    D. Hill...$6
1988 Team helmet, field............................$6
1989 Team helmet....................................$6
1990 E. Givins, D. Hill, W. Moon................$6
1991 Warren Moon....................................$6
1992 Jack Pardee.....................................$6
1993 Bruce Matthews, Mike Munchak........$6
1994 Player collage..................................$6
1995 Oilers helmet and Texas flag..............$6
1996 Collage of team history.....................$6
Become Tennesee Oilers
1997 Player collage, Oilers logo................$6
1998 Steve McNair, Eddie George.............$6
Become Tennesee Titans
1999 Photo of stadium............................$15
2000 J. Kearse, S. McNair, others............$15
2001 B. Bishop, J. Kearse, R. Godfrey......$15
2002 S. McNair, K. Dyson, D. Mason.........$6

Washington Redskins

1946 Redskins head logo.........................$50
1947 Name, Indian mascot.......................$50
1948 Indian mascot and 1948...................$50
1949 Indian mascot and 1949...................$50
1950 Indian mascot and 1950...................$40
1951 Indian mascot and 1951...................$40

1952 Indian mascot and 1952	$40	
1953 Indian mascot and 1953	$40	
1954 Indian mascot and 1954	$40	
1955 Redskins in action	$40	
1956 Redskins in action	$40	
1957 Redskins in action	$40	
1958 Year and 1958	$40	
1959 Team helmet, pennant	$40	
1960 Football and 1960	$27	
1961 Silver Anniversary	$27	
1962 Football	$27	
1963 Capitol building	$27	
1964 Tomahawk and drum	$27	
1965 Team helmet	$27	
1966 Tepee, D.C. Stadium	$27	
1967 Tepee, D.C. Stadium	$27	
1968 Tepee, D.C. Stadium	$27	
1969 Tepee, D.C. Stadium	$27	

1970 Tepee, D.C. Stadium	$13
1971 Tepee, D.C. Stadium	$13
1972 Team helmet	$13
1973 Team logo, D.C. sites	$13
1974 Team helmet, Capitol	$13
1975 Pregame huddle	$13
1976 Team logo, George Allen	$13
1977 Redskins in action	$13
1978 Mark Moseley	$13
1979 Indian, Redskins in action	$13
1980 Team helmet	$6
1981 Team logo	$6
1982 "Redskins" and helmet	$6
1983 Helmet, Super Bowl trophy	$8
1984 Joe Theismann	$7
1985 John Riggins, Joe Theismann	$8
1986 50th Anniversary logo	$6
1987 Gary Clark, Art Monk	$8

1988 Super Bowl XXII ring	$8
1989 Art Monk in action	$8
1990 Charles Mann	$6
1991 Darrell Green	$6
1992 Art Monk catching a pass	$6
1993 Jim Lachey	$6
1994 Previous press guides	$6
1995 Redskins Pro Bowlers	$6
1996 Brian Mitchell, Redskins Stadium	$6
1997 Terry Allen	$6
1998 Darrell Green, Cris Dishman	$6
1999 Helmet and Vintage Photos	$6
2000 Logo	$6
2001 Helmet	$6
2002 70th Anniversary Logo & Three Vintage Photos	$6

FOOTBALL YEARBOOKS

Arizona Cardinals

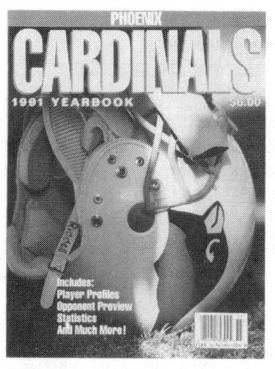

St. Louis Cardinals

1967 Team photo	$35
1968 Team photo	$35
1969	$35
1976	$15

Phoenix Cardinals

1988	$6
1989 Team helmet in the desert	$6
1990	$6
1991 Team helmet	$6
1992 Closeup of player holding football	$6
1993 M. Bankston, R. Davis, M. Jones, K. Rucker, E. Swann	$6

Become Arizona Cardinals

1994 Buddy Ryan, generic player	$6
1995	$6
1996	$6
1997	$6
1998	$6
1999 Jake Plummer, others	$6
2000 Tillman, Pittman, others	$6
2001 Plummer, Coach McGinnis, others	$6
2002 L.J. Shelton, others	$6

Atlanta Falcons

1966 Team logo and 1966	$45
1967 Team logo and 1967	$35
1968 Team logo and 1967	$30
1969 Team logo and 1969	$25
1970	$25
1971	$25
1972 Bob Berry, others	$20
1973 Dave Hampton, team helmet	$20
1974 Tommy Nobis	$20

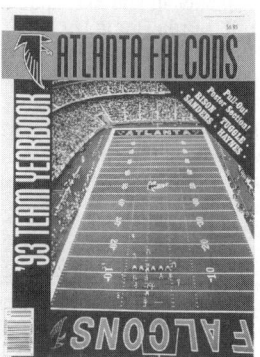

1975	$15
1976 Steve Bartkowski, others	$15
1977	$15
1992 Exterior of Georgia Dome	$8
1993 Georgia Dome field	$8
1995 J. George, B. Emanuel	$8
1997 T. Hall, M. Andersen, others	$8
1998 M. Andersen, J. Tuggle, C. Chandler	$8
1999 M. Anderson, NFC Trophy	$8
2000 Collage of Past & Present Players	$8
2001 Falcon Bird & NFL Football	$8
2002 M. Vick, K. Brooking, owner Arthur Blank, coach D. Reeves	$8

Baltimore Ravens

1999 Inaugural, C. Palmer, others	$6

Buffalo Bills

1965 Bills vs. Chiefs in action	$35
1968 J. Kemp, B. Byrd, P. Maguire	$45
1969 Gary McDermott	$45

1971 O. J. Simpson	$40
1972 O. J. Simpson	$40
1984 Joe Ferguson	$20
1989 Team logo, Bills in action	$6
1990 Bills red helmet	$6
1991 Helmet, AFC Championship trophy	$6
1992 Bills flag flying at Rich Stadium	$6
1993 View inside Rich Stadium	$6
1994 Bills memorabilia	$6
1995 Bills logo, several players	$6
1996 Helmet, 3 Pro Bowl players	$6
1997 B. Smith tackling Broncos runner	$6
1998 W. Phillips, T. Washington, others	$6
1999 E. Moulds, D. Flutie, others	$6
2000 R. Johnson, E. Moulds, others	$6
2001 Johnson, Moulds, S. Cowart	$6
2002 Bledsoe, Moulds, L. Fletcher	$6

Carolina Panthers

1995 K. Collins, S. Mills, D. Capers	$8
2001 Mike Minter	$8

Chicago Bears

1952 Growling bear	$40
1955 Rams players tackling a Bear	$35
1956 Kicker and holder	$35
1960 Artwork of player, bear	$25
1964 Helmet	$20
1983 Helmet	$12
1986 Locker with Super Bowl Trophy	$10
1987 Helmet, reflection of city skyline	$12
1988 Huge red bear looking over huddle	$10
1989 Player introductions, helmet	$8
1990 Bears defense vs. Packers	$8
1991	$8
1992 N. Anderson,, W. Perry, T. Armstrong	$8

1993 M. Carrier, R. Dent, J. Morrissey $8
1994 Bears memorabilia $8
1995 Flag, A. Spellman, C. Zorich, others ..$8
1996 ....$8
1997 ....$8
1998 ....$8
1999 D. Jauron, G. Halas, others $8
2000 D. Jauron and players.........................$8
2001 J. Allen, M. Brown, Urlacher, others ..$8
2002 Urlacher, M. Booker, others...............$8

Cleveland Browns

1987 Bernie Kosar....................................$8
1988 B. Kosar, E. Byner $8
1989 Bernie Kosar....................................$8
1990 Langhorne, Slaughter.........................$8
1991 ....$8
1992 Artwork of hand and helmet $8
1993 Clay Matthews..................................$8
1994 Eric Metcalf $6
1995 Pepper Johnson $6
2001 Art rendering of various players $8
2002 Art rendering of various players $8

Dallas Cowboys

1967 Don Meredith....................................$45
1968 Bob Hayes $40
1969 Bob Lilly...$40
1970 Calvin Hill $30
1971 Walt Garrison $30
1972 Roger Staubach $30
1973 Tom Landry $25
1980 T. Dorsett, T. Landry, Cheerleaders..$20
1982 Danny White......................................$15
1992 Cowboys greats, "Return to Glory"....$10
1993 Troy Aikman, Super Bowl photos $10
1994 Four Super Bowl trophies, helmet $10
1995 Collage with Aikman, Haley, others..$10
1996 Five Super Bowl Trophies, helmet $10
1997 T. Aikman, E. Smith...........................$10
1998 Collage with D. Sanders, others $10
1999 Emmitt Smith, Troy Aikman $10
2000 Aikman, L. Allen, E. Smith, others....$10
2001 Emmitt Smith $10
2002 Emmitt Smith $10

Denver Broncos

1974 The Making of a Contender.............$20
1978 Craig Morton $10
1986 Louis Wright $7
1987 John Elway $7
1988 ....$7
1989 ....$7
1991 Fireworks over stadium $7
1992 Broncos defense in action $7
1993 John Elway $8
1994 John Elway $8
1995 John Elway $8
1996 ....$8

1997 Broncos helmet, Elway Tribute $8
1998 ....$9
1999 Shanahan, Sharpe, T. Davis, Elway ...$9
2000 Collage of history $8
2001 Rod Smith, Ed McCaffrey..................$8
2002 Coach Mike Shanahan $8

Detroit Lions

1984 ....$10
1985 Player No. 35....................................$10
1991 Barry Sanders $10
1992 ....$10
1993 Barry Sanders and others $10
1994 Barry Sanders $10
1995 Barry Sanders $10
1996 Barry Sanders $8
1997 B. Sanders, H. Moore, K. Glover $8
1998 ....$8
1999 Barry Sanders in action....................$8
2000 Five Pro Bowl players $8
2001 Matt Millen, team huddle, head coach$8
2002 Ford Field $8

Green Bay Packers

1960 Paul Hornung, Jerry Kramer $300
1961 Forrest Gregg $250
1962 Vince Lombardi $200
1963 Jim Taylor $150
1964 Bart Starr..$125
1965 Curly Lambeau, Vince Lombardi....$125
1966 Willie Davis $100
1967 Packers vs. Kansas City Chiefs......$100
1968 Ray Nitschke $75

1969 Donny Anderson..............................$40
1970 Travis Williams................................$35
1971 Dan Devine.......................................$35
1972 John Brockington..............................$30
1973 Chester Marcol, Ron Widby $30
1974 Jerry Tagge $25
1975 Bart Starr...$30
1976 Fred Carr $20
1977 Lynn Dickey $20
1978 Johnnie Gray $15
1979 T. Middleton, D. Whitehurst $10
1980 Rich Wingo $10
1981 Gerry Ellis, Eddie Lee Ivery.............$10
1982 John Jefferson, James Lofton $15
1983 Mike Douglass..................................$10
1984 25th Anniversary, Forrest Gregg $12
1985 Paul Coffmann..................................$9
1986 Randy Scott......................................$6
1987 Randy Wright $6
1988 Lindy Infante $6
1989 Tim Harris...$6
1990 Don Majkowski..................................$6
1991 Sterling Sharpe $7
1992 Mike Holmgren $6
1993 Brett Favre $8
1994 Reggie White....................................$8
1995 Edgar Bennett $7
1996 Brett Favre $9
1997 Super Bowl XXXI trophy $8
1998 Antonio Freeman, Robert Brooks.......$8
1999 B. Favre, R. Rhodes, others $8
2000 Mike Sherman $8
2001 Brett Favre $8
2002 Ahman Green $8

Indianapolis Colts

Baltimore Colts
1953 10th Anniversary helmet $60
1958 Memorial Stadium $45
1959 ....$45
1960 ....$40
1961 Weeb Eubank, Colts sideline $40
1962 Team helmet.....................................$40
1963 ....$35
1964 Johnny Unitas...................................$35
1978 Bert Jones $10

Indianapolis Colts
1988 Eric Dickerson $8
1989 ....$8
1991 Jack Herrod $8
1992 Q. Coryatt, S. Emtman, T. Marchibroda..$8
1993 10th Celebration logo $8
1994 ....$8
1995 ....$8
1996 ....$8
1997 ....$8
1998 ....$8
2001 P. Manning, E. James, M. Harrison $8

Jacksonville Jaguars

1995 T.Coughlin, M. Brunell, W.Moore, J.Lageman $10
1996 T. Coughlin, K. Hardy, M. Brunell $10
1997 M. BrunellK. Hardy $10
1998 M. Brunell, T. Boselli, J. Smith, M. Hollis, B. Barker...$10
1999 Tony Boselli, Fred Taylor $8
2000 A. Beasley, K. Hardy, F. Bryant..........$8
2001 M. Brunell, McCardell, F. Taylor.........$8
2002 J. Smith, T. Brackens, M. Brunell........$8

Kansas City Chiefs

1968 ....$40
1969 ....$40
1970 Hank Stram $35
1971 H. Stram, L. Dawson, others $35
1972 Ed Podolak $20
1990 Silver Anniversary Season $10
1994 Joe Montana $10
1996 Neil Smith $8
1997 ....$8
1999 Tony Gonzalez...................................$8

Miami Dolphins

1984 Topps card collage $25
1985 Dan Marino.......................................$20
1986 Dolphins helmet, jacket $15
1987 ....$10
1988 Dan Marino.......................................$10
1990 Silver Anniv. Season $20
1993 J.B. Brown, B. Cox, D. Griggs, J. Offerdahl, L. Oliver, T. Vincent $8
1994 Dan Marino...$8
1995 Team photo $8
1996 ....$8
1997 ....$8
1998 ....$9
1999 Zach Thomas $8
2000 Sam Madison $8
2001 Jason Taylor $8
2002 Jay Fiedler...$8

Minnesota Vikings

1961 Vikings cartoon and referee $55
1975 ....$15
1976 Viking artwork...................................$15
1991 ....$8
1992 D. Green, R. McDaniel, others $8
1993 Artwork by Allen J. Peterson $8
1994 ....$8
1995 Cris Carter...$8
1996 ....$8
1997 Brad Johnson $8
1998 John Randle $8
1999 Cris Carter $8
2000 40th Anniversary $8
2001 Randy Moss $8
2002 Daunte Culpepper $8

New England Patriots

Boston Patriots

1964 Cartoon $40
1965 Gino Cappelletti, Babe Parilli...........$35
1966 J.D. Garrett, Jim Nance $35
1967 Jim Nance $35

New England Patriots

1978 ....$13
1979 Sam Cunningham, others $10
1980 Rod Shoate $13
1981 Vagas Ferguson $10
1985 Tony Eason, Craig James, others.......$6
1986 ....$7
1987 ....$6
1988 Player pileup......................................$6
1989 Defense vs. Bills $6
1991 ....$6
1992 View of Stadium during a game $6
1993 Bledsoe, Parcells, others...................$6
1994 Drew Bledsoe $8
1995 Parcells, Bledsoe, Coates $8
1996 ....$8
1997 D. Bledsoe, T. Glenn..........................$8
1998 C. Slade, T. Johnson, W. McGinist $8
1999 Drew Bledsoe $8
2000 Lawyer Milloy $8
2001 Collage of players, including Bledsoe.$8
2002 Lombardi Trophy and six players........$8

New Orleans Saints

1968 Dan Abramowicz $25
1988 Helmet, musical instuments $8
1991 25th Anniversary $8
1992 Bobby Hebert $8
1993 Saints defense making tackle.............$8
1994 ....$8
1995 ....$8
1996 ....$8
1997 Mike Ditka $8
1998 Mike Ditka...$8
2000 J. Blake, R. Williams, others...............$8
2001 J. Horn, L. Glover, others $8
2002 A. Brooks, D. McAllister, others $8

New York Giants

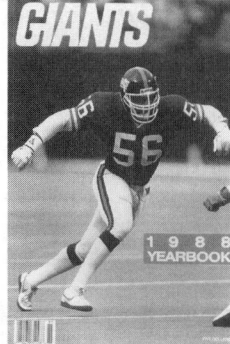

1963 Y. A. Tittle $95
1964 Y.A. Tittle, Alex Webster $40
1965 Giants offensive line $40
1966 Tucker Frederickson $40
1967 Giants vs. St. Louis Cardinals $35
1968 Fran Tarkenton $30
1969 Fran Tarkenton $30
1970 Joe Morrison $30
1971 Giants defense vs. Rams $10
1974 ....$25
1975 ....$20
1976 John Mendenhall $20
1985 ....$10
1986 Phil Simms $10

1987 Lombardi Trophy, helmet $10
1988 Lawrence Taylor $10
1989 M. Bavaro, C. Banks..........................$10
1990 Lawrence Taylor in action $10
1991 Ottis Anderson....................................$10
1992 Leonard Marshall.................................$8
1993 Phil Simms $8
1994 70th Anniversary artwork $8
1995 Player looking through helmet............$8
1996 Championship anniversary art $8
1997 Giants helmet and footballs $8
1998 ....$8
1999 75th Anniversary, helmets $8
2001 K. Collins, T. Barber, M. Strahan $8

New York Jets

1960 ....$80
1961 Titans AFL...$70
1962 ....$60
1963 ....$60
1964 L. Grantham, W. McDaniel, M. Snell $60
1965 Matt Snell $60
1966 Joe Namath $60
1967 Jets vs. Chargers $35
1968 Emerson Boozer, Joe Namath $35
1969 Joe Namath $75
1970 Don Maynard $20
1971 Action photo vs. Giants $15
1972 Joe Namath, John Riggins $15
1973 Artwork collage $15
1974 Charles Winner, Joe Namath $15
1975 Jets in action artwork $15
1976 ....$15
1977 Greg Buttle, Clark Gaines, Richard Todd, others...$15
1978 Richard Todd, others $15
1979 Richard Todd, others $15
1980 R. Todd, Statue of Liberty.................$15
1981 F. McNeil, B. Harper, M. Powell $15
1982 J, . Klecko, M. Gastineau...................$15
1983 Freeman McNeil artwork $15
1984 Helmet, Silver Anniversary $12
1985 Namath, McNeil, Gastineau $12
1986 O'Brien, McNeil, others $10
1987 D. Maynard, others $10
1988 Snapshots on jersey background $10
1989 Al Toon, others $10
1990 B. Coslett, Toon, others $10
1991 B.Thomas, Namath, Boozer, others ...$8
1992 Jets soaring over stadium $8
1993 Player #93 holding helmet..................$8
1994 J. Johnson, B. Washington..................$8
1995 Mo Lewis $8
1996 ....$8
1997 B. Parcells, A, Murrrell, W. Chrebet....$8
1998 ....$8
1999 Bill Parcells, others $8
2000 Coach Al Groh.....................................$8
2001 H. Edwards, V. Testaverde, others.....$8
2002 Group of players with hands in air $8

Oakland Raiders

Oakland Raiders
1968 Raider ballcarrier $25
Los Angeles Raiders
1982 Raider player on the sidelines $8
1983 Raiders in action $8
1984 Super Bowl XVIII ring $8
1985 Helmet, three Super Bowl trophies.....$8
1986 Team logo..$6
1987 Matt Millen $6
1988 Van McElroy $6
1989 Team helmet $6
1990 Team helmet $6
1991 ....$6
1992 "Tradition of Greatness".....................$6
1993 ....$6
1994 ....$6
Oakland Raiders
1995 Super Bowl trophies $6
1996 Trophies, Raiders helmet....................$6
1997 ....$6
1998 ....$6
1999 Trophies and Team Helmet.................$6
2000 Trophies and Team Helmet.................$6
2001 Trophies and Team Helmet.................$6
2002 Trophies and Team Helmet.................$6

Philadelphia Eagles

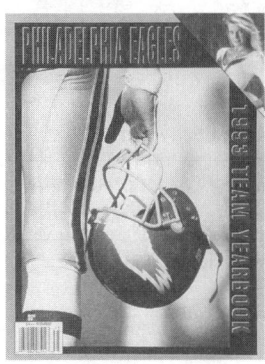

1972 Eagles vs. Dallas Cowboys $25
1973 Eagles vs. Kansas City Chiefs $20
1974 H. Carmichael, R. Gabriel $20
1975 Eagles in action $20
1976 Dick Vermiel $20
1977 ....$20
1978 ....$20
1979 "Winners"...$20
1980 "The Eagles have Arrived"................$15
1981 NFC Champions ring.........................$10
1982 Eagles memorabilia...........................$10
1983 H. Carmichael, W. Montgomery $10
1984 Ron Jaworski $10
1985 ....$10
1986 Mike Quick.......................................$10
1987 Reggie White.....................................$10

1988 Mike Quick.......................................$10
1989 William Frizzell, others $10
1990 Randall Cunningham..........................$10
1991 Player raising football over head $8
1992 Eagles on defense.............................$8
1993 Player holding a helmet at his side.....$8
1994 Four Eagle defenders $8
1995 Ricky Watters $7
1996 Eagles defense in action $7
1997 Ray Rhodes, Irving Fryar $7
1998 Bobby Hoying, Tommy McDonald $7

Pittsburgh Steelers

1978 Super Bowl trophies $10
1979 T. Bradshaw, J. Greene $10
1980 T. Bradshaw, others $10
1990 B. Brister, L. Lipps, R. Woodson, others . $8
1991 Team helmet $8
1992 Steelers greats $8
1993 Bill Cowher, action scenes $8
1994 Night scene of city, helmet $8
1995 N. O'Donnell, B. Cowher, others $8
1996 Bill Cowher holding trophy..................$8
1997 Team helmet $8
1998 Crowded stadium during game $8
1999 J. Bettis, K. Stewart, others $8
2000 Millennium Edition $8
2001 Three Rivers Stadium........................$8
2002 Collage of Players - 70 seasons.........$8

St. Louis Rams

Los Angeles Rams
1958 Cartoon running back.......................$40
1959 Cartoon mascot on a ram.................$40
1960 Cartoon ram, helmet $35
1961 Cartoon ram $35
1962 Jon Arnett..$35
1963 Dick Bass $35
1983 Rams offense $10
1984 Quarterback taking snap $10
1985 Football cards of Rams greats $10
1987 Ram's head, helmet $10
1988 Rams '88 with action photos inside ..$10
1989 10th Anniversary in Anaheim $10
1990 Newspaper headlines........................$8
1991 ....$8
1992 ....$8
1993 ....$8
1994 Jerome Bettis $5
St. Louis Rams
1995 Bern Bostek......................................$8
1999 Trent Green $8
2000 Kurt Warner, M. Faulk $8
2001 Marshall Faulk $8
2002 K. Warner, A. Williams, M. Faulk $8

San Diego Chargers

1984 Dan Fouts..$15
1988 Player artwork $10

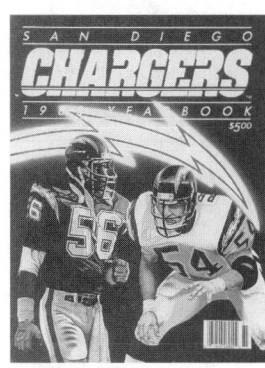

1989 Chargers helmet...............................$10
1991 Football flying over stadium...............$8
1992 Marion Butts $8
1993 B. Ross, J. Seau, R. Harmon, others . $8
1994 Junior Seau in action.........................$8
1995 AFC Championship ring $8
1996 ....$8
1997 ....$8
1998 Ryan Leaf, J. Seau, others $8
1999 Junior Seau $8
2000 L. Alworth, J. Seau, D. Fouts, others ..$8
2001 D. Flutie, J. Seau, R. Harrison $8
2002 J. Seau...$8

San Francisco 49ers

1958 Team mascot shooting guns.............$50
1963 John Brodie $40
1982 ....$20
1983 ....$15
1984 B. Walsh, J.. Montana, others $15
1985 Bill Walsh, Super Bowl celebration...$10
1986 Joe Montana.....................................$15
1987 J. Montana, R. Francis $15
1988 Red Porsche, Golden Gate Bridge $9
1989 Three Super Bowl trophies.................$9
1990 Super Bowl trophies $9
1991 Winning Tradition Continues...............$9
1992 J. Montana, J. Rice............................$9
1993 Steve Young $9
1994 Jerry Rice $8
1995 Five Time World Champions $8
1996 50th Anniversary $8
1997 New Era Begins.................................$8
1998 Rice, J.J. Stokes, T. Owens $8
2001 Jeff Garcia, Terrell Owens $8
2002 Group Picture $8

Seattle Seahawks

1976 Team helmet, NFL pennants $25
1987 E. Robinson, others..........................$10
1988 Team helmet.....................................$8
1989 Team helmet.....................................$8
1993 Defense gang tackling a Falcon $8
1994 Rick Mirer $8

1997 Defensive pileup $8
1998 Warren Moon $8
2000 Coach Mike Holmgren $8
2001 Husky Stadium $8

Tampa Bay Buccaneers

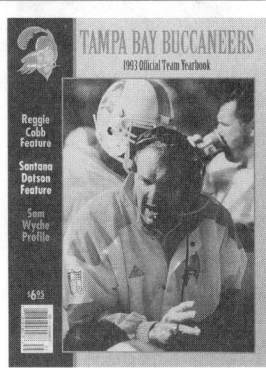

1992 Center snapping ball to quarterback ..$8
1993 Sam Wyche $8
1994 ....$6
1995 ....$6
1996 ....$6
1997 ....$6
1998 T. Dilfer, H. Nickerson $6
1999 M. Alstott, R. Brooks $10
2000 Collage of players $8
2001 Collage of players $8

Tennessee Titans

Houston Oilers
1965 Oilers vs. San Diego Chargers $40
1968 ....$30
1970 ....$30
1990 ....$8
1991 Warren Moon $8
1992 Jack Pardee $8
1993 C. Duncan, E. Givens, H. Jeffires,
    W. Slaughter $8
1994 Ray Childress $8
1995 Graphics, generic player photo $8

Tennessee Oilers

1998 Eddie George, Steve McNair $8

Tennesee Titans

1999 Eddie George $8
2000 B. Adams, B. Matthews, others $8
2001 Kevin Carter, Jevon Kearse $8
2002 Steve McNair $8

Washington Redskins

1973 George Allen, Chris Hanburger $25
1974 George Allen, others $20
1976 Redskins' field goal attempt $20
1977 ....$20
1986 50th Anniversary logo $10
1987 Doug Williams $10
1988 Super Bowl action photos $10
1989 K. Bryant, M. Rypien, R. Sanders,
    D. Williams $8

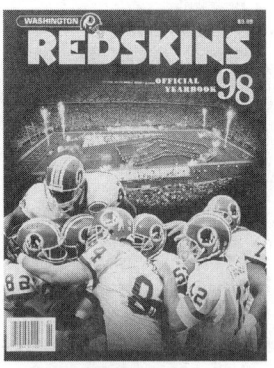

1990 Art Monk, others $8
1991 Game action $8
1992 A. Monk, R. Grimm, J. Jacoby, others ... $8
1993 Redskins defense $8
1994 Norv Turner, Heath Schuler $7
1995 B. Mitchell, H. Schuler $7
1996 Norv Turner, player collage $7
1997 Collage of players $7
1998 Players celebrating, marching band ...$7
1999 Collage of players $7
2000 D. Sanders, B. Smith, D. Green $7
2001 Collage of players $7
2002 Steve Spurrier, Marvin Lewis $7

HOCKEY MEDIA GUIDES

Anaheim Mighty Ducks

1993-94 Inaugural season $12
1994-95 Guy Hebert goalie mask $8
1995-96 O. Tverdovsky, P. Kaiya $8
1996-97 P. Kariya, T. Selanne $8
1997-98 Crowd scenes, players celebrating...$8
1998-99 P. Kariya, T. Selanne $8
1999-00 Collage of photos $10
2000-01 P. Kariya, T. Selanne, S. Rucchin ..$8
2001-02 Kariya, Selanne, others $8
2002-03 10th Season Memorabilia $8

Atlanta Thrashers

2000-01 Player celebration $10
2001-02 Ray Ferraro $8
2002-03 Dany Heatley with trophy $8

Boston Bruins

1946-47 ....$150
1947-48 ....$125
1948-49 ....$100
1949-50 ....$75
1950-51 ....$50

1951-52 Team logo and year $50
1952-53 Bear's head artwork $50
1953-54 Bear's head artwork $50
1954-55 Bear"s head artwork $50
1955-56 Bruins name and year $50
1956-57 Bruins name and year $50
1957-58 Bruins name and year $50
1958-59 Bruins name and year $50
1959-60 Bear cartoon $40
1960-61 Bruin cartoon $30
1961-62 Bruins mascot and year $30
1962-63 Wayne Connelly $30
1963-64 John Bucyk $75
1964-65 Gary Dornhofer, Bobby Leiter $50
1965-66 Ed Johnston $50
1966-67 Murray Oliver $45
1967-68 Bobby Orr $60
1968-69 Bruins action vs. Montreal $45
1969-70 Esposito, Hodge vs. Blackhawks....$45
1970-71 Bruins vs. Blackhawks $45
1971-72 Pregame anthems with Montreal ...$40
1972-73 Stanley Cup trophy $40
1973-74 50th Anniversary w, Esposito, Orr ..$30
1974-75 John Bucyk $30
1975-76 Terry O'Reilly $25
1976-77 Don Cherry, Park, Ratelle $25
1977-78 Gerry Cheevers $25
1978-79 Bob Schmautz $15
1979-80 Rick Middleton $15
1980-81 Ray Bourque $12
1981-82 Wayne Cashman $12
1982-83 Steve Kasper with Selke Trophy $9
1983-84 60th Anniversary, Peter Peeters
    with Vezina Trophy $9
1984-85 Barry Pederson $9
1985-86 Bruins hockey pucks $9
1986-87 Gord Kluzak $9
1987-88 Ray Bourque with Norris Trophy ...$9

1988-89 Cam Neely $9
1989-90 Rejean Lemelin, Andy Moog $9
1990-91 Team artwork $9
1991-92 Ray Bourque $9
1992-93 Fred Cusick $9
1993-94 Adam Oates $9
1994-95 "Thanks for the Memories" $8
1995-96 M. Czerkawski, J. Rohloff, B. Lacher $7
1996-97 T. Donato, R. Bourque, others $7
1997-98 Ray Bourque $7
1998-99 Bruins' Calder Trophy winners $7
1999-00 Ray Bourque $7
2000-01 D. Sweeney, B. Dafoe, others $7
2001-02 Joe Thornton $7
2002-03 Brian Rolston, Glen Murray $7

Buffalo Sabres

1970-71 Team logo and year $85
1971-72 Action photo $30
1972-73 Roger Crozier $25
1973-74 Gil Perreault $25
1974-75 Richard Martin $20
1975-76 Rene Robert $20
1976-77 Danny Gare $15
1977-78 Gerry Desjardins $15
1978-79 Don Edwards $10
1979-80 Craig Ramsay $9
1980-81 Danny Gare $9
1981-82 Danny Gare, others $9
1982-83 Gil Perreault $9
1983-84 Mike Ramsey $9
1984-85 Tom Barrasso $9
1985-86 Tom Barrasso, Bob Sauve $9
1986-87 Sabres in action $9
1987-88 Team logo and bench $9
1988-89 Tom Barrasso $9
1989-90 Phil Housley $9
1990-91 Pierre Turgeon $9

1991-92 Dave Andreychuk $9
1992-93 Pat LaFontaine $9
1993-94 LaFontaine, Hasek, Mogilny, May.....$9
1994-95 25th Anniversary logo $7
1995-96 Memorabilia collage $7
1996-97 Sabres logo on jersey $7
1997-98 M. Barnaby, D. Audette, D. Hasek $7
1998-99 Dominick Hasek $7

Calgary, Atlanta Flames

Atlanta Flames
1972-73 Team logo $45
1973-74 Team logo, Phil Myre...................$35
1974-75 Flames and Flyers fighting..........$30
1975-76 Team logo, photos.......................$20
1976-77 Daniel Bouchard $20
1977-78 Tom Lysiak, Willi Plett, Eric Vail ..$20
1978-79 Team uniform, puck, equipment ..$20
1979-80 Guy Chouinard.............................$20

Calgary Flames
1980-81 Team logo $20
1981-82 Kent Nilsson $12
1982-83 Team logo $6
1983-84 Lanny McDonald $10
1984-85 Lanny McDonald $10
1985-86 Goalie gloves a puck $8
1986-87 Campbell Conference trophy $9
1987-88 Joe Mullen.....................................$9
1988-89 Hakan Loob, Joe Nieuwendyk $9
1989-90 Stanley Cup trophy.......................$9
1990-91 Al MacInnis, Sergei Makarov $9
1991-92 ....$9
1992-93 Gary Roberts $9
1993-94 Art of Flames celebrating..............$9
1994-95 Olympic Saddledome.....................$8
1995-96 Trevor Kidd action photo $6
1996-97 G. Roberts with Masterton Trophy $6
1997-98 Collage of "Young Guns" $6
1998-99 V. Bure, J. Wiemer, others.............$6
1999-00 Player Collage...............................$6
2000-01 Photos of four players $6
2001-02 Collage of photos $6
2002-03 Photos of three players $6

Carolina Hurricanes

1997-98 Hurricanes Player.........................$7
1998-99 Trevor Kidd $6
2000-01 Action photos $6
2001-02 Jeff O'Neill...................................$6
2002-03 Ron Francis $7

Chicago Blackhawks
1960-61 ....$75
1961-62 ....$50
1962-63 ....$45
1963-64 Team logo and year....................$45
1964-65 ....$45
1965-66 Team logo and year....................$45
1966-67 ....$45
1967-68 B. Hull, S. Mikita, A. Wirtz $45
1968-69 B. Hull, S. Mikita, W. Wirtz $45
1969-70 Team logo and year....................$30
1970-71 Team mascot, Wales Trophy $30
1971-72 Team logo and year, Western
    Division Champions.............................$30
1972-73 Team mascot................................$25
1973-74 Team logo, artwork......................$25
1974-75 Team artwork $25
1975-76 50th Anniversary artwork $25
1976-77 Team logo and year.....................$15
1977-78 Team logo, artwork......................$15
1978-79 Team logo and crossed sticks $15
1979-80 Team logo.....................................$15
1980-81 Tony Esposito, others $12
1981-82 Denis Savard, Darryl Sutter $12
1982-83 Doug Wilson and Norris Trophy $4
1983-84 Celebration photos $9
1984-85 Denis Savard, Al Secord, others ...$9
1985-86 Chicago has Fans slogan..............$9
1986-87 R. Murray, D. Savard, Al Secord....$9
1987-88 Bob Murdock, other coaches $9
1988-89 Denis Savard photos and locker ...$9
1989-90 Celebration photos $9
1990-91 All-Star Game logo........................$9
1991-92 J Roenick, C. Chelios, others........$9
1992-93 Action photos $9
1993-94 Chicago Stadium art $6
1994-95 Logo from draped uniform.............$6
1995-96 Logo and "Cold Steel on Ice" $6
1996-97 Chris Chelios.................................$6
1997-98 Tony Amonte $6
1998-99 Blackhawks logo $6
1999-00 ....$6
2000-01 75th anniversary $6
2001-02 Indian head logo $6
2002-03 Players, crowd, american flag $6

Colorado Avalanche
1995-96 Avalanche logos $7
1996-97 Stanley Cup, Denver skyline $7
1997-98 Closeup of team logo on jersey.....$7
1998-99 Mountain scene with avalanche $7

1999-00 The Pepsi Center $10
2000-01 NHL All-Star logo $10
2001-02 Stanley Cup.................................$10
2002-03 Team Banners-Pursuing History ...$8

Colorado Rockies
1976-77 Team logo.....................................$40
1977-78 Mountains photo, team logo........$35
1978-79 Mountains, stream, team logo.....$25
1979-80 Don Cherry...................................$25
1980-81 Lanny McDonald $30
1981-82 Action photos, team logo............$40
Became New Jersey Devils in 1982-83

Columbus Blue Jackets
2000-01 Logo $12
2001-02 Collage of players $8
2002-03 E. Knutson, R. Whitney, R. Klesla.... $8

Dallas Stars

As Minnesota North Stars
1967-68 Team logo.....................................$35
1968-69 Cesare Maniago...........................$35
1969-70 Danny Grant, Calder Trophy........$35
1970-71 Danny O'Shea...............................$25
1971-72 North Stars vs. Boston Bruins.....$25
1972-73 Cesare Maniago, G. Worsley $25
1973-74 Dennis Hextall $25
1974-75 Bill Goldsworthy $20
1975-76 North Stars in action $15
1976-77 North Stars vs. Calgary Flames ..$15
1977-78 R. Eriksson, S. Jensen, A. Pirus,
    G.Sharpley..$15
1978-79 North Stars uniforms $15
1979-80 Action artwork $12
1980-81 Al MacAdam, Steve Payne..........$12
1981-82 Don Beaupre, others....................$12
1982-83 Celebrating vs. St. Louis Blues $9
1983-84 John Mariucci artwork $9
1984-85 Neal Broten $9
1985-86 A. Shaver, action photos $9
1986-87 Neal Broten with trophies.............$9
1987-88 Dino Ciccarelli $9
1988-89 Celebration photo.........................$9

1989-90 Player in action.............................$9
1990-91 B. Bellows, N. Broten, J. Casey $9
1991-92 Memorabilia................................$9
1992-93 ....$9

As Dallas Stars

1993-94 Artwork of Dallas city skyline $12
1994-95 Mike Modano illustration $8
1995-96 Andy Moog...................................$6
1996-97 J. Nieuwendyk, M. Modano $6
1997-98 Spotlighted logo, action photos $6
1998-99 President's Trophy..........................$6
1999-00 Player shot holding the Cup $6
2000-01 M. Modano, Belfour, skyline $6
2001-02 Modano, Turgeon, Nieuwendyk.....$6
2002-03 10th Season Dallas Collage..........$6

Detroit Red Wings

1960-61 Cartoon $125
1961-62 ....$100
1962-63 Team logos................................$100
1963-64 ....$100
1964-65 ....$75
1965-66 ....$75
1966-67 R. Crozier, A. Delvecchio, G. Howe. $75
1967-68 ....$65
1968-69 Gordie Howe $65
1969-70 ....$50
1970-71 Gordie Howe $50
1971-72 Alex Delvecchio............................$30
1972-73 Alex Delvecchio............................$30
1973-74 A. Delvecchio, M. Redmond........$30
1974-75 Alex Delvecchio............................$20
1975-76 Goalie mask.................................$20
1976-77 50th Anniversary photos $15
1977-78 Goalie mask, logos $15
1978-79 Action photos with headlines $15
1979-80 Olympia Stadium, Joe Louis Arena. $15
1980-81 Red Wings in action $15
1981-82 Reed Larson.................................$15
1982-83 Team artwork $9
1983-84 Goalie net, team jersey $9
1984-85 Team logo, action photos $9
1985-86 John Ogrodnick.............................$9
1986-87 J. Demers, P. Klima, S. Yzerman ..$9

1987-88 J. Demers, celebration photos $9
1988-89 J. Demers, G. Gallant, S. Yzerman ... $9
1989-90 Team logo and management.........$9
1990-91 Shawn Burr, Steve Yzerman $9
1991-92 S. Fedorov, M. Ilitch......................$9
1992-93 Y. Racine, P. Ysebaert, others......$9
1993-94 Yzerman, Fedorov, Bowman $9
1994-95 Sergei Ferorov w, trophies $8
1995-96 Team celebration, 70th Anniv. $8
1996-97 "Hockeytown" winged wheel logo ...$8
1997-98 "Hockeytown" winged wheel logo ...$8
1998-99 Stanley Cup, "Hockeytown"...........$8
1999-00 Red Wings logo............................$8
2000-01 Red Wings logo............................$8
2001-02 Nicklas Lidstrom...........................$8
2002-03 Stanley Cup..................................$10

Edmonton Oilers

1975-76 Fight vs. Cleveland......................$50
1976-77 Oilers in action $40
1977-78 ....$40
1978-79 Dave Dryden, Hamilton $40
1979-80 Dave Dryden, Wayne Gretzky.....$40
1980-81 Wayne Gretzky, Blair McDonald..$35
1981-82 Wayne Gretzky, Andy Moog........$35
1982-83 Oilers puck..................................$20
1983-84 Mark Messier, Andy Moog $20
1984-85 Team uniforms, Stanley Cup $20
1985-86 Wayne Gretzky with trophies.......$25
1986-87 P. Coffey, W. Gretzky with trophies. $12
1987-88 Gretzky, Stanley Cup celebration ...$12
1988-89 10th Anniversary logo $12
1989-90 Team logo....................................$12
1990-91 Mark Messier, trophy...................$12
1991-92 T. Green, coaching staff $12
1992-93 Stanley Cup memorabilia $12
1993-94 Oilers road jersey $12
1994-95 Jason Arnott.................................$6
1995-96 Oilers logo $5
1996-97 Oil pipeline with team logo $5
1997-98 Oilers logo, goaltenders mask.......$5
1998-99 Art collage, 20th Anniversary logo . $5
1999-00 ....$5
2000-01 Tommy Salo $5
2001-02 Goalie's Pads with Oilers Logo $5
2002-03 Hockey Sticks with Oilers Logo $5

Florida Panthers

1993-94 Logo, player on beach...................$9
1994-95 Awards nominees...........................$8
1995-96 Collage of Florida postcards $6
1996-97 Prince of Wales Trophy $6
1997-98 Panthers memorabilia $6
1998-99 Five original Panthers $6
1999-00 P. Bure, V. Kozlov, R. Whitney $6
2000-01 Pavel Bure, Group Shot $6
2001-02 Pavel Bure....................................$6
2002-03 Roberto Luongo, others $6

New England, Hartford Whalers

1972-73 ....$45
1973-74 Ted Green with WHA trophy........$40
1974-75 Al Smith, Hartford Civic Center ...$40

Hartford Whalers

1975-76 Number 5 with Whaler photos.....$35
1976-77 Rick Ley, Webster, others...........$35
1977-78 ....$30
1978-79 Gordie Howe $25
1979-80 Rick Ley $25
1980-81 Dave Keon...................................$10
1981-82 Larry Pleau...................................$10
1982-83 Whalers pucks..............................$10
1983-84 R. Francis, Johnson, B. Stoughton. $10
1984-85 Team logo, Greg Millen $10

1985-86 Ron Francis $10
1986-87 K. Dineen, R. Francis, M. Liut $10
1987-88 Mike Liut......................................$10
1988-89 Ulf Samuelsson, Dave Tippett.....$10
1989-90 Kevin Dineen $10
1990-91 Ron Francis $10
1991-92 ....$10
1992-93 Team jersey..................................$10
1993-94 ....$8
1994-95 C. Pronger, S. Burke, G. Sanderson .$8
1995-96 ....$6

Become Carolina Hurricanes

Los Angeles Kings

1966-67 ....$75
1967-68 ....$75
1968-69 Kings artwork $50
1969-70 Gerry Desjardins $40
1970-71 Team logo $35
1971-72 Bob Pulford $25
1972-73 Butch Goring $25
1973-74 Go Kings artwork $20
1974-75 Butch Goring $15
1975-76 M. Dionne, B. Pulford, R. Vachon ..$15
1976-77 Butch Goring $15
1977-78 M. Dionne, B. Goring, R. Vachon ...$15
1978-79 Marcel Dionne $15
1979-80 M. Dionne, B. Goring, D. Taylor,
R. Vachon $15
1980-81 M. Dionne, C. Simmer,D. Taylor ..$15
1981-82 Mario Lessard $9
1982-83 Steve Bozek $9
1983-84 Marcel Dionne jersey, photos........$9
1984-85 Pat Quinn, Rogie Vachon $9
1985-86 M. Dionne, B. Nicholls, D. Taylor,
others...$9
1986-87 20th Anniversary logo $9
1987-88 B. Nicholls, L. Robitaille, others.....$9
1988-89 Wayne Gretzky, Luc Robitaille.......$9
1989-90 Team logo.....................................$9
1990-91 Fan photos, team logo...................$9
1991-92 Silver season hologram.................$9
1992-93 B. Melrose, N. Beverley.................$9
1993-94 Gretzky, Robitaille, others $9
1994-95 Illustration of unidentified player....$8
1995-96 Wayne Gretzky...............................$6
1996-97 Kings logo and 1996-97 ....$6
1997-98 Kings logo and 1997-98 ....$6
1998-99 Logo, player at faceoff $6
1999-00 ....$6
2000-01 Kings jersey..................................$6
2001-02 Norstrom, Palffy, others................$6
2002-03 Crown logo jersey $6

Minnesota Wild

2000-01 Wild Logo in patch form $10
2001-02 Wild Logo in jersey form...............$8
2002-03 Wild memorabilia photo................$8

Montreal Canadiens

1953-54 Team logo...................................$150
1954-55 Team logo...................................$125
1955-56 Team logo.....................................$75
1956-57 ....$40
1957-58 ....$30
1958-59 ....$25
1959-60 ....$25
1960-61 ....$25
1961-62 ....$125
1962-63 Claude Provost, Henri Richard..$100
1963-64 Jean Beliveau..............................$45
1964-65 ....$45
1965-66 ....$45
1966-67 ....$45

1967-68 ....$45
1968-69 ....$45
1969-70 ....$45
1970-71 Team artwork $30
1971-72 Team logo $30
1972-73 Team logo $30
1973-74 Team artwork $30
1974-75 50th Anniversary artwork $15
1975-76 S. Bowman, G. Lafleur, Pollock...$15
1976-77 Y. Cournoyer, K. Dryden, G. Lafleur $15
1977-78 Serge Savard $15
1978-79 Yvan Cournoyer $15
1979-80 Serge Savard $15
1980-81 Guy Lafleur, Pierre Larouche $15
1981-82 Bob Gainey $12
1982-83 Guy Lafleur, others $12
1983-84 Mario Tremblay..........................$12
1984-85 Guy Carbonneau.........................$12
1985-86 Steve Penney $12
1986-87 Stanley Cup celebration $12
1987-88 Mats Naslund $12
1988-89 M. Nasland, S. Richer, P. Roy,
   others...$12
1989-90 Stanley Cup celebration $12
1990-91 Stephane Richer, Patrick Roy $12
1991-92 ....$12
1992-93 Patrick Roy $12
1993-94 Stanley Cup celebration $12
1994-95 Patrick Roy $9
1995-96 Montreal Forum $9
1996-97 Collage of action photos $9
1997-98 V. Damphousse, M. Recchi, S. Koivu.$9
1998-99 Photo of goalie and net $9
1999-00 ....$9
2000-01 Team logo $9
2001-02 Saku Koivu $9
2002-03 Saku Koivu, Jose Theodore $9

Nashville Predators

1998-99 Memorabilia collage $8
1999-00 Collage of players $8
2000-01 C. Ronning, T. Fitzgerald, others...$8
2001-02 M. Dunham, K. Timonen $8
2002-03 Collage of players $8

New Jersey Devils

1982-83 Devils artwork $20
1983-84 Team in tuxes..............................$12
1984-85 Mel Bridgman...............................$12
1985-86 G. Adams, T. Higgins, D. Sulliman..$12
1986-87 Kirk Muller $12
1987-88 Devils' kids' artwork $12
1988-89 Aaron Broten, Kirk Muller............$12
1989-90 Sean Burke $12
1990-91 John MacLean $12
1991-92 10th Anniversary, action photos ..$10
1992-93 Scott Stevens $10
1993-94 Jacques LeMaire..........................$10
1994-95 Devils' award winners..................$10

1995-96 ....$10
1996-97 15th Anniversary, J. MacLean $10
1997-98 M. Brodeur, others $10
1998-99 Scott Stevens, M. Brodeur $10
1999-00 Arena painting with jerseys $10
2000-01 Scott Stevens w, Stanley Cup $10
2001-02 Devils logo...................................$8
2002-03 Devils logo...................................$8

New York Islanders

1972-73 Team logo...................................$45
1973-74 Billy Harris.................................$30
1974-75 Syl Apps, Denis Potvin................$30
1975-76 Playoff action vs. N.Y. Rangers ...$30
1976-77 Denis Potvin, Chico Resch..........$30
1977-78 Ed Westfall $25
1978-79 Mike Bossy..................................$25
1979-80 Bryan Trottier..............................$25
1980-81 Stanley Cup Champions $20
1981-82 Stanley Cup Champions $15
1982-83 B. Trottier with the Stanley Cup...$12
1983-84 D. Potvin, B. Smith, J. Tonelli,
   B. Trottier $12
1984-85 Mike Bossy 400th goal $12
1985-86 M. Bossy, B. Sutter, J. Tonelli,
   B. Trottier $12
1986-87 Al Arbour, Terry Simpson $12
1987-88 ....$12
1988-89 P. LaFontaine, B. Trottier, others.....$12
1989-90 David Volek $12
1990-91 Pat LaFontaine $12
1991-92 M. Bossy, D. Potvin $12
1992-93 The New Ice Age.........................$9
1993-94 Pierre Turgeon.............................$9
1994-95 Lorne Henning $8
1995-96 Islanders jerseys, M. Milbury.........$6
1996-97 25th anniversary, player photos ...$6
1997-98 Berard, Palffy, McCabe $6
1998-99 Kenny Johnson $6
1999-00 Collage of players $6
2001-02 Michael Peca, Alexei Yashin..........$6
2002-03 Michael Peca................................$6

New York Rangers

1947-48 Inside the Blue Shirt.................$200

1948-49 Buddy O'Connor.......................$175
1949-50 Edgar Laprade $125
1950-51 C. Rayner, 25th Anniversary $125
1951-52 Don Raleigh $75
1952-53 ....$50
1953-54 ....$50
1954-55 Muzz Patrick, Ivan Irwin $50
1955-56 ....$40
1956-57 ....$40
1957-58 ....$40
1958-59 ....$40
1959-60 ....$40
1960-61 ....$40
1961-62 ....$40
1962-63 ....$40
1963-64 Jacques Plante...........................$40
1964-65 Rod Gilbert $40
1965-66 Harry Howell vs. Stan Mikita $40
1966-67 Bob Nevin..................................$40
1967-68 Ed Giacomin...............................$40
1968-69 Jean Ratelle $40
1969-70 Arnie Brown vs. Bobby Hull.........$35
1970-71 Ed Giacomin, Brad Park..............$35
1971-72 Ed Giacomin, Gilles Villemure.....$30
1972-73 Vic Hadfield 50th goal $30
1973-74 Ed Giacomin...............................$30
1974-75 Ted Irvine, Brad Park...................$25
1975-76 50th Anniversary logo $25
1976-77 Rangers jersey artwork $20
1977-78 Phil Esposito, others $20
1978-79 Fred Shero $20
1979-80 John Davidson $15
1980-81 Rangers in action $15
1981-82 Rangers in action $10
1982-83 Rangers in action $6
1983-84 Madison Square Garden..............$10
1984-85 Team jersey.................................$6
1985-86 Empire State Building..................$10
1986-87 Statue of Liberty........................$10
1987-88 J. Bergeron, P. Esposito $10
1988-89 Rangers in action $10
1989-90 Tony Granato, Brian Leetch.........$10
1990-91 M. Gartner, B. Leetch, B. Nicholls.... $9
1991-92 B. Leetch, M. Richter....................$9
1992-93 ....$9
1993-94 B. Leetch, M. Messier $9
1994-95 M. Messier holding Stanley Cup ...$8
1995-96 70th anniversary memorabilia
   collage..$8
1996-97 W. Gretzky, M. Messier $10
1997-98 Brian Leetch $8
1998-99 Statue of Liberty, illustration..........$8
1999-00 Madison Square Garden.............$10
2000-01 75th Anniversary logo $10
2001-02 M. Richter, M. Messier, others $8
2002-03 B. Leach, E. Lindros, P. Bure,
   M. Messier, M. Richter............................$8

Oakland, California Golden Seals

Oakland Seals

1968-69 Seals in action............................$35
1969-70 Seals artwork $25
1970-71 Team artwork $20

California Golden Seals

1971-72 Seals artwork $15
1972-73 Seals artwork $10
1973-74 Goaltender artwork $10
1974-75 Closeup of Goalie mask.............$10
1975-76 Seals in action............................$10

Ottawa Senators

1992-93 Artwork collage $9
1993-94 A. Daigle, A. Yashin......................$7
1994-95 Overhead photo of Senator players..$7
1995-96 ....$7
1996-97 Daniel Alfredsson $7
1997-98 Photographic slides of action $7
1998-99 Senators patch on jersey $7
1999-00 Ted Saunders (original player) ...$10
2000-01 Senators logo $10
2001-02 10th Anniversary Season.............$10
2002-03 Senators Logo, celebrating $8

Philadelphia Flyers

1967-68 Team artwork $35
1968-69 Campbell Trophy $35
1969-70 Flyers artwork $35
1970-71 Team logo, NHL pucks $30
1971-72 TV camera....................................$30
1972-73 Dan Earle, G. Hart $30
1973-74 Flyers artwork $25
1974-75 Stanley Cup artwork.....................$25
1975-76 Trophies $20
1976-77 B. Barber, B. Clarke, R. Leach $20
1977-78 Flyers equipment..........................$20
1978-79 Flyers artwork $20
1979-80 Action photos $6
1980-81 Team logo, photos $15
1981-82 Players' faces $15
1982-83 Action photos $6
1983-84 Bobby Clarke................................$10
1984-85 Brian Propp $10
1985-86 Pelle Lindbergh $10
1986-87 Mark Howe $10
1987-88 Ron Hextall....................................$10
1988-89 Flyers artwork $10
1989-90 Flyers artwork $10
1990-91 Team equipment $9
1991-92 Player illustrations $9
1992-93 Eric Lindros, others $10
1993-94 Eric Lindros, three others..............$9
1994-95 Eight player photos $8
1995-96 M. Renberg, E. Desjardins, others....$8
1996-97 Action scenes, 30th Anniv. logo $9
1997-98 Lindros, Brind 'Amor, Leclair, Coffey $8
1998-99 E. Lindros, R. Brind'Amor, others..$8
1999-00 Six players.....................................$8
2000-01 Collage of players $8

2001-02 Flyers logo with players...............$8
2002-03 Flyers logo with players...............$8

Phoenix Coyotes

1996-97 Coyotes new logo..........................$7
1997-98 Coyotes head logo $7
1998-99 Tkachuk, Roenick, Tocchet,
  others...$7
1999-00 Team logo.......................................$7
2000-01 Team logo.......................................$7
2001-02 Wayne Gretzky...............................$7
2002-03 Collage of players $7

Pittsburgh Penguins

1968-69 Les Binkley....................................$40
1969-70 Team artwork $40
1970-71 Red Kelly $40
1971-72 Team logo......................................$35
1972-73 Team logo......................................$35
1973-74 Ken Schinkel $20
1974-75 Syl Apps..$15
1975-76 Ron Schock....................................$20
1976-77 S. Apps, J. Pronovost, P. Larouche $20
1977-78 Syl Apps..$20
1978-79 Orest Kindrachuk $20
1979-80 Randy Carlyle, George Ferguson .$6
1980-81 Rick Kehoe $15
1981-82 Randy Carlyle, Rick Kehoe $15
1982-83 Michael Dion $6
1983-84 Goal celebration $10
1984-85 Mike Bullard $10
1985-86 Mario Lemieux $10
1986-87 Team memorabilia.........................$10
1987-88 Mario Lemieux $10
1988-89 Mario Lemieux $10
1989-90 T. Barrasso, R. Brown, P. Coffey,
  M. Lemieux..$10
1990-91 S. Bowman, B. Johnson, C. Patrick..$9
1991-92 Stanley Cup celebration $9
1992-93 Lemieux, 1991 Stanley Cup $9
1993-94 Lemieux, Barrasso, others $9
1994-95 Jagr, Barrasso, Francis................$10
1995-96 R. Francis, J. Jagr........................$8
1996-97 30th anniv., Jagr, Lemieux $8
1997-98 R. Constantine, Jagr, Lemieux $8
1998-99 Jaromir Jagr $8
1999-00 Mario Lemieux, Jaromir Jagr.........$8
2000-01 Jaromir Jagr $8
2001-02 Mario Lemieux, Andy Bathgate.....$8
2002-03 Collage of players $8

Quebec Nordiques

1974-75 ....$30
1975-76 ....$25
1976-77 Nordiques fleur-de-lis logo $25
1977-78 ....$25
1978-79 ....$25
1979-80 Nordiques art $20
1980-81 Nordiques art $15
1981-82 Anton and Peter Stastny $15

1982-83 Nordiques art $12
1983-84 M. Goulet, D. Hunter, others........$12
1984-85 Nordiques memorabilia $10
1985-86 Nordiques art $10
1986-87 Team logo......................................$10
1987-88 Nordiques in action $10
1988-89 Goal celebration $10
1989-90 Media equipment..........................$10
1990-91 G. Lafleur, M.Petit, J. Sakic.........$10
1991-92 J. Sakic, celebrating $10
1992-93 O. Nolan, J. Sakic, M. Sundin $10
1993-94 Artwork of generic player $10
1994-95 Quebec skyline, action scenes......$8

Become Colorado Avalanche

San Jose Sharks

1991-92 Sharks memorabilia $15
1992-93 Die cut shark fin $15
1993-94 Shark fin cutting through land $12
1994-95 Hockey equipment.........................$8
1995-96 Puck and ticket stubs $8
1996-97 Blurred battle on ice $7
1997-98 V. Kozlov, O. Nolan, J. Friesen $7
1998-99 D. Sutter, O. Nolan, others $7
1999-00 NHL and Sharks logo on black......$7
2000-01 10th Anniversary Collage $7
2001-02 Hockey with Mega Bite.................$7
2002-03 Seven players & Banner...............$7

St. Louis Blues

1967-68 Keenan, Martin, Schock, others ..$40
1968-69 Glenn Hall $35
1969-70 Vezina and Campbell trophies $35
1970-71 Campbell Trophy $35
1971-72 Team action photos $35
1972-73 St. Louis Arena.............................$35
1973-74 Action photos $30
1974-75 Andy Hebenton, Garry Unger $25
1975-76 Gratton, G. Hall, E. Johnston,
  others...$25
1976-77 Emile Francis................................$20
1977-78 Team artwork $15
1978-79 Team artwork $15
1979-80 Ed Staniowski................................$10

1980-81 Team art......................................$15
1981-82 Mike Liut......................................$9
1982-83 Emile Francis $9
1983-84 Brian Sutter.................................$9
1984-85 Team jersey.................................$9
1985-86 Team logo $9
1986-87 Team memorabilia.......................$9
1987-88 Team artwork $9
1988-89 Berry, Micheletti, Brian Sutter $9
1989-90 Dan Kelly.....................................$9
1990-91 Brett Hull, Rick Meagher $9
1991-92 Artwork of Blues greats.................$9
1992-93 Brett Hull $9
1993-94 Curtis Joseph $9
1994-95 Mike Keenan................................$8
1995-96 Blues team logo $7
1996-97 B. Hull, A. MacInnis, G. Fuhr.........$7
1997-98 Blues memorabilia.......................$7
1998-99 P. Turgeon, C. Pronger, C. Conroy....$7
1999-00 ....$7
2000-01 Chris Pronger...............................$7
2001-02 Various players in action poses.....$7
2002-03 Blues Logo $7

Tampa Bay Lightning

1992-93 Logo, small photos $15
1993-94 Terry Crisp, others.......................$10
1994-95 C. Gratton, D. Puppa, R. Hamrlik..$8
1995-96 Roman Hamrlik $7
1996-97 Three players celebrating a goal...$7
1997-98 Jason Wiemer, others $10
1998-99 Lightning bolt design, jerseys........$8
2000-01 Three Lightning players................$8

Toronto Maple Leafs

1962-63 George Armstrong $75
1963-64 Frank Mahovlich..........................$75
1964-65 Action photos $75
1965-66 Johnny Bower $75
1966-67 Dave Keon....................................$60
1967-68 Dave Keon....................................$60
1968-69 ....$50
1969-70 Maple Leafs in action $50
1970-71 Maple Leafs artwork....................$45

1971-72 Maple Leafs artwork....................$20
1972-73 Maple Leafs Garden, team logo..$20
1973-74 ....$20
1974-75 Team logo....................................$15
1975-76 Team logo....................................$15
1976-77 B. Salming, D. Sittler, others $15
1977-78 T. Horton, B. Salming, D. Sittler,
   others..$15
1978-79 Darryl Sittler $15
1979-80 Borje Salming..............................$15
1980-81 Borje Salming..............................$15
1981-82 50th Anniversary photos $9
1982-83 Rick Vaive 50th goal.....................$9
1983-84 G. Gingras, R. Vaive, W. Poddubny,
   others..$9
1984-85 Allen Bester, Rick Vaive $9
1985-86 Maple Leafs in action $9
1986-87 Goal celebration $9
1987-88 Wendell Clark...............................$9
1988-89 Team logo.....................................$9
1989-90 Vincent Damphousse...................$9
1990-91 V. Damphousse, G. Leeman,
   E Olczyk $6
1991-92 Collage of Maple Leafs greats $9
1992-93...$9
1993-94 Newspaper clippings, souvenirs....$9
1994-95 Logo, goal celebration $8
1995-96 Maple Leafs sweaters $6
1996-97...$6
1997-98...$6
1998-99 Maple Leaf greats $6
1999-00 Collage of players $6
2002-03...$6

Vancouver Canucks

1970-71 Team logo, action photo $60
1971-72 Team logo, action artwork $50
1972-73 Team logo....................................$45
1973-74 Team puck, stick..........................$25
1974-75 Celebration vs. Blackhawks $20
1975-76 Team artwork $20
1976-77 Action photos $20
1977-78 Don Lever, others $15
1978-79 New team logo $15
1979-80 Glen Hanlon $15
1980-81 Canucks vs. North Stars $9
1981-82 Darcy Rota vs. Capitals................$9
1982-83 Fans celebrating...........................$9
1983-84 Action photos $9
1984-85 Team logo.....................................$9
1985-86 Canucks new uniform artwork.......$9
1986-87 Action photos $9
1987-88 B. Burke, B. McCammon, P. Quinn ..$9
1988-89 Stan Smyl.....................................$9
1989-90 Trevor Linden.................................$9
1990-91 Team jerseys, equipment $9
1991-92 Painting of Trevor Linden...............$9
1992-93 P. Bure, K. McLean, P. Quinn $10
1993-94 P. Bure, city in background............$9
1994-95 Photo montage..............................$8
1995-96 P. Bure, K. McLean, P. Quinn $8
1996-97 Lumme, Linden, Bure, Mogilny $8
1997-98 New logo on a jersey.....................$8
1998-99 M. Messier, T. Bertuzzi, others......$8
1999-00 Collage of players, logo.................$8
2000-01 Collage of players $8

Washington Capitals

1974-75 Team locker room.........................$60
1975-76 Ron Low $50
1976-77 Tony White $25
1977-78 Team artwork $25
1978-79 Guy Charron $25
1979-80 Ryan Walter...................................$9

1980-81 M. Gartner, D. Maruk, others.......$20
1981-82 Mike Palmateer $20
1982-83 Dennis Maruk................................$9
1983-84 Rod Langway $12
1984-85 Rod Langway, others.....................$9
1985-86 Bobby Carpenter, Mike Gartner $9
1986-87 Capital building, team puck $9
1987-88 Bobby Gould, Larry Murphy $9
1988-89 15th Anniversary, Scott Stevens ...$9
1989-90 D. Ciccarelli,, R. Courtnall, M. Ridley $9
1990-91 John Druce, Rod Langway............$9
1991-92 Silhoutte of Capitol building..........$9
1992-93 Dale Hunter..................................$9
1993-94 Kevin Hatcher...............................$9
1994-95 Player drawing, Joe Juneau...........$8
1995-96 Bondra, Schoenfeld, Carey $7
1996-97 Bondra, Hunter, Carey, others.......$7
1997-98 Map of downtown DC....................$7
1998-99 Eastern Conference trophy $7
1999-00 Collage of players $7
2001-02 "Caps Intensity"............................$7
2002-03 Logo, goalie photo........................$7

Winnipeg Jets

1972-73 Logo, action artwork....................$35
1973-74...$25
1974-75...$25
1975-76 Jets team photos..........................$25
1976-77 ....$25
1977-78 ....$25
1978-79 WHA Championship trophy.........$25
1979-80 Lars-Erik Sjoberg with WHA trophy $20
1980-81 Dave Christian...............................$20
1981-82 Dave Babych $15
1982-83 Dale Hawerchuk, Calder Trophy $9
1983-84 Dale Hawerchuk, others..............$15
1984-85 L. Boschman, R. Carlyle,
   D. Hawerchuk $9
1985-86 Dale Hawerchuk, Jets puck.........$10
1986-87 Action photos $10
1987-88 Lightning on Ice...........................$10
1988-89 Winnipeg skyline $10
1989-90 B. Ashton, P. Elynuik, others $10
1990-91 Winnipeg Style.............................$10
1991-92 Phil Housley, Shawn Cronin $9
1992-93 Troy Murray, Bob Essensa............$9
1993-94 Tie Domi.......................................$9
1994-95 Goal celebration $7
1995-96 T. Steen, Jets farewell $7
Become Phoenix Coyotes

Chapter 5

PROGRAMS

Many fans purchase a souvenir program to keep score when they attend a game. Others, however, just purchase the program as reading material, or perhaps to secure autographs, which increases the program's value. Although unscored programs are preferred, a scored program, if done neatly, does have intrinsic value; it provides a history of what happened for that particular game, and can trigger fond memories for fans who were there. Programs from games when a record was broken or a significant event happened command premium values, as do those from playoff, championship and all-star games.

Program design and attractiveness add to the value of a program, especially the front cover. Condition is an important factor in determining a program's value. Most collectors want them to be in nice condition, hence it will have a higher value than one which is torn, stained or missing pages. Values given in this guide are for programs in excellent condition, those which show little wear and tear. Other factors in determining a program's value include scarcity and rarity.

Program collecting is a huge hobby. And thanks to online auction sites such as eBay and Yahoo, collectors, dealers and sellers have benefitted by the supply and demand.

Pro football programs from the 1930s draw premium prices and interests. But it's the colorful editions of the 1940s and '50s that add the most artistic value to program collecting. Programs from the old AFL and All-America Football Conference draw remarkable prices, especially for teams no longer in existence.

But there is a growing market for older hockey programs, and also for exhibition games from barnstorming tours by all pro sports teams from the 1930s to '50s. Many times these programs are much more scarce.

Vintage World Series, Super Bowl, Stanley Cup and NBA Championship programs still have high demand. But because of extended playoff series, the market for postseason programs of the past 25 years has flatlined. Some dealers say program collectors, in general, have declined.

WORLD SERIES PROGRAMS

World Series programs have been produced since 1903 when Boston (A.L.) defeated Pittsburgh (N.L.) five games to three. Programs have been produced and saved as souvenirs each year since with the exception of 1904 (when John J. McGraw refused to allow his New York Giants to play an "inferior" team from the American League) and 1994 (MLB strike season).

In general, World Series programs, especially from championship teams, are in more demand than those from All-Star games and regular season games.

Since 1974, only one program has been produced for the World Series for both American and National League teams.

Like any other collectible, the better the condition, the more valuable the program. Programs that are unscored, not torn or faded and containing the original inserts, are more valuable.

Year	Team	Price
1903	Pittsburgh	$15,000/$30,000
1903	Boston	$15,000/$30,000
1904	No series	
1905	Philadelphia	$7,000/$16,000
1905	New York Giants	$7,000/$10,000
1906	Chicago Cubs	$7,000/$10,000
1906	Chicago White Sox	$7,000/$7,500

1917 World Series program

1926 World Series program

1927 World Series program

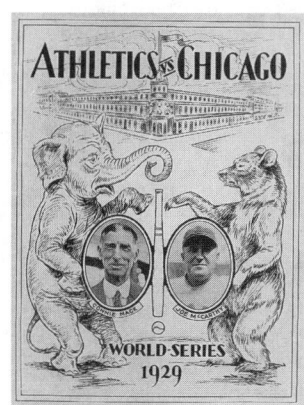

1929 World Series program

1931 World Series program

1933 World Series program

1939 World Series program

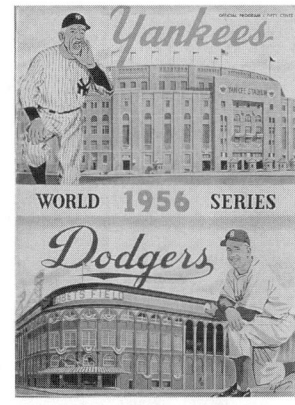
1956 World Series program

Year	Team	Price
1907	Detroit	$10,000/$14,000
1907	Chicago Cubs	$7,000/$10,000
1908	Detroit	$8,000/$12,000
1908	Chicago Cubs	$8,000/$12,500
1909	Detroit	$8,000/$10,000
1909	Pittsburgh	$6,000/$10,000
1910	Chicago Cubs	$5,000/$7,500
1910	Philadelphia A's	$5,000/$10,000
1911	Philadelphia A's	$5,000/$6,000
1911	New York Giants	$3,000/$4,000
1912	New York Giants	$2,000/$4,000
1912	Boston Red Sox	$1,500/$3,000
1913	New York Giants	$2,000/$3,500
1913	Philadelphia A's	$2,000/$4,500
1914	Boston Braves	$3,000/$5,000
1914	Philadelphia	$2,000/$3,500
1915	Philadelphia A's	$2,500/$3,500
1915	Boston Red Sox	$2,000/$3,500
1916	Brooklyn	$2,000/$5,000
1916	Boston Red Sox	$2,000/$4,000
1917	New York Giants	$1,500/$3,500
1917	Chicago White Sox	$3,500/$5,000
1918	Boston Red Sox	$5,000/$10,000
1918	Chicago Cubs	$3,000/$5,000
1919	Cincinnati	$2,500/$4,000
1919	Chicago White Sox	$5,000/$9,000
1920	Brooklyn	$2,000/$5,000
1920	Cleveland	$3,000/$7,000
1921	New York Yankees	$1,500/$3,000
1921	New York Giants	$1,500/$3,000
1922	New York Yankees	$1,500/$2,500
1922	New York Giants	$1,500/$2,500
1923	New York Yankees	$1,500/$4,000
1923	New York Giants	$1,500/$3,500
1924	New York Giants	$1,500/$3,000
1924	Washington	$1,000/$2,000
1925	Pittsburgh	$3,000/$5,000
1925	Washington	$500/$1,000
1926	St. Louis Cardinals	$1,000/$2,000
1926	New York Yankees	$700/$1,500
1927	Pittsburgh	$2,000/$5,000
1927	New York Yankees	$2,000/$3,000
1928	St. Louis Cardinals	$1,000/$1,500
1928	New York Yankees	$1,500/$2,750
1929	Chicago Cubs	$500/$1,000
1929	Philadelphia A's	$1,000/$1,500
1930	St. Louis Cardinals	$400/$750
1930	Philadelphia A's	$500/$1,000
1931	St. Louis Cardinals	$350/$750
1931	Philadelphia A's	$450/$750
1932	Chicago Cubs	$700/$1,000
1932	New York Yankees	$750/$1,250
1933	New York Giants	$700/$1,000

Year	Team	Price
1933	Washington	$550/$700
1934	St. Louis Cardinals	$350/$600
1934	Detroit	$450/$600
1935	Chicago Cubs	$350/$500
1935	Detroit	$500/$700
1936	New York Giants	$200/$400
1936	New York Yankees	$375/$400
1937	New York Giants	$275/$350
1937	New York Yankees	$250/$375
1938	Chicago Cubs	$250/$350
1938	New York Yankees	$200/$400
1939	Cincinnati Reds	$275/$350
1939	New York Yankees	$300/$350
1940	Cincinnati	$300/$350
1940	Detroit	$250/$325
1941	Brooklyn	$200/$400
1941	New York Yankees	$125/$250
1942	St. Louis Cardinals	$125/$250
1942	New York Yankees	$125/$250
1943	St. Louis Cardinals	$200/$250
1943	New York Yankees	$200/$250
1944	St. Louis Cardinals	$175/$250
1944	St. Louis Browns	$200/$350
1945	Chicago Cubs	$150/$200
1945	Detroit	$225/$350
1946	St. Louis Cardinals	$175/$200
1946	Boston Red Sox	$175/$225
1947	Brooklyn	$250/$300
1947	New York Yankees	$175/$250
1948	Boston Braves	$150/$175
1948	Cleveland	$100/$175
1949	Brooklyn	$200/$250
1949	New York Yankees	$175/$200
1950	Philadelphia Phillies	$125/$200
1950	New York Yankees	$150/$225
1951	New York Giants	$150/$225
1951	New York Yankees	$150/$225
1952	Brooklyn	$200/$275
1952	New York Yankees	$150/$200
1953	Brooklyn	$225/$325
1953	New York Yankees	$150/$200
1954	New York Giants	$200/$250
1954	Cleveland	$125/$200
1955	Brooklyn	$250/$300
1955	New York Yankees	$150/$225
1956	Brooklyn	$175/$300
1956	New York Yankees	$125/$200
1957	Milwaukee	$100/$175
1957	New York Yankees	$100/$175
1958	Milwaukee	$100/$175
1958	New York Yankees	$100/$175
1959	Los Angeles	$75/$125
1959	Chicago White Sox	$150/$200

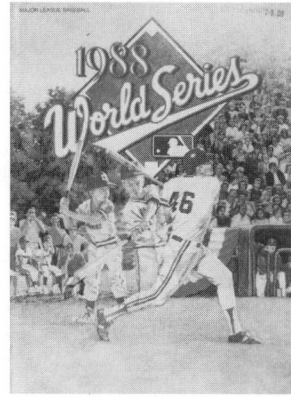

| 1965 World Series program | 1975 World Series program | 1987 World Series program | 1988 World Series program |

Year	Team	Price	Year	Team	Price
1960	Pittsburgh	$100/$125	1974	Oakland/Los Angeles	$15/$35
1960	New York Yankees	$75/$100	1975	Cincinnati/Boston	$25/$50
1961	Cincinnati	$100/$125	1976	Cincinnati/New York Yankees	$15/$30
1961	New York Yankees	$100/$150	1977	New York Yankees/Los Angeles	$10/$25
1962	San Francisco	$150/$225	1978	New York Yankees/Los Angeles	$10/$20
1962	New York Yankees	$75/$100	1979	Pittsburgh/Baltimore	$10/$15
1963	Los Angeles	$60/$75	1980	Philadelphia/Kansas City	$10/$15
1963	New York Yankees	$60/$75	1981	Los Angeles/New York Yankees	$12/$18
1964	St. Louis	$100/$125	1982	St. Louis/Milwaukee	$15
1964	New York Yankees	$60/$75	1983	Philadelphia/Baltimore	$15
1965	Los Angeles	$30/$40	1984	Detroit/San Diego	$10
1965	Minnesota	$75/$100	1985	Kansas City/St. Louis	$10
1966	Los Angeles	$40/$50	1986	New York Mets/Boston	$10
1966	Baltimore	$85/$125	1987	Minnesota/St. Louis	$10
1967	St. Louis	$100/$125	1988	Los Angeles/Oakland	$10
1967	Boston	$100/$125	1989	Oakland/San Francisco	$10
1968	St. Louis	$100/$125	1990	Cincinnati/Oakland	$10
1968	Detroit	$125/$225	1991	Minnesota/Atlanta	$10
1969	New York Mets	$125/$150	1992	Atlanta/Toronto	$10
1969	Baltimore	$50/$75	1993	Toronto/Philadelphia	$10
1970	Cincinnati	$50/$75	1995	Atlanta/Cleveland	$10
1970	Baltimore	$25/$55	1996	New York Yankees/Atlanta	$10
1971	Pittsburgh	$75/$100	1997	Florida/Cleveland	$10
1971	Baltimore	$40/$50	1998	New York Yankees/San Diego	$10
1972	Cincinnati	$50/$75	1999	New York Yankees/Atlanta	$10
1972	Oakland	$60/$75	2000	New York Yankees/New York Mets	$10
1973	New York Mets	$20/$60	2001	Arizona Diamondbacks/New York Yankees	$10
1973	Oakland	$60/$75	2002	Anaheim Angels/San Francisco Giants	$10

PLAYOFF PROGRAMS

The best-of-five League Championship series was initiated in 1969 and expanded to best-of-seven in 1985. With these additional playoff games came the usual parade of collectibles, including programs. These items, and their Division series counterparts, are the least popular of the post-season game programs. As with World Series programs, the programs from the winning team are generally more valuable.

American League

Championship programs

1969 Baltimore		$60-$65
1969 Minnesota		$60-$125
1970 Baltimore		$30-$50
1970 Minnesota		$100-$150
1971 Baltimore		$30-$50
1971 Oakland		$25-$50
1972 Detroit		$85-$115
1972 Oakland		$25-$50
1973 Baltimore		$30-$40
1973 Oakland		$20-$50
1974 Baltimore		$15-$40

Championship programs

1974 Oakland		$300-$350
1975 Boston		$40-$50
1975 Oakland		$40-$50
1976 New York		$10-$15
1976 Kansas City		$7-$15
1977 New York		$12-$15
1977 Kansas City		$10-$20
1978 New York		$7-$15
1978 Kansas City		$10-$20
1979 Baltimore		$60-$85
1979 California		$7-$15
1980 New York		$7-$10

1974 A.L. Playoff program

1976 A.L. Playoff program

1983 A.L. Playoff program

1985 A.L. Playoff program

Championship programs

1980 Kansas City	$7-$12
1981 New York at Oakland	$10-$20
1981 Oakland at New York	$10-$15
1981 K.C. at Oakland	$10-$20
1981 Oakland at K.C.	$40-$60
1981 Milwaukee at New York	$10-$15
1981 New York at Milwaukee	$40-$50
1982 Milwaukee	$60-$85
1982 California	$7-$10
1983 Baltimore	$7-$15
1983 Chicago	$10-$20
1984 Detroit	$7-$15
1984 Kansas City	$15-$20
1985 Toronto	$25-$35
1985 Kansas City	$25-$35
1986 Boston	$7-$15
1986 California	$20-$35
1987 Detroit	$6-$15
1987 Minnesota	$10-$20
1988 Boston	$6-$10
1988 Oakland	$75-$125
1989 Toronto	$20-$30
1989 Oakland	$20-$30
1990 Boston	$20-$30
1990 Oakland	$20-$30
1991 Toronto	$20-$30
1991 Minnesota	$20-$30
1992 Toronto	$20-$30
1992 Oakland	$20-$30
1993 Toronto	$10-$20
1993 Chicago	$10-$20
1995 Cleveland	$10-$20
1995 Seattle	$10-$20
1996 New York	$10-$15
1996 Baltimore	$8-$12
1997 Cleveland	$8-$12
1997 Baltimore	$8-$12
1998 New York	$10-$15
1998 Cleveland	$8-$12
1999 New York	$8-$12
2000 New York	$8-$12
2001 New York	$8-$12
2002 Anaheim	$8-$12

National League

Championship programs

1969 New York	$100-$350
1969 Atlanta	$40-$65
1970 Pittsburgh	$300
1970 Cincinnati	$50-$75
1971 Pittsburgh	$30-$40
1971 San Francisco	$1,000
1972 Pittsburgh	$25-$40

1972 Cincinnati	$20-$30
1973 New York	$50-$75
1973 Cincinnati	$100-$175
1974 Pittsburgh	$200-$250
1974 Los Angeles	$150-$325
1975 Pittsburgh	$7-$15
1975 Cincinnati	$7-$15
1976 Philadelphia	$7-$15
1976 Cincinnati	$50-$75
1977 Philadelphia	$7-$15
1977 Los Angeles	$50-$75
1978 Philadelphia	$7-$12
1978 Los Angeles	$7-$15
1979 Pittsburgh	$7-$12
1979 Cincinnati	$12-$15
1980 Philadelphia	$10-$15
1980 Houston	$40-$50
1981 Houston at Los Angeles	$10-$15
1981 Philadelphia at Montreal	$15-$25
1981 Montreal at Philadelphia	$20-$25
1981 Los Angeles at Montreal	$30-$40
1981 Montreal at Los Angeles	$7-$30
1982 St. Louis	$15-$25
1982 Atlanta	$7-$10
1983 Philadelphia	$5-$15
1983 Los Angeles	$60-$85
1984 Chicago	$15-$20
1984 San Diego	$20-$25
1985 St. Louis	$25-$45
1985 Los Angeles	$50-$60
1986 Houston	$10-$20
1986 New York	$15-$30
1987 St. Louis	$6-$10
1987 San Francisco	$15-$30
1988 New York	$6-$10
1988 Los Angeles	$6-$10

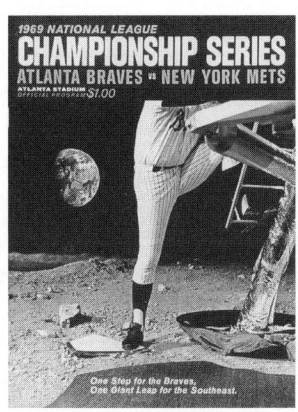
1969 N.L. Playoff program

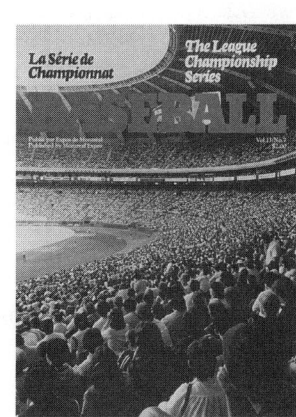
1981 N.L. Playoff program

1989 Chicago	$10-$15
1989 San Francisco	$10-$15
1990 Pittsburgh	$15-$20
1990 Cincinnati	$15-$20
1991 Pittsburgh	$10-$20
1991 Atlanta	$40-$50
1992 Pittsburgh	$10-$20
1992 Atlanta	$40-$50
1993 Philadelphia	$10-$20
1993 Atlanta	$10-$20
1995 Atlanta	$10-$20

1995 Cincinnati	$10-$20
1996 Atlanta	$10-$15
1996 St. Louis	$10-$12
1997 Florida	$10-$12
1997 Atlanta	$10-$12
1998 San Diego	$10-$12
1998 Atlanta	$10-$12
1999 Atlanta	$10-$12
2000 New York Mets	$10-$12
2001 Arizona	$8-$12
2002 San Francisco	$8-$12

LANDMARK GAMES

Programs and tickets from landmark games warrant a premium above the values of other regular-season programs and tickets from the same year. These include games in which a record was broken, a no-hitter was thrown or a milestone was reached.

The tickets from the games in which Cal Ripken Jr. tied and broke the consecutive games record weren't torn at the gate, so only full tickets are available. The same is true of Eddie Murray's 500th home run game. For other games, particularly those that took place decades ago, full tickets are scarce, so a value for the stubs is given. These tickets are denoted with an (S) after the value.

The following price list includes programs and tickets from some monumental games in baseball history.

ALL-TIME LEADERS

DATE	GAME/PLAYER	TICKET	PROGRAM
7/1/41	Joe DiMaggio ties consecutive games w/hit record	$650 (S)	$400
7/2/41	Joe DiMaggio breaks consecutive games w/hit record	1,000 (S)	800
7/17/41	Joe DiMaggio's hitting streak ends	2,500	700
9/26/61	Roger Maris hits record-tying 61st home run	600 (S)	250
10/1/61	Roger Maris hits record 61st home run	1,000 (S)	1,000
4/1/74	Hank Aaron ties all-time home run record	600	100
4/8/74	Hank Aaron breaks all-time home run record	1,500	100
4/27/83	Nolan Ryan breaks all-time strikeout record	200	20
9/11/85	Pete Rose breaks all-time hit record	250	30
5/1/91	Rickey Henderson breaks all-time stolen base record	150	20
9/5/95	Cal Ripken Jr. ties all-time consecutive games played record	100	15
9/6/95	Cal Ripken Jr. breaks all-time consecutive games played record	200	20
9/6/95	Cal Ripken Jr. 2,131 consecutive games (commemorative)	100	30
6/14/96	Cal Ripken Jr. breaks world consecutive games played record	35	20

3,000th HIT GAMES

DATE	PLAYER	TICKET	PROGRAM
9/30/72	Roberto Clemente	$1,000	$75
5/5/78	Pete Rose	200	20
9/12/79	Carl Yastrzemski	100	20
8/4/85	Rod Carew	100	15
9/9/92	Robin Yount	150	22
9/30/92	George Brett	200	22
9/16/93	Dave Winfield	55	20
6/30/95	Eddie Murray	50	15
9/16/96	Paul Molitor	30	12
8/6/99	Tony Gwynn	25	15
8/7/99	Wade Boggs	20	10
4/15/00	Cal Ripken Jr.	30	15

500th HOME RUN GAMES

DATE	PLAYER	TICKET	PROGRAM
5/12/70	Ernie Banks	$200	$25
6/30/78	Willie McCovey	150	12

500th HOME RUN GAMES

DATE	PLAYER	TICKET	PROGRAM
9/17/84	Reggie Jackson	175	25
4/18/87	Mike Schmidt	150	15
9/6/96	Eddie Murray	100	12
8/5/99	Mark McGwire	100	12
4/17/01	Barry Bonds	50	15

300th WIN GAMES

DATE	PLAYER	TICKET	PROGRAM
5/6/82	Gaylord Perry	$100	$12
9/23/83	Steve Carlton	80	12
8/4/85	Tom Seaver	150	18
10/6/85	Phil Niekro	100	12
6/18/86	Don Sutton	100	12
7/30/90	Nolan Ryan	125	15
7/30/90	Nolan Ryan (commemorative)	n/a	20

NO-HIT GAMES

DATE	PLAYER	TICKET	PROGRAM
5/15/73	Nolan Ryan-California	$800	$100
7/15/73	Nolan Ryan-California	700	75
9/28/74	Nolan Ryan-California	400	75
6/1/75	Nolan Ryan-California	400	75
5/30/77	Dennis Eckersley-Cleveland	125	30
6/16/78	Tom Seaver-Cincinnati	125	30
9/26/81	Nolan Ryan-Houston	800	100
6/2/90	Randy Johnson-Seattle	150	30
6/11/90	Nolan Ryan-Texas	125	40
5/1/91	Nolan Ryan-Texas	225	75
7/28/91	Dennis Martinez-Montreal	25	8
9/8/93	Darryl Kile-Houston	25	8
9/17/96	Hideo Nomo-Los Angeles	35	8
5/14/96	Dwight Gooden-New York Yankees	25	8
5/11/96	Al Leiter-Florida	25	8

PERFECT GAMES

DATE	PLAYER	TICKET	PROGRAM
10/8/56	Don Larson-Yankees (World Series)	$500 (S)	$400
9/9/65	Sandy Koufax-Dodgers	400 (S)	100
5/8/68	Jim "Catfish" Hunter-Oakland	250	50
5/15/81	Len Barker-Cleveland	25	10
9/30/84	Mike Witt-California	25	10
9/16/88	Tom Browning-Cincinnati	25	10
7/28/91	Dennis Martinez-Montreal	25	8
7/28/94	Kenny Rogers-Texas	25	8

WORLD SERIES SPECIALS

DATE	GAME/PLAYER	TICKET	PROGRAM
9/29/54	Willie Mays catch	$1,000	$350
10/21/75	Carlton Fisk's HR in 12th inning of Game 6	100	55
10/18/77	Reggie Jackson hits 3 consecutive HRs in Game 6	125	55
10/25/86	Buckner boots grounder in Game 6	75	20
10/15/88	Kirk Gibson's pinch-hit home run Game 1	50	20

SPECIAL REGULAR SEASON GAMES

DATE	GAME/PLAYER	TICKET	PROGRAM
4/18/23	First game at Yankee Stadium	$800 (S)	$800
7/4/41	Lou Gehrig Memorial Day	1,500	100
4/15/47	Jackie Robinson's first Dodgers games	1,000	500
4/27/47	Babe Ruth Day	1,000	200
10/1/51	Bobby Thomson's "Shot Heard Around the World"	800 (S)	750
4/30/52	Ted Williams Day	800	400
4/16/57	Roger Maris' first game	700	100
9/24/57	Last game at Ebbets Field	2,000	1,500
5/7/59	Exhibition game honoring Roy Campanella	450	100
9/29/59	Playoff between Los Angeles and Milwaukee Game 2	250	50
4/10/62	First game at Dodger Stadium	900	150
4/13/62	New York Mets first home game (Polo Grounds)	900	200
10/3/62	Playoff between Los Angeles and San Francisco Game 3	200	40

DATE	GAME/PLAYER	TICKET	PROGRAM
4/8/63	Pete Rose's first Major League game	500	200
9/29/63	Stan Musial's last game	450	400
4/8/69	San Diego Padres' first game (San Diego Stadium)	700	150
4/14/69	Montreal Expos' first home game	250	60
6/8/69	Mickey Mantle Day	1,000	100
6/30/70	First game at Riverfront Stadium	150	35
10/1/70	Last game at Shibe Park	300 (S)	80
4/6/77	Seattle Mariners' first game	75	20
4/7/77	Toronto Blue Jays' first game	100	50
10/2/78	Bucky Dent's three-run homer in playoff vs. Red Sox	200	50
8/1/79	Thurman Munson's last game	400 (S)	25
4/18/81	Tom Seaver's 3,000th strikeout	125	25
7/24/83	George Brett pine tar incident	250	20
4/29/86	Roger Clemens strikes out 20 batters	125	25
9/22/89	Nolan Ryan's 5,000th strikeout	100	18
9/14/90	Ken Griffey Sr. and Jr. hit back-to-back home runs	50	15
4/6/92	First game at Camden Yards	40	20
4/5/93	Colorado Rockies' first game	100	20
4/5/93	Florida Marlins' first game	85	30
4/5/93	Florida Marlins' first game commemorative ticket (2,500 made)	150	n/a
4/9/93	Colorado Rockies' first home game	85	25
9/22/93	Nolan Ryan's last game pitched	35	10
4/4/94	First game at Jacobs Field	75	20
9/18/96	Roger Clemens strikes out 20 batters	45	15
4/15/97	Jackie Robinson Day (Shea Stadium)	25	10

ALL-STAR GAME PROGRAMS

All-Star Game programs are generally scarcer than World Series programs since (with the exception of four years) there has been just one All-Star Game annually rather than a four-to-seven game World Series.

All-Star programs have been printed each year with the exception of 1945 when no game was played due to World War II. Programs from 1934, 1936 and 1942 are particularly scarce.

1933 Chicago	$1,300-$2,500
1934 New York N.L.	$1,500-$3,000
1935 Cleveland	$450-$600
1936 Boston	$3,500-$5,500
1937 Washington	$500-$850
1938 Cincinnati	$700-$1,000
1939 New York A.L.	$800-$1,000
1940 St. Louis	$800-$900
1941 Detroit	$600-$850
1942 New York N.L.	$4,000-$4,500
1943 Philadelphia	$450-$700
1944 Pittsburgh	$1,000-$1,250

1945	no game
1946 Boston	$850-$1,100
1947 Chicago N.L.	$400-$550
1948 St. Louis	$300-$550
1949 Brooklyn	$900-$1,000
1950 Chicago A.L.	$250-$500
1951 Detroit	$150-$300
1952 Philadelphia	$150-$250
1953 Cincinnati	$175-$300
1954 Cleveland	$175-$250
1955 Milwaukee	$125-$175
1956 Washington	$150-$200

1935, Cleveland

1937, Washington

1941, Detroit

1946, Boston

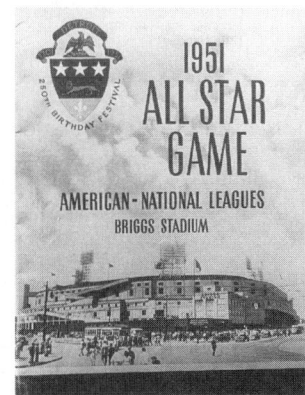

1951, Detroit

1955, Milwaukee

1960, Kansas City

1961, San Francisco

1957 St. Louis	$150-$250
1958 Baltimore	$200-$250
1959 Pittsburgh	$200-$250
1959 Los Angeles	$75-$100
1960 Kansas City	$125-$175
1960 New York A.L.	$75-$100
1961 San Francisco	$350-$500
1961 Boston	$300-$600
1962 Washington	$150-$250
1962 Chicago N.L.	$150-$200
1963 Cleveland	$75-$125
1964 New York N.L.	$200-$325
1965 Minnesota	$75-$125
1966 St. Louis	$150-$250
1967 California	$100-$200
1968 Houston	$75-$150
1969 Washington	$50-$85
1970 Cincinnati	$75-$150
1971 Detroit	$100-$200
1972 Atlanta	$20-$40
1973 Kansas City	$150-$200
1974 Pittsburgh	$20-$40
1975 Milwaukee	$40-$65
1976 Philadelphia	$15-$25
1977 New York A.L.	$7-$20
1978 San Diego	$30-$50
1979 Seattle	$10-$25
1980 Los Angeles	$20-$40
1981 Cleveland	$7-$20
1982 Montreal	$25-$40
1983 Chicago A.L.	$10-$15
1984 San Francisco	$5-$15
1985 Minnesota	$5-$15
1986 Houston	$5-$15
1987 Oakland	$10-$15
1988 Cincinnati	$10-$15

1989 California	$10-$15
1990 Chicago N.L.	$10-$15
1991 Toronto	$10-$15
1992 San Diego	$10-$15
1993 Baltimore	$12-$15
1994 Pittsburgh	$10
1995 Texas	$10
1996 Philadelphia	$10
1997 Cleveland	$10
1998 Colorado	$10
1999 Boston	$10
2000 Atlanta	$10
2001 Seattle	$10
2002 Milwaukee	$10
2003 Chicago A.L.	$10

1982, Montreal

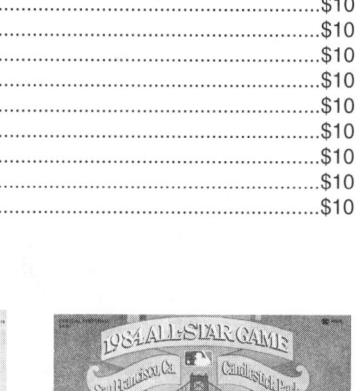

1984, San Francisco

1968, Houston

1974, Pittsburgh

1978, San Diego

1979, Seattle

Football Programs

AFL Championship programs

1960 Houston Oilers vs. Los Angeles
Chargers...$800

1961 San Diego Chargers vs. Houston...$300
1962 Houston Oilers vs. Dallas Texans...$700

1963 San Diego Chargers vs.
Boston .... $150-$200

1964 Buffalo vs. San Diego.....................$250

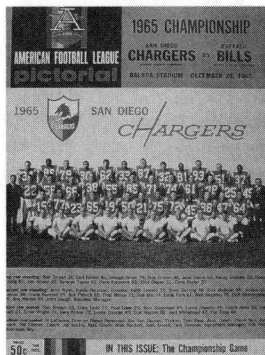

1965 San Diego vs. Buffalo.....................$200

1966 Kansas City vs. Buffalo .... $100-$250
1967 Oakland vs. Houston.....................$125
1968 New York Jets vs. Oakland.............$200
1969 Kansas City vs. New York Jets.......$295

NFL Championship programs

1938 New York vs. Green Bay.............$2,000
1941 Chicago vs. New York $950
1942 Washington vs. Chicago................$900
1943 Washington vs. Chicago....... $700-$900
1944 N.Y. Giants vs. Green Bay.... $600-$750
1945 Cleveland Rams vs.
Washington.............................. $600-$1,000
1946 New York Giants vs. Chicago
Bears .... $600-$700
1947 Philadelphia vs. Chicago Cardinals...$500
1948 Philadelphia vs. Chicago Cardinals...$500
1949 Los Angeles Rams vs. Philadelphia ..$450
1950 Cleveland Browns vs. Los Angeles
Rams $350
1951 Los Angeles Rams vs. Cleveland
Rams .... $250-$350
1952 Detroit vs. Cleveland .... $250-$450
1953 Cleveland vs. Detroit $450

1954 Cleveland vs. Detroit. $300
1955 Los Angeles Rams vs. Cleveland...$250
1956 New York Giants vs. Chicago $325
1957 Cleveland vs. Detroit .... $295-$450
1958 Baltimore vs. New York Giants $400
1959 Baltimore vs. New York Giants $350
1960 Philadelphia vs. Green Bay $300
1961 New York Giants vs. Green Bay $175-$250
1962 New York Giants vs. Green Bay $150-$250
1963 New York Giants vs. Chicago $200
1964 Cleveland vs. Baltimore.................$200
1965 Cleveland vs. Green Bay ...... $125-$200
1967 Green Bay vs. Dallas.....................$250

Super Bowl programs

Early Super Bowl programs are prized collectibles. The first two programs in which the Green Bay Packers were victorious have always been in demand. The Super Bowl III program, in which the New York Jets defeated the Baltimore Colts, as Joe Namath guaranteed, has also increased in value.

Another program that is always high in demand is from Super Bowl V. Plenty of programs were printed for the game; however, a few days prior to the game a truck that was delivering the programs ran off an icy highway and most of the programs were destroyed. Vendors ran out of programs before the game even started.

I at Los Angeles, Jan. 15, 1967 (Green Bay
Packers vs. Kansas City Chiefs).....$275-$395
II at Miami, Jan. 14, 1968 (Green Bay Packers
vs. Oakland Raiders) .... $350-$400
III at Miami, Jan. 12, 1969 (New York Jets vs.
Baltimore Colts) .... $225-$325
IV at New Orleans, Jan. 11, 1970 (Minnesota
Vikings vs. Kansas City Chiefs).. $175-$225
V at Miami, Jan. 17, 1971 (Baltimore Colts vs.
Dallas Cowboys) .... $350-$400

VI at New Orleans, Jan. 16, 1972 (Dallas
Cowboys vs. Miami Dolphins)..... $125-$200
VII at Los Angeles, Jan. 14, 1973 (Miami Dol-
phins vs. Washington Redskins)....$125- $200
VIII at Houston, Jan. 13, 1974 (Minnesota
Vikings vs. Miami Dolphins)........ $125-$200
IX at New Orleans, Jan. 12, 1975 (Pittsburgh
Steelers vs. Minnesota Vikings)......$125-$175

X at Miami, Jan. 18, 1976 (Dallas Cowboys
vs. Pittsburgh Steelers)............... $125-$195
XI at Pasadena, Jan. 9, 1977 (Oakland
Raiders vs. Minnesota Vikings) ...... $65-$95
XII at New Orleans, Jan. 15, 1978 (Dallas
Cowboys vs. Denver Broncos)............$65-$95
XIII at Miami, Jan. 21, 1979 (Pittsburgh Steelers
vs. Dallas Cowboys)...........................$65-$95
XIV at Pasadena, Jan. 20, 1980 (Los Angeles
Rams vs. Pittsburgh Steelers) .... $35-$70
XV at New Orleans, Jan. 25, 1981 (Oakland
Raiders vs. Philadelphia Eagles).... $25-$45
XVI at Pontiac, Jan. 24, 1982 (San Francisco
49ers vs. Cincinnati Bengals) .... $25-$40
XVII at Pasadena, Jan. 30, 1983 (Miami
Dolphins vs. Washington Redskins) ...$25-$40
XVIII at Tampa, Jan. 22, 1984 (Washington
Redskins vs. Los Angeles Raiders)....$25-$35
XIX at Palo Alto, Jan. 20, 1985 (Miami Dolphins
vs. San Francisco 49ers).....................$20-$30

XX at New Orleans, Jan. 26, 1986 (Chicago Bears vs. New England Patriots) .... $20-$30
XXI at Pasadena, Jan. 25, 1987 (Denver Broncos vs. New York Giants) .... $15-$25
XXII at San Diego, Jan. 31, 1988 (Washington Redskins vs. Denver Broncos) .... $15-$25

XXIII at Miami, Jan. 22, 1989 (Cincinnati Bengals vs. San Francisco 49ers) .. $15-$25
XXIV at New Orleans, Jan. 28, 1990 (San Francisco 49ers vs. Denver Broncos) .... $15-$25
XXV at Tampa, Jan. 27, 1991 (Buffalo Bills vs. New York Giants) .... $15-$25
XXVI at Minneapolis, Jan. 26,1992 (Washington Redskins vs. Buffalo Bills) .... $15-$25

XXVII at Pasadena, Jan. 31, 1993 (Buffalo Bills vs. Dallas Cowboys) .... $15-$25

XXVIII at Atlanta, Jan. 30, 1994 (Dallas Cowboys vs. Buffalo Bills)............. $15-$25
XXIX at Miami, Jan. 29, 1995 (San Francisco 49ers vs. San Diego Chargers) .... $15-$20
XXX at Phoenix, Jan. 28, 1996 (Dallas Cowboys vs. Pittsburgh Steelers) ... $15-$20
XXXI at New Orleans, Jan. 26, 1997 (Green Bay Packers vs. New England Patriots) .... $15-$25
XXXII at San Diego, Jan. 25, 1998 (Denver Broncos vs. Green Bay Packers).... $15-$20
XXXIII at Miami, Jan. 31, 1999 (Denver Broncos vs. Atlanta Falcons) $15
XXIV at Atlanta, Jan. 30, 2000 (St. Louis Rams vs. Tennessee Titans) .... $15-$20
XXXV at Tampa, Jan. 28, 2001 (Baltimore Ravens vs. New York Giants) .... $15-$20
XXXVI at New Orleans, Feb. 4, 2002 (New England Patriots vs. St. Louis Rams) .... $15-$20
XXXVII at San Diego, Jan. 26, 2003 (Tampa Bay Buccaneers vs. Oakland Raiders) .... $15-$20

Football playoff game programs

Dec. 22,1968 NFL Western Conference Championship (Minnesota vs. Baltimore)............$50
Dec. 22, 1968 AFL Western Division playoff (Oakland vs. Kansas City) $50
Dec. 20, 1969 inter-division playoff (New York Jets vs. Kansas City).............$65
Dec. 21, 1969 AFL division playoff (Oakland vs. Houston)...........................$45
Dec. 27, 1969 Western Conference Championship (Minnesota vs. Los Angeles).......$40
Dec. 28, 1969 Eastern Conference Championship (Dallas vs. Cleveland) $75
Dec. 26, 1970 AFC divisional playoff (Baltimore vs. Cincinnati)........................$40
Dec. 26, 1970 NFC divisional playoff (Dallas vs. Detroit) $40
Dec. 27,1970 AFC divisional playoff (Oakland vs. Miami)...............................$40
Dec. 27, 1970 NFC divisional playoff (Minnesota vs. San Francisco) $40
Jan. 3, 1971 NFC Championship (San Francisco vs. Dallas).....................$75
Dec. 25, 1971 NFC divisional playoff (Minnesota vs. Dallas) $45
Dec. 25, 1971 AFC divisional playoff (Miami vs. Kansas City).......................$125
Dec. 26, 1971 NFC divisional playoff (San Francisco vs. Washington) $40
Dec. 26,1971 AFC divisional playoff (Cleveland vs. Baltimore)........................$40
Jan. 2,1972 NFC championship (Dallas vs. San Francisco).....................$75
Jan. 2, 1972 AFC championship (Baltimore vs. Miami)..............................$75

Dec. 23, 1972 AFC divisional playoff (Pittsburgh vs. Oakland) $90
Dec. 23, 1972 NFC divisional playoff (San Francisco vs. Dallas) $65
Dec. 24,1972 AFC divisional playoff (Miami vs. Cleveland) $35
Dec. 24, 1972 NFC divisional playoff (Washington vs. Green Bay).................$35
Dec. 31, 1972 NFC divisional playoff (Washington vs. Dallas) $75
Dec. 31, 1972 AFC divisional playoff (Miami vs. Pittsburgh) $65
Dec. 22,1973 AFC divisional playoff (Miami vs. Cincinnati) $35
Dec. 23, 1973 NFC divisional playoff (Los Angeles vs. Dallas) $65
Dec. 23, 1973 AFC divisional playoff (Cincinnati vs. Miami) $35
Dec. 30, 1973 NFC championship (Dallas vs. Minnesota) $65
Dec. 21, 1974 NFC divisional playoff (Minnesota vs. St. Louis) $35
Dec. 22, 1974 AFC divisional playoff (Pittsburgh vs. Buffalo) $35
Dec. 22, 1974 NFC divisional playoff (Los Angeles vs. Washington) $35
Dec. 29, 1974 NFC championship (Minnesota vs. Los Angeles) $45
Dec. 29, 1974 AFC championship (Pittsburgh vs. Oakland $65
Jan. 4, 1975 NFC championship (Los Angeles vs. Dallas) $60
Dec. 27, 1975 NFC divisional playoff (Los Angeles vs. St. Louis) $35
Dec. 28, 1975 NFC divisional playoff (Minnesota vs. Dallas) $75
Dec. 28, 1975 AFC divisional playoff (Cincinnati vs. Oakland) $35
Jan. 4, 1976 AFC championship (Pittsburgh vs. Oakland) $65
Dec. 18,1976 AFC divisional playoff (New England vs. Oakland) $35
Dec. 18, 1976 NFC divisional playoff (Washington vs. Minnesota) $35
Dec. 19, 1976 AFC divisional playoff (Pittsburgh vs. Baltimore) $35
Dec. 19, 1976 NFC divisional playoff (Los Angeles vs. Dallas) $35
Dec. 26,1976 NFC championship (Los Angeles vs. Minnesota) $45
Dec. 24,1977 AFC divisional playoff (Baltimore vs. Oakland) $35
Dec. 24, 1977 AFC divisional playoff (Pittsburgh vs. Denver) $25
Dec. 26,1977 NFC divisional playoff (Chicago vs. Dallas) $25
Dec. 26, 1977 NFC divisional playoff (Minnesota vs. Los Angeles) $25
Jan. 1, 1978 AFC championship (Oakland vs. Denver) $45
Jan. 1, 1978 NFC championship (Minnesota vs. Dallas) $45
Dec. 24, 1978 AFC wildcard (Houston vs. Miami)...............................$25
Dec. 24, 1978 NFC wildcard (Philadelphia vs. Atlanta).......................$25
Dec. 30, 1978 AFC divisional playoff (Pittsburgh vs. Denver) $25
Dec. 30, 1978 NFC divisional playoff (Atlanta vs. Dallas) $25
Dec. 31, 1978 AFC divisional playoff (Houston vs. New England) $25
Dec. 31, 1978 NFC divisional playoff (Minnesota vs. Los Angeles) $25

Jan. 7, 1979 AFC championship
(Houston vs. Pittsburgh) $45

Jan. 7, 1979 NFC championship
(Dallas vs. Los Angeles) $45

Dec. 23, 1979 NFC wildcard
(Philadelphia vs. Chicago) $25

Dec. 23, 1979 AFC wildcard
(Denver vs. Houston) $65

Dec. 29, 1979 NFC divisional playoff
(Philadelphia vs. Tampa Bay) $25

Dec. 29, 1979 AFC divisional playoff
(Houston vs. San Diego) $35

Dec. 30, 1979 NFC divisional playoff
(San Francisco vs. Washington) $40

Dec. 30, 1979 AFC divisional playoff
(Dallas vs. Los Angeles) $25

Jan. 6, 1980 NFC championship
(Los Angeles vs. Tampa Bay) $45

Jan. 6, 1980 AFC championship
(Houston vs. Pittsburgh) $45

Dec. 28, 1980 AFC wildcard
(Houston vs. Oakland) $25

Dec. 28, 1980 NFC wildcard
(Los Angeles vs. Dallas) $25

Jan. 3, 1981 NFC divisional playoff
(Philadelphia vs. Minnesota) $25

Jan. 4, 1981 NFC divisional playoff
(Dallas vs. Atlanta) $25

Dec. 27 1981 AFC wildcard
(Buffalo vs. New York Jets) $35

Jan. 2, 1982 NFC divisional playoff
(Tampa Bay vs. Dallas) $25

Jan. 3, 1982 AFC divisional playoff
(Buffalo vs. Cincinnati) $35

Jan. 10, 1982 AFC championship
(San Diego vs. Cincinnati) $75

Jan. 8, 1983 NFC 1st round
(St. Louis vs. Green Bay) $25

Jan. 9, 1983 AFC 1st round
(San Diego vs. Pittsburgh) $25

Jan. 9, 1983 NFC 1st round
(Dallas vs. Tampa Bay) $25

Jan. 15, 1983 AFC 2nd round
(Raider vs. New York) $25

Jan. 16, 1983 AFC 2nd round
(San Diego vs. Miami) $25

Jan. 23,1983 AFC championship
(Miami vs. New York) $25

Dec. 26, 1983 NFC wildcard
(Dallas vs. Los Angeles) $25

Jan. 1, 1984 NFC divisional playoff
(Washington vs. Los Angeles) $25

Dec. 22, 1984 AFC wildcard
(Seattle vs. Raiders) $25

Dec. 29, 1984 AFC divisional
(Miami vs. Seattle) $25

Dec. 30, 1984 NFC divisional
(Chicago vs. Washington) $25

Dec. 28, 1985 AFC wildcard
(New York Jets vs. New England) $25

Dec. 29, 1985 NFC wildcard
(New York Giants vs. San Francisco) $35

Jan. 4, 1986 AFC divisional
(Miami vs. Cleveland) $25

Jan. 4, 1986 NFC divisional
(Dallas vs. Los Angeles) $25

Jan. 5, 1986 NFC divisional
(Chicago vs. New York) $35

Jan. 12, 1986 NFC championship
(Chicago vs. Los Angeles) $45

Jan. 12,1986 AFC championship
(Miami vs. New England) $45

Dec. 28,1986 AFC wildcard
(Miami vs. Seattle)................................$25

Dec. 28, 1986 NFC wildcard
(Los Angeles vs. Washington) $25

Jan. 3, 1987 AFC divisional
(New York vs. Cleveland) $25

Jan. 3, 1987 NFC divisional
(Chicago vs. Washington) $25

Jan. 11, 1987 NFC championship
(New York vs. Washington) $45

Jan. 11, 1987 AFC championship
(Cleveland vs. Denver) $45

Jan. 3, 1988 NFC wildcard
(New Orleans vs. Minnesota) $20

Jan. 9, 1988 AFC divisional
(Cleveland vs. Indianapolis) $25

Jan. 10, 1988 AFC divisional
(Denver vs. Houston) $35

Jan. 10, 1988 NFC divisional
(Chicago vs. Washington) $25

Jan. 17, 1988 AFC championship
(Denver vs. Cleveland) $45

Dec. 26, 1988 NFC wildcard
(Minnesota vs. Los Angeles) $20

Dec. 31, 1988 AFC divisional
(Cincinnati vs. Seattle) $20

Dec. 31, 1988 NFC divisional
(Chicago vs. Philadelphia) $20

Jan. 1, 1989 AFC divisional
(Buffalo vs. Houston) $25

Jan. 1, 1989 NFC divisional
(San Francisco vs. Minnesota) $20

Jan. 8, 1989 NFC championship
(Chicago vs. San Francisco)...................$35

Dec. 31, 1989 NFC wildcard
(Philadelphia vs. Los Angeles) $20

Jan. 6, 1990 AFC divisional
(Buffalo vs. Cleveland) $25

Jan. 7, 1990 NFC divisional
(New York vs. Los Angeles) $25

Jan. 14, 1990 AFC championship
(Denver vs. Cleveland) $40

Jan. 5, 1991 NFC wildcard
(Philadelphia vs. Washington) $20

Jan. 6, 1991 NFC wildcard
(New Orleans vs. Chicago).....................$20

Jan. 12, 1991 NFC divisional
(San Francisco vs. Washington) $25

Jan. 13, 1991 NFC divisional
(Chicago vs. New York) $25

Dec. 28, 1991 NFC wildcard
(Atlanta vs. New Orleans) $20

Dec. 29, 1991 AFC wildcard
(Houston vs. New York) $20

Dec. 29, 1991 NFC wildcard
(Chicago vs. Dallas) $20

Jan. 5, 1992 AFC divisional
(Buffalo vs. Kansas City) $25

Jan. 12, 1992 AFC championship
(Buffalo vs. Denver) $35

Jan. 3, 1993 NFC wildcard
(New Orleans vs. Philadelphia) $15

Jan. 15, 1994 NFC divisional
(San Francisco vs. New York Giants) $15

Jan 16, 1994 NFC divisional
(Dallas vs. Green Bay) $15

Jan. 23, 1994 AFC championship
(Buffalo vs. Kansas City) $15

Jan. 23, 1994 NFC championship
(Dallas vs. San Francisco) $15

Dec. 31, 1994 AFC wildcard
(Miami vs. Kansas City) $12

Jan. 1, 1995 AFC wildcard
(Cleveland vs. New England)...................$12

Dec. 31, 1994 NFC wildcard
(Green Bay vs. Detroit) $12

Jan. 1, 1995 NFC wildcard
(Chicago vs. Minnesota) $12

Jan. 7, 1995 AFC divisional
(Pittsburgh vs. Cleveland) $12

Jan. 7, 1995 NFC divisional
(San Francisco vs. Chicago) $12

Jan. 8, 1995 AFC divisional
(San Diego vs. Miami) $12

Jan. 8, 1995 NFC divisional
(Dallas vs. Green Bay)...........................$12

Jan. 15, 1995 AFC championship
(San Diego vs. Pittsburgh) $12

Jan. 15, 1995 NFC championship
(San Francisco vs. Dallas) $12

Dec. 30, 1995 AFC wildcard
(Buffalo vs. Miami) $10

Dec. 31, 1995 AFC wildcard
(Indianapolis vs. San Diego) $10

Dec. 30, 1995 NFC wildcard
(Philadelphia vs. Detroit) $10

Dec. 31, 1995 NFC wildcard
(Green Bay vs. Atlanta) $10

Jan. 6, 1996 AFC divisional
(Pittsburgh vs. Buffalo) $10

Jan. 7, 1996 AFC divisional
(Indianapolis vs. Kansas City) $10

Jan. 6, 1996 NFC divisional
(Green Bay vs. San Francisco) $12

Jan. 7, 1996 NFC divisional
(Dallas vs. Philadelphia) $12

Jan. 14, 1996 AFC championship
(Pittsburgh vs. Indianapolis) $10

Jan. 14, 1996 NFC championship
(Dallas vs. Green Bay)...........................$12

Dec. 28, 1996 AFC wildcard
(Jacksonville vs. Buffalo) $10

Dec. 29, 1996 AFC wildcard
(Pittsburgh vs. Indianapolis) $10

Dec. 28, 1996 NFC wildcard
(Dallas vs. Minnesota) $10

Dec. 29, 1996 NFC wildcard
(San Francisco vs. Philadelphia) $10

Jan. 4, 1997 AFC divisional
(Jacksonville vs. Denver) $10

Jan. 4, 1997 NFC divisional
(Green Bay vs. San Francisco)...............$10

Jan. 5, 1997 AFC divisional
(New England vs. Pittsburgh) $10

Jan. 5, 1997 NFC divisional
(Carolina vs. Dallas) $10

Jan. 12, 1997 AFC championship
(New England vs. Jacksonville) $10

Jan. 12, 1997 NFC championship
(Green Bay vs. Carolina) $10

Jan. 3, 1998 AFC divisional
(Pittsburgh vs. New England) $10

Jan. 3, 1998 NFC divisional
(Minnesota vs. San Francisco) $10

Jan. 4, 1998 AFC divisional
(Denver vs. Kansas City) $10

Jan. 4, 1998 NFC divisional
(Tampa Bay vs. Green Bay)....................$10

Jan. 11, 1998 AFC championship
(Denver vs. Pittsburgh) $10

Jan. 11, 1998 NFC championship
(Green Bay vs. San Francisco)..............$10

Jan. 9, 1999 AFC divisional
(Miami vs. Denver)................................$10

Jan. 9, 1999 NFC divisional
(San Francisco vs. Atlanta) $10

Jan. 10, 1999 AFC divisional
(New York Jets vs. Jacksonville).............$10

Jan. 10, 1999 NFC divisional
(Arizona vs. Minnesota) $10

Jan. 17, 1999 AFC championship (New York Jets vs. Denver Broncos) $10
Jan. 17, 1999 NFC championship (Atlanta vs. Minnesota) $10
Jan. 15, 2000 AFC divisional (Jacksonville vs. Miami) $10
Jan. 15, 2000 NFC divisional (Tampa Bay vs. Washington) $10
Jan. 16, 2000 AFC divisional (Tennessee vs. Indianapolis) $10
Jan. 16, 2000 NFC divisional (St. Louis vs. Minnesota) $10
Jan. 23, 2000 AFC championship (Tennessee vs. Jacksonville) $10
Jan. 23, 2000 NFC championship (Tampa Bay vs. St. Louis) $10
Jan. 6, 2001 AFC divisional (Miami vs. Oakland) $10
Jan. 6, 2001 NFC divisional (New Orleans vs. Minnesota) $10
Jan. 7, 2001 AFC divisional (Baltimore vs. Tennessee) $10
Jan. 7, 2001 NFC divisional (Philadelphia vs. New York Giants) $10
Jan. 14, 2001 AFC championship (Baltimore vs. Oakland) $10
Jan. 14, 2001 NFC championship (Minnesota vs. New York Giants) $10
Jan. 19, 2002 AFC divisional (Oakland vs. New England) $10
Jan. 19, 2002 NFC divisional (Philadelphia vs. Chicago) $10
Jan. 20, 2002 AFC divisional (Baltimore vs. Pittsburgh) $10
Jan. 20, 2002 NFC divisional (Green Bay vs. St. Louis) $10
Jan. 27, 2002 AFC championship (New England vs. Pittsburgh) $10
Jan. 27, 2002 NFC championship (Philadelphia vs. St. Louis) $10
Jan. 11, 2003 AFC divisional (Pittsburgh vs. Tennessee) $10
Jan. 11, 2003 NFC divisional (Atlanta vs. Philadelphia) $10
Jan. 12, 2003 AFC divisional (New York Jets vs. Oakland) $10
Jan. 12, 2003 NFC divisional (San Francisco vs. Tampa Bay) $10
Jan. 19, 2003 AFC championship (Tennessee vs. Oakland) $10
Jan. 19, 2003 NFC championship (Tampa Bay vs. Philadelphia) $10

Pro Football Hall of Fame Game Programs

Aug. 11, 1962 New York Giants vs. St. Louis Cardinals $75
Sept. 7, 1963 Pittsburgh Steelers vs. Cleveland Browns $60

Sept. 6, 1964 Baltimore Colts vs. Pittsburgh Steelers $50
Sept. 11, 1965 Detroit Lions vs. Washington Redskins $50
1966 No game was played ....N/A
Aug. 5, 1967 Cleveland Browns vs. Philadelphia Eagles $55
Aug. 2, 1968 Dallas Cowboys vs. Chicago Bears $50
Aug. 12, 1969 Atlanta Falcons vs. Green Bay Packers $45
Aug. 8, 1970 Minnesota Vikings vs. New Orleans Saints $45
July 31, 1971 Houston Oilers vs. Los Angeles Rams $45
July 27, 1972 Kansas City Chiefs vs. New York Giants $45
July 28, 1973 New England Patriots vs. San Francisco 49ers $40
July 27, 1974 Buffalo Bills vs. St. Louis Cardinals $40
Aug. 2, 1975 Washington Redskins vs. Cincinnati Bengals $40
July 24, 1976 Denver Broncos vs. Detroit Lions $30
July 30, 1977 Chicago Bears vs. New York Jets $35
July 29, 1978 Miami Dolphins vs. Philadelphia Eagles $35
July 28, 1979 Dallas Cowboys vs. Oakland Raiders $35
Aug. 2, 1980 Green Bay Packers vs. San Diego Chargers $30
Aug. 1, 1981 Cleveland Browns vs. Atlanta Falcons $30
Aug. 7, 1982 Minnesota Vikings vs. Baltimore Colts $30
July 30, 1983 Pittsburgh Steelers vs. New Orleans Saints $25
July 28, 1984 Tampa Bay Buccaneers vs. Seattle Seahawks $30
July 30, 1985 New York Giants vs. Houston Oilers $25
Aug. 2, 1986 New England Patriots vs. St. Louis Cardinals $25

Aug. 8, 1987 San Francisco 49ers vs. Kansas City Chiefs $25
July 30, 1988 Cincinnati Bengals vs. Los Angeles Rams $25
Aug. 5, 1989 Washington Redskins vs. Buffalo Bills $20
Aug. 4, 1990 Cleveland Browns vs. Chicago Bears $20
July 27, 1991 Detroit Lions vs. Denver Broncos $20

Aug. 1, 1992 Philadelphia Eagles vs. New York Jets $20
July 31, 1993 Green Bay Packers vs. Los Angeles Raiders $15
July 30, 1994 San Diego Chargers vs. Atlanta Falcons $15
July 29, 1995 Carolina Panthers vs. Jacksonville Jaguars $15
July 27, 1996 Indianapolis Colts vs. New Orleans Saints $12
July 26, 1997 Minnesota Vikings vs. Seattle Seahawks $12
Aug. 1, 1998 Pittsburgh Steelers vs. Tampa Bay Buccaneers $10
Aug. 9, 1999 Cleveland Browns vs. Dallas Cowboys $10
Aug. 9, 2000 New England Patriots vs. San Francisco 49ers $10
Aug. 6, 2001 St. Louis Rams vs. Miami Dolphins $10
Aug. 5, 2002 New York Giants vs. Houston Texans $10
Aug. 4, 2003 Kansas City Chiefs vs. Green Bay Packers $10

College Bowl Games

Rose Bowl

1925 Notre Dame vs. Stanford $2,800
1926 Alabama vs. Washington $2,000
1927 Alabama vs. Stanford $1,800
1928 Stanford vs. Pitt $950
1929 Georgia Tech vs. California $850
1930 Pitt vs. USC $700
1931 Alabama vs. Washington State $950

1932 Tulane vs. USC $600
1933 Pitt vs. USC $450
1934 Columbia vs. Stanford $495
1935 Alabama vs. California $700
1936 SMU vs. Stanford $275
1937 Pitt vs. Washington $225
1938 Alabama vs. California $250
1939 Duke vs. USC $250
1940 Tennessee vs. USC $225

1941 Nebraska vs. Stanford $300
1942 Duke vs. Oregon State $1,000
1943 Georgia vs. UCLA $150
1944 Washington vs. USC $135
1945 Tennessee vs. USC $135
1946 Alabama vs. Stanford $125
1947 Illinois vs. UCLA $125
1948 Michigan vs. USC $125
1949 Northwestern vs. California $125

1950 Ohio State vs. California....................$95
1951 Michigan vs. California $95
1952 Illinois vs. Stanford $85
1953 Wisconsin vs. USC...........................$85
1954 Michigan State vs. UCLA $75
1955 Ohio State vs. USC...........................$75
1956 Michigan State vs. UCLA $65
1957 Iowa vs. Oregon State.......................$85
1958 Ohio State vs. Oregon.......................$85
1959 Iowa vs. California $65
1960 Wisconsin vs. Washington $75
1961 Minnesota vs. Washington $65

1962 Minnesota vs. UCLA..........................$65
1963 Wisconsin vs. USC............................$75
1964 Illinois vs. Washington......................$65
1965 Michigan vs. Oregon State $65
1966 Michigan State vs. UCLA $65
1967 Purdue vs. USC.................................$90
1968 Indiana vs. USC $90
1969 Ohio State vs. USC $65
1970 Michigan vs. USC..............................$60
1971 Ohio State vs. USC $60
1972 Michigan vs. Stanford.......................$70
1973 Ohio State vs. USC $60
1974 Ohio State vs. USC $60
1975 Ohio State vs. USC $60
1976 Ohio State vs. UCLA $50
1977 Michigan vs. USC..............................$45
1978 Michigan vs. Washington $45
1979 Michigan vs. USC..............................$45
1980 Ohio State vs. USC $35
1981 Michigan vs. Washington $30
1982 Iowa vs. Washington $30
1983 Michigan vs. UCLA $30
1984 Illinois vs. UCLA $30
1985 Ohio State vs. USC $30
1986 Iowa vs. UCLA...................................$25
1987 Michigan vs. Arizona State...............$25
1988 Michigan State vs. USC $25
1989 Michigan vs. USC..............................$25
1990 Michigan vs. USC..............................$25
1991 Iowa vs. Washington $25
1992 Michigan vs. Washington $25
1993 Michigan vs. Washington $20
1994 Wisconsin vs. UCLA $20
1995 Oregon vs. Penn State $20
1996 USC vs. Northwestern......................$20
1997 Ohio State vs. Arizona State $20
1998 Michigan vs. Washington State $20
1999 Wisconsin vs. UCLA $20
2000 Wisconsin vs. Stanford.....................$20
2001 Washington vs. Purdue $20
2002 Miami vs. Nebraska..........................$25
2003 Oklahoma vs. Washington St. $15

Sugar Bowl

1935 Temple vs. Tulane......................$1,050
1936 TCU vs. LSU $950
1937 Santa Clara vs. LSU......................$450

1938 Santa Clara vs. LSU......................$400
1939 Carnegie Tech vs. TCU $400
1940 Texas A&M vs. Tulane...................$450
1941 Boston College vs. Tennessee.......$400
1942 Fordham vs. Missouri $200
1943 Tulsa vs. Tennessee......................$275
1944 Georgia Tech vs. Tulsa $175
1945 Alabama vs. Duke $165
1946 St. Marys vs. Oklahoma A&M $160
1947 North Carolina vs. Georgia.............$170
1948 Alabama vs. Texas $170
1949 N. Carolina vs. Oklahoma $125
1950 Oklahoma vs. LSU $110
1951 Oklahoma vs. Kentucky...................$95
1952 Maryland vs. Tennessee $95
1953 Georgia Tech vs. Mississippi..........$135
1954 Georgia Tech vs. West Virginia $95
1955 Navy vs. Mississippi $85
1956 Georgia Tech vs. Pittsburgh $85
1957 Baylor vs. Tennessee $145
1958 Texas vs. Mississippi $85
1959 Clemson vs. LSU.............................$85
1960 Mississippi vs. LSU $75
1961 Mississippi vs. Rice $75
1962 Alabama vs. Arkansas $75
1963 Mississippi vs. Arkansas $75
1964 Alabama vs. Mississippi $75
1965 LSU vs. Syracuse............................$65
1966 Florida vs. Missouri $95
1967 Alabama vs. Nebraska $110
1968 LSU vs. Wyoming............................$65
1969 Georgia vs. Arkansas $65
1970 Mississippi vs. Arkansas $60
1971 Tennessee vs. Air Force $60
1972 Auburn vs. Oklahoma $60
1973 Oklahoma vs. Penn State................$60
1974 Alabama vs. Notre Dame $60
1975 Florida vs. Nebraska $80
1976 Alabama vs. Penn State $60
1977 Georgia vs. Pittsburgh.....................$50
1978 Alabama vs. Ohio State...................$50
1979 Alabama vs. Penn State $50
1980 Alabama vs. Arkansas $50
1981 Georgia vs. Notre Dame..................$60
1982 Georgia vs. Pittsburgh.....................$45
1983 Georgia vs. Penn State $45
1984 Michigan vs. Auburn.......................$40
1985 LSU vs. Nebraska $35

1986 Miami vs. Tennessee.........................$30
1987 LSU vs. Nebraska $30
1988 Auburn vs. Syracuse $25
1989 FSU vs. Auburn $25
1990 Miami vs. Alabama $25
1991 Virginia vs. Tennessee $25
1992 Florida vs. Notre Dame $25
1993 Alabama vs. Miami $25
1994 Florida vs. West Virginia...................$20
1995 Florida vs. Florida State $20
1996 Texas vs. Virginia $20

1997 Florida vs. Florida State $20
1998 Florida State vs. Ohio State $15
1999 Ohio State vs. Texas A&M................$20
2000 Virginia Tech vs. Florida State..........$15
2001 Miami vs. Florida $15
2002 LSU vs. Illinois $12
2003 Georgia vs. Florida State.................$15

Cotton Bowl

1943 Texas vs. Georgia Tech $290
1944 Texas vs. Randolph Field $290
1945 Oklahoma A&M vs. TCU $195
1946 Missouri vs. Texas $200
1947 Arkansas vs. LSU $450
1948 Penn State vs. SMU $150
1949 Oregon vs. SMU $135
1950 North Carolina vs. Rice $125

1951 Tennessee vs. Texas $115
1952 Kentucky vs. TCU $95
1953 Tennessee vs. Texas $85
1954 Alabama vs. Rice $95
1955 Georgia Tech vs. Arkansas $85
1956 Mississippi vs. TCU $85
1957 Syracuse vs. TCU $85
1958 Navy vs. Rice $75
1959 Air Force vs. TCU $75
1960 Syracuse vs. Texas...........................$70
1961 Duke vs. Arkansas $70
1962 Mississippi vs. Texas $70
1963 LSU vs. Texas..................................$70
1964 Navy vs. Texas $115
1965 Arkansas vs. Nebraska $135
1966 LSU vs. Arkansas $120
1967 Georgia vs. Wyoming $65
1968 Alabama vs. Texas A&M...................$100
1969 Tennessee vs. Texas $65
1970 Notre Dame vs. Texas $125
1971 Notre Dame vs. Texas $125
1972 Penn State vs. Texas $60
1973 Texas vs. Alabama $60
1974 Nebraska vs. Texas $60
1975 Penn State vs. Baylor $60
1976 Georgia vs. Arkansas $50
1977 Maryland vs. Houston $50
1978 Notre Dame vs. Texas $75
1979 Notre Dame vs. Houston $75
1980 Nebraska vs. Houston $45
1981 Alabama vs. Baylor $45
1982 Alabama vs. Texas $45
1983 Pittsburgh vs. SMU $45
1984 Georgia vs. Texas $40
1985 Boston College vs. Houston $40
1986 Auburn vs. Texas A&M $35
1987 Ohio State vs. Texas A&M..................$30
1988 Notre Dame vs. Texas A&M $30
1989 UCLA vs. Arkansas $25
1990 Tennessee vs. Arkansas $25
1991 Miami vs. Texas................................$25
1992 FSU vs. Texas A&M...........................$25

1993 Notre Dame vs. Texas A&M $25
1994 Notre Dame vs. Texas A&M $25
1995 USC vs. Texas Tech $20

1996 Colorado vs. Oregon $20
1997 BYU vs. Kansas State $20
1998 UCLA vs. Texas A&M $15
1999 Texas vs. Mississippi State...............$15
2000 Arkansas vs. Texas $12
2001 Kansas State vs. Tennessee $12
2002 Oklahoma vs. Arkansas $12
2003 Texas vs. LSU $12

Orange Bowl

1935 Bucknell vs. Miami.....................$1,295
1936 Catholic vs. Ole Miss.................$1,000
1937 Duquesne vs. Mississippi St...........$900
1938 Auburn vs. Michigan St. $950
1939 Oklahoma vs. Tennessee $595
1940 Georgia Tech vs. Missouri.............$275
1941 Mississippi vs. Georgetown...........$250
1942 TCU vs. Georgia.........................$350
1943 Alabama vs. Boston College $400
1944 LSU vs. Texas $400
1945 Georgia Tech vs. Tulsa $200
1946 Holy Cross vs. Miami....................$250
1947 Tennessee vs. Rice $200
1948 Georgia Tech vs. Kansas $150
1949 Texas vs. Georgia........................$150
1950 Santa Clara vs. Kentucky $100
1951 Clemson vs. Miami.......................$125
1952 Georgia Tech vs. Baylor $100
1953 Alabama vs. Syracuse...................$100
1954 Oklahoma vs. Maryland $95
1955 Duke vs. Nebraska $125
1956 Maryland vs. Oklahoma $95
1957 Clemson vs. Colorado $115
1958 Duke vs. Oklahoma $110

1959 Syracuse vs. Oklahoma $95
1960 Georgia vs. Missouri $85
1961 Navy vs. Missouri $85
1962 LSU vs. Colorado $85
1963 Alabama vs. Oklahoma $350
1964 Auburn vs. Nebraska.....................$110
1965 Texas vs. Alabama $300

1966 Alabama vs. Nebraska $300
1967 Georgia Tech vs. Florida $200
1968 Oklahoma vs. Tennessee $75
1969 Penn State vs. Kansas $75
1970 Penn State vs. Missouri $60
1971 LSU vs. Nebraska $100
1972 Alabama vs. Nebraska $100
1973 Notre Dame vs. Nebraska $110
1974 Penn State vs. LSU $60
1975 Notre Dame vs. Alabama $60
1976 Michigan vs. Oklahoma $60
1977 Ohio State vs. Colorado $50
1978 Arkansas vs. Oklahoma $50
1979 Nebraska vs. Oklahoma $50
1980 FSU vs. Oklahoma $45
1981 FSU vs. Oklahoma $45
1982 Clemson vs. Nebraska $50
1983 LSU vs. Nebraska $50
1984 Miami vs. Nebraska $50
1985 Washington vs. Oklahoma $45
1986 Penn State vs. Oklahoma $45
1987 Arkansas vs. Oklahoma $45
1988 Miami vs. Oklahoma $25
1989 Miami vs. Nebraska $25
1990 Notre Dame vs. Colorado $20
1991 Colorado vs. Notre Dame $20
1992 Miami vs. Nebraska $20
1993 Nebraska vs. Florida State $20
1994 Florida State vs. Nebraska $20
1995 Nebraska vs. Miami (Florida) $20
1996 Florida State vs. Notre Dame $20
1997 Nebraska vs. Virginia Tech $20
1998 Nebraska vs. Tennessee $20
1999 Florida vs. Syracuse.....................$15
2000 Michigan vs. Alabama $15
2001 Oklahoma vs. Florida State $15
2002 Florida vs. Maryland......................$15
2003 USC vs. Iowa..............................$15

Liberty Bowl

1959 Penn State vs. Alabama $95
1960 Penn State vs. Oregon $75
1961 Syracuse vs. Miami $65
1962 Oregon State vs. Villanova..............$65
1963 Mississippi State vs. N.C. State $65
1964 Utah vs. West Virginia $65
1965 Mississippi vs. Auburn $60
1967 N.C. State vs. Georgia $60
1968 Mississippi vs. Virginia Tech $50
1969 Colorado vs. Alabama $60
1970 Tulane vs. Colorado......................$50
1971 Tennessee vs. Arkansas $50
1972 Georgia Tech vs. Iowa State $50
1973 N.C. State vs. Kansas $50
1974 Tennessee vs. Maryland $50
1975 USC vs. Texas A&M $50
1976 Alabama vs. UCLA $50
1977 North Carolina vs. Nebraska $75
1978 LSU vs. Missouri $45
1979 Penn State vs. Tulane $45
1980 Purdue vs. Missouri.......................$45
1981 Ohio State vs. Navy.......................$45
1982 Alabama vs. Illinois.......................$45
1983 Notre Dame vs. Boston College $45
1984 Auburn vs. Arkansas $40
1985 LSU vs. Baylor $40
1986 Tennessee vs. Minnesota................$35
1987 Georgia vs. Arkansas $30
1988 South Carolina vs. Indiana $25
1989 Mississippi vs. Air Force $25
1990 Air Force vs. Ohio State $20
1991 Air Force vs. Mississippi State $20
1992 Air Force vs. Mississippi..................$20
1993 Louisville vs. Michigan State $15

1994 Illinois vs. E. Carolina $15
1995 E. Carolina vs. Stanford $12
1996 Syracuse vs. Houston $12
1997 So. Mississippi vs. Pittsburgh $12
1998 Tulane vs. BYU $12
1999 S. Mississippi vs. Colorado St. $12
2000 Louisville vs. Colorado State $12
2001 Louisville vs. BYU.........................$12
2002 TCU vs. Colorado State $12

Fiesta Bowl

1971 Arizona State vs. Florida State........$50
1972 Arizona State vs. Missouri...............$45
1973 Arizona State vs. Pittsburgh $45
1974 Oklahoma State vs. BYU................$45
1975 Arizona State vs. Nebraska $45
1976 Oklahoma vs. Wyoming..................$45
1977 Penn State vs. Arizona State...........$45
1978 Arkansas vs. UCLA $45
1979 Pittsburgh vs. Arizona $45
1980 Penn State vs. Ohio State $45
1982 Penn State vs. USC.......................$40
1983 Arizona State vs. Oklahoma.............$35
1984 Pittsburgh vs. Ohio State $35
1985 Miami vs. UCLA $35
1986 Michigan vs. Nebraska $35
1987 Penn State vs. Miami.....................$30
1988 Florida State vs. Nebraska $25
1989 Notre Dame vs. West Virginia $20
1990 Florida State vs. Nebraska $15
1991 Louisville vs. Alabama....................$15
1992 Penn State vs. Tennessee...............$15
1993 Syracuse vs. Colorado $15
1994 Miami vs. Arizona $15

1995 Nebraska vs. Florida $15
1996 Penn State vs. Texas $15
1997 Kansas State vs. Syracuse $15
1998 Kansas State vs. Texas $12
1999 Tennessee vs. Florida State.............$12
2000 Nebraska vs. Tennessee $12
2001 Notre Dame vs. Oregon St. $12
2002 Oregon vs. Colorado $12
2003 Ohio State vs. Miami $18

Hall of Fame Bowl

1977 Maryland vs. Minnesota $45
1978 Texas A&M vs. Iowa State...............$35
1979 South Carolina vs. Missouri.............$30
1980 Tulane vs. Arkansas $25
1981 Mississippi State vs. Kansas $25
1982 Air Force vs. Vanderbilt $25
1984 Wisconsin vs. Kentucky...................$25
1986 Georgia vs. Boston College..............$20
1988 Alabama vs. Michigan $20
1989 Syracuse vs. LSU.........................$20
1990 Ohio State vs. Auburn $15
1991 Clemson vs. Illinois........................$15
1992 Ohio State vs. Syracuse $15
1993 Tennessee vs. Boston College $15

1994 Michigan vs. North Carolina State....$15
1995 Wisconsin vs. Duke $15
1996 Auburn vs. Penn State.....................$15
1997 Michigan vs. Alabama $15
1998 Georgia vs. Wisconsin......................$15

Outback Bowl

1999 Colorado vs. Oregon $12
2000 Penn State vs. Kentucky...................$12
2001 South Carolina vs. Ohio State..........$12
2002 South Carolina vs. Ohio State..........$12
2003 Michigan vs. Florida $12

Aloha Bowl

1982 Washington vs. Maryland.................$35
1983 Washington vs. Penn State $30
1984 Notre Dame vs. SMU $30
1985 Alabama vs. USC $25
1986 North Carolina vs. Arizona $20
1987 Florida vs. UCLA $20
1988 Washington State vs. Hawaii............$20
1989 Michigan State vs. Hawaii $20
1990 Syracuse vs. Arizona........................$15
1991 Georgia Tech vs. Stanford................$15
1992 Kansas vs. BYU $15
1993 Colorado vs. Fresno State................$15
1994 Boston College vs. Kansas State $15
1995 UCLA vs. Kansas $15
1996 Navy vs. California $15
1997 Washington vs. Michigan State $12
1999 Wake Forest vs. Arizona State $12
2000 Boston College vs. Arizona St..........$12

Peach Bowl

1968 LSU vs. Florida State $85
1969 South Carolina vs. West Virginia......$65
1970 North Carolina vs. Arizona State......$65
1971 Georgia Tech vs. Mississippi $55
1972 N.C. State vs. West Virginia $50
1973 Georgia vs. Maryland $50
1974 Vanderbilt vs. Texas Tech $50
1975 N.C. State vs. West Virginia $50
1976 North Carolina vs. Kentucky.............$50
1977 N.C. State vs. Iowa State $45
1978 Georgia Tech vs. Purdue..................$45
1979 Clemson vs. Baylor $45
1980 Virginia Tech vs. Miami.....................$65
1981 Florida State vs. North Carolina $40
1982 Tennessee vs. Iowa $45
1983 Florida State vs. N.C. State.............$40
1984 Virginia vs. Purdue $40
1985 Army vs. Illinois $35
1986 Virginia Tech vs. N.C. State $30
1987 Indiana vs. Tennessee.....................$30
1988 Iowa vs. N.C. State...........................$25
1989 Syracuse vs. Georgia $20
1990 Auburn vs. Indiana $20
1991 East Carolina vs. N.C. State.............$20
1992 North Carolina vs. Miss. State.........$20
1993 Clemson vs. Kentucky......................$20
1994 N.C. State vs. Mississippi St $20
1995 Virginia vs. Georgia $20
1996 LSU vs. Clemson..............................$15
1997 Auburn vs. Clemson $15
1998 Georgia vs. Virginia $12
1999 Mississippi St. vs. Clemson..............$12
2000 LSU vs. Georgia Tech $12
2001 North Carolina vs. Auburn................$12

2002 Maryland vs. Tennessee $12

Gator Bowl

1954 Auburn vs. Baylor $200
1960 Florida vs. Baylor.............................$150
1961 Penn State vs. Georgia Tech............$90
1962 Florida vs. Penn State $90
1963 North Carolina vs. Air Force $90
1964 Florida State vs. Oklahoma $90
1965 Georgia Tech vs. Texas Tech............$90
1966 Tennessee vs. Syracuse $90
1967 Penn State vs. Florida State $75
1968 Alabama vs. Missouri $75
1969 Florida vs. Tennessee $75
1970 Mississippi vs. Auburn......................$65
1971 North Carolina vs. Georgia $65
1972 Auburn vs. Colorado.........................$65
1973 Tennessee vs. Texas Tech................$60
1974 Texas vs. Auburn $60
1975 Florida vs. Maryland $60
1976 Notre Dame vs. Penn State..............$60
1977 Clemson vs. Pitt $50
1978 Ohio State vs. Clemson....................$65
1979 Michigan vs. North Carolina $50
1980 South Carolina vs. Pitt.....................$45
1981 North Carolina vs. Arkansas $40
1982 Florida State vs. West Virginia $40
1983 Florida vs. Iowa $40
1984 South Carolina vs. Okla. State.........$35
1985 Florida State vs. Oklahoma $35
1986 Stanford vs. Clemson $35
1987 South Carolina vs. LSU $30
1988 Georgia vs. Michigan State $25
1989 West Virginia vs. Clemson $20
1990 Michigan vs. Mississippi $20
1991 Oklahoma vs. Virginia $15
1992 North Carolina State vs. Florida.......$15
1993 Alabama vs. North Carolina $15
1994 Tennessee vs. Virginia Tech..............$15
1996 Clemson vs. Syracuse......................$15
1997 North Carolina vs. West Virginia $15
1998 North Carolina vs. Virginia $15
1999 Georgia Tech vs. Notre Dame $15
2000 Miami vs. Georgia Tech....................$12
2001 Virginia Tech vs. Clemson $12
2002 Florida St. vs. Virginia Tech..............$12
2003 N.C. State vs. Notre Dame..............$12

Sun Bowl

1936 Hardin-Simmons vs. N. Mexico St..$195
1937 Hardin-Simmons vs. UTEP $185
1938 West Virginia vs. Texas Tech..........$145
1939 Utah vs. New Mexico......................$155

1940 Arizona St. vs. Catholic $145
1941 Case Reserve vs. Arizona St. $125
1942 Tulsa vs. Texas Tech.......................$135
1943 Air Force vs. Hardin-Simmons $120
1944 SW Texas St. vs. New Mexico........$115
1945 SW Texas St. vs. U. of Mexico........$115
1946 New Mexico vs. Denver $115
1947 Cincinnati vs. Virginia Tech $115
1948 Miami Ohio vs. Texas Tech............$110
1949 West Virginia vs. UTEP $95
1950 UTEP vs. Georgetown.....................$95
1951 West Texas A&M vs. So. Miss. $95
1952 Texas Tech vs. Pacific $95
1953 Pacific vs. So. Mississippi...............$95
1954 UTEP vs. S. Mississippi $95
1955 UTEP vs. Florida St........................$115
1956 Wyoming vs. Texas Tech $95
1957 G. Washington vs. UTEP................$90
1958 Wyoming vs. Hardin-Simmons $85
1959 New Mexico St. vs. North Texas.......$80
1960 New Mexico St. vs. Utah St. $80
1961 Villanova vs. Wichita St. $80
1962 West Texas A&M vs. Ohio................$85
1963 Oregon vs. SMU $90
1964 Georgia vs. Texas Tech $90
1965 TCU vs. UTEP.................................$65
1966 Wyoming vs. Florida State $65
1967 Mississippi vs. UTEP $65
1968 Auburn vs. Arizona $65
1969 Nebraska vs. Georgia $65
1970 Georgia Tech vs. Texas Tech............$60
1971 Iowa State vs. LSU $60
1972 North Carolina vs. Texas Tech..........$60
1973 Auburn vs. Missouri $60
1974 N. Carolina vs. Mississippi State $50
1975 Pitt vs. Kansas.................................$50
1976 Texas A&M vs. Florida.....................$50
1977 Stanford vs. LSU $50
1978 Texas vs. Maryland..........................$45
1979 Texas vs. Washington......................$45
1980 Mississippi State vs. Nebraska.........$40
1981 Oklahoma vs. Houston $40
1982 Texas vs. North Carolina $40
1983 Alabama vs. SMU.............................$40
1984 Tennessee vs. Maryland $35
1985 Georgia vs. Arizona $30
1986 Alabama vs. Washington..................$30
1987 West Virginia vs. Oklahoma State $25
1988 Army vs. Vanderbilt $25
1989 Texas A&M vs. Pitt...........................$20
1990 Michigan State vs. USC $20
1991 Illinois vs. UCLA $15
1992 Baylor vs. Arizona $15
1993 Oklahoma vs. Texas Tech................$15
1994 Texas vs. North Carolina $15
1995 Washington vs. Iowa $15
1996 Stanford vs. Michigan State $15
1997 Iowa vs. Arizona State.....................$15
1998 TCU vs. Southern California.............$12
1999 Minnesota vs. Oregon $12
2000 Wisconsin vs. UCLA........................$12
2001 Washington St. vs. Purdue...............$12
2002 Purdue vs. Washington $12

Basketball Programs

NBA All-Star Game programs

1951 Boston $800
1952 Boston $600
1953 Fort Wayne $600
1954 New York $550
1955 New York $495
1956 Rochester..$495

1957 Boston $325
1958 St. Louis $225
1959 Detroit..$195
1960 Philadelphia.....................................$225
1961 Syracuse $195
1962 St. Louis $195
1963 Los Angeles $195

1964 Boston $175
1965 St. Louis $175
1966 Cincinnati $75
1967 San Francisco .... $150-$175
1968 New York $125
1969 Baltimore $110
1970 Philadelphia.......................................$90
1971 San Diego $125
1972 Los Angeles $110
1973 Chicago $70

1974 Seattle $60
1975 Phoenix $70
1976 Philadelphia......................................$35
1977 Milwaukee $50
1978 Atlanta $50
1979 Detroit..$50
1980 Washington $40
1981 Cleveland $40
1982 New Jersey $40
1983 Los Angeles $40
1984 Denver $40
1985 Indiana $40
1986 Dallas $40
1987 Seattle $40

1988 Chicago $25
1989 Houston $25
1990 Miami $25
1991 Charlotte $25
1992 Orlando $25
1993 Salt Lake City $20
1994 Minneapolis $20

1995 Phoenix $15
1996 San Antonio.....................................$15
1997 Cleveland $10
1998 New York $10

1999 No game
2000 Oakland $10
2001 Washington $10
2002 Philadelphia.....................................$10
2003 Atlanta $10

ABA All-Star Game programs

1968 Indianapolis $195
1969 Louisville.......................................$175
1971 Greensboro, N.C. $150
1972 Kentucky.......................................$125
1973 Salt Lake City $125
1974 Norfolk, Va. $100
1975 San Antonio....................................$95
1976 Denver...$85

NBA Finals programs

1960-61 Syracuse at Boston $400
1962-63 Boston at Los Angeles $300
1963-64 San Francisco at Boston $250
1964-65 Boston at Los Angeles $250
1965-66 Boston at Los Angeles $200
1967-68 Boston at Los Angeles $200
1968-69 Los Angeles at Boston $150
1968-69 Boston at Los Angeles $150
1969-70 Los Angeles at New York $125
1969-70 New York at Los Angeles $150
1971-72 Los Angeles at New York $125
1971-72 New York at Los Angeles $100
1972-73 Los Angeles at New York $100
1973-74 Milwaukee at Boston $100
1974-75 Golden State at Washington ...$100
1975-76 Phoenix at Boston $100
1976-77 Philadelphia at Portland $100
1978-79 Washington at Seattle $100
1979-80 Philadelphia at Los Angeles......$100
1980-81 Houston at Boston...................$75
1981-82 Philadelphia at Los Angeles....$75
1983-84 Boston at Los Angeles $75
1984-85 Boston at Los Angeles $75
1993-94 Houston at New York...............$25
1994-95 Houston vs. Orlando $15
1995-96 Chicago vs. Seattle $50
1996-97 Chicago vs. Utah......................$65
1997-98 Chicago vs. Utah......................$75
1998-99 San Antonio vs. New York...........$20
1999-2000 LA Lakers vs. Indiana............$25
2000-01 LA Lakers vs. Philadelphia.........$20
2001-02 LA Lakers vs. New Jersey.........$20
2002-03 San Antonio vs. New Jersey $20

NBA playoff programs

1947 Philadelphia at New York...............$300
1951 Boston at New York $200
1955 Boston at New York $150
1956 Syracuse at Boston $125
1956 Syracuse at Philadelphia...............$125
1958 Boston at Philadelphia...................$100
1958 Syracuse at Philadelphia...............$100
1959 Syracuse at Boston $45
1962 Boston at Philadelphia.....................$45
1962 Los Angeles at Detroit $60
1964 Cincinnati at Philadelphia................$45
1965 Philadelphia at Boston.....................$45
1965 Baltimore at Los Angeles $50
1966 St. Louis at Los Angeles..................$45
1966 Philadelphia at Boston.....................$40
1966 Boston at Philadelphia............. $40-$65
1967 Philadelphia at Boston.....................$40
1967 Los Angeles at San Francisco..........$40
1967 St. Louis at San Francisco................$40

1967 Boston at New York $40
1968 St. Louis at San Francisco $35
1968 San Francisco at Los Angeles..........$35
1968 Los Angeles at San Francisco..........$35
1968 Chicago at Los Angeles $35
1968 Los Angeles at Chicago $45
1968 Philadelphia at Boston .... $35-$65
1968 Philadelphia at New York.................$35
1969 Atlanta at San Diego $45
1969 Boston at Philadelphia $35
1969 Atlanta at Philadelphia $35
1969 Boston at New York $35
1969 Baltimore at New York $35
1969 New York at Baltimore $40
1969 New York at Boston $40
1970 Philadelphia at Milwaukee...............$35
1970 New York at Philadelphia.................$35
1970 Milwaukee at Philadelphia...............$35
1970 Milwaukee at New York $30
1970 Baltimore at New York $30
1970 New York at Baltimore $30
1970 Phoenix at Los Angeles $35
1971 Milwaukee at Los Angeles...............$40
1971 New York at Baltimore $40
1971 Milwaukee at San Francisco.............$30
1971 Atlanta at New York $30
1971 Baltimore at New York $30
1972 Chicago at Los Angeles $35
1972 Milwaukee at Golden State $35
1972 New York at Baltimore .... $30-$35
1972 Los Angeles at Milwaukee................$35
1972 Boston at Atlanta..............................$35
1972 New York at Boston $35
1972 Baltimore at New York $30
1972 Boston at New York $30
1972 Los Angeles at Chicago $30
1972 Los Angeles at New York $100
1972 New York at Los Angeles $100
1973 Los Angeles at Golden State $35
1973 Milwaukee at Golden State $35
1973 New York at Baltimore $35
1973 New York at Boston $30
1973 Atlanta at Boston.............................$30
1973 Boston at New York $30
1973 Baltimore at New York $30
1973 Chicago at Los Angeles $30
1973 Los Angeles at New York $100
1973 New York at Los Angeles $100
1974 Milwaukee at Los Angeles........ $25-$30
1974 Los Angeles at Milwaukee................$30
1974 Chicago at Milwaukee $30
1974 Detroit at Chicago $30

1974 Boston at Buffalo $30
1974 Detroit at Chicago $30
1974 New York at Washington $30
1974 Boston at New York $25
1974 Washington at New York $25
1974 Chicago at Detroit $25
1974 Buffalo at Boston $25

1974 New York at Boston $25
1975 Chicago at Kansas City $25
1975 Seattle at Detroit .... $20-$25
1975 Buffalo at Washington $25
1975 Chicago at Golden State $25
1975 Houston at Boston............................$25
1975 Boston at Houston............................$25
1975 Washington at Boston $25
1975 New York at Houston........................$25
1975 Washington at Buffalo $25
1975 Boston at Washington $25
1975 Houston at Boston............................$25
1976 Cleveland at Washington..................$25
1976 Detroit at Golden State $25
1976 Washington at Cleveland..................$25
1976 Cleveland at Boston $25
1976 Golden State at Detroit.....................$25
1976 Buffalo at Boston .... $20-$25
1976 Boston at Buffalo $25
1976 Boston at Cleveland $25
1976 Philadelphia at Buffalo $25
1976 Buffalo at Philadelphia $25
1976 Detroit at Milwaukee........................$25
1976 Seattle at Phoenix $25
1977 Los Angeles at Portland $25
1977 Denver at Portland $25
1977 Los Angeles at Golden State $25
1977 Washington at Cleveland..................$25
1977 Portland at Chicago..........................$25
1977 Philadelphia at Boston $25
1977 Washington at Houston $25
1977 Houston at Washington $25
1977 Golden State at Los Angeles $25
1977 San Antonio at Boston $25
1977 Washington at Cleveland..................$25
1977 Detroit at Golden State $25
1977 Portland at Los Angeles $25
1977 Portland at Denver $25
1978 Philadelphia at New York..................$20
1978 Cleveland at New York $20
1978 Los Angeles at Seattle $20
1978 Seattle at Portland............................$20
1978 New York at Cleveland $20
1978 Philadelphia at Washington..............$20
1979 Seattle at Phoenix $20
1979 Phoenix at Seattle............................$20
1979 Philadelphia at New Jersey $20
1979 Houston at Atlanta............................$20
1979 Washington at Seattle $75
1980 Milwaukee at Seattle $20
1980 Philadelphia at Boston .... $20-$25
1980 Washington at Philadelphia..............$20
1980 Philadelphia at Atlanta $20
1980 Houston at Boston............................$20
1981 Kansas City at Portland....................$20
1981 Philadelphia at Boston $20
1982 Washington at Boston $20
1982 Philadelphia at Boston $20
1984 Philadelphia at New Jersey Nets......$20
1984 Boston at New York $20
1985 Philadelphia at Boston $20
1986 San Antonio at Los Angeles.............$20
1988 Detroit at Boston $20
1990 Boston at New York $15
1990 Houston at Los Angeles $15
1994 Houston at New York........................$25

ABA playoff programs

1969 Indiana at Miami..............................$45
1970 Los Angeles at Indiana (Finals)......$150
1970 Indiana at Los Angeles (Finals)......$150
1971 New York at Virginia $35
1971 Miami at Kentucky $30
1972 Indiana at New York (Finals) $125

1972 New York at Indiana (Finals) $125
1973 Indiana at Kentucky (Finals)...........$125
1973 Kentucky at Indiana (Finals)...........$125
1974 New York at Virginia $30
1974 San Diego at Utah............................$25
1975 Indiana at San Antonio.....................$25
1975 Denver at Indiana $25
1975 Indiana at Kentucky (Finals)...........$100

Hockey Programs
Stanley Cup Finals programs

1929-30 Montreal/Boston....................$1,500
1930-31 Montreal/Chicago $1,500
1931-32 Toronto/New York Rangers $1,200
1932-33 New York Rangers/Toronto $1,000
1933-34 Chicago/Detroit $800
1934-35 Montreal/Toronto $800
1935-36 Detroit/Toronto..........................$700
1936-37 Detroit/New York Rangers $700
1937-38 Chicago/Toronto $600
1938-39 Boston/Toronto $600
1939-40 New York Rangers/Toronto $700
1940-41 Boston/Detroit $700
1941-42 Toronto/Detroit $700
1942-43 Detroit/Boston $600
1943-44 Montreal/Chicago $700
1944-45 Toronto/Detroit $500
1945-46 Montreal/Boston $600
1946-47 Toronto/Montreal $500
1947-48 Toronto/Detroit...........................$450
1948-49 Toronto/Detroit...........................$450
1949-50 Detroit/New York Rangers.........$400
1950-51 Toronto/Montreal $350
1951-52 Detroit/Montreal.........................$350
1952-53 Montreal/Boston $400
1953-54 Detroit/Montreal.........................$275
1954-55 Detroit/Montreal.........................$275
1955-56 Montreal/Boston $300
1957-58 Boston/Montreal $300
1958-59 Montreal/Toronto $300
1959-60 Toronto/Montreal $300
1060-61 Chicago/Detroit $250
1961-62 Toronto/Chicago $200
1962-63 Toronto/Detroit...........................$200
1963-64 Toronto/Detroit...........................$200
1964-65 Chicago/Montreal $250
1965-66 Detroit/Montreal.........................$250
1966-67 Toronto/Montreal $200
1967-68 St. Louis/Montreal $200
1968-69 Montreal/St. Louis $150
1969-70 Boston/St. Louis $125
1970-71 Montreal/Chicago $125
1971-72 Boston/New York Rangers $125
1972-73 Chicago/Montreal $150
1973-74 Philadelphia/Boston $100
1974-75 Philadelphia/Buffalo $100
1975-76 Montreal/Philadelphia..................$75
1976-77 Montreal/Boston $75
1977-78 Montreal/Boston $75
1978-79 Montreal/New York Rangers $75
1979-80 New York Islanders/Philadelphia ..$75
1980-81 New York Islanders/Minnesota....$40
1981-82 New York Islanders/Vancouver....$40
1982-83 New York Islanders/Edmonton $45
1983-84 Edmonton/New York Islanders $45
1984-85 Edmonton/Philadelphia $45
1985-86 Montreal/Calgary.........................$45
1986-87 Edmonton/Philadelphia $45
1987-88 Boston/Edmonton.........................$75
1988-89 Calgary/Montreal.........................$45
1990-91 Minnesota/Pittsburgh $45
1991-92 Pittsburgh/Chicago $25
1992-93 Los Angeles/Pittsburgh $25

1993-94 Vancouver/New York Rangers.....$15
1994-95 New Jersey/Detroit.....................$12
1995-96 Colorado/Florida $12
1996-97 Detroit/Philadelphia....................$12
1997-98 Detroit/Washington.....................$10
1998-99 Dallas/Buffalo $10
1999-2000 New Jersey/Dallas $10
2000-2001 Colorado/New Jersey.............$10
2001-2002 Detroit/Carolina $10
2002-2003 New Jersey/Anaheim $10

NHL All-Star Game programs

1947-48 Toronto $500
1948-49 Chicago.......................... $300-$350
1949-50 Toronto .... $300-$350
1950-51 Detroit .... $225-$250
1951-52 Toronto $200
1952-53 Detroit $200
1953-54 Montreal $200
1954-55 Detroit $150
1955-56 Detroit $150
1956-57 Montreal $150
1957-58 Montreal $150
1958-59 Montreal $150
1959-60 Montreal $150
1960-61 Montreal $100
1961-62 Chicago $75
1962-63 Toronto $50
1963-64 Toronto $50
1964-65 Toronto $50
1965-66 Montreal $75
1966-67 Montreal $75
1967-68 Toronto $50
1968-69 Montreal $50
1969-70 St. Louis $50
1970-71 Boston..$40
1971-72 Minnesota $35
1972-73 New York $35
1973-74 Chicago $35
1974-75 Montreal $35
1975-76 Philadelphia $30
1976-77 Vancouver $30
1977-78 Buffalo $30
1978-79 New York $50

1979-80 Detroit $30
1980-81 Los Angeles $20
1981-82 Washington $20

1982-83 New York $20
1983-84 New Jersey $20

1984-85 Calgary.......................................$20
1985-86 Hartford $20
1986-87 Quebec $25
1987-88 St. Louis $18
1988-89 Edmonton...................................$20
1989-90 Pittsburgh $17

1990-91 Chicago $15
1991-92 Philadelphia................................$10
1992-93 Montreal $10
1993-94 New York $10
1994-95 Game Cancelled

1995-96 Boston...$8
1996-97 San Jose $8
1997-98 Vancouver $8
1998-99 Tampa $8
1999-00 Toronto 50th Anniversary $12
2000-01 Denver...$8
2001-02 Los Angeles $8
2002-03 Florida $8

Boxing Programs

Heavyweight Bouts

Date	Opponents	Price
07/04/19	Dempsey vs. Willard	$4,500
07/02/21	Dempsey vs.Carpentier	$1,200
07/04/23	Dempsey vs. Gibbons	$1,100

09/14/23 Dempsey vs. Firpo $1,000
09/23/26 Tunney vs. Dempsey $2,500

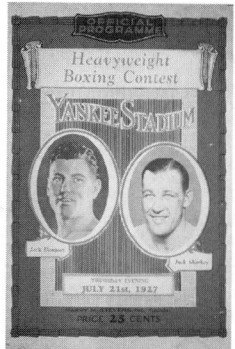

07/21/27 Dempsey vs. Sharkey............$1,500
09/22/27 Tunney vs. Dempsey $3,500
06/12/30 Schmeling vs. Sharkey $600
07/03/31 Schmeling vs. Stribling $750
06/21/32 Sharkey vs. Schmeling $650
06/25/35 Louis vs. Carnera $700
09/24/35 Louis vs. Baer.........................$775
06/19/36 Schmeling vs. Louis $2,525

08/18/36 Louis vs. Sharkey $800
06/22/37 Louis vs. Braddock $2,000

06/22/38 Louis vs. Schmeling $3,500
11/17/39 Conn vs. Lesnevich $250
06/05/40 Conn vs. Lesnevich $250
05/23/41 Louis vs. Baer...........................$875
06/18/41 Louis vs. Conn...........................$775
01/09/42 Louis vs. Baer.......................... $850

06/19/46 J. Louis vs. Conn.......................$600
12/05/47 Louis vs. Walcott $665
06/25/48 Louis vs. J. Walcott...................$650
06/22/49 Charles vs. Walcott $250
09/27/50 Charles vs. Louis.......................$300
03/07/51 Charles vs. Walcott $350
07/18/51 Walcott vs. Charles $350
10/26/51 Marciano vs. Louis $3,500
06/05/52 Walcott vs. Charles $350
09/23/52 Marciano vs. Walcott $2,500
05/15/53 Marciano vs. Walcott $2,500
06/17/54 Marciano vs. Charles $600
09/17/54 Marciano vs. Charles $600
05/16/55 Marciano vs. Cockell $600
09/21/55 Marciano vs. Moore..................$500
11/30/56 Patterson vs. Moore $400
06/26/59 Johansson vs. Patterson $300
06/20/60 Patterson vs. Johansson $275
03/13/61 Patterson vs.Johansson $275
09/25/62 Liston vs. Patterson $300
11/15/62 Clay vs. Moore $2,500
07/22/63 Liston vs. Patterson $310

02/25/64 Clay vs. Liston $3,500

05/25/65 Ali vs. Liston $700
11/22/65 Ali vs. Patterson $575
03/04/68 Frazier vs. Mathis $235
11/28/70 Frazier vs. Foster.....................$250
03/08/71 Frazier vs. Ali........................$1,000
09/20/72 Ali vs. Patterson $565
11/21/72 Ali vs. Foster...........................$850
01/22/73 Foreman vs. Frazier $365
03/31/73 Norton vs. Ali..........................$560
09/01/73 Foreman vs. Roman.................$200
09/10/73 Ali vs. Norton $250
01/28/74 Ali vs. Frazier..........................$500
03/26/74 Foreman vs. Norton.................$550
10/30/74 Ali vs. Foreman $5,000
10/01/75 Ali vs. Frazier $5,000
09/15/76 Foreman vs. Frazier $500
09/28/76 Ali vs. Norton.........................$235
09/29/77 Ali vs. Shavers.......................$450
02/15/78 Spinks vs. Ali.........................$450
06/09/78 Holmes vs. Norton..................$300
09/15/78 Ali vs. L.Spinks......................$340
10/02/80 Holmes vs. Ali........................$130
06/12/81 L. Holmes vs. L. Spinks...........$150
06/11/82 Holmes vs. Cooney.................$100
05/20/83 Holmes vs. Witherspoon $75
09/21/85 M. Spinks vs. Holmes..............$75
04/19/86 M. Spinks vs. Holmes..............$70
11/22/86 Tyson vs. Berbick $400
03/07/87 Tyson vs. Bonecrusher Smith.....$45
05/30/87 Tyson vs. Thomas $250
05/30/87 Tucker vs. Douglas $250
08/01/87 Tyson vs.Tucker $150
10/16/87 Tyson vs. Biggs $100
01/22/88 Tyson vs. Holmes $75
03/20/88 Tyson vs. Tubbs.......................$200

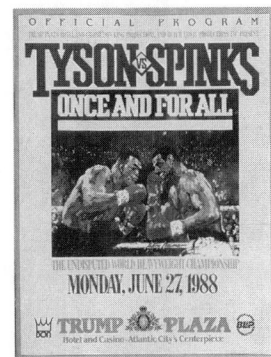

06/27/88 Tyson vs. Spinks........................$75
02/25/89 Tyson vs. Bruno.........................$50
07/21/89 Tyson vs. C. Williams $50

01/15/90 Forman vs. Cooney $40
10/25/90 Holyfield vs. Douglas...............$100
03/18/91 Tyson vs. Ruddock $60
04/19/91 Holyfield vs. Foreman................$45
06/28/91 Tyson vs. Ruddock $65
10/18/91 Mercer vs. Morrison $30

11/23/91 Holyfield vs. Cooper $30
02/07/92 Holmes vs. Mercer $20
05/15/92 Moorer vs.Cooper.....................$15
06/19/92 Holyfield vs. Holmes..................$25
07/18/92 Bowe vs. Coetzer $20
07/28/92 Dokes vs. Ferguson....................$10
10/31/92 Lewis vs. Ruddock.....................$50
11/13/92 Bowe vs. Holyfield $50

06/07/93 Morrison vs. Foreman $35

04/22/94 Holyfield vs. Moorer....................$70
09/24/94 L. Lewis vs. McCall.....................$35
11/05/94 Foreman vs. Moorer $100
11/09/96 Tyson vs. Holyfield.....................$25

06/28/97 Holyfield vs. Tyson.....................$25
03/14/99 Holyfield vs. L. Lewis.................$75

Chapter 6

PERIODICALS

Because of their affordability, sports publications have been gaining popularity with collectors. Collecting periodicals can encompass such magazines as well known sports periodicals like *Sport*, *Sports Illustrated*, *The Sporting News*, *Inside Sports*, *Dell Sports* or *Street & Smith's*. Other opportunities and challenges are available to collectors with sports-related covers on general interest magazines such as *Time*, *Newsweek*, *Life* and *Boy's Life*.

To determine pricing for autographed magazine covers, a general guideline is to add the current value of the periodical and the price of the athlete's signature (many are found in Chapter 1).

Sports Illustrated

The premiere issue of publishing mogul Henry Luce Booth's weekly *Sports Illustrated* with Eddie Mathews pictured on the cover is a favorite of collectors. That issue, and the second issue as well (which is even more valuable), includes fold-out pages of 1954 Topps baseball cards printed on thin paper stock.

Since then, *SI* has been recognized as a leading name in sports publishing.

The attractive cover photos are generally what drives the collectibility of *SI*s. A popular athlete's first appearance on a cover is also desirable.

Autographed covers are also popular. Generally, prices for autographed issues are worth the price of the magazine, plus the value of the athlete's signature on an 8x10 photo.

Date	Cover Subject	VG	EX	NM
1954				

Date	Cover Subject	VG	EX	NM
08/16	Eddie Mathews	$150	$225	$350
08/23	Golf Bags	200	300	475
08/30	Vacationing	10	18	30
09/06	Sailing	8	15	25
09/13	Sports Car	8	15	25
09/20	Rodeo	8	15	25
09/27	Calvin Jones	8	15	25
10/04	Horserider, Colorado	8	15	25
10/11	Oklahoma Band	8	15	25
10/18	Steeplechase	8	15	25
10/25	English Setter	8	15	25
11/01	Oklahoma Football	8	15	25
11/08	Surfcasting	8	15	25
11/15	Spoonbill Duck	8	15	25
11/22	Y.A. Tittle	18	30	40
11/29	1900 Peugot	6	12	18
12/06	Lion in the Bush	6	12	18
12/13	Royal Horse Show	6	12	18
12/20	Ken Sears	6	12	18
12/27	Ski Resort	6	12	18
1955				
01/03	Roger Bannister	$5	$8	$12
01/10	Santa Anita Horseracing	5	8	12
01/17	R. Rodriguez: Bullfighting	5	8	12
01/24	Hedberg/Karten: Gymnastics	5	8	12
01/31	Jill Kilmont	5	8	12
02/07	Carol Heiss	5	8	12
02/14	Great Dane Dog	5	8	12
02/21	Swimsuit Edition (Betty di Bugnano)	5	8	12
02/28	Hialeah Park Horseracing	5	8	12
03/07	Jo Alston: Badminton	5	8	12
03/14	Buddy Werner	5	8	12
03/21	Parry O'Brien	5	8	12
03/28	Bowling	5	8	12
04/04	Ben Hogan	6	12	18

Date	Cover Subject	VG	EX	NM
04/11	W. Mays/L. Durocher	90	120	150
04/18	Al Rosen	60	90	120
04/25	Mountain Climber	5	8	12
05/02	Tom Courtney: Track	5	8	12
05/09	Hot Air Ballooning	5	8	12
05/16	Bird Watching	5	8	12
05/23	Zale Perry: Skindiver	5	8	12
05/30	Herb Score	8	15	25
06/06	Trout Fishing	5	8	12
06/13	Ocean Racing	5	8	12
06/20	Ed Furgol U.S. Open	5	8	12
06/27	Duke Snider	35	60	90
07/04	Bulldog	5	8	12
07/11	Yogi Berra	18	30	60
07/18	Swaps	5	8	12

Date	Cover Subject	VG	EX	NM
07/25	Alpine Vacation	5	8	12

Date	Cover Subject	VG	EX	NM
08/01	Ted Williams	60	90	120
08/08	Archery	5	8	12
08/15	1st Anniversary Issue	5	8	12
08/22	Don Newcombe	8	15	25
08/29	Tony Trabert	5	8	12
09/05	Spearfishing	5	8	12
09/12	Bud Wilkinson	6	12	18
09/19	Rocky Marciano	10	18	30
09/26	Walter Alston	10	18	30
10/03	Doak Walker	6	12	18
10/10	Gamebirds	5	8	12
10/17	Princeton Marching Band	5	8	12
10/24	Hopalong Cassidy	6	12	18
10/31	Horse Review	5	8	12
11/07	Bob Pellegrini	5	8	12
11/14	Ernest Burton	5	8	12
11/21	Ske Werner	5	8	12
11/28	Don Hollander	5	8	12
12/05	Louise Dyer: Fencing	5	8	12
12/12	Dachshunds	5	8	12
12/19	Ski Resort	5	8	12
12/26	Jim Swink	5	8	12

1956

Date	Cover Subject	VG	EX	NM
01/02	Johnny Podres	$18	$30	$40
01/09	Bob Cousy	15	28	50
01/16	Mike Souchak: Crosby	6	12	18
01/23	Jean Beliveau	12	25	35
01/30	Jenkins and Albright	5	8	12
02/06	Ralph Miller	5	8	12
02/13	C. Maute: Indoor Track	5	8	12
02/20	White Heron	5	8	12
02/27	Hialeah	5	8	12
03/05	Stan Musial	25	35	60
03/12	Champion Afgan	5	8	12
03/19	Marlin Champion	5	8	12
03/26	Jim Kimberly Sebring	5	8	12
04/02	Al Wiggins: Swimming	5	8	12
04/09	Special Baseball Issue	6	12	18
04/16	Barbara Womack	5	8	12
04/23	Billy Martin	18	30	40
04/30	Trout Fishing	5	8	12
05/07	Kentucky Derby	5	8	12

Date	Cover Subject	VG	EX	NM
05/14	A.Kaline/H. Kuenn	15	28	40
05/21	John Landy	5	8	12
05/28	Bob Sweikert	5	8	12
06/04	Floyd Patterson	10	18	30
06/11	Sam Snead	10	18	30

Date	Cover Subject	VG	EX	NM
06/18	Mickey Mantle	110	170	240
06/25	Warren Spahn	18	30	40
07/02	Sime and Morrow	5	8	12
07/09	All Star Game	12	25	35

Date	Cover Subject	VG	EX	NM
07/16	Reds' Musclemen	30	40	75
07/23	Adios Harry Fastest Pacer	5	8	12
07/30	Joe Adcock	6	12	18
08/06	Jeane Stunyo	5	8	12
08/13	Sailing in the Olympics	5	8	12
08/20	2nd Anniv. Issue	6	12	18
08/27	Doris and Ruth Gissy	5	8	12
09/03	Lew Hoad Forest Hills	5	8	12
09/10	Whitey Ford	25	35	60
09/17	Willie Hartack	5	8	12
09/24	Special Football Issue	6	12	18
10/01	M. Mantle: World Series	60	90	120
10/08	Paul Brown	10	18	30
10/15	Harold S. Vanderbilt	5	8	12
10/22	Duck Hunting	5	8	12
10/29	Paul Hornung	15	25	50

Date	Cover Subject	VG	EX	NM
11/05	Yale Bulldog	5	8	12
11/12	Michigan Football	6	12	18
11/19	Olympic Preview	5	8	12
11/26	USC vs. UCLA Football	6	12	18
12/03	Charlie Conerly	6	12	18
12/10	Olympic Track	5	8	12
12/17	Elizabeth Guest: Skiing	5	8	12
12/24	Bowl Previews	6	12	18

1957

Date	Cover Subject	VG	EX	NM
01/07	Bobby Morrow	$6	$12	$18
01/14	Western Skiing	5	8	12
01/21	Johnny Lee	5	8	12
01/28	Boston Bruins	8	15	25
02/04	Hugh Shadelee: Sailboat	5	8	12
02/11	Boxer Dog	5	8	12
02/18	Jim Krebs	5	8	12
02/25	Saxton/Basilio: Boxing	6	12	18
03/04	Mantle: Spring Training	60	90	120
03/11	Ben Hogan	15	25	50
03/18	G. Howe/T. Lindsey	8	15	25
03/25	Sebring	5	8	12
04/01	Dan Hodge	5	8	12
04/08	Trout Fishing	5	8	12
04/15	Spring Baseball	12	25	35

Date	Cover Subject	VG	EX	NM
04/22	Wally Moon	6	12	18
04/29	Fullmer vs. Robinson	6	12	18
05/06	Kentucky Derby	5	8	12
05/13	Billy Pierce	6	12	18
05/20	Gussie Busch	5	8	12
05/27	Indy 500	5	8	12
06/03	Clem Labine	6	12	18
06/10	Cary Middlecoff	5	8	12
06/17	Eddie Arcaro	5	8	12
06/24	Bob Gutkowski	5	8	12
07/01	Yachting	5	8	12
07/08	T. Williams/S. Musial	60	90	120
07/15	Animal Moods	5	8	12
07/22	Hank Bauer	6	12	18
07/29	Floyd Patterson	5	8	12
08/05	Physical Fitness	5	8	12
08/12	Russell Schleeh	5	8	12
08/19	Hambletonian	5	8	12
08/26	Countess Consuelo Crespi	5	8	12
09/02	Althea Gibson	5	8	12
09/09	Roy McMillan	6	12	18
09/16	Carmen Basilio	6	12	18
09/23	Football Preview	6	12	18
09/30	World Series Issue	10	18	30
10/07	Ollie Matson	8	15	25
10/14	Charles Goren	5	8	12
10/21	Waterfowl Season	5	8	12
10/28	Autumn Trees	5	8	12

Date	Cover Subject	VG	EX	NM
11/04	Bobby Cox	5	8	12
11/11	Lemon Drop Kid	5	8	12
11/18	Oklahoma Football	6	12	18
11/25	Ski Revolution	5	8	12
12/02	Russian Physical Fitness	5	8	12
12/09	College Basketball	5	8	12
12/16	Ski Fashion	5	8	12
12/23	Stan Musial	15	28	50

1958

Date	Cover Subject	VG	EX	NM
01/06	Nassau Family Fun	$5	$8	$12
01/13	Bill Mauldin/Caribbean	5	8	12
01/20	NBA All Star Game	6	12	18
01/27	Willie Shoemaker	6	12	18
02/03	Seals	5	8	12
02/10	H. Salaun/D. Mateer	5	8	12
02/17	Jacques Plante	10	18	30
02/24	Phil Reavis - Polevault	5	8	12
03/03	Yankee Spring Training	8	15	25
03/10	Australian Surfers	5	8	12
03/17	Sal Maglie	6	12	18
03/24	Basilio vs. Robinson	5	8	12
03/31	Roy Sievers	6	12	18
04/07	The Masters	5	8	12
04/14	Baseball Special	6	12	18
04/21	Del Crandall	6	12	18
04/28	Silky Sullivan	5	8	12
05/05	Gil McDougald	6	12	18
05/12	America's Cup	5	8	12
05/19	Richie Ashburn	6	12	18
05/26	Pat O'Conner	5	8	12
06/02	Eddie Mathews	12	25	40
06/09	Dick Mayer:U.S. Open	5	8	12
06/16	Hoad vs.Gonzalez	5	8	12
06/23	Jackie Jensen	6	12	18
06/30	Mixed Doubles Tennis	5	8	12

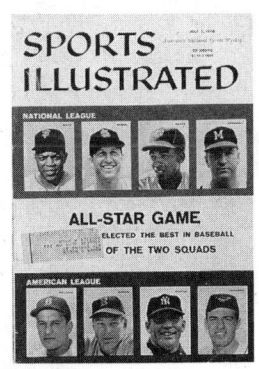

Date	Cover Subject	VG	EX	NM
07/07	All Stars Mays/Mantle	15	28	50
07/14	Educating Your Dog	5	8	12
07/21	Chris Von Sakltza	5	8	12
07/28	Frank Thomas	6	12	18
08/04	Nantucket: Vacation	5	8	12
08/11	Clare Boothe Luce	5	8	12
08/18	Roy Harris	5	8	12
08/25	Pine Valley Golf	5	8	12
09/01	F. Patterson/Harris	8	15	25
09/08	Salmon Fishing	5	8	12
09/15	America's Cup Racing	5	8	12
09/22	College Football	6	12	18
09/29	World Series	6	12	18
10/06	Goose Hunting	5	8	12
10/13	Ohio State Football	6	12	18
10/20	James McCarthy	5	8	12
10/27	Chick Zimmerman	5	8	12

Date	Cover Subject	VG	EX	NM
11/03	Hugh Wiley	5	8	12
11/10	Herb Elliott	5	8	12
11/17	John Olin: Hunting	5	8	12
11/24	Dawkins Army Football	5	8	12
12/01	Ski Preview	5	8	12
12/08	College Basketball	5	8	12
12/15	B. Wagner/B. Paul	5	8	12
12/22	Holiday Issue	5	8	12

1959

Date	Cover Subject	VG	EX	NM
01/05	Rafer Johnson: UCLA	$6	$12	$18
01/12	Andy Bathgate	6	12	18
01/19	Pheasant Shoot	5	8	12
01/26	Hialeah	5	8	12
02/02	Ron Delany	5	8	12
02/09	Winter Fun in Colorado	5	8	12
02/16	Johnny Longden	5	8	12
02/23	Small Boat Sailing	5	8	12
03/02	Casey Stengel	12	25	35
03/09	Ed Sullivan	5	8	12
03/16	Phil Hill Sebring	5	8	12
03/23	Aly Khan: Sporting Prince	5	8	12
03/30	Tommy Armour	5	8	12
04/06	Bobby Jones	5	8	12
04/13	Willie Mays	25	35	60
04/20	Billy Talbert	5	8	12
04/27	Kentucky Derby	5	8	12
05/04	Bob Turley	6	12	18
05/11	Gambling at Las Vegas	5	8	12
05/18	Bob/ Bus Mosbacher	5	8	12
05/25	Indianapolis 500	5	8	12
06/01	Gary Cooper	6	12	18
06/08	Tommy Bolt	5	8	12
06/15	Los Angeles Coliseum	5	8	12
06/22	Ingemar Johannson	6	12	18
06/29	Golden Eagle	5	8	12
07/06	Patterson/I. Johannsen	8	15	25
07/13	Becky Collins	5	8	12
07/20	USA/USSR Track Meet	5	8	12
07/27	Toots Shor	5	8	12
08/03	Trotting	5	8	12
08/10	L. Aparicio/ N. Fox	25	35	60
08/17	Anne Quast	5	8	12
08/24	Yachting	5	8	12
08/31	Parry O'Brien	5	8	12
09/07	Alex Olmeto	5	8	12
09/14	Sebastian Coe	5	8	12
09/21	Football Special	5	8	12
09/28	Chicago White Sox	6	12	18
10/05	Johnny Unitas	12	25	35
10/12	Duck Hunting	5	8	12
10/19	Autumn at Lime Rock	5	8	12
10/26	George Izo	5	8	12
11/02	Ryder Cup Golf	5	8	12
11/09	College Football	5	8	12
11/16	Daytona Sports cars	5	8	12
11/23	Alta, Utah Ski Season	5	8	12
11/30	Hunting Dog	5	8	12
12/07	College Basketball	5	8	12
12/14	Tom Watson Family	5	8	12
12/21	Holiday Issue	5	8	12

1960

Date	Cover Subject	VG	EX	NM
01/04	Ingemar Johannson	$5	$10	$15
01/11	Jerry Lucas	5	10	15
01/18	Art Wall	4	6	10
01/25	Hockey USSR	4	6	10
02/01	Betsy Snite	4	6	10

Date	Cover Subject	VG	EX	NM
02/08	Dog Show	4	6	10
02/15	Olympic Review	4	6	10
02/22	Sword Dancer	4	6	10
03/01	Squaw Valley	4	6	10
03/07	Spring Training	5	10	15
03/14	Family Bowling	4	6	10
03/21	Maurice Richard	5	10	15
03/28	Fishing	4	6	10
04/04	The Masters	4	6	10
04/11	Baseball Annual	5	10	15
04/18	Carin Cone: Swimmer	4	6	10
04/25	Dallas Long	4	6	10
05/02	Kentucky Derby	4	6	10
05/09	Alaska	4	6	10
05/16	Australia	4	6	10
05/23	C. Goren Bridge	4	6	10
05/30	Herb Elliot/Burleson	4	6	10
06/06	Red Schoendienst	6	12	20
06/13	Arnold Palmer	6	12	20
06/20	Ingemar Johannson	5	10	15
06/27	Glenn Davis	5	10	15
07/04	Comisky Park Fireworks	5	10	15
07/11	Jim Beatty	4	6	10
07/18	Candlestick Park	4	6	10
07/25	Sailing	4	6	10
08/01	Mike Troy	4	6	10
08/08	Dick Groat	6	12	20
08/15	Olympics	4	6	10
08/22	Barbara McIntire	4	6	10
08/29	Mountain Climbing	4	6	10
09/05	Olympics/Rome	4	6	10
09/12	Jack Nicklaus	10	20	30
09/19	Football Special	5	10	15
09/26	Jim Brown	11	21	35
10/03	Bob Schordt	4	6	10
10/10	Vernon Law	4	6	10
10/17	Sportswear	4	6	10
10/24	Football Violence	4	6	10
10/31	Jack Brabham	4	6	10
11/07	Gourmets	4	6	10
11/14	Bobby Hull	7	15	25
11/21	Ski Sportswear	4	6	10
11/28	Joe Bellino	4	6	10
12/05	Sam Snead	5	10	15
12/12	Basketball Special	5	10	15
12/19	Norm Van Brocklin	6	12	20
12/26	President /Mrs. Kennedy	12	22	40

1961

Date	Cover Subject	VG	EX	NM
01/09	Arnold Palmer	$7	$15	$25
01/16	Bob Cousy	6	12	20
01/23	Pebble Beach/Crosby	4	6	10
01/30	Safe Driving	4	6	10
02/06	Indoor Track	4	6	10
02/13	Laurence Owen Skating	4	6	10
02/20	Billy Casper	4	7	12
02/27	Bobsled Championship	4	6	10
03/06	Spring Training/Reds	5	10	15
03/13	Floyd Patterson	5	10	15
03/20	Parachute Jumper	4	6	10
03/27	Basketball's Championship	4	7	12
04/03	The Masters	4	6	10
04/10	Baseball Issue	5	10	15
04/17	Golden Gate Fishing	4	6	10
04/24	Hot Rod Cult	4	6	10
05/01	Kentucky Derby	4	6	10
05/08	Gary Player	4	7	12

Date	Cover Subject	VG	EX	NM
05/15	Cookie Lavagetto	4	7	12
05/22	Our Beaches	4	6	10
05/29	Indianapolis 500	4	6	10
06/05	Ocean Racing	4	6	10
06/12	U.S.Open	4	6	10
06/19	Earl Long	4	6	10
06/26	W. Mays/E. Broglio	6	12	20
07/03	Underwater Swimmer	4	6	10
07/10	World Tennis Crisis	4	6	10
07/17	Valerie Brumel	4	6	10
07/24	Fishing	4	6	10
07/31	Split-Second Baseball	4	7	12
08/07	Chess	4	6	10
08/14	Murray Rose, Mays	5	10	20
08/21	Judy Torluemke	4	6	10
08/28	John Sellars	4	6	10
09/04	Forest Hills	4	6	10
09/11	Deane Beman	4	6	10
09/18	College Football	4	7	12
09/25	Bart Starr	10	20	30
10/02	Roger Maris	12	22	40
10/09	Joey Jay	4	7	12
10/16	Terry Baker	4	6	10
10/23	Jon Arnett	4	7	12
10/30	Wilt Chamberlain	10	20	30
11/06	Kelso	4	6	10
11/13	Tom McNeeley	4	6	10
11/20	Y. A. Tittle	6	12	20
11/27	Jimmy Saxton	4	6	10
12/04	Speed on Skis	4	6	10
12/11	Basketball	4	7	12
12/18	Dan Currie: Packers	4	7	12
12/25	Francine Bre'aud	4	6	10

1962

Date	Cover Subject	VG	EX	NM
01/08	Jerry Lucas	$6	$12	$20
01/15	Boston Bruins	5	10	15
01/22	Doug Sanders	4	6	10
01/29	Chet Jastremski	4	6	10
02/05	Joan Hannah	4	6	10
02/12	Sonny Liston	5	10	15
02/19	Mickey Wright	4	6	10
02/26	John Uelses	4	6	10
03/05	Casey Stengel	10	20	30
03/12	Kentucky Derby Favorites	4	6	10
03/19	UCLA Bruins	5	10	15
03/26	Ricardo Rodriguez	4	6	10
04/02	Arnold Palmer	6	12	20
04/09	Frank Lary	4	7	12
04/16	Donna De Varona	4	6	10
04/23	Jerry Schmidt	4	6	10
04/30	Luis Aparicio	8	15	25
05/07	Kentucky Derby	4	6	10
05/14	Gene Littler	4	6	10
05/21	Fun on the Water	4	6	10
05/28	Floyd Patterson	5	10	15
06/04	Willie Mays	11	21	35
06/11	U.S.Open Preview	4	6	10
06/18	Cornell's Rowing Crew	4	6	10
06/25	Jack Nicklaus	8	15	25
07/02	Mickey Mantle	55	80	125
07/09	Greter Invades Australia	4	6	10
07/16	Igor Ter-Ovanesyan	4	6	10
07/23	Barbara McAlister	4	6	10
07/30	Ken Boyer	6	12	20
08/06	Paul Runyan	4	6	10
08/13	Dick Fortenberry	4	6	10

Date	Cover Subject	VG	EX	NM
08/20	Don Drysdale	10	20	30
08/27	Helga Schultze	4	6	10
09/03	Beach Explosion in Calif.	4	6	10
09/10	Jim Taylor	9	20	35
09/17	Sonny Liston	5	10	15
09/24	College Football	4	7	12
10/01	World Series	6	12	20
10/08	Tommy McDonald	5	10	15
10/15	Sonny Gibbs of TCU	4	6	10
10/22	Big Game Hunting	4	6	10
10/29	Fran Tarkenton	10	20	30
11/05	Calif. Gold Divers	4	6	10
11/12	A. Palmer/S.Snead	10	20	30
11/19	Nick Pietrosante	4	7	12
11/26	Paul Dietzel	4	6	10
12/03	Winter in Montana	4	6	10
12/10	Cotton Nash	5	10	15
12/17	Frank Gifford	9	20	35
12/24	The Bold American	4	6	10

1963

Date	Cover Subject	VG	EX	NM
01/07	Terry Baker	$4	$7	$12
01/14	Phil Rodgers	4	6	10
01/21	Resorts	4	6	10
01/28	Howie Young	4	7	12
02/04	Valerie Brumel	4	6	10
02/11	Cathy Nagel	4	6	10
02/18	Jerry Barber	4	6	10
02/25	Rex Ellsworth	4	6	10
03/04	Sandy Koufax	14	23	45
03/11	Chuck Ferris	4	6	10
03/18	Basketball's Championship	4	7	12
03/25	Sonny Liston	4	7	12
04/01	Master's Preview	4	6	10
04/08	Harmon Killebrew	10	20	30
04/15	Tennis Clubs	4	6	10
04/22	Marlin Fishing	4	6	10
04/29	Art Mahaffey	4	7	12
05/06	Kentucky Derby Preview	4	6	10
05/13	Cruise Ship	4	6	10
05/20	Paul Hornung	10	20	30
05/27	Dan Gurney	4	6	10

Date	Cover Subject	VG	EX	NM
06/03	Bob Hope	5	10	15
06/10	Cassius Clay	12	22	40
06/17	Jack Nicklaus	6	12	20
06/24	Roy Face	4	7	12
07/01	Julius Boros	4	7	12
07/08	Casting	4	6	10
07/15	Arnold Palmer	6	12	20
07/22	Dick Groat	5	10	15
07/29	Sonny Liston	5	10	15
08/05	Nancy Vonderheide	4	6	10
08/12	Alfred G. Vanderbilt	4	6	10

Date	Cover Subject	VG	EX	NM
08/19	Ron Vanderkelen	4	6	10
08/26	Dennis Ralston	4	6	10
09/02	Ron Fairly	4	7	12
09/09	Dallas Cowboys	5	10	15
09/16	Yachting	4	6	10
09/23	George Mira	4	6	10
09/30	Whitey Ford	8	15	25
10/07	Deer Hunting	4	6	10
10/14	Ronnie Bull	4	7	12
10/21	Duke Carlisle	4	6	10
10/28	Jerry Lucas/Art Heyman	5	10	15
11/04	Northwestern Line	4	6	10
11/11	Pro Football Roughness	4	6	10
11/18	Skiing in Vermont	4	6	10
11/25	Willie Galimore	4	7	12
12/02	Roger Staubach	10	20	30
12/09	College Basketball	4	6	10
12/16	Kyle Rote	5	10	15
12/23	C.K.Yang	4	6	10

1964

Date	Cover Subject	VG	EX	NM
01/06	Pete Rozelle	$4	$7	$12
01/13	Jack Dempsey	6	12	20
01/20	Ist Swimsuit Issue	9	20	35
01/27	Buddy Werner	3	5	8
02/03	Bobby Hull	6	12	20
02/10	Egon Zimmermann	3	5	8
02/17	Bridge by Charles Goren	3	5	8
02/24	Cassius Clay	9	20	35
03/02	Y. Berra/C. Stengel	10	20	30
03/09	C. Clay/S. Liston	10	20	30
03/16	Gordie Howe	8	15	25
03/23	Tony Lema	3	5	8
03/30	Walt Hazzard	4	6	10
04/06	Jack Nicklaus	5	10	15
04/13	Sandy Koufax	10	20	30
04/20	Texas Girls Track	3	5	8
04/27	Claude Harmon	3	5	8
05/04	Kentucky Derby	3	5	8
05/11	Al Kaline	6	12	20
05/18	Joey Giardello	4	7	12
05/25	Frank Howard	4	7	12
06/01	A.J. Foyt	4	6	10
06/08	Bill Hartack	4	6	10
06/15	U.S.Open	3	5	8
06/22	Tom O'Hara	3	5	8
06/29	Ken Venturi	4	6	10
07/06	Alvin Dark	4	7	12
07/13	Bill Talbert	3	5	8
07/20	Shirley McClain	4	6	10
07/27	Tommy McDonald	5	10	15
08/03	Betsy Rawls	3	5	8
08/10	Johnny Callison	4	6	10
08/17	Don Trull	3	5	8
08/24	Yachting	3	5	8
08/31	Brooks Robinson	6	12	20
09/07	Y.A.Tittle	6	12	20
09/14	J. Ryun: Olympic Trials	3	5	8
09/21	College Football	4	6	10
09/28	Tommy Mason	4	6	10
10/05	Billy Mills	3	5	8
10/12	Dick Butkus	10	20	30
10/19	Tokyo Olympics Begin	3	5	8
10/26	Tommy Heinsohn	6	12	20
11/02	John Huarte	4	6	10
11/09	John David Crow	5	10	15
11/16	Clay vs. Liston	6	12	20

Date	Cover Subject	VG	EX	NM
11/23	Skiing	3	5	8
12/07	Bill Bradley	6	12	20
12/14	Charley Johnson	4	7	12
12/21	Ken Venturi	4	6	10

1965

Date	Cover Subject	VG	EX	NM
01/04	Frank Ryan	$4	$6	$10
01/11	Ernie Koy	3	5	8
01/18	Swimsuit Edition (Sue Peterson)	10	20	30
01/25	Bobby Hull	6	12	20
02/01	George Chuvalo	4	6	10
02/08	Jerry West	6	12	20
02/15	Best 18 in America (1st 9)	3	5	8
02/22	Best 18 in America (2nd 9)	3	5	8
03/01	J. Bunning/B. Belinsky	5	10	15
03/08	Billy Kidd	4	6	10
03/15	Tony Lema	3	5	8
03/22	Willie Pastrano	4	7	12
03/29	Gail Goodrich	5	10	15
04/05	J. Nicklaus/A. Palmer	6	12	20
04/12	Wilt Chamberlain	8	15	25
04/19	Baseball 1965	5	10	15
04/26	Sonny Liston	5	10	15
05/03	Kentucky Derby	3	5	8
05/10	Marie Mulder/Janell Smith	3	5	8
05/17	Bill Veeck	4	7	12
05/24	Clay vs. Liston	8	15	25
05/31	Indianapolis 500	3	5	8
06/07	C. Clay/S. Liston	8	15	25
06/14	U.S. Open	3	5	8
06/21	Mickey Mantle	12	22	40
06/28	Harvard Crew	3	5	8
07/05	Bill Talbert	3	5	8
07/12	Maury Wills	5	10	15
07/19	Joe Namath	9	20	35
07/26	Arnold Palmer	5	10	15
08/02	Power Boating	3	5	8
08/09	Juan Marichal	6	12	20
08/16	Y.A.Tittle	5	10	15
08/23	Tony Oliva	5	10	15
08/30	Michael Jazy	3	5	8
09/06	Sugar Ray Robinson	6	12	20
09/13	Fran Tarkenton	5	10	15
09/20	Frank Solich	3	5	8
09/27	Frank Ryan	3	5	8
10/04	Zoilo Versalles	4	7	12
10/11	49ers on the Move	4	7	12
10/18	Tommy Nobis	4	7	12

Date	Cover Subject	VG	EX	NM
10/25	Bill Russell	6	12	20
11/01	C. Johnson/ S.Randle	5	10	15
11/08	Harry Jones	3	5	8
11/15	Skier	3	5	8

Date	Cover Subject	VG	EX	NM
11/22	Clay vs. Patterson	8	15	25
11/29	Dennis Gabatz	3	5	8
12/06	UCLA Basketball	4	6	10
12/13	Lance Alworth	5	10	15

Date	Cover Subject	VG	EX	NM
12/20	Sandy Koufax	8	15	25

1966

Date	Cover Subject	VG	EX	NM
01/03	College Bowls	$3	$5	$8
01/10	Jim Taylor	6	12	20
01/17	Swimsuit Edition (Sunny Bippus)	8	15	25
01/24	Iowa of The Big Ten	3	5	8
01/31	Stan Mikita	5	10	15
02/07	Billy Casper	4	6	10
02/14	Rick Mount	3	5	8
02/21	Jean Claude Killy	4	6	10
02/28	L. Durocher/E. Stanky	5	10	15
03/07	Adolph Rupp	4	6	10
03/14	Richmond Flowers	3	5	8
03/21	Gary Player	4	7	12
03/28	P. Riley/H. Flournoy	3	5	8
04/04	Nicklaus/Palmer	6	12	20
04/11	Clay/Chuvalo	6	12	20
04/18	Dick Groat	5	10	15
04/25	Hawks/RedWings	4	7	12
05/02	Peggy Fleming	4	6	10
05/09	John Havlicek	6	12	20
05/16	Kentucky Derby	3	5	8
05/23	Sam McDowell	4	7	12
05/30	Indianapolis 500	3	5	8
06/06	J.Morgan/S.Jackson	5	10	15
06/13	U.S.Open/Ken Venturi	4	6	10
06/20	Jim Ryun	3	5	8
06/27	U.S.Open/Billy Casper	4	6	10
07/04	Ocean Sailing	3	5	8
07/11	Andy Etchebarren	4	6	10
07/18	Surfing	3	5	8
07/25	O. Graham/E. B. Williams	5	10	15
08/01	Jim Ryun	3	5	8
08/08	Frank Emanuel	3	5	8
08/15	Bear Bryant	5	10	15
08/22	Hornung/Taylor	6	12	20
08/29	Arthur Ashe	4	6	10
09/05	Harry Walker	4	7	12
09/12	Gale Sayers	8	15	25
09/19	Gary Beban of UCLA	4	6	10
09/26	Gaylord Perry	5	10	15
10/03	Roman Gabriel	5	10	15
10/10	Brooks/F. Robinson	8	15	25
10/17	Joe Namath	8	15	25
10/24	Elgin Baylor	6	12	20
10/31	Bart Starr	6	12	20
11/07	Terry Hanratty	4	7	12

Date	Cover Subject	VG	EX	NM
11/14	Super Ski Runs	3	5	8
11/21	Ross Fichtnel	3	5	8
11/28	Notre Dame/Mich. State	4	6	10
12/05	Lew Alcindor	10	20	30
12/12	Jim Nance	4	6	10
12/18	Jim Ryun	3	5	8

1967

Date	Cover Subject	VG	EX	NM
01/02	Kitty McManus	$3	$5	$8
01/09	Bart Starr	6	12	20
01/16	Swimsuit Edition (Lynn Tindall)	8	12	25
01/23	Max McGee	5	10	15
01/30	Rod Gilbert	4	7	12
02/06	Clay vs. Terrell	6	12	20
02/13	Rick Barry	5	10	15
02/20	Bob Seagren	4	6	10
02/27	G. Walters/C.Thoimforde	3	5	8
03/06	Arnold Palmer & Wife	5	10	15
03/13	Jim Nash	3	5	8
03/20	Stan Mikita	5	10	15
03/27	Jean-Claude Killy	4	6	10
04/03	Lew Alcindor: UCLA	6	12	20
04/10	Jack Nicklaus	5	10	15
04/17	Maury Wills	5	10	15
04/24	Rick Barry	5	10	15
05/01	Jim Hall	4	6	10
05/08	Mickey Mantle	9	22	35
05/15	Koufax/Drysdale/Wills	10	20	30
05/22	Tommy Smith	3	5	8
05/29	Indianapolis 500	3	5	8
06/05	Al Kaline	5	10	15
06/12	Billy Casper	4	6	10
06/19	Gypsy Joe Harris	3	5	8
06/26	Jack Nicklaus	4	7	12
07/03	Roberto Clemente	10	20	30
07/10	Muhammad Ali	8	15	25
07/17	Fran Tarkenton	5	10	15
07/24	Surfers in Hawaii	3	5	8
07/31	The Spitball	4	6	10
08/07	Gay Brewer	3	5	8
08/14	J.Taylor/G. Cuozzo	5	10	15
08/21	Carl Yastrzemski	6	12	20
08/28	Intrepid	3	5	8
09/04	Tim McCarver	4	7	12
09/11	College Football	4	6	10
09/18	Tommy Mason	4	7	12
09/25	Nino Benvenutti	4	6	10
10/02	USC vs. Texas	4	6	10
10/09	Mike Phipps: Purdue	4	6	10

Date	Cover Subject	VG	EX	NM
10/16	Lou Brock	6	12	20
10/23	Pro Basketball Issue	4	7	12
10/30	Ala. vs. Tenn.	4	6	10

Date	Cover Subject	VG	EX	NM
11/06	Dan Reeves	4	7	12
11/13	The Ski Scene	3	5	8
11/20	O.J. Simpson	5	10	15
11/27	Jim Hart	4	7	12
12/04	College Basketball	4	6	10
12/11	Bobby Orr	6	12	20
12/18	Roman Gabriel	4	7	12
12/25	Carl Yastrzemski	6	12	20

1968

Date	Cover Subject	VG	EX	NM
01/08	Packer and Raiders	$6	$12	$20
01/15	Swimsuit Edition (Turia Mau)	6	12	20
01/22	Vince Lombardi	10	20	30
01/29	Lew Alcindor	8	12	25
02/05	Billy Kidd/Jimmy Heuga	3	5	8
02/12	Bobby Hull	5	10	15
02/19	Peggy Fleming	4	6	10
02/26	Curtis Turner	3	5	8

Date	Cover Subject	VG	EX	NM
03/04	Pete Maravich	6	12	20
03/11	Johnny Bench	8	12	25
03/18	Bill Bradley	5	10	15
03/25	Julius Boros	4	6	10
04/01	Lew Alcindor	6	12	20

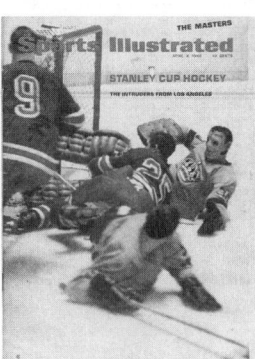

Date	Cover Subject	VG	EX	NM
04/08	Kings in Stanley Cup	4	6	10
04/15	Lou Brock	5	10	15
04/22	B. Goalby/R. De Vicenzo	3	5	8
04/29	J. West/Elgin Baylor	6	12	20
05/06	Ron Swoboda	4	6	10
05/13	Indianapolis 500	3	5	8
05/20	Derby Drug Mystery	3	5	8

Date	Cover Subject	VG	EX	NM
05/27	Pete Rose	8	12	25
06/03	Dave Patrick	3	5	8
06/10	U.S. Open	3	5	8
06/17	Don Drysdale	6	12	20
06/24	Lee Trevino	4	7	12
07/01	The Black Athlete	4	6	12

Date	Cover Subject	VG	EX	NM
07/08	Ted Williams	10	20	30
07/15	Ray Nitschke	6	12	20
07/22	Mark Spitz	4	7	12
07/29	Denny McLain	5	10	15
08/05	Nevele Pride	3	5	8
08/12	Paul Brown	4	7	12
08/19	Curt Flood	5	10	15
08/26	Rod Laver	3	5	8
09/02	Ken Harrelson	3	5	8
09/09	Leroy Keyes	3	5	8
09/16	Don Meredith	5	10	15
09/23	D. McLain/ A. Kaline	5	10	15
09/30	Mexico Olympics	3	5	8
10/07	St. Louis Cardinals	5	10	15
10/14	O.J.Simpson	5	10	15
10/21	Olympic Preview	3	5	8
10/28	F. Gregg/B. Brown	5	10	15

Date	Cover Subject	VG	EX	NM
11/04	Earl Monroe	5	10	15
11/11	Bruce Jankowski	3	5	8

Date	Cover Subject	VG	EX	NM
11/18	Ski My Way by Killy	3	5	8
11/25	Earl Morrall	4	6	10
12/02	Challenge to UCLA	3	5	8

Date	Cover Subject	VG	EX	NM
12/09	Joe Namath	8	12	25
12/16	Donnie Anderson	4	7	12

Date	Cover Subject	VG	EX	NM
12/23	Bill Russell	6	12	20

1969

Date	Cover Subject	VG	EX	NM
01/06	Tom Matte	$4	$7	$12
01/13	Swimsuit Edition	8	12	25
01/20	Joe Namath	8	12	25
01/27	Wilt Chamberlain	10	15	20
02/03	Bobby Orr	10	15	20
02/10	Bud Ogden: Santa Clara	3	5	8
02/17	Bob Lunn	3	5	8
02/24	Dave DeBusschere	4	7	12
03/03	Vince Lombardi	8	12	25
03/10	Track Scandal	3	5	8
03/17	Ted Williams	8	15	25
03/24	Jeff Mullins/R. Guerin	4	6	10
03/31	Lew Alcindor: UCLA	8	12	25
04/07	Red Berenson	3	5	8
04/14	Bill Freehan	4	7	12
04/21	Tommy Archer	3	5	8
04/28	Bill Russell	6	12	20
05/05	Muhammad Ali	8	12	25
05/12	John Havlicek	5	10	15
05/19	Walter Alston	6	12	20
05/26	Grizzly	3	5	8
06/02	Fun on the Water	3	5	8
06/09	Lee Trevino	5	10	15
06/16	Joe Namath	8	12	25
06/23	Drug Scandal	3	5	8
06/30	Ron Santo	5	10	15
07/07	Reggie Jackson	8	12	25

Date	Cover Subject	VG	EX	NM
07/14	O.J. Simpson	5	10	15
07/21	Billy Martin	5	10	15
07/28	S. Jurgensen/V. Lombardi	10	15	20
08/04	Bill Russell	10	15	20
08/11	Joe Namath	8	12	25
08/18	Hank Aaron	8	12	25
08/25	O.J. Simpson	5	10	15
08/31	Lew Alcindor: UCLA	6	12	20
09/01	Arnold Palmer	5	10	15
09/08	P. Rose/E. Banks	6	12	20
09/15	Rex Kern	3	5	8
09/22	Jim Turner	4	6	10
09/29	Jimmy Jones: USC	4	7	12
10/06	Frank Robinson	5	10	15
10/13	Bruce Kemp: Georgia	3	5	8
10/20	Brooks Robinson	5	10	15
10/27	Lew Alcindor	10	15	20
11/03	Minnesota Vikings	4	6	10
11/10	Steve Owens	4	6	10
11/17	Skiing in Italy	3	5	8

Date	Cover Subject	VG	EX	NM
11/24	L. Dawson/Chiefs	5	10	15
12/01	Pete Maravich	6	12	20
12/08	Walt Frazier	5	10	15
12/15	Slick Street	3	5	8

Date	Cover Subject	VG	EX	NM
12/22	Tom Seaver	10	20	30

1970

Date	Cover Subject	VG	EX	NM
01/05	Dave Osborn	$3	$5	$8
01/12	Swimsuit Edition (Cheryl Tiegs)	8	15	25
01/19	Len Dawson	10	20	30

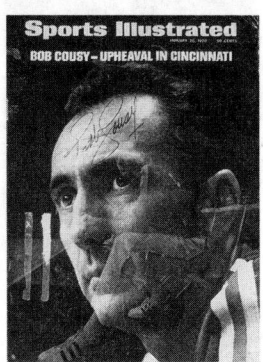

Date	Cover Subject	VG	EX	NM
01/26	Bob Cousy	4	6	10
02/02	Last Chance	2	4	7
02/09	Terry Bradshaw	4	6	10
02/16	Tom McMillan	3	5	8
02/23	Denny McLain	4	6	10
03/02	Eddie Giacomin	2	4	7
03/09	Lew Alcindor	4	7	12
03/16	Dan Issel	4	6	10
03/23	Dick Allen	4	6	10
03/30	Artis Gilmore	3	5	8
04/06	Keith Magnuson	2	4	7
04/13	Jerry Koosman	4	7	12
04/20	Billy Casper	3	5	8
04/27	L. Alcindor/W. Reed	4	7	12
05/04	Bobby Orr	4	7	12
05/11	Super Hippie	2	4	7
05/18	Dave DeBusschere	3	5	8
05/25	Hank Aaron	4	7	12
06/01	A. Palmer/J. Nicklaus	3	5	8
06/08	Al Unser: Indy Victory	3	5	8
06/15	Steve Prefontaine	2	4	7
06/22	Tony Conigliaro	4	7	12
06/29	Tony Jacklin	2	4	7
07/06	George Frenn	2	4	7

Date	Cover Subject	VG	EX	NM
07/13	Johnny Bench	4	7	12
07/20	Joe Kapp	3	5	8
07/27	Willie Mays	4	7	12
08/03	Frank Shorter	2	4	7
08/10	Mike Garrett	2	4	7
08/17	Joe Namath	4	7	12
08/24	Rick Barry	3	5	8
08/31	Les Shy	2	4	7
09/07	Bud Harrelson	3	5	8
09/14	Archie Manning	3	5	8

Date	Cover Subject	VG	EX	NM
09/21	Dick Butkus	4	6	10
09/28	L. Durocher/D. Murtaugh	3	5	8
10/05	Colorado/Penn State	2	4	7
10/12	Alex Karras	3	5	8
10/19	Brooks Robinson	4	6	10
10/26	Oscar Robertson	3	5	8
11/02	Monday Night Football	2	4	7
11/09	Theismann/Tatum/Wooster	3	5	8
11/16	Calvin Murphy	3	5	8
11/23	George Blanda	3	5	8
11/30	Sidney Wicks	2	4	7
12/07	Roman Gabriel	3	5	8
12/14	Woo Woo Worster	2	4	7
12/21	Bobby Orr	3	5	8

1971

Date	Cover Subject	VG	EX	NM
01/04	John Roche	$2	$4	$7
01/11	Joe Theismann	3	5	8
01/18	Craig Morton	3	5	8
01/25	Jim O'Brien	2	4	7
02/01	Swimsuit Edition (Tannia Rubiano)	6	12	20
02/08	Alcindor/W. Reed	4	6	10
02/15	Jim Plunkett	3	5	8
02/22	Del Meriwether	2	4	7
03/01	Ali/Frazier	5	10	15
03/08	Jack Nicklaus	3	5	8
03/15	Muhammad Ali	5	10	15
03/22	Wes Parker	2	4	7

Date	Cover Subject	VG	EX	NM
03/29	Tony/Phil Esposito	3	5	8
04/05	Steve Patterson	2	4	7
04/12	Boog Powell	3	5	8
04/19	Knicks/Bucks	2	4	7
04/26	Derek Sanderson	2	4	7
05/03	D. Duncan /J. Fregosi	3	5	8

Date	Cover Subject	VG	EX	NM
05/10	Oscar Robertson	4	6	10
05/17	James McCalister	2	4	7
05/24	Jim Ryun/Marty Liquori	2	4	7
05/31	Vida Blue	3	5	8
06/07	A. Unser/P. Revson	2	4	7

Date	Cover Subject	VG	EX	NM
06/14	Canonero	2	4	7
06/21	Jerry Grote	3	5	8
06/28	Lee Trevino	3	5	8
07/05	Alex Johnson	2	4	7
07/12	Evonne Goolagong	2	4	7
07/19	George Blanda	3	5	8
07/26	Muhammad Ali	4	6	10
08/02	Willie Stargell	3	5	8
08/09	Mike Patterson	2	4	7
08/16	Calvin Hill	3	5	8
08/23	Steve McQueen	3	5	8

Date	Cover Subject	VG	EX	NM
08/30	Ferguson Jenkins	3	5	8
09/06	Jackie Stewart	2	4	7
09/13	Tommy Casanova	2	4	7
09/20	John Brodie	3	5	8
09/27	Maury Wills	3	5	8
10/04	Sonny Sixkiller	2	4	7
10/11	Mean Joe Greene	3	5	8

Date	Cover Subject	VG	EX	NM
10/18	Frank Robinson	3	5	8
10/25	G. Johnson/DeBusschere	3	5	8
11/01	Ed Marinaro	3	5	8
11/08	Norm Bulach	2	4	7
11/15	Olympics	2	4	7
11/22	Oklahoma/Nebraska	2	4	7
11/29	Tom Burleson	2	4	7
12/05	Johnny Musso	2	4	7
12/13	Gail Goodrich	3	5	8
12/20	Lee Trevino	3	5	8

1972

Date	Cover Subject	VG	EX	NM
01/03	Garo Yepremian	$3	$5	$8
01/10	Nebraska Football	2	4	7
01/17	Swimsuit Edition (Sheila Roscoe)	6	12	20
01/24	Duane Thomas	3	5	8
01/31	Ann Henning	2	4	7
02/07	W. Frazier/D. Cowens	3	5	8

Date	Cover Subject	VG	EX	NM
02/14	Ken Dryden	2	4	7
02/21	Allie McGuire	2	4	7
02/28	A.J. Foyt	2	4	7
03/06	Bill Walton: UCLA	3	5	8
03/13	Johnny Bench	3	5	8
03/20	NCAA Champions	2	4	7

Date	Cover Subject	VG	EX	NM
03/27	Vida Blue	2	4	7
04/03	Bill Walton	3	5	8
04/10	Joe Torre	4	6	10
04/17	Jack Nicklaus	3	5	8
04/24	Lew Alcindor	3	5	8
05/01	Willie Davis	2	4	7
05/08	P. Esposito/B. Orr	3	5	8
05/15	Wilt Chamberlain	3	5	8
05/22	Willie Mays	4	6	10
05/29	Louie Jacobs	2	4	7
06/05	Mark Donohue	2	4	7

Date	Cover Subject	VG	EX	NM
06/12	Dick Allen	3	5	8
06/19	Bobby Hull	4	6	10
06/26	Jack Nicklaus	3	5	8
07/03	Steve Blass	2	4	7
07/10	Johnny Unitas	4	6	10
07/17	Jim Ryun	2	4	7
07/24	Tommy Prothro	2	4	7
07/31	Robyn Smith	2	4	7

Date	Cover Subject	VG	EX	NM

Date	Cover Subject	VG	EX	NM
08/07	Csonka and Kiick	3	5	8
08/14	Bobby Fisher	2	4	7
08/21	Sparky Lyle	3	5	8
08/28	Olympics	2	4	7
09/04	Mark Spitz	2	4	7
09/11	Bob Devaney	2	4	7
09/18	Walt Garrison	2	4	7
09/25	Carlton Fisk	3	5	8
10/02	Greg Pruitt	2	4	7
10/09	Joe Namath	4	6	10
10/16	Wilt Chamberlain	3	5	8
10/23	Catfish Hunter	3	5	8
10/30	Dave & Don Buckley	2	4	7
11/06	Larry Brown	2	4	7
11/13	John Havlicek	3	5	8
11/23	Terry Davis	2	4	7
11/27	Walter Luckett	2	4	7
12/04	Steve Spurrier	2	4	7
12/11	Campy Russell	2	4	7
12/18	Leroy Jordan	2	4	7
12/25	J.Wooden/B.J. King	3	5	8

1973

Date	Cover Subject	VG	EX	NM
01/08	Mercury Morris	$3	$5	$8
01/15	Doug Collins	2	4	7
01/22	Bob Griese	4	6	10
01/29	Swimsuit Edition (Dayle Haddon)	6	12	20
02/05	Bill Walton	3	5	8
02/12	Steve Smith	2	4	7
02/19	Abdul-Jabbar	3	5	8
02/26	Gil Perreault	2	4	7
03/05	Rugby	2	4	7
03/12	Bill Melton	3	5	8
03/19	Olga Korbut	2	4	7
03/26	Bill Walton	3	5	8
04/02	Henri Richard	3	5	8
04/09	Steve Carlton	3	6	10
04/16	Earl Monroe	3	5	8
04/23	Muhammad Ali	4	7	12
04/30	Chris Speier	3	5	8
05/07	W. Frazier/J. West	3	5	8
05/14	Mark and Suzy Spitz	2	4	7
05/21	Bobby Riggs	2	4	7
05/28	Women/Raw Deal	2	4	7
06/04	Wilbur Wood	3	5	8
06/11	Secretariat	2	4	7
06/18	George Foreman	4	6	10
06/25	Jack Nicklaus	3	5	8
07/02	B.Murcer/R.Blomberg	3	5	8
07/09	George Allen	3	5	8
07/16	Billie Jean King	2	4	7
07/23	Tom Weiskopf	2	4	7

Date	Cover Subject	VG	EX	NM
07/30	Carlton Fisk	4	6	10
08/06	John Matuszak	3	5	8
08/13	Dirt Bike Racing	2	4	7
08/20	Dodgers/Russell/Osteen	4	6	10
08/27	Duane Thomas	2	4	7
09/03	Bob Rigby	2	4	7
09/10	Texas Football	3	5	8
09/17	Larry Csonka	3	5	8
09/24	Danny Murtaugh	3	5	8
10/01	USC's Anthony Davis	3	5	8
10/08	Fran Tarkenton	4	6	10
10/15	Tiny Archibald	3	5	8
10/22	Bert Campaneris	3	5	8
10/29	O.J. Simpson	3	5	8
11/05	Notre Dame/USC	3	5	8
11/12	Pete Maravich	4	6	10
11/19	Phil Esposito	3	5	8
11/26	David Thompson	3	5	8
12/03	Alabama Football	2	4	7
12/10	L. Elmore/ B.Walton	3	5	8
12/17	Raiders/ Chiefs	3	5	8
12/24	Jackie Stewart	2	4	7

1974

Date	Cover Subject	VG	EX	NM
01/07	Fran Tarkenton	$3	$5	$8
01/14	Julius Erving	4	6	10
01/21	Larry Csonka	3	5	8
01/28	Swimsuit Edition (Ann Simonton)	6	12	20
02/04	Muhammad Ali	4	6	10
02/11	Ben Crenshaw	2	4	7
02/18	John Havlicek	3	5	8
02/25	UCLA: Bill Walton	3	5	8
03/04	Jimmy Connors	2	4	7

Date	Cover Subject	VG	EX	NM
03/11	Gordie Howe	4	6	10
03/18	Babe Ruth	4	6	10
03/25	UCLA vs. NC State	3	5	8
04/01	NC State/UCLA	3	5	8
04/08	Pete Rose	4	6	10

Date	Cover Subject	VG	EX	NM
04/15	Hank Aaron	6	12	20

Date	Cover Subject	VG	EX	NM
04/22	Gary Player	2	4	7
04/29	Bruce Hardy	2	4	7
05/06	Hockey: Phil/NY	2	4	7
05/13	Kentucky Derby	2	4	7
05/20	Havlicek/Jabbar	3	5	8
05/27	Jim Wynn	2	4	7
06/03	Johnny Rutherford	2	4	7
06/10	Johnny Miller	2	4	7
06/17	Reggie Jackson	4	6	10
06/24	Hale Irwin	2	4	6

Date	Cover Subject	VG	EX	NM
07/01	Rod Carew	3	5	8
07/08	Gerald Ford	3	5	8
07/15	Connors/Evert	2	4	7
07/22	Lou Brock	3	5	8

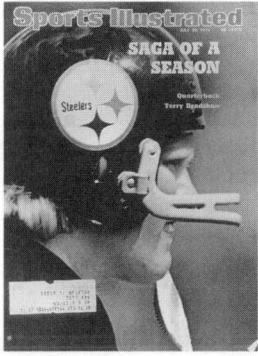

Date	Cover Subject	VG	EX	NM
07/29	Terry Bradshaw	3	5	8
08/05	Pro Football Strike	2	4	7
08/12	Mike Marshall	2	4	7
08/19	Lee Trevino	2	4	7
08/26	John Newcombe	2	4	7
09/02	Evel Knievel	2	4	7
09/09	Archie Griffin	2	4	7

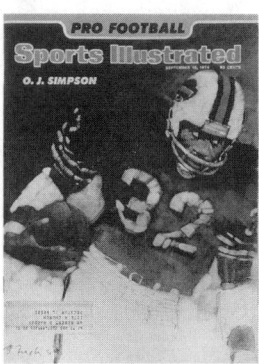

Date	Cover Subject	VG	EX	NM
09/16	O. J. Simpson	3	5	8
09/23	Joe Gilliam	2	4	7
09/30	Tom Clements	2	4	7
10/07	Catfish Hunter	3	5	8

Date	Cover Subject	VG	EX	NM
10/14	Walton/Jabbar	3	5	8
10/21	A's/ Dodgers	3	5	8
10/28	Ali/Foreman	4	6	10
11/04	Oklahoma Controversy	2	4	7
11/11	Muhammad Ali	4	6	10
11/18	Woody Green	2	4	7
11/25	Ken Dryden	2	4	7
12/02	College Basketball	2	4	7
12/09	Anthony Davis	2	4	7
12/16	Rick Barry	2	4	7
12/23	Muhammad Ali	4	6	10

1975

Date	Cover Subject	VG	EX	NM
01/06	Franco Harris	$3	$5	$8
01/13	Bill Tilden	2	4	7
01/20	Terry Bradshaw	3	5	8
01/27	Swimsuit Edition (Cheryl Tiegs)	6	12	20
02/03	John Laskowski	2	4	7
02/10	Roggie Vachon	2	4	7
02/17	David Meyers	2	4	7
02/24	Dog Show	2	4	7
03/03	Reds Spring Training	4	6	10
03/10	Lee Elder	2	4	7
03/17	Phil Ford	2	4	7
03/24	Chuck Wepner	2	4	7
03/31	Wildcats: Final Four	2	4	7
04/07	Steve Garvey	3	5	8
04/14	Vasilli Alexyev	2	4	7
04/21	Jack Nicklaus	3	5	8
04/28	Garfield Heard	2	4	7
05/05	Jimmy Connors	2	4	7
05/12	Kentucky Derby	2	4	7
05/19	A.J. Foyt	2	4	7
05/26	Jimmy Wynn	2	4	7
06/02	Billy Martin	3	5	8
06/09	Rocky Bleier	3	5	8
06/16	Nolan Ryan	4	7	12
06/23	Pele	2	4	7
06/30	Lou Graham	2	4	7
07/07	Fred Lynn	3	5	8
07/14	Arthur Ashe	2	4	7
07/21	T. Seaver /J.Palmer	4	6	10
07/28	Warfield/Csonka/Kiick	3	5	8
08/04	Tim Shaw	2	4	7
08/11	Baseball Boom	3	5	8
08/18	Jack Nicklaus	3	5	8
08/25	Bart Starr	3	5	8
09/01	Brian Oldfield	2	4	7
09/08	College Football	2	4	7
09/15	Ali/Frazier in Manila	4	6	10
09/22	Mean Joe Green	3	5	8
09/29	Rick Slager	2	4	7

Date	Cover Subject	VG	EX	NM
10/06	Reggie Jackson	4	6	10
10/13	Ali/Frazier:Epic Battle	5	10	15
10/20	J.Bench/L. Tiant	4	6	10
10/27	George McGinnis	2	4	7
11/03	J. Bench/W.McEnaney	3	5	8
11/10	Fran Tarkenton	3	5	8
11/17	Hockey Violence	2	4	7
11/24	Chuck Muncie	2	4	7
12/01	Kent Benson	2	4	7
12/08	Bubba Bean	2	4	7
12/15	G. Foreman/M. Ali	4	6	10

Date	Cover Subject	VG	EX	NM
12/22	Pete Rose	4	6	10

1976

Date	Cover Subject	VG	EX	NM
01/05	Preston Pearson	$3	$5	$8
01/12	Franco Harris	3	5	8
01/19	Swimsuit Edition (Yvette Sylander, Yvonne Sylander)	6	12	20
01/26	Lynn Swann	3	5	8
02/02	SheilaYoung	2	4	7
02/09	E. Grunfeld/B. King	2	4	7
02/16	Franz Klammer	2	4	7
02/23	Bobby Clarke	2	4	7
03/01	Muhammad Ali	3	5	8
03/08	Bob McAdoo	2	4	7
03/15	Bill Veeck	2	4	7
03/22	Tracey Austin	2	4	7
03/29	Kent Benson	2	4	7
04/05	Scott May	2	4	7
04/12	Joe Morgan	3	5	8
04/19	Ray Floyd	2	4	7
04/26	Evonne Goolagong	2	4	7
05/03	Mike Schmldt	3	5	8
05/10	Angel Cordero	2	4	7
05/17	Julius Erving	3	5	8
05/24	Larry Robinson	2	4	7
05/31	C. Fisk/L. Piniella	3	5	8
06/07	A. Adams/D. Cowens	2	4	7
06/14	Dwight Stones	2	4	7
06/21	George Brett	4	6	10
06/28	Bowie Kuhn	2	4	7
07/05	Frank Shorter	2	4	7
07/12	Randy Jones	2	4	7
07/19	Scott May/F.Shorter	2	4	7
07/26	Montreal Olympics	2	4	7
08/02	Nadia Comeneci	2	4	7
08/09	Bruce Jenner	2	4	7
08/16	Calvin Hill	3	5	8
08/23	Steve Spurrier	2	4	7
08/30	Reggie Jackson	4	6	10
09/06	Rick Leach	2	4	7
09/13	Bert Jones	2	4	7
09/20	Jimmy Connors	2	4	7

Date	Cover Subject	VG	EX	NM
09/27	Ken Norton	2	4	7
10/04	Mark Manges	2	4	7
10/11	George Foster	3	5	8
10/18	Chuck Foreman	3	5	8
10/25	J. Erving/D. Cowens	3	5	8
11/01	Johnny Bench	4	6	10
11/08	Tony Dorsett	3	5	8
11/15	David Thompson	2	4	7
11/22	Walter Payton	4	6	10
11/29	Ricky Green	2	4	7
12/06	Rocky Bleier	3	5	8
12/13	Bill Walton	3	5	8
12/20	Chris Evert	2	4	7

1977

Date	Cover Subject	VG	EX	NM
01/03	Clarence Davis	$2	$4	$7
01/10	Tony Dorsett	3	5	8
01/17	Ken Stabler	3	5	8
01/24	Swimsuit Edition (Lena Hansbod)	6	12	20
01/31	Bill Cartwright	2	4	7
02/07	Guy LaFleur	2	4	7
02/14	Kareem Abdul-Jabbar	3	5	8
02/21	NBC's Olympic Deal	2	4	7
02/28	Cale Yarborough	2	4	7
03/07	Steve Cauthen	2	4	7
03/14	Tommy Lasorda	3	5	8
03/21	George McGinnis	2	4	7
03/28	Bump Wills	2	4	7
04/04	Butch Lee	2	4	7
04/11	Joe Rudi	3	5	8
04/18	Tom Watson	2	4	7
04/25	Sidney Wicks	2	4	7
05/02	Reggie Jackson	4	6	10
05/09	Brad Park	2	4	7
05/16	Seattle Slew	2	4	7
05/23	B. Walton/Abdul-Jabbar	3	5	8
05/30	Dave Parker	3	5	8
06/06	Mark Fidrych	3	5	8
06/13	Bill Walton	3	5	8
06/20	Seattle Slew	2	4	7
06/27	Tom Seaver	4	6	10
07/04	Ted Turner	2	4	7
07/11	Bjorn Borg	2	4	7

Date	Cover Subject	VG	EX	NM

07/18 .... R. Carew/T. Williams .... 4 .... 6 10

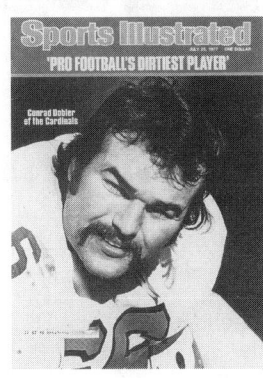

Date	Cover Subject	VG	EX	NM
07/25	Conrad Dobler	2	4	7
08/01	Colorado Rapids	2	4	7
08/08	Carlos Monzon	2	4	7
08/15	Sadaharu Oh	3	5	8
08/22	Lanny Wadkins	2	4	7
08/29	Greg Luzinski	2	4	7
09/05	Ross Browner	2	4	7
09/12	Alberto Juantoren	2	4	7
09/19	Ken Stabler	3	5	8
09/26	Roberto Duran	2	4	7
10/03	Billy Sims	2	4	7
10/10	M. Ali/E. Shavers	3	5	8
10/17	Rubin Carter	2	4	7
10/24	World Series	3	5	8
10/31	Maurice Lucas	2	4	7
11/07	Burt Reynolds	3	5	8
11/14	Belmont Horse Racing	2	4	7
11/21	AFC/NFC Rivalry	2	4	7
11/28	Larry Bird	4	6	10
12/05	Earl Campbell	3	5	8
12/12	Brian Trottier	2	4	7
12/19	Steve Cauthen	2	4	7

1978

Date	Cover Subject	VG	EX	NM
01/02	Mark Van Eeghan	$2	$4	$7
01/09	Terry Eurick	2	4	7
01/16	Swimsuit Edition (Maria Joao)	6	12	20
01/23	R.White/H.Martin	3	5	8
01/30	Duran Beats DeJesus	2	4	7
02/06	Buerkle Beats Bayi	2	4	7
02/13	Sidney Moncrief	3	5	8
02/20	Walter Davis	2	4	7
02/27	Leon Spinks	2	4	7
03/06	Houston McTear	2	4	7
03/13	Gene Banks	2	4	7
03/20	Clint Hurdle	2	4	7
03/27	Jack Nicklaus	2	4	7

Date	Cover Subject	VG	EX	NM
04/03	Goose Givens	2	4	7
04/10	R. Carew/G. Foster	3	5	8
04/17	Gary Player	2	4	7
04/24	Mark Fidrych	3	5	8
05/01	Gary Player	2	4	7
05/08	Elvin Hayes	3	5	8
05/15	Affirmed Wins Derby	2	4	7
05/22	Marvin Webster	2	4	7
05/29	L. Robinson/K. Dryden	2	4	7
06/05	Al Unser	2	4	7
06/12	Ken Norton	2	4	7
06/19	Affirmed/Alydar	2	4	7
06/26	Andy North	2	4	7
07/03	The World Cup	2	4	7
07/10	Nancy Lopez	2	4	7
07/17	Money Report	2	4	7
07/24	Nicklaus Wins Again	2	4	7

Date	Cover Subject	VG	EX	NM
07/31	Billy Martin	3	5	8
08/07	Pete Rose's Streak	4	6	10
08/14	Football Brutality	2	4	7
08/21	Bill Walton	3	5	8
08/28	Ballooning	2	4	7
09/04	Roger Staubach	3	5	8
09/11	Lou Holtz	2	4	7
09/18	Jimmy Connors	2	4	7
09/25	Muhammad Ali	3	5	8
10/02	Charles White	2	4	7
10/09	Terry Bradshaw	3	5	8
10/16	Marvin Webster	2	4	7
10/23	Lee Lacy/Brian Doyle	2	4	7
10/30	Bill Rodgers	2	4	7
11/06	Fixer	2	4	7
11/13	Chuck Fusina	2	4	7
11/20	Rick Berns	2	4	7
11/27	Magic Johnson	4	6	10
12/04	Earl Campbell	3	5	8
12/11	Jeff Love	2	4	7
12/18	John McEnroe	2	4	7
12/25	Jack Nicklaus	3	5	8

1979

Date	Cover Subject	VG	EX	NM
01/08	Bowl Games	$2	$4	$7
01/15	Terry Bradshaw	3	5	8
01/22	College Basketball	2	4	7
01/29	Rocky Bleier	3	5	8
02/05	Swimsuit Edition (Christie Brinkley)	6	12	20
02/12	Danny Lopez	2	4	7
02/15	Year in Sports	2	4	7
02/19	Moses Malone	2	4	7
02/26	Eamonn Coghlan	2	4	7
03/05	Spring Training	3	5	8
03/12	Dudley Bradley	2	4	7

Date	Cover Subject	VG	EX	NM
03/19	Harry Chappas	2	4	7
03/26	Larry Bird	4	6	10
04/02	Earvin Johnson	4	6	10
04/09	J. Rice/D. Parker	3	5	8
04/16	Denis Potvin	2	4	7
04/23	Fuzzy Zoeller	2	4	7
04/30	George Bamberger	2	4	7
05/07	Elvin Hayes	2	4	7
05/14	Kentucky Derby	2	4	7
05/21	Giorgio Chinaglia	2	4	7
05/28	Pete Rose: Phillies	3	5	8
06/04	Tom Watson	2	4	7
06/11	Gus Williams	2	4	7
06/18	Earl Weaver	3	5	8
06/25	Hale Irwin	2	4	7
07/02	Duran/Palomino	2	4	7
07/09	Eamonn Coghlan	2	4	7
07/16	Bjorn Borg	2	4	7

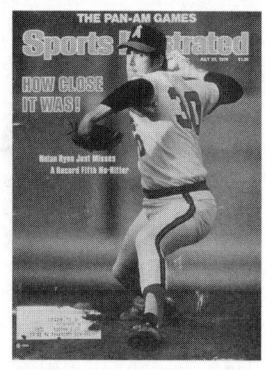

Date	Cover Subject	VG	EX	NM
07/23	Nolan Ryan	4	7	12
07/30	Sebastian Coe	2	4	7
08/06	Ken Stabler	3	5	8
08/13	Silver Anniversary	4	6	10
08/20	John Jefferson	2	4	7
08/27	BB'S Golden Oldies	4	6	10
09/03	Earl Campbell	3	5	8
09/10	Sims/White/Walker	3	5	8
09/17	Tracy Austin	2	4	7
09/24	Vagas Ferguson	2	4	7
10/01	Dewey Selmon	2	4	7
10/08	Larry Holmes	3	5	8
10/15	Bill Walton	2	4	7
10/22	D. DeCinces/P. Garner	2	4	7
10/29	Bill Rogers	2	4	7
11/05	Franco Harris	3	5	8
11/12	College Football	2	4	7
11/19	Magic Johnson	3	5	8
11/26	Art Schlichter	2	4	7
12/03	College Basketball	2	4	7
12/10	Sugar Ray Leonard	4	6	10
12/17	Ralph Sampson	2	4	7
12/24	Stargell/Bradshaw	3	5	8

1980

Date	Cover Subject	VG	EX	NM
01/07	Ricky Bell	$2	$4	$7
01/14	Greenwood/Pastorini	2	4	7
01/21	Gordie Howe	3	5	8
01/28	John Stallworth	2	4	7
02/04	Swimsuit Edition (Christie Brinkley)	6	12	20
02/11	Eric Heiden	2	4	7
02/18	Mary Decker	1	3	6
02/25	Eric Heiden	1	3	6
03/03	USA Hockey Team	3	5	8

Date	Cover Subject	VG	EX	NM
03/10	Jim Craig	3	5	8
03/17	Albert King	2	4	7
03/24	Kirk Gibson	3	5	8
03/31	Griffith/Louisville	1	3	6
04/07	Keith Hernandez	3	5	8
04/14	Muhammad Ali	4	6	10
04/21	Seve Ballesteros	1	3	6
04/28	Dr. J./Larry Bird	3	5	8

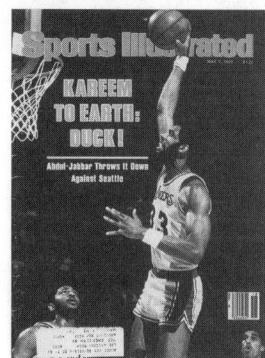

Date	Cover Subject	VG	EX	NM
05/05	Kareem Abdul-Jabbar	3	5	8
05/12	Kentucky Derby	1	3	6
05/19	Shame or Education?	1	3	6
05/26	Magic Johnson	3	5	8
06/02	Johnny Rutherford	1	3	6
06/09	Darryl Porter	2	4	7
06/16	Roberto Duran	2	4	7
06/23	Jack Nicklaus	2	4	7
06/30	Duran/Leonard	3	5	8
07/07	Steve Scott	1	3	6
07/14	Bjorn Borg	2	4	7
07/21	Steve Carlton	3	5	8
07/28	Olympics	1	3	6
08/04	Reggie Jackson	4	6	10
08/11	Sebastian Coe	1	3	6
08/18	J.R. Richard	2	4	7
08/25	Baltimore Orioles	3	5	8
09/01	Hugh Green	2	4	7
09/08	Pro Football	2	4	7
09/15	John McEnroe	1	3	6
09/22	Billy Sims	2	4	7
09/29	Muhammad Ali	3	5	8
10/06	Gary Carter	2	4	7
10/13	Muhammad Ali	3	5	8
10/20	Paul Westphal	2	4	7
10/27	Schmidt/Porter	3	5	8
11/03	Alberto Salazar	1	3	6
11/10	L.C. Greenwood	2	4	7
11/17	Herschel Walker	2	4	7

Date	Cover Subject	VG	EX	NM
11/24	Sugar Ray Leonard	3	5	8

Date	Cover Subject	VG	EX	NM
12/01	Aguirre/Sampson/King	2	4	7
12/08	Vince Ferragamo	2	4	7
12/15	Lloyd Free	2	4	7
12/22	U.S. Hockey	3	5	8

1981

Date	Cover Subject	VG	EX	NM
01/05	Dave Winfield	$3	$5	$8
01/12	Chuck Muncie	2	4	7
01/19	Mark Van Eeghan	2	4	7
01/26	Bobby Knight	3	5	8
02/02	Rod Martin	1	3	6
02/09	Swimsuit Edition (Christie Brinkley)	6	12	20
02/16	Point Shaving Scheme	1	3	6
02/23	Bobby Carpenter	1	3	6
03/02	J.R. Richard	2	4	7
03/09	Earvin Johnson	3	5	8
03/16	Rollie Fingers	3	5	8
03/23	Rolando Blackman	2	4	7
03/30	Ralph Sampson	2	4	7
04/06	Isiah Thomas	3	5	8
04/13	G. Brett/M. Schmidt	4	6	10
04/20	Tom Watson	2	4	7
04/27	Oakland's 5 Aces	2	4	7
05/04	Gerry Cooney	2	4	7
05/11	K. McHale/L. Bird	3	5	8
05/18	Fernando Valenzuela	3	5	8
05/25	A.J. Foyt	2	4	7
06/01	Marvis and Joe Frazier	2	4	7
06/08	Greg Luzinski	2	4	7
06/15	Bjorn Borg	1	3	6
06/22	Strike	1	3	6
06/29	David Graham	1	3	6
07/06	Sugar Ray Leonard	3	5	8
07/13	John McEnroe	1	3	6
07/20	Vince Ferragamo	2	4	7
07/27	Tom Seaver	3	5	8
08/03	John Hannah	2	4	7
08/10	Brett/Schmidt	3	5	8
08/17	Gary Carter	2	4	7
08/23	Wendell Tyler	2	4	7
08/30	Herschel Walker	3	5	8
09/07	Jim Plunkett	2	4	7
09/14	Thomas Hearns	2	4	7
09/21	John McEnroe	1	3	6
09/28	Sugar Ray Leonard	3	5	8
10/05	Marcus Allen	2	4	7
10/12	Wayne Gretzky	3	5	8
10/19	College Football	2	4	7

Date	Cover Subject	VG	EX	NM
10/26	Graig Nettles	2	4	7
11/02	World Series	2	4	7
11/09	Larry Bird	3	5	8
11/16	Holmes/Snipes	2	4	7

Date	Cover Subject	VG	EX	NM
11/23	Bear Bryant	3	5	8
11/30	S.Perkins/J. Worthy	2	4	7
12/07	Tony Dorsett	2	4	7
12/14	Cris Collinsworth	2	4	7
12/21	Earl Cooper	2	4	7
12/28	Sugar Ray Leonard	3	5	8

1982

Date	Cover Subject	VG	EX	NM
01/11	Perry Tuttle	$1	$3	$5
01/18	Dwight Clark/The Catch	4	6	10
01/25	Joe Montana	4	6	10
02/01	Earl Cooper	2	4	7
02/08	Swimsuit Edition (Carol Alt)	6	12	20
02/15	Wayne Gretzky	4	6	10
02/22	Sidney Moncrief	3	5	8
03/01	Herschel Walker	2	4	7
03/08	Surfing	1	3	6
03/15	Reggie Jackson	3	5	8
03/22	Pat Ewing: Georgetown	3	5	8
03/29	Sam Perkins	2	4	7
04/05	James Worthy	2	4	7
04/12	Steve Garvey	3	5	8
04/19	Craig Stadler	1	3	6
04/23	Renaldo Nehemiah	1	3	6
05/03	Jack Sikma	3	5	8
05/10	Georgia Frontiere/Jones	1	3	6
05/17	Gaylord Perry	2	4	7
05/24	Magic Johnson	3	5	8
05/31	Julius Erving	3	5	8
06/07	Gerry Cooney	2	4	7
06/14	Cocaine	1	3	6
06/21	Cooney/Holmes	2	4	7
06/28	Tom Watson	2	4	7
07/05	Kent Hrbek	2	4	7
07/12	Jimmy Connors	1	3	6
07/19	Rose/Yaz	3	5	8
07/26	Mary Decker	1	3	6
08/02	Ray Mancini	2	4	7
08/09	Dale Murphy	3	5	8
08/16	Walter Payton	3	5	8
08/23	Franco Harris	3	5	8
08/30	Tom Cousineau	1	3	6
09/06	Rickey Henderson	3	5	8
09/13	Wayne Peace	1	3	6
09/20	Jimmy Connors	1	3	6
09/27	Pro Football	2	4	7
10/04	Todd Blackledge	2	4	7
10/11	Robin Yount	4	6	10
10/18	Marvin Hagler	2	4	7
10/25	Yount/Smith	3	5	8
11/01	Moses Malone	2	4	7
11/08	John Elway	4	6	10
11/15	Sugar Ray Leonard	3	5	8
11/22	Ray Mancini	2	4	7
11/29	Sampson/Ewing	3	5	8
12/06	Redskins/Eagles	2	4	7
12/13	Marcus Allen	3	5	8
12/20	Ralph Sampson	2	4	7
12/27	Wayne Gretzky	3	5	8

1983

Date	Cover Subject	VG	EX	NM
01/10	College Football	$2	$4	$7
01/17	Chuck Muncie	2	4	7
01/23	Andra Franklin	1	3	6
01/30	Darryl Grant	1	3	6
02/07	John Riggins/SB XVI	3	5	8

Date	Cover Subject	VG	EX	NM
02/14	Swimsuit Edition (Cheryl Tiegs)	6	12	20
02/21	Terry Cummings	2	4	7
02/28	Julius Erving	3	5	8
03/07	Herschel Walker	2	4	7
03/14	Rose/Morgan/Perez	4	6	10
03/21	St. Johns	1	3	6
03/28	M. Spinks/Braxton	2	4	7
04/04	Gary Carter	2	4	7
04/11	NC State/Champs	2	4	7
04/18	Tom Seaver	3	5	8
04/25	Steve Garvey	3	5	8
05/02	Larry Bird: NBA Playoffs	3	5	8
05/09	Kareem Abdul-Jabbar	3	5	8
05/16	Kentucky Derby	1	3	6
05/23	Billy Smith	1	3	6
05/30	Larry Holmes	2	4	7
06/06	Moses Malone	2	4	7
06/13	Rod Carew	3	5	8
06/20	Marcus Dupree	2	4	7
06/27	Duran/Moore	2	4	7
07/04	Dale Murphy	3	5	8
07/11	John McEnroe	1	3	7
07/18	A. Dawson/D. Stieb	3	5	8
07/25	Tom Watson	2	4	7
08/01	Richard Todd	2	4	7
08/08	Howard Cosell	2	4	7
08/15	John Elway	4	6	10
08/22	Carl Lewis	2	4	7
08/29	Tony Dorsett	3	5	8
09/05	Mike Rozier	2	4	7
09/12	Edwin Moses	1	3	6
09/19	Martina Navartilova	1	3	6
09/26	Doug Flutie	3	5	8
10/03	Steve Carlton	3	5	8
10/10	Joe Washington	2	4	7
10/17	Eric Dickerson	3	5	8
10/24	Rick Dempsey	2	4	7
10/31	Ralph Sampson	2	4	7
11/07	Hagler/Duran	2	4	7
11/14	Dan Marino	4	6	10
11/21	Hagler/Duran	2	4	7
11/28	Michael Jordan	15	25	35
12/05	Sam Bowie	2	4	7
12/12	Jim Brown	3	5	8
12/19	John Riggins	2	4	7
12/26	Mary Decker	1	3	6

1984

Date	Cover Subject	VG	EX	NM
01/09	Keith Griffin	$1	$3	$6
01/16	Joe Theisman	3	5	8
01/23	Wayne Gretzky	3	5	8
01/30	Jack Squimb/SB XVII	2	4	7
02/06	Winter Olympics	1	3	6
02/13	Swimsuit Edition (Paulina Porizkova)	5	10	15
02/20	Debbie Armstrong	1	3	6
02/27	Bill Johnson	1	3	6
03/05	Magic Johnson	3	5	8
03/12	George Brett	3	5	8
03/19	Patrick Ewing	3	5	8
03/26	Sam Perkins	2	4	7
04/02	Yogi Berra	3	5	8
04/09	Georgetown/Houston	2	4	7

Date	Cover Subject	VG	EX	NM
04/16	Gossage/Nettles	3	5	8
04/23	Darryl Strawberry	3	5	8
04/30	American Tragedy	1	3	6
05/07	Bernard King	2	4	7
05/14	Mike Bossy	2	4	7
05/21	Soviet Boycott	1	3	6
05/28	Alan Trammell	3	5	8
06/04	Magic Johnson	3	5	8
06/11	Leon Durham	2	4	7
06/18	Martina Navratilova	1	3	6
06/26	Carl Lewis	2	4	7
07/02	Dwight Stones	1	3	6
07/09	Jeff Float	1	3	6
07/16	John McEnroe	1	3	6
07/23	Michael Jordan	10	20	30
07/30	Jack Lambert	3	5	8
08/06	Rafer Johnson	2	4	7
08/13	Mary Lou Retton	2	4	7
08/20	Carl Lewis	2	4	7
08/27	Pete Rose	3	5	8
09/03	Joe Theismann	2	4	7
09/10	Dolphins/Redskins	2	4	7
09/17	John McEnroe	1	3	6
09/24	Gooden/Sutcliffe	3	5	8
10/01	Jeff Smith	1	3	6
10/08	Sammy Winder	1	3	6
10/15	Walter Payton	3	5	8
10/22	Alan Trammell	2	4	7
10/29	Russell/Bird	3	5	8
11/05	Jerry Faust	1	3	6
11/12	What's Wrong With NFL	1	3	6
11/19	Mark Duper	2	4	7
11/26	Reagan/Ewing/Thompson	3	5	8
12/03	Doug Flutie	2	4	7
12/10	Michael Jordan	6	12	20
12/17	Eric Dickerson	3	5	8
12/24	Moses/Retton	1	3	6

1985

Date	Cover Subject	VG	EX	NM
01/07	Walter Abercrombie	$1	$3	$6
01/14	Dan Marino/SB XVIII	4	6	10
01/21	Marino/Montana	4	6	10
01/28	Roger Craig: 49ers	3	5	8
02/04	Walter Berry	1	3	6
02/11	Swimsuit Edition (Paulina Porizkova)	5	10	15
02/18	Wayne Gretzky	3	5	8
02/25	Doug Flutie	3	5	8
03/04	Schmidt/Millionaires	3	5	8
03/11	Jack/Gary Nicklaus	2	4	7
03/18	Fred Lynn	2	4	7

Date	Cover Subject	VG	EX	NM

Date	Cover Subject	VG	EX	NM
03/25	Mantle/Mays/Ueberroth	5	10	15
04/01	McLain/Mullin/Ewing	2	4	7
04/08	Villanova/Georgetown	2	4	7
04/15	Dwight Gooden	3	5	8
04/22	Hagler/Hearns	2	4	7
04/29	Hulk Hogan	3	5	8

Date	Cover Subject	VG	EX	NM
05/06	Billy Martin	3	5	8
05/13	Magic Johnson	3	5	8
05/20	Patrick Ewing	3	5	8
05/27	Herschel Walker	2	4	7
06/03	Danny Sullivan	1	3	6
06/10	K.Jabbar/L.Bird	3	5	8
06/17	Jabbar/Evert	3	5	8
06/24	North/Weaver	1	3	6
07/01	Larry Holmes	2	4	7
07/08	Fernando Valenzuela	3	5	8
07/15	Boris Becker	1	3	7
07/22	Howie Long	3	5	8
07/29	Decker-Slaney/Zola	1	3	6
08/05	Pedro Guerrero	2	4	7
08/12	Tony Dorsett	3	5	8
08/19	Pete Rose	3	5	8
08/26	Bernie Kosar	2	4	7
09/02	Dwight Gooden	3	5	8
09/09	Bill Elliot	1	3	6
09/16	Joe Louis	2	4	7

Date	Cover Subject	VG	EX	NM
09/23	Ozzie Smith	3	5	8

Date	Cover Subject	VG	EX	NM
09/30	Spinks/Holmes	2	4	7
10/07	Tony Robinson	1	3	6
10/14	Eddie Robinson	2	4	7
10/21	Jim McMahon	3	5	8
10/28	Ozzie Smith	3	5	8
11/04	K.C. Royals	2	4	7
11/11	Florida/Penn State	2	4	7
11/18	Dale Brown	1	3	6
11/25	White/Singletary/Duerson	2	4	7
12/02	Bo Jackson/Long/Dudek	3	5	8
12/09	Kirk Gibson	2	4	7
12/16	Marcus Allen	2	4	7
12/23	Kareem Abdul-Jabbar	3	5	8

1986

Date	Cover Subject	VG	EX	NM
01/06	Mike Tyson	$2	$4	$7
01/13	Craig Powers	1	3	6
01/20	Jim McMahon	3	5	8
01/27	Mike Singletary	2	4	7
02/03	Chicago Bears	2	4	7
02/10	Swimsuit Edition (Elle MacPherson)	6	12	20
02/17	Danny Manning	2	4	7
02/24	Networks	1	3	6
03/03	Larry Bird: Living Legend	3	5	8
03/10	Gambling	1	3	6
03/17	Mark Alaire	1	3	6
03/24	Galer/Mugabi	1	3	6
03/31	Final Four	2	4	7
04/07	Pervis Ellison	2	4	7
04/14	Wade Boggs	3	5	8
04/21	Jack Nicklaus	2	4	7
04/28	Dominique Wilkins	2	4	7
05/05	Ernest Hemingway	2	4	7

Date	Cover Subject	VG	EX	NM
05/12	Roger Clemens	4	6	10
05/19	James Worthy	2	4	7
05/25	Olajuwon/Navratilova	2	4	7
06/02	Montreal Canadiens	2	4	7
06/09	Larry Bird	3	5	8
06/16	Kevin McHale	2	4	7
06/23	Ray Floyd	1	3	6
06/30	Len Bias	2	4	7
07/07	Diego Maradona	1	3	6
07/14	Bo Jackson	3	5	8
07/21	Jim Kelly	2	4	7
07/28	Rickey Henderson	3	5	8
08/04	Oil Can Boyd	2	4	7
08/11	Too Tall Jones	2	4	7
08/18	Herschel Walker	2	4	7
08/25	Ron Darling	2	4	7
09/01	Kristie Phillips	1	3	6
09/08	Sugar Ray Leonard	3	5	8
09/15	Ivan Lendl	1	3	6

Date	Cover Subject	VG	EX	NM
09/22	L. Taylor/M. Gastineau	3	5	8
09/29	Michigan/Notre Dame	2	4	7
10/06	Daryll Strawberry	3	5	8
10/13	John Elway	3	5	8
10/20	DeCinces/Grich	2	4	7
10/27	Rice/Carter	2	4	7
11/03	Ray Knight	2	4	7
11/10	NFL Injury	1	3	6
11/17	Michael Jordan	6	12	20
11/24	Vinny Testaverde	2	4	7
12/01	Mike Tyson	2	4	7
12/08	Walter Payton: Bears	3	5	8
12/15	Mark Bavaro	2	4	7
12/23	Joe Paterno	3	5	8

1987

Date	Cover Subject	VG	EX	NM
01/05	Brian Bosworth	$2	$4	$7
01/12	Ozzie Newsome	2	4	7
01/19	Rich Karlis	2	4	7
01/26	Lawrence Taylor	3	5	8
02/02	Phil Simms: SB XX	3	5	8
02/09	Swimsuit Edition (Elle MacPherson)	6	12	20
02/16	Dennis Connor/Reagan	3	5	8
02/23	Magic Johnson	3	5	8
03/02	J.R. Ried	2	4	7
03/09	Ripken Family	3	5	8
03/16	Gary McLain	1	3	6
03/23	Bobby Knight	2	4	7
03/30	Hagler/Leonard	3	5	8
04/06	Carter/Snyder: BB Issue	3	5	8
04/13	Hagler/Leonard	3	5	8
04/20	Player Salaries	1	3	6
04/27	Rob Deer	2	4	7
05/04	Julius Erving	3	5	8
05/11	Reggie Jackson	4	6	10
05/18	Isiah Thomas	3	5	8
05/25	Eric Davis	2	4	7
06/01	Wayne Gretzky	3	5	8
06/08	Larry Bird: Celtic Pride	3	5	8
06/15	L.A./Boston	2	4	7

Date	Cover Subject	VG	EX	NM
06/22	Kareem Abdul-Jabbar	3	5	8
06/29	Watson/Simpson	2	4	7
07/06	One Day in Baseball	2	4	7
07/13	Strawberry/Mattingly	4	6	10
07/20	Andre Dawson	3	5	8
07/27	Pit Bull	1	3	6
08/03	Vinnie Testaverde	2	4	7
08/10	Mike Tyson	2	4	7
08/17	Alan Trammell	2	4	7
08/24	Jim McMahon	3	5	8
08/31	Tim Brown	2	4	7
09/07	Surf's Up	1	3	6

Date	Cover Subject	VG	EX	NM
09/14	Jackie Joyner-Kersee	2	4	7
09/21	John Elway	3	5	8
09/28	Ozzie Smith	3	5	8
10/05	Lloyd Moseby	2	4	7
10/12	Steve Walsh	2	4	7
10/19	Twins/World Series	3	5	8
10/26	Dan Gladden	2	4	7
11/02	Minnesota Twins	3	5	8
11/09	Eric Dickerson	2	4	7
11/16	Rodney Anderson	1	3	6
11/23	Dexter Manley	2	4	7
11/30	Oklahoma/Nebraska	2	4	7
12/07	Arnold Schwarzenegger	2	4	7
12/14	Bo Jackson	3	5	8
12/21	Athletes Who Care	2	4	7
12/28	Michael Jordan	6	12	20

1988

Date	Cover Subject	VG	EX	NM
01/11	Miami	$2	$4	$7
01/18	Anthony Carter	2	4	7
01/25	John Elway	3	5	8
02/01	Mike Tyson	3	5	8

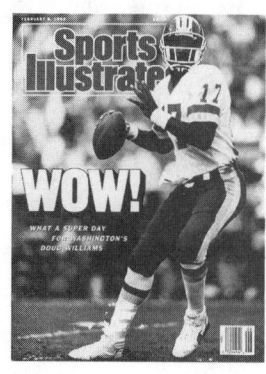

Date	Cover Subject	VG	EX	NM
02/08	Doug Williams	3	5	8
02/15	Swimsuit Edition (Elle MacPherson)	6	12	20
02/22	Chamberlain/Russell	4	6	10
03/01	Brian Boitano	2	4	7
03/07	Kirk Gibson	2	4	7
03/14	Pam Postema	1	3	6
03/21	Larry Bird	3	5	8
03/28	Mark Macon	1	3	6
04/04	M.McGwire/W. Clark	4	6	10
04/11	Danny Manning	2	4	7
04/18	Magic Johnson	3	5	8
04/25	Muhammad Ali	4	6	10
05/02	Billy Ripken	2	4	7
05/09	Pete Rose: Super Red	3	5	8
05/16	Michael Jordan	5	10	15
05/23	Magic Johnson	3	5	8
05/30	Wayne Gretzky	3	5	8
06/06	Fired Coaches/Managers	2	4	7
06/13	MikeTyson/Robin Givens	2	4	7
06/20	Michael Spinks	2	4	7
06/27	M. Johnson/B. Laimbeer	3	5	8
07/04	Mike Tyson	2	4	7
07/11	Darryl Strawberry	3	5	8
07/18	Casey at the Bat	2	4	7
07/25	Florence Joyner	2	4	7
08/01	Tony Dorsett	3	5	8
08/08	Beer	1	3	6
08/15	Sports in China	1	3	6
08/22	Gretzky/Magic Johnson	3	5	8
08/29	Bernie Kosar	2	4	7

Date	Cover Subject	VG	EX	NM
09/05	Florida Football	2	4	7
09/12	Jim McMahon	3	5	8
09/19	Steffi Graf	1	3	6
09/26	Dwight Evans	2	4	7
10/03	Ben Johnson	1	3	6
10/10	Flo-Jo/Jackie Joyner	2	4	7

Date	Cover Subject	VG	EX	NM
10/17	Jose Canseco	3	5	8
10/24	Tony Rice	1	3	6
10/31	Orel Hershiser	2	4	7
11/07	Karl Malone	3	5	8
11/14	Landry/Noll	3	5	8

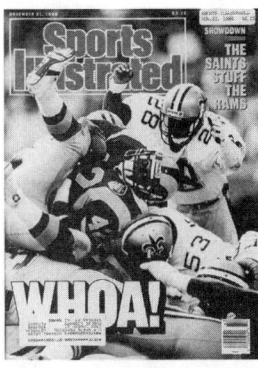

Date	Cover Subject	VG	EX	NM
11/21	Saints/Rams	2	4	7
11/28	Rodney Peete	2	4	7
12/05	Tony Rice	1	3	6

Date	Cover Subject	VG	EX	NM
12/12	Charles Barkley	3	5	8
12/19	Orel Hershiser	2	4	7
12/26	Florence Joyner	2	4	7

1989

Date	Cover Subject	VG	EX	NM
01/09	Rice/Notre Dame	$2	$4	$7
01/16	Ickey Woods	2	4	7

Date	Cover Subject	VG	EX	NM
01/23	Kareem Abdul Jabbar	3	5	8
01/30	Jerry Rice	4	6	10
02/06	Mario Lemieux	4	6	10
02/07	Swimsuit : 25th Ann. Issue (Kathy Ireland)	6	12	20
02/13	Patrick Ewing	3	5	8
02/20	Chris Jackson	1	3	6
02/27	Charles Thompson	1	3	6
03/06	Wade Boggs	3	5	8
03/13	Michael Jordan	6	12	20
03/20	Jimmy Johnson	2	4	7
03/27	Steffi Graf	1	3	6
04/03	Pete Rose: BB Issue	4	6	10
04/10	Univ. of Michigan	2	4	7
04/17	Nick Faldo	1	3	6
04/24	Tony Mandarich	1	3	6
05/01	Nolan Ryan: Texas Heat	5	10	15
05/08	John Peters	1	3	6
05/15	M. Jordan/Ragin' Bull	6	12	20
05/22	Julie Krone	1	3	6
05/29	Kentucky Shame	1	3	6
06/05	James Worthy	2	4	7
06/12	Bo Jackson	3	5	8
06/19	Leonard/Hearns	3	5	8
06/26	Curtis Strange	1	3	6
07/03	Pete Rose	3	5	8
07/10	Rick Rueschel	2	4	7
07/17	George Foreman	3	5	8
07/24	Gregg Jefferies	2	4	7
07/31	Greg Lemond	2	4	7
08/07	Boomer Esiason	3	5	8
08/14	Michael Jordan	5	10	15
08/21	Troy Aikman	4	6	10
08/28	Chris Evert	1	3	6
09/04	College Football	2	4	7
09/11	Randall Cunningham	3	5	8
09/18	Boris Becker	1	3	6
09/25	Rocket Ismail	2	4	7
10/02	Joe Montana	4	6	10
10/09	Sergei Starikov	1	3	6
10/16	Rickey Henderson	3	5	8
10/23	Herschel Walker	2	4	7
10/30	Earthquake	1	3	6
11/06	Dumars/Jordan	5	10	15
11/13	Deion Sanders	4	6	10
11/20	Rumeal Robinson	2	4	7
11/27	Heisman	2	4	7
12/04	Steve McGuire	1	3	6
12/11	Larry Bird	3	5	8
12/18	Montana/Johnson/Gretzky	3	5	8
12/25	Greg Lemond	2	4	7

1990

Date	Cover Subject	VG	EX	NM
01/08	Miami football	$2	$4	$7
01/15	Jerry Rice	1	3	6
01/22	John Elway	1	3	6
01/29	David Robinson	2	4	7
02/05	Joe Montana	3	5	8
02/12	Swimsuit Edition (Judit Masco)	4	5	10
02/19	Mike Tyson	1	3	6
02/26	Buster Douglas	1	3	6
03/05	Gary Payton	1	3	6
03/12	Tony LaRussa	-	2	5
03/19	Jennifer Capriati	-	2	5
03/25	Bo Kimble	-	2	5
04/02	UNLV	-	2	5
04/09	UNLV Wins NCAA	1	3	6

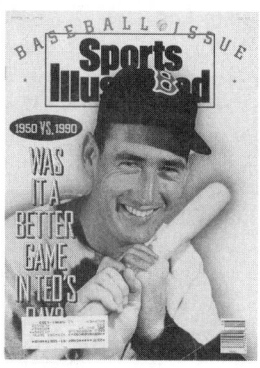

Date	Cover Subject	VG	EX	NM
04/16	Ted Williams	2	4	7
04/25	Tomas Sandstrum	-	2	5
04/30	Jeff George	-	2	5
05/07	Ken Griffey, Jr.	5	8	15
05/14	Sneakers	-	2	5
05/21	M. Jordan/Showtime	4	7	12
05/28	Will Clark	-	2	5
06/04	Len Dykstra	-	2	5
06/11	Isiah Thomas	-	2	5
06/18	Monica Seles	-	2	5
06/25	Hale Irwin	-	2	5
07/02	Marvin Hagler	-	2	5
07/09	Darryl Strawberry	-	2	5
07/16	Martina Navratilova	-	2	5
07/23	Minor League Baseball	1	3	6
07/30	Greg Lamond	-	2	5
08/06	Joe Montana	2	4	7
08/13	Autographs	1	3	6
08/20	Jose Canseco	1	3	6
08/27	Troy Aikman	3	5	8
09/03	Todd Marinovich	1	3	6
09/10	Barry Sanders	2	4	7
09/17	Pete Sampras	-	2	5
09/24	Rick Mirer	-	2	5
10/01	Bobby Bonilla	1	3	6
10/08	O.J. Simpson	1	3	6
10/15	Burt Grossman	-	2	5
10/22	Dennis Eckersley	1	3	6
10/29	Chris Sabo	2	4	7
11/05	Bill Laimbeer	-	2	5
11/12	William Bell	-	2	5
11/19	S. Augman/L. Johnson	3	5	8
11/26	Notre Dame	1	3	6
12/03	Magic Johnson:	3	5	8
12/10	Ty Detmer	1	3	6

Date	Cover Subject	VG	EX	NM
12/17	Michael Jordan	5	10	15
12/24	Joe Montana	2	4	7
12/31	Pictures of 1990	-	2	5

1991

Date	Cover Subject	VG	EX	NM
01/14	Dan Marino	$2	$4	$7
01/21	Shaquille O'Neal	5	10	15
01/28	Ottis Anderson	3	5	8
02/04	Everson Walls	3	5	8
02/11	Swimsuit Edition (Ashley Montana)	4	6	10
02/18	Jordan: Dream Team	6	12	20
02/25	Rocket Ismail	-	2	5
03/04	Darryl Strawberry	-	2	5
03/11	Robert Parish	-	2	5
03/18	Brett Hull	2	4	7
03/25	Mike Tyson	1	3	6
04/01	Mark Randall	-	2	5
04/08	Grant Hill	4	7	12
04/15	N. Ryan: Baseball '91	3	5	8
04/22	Ian Woosman	-	2	5
04/29	Evander Holyfield	1	3	6
05/06	Bjorn Borg	-	2	5
05/13	Roger Clemens	4	7	7
05/20	Michael Johnson	-	2	5
05/27	M. Mantle/R. Maris	4	6	10
06/03	Michael Jordan	6	12	20
06/10	Magic and Michael	5	10	15
06/17	M. Jordan Air Power	5	10	15
06/24	Mike Tyson	1	3	6
07/01	Orel Hershiser	-	2	5
07/08	Lyle Alzado	-	2	5
07/15	Steffi Graf	-	2	5
07/22	A Fan's World	-	2	5

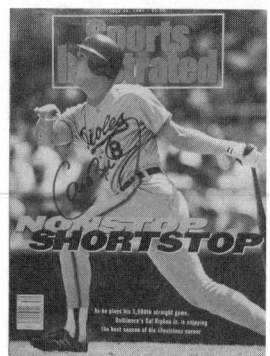

Date	Cover Subject	VG	EX	NM
07/29	Cal Ripken Jr.	5	10	15
08/05	Black Athlete	1	3	6
08/12	Eric Dickerson	-	2	5
08/19	John Daly	2	4	7
08/26	David Klingler	-	2	5
09/02	Bruce Smith	1	3	6
09/09	Mike Powell	-	2	5
09/16	Jimmy Conners	-	2	5
09/23	Desmond Howard	-	2	5
09/30	Ramon Martinez	1	3	6
-	Special Issue: Red Grange	4	6	10
-	25 Unforgettable Moments	4	7	12
10/07	Bobby Hebert	-	2	5
10/14	Gary Clark	-	2	5
10/21	Kirby Puckett	3	5	8
10/28	Twins/Braves Series	2	4	7
11/04	Twins Win Series	3	5	8
11/11	Jordan/Pippen/Jackson	4	7	12
11/18	Magic Johnson	3	5	8

Date	Cover Subject	VG	EX	NM
11/25	Christian Laettner	1	3	6
12/02	Jim McMahon	1	3	6
12/09	Desmond Howard	-	2	5
12/16	Bills/Raiders	1	3	6
12/23	M. Jordan Hologram	5	10	15
12/30	Photos of 1991	1	3	6

1992

Date	Cover Subject	VG	EX	NM
01/13	Muhammad Ali	$3	$5	$8
01/20	Thurman Thomas	1	3	6
01/27	Winter Olympics	1	3	6
02/03	Mark Rypien	2	4	7
02/10	Patrick Ewing	2	4	7
02/17	Mike Tyson	1	3	6
02/24	Bonnie Blair	-	2	5
03/02	Kristi Yamaguchi	-	2	5
03/09	Swimsuit Edition (Kathy Ireland)	4	6	10
03/16	Ryne Sandberg	4	7	12
03/23	Larry Bird	1	3	6
03/30	Malcolm Mackey	-	2	5
04/06	K. Puckett: Baseball '92	2	4	7
04/13	Bobby Hurley	4	6	10
04/20	Fred Couples	-	2	5
04/27	Deion Sanders	1	3	6
05/04	Barry Bonds	3	5	8
05/11	M. Jordan/C. Drexler	4	7	12
05/18	Baseball '92	-	-	5
05/25	Michael Jordan	5	10	15
06/01	Mark McGwire	3	5	8
06/08	Mario Lemieux	2	4	7
06/15	Michael Jordan	5	10	15
06/22	Michael Jordan	5	10	15
06/29	Tom Kite	-	2	5
07/06	Steve Palermo	-	2	5
07/13	Andre Agassi	-	2	5
07/22	Jackie Kersee	-	2	5
07/27	Joe Montana	2	4	7
08/03	Nelson Diebe	-	2	5
08/10	Gail Devers	-	2	5
08/17	Carl Lewis	1	3	6
08/24	Deion Sanders	1	3	6
08/31	College Football '92	1	3	6
09/07	Jerry Rice	2	4	7
09/14	Jim Harbaugh	-	2	5
09/21	Stefan Edberg	-	2	5
09/28	Tony Mandarich	-	2	5
10/05	George Brett	1	3	6
10/12	Randall Cunningham	1	3	6
10/19	Dave Winfield	1	3	6
10/26	R. Alomar/J. Smoltz	2	4	7
Fall Sp	Willie Mays	2	4	7
11/02	Toronto Blue Jays	2	4	7

Date	Cover Subject	VG	EX	NM
11/09	Charles Barkley	2	4	7
11/16	Dallas Defense	1	3	6
11/23	Riddick Bowe	1	3	6
11/30	Shaquille O'Neal	4	7	12
12/07	Carnage Games	-	2	5
12/14	L. Bird/ M. Johnson	2	4	7
12/21	Arthur Ashe	1	3	6

1993

Date	Cover Subject	VG	EX	NM
01/11	Jim Valvano	$1	$3	$6
01/18	Steve Young	1	3	6
01/25	Emmitt Smith	3	5	8
02/01	Super Bowl Preview	-	2	5
02/08	Troy Aikman	2	4	7
02/15	Arthur Ashe	-	2	5
02/22	Swimsuit Edition (Vendela)	4	6	10
03/01	George Steinbrenner	-	2	5
03/08	Brian Reese: N. Carolina	-	2	5
03/15	Reggie White	1	3	6
03/22	Dwight Gooden	1	3	6
03/29	Jason Kidd	4	6	10
04/05	David Cone	1	3	6
04/12	Eric Montross	2	4	7
04/19	Mario Lemieux	1	3	6
04/26	Joe Montana	2	4	7
05/03	Joe DiMaggio	4	6	10
05/10	Monica Seles	-	2	5
05/17	Hakeem Olajuwon	1	3	6
05/24	Barry Bonds	1	3	6
05/31	Patrick Ewing	1	3	6
06/07	Michael Jordan	5	10	15
06/14	Canadiens: Stanley Cup	-	2	5
06/21	Michael Jordan	5	10	15
06/29	Michael Jordan	5	10	15
07/05	Mike Piazza	1	3	6
07/12	Laurie Crews/Pat Olin	-	2	5
07/19	B. Gibson/D. McLain	1	3	6
07/26	Greg Norman	-	2	5
08/02	J. Elway/D. Reeves	2	4	7
08/09	Reggie Lewis	1	3	6
08/16	Nike Boss: Phil Knight	-	2	5
08/23	Mary Pierce	-	2	5
08/30	Scott Bentley	-	2	5
09/06	Junior Seau	1	3	6
09/13	Joe Montana	2	4	7
09/20	Pernell Whitaker	-	2	5
09/27	Ron Gant	-	2	5
10/04	Boomer/Gunner Esiason	1	3	6
10/11	Chuck Cecil	-	2	5
10/18	Michael Jordan	4	7	12
10/25	Michael Irvin	1	3	6
11/01	Joe Carter	1	3	6
11/08	A.Mourning/B.Russell	2	4	7
11/15	Evander Holyfield	1	3	6
11/22	Jim Flanagan	-	2	5
11/29	Boston College	-	2	5
12/06	Jeff Lageman	-	2	5
12/13	Damon Bailey	-	2	5
12/20	Don Shula	2	4	7
12/27	93 Things From 1993	-	2	5

1994

Date	Cover Subject	VG	EX	NM
01/10	Florida State	$-	$2	$5
01/17	Nancy Kerrigan	-	2	5
01/24	Joe Montana	2	4	7
01/31	Emmitt Smith	3	5	8

Date	Cover Subject	VG	EX	NM
02/07	Emmitt Smith	3	5	8
02/14	Swimsuit Edition (Rachel Hunter, Kathy Ireland, Elle Macpherson)	5	10	15
02/21	Tommy Moe	-	2	5
02/28	Dan Jansen/B. Blair	-	2	5
03/07	David Robinson	1	3	6

Date	Cover Subject	VG	EX	NM
03/14	Michael Jordan	5	10	15
03/21	Bill Clinton	1	3	6
03/28	Boston College	-	2	5
04/04	K. Griffey/M. Piazza	3	5	8
04/11	Corliss Williamson	1	3	6
04/18	Mickey Mantle	4	6	10
04/25	Dan Wilkinson	-	2	5
05/02	Gary Payton	1	3	6
05/09	Tennis in Crisis	-	2	5
05/16	Florida Football	-	2	5
05/23	Braves vs. Mets	1	3	6
05/30	John Starks	1	3	6
06/06	Ken Griffey Jr.		6	10
06/13	Mark Messier	1	3	6
06/20	M. Richter/P. Ewing	1	3	6
06/27	O.J. Simpson	1	3	6
07/04	Ernie Stewart: Soccer	-	2	5
07/11	Pete Sampras	-	2	5
07/18	Mussina/McDonald	1	3	6
07/25	Via Brazil	-	2	5
08/01	Emmitt Smith	2	4	7
08/08	Frank Thomas	2	4	7
08/15	Ed Mathews: 40th Anniv.	3	5	8
08/22	Baseball Strike	-	2	5
08/29	Arizona Wildcats	-	2	5
09/05	Will Wolford	-	2	5
09/12	Dan Marino	2	4	7
09/19	Muhammad Ali	3	5	8
09/26	Steve McNair	1	3	6
10/03	Michael Westbrook	1	3	6
10/10	Pernell Whitaker	-	2	5
10/17	Natrone Means	1	3	6
10/24	Freddie Scott	-	2	5
10/31	Hisanobu Watanabe	-	2	5
11/07	Charles Barkley	1	3	6
11/14	George Foreman	1	3	6
11/21	Ricky Watters	1	3	6
11/28	Felipe Lopez	-	2	5
12/05	Steelers/Raiders	1	3	6
12/12	Emmitt Smith/Others	1	3	6
12/19	B. Blair/Johann Koss	-	2	5
12/26	Jerry Rice	2	4	7

1995

Date	Cover Subject	VG	EX	NM
01/09	Tom Osborne	$-	$2	$5
01/16	T. Aikman/S. Young	2	4	7
01/23	Steve Young	1	3	6

Date	Cover Subject	VG	EX	NM
01/30	Derrick Coleman	1	3	6
02/06	S.Young: SB MVP	1	3	6
02/13	Penny Hardaway	2	4	7
02/20	Swimsuit Edition (Daniela)	4	6	10
02/27	Gooden/Strawberry	1	3	6
03/06	Jerry Stackhouse	1	3	6
03/13	Andre Agassi	-	2	5
03/20	Michael Jordan	4	7	12
03/27	Michael Jordan	4	7	12
04/03	Arkansas Basketball	-	2	5
04/10	Ed O'Bannon	-	2	5
04/17	Ben Crenshaw	-	2	5
04/24	Joe Montana	2	4	7
05/01	Cal Ripken Jr.	3	5	8
05/08	Vlade Divac	-	2	5
05/15	Erickson/Mueller/Cox	-	2	5
05/22	M. Jordan/S. O'Neal	4	7	12
05/29	Dennis Rodman	2	4	7
06/05	Matt Williams	1	3	6
06/12	University of Miami	-	2	5
06/19	Clyde Drexler	1	3	6
06/26	Kevin Garnett	2	4	7
07/03	Mike Tyson	1	3	6
07/10	Hideo Nomo	1	3	6
07/17	Monica Seles	-	2	5
07/24	Auto Racing	-	2	5
07/31	John Daly	-	2	5

Date	Cover Subject	VG	EX	NM
08/07	Cal Ripken Jr.	3	5	8
08/14	Greg Maddux	2	4	7
08/21	Mickey Mantle	4	6	10
08/28	Keyshawn Johnson	3	5	8
09/04	Dan Marino	2	4	7
09/11	Cal Ripken Jr.	3	5	8
09/18	Emmitt Smith	2	4	7
09/25	Danny Wuerfel	-	2	5
10/02	Mo Vaughn	1	3	6
10/09	Deion Sanders	1	3	6
10/16	Ken Griffey Jr.	3	5	8
10/23	Jordan/Rodman	4	7	12
10/30	Bo Jackson	1	3	6
11/07	Greg Maddux	1	3	6
11/13	Northwestern	-	2	5
11/20	Elvis	2	4	7
11/27	Jacque Vaughn	-	2	5
12/11	Pat Riley/ Don Shula	1	3	6
12/18	Cal Ripken Jr.	3	5	8
12/25	Shaquille O'Neal	3	5	8

1996

Date	Cover Subject	VG	EX	NM
01/01	Steve Tasker	$-	$2	$5
01/08	Billy Payne	-	2	5

Date	Cover Subject	VG	EX	NM
01/15	Brett Favre	3	5	8
01/22	Emmitt Smith	2	4	7
01/29	Swimsuit Edition (Tyra Banks, Valeria Mazza)	4	6	10
02/05	Emmitt Smith	2	4	7
02/12	Magic Johnson	2	4	7
02/19	Marcus Stroud	-	2	5
02/26	Rick Pittino	-	2	5
03/04	Dennis Rodman	2	4	7
03/11	W.Gretzky/N. O'Donnell	2	4	7
03/18	Jay Buhner	1	3	6
03/25	Texas Tech	-	2	5
04/01	Manny Ramirez	2	4	7
04/08	Antoine Walker	1	3	6
04/15	Christy Martin	-	2	5
04/22	Greg Norman	-	2	5
04/29	David Robinson	1	3	6
05/06	Albert Belle	-	2	5
05/13	D. Marino/J. Johnson.	-	3	6
05/20	Marge Schott	-	2	5
05/27	P. Jackson/M. Jordan	4	7	12
06/03	Michael Jordan	4	7	12
06/10	Gary Payton	-	2	5
06/17	Michael Jordan	4	7	12
95/96	Special Comm. Ed. Bulls Championship	4	6	10
06/24	Richie Parker	-	2	5
07/01	Emmitt Smith	2	4	7
07/08	Alex Rodriguez	4	6	10
07/15	Drew Rosenhaus	-	2	5
07/22	Olympic Preview	-	2	5
07/29	Tom Dolan	-	2	5
08/05	Carl Lewis	-	2	5
08/12	Michael Johnson	-	2	5
08/19	Al Simmons	1	3	6
09/02	Green Bay Packers	2	4	7
09/09	Miami Dolphins	1	3	6
09/16	Ahman Green	-	2	5
09/23	Ron Powlus	-	2	5
09/30	Ali/Frazier	3	5	8
10/07	Gretzky/Messier	2	4	7
10/14	Roberto Alomar	1	3	6
10/21	Derek Jeter	3	5	8
11/04	Joe Girardi	-	2	5
11/11	Shaq/Kareem/Mikan	2	4	7
11/18	Evander Holyfield	1	3	6
11/25	Ted Williams	2	4	7
12/02	Danny Fortson	-	2	5
12/09	Warrick Dunn	1	3	6
12/16	Brett Favre	3	5	8
12/23	Tiger Woods	2	4	7
12/30	John Elway	3	5	8
-	Special: Champion Yanks	4	6	10
-	Special: Atlanta Olympics	1	3	6

1997

Date	Cover Subject	VG	EX	NM
01/06	John Elway	$2	$4	$7
01/13	M. Brunell/K. Collins	1	3	6
01/20	Antonio Freeman	1	3	6
01/27	B. Favre/M. Holmgren	2	4	7
02/03	Desmond Howard	1	3	6
02/10	Terrell Brandon	-	2	5
02/17	NFL Success	-	2	5
02/21	Swimsuit Edition (Tyra Banks)	4	6	10
03/03	Sugar Ray Leonard	1	3	6
03/10	Jamila Wideman	-	2	5

Date	Cover Subject	VG	EX	NM
03/24	Kansas Sweet 16	-	2	5
03/31	Randy Johnson	-	2	5
04/07	Miles Simon: Arizona	1	3	6
04/14	Michelle Smith	-	2	5
04/21	Tiger Woods	1	3	6
04/28	Top 50 Jock Schools	-	2	5
06/09	Michael Jordan	4	7	12
06/23	Michael Jordan Dynasty	4	7	12
97/98	Special Comm. Ed. Bulls (Jordan)	5	10	15
06/30	Mike Tyson	2	4	7
07/07	Tyson/Holyfield	2	4	7
07/14	Pete Sampras	2	4	7
07/21	Frank Gifford	4	6	10
07/28	Tony Gwynn	3	5	8
08/04	Steve Young	3	5	8
08/11	Pudge Rodriquez	1	3	6
09/01	K. Stewart/Other QB's	2	4	7
09/08	Steve Young	1	3	6
09/15	Venus Williams	-	2	5
09/22	Peyton Manning	3	5	8
09/29	Warrick Dunn	1	3	6
10/06	Tiger Woods	1	3	6
10/13	Emmitt Smith	2	4	7
10/20	Kevin Faulk/LSU	-	2	5
10/27	Larry Bird	2	4	7
11/03	Edgar Renteria	1	3	6
11/10	Grant Hill	2	4	7
11/17	S. Wojciechowski	-	2	5
11/24	Jerome Bettis	1	3	6
12/01	Michigan vs. Ohio State	-	-	25
12/15	Latrell Sprewell	1	3	6
-	Bulls Comm. Edition			
-	Jordan: 5 NBA Championships	4	7	12

1998

Date	Cover Subject	VG	EX	NM
01/12	Brent Jones	$-	$2	$5
02/02	John Elway	2	4	7
02/16	Michael Jordan	4	7	12
02/20	Swimsuit Edition (Heidi Klum)	4	6	10
02/23	Olympics	-	2	5
03/02	Pat Summitt	-	2	5
03/30	Nazr Mohammad	-	2	5
04/06	Kentucky Wildcats	-	2	5
04/20	Pedro Martinez	1	3	6
04/27	Kobe Bryant/Magic	3	5	8
05/04	Khalid Minor	-	2	5
05/25	Mike Piazza	1	3	6
06/01	John Stockton	1	3	6
06/08	M. Jordan/S. Pippen	4	6	10
06/15	Michael Jordan	4	7	12
06/22	M. Jordan "The Shot"	4	7	12
97/98	Bulls Comm. Issue	4	6	10
06/20	Sammy Sosa	4	6	10
07/06	Alex Rodriguez	3	5	8
07/20	Mike Ditka	1	3	6
07/27	Mark O'Meara	-	2	5
08/03	Mark McGwire	4	7	12
08/17	Brett Favre	3	5	8

Date	Cover Subject	VG	EX	NM

Date	Cover Subject	VG	EX	NM
08/24	Babe Ruth	2	4	7
08/31	Andy Katzenmoyer	-	2	5
09/07	McGwire & Son	4	7	12

09/14	McGwire: "The Record"	4	7	12
09/14	SI Extra Edition Mark McGwire "62!"	4	7	12
09/21	Sammy Sosa	4	6	10
09/28	Terrell Davis	2	4	7
10/05	Mark McGwire	4	7	12
10/07	Special Comm. Ed McGwire/Sosa	5	10	15
10/12	Greg Vaughn	1	3	6
10/19	"Kill the Umps"	-	2	5
10/28	NFL's Dirtiest Players	-	2	5
11/02	Yankees celebration	2	4	7
11/09	Doug Flutie	1	3	6
11/16	Ricky Williams	3	5	8
11/23	Arthur Lee	-	2	5
11/30	John Elway	2	4	7
12/07	Randall Cunningham	1	3	6
12/14	Bill Parcells	1	3	6
12/21	Sportmen of the Year	-	2	5

1999

01/11	Peerless Price	$1	$3	$6
01/18	Keyshawn Johnson	1	3	6
01/25	Michael Jordan	4	7	12
02/01	Shannon Sharpe	1	3	6
02/08	John Elway	2	4	7
02/12	Swimsuit Edition (Rebecca Romijn-Stamos)	4	6	10
02/15	Scottie Pippen	1	3	6
02/22	Duke	1	2	5
03/01	Roger Clemens	1	2	5
03/08	Dennis Rodman	1	2	5
03/15	March Madness	1	2	5
03/22	Wally Szczerbiak	1	2	5
03/29	Kevin Brown	1	1	5
04/05	Ricky Moore	1	1	4
04/12	David Duval	2	3	5

04/19	NFL Draft Preview	2	3	5
04/26	Wayne Gretzky	4	7	12
05/03	Kevin Garnett	2	3	5
05/10	Bill Russell	3	5	7
05/17	Ken Griffey Jr.	2	3	5
05/24	Jocks and Rock	1	2	4
05/31	Tim Duncan	2	3	5
06/07	Latrell Sprewell	1	2	4
06/14	Andre Agassi	1	2	4
06/21	Derek Jeter	3	5	7
06/28	NBA Finals	1	2	4
07/05	David Robinson	2	3	5
07/12	Sandy Koufax	3	6	10
07/19	Brandi Chastain	3	6	10
07/26	Muhammad Ali	4	7	12
08/09	Barry Sanders	3	6	10
08/16	College Football Preview	1	2	4
08/23	Tiger Woods	4	7	12
08/30	1999 NFL Preview	1	2	4
09/06	Mets Infield	1	2	4
09/13	Who's coaching your kid?	1	2	4
09/20	Serena Williams	2	4	6
09/27	Bottoms Up	1	2	4
10/04	Ryder Cup	2	4	6
10/11	Denver Broncos	2	4	6
10/18	Kurt Warner	2	4	7
10/25	Scott Brosius	2	4	7
11/01	Phil Jackson	2	4	6
11/08	Walter Payton	4	7	12
11/15	College Basketball Preview	1	2	4
11/22	Peyton Manning	2	4	6
11/29	20th Century Celebration	4	7	12
12/06	Virginia Tech	2	4	6
12/13	Dan Marino	3	6	10
12/20	Sportswoman of Year	1	3	5
12/27	50 Greatest	2	4	6

2000

01/10	Peter Warrick	$1	$3	$6
01/17	Shaquille O'Neal	1	3	6
01/24	Isaac Bruce	1	3	5
01/31	Jevon Kearse	1	3	5
02/01	Swimsuit Edition (Daniela Pestova)	4	6	10
02/07	Kurt Warner	1	3	5
02/14	Michael Jordan	4	7	12
02/21	Ken Griffey Jr.	1	3	5
02/28	Vince Carter	1	3	5

03/06	McGwire, Sosa, Griffey	2	5	8
03/13	Frank Thomas	1	3	5
03/20	NCAA Tournament	1	3	5
03/27	Baseball Preview	1	3	5

Date	Cover Subject	VG	EX	NM
04/03	Tiger Woods	4	7	12
04/10	Mateen Cleaves	1	3	5
04/17	The Clippers	1	3	5
04/24	Keyshawn Johnson	2	4	6
05/01	Vladimir Guerrero	1	3	5
05/08	Randy Johnson	2	4	6
05/15	Ticket Prices	1	3	5
05/22	Bob Knight	2	4	6
05/29	Postseason Wars	1	3	5
06/05	Anna Kournikova	2	4	6
06/12	Kobe Bryant	2	4	6
06/19	New Jersey Devils	1	3	5
06/26	Tiger Woods	4	7	12
07/03	Dennis Miller	1	3	5
07/10	David Wells	2	4	6
07/17	Jason Giambi	1	3	5
07/24	Lance Armstrong	1	3	5
07/31	William Perry	1	3	5
08/14	College Football Preview	1	3	5
08/21	Mike Piazza	1	3	5
08/28	Tiger Woods	4	6	10
09/04	Ryan Leaf	1	3	5
09/11	Olympic Preview	2	4	6
09/18	Bob Knight	2	4	6
09/25	Megan Quann	1	3	5
10/02	Marion Jones	2	4	6
10/09	Kurt Warner	1	3	5
10/16	Jim Edmonds	1	3	5
10/23	Rich Gannon	1	3	5
10/30	Kevin Garnett, Darius Miles	1	3	5
11/06	Quentin Griffin	1	3	5
11/13	Eddie George	1	3	5
11/20	College Basketball Review	1	3	5
11/27	Decision 2000	1	3	5
12/04	Daunte Culpepper	1	3	5
12/18	Tiger Woods	4	7	10
12/25	Chris Rock	1	3	5

2001

Date	Cover Subject	VG	EX	NM
01/08	Quentin Griffin	$1	$3	$6
01/15	Corey Harris	1	3	5
01/22	Amani Toomer	1	3	5
01/29	Tony Siragusa, Michael Strahan	1	3	5
02/05	Super Bowl XXXV	1	3	5
02/12	XFL Football	2	5	8
02/19	NBA Midseason Report	1	3	5
02/26	Dale Earnhardt	4	7	12
03/01	Swimsuit Edition (Elsa Benitez)	4	6	10
03/05	Nomar Garciaparra	1	3	5
03/12	Marion Lemieux	2	5	8
03/19	March Mayhem	1	3	5
03/27	Baseball Preview 2001	1	3	5
04/02	Final Four	1	3	5
04/09	NCAA Champs: Duke	1	3	5
04/16	Tiger Woods	2	5	8
04/23	Allen Iverson	1	3	5
04/30	Matt Lawton	1	3	5
05/07	Johnny Unitas	2	4	6
05/14	Vince Carter, Allen Iverson	1	3	5
05/21	Charlotte Hornets	1	3	5
05/28	Ichiro Suzuki	2	5	8
06/04	Shaquille O'Neal	1	3	5
06/11	Larry Walker	1	3	5
06/18	Ray Bourque	2	5	8
06/25	Shaquille O'Neal, Kobe Bryant	1	3	5

Date	Cover Subject	VG	EX	NM
07/02	Dallas Cowboys Cheerleaders	1	3	5
07/16	Bret Boone	1	3	5
07/23	Bob Kalsu	1	3	5
07/30	David Duval	1	3	5
08/06	Lance Armstrong	1	3	5
08/13	College Football Preview	1	3	5
08/20	Magic Johnson	1	3	5
08/27	Overrated and Underrated	1	3	5
09/03	Marshall Faulk	1	3	5
09/10	Roger Clemens	1	3	5
09/17	David Carr	1	3	5
09/24	Week That Sports Stood Still	2	4	6
10/01	Jay Fiedler	1	3	5
10/08	Barry Bonds	2	4	6
10/15	Oklahoma Football	1	3	5
10/22	Derek Jeter	2	4	7
10/29	Michael Jordan	4	7	12
11/05	Randy Johnson	1	3	5
11/12	Arizona Diamondbacks	1	3	5
11/19	Jason Williams	1	3	5
11/26	Eric Crouch	1	3	5
12/03	Stephen Davis	1	3	5
12/10	Kordell Stewart	1	3	5
12/17	R. Johnson/C. Schilling	1	3	5
12/24	Year-End Issue	1	3	5

2002

Date	Cover Subject	VG	EX	NM
01/07	Clinton Portis	1	3	5
01/14	Michael Jordan	4	4	12
01/21	SI Jinx	1	3	5
01/28	Jason Kidd	1	3	5
02/01	Swimsuit Edition (Yamila Diaz-Rahi)	4	6	10
02/04	Apolo Anton Ohno	1	3	5
02/11	Super Bowl XXXVI	1	3	5
02/18	LeBron James	4	6	10
02/25	Chris Witty	1	3	5
03/04	Sarah Hughes	1	3	5
03/11	Charles Barkley	2	4	6
03/18	Jason Williams	1	3	5
03/25	Jason Giambi	1	3	5
04/01	E. Knutsen, B. Cecil	-	2	5
04/08	Juan Dixon	1	3	5
04/15	Tom Brady, Barry Bonds	2	5	8
04/22	Tiger Woods	4	7	12
04/29	Kenyon Martin	1	3	5
05/06	Dirk Nowitzki	1	3	5
05/13	Trevor Hoffman	1	3	5
05/20	Mike Tyson	2	4	6
05/27	Clint Mathis	-	2	4
06/03	Steroids In Baseball	1	3	5
06/10	Kobe Bryant, Jason Kidd	2	5	8
06/17	Shaquille O'Neal	2	4	6
06/24	World Cup Soccer	-	1	5
07/01	Dale Earnhardt Jr.	1	3	5
07/08	Ichiro Suzuki	2	5	8
07/15	Ted Williams	3	6	10
07/29	John Madden	1	3	5
08/05	Lance Armstrong	1	3	5
08/12	College Football Preview	1	3	5
08/19	David Carr	1	3	5
08/26	Alfonso Soriano	1	3	5
09/02	Randy Moss	1	3	5
09/09	Jon Gruden, W. Sapp	1	3	5
09/16	Football Odyssey	1	3	5
09/23	Johnny Unitas	2	5	8

Date	Cover Subject	VG	EX	NM
09/30	Notre Dame Football	1	3	5
10/07	Sports Colleges	1	3	5
10/14	NHL Preview/Red Wings	1	3	5
10/21	Trent Smith	-	2	5
10/28	Yao Ming	3	5	8
11/04	John Lackey	1	3	5
11/11	Joey Harrington	1	3	5
11/18	High School Sports	-	2	5
11/25	J. Gardner, L. Walton	1	3	5
12/02	Maurice Clarett	1	3	5
12/09	Ricky Williams	2	4	6
12/16	Lance Armstrong	1	3	5
12/23	Brett Favre	2	4	6
12/30	Stories of the Year	2	4	6

2003

Date	Cover Subject	VG	EX	NM
01/13	Craig Krenzel	1	3	5
01/20	Rich Gannon	1	3	5
01/27	R. Gannon, W. Sapp	1	3	5
02/03	Super Bowl XXXVII	1	3	5
02/10	Yao Ming	2	5	8
02/17	Michael Jordan	3	6	12
02/18	Swimsuit Edition (Petra Nemcova)	4	6	10

Date	Cover Subject	VG	EX	NM
02/24	Spring Training	1	3	5
03/03	Kobe Bryant	3	6	12
03/10	Cliff Hawkins	-	2	5
03/17	Kirby Puckett	1	3	5
03/24	March Madness	1	3	5
03/31	New York Yankees	1	3	5
04/07	Final Four	1	3	5
04/14	Carmelo Anthony	1	3	5
04/21	Mike Weir	-	2	5
04/28	Carson Palmer	1	3	5
05/05	101 Most Influential Minorities in Sports	1	3	5
05/12	Bobby Jackson	1	3	5
05/19	Jason Kidd	1	3	5
05/26	Serena Williams	1	3	5
06/02	Roger Clemens	2	4	6
06/09	Tim Duncan	2	4	6
06/16	P. Ferreras, A. Mestre	-	2	5
06/23	David Robinson	1	3	5
06/30	Bo Jackson	1	3	5
07/07	Kerry Wood, Mark Prior	1	3	5
07/14	50th Anniversary	3	6	10
07/28	Kobe Bryant	3	6	12

Sport

Published by MacFadden from Sept., 1946 until 1988, with the exception of one month (Jan. 1952). *Sport* magazine is noted for its beautiful full color photography of the stars on its covers and feature stories which usually numbered 5-6 pages per issue. Many of the beautiful color photographs in the magazine's early years were taken by acclaimed photographer Ozzie Sweet.

1946

Date	Cover Subject	VG	EX	NM
Sep	J. DiMaggio	$300	$450	$750
Oct	G. Davis/D. Blanchard	100	250	300
Nov	Lujack/ Leahy	60	90	150
Dec	Tom Harmon	60	90	150

1947

Date	Cover Subject	VG	EX	NM
Jan	Andy Phillips	$20	$35	$60
Feb	Bently Brothers	20	35	60

Date	Cover Subject	VG	EX	NM
Mar	Alex Groza	20	35	60
Apr	Leo Durocher	20	35	60
May	Horse Racing	20	35	60
Jun	Bob Feller	25	40	70
Jul	E. Dyer/J. Cronin	20	35	60
Aug	Ted Williams	40	60	100
Sep	Joe/Dom DiMaggio	45	75	120
Oct	Harry Gilmer	10	20	30
Nov	Johnny Lujack	12	24	35
Dec	Charlie Trippi	10	20	30

1948

Date	Cover Subject	VG	EX	NM
Jan	Ralph Beard	$10	$20	$30
Feb	Frank Brimsek	10	20	30
Mar	George Kaftan	10	20	30
Apr	Ted Williams	30	50	70
May	Babe Ruth	20	30	60
Jun	Joe Louis	15	25	40

Date	Cover Subject	VG	EX	NM
Jul	Ewell Blackwell	10	20	30
Aug	Stan Musial	30	50	70

Date	Cover Subject	VG	EX	NM
Sep	J. DiMaggio/T. Williams	40	60	100
Oct	Lou Gehrig	30	50	70
Nov	Doak Walker	12	24	35
Dec	Johnny Lujack	10	20	30

1949

Date	Cover Subject	VG	EX	NM
Jan	Ed Macauly	$10	$20	$30
Feb	Lou Boudreau	10	20	30
Mar	Ralph Beard	10	20	30
Apr	Bob Feller	20	30	60
May	Enos Slaughter	15	25	40
Jun	Hal Newhouser	15	25	40
Jul	Boudreau/Gordon	15	25	40
Aug	Jackie Robinson	30	50	70
Sep	Joe DiMaggio	60	90	150
Oct	Christy Mathewson	15	25	40
Nov	Charlie Justice	10	20	30
Dec	J. Lujack/S. Luckman	12	25	40
Annual	Boudreau/Louis/Walker	12	25	35

1950

Date	Cover Subject	VG	EX	NM
Jan	Don Lofgran/R. Herrerias	$10	$20	$30
Feb	Tommy Henrich	12	24	35
Mar	George Mikan	15	25	40
Apr	Casey Stengel	15	25	40
May	Ralph Kiner	15	25	40
Jun	Bob Lemon	15	25	40

Date	Cover Subject	VG	EX	NM
Jul	Stan Musial	20	30	60
Aug	Art Houtteman	10	20	30
Sep	Don Newcombe	15	25	40
Oct	World Series	12	24	35
Nov	Harry Agganis	12	14	35
Dec	Football Pictorial	10	20	30
Dec	Sport Annual	15	25	40

1951

Date	Cover Subject	VG	EX	NM
Jan	Basketball	$10	$20	$30
Feb	Nat Holman	10	20	30
Mar	Special Sports	10	20	30
Apr	Baseball	12	24	35

Date	Cover Subject	VG	EX	NM
May	Baseball Jubilee	12	24	35
Annual	HOF Picture	12	24	35
Jun	Sugar Ray Robinson	10	20	30
Jul	Ewell Blackwell	10	20	30
Aug	Yogi Berra	15	25	40

Date	Cover Subject	VG	EX	NM
Sep	Ted Williams	25	40	70

Date	Cover Subject	VG	EX	NM
Oct	Jackie Robinson	25	40	70
Nov	Bill McColl	10	20	30
Dec	Johnny Lujack	10	20	30

1952

Date	Cover Subject	VG	EX	NM
Jan	No Issue	-	-	-
Feb	Sugar Ray Robinson	$10	$20	$30
Mar	Gil McDougald	10	20	30
Apr	Chico Carrasquel	10	20	30
May	Alvin Dark	10	20	30
Jun	Ralph Kiner	15	25	40
Jul	Stan Musial	20	30	60
Aug	A. Reynolds/Y. Berra	15	25	40
Sep	Mike Garcia	10	20	30
Oct	J. Robinson/ Reese	25	40	70
Nov	J. Robinson/A. Reynolds	20	35	60
Dec	Johnny Olszewski	10	20	30

1953

Date	Cover Subject	VG	EX	NM
Jan	Rocky Marciano	$15	$25	$40
Feb	Bobby Shantz	10	20	30
Mar	Bob Cousy	15	25	40
Apr	Mickey Mantle	75	100	125
May	Bob Lemon	5	10	15
Jun	Hank Sauer	5	10	15
Jul	Ferris Fain	5	10	15

Date	Cover Subject	VG	EX	NM

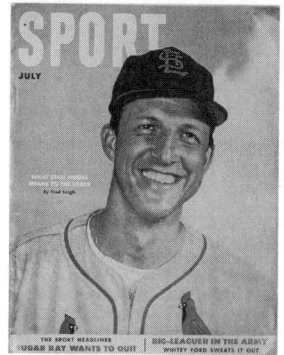

Date	Cover Subject	VG	EX	NM
Aug	Warren Spahn	6	12	20
Sep	Robin Roberts	6	12	20
Oct	Roy Campanella	8	15	25
Nov	Phil Rizzuto	8	15	25
Dec	Michigan State FB	5	10	15

1954

Date	Cover Subject	VG	EX	NM
Jan	Eddie Lebaron	$5	$10	$15
Feb	Eddie Mathews	15	25	35
Mar	Casey Stengel	6	12	20
Apr	Don Newcombe	6	12	20
May	Ted Kluszewski	8	15	25
Jun	Rocky Marciano	8	15	25

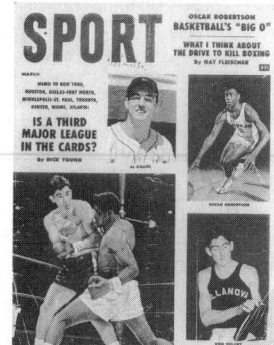

Date	Cover Subject	VG	EX	NM
Jul	Stan Musial	12	20	40
Aug	Minnie Minoso	6	12	20
Sep	Duke Snider	15	25	35
Oct	Al Rosen	5	10	20
Nov	Larry Morris	4	6	10
Dec	Pete Vann	4	6	10

1955

Date	Cover Subject	VG	EX	NM
Jan	Pete Pihos	$4	$6	$10
Feb	Alvin Dark	4	6	10
Mar	Rocky Marciano	5	10	15
Apr	Bob Turley	5	10	15
May	Bobby Thomson	5	10	15
Jun	Johnny Antonelli	4	7	12
Jul	Ned Garver	4	6	10
Aug	Paul Richards	4	6	10
Sep	Duke Snider	8	15	25
Oct	Yogi Berra	6	12	20
Nov	Eddie Erdelatz	4	6	10
Dec	Hugh McElhenny	4	7	12

1956

Date	Cover Subject	VG	EX	NM
Jan	Doak Walker	4	7	12
Feb	Sihogo Green	4	6	10
Mar	Walter Alston	4	7	12
Apr	Larry Doby	5	10	15
May	Bob Lemon	6	12	20
Jun	Willie Mays	8	15	25
Jul	Ted Williams	15	25	40

Date	Cover Subject	VG	EX	NM
Aug	Wilmer Mizell	4	6	10
Sep	10th Anniversary	5	10	15
Oct	Mickey Mantle	20	35	60
Nov	Paul Hornung	6	12	20
Dec	Bobby Morrow	4	6	10

1957

Date	Cover Subject	VG	EX	NM
Jan	Wilt Chamberlain	6	12	20
Feb	Jacques Plante	5	10	15
Mar	Mickey Mantle	15	25	50
Apr	Eddie Mathews	6	12	20
May	Campanella/Spahn/Roberts	6	12	20
Annual	Kluszewski	6	12	20
Jun	Early Wynn	12	22	40
Jul	Al Kaline	15	25	35
Aug	Joe Adcock	6	12	20
Sep	Duke Snider	15	25	35
Nov	Don Stephenson	4	6	10
Dec	Chicago Bears	5	10	15

1958

Date	Cover Subject	VG	EX	NM
Jan	Baseball Stars: Mays/Snider/Others	$6	$12	$20
Feb	Carmen Basilio	5	10	15
Mar	Lew Burdette	5	10	15
Apr	Nellie Fox	6	12	20
May	Yogi Berra	6	12	20
Jun	Willie Mays	8	15	25
Jul	Herb Score	5	10	15
Aug	Billy Martin	5	10	15
Sep	Eddie Mathews	6	12	20
Oct	B.Turley/H.Aaron/Snead	4	7	12
Nov	Bob Anderson	3	5	8
Dec	Johnny Unitas	6	12	20

1959

Date	Cover Subject	VG	EX	NM
Jan	Maurice Richard	$4	$7	$12
Feb	Rafer Johnson/L. Burdette	4	6	10

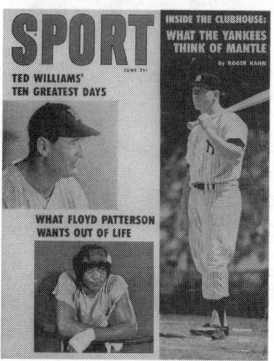

Date	Cover Subject	VG	EX	NM
Mar	A. Kaline/O.Robertson/ F. Patterson	10	20	30
Apr	Rocky Colavito	10	20	30
May	Hank Bauer	4	7	12
Jun	Mantle, T. Williams	15	25	50

Date	Cover Subject	VG	EX	NM
Jul	Jimmy Piersall	4	6	10
Aug	Mantle/others	10	20	30
Sep	T. Williams/S. Musial	12	22	40
Oct	Warren Spahn	6	12	20
Nov	Paul Dietzel/ B. Cannon	4	6	10

Date	Cover Subject	VG	EX	NM
Dec	Johnny Unitas	6	12	20

1960

Date	Cover Subject	VG	EX	NM
Jan	Bob Cousy	$5	$10	$15
Feb	Ingemar Johansson	3	5	8
Mar	Willie Mays/Others	5	10	15
May	Harmon Killebrew	8	15	25
Jun	Don Drysdale	8	15	15
Jul	L. Aparicio/F. Howard	6	12	20
Aug	Mickey Mantle	12	22	40
Sep	R. Colavito/Mays/Fox	8	15	25
Oct	B. Ruth/L. Sherry	4	6	10
Nov	Roger Maris	10	20	30
Dec	John Unitas	6	12	20

1961

Date	Cover Subject	VG	EX	NM
Jan	Bobby Layne	$5	$10	$15
Feb	Danny Murtaugh	4	6	10
Mar	O. Robertson/J.Twyman	4	6	10
Apr	Frank Howard	4	6	10
May	D. Groat/Mantle Insert	5	10	15
Jun	Willie Mays	5	10	15
Jul	Rocky Colavito	8	15	25
Aug	Spahn/Boyer	5	10	15

Date	Cover Subject	VG	EX	NM
Sep	J. DiMaggio/Mantle	12	22	40
Oct	Wally Moon	4	6	10

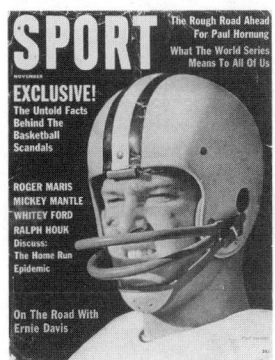

Date	Cover Subject	VG	EX	NM
Nov	Paul Hornung	6	12	20
Dec	Sam Huff	4	6	10

1962

Date	Cover Subject	VG	EX	NM
Jan	Jim Brown	$6	$12	$20
Feb	Roger Maris	8	15	25
Mar	Wilt Chamberlain	4	7	12
Apr	N. Cash/V.Pinson	4	6	10
May	Baseball Sluggers	4	7	12
Jun	Hank Aaron	6	12	20
Aug	Colavito/Kuenn	6	12	20
Sep	Boyer/Musial	6	12	20
Oct	Willie Mays	5	10	15
Nov	Jim Taylor/T.Davis	4	7	12
Dec	John Unitas/Jim Brown	6	12	20

1963

Date	Cover Subject	VG	EX	NM
Jan	Paul Hornung	$6	$12	$20
Feb	Maury Wlills	3	5	8
Mar	Bob Cousy	4	6	10
Apr	S. Musial/ W. Chamberlain	4	6	10
May	Berra/Mantle	12	22	40
Jun	Maury Wills	3	5	8

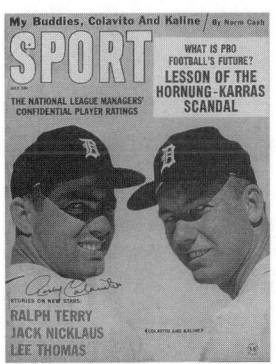

Date	Cover Subject	VG	EX	NM
Jul	Kaline/Colavito	10	20	30
Aug	Willie Mays	5	10	15
Sep	Sandy Koufax	6	12	20
Oct	Mickey Mantle	10	20	30
Nov	Whitey Ford	5	10	15
Dec	Del Shofner	3	5	8
Annual	Mantle,Chamberlain,Hornung	6	12	20

1964

Date	Cover Subject	VG	EX	NM
Jan	Jim Taylor	$6	$12	$20
Feb	Sandy Koufax	5	10	15
Mar	Cassius Clay	8	15	25
Apr	Oscar Robertson	5	10	15
May	Warren Spahn	4	7	12
Jun	Dick Stuart	3	5	8
Jul	Yastrzemski/Davis/Tresh	3	5	8
Aug	J. DiMaggio,/W. Mays	6	12	20
Sep	Mickey Mantle	10	20	30

Date	Cover Subject	VG	EX	NM
Oct	Willie Mays	5	10	15
Nov	Harmon Killebrew	5	10	15
Dec	Jimmy Brown	6	12	20

1965

Date	Cover Subject	VG	EX	NM
Jan	John Unitas	$4	$7	$12
Feb	Fred Hutchinson	1	3	58
Mar	Jerry West	4	7	12
Apr	Dean Chance	3	5	8
May	Sandy Koufax	5	10	15
Jun	Willie Mays	4	7	12
Jul	Johnny Callison	4	6	10
Aug	Mickey Mantle	10	20	30
Sep	Gehrig/DiMaggio	6	12	20
Oct	S. Koufax/Wills	4	7	12
Nov	J. Unitas/T.Mason	4	6	10
Dec	Fran Tarkenton	3	5	8

1966

Date	Cover Subject	VG	EX	NM
Jan	Charley Johnson	$3	$5	$8
Feb	Sandy Koufax	4	7	12
Apr	W. Mays/P. Hornung	4	6	10
May	Maury Wills	3	5	8
Jun	Joe Namath	5	10	15
Jul	Mickey Mantle	8	15	25
Aug	Frank Robinson	3	5	8
Sep	Willie Mays	4	7	12
Oct	Sandy Koufax	4	7	12
Nov	John Brodie	3	5	8
Dec	Gale Sayers	5	10	15

1967

Date	Cover Subject	VG	EX	NM
Jan	Don Meredith	$3	$5	$8
Feb	Frank Robinson	3	5	8
Mar	Wilt Chamberlain	3	5	8
Apr	Lew Alcindor	4	6	10
May	Mickey Mantle	8	15	25
Jun	Willie Mays	4	6	10
Jul	Richie Allen/J.Ryun	1	3	6

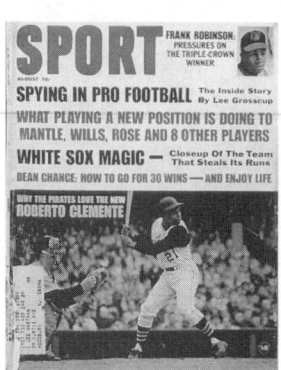

Date	Cover Subject	VG	EX	NM
Aug	Roberto Clemente	10	20	30
Sep	Pete Rose	6	12	20
Oct	John Unitas	3	5	8
Nov	Joe Namath	4	6	10
Dec	Bart Starr	4	6	10

1968

Date	Cover Subject	VG	EX	NM
Jan	Mike Garrett	$1	$3	$6
Feb	Carl Yastrzemski	4	6	10
Mar	Lew Alcindor	3	5	8
Apr	Bobby Hull	4	6	10
May	Willie Mays	3	5	8
Jun	Carl Yastrzemski	4	6	10

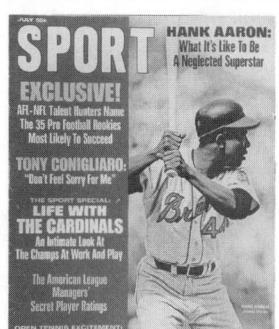

Date	Cover Subject	VG	EX	NM
Jul	Hank Aaron	4	6	10
Aug	Pete Rose	4	7	12
Sep	Don Drysdale	3	5	8
Oct	Fran Tarkenton	1	3	6
Nov	Don Meredith	1	3	6
Dec	O.J. Simpson	4	6	10
Annual	Yastrzemski/Chamberlain/ Nicklaus	5	10	15

1969

Date	Cover Subject	VG	EX	NM
Jan	Deacon Jones	$3	$5	$8
Feb	John Havlicek	1	3	6
Mar	West/ Baylor/Chamberlain	3	5	8
Apr	Mickey Mantle	10	20	30
May	Koufax/DiMaggio/Ruth/Mays	1	3	6
Jun	Ted Williams	4	7	12
Jul	Tony Conigliaro	5	10	15
Aug	O. J. Simpson	4	6	10
Sep	Durocher/Banks/Santo	6	12	20
Oct	Sonny Jurgensen	1	3	6
Nov	Gale Sayers	5	10	15
Dec	Orr/ Simpson,/McLain	3	5	8
Annual	O.J.Simpson/Gibson	4	7	12

1970

Date	Cover Subject	VG	EX	NM
Jan	Calvin Hill	$3	$5	$8
Feb	Lew Alcindor	3	5	8
Mar	Jerry West	3	5	8
Apr	Willis Reed	3	5	8
May	Tom Seaver	4	6	10
Jun	Harmon Killebrew	4	6	10
Jul	Starr/Unitas	3	5	8
Aug	Hank Aaron	4	6	10
Sep	Johnny Bench	4	7	12
Oct	Manning/Theismann/ Plunkett	3	6	8
Nov	Dick Butkus	6	12	20
Dec	Roman Gabriel	1	3	6
Annual	Mets Players WS		5	1015

1971

Date	Cover Subject	VG	EX	NM
Jan	Mike Lucci	$1	$3	$6
Feb	Bobby Orr	8	15	25
Feb	Dave Bing	1	3	6
Mar	Pete Maravich	5	10	15
Apr	John Havlicik	3	5	8
May	T. Williams/ McLain/Flood	5	10	15
Jun	Boog Powell	3	5	8
Jul	Carl Yastrzemski	4	6	10
Aug	Mike Curtis	1	3	6

Date	Cover Subject	VG	EX	NM

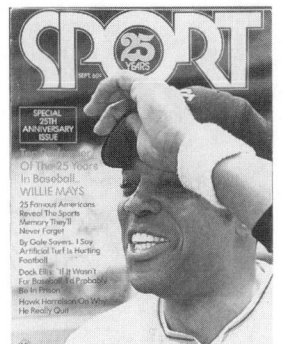

Date	Cover Subject	VG	EX	NM
Sep	Willie Mays	4	6	10
Oct	Vida Blue	1	3	6
Nov	Ken Willard	5	10	15
Dec	Bob Griese	3	5	8

1972

Date	Cover Subject	VG	EX	NM
Jan	Larry Brown	1	3	6
Feb	Tony Esposito	4	7	12
Feb	Spencer Haywood	1	3	6
Mar	Wilt Chamberlain	3	5	8
Apr	Bobby Orr	5	10	15
May	Bobby Hull	4	6	10
Jun	Brooks Robinson	4	6	10
Jul	Joe Namath	4	6	10

Date	Cover Subject	VG	EX	NM
Aug	Tom Seaver	4	7	12
Sep	Frank Robinson	3	5	8
Oct	Johnny Bench	5	10	15
Oct	Jim Plunkett	3	5	8
Nov	Otis Taylor	1	3	6
Dec	Fran Tarkenton	3	5	8

1973

Date	Cover Subject	VG	EX	NM
Jan	Merlin Olsen	$1	$3	$6
Feb	Rick Barry	1	3	6
Mar	Ken Dryden	1	3	6
Apr	Oscar Robertson	3	5	8
May	Dave Cowens	1	3	6
Jun	A.J. Foyt	1	3	6
Jul	George Foreman	1	3	6
Aug	Bobby Murcer	3	5	8
Sep	Gaylord Perry	3	5	8
Oct	Pete Rose/Others	5	5	8
Nov	Franco Harris	0	5	8
Dec	Joe Namath	0	6	10

1974

Date	Cover Subject	VG	EX	NM
Jan	L. Little/Fernandez	$1	$3	$6
Feb	K. Abdul-Jabbar	3	5	8
Mar	Russell/Chamberlain	1	3	6
Apr	Dave DeBusschere	1	3	6
May	Hank Aaron #715	5	10	15

Date	Cover Subject	VG	EX	NM
Jun	Pete Rose	4	6	10
Jul	Chris Evert/J. Connors	1	3	6
Aug	Larry Csonka	4	7	12
Sep	Muhammad Ali	5	10	15
Oct	Reggie Jackson	4	7	12
Dec	O.J. Simpson	3	5	8

1975

Date	Cover Subject	VG	EX	NM
Jan	Fran Tarkenton	$3	$5	$8
Feb	Muhammad Ali	4	6	10
Mar	Julius Erving	4	6	10
Apr	Rick Barry	1	3	6
May	Frank Robinson	3	5	8
Jun	Johnny Miller	1	3	6
Jul	Bobby Bonds	3	5	8
Aug	Billy Martin	4	6	10
Sep	Jimmy Conners	1	3	6
Oct	James Harris	1	3	6
Nov	Joe Namath	4	6	10
Dec	Joe Green	4	6	10

1976

Date	Cover Subject	VG	EX	NM
Jan	Super Bowl Preview	$3	$5	$8
Feb	Fran Tarkenton	3	5	8
Mar	George MacGinnis	1	3	6
Apr	Steve Garvey	4	6	10
May	Bruce Jenner	4	6	10
Jun	White House Cartoon	1	3	6
Jul	Bruce Jenner	1	3	6
Aug	Rose/Morgan	5	10	15
Sep	Franco Harris	4	6	10
Oct	Bert Jones	1	3	6
Nov	O.J. Simpson	3	5	8
Dec	Pill Popping	1	3	6

1977

Date	Cover Subject	VG	EX	NM
Jan	Roger Staubach	$4	$6	$10
Feb	Julius Erving	4	7	12
Mar	Namath, Simpson, Orr	4	6	10
Apr	Bill Walton	3	5	8
May	Jan Stephenson	4	7	12
Jun	Greed	1	3	6
Jul	Mark Fidrych	3	5	8
Aug	Boxing	1	3	6
Sep	Vikings/Raiders	1	3	6

Date	Cover Subject	VG	EX	NM
Oct	Rod Carew	1	3	6
Nov	Earl Monroe	3	5	8
Dec	Ken Stabler	3	5	8

1978

Date	Cover Subject	VG	EX	NM
Jan	Tony Dorsett	$3	$5	$8
Feb	K. Abdul-Jabbar	3	5	8
Mar	Maurice Lucas	1	3	6
Apr	S. Lyle/Gossage	3	5	8
May	Graig Nettles	3	5	8
Jun	Julius Erving	4	6	10

Date	Cover Subject	VG	EX	NM
Jul	Jim Rice	3	5	8
Aug	Tom Seaver	4	6	10
Sep	Cliff Branch	1	3	6
Oct	Carl Yastrzemski	3	5	8
Nov	O.J. Simpson	1	3	6
Dec	Jack Lambert	4	7	12

1979

Date	Cover Subject	VG	EX	NM
Jan	Harvey Martin	$1	$3	$6
Feb	Julius Erving	4	6	10
Mar	John Drew	1	3	6
Apr	Pete Rose	4	6	10
May	Ron Guidry	1	3	6
Jun	Dave Parker	1	3	6
Jul	Graig Nettles	1	3	6
Aug	Rod Carew	3	5	8
Sep	Jack Lambert	3	5	8

Date	Cover Subject	VG	EX	NM
Oct	Reggie Jackson	4	6	10
Nov	Raiders	3	5	8
Dec	Pat Haden	1	3	6

1980

Date	Cover Subject	VG	EX	NM
Jan	Jack Ham	$1	$3	$6
Feb	Magic Johnson	4	7	12
Mar	Larry Bird	5	10	15
Apr	Willie Stargell	3	5	8
Apr	Nolan Ryan	6	12	20
May	George Brett	5	10	15
Jun	Bill Russell	1	3	6
Jul	Gorman Thomas	1	3	6
Aug	Terry Bradshaw	3	5	8
Sep	Art Schlicter	-	2	5
Oct	Earl Campbell	3	5	8
Nov	Lee Roy Selmon	1	3	6
Dec	Football Special Teams	1	3	6

1981

Date	Cover Subject	VG	EX	NM
Jan	Billy Simms	$1	$3	$6
Feb	Danny White	1	3	6
Mar	Kelly Tripucka	-	2	5
Apr	George Brett	3	5	8
May	Billy Martin	1	3	6
Jun	Dave Parker	1	3	6
Jul	Bruce Sutter	-	2	5
Aug	Jim Plunkett	1	3	6
Sep	Earl Campbell	1	3	6
Oct	Doug Plank	-	2	5
Nov	Lester Hayes	-	2	5
Dec	Steve Bartkowski	-	2	5

1982

Date	Cover Subject	VG	EX	NM
Jan	Tony Dorsett	$1	$3	$6
Feb	Magic Johnson	3	5	8
Mar	Gerry Cooney	-	2	5
Apr	Fernando Valenzuela	1	3	6

Date	Cover Subject	VG	EX	NM
May	Reggie Jackson	3	5	8
Jun	Tom Seaver	3	5	8

Date	Cover Subject	VG	EX	NM
Jul	Billy Martin	1	3	6
Aug	Joe Montana	3	5	8
Sep	Herschel Walker	1	3	6
Oct	L.A Rams RB	-	2	5
Nov	L. Taylor/M. Johnson	1	3	6
Dec	Patrick Ewing	1	3	6

1983

Date	Cover Subject	VG	EX	NM
Jan	Herschel Walker	$1	$3	$6
Feb	Tony Dorsett	1	3	6
Mar	Moses Malone, G. Carter	1	3	6
Apr	Steve Garvey	1	3	6
May	Steve Carlton	3	5	8
Jun	Schmidt/Dawson/Yount	3	5	8

Date	Cover Subject	VG	EX	NM
Jul	Reggie Jackson	3	5	8
Aug	Marcus Allen	1	3	6
Sep	Marcus Dupree	-	2	5
Oct	Mark Gastineau	1	3	6
Nov	Franco Harris	1	3	6
Dec	Lyle Alzado	-	2	5

1984

Date	Cover Subject	VG	EX	NM
Jan	Dan Marino	$3	$5	$8
Feb	Dickerson/Ewing	1	3	6
Mar	M.Johnson/Salaries	1	3	6

Date	Cover Subject	VG	EX	NM
Apr	Cal Ripken	3	5	8
May	Wayne Gretzky	3	5	8
Jun	Dale Murphy	1	3	6
Jul	Tommy Lasorda/Others	-	2	5
Aug	Eric Dickerson	1	3	6
Sep	Darryl Clark	-	2	5
Oct	Walter Payton	3	5	8
Nov	Football Betting	-	2	5
Dec	Mullins/Ewing	-	2	5

1985

Date	Cover Subject	VG	EX	NM
Jan	Dan Marino	$3	$5	$8
Feb	D. Gooden/Others	1	3	6

Date	Cover Subject	VG	EX	NM
Mar	Joe Montana, M. Johnson	3	5	8
Apr	Doc Gooden	1	3	6
May	Keith Hernandez/G. Matthews	-	2	5
Jun	George Brett	3	5	8
Jul	Kirk Gibson	1	3	6
Aug	Joe Montana	3	5	8
Sep	Maryland Terps	-	2	5
Oct	Dan Marino	3	5	8
Nov	Marcus Allen/L. Taylor	1	3	6
Dec	Ewing/ R. Auerbach	-	2	5

1986

Date	Cover Subject	VG	EX	NM
Jan	Jim McMahon	$1	$3	$6
Feb	William Perry	1	3	6
Mar	Swimsuit	4	6	10
Apr	Bret Saberhagen	1	3	6
Apr	Dwight Gooden	1	3	6

Date	Cover Subject	VG	EX	NM
May	George Brett	3	5	8
Jun	A. Jabbar/Salaries	1	3	6
Jul	R. Jackson/P. Rose	3	5	8
Aug	Howie Long	1	3	6
Sep	Jim Harbaugh	-	2	5
Oct	Dan Marino	3	5	8
Nov	Pervis Ellison	-	2	5

Date	Cover Subject	VG	EX	NM
Dec	Multiple Covers	-	2	5

1987

Date	Cover Subject	VG	EX	NM
Jan	John Elway	$3	$5	$8
Feb	Special Ed. - Montana	3	5	8
Mar	R. Clemens, Schmidt	1	3	6
Apr	Darryl Strawberry	1	3	6
May	Dominique Wilkins	-	2	5
Jun	Jordan Et. Al	4	6	10
Jul.	Dave Parker	1	3	6
Aug	Roger Craig	1	3	6
Sep	Lawrence Taylor	1	3	6
Oct	Dan Marino	3	5	8
Nov	L. Bird/M. Johnson	3	5	8
Dec	P. Simms/Etc	-	2	5

1988

Date	Cover Subject	VG	EX	NM
Jan	Boomer Esiason	$1	$3	$6
Feb	Madden & Coaches	-	2	5
Mar	G. Jefferies/J. McDowell	-	2	5
Apr	Don Zimmer	1	2	5
May	Isiah Thomas	1	3	6
Jun	Tyson/Gibson	-	2	5
Jul	Mike Tyson	-	2	5
Aug	Oakland Raiders	-	2	5
Sep	Troy Aikman	1	3	6
Oct	Cornelius Bennett	-	2	5
Nov	M. Jordan	4	6	10
Dec	Stacy King	-	2	5

1989

Date	Cover Subject	VG	EX	NM
Jan	Dennis Gentry	$-	$2	$5
Feb	Swimsuit/Cindy Crawford	4	7	12
May	Orel Hershiser	1	3	6
Apr	K. Gibson/ Mattingly	3	5	8
May	Magic Johnson	1	3	6
Jun	Dan Marino/ R. Clemens	1	3	6
Jul	Jose Canseco	1	3	6
Aug	Joe Montana	3	5	8
Sep	Emmitt Smith	1	3	6
Oct	Marino/Gooden	1	3	6
Nov	Bird/M. Johnson/Jordan	3	5	8
Dec	Alonzo Mourning	1	3	6

1990

Date	Cover Subject	VG	EX	NM
Jan	Jim Everett	$-	$2	$5
Feb	Swimsuit Issue	4	6	10
Mar	Bo Jackson	1	3	6
Apr	J. Canseco/Others	1	3	6
May	Baseball Preview	1	3	6
Jun	Salaries	-	2	5
Jul	Will Clark	1	3	6
Jul	Joe Montana	1	3	6
Aug	Neal Anderson	-	2	5
Aug	Joe Montana	1	3	6
Aug	Barry Sanders	1	3	6

Date	Cover Subject	VG	EX	NM
Sep	Bo Jackson/ Others	-	2	5
Oct	100 Best in Sports	1	3	6
Nov	Joe Montana	1	3	6
Dec	R. Cunningham/ L.Taylor	-	2	5

1991

Date	Cover Subject	VG	EX	NM
Jan	Michael Jordan	$4	$6	$10
Feb	Swimsuit Issue	4	6	10
Mar	Ken Griffey Jr.	3	5	8
Apr	Jose Canseco	1	3	6
May	H. Johnson, J. Reardon	-	2	5
Jun	Darryl Strawberry	1	3	6
Jul	Joe Montana/Others	1	3	6
Aug	Ronnie Lott	-	2	5
Sep	J. Montana/Others	1	3	6
Oct	Bo Jackson	1	3	6
Nov	Michael Jordan	4	6	10
Dec	Michael Jordan	4	6	10

1992

Date	Cover Subject	VG	EX	NM
Jan	Jim Kelly	$1	$3	$6
Feb	Charles Barkley	1	3	6
Mar	Swimsuit	4	6	10
Apr	Bo Jackson, F. Thomas	1	3	6
May	Cal Ripken	3	5	8
Jun	M. Jordan, S. Pippin	3	5	8
Jul	Troy Aikman	1	3	6
Aug	Mark Rypien	-	2	5
Sep	Barry Sanders, J. Elway	3	5	8
Oct	Larry Johnson	-	2	5
Nov	Tim Hardaway	-	2	5
Dec	Rod Woodson	-	2	5

1993

Date	Cover Subject	VG	EX	NM
Jan	Sport Top 40/Jordan	$3	$5	$8
Feb	Swimsuit	4	6	10
Mar	Baseball '93	1	3	6
Apr	Bonds/Bonilla/Clemens	1	3	6
May	Jordan/P. Ewing	3	5	8
Jun	Michael Jordan	4	6	10
Jul	Troy Aikman	1	3	6
Aug	J.Montana/Young	1	3	6
Sep	Joe Montana	3	5	8
Oct	Steve Young	1	3	6
Nov	M. Jordan/S. O'Neal/Barkley	1	3	6
Dec	Michael Jordan	4	6	10

1994

Date	Cover Subject	VG	EX	NM
Jan	Steve Young	$1	$3	$6
Feb	Joe Montana	1	3	6
Mar	Swimsuit	4	6	10
Apr	Barry Bonds	-	2	5
May	Mike Piazza	1	3	6
Jun	Scottie Pippen	1	3	6
Jul	T. Aikman/E. Smith	1	3	6
Aug	Dan Marino	1	3	6
Sep	Troy Aikman	1	3	6
Oct	Marcus Allen	1	3	6
Nov	Michael Jordan	4	6	10

Date	Cover Subject	VG	EX	NM
Dec	Shaquille O'Neal	3	5	8

1995

Date	Cover Subject	VG	EX	NM
Jan	Frank Thomas	$1	$3	$6
Feb	Jerry Rice	1	3	6
Mar	Swimsuit	3	5	8
Apr	Michael Jordan	4	6	10
May	Charles Barkley	1	3	6
Jun	Michael Jordan	4	6	10
Jul	Steve Young	1	3	6
Aug	E.Smith/S. Young/Elway	1	3	6
Sep	Steve Young	1	3	6
Oct	Marino/Young/Aikman	1	3	6
Nov	M.Jordan/S. O'Neal/Others	3	5	8
Dec	Michael Jordan	4	6	10

1996

Date	Cover Subject	VG	EX	NM
Jan	Michael Jordan	$4	$6	$10
Feb	Dan Marino/Troy Aikman	3	5	8
Mar	Swimsuit	3	5	8
Apr	Anfernee Hardaway	1	3	6
May	Jordan/Magic/Rodman	3	5	8
Jun	Jordan/Pippen/Rodman	3	5	8
Jul	S. Young/J. Rice	1	3	6
Aug	Favre/Marino/Seau,Smith	1	3	6
Sep	Jordan: Sport 50th	4	7	12
Oct	D. Marino/T. Aikman	1	3	6
Nov	M. Jordan, others	3	5	8
Dec	Shaquille O'Neal	3	5	8

1997

Date	Cover Subject	VG	EX	NM
Jan	Emmitt Smith	$3	$5	$8
Feb	B. Favre, J. Elway	3	5	8
Mar	Swimsuit	3	5	8
Apr	Dennis Rodman	-	2	5
May	Grant Hill	1	3	6
Jun	Michael Jordan	4	7	12
Jul	Tim Duncan	1	3	6
Aug	Brett Favre	3	5	8
Sep	Troy Aikman	1	3	6
Oct	B. Favre/D. Marino	3	5	8
Nov	Michael Irvin	-	2	5
Dec	Michael Jordan	4	6	10

1998

Date	Cover Subject	VG	EX	NM
Jan	Dominators of '97	$-	$2	$5
Feb	Dorsey Levens	-	2	5
Mar	Swimsuit	3	5	8
Apr	Dick Vitale	-	2	5
May	Baseball's Best/Worst Values	-	2	5
Jun	S. O'Neal/K. Bryant	1	3	6
Jul	Chipper Jones	1	3	6
Aug	Brett Favre	1	3	6
Sep	Barry Sanders	1	3	6
Oct	Favre/Aikman/Elway/ K. Stewart	1	3	6
Nov	Mutombo/Jeter/Aikman/ Cooper/Agassi	-	2	5
Dec	Terrell Davis	1	3	6

The Sporting News

The first issue of *The Sporting News*, an eight-page newspaper, was published by Alfred Henry Spink of St. Louis in 1886. Although other professional and collegiate sports are covered, baseball has always been *TSN*s primary attraction, with each weekly issue devoting coverage to every major league team.

Often called the Bible of Baseball, *The Sporting News* has included box scores of all major league games, and has offered several attractive baseball-related photographic and artistic covers throughout the years. In the late 1960s, *TSN* began using color on its covers.

During the 1970s, most front covers were devoted to baseball players, with collegiate and professional football and basketball following. This continued throughout the decade, until the 1980s, when the paper began featuring more than one sport on its covers.

Those who collect *TSN*s, which should have their pages intact and be at least in Very Good condition, often seek those which feature one player, members of one team, or superstars. Some people collect issues from an entire memorable season, or try to collect as many issues as possible, for the publication's historical information.

Many times collectors have the covers autographed and framed. *TSN* did not start putting mailing labels on the front cover until the Nov. 28, 1981, issue. However, the labels are positioned so as not to detract from the cover photo.

TSN has also devoted space to the sports memorabilia hobby, with occasional ads for sports books, publications, baseball cards and memorabilia, and baseball card shows.

Common issues from the 1910s in Very Good condition sell for about $50 each; all issues thereafter until the 1960s fall in a range from $10-$30. Issues from the 1970s-1990s generally sell for $15 or less.

Issues during the regular season (April-October), as well as commemorative, Opening Day, All-Star and World Series and superstar issues, generally have higher prices than those from the off-season (November-March) and have more investment potential.

It wasn't until 1964 that cover photos and illustrations were standard on the front cover; prior to then, the front pages were designed like a regular newspaper.

1932

01/02/32 Bud Tinning $30
01/14/32 Les Mallon $30
01/21/32 Oscar Roettger $30
01/28/32 Joyner White $30
02/04/32 Horace Ford.. $30
02/11/32 Lee Mangum $30
02/18/32 Cubs prepare for Catalina Island.......... $30
02/25/32 Marv Olson, Bill Terry $35
03/03/32 Sam Gibson, Waite Hoyt $35
03/10/32 Edward Madjeski $30
03/17/32 Leonard Koenecke $30
03/24/32 William Brenzel $30
03/31/32 Smead Jolley $32
04/07/32 Burleigh Grimes................................... $35
04/14/32 Monte Weaver $30
04/21/32 Harold Anderson.................................. $30
04/28/32 Samuel Byrd $30
05/05/32 William Rogell $30
05/12/32 Walter Betts $30
05/19/32 Ernie Lombardi $35
05/26/32 Bill Dickey $50
06/02/32 Fritz Knothe, Pie Traynor $35
06/09/32 Jimmie Foxx, Bill Terry........................ $65
06/16/32 Mel Ott.. $65
06/23/32 Dizzy Dean $75
06/30/32 Lefty Gomez $50
07/07/32 William Clark $30
07/14/32 Larry French $30
07/21/32 Oscar Melillo $30
07/28/32 Lloyd Brown $30
08/04/32 Earl Grace $30
08/11/32 John Jones $30
08/18/32 Ernie Orsatti $30
08/25/32 Baxter Jordan $30
09/01/32 Pepper Martin, Red Ruffing................. $45
09/08/32 Tony Freitas $30
09/15/32 Billy Herman, Joe Medwick $35
09/22/32 Evar Swanson $30
09/29/32 Yankees vs. Cubs $150
10/06/32 L. Gehrig, B. Ruth................................ $350
10/13/32 Joe Cronin, Hal Smith.......................... $32
10/20/32 Howard Maple $30
10/27/32 John Hogan $30
11/03/32 Del Bissonette $30
11/10/32 Fred Lindstrom $32
11/17/32 George Susce $30
11/24/32 George Grantham................................ $30
12/01/32 Harry Taylor $30
12/08/32 Babe Herman $32
12/15/32 Travis Jackson $32

12/22/32 Hal Rhyne.. $30
12/29/32 Sam West $30

1933

01/05/33 Henry Johnson $30
01/12/33 Gus Mancuso $30
01/19/33 Paul Andrews $30
01/26/33 Woody English...................................... $30
02/02/33 Ossie Bluege $30
02/09/33 Joe Moore, Honus Wagner $35
02/16/33 Harry Rice $30
02/23/33 Carl Reynolds $30
03/02/33 Bud Parmelee $30
03/09/33 Bob Boken $30
03/16/33 Beryl Richmond $30
03/23/33 Hal Schumacher, Luke Appling $35
03/30/33 Don Brennan $30
04/06/33 Frank Reiber $30
04/13/33 Bill Werber $30
04/20/33 Schoolboy Rowe.................................. $35
04/27/33 Clinton Brown $30
05/04/33 Carl Hubbell, Luke Appling $45
05/11/33 Pete Fox, Schoolboy Rowe.................. $35
05/18/33 Russell Van Atta $30
05/25/33 Wally Berger $32
06/01/33 Jake Miller $30
06/08/33 Bobby Coombs $30
06/15/33 Harley Boss $30
06/22/33 Bill McAfee $30
06/29/33 John Jackson $30
07/06/33 First All-Star issue $300
07/13/33 Chuck Fullis $30
07/20/33 Dib Williams $30
07/27/33 Rogers Hornsby, Sam Leslie $45
08/03/33 Dizzy Dean $50
08/10/33 Carl Hubbell, Monte Pearson $40
08/17/33 D. Chapman (Nationals), Mel Ott........ $40
08/24/33 Dolph Camilli $32
08/31/33 Dizzy and Paul Dean $50
09/07/33 Gus Mancuso $30
09/14/33 Travis Jackson $32
09/21/33 Joey Kuhel $30
09/28/33 Al Lopez $32
10/05/33 World Series, Nationals/Giants............ $125
10/12/33 Giants team photo $85
10/19/33 Babe Phelps $30
10/26/33 Fritz Ostermueller $30
11/02/33 Tony Piet $30
11/09/33 Red Rolfe $35
11/16/33 John Pomorski $30
11/23/33 Spud Davis $30
11/30/33 George Steinback.................................. $30

12/07/33 Reggie Grabowski $30
12/14/33 Raymond Prim $30
12/21/33 John Stone $30
12/28/33 Joseph Glenn $30

1934

01/04/34 Lou Chiozza $28
01/11/34 Pete Fox $28
01/18/34 Benny Tate $28
01/25/34 Glenn Spencer $28
02/01/34 Forrest Twogood $28
02/08/34 Edward Baecht $28
02/15/34 Henry Johnson $28
02/22/34 Cy Blanton $28
03/01/34 Dick Ward $28
03/08/34 John Krider $28
03/15/34 Giants catchers $28
03/22/34 Otho Nitcholas, Lee Stine $28
03/29/34 Al Lopez $30
04/05/34 Bill and George Dickey $40
04/12/34 Augie Galan $28
04/19/34 Jack Rothrock $28
04/26/34 Johnny Pasek $28
05/03/34 Al Spohrer $28
05/10/34 Daniel MacFayden $28
05/17/34 Carl Reynolds $28
05/24/34 Joe Cascarella $28
05/31/34 Curt Davis $28
06/07/34 Linus Frey $28
06/14/34 Al Benton $28
06/21/34 William Urbanski $28
06/28/34 Billy Knickerbocker $28
07/05/34 Second All-Star issue $250
07/12/34 Johnny Broaca $28
07/19/34 Fred Ostermueller $28
07/26/34 Hal Lee $28
08/02/34 James Weaver $28
08/09/34 Alex Kampouris $28
08/16/34 Bill Myers $28
08/23/34 Zeke Bonura $28
08/30/34 Buzz Boyle $28
09/06/34 Jo Jo White $28
09/13/34 Leslie Tietje $28
09/20/34 Johnny McCarthy $28
09/27/34 Beryl Richmond $28
10/04/34 World Series, Tigers/Cardinals $25
10/11/34 Cards win World Series $75
10/18/34 George Hockette $28
10/25/34 Pat Malone $28
11/01/34 Oscar Melillo $28
11/08/34 Lynford Lary $28
11/15/34 George Watkins $28
11/22/34 Dick Bartell, Johnny Vergez $28
11/29/34 Joe DiMaggio, Al Todd $50
12/06/34 George Stumpf $28
12/13/34 Bill Dietrich $28
12/20/34 Dutch Leonard $28
12/27/34 Marvin Duke $28

1935

01/03/35 Wally Moses $28
01/10/35 Steve Sundra $28
01/17/35 Roy Hansen $28
01/24/35 Hal Finney $28
01/31/35 Walter Millies $28
02/07/35 Francis Parker $28
02/14/35 Larry Bettencourt $28
02/21/35 Edward Durham $28
02/28/35 Eugene Schott $28

03/07/35 Leon Chagnon $28
03/14/35 Cliff Bolton $28
03/21/35 Todd Moore $28
03/28/35 Luke Sewell $28
04/04/35 Clyde Hatter $28
04/11/35 Babe Dahlgren $28
04/18/35 Leslie Tietje $28
04/25/35 Tony Lazzeri $35
05/02/35 Joseph Stripp $28
05/09/35 Johnny Whitehead $28
05/16/35 Dolph Camilli $30
05/23/35 Whitey Whitehead $28
05/30/35 Bucky Harris, Bobo Newsom $30
06/06/35 Whitey Wilshere $28
06/13/35 Pep Young $28
06/20/35 Leon Chagnon $28
06/27/35 Tommy Bridges $28
07/04/35 Cleveland All-Star issue $50
07/11/35 Slick Castleman $28
07/18/35 William Myers $28
07/25/35 Pete Fox $28
08/01/35 Roy Henshaw $28
08/08/35 Lewis Riggs $28
08/15/35 Jose Gomez $28
08/22/35 Joe Vosmik $28
08/29/35 Joseph Bowman $28
09/05/35 Roxie Lawson $28
09/12/35 Bud Hafey $28
09/19/35 Ivy Andrews $28
09/26/35 Paul Derringer $28
10/03/35 World Series, Tigers/Cubs $95
10/10/35 Tigers win World Series $75
10/17/35 Hal Lee $28
10/24/35 William McGee $28
10/31/35 Henry Coppola $28
11/07/35 Eugene Lillard $28
11/14/35 Dennis Galehouse $28
11/21/35 Frank Pytlok $28
11/28/35 Whitey Whitehead $28
12/05/35 Donald McNair $28
12/12/35 Leroy Parmelee $28
12/19/35 Marcellus Monte Pearson $28
12/26/35 Monte Pearson $28

1936

01/02/36 George McQuinn $28
01/09/36 Frank Gabler $28
01/16/36 Jack Knott $28
01/23/36 Roy Johnson $28
01/30/36 Babe Phelps $28
02/06/36 Elburt Fletcher $28
02/13/36 James DeShong $28
02/20/36 Orville Jorgens $28
02/27/36 Roy Hughes $28
03/05/36 Samuel Leslie $28
03/12/36 Rudy York $28
03/19/36 Alfred Todd $28
03/26/36 James Oglesby $28
04/02/36 Hank Greenberg $50
04/09/36 Lee John Norris $28
04/16/36 Albert Butcher $28
04/23/36 Charlie Grimm $28
04/30/36 Bill and George Dickey $45
05/07/36 Bill Terry $40
05/14/36 Dusty Rhodes $28
05/21/36 50th Anniversary issue $75
05/28/36 Frankie Frisch $40
06/04/36 Steve O'Neill $28

06/11/36 Stuart Martin......................................$28
06/18/36 Gabby Hartnett $35
06/25/36 Monte Pearson $28
07/02/36 All-Star Game issue.........................$50
07/09/36 Augie Galan, Lou Gehrig................$85
07/16/36 Jimmie Foxx, Lefty Grove...............$75
07/23/36 Dizzy Dean $45
07/30/36 Jimmie Foxx....................................$50
08/06/36 Tom Yawkey $28
08/13/36 Italo Chelini.....................................$28
08/20/36 Rip Radcliff......................................$28
08/27/36 Women baseball fans $28
09/03/36 Jimmie Foxx, Joe McCarthy............$50
09/10/36 Bob Feller $100
09/17/36 Branch Rickey..................................$35
09/24/36 John McCarthy.................................$28
10/01/36 Yankees (Gehrig) vs. Giants............$200
10/08/36 Gehrig, Yankees win Series.............$50
10/15/36 James Mosolf..................................$28
10/22/36 Earl Averill, other Indians................$35
10/29/36 Joe DiMaggio, family.......................$25
11/05/36 Six comeback players $28
11/12/36 Burleigh Grimes..............................$32
11/19/36 American League officials $28
11/26/36 Lou Gehrig, Lefty Gomez $100
12/03/36 George Caster..................................$28
12/10/36 Winter meetings...............................$28
12/17/36 Cookie Lavagetto $30
12/24/36 Cronin, D. Dean, Ruth $30
12/31/36 Hubbell, McCarthy, Rickey, Vander Meer............. $100

1937

01/07/37 Cuyler, Frisch, Goslin, others $40
01/14/37 M. Cochrane, P. Dean, other injured players $35
01/21/37 Ival Goodman $26
01/28/37 Paul Dean, Branch Rickey $30
02/04/37 V. DiMaggio, other minor leaguers.....$28
02/11/37 P. Dean, Goslin, P. Waner................$40
02/18/37 Gabby Hartnett $28
02/25/37 St. Louis Browns..............................$28
03/04/37 Giants in Havana $28
03/11/37 Bob Feller $75
03/18/37 A's, White Sox in spring training $26
03/25/37 DiMaggio, Greenberg, others...........$75
04/01/37 Jeff Heath $26
04/08/37 Pepper Martin $28
04/15/37 Roxie Lawson $26
04/22/37 Hefty ballplayers $36
04/29/37 DiMaggio, Doerr, Gehrig, Mungo........$100
05/06/37 M. Cochrane, H. Greenberg $50
05/13/37 Lamar Newsome $26
05/20/37 Gerry Walker $26
05/27/37 Cubs trainer $26
06/03/37 Lloyd Waner.....................................$35
06/10/37 Branch Rickey..................................$28
06/17/37 Dick Bartell $26
06/24/37 Jimmy Dykes $26
07/01/37 Griffith Stadium, All-Star issue $100
07/08/37 Paul Dean, Carl Hubbell...................$40
07/15/37 Gabby Hartnett, Charlie Root $28
07/22/37 Bucky Jordan $26
07/29/37 Del Baker $26
08/05/37 Heinie Manush..................................$28
08/12/37 John Wilson $26
08/19/37 Gabby Hartnett, Mel Ott $40
08/26/37 Jim Turner..$26
09/02/37 Rudy York...$26
09/09/37 Joe Medwick $30

09/16/37 Kid fans...$26
09/23/37 Lou Gehrig.......................................$100
09/30/37 Body parts of the stars: DiMaggio's eyes,
    Gehrig's legs, etc. $75
10/07/37 Yankees vs. Giants..........................$50
10/14/37 Yankees win World Series................$100
10/21/37 Major League trainers $26
10/28/37 Ossie Vitt $26
11/04/37 Pirate bosses $26
11/11/37 Charlie Gehringer $35
11/18/37 Dodger bosses $26
11/25/37 Joe DiMaggio, Tony Lazzeri $60
12/02/37 Indian bosses $26
12/09/37 Milwaukee winter meetings $26
12/16/37 More winter meetings $26
12/23/37 Joe Medwick MVP celebration $30
12/30/37 J.T. Allen, Keller, Barrow.................$75

1938

01/06/38 Florida players at home $26
01/13/38 Like father, like son $26
01/20/38 Grover Alexander HOF election..........$35
01/27/38 Cecil Travis $26
02/03/38 St. Petersburg players at home $26
02/10/38 August Mancuso $26
02/17/38 Joe Gordon, other rookies $35
02/24/38 Harry Danning $26
03/03/38 Lefty Gomez $32
03/10/38 Cubs at Catalina Island $26
03/17/38 Indians in New Orleans $26
03/24/38 St. Louis Browns players $26
03/31/38 Spalding factory making balls.............$26
04/07/38 Vince DiMaggio, other Bees $28
04/14/38 Clay Bryant $26
04/21/38 First pitch presidents $32
04/28/38 Bobby Doerr $30
05/05/38 Bobo Newsom $26
05/12/38 Bob Feller in action $65
05/19/38 Three umpires $26
05/26/38 Bill Dickey $35
06/02/38 Tot Pressnell $26
06/09/38 C. Stengel managing Bees $45
06/16/38 Sam Chapman, Dick Siebert $26
06/23/38 Babe Ruth, Dodger coach $125
06/30/38 All-Star issue $150
07/07/38 Crosley Field....................................$26
07/14/38 John Gee, Babe Ruth $25
07/21/38 Fastest ballplayers $26
07/28/38 Ballplayers' wives $28
08/04/38 Hank Greenberg $45
08/11/38 Ernie Lombardi $30
08/18/38 Major League musicians $26
08/25/38 Joe Glenn $26
09/01/38 Lynn Myers $26
09/08/38 Vance Page $26
09/15/38 Miguel Gonzalez...............................$26
09/22/38 Red Ruffing $35
09/29/38 Hank Greenberg $40
10/06/38 Yankee team picture.........................$100
10/13/38 Faces in World Series crowd, with Ruth...............$75
10/20/38 Major league scouts $26
10/27/38 Off-season hunting, with Jimmie Foxx...................$35
11/03/38 Jimmie Foxx, Ernie Lombardi $35
11/10/38 Macks 1913 $100,000 infield............$28
11/17/38 PCL presidents $26
11/24/38 Gehrig, Goslin, Simmons, vets............$75
12/01/38 New Orleans winter meetings $26
12/08/38 MLB President Bramham $26

06/19/41 Ted Williams $75
06/26/41 Appling, Boudreau, Reese, Rizzuto, others.......... $45
07/03/41 Briggs Stadium, All-Star issue $85
07/10/41 Jeff Heath $24
07/17/41 Sportsmans Park scoreboard $24
07/24/41 Foxx, Gehrig, Mize, others $80
07/31/41 300 game winners: Grove, Johnson,
  Mathewson, Young, others $50
08/07/41 Relief pitchers $24
08/14/41 Honus Lobert $24
08/21/41 All-Star Noisomatics $24
08/28/41 Joe Gordon, Phil Rizzuto $30
09/04/41 Lon Warneke $24
09/11/41 Hal Chase $24
09/18/41 Hal Chase $24
09/25/41 Joe McCarthy $28
10/02/41 World Series issue $75
10/09/41 World Champion Yankees $75
10/16/41 Baker, Roffe, Traynor, others $28
10/23/41 John Wyatt $24
10/30/41 Minor league managers $24
11/06/41 Dolph Camilli $24
11/13/41 Joe DiMaggio $100
11/20/41 Cobb, Hornsby, Jackson, T. Williams, others $75
11/27/41 Jacksonville winter meetings $24
12/04/41 Lou Boudreau $35
12/11/41 Winter meetings $24
12/18/41 Hank Greenberg $40
12/25/41 Rogers Hornsby $35

1942
01/01/42 Ted Williams, others $100
01/08/42 Mel Ott $40
01/15/42 Frisch, Gehringer, Hornsby, others $40
01/22/42 FDR to Landis: Keep Playing $30
01/29/42 Ted Williams $75
02/05/42 Musial, others as minor leaguers $35
02/12/42 Jimmie Foxx, others $40
02/19/42 M. Cochrane, B. Dickey, others $35
02/26/42 Bill McKechnie $24
03/05/42 Yankee pitchers $24
03/12/42 Bruce Campbell $24
03/19/42 Lou Boudreau, Burt Shotton $28
03/26/42 Mrs. McGraw, Mel Ott $35
04/02/42 Ty Cobb $45
04/09/42 Nine major league coaches $24
04/16/42 FDR: Play Ball $28
04/23/42 Vern Stephens $24
04/30/42 Player-managers: Boudreau, Cronin, Ott, others .. $35
05/07/42 Bob Feller, Hank Greenberg, others $40
05/14/42 Navy photos $24
05/21/42 Four players wearing #3 .... $24
05/28/42 Bobby Doerr $26
06/04/42 Three Phillies with glasses $24
06/11/42 Joe Gordon $26
06/18/42 Edgar Smith $24
06/25/42 Paul Waner $26
07/02/42 All-Star issue: Gehrig, Foxx, Ruth $50
07/09/42 Don Gutteridge $24
07/16/42 Players at new positions $24
07/23/42 Chet Laabs $24
07/30/42 Rollie Hemsley $24
08/06/42 Lou Boudreau, others $30
08/13/42 Hitting pitchers: Ruth, others $60
08/20/42 Headhunting cartoon $24
08/27/42 Lou Novikoff caricature $24
09/03/42 Reese, Rizzuto, others $30
09/10/42 Close plays $24

09/17/42 James Sewell $24
09/24/42 Joe Jackson $50
10/01/42 World Series issue, J. McCarthy $100
10/08/42 Famous Babes: Ruth, others $65
10/15/42 Stan Musial $40
10/22/42 Ossie Bluege $24
10/29/42 Mort Cooper $24
11/05/42 Branch Rickey $26
11/12/42 Bobo Newsom $24
11/19/42 Sam Breadon $24
11/26/42 Nick Altrock $24
12/03/42 Judge Landis $26
12/10/42 Al Schacht $24
12/17/42 Lefty Grove $28
12/24/42 Major leaguers' war efforts $24
12/31/42 Southworth, Veeck, Williams, others $100

1943
01/07/43 Steve O'Neill $22
01/14/43 Map of Northeastern U.S. $22
01/21/43 Sylvester Goedde $22
01/28/43 Bob Feller in Navy uniform $40
02/04/43 Ty Cobb as WWI captain $30
02/11/43 Cubs uniform changes $22
02/18/43 Joe Cronin $22
02/25/43 Joe DiMaggio joins the Army $75
03/04/43 Griffith, Harris, Hornsby $30
03/11/43 Bear Mountain (Dodgers training site) $22
03/18/43 Babe Dahlgren $22
03/25/43 Paul, Lloyd Waner $22
04/01/43 Joe DiMaggio $60
04/08/43 Carl Hubbell $35
04/15/43 Franklin D. Roosevelt $30
04/22/43 Soldier reading sports page $22
04/29/43 Case, Johnson, Spence $22
05/06/43 Etten, Gordon, Johnson, Stirnweiss $25
05/13/43 Front-Row Hits for Home Fronters $22
05/20/43 Garbs, Simmons, Weatherly $24
05/27/43 Five new Cardinals $22
06/03/43 Jesse S. Flores $22
06/10/43 Dutch Leonard with rookies $22
06/17/43 Army (DiMaggio, Slaughter) vs. Navy
  (Mize, Williams) $75
06/24/43 Dixie, Harry, G. Walker $22
07/01/43 American flag $22
07/08/43 Shibe Park: All-Star issue $24
07/15/43 Durocher, Newsom, Rickey $22
07/22/43 Dodger Bum, Giant $25
07/29/43 Gus Mancuso $22
08/05/43 Mike Naymick $22
08/12/43 Ford Frick $22
08/19/43 Nick Etten $22
08/26/43 Dodger Bum playing with kids $24
09/02/43 Howie Schultz, Dodgers $22
09/09/43 Beauregard, W. Johnson $22
09/16/43 Cardinals team photo $75
09/23/43 World Series issue, M. Cooper $45
09/30/43 Joe McCarthy, Billy Southworth $25
10/07/43 Red Barber $35
10/14/43 Joe McCarthy, World Series $95
10/21/43 Break up the Yanks! $75
10/28/43 Judge Landis, Babe Ruth $65
11/04/43 Stan Musial $50
12/02/43 Winter meetings $22
12/09/43 Frisch, Musial, Walker $35
12/16/43 Herb Pennock $22
12/30/43 Chandler, Griffith, McCarthy, others $60

1944

01/06/44 Carl Hubbell $35
01/13/44 Wrigley Field, Los Angeles $22
01/20/44 Branch Rickey, other owners $25
01/27/44 Babe Dahlgren, Bobo Newsom $22
02/03/44 Baseball team owners $22
02/10/44 Little Lamzeetivee $22
02/17/44 Clark Griffith $25
02/24/44 Ty Cobb $45
03/02/44 1944 A.L. schedule $22
03/09/44 1994 N.L. schedule $22
03/16/44 Durocher, C. Mack, McCarthy $30
03/23/44 Ralph Siewart, Joe Wood $22
03/30/44 Giants jogging $22
04/06/44 Spring training photos $22
04/13/44 Full page soldier cartoon $22
04/20/44 Stadium photo $22
04/27/44 Servicemen at a game $22
05/04/44 J. DiMaggio in an Army helmet $60
05/11/44 Scorecard vendor $22
05/18/44 Nick Etten $22
05/25/44 No-hit Hall of Fame $25
06/01/44 Thomas Edison and night ball $30
06/08/44 George Sisler $22
06/15/44 Dixie Walker $22
06/22/44 Cy Young $40
06/29/44 Browns mascot $22
07/06/44 Pirates mascot, All-Star issue $75
07/13/44 Stan Musial, Dixie Walker $50
07/20/44 Dodger Bum $22
07/27/44 Team mascots playing cards $22
08/03/44 Connie Mack $25
08/10/44 Browns mascot $22
08/17/44 Mel Ott $35
08/24/44 Browns mascot $22
08/31/44 Hal Newhouser, Dizzy Trout $30
09/07/44 Browns mascot $22
09/14/44 A.L. pennant race $22
09/21/44 Newhouser, ONeill, Trout $28
09/28/44 Cardinals end season $22
10/05/44 Browns mascot $65
10/12/44 Browns mascot getting shot $50
10/19/44 Marty Marion, Vern Stephens $35
11/02/44 Doc Blanchard $26
11/09/44 Dodger Bum $24
11/23/44 Marty Marion $24
11/30/44 Judge Landis dies $35
12/14/44 Baseball winter meetings $22
12/28/44 M. Marion, L. Sewell, others $50

1945

01/04/45 Dodger Bum This IS Next Year! $25
01/11/45 Hall of Fame balloting process $20
01/18/45 Willard Mullin cartoon $20
01/25/45 American Legion cartoon $20
02/01/45 Larry MacPhail $20
02/08/45 Abbott and Costello, Durocher, McCarthy, Ott $35
02/15/45 Commissioner search committee $20
02/22/45 Search for a new commissioner $20
03/01/45 Dodger Bum $22
03/08/45 Lou Novikoff $20
03/15/45 1945 A.L. schedule $20
03/22/45 1945 N.L. schedule $20
03/29/45 Larry MacPhail $20
04/05/45 Leo Durocher $25
04/12/45 Browns mascot $20
04/19/45 Presidents at baseball games $20
04/26/45 Yankee and Brown mascots $20

05/03/45 Happy Chandler, Judge Landis $22
05/10/45 New York Giants $20
05/17/45 Phillie rhubarb $20
05/24/45 Giants mascot $22
05/31/45 Mort Cooper $20
06/07/45 Dave Ferriss $20
06/14/45 Howard Schultz $20
06/21/45 Indian with tomahawk $20
06/28/45 Dodger Bum $22
07/05/45 Hank Greenberg $35
07/12/45 Fans discuss the All-Star Game $50
07/19/45 Al Benton $20
07/26/45 Charlie Grimm $20
08/02/45 Larry MacPhail $20
08/09/45 Major League managers $20
08/16/45 Al Rosen $25
08/23/45 Joe McCarthy $24
08/30/45 Bob Feller $35
09/06/45 Leo Durocher $25
09/13/45 Browns, Indians, Senators, Tigers, Yankees
          mascots $20
09/20/45 Dick Fowler $20
09/27/45 Happy Chandler $22
10/04/45 Briggs Stadium, D. Eisenhower $85
10/11/45 Tiger licking Cubs bones, World Series $70
10/25/45 Clarence Ace Parker $20
11/01/45 Bill Veeck $25
11/08/45 Breadon, Musial, Slaughter, others $35
11/15/45 Happy Chandler $22
11/29/45 Happy Chandler, Muddy Ruel $20
12/06/45 Player returning from war $25
12/13/45 Two baseball owners $20
12/27/45 H. Newhouser, Player of the Year $30

1946

01/03/46 Hall of Fame elections $22
01/10/46 Sam Breadon $20
01/17/46 Larry MacPhail $22
01/24/46 Happy Chandler $22
01/31/46 Joe DiMaggio, Ted Williams $50
02/07/46 Mel Ott $25
02/14/46 Grapefruit League $20
02/21/46 Hank Greenberg $30
02/28/46 Mexican League $20
03/07/46 Bob Feller $30
03/14/46 Ted Williams $50
03/21/46 Leo Durocher $25
03/28/46 Cardinal outfielders $20
04/04/46 Johnny Mize $25
04/11/46 Mickey Owen $20
04/18/46 Peacetime baseball begins $50
04/25/46 Spud Chandler $25
05/02/46 Tommy Henrich $25
05/09/46 Joe Cronin, Joe McCarthy $25
05/16/46 1946 Red Sox sluggers $25
05/23/46 Ted Williams $30
06/05/46 Bill Dickey, Ted Lyons $28
06/12/46 Babe Ruth $50
06/19/46 Red Sox tear apart the league $20
06/26/46 Joe Garagiola $25
07/03/46 Veeck buys the Indians $20
07/10/46 Bill Veeck, All-Star issue $50
07/17/46 Ted Williams $40
07/24/46 Larry MacPhail $20
07/31/46 Hal Newhouser $25
08/07/46 Dizzy Dean $25
08/14/46 M. Owen, Mexican League $20
08/21/46 Mickey Owen $20

08/28/46 Feller's 98 mph pitch	$30
09/04/46 Larry MacPhail	$20
09/11/46 Jackie Robinson	$50
09/18/46 Mickey Vernon, Ted Williams	$30
09/25/46 Stan Musial, Ted Williams	$60
10/02/46 Eddie Collins	$20
10/09/46 Frankie Frisch, World Series	$60
10/16/46 DiMaggio, Gordon, MacPhail	$50
10/23/46 Harry Brecheen, World Series	$50
10/30/46 TSN 60-year chronology	$250
11/06/46 Bob Feller	$25
11/13/46 Bucky Harris	$20
11/20/46 Ted Williams MVP	$50
11/27/46 Stan Musial MVP	$50
12/04/46 Leo Durocher	$40
12/18/46 Walter Johnson	$40
12/25/46 Billy Evans	$20

1947

01/01/47 Dyer, Musial, Yawkey	$60
01/08/47 Little stars	$20
01/15/47 Joe DiMaggio	$40
01/22/47 Branch Rickey	$30
01/29/47 Bob Feller	$30
02/05/47 Pepper Martin	$25
02/12/47 Sam Breadon, Stan Musial	$25
02/19/47 Hank Greenberg	$25
02/26/47 Hornsby, McKechnie, Speaker	$25
03/05/47 Stan Musial, Ted Williams	$40
03/12/47 Leo Durocher, Happy Chandler	$40
03/19/47 Leo Durocher, Larry MacPhail	$40
03/26/47 Chandler, Durocher, MacPhail	$40
04/02/47 Hank Greenberg	$30
04/09/47 Yogi Berra, Joe Medwick	$25
04/16/47 Leo Durocher	$60
04/23/47 Babe Ruth	$300

04/30/47 Pete Reiser	$20
05/07/47 Babe Ruth Day	$50
05/14/47 Hank Greenberg	$25
05/21/47 Johnny Mize	$25
05/28/47 Hal Chase	$20
06/04/47 Dugout jockeys	$20
06/11/47 George McQuinn	$20
06/18/47 Bobby Thomson	$22
06/25/47 Warren Spahn	$35
07/02/47 Ewell Blackwell	$20
07/09/47 Phil Wrigley, All-Star issue	$60
07/16/47 Larry Doby	$60
07/23/47 Bobo Newsom	$25
07/30/47 Hall of Fame inductees	$25
08/06/47 Burt Shotton	$20
08/13/47 Harry The Hat Walker	$20
08/20/47 Stan Musial	$35
08/27/47 Connie Mack	$25
09/03/47 Dan Bankhead	$25

09/10/47 Frank McCormick	$20
09/17/47 Jackie Robinson	$75
09/24/47 Dixie and Harry Walker	$20
10/01/47 Bucky Harris, Burt Shotton	$75
10/08/47 Joe McCarthy, Tom Yawkey	$60

10/15/47 George Weiss	$50
10/22/47 Joe Kuhel	$20
10/29/47 Larry MacPhail	$20
11/05/47 Red Ruffing	$20
11/12/47 Muddy Ruel, Zack Taylor	$20
11/19/47 Snuffy Stirnweiss	$20
11/26/47 Bob Elliott	$20
12/03/47 Joe DiMaggio	$50
12/10/47 Sam Breadon	$25
12/17/47 Leo Durocher	$25
12/24/47 Hugh Casey	$20
12/31/47 Harris, Rickey, T. Williams	$75

1948

01/07/48 Phil Masi	$35
01/14/48 Stars' salaries	$20
01/21/48 Sam Breadon	$20
01/28/48 Bob Feller, Bill Veeck	$30
02/04/48 Joe McCarthy	$20
02/11/48 Herb Pennock	$20
02/18/48 Eddie Miller	$20
02/25/48 Spring training	$20
03/03/48 Herb Pennock, Pie Traynor	$25
03/10/48 Joe McCarthy	$22
03/17/48 Pat Seerey	$20
03/24/48 Babe Ruth	$30
03/31/48 Pesky, McCarthy, Stephens	$22
04/07/48 Hank Greenberg	$30
04/14/48 Joe McCarthy	$22
04/21/48 1948 predictions	$50
04/28/48 Dixie Walker	$20
05/05/48 Schoolboy Rowe	$20
05/12/48 Bill Meyer	$20
05/19/48 Blackwell, Branca, Feller, Newhouser	$30
05/26/48 Ken Keltner	$20
06/02/48 Stan Musial	$35
06/09/48 50 Home Run Club	$30
06/16/48 Yankee Stadium's 25th anniversary	$25
06/23/48 Babe Ruth	$300
06/30/48 Ted Williams	$40
07/07/48 Bob Lemon	$20
07/14/48 Roy Campanella	$40
07/21/48 Vic Raschi	$25
07/28/48 Leo Durocher	$22
08/04/48 Joe Tinker	$20
08/11/48 Tinker, Evers, Chance	$22
08/18/48 Lou Boudreau	$24
08/25/48 Babe Ruth	$500
09/01/48 Carl Erskine	$100

09/08/48 Phil Rizzuto... $22
09/15/48 Richie Ashburn $22
09/22/48 Satchel Paige $25
09/29/48 B. Southworth, G. Stallings $20
10/06/48 1914 Braves, World Series $50
10/13/48 TSN All-Star team, World Series $50
10/20/48 Casey Stengel, George Weiss $20
10/27/48 Casey Stengel $25
11/03/48 Happy Chandler $20
11/10/48 Lefty Gomez $20
11/17/48 Steve O'Neill $20
11/24/48 Red Rolfe..................................... $20
12/01/48 Lou Boudreau $25
12/08/48 Stan Musial $35
12/15/48 Baseball winter meetings $20
12/22/48 Baseball winter meetings $20
12/29/48 Boudreau, Meyer, Veeck................... $40

1949
01/05/49 Pete Reiser $30
01/12/49 20 game winners $18
01/19/49 Earl Torgeson $18
01/26/49 Dick Manville $18
02/02/49 Bill Veeck $20
02/09/49 Murray Dickson $18
02/16/49 Joe DiMaggio, Bob Feller $30
02/23/49 Spring training $18
03/02/49 Honus Wagner $20
03/09/49 Casey Stengel, 1949 Yankees........... $20
03/16/49 Fred Sanford $18
03/23/49 George Earnshaw $18
03/30/49 Joe McCarthy $18
04/06/49 Gene Woodling............................... $18
04/13/49 Joe DiMaggio, Ted Williams $200
04/20/49 Joe DiMaggio................................. $50
04/27/49 Lou Boudreau $20
05/04/49 Chuck Connors $18
05/11/49 Charlie Gehringer $20
05/18/49 Bobby Shantz $18
05/25/49 Sam Breadon $18
06/01/49 Sam Breadon $18
06/08/49 Sam Breadon $18
06/15/49 Mexican Leaguers reinstated $18
06/22/49 Frankie Frisch $18
06/29/49 Ray Boone $18
07/06/49 Joe DiMaggio................................. $50
07/13/49 Ebbets Field, All-Star issue $50
07/20/49 Billy Southworth............................. $20
07/27/49 Casey Stengel $25
08/03/49 Stan Musial $30
08/10/49 Joe Page $25
08/17/49 Luke Appling.................................. $20
08/24/49 Yogi Berra $25
08/31/49 Connie Mack Day $18
09/07/49 Joe DiMaggio................................. $50
09/14/49 Bill Klem...................................... $18
09/21/49 Enos Slaughter $22
09/28/49 Billy Southworth............................. $18
10/05/49 Enos Slaughter, Ted Williams $50
10/12/49 Casey Stengel, World Series............. $45
10/19/49 Branch Rickey, World Series $50
10/26/49 Casey Stengel $30
11/02/49 Phil Rizzuto................................... $20
11/09/49 Leo Durocher $18
11/16/49 Yogi Berra, Joe Garagiola................. $25
11/23/49 Jackie Robinson $40
11/30/49 Ted Williams $40
12/07/49 Vern Stephens, Ted Williams............. $25

12/14/49 Bobby Thomson $18
12/21/49 TSN All-Star team $20
12/28/49 Carpenter, Stengel, Williams............. $60

1950
01/04/50 Joe DiMaggio $35
01/11/50 Branch Rickey $18
01/18/50 Bob Dillinger $18
01/25/50 Virgil Trucks $18
02/01/50 Jackie Robinson $25
02/08/50 Gerry Priddy $18
02/15/50 Ty Cobb $30
02/22/50 Spiraling salaries $18
03/01/50 Hank Greenberg $22
03/08/50 Del Crandall.................................. $20
03/15/50 Branch Rickey $20
03/22/50 Connie Mack.................................. $20
03/29/50 Sam Jethroe $20
04/05/50 Connie Mack.................................. $20
04/12/50 Jackie Jensen, Billy Martin $25
04/19/50 B. Rickey, Jackie Robinson................ $35
04/26/50 Luke Easter $20
05/03/50 Jack Banta $20
05/10/50 Yogi Berra $25
05/17/50 Edward Barrow $18
05/24/50 Ty Cobb $25
05/31/50 Robin Roberts, Curt Simmons $20
06/07/50 Phil Rizzuto $20
06/14/50 Bob Feller $25
06/21/50 Boston 29, Browns 4 .... $18
06/28/50 Joe McCarthy $20
07/05/50 George Kell $20
07/12/50 Babe Ruth, All-Star game.................. $50
07/19/50 Luke Easter $25
07/26/50 Ty Cobb, Babe Ruth $30
08/02/50 Casey Stengel $25
08/09/50 Eddie Collins, Larry Lajoie................ $18
08/16/50 Sam Jethroe $18
08/23/50 Vern Bickford $25
08/30/50 Preacher Roe $20
09/06/50 Hank Bauer $18
09/13/50 Gil Hodges.................................... $20
09/20/50 Lou Boudreau $20
09/27/50 Sal Maglie.................................... $20
10/04/50 Branch Rickey, World Series $50
10/11/50 Whitey Ford, World Series................. $50
10/18/50 Jerry Coleman, World Series $40
10/25/50 Connie Mack.................................. $18
11/01/50 Walter O'Malley, Branch Rickey........... $25
11/08/50 Jim Konstanty, Phil Rizzuto $20
11/15/50 Grover Cleveland Alexander............... $30
11/22/50 Honus Wagner................................ $22
11/29/50 Al Lopez $18
12/06/50 Baseball winter meetings $18
12/13/50 Marty Marion $18
12/20/50 Happy Chandler............................... $18
12/27/50 Happy Chandler............................... $18

1951
01/03/51 Rizzuto, Rolfe, Weiss....................... $40
01/10/51 Yogi Berra, Phil Rizzuto $25
01/17/51 Phil Rizzuto $20
01/24/51 Tom Henrich $18
01/31/51 Mickey Mantle................................ $100
02/07/51 Jimmie Foxx, Mel Ott........................ $25
02/14/51 National Leagues 75th $25
02/21/51 Happy Chandler............................... $18
02/28/51 Stan Musial $25
03/07/51 Red Ruffin $18

03/14/51 Stan Musial..................................... $25	06/18/52 Rogers Hornsby, Bill Veeck.................. $18
03/21/51 Happy Chandler............................. $18	06/25/52 Jimmy Piersall............................... $15
03/28/51 Fred Clarke.................................... $18	07/02/52 Carl Erskine.................................. $15
04/04/51 Mickey Mantle.............................. $50	07/09/52 Leo Durocher, Casey Stengel............ $35
04/11/51 Bobby Avila................................... $25	07/16/52 Solly Hemus................................. $20
04/18/51 Play Ball....................................... $40	07/23/52 Clark Griffith................................ $16
04/25/51 Mickey Mantle............................. $300	07/30/52 Clark Griffith................................ $16
05/02/51 Grover Alexander.......................... $25	08/06/52 Clark Griffith................................ $16
05/09/51 Leo Durocher............................... $18	08/13/52 Jackie Jensen............................... $16
05/16/51 Gil McDougald.............................. $18	08/20/52 Bill Veeck................................... $18
05/23/51 Leo Durocher............................... $20	08/27/52 Bill Loes.................................... $16
05/30/51 Furillo, Hodges, Robinson, Snider......... $35	09/03/52 Robin Roberts.............................. $16
06/06/51 Branch Rickey............................... $18	09/10/52 Early Wynn.................................. $18
06/13/51 Ed Lopat...................................... $18	09/17/52 Hank Sauer.................................. $16
06/20/51 Minnie Minoso.............................. $18	09/24/52 Joe Black, Clint Courtney................. $16
06/27/51 Walter OMalley, Buzzie Bavasi........... $20	10/01/52 1941 Dodgers, World Series.............. $40
07/04/51 1926 Cardinals.............................. $18	10/08/52 1952 Yankees, 1952 Dodgers............ $40
07/11/51 Cobb, Cochrane, Gehringer............... $50	10/15/52 Johnny Mize, World Series................ $40
07/18/51 Roy Campanella............................ $25	10/22/52 Mickey Mantle.............................. $40
07/25/51 Allie Reynolds............................... $18	10/29/52 Phil Rizzuto................................. $18
08/01/51 Dizzy and Paul Dean...................... $20	11/05/52 Frank Lane, Bill Veeck.................... $16
08/08/51 1951 Dodgers............................... $25	11/12/52 Mickey Mantle.............................. $50
08/15/51 Willie Mays.................................. $50	11/19/52 Duke Snider................................. $25
08/22/51 Charlie Gehringer.......................... $30	11/26/52 TSN All-Star team.......................... $20
08/29/51 Bob Feller.................................... $30	12/03/52 Del Webb................................... $16
09/05/51 Casey Stengel.............................. $30	12/10/52 Jackie Robinson............................ $25
09/12/51 Johnny Sain................................. $18	12/17/52 Ferris Fain.................................. $16
09/19/51 Bobby Thomson............................ $25	12/24/52 Johnny Allen................................ $16
09/26/51 Bill Klem..................................... $18	12/31/52 Roberts, Stanky, Weiss................... $30

1953

10/03/51 Home Run Baker, World Series............ $50	01/07/53 1952 Baseball thrills section.............. $30
10/10/51 Fain, Feller, Musial, Roe................. $200	01/14/53 Johnny Mize................................. $18
10/17/51 Warren Giles, World Series................ $45	01/21/53 Eddie Stanky............................... $16
10/24/51 Gabe Paul.................................... $18	01/28/53 Johnny Mize................................. $18
10/31/51 Lou Boudreau............................... $20	02/04/53 Dizzy Dean, Al Simmons................. $20
11/07/51 Alvin Dark.................................... $18	02/11/53 Ed Yost.................................... $16
11/14/51 Stan Musial, Ted Williams................ $45	02/18/53 Eddie Robinson............................ $16
11/21/51 Yogi Berra.................................... $25	02/25/53 August A. Busch Jr........................ $16
11/28/51 Gil Hodges................................... $20	03/04/53 Russ Meyer................................. $16
12/05/51 Bill Bevins................................... $18	03/11/53 Mickey Grasso............................. $16
12/12/51 Minnie Minoso.............................. $25	03/18/53 Browns move to Baltimore, Braves move to
12/19/51 Joe DiMaggio.............................. $100	Milwaukee.................................... $16
12/26/51 Joe DiMaggio............................... $40	03/25/53 Braves and Browns shift.................. $16

1952

01/02/52 Durocher, Musial, Weiss................... $75	04/01/53 Garcia, Lemon, Wynn...................... $20
01/09/52 Leo Durocher, Eddie Stanky............. $18	04/08/53 Casey Stengel............................. $18
01/16/52 Tommy Holmes.............................. $16	04/15/53 Play Ball................................... $30
01/23/52 Walter Briggs................................ $16	04/22/53 Milwaukee opener.......................... $16
01/30/52 Gus Zernial.................................. $16	04/29/53 Mickey Mantle.............................. $100
02/06/52 Negro ballplayers........................... $30	05/06/53 Clint Courtney, Billy Martin.............. $16
02/13/52 Ralph Branca, Bobby Thomson........... $30	05/13/53 Bobo Holloman............................ $16
02/20/52 Johnny Mize................................. $20	05/20/53 Cobb, Mize, Slaughter.................... $20
02/27/52 Paul Waner.................................. $16	05/27/53 Dave Philley............................... $16
03/05/52 Casey Stengel.............................. $18	06/03/53 Roy Campanella............................ $25
03/12/52 Dickey, DiMaggio, Ruth................... $30	06/10/53 Hoyt Wilhelm............................... $16
03/19/52 Ty Cobb..................................... $25	06/17/53 Mickey Mantle.............................. $45
03/26/52 Ty Cobb..................................... $25	06/24/53 1953 Yankees winning streak............. $16
04/02/52 Clem Labine................................. $16	
04/09/52 Monte Irvin.................................. $18	
04/16/52 Play Ball..................................... $40	
04/23/52 Wilmer Mizell............................... $16	
04/30/52 Walter O'Malley............................. $20	
05/07/52 Walter O'Malley............................. $20	
05/14/52 Ty Cobb..................................... $22	
05/21/52 Jackie Jensen............................... $15	
05/28/52 Dale Mitchell................................ $15	
06/04/52 Davey Williams.............................. $15	
06/11/52 Ty Cobb, Rogers Hornsby................. $25	

07/01/53 Mickey Mantle, Ed Mathews $45
07/08/53 Doby, Easter, Rosen $20
07/15/53 C. Dressen, C. Stengel $30
07/22/53 Carl Furillo, Monte Irvin $20
07/29/53 Robin Roberts $18
08/05/53 Ted Williams $30
08/12/53 Mickey Vernon $18
08/19/53 Allie Reynolds $18
08/26/53 1953 Dodger sluggers $20
09/02/53 Vic Raschi, Preacher Roe $18
09/09/53 Red Schoendienst $18
09/16/53 Ed Mathews $25
09/23/53 Yankees, Dodgers clinch $20
09/30/53 1949-53 Yankees, World Series issue $45
10/07/53 Junior Gilliam, Harvey Kuenn $20
10/14/53 Bill Veeck, World Series $40
10/21/53 Rogers Hornsby $18
10/28/53 Rogers Hornsby $18
11/04/53 Jimmy Piersall $18
11/11/53 Nap Lajoie $18
11/18/53 Jimmie Dykes $18
11/25/53 Eddie Joost $18
12/02/53 Atlanta Crackers $16
12/09/53 Walter Alston $18
12/16/53 Bob Feller $20
12/23/53 Ed Barrow $16
12/30/53 Perini, Rosen, Stengel $35

1954

01/06/54 1953 Baseball thrills $20
01/13/54 Bobo Newsom $16
01/20/54 Danny O'Connell $16
01/27/54 Dickey, Maranville, Terry $20
02/03/54 Spring training $16
02/10/54 Bobby Thomson $18
02/17/54 Paul Krichell $16
02/24/54 Willie Mays $30
03/03/54 Enos Slaughter $16
03/10/54 Johnny Antonelli $16
03/17/54 Walter Alston $18
03/24/54 J.A. Robert Quinn $16
03/31/54 Don Newcombe $18
04/07/54 1954 Dodgers $16
04/14/54 Baseball returns to Baltimore $35
04/21/54 Ted Williams $30
04/28/54 Hal Jeffcoat $16
05/05/54 Bucky Harris $16
05/12/54 Stan Musial $75
05/19/54 Johnny Temple $16
05/26/54 Gene Baker, Ernie Banks $22
06/02/54 Art Houtteman $16
06/09/54 Ed Lopat $16
06/16/54 Roy Campanella $25
06/23/54 Hornsby, Musial, Wagner $25
06/30/54 Frank Thomas $16

07/07/54 Willie Mays, Duke Snider $45
07/14/54 Dusty Rhodes, All-Star issue $30
07/21/54 Willie Mays $35
07/28/54 Eddie Stanky $16
08/04/54 Bob Feller $25
08/11/54 Branch Rickey $16
08/18/54 Bob Lemon $16
08/25/54 Don Mueller $16
09/01/54 Jack Harshman $16
09/08/54 Smokey Burgess $16
09/15/54 Johnny Antonelli, Willie Mays $50
09/22/54 Casey Stengel $18
09/29/54 L. Durocher, A. Lopez $45
10/06/54 B. Grim, W. Moon, World Series $25
10/13/54 Antonelli, Avila, Lemon, Mays $100
10/20/54 Pinky Higgins $16
10/27/54 Connie Mack $16
11/03/54 Joe McCarthy $16
11/10/54 Joe McCarthy $16
11/17/54 A's move to Kansas City $16
11/24/54 Joe Garagiola $16
12/01/54 Bob Turley $16
12/08/54 Bob Feller $15
12/15/54 TSN All-Star team $20
12/22/54 Ted Kluszweski $18
12/29/54 Stan Lopata $16

1955

01/05/55 Durocher, Mays, Stoneham $60
01/12/55 Nellie Fox $16
01/19/55 Ken Boyer $18
01/26/55 Joe Nuxhall $16
02/02/55 DiMaggio, Hartnett, Lyons, Vance $25
02/09/55 Home Run Baker, Ray Schalk $16
02/16/55 Home Run Baker $16
02/23/55 Sad Sam Jones $16
03/02/55 Roy Campanella $20
03/09/55 Jim Busby $16
03/16/55 Gil Hodges $18
03/23/55 Herb Score $16
03/30/55 Mike Higgins $16
04/06/55 Warren Spahn $20
04/13/55 Ken Boyer, Herb Score $35
04/20/55 Ralph Kiner $18
04/27/55 25 game winners $16
05/04/55 1955 Yankees $20
05/11/55 Don Mueller $16
05/18/55 Harvey Kuenn $16
05/25/55 Duke Snider $20
06/01/55 Harry Chiti $16
06/08/55 Al Kaline $25
06/15/55 Yogi Berra, Roy Campanella $25
06/22/55 Don Newcombe $25
06/29/55 Jim Konstanty $16
07/06/55 Dick Donovan $16
07/13/55 Stan Musial, All-Star issue $30
07/20/55 Ernie Banks $25
07/27/55 Preacher Roe $20
08/03/55 Sherm Lollar $50
08/10/55 Spitball debate $16
08/17/55 Jimmy Piersall $16
08/24/55 Del Ennis $16
08/31/55 Hank Bauer $18
09/07/55 Al Smith $16
09/14/55 Mickey Mantle $30
09/21/55 Don Mossi, Ray Narleski $18
09/28/55 Previous Yankees/Dodgers World Series $60
10/05/55 Herb Score, Bill Virdon $25

10/12/55 Johnny Podres, World Series $200
10/19/55 Ford, Kaline, Roberts, Snider $35
10/26/55 Roy Campanella $20
11/02/55 Clark Griffith $16
11/09/55 Bobby Bragan $16
11/16/55 Cy Young $18
11/23/55 Double play combos $16
11/30/55 Bucky Walters $16
12/07/55 TSN All-Star team $18
12/14/55 Roy Campanella $20
12/21/55 Earl Torgeson $16
12/28/55 Bob Feller $20

1956

01/04/56 Alston, O'Malley, Snider............................ $60
01/11/56 Gil Coan $14
01/18/56 Randy Jackson $14
01/25/56 Pepper Martin $14
02/01/56 Joe Cronin, Hank Greenberg $15
02/08/56 Joe Cronin, Hank Greenberg $18
02/15/56 Connie Mack... $16
02/22/56 Calvin Griffith $14
02/29/56 Robin Roberts $16
03/07/56 Hank Greenberg $18
03/14/56 Vern Law $14
03/21/56 Greatest players from 1946-55 .... $25
03/28/56 Stan Musial $25
04/04/56 Earl Averill $14
04/11/56 Marty Marion $14
04/18/56 Yankees vs. Dodgers $35
04/25/56 Minnie Minoso $14
05/02/56 Top relievers $14
05/09/56 Bob Friend $14
05/16/56 Bill Sarni $14
05/23/56 Vic Wertz $14
05/30/56 Dale Long $14
06/06/56 Murray Dickson....................................... $14
06/13/56 Mickey Mantle $75
06/20/56 Gabe Paul... $14
06/27/56 Alvin Dark $14
07/04/56 DiMaggio, Musial, Williams........................ $100
07/11/56 Stan Musial $100
07/18/56 Gabe Paul, All-Star issue $20
07/25/56 Tigers sold for $5.5 million...................... $20
08/01/56 Bill Skowron $20
08/08/56 Fred Haney $14
08/15/56 Ted Williams $25
08/22/56 Braves pitchers $20
08/29/56 Joe Adcock $20
09/05/56 Luis Aparicio, Frank Robinson $25
09/12/56 The home run $20
09/19/56 Birdie Tebbetts $25
09/26/56 Babe Ruth $45
10/03/56 C. Stengel, World Series issue $60
10/10/56 Aaron, Mantle, Newcombe, Pierce $50
10/17/56 Don Larsen $400
10/24/56 Luis Aparicio, Frank Robinson $20
10/31/56 No-hit pitchers $14
11/07/56 Al Lopez $14
11/14/56 Mickey Mantle $30
11/21/56 Frank Lary $30
11/28/56 Mickey Mantle $30
12/05/56 Baseball's 5 greatest feats........................ $15
12/12/56 Bob Scheffing $14
12/19/56 Jackie Robinson $14
12/26/56 Harvey Kuenn.. $14

1957

01/02/57 Mantle, Paul, Tebbetts $75

01/09/57 Bob Feller $18
01/16/57 Jackie Robinson $20
01/23/57 Mickey Mantle, George Weiss........................ $30
01/30/57 Duke Snider... $18
02/06/57 Stan Musial $20
02/13/57 Sam Crawford, Joe McCarthy $15
02/20/57 Ted Williams $25
02/27/57 Yankees/A's trade $14
03/06/57 Phil Rizzuto $15
03/13/57 Gil Hodges.. $15
03/20/57 Frank Sullivan $14
03/27/57 Marv Throneberry $14
04/03/57 Ty Cobb $16
04/10/57 Ted Williams $20
04/17/57 Tony Kubek, Andre Rodgers $30
04/24/57 Roy Campanella $20
05/01/57 Roger Maris $25
05/08/57 Tom Yawkey $14
05/15/57 Ted Williams $25
05/22/57 Ted Williams $20
05/29/57 Whitey Ford $18
06/05/57 Dodgers, Giants to move.............................. $25
06/12/57 Walter O'Malley $14
06/19/57 Stan Musial $20
06/26/57 Baseball brawls, beanballs $14
07/03/57 Danny McDevitt $14
07/10/57 Stan Musial, Ted Williams $30
07/17/57 Ford Frick.. $15
07/24/57 Yankees' success system $14
07/31/57 Giants to move to San Francisco.................... $14
08/07/57 Polo Grounds history $15
08/14/57 Polo Grounds history $20
08/21/57 Roy Sievers $14
08/28/57 Giants shift $14
09/04/57 Nellie Fox $14
09/11/57 Frank Malzone $14
09/18/57 Walt Moryn $14
09/25/57 Al Kaline $20
10/02/57 W. Spahn, World Series issue $35
10/09/57 Stan Musial, Ted Williams $35
10/16/57 Dodgers to move to L. A............................. $30
10/23/57 Lew Burdette $14
10/30/57 L.A. franchise battle................................ $15
11/06/57 Yogi Berra $18
11/13/57 Yogi Berra $18
11/20/57 Frank Lane $14
11/27/57 Frank Lane $20
12/04/57 Baseball winter meetings $14
12/11/57 MVP balloting $14
12/18/57 Al Lopez $14
12/25/57 L.A. Dodgers $15

1958

01/01/58 Hutchinson, Lane, Williams $35
01/08/58 Mickey Mantle, Ted Williams........................ $15
01/15/58 Ed Mathews $18
01/22/58 Frank Lane, George Weiss $14
01/29/58 L.A. Dodgers $14
02/05/58 Roy Campanella $20
02/12/58 Stars salaries then and now $14
02/19/58 Billy Martin $15
02/26/58 Willie Mays $20
03/05/58 Gil Hodges, Duke Snider $18
03/12/58 Deron Johnson $14
03/19/58 Leadoff hitters...................................... $14
03/26/58 1958 Braves $15
04/02/58 1958 Giants $15
04/09/58 1958 batting race.................................... $15

04/16/58 California here we come $30
04/23/58 Eisenhower at season opener $14
04/30/58 L.A. Dodgers $16
05/07/58 Chinese home runs $14
05/14/58 Stan Musial... $60
05/21/58 Branch Rickey $14
05/28/58 1958 Yankee pitchers $14
06/04/58 San Francisco Giants $14
06/11/58 Ryne Duren $14
06/18/58 Yankees/Kansas City trades $14
06/25/58 Walter O'Malley $14
07/02/58 Gabe Paul... $14
07/09/58 All-Time All-Stars............................... $25
07/16/58 Casey Stengel $15
07/23/58 Jackie Jensen $14
07/30/58 Phil Wrigley.. $14
08/06/58 Bob Turley... $14
08/13/58 Philly Whiz Kids $14
08/20/58 Yankees old-timers $15
08/27/58 Ted Williams $25
09/03/58 Ernie Banks $18
09/10/58 Banks, Jensen, Spahn, Turley $16
09/17/58 Pete Runnels $14
09/24/58 Aaron, Ashburn, Mays, Musial............. $35
10/01/58 G. Weiss, World Series issue $30
10/08/58 Top Rookies in 1958 .... $16
10/15/58 Player/managers, World Series $25
10/22/58 Mighty Mites $14
10/29/58 Casey Stengel $15
11/05/58 Stan Musial.. $20
11/12/58 Max Carey $14
11/19/58 Lee MacPhail $14
11/26/58 Houston bids for franchise $14
12/03/58 Baseball winter meetings..................... $14
12/10/58 Will Harridge $14
12/17/58 Joe Cronin, Will Harridge $14
12/24/58 New York Yankees' homes $14
12/31/58 Brown, Stengel, Turley......................... $25

1959
01/07/59 Will Harridge $14
01/14/59 Marty Marion $14
01/21/59 Bill Norman.. $14
01/28/59 Willie Mays $20
02/04/59 Soaring player salaries $14
02/11/59 Zack Wheat $14
02/18/59 Spring training $14
02/25/59 Bill Veeck $15
03/04/59 Durocher, Frisch, McGraw, Stallings...... $15
03/11/59 Solly Hemus $14
03/18/59 Frank Lary $14
03/25/59 Ty Cobb $18
04/01/59 Don Mossi, Ray Narleski $14
04/08/59 Play Ball... $25
04/15/59 HOF historian Lee Allen $14
04/22/59 Clint Courtney $14
04/29/59 Woodie Held $14
05/06/59 Paul Richards $14
05/13/59 1959 Yankees' woes $14
05/20/59 Ernie Banks $18
05/27/59 1925 Yankees $14
06/03/59 Hank Aaron $20
06/10/59 Rocky Colavito, Ed Mathews $16
06/07/59 Hoyt Wilhelm $14
06/24/59 Roy Face $14
07/01/59 Harmon Killebrew $15
07/08/59 Carl Hubbell, Ted Williams................... $25
07/15/59 Billy Jurges $14

07/22/59 Senators sluggers $14
07/29/59 Orioles staff $14
08/05/59 Don Drysdale...................................... $15
08/12/59 Willie McCovey $20
08/19/59 Eppa Rixey $14
08/26/59 Al Lopez $14
09/02/59 Ty Cobb $18
09/09/59 1959 White Sox, Bill Veeck $20
09/16/59 Tony Cuccinello, Al Lopez $14
09/23/59 1959 Yankees fall................................ $15
09/30/59 Bill Veeck, World Series issue $30
10/07/59 Early Wynn $15
10/14/59 1959 World Series summary $25
10/21/59 Larry Sherry $14
10/28/59 Wally Moon $14
11/04/59 Chuck Dressen $14
11/11/59 TSNs 1959 All-Stars $18
11/18/59 Nellie Fox... $15
11/25/59 Bob Allison $14
12/02/59 Baseball winter meetings $14
12/09/59 Stan Musial, Ted Williams $15
12/16/59 Billy Jurges $15
12/23/59 Hall of Fame first basemen.................. $18
12/30/59 Alston, Bavasi, Wynn........................... $30

1960
01/06/60 Walter Alston $14
01/13/60 Joe Cronin $12
01/20/60 Willie Mays $25
01/27/60 Clark Griffith $12
02/03/60 Johnny Temple $12
02/10/60 Rice, Rixey, Roush $12
02/17/60 Ernie Banks $18
02/24/60 Walter O'Malley $12
03/02/60 Pete Reiser $12
03/09/60 1960 White Sox $12
03/16/60 Walter Alston $12
03/23/60 Chuck Dressen $12
03/30/60 1960 Yankees analysis $15
04/06/60 Eddie Lopat $12
04/13/60 Play Ball... $25
04/20/60 Johnson, Mathewson, Spahn, Wynn, Young $20
04/27/60 Rocky Colavito, Harvey Kuenn $14
05/04/60 Bill DeWitt.. $12
05/11/60 Ken Boyer $12
05/18/60 Lou Boudreau $12
05/25/60 Roger Maris $25
06/01/60 Bill Veeck $12
06/08/60 Frank Howard $12
06/15/60 Bill Mazeroski $13
06/22/60 Comiskey dynasty $12
06/29/60 Ted Williams $40
07/06/60 Roberto Clemente $25
07/13/60 Roger Maris, All-Star issue................... $25
07/20/60 New franchises for 1962 .... $15
07/27/60 Del Crandall $12
08/03/60 Cookie Lavagetto $12
08/10/60 Jim Piersall, Casey Stengel $12
08/17/60 Ted Williams $100
08/24/60 Dick Groat.. $12
08/31/60 Dick Groat, Roger Maris $20
09/07/60 Roy Sievers $12
09/14/60 1890s stars $12
09/21/60 Hemus, Lavagetto, Murtaugh, Richards $12
09/28/60 Stan Musial... $25
10/05/60 '27 Yankees, World Series issue $30
10/12/60 M. Fornieles, L. McDaniel $15
10/19/60 B. Richardson, World Series $25

10/26/60 Casey Stengel $15
11/02/60 American League expansion $12
11/09/60 George Weiss $12
11/16/60 Roger Maris $25
11/23/60 Roy Harney $12
11/30/60 Baseball winter meetings........................ $12
12/07/60 Ralph Houk $12
12/14/60 Los Angeles Angels $12
12/21/60 John Galbreath $12
12/28/60 Billy Bruton $12

1961

01/04/61 Mazeroski, Murtaugh, Weiss $30
01/11/61 Ted Kluszewski $13
01/18/61 Dazzy Vance, Johnny Vander Meer........ $12
01/25/61 Max Carey, Billy Hamilton $12
02/01/61 Walter Alston $12
02/08/61 Lindy McDaniel $12
02/15/61 Stars' swan songs $14
02/22/61 Max Carey $12
03/01/61 Ralph Houk $12
03/08/61 Leo Durocher.. $13
03/15/61 Yankees, Tigers outfielders.................... $15
03/22/61 Joe DiMaggio.. $18
03/29/61 Mickey Mantle $30
04/05/61 1961 managers $12
04/12/61 Presidents/Opening Day......................... $40
04/19/61 Willie Davis, Carl Yastrzemski $30
04/26/61 Whitey Ford $16
05/03/61 Babe Herman $14
05/10/61 Wally Moon $25
05/17/61 Jim Gentile... $14
05/24/61 Alvin Dark $14
05/31/61 Charles Finley... $14
06/07/61 Pitching coach Jim Turner $14
06/14/61 Johnny Temple $14
06/21/61 Sandy Koufax $20
06/28/61 Mickey Mantle, Roger Maris $100
07/05/61 300 game winners $20
07/12/61 Cash, Cepeda, Ford, Jay, Koufax, Mantle,
   Maris, F. Robinson $60
07/19/61 George Weiss $20
07/26/61 Ty Cobb $50
08/02/61 Red Sox immortals $40
08/09/61 Ford Frick $25
08/16/61 Elston Howard $15
08/23/61 Whitey Ford $25
08/30/61 Top 1961 rookies $30
09/06/61 Mickey Mantle, Roger Maris $75
09/13/61 Arroyo, Ford, Spahn............................... $40
09/20/61 Ralph Houk $40
09/27/61 Mantle, Maris, Ruth $100
10/04/61 1939 Yanks vs. Reds, World Series........ $50
10/11/61 Casey Stengel, N.Y. Mets $200
10/18/61 Hail to the champs $45
10/25/61 Yogi Berra $15
11/01/61 Top 1961 rookies $15
11/08/61 Ron Santo $12
11/15/61 Johnny Temple $12
11/22/61 Roger Maris $60
11/29/61 Baseball winter meetings........................ $12
12/06/61 Walter O'Malley $12
12/13/61 Ty Cobb $14
12/20/61 Best No. 2 hitters $14
12/27/61 George Sisler.. $12

1962

01/03/62 Houk, Maris, Spahn, Topping $40
01/10/62 Al Kaline $18

01/17/62 Rogers Hornsby $14
01/24/62 Hall of Fame candidates......................... $15
01/31/62 Pie Traynor $12
02/07/62 Elston Howard $13
02/14/62 Gil Hodges $13
02/21/62 Sophomore jinx $12
02/28/62 Roger Maris $18

03/07/62 Mantle, Mays, Musial, Spahn, Williams $50
03/14/62 Hall of Famers who stayed with one team............ $25
03/21/62 Braves infielders $12
03/28/62 Ray Schalk $12
04/04/62 Minnie Minoso $12
04/11/62 Play Ball.. $20
04/18/62 1962 Giants $12
04/25/62 Ford Frick $12
05/02/62 Felipe and Matty Alou... $12
05/09/62 Casey Stengel $12
05/16/62 Ralph Terry $12
05/23/62 Sandy Koufax $15
06/02/62 Luis Aparicio, Dick Howser $12
06/09/62 1962 Giants pitchers $12
06/16/62 Bob Purkey $12
06/23/62 Carl Sawatski... $12
06/30/62 Don Drysdale... $14
07/07/62 All-Star goats $18
07/14/62 Maury Wills $12
07/21/62 Davis, Mantle, Mays, Wagner $25
07/28/62 Chicago Cubs immortals $20
08/04/62 Bob Gibson $20
08/11/62 1962 Reds $12
08/18/62 Yogi Berra $20
08/25/62 Juan Marichal $20
09/01/62 Tom Tresh $12
09/08/62 New York Mets $20
09/15/62 Ron Fairly, Frank Howard $12
09/22/62 Donovan, Mantle, Marichal, Wills $20
09/29/62 George Weiss $12
10/06/62 W. O'Malley, World Series issue $20
10/13/62 Ralph Houk $20
10/20/62 1962 baseball thrills.. $20
10/27/62 Ken Hubbs, Tom Tresh $20
11/03/62 Birdie Tebbetts... $12
11/10/62 Brooks and Frank Robinson $30
11/17/62 Don Drysdale $14
11/24/62 Stan Musial.. $18
12/01/62 George Sisler Jr.. $12
12/08/62 Tom Tresh $12
12/15/62 Jack Sanford $12
12/22/62 Walter O'Malley $12
12/29/62 Don Drysdale, Maury Wills................................... $25

1963

01/05/63 1962 World Series Game 7 .... $12-$15
01/12/63 Top rookie prospects .... $10-$14

01/19/63 Jim Piersall $12
01/26/63 Dean Chance .... $10-$12
02/02/63 Sam Mele .... $10-$12
02/09/63 Chicago White Sox $12
02/16/63 Sandy Koufax .... $15-$16
02/23/63 Johnny Pesky .... $10-$12
03/02/63 Dan Topping .... $10-$12
03/09/63 Johnny Sain $12
03/16/63 Mickey Mantle, Willie Mays $35
03/23/63 1963 Yankees .... $12-$15
03/30/63 Ralph Terry $12
04/06/63 Don Hoak $12
04/13/63 Play Ball .... $15-$18
04/20/63 Duke Snider .... $14-$15
04/27/63 Ernie Broglio .... $12-$14
05/04/63 T. Kubek, B. Richardson $14
05/11/63 Luis Aparicio, Al Smith .... $12-$13
05/18/63 Cubs pitchers $12
05/25/63 Sandy Koufax .... $15-$16
06/01/63 Ron Fairly $12
06/08/63 Jim Piersall, Casey Stengel .... $12-$15
06/15/63 Gil Hodges .... $13-$15
06/22/63 Billy O'Dell $12
06/29/63 Juan Marichal .... $12-$14
07/06/63 New York Yankees .... $12-$14
07/13/63 Casey Stengel, All-Star issue .... $18-$20
07/20/63 Aaron, Ford, Koufax, Wagner $20
07/27/63 Hal Woodenshick $12
08/03/63 Rich Rollins $12
08/10/63 Frank Malzone, Carl Yastrzemski ... $15-$16
08/17/63 Dick Ellsworth $12
08/24/63 1963 Dodgers $12
08/31/63 Warren Spahn .... $14-$15
09/07/63 Dick Groat $12
09/14/63 Jimmy Hall $12
09/21/63 1963s top rookies .... $14-$15
09/28/63 20 game winners .... $12-$15
10/05/63 Yankees vs. Dodgers/prior World Series .... $20-$25
10/12/63 Aaron, Ford, Kaline, Koufax .... $20-$30
10/19/63 Dodgers sweep the Yankees .... $20-$25
10/26/63 Pete Rose $30
11/02/63 Dick Stuart $12
11/09/63 Yogi Berra .... $14-$15
11/16/63 Carl Yastrzemski .... $15-$16
11/23/63 Hank Aaron .... $12-$18
11/30/63 Elston Howard $12
12/07/63 Rocky Colavito .... $12-$15
12/14/63 Sandy Koufax $25
12/21/63 Leon Wagner $12
12/28/63 Jim Bouton $12

1964

01/04/64 1963 Los Angeles Dodgers $20
01/11/64 Albie Pearson .... $10-$12
01/18/64 Sandy Koufax .... $18-$20
01/25/64 Walter Alston .... $10-$12
02/01/64 Jim Mudcat Grant .... $10-$12
02/08/64 Lum Harris .... $12-$15
02/15/64 Chuck Hinton .... $10-$12
02/22/64 Eddie Mathews .... $12-$15
02/29/64 Casey Stengel .... $12-$15
03/07/64 Burleigh Grimes .... $10-$12
03/14/64 Al Kaline .... $15-$20
03/21/64 Willie McCovey .... $14-$15
03/28/64 Branch Rickey .... $10-$12
04/04/64 Jim Gilliam .... $10-$12
04/11/64 Don Drysdale, Sandy Koufax $20
04/18/64 Play Ball .... $15-$18

04/25/64 Aaron, Mathews, Spahn $20
05/02/64 Cepeda, Mays, McCovey .... $20-$25
05/09/64 Frank Howard .... $10-$12
05/16/64 Tony Oliva $12
05/23/64 Richie Allen $12
05/30/64 Ron Hansen .... $10-$12
06/06/64 Dave Wickersham .... $10-$12
06/13/64 Ron Santo .... $10-$15
06/20/64 Wally Bunker .... $10-$12
06/27/64 Whitey Ford $15
07/04/64 Billy Williams $12
07/11/64 Willie Mays $25
07/25/64 Gene Mauch .... $10-$12
08/01/64 Boog Powell .... $10-$15
08/08/64 Ron Hunt .... $10-$12
08/15/64 Bill Freehan .... $10-$12
08/22/64 Johnny Callison .... $10-$15
08/29/64 B. Allison, H. Killebrew $15
09/05/64 Roberto Clemente .... $20-$30
09/12/64 Elston Howard .... $12-$15
09/19/64 Brooks Robinson .... $15-$20
09/26/64 Ken Boyer .... $12-$15
10/03/64 Dean Chance .... $10-$12
10/10/64 Allen, Bunker, Oliva, World Series $20
10/17/64 Yanks vs. Cardinals, World Series $20
10/24/64 Bing Devine, World Series $20
10/31/64 Johnny Keane .... $10-$15
11/07/64 Ara Parseghian $15
11/14/64 Dick Butkus .... $12-$15
11/21/64 Johnny Unitas .... $12-$15
11/28/64 Bob Pettit $14
12/05/64 Mel Stottlemyre, Harry Walker $10
12/12/64 Jim Brown .... $12-$15
12/19/64 Gino Capelletti $10
12/26/64 Jerry Hill, Jim Parker $9

1965

01/02/65 Ken Boyer, Bob Gibson .... $16-$20
01/09/65 Don Shula, Johnny Unitas .... $14-$18
01/16/65 Red Auerbach $12
01/23/65 Bill Bradley $25
01/30/65 Jerry West .... $12-$15
02/06/65 Baseball to select new commissioner ... $10-$12
02/13/65 Walt Hazzard, Sam Jones $10
02/20/65 Joe Lapchick $9
02/27/65 Spring training .... $10-$15
03/06/65 Bill Bradley $25
03/20/65 Rocky Colavito .... $10-$15
03/13/65 Bill Russell .... $12-$15
03/27/65 Juan Marichal $15
04/03/65 Bo Belinsky, Dick Stuart .... $10-$12
04/10/65 Houston Astrodome .... $10-$12
04/17/65 Play Ball $15
04/24/65 President Johnson visits the Astrodome $12
05/01/65 John Romano .... $10-$12

05/08/65 Eddie Mathews .... $12-$15

05/15/65 Tony Conigliaro .... $10-$20
05/22/65 Frank Robinson $15
05/29/65 White Sox pitchers .... $10-$15
06/05/65 Bob Gibson $15
06/12/65 Felix Mantilla .... $10-$12
06/19/65 Wes Parker .... $10-$12
06/26/65 Vic Davalillo .... $10-$12
07/03/65 Hank Aaron .... $12-$18
07/10/65 Eddie Fisher .... $10-$20
07/17/65 D. Drysdale, S. Koufax .... $20-$30
07/24/65 Willie Horton .... $10-$15
07/31/65 Deron Johnson .... $10-$12
08/07/65 Sonny Siebert .... $10-$12
08/14/65 Richie Allen $12
08/21/65 Pete Rose .... $25-$40
08/28/65 Curt Blefary .... $10-$12
09/04/65 Vern Law .... $10-$12
09/11/65 Sam McDowell .... $10-$12
09/18/65 Jim Bunning .... $10-$15
09/25/65 Sandy Koufax $25
10/02/65 Willie McCovey .... $12-$20
10/09/65 Mudcat Grant, World Series $15
10/16/65 Lou Johnson .... $10-$15
10/23/65 Maury Wills, World Series .... $12-$15
10/30/65 Grant, Koufax, Mays, Oliva .... $20-$25
11/06/65 Cal Griffith $10
11/13/65 Charlie Johnson $10
11/20/65 Paul Lowe $9
11/27/65 Mike Garrett $9
12/04/65 D. Anderson, J. Grabowski $10
12/11/65 All-American Offense $10
12/18/65 Jim Brown $15
12/25/65 Gale Sayers $15

1966

01/01/66 Joe Namath .... $20-$25
01/08/66 Sandy Koufax .... $20-$25
01/15/66 Packers, Vince Lombardi $15
01/22/66 Ted Williams .... $10-$15
02/05/66 Cazzie Russell .... $10-$12
02/12/66 Guy Rodgers $10
02/26/66 Wilt Chamberlain $15
03/05/66 Hank Aguirre .... $10-$12
03/12/66 Cazzie Russell .... $10-$12
03/19/66 Dick Stuart .... $10-$12
03/26/66 Willie Davis .... $10-$12
04/02/66 Camilo Pascual .... $10-$12
04/09/66 Brooks and Frank Robinson .... $20-$25
04/16/66 Atlanta and Anaheim stadiums $15
04/30/66 Braves move to Atlanta .... $10-$12
05/07/66 Larry Brown, Fred Whitfield .... $10-$12
05/14/66 Don Sutton .... $10-$15
05/21/66 Willie Mays .... $20-$25
05/28/66 Luis Tiant .... $10-$15
06/04/66 Rick Reichardt .... $10-$12
06/11/66 Joe Morgan .... $12-$15
06/18/66 Koufax, Marichal .... $18-$25
06/25/66 Sonny Siebert .... $10-$12
07/02/66 Richie Allen .... $10-$12
07/09/66 Jim Northrup .... $10-$15
07/16/66 August A. Busch Jr. .... $12-$15
07/23/66 Gaylord Perry .... $12-$15
07/30/66 Jack Aker .... $10-$15
08/06/66 Woodie Fryman .... $10-$12
08/13/66 Boog Powell .... $10-$15
08/20/66 Orlando Cepeda .... $10-$15
08/27/66 Baltimore Orioles .... $12-$15
09/03/66 Phil Regan .... $10-$12

09/10/66 Jim Kaat .... $10-$12
09/17/66 Willie Stargell .... $14-$15
09/24/66 Felipe and Matty Alou .... $10-$15
10/01/66 Jim Nash .... $10-$12
10/08/66 Hank Bauer, World Series .... $15-$20
10/15/66 Jim Lefebvre .... $10-$20
10/22/66 Luis Aparicio .... $12-$20
10/29/66 Don Meredith .... $12-$15
11/05/66 Terry Hanratty .... $10-$12
11/12/66 George Gross, Keith Lincoln $10
11/19/66 Larry Wilson $10
11/26/66 Johnny Robinson $10
12/03/66 Bob Gladieux $10
12/10/66 Steve Spurrier $15
12/17/66 Bill Russell .... $12-$14
12/24/66 Elijah Pitts $10
12/31/66 Rick Barry $12

1967

01/07/67 Bart Starr $12
01/14/67 Hank Stram $10
01/21/67 Lew Alcindor $12
01/28/67 Alex Hannum $10
02/04/67 Tom & Dick Van Arsdale $10
02/11/67 Mendy Rudolph $12
02/18/67 Harry Howel $12
02/25/67 Baseball cartoons .... $10-$15
03/04/67 Bob Cousy $15
03/11/67 Stan Mikita $15
03/18/67 Hoyt Wilhelm .... $8-$15
03/25/67 Andy Etchebarren .... $8-$12
04/01/67 Chance, Grant, Kaat .... $9-$15
04/08/67 Frank Robinson $15
04/15/67 Play Ball .... $12-$15
04/22/67 Jim Fregosi .... $8-$12
04/29/67 Roger Maris .... $25-$30
05/06/67 Whitey Ford .... $12-$20
05/13/67 Steve Hargan .... $8-$12
05/20/67 Rick Reichardt .... $8-$12
05/27/67 Walter Alston .... $8-$12
06/03/67 Gary Nolan .... $8-$12
06/10/67 Rod Carew .... $10-$20
06/17/67 Juan Marichal .... $9-$15
06/24/67 Al Dark, Eddie Stanky .... $8-$12
07/01/67 Jim Lonborg .... $8-$15
07/08/67 Bob Veale .... $8-$12
07/15/67 J. McGlothlin, All-Star issue .... $12-$15
07/22/67 Tim McCarver .... $10-$15
07/29/67 Tommy John, Gary Peters .... $8-$12
08/05/67 Dick Williams .... $8-$12
08/12/67 Joe Torre .... $9-$12
08/19/67 Paul Blair .... $8-$12
08/26/67 Mike McCormick .... $8-$12
09/02/67 Gil Hodges, Frank Howard .... $9-$15
09/09/67 Rusty Staub .... $8-$15
09/23/67 Carl Yastrzemski .... $15-$30
09/30/67 Earl Wilson .... $8-$12
10/07/67 S. Musial, R. Schoendienst .... $12-$20
10/14/67 Carl Yastrzemski .... $25-$30
10/21/67 Jim Lonborg, World Series .... $15-$20
10/28/67 Bob Gibson, World Series .... $20-$25
11/04/67 Len Dawson $10
11/11/67 Jim Hart $10
11/18/67 Gary Beban $10
11/26/67 Fran Tarkenton $10
12/02/67 Leroy Kelly $10
12/09/67 Lew Alcindor $12
12/16/67 Vince Lombardi $12

12/23/67 Darryl LaMonica $10
12/30/67 Roman Gabriel $10

1968

01/06/68 Green Bay Packers $12
01/13/68 Vince Lombardi, Bart Starr $12
01/20/68 Wes Unseld $10
01/27/68 Donny Anderson $10
02/03/68 Phil Esposito $15
02/10/68 Len Wilkins $10
02/17/68 Don May $10
02/24/68 Elvin Hayes $10
03/02/68 Carl Yastrzemski .... $15-$30
03/09/68 Dick Hughes .... $8-$10
03/16/68 Mark Belanger .... $8-$12
03/23/68 Jim Bunning .... $8-$15
03/30/68 Don Wert .... $8-$12
04/06/68 Mickey Mantle and family .... $25-$35
04/13/68 Lou Brock .... $12-$20
04/20/68 Pete Rose .... $25-$35
04/27/68 Jim Fregosi, Bobby Knoop .... $8-$12
05/04/68 Harmon Killebrew .... $12-$20
05/11/68 Jerry Koosman .... $8-$15
05/18/68 Mickey Lolich .... $8-$15
05/25/68 Orlando Cepeda .... $9-$15
06/01/68 Frank Howard .... $8-$12
06/08/68 Don Drysdale .... $9-$15
06/15/68 Woody Fryman .... $8-$10

06/22/68 Jim Hardin .... $8-$12
06/29/68 Tony Horton .... $8-$10
07/06/68 Denny McLain .... $8-$15
07/13/68 Willie McCovey, All-Star issue $15
07/20/68 Willie Horton .... $9-$15
07/27/68 Matty Alou .... $8-$12
08/03/68 Luis Tiant .... $8-$12
08/10/68 Glenn Beckert .... $8-$12
08/17/68 R. Jackson, R. Monday .... $25-$35
08/24/68 Dal Maxvill .... $8-$12
08/31/68 Ted Uhlaender .... $8-$12
09/07/68 Phil Regan .... $8-$12
09/14/68 Roman Gabriel $10
09/21/68 Bill Freehan .... $8-$15
09/28/68 Mike Shannon .... $8-$15
10/05/68 D. McLain, L. Grove, World Series $15
10/12/68 R. Maris and family, World Series $35
10/19/68 Bob Gibson, World Series .... $10-$20
10/26/88 Don Meredith $15
11/02/88 Sonny Jurgensen $10
11/09/68 Terry Hanratty $10
11/16/68 B. Bell, J. Lynch, W. Lanier $10
11/23/68 Bart Starr $10
11/30/68 Earl Morrall $10
12/07/68 College Basketball Preview $10
12/14/68 O.J. Simpson $12
12/21/68 John Hadl $10

12/28/68 Joe Namath $20

1969

01/04/69 Denny McLain $12
01/11/69 John Mackey $8
01/18/69 Elvn Hayes $8
01/25/69 Joe Namath $15
02/01/69 Norm Ullman $8
02/08/69 Bobby Hull $15
02/15/69 Phil Esposito $15
02/22/69 Gordie Howe $15
03/01/69 Willie Mays .... $15-$20
03/08/69 Billy Casper $8
03/15/69 Ted Williams $15
03/22/69 Denny McLain $12
03/29/69 Tony Conigliaro $12
04/05/69 100 Years of Baseball $15
04/12/69 Brock, Flood, Pinson $15
04/19/69 Don Buford $10
04/26/69 Tug McGraw $10
05/03/69 Mel Stottlemyre $10
05/10/69 Bill Sudakis $10
05/17/69 Dave McNally $10
05/24/69 Richie Hebner $10
05/31/69 Bobby Murcer $10
06/07/69 Don Kessinger $10
06/14/69 Blue Moon Odom $10
06/21/69 Lee May $10
06/28/69 Ray Culp $10
07/05/69 Ken Holtzman $10
07/12/69 Rod Carew $15
07/19/69 Powell, B. Robinson, F. Robinson $20
07/26/69 Reggie Jackson $30
08/02/69 Matty Alou $10
08/09/69 Willie McCovey $15
08/16/69 Rico Petrocelli $10
08/23/69 Phil Niekro $12
08/30/69 Steve Carlton .... $12-$15
09/06/69 Ron Santo $12
09/13/69 Mike Cuellar $10
09/27/69 Bobby Tolan $10
10/04/69 Billy Martin $15
10/11/69 Tom Seaver $20
10/18/69 Boog Powell $15
10/25/69 Harmon Killebrew $15
11/01/69 David (Mets)/Goliath (Orioles) $20
11/08/69 Rex Kern $8
11/15/69 George Allen $8
11/22/69 Garrett, Holmes, McVea $8
11/29/69 Mike Phipps $8
12/06/69 Rick Mount $8
12/13/69 Bobby Orr $20
12/20/69 Darryl Lamonica $10
12/27/69 Roman Gabriel $7

1970

01/03/70 James Street	$10
01/10/70 Bill Bradley	$20
01/17/70 Willie Mays	$15
01/24/70 R. Vachon	$7
01/31/70 Mike Pratt	$7
02/07/70 Lou Hudson	$7
02/14/70 Pete Maravich	$15
02/21/70 Tony Esposito	$7
02/28/70 Roberto Clemente	$20
03/07/70 John Valley	$7
03/14/70 Bill Russell	$8
03/21/70 Stan Mikita	$8
03/28/70 Lew Alcindor	$8
04/04/70 Arnold Palmer	$10
04/11/70 T. Conigliaro, R. Smith, C. Yastrzemski	$25
04/18/70 Johnny Bench	$20
04/25/70 Bert Campaneris	$7
05/02/70 Rusty Staub	$8
05/09/70 Brant Alyea	$7
05/16/70 Tony Perez	$10
05/23/70 Hank Aaron	$15
05/30/70 Dave Johnson	$7
06/06/70 Richie Allen	$8
06/13/70 Vada Pinson	$8
06/20/70 Jim Merritt	$7
06/27/70 Danny Walton	$8
07/04/70 Rico Carty	$8
07/11/70 Felipe Alou	$7
07/18/70 Pete Rose	$20
07/25/70 Willie Mays	$15
08/01/70 Billy Grabarkewitz	$7
08/08/70 Al Kaline	$15-$20
08/15/70 Ray Fosse	$7
08/22/70 Roy White	$7
08/29/70 Dave Giusti	$7
09/05/70 Bud Harrelson	$7
09/12/70 Bernie Carbo	$7
09/26/70 Joe Pepitone	$7
10/03/70 Gaylord Perry/Jim Perry	$10
10/10/70 Danny Murtaugh	$7
10/17/70 Cuellar, McNally, Palmer	$12

10/24/70 Johnny Bench	$15
10/31/70 World Series wrap-up	$10
11/07/70 Archie Manning	$10
11/14/70 Bill Munson	$7
11/21/70 Jim Johnson	$7
11/28/70 Joe Theismann	$7
12/05/70 Gary Cuozzo	$7
12/12/70 Austin Carr	$7
12/19/70 Keith Magnuson	$7
12/26/70 Johnny Robinson	$7

1971

01/02/71 Rex Kern	$5
01/09/71 John Wooden	$5
01/16/71 Johnny Unitas	$7
01/23/71 Dan Issel	$5
01/30/71 Super Bowl V	$6
02/06/71 Brad Park	$7
02/13/71 Lew Alcindor	$7
02/20/71 Phil Esposito	$7
02/27/71 Bamberger, Etchebarren, Palmer	$10
03/06/71 Pete Maravich	$10
03/13/71 Sidney Wicks	$7
03/20/71 John Havlicek	$7
03/27/71 Mel Daniels	$5
04/03/71 Yvonne Cournoyer	$5
04/10/71 Johnny Bench, Boog Powell	$10
04/17/71 Reggie Jackson	$15
04/24/71 Tony Conigliaro	$10
05/01/71 Manny Sanguillen	$5
05/08/71 Steve Carlton	$10
05/15/71 Kentucky Derby (Canonero II)	$5
05/22/71 Willie Stargell	$8
05/29/71 Indianapolis 500	$5
06/05/71 Vida Blue	$5
06/12/71 Jerry Grote	$5
06/19/71 Sonny Siebert	$5
06/26/71 Dick Dietz	$5
07/03/71 Fergie Jenkins	$8
07/10/71 Bobby Murcer	$8
07/17/71 Willie Mays	$12
07/24/71 Joe Torre	$5
07/31/71 Frank Robinson	$8
08/07/71 Tony Oliva	$7
08/14/71 Amos Otis	$5
08/21/71 Dock Ellis	$5
08/28/71 Jack Nicklaus	$8
09/04/71 Bill Melton	$5
09/11/71 College Football Review	$5
09/18/71 John Brodie	$5
09/25/71 Mickey Lolich	$8
10/02/71 Wilbur Wood	$5
10/09/71 Al Downing	$5
10/16/71 Brooks Robinson	$12
10/23/71 Joe Torre	$5
10/30/71 Roberto Clemente	$15
11/06/71 Walt Patulski	$5
11/13/71 Billy Kilmer	$5
11/20/71 Terry Easley, Pat Sullivan	$5
11/27/71 Greg Pruitt	$5
12/04/71 Bob Griese	$5
12/11/71 Otis Taylor	$5
12/18/71 Allan Hornyak & Luke Witte	$5
12/25/71 Garry Unger	$5

1972

01/01/72 Jerry Tagge	$10
01/08/72 Lee Trevino	$5
01/15/72 Roger Staubach	$6
01/22/72 W. Chamberlain, Gail Goodrich	$6
01/29/72 Artis Gilmore	$5
02/05/72 Tyler Palmer	$5
02/12/72 Ted Harris	$5

02/19/72 Dave Cowens $5
02/26/72 Jean Ratelle $6
03/04/72 Cuellar, Dobson, McNally, Palmer $8
03/11/72 Chris Evert... $6
03/18/72 Bill Walton.. $6
03/25/72 Marc Tardif $5
04/01/72 Jack Nicklaus.. $8
04/08/72 Roberto Clemente $15
04/15/72 Kareem Abdul-Jabbar $5
04/22/72 Bobby Hull $8
04/29/72 Play Ball.. $7

05/06/72 Gary Cheevers $5
05/13/72 Don Sutton $7
05/20/72 Kentucky Derby (Riva Ridge) $5
05/27/72 Milt Wilcox $5
06/03/72 Dave Kingman $5
06/10/72 Mickey Lolich $7
06/17/72 Gary Nolan $5
06/24/72 D. Baylor, T. Crowley, Grich $7
07/01/72 Danny Frisella, Tug McGraw.............................. $6
07/08/72 Lou Piniella $6
07/15/72 Manny Sanguillen $5
07/22/72 Joe Rudi $5
07/29/72 Hank Aaron .... $10-$15
08/05/72 Jack Nicklaus.. $7
08/12/72 Sparky Lyle... $5
08/19/72 Cesar Cedeno $5
08/26/72 Mark Spitz $5
09/02/72 Steve Carlton $10
09/09/72 Bob Devaney $5
09/16/72 Len Dawson.. $5
09/23/72 Carlton Fisk $8
09/30/72 Al Oliver $5
10/14/72 Luis Tiant $6
10/21/72 Billy Williams... $7
10/28/72 Johnny Bench $12
11/04/72 Dick Williams $5
11/11/72 Jerrel Wilson $5
11/18/72 Larry Csonka $5
11/25/72 Larry Brown $5

12/02/72 Guy Perreault $5
12/09/72 Terry Bradshaw $5

12/16/72 Bill Walton... $5
12/23/72 Jacques LeMaire $5
12/30/72 Nate Archibald.. $5

1973

01/06/73 Charlie Finley $5
01/13/73 Super Bowl VII.. $6
01/20/73 Jean-Paul Parise $5
01/27/73 Spencer Haywood $5
02/03/73 Zelmo Beaty $5
02/10/73 Mickey Redmond.. $5
02/17/73 UCLA Bruins $6
02/24/73 George McGinnis $5
03/03/73 Rollie Fingers .... $6-$10
03/10/73 Bobby Clarke $8
03/17/73 Bill Walton, John Wooden $5
03/24/73 Nate Archibald... $5
03/31/73 Billy Cunningham $5
04/07/73 Jack Nicklaus... $6
04/14/73 Steve Carlton... $10
04/21/73 Phil Esposito.. $6
04/28/73 Chris Speier... $5
05/05/73 Nolan Ryan $15
05/12/73 Fred Patek, Cookie Rojas $5
05/19/73 Joe Morgan $7
05/26/73 Indianapolis 500 .... $5
06/02/73 Wilbur Wood $5
06/09/73 Joe Ferguson... $5
06/16/73 Joe Coleman $5
06/23/73 Ron Santo $6
06/30/73 Ron Blomberg $5
07/07/73 Bobby Bonds $5
07/14/73 John Mayberry $5
07/21/73 Bob Watson $5
07/28/73 Bench, Morgan, Rose.. $15
08/04/73 Bert Byleven $5
08/11/73 Bobby Bonds $5
08/18/73 Thurman Munson $15
08/25/73 Del Unser $5
09/01/73 Orlando Cepeda $5
09/08/73 Darrell Evans $5
09/15/73 Gradishar, Hayes & Hicks $5
09/22/73 Larry Csonka $5
09/29/73 Lou Brock $8
10/06/73 Willie Mays .... $10-$15
10/13/73 Jim Palmer... $8
10/20/73 Blue, Holtzman, Hunter $10
10/27/73 Jon Matlack $5
11/03/73 Mike Andrews $5
11/10/73 John Hadl $5
11/17/73 Fran Tarkenton $5
11/24/73 Archie Griffin.. $5

12/01/73 Tom Clements..................................$5	03/08/75 Bobby Bonds, Jim Hunter...............$7-$12
12/08/73 Bill Walton.....................................$5	03/15/75 Julius Erving...................................$7
12/15/73 Bob Lee..$5	03/22/75 Dave Cowens...............................$4
12/22/73 O. J. Simpson...............................$6	03/29/75 George McGinnis..........................$4
12/29/73 Nick Buoniconti.............................$5	04/05/75 Rogie Vachon...............................$4

1974

01/05/74 Pete Maravich...............................$7	04/12/75 Opening Day.................................$5
01/12/74 Julius Erving.................................$7	04/19/75 Elvin Hayes..................................$4
01/19/74 Bob Griese....................................$5	04/26/75 Dave Concepcion...........................$5
01/26/74 David Thomspon.............................$4	05/03/75 Frank Robinson..............................$6
02/02/74 George Gervin...............................$4	05/10/75 Greg Luzinski................................$5
02/09/74 Kerry & Kim Hughes.......................$4	05/17/75 Nolan Ryan...............................$12-$20
02/16/74 Johnny Miller................................$4	05/24/75 Ken Reitz.....................................$4
02/23/74 Bill Walton....................................$4	05/31/75 Jim Palmer...................................$6
03/02/74 Dick Green....................................$4	06/07/75 Madlock, Monday, Morales...............$6
03/09/74 John Schumate..............................$$	06/14/75 Ron LeFlore..................................$5
03/16/74 Dave Schultz.................................$4	06/21/75 Andy Messersmith.........................$4
03/23/74 Bob McAdoo..................................$4	06/28/75 Hal McRae....................................$4
03/30/74 Rick Barry.....................................$4	07/05/75 Joe Morgan...................................$6
04/06/74 Play Ball.......................................$6	07/12/75 Fred Lynn.....................................$6
04/13/74 Jack Nicklaus................................$6	07/19/75 Mays, Musial, Ruth, Williams, Feller, Hubbell,
04/20/74 Hank Aaron, Babe Ruth.............$15-$25	Kaline, Marichal...............................$10
04/27/74 Ted Simmons................................$4	07/26/75 Robin Yount.................................$15
05/04/74 Roy White....................................$4	08/02/75 Dave Parker..................................$5
05/11/74 Jim Wynn.....................................$4	08/09/75 Claudell Washington......................$4
05/18/74 Jeff Burroughs...............................$4	08/16/75 Al Hrabosky..................................$4
05/25/74 Ken Singleton...............................$4	08/23/75 Jim Kaat......................................$4
06/01/74 John Hiller....................................$4	08/30/75 Larry Bowa, Dave Cash..................$4
06/08/74 Mike Schmidt...........................$15-$20	09/06/75 Randy Jones.................................$4
06/15/74 Gaylord Perry...............................$5	09/20/75 John Mayberry..............................$4
06/22/74 Tommy John.................................$5	09/27/75 Terry Bradshaw.............................$5
06/29/74 Rod Carew...............................$7-$15	10/04/75 Fingers, Lindblad, Todd...................$6
07/06/74 Ralph Garr....................................$4	10/11/75 Sparky Anderson............................$5
07/13/74 Carlton Fisk..................................$6	10/18/75 Fred Lynn.....................................$6
07/20/74 Dick Williams................................$4	10/25/75 Rick Barry....................................$4
07/27/74 Mike Marshall................................$4	11/01/75 Roger Staubach.............................$5
08/03/74 Steve Busby.................................$4	11/08/75 Pete Johnson................................$4
08/10/74 Greg Gross...................................$4	11/15/75 Curley Culp...................................$4
08/17/74 Reggie Jackson............................$12	11/22/75 Lynn Swann...................................$5
08/24/74 Jorge Orta....................................$4	11/29/75 Fran Tarkenton..............................$5
09/07/74 Cornelius Greene, Archie Griffin........$4	12/06/75 Jim Bakken...................................$4
09/14/74 Richie Zisk...................................$4	12/13/75 Richard Washington........................$4
09/21/74 O.J. Simpson................................$4	12/20/75 Bert Jones....................................$4
09/28/74 Reggie Smith................................$4	12/27/75 Ray Guy.......................................$4
10/05/74 Rod Shoate..................................$4	

1976

10/12/74 Jim Plunkett..................................$4	01/03/76 John Sciarra..................................$4
10/19/74 Bill Virdon....................................$4	01/10/76 Archie Griffin................................$4
10/26/74 Steve Garvey................................$7	01/17/76 Adrian Dantley..............................$4
11/02/74 Brock, Burroughs, Hunter, M. Marshall.........$7	01/24/76 Franco Harris................................$4
11/09/74 John Hart.....................................$4	01/31/76 Scot May......................................$4
11/16/74 Reggie McKenzie...........................$4	02/07/76 Alvan Adams.................................$4
11/23/74 Dennis Franklin..............................$4	02/14/76 Kareem Abdul-Jabbar......................$5
11/30/74 George Blanda...............................$5	02/21/76 John Lucas...................................$4
12/07/74 Kenny Anderson.............................$$	02/28/76 George McGinnis..........................$4
12/14/74 Monte Towe..................................$4	03/06/76 Fred Lynn.....................................$6
12/21/74 Marv Hubbard................................$4	03/13/76 David Thompson............................$4
12/28/74 Rick Barry.....................................$5	03/20/76 Cleamons, Fitch, Smith, Snyder.........$4

1975

	03/27/76 Phil Smith.....................................$4
01/04/75 Lou Brock.....................................$6	04/03/76 John Havlicek................................$5
01/11/75 Bob McAdoo..................................$4	04/10/76 Fergie Jenkins...............................$5
01/18/75 T. Bradshaw, F. Tarkenton................$5	04/17/76 Don Gullett...................................$4
01/25/75 Swen Nater...................................$$	04/24/76 Frank Tanana.................................$4
02/01/75 Guy Lafleur...................................$4	05/01/76 Larry Bowa...................................$4
02/08/75 Steve Green...................................$4	05/08/76 Dave Kingman..............................$4
02/15/75 Walt Frazier...................................$5	05/15/76 Toby Harrah...................................$4
02/22/75 Steve Vickers................................$$	05/22/76 Willie Horton..................................$8
03/01/75 Adrian Dantley..............................$5	05/29/76 Ron Cey......................................$5
	06/05/76 George Brett...........................$12-$15

06/12/76 Chris Chambliss $4
06/19/76 Randy Jones $4
06/26/76 Ron LeFlore $5
07/03/76 George Foster $4
07/10/76 John Montefusco $4
07/17/76 Johnny Bench $8
07/24/76 Jim Slaton $4
07/31/76 Al Oliver $4
08/07/76 Dennis Leonard $4
08/14/76 Mark Fidrych $5
08/21/76 Dave Cash $4
08/28/76 Rico Carty $4
09/04/76 Tony Dorsett $6
09/11/76 Jack Lambert $4
09/18/76 Rick Rhoden $4
09/25/76 Mickey Rivers $4
10/02/76 Rick Leach $5
10/09/76 Billy Kilmer $4
10/16/76 Rawly Eastwick $4
10/23/76 Cincinnati's Big Red Machine $15
10/30/76 Jo Jo White $4
11/06/76 Steve Grogan $4
11/13/76 Ricky Bell $4
11/20/76 Conrad Dobler $4
11/27/76 Wally Chambers $4
12/04/76 Marques Johnson $4
12/11/76 Dave Caspar $4
12/18/76 Isaac Curtis $4
12/25/76 Bert Jones $4

1977

01/01/77 Tony Dorsett $6
01/08/77 David Thompson $4
01/15/77 Kenny Stabler $5
01/22/77 Bill Walton $5
01/29/77 Rudy Tomlanovich $4
02/05/77 Reggie Robey $4
02/12/77 Julius Erving $6
02/19/77 Pete Maravich $8
02/26/77 Billy Knight $4
03/05/77 Baylor, Grich, Rudi $5
03/12/77 Paul Westphal $4
03/19/77 Elvin Hayes $4
03/26/77 Wayne Garland $4
04/02/77 Mike Schmidt $10
04/09/77 Don Gullett, Reggie Jackson $10
04/16/77 Bert Campaneris $4
04/23/77 Rick Monday $4
04/30/77 Rollie Fingers $4
05/07/77 Amos Otis $4
05/14/77 Joe Rudi $4
05/21/77 Ted Simmons $4
05/28/77 Ron Cey $4
06/04/77 Mitchell Page $4
06/11/77 Dave Parker $4
06/18/77 Richie Zisk $4
06/25/77 Bruce Sutter $4
07/09/77 Butch Wynegar $4
07/16/77 Jeff Burroughs $4
07/23/77 Frank Tanana $4
07/30/77 Steve Carlton $7
08/06/77 Joe Morgan $6
08/13/77 Jim Rice $6
08/20/77 Cromartie, Dawson, Valentine $6
08/27/77 Billy Hunter, Bump Wills $4
09/03/77 Tommy John $4
09/10/77 Russ Browner $4
09/17/77 Tony Dorsett $5

09/24/77 Graig Nettles $5
10/01/77 Greg Luzinski $5
10/08/77 Al Cowens $4
10/15/77 Rod Carew $7
10/22/77 Baker, Cey, Garvey, Smith $8
10/29/77 Pete Maravich $8
11/05/77 Earl Campbell $7
11/12/77 Craig Morton $4
11/19/77 Walter Payton $12
11/26/77 Drew Pearson $4
12/03/77 Reggie Theus $4
12/10/77 Jack Ham $4
12/17/77 Pat Haden $4
12/24/77 Bob Griese $4
12/31/77 Bear Bryant, Woody Hayes $6

1978

01/07/78 Steve Cauthen $4
01/14/78 Butch Lee $4
01/21/78 Craig Morton & Roger Staubach $5
01/28/78 Dave Twardzik $4
02/04/78 Jack Givens $4
02/11/78 Julius Erving $7
02/18/78 Walter Davis $5
02/25/78 Larry Bird $15
03/04/78 Rod Carew, George Foster $7
03/11/78 David Greenwood, Roy Hamilton $4
03/18/78 David Thompson $4
03/25/78 Kareem Abdul-Jabbar $4
04/01/78 Bernard King $4
04/08/78 Salute To 1978 Season $4
04/15/78 Lyman Bostock $4
04/22/78 Garry Templeton $4
04/29/78 Steve Kemp, Jason Thompson $4
05/06/78 Don Money $4
05/13/78 Ross Grimsley $4
05/20/78 Pete Rose $9
05/27/78 Jim Rice $6
06/03/78 Barr, Blue, Knepper, Montefusco $5
06/10/78 Gary Alexander $4
06/17/78 Ron Guidry $6
06/24/78 Vic Davalillo, Manny Mota $4
07/01/78 Paul Splittorff $4
07/08/78 Flanagan, Martinez, McGregor, Palmer $7
07/15/78 Carew, Foster, Garvey, Guidry, Seaver, Rice $8
07/22/78 Larry Bowa $4
07/29/78 Jim Sundberg $4
08/05/78 Terry Puhl $4
08/12/78 Paul Molitor $8
08/19/78 Jack Clark $4
08/26/78 Davey Lopes $4
09/02/78 Roger Staubach $4
09/09/78 Joe Montana $15
09/16/78 Carlton Fisk $6
09/23/78 Dave Parker $4
09/30/78 Rich Gossage $5
10/07/78 Chuck Fusina $5
10/14/78 Elvin Hayes $4
10/21/78 Steve Garvey $5
10/28/78 Ron Guidry $6
11/04/78 Joe Theismann $4
11/11/78 Billy Sims $4
11/18/78 Jack Thompson $4
11/25/78 Terry Bradshaw $5
12/02/78 Mike Gminski $4
12/09/78 Earl Campbell $6
12/16/78 Steve Grogan $4

12/23/78 Matt Bahr $4
12/30/78 Jeff Rutledge $4

1979

01/06/79 Ron Guidry $6
01/13/79 Kelly Tripucka $4
01/20/79 Walter Davis & Paul Westphal $4
01/27/79 Franco Harris $4
02/03/79 Moses Malone $4
02/10/79 George Gervin $4
02/17/79 Lloyd Free & Randy Smith $4
02/24/79 John Drew $4
03/03/79 Spring Training issue $5
03/10/79 Lloyd Free & Randy Smith $4
03/17/79 Larry Bird $15
03/24/79 Phil Ford $4
03/31/79 Magic Johnson $15
04/07/79 Guidry, Madlock, Perry, Rice $6
04/14/79 Bob Dandridge $4
04/21/79 Pete Rose $7
04/28/79 Rod Carew $6
05/05/79 Reggie Jackson $8
05/12/79 Vida Blue $4
05/19/79 Al Oliver $4
05/26/79 J.R. Richard $4
06/02/79 Mike Marshall $4
06/09/79 Gary Carter $7
06/16/79 Fred Lynn $6
06/23/79 Brock, Hendrick, Hernandez, Simmons, Templeton $7
06/30/79 Tommy John $4
07/07/79 Roy Smalley $4
07/14/79 Terry Bradshaw $5
07/21/79 Brett, Lynn, Parker, Rose $8
07/28/79 Joe Niekro $4
08/04/79 Don Baylor $4
08/11/79 Willie Stargell $6
08/18/79 Mike Flanagan $4
08/25/79 Dave Kingman, Mike Schmidt $8
09/01/79 Walter Payton $10
09/08/79 Mark Herrmann $4
09/15/79 Carl Yastrzemski $7
09/22/79 Lou Brock $6
09/27/79 Tom Seaver $8
10/06/79 Darrell Porter $4
10/13/79 Steve Johnson $4
10/20/79 Bench, Dent, Fingers, Jackson, Rose $8
10/27/79 Wilbert Montgomery $4
11/03/79 Art Schlichter $4
11/10/79 Paul McDonald $4
11/17/79 Dan Fouts $4
11/24/79 Lee Roy Selmon $4
12/01/79 Gminski, Griffith & O'Koren $4
12/08/79 Ottis Anderson $4
12/15/79 John Stallworth $4
12/22/79 Brian Sipe $4
12/29/79 Pete Rose $8

1980

01/05/80 Steadman Shealey $4
01/12/80 Willie Stargell $5
01/19/80 Kyle Macy $4
01/26/80 Jack Lambert, Jack Youngblood $4
02/02/80 Billy Cunningham, Lynn Swann $4
02/09/80 Larry Bird $15
02/16/80 Joe Barry Carroll $4
02/23/80 Truck Robinson $4
03/01/80 Mark Aguirre, Ray Meyer $4
03/08/80 Keith Hernandez $5
03/15/80 Magic Johnson $15

03/22/80 Darrell Griffith $4
03/29/80 Joe Barry Carroll $4
04/05/80 Bobby Clarke, Guy LaFleur .... • $5
04/12/80 Mike Flanagan, Dave Winfield $6
04/19/80 Nolan Ryan $12
04/26/80 George Brett $10
05/03/80 Billy Sims, Marc Wilson $4
05/10/80 Kent Tekulve $4
05/17/80 George Foster $4
05/24/80 Gorman Thomas $4
05/31/80 Ken Reitz, Champ Summers $4
06/07/80 Dave Kingman $4
06/14/80 Carlton Fisk $6
06/21/80 Steve Carlton $7
06/28/80 Reggie Smith $4
07/05/80 Billy Martin $6
07/12/80 Steve Garvey $6
07/19/80 Franco Harris $4
07/26/80 Jim Palmer, Earl Weaver $6
08/02/80 Reggie Jackson $8
08/09/80 Willie Wilson $4
08/16/80 Lee Mazzilli $4
08/23/80 Jim Bibby, Steve Stone $4
08/30/80 Andre Dawson, Ron LeFlore $5
09/06/80 Kenny Stabler $4
09/13/80 Hugh Green & Major Ogilvie $4
09/20/80 George Brett $8
09/27/80 Jose Cruz, Walter Payton .... • $10
10/04/80 Pete Rose $8
10/11/80 Abdul-Jabbar, Magic Johnson $12
10/18/80 Ron Jaworski $4
10/25/80 Dan Quisenberry, Mike Schmidt $8
11/01/80 Willie Aikens $4
11/08/80 John Jefferson $4
11/15/80 Bear Bryant, Vince Ferragamo $6
11/22/80 Herschel Walker $5
11/29/80 Conrad Dobler $4
12/06/80 Albert Kino $4
12/13/80 Steve Bartkowski $4
12/20/80 Joe Cribbs & Billy Sims $4
12/27/80 Earl Campbell $6

1981

01/03/81 Bob Crable, Herschel Walker $6
01/10/81 George Brett $8
01/17/81 Tommy Kramer, Jerry Robinson $4
01/24/81 W. Montgomery, Jim Plunkett $4
01/31/81 Bill Bergey, Ted Hendricks $4
02/07/81 Jim Plunkett $4
02/14/81 Steve Johnson, Ralph Sampson $4
02/21/81 The NBA Shattering Headache $4
02/28/81 Bossy, Potvin, Trottier $7
03/07/81 Rick Langford, Billy Martin $5
03/14/81 J. B. Carroll, L. Free, B. King $4
03/21/81 Mark Aguirre $4
03/28/81 Fred Lynn, Don Sutton $5
04/04/81 Jeff Lamp, Isiah Thomas $6
04/11/81 Cooper, Oglivie, Simmons, Thomas, Yount $8
04/18/81 Ty Cobb, Nap Lajoie $4
04/25/81 Bruce Sutter $5
05/02/81 Bum Phillips $4
05/09/81 Tony Armas, Matt Keough $4
05/16/81 Fisk, LeFlore, Luzinski $6
05/23/81 T. Raines, F. Valenzuela $5
05/30/81 R. Grebey, B. Kuhn, Marvin Miller $4
06/06/81 Gary Matthews $4
06/13/81 Ken Singleton $4
06/20/81 Stan Musial, Pete Rose $8

06/27/81 On Strike.. $4
07/04/81 David Graham $4
07/11/81 Tony Dorsett $4
07/18/81 C. Evert Lloyd, J. McEnroe $4
07/25/81 Chuck Tanner $4
08/01/81 H. Green, E. J. Junior, L. Taylor............... $8

08/07/81 R. Foster, B. Gibson, Mize......................... $4
08/14/81 Baseball's Back $4
08/22/81 Goose Gossage $4
08/29/81 Bench, Concepcion, Seaver $6
09/05/81 Anthony Carter $4
09/12/81 Kellen Winslow $4
09/17/81 Sugar Ray Leonard $4
09/26/81 David Woodley.. $4
10/03/81 Doug James & Tim Koegel $4
10/10/81 Nolan Cromwell $4
10/17/81 Ed Jones & Harvey Martin.......................... $6
10/24/81 Bennett, Knox & Vermeil............................ $4
10/31/81 Dave Winfield $6
11/07/81 Larry Bird, Cedric Maxwell $10
11/14/81 Tommy Kramer $4
11/21/81 Fred Dean, Joe Montana............................ $15
11/28/81 Dan Marino $15
12/05/81 D. Crum, J. Eaves, D. Smith $4
12/12/81 Ken Anderson.. $4
12/19/81 Marcus Allen... $5
12/26/81 Mark Gastineau, Joe Klecko...................... $5

1982
01/02/82 Herschel Walker $5
01/09/82 Wayne Gretzky $15
01/16/82 Dan Fouts $4
01/23/82 Anderson, Johnson, Lott $4
01/30/82 K. Anderson, J. Montana $12
02/06/82 Joe Montana.. $12
02/13/82 Sam Perkins $6
02/20/82 Isiah Thomas $4
02/27/82 Moses Malone $4
03/06/82 Steve Garvey $5
03/13/82 Lafleur, Bossy, Trottier, Smith $7
03/20/82 Ralph Sampson $4
03/27/82 Ozzie Smith, Garry Templeton $4
04/03/82 Final Four Preview $4
04/10/82 Perry, Rose, Stargell, Yastrzemski............ $8
04/17/82 Collins, Foster, Griffey $4
04/24/82 Al Oliver $4
05/03/82 Rafael Ramirez $4
05/10/82 Eddie Murray $6
05/17/82 Keith Hernandez $5
05/24/82 Craig Stadler.. $4
05/31/82 LaMarr Hoyt, Keith Moreland...................... $4
06/07/82 Gerry Cooney, Larry Holmes $4
06/14/82 Rickey Henderson $7
06/21/82 John McEnroe $4
06/28/82 Carl Yastrzemski... $6

07/05/82 Gene Mauch $4
07/12/82 Gary Carter, Andre Dawson $6
7/19/82 Mike Ditka & Frank Kush $4
07/26/82 Earl Weaver $4
08/02/82 Aaron, Chandler, T. Jackson, F. Robinson............. $6
08/09/82 Cecil Cooper, Robin Yount......................... $7
08/16/82 Vince Ferragamo, Bert Jones $4
08/23/82 Reggie Jackson, Steve Sax........................ $7
08/30/82 Herschel Walker $5
09/06/82 Randy White $4
09/13/82 Marcus Allen.. $4
09/06/82 Rickey Henderson $4
09/20/82 Dale Murphy $4
09/27/82 John Elway $7
10/04/82 Todd Blackledge $4
10/11/82 Don Sutton, Robin Yount $7
10/18/82 Cecil Cooper, Bruce Sutter $4
10/25/82 Lonnie Smith, Robin Yount $7
11/01/82 Julius Erving, Moses Malone...................... $6
11/08/82 Pitt Panthers of Defense $4
11/15/82 Gerry Faust.. $4
11/22/82 Sugar Ray Leonard $4
11/29/82 Neil Lomax, John Stuckey $4
12/06/82 Terry Bradshaw $4

12/13/82 Herschel Walker $5
12/20/82 Kenny Stabler $4

12/27/82 J. Brooks, B. Harper $4

1983
01/03/83 Whitey Herzog $4
01/10/83 Moseley, Riggins & Theismann $6
01/17/83 Tom Landry & Don Shula $6
01/24/83 John Riggins $6
01/31/83 A.J. Duhe & Dexter Manley $6
02/07/83 Russ Grimm & John Riggins $6
02/14/83 Wayman Tisdale $4
02/21/83 Wayne Gretzky & Pete Peeters $15
02/28/83 Cheeks, Moncrief & Paxson $4
03/07/83 Billy Martin.. $4
03/14/83 Granger, Minifield & Sundvold $4
03/21/83 Steve Garvey... $4

03/28/83 Michael Jordan $20
04/04/83 Porter, L. Smith, O. Smith, Sutter $4
04/11/83 Carl Yastrzemski $6
04/18/83 Steve Kemp $4
04/25/83 John Elway $6
05/02/83 Reggie Jackson $7

05/09/83 Nolan Ryan $10
05/16/83 George Brett $7
05/23/83 Greg Brock, Mike Marshall $4
05/30/83 Abdul-Jabbar, Moses Malone $5
06/06/83 Steve Carlton $6
06/13/83 Dave Stieb $4
06/20/83 Rod Carew $6
06/27/83 Darrell Evans $4
07/04/83 TSNs All-Time All-Stars $6
07/11/83 Fernando Valenzuela $4
07/18/83 Joe Montana $15
07/25/83 Pete Rose $7
08/01/83 Alston, Kell, Marichal, B. Robinson $6
08/08/83 Brett, MacPhail, Martin, McClelland $5
08/15/83 Franco Harris, Jack Lambert $4
08/22/83 Ray Knight, Nancy Lopez $4
08/29/83 B. Kiel $4
09/05/83 Jones, Todd & Walker $5
09/12/83 Floyd Bannister $4
09/19/83 Walter Payton $10
09/26/83 Cecil Cooper, Andre Dawson $5
10/03/83 Danny White $4
10/10/83 Alexander, Fisk, Larsen, Mazeroski $5
10/17/83 Lyle Alzado, Ted Hendricks $4
10/24/83 Cal Ripken Jr., Lenn Sakata $10
10/31/83 Ralph Sampson $4
10/31/83 Marvin Hagler $4
11/14/83 Eric Dickerson $4
11/21/83 Mike Rozier $4
11/28/83 Hakeem Olajuwon $6
12/05/83 Dan Marino $12
12/12/83 R. Green $4
12/19/83 Mike Rozier $4
12/26/83 John Riggins $6

1984

01/02/84 Bowie Kuhn $4
01/09/84 Dave Krieg $4
01/16/84 John Riggins $5
01/23/84 Mark Aguirre $5
01/30/84 Jenson, Hayes $5
02/06/84 Iafrate, Jensen, LaFontaine, Vairo $5
02/13/84 Michael Jordan & Sam Perkins $15
02/20/84 Larry Bird & Robert Parrish $12
02/27/84 Mike Rozier $4
03/05/84 Cal Ripken Jr. $10
04/02/84 Pete Rose $7
04/09/84 Goose Gossage $4
04/16/84 Kareem Abdul-Jabbar $4

04/23/84 Wade Boggs $6
04/30/84 Bill Madlock $4
05/07/84 Phil Niekro, Jose Rijo $5
05/14/84 Dave Kingman $5
05/21/84 Darryl Strawberry $8
05/28/84 Lemon, Parrish, Trammell, Whitaker $8
06/04/84 USFL $4
06/11/84 Mike Schmidt $8
06/18/84 Leon Durham $4
06/25/84 Eddie Murray $6
07/02/84 Rickey Henderson $6
07/09/84 Cronin, Foxx, Gehrig, Hubbell, Simmons, Ruth $6
07/16/84 Warren Moon $8
07/23/84 Tony Gwynn $8
07/30/84 Carl Lewis $4
08/06/84 Aparicio, Drysdale, Killebrew, Reese $10
08/13/84 Hogshead, Johnson, Steinseifer, Torres $4
08/20/84 Ryne Sandberg $10
08/27/84 Texas is #1 .... $4
09/03/84 E. Jones, T. Landry, D. White $5
09/10/84 Bracelin, Dickey & McMillan $4
09/17/84 Kirk Gibson, Willie Hernandez $7
09/24/84 Kirby Puckett $10
10/01/84 Walter Payton $8
10/08/84 Willie Mays $7
10/15/84 Steve Garvey, Alan Trammell $7
10/22/84 Gibson, Trammell, Whitaker $7
10/29/84 Michael Jordan $15
11/05/84 Dan Marino $10
11/12/84 Doug Flutie $4
11/19/84 Mark Gastineau $5
11/26/84 Wayman Tisdale $4
12/03/84 Bryant, Butler, Harris, Nash, Robinson $4
12/10/84 Eric Dickerson $4
12/17/84 Roger Craig & Bill Walsh $8
12/31/84 Peter Ueberroth $4

1985

01/07/85 William Bennett $4
01/14/85 Mark Clayton $4
01/21/85 Joe Montana $12
01/28/85 Joe Montana, Wendall Tyler $12
02/04/85 Wayne Gretzky $12
02/11/85 Berra, Henderson, Steinbrenner, Armstrong,
         Montefusco, Torborg $4
02/18/85 Chris Mullin $6
02/25/85 Larry Bird $10
03/04/85 Ryne Sandberg $8
03/11/85 H. Olajuwon, R. Sampson $8
03/18/85 Carpenter, Christian, Langway $4
03/25/85 Bruce Sutter $4
04/01/85 Patrick Ewing $6
04/08/85 Rickey Henderson, Don Mattingly $8
04/15/85 Anderson, Gibson, Hernandez, Morris, Trammell ... $7
04/22/85 LaMarr Hoyt $4
04/29/85 Dale Murphy $4
05/06/85 Magic Johnson, James Worthy $12
05/13/85 Armas, Boggs, Easler, Evans, Rice $4
05/20/85 Billy Martin $4
05/27/85 Terry Whitfield $4
06/03/85 Anderson, Bryant, Kelly, Walker $5
06/10/85 Brett, Quisenberry, Schuerholz, Wilson $4
06/17/85 Joaquin Andujar, Mario Soto $4
06/24/85 J. Clark, D. Green baseball cards $4
06/31/85 Dale Murphy, Eddie Murray $5
07/08/85 Vince Coleman $4
07/15/85 Bill Caudill, Gary Lavelle $4
07/22/85 NFL Training Camp Issue $4

07/29/85 Gooden, Brock, Slaughter, Vaughan, Wilhelm $7
08/05/85 Namath, Simpson, Staubach................................. $5
08/12/85 Tom Seaver $5
08/19/85 Peter Ueberroth $4
08/26/85 Bo Jackson $6
09/02/85 Curt Warner $4
09/09/85 Pittsburgh Pirates franchise.................................. $4
09/16/85 Pete Rose $7
09/23/85 Neil Lomax.. $4
09/30/85 Mets-Yankees battle for Big Apple $6
10/07/85 Pedro Guerrero.. $5

10/14/85 Cardinals celebrate pennant.................................. $4
10/21/85 .... $6
10/28/85 Jim McMahon $8
11/04/85 George Brett, Bret Saberhagen $6
11/11/85 Chuck Long $4
11/18/85 Cromwell, Green, Irvin, Johnson $4
11/25/85 Jerry Faust $4
12/02/85 F. McNeil, L. Taylor $6
12/09/85 Kirk Gibson $5
12/16/85 Allen, Craig, Payton, Wilder $8
12/23/85 Who will be #1? $4

1986
01/06/86 Pete Rose, Whitey Herzog $6
01/13/86 Dan Marino $8
01/20/86 S. Brock. R. Dent $4
01/27/86 Hakeem Olajuwon $6
02/03/86 Hampton, Marshall & Wilson $6
02/10/86 Ken "Hawk" Harrelson $4
02/17/86 Candlestick Park... $4
02/24/86 Dawkins, Ferrell & Smith $4
03/03/86 Brett, J. Clark, R. Henderson............................... $6
03/10/86 Manute Bol $4
03/17/86 Reggie Jackson, Danny Manning $4
03/24/86 Dave Parker, Darryl Strawberry $4
03/31/86 Larry Bird, Magic Johnson.................................... $12
04/07/86 Ozzie Smith $6
04/14/86 Anderson, Coffey, Gretzky, Kurri........................... $8
04/21/86 Canseco, W. Clark, Galarraga, Incaviglia, Carew.... $7
04/28/86 Hoyt, D. Williams, Guidry...................................... $4
05/05/86 Bill Walton $4
05/12/86 Boone, R. Jackson, Sutton $6
05/19/86 P. Niekro, Martin, Schmidt $4
05/26/86 Carlton, Rose, Ryan, Puckett $6
06/02/86 Robin Yount, Hubie Brooks $6
06/16/86 Bill Walton $4
06/23/86 Ray Floyd.. $4
06/30/86 Len Bias $6
06/09/86 Gooden, K. Hernandez, Leonard $7
06/16/86 Don Sutton $4
06/23/86 Hal Lanier, Bobby Valentine $4
06/30/86 George Steinbrenner.. $6
07/07/86 Mike Krukow $4
07/14/86 Wade Boggs, Bo Jackson $7

07/21/86 Darling, Fernandez, Orosco $4
07/28/86 Bankhead, Clark, McDowell, Snyder, Witt, Clemens$6
08/04/86 Glenn Davis, Mike Scott $6
08/18/86 Jose Canseco, Tim Raines..................................... $6
08/25/86 Earl Weaver, Tom Lasorda $4
09/01/86 D. Mattingly, R. Henderson $8
09/08/86 Jack Morris, Jay Schroeder $4
09/15/86 Rob Deer, Herschel Walker $5
09/16/86 Football Special $5
09/22/86 Lou Holtz $4
09/29/86 G. Carter, Clemens, Ashburn $8
10/06/86 Vinny Testaverde $4
10/13/86 G. Davis, DeCinces, K. Hernandez, Rice $6
10/20/86 John Elway $6
10/27/86 Len Dykstra, Mike Schmidt $5
11/03/86 Marty Barrett, Gary Carter $4
11/24/86 Lance Parrish $5
11/10/86 Jim McMahon $6
11/11/86 Basketball Special $6
11/17/86 Lawrence Taylor $8
11/24/86 Eric Dickerson $5
11/25/86 College Basketball Preview $4
12/01/86 Vinny Testaverde $4
12/08/86 Joe Montana... $8
12/15/86 Roger Clemens $5
12/22/86 Bernie Kosar... $6

1987
01/05/87 Larry Bird.. $10
01/12/87 Penn State football $4
01/19/87 Jim Burt, Leonard Marshall $4
01/26/87 John Elway $5
02/02/87 Phil McConkey... $4
02/09/87 Los Angeles Clippers $4
02/16/87 Bobby Knight $5
02/23/87 David Robinson $10
03/02/87 Dwight Gooden... $3-$4
03/09/87 Steve Alford $4
03/16/87 Tito Horford, J.R. Reid $4
03/23/87 Julius Erving, Michael Jordan................................. $8
03/30/87 Mike Schmidt .... $4-$5
04/06/87 Reggie Jackson .... $4-$5
04/13/87 Ron Guidry .... $3-$4
04/27/87 Magic Johnson $8
05/11/87 Andre Dawson $4
05/18/87 Pete Rose .... $4-$5
05/25/87 Bret Saberhagen $4
06/01/87 R. Henderson, Charles Hudson $4
06/08/87 Jack Clark $3
06/15/87 Eric Davis $3
06/22/87 Kareem Abdul-Jabbar.. $7
07/06/87 Harold Baines, Jody Davis $3
07/13/87 Jack Morris, Alan Trammell .... $3-$4
07/27/87 Bert Blyleven, Jeff Reardon............................... $3-$4
08/03/87 Whitey Herzog $3
08/10/87 Coleman, Durham, Guidry, R. Henderson,
          Pettis, Strawberry $4
08/17/87 L. Dawson, J. Greene, J. McMahon $5
08/24/87 Cal Ripken Sr. $3
08/31/87 G. Bell, J. Clark, E. Davis, Dawson, Mattingly,
          McGwire $4
09/07/87 Will Clark $4
09/14/87 Jamelle Holieway.. $4
09/21/87 B. Bosworth, V. Testaverde................................... $4
09/28/87 Baltimore: Life After Football $4
10/05/87 George Bell, Alan Trammell................................ $3-$4
10/12/87 Wayne Gretzky $8
10/19/87 Boston Red Sox, New York Mets............................ $3

10/26/87 Greg Gagne, Willie McGee.....................................$3
11/02/87 Kent Hrbek, Kirby Puckett...............................$4-$5
11/09/87 Gaston Green, Danny White $4
11/23/87 Ozzie Newsome, Walter Payton, D. Sanders $5
11/30/87 Emmitt Smith.......................................$10
12/07/87 Bo Jackson, Pat LaFontaine $5
12/14/87 George Bell, Manute Bol, Tim Brown $5
12/21/87 Bobby Hebert, T. Richmond.........................$4

1988

01/04/88 Jerry Rice $10
01/11/88 Jimmy Johnson......................................$5
01/18/88 Joe Bostic, William Perry, Doug Williams $4
01/25/88 John Elway, Doug Williams...................$6
02/01/88 Yankees, Mets hats...............................$3
02/08/88 Rulon Jones, Raleigh McKenzie, Doug Williams.....$4
02/15/88 Ron Hextall $4
02/22/88 Charles Barkley, Magic Johnson $8
02/29/88 Danny Ferry, J.R. Reid $4
03/07/88 Kirk Gibson, Tommy Lasorda $3
03/14/88 Paul Coffey, Mario Lemieux.........................$6
03/21/88 Danny Ainge $4
03/28/88 Hersey Hawkins $4
04/04/88 Stacey King $4
04/11/88 Kent Hrbek, Wayne Garland $3
04/25/88 Eddie Murray, Frank Robinson ....$3-$4
05/02/88 Billy Martin, Dave Winfield ....$4-$5
05/09/88 Roger Clemens.................................$4-$5
05/16/88 Canseco, Parker, McGwire ....$4-$5
05/23/88 Larry Bird, Dennis Johnson $7
05/30/88 Wrigley Field.......................................$3
06/06/88 Gooden, D. Robinson, Ryan ....$6-$7
06/20/88 Greg Maddux, Mark Grace ....$4-$5
07/04/88 Andres Galarraga, Billy Martin $4
07/11/88 Baseball cards, Andy Van Slyke.................$3-$4
07/18/88 Tony Dorsett $5
07/25/88 Brett, Sabo, Steinbach.........................$3-$4
08/01/88 Frank Viola $3
08/08/88 Darryl Strawberry $3
08/15/88 Joe Morgan, Darryl Stingley ....$3-$4
08/22/88 Alan Trammell...................................$3-$4
09/05/88 Kirby Puckett, Dennis Rasmussen ....$4-$5
09/12/88 Jack Cooke, Bobby Beathard, Joe Gibbs $4
09/19/88 Cornelius Bennett..............................$5
09/26/88 Michael Irvin $8
10/17/88 Boggs, Canseco, Gibson, Strawberry....................$4
10/24/88 Kirk Gibson, Orel Hershiser $4
10/31/88 Orel Hershiser $4
11/07/88 Larry Bird, Magic Johnson.........................$8
11/14/88 Dick Shultz, Vinny Testaverde, Broderick Thomas........$6
11/21/88 Boomer Esiason $6
11/28/88 L. Holtz, T. Landry, C. Noll $5
12/05/88 Notre Dame football............................$4
12/12/88 Neil Lomax, J.T. Smith $4
12/19/88 Barry Sanders $8

1989

01/09/89 Neal Anderson.....................................$4
01/16/89 Boomer Esiason, Joe Montana $7
01/23/89 J. Bench, C. Yastrzemski ....$4-$5
01/30/89 David Fulcher, Jerry Rice $6
02/06/89 Wayne Gretzky $7
02/13/89 M. Allen, N. Anderson, K. Malone $6
02/20/89 Wayne Gretzky, Chris Jackson $7
02/27/89 Sean Elliott, Pervis Ellison, Danny Ferry,
　　Stacey King.....................................$5
03/06/89 Molitor, Murray, Valentine, Van Slyke......................$5
03/13/89 Stacey King $3
03/20/89 C. Barkley, M. Jordan $8

03/27/89 Stacey King, Chris Mullin $4
04/03/89 J. Clark, Hurst, McKeon..$3

04/10/89 Ken Griffey Jr., Ken Griffey Sr......................................$8
04/17/89 Troy Aikman..$6
04/24/89 Terry Cummings $4
04/24/89 Ellis Burks, Pete Rose ....$4-$5
05/01/89 Gregg Jefferies $4
05/08/89 Kevin Mitchell $3
05/15/89 B. Anderson, Cal Ripken Jr. ....$4-$5
05/22/89 Tommy John, Jose DeLeon $3
05/29/89 Dennis Rodman, Isiah Thomas $6
06/05/89 Ernie Whitt, Fred McGriff $4
06/12/89 Blyleven, D. Sanders, Schmidt $4
06/26/89 J. Edwards, A.C. Green, J. Salley $4
07/03/89 Neil Lomax, Barry Switzer $4
07/10/89 Pervis Ellison, David Stern $4
07/03/89 John Franco, Don Zimmer $3
07/24/89 O. Hershiser, H. Johnson $4
07/31/89 J. Franco, Palmeiro, Sierra $4
08/07/89 Lonnie Smith $3
08/14/89 Will Clark, Kevin Mitchell $4
08/21/89 Nolan Ryan..$5-$6
08/28/89 Jose Oquendo, Mike Scott $3
09/04/89 Pete Rose...$4-$5
09/11/89 B. Schembechler, M. Schottenheimer $4
09/18/89 Wade Boggs, Tony Gwynn ....$4-$5
09/25/89 Notre Dame vs. Michigan $4
10/02/89 Tim Krumrie, Jim McMahon $6
10/09/89 Randall Cunningham, Mario Lemieux,
　　Reggie White $6
10/16/89 McGriff, McGwire, Mitchell, Sandberg.....................$5
10/23/89 Terry Kennedy, Terry Steinbach $3
10/30/89 San Francisco earthquake............................$4
11/06/89 Oakland A's $3
11/13/89 Phil Simms, Emmitt Smith $7
12/04/89 D. Hawkins, Todd Marinovich $4
12/11/89 Kevin Mitchell $3
12/18/89 Steve Largent $5

1990

01/01/90 Joe Montana..$8
01/08/90 J. Carter, M. Davis, Langston, Parker.....................$4
01/15/90 P. Ewing, B. Sanders, P. Simms $6
01/22/90 John Elway, Joe Montana............................$8
01/29/90 Mike Schmidt...$4-$5
02/05/90 Joe Montana $8
02/12/90 Paul Tagliabue $4
02/19/90 Brett Hull, Alonzo Mourning $6
02/26/90 Chris Jackson, Isiah Thomas $5
03/05/90 Baseball lockout $3
03/12/90 Dwight Gooden, Pete Rose ....$3-$4
03/26/90 Charles Barkley, Dennis Scott $5
04/02/90 Alaa Abdelnaby $4
04/09/90 J. McKeon, Darryl Strawberry.........................$3

04/16/90 Blair Thomas $4
04/23/90 David Robinnson $7
04/30/90 G. Davis, Hrbek, Puckett ....$3-$4
05/07/90 E. Davis, Larkin, O'Neill, Piniella, Sabo $4
05/14/90 Mark Jackson, Magic Johnson $6
05/28/90 Michael Jordan $8
05/21/90 Jose Canseco, Will Clark $4
06/04/90 Cecil Fielder $4
06/11/90 Schooler, Viola, M. Williams $4
06/18/90 Len Dykstra $4
06/25/90 Nolan Ryan, Bill Laimbeer ....$4-$5
07/02/90 Barry Bonds, Charlie Fox $4
07/09/90 Dwight Gooden, Bret Saberhagen $3
07/16/90 Mouse Davis, Lyle Alzado $4
07/23/90 Bert Blyleven, Don Drysdale $4
07/30/90 M. Davis, Heaton, Parker, Wells $3
08/06/90 Gant, Strawberry, Tapani $3
08/13/90 Nolan Ryan, George Steinbrenner $4
08/20/90 Comiskey Park, Hurst, Mattingly $4
08/27/90 Bob Welch, John Elway $3
09/03/90 Jeff Ballard, Ramon Martinez $3
09/10/90 Jose Canseco, Barry Larkin $4
09/17/90 Jeff George $4
09/24/90 Rickey Henderson $3
10/01/90 Baines, Canseco, Lansford, McGee, McGwire,
   Welch, Weiss $3
10/15/90 Chris Sabo, Andy Van Slyke $3
10/22/90 Dennis Eckersley ....$3-$4
10/29/90 Rob Dibble, Lou Piniella $3
11/12/90 Warren Moon $6
11/19/90 P. Westhead, O. Woolridge $4
11/26/90 Wayne Gretzky $7
12/03/90 Joe Montana, Lawrence Taylor $8
12/10/90 Clyde Drexler, Boomer Esiason $5
12/17/90 Joe Carter, Fred McGriff ....$3-$4
12/24/90 Norm Ellenberger, Bobby Knight, Pete Peeters,
   Jerry Rice $5
12/31/90 Glove of money $3

1991

01/07/91 Nolan Ryan $4
01/14/91 George Ackles, Ed Belfour $3
01/21/91 Brett Hull, Buddy Ryan, J. Williams $4
01/28/91 Scott Radecic, Darryl Talley $3
02/04/91 James Lofton, Everson Walls, P. Williams $4
02/11/91 Kevin Johnson, Magic Johnson $6
02/18/91 Sam Perkins, Rick Pitino $4
02/25/91 Bernard King, L. Robinson $4
03/04/91 Michael Jordan, Scottie Pippen $7
03/04/91 Dave Parker $3
03/11/91 Jim Palmer $4
03/25/91 Richmond Spiders basketball team $3
04/01/91 Umpire Bruce Froemming $3
04/08/91 Christian Laettner $4
04/22/91 G. Bell, J. Clark, R. Henderson, Sanderson $3
04/29/91 Portland Trailblazers $4
05/13/91 Rickey Henderson, Nolan Ryan ....$4-$5
05/20/91 Rob Dibble ....$2-$3
05/27/91 Dave Justice $3
06/03/91 Mario Lemieux $6
06/10/91 M. Johnson, M. Jordan $7
06/17/91 Andre Dawson ....$3-$4
06/24/91 Michael Jordan $7
07/01/91 Gambling in baseball ....$2-$3
07/08/91 Hundley, Lankford, Van Poppel $2
07/15/91 Roger Craig, Ronnie Lott $5
07/22/91 Michael Jordan $7
07/29/91 Peter Ueberroth ....$2-$3

08/05/91 Tiger Stadium ....$2-$3
08/12/91 Lineups, Dennis Martinez ....$2-$3
08/19/91 Wounded baseball ....$2-$3
08/26/91 Pedro Guerrero, David Klingler ....$2-$3
09/09/91 Bobby Cox, R. Cunningham ....$2-$3
09/16/91 Bobby Bonilla, Jackie Sherrill $3
09/23/91 Terry Pendleton, Don Shula $3
09/30/91 Rocket Ismail, Wayne Gretzky $5
10/07/91 Sam Mills $3
10/14/91 John Smoltz $3
10/21/91 Kirby Puckett, Jim Mora ....$3-$4
10/28/91 Ray Handley, Jeff Hostetler $4
11/04/91 Jack Morris, Ty Detmer $3
11/11/91 Bobby Bonilla $3
11/18/91 Magic Johnson $6
12/02/91 Tom Rathman $4
12/09/91 K. Loughery, Derrick Thomas $4
12/16/91 Bobby Bonilla $3
12/23/91 Steve Palermo, Whitey Herzog ....$2-$3
12/30/91 Mark Rypien $4

1992

01/06/92 Michael Jordan $6
01/13/92 John Elway, Tim Hardaway $5
01/20/92 R. Hextall, B. Smith, J. Wright $4
01/27/92 Kenny Smith, Thurman Thomas $4
02/03/92 B. Edwards, Alexander Mogilny, Andre Reed $4
02/10/92 Jerry Tarkanian $4
02/17/92 W. Gretzky, M. Jordan, A. Mourning $6
02/24/92 Charles Barkley $6
03/02/92 Tom Glavine $3
03/02/92 Sam Wyche $3
03/09/92 Kirby Puckett, C. Laettner ....$3-$4
03/16/92 George Brett, D. Rodman ....$3-$4
03/23/92 Mark Messier, Shaquille O'Neal $5
03/30/92 Cal Ripken Jr., Jim Jackson ....$3-$4
04/06/92 Joe Carter, Rob Dibble ....$2-$3
04/13/92 Jose Canseco, C. Laettner $3
04/20/92 Camden Yards ....$2-$3
04/27/92 Butch Hobson, S. Pippen $2
05/04/92 Barry Bonds, S. Emtman $3
05/11/92 Tony Gwynn, J. Bagley $3
05/18/92 Craig Biggio, C. Drexler ....$2-$3
05/25/92 Lenny Harris $2
06/01/92 T. Hundley, T. Porter, C. Miller $2
06/08/92 Jeff Reardon, S. Pippen $2
06/15/92 Gary Sheffield, M. Jordan $6
06/22/92 David Cone, Chicago Bulls ....$2-$3
06/29/92 Leo Durocher, Willie Randolph $3
07/06/92 Norm Charlton, Rob Dibble $2
07/20/92 Carlton Fisk, C. Barkley ....$2-$3
07/27/92 Robin Yount, J. George $3
08/03/92 El Beisbol $2
08/24/92 Bill Walsh $3
08/31/92 John Smoltz, L. Bird $3
09/14/92 Joe Carter $3
09/07/92 Randall Cunningham $4
09/14/92 Minnesota Vikings $3
09/21/92 Paul Tagliabue, Fay Vincent $3
09/28/92 J. Bell, D. Fletcher, D. Krieg $2
10/05/92 T. Glavine, F. Thomas, E. Lindros ....$3-$4
10/12/92 Dennis Eckersley $3
10/19/92 Steve Avery, D. Majkowski ....$2-$3
10/26/92 Ed Sprague, D. Marino $2
11/02/92 Joe Carter, Otis Nixon ....$2-$3
11/09/92 Frank Boyles, Robert Parish $4
11/16/92 Jimmy Johnson, Gino Torretta $3
11/23/92 Mark McGwire, Football helmet $5

11/30/92 Elvis Grbac, Jamal Mashburn $4
12/07/92 Bill Bidwell, Dennis Rodman $3
12/14/92 Dick Butkus, Mike Singletary $5
12/21/92 Paul Tagliabue $3
12/28/92 Mike Kryzyewski $3

1993

01/11/93 Steve Young $5
01/18/93 C. Barkley, O. Harrington $4
01/25/93 M. Lemieux, E. Smith $5
02/01/93 George Brett $4
02/08/93 Dallas Cowboys Dynasty $4
02/15/93 C. Mullin, S. O'Neal $5
02/22/93 How We'd Fix Baseball $2
03/01/93 Joe Siddall $2
03/08/93 Kentucky vs. Indiana $3
03/15/93 Shawn Kemp $5
03/22/93 Thomas Hill, Eric Montross $3
03/29/93 John Lucas $3
04/05/93 Dave Winfield $3
04/12/93 Eric Montross, Chris Webber $4
04/19/93 Roger Clemens $3
04/26/93 Mario Lemieux $4
05/03/93 D. Ainge, C. Barkley, K. Johnson $4
05/10/93 Bobby Beathard, Darrien Gordon $3
05/17/93 Carlton Fisk $3
05/24/93 H. Olajuwon vs. 76ers $4
05/31/93 Gregg Jefferies .... $2-$3
06/07/93 C. Barkley, O. Miller $5
06/14/93 Barry Bonds $4
06/21/93 C. Barkley, S. Pippen $5
06/28/93 Danny Ainge, Michael Jordan $6
07/05/93 Barry Bonds $4
07/12/93 Reggie White $5
07/19/93 Jim Abbott .... $2-$3
07/26/93 Jack McDowell $3
08/02/93 Dave Justice $3
08/09/93 Wade Boggs, Chad Kreuter $3
08/16/93 Nolan Ryan, Robin Ventura $5
08/23/93 Gene Stallings $3
08/30/93 Don Mattingly .... $3-$4
09/06/93 Joe Montana $5
09/13/93 John Elway $5
09/20/93 Frank Thomas $5
09/27/93 Rick Mirer $3
10/04/93 Junior Seau $4
10/11/93 John Kruk $3
10/18/93 Michael Jordan $6
10/25/93 Len Dykstra $3
11/01/93 Jays Celebrate $3
11/08/93 Shaquille O'Neal $6
11/15/93 Phil Simms $4
11/22/93 John Covington $3
11/29/93 Eric Montross $3
12/06/93 Richard Dent, Ken Ruettgers $4
12/13/93 Charlie Ward $3
12/20/93 Jerry Rice $5

1994

01/04/94 Ted Turner .... $2-$3
01/10/94 Scott Bentley, Dan Kannel $2
01/17/94 Warren Moon $3
01/24/94 Chris Webber $3

01/31/94 Thurman Thomas $4
02/07/94 Emmitt Smith $4
02/21/94 Corliss Williamson $2
02/28/94 Denis Boucher $2
03/14/94 Don Baylor $3
03/28/94 Charles Barkley $3
04/04/94 Ken Griffey Jr. $5
04/11/94 C. Laettner, C. Williamson .... $2-$3
04/18/94 Deion Sanders $4
04/25/94 Danny Manning .... $2-$3
05/02/94 Curtis Pride .... $2-$3
05/09/94 Shaquille O'Neal .... $3-$4
05/16/94 Mark Messier $3
05/23/94 Charles Oakley, Scottie Pippen $3
05/30/94 Bob Tewksbury $2
06/05/94 Carlos Delgado $2
06/13/94 Hakeem Olajuwon $3
06/20/94 Patrick Ewing .... $2-$3
07/04/94 Albert Belle .... $3-$4
07/11/94 Greg Maddux $4
07/18/94 Dan Marino .... $3-$4
07/25/94 Ozzie Guillen, Kenny Lofton $3
08/01/94 Barry Larkin $4
08/08/94 R. Ravitch, K. Rogers, D. Fehr $2
08/15/94 Hickory Crawdads fans $2
08/22/94 Baseball strike photo $2
08/29/94 Rohan Marley $2
09/05/94 E. Smith, T. Thomas $3
09/12/94 Emmitt Smith $3
09/19/94 Steve Young $3
09/26/94 Baseball strike squabbles $2
10/03/94 Mike Keenan $2
10/10/94 Fuzzy Thurston .... $2-$3
10/17/94 Natrone Means .... $2-$3
10/31/94 Joe Carter $3
11/14/94 Ted Williams $4
11/21/94 Jerry Rice .... $3-$4
11/28/94 Felipe Lopez .... $2-$3
12/05/94 Charles Haley $3
12/12/94 S. Bowman, E. Robinson, L. Wilkens .... $2-$3
12/19/94 Emmitt Smith .... $3-$4
12/26/94 V. Maxwell, Reggie Miller .... $2-$3

1995

02/27/95 Who's on First? .... $2-$3
04/10/95 Cal Ripken Jr. $4
05/01/95 Tom Glavine $3
05/08/95 Frank Thomas $4
06/05/95 Sandy Koufax, Nolan Ryan .... $4-$5
06/19/95 Baseball fans .... $2-$3
07/03/95 Eddie Murray $3
07/10/95 Lee Smith .... $2-$3
08/07/95 Clemens, Gant, R. Jackson, Mays $3
08/28/95 Benito Santiago, Eric Young .... $2-$3
09/11/95 Lou Gehrig, Cal Ripken .... $4-$5
10/09/95 Greg Maddux .... $3-$4
10/30/95 Mark Lemke, Kenny Lofton $3
11/06/95 Atlanta Braves celebrate $3
12/18/95 Cal Ripken Jr. $4

Note: Sporting News issues from 1996 on are priced at $2-$4.

Baseball Digest

Baseball Digest is the nation's oldest active and continuously published magazine devoted to baseball. The magazine was founded in 1942 by Herbert F. Simmons, a member of the Baseball Writers Association of America, as a collection of baseball articles from around the country. The original cover price was 15 cents. In the early years, *Baseball Digest* printed only 10 issues a year—typically not issuing a November or December issue. Starting in 1969, its frequency changed to 12 issues per year.

Today, the magazine continues in the direction that its loyal readers demand: entertaining features, easily digestible anecdotes, and loads of stats and stats analysis.

Baseball Digest has a relatively small following (compared to *Sports Illustrated*) among publications collectors, so the secondary values of most issues are lower than those for other sports magazines. But as this area of the baseball memorabilia hobby continues its steady growth in popularity, the values of *Baseball Digest* back issues should grow as well. In fact, issues with Hall of Famer covers usually attract healthy amounts of attention in Internet auctions. Certain issues that normally book for around $10—a June 1952 (Pee Wee Reese) or an April 1954 (Whitey Ford), for example—can sell for $15-$20 at such sites as eBay.

The following prices are for magazines in Excellent/Near-Mint condition.

Year	Month	Cover	Price

Year	Month	Cover	Price
1942	August	Hit and run	$250
1942	October	Pete Reiser	$100
1942	November	Double play	$75
1942	December	Joe DiMaggio/Billy Southworth	$125
1943	February	At bat in Iceland	$25
1943	March	Back to school	$10
1943	April	Get two	$10
1943	May	Catching a popup	$20
1943	July	Play at second base	$10
1943	August	Safe at the plate	$10
1943	September	Stan Musial	$40
1943	October	Spud Chandler	$10
1943	November	Johnny Lindell	$10
1944	February	Bill Johnson	$15
1944	March	Bill Nicholson/Rip Sewell	$15
1944	April	Dixie Ward	$15
1944	May	Lou Boudreau	$20
1944	July	Vern Stephens	$10
1944	August	Bucky Walters	$15
1944	September	Charlie Grimm	$10
1944	October	Walker Cooper	$10
1944	November	Marty Marion	$10
1945	February	Hal Newhouser	$15
1945	March	George McQuinn	$15
1945	April	Dixie Walker	$15
1945	May	Bill Voiselle	$15
1945	July	Hank Borowy	$15
1945	August	Tommy Holmes	$15
1945	September	Stan Hack	$15
1945	October	Hank Greenberg	$15
1945	November	Al Lopez	$15
1946	February	Charlie Keller	$15
1946	March	Play at the Plate	$10
1946	April	Bobby Doerr	$15
1946	May	Bob Feller	$15

Year	Month	Cover	Price
1946	July	Joe DiMaggio/Ted Williams	$50
1946	August	Joe Cronin	$15
1946	September	Hank Wyse	$15
1946	October	Dave Ferris	$15
1946	November	Johnny Pesky/Red Schoendienst	$15
1947	February	Bucky Harris	$10
1947	March	Johnny Rigney	$10
1947	April	Johnny Van Cuyk	$10
1947	May	Hank Greenberg/Billy Herman	$10

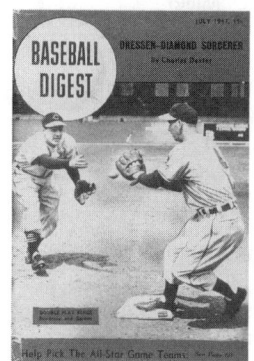

Year	Month	Cover	Price
1947	July	Lou Boudreau/Joe Gordon	$15
1947	August	Buddy Kerr	$10
1947	September	Ewell Blackwell	$10
1947	October	Joe DiMaggio	$50
1947	November	Ralph Lapointe	$10
1948	January	Joe Page	$10
1948	February	Leo Durocher/Branch Rickey	$10
1948	March	Ennis/Hubbard/Meyer	$10
1948	April	Joe McCarthy	$10
1948	May	Art Houtteman	$10
1948	June	Willard Marshall	$10
1948	July	Ralph Kiner	$10
1948	August	Lou Boudreau	$10
1948	September	Stan Musial	$25
1948	October	Hank Sauer	$10
1948	November	Paul Fagen	$10
1949	January	Jim Hegan	$10
1949	February	Red Rolfe	$10
1949	March	Ted Williams	$25
1949	April	Joe DiMaggio	$25
1949	May	Play at the plate	$10
1949	June	Robin Roberts	$15
1949	July	Johnny Groth	$10
1949	August	Frankie Frisch	$10
1949	September	Vic Raschi	$10
1949	October	Mel Parnell/Birdie Tebbets	$10

Year	Month	Cover	Price
1949 ... November	......	Tommy Henrich/Allie Reynolds	$10
1950 ... January	....	Richie Ashburn/Roy Smalley	$15
1950 ... February	....	Dave Koslo	$10
1950 ... March	....	50 Baseball Rules	$10
1950 ... April	....	Bob Feller	$15
1950 ... May	....	Dark/Kramer/Stankey	$10
1950 ... June	....	Joe DiMaggio	$25
1950 ... July	....	Phil Rizzuto	$10
1950 ... August	....	Dick Sisler	$10

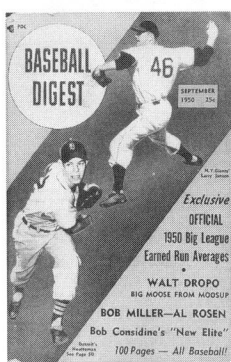

Year	Month	Cover	Price
1950 ... September	.....	Art Houtteman/Larry Jansen	$10
1950 ... October	....	Hoot Evans	$10
1950 ... November	......	Jim Konstanty	$10
1951 ... January	....	Yogi Berra/Whitey Ford	$15
1951 ... February	....	Gil Hodges	$10

Year	Month	Cover	Price
1951 ... March	....	Eddie Yost	$10
1951 ... April	....	Joe DiMaggio	$25
1951 ... May	....	George Earnshaw	$10
1951 ... June	....	Ted Williams	$25
1951 ... July	....	Irv Noren	$10
1951 ... August	....	Nellie Fox/Paul Richards	$15
1951 ... September	.....	Stan Musial	$15
1951 ... October	....	Gil McDougald	$10
1951 ... November	......	Charlie Dressen	$10
1952 ... January	....	Eddie Lopat/Phil Rizzuto	$10
1952 ... February	....	Eddie Stanky	$10
1952 ... March	....	Sid Gordon	$10
1952 ... April	....	Mike Garcia	$10
1952 ... May	....	George Staley	$10
1952 ... June	....	Pee Wee Reese	$10
1952 ... July	....	Ted Kluszewski	$10
1952 ... August	....	Bobby Shantz	$10
1952 ... September	.....	Sal Maglie	$10

Year	Month	Cover	Price
1952 ...	October	Carl Erskine	$10
1952 ...	November	Duke Snider	$10
1953 ...	January	Robin Roberts	$10

Year	Month	Cover	Price
1953 ...	February	Eddie Mathews	$15
1953 ...	March	Billy Martin	$15
1953 ...	April	Hornsby/Mantle/Musial	$25
1953 ...	May	Carl Furillo	$10
1953 ...	June	Bob Lemon	$10
1953 ...	July	Dorish/Kellner/Logan	$10
1953 ...	August	Robin Roberts	$10
1953 ...	September	O'Connell/Strickland/Trucks	$10
1953 ...	October	Casey Stengel	$10
1954 ...	January	Billy Martin	$10
1954 ...	March	Jimmy Piersall	$10
1954 ...	April	Whitey Ford	$10
1954 ...	May	Harvey Kuenn	$10
1954 ...	June	Eddie Mathews/Bobby Morgan	$10
1954 ...	July	Bob Turley	$10
1954 ...	August	Bob Keegan	$10
1954 ...	September	Willie Mays	$10
1954 ...	October	World Series	$10
1954 ...	November	Dusty Rhodes	$10
1955 ...	January	Ralph Kiner	$10

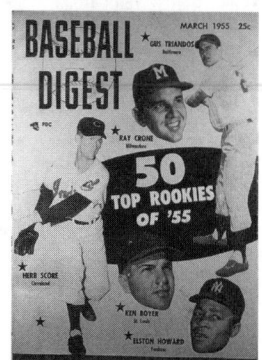

Year	Month	Cover	Price
1955 ...	March	Rookies of '55	$10
1955 ...	April	Alvin Dark	$10
1955 ...	May	Bob Lemon/Don Mueller	$10
1955 ...	June	Bobby Avila	$10
1955 ...	July	Bill Skowron	$10

Year	Month	Cover	Price
1955 ...	August	Roy McMillan/Al Smith	$10
1955 ...	September	Don Newcombe	$10
1955 ...	October	Walt Alston/Tommy Byrne	$10
1955 ...	November	Johnny Podres	$10
1956 ...	February	Al Kaline	$10
1956 ...	March	Rookie Report	$15
1956 ...	April	Luis Aparicio	$10
1956 ...	May	Mike Higgins	$10
1956 ...	June	Clem Labine	$10
1956 ...	July	Mickey Mantle	$25
1956 ...	August	Dale Long	$10
1956 ...	September	Yogi Berra	$15
1956 ...	October	World Series	$10
1956 ...	November	Don Larsen	$15
1957 ...	January	Robin Roberts	$10

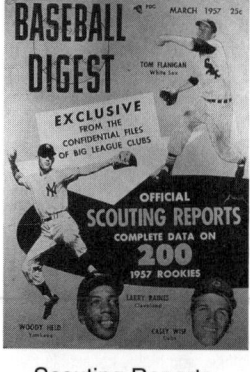

Year	Month	Cover	Price
1957 ...	March	Scouting Reports	$10
1957 ...	April	Farrell/Scheffing/Tighe	$10
1957 ...	May	Don Blasingame	$10
1957 ...	June	Breaking up double play	$10
1957 ...	July	Don Hosak	$10
1957 ...	August	Stan Musial	$15
1957 ...	September	Bobby Shantz	$10
1957 ...	October	Babe Ruth	$10
1958 ...	January	Lew Burdette	$10
1958 ...	February	Lindy McDaniel	$10
1958 ...	March	Scouting Reports	$10
1958 ...	April	Willie Mays/Duke Snider	$10
1958 ...	May	Ted Williams	$20
1958 ...	June	Stan Musial	$25
1958 ...	July	Warren Spahn	$10
1958 ...	August	Bob Turley	$10
1958 ...	September	Pete Runnels	$10
1958 ...	October	World Series	$10
1959 ...	January	Jensen/Roberts/Truly	$10
1959 ...	February	Baseball's Darling Daughters	$10
1959 ...	March	Scouting Reports	$10
1959 ...	April	Ernie Banks	$10
1959 ...	May	Juan Pizarro	$10

Year	Month	Cover	Price
1959 ...	June	Antonelli/Landis/Pascual	$10
1959 ...	July	Vada Pinson	$10
1959 ...	August	Hoyt Wilhem	$10
1959 ...	September	Rocky Colavito/Roy Face	$10
1959 ...	October	World Series	$10
1960 ...	January	John Roseboro/Larry Sherry	$8
1960 ...	February	Harvey Kuenn	$8
1960 ...	March	Scouting Reports	$8
1960 ...	April	Jim Landis/Charlie Neal	$8
1960 ...	May	Early Wynn	$8
1960 ...	June	Bunning/Francona/McDaniel	$8
1960 ...	July	Vern Law	$8
1960 ...	August	Dick Gary/Dick Stuart	$8
1960 ...	September	Ron Hansen	$8
1960 ...	October	Dick Groat	$8
1961 ...	January	Bill Virdon	$8
1961 ...	February	Ralph Houk	$8
1961 ...	March	Scouting Reports	$8
1961 ...	April	Tony Kubek/Al Sprangler	$8
1961 ...	May	Glenn Hobbie	$8
1961 ...	June	Earl Battey	$8
1961 ...	July	Wally Moon	$8
1961 ...	August	Norm Cash	$8
1961 ...	September	Whitey Ford	$8

Year	Month	Cover	Price
1961 ...	October	Koufax/Mantle/Maris/F. Robinson	$25
1962 ...	January	Elston Howard/Ralph Terry	$8
1962 ...	February	Joey Jay	$8
1962 ...	March	Scouting Reports	$8
1962 ...	April	Orlando Cepeda	$8
1962 ...	May	Jim Landis	$8
1962 ...	June	Mickey Mantle	$25
1962 ...	July	Dick Donovan	$8
1962 ...	August	$20 home runs	$8
1962 ...	September	Rich Rollins	$8
1962 ...	October	Tom Tresh/Frank Howard	$8
1963 ...	January	Ralph Terry	$8
1963 ...	February	Ty Cobb/Maury Wills	$8
1963 ...	March	Scouting Reports	$10
1963 ...	April	Rosters	$8
1963 ...	May	Drysdale/Dean/Grove	$8
1963 ...	June	Al Kaline	$8
1963 ...	July	Jim O'Toole	$8
1963 ...	August	Jim Bouton	$8
1963 ...	September	Denny Lemaster	$8
1963 ...	October	Al Downing	$8
1964 ...	January	Dodgers' Aces	$8
1964 ...	February	Roger Maris	$10
1964 ...	March	Scouting Reports	$8
1964 ...	April	Sandy Koufax	$10
1964 ...	May	Harmon Killebrew	$8
1964 ...	June	Tommy Davis/Carl Yastrzemski	$8

Year	Month	Cover	Price
1964 ...	July	Jim Maloney	$8
1964 ...	August	Dave Nicholson	$8
1964 ...	September	Dennis Bennett/Willie Smith	$8
1964 ...	October	Miracle Braves	$8
1965 ...	January	Dick Groat	$8
1965 ...	February	Winter Trades	$8
1965 ...	March	Scouting Reports	$8
1965 ...	April	Which tag is phoney?	$8
1965 ...	May	Bill Freehan	$8
1965 ...	June	Tony Conigliaro	$8
1965 ...	July	Yankees' Six Mistakes	$10
1965 ...	August	Don Drysdale	$8
1965 ...	September	Pete Ward/Joe Morgan	$8
1965 ...	October	Biggest World Series mysteries	$8
1966 ...	January	Sandy Koufax	$10

Year	Month	Cover	Price
1966 ...	February	Willie Mays	$8
1966 ...	March	Scouting Reports	$8
1966 ...	April	Rosters	$8
1966 ...	May	Sam McDowell	$8
1966 ...	June	Should the rules be changed?	$8
1966 ...	July	Juan Marichal	$8
1966 ...	August	Gene Alley/Bill Mazeroski	$8
1966 ...	September	George Scott	$8
1966 ...	October	World Series	$8
1967 ...	January	Bunker/Drabowsky/Palmer	$8
1967 ...	February	Allison/Drysdale/Mathews	$10
1967 ...	March	Scouting Reports	$8
1967 ...	April	Rosters	$8
1967 ...	May	Roger Maris	$10
1967 ...	June	Gaylord Perry/Juan Marichal	$8
1967 ...	July	Denny McLain	$8
1967 ...	August	Joe Horlen	$8
1967 ...	September	Tim McCarver	$8
1967 ...	October	World Series	$8

Year	Month	Cover	Price
1968 ...	January	Bob Gibson	$8
1968 ...	February	Billy Williams	$8
1968 ...	March	Scouting Reports	$8

Year	Month	Cover	Price
1968 ...	April	Rosters	$8
1968 ...	May	Rod Carew/Jay Johnstone	$8
1968 ...	June	Cookie Rojas/Nellie Briles	$8
1968 ...	July	Jerry Koosman	$8

Year	Month	Cover	Price
1968 ...	August	Andy Kosco	$8
1968 ...	September	Matty Alou/Ken Harrelson	$8
1968 ...	October	World Series	$8
1969 ...	January	Lou Brock/Bill Freehan	$8
1969 ...	February	Mickey Mantle	$25

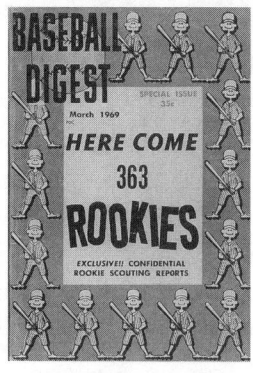

Year	Month	Cover	Price
1969 ...	March	Rookie/Scouting Reports	$8
1969 ...	April	Rosters	$8
1969 ...	May	Al Lopez	$8
1969 ...	June	Ernie Banks	$8
1969 ...	July	Tony Conigliaro	$8
1969 ...	August	Frank Robinson	$8
1969 ...	September	Brushback Tragedy	$8
1969 ...	October	World Series	$8
1969 ...	November	Future Superstars	$8
1969 ...	December	Tom Seaver	$10
1970 ...	January	Harmon Killebrew	$5
1970 ...	February	Joe Pepitone	$5
1970 ...	March	Gene Alley	$5
1970 ...	April	Tony Perez	$5
1970 ...	May	Roberto Clemente	$10
1970 ...	June	Mel Stottlemyre	$5
1970 ...	July	Ken Holtzman	$5
1970 ...	August	Sal Bando	$5
1970 ...	September	Tony Perez	$5
1970 ...	October	Jim Palmer	$5
1970 ...	November	Johnny Bench	$5
1970 ...	December	Billy Williams	$5
1971 ...	January	Brooks Robinson	$5
1971 ...	February	Sal Bando/Juan Marichal	$5

Year	Month	Cover	Price
1971 ...	March	Carl Yastrzemski	$5
1971 ...	April	Bob Gibson	$5
1971 ...	May	Willie Mays	$5
1971 ...	June	Tony Oliva	$5
1971 ...	July	Hank Aaron	$5
1971 ...	August	Vida Blue	$5
1971 ...	September	Joe Pepitone	$5
1971 ...	October	World Series	$5
1971 ...	November	Bobby Murcer	$5
1971 ...	December	Joe Torre	$5
1972 ...	January	Steve Blass	$5
1972 ...	February	Earl Williams	$5
1972 ...	March	Frank Robinson	$5
1972 ...	April	Bill Melton	$5
1972 ...	May	Rosters	$5
1972 ...	June	Reggie Jackson	$8
1972 ...	July	Richie Allen	$5
1972 ...	August	Bud Harrelson	$5
1972 ...	September	Roberto Clemente	$10
1972 ...	October	World Series	$5
1972 ...	November	Carlton Fisk	$5
1972 ...	December	Richie Allen	$5
1973 ...	January	Pete Rose	$5
1973 ...	February	Cesar Cedeño	$5
1973 ...	March	Harmon Killebrew	$5
1973 ...	April	Don Kessinger	$5
1973 ...	May	Nolan Ryan	$15
1973 ...	June	Tom Seaver	$10
1973 ...	July	Pete Rose	$5
1973 ...	August	Allen/May/Melton	$5
1973 ...	September	Ken Holtzman	$5
1973 ...	October	Bill Russell	$5
1973 ...	November	Jose Cardenal	$5
1973 ...	December	Willie Stargell	$5
1974 ...	January	World Series	$5
1974 ...	February	Bobby Bonds	$5
1974 ...	March	Bobby Grich	$5
1974 ...	April	Hank Aaron	$5
1974 ...	May	Ted Sizemore	$5
1974 ...	June	Felix Millan	$5
1974 ...	July	Brooks Robinson	$5
1974 ...	August	Gaylord Perry	$5
1974 ...	September	Tommy John	$5
1974 ...	October	Richie Allen	$5
1974 ...	November	Bando/Campaneris/Jackson	$8

Year	Month	Cover	Price

Year	Month	Cover	Price
1974 ...	December	Lou Brock	$5
1975 ...	January	Rollie Fingers	$5
1975 ...	February	Steve Garvey	$5
1975 ...	March	Jeff Burroughs	$5
1975 ...	April	Jim "Catfish" Hunter	$5
1975 ...	May	Mike Schmidt	$8
1975 ...	June	Rod Carew	$5
1975 ...	July	Nolan Ryan	$15
1975 ...	August	Rick Monday	$5
1975 ...	September	Johnny Bench	$5
1975 ...	October	Vida Blue	$5
1975 ...	November	Fred Lynn	$5
1975 ...	December	Joe Morgan	$5
1976 ...	January	Pete Rose	$5
1976 ...	February	Jim Palmer	$5
1976 ...	March	George Brett	$5
1976 ...	April	Carlton Fisk	$5
1976 ...	May	Frank Tanana	$5
1976 ...	June	Rick Manning	$5
1976 ...	July	Bill Madlock	$5
1976 ...	August	Randy Jones	$5
1976 ...	September	Larry Bowa	$5
1976 ...	October	Mickey Rivers	$5
1976 ...	November	Mark Fidrych	$5
1976 ...	December	Joe Morgan	$5
1977 ...	January	World Series	$5
1977 ...	February	Thurman Munson	$5
1977 ...	March	Amos Otis	$5
1977 ...	April	Mark Fidrych	$5
1977 ...	May	John Montefusco	$5
1977 ...	June	Steve Carlton	$5
1977 ...	July	Dave Parker	$5
1977 ...	August	Ivan DeJesus/Manny Trillo	$5
1977 ...	September	Carl Yastrzemski	$5
1977 ...	October	Steve Garvey	$5
1977 ...	November	Bump Wills	$5
1977 ...	December	George Foster	$5
1978 ...	January	Reggie Jackson	$5
1978 ...	February	Willie McCovey	$5
1978 ...	March	Rod Carew	$5
1978 ...	April	Tom Seaver	$10
1978 ...	May	Cesar Cedeño	$5
1978 ...	June	Garry Templeton	$5
1978 ...	July	Dave Kingman	$5
1978 ...	August	Jim Rice	$5
1978 ...	September	Ron Guidry	$5
1978 ...	October	Rich Gale/Clint Hurdle	$5
1978 ...	November	Reggie Smith	$5
1978 ...	December	Dave Parker	$5
1979 ...	January	World Series	$5
1979 ...	February	Dave Winfield	$5

Year	Month	Cover	Price
1979 ...	March	Greg Luzinski	$5
1979 ...	April	Rich Gossage	$5
1979 ...	May	Jack Clark	$5
1979 ...	June	Steve Garvey	$5
1979 ...	July	Al Oliver	$5
1979 ...	August	Bill Buckner	$5
1979 ...	September	Tommy John	$5
1979 ...	October	Mike Schmidt	$5
1979 ...	November	Omar Moreno	$5
1979 ...	December	George Brett	$5
1980 ...	January	World Series	$5
1980 ...	February	Paul Molitor	$5
1980 ...	March	Gary Carter	$5
1980 ...	April	Willie Stargell	$5
1980 ...	May	Don Baylor	$5
1980 ...	June	J.R. Richard/Nolan Ryan	$5
1980 ...	July	Baumgarten/Burns/Trout	$5
1980 ...	August	Ken Landreaux	$5
1980 ...	September	Steve Carlton	$5

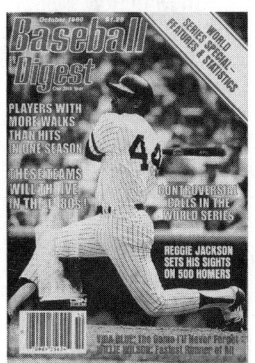

Year	Month	Cover	Price
1980 ...	October	Reggie Jackson	$5
1980 ...	November	Joe Charboneau	$5
1980 ...	December	George Brett	$5
1981 ...	January	Tug McGraw	$5
1981 ...	February	Eddie Murray	$5
1981 ...	March	Rickey Henderson	$5
1981 ...	April	Mike Schmidt	$5
1981 ...	May	Gary Carter	$5
1981 ...	June	Cecil Cooper	$5
1981 ...	July	Carlton Fisk	$5
1981 ...	August	Fernando Valenzuela	$5
1981 ...	September	Danny Darwin	$5
1981 ...	October	Ron Davis	$5
1981 ...	November	Pete Rose	$5
1981 ...	December	Tim Raines	$5
1982 ...	January	Steve Garvey	$5
1982 ...	February	Carney Lansford	$5
1982 ...	March	Rollie Fingers	$5
1982 ...	April	Dave Winfield	$5
1982 ...	May	Nolan Ryan	$15
1982 ...	June	Jerry Reuss	$5
1982 ...	July	Salome Barojas	$5
1982 ...	August	Dale Murphy	$5
1982 ...	September	Rickey Henderson	$5
1982 ...	October	Robin Yount	$5
1982 ...	November	Kent Hrbek	$5
1982 ...	December	Lonnie Smith/Ozzie Smith	$5
1983 ...	January	Darrell Porter	$5
1983 ...	February	Mario Soto	$5
1983 ...	March	Doug DeCinces	$5
1983 ...	April	Willie McGee	$5
1983 ...	May	Pete Vuckovich	$5
1983 ...	June	Cal Ripken Jr.	$5

Year	Month	Cover	Price
1983	July	Tony Peña	$5
1983	August	Dave Stieb	$5
1983	September	Chris Chambliss	$5
1983	October	Ron Kittle	$5
1983	November	Steve Carlton	$5
1983	December	Carlton Fisk	$5
1984	January	Rick Dempsey	$5
1984	February	Wade Boggs	$5
1984	March	Dale Murphy	$5
1984	April	Mike Boddicker	$5
1984	May	Andre Dawson	$5
1984	June	Lance Parrish	$5
1984	July	Bill Madlock	$5
1984	August	Leon Durham	$5
1984	September	Gwynn/Martinez/McReynolds	$5
1984	October	Ryne Sandberg	$5
1984	November	Keith Hernandez	$5
1984	December	Mark Langston	$5
1985	January	Alan Trammell	$5
1985	February	Don Mattingly	$5
1985	March	Frank Viola	$5
1985	April	Jack Morris	$5
1985	May	Tony Gwynn	$5
1985	June	Dwight Gooden	$5
1985	July	Bruce Sutter	$5
1985	August	Pete Rose	$5
1985	September	Lee Smith	$5
1985	October	Ron Guidry	$5
1985	November	Pedro Guerrero	$5
1985	December	Dwight Gooden	$5
1986	January	Willie McGee	$5
1986	February	Bret Saberhagen	$5
1986	March	Tom Browning	$5
1986	April	Harold Baines	$5
1986	May	Darryl Strawberry	$5
1986	June	Eddie Murray	$5
1986	July	Bert Blyleven	$5
1986	August	Roger Clemens	$10
1986	September	Gary Carter	$5
1986	October	Jose Canseco/Wally Joyner	$5
1986	November	Bill Doran	$5
1986	December	Roger Clemens/Teddy Higuera	$5
1987	January	Wade Boggs/Don Mattingly	$5
1987	February	Sid Fernandez	$5
1987	March	Mike Scott	$5
1987	April	Chris Brown	$5
1987	May	Pete O'Brien	$5
1987	June	Eric Davis/Jody Davis	$5
1987	July	Mike Witt	$5
1987	August	Rickey Henderson	$5
1987	September	Jack Clark/Ozzie Smith	$5
1987	October	Mark McGwire	$5
1987	November	George Bell	$5
1987	December	Kevin Seitzer	$5
1988	January	Andre Dawson	$5
1988	February	Frank Viola	$5
1988	March	Jimmy Key	$5
1988	April	Kevin McReynolds/Mike Pagliarulo	$5
1988	May	Eric Davis	$5
1988	June	Royals Pitchers	$5
1988	July	Andy Van Slyke	$5
1988	August	Dave Winfield	$5
1988	September	Greg Maddux	$5
1988	October	Kirby Puckett	$5
1988	November	Jose Canseco	$5
1988	December	Tony Gwynn	$5

Year	Month	Cover	Price
1989	January	Jose Canseco	$5
1989	February	Orel Hershiser	$5
1989	March	Greg Jefferies	$5
1989	April	Kirk Gibson	$5
1989	May	Cory Snider	$5
1989	June	Fred McGriff	$5
1989	July	Will Clark	$5
1989	August	Nolan Ryan	$12
1989	September	Bo Jackson	$5
1989	October	Dave Stewart	$5
1989	November	Howard Johnson	$5
1989	December	Jerome Walton/Dwight Smith	$5
1990	January	Abbott/Clark/Ryan	$8
1990	February	Ruben Sierra	$5

Year	Month	Cover	Price
1990	March	Ken Griffey Jr.	$12
1990	April	Canseco/McGwire/Steinbach	$5
1990	May	Gibson/Strawberry/Winfield	$5
1990	June	Mark Grace	$5
1990	July	Bill Geren/Lou Whitaker	$5
1990	August	Bobby Bonilla/Frank Viola	$5
1990	September	Rickey Henderson	$5
1990	October	Ozzie Guillen	$5
1990	November	Cecil Fielder	$5
1990	December	Sandy Alomar/Dave Justice	$5
1991	January	Bob Welch	$3
1991	February	Chris Sabo	$3
1991	March	Ray Lankford	$3
1991	April	Charlton/Dibble/Myers	$3
1991	May	Darryl Strawberry	$3
1991	June	Tim Raines	$3
1991	July	Kevin Mitchell	$3

Year	Month	Cover	Price
1991	August	Roger Clemens	$3
1991	September	Robin Yount	$3
1991	October	Cal Ripken Jr.	$8
1991	November	Rafael Palmeiro	$3
1991	December	Chuck Knoblauch	$3

Year	Month	Cover	Price

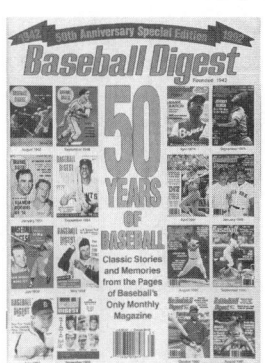

Year	Month	Cover	Price
1992	January	Steve Avery	$3
1992	February	Kirby Puckett	$3
1992	March	'92 Rookies	$3
1992	April	Frank Thomas	$3
1992	May	Wade Boggs	$3
1992	June	Dan Gladden/Greg Olson	$3
1992	July	Howard Johnson	$3
1992	August	Mark McGwire	$3
1992	September	Juan Guzman	$3
1992	October	Kirby Puckett	$3
1992	November	Dennis Eckersley/Tom Glavine	$3
1992	December	Pat Listach	$3
1993	January	Roberto Alomar	$3
1993	February	Gary Sheffield	$3
1993	March	Tim Wakefield	$3
1993	April	Jose Canseco	$3
1993	May	Curt Schilling	$3
1993	June	Robin Ventura	$3
1993	July	Juan Gonzalez	$3
1993	August	Barry Bonds	$3
1993	September	Joe Carter	$3
1993	October	John Kruk	$3
1993	November	Frank Thomas	$6
1993	December	Mike Piazza	$6
1994	January	Paul Molitor	$3
1994	February	Randy Johnson	$3
1994	March	Greg Maddux	$3
1994	April	Carlos Baerga	$3
1994	May	Lenny Dykstra	$3
1994	June	Rafael Palmeiro	$3
1994	July	Lance Johnson	$3
1994	August	Matt Williams	$3
1994	September	Kirby Puckett	$3
1994	October	Ozzie Smith	$3
1994	November	Jimmy Key	$3
1994	December	Bob Hamelin	$3
1995	January	Jeff Bagwell	$3
1995	February	Tony Gwynn	$3
1995	March	Raul Mondesi	$3
1995	April	Kenny Lofton	$3
1995	May	Don Mattingly	$3
1995	June	Fred McGriff	$3
1995	July	Cal Ripken Jr.	$8
1995	August	Eddie Mathews	$3
1995	September	John Valentin	$3
1995	October	Barry Larkin	$3
1995	November	Mickey Mantle	$15
1995	December	Hideo Nomo	$3
1996	January	Albert Belle	$3
1996	February	Tom Glavine	$3
1996	March	Tim Salmon	$3
1996	April	Dante Bichette	$3
1996	May	Edgar Martinez	$3
1996	June	Roberto Alomar	$3
1996	July	Mike Piazza	$3
1996	August	Jason Giambi	$3
1996	September	Harold Baines	$3
1996	October	John Smoltz	$3
1996	November	Mark McGwire	$3
1996	December	Derek Jeter	$3
1997	January	Alex Rodriguez	$3
1997	February	Ken Caminiti	$3
1997	March	Andruw Jones	$3
1997	April	Ken Griffey Jr.	$3
1997	May	Albert Belle/Frank Thomas	$3
1997	June	Brown/Fernandez/A. Leiter	$3
1997	July	Ivan Rodriguez	$3
1997	August	Larry Walker	$3
1997	September	Roger Clemens	$3
1997	October	Tino Martinez	$3
1997	November	Chipper Jones	$3
1997	December	Nomar Garciaparra	$3
1998	January	Tony Gwynn	$3
1998	February	Charles Johnson	$3
1998	March	Curt Schilling	$3
1998	April	Jay Bell/Matt Williams	$3
1998	May	Paul O'Neill	$3
1998	June	Mike Mussina	$3
1998	July	Jeromy Burnitz	$3
1998	August	Kerry Wood	$3
1998	September	Mark McGwire	$5
1998	October	Derek Jeter	$4
1998	November	Greg Vaughn	$3
1998	December	Sammy Sosa	$3
1999	January	Wells/Clemens/Brown	$3
1999	February	Omar Vizquel	$3
1999	March	Juan Gonzalez	$3
1999	April	Mark McGwire	$5
1999	May	Vladimir Guerrero	$3
1999	June	Roger Clemens	$3
1999	July	Thomas/Ripken Jr./Gwynn	$4
1999	August	Jose Canseco	$3
1999	September	Pedro Martinez	$3
1999	October	Manny Ramirez	$3
1999	November	Ventura/Piazza	$3
1999	December	Williams/Ruth/Mays	$5
2000	January	Ivan Rodriguez	$3
2000	February	Mariano Rivera	$3
2000	March	Randy Johnson	$3
2000	April	Chipper Jones	$3
2000	May	McGwire/Griffey Jr./Sosa	$5
2000	June	Nomar Garciaparra	$3
2000	July	Jim Edmonds	$3
2000	August	Greg Maddux	$3
2000	September	Todd Helton	$3
2000	October	Magglio Ordonez	$3
2000	November	Edgar Martinez	$3
2000	December	Bonds/Piazza/Delgado	$3
2001	January	Pedro Martinez	$3
2001	February	Derek Jeter	$4
2001	March	Edgardo Alfonzo	$3
2001	April	Mark McGwire/Jason Giambi	$4
2001	May	Andruw Jones	$3
2001	June	Jeff Kent	$3
2001	July	Mike Mussina	$3
2001	August	Kevin Brown	$3

Baseball Magazine

Baseball Magazine, launched in 1908, was our nation's premier baseball publication for its first few decades of life. By the middle of the 20th century, such competitors as *The Sporting News*, *Sport* and *Sports Illustrated* started grabbing market share. Ultimately, 1953 was the beginning of the end for *Baseball Magazine*. Only eight issues appeared that year, followed by four each in '54 and '55, five in '56, and two final issues in 1957. An attempt to revive the magazine in 1964 and '65 was short-lived, and a lack of interest forced *Baseball Magazine* to vanish for good after its April 1965 issue.

Today, vintage copies of *Baseball Magazine* are the most valuable of all baseball publications in the hobby. Finding a Near Mint issue is almost impossible because the magazine has been out of print so long. Plus, relatively few fans saved their issues.

In our *Baseball Magazine* pricing section, we don't list cover subjects because most of the publication's covers were illustrations of baseball scenes, fans or action. The publisher rarely used photography of baseball stars on the cover.

The prices below reflect magazines in Excellent condition.

April 1912	Player	$90
May 1912	Opening Day	$90
December 1912	Football player	$90
March 1913	Frank Chase	$90
April 1915	Walter Johnson	$150
May 1916	Joe Jackson	$150
September 1916	Brown paper (no cover)	$20
October 1916	Brown paper (no cover)	$40
November 1916	Brown paper (no cover)	$40
January 1917	John McGraw	$35
February 1917	St. Louis players	$50
March 1917	Tris Speaker	$95
November 1917	Baseball fans	$65

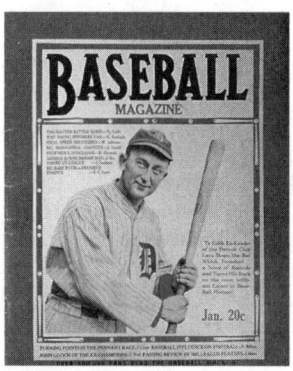

January 1919	Ty Cobb	$200
March 1920	Pat Moran	$75
September 1920	Cleveland player	$90
October 1922	Play at third	$35
March 1923	Batter and catcher	$45
November 1924	Batter	$45
May 1925	Pitcher	$35
November 1925	Pitcher, World Series	$50
February 1926	Fielder	$35
April 1926	Play at the plate	$45
May 1926	Pitcher	$35
August 1926	Eddie Collins, George Sisler	$35
September 1926	Catcher	$45
February 1927	Batter	$40
April 1927	Play at first	$35
July 1927	Robert O'Farrell	$35

August 1927	Catcher	$35

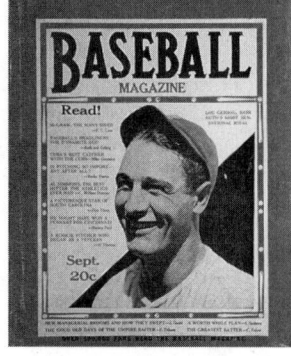

September 1927	Lou Gehrig	$50
October 1927	Joe McCarthy	$30
May 1928	Pitcher	$35
June 1928	First baseman	$45
July 1928	Batter and catcher	$35
August 1928	Batter	$45
September 1928	Play at third	$35
January 1929	Play at plate	$40
February 1929	Sliding into base	$40
March 1929	Catcher	$40
April 1929	Base runner	$40
May 1929	Pitcher	$40
June 1929	Batter	$35
July 1929	Play at second	$40
August 1929	Mickey Cochrane	$40
September 1929	Batter	$40
January 1930	Pitcher illustration	$30
February 1930	Pitcher illustration	$30
March 1930	Lefty Grove	$30
April 1930	Batter illustration	$40
May 1930	Al Simmons	$40
June 1930	Batter illustration	$40
July 1930	Grover Alexander	$35
August 1930	Pitcher illustration	$25
September 1930	Play at the plate	$40
October 1930	Pitcher illustration	$40
November 1930	World Series crowd	$25
January 1931	Pitcher illustration	$35
March 1931	Fielder illustration	$30
April 1931	Play at second	$35
May 1931	1930-31 Champions banner	$35
June 1931	Batter illustration	$35
July 1931	Catcher and batter	$25
August 1931	Rabbit Maranville	$30
September 1931	Play at second	$30
October 1931	Wes Ferrell	$35
November 1931	World Series number	$25

December 1931	Fielder	$30
January 1932	Unknown	$35
February 1932	Chuck Klein	$45
March 1932	Play at the plate	$75
April 1932	Pepper Martin	$35
May 1932	Play ball	$35
June 1932	Max Carey	$35
July 1932	Fielder illustration	$30
August 1932	Catcher illustration	$35
September 1932	George Earnshaw	$35
October 1932	Earl Averill	$50
November 1932	World Series number	$35
December 1932	J. McCarthy, President Roosevelt	$75
February 1933	Jimmie Foxx	$45
March 1933	John Heydler	$35
April 1933	Dale Alexander	$35
May 1933	25th Anniversary issue	$45
June 1933	Bill Terry	$45
July 1933	Red Faber	$35
August 1933	Play at second	$35
February 1934	William Harridge	$40
May 1934	Play at the plate	$35
June 1934	Bob O'Farrell	$35
July 1934	Jimmy Dykes	$35
September 1934	Mel Harder	$30
January 1935	Ford Frick	$35
July 1935	Charles Dressen	$30
September 1935	Mel Ott	$45
October 1935	Hank Greenberg	$45
January 1936	Buddy Myers	$30
February 1936	Gabby Hartnett	$40
March 1936	Steve O'Neill	$35
May 1936	Play Ball	$35
June 1936	Roger Cramer	$35
July 1936	Joe Medwick	$75

April 1938	Catchers mask	$30
June 1938	Gus Mancuso	$30
July 1938	Frank Crosetti	$30
August 1938	Gabby Hartnett, umpire	$75
September 1938	Red Rolfe	$30
October 1938	World Series issue	$75
November 1938	Gabby Hartnett, Joe McCarthy	$30
December 1938	Dizzy Dean	$30
January 1939	Ernie Lombardi	$35
February 1939	Bob Feller	$35
March 1939	Play at the plate	$35
April 1939	Bobby Doerr	$35
May 1939	D. Bartell, H. Leiber, G. Mancuso	$30
June 1939	Abner Doubleday	$75
July 1939	Baseball action photos	$75
September 1939	Dodgers on the mound	$35
October 1939	Red Rolfe	$50
November 1939	Bucky Walters, Joe DiMaggio	$50
December 1939	Ted Williams	$50
January 1940	Terry Moore	$25
February 1940	Baseball close-up	$25
March 1940	P. Coscarart, C. Dressen, L. Durocher	$25
April 1940	Joe Gordon	$25
May 1940	Umpire Bill Klem	$25
June 1940	B. Feller, R. Hemsley, O. Vitt	$35
July 1940	Ernie Lombardi, Johnny Mize	$35
August 1940	Flash Gordon	$25
September 1940	Harry Danning	$25
October 1940	Joe DiMaggio	$50
November 1940	Reds team photo	$30
December 1940	Tigers/Reds World Series	$30
January 1941	Jimmy Wilson	$25

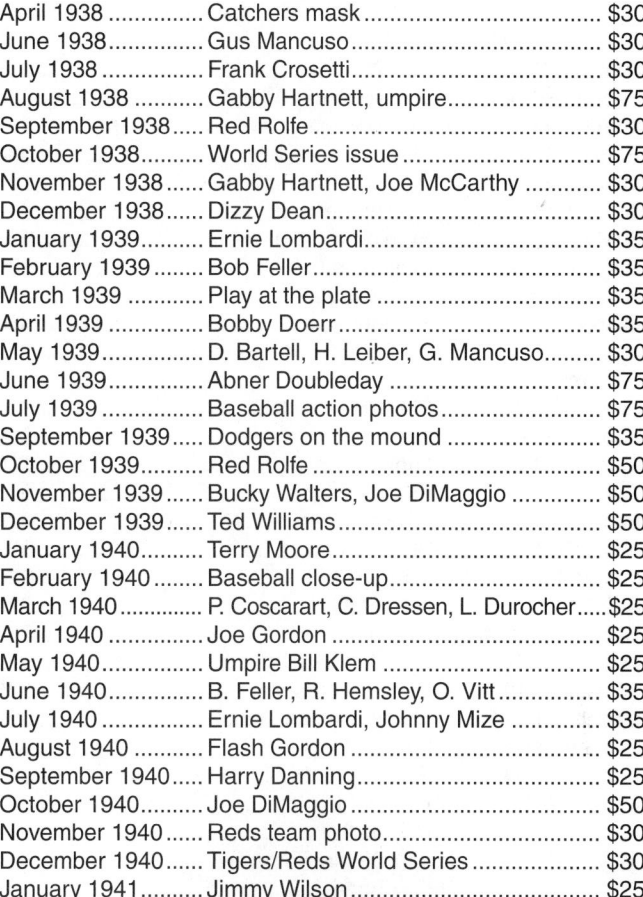

February 1941	Connie Mack	$25
March 1941	Babe Young	$25
April 1941	Joe McCarthy	$25
May 1941	Bucky Walters	$25
June 1941	Jake Early, Ban Johnson	$25
July 1941	Johnny Hopp, Babe Young	$25
August 1941	Ted Williams	$45
September 1941	Dolph Camilli, Enos Slaughter	$25
October 1941	Umpire Bill Summers	$30
November 1941	Yankees team	$30
December 1941	Billy Herman	$30
January 1942	Lou Boudreau	$50
February 1942	Mel Ott, team executives	$40
March 1942	Play at the plate	$35
April 1942	Ebbets Field	$35
May 1942	Hank Greenberg	$45
June 1942	Enos Slaughter	$35
July 1942	Play at the plate	$35
August 1942	Paul Waner	$35
September 1942	Joe Gordon, Elmer Valo	$35
October 1942	Play at the plate	$35

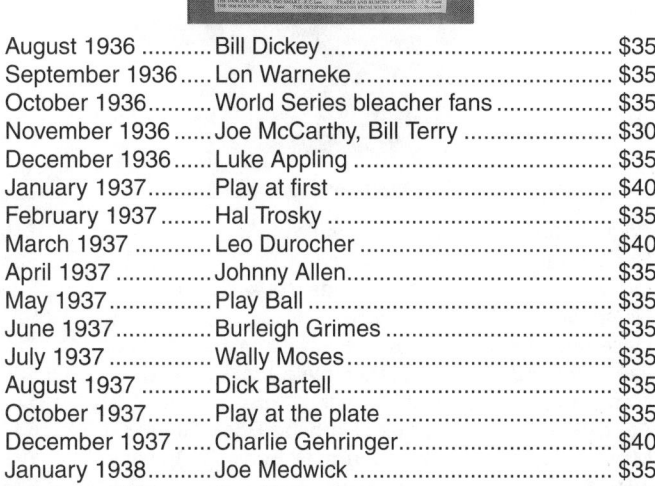

August 1936	Bill Dickey	$35
September 1936	Lon Warneke	$35
October 1936	World Series bleacher fans	$35
November 1936	Joe McCarthy, Bill Terry	$30
December 1936	Luke Appling	$35
January 1937	Play at first	$40
February 1937	Hal Trosky	$35
March 1937	Leo Durocher	$40
April 1937	Johnny Allen	$35
May 1937	Play Ball	$35
June 1937	Burleigh Grimes	$35
July 1937	Wally Moses	$35
August 1937	Dick Bartell	$35
October 1937	Play at the plate	$35
December 1937	Charlie Gehringer	$40
January 1938	Joe Medwick	$35
February 1938	Gee Walker	$30
March 1938	Play at the plate	$30

November 1942	J. McCarthy, B. Southworth	$35
December 1942	Cal Griffith	$35
January 1943	Pee Wee Reese	$35
February 1943	Johnny Pesky, Phil Rizzuto	$35
March 1943	Jimmy Brown	$30
April 1943	Play at the plate	$30
May 1943	Play at the plate	$25
June 1943	Play at the plate	$30
July 1943	Arguing with an umpire	$30
August 1943	Play at first	$30
September 1943	Arky Vaughan	$30
October 1943	Bill Johnson	$50
November 1943	J. McCarthy, B. Southworth	$30
December 1943	Frank Crosetti	$25
January 1944	Play at the plate	$25
February 1944	Play at third	$20
March 1944	Yankees bat boy	$20
April 1944	Pirates player	$25
May 1944	Senators pitchers	$25
June 1944	Buy Bonds	$25
July 1944	Jimmie Foxx	$35
August 1944	Play at third	$20
September 1944	Play at the plate	$25
October 1944	The Cooper brothers	$25
November 1944	Detroit Tigers players	$25
December 1944	Cardinals team photo	$25
January 1945	Play at the plate	$25
February 1945	Ford Frick, William Harriot	$25
March 1945	Play at the plate	$25
April 1945	Play Ball	$25
May 1945	Joe Cronin, Tom Yawkey	$15
June 1945	Buy Bonds	$25
July 1945	Happy Chandler	$25
August 1945	Rundown play	$25
September 1945	Boston Braves players	$25
October 1945	Chicago Cubs players	$25
November 1945	Chief Bender, Connie Mack	$25
December 1945	Charlie Grimm, Steve O'Neill	$25
January 1946	Play at the plate	$25
February 1946	Play at the plate	$25
March 1946	Play at the plate	$25
April 1946	L. Durocher, J. McCarthy, M. Ott	$35
May 1946	Lou Boudreau, Bob Feller	$35
June 1946	President Truman	$25
July 1946	Pee Wee Reese, Pete Reiser	$35
August 1946	Rudy York	$25
September 1946	Play at third	$25
October 1946	Bobby Doerr, Ted Williams	$45
November 1946	Bob Feller, Hal Newhouser	$40
December 1946	Cardinals team photo	$25
January 1947	Johnny Pesky	$25
February 1947	George Case	$25
March 1947	Happy Chandler	$25
April 1947	Play at the plate	$25
May 1947	Eddie Stanky	$45
June 1947	Ted Williams	$45
July 1947	Pete Reiser, Andy Seminick	$35
August 1947	Luke Appling	$25
September 1947	Ewell Blackwell	$25
October 1947	Cincinnati Reds	$25
November 1947	Ralph Kiner, Johnny Mize	$30
December 1947	Jackie Robinson	$45
January 1948	Play at third	$25
February 1948	Joe Cronin, Joe McCarthy	$35
March 1948	Yogi Berra, Jack Conway	$30
April 1948	Play at the plate	$25

May 1948	T. Holmes, D. Litwhiler, C. Ryan	$25
June 1948	President Truman	$20
July 1948	Clyde Kluttz, Johnny Mize	$25
August 1948	Steve O'Neill, Dizzy Trout	$25
September 1948	Stan Musial	$35
October 1948	Lou Boudreau, Mike Guerra	$50
November 1948	Connie Mack	$20
December 1948	Lou Boudreau	$25
January 1949	Joe DiMaggio, Bobby Doerr, Ted Williams	$60
February 1949	Gil Coan, Joe Dobson	$25
March 1949	Pat Mullin	$25
April 1949	Bob Swift, Birdie Tebbetts	$25
June 1949	Griffith Stadium	$25
July 1949	Ralph Branca	$25
August 1949	Del Rice	$25
September 1949	Casey Stengel	$25
October 1949	Richie Ashburn, Clyde McCullough, Andy Seminick	$35
November 1949	Connie Mack	$30
December 1949	Ford Frick, William Harridge, Casey Stengel	$20
January 1950	Red Sox pitchers	$20
February 1950	Roy Sievers	$20
March 1950	T. Henrich, J. Mize, C. Stengel	$20
April 1950	Sherm Lollar, Birdie Tebbetts	$20
May 1950	Stan Musial	$25
June 1950	Earl Torgeson	$20
July 1950	Connie Mack	$25
August 1950	Eddie Sawyer	$20
September 1950	Johnny Lipon	$20
October 1950	Richie Ashburn	$35
December 1950	Yankee Stadium	$35
January 1951	Play at second	$20
February 1951	Billy Goodman	$20
March 1951	Braves vs. Cubs	$20
April 1951	Joe Garagiola	$15
May 1951	Vern Bickford, Johnny Sain, Warren Spahn	$20
June 1951	Casey Stengel	$20
July 1951	Eddie Sawyer, Casey Stengel	$15

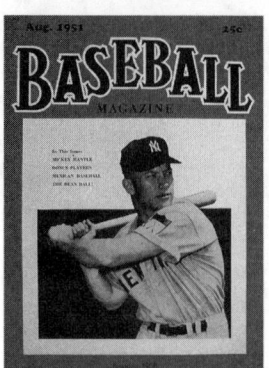

August 1951	Mickey Mantle	$45
September 1951	Gil Hodges	$35
October 1951	World Series issue	$25
November 1951	Bob Feller	$25
December 1951	Cy Young	$25
January 1952	Out at the plate	$20
March 1952	Ned Garver	$20
April 1952	Rogers Hornsby, Eddie Stanky	$40
May 1952	R. Ashburn, D. Ennis, T. Brown	$35
June 1952	Willie Mays	$35
July/August 1952	All-Star Game issue	$20

September 1952	Babe Ruth anniversary issue	$35
October 1952	Pennant issue	$45
November/December 1952	World Series issue	$20
April 1953	Pee Wee Reese, Hank Sauer, Bobby Shantz	$35
May 1953	Solly Hemus, Johnny Mize	$20
June 1953	Joe DiMaggio, Hoot Evers, Allie Reynolds	$40
July 1953	Billy Bruton, Mickey Mantle	$45
August 1953	L. Appling, R. Boone, D. Gernert	$15
September 1953	Karl Drews, Mickey Vernon, Del Wilber	$20
October 1953	Gus Bell, Gil Hodges	$35
November 1953	Reese, Rizzuto, Roberts, Schoendienst	$35
August 1954	Mickey Mantle	$20
September 1954	Casey Stengel	$10
October 1954	World Series issue	$10
March 1955	Connie Mack	$15
May 1955	Illustration	$10
June 1955	Illustration	$10
July 1955	All-Star Game issue	$15
May 1956	Play Ball	$25
June 1956	Ted Williams	$30
July 1956	Mickey Mantle	$40
August 1956	Bob Friend	$20
October 1956	Casey Stengel	$20
May 1957	Don Larsen	$20
September 1957	Bob Feller	$20
November 1964	Johnny Callison	$30
December 1964	Brooks Robinson	$30
January 1965	Cardinals team photo	$20
February 1965	Cleveland's Municipal Stadium	$20
March 1965	Frank Howard	$30
April 1965	Wally Bunker	$20

American League Red Books

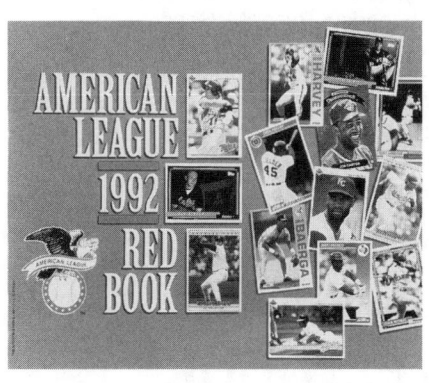

1943 Blue V, (First Red Book)	$25-$75
1944 Blue baseball with red seams	$25-$50
1945 Blue baseball with red seams	$25-$50
1946 Blue baseball with title	$25-$45
1947 Baseball in right corner	$25-$40
1948 Title and 1948	$25-$40
1949 Title and 1949	$25-$40
1950 Title and 1950 (1st glossy cover)	$20-$35
1951 A.L. Golden Anniversary	$20-$35
1952 Play Ball!, Ted Williams	$20-$35
1953 Shantz, Fox, Wynn, others	$20-$35
1954 Vernon, Kuenn, Stengel, Rose	$20-$35
1955 All-Star Team photo	$20-$35
1956 Lemon, Stengel, managers	$20-$30
1957 Team logos	$17-$30
1958 50th Anniversary of BBWAA	$17-$30
1959 Tiger sliding into home	$17-$30
1960 Cobb, DiMaggio, Fox, Ruth, Gehrig, others	$20-$35
1961 Four players with arms linked	$17-$30

1962 Mantle, Maris, A.L. HR Leaders	$20-$35
1963 Team pennants	$17-$25
1964 Killebrew, Yastrzemski, others	$15-$25
1965 D. Chance, Powell, Oliva, others	$12-$22
1966 McDowell, T. Conigliaro, others	$14-$24
1967 Frank Robinson Triple Crown	$14-$24
1968 Yastrzemski MVP/Triple Crown	$14-$24
1969 Cobb, Ruth, HOF plaques	$14-$24
1970 Harmon Killebrew	$10-$20
1971 Boog Powell	$10-$20
1972 Team, Major League logos	$10-$20
1973 Team hats with Oakland in center	$10-$20
1974 Team, Major League logos	$10-$20
1975 Team logos	$10-$15
1976 Carlton Fisk Series homer	$10-$15
1977 Team logos, with Seattle and Toronto	$10-$15
1978 Carew, Nettles, Murray, others	$10-$15
1979 Guidry, Rice, Carew, others	$10-$15
1980 Orioles and Eddie Murray	$7-$12
1981 Boddicker, Charboneau, Brett	$7-$12
1982 1981 Playoffs team pictures	$7-$12
1983 Vuckovich, Yount, Ripken	$7-$12
1984 L. Hoyt, Ripken, Quisenberry, Kittle	$7-$12
1985 Stars and Detroit Tigers Series celebration	$7-$8
1986 Newspaper headlines (Boggs, Seaver, others)	$7
1987 Mattingly, Canseco, Clemens, others	$7
1988 Twins World Series celebration	$7
1989 1988 A.L. media guide covers	$7
1990 1980s Red Book covers	$7
1991 League trophies, awards	$7
1992 Baseball cards	$7
1993 George Brett, Robin Yount	$7

National League Green Books

1935 Jan. 30, 1935 (First Green Book)	$30-$60
1936 60th Birthday edition, Feb. 2, 1936	$30-$50
1937 Title and Feb. 5, 1937	$30-$50
1938 Title and 1938	$30-$50
1939 Centennial edition 1839-1939	$30-$45

1940 Title and 1940	$25-$40
1941 Title and 1941	$25-$35
1942 Baseball diamond	$25-$60
1943 Title and 1943	$25-$60
1944 Title and 1944	$25-$60

1945 Title and 1945	$25-$50
1946 BBWAA logo	$25-$50
1947 Title and 1947 in diamond shape	$25-$40
1948 Runner thrown out at first base	$25-$35
1949 Team logos, pennants	$25-$35
1950 Team logos, pennants	$20-$30
1951 75th Anniversary, ball in glove	$30-$30
1952 National League cities	$20-$30
1953 National League cities	$20-$30
1954 All-Star Team, 1st glossy cover	$20-$30
1955 Eight stars (Mays, Musial, Spahn)	$20-$30
1956 Dodgers celebration photos	$20-$30
1957 National League	$17-$25
1958 N.L. salutes the BBWAA	$17-$25
1959 Spahn/Musial clippings	$17-$25
1960 Snider, McCovey, Musial, others	$17-$25
1961 Spahn, Howard, F. Robinson, etc.	$14-$20
1962 Map of U.S., team logos	$14-$20

1963 1958-62 League Champs parks	$14-$20
1964 Stan Musial	$14-$20
1965 List of past N.L. Champions	$12-$20
1966 Stadiums of 1960s, seven	$12-$20
1967 1962-66 Attendance figures	$12-$20
1968 1967 Highlights/news clippings	$12-$15
1969 1869 Cincinnati Red Stockings	$12-$15
1970 Hodges, Rose, McCovey, Mets	$12-$15
1971 Baseball with team names	$12-$15
1972 12 bats with team names	$12-$15
1973 Roberto Clemente memorial	$12-$15
1974 Hank Aaron/Babe Ruth bust	$12-$15
1975 Aaron, Brock, Schmidt, others	$12-$15
1976 Reds World Series celebration	$12-$15
1977 Team logos	$12-$15
1978 12 league stars	$12-$15
1979 League helmets, four bats	$10-$12
1980 Baseball	$7
1981 Schmidt, McGraw, All-Stars, Astros	$7
1982 Valenzuela, Ryan, Schmidt, Rose	$7
1983 Sax, D. Murphy, Carlton, others	$7
1984 Team pennants	$7
1985 Garvey, Sandberg, Gooden, Sutcliffe	$7
1986 Rose, Gooden, Ryan, McGee	$7
1987 Worrell, Scott, Mets, Schmidt, Raines	$7
1988	$7
1989 Los Angeles celebration	$7
1990 1980s MVPs and Cy Youngs	$7
1991 Reds celebration, others	$7
1992 Braves celebration	$7
1993 U.S. map with team logos	$7

Famous Sluggers of...
Famous Slugger Yearbook

Illustrated artwork was used for the years which do not appear in this list.

1928 Illustration	$200
1931 Illustration	$65
1932 Illustration	$50
1933 Jimmie Foxx, Chuck Klein	$50
1934 Lou Gehrig, Paul Waner	$50
1935 Arky Vaughan, Buddy Myer	$40
1936 Lou Gehrig, Mel Ott	$50
1937 Charlie Gehringer, Joe Medwick	$40
1938 Illustration	$35
1939 Jimmie Foxx, Ernie Lombardi	$40
1940 Joe DiMaggio	$40
1941 Joe DiMaggio, others	$40
1942 Joe DiMaggio, Ted Williams	$45
1943 Ted Williams, Ernie Lombardi	$40
1944 Stan Musial	$35
1945 Dixie Walker, Lou Boudreau	$30
1947 Stan Musial, Mickey Vernon	$30
1948 Lefty O'Doul	$25
1949 Ted Williams, Stan Musial	$35
1950 Jackie Robinson, Ted Williams	$35
1951 Ralph Kiner	$25
1952 Illustration	$20
1953 Illustration	$20
1954 Illustration	$20

1955 Ted Williams	$25
1956 Al Kaline, Richie Ashburn	$25
1957 M. Mantle, H. Aaron, T. Kluszewski	$25
1958 Ted Williams	$25
1959 Stan Musial	$25
1960 Rocky Colavito, others	$20
1961 Ernie Banks	$20
1962 Roger Maris	$25
1963 Tommy Davis, Pete Runnels	$15
1964 Tommy Davis, Carl Yastrzemski	$15
1965 Roberto Clemente, Tony Oliva	$15
1966 Roberto Clemente, Tony Oliva	$15
1967 Frank Robinson, Matty Alou	$15
1968 Roberto Clemente, Carl Yastremski	$15
1969 Pete Rose, Carl Yastrzemski	$12
1970 Pete Rose, Rod Carew	$12
1971 Johnny Bench, Alex Johnson	$12
1972 Willie Stargell, others	$12
1973 Dick Allen	$10
1974 Hank Aaron	$10
1975 Johnny Bench	$10
1976 Salute to the National League	$10
1977 Yankee Stadium	$10
1978 Illustration	$10

Inside Sports

Date	Cover Subject	Price
Oct. 1979	Bob Lemon	$20-$30
Apr. 1980	Nolan Ryan	$30-$40
May 1980	M. Fidrych, J. Bench, Magic Johnson	$10-$15
July 1980	Ken Reitz	$5-$7
Aug. 1980	W. Randolph, S. Garvey, Roberto Duran	$6-$7
Sept.1980	Art Schlichter, Ken Stabler	$7-$10
Oct. 1980	Howard Cosell, Frank Gifford, Don Meredith	$5-$10
Dec. 1980	"Bear" Bryant, Ray Meyer	$5-$7

Date	Cover Subject	Price
Feb. 1981	First swimsuit issue	$15
April 1981	George Brett	$7
May 1981	Outlaw Pitchers	$4-$7

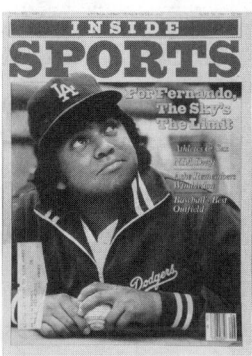

Date	Cover Subject	Price
Jun. 1981	Fernando Valenzula	$5-$7
Jul. 1981	Joe Namath	$7-$15
Aug. 1981	Salary Survey (Pete Rose)	$6-$7
Sep. 1981	Herschel Walker	$4-$7
Oct. 1981	John Matuszek	$5-$7
Nov. 1981	Tony Dorsett	$7-$10
Dec. 1981	Terry Bradshaw	$7-$10
Jan. 1982	Randy White	$4-$7
April 1982	Steve Garvey	$5-$7
May 1982	Pete Rose	$6-$7
Aug. 1982	Joe Montana	$10-$15
Sep. 1982	Kellen Winslow	$5-$7
Oct. 1982	Jack Lambert	$5-$7
Nov. 1982	Ed "Too Tall" Jones	$5-$7
Oct. 1983	John Riggins	$7
Nov. 1983	Lawrence Taylor	$7
Jan. 1984	Ken Stabler	$7
Mar. 1984	Darryl Strawberry	$6-$7
Apr. 1984	C. Ripken Jr., C. Fisk, E. Murray, O. Smith	$10
May 1984	Fernando Valenzuela	$5-$7

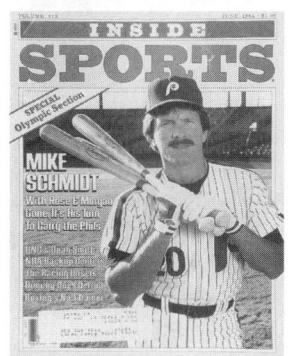

Date	Cover Subject	Price
Jun. 1984	Mike Schmidt	$5-$7
Jul. 1984	Steve Garvey, Rich Goosage	$5-$7
Aug. 1984	D. Winfield, G. Steinbrenner	$5-$7
Sep. 1984	Danny White	$7
Oct. 1984	Walter Payton	$15
Nov. 1984	Joe Theismann	$7
Dec. 1984	Marcus Allen, E. Dickerson	$7
Jan. 1985	Joe Montana	$10
Apr. 1985	K. Gibson, R. Sandberg, S. Garvey, D. Quisenberry	$5-$7
May 1985	Rick Sutcliffe, Gary Carter	$4-$6
Jun. 1985	R. Henderson, six Dodgers	$5-$7
Jul. 1985	T. Seaver, N. Ryan, J. Koosman	$9
Aug. 1985	NFL ratings	$7
Sep. 1985	NFL & College Football preview	$15
Oct. 1985	Mark Gastineau	$7
Nov. 1985	P. Ewing, M. Jordan	$25
Dec. 1985	College All-Americans	$7
Jan. 1986	Jim McMahon	$10
Mar. 1986	Baseball's Best Player (Rickey Henderson)	$8
Apr. 1986	1986 Baseball Preview	$4-$6
May 1986	Baseball ratings and Inside Stuff	$6-$8
Jun. 1986	Larry Bird, Magic Johnson	$10
Jul. 1986	Walter Payton	$12
Aug. 1986	Football ratings	$12
Sep. 1986	NFL & college football preview	$12
Oct. 1986	Football's best players	$12
Nov. 1986	L. Bird, J. Erving, M. Johnson, M. Jordan	$15
Dec. 1986	S. Alford, D. Robinson	$10
Jan. 1987	NFL playoffs	$10
Mar. 1987	Baseball's Best by Position	$6-$8
Apr. 1987	1987 Baseball preview	$3-$6
May 1987	Baseball ratings and Inside Stuff	$6
Jun. 1987	Michael Jordan	$12
Jul. 1987	Jim McMahon, Phil Simms	$10
Aug. 1987	Football ratings	$12
Sep. 1987	NFL and college football preview	$7
Oct. 1987	Football's best players	$7
Nov. 1987	NBA and college basketball review	$7
Dec. 1987	Basketball ratings	$12

Date	Cover Subject	Price

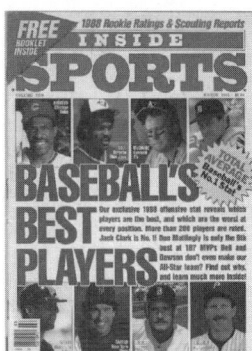

Date	Cover Subject	Price

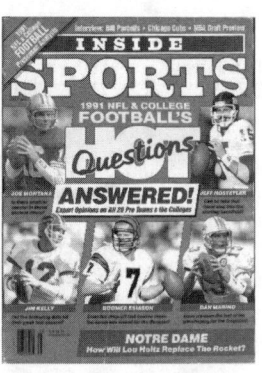

Mar. 1988 Baseball's Best Players .... $4-$6
Apr. 1988 1988 Baseball Preview .... $3-$6
May 1988 P. Ewing, Magic Johnson $12
Jun. 1988 Baseball Ratings, Inside Stuff .... $3-$6
Jul. 1988 100 football questions $12
Aug. 1988 Football ratings $7
Sep. 1988 B. Kosar, Rodney Peete, Phil Simms, S. Smith .. $7
Oct. 1988 NFL defenses $7
Nov. 1988 L. Bird, M. Johnson, M. Jordan $12
Dec. 1988 Mark Jackson, Magic Johnson $7
Mar. 1989 Total Average .... $3-$6
Apr. 1989 Baseball Preview .... $3-$6
May 1989 NBA playoff preview $5
Jul. 1989 J. Montana, J. Rice, J. Johnson $6
Aug. 1989 Troy Aikman, Mike Singletary $6
Sep. 1989 R. Cunningham, W. Moon $5
Oct. 1989 Michael Jordan .... $7-$10
Nov. 1989 M. Johnson, M. Jordan .... $7-$10
Dec. 1989 Akeem Olajuwon $8
Jan. 1990 R. Cunningham, J. Elway, B. Esiason, J. Everett,
     B. Kosar, D. Marino, J. Montana, P. Simms ...... $5-$7
Feb. 1990 W. Gretzky, Bo Jackson, M. Jordan, M. Lemieux,
     K. Malone, W. Moon, J. Rice, others $10
Feb. 1990 Henderson, Clark, Bo Jackson, G. Carter $4
Apr. 1990 B. Jackson, Hershiser, McGriff, H. Johnson, Clark,
     Grace, Boggs $5
May 1990 Michael Jordan $10
Jun. 1990 Wayne Gretzky, Magic Johnson,
     Joe Montana, others $10
Jul. 1990 Joe Montana, Bill Walsh $10
Aug. 1990 Jeff George, Lou Holtz, Bernie Kosar,
     Phil Simms .... $5-$6
Sep. 1990 C. Erickson, B. Esiason, J. Everett, R. Ismail ..... $5-$6
Oct. 1990 R. Bourque, B. Hull, M. Jordan, A. MacInnis,
     M. Messier, B. Nicholls, J. Otto $6
Nov. 1990 T. Chambers, L. Johnson, M. Jordan,
     A. Mourning .... $5-$7
Dec. 1990 C. Barkely, J. Dumars, P. Ewing, M. Johnson,
     M. Jordan $10
Jan. 1991 B. Jackson, J. Montana, M. Singletary, L. Taylor $8
Feb. 1991 Clemens, Canseco, Stewart, Rijo, Gooden,
     Fielder $4
Apr. 1991 Top salaries Canseco Strawberry, Clemens $4
Apr. 1991 W. Gretzky, Brett Hull, M. Jordan, J. Montana,
     D. Robinson, L. Taylor, others $7
May 1991 L. Bird, C. Drexler, M. Johnson, M. Jordan ...... $8-$10
Jun. 1991 Bo Jackson $7

Jul. 1991 Boomer Esiason, Jeff Hostetler, Jim Kelly,
     Dan Marino, Joe Montana .... $6-$8
Aug. 1991 Elvis Grbac, Amp Lee, Phil Simms, Derrick
     Thomas $5
Sep. 1991 Joe Montana .... $8-$10
Oct. 1991 Michael Jordan $10
Nov. 1991 C. Cheaney, C. Drexler, M. Jordan,
     C. Laettner .... $5-$7
Dec. 1991 Charles Barkley, Larry Bird, Magic Johnson,
     Michael Jordan, Karl Malone, Hakeem Olajuwon,
     David Robinson .... $8-$10
Jan. 1992 S. DeBerg, J. Elway, B. Hebert, J. Kelly, W. Moon,
     M. Rypien .... $5-$7
Feb. 1992 Larkin, Bonds, Clark, Sandberg, Canseco,
     Puckett $5
Mar. 1992 Lee Smith, J. Carter, S. Avery, R. Henderson $4
Apr. 1992 David Cone, Greg Maddux $5
May 1992 M. Jordan, K. Malone $10

Jun. 1992 Dream Team — C. Barkley, L. Bird, C. Daly,
     P. Ewing, M. Johnson, M. .Jordan, M. Krzyzewski,
     K. Malone $10
Jul. 1992 B. Sanders, T. Thomas $7
Aug. 1992 R. Cunningham, E. Dickerson, D. Howard,
     M. Rypien .... $5-$6
Sep. 1992 R. Cunningham, M. Rypien $6
Oct. 1992 B. Hurley, M. Jordan, M. Lemieux $7
Nov. 1992 C. Drexler, M. Jordan, S. O'Neal, P. Riley $8
Dec. 1992 W. Chamberlain, M. Jordan .... $7-$8
Jan. 1993 T. Aikman, R. Cunningham, S. Young $8
Feb. 1993 C. Barkley, P. Ewing, M. Jordan, K. Malone, S. O'Neal,
     S. Pippen, D. Robinson, J. Stockton $8
Apr. 1993 David Cone, Greg Maddux $5
May 1993 C. Barkley, C. Drexler, P. Ewing, S. Kemp,
     M. Jordan, S. O'Neal, M. Price .... $5-$7
Jun. 1993 Shaquille O'Neal $8
Jul. 1993 M. Ditka, W. Moon, B. Parcells, D. Sanders,
     E. Smith, R Woodson .... $5-$7
Aug. 1993 J. Montana, T. Vanover, T. Wheatley, R. White ... $6

Date	Cover Subject	Price
Sep. 1993	T. Aikman, J. Kelly, D. Marino, W. Moon, J. Montana, S. Young	$6
Oct. 1993	Shaquille O'Neal	$8
Nov. 1993	C. Barkley, M. Jordan	$7
Dec. 1993	L. Johnson, S. Kemp, C. Laettner, S. O'Neal, I. Thomas, J. Worthy	$6
Jan. 1994	T. Aikman, J. Kelly, J. Montana, B. Sanders, P. Simms, W Wilson	$4
Feb. 1994	C. Barkley, C. Drexler, P. Ewing, S. Kemp, L. Johnson, M. Price	$4
Apr. 1994	J. Kidd, E. Montross, G. Robinson, J. Rose, C. Williamson	$4
May 1994	Glavine, Bonds, Thomas, Gywnn, Canseco	$4
Jun. 1994	Barry Bonds, other sports stars	$4
Jul. 1994	J. Johnson, J. Jones, E. Smith, B. Switzer, T. Thomas	$4
Aug. 1994	D. Marino, J. Montana, E. Smith, S. Young	$5
Sep. 1994	D. Bledsoe, R. Cunningham, B. Esiason, D. Marino, B. Sanders, T. Thomas	$4
Oct. 1994	A. Davis, J. Johnson, D. Marino, K. Norton, J. Rice, B. Ryan, S. Young	$4
Nov. 1994	C. Barkley, P. Ewing, R. Miller, H. Olajuwon, S. O'Neal, S. Pippen	$4
Dec. 1994	C. Barkley, L. Johnson, M. Jordan, S. O'Neal, P. Riley	$4
Jan.1995	Troy Aikman	$3
Feb. 1995	Anfernee Hardaway	$3
Mar. 1995	Reggie Miller	$3
Apr. 1995	Swimsuit	$6
May 1995	NFL's Perfect Man	$3
Jun. 1995	Shaquille O'Neal	$4
Jul. 1995	Troy Aikman, Jack McDowell	$3
Aug. 1995	Deion Sanders	$3

Date	Cover Subject	Price
Sep. 1995	Dan Marino	$4
Oct. 1995	Herschel Walker	$3
Nov. 1995	NBA preview	$3
Dec. 1995	M. Jordan/D. Rodman	$5
Jan. 1996	Cowboys/49ers	$3
Feb. 1996	Dennis Rodman	$3
Mar 1996	Swimsuit: Gena Lee Nolan	$6
Apr. 1996	M. Jordan/others	$5
May 1996	NFL's Perfect Man	$3
Jun. 1996	Jordan/Rodman/Pippen	$5
Jul. 1996	Dan Marino	$4
Aug. 1996	T. Aikman/S. Young	$4
Sep. 1996	Neil O'Donnell	$3
Oct. 1996	Larry Johnson	$3
Nov. 1996	Michael Jordan	$6
Dec. 1996	Shaquille O'Neal	$4
Jan. 1997	Cowboys/49ers	$3
Feb. 1997	M. Jordan/others	$5
Mar. 1997	Swimsuit: Donna S'Errico	$6
Apr. 1997	Baseball Preview	$3
May 1997	NFL's Perfect Man	$3
Jun. 1997	Alex Rodriguez	$4
Jul. 1997	Chipper Jones	$3
Aug. 1997	Troy Aikman	$3
Sep. 1997	Fox NFL Sunday	$3
Oct. 1997	Dermontti Dawson	$3
Nov. 1997	M. Jordan/others	$5
Jan. 1998	Michael Jordan	$6
Feb. 1998	B. Favre/J. Elway/S. Young	$4
Mar. 1998	Kobe Bryant	$4
Apr. 1998	Baseball preview	$3
May 1998	NFL's Perfect Man	$3
Jun. 1998	Swimsuit: Carmen Electra	$6

Football Magazines

AFL Yearbook

1960 Handoff artwork	$50
1961	$45
1962 Pro Bowl photo	$30
1963	$25
1964 Kansas City Chiefs vs. Houston Oilers	$20
1965 George Blanda	$25
1966 Action photos	$20
1967	$15
1968 AFL autograph handbook	$15
1969 Matt Snell	$20

All-Pro Football
(Maco Magazine)

1957 Scrambling quarterback	$45
1958	$35
1959 Johnny Unitas	$45
1960	$25
1961 Kyle Rote	$20
1962 Y.A. Tittle	$20
1963 Bart Starr	$25
1964 Johnny Unitas	$20
1965 Fran Tarkenton	$25
1966 Frank Ryan	$15
1967 Carroll Dale	$10
1968	$12
1969 Joe Namath	$25

All-Pro Football
Exclusive: Pete Rozelle On The Betting Scandal
Is Y. A. Tittle Destined To Lose The Big Ones?

Are The Packers The Best Ever? • Who's The All-Time Fullback?
Revelations Of A Linebacker • Scouting Reports On The NFL, AFL

1970 Hank Stram	$12
1971 John Brodie	$10
1972	$10
1973 Fran Tarkenton	$15
1974 Fran Tarkenton	$15

Athlon's Pro Football

1983 John Riggins	$15
1984 Brian Sipe	$12
All other covers	$12
1985 All covers	$12
1986 All covers	$12
1987 Bernie Kosar	$13
All other covers	$10

1988 Bernie Kosar $10
 All other covers $8
1989 All covers $10
1990 Eric Metcalf $8
 All other covers $8

Complete Sports
AFL & NFL Yearbook

1964 Jim Brown $30
1965 Charlie Hennigan, Johnny Morris $25
1966 Jim Brown, Jack Kemp $30
1967 Gale Sayers $25
1968 Roman Gabriel $15
1969 Sonny Jurgensen, Matt Snell $15
1970 Curley Culp $12
1971 Dick Butkus $18
1972 Larry Csonka, Jim Plunkett $15
1973 .... $12
1974 .... $12
1975 .... $13
1976 .... $14

Cord Sportfacts' Pro Football Guide

1969 John Mackey $17
1970 Joe Kapp $17
1971 Mike Curtis $15
1972 Joe Namath $25
1973 Larry Brown $12
1974 Larry Csonka $15
1975 Franco Harris $18
1976 Franco Harris $18
1977 O. J. Simpson $15
1978 Tony Dorsett $15
1979 .... $15
1980 Terry Bradshaw $12
1981 Jack Lambert $15

Cord Sportfacts' Pro Football Report

1969 Sonny Jurgensen $10
1970 Joe Namath $15
1971 Ron Johnson $10
1972 Dick Butkus $14
1973 Larry Csonka $14
1974 O.J. Simpson $15

Dell Sports' Pro Football Preview

1958 Bobby Layne $80
1959 Johnny Unitas $75
1960 Charlie Conerly, Don Meredith $60
1961 Paul Hornung $55
1962 Jim Brown, Jim Taylor $60
1963 Y.A. Tittle $45
1964 Jim Brown $55
1965 Joe Namath, Johnny Unitas $55
1966 Gale Sayers $35
1967 Bart Starr $35
1968 Donny Anderson $30
1969 Leroy Kelly $30
1970 Johnny Unitas $25
1971 Joe Namath $30
1972 Roger Staubach $30
1973 Bob Griese $20
1974 Larry Csonka $20

Fawcett's Pro Football

1961 Paul Hornung $30
1962 Jim Taylor $25
1963 Jim Taylor $20

Football Digest
Simons Publishing

1947 Johnny Lujack .... $35-$70
1948 Chuck Bednarik .... $25-$40
1949 Sammy Baugh .... $30-$55
1950 Gordon Soltau .... $25-$40
1951 Fred Benners, Sonny Gandee .... $25-$40
1952 Hugh McElhenny .... $25-$40

Digest Publishing Corp.

Dec. 1967 Don Perkins $30
Feb. 1968 .... $25
April 1968 Bart Starr $30
Aug. 1968 Bobby Bell $25
Oct. 1968 Leroy Kelly $20
Nov. 1968 Dave Parks $15
Dec. 1968 Noland Smith $15

Century Publishing Co.

Sept. 1971 Gene Washington .... $50-$60
Oct. 1971 Sonny Jurgensen .... $10-$12
Nov. 1971 Greg Landry .... $7-$12
Dec. 1971 Dick Gordon .... $7-$12
Jan. 1972 John Brodie .... $10-$12
Feb. 1972 Dave Osborn .... $10-$12
March 1972 John Brockington .... $7-$8
April 1972 Duane Thomas .... $10-$12
May 1972 Fran Tarkenton .... $10-$12
July 1972 Daryle Lamonica .... $7-$8
Sept. 1972 Dick Butkus .... $10-$12

Oct. 1972 Len Dawson .... $10-$12
Nov. 1972 Joe Namath .... $15-$20
Dec. 1972 Mercury Morris .... $10-$12
Jan. 1973 Larry Brown, Dick Butkus, Tommy Nobis ...... $10-$12
Feb. 1973 Terry Bradshaw .... $10-$12
March 1973 John Brockingon .... $7-$8
April 1973 Bob Griese .... $10-$12
May 1973 Norm Snead .... $7-$8
July 1973 O.J. Simpson .... $15-$20
Aug. 1973 Larry Csonka .... $10-$12
Sept. 1973 Mean Joe Greene .... $10-$12
Nov. 1973 Bobby Douglass .... $7-$8
Dec. 1973 Daryle Lamonica .... $7-$8
Jan. 1974 Chuck Foreman .... $10-$12
Feb. 1974 John Hadl .... $7-$8
March 1974 O.J Simpson .... $15-$20
April 1974 Larry Csonka .... $10-$12
May 1974 Calvin Hill .... $10-$12
July 1974 Archie Manning .... $15-$16
Sept. 1974 Bob Griese, John Hadl .... $10-$12
Oct. 1974 Roger Staubach .... $10-$12
Nov. 1974 Fran Tarkenton .... $10-$12
Dec. 1974 John Brockingion .... $7-$8
Jan. 1975 Ken Stabler .... $7-$8
Feb. 1975 Jim Hart .... $7-$8
March 1975 Ken Stabler .... $7-$8
April 1975 Franco Harris, Chuck Noll .... $10-$12
May 1975 Ken Anderson .... $7-$8
July 1975 Otis Armstrong .... $7-$8
Sept. 1975 Terry Bradshaw .... $10-$12
Oct. 1975 Jim Plunkett .... $10-$12
Nov. 1975 Wally Chambers .... $7-$8
Dec. 1975 Joe Namath .... $15-$20
Jan. 1976 Mercury Morris .... $10-$12
Feb. 1976 Jeff Siemon .... $7-$8
March 1976 O.J. Simpson .... $15-$20
April 1976 Lynn Swann .... $10-$12
May 1976 Dan Pastorini .... $7-$8
July 1976 Bert Jones .... $7-$8
Sept. 1976 Jack Lambert, Roger Staubach .... $10-$12
Oct. 1976 Roger Staubach .... $10-$12
Nov. 1976 Terry Metcalf .... $7-$8
Dec. 1976 Billy Kilmer .... $7-$8
Jan. 1977 Fran Tarkenton .... $10-$12
Feb. 1977 Jim Langer .... $10-$12
March 1977 Ken Stabler .... $10-$12
April 1977 Clarence Davis .... $10-$12
May 1977 Steve Grogan .... $7-$8
July 1977 Greg Pruitt .... $7-$8
Sept. 1977 Joe Namath .... $15-$20
Oct. 1977 Terry Bradshaw, Ken Stabler .... $10-$12
Nov. 1977 Walter Payton .... $15-$20
Dec. 1977 Ken Anderson .... $7-$8
Jan. 1978 Steve Bartkowski, Jack Youngblood .... $7-$8
Feb. 1978 Bert Jones .... $7-$8
March 1978 Tony Dorsett .... $15-$16
April 1978 Craig Morton, Randy White .... $10-$12
May 1978 Jim Zorn .... $7-$8
July 1978 Roger Staubach .... $10-$12
Sept. 1978 Chuck Foreman .... $8-$10
Oct. 1978 Ron Jaworski .... $7-$8
Nov. 1978 O.J. Simpson .... $10-$15
Dec. 1978 Franco Harris .... $10-$12
Jan. 1979 Pat Haden .... $7-$8
Feb. 1979 Don Shula .... $10-$12
March 1979 Earl Campbell .... $10-$12
April 1979 Terry Bradshaw .... $10-$12

May 1979 Archie Manning .... $15-$16
July 1979 Craig Morton .... $10-$12
Sept. 1979 Steve Grogan .... $7-$8
Oct. 1979 Bill Bergey .... $10-$12
Nov. 1979 Dan Fouts .... $10-$12
Dec. 1979 David Whitehurst .... $7-$8
Jan. 1980 Larry Csonka .... $8-$10
Feb. 1980 Terry Bradshaw .... $10-$12
March 1980 Dan Fouts .... $8-$10
April 1980 Lynn Swann .... $5-$7
May 1980 Lee Roy Selmon .... $5-$7
July 1980 Vince Ferragamo .... $5-$7
Sept. 1980 Ken Stabler .... $7-$8
Oct. 1980 Harry Carson .... $8-$10
Nov. 1980 Walter Payton .... $12-$15
Dec. 1980 Russ Francis .... $5-$7
Jan. 1981 Wilbert Montgomery .... $5-$7
Feb. 1981 Bert Jones .... $5-$7
March 1981 Brian Sipe .... $8-$10
April 1981 Billy Sims .... $10-$12
May 1981 Steve Bartkowski .... $5-$7
July 1981 Joe Ferguson .... $5-$7
Sept. 1981 Jim Plunkett .... $7-$8
Oct. 1981 Tommy Kramer .... $5-$7
Nov. 1981 O.J. Anderson .... $7-$8
Dec. 1981 Dan White .... $8-$10
Jan. 1982 David Woodley .... $8-$10
Feb. 1982 Ron Jaworski .... $5-$7
March 1982 George Rogers .... $5-$7
April 1982 Ken Anderson .... $5-$7
May 1982 Joe Montana .... $15-$20
July 1982 Joe Theismann .... $8-$10
Sept. 1982 Bert Jones .... $5-$7
Oct. 1982 Joe Klecko .... $6-$10
Nov. 1982 Terry Bradshaw .... $8-$10
Dec. 1982 Joe Montana, Bill Walsh .... $20-$25
Jan. 1983 Dan Fouts $8
Feb. 1983 William Andrews .... $5-$7
March 1983 Randy White $8
April 1983 Marcus Allen $10
May 1983 John Riggins $8
July 1983 Herschel Walker .... $8-$10
Sept. 1983 Lawrence Taylor .... $10-$15
Oct. 1983 Doug Williams $6
Nov. 1983 Kellen Winslow $5
Dec. 1983 Lynn Dickey .... $5-$7
Jan. 1984 Brian Sipe .... $6-$10
Feb. 1984 Danny White $8
March 1984 Eric Dickerson .... $7-$8
April 1984 Joe Theismann $6
May 1984 Dan Marino $15
July 1984 Curt Warner .... $5-$7
Sept. 1984 Marcus Allen .... $6-$7
Oct. 1984 Franco Harris $8
Nov. 1984 John Elway .... $8-$10
Dec. 1984 Billy Sims $5
Jan. 1985 Tony Dorsett $8
Feb. 1985 Joe Montana .... $15-$20
March 1985 Walter Payton .... $12-$15
April 1985 Dan Marino .... $15-$20
May 1985 Eric Dickerson .... $7-$8
July 1985 Doug Flutie $5
Sept. 1985 Dave Krieg .... $5-$7
Oct. 1985 Danny White .... $5-$7
Nov. 1985 Mark Gastineau $5
Dec. 1965 Neil Lomax $5
Jan. 1986 Howie Long $6

Feb. 1986 Jim McMahon .... $5-$8
March 1986 Dieter Brock $5
April 1986 Marcus Allen $6
May 1986 Tony Eason, Otis Wilson $8
July 1986 Joe Morris $5
Sept. 1986 Jim McMahon $5
Oct. 1986 Louis Lipps $5
Nov. 1986 James Lofton .... $5-$7
Dec. 1986 Dan Fouts $6
Jan. 1987 Herschel Walker $6
Feb. 1987 Walter Paylon $10
March 1987 Jay Schroeder $5
April 1987 Lawrence Taylor $8
May 1987 Phil Simms $8
July 1987 Dan Marino $10
Sept. 1987 Bernie Kosar .... $5-$7
Oct. 1987 Tommy Kramer $5
Nov. 1987 Tony Eason $5
Dec. 1987 Curt Warner $5
Jan. 1988 Joe Montana $10
Feb. 1988 Walter Payton $10
March 1988 Eric Dickerson $6
April 1988 Jerry Rice $8
May 1988 Doug Williams $8
July 1988 John Elway $6
Sept. 1988 Phil Simms $5
Oct. 1988 Morten Andersen $5
Nov. 1988 Cornelius Bennett, Shane Conlan $6
Dec. 1988 Chris Doleman $5
Jan. 1989 Brian Bosworth $5
Feb. 1989 Mike Singletary .... $6-$7
March 1989 Keith Jackson $6
April 1989 Boomer Esiason $6
May 1989 Troy Aikman $8
July 1989 Warren Moon $5
Sept. 1989 Jim Everett $5
Oct. 1989 Vinny Testaverde $5
Nov. 1989 Jim Kelly $6
Dec. 1989 Lawrence Taylor $6
Jan. 1990 Roger Craig $3
Feb. 1990 John Elway $3
March 1990 Barry Sanders $4
April 1990 Joe Montana $6
May 1990 Keith McCants $3
July 1990 Christian Okoye $3
Sept. 1990 James Brooks $3
Oct. 1990 Bill Fralic $3
Nov. 1990 Randall Cunningham $3
Dec. 1990 Bo Jackson $5
1991-1999 are .... $3-$5

Football Forecast
(Fawcett Publishing)

1962 Y.A. Tittle $25
1963 Bart Starr $20

Game Plan Pro Football

1971 George Banda $18
1972 Roger Staubach $20
1973 Larry Csonka $15
1974 Fran Tarkenton $14
1975 Franco Harris $17
1976 Roger Staubach $17
1977 Walter Payton $20
1978 Bert Jones $15
1979 Archie Manning $10
1980 Joe Ferguson $10

1981 Ricky Bell $8
1982 Steve Bartkowski $10
1983 Richard Todd $8
1984 Jim Plunkett/Marcus Allen $10
1985 John Elway $15
1986 Phil Simms $10
1987 Jim Everett, John Elway, Phil Simms $12
1988 .... $10
1989 .... $7
1990 Dan Marino $10

Goal Post Pro Football

1975 Sedrick McIntyre $12
1975 O.J. Simpson $20
1976 Ricky Bell $12
1976 Chuck Foreman, Fran Tarkenton $12
1977 Lawrence McCutcheon $10
1977 George Woodard $12
1978 I. M. Hipp $12
1978 Craig Morton $12
1979 Billy Sims $12
1979 Brian Sipe $8
1980 Terry Bradshaw $12
1981 Joe Ferguson $10
1982 Jim Kelly $12
1982 Ken Anderson $12
1983 Wayne Peace $10

Inside Football
(Sport Magazine)

1961 Ernie Davis, Johnny Unitas $30
1962 Jim Taylor $25
1963 Jim Brown, George Mira $20
1964 Roger Staubach $25
1965 Joe Namath $25
1966 Johnny Unitas $20
1967 Terry Hanratty $20
1968 O. J. Simpson $15
1969 Sonny Jurgensen, Vince Lombardi $15
1970 Gale Sayers $20

Kickoff

1956 Jim Swink (TCU) $30
1957 Walt Lowalczyk (Michigan State) $25
1958 Bob Anderson (Army) $20
1959 Billy Cannon (LSU) $20
1960 Alan Ameche $20
1961 Ernie Davis $15
1962 George Mira (Miami) $15
1963 George Mira, Roger Staubach $25

Popular Library

1964 .... $10
1965 Floyd Little, Tommy Nobis $15
1966 .... $10

1967 Terry Hanratty (Notre Dame) $20
1968 O.J. Simpson (USC) $25
1969 Rex Kern (Ohio State), O.J. Simpson (USC) $25
1970 .... $10
1971 Ed Marinaro (Cornell) $10
1972 John Hufnagel (Penn State) $10
1973 A. Davis (USC) $12
1974 Archie Griffin $15

Lindy's Pro Football

1987 Boomer Esiason, Bernie Kosar $8
   Phil Simms, Al Toon $7
1988 Tommy Kramer, Randy Wright $6
1989 Boomer Esiason, Bernie Kosar $7
1990 Boomer Esiason, Eric Metcalf $6

NFL Yearbook

1953 Quarterback and team logos $75
1954 Player in 3-point stance $60
1955 Wide receiver $50
1956 .... $40
1957 .... $35
1958 .... $30
1959 Black-and-white cartoon $25
1960 Ball carrier $25
1961 Player catching ball $20
1962 .... $20
1963 .... $20
1964 .... $15
1965 .... $15
1966 Fran Tarkenton $20
1967 Donny Anderson $20
1968 Now "NFL autograph handbook" $15
1969 Roman Gabriel $10

Official NFL Annuals
Pro Football Yearbook

1979 Earl Campbell, Tony Dorsett, Walter Payton $12
1980 Terry Bradshaw, Dan Fouts, Walter Payton $12

NFL Team Book

1986 William Perry $7

Preview

1989 Joe Montana $10

Petersen's Football

1956 Ron Waller .... $35-$60
1957 Frank Gifford .... $25-$40
1958 Jon Arnett, Tom Wilson .... $25-$40
1959 Lenny Moore .... $25-$40
1960 Pro Bowl scene .... $25-$30
1961 Bill Anderson .... $20-$30
1962 Jim Brown $45
1963 Y.A. Tittle .... $25-$35

1964 Jim Brown, George Halas .... $25-$35
1970 Roman Gabriel .... $15-$20
1971 George Blanda, John Brodie, Bart Starr .... $15-$20
1972 Washington Redskins vs. Los Angeles Rams .... $15-$20
1973 Larry Brown, Larry Csonka, Bob Greise, Jim Kiick ....$15-$20
1974 O.J. Simpson .... $15-$25
1975 Jack Lambert, Dwight White .... $12-$16
1976 Bert Jones .... $12-$16
1977 John Madden, Ken Stabler .... $12-$16
1978 Ed "Too Tall" Jones, Roger Staubach .... $12-$16
1979 Terry Bradshaw .... $12-$16
1980 Vince Ferragamo, Pat Haden .... $10-$12
1981 Jim Plunkett, O.J. Simpson, Johnny Unitas .... $10-$12
1982 Joe Montana .... $15-$20
1983 Joe Theismann, John Riggins .... $10-$12
1984 Wendell Tyler .... $10-$12
1985 Calvin Muhammad .... $10-$12
1986 Walter Payton .... $12-$15
1987 Warren Moon, Herschel Walker .... $10-$12
1988 .... $8
1989 .... $7
1990 Joe Montana $20

Pro Football Annual
(Reliance Publishing)

1979 Terry Bradshaw, Earl Campbell $17
1980 Terry Bradshaw, Earl Campbell $15
1981 Earl Campbell, Jim Plunkett, Billy Sims $10
1982 Dan Fouts, Joe Montana $15
1983 Marcus Allen, John Riggins $12

Pro Football Annual
(Sport Magazine)

1964 Jim Brown $35
1965 Johnny Unitas $30
1966 .... $25
1967 Bart Starr $25
1968 Sonny Jurgensen, Johnny Unitas $20
1969 Joe Namath, Gale Sayers $25
1970 Roman Gabriel, Joe Namath $20
1971 Joe Namath $20

Pro Football Illustrated
(Elbak Publishing)

1941 New York Giants $200
1942 Ball carrier in action $175
1943 Sammy Baugh $175
1944 Over-the-shoulder catch $140
1945 Ball carrier in action $140
1946 Wilbur Moore $125
1947 Pat Harder $125
1948 Bosh Pritchard $100
1949 Clyde Goodnight $100
1950 Fred Gehrke $75
1951 Billy Vessels $75

Becomes Sports Review

1952 Action shot $75
1953 Leon Hart, Perry Lowell $65
1954 UCLA vs. USC $65
1955 Notre Dame vs. Texas $65
1956 Ted Kress (Michigan) $65
1957 Hugh McElhenny, Clendon Thomas $60
1958 Blanche Martin, Sam Williams $60
1959 Jeff Langston, Donald Norton $50
1960 Johnny Unitas $60
1961 Baltimore Colts vs. New York Giants $60

1962 Baltimore Colts vs. Chicago Bears $60
1965 Johnny Unitas.. $60

Pro Football Illustrated
(Complete Sports)

1961 Johnny Unitas.. $35
1962 Paul Hornung.. $30
1963 Jim Brown.. $35
1964 Jim Brown.. $35
1967 Joe Namath, Johnny Unitas $30
1968 Joe Namath $30
1969 Roman Gabriel, Joe Namath $25
1970 Gale Sayers, Leroy Kelly $20
1971 John Brodie, Joe Namath $25
1972 Joe Namath, Fran Tarkenton $25
1973 Larry Csonka $20
1974 O.J. Simpson $25
1975 O.J. Simpson, Chuck Foreman...................................... $20
1976 Ken Anderson, Fran Tarkenton $15
1977 O.J. Simpson $12
1978 Walter Payton $15
1980 O.J. Anderson $15
1981 Billy Sims $12
1983 Tony Dorsett, Freeman McNeil $15

New Publisher - Lexington Library

1985 John Elway, Dan Marino, Joe Montana $15
1986 Jim McMahon $10
1987 John Elway, Dan Marino, Phil Simms $12
1988 Herschel Walker $8
1989 Boomer Esiason $8
1990 Joe Montana.. $10

Pro Football Stars
(Whitestone Publishing)

1957 Frank Gifford.. $75
1960 Johnny Unitas.. $45
1961 Jim Brown.. $50
1962 Bart Starr $40
1963 Jim Taylor $35
1964 Paul Hornung.. $30

Becomes Pro & College Football

1965 .... $30
1968 Joe Namath $35
1969 Cleveland Browns vs. New York Giants...................... $20
1970 Leroy Kelly $15
1971 Duane Thomas $15

Pro Football Weekly

11/17/67 Bart Starr $25
11/24/67 Mike Farr $8
10/05/67 Bart Starr $12
10/12/67 Cowboys, Packers $12
10/19/67 Johnny Unitas $15
10/26/67 Don Maynard $10
11/02/67 Colts vs. Vikings $8
11/09/67 B. Thompson $8
11/16/67 John Mackey, Willie Wood $8
11/23/67 Walter Johnson, Elijah Pitts $8
11/30/67 Jerry Logan, Ron Porter $8
12/07/67 Vince Lombardi, Bart Starr $12
12/14/67 Joe Morrison.. $10
12/21/67 George Allen, Paul Warfield $8
12/28/67 Deacon Jones, Johnny Unitas $10
01/04/68 Bob Jeter, Vince Lombardi $10
11/11/68 Packers, Raiders $10

11/18/68 Daryle Lamonica, Bart Starr.................................... $10
11/25/68 Green Bay Packers Champions $17
Feb. 1968 Roman Gabriel, Les Josephson $8
March 1968 Joe Namath $15
April 1968 Jack Concannon $8
May 1968 Don Meredith $12
June 1968 Len Dawson $10
July 1968 Ray Nitschke $10
Aug. 1968 George Halas, Vince Lombardi $10
08/15/68 Bears, Cowboys $7
08/22/68 Tucker Frederickson, Bart Starr $10
08/29/68 Leroy Kelly $8
09/05/68 Chargers, Rams $7
09/12/68 Len Dawson, Otis Taylor $8
09/19/68 Dennis Partee $7
09/26/68 Otto Graham, Gale Sayers $10
10/03/68 Lee Roy Caffey $8
10/10/68 Charlie Taylor $7
10/17/68 Hewritt Dixon $7
10/24/68 Ray Nitschke, Dave Robinson $7
10/31/68 O.J. Simpson $15
11/07/68 Mike Garrett $7
11/14/68 Ray Nitschke $8
11/21/68 Johnny Unitas $10
11/28/68 Ben Davidson $8
12/05/68 Bruce Gossett, Ed Meador $7
12/12/68 Don Meredith $10
12/19/68 Bart Starr, Johnny Unitas $12
12/16/68 Len Dawson, Jacky Lee $8
01/02/69 Lindsey, Don Meredith $10
01/09/69 Joe Namath $12
01/16/69 Joe Namath $12
01/23/69 New York Jets champions $17
01/30/69 Jim Kiick, Ken Willard $8
02/13/69 O.J. Simpson $12
12/20/69 Vince Lombardi $12
April 1969 Gale Sayers $9
May 1969 Paul Brown.. $7
June 1969 Pete Rozelle $7
July 1969 Billy Kilmer $7
08/14/69 Sonny Jurgensen, Vince Lombardi........................ $8
08/21/69 Joe Namath, Fran Tarkenton $10
08/28/69 O.J. Simpson $15
09/04/69 Browns vs. Chargers $7
09/11/69 Ed Meador, Ron Smith $7
09/18/69 Kansas City Chiefs $7
09/25/69 Pete Beathard, Tom Keating.................................... $7
10/02/69 John Brodie $8
10/09/69 Lance Alworth $8
10/16/69 Joe Kapp $7
10/23/69 Tommy Hart $7
10/30/69 Bob Griese $9
11/06/69 Fran Tarkenton $9
11/13/69 Roman Gabriel $7
11/20/69 Jim Marshall $7
11/27/69 Dick Butkus $9
12/04/69 Chiefs, Raiders $7
12/11/69 Maxie Baughan, Sonny Jurgensen........................ $7
12/18/69 Rams, Vikings $7
12/25/69 Daryle Lamonica $7
01/01/70 Joe Namath $9
01/08/70 Leroy Kelly, Craig Morton $7
01/15/70 Len Dawson, Joe Kapp $7
01/22/70 Len Dawson, Chiefs champs.................................... $12
01/29/70 Terry Bradshaw $9
Feb. 1970 Mike McCoy, Steve Owens $7

March 1970 Bruce Gossett, Johnny Unitas $8
April 1970 Vince Lombardi, Hank Stram $9
May 1970 Allie Sherman $7
June 1970 Joe Kapp $7
July 1970 Lance Alworth, Dick Butkus $9
Aug. 1970 Jim Otis $7
08/15/70 Jan Stenerud $7
08/22/70 Joe Kapp, Joe Namath $9
08/29/70 Roman Gabriel, Calvin Hill $6
09/05/70 Walt Garrison, Don Shula $7
09/12/70 Paul Guidry $7
09/19/70 Vince Lombardi $10
09/26/70 Les Josephson $6
10/03/70 Bill Munson $6
10/10/70 Bob Griese $8
10/17/70 Ray Nitschke $7
10/24/70 Kermit Alexander, Joe Kapp $6
10/31/70 Bill Nelsen, Bob Brown $6
11/07/70 George Blanda, Landry $8
11/14/70 Lance Alworth $8
11/21/70 Rick Dempsey $6
11/28/70 Mike Phillips $6
12/05/70 Bart Starr $9
12/12/70 John Hadl $6
12/19/70 Fred Cox $6
12/26/70 Browns, Cowboys $8
01/02/71 John Brodie, Daryle Lamonica $7
01/09/71 Alan Page $7
01/16/71 Johnny Unitas, Duane Thomas $8
01/23/71 Craig Morton, Johnny Unitas $7
01/30/71 Chuck Howley $7
02/13/71 Mike Curtis, MacArthur Lane $6
02/20/71 Archie Manning, Jim Plunkett $6
April 1971 Don Meredith, Dan Reeves $8
May 1971 Gale Sayers $8
June 1971 Johnny Unitas $8
July 1971 Joe Namath $9
Aug. 1971 Jim Plunkett $6
08/14/71 Eddie Hinton $7
08/21/71 Joe Namath $10
08/28/71 Willie Lanier $7
09/04/71 J. Reynolds $7
09/11/71 Tody Smith $7
09/18/71 Emmitt Thomas $7
09/25/71 Carl Eller $7
10/02/71 Dan Devine $7
10/09/71 Dick Butkus, Kent Nix $9
10/16/71 Ken Anderson $7
10/23/71 Jerry Sherk $7
10/30/71 Archie Manning $8
11/06/71 Bill Nelsen $7
11/13/71 George Blanda $9
11/20/71 John Brockington, Dick Butkus $8
11/27/71 Len Dawson, Otis Taylor $7
12/04/71 Pettis Norman $7
12/11/71 Bob Gresham $7
12/18/71 Tom Dempsey $7
12/25/71 George Blanda $8
01/01/72 Charlie Durkee $7
01/08/72 Don Nottingham, Johnny Unitas $8
01/15/72 John Brodie, Johnny Unitas $9
01/22/72 Bob Griese, Roger Staubach $9
01/29/72 Roger Staubach $15
Feb. 1972 John Reaves $7
March 1972 Alan Page, Fran Tarkenton $9
April 1972 Who is the best QB? $7

May 1972 Willie Ellison $7
June 1972 Alan Page $8
July 1972 49ers, Lions, Bears $7
Aug. 1972 Calvin Hill $8
08/12/72 Ron Johnson $6
08/19/72 Daryle Lamonica $7
08/26/72 Roger Staubach $8
09/02/72 Billy Kilmer $8
09/09/72 Mike Lucci $7
09/16/72 Jim Lynch $6
09/23/72 Len Dawson, Otis Taylor $8
09/30/72 Joe Greene $8
10/07/72 Joe Namath $9
10/14/72 John Brockington, Vern Vandy $6
10/21/72 Leroy Kelly $6
10/28/72 Bob Griese $8
11/04/72 Mel Farr $7
11/11/72 Dan Pastorini $6
11/18/72 Steve Spurrier $6
11/25/72 Dick Butkus $8
12/02/72 Earl Morrall $7
12/09/72 John Mackey, Dan Pastorini $6
12/16/72 Tom Landry $8
12/23/72 Ken Willard $6
12/30/72 Roman Gabriel $6
01/06/73 Larry Brown $6
01/13/73 L.C. Greenwood $7
01/20/73 George Allen, Don Shula $7
01/27/73 Larry Csonka, Bob Griese, Dolphins champs $15
Feb. 1973 O.J. Simpson $9
March 1973 John Matuszak $8
April 1973 McCafferty $6
May 1973 Don Shula $7
June 1973 O.J. Simpson $9
July 1973 Dick Butkus $8
Aug. 1973 John McKay, Don Shula $7
08/11/73 49ers, Patriots $6
08/18/73 Calvin Hill $6
08/25/73 B. Brunet $6
09/01/73 Johnny Unitas $9
09/08/73 John Riggins $8
09/15/73 Jim Files $6
09/22/73 Sonny Jurgensen, Billy Kilmer $7
09/29/73 O.J. Simpson $10
10/06/73 Redskins, Cardinals $6
10/13/73 Rams, 49ers $6
10/20/73 Ed Podolak $6
10/27/73 Terry Bradshaw $8
11/03/73 Rich McGeorge $7
11/10/73 Gene Hickerson $6
11/17/73 Bobby Douglass $6
11/24/73 Daryle Lamonica $7
12/01/73 John Madden $7
12/08/73 Greg Pruitt $6
12/15/73 Pete Athas $6
12/22/73 Cowboys, Redskins $9
12/29/73 Terry Bradshaw, O.J. Simpson $9
01/05/74 Mercury Morris $6
01/12/74 Bob Hayes $8
01/19/74 Bob Griese, Fran Tarkenton $9
01/26/74 Larry Csonka, Dolphins champs $12
Feb. 1974 Garo Yepremian $7
March 1974 Joe Theismann $9
April 1974 Bob Griese $9
May 1974 Larry Csonka, Jim Kiick $7
June 1974 Paul Warfield $7

July 1974 Dallas Cowboys	$8		08/09/76 Jets, Cardinals	$7
Aug. 1974 Jake Scott	$6		08/16/76 Mike Livingston	$6
08/10/74 M. Botts	$6		08/23/76 Walter Payton	$8
08/17/74 Charlie Napper	$7		08/30/76 Chiefs, Redskins	$6
08/24/74 J. Johnson	$6		09/06/76 R. Davis	$6
08/31/74 Ken Stabler	$7		09/13/76 Richard Todd	$7
09/07/74 Don Strock	$6		09/20/76 Mike Thomas	$6
09/14/74 R. Moscati	$6		09/27/76 Joe Greene	$7
09/21/74 Chuck Knox, Don Shula	$7		10/04/76 Haskel Stanback	$6
09/28/74 Jim Plunkett	$5		10/11/76 Billy Kilmer	$7
10/05/74 Emerson Boozer	$7		10/18/76 Craig Clemons	$6
10/12/74 Chester Marcol	$6		10/25/76 Hugh McKinnis	$6
10/19/74 Charlie Johnson	$6		11/01/76 John Hicks	$6
10/26/74 Sonny Jurgensen	$7		11/08/76 Chip Myers	$6
11/02/74 O.J. Simpson	$9		11/15/76 Rocky Bleier	$6
11/09/74 Larry Csonka	$8		11/22/76 Lynn Dickey	$6
11/16/74 Dave Osborn	$6		11/29/76 Carlos Brown	$6
11/23/74 Ken Anderson	$6		12/06/76 Roger Staubach	$7
11/30/74 O.J. Simpson	$9		12/13/76 Jack Lambert	$7
12/07/74 Duane Thomas	$6		12/20/76 Gordon Bell	$6
12/14/74 J. Kenworth	$6		12/27/76 Ken Stabler	$7
12/21/74 Joe Namath	$9		Jan. 1977 Wally Hilgenberg, Ken Stabler	$7
12/28/74 Ken Grandberry	$6		Feb. 1977 John Madden	$11
01/04/75 Art Thoms	$6		March 1977 Fran Tarkenton	$8
01/11/75 Dave Osborn	$6		April 1977 Ron Jaworski	$7
01/18/75 George Blanda, Joe Greene	$8		May 1977 Bears, 49ers	$6
01/25/75 Joe Greene, Steelers champs	$12		June 1977 Ricky Bell	$6
Feb. 1975 Joe Greene, Jim Hart	$7		July 1977 Steelers, Vikings	$6
March 1975 Walter Payton	$8		08/15/77 Dan Pastorini, Mike Phipps	$6
April 1975 Ken Stabler	$7		Aug. 1977 Chuck Noll	$6
May 1975 Joe Greene, L.C. Greenwood	$7		08/15/77 Greg Latta	$6
June 1975 Raiders vs. Colts	$6		08/22/77 Henry Marshall	$6
July 1975 Joe Namath	$9		08/29/77 Ron East	$6
Aug. 1975 Virgil Livers	$6		09/05/77 Tony Reed, Eckern	$6
08/12/75 Terry Bradshaw	$8		09/12/77 Lawrence McCutcheon	$6
08/19/75 MacArthur Lane	$6		09/19/77 Bert Jones	$6
08/26/75 Merlin Olsen	$7		09/26/77 Preston Pearson	$7
09/02/75 New Orleans Saints Superdome	$7		10/03/77 David Lewis	$6
09/09/75 Cullen Bryant	$6		10/10/77 Pat Leahy	$6
09/16/75 Roman Gabriel	$6		10/17/77 Tom MacLeod	$6
09/23/75 Lawrence McCutcheon	$6		10/24/77 Don McCauley	$6
09/30/75 Archie Manning	$7		10/31/77 John James	$6
10/07/75 Gary Huff	$6		11/07/77 Don Hardeman	$6
10/14/75 Norm Snead	$6		11/14/77 O.J. Simpson	$8
10/21/75 Essex Johnson	$6		11/21/77 Walter Payton	$8
10/28/75 O.J. Simpson	$9		11/28/77 Walter Payton	$8
11/04/75 Rocky Bleier	$6		12/05/77 Terry Bradshaw, Joe Klecko	$8
11/11/75 Don Hardeman	$6		12/12/77 Delvin Williams	$6
11/18/75 Robert Miller	$6		12/19/77 Rocky Bleier	$6
11/25/75 Pat Sullivan	$6		12/26/77 Larry Csonka	$8
12/02/75 George Blanda	$8		01/02/78 John Matuszak	$8
12/09/75 Boobie Clark	$6		Jan. 1978 Cowboys, Broncos	$7
12/16/75 Billy Kilmer	$8		Feb. 1978 Ed Jones, Cowboys champs	$12
12/23/75 Bert Jones	$7		March 1978 Ken Houston, Greg Pruitt	$6
12/30/75 Lydell Mitchell	$6		April 1978 Terry Metcalf	$6
01/06/76 Ron Jaworski	$7		May 1978 John Dutton, B. Williams	$6
01/13/76 Dave Edwards	$7		June 1978 Earl Campbell	$7
01/20/76 Tom Landry	$7		July 1978 Bob Griese, Roger Staubach	$8
01/27/76 L.C. Greenwood, Steelers champs	$12		07/15/78 Coy Bacon	$5
Feb. 1976 Joe Namath	$9		08/07/78 Steve Schubert	$6
March 1976 John Riggins	$7		08/14/78 Craig Colquitt	$5
April 1976 John Hadl	$6		10/02/78 Richard Todd	$5
May 1976 Lee Roy Selmon	$6		10/09/78 Tony Galbreath	$5
June 1976 Kenny Stabler	$8		10/16/78 Bubba Bean	$5
July 1976 Texas A&M	$6		10/23/78 Lawrence McCutcheon	$5
Aug. 1976 Steelers, college season	$6		10/30/78 Joe Pisarcik	$5

11/06/78 T. Daykin	$5
11/13/78 Joe Federspiel	$5
11/27/78 Don Macek	$5
12/04/78 Rick Kane	$5
12/11/78 Joe Theismann	$7
12/18/78 Dexter Bussey	$5
12/25/78 Ricky Thompson	$5
01/01/78 Bum Phillips, Don Shula	$6
01/08/78 Jack Dolbin	$5
01/15/78 Terry Bradshaw, Roger Staubach	$8

Profile

1974 O.J. Simpson	$25
1975 Ken Stabler	$17

Prolog Official NFL Annual

1971 Logo and 1971 (hardcover)	$25
Logo and 1971 (paperback)	$20
1972 Miami vs. Dallas (hardcover)	$15
Miami vs. Dallas (paperback)	$15
1973 Larry Brown (hardcover)	$20
Larry Brown (paperback)	$15
1974 Mercury Morris	$15
1975 Terry Bradshaw, Franco Harris	$15
1976 Fran Tarkenton	$15
1977 Bert Jones	$15
1978 Walter Payton	$15
1979 Terry Bradshaw	$15
1980 Jack Youngblood	$15
1981 Jim Plunkett	$15
1982 Joe Montana	$20
1983 Freeman McNeil	$15
1984 Eric Dickerson	$15
1985 Walter Payton	$20
Joe Montana	$20
1986 Marcus Allen	$15
Joe Morris	$15
Mike Singletary	$15
1987 Phil Simms	$15
Walter Payton	$20
1988 Anthony Carter, Bernie Kosar, Jim McMahon	$10
Jerry Rice	$15
1989 Tim Brown, Joe Montana, J.L. Williams	$10
1990 Bo Jackson, Joe Montana, Lawrence Taylor	$15

The Sporting News AFL Guide

1962 Dick Harris	$75-$100
1963 Charlie Hennigan	$65-$90
1964 Curtis McClinton	$40-$75
1965 Tobin Rote	$40-$60
1966 Buck Buchanan, Paul Lowe	$30-$60
1967 Bobby Burnett, Jack Kemp	$35-$60
1968 George Blanda, Dayle Lamonica, Jim Nance, George Sauer	$20-$55
1969 Matt Snell	$20-$35
1970 Lance Alworth	$20-$30

The Sporting News Football Guide

1970 Hank Stram	$45
1971 Jim Bakken	$35-$40
1972 Roger Staubach	$35-$40
1973 Mercury Morris	$32-$35
1974 Larry Csonka	$32-$35
1975 Franco Harris	$28-$35
1976 Lynn Swann	$25-$30
1977 Ken Stabler	$25-$30
1978 Roger Staubach	$25-$30

1979 Terry Bradshaw	$25-$30
1980 John Stallworth, Lynn Swann	$20-$25
1981 Billy Sims	$20-$25
1982 Ken Anderson	$20-$25
1983 Mark Moseley	$20-$25
1984 Eric Dickerson	$20-$25
1985 Dan Marino	$25
1986 Marcus Allen	$15-$20
1987 Phil Simms	$15-$20
1988 John Elway	$15-$20
1989 Steve Largent	$15-$20
1990 Joe Montana	$15-$20
1991 Warren Moon	$15

The Sporting News Football Record & Rule Book

1945 Wide receiver	$40
1946 A.A. Stagg	$35
1947 Pop Warner	$35
1948 Frank Leahy	$30
1949 Sammy Baugh	$30
1950 Earle "Greasy" Neale	$25

The Sporting News Football Register

1966 St. Louis defense	$45-$60
1967 Curt McClinton	$35-$45
1968 George Mira	$35-$45
1969 Bart Starr	$40
1970 Roman Gabriel	$30
1971 Sonny Jurgensen	$30
1972 Philadelphia Eagles vs. St. Louis Cardinals	$30
1973 Terry Bradshaw	$30
1974 O.J. Simpson	$40
1975 Ken Stabler	$25
1976 Fran Tarkenton	$20-$25
1977 Bert Jones	$15-$20
1978 Walter Payton	$25-$30
1979 Earl Campbell	$20-$25
1980 Dan Fouts	$15-$20
1981 Brian Sipe	$15-$20
1982 George Rogers	$15-$20
1983 Marcus Allen	$15-$20
1984 Dan Marino	$20
1985 Walter Payton	$15-$20
1986 Eddie Brown	$10-$15
1987 Rueben Mayes	$10-$15
1988 Jerry Rice	$15
1989 Boomer Esiason	$10-$15
1990 Barry Sanders	$15

The Sporting News Pro Yearbook

1981 Brian Sipe	$20
1982 Kellen Winslow	$15
1983 John Riggins	$15
1984 Ken Anderson, Tom Cousineau	$20

All other covers $15
1985 Dan Marino, Joe Montana $35
1986 Jim McMahon $15
    All other covers $12
1987 Boomer Esiason, Bernie Kosar $15
    All other covers $12
1988 Eric Dickerson $10
    All other covers $10
1989 Reggie Williams $8
    All other covers $10
1990 All covers $8

The Sporting News Super Bowl Book

1981 Jim Plunkett $15
1982 Joe Montana $20
1983 Russ Grimm, John Riggins $15
1984 Raiders blocking Redskins punt $10
1985 Joe Montana $20
1986 Dan Hampton $10
1987 Mark Bavaro, Phil McConkey $10
1988 Doug Williams $10
1989 Jerry Rice $10
1990 Joe Montana $10
1991 Jeff Hostetler $10

Sports All Stars
(Maco Magazine)

1958 Rams running back $35
1959 .... $30
1960 Johnny Unitas $35
1961 .... $20
1962 .... $25
1963 Jim Taylor $20
1964 Jim Brown $25
1965 Charley Johnson $15
1966 Dick Butkus $25
1967 Gale Sayers $25
    All others $20
1968 Johnny Unitas $25
1968 Roman Gabriel $15
    All others $12
1969 Fran Tarkenton $15
1969 Leroy Kelly $14
    All others $12
1970 Don Maynard $15
1971 .... $12
1972 Jim Plunkett $12
1973 Mercury Morris $10
1974 Roger Staubach $15
1975 Terry Bradshaw $15
1976 Terry Bradshaw $15
1977 .... $12
1978 .... $12
1979 Ken Anderson $10

Sports Quarterly

1968 Donny Anderson $15
1969 Joe Namath $20
1970 Sonny Jurgensen $17
1971 .... $12
1972 Oakland Raiders vs. Los Angeles Rams $15
1973 Larry Csonka, Bob Griese, Jim Kiick ... $15
1974 O.J Simpson $25
1975 Minnesota Vikings vs. Pittsburgh Steelers ... $15
1976 Lynn Swann $20
1977 .... $12
1978 Lyle Alzado $12
1979 Terry Bradshaw $15

Sports Review

1967 Bart Starr $25
1968 Bart Starr, Johnny Unitas $20
1969 Joe Namath $25
1970 Joe Kapp $15
1971 Baltimore Colts vs. Dallas Cowboys ... $15
1972 .... $15
1973 Billy Kilmer $15

Sports Stars Of Pro & College Football

1972 Jim Plunkett $17
1973 Bob Griese $15
1974 Larry Csonka $18
1975 Ken Stabler $15

Sports Stars Of Pro Football

1968 Bart Starr $25
1969 Joe Namath $30
1970 .... $15
1971 .... $15
1972 Joe Namath $25
1973 Larry Brown $15
1974 Bob Griese $18
1975 Terry Bradshaw $20

Sports Today

1971 Joe Namath $25
1972 Roger Staubach $20
1973 Joe Namath $20
1974 O.J. Simpson $25

Street & Smith's College Football

1940 Center hiking the ball .... $175-$250
1941 Frankie Albert (Stanford) .... $75-$150
1942 Alan Cameron (Navy) .... $75-$150
1943 Steve Juzwik .... $75-$150
1944 Bob Kelly (Notre Dame) .... $75-$150
1945 Bob Jenkins (Navy) .... $65-$100
1946 John Ferraro (USC) .... $65-$100
1947 George Connor (Notre Dame) $65-100
1948 Jack Cloud (William & Mary) .... $65-$100
1949 Charley Justice (N. Carolina) .... $65-$100
1950 Leon Heath (Oklahoma) .... $50-$85
1951 Bob Smith (Texas A&M) .... $50-$85
1952 Johnny Olszewskj (California) .... $50-$85
1953 "Ike" Eisenhauer (Navy) .... $75-$100
1954 Ralph Guglielmi (Notre Dame) ...... $50-$85
1955 Howard Cassidy (Ohio State) $75-100
1956 Jim Swink (TCU) .... $50-$85
1957 Clendon Thomas, Oklahoma .... $75-$100
1958 Bob White (Ohio State) .... $50-$85
1959 Brennan, Izo, Kuharich (Notre Dame) ..... $50-$85
1960 Rich Mayo (Air Force) .... $40-$60
1961 Ronnie Bull (Baylor) .... $40-$60
1962 Jay Wilkinson (Duke) .... $40-$60
1963 Tom Myers (Northwestern) .... $35-$60
    Pete Beathard, Hal Bedsole (USC) ..... $40-$60
    Paul Martha (Pitt) .... $40-$60
1964 Roger Staubach (Navy) .... $50-$75
    Dick Butkus (Illinois) .... $40-$60
    Craig Morton (California) .... $35-$60
1965 Roger Bird (Kentucky) .... $35-$45
    Phil Sheridan (Notre Dame) .... $35-$45
    Ray Handley (Stanford) .... $35-$45
1966 Steve Spurrier (Florida) .... $35-$50
    Bob Griese (Purdue) .... $45-$60
    Gary Beban (UCLA) .... $35-$45

1967 Ted Hendricks (Miami) .... $30-$45
  Terry Hanratty (Notre Dame) .... $30-$45
  Ron Drake (USC) .... $30-$45
1968 O.J. Simpson (USC) .... $50-$60
  Chris Gilbert (Texas) .... $30-$45
  Larry Smith (Florida) .... $30-$45
1969 Rex Kern (Ohio State) .... $30-$35
  Billy Main .... $25-$30
  Steve Kiner (Tennessee) .... $30-$45
1970 Jim Plunkett (Stanford) .... $35-$45
  Archie Manning (Mississippi) .... $40-$45
  Steve Worster (Texas) .... $30-$35
1971 Pat Sullivan (Auburn) .... $25-$30
  Joe Ferguson (Arkansas) .... $25-$30
  Sonny Sixkiller (Washington) .... $25-$30
1972 Brad Van Pelt (Michigan State) .... $25-$30
  John Hufnagel (Penn State) .... $20-$25
  Pete Adams (USC) .... $25-$30
1973 Champ Henson (Ohio State) .... $20-$25
  Kermit Johnson (UCLA) .... $20-$25
  Wayne Wheeler (Alabama) .... $20-$25
1974 Tom Clements (Notre Dame) .... $20-$25
  Pat Haden (USC) .... $20-$25
  Brad Davis (LSU) .... $20-$25
1975 Archie Griffin (Ohio State) .... $20-$25
  Richard Todd (Alabama) .... $20-$25
  John Sciarra (UCLA) .... $25-$30
1976 Tony Dorsett (Pittsburgh) .... $28-$32
  Rob Lytle (Michigan) .... $20-$24
  Ricky Bell (USC) .... $20-$24
1977 Guy Benjamin (Stanford) .... $20-$24
  Ken MacAfee (Notre Dame) .... $20-$24
  Ben Zambiasi (Georgia) .... $20-$24
1978 Rick Leach (Michigan) .... $20-$24
  Jack Thompson (Wash. State) .... $20-$24
  Jeff Rutledge (Alabama) .... $20-$24
1979 Charles White (USC) .... $20-$24
  Mark Herrmann (Purdue) .... $20-$24
  Jeff Pyburn (Georgia) .... $20-$24
1980 Art Schlichter (Ohio State) $20
  Rich Campbell (California) $20
  Scott Woerner (Georgia) $20
1981 Bear Bryant, Herschel Walker $18
  Anthony Carter, Bob Crable $15
  Dan Marino, Joe Morris $30
  John Elway (Stanford) $25
1982 Herschel Walker (Georgia) $25
  John Elway (Stanford) $20
  Dan Marino, Curt Warner $25
  Tony Eason, Marcus Marek $15
1983 Mike Rozier (Nebraska) $15
  Jacque Robinson (Washington) $15
  Kenny Jackson (Penn State) $15
  Marcus Dupree (Oklahoma) $15
1984 Bo Jackson (Auburn) $30
  Doug Flutie (Boston College) $15
  Jack Trudeau (Illinois) $15
1985 Keith Byars (Ohio State) .... $10-$15
  D.J. Dozier (Penn State) $15
  Robbie Bosco (Brigham Young) .... $10-$15
  Jeff Wickersham (LSU) $10
1986 Vinny Testaverde (Miami) .... $10-$15
  Lorenzo White (Michigan State) .... $10-$15
  D.J. Dozier, Joe Paterno .... $10-$15
  UCLA Bruins $12
1987 Tim Brown (Notre Dame) $15
  Gaston Green (UCLA) $10

  Kerwin Bell (Florida) $15
  Gordie Lockbaum (Holy Cross) $12
  Joe Paterno (Penn State) $12
  Jamelle Holieway (Oklahoma) $10
1968 Troy Aikman, Rodney Peete $15
  Bobby Humphrey (Alabama) $10
  Steve Taylor (Nebraska) $10
  Todd Ellis (South Carolina) $10
  Mike Power (Boston College) $10
1989 Emmitt Smith (Florida) $20
  Mark Carrier (USC) $10
  Tony Rice (Notre Dame) $15
  Troy Taylor (California) $10
  Major Harris (West Virginia) $10
  Demetrius Brown (Michigan) $10
  Bill Musgrave (Oregon) $10
  Mike Gundy (Oklahoma State) $10
1990 50th Anniversary $10
1991 Klingler/Hagan/Detmer/Van Pelt $10

Street & Smith's Pro Football

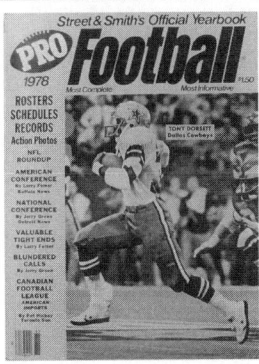

1963 Y.A. Tittle $90
  Milt Plum .... $60-$90
  Roman Gabriel .... $60-$90
1964 Bart Starr .... $40-$60
  Jim Katcavage .... $40-$60
  Terry Baker .... $40-$60
1965 Johnny Unitas $75
  Frank Ryan .... $40-$60
  Dick Bass .... $40-$60
1966 J. Hillebrand, R. LaLonde .... $40-$60
  Ken Willard .... $40-$60
  Charley Johnson .... $40-$60
1967 Mike Rabold, Gale Sayers .... $35-$60
  Dick Bass .... $35-$45
  Tony Lorick, Bob Vogel .... $35-$45
1968 Don Meredith .... $35-$55
  Norm Snead .... $35-$45
  Hewritt Dixon .... $35-$45
1969 Joe Namath .... $45-$75
  John Brodie .... $35-$45
  Jack Concannon, George Seals .... $35-$45
1970 Joe Namath .... $40-$75
  Roman Gabriel .... $30-$40
  Joe Kapp .... $30-$35
1971 Ralph Neely, Duane Thomas .... $25-$30
  Earl Morrall .... $25-$30
  John Brodie, Ken Willard .... $25-$30
1972 R. Staubach, D. Thomas .... $25-$35
  Bob Griese .... $25-$30
  John Hadl .... $25-$30
1973 Larry Csonka .... $25-$30
  Chester Marcol .... $25-$30
  Steve Spurrier .... $35-$40

1974 Roger Staubach .... $25-$35
    O.J. Simpson .... $30-$40
    Jim Bertelsen .... $25-$30
1975 Franco Harris .... $20-$30
    Jim Hart .... $20-$25
    Lawrence McCutcheon .... $20-$25
1976 Roger Staubach .... $25-$30
    Terry Bradshaw .... $25-$30
    Ken Stabler .... $20-$25
1977 Walter Payton .... $30-$40
    Bert Jones .... $20-$25
    John Cappelletti .... $20-$25
1978 Tony Dorsett $20
    Bob Griese .... $20-$28
    Mark Van Eeghen .... $20-$25
1979 Roger Staubach .... $25-$30
    Terry Bradshaw .... $20-$25
    Jim Zorn .... $20-$25
1980 Walter Payton .... $25-$30
    Terry Bradshaw .... $15-$20
    Dan Fouts $15
1981 Tommy Kramer, Brian Sipe $15
    Jim Plunkett, Jim Zorn $15
    Steve Bartkowski, Earl Campbell $15
    Joe Ferguson, Ron Jaworski $15
1982 Joe Montana $30
    Lawrence Taylor .... $15-$20
    Tony Dorsett .... $15-$20
    Ken Anderson .... $12-$15
1983 Marcus Allen $20
    Joe Theismann .... $12-$15
    Ken Anderson .... $12-$15
    A.J. Duhe .... $12-$15
1984 Walter Payton .... $20-$25
    Dan Marino $25
    Marcus Allen $20
    John Riggins .... $12-$15
1985 Joe Montana .... $18-$20
    Walter Payton .... $12-$15
    Dan Marino $15
    Phil Simms $12
1986 Dan Marino .... $15-$18
    Eric Dickerson .... $10-$12
    Mike Singletary .... $10-$12
    Joe Morris .... $10-$12
1987 Dan Marino $15
    Tony Dorsett $10
    John Elway .... $10-$12
    Phil Simms .... $10-$12
    Bernie Kosar .... $10-$12
1988 Jerry Rice $15
    Warren Moon $10
    John Offerdahl $8
    Doug Williams $8
    Anthony Carter $8
    Ozzie Newsome $10
1989 Boomer Esiason $10
    Jim Everett $10
    Roger Craig $10
    Jim Kelly .... $10-$12
    Randall Cunningham $10
    Mike Singletary .... $10-$12
    Herschel Walker $10
    Morten Andersen $10
1990 Joe Montana .... $14-$18
1991 Lawrence Taylor $12

1992 Lawrence Taylor $12
    Randall Cunningham $10
1993 Phil Simms $10
    Dan Marino $20
    Joe Montana/Brett Favre $15
1994 Reggie White $12
    Eric Metcalf/Reggie Brooks $10
    Emmitt Smith $12
1995 Doug Brown $10
    Drew Bledsoe $12
    Junior Seau/Eric Hill $10
    Jim Everett/Jeff George $10
    Ricky Ervins $10
    Chris Warren $10
    Neil O'Donnell/Randall Cunningham $12
    Frank Reich $10
    Brett Favre/Warren Moon $12
    Chris Zorich $10
    John Elway/Jeff Hostetler $12
    Steve Young $12
    Vinnie Testaverde $12
    Troy Aikman $12
1996 Barry Sanders/Rashan Salaam $12
    Rodney Hampton $10
    Brett Favre $12
    Greg Lloyd $12
    Emmitt Smith $12
    Curtis Martin $12
    Jerry Rice $12
1997 Keyshawn Johnson $12

Touchdown All-Pro

1964 Ron Bull $40
1967 Fran Tarkenton $30
1968 Donny Anderson, Daryle Lamonica $25
1969 Joe Namath $30
1970 Roman Gabriel, Calvin Hill $15
1971 Mike Curtis, Fran Tarkenton $20
1972 Calvin Hill $17
1973 Larry Brown $17
1974 O.J. Simpson $25

True Football Yearbook

1950 Punter in action $75
1951 Kyle Rote $70
1952 Otto Graham $65
1953 Johnny Lattner $60
1956 Defender blocking punt $25
1957 Running back $25
1958 Jim Brown/Joe Schmidt $25
1959 Johnny Unitas $30
1960 Ernie Davis $25
1961 Roman Gabriel $20
1962 Paul Hornung $25
1963 Herb Adderly $25
1964 Jim Brown $30
1965 Johnny Unitas $30
1966 Bart Starr $20
1967 Bart Starr $20
1968 John Unitas $20
1969 Earl Morrall $12
1970 Len Dawson $15
1971 Tom Nowatzke $10
1972 Alan Page, Roger Staubach $20
1978 Roger Staubach $18
1979 Earl Campbell $15
1980 Mean Joe Greene $15
1981 Jim Plunkett $12

Woodward's Football Yearbook

1949 Dan Foldberg .... $35-$75
1950 Bobby Williams .... $25-$40
1951 Bob Smith .... $25-$40
1952 Harry Agganis .... $25-$40
1953 Bob Burkhart .... $25-$40
1954 Ralph Gugliemi .... $25-$40
1955 George Welsh .... $25-$40
1956 Tommy McDonald .... $25-$40
1957 Bobby Cox .... $25-$40
1958 Bob Reifsnyder .... $25-$40
1959 Bob Anderson .... $25-$40
1960 Bob Schloredt .... $20-$30
1961 Joe Romig .... $20-$30

Pocket Pro Football Annuals
Complete Handbook Of Pro Football
(Lancer Books)

1971 Fran Tarkenton $15
1972 Roger Staubach $20
1973 Bob Griese $15
1974 O.J. Simpson $20
1975 Mean Joe Greene $15
1976 Terry Bradshaw $15
1977 Ken Stabler $15
1978 Walter Payton $15
1979 Pittsburgh Steelers $12
1980 Lynn Swann $12
1981 Jim Plunkett $10
1982 Joe Montana $20
1983 John Riggins Joe Theismann $10
1984 Marcus Allen $10
1985 Joe Montana $18
1986 Jim McMahon $10
1987 Phil Simms $10
1968 Bo Jackson $10
1989 Jerry Rice $15
1990 Terry Bradshaw, Joe Montana $10

NFL Report

1972 Jim Plunkett (Signet) $15
1973 Terry Bradshaw, Franco Harris (Signet) $20
1974 Larry Csonka (Signet) $15

1975 Lawrence McCutcheon (Dell) $10
1976 Franco Harris (Dell) $15
1977 Ken Stabler (Dell) $12
1978 Mark Van Eeghen (Dell) $8
1979 Tony Dorsett (Dell) $15
1980 Earl Campbell (Dell) $12
1981 Wilbert Montgomery (Dell) $7
1982 Kellen Winslow (Dell) $9
1983 James Lofton (Dell) $8
1984 Todd Christensen (Dell) $7
1987 Eric Dickerson (Signet) $8
1988 John Elway (Signet) $10

Pro Football (Ballantine Books)

1976 Lynn Swann $15
1977 O.J. Simpson $25

Pro Football Almanac
(Fawcett Gold Medal Books)

1964 Jim Brown $30
1965 Bill Brown, Fran Tarkenton $20

Pro Football Handbook
(Pocket Books)

1960 Johnny Unitas $35
1961 Sonny Jurgensen $30
1962 Football action $25
1963 Cleats and ball $20
1964 Ball carrier $15
1965 Jim Brown $30
1966 .... $15
1967 Ball bursting through paper $35
1968 White helmet $10
1969 Jets wool cap on a football $10

Becomes: The Pocket Book Of Pro Football

1974 O.J. Simpson $25
1975 Mean Joe Greene $15
1976 Terry Bradshaw $15
1977 Ken Stabler $12
1978 Walter Payton $15
1979 Terry Bradshaw $15
1980 Earl Campbell $12

Basketball Magazines

All-Pro Basketball Stars

1976 Rick Barry $8
1977 John Havlicek $10
1978 Julius Erving $12
1979 David Thompson $8
1981 Larry Bird, Julius Erving $20
1982 Julius Erving $10

Basketball Annual
(Complete Sports)

1970-71 Lew Alcindor $20
1971-72 Pete Maravich $15
1972-73 .... $10
1973-74 Bill Walton $10
1974-75 David Thompson $8
1975-76 Rick Barry $8
1976-77 .... $8
published by Tiger Press

1977-78 .... $15
1978-79 Artis Gilmore $15
1979-80 Mike Gminski, Mike O'Koren, Kelly Tripucka $15
1980-81 Mark Aguirre, Rod Foster, Kelly Tripucka $15
1981-82 John Bagley, John Paxson, Ralph Sampson $15
1982-83 Ralph Sampson $15
1983-84 .... $12
1984-85 .... $12
1985-86 .... $12
1986-87 David Robinson $18
1987-88 Charles Barkley, Magic Johnson, Michael Jordan.. $20
1988-89 Magic Johnson, Isiah Thomas $15
1989-90 .... $10
1990-91 .... $10

Basketball Digest

Nov. 1973 Artis Gilmore $45
Dec. 1973 Jerry West $15
Jan. 1974 Norm Van Lier $10

Feb. 1974 Kareem Abdul-Jabbar $12
March 1974 Walt Frazier $12
April 1974 Dave DeBusschere $12
Nov. 1974 John Havlicek $12
Dec. 1974 Bob McAdoo $12
Jan. 1975 Bob Lanier $10
Feb. 1975 Bill Walton $12
March 1975 Nate Thurmond $10
April 1975 Rick Barry $10
Nov. 1975 Kareem Abdul-Jabbar $12
Dec. 1975 Walt Frazier $12
Jan. 1976 Pete Maravich $15
Feb. 1976 Julius Erving $15
March 1976 Elvin Hayes $10
April 1976 Dave Cowens $10
Nov. 1976 Bob McAdoo $10
Dec. 1976 Julius Erving, David Thompson $15
Jan. 1977 Artis Gilmore $10
Feb. 1977 George McGinnis $10
March 1977 Earl Monroe $10
April 1977 Bill Walton $10
May 1977 Jo Jo White $10
June 1977 Kareem Abdul-Jabbar $10
Nov. 1977 Maurice Lucas $10
Dec. 1977 Rick Barry $10
Jan. 1978 Darryl Dawkins, Moses Malone $10
Feb. 1978 Alvan Adams $10
March 1978 Dan Issel $10
April 1978 Dave Cowens $10
May 1978 Bob Lanier $10
June 1978 Bill Walton $10
Nov. 1978 Marvin Webster $10
Dec. 1978 George Gervin $10
Jan. 1979 David Thompson $10
Feb. 1979 Pete Maravich $15
March 1979 Bob McAdoo $10
April 1979 Elvin Hayes $10
May 1979 Artis Gilmore $10
June 1979 Moses Malone $10
Nov. 1979 Dennis Johnson $10
Dec. 1979 Kareem Abdul-Jabbar $10
Jan. 1980 Paul Westphal $10
Feb. 1980 Julius Erving $15
March 1980 Larry Bird $20
April 1980 Marques Johnson $8
May 1980 Lloyd Free $8
June 1980 Julius Erving, Magic Johnson $25
Nov. 1980 Magic Johnson $20
Dec. 1980 Phil Ford $8
Jan. 1981 Bill Cartwright $10
Feb. 1981 Walter Davis $8
March 1981Darryl Dawkins $8
April 1981 Adrian Dantley, Darrell Griffith $8
May 1981George Gervin $8
June 1981 Julius Erving $15
Nov. 1981 Larry Bird $15
Dec. 1981 Moses Malone $10
Jan. 1982 Joe Barry Carroll $8
Feb. 1982 Isiah Thomas $10
March 1982 Reggie Theus $8
April 1982 Sidney Moncrief $8
May 1982 Alex English $8
June 1982 Kareem Abdul-Jabbar $20
Nov. 1982 Magic Johnson $20
Dec. 1982 Buck Williams $8
Jan. 1983 Robert Parish $10

Feb. 1983 Kelly Tripucka $8
March 1983 Gus Williams $8
April 1983 Bernard King $10
May 1983 Artis Gilmore $10
June 1983 Moses Malone $10
Nov. 1983 Julius Erving $15
Dec. 1983 Kiki Vandeweghe $8
Jan. 1984 Larry Bird $15
Feb. 1984 Mark Aguirre $10
March 1984 Maurice Lucas $8
April 1984 Jim Paxson $8
May 1984 Magic Johnson $15
June/July 1984 Ralph Sampson $8
Nov. 1984 Larry Bird $15
Dec. 1984 Jack Sikma $10
Jan. 1985Bernard King $7
Feb. 1985 Isiah Thomas $8
March 1985 Jeff Ruland $4
April 1985 Hakeem Olajuwon $8
May 1985 Kareem Abdul-Jabbar $7
June/July 1985 Michael Jordan $15
Nov. 1985 Patrick Ewing $10
Dec. 1985 Rolando Blackman $4
Jan. 1986 Kevin McHale $7
Feb. 1986 Dominique Wilkins $7
March 1986 Ralph Sampson $5
April 1986 Charles Barkley $8
May 1986 Magic Johnson $8
June/July 1986 Larry Bird $8
Nov. 1986 Hakeem Olajuwon $8
Dec. 1986 Xavier McDaniel $4
Jan. 1987 Michael Jordan $10
Feb. 1987 Moses Malone $6
March 1987 Terry Cummings $4
April 1987 Julius Erving $6
May 1987 Kevin McHale, Kevin Willis $6
June/July 1987 Magic Johnson $8
Nov. 1987 Larry Bird $7
Dec. 1987Isiah Thomas $5
Jan. 1988 Karl Malone $5
Feb. 1988 Charles Barkley $6
March 1988 Rolando Blackman, Derek Harper $4
April 1988 Michael Jordan $8
May 1988 Adrian Dantley $5
June/July 1988 Magic Johnson $7
Nov. 1988 Larry Bird $8
Dec. 1988 Kevin Duckworth $4
Jan. 1989 Moses Malone, Reggie Theus $4
Feb. 1989 Kareem Abdul-Jabbar $6
March 1989 Brad Daugherty, Patrick Ewing $5
April 1989 Michael Adams $4
May 1989 Karl Malone,Hakeem Olajuwon $5
June/July 1989 Michael Jordan $6
Nov. 1989 Joe Dumars $4
Dec. 1989 Chris Mullin $4
Jan. 1990 Patrick Ewing, Michael Jordan, Trent Tucker $6
Feb. 1990 Dennis Rodman $4
March 1990 Charles Barkley $6
April 1990 Terry Porter $4
May 1990 Michael Jordan $6
June/July 1990 David Robinson $8
Nov. 1990 Kevin Johnson $4
Dec. 1990 Mark Price $4
Jan. 1991 Charles Smith $3
Feb. 1991 Bill Laimbeer $3
March 1991 Hakeem Olajuwon, David Robinson $6

April 1991 Kevin McHale, Brian Shaw $4
May 1991 Clyde Drexler $4
June/July 1991 Michael Jordan $7

Basketball Forecast

1985-86 Larry Bird, Michael Jordan $12
1986-87 Patrick Ewing, H. Olajuwon $8
1987-88 Magic Johnson $9
1988-89 Michael Jordan $10
1989-90 Magic Johnson $8

Basketball News Yearbook

1973 Archibald, Cunninghan, Russell $15
1974 Julius Erving $15
1975 Walt Frazier, John Havlicek $13
1976 Rick Barry $12
1977 Julius Erving $15
1978 Pete Maravich, Willis Reed, Bill Walton $15
1979 Nancy Lieberman, Wes Unseld, Bill Walton $10
1980 Jack Sikma $12
1981 Larry Bird $17

Basketball Scene

1979-80 .... $10
1980-81 Larry Bird, Magic Johnson $15
1981-82 .... $10
1982-83 .... $8
1983-84 .... $8
1984-85 .... $8
1985-86 Patrick Ewing $8
1986-87 Larry Bird, Michael Jordan, Hakeem Olajuwon,
   Dominique Wilkins $8
1987-88 .... $6
1988-89 .... $6
1989-90 .... $5
1990-91 .... $4
1991-92 Larry Bird, Magic Johnson, Michael Jordan ... $4

Basketball Sports Stars (Hewfred)

1969 Lew Alcindor, Bill Bradley, Earl Monroe $20
1970 Lew Alcindor $15
1971 Jerry West .... $13-$15
1972 Pete Maravich $20
1973 Wilt Chamberlain .... $13-$15
1974 Walt Frazier $15
1975 Dave Cowens, John Havlicek $15
1976 Rick Barry $15

Basketball Weekly

12/04/67 Lew Alcindor, Will NBA Survive? $25
12/11/67 Butch Van Breda Kolff $15
12/21/67 Walter Kennedy, No War With ABA $15
12/31/67 Dave Bing, College holiday tournaments $15
01/08/68 Calvin Murphy, UCLA wins 42nd straight $15
01/15/68 Doug Moe, First ABA All-Star game $15
01/22/68 Houston (Elvin Hayes) vs. UCLA $15
01/29/68 Houston (Elvin Hayes) vs. UCLA $15
02/05/68 Wilt Chamberlain, NBA expansion $15
02/12/68 Dean Smith, NCAA conference races $15
02/19/68 Dave Bing, 76ers won't lose Hannum $15
02/26/68 Clark, Miller, Scott, NCAA tournament $15
03/11/68 NCAA All-Americans $15
03/18/68 Howard, Nelson, Kentucky, UNC as dark horses .. $15
03/25/68 Elvin Hayes, Can Houston do it again? $15
04/30/68 Wilt Chamberlain, Bill Russell, All-NBA team $15
11/01/68 Wilt Chamberlain, Jerry West $17
12/02/68 John Wooden, UCLA preseason #1 .... $15

12/12/68 Rick Barry, Earl Monroe, Wes Unseld $15
12/23/68 Steve Patterson, UCLA after Lew Alcindor $15
12/30/68 Charlie Scott, NCAA holiday tournaments $15
01/06/69 Wilt Chamberlain $17
01/13/69 Oscar Robertson, NBA All-Stars $15
01/20/69 Kevin Loughery, Bullets as most improved team ... $15
02/03/69 NBA referees $15
02/10/69 Who's #2 behind UCLA? $15
02/17/69 LaSalle on NCAA probation $15
02/24/69 NCAA basketball upsets $15
03/03/69 Scouting reports, Lew Alcindor $15
03/10/69 NCAA All-Americans $15
03/17/69 John Wooden, Who will challenge UCLA? $15
04/01/69 Lew Alcindor, UCLA shoots for #3 .... $15
05/01/69 All-NBA Team $15
11/22/69 Rick Barry, Spencer Haywood, NBA vs. ABA $13
12/08/69 Charlie Scott, Many try to succeed UCLA $13
12/19/69 Bill Bradley, Willis Reed, Kentucky #1 .... $13
12/29/69 M. Hauer, College holiday tournaments $13
01/05/70 Dan Issel, Pratt, Steele, Kentucky is #1 ..... $13
01/12/70 Hall, Taylor, Kentucky #1, UCLA #2 .... $13
01/19/70 Lew Alcindor, Jerry West, NBA All-Stars $13
01/26/70 Walter Kennedy, No merger for the NBA, ABA ... $13
02/02/70 Pistol Pete Maravich $16
02/09/70 Charlie Scott, ABA makes "war plans" $13
02/16/70 Bob Lanier, St. Bonaventure $13
02/23/70 Rick Mount $13
03/02/70 Kentucky, UCLA tied in poll $13
03/09/70 Dan Issel, NCAA All-Americans $13
03/16/70 Adolph Rupp, NCAA tournament preview $13
03/23/70 J. Williams, UCLA shoots for 4th title $13
04/06/70 Pro basketball war continues $13
05/10/70 Wilt Chamberlain, Willis Reed, Lakers vs. Knicks . $13
11/23/70 Red Holzman, NBA vs. ABA $12
11/30/70 UCLA is preseason #1 .... $12
12/10/70 Frank Ramsey, ABA/NBA merger gap widens ... $12
12/21/70 Larry Costello, Bucks set record pace $12
01/04/71 McGuire, Kraft, College holiday tournaments .. $12
01/11/71 Pistons are for real $12
01/18/71 Wilt Chamberlain, Jerry West, NBA All-Star game ... $12
01/25/71 Mel Daniels, Dan Issel, ABA All-Star game $12
02/01/71 Sidney Wicks, UCLA $12
02/08/71 Bing, McGlocklin, #2 USC vs. #1 UCLA $12
02/15/71 John Wooden, UCLA is #1 .... $12
02/22/71 Parity in the ABA $12
02/29/71 Who can beat UCLA? $12
03/01/71 Who's the #1 Pick? $12
03/08/71 NCAA All-Americans $12
03/15/71 Al McGuire, NCAA tournament $12
03/22/71 Adolph Rupp, Kentucky $12
05/15/71 Italy attracts U.S. players $12
11/23/71 ABA/NBA start new seasons $12
11/30/71 USC becomes new #1 .... $12
12/10/71 Wilt Chamberlain $10
12/21/71 UCLA is #1 .... $10
01/11/72 Jim Chones, Marquette $10
01/18/72 Kareem Abdul-Jabbar, Walt Frazier, Jerry West, NBA
   All-Star game $10
01/25/72 Ivy League, UCLA is #1 .... $10
02/01/72 Gilmore, Issel, Simpson, ABA All-Star game $10
02/08/72 Denny Crum, ABA draft $10
02/15/72 Proposed division after merger $10
02/22/72 UCLA favored again $10
02/29/72 Jim McDaniels $10
03/07/72 Julius Erving to jump leagues? $10
03/14/72 Bill Walton $10

04/15/79 Dick Motta.. $6
06/15/79 Class of '83, Ralph Sampson $7
11/28/79 Kareem Abdul-Jabbar, Julius Erving, John Havlicek.....$6
12/12/79 Ohio State is #1 .... $6
12/12/79 Prep stars $6
12/26/79 Doug Collins, Julius Erving $6
01/03/80 Ray Meyer $6
01/10/80 Larry Brown $6
01/17/80 Hubie Brown, John Drew...................................... $6
01/24/80 Darrell Griffith $6
01/31/80 Moses Malone $6
02/07/80 Larry Bird... $7
02/14/80 Danny Ainge $6
02/21/80 Dennis Johnson, Gus Williams................................. $6
02/28/80 Frank McGuire $6
03/07/80 NCAA All-Americans: Mark Aguirre, others............. $6
03/14/80 Mark Aguirre $6
03/21/80 Denny Crum $6
03/28/80 NCAA Final Four $6
04/15/80 NBA Playoffs $6
11/28/80 NCAA Preview $6
12/12/80 Walter Davis $6
12/26/80 Magic Johnson $7
01/08/81 Albert King, Maryland... $5
01/15/81 New York Knicks $5
01/22/81 Oregon State $5
12/29/81 Ray Meyer $5
02/05/81 Marques Johnson $5
02/12/81 David Thompson $5
02/26/81 Billy Cunningham $5
03/05/81 Durand Macklin, LSU... $5
03/12/81 Larry Bird, Robert Parish..................................... $6
03/19/81 NCAA All-Americans: Ralph Sampson, Isiah Thomas..$5
03/26/81 Ralph Miller, Oregon State $5
04/02/81 Ralph Sampson $5
04/15/81 Paul Westhead $5
06/15/81 Patrick Ewing, Georgetown $5
11/20/81 Otis Birdsong, Mitch Kupchak $5
11/27/81 Larry Farmer, UCLA $5
12/04/81 Billy Thompson, Camden $5
12/19/81 Adrian Dantley $5
12/26/81 Wes Unseld $7
01/07/82 Antoine Carr, Wichita State $5
01/21/82 Scooter McCray, Rodney McCray................................. $5
01/28/82 Julius Erving, Darryl Dawkins $7
02/04/82 Sleepy Floyd, Georgetown $5
02/11/82 Bill Fitch $5
02/18/82 Michael Cooper, Kevin McHale.................................. $5
02/25/82 Steve Stipanovich, Missouri................................... $5
03/04/82 James Worthy, North Carolina.................................. $5
03/11/82 George Gervin $5
03/18/82 Dominique Wilkins, James Worthy,
    NCAA All-Americans $5
03/25/82 Ralph Sampson, Virginia $5
04/01/82 Dana Kirk... $5
05/08/82 NCAA Final Four $8
05/15/82 Julius Erving, Magic Johnson $7
06/15/82 Norm Nixon $5
11/14/82 Moses Malone $6
11/21/82 Patrick Ewing, Sam Perkins, Ralph Sampson $7
12/09/82 Reggie Williams $5
12/23/82 Gus Williams.. $5
01/03/83 Dean Smith, North Carolina $5
01/13/83 Rollie Massimino, Villanova $5
01/20/83 UCLA vs. Jackson Wright....................................... $5
01/27/83 Kareem Abdul-Jabbar, Robert Parish...................... $5

02/03/83 Melvin Turpin, Kentucky....................................... $5
02/10/83 Julius Erving, Moses Malone................................... $7
02/17/83 Marques Johnson $5
02/24/83 Larry Brown, Buck Williams.................................... $5
03/03/83 Ralph Sampson, others $5
03/10/83 Maurice Lucas $5
03/17/83 Troy Taylor, Randy Wittman, Indiana $5
03/24/83 Michael Jordan, NCAA All-Americans...................... $8
03/31/83 Ralph Sampson $5
04/07/83 Guy Lewis.. $5
04/14/83 Derrick Floyd $5
05/15/83 Moses Malone $5
11/14/83 New NBA coaches... $5
11/28/83 Patrick Ewing, Georgetown $6
12/12/83 Denny Crum, Jack Sikma $4
12/19/83 Adrian Dantley, NCAA coaches $4
01/03/84 World Free, others $4
01/16/84 Julius Erving $6
01/23/84 Ralph Sampson, Steve Stipanovich $4
01/30/84 Michael Cage $4
02/06/84 Isiah Thomas, Kelly Tripucka $4
02/13/84 Terry Holland, Othell Wilson $4
02/20/84 Wayman Tisdale $4
02/27/84 Kevin McHale, Mark Price $4
03/05/84 Magic Johnson, Isiah Thomas................................... $4
03/12/84 Michael Jordan, Sam Perkins $6
03/19/84 Michael Jordan, Chris Mullin, NCAA All-Americans $6
03/26/84 NCAA tournament $5
04/02/84 Billy Tubbs, Oklahoma $5
04/09/84 Hakeem Olajuwon, Final Four $5
05/21/84 Moses Malone $5
06/18/84 Kareem Abdul-Jabbar, Robert Parish...................... $6
11/12/84 Magic Johnson, David Stern $5
11/26/84 Chris Mullin, Wayman Tisdale, Pearl Washington ... $4
12/10/84 High school basketball.. $4
12/17/84 Patrick Ewing, Georgetown $6
12/31/84 Larry Bird.. $5
01/14/85 Orlando Woolridge $4
01/21/85 Hakeem Olajuwon $5
01/28/85 Dominique Wilkins $5
02/04/85 James Worthy.. $5
02/11/85 Danny Manning, Kansas $4
02/18/85 Kareem Abdul-Jabbar, Julius Erving $5
02/25/85 Ed Pickney, Villanova $4
03/04/85 John Williams $4
03/11/85 Terry Cummings, Danny Ferry, Larry Nance $4
03/18/85 Patrick Ewing, Chris Mullin, NCAA All-Americans $5
03/25/85 Patrick Ewing... $5
04/01/85 Bill Frieder $5
04/08/85 Patrick Ewing, Keith Lee, Chris Mullin, Ed Pickney.......$5
05/20/85 Larry Bird, Robert Parish..................................... $5
06/24/85 Chris Mullin, Wayman Tisdale $4
11/11/85 Dave DeBusschere, Patrick Ewing, David Stern $5
11/25/85 Brad Daugherty, Dean Smith.................................... $4
11/16/85 J.R. Reid $4
01/06/86 Kareem Abdul-Jabbar... $5
01/20/86 M. Martin, J. McCaffrey....................................... $4
01/27/86 Reggie Lewis $4
02/03/86 Julius Erving, Geroge Gervin $5
02/10/86 Dana Kirk, others... $4
02/17/86 Magic Johnson, Guy Lewis, Olden Polynice $4
02/24/86 Manute Bol, Rick Pitino, Spud Webb $4
03/03/86 Hakeem Olajuwon, Ron Harper $5
03/10/86 Mark Alarie, Johnny Dawkins $4
03/17/86 NCAA All-Americans: Brad Daugherty, others $4
03/24/86 Walter Berry $4

03/31/86 Mike Krzyzewski $5
04/07/86 NCAA Final Four coaches $4
04/21/86 High School All-Americans: J.R. Reid, others $4
05/19/86 Larry Bird $5
06/23/86 NBA draft preview: Len Bias, others $4
12/01/86 Rex Chapman, Kentucky $4
12/21/86 Alonzo Mourning, Billy Owens, others $5
01/04/88 Bobby Knight, Dick Vitale $4
01/11/88 David Robinson $5
01/25/88 Pete Maravich $4
02/01/88 Walt Hazzard, Michael Ray Richardson $4
02/08/88 NBA All-Stars: Magic Johnson, Michael Jordan $5
02/15/88 Michael Jordan, Billy Packer, Malik Sealy $5
02/22/88 Michael Smith $3
03/29/88 John Chaney $3
03/07/88 Hersey Hawkins, others $3
03/14/88 Bobby Hurley, others $3
03/21/88 NCAA All-Americans: Sean Elliott, Danny Manning $3
03/28/88 Danny Manning $3
04/04/88 Lute Olson $3
04/11/88 NCAA Final Four picks $3
05/02/88 Alonzo Mourning, Billy Owens $4
05/16/88 Mark Jackson, Michael Jordan, Pat Riley $4
06/20/88 NBA draft: Danny Manning, Rony Seikaly $3
11/15/88 Danny Manning $3
12/06/88 Duke #1, Danny Ferry, Mike Krzyzewski $3
12/20/88 Kenny Anderson $3
01/03/89 Michael Jordan, Jerry Tarkanian $5
01/10/89 Jerry West $3
01/24/89 Randy White, Louisiana Tech $2
01/31/89 Tom Hammonds, Dominique Wilkins $2
02/07/89 Brad Daugherty, Ron Harper, others $1
02/14/89 NBA All-Stars: Hakeem Olajuwon $2
02/21/89 Mookie Blaylock, Stacey King $1
02/28/89 Terry Cummings $1
03/07/89 Chris Jackson $1
03/14/89 Tom Chambers, Kevin Johnson $2
03/21/89 Lute Olson $1
03/27/89 NCAA All-Americans: Sean Elliott, Stacey King,
   others $1
04/03/89 Sean Elliott $1
04/10/89 Final Four preview $1
05/29/89 Michigan's Glen Rice, Rumeal Robinson $1
05/16/89 Can Los Angeles win three in a row? $1
06/20/89 Draft preview: Sean Elliott, Danny Ferry, others $1
11/14/89 Isiah Thomas $2
12/05/89 Todd Day, Lee Mayberry, Arkansas #1 .... $1
12/19/89 Shawn Bradley, Eric Montross $2
01/02/90 Basketball cards $1
01/10/90 Chuck Daley $1
01/23/90 Gary Payton, others $1
01/30/90 Alonzo Mourning $2
02/13/90 Doug Smith, NBA All-Stars $1
02/20/90 Karl Malone $2
02/27/90 Georgia Tech's Dennis Scott, Bobby Cremins $1
03/06/90 Charles Barkley $3
03/13/90 Chris Smith, University of Connecticut $1
03/20/90 Hakeem Olajuwon, others $2
03/26/90 NCAA All-Americans: Derrick Coleman, Gary Payton,
   others $2
04/02/90 Lionel Simmons $1
04/09/90 Leather, Anderson, others $2
05/01/90 UNLV'S Stacey Augmon, Larry Johnson,
   Jerry Tarkanian $3
05/15/90 NBA playoffs preview $1
06/01/90 Draft preview: Derrick Coleman, Dennis Scott $1
11/13/90 Michael Jordan $3

11/27/90 Arizona's Sean Rooks, Ed Stokes, Brian Williams $1
12/10/90 Chris Webber $2
15/17/90 Paul Westhead $1
01/14/91 Shaquille O'Neal $4
02/04/91 Denny Crum, Rick Pitino $1
02/11/91 Bernard King $1
02/18/91 Stacey Augmon, Lee Mayberry $1
02/25/91 Michael Jordan $3
03/04/91 Calbert Cheaney, Jim Jackson $1
03/11/91 Maurice Cheeks, Alex English, Moses Malone $1
03/18/91 Terry Dehere, David Booth, others $1
03/25/91 NCAA All-Americans: Larry Johnson,
   Shaquille O'Neal $3
04/01/91 Larry Johnson $2
04/08/91 Final Four Preview $1
04/29/91 Chris Webber $2
05/13/91 Michael Jordan, playoff preview $2
07/08/91 Larry Johnson, Dikembe Mutombo, Billy Owens $2
11/19/91 Clyde Drexler $2
12/03/91 UCLA's Don MacLean, Gerald Madkins,
   Darrick Martin $1
01/07/92 Mike Krzyzewski $2
03/10/92 LaPhonso Ellis $2
05/12/92 Michael Jordan $4
07/06/92 Magic Johnson $3
11/17/92 Patrick Ewing, NBA preview $3

Basketball's Best

1951-52 Harry Boykoff $60
1952-53 George Mikan $75
1953-54 Bob Cousy, George Mikan, Dolph Schayes $75
1954-55 Bob Cousy, George Mikan, Dolph Schayes $75
1955-56 Red Rocha $30
1956-57 Hand palming a basketball $25
1957-58 Bob Cousy $45
1958-59 Tom Heinsohn, Bill Russell $45
1959-60 Frank Ramsey $20
1960-61 Elgin Baylor $25
1961-62 Wilt Chamberlain $30
1962-63 Elgin Baylor, Wilt Chamberlain, Jerry West $30
1963-64 Jerry West $25
1964-65 Wilt Chamberlain $25
1965-66 Elgin Baylor $20
1966-67 Rick Barry $15
1967-68 Wilt Chamberlain, Bill Russell $20
1968-69 John Havlicek, Bailey Howell $15
1969-70 Lew Alcindor, Willis Reed $35
1970-71 Wilt Chamberlain, Willis Reed $15
1971-72 Lew Alcindor, Willis Reed $15
1972-73 Lew Alcindor, Wilt Chamberlain $20

Complete Sports Basketball

1961-62 Bill Russell $25
1962-63 .... $25
1963-64 Jerry West $25

becomes Pro Basketball Illustrated

1964-65 Oscar Robertson	$20
1965-66 Wilt Chamberlain	$20
1966-67 Bill Russell	$15
1967-68 Bill Bradley	$15
1968-69 Baylor, Chamberlain, West	$15
1969-70 Lew Alcindor	$15
1970-71 Lew Alcindor	$15
1971-72 Lew Alcindor	$15
1972-73 John Havlicek	$15
1973-74 Dave Cowens	$15
1974-75 Julius Erving	$20
1975-76 Bob McAdoo	$15
1976-77 Julius Erving	$20
1977-78 Julius Erving	$20
1978-79	$10
1979-80 Larry Bird, Magic Johnson	$20

published by Lexington Library

1980-81	$15
1981-82	$10
1982-83	$10
1983-84 Julius Erving	$15
1984-85	$10
1985-86 Larry Bird, Michael Jordan	$12
1986-87 Magic Johnson	$10
1987-88 Michael Jordan	$10
1988-89	$8
1989-90 Michael Jordan	$10
1990-91	$8

Cord Sportfacts
Pro Basketball Guide

1972 Lew Alcindor	$15
1973 Kareem Abdul-Jabbar, Jerry West	$15
1974 Walt Frazier	$15
1975 Kareem Abdul-Jabbar, Dave Cowens	$15
1976 Rick Barry	$15

Courtside

March 1989 Kelly Tripucka	$4
April 1989 Hakeem Olajuwon	$7
May 1989 Kiki Vandeweghe	$4
Nov. 1989 David Robinson, Season preview	$8
Dec. 1989 Magic Johnson	$10
Jan. 1990 Tom Chambers	$4
Feb. 1990 Mr. and Mrs. Bill Laimbeer	$3
March 1990 Alexander Volkov	$3
April 1990 Sherman Douglas	$3
May 1990 Magic Johnson, Isiah Thomas	$8
Nov. 1990 Terry Cummings, Dennis Rodman, Season preview	$4
Dec. 1990 Moses Malone, Alvin Robertson	$4
Jan. 1991 Reggie Lewis	$4
Feb. 1991 Mr. and Mrs. Sarunas Marciulionis	$3
March 1991 Patrick Ewing, Moses Malone	$4
May 1991 Joe Dumars, Jerome Kersey, Dan Majerle, Scottie Pippen	$6
Dec. 1991 Kevin McHale, David Robinson, Season preview	$5

Dell Basketball
Woodward's 1951

1950 Don Logfran, University of San Francisco	$45
1951 Bob Zawoluk, St. John's	$40
1952	$30
1953	$25
1954 Bob Cousy	$45

1955 Tom Gola, LaSalle	$40
1956 Tom Heinsohn, Hot Rod Hundley, Bill Russell	$40
1957 Wilt Chamberlain, Hot Rod Hundley, Bob Pettit	$40
1958 Wilt Chamberlain	$40
1959 Connie Hawkins, Oscar Robertson, Jerry West	$40
1960 Wilt Chamberlain, Jerry West	$35
1961 Jerry Lucas, Ohio State	$35
1962 Wilt Chamberlain, Bill Russell	$35
1963 Oscar Robertson	$35
1964 Barry Kramer, NYU	$30
1965 Bill Bradley	$30
1966 Cazzie Russell	$30
1967 Bill Russell	$30
1968 Lew Alcindor	$30

Fast Break
(Popular Library)

1969 Dave Bing, Jerry West	$15
1970 Lew Alcindor, John Havlicek, Bill Russell, Jerry West	$15
becomes Basketball's All-Pro Annual	
1971 Lew Alcindor, Pete Maravich, Rick Mount, Willis Reed	$15
1972	$10
1973 Wilt Chamberlain, Kareem Abdul-Jabbar	$15
1974	$10
1975 John Havlicek	$10

Game Plan College Basketball Yearbook

1977-78 Phil Ford, North Carolina	$20
1978-79 Larry Bird, David Greenwood, Magic Johnson	$30
1980-81 Kyle Macy	$20
1981-82 Albert King	$20
1982-83 Sleepy Floyd	$20
1983-84 Sam Perkins	$20
1984-85 Keith Lee	$20
1985-86 Wayman Tisdale	$20
1987-88 Charles Smith, Pitt	$20
1988-89	$15
1989-90 Jim Boeheim, Derrick Coleman, Billy Owens	$15
1990-91	$15

Game Plan Pro Basketball Yearbook

1977-78 Julius Erving	$25
1978-79 Doug Collins	$20
1986-87 Mark Price, Kenny Smith	$12
1987-88 David Robinson	$15
1988-89	$10
1989-90	$10
1990-91	$10

Hoop Basketball Yearbook

1985-86 Patrick Ewing	$15
1986-87 Charles Barkley, Larry Bird	$12
1987-88 Magic Johnson, Kevin McHale	$12
1988-89	$10
1989-90	$10
1990-91	$10

Hoop NBA Today Edition

Nov. 1984 Larry Bird	$12
Dec. 1984 Bernard King	$6
Jan. 1985 Michael Jordan	$15
Feb. 1985 Reggie Theus	$5
March 1985 Kareem Abdul-Jabbar, Bill Walton	$7
April 1985 Isiah Thomas	$7
May 1985 Larry Bird	$8
July 1985 Kareem Abdul-Jabbar, Larry Bird	$8
Nov. 1985 Patrick Ewing	$7
Dec. 1985 Julius Erving	$7

Jan. 1986 Terry Cummings..............................$5
Feb. 1986 Rolando Blackman, Detlef Schrempf, others.........$4
March 1986 Derek Smith..............................$4
April 1986 Dominique Wilkins..............................$6
May 1986 Magic Johnson..............................$12
June 1986 Larry Bird..............................$8
Nov. 1986 Hall of Fame special edition $7
Dec. 1986 Larry Bird, Moses Malone $7
Jan. 1987 Michael Jordan..............................$10
Feb. 1987 Hakeem Olajuwon $7
March 1987 Kiki Vandeweghe $4
April 1987 ....$4
May 1987 Julius Erving $8
June 1987 Trophy ball, shoe and towel $4
July 1987 Magic Johnson $8
Dec. 1987 Michael Jordan...............$10
Jan. 1988 Kareem Adbul-Jabbar $6
Feb. 1988 Buck Williams $4
March 1988 Karl Malone $5
April 1988 Isiah Thomas...............$5
May 1988 Charles Barkley $6
June 1988 Championship trophy $4
July 1988 Kareem Abdul-Jabbar, Magic Johnson,
James Worthy $7
Dec. 1988 Danny Manning $4
Jan. 1989 Moses Malone, Reggie Theus,
Dominique Wilkins $4
Feb. 1989 Roy Tarpley...............$4
March 1989 Chris Mullin...............$5
April 1989 Larry Nance $4
May 1989 Kareem Abdul-Jabbar, Bill Laimbeer $5
June 1989 Trophy and ball...............$4
July 1989 Isiah Thomas...............$4
Dec. 1989 David Robinson...............$7
Jan. 1990 Mark Aquirre $4
Feb. 1990 Karl Malone $4
March 1990 Kevin Johnson $4
April 1990 Patrick Ewing...............$4
May 1990 Fat Lever $3
June 1990 Trophy and basketballs $3
July 1990 Bill Laimbeer, Dennis Rodman, Buck Williams $3
Dec. 1990 Jerome Kersey, Buck Williams $3
Jan. 1991 Charles Barkley, Larry Bird...............$6
Feb. 1991...............$4
March 1991 Michael Jordan, Dennis Rodman, John Salley $7
April 1991 Shawn Kemp $6
May 1991 Karl Malone, Mychal Thompson $4
June 1991 Isiah Thomas $4
July 1991 Michael Jordan with trophy $7
Dec. 1991 Michael Jordan...............$6

Inside Basketball
(Sport Magazine)

1964 Wilt Chamberlain, Bill Russell $20
1965 Oscar Robertson $20
1966 Bill Russell $15
1967 Lew Alcindor, Wilt Chamberlain...............$15
1968 Lew Alcindor $15
1969 Lew Alcindor $15
1970 Pete Maravich, Rick Mount, Calvin Murphy...............$15
1971 Walt Frazier, Jerry West $15

Petersen's Pro Basketball

1978-79 Elvin Hayes $20
1979-80 Kareem Abdul-Jabbar, Dennis Johnson...............$20
1980-81 Magic Johnson $20
1982-86 Not published

1987-88 Sleepy Floyd, Magic Johnson $20
Tom Chambers, Clyde Drexler, Xavier McDaniel.............$12
Mark Aguirre, Hakeem Olajuwon $15
Charles Barkley, Dominique Wilkins $15
Charles Barkley, Moses Malone $15
Larry Bird, Patrick Ewing $15
Michael Jordan, Isiah Thomas $15
Larry Bird, Magic Johnson $15
1988-89 Magic Johnson, Michael Jordan...............$12
Magic Johnson, Ralph Sampson $8
Clyde Drexler, Dale Ellis $6
Hakeem Olajuwon, Roy Tarpley $7
Michael Jordan, Dominique Wilkins $7
Larry Bird, Patrick Ewing $7
Terry Cummings, Isiah Thomas $6
Alex English, Karl Malone $6
1989-90 Magic Johnson, Chris Mullin $7
Charles Barkley, Kelly Tripucka $7
Magic Johnson, Michael Jordan $10
Dale Ellis, Karl Malone $6
Michael Jordan, Moses Malone $7
Ron Harper, Isiah Thomas $6
Adrian Dantley, Hakeem Olajuwon $6
Robert Parish, Patrick Ewing $6
1990-91 Magic Johnson, Michael Jordan...............$12
Clyde Drexler, Magic Johnson $9
Tom Chambers, Karl Malone $6
Hakeem Olajuwon, David Robinson $8
Rony Seikaly, Dominique Wilkins $6
Larry Bird, Patrick Ewing $8
Charles Barkley, Muggsy Bogues $7
Michael Jordan, Isiah Thomas...............$10

Popular Library
Basketball Yearbook

1960 Jerry West $25
1961 Jerry Lucas $25
1962 Jerry Lucas $25
1963 Ron Bonham, Cincinnati...............$25
1964 Gary Bradds, Ohio State $20
1965 Bill Bradley, Oscar Robertson...............$20
1966 Cazzie Russell, Jerry West $15
1967 Lew Alcindor $15
1968 Lew Alcindor, Rick Barry, Bill Bradey...............$15
1969 Lew Alcindor, Elvin Hayes, John Havlicek $15
1970 Walt Frazier, Rick Mount...............$15
1971 Lew Alcindor, Willis Reed $15
1972 Lew Alcindor, Tom McMillen $15
1973 Bill Walton...............$15
1974 Bill Walton...............$15
1975 Dave Cowens, John Havlicek $12
1976 Rick Barry...............$15
1977 Julius Erving $20
1978 Bill Walton...............$15
1979 Bill Walton...............$15
1980 Larry Bird...............$20
1981 Kareem Abdul-Jabbar, Magic Johnson...............$15

Pro Basketball Almanac

1968 Wilt Chamberlain, Bill Russell $18
1969 Wilt Chamberlain, Bill Russell $15
1970 John Havlicek $15
1971 Pete Maravich $20
1972 Lew Alcindor, Willis Reed $15

The Sporting News
College & Pro Yearbook

1982-83 Kareem Abdul-Jabbar, Patrick Ewing,
Ralph Sampson $20
1983-84 Kareem Abdul-Jabbar, Michael Jordan, Keith Lee $35
1984-85 Ralph Sampson, Wayman Tisdale $20
   Steve Alford, Dallas Comegys, Bobby Knight $20
   Larry Bird, Patrick Ewing $25
   Patrick Ewing, Magic Johnson $20
   Keith Lee, James Worthy $20
1985-86 Mark Price, Kenny Walker $15
   Magic Johnson, Mark Price $20
   Michael Jordan, David Rivers $35
   Kevin McHale, Pearl Washington $20
1986-87 Charles Barkley, Reggie Miller $25
   Steve Alford, Danny Manning $12
   Charles Barkley, Pervis Ellison $25
   Charles Barkley, David Robinson $15
1988-89 Mark Aquirre, Magic Johnson, Isiah Thomas $15

The Sporting News College Yearbook

1987-88 Rex Chapman $6
   Fennis Denbo $5
   David Rivers $5
   Rony Seikaly $6
   Danny Manning $7.50
1988-89 Mookie Blaylock, Stacey King $6
   Danny Ferry $6
   Patrick Ewing, Alonzo Mourning $12
   B.J. Armstrong $7
   Dyron Nix, Dwayne Schintzius $5
   Sean Elliott, Todd Lichti $7
1989-90 Chris Jackson $5
   Greg Anthony, Stacey Augmon, Jerry Tarkanian $7
   Derrick Coleman, Billy Owens, others $8
   Rumeal Robinson $5
   Chris Corchiani, Rodney Monroe $5
1990-91 Kenny Anderson, Rodney Monroe $7.50
   Shaquille O'Neal, Allan Houston $15
   Stacey Augmon, Larry Johnson, Chris Mills $7
   Eric Anderson, Jimmy Jackson, Steve Smith $6
   Jim Calhoun, Billy Owens, Chris Smith $6
   Alonzo Mourning, Billy Owens $8
   Todd Day, Lee Mayberry, Shaquille O'Neal $15
   Henry Iba, Mark Randall, Doug Smith $4
1990-91 Alonzo Mourning, Billy Owens $15

The Sporting News
Official ABA Guide

1968-69 Rick Barry $75
1969-70 Warren Armstrong, Mel Daniels $45
1970-71 Official ABA ball $50
1971-72 Mel Daniels, Julius Keye $45
1972-73 Artis Gilmore $45
1973-74 Billy Cunningham $45
1975-76 Artis Gilmore $40

The Sporting News
Official NBA Guide

1958-59 Bob Pettit $75
1959-60 Bill Russell $60
1960-61 Referee artwork $50
1961-62 Bob Pettit $50
1962-63 Tom Heinsohn $50
1963-64 Hawks vs. Royals $25
1964-65 John Havlicek $45

1965-66 Bill Russell, Jerry West $45
1966-67 Gene Wiley, Los Angeles Lakers $25
1967-68 Wilt Chambelain, Nate Thurmond $35
1968-69 Oscar Robertson, Jerry West $30
1969-70 Team logos $30
1970-71 Wilt Chamberlain, Willis Reed $25
1971-72 Lew Alcindor, Wes Unseld $25
1972-73 Wilt Chamberlain $25
1973-74 Willis Reed $25
1974-75 John Havlicek $25
1975-76 Rick Barry .... $16-$20
1976-77 Jo Jo White .... $16-$20
1977-78 Bill Walton .... $17-$20
1978-79 Wes Unseld .... $15-$20
1979-80 Elvin Hayes .... $16-$20
1980-81 Larry Bird, Magic Johnson $45
1981-82 Cedric Maxwell $20
1982-83 Magic Johnson $25
1983-84 Kareem Abdul-Jabbar, Julius Erving $20
1984-85 Larry Bird $25
1985-86 Larry Bird, Michael Jordan $30
1986-87 Larry Bird $25
1987-88 Magic Johnson $25
1988-89 Michael Jordan $30
1989-90 Joe Dumars $20
1990-91 Isiah Thomas $20

The Sporting News
Official NBA Register

1980-81 Kareem Abdul-Jabbar $20
1981-82 Julius Erving $20
1982-83 Moses Malone $20
1983-84 Moses Malone $20
1984-85 Kareem Abdul-Jabbar, Ralph Sampson $20
1985-86 Kareem Abdul-Jabbar, Robert Parish $20
1986-87 Larry Bird, Hakeem Olajuwon, Bill Walton $20
1987-88 Michael Jordan $20
1988-89 James Worthy $20
1989-90 Karl Malone $20
1990-91 Patrick Ewing, David Robinson $20

The Sporting News
Pro Basketball Yearbook

1987-88 Magic Johnson	$15
Dominique Wilkins	$8
Ralph Sampson	$5
Michael Jordon	$15
Larry Bird	$15
1988-89 Kevin McHale	$10
Mark Aguirre, Magic Johnson, Isiah Thomas	$10
1989-90 Mark Jackson	$5
Joe Dumars	$7
Robert Parish	$7
Michael Jordan	$12
Hakeem Olajuwon	$12
Karl Malone	$10
1990-91 Larry Bird, Patrick Ewing, Karl Malone	$8
Magic Johnson, Michael Jordan	$10
Magic Johnson, David Robinson	$8
Michael Jordan, Bill Laimbeer	$8
Hakeem Olajuwon, David Robinson	$8

Sports Quarterly
Pro Basketball Special

1968-69 Bill Bradley	$15
1969-70 Lew Alcindor, Bob Cousy	$15
1970-71 Pete Maravich, Willis Reed	$15
1971-72 Lew Alcindor	$15
1972-73 Walt Frazier	$15
1973-74 Wilt Chamberlain	$8
1974-75 Julius Erving, John Havlicek	$15
1975-76 Rick Barry	$15
1976-77 Alvan Adams, JoJo White	$15
1977-78 Julius Erving, Bill Walton	$15

Street & Smith's Basketball

1957 Charlie Tyra, Louisville	$125
1958 Tommy Kearns, North Carolina	$100
1970-71 Lew Alcindor, Willis Reed	$40
Austin Carr, Rudy Tomjanovich	$40
Wes Unseld, Jerry West	$40
1971-72 Kareem Abdul-Jabbar, Willis Reed	$40
1972-73 Kareem Abdul-Jabbar, Dave Cowens	$40
Gail Goodrich, John McGlockin	$30
Bill Walton	$40
1973-74 John Havlicek, Pete Maravich	$40
Oscar Robertson, Jerry West	$40
Gail Goodrich	$30
1974-75 Julius Erving	$35
1974-75 Dave Cowens, Kareem Abdul-Jabbar	$35
1975-76 Julius Erving	$35
Adrian Dantley, Marques Johnson	$35
Rick Barry, Paul Silas	$35
1976-77 John Havlicek	$30
Pete Maravich	$30
Alvan Adams, Dave Cowens, Paul Westphal	$30

1977-78 Melvin Bennett, Julius Erving	$25
1977-78 Bill Walton	$30
1978-79 Kyle Macy	$20
Kareem Abdul-Jabbar	$25
Gene Banks, Kelly Tripucka	$25
1979-80 Gene Banks, Mike O'Koren	$20
Darnell Valentine	$20
Bill Walton	$25
1980-81 Larry Bird, Julius Erving	$25
Sam Bowie, Julius Erving, Al Wood	$20
1981-82 Sam Bowie	$15
Rod Foster, John Paxson	$15
Kareem Abdul-Jabbar, Magic Johnson	$30
Rod Foster, Moses Malone	$20
Larry Bird	$30
1982-83 Sam Perkins	$20
John Paxson	$20
Larry Bird, Julius Erving, Patrick Ewing	$30
1983-84 Patrick Ewing	$15
Bobby Knight	$15
A.C. Green	$15
1984-85 Chris Mullin	$15
Milt Wagner	$5
Wayman Tisdale	$15
Magic Johnson	$20
1985-86 Pearl Washington	$10
Danny Manning	$15
James Worthy	$15
1986-87 Kenny Smith	$10
Michael Jordan	$30
Hakeem Olajuwon	$15
Larry Bird, David Robinson	$20
1987-88 Larry Bird	$20
Magic Johnson	$20
Bob Knight, Keith Smart	$15
Dominique Wilkins	$15
Hakeem Olajuwon	$15
J.R. Reid	$10
1988-89 Sherman Douglas, Mark Macon	$10
Danny Ferry	$5
Stacey King	$5
Tom Hammonds	$5
(Pro) Larry Bird, Magic Johnson, Michael Jordan	$30
1989-90 Hank Gathers	$15
Rumeal Robinson	$12
Alonzo Mourning	$15
Chris Jackson	$12
Patrick Ewing	$20
(Pro) Isiah Thomas	$15
(Pro) Karl Malone	$15
(Pro) Michael Jordan	$25
1990-91 Doug Smith	$10
Chris Smith	$5
Steve Smith	$7
Kenny Anderson, Bobby Hurley	$15
Don MacLean, Harold Miner	$7
Larry Johnson	$10
(Pro) Michael Jordan	$20
1991-92 Shaquille O'Neal	$15
Michael Jordan	$20
Terry DeHere, Alonzo Mourning	$12
1993-94 Shaquille O'Neal	$12

Vitale's Basketball

1983-84 Michael Jordan, North Carolina	$35
Moses Malone	$10
Magic Johnson	$35

1985-86 Kareem Abdul-Jabbar $15
  Mark Price, Kenny Smith $10
  Michael Jordan $20
  Patrick Ewing, Bernard King $15
1986-87 David Robinson, Navy $20
  Larry Bird, Magic Johnson $20
  Dominique Wilkins $12
  Kenny Smith, North Carolina $8
  Kareem Abdul-Jabbar, Ralph Sampson $12
  James Blackmon, Pervis Ellison $7
  Steve Alford, Danny Manning $8
1987-88 Derrick Coleman, J.R. Reid $12
  Larry Bird $15
  James Worthy $10
  Dominique Wilkins $10
  Xavier McDaniel, Kiki Vandeweghe $7
  Derrick Chievous, Danny Manning $7
  Bob Knight, Everette Stephens $6
  Isiah Thomas $10
  Michael Jordan $12
  Moses Malone $8
  Rex Chapman, Charles Smith $5
  Mark Aguirre, Rodney McCray $6
1988-89 Mark Jackson $5
  Sherman Douglas, John Thompson $7
  Michael Jordan, Isiah Thomas $15
  Danny Ferry, J.R. Reid $6
  B.J. Armstrong, Stacey King $6
  Pervis Ellison, Dwayne Schintzius $5
  Sean Elliott, Todd Lichti $6
  James Worthy $7
1989-90 Magic Johnson, Jerry Tarkanian $12
  Joe Dumars, Rumeal Robinson $7
  Patrick Ewing, Alonzo Mourning $10
  Michael Jordan, Kendall Gill $10
  Kevin Johnson, Lute Olson $7
  Chris Jackson, Hakeem Olajuwon $8
  Chris Mullin, John Stockton $8
  Rex Chapman, Scott Williams $4
1990-91 Charles Oakley, Billy Owens $6
  Larry Bird, Magic Johnson $10
  Kenny Anderson, Rodney Monroe $7

Michael Jordan, Doug Smith $10
Reggie Miller, LaBradford Smith $7
Tom Chambers, Buck Williams $5
Steve Smith, Isiah Thomas $7
Shaquille O'Neal, David Robinson $10

Basketball Stars Of...

1961 Wilt Chamberlain $20
1962 Bob Cousy $20
1963 Duquesne vs. Bradley $20
1964 Wilt Chamberlain $20
1965 Bill Russell $20
1966 Bill Russell $20
1967 Willis Reed, Bill Russell $15
1968 Wilt Chamberlain $15
1969 Willis Reed $15
1970 Lew Alcindor $15
1971 Willis Reed $15
1972 Lew Alcindor $15
1973 Jerry West $15
1974 Dave Cowens, Walt Frazier $15
1975 Kareem Abdul-Jabbar, Dave Cowens, John Havlicek $15

The Complete Handbook of Pro Basketball

1975 Julius Erving, John Havlicek $15
1976 Jerry West $10
1977 Julius Erving $15
1978 Bill Walton $10
1979 Elvin Hayes $7
1980 Dennis Johnson $6
1981 Magic Johnson $20
1982 Larry Bird, Julius Erving $20
1983 Julius Erving, Magic Johnson $20
1984 Kareem Abdul-Jabbar, Moses Malone $10
1985 Larry Bird $15
1986 Patrick Ewing $10
1987 Larry Bird $10
1988 Magic Johnson $12
1989 Magic Johnson, Isiah Thomas $15
1990 Kareem Abdul-Jabbar, Joe Dumars, Magic Johnson,
  James Worthy $10
1991 Michael Jordan, Bill Laimbeer $8

Hockey Magazines

Action Sports Hockey

Jan. 1972 Dave Keon $12
Feb. 1972 Keith Magnuson $7
March 1972 Jean Ratelle $8
April 1972 Frank and Pete Mahovlich $10
May 1972 Bobby Hull $12
Oct. 1972 Brad Park $12
Nov. 1972 Bobby Orr $12
Dec. 1972 Marcel Dionne $8
Jan. 1973 Bobby Clarke $8
Feb. 1973 Garry Unger $7
March 1973 Bobby Hull $10
April 1973 .... $7

May 1973 Jacques Lemaire $7
Nov. 1973 Bobby Clarke $8
Dec. 1973 Brad Park $9
Jan. 1974 Tony Esposito $7
Feb. 1974 Paul Henderson $6
March 1974 Phil Esposito $7
April 1974 Bobby Orr $8
May 1974 Yvan Cournoyer $7
Dec. 1974 Bobby Clarke $8
Jan. 1975 .... $6
Feb. 1975 Derek Sanderson $6
March 1975 Bobby Orr, Brad Park $8

April 1975 New York Rangers vs. Montreal Canadiens.......... $5
May 1975.. $5
Dec. 1975 Guy Lafleur.. $7
Jan. 1976.. $5
Feb. 1976 Denis Potvin... $5
March 1976 Phil Esposito, Brad Park $7
April 1976 .... $5
May 1976 Philadelphia Flyers vs. USSR $4
Nov. 1976 Guy Lafleur, Reggie Leach $6
Jan. 1977 Darryl Sittler $5
Feb. 1977 Bobby Orr, Denis Potvin $5
March 1977 Ken Dryden, Pete McNab $5
April 1977 .... $5
May 1977 Bobby Clarke, Brad Park $5
Nov. 1977 Guy Lafleur $6
Jan. 1978 Borje Salming $5
Feb. 1978 Gil Perreault.. $6
March 1978 Larry Robinson $5
April 1978 Gordie Howe, Mike Palmateer............................. $7
Nov. 1978 Tiger Williams $5
Jan. 1979 Guy Lafleur $6
Feb. 1979 Ken Dryden.. $5
March 1979 Borje Salming $5
April 1979 Terry O'Reilly $5
Nov. 1979 Guy Lafleur $5
Jan. 1980 Ulf Nilsson $4
Feb. 1980 Darryl Sittler.. $5
March 1980 Chicago Blackhawks vs. New York Islanders $4
April 1980 Marcel Dionne $5

Complete Handbook Of Pro Hockey

1971-72 Chicago Blackhawks vs. Boston Bruins $12
1972-73 New York Rangers vs. Boston Bruins...................... $8
1973-74 New York Rangers vs. Montreal Canadiens............. $8
1974-75 Bobby Clarke $10
1975-76 .... $7
1976-77 Paul Newman in the movie Slapshot...................... $10
1977-78 Guy Lafleur.. $10
1978-79 Montreal Canadiens vs. Boston Bruins $7
1979-80 Bob Gainey.. $8
1980-81 New York Islanders with the Stanley Cup................ $7
1981-82 Wayne Merrick.. $5
1982-83 Wayne Gretzky... $12
1983-84 Billy Smith.. $5
1984-85 Wayne Gretzky, Edmonton Oilers with Stanley Cup $10
1985-86 Wayne Gretzky... $10
1986-87 Philadelphia Flyers vs. Calgary Flames $4
1987-88 Ron Hextall $4

Cord Sportfacts Hockey Guide

1969-70 Norm Ullman $15
1970-71 Bobby Orr $20
1971-72 Bobby Orr $20
1972-73 Bobby Orr $20
1973-74 Frank Mahovlich $10

Hockey Blueline Magazine

Oct. 1954 Gordie Howe $200
Nov. 1954 Maurice Richard $100
Dec. 1954 Al Rollins $80
Jan. 1955 Milt Schmidt $80
Feb. 1955 Jim Thomson $60
March 1955 Jean Beliveau $80
April 1955 Bob Goldham $60
May 1955 Edgar Laprade $50
June 1955 Bill Quackenbush $80
Oct. 1955 Toe Blake $80

Nov. 1955 Tony Leswick $50
Dec. 1955 Jacques Plante.. $80
Jan. 1956 Ted Lindsay $75
March 1956 Gil Mayer $50
April 1956 Jean Beliveau $80
May 1956 Toe Blake, Bernie Geoffrion, Dickie Moore,
    Jacques Plante $75
Sept. 1956 Maurice Richard $80
Oct. 1956 Gordie Howe... $100
Nov. 1956 Maurice Richard $80
Dec. 1956 Ted Sloan $50
Jan. 1957 Ted Lindsay $50
Feb. 1957 Doug Mohns $50
March 1957 Jean Beliveau.. $75
April 1957 Gump Worsley.. $60
May 1957 Gordie Howe $80
Nov. 1957 Ed Litzenberger $40
Dec. 1957 Bernie Geoffrion $50
Jan. 1958 Lou Fontinato $40
Feb. 1958 Don McKenney $30
March 1958 Andy Bathgate $50
April 1958 Frank Mahovlich $50
May 1958 Maurice Richard.. $45
Oct. 1958 Henri Richard $45
Nov. 1958 Fleming Mackell $30
Nov. 1958 Bill Gadsby $45
Jan. 1959 Dickie Duff $50
Feb. 1959 Andy Bathgate $45
March 1959 Hockey fights $40
April 1959 Jean Beliveau... $50
May 1959 Andy Bathgate, Jean Beliveau, Jacques Plante,
    others... $50

Hockey Digest

Nov. 1972 Bobby Orr .... $45-$60
Dec. 1972 Ken Dryden .... $20-$24
Jan. 1973 Minnesota North Stars vs. New York Rangers.... $12-$16
Feb. 1973 Keith Magnuson... $10-$12
March 1973 Brad Park.. $12-$16
April 1973 Derek Sanderson $10
May 1973 Garry Unger.. $10-$12
June 1973 Phil Esposito .... $12-$16
Nov. 1973 Rick MacLeish .... $10-$12
Dec. 1973 Henri Richard .... $10-$12
Jan. 1974 Bobby Hull .... $15-$20
Feb. 1974 Mickey Redmond... $10-$12
March 1974 Gil Perreault .... $10-$12
April 1974 Steve Vickers.. $10-$12
May 1974 Tony Esposito .... $10-$12
June 1974 Tom Lysiak.. $10-$12
Nov. 1974 Dave Schultz .... $10-$12
Dec. 1974 Mike Walton .... $10-$12
Jan. 1975 Bobby Orr .... $15-$20

Feb. 1975 Stan Mikita.............................$12-$16
March 1975 Marcel Dionne ....$10-$12
April 1975 Rick Martin ....$10-$12
May 1975 Derek Sanderson......................$10-$16
June 1975 Guy Lafleur ....$10-$12
Nov. 1975 Bobby Clarke ....$10-$12
Dec. 1975 Gil Perreault ....$10-$12
Jan. 1976 Denis Potvin ....$8-$10
Feb. 1976 Bobby Hull ....$12-$16
March 1976 Bobby Sheehan ....$8-$10
April 1976 Garry Unger ....$8-$10
May 1976 Jean Ratelle ....$8-$10
June 1976 Ken Dryden ....$10-$12
Nov. 1976 Bobby Orr ....$15-$20
Dec. 1976 Phil Esposito ....$12-$16
Jan. 1977 Larry Robinson, Guy Lafleur......$10-$12
Feb. 1977 Dave Schultz.................................$8
March 1977 Peter McNab ....$8-$10
April 1977 Steve Shutt..............................$8-$10
May 1977 Borje Salming ....$8-$10
June 1977 Glenn Resch ....$8-$10
Nov. 1977 Serge Savard...........................$10-$12
Dec. 1977 Willi Plett ....$8-$10
Jan. 1978 Rick MacLeish $12
Feb. 1978 Wayne Cashman $8
March 1978 Mike Bossy $12
April 1978 Rick Martin ....$8-$10
May 1978 Darryl Sittler ....$10-$12
June 1978 Guy Lafleur ....$10-$12
Nov. 1978 Terry O'Reilly ....$8-$12
Dec. 1978 Anders Hedberg, Ulf Nilsson........$8-$10
Jan. 1979 Danny Gare ....$8-$10
Feb. 1979 Dale McCourt ....$8-$10
March 1979 Clark Gillies ....$8-$10
April 1979 New York Rangers vs. Philadelphia Flyers............$8
May 1979 Ken Dryden, Bryan Trottier ....$10-$12
June 1979 Guy Lafleur ....$10-$12
Nov. 1979 New York Rangers vs. Montreal Canadiens...$8-$10
Dec. 1979 Marcel Dionne ....$10-$12
Jan. 1980 Bobby Clarke $8
Feb. 1980 New York Islanders vs. Edmonton Oilers..........$5-$7
March 1980 Phil Esposito............................$8-$10
April 1980 Gil Perreault $6
May 1980 Wayne Gretzky ....$25-$40
June 1980 Tony Esposito ....$6-$10
Nov. 1980 New York Islanders with the Stanley Cup.............$5
Dec. 1980 Ray Bourque ....$5-$7
Jan. 1981 Clark Gillies.................................$5-$7
Feb. 1981 Philadelphia Flyers vs. St. Louis Blues................$5
March 1981 Mike Bossy $8
April 1981 Phil Esposito, Bob Gainey $6
May 1981 Charlie Simmer ....$5-$7
June 1981 Denis Savard ....$5-$7
Nov. 1981 Wayne Gretzky ....$25-$30
Dec. 1981 Bryan Trottier ....$6-$10
Jan. 1982 Rick Kehoe ....$5-$7
Feb. 1982 Reed Larson ....$5-$7
March 1982 Bobby Smith ....$5-$7
April 1982 Normand Leveille ....$5-$7
May 1982 Wayne Gretzky ....$25-$30
June 1982 Mark Acton.................................$5-$7
Nov. 1982 Bryan Trottier ....$6-$10
Dec. 1982 Doug Wilson $5
Jan. 1983 Bobby Carpenter..........................$4-$5
Feb. 1983 Peter Stastny $5
March 1983 Denis Savard $5

April 1983 Dino Ciccarelli ....$4-$5
May 1983 Pete Peeters ....$4-$5
June 1983 Wayne Gretzky ....• $20
Nov. 1983 Billy Smith.....................................$5
Dec. 1983 Barry Pederson ....$5-$7
Jan. 1984 Phil Housley...................................$5
Feb. 1984 Mark Pavelich ....$5-$7
March 1984 Richard Brodeur $5
April 1984 Larry Robinson $5
May 1984 Wayne Gretzky ....$20-$25
June 1984 Denis Potvin ....$5-$7
Nov. 1984 Mark Messier $6
Dec. 1984 Tom Barrasso ....$4-$5
Jan. 1985 Michel Goulet $5
Feb. 1985 Dino Ciccarelli $5
March 1985 Herb Brooks ....$4-$5
April 1985 Tim Kerr......................................$5
May 1985 Mike Bossy $8
June 1985 Wayne Gretzky $20
Nov. 1985 Paul Coffey $5
Dec. 1985 Pelle Lindbergh $8
Jan. 1986 Rod Langway $5
Feb.1986 Marcel Dionne $6
March 1986 Mario Lemieux.............................$25
April 1986 Barry Pederson $5
May 1986 Kelly Hrudey $5
June 1986 Wayne Gretzky $5
Nov. 1986 Patrick Roy $8
Dec. 1986 John Vanbiesbrouck $5
Jan. 1987 Wendel Clark $5
Feb. 1987 Bernie Federko $5
March 1987 Mark Howe $8
April 1987 Scott Stevens $5
May 1987 Mike Bossy $8
June 1987 Wayne Gretzky $20
Nov. 1987 Ron Hextall $5
Dec. 1987 Glen Hanlon $5
Jan. 1988 Dale Hawerchuk $6
Feb. 1988 Mario Lemieux $20
March 1988 Kevin Dineen $5
April 1988 Denis Potvin $5
May 1988 Montreal Canadiens vs. Boston Bruins.................$5
June 1988 Grant Fuhr $5
Nov. 1988 Wayne Gretzky $15
Dec. 1988 Sean Burke $5
Jan. 1989 Mike Keenan $5
Feb. 1989 Al MacInnis $5
March 1989 Cam Neely $5
April 1989 Brian Leetch $5
May 1989 Steve Yzerman $5
June 1989 Mario Lemieux $15
Nov. 1989 Joe Mullen $5
Dec. 1989 Wayne Gretzky $15
Jan. 1990 Chris Chelios $3
Feb. 1990 Kevin Hatcher, Mick Vukota $3
March 1990 Sergei Makarov $4
April 1990 Doug Wilson $3
May 1990 Philadelphia Flyers vs. New York Rangers $3
June 1990 Ray Bourque $4
Nov. 1990 Mark Messier $4
Dec. 1990 John Druce....................................$3
Jan. 1991 Jon Casey $3
Feb. 1991 Dale Hawerchuk $4
March 1991 Brett Hull $5
April 1991 John Vanbiesbrouck $3
May 1991 Chris Chelios $3

June 1991 Wayne Gretzky $10
Nov. 1991 Mario Lemieux.. $8
Dec. 1991 Stephane Richer $3
to date - $3-$5 each

Hockey Illustrated

Nov. 1962 Jacques Plante $60
Dec. 1962 Andy Bathgate $35
Jan. 1963 Jean Beliveau $35
Feb. 1963 Bobby Hull $45
March 1963 Gordie Howe.. $50
Nov. 1963 .... $30
Dec. 1963 Dave Keon, Terry Sawchuck $25
Jan. 1964 Boom Boom Geoffrion $25
Feb. 1964 Henri Richard $20
March 1964 Glenn Hall, Elmer Vasko............................... $20
April 1964 Bobby Hull $40
Nov. 1964 .... $20
Dec. 1964 Johnny Bower, Marcel Pronovost..................... $20
Jan. 1965 Jean Beliveau $20
Feb. 1965 Dave Keon $20
March 1965 Montreal Canadiens vs. Chicago Blackhawks.. $18
April 1965 Bobby Hull $35
Nov. 1965 Jean Beliveau $20
Dec. 1965 Bobby Hull, Frank Mahovlich, Henri Richard....... $20
Jan. 1966 Gordie Howe.. $45
Feb. 1966 Johnny Bower, Bobby Hull................................ $20
March 1966 Henri Richard $18
April 1966 Jean Beliveau... $20
Nov. 1966 Henri Richard $18
Dec. 1966 Bobby Hull, Gordie Howe................................. $45
Jan. 1967 Bobby Hull $25
Feb. 1967 Jean Beliveau $20
March 1967 Bobby Rousseau $18
April 1967 Dave Keon, Henri Richard................................ $18
Nov. 1967 Bobby Hull $25
Dec. 1967 Henri Richard $18
Jan. 1968 Ed Giacomin $18
Feb. 1968 Bobby Hull $20
March 1968 Gordie Howe.. $30
April 1968 Frank Mahovlich $20
May 1968 Bobby Hull... $20
Nov. 1968 Jean Beliveau $20
Dec. 1968 Bobby Hull $20
Jan. 1969 Rod Gilbert $18
Feb. 1969 Gordie Howe $30
March 1969 Bobby Orr $30
April 1969 Bobby Hull $20
May 1969 Jean Beliveau $20
Nov. 1969 .... $20
Dec. 1969 Gordie Howe $30
Jan. 1970 Bobby Hull $18
Feb. 1970 Stan Mikita.. $15

March 1970 Alex Delvecchio $15
April 1970 Bobby Orr $20
May 1970 Ed Giacomin $15
Nov. 1970 Bobby Orr $20
Dec. 1970 Tony Esposito $15
Jan. 1971 Gordie Howe.. $20
Feb. 1971 Keith Magnuson $12
March 1971 Jean Beliveau, Yvan Cournoyer $15
April 1971 Brad Park, Ed Westfall $15
May 1971 Derek Sanderson $15
Nov. 1971 Ken Dryden $15
Dec. 1971 Phil Esposito $18
Jan. 1972 Gil Perreault.. $15
Feb. 1972 Dennis Hull $12
March 1972 Garry Unger.. $12
April 1972 Rod Gilbert, Vic Hadfield, Jean Ratelle.............. $12
May 1972 Gump Worsley $15
June 1972 John McKenzie $10
Nov. 1972 Walt Tkaczuk $15
Dec. 1972 Phil Esposito $15
Jan. 1973 Marcel Dionne $15
Feb. 1973 Paul Henderson $10
March 1973 Dennis Hull $12
April 1973 Derek Sanderson $15
May 1973 Rick Martin, Gil Perreault.................................. $12
June 1973 Bobby Orr $15
Nov. 1973 .... $10
Dec. 1973 .... $10
Jan. 1974 Yvan Cournoyer, Rene Robert........................... $10
Feb. 1974 Doug Favell, Bobby Orr $12
March 1974 Rod Gilbert, Bobby Hull, Dave Schultz........... $12
April 1974 Tony Esposito $12
May 1974 Gil Perreault, Norm Ullman $12
June 1974 Rick Martin, Brad Park, Henri Richard............... $12
Jan. 1975 Bobby Orr $15
Feb. 1975 Ken Dryden $12
March 1975 Bobby Clarke $12
April 1975 Phil Esposito $12
May 1975 RogieVachon $12
Jan. 1976 Bobby Orr $15
Feb. 1976 Guy Lafleur $12
March 1976 Tony Esposito $12
April 1976 Ken Dryden $12
May 1976 Bobby Clarke, Guy Lafleur $12
Jan. 1977 Denis Potvin $10
Feb. 1977 Darryl Sittler.. $10
March 1977 Larry Robinson $10
April 1977 Bernie Parent $10
May 1977 Guy Lafleur $10
Jan. 1978 Rick Martin $10
Feb. 1978 Ken Dryden $10
March 1978 Bobby Clarke $12
April 1978 Rogie Vachon $10
May 1978 Guy Lafleur $10
Jan. 1979 Jacques Lemaire $10
Feb. 1979 Darryl Sittler.. $10
March 1979 Marcel Dionne $10
April 1979 Bryan Trottier.. $10
Jan. 1980 Mike Palmateer... $8
Feb. 1980 Real Cloutier.. $8
March 1980 Reggie Leach $8
April 1980 Anders Hedberg $8
Jan. 1981 Jim Schoenfeld $8
Feb. 1981 Bobby Smith $7.50
March 1981 Borje Salming $7.50
April 1981 Mike Bossy $5

Feb. 1984 Kent Nilsson $5
Feb. 1985 Mark Messier $7
March 1985 Brent Sutter $5
May 1985 Mike Bossy, Wayne Gretzky, Kent Nilsson $5
Feb. 1986 Paul Coffey, Rick Vaive $5
Feb. 1987 Wendel Clark $5
Feb. 1989 Wayne Gretzky, Denis Savard $5
April 1989 Wayne Gretzky, Brian Leetch $5

Hockey Illustrated Yearbook

1961-62 Bernie Geoffrion $30
1962-63 .... $20
1963-64 .... $20
1964-65 Eddie Shack $20
1965-66 .... $18
1966-67 .... $15
1967-68 .... $15
1968-69 .... $15
1969-70 .... $12
1970-71 .... $12
1971-72 .... $15
1972-73 .... $10
1973-74 Bobby Clarke $12
1974-75 Bernie Parent $10
1975-76 Bobby Clarke $10
1976-77 Ken Dryden $10
1977-78 Guy Lafleur $10
1978-79 Mike Bossy $8
1979-80 Guy Lafleur $8
1980-81 Wayne Gretzky $18
1981-82 .... $8
1982-83 Wayne Gretzky $15
1983-84 Wayne Gretzky $10
1986-87 Wayne Gretzky $10

Hockey News Yearbook

1982-83 Wayne Gretzky $12
1983-84 Wayne Gretzky, Pete Peeters $10
1984-85 .... $7
1985-86 .... $7
1986-87 Paul Coffey, Wayne Gretzky, Claude Lemieux $10
1987-88 .... $7
1988-89 Mario Lemieux $8
1989-90 Wayne Gretzky, Mario Lemieux, Al MacInnis $8
1990-91 .... $5

Hockey Pictorial

Oct. 1955 Jean Beliveau, others $100
Nov. 1955 Red Kelly, others $80
Dec. 1955 Leo Labine $70
Jan. 1956 Tod Sloan, others $60
Feb. 1956 Andy Bathgate $70
March 1956 Henri and Maurice Richard $75
April 1956 Glenn Hall $60
May 1956 Henri Richard, Stanley Cup $70
Oct. 1956 Jean Beliveau, Gordie Howe, Ted Lindsay $80
Nov. 1956 Gordie Howe, Norm Ullman, Gump Worsley $65
Dec. 1956 Jean Beliveau $60
Jan. 1957 Leo Labine $40
Feb. 1957 Gordie Howe, Ted Lindsay $65
March 1957 Doug Harvey $55
April 1957 Doug Harvey, Gordie Howe, Ted Lindsay $55
May 1957 Henri Richard $50
Oct. 1957 Rocket Richard $50
Nov. 1957 Bill Gadsby $50
Dec. 1957 Gordie Howe $70
Jan. 1958 Real Chevrefils $30

Feb. 1958 Camille Henry $30
March 1958 Ed Chadwick $30
April 1958 Henri Richard $40
May 1958 Allan Stanley $40
Oct. 1958 Frank Mahovlich $40
Nov. 1958 Ed Litzenberger $30
Dec. 1958 Norm Ullman $32
Jan. 1959 Andy Bathgate $35
Feb. 1959 Doug Mohns $30
March 1959 Tom Johnson $30
April 1959 Glenn Hall $30
May 1959 Montreal Canadiens, Stanley Cup $30
Oct. 1959 Dickie Moore $30
Nov. 1959 Bobby Hull $55
Dec. 1959 Alex Delvecchio $32
Jan. 1960 Carl Brewer $25
Feb. 1960 Vic Stasiuk $25
March 1960 "Kid Hockey Flourishes" $20
April 1960 Jean Beliveau $35
Sept. 1960 Bob Pulford $20
Oct. 1960 Dean Prentice $22
Nov. 1960 Billy Hay $20
Dec. 1960 Don McKenney $20
Jan. 1961 Murray Oliver $20
Feb. 1961 Ralph Backstrom $22
March 1961 Bobby Hull $40
April 1961 Frank Mahovlich $28
Sept. 1961 Bernie Geoffrion $28
Oct. 1961 Dave Keon $24
Nov. 1961 Doug Mohns $22
Dec. 1961 Jean Beliveau, Glenn Hall, others $24
Jan. 1962 Bernie Geoffrion, Glenn Hall, Andre Pronovost,
  others $24
Feb. 1962 Carl Brewer $20
March 1962 Boston, Detroit, Montreal, Toronto $20
April 1962 Red Kelly, Jacques Plante, Bob Pulford $20
Sept. 1962 Toronto Maple Leafs vs. Boston Bruins $20
Oct. 1962 Henri Richard $20
Nov. 1962 Chicago Blackhawks vs. Montreal Canadiens $20
Dec. 1962 Chicago Blackhawks vs. Toronto Maple Leafs $20
Jan. 1963 Gordie Howe $35
Feb. 1963 Stan Mikita $30
March 1963 Don Simmons $20
April 1963 Bobby Hull $28
Sept. 1963 Johnny Bower, Bobby Hull $25
Oct. 1963 Jacques Plante $24
Nov. 1963 Gordie Howe $40
Dec. 1963 Chicago Blackhawks bench $20
Jan. 1964 Leo Boivin, Milt Schmidt $24
Feb. 1964 Jean Beliveau $24
March 1964 Pierre Pilote $20
April 1964 Jacques Laperriere $16
Sept. 1964 Charlie Hodge $16
Oct. 1964 All-Star Game $18
Nov. 1964 .... $15
Dec. 1964 Harry Howell $18
Jan. 1965 Elmer Vasko $16
Feb. 1965 Toronto vs. Montreal $16
March 1965 New York Rangers $18
April 1965 Ron Ellis, Charlie Hodge $16
May 1965 Gordie Howe, Norm Ullman $25
Oct. 1965 Frank Mahovlich, Henri Richard $20
Nov. 1965 Rod Gilbert $22
Dec. 1965 Bill Gadsby, Gordie Howe $27
Jan. 1966 Frank Mahovlich $22
Feb. 1966 Stan Mikita $25
March 1966 Roger Crozier $18

April 1966 Glenn Hall, Bobby Hull, Stan Mikita, Pierre Pilote.....$25
May 1966 .... $15
Oct. 1966 Montreal Canadiens goalies $20
Nov. 1966 Bob Pulford.. $15
Dec. 1966 Alex Delvecchio, Gordie Howe $24
Jan. 1967 Gerry Cheevers $18
Feb. 1967 Ed Giacomin $18
March 1967 Bobby Rousseau... $14
April 1967 Bobby Hull.. $24
Oct. 1967 NHL expansion $20
Nov. 1967 Bobby Orr... $30
Dec. 1967 Hank Bassen, Terry Crisp, Jim Roberts $15
Jan. 1968 Cesare Maniago, Bob Woytowich $14
Feb. 1968 Stan Mikita... $20
March 1968 Paul Henderson, Bruce MacGregor,
    Norm Ullman... $15
April 1968 Stanley Cup... $15
Oct. 1968 St. Louis Blues $20
Nov. 1968 Claude Ruel.. $14
Dec. 1968 Wren Blair, Wayne Connelly.............................. $12
Jan. 1969 Gump Worsley $15
Feb. 1969 Stan Mikita... $18
March 1969 Gordie Howe, Brad Park.................................. $20
April 1969 J.C. Tremblay... $12
Nov. 1969 Montreal Canadiens vs. St. Louis Blues............. $20
Dec. 1969 Ken Hodge $15
Jan. 1970 .... $12
Feb. 1970 Yvan Cournoyer $14
March 1970 Bobby Orr $20
April 1970 Mike Laughton, Juha Widing $13
May 1970 St. Louis Blues $13
Nov. 1970 Carol Vadnais $15
Dec. 1970 Tony Esposito $14
Jan. 1971 Roger Crozier $13
Feb. 1971 Phil Esposito $21
March 1971 Keith Magnuson.. $10
April 1971 Bobby Orr $20
May 1971 Ken Dryden $18
Nov. 1971 Chicago Blackhawks vs. Montreal Canadiens..... $15
Dec. 1971 Norm Ullman $14
Jan. 1972 Bill White... $10
Feb. 1972 Frank Mahovlich, Jacques Plante........................ $14
March 1972 Carol Vadnais $10
April 1972 Tony Esposito, Bobby Hull, Pete Mahovlich $14
May 1972 Rod Gilbert.. $14
Nov. 1972 1972-73 Preview.. $15
Dec. 1972 Brad Park.. $16
Jan. 1973 Jim Neilson, Gilles Villemure $12
Feb. 1973 Richard Martin, Gil Perreault $16
March 1973 Dan Awrey, Phil Esposito.................................. $16
April 1973 Ken Dryden, Murray Oliver, Dean Prentice $14
May 1973 Bobby Orr... $18
Nov. 1973 Gil Perreault.. $14
Dec. 1973 Jim Neilson, Steve Vickers................................. $12
Jan. 1974 Bobby Orr $18
Feb. 1974 Dave Keon $14
March 1974 Richard Martin $14
April 1974 Tony Esposito $12
May 1974 Frank Mahovlich $12
Nov. 1974 Phil Esposito $16
Dec. 1974 Denis Potvin $12
Jan. 1975 Bobby Orr $15
Feb. 1975 Gary Smith $10
March 1975 Phil Russell... $10
April 1975 Danny Grant... $10
May 1975 Ken Dryden $12

Nov. 1975 Rod Gilbert $12
Dec. 1975 Stan Mikita $12
Jan. 1976 Bobby Clarke $15
Feb. 1976 Phil Esposito.. $12
March 1976 Rogie Vachon $10
April 1976 Gerry Cheevers $10
May 1976 Bobby Clarke $15
Nov. 1976 Bobby Clarke $15
Dec. 1976 Phil Esposito $12
Jan. 1977 Brad Park.. $12
Feb. 1977 Don Murdoch $10
March 1977 Marcel Dionne $12
April 1977 Steve Shutt $10
May 1977 Reggie Leach $10
June 1977 Guy Lafleur $14
Oct. 1977 Larry Robinson $12
Nov. 1977 Lanny McDonald $10
Dec. 1977 Denis Potvin $10
Jan. 1978 Guy LaPointe, Richard Martin.............................. $10
Feb. 1978 Bryan Trottier $10
March 1978 Keith Magnuson... $10
April 1978 Gil Perreault $10
May 1978 Guy Lafleur $10
Oct. 1978 Guy Lafleur $12
Nov. 1978 Terry O'Reilly $10
Dec. 1978 Bobby Orr, Brad Park, Borje Salming................. $12
Jan. 1979 Anders Hedberg, Glenn Resch, Joe Watson....... $10
Feb. 1979 Dale McCourt, Larry Robinson, Vladislav Tretiak $10
March 1979 Tony Esposito, Tom Lysiak, Gary Sargent,
    Rogie Vachon $10
April 1979 Mike Bossy, Garry Unger $12
May 1979 Stan Mikita, Denis Potvin..................................... $12
Oct. 1979 1979-80 Preview... $12
Nov. 1979 Darryl Sittler $10
Dec. 1979 Mike Milbury $10
Jan. 1980 Don Edwards $8
Feb. 1980 Mark Howe $10
March 1980 Brian Propp $8
April 1980 Brian Sutter $8

Hockey Times

Nov. 1970 Gordie Howe, Bobby Orr $20
Dec. 1970 Ken Hodge $10
Jan. 1971 Boston Bruins vs. Chicago Blackhawks $8
Feb. 1971 Bobby Orr.. $15
March 1971 St. Louis Blues vs. Boston Bruins $8
April 1971 Boston Bruins with the Stanley Cup.................... $10
May 1971 Eddie Johnston.. $8
June 1971 Montreal Canadiens with the Stanley Cup......... $10
July 1971 Jean Beliveau... $12
Aug. 1971 Tony Esposito, Gordie Howe $12
Sept. 1971 Bobby Orr.. $12
Oct. 1971 Bobby Orr.. $12

Nov. 1971 Phil Esposito...$12
Dec. 1971 Derek Sanderson $8
Jan. 1972 Reggie Leach $8
Feb. 1972 Ken Hodge, Bobby Hull, Bobby Orr $15
March 1972 Montreal Canadiens vs. Boston Bruins $10
April 1972 Ken Dryden $10
May 1972 Bobby Orr...$12
June 1972 Bobby Orr $12
July 1972 Boston Bruins executives $7
Aug. 1972 Eddie Johnston $7
Sept. 1972 Bobby Orr..$12
Oct. 1972 John Bucyk $10
Nov. 1972 Bobby Orr $12
Dec. 1972 Tony Esposito $8
Jan. 1973 Boston Bruins artwork $7
Feb. 1973 Fred Stanfield $7
March 1973 Bobby Orr $10
April 1973 Bobby Orr $10
May 1973 Ted Green $7
June 1973 ....$7
July 1973 ....$7
Aug. 1973 ....$7
Sept. 1973 ....$7

Hockey Today
Published by CAHA

1977-78 Darryl Sittler $18
1978-79 Guy Lafleur $15
1979-80 ....$12
1980-81 Bobby Smith $10
1981-82 ....$12
1982-83 ....$12
1983-84 Wayne Gretzky, James Patrick, Bryan Trottier........$15
1984-85 ....$8
1985-86 Lanny McDonald $7
1986-87 ....$7
1987-88 Wayne Gretzky, Mario Lemieux...........................$12
1988-89 Sean Burke..$6
1989-90 Wayne Gretzky, Gordie Howe $10
1990-91 Eric Lindros, Mark Messier, Mike Ricci.................$8

Hockey World

May 1966 Jean Beliveau $60
Oct. 1966 Boom Boom Geoffrion $35
Nov. 1966 Bobby Hull, Stan Mikita, Billy Reay $35
Jan. 1967 Bruce MacGregor, Norm Ullman, Gump Worsley $25
Feb. 1967 Rod Gilbert, Phil Goyette, Don Marshall.............$22
March 1967 Yvan Cournoyer..$22
April 1967 Bobby Hull, Bobby Orr...................................$35
May 1967 Henri Richard...$25
Oct. 1967 Glenn Hall $20
Nov. 1967 Eddie Johnston, Dave Keon $20
Dec. 1967 New York Rangers vs. Toronto Maple Leafs $18
Jan. 1968 Bobby and Dennis Hull $25
Feb. 1968 Eddie Shack $18
March 1968 Bernie Parent..$18
April 1968 Doug Favell, Bobby Hull, Bobby Orr,
    Ed Vam Impe $22
May 1968 Jean Beliveau, Bobby Hull, Stan Mikita,
    Bobby Orr $24
Oct. 1968 1968-69 Preview $22
Nov. 1968 Bobby Orr $35
Dec. 1968 Stan Mikita $25
Jan. 1969 Bob Nevin $20
Feb. 1969 Red Berenson $20
March 1969 All-Star Game $20
April 1969 Stanley Cup playoffs.....................................$22

Oct. 1969 1969-70 Preview $22
Nov. 1969 Ed Giacomin $20
Dec. 1969 Phil Esposito, Bill Flett..................................$20
Jan. 1970 Keith Magnuson, Danny O'Shea.......................$14
Feb. 1970 Gary Smith $10
March 1970 Tony Esposito $18
April 1970 Bobby Hull, Bobby Orr...................................$25
May 1970 Stanley Cup playoffs $20
Oct. 1970 1970-71 Preview $17
Nov. 1970 Jacques Plante $17
Dec. 1970 Vic Hadfield, Jean Ratelle $14
Jan. 1971 Garry Unger..$14
Feb. 1971 Dennis Hull $14
March 1971 Gil Perreault $14
April 1971 Stanley Cup playoffs.....................................$17
May 1971 Gerry Cheevers, Jean Ratelle..........................$17
Oct. 1971 Garry Unger $12
Nov. 1971 Gerry Cheevers $14
Dec. 1971 Gil Perreault $12
Jan. 1972 John Bucyk $12
March 1972 Doug Favell..$12
April 1972 Stanley Cup playoffs.....................................$15
May 1972 Walter Tkaczuk $14
Jan. 1972 Minnesota North Stars in action $15
Nov. 1972 Ken Dryden $14
Dec. 1972 Dunc Wilson $10
Jan. 1973 Yvan Cournoyer, Eddie Johnston $12
March 1973 Bobby Orr $20
April 1973 Stanley Cup playoffs.....................................$17
May 1973 Keith Magnuson $14
Oct. 1973 1973-74 Preview $17
Nov. 1973 Tony Esposito $14
Dec. 1973 Rick MacLeish $14
Jan. 1974 Stan Mikita $14
March 1974 Bill Goldsworthy...$14
April 1974 Syl Apps $12
May 1974 Bobby Orr $20
Oct. 1974 Bobby Clarke $15
Nov. 1974 Darryl Sittler $12
Dec. 1974 Garry Unger $10
Jan. 1975 Dick Redmond $10
March 1975 Tom Lysiak...$10
April 1975 Dennis Hextall $10
May 1975 Phil Esposito $12
Oct. 1975 Bernie Parent $12
Nov. 1975 Bobby Orr $15
Jan. 1976 Phil Esposito $14
Feb. 1976 Danny Gare $10
March 1976 Darryl Sittler...$10
April 1976 Tony Esposito $10
May 1976 Stanley Cup playoffs $14

Inside Hockey

Nov. 1987 Dale Hawerchuk $5
Jan. 1988 Mark Messier $6
March 1988 Scott Stevens $4
May 1988 Stephane Richer $4
Oct. 1988 Sean Burke $4
Nov. 1988 Hockey violence $3
Jan. 1989 Mats Nashlund, Larry Robinson $4
Feb. 1989 Glenn Anderson $3
April 1989 Claude Lemieux $3
May 1989 25 People You Should Know...............................$6
Oct. 1989 Darryl Sittler $3
Nov. 1989 Wayne Gretzky $7
Dec. 1989 Trevor Linden $4
Jan. 1990 Paul Coffey, Mike Ricci $4

Feb. 1990 Tomas Sandstrom...$3
April 1990 Hockey fighting $5
May 1990 Doug Gilmour, Mark Messier, Adam Oates $5
Oct. 1990 Ray Bourque, Brett Hull $7
Nov. 1990 Eric Lindros (Canada) $10
    Kirk Muller (United States)...$5
Jan. 1991 Esa Tikkanen..$5
Feb. 1991 Chris Chelios $5
April 1991 Theoren Fleury..$4
May 1991 Don Cherry (Canada) $3
    Brett Hull (United States)...$5
Oct. 1991 Ed Belfour, Dave Gagner, Mark Recchi $5
Nov. 1991 Mario Lemieux...$6
Dec. 1991 Joe Sakic...$5
Jan. 1992 Pavel Bure $5
Feb. 1992 Sergei Fedorov $5
April 1992 Jeremy Roenick...$5
Sept. 1992 Mario Lemieux, Mark Messier, Patrick Roy.........$5
Nov. 1992 Eric Lindros $5
Dec. 1992 Patrick Roy $5
Feb. 1993 Ron Hextall $5
April 1993 Doug Gilmour $5

Official NHL Guide

1932-33 Howie Morenz $450
1933-34 ....$400
1934-35 ....$300
1935-36 Action artwork $250
1936-37 ....$200
1937-38 ....$200
1938-39 ....$200
1939-40 ....$200
1940-41 ....$200
1941-42 ....$150
1942-43 ....$150
1943-44 ....$150
1944-45 ....$150
1945-46 Action artwork $150
1946-47 Elmer Lach $150
1947-48 Max Bentley...$150
1948-49 Maurice Richard $175
1949-50 Buddy O'Connor $125
1950-51 Sid Abel $100
1951-52 Chuck Rayner $100
1952-53 NHL logo $100
1953-54 NHL logo $100
1954-55 NHL logo $100
1955-56 NHL logo $100
1956-57 NHL logo $100
1957-58 NHL logo $100
1958-59 NHL logo $100
1959-60 NHL logo $100
1960-61 NHL logo $80
1961-62 NHL logo $80
1962-63 NHL logo $80
1963-64 NHL logo $80
1964-65 NHL logo $80
1965-66 NHL logo $60
1966-67 50th Anniversary NHL logo $60
1967-68 NHL logo $60
1968-69 NHL logo $60
1969-70 Phil Esposito, Serge Savard, Gump Worsley $50
1970-71 Clarence Campbell, Gordie Howe..........................$35
1971-72 John Bucyk, Phil Esposito, Bernie Geoffrion,
    Bobby Hull, Maurice Richard $30
1972-73 Phil Esposito, Gump Worsley $25
1973-74 Bobby Clarke, Yvan Cournoyer, Phil Esposito,
    Bobby Orr $30

1974-75 Bobby Clarke, Phil Esposito $30
1975-76 Ken Dryden, Ed Westfall $20
1976-77 Curt Bennett, Garry Unger $17
1977-78 Clarence Campbell...$16
1978-79 Bob Gainey, the Selke Trophy $16
1979-80 NHL team logos $15
1980-81 Wayne Gretzky...$30
1981-82 Mike Liut $12
1982-83 Wayne Gretzky..$25
1983-84 New York Islanders..$12

Becomes: Official NHL Guide & Record Book

1984-85 Gretzky, Oilers, with Stanley Cup $20
1985-86 Paul Coffey, Wayne Gretzky..................................$16
1986-87 Bob Gainey, Larry Robinson $10
1987-88 Michel Goulet, Wayne Gretzky, Gordie Howe $15
1988-89 Wayne Gretzky, Mario Lemieux..............................$15
1989-90 Lanny McDonald, Stanley Cup $8
1990-91 Ray Bourque, Brett Hull, Mark Messier...................$7

Official NHL Record Book

1948-49 Bill Durnan...$70
1949-50 ....$70
1950-51 Terry Sawchuck $50
1951-52 ....$50
1952-53 ....$50
1953-54 ....$50
1954-55 ....$50
1955-56 ....$50
1956-57 ....$50
1957-58 Jean Beliveau, Bill Gadsby, Gordie Howe, others $50
1958-59 Andy Bathgate, Glenn Hall, Gordie Howe, others $50
1959-60 ....$50
1960-61 Bernie Geoffrion, Gordie Howe, Bobby Hull, others $45
1961-62 ....$36
1962-63 ....$36
1963-64 Jean Beliveau, Gordie Howe, Stan Mikita, others ..$45
1964-65 ....$36
1965-66 John Bucyk, Jean Beliveau, Gordie Howe, Bobby Hull
    others...$36
1966-67 ....$30
1967-68 ....$30
1968-69 ....$30
1969-70 ....$30
1970-71 ....$20
1971-72 ....$20
1972-73 ....$20
1973-74 ....$20
1974-75 ....$16
1975-76 ....$16
1976-77 ....$16
1977-78 ....$16
1978-79 ....$16
1979-80 ....$16
1980-81 ....$10
1981-82 ....$10
1982-83 NHL logo and year $10
1983-84 Wayne Gretzky..$20

Becomes Official NHL Guide & Record Book
Rinkside

Nov. 1989 Calgary Flames $5
Dec. 1989 Tom Barrasso..$4
Jan. 1990 Mario Lemieux..$7
Feb. 1990 Kevin Dineen $3
March 1990 Bob Kudelski..$3
April 1990 Don Beaupre $3

Nov. 1990 Paul Cavallini $3
Dec. 1990 Luc Robitaille... $4
Jan. 1991 Doug Wilson $3
Feb. 1991 Bobby Holik $3
March 1991 Jimmy Carson....................................... $4
April 1991 Playoff Preview.. $3

The Sporting News Hockey Yearbook

1990-91 Pat LaFontaine, Brian Leetch $7
    Brett Hull, Mike Keenan $7
    Wayne Gretzky, Mario Lemieux $10
    Ray Bourque, Patrick Roy................................ $7
    Mark Messier, Patrick Roy $7
1991-92 Brian Leetch $7
1992-93 Eric Lindros $10
1993-94 Pierre Turgeon/Mike Gartner.................... $7
1994-95 John LeClair... $7

The Sporting News NHL Guide

1967-68 Detroit goalie .... $125-$175
1968-69 Johnny Bower, Bobby Hull............................ $60-$90
1969-70 Bobby Orr .... $50-$75
1970-71 Gordie Howe .... $40-$60
1971-72 Phil Esposito.................................... $40-$60
1972-73 Bobby Orr .... $45-$60
1973-74 Yvan Cournoyer .... $35-$45
1974-75 Bernie Parent .... $35-$45
1975-76 Bobby Clarke .... $25-$40
1976-77 Ken Dryden .... $20-$40
1977-78 Guy Lafleur... $40
1978-79 Larry Robinson, Canadiens with the Stanley
    Cup .... $25-$35
1979-80 Bob Gainey....................................... $25-$35
1980-81 Denis Potvin .... $20-$30
1981-82 Mike Bossy .... $15-$25
1982-83 Wayne Gretzky .... $30-$40
1983-84 Wayne Gretzky .... $30-$35
1984-85 Wayne Gretzky .... $30-$35
1985-86 Paul Coffey, Wayne Gretzky, Jari Kurri .... $30-$35
1986-87 Claude Lemieux .... $25-$30

1987-88 Ron Hextall.. $20-$30
1988-89 Mario Lemieux.. $25
1989-90 .... $15
1990-91 .... $10

The Sporting News NHL Register

1972-73 Rick Martin .... $35-$40
1973-74 Bobby Clarke... $30
1974-75 Stan Mikita .... $20-$30
1975-76 Rick Martin, Gil Perreault, Rene Robert .... $25-$30
1976-77 Marcel Dionne .... $20-$25
1977-78 Borje Salming $25
1978-79 Denis Potvin $25
1979-80 Bryan Trottier.. $20-$25
1980-81 Wayne Gretzky.................................... $30-$40
1981-82 Mike Liut $15
1982-83 Mike Bossy .... $10-$15
1983-84 Pete Peeters.. $15-$20
1984-85 Ron Langway $15
1985-86 Tim Kerr, New York Islanders .... $15-$20
1986-87 Mario Lemieux.. $25
1987-88 Wayne Gretzky....................................... $25
1988-89 Grant Fuhr .... $10-$15
1989-90 .... $10
1990-91 .... $8

Life Magazine

Life magazine was published between 1936 and 1972 as a general interest newsmagazine. It was widely distributed and covered a variety of topics. Unlike *Newsweek*, which is also a weekly newsmagazine, *Life* was generally saved more often because of its compelling photography and covers.

Prices listed are for magazines in excellent condition.

Date	Cover	Sport	Price
10/11/37	Chuck Williams	Football	$15

Date	Cover	Sport	Price

| 10/24/38 | Sid Luckman | Football | $25 |

05/01/39	Joe DiMaggio	Baseball	$150
08/28/39	Alice Marble	Tennis	$10
10/09/39	Child Player	Football	$10

Date	Cover	Sport	Price
01/15/40	R. Vaughn/T. McGarvin	Basketball	$15
04/01/40	John Rucker	Baseball	$15

Date	Cover	Sport	Price
11/11/40	Tom Harmon	Football	$25

Date	Cover	Sport	Price
09/01/41	Ted Williams	Baseball	$150
11/17/41	Texas Players	Football	$10
01/22/45	Bill Kotsores/Ivor	Basketball	$15
10/22/45	Paul Sarringhaus	Football	$10
04/01/46	Red Barrett	Baseball	$15
09/16/46	G.Davis/D. Blanchard	Football	$25
09/29/47	Johnny Lujack	Football	$15
04/05/48	Dodgers Rookies	Baseball	$20
09/27/48	Doak Walker	Football	$25
05/02/49	Arnold Galiffa	Baseball	$10

Date	Cover	Sport	Price
08/01/49	Joe DiMaggio	Baseball	$100
10/03/49	Charlie Justice	Football	$15

Date	Cover	Sport	Price
05/08/50	Jackie Robinson	Baseball	$85
11/13/50	Kyle Rote	Football	$10
06/08/53	Roy Campanella	Baseball	$50
09/14/53	Casey Stengel	Baseball	$40

Date	Cover	Sport	Price
06/25/56	Mickey Mantle	Baseball	$125
10/14/57	Braves victory parade	Baseball	$20
04/05/58	Sugar Ray Robinson	Boxing	$15
04/28/58	Willie Mays	Baseball	$35
07/21/58	Roy Campanella	Baseball	$35
07/06/59	Gardner McKay	Tennis	$10
07/20/59	Johansson/Lundgren	Boxing	$10
12/05/60	Pro Football Kickoff	Football	$5

Date	Cover	Sport	Price
08/18/61	M. Mantle/R. Maris	Baseball	$125
11/17/61	Minnesota Vikings	Football	$15
04/13/62	Richard Burton/Liz Taylor (Mantle & Maris Cards)	Baseball	$150
09/28/62	Don Drysdale	Baseball	$25
08/02/63	Sandy Koufax	Baseball	$35

Date	Cover	Sport	Price

Date	Cover	Sport	Price

03/06/64	Cassius Clay	Boxing	$50
07/30/65	Mickey Mantle	Baseball	$50
08/08/65	Ben Hogan	Golf	$75
12/10/65	Tommy Nobis	Football	$10
04/08/66	Pete Dawkins	Football	$15
10/14/66	Packers vs. Browns	Football	$10
09/08/67	Carl Yastrzemski	Baseball	$25
09/20/68	Arthur Ashe	Tennis	$15
12/13/68	Baltimore Colts	Football	$10
06/20/69	Joe Namath	Football	$15

09/26/69	Jerry Koosman	Baseball	$15
10/23/70	Muhammad Ali	Boxing	$25
03/05/71	Ali/Frazier	Boxing	$15
03/19/71	Ali/Frazier	Boxing	$15
12/03/71	Baltimore Colts	Football	$10
01/14/72	Staubach/Landry	Football	$15
03/24/72	Jabbar/Chamberlain	Basketball	$15
10/06/72	Tough Guys/Bob Lilly	Football	$10
11/03/72	Joe Namath	Football	$15
01/19/81	Muhammad Ali	Boxing	$10

Collier's

Date	Cover	Sport	Price
10/12/42	Football action scene	Football	$12
11/14/42	Referee on cover, inside has Jim Thorpe story	several	$15

| 07/27/46 | Joe DiMaggio | Baseball | $60 |

Date	Cover	Sport	Price

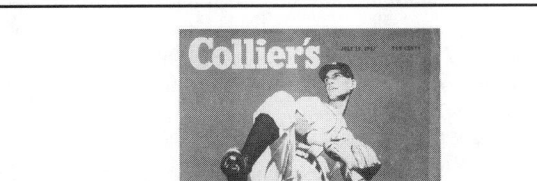

| 07/19/47 | Hal Newhouser | Baseball | $30 |
| 06/21/52 | Jackie Jensen family | Baseball | $15 |

Look

Date	Cover	Sport	Price
10/10/39	Joe DiMaggio	Baseball	$95
04/30/46	Hank Greenberg	Baseball	$40
10/15/46	Ted Williams	Baseball	$80
09/14/48	Doak Walker	Football	$200
04/26/49	Joe DiMaggio Sr.& Jr.	Baseball	$80
09/12/50	B. Williams: Notre Dame	Football	$15
04/24/51	Phil Rizzuto	Baseball	$45
05/22/51	J. DiMaggio, others	Baseball	$50
07/31/51	S. Musial, others	Baseball	$35

Date	Cover	Sport	Price
09/25/51	R. Campanella, others	Baseball	$25
10/09/51	T. Williams, others	Baseball	$45
03/11/52	Bob Feller	Baseball	$25
04/22/52	Casey Stengel	Baseball	$20
06/17/52	R. Hornsby, others	Baseball	$20
07/15/52	Al Rosen, others	Baseball	$20
08/12/52	M. Mantle, others	Baseball	$90
05/03/55	Willie Mays, others	Baseball	$30

Saturday Evening Post

Date	Cover	Sport	Price
05/11/63	Leo Durocher	Baseball	$15
09/21/68	Fran Tarkenton	Football	$12
Nov./74	Roosevelt Grier and his needlepoint	Football	$9

Newsweek

Date	Cover	Sport	Price
04/15/33	Play at home	Baseball	$50
04/29/33	Carl Hubbell	Baseball	$75
09/09/33	Connie Mack	Baseball	$75
09/30/33	Clark Griffith	Baseball	$60
12/23/33	Judge Landis	Baseball	$75
02/17/34	Babe Ruth	Baseball	$200
03/17/34	Mel Ott	Baseball	$75
10/06/34	Mickey Cochrane	Baseball	$75
04/20/35	Judge Landis	Baseball	$50
10/03/36	Carl Hubbell	Baseball	$50
10/11/37	Carl Hubbell	Baseball	$35
04/18/38	Rudy York	Baseball	$30
06/13/38	Henry Armstrong	Boxing	$35
10/10/38	Yankees/Cubs	Baseball	$30
06/19/39	Abner Doubleday	Baseball	$100
07/17/39	Bobby Riggs	Tennis	$50
09/16/46	Ted Williams	Baseball	$100
10/06/47	Branch Rickey	Baseball	$50
09/24/47	Bob Feller	Baseball	$50
10/05/47	Dodgers in W. S.	Baseball	$45
04/26/48	J. McCarthy, Southworth	Baseball	$45
04/26/48	Billy Southworth	Baseball	$45
10/25/48	Sonja Henie	Figure Skating	$25
06/20/49	Harrison Dillard	Track	$25
08/08/49	Branch Rickey	Baseball	$20
04/17/50	Mel Parnell	Baseball	$15
10/04/54	Feller, Lemon	Baseball	$25
10/03/55	Baseball, TV	Baseball	$8
01/25/56	Mickey Mantle	Baseball	$125
07/01/57	Stan Musial	Baseball	$25
08/03/59	Casey Stengel	Baseball	$20
08/04/60	Home runs	Baseball	$10
08/14/61	Mickey Mantle	Baseball	$75
10/13/61	Pro Football	Football	$10
10/30/61	Paul Hornung	Football	$25
04/26/65	Houston Astrodome	Baseball	$30

Date	Cover	Sport	Price
10/11/65	Sandy Koufax	Baseball	$40
07/25/66	Jim Ryun	Track	$25
05/29/67	Mario Andretti	Auto Racing	$25
10/02/67	Carl Yastrzemski	Baseball	$40
09/15/69	Joe Namath	Football	$45
12/15/69	W. Reed/W. Frazier	Basketball	$25
10/05/70	Terry Bradshaw	Football	$35
11/09/70	Muhammad Ali	Boxing	$45
07/19/71	Lee Trevino	Golf	$25
11/01/71	George Allen	Football	$20
02/14/72	Winter Olympics	Olympics	$15
06/26/72	Chris Evert	Tennis	$15
09/11/72	'72 Olympics	Olympics	$10
10/02/72	Howard Cosell	All Sports	$10
12/04/72	Larry Brown	Football	$15
06/11/73	Secretariat	Horse Racing	$50
08/13/73	H. Aaron/B. Ruth	Baseball	$35
06/03/74	Mary Bacon	Horse Racing	$10
07/01/74	Bjorn Borg	Tennis	$15
02/03/75	Jack Nicklaus	Golf	$25

Date	Cover	Sport	Price
02/03/75	Johnny Miller	Golf	$25

Date	Cover	Sport	Price
06/16/75	Nolan Ryan	Baseball	$45
06/28/76	Vida Blue	Baseball	$15
01/03/77	Nadia Comaneci	Olympics	$10
01/22/79	Bradshaw, Henderson	Football	$30
06/23/80	Sugar Ray Leonard	Boxing	$15
09/07/81	John McEnroe	Tennis	$15
01/25/82	J. Montana, K. Anderson	Football	$20
09/20/82	Gene Upshaw	Football	$20
05/28/84	Robert Redford "The Natural"	Baseball	$15
07/30/84	Carl Lewis	Olympics	$10
08/13/84	Mary Lou Retton	Olympics	$8
08/20/84	Olympic Team	Olympics	$10
05/14/90	Jennifer Capriati	Tennis	$7
08/06/90	G. Steinbrenner	Baseball	$5

Date	Cover	Sport	Price
11/18/91	Magic Johnson	Basketball	$10
01/24/92	Tonya Harding	Olympics	$4
02/10/92	Kristy Yamaguchi	Olympics	$7
07/06/92	Jordan, Bird, Magic	Basketball	$15
10/11/93	Michael Jordan	Basketball	$20
02/21/94	Tonya Harding	Olympics	$4
03/20/95	Michael Jordan	Basketball	$6
09/14/98	McGwire, Sosa	Baseball	$15
02/15/99	Drugs In Sports	Olympics	$2

Date	Cover	Sport	Price
03/22/99	Joe DiMaggio	Baseball	$10
07/19/99	Brandi Chastain	Soccer	$15
10/25/99	Muhammad Ali	Legends	$12
09/11/00	Marion Jones	Olympics	$5
10/30/00	Jeter-Piazza	Baseball	$10
06/18/01	Tiger Woods	Golf	$12

Time

Time, the popular weekly newsmagazine which is still being published, has had a number of sports figures on its covers. Unlike Life, which was saved more often, issues of *Time* were often thrown away, and are considerably scarcer.

Date	Cover	Sport	Price
09/17/23	Jack Dempsey	Boxing	$500
03/30/25	George Sisler	Baseball	$1,000
08/30/25	Bobby Jones	Golf	$1,500
10/05/25	Red Grange	Football	$400
08/30/26	James Tunney	Boxing	$400
04/11/27	Connie Mack	Baseball	$300
06/27/27	John McGraw	Baseball	$400
11/07/27	Knute Rockne	Football	$400
06/24/29	Max Schmeling	Boxing	$250
07/29/29	Jimmie Foxx	Baseball	$350
10/14/29	William Wrigley	Baseball	$150
08/25/30	Wilbert Robinson	Baseball	$125
09/21/30	Bobby Jones	Golf	$600
10/01/31	Primo Carnero	Boxing	$100
04/28/32	Gabby Street	Baseball	$100
08/31/32	Ellsworth Vines Jr.	Tennis	$25
09/04/33	Jack Crawford	Tennis	$25
07/09/34	Lefty Gomez	Baseball	$100
02/11/35	Lorne Cabot	Hockey	$35
04/15/35	Dizzy Dean	Baseball	$125
09/02/35	Don Budge	Tennis	$25
10/07/35	Mickey Cochrane	Baseball	$150
07/13/36	Joe DiMaggio	Baseball	$350
10/05/36	Gehrig/Hubbell	Baseball	$3,000

Date	Cover	Sport	Price
4/19/37	Bob Feller	Baseball	$100
10/25/37	Duke's Wade	Football	$30
03/14/38	David Kerr	Hockey	$35
08/01/38	Happy Chandler	Baseball	$30
06/06/38	Johnny Goodman	Golf	$35
07/17/39	Sonja Henie	Olympics	$45
11/06/39	Tom Harmon	Football	$40
08/21/39	Eleanor Holm	Swimming	$25
09/29/41	Joe Louis	Boxing	$125
07/02/45	Mel Ott	Baseball	$100
11/12/45	Davis/Blanchard	Football	$35
09/02/46	Pauline Betz	Tennis	$15
10/14/46	Frank Leahy	Football	$30
04/14/47	Leo Durocher	Baseball	$75
09/01/47	Jake Kramer	Tennis	$15

Date	Cover	Sport	Price

Date	Cover	Sport	Price
09/22/47	Jackie Robinson	Baseball	$200
11/03/47	Bob Chappuis	Football	$35
05/17/48	Eddie Arcaro	Jockey	$25
08/02/48	Mel Patton	Olympics	$15
10/04/48	Joe DiMaggio	Baseball	$275
01/10/49	Ben Hogan	Golf	$100
05/30/49	Ben Jones	Horse Racing	$10
09/05/49	Stan Musial	Baseball	$150
04/10/50	Ted Williams	Baseball	$200
06/25/51	Sugar Ray Robinson	Boxing	$75
08/27/51	Dick Savitt	Tennis	$10
10/01/51	Bert Lahr	Baseball	$30
11/19/51	Richard Kazmaier	Football	$35

04/28/52	Eddie Stanky	Baseball	$35
07/21/52	Bob Mathias	Track	$10
06/13/53	Mickey Mantle	Baseball	$200
11/09/53	John Lattner	Football	$35
04/26/54	Briggs Cunningham	Auto Racing	$10
06/21/54	Sam Snead	Golf	$45

07/26/54	Willie Mays	Baseball	$75
11/29/54	Bobby Layne	Football	$25
07/11/55	August Busch Jr.	Baseball	$25
08/08/55	Roy Campanella	Baseball	$65
10/03/55	Casey Stengel	Baseball	$40
05/28/56	Robin Roberts	Baseball	$40
10/08/56	Duffy Daugherty	Football	$15

Date	Cover	Sport	Price
12/03/56	Parry O'Brien	Track	$10
07/08/57	Birdie Tebbetts	Baseball	$15
08/26/57	Althea Gibson	Tennis	$15
02/10/58	Willie Hartack	Horse Racing	$10
04/28/58	Walter O'Malley	Baseball	$25
10/20/58	Amos A. Stagg	Football	$25
02/09/59	Alex Cushing	Skiing	$10
08/04/59	Rocky Colavito	Baseball	$30
11/30/59	Sam Huff	Football	$35
05/02/60	Arnold Palmer	Golf	$35
08/29/60	Rafer Johnson	Track	$10

02/17/61	Oscar Robertson	Basketball	$30
06/29/62	Jack Nicklaus	Golf	$35
08/03/62	Del Webb	Baseball	$10
12/21/62	Vince Lombardi	Football	$35
03/22/63	Cassius Clay	Boxing	$75
10/18/63	Roger Staubach	Football	$25
09/11/64	Hank Bauer	Baseball	$30
11/20/64	Ara Parseghian	Football	$25
07/09/65	Jim Clark	Racing	$10
11/26/65	Jim Brown	Football	$50
06/10/66	Juan Marichal	Baseball	$35
10/28/66	Seymour/Hanratty	Football	$20
09/13/68	Denny McLain	Baseball	$20

03/01/68	Bobby Hull	Hockey	$35
09/13/69	Mets/D. McLain	Baseball	$30
03/08/71	Ali/Frazier	Boxing	$40
07/19/71	Lee Trevino	Golf	$15
08/23/71	Vida Blue	Baseball	$15
01/17/72	Staubach/Griese	Football	$25
07/10/72	Johnny Bench	Baseball	$15
09/11/72	Mark Spitz	Olympics	$10
10/16/72	Joe Namath	Football	$35
12/11/72	Don Shula	Football	$20
06/11/73	Secretariat	Horse Racing	$25
09/10/73	Bobby Riggs	Tennis	$10
06/03/74	Reggie Jackson	Baseball	$30
02/24/75	Bernie Parent	Hockey	$15
04/28/75	Jimmy Conners	Tennis	$10

Date	Cover	Sport	Price
08/18/75	Charlie Finley	Baseball	$15
12/08/75	Pitt's Front Four	Football	$10
02/02/76	Dorothy Hamill	Olympics	$10
04/26/76	Babe Ruth	Baseball	$15
08/02/76	Nadia Comaneci	Olympics	$10
01/10/77	Super Bowl	Football	$5

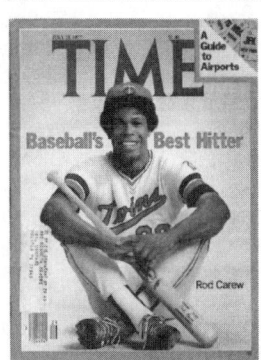

Date	Cover	Sport	Price
07/18/77	Rod Carew	Baseball	$15
01/16/78	Super Bowl XII	Football	$20
02/27/78	Muhammad Ali	Boxing	$25
05/29/78	Steve Cauthen	Horse Racing	$5
06/26/78	Women in Sports	Multi-Sport	$5
02/11/80	Eric Heiden	Olympics	$10
06/30/80	Bjorn Borg	Tennis	$10
09/29/80	Bear Bryant	Football	$15
05/11/81	Billy Martin	Baseball	$10
01/25/82	Joe Montana	Football	$35
06/14/82	Cooney/Stallone	Boxing	$10
10/17/83	Peter Uberroth	Olympics	$5
01/30/84	Mahre/McKinney	Olympics	$5
07/30/84	Carl Lewis	Olympics	$10
03/18/85	Gretzky/Bird	Multi-Sport	$30
08/19/85	Pete Rose	Baseball	$15

Date	Cover	Sport	Price
01/27/86	W. Payton/W. Perry	Football	$10
04/07/86	Dwight Gooden	Baseball	$5
02/09/87	Dennis Conner	Yacht Racing	$5
06/27/88	Mike Tyson	Boxing	$10
09/19/88	Joyner-Kersee	Olympics	$5
04/03/89	College Trap	College Sports	$5
07/10/89	Pete Rose	Baseball	$10
07/27/92	Kim Zmeskal	Olympics	$5
02/21/94	Kerrigan/Harding	Olympics	$5
06/27/94	O.J. Simpson	Football	$5
02/12/96	Cal Ripken/M. Johnson	Baseball/Basketball	$5
01/27/97	R. White/B. Favre	Football	$5
02/17/97	O.J. Simpson	Football	$5

Date	Cover	Sport	Price
06/22/98	Michael Jordan	Basketball	$8
07/27/98	Griffey/McGwire	Baseball	$5
07/19/99	Women's Soccer	Soccer	$5
09/11/00	Marion Jones	Olympics	$5
03/05/01	Dale Earnhardt	Racing	$10
09/03/01	S & V Williams	Tennis	$6
02/11/02	Sarah Hughes	Olympics	$5
02/25/02	J. Sale/D. Pelletier	Olympics	$5

Boys' Life

Boys' Life, the official magazine for the Boy Scouts of America, has had numerous sports-related covers since its inception in 1911. Most copies of *Boys' Life* are relatively inexpensive for collectors.

Date	Cover	Sport	Price
Aug 1959	Mickey Mantle	Baseball	$60

Date	Cover	Sport	Price
Apr. 1963	Yogi Berra	Baseball	$30
Nov. 1963	Roger Staubach	Football	$25
Mar. 1966	Willie Mays	Baseball	$20
Mar. 1967	Indy 500	Auto Racing	$10
Mar. 1968	R. Clemente	Baseball	$25

Date	Cover	Sport	Price
Mar. 1969	Ron Santo	Baseball	$15
Jun. 1969	M. Mantle Sr. & Jr.	Baseball	$30
Mar. 1970	Mike Hegan	Baseball	$8
Sep. 1970	Calvin Hill	Football	$10

Date	Cover	Sport	Price
Oct. 1970	Bill Bradley	Basketball	$20
Dec. 1970	Bobby Orr	Hockey	$30
Jul. 1971	Johnny Bench	Baseball	$20
Sep. 1971	B. Robinson	Baseball	$20
Oct. 1971	Sonny Sixkiller	Football	$10
Jan. 1972	Wes Unseld	Basketball	$10
Mar. 1972	Hank Aaron	Baseball	$20
Oct. 1972	Greg Pruett	Football	$6
Dec. 1972	Jean Ratelle	Hockey	$6
Jan. 1973	Dave Cowens	Basketball	$8
Mar. 1973	Fergie Jenkins	Baseball	$10
Jan. 1974	Tiny Archibald	Basketball	$8
Nov. 1974	O.J. Simpson	Football	$13
Jul. 1975	Andy Coan	Swimming	$5
Sep. 1975	Dave Concepcion	Baseball	$8
Oct. 1975	Jim Plunkett	Football	$8
Jan. 1976	Rick Barry	Basketball	$11
Jan. 1976	Steve Williams	Track	$5
Sep. 1976	Aaron, Oliva, Horton	Baseball	$10
Nov. 1976	Bert Jones	Football	$8

Date	Cover	Sport	Price
Nov. 1977	R. Staubach	Football	$12
Jun. 1978	Rod Carew	Baseball	$12
Nov. 1978	K. Abdul-Jabbar	Basketball	$15
Mar. 1979	John McEnroe	Tennis	$10
Nov. 1979	T. Bradshaw	Football	$10
Mar. 1980	Jim Rice	Baseball	$5
Sep. 1980	Dave Parker	Baseball	$4
Nov. 1980	Dan Fouts	Football	$10
Sep. 1981	Keith Hernandez	Baseball	$6
Apr. 1982	George Brett	Baseball	$10
Nov. 1982	Joe Montana	Football	$35
Jul. 1983	Carl Lewis	Olympics	$6
Nov. 1983	Jim Zorn	Football	$3
Jun. 1985	Pete Rose	Baseball	$12
Aug. 1985	Ryne Sandberg	Baseball	$11
Oct. 1985	Sidney Moncrief	Basketball	$5
Nov. 1985	Robert Jackson	Football	$1
Sep. 1986	Doc Gooden	Baseball	$5
Jan. 1987	Paul Coffey	Hockey	$3
Oct. 1988	Reggie White	Football	$5
Jul. 1989	Orel Hershiser	Baseball	$2
Sep. 1990	Andre Dawson	Baseball	$2
Feb. 1991	Magic Johnson	Basketball	$8
Apr. 1991	Nolan Ryan	Baseball	$10
Nov. 1991	Matt Bahr	Football	$1
Apr. 1992	Ken Griffey Jr.	Baseball	$10
Nov. 1992	Emmitt Smith	Football	$6
Jan. 1993	Kevin Johnson	Basketball	$2
Apr. 1993	Kirby Puckett	Baseball	$3
Oct. 1993	Troy Aikman	Football	$3
May 1994	Juan Gonzalez	Baseball	$3
Apr. 1998	Nomar Garciaparra	Baseball	$5
Mar. 1999	Justin Labonte	Racing	$5

Baseball Comic Books

Note: Prices are for Comic Books that are in Excellent + condition with no lables.

A-1 Comics
Magazine Enterprises
1944-1955
89) Home Run, Stan Musial $100

All-Pro Sports
1) Unauthorized bio—Bo Jackson, baseball (black and white) $2

The All-Star Story of the Dodgers
Stadium Communications
April 1979
1F) Roy Campanella, Sandy Koufax, Jackie Robinson $2

All-Time Sports Comics
Hillman Periodicals
Oct.-Nov. 1949
5) Baseball $50
7) Baseball $50

The Amazing Willie Mays
Famous Funnies Publications
September 1954
1) Willie Mays $350

The Amazon of the Ozarks
Prize/Headline Feature
June-July 1948
2) Baseball $30

Babe Ruth Sports Comics
Harvey Publications
April 1949-February 1951
1) Basketball $150
2) Baseball $125
3) Joe DiMaggio $125
4) Bob Feller $75
8) Yogi Berra $75
9) Stan Musial $50

Baseball Classics
Personality
1) Willie Mays $3
1a) Willie Mays with trading cards $5
2) Lou Gehrig $3
2a) Lou Gehrig with trading cards $5

Baseball Comics
Will Eisner Productions
Spring 1949
1) Rube Rooky $100

Baseball Comics
Personality

1) Frank Thomas $3
1a) Frank Thomas with cards $5
2) Rickey Henderson $3
2a) Rickey Henderson with cards $5
3) Nolan Ryan $3
3a) Nolan Ryan with cards $5
4) Cal Ripken Jr. $3
4a) Cal Ripken Jr. with cards $5

Baseball Greats
Dark Horse
1) Jimmy Piersall story $3

Baseball Heroes
Fawcett Publications
1952
Babe Ruth/Hall of Fame Biographies ..$400

Baseball Legends
Revolutionary
1) Babe Ruth $3
2) Ty Cobb $3
3) Ted Williams $3
4) Mickey Mantle $3
5) Joe DiMaggio $3
6) Jackie Robinson $3
7) Sandy Koufax $3
8) Willie Mays $3
9) Honus Wagner $3

10) Roberto Clemente $3
11) Yogi Berra $3
13) Hank Aaron $3
14) Carl Yastrzemski $3
15) Satchel Paige $3
16) Johnny Bench $3
17) Shoeless Joe Jackson $3
18) Lou Gehrig $3

Baseball Sluggers
Personality Comics
1) Ken Griffey Jr. $2.75
1a) limited edition $5
2) Dave Justice $2.75
2a) limited edition $5
3) Frank Thomas $2.75
3a) limited edition $5
4) Don Mattingly $2.75
4a) limited edition $5

Baseball Superstars
Revolutionary
Hank Aaron; Jim Abbott; Alomar broth-
ers; Steve Avery, Tom Glavine;
Johnny Bench; Yogi Berra; George
Brett; Jose Canseco; Roger Clemens;
Joe DiMaggio; Dennis Eckersley;
Carlton Fisk; Lou Gehrig; Ken Griffey
Jr.; Rickey Henderson; Bo Jackson;
Mickey Mantle; Billy Martin; Willie
Mays; Mark McGwire; Kirby Puckett;
Cal Ripken Jr.; Pete Rose; Nolan
Ryan; Babe Ruth; Ryne Sandberg;
Darryl Strawberry; Frank Thomas;
Honus Wagner; Ted Williams; Dave
Winfield; Carl Yastrzemski; Annual #1
Nolan Ryan. .... $3 ea.

Baseball Thrills
Ziff-Davis Publishing Co.
1951-1952
1) Bob Feller $100
2) Yogi Berra $100
3) Joe DiMaggio $150

Baseball Thrills 3-D
3-D Zone
May 1990
1) Ty Cobb, Ted Williams ....cover

Best Pitchers
Personality
1) Nolan Ryan ....cover
1a) Nolan Ryan with cards ....cover
2) Dwight Gooden ....cover
2a) Dwight Gooden with cards ....cover
3) Roger Clemens ....cover
3a) Roger Clemens with cards ....cover

Bill Sterns Sports Book
Ziff-Davis Publishing Co.
1951-1952
1) Ewell Blackwell $40

Blue Bolt
Funnies Inc./Novelty Press/Premium
Group of Comics 1940-1949
8-1 Baseball cover $15

9-1 Baseball cover $15
10-1 Baseball cover $15

Blue Devil
DC Comics
1984-1986
26) Special baseball issue $2

Brooks Robinson
Magnum
May 1992
1) Photo $2

Calling All Boys
Parents Magazine Institute
1946-1948
7) Baseball $14
12) Baseball $20

Comics Revue
St. John Publishing Co.
1947-48
3) Iron Vic baseball cover $15

Daredevil Comics
Lev Gleason Publications
July 1941-Sept. 1956
25) Baseball cover $50

DC Superstars
National Periodical Publications/DC
Comics
1976-1978
10) Superhero Baseball Special $4

Don Newcombe
Fawcett Publications
1950

1) Baseball Star $200

Famous Funnies
Eastern Color
1933-1955
22) Baseball cover $200
58) Baseball cover $100

Parents Institute
1947-1949
7) Baffling Mystery on the Diamond $25

Jackie Robinson
Fawcett Publications
1950-1952

Famous Plays of Jackie Robinson .. $450
2) Famous Plays of Jackie
   Robinson $300
3) Famous Plays of Jackie
   Robinson $250
4) Famous Plays of Jackie
   Robinson $250
5) Famous Plays of Jackie
   Robinson $250
6) Famous Plays of Jackie
   Robinson $300

King Comics
David McKay Publications
Starring Popeye
1936-1952
39) Baseball $100
61) Phantom Baseball $50
156) Baseball $35

Krazy Komics
Timely
1942-1948
24) Baseball $40

Larry Doby, Baseball Hero
Fawcett Publications
1950
1) Baseball $150

Lil' Abner
Harvey Publications
1947-1955
83) Baseball $40

Mel Allen Sports Comics
Visual Editions
1949-1950

2) Lou Gehrig $150

Mickey Mantle Comics
Magnum

1) Rise to Big Leagues $3

Negro Heroes
Parents Magazine Institute
1947-1948

2) Jackie Robinson $375

Phil Rizzuto
Fawcett Publications
1951

The Sensational Story of the American
Leagues MVP $250

Power Pack
1984-1991

13) Baseball issue $2

The Pride of the Yankees
Magazine Enterprises

No # The Life of Lou Gehrig $425

Ralph Kiner, Home Run King
Fawcett Publications
1950

No # Life Story of the Famous Pittsburgh
Slugger $100

Real Heroes Comics
Parents Magazine Institute
1941-1946

6) Lou Gehrig $100
14) Pete Gray $30

Real Life Comics
Nedor/Better/Standard Publications
1941-1952

24) Babe Ruth $100
41) Jimmie Foxx $50

Roy Campanella, Baseball Hero
Fawcett Publications
1950

No # Life Story of the Battling Dodgers
Catcher $325

Sport Comics
Street & Smith Publications
1940-1941

1) Lou Gehrig $300
3) Phil Rizzuto $125

Sports Action
Marvel Comics
1950-1952

3) Hack Wilson $50
7) Jim Konstanty $35
8) Ralph Kiner $35

Sports Classics
Personality Comics

1) Babe Ruth $3
1a) with trading cards $5
2) Mickey Mantle $3
2a) with trading cards $5
3) Ty Cobb $3
3a) with trading cards $5
4) Ted Williams $3
4a) with trading cards $5
5 Jackie Robinson $3
5a) with trading cards $5

Sports Personalities
Personality Comics
1992

2) Nolan Ryan................................. $3
2a) limited edition $5
3) Rickey Henderson $3
3a) limited edition $5
8) George Brett............................... $3
8a) limited edition $5
12) Ken Griffey Jr............................ $3
12a) with trading cards $5
14) Pete Rose................................. $3
14a) with trading cards $5

Sports Stars
Parents Magazine Institute
1946

2) Baseball Greats........................... $125

Sport Thrills
Star Publications
1950-1951

11) Ted Williams, Ty Cobb $150
12) Joe DiMaggio, Phil Rizzuto $150
14) baseball cover $50
15) baseball cover $50

Supersnipe Comics
Street & Smith's Publications
1942-1949

2-4 Baseball $100
3-3 Baseball $75
3-11 Baseball Pitcher $75
4-8 Baseball Star $75

Target Comics
Funnies Inc./Novelty Publishing/
Star Publications
1940-1949

9-5 Baseball $30

Thrilling True Story of the Baseball Giants
Thrilling True Story of the Baseball Yankees
Fawcett Publications
1952

Famous Giants of the Past $250
Baseball Yankees $350

True Comics
True Comics/Parents Magazine Press
1941-1950

3) Baseball Hall of Fame $100
6) Baseball World Series $95
15) Bob Feller $45
37) Baseball $25
44) El Senor Goofy, baseball........... $25
49) Baseball $20
71) The Story of Joe DiMaggio........ $25
77) Lou Boudreau $25
78) Stan Musial $25
84) Includes baseball $15

True Sport Picture Stories
Street & Smith Publications
1942-1949

1-5 Joe DiMaggio $160
1-7 Mel Ott................................. $85
2-3 Carl Hubbell $70
2-7 Stan Musial $75
2-10 Connie Mack $70
3-2 The Philadelphia Athletics.......... $60
3-3 Leo Durocher $60
3-12 Red Sox vs. Senators.............. $35
4-1 Spring Training in full spring....... $35
4-2 How to Pitch 'Em Where They
Can't Hit 'Em.............................. $35

Vic Verity Magazine
Vic Verity Publications
1945

5) Championship Baseball Game..... $35

WOW Comics
Fawcett Publications
1940-1948

69) Tom Mix Baseball $50

Yogi Berra
Fawcett Publications
1957

1) Yogi Berra................................ $150

Young All-Stars
DC Comics
June 1987

7) Baseball Game...........................cover

Chapter 7

BOOKS

Four main factors determine the value of a used sports book: scarcity, desirability, condition, and edition. Generally, scarcity adds to the value of a book, but not significantly unless the book is considered desirable in the first place. Hundreds of fairly hard-to-find sports books are not particularly valuable because there is no demand for them. However, desirable books that are scarce always command premium prices.

Desirability is ultimately in the eye of the reader/buyer, but the author, the subject, the degree of originality, and the overall quality or "readability" of the book are the main factors that determine a book's standing with collectors. Sports card collectors should have little trouble understanding that condition greatly affects the value of books. Torn or missing pages, lack of a dust jacket, cup or glass rings on the cover, general wear and tear on the spine and other such defects greatly reduce any book's value.

Three particularly important aspects of condition to be aware of are:

1.) "ex libre" books, i.e. discards from libraries, are considered damaged goods and are shunned by collecting purists;

2.) a lack of a dust jacket (if issued) significantly reduces the value of a book, sometimes up to 50 percent or more.

3.) To be worth top dollar a book should be a first printing of a first edition. Subtract 25 percent for a later printed book.

Two other influences on value are worth noting. First, although an autograph normally lessens the value of a premier sports card, it enhances a sports book, whether the book is signed by the author or the subject(s), or both. Second, a biography is not necessarily valuable because the subject is a superstar. It often depends on scarcity; a hard-to-find biography of a lesser player could be considered more valuable.

Of course, there is no guarantee that any sports book will appreciate dramatically, so the average collector would be well advised to collect books they enjoy for their own sake.

Because there are so many sports books, with a few hundred new ones published annually, most collectors should consider specializing. Four common approaches to specialization are collecting by quality, team, genre (e.g., record books, fiction, picture books, general histories), or topic.

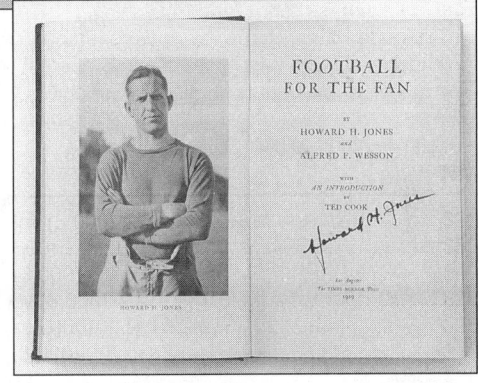

Finally, there is a wide variety of sources for used sports books—garage sales, card shows, library sales, antiquarian book sales, hobby periodicals (such as *Sports Collectors Digest*), used book stores, and used book dealers who issue mail-order catalogs. Remaindered books at cut-rate prices can also be found in new-book book stores, but these offerings will always be recently published books that either didn't sell well or were over-printed.

Thousands of used and out-of-print sports books, common and rare, are available on the Internet. The most complete listing is found at Web site www.abebooks.com. You may search by author or title or browse at "Sports." Books can also be purchased at auction on www.ebay.com or other auction sites.

The following list is by no means comprehensive, but should offer collectors a snapshot of some of the more popular titles among book collectors. Unless noted otherwise, the price given is for first-edition printing, hard cover, with the book and original dust jacket in Very Good condition. Subtract about 50 percent if the book is missing its dust jacket and 25 percent for a later edition.

Symbols — SC means soft cover, No DJ Issued means hard cover that never had a dust jacket.

Best of Baseball Books

Here are some of the best baseball books ever published, classic books that would form the foundation of any collection. First editions of many of these titles are becoming quite scarce.

A Ball Player's Career, Adrian C, "Cap" Anson, Era Publishing, (1900), No DJ Issued $250

America's National Game, A.G. Spalding, American Sports Publishing, (1911), No DJ Issued .... $300-$400
Hall of Fame pitcher relates baseball's early history with photos and four dramatic fold-outs.

Babe, The Legend Comes to Life, Robert Creamer, Simon & Schuster, (1974) $15
Considered by many as the best sports biography ever written, Babe increases our affection and respect for baseball's foremost hero.

Ball Four, Jim Bouton, World Publishing, (1970) $30
Although rather tame by today's standards, Bouton's tell-all shocker of 1970 is still the funniest baseball book in captivity.

The Ballparks, Bill Shannon, Hawthorne Books, (1965) $100
This photo-history, the first book on its subject, is tough to find and high on many collectors' want-lists.

Baseball: The Early Years (1960); Baseball: The Golden Age (1971), Harold Seymour, and *Baseball: The Peoples Game*, Oxford University Press, (1990) $75, $75, $20
This triology ranks as baseball literature's most highly regarded general history.

Baseball I Gave You All the Best Years of My Life, edited by Richard Grossinger and Kevin Kerrane, North Atlantic, (1977), SC ... $35
A mind-bending anthology of eclectic poetry and prose.

Baseball Uniforms of the 20th Century, Mark Okkonen, Sterling, (1991) .... $90-$125
First book devoted entirely to baseball uniforms, design changes for each year, each team

The Boys of Summer, Roger Kahn, Harper & Row, (1972) $50
The book that immortalized that Brooklyn Dodgers of the early 1950s, *The Boys of Summer* is the quintessential classic baseball book.

Robert Obojski

Bush League, Robert Obojski, MacMillan (1975) $25

Conceived as a companion to *The Baseball Encyclopedia*, *Bush League* was published in 1975, but it is still the best reference book on the minors.

The Celebrant, Eric Rolfe Greenberg, Everett House, (1983) .... more than $90
A novel about Christy Mathewson and his biggest fan, *The Celebrant* is a scarce book with a big following.

The Cincinnati Game, Lonnie Wheeler, Orange Frazer Press, (1988) .... $175-$300
This is the most innovative team history ever, but only 3,000 copies of the hardback were published.

The Chrysanthemum and the Bat, Robert Whiting, Dodd Mead, (1977) $200
The first major treatment of Japanese baseball, this is also a book about the clash of two cultures.

Eight Men Out, Eliot Asinof, Holt Reinhart, (1963) $250
This is the best book about baseball's most infamous scandal, the fixed 1919 World Series.

False Spring, Pat Jordan, Dodd Mead, (1975) $50
This beautifully written coming-of-age autobiography about failure in the minor leagues reads like a novel.

The Fireside Book of Baseball, Vol. I, II, III & IV (SC), edited by Charles Einstein, Simon & Schuster (1956, 1958, 1968, 1989) $50, $50, $75, $15
These are the first great (and still unsurpassed) anthologies of baseball literature.

The Glory of Their Times, Lawrence Ritter, MacMillan, (1966).. $85
This collection of first-person accounts by players from the '20s was a pioneer in baseball oral histories.

The Great American Baseball Card Flipping, Trading and Bubble Gum Book, Brendan C. Boyd and Fred C. Harris $25
This most nostalgic of all baseball books was the first to demonstrate the enormous appeal of baseball cards.

The Heart of the Order, by Tom Boswell, Doubleday (1989) $10

The Hidden Game of Baseball, John Thorn and Pete Palmer, Doubleday, (1984) $40
Creative new ways to evaluate a player's performance.

The Hot Stove League, Lee Allen, A.S. Barnes, (1955).. $100-$150
Literate collection of baseball anecdote, often obscure, always interesting.

The Image of Their Greatness, by Lawrence Ritter and Donald Honig, Crown, (1979) $10

How Life Imitates the World Series, by Tom Boswell, Doubleday (1982) .... $70-$100

Late Innings, by Roger Angell, Simon & Schuster (1982) .. $15-$30

The Long Season, and *Pennant Race*, Jim Brosnan, Harper Brothers, (1960, 1962) .... $60-$75 each
Great inside looks at Major League Baseball, Brosnan's diaries remain the only books to be entirely written by an active Major League player.

Lords of the Realm, John Helyar, Villard, (1994) $20
Best available history of the business of baseball, and its owners, past and present. Casey Award Winner.

The National Game, Alfred E. Spink, National Game Publishing, (1910), No DJ Issued .... $800-$1,000
Classic early history packed with key data.

New Bill James Historical Baseball Abstract, Bill James, Simon & Schuster, (2001) $25

Only the Ball Was White, Robert Peterson, Prentice Hall, (1970) $125
This pioneering history of Negro League baseball is a must for anyone interested in this popular topic.

Season Ticket, by Roger Angell, Houghton-Mifflin, (1988) $15

Shoeless Joe, W. P. Kinsella, Houghton Mifflin, (1982) .. more than $75

The novel that *Field of Dreams* was based on, *Shoeless Joe* is highly sought-after by collectors of American fiction as well as collectors of great baseball books.

The Summer Game, by Roger Angell, Viking (1972) .... $40-$80

Ty Cobb, Charles C. Alexander, Oxford University Press, (1984) $50
This great biography of baseball's fiercest immortal was underestimated and underprinted by its original publisher.

The Ultimate Baseball Book, edited by Dan Okrent and Harry Levine, Houghton Mifflin, (1979).. $75
Great photos and superb writing by an all-star lineup highlight this coffee-table spectacular.

Veeck as in Wreck, Bill Veeck and Ed Linn, Putman, (1962) . $75-$100
Baseball's maverick promoter tells how it's done in a consistently entertaining and seldom-offered-for-sale book.

Who's Who in Major League Baseball, Harold Johnson, Buxton Publishing, (1933) .... $400-$600
Full page sepia studio photos of all players in civilian clothes with brief biography. One of a kind, proved too expensive to reissue annually as was planned.

Why Time Begins on Opening Day, by Tom Boswell, Doubleday (1984) $20

Biographies/Autobiographies
(arranged by subject's name)

I Had a Hammer, by Hank Aaron with Lonnie Wheeler, Harper/Collins (1991) $10

The Hank Aaron Story, by Milton Shapiro, Messner (1961) $15

Aaron R.F., by Henry Aaron and Furman Bisher, World (1968) .... $75-$100

Hank Aaron—Quiet Superstar, by Al Hirshberg, Putnam (1974) $75

Hank Aaron 715, by Pat Reshen, Arco (1974) $30

The Man Who Made Milwaukee Famous, by Don Money (Hank Aaron), Agape (1976) $45

Ol' Pete: The Grover Cleveland Alexander Story, by Jack Kavanagh, Diamond Communications (1996) $18

Crash, by Tom Whitaker and Dick Allen, Ticknor & Fields (1989) .... $15-$25

You Can't Beat the Hours, by Mel Allen and Ed Fitzgerald, Harper (1964) $45

The Bob Allison Story, by Hal Butler, Messner (1967)................ $75

My Life in Baseball, by Felipe Alou with Herm Weiskopf, Word (1967) $30

Alston and the Dodgers, Walter Alston with Si Burick, Doubleday (1966).. $30

A Year at a Time, by Walt Alston and Jack Tobin, Word (1976) $25

Bless You Boys, Sparky Anderson with Dan Ewald (1984 season recap), Contemporary (1984) $25

Sparky!, by Sparky Anderson with Dan Ewald, Prentice Hall (1990).. $40

They Call Me Sparky, by Sparky Anderson and Dan Ewald, Sleeping Bear Press (1999) $18

Sleeper Cars and Flannel Uniforms: A Lifetime of Memories, by Elden Auker with Tom Keegan, Triumph (2001) $15

Mr. Cub, by Ernie Banks and Jim Enright, Follet (1971) $75

My Fifty Years in Baseball, by Edward Barrow and James Kahn, Coward McCann (1951) $75

Rowdy Richard, by Dick Bartell and Norman Macht, North Atlantic (1987) $25

Don Baylor, by Don Baylor and Claire Smith, St. Martins (1989) $10

Bo—Pitching and Wooing, by Maury Allen (Bo Belinsky), Dial (1973).. $30

Hardball, by George Bell with Bob Elliot, Key Porter (1990) $25

From Behind the Plate, by Johnny Bench with George Kalinsky, Rutledge (1972) $30

Johnny Bench—King of the Catchers, by Lou Sabin, Putnam (1977) $75

Catch You Later, by Johnny Bench with William Brashler, Harper & Row (1979).. $30

Moe Berg—Athlete, Scholar, Spy, by Lewis Kaufman, et. al., Little, Brown (1974) $50

The Catcher Was a Spy, by Nicholas Dawidoff (Moe Berg), Pantheon (1994) $12

Yogi Berra—The Muscle Man, by Ben Epstein, Barnes (1951) $150

Yogi Berra, by Joe Trimble, Barnes (1952)................................. $75

The Yogi Berra Story, by Gene Roswell, Messner (1958) $75

Yogi, Yogi Berra with Ed Fitzgerald, Doubleday (1961) $20

The Story of Yogi Berra, by Gene Schoor, Doubleday (1976), HC $50

Yogi, It Ain't Over, Yogi Berra with Tom Horton, McGraw Hill (1989).. $10

When You Come to a Fork in the Road, Take It! Inspiration and Wisdom from One of Baseball's Greatest Heroes, by Yogi Berra with David Kaplan, Hyperion (2001) $10

The Wit and Wisdom of Yogi Berra, by Phil Pepe, Hawthorn (1974).. $20

Ewell Blackwell, by Lou Smith, Barnes (1951) $65

Vida, His Own Story, by Vida Blue and Bill Libby, Prentice Hall (1972).. $25

Vida Blue—Coming Up Again, by Don Kowet, Putnam (1974)........$12

Barry Bonds: Baseball's Super Star, by Steven Travers, Sports Publishing (2002) $18

This Gracious Season: Barry Bonds and the Greatest Year in Baseball, by Josh Suchon, Winter Publications (2002)......... $25

Lou Boudreau, Covering All the Bases, by Lou Boudreau and Russell Schneider, Sagamore (1993) $22

Player-Manager, Lou Boudreau with Ed Fitzgerald, Little, Brown (1949) $75

I'm Glad You Didn't Take It Personally, by Jim Bouton with Leonard Schecter, Morrow (1971) $12

I Managed Good, But Boy Did They Play Bad, Jim Bouton with Neil Offen, Playboy (1973) $12

Ball Four Plus Five: An Update (1970-80), by Jim Bouton, Stein & Day (1981) $15

Ken Boyer, by Jack Zanger, Nelson (1965) $75

You Can't Hit the Ball With the Bat on Your Shoulder, by Bobby Bragan and Jeff Guinn, Summit (1992) $25

George Brett: Last of a Breed, by Steve Cameron, Taylor Publishing (1993) $20

The George Brett Story, by John Garrity, Coward McCann & Geoghegan (1981) $35

Stealing Is My Game, by Lou Brock with Franz Schulze, Prentice Hall (1976) $65

Jim Bunning, by Frank Dolson, Temple (1998) $30

The Jim Bunning Story, by Jim Bunning and Ralph Bernstein, Lippincott (1965) $40

Roy Campanella, by Dick Young, Grosset & Dunlap (1952) $75

It's Good to Be Alive, by Roy Campanella, Little, Brown (1959) $45

Roy Campanella—Man of Courage, by Gene Schoor, Putnam (1959) $75

Carew, by Rod Carew and Ira Berkow, Simon & Schuster (1979) ...$25

A Dream Season, by Gary Carter and John Hough Jr. (recaps 1986 season), HBJ (1987) $10

The Gamer, by Gary Carter, Word (1993) $30

Baby Bull: From Hardball to Hard Time and Back, by Orlando Cepeda with Herb Fagen, Taylor, (1998) $20

The Orlando Cepeda Story, by Bruce Markusen, Arte Publico Press (2001) $12

My Ups & Downs in Baseball, by Orlando Cepeda, Putnam (1968) $75

Orlando Cepeda, by Bob Stevens and Richard Keller, Woodford (1987) $25

Hal Chase, by Martin D. Kohout, McFarland (2001), SC $25

Rocket Man, by Roger Clemens with Peter Gammons, S. Greene (1987) .... $40-$50

Clemente, by Kal Wagenheim (Roberto Clemente), Praeger (1973) $35

The Life of Roberto Clemente, by Paul Robert Walker, HBJ (1988) $10

Roberto Clemente, The Great One, by Bruce Markusen, Sports Publishing (1998) $20

Who Was Roberto, by Phil Musick, Doubleday (1974).............. $65

Ty Cobb—Idol of Baseball Fandom, by Sverre Braathen, Avondale (1928), No DJ Issued $800

The Tiger Wore Spikes, by John McCallum (Ty Cobb), Barnes (1956) $45

My Life in Baseball—The True Record, by Ty Cobb with Al Stump, Doubleday (1961) .... $40-$75

The Ty Cobb Scrapbook, by Marc Okkonen, Sterling (2001) $15

Ty Cobb—The Greatest, by Robert Rubin, Putnam (1978)........ $75

Mickey Cochrane, by Charlie Bevis, McFarland (1998), SC....... $25

Don't Knock the Rock, by Gordon Cobbledick (Rocky Colavito), World (1966) .... $150-$300

Commy, The Life Story of the Grand Old Roman of Baseball, by G.W. Axelson and Charles A. Comiskey, The Reilly & Lee Co. (1919).. $150-$250

A Pitcher's Story: Innings With David Cone, by Roger Angell, Warner (2001) $8

Seeing It Through, by Tony Conigliaro with Jack Zanger, MacMillan (1970)... $15

Tony C: The Triumph and Tragedy of Tony Conigliaro, by David Cataneo, Rutledge Hill (1997) $15

Jocko, by Jocko Conlon and Robert Creamer, Lippincott (1967) $25

Inside Pitch, by Roger Craig and Vern Plagenhoef (pitching coach recaps 1984 Detroit Tigers season, Eerdmans (1984), SC . $10

Slugging It Out in Japan, by Warren Cromartie and Robert Whiting, Kodansha Intl. (1991).. $20

When in Doubt, Fire the Manager, by Alvin Dark and John Underwood, Dutton (1980).. $20-$25

Born to Play: The Eric Davis Story, by Eric Davis and Ralph Wiley, Viking (1999) $6

The Tommy Davis Story, by Patrick Russell, Doubleday (1969)........$75

America's Dizzy Dean, by Curt Smith, Bethany Press (1978)... $17-$25

Diz, by Robert Gregory, Viking (1992) $15

Ol' Diz, by Vince Staten, HarperCollins (1992) $12

Real Grass, Real Heroes, by Dom DiMaggio and Bill Gilbert, Zebra Books (1990) $15

DiMaggio: Setting the Record Straight, by Morris Engelberg and Marv Schneider, MBI (2003) $20

Joe DiMaggio, The Hero's Life, by Richard Ben Cramer, Simn & Schuster (2000)... $15

Joe DiMaggio, Yankee Clipper, by Tom Meany, Barnes (1951) .. $65

Where Have You Gone Joe DiMaggio?, by Maury Allen, Dutton (1975) $25

The DiMaggio Albums, by Richard Whittingham (two volumes), Putnam (1982) .... $25-$40

Joe DiMaggio, by George DeGregorio, Scarborough (1981) $30

Joe DiMaggio: Baseball's Yankee Clipper, by Jack B. Moore, Praeger (1987), SC $15

Pride Against Prejudice, by Joseph Thomas Moore (Larry Doby), Praeger (1988), SC $20

One Last Round for the Shuffler, by Tom Clark (Shufflin Phil Douglas), Truck Books (1979), SC $35

The Don Drysdale Story, by Milton Shapiro, Messner (1964) $75

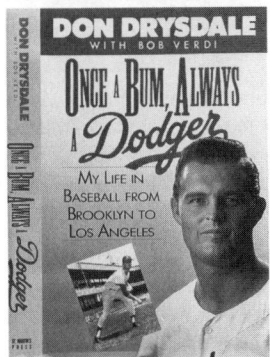

Once a Bum, Always a Dodger, by Don Drysdale with Bob Verdi, St. Martins (1990) $10

The Comeback, by Ryne Duren and Robert Drury, Lorenz (1978), HC $45

The Leo Durocher Story, by Gene Schoor, Messner (1955) $10

The Lip: A Biography of Leo Duracher, by Gerald Eskenazi, Morrow (1993) $10

Nice Guys Finish Last, by Leo Durocher and Ed Linn, Simon & Schuster (1975) $35

Nails, Lenny Dykstra with Marty Noble, Doubleday (1987) $25

Dock Ellis in the Country of Baseball, by Dock Ellis and Donald Hall, Coward McCann (1976) .... $20-$25

Umpiring From the Inside, by Billy Evans, self-published (1947) .. $150

Strikeout Story, by Bob Feller, Barnes (1947) .... $50-$90

Bob Feller, by Gene Schoor, Doubleday (1962) .... $50-$60

Now Pitching, Bob Feller/A Baseball Memoir, by Bob Feller with Bill Gilbert, Birch Lane Press (1990) $15

No Big Deal, by Mark Fidrych with Tom Clark, Lippincott (1977) $20

Yankee Stranger, by Ed Figueroa and Dorothy Harshman, Exposition Press (1982) .... $35-$50

The Way It Is, by Curt Flood, Pocket Books (1972) $60

Slick, by Whitey Ford and Phil Pepe, Morrow (1987) $40

Whitey and Mickey, by Whitey Ford, Mickey Mantle and Joe Durso, Viking (1977) $15

The George Foster Story, by Malka Drucker with George Foster, Holiday House (1979) $25

The Best Pitcher in Baseball: The Life of Rube Foster, Negro League Giant, by Robert Charles Cottrell, New York University Press (2001) $25

Little Nel: The Nellie Fox Story, by David Gough and Jim Bard, Megbec Publishing (2000), SC $20

Double X: Jimmie Foxx Baseball's Forgotten Slugger, by Bob Gorman, Holy Name Society (1990) $15

Jimmie Foxx, by W. Harrison Daniel, McFarland (1996) $25

Behind the Mask, by Bill Freehan, World (1970) $30

Frank Frisch—The Fordham Flash, by Frank Frisch and J. Roy Stockton, Doubleday (1962) $65

Garvey, by Steve Garvey with Skip Rozin, Times (1986) $12

Lou Gehrig—Pride of the Yankees, by Paul Gallico, Grosset & Dunlap (1942) $35

Lou Gehrig—Boy of the Sand Lots, by Guernsey Van Riper, Bobbs-Merrill (1949) $25

Iron Horse, by Ray Robinson (Lou Gehrig), Norton (1990) $17

Take Time for Paradise, by A. Bartlett Giamatti, Summit (1989) $10

From Ghetto to Glory, by Bob Gibson with Phil Pepe, Prentice Hall (1968) $50

A Stranger to the Game, by Bob Gibson with Lonnie Wheeler, Viking (1994) .... $20-$30

Josh Gibson, by William Brashler, Harper & Row (1978).... $75-$95

None but the Braves, by Tom Glavine with Nick Cafardo, HarperCollins (1996) $10

Rookie, by Richard Woodley (Dwight Gooden), Doubleday (1985) . $10

Dwight Gooden—Strikeout King, by Nathan Aaseng, Lerner (1988) .$8

One Armed Wonder, by William C. Kashatus (Pete Gray), McFarland (1995), SC $18

The Story of My Life, by Hank Greenberg with Ira Berkow, Times Books (1989) .... $22-$30

Calvin: Baseball's Last Dinosaur, by Jon Kerr (Calvin Griffith), William C. Brown (1990) SC $15

Jolly Cholly's Story, by Charlie Grimm and Ed Prell, Regnery (1968) .... $25-$40

Lefty Grove, by Jim Kaplan, SABR (2000), SC $13

Guidry, by Ron Guidry and Peter Golenbock, Prentice Hall (1980) $20

Tony!, by Tony Gwynn and Jim Geschke, Contempory (1986) $25

Hawk, by Ken Harrelson and Al Hirshberg, Viking (1969) $25

Off Base, by Rickey Henderson with John Shea, Harper/Collins (1992) $10

If at First, by Keith Hernandez and Mike Bryan, McGraw Hill (1986) $15

The Duke of Havana, by Steve Fainaru and Ray Sanchez, Villard (2001), Orlando Hernandez $15

Out of the Blue, by Orel Hershiser and Jerry Jenkins, Wolgemuth & Hyatt (1989) $8

White Rat, by Whitey Herzog with Kevin Horrigan, Harper & Row (1987) $10

The High Hard One, by Kirby Higbe and Martin Quigley, Viking (1967) .... $40-$50

Gil Hodges: The Quiet Man, by Marino Amoruso, Erickson (1991) .. $25

My War With Baseball, by Rogers Hornsby with Bill Surface, Coward-McCann (1962) $70

The Willie Horton Story, by Hal Butler, Messner (1970) $25

The Jocks Itch, by Tom House, Contemporary (1989) $15

Elston and Me: The Story of the First Black Yankee, by Arlene Howard and Ralph Wimbish, University of Missouri Press (2001), Elston Howard $25

Frank Howard: The Gentle Giant, by Al Hirshberg, Putnam (1973) .. $40

Between the Lines, by Steve Howe with Jim Greenfield, Masters (1989) $12

Catfish, Million Dollar Pitcher, by Bill Libby (Jim Hunter), Coward McCann (1976) $12

Catfish Hunter, by Irwin Stambler, Putnam (1976) $20

Catfish, by Jim Catfish Hunter and Armen Keteyian, McGraw Hill (1988) $10

Bo Knows Bo, by Bo Jackson with Dick Schaap, Doubleday (1990) ..$8

Reggie Jackson, The $3 Million Man, by Maury Allen, Harvey (1978) $15

The Reggie Jackson Story, by Bill Libby, Lothrop (1979) $20

Reggie, by Reggie Jackson with Mike Lupica, Villard (1984) $15

Mr. October, by Maury Allen (Reggie Jackson), Times (1981) .. $20

Say It Ain't So Joe—The Story of Shoeless Joe Jackson, by Donald Gropman, Little, Brown (1979) .... $50-$60

Shoeless Joe and Ragtime Baseball, by Harvey Frommer (Shoeless Joe Jackson), Taylor (1992) $15

Shoeless, The Life and Times of Joe Jackson, by David L. Fleitz, McFarland (2001), SC $25

Like Nobody Else, by Ferguson Jenkins and George Vass, Regnery (1973) $30

The Golden Boy: A Biography of Jackie Jensen, by George I. Martin, Randall (2000), SC $14

Derek Jeter: The Life You Imagine, by Derek Jeter and Jack Curry, Crown (2000) $15

The Tommy John Story, by Tommy and Sally John with Joe Muser, Revell (1978) $8

Ban Johnson, by Gene Murdock, Greenwood (1982) $75

Walter Johnson, by Roger Treat, Messner (1948) $100

Walter Johnson, A Life, by Jack Kavanagh, Diamond Communications (1996), SC, MacMillan/SABR Research Award winner $15

Walter Johnson—Baseball's Big Train, by Henry Thomas, Phenom (1995) .... $30-$40

Temporary Insanity, by Jay Johnstone with Rick Talley, Contemporary (1985) $10

Over the Edge, by Jay Johnstone with Rick Talley, Contemporary (1987) $10

Cleon, by Cleon Jones with Ed Hershey, Coward McCann (1970) . $25

Addie Joss: King of Pitchers, by Scott Longert, SABR (1998), SC $15

The Al Kaline Story, by Al Hirshberg, Messner (1964) ...... $60-$100

Al Kaline and the Detroit Tigers, by Hal Butler, Regnery (1973) $70

Still Pitching, by Jim Kaat, Triumph (2003) $18

Hello Everybody, I'm George Kell, by George Kell with Dan Ewald, Sports Publishing (1998) $25

Slide, Kelly, Slide: The Wild Life of Mike "King" Kelly, by Marty Appel, Scarecrow (1996), Casey Award Winner $35

The Harmon Killebrew Story, by Hal Butler, Messner (1966) $95

Harmon Killebrew, Baseball's Superstar, Deseret (1971).......... $85

Ralph Kiner, The Heir Apparent, by Tom Meany, Barnes (1951).....$45

Kiner's Korner, by Ralph Kiner and Joe Gergen, Arbor (1987)... $10

Jim Konstanty, by Frank Yeutter, Barnes (1951) $75

Sandy Koufax: A Lefty's Legacy, by Janet Leavy, HarperCollins (2002) $12

Sandy Koufax—Strikeout King, Arnold Hano, Putnam (1964) ... $70

Koufax, by Sandy Koufax with Ed Linn, Viking (1966)......... $50-$85

Hardball, by Bowie Kuhn, Times (1987) $10

Judge Landis and 25 Years of Baseball, by J.G. Taylor Spink, Crowell (1947) $22

The Perfect Yankee: The Incredible Story of the Greatest Miracle in Baseball, by Don Larsen and Mark Shaw, Sports Publishing (2001) $13

The Artful Dodger, by Tommy Lasorda with David Fisher, Arbor House (1985) $15

The Wrong Stuff, by Bill Lee with Dick Lally, Viking (1984) $20

Breakout, by Ron LeFlore with Jim Hawkins, Harper & Row (1978) $15

Prophet of the Sandlots, by Mark Winegardner (scout Tony Luccadello), Atlantic Monthly (1990) $15

Al Lopez, by Wes Singletary, McFarland (1999), SC $25

Fred Lynn, Young Star, by Bill Libby, Putnam (1977)................. $15

Fred Lynn, The Hero from Boston, by Ed Dolan and Richard Lyttle, Icarus (1982) $25

My 66 Years in the Big Leagues, by Connie Mack, Winston (1950) .... $50-$75

The MacPhails: Baseball's First Family of the Front Office, by G. Richard McKelvey, McFarland (2000), SC $22

My Nine Innings, by Lee MacPhail, Meckler (1989) $15

Close Shave: The Life and Times of Baseball's Sal Maglie, by James D. Szalontai, McFarland (2002), SC $25

The Sal Maglie Story, by Milton Shapiro, Messner (1957) ..... $75-$100

The Mickey Mantle Story, by Mickey Mantle and Ben Epstein, Holt (1953) $150

My Favorite Summer 1956, by Mickey Mantle and Phil Pepe, Doubleday (1991).. $10

Mickey Mantle—Yankee Slugger, by Milton Shapiro, Messner (1962) .... $100-$150

Mickey Mantle: America's Prodigal Son, by Tony Castro, Brassey's (2002).. $20

Mickey Mantle—Mr. Yankee, by Al Silverman, Putnam (1963)... $75-$100

The Quality of Courage, by Mickey Mantle, Doubleday (1964)... $50-$60

The Mick, by Mickey Mantle with Herb Gluck, Doubleday
(1985) $25
A Pitcher's Story, by Juan Marichal with Charles Einstein,
Doubleday (1967) $50
Roger Maris: A Man for All Seasons, by Maury Allen, Donald Fine &
Co. (1986) .... $30-$50
Roger Maris: A Title to Fame, by Harvey Rosenfeld, Praire House
(1991) $15
Rube Marquard, by Larry D. Mansch, McFarland (1998), SC $22
The Return of Billy the Kid, by Norman Lewis Smith
(Billy Martin), Coward McCann (1977) $17

Billy Martin, by Gene Schoor, Doubleday (1980) $17
Billyball, Billy Martin with Phil Pepe, Doubleday (1987) $10
The Last Yankee, by David Falkner (Billy Martin), Simon & Schuster
(1992) $20
Wild, High and Tight, by Peter Golenbock (Billy Martin),
St. Martins (1994) $10
The Eddie Mathews Story, by Al Hirshberg, Messner
(1961) .... $75-$125

Eddie Mathews and the National Pastime, by Eddie Mathews and
Bob Buege, Douglas American (1994) $25
Pitching in a Pinch, by Christy Mathewson, Putnam (1912) $350
Christy Mathewson, by Gene Schoor with Henry Gilfond, Messner
(1953) .... $90-$125
They Call Me Sarge, by Fred Mitchell with Gary Matthews, Bonus
(1985), SC $35
The Willie Mays Story, by Ken Smith, Greenberg (1954) $100
Born to Play Ball, Willie Mays and Charles Einstein, Putnam
(1955) .... $45-$65

Willie Mays Story, by Milton Shapiro, Messner (1960) ...... $75-$100

Mays, Mantle, Snider/A Celebration, by Donald Honig,
MacMillan (1987) .... $30-$40
The Willie Mays Album, by Howard Liss, Hawthorn (1966) $65
My Life In and Out of Baseball, by Willie Mays and Charles
Einstein, Dutton (1966) .... $30-$40
Willie Mays—Baseball Superstar, by Sam and Beryl Epstein,
Garrard (1975) .... $40-$60
Willie's Time, by Charles Einstein (Willie Mays), Lippincott (1979)..$15
Say Hey, Willie Mays, with Lou Sahadi, Simon & Schuster (1988)..$10
Oh, Baby, I Love It, by Tim McCarver with Ray Robinson, Villard
(1987) $8
A Funny Thing Happened on the Way to Cooperstown, by Mickey
McDermott with Eisenberg, Triumph (2003) $20
John McGraw, by Charles C. Alexander, Viking (1988) $10
Screwball, by Tug McGraw and Joe Durso, Houghton-Mifflin
(1974) $10
Mark McGwire: Home Run Hero, by Rob Rains, St. Martins
(1998) $10
Nobody's Perfect, by Denny McLain with Dave Diles, Dial
(1975) $15
Strikeout, by Denny McLain with Mike Nahrstedt, Sporting News
(1988) $10
Safe by a Mile, by Charlie Metro with Tom Altherr, University of
Nebraska Press (2002), SC $25
Joe Morgan: A Life in Baseball, by Joe Morgan with David Falkner,
Norton (1993) $8
Thurman Munson—Pressure Player, by Bill Libby, Putnam
(1978) .... $30-$50
Thurman Munson, by Thurman Munson with Martin Appel, Coward
McCann (1978) $35
Thurman Munson, by Christopher Devine, McFarland (2001), SC..$25
Ask Dale Murphy, by Dale Murphy with Curtis Patton, Algonquin
(1987) $12

Stan Musial—The Man, by Tom Meany, Barnes (1951) $40
The Stan Musial Story, by Gene Schoor and Henry Gilfond,
Messner (1955) $35
Stan Musial—The Man, by Irv Goodman, Nelson (1961) $30
Stan Musial, by Ray Robinson, Putnam (1963) .... $75-$100

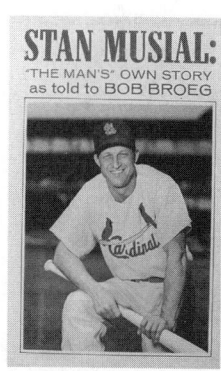

Stan Musial—The Man's Own Story, by Stan Musial and Bob Broeg, Doubleday (1964) ....$40-$50

The Man, Stan Musial, Then and Now, Stan Musial and Bob Broeg, Bethany (1977) $45

Musial: From Stash to Stan the Man, by James N. Giglio, University of Missouri Press (2001) $35

A Tiger in His Time, by David Jordan, Diamond (1990), (Hal Newhouser) $25

Knuckler—The Phil Niekro Story, Wilfred Binette, Hallux Bros. (1970) $20

Knuckleballs, by Phil Niekro and Tom Bird, Freundlich (1986) ... $15

Sadahura Oh, by Sadahura Oh and David Falkner, Times (1984) ..$30

Baseball's Best Kept Secret: Al Oliver and his time in Baseball, by Al Oliver and Andrew O'Toole, City of Champions (1997).....$25

Mel Ott, by Fred Stein, McFarland (1999), SC $25

Don't Look Back: Satchel Paige in the Shadows of Baseball, by Mark Ribowsky, Simon & Schuster (1994) $12

Pitchin' Man, by Satchel Paige and Hal Lebovitz, Cleveland News (1948), SC $35

Maybe I'll Pitch Forever, by Satchel Paige and David Lipman, Doubleday (1962) $65

Andy Pafko—The Solid Man, by John Hoffman, Barnes (1951) $65

Behind the Mask, by Dave Pallone and Alan Steinberg, Viking (1990) $8

Out at Home, by Milt Pappas and Larry Names, Angel Press (2000) $20

Joe, You Coulda Made Us Proud, by Joe Pepitone and Barry Stainback, Playboy (1975).....................................$25

Me and the Spitter, by Gaylord Perry and Bob Sudyk, Sunday Review Press (1974) $45

Fear Strikes Out, by Jim Piersall and Al Hishberg, Little Brown (1955) $50

The Truth Hurts, by Jimmy Piersall, Contemporary (1984) $15

Sweet Lou, by Lou Piniella and Maury Allen, Putnam (1986) $15

Snap Me Perfect, by Darrell Porter and William Deerfield, Nelson (1984) $8

Kirby Puckett—Fan Favorite, by Ann Bauleke (biography for younger readers), Lerner (1993) $15

I Love This Game, by Kirby Puckett with Mike Bryan, Harper/Collins (1993) $8

Ted Double Duty Radcliffe, by Kyle McNary, McNary (1994), SC $30

Phil Regan, by Phil Regan and James Hefley, Zondervan (1968)...$30

The Bobby Richardson Story, by Bobby Richardson, Revell (1965).$15

Branch Rickey, by Arthur Mann, Houghton-Mifflin (1957) $30

Branch Rickey, by Murray Polner, Atheneum (1982) $45

Branch Rickey in Pittsburgh, by Andrew O'Toole, McFarland (2000), SC $23

Iron Man: The Cal Ripken, Jr. Story, by Harvey Rosenfeld, St. Martins (1995) $10

The Only Way I Know, by Cal Ripken Jr. and Mike Bryan, Viking (1997) $10

Phil Rizzuto, by Joe Trimble, Barnes (1951) $30

Phil Rizzuto: A Yankee Tradition, by Dan Hirshberg, Sagamore (1993) $25

O Holy Cow! The Selected Verse of Phil Rizzuto, by Hart Seely and Tom Peyer, Ecco (1993) $10

The Brooks Robinson Story, by Jack Zanger, Messner (1967) .. $15

Putting It All Together, by Brooks Robinson and Fred Bauer, Hawthorn (1971) ....$20-$30

Third Base Is My Home, by Brooks Robinson and Jack Tobin, Word (1974)..$20-$30

Extra Innings, by Frank Robinson and Berry Stainback, McGraw-Hill (1988) $15

My Life in Baseball, by Frank Robinson and Al Silverman, Doubleday (1975)..$15-$20

Jackie Robinson, by Arnold Rampersand, Knopf (1997) $15

Jackie Robinson: Race, Sports, and the American Dream, by Joseph Dorinson and Joram Warmund, M.E. Sharpe (1998) $30

My Own Story, by Jackie Robinson and Wendell Smith, Greenberg (1948) ....$200-$300

The Jackie Robinson Story, by Arthur Mann, FJ Low (1950), SC $55

Wait Till Next Year, by Jackie Robinson and Carl Rowan, Random House (1960)..$50-$70

Jackie Robinson of the Brooklyn Dodgers, by Milton Shapiro, Messner (1957)..$40

Jackie Robinson—Baseball's Gallant Fighter, by Sam and Beryl Epstein, Garrard (1974) $45

Jackie Robinson—A Life Remembered, by Maury Allen, Watts (1987)..$25

I Never Had It Made, by Jackie Robinson and Alfred Duckett, Putnam (1972) $35

Uncle Robbie, by Jack Kavanagh and Norman Macht, SABR (1999), SC, Wilbert Robinson $15

The Pete Rose Story, by Pete Rose, World (1970) $27

Pete Rose, They Call Him Charlie Hustle, by Bill Libby, Putnam (1972)..$20

Charlie Hustle, by Pete Rose with Bob Hertzel, Prentice Hall (1975) $10

Collision at Home Plate, by James Reston, Jr., Burlingame (1991), (Pete Rose) $75

Pete Rose, Mr. .300, by Keith Brandt, Putnam (1977) $12

Pete Rose, My Life in Baseball, by Pete Rose, Doubleday (1979) ..$25

Pete Rose: My Story, by Pete Rose with Roger Kahn, MacMillan (1989) $7.50

Hustle: The Myth, Life and Lies of Pete Rose, by Michael Y. Sokolove, Simon & Schuster (1990).................... $15

Glory Days With the Dodgers, by John Roseboro and Bill Libby, Atheneum (1978) $30

Super Scout—Thirty Five Years of Major League Scouting, by Jim Russo and Bob Hammel, Bonus (1992) $15

Babe Ruth, by Tom Meany, Barnes (1947) .... $30-$50

The Babe Ruth Story, by Babe Ruth and Bob Considine, Dutton (1948) $50

Babe Ruth—Baseball Boy, by Guernsey Van Riper, Bobbs-Merrill (1954) $25

Babe Ruth, His Story in Baseball, by Lee Allen, Putnam (1966) $17.50

Babe Ruth's America, by Robert Smith, Crowell (1974)............. $40

Babe Ruth: His Life and Legend, by Karl Wagenheim, Praeger (1974) .... $25-$35

The Life That Ruth Built, by Marshall Smelser (Babe Ruth), Quadrangle (1975) $50

Babe Ruth—Sultan of Swat, by Lois P. Nicholson, Goodwood (1994) $20

Nolan Ryan - Fireballer, by Bill Libby, Putnam (1975) .... $75-$100

Nolan Ryan: The Road to Cooperstown, by Nolan Ryan and T.R. Sullivan, Addax (1999) $20

Throwing Heat, by Nolan Ryan and Harvey Frommer, Doubleday (1988) $15

Miracle Man: Nolan Ryan, by Nolan Ryan with Jerry Jenkins, Word (1992) $10

Second to None, by Ryne Sandberg and Barry Rozner, Bonus (1995) $20

Ron Santo: For Love of Ivy, by Ron Santo with Randy Minkoff, Bonus (1993) $15

Sax!, by Steve Sax and Steve Delsohn, Contemporary (1986) .. $15

Clowning Through Baseball, by Al Schact, Barnes (1941) $30

Mike Schmidt, by William C. Kashatus, McFarland (2000), SC .. $22

Red, A Baseball Life, by Red Schoendienst with Rob Rains, Sports Publishing (1998) $12

Tom Seaver of the Mets, by George Sullivan, Putnam (1971).... $20

Inside Corner—Talks with Tom Seaver, by Joel Cohen, Atheneum (1974) $30

Tom Seaver—Portrait of a Pitcher, by Malka Drucker with Tom Seaver, Holiday (1978) $20

Seaver, by Gene Schoor (Tom Seaver), Contemporary (1986) .. $10

The Blooper Man, by Elson Smith (Rip Sewell), J. Pohl (1981), SC. $20

The Ted Simmons Story, by Jim Brosnan, Putnam (1977) $20

Country Hardball, by Enos Slaughter and Kevin Reid, Tudor (1981) $90

Wizard, by Ozzie Smith with Rob Rains, Contemporary (1982). $25

The Duke Snider Story, by Irwin Winehouse, Messner (1964) ... $30

The Duke of Flatbush, by Duke Snider with Bill Gilbert, Zebra (1988) $10

Indian Summer, by Brian McDonald, Rodale (2003), Louis Sockalexis $18

Louis Sockalexis: The First Cleveland Indian, by David Fleitz, McFarland (2002), SC $20

Sosa, by Sammy Sosa with Marcos Breton, Warner (2000) $6

A.G. Spalding and the Rise of Baseball, by Peter Levine, Oxford (1985) $15

Willie Stargell, by Bill Libby, Putnam (1973) $10

Willie Stargell—An Autobiography, by Willie Stargell and Tom Bird, Harper & Row (1984) $25

Rusty Staub of the Expos, by John Robertson, Prentice Hall (1971) $45

Casey Stengel—Baseball's Greatest Manager, by Gene Schoor, Messner (1953) .... $75-$90

Casey Stengel, by Frank Graham Jr., John Day (1958) $30

Casey at the Bat, by Casey Stengel and Harry T. Paxton, Random House (1962) $25

Casey, by Joseph Durso (Casey Stengel), Prentice Hall (1967)... $25-$35

Casey Stengel, by Norman MacLean, Drake (1976)................. $40

Stengel: His Life and Times, by Robert W. Creamer, Simon & Schuster (1984).. $10

Tomorrow, I'll Be Perfect, by Dave Stieb and Kevin Boland, Doubleday (1986) $20

Darryl, by Darryl Strawberry and Art Rust Jr., Bantam (1992) $8

Sunday at the Ballpark: Billy Sunday's Professional Baseball Career 1883-1890, by Wendy Knickerbocker, Scarecrow Press (2000) $30

Birdie: Confessions of a Baseball Nomad, by Birdie Tebbetts with James Morrison $15

Triumph Born of Tragedy, by Andre Thornton and Al Janssen, Harvest House (1983) $25

El Tiante, by Luis Tiant and Joe Fitzgerald, Doubleday (1976).. $35

Fernando!, by Mike Littwin (Fernando Valenzuela), Bantam (1981) .$10

The Hustlers Handbook, by Bill Veeck with Ed Linn, Putnam (1965) $35

The Kid from Cuba, James Terzian (Zoilo Versailles), Doubleday (1967)... $40-$50

The Ginger Kid, by Irving Stein (Buck Weaver), Brown and Benchmark (1992) $25

It's What You Learn After You Know It All That Counts, by Earl Weaver and Barry Stainback, Doubleday (1982) .... $25-$35

The Last Commissioner, by Fay Vincent, Simon & Schuster (2002) $18

Omar: My Life on and off the Field, by Omar Vizquel and Bob Dyer, Gray & Company (2002) $20

Rube Waddell, by Alan H. Levy, McFarland (2000), SC $25

Honus Wagner, by Arthur D. Hittner, McFarland (1996), Seymour Medal winner $35

Honus Wagner, by Dennis and Jeanne DeValeria, Henry Holt (1996) $12

Big and Little Poison, by Clifton Blue Parker (Paul and Lloyd Waner), McFarland (2002), SC $25

Baseball's Radical for all Seasons: A Biography of John Montgomery Ward, by David Stevens, Scarecrow (1998)...................... $35

A Clever Base-Ballist: The Life and Times of John Montgomery Ward, by Brian DiSalvatore, Pantheon (1999) $18

Five O'Clock Comes Early, by Bob Welch and George Vecsey, Morrow (1982).. $20

Memories of a Ballplayer: Bill Werber and Baseball in the 1930s, by Bill Werber and C. Paul Rogers III, University of Nebraska Press (2001), SC.. $12

Billy, the Classic Hitter, by Billy Williams and Irv Haag, Rand McNally (1974) $50

Ted Williams, by Arthur Sampson, Barnes (1950) $45

My Turn at Bat, by Ted Williams with John Underwood, Simon & Schuster (1969).. $45

Ted Williams: Seasons of the Kid, by Richard Cramer, Prentice Hall (1991).. $45

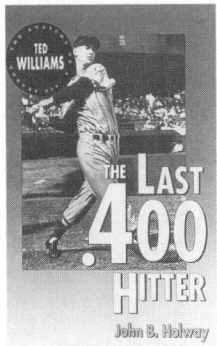

The Last .400 Hitter, by John B. Holway (Ted Williams), William C. Brown (1991)... $20

Ted Williams—A Baseball Life, by Michael Seidel, Contemporary (1991) $20

It Pays to Steal, by Maury Wills and Steve Gardner, Prentice Hall (1963) $20

How to Steal a Pennant, by Maury Wills and Don Freeman, Putnam (1976) $12

On the Run, by Maury Wills and Mike Celizic, Carroll & Graf (1991) $15

Fouled Away: Baseball Tragedy of Hack Wilson, by Clifton Blue Parker, McFarland (2000), SC $25

Hack, by Robert Boone and Gerald Grunska (Hack Wilson), Highland Press (1978) .... $40-$50

Dave Winfield—23 Million Dollar Man, by Gene Schoor, Stein & Day (1982) $30

Winfield—A Player's Life, by Dave Winfield with Tom Parker, Norton (1988) $8

Dave Winfield—3,000 and Counting, by the St. Paul Pioneer Press, Andrews & McMeel (1993) $15

Philip K. Wrigley, by Paul Angle, Rand McNally (1975) $65

Yaz, by Carl Yastrzemski with Al Hirshberg, Viking (1968) $20

Yaz, Baseball, the Wall and Me, by Carl Yastrzemski and Gerald Eskanazk, Doubleday (1990) $15

Batting, by Carl Yastrzemski with Al Hirshberg, Viking (1972), HC .. $20

Cy Young: A Baseball Life, by Reed Browning, University of Massachusetts Press (2000), Casey Award Winner $25

Zim: A Baseball Life, by Don Zimmer with Bill Madden, Total Sports (2001) $12

Historical

A Yankee Century: A Celebration of the First Hundred Years of Baseball's Greatest Teams, by Harvey Frommer, (2002) $22

The Autobiography of Baseball: The Inside Story from the Stars Who Played the Game, by Joseph Wallace and Ira Berkow, Abradale Press (2000) $18

After the Miracle, by Maury Allen (1969 Mets, 20 years later), Watts (1989) $20

All Roads Lead to October: Boss Steinbrenner's 25-year Reign of the New York Yankees, by Maury Allen, St. Martin's (2000).. $20

A Legend in the Making: The New York Yankees in 1939, by Richard Tofel, Ivan R. Dee (2002) $20

American Baseball: From Gentleman's Sport to the Commissioner System, Vol. I (1966); *From The Commissioner's to Continental Expansion, Vol. II* (1970); *From Postwar Expansion to the Electronic Age, Vol. III* (1983), by David Quentin Voight, University of Oklahoma Press $40, $30, $30

The Armchair Book of Baseball, by John Thorn, Scribners (1985)....$8

A Thinking Man's Guide to Baseball, by Leonard Koppett, MacMillan, (1970) $25

A Tour to End All Tours, by James E. Elfers, University of Nebraska Press, (2003), Major League Baseball's 1912-1924 World Tour. $20

Backstage at the Mets, by Lindsey Nelson and Al Hirshberg, Viking (1966) $10

Ballplayers Are Human Too, by Ralph Houk and Charles Dexter, Putnam (1962) $20

Banks to Sandberg to Grace: Five Decades of Love and Frustration with the Chicago Cubs, by Carrie Muskat, Contemporary, (2001) $15

Baseball As I Have Known It, by Fred Lieb, Coward McCann, (1977) $20

Baseball Between the Lines, by Donald Honig, Coward McCann (1976) $20

Baseball, Chicago Style: A Tale of Two Teams, One City, by Jerome Holtzman and George Vass, Bonus Books, (2001) $20

Baseball Confidential, by Arthur Mann, McKay, (1951), Brooklyn Dodgers front office man tells about Dodgers in 1940s and Jackie Robinson's joining the club $40

Baseball Is a Funny Game, by Joe Garagiola with Martin Quigley, Lippincott (1960) $30

Baseball in '41, by Robert Creamer, Viking, (1991) $18

Baseball Rookies Who Made Good, by M.G. Bonner (Mantle, Williams, Ruth, etc.), Knopf (1954) $30

Baseball Through a Knothole, by Bill Borst (history of baseball in St. Louis), Krank (1980), SC $15

Baseball When the Grass Was Real, by Donald Honig, Coward McCann (1975), Oral history of 1920s-1940s $25

Baseball's Back in Town, by Louis Cauz, Controlled Media, (1977), Blue Jays arrive in Toronto $40

Baseball's Great Experiment, by Jules Tygiel, Oxford, (1983), Jackie Robinson and Branch Rickey $40

Baseball's 100, by Maury Allen (his picks as the best), Galahad (1982) $17

Bats, by Davey Johnson and Peter Golenbock (New York Mets' 1985 season), Putnam (1986) $8

Basepaths, by Marc Gunther, Scribners, (1984), Player development in minor leagues $15

Beating the Bushes, by Frank Dolson (life in the minors), Icarus (1982) $20

Before They Were the Bombers: The New York Yankees' Early Years, 1903-1915, by Jim Reisler, McFarland, (2002) $28

The Best Seat in Baseball, But You Have to Stand, by Lee Gutkind (1974 season from an umpiring crews viewpoint), Dial (1975)... $30-$40

Beyond the Shadow of the Senators: The Untold Story of the Homestead Grays and the Integration of Baseball, by Brad Synder, Contemporary, (2003)..................................... $20

Beyond the Sixth Game, by Peter Gammons (Boston Red Sox from the sixth game of the 1975 World Series on), Houghton-Mifflin (1985) $15

Big Red Dynasty, by Greg Rhodes and John Erardi, Road West (1997), Cincinnati Reds of the 1970s..................... $30

Blackball Stars, by John Holway, Meckler, (1988), Biographical essays on Negro Leaguers $20

Black Baseball's National Showcase: The East-West All-Star Game, 1933-1953, by Larry Lester, University of Nebraska Press, (2002) $35

Black Diamonds, by John Holway, Meckler (1989)................... $20

Bleachers—A Summer in Wrigley Field, by Lonnie Wheeler, Contemporary (1988) $30

The Boston Red Sox, by Tom Meany, Barnes (1956) $35

The Boys of October, by Doug Hornig, Contemporary, (1975), 1975 Red Sox season.. $18

The Boys of Summer, by Roger Kahn, Harper & Row (1972).... $40

The Boys Who Would Be Cubs, by Joseph Bosco (a year with the Class A Peoria Cubs), Morrow (1990)..................... $12-$20

Breaking the Slump: Baseball in the Depression Era, by Charles C. Alexander, Columbia University Press (2002).................. $25

The Broadcasters, by Red Barber, Dial (1970) $30

The Bronx Zoo, by Sparky Lyle and Peter Golenbock, Crown (1979)... $10

The Business of Major League Baseball, by Gerald Scully, University of Chicago (1989), How the game on the field is affected by baseball's economic structure $25

Can't Anybody Here Play This Game?, by Jimmy Breslin (New York Mets' first year), Viking (1963) $60

Catch—A Major League Life, by Ernie Whitt and Greg Cable (Blue Jays 1988 season as seen by team's catcher), McGraw Hill - Ryerson $20

Champagne and Baloney, by Tom Clark (recaps Oakland's prominence in the 1970s), Harper & Row (1976) $15

Charlie O & the Angry A's, by Bill Libby, Doubleday (1975) $20

The Chrysanthemum and the Bat, by Robert Whiting (baseball in Japan), Dodd, Mead (1977) .... $75-$90

The Cincinnati Reds, by Ritter Collett, Jordan-Powers (1976) ... $45

Colorado Rockies—The Inaugural Season, by Rich Clarkson and Bob Baron, Fulcrum (1993) $40

Cooperstown: Baseball's Hall of Fame, by Lowell Reidenbaugh, (1999) $10

The Crooked Pitch, by Martin Quigley, Algonquin (1984) $35

The Cubs of '69, by Rick Talley (recaps the bittersweet 1969 season), Contemporary (1989) $20

A Cunning Kind of Ploy: The Cubs-Giants Rivalry, 1876-1932, by Warren Wilbert, McFarland (2002) $23

The Curse of the Bambino, by Dan Shaughnessy, Dutton (1990) ...$25

The Diamond in the Bronx, Yankee Stadium and the Politics of New York, by Neil Sullivan, Oxford (2001) $25

The Dizziest Season, by G.H. Fleming, Morrow (1984), 1934 season $40

Dizzy and the Gashouse Gang, by Doug Feldmann, McFarland (2000), SC $23

Dollar Sign on the Muscle, by Kevin Kerrane, Beaufort (1984), World of baseball scouts $30

Durocher's Cubs: The Greatest Team That Didn't Win, by David Claerbaut, Taylor Publishing (2000) $18

Epic Season: The 1948 American League Pennant Race, by David Kaiser, University of Massachusetts Press (1998), SC $14

Even the Browns, by William Mead, Contemporary (1978), Baseball during World War II $15

Fair Ball, A Fan's Case for Baseball, by Bob Costas, Bantam Books (2000) $5

Few and Chosen: Defining Yankee Greatness Across the Eras, by Whitey Ford and Phil Pepe, Triumph (2001), Ford ranks the five best Yankees all-time at each position $22

Few and Chosen: Defining Cardinal Greatness Across the Eras, by Tim McCarver with Phil Pepe, Triumph (2003) $22

Fleeter Than Birds: The 1985 St. Louis Cardinals, by Doug Feldmann, McFarland (2002), SC $22

The Gashouse Gang, by Robert Hood, Morrow (1976) $40

The Giants of the Polo Grounds, by Noel Hynd, Doubleday (1988) $20

The Greatest Game Ever Played, by Jerry Izenberg, Holt (1987), Sixth playoff game of Mets vs Astros in 1986 .... $25

The Greatest of All, by John Mosedale, Dial (1974), The 1927 Yankees $65

The Home Run Heard Round the World, by Ray Robinson, Harper-Collins (1991), Giants vs. Dodgers in 1951 ends with Bobby Thomson home run $12

July 2, 1903, by Mike Sowell, MacMillan (1992), Mysterious death of Big Ed Delahanty $40

The Last Great Season, by Michael Shapiro, Doubleday (2003), Season of 1956 .... $20

The League That Failed, by David Voigt, Doubleday (2003), Brief but important Player's League 1892-1899 .... $38

Legends of the Tribe, An Illustrated History of the Cleveland Indians, by Morris Eckhouse, Taylor Publishing (2000) $30

Lightning in a Bottle, by Herbert F. Crehan with James W. Ryan (1967 Boston Red Sox), Branden (1992), SC $20

Louisville Slugger, by Jan Arrow (history of bat making), Pantheon (1984) $30

Love Letters to the Mets, by Bill Adler, Simon & Schuster (1965) ...$50

The Man in the Crowd—Confessions of a Sports Addict, by Stanley Cohen, Random House (1981) $8

The Man in the Dugout, by Donald Honig, Follett (1977) $15

The Man Who Stole First Base, by Eric Nadel and Craig R. Wright (135 off-beat stories), Taylor (1989) $12

Men at Work, by George F. Will, MacMillan (1990) $8

The Men in Blue, by Larry Gerlach, Viking (1980) $25

The Men of Autumn, by Dom Forker (1949-53 New York Yankees), Taylor (1989) $10

Men of the Reds Machine, by Ritter Collett (1970s Cincinnati Reds), Landfall (1976) $20

The Mets Will Win the Pennant, by William Cox, Putnam (1964) ...$40

The Million-To-One Team: Why the Chicago Cubs Haven't Won a Pennant Since 1945, by George Castle, Diamond (2000) $22

The Milwaukee Braves, a Baseball Eulogy, by Bob Buege, Douglas (1988) $65

The Minors, by Neil J. Sullivan (historical overview of the minor leagues), St. Martins (1990) $25

Miracle at Coogans Bluff, by Thomas Kiernan (1951 Giants), Crowell (1975) $30

Miracle in Atlanta, by Furman Bisher, World (1966), Braves move to Atlanta $25

Misfits!, J. Thomas Hetrick (1899 Cleveland Spiders), McFarland (1991), No DJ Issued $25

More Than Merkle, by David Anderson, University of Nebraska Press (2000), Exciting season of 1908 and the last World Series win of the Cubs $25

My Baseball Diary, by James Farrell (novelist's viewpoint on the game he followed all his life), Barnes (1957) .... $40-$50

My Baseball Scrapbook, by Bob Broeg (St. Louis Cardinal beat writer), River City (1983) $45

The National Game: Baseball and American Culture, by John P. Rossi, Ivan Dee (2000) $20

The Negro Leagues, by Leslie Heaphy, McFarland (2003), Solid, comprehensive history $40

The Neighborhood of Baseball, by Barry Gifford (Chicago Cubs from the 1950s-80s), Dutton (1981) $12

New York City Baseball, by Harvey Frommer (1947-57 baseball in New York), MacMillan (1980) $10

Nine Innings, by Daniel Okrent (1982 Brewer/Orioles game), Ticknor & Fields (1985) $8

1947: When All Hell Broke Loose in Baseball, by Red Barber, Doubleday (1982) $20

1951: When Giants Played the Game, by Kerry Kerrane, McFarland (2001), SC $12

1960: The Last Pure Season, by Kerry Kerrane, Sports Publishing (2000) $20

No Cheering in the Press Box, by Jerome Holtzman, Holt, Rinehart & Winston (1974) $8

No Joy in Mudville, by Ralph Andreano, Schenkman (1965) $10

Occasional Glory: A History of the Philadelphia Phillies, by David M. Jordan, McFarland (2002), SC $23

October Men, by Roger Kahn, Harcourt (2003), 1978 Yankees miraculous season $18

October 1964, by David Halberstam (recaps pennant race and World Series), Villard (1994) $5

One Strike Away, by Dan Shaughnessy (1986 Red Sox season), Beaufort (1987) $25

The Only Ticket Off the Island, by Gare Joyce (a season in the Dominican Republic's Winter League), Lester & Orpen Dennys (1990) $20

Our Game, by Charles C. Alexander (history of the game), Holt (1991) $10

Out of My League, by George Plimpton, Harper (1961) $25

Past Time: Baseball as History, by Jules Tygiel, Oxford (2000), Seymour Medal Winner $15

Pen Men, by Bob Cairns (life in the bullpen), St. Martins (1992) $10

The Perfect Game, by Tom Seaver and Dick Schaap (1969 Mets), Dutton (1970) $15

The Philadelphia Phillies—The Team that Wouldn't Die, by Hal Bodley (1981) $45

Pine Tarred and Feathered, by Jim Kaplan (Sports Illustrated writer), Algonquin (1985) $8

Pinstripe Pandemonium, by Geoffrey Stokes (Yankees 1983 season), Harper & Row (1984) $8

The Pirates—We Are Family, Lou Sahadi, Times (1980) $20

Pitchers Do Get Lonely, by Ira Berkow, Atheneum (1988) $10

The Pitch That Killed, by Mike Sowell, MacMillan (1989), Casey Award Winner $75

The Pittsburgh Crawfords, by Jim Bankes, McFarland (2001), Five Hall of Famers on one of the greatest teams ever, SC $23

Play Ball, by John Feinstein (baseball's troubled times), Villard (1993) $8

Playing Around, by Donald Hall, et. al. (1973 spring training with the Pittsburgh Pirates), Little, Brown (1974) $25

POW Baseball in World War II, by Tim Wolter, McFarland (2002), Baseball behind barbed wire, SC $22

The Pride of Havana: A History of Cuban Baseball, by Robert Echevarria, Oxford (2001) $12

Pride of October, by Bill Madden, Warner (2003), What it was like to be a New York Yankee, interviews with 17 former players..... $20

The Psychologist at Bat, by David F. Tracy (team psychologist for the St. Louis Browns), Sterling (1951) $50

Roger Maris at Bat, by Roger Maris and Jim Ogle, Duell (1961 season), Sloan and Pearce (1962) $125

The Rookies, by Ed Walton, Stein & Day (1982) $12

Safe at Home, by Sharon Hargrove (baseball wife tells her story), by Texas A&M (1989) $17

Saying It's So: A Cultural History of the Black Sox Scandal, by Daniel A. Nathan, University of Illinois Press (2003) $35

A Season in the Sun, by Roger Kahn, Harper & Row (1977)...... $5

Season of Dreams, by Tom Kelly and Ted Robinson (Minnesota Twins 1991 season), Voyager Press (1992) $25

The Seasons: Ten Memorable Years in Baseball and in America, by Bill Gilbert, Citadel Press (2003) $22

The Seattle Pilots Story, by Carson Van Lindt, Marabou (1993), SC $40

The Short Season, by David Falkner (spring training atmosphere), Times (1986) $25

Sixty-One, by Tony Kubek, MacMillan (1987) $50

Slouching Toward Fargo, by Neal Karlen, Avon (1999), Two years with the St. Paul Saints in the independent Northern League, Casey Award Winner $20

Some Are Called Clowns, Bill Heward and Dimitri Gat (season with pitcher/manager of the 1973 Indianapolis Clowns), Crowell (1974) .... $50-$60

Streak: Joe DiMaggio and the Summer of 1941, by Michael Seidel, McGraw Hill (1988) $20

Strength Down the Middle: The Story of the 1958 Chicago White Sox, by Larry Kalas, Donnelley & Sons (2000) $18

The Suitors of Spring, by Pat Jordan, Dodd Mead (1973) $15

Summer of '98, by Mike Lupica, Putman (1999) $15

Summer of '64: A Pennant Lost, by William Cook, McFarland (2002), SC $22

Sunday Baseball, by Charlie Bevis, McFarland (2003), Controversy over Major League Baseball on Sunday, SC $20

Superstars and Screwballs, by Richard Goldstein (baseball in Brooklyn), Dutton (1991) $10

Sweet Seasons, by Dom Forker (1955-64 New York Yankees), Taylor (1990) $10

Take Me Out to the Cubs Game, by John C. Skipper, McFarland (2000), 35 former Cubs talk about losing at Wrigley Field, SC $20

The Teammates: A Portrait of a Friendship, by David Halberstam, Hyperion (2003), Red Sox teammates Ted Williams, Dom DiMaggio, Johnny Pesky and Bobby Doerr $20

Ted Williams—The Golden Year 1957, by Edwin Pope, Prentice Hall (1970) $75

The Twenty-Four Inch Home Run, by Michael Bryson (baseball oddities and anecdotes), Contemporary (1990) $15

The 26th Man, by Steve Fireovid and Mark Winegardner (story of a veteran minor leaguer), MacMillan (1991) $8

They Kept Me Loyal to the Yankees, by Victor Debs (tribute to former Yankees), Rutledge (1993) $18

Tomahawked, by Bill Zack (1992 Braves season), Simon & Schuster (1993) $10

Two Spectacular Seasons, by William B. Mead (1930 and 1968 seasons recapped), Macmillan (1990) $8

Up From the Minor Leagues, by Donald Honig, Cowles (1970) . $40

View From the Dugout, Ed Richter (1963 Philadelphia Phillies season), Chilton (1964) .... $75-$95

Voices From the Great Black Baseball Leaguers, by John Holway, Dodd Mead (1975) $50

Voices of the Game, by Curt Smith (chronicles baseball broadcasting), Diamond (1987) .... $75-$95

Wait Til Next Year, by Chris Jennison (New York City baseball from the 1940s and '50s), Norton (1974) $30

We Won Today, by Kathleen Parker (diary of a 1976 Mets fan), Doubleday (1977) $25

When Boston Won the World Series, by Bob Ryan, Running Press (2003), World Series of 1903 .... $15

When the Cheering Stops, by Lee Heiman, Dave Weiner and Bill Gutman (profiles 21 players from the 1950s and 1960s), MacMillan (1990) $8

The Whiz Kids, by Harry Paxton (1950 Phillies), McKay (1950) $175

The Whiz Kids and the 1950 Pennant, by Robin Roberts and Paul C. Rogers III, Temple University Press (1996) $25

Winning, by Earl Weaver and John Sammis, Morrow (1972) $20

Wild and Outside, by Stefan Fatsis (1994 season of the independent Northern League of Professional Baseball), Walker (1995)........ $12

Yankee Batboy, by Joe Carrieri and Zander Hollander, Barnes (1945) $20

The Year of the Tiger, by Jerry Green, Coward McCann (1969) $40

The Year the Mets Lost Last Place, by Paul Zimmerman and Dick Schaap, World (1969)... $10

The Year They Called Off the World Series, by Benton Stark (details the 1904 season), Avery (1991)................................ $8

You Gotta Have Wa, by Robert Whiting (baseball in Japan), MacMillan (1989).. $15

Team Histories Series

G.P. Putman series - 1944-1955

The Baltimore Orioles: The History of a Colorful Team in Baltimore and St. Louis, by Fred Lieb (1955) .... $325-$400

The Boston Braves, by Harold Kaese (1948) .... $100-$150

The Boston Red Sox, by Fred Lieb (1947) $60

The Brooklyn Dodgers, by Frank Graham (1945)............ $125-$150

The Chicago Cubs, by Warren Brown (1946) $65

The Chicago White Sox, by Warren Brown (1952) $80

The Cincinnati Reds, by Lee Allen (1948) $135

The Cleveland Indians, by Franklin Lewis (1949) .... $75-$120

Connie Mack, by Fred Lieb (Philadelphia Athletics history) (1945)..$65

The Detroit Tigers, by Fred Lieb (1946)........................ $80-$120

The Milwaukee Braves, by Harold Kaese and Russell G. Lynch (1954) .... $80-$120

The New York Giants, by Frank Graham (1952)................ $60-$120

The New York Yankees, by Frank Graham (1948)................... $200

The Philadelphia Phillies, by Fred Lieb and Stan Baumgartner (1953) $225

The Pittsburgh Pirates, by Fred Lieb (1948)........................ $125

The St. Louis Cardinals, by Fred Lieb (1944) $50

The Washington Senators, by Shirley Povich (1954) $400

The Coward-McCann Sports Library series

The Go-Go Chicago White Sox, by Dave Condon (1960) $25

The Los Angeles Dodgers, by Paul Zimmerman (1960) $35

The World Champion Pittsburgh Pirates, by Dick Groat and Bill Surface (1961) $45

Bruce Chadwick and David Spindel Memories and Memorabilia series, Abbeville Publishing

The Boston Red Sox, (1992), No DJ Issued .... $30-$40

The Bronx Bombers, (1992)..................................... $25-$30

The Chicago Cubs, (1994) $20

The Cincinnati Reds, (1994)....................................... $25

The Dodgers, (1993).. $18

The Giants, (1993).. $15

MacMillan Baseball's Great Teams series

The Boston Red Sox, by Henry Berry (1975)...................... $25

The Chicago Cubs, by Jim Enright (1975)......................... $25

The Dodgers, by Thomas Holmes (1975) $40

The Detroit Tigers, by Joe Falls (1975) $25

Peter Golenbock oral history series

Amazin', St. Martin's Press (2002), New York Mets $23

Bums, Putman (1984), Brooklyn Dodgers, Casey Award winner.. $25

Dynasty, Prentice-Hall (1975), New York Yankees (1949-1964) $35-$45

Fenway, Putman (1992), Boston Red Sox........................... $25

The Spirit of St. Louis, Spike (2000), St. Louis Browns & Cardinals) $15

Wrigleyville, St. Martin's Press (1996), Chicago Cubs........ $20-$30

Others

The California Angels, by Ross Newhan, Simon & Schuster (1982)... $25

From 33rd Street to Camden Yards, by John Eisenberg, Contemporary (2001), Oral history of the Baltimore Orioles $16

The New York Mets, by Leonard Koppett, MacMillan (1970) $40

Redleg Journal, by Greg Rhodes and John Snyder, Road West Publishing (2000), Year by Year and Day by Day with the Cincinnati Reds since 1866, Magnus opus, SC..................................... $30

The Red Sox Century, by Glenn Stout and Richard Johnson, Houghlin Mifflin (2000).. $30

The Washington Senators 1901-1971, by Tom Deveaux, McFarland (2001), No DJ Issued $38

Ballparks

The Ballpark Book, by Ron Smith and Kevin Belford, Sporting News (2000), Colorful design to describe 46 parks, old and new... $32

Ballparks, by Robert Von Goeben and Red Howard, Metro Books (2000).. $15

Ballparks of North America, by Michael Benson, McFarland (1989), Comprehensive reference to hundreds of "grounds, yards and stadiums" across America from 1845 .... $50-$65

Diamonds, The Evolution of the Ball Park, by Michael Gershman, Houghton Mifflin (1993), Casey Award Winner $25

Green Cathedrals, by Philp J. Lowry, Addison Wesley (1992) ... $15

Lost Ballparks, by Lawrence Ritter, Villard (1992), History of 20 now defunct, great in their day, ballparks..................................... $25

Storied Stadiums, by Curt Smith, Carroll & Graf (2001), Baseball's history through its ballparks....................................... $25

Take Me Out to the Ballgame: An Illustrated Guide to Baseball Parks Past & Present, by Josh Leventhal, Black Dog 7 Leventhal (2000) $30

To Everything a Season, by Bruce Kuklick, (Shibe Park, Philadelphia), Princeton (1991), Casey Award Winner $25

The New York Mets, by Leonard Koppett, Macmillan (1970) $40

Classic Books of Baseball Art and Photographs

The American Diamond, by Branch and Robert Riger, Simon & Schuster (1965), Rickey provides text illustrated by spectacular Riger drawings and photos $85

The Art of Baseball, by Shelly Mehlman Dinhoffer, Harmony Books (1990), History of American Game in painting, sculpture and folk art in splendidly designed pages... $30

Babe: A Life in Pictures, by Lawrence Ritter and Mark Rucker, Ticknor & Fields (1988), Vintage photos cover every aspect of Babe Ruth's life and career $45

The Baseball Anthology: 125 Years of Stories, Poems, Articles, Photographs, Drawings, Interviews, Cartoons and Other Memorabilia, by Joseph Wallace, Abradale Press (1998) $25

Baseball: A Treasury of Art and Literature, by Michael Ruscoe, editor, Lauter Levin (1993), Oversized, 400 pages of the best work of great artists $45

Baseball's Golden Age, by Neal and Constance McCabe, Abrams (1993), Glorious photos of Charles M. Conlan reproduced from original plates... $15

Baseball Memories: 1900-1909, Baseball Memories: 1930-1939, Baseball Memories: 1950-1959, by Marc Okkonen, Sterling (1992, 1994, 1993), Important books, not for the quality of the photos, many of them photo copies, but for their quantity. Many are the only published photo of the subject. Almost all of the players and managers of the given decade plus photos of the cities and ballparks are pictured $30, $35, $35

Cardinals Collection, by Mark Stang, Orange Frazer (2002), 100 years of St. Louis Cardinals photo images........................... $25

Cubs Collection, by Mark Stang, Orange Frazer, (2001), 100 years of Chicago Cubs photo images $25

Diamonds Are Forever: Artists and Writers on Baseball, by Peter Gordon, editor, Chronicle Books (1987), Handsome book records materials that toured the country as a Smithsonian Institution Traveling Exhibition $30

The Game That Was, by Richard Cahan and Mark Jacob, Contemporary Books (1996), Stunning George Brace Baseball Photo Collection.. $25

Indians Illustrated, by Mark Stang, Orange Frazer, (2000), 100 years of Cleveland Indians photos...$25

The Reds in Black and White, by Greg Rhodes and Mark Stang, Road West Publishing (1999), 100 years of Cincinnati Reds photo images... $25

Shadows of Summer, by Donald Honig, Viking (1994), Coffee table book with mostly full page sepia vintage photos from 1869-1947 .... $35

Football Books

Hard covers

A War in Dixie: Alabama vs. Auburn, by Ivan Maisel and Kelly Whiteside (2001) $15

About Three Bricks Shy of a Load, by Roy Blount Jr. (1974) $15

Against the Grain, by Eugene "Mercury" Morris and Steve Fiffer (1988) $18

Always on the Run, by Larry Csonka and Jim Kiick with Dave Anderson (1973).. $20

A Matter of Style, by Joe Namath with Bob Oates Jr. (1973) $35

An Odd Steelers Journey, by Andy Russell (2002) $20

The Art of Quarterbacking, by Kenny Anderson with Jack Clancy (1984) $18

Audibles, by Joe Montana and Bob Raissman (1986)................ $18

The Best of the Athletic Boys - The White Man's Impact on Jim Thorpe, by Jack Newcombe $25

Best Plays of the Year, by Robert Riger (1962) $25

Blanda: Alive and Kicking, by Wells Twombley $25

Bo Knows Bo, Bo Jackson and Dick Schaap (1990) $8

Bootlegger's Boy, by Barry Switzer (1990) $8

Born to Referee, My Life on the Gridiron, by Jerry Markbreit with Alan Steinberg (1988) $18

Born to Run, The O.J. Simpson Story, by Larry Fox.................... $20

The Boz: Confessions of a Modern Anti-Hero, by Brian Bosworth with Rick Reilly (1988) $8

Brian Piccolo: A Short Season, by Jeannie Morris (1971), basis for the movie "Brian's Song" $10

Broadway Joe and his Super Jets, by Larry Fox (1969), 1968-69 New York Jets season $20

Broken Patterns, the Education of a Quarterback, by Fran Tarkenton and Brock Yates (1971).. $18

Bud: The Other Side of the Glacier, by Bill McGrane (1986), Bud Grant $30

Building a Champion, by Bill Walsh with Glenn Dickey (1990) ... $15

By a Nose: The Off-Center Life of Football's Funniest Lineman, by Fred Smerlas and Vic Carucci, Simon & Schuster, 1990 ..... $15

Calling the Shots, by Mike Singletary with Armen Keteyian (1984) .$18

Cleveland Browns: A-Z, by Roger Gordon (2002) $20

Coach: A Season With Lombardi, by Tom Dowling (1970)......... $25

Coaching: The Way of A Winner, by Knute Rockne (1929) $65

Dennis Byrd, Rise and Walk, by Dennis Byrd with Michael D'Orso (1993) $8

Distant Replay, by Jerry Kramer with Dick Schaap (1985) $20

Ditka, An Autobiography, by Mike Ditka with Don Pierson (1986)....$15

Ditka: Monster of the Midway, by Armen Keteyian (1992) $15

Earl Campbell: The Driving Force, by Sam Blair (1980)............. $15

The End of Autumn, by Michael Oriard (1982), former Kansas City Chiefs/Notre Dame player reflects on his football career $15

Even Big Guys Cry, by Alex Karras with Herb Gluck (1977)....... $18

Fatso, Football When Men Were Really Men, Arthur J. Donovan Jr. and Bob Drury (1987)... $14

Favre: For the Record, by Brett Favre, Chris Havel (1997), Doubleday $17

Fighting Back, by Rocky Bleier with Terry O'Neil (1975) $25

Football and the Single Man, by Paul Hornung (1965) $15

Frank Gifford: The Golden Year 1956, by William Wallace......... $20

The Glory of Titletown: The Classic Green Bay Packers Photography of Vernon J. Biever, by Peter Strupp and Vernon J. Biever, (1997) Taylor Publishing... $30

Great Pass Receivers of the NFL, by Dave Anderson (1966)...... $8

The Green Bay Packers, by Arch Ward (1946) $30

The Green Bay Packers: Pro Football's Pioneer Team, by Chuck Johnson (1961) $35

Halas on Halas, by George Halas (1979).................................. $25

Happy To Be Alive, by Darryl Stingley with Mark Mulvoy (1983).....$25

Hard Nose: The 1986 New York Giants, by Jim Burt (1987) $25

Hard Knox: The Life of an NFL Coach, by Chuck Knox and Bill Plaschke (1988) $25

Hearing the Noise: My Life in the NFL, by Preston Pearson (1985).. $30

Heart of a Lion, the Wild and Woolly Life of Bobby Layne, by Bob St. John (1991).. $20

Hey! Wait a Minute (I Wrote a Book), by John Madden with Dave Anderson (1984) $8

The Hundred Yard Lie: The Corruption of College Football, by Rick Telander (1989) $9

I Can't Wait Until Tomorrow Cause I Get Better Looking Every Day, by Joe Namath with Dick Schaap (1969) $20

I Am Third, by Gale Sayers with Al Silverman (1970) $20

I Remember Tom Landry, by Denne H. Freeman and Jaime Aron (2001), Longtime Landry colleagues talk of his career $12

I'm Still Scrambling, by Randall Cunningham with Steve Wartenberg (1993) $20

Inside Football, by George Allen (1970) $16

Inside Pro Football, by J. King (1958) $11

Inside the Pressure Cooker, by Sid Gilman (1974), about the New York Jets $30

Instant Replay: The Green Bay Diary of Jerry Kramer, by Dick Schaap (1968) $15

In the Pocket: My Life As A QB: Earl Morrall (1969) $25

Iron Men: Bucko, Crazylegs and the Boys Recall the Golden Days of Pro Football, by Stuart Leuthner (1988) $10

It's Only a Game, (2001) by Terry Bradshaw with David Fisher $20

Jerry Kramer's Farewell to Football, by Dick Schaap (1969) $15

Jets: Broadway's 30-Year Guarantee, by Editors of The New York Daily News (1998), Sport Publishing $30

Jim Otto: The Pain of Glory, by Jim Otto, Dave Newhouse (2000) $15

The Jim Plunkett Story, by Jim Plunkett and Dave Newhouse (1981) $20

Kansas City Chiefs Encyclopedia, by Mark Stallard (2002) $35

Knute Rockne: Man Builder, by Harry Stuhldreher (1931) $60

Last Call: Memoirs of an NFL Referee, by Jerry Markbreit and Alan Steinberg (2002) $20

The Last Season of Weeb Ewbank, by Paul Zimmerman (1974) $25

Little Men of the NFL, by Bob Rubin (1974) $8

Lombardi: Winning Is the Only Thing, by Jerry Kramer (1971) .. $20

Looking Deep, by Terry Bradshaw with Buddy Martin (1989) $20

LT, Living on the Edge, by Lawrence Taylor with David Falkner $15

The Man Inside, (Tom) Landry, by Bob St. John (1979) $18

McMahon!, by Jim McMahon and Bob Verdi (1986) $40

Mean Joe Greene and the Steelers Front Four, by Larry Fox (1975) $30

Nitschke, with Robert W. Wells (1973) $15

The Miami Dolphins, by Morris McLemore (1972) $15

My Greatest Day in Football, by Murray Goodman and Leonard Lewin $10

My Life with the Redskins, by Corinne Griffith $12

My Story (And I'm Sticking to It), by Alex Hawkins (1989) $22

My Sunday Best, by J. Fleischer $10

The New York Giants, by Al Derogatis (1964) $25

Never Die Easy, the autobiography of Walter Payton by Walter Payton with Don Yaeger (2000), Villard $25

NFL Pro Football Hall of Fame All Time Greats, by Donald R. Smith $10

The 1960 Philadelphia Eagles, by Robert Gordon (2001), SC... $14

Nose to Nose: Survival in the Trenches of the NFL, by Joe Klecko and Joe Fields with Greg Logan (1989) $25

Nothing to Kick About: The Autobiography of a Modern Immigrant, by Pete Gogolack with Joseph Carter (1973) $10

Off My Chest, by Jimmy Brown with Myron Cope (1964) $30

The $1 League, by Jim Byrne (1986), history of the USFL ...... $50-$70

One Giant League, by Jeff Hostetler with Ed Fitzgerald (1991) $20

Once a Cowboy, by Walt Garrison with John Tullius (1988) $25

One Knee Equals Two Feet, by John Madden and Dave Anderson (1986) $14

Open Field, by John Brodie with James D. Houston (1974) $14

The other league; the fabulous story of the American Football League, by Jack Horrigan .... $50-$65

Out of Control, by Thomas "Hollywood" Henderson and Peter Knobler (1987) $5

Over the Hill to the Super Bowl, by Owens (1973), HC, about the 1973 Redskins $35

Packer Dynasty, Phil Bengston with Todd Hunt (1968), ... $35

Paper Lion, by George Plimpton (1966) $30

Pittsburgh Steelers - Great Teams, Great Years, by Ray Didinger (1974) $20

The Players, by Tex Maule (1967) $15

Quarterbacks Have all the Fun, by Dick Schaap (1974) $18

The Red Grange Story, by Red Grange (1953) .... $30-$40

Roger Craig: Strictly Business, by Garry Niver (1992) $35

Roger Staubach: A Special Kind of QB, by Sullivan (1974) $15

Rosey: The Gentle Giant, by Rosey Grier with Dennis Baker (1986) $20

Running Tough: Memoirs of a Football Maverick, by Tony Dorsett and Harvey Frommer (1989) $8

Run to Daylight, by Vince Lombardi (1971) $25

Seven Days to Sunday, by Asinoff (1968) $30

Shark Among Dolphins: Inside Jimmy Johnson's Transformation of the Miami Dolphins, by Steve Hubbard $10

Simms To McConkey: Blood, Sweat and Gatorade, by Phil McConkey and Phil Simms (1987) $7

Simply Devine: Memoirs of a Hall of Fame Coach, by Dan Devine and Michael R. Steele (2000) $16

Singletary on Singletary, by Mike Singletary and Jerry Jenkins (1991) $20

Starr - My Life in Football, by Bart Starr with Murray Olderman (1987) $13

Steelers, Team of the Decade, by Lou Sahadi (1979) $45

Super Bowl Chronicles : A Sportswriter Reflects on the First 25 Years of America's Game, by Jerry Green $16

Super Bowl: Of Men, Myths and Moments, by Marty Ralbovsky (1971) $13

Super Bowl Sunday: The Day America Stops, by CBS Sports (2000) $12

Tarkenton, by Jim Klobuchar and Fran Tarkenton (1976) $15

Terry Bradshaw, Man of Steel, by Terry Bradshaw with David Diles (1979) $30

Texas Triology: A Season in the Lone Star State, by Mitchell Krugel, SC (2002) $20

The Whole Ten Yards, by Frank Gifford and Harry Waters (1993) $7

The Winning Edge, by Don Shula (1973) $20

They Call It A Game, by Bernie Parrish (1971) $10

They Call Me Assassin, by Jack Tatum with Bill Kushner (1979).....$15

They Call Me Dirty, by Conrad Dobler and Vic Carucci (1988) $15

They're Playing My Game, by Hank Stram with Lou Sahadi (1986) ..$5

Tom Landry, by Tom Landry and Gregg Lewis (1990) $15

Total Impact, Straight Talk from Football's Hardest Hitter, by Ronnie Lott with Jill Lieber (1991) $20

Vikes, Mikes and Something on the Backside, by Ahmad Rashad with Peter Bodo (1988) $25

Vince, A Personal Biography of Vince Lombardi, by Michael O'Brien (1987) $22

Weeb Ewbank's The Football Way, by Lud Duroska (1967)....... $20

When the Grass was Real (Ten Best Years of Pro Football), by Bob Carroll (1993) $20

Y.A. Tittle: I Pass, by Don Smith (1964) $25

Basketball Books

Against the World, by Kerry Eggers and Dwight Jaynes (1993), recaps the Portland Trailblazers' 1991-92 season................. $12

A Season Inside: One Year in College Basketball, by John Feinstein $8

A Season On The Brink: A Year with Bob Knight and the Indiana Hoosiers, by John Feinstein (1986) $6

A View From Above, by Wilt Chamberlain (1991)...................... $15

A View From the Bench, Red Holzman with Leonard Lewin (1980) $25

A View From the Rim: Willis Reed on Basketball, by Willis Reed and Phil Pepe (1971) $20

Boston Celtic Encyclopedia, by Peter Bjarkman (2000) $30

Bill Bradley: One to Remember, by Halter (1975) $25

Bill Walton, Nothing but Net, by Bill Walton with Gene Wojciechowski (1994) $20

Bird: The Making of An American Sports Legend, by Lee Daniel Levine (1988) $20

The Chicago Bulls Encyclopedia, by Alex Sachare (1998) $25

The Cockroach Basketball League, by Charles Rosen (1992) $18

Cousy on the Celtic Mystique, by Bob Cousy with Bob Ryan (1988) $20

Dean Smith: A Tribute, by Ken Rosenthal (2001), More than 100 notables reflect on Smith's career $12

Drive, The Story of My Life, Larry Bird with Bob Ryan (1989).... $15

Fighting Illini Basketball: A Hardwood History, from the archives of the Champaign News Gazette (2000) $14

Forty-Eight Minutes, A Night in the Life of the NBA, by Bob Ryan and Terry Pluto (1987) $20

Foul! The Connie Hawkins Story, by David Wolf (1972) $20

The Franchise, by Cameron Stauth (1990) $18

George McGinnis: Basketball Superstar, by James Haskins $8

Giant Steps, by Kareem Abdul-Jabbar and Peter Knobler (1983) ...$15

Go Up For Glory, by Bill Russell and William McSweeney (1966) ...$25

Hang Time, Days & Dreams with Michael Jordan, by Bob Greene (1992) $30

Heir to a Dream, by Pete Maravich and Darrel Campbell (1987).....$30

Holzman's Basketball: Winning Strategy and Tactics, by Red Holzman (1973).. $15

Hondo, Celtic Man In Motion, by Bob Ryan (1977), biography of John Havlicek $30

Indiana University Basketball: For the Thrill of It, by Melanie Tolliver (2002) $30

In the Land of the Giants, My Life in Basketball, by Tyrone "Muggsy" Bogues and David Levine (1994) $20

Jim O'Brien: Bucking the Odds, by Ralph Paulk (2001) $15

The Jordan Rules, by Sam Smith (1992) $15

John Wooden: They Call Me Coach, by Jack Tobin (1973)........ $25

Kareem, by Kareem Abdul-Jabbar with Mignon McCrthy (1990) $12

The Killer Instinct, by Bob Cousy with Jim Devaney (1975) $35

Krazy about the Knicks, by Marv Albert (1971) $35

The Last Loud Roar, by Bob Cousy with Ed Linn (1964) $30

Life on the Run, by Bill Bradley (1976) $18

Loose Balls, by Terry Pluto (1990), traces the history of the ABA....$15

Magic's Touch, by Earvin "Magic" Johnson Jr. and Roy S. Johnson.. $20

Michael Jordan Speaks: Lessons from the World's Greatest Champion, by Janet Lowe (1999) $10

Mr. Basketball, by George Mikan and Bill Carlson (1951).......... $35

Mr. Clutch: The Jerry West story, by Jerry West and Bill Libby (1969)... $35

My Life, by Earvin "Magic" Johnson with William Novak (1992) $10

Nothing but Net: Just Give Me the Ball and Get Out of the Way, by Bill Walton (1994), Hyperion $20

Obsession - Timberwolves Stalk the NBA, by Bill Heller (1989), traces startup of the Minnesota Timberwolves basketball team...........$10

One Basketball and Glory, by Newt Oliver (1969), the Bevo Francis story $15

The Open Man: A championship diary, by Dave DeBusschere with Paul Zimmerman and Dick Schaap (1970) $25

Pistol Pete Maravich, The making of a basketball star, by Bill Gutman (1972) $25

The Punch: One Night, Two Lives, and the Fight That Changed Basketball Forever, by John Feinstein, Little Brown, (2002), Rudy Tomjanovich and Kermit Washington $18

Rebound: K.C. Jones Autobiography, by Jack Warner (1986) ... $15

Red on Red, Red Holzman and Harvey Frommer (1987) $18

Sacred Hoops, Spiritual Lessons of a Hardboard Warrior, by Phil Jackson and Hugh Delehanty (1996) $18

Second Wind, the Memoirs of an Opinionated Man, by Bill Russell with Taylor Branch (1979) $25

Shaq Attaq!, by Shaquille O'Neal with Jack McCallum (1993)........$12

Show Time: Inside the Lakers' Breakthrough Season, by Pat Riley (1988).. $18

Stand Tall, the Lew Alcindor Story, by Phil Pepe (1970) $25

Sweet Redemption, by Gary Williams and David Vise (2002),
Maryland wins the NCAA Championship $20

Tall Tales - Glory Years of the NBA, by Terry Pluto (1992) $25

They Cleared the Lane: The NBA's Black Pioneers, by Ron Thomas (2002) $25

Trial by Basketball: The Life and Times of Tex Winter, by Mark Bender (2000) $15

24 Seconds to Shoot: Informal History of the NBA, by Leonard Koppett (1968) $25

To The Brink: Stockton, Malone and the Utah Jazz's Climb to the Edge of Glory, by Michael C. Lewis (1998) $15

Unfinished Business, by Jack McCallum (1992), recaps the 1990-91 Celtics season $20

The View From Section III, by Mike Shatzkin (1970), recaps the Knicks' 1969-70 season $30

Vitale, by Dick Vitale (1988) $10

Walt Frazier: One Magic Season and a Basketball Life, by Walt Frazier and Neil Offen (1988) $15

The Walton Gang, by Bill Libby (1974) $10

Willis Reed, The Knicks Take Charge Man, by Larry Fox (1970) $30

Wilt, by Wilt Chamberlain and David Shaw (1973) $20

The Winner Within, A Life Plan for Team Players, by Pat Riley (1993) $20

Hockey Books

And ...Howe! : An Authorized Autobiography, by Gordie Howe, Colleen Howe, Tom Delisle $8

Andy Bathgate's Hockey Secrets, by Andy Bathgate (1964) $5

A Spin of the Wheel: Birth of the Buffalo Sabres, by R. Brewitt (1975) $23

Bernie! Bernie! Bernie!, by Bernie Parent with Bill Fleischman and Sonny Schwartz (1975) $20

Bobby Clarke, by Edward Dolan and Richard Lyttle (1977) $25

Bobby Clarke and the Ferocious Flyers, by Stan Fischler (1974) $35

Bobby Orr and the Big Bad Bruins, by Stan Fischler (1969) $18

Bobby Orr: Lightning On Ice, by Howard Liss (1975) $17

Bobby Orr: My Game, by Bobby Orr and Mark Mulvoy (1974) ... $20

Chicago's Black Hawks, by Stan Fischler $8

Cowboy on Ice, by Phil Lorange (1975), biography of Howie Young $20

Cyclone Taylor: A Hockey Legend, by Eric Whitehead (1977) ... $10

The Detroit Red Wings: Greatest Moments and Players, by Steve Fischler (2002) $22

The Detroit Red Wings: The Illustrated History, by Richard Bak (1998) $18

Eddie: A Goalie's Story, by H. Delano (1976), biography of Eddie Giacomin, ... $18

Face-Off at the Summit, by Ken Dryden (1973) $15

The Fastest Sport, by Gerald Eskenazi (1974) $15

The Flying Frenchmen, Hockey's Greatest Dynasty, by Maurice "Rocket" Richard and Stan Fischler (1971) $20

The Game, by Ken Dryden (1983) $12

Garry Unger and the Battling Blues, by Stan Fischler (1976) $15

Goaltender, by Gerry Cheevers (1971) $18

Gordie Howe, by Stan Fischler (1967) $15

Gordie Howe: Number 9, by Jim Vipond (1968) $15

Great Upsets of Stanley Cup Hockey, by John Devaney (1976) $15

Gretzky, An Autobiography, by Wayne Gretzky with Rick Reilly (1990) $25

The Hammer, by Dave Schultz with Stan Fischler (1981) $10

Dominik Hasek: The Dominator, by Randy Schultz (2002) $20

High Stick, by Ted Green (1971) $18

The Hockey Compendium: NHL Facts, Stats, and Theories, by Jeff Z. Klein and Karl-Ear Reif (2001) $15

Hockey In My Blood, by Johnny Bucyk with Russ Conway (1972) $18

Hockey Is A Battle, by Punch Imlach (1969) $17

Hockey Is My Game, by Bobby Hull (1967) $25

Hockey Is My Life, by Phil Esposito with Gerald Eskenazi (1972) $15

The Hockey News Century of Hockey, by Steve Dryden (2000) $20

I Play to Win, by Stan Mikita (1969) $20

Larinov, by Igor Larinov, Jim Taylor and Leonid Reizer (1990), saga of Russian player pursuing NHL career $10

The Men in the Nets, by J. Hunt (1967) $20

Mr. Hockey: The World of Gordie Howe (1975) $19

My Three Hockey Players, by Colleen Howe (1972) $25

My 26 Stanley Cup: Memories of a Hockey Life, by Dick Irving (2001) $25

The New York Rangers: Broadway's Longest Running Hit, by John Kreiser and Lou Friedman (1996) $25

None Against!, by Keith Magnuson (1973) $20

One Hundred and One Years of Hockey: The Chronicle of a Century on Ice, edited by Al Strachan and Eric Duhatschek, (2001) $25

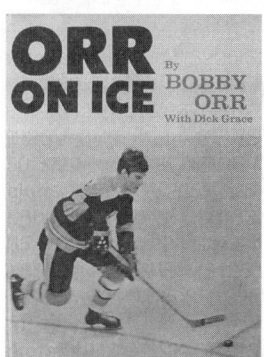

Orr on Ice, by Bobby Orr (1970) with Dick Grace $25

Play the Man, by Brad Park with Stan Fischler (1971) $20

Power Play: The Story of the Toronto Maple Leafs, by Stan Fischler (1972) $20

Rocket Richard, by Andy O'Brien (1969) $18

Strength Down Centre, by Hugh Hood (1970), biography of Jean Beliveau $27

They Call Me Gump, by Lorne "Gump" Worsley with Tim Moriarity (1975) $20

Those Were the Days, by Stan Fischler (1976) $15

We Love You Bruins: Boston's Gashouse Gang from Eddie Shore to Bobby Orr, by John Devaney $20

Whos Who in Hockey, by Stan and Shirley Fischler, SC, Comprehensive listing of all NHL players with profiles, histories, (2002) $20

Chapter 8

COMMEMORATIVES

Commemorative covers and postcards is a category that is ideally suited for sports collecting. Famous athletic events and individual player accomplishments can be celebrated and remembered long after they occur.

Commemorative covers or cachets usually depict an achievement and often contain a postmark from the nearest U.S. Post Office. Autograph(s) can add extra value and importance to the items.

Also included in this category are Hall of Fame art postcards and commemorative sheets.

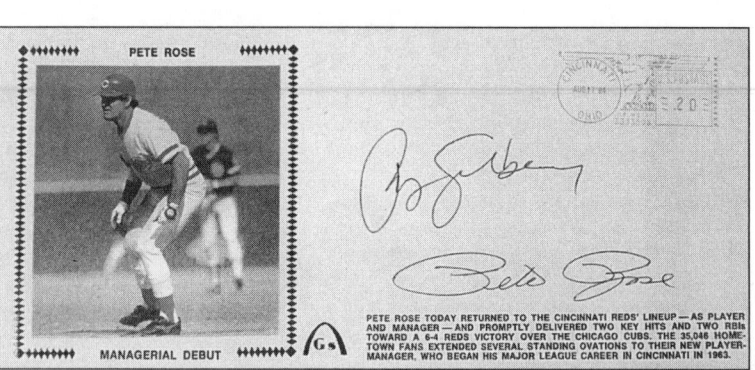

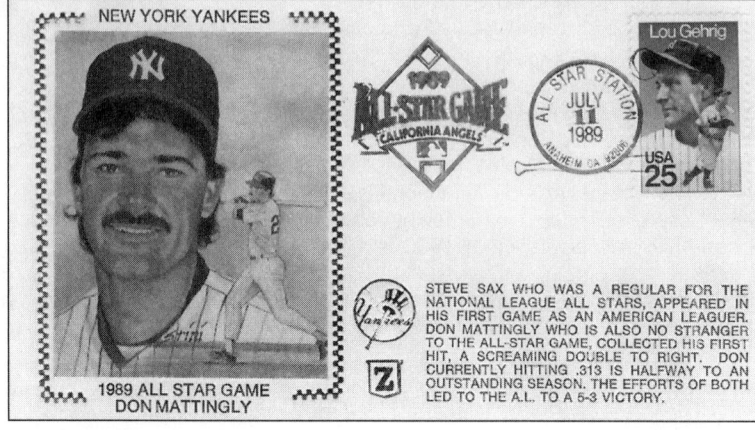

Perez-Steele Postcards

Baseball Hall of Fame Art Postcards

In its first postcard set issued in 1980, Perez-Steele Galleries of Fort Washington, Pa., produced the first of four limited-edition sets. The first set is devoted to members of the Hall of Fame and is updated every two years to add the new inductees. The 10,000 numbered sets of postcards produced each time are generally collected autographed. "I" means it's impossible that the player could have signed the postcard. Generally, unsigned postcards range from $2-$35.

In September of 2003, Peggy Steele announced that the Perez-Steele franchise was ending after nearly a quarter-century of creating stunning artwork for the hobby. Virtually all of the remaining Perez-Steele inventory was transferred to the Baseball Hall of Fame, which has had a business arrangement with Frank and Peggy Steele and artist Dick Perez since 1980.

As the official portrait artist for the Hall of Fame, Perez was slated to continue creating the original artwork of new Hall of Famers, but there are no announced plans at the moment for any continuation of the acclaimed Perez-Steele Hall of Fame Postcard set. Fifteen series have been produced from 1980 to 2001; there are no cards from 2002 inductee Ozzie Smith and 2003 inductees Gary Carter and Eddie Murray.

Though halting production of the Postcard series could ultimately lead to some downward price pressure, hobby insiders have theorized that at some point in the future the series could be resumed, perhaps not with the individual card serial numbering but at least in editions of 10,000 for each player to match the first 15 series.

First Series (Brown, 1980)

1. Ty Cobb .... $30 un, I
2. Walter Johnson.. $10 un, I
3. Christy Mathewson .... $10 un, I
4. Babe Ruth .... $40 un, I
5. Honus Wagner .... $15 un, I
6. Morgan Bulkeley .... $2 un, I
7. Ban Johnson .... $2 un, I
8. Nap Lajoie .... $5 un, I
9. Connie Mack.. $5 un, I
10. John McGraw .... $5 un, I
11. Tris Speaker.. $15 un, I
12. George Wright .... $2 un, I
13. Cy Young .... $10 un, I
14. Grover Alexander.. $5 un, I
15. Alexander Cartwright .... $2 un, I
16. Henry Chadwick .... $2 un, I
17. Cap Anson .... $2 un, I
18. Eddie Collins... $5 un, I
19. Candy Cummings .... $2 un, I
20. Charles Comiskey .... $2 un, I
21. Buck Ewing .... $2 un, I
22. Lou Gehrig.. $30 un, I
23. Willie Keeler .... $2 un, I
24. Hoss Radbourne .... $2 un, I
25. George Sisler... $15 un, I
26. A.G. Spalding .... $2 un, I
27. Rogers Hornsby .... $10 un, I
28. Kenesaw Landis .... $2 un, I
29. Roger Bresnahan .... $2 un, I
30. Dan Brouthers .... $2 un, I

Second Series (Green, 1980)

31. Fred Clarke... $2 un, I
32. Jimmy Collins .... $2 un, I
33. Ed Delahanty .... $2 un, I
34. Hugh Duffy .... $2 un, I
35. Hughie Jennings... $2 un, I
36. King Kelly .... $2 un, I
37. Jim O'Rourke .... $2 un, I
38. Wilbert Robinson .... $2 un, I
39. Jesse Burkett .... $2 un, I
40. Frank Chance .... $5 un, I
41. Jack Chesbro .... $2 un, I
42. Johnny Evers .... $5 un, I
43. Clark Griffith .... $2 un, I
44. Thomas McCarthy .... $2 un, I
45. Joe McGinnity.. $2 un, I
46. Eddie Plank .... $5 un, I
47. Joe Tinker... $5 un, I
48. Rube Waddell .... $2 un, I
49. Ed Walsh .... $2 un, I
50. Mickey Cochrane... $5 un, I

51. Frankie Frisch.. $5 un, I
52. Lefty Grove .... $10 un, I
53. Carl Hubbell.. $10 un, $70
54. Herb Pennock .... $2 un, I
55. Pie Traynor .... $2 un, I
56. Mordecai Brown .... $2 un, I
57. Charlie Gehringer .... $10 un, $55
58. Kid Nichols .... $2 un, I
59. Jimmie Foxx .... $15 un, I
60. Mel Ott... $10 un, I

Third Series (Blue, 1980)

61. Harry Heilmann .... $2 un, I
62. Paul Waner .... $5 un, I
63. Edward Barrow .... $2 un, I
64. Chief Bender .... $5 un, I
65. Tom Connolly .... $2 un, I
66. Dizzy Dean .... $10 un, I
67. Bill Klem .... $2 un, I
68. Al Simmons .... $5 un, I
69. Bobby Wallace .... $2 un, I
70. Harry Wright .... $2 un, I
71. Bill Dickey .... $10 un, $75
72. Rabbit Maranville .... $2 un, I
73. Bill Terry.. $10 un, $75
74. Frank Baker .... $5 un, I

75. Joe DiMaggio .... $25 un, $245
76. Gabby Hartnett... $2 un, I

77. Ted Lyons .... $10 un, $225

78. Ray Schalk .... $2 un, I
79. Dazzy Vance..................................... $2 un, I
80. Joe Cronin .... $10 un, $750

81. Hank Greenberg............................. $10 un, $350
82. Sam Crawford................................. $5 un, I
83. Joe McCarthy .... $10 un, I
84. Zack Wheat .... $5 un, I
85. Max Carey .... $8 un, I
86. Billy Hamilton.................................. $2 un, I
87. Bob Feller .... $10 un, $20
88. Bill McKechnie .... $2 un, I
89. Jackie Robinson .... $15 un, I
90. Edd Roush...................................... $10 un, $85

Fourth Series (1981, Red)

91. John Clarkson .... $2 un, I
92. Elmer Flick..................................... $2 un, I
93. Sam Rice .... $5 un, I
94. Eppa Rixey .... $2 un, I
95. Luke Appling................................... $8 un, $45
96. Red Faber....................................... $2 un, I

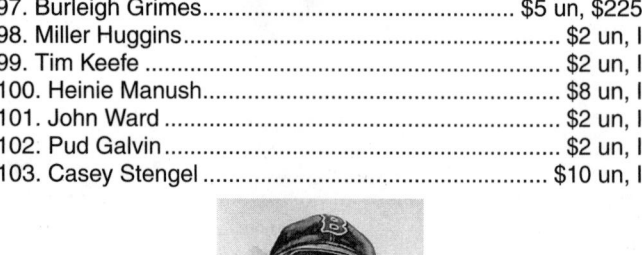

97. Burleigh Grimes............................... $5 un, $225
98. Miller Huggins................................. $2 un, I
99. Tim Keefe .... $2 un, I
100. Heinie Manush................................ $8 un, I
101. John Ward..................................... $2 un, I
102. Pud Galvin..................................... $2 un, I
103. Casey Stengel .... $10 un, I

104. Ted Williams .... $45 un, $225

105. Branch Rickey .... $2 un, I
106. Red Ruffing .... $5 un, $450

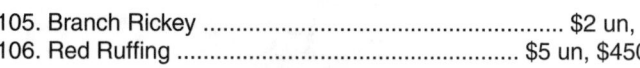

107. Lloyd Waner .... $5 un, $2,000
108. Kiki Cuyler .... $5 un, I
109. Goose Goslin .... $5 un, I
110. Joe Medwick.................................. $10 un, I
111. Roy Campanella .... $10 un, $325
112. Stan Coveleski................................ $5 un, $450
113. Waite Hoyt.................................... $5 un, $450

114. Stan Musial.................................... $25 un, $75
115. Lou Boudreau................................. $10 un, $20
116. Earle Combs................................... $5 un, I
117. Ford Frick...................................... $2 un, I
118. Jesse Haines.................................. $8 un, I
119. David Bancroft .... $2 un, I
120. Jake Beckley................................... $2 un, I

Fifth Series (1981, Yellow)

121. Chick Hafey .... $5 un, I
122. Harry Hooper.................................. $5 un, I
123. Joe Kelley .... $2 un, I
124. Rube Marquard .... $5 un, I
125. Satchel Paige .... $15 un, $2,500
126. George Weiss .... $2 un, I
127. Yogi Berra .... $15 un, $40
128. Josh Gibson .... $5 un, I
129. Lefty Gomez .... $10 un, $65
130. William Harridge .... $2 un, I

131. Sandy Koufax .... $15 un, $95
132. Buck Leonard .... $10 un, $35
133. Early Wynn .... $10 un, $25
134. Ross Youngs .... $2 un, I
135. Roberto Clemente .... $25 un, I
136. Billy Evans .... $2 un, I
137. Monte Irvin.. $10 un, $15
138. George Kelly .... $5 un, $300

139. Warren Spahn .... $10 un, $20
140. Mickey Welch.. $2 un, I
141. Cool Papa Bell .... $10 un, $70
142. Jim Bottomley .... $5 un, I
143. Jocko Conlan .... $5 un, $35
144. Whitey Ford .... $10 un, $40
145. Mickey Mantle..................................... $50 un, $250
146. Sam Thompson .... $2 un, I
147. Earl Averill .... $10 un, $450
148. Bucky Harris .... $2 un, I
149. Billy Herman .... $5 un, $25
150. Judy Johnson .... $10 un, $65

Sixth Series (1981, Orange)

151. Ralph Kiner... $10 un, $15
152. Oscar Charleston .... $5 un, I

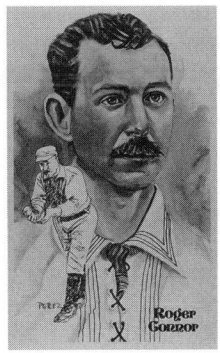

153. Roger Connor .... $2 un, I
154. Cal Hubbard .... $2 un, I
155. Bob Lemon .... $10 un, $20
156. Freddie Lindstrom................................. $2 un, I
157. Robin Roberts .... $10 un, $15

158. Ernie Banks.. $10 un, $35
159. Martin DiHigo .... $5 un, I
160. John Lloyd .... $5 un, I
161. Al Lopez .... $10 un, $55
162. Amos Rusie .... $2 un, I
163. Joe Sewell .... $10 un, $45
164. Addie Joss .... $2 un, I
165. Larry MacPhail .... $2 un, I
166. Eddie Mathews .... $10 un, $35
167. Warren Giles.. $2 un, I

168. Willie Mays .... $20 un, $95
169. Hack Wilson.. $5 un, I
170. Al Kaline .... $10 un, $20
171. Chuck Klein .... $2 un, I
172. Duke Snider.. $10 un, $40
173. Tom Yawkey .... $2 un, I
174. Rube Foster .... $2 un, I
175. Bob Gibson .... $10 un, $20
176. Johnny Mize .... $10 un, $25
A. Abner Doubleday .... $5 un, I
B. Stephen C. Clark................................. $2 un, I
C. Paul S. Kerr .... $2 un, I
D. Edward W. Stack .... $8 un, $12

Seventh Series (1983, Brown)

177. Hank Aaron .... $15 un, $75

178. Happy Chandler.. $5 un, $25
179. Travis Jackson .... $5 un, $75

180. Frank Robinson .... $10 un, $25
181. Walter Alston .... $10 un, $650
182. George Kell.. $5 un, $10
183. Juan Marichal .... $5 un, $15
184. Brooks Robinson .... $10 un, $20

Eighth Series (1985, Green)

185. Luis Aparicio... $10 un, $20
186. Don Drysdale.. $5 un, $30

187. Rick Ferrell .... $5 un, $15
188. Harmon Killebrew .... $10 un, $25

189. Pee Wee Reese.. $10 un, $40

190. Lou Brock .... $8 un, $20

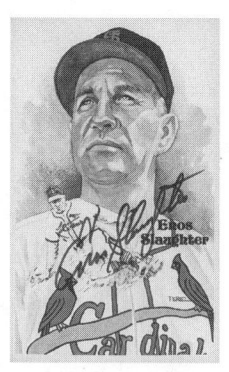

191. Enos Slaughter... $5 un, $15
192. Arky Vaughan .... $5 un, I

193. Hoyt Wilhelm .... $5 un, $15

Ninth Series (1987, Blue)

194. Bobby Doerr .... $5 un, $8
195. Ernie Lombardi .... $5 un, I
196. Willie McCovey .... $5 un, $25
197. Ray Dandridge .... $5 un, $12
198. Catfish Hunter .... $5 un, $25
199. Billy Williams .... $5 un, $12
E. Perez-Steele "Family".. $2 un, $6

Tenth Series (1989, Red)

200. Willie Stargell.. $5 un, $25
201. Al Barlick .... $2 un, $15
202. Johnny Bench.. $5 un, $40
203. Red Schoendienst .... $5 un, $15
204 .Carl Yastrzemski.. $5 un, $35
F. President Bush & Ed Stack................................... $5 un, $200

Eleventh Series (1991)

205. Joe Morgan .... $5 un, $40
206. Jim Palmer... $5 un, $35
207. Rod Carew... $5 un, $35
208. Ferguson Jenkins .... $5 un, $20
209. Tony Lazzeri .... $2 un, I
210. Gaylord Perry .... $5 un, $20
211. Bill Veeck .... $2 un, I

Twelfth Series

212. Steve Carlton .... $5 un, $30
213. Leo Durocher.. $5 un, I
214. Rollie Fingers .... $5 un, $15
215. Reggie Jackson.. $5 un, $25
216. Bill McGowan.. $5 un, I
217. Hal Newhouser.. $5, $15-$20
218. Phil Rizzuto .... $15 un, $35
219. Tom Seaver $15, $35

Thirteenth Series

220. Richie Ashburn .... $10 un, $100
221. Jim Bunning... $5 un, $15
222. Leon Day .... $5 un, I
223. Bill Foster .... $5 un, I
224. Ned Hanlon .... $5 un, I
225. William Hulbert .... $5 un, I
226. Mike Schmidt.................................... $10 un, $25-$30
227. Earl Weaver .... $5 un, $15
228. Vic Willis .... $5 un, I

Fourteenth Series

229. Nellie Fox.. $5 un, I
230. Tom Lasorda.. $5 un, $65
231. Phil Niekro .... $5 un, $40
232. Willie Wells .... $3 un, I
233. George Davis.. $2 un, I

234. Larry Doby... $10 un, $45
235. Lee MacPhail... $10 un, $45
236. Joe Rogan .... $5 un, I

237. Don Sutton .... $10 un, $40

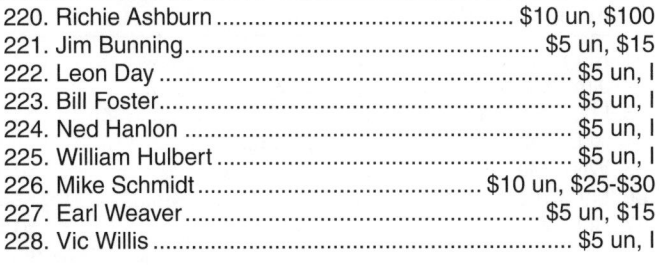

238. George Brett.. $10 un, $90
239. Orlando Cepeda .... $10 un, $45
240. Nestor Chylak .... $2 un, I
241. Nolan Ryan.. $15 un, $90
242. Frank Selee .... $2 un, I
243. Joe Williams .... $3 un, I
244. Robin Yount .... $10 un, $80

Fifteenth Series

245. Sparky Anderson... $10 un, $45
246. Carlton Fisk .... $10 un, $75
247. Bid McPhee .... $3 un, I
248. Tony Perez .... $10 un, $45
249. Turkey Stearnes .... $3 un, I
250. Bill Mazeroski .... $10 un, $35
251. Kirby Puckett .... $10 un, $90
252. Hilton Smith .... $3 un, I
253. Dave Winfield .... $10 un, $75
G. Franklin A. Steele .... $5 un

Perez-Steele Great Moments

In 1985, Perez-Steele Galleries offered 5,000 numbered sets of Great Moments postcards, with periodical updates. These cards are generally purchased for the autograph, or to be autographed; the prices listed are for signed postcards. "I" means it's impossible that the player could have signed the card. Generally, unsigned cards sell for about $5-$15 each, except for higher priced cards for players such as Babe Ruth, Lou Gehrig, Ted Williams, Mickey Mantle, Stan Musial and Charlie Gehringer.

First Series (1985)

1. Babe Ruth .... $15 un, I
2. Al Kaline $20
3. Jackie Robinson .... $10 un, I
4. Lou Gehrig.. $10 un, I
5. Whitey Ford $35
6. Christy Mathewson .... $5 un, I
7. Roy Campanella .... $8 un, $200
8. Walter Johnson.. $5 un, I
9. Hank Aaron $55
10. Cy Young .... $5 un, I
11. Stan Musial.. $55
12. Ty Cobb .... $15 un, I

Second Series (1987)

13. Ted Williams $175
14. Warren Spahn $20
15. The Waner Brothers I
16. Sandy Koufax $75
17. Robin Roberts $15
18. Dizzy Dean .... $5 un, I
19. Mickey Mantle.. $195
20. Satchel Paige .... $10 un, I
21. Ernie Banks $35
22. Willie McCovey $25

23. Johnny Mize $20
24. Honus Wagner.. $5 un, I

Third Series (1988)

25. Willie Keeler.. I
26. Pee Wee Reese $45
27. Monte Irvin.. $10
28. Eddie Mathews $25
29. Enos Slaughter $15
30. Rube Marquard I
31. Charlie Gehringer $45

32. Roberto Clemente .... $15 un, I

33. Duke Snider...$25
34. Ray Dandridge..$15
35. Carl Hubbell..$50
36. Bobby Doerr $6

Fourth Series (1988)

37. Bill Dickey $45
38. Willie Stargell...$30
39. Brooks Robinson $15
40. Tinker-Evers-Chance..$5 un, I
41. Billy Herman $15
42. Grover Alexander...$2 un, I
43. Luis Aparicio $12
44. Lefty Gomez $35
45. Eddie Collins...I
46. Judy Johnson ....$5 un, I
47. Harry Heilmann I
48. Harmon Killebrew $25

Fifth Series (1990)

49. Johnny Bench...$35
50. Max Carey I
51. Cool Papa Bell..$5 un, $80
52. Rube Waddell I
53. Yogi Berra $20

54. Herb Pennock...I

55. Red Schoendienst $15
56. Juan Marichal $15
57. Frankie Frisch I
58. Buck Leonard $35
59. George Kell...$15

60. Chuck Klein I

Sixth Series (1990)

61. King Kelly I
62. Jim Hunter $35
63. Lou Boudreau $15
64. Al Lopez $45
65. Willie Mays $75
66. Lou Brock $25
67. Bob Lemon $15
68. Joe Sewell ....$2 un, I
69. Billy Williams $15
70. Rick Ferrell $10
71. Arky Vaughan I
72. Carl Yastrzemski $35

Seventh Series (1991)

73. Tom Seaver $45
74. Rollie Fingers $25
75. Ralph Kiner $20
76. Frank Baker I
77. Rod Carew $45
78. Goose Goslin I
79. Gaylord Perry $20
80. Hack Wilson..I
81. Hal Newhouser $55
82. Early Wynn $55
83. Bob Feller $15
84. Branch Rickey ....$5 un, I

Eighth Series (1992)

85. Jim Palmer..$35
86. Al Barlick $35
87. Willie, Mickey & Duke ....$15 un
88. Hank Greenberg ....$5 un, I
89. Joe Morgan $35
90. Chief Bender I
91. Reese, Robinson $95
92. Jim Bottomley I
93. Ferguson Jenkins $20
94. Frank Robinson $35
95. Hoyt Wilhelm $35
96. Cap Anson..I

Ninth Series (1992)

97. Jim Bunning..$35
98. Richie Ashburn ....$5 un, signed very rare
99. Steve Carlton $35
100. Mike Schmidt...$75
101. Nellie Fox..$5 un, I
102. Tommy Lasorda $65
103. Leo Duracher ....$5 un, I
104. Reggie Jackson $65
105. Phil Niekro $35
106. Phil Rizzuto $30
107. Willie Wells I
108. Earl Weaver $25

Perez-Steele Celebration Cards

This 45-card set was issued in 1989 to commemorate the 50th anniversary of the Baseball Hall of Fame and the Galleries' 10th anniversary. There were 10,000 sets made. The set will not be updated; a complete set has 44 Hall of Famers and one checklist. Cards are 3 1/2-by-5 1/4 inches in size. "I" means it is impossible that the player could have signed the card. Unsigned cards are generally about $8-$10 each, but are generally more for players such as Mickey Mantle, Stan Musial and Ted Williams.

15. Charlie Gehringer		$5 un, $35
16. Lefty Gomez		$3 un, I
17. Billy Herman		$3 un, $15
18. Catfish Hunter		$3 un, $30
19. Monte Irvin		$3 un, $15
20. Judy Johnson		$3 un, I
21. Al Kaline		$3 un, $20

1. Hank Aaron		$3 un, $45
2. Luis Aparicio		$3 un, $12
3. Ernie Banks		$2 un, $25
4. Cool Papa Bell		$5 un, $55
5. Johnny Bench		$3 un, $35
6. Yogi Berra		$5 un, $30
7. Lou Boudreau		$3 un, $12
8. Roy Campanella		$3 un, $200
9. Happy Chandler		$3 un, $25
10. Jocko Conlan		$3 un, $450
11. Ray Dandridge		$5 un, $20
12. Bill Dickey		$3 un, $55
13. Bobby Doerr		$3 un, $10
14. Rick Ferrell		$3 un, $15

22. George Kell		$3 un, $10
23. Harmon Killebrew		$3 un, $20
24. Ralph Kiner		$3 un, $15
25. Bob Lemon		$3 un, $10
26. Buck Leonard		$3 un, $20
27. Al Lopez		$3 un, $55
28. Mickey Mantle		$15 un, $150
29. Juan Marichal		$2 un, $10
30. Eddie Mathews		$3 un, $25
31. Willie McCovey		$3 un, $25
32. Johnny Mize		$3 un, $15
33. Stan Musial		$5 un, $45
34. Pee Wee Reese		$3 un, $30
35. Brooks Robinson		$3 un, $12
36. Joe Sewell		$3 un, $30
37. Enos Slaughter		$3 un, $10
38. Duke Snider		$5 un, $30
39. Warren Spahn		$3 un, $15
40. Willie Stargell		$3 un, $12
41. Bill Terry		$3 un, I
42. Billy Williams		$3 un, $10
43. Ted Williams		$10 un, $95
44. Carl Yastrzemski		$3 un, $15

Perez-Steele Master Works

This 50-card set was produced in two 25-card series beginning in 1990 and features 10 players on five different postcard styles. The players are Charlie Gehringer, Mickey Mantle, Willie Mays, Duke Snider, Warren Spahn, Yogi Berra, Johnny Mize, Willie Stargell, Ted Williams and Carl Yastrzemski. Four designs are modeled after the 1888 Goodwin Champions baseball card set, the 1908 Rose cards, the Ramly 1909 set and the 1911 gold-bordered T205 set. The last design was created by the artist, Dick Perez. There were 10,000 sets produced. Prices are for individual cards.

Charlie Gehringer

1. Ramly	($6 unsigned, $50 signed)
2. Goodwin	($6 unsigned, $50 signed)
3. Rose	($6 unsigned, $50 signed)
4. Gold Border	($6 unsigned, $50 signed)
5. Perez-Steele	($6 unsigned, $50 signed)

Mickey Mantle

6. Ramly .... ($20 unsigned, $150 signed)
7. Goodwin .... ($20 unsigned, $150 signed)
8. Rose .... ($20 unsigned, $150 signed)
9. Gold Border .... ($20 unsigned, $150 signed)
10. Perez-Steele .... ($20 unsigned, $150 signed)

Willie Mays

11. Ramly .... ($7 unsigned, $35 signed)
12. Goodwin .... ($7 unsigned, $35 signed)
13. Rose .... ($7 unsigned, $35 signed)
14. Gold Border .... ($7 unsigned, $35 signed)
15. Perez-Steele .... ($7 unsigned, $35 signed)

Duke Snider

16. Ramly .... ($6 unsigned, $20 signed)
17. Goodwin .... ($6 unsigned, $20 signed)
18. Rose .... ($6 unsigned, $20 signed)
19. Gold Border .... ($6 unsigned, $20 signed)
20. Perez-Steele .... ($6 unsigned, $20 signed)

Warren Spahn

21. Ramly .... ($6 unsigned, $20 signed)
22. Goodwin .... ($6 unsigned, $20 signed)
23. Rose .... ($6 unsigned, $20 signed)
24. Gold Border .... ($6 unsigned, $20 signed)
25. Perez-Steele .... ($6 unsigned, $20 signed)

Yogi Berra

26. Ramly .... ($7 unsigned, $25 signed)
27. Goodwin .... ($7 unsigned, $25 signed)

28. Rose .... ($7 unsigned, $25 signed)
29. Gold Border .... ($7 unsigned, $25 signed)
30. Perez-Steele .... ($7 unsigned, $25 signed)

Johnny Mize

31. Ramly .... ($6 unsigned, $35 signed)
32. Goodwin .... ($6 unsigned, $35 signed)
33. Rose .... ($6 unsigned, $35 signed)
34. Gold Border .... ($6 unsigned, $35 signed)
35. Perez-Steele .... ($6 unsigned, $35 signed)

Willie Stargell

36. Ramly .... ($6 unsigned, $20 signed)
37. Goodwin .... ($6 unsigned, $20 signed)
38. Rose .... ($6 unsigned, $20 signed)
39. Gold Border .... ($6 unsigned, $20 signed)
40. Perez-Steele .... ($6 unsigned, $20 signed)

Ted Williams

41. Ramly .... ($20 unsigned, $125 signed)
42. Goodwin .... ($20 unsigned, $125 signed)
43. Rose .... ($20 unsigned, $125 signed)
44. Gold Border .... ($20 unsigned, $125 signed)
45. Perez-Steele .... ($20 unsigned, $125 signed)

Carl Yastrzemski

46. Ramly .... ($10 unsigned, $30 signed)
47. Goodwin .... ($10 unsigned, $30 signed)
48. Rose .... ($10 unsigned, $30 signed)
49. Gold Border .... ($10 unsigned, $30 signed)
50. Perez-Steele .... ($10 unsigned, $30 signed)

Goal Line Hall of Fame Art Cards

These gorgeous postcard-sized cards by artist Gary Thomas feature full-color paintings of all members of the Pro Football Hall of Fame. Many believe the Goal Line set is among the most beautiful artwork in sports memorabilia. The set is especially poignant for collectors of teams because it provides a rare yet exact color and image reference to stars of yore, such as Cliff Battles, Bronko Nagurski, Ace Parker and Mel Hein.

Started in 1989, these limited-edition (numbered to 5,000) cards were issued in six sets. Since 1995, each year's Hall inductees have constituted the set with the exception of 1997, when the long-awaited Johnny Unitas card withheld from Series 6 was included in the set with the 1997 Hall inductees.

Each player receives 50 hand-numbered cards stamped "proof." The player can keep the cards or sign them and return as a donation to the Hall of Fame gift shop for $1,000. These "proofs" generally are not worth more than 10 to 20 percent than that of the regularly signed edition.

GL Art is a very popular item to have signed by the HOFers. Some of the cards have proved to be more collectible than others. For example, the first series of 30 cards has long been sold out, but many of the individual cards can still be bought. Also, cards of those players known to be popular signers are generally more difficult to find because collectors have gobbled up the cards to secure autographs. Example: Sammy Baugh.

Most of the cards sell for $2 to $6. The cards are issued in alphabetical order according to set. Goal Line Art also lists the cards in numerical order for the purpose of listing. Signed cards are generally priced as the value of the card plus the player's signature. But there are exceptions.

Some players (such as Deacon Jones) have been reluctant to sign the cards because the limited edition has made the signed pieces fairly valuable. Coaches Joe Gibbs and Don Shula have been known to sign GL Art only at charity functions, thus limiting availability. Lynn Swann is leary of the autograph hobby. And Alex Wojciechowicz died about a month after his card was issued, limiting the number of signatures on GL Art.

The most desired signed GL Art is that of Dan Fortmann, who suffered from Parkinson's Disease and died in 1995. Given Fortmann's health condition, authenticators have had a difficult time verifying his few available signatures on the cards. It's a widely held belief that his wife might have signed some of the cards.

All of these factors are considered by dealers and collectors when selling, buying and pricing Goal Line Art. For pricing of signed Goal Line Hall of Fame art cards, see the Football Hall of Fame autograph pricing in Chapter 1.

	MT
Complete Set (221):	$800
Uncut sheet of Series I	$2,100

1989, Series 1 (30)—Keys: Terry Bradshaw, Jim Brown, Frank Gifford, Otto Graham, Red Grange, Jim Thorpe ... $150

1990, Series 2 (30)—Keys: Paul Brown, Dan Fortmann, Paul Hornung, Bronko Nagurski, Joe Namath, Ray Nitschke ... $85

1991, Series 3 (30)—Keys: Dick Butkus, Earl Campbell, Don Hutson, Vince Lombardi, Roger Staubach ... $85

1992, Series 4 (30)—Keys: Sammy Baugh, Al Davis, Mel Hein, Bob Lilly, John Riggins, Alex Wojciechowicz ... $85

1993 Series 5 (30)—Keys: George Blanda, Bob Griese, Lamar Hunt, Jack Lambert, Tom Landry, Walter Payton ... $85

1994 Series 6 (24)—Keys: Tony Dorsett, Franco Harris, Curly Lambeau, O.J. Simpson, Bart Starr ... $85

1995 (5)—Jim Finks, Henry Jordan, Steve Largent, Lee Roy Selmon and Kellen Winslow ... $28

1996 (5)—Lou Creekmur, Dan Dierdorf, Joe Gibbs, Charlie Joiner and Mel Renfro. ... $28

1997 (5)—Mike Haynes, Wellington Mara, Don Shula and Mike Webster, plus the issue of Johnny Unitas withheld from Series 6. ... $28

1998 (5)—Paul Krause, Tommy McDonald, Anthony Munoz, Mike Singletary and Dwight Stevensen ... $28

1999 (5)—Eric Dickerson, Tom Mack, Ozzie Newsome, Billy Shaw and Lawrence Taylor ... $28

2000 (5)—Howie Long, Ronnie Lott, Joe Montana, Dan Rooney, and Dave Wilcox.. ... $24

2001 (7)—Nick Buoniconti, Marv Levy, Mike Munchak, Jackie Slater, Lynn Swann, Ron Yary and Jack Youngblood ... $25

2002 (5)—George Allen, Dave Casper, Dan Hampton, Jim Kelly and John Stallworth ... $25

2003 (5)—Marcus Allen, Elvin Bethea, Joe DeLamielleure, James Lofton and Hank Stram ... $25

Unsigned	Mint
1 Lance Alworth	$6

Unsigned	Mint
2 Morris (Red) Badgro	$2.50
3 Cliff Battles	$2.50

Unsigned	MT
4 Mel Blount	$2.50
5 Terry Bradshaw	$15
6 Jim Brown	$15
7 George Connor	$2.50
8 Turk Edwards	$2.50
9 Tom Fears	$2.50
10 Frank Gifford	$10
11 Otto Graham	$15
12 Red Grange	$5
13 George Halas	$4
14 Clarke Hinkle	$2.50
15 Robert (Cal) Hubbard	$2.50
16 Sam Huff	$2.50
17 Frank (Bruiser) Kinard	$2.50
18 Dick (Night Train) Lane	$2.50
19 Sid Luckman	$6
20 Bobby Mitchell	$2.50
21 Merlin Olsen	$4
22 Jim Parker	$2.50
23 Joe Perry	$3
24 Pete Rozelle	$3
25 Art Shell	$3
26 Fran Tarkenton	$9
27 Jim Thorpe	$6
28 Paul Warfield	$3
29 Larry Wilson	$2.50
30 Willie Wood	$2.50
31 Doug Atkins	$2
32 Bobby Bell	$2
33 Raymond Berry	$3
34 Paul Brown	$2
35 Guy Chamberlin	$2

Unsigned	MT		Unsigned	MT
36 Earl (Dutch) Clark	$2		67 Ray Flaherty	$2
37 Jimmy Conzelman	$2		68 Forrest Gregg	$2.50
38 Len Dawson	$3		69 Lou Groza	$3
39 Mike Ditka	$8		70 John Hannah	$2
40 Dan Fortmann	$2		71 Don Hutson	$2.50
41 Frank Gatski	$2		72 David (Deacon) Jones	$2
42 Bill George	$2		73 Stan Jones	$2
43 Elroy Hirsch	$3		74 Sonny Jurgensen	$3
44 Paul Hornung	$4		75 Vince Lombardi	$3
45 John Henry Johnson	$2		76 Tim Mara	$2
46 Walt Kiesling	$2		77 Ollie Matson	$2
47 Yale Lary	$2		78 Mike McCormack	$2
48 Bobby Layne	$3		79 John (Blood) McNally	$2
49 Tuffy Leemans	$2		80 Marion Motley	$2
50 Geo. Preston Marshal	$12		81 George Musso	$2
51 George McAfee	$2		82 Earle (Greasy) Neale	$2
52 Wayne Millner	$2		83 Clarence (Ace) Parker	$2
53 Bronko Nagurski	$4		84 Pete Pihos	$2
54 Joe Namath	$10		85 Tex Schramm	$2
55 Ray Nitschke	$3		86 Roger Staubach	$12
56 Jim Ringo	$2		87 Jan Stenerud	$2
57 Art Rooney	$2		88 Y.A. Tittle	$3
58 Joe Stydahar	$2		89 Clyde (Bulldog) Turner	$2
59 Charley Taylor	$2		90 Steve Van Buren	$2
60 Charlie Trippi	$2		91 Herb Adderley	$2
61 Fred Biletnikoff	$3		92 Lem Barney	$2
62 Buck Buchanan	$2		93 Sammy Baugh	$10
63 Dick Butkus	$6		94 Chuck Bednarik	$3
64 Earl Campbell	$8		95 Charles W. Bidwill	$2
65 Tony Canadeo	$2		96 Willie Brown	$2
66 Art Donovan	$3		97 Al Davis	$4

Unsigned	MT
98 Bill Dudley	$2
99 Weeb Ewbank	$2
100 Len Ford	$2
101 Sid Gillman	$2
102 Jack Ham	$2
103 Mel Hein	$2
104 Bill Hewitt	$2
105 Dante Lavelli	$2
106 Bob Lilly	$3
107 John Mackey	$2
108 Hugh McElhenny	$3
109 Mike Michalske	$2
110 Ron Mix	$2
111 Leo Nomellini	$2
112 Steve Owen	$2
113 Alan Page	$2.50
114 Dan Reeves	$2
115 John Riggins	$3
116 Gale Sayers	$6
117 Ken Strong	$2
118 Gene Upshaw	$3
119 Norm Van Brocklin	$4
120 Alex Wojciechowicz	$2
121 Bert Bell	$2
122 George Blanda	$4
123 Joe Carr	$2
124 Larry Csonka	$4
125 John (Paddy) Driscoll	$2
126 Dan Fouts	$3
127 Bob Griese	$4
128 Ed Healy	$2
129 Wilbur (Fats) Henry	$2
130 Ken Houston	$2
131 Lamar Hunt	$2
132 Jack Lambert	$2.50
133 Tom Landry	$4
134 Willie Lanier	$2
135 Larry Little	$2
136 Don Maynard	$3
137 Lenny Moore	$3
138 Chuck Noll	$3
139 Jim Otto	$2
140 Walter Payton	$10
141 Hugh (Shorty) Ray	$2
142 Andy Robustelli	$2
143 Bob St. Clair	$2
144 Joe Schmidt	$3
145 Jim Taylor	$3
146 Doak Walker	$3
147 Bill Walsh	$3
148 Bob Waterfield	$3
149 Arnie Weinmeister	$2
150 Bill Willis	$2
151 Roosevelt Brown	$2
152 Jack Christiansen	$2
153 Willie Davis	$3
154 Tony Dorsett	$6
155 Bud Grant	$2
156 Joe Greene	$5
157 Joe Guyon	$2
158 Franco Harris	$4
159 Ted Hendricks	$2
160 Arnie Herber	$2

	MT
161 Jimmy Johnson	$2
162 Leroy Kelly	$2

Unsigned	MT
163 Curly Lambeau	$2
164 Jim Langer	$2
165 Link Lyman	$2
166 Gino Marchetti	$3
167 Ernie Nevers	$3
168 O.J. Simpson	$12
169 Jackie Smith	$2
170 Bart Starr	$12
171 Ernie Stautner	$2.50
172 George Trafton	$2
173 Emlen Tunnell	$2
174 Johnny Unitas	$5
175 Randy White	$2.50
176 Jim Finks	$2
177 Henry Jordan	$2.50
178 Steve Largent	$3
179 Lee Roy Selmon	$2.50
180 Kellen Winslow	$2.50
181 Lou Creekmur	$2
182 Dan Dierdorf	$2
183 Joe Gibbs	$2
184 Charlie Joiner	$2
185 Mel Renfro	$2
186 Mike Haynes	$2
187 Wellington Mara	$2
188 Don Shula	$3
189 Mike Webster	$2
190 Paul Krause	$2
191 Tommy McDonald	$2
192 Anthony Munoz	$2
193 Mike Singeltary	$2
194 Dwight Stevensen	$2
195 Eric Dickerson	$2
196 Tom Mack	$2
197 Ozzie Newsome	$2
198 Billy Shaw	$2
199 Lawrence Taylor	$3
200 Howie Long	$2
201 Ronnie Lott	$2
202 Joe Montana	$2
203 Dan Rooney	$2
204 Dave Wilcox	$2
205 Nick Buoniconti	$2
206 Marv Levy	$2
207 Mike Munchak	$2
208 Jackie Slater	$2
209 Lynn Swann	$3
210 Ron Yary	$2
211 Jack Youngblood	$2
212 George Allen	$2
213 Dave Casper	$2
214 Dan Hampton	$2
215 Jim Kelly	$2
216 John Stallworth	$2
217 Marcus Allen	$2
218 Elvin Bethea	$2
219 Joe Delamielleure	$2
220 James Lofton	$2
221 Hank Stram	$2

Commemorative Historic Limited Editions
Z Silk Cachets

When Don Mattingly tied Dale Long's record of eight homers in eight consecutive games, Historic Limited Editions was there to capture the event on a silk-cacheted philatelic cover. The process begins with a staff artist who does an original painting of a ballplayer or event. The painting is then reproduced on specially-manufactured silk-like cloth in full color. These silk cachets are then applied by hand to envelopes which have been stamped and postmarked by the post office in the corresponding city where the event occurred.

In the case of the Mattingly record, company president John Zaso, with a few minutes to spare before a midnight deadline, flew to Arlington, Texas, to secure a postmark with the date of the event — July 18, 1987. Six hundred envelopes were created. Generally, 200 to 600 covers are produced per event, depending on the player and/or event involved and potential demand by collectors. Mattingly has been one of the more popular players. Several events, including the World Series, playoffs, All-Star games and Hall of Fame inductions, are commemorated annually. Year-end award winners are also recognized.

The covers are suitable for autographing, although the company does offer a limited number already signed by the players. Investment potential varies, but some command far more than the original issue price. For example, the cachet honoring Reggie Jackson's 500th home run had an issue price of $4 but is now up to $150 autographed. Historic Limited Editions is located in New Canaan, Conn.

In the following checklist, based on Mint condition, an "a" after the value means the item is autographed. The prices are the current market prices.

Subject/Description	Value
Abbott, Jim - No-Hitter at Yankee Stadium	$7
Abbott, Jim - No-Hitter - Different Cachet	$7
Aaron, Hank - Retired Uniform, Atlanta	$5
Abrams, Cal - Brooklyn Dodger Hall of Fame	$7
Aguilera, Rick - 25th Anniversary Mets	$5
Allen, Mel - Historic Cooperstown	$7
1983 All-Star Game - 50th Anniversary All-Star Game on 8 Ruth First Day Covers	$55
1990 All-Star Game - Chicago	$5
1992 All-Star Game - San Diego	$5
1995 All-Star Game - Arlington	$5
1996 All-Star Game - Philadelphia	$5
1996 All-Star Game Fanfest - Philadelphia	$5
Alomar, Sandy - 1991 All-Star Game Toronto, Canada	$5
Alomar, Sandy - 1997 All-Star Game MVP	$5
Alomar, Sandy - 1997 World Series Game 2	$8
Alomar, Roberto - 1992 World Series Game 3	$10
Alomar, Roberto and Darren Daulton - 1993 World Series Game	$7
Alou, Moises - 1997 World Series Game 5	$8
Alston, Walter - 1983 Hall of Fame Induction	$8
Alston, Walter	$5
Amoros, Sandy - 1955 World Series Catch	$5
Amoros, Sandy - 1955 Series	$5
Aparicio, Luis - Big Apple III Show Cover	$5
Aparicio, Luis - Big Apple IV Show Cover	$5
Aparicio, Luis - Big Apple III Show Card	$3
Aparicio, Luis - Big Apple IV Show Card	$4
Aparicio, Luis - Heroes of Baseball - Argentina Honors	$7
Arroyo, Luis - Salute to '61 Yankees	$6
Arroyo, Luis - Old Timer's Day	$5
Ashburn, Richie - Retired Uniform	$5

Subject/Description	Value
Ashburn, Richie - Hall of Fame Induction Phillies Uniform	$8
Ashburn, Richie - Hall of Fame Induction Mets Uniform	$5
Ashburn, Richie - Dies	$5
Aspromonte, Bob	$5
Backman, Wally - Mets 25th Anniversary	$5
Bagwell, Jeff - 1991 N.L. Rookie of the Year	$9
Bagwell, Jeff - Frank Thomas 1994 MVP's	$5
Bagwell, Jeff - 1994 Gold Glove	$8
Baltimore Orioles - 1993 Opening Day	$5
Bankhead Dan	$5
Banta, Jack	$5
Barber, Red - Dodger Announcer	$5
Barber, Red - First T.V. Game Interviewing Leo Durocher	$5
Barfield, Jesse - Traded to Yanks	$5
Barlick, Al - 1989 Hall of Fame Election	$5
Barlick, Al - 1989 Hall of Fame Induction	$5
Barney, Rex	$5
Barrett, Marty - 1989 Playoffs	$5
Barrow, Ed - Yankee Memorial Park	$5
Baseball Strike 1985	$4
Baseball Strike Settlement 1985	$4
Bauer, Hank - Old Timer's Day 1985	$5
Bauer, Hank - Old Timer's Day 1991	$5
Bauer, Hank - Queens New York Card Show	$5
Bauer, Hank - Queens New York Card Show Card	$4
Baylor, Don - Breaks Minoso Record	$7
Baylor, Don - Received the Roberto Clemente Award	$6
Bedrosian, Steve - 1987 N.L. Cy Young Award	$6
Behrman, Hank	$5
Bench, Johnny & Carl Hubbell 50th Anniversary of All-Star Game Cachet	$10

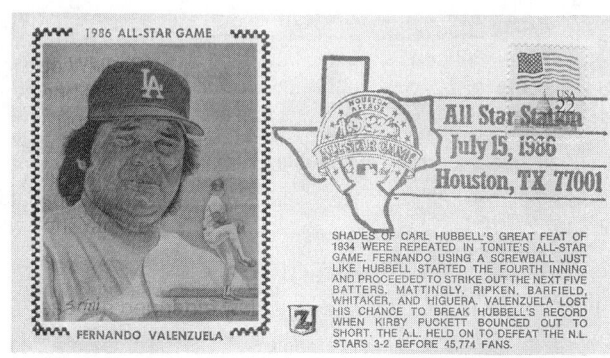

Subject/Description	Value
Bench, Johnny - Elected for Induction to Hall of Fame	$8
Bench, Johnny - Hall of Fame Induction	$10
Berra, Dale - Traded to Yankees	$4
Berra, Yogi - Named Yankee Manager 1983	$8
Berra, Dale & Yogi - Father and Son Team	$5
Berra, Yogi - Dismissed	$5
Berra, Yogi - Memorial Park	$8
Berra, Yogi - Salute to the '69 Mets	$6
Berra, Yogi - Salute to the '61 Yankees	$8
Berra, Yogi - New Brunswick Card Show	$5
Berra, Yogi - New Brunswick Show Postmarked Show Card	$4
Berra, Dandridge, Mathews at Hall of Fame Show	$35
Berryhill, Damon - '92 World Series Game 1	$7
Bessent, Don - Dodgers Win 56 Pennant	$5
Bevacqua, Kurt - 1984 World Series Game 2	$8
Black, Joe	$5
Blanchard, Johnny - Salute to '61 Yankees	$6
Blanchard, Johnny - Old Timer's Day	$5
Boddicker, Mike - Columbia MD Show	$4
Boddicker, Mike - Columbia MD Show Postmarked Show Card	$4
Boddicker, Mike - 1983 World Series Game 3	$10
Boggs, Wade - Card Show Postmarked Show Card	$6
Boggs, Wade - 1986 World Series Game 2	$10
Boggs, Wade - 1987 Batting Title	$7
Boggs, Wade - 200 Hits in 6 Seasons	$8
Boggs, Wade - 1993 All-Star Game	$6
Boggs, Wade - 1995 All-Star Game	$6
Bonds, Barry - 1992 N.L. MVP	$8
Bonds, Barry - Frank Thomas 1993 N.L. MVP's	$5
Bonds, Barry - 1993 Gold Glove	$7
Bonds, Barry, Williams & Lewis 1994 Gold Glove	$6
Bonds, Barry - 1997 Gold Glove	$6
Bonilla, Bobby - 1993 Mets Opening Day	$6
Boone, Bob - All Time Record For Games Caught 1919	$10
Borders, Pat - 1992 World Series Game 6	$7
Borders, Pat - 1992 World Series MVP	$5
Borowy, Hank - Show Cover	$4
Borowy, Hank - Show Card	$4
Boyer, Clete - Old Timer's Day	$5
Boyer, Clete - Salute to the '61 Yankees	$6
Boswell, Ken - Salute to the '69 Mets	$5
Branca, Ralph - Shot Heard Round the World	$5
Branca, Ralph - Hasbrouck Heights Show, Show Card	$4
Bragan, Bobby - Dodger Symphony Band	$5
Brett, George - 1985 World Series Game 7	$10
Brett, George - 1985 A.L. Playoffs	$10
Brett, George - 3,000 Hit	$10
Brett, George - Opening Day	$7
Brett, George - Set of 2 Covers Pine Tar Game and Playoff	$40
Bridges, Rocky	$5
Brock, Lou - Elected into the Hall of Fame 1985	$8
Brock, Lou - Inducted into the Hall of Fame 1985	$10
Brock, Lou - Arlington Texas Show Cover	$5
Brock, Hunter, Jenkins on Hall of Fame Show Cover	$35
Brooks, Hubie - 100th RBI 1985	$5
Brown, Don - Traded to the New York Mets	$5
Brown, Tommy	$5
Browning, Tom - Pitches a Perfect Game 1988	$10
Bunning, Jim - Hall of Fame Induction - Phillies Uniform	$8
Bunning, Jim - Hall of Fame Induction - Detroit Uniform	$8
Byrne, Tommy - Old Timer's Day Game	$5
Cabrera, Francisco - 1992 N.L. Playoffs	$5
Callison, Johnny - Valley Forge Show Cover	$5
Callison, Johnny - Valley Forge Show Card	$4
Camilli, Dolph	$5
Caminiti, Ken and Juan Gonzalez - 1996 MVP Award	$5
Campanella, Roy - 1949 All-Star Game	$7
Campanella, Roy - 6th National Card Show	$6

Subject/Description	Value
Campanella, Roy - Uniform Retired	$5
Campanella, Roy - Paralyzed Following Auto Accident	$5
Campanella, Roy - Last Game at Ebbits Field	$5
Campanella, Roy - Received the 1955 MVP Award	$6
Candelario, John - 1989 Exhibition Game	$5
Canseco, Jose - 1988 A.L. Playoffs	$6
Canseco, Jose - 1988 A.L. MVP	$7
Cardwell, Don - Salute to the '69 Mets	$5
Carew, Rod - Record Hit #3024	$9
Carew, Rod - Hall of Fame Induction 1991	$6
Carey, Andy - Plainview N.Y. Card Show Cover	$4
Carey, Andy - Plainview N.Y. Card Show Postmarked Show Card	$4
Carlton, Steve - 1983 N.L. Playoffs	$12
Carlton, Steve - Induction Day	$8
Carlton, Steve - Induction Day, Black and White Cachet	$5
Carlton, Steve - Retired Uniform	$5
Carlton, Niekro, Spahn, Perry - Dearborn Michigan Show	$6
Carter, Gary - '85 Mets Opening Day	$5
Carter, Gary - Catches in 1800th Game - Record	$8
Carter, Gary - 300th Home Run	$8
Carter, Gary - Traded to the Mets 1984	$5
Carter, Gary - 1986 World Series Game 4	$8
Carter, Gary - 25th Anniversary of the Mets	$6
Carter, Gary - Retired Uniform	$5
Castillo, Marty - 1984 World Series Game 3	$8
Cedeno, Cesar - 1985 World Series Game 1	$6
Cerone, Rick - Opening Day	$5
Chambliss, Chris - Old Timer's Day	$5
Charles, Ed - Salute to the '69 Mets	$6
Chester, Hilda - Brooklyn Dodger Cow Bell Lady	$5
Cimoli, Gino	$5
Clark, Allie - 1984 Parsippany Show Cover	$5
Clark, Allie - 1984 Parsippany Show Postmarked Card	$4
Clark, Jack - Designated Hitter	$5
Clark, Will - 1989 N.L. Playoffs	$8
Clark, Will - 1991 All-Star Game	$8
Clemens, Roger - 1986 A.L. MVP Award	$25
Clemens, Roger - 1986 Cy Young Award	$20
Clemens, Roger - 1987 Cy Young Award	$15
Clemens & Glavine - 1991 Cy Young Winners	$15
Clemens, Roger - 200th Win	$10
Clemens, Roger-Pedro Martinez - 1997 Cy Young	$6
Clemente, Roberto - Statue Dedication	$6
Clemente, Roberto - Argentina Salutes Heroes of Baseball	$8
Clemente, Roberto - Forbes Field Special Cancel	$8
Clemente, Roberto - Forbes Field Special Cancel Diff. Cachet	$6
Clemente, Roberto - Retired Uniform	$5
Clemente, Roberto - 25th Anniversary	$8
Clemente, Roberto - Clemente Night at Three Rivers Stadium	$8
Clemente, Roberto - 3,000 Hit and Other Records	$8
Clendenon, Don - Salute to '69 Mets	$6
Coates, Jim - Salute to '61 Yankees	$6
Coleman, Vince - '87 World Series Game 3	$7
Coleman, Vince - 1985 Rookie of the Year	$10
Collins, Joe - 1984 Hasbrouck Heights Show Cover	$5
Collins, Joe - Hasbrouck Heights Show Postmarked Show Card	$4
Connors, Chuck - Commemorating His Only Brooklyn Game	$7
Colorado Rockies - Expansion Draft	$10
Colorado Rockies - Opening Day	$5
Cone and Maddux - 1994 Cy Young Winners	$6
Cone, David - Yankees Clinch American League East	$8
Cone, David - 1996 World Series Game 6	$7
Cox, Billy	$5
Cordova, Marty - Hideo Nomo 1995 Rookie of the Year	$5
Cracker Jax Classics - 1984	$5
Craig, Roger - 1955 World Series	$5

Subject/Description	Value	Subject/Description	Value
Cuccinello, Tony	$5	Doerr, Stargell, and Herman - Hall of Fame Game	$35
Daley, Bud - Salute to the 1961 Yankees	$6	Doerr, Bobby - 1986 Hall of Fame Election	$6
Dandridge, Ray - Elected to the Hall of Fame	$6	Doerr, Bobby - 1986 Hall of Fame Induction	$8
Dandridge, Ray - Inducted to the Hall of Fame	$6	Downing, Al - Salute to the 1961 Yankees	$8
Dandridge, Mathews, Berra - Hall of Fame Show Cover	$35	Dressen, Chuck	$5
Dark, Al - Saddlebrook Show Cover	$5	Dropo, Walt - New York Show Cover	$4
Dark, Al - Saddlebrook Show Postmarked Show Card	$4	Dropo, Walt - New York Show Postmarked Show Card	$4
Darling, Ron - 25th Anniversary of the Mets	$5	Drysdale, Don - Opening Day 1956	$7
Darling, Ron - 2nd Consecutive Shutout	$5	Duren, Ryne - Salute to the 1961 Yankees	$6
Darling, Ron - Mets Win Divisional Title	$5	Durocher, Leo - Induction Day	$6
Darling, Ron - Flushing New York Card Show Cover	$5	Durocher, Leo - Induction Day in Giants Uniform	$6
Darling, Ron - Flushing New York Show Postmarked Card	$4	Durocher, Leo - First T.V. Game	$5
Darling, Ron - Freehold New Jersey Show	$4	Durocher, Leo - 7th National (Dodger Uniform)	$6
Darling, Ron - Freehold New Jersey Show Postmarked Show Card	$4	Durocher, Leo - 7th National (Giants Uniform)	$6
Dauer, Rick - 1983 World Series Game 4	$8	Dyer, Duffy - Salute to the 1969 Mets	$6
Daulton, Darren & Roberto Alomar - Game 2 1993 World Series	$6	Dykstra, Len - 25th Anniversary of the Mets	$5
Davis, Alvin - 1984 A.L. Rookie of the Year	$5	Dykstra, Len - Exhibition Game	$5
Davis, Eric - 1990 World Series Game 1	$10	Dykstra, Len - 1986 World Series Game 3	$8
Davis, Mark - 1989 N.L. Cy Young	$5	Dykstra, Len - Thompson Game One 1993 World Series	$6
Dawson, Andre - 300th Career Stolen Base	$8	Dykstra, Len - Game 6 1993 World Series	$7
Dawson, Andre - 1987 N.L. MVP	$8	Ebbets Field Opens	$6
Day, Leon - Hall of Fame Induction	$8	Ebbets Field Demolished	$5
Dempsey, Rick - 1983 World Series Game 5	$8	Eckersley, Dennis - 1989 A.L. Playoffs	$5
Dent, Bucky - New Yankee Manager	$5	Eckersley, Dennis - 1990 A.L. Playoffs	$6
Dent, Bucky - Yankee Old Timer's Day	$5	Eckersley, Dennis - 1992 A.L. MVP	$5
Dent, Bucky - Saddle Brook Show Cover	$4	Eckersley, Dennis - 1992 A.L. Cy Young Award	$5
Dent, Bucky - Saddle Brook Show Postmarked Show Card	$4	Edwards, Bruce	$5
Devereaux, Mike - 1995 National League Playoffs	$5	Ennis, Del - Philadelphia Card Show	$4
Dibble, Ron - 1990 N.L. Playoffs-MVP	$7	Ennis, Del - Philadelphia Show Postmarked Card	$4
Dickey, Bill - Yankee Memorial Park	$8	Erskine, Carl - First No-Hitter	$7
Dickey, Bill - Retired Uniform	$5	Erskine, Carl - Second No-Hitter	$7
DiLauro, Jack - Salute to the 1969 Mets	$5	Everett, Carl - Mets Opening Day	$5
DiMaggio Brothers - Joe, Vince and Dom	$15	Face, Roy - New York Show Cover	$5
DiMaggio, Joe - Pride of the Yankees	$15	Face, Roy - New York Show Postmarked Card	$5
DiMaggio, Joe - Heroes of New York Baseball	$15	Feller, Bob - 50th Anniversary of His No-Hitter	$10
DiMaggio, Joe - 1991 All-Star Game	$15	Feller, Bob - 1985 Cracker Jack Classic	$6
DiMaggio, Joe - Joe DiMaggio Day at Yankee Stadium	$15	Fernandez, Sid - Signs With Mets	$5
DiMaggio, Joe - 1983 Old Timer's Day	$15	Fernandez, Sid - 25th Anniversary of the Mets	$5
DiMaggio, Joe - Memorial Park	$20	Fernandez, Sid - 1986 All-Star Game	$6
DiMaggio, Joe - Second East Coast National	$15	Fielder, Cecil - 11th Member of the 50 Home Run Club	$7
DiMaggio, Joe - Set of 2 Covers Batting Streak, Start and Finish	$25	Fingers, Rollie - 1992 Hall of Fame Induction	$8
DiMaggio, Joe - Rody II Show Cover	$8	Fingers, Rollie - New York Show Cover	$5
DiMaggio, Joe - Uniform Retired	$8	Fingers, Rollie - New York Show Postmarked Card	$4
DiMaggio, Joe - DiMaggio Honors Rizzuto at Phil Rizzuto Day	$5	Fisk, Carlton - 1991 All-Star Game	$8
DiMaggio, Joe - Ted Williams 1941 Incredible Season - All-Star Game	$10	Florida Marlins - Expansion Draft	$10
DiMaggio, Joe - With Ted Williams at Toronto All-Star Game	$10	Florida Marlins - Opening Day	$6
Ditmar, Art - Salute to the 1961 Yankees	$8	Ford, Whitey - Old Timer's Game 1983	$10
Dodgers - First T.V. Transmission	$5	Ford, Whitey - Old Timer's Game 1984	$10
Dodgers Symphony Band Led by Bragen	$5	Ford, Whitey - Salute to the 1961 Yankees	$7
Dodgers Win 1941 Pennant	$5	Ford, Whitey - Honored by Yankees	$6
		Ford, Whitey - Memorial Park	$8
		Ford, Whitey - 7th National Card Show	$7
		Ford, Whitey - Hasbrouck Heights Card Show Cover	$10
		Ford, Whitey - Hasbrouck Heights Show Postmarked Card	$8

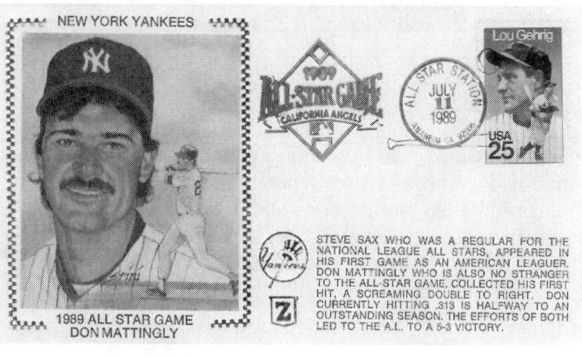

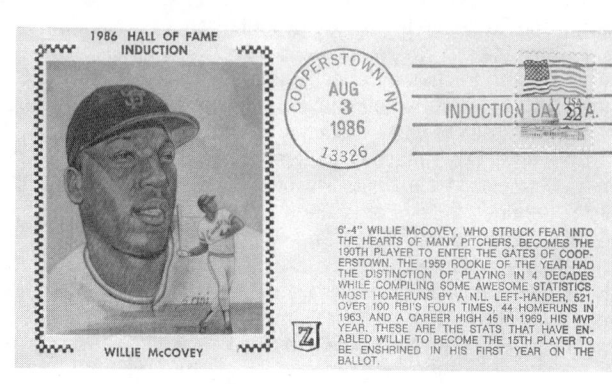

Subject/Description	Value
Ford, Curt - 1987 World Series Game 5	$6
Foster, Willie - 1996 Hall of Fame Induction	$5
Foster, Willie - 1996 Hall of Fame Induction, Different Cachet	$5
Fox, Nellie - 1997 Hall of Fame Election	$7
Fox, Nellie - 1997 Hall of Fame Induction	$8
Franco, John - Traded to the Mets	$5
Frederick, Johnny	$5
Furillo, Carl - 1955 World Series	$5
Furillo, Carl	$5
Gaetti, Gary - 1987 Playoffs	$5
Gagne, Greg - 1987 World Series Game 7	$6
Gagne, Greg - 1991 World Series Game 1	$7
Galan, Augie	$5
Garagiola, Lazzeri & Veeck - 1991 Hall of Fame Induction	$6
Garagiola, Joe - 6th National Convention	$6
Garagiola, Joe - 1985 Cracker Jax Classic	$6
Garciaparra - Rolan - Rookies of the Year	$6
Gaspar, Rod - Salute to the 1969 Mets	$5
Gardner, Billy - Salute to the 1961 Yankees	$6
Garvey, Steve - 1984 N.L. Playoffs	$10
Garrett, Wayne - Salute to the 1969 Mets	$5
Gehrig, Lou and Carl Yastrzemski - 50th Anniversary All-Star Game on Ruth F.D.C.	$7
Gehrig, Lou - Memorial Park	$8
Gehrig, Lou - Retired Uniform	$8
Gehrig, Lou - Set of 10 First Day Covers Covering Career	$60
Gehrig, Lou - Single First Day Cover From Set	$8
Gentry, Gary - Salute to the 1969 Mets	$5
Gentile, Jim	$5
Gibbons, John - 25th Anniversary of the Mets	$5
Gibson, Kirk - 1984 A.L. Playoffs	$12
Gibson, Kirk - 1984 World Series Game 5	$10
Gibson, Kirk - 1988 World Series Game 1	$10
Gibson, Kirk - 1988 N.L. MVP	$8
Gibson, Bob - 7th National Convention Cover	$5
Gilliam, Junior	$5
Gionfriddo, Al	$5
Girardi, Joe - 1996 World Series Game 6	$7
Glavine, Tom, Roger Clemens - 1991 Cy Young	$7
Glavine, Tom - 1995 World Series MVP	$5
Glavine, Tom - 1996 N.L. Playoffs	$5
Glavine, Tom - 1997 N.L. Playoffs	$5
Gomez, Lefty - Lake Harmoney Show	$6
Gomez, Lefty - Memorial Park	$6
Gomez, Lefty - Pride of the Yankees	$6
Gomez, Lefty & Dave Stieb - 50th Anniversary All-Star Game on Ruth F.D.C.	$6
Gonzalez, Juan & Ken Caminiti - 1996 MVP	$5
Gooden, Dwight & Darryl Strawberry - Back to Back Rookies	$6
Gooden, Dwight - Rookie Strike Out Record	$7
Gooden, Dwight - Opening Day 1986	$5
Gooden, Dwight - 25th Anniversary of the Mets	$5
Gooden, Dwight - Mets 25th Anniversary, Different Cachet	$5
Gooden, Dwight - 1988 All-Star Game	$5
Gooden, Dwight - 1,000 Strikeouts	$5
Gooden, Dwight - Mets Clinch N.L. East	$6
Gooden, Dwight - Receives Rookie of the Year Award	$6
Gooden, Dwight - 1985 Cy Young Award	$8
Gooden, Dwight - 1984 N.L. Strikeout Record	$14
Gooden, Dwight - 1985 "K" Day	$6
Gooden, Dwight - 20 Wins Under 20 Years Old 1985	$7
Gooden, Dwight - Catch A Rising Star Show Postmarked Show Card	$10
Gooden, Dwight - Yankee No-Hitter	$8
Green, Dallas - New York Manager	$5
Griffey, Ken, Jr. - 1991 All-Star Game	$8
Griffey, Ken, Jr. - 1992 Gold Glove	$10
Griffey, Ken, Jr. - 1994 All-Star Game	$7

Subject/Description	Value
Griffey, Ken, Jr. - 1997 Gold Glove	$7
Griffey, Ken, Jr. & Larry Walker - 1997 MVP's	$5
Groat, Dick - New York Show Cover	$5
Groat, Dick - New York Show Postmarked Show Card	$4
Grote, Jerry - Salute to the 1969 Mets	$5
Grote, Jerry & Duke Snider - First East Coast National	$10
Guidry, Ron - Career Milestones	$7
Guidry, Ron - 1985 Gold Glove Award	$6
Guidry, Ron - 1987 Gold Glove Award	$6
Guidry, Ron - Old Timer's Day 1989	$5
Guidry, Ron - Retires, 1989	$5
Guillen, Ozzie - 1985 A.L. Rookie of the Year	$7
Gwynn, Tony - 1991 Opening Day	$7
Gwynn, Tony - 1994 All-Star Game	$7
Hallahan, Bill & Mario Soto - 50th Anniversary All-Star Game on Ruth F.D.C.	$6
Hamelin, Bob & Raul Mondesi - 1994 Rookies of the Year	$5
Hale, Bob - Salute to the 1961 Yankees	$6
Hanlon, Ned - 1986 Hall of Fame Induction	$5
Hanlon, Ned - 1986 Hall of Fame Induction, Different Cachet	$5
Hall of Fame Exhibition Game 1990 - Orioles vs. Expos	$5
Hall of Fame Exhibition Game 1992 - Mets vs. White Sox	$5
Hall of Fame Exhibition Game 1992 - White Sox vs. Mets	$5
Hall of Fame Exhibition Game 1992 - Willie Randolph	$5
Hall of Fame Exhibition Game 1993 - Indians vs. Dodgers	$5
Hall of Fame Exhibition Game 1993 - Dodgers vs. Indians	$5
Hall of Fame Exhibition Game 1995 - Cubs vs. Tigers	$5
Hall of Fame Induction - Class of 1996 - Hanlon, Foster, Weaver, Bunning	$6
Harrelson, Bud - Old Timer's Day 1988	$5
Harrelson, Bud - Salute to the 1969 Mets	$6
Hassett, Buddy	$5
Hattan, Joe	$5
Hawkins, Andy - 15th Win	$5
Head, Ed	$5
Hearn, Ed - 25th Anniversary of the Mets	$5
Heep, Danny - 25th Anniversary of the Mets	$5
Henderson, Rickey - Yankee Debut	$8
Henderson, Rickey - Scores His 138th H.R. Passing Henrich's Record	$12
Henderson, Rickey - 1985 All-Star Game	$10
Henderson, Rickey - 1988 All-Star Game	$6
Henderson, Rickey - Opening Day 1988	$5
Henderson, Rickey - 1985 Stolen Base Record	$16
Henderson, Rickey - 1988 Yankee Stolen Base Record	$8
Henderson, Rickey - Lead Off Home Run Record	$8
Henderson, Rickey - 1990 Ties Ty Cobb's Stolen Base Record	$15
Henderson, Rickey - 1990 Breaks Ty Cobb's Stolen Base Record	$20
Henderson, Rickey - 1991 Ties Lou Brock's Stolen Base Record	$14
Henderson, Rickey - 1991 Breaks Lou Brock's Stolen Base Record	$20
Henderson, Rickey - 1989 A.L. Playoffs MVP	$8
Henderson, Rickey - 1989 World Series Game 3	$8
Henderson, Rickey - 1990 A.L. Playoffs	$6
Henderson, Rickey - 1991 All-Star Game	$5
Henrich, Tommy - 1987 Pride of the Yankees	$5
Henrich, Tommy - 1984 Queens N.Y. Postmarked Show Card	$4
Henrich, Tommy - 1941 World Series	$5
Hentgen, Pat & John Smoltz - 1996 Cy Young Award	$5
Herman, Billy	$5
Herman, Billy - National Old Timer's Day 1986	$5
Herman, Billy - Queens N.Y. Show Postmarked Card	$4
Herman, Babe	$5
Herman, Doerr, Stargell - H.O.F. Show	$35
Hermanski, Gene	$7
Hermanski, Gene - Parsippany N.J. Postmarked Show Card	$4
Hermanski, Gene - Parsippany N.J. Show Cover	$5

Subject/Description	Value
Hernandez, Willie - 1984 A.L. Cy Young Award Winner	$7
Hernandez, Willie - 1984 A.L. MVP	$7
Hernandez, Keith - 1985 Gold Glove Award	$5
Hernandez, Keith - 1985 Silver Slugger	$5
Hernandez, Keith - 1987 2,000 Hit Mark	$6
Hernandez, Keith - 1988 Gold Glove	$5
Hernandez, Keith - 25th Anniversary of the Mets	$5
Hernandez, Keith - Flushing N.Y. Show Cover	$5
Hernandez, Keith - Flushing N.Y. Show Postmarked Card	$4
Hernandez, Livan - 1997 National League Playoffs	$5
Hernandez, Livan - 1997 World Series Game 1	$7
Hershiser, Orel - 1988 N.L. Playoffs	$6
Hershiser, Orel - 1988 N.L. Cy Young Award	$6
Hershiser, Orel - 1988 World Series Game 1	$8
Hershiser, Orel - 1988 World Series Game 5	$8
Hershiser, Orel - 1995 A.L. Playoffs	$5
Herzog, Whitey - 1983 Man of the Year	$5
Herzog, Whitey & John McGraw - 50th Anniversary All-Star Game	$6
Higbe, Kirby	$5
Hoak, Don	$5
Hodges, Gil - 1955 World Series	$6
Hodges, Gil - Salute to the 1969 Mets	$8
Hodges, Gil - 4 H.R.'s in a Single Game	$5
Holland, Al - Philadelphia Pa. Show Cover	$5
Holland, Al - Philadelphia Pa. Postmarked Show Card	$4
Hollandsworth, Todd & Derek Jeter - 1996 R.O.Y.	$5
Holmes, Tommy - Brooklyn Dodger Serie	$5
Houk, Ralph - National Old Timers Day	$5
Houk, Ralph - Salute to the 1961 Yankees	$8
Howard, Elston - 1984 Yankee Old Timer's Day	$6
Howard, Elston - Memorial Park	$5
Howard, Elston - Howard's Wife Arlene Throws Out First Ball	$5
Howard, Elston - Pride of the Yankees Award	$5
Howard, Elston - Salute to the 1961 Yankees	$8
Howell, Jay - 1988 World Series Game 4	$6
Howell, Dixie	$5
Howser, Dick - Memorial Tribute	$5
Hoyt, Lamar - 1985 All-Star MVP	$5
Hrbek, Kent - 1987 World Series Game 6	$8
Hrbek, Kent - New York Show Cover	$4
Hrbek, Kent - New York Show Postmarked Card	$4
Hundley, Todd - Breaks Catchers H.R. Record	$5
Hudson, Charles - Yankee Opening Day 1987	$5
Huggins, Miller - Memorial Park	$5
Hulbert, William - 1995 Hall of Fame Induction	$5
Hunter, Catfish - 1987 Hall of Fame Election	$6
Hunter, Catfish - 1987 Hall of Fame Induction	$8
Hunter, Catfish - Yankees Honor Him with Catfish Hunter Day	$5
Hunter, Catfish - Hall of Fame Induction in Suit Not Uniform	$8
Hunter, Catfish - 1986 Old Timer's Day	$6
Hunter, Catfish - 1987 Old Timer's Day	$6
Hunter, Jenkins, Brock - Hall of Fame Show	$35
Hurst, Bruce - 1986 World Series Game 1	$6
Hurst, Bruce - 1986 World Series Game 5	$6
Irvin, Killebrew, Slaughter, Robinson - Hall of Fame Show	$35
Jackson, Danny - 1985 World Series Game 5	$6
Jackson, Ransom	$5
Jackson, Reggie - 1993 Hall of Fame Induction, Yankee Uniform	$8
Jackson, Reggie - Combination Cover 2 Cancels H.O.F. and Jackson Day	$16
Jackson, Reggie - 1993 Hall of Fame Induction, Oakland Uniform	$7
Jackson, Reggie - 1993 Hall of Fame Induction, Orioles Uniform	$7
Jackson, Reggie - 1993 Hall of Fame Induction, Angels Uniform	$7
Jackson, Reggie - 1993 Pride of the Yankees	$6
Jackson, Reggie - Yankees Retire His #44	$7
Jackson, Reggie - Combination Cover 2 Postmarks H.O.F. & #44 Retired	$16

Subject/Description	Value
Jackson, Reggie - 399th Career Home Run	$30
Jackson, Reggie - 500th Career Home Run	$50
Jackson, Reggie - 1985 1,000 Extra Base Hits	$20
Jackson, Reggie - Last Game Played at Yankee Stadium	$10
Jackson, Reggie - Hall of Fame Induction Pictured With His Father	$7
Jackson, Reggie - Old Timer's Day 1991	$5
Jackson, Reggie - New York Show Cover	$5
Jackson, Reggie - New York Show Postmarked Card	$4
Jackson, Reggie - New York Show Combination with N.Y. Marathon	$10
Jackson, Reggie - New York Show Combination Card with Marathon	$10
James, Johnny - Salute to the 1961 Yankees	$6
Jefferies, Gregg - Debut	$5
Jenkins, Ferguson - 1991 Hall of Fame Induction	$6
Jenkins, Brock, Hunter - Hall of Fame Show	$35
Jenkins, Ferguson - New York Show Postmarked Show Card	$4
Jeter, Derek & Todd Hollandsworth - 1996 R.O.Y.	$8
Jeter, Derek - Jeter Home Run Catch by Jeff Maier Saves Game	$7
Jeter, Derek - Pride of the Yankees 1998	$6
Jethroe, Sam - New York Show Cover	$5
Jethroe, Sam - New York Show Postmarked Show Card	$4
John, Tommy - All Time Win List	$7
Johnson, Davey - 25th Anniversary of the Mets	$5
Johnson, Davey - Manager of the 25th Anniversary Mets	$5
Johnson, Howard - 1989 All-Star Game	$5
Johnson, Howard - 1991 All-Star Game	$5
Johnson, Howard - 1989 Silver Slugger	$5
Johnson, Randy & Greg Maddux - Win 1995 Cy Young Award	$5
Jones, Andruw - 1996 World Series Game 1	$7
Jones, Cleon - Salute to the 1969 Mets	$5
Jorgensen, Johnny	$5
Joyner, Wally - Yankees Old Timer's Day Game	$5
Justice, Dave - 1991 World Series Game 3	$9
Justice, Dave - 1995 World Series Game 6	$7
Karros, Eric - 1992 N.L. Rookie of the Year	$5
Kell, George - 1983 Hall of Fame Induction	$8
Kell, Kaline, Marichal & Boudreau - Hall of Fame Show	$35
Kellert, Frank	$5
Keller, Charlie - Queens New York Show Cover	$5
Keller, Charlie - Queens New York Postmarked Show Card	$4
Killebrew, Slaughter, Brooks Robinson, Irvine - Hall of Fame Show	$35
Klesko, Ryan - 1995 World Series Game 4	$6
Kent, Jeff - Mets 1994 Season Opener	$5
Key, Jimmy - 1992 World Series Game 4	$6
Kiner, Ralph - Salute to the 1969 Mets	$6
King, Clyde - First Brooklyn Game	$5
King, Clyde	$5
Knight, Ray - 1986 World Series MVP	$5
Knight, Ray - 25th Anniversary of the Mets	$5
Knoblauch, Chuck - A.L. Rookie of the Year	$7
Koonce, Cal - Salute to the 1969 Mets	$5
Koosman, Jerry - Mets Hall of Fame	$5
Koosman, Jerry - Salute to the 1969 Mets	$6
Koufax, Sandy - 1955 Inaugural Appearance	$5
Koufax, Sandy	$5
Kranepool, Ed - Salute to the 1969 Mets	$5
Kubek, Tony - Yankee Old Timer's Day	$5
Kubek, Tony - Salute to the 1961 Yankees	$8
Kucks, Johnny - Parsippany Card Show	$5
Kucks, Johnny - Parsippany Show Postmarked Card	$4
Kucks, Johnny - New York Show Postmarked Card	$4
Kuhn, Bowie & Judge Landis - 50th Anniversary of All-Star Game On Ruth F.D.C.	$6
Labine, Clem - Pitches First Complete Game	$6
Landrum, Tito - 1985 World Series Game 4	$8

Subject/Description	Value
Larkin, Barry - 1990 World Series Game 2	$8
Larkin, Barry & Mo Vaughn - 1995 MVP's	$5
Larsen, Don - Perfect Game 30th Anniversary 1986	$10
Lasorda, Tom - 1985 Opening Day	$7
Lasorda, Tom - First Brooklyn Game	$6
Lasorda, Tom - Induction into the Hall of Fame (L.A. Dodgers Uniform)	$10
Lasorda, Tom - Induction - H.O.F. (Brooklyn Dodger Uniform)	$10
Lasorda, Tom - Class of '97, Four 1997 Inductees into H.O.F.	$10
Last Game at Ebbets Field	$5
Laudner, Tim - 1987 World Series Game 2	$6
Lavagetto, Cookie - Breaks Up No-Hitter	$6
Lavagetto, Cookie - Inducted Brooklyn Dodger Hall of Fame	$5
Lavagetto, Cookie - Ends Bevens No-Hitter	$5
Lawless, Tom - 1987 World Series Game 4	$6
Leiter, Al - Yankee Debut	$7
Leiter, Al - Yankee First Season Win	$5
Leius, Scott - 1991 World Series Game 2	$8
Lemke, Mark - 1991 World Series Game 4	$8
Lemon, Bob - 1987 Yankee Old Timer's Day	$5
Leonard, Buck - 1983 New York Show Cover	$10
Leonard, Buck - 1983 New York Postmarked Show Card	$8
Leonard, Jeffrey - 1987 N.L. Playoffs	$5
Leonard, Jeffrey - 1987 N.L. Playoffs MVP	$5
Lewis, Darren, Bonds & Williams - 1994 Gold Glove Winners	$5
Leyland, Jim - 1997 World Series Game 7	$7
Leyritz, Jim - 1996 World Series Game 4	$7
Linz, Phil - Queens New York Card Show Cover	$5
Linz, Phil - Queens New York Postmarked Show Card	$4
Listach, Pat - 1992 A.L. Rookie of the Year	$5
Loes, Billy	$5
Lolich, Mickey - Saddle Brook N.J. Show Card	$5
Lolich, Mickey - Saddle Brook N.J. Postmarked Show Card	$4
Lombardi, Ernie - 1986 Hall of Fame Election	$5
Lombardi, Ernie - 1986 Hall of Fame Induction	$5
Lombardi, Phil - Stadium Home Game	$5
Lombardi, Vic - Brooklyn Dodger Series	$5
Lopat, Eddie - 1985 Yankee Old Timer's Day	$5
Lopat, Eddie - 5th National Postmarked Show Card	$4
Lopez, Arturo - 5th National Show Cover	$5
Lopez, Arturo - 5th National Postmarked Show Card	$4
Lopez, Al - Argentina Salutes Baseball Heroes	$7
Lopez, Hector - Salute to the 1961 Yankees	$6
Lyle, Sparky - 1988 Old Timer's Day	$7
Mass, Duke - Salute to the 1961 Yankees	$8
Mack, Connie & Harvey Kuehn - 50th Anniversary of the All-Star Game	$6
MacPhail, Larry - 1941 World Series	$5
MacPhail, Lee Jr. - Hall of Fame Induction 1998	$6
Maddox, Gary - 1983 World Series Game 1	$10
Maddux, Greg - 1992 N.L. Cy Young	$5
Maddux, Greg & Jack McDowell - 1993 Cy Young Award Winners	$5
Maddux, Greg & David Cone - 1994 Cy Young Award Winners	$5
Maddux, Greg & Randy Johnson - 1995 Cy Young Award Winners	$5
Maddux, Greg - 1995 World Series Game 1	$6
Maddux, Greg - 1996 World Series Game 2	$7
Maglie, Sal - Anniversary of No-Hitter	$5
Malkmus, Bobby - 5th National Convention Cover	$5
Malkmus, Bobby - 5th National Postmarked Show Card	$4
Mantle, Mickey - Diamond Legends Show Cover	$10
Mantle, Mickey - Raritan Center I Show Cover	$25
Mantle, Mickey - Raritan Center II Show Cover	$22
Mantle, Mickey - Reinstated Into Baseball	$10
Mantle, Mickey - Old Timer's Day	$10
Mantle, Mickey - Salute to the 1961 Yankees	$8
Mantle, Mickey - Heroes of N.Y. Baseball	$5

Subject/Description	Value
Mantle, Mickey - 3rd East Coast National Card Show Cover	$12
Mantle, Mickey - 4th East Coast National Card Show Cover	$12
Mantle, Mickey - Throws First Ball 1985 Opening Day	$12
Mantle, Mickey - 7th National Card Show Arlington, Texas	$10
Mantle, Mickey - 2nd East Coast National Card Show	$15
Mantle, Mickey - New Brunswick, N.J. Postmarked Show Card	$15
Mantle, Mickey - Press Conference Following Liver Transplant	$8
Mantle, Mickey - Returns Home After Liver Transplant	$8
Mantle, Mickey - Mantle Dies	$8
Mantle, Mickey - A Legend Dies	$8
Mantle, Mickey - Honored at Funeral By Fellow Players	$6
Mantle, Mickey - Funeral	$6
Mantle, Mickey - Laid to Rest Following Funeral	$6
Mantle, Mickey - His Uniform Number Retired	$6
Mantle, Mickey - Monument Dedicated at Yankee Stadium	$8
Mantle, Mickey - Historic Cooperstown	$8
Mantle, Mickey - Honored by Argentina	$7
Mantle, Mickey, Willie Mays & Duke Snider - Atlantic City Show	$8
Mantle, Mickey, Willie Mays & Duke Snider - East Coast National	$8
Marichal, Juan - 1983 Hall of Fame Induction	$12
Marichal, Juan - Argentina Salutes Heroes of Baseball	$7
Marichal, Juan, Boudreau, Kell, Kaline - Hall of Fame Show	$35
Maris, Roger - 1983 Yankee Old Timers Game	$8
Maris, Roger - 1984 Yankee Old Timers Game	$7
Maris, Roger - Honored	$7
Maris, Roger - Memorial Park	$8
Maris, Roger - Salute to the 1961 Yankees	$8
Maris, Roger - 25th Anniversary of the 61st Home Run	$10
Maris, Roger - Dies	$6
Maris, Roger - Final Tribute	$6
Marlins - Draft Pick	$10
Marlins - Opening Day - First Game	$5
Marlins Win 1997 World Series. Set of 7 Covers, One For Each Game	$35
Marshall, Mike - Traded	$5
Marshall, Willard - 5th National Convention	$5
Martin, Billy - Billy is Back IV	$8
Martin, Billy - Billy is Back V	$6
Martin, Billy - Billy Martin Day at Yankee Stadium	$6
Martin, Billy - 1987 Yankee Old Timers Day	$6
Martin, Billy - Memorial Following His Death	$6
Martin, J.C. - Salute to the 1969 Mets	$5
Martinez, Tino - 1997 All-Star Game	$8
Martinez, Tippy - Baltimore-Washington Card Show	$5
Martinez, Tippy - Baltimore-Maryland Postmarked Show Card	$4
Mathews, Eddie - Uniform Retired	$5
Mathews, Berra & Dandridge - Hall of Fame Show	$35
Mattingly, Don - 1984 A.L. Batting Title	$20
Mattingly, Don - Ties Lou Gehrig's Doubles Record	$18
Mattingly Don - Breaks Roger Maris RBI Record	$18
Mattingly, Don - 145 RBI's	$25
Mattingly, Don - 1985 MVP	$45
Mattingly, Don - 1985 Gold Glove Award	$10
Mattingly, Don - 200 Hits on Nov. 9, 1986	$20
Mattingly, Don - 100 Career Home Runs	$15
Mattingly, Don - Gold Glove Award 7-10-87	$15
Mattingly, Don - Ties Consecutive Home Run Record	$15
Mattingly, Don - Breaks Ruth's Record	$15
Mattingly, Don - 6th Grand Slam Home Run	$15
Mattingly, Don - Gold Glove Award 12-2-87	$15
Mattingly, Don - Opening Day 1988	$6
Mattingly, Don - 1988 Gold Glove Award 12-7-88	$6
Mattingly, Don - 1989 Opening Day	$6
Mattingly, Don - 1989 All-Star Game	$6
Mattingly, Don - Last Season Game 1989	$6
Mattingly, Don - 1992 Gold Glove Winner	$6

Subject/Description	Value
Mattingly, Don - Closing Day 1993	$6
Mattingly, Don - Opening Day 1994	$6
Mattingly, Don - 2,000 Hits	$10
Mattingly, Don - 1993 Gold Glove	$7
Mattingly, Don - 1994 Gold Glove	$7
Mattingly, Don - Mattingly Retires	$8
Mattingly, Don - Mattingly Officially Retires	$6
Mattingly, Don - 1997 Pride of the Yankees	$8
Mattingly, Don - Mattingly's Number is Retired	$5
Mattingly, Don - Flag Raising on Opening Day	$8
Mattingly, Don - Don Mattingly Day at Yankee Stadium	$8
Mauch, Gene - 1985 Angels Opening Day	$5
Mays, Willie - Uniform Retired	$6
Mays, Snider - Brooklyn Dodger Series	$5
Mays, Willie - First Inter League Texas Ranger Game	$8
Mays, Willie, Mickey Mantle, Duke Snider - Atlantic City Show	$8
Mays, Willie, Mickey Mantle, Duke Snider - East Coast National	$8
Mays, Willie - Reinstated into Baseball	$8
Mazzilli, Lee - Consecutive Game Streak	$5
Mazzilli, Lee - 25th Anniversary Team of the Mets	$5
McAndrew, Jim - Salute to the 1969 Mets	$5
McCarthy, Joe - Memorial Park	$5
McCovey, Willie - 1986 Hall of Fame Election	$8
McCovey, Willie - 1986 Hall of Fame Induction	$9
McCovey, Willie - Retired Uniform	$5
McCovey, Willie - 1983 New York Show Postmarked Show Card	$4
McCormick, Mike	$5
McDevitt, Danny	$5
McDowell, Roger - 25th Anniversary Team of the Mets	$5
McDowell, Jack - 1993 A.L. Cy Young	$5
McDowell, Jack - 1995 Yankee Season Opener	$5
McGee, Willie - 1985 N.L. MVP	$6
McGraw, Tug - Salute to the 1969 Mets	$5
McReynolds, Kevin - Known as the Mets "Quiet Man"	$5
Mets - First Inter League Game - Subway Series	$6
Mets Championship Trophy - 1969 World Series	$5
Mets - 1993 Opening Day	$5
Medwick, Ducky - Felled by a Pitch	$5
Meyer, Russ - Brooklyn Dodger Series	$5
Mlicki, Dave - Pitches First Inter League Game at Yankee Stadium	$6
Miksis, Eddie	$5
Minner, Paul	$5
Mitchell, Kevin - 1989 N.L. MVP Award	$6
Mitchell, Kevin - 25th Anniversary Team of the Mets	$5
Molitor, Paul - 3 Stolen Bases Record Tied	$8
Molitor, Paul - Hitting Streak	$8
Molitor, Paul - 1993 World Series Game 3	$8
Monbouquette, Bill - 5th Old Timer's Day Classic	$5
Mondes, Raul & Bob Hamelim - 1994 R.O.Y.	$5
Morgan, Joe & Jim Palmer - 1990 Hall of Fame Induction	$7
Morgan, Joe - 1990 Hall of Fame Induction	$5
Morgan, Joe - 1985 New York Show Postmarked Card	$4
Morgan, Bobby - Brooklyn Dodger Series	$5
Morris, Jack - 1984 World Series Game 1	$10
Morris, Jack - 1991 World Series Game 7	$8
Mueller, Don - New York Show Cover	$5
Mueller, Don - New York Show Postmarked Show Card	$4
Munson, Thurman - Memorial Park	$20
Munson, Thurman - Mrs. Diane Munson Throws First Ball Opening Day	$7
Munson, Thurman - Pride of the Yankees	$7
Murcer, Bobby - 1987 Yankee Old Timer's Day	$5
Murcer, Bobby - 1989 Yankee Old Timer's Day	$5
Murphy, Bob - Salute to the 1969 Mets	$6
Murray, Eddie - 500th Home Run Special Postmark	$8
Murray, Eddie - 500th Home Run-Cover Postmarked Day of H.R. 156 Issued	$25
Musial, Stan - Freehold N.J. Postmarked Show Card	$5

Subject/Description	Value
Musial, Stan - Retired Uniform	$5
Myers, Randy - 1990 N.L. Playoffs MVP	$7
Neal, Charlie	$5
Nelson, Lindsey - Salute to the 1969 Mets	$6
Nelson, Rocky	$5
Nettles, Graig - 1991 Yankee Old Timer's Day	$6
Nettles, Graig - 1985 New York Show Cover	$5
Nettles, Graig - 1985 New York Postmarked Show Card	$4
Newcombe, Don - 1955 World Series	$6
Newcombe, Don - Big Apple IV New York Show Cover	$5
Newcombe, Don - Big Apple V New York Show Cover	$5
Newcombe, Don - Big Apple V Postmarked Show Card	$4
Newcombe, Don - Receives 1956 MVP and Cy Young Awards	$5
Newhauser, Hal - 1992 Hall of Fame Induction	$6
Newhauser, Hal - Big Apple IV New York Card Show	$5
Newhauser, Hal - Big Apple IV Postmarked Show Card	$4
Niekro, Phil & Joe Niekro - Combined Victories by Both Brothers 530	$8
Niekro, Phil - 300 Wins	$12
Niekro, Phil - Inducted into the Hall of Fame (Braves Uniform)	$8
Niekro, Phil - Inducted into the Hall of Fame (Yankees Uniform)	$8
Niekro, Carlton, Spahn, Perry - Dearborn 300 Winners Show Cover	$6
Neimann, Randy - 25th Anniversary of the Mets Team	$5
Nomo, Hideo & Marty Cordova - 1995 R.O.Y.	$7
Nomo, Hideo - 1995 All-Star Game - Arlington	$7
Oakland Athletics Opening Day - 1993	$5
Ojea, Chad - Game Six 1997 World Series	$7
Ojeda, Bob - 25th Anniversary of the Mets Team	$5
Olivia, Tony - 1985 New York Show Cover	$5
Olivia, Tony - 1965 New York Postmarked Show Card	$4
Olmo, Luis	$5
Olson, Gregg - 1989 A.L. Rookie of the Year	$6
O'Malley, Walter - Last Game at Ebbets Field	$5
O'Neill, Paul - Day 1994 Yankees Opening Day	$5
Orosco, Jesse - 1986 World Series Game 7	$8
Orosco, Jesse - 25th Anniversary of the Mets Team	$5
Owen, Mickey - Brooklyn Dodger Hall of Fame	$5
Pafko, Andy - Traded	$5
Pagliarulo, Mike - Yankee Exhibition Game	$5
Pagliarulo, Mike - 1988 Yankee Opening Day	$5
Pagliarulo, Mike - New York Sports Show Cover	$5
Palica, Erv	$5
Piazza, Mike - 1993 N.L. Rookie of the Year	$8
Palmer, Jim - 1983 World Series Game 3	$10
Palmer, Jim - 1983 A.L. Playoffs	$12
Palmer, Jim - 1990 Hall of Fame Induction	$6
Palmer, Jim - Ireland Salutes Heroes of American Baseball	$7
Parrott, Harold - Brooklyn Dodger Reporter	$5
Pena, Alejandro - Traded to the Mets	$5
Pendleton & Ripken - 1991 MVP Awards	$10
Pendleton, Terry - 1985 World Series Game 2	$10
Pendleton, Terry - 1991 World Series Game 5	$9
Pepitone, Joe - 1989 Old Timer's Day Game	$5
Perry, Gaylord - 1991 Hall of Fame Induction	$6
Perry, Gaylord - Manhattan N.Y. Show Cover	$5
Perry, Gaylord - Manhattan N.Y. Postmarked Show Card	$4
Perry, Gaylord - Houston, TX Show Cover	$5
Perry, Gaylord - Houston, TX Card Show Cover	$4
Perry, Carlton, Niekro, Spahn - 300 Game Winners, Dearborn Show	$6
Perry, Jim - Manhattan, New York Card Show Cover	$5
Perry, Jim - Manhattan, New York Postmarked Show Card	$4
Peterson, Fritz - New York Show Cover	$5
Peterson, Fritz - New York Postmarked Show Card	$4
Phifer, Bill - Brooklyn Dodger Bat Boy	$5
Piazza, Mike - 1993 N.L. ROY	$8
Piazza, Mike - 1995 All-Star Game	$8
Pierce, Billy - Manhattan, New York Card Show	$5
Pierce, Billy - Manhattan, New York Postmarked Show Card	$4

Subject/Description	Value
Pignatano, Joe - Salute to the 1969 Mets	$5
Piniella, Lou - Lou Retires 1984	$6
Piniella, Lou - Named Yankee Manager 1985	$6
Piniella, Lou - Opening Day 1986	$6
Piniella, Lou - Named Yankee Manager 1988	$6
Pittsburgh Pirates - Opening Day 1994	$5
Pitler, Jake	$5
Playoffs - 1993 American League	$5
Playoffs - 1993 National League	$5
Podres, Johnny - First Series Win For Dodgers	$8
Podres, Johnny - Manhattan, New York Card Show	$5
Podres, Johnny - Manhattan, N.Y. Postmarked Show Card	$4
Podbielan, Bud	$5
Pope John Paul II - Memorial Park	$7
Pope Paul VI - Memorial Park	$6
General Powell - Throws First Ball at 1991 Season Opener	$8
Puckett, Kirby - 1991 World Series Game 6	$10
Raines, Tim - 1987 MVP	$5
Ramirez, Manny - 1995 World Series Game 3	$6
Randolph, Willie - Yankee Opening Day	$5
Randolph, Willie - Hall of Fame Game	$5
Rasmussen, Dennis - First at Home Game	$5
Reese, Pee Wee - 1984 Hall of Fame Induction	$10
Reese, Pee Wee - Joins Military in W.W.II (B&W Cachet)	$5
Reese, Pee Wee - Retired Uniform	$5
Reese, Pee Wee - 1985 New York Show Cover	$6
Reese, Pee Wee - 1985 New York Postmarked Show Card	$5
Reed, Jack - Salute to the 1961 Yankees	$5
Reiser, Pete	$5
Reniff, Hal - Salute to the 1961 Yankees	$6
Reynolds, Allie - 35th Anniversary of His No-Hitter	$7
Reynolds, Allie - Memorial Park	$5
Rhoden, Rick - Last Season Game	$5
Rhoden, Rick - Yankee Debut	$5
Richardson, Bobby - Cracker Jack Classic	$5
Richardson, Bobby - Salute to the 1961 Yankees	$6
Richardson, Bobby - Queens New York Show Cover	$5
Righetti, Dave - 1986 All-Star Game	$10
Righetti, Dave - Yankee 1986 Opening Day	$6
Righetti, Dave - Yankee Rolaids Relief Man	$5
Righetti, Dave - No Hitter, July 4, 1983	$12
Rijo, Jose - World Series Game 4	$8
Rijo, Jose - 1990 World Series MVP	$5
Ripken, Cal - 1990 All-Star Game	$8
Ripken, Cal - 1992 All-Star Game	$10
Ripken, Cal - 1990 Hall of Fame Game	$10
Ripken, Cal - Camp Hill, PA Show Cover Very Limited Issue	$85
Ripken, Cal - Camp Hill, PA Postmarked Show Card (Limited)	$60
Ripken, Cal - 2,000 Consecutive Game	$15
Ripken, Cal - Freehold, New Jersey Postmarked Show Card	$20
Ripken, Cal - Ties Gehrig Record	$12
Ripken, Cal - Breaks Gehrig Record	$12
Ripken, Cal - "2131" Wheaties Silk Cachet of Postmarked 5x7 Card	$12
Ripken, Cal - 1996 All-Star Game	$10

Subject/Description	Value
Ripken, Cal - Throws First Ball in 1995 World Series	$10
Ripken, Cal - Ties Kinugasa International Record	$9
Ripken, Cal - Breaks Kinugasa International Record	$10
Ripken, Cal - 1997 Season Opener	$8
Ripken, Cal - 1997 All-Star Game	$8
Ripken, Cal - 1997 World Series Playoffs	$8
Rivers, Mickey - 1988 Old Timer's Day	$5
Rizzuto, Phil - Game Announcer	$5
Rizzuto, Phil - Induction Day	$8
Rizzuto, Phil - Hall of Fame Induction	$8
Rizzuto, Phil - 1983 Old Timer's Day	$10
Rizzuto, Phil - 1984 Old Timer's Day	$10
Rizzuto, Phil - Phil Rizzuto Day 1985	$8
Rizzuto, Phil - Phil Rizzuto Day 1994	$5
Rizzuto, Phil - Pride of the Yankees	$5
Rizzuto, Phil - Honored by the Yankees	$5
Rizzuto, Phil - Honored by the Joe DiMaggio at Stadium	$6
Rizzuto, Phil - Memorial Park	$8
Rizzuto, Phil - Uniform Retired	$5
Rizzuto, Phil - 1985 Freehold New Jersey Card Show	$5
Robinson, Brooks - 1983 Hall of Fame Induction	$10
Robinson, Jackie - 1947 World Series	$5
Robinson, Jackie - 1949 MVP	$6
Robinson, Jackie - Retires	$5
Robinson, Jackie - 50th Anniversary of the Hall of Fame	$7
Robinson, Jackie - Selig Retires All #42's in Baseball	$7
Robinson, Jackie - Mets Salute Robinson's 50th Anniversary	$6
Robinson, Jackie - 50th Anniversary - L.A. Season Opener	$6
Robinson, Jackie - 50th Anniversary - Angels Season Opener	$6
Robinson, Jackie - 50th Anniversary - President Clinton at Shea	$7
Robinson, Jackie - 50th Anniversary Hall of Fame Exhibition	$7
Robinson, Jackie - Retired Uniform	$5
Robinson, Frank - Retired Uniform	$5
Robinson, Irvine, Killebrew, Slaughter - Hall of Fame Show	$35
Roberts, Robin - Retired Uniform	$5
Roberts, Robin - Billy Williams Hall of Fame Show	$35
Roe, Preacher - 1949 World Series	$5
Roebuck, Ed	$5
Rolen, Scott & Nomar Garciaparra - 1997 Rookie of the Year	$5
Rose, Pete - Tie and Breaks Cobbs Record (Set of 2 Covers)	$50
Rose, Pete - Banned From Baseball	$10
Roseboro, John	$5
Rojek, Stan	$5
Ruppert, Jacob - Yankee Memorial Park	$5
Ruth, Babe & Fred Lynn - 50th Anniversary All-Star Game	$6
Ruth, Babe - First Day Cover	$7
Ruth, Babe & Mickey Mantle - Mantle Breaks Ruth W.S. Home Run Record	$10
Ruth, Babe - Uniform Retired	$6
Ruth, Babe - Yankee Memorial Park	$7
Ruth, Babe - 50th Anniversary of the All-Star Game - Special Show Postmark	$5
Ruth, Stainback, Hassett & Cuyler Dodger Coaches	$5
Ruth, Babe - 100th Anniversary of His Birth (Large Postmark)	$8
Ryan, Nolan - Salute to the 1969 Mets	$8
Ryan, Nolan - Ryan Retires, Set of 4	$35
Ryan, Nolan - Ryan Retires	$8
Ryan, Nolan - Alvin Express Station	$5
Ryan, Nolan - 1991 Opening Day	$7
Ryan, Nolan - 3,000 Strikeouts	$12
Ryan, Nolan - 300 Wins	$15
Ryan, Nolan - Opening Day, President Bush Throws Out First Ball	$8
Ryan, Nolan - Major League Record	$10
Ryan, Nolan - Rangers Opening Day 1993	$6
Ryan, Nolan - 5,000 Strikeouts	$75
Ryan, Nolan - 7th No-Hitter	$20
Ryan, Nolan & George Brett - Retired Same Day	$15
Ryan, Nolan - Set of 7 Covers - No Hitters Comm. Celebration Week	$35

REGGIE JACKSON BECAME ONLY THE 13th PLAYER IN MAJOR LEAGUE HISTORY TO REACH 500 CAREER HOMERUNS, WHEN HE CONNECTED IN THE SEVENTH INNING OFF OF ROYALS STARTER BUD BLACK. IT WAS THE 22nd HOMERUN OF THE SEASON FOR THE 38 YEAR OLD SLUGGER. HANK AARON HEADS A LIST OF 11 HALL OF FAMERS WHO HAVE PASSED THE 500 PLATEAU. REGGIE IS SURE TO BE ENSHRINED AND JOIN THE RANKS OF THE HALL OF FAMES ALL-TIME SLUGGERS.

Subject/Description	Value
Ryan, Nolan - St. Vincent Non-Silk First Day Cover	$7
Ryan, Nolan - Rangers Retire His Jersey	$6
Ryan, Nolan - Houston Astros Retire His Jersey	$6
Saberhagen, Bret - 1985 A.L. Cy Young Award	$7
Saberhagen, Bret - 1985 World Series MVP	$6
Saberhagen, Bret - 1985 World Series Game 3	$8
Saberhagen, Bret - 1989 A.L. Cy Young	$5
Sabo, Chris - 1990 World Series Game 3	$9
Sabo, Chris - 1988 Rookie of the Year	$6
Salmon, Tim & Mike Piazza - 1993 Rookie of the Year	$5
Samuel, Juan - Traded to the Mets	$5
Samuel, Juan - Philadelphia Show Cover	$5
Samuel, Juan - Philadelphia Postmarked Show Card	$4
Santana, Rafael - 25th Anniversary of the Mets	$5
Santiago, Benito - 1987 N.L. Rookie of the Year	$6
Schilling, Curt - 300th Strikeout	$7
Schmidt, Mike - 1988 Ties Mantle All Time Home Run Record	$12
Schmidt, Mike - 1990 #20 Retired by Phillies	$12
Schmidt, Mike - 1990 #20 Retired (Different Cachet)	$12
Schmidt, Mike - Elected to the Hall of Fame	$7
Schmidt, Mike - Inducted Into the Hall of Fame	$8
Schmidt, Mike - Inducted Into the Hall of Fame (Different Cachet)	$8
Schmidt, Mike - Retired Uniform	$5
Schoendienst, Red - Elected to the Hall of Fame - 1989	$5
Schoendienst, Red - Inducted Into the Hall of Fame - 1989	$5
Scott, Mike - 1986 National League Cy Young	$6
Scott, Mike - 1986 N.L. Playoffs	$6
Seaver, Tom - 1985 - 300 Wins	$12
Seaver, Tom - 300 Win Combo Cover Also Postmarked H.O.F. Induction	$15
Seaver, Tom - 1985 15th Record Start	$7
Seaver, Tom - 1983 Returns to the Mets	$8
Seaver, Tom - 1987 Returns to the Mets	$8
Seaver, Tom - Retires	$6
Seaver, Tom - Salute to the 1969 Mets	$6
Seaver, Tom - Inducted Into the Hall of Fame - 1992	$8
Seaver, Tom - Number 41 Retired	$10
Seaver, Tom - 2nd East Coast National	$12
Seaver, Tom - Tom Seaver Day at Shea Stadium	$6
Seaver, Tom - Uniform Retired	$5
Seaver, Tom - 3rd East Coast National	$10
Shamsky, Art - Salute to the 1969 Mets	$6
Shea Stadium - Salute to the 1969 Mets	$7
Sheffield, Gary - 1997 World Series Game 3	$7
Sheldon, Rollie - Salute to the 1961 Yankees	$6
Shotton, Barney	$5
Shuba, George - Brooklyn Dodger Hall of Fame	$5
Simmons, Ted - New York Show Cover	$5
Simmons, Ted - New York Show Postmarked Show Card	$4
Sisk, Doug - 25th Anniversary of the Mets	$6
Sixth Annual National Sports Collectors Convention	$6
Skowron, Bill - 1991 Yankee Old Time'rs Day	$5
Skowron, Bill - 1986 National Old Timer's Day Held in Washington	$5
Skowron, Bill - Salute to the 1961 Yankees	$6
Skowron, Bill - Queens New York Show Cover	$5
Skowron, Bill - Queens New York Postmarked Show Card	$5
Slaughter, Enos - Elected to the Hall of Fame 1985	$6
Slaughter, Enos - Inducted into the Hall of Fame 1985	$8
Slaughter, Enos - 1991 Yankee Old Timer's Day	$5
Slaughter, Robinson, Irvin & Killebrew - Hall of Fame Show	$35
Smith, Lonnie - 1992 World Series Game 5	$7
Smith, Ozzie - 1985 N.L. Playoffs	$7
Smith, Ozzie - Retires	$8
Smoltz, John & Pat Hentgen - 1996 Cy Young Award	$5
Snider, Duke & Jerry Grote - First East Coast National Show	$10
Snider, Duke - Heroes of New York Baseball	$7
Snider, Duke - Brooklyn Show Cover	$6
Snider, Duke - 1984 Brooklyn Show Postmarked Show Card	$5
Snider, Duke - Retired Uniform	$5

Subject/Description	Value
Snider, Duke & Willie Mays - Brooklyn Dodger Series	$5
Snider, Duke - 4 Home Runs in the 1952 Series	$5
Snider, Duke, Mantle, Mays - Atlantic City Show	$8
Snider, Duke, Mantle, Mays - East Coast National Show	$8
Spahn, Carlton, Niekro, Perry - Dearborn Mi. 300 Winners Card Show Cachet	$6
Spooner, Karl	$5
Sprague, Ed - 1992 World Series Game 2	$6
Stafford, Bill - Salute to the 1961 Yankees	$6
Stanky, Eddie	$5
Stanley, Mike - 1994 Yankee Opening Day	$5
Stargell, Willie - 1988 Hall of Fame Election	$6
Stargell, Willie - 1988 Hall of Fame Induction	$8
Stargell, Willie - New York Show Cover	$5
Stargell, Willie - New York Show Postmarked Show Card	$4
Stargell, Herman, Doerr - Hall of Fame Show	$35
Staub, Rusty - Ties Ty Cobbs Record	$7
Steib, Dave & Lefty Gomez - 50th Anniversary All-Star Game on Ruth F.D.C.	$7
Steinbach, Terry - 1989 World Series Game 2	$8
Stengel, Casey - Memorial Park	$6
Stengel, Casey - Brooklyn Dodger Manager	$5
Stewart, Dave - 1989 World Series Game 3	$8
Stewart, Dave - 1989 World Series MVP	$5
Stone, Jeff - Lancaster, Pa. Show Cover	$5
Stone, Jeff - Lancaster, Pa. Postmarked Show Card	$4
Strawberry, Darryl - Opening Day 1991	$6
Strawberry, Darryl & Dwight Gooden - 1984 Back to Back Rookies	$6
Strawberry, Darryl - Back to Back to Back Home Runs	$6
Strawberry, Darryl - 1985 All-Star Game	$8
Strawberry, Darryl - 1986 All-Star Game	$7
Strawberry, Darryl - 1988 All-Star Game	$6
Strawberry, Darryl - 25th Anniversary of the Mets	$5
Strawberry, Darryl - Yankee Debut	$6
Strike - 1985 Baseball Strike	$5
Strike - 1985 Baseball Strike Settlement	$5
Strike - 1994 Baseball Strike - Cover Lists Player Rep. From Each A.L. Team	$5
Strike - 1994 Baseball Strike - Cover Lists Player Rep. From Each N.L. Team	$5
Sukeforth, Clyde	$5
Sundberg, Jim - 1985 World Series Game 6	$8
Sutcliffe, Rick - 1984 Cy Young	$9
Sutton, Don - 300 Wins	$10
Tartabull, Danny - 1993 Closing Day	$5
Taylor, Ron - Salute to the 1969 Mets	$5
Terry, Ralph - Salute to the 1961 Yankees	$6
Teufel, Tim - 25th Anniversary of the Mets	$5
Thomas, Frank - 1993 All-Star Game	$6
Thomas, Frank & Barry Bonds - 1993 MVP's	$5
Thomas, Frank & Jeff Bagwell - 1994 MVP's	$5
Thomas, Frank - (The Pittsburgh Frank Thomas) Postmarked Card	$4
Thomas, Leroy - Salute to the 1961 Yankees	$8
Thome, Jim - 1995 World Series Game 5	$6
Thomson, Bobby - Hasbrouck Heights Show Cover	$4
Thomson, Bobby - Hasbrouck Heights Postmarked Show Card	$5
Thomson, Bobby - 5th National Sports Collectors Convention	$5
Thomson, Bobby - 5th National Sports Convention Postmarked Show Card	$4
Thompson, Milt & Len Dykstra - 1993 World Series Game 1	$7
Tolleson, Wayne - 1987 Yankee Opening Day	$5
Torgeson, Earl - Salute to the 1961 Yankees	$7
Toronto Blue Jays - 1989 Playoffs	$5
Torre, Joe - Yankee Manager - Yankees Win Pennant	$5
Trammel, Alan - 1984 World Series Game 4	$10
Tresh, Tom - Salute to the 1961 Yankees	$6
Tresh, Tom - Queens Card Show	$5
Tresh, Tom - Queens New York Postmarked Show Card	$4
Trucks, Virgil - Arlington Classic	$5

Subject/Description	Value
Turley, Bob - Salute to the 1961 Yankees	$6
Twenty-Fifth Anniversary of the Mets	$5
Valenzuela, Fernando - 1986 All-Star Game	$6
Valo, Elmer	$5
Van Cuyk, Chris	$6
Van Cuyk, Chris - 15th Run Inning	$5
Van Lingle, Mungo - New York Show Cover	$5
Vander Meer, Johnny - First Game at Ebbets Field	$8
Vaughan, Floyd - 1985 Hall of Fame Election	$5
Vaughan, Floyd - 1985 Hall of Fame Induction	$5
Vaughan, Mo & Barry Larkin - 1995 MVP's	$5
Versailles, Zoilo - New York Show Cover	$5
Versailles, Zoilo - New York Show Postmarked Show Card	$4
Viola, Frank, - 1987 World Series MVP	$5
Viola, Frank - 1988 A.L. Cy Young Award	$6
Virdon, Bill - 1985 Cracker Jack Classic	$5
Vizcaino, Jose - 1994 Mets Season Opener	$5
Walker, Dixie	$5
Walker, Rube - 1951 Dodgers	$5
Walker, Rube - Salute to the 1969 Mets	$5
Walton, Jerome - 1989 A.L. Rookie of the Year	$5
Ward, Gary - 1988 Yankee Opening Day	$5
Washington, Claudell - Yankee Series	$5
Weaver, Earl - 1996 Hall of Fame Induction	$7
Weaver, Earl - 1996 Hall of Fame Induction (Different Cachet)	$7
Weiss, Walt - 1988 A.L. Rookie of the Year	$6
Weiss, Walt - 1989 World Series Game 1	$8
Weis, Al - Salute to the 1969 Mets	$5
Welch, Bob - 1988 World Series Game 3	$8
White, Bill - Announcer	$5
Williams, Ted & Joe DiMaggio - Honored at the 1991 All-Star Game	$8
Wyatt, Whitlow	$5
Wyatt, Whitlow - Dodgers Clinch Flag	$5
Wilhelm, Hoyt - 1985 Hall of Fame Election	$6
Wilhelm, Hoyt - 1985 Hall of Fame Induction	$6
Wilhelm, Hoyt - 1985 New York Card Show	$5
Williams, Matt, Barry Bonds & Darren Lewis - 1994 Gold Glove	$5
Williams, Billy - 1987 Hall of Fame Election	$8
Williams, Billy - 1987 Hall of Fame Induction	$8
Williams, Billy & Robin Roberts - Hall of Fame Show	$35
Williams, Dick	$5
Williams & DiMaggio - Postmarked Show Card	$15
Williams, Ted - Final Game & Home Run	$15
Williams, Ted - World Ward II Pilot	$8
Williams, Ted & Joe DiMaggio - Honoring Boston's Greatest	$10
Williams, Ted - Leaves For Korean War	$8
Williams, Ted - 1991 All-Star Game	$8
Williams & DiMaggio - 1991 All-Star Game - Canada	$10
Williams, Ted - Retired Uniform	$5
Williams, Ted - Rody II Postmarked Show Card	$6
Williams, Ted - King of Prussia Postmarked Show Card	$6
Williams, Bernie - 1996 Playoff MVP	$6
Williams, Bernie - 1997 Gold Glove Award	$6
Williams, Bernie - 1997 All-Star Game	$6
Williams, Mitch - 1993 World Series Game 5	$6
Williams, Matt - Indians Opening Day 1997	$7
Willie, Mickey & The Duke - 1990 Atlantic City Show Cover	$8
Willie, Mickey & The Duke - East Coast National Show	$8
Wilson, Glen - King of Prussia Show	$5
Wilson, Glen - King of Prussia Postmarked Show Card	$4
Wilson, Mookie - 25th Anniversary of the Mets	$5
Wilson, Mookie - 1,000 Career Hits	$7
Wilson, Mookie - Home Run #564 Mets Record	$5
Wilson, Mookie - Flushing N.Y. Show Cover	$5
Wilson, Mookie - Flushing N.Y. Postmarked Show Card	$4

Subject/Description	Value
Wilson, Mookie - 1986 World Series Game 6	$8
Winfield, Dave - 100th R.B.I.	$6
Winfield, Dave - 300th Home Run	$6
Winfield, Dave - 200th Home Run As A Yankee	$6
Winfield, Dave - 1985 Gold Glove Award	$6
Winfield, Dave - 1987 Gold Glove Award	$6
Winfield, Dave - Opening Day 1987	$6
Winfield, Dave - R.B.I. Mark	$6
Winfield, Dave - 1985 All-Star Game	$6
Winfield, Dave - 1986 All-Star Game	$6
Winfield, Dave - 1987 All-Star Game	$6
Winfield, Dave - 1988 All-Star Game	$6
Winfield, Dave - Freehold New Jersey Show Cover	$5
Winfield, Dave - Freehold New Jersey Postmarked Show Card	$4
Winfield, Dave - Winfield Retires	$6
Woodling, Gene - Yankee Old Timer's Day	$5
World Series - Game 3 Cancelled Due to San Francisco Earthquake	$10
Worrell, Todd - 1986 Rookie of the Year	$5
Wynegar, Butch - Yankee Opening Day 1985	$5
Wynn, Early - 1985 Saddle Brook N.J. Postmarked Show Card	$4
Yankees 1993 Opening Day - Official Yankee Logo On Cover	$5
Yankees Clinch the 1996 American League East	$6
Yankees 1996 World Series Champs - Receive N.Y. Ticker Tape Parade	$6
Yankees 1996 World Series Champs - Receive New York Key to the City	$6
Yankees - First Inter League Game - Subway Series	$6
Yankee Stadium - 60th Anniversary Shown With Stadium & Babe Ruth	$20
Yastrzemski, Carl - Elected to the Hall of Fame 1989	$8
Yastrzemski, Carl - Inducted Into the Hall of Fame 1989	$10
Yastrzemski, Carl - Hyannis Mass. Show Cover	$5
Yastrzemski, Carl - Hyannis Mass. Postmarked Show Card	$4
Yastrzemski, Carl - Lake Harmony Pa. Show Cover	$5
Yastrzemski, Carl - Dearborn Mich. Show Cover	$5
Yastrzemski, Carl - Foxboro, Mass. Postmarked Show Card	$4
Yastrzemski, Carl - Retired Uniform	$5
Yvars, Sal - 5th National Card Show	$5
Yvars, Sal - 5th National Postmarked Show Card	$4
Yount, Robin - 3,000 Hits	$10
Yount, Robin - 1989 A.L. MVP	$8
Yount, Robin - 1985 New York Show Cover	$5
Yount, Robin - 1985 New York Postmarked Show Card	$4
Yost, Eddie - Salute to the 1969 Mets	$5
Zimmer, Don	$5
1983 Orioles - Phillies Series - 5 Covers	$40
1984 Padres - Tigers Series - 5 Covers	$35
1985 St. Louis - Kansas City Series - 7 Covers	$35
1986 Mets - Red Sox Series - 7 Covers	$35
1987 St. Louis - Minnesota Series - 7 Covers	$40
1988 Oakland - Los Angeles Series - 5 Covers	$25
1989 San Francisco - Oakland Series - 4 Covers	$20
1990 Cincinnati - Oakland Series - 4 Covers	$20
1991 Minnesota - Atlanta Series - 7 Covers	$35
1992 Atlanta - Toronto Series - 6 Covers	$30
1993 Phillies - Toronto Series - 6 Covers	$30
1995 Atlanta - Cleveland Series - 6 Covers	$30
1996 Atlanta - Yankees Series - 6 Covers	$35
1996 Cleveland - Marlins Series - 7 Covers	$40
1985 Baseball Strike	$5
1985 Baseball Settlement	$5
1994 Strike A.L. Teams	$5
1995 Strike N.L. Teams	$5

Gateway Stamp Co.

Gateway Stamp Co., of Florissant, Mo., has been producing its full-color "silk" commemorative cachets since 1977. The company has covered all the primary sports, with baseball as its main subject.

The limited-edition envelopes are postmarked on the historic dates by the United States Postal Service, which only dates items submitted before midnight. Gateway has employees who track a player's progress toward a milestone accomplishment; they also follow the player, with a determined number of stamped cachets to be postmarked, until the event has occurred. When the event has happened, the employee has the post office in that city hand-cancel the envelopes. Whenever possible, Gateway also incorporates philatelic cancellations on the envelopes.

The cachets feature gold borders, biographical information and full-color silk cachets, which are actual event photos, publicity photos, or artists' renditions. A primary attraction of the cachets is that Gateway has designed the envelopes to be autographed, and obtains the signatures of the players represented on them.

Values of the covers are determined by condition (cleanliness, crispness of corners, centering, positioning of copy, clarity of postmarks) and autographs - quality and player represented. In the following checklist, based on Mint condition, the values are for unsigned cachets, unless they were issued autographed. An "a" after the price indicates an autographed cachet.

Baseball

Hank Aaron Hall of Fame Induction, 8/1/82	$40
All-Star logo, 1979 in Seattle, 7/17/79	$10
All-Star logo, 1983 in Chicago (AL), 7/6/83	$15a
All-Star logo, 1989 in Anaheim, 7/11/89	$5
Walter Alston Hall of Fame induction, 7/31/83	$60a
Anaheim Stadium 25th anniversary, 4/19/91	$5
100 autographed by Rick Reichardt, who hit first home run there	$15
100 autographed by Jimmy Piersall,	$15
Marcelino Lopez, Jay Johnstone and Clyde Wright	$30
Sparky Anderson 100 wins both leagues, 9/23/84	$17a
Luis Aparicio Hall of Fame induction, 8/12/84	$25a
Luke Appling 50th anniversary of Hall of Fame, 6/12/89	$5
100 autographed by Chico Carrasquel and Don Kolloway	$25
Arlington Stadium last game played	$5
Astrodome 25th anniversary, 4/12/90	$5
150 autographed by Dick Allen, who hit the first home run there	$20
Atlanta-Fulton County Stadium 25th anniversary, 4/12/90	$5
Carlos Baerga home run record, 4/8/93	$20a
Baltimore Memorial Stadium last game, 10/6/91	$5
Baltimore Orioles losing streak ends, 4/29/88, signed by Frank Robinson	$25
Ernie Banks 50th anniversary All-Star Game, 7/6/83	$60a
Bret Barberie Florida Marlins first hit	$20a
Len Barker perfect game, 5/15/81	$35
Al Barlick Hall of Fame induction, 7/23/89	$20a
Cool Papa Bell Black Heritage 50th, 9/16/83	$95
Johnny Bench Hall of Fame induction, 7/23/89	$40a
Bert Blyleven 3,000 strikeouts, set of 2, 8/1/86	limited availability
Bob Boone all-time catching record, 9/16/87	$20a
Lou Boudreau 50th anniversary Hall of Fame, 6/12/89	$17a
Lou Brock 3,000 hits set of 2, 8/14/79	$20a
Lou Brock Hall of Fame induction, 7/28/85	$20a
Tom Browning perfect game, 9/16/88	$17a
Busch Stadium 25th anniversary, 5/12/91	$5
Camden Yards inaugural game, 4/6/92	$5
Roy Campanella 50th anniversary of Hall of Fame, 6/12/89	$650a
Canada FDI 150th anniversary of baseball in Canada, 9/14/88	$5
Candlestick Park 30th anniversary, 4/12/90	$5
Jose Canseco 40 home runs/40 stolen bases, 9/23/88	$75a
Rod Carew 3,000 hits, set of 2, 8/4/84	$30a
Rod Carew Hall of Fame induction	$40a
Steve Carlton 1979 All-Star Game, 7/17/79	$30a
Steve Carlton 3,000 strikeouts, set of 2, 4/29/81	limited availability
Steve Carlton all-time strikeout record, 6/7/83	$40a
Steve Carlton 300 wins, 9/23/83	$20
Steve Carlton 4,000 strikeouts, 8/5/86	$30a
Steve Carlton left-handed strikeout record, 7/6/90	$100a
Happy Chandler Hall of Fame induction, 8/1/82	$75a
Cincinnati Reds 14-run first inning, with 10 autographs	$150a

Will Clark 1988 All-Star logo, 7/12/88	$25a
Will Clark 1989 All-Star logo, 7/11/89	$25a
Will Clark 1991 All-Star Game	$5
Roger Clemens 20 strikeouts in a game, 4/29/86	$250a
Roberto Clemente FDI of Clemente stamp, 8/17/84	$5
Cleveland Stadium last game played, 4/3/93	$5
autographed by Mel Harder	$15a
Vince Coleman rookie stolen base record, 8/15/85	$19a
Comiskey Park last game played, 9/30/90	$6
Comiskey Park first game played, 4/18/91	$5
Jocko Conlon 50th anniversary Hall of Fame, 6/12/89	$5
Joe Cowley no hitter, 9/16/86	$75a
Ray Dandridge Hall of Fame induction, 7/26/87	$25a
Eric Davis three grand slams in a month, 5/30/87	$20a
Jim Deshaies strikeout record, 9/23/86	$15a
Bill Dickey 50th anniversary of All-Star Game, 1983	$95a
Joe DiMaggio 40th anniversary of 56-game hitting streak 7/16/81	limited availability
Joe DiMaggio 50th anniversary of 56-game hitting streak, 7/16/91	$25
Dodger Stadium 25th anniversary, 4/13/87	$10
Bobby Doerr Hall of Fame induction, 8/3/86	$17a
Don Drysdale Hall of Fame induction, 8/12/84	$50a
Earthquake 1989 World Series interruption, 10/17/89	$5
100 autographed by Giants Manager Roger Craig	$15
Ebbets Field 80th anniversary of opening, 4/4/93	$5
Darrell Evans oldest player to hit 40 home runs, 10/2/85	$50a
Darrell Evans 400th home run, 9/22/88	$17a
Bob Feller 50th anniversary of first game, 8/23/86	$17a
Fenway Park 75th anniversary, 4/20/87	limited availability
Rick Ferrell Hall of Fame induction, 8/12/84	$25a
Cecil Fielder over the roof home run at Tiger Stadium	$40a
Cecil Fielder 50 home run season, 10/3/90	$25a
Rollie Fingers all-time saves record, 4/13/85	$20a
Rollie Fingers Hall of Fame induction, 8/2/92	$20a
Carlton Fisk 1,807 games caught, 8/19/88	limited availability
500 Home Run Club signed by all 12 living members	$750a
Whitey Ford Hall of Fame induction, 6/12/79	$80a
Bob Forsch 1st no hitter, 4/16/78	$15
Bob Forsch 2nd no hitter, 9/26/83	$20a
Eddie Gaedel 40th anniversary of pinch hit appearance, 8/19/91, autographed by pitcher Bob Cain	$15a
Andres Galarraga First Colorado Rockies hit	$25a
Billy Gardner salute to 1961 Yankees, 8/26/94	$5
Steve Garvey 1,000 consecutive games, 6/7/82	$20a
Steve Garvey 1,118 consecutive games, 6/16/83	$20a
Steve Garvey Padres retire uniform, 4/16/88	$20a
Lou Gehrig FDI of Gehrig stamp, 6/10/89	$8
Lou Gehrig 50th anniversary of retirement, 7/4/89	limited availability
500 autographed by Yankee first baseman Don Mattingly	$60
Charlie Gehringer 50th anniversary of All-Star Game, 4/16/83	$175a
Bob Gibson Hall of Fame induction, 8/12/81	$25a

Kirk Gibson 1988 World Series MVP, 10/15/88 .... $25a
Lefty Gomez 50th anniversary of All-Star Game, 4/16/83 .... $60a
Doc Gooden rookie strikeout record, 9/26/84.......................... $30a
Doc Gooden youngest 20-game winner, 8/25/85 .... $30a
Goose Gossage 300th career save, 8/6/88.............................. $17a
Ron Guidry 1979 All-Star Game, 7/17/79 .... $5
Ken Griffey Jr. and Sr. Juniors major league debut, set of two $50a
Ken Griffey Jr. and Sr. father/son on same team $50a
Harvey Haddix 30th anniversary of perfect game, 5/26/94 ...... $30a
Ernie Harwell Hall of Fame induction $17a
Andy Hawkins no hitter, 7/1/90.. $15a
Rickey Henderson stolen base record, 8/27/82 .... $40a
Rickey Henderson all-time stolen bases, 5/1/91 .... $50a
Billy Herman 50th anniversary of Hall of Fame, 6/12/89 .... $30a
Orel Hershiser 59 scoreless innings, 9/28/88......................... $75a
Bob Horner four home runs in a game, 7/6/86 .... $18a
Charlie Hough Florida Marlins first pitch $20a
Carl Hubbell 50th anniversary of All-Star feat, 7/10/84 .... $95a
Catfish Hunter Hall of Fame induction, 7/26/87 .... $20a
Monte Irvin 50th anniversary of Hall of Fame, 6/12/89 .... $17a
Bo Jackson 1989 All-Star Game $75a
Reggie Jackson 1977 World Series, three home runs, 10/18/77 . $300a
Reggie Jackson 1979 All-Star appearance $50a
Reggie Jackson 400th home run, 8/11/80.............................. $50a
Reggie Jackson 500th home run, 9/17/84.............................. $150a
Reggie Jackson 500th home run, numbered version $200a
Travis Jackson Hall of Fame induction, 8/1/82 .... $60a
Jacobs Field, Cleveland inaugural game, 4/4/94 .... $5
Fergie Jenkins 3,000 strikeouts, set of 2, 5/25/83 .... $20a
Fergie Jenkins Canadian Hall of Fame induction, 11/19/87 .... $5
Judy Johnson Black Heritage 50th anniversary, 9/16/83 .... $75a
Walter Johnson all-time strikeout leader $25a
Wally Joyner rookie All-Star, 7/15/86...................................... $20a
Jim Kaat 25 years, 4/5/83 .... $15a
Al Kaline Hall of Fame induction, 8/30/80............. limited availability
George Kell Hall of Fame induction, 7/31/83........................... $25a
Harmon Killebrew Hall of Fame induction, 8/12/84 .... $25a
Ralph Kiner 50th anniversary of Hall of Fame, 6/12/89 .... $17a
Dave Kingman 400th home run, 8/10/85 .... $30a
Sandy Koufax 50th anniversary of Hall of Fame, 6/12/89 .... $40a
Rick Langford 21 complete games, 9/6/80 .... $150a
Rick Langford 22 complete games, 9/12/80 .... $35a
Don Larsen 30th anniversary of World Series perfect game
   10/8/86 .... $20a
Tony Lazzeri Hall of Fame induction, 7/21/91........................... $5
   100 autographed by Frank Crosetti $17a
Bob Lemon 50th anniversary of Hall of Fame, 6/12/89 .... $17a
Buck Leonard Black Heritage 50th anniversary, 9/16/83 .... $30a
Al Lopez 50th anniversary of the Hall of Fame, 6/12/89........... $80a
Fred Lynn 1979 All-Star Game, 7/17/79 .... $20a
Willie McGee NL switch-hitting record, 10/6/85 .... $18a
Mantle/Maris anniversary of 1961 season, autographed by Mantle $125
Mickey Mantle 40th anniversary of Hall of Fame, 6/12/79 ..... $175a
Juan Marichal Hall of Fame induction, 7/31/83 .... $20a
Billy Martin remembrance, 12/29/89... $5
Eddie Mathews 50th anniversary of Hall of Fame, 6/12/89 ...... $20a
Don Mattingly batting record, 10/5/86 .... $35a
Don Mattingly consecutive home runs, 7/18/87...................... $35a
Don Mattingly grand slams, 9/29/87 .... $150a
Willie Mays induction, 8/2/79.. $150a
Willie McCovey 500th home run, set of 2, 6/3/78 .... $125a
Willie McCovey Hall of Fame induction, 8/3/86 .... $25a
Mark McGwire rookie home run record, 8/14/87 .... $40a
Mark McGwire five home runs in two games, 6/28/87 .... $50a
Mile High Stadium/Denver first Colorado game $5
Minnie Minoso five decades of baseball, 10/4/80 .... $300a
Johnny Mize Hall of Fame induction, 8/2/81........................... $25a
Paul Molitor 39-game hitting streak, 8/25/87 .... $30a
Joe Morgan Hall of Fame induction, 8/6/90............................ $15a
Jack Morris no hitter, 4/7/84 .... $22a
Dale Murphy 1983 All-Star Game .... limited availability

Eddie Murray 1,500 RBI, 5/23/95 .... $40a
Stan Musial hit record broken, 8/10/81 .... $40a
Hal Newhouser Hall of Fame induction, 8/2/92 .... $20a
Phil Niekro 3,000 strikeouts, set of 2, 7/4/84 .... $20a
Phil Niekro 300 wins, 6/10/85 .... $20a
Phil Niekro/Steve Carlton 300-game winner teammates, 4/9/87,
   signed by both $50
Phil Niekro/Don Sutton 300-game winners, 8/28/86, signed by
   both $60a
Phil Niekro/Joe Niekro winningest brother combination, signed by
   both $25a
Juan Nieves no hitter, 4/15/87.. $20a
Oakland/Alameda/ 25th anniversary, 4/17/93 .... $5
Olympic baseball team 1984 team reunited, 21 autographs ... $200
Olympic baseball team 1988 team reunited, 22 autographs ... $200
Dave Palmer 5-inning perfect game, 4/22/84 .... $15a
Jim Palmer Hall of Fame induction, 8/5/90.............................. $5
Satchel Paige 40th anniversary Hall of Fame, 6/12/79 .... $400a
Chan Ho Park major league debut, 4/8/94.............................. $30a
Dave Parker 1979 All-Star Game, 7/17/79 .... $20a
Gaylord Perry 300 wins, set of 2, 5/6/82 .... $20a
Gaylord Perry Hall of Fame induction, as a Giant or an Indian $20a
Gaylord Perry/Jim Perry winningest brother combination,
   autographed by both $40a
Kirby Puckett 10 consecutive hits, 8/30/87............................. $40a
Jeff Reardon 40 saves both leagues, 9/30/88......................... $17a
Pee Wee Reese Hall of Fame induction, 8/12/84...................... $5
Jim Rice 1983 All-Star Game.. $20a
Dave Righetti no hitter, 7/4/83 .... $20a
Cal Ripken Jr. consecutive innings played, 9/14/87 .... $20
Cal Ripken Jr. 2,131 consecutive games played $25
Robin Roberts 50th anniversary of the Hall of Fame, 6/12/89 .... $17a
Brooks Robinson Hall of Fame induction, 7/31/83 .... $20a
Frank Robinson Hall of Fame induction, 8/1/82 .... $25a
Jackie Robinson 40th anniversary of first game played $5
   100 autographed by Johnny Sain, first pitcher Robinson faced $15
   100 autographed by Dick Littlefield, only player to be
      traded for Robinson $25
Jackie Robinson First Day Issue of stamp, 8/2/82 .... $5
Pete Rose all-time NL hit record, set of 2, 6/10/85 .... $35a
Pete Rose 3,000 hits, set of 2, 5/5/78 .... $50a
Pete Rose 44-game hitting streak, game 37, 7/24/78 .... $35
Pete Rose 44-game hitting streak, game 38, 7/25/78 .... $35
Pete Rose 44-game hitting streak, game 44, 7/31/78 .... $50
Pete Rose 44-game hitting streak, night it ended, 8/1/78 .... $75
Pete Rose 4,000 hits, 4/13/84 .... $75a
Pete Rose 3,309 games played, 6/29/84 .... $60a
Pete Rose managerial debut, 8/17/84...................................... $15
Pete Rose 4,192 hits, all-time record, set of 4, 9/1/94 .... $75a
Pete Rose banishment, 8/24/89 .... $30
Edd Roush 70th anniversary of batting title, 9/30/87 .... $5
Babe Ruth FDI of Ruth stamp, 7/6/83 .... $10
Nolan Ryan 3,000 strikeouts, set of 2, 7/4/80 .... $50a
Nolan Ryan 5th no hitter, 9/26/81 .... $300a
Nolan Ryan 3,509 strikeouts, 4/27/83 .... $50a
Nolan Ryan 4,000 strikeouts, 7/11/85 .... $50a
Nolan Ryan 5,000 strikeouts, 8/22/89 .... $150a
Nolan Ryan 6th no hitter, 6/11/90 .... $50a
Nolan Ryan 300 wins, 7/31/90 .... $50a
Nolan Ryan 7th no hitter, 5/1/91 .... limited availability
Nolan Ryan 27th season, 4/9/93 .... $50a
St. Louis Browns 40th anniversary of last game in St. Louis $5
San Diego Padres three home runs to start the game, autographed
   by Marvell Wynne, Tony Gwynn and John Kruk, 4/13/87 ..... $75
San Diego Padres 20th anniversary, autographed by Randy Jones. $17
Benito Santiago rookie hit streak, 10/2/87 .... $20a
Mike Schmidt 400th home run, 5/15/85 .... $50a
Mike Schmidt 500th home run, 4/18/87 .... $50a
Red Schoendienst Hall of Fame induction, 7/23/89 .... $20a
Mike Scott no hitter, 9/25/86.. $17a
Tom Seaver 3,000 strikeouts, set of 2, 4/18/81 .... $30a

Tom Seaver uniform retirement, 7/24/84 .... $30a
Tom Seaver Opening Day record, 4/9/85 .... $30a
Tom Seaver 300 wins, 8/4/85 .... $30a
Tom Seaver Hall of Fame induction, 8/2/92 .... $40a
Tom Seaver no hitter $15
Joe Sewell 50th anniversary of Hall of Fame, 6/12/89 .... $5
Shea Stadium 25th anniversary, 4/17/89 .... $10
Sheffield/McGriff back-to-back home runs in consecutive innings,
   8/6/92, autographed by both $40
Enos Slaughter Hall of Fame induction, 7/28/85 .... $25a
Lee Smith 300th save, 8/25/91 .... $22a
Lee Smith all-time save record, 4/13/93 .... $22a
Ozzie Smith 10th straight All-Star Game, 7/14/92 .... $25a
Duke Snider Hall of Fame induction, 8/3/80 .... $25a
Warren Spahn 300 wins, 5/6/82 .... $50a
Willie Stargell Hall of Fame induction, 7/31/88 .... $20a
Rusty Staub 100 pinch hits, 9/21/83 .... $20a
Rusty Staub last game, set of 2, 7/13/86 .... $30a
Dave Stewart no hitter, 6/29/90 .... $25a
Terry Steinbach 1988 All-Star Game $15a
Don Sutton 3,000 strikeouts, set of 2, 6/24/83 .... $20a
Don Sutton 300 wins, 6/18/86 .... $20a
Ralph Terry 50th annivesary of All-Star Game $100
Texas Trio home run record, signed by Juan Gonzalez, Rafael
   Palmeiro and Dean Palmer .... limited availability
Bobby Thomson 40th anniversary of 1951 playoffs............... $17a
Jim Thorpe FDI of Thorpe stamp, 5/24/84 .... $5
Three Rivers Stadium 25th anniversary $5
Tiger Stadium 80th anniversary $5
Triple Crown autographed by Ted Williams, Mickey Mantle, Frank
   Robinson, Carl Yastrzemski $400a
Fernando Valenzuela ERA record, 4/28/85 .... $35a
Johnny VanderMeer back-to-back no hitters, set of 2 . limited availability
Andy Van Slyke 1988 All-Star Game $25a
Arky Vaughn Hall of Fame induction, 7/8/85 .... $5
Mark Whiten four home runs in a game, 9/8/93 .... $20a
Hoyt Wilhelm Hall of Fame induction, 7/28/85...................... $20a
Billy Williams Hall of Fame induction, 7/26/86 .... $5
Ted Williams 50th anniversary of .400 season, 9/28/91 .... $20
Todd Worrell rookie saves record, 8/10/86 .... $17a
Wrigley Field first night game, set of 2, 8/8/88 .... $10
Early Wynn 300 wins, 5/6/82 .... $50a
Yankee Stadium 70th anniversary photo $5
Yankee Stadium 70th anniversary art...................................... $5
Carl Yastrzemski 3,000 hits, 9/12/79 .... $100a
Carl Yastrzemski Hall of Fame induction, 7/23/89.......limited availability
Eric Young first rookie home run $20a
Robin Yount 3,000 hits, 9/9/92... $40a
Willie, Mickey and the Duke autographed by Mays, Mantle and
   Snider, 1/14/89 .... $300
Maury Wills 25th anniversary of 104 stolen bases, 10/3/87 .... $17a
Dave Winfield 1979 All-Star Game $30a
Dave Winfield 400th home run, 8/14/91 .... $30a
Dave Winfield 3,000th hit, 9/16/93 .... $35a
Mike Witt perfect game, 9/30/84 .... $17a

Gateway World Series cachets

A is autographed, U is unautographed

1978

Game 1: Oct. 10, 1978, Los Angeles, Calif. Stadium artwork. A by
   Reggie Jackson ($75), Steve Garvey ($60), Ed Figueroa ($40).
Game 2: Oct. 11, 1978, Los Angeles, Calif. Ron Cey and Davey
   Lopes. A by Cey, Lopes or Don Sutton ($45), Garvey ($60), Sut-
   ton and Catfish Hunter ($75), Garvey and Hunter ($80).
Game 3: Oct. 13, 1978, Bronx, N.Y. Graig Nettles. A by Ron Guidry
   ($50), Nettles ($45).
Game 4: Oct. 14, 1978, Bronx, N.Y. Tommy Lasorda, Cey and
   Garvey. A by Lasorda ($50), Reggie Jackson ($75), Reggie
   Smith ($45), Garvey ($60).
Game 5: Oct. 15, 1978, Bronx, N.Y. Thurman Munson. U ($35).

Game 6: Oct. 17, 1978, Los Angeles, Calif. World Series trophy. A
   by Hunter ($50), Yogi Berra ($60).

1979

Game 1: Oct. 10, 1979, Baltimore, Md. Stadium artwork. A by Mark
   Belanger ($20), Eddie Murray ($25), Frank Robinson ($25),
   Willie Stargell ($25), John Lowenstein ($20).
Game 1: Mike Flanagan. U ($20).
Game 2: Oct. 11, 1979, Baltimore, Md. Jim Palmer. A by Palmer ($25).
Game 2: Kent Tekulve. U ($10).
Game 3: Oct. 12, 1979, Pittsburgh, Pa. Kiko Garcia. U ($10).
Game 4: Oct. 13, 1979, Pittsburgh, Pa. Earl Weaver. A by Weaver
   ($20), U ($10).
Game 5: Oct. 14, 1979, Pittsburgh, Pa. Dave Parker and Rick
   Dempsey. A by Parker ($25), Dempsey or Bill Madlock ($20),
   Mike Flanagan or Tim Foli ($15).
Game 6: Oct. 16, 1979, Baltimore, Md. Kent Tekulve. U ($10).
Game 6: Oct. 16, 1979, Baltimore, Md. Jim Palmer. A by Palmer
   ($25), U ($10).
Game 7: Oct. 17, 1979, Baltimore, Md. Willie Stargell and Bill Rob-
   inson. A by Stargell ($25), Robinson ($20), U ($10).

1980

Game 1: Oct. 14, 1980, Philadelphia, Pa. Stadium artwork. A by
   Bob Boone, Bake McBride or Frank White ($20).
Game 2: Oct. 15, 1980, Philadelphia, Pa. Steve Carlton. A by Carl-
   ton ($35), U ($15).
Game 3: Oct. 17, 1980, Kansas City, Kan. George Brett. A by Brett
   ($50), Amos Otis ($20), U ($15).
Game 4: Oct. 18, 1980, Kansas City, Kan. Willie Mays Aikens. U
   ($10), A by Larry Christenson ($20).
Game 5: Oct. 19 1980, Kansas City, Kan. Bob Boone and Darrell
   Porter. A by Manny Trillio, Del Unser or Tug McGraw ($20).
Game 6: Oct. 21, 1980, Philadelphia, Pa. Mike Schmidt. A by
   Schmidt ($50), U ($15).

1981

Game 1: Oct. 20, 1981, Bronx, N.Y. Stadium artwork. A by Ron
   Guidry, Bob Lemon or Dave Righetti ($15), U ($10).
Game 2: Oct. 21, 1981, Bronx, N.Y. Goose Gossage. A by Gossage
   ($15).
Game 3: Oct. 23, 1981, Los Angeles, Calif. Fernando Valenzuela.
   U ($10).
Game 3: Oct. 23, 1981, Los Angeles, Calif. Ron Cey. A by Cey and
   Tommy Lasorda ($30), U ($10).
Game 4: Oct. 24, 1981, Los Angeles, Calif. Steve Garvey. A by
   Garvey ($20).
Game 5: Oct. 25, 1981, Los Angeles, Calif. Jerry Reuss. A by
   Reuss ($15), U ($10).
Game 6: Oct. 28, 1981, Bronx, N.Y. Steve Yeager and Steve Howe.
   A by Yeager, Cey or Dusty Baker ($15), U ($10).

1982

Game 1: Oct. 12, 1982, St. Louis, Mo. Stadium artwork. A by
   Tommy Herr ($15), U ($10).
Game 2: Oct. 13, 1982, St. Louis, Mo. Darrell Porter. A by Porter
   ($15), U ($10).
Game 2: Oct. 13, 1982, St. Louis, Mo. Ted Simmons. A by Sim-
   mons ($15), U ($10).
Game 3: Oct. 15, 1982, Milwaukee, Wis. Joaquin Andujar. A by
   Willie McGee ($15), U ($10).
Game 4: Oct. 16, 1982, Milwaukee, Wis. Cecil Cooper. A by Cooper
   ($15), Ozzie Smith ($25), U ($10).
Game 5: Oct. 17, 1982, Milwaukee, Wis. Robin Yount. A by Yount
   ($35), or U ($20).
Game 6: Oct. 19, 1982, St. Louis, Mo. Keith Hernandez. A by Her-
   nandez ($15), U ($10).
Game 6: Oct. 19, 1982, St. Louis, Mo. Darrell Porter. A by Porter
   ($15), U ($10).
Game 7: Oct. 20, 1982, St. Louis, Mo. Bruce Sutter. A by Sutter,
   McGee or Lonnie Smith ($15), U ($10).

1983

Game 1: Oct. 11, 1983, Baltimore, Md. Stadium artwork. A by Joe Morgan ($25), Al Holland ($15).

Game 2: Oct. 12, 1983, Baltimore, Md. Mike Boddicker. A by Boddicker ($15), U ($7.50).

Game 3: Oct. 14, 1983, Philadelphia, Pa. Rick Dempsey. A by Dempsey ($15), U ($7.50).

Game 3: Oct. 14, 1983, Philadelphia, Pa. Joe Morgan. A by Morgan ($25).

Game 4: Oct. 15, 1983, Philadelphia, Pa. John Denny. A by Denny ($15), U ($7.50).

Game 5: Oct. 16, 1983, Philadelphia, Pa. Rick Dempsey. A by Dempsey ($15), U ($7.50).

Game 5: Oct. 16, 1983, Philadelphia, Pa., Eddie Murray. A by Murray ($25), U ($7.50).

1984

Game 1: Oct. 9, 1984, San Diego, Calif. Stadium artwork. U ($7.50).

Game 2: Oct. 10, 1984, San Diego, Calif. Kurt Bevacqua and Terry Kennedy. A by Kennedy ($15), U ($7.50).

Game 3: Oct. 12, 1984, Detroit, Mich. Willie Hernandez. A by Hernandez ($15), U ($7.50).

Game 4: Oct. 13, 1984, Detroit, Mich. Alan Trammell. A by Trammell ($15), U ($7.50).

Game 5: Oct. 14, 1984, Detroit, Mich. Kirk Gibson. A by Gibson ($25), U ($7.50).

1985

Game 1: Oct. 19, 1985, Kansas City, Mo. Stadium artwork. A by Ozzie Smith ($25), U ($7.50).

Game 2: Oct. 20, 1985, Kansas City, Mo. Terry Pendleton. A by Pendleton ($15), U ($7.50).

Game 3: Oct. 22, 1985, St. Louis, Mo. Frank White photo. A by White ($15), U ($7.50).

Game 4: Oct. 23, 1985, St. Louis, Mo. John Tudor. A by Tudor ($15), U ($7.50).

Game 5: Oct. 24, 1985, St. Louis, Mo. Willie Wilson. U ($7.50).

Game 6: Oct. 26, 1985, Kansas City, Mo. Charlie Leibrandt. A by Leibrandt ($15), U ($7.50).

Game 7: Oct. 27, 1985, Kansas City, Mo. Bret Saberhagen and George Brett. A by Saberhagen ($25), by Saberhagen and Brett ($75).

1986

Game 1: Oct. 18, 1986, New York, NY. Stadium artwork. A by Davey Johnson or Bill Buckner ($15), U ($7.50).

Game 2: Oct. 19, 1986, New York, N.Y. Dwight Gooden. A by Gooden ($25), U ($10).

Game 2: Oct. 19, 1986, New York, N.Y. Roger Clemens. A by Clemens ($35), U ($10).

Game 3: Oct. 21, 1986, Boston, Mass. Lenny Dykstra. A by Dykstra ($20), U ($7.50).

Game 4: Oct. 22, 1986, Boston, Mass. Gary Carter. A by Carter ($20), U ($10).

Game 5: Oct. 23, 1986, Boston, Mass. Bruce Hurst. A by Hurst ($15), U ($7.50).

Game 6: Oct. 25, 1986, New York, N.Y. Keith Hernandez. A by Hernandez ($15), U ($7.50).

Game 6: Oct. 25, 1986, New York, N.Y. Wade Boggs. A by Boggs ($25), U ($10).

Game 7: Oct. 27, 1986, New York, N.Y. Ray Knight. A by Knight ($15), U ($7.50).

1987

Game 1: Oct. 17, 1987, Minneapolis, Minn. Stadium artwork. A by Kirby Puckett ($30), Tom Brunansky ($15), U ($7.50).

Game 2: Oct. 18, 1987, Minneapolis, Minn. Bert Blyleven. A by Blyleven ($15), U ($7.50).

Game 3: Oct. 20, 1987, St. Louis, Mo. Vince Coleman. A by Coleman ($15), U ($7.50).

Game 4: Oct. 21, 1987, St. Louis, Mo. Tom Lawless. A by Lawless ($15).

Game 5: Oct. 22, 1987, St. Louis, Mo. Ozzie Smith. A by Smith ($25), U ($10).

Game 6: Oct. 24, 1987, Minneapolis, Minn. Kent Hrbek. A by Hrbek ($15).

Game 7: Oct. 25, 1987, Minneapolis, Minn. Frank Viola. A by Viola ($15), U ($7.50).

1988

Game 1: Oct. 15, 1988, Los Angeles, Calif. Stadium artwork. A by Jose Canseco ($25), U ($7.50).

Game 2: Oct. 16, 1988, Los Angeles, Calif. Orel Hershiser. A by Hershiser ($20), U ($7.50).

Game 3: Oct. 18, 1988, Oakland, Calif. Mark McGwire. A by McGwire ($20).

Game 4: Oct. 19, 1988, Oakland, Calif. Mike Scioscia. A by Scioscia ($15), U ($7.50).

Game 5: Oct. 20, 1988, Oakland, Calif. Mickey Hatcher. A by Hatcher ($15), U $7.50.

1989

Game 1: Oct. 14, 1989, Oakland, Calif. Stadium artwork. A by Matt Williams ($20), U ($7.50).

Game 2: Oct. 15, 1989, Oakland, Calif. Rickey Henderson. A by Henderson ($25), U ($7.50).

Earthquake: Oct. 17, 1989, San Francisco, Calif. Earthquake artwork. A by Roger Craig ($15), U ($7.50).

Game 3: Oct. 27, 1989, San Francisco, Calif. Dave Stewart. A by Stewart ($20), U ($7.50).

Game 4: Oct. 28, 1989, San Francisco, Calif. Mike Moore. A by Moore ($15), U ($7.50).

1990

Game 1: Oct. 16, 1990, Cincinnati, Ohio. Stadium artwork. A by Lou Piniella or Eric Davis ($15), U ($7.50).

Game 2: Oct. 17, 1990, Cincinnati, Ohio. Billy Hatcher and Carney Lansford. A by Hatcher ($15), U ($7.50).

Game 3: Oct. 19, 1990, Oakland, Calif. Chris Sabo. A by Sabo ($15).

Game 3: Oct. 19, 1990, Oakland, Calif. Rob Dibble. A by Dibble and Norm Charlton ($25), U ($10).

Game 4: Oct. 20, 1990, Oakland, Calif. Jose Rijo. A by Rijo ($15).

1991

Game 1: Oct. 19, 1991, Minneapolis, Minn. Stadium artwork. A by Tom Glavine ($15).

Game 2: Oct. 20, 1991, Minneapolis, Minn. Ron Gant. A by Gant ($15), U ($7.50).

Game 3: Oct. 22, 1991, Atlanta, Ga. Steve Avery. A by Avery ($15), U ($7.50).

Game 4: Oct. 23, 1991, Atlanta, Ga. Lonnie Smith and Brian Harper. U ($7.50).

Game 5: Oct. 24, 1991, Atlanta, Ga. Mark Lemke. A by Lemke ($15), U ($7.50).

Game 6: Oct. 26, 1991, Minneapolis, Minn. Kirby Puckett. U ($7.50).

Game 7: Oct. 27, 1991, Minneapolis, Minn. Jack Morris. U ($7.50).

Gateway
Football

GS53 Super Sunday: Postmarked Jan. 20, 1980, Pasadena, Calif., featuring artwork by Scott Forst. 2,000 issued, some autographed by Cullen Bryant, L.C. Greenwood, John Stallworth or Wendell Tyler $25

GS54 Los Angeles Rams: Postmarked Jan. 20, 1980, Pasadena, Calif. 2,000 issued, featuring photo of Vince Ferragamo and Rich Saul. Some autographed by Vince Ferragamo, Rich Saul, Cullen Bryant or Wendell Tyler $20

GS55 Pittsburgh Steelers: Postmarked Jan. 20, 1980, Pasadena, Calif. 2,000 issued, featuring photo of Franco Harris and Fred Dryer. Some autographed by Franco Harris, L.C. Greenwood or John Stallworth $30

GS73 New Orleans: Postmarked Jan. 25, 1981, New Orleans, La., site of the 1981 Super Bowl between the Oakland Raiders and Philadelphia Eagles. 2,000 issued $20

GS74 Oakland: Postmarked Jan. 25, 1981, New Orleans, La., site of the 1981 Super Bowl between Oakland and Philadelphia. 2,000 issued $20

GS75 Philadelphia: Postmarked Jan. 25, 1981, New Orleans, La., site of the 1981 Super Bowl between Oakland and Philadelphia. 2,000 issued $20

GS97 Bear Bryant: Postmarked Dec. 29, 1982, Memphis, Tenn., upon Bryant's last collegiate game, a victory for an all-time record of 323 wins. Bryant photo. 2,000 issued $50

GS165 Jim Thorpe First Day of Issue: Postmarked "First Day of Issue" May 24, 1984, Broken Arrow, Okla. 3,500 issued. Bill Perry artwork. 50 hand-cancellations ....Undetermined.

GS182 Walter Payton Rushing Record: Postmarked Oct. 7, 1984, Chicago, Ill. 1,500 issued, autographed $50

GS188 Eric Dickerson Single-Season Rushing Record: Postmarked Dec. 9, 1984, Anaheim, Calif. 1,500 issued, autographed $30

GS189 Dan Marino Passing Record: Postmarked Dec. 18, 1984, commemorating Marino's single-season record of 5,000 yards passing. 1,000 issued $35

GS193 Super Bowl, Palo Alto: Postmarked Jan. 20, 1985, Palo Alto, Calif., with pictorial Super Bowl XIX postmark. 1,100 issued with Scott Forst artwork. Issued autographed by various players or Bill Walsh $15

GS194 Super Bowl Dolphins: Postmarked Jan. 20, 1985, Palo Alto, Calif., with pictorial Super Bowl XIX postmark. 1,100 issued, autographed by Dan Marino $25

GS195 Super Bowl 49ers: Postmarked Jan. 20, 1985, Palo Alto, Calif., with pictorial Super Bowl XIX postmark. 1,100 issued autographed by Joe Montana, with action photo $50

GS209 Roger Staubach Hall of Fame Induction: Postmarked Aug. 3, 1985, Canton, Ohio, with a special Hall of Fame Induction Day postmark. 1,500 issued, autographed. Bill Perry artwork $25

GS210 O.J. Simpson Hall of Fame Induction: Postmarked Aug. 3, 1985, Canton, Ohio. 1,000 issued, autographed. Bill Perry artwork.. $50

GS211 Joe Namath Hall of Fame Induction: Postmarked Aug. 3, 1985, Canton, Ohio. 1,500 issued, autographed. Bill Perry artwork.. $50

GS222 Eddie Robinson Coaching Record: Postmarked Oct. 5, 1985, Dallas, Texas, as Grambling University's Robinson passed Paul "Bear" Bryant as the winningest coach in college football history. 1,000 issued, autographed $20

GS237 1986 Super Bowl, Superdome: Postmarked Jan. 26, 1986, New Orleans, La., with large U.S.P.S. pictorial Super Bowl XX cancellation. Stadium artwork by Scott Forst. 800 issued unautographed or autographed by Mike Singletary or Richard Dent $15

GS238 1986 Super Bowl, Chicago Offense: Postmarked Jan. 26, 1986, New Orleans, La., with large pictorial Super Bowl XX postmark. 800 issued picturing Jim McMahon, 500 autographed $20

GS239 1986 Super Bowl, Chicago Defense: Postmarked Jan. 26, 1986, New Orleans, La., with large pictorial Super Bowl XX cancellation. 800 issued picturing William "Refrigerator" Perry. 500 autographed by Perry, 300 autographed by Richard Dent $20

GS290 Paul Hornung Hall of Fame Induction: Postmarked Aug. 3, 1986, Canton, Ohio, with pictorial philatelic postmark. 1,000 issued, autographed. Bill Perry artwork.................................$20

GS317 1987 Super Bowl, Pasadena: Postmarked Jan. 25, 1987, Pasadena, Calif., with large Super Bowl XXI U.S.P.S. cancellation. Vince Lombardi trophy artwork by Scott Forst. 800 issued with various New York Giants autographs, including Jim Burt, Harry Carson and Lawrence Taylor..................................... $15

GS318 1987 Super Bowl, New York: Postmarked Jan. 25, 1987, Pasadena, Calif., with large Super Bowl XXI cancellation. 800 issued picturing Phil Simms, autographed by Simms or Simms and Joe Morris... $35

GS319 1987 Super Bowl, Denver: Postmarked Jan. 25, 1987, Pasadena, Calif., with large Super Bowl XXI cancellation. 800

issued picturing John Elway and Bobby Humphrey. Autographed by Elway $30

GS378 1988 Super Bowl, Jack Murphy Stadium: Postmarked Jan. 31, 1988, San Diego, Calif., with large U.S.P.S. pictorial Super Bowl XXII cancellation. 800 issued with Scott Forst stadium artwork. 500 autographed by Art Monk $15

GS379 1988 Super Bowl, Washington: Postmarked Jan. 31, 1988, San Diego, Calif., with large Super Bowl XXII cancellation. 800 issued, autographed, picturing Doug Williams $20

GS380 1988 Super Bowl, Denver: Postmarked Jan. 31, 1988, San Diego, Calif., with large Super Bowl XXII cancellation. 800 issued, autographed, picturing John Elway: $25

GS390 Mike Ditka, Hall of Famer: Postmarked July 30, 1988, Canton, Ohio, on Ditka's induction into the Football Hall of Fame. 1,000 issued, autographed. Bill Perry artwork $30

GS391 Fred Biletnikoff, Hall of Famer: Postmarked July 30, 1988, Canton, Ohio, on Biletnikoff's induction into Football Hall of Fame. 600 issued, autographed. Bill Perry artwork $25

GS419 1989 Super Bowl, Miami: Postmarked Jan. 22, 1989, Opa Locka, Fla. 650 issued, bearing Scott Forst artwork of Joe Robbie Stadium. 300 autographed by Ickey Woods, 100 autographed by Jerry Rice, Ronnie Lott and Roger Craig $100

GS420 1989 Super Bowl, San Francisco: Postmarked Jan. 22, 1989, Opa Locka, Fla. 650 issued, autographed, picturing Joe Montana $125

GS451 Terry Bradshaw Hall of Fame Induction: Postmarked Aug. 22, 1989, Canton, Ohio, with large pictorial Hall of Fame postmark. 1,000 issued, autographed, featuring Bill Perry artwork $25

GS467 1990 Super Bowl, Superdome: Postmarked Jan. 28, 1990, New Orleans, La., with special philatelic Super Bowl XXIV postmark. 800 issued featuring Scott Forst Superdome stadium artwork. 100 autographed by Jerry Rice $15

GS468 1990 Super Bowl, San Francisco: Postmarked Jan. 28, 1990, New Orleans, La. 800 issued, autographed, bearing action photo of Joe Montana. All bear Super Bowl XXIV postmarks, while 500 have "Montana" statehood anniversary postage stamps....................$50

GS469 1990 Super Bowl, Denver: Postmarked Jan. 28, 1990, New Orleans, La., with Super Bowl XXIV philatelic postmark. 800 issued, autographed, with John Elway photo $25

GS483 Tom Landry Hall of Fame Induction: Postmarked Aug. 8, 1990, Canton, Ohio, with pictorial Hall of Fame postmark. 1,200 issued, autographed, featuring Bill Perry artwork $20

GS484 Bob Griese Hall of Induction: Postmarked Aug. 8, 1990, with pictorial Hall of Fame postmark. 1,000 issued, autographed, featuring Bill Perry artwork $20

Basketball

GS538 Basketball First Day of Issue: Postmarked Aug. 28, 1991, Springfield, Mass., "First Day of Issue" on the 29-cent commemorative basketball postage stamp. 1,000 issued, 50 hand-cancellations acquired $30

GS539 Larry Bird: Postmarked Aug. 28, 1991, Springfield, Mass., on the 29-cent basketball stamp. 500 issued, autographed . $65

Michael Jordan returns to NBA, postmarked 3/19/95, autographed $90

Bill Walton, Basketball Centennial, Aug 28, 1991, autographed $50

Hockey

GS98 Wayne Gretzky 77 Goals: Postmarked Feb. 24, 1982, Buffalo, N.Y., as Gretzky broke Phil Esposito's all-time single-season goal scoring record. 500 issued, autographed $350

GS120 Wayne Gretzky Points Record: Postmarked Dec. 5, 1982, Edmonton, Alberta, Canada, as Gretzky scored a point in his 29th consecutive game, a new single season record. 2,000 issued with Gretzky action photo, autographed $250

GS464 Mario Lemieux Pittsburgh: Postmarked Jan. 21, 1990, Pittsburgh, Pa., upon the 1990 NHL All-Star Game. 500 issued, autographed, picturing Lemieux in action, with Wayne Gretzky in the background $65

Chapter 9

MEDALLIONS

LIMITED EDITION

In an effort to attract collectors looking for a rare, high-end collectible, several companies have produced various precious-metal-based collectibles over the years. This group of collectibles is commonly referred to by the generic name of "limited-edition collectibles." While the print runs for these items don't always qualify as being "rare," they are generally produced in a publically announced quantity, hence the limited-edition designation.

While medallions make up the largest segment of the LEC category, precious metal trading cards have also been issued on numerous occasions in recent years.

As a rule, most LEC releases are produced and purchased as commemorative items which salute a specific event or individual accomplishment. Most collectors pick and choose which items they like based on their player or team preferences, but rarely purchase everything from a given company's print run. An active secondary market for these collectibles has never materialized, meaning most LEC releases maintain a value consistent with their original sale price.

BLEACHERS

Bleachers began releasing 23 Karat Gold Cards in 1993. The first cards were a tribute to a legend, Nolan Ryan, and the recognition of a future star, Ken Griffey Jr. In 1995, Bleachers joined dozens of other manufacturers in celebrating the record-breaking streak of Cal Ripken Jr. by issuing two cards. Other milestones honored by Bleachers include Eddie Murray's 500 home run and 3,000 hit plateau, and Griffey's chase of Roger Maris' record 61 home runs in a season. Most of these cards carry a suggested retail price of $30. The company is no longer in business.

Year	Player	Mintage	Price
1993	Griffey Jr., Ken #1 (Mega Star)	10,000	$30
1993	Ryan, Nolan #1 (27 Seasons)	10,000	$30
1993	Ryan, Nolan #2 (Strikeout King)	5,714	$90
1995	Griffey Jr., Ken #2 (silver/gold)	10,000	$30
1995	Ripken Jr., Cal #1 (Iron Man)	75,000	$30
1995	Ripken Jr., Cal/Gehrig, Lou (Iron Men)	20,000	$30
1995	Thomas, Frank	10,000	$30
1996	Ford, Whitey	25,000	$30
1996	Mantle, Mickey #1 (Baseball's All-Time Great)	25,000	$30
1996	Mantle, Mickey #2 (MVP)	10,000	$30
1996	Mantle, Mickey #3 (Triple Crown)	10,000	$30
1996	Mantle, Mickey #4 (#7)	10,000	$30
1996	Mantle, Mickey #5 (Commerce Comet)	10,000	$30
1996	Mantle, Mickey (Diamond Star)	10,000	$30
1996	Murray, Eddie #1 (500 HRs)	10,000	$30
1996	Murray, Eddie #2 (3,000 Hits & 500 HRs)	5,000	$30
1996	Ripken Jr., Cal #2 (World Record)	10,000	$30
1996	Ripken Jr., Cal (Diamond Star)	21,310	$30
1996	Ripken Jr., Cal (Japanese)	10,000	$30
1996	Rodriguez, Alex (black facsimile autograph)	5,000	$30
1996	Rodriguez, Alex (pearl facsimile autograph)	5,000	$30
1996	Ryan, Nolan (Diamond Star)	10,000	$30
1996	Ryan, Nolan (laser cut Diamond Star)	10,000	$30
1996	Thomas, Frank (Diamond Star)	10,000	$30
1996	Williams, Ted	25,000	$30
1996	Williams, Ted (Diamond Star)	10,000	$30
1997	Clemente, Roberto (Diamond Star)	10,000	$30
1997	Gehrig, Lou/Ruth, Babe (Avon)	50,000	$30
1997	Griffey Jr., Ken #3 (triple image)	10,000	$30
1997	Griffey Jr., Ken #4 (name in teal)	10,000	$30
1997	Griffey Jr., Ken w/Chasing 62 HRs logo #1	4,997	$40
1997	Griffey Jr., Ken w/Chasing 62 HRs logo #2	4,997	$40
1997	Griffey Jr., Ken w/Chasing 62 HRs logo #3	4,997	$40
1997	Jeter, Derek	10,000	$30
1997	Ruth, Babe (Diamond Star)	10,000	$30

Chicago Processing Enviromint Medallions

Chicagoland first produced medallions in 1985 and continued through 1998. The company named its product Enviromint because the silver medallions are made from recycled silver taken from film scraps. Each coin issued commemorates a specific milestone or event, like George Brett's 3,000th hit, All-Star games, or division championship winners.

Starting in 1995, the coins were produced in bronze, silver, gold, and 24K versions, as well as proof sets. Mintage for these medallions ranged from 95 for some of the gold medallions to 25,000 for some of the first produced. The coins are individually numbered and are licensed by Major League Baseball.

Two of the most sought-after medallions are the 1990 Nolan Ryan 300th victory (limited to 1,500 coins and selling for $75), and the 1990 Ken Griffey Sr. and Jr. two piece set (3,300, $85).

Prices are for coins in mint condition. Listings below indicate the medallion, year, mintage and value.

World Series Champions

New York Mets, 1986, 25,000	$45
Minnesota Twins, 1987, 25,000	$45
Los Angeles Dodgers, 1988, 25,000	$35
Oakland Athletics, 1989, 6,550	$35
Cincinnati Reds, 1990, 25,000	$35
Toronto Blue Jays, 1992, 25,000	$60
Atlanta Braves Silver, 1995, 10,000	$40
Atlanta Braves 24K, 1995, 5,000	$60
Atlanta Braves 3-pc. Proof Set, 1995, 1,995	$140
Atlanta Braves Gold, 1995, 1,995	$850
New York Yankees Silver, 1996, 10,000	$40
New York Yankees 24K, 1996, 3,000	$60
New York Yankees 3-pc. Proof Set, 1996, 1,000	$140
New York Yankees Gold, 1996, 96	$850
Florida Marlins 6-pc. Photo/Coin Set, 1997	$500
Florida Marlins Silver, 1997, 25,000	$35
Florida Marlins 24K, 1997, 7,500	$50
Florida Marlins 3-pc. Proof Set, 1997, 1,000	$125
Florida Marlins Gold, 1997, 197	$850

American League Champions

Minnesota Twins, 1987, 5,000	$45
Oakland Athletics, 1988, 4,250	$32
Oakland Athletics, 1989, 6,550	$32
Oakland Atheltics, 1990, 10,000	$30
Minnesota Twins, 1991, 10,000	$30
Toronto Blue Jays, 1992, 10,000	$55
Cleveland Indians Silver, 1995, 10,000	$35
Cleveland Indians 24K, 1995, 3,000	$40
Cleveland Indians 3-pc. Proof Set, 1995, 250	$140
Cleveland Indians Gold, 1995, 95	$850
New York Yankees Silver, 1996, 10,000	$40
New York Yankees 24K, 1996, 3,000	$60
NewYork Yankees 3-pc. Proof Set, 1996, 250	$140
Cleveland Indians Silver, 1997, 10,000	$35
Cleveland Indians 24K, 1997, 1,000	$50
Cleveland Indians 10-pc. Proof Set, 1997, 500	$125
Cleveland Indians 6-pc. WS Photo/Coin Set, 1997, 500	$300

National League Champions

St. Louis Cardinals, 1987, 5,000	$45
Los Angeles Dodgers, 1988, 4,050	$30
San Francisco Giants, 1989, 8,100	$30
Philadelphia Phillies, 1993, 10,000	$45
Cincinnati Reds, 1996, 10,000	$30
Atlanta Braves, 1992, 10,000	$45
Atlanta Braves Gold, 1994, 95	$850
Atlanta Braves Silver, 1995, 10,000	$40
Atlanta Braves 24K, 1995, 3,000	$60
Atlanta Braves 3-pc. Proof Set, 1995, 95	$140
Florida Marlins Silver, 1997, 10,000	$35
Florida Marlins 24K, 1997, 3,000	$45
Florida Marlins 10-pc. Proof Set, 1997, 500	$125

American League East Division Winners

Detroit Tigers, 1987, 1,800	$35
Boston Red Sox, 1988, 500	$45
Toronto Blue Jays, 1989, 2,300	$70
Boston Red Sox, 1990, 450	$50
Toronto Blue Jays, 1991, 5,000	$70
Toronto Blue Jays, 1992, 5,000	$55
Boston Red Sox Silver, 1995, 5,000	$40
Boston Red Sox 24K, 1995, 1,995	$60
Boston Red Sox Bronze, 1995, 500	$20
Boston Red Sox 3-pc. Proof Set, 1995, 95	$140
Baltimore Orioles Silver, 1997, 1,997	$35
Baltimore Orioles 24K, 1997, 500	$50
Baltimore Orioles 3-pc. Proof Set, 1997, 197	$125

American League West Division Winners

Minnesota Twins, 1987, 3,000	$35
Oakland Athletics, 1988, 800	$35
Oakland Athletics, 1989, 500	$35
Oakland Athletics, 1990, 150	$75
Minnesota Twins, 1991, 5,000	$30
Seattle Mariners Silver, 1995, 5,000	$40
Seattle Mariners 24K, 1995, 1,995	$60
Seattle Mariners Bronze, 1995, 500	$20

Seattle Mariners 3-pc. Proof Set, 1995, 95 .... $140
Texas Rangers Silver, 1996, 1,996 .... $35
Texas Rangers 24K, 1996, 500 .... $55
Texas Rangers 3-pc. Proof Set, 1996, 196 .... $130
Seattle Mariners Silver,1997, 1,997 .... $35
Seattle Mariners 24K, 1997, 500 .... $50
Seattle Mariners 3-pc. Proof Set, 1997, 197 .... $125

National League East Division Winners

St. Louis Cardinals, 1987, 1,500 .... $35
New York Mets, 1988, 1,100 .... $35
Chicago Cubs, 1989, 6,200 .... $35
Chicago Cubs, 1989, 10,000 .... $35
Pittsburgh Pirates, 1990, 1,300 .... $35
Pittsburgh Pirates, 1991, 450 .... $45
Atlanta Braves Silver, 1995, 5,000 .... $40
Atlanta Braves 24K, 1995, 1,995 .... $60
Atlanta Braves Bronze, 1995, 500 .... $20
Atlanta Braves 3-pc. Proof Set, 1995, 95 .... $125
Atlanta Braves Silver, 1997, 1,997 .... $35
Atlanta Braves 24K, 1997, 500 .... $50
Atlanta Braves 3-pc. Proof Set, 1997, 197 .... $125

National League East Division Winners

San Francisco Giants, 1987, 1,000 .... $35
Los Angeles Dodgers, 1988, 800 .... $35
San Francisco Giants, 1989, 600 .... $35
Cincinnati Reds, 1990, 1,050 .... $55
Atlanta Braves, 1991, 5,000 .... $32
Atlanta Braves, 1992, 5,000 .... $34
Los Angeles Dodgers Silver, 1995, 5,000 .... $40
Los Angeles Dodgers 24K, 1995, 1,995 .... $60
Los Angeles Dodgers Bronze, 1995, 500 .... $20
Los Angeles Dodgers 3-pc. Proof Set, 1995, 95 .... $125
San Francisco Giants Silver, 1997, 1,997 .... $35
San Francisco Giants 24K, 500 .... $50
San Francisco Giants 3-pc. Proof Set, 1997, 197 .... $125

American League Central Division Winners

Cleveland Indians Silver, 1995, 5,000 .... $40
Cleveland Indians 24K, 1995, 1,995 .... $60
Cleveland Indians 3-pc. Proof Set, 1995, 95 .... $125
Cleveland Indians Silver, 1997, 1,997 .... $35
Cleveland Indians 24K, 1997, 500 .... $50
Cleveland Indians 3-pc. Proof Set, 1997, 197 .... $125

National League Central Division Winners

Cincinnati Reds Silver, 1995, 5,000 .... $40
Cincinnati Reds 24K, 1995, 1,995 .... $60
Cincinnati Reds Bronze, 1995, 500 .... $20
Cincinnati Reds 3-pc. Proof Set, 1995, 95 .... $125
Houston Astros Silver, 1997, 1,997 .... $40
Houston Astros 24K, 1997, 500 .... $60
Houston Astros 3-pc. Proof Set, 1997, 197 .... $125

All-Star Game

Cincinnati, 1988, 2,000 .... $45
Anaheim,1989, 2,000 .... $45
Toronto, 1991, 5,000 .... $60
San Diego, 1992, 5,000 .... $40
Baltimore, 1993, 5,000 .... $35
Pittsburgh Silver, 1994, 5,000 .... $40
Pittsburgh 24K, 1994, 500 .... $60
Texas Silver, 1995, 5,000 .... $40
Texas 24K, 1995, 1,000 .... $60
Texas Bronze, 1995, 5,000 .... $20
Texas 3-pc. Proof Set, 1995, 95 .... $125
Philadelphia Silver, 1996, 1,996 .... $40
Philadelphia 24K, 1996, 500 .... $60
Philadelphia 3-pc. Proof Set, 1996, 196 .... $125
Philadelphia Ball/Coin, 1996, 500 .... $50
Philadelphia Ball/Coin, 1996, 500 .... $80
Cleveland Silver, 1997, 1,997 .... $30
Cleveland 24K, 1997, 500 .... $50
Cleveland 3-pc. Proof Set, 1997, 197 .... $125
Cleveland Ball/Coin with Case, 1997, 1,997 .... $125
Colorado Silver, 1998, 1,998 .... $35
Colorado 24K, 1998, 500 .... $50
Colorado 3-pc. Proof Set, 1998, 198 .... $125

Player Coins

Roberto Alomar Silver, 1995, 1,500 .... $35
Roberto Alomar 24K, 1995, 125 .... $60
Roberto Alomar Bronze, 1995, 500 .... $20
Roberto Alomar Silver/All-Star, 1995, 1,995 .... $35
Roberto Alomar 24K/All-Star, 1995, 500 .... $60
Roberto Alomar Bronze/All-Star, 1995, 1,995 .... $20
Roberto Alomar All-Star 3-pc. Proof Set, 1995, 95 .... $125
Roberto Alomar All-Star Ball/Coin Set, 1996, 100 .... $125
Roberto Alomar All-Star Photo/Coin Set, 1997, 500 .... $50
Roberto Alomar 3-pc. Photo/Coin Set, 1997, 197 .... $150
Sandy Alomar WS Photo/Coin Set, 1997, 1,997 .... $45
Moises Alou All-Star Photo/Coin Set 1997, 197 .... $150
Moises Alou WS Photo/Coin Set 1997, 1,997 .... $50
Brady Anderson All-Star Photo/Coin Set, 1997, 500 .... $50
Brady Anderson 3-pc. Photo/Coin Set, 1997, 197 .... $140
Paul Assenmacher WS Photo/Coin Set, 1997, 1,997 .... $45
Carlos Baerga Silver/All-Star, 1995 1,995 .... $35
Carlos Baerga 24K/All-Star, 1995, 500 .... $50
Carlos Baerga Bronze/All-Star 1995 1,995 .... $20
Carlos Baerga All-Star 3-pc. Proof Set 1995, 95 .... $130
Jeff Bagwell Silver, 1996, 1,996 .... $30
Jeff Bagwell 24K Select, 1996, 500 .... $50
Jeff Bagwell 3-pc. Proof Set, 1996, 196 .... $125
Jeff Bagwell All-Star Ball/Coin Set, 1996, 100 .... $125
Jeff Bagwell All-Star 3-pc. Photo Set, 1997, 197 .... $150
Albert Belle Silver, 1995, 1,500 .... $35
Albert Belle 24K, 1995, 125 .... $60

Albert Belle Bronze, 1995, 500..................................... $20
Albert Belle Silver/All-Star, 1995, 1,995 .... $35
Albert Belle 24K/All-Star, 1995, 500 .... $60
Albert Belle Bronze/All-Star, 1995, 1,995 .... $20
Albert Belle All-Star 3-pc. Proof Set, 1995, 95 ...... $130
Albert Belle All-Star Ball/Coin Set, 1996, 100 .... $130
Albert Belle Framed Photo/Coin Set, 1996, 96.................. $130
Albert Belle Silver, 1997, 1,997 .... $35
Albert Belle 24K/All-Star, 1997, 500 .... $50
Albert Belle 3-pc. Proof Set, 1997, 197 .... $125
Albert Belle All-Star Photo/Coin Set, 1997, 500 ...... $50
Albert Belle 3-pc. All-Star Photo/Coin Set, 1997, 197 .... $150
Johnny Bench Silver/Hall of Fame, 1989, 15,000.............. $45
Dante Bichette Silver/All-Star, 1995, 1,995 .... $35
Dante Bichette 24K/All-Star, 1995, 500 .... $60
Dante Bichette Bronze/All-Star, 1995, 1,995 .... $20
Dante Bichette All-Star 3-pc. Proof Set, 1995, 95 .... $130
Dante Bichette All-Star Ball/Coin Set, 1996, 100 ...... $125
Dante Bichette, Framed Photo/Coin Set 1996, 96....... $125
Dante Bichette NL Photo/Coin Set 1997, 500 .... $50
Craig Biggio All-Star Photo/Coin Set, 1997, 500 ...... $50
Craig Biggio 3-pc. Photo/Coin Set, 1997, 197 .... $150
Jeff Blauser All-Star Photo/Coin Set, 1997, 500 .... $50
Jeff Blauser All-Star Photo/Coin Set, 1997, 197 .... $150
Wade Boggs Batting Title, 1993, 1,249 .... $50
Wade Boggs 1993, 13,751 .... $45
Wade Boggs, Silver/All-Star, 1995, 1,995 .... $35
Wade Boggs, 24K/All-Star, 1995, 500 .... $60
Wade Boggs, Bronze/All-Star, 1995, 1,995 .... $20
Wade Boggs All-Star 3-pc. Proof Set, 1995, 95 .... $130
Wade Boggs All-Star Ball/Coin Set, 1996, 100 .... $130
Wade Boggs WS Reverse, 1996, 500 .... $30
Wade Boggs, WS 3-pc. Proof Set, 1996, 96 .... $125
Wade Boggs, WS Combo, 1996, 196 .... $125
Wade Boggs, Framed Photo/Coin Set, 1996, 96.......... $125
Barry Bonds Silver/NL MVP, 1993, 1,500 .... $40
Barry Bonds 24K/NL MVP, 1993, 125 .... $25
Barry Bonds Bronze/NL MVP, 1993, 500.................... $20
Barry Bonds Silver/All-Star, 1995, 1,995 .... $40
Barry Bonds 24K/All-Star, 1995, 500........................ $60
Barry Bonds Bronze/All-Star, 1995, 1,995 .... $20
Barry Bonds All-Star 3-pc. Proof Set, 1995, 95 .... $125
Barry Bonds All-Star Ball/Coin Set, 1996, 100 .... $125
Barry Bonds All-Star Photo/Coin Set, 1997, 500........ $50
Barry Bonds All-Star 3-pc. Photo/Coin Set, 1997, 197......... $50
Bobby Bonilla WS Photo/Coin Set, 1997,1,997........... $50
George Brett Silver/3 Decades of Baseball, 1991, 2,033 ..... $45
George Brett Silver/3,000th Hit, 1992, 6,273 .... $45
George Brett/RobinYount 2-pc. Set, 1992, 1,000 .... $50
George Brett Silver 1992, 15,000 .... $40
George Brett Silver/3,000 Hits, 1992, 15,000.............. $40
Jay Buhner Silver, 1995, 1,995................................ $35
Jay Buhner 24K,1995, 500 .... $60
Jay Buhner Bronze, 1995, 1,995 .... $20
Jay Buhner 3-pc. Proof Set, 1995, 95 .... $130
Jay Buhner All-Star Ball/Coin Set, 1996, 100 .... $130
Ken Caminiti NL MVP 3-pc. Proof Set, 1996, 196.............. $130
Ken Caminiti All-Star Photo/Coin Set, 1997, 500 .... $50
Ken Caminiti All-Star 3-pc. Photo/Coin Set, 1997, 197 ...... $150
Jose Canseco Silver/40-40, Athletics, 1990, 6,000 .... $45
Jose Canseco Silver/40-40, Rangers, 1992, 9,000 .... $40
Jose Canseco Silver, 1995, 1,995 .... $35
Jose Canseco 24K, 1995, 500 .... $60
Jose Canseco Bronze, 1995, 1,995 .... $20
Jose Canseco 3-pc. Proof Set, 1995, 95................... $125
Steve Carlton 4 Cy Youngs, 1990, 15,000.................. $45
Joe Carter Silver, 1995, 1,500................................ $35

Joe Carter 24K, 1995, 125 .... $60
Joe Carter Bronze, 1995, 500................................. $20
Joe Carter Silver, 1995, 1,995 .... $35
Joe Carter 24K, 1995, 500 .... $60
Joe Carter Bronze, 1995, 1,995 .... $20
Joe Carter 3-pc. Proof Set, 1995, 95 .... $130
Joe Carter All-Star Ball/Coin Set, 1996, 100 .... $125
Vinny Castilla Silver/All-Star, 1995, 1,995 .... $35
Vinny Castilla 24K/All-Star, 1995, 500...................... $60
Vinny Castilla Bronze/All-Star, 1995, 1,995............... $20
Vinny Castilla All-Star 3-pc. Proof Set, 1995, 95 .... $130
Will Clark 1990, 2,389 .... $42
Will Clark Silver, 1995, 15,000................................ $35
Will Clark Silver, 1995, 1,995 .... $40
Will Clark 24K, 1995, 500 .... $60
Will Clark Bronze, 1995, 1,995 .... $20
Will Clark 3-pc. Proof Set, 1995, 95 .... $130
Will Clark, All-Star Photo/Coin Set, 1997, 500 .... $50
Roger Clemens Silver/'86-'87 Cy Young, 1990, 740 .... $60
Roger Clemens Silver, 1995, 1,995 .... $40
Roger Clemens 24K, 1995, 500 .... $60
Roger Clemens Bronze, 1995, 1,995 .... $20
Roger Clemens 3-pc. Proof Set, 1995, 95 .... $135
R. Clemens Cy Young Photo/Coin Set, 1997, 500 ...... $50
Roger Clemens 24K/Cy Young, 1997, 1,000 .... $35
Roberto Clemente Silver/1973 HOF, 1998, 15,000 .... $55
R. Clemente Silver/All-Star Game, 1994, 5,000 .... $40
Roberto Clemente 24K/All-Star Game, 1994, 1,000 .... $75
Roberto Clemente Silver/Career, 1995, 5,000 .... $40
Roberto Clemente 24K/Career 1995, 1,000 .... $75
Roberto Clemente Silver/Card, 1995, 1,973 .... $225
Roberto Clemente 24K/Card, 1995, 500 .... $350
Roberto Clemente Silver Coin/Card Set, 1995, 500........... $275
Roberto Clemente 24K Coin/Card Set, 1995, 100 .... $400
Ty Cobb 1988, 1,093 .... $45
Ty Cobb Saver, 1995, 15,000 .... $30
Jeff Conine WS Photo/Coin Set, 1997, 1,997 .... $50
Craig Counsell WS Photo/Coin Set, 1997, 1,997 .... $50
Darren Daulton Silver, 1995, 1,500 .... $35
Darren Daulton 24K, 1995, 125............................... $70
Darren Daulton Bronze, 1995, 500 .... $20
Darren Daulton Silver/All-Star, 1995, 1,995................ $30
Darren Daulton 24K/All-Star, 1995, 500.................... $60
Darren Daulton Bronze/All-Star, 1995, 1,995 .... $20
Darren Daulton All-Star 3-pc. Proof Set, 1995, 95 ..... $130
Mark Davis 1989 Cy Young, 1989, 270 .... $65
Andre Dawson 1987 MVP, 1990, 10,900.................... $32.50
Andre Dawson 1993, 4,100 .... $45
Jason Dickson All-Star Photo/Coin Set, 1997, 500 ..... $50
Jason Dickson 3-pc. Photo/Coin Set, 1997, 197 .... $150
Larry Doby Silver, 1997, 500 .... $38
Larry Doby 24K, 1997, 500 .... $55
Larry Doby 3-pc. Proof Set, 1997, 19 .... $130
Lenny Dykstra 24K, 1995, 125 .... $60
Lenny Dykstra Bronze, 1995, 500 .... $20
Lenny Dykstra Silver/All-Star, 1995, 1,995 .... $40
Lenny Dykstra 24K/All-Star, 1995, 500..................... $60
Lenny Dykstra Bronze/All-Star, 1995, 1,995.............. $20
Lenny Dykstra All-Star 3-pc. Proof Set, 1995, 95 ...... $130
Dennis Eckersley 40 saves/3 years, 1992, 400........... $50
Dennis Eckersley 1992 Cy Young, 1992, 15,000.......... $35
Dennis Eckersley Silver, 1995, 1,995 .... $40
Dennis Eckersley 24K, 1995, 500 .... $60
Dennis Eckersley Bronze, 1995, 1,995...................... $20
Dennis Eckersley 3-pc. Proof Set, 1995, 95............... $130
Shawn Estes 3-pc. Photo/Coin Set, 1997, 197 .... $150
Alex Fernandez, WS Photo/Coin, 1997, 1,997............. $50

Alex Fernandez, WS Photo/Coin Set, 1997, 1,997 .... $50
Tony Fernandez WS Photo/Coin Set, 1997, 1,997 .... $50
Cecil Fielder AL HR/RBI Leader, 1991, 15,000 .... $30
Cecil Fielder Silver, 1996, 1,996 .... $30
Cecil Fielder 24K, 1996, 500 .... $50
Cecil Fielder 3-pc. Proof Set, 1996, 196 .... $125
Cecil Fielder WS Reverse Silver, 1996, 500 .... $30
Cecil Fielder WS 3-pc. Proof Set, 1996, 96 .... $130
Cecil Fielder WS Combo, 1996, 196 .... $130
Cecil Fielder WS 24K, 1996, 196 .... $50
Rollie Fingers Silver/Hall of Fame, 1995, 15,000 .... $38
Carlton Fisk Most Hits by Catcher, 1990, 15,000 .... $38
Andres Gallaraga Silver, 1995, 1,500 .... $40
Andres Gallaraga Bronze, 1993, 500 .... $20
Andres Gallaraga 24K, 1993, 125 .... $60
Andres Gallaraga Silver, 1995, 1,995 .... $40
Andres Gallaraga 24K, 1995, 500 .... $60
Andres Gallaraga Bronze, 1995, 1,995 .... $20
Andres Gallaraga 3-pc. Proof Set, 1995, 95 .... $130
Andres Gallaraga Photo/Coin Set, 1996, 96 .... $125
A. Gallaraga All-Star Photo/Coin Set, 1997, 197 .... $150
Nomar Garciaparra 24K/ROY, 1997, 1,000 .... $35
Nomar Garciaparra ROY Bronze Photo/Coin Set, 1997, 500 ... $50
Steve Garvey 1,207 Consecutive Games, 1989, 15,000 ...... $35
Lou Gehrig 2,130 Consecutive Games, 1987, 1,352 .... $45
Kirk Gibson 1988 MVP, 1988, 600 .... $45
Kirk Gibson Silver, 1995, 1,995 .... $40
Kirk Gibson 24K, 1995, 500 .... $60
Kirk Gibson Bronze, 1995, 1,995 .... $20
Kirk Gibson 3-pc. Proof Set, 1995, 95 .... $130
Tom Glavine Silver/'91 Cy Young, 1991, 15,000 .... $35
Tom Glavine Silver, 1995, 1,995 .... $40
Tom Glavine 24K, 1995, 500 .... $60
Tom Glavine Bronze, 1995, 1,995 .... $20
Tom Glavine 3-pc. Proof Set, 1995, 95 .... $130
Tom Glavine All-Star Ball/Coin Set, 1996, 100 .... $20
Tom Glavine Silver/WS, 1996, 500 .... $30
Tom Glavine 24K/WS, 1996, 196 .... $50
Tom Glavine, WS 3-pc. Proof Set, 1996, 96 .... $125
Tom Glavine, WS Combo Set, 1996, 196 .... $125
Tom Glavine, All-Star 3-pc. Photo/Coin Set, 1997, 197 ..... $150
Juan Gonzalez, Bronze, 1995 .... $20
Juan Gonzalez, Silver, 1995, 1,500 .... $40
Juan Gonzalez 24K, 1995, 125 .... $60
Juan Gonzalez Silver, 1995, 1,995 .... $40
Juan Gonzalez 24K, 1995, 500 .... $60
Juan Gonzalez Bronze, 1995, 1,995 .... $20
Juan Gonzalez 3-pc. Proof Set, 1995, 95 .... $130
Juan Gonzalez Silver/AL MVP, 1996, 1,996 .... $40
Juan Gonzalez 24K/AL MVP, 1996, 500 .... $60
Juan Gonzalez AL MVP 3-pc. Proof Set, 1996, 196 .... $130
Juan Gonzalez AL Photo/Coin Set, 1997, 500 .... $50
Dwight Gooden Silver, 1995, 15,000 .... $35
Mark Grace Silver, 1995, 1,500 .... $35

Mark Grace 24K, 1995, 125 .... $60
Mark Grace Bronze, 1995, 500 .... $20
Mark Grace Silver/All-Star, 1995, 1,995 .... $40
Mark Grace 24K/All-Star, 1995, 500 .... $60
Mark Grace Bronze/All-Star, 1995, 1,995 .... $20
Mark Grace All-Star 3-pc. Proof Set, 1995, 95 .... $130
Mark Grace Framed Photo/Coin Set, 1996, 96 .... $130
Ken Griffey Jr. & Sr., 1990, 3,700 .... $65
Ken Griffey Jr. & Sr., 1990, 3,300 .... $85
Ken Griffey Jr. & Sr. Silver, 1995, 15,000 .... $35
Ken Griffey Jr. Silver, 1995, 1,500 .... $45
Ken Griffey Jr. 24K, 1995, 125 .... $80
Ken Griffey Jr. Bronze, 1995, 500 .... $25
Ken Griffey Jr. Silver/All-Star, 1995, 1,995 .... $45
Ken Griffey Jr. 24K/All-Star, 1995, 500 .... $65
Ken Griffey Jr. Bronze/All-Star, 1995, 1,995 .... $25
Ken Griffey, Ken Jr. All-Star 3-pc. Proof Set, 1995, 95 .... $140
Ken Griffey Ken Jr. All-Star Ball/Coin Set, 1996, 100 .... $149
Ken Griffey Jr. Framed Photo/Coin Set, 1996, 96 .... $140
Ken Griffey Jr. All-Star Photo/Coin Set, 1996, 500 .... $65
Ken Griffey, Jr. MVP Photo/Coin Set, 1997, 500 .... $65
Ken Griffey Jr. 24K/MVP, 1997, 1,000 .... $45
Ken Griffey Jr. HR Leader Photo/Coin Set, 1997, 500 .... $65
Ken Griffey Jr. 24K/HR Leader, 1997, 1,000 .... $45
Ken Griffey Jr. 24K HR/MVP 2-pc. Set, 1997, 97 .... $140
Ken Griffey Jr. Bronze HR/MVP 2-pc. Set, 1997, 197 .... $95
Tony Gwynn Batting Title '87, '88, '89, 1990, 1,075 .... $50
Tony Gwynn Silver/All-Star, 1995, 1,995 .... $40
Tony Gwynn 24K/All-Star, 1995, 500 .... $60
Tony Gwynn Bronze/All-Star, 1995, 1,995 .... $20
Tony Gwynn All-Star 3-pc. Proof Set, 1995, 95 .... $130
Tony Gwynn All-Star Ball/Coin Set, 1996, 100 .... $125
Tony Gwynn Framed Photo/Coin Set, 1996, 96 .... $125
Tony Gwynn Batting Title Photo/Coin Set, 1997, 500 .... $50
Tony Gwynn 24K Batting Title, 1997, 1,000 .... $35
Tony Gwynn/Frank Thomas 24K 2-pc. Set, 1997, 97 .... $130
Tony Gwynn /Frank Thomas Bronze 2-pc. Set, 1997, 197 ...... $80
Rickey Henderson, Stolen Bases, 1990, 7,109 .... $45
Rickey Henderson 1993, 7,981 .... $40
Rickey Henderson Silver, 1995, 1,995 .... $40
Rickey Henderson 24K, 1995, 500 .... $60
Rickey Henderson Bronze, 1995, 1,995 .... $20
Rickey Henderson 3-pc. Proof Set, 1995, 95 .... $130
Pat Hentgen Silver/AL Cy Young, 1996, 1,996 .... $35
Pat Hentgen 24K/AL Cy Young, 1996, 500 .... $50
Pat Hentgen AL Cy Young 3-pc. Proof Set, 1996, 196 .... $125
Livan Hernandez WS Photo/Coin Set, 1997, 1,997 .... $50
Livan Hernandez WS MVP Photo/Coin Set, 1997, 1,997 .... $50
Livan Hernandez 2-pc. Card/Coin Set, 1997, 197 .... $180
Orel Hershiser 1988 Cy Young, 1989, 600 .... $45
Orel Hershiser Silver, 1997, 1,995 .... $40
Orel Hershiser 24K, 1995, 500 .... $60
Orel Hershiser Bronze, 1995, 1,995 .... $20
Orel Hershiser 3-pc. Proof Set, 1995, 95 .... $130
Orel Hershiser WS Photo/Coin Set, 1,997, 1,997 .... $50
Todd Hollandsworth Silver/ROY 1996, 1,996 .... $35
Todd Hollandsworth 24K/ROY, 1996, 500 .... $50
Todd Hollandsworth ROY 3-pc. Proof Set, 1996, 196 .... $125
Bo Jackson Raiders/Royals, 1990, 4,400 .... $45
Bo Jackson Raiders/White Sox, 1991, N/A $35
Reggie Jackson 1993 HOF Gold, 1993, 44 .... $850
Reggie Jackson HOF 2-pc. Set, 1993, 100 .... $125
Derek Jeter Silver/WS Reverse, 1996, 500 .... $40
Derek Jeter WS Ball/Coin Set, 1996, 96 .... $130
Derek Jeter 24K/WS, 1996, 196 .... $60
Derek Jeter WS 3-pc. Proof Set, 1996, 96 .... $125

Derek Jeter Framed Photo/Coin Set, 1996, 96 .... $125
Derek Jeter Silver/ROY, 1996, 1,996 .... $30
Derek Jeter 24K/ROY, 1996, 500 .... $50
Derek Jeter ROY 3-pc. Proof Set, 1996, 196 .... $125
Fergie Jenkins 1991 HOF, 1991, 15,000 .... $35
Charles Johnson WS Photo/Coin Set, 1997, 1,997 .... $50
Howard Johnson HR/RBI Champ, 680 .... $35
Randy Johnson Silver, 1995, 1,500 .... $40
Randy Johnson 24K, 1995, 125 .... $60
Randy Johnson Bronze, 1995, 500 .... $20
Randy Johnson Silver/All-Star, 1995, 1,995 .... $40
Randy Johnson 24K/All-Star, 1995, 500 .... $60
Randy Johnson Bronze/All-Star, 1995, 1,995 .... $20
Randy Johnson All-Star 3-pc. Proof Set, 1995, 95 .... $130
Randy Johnson Silver/Cy Young, 1995, 1,995 .... $45
Randy Johnson 24K/Cy Young, 1995, 500 .... $65
Randy Johnson Bronze/Cy Young, 1995, 1,995 .... $50
R. Johnson Cy Young 3-pc. Proof Set, 1995, 95 .... $135
Randy Johnson Framed Photo/Coin Set, 1996, 96 .... $130
Randy Johnson 3-pc. Photo/Coin Set, 1997, 197 .... $160
Chipper Jones Silver, 1995, 1,995 .... $40
Chipper Jones 24K, 1995, 500 .... $60
Chipper Jones Bronze, 1995, 1,995 .... $20
Chipper Jones 3-pc. Proof Set, 1995, 95 .... $130
Chipper Jones All-Star Ball/Coin Set, 1996, 100 .... $125
Chipper Jones 24K/WS, 1996, 196 .... $50
Chipper Jones WS 3-pc. Proof Set, 1996, 96 .... $130
Chipper Jones WS Combo, 1996, 196 .... $125
Chipper Jones Framed Photo/Coin Set, 1996, 96 .... $125
Chipper Jones All-Star 3-pc. Photo/Coin Set, 1997, 197 ... $150
Bobby Jones All-Star Photo/Coin Set, 1997, 500 .... $50
Bobby Jones All-Star Photo/Coin Set, 1997, 197 .... $150
David Justice 1990 Rookie of Year, 1991, 15,000 .... $38
David Justice Silver, 1995, 1,995 .... $40
David Justice 24K, 1995, 500 .... $60
David Justice Bronze, 1995, 1,995 .... $20
David Justice 3-pc. Proof Set, 1995, 95 .... $125
David Justice Silver/WS, 1996, 500 .... $30
David Justice 24K/WS, 1996, 196 .... $50
David Justice WS 3-pc. Proof Set, 1996, 96 .... $125
David Justice WS Combo, 1996, 196 .... $125
David Justice Framed Photo/Coin Set 1996, 96 .... $125
David Justice All-Star Photo/Coin Set, 1997, 500 .... $50
David Justice 3-pc. Photo/Coin Set, 1997, 197 .... $150
David Justice WS Photo/Coin Set, 1997, 1,997 .... $50
Harmon Killebrew 1984 Hall of Fame, 1991, 15,000 .... $45
Chuck Knoblauch 1993, 15,000 .... $40
Chuck Knoblauch Silver, 1995, 1,995 .... $40
Chuck Knoblauch 24K, 1995, 500 .... $60
Chuck Knoblauch Bronze, 1995, 1,995 .... $20
Chuck Knoblauch 3-pc. Proof Set, 1995, 95 .... $130
Chuck Knoblauch All-Star Ball/Coin Set, 1996, 100 .... $130
Chuck Knoblauch 3-pc. Photo/Coin Set, 1997, 197 .... $150
Barry Larkin Bronze/All-Star, 1995, 1,995 .... $20
Barry Larkin All-Star 3-pc. Proof Set, 1995, 95 .... $130
Barry Larkin All-Star Photo/Coin Set, 1997, 500 .... $60
Barry Larkin All-Star 3-pc. Photo/Coin Set, 1997, 197 ...... $150
Kenny Lofton Silver/All-Star, 1995, 1,995 .... $40
Kenny Lofton 24K/All-Star, 1995, 500 .... $60
Kenny Lofton Bronze/All-Star, 1995, 1,995 .... $20
Kenny Lofton 3-pc. Proof Set 1995, 95 .... $130
Kenny Lofton All-Star Ball/Coin Set 1996, 100 .... $130
Kenny Lofton Framed Photo/Coin Set 1996, 96 .... $130
Kenny Lofton All-Star Photo/Coin Set 1997, 500 .... $50
Kenny Lofton 3-pc. Photo/Coin Set 1997, 197 .... $150
Greg Maddux Silver/Cy Young, 1992, 15,000 .... $40
Greg Maddux Silver/Cy Young, 1993, 1,500 .... $65

Greg Maddux Bronze/Cy Young, 1993, 500 .... $40
Greg Maddux 24K/Cy Young, 1993, 125 .... $100
Greg Maddux Silver/All-Star, 1995, 1,995 .... $45
Greg Maddux, 24K/All-Star, 1995, 500 .... $65
Greg Maddux, Bronze/All-Star, 1995, 1,995 .... $25
Greg Maddux All-Star 3-pc. Proof Set, 1995, 95 .... $140
Greg Maddux Silver/4-Time Cy Young Winner, 1995, 1,995 ..... $45
Greg Maddux 24K/4 Time Cy Young Winner, 1995, 500 ...... $65
Greg Maddux Bronze/4 Time, 1995, Cy Young Winner,
    1,995 .... $25
Greg Maddux 4 Time Cy Young Winner 3-pc. Proof Set, 1995,
    95 .... $130
Greg Maddux All-Star Ball/Coin Set, 1996, 100 .... $135
Greg Maddux WS Combo 1996, 196 .... $135
Greg Maddux Framed Photo/Coin Set, 1996, 96 .... $135
Greg Maddux All-Star 3-pc. Photo/Coin Set, 1997, 197 .... $150
Mickey Mantle Silver, 1997, 10,000 .... $45
Mickey Mantle 24K, 1997, 1,956 .... $75
Mickey Mantle Bronze, 1997, 25,000 .... $25
Mickey Mantle 3-pc. Proof Set, 1997, 1,000 .... $150
Mickey Mantle Gold, 1997, 100 .... $850
Mickey Mantle Card/Coin 2-pc. Set, 1997, 1,956 .... $65
Pedro Martinez All-Star Photo/Coin Set, 1997, 500 .... $50
Pedro Martinez All-Star 3-pc. Photo/Coin Set, 1997, 197 .... $150
Pedro Martinez Cy Young 24K Bronze 1997, 1,000 .... $35
Tino Martinez Silver, 1995, 1,995 .... $40
Tino Martinez 24K, 1995, 500 .... $60
Tino Martinez Bronze, 1995, 1,995 .... $20
Tino Martinez 3-pc. Proof Set, 1995, 95 .... $130
Tino Martinez All-Star Photo/Coin Set, 1997, 500 .... $50
Tino Martinez 3-pc. Photo/Coin Set, 1997, 197 .... $150
Edgar Martinez Silver/All-Star, 1995, 1,995 .... $40
Edgar Martinez 24K/All-Star, 1995, 500 .... $60
Edgar Martinez Bronze/All-Star, 1995, 1,995 .... $20
Edgar Martinez All-Star 3-pc. Proof Set, 1995, 95 .... $130
Edgar Martinez All-Star Ball/Coin Set, 1996, 100 .... $125
Edgar Martinez Framed Photo/Coin Set, 1996, 96 .... $125
Edgar Martinez All-Star Photo/Coin Set, 1997, 500 .... $50
Edgar Martinez 3-pc. Photo/Coin Set, 1997, 197 .... $150
Dennis Martinez Silver/All-Star, 1995, 1,995 .... $40
Dennis Martinez 24K/All-Star 1995, 500 .... $60
Dennis Martinez Bronze/All-Star, 1995, 1,995 .... $20
D. Martinez, All-Star 3-pc. Proof Set, 1995, 95 .... $130
Don Mattingly Most Grand Slams, 1988, 15,000 .... $40
Don Mattingly Silver, 1995, 1,995 .... $60
Don Mattingly 24K, 1995, 500 .... $80
Don Mattingly Bronze, 1995, 1,995 .... $20
Don Mattingly, 3-pc. Proof Set, 1995, 95 .... $130
Jack McDowell Silver/1993 Cy Young, 1994, 1,500 .... $40
Jack McDowell 24K/1993 Cy Young, 1994, 125 .... $60
Jack McDowell Bronze/ 1993 Cy Young, 1994, 500 .... $20
Jack McDowell/Frank/Thomas 2-pc. set, 1994, 100 .... $85
Jack McDowell Silver, 1995, 1,995 .... $40
Jack McDowell 24K, 1995, 500 .... $60
Jack McDowell Bronze, 1995, 1,995 .... $20
Jack McDowell 3-pc. Proof Set, 1,995, 95 .... $130
Fred McGriff Silver/All-Star, 1995, 1,995 .... $40
Fred McGriff 24K/All-Star, 1995, 500 .... $60
Fred McGriff Bronze/All-Star, 1995, 1,995 .... $20
Fred McGriff 3-pc. Proof Set, 1995, 95 .... $130
Fred McGriff All-Star Ball/Coin Set, 1996, 100 .... $125
Fred McGriff WS Silver, 1996, 500 .... $30
Fred McGriff WS 24K, 1996, 196 .... $50
Fred McGriff WS 3-pc. Proof Set, 1996, 96 .... $125
Fred McGriff WS Combo Set, 1996, 196 .... $125
Fred McGriff NL Photo/Coin Set, 1997, 500 .... $50
Mark McGwire 30 HR/4 season, 1991, 15,000 .... $45

Mark McGwire Silver/All-Star, 1995, 1,995.................. $45
Mark McGwire 24K/All-Star, 1995, 500 .... $65
Mark McGwire Bronze/All-Star, 1995, 1,995 .... $25
Mark McGwire All-Star 3-pc. Proof Set, 1995, 95 .... $135
Mark McGwire All-Star Ball/Coin Set, 1996, 100.............. $125
Mark McGwire Framed Photo/Coin Set, 1996, 96 .... $125
Mark McGwire 3-pc. All-Star Photo/Coin Set, 1997, 197 ... $150
Mark McGwire HR Leader, 1997, 500 .... $50
Mark McGwire 24K Bronze/HR Leader, 1997, 1,000 .... $35
Jose Mesa WS Photo/Coin Set, 1997, 1,997 .... $50
Kevin Mitchell 1989 MVP, 1990, 1,200 .... $35
Kevin Mitchell 1992, 108.. $60
Kevin Mitchell 1993, 13,692..................................... $32
Paul Molitor 39-Game Hitting Streak, 1990, 11,001 .... $35
Joe Morgan 1990 HOF, 1990, 15,000 .... $45
Eddie Murray Silver/3,000 Hits, 1995, 3,000 .... $45
Eddie Murray 24K/3,000 Hits, 1995, 1,995 .... $65
Eddie Murray Gold/3,000 Hits, 1995, 100.................. $850
Eddie Murray 3,000 Hits 3-pc. Proof Set, 1995, 95 .... $130
Eddie Murray Silver/500th Home Run, 1996, 1,996 .... $35
Eddie Murray 24K/500th Home Run, 1996, 1,000 .... $55
Eddie Murray 500th Home Run 3-pc. Proof Set, 1996, 196.... $125
Eddie Murray Gold/500th Home Run, 1996, 33 .... $850
Eddie Murray 500th HR/3,000th Hit 2-pc. Silver, 1996, 500...... $85
Eddie Murray 500th HR/3,000th Hit 2-pc. 24K, 1996, 100 ...... $140
Randy Myers Silver/All-Star, 1995, 1,995................. $40
Randy Myers 24K/All-Star, 1995, 500 .... $60
Randy Myers Bronze/All-Star, 1995, 1,995 .... $20
Randy Myers All-Star 3-pc. Proof Set, 1995, 95 .... $130
Charles Nagy AL Photo/Coin Set, 1997, 500 .... $50
Charles Nagy WS Photo/Coin Set, 1997, 1,997 .... $50
C. Nagy 3-pc. All-Star Photo/Coin Set, 1997, 500 .... $150
Robb Nen WS Photo/Coin Set 1997, 1,997 .... $50
Hideo Nomo Silver/All-Star, 1995, 1,995................. $40
Hideo Nomo 24K/All-Star, 1995, 500 .... $60
Hideo Nomo Bronze/All-Star, 1995, 1,995 .... $20
Hideo Nomo All-Star 3-pc. Proof Set 1995, 95 .... $130
Hideo Nomo Silver 1995, 1,995............................... $40
Hideo Nomo 24K 1995, 500 .... $60
Hideo Nomo Bronze, 1995, 1,995 .... $20
Hideo Nomo Silver/Rookie, 1995, 1,995 .... $40
Hideo Nomo 24K/Rookie, 1995, 500 .... $60
Hideo Nomo, Bronze/Rookie, 1995, 1,995 .... $20
Hideo Nomo, Rookie 3-pc. Proof Set, 1995, 95 .... $130
Hideo Nomo, Framed Photo/Coin Set, 1995, 96 .... $130
John Olerud Silver, 1993, 1,500 .... $40
John Olerud 24K, 1993, 125 .... $60
John Olerud Bronze, 1993, 500................................ $20
John Olerud Silver, 1995, 1,995.............................. $40
John Olerud 24K, 1995, 500 .... $60
John Olerud Bronze, 1995, 1,995............................ $20
John Olerud 3-pc. Proof Set, 1995, 95 .... $130
Gregg Olson '89 Rookie of the Year, 1990, 15,000 .... $35
Paul O'Neill Silver/All-Star, 1995, 1,995.................. $40
Paul O'Neill 24K/All-Star, 1995, 500....................... $60
Paul O'Neill Bronze/All-Star, 1995, 1,995................ $20
Paul O'Neill All-Star 3-pc. Proof Set, 1995, 95 .... $130
Terry Pendleton 1991 Batting Title, 1991, 900 .... $45
Terry Pendleton, 1991 NL MVP, 1991, 15,000.................. $40
Terry Pendleton Silver, 1995, 1,995........................ $40
Terry Pendleton 24K, 1995, 500............................. $60
Terry Pendleton Bronze, 1995, 1,995 .... $20
Terry Pendleton 3-pc. Proof Set, 1995, 95 .... $130
Andy Pettitte Silver WS Reverse, 1996, 500 .... $35
Andy Pettitte WS Ball/Coin Set, 1996, 96................. $125
Andy Pettitte WS 24K, 1996, 196............................ $55
Andy Pettitte WS 3-pc. Proof Set, 1996, 96 .... $125

Mike Piazza Silver, 1993, 1,500 .... $50
Mike Piazza 24K, 1993, 125................................... $75
Mike Piazza Bronze, 1993, 500.............................. $25
Mike Piazza Silver/All-Star, 1995, 1,995................. $40
Mike Piazza 24K/All-Star, 1995, 500...................... $60
Mike Piazza Bronze/All-Star, 1995, 1,995 .... $20
Mike Piazza All-Star 3-pc. Proof Set, 1995, 95 .... $130
Mike Piazza All-Star Ball/Coin Set, 1996, 100.................. $125
Mike Piazza Framed Photo/Coin Set, 1996, 96 .... $125
Mike Piazza 3-pc. Photo/Coin Set, 1997, 197 .... $150
Kirby Puckett AL Batting Champ, 1990, 2,200 .... $50
Kirby Puckett Silver/All-Star, 1995, 1,995................ $40
Kirby Puckett 24K/All-Star, 1995, 500 .... $60
Kirby Puckett Bronze/All-Star, 1995, 1,995 .... $20
Kirby Puckett All-Star 3-pc. Proof Set, 1995, 95 .... $130
Kirby Puckett Silver/Retirement, 1996, 1,996 .... $35
Kirby Puckett 24K/Retirement, 1996, 500 .... $55
Kirby Puckett Retirement 3-pc. Proof Set, 1996, 196......... $130
Kirby Puckett Gold/Retirement 1996, 34 .... $850
Kirby Puckett Framed Photo/Coin Set, 1996, 96 .... $125
Manny Ramirez Silver/All-Star, 1995, 1,995............. $40
Manny Ramirez 24K/All-Star, 1995, 500 .... $60
Manny Ramirez Bronze/All-Star, 1995, 1,995 .... $20
Manny Ramirez All-Star 3-pc. Proof Set, 1995, 95............. $130
Manny Ramirez Framed Photo/Coin Set, 1996, 96 .... $130
Manny Ramirez WS Photo/Coin Set, 1997, 1,997 ...... $50
Edgar Renteria, WS Photo/Coin Set, 1997, 1,997 ...... $50
Cal Ripken 1991 MVP, 1992, 15,000 .... $40
Cal Ripken Silver, 1995, 1,500 .... $50
Cal Ripken 24K, 1995, 125 .... $80
Cal Ripken Bronze 1995, 500................................. $30
Cal Ripken Silver/All-Star, 1995, 1,995................... $40
Cal Ripken 24K/All-Star, 1995, 500 .... $60
Cal Ripken Bronze/All-Star, 1995, 1,995 .... $20
Cal Ripken All-Star 3-pc. Proof Set, 1995, 95 .... $130
Cal Ripken Silver/2,131 Coin, 1996, 10,000 .... $40
Cal Ripken 24K/2,131 Coin, 1996, 2,131 .... $75
Cal Ripken Jr. Gold/2,131 Coin, 1996, 95 .... $850
Cal Ripken 2,131 Coin 3-pc. Proof Set, 1996, 500........... $135
Cal Ripken All-Star Ball/Card Set, 1996, 100 .... $125
Cal Ripken All-Star Photo/Coin Set, 1997, 500 .... $150
Brooks Robinson 1983 HOF, 1991, 15,000 .... $35
Alex Rodriguez All-Star Ball/Coin Set, 1996, 100.............. $125
Alex Rodriguez Silver, 1996, 1,996 .... $40
Alex Rodriguez 24K, 1996, 500.............................. $60
Alex Rodriguez Bat. Champ. 3-pc. Proof Set, 1996, 196 ... $125
Alex Rodriguez All-Star Photo/Coin Set, 1997, 500 .... $50
Ivan Rodriguez, Silver/All-Star, 1995, 1,995............ $40
Ivan Rodriguez, 24K/All-Star, 1995, 500 .... $60
Ivan Rodriguez, Bronze/All-Star, 1995, 1,995 .... $20
Ivan Rodriguez All-Star 3-pc. Proof Set 1995, 95 .... $130
Ivan Rodriguez All-Star Ball/Coin Set, 1996, 100............. $125
Ivan Rodriguez All-Star Photo/Coin Set, 1997, 500 .... $50
Ivan Rodriguez 3-pc. Photo/Coin Set, 1997, 197 .... $150
Scott Rolen ROY Photo/Coin Set, 1997, 500 .... $50
Scott Rolen ROY 24K Bronze, 1997, 1,000.................... $35
Pete Rose All-Time Hit Leader, 1985, 25,000 .... $65
Babe Ruth 1987, 15,000 .... $50
Nolan Ryan 5,000th Strikeout, 1989, 1,500 .... $75
Nolan Ryan 300th Victory, 1990, 1,500 .... $75
Nolan Ryan 7th No-Hitter, 1991, 1,500 .... $65
Nolan Ryan Silver/Retirement, 1993, 15,000 .... $45
Nolan Ryan Gold/Retirement, 1993, 100.................... $850
Nolan Ryan Bronze/Retirement, 1993, 25,000.................. $20
Nolan Ryan Retirement 2-pc. set, 1993, 500 .... $145
Nolan Ryan Bat w/Silver Coin Set, 1993, 1,993 .... $175
Nolan Ryan Bat w/24K Coin Set, 1993, 500...................... $250

Nolan Ryan Silver/Jersey Retirement, 1996, 1,996 .... $35
Nolan Ryan 24K/Jersey Retirement, 1996, 500 .... $55
N. Ryan Jersey Retirement 3-pc. Proof Set, 1996, 196 ..... $135
Bret Saberhagen 1998 Cy Young, 1990, 300 .... $65
Bret Saberhagen Silver, 1995, 1,995 .... $40
Bret Saberhagen 24K, 1995, 500 .... $60
Bret Saberhagen Bronze, 1995, 1,995 .... $20
Bret Saberhagen 3-pc. Proof Set, 1995, 95 .... $130
Chris Sabo '88 NL ROY, 1989, 1,315 .... $45
Tim Salmon Silver, 1993, 1,500 .... $45
Tim Salmon 24K, 1993, 125 .... $65
Tim Salmon Bronze, 1993, 500 .... $25
Tim Salmon Silver, 1995, 1,995 .... $50
Tim Salmon 24K, 1995, 500 .... $60
Tim Salmon Bronze, 1995, 1,995 .... $20
Tim Salmon 3-pc. Proof Set, 1995, 95 .... $130
Ryne Sandberg Errorless Streak, 1990, 15,000 .... $38
Ryne Sandberg Framed Photo/Coin Set, 1996, 96 .... $125
Ryne Sandberg Silver, 1996, 1,996 .... $35
Ryne Sandberg 24K, 1996, 500 .... $50
Ryne Sandberg 3-pc. Proof Set, 1996, 196 .... $125
Ryne Sandberg Silver/HRs Record, 1997, 1,997 .... $35
Ryne Sandberg 24K/HRs Record, 1997, 500 .... $50
Ryne Sandberg HRs Record 3-pc. Proof Set, 1997, 197 ... $125
Deion Sanders 1992, 15,000 .... $32
Deion Sanders Silver, 1997 1,997 .... $35
Deion Sanders 24K, 1997, 500 .... $50
Deion Sanders 3-pc. Proof Set, 1997, 197 .... $125
Tony Saunders, WS Photo/Coin Set, 1997, 1,997 .... $50
Mike Schmidt Player of Decade, 1990, 10,000 .... $45
Mike Schmidt Silver/Hall of Fame, 1995, 5,000 .... $65
Mike Schmidt, 24K/Hall of Fame, 1995, 1,995 .... $85
Mike Schmidt, Gold/Hall of Fame, 1995, 95 .... $850
Mike Schmidt, Bronze/Hall of Fame, 1995, 5,000 .... $25
Curt Schilling, All-Star Photo/Coin Set, 1997, 500 .... $50
Curt Schilling All-Star 3-pc. Photo Set, 1997, 197 .... $150
Tom Seaver 1992 HOF, 1992, 15,000 .... $40
Gary Sheffield WS Photo/Coin Set, 1997, 1,997 .... $50
Ozzie Smith Silver, 1995, 1,500 .... $50
Ozzie Smith 24K, 1995, 125 .... $70
Ozzie Smith Bronze, 1995, 500 .... $25
Ozzie Smith Silver/All-Star, 1995, 1,995 .... $40
Ozzie Smith 24K/All-Star, 1995, 500 .... $60
Ozzie Smith Bronze/All-Star, 1995, 1,995 .... $20
Ozzie Smith All-Star 3-pc. Proof Set, 1995, 95 .... $130
Ozzie Smith All-Star Ball/Coin Set, 1996, 100 .... $125
Ozzie Smith Framed Photo/Coin Set, 1996, 96 .... $125
John Smoltz All-Star Ball/Coin Set, 1996, 100 .... $125
John Smoltz Silver, 1996, 1,996 .... $35
John Smoltz 24K, 1996, 500 .... $55
John Smoltz 3-pc. Proof Set, 1996, 196 .... $130
John Smoltz 24K/WS, 1996, 196 .... $50
John Smoltz WS 3-pc. Proof Set, 1996, 96 .... $125
John Smoltz Silver/NL Cy Young, 1996, 1,996 .... $35
John Smoltz 24K/NL Cy Young, 1996, 500 .... $50
John Smoltz NL Cy Young 3-pc. Proof Set, 1996, 196 ...... $125
John Smoltz NL Photo/Coin Set, 1997, 500 .... $50
Sammy Sosa Bronze/All-Star, 1995, 1,995 .... $20
Sammy Sosa 24K/All-Star, 1997, 500 .... $50
Darryl Strawberry 1990, 1,200 .... $45
Darryl Strawberry 1995, 13,800 .... $32
Darryl Strawberry WS, 1996, 500 .... $30
Darryl Strawberry WS 3-pc. Proof Set, 1996, 96 .... $125
Frank Thomas Silver/AL MVP, 1993, 1,500 .... $50
Frank Thomas 24K/AL MVP, 1993, 125 .... $80
Frank Thomas Bronze/AL MVP, 1993, 500 .... $28
Frank Thomas Silver/MVP, 1994, 1,500 .... $50

Frank Thomas 24K/MVP, 1994, 125 .... $80
Frank Thomas Bronze/MVP, 1994, 500 .... $28
Frank Thomas Silver/All-Star, 1995, 1,995, ... $40
Frank Thomas 24K/All-Star, 1995, 500 .... $60
Frank Thomas Bronze/All-Star, 1995, 1,995 .... $20
Frank Thomas All-Star 3-pc. Proof Set, 1995, 95 .... $120
Frank Thomas All-Star Ball/Coin Set, 1996, 100 .... $125
Frank Thomas All-Star Photo/Coin Set, 1997, 197 .... $140
Jim Thome WS Photo/Coin Set, 1997, 1,997 .... $50
Mo Vaughn Silver/All-Star, 1995, 1,995 .... $40
Mo Vaughn 24K/All-Star, 1995, 500 .... $60
Mo Vaughn Bronze/All-Star, 1995, 1,995 .... $20
Mo Vaughn All-Star 3-pc. Proof Set, 1995, 95 .... $130
Mo Vaughn All-Star Ball/Coin Set, 1996, 100 .... $125
Mo Vaughn AL Photo/Coin Set, 1997, 500 .... $50
Frank Viola, '88 Cy Young, 1988, 15,000 .... $32
Omar Vizquel WS Photo/Coin Set, 1997, 1,997 .... $50
Larry Walker MVP Photo/Coin Set, 1997, 500 .... $50
Larry Walker 24K Bronze MVP, 1997, 1,000 .... $35
Jerome Walton '89 NL ROY, 1990, 900 .... $55
John Wetteland Silver/WS MVP, 1996, 500 .... $30
John Wetteland 24K/WS MVP, 1996, 196 .... $50
John Wetteland WS MVP 3-pc. Proof Set, 1996, 96 .... $125
Devon White WS Photo/Coin Set 1997, 1,997 .... $45
Bernie Williams Silver/WS Reverse, 1996, 500 .... $30
Bernie Williams 24K/WS, 1996, 196 .... $50
Bernie Williams WS 3-pc. Proof Set, 1996, 96 .... $125
Bernie Williams Photo/Coin Set, 1997, 500 .... $40
Billy Williams 1987 HOF, 1991, 15,000 .... $35
Matt Williams Silver, 1995, 1,500 .... $40
Matt Williams 24K, 1995, 125 .... $65
Matt Williams Bronze 1995, 500 .... $22
Matt Williams Silver/All-Star 1996, 1,995 .... $30
Matt Williams 24K/All-Star 1996, 500 .... $50
Matt Williams Bronze/All-Star, 1996, 1,995 .... $20
Matt Williams All-Star 3-pc. Proof Set, 1996, 95 .... $125
Matt Williams AL Photo/Coin Set, 1997, 500 .... $50
Matt Williams WS Photo/Coin Set, 1997, 1,997 .... $50
Dave Winfield 1992, 389 .... $60
Dave Winfield Twins, 1993, 14,611 .... $40
Dave Winfield Silver, 1995, 1,995 .... $40
Dave Winfield 24K, 1995, 500 .... $60
Dave Winfield Bronze 1995, 1,995 .... $20
Dave Winfield 3-pc. Proof Set, 1995, 95 .... $130
Bobby Witt AL Photo/Coin Set 1997, 500 .... $45
Mark Wohlers NL Photo/Coin Set, 1997, 500 .... $45
Jaret Wright WS Photo/Coin Set, 1997, 500 .... $50
Robin Yount 1989 MVP, 1990, 2,387 .... $50
Robin Yount 3,000th Hit, 1992, 12,632 .... $35

Team Commemorative Coins

Arizona Diamondbacks Silver, 1998, 5,000 .... $30
Arizona Diamondbacks 24K, 1998, 500 .... $50
Arizona Diamondbacks Silver Inaugural, 1998, 1,998 .... $40
Arizona Diamondbacks 24K Inaugural, 1998, 500 .... $50
Arizona Diamondbacks Inaugural 1998 3-pc. Proof Set, 1998,
    198 .... $125
New Arlington Stadium Silver, 1995, 5,000 .... $40
New Arlington Stadium 24K, 1995, 500 .... $60
New Arlington Stadium Gold, 1995, 100 .... $850
Old Arlington Stadium Silver, 1995, 5000 .... $40
Old Arlington Stadium 24K, 1995, 500 .... $60
Old/New Arlington Stadium 1995, 1,000 .... $85
Old/New Arlington Stadium 2-pc. Silver Set , 1993, 1,000 ... $75
Old/New Arlington Stadium 2-pc. 24K Set, 1995, 100 .... $135
Atlanta Braves Silver Generic Coin, 1995, 1,000 .... $30
Baltimore Orioles Silver Generic Coin, 1995, 1,000 .... $30

Baltimore Orioles Silver/AL Wild Card, 1996, 1,996............ $30
Baltimore Orioles 24K/AL Wild Card, 1996, 500 .... $50
Baltimore Orioles AL Wild Card, 1996, 196....................... $125
Camden Yards/Orioles Silver, 1996, 1,000...................... $30
Chicago Cubs Silver Generic Coin, 1991, 1,500 .... $50
Chicago Cubs 24K/1984 Division Heir, 1990, 1,500 .... $50
Chicago Cubs 24K/1989 Division Heir, 1990, 1,500 .... $50
Chicago Cubs Silver/Wrigley Field, 1988, 39,012 .... $30
First Night Game Chicago Cubs 24K/Wrigley Field, 1,500... $60
Chicago Cubs/Wrigley 75th Anniversary 1990, 10,000....... $40
Chicago White Sox Silver Generic Coin, 1995, 1,000 .... $45
Cleveland Indians Stadium Gold 1995, 61 .... $850
Cleveland Indians/Eddie Murray 1995, 400 .... $85
Cleveland Indians/Eddie Murray, 2-pc. Silver Set 1995, 100... $135
Cleveland Indians 2-pc. 24K Set, 1,000 .... $30
Cleveland Indians Silver Generic Coin, 1995, 1,000 .... $30
Cleveland Indians Silver, 1995, 1,000 .... $60
Cleveland Indians 24K, 1995, 196................................... $85
Cleveland Indians Back-to-Back 2-pc. Set, 1996, 10,000 .... $40
Colorado Rockies Franchise, 1991, 10,000...................... $40
Colorado Rockies Inaugural, 1993, 5,000 .... $30
Colorado Rockies Silver/Record Attendance 1995, 5,000.... $40
Colorado Rockies Silver/1995 Wildcard, 1,995 .... $60
Colorado Rockies 24K/1995 Wildcard, 1995, 500............... $20
Colorado Rockies Bronze/'95 Wildcard, 1995, 95 .... $130
Colorado Rockies 3-pc. Proof Set, 680 .... $75
Comiskey Park 75th Anniversary, 1985, 43,931 .... $35
Old/New Comiskey Park, 1990, 195................................ $185
Coors Field Silver 2-pc. Card/Coin Set, 1995 .... $125
Coors Field 24K 2-pc. Card/Coin Set, 1995, 95 .... $50
Coors Field Inaugural Silver, 1995, 1,999 .... $75
Coors Field Inaugural Gold, 1995.................................. $850
Florida Marlins Franchise, 1991, 10,000 .... $40
Florida Marlins Inaugural, 1993, 10,000.......................... $40
Florida Marlins Silver/Wild Card, 1,997 .... $40
Florida Marlins 24K/Wild Card, 1997, 197....................... $139
Florida Marlins Wild Card 3-pc. Proof Set, 1997, 500 .... $400
Florida Marlins 10pc. Framed Set, 1997, 1,000 .... $30
Houston Astros Silver Generic Coin, 1995, 5,000 .... $40
Interleague Play 24K/Yankees-Mets, (Yankees side) 1,997 ...... $60
Interleague Play/Yankees-Mets 3-pc.Set, 1997, (Yankees side)
    500.. $125
Interleague Play/Yankees-Mets 24K, 1997,
    (Mets side), 1,997 .... $60
Interleague Play/Yankees-Mets 1997, 3-pc. Set (Mets side),
    500.. $125
Interleague Play Silver/Cubs-White Sox, 1997, 5,000.......... $40

Interleague Play 24K/Cubs-White Sox, 1997, Cubs side),
    1,997... $60
Interleague Play Cubs-White Sox, 1997, 3-pc. Set (Cubs side),
    500.. $125
Interleague Play 24K Cubs-White Sox, 1997, (White Sox side),
    1,997... $60
Interleague Play Cubs/White Sox, 1997, 3-pc. Set
    (White Sox side), 500 .... $125
Kansas City Royals 25th Anniversary, 1993, 5,000............. $40
Kansas City Royals Silver Generic Coin 1995, 1,000 .... $30
Los Angeles Dodgers 100th Anniversary 1990, 5,000 .... $65
Los Angeles Silver Generic Coin, 1995, 1,000.................. $30
Los Angeles Dodgers Silver/Rookies, 1995, 1,995 .... $40
Los Angeles Dodgers 24K/Rookies 1995, 500.................. $60
Los Angeles Dodgers Bronze/Rookies, 1995, 1,995........... $20
Los Angeles Dodgers Rookies, 1995, 3-pc. Proof Set, 95.......$130
Los Angeles Dodgers Silver/Wild Card, 1996, 1,996 .... $40
Los Angeles Dodgers 24K/Wild Card, 1996, 500................ $60
Los Angeles Dodgers Wild Card, 1996, 3-pc. Proof Set,
    1,996.. $125
Montreal Expos 25th Anniversary, 1993, 5,000.................. $45
Montreal Expos Silver Generic Coin, 1995, 1,000 .... $30
Milwaukee Brewers Silver Generic Coin, 1995, 1,000.......... $30
Milwaukee Brewers Silver/25th Anniversary, 1995, 5,000.... $30
Milwaukee Brewers 24K/25th Anniversary, 1995, 1,000 ...... $50
Minnesota Twins Silver Generic Coin, 1995, 1,000............. $30
New York Yankees Silver/Wildcard, 1995, 5,000................ $40
New York Yankees 24K/Wildcard, 1995, 1,995................... $60
New York Yankees Bronze/Wildcard 1995, 500.................. $20
New York Yankees Wildcard, 1995, 3-pc. Proof Set, 95 ..... $130
New York Yankees Silver/Wildcard, 1997, 1,997 .... $35
New York Yankees 24K/Wildcard 1997, 500...................... $50
New York Yankees Wild Card, 1997, 3-pc. Proof Set, 1,997....$125
Philadelphia Phillies Silver Generic Coin, 1995, 1,000 .... $30
Rookies Mark McGwire/Jose Canseco, 1990, 15,000.......... $65
Seattle Mariners Silver Generic Coin, 1995, 1,000 .... $30
St. Louis Cardinals 100th Anniversary, 1992, 5,000............ $50
Tampa Bay Devil Rays Silver/Inaugural, 1998, 1,998.......... $38
Tampa Bay Devil Rays 24K/Inaugural, 1998, 500 .... $50
Tampa Bay Devil Rays Inaugural, 1998, 3-pc. Proof Set,
    198.. $125
Texas Rangers Silver Generic Coin 1995, 1,000 .... $30
Toronto Blue Jays Alomar/Carter/White, 1992, 15,000 .... $45
Toronto Blue Jays Back-to-Back 2-pc. Set, 1993, 400 .... $175
World Series 3-Pc. set, 1992, 500................................... $290
World Series 3-Pc. set, 1993, 500................................... $255

Chicagoland Processing Enviromint medallions
Basketball, Football, Hockey

1994-95 NBA releases

Atlanta Hawks,1994 Central Division Champs, regular and 24k $30, $50
Boston Garden/Fleet Center Old/New,1995 regular and 24k $30, $50
Boston Celtics Final Game at the Boston Garden,1995, regular and 24k $30, $50
Boston Celtics/Boston Garden,1995, two-piece silver set and two-piece 24k set $60, $100
Houston Rockets 1995 World Champions double clutch city, 24k and one-ounce gold $30, $50
Houston Rockets 1995 World Champions three-piece proof set, three-piece silver set and three-piece 24k set $90, $150
Houston Rockets 1994-95 two-piece Back-to-Back silver set and Back-to-Back 24k set $60, $90
Houston Rockets 1995 Western Conference Champs regular and 24k $30, $50
Houston Rockets 1994 World Champions regular, 24k and one-ounce gold $65, $150
Houston Rockets 1994 World Champions three-piece set and three-piece 24k set $90, $150
Houston Rockets 1994 World Champions/Hakeem Olajuwon MVP, two-piece set .... $50 each
Houston Rockets 1994 Western Conference Champs, regular and 24k $50, $90
Houston Rockets 1994 Midwestern Division Champs, regular and 24k $30, $50
New York Knicks 1994 Eastern Conference Champs, regular and 24k $30, $50
New York Knicks 1994 Atlantic Division Champs, regular and 24k $30, $50
Orlando Magic 1995 Eastern Conference Champs, regular and 24k $30, $50
Orlando Magic 1995 Eastern Conference Champs, three-piece set $75
Seattle Supersonics 1994 Pacific Division Champs, regular and 24k $30, $50
Toronto Raptors New Franchise regular and 24k $30, $50
Toronto Raptors Inaugural Season $30
Vancouver Grizzlies New Franchise regular and 24k ... $30, $50
Raptors/Grizzlies two-piece set $90
1995 NBA All-Star Game, Phoenix All-NBA Team five-piece silver set and five-piece 24k set $150, $350

1994 NBA releases

1994 NBA All-Star Game, 1994, 5,000 .... $30
1994 USA Basketball, 1994, team set silver (83/at $595/so) and 24k set (17/at $875/so)

1993 NBA releases

Chicago Bulls Consecutive Champs, three-pc. set, 1993, 1,000 .... $175
Chicago Bulls World Champs, three-pc. set,1993, 500 ...... $125
1993 Chicago Bulls NBA World Champs, 1993, 25,000 ...... $30
1993 Chicago Bulls NBA World Champs, 1993, 193 .... $850
1993 Chicago Bulls Eastern Conference Champs, 1993, 10,000 .... $30
1993 Chicago Bulls Central Division Champs, 1993, 5,000 . $30
1993 Houston Rockets Midwest Division Champs, 1993, 5,000 .... $30
1993 NBA All-Star Game, 1993, 5,000 .... $30
1994 NBA All-Star Game - Minnesota Timberwolves, 1993, 5,000 .... $30
1993 New York Knicks Atlantic Division Champs, 1993, 42 . $75
1993 Phoenix Suns Western Conference Champs, 1993, 10,000 .... $30
1993 Phoenix Suns Pacific Division Champs, 1993, 5,000 .. $30
1993 USA Basketball Team $35

1992 NBA releases

All 27 NBA basic team commemoratives, 1992, 1,000 each..... $30
Atlanta Hawks 25th Anniversary, 1992, 5,000 .... $30
Basketball Tournament of Americas, 1992, 5,000 .... $30
1992 Boston Celtics Atlantic Division Champs, 1992, 5,000 .....$30
1992 Chicago Bulls NBA World Championship, 1992, 25,000..$30
1992 Chicago Bulls Central Division Champs, 1992, 1,053 ......$40
1992 Chicago Bulls Eastern Conference Champs, 1992, 1,543 .... $40
Chicago Bulls Back-to-Back Champs, 1992, 1,000 .... $83
Complete Eastern/Western Conference (27-pc. matched set), 1992, 100 .... $900
Denver Nuggets 25th Anniversary, 1992, 5,000 .... $30
Indiana Pacers 25th Anniversary, 1992, 5,000 .... $30
1992 NBA All-Star Game, 1992, 10,000 .... $30
Phoenix Suns 25th Anniversary, 1992, 5,000 .... $30
1992 Portland Trailblazers Western Conference Champs, 1992, 10,000 .... $30
1992 Portland Trailblazers Pacific Division Champs, 1992, 5,000 .... $30
Seattle Supersonics 25th Anniversary, 1992 .... $30
USA Basketball, 10-coin set, 1992, 250 .... $500
USA Basketball, 12-coin set, 1992, 750 .... $700
USA Basketball, two 6-pc. sets, 1992, 475 .... $600
1992 Utah Jazz Midwest Division, 1992, 5,000 .... $30
1992 World Championship, three-pc. set, 1992, 500 .... $125

1991 NBA releases

1991 Chicago Bulls NBA World Championship, 1991, 25,000 ...$30
1991 Chicago Bulls Central Division Champs, 1991, 1,500 ......$35
1991 Chicago Bulls Eastern Conference Champs, 1991,
1,500 .... $50
Chicago Bulls 25th Anniversary, 1991, 5,000 .... $30

NBA Players

Charles Barkley - 1993 NBA MVP, 1993, 15,000 .... $30
USA Charles Barkley, 1992, 2,750 .... $50
USA Larry Bird, 1992, 5,150 .... $60
USA Derrick Coleman, 1994 silver (45) and 24k .... (5 at $50 each)
Derrick Coleman - 1991 Rookie of the Year, 1992, 15,000 .. $30
Clyde Drexler - 1995 Houston Rockets regular and 24k $30
USA Clyde Drexler, 1992, 2,950 .... $45
USA Joe Dumars, 1994 silver (45) and 24k ...... (5 at $50 each)
Patrick Ewing - New York Knicks, 1995, regular and
24k $30, $50
USA Patrick Ewing, 1992, 2,500 .... $50
Anfernee Hardaway, 1995, All-NBA Team regular and
24k $30, $50
USA Tim Hardaway,1994, silver (95) and 24k .. (5 at $50 each)
Grant Hill/Jason Kidd, 1995, two-piece silver rookie set and
two-piece 24k rookie set ....$50, $120 each
Grant Hill -1995 Co-Rookie of the year regular and
24k $30, $50
USA Kevin Johnson,1994 silver (75) and 24k . (20 at $50 each)
USA Larry Johnson, 1994, silver (55) and 24k ....(20 at $50 each)
Larry Johnson - 1992 Rookie of the Year, 1992, 15,000 ...... $30
USA Magic Johnson,1992, 5,000 .... $55
Magic Johnson - All-Time Assists, 1991, 3,583.................... $30
USA Michael Jordan, 1992, 7,500... $75
Michael Jordan - 1992 MVP, 1992, 3,905............................. $85
Michael Jordan - 1991 MVP, 1991, 13,299 .... $75
USA Shawn Kemp, 1994, silver (60) and 24k ......(14 at $50 each)
Jason Kidd - 1995 Co-Rookie of the year regular and
24k $30, $50
USA Christian Laettner, 1992 , 2,600 .... $32
Jim Les - 3-Point Field Goal Percentage, 1991, 15,000 ...... $30
USA Dan Majerle, 1994, silver (76) and 24k ....(30 at $50 each)
Karl Malone -1995 All-NBA Team regular and 24k $30
USA Karl Malone, 1992, 2,450 .... $50
Reggie Miller - Indiana Pacers, 1995, regular and 24k $30, $50
USA Reggie Miller, 1994, silver (75) and 24k ......(20 at $50 each)
Reggie Miller-Free Throw Percentage, 1991, 15,000 .... $30
USA Chris Mullin, 1992, 2,500 .... $43
USA Alonzo Mourning, 1994, silver (55) and
24k .... (20 at $50 each)
Hakeem Olajuwon - 1994 NBA MVP, 1994, regular and 24k,
125 ....$65 each
Hakeem Olajuwon - Blocked Shots, 1992, 144 .... $125
USA Shaquille O'Neal, 1994, silver (507) and
24k .... (215 at $50 each)

Shaquille O'Neal - 1992 1st Round Draft Pick, 1993,
15,000.. $30
Shaquille O' Neal/Chris Webber (two-piece set), 1993,
1,000.. $83
Scottie Pippen - All-NBA Team, 1995, regular and 24k $30, $50
USA Scottie Pippen, 1992, 3,100 .... $50
USA Mark Price,1994, silver (74) and 24k ....5 at $50 each
David Robinson - All-NBA Team, regular and 24k........ $30, $50
David Robinson - San Antonio Spurs, 1994, regular............ $30
USA David Robinson, 1992, 2,750 .... $50
David Robinson - Rebounding Champ, 1991, 15,000 .... $40
Glenn Robinson - Milwaukee Bucks, 1995, two-piece silver set
and two-piece 24k set.. $30
Glenn Robinson - 1994 1st Round Draft Pick, 1994, regular and
24k $30, $50
USA Steve Smith, 1994, silver (45) and 24k .... (5 at $50 each)
John Stockton - NBA Assists All-Time Leader, 1995,
regular and 24k.. ($30, $50)
John Stockton - All-NBA Team, 1995, regular and
24k .... ($30 each, $50 each)
USA John Stockton, 1992, 2,500 .... $43
John Stockton - 1994 NBA Assists, 1994, 75 .... $30
John Stockton,- Assists, 1992, 15,000 .... $30
Isiah Thomas, 1994, silver (45) and 24k .... (20 at $50 each)
Chris Webber - Washington Bullets, 1994, regular............... $30
Chris Webber - 1993 1st Round Draft Pick, 1993, 1,255 .... $30
Buck Williams - Field Goal Percentage, 1991, 15,000 .... $30
USA Dominique Wilkins,1994, silver (50) and
24k .... (5 at $50 each)

NHL 1994-95 releases

Boston Bruins Final Game at the Boston Garden, 1995, regular
and 24k... $30, $50
Boston Bruins/Boston Garden, 1995, two-piece silver and
two-piece 24k $60, $90
Detroit Red Wings 1995 Western Conference Champs,1995
regular and 24k... $30, $50
Detroit Red Wings 1995 Western Conference Champs,1995
three-piece set.. $120
New Jersey Devils 1995 Eastern Conference Champs,1995,
regular and 24k... $30, $50
New Jersey Devils 1995 Eastern Conference Champs,1995,
three-piece proof set.. $125
New Jersey Devils 1995 Stanley Cup Champs,1995, regular,
24k and one-ounce... $30, $50, $120
New Jersey Devils 1995 Stanley Cup Champs, 1995, three-
piece proof set, three-piece regular and three-
piece 24k $60, $90, $130

1994 NHL releases

Calgary Flames 1994 Pacific Division Champs, 1994, regular
and 24k... $30, $50
Detroit Red Wings 1994 Central Division Champs, 1994, regular
and 24k...$30, $50
New York Rangers 1994 Atlantic Division Champs, 1994, regular
and 24k...$30, $50
New York Rangers 1994 Eastern Conference Champs, 1994,
regular and 24k... $30, $50
New York Rangers 1994 Stanley Cup Champs,1994, regular,
24k and one-ounce gold... $30, $50
New York Rangers 1994 Stanley Cup Champs,1994, three-
piece regular set and three-piece 24k set $80, $150
Opening Night - Fleet Center (Boston Bruins), 1994, regular
and 24k... $30, $50
Pittsburgh Penguins Northeast Division Champs,1994, regular
and 24k... $30, $50

St. Louis Blues - Kiel Center Inaugural Season 1994-95,1994, regular $30

Vancouver Canucks 1994 Western Conference Champs, 1994, regular and 24k.. $30, $50

1993 NHL releases

1993 Adams Division Playoff Champion Montreal Canadiens, 1993, 5,000.. $30

1993 Adams Division - Boston Bruins, 1993, 5,000 .... $30

1993 Campbell Conference - Los Angeles Kings, 1993, 10,000.. $30

Dallas Stars Inaugural, 1993 , 5,000, ... $30

Ducks/Panthers Inaugural (two-piece set), 1993, 500 .... $85

Florida Panthers - Inaugural Season, 1993, 1,500.............. $30

Mighty Ducks of Anaheim - Inaugural Season, 1993, 1,500 .....$55

NHL 45th New York Rangers All-Star Game, 1993, 5,000 ... $30

NHL 44th Montreal Canadiens All-Star Game, 1993, 5,000 .....$30

1993 Norris Division Playoff Champion Toronto Maple Leafs,1993, 5,000 .... $30

1993 Norris Division - Chicago Blackhawks, 1993, 5,000 .... $30

1993 Patrick Division Playoff Champion New York Islanders, 1993, 5,000.. $30

1993 Patrick Division - Pittsburgh Penguins, 1993, 211 ...... $30

San Jose Sharks New Arena Inaugural, 1993, 5,000........... $30

1993 Smythe Division Playoff Champion Los Angeles Kings, 1993, 5,000.. $30

1993 Smythe Division - Vancouver Canucks, 1993, 5,000 ... $30

1993 Stanley Cup - Montreal Canadiens, 1993, 25,000....... $30

1993 Stanley Cup set (three-pieces),1993, 500 .... $125

1993 Stanley Cup Centennial, 1993, 500........................... $125

1993 Wales Conference - Montreal Canadiens, 1993, 10,000.. $30

1992 NHL releases

All 24 NHL basic team commemoratives, 1992, 1,000 each......$30

Complete Wales/Campbell Conference (24-piece set), 1992, 100.. $900

1992 Adams Division - Montreal Canadiens, 1992, 5,000 ....$30

1992 Campbell Conference - Chicago Blackhawks, 1992, 10,000.. $30

1992 Norris Division - Detroit Red Wings, 1992 .... $55

Ottawa Senators - Inaugural, 1992, 5,000........................... $30

1992 Patrick Division - New York Rangers, 1992, 366 .... $30

Pittsburgh Penguins Back-to-Back Champs (two piece set), 1992, 1,000.. $83

Pittsburgh Penguins 25th Anniversary, 1992, 5,000............. $30

1992 Smythe Division - Vancouver Canucks, 1992, 378 .... $55

1992 Stanley Cup set (three-pieces), 1992, 500 .... $30

1992 Stanley Cup - Pittsburgh Penguins, 1992, 25,000....... $30

St. Louis Blues 25th Anniversary, 1992, 5,000.................... $30

Tampa Bay Lightning - Inaugural, 1992, 5,000..................... $30

1992 Wales Conference - Pittsburgh Penguins,1992, 10,000.. $30

1991 NHL releases

1991 Adams Division - Boston Bruins, 1991, 300 .... $75

1991 Campbell Conference - Minnesota North Stars, 1991, 800.. $30

Labatt-Coupe Canada Cup - Canada, 1991, 10,000........... $50

Labatt-Coupe Canada Cup - Czechoslovakia, 1991, 1,000 ......$30

Labatt-Coupe Canada Cup - Finland, 1991, 1,000 .... $50

Labatt-Coupe Canada Cup - Sweden, 1991, 1,000 .... $50

Labatt-Coupe Canada Cup - United States, 1991, 10,000... $30

Labatt-Coupe Canada Cup - U.S.S.R., 1991, 1,000 .... $100

Los Angeles Kings 25th Anniversary, 1991, 5,000, ... $30

NHL 43rd Philadelphia Flyers All-Star Game, 1991 .... $30

1991 Norris Division Playoffs - Minnesota North Stars, 1991, 900.. $30

1991 Norris Division - Chicago Blackhawks, 1991, 300 ...... $75

1991 Patrick Division - Pittsburgh Penguins, 1991, 3,525 ... $55

San Jose Sharks Inaugural Year, 1991, 10,000 .... $30

1991 Smythe Division - Los Angeles Kings, 1991, 5,000..... $30

1991 Stanley Cup - Pittsburgh Penguins, 1991, 25,000....... $30

1991 Wales Conference - Pittsburgh Penguins, 1991, 3,000 .... $55

1990 NHL releases

NHL 42nd Chicago Blackhawks All-Star Game, 1990, 1,500 ...$50

1990 Norris Division - Chicago Blackhawks, 1990, 500 ...... $60

1990 Patrick Division - New York Rangers, 1990, 300 .... $55

1990 Stanley Cup - Edmonton Oilers, 1990, 5,000 .... $30

1989 NHL releases

1989 Campbell Conference - Calgary Flames, 1989, 5,000 .....$75

NHL 41st Annual All-Star Game, 1989, 500 .... $50

1989 Stanley Cup - Calgary Flames, 1989, 5,000 .... $30

1989 Wales Conference - Montreal Canadiens, 1989, 300 ......$75

1988 NHL releases

1988 Campbell Conference - Edmonton Oilers, 1988, 300 ......$70

1988 Norris Division - Detroit Red Wings, 1988, 400 .... $60

1988 Patrick Division - New Jersey Devils, 1988, 500 .... $50

1988 Stanley Cup - Edmonton Oilers, 1988, 5,000 .... $30

1988 Wales Conference - Boston Bruins, 1988, 300 .... $55

NHL Players

Dave Andreychuk - Toronto Maple Leafs, 1995, regular, 24k and bronze.. $30, $60, $20

Ed Belfour - Chicago Blackhawks, 1995, 24k gold select set (500) $250

Ed Belfour - Vezina and Calder trophies, 1991, 5,000 .... $30

Ray Bourque - Boston Bruins,1995, 24k gold select set (500) ....$85 each

Ray Bourque - Norris Trophy, 1991, 5,000 .... $30

Pavel Bure - Vancouver Canucks, 1994, 24k gold select set .... (125 at $50 each)

Pavel Bure - Vancouver Canucks, 1992, 5,000 .... $30

Guy Charbonneau - Montreal Canadiens, 1993, 5,000........ $30

Chris Chelios - Chicago Blackhawks, 1995, regular, 24k and bronze.. $30, $50, $20

Wendel Clark - Toronto Maple Leafs, 1995, regular, 24k and bronze.. $30, $50, $20

Paul Coffey - Detroit Red Wings, 1995, regular.................... $30

Paul Coffey - Detroit Red Wings, 1995, 24k gold select set (500) $65

Paul Coffey - Los Angeles Kings, 1992, 4,250 .... $30

Paul Coffey - Leading Defenseman, Penguins, 1991, 750 ... $55

Sergei Fedorov - Detroit Red Wings, 1995, regular, 24k and bronze.. $30, $50, $20

Grant Fuhr - Toronto Maple Leafs, 1995, 24k gold select set (500) $30, $50, $20

Grant Fuhr - Vezina Trophy, 1992, 5,000............................ $30

Doug Gilmour - Toronto Maple Leafs, 1995, 24k gold select set (500) $85

Doug Gilmour - Toronto Maple Leafs Most Goals, 1993, 5,000 .... $30

Wayne Gretzky - All-Time Goals,1994,one-ounce silver (25,000), one-ounce gold (199) and 1¼4-ounce gold (1,851) $75

Wayne Gretzky - All-Time Goals,1994 24k gold select (5,000), bronze (50,000) $60, $20

Wayne Gretzky - All-Time Goals, 1994, two-piece set (802) ....$30 each

Wayne Gretzky - All-Time Goals, 1994, three-piece set, (999) ....$30 each

Wayne Gretzky - All-Time Goals,1994 1/2-pound, (1,851).........$85

Wayne Gretzky - All-Time Points, 1994, regular and one-ounce pure gold,(99) $85

Wayne Gretzky - Canadian Edition, 1989, 18,510 .... $85

Wayne Gretzky - Domestic Edition, 1989, 10,893 .... $55

Brett Hull/Bobby Hull, 1995, 24k gold select, (500) $85

Brett Hull/Bobby Hull - Father/Son Commemorative, 1991, 15,000 .... $30

Jaromir Jagr - Pittsburgh Penguins, 1995, 24k gold select, 500 .... $65

Jaromir Jagr - Pittsburgh Penguins, 1992, 5,000................. $30

Jari Kurri - Los Angeles Kings, 1995, regular, 24k and bronze $60, $20

Pat LaFontaine - New York Islanders,1993, 5,000................. $30

Steve Larmer - New York Rangers, 1995, regular and 24k gold select (500) $30, $60

Steve Larmer - Chicago Blackhawks,1992, 5,000................. $30

Brian Leetch - New York Rangers, 1994, regular, 24k (125 at $65) and bronze... $20

Brian Leetch - 1994 Conn Smythe Trophy, 1994, 24k and bronze... $50, $20

Mario Lemieux - 1992 Conn Smythe Trophy, 1992, 5,000.... $30

Mario Lemieux - 1992 Conn Smythe Trophy, heirloom 24k .. $85

Mario Lemieux - Conn Smythe Trophy, 1991, 5,000 .... $60

Mario Lemieux - 1991 Conn Smythe Trophy, heirloom 24k .. $75

Eric Lindros - Philadelphia Flyers, 1994, regular, 24k (125 at $50 each,) and bronze..................................... $25

Al MacInnis - Calgary Flames Norris Trophy, 1993, 5,000 ... $30

Mark Messier - New York Rangers, 1995, 24k (500)........... $75

Mark Messier - Hart, Conn, Smythe, Pearson, 1992, 5,000.......$30

Adam Oates - Boston Bruins,1995, regular, 24k and bronze.. $30, $50, $20

Felix Potvin - Toronto Maple Leafs,1994 regular, 24k, 125 and bronze.. $30, $50, $20

Mike Richter - New York Rangers,1995, regular, 24k and bronze.. $30, $50, $20

Luc Robitaille - Los Angeles Kings, 1993, 5,000 .... $30

Patrick Roy - Montreal Canadiens,1994, 24k gold select .... (125 at $50 each)

Patrick Roy - 1993 Conn Smythe Trophy, 1993, 5,000, ... $30

Patrick Roy - Montreal Canadiens, 1992, 5,000 .... $30

Joe Sakic - Quebec Nordiques, 1995, 24k gold select (500) $50

Joe Sakic - Quebec Nordiques, Team Scoring, 1993, 5,000 .....$30

Teemu Selanne - Winnipeg Jets, 1995, 24k gold select (500) $50

Teemu Selanne - 1993 Calder Trophy, 1993, 5,000 .... $30

John Vanbiesbrouck - Florida Panthers, 1995, regular, 24k and bronze... $30, $25

Steve Yzerman - Detroit Red Wings, 1995, 24k gold select (500) $55

Steve Yzerman - Detroit Red Wings, 1992, 5,000................. $30

NFL
1994-95 releases

Buffalo Bills 35th Anniversary regular and 24k... (100 at $135 each)

Carolina Panthers Inaugural Season regular and 24k ($30, $60)

Carolina Panthers flip coin 24k... $50

Chicago Bears coin-art regular, and 24k.................. ($30, $65)

Chicago Bears Super Bowl XX Champs heirloom $30

Chicago Bears Super Bowl XX/Walter Payton Rushing Record two-piece heirloom 24k set $65

Chicago Bears 75th Anniversary regular and 24k........ $30, $60

Chicago Bears/Mike Ditka/Walter Payton three-piece 24k gold set $130

Dallas Cowboys 1994 NFC Eastern Division regular and 24k... $30, $60

Green Bay Packers 1994 NFC Wild Card regular and 24k... $30, $60

Jacksonville Jaguars coin-art, regular and 24k $30, $50

Jacksonville Jaguars Inaugural Season regular and 24k... $30, $50

Jacksonville Jaguars flip coin 24k.. $30

Jacksonville Jaguars Franchise/new logo........................... $30

Jaguars/Panthers Inaugural season two-piece silver set and two-piece 24k set....................... $60, $120

Jaguars/Panthers flip coin 24k $60

Jaguars/Panthers matched two-piece set.......................... $65

New Jaguars/Panthers matched two-piece set $60

Miami Dolphins 1994 AFC Eastern Division, regular and 24k... $30, $60

Minnesota Vikings 1994 NFC Central Division, regular and 24k... $30, $65

Monday Night Football 25th Anniversary, regular and 24k... $30, $65

Pittsburgh Steelers 1994 AFC Central Division, regular and 24k... $30, $65

San Diego Chargers AFC/Super Bowl XXIX, two-piece regular set and two-piece 24k set....................... $60, $120

San Diego Chargers 1994 AFC Champions, regular and 24k .... (1,000 at $50 each)

San Diego Chargers 1994 AFC Western Division regular and 24k... $30, $50

San Francisco 49ers NFC/Super Bowl XXIX, two-piece regular set and two-piece 24k set....................... $30, $50

San Francisco 49ers 1994 NFC Champions, regular and 24k... $30, $60

San Francisco 49ers 1994 NFC Western Division regular and 24k... $30, $50

Super Bowl XXIX/Joe Robbie Stadium commemorative, regular and 24k... $30, $60

Super Bowl XXIX Champions - San Francisco 49ers regular, 24k and one-ounce....................... $30, $60, $125

Super Bowl XXIX Champions - San Francisco 49ers three-piece set regular and three-piece 24k set $120, $225

Super Bowl XXVIII Champions - Dallas Cowboys, three-piece set (500) $125

Super Bowl XXVIII Champions - Dallas Cowboys regular, one-ounce gold (194) and 24k gold select $100, $60

1993 NFL releases

Buffalo Bills 1993 AFC Champions, 1993 .... $30

Buffalo Bills 1993 AFC Western Division, 1993 .... $30

Carolina Panthers Franchise, 1993 .... $30

Dallas Cowboys Super Bowl XXVII, 25,000 .... $30

Dallas Cowboys 1993 NFC Champions, 1993 .... $30

Dallas Cowboys 1993 NFC Eastern Division, 1993, 265 ..... $30

Detroit Lions 1993 NFC Central Division, 1993................... $30

Green Bay Packers 75th Anniversary, 1993, 5,000 .... $30

Green Bay Packers/Bart Starr (two-piece set) ,1993, 500 .. $83

Houston Oilers 1993 AFC Eastern Division, 1993 .... $30

Jacksonville Jaguars Franchise, 1993, 1,922 .... $30

Kansas City Chiefs 1993 AFC Western Division, 1993........ $30

San Francisco 49ers 1993 NFC Western Division, 1993, 89 ....$30

Super Bowl XXVII (three-piece set), 1993, 500 .... $125

1992 NFL releases

All 28 NFL basic team commemoratives, 1992, 1,000 each......$30
Complete 28-piece AFC/NFC matched set, 1992, 100 ...... $900
100th Anniversary of Professional Football, 1992, 1,000 .... $30
1992 Buffalo Bills AFC Champions,1992, 2,050 .... $35
1992 Dallas Cowboys NFC Champions, 1992, 1,644 .... $35
1992 Dallas Cowboys NFC Eastern Division, 1992, 499 ... $45
1992 Miami Dolphins AFC Eastern Division, 1992, 180...... $30
1992 Minnesota Vikings NFC Central Division, 1992, 139 .... $30
1992 Pittsburgh Steelers AFC Central Division, 1992, 330 .... $35
1992 San Diego Chargers AFC Western Division, 1992, 574 .... $30
1992 San Francisco 49ers NFC Western Division, 1992, 118 .... $55
1992 Washington Redskins NFC Champions, 1992, 1,000......$30

1991 NFL releases

1991 Buffalo Bills AFC Champions, 1991, 10,000 .... $55
1991 Buffalo Bills AFC Eastern Division, 1991, 5,000 .... $40
1991 Denver Broncos AFC Western Division, 1991, 5,000.. $30
1991 Detroit Lions NFC Central Division, 1991, 5,000...... $30
1991 Houston Oilers AFC Central Division, 1991, 300 .... $30
1991 New Orleans Saints NFC Western Division, 1991, 5,000.. $30
1991 Washington Redskins NFC Eastern Division, 1991, 5,000.. $30
Washington Redskins Super Bowl XXVI Champs, 1991, 25,000.. $30

1990 NFL releases

1990 Buffalo Bills AFC Champions, 1990, 2,800 .... $85
1990 Buffalo Bills AFC East Division, 1990, 1,400 .... $65
1990 Chicago Bears NFC Central Division, 1990, 5,000 .... $50
Chicago Bears 70th Anniversary, 1990, 7,500 .... $35
1990 Cincinnati Bengals AFC Central Division, 1990, 5,000.....$30
1990 Los Angeles Raiders AFC Western Division, 1990, 5,000.. $30
New York Giants Super Bowl XXV Champions, 1990, 10,000..$30
1990 New York Giants 1990 NFC Champions, 1990, 1,400......$50
1990 New York Giants NFC Eastern Division, 1990, 5,000.. $30
1990 San Francisco 49ers NFC Western Division, 1990, 5,000 .... $45

1989 NFL releases

1989 Buffalo Bills AFC Eastern Division, 1989, 2,000 .... $225
1989 Cleveland Browns AFC Central Division, 1989, 3,400 .....$50
1989 Denver Broncos AFC Champions, 1989, 10,000 .... $30
1989 Denver Broncos AFC Western Division, 1989, 5,000 .... $30
1989 Minnesota Vikings NFC Central Division, 1989, 5,000......$30
1989 New York Giants NFC Eastern Division, 1989, 5,000 .... $34
San Francisco 49ers Super Bowl XXIV Champions, 1989, 10,000.. $30
1989 San Francisco 49ers NFC Champions, 1989, 10,000.......$45

1989 San Francisco 49ers NFC Western Division, 1989, 5,000 .... $45

1988 NFL releases

1988 Buffalo Bills AFC Eastern Division, 1988, 1,800 ...... $350
1988 Chicago Bears NFC Central Division, 1988, 900 .... $75
1988 Cincinnati Bengals AFC Champions, 1988, 1,400 ..... $40
1988 Cincinnati Bengals AFC Central Division 1988, 900 , . $55
1988 Philadelphia Eagles NFC Eastern Division, 1988, 300 $70
San Francisco 49ers Super Bowl XXIII Champions, 1988, 10,000.. $50
1988 San Francisco 49ers NFC Champions, 1988, 1,300 .. $55
1988 San Francisco 49ers NFC Western Division, 1988, 100 .... $150
1988 Seattle Seahawks AFC Western Division, 1988, 700 ......$65

1987 NFL releases

1987 Chicago Bears NFC Central Division, 1987, 500 .... $75
1987 Cleveland Browns AFC Central Division, 1987, 2,400 $75
1987 Denver Broncos AFC Champions, 1987, 3,100 .... $35
1987 Denver Broncos AFC Western Division, 1987, 900 .... $75
Houston Oilers 1987 AFC Playoff Wild Card, 1987, 100 ... $225
1987 Indianapolis Colts AFC Eastern Division, 1987, 700 .. $50
Minnesota Vikings 1987 NFC Playoff Wild Card, 1987, 1,300.. $40
New Orleans Saints 1987 NFC Playoff Wild Card,1987, 500 .... $55
1987 San Francisco 49ers NFC Western Division,1987, 500 .... $55
Seattle Seahawks 1987 AFC Playoff Wild Card, 1987, 100 ...$250
Washington Redskins Super Bowl XXII Champs, 1987, 7,200.. $30
1987 Washington Redskins NFC Champions, 1987, 2,000 .....$45
1987 Washington Redskins NFC Eastern Division, 1987, 1,500.. $45

1986 NFL releases

1986 Cleveland Browns AFC Central Division, 1986, 4,450 .....$50
Dallas Cowboys NFL Champs 1971 and 1977, 1986, 1,200 ....$45
1986 Denver Broncos AFC Champions, 1986, 4,250 .... $50
New York Giants Super Bowl XXI Champions, 1986, 10,000 .... $55
1986 New York Giants NFC Champions, 1986, 4,500 .... $45
Pittsburgh Steelers Super Bowls IX, X, XIII and XIV, 1986, 800 .... $175
Washington Redskins 50th Anniversary, 1986, 586 .... $250

1985 NFL releases

Chicago Bears Super Bowl XX Champions, 1985, 8,918... $125
1985 Chicago Bears NFC Champions, 1985, 7,000 .... $55
1985 New England Patriots AFC Champions, 1985, 4,000 .....$45

NFL Players

Troy Aikman - Dallas Cowboys, 1992, 2,386 .... $40
Troy Aikman - Dallas Cowboys (#2) and 24k............... $35, $65

Marcus Allen - Kansas City Chiefs, regular and 24k $30, $55
Jerome Bettis - Los Angeles Rams regular and 24k ... $30, $55
Mark Carrier - 1990 Defensive Rookie of the Year, 35 .... $45
Randall Cunningham - Philadelphia Eagles, regular and
    24k... $30, $55
Mike Ditka - 1988 NFL Hall of Fame, 1988, 15,000.............. $30
Mike Ditka - Chicago Bears, regular..................................... $30
John Elway - Denver Broncos , 1992, 1,144 .... $40
John Elway - Denver Broncos (#2) regular and 24k..... $30, $55
Boomer Esiason - New York Jets, 1993, 30 .... $65
Boomer Esiason - Cincinnati Bengals, 1990, 624 .... $50
Brett Favre - Green Bay Packers, regular and 24k....... $35, $60
Brett Favre, Sterling Sharpe, Reggie White three-piece silver
    set (100 at $125) and three-piece 24k set.................... $150
Dan Hampton - 4-Time Pro Bowl, 1990, 155...................... $35
Michael Irvin - Dallas Cowboys, 1992, 1,393 .... $35
Bo Jackson - Baseball/Football, 1990, 15,000 .... $30
Jim Kelly - Buffalo Bills, 1992, 1,640 .... $40
Jim Kelly - Buffalo Bills (#2) regular and 24k................ $30, $55
Jim Kelly/Buffalo Bills 35th Anniversary two-piece silver set and
    two-piece 24k set.. $60, $90
Bernie Kosar - Cleveland Browns, 1990, 1,065 .... $40
Bernie Kosar - Miami Dolphins regular................................ $30
Tom Landry, 1988, 4,083 .... $30
Vince Lombardi - 1971 NFL Hall of Fame, 1987, 2,535 ...... $50
Dan Marino - Miami Dolphins, 1992, 1,710 .... $40
Dan Marino - Miami Dolphins (#2) regular and 24k...... $35, $60
Art Monk - All-Time NFL Receptions,1992, 1,178............... $35

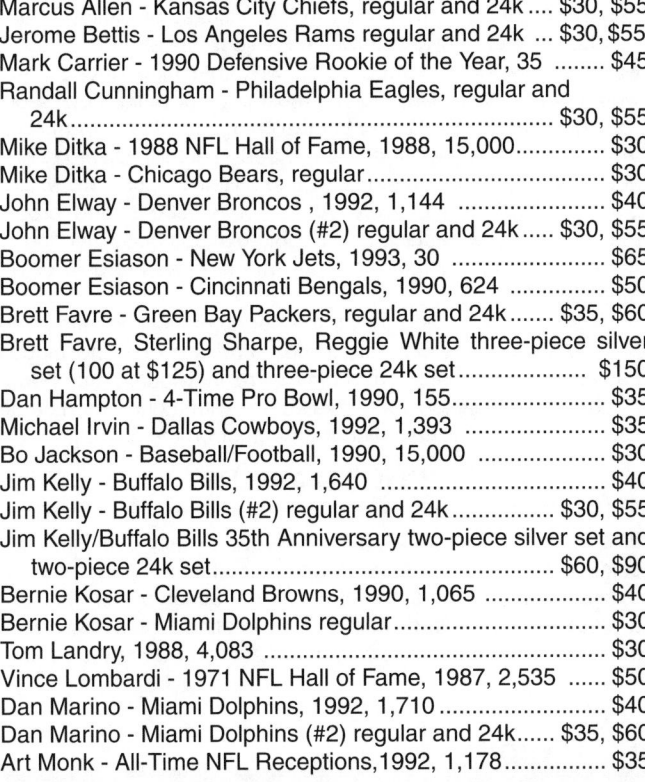

Joe Montana - Retirement two-piece card and coin set $35
Joe Montana - Kansas City Chiefs, 1993, 7,000 .... $30
Joe Montana - Kansas City Chiefs (#2), 1994, regular and
    24k $30, $60
Joe Montana - Kansas City Chiefs 1-ounce pure gold, 1993,
    100.. $850
Joe Montana - card/medallion, (two-piece set), 1993, 367 ......$120
Joe Montana - Player of the Decade, 49ers, 1990, 8,000 ... $65
Joe Montana/Marcus Allen two-piece silver set and two-piece
    24k set $30, $60
Warren Moon - Minnesota Vikings regular and 24k $30, $50
Warren Moon - 1991 AFC Player of the Year, 1991, 702 .... $55
Neil O'Donnell -Pittsburgh Steelers, regular........................ $30
Walter Payton-two-piece matched set $60
Walter Payton-24k gold select $55
Walter Payton - 1993 Hall of Fame, 1993, 16,726.............. $35
Walter Payton - 1993 Hall of Fame Gold, 1993, 110 .... $850
Walter Payton - All-Time Leading Rusher 1987, 16,726 ..... $45
Walter Payton - commemorative card set, 1987, 16,726...... $65
Jerry Rice - 101 Touchdowns, 1992, 336 .... $60
Jerry Rice - San Francisco 49ers/127 touchdowns, regular
    (900) and 24k $30, $55
Jerry Rice/Steve Young two-piece silver set and two-piece 24k
    set.. $60, $110
Barry Sanders - 1989 Rookie of the Year, 1992, 1,307 .... $40
Barry Sanders - Detroit Lions (#2), regular and 24k..... $30, $60
Deion Sanders - San Francisco 49ers, regular and 24k $30, $50
Sterling Sharpe - Green Bay Packers regular and 24k $30, $50
Mike Singletary - Retirement, 1992, 681 .... $45
Emmitt Smith - Dallas Cowboys, 1992, 2,191 .... $40
Emmitt Smith - Dallas Cowboys (#2), regular (900) and
    24k $30, $55
Emmitt Smith, Troy Aikman, Michael Irvin (three-piece set),
    1992, 710 .... $125, $145
Emmitt Smith, Troy Aikman, Michael Irvin three-piece set
    (#2), and 24k set... $125
Bart Starr - Green Bay Packers, 1993, 5,000, ... $30
Lawrence Taylor - Defensive Player of the Decade, 1990,
    2,238.. $45
Reggie White - Green Bay Packers, regular and 24k ... $30, $50
Steve Young - San Francisco 49ers, regular and 24k... $30, $55
Steve Young - Super Bowl XXIX MVP, regular and 24k $30, $50

HIGHLAND MINT

LIMITED-EDITION TRADING CARDS

In 1992, Highland Mint issued reproductions of popular trading cards in bronze and silver. The cards are etched in remarkable detail to look exactly like the player's rookie card and recent-year issues. The cards retailed for $50 (bronze) and $235 (silver), but the prices didn't stay that low for long. Cards that sold out of the bronze and silver editions were reproduced in an extremely limited gold edition that retailed for $500 and also quickly grew in value.

The original license allowed for the reproduction only of Topps cards. In 1994, Pinnacle got into the mix, and in 1995, Highland Mint replicated an Upper Deck card of Michael Jordan playing baseball. This Jordan card was Highland Mint's last card release, as collector demand shifted to the company's less expensive line of coins.

In 1995, Highland Mint experimented with mini-cards, releasing a Cal Ripken Jr. and Lou Gehrig double mini-set to coincide with the consecutive game record held by Gehrig and about to be broken by Ripken. The set went over so well that four other pairings were introduced, including Greg Maddux and Cy Young, commemorating Maddux's fourth straight Cy Young Award.

MEDALLIONS

In 1994, Highland Mint built on the success of its limited edition cards with a line of sports medallions. The concept was the same, in that the company started with bronze and silver editions and didn't offer gold until later. The bronze mintage was 25,000 with a retail price of $9.99, while silver's numbers were 5,000 and $19.95. The gold line of the Gold Signature Series—featured silver coins with gold overlays of the featured players. Mintage was 1,500 of each, retailing for $49.95. All three of these products came encased in hard plastic capsules in velvet-lined jewelery boxes.

At the outset, the coins were red hot—medallion prices were rising within weeks of release. To further capitalize on the popu-larity, Highland Mint started offering collectors something different: jumbo medallions. The Magnum Series kicked off with Cal Ripken Jr. and Ken Griffey Jr., each depicted on bronze and silver medallions 2.5 inches in diameter—more than twice the size of the regular medallions. Each coin was packaged in a velvet box that opened like a book. Mintage was 3,500 bronze ($35 retail) and 750 silver ($150 retail). Like the cards, when bronze and silver sold out, gold versions were introduced (375 mintage, $250 apiece).

In 1997, Highland Mint showered the market with several new series, most in response to the success of these in other sports. Sets of two and three medallions encased in one box were issued. Bronze medallions with matching phone cards were introduced late in '97. The most popular of the new issues was the Elite Series. Griffey led the charge for these 44-millimeter medallions, issued in bronze (5,000 mintage), silver (2,500), and gold signature versions (1,000). Retail prices were $20, $40, and $80, respectively. As a bonus, 500 of the bronze medallions were replaced with gold-plated coins. Secondary market values have risen to the same level as the gold signature versions.

The player selection for all the series is stocked with baseball's big boys, the hottest rookies, and some of the biggest names from the past. The coins were individually numbered. Each of the medallions and sets comes with a numbered certificate of authenticity, matching the number on the coin(s).

PHOTO-MINTS

In 1999, The Highland Mint introduced a new line of collectibles entitled Photo-Mints. These pieces usually consisted of a color photo of an individual player (sometimes autographed), a medallion describing some of his career accomplishments, and a piece of game-used memorabilia relating to the athlete. All three items were contained within a framed and matted setting.

HIGHLAND MINT CARDS

Pinnacle
Bronze

Yr	Player	NM
'94	Jeff Bagwell (2,500)	$75
'94	Greg Maddux (2,500)	$80
'94	Mickey Mantle (5,000)	$180
'94	Nolan Ryan (5,000)	$175

Silver

Yr	Player	NM
'94	Jeff Bagwell (750)	$250
'94	Greg Maddux (750)	$300
'94	Mickey Mantle (1,000)	$800
'94	Nolan Ryan (1,000)	$600

Gold

Yr	Player	NM
'94	Mickey Mantle (500)	$1,300
'94	Nolan Ryan (500)	$1,200

Topps
Bronze

Yr	Player	NM
'92	Roberto Alomar (928)	$80
'94	Ernie Banks (920)	$75
'94	Johnny Bench (1,384)	$480
'92	Barry Bonds (2,677)	$100
'92	George Brett (3,560)	$90
'92	Will Clark (1,044)	$80
'92	Roger Clemens (1,789)	$90
'92	Juan Gonzalez (1,899)	$90
'92	Ken Griffey Jr. (5,000)	$150
'94	David Justice (1,396)	$75
'92	Don Mattingly (1,550)	$80
'94	Paul Molitor (639)	$125
'93	Mike Piazza (2,500)	$80
'92	Kirby Puckett (1,723)	$125
'92	Cal Ripken (4,065)	$225
'92	Brooks Robinson (2,043)	$75
'92	Nolan Ryan (5,000)	$250
'94	Tim Salmon (768)	$80
'92	Ryne Sandberg (1,932)	$80
'94	Deion Sanders, (668)	$55
'94	Mike Schmidt (1,641)	$75
'92	Ozzie Smith (1,088)	$100
'92	Frank Thomas (5,000)	$125
'92	Dave Winfield (1,216)	$75
'94	Carl Yastrzemski (1,072)	$75
'92	Robin Yount (1,564)	$80

Bronze Autograph

Yr	Player	NM
'92	Brooks Robinson (350)	$150

Silver

Yr	Player	NM
'92	Roberto Alomar (214)	$325

'94	Ernie Banks (437)	$350
'94	Johnny Bench (500)	$400
'92	Barry Bonds (596)	$400
'92	George Brett (999)	$325
'92	Will Clark (150)	$450
'92	Roger Clemens (432)	$350
'92	Juan Gonzalez (365)	$300
'92	Ken Griffey Jr. (1,000)	$600
'94	David Justice (265)	$300
'92	Don Mattingly (414)	$350
'94	Paul Molitor (260)	$350
'93	Mike Piazza (750)	$450
'92	Kirby Puckett (359)	$500
'92	Cal Ripken (1,000)	$800
'92	Brooks Robinson (796)	$350
'92	Nolan Ryan (999)	$1,200
'94	Tim Salmon (264)	$300
'92	Ryne Sandberg (430)	$325
'94	Deion Sanders (187)	$250
'94	Mike Schmidt (500)	$350
'92	Ozzie Smith (211)	$400
'92	Frank Thomas (1,000)	$600
'92	Dave Winfield (266)	$325
'94	Carl Yastrzemski (500)	$300
'92	Robin Yount (349)	$300

Silver Autograph

'92	Brooks Robinson (150)	$400

Gold

'92	Ken Griffey Jr. (500)	$1,300
'93	Mike Piazza (374)	$1,000
'92	Frank Thomas (500)	$1,200

Mini-Cards
Bronze

Yr	Player	NM
'96	Griffey/Thomas (5,000)	$100
'96	Johnson/Ryan (2,500)	$85
'96	Maddux/Young (2,500)	$85
'96	Piazza/Campaneris (2,500)	$75
'95	Ripken/Gehrig (2,500)	$180

Silver

'96	Griffey/Thomas (1,000)	$200
'96	Johnson/Ryan (500)	$175
'96	Maddux/Young (500)	$175
'96	Piazza/Campaneris (500)	$175
'95	Ripken/Gehrig (500)	$400

Gold

'96	Griffey/Thomas (500)	$300
'95	Ripken/Gehrig (375)	$700

HIGHLAND MINT MEDALLIONS

Bronze

Yr	Player	NM
'96	Jeff Bagwell (25,000)	$15
'98	Nomar Garciaparra (15,000)	$20

'94	Ken Griffey Jr. (25,000)	$40
'98	Ken Griffey Jr. .5lb (2,500)	$60
'98	Ken Griffey Jr. (15,000)	$25
'97	Derek Jeter (25,000)	$20
'96	Chipper Jones (25,000)	$20
'94	Greg Maddux (25,000)	$18
'97	Mickey Mantle (25,000)	$30
'94	Don Mattingly (25,000)	$22
'98	Mark McGwire .5lb (2,500)	$60
'98	Mark McGwire (25,000)	$20
'99	Mark McGwire (3-pc. 2,500)	$75
'99	Mark McGwire 500 HR (10,000)	$20
'94	Mike Piazza (25,000)	$18
'94	Cal Ripken (25,000)	$20
'96	Cal Ripken (15,000)	$20
'99	Cal Ripken .5lb. (1,500)	$60
'96	Alex Rodriguez (25,000)	$20
'94	Frank Thomas (25,000)	$18

Silver

Yr	Player	NM
'96	Roberto Alomar (5,000)	$30
'94	Jeff Bagwell (5,000)	$30
'95	Albert Belle (5,000)	$25
'94	Wade Boggs (5,000)	$25
'99	Wade Boggs 3000 hit (5,000)	$30
'94	Barry Bonds (5,000)	$30
'95	Jose Canseco (5,000)	$25
'95	Will Clark (5,000)	$20
'94	Roger Clemens (5,000)	$40

'99...... J.D. Drew (1,999) $30
'96...... Cecil Fielder (5.000) $20
'98...... Juan Gonzalez (5,000) $30
'94...... Ken Griffey Jr. (5,000) $55
'98...... Ken Griffey Jr. .5lb (1,500) $170
'95...... Tony Gwynn (5,000) $25
'97...... Hideo Irabu (5.000) $25
'96...... Derek Jeter (5,000) $45
'97...... Andruw Jones (5.000) $30
'95...... Chipper Jones (5,000) $45
'94...... Greg Maddux (5,000) $40
'94...... Don Mattingly (5,000) $50
'97...... Mark McGwire (5.000) $50
'98...... Mark McGwire .5lb (1,500) $150
'98...... Mark McGwire 70 HRs (7,500) $50
'99...... Mark McGwire (3-pc. 1,500) $130
'99...... Mark McGwire 500 HR (5,000) $40
'97...... Raul Mondesi (5,000) $30
'96...... Eddie Murray (5,000) $35
'95...... Hideo Nomo (5,000) $30
'94...... Mike Piazza (5,000) $40
'95...... Kirby Puckett (5,000) $35
'94...... Cal Ripken (5,000) $75
'96...... Alex Rodriguez (5,000) $40
'98...... Babe Ruth (5,000) $40
'96...... Ryne Sandberg (5,000) $35
'95...... Ozzie Smith (5,000) $30
'98...... Sammy Sosa (5,000) $40
'94...... Frank Thomas (5,000) $35
'96...... Mo Vaughn (5,000) $20

Gold

'99...... Mark McGwire (3-pc. 500) $225

Gold Signature

'99...... Wade Boggs 3,000 hit (1,000) $50
'95...... Barry Bonds (1,500) $85
'95...... Ken Griffey Jr. (1,500) $125
'96...... Derek Jeter (1,500) $85
'96...... Chipper Jones (1,500) $85
'95...... Greg Maddux (1,500) $90
'98...... Mark McGwire, (1,273) $125
'98...... Mark McGwire Err (227) $125
'98...... Mark McGwire, .5lb (500) $250
'99...... Mark McGwire 500 HR (1,000) $70
'95...... Hideo Nomo (1,500) $50
'96...... Mike Piazza (1,500) $100
'96...... Kirby Puckett (1,500) $70
'95...... Cal Ripken (1,500) $125
'96...... Alex Rodriguez (1,500) $80
'98...... Sammy Sosa (1,500) $75
'95...... Frank Thomas (1,500) $85

Proof Set

'99...... Mark McGwire (9-pc. 250) $550

Elite Series

Yr	Player	NM

Bronze

'97	Ken Griffey Jr. (4,500)	$40
'97	Chipper Jones (4,500)	$25
'98	Mickey Mantle (4,500)	$55
'97	Cal Ripken (4,500)	$35
'97	Alex Rodriguez (4,500)	$30
'97	Frank Thomas (4,500)	$30

Silver

'97	Ken Griffey Jr. (2,500)	$60
'97	Chipper Jones (2,500)	$40
'98	Mickey Mantle (2,500)	$65

'97 ......Cal Ripken (2,500) $65
'97 ......Alex Rodriguez (2,500) $40
'97 ......Frank Thomas (2,500) $40

Gold Signature

'97 ......Ken Griffey Jr. (1,000) $120
'97 ......Chipper Jones (1,000) $80
'98 ......Mickey Mantle (1,000) $130
'97 ......Cal Ripken (1,000) $120
'97 ......Alex Rodriguez (1,000) $80
'97 ......Frank Thomas (1,000) $75

Gold Plated Random Inserts

'97 ......Ken Griffey Jr. (500) $200
'97 ......Chipper Jones (500) $160
'97 ....Cal Ripken (500) $250
'97 ......Alex Rodriguez (500) $130
'97 ......Frank Thomas (500) $100

Proof Sets

'97 ......Ken Griffey Jr. (350) $350
'97 ......Chipper Jones (350) $170
'98 ......Mickey Mantle (350) $200
'97 ......Cal Ripken (350) $250
'97 ......Alex Rodriguez (350) $175
'97 ......Frank Thomas (350) $150

Magnum

Yr	Player	NM

Bronze

'96	Ken Griffey Jr. (5,000)	$100
'96	Mickey Mantle (3,500)	$110
'96	Cal Ripken (3,000)	$120
'97	Alex Rodriguez (3,000)	$65
'96	Babe Ruth (3,500)	$80
'96	Nolan Ryan (3,500)	$75
'97	Frank Thomas (3,000)	$60

Silver

'96	Ken Griffey Jr. (750)	$200
'96	Cal Ripken (750)	$200
'99	Cal Ripken .5lb. (500)	$130
'97	Alex Rodriguez (750)	$150
'96	Babe Ruth (750)	$150
'96	Nolan Ryan (750)	$175
'97	Frank Thomas (750)	$140

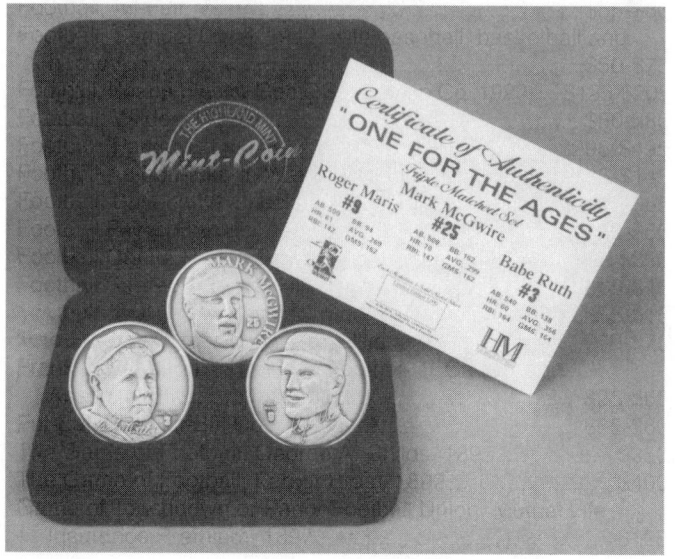

Gold

'96	Ken Griffey Jr. (375)	$350
'96	Cal Ripken (375)	$350
'96	Babe Ruth (375)	$200
'98	Nolan Ryan (375)	$300
'97	Mickey Mantle (375)	$400

Magnum/Motion Set

'96	Babe Ruth (1,000)	$130

MOTION MINTS

Yr	Player	NM

Bronze

'98	Mickey Mantle 500 HR (2,500)	$100

Nickel

'98	Mickey Mantle #6 (2,500)	$120
'99	Mark McGwire 62 HR (1,000)	$75
'99	Mark McGwire 70 HR (1,500)	$750

Gold

'99	Mark McGwire 62 HR (500)	$150
'99	Mark McGwire 70 HR (500)	$120

PHOTO-MINTS

Yr	Player	NM

'99	Ken Griffey Jr. (w/piece of glove)	$160
'99	Mark McGwire (w/piece of bat)	$160
'99	Roberto Clemente (w/piece of jersey)	$160
'99	Ken Griffey Jr. (2,500)	$75
'99	Nomar Garciaparra (2,500)	$75
'99	Derek Jeter (2,500)	$75
'99	Mark McGwire (2,500)	$100
'99	Sammy Sosa (2,500)	$80
'99	Sosa/McGwire 2 Coins (2,500)	$100
'99	Mickey Mantle (2,500)	$80
'99	Nolan Ryan (2,500)	$70
'99	Yankees WS (2,500)	$80
'00	Stan Musial auto	$100
'00	Babe Ruth	$200
'00	Ty Cobb	$200
'00	Joe DiMaggio w/bat	$200
'00	Derek Jeter w/bat	$150
'00	Dave Winfield w/bat (525)	$75
'00	Dave Winfield autographed (200)	$160
'01	Jimmie Foxx w/bat (250)	$120

'01	Nomar Garciapara w/jersey	$130
'01	Ken Griffey Jr. w/bat	$130
'01	Ken Griffey Jr. Home Run Hero	$130
'01	Tony Gwynn auto w/bat	$200
'01	Tony Gwynn w/bat	$80
'01	Shoeless Joe Jackson w/bat	$275
'01	Reggie Jackson "New York" w/bat	$100
'01	Reggie Jackson HOF w/bat	$100
'01	Pedro Martinez "Cy Young" w/jersey	$120
'01	Don Mattingly "Captain" auto w/bat	$175
'01	Don Mattingly "MVP" w/bat	$100
'01	Stan Musial HOF auto w/bat	$150
'01	Stan Musial "7 batting titles" w/bat	$110
'01	Stan Musial MVP w/bat	$110
'01	Willie Mays auto w/bat	$325
'01	Willie Mays "660" w/bat	$130
'01	Mays/Bonds w/bats	$250
'01	Kirby Puckett auto w/bat	$250
'01	Kirby Puckett w/bat	$95
'01	Cal Ripken 1983 MVP w/bat	$140
'01	Cal Ripken All-Star w/bat	$140
'01	Pete Rose auto w/bat	$180
'01	Pete Rose w/bat	$115
'01	Nolan Ryan auto w/bat	$270
'01	Nolan Ryan w/jersey	$150
'01	Mike Schmidt auto w/bat	$270
'01	Mike Schmidt MVP w/bat	$150
'01	Mike Schmidt 500 HR w/bat	$45
'01	Sammy Sosa w/bat	$130
'01	Dave Winfield "Yankees" auto w/bat	$200
'01	Dave Winfield "Minnesota" w/bat	$125
'01	Carl Yastrzemski auto w/jersey	$160
'01	Carl Yastrzemski w/jersey	$140

Rare Metal

Yr	Player	NM

Silver

'98	Ken Griffey Jr. (2,500)	$40
'98	Cal Ripken (2,500)	$35

Signature Series

'99	Ken Griffey Jr. (1,000)	$60

Sculpt Monu-Mint

Yr	Player	NM

Bronze

'98	Mickey Mantle (536)	$400
'99	Mark McGwire (500)	$350
'98	Cal Ripken (250)	$350
'99	Nolan Ryan (324)	$300

Silver

'98	Mickey Mantle (18)	$550
'99	Mark McGwire (70)	$500
'99	Nolan Ryan (27)	$600

Team 2000

Yr	Player	NM

'99	Ken Griffey Jr. (2,000)	$40
'99	Derek Jeter (2,000)	$40
'99	Alex Rodriguez (2,000)	$35

Medallion Sets

Yr	Player	NM

Litho-Mints

'98	Ken Griffey (2,500)	$90
'98	Tony Gwynn (2,500)	$90

'98......	Derek Jeter (2,500)	$70
'98......	Chipper Jones (2,500)	$70
'98......	Greg Maddux (2,500)	$70
'98......	Mark McGwire (2,500)	$150
'98......	Mike Piazza (2,500)	$70
'98......	Cal Ripken (2,500)	$80
'98......	Alex Rodriguez (2,500)	$70
'98......	Frank Thomas (2,500)	$50

Silver Motion Mints

| '98...... | Mickey Mantle (2,500) | $80 |
| '99...... | Mark McGwire 70th HR (2,500) | $50 |

Gold Motion Mints

| '99...... | Mark McGwire 70th HR (500) | $80 |

Tele-Mints

'97......	Ken Griffey (1,743)	$60
'97......	Derek Jeter (748)	$45
'97......	Chipper Jones (748)	$40
'97......	Greg Maddux (490)	$45
'97......	Mike Piazza (494)	$40
'97......	Cal Ripken (1,445)	$50
'97......	Alex Rodriguez (669)	$45
'97......	Frank Thomas (493)	$35

Ring and Coin Set

Yr	Player	NM
'98......	Roger Clemens (2,500)	$60
'99......	Nomar Garciaparra (2,500)	$65
'98......	Ken Griffey (2,500)	$70
'98......	Derek Jeter (2,500)	$70
'98......	Chipper Jones (2,500)	$60

'98	Mark McGwire (2,500)	$90
'98	Mike Piazza (2,500)	$60
'98	Cal Ripken (2,500)	$70
'98	Alex Rodriguez (2,500)	$65
'98	Sammy Sosa (500)	$65

SETS

Yr	Player	NM

Bronze/Silver Set

| '98 ...... | Ken Griffey Jr. .5lb (250) | $200 |
| '98 ...... | Mark McGwire .5lb (250) | $225 |

Bronze/Silver/Gold Set

| '98 ...... | Mark McGwire (500) | $130 |

Bronze

'99	Atlanta Braves Cy Young (2,500) (Glavine/Maddux/Smoltz)	$40
'98	Chicago Connection (1,500) (Sosa/Wood)	$35
'97	Pacific Power (2,500) (Rodriguez/Johnson/Griffey)	$40
'97	Pinstripe Heroes (2,500) Mattingly/Mantle/Jeter	$70
'97	Southern Pride (2,500) (C. Jones/A. Jones/Maddux)	$40

Silver

Yr	Player	NM
'99	Atlanta Braves Cy Young (250) (Glavine/Maddux/Smoltz)	$130
'99	Chicago Connection (500) (Sosa/Wood)	$70

Gold

Yr	Player	NM
'99	Chicago Connection (250) (Sosa/Wood)	$130

Bronze

'97	Belle/Thomas (2,500)	$25
'97	Griffey/Thomas (2,500)	$50
'97	Young Guns (2,500) (Jeter/Jones/Rodriguez)	$45

Silver

'97	Home Run Heroes (1,000) (McGwire/Griffey)	$100
'98	McGwire/Maris (2,500)	$75
'98	One for the Ages Nickel McGwire/Maris/Ruth (5,000)	$100
'98	Sosa/Maris (2,500)	$65

Gold

| '98 ...... | McGwire/Maris (250) | $175 |
| '98 ...... | Sosa/Maris (250) | $125 |

Gold Magnum

| '99 ...... | Pure Power Cubed (100) Ruth/Mantle/McGwire | $300 |

Basketball, Football, Hockey, Racing

Basketball Cards

Bronze Fleer

Yr	Player	NM
1996 Charles Barkley (5,000)		$50

Bronze Hoops

Yr	Player	NM
1996 Magic Johnson (5,000)		$60
1998 David Robinson (5,000)		$45
1996 Jerry Stackhouse (2,500)		$40
1996 Damon Stoudamire (2,500)		$50

Bronze Legends

Yr	Player	NM
1996 Kareem Abdul-Jabbar (5,000)		$50
1995 Larry Bird (5,000)		$100
1996 Hakeem Olajuwon (1,500)		$45
1995 Jerry West (2,500)		$50

Bronze Skybox

Yr	Player	NM
1997 Kevin Garnett (1,000)		$50
1997 Grant Hill (ST) (2,500)		$70

Bronze Upper Deck

Yr	Player	NM
1996 Anfernee Hardaway (2,500)		$50
1996 Michael Jordan (5,000)		$175

Silver Fleer

Yr	Player	NM
1996 Charles Barkley (1,000)		$200

Silver Hoops

Yr	Player	NM
1996 Magic Johnson (1,000)		$200
1996 David Robinson (1,000)		$200
1996 Jerry Stackhouse (500)		$190
1996 Damon Stoudamire (500)		$200

Silver Legends

Yr	Player	NM
1996 Kareem Abdul-Jabbar (1,000)		$200
1995 Larry Bird, (1,000)		$375
1996 Hakeem Olajuwon (250)		$200
1995 Jerry West (500)		$200

Silver Skybox

Yr	Player	NM
1997 Kevin Garnett (150)		$200
1997 Grant Hill (ST) (500)		$230

Silver Upper Deck

Yr	Player	NM
1996 Anfernee Hardaway (500)		$225
1996 Michael Jordan (1,000)		$500

Gold Legends

Yr	Player	NM
1995 Larry Bird (500)		$700

Gold Upper Deck

Yr	Player	NM
1996 Michael Jordan (500)		$900

Mini-Cards Bronze

Yr	Player	NM
1996 Hill/Kidd (2,500)		$65
1996 Jordan (5,000)		$100

Mini-Cards Silver

Yr	Player	NM
1996 Hill/Kidd (500)		$150
1996 Michael Jordan (1,000)		$225

Mini-Cards Gold

Yr	Player	NM
1996 Michael Jordan (500)		$350

Basketball Medallions

Bronze

Yr	Player	NM
1997 Kobe Bryant (25,000)		$20
1997 Kevin Garnett (25,000)		$12
1996 Anfernee Hardaway (25,000)		$15
1997 Anfernee Hardaway (4c) (10,000)		$15
1995 Michael Jordan (25,000)		$25
1996 Scottie Pippen (25,000)		$12
1996 Dennis Rodman (GX12,500)		$20
1996 Dennis Rodman (YX12,500)		$20
1996 Dennis Rodman (3-pc.) (2,500)		$45

Silver

Yr	Player	NM
1997 Charles Barkley (5,000)		$20
1995 Larry Bird (7,500)		$35
1997 Kobe Bryant (3,000)		$40
1996 Marcus Camby (3,000)		$20
1997 Clyde Drexler (5,000)		$25
1997 Tim Duncan (3,000)		$40
1996 Kevin Garnett (7,500)		$30
1996 Anfernee Hardaway (3,000)		$30
1997 Anfernee Hardaway (4c) (5,000)		$30
1997 Grant Hill (5,000)		$30
1996 Allen Iverson (3,000)		$20
1996 Larry Johnson (7,500)		$15
1995 Michael Jordan (7,500)		$60
1998 Michael Jordan 5x MVP (4,500)		$30
1996 Shawn Kemp (7,500)		$20
1997 Stephon Marbury (3,000)		$25
1997 Hakeem Olajuwon (5,000)		$20
1998 Shaquille O'Neal (5,000)		$25
1996 Scottie Pippen (7,500)		$25
1996 Dennis Rodman (RX7,500)		$30
1996 John Stockton (7,500)		$25
1996 Nick Van Exel (7,500)		$15
1998 Keith Van Horn (3,000)		$30

Gold

Yr	Player	NM
1997 Anfernee Hardaway (4c) (1,500)		$60
1995 Michael Jordan (100)		$1,250

Gold Signature

Yr	Player	NM
1995 Anfernee Hardaway (1,500)		$90
1995 Michael Jordan (1,000)		$140
1997 Scottie Pippen (1,500)		$70
1996 Mitch Richmond (1,000)		$50

3-Piece Proof Set

Yr	Player	NM
1998 Michael Jordan 5x MVP (500)		$120

Back to Back Silver

Yr	Player	NM
1997 Garnett/Bryant (1,500)		$30

Elite Bronze

Yr	Player	NM
1997 Patrick Ewing (5,000)		$20
1997 Anfernee Hardaway (5,000)		$20
1997 Grant Hill (5,000)		$25
1997 Michael Jordan (4,500)		$25

Elite Series Silver

Yr	Player	NM
1997 Patrick Ewing (2,500)		$35
1997 Anfernee Hardaway (2,500)		$35
1997 Grant Hill (2,500)		$40
1997 Michael Jordan (2,500)		$50

Elite Series Gold

Yr	Player	NM
1997 Patrick Ewing (1,000)		$75
1997 Anfernee Hardaway (1,000)		$75
1997 Grant Hill (1,000)		$80
1997 Michael Jordan (1,000)		$90

Elite Series Gold Plated

Yr	Player	NM
1997 Patrick Ewing (500)		$70
1997 Anfernee Hardaway (500)		$70
1997 Grant Hill (500)		$75
1997 Michael Jordan (500)		$80

Elite Series Proof Set

Yr	Player	NM
1997 Patrick Ewing (350)		$140
1997 Anfernee Hardaway (350)		$140
1997 Grant Hill (350)		$160
1997 Michael Jordan (350)		$180

Extreme Medal Gold Plated

Yr	Player	NM
1998 Kobe Bryant (500)		$100

Extreme Medal 3-Piece Proof Set

Yr	Player	NM
1998 Kobe Bryant (100)		$300

Hardcourt Bronze

Yr	Player	NM
1997 Ray Allen (500)		$12
1997 Karl Malone (500)		$15
1997 Reggie Miller (500)		$12
1997 Alonzo Mourning (500)		$12
1997 Dikembe Mutumbo (500)		$12
1997 Chris Webber (500)		$12

Hardcourt Silver

Yr	Player	NM
1997 Ray Allen (250)		$20
1997 Karl Malone (250)		$25
1997 Reggie Miller (250)		$20
1997 Alonzo Mourning (250)		$20
1997 Dikembe Mutumbo (250)		$20
1997 Chris Webber (250)		$20

Hardcourt Gold

Yr	Player	NM
1997 Ray Allen (100)		$65
1997 Karl Malone (100)		$70
1997 Reggie Miller (100)		$65
1997 Alonzo Mourning (100)		$65
1997 Dikembe Mutumo (100)		$65
1997 Chris Webber (100)		$65

Magnum Bronze

Yr	Player	NM
1997 Bulls NBA Champs (1,500)		$70
1996 Michael Jordan (3,000)		$85
1998 Shaquille O'Neal (3,000)		$45

Magnum Silver

Yr	Player	NM
1997 Bulls NBA Champs (250)		$175
1996 Michael Jordan (500)		$300

Team Coins Bronze

Yr	Player	NM
1997 Bulls (4-pc set) (5,000)		$40
1997 Bulls Trio (2,500) (Jordan/Pippen/team)		$50
1997 Bulls Eastern Confer. (1,500)		$20
1997 Bulls NBA (Champs (7,500)		$20
1997 Bulls Central Champs (1,500)		$12
1998 Bulls Trio (1,998) (Jordan/Pippen/team)		$30
1998 Heat Atlantic Champs (1,500)		$12
1998 Jazz Midwest Champs (1,500)		$12
1998 Lakers Pacific Champs (1,500)		$12
1997 Rockets Trio (2,500) (Olajuwon/Barkley/Drexler)		$30

Team Coins Silver

Yr.	Player	NM
1996 Bulls/Sonics Set (500)		$70
1996 Bulls 70 Wins (2,500)		$65
1996 Bulls Win Division (1,000)		$45
1996 Bulls Win Conference (5,000)		$45
1996 Bull Champs (5,000)		$45
1996 Bulls Win Finals (7,500)		$45
1997 Bulls Eastern Confer. (750)		$45
1997 Bulls NBA Champs (1,500)		$60
1998 Bulls Central Champs (500)		$30
1998 Bulls Eastern Champs (2,500)		$30
1997 Jazz West Confer. (1,500)		$25
1998 Jazz Midwest Champs (500)		$30
1998 Jazz Western Champs (2,500)		$30
1998 Bulls 6x Champs (5,000)		$30
1998 Bulls 6x Champs (.5lb 1,998)		$130
1996 Magic Team (5,000)		$35
1996 Magic Win Division (1,000)		$20
1996 Sonics Win Confer. (5,000)		$20
1996 Sonics Win Division (1,000)		$20
1996 Spurs Win Division (1,000)		$20
1998 Heat Atlantic Champs (500)		$30

Team Coins Gold

Yr.	Player	NM
1998 Bulls Eastern Champs (1,000)		$65

1998 Bulls Champs 1 lb. (9) $10,000
1998 Jazz Western Champs (1,000) $85

Team Coins
Gold Signature

Yr.	Player	NM
1996 Bulls (2-pc) (1,500)		$125
1997 Bulls East Conference (750)		$45
1997 Bulls NBA Champs (1,500)		$60
1998 Bulls Central Champ (100)		$65
1998 Bulls Champs 1 lb. (9)		$10,000
1997 Chicago Bulls (7,500)		$60
1998 Heat Atlantic Champs (100)		$65
1997 Jazz West Conference (750)		$45
1998 Jazz Midwest Champs (100)		$65
1997 Utah Jazz (7,500)		$60
1998 Lakers Pacific Champs (100)		$65

Football Cards
Bronze Legends

Yr.	Player	NM
1995 Joe Namath (5,000)		$60
1995 Roger Staubach (2,500)		$75
1995 Johnny Unitas (5,000)		$65

Bronze Pinnacle

Yr.	Player	NM
1997 Kerry Collins (1,500)		$35
1995 Dan Marino (5,000)		$150
1997 Dan Marino (PZ, ST) (3,500)		$80
1995 Erict Rhett (2,500)		$30
1996 Jerry Rice (2,500)		$50
1996 Rashan Salaam (2,500)		$30
1995 Heath Shuler (2,500)		$30

Bronze Score

Yr.	Player	NM
1995 Troy Aikman (5,000)		$80
1995 Drew Bledsoe (5,000)		$75
1996 Brett Favre (SE) (1,500)		$80
1996 Curtis Martin (2,500)		$80
1996 Barry Sanders (1,500)		$100
1995 Emmitt Smith (5,000)		$150
1996 Kordell Stewart (2,500)		$80

Bronze Topps

Yr.	Player	NM
1993 Troy Aikman (2,500)		$150
1994 Marcus Allen (549)		$55
1994 Jerome Bettis (1,566)		$75
1994 Drew Bledsoe (2,500)		$125
1993 John Elway (2,020)		$100
1995 Marshall Faulk (2,500)		$50
1994 Brett Favre (714)		$100
1994 Michael Irvin (1,833)		$50
1994 Jim Kelly (1,165)		$60
1993 Dan Marino (2,500)		$300
1995 Natrone Means (1,026)		$30
1994 Rick Mirer (1,982)		$30
1994 Jerry Rice (2,500)		$125
1994 Barry Sanders (2,500)		$110
1994 Deion Sanders (1,033)		$70
1994 Sterling Sharpe (901)		$50
1994 Emmitt Smith (2,500)		$225
1994 Lawrence Taylor (1,630)		$50
1993 Steve Young (2,500)		$110

Bronze Upper Deck

Yr.	Player	NM
1994 Joe Montana (5,000)		$150

Silver Legends

Yr.	Player	NM
1995 Joe Namath (1,000)		$235
1995 Roger Staubach (500)		$235
1995 Johnny Unitas (1,000)		$235

Silver Pinnacle

Yr.	Player	NM
1997 Kerry Collins (250)		$175
1995 Dan Marino (1,000)		$600
1997 Dan Marino (PZ, ST) (500)		$250
1995 Erict Rhett (500)		$175
1996 Jerry Rice (500)		$235
1996 Rashan Salaam (500)		$175
1995 Heath Shuler (500)		$200

Silver Score

Yr.	Player	NM
1995 Troy Aikman (1,000)		$235
1995 Drew Bledsoe (1,000)		$265
1996 Brett Favre (SE) (250)		$300
1996 Curtis Martin (500)		$250
1996 Barry Sanders (250)		$250
1995 Emmitt Smith (1,000)		$275
1996 Kordell Stewart (500)		$235

Silver Topps

Yr.	Player	NM
1993 Troy Aikman (500)		$500
1994 Marcus Allen (88)		$250
1994 Jerome Bettis (301)		$250
1994 Drew Bledsoe (500)		$450
1993 John Elway (500)		$300
1995 Marshall Faulk (530)		$350
1994 Brett Favre (110)		$325
1994 Michael Irvin (509)		$350
1994 Jim Kelly (419)		$235
1993 Dan Marino (500)		$800
1995 Natrone Means (136)		$235
1994 Rick Mirer (384)		$235
1994 Jerry Rice (750)		$700
1994 Barry Sanders (750)		$500
1994 Deion Sanders (191)		$235
1994 Sterling Sharpe (171)		$235
1994 Emmitt Smith (750)		$1,000
1994 Lawrence Taylor (585)		$235
1993 Steve Young (500)		$450

Silver Upper Deck

Yr.	Player	NM
1994 Joe Montana (1,000)		$400

Gold Pinnacle

Yr.	Player	NM
1995 Dan Marino (500)		$700
1997 Dan Marino (PZ, ST) (250)		$400

Gold Score

Yr.	Player	NM
1995 Emmitt Smith (500)		$750

Gold Topps

Yr.	Player	NM
1993 Troy Aikman (375)		$1,000

Yr. Player	NM
1994 Drew Bledsoe (375)	$1,000
1993 Dan Marino (375)	$1,250
1994 Jerry Rice (375)	$1,000
1994 Barry Sanders (375)	$850
1994 Emmitt Smith (375)	$1,700
1993 Steve Young (375)	$900

Gold Upper Deck

Yr. Player	NM
1994 Joe Montana (500)	$1,000

Football Medallions

Bronze

Yr. Player	NM
1995 Troy Aikman (25,000)	$20
1994 Drew Bledsoe (25,000)	$18
1998 Mark Brunell (15,000)	$15
1998 John Elway (25,000)	$20
1997 Brett Favre (25,000)	$15
1996 Brett Favre (25,000)	$20
1997 Brett Favre (MVP) (15,000)	$15
1994 Dan Marino (25,000)	$20
1995 Joe Montana (25,000)	$18
1999 Randy Moss ROY (25,000)	$15
1994 Jerry Rice (25,000)	$15
1996 Deion Sanders (2,500)	$15
1994 Emmitt Smith (25,000)	$20
1996 Steve Young (22,500)	$12
1994 Steve Young (25,000)	$15
1997 Dan Marino (25,000)	$20

Silver

Yr. Player	NM
1994 Troy Aikman (7,500)	$40
1996 Jerome Bettis (Rams) (2,100)	$30
1996 Jerome Bettis (Steelers) (5,400)	$30
1994 Drew Bledsoe (7,500)	$50
1996 Ki-Jana Carter (7,500)	$15
1996 Kerry Collins (7,500)	$15
1996 Trent Dilfer (7,500)	$20
1995 John Elway (7,500)	$40
1994 Marshall Faulk (7,500)	$30
1995 Brett Favre (7,500)	$50
1997 Brett Favre (MVP) (3,500)	$40
1999 Doug Flutie (5,000)	$30
1996 Eddie George (5,000)	$40
1997 Terry Glenn (7,500)	$30
1995 Michael Irvin (7,500)	$20
1995 Jim Kelly (7,500)	$30
1998 Ryan Leaf (5,000)	$30
1998 Peyton Manning (5,000)	$30
1994 Dan Marino (7,500)	$50
1996 Curtis Martin (7,500)	$30
1996 Natrone Means (7,500)	$20
1994 Rick Mirer (7,500)	$10
1995 Joe Montana (7,500)	$40
1998 Randy Moss (5,000)	$30
1999 Randy Moss ROY (5,000)	$30
1996 Joe Namath (7,500)	$30
1994 Jerry Rice (7,500)	$35
1996 Rashan Salaam (7,500)	$15
1995 Barry Sanders (7,500)	$50
1994 Deion Sanders (49ers) (2,690)	$30
1994 Deion Sanders (Dallas) (4,810)	$35
1995 Junior Seau (7,500)	$25
1995 Heath Shuler (7,000)	$10
1994 Emmitt Smith (7,500)	$50
1996 Kordell Stewart (7,500)	$40
1997 Reggie White (7,500)	$25

Yr. Player	NM
1996 Rod Woodson (7,500)	$25
1994 Steve Young (7,500)	$35

Gold

Yr. Player	NM
1995 Dan Marino (100)	$1,350
1995 Joe Montana (100)	$1,350
1994 Emmitt Smith (100)	$1,350

Gold Signature

Yr. Player	NM
1996 Troy Aikman (1,500)	$90
1997 Drew Bledsoe (1,500)	$80
1996 John Elway (1,500)	$85
1996 Brett Favre (1,500)	$100
1996 Dan Marino (1,500)	$100
1999 Randy Moss ROY (1,500)	$50
1996 Jerry Rice (1,500)	$75
1998 Barry Sanders (1,500)	$50
1996 Emmitt Smith (1,500)	$100

Elite Bronze

Yr. Player	NM
1997 Troy Aikman (4,500)	$20
1997 Dan Marino (4,500)	$20

Elite Series Silver

Yr. Player	NM
1997 Troy Aikman (2,500)	$40
1997 Dan Marino (2,500)	$40

Elite Series Gold

Yr. Player	NM
1997 Troy Aikman (1,000)	$80
1997 Dan Marino (1,000)	$80

Elite Series Gold Plated

Yr. Player	NM
1997 Troy Aikman (500)	$75
1997 Dan Marino (500)	$75

Elite Series Proof Set

Yr. Player	NM
1997 Troy Aikman (350)	$150
1997 Dan Marino (350)	$150

Football Coin Bronze

Yr. Player	NM
1997 Dan Marino (25,000)	$20

Football Coin Silver

Yr. Player	NM
1996 Troy Aikman (4,500)	$50
1996 Brett Favre (4,500)	$60
1996 Dan Marino (7,500)	$60
1996 Jerry Rice (7,000)	$50
1996 Emmitt Smith (7,000)	$60

Football Coin Silver with Earring

Yr. Player	NM
1996 Troy Aikman (500)	$150
1996 Brett Favre (500)	$150
1996 Jerry Rice (500)	$150
1996 Emmitt Smith (500)	$150

Magnum Bronze

Yr. Player	NM
1997 Brett Favre (2,500)	$50

1997 Dan Marino (2,500) $50
1997 Barry Sanders (2,500) $55
1997 Emmitt Smith (2,500) $45
1997 John Elway (2,500) $40

Magnum Silver

Yr.	Player	NM
1997 Brett Favre (500)		$150
1997 Dan Marino (500)		$160
1997 Barry Sanders (500)		$160
1997 Emmitt Smith (500)		$150
1998 John Elway (500)		$130

Magnum Gold

Yr.	Player	NM
1997 Brett Favre (250)		$250
1997 Dan Marino (250)		$260
1997 Barry Sanders (250)		$260
1997 Emmitt Smith (250)		$250

Magnum Gold Signature

Yr.	Player	NM
1998 Barry Sanders (250)		$250
1998 Emmitt Smith (250)		$250

Bronze Medallion with Lithograph

Yr.	Player	NM
1997 Troy Aikman (2,500)		$50
1997 John Elway (2,500)		$50
1997 Brett Favre (2,500)		$50
1998 Brett Favre (2,500)		$40
1998 Favre/White/Brooks (2,500)		$65
1997 Mark Brunell (2,500)		$65
1997 Dan Marino (2,500)		$55
1997 Jerry Rice (2,500)		$50
1997 Barry Sanders (2,500)		$50
1997 Emmitt Smith (2,500)		$50
1997 Steve Young (2,500)		$50

Bronze Medallion with Photo

Yr.	Player	NM
1999 John Elway (2,500)		$65

Bronze Medallion with Motion Card

Yr	Player	NM
1998 Troy Aikman (2,500)		$35
1998 Drew Bledsoe (1,500)		$35
1998 Terrell Davis (1,500)		$40
1998 Brett Favre (2,500)		$40
1998 Eddie George (1,500)		$35
1998 Dan Marino (2,500)		$35
1998 Emmitt Smith (2,500)		$35
1998 Kordell Stewart (1,500)		$45

Bronze Medallion with Phone Card

Yr.	Player	NM
1997 Drew Bledsoe (2,500)		$35
1997 John Elway (2,500)		$40
1997 Brett Favre (2,500)		$40
1998 Dan Marino (2,500)		$40
1998 Jerry Rice (2,500)		$35
1998 Barry Sanders (2,500)		$35
1998 Kordell Stewart (2,500)		$35
1998 Super Bowl XXXII (250)		$65
1998 Steve Young (2,500)		$35

Two-Tone Medallion with Ring Weight

Yr.	Player	NM
1998 Troy Aikman (2,500)		$60
1998 Mark Brunell (2,500)		$60
1998 Terrell Davis (2,500)		$60
1998 John Elway (2,500)		$60
1998 Dan Marino (2,500)		$60
1998 Jerry Rice (2,500)		$60
1998 Emmitt Smith (2,500)		$60
1999 Kordell Stewart (2,500)		$60

Back-to-Back Silver

Yr.	Player	NM
1998 Barry Sanders/Favre (1,500)		$40
1998 J. Bettis/K. Stewart (1,500)		$35
1998 John Elway/Terrell Davis (1,500)		$40

Mini-Mints Silver

Yr.	Player	NM
1998 John Elway (5,000)		$25
1998 Brett Favre (5,000)		$20
1998 Dan Marino (5,000)		$20
1998 Jerry Rice (5,000)		$20
1998 Emmitt Smith (5,000)		$20

Mini-Mints Silver with Gold Overlay

Yr.	Player	NM
1998 John Elway (1,000)		$35
1998 Brett Favre (1,000)		$35
1998 Dan Marino (1,000)		$35
1998 Jerry Rice (1,000)		$35
1998 Emmitt Smith (1,000)		$35

Team Coins Bronze

Yr.	Player	NM
1996 49er Trio (2,500) (Montana/Young/Rice)		$50
1996 Cowboy Trio (2,500) (Aikman/Emmitt/Sanders)		$55
1997 Packer Trio (2,500) (Favre/White/Chmura)		$45
1997 Packers SB XXXII (25,000)		$25

Team Coins Silver

Yr.	Team	NM
1997 49er Div Champs (2,500)		$25
1999 Bronco Div Champs (2,500)		$30
1999 Broncos AFC Champs (5,000)		$30
1999 Cowboys Div Champs (2,500)		$30
1999 Falcons NFC Champs (5,000)		$30
1997 Giants Div Champs (2,500)		$20
1999 Jaguars Div Champs (2,500)		$30
1999 Jets Div Champs (2,500)		$30
1997 Packers Div Champs (2,500)		$25
1997 Packers SB XXXI (10,000)		$40
1998 Packers NFC Champs (2,500)		$30
1996 Ravens Inaugural (1,500)		$35
1999 Vikings Div Champs (2,500)		$30

Team Coins Gold

Yr.	Team	NM
1997 49er Div Champs (500)		$65
1998 Bronco AFC Champs (500)		$65
1999 Broncos AFC Champs (2,500)		$70
1999 Falcons NFC Champs (2,500)		$70
1997 Packer Div Champs (500)		$65
1997 Packer SB XXXI (2,500)		$60
1998 Packer NFC Champs (500)		$65

Miscellaneous Bronze

Yr.	Player	NM
1997 Balfour SB XXXI (25,000)		$30
1998 Balfour SB XXXII (20,000)		$35
1999 Balfour SB XXXIII (10,000)		$35

Miscellaneous Silver

Yr.	Player	NM
1999 AFC/NFC Champs Broncos/Falcons (500)		$60
1997 Balfour SB XXXI (7,500)		$50
1998 Balfour SB XXXII (7,500)		$50
1999 Balfour SB XXXIII (7,500)		$50

Miscellaneous Gold

Yr.	Player	NM
1999 AFC/NFC Champs Broncos/Falcons (250)		$140
1997 Balfour SB XXXI (2,500)		$80
1998 Balfour SB XXXII (2,500)		$80
1999 Balfour SB XXXIII (2,500)		$80

Miscellaneous

Gold Signature

Yr.	Player	NM
1998 Balfour SB XXXII (7,500)		$69
1999 Balfour SB XXXIII (7,500)		$60

Hockey Cards

Bronze

Yr.	Player	NM
1994 Ray Bourque (634)		$75
1996 Martin Brodeur (1,500)		$50
1994 Pavel Bure (1,519)		$75
1996 Alexander Daigle (1,500)		$50
1994 Serge Fedorov (914)		$100
1994 Doug Gilmour (461)		$100
1993 Wayne Gretzky (5,000)		$210
1993 Gordie Howe (5,000)		$75
1996 Bobby Hull (2,500		$50
1994 Brett Hull (1,202)		$75
1995 Jaromir Jagr (2,500)		$75
1995 Paul Karyia (1,500)		$50
1996 Pat LaFontaine (1,500)		$50
1993 Mario Lemieux (3,557)		$150
1997 Mario Lemieux (1,500)		$75
1994 Eric Lindros (2,668)		$90
1994 Mark Messier (1,034)		$75
1995 Cam Neely (1,500)		$50
1995 Bobby Orr (5,000)		$50
1994 Felix Potvin (9,020)		$100
1995 Jeremy Roenick (2,500)		$50
1994 Patrick Roy (1,986)		$110
1994 Teemu Selenne (537)		$100
1994 Steve Yzerman (926)		$125

Silver

Yr.	Player	NM
1994 Ray Bourque (128)		$250
1996 Martin Brodeur (250)		$235
1994 Pavel Bure (414)		$250
1996 Alexander Daigle (250)		$235
1994 Serge Fedorov (208)		$300
1994 Doug Gilmour (101)		$275
1993 Wayne Gretzky (1,000)		$850
1995 Gordie Howe (1,000)		$235
1996 Bobby Hull (500)		$235
1994 Brett Hull (500)		$350
1995 Jaromir Jagr (500)		$250
1995 Paul Karyia (250)		$235
1996 Pat LaFontaine (250)		$235
1996 Mario Lemieux (999)		$325
1997 Mario Lemieux (250)		$250
1994 Eric Lindros (694)		$300
1994 Mark Messier (280)		$300
1995 Cam Neely (250)		$235
1995 Bobby Orr (1,000)		$235
1994 Felix Potvin (210)		$250
1995 Jeremy Roenick (500)		$235
1994 Patrick Roy (500)		$425
1994 Teemu Selenne (131)		$275
1994 Steve Yzerman (233)		$275

Hockey Medallions

Bronze

Yr.	Player	NM
1996 Mario Lemieux (25,000)		$20
1997 Steve Yzerman (25,000)		$15

Silver

Yr.	Player	NM
1996 Ray Bourque (5,000)		$25
1994 Pavel Bure (5,000)		$30
1994 Serge Fedorov (5,000)		$30
1997 Peter Forsberg (5,000)		$25
1998 Dominik Hasek (5,000)		$30
1996 Brett Hull (5,000)		$25
1996 Jaromir Jagr (5,000)		$35
1994 Mario Lemieux (5,000)		$40
1995 Eric Lindros (5,000)		$40
1995 Bobby Orr (3,500)		$20
1995 Bobby Orr (error) (1,500)		$40
1996 Orr & Bourque (500)		$50
1996 Chris Osgood (5,000)		$30
1996 Patrick Roy (5,000)		$30
1997 Joe Sakic (5,000)		$25
1996 Teemu Selanne (5,000)		$25
1996 John Vanbiesbrouck (5,000)		$30
1996 Steve Yzerman (5,000)		$30

Goal Signature

Yr.	Player	NM
1997 Jaromir Jagr (1,000)		$60
1996 Mario Lemieux (1,000)		$90
1996 Eric Lindros (1,000)		$85
1997 Bobby Orr (1,500)		$60
1997 Patrick Roy (1,000)		$55

Elite Bronze

Yr.	Player	NM
1998 Jaromir Jagr (3,000)		$25
1998 Paul Karyia (3,000)		$20
1997 Mario Lemieux (3,000)		$30
1997 Eric Lindros (3,000)		$25
1997 Mark Messier (3,000)		$25
1997 Patrick Roy (3,000)		$30

Elite Series Silver

Yr.	Player	NM
1998 Jaromir Jagr (1,000)		$45
1998 Paul Karyia (1,000)		$40
1997 Mario Lemieux (1,000)		$50
1997 Eric Lindros (1,000)		$50
1997 Mark Messier (1,000)		$50
1997 Patrick Roy (1,000)		$40

Elite Series Gold

Yr.	Player	NM
1998 Jaromir Jagr (250)		$80
1998 Paul Karyia (250)		$80
1997 Mario Lemieux (250)		$90
1997 Eric Lindros (250)		$85
1997 Mark Messier (250)		$85
1997 Patrick Roy (250)		$80

Elite Series Proof

Yr.	Player	NM
1998 Paul Karyia (150)		$150
1997 Mario Lemieux (150)		$185
1997 Eric Lindros (150)		$175
1997 Mark Messier (150)		$175
1997 Patrick Roy (150)		$175

Magnum Bronze

Yr.	Team	NM
1996 Avalanche (1,000)		$55
1987 Red Wings Stan. Cup (1,500)		$45
1998 Red Wings Stan. Cup (1,500)		$45

Magnum Silver

Yr.	Team	NM
1996 Avalanche (250)		$150
1997 Red Wings Stan. Cup (250)		$150
1998 Red Wings Stan. Cup (250)		$150

Team Coins Bronze

Yr.	Team	NM
1997 Red Wings Trio (25,000) (Yzerman/Federov/team)		$40
1997 Penguins Trio (25,000) (Lemieux/Jagr/team)		$35

Team Coins Silver

Yr.	Team	NM
1998 Capitals Eastern (2,500)		$30

Yr.	Team	NM
1997 Red Wings Stan. Cup (5,000)		$25
1998 Red Wings Western (2,500)		$30
1998 Red Wings S.C. (5,000)		$30
1998 Red Wings S.C. (5lb. 1,998)		$30

Team Coins Gold

Yr.	Team	NM
1998 Captals Eastern (1,000)		$85
1998 Red Wings S.C. (1lb. 9)		$10,000
1998 Red Wings Western (1,000)		$65

Racing Cards

Bronze

Yr.	Driver	NM
1994 Dale Earnhardt (5,000)		$100
1985 Bill Elliot (5,000)		$50
1994 Jeff Gordon (5,000)		$100
1994 Ernie Irvan (5,000)		$50
1995 Mark Martin (5,000)		$60
1994 Rusty Wallace (2,500)		$60

Silver

Yr.	Driver	NM
1994 Dale Earnhardt (1,000)		$300
1995 Bill Elliot (1,000)		$235
1994 Jeff Gordon (1,000)		$250
1994 Ernie Irvan (1,000)		$235
1995 Mark Martin (1,000)		$235
1994 Rusty Wallace (500)		$235

Gold

Yr.	Driver	NM
1994 Dale Earnhardt (500)		$1,000

Chapter 10

PRESS PINS AND BADGES

Press pins, which have been issued since 1911, are distributed to members of the media by the host teams for World Series and baseball All-Star games. The lapel pins provide the reporters legitimate access to cover the game.

Enamel pins have replaced the fairly ornate pins, with ribbons and medals, of the early years. Many are quite simple in their designs, which is a factor in the value of the pin; generally, the better-looking, better-conditioned pins are more valuable. Also, pins for the teams which lost usually cost less than those of the winners. But rarity and the reputation of the team are the main factors. Each team, except the 1918 Chicago Cubs, has issued a pin.

Phantom pins are those which are created by teams which might end up in post-season play, but don't, by failing to make the World Series; teams must decide to produce pins before the season is over. Several major league teams already have unused, undated pins available for future use.

All-Star pins first appeared in 1938, skipping 1939, 1940, 1942, 1944 and 1945, and then running consecutively since 1946. There are usually fewer All-Star pins available for collectors,

because not as many have been made; fewer reporters cover this game compared to the number who cover the World Series.

National Baseball Hall of Fame pins were first produced in 1982 by L.B. Balfour Co., to honor Hall of Fame inductees. Those players have their names featured on the pins, which are given to the media and dignitaries who attend the induction ceremonies.

The following pin listings show the year, the manufacturer, type of fastener, color and value.

In general, here's a price range for World Series pins for each decade:

1910s	$2,500-$18,000
1920s	$375-$4,000
1930s	$225-$5,000
1940s	$250-$2,400
1950s	$125-$500
1960s	$50-$300
1970s	$50-$375
1980s	$25-$175
1990s	$50-$150

Press Pins

World Series Pins

1911 Philadelphia Athletics: Allen A. Kerr; brooch; blue ....$13,850-$18,000

1912 New York Giants: Whitehead & Hoag; brooch; blue ....$6,500-$12,500

1912 Boston Red Sox: Unknown; threaded post; red ....$3,500-$5,000

1913 New York Giants: Whitehead & Hoag; threaded post; blue ....$5,000-$10,000

1913 Philadelphia Athletics: J.E. Caldwell; brooch; blue/green ....$6,000-$6,500

1914 Boston Braves: Bent & Bush; threaded post; blue $5,000-$5,500

1914 Philadelphia Athletics: J.E. Caldwell; brooch; blue/white/green ....$6,500-$11,000

1915 Philadelphia Phillies: J.E. Caldwell; brooch; red ....$6,000-$11,000

1915 Boston Red Sox: Bent & Bush; threaded post; gold..................$4,000-$5,500

1916 Brooklyn Dodgers: Dieges & Clust; threaded post; blue/white ....$4,000-$4,400

1916 Boston Red Sox: Bent & Bush; threaded post; red/blue ....$4,000-$5,000

1917 New York Giants: Unknown; brooch; gold ....$4,500-$7,000

1917 Chicago White Sox, with banner: Greenduck; threaded post; blue ....$4,000-$9,500

1918 Boston Red Sox: Bent & Bush; threaded post; gold ....$3,000-$5,500

1919 Cincinnati Reds: Gustave Fox; threaded post; gold$2,500-$4,750

1919 Chicago White Sox, with banner: Greenduck; threaded post; gold ....$5,000-$12,000

1920 Brooklyn Dodgers: Unknown; threaded post; red .$2,500-$3,000

1920 Cleveland Indians, enamel: Unknown; threaded post; green/white ....$1,500-$3,000

1920 Cleveland Indians celluloid button: Unknown; safety brooch; black/white ....$2,500-$3,500

1921 New York Yankees/Giants: Whitehead & Hoag; brooch; blue/white ....$2,000-$2,500

1922 New York Yankees/Giants: Whitehead & Hoag; brooch; blue/white ....$3,000-$4,000

1923 New York Yankees: Dieges & Clust; threaded post; red/white/blue..................$2,300-$3,800

1924 New York Giants: Dieges & Clust; threaded post; blue ....$845-$1,500

1924 Washington Senators: Dieges & Clust; threaded post; red/white/blue ....$1,000-$1,500

1925 Pittsburgh Pirates: Whitehead & Hoag; threaded post;
   black/white..$1,500-$2,500
1925 Washington Senators: Dieges & Clust; threaded post;
   blue...$1,375-$2,000
1926 St. Louis Cardinals: Unknown; threaded post; red $1,300-$2,400
1926 New York Yankees: Dieges & Clust; threaded post;
   red/white/blue ....$1,200-$1,500
1927 Pittsburgh Pirates: Whitehead & Hoag; threaded post;
   black/white...$1,100-$2,000
1927 New York Yankees: Dieges & Clust; threaded post;
   red/white/blue ....$2,000-$2,300
1928 St. Louis Cardinals: St. Louis Button; threaded post;
   red/white/blue ....$875-$1,200
1928 New York Yankees: Dieges & Clust; threaded post;
   red/white/blue ....$1,850-$2,400
1929 Chicago Cubs: Hipp & Coburn; threaded post;
   red/white/blue ....$1,500-$2,350
1929 Philadelphia Athletics: Unknown; threaded post;
   blue/white ....$375-$800
1930 St. Louis Cardinals: St. Louis Button; threaded post;
   red/white/blue ....$500-$1,000
1930 Philadelphia Athletics: Unknown; threaded post;
   blue/white ....$3,000-$5,000
1931 St. Louis Cardinals: St. Louis Button; threaded post;
   red/white/blue ....$650-$900
1931 Philadelphia Athletics: Unknown; threaded post;
   blue/white ....$1,300-$1,500
1932 Chicago Cubs: Dieges & Clust; threaded post;
   black/white...$1,900-$2,200
1932 New York Yankees: Dieges & Clust; threaded post;
   gold ....$1,000-$1,200
1933 New York Giants: Dieges & Clust; threaded post;
   red/green/blue ....$235-$700
1933 Washington Senators: Dieges & Clust; threaded post;
   gold..$700-$950
1934 St. Louis Cardinals: St. Louis button; threaded post;
   red/white...$650-$800
1934 Detroit Tigers: Dieges & Clust; threaded post;
   black/white...$600-$750
1935 Chicago Cubs: S.D. Childs; brooch; red/white/blue $2,200-$3,000
1935 Detroit Tigers: Unknown; threaded post; black.......$600-$800
1936 New York Giants: Dieges & Clust; threaded post;
   black/white/orange...$275-$400
1936 New York Yankees: Dieges & Clust; threaded post;
   red/white/blue ....$550-$800
1937 New York Giants: Dieges & Clust; threaded post;
   black/orange ....$225-$350
1937 New York Yankees: Dieges & Clust; threaded post;
   red/white/blue ....$450-$600
1938 Chicago Cubs: Lambert Bros.; brooch;
   red/white/blue ....$1,400-$2,250
1938 New York Yankees: Dieges & Clust; threaded post;
   red/white/blue ....$475-$750
1939 Cincinnati Reds: Bastian Bros.; threaded post, brooch;
   red/white/blue ....$275-$425
1939 New York Yankees: Dieges & Clust; threaded post;
   red/white/blue ....$400-$750
1940 Cincinnati Reds: Bastian Bros.; threaded post, brooch;
   red/white/blue ....$350-$425

1940 Detroit Tigers: Unknown; threaded post; gold........$475-$650
1941 Brooklyn Dodgers: Dieges & Clust; threaded post;
   red/white/blue ....$450-$725
1941 New York Yankees: Dieges & Clust; threaded post;
   red/white/blue ....$275-$475
1942 St. Louis Cardinals: St. Louis button; safety brooch;
   red/white/black ....$2,000-$2,400
1942 New York Yankees: Dieges & Clust; threaded post, brooch;
   silver..$275-$400
1943 St. Louis: St. Louis button; safety brooch;
   red/black/white ....$1,000-$2,000
1943 New York Yankees: Dieges & Clust; threaded post, brooch;
   silver..$300-$500
1944 St. Louis Cardinals: St. Louis button; threaded post;
   copper ....$450-$575
1944 St. Louis Browns: St. Louis button; threaded post;
   copper ....$500-$575
1945 Chicago Cubs: Unknown; threaded post;
   red/white/blue ....$400-$550
1945 Detroit Tigers: Unknown; threaded post; red/blue..$400-$500
1946 St. Louis Cardinals: St. Louis button; threaded post;
   red/white/silver ....$350-$500
1946 Boston Red Sox: Balfour; threaded post; red/white ....$300-$575
1947 Brooklyn Dodgers: Dieges & Clust; threaded post, brooch;
   blue ....$400-$800
1947 New York Yankees: Dieges & Clust; threaded post;
   red/white/blue ....$500-$600
1948 Boston Braves: Balfour; threaded post; red/white/
   copper ....$400-$475
1948 Cleveland Indians: Balfour; threaded post; red/white
   black...$250-$400
1949 Brooklyn Dodgers: Dieges & Clust; threaded post, brooch;
   blue ....$350-$400
1949 New York Yankees: Dieges & Clust; threaded post, brooch
   red/white/blue ....$300-$400
1950 Philadelphia Phillies: Martin; needle post; red/silver ...$250-$350
1950 New York Yankees: Dieges and Clust; threaded post, brooch
   red/white/blue ....$250-$375
1951 New York Giants: Dieges & Clust; threaded post;
   black/white ....$150-$175
1951 New York Yankees: Dieges & Clust; threaded post, brooch;
   red/white/blue ....$125-$175
1952 Brooklyn Dodgers: Dieges & Clust; threaded post, brooch;
   red/blue ....$300-$400
1952 New York Yankees: Balfour; threaded post, brooch;
   red/white/blue ....$200-$300
1953 Brooklyn Dodgers: Dieges & Clust; threaded post, brooch;
   white/blue ....$275-$350
1953 New York Yankees: Balfour; threaded post and brooch;
   red/white/blue ....$250-$325
1954 New York Giants: Dieges and Clust; threaded post;
   black/white ....$150-$200
1954 Cleveland Indians: Balfour; threaded post; red/white/blue/
   black...$250-$300
1955 Brooklyn Dodgers: Dieges & Clust; threaded post, brooch;
   silver/white/blue ....$500-$800
1955 New York Yankees: Balfour; threaded post, brooch;
   red/white/blue ....$125-$275

1956 Brooklyn Dodgers: Dieges & Clust; clasps; silver/white/
blue .... $500-$750
1956 New York Yankees: Balfour; threaded post, brooch;
red/white/blue .... $200-$300
1957 Milwaukee Braves: Balfour; threaded post; copper/
red .... $150-$200
1957 New York Yankees: Balfour; threaded post, brooch
red/white/blue .... $150-$200
1958 Milwaukee Braves: Balfour; threaded post; black/
white .... $200-$275
1958 New York Yankees: Balfour; threaded post, brooch, white/
blue .... $175-$200
1959 Los Angeles Dodgers: Balfour; threaded post, charm, brooch;
white/blue .... $125-$250
1959 Chicago White Sox: Balfour; threaded post, brooch;
blue/green .... $175-$275
1960 Pittsburgh Pirates: Josten; threaded post; black/
white .... $175-$250
1960 New York Yankees: Balfour; threaded post, brooch white/
blue .... $100-$150
1961 Cincinnati Reds: Balfour; threaded post, charm
red/white/blue .... $100-$175
1961 New York Yankees: Balfour; threaded post, brooch;
red/white/blue .... $125-$225
1962 San Francisco Giants: Balfour; threaded post; white .. $200-$275
1962 New York Yankees: Balfour; threaded post, brooch;
red/white/blue .... $100-$150
1963 Los Angeles Dodgers: Balfour; threaded post; blue.... $125-$150
1963 New York Yankees: Balfour; needle post, brooch;
red/white/blue .... $100-$175
1964 St. Louis Cardinals: Josten; threaded post, brooch;
red .... $125-$200
1964 New York Yankees: Balfour; needle post; red/white/
blue .... $175-$200
1965 Los Angeles Dodgers: Balfour; needle post, charm;
blue .... $50-$150
1965 Minnesota Twins: Balfour; needle post; red/white/blue . $50-$125
1966 Los Angeles Dodgers: Balfour; needle post, charm;
blue .... $50-$150
1966 Baltimore Orioles: Balfour; needle post, clasp, charm, brooch;
black/white/orange...................................... $175-$200
1967 St. Louis Cardinals: Balfour; needle post, charms;
red/white/black .... $75-$100
1967 Boston Red Sox: Balfour; needle post, charm; red/white/
blue .... $150-$200
1968 St. Louis Cardinals: Balfour; needle post, charms;
red/white/black... $75-$125
1968 Detroit Tigers: Balfour; needle post, charms; blue . $125-$200
1969 New York Mets: Balfour; needle post, charm; blue/
orange .... $200-$300
1969 Baltimore Orioles: Balfour; needle post, charms, clasp,
brooch; black/white/orange.......................... $150-$200
1970 Cincinnati Reds: G.B. Miller; needle post, charms;
red/white/black... $125-$150
1970 Baltimore Orioles: Jenkins; needle post, clasp, charm,
brooch; black/white/orange.......................... $100-$150
1971 Pittsburgh Pirates: Balfour; needle post; black......... $75-$150
1971 Baltimore Orioles: Balfour; needle post, clasp, brooch;
black/white/orange...................................... $100-$150

1972 Cincinnati Reds: Balfour; needle post, charm; red/
white .... $100-$150
1972 Oakland A's: Balfour; needle post, charm; green/white.$125-$250
1973 New York Mets: Balfour; needle post, charm; orange/
blue .... $125-$150
1973 Oakland A's: Josten; needle post, charms; green/
white .... $200-$275
1974 Los Angeles Dodgers: Balfour; needle post, charms;
blue .... $125-$150
1974 Oakland A's: Josten; needle post; green/white ...... $300-$375
1975 Cincinnati Reds: Balfour; needle post, charms; red ..... $100-$200
1975 Boston Red Sox: Balfour; needle post, charms; red/
white.. $125-$200
1976 Cincinnati Reds: Balfour; needle post, charms; red$125-$175
1976 New York Yankees: Balfour; needle post; red/white/
blue .... $125-$175
1977 Los Angeles Dodgers: Balfour; needle post, charms;
red/white/blue... $125-$150
1977 New York Yankees: Balfour; needle post, charms; blue $75-$125
1978 Los Angeles Dodgers: Balfour; needle post, charms;
blue/white .... $75-$100
1978 New York Yankees: Balfour; needle post, charms; red/
white/blue .... $50-$125
1979 Pittsburgh Pirates: Balfour; needle post; gold .... $50-$125
1979 Baltimore Orioles: Balfour; needle post, clasp, charm, brooch;
white/black/orange .... $50-$100
1980 Philadelphia Phillies: Balfour; needle post; gold .... $50-$75
1980 Kansas City Royals: Green Co.; needle post, charms;
blue/white .... $50-$175
1981 Los Angeles Dodgers: Balfour; needle post, charms;
red/white/blue... $50-$100
1981 New York Yankees: Balfour; needle post; blue .... $75-$100
1982 St. Louis Cardinals: Balfour; needle post, charms; red... $50-$75
1982 Milwaukee Brewers: Balfour; needle post, charms; blue $50-$100
1983 Philadelphia Phillies: Balfour; needle post, charms; red/
white/green... $40-$75
1983 Baltimore Orioles: Balfour; needle post, charm, brooch;
orange/white/black .... $65-$100
1984 San Diego Padres: Balfour; needle post, charms; brown/
white.. $25-$75
1984 Detroit Tigers: Balfour; needle post, charms; blue ..... $45-$75
1985 Kansas City Royals: Green Co.; needle post, charms;
blue/white .... $75-$100
1985 St. Louis Cardinals: Balfour; needle post, charms;
red/black .... $75-$100
1986 New York Mets: Balfour; needle post, charms;
blue/orange .... $100-$135
1986 Boston Red Sox: Balfour; needle post, charms; red/white/
blue .... $75-$125
1987 St. Louis Cardinals: Balfour; needle post, charms;
red/white/gold... $100-$125
1987 Minnesota Twins: Josten; needle post, charms; gold.... $75-$125
1988 Oakland A's .... $60-$75
1988 Los Angeles Dodgers................................... $50-$75
1989 San Francisco Giants .... $75-$100
1989 Oakland A's .... $75-$100
1990 Cincinnati Reds .... $125-$150
1990 Oakland A's .... $75-$100
1991 Atlanta Braves .... $60-$100

1991 Minnesota Twins .... $60-$100
1992 Atlanta Braves .... $100-$125
1992 Toronto Blue Jays .... $125-$150
1993 Philadelphia Phillies .... $50-$100
1993 Toronto Blue Jays .... $125-$150
1995 Atlanta Braves .... $100-$150
1995 Cleveland Indians .... $100-$150
1999 New York Yankees .... $100-$150

Phantom Press Pins

1938 Pittsburgh Pirates: Whitehead & Hoag; threaded post; red/white/black .... $500-$1,000
1944 Detroit Tigers: Unknown; threaded post; red/white/blue .... $375-$500
1945 St. Louis Cardinals: St. Louis button; threaded post; red/white .... $475-$600
1946 Brooklyn Dodgers: Dieges & Clust; threaded post, brooch .... $125-$275
1948 Boston Red Sox: Balfour; threaded post; red/white/blue .... $1,200-$1,800
1948 New York Yankees: Dieges & Clust, threaded post; red/white/blue .... $1,600-$1,800
1949 St. Louis Cardinals: Unknown; threaded post; red/white/black .... $450-$725
1949 Boston Red Sox: Balfour; threaded post; red/white/blue .... $950-$1,400
1950 Brooklyn Dodgers: Balfour; threaded post; red/white/blue .... $1,600-$2,400
1951 Cleveland Indians: Balfour; threaded post; red/white/black .... $1,200-$1,750
1951 Brooklyn Dodgers: Dieges & Clust; threaded post, brooch; red/white/blue .... $125-$400
1952 New York Giants: Dieges & Clust; threaded post, brooch; white/black .... $275-$350
1955 Chicago White Sox: Unknown; threaded post; red/white/blue .... $800-$1,400
1955 Cleveland Indians: Balfour; threaded post; red/white/blue/black .... $600-$800
1956 Milwaukee Braves: Balfour; threaded post; red/copper. $100-$150
1959 San Francisco Giants: Balfour; threaded post; white/black .... $550-$800
1959 Milwaukee Braves: Balfour; threaded post, charm; red/copper .... $400-$500
1960 Chicago White Sox: Balfour; threaded post; red/white .... $1,200-$1,600
1960 Baltimore Orioles: Balfour; threaded post; red/green/black .... $800-$1,250
1963 St. Louis Cardinals: Josten; threaded post; red .... $75-$150
1964 Philadelphia Phillies: Martin; needle post; red/blue .... $15-$30
1964 Chicago White Sox: Balfour; needle post; red/white/blue .... $800-$1,100
1964 Baltimore Orioles: Balfour; needle post; orange/white/black .... $625-$850
1964 Cincinnati Reds: Balfour; needle post, brooch; red/white/black .... $200-$250
1965 San Francisco Giants: Balfour; threaded post; white/black .... $125-$150
1966 Pittsburgh Pirates: Balfour; needle post; black .... $375-$450

1966 San Francisco Giants: Balfour; threaded post; white/black .... $950-$1,200
1967 Minnesota Twins: Balfour; needle post; red/white/blue..$50-$60
1967 Chicago White Sox: Balfour; needle post; red/white/blue .... $75-$100
1969 San Francisco Giants: Balfour; needle post; white/black .... $100-$150
1969 Atlanta Braves: Josten; needle post, charm; blue ...... $45-$75
1969 Minnesota Twins: Balfour; needle post; red/white/blue....$75-$150
1970 California Angels: Balfour; needle post; red/white/blue .... $450-$500
1970 Chicago Cubs: Balfour; needle post; blue/white .... $450-$500
1971 San Francisco Giants: Balfour; needle post; black .... $125-$150
1971 Oakland A's (smaller pin): Unknown; needle post; green/white .... $100-$150
1971 Oakland A's (larger pin): Balfour; needle post, charm; green/white .... $650-$750
1972 Chicago White Sox: Balfour; needle post; red/white/blue .... $875-$1,000
1972 Pittsburgh Pirates: Balfour; needle post; no color .... $600-$750
1974 Texas Rangers: Balfour; needle post; red/white/blue/gold .... $400-$550
1975 Oakland A's: Josten; needle post; green/white ...... $300-$450
1976 Philadelphia Phillies: Balfour; needle post; no color ....$35-$75
1977 Boston Red Sox: Balfour; needle post, charm; red/blue ...$50-$75
1978 San Francisco Giants: Balfour; needle post; black/orange .... $30-$50
1978 Cincinnati Reds: Balfour; needle post, charm; red .... $75-$100
1978 Milwaukee Brewers .... $50-$75
1979 Montreal Expos: Balfour; needle post; no color .... $50-$75
1979 California Angels: Balfour; needle post; red/white/blue $200-$250
1979 Houston Astros: Balfour; needle post; white/blue .... $850-$900
1980 Houston Astros: Balfour; needle post, charm; blue/orange .... $150-$200
1981 Oakland A's: Balfour; needle post, charm; green ...... $55-$85
1981 Chicago Cubs: Balfour; needle post; red/white/blue ..... $175-$200
1981 Philadelphia Phillies: Balfour; needle post; red/white........ $45-$75
1982 Los Angeles Dodgers: Balfour; needle post, charm; red/white/blue .... $125-$150
1983 Milwaukee Brewers: Balfour; needle post; white/black . $200-$250
1983 Chicago White Sox: Balfour; needle post; red/blue.......... $40-$50
1983 Pittsburgh Pirates: Balfour; needle post; black .... $200-$275
1984 Chicago Cubs: Balfour; needle post, charm; red/black. $125-$200
1985 Toronto Blue Jays: Balfour; needle post, charm; red/white/blue .... $200-$250
1986 California Angels: Gem Peddler; needle post, charm; no color... $175-$200
1986 Houston Astros: Balfour; needle post, charm; red/blue .. $75-$150
1987 Detroit Tigers: Balfour; needle post; blue/white/gold..... $125-$175
1987 New York Yankees: Balfour; threaded post; blue/white/gold... $175-$200
1987 New York Mets: Balfour; needle post; orange/black/white/gold.. $200-$225
1987 San Francisco Giants: Balfour; needle post; black/white/gold... $75-$100
1987 Boston Red Sox .... $150-$175
1988 Boston Red Sox .... $75-$100
1990 Pittsburgh Pirates.. $300-$350
1990 Boston Red Sox .... $60-$75

All-Star Pins

1938 Cincinnati: Bastian Brothers; safety pin; red/white/blue .... $7,000-$8,000
1941 Detroit: Dodge; threaded post; blue .... $2,200-$2,500
1943 Philadelphia: Unknown; threaded post; silver .. $1,200-$1,500
1946 Boston: Balfour; threaded post; red .... $575-$1,000
1947 Chicago: Unknown; threaded post; red/white/blue $1,100-$1,850
1948 St. Louis: St. Louis button; threaded post; brown/white.. $650-$2,250
1949 Brooklyn: Balfour; threaded post, brooch; blue ...... $325-$400

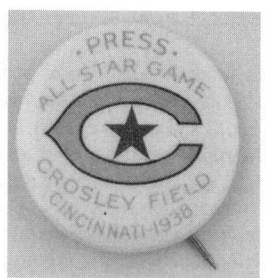

1950 Chicago: Balfour; threaded post, brooch; red/white $150-$325
1951 Detroit: Unknown; threaded post, brooch; red/white/blue .... $250-$375
1952 Philadelphia: Martin; needle post; red/white/blue ... $175-$400
1953 Cincinnati: Robbins; threaded post; red/white/black.... $225-$375
1954 Cleveland: Balfour; threaded post; red/white/black $250-$375
1955 Milwaukee: Balfour; brooch; gold .... $175-$350
1956 Washington: Balfour; threaded post, clasp; red/white/blue .... $225-$350
1957 St. Louis: Balfour; threaded post, brooch; black/red .. $300-$350
1958 Baltimore: Balfour; threaded post, charm; black/white/orange .... $400-$650
1959 Los Angeles: Balfour; threaded post, brooch; blue/white .... $100-$150
1959 Pittsburgh: Balfour; threaded post; red/white/black $225-$400
1960 Kansas City: Balfour; threaded post; red .... $125-$200
1960 New York Yankees: Balfour; threaded post; red/white/blue .... $200-$400
1961 Boston: Balfour; needle post; red/white/blue .... $400-$500
1961 San Francisco: Balfour; threaded post; white .... $475-$600
1962 Chicago: Balfour; needle post; red/white/blue .... $250-$350
1962 Washington: Balfour; threaded post, clasp; white/blue .... $200-$250
1963 Cleveland: Balfour; threaded post; red/white/blue/black .... $75-$150
1964 New York (Shea Stadium): Balfour; needle post, charm; blue/orange .... $200-$250
1965 Minnesota: Balfour; needle post; red/white/blue ..... $100-$175
1966 St. Louis: Balfour; needle post; red .... $35-$80
1967 California: Balfour; needle post, charm; blue/white .. $50-$150
1968 Houston: Balfour; needle post, charm; blue/white .. $100-$125
1969 Washington: Balfour; needle post, clasp; blue .... $75-$150
1970 Cincinnati: Balfour; needle post, charm; red/white/black $75-$100
1971 Detroit: Balfour; needle post, charms; red/white/blue.. $100-$175
1972 Atlanta: Balfour; needle post, charm; red/blue .... $75-$125
1973 Kansas City: Balfour; needle post, charm; blue ...... $75-$150
1974 Pittsburgh: Balfour; needle post; gold .... $175-$275
1975 Milwaukee: Unknown; brooch; gold .... $50-$100
1976 Philadelphia: Balfour; needle post; gold .... $50-$75
1977 New York Yankees: Balfour; pin .... $100-$125
1977 New York: Balfour; charm; gold .... $30-$50
1978 San Diego: Balfour; needle post, charm, brooch; brown/blue .... $40-$80
1979 Seattle: Balfour; needle post, charm, brooch; blue/white $30-$60
1980 Los Angeles: Balfour; needle post, charm; gold .... $30-$60
1981 Cleveland: Balfour; needle post, charm; red/white/blue .. $25-$50
1982 Montreal: Balfour; needle post, straight pin; gold .... $60-$75
1983 Chicago: Balfour; needle post, charms; red/blue .... $25-$50
1984 San Francisco: Balfour; needle post, charm; orange/black/white .... $20-$35
1985 Minnesota: Peter David; needle post, charms; red/white/blue .... $20-$25
1986 Houston: Balfour; needle post, charms; red/white/blue/silver .... $65-$125
1987 Oakland: Josten; needle post; copper .... $75-$90
1988 Cincinnati: Josten; needle post; red/white/blue/silver .... $75-$100
1989 California .... $55-$75
1990 Chicago .... $125-$150

1991 Toronto .... $100-$125
1992 San Diego .... $20-$100
1993 Baltimore .... $100-$150
1994 Pittsburgh .... $75-$125
1995 Texas .... $50-$100
1996 Philadelphia .... $50-$100
1997 Cleveland .... $50-$100
1998 Denver .... $50-$100
1999 Boston .... $100-$150
2000 Atlanta .... $75-$100
2001 Seattle .... $75-$100
2002 Milwaukee .... $75-$100
2003 Chicago .... $50-$100

Hall of Fame Press Pins

1982: Balfour; charms and standard needle post: Hank Aaron, Happy Chandler, Travis Jackson, Frank Robinson ..... $400-$700
1983: Balfour; charms and standard needle post: Walter Alston, George Kell, Juan Marichal, Brooks Robinson .... $400-$525
1984: Balfour; charms and standard needle post: Luis Aparicio, Don Drysdale, Harmon Killebrew, Rick Ferrell, Pee Wee Reese .... $225-$375
1985: Balfour; charms and standard needle post: Lou Brock, Enos Slaughter, Arky Vaughan, Hoyt Wilhelm .... $250-$350
1986: Balfour; charms and standard needle post: Bobby Doerr, Ernie Lombardi, Willie McCovey .... $225-$350
1987: Balfour; charms and standard needle post: Ray Dandridge, Jim Hunter, Billy Williams .... $500-$650
1988: Balfour; charms and standard needle post: Willie Stargell .... $500-$650
1989: Al Barlick, Johnny Bench, Red Schoendienst, Carl Yastrzemski .... $500-$650
1989: 50th Anniversary Medallion: Al Barlick, Johnny Bench, Red Schoendienst, Carl Yastrzemski .... $650-$700
1990: Joe Morgan, Jim Palmer .... $450-$650
1990: (1936 inductees) Ty Cobb, Walter Johnson, Christy Mathewson, Babe Ruth, Honus Wagner $750
1991: Rod Carew, Fergie Jenkins, Gaylord Perry, Tony Lazzeri, Bill Veeck .... $375-$575
1991: (1937 inductees) Morgan Bulkeley, Ban Johnson, Nap Lajoie, Connie Mack, John McGraw, Tris Speaker, George Wright, Cy Young $700
1992: Rollie Fingers, Bill McGowan, Hal Newhouser, Tom Seaver $400
1992: (1938 inductees) Grover Cleveland Alexander, Alexander Cartwright, Henry Chadwick $375

1992: (1955 inductees) Frank Baker, Joe DiMaggio, Gabby Hartnett, Ted Lyons, Ray Schalk, Dazzy Vance $495

1993: Reggie Jackson $450

1993: (1939 inductees) Charles Comiskey, Buck Ewing, Cap Anson, Candy Cummings, Eddie Collins $400

1993: (1939 inductees) Charles Radbourne, George Sisler, Al Spalding, Lou Gehrig, Wee Willie Keeler $500

1994: Steve Carlton, Leo Durocher, Phil Rizzuto ....$425-$450

1994: (1942 inductee) Rogers Hornsby $375

1994: (1966 inductees) Casey Stengel, Ted Williams $375

1995: Richie Ashburn, Leon Day, William Hulbert, Mike Schmidt, Vic Willis $375

1995: (1944 inductee) Kenesaw Mountain Landis $375

1995: (1969 inductees) Roy Campanella, Stan Coveleski, Waite Hoyt, Stan Musial $375

1996: Jim Bunning, Earl Weaver, Ned Hanlon, B. Foster.........$375

1996: (1974 inductees) Cool Papa Bell, Jim Bottomley, Jocko Conlan, Whitey Ford, Mickey Mantle, Sam Thompson.....................$375

1997: Tommy Lasorda, Phil Niekro, Nellie Fox, Willie Wells $350

1997: (1962 inductees) Bob Feller, Bill McKechnie, Jackie Robinson, Edd Roush...$350

1997: (1962 inductees) Yogi Berra, Josh Gibson, Lefty Gomez, Will Harridge, Sandy Koufax, Buck Leonard, Early Wynn, Ross Youngs $350

1998: Don Sutton, Larry Doby pin..................................$100-$150

PM10 Stadium Photo issues

These pins were issued in various sizes and were sold at ball parks around the country; the most popular pin size is 1 3/4". All of the pins have black-and-white photos on various color backgrounds, as noted after the players names.

1. Hank Aaron, blue..$275
2. Sandy Amoros, blue $50
3. Harry Anderson, black..$75
4. Johnny Antonelli, white/N.Y..................................$45
   Johnny Antonelli, black, white/S.F...........................$25
5. Richie Ashburn, gray...$135
6. Dick Bartell, photo in circle................................$15
7. Gus Bell, white $85
8. Yogi Berra, blue $50
   Yogi Berra, white $75
   Yogi Berra, gray more expensive $95
9. Joe Black, white/profile......................................$95
   Joe Black, white/portrait.....................................$50
   Joe Black, black/white..$25
10. Don Bollweg, gray..$20
11. Lou Boudreau, white..$15
    Lou Boudreau, cap is red/blue...............................$250
12. Eric Bressoud, gray..$20
13. Billy Bruton, white..$25
14. Dolph Camilli, white...$15
15. Roy Campanella, white..$75
    Roy Campanella, blue..$100
    Roy Campanella, ivory..$75
16. Chico Carrasquel, White Sox $125
17. Phil Cavaretta, stars in border.............................$150
18. Orlando Cepeda, dirty white..................................$45
    Orlando Cepeda, railing......................................$50
19. Roberto Clemente, We remember...............................$30
20. Gerry Coleman, gray..$15
21. Tony Conigliaro, gray..$50
    Tony Conigliaro, gray/teeth showing $50
22. Morton Cooper, white/black...................................$15
23. Billy Cox, white...$15
    Billy Cox, ivory...$45
24. Al Dark, white...$15
25. Jim Davenport, gray..$95
    Jim Davenport, ivory...$95
26. Jerome (Dizzy) Dean, black...................................$60
27. Bill Dickey, Yankees...$150
28. Dom DiMaggio, black..$50
    Dom DiMaggio, ivory..$20
29. Joe DiMaggio, green $280
    Joe DiMaggio, black...$280
    Joe DiMaggio, white...$280
    Joe DiMaggio, light blue.....................................$65
    Joe DiMaggio, white circle..................................$320
    Joe DiMaggio, autograph.....................................$275
30. Larry Doby, white..$15
    Larry Doby, black..$65

    Larry Doby, Congratulations $85
31. Luke Easter, Indians...$65
32. Del Ennis, dirty gray..$95
    Del Ennis, brown...$95
33. Carl Erskine, white..$35
34. Bob Feller, white..$15
    Bob Feller, autograph.......................................$175
35. Whitey Ford, white...$70
36. Nelson Fox, foxes...$250
37. Carl Furillo, black/white, facing right.....................$125
    Carl Furillo, black/white, facing left.......................$95
    Carl Furillo, ivory...$125
    Carl Furillo, blue..$145
38. Len Gabrielson, SF...$75
39. Ned Garver, white...$125
40. Lou Gehrig, photo in circle.................................$300
41. Junior Gilliam, small print..................................$95
    Junior Gilliam, large print..................................$95
42. Lefty Gomez, Yankees..$125
43. Ruben Gomez, black/white, photo in circle $15
44. Billy Goodman, white...$65
45. Granny Hamner, gray...$125
46. Jim Hart, ear missing.......................................$125
47. Gabby Hartnett, black..$50
48. Grady Hatton, Reds...$75
49. Jim Hegan, name in red......................................$250
50. Tom Henrich, light gray......................................$50
    Tom Henrich, white...$20
51. Mike Higgins, black..$15
52. Gil Hodges, white/eyes left..................................$75
    Gil Hodges, white/eyes front................................$125
    Gil Hodges, black/white......................................$75
    Gil Hodges, orange...$75
53. Elston Howard, white...$25
54. Carl Hubbell, photo in circle...............................$125
    Carl Hubbell, white circle...................................$25
55. Monte Irvin, black...$40
    Monte Irvin, white circle...................................$125
    Monte Irvin, white..$125
56. Forrest Spook Jacobs, black/white............................$20
57. Jackie Jensen, black...$25
    Jackie Jensen, natural.......................................$50
    Jackie Jensen, white...$95
58. Walter Johnson, Senators....................................$250
59. Willie Jones, gray...$85
60. Harmon Killebrew, natural...................................$175
61. Ralph Kiner, white circle...................................$175
62. Ted Kluszewski, white..$75
63. Jim Konstanty, gray...$145

64. Ed Kranepool, white	$20	
65. Hal Lanier, black circle	$125	
66. Big Bill Lee, black/gray	$15	
67. Bob Lemon, white	$15	
Bob Lemon, white circle	$145	
68. Jim Lemon, white circle	$125	
69. Whitey Lockman, black/white	$15	
70. Stan Lopata, gray	$125	
71. Sal Maglie, black/white	$45	
72. Frank Malzone, ivory	$45	
Frank Malzone, natural	$15	
73. Mickey Mantle, blue/ear missing	$250	
Mickey Mantle, ivory, baseball style	$175	
Mickey Mantle, blue, name at wrist	$135	
Mickey Mantle, white/name at elbow	$125	
Mickey Mantle, white/both hands visible	$40	
Mickey Mantle, white/eyes closed	$300	
Mickey Mantle, with Teresa Brewer	$50	
74. Juan Marichal, black	$135	
75. Marty Marion, white circle	$135	
76. Roger Maris, yellow	$25	
Roger Maris, pink	$50	
Roger Maris, orange	$25	
Roger Maris, white	$125	
77. Willie Mays, gray/S.F.	$175	
Willie Mays, white/N.Y.	$45	
Willie Mays, gray/N.Y.	$195	
Willie Mays, natural/S.F.	$145	
Willie Mays, S.F./stands	$275	
Willie Mays, white circle	$175	
Willie Mays, turquoise	$250	
78. Willie McCovey, gray	$50	
79. Gil McDougald, dirty gray	$15	
80. Clift Melton, photo in circle	$15	
81. Bill Meyer, white circle	$125	
82. Orestes Minoso, white circle	$145	
83. Bill Monbouquette, gray	$15	
84. Don Mueller, white	$15	
85. Bobby Murcer, white	$15	
86. Danny Murtaugh, white circle	$150	
87. Stan Musial, yellow	$45	
Stan Musial, white	$250	
Stan Musial, white/ear noticeable	$225	
88. Don Newcombe, ivory	$25	
Don Newcombe, blue	$75	
Don Newcombe, white/mouth open	$30	
89. Dan O'Connell, photo in a white border	$15	
90. Andy Pafko, black	$145	
91. Joe Page, ivory	$35	
92. Leroy Paige, ivory	$175	
93. Mel Parnell, white	$15	
94. Joe Pepitone, white	$20	
95. Gaylord Perry, white	$50	
96. Johnny Pesky, white	$65	
97. Rico Petrocelli, gray	$50	
98. Jimmy Piersall, ivory	$30	
99. Johnny Podres, white	$45	

100. Johnny Pramesa, dirty gray	$75	
101. Dick Radatz, gray	$30	
102. Vic Raschi, white	$45	
103. Pee Wee Reese, white	$75	
Pee Wee Reese, gray/B on cap	$45	
Pee Wee Reese, gray/ear missing	$125	
Pee Wee Reese, light gray	$75	
104. Pete Reiser, photo in circle	$15	
105. Bill Rigney, black/white	$15	
106. Phil Rizzuto, ivory	$50	
107. Robin Roberts, black/white	$20	
Robin Roberts, brown	$125	
108. Jackie Robinson, yellow	$50	
Jackie Robinson, red	$250	
Jackie Robinson, ROY	$125	
Jackie Robinson, blue	$125	
Jackie Robinson, gray/white	$275	
Jackie Robinson, white	$275	
Jackie Robinson, white/ear missing	$300	
Jackie Robinson, natural	$125	
109. Preacher Roe, white	$125	
110. Saul Rogovin, photo in circle	$15	
111. Stan Rojek, white circle	$125	
112. Al Rosen, white	$15	
113. Charles Herbert Ruffing, gray	$25	
114. Babe Ruth, black	$400	
115. Chuck Schilling, white	$65	
Chuck Schilling, white	$65	
116. George Scott, white	$15	
117. Andy Seminick, gray	$125	
118. Bobby Shantz, white	$20	
Bobby Shantz, gray	$125	
119. Frank Shea, black/white	$15	
120. Curt Simmons, brown	$125	
121. Enos Slaughter, black	$85	
122. Roy Smalley, white circle	$125	
123. Duke Snider, dirty gray	$45	
Duke Snider, blue	$175	
Duke Snider, black	$95	
124. Dick Stuart, gray	$50	
125. Hank Thompson, white circle	$45	
126. Bobby Thomson, ivory	$40	
127. Gus Triandos, light gray	$70	
128. Robert Lee Trice, natural	$75	
129. Eddie Waitkus, gray	$125	
130. Dixie Walker, white circle	$45	
131. Bill Werle, white circle	$145	
132. Sam White, white	$15	
133. Ted Williams, black/white, name on bottom	$75	
Ted Williams, black/white, name on top	$175	
Ted Williams, black	$175	
Ted Williams, white	$175	
Ted Williams, white	$175	
Ted Williams, natural, name at bottom	$75	
134. Gene Woodling, natural	$145	
135. Whitlow Wyatt, photo in circle	$15	
136. Carl Yastrzemski, gray	$150	
Carl Yastrzemski, white	$150	
137. Gus Zernial, gray	$125	

Super Bowl Press Pins

Note: Press pins for Super Bowls I, II and III were issued as tie bars. Formal press pins were not issued for Super Bowls IV and V, instead patches were issued for the media personnel. Super Bowl IV patch is valued at $85, while the Super Bowl V patch is listed at $90.

I at Los Angeles, Jan. 15, 1967 (Green Bay Packers vs. Kansas City Chiefs) $1,450

II at Miami, Jan. 14, 1968 (Green Bay Packers vs. Oakland Raiders) $1,250

III at Miami, Jan. 12, 1969 (New York Jets vs. Baltimore Colts) ..$2,300

IV at New Orleans, Jan. 11, 1970 (Minnesota Vikings vs. Kansas City Chiefs) .... patch $85

V at Miami, Jan. 17, 1971 (Baltimore Colts vs. Dallas Cowboys).. patch $90

VI at New Orleans, Jan. 16, 1972 (Dallas Cowboys vs. Miami Dolphins) $400

VII at Los Angeles, Jan. 14, 1973 (Miami Dolphins vs. Washington Redskins) $375

VIII at Houston, Jan. 13, 1974 (Minnesota Vikings vs. Miami Dolphins) $375

IX at New Orleans, Jan. 12, 1975 (Pittsburgh Steelers vs. Minnesota Vikings) $285

X at Miami, Jan. 18, 1976 (Dallas Cowboys vs. Pittsburgh Steelers) $325

XI at Pasadena, Jan. 9, 1977 (Oakland Raiders vs. Minnesota Vikings).. $250

XII at New Orleans, Jan. 15, 1978 (Dallas Cowboys vs. Denver Broncos) ....$275-$295

XIII at Miami, Jan. 21, 1979 (PIttsburgh Steelers vs. Dallas Cowboys).. $250

XIV at Pasadena, Jan. 20, 1980 (Los Angeles Rams vs. Pittsburgh Steelers) $200

XV at New Orleans, Jan. 25, 1981 (Oakland Raiders vs. Philadelphia Eagles) $175

XVI at Pontiac, Jan. 24, 1982 (San Francisco 49ers vs. Cincinnati Bengals) $150

XVII at Pasadena, Jan. 30, 1983 (Miami Dolphins vs. Washington Redskins) $275

XVIII at Tampa, Jan. 22, 1984 (Washington vs. Los Angeles Raiders)... $135

XIX at Palo Alto, Jan. 20, 1985 (Miami vs. San Francisco) $125

XX at New Orleans, Jan. 26, 1986 (Chicago Bears vs. New England Patriots) $135

XXI at Pasadena, Jan. 25, 1987 (Denver Broncos vs. New York Giants)... $120

XII at San Diego, Jan. 31, 1988 (Washington Redskins vs. Denver Broncos) $125

XXIII at Miami, Jan. 22, 1989 (Cincinnati Bengals vs. San Francisco 49ers) $125

XXIV at New Orleans, Jan. 28, 1990 (San Francisco 49ers vs. Denver Broncos) $125

XXV at Tampa, Jan. 27, 1991 (Buffalo Bills vs. New York Giants) ...$95

XXVI at Minneapolis, Jan. 26, 1992 (Washington Redskins vs. Buffalo Bills) $125

XXVII at Pasadena, Jan. 31, 1993 (Buffalo Bills vs. Dallas Cowboys) $95

XXVIII at Minneapolis, Jan. 29, 1994 (Buffalo Bills vs. Dallas Cowboys) $125

XXIX at Miami, Jan. 29, 1995 (San Francisco 49ers vs. San Diego Chargers) $200

XXX at Phoenix, Jan. 28, 1996 (Dallas Cowboys vs. Pittsburgh Steelers) $135

XXXI at New Orleans, Jan 26, 1997 (Green Bay Packers vs. New England Patriots) $175

XXXII at San Diego, Jan. 25, 1998 (Denver Broncos vs. Green Bay Packers) $135

XXXIII at Miami, Jan. 31, 1999 (Denver Broncos vs. Atlanta Falcons) $135

XXXVI at Atlanta, Jan. 30, 2000 St. Louis Rams vs. Tennessee Titans) $125

XXV at Tampa, Jan. 28, 2001 (Baltimore Ravens vs. N.Y. Giants) $105

Chapter 11

TICKETS

Ticket stubs do not command high prices unless they are from World Series, All-Star or playoff games, or from a game in which a significant achievement or record occurred. Generally, the stubs are in either Poor or Fair condition, because they have been bent and are worn, or rated very good to excellent because they have been preserved. Full, unused tickets are worth more than stubs, and are generally for seats which went unsold for a playoff or World Series game, or one in which a baseball milestone occurred. Shortly after Nolan Ryan won his 300th game in 1990, unused tickets were being offered for $60; an unused ticket and program were priced at $75. Special commemorative certificates, printed by the respective teams, also add to the value and make for an attractive display.

Other tickets which would command premium prices would be those for games such as when Reggie Jackson hit three homers in the sixth game of the 1977 World Series, and the 1956 World Series game when Don Larsen pitched a perfect game against the Brooklyn Dodgers. One ticket stub from that game sold for $532 in a 1992 auction. It was autographed, framed and matted and included a photo of the final pitch and a copy of the box score.

Other examples from auction results have shown prices realized from games from the 1922 and 1923 World Series (at the Polo Grounds and Yankee Stadium) were between $177-$296, while a 1920 Cleveland Indians full ticket from Game 4 sold for $967. A full ticket from Stan Musial's last game, Sept. 29, 1963, at St. Louis, sold for $242, while a full ticket from Catfish Hunter's perfect game on May 8, 1968, at Oakland, sold for $370. A 1978 All-Star Game full ticket from San Diego sold for $77. But in general, ticket stubs shouldn't cost more than $30.

The most valuable ticket stubs have seat numbers, which are generally printed in a different ink color in a separate press run. Those without, generally from the 1940s and 1950s, and sold in large blocks, are usually of little or no value because they are artist's proofs.

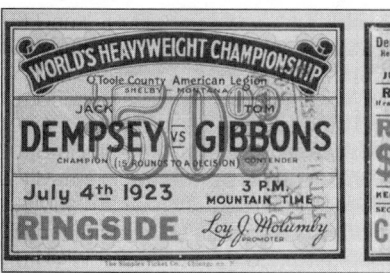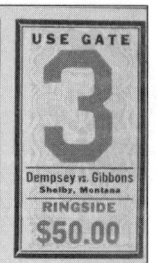

Baseball Tickets

Year	Price
Pre-1900s*...	$100-$350
1900-1910..	$75-$100
1911-1920..	$50-$75
1921-1930..	$35-$50
1931-1940..	$25-$35
1941-1950..	$20-$25
1951-1960..	$15-$20
1961-1970..	$10-$15
1971-1980..	$5-$8
1981-1990..	$4-$6
1991-present..	$3-$5

*Pre-1900 tickets and stubs are available from only a very limited number of teams.

There can be a wide range in values even among tickets from the same team in the same era. For instance, tickets from the 1960-64 Chicago White Sox feature player photographs, and range in value from $5 for common players to $20 for Luis Aparicio.

Note: The first ticket price is for a full ticket, the second is a stub. A means All-Star, P means league championship series game, WS means World Series.

Boston Braves tickets: 1936 A ($450/$225); 1914 WS ($1,800/$900); 1948 WS ($225/$125-$175).

Brooklyn Dodgers tickets: 1949 A ($170/$85); 1916 WS ($1,400/$650-$800); 1920 WS ($900/$450); 1941-47-49 WS ($225-$275/$85-$225); 1952-53-56 WS ($150-$175/$85-$175); 1955 WS ($250/$95-$125).

Colorado Rockies tickets: 1998 A ($100/$50).

Florida Marlins tickets: 1997 P ($10/$5); 1997 WS ($20/$10).

Houston Colt .45s tickets: None.

Kansas City A's tickets: 1960 A ($70/$35).

Milwaukee Braves tickets: 1955 A ($175/$85-$175); 1957-58 WS ($175-$225/$50-$85).

New York Giants tickets: 1934 A ($450/$225); 1942 A ($225/$125); 1905 WS ($2,600/$1,400); 1911-12-13 WS ($1,800/$650-$900); 1917 WS (1,400/$650); 1921-22-23-24 WS ($900/$450); 1933-36-37 WS ($450/$140-$225); 1951 WS ($175/$85-$140).

Philadelphia A's tickets: 1943 A ($225/$125); 1905 WS ($2,700/$1,400); 1910-11-13-14 WS ($1,800/$900); 1915 WS ($1,400/$650); 1930-31 WS ($450/$175-$275).

St. Louis Browns tickets: 1948 A ($225/$125); 1944 WS ($225/$85-$150).

Seattle Pilots tickets: None.

Washington Senators tickets: 1937 A ($450/$225); 1956 A ($175/$85); 1962 A ($85/$40-$85); 1969 A ($85/$40); 1924-25 WS ($900/$450); 1933 WS ($450/$85-$225).

Atlanta Braves tickets: 1972 A ($60/$20); 2000 A ($100/$50); 1969 P ($35/$20); 1982 P ($20/$5); 1991-92-95-96-97-98-99-01 P ($10/$5); 1991-92-95-96-99 WS ($20/$10).

Cincinnati Reds tickets: 1938 A ($450/$225); 1953 A ($175/$85-$200); 1970 A ($50/$25-$60); 1988 A ($40/$20-$60); 1970-72-73-75-76-79 P ($40-$85/$25-$65); 1990 P ($20/$10); 1993-95 P ($125/$40-$70); 1995 P ($10/$5); 1919 WS ($2,250/$1,150); 1939 WS ($450/$225); 1940 WS ($225/$125-$150); 1961 WS ($80/$40-$85); 1970-75-76 WS ($50-$155/$15-$70); 1990 WS ($125/$45).

Houston Astros tickets: 1968 A ($80/$40-$125); 1986 A ($40/$20); 1981-86 P ($30/$15).

Arizona Diamondbacks tickets: 2001 P ($10/$5); 2001 WS ($20/$10)

Los Angeles Dodgers tickets: 1959 A ($175/$125-$200); 1980 A ($40/$20-$30); 1974-77-78 P ($55/$25); 1981-83-85-88 P ($55/$30); 1959 WS ($175/$85); 1963-65-66 WS ($70-$150/$50-$60); 1974-77-78 WS ($85-$150/$40-$70); 1981-88 WS ($35-$85/$20-$50).

San Diego Padres tickets: 1978 A ($50/$25); 1992 A ($25/$15); 1984 P ($30/$15); 1998 P ($10/$5); 1984 WS ($85/$75); 1998 WS ($20/$10).

San Francisco Giants tickets: 1961 A ($80/$40); 1984 A ($35/$15); 1971 P ($40/$15); 1987-89 P ($30/$15); 2002 P ($10/$5); 1962 WS ($325/$75-$150); 1989 WS ($35/$15); 2002 WS $20/$10).

Chicago Cubs tickets: 1947 A ($200-$225/$150); 1962 A ($175-$225/$40); 1990 A ($150/$70); 1984 P ($40/$15); 1989 P ($35/$15); 1906-07-08 WS ($2,250/$1,150); 1910 WS ($1,800/$900); 1918 WS ($1,400/$650); 1929 WS ($650/$275-$325); 1932-35-38 WS ($450/$175-$225); 1945 WS ($225/$125).

Montreal Expos tickets: 1982 A ($200/$125); 1981 P ($30/$15).

New York Mets tickets: 1964 A ($70/$40); 1969 P ($75/$60); 1973 P ($150/$40); 1986-88 P ($30/$15); 1999-00 P ($10/$5); 1969 WS ($375/$110); 1973 WS ($250/$50-$85); 1986 WS ($275/$85-$125); 2000 WS ($20/$10).

Philadelphia Phillies tickets: 1952 A ($175/$85); 1976 A ($50/$20); 1996 A ($100/$50); 1976-77-78 P ($40/$25-$40); 1980-83 P ($70/$30); 1993 P ($40/$20); 1915 WS ($1,400/$650); 1950 WS ($275/$125-$160); 1980-83 WS ($35/$15); 1993 WS ($100/$40).

Pittsburgh Pirates tickets: 1944 A ($225/$125); 1959 A ($175/$85); 1974 A ($125-$150/$35-$50); 1994 A ($100/$50); 1970-71-72-74-75-79 P ($85/$25-$50), 1990-91-92 P ($18/$10); 1903 WS ($6,750/$3,500); 1909 WS ($2,250/$1,150); 1925 WS ($900/$450); 1927 WS ($650/$325); 1960 WS ($80/$45-$125); 1971-79 WS ($85-$125/$25-$50).

St. Louis Cardinals tickets: 1940 A ($225/$125); 1957 A ($100-$175/$45); 1966 A ($80/$40); 1982-85-87 P ($30/$15); 1996-00-02 P ($10/$5); 1926-28 WS ($650/$325-$400); 1930-31-34 WS ($450/$200-$225); 1942-43-44-46 WS ($225/$125); 1964-67-68 WS ($80/$50-$85); 1982-85-87 WS ($85-$125/$40-$50).

Baltimore Orioles tickets: 1958 A ($225/$125); 1993 A ($175/$50); 1969 P ($60-$85/$30-$60); 1970-71 P ($35-$75/$15-$45); 1973-74 P ($25-$60/$35-$45); 1979 P ($25/$7); 1983 P ($18/$5); 1995-97 P ($10/$5); 1966 WS ($125/$45); 1969-70 WS ($80/$40-$50); 1971 WS ($60/$25-$50); 1979 WS ($125/$45); 1983 WS ($60/$35).

Boston Red Sox tickets: 1946 A ($225/$125); 1961 A ($85/$40); 1999 A ($100/$50); 1975 P ($50/$25); 1986-88 P ($100/$15-$30); 1990 P ($25/$10); 1999 P ($10/$5); 1903 WS ($6,750/$3,500); 1915-16-18 WS ($1,400/$650); 1946 WS ($125/$80); 1967 WS ($80-$125/$45-$90); 1975 WS ($45/$25); 1986 WS ($35/$15).

A ticket from the 1957 World Series in Milwaukee

A ticket stub from 1945 Wrigley Field

A ticket from the Oct. 1, 1939 World Series game at Yankee Stadium

A phantom World Series ticket from 1960

Cleveland Indians tickets: 1935 A ($450/$225); 1954 A ($175/$85-$150); 1963 A ($80/$40); 1981 A ($35/$15); 1997 A ($100/$50); 1995-97-98 P ($10/$5); 1920 WS ($900/$225-$375); 1948 WS ($225/$85-$175); 1954 WS ($175/$65-$100); 1995-97 WS ($20/$10).

Detroit Tigers tickets: 1941 A ($225/$125); 1951 A ($175/$85); 1971 A ($45/$25); 1972 P ($40/$20); 1984-87 P ($35-$60/$35); 1908-09 WS ($2,250/$1,150); 1934-35 WS ($450/$175-$225); 1940-45 WS ($225/$125-$150); 1968 WS ($75/$50); 1984 WS ($35-$60/$35).

Milwaukee Brewers tickets: 1975 A ($50/$25); 2002 A ($100/$50); 1982 P ($30/$15-$25); 1982 WS ($85-$125/$40).

New York Yankees tickets: 1939 A ($300-$450/$225); 1960 A ($75/$40); 1977 A ($45/$25); 1976-77-78 P ($40/$15-$25); 1980-81 P ($30/$15-$25); 1995-98-99-00-01 P ($10/$5); 1921-22-23 WS ($900/$450); 1926-27-28 WS ($650/$250-$325); 1932-36-37-38-39 WS ($450/$150-$225); 1941-42-43-47-49 WS ($225/$100-$175); 1950-51-52-53-55-56-57-58 WS ($150-$175/$85-$150); 1960-61-62-63-64 WS ($225/$40-$85); 1976-77-78 WS ($45/$30); 1981 WS ($35/$15); 1996-98-99-00-01 WS ($20/$10).

Toronto Blue Jays tickets: 1991 A ($175-$65); 1985-89 P ($30-$40/$15); 1991-92 P ($20-$65/$10); 1993 P ($45/$20); 1992-93 WS ($100-$200/$15-$50).

Anaheim Angels tickets: 2002 P ($10/$5); 2002 WS ($20/$10)

California Angels tickets: 1967 A ($175/$100); 1989 A ($35-$70/$15-$50); 1979-82 P ($35/$15-$35); P 1986 ($30/$10).

Chicago White Sox tickets: 1933 A ($450/$225-$275); 1950 A ($175/$85); 1983 A ($35-$85/$15); 2003 A ($100/$50); 1986 P ($15/$5); 1993 P ($70/$15); 1906 WS ($2,250/$1,150); 1917 WS ($1,400/$650); 1919 WS ($3,500/$1,600); 1959 WS ($175/$85-$100).

Kansas City Royals tickets: 1973 A ($45/$25); 1976-77-78 P ($40/$20); 1980-81-84-85 P ($30/$15); 1980-85 WS ($125-$150/$45-$50).

Minnesota Twins tickets: 1965 A ($80-$150/$40); 1985 A ($35/$15-$25); 1969 P ($75/$35); 1970-87 P ($40-$75/$15-$30); 1991 P ($20-$45/$10-$20); 2002 P ($10/$5); 1965 WS ($125-$175/$40-$60); 1987 WS ($85-$125/$40-$70); 1991 WS $100/$35-$50).

Oakland A's tickets: 1987 A ($35/$15); 1971-72-73-74-75 P ($40/$25-$35); 1988-89 P ($60-$75/$15-$25); 1990-92 P ($18/$10); 1972-73-74-75 WS ($85-$150/$45-$75); 1988-89 WS ($125-$150/$15-$50); 1990 WS ($20/$10).

Seattle Mariners tickets: 2001 A ($100/$50); 1995-00-01 P ($10/$5).

Texas Rangers tickets: 1995 A ($100/$50).

Full Ticket Sheets

Seattle Mariners tickets: 1979 A ($40/$20).
Texas Rangers tickets: 1995 A ($125/$50-$75).

1965 Minnesota Twins: WS 1, 2, 6, 7... $265
1982 St. Louis Cardinals: WS 1, 2, 6, 7..................................... $525
1982 Chicago White Sox (yellow): ALCS 1, 2; WS 3, 4, 5 .... $25
1982 Chicago White Sox (tan): ALCS 1, 2; WS 3, 4, 5 .... $25
1982 Chicago White Sox (green): ALCS 1, 2; WS 3, 4, 5 .... $25
1982 Chicago White Sox (orange): ALCS 1, 2; WS 3, 4, 5 .... $25
1982 Chicago White Sox (purple): ALCS 1, 2; WS 3, 4, 5 .... $25
1984 Minnesota Twins: ALCS 1, 2; WS A, B, C, D.................... $40
1987 St. Louis Cardinals: NLCS 1, 2, 6, 7; WS 3, 4, 5 .... $595
1989 San Francisco Giants: WS 3, 4, 5 .... $295
1992 Minnesota Twins: ALCS 3, 4, 5; WS 3, 4, 5 .... $50

Miscellaneous Tickets/Stubs

Tickets increase in value due to significant home runs, wins, etc.
•Arizona Diamondbacks inaugural season Opening Day ticket stub, 1998 .... $40
•American League pocket schedule $50
•Chicago Cubs first night game full ticket, Aug. 8, 1988............ $85
•Colorado Rockies inaugural season Opening Day ticket stub $50
•Hank Aaron hits #714, opening day ticket in Cincinnati, 1974 ...... $145
•Hank Aaron hits #715, ticket in Atlanta, 1974 .... $300
•Barry Bonds hits #500, full ticket, April 17, 2001 .... $25
•Rod Carew 3,000th hit full ticket, $95, signed $150
•Steve Carlton 300th win ticket stub, signed $75
•Roger Clemens 3,000th strikeout, full ticket............................ $40
•Florida Marlins inaugural season Opening Day ticket stub $45
•Tony Gwynn's 3,000th hit Aug. 6, 1999, ticket stub................. $15
•Reggie Jackson 500th home run full ticket, $175, signed $250
•Sandy Koufax's 1964 no-hitter ticket stub, June 4, 1964, with newspaper clippings.. $225
•Roger Maris' 60th home run ticket stub, Sept. 26, 1961 .... $475
•Mark McGwire's 62nd home run full ticket $90
•Mark McGwire's 70th home run full ticket (original) $150
•Mark McGwire's 70th home run full ticket (souvenir reprint) $15
•Mark McGwire's 500th home run, Aug. 5, 1999...................... $20
•Montreal Expos inaugural season Opening Day ticket $100
•Paul Molitor 3,000th hit ticket stub $50
•Eddie Murray's 500th home run ticket stub $60
•Eddie Murray's 3,000th hit ticket stub $55
•Phil Niekro's 300th win ticket stub.. $40
•Gaylord Perry's 300th win ticket $50
•Pittsburgh Pirates pocket mirror/schedule, has schedule on the celluloid front and a mirror on the back $400
•Cal Ripken Jr. embossed ticket from Sept. 5, 1995 .... $90
•Cal Ripken Jr. embossed ticket from Sept. 6, 1995 .... $160
•Cal Ripken Jr. ticket from April 15, 2000 3,000th hit game $50
•Cal Ripken's Last Game, Oct. 6, 2001 .... $200
•Pete Rose 4,000 hit certificate, says "I Was There," signed $40

An opening day ticket from the inaugural season (1993) for the Colorado Rockies.

A ticket from the April 17, 2001, game in which Barry Bonds hit his 500th home run.

A ticket stub from the Oct. 1, 1961 game at Yankee Stadium in which Roger Maris hit his 61st home run.

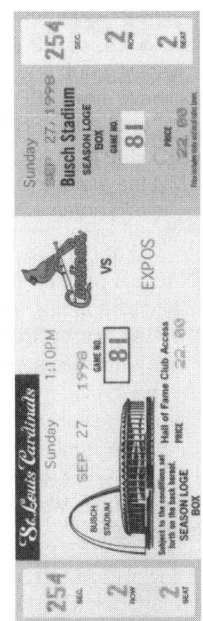

A ticket from the Sept. 27, 1998, game in which Mark McGwire hit his 69th and 70th home runs.

- Pete Rose's 4,192nd hit ticket, Sept. 11, 1985, signed........... $225
- Pete Rose's 4,192nd hit full ticket, framed, signed and matted with an autographed photo from the game, Sept. 11, 1985 .... $325
- Nolan Ryan 6th no-hitter full ticket, framed and matted with an autographed photo from the game............................... $225
- Nolan Ryan 7th no-hitter full ticket, May 13, 1991, unsigned, $65, signed... $125
- Nolan Ryan 300th win full ticket, May 13, 1991 .... $75
- Nolan Ryan 300th win full ticket, May 13, 1991, autographed $150
- Nolan Ryan first attempt at 300 wins, July 25, 1990, ticket vs. New York Yankees.. $35
- Nolan Ryan's last game full ticket, Sept. 22, 1993.................... $35
- Sammy Sosa's 62nd home run full ticket $60
- Sammy Sosa's 66th home run ticket... $65
- Mike Schmidt's 500th home run, ticket, April 18, 1987, signed.....$165
- Tom Seaver's 300th win ticket stub $100
- Don Sutton's 300th win ticket stub $45
- Tampa Bay Devil Rays inaugural season Opening Day ticket, 1998 .... $35
- Toronto Blue Jays inaugural season Opening Day ticket, 1977....$100
- Dave Winfield's 3,000th hit ticket stub...................................... $55
- Robin Yount's 3,000th hit full ticket $60

Baseball Schedules

If you search through the scrapbooks, wallets and shoe boxes of memorabilia long enough, inevitably you'll find an annual schedule or two for a favorite team of yesteryear.

Schedules, or skeds for short, offer collectors an inexpensive alternative to the big-ticket items which anchor any fan's collection. The limits are endless.

Although the most common form is a pocket schedule, skeds come in all shapes, sizes and for all sports. Collegiate sports such as baseball, football and hockey often utilize sked-cards, which are usually a single piece of paper or tagboard stock with artwork on one side and a game schedule on the back. Professional sports teams generally use folded skeds, similar to sked-cards, but with multiple panels separated by folds. These types of schedules are commonly provided by the Major League teams' ticket offices. Other schedule varieties include match-book covers, schedule cups, ticket brochures, decals, magnets, rulers, napkins, place mats, stickers, key chains, plastic coin purses and poster skeds.

The easiest way to begin or add to a schedule collection is to contact professional teams for ticket information. You'll usually get a response, especially if you send a self-addressed stamped envelope, which means the team isn't paying postage and already has a pre-addressed envelope to send back. When mailing to Canada, remember that any SASEs sent to the Montreal Expos or Toronto Blue Jays require Canadian postage.

Because schedules are primarily advertising pieces through which the sponsors can reach a wide, varying target audience, the sponsors themselves can be a source for schedules. Other possible sources can be found by determining who advertises in the team's yearbook and programs. Radio and television sponsors, and stations which carry the broadcasts, also often produce skeds, as may those who advertise on the television and radio broadcasts.

Off-the-wall skeds can be found in a variety of locations, such as restaurants (which often offer matchbook schedules) liquor stores, sporting goods stores, museums, banks and credit unions, motels and hotels, and ticket offices. When traveling, remember to check gas stations, convenience stores, and kiosks which are located along interstate rest stops.

Another way to obtain schedules is by trading, searching for prospective partners in classified ads in hobby publications such as Sports Collectors Digest and sked newsletters.

If the conventional shoe box or scrapbook is not used for displaying schedules, many pocket schedules will fit into eight- or nine-pocket baseball card plastic sheets which are held together in an album. These sheets protect the skeds from getting dinged and folded. Oversized schedules may fit into a 5-by-7 inch, dollar bill-sized, or postcard-sized plastic sheets.

Condition is not a critical factor in determining a schedule's value, but it is important. It's more valuable if it isn't damaged, ripped or torn, or marked on. Schedules for defunct teams carry a slight premium value compared to other schedules of the same year, as do localized, scarcer schedules and those featuring team or player photos.

Schedules and their general values: 1901-1909 ($150); 1910-19 ($100); 1920-29 ($75); 1930-39 ($35); 1940-49 ($30); 1950-59 ($25); 1960-69 ($15); 1970-79 ($10); 1980-85 ($2); 1986-on ($1).

Super Bowl Tickets, Stubs

With all the added attention on Super Bowl memorabilia from collectors and fans, it has made it especially hard on dealers to find the collectibles. Super Bowl attendees aren't willing to unload their ticket stubs for a song.

Dealers have had to dig deeper into their pockets to get their hands on ticket stubs or full tickets. It's tougher for dealers to buy ticket stubs from people after the game.

On the flipside, it is now easier to find ticket stubs in better condition because fans are making sure they put their ticket stubs in plastic holders.

They tell ticket tearers to be very careful and after the stub was torn off, they put it in a protective holder.

One example where collectors would be hard-pressed to find a ticket stub in very good shape is Super Bowl IV, which was played at Tulane Stadium in New Orleans.

It seems college students hired as ticket rippers for that game weren't too concerned with tearing them on the perforation. It's estimated that a good 95 percent of all those stubs were just torn right in half, which makes a clean tear for that stub all that much more collectible.

Tickets and stubs from Super Bowl III, the game in which Joe Namath predicted the underdog New York Jets victory over the Baltimore Colts, are also highly prized by collectors.

Also: stubs from Super Bowls involving the Packers, Cowboys and 49ers excite collectors because of those teams' vast fan base.

Note: All values based on the ticket /stub in EX or better condition.

Ticket Stubs/Full Tickets

Super Bowl I	$400-$1,200/$1,600
Super Bowl II	$500-$700/$8,500
Super Bowl III	$500-$800/$3,400
Super Bowl IV	$300-$475/$1,100
Super Bowl V	$250-$350/$2,500
Super Bowl VI	$150-$250/$1,600
Super Bowl VII	$200-$275/$700-$900
Super Bowl VIII	$150-$200/$450-$550
Super Bowl IX	$175-$225/$400-$500
Super Bowl X	$150-$175/$300-$400
Super Bowl XI	$100-$150/$300-$400
Super Bowl XII	$300-$575/$9,000
Super Bowl XIII	$125-$175/$500-$600
Super Bowl XIV	$75-$125/$300-$400
Super Bowl XV	$75-$125/$300-$400
Super Bowl XVI	$100-$150/$350-$500
Super Bowl XVII	$100-$150/$300-$450
Super Bowl XVIII	$100-$150/$300-$450
Super Bowl XIX	$100-$150/$300-$400
Super Bowl XX	$100-$150/$300-$400
Super Bowl XXI	$100-$150/$295-$450
Super Bowl XXII	$50-$100/$225-$400
Super Bowl XXIII	$50-$100/$240-$400
Super Bowl XXIV	$50-$100/$235-$400
Super Bowl XXV	$100-$150/$225-$350
Super Bowl XXVI	$75-$125/$200-$350
Super Bowl XXVII	$50-$100/$225-$350
Super Bowl XXVIII	$60-$110/$295-$400
Super Bowl XXIX	$50-$100/$295-$350
Super Bowl XXX	$50-$100/$275-$300
Super Bowl XXXI	$75-125/$250-$300

Super Bowl I

Super Bowl XXVII

Super Bowl XXXII	$75-125/$250-$300
Super Bowl XXXIII	$50-100/$275-$300
Super Bowl XXXIV	$75-125/$250-$300
Super Bowl XXXV	$50-100/$275-$300
Super Bowl XXXVI	$50-100/$275-$300
Super Bowl XXXVII	$50-100/$275-$300

Boxing Tickets

Boxing is one of the most ancient of all sports. Formal matches have been traced to the Twenty-third Olympiad held near Athens in 688 B.C. As it grew in popularity, admission requirements to major events became necessary. When and where these requirements first included a ticket, or a remuneration to associated individuals, in any shape or form, is not known. There is not an overabundance of boxing tickets available to collectors for fights held prior to 1900.

A popular starting point for many serious collectors of boxing tickets has been the James J. Corbett versus John L. Sullivan Heavyweight Championship fight of Sept. 7, 1892. It was one of boxing's greatest bouts. The 10,000 fans who witnessed the fight paid $15 for a ticket. Upon entering the arena the ticket was punched leaving three small holes on a now "used" ticket. In spite of his loss Sullivan was arguably the most beloved sporting figure of the 19th century. Many of those who attended the fight honorably adhered their used ticket into a scrapbook or set it aside for safekeeping. The popularity of the fighters, the admission fee —considered exorbitant at the time — and the importance of the event contributed significantly to the survival of some fine examples of this ticket. Collectors have also found an aesthetic appeal to the tickets design — exemplary artwork from this era. Purchasing an excellent example of this ticket today can cost collectors around $2,000.

Ticket Forms & Types

Boxing tickets are typically found in three forms: full boxing ticket, boxing ticket without stub and ticket stub. Full boxing tickets are preferred by collectors because they are usually unaltered. A ticket in this state is assumed to be unused. Since most individuals who purchase admission tickets generally attend the fight, altered boxing tickets are the most common form found by collectors.

Selected Boxing Tickets

1884
Kilrain vs. Cleary Ticket Stub, VG.............................. $900
1890
Corbett vs. McCaffrey, EX $5,500
1892
Sullivan vs. Corbett VG....................................... $2,000
Dixon vs. Skelly, 9/6, rare, VG $1,000
1897
Mysterious Billy Smith, from Tuxedo Athletic Club $750
Sullivan vs. Kaigh, VG $625
1902
Corbett vs. McGovern, Fair.................................... $450
Erne vs. Gans Ticket Stub, G, minor creases................. $400
Ryan vs. Carter, EX.. $950

Altered tickets are commonly differentiated from unused by the lack of a ticket portion, such as a stub. The stub, which is usually smaller than the main portion of the ticket, normally detaches at the perforation or perforation line. Boxing ticket stubs often have little aesthetic appeal and in many cases even fail to include the fighters' names. It is the main portion of the ticket that fascinates collectors most. This section usually has an attractive design, the fighters' names or perhaps a photograph, and venue information.

Illustrated tickets, or tickets that include photos of the fighters have greater aesthetic appeal, but not necessarily more value. Placing photographic images of the fighters on tickets, usually just a portrait, became popular during the end of the first decade of the 1900s. Some early examples of this technique, include the Johnson versus Jefferies heavyweight championship ticket (1910) and the Jim Flynn versus Jack Johnson world championship ticket (1912).

Older tickets were often "hole punched" during admittance into the arena. This practice remained common into the 1930s, despite the inclusion of a stub into the ticket's design. Improved perforation equipment eventually made it easier for ticket takers to remove the stubs rather than punch the tickets. Punch size, design, and placement can vary. For example, tickets used for the Johnny Dundee versus Benny Leonard fight were punched with a star shape, also tickets used for the Patterson versus Harris fight (8/18/58) had a stub removed and were punched with a variety of shapes (round and "E").

*Prices listed are for full tickets unless noted.

1904
Britt vs. Corbett Ticket Stub, minor creases, G $400
Ryan vs. O'Brien, EX $975
Ryan vs. Root EX $975
1907
Gans vs. Britt II Ticket Stub, VG.................................... $375
1909
Nelson vs. Hyland , EX $775
Johnson vs. O'Brien, Ticket Stub, (Fighters' names do not appear.), G $125
Attell vs. Weeks, Ticket Stub, VG $295
1910
Jeffries vs. Johnson, EX.. $1,500
Nelson vs. Moran, Ticket Stub, EX.................................. $400
1912
Flynn vs. Johnson, rare, EX $950

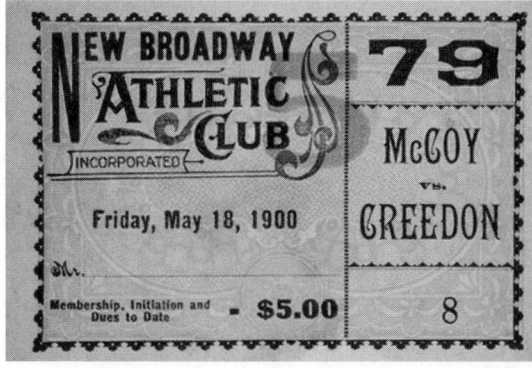

Ticket stub from the May 18, 1900 McCoy/Creedon bout.

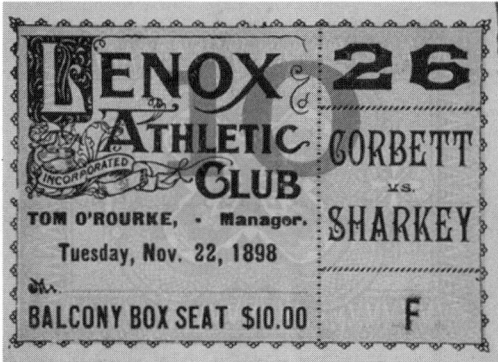

Stub from the November 22, 1898 Corbett/ Sharkey bout.

1913

Burns vs. McCarty, rare, EX	$1,400
Ritchie vs. Rivers, rare, EX	$750

1919

Leonard vs. Dundee, EX	$180
Leonard vs. White, EX	$180
Willard vs. Dempsey, NM	$600
Unused, set of 5, printer's proofs	$450

1921

Dempsey vs. Carpentier, Ticket without stub, EX	$100

1922

Leonard vs. White, NM	$125

1923

Criqui vs. Dundee, EX	$150
NM	$175
Dempsey vs. Firpo Ticket Stub, G,	$225
(Fighters not named)	$60
Dempsey vs. Gibbons, EX	$300
Kilbane vs. Criqui, EX	$140
Wilde vs. Villa, NM	$150

1924

Carpentier vs. Gibbons, NM	$175
Firpo vs. Wills Stub, EX	$60

1925

McTigue vs. Berlenbach, G	$125
Berlenbach vs. Delaney II, VG, postponed until Dec.	$175
Walker vs. Shade, NM	$250

1926

Carpentier vs. Loughran, Ticket without stub, NM	$125
Flowers vs. Walker, Ticket without stub, VG	$115

1927

Sharkey vs. Maloney, NM	$225
Dempsey vs. Sharkey, Ticket Stub, G	$55
Dempsey vs. Tunney, EX	$300

1929

Fields vs. Dundee, VG	$125
Loughran vs. Braddock, NM	$265
Schmeling vs. Uzcudon, (Paolino on ticket - boxer's first name), EX	$185
Sharkey vs. Loughran I, NM	$230
Singer vs. Chocolate, NM	$150
EX, punched	$125

1930

Carnera vs. Christner, EX	$195
Carnera vs. Godfrey, Ticket (with detached stub), EX	$250
Chocolate vs. Berg, EX	$135
Mandell vs. Singer, EX	$110
Sharkey vs. Campolo, NM	$210
Singer vs. McLarnin, NM	$95

1931

Canzoneri vs. Berg, EX	$200
VG	$175

1932

Jack Dempsey "All Star Fight Card," 11/18, NM	$150
Schmeling vs. Stribling, VG	$185

1932

Canzoneri vs. Petrolle, G	$110
Dempsey vs. Wine Ticket Stub, EX	$120
Schaaf vs. Gross, NM	$100
McLarnin vs. Brouillard Boxing Ticket, EX	$90

1933

Corbett vs. McLarnin, NM	$150

1934

Baer vs. Carnera Ticket Stub, (Fighters are not named), EX	$55
Ticket without stub, EX	$90
Rodak vs. Chocolate , NM, postponed	$85
Rosenbloom vs. Knight, NM	$95

1935

Baer vs. Willis, Exhibition, EX	$155
Baer vs. Braddock Ticket Stub, VG	$80
Canzoneri vs. Klick, EX	$150
NM	$175
Jack Dempsey "Boxing Show," 6/17, NM	$95
Louis vs. Baer, EX	$500
Louis vs. Levinsky, EX	$400
Louis vs. Ramage, EX	$200

1936

Louis vs. Sharkey, NM	$400
Schmeling vs. Joe Louis I Ticket Stub, (Fighters are not named.), EX	$100
EX, printer's proofs	$400

1937

Baer vs. Farr Ticket Stub, NM	$75
Baer vs. Foord Ticket Stub, VG	$60
Carnival of Champions Ambers/Montanez, Ross/Garcia, NM	$135
Louis vs. Farr, NM	$350
Steele vs. Overlin, EX	$70
Steele vs. Williams, NM	$115
Braddock vs. Louis, EX	$325
Ticket Stub	$65
Galento vs. Nova, VG	$100

1938

Ambers vs. Armstrong, EX	$175
Farr vs. Nova, M	$110
Galento vs. Lewis, 7/13, EX	$130
Galento vs. Thomas , VG	$145

1939

Ambers vs. Arizmendi, NM	$100
Apostoli vs. Conn, NM	$135
Archibald vs. Jeffra, NM	$120
Archibald vs. Rodak, NM	$120
Armstrong vs. Fontaine, NM	$165
Baer vs. Nova "Dressing Room Pass," NM	$200
Conn vs. Lesnevich, NM	$135
Escobar vs. Morgan, NM	$110
Galento vs. Bresica, NM	$80
Louis vs. Lewis, VG	$245

![Ticket from May 4, 1900 Smith/Joe Walcott bout.]

Ticket from May 4, 1900 Smith/Joe Walcott bout.

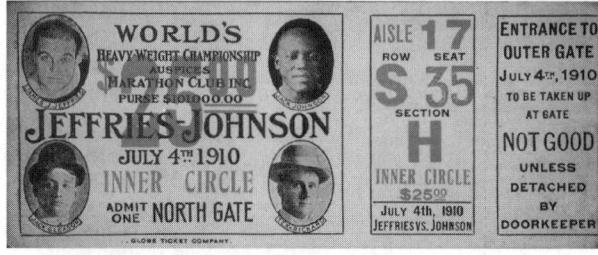

Ticket from July 4, 1910 Jim Jefferies/Jack Johnson bout.

Mann vs. Knox , NM $75

1940

Ambers vs. Jenkins, EX $140
   VG $100
Archibald vs. Jeffra, NM $115
Armstrong vs. Montanez, NM... $145
Armstrong vs. Zivic, NM, 10/4, Sugar Ray Robinson Pro Debut....$325
Angott vs. Day , NM... $60
Conn vs. Pastor, "Working Press," EX $145
   NM $150
Conn vs. Savoid, EX.. $150
Hostak vs. Zale, NM.. $140
Garcia vs. Armstrong, EX $110
Garcia vs. Belloise, VG $60
Jenkins vs. Armstrong, "Club Official," NM $140
Jenkins vs. Lello, EX $95
Louis vs. Godoy, EX, printer's proofs $250
Mann vs. Baer, EX... $100

1941

Baer vs. Louis, EX, printer's proofs $175
Jenkins vs. Tribuani, NM... $110
Jenkins vs. Cochrane, EX $115
Louis vs. Conn I, NM $350
Louis vs. Nova, NM $250
Soose vs. Vigh, EX... $85
Zivic vs. Davis, NM, proofs $90

1942

Angott vs. Montgomery, EX $115
Louis vs. Conn, NM, postponed, 10/12 .... $125
Overlin vs. Apostoli, NM $110
Salica vs. Ortiz Boxing Ticket, NM $80

1943

Pep vs. Angott, "Working Press," EX $135

1944

Armstrong vs. Davis, NM... $130
Montgomery vs. Jack, EX.. $115

1946

Louis vs. Conn II, NM $325
Louis vs. Mauriello, NM.. $190
Robinson vs. Sebastian, EX... $175
Servo vs. Robinson, NM, fight postponed $275

1947

Graziano vs. Zale, Ticket without stub, EX $125

1948

Graziano vs. Zale, NM.. $300
Louis vs. Foxworth, Ticket Stub, EX $85
Williams vs. Flores,Robinson/Gavilan, G $125

1949

Charles vs. Valentino, Ticket without stub, NM....................... $85
Charles vs. Walcott "Official Pass," VG $60
LaMotta vs. Cerdan, "Photographer," NM $160
Graziano vs. Fusari, NM.. $130
   "Dressing Room Pass" $55

1950

Graziano vs. Curcio, NM $150
LaMotta vs. Mitri, NM $135
Louis vs. Charles, NM... $240
Pep vs. Famechon, EX $105
Pep vs. Saddler, NM.. $150

1951

Charles vs. Maxim, scarce, EX $210
Louis vs. Marciano, postponed for two weeks, 11/11, M........ $350
Pep vs. Saddler, NM.. $170
Turpin vs. Robinson, EX $160

1952

Gavilan vs. Dykes, NM $120
Graziano vs. Davey, Ticket without stub, EX $85
Marciano vs. Mathews, NM $260
Maxim vs. Moore , NM $100
Robinson vs. Maxim $130
   EX, printer's proof $150
Walcott vs. Charles, "Dressing Room Pass," EX $160
Walcott vs. Marciano "Dressing Room Pass," NM $150
   EX $295
Ticket Stub, EX $45

1953

Gavilan vs. Bratton. Ticket without stub, NM $60
Gavilan vs. Davey, Ticket without stub, EX............................. $70
Marciano vs. Lastarza, NM $125
Marciano vs. Walcott II, NM $150

1956

Basilio vs. Saxton, 3/14 .... $110
Charles vs. Richardson, Ticket without stub, NM $60
Saxton vs. Basillo, NM, 9/12 .... $125

1957

Gavilan vs. Martinez, NM $110

1958

Max Baer Television Show Full Ticket, NM $70
Robinson vs. Basilio Full Closed-Circuit Ticket, NM $65
   EX $185
Napoles vs. Cobblah, G $35

1959

Aikins vs. Jordan, NM $60
Basilio vs. Fullmer, Ticket VG.. $70
Patterson vs. London, NM... $160

1960

Tournament of Champions Press Pass, Golden Gloves,
   Cassius Clay, 3/2... $350
U.S. Olympic Amateur Finals, 5/8 Cassius Clay, small size
   (1.25"x4"), EX... $600
Fullmer vs. Robinson Boxing Ticket without stub, M $100
Paret vs. Thompson, NM.. $135
Johansson vs. Patterson II Ticket Stub, EX* $65

1961

Liston vs. Westphal, NM.. $200
Patterson vs. McNeeley, NM, postponed three weeks $120

Ticket from July 4, 1923 Jack Dempsey/Tom Gibbons bout.

Ticket from June 19, 1946 Joe Louis/Billy Conn bout.

Pender vs. Downes..$95

1962

Clay vs. Lavorante Ticket Stub, EX.......................................$220
   VG $400
Gavilan vs. Dykes, NM $95
Patterson vs. Liston I, G $125

1963

Clay vs. Cooper, Ticket without stub, NM $400
Liston vs. Patterson, M $120
4/4, postponed $50
Liston vs. Patterson II, EX $225

1964

Joe Frazier vs. Buster Mathis, Sr., Griffith/Benvenuti, EX...........$90
Griffith vs. Charnley, Ticket without stub, EX $35
Griffith vs. Rodriguez, NM $60
"Dressing Room Pass," EX $25
Liston vs. Clay "Interview Room" Pass, 2/25, NM $300
   Full Ticket, 11/16 "Dressing Room," post poned, NM.........$300
   Full Ticket, 11/16 "Weigh-in," postponed, NM $300
Patterson vs. Powell, NM $170

1965

Clay vs.Patterson Interview Area Pass, scarce, NM.................$325
Perkins vs. Hernandez, Ticket, EX $35

1966

Ali vs. Cooper II Boxing Ticket without stub, NM $300
   Weigh-in, EX $150
Ali vs. Terrell, NM, fight postponed $100
Ali vs. C. Williams Boxing Ticket without stub, EX $150
"Working Press Pass," NM..$160
"Dressing Room Pass," VG $115
Burruni vs. McGowan Boxing Ticket without stub, G $35
Giardello vs. White, NM $100
Griffith vs. Archer, NM $110
Tiger vs. Griffith, EX, "Press" $60
Torres vs. Thornton, "Employee," EX $70

1967

Ali vs. Terrell Boxing Ticket without stub, EX $150
   "Pre-fight Pass," EX $175
   "Clubhouse Pass," NM $175
   "Working Press Pass," EX $175
Benvenuti vs. Griffith II, VG $120
Patterson vs. Johnson, EX $40
Quarry vs. Patterson, NM $175

1969

Castillo vs. Jangalay Ticket without stub, VG $25
Ellis vs. Cooper, NM, postponed $130
Napoles vs. Cokes Ticket without stub, G $30
Olivares vs. Castillio I, Ticket, EX $35

1971

Ali vs. Ellis Closed-Circuit Ticket, NM.................................$40
Ali vs. Mathis, Sr. Closed-Circuit Ticket, EX $35
Backus vs. Napoles Ticket without stub, VG $60
Frazier vs. Ali I, Closed-Circuit Ticket..................................$60

1972

Foster vs. Finnegan, Ticket without stub, EX $40
Foster vs. Rondon, NM $105
Monzon vs. Briscoe, EX $125

1973

Ali vs. Norton, "Dressing Room"...$160
Otero vs. Buchanan, NM $50
Ali Exhibition, 10/24, NM..$500

1974

Quarry vs. Frazier, NM $200

1975

Ali vs. Wepner Circuit Boxing Ticket, EX.............................$150
"Press," NM $185
Ali vs. Lyle, EX $550
Ali vs. Frazier NM $300
Frazier vs. Ellis Boxing Ticket without stub, NM $100

1976

Boxing Writers Assoc., EX $15
Foreman vs. Frazier II, Full Closed-Circuit Ticket, NM $50

1977

Ali vs. Evangelista, Ticket without stub, NM $400
   "Dressing Room" $160
   "Working Press" $160
Ali vs. Shavers, EX $150
   NM $225

1978

L. Spinks vs. Ali, NM $600
"Press Ringside," Full Boxing Pass, autographed by Ali...........$550
Galindez vs. Lopez, NM $105
Holmes vs. Shaver, NM $175
Holmes Exhibition, NM..$125

1979

Ali vs. Alzado, EX $400
Holmes vs. Weaver, NM $215
Benitez vs. Leonard Boxing Ticket without stub, EX $35
Leonard vs. Marcotte, (Marcotte not named), NM.................$100
Lopez vs. Ayala, NM $50

1980

Antuofermo vs. Minter Partial Ticket, VG $40
Leonard vs. Duran, Ticket Stub VG $200
Tate vs. Weaver, NM $120
Hearns vs. Cuevas Ticket without stub, NM.........................$70
Holmes vs. Ali, NM $175
Watt vs. O'Grady, NM $45

1981

Chandler vs. Lujan, NM $15
Cooney vs. Norton, EX $100
Duran vs. Minchillo, NM $100
Hearns vs. Shields "Official's Pass," NM $20
Holmes vs. Berbick, NM $125
Holyfield vs. Edleon, NM $100

Ticket from December 5, 1947 Joe Louis/Jersey Joe Walcott bout.

Ticket from September 26, 1951 Sandy Saddler/Willie Pep bout.

1982

Holmes vs. Cooney, "Complimentary, no refund," NM $75
Mancini vs. Kim, NM $200
Benitez vs. Duran, NM $110
Witherspoon vs. Snipes, NM $50

1983

Hagler vs. Duran Boxing Ticket without stub, NM $60
Hagler vs. Scypion, EX $60
Hagler vs. Mamby, EX $32
Holmes vs. M. Frazier, NM $150

1984

Witherspoon vs. Thomas, EX $100
Hearns vs Duran, NM $125
Ticket without stub, NM $75

1985

Hagler vs. Hearns, NM $150
Holmes vs. Bey, NM $100

1986

Berbick vs. Tyson Full Ticket Stub, NM $300
Hagler vs. Mugabi Hearns/Shuler , NM $125
Full Closed-Circuit Ticket, NM $35
M. Spinks vs. Holmes II, VG $100

1987

Hagler vs. Leonard, NM $175
Hearns vs. Andries"Ref's Pass," NM $60
Hearns vs. Roldan, NM $60
Holyfield vs. Ocasio, NM $65
Tyson vs. Biggs, NM $100

1988

Hearns vs. Barkley, NM $75
Foreman vs. Qwai, NM $125
Holyfield vs. DeLeon, NM $90
Leonard vs. LaLonde, NM $100
Tyson vs. Michael Spinks, NM $150
   "Press Pass," coated, NM $75
   Full Closed-Circuit Ticket, NM $15
Tyson vs. Holmes, NM $175

1989

Chavez vs. Fuentes, NM $60
Dokes vs. Holyfield, NM $100
B. Mitchell vs. I. Mitchell, NM $25

1990

Foreman vs. Cooney, NM $150
Douglas vs. Holyfield, NM $150

1991

Brown vs. McGrits, NM $45
Holmes vs. Anderson, NM $45
Tyson vs. Ruddock, NM $225
Tyson vs. Ruddock II, NM $200

1992

Bowe vs. Coetzer, NM $65
Czyz vs. Lalonde, NM $35
Holyfield vs. Bowe, NM $100

1993

Bowe vs. Dokes, NM $60
L. Lewis vs. T. Tucker, NM $60
Bowe vs. J. Ferguson, NM $60

L. Lewis vs. Bruno, NM $60
Holyfield vs. Rowe, NM $60

1994

Moorer vs. Holyfield, NM $65
L. Lewis vs. P. Jackson, NM $60
McCall vs. L. Lewis, NM $65
Foreman vs. Moorer $100

1995

McCall vs. Holmes, NM $60
Seldon vs. T. Tucker, NM $60
Foreman vs. A. Schulz, NM $110
LaRosa vs. Hinton, NM $50
Seldon vs. Hipp, NM $50
Bruno vs. McCall, NM $50
Botha vs. Schulz, NM $50

1996

Nielsen vs. LaRosa, NM $50
Tyson vs. Bruno, NM $50
Nielsen vs. P. Jackson, NM $50
Nielsen vs. Hunter, NM $50
Moorer vs. Schulz, NM $50
Tyson vs. Seldon, NM $50
Holyfield vs. Tyson, NM $60
Moorer vs. Botha, NM $50

1997

Nielsen vs.Holmes, NM $50
L. Lewis vs. McCall, NM $50
Moorer vs. Bean, NM $50
Holyfield vs. Tyson, NM $50
L. Lewis vs. Akinwande, NM $50
L. Lewis vs. Golota, NM $50
Holyfield vs. Moorer, NM $50
Nielsen vs. Steele, NM $50

1998

L. Lewis vs. Briggs, NM $40
Nielsen vs. Butler, NM $40
Holyfield vs. Bean, NM $40
L. Lewis vs. Mavrovic, NM $40

1999

L. Lewis vs. Holyfield, NM $50
L. Lewis vs. Holyfield, NM $50

2000

L. Lewis vs. Grant, NM $40
L. Lewis vs. Botha, NM $40
Holyfield vs. Ruiz, NM $40
L. Lewis vs. Tua, NM $40

2001

Ruiz vs. Holyfield, NM $35
Rahman vs. L. Lewis, NM $35
L. Lewis vs. Rahman, NM $35
Ruiz vs. Holyfield, NM $35

2002

L. Lewis vs. Tyson, NM $50
Ruiz vs. K. Johnson, NM $35
Byrd vs. Holyfield, NM $35

2003

Jones Jr. vs. Ruiz, NM $35

Chapter 12

PENNANTS

Since almost every kid who had a felt pennant tacked it up on his bedroom wall, it's unusual to find a vintage pennant in well-preserved, investment grade condition. Most, measuring 12-by-30 inches, have pin holes in them and can be purchased for less than $50. Today's versions, often available at stadiums and arenas, are made in large quantities, so look for pennants prior to 1960, and concentrate on pennants for popular teams, championship teams, teams that no longer exist, or those which commemorate a specific event. Stacks of pennants are almost always available at larger card shows or through sports auctions. But sometimes a pennant or two will turn up in an antique shop or flea market. Although it probably isn't going to offer big returns as an investment piece, a pennant can still add a nice decorative touch to any memorabilia display.

BASEBALL PENNANTS

The history of baseball pennants is perhaps the most difficult to track of all memorabilia. While a good deal is known about recent pennants, it's virtually impossible to determine how many were produced prior to 1970.

The first known baseball pennants appeared at ballparks around the turn of the century. From 1905-1910 the first pennants bearing team or city names were produced. The first commemorative pennant—celebrating the World Champion Boston Braves—appeared in 1914. By 1986, the market had grown considerably, as fans of the New York Mets had a selection of eight banners to choose from at Shea Stadium souvenir stands. Championship and single-season pennants through the years have evolved to include team rosters, facsimile signatures and team photos.

But the earliest pennants were not always season-specific. In the early years, fans might find the same pennants for sale at the ballpark for several years in a row. And these pennants were generally made with excess and scrap felt, so sizes and colors would differ at each stadium. Manufacturer labels can often be found sewn on the back of pennants produced before 1940, but for pennants issued between 1940 and 1970 it's nearly impossible to determine a specific producer.

Technology in the 1970s brought a change to the traditional felt pennants. Synthetics were added to the fabric, making pennants thinner, more rigid and less expensive to produce. Two companies—Trench Manufacturers of Buffalo and WinCraft of Winona, Minn.—established licensing agreements and have been the major players in the industry since 1970.

Event-specific and commemorative pennants seem to be the easiest to track, as well as being the most popular with collectors. They're often limited editions sold only at ballparks involved in the event. Pennants from the World Series, ballpark openings and retirement ceremonies fall into this category.

Attaching values to pennants is extremely difficult. Before the early 1990s, there were no checklists available, and previously unknown specimens are continually being discovered. The best places to find vintage pennants are in the traditional baseball cities, at card shows or through auctions.

In general, collectors prefer attractive pennants that can easily be displayed. Vibrant, colorful pennants, especially of the pre-1970 variety, are the most valuable and hardest to find. Many older pennants are faded, missing tassels or have pinholes around the tip—all direct results of being hung on bedroom walls.

Selected Pennants

Teams

1920s Cleveland Indians, red with white letters $135

1930s Boston Braves, batting scene, red $125

1930s Boston Red Sox, 3/4 size pennant .... $75-$125

1934-35 Detroit Tigers, black-and-white on orange $375

1935 Detroit Tigers World Champs scroll pennant, orange on
    black $350

Early-1940s Boston Red Sox, large baseball over the stadium, gray
    and red $100

Early-1940s Brooklyn Dodgers, batter and catcher, white on red .. $285

Early-1940s Brooklyn Dodgers, Brooklyn Dodgers: Our Champs,
    white on purple $395

Mid-1940s Boston Red Sox, batter hitting pitched ball, white on
    red $135

Late-1940s Brooklyn Dodgers, shows catcher and batter from
    backside, white on blue $175

Late-1940s New York Yankees, player sliding into tag, white on
    blue $95

Late-1940s Philadelphia Phillies signature, Fightin Phillies, white
    and red $195

Late-1940s St. Louis Cardinals, two birds on a bat, red, yellow and
white on red $65

Late-1940s St. Louis Browns, player making a catch, orange on
    blue $175

1940s Boston Red Sox, runner sliding into base, white on red $145

1940s Brooklyn Dodgers, player sliding into tag, blue on white $150

1940s Chicago Cubs, large C in Chicago, white on blue $110

1940s Chicago Cubs, player sliding into a tag, black on orange $95

1940s Chicago White Sox, infield play in progress, white on
    dark blue $125

1940s Cincinnati Reds, Cincinnati in Gothic letters, white and red. $150

1940s Cleveland Indians, Indian with full headdress, white on red .. $80

1940s Detroit Tigers, black tiger head on orange $85

1940s New York Giants, batter, catcher and umpire, white and
    blue $125

Early-1950s Brooklyn Dodgers, red, white and blue $295

Early-1950s Philadelphia A's, white on blue $85

Mid-1950s Chicago Cubs Wrigley Field, Cub playing with a ball,
    white on blue .... $90-$125

Mid-1950s Baltimore Orioles, bird on a baseball, white and pink on
    red $100

Mid-1950s New York Yankees, Uncle Sam, multi-color on blue . $125

Late-1950s Baltimore Orioles, bird pitching over Memorial
    Stadium $95

Late-1950s San Francisco Giants, mascot on the bridge, white,
    gray and pink and green $85

1950s Chicago Cubs, two cubs standing, white and peach on
    blue $55

1950s Chicago White Sox, winged foot, white and yellow on
    blue $75

1950s Detroit Tigers, Tiger head inside Tiger Stadium $60

1950s New York Giants, orange and white on black $60

1950s New York Yankees, Yankee logo, red and blue on white .. $95

1950s Philadelphia Phillies, Go Phillies Go with batting scene .. $60

1950s Philadelphia Phillies, elephant with a ball in its trunk, white
    and blue $125

1950s-60s Pittsburgh Pirates, black with Pirate head with a sword
    in his mouth $90

1950 Philadelphia Phillies, Fightin Phillies, with tag scene, players
    names $165

1950 Philadelphia, "Fightin' Phillies", player and bat, red St. Louis
    Cardinals, Sportman's Park .... $90-$135

Early-1960s Chicago Cubs, Wrigley Field, multi-color on blue . $55

Early-1960s Houston Colt 45s, blue and orange on white $65

Early-1960s New York Mets, skyline, team logo, blue and white on
    dark blue $85

Early-1960s New York Yankees .... $75-$95

Mid-1960s Chicago Cubs, Cub bear in Wrigley Field .... $70-$90

Mid-1960s San Francisco Giants, SF in block, Giants logo, bat,
    black on orange $65

Late-1960s Baltimore Orioles, bird on top of an O, bat and glove,
    black on orange $65

Late-1960s New York Mets, shows Shea, Mr. Met and Liberty on
    blue $45

Late-1960s Washington Senators, white on red $60

1960s Atlanta Braves, multi-color on navy $35

1960s Kansas City A's stadium pennant .... $90-$125

1960s Pittsburgh Pirates, multi-color on black $40

1960s St. Louis Cardinals, multi-color on red $40

1960s San Francisco Giants, play at the plate, black on orange $85

1960s Washington Senators, pitcher and capital, red, white and
    blue $75

1960 St. Louis Browns, shows batter, white on brown $55

1961 Cincinnati Reds picture pennant $135

1961 Cincinnati Reds National League Champions, players names,
    red and blue on white $110

1961 New York Yankees picture pennant $250

1963 New York Mets black-and-white picture pennant $155

1964 Philadelphia Phillies picture pennant $85

1965 Houston Colt .45s/Houston Astrodome, double-sided
    pennant $150

1966 Baltimore Orioles team picture pennant $100

1966 Chicago White Sox team picture pennant, red and blue on
    white $110

1966 New York Mets team picture pennant $135

1966-67 California Angels, Anaheim Stadium $55

1967 St. Louis Cardinals National League Champions $40

1968 Chicago White Sox picture pennant $85

1969 Boston Red Sox picture pennant $55

1969 Cincinnati Reds picture pennant $95

1969 Houston Astros $20

1969 Kansas City Royals $40

1969 Montreal Expos $35

1969 Seattle Pilots, MLB logo, Seattle in script, multi-colored on
    red .... $75-$100

1969 Seattle Pilots, multi-color on white felt .... $125-$150

1969-71 Washington Senators, red and blue on white $75

Early-1970s Chicago White Sox, batter on sock in red circle $45

1970s Cleveland Indians, Chief Wahoo with bat and ball, black $45

Early-1970s Minnesota Twins, TC in dot over I in Minnesota,
    white on blue $35

1942 St. Louis Cardinals World Series pennant

Boston Red Sox pennant

1970s Baltimore Orioles $10
1970s Houston Astros $10
1970s Milwaukee Brewers.. $10
1970s St. Louis Cardinals $10
1970s San Diego Padres, crossed bats with padre, white on
    brown.. $55
1970s San Francisco Giants $10
1970 Baltimore Orioles picture pennant .... $75-$90
1970 Milwaukee Brewers, barrel man swinging a bat, gold on
    blue $55
1971 Pittsburgh Pirates color team photo pennant $95
1973 Boston Red Sox Fenway Park, white and green on red $50
1974 Cincinnati Reds picture pennant .... $60-$75

Events

1962 Dodger Stadium grand opening, blue and red vertical
    pennant $75
1969 Mickey Mantle Day at Yankee Stadium, red $55
1969 San Diego Padres first year.................................... $30-$45
1974 Hank Aaron "Home Run King, 1974"................................ $45
1974 Hank Aaron, "All Time Home Run Champion" $45
1978 Do it Pete! Do it Pete! Rose's hitting streak, 7/25/78 at Shea
    Stadium $55
1978 Go For It Pete! 4192 Hits, Tie-Breaker $55
1979 Carl Yastrzemski, "Yaz 1979, 400 HR, 3000 Hits" $45
1983 Carl Yastrzemski, "Yaz, #8", stats, retirement day
    pennant .... $20-$35
1993 Florida Marlins Opening Day... $10
2001 Camden Yards 10th Anniversary $8

Recent World, League and Division Championships

1948 Cleveland Indians American League Champs/World Series,
    multi-color on dark red.. $195
1955 Brooklyn Dodgers National League Champs, scroll, Bum,
    blue $200
1957 Milwaukee Braves World Champions, names of players, white
    and purple $250
1958 Milwaukee Braves National League Champs, Indian dancing,
    player names, white and red $110
1958 Milwaukee Braves 1958 National League Champs scroll
    pennant $100
1959 Chicago White Sox American League Champs, white on
    blue $125
Early 1960s New York Yankees American League Champs, player
    names on scroll .... $125-$175
1960 Pittsburgh Pirates 1960 National League Champions, pirate
    holding a sword $135
1961 Cincinnati 1961 National League Champions, player's names
    on scroll .... $70-$100
1961 Cincinnati, World Series, picture, ... $100
1963 World Series, LA Dodgers vs. NYY, blue felt.................... $75
1965 World Series Los Angeles Dodgers vs. Minnesota Twins,
    blue felt $75
1966 World Series Los Angeles Dodgers vs. Baltimore Orioles,
    Dodger Stadium, blue felt $65
1967 World Series, Red Sox vs. Cardinals, Fenway Park, black
    and red on white.. $75

1967 St. Louis Cardinals National League Champions.............. $40
1968 Detroit Tigers American League Champions, black and
    orange on white.. $125-$150
1968 St. Louis Cardinals National League Champions/World
    Series, white and pink on red... $65
1969 Baltimore Orioles World Series picture pennant $95
1969 New York Mets World Champions, orange on blue $95
1970 AL Champs, Orioles, players scroll $75
1970 World Champs, Orioles, team picture, orange and black on
    white $75
1971 World Champions, Pittsburgh, player scroll (Mazeroski,
    Clemente, Stargell) $70
1971 Pittsburgh Pirates National League Champs scroll, black and
    gold on white.. $60
1973 Chicago White Sox American League Western Division
    Champions.. $30
1973 New York Mets World Champs signature pennant .... $60-$90
1973 New York Mets You Gotta Believe, Mets #1 Again, 1973
    Champions, blue on white.. $75
1973 New York Mets Eastern Division Champs scroll pennant,
    white and orange on blue.. $70-$85
1973 Oakland As American League Champs scroll pennant..... $45
1974 NL Champions, LA Dodgers $40
1974 Los Angeles Dodgers World Series signature pennant $50
1975 Dodgers Team photo... $40
1975 AL Eastern Division Champs, Red Sox........................... $40
1975 AL Playoffs, Boston vs. Oakland $55
1975 World Series, NL Champions, Cincinnati, player scroll
    (Rose, Concepcion, Bench, Morgan) $45
1975 World Series, AL Champions, Boston, player scroll
    (Fisk, Yastrzemski) $45
1975 World Series, Boston vs. Cincinnati $40
1976 Cincinnati Reds World Champs trophy $45
1977 NL Champions, Dodgers, Dodger Stadium, signatures $40
1977 World Series, Dodgers, Dodger Stadium, signatures........ $35
1977 World Series, LA Dodgers vs. NYY................................. $30
1978 World Series, NL Champions, LA, player scroll (Garvey), blue
    or red left border.. $35
1978 NL Champions, LA $30
1978 World Series AL Champions, NYY, player scroll (Hunter), blue
    or red left border $30
1978 NL Eastern Division Champs, Phillies, player scroll (Schmidt,
    Maddox, Carlton)... $30
1979 World Champs, Pirates, Three Rivers Stadium................ $25
1979 World Champs, Pirates, player scroll (Stargell)............... $45
1979 World Champion, Orioles (phantom) $20
1980 Kansas City World Series scroll pennant, blue and gold
    on white... $35
1980 World Series, NL Champs, Phillies, player scroll ...... $30-$40
1980 World Champs, Phillies, "P" $20
1980 World Champions, Phillies, "We're #1", player scroll (Maddox,
    Schmidt, Rose, Carlton) $30
1981 AL Champions, NYY, player scroll (Winfield) .... $25-$35
1981 World Series, Dodgers vs. Yankees $30
1981 World Champions, Dodgers $20
1982 AL Champions, Milwaukee.. $20
1982 World Champions, St. Louis, player scroll........................ $20

1940s Brooklyn Dodgers pennant

1957 Milwaukee Braves pennant

1963 National League All-Stars pennant

Chicago White Sox pennant

1983 AL Eastern Division Champs, Orioles, signatures (Murray, Ripken) $35
1983 AL Western Division Champs, Chicago, player scroll (Fisk) $10
1983 AL Western Division Champions, White Sox, team photo $10
1983 AL Eastern Division Champions, Baltimore, player scroll (Murray, Ripken) $35
1983 NL Eastern Division Champions, Phillies $15
1983 NL Eastern Division Champions, Philadelphia, player scroll.. $15
1983 AL Champions, Orioles, Memorial Stadium $25
1983 AL Champs, Orioles, dates, stadium, ARA....................... $15
1983 AL Champions, Orioles, "Milk's the One".......................... $15
1983 World Series, AL Champions, Baltimore, player scroll (Murray, Ripken) $25
1983 World Series, NL Champions, Philadelphia, player scroll.. $15
1983 World Series, Orioles vs. Phillies, "I Was There!".............. $20
1983 World Series Champions, Baltimore, player scroll ..... $30-$40
1984 Eastern Division Champs, Cubs, swinging bear, player scroll $20
1984 World Series, NL Champions, Cubs, player scroll (Sandberg, Eckersley).. $31
1984 Detroit Tigers World Champions scroll pennant, blue and orange on black ....$25-$40
1985 NL Eastern Division Champions, St Louis $15
1985 World Series, NL Champions, St Louis, player scroll $15
1985 World Series, NL Champions, St Louis $15
1985 World Champions, KC Royals, player scroll $15
1986 AL Eastern Division Champions, Red Sox, player scroll ... $25
1986 NL Eastern Division Champions, Mets, player scroll $25
1986 AL Western Division Champions, Angels $20
1986 AL Championship, Red Sox vs. Angels, Fenway Park $35
1986 NL Champions, Mets, signatures $30
1986 AL Champions, Red Sox, signatures $30
1986 AL Champions, Red Sox, player scroll (Seaver, Clemens, Boggs) $30
1986 World Series, Red Sox vs., Mets $25
1986 World Champions, Mets, player scroll $25
1986 New York Mets World Champs signature pennant $35
1987 AL Western Division Champions, Minnesota, player scroll (Puckett) $15
1987 AL Eastern Division Champions, Detroit, player scroll $15
1987 AL Champions, Minnesota, 1987 World Series................. $15
1987 World Series, Minnesota vs. St Louis............................... $15

1987 World Series, AL Champions, Minnesota, signatures (Puckett) $15
1988 World Series, LA vs. Oakland, logo................................. $10
1988 World Series Champions, LA Dodgers, 1988 National League $10
1989 AL Eastern Division Champions, Orioles, player scroll, Trench $25
1989 World Series, "Battle of the Bay" $10
1989 Chicago Cubs N. L. East Champs $10
1990 World Series Champions, Cincinnati, signatures $10
1990 World Series, AL Champions, Oakland............................ $10
1991 World Series, Minnesota vs. Atlanta, WinCraft $10
1991 World Series Champs, Minnesota, first WinCraft player drawings $25
1991 World Series Champions, Minnesota, signatures $10
1992 NL Easter Division Champions, Pittsburgh, "3 in a Row!" WinCraft $15
1992 NL Eastern Division Champions, Pirates, player list, Trench... $15
1992 AL Champions, Blue Jays, signatures, Trench $8
1992 NL Champions, Braves, signatures, "Back '91 to '92 Back", Trench $10
1992 World Series, Atlanta vs. Toronto, WinCraft $8
1992 World Series, Braves vs. Blue Jays, Trench $8
1992 World Champions, Toronto, WinCraft................................ $8
1992 World Series Champions, Toronto, player drawings, WinCraft.$15
1993 NL Western Division Champions, Atlanta, "3Peat", Trench.... $10
1993 AL Western Division Champions, Chicago, WinCraft....... $10
1993 NL Western Division Champions, Atlanta, names scrolled, Trench $10
1993 NL Eastern Division Champions, Philadelphia, names scrolled, Trench $10
1993 NL Champions, Philadelphia, signatures, Trench.............. $8
1993 NL Champions, Philadelphia Phillies, WinCraft $8
1993 World series, Phillies vs. Blue Jays, WinCraft $8
1993 World Series Champions, Toronto, WinCraft..................... $10
1995 NL Eastern Division Champions, Braves $8
1995 AL Eastern Division Champions, Red Sox......................... $8
1995 AL Division Series, Tag $10
1995 AL Champions, Cleveland, WinCraft................................ $10
1995 AL Champions, Cleveland, player drawings, WinCraft, rare ...$55
1995 World Series Champions, Atlanta, Tag $8
1995 World Champions, Atlanta, WinCraft................................ $10

1969 New York Yankees Mickey Mantle Day pennant

1969 Seattle Pilots pennant

1970 Pittsburgh Pirates N.L. Championship pennant

1995 World Series Champions, Atlanta, player drawings,
   WinCraft $15
1996 Division Series, Cleveland, "Back to Back", Tag..............$10
1996 AL Championship Series, Orioles, Tag............................$15
1996 AL Championship Series, Orioles vs. NYY, Tag $15
1996 Eastern Division Champions, NYY, WinCraft $10
1996 Championship Series, Orioles, signatures, WinCraft $15
1996 NL Champions, Atlanta, WinCraft $10
1996 AL Champions, NYY, WinCraft $10
1996 World Series, NYY vs. Atlanta Braves, WinCraft..............$10
1996 World Champions NYY, The Fall Classic, WinCraft $10
1996 NYY World Champions, player drawings, vertical, WinCraft...$15
1997 NL Championship Series, Braves vs. Marlins, WinCraft ...$15
1997 AL Championship Series, Indians vs. Orioles, WinCraft ..$15
1997 AL Championship Series, Cleveland vs. Baltimore, Tag......$8
1997 AL Western Division Champions, Seattle, WinCraft $8
1997 AL East Division Champs Orioles, Tag.............................$8
1997 Eastern Division Champions, Orioles, WinCraft $8
1997 AL Wild Card Yankees, WinCraft $15
1997 League Championship Series, AL Champions, WinCraft..$15
1997 League Championship Series, NL Champions, WinCraft..$15
1997 World Series Champions, WinCraft $8
1997 World Series, Indians vs. Marlins, WinCraft $8
1997 World Series, "Florida versus Cleveland", Tag $8
1997 World Champions Signature, Marlins, WinCraft...............$10
1997 World Series Champions, Marlins, player drawings, WinCraft $10
1998 World Series Champions, NYY, signatures, WinCraft $10
1998 World Series Champions, NYY, photos, WinCraft $10
1999 World Series, "1999 Fall Classic, Yankee Stadium", Tag $8
2000 Seattle Mariners League Championship Series, WinCraft $8

Recent All-Star Games

1961 All-Star Game, Fenway Park ....$150-$175
1972 All-Star Game in Atlanta, red and blue on white................$55
1973 All-Star, KC, stadium $45
1975 All-Star, Milwaukee, AL vs. NL $30
1976 All-Star, Philadelphia, AL, players scroll, ...$30
1977 All-Star, New York, stadium, red, AL vs. NL $30
1979 All-Star, Seattle, dome...$20
1981 All-Star, Cleveland, logo $20
1983 All-Star, Chicago, logo $20
1983 All-Star, Chicago, written names $15
1985 All-Star, Minnesota, logo $15
1986 All-Star, Houston, Round-Up, pin stripes..........................$15
1986 All-Star, Houston, Round-Up, solid $15
1987 All-Star, Oakland, logo..$15
1988 All-Star, Cincinnati, logo, WinCraft $15
1989 All-Star, California, logo $12
1990 All-Star, Chicago, logo $12
1991 All-Star, Toronto, WinCraft $12
1992 All-Star, San Diego, logo, WinCraft $11
1993 All-Star Game, Baltimore, logo, green, Trench $10
1993 All-Star Game, Baltimore, logo, stars, WinCraft $10
1993 All-Star Game, Baltimore, limited 10,000, WinCraft $10
1994 All-Star Game in Pittsburgh, WinCraft $10
1995 All-Star Game, Texas, logo, WinCraft $8
1996 All-Star Game, Philadelphia, July 9, WinCraft.....................$8
1996 All-Star Game, Philadelphia, Tag..$8

1996 All-Star Game, Philadelphia, signatures, WinCraft (Ripken).. $15
1997 All-Star Game, Cleveland, All-Star Week, Tag $8
1997 All-Star Game, Cleveland, tickets, WinCraft $8
1998 All-Star Game Colorado, The 69th Annual, WinCraft $8
2001 All-Star Game Seattle, logo, WinCraft................................$8
2001 All-Star Game, Seattle, July 10, Tag $8
2001 All-Star Game, Seattle, Signatures, WinCraft (Ripken)....$10

1950 American Nut & Chocolate Pennants

Although there is nothing on these small (1 7/8 by 4) felt pennants to identify the issuer, surviving ads show that the American Nut & Chocolate Co. of Boston sold them as a set of 22 for 50 cents. The pennants of American League players are printed in blue on white, while National Leaguers are printed in red on white. The pennants feature crude line-art drawings of players on the left, along with a facsimile autograph. The pennants carry an American Card Catalog designation of F510. The complete set of 22 pennants is worth $350 in Near Mint condition.

Ewell Blackwell, ...$15
Harry Brecheen $15
Phil Cavarretta $15
Bobby Doerr...$17
Bob Elliott...$15
Boo Ferris...$15
Joe Gordon...$15
Tommy Holmes $15
Charles Keller...$15
Ken Keltner...$15
Whitey Kurowski $15
Ralph Kiner $20
Johnny Pesky $15
Pee Wee Reese $35
Phil Rizzuto...$30
Johnny Sain $17
Enos Slaughter $17
Warren Spahn $30
Vern Stephens $15
Earl Torgeson $15
Dizzy Trout..$15
Ted Williams..$70

1962-64 Bazooka Team Pennants

These brightly colored 14 1/2-inch pennants were redeemable with Bazooka bubble gum wrappers.

Complete set: (20).. $200
Chicago Cubs .... $10-$12
Cincinnati Reds .... $8-$10
Houston Colt .45s .... $8-$10
Los Angeles Dodgers .... $12-$15
Milwaukee Braves .... $12-$15
New York Mets .... $12-$15
Philadelphia Phillies .... $8-$10
Pittsburgh Pirates .... $8-$10
San Francisco Giants .... $8-$10
St. Louis Cardinals .... $10-$12
Baltimore Orioles .... $8-$10
Boston Red Sox .... $10-$12
Chicago White Sox .... $8-$10
Cleveland Indians .... $8-$10
Detroit Tigers .... $8-$10
Kansas City Athletics .... $8-$10
Los Angeles Angels .... $8-$10
Minnesota Twins .... $8-$10
New York Yankees .... $15-$20

Players

These are pennants with player caricatures drawn by Mudge. As a group, they are very distinct and unique in design, and represent the "rookie" pennants for many recent players and Hall of Fame stars.

When collecting current pennants, hobbyists can look to three manufacturers—Mitchell & Ness, Tag Express and Win-Craft. Through extensive research, Mitchell & Ness has produced a line of replica pennants similar to those produced from 1907-1970. Each season, WinCraft produces a new pennant for every Major League team, but their specialty is a line of pennants featuring player caricatures. Recently WinCraft has begun to produce wool team pennants that feature current team logos. Tag Express, the company that purchased Trench, specializes in event- and ballpark-specific pennants.

Here is a list of some of the WinCraft caricature pennants with their latest secondary market values.

Frank Thomas pennant

1991-1992 WinCraft

Player	Team	Quantity	Price
George Brett	Royals	Less than 5,000	$10
Jose Canseco	A's	Less than 5,000	$15
Roger Clemens	Red Sox	Less than 5,000	$7
Ken Griffey Sr. & Jr.	Mariners	More than 5,000	$10
Ken Griffey Jr.	Mariners	More than 5,000	$10
Tony Gwynn	Padres	Less than 5,000	$8
Don Mattingly	Yankees	More than 5,000	$7
Mark McGwire	A's	Less than 5,000	$6
Paul Molitor	Brewers	Less than 5,000	$5
Cal Ripken Jr.	Orioles	Est. 25,000	$8
Cal Ripken Jr. (MVP)	Orioles	More than 5,000	$10
Nolan Ryan	Rangers	Est. 8,922	$10
Nolan Ryan (Texas Heat)	Rangers	Est. 6,780	$10
Nolan Ryan (5,000 Ks)	Rangers	Est. 11,093	$8
World Champ '91	Twins	More than 5,000	$8
World Champ '92	Blue Jays	Less than 5,000	$6

1993 WinCraft

WinCraft began numbering its pennants in 1993.

No.	Player	Team	Quantity	Price
100	Kirby Puckett	Twins	More than 5,000	$6
103	Ken Griffey Jr.	Mariners	More than 5,000	$10
105	Mark McGwire	A's	Less than 5,000	$7
106	George Brett	Royals	Less than 5,000	$7
107	Ozzie Smith	Cardinals	Less than 5,000	$6
108	Braves Fever	Braves	More than 5,000	$5
112	Chiefs of Staff	Braves	Less than 5,000	$5
117	Barry Bonds	Giants	More than 5,000	$6
118	Nolan Ryan (Farewell)		More than 5,000	$8
120	George Brett (Thanks)	Royals	Est. 5,000	$8

1994-1998 WinCraft

Quantities not available.

	Player	Team	Price
121	Miracle Mets 25th Anniversary	Mets	$10
123	Frank Thomas (MVP)	White Sox	$10
128	Dave Winfield	Twins	$5
129	Mike Piazza	Dodgers	$7
134	Cleveland Tribe	Indians	$5
135	Barry Bonds	Giants	$6
138	David Cone	Royals	$5
139	Greg Maddux	Braves	$8
140	Randy Johnson	Mariners	$6
142	Nolan Ryan	Rangers	$8
147	Gary Sheffield	Marlins	$5
148	Roberto Clemente	Pirates	$10
150	Cal Ripken Jr.	Orioles	$10
151	Ken Griffey Jr.	Mariners	$10
156	Cal Ripken Jr.	Orioles	$10
158	Barry Bonds	Giants	$6

	Player	Team	Price
159	Mike Piazza	Dodgers	$7
160	Mo Vaughn	Red Sox	$5
161	Red Schoendienst— Stadium Exclusive	Cardinals	$6
162	Big Bats II	Rockies	$5
164	The Big Three	Rockies	$5
168	Cal Ripken Jr.	Orioles	$10
169	Cal Ripken Jr.	Orioles	$10
170	Mo Vaughn (MVP)	Red Sox	$6
171	Kirby Puckett	Twins	$6
172	Albert Belle	Indians	$6
173	Ken Griffey Jr.	Mariners	$10
174	David Cone	Yankees	$5
176	Paul Molitor	Twins	$5
177	Marty Cordova (ROY '95)	Twins	$5
178	Hideo Nomo (ROY '95)	Dodgers	$7
179	Barry Larkin ('95 NL MVP)	Reds	$5
180	Ryne Sandberg	Cubs	$6
184	Cal Ripken Jr.	Orioles	$10
186	Chipper Jones	Braves	$8
189	Greg Maddux (4-time Cy Young)	Braves	$8
192	Blake Street Bombers	Rockies	$5
195	Rey Ordonez	Mets	$5
198	White Sox Signature Pennant	White Sox	$8
199	Rockies Signature Pennant	Rockies	$6
200	Reds Signature Pennant	Reds	$6
203	All-Star Game Signature	Pennant	$10
204	Alex Rodriguez	Mariners	$7
205	Eddie Murray (3,000 hits)	Orioles	$7
206	Paul Molitor (3,000 hits)	Twins	$7
207	Ken Griffey Jr.	Mariners	$10
208	Cal Ripken Jr.	Orioles	$10
209	Albert Belle	White Sox	$6
210	Frank Thomas	White Sox	$10
211	Mike Piazza	Dodgers	$8
215	Derek Jeter	Yankees	$7
216	Cal Ripken Jr. (Stadium Exclusive)	Orioles	$12
218	Mo Vaughn	Red Sox	$6
219	Roberto Clemente	Pirates	$10
220	Mark McGwire	A's	$7
225	Rockies Signature Pennant	Rockies	$6
226	Don Mattingly	Yankees	$6
231	Mark McGwire	Cardinals	$5
232	Roger Clemens (Cy Young)	Blue Jays	$7
233	Ken Griffey Jr. (MVP)	Mariners	$10
235	Nomar Garciaparra	Red Sox	$7
236	Albert Belle	White Sox	$5
237	Barry Bonds	Giants	$5
241	Cal Ripken Jr.	Orioles	$10
242	Frank Thomas	White Sox	$10

1989 Salem, Dated

Nolan Ryan, 5000Ks		$35
Jim Abbott, California		$10
Wade Boggs, Boston		$25
Jose Canseco, Oakland		$25

Roger Clemens, Boston $30
Andre Dawson, Chicago.. $10
Dwight Gooden, New York... $10
Mark Grace, Chicago.. $10
Mike Greenwell, Boston.. $10
Ken Griffey Jr., Seattle $25
Ken Griffey Jr. and SRT, All in the Family, Seattle $25
Rickey Henderson, Oakland $10
Orel Hershiser, LA $10
Bo Jackson, KC $20
Don Mattingly, New York $20
Mark McGwire, Oakland $25
Kevin McReynolds, New York $10
Cal Ripken, Baltimore... $35
Nolan Ryan, Texas $35
Ryne Sandberg, Chicago $20
Ozzie Smith, St Louis $10
Alan Trammell, Detroit $10
Andy VanSlyke, Pittsburgh $10

Salem, Undated

Darryl Strawberry, LA $15
Bo Jackson, Chicago $10
Kent Hrbek, Minnesota $10

1992 and later, WinCraft, Dated

Nolan Ryan, Farewell to a Legend, WinCraft #118 .... $10
Nolan Ryan, Texas Heat $20
Cecil Fielder, Detroit $20
Robin Yount, Milwaukee $25
Kevin Mitchell, Seattle $10

Cal Ripken

It's only fitting that one of the most popular players in history also has a large selection of pennants to help commemorate his career. Some, especially concerning his breaking of Lou Gehrig's consecutive-games streak and his retirement, are extremely rare:

Cal Ripken, 1989, Salem $35
Cal Ripken, 1991 & 1983 AL MVP $25
Cal Ripken, "Iron Man", WinCraft #150 .... $15
Cal Ripken, "2131 Consecutive Games", WinCraft #156, very
    difficult, limited 5000, numbered .... $75+
Cal Ripken, exclusive for Camden Yards, WinCraft #169.......... $15
Cal Ripken, "2131 Consecutive Games", vertical, WinCraft #168 ...$10
Cal Ripken, vertical, WinCraft #184 .... $10
Cal Ripken, vertical, WinCraft #208 .... $10
Cal Ripken, vertical, WinCraft #216 .... $10
Cal Ripken, vertical, WinCraft #241 .... $10
Cal Ripken, 2632, Record Breaking, horizontal, WinCraft, limited
    2632, unnumbered $25
Cal Ripken, 2632, Record Breaking, horizontal, WinCraft #286......$15
Cal Ripken, 2632, Record Breaking, vertical, WinCraft #286, limited
    2632, numbered $35
Cal Ripken, classic, WinCraft #292 .... $10
Cal Ripken, #8, 2001 WinCraft #371 .... $10
Cal Ripken, "Thanks Cal", WinCraft, horizontal............ $10
Cal Ripken, Iron Man "Thanks Cal for the Memories", WinCraft,
    vertical... $10
Cal Ripken, "Final Home Series", Sept. 21-23, limited 5000...... $20
Cal Ripken, "Final Series, Orioles vs. Red Sox, Oct. 4-6", limited
    2000 .... $35

Basketball Pennants

Baltimore Bullets late 1960s pennant............................ $55
Boston Celtics 1960s, green on white $55
Boston Celtics 1983-84 world champions pennant, with player
    names on a scroll .... $20-$40
Buffalo Braves, black/light blue on white $55
Chicago Bulls pennant signed by 12 of the 1990-91 world champions,
    including Bill Cartwright, Michael Jordan and Scottie Pippen...$250
Dallas Mavericks 1991-92 team autographed pennant $60
Harlem Globetrotters pennant, 1970s, shows three players holding
    basketballs in between the letters .... $40-$50
Houston Rockets 1994-95 NBA Champions $5
Kansas City Kings 1970s pennant, 12x30, red/white/blue $25
Los Angeles Clippers 1986-87 autographed team pennant, signed
    by 10 players, including Elgin Baylor and Norm Nixon $50
Milwaukee Bucks 1960s pennant, buck's head with basketball in
    the antlers, green on white .... $30-$50
1982 National Basketball Championship (UNC, Michael Jordan win
    championship) .... $35-$50
New York Knicks late 1950s, player dunking, orange/blue on white $95
New York Knicks 1960s, large basketball, blue on orange $55
New York Knicks 1969 pennant, 12x30, white/orange/blue........ $45
New York Nets, ABA logo, red and light blue on white $55
Philadelphia 76ers 1960s pennant, red letters with a basketball
    player in action $25

Philadelphia 76ers 1982-83 World Championship pennant, 12x30,
    red/white/blue.. $30-$50
Philadelphia 76ers 1984-85 pennant, 12x20, red/white/blue with
    players' names $45
Portland Trailblazers 1991-92 team autographed pennant........ $70
Sacramento Kings 1986-87 autographed team pennant, signed by
    11 players, including Reggie Theus and Otis Thorpe $50
San Antonio Spurs 1986-87 autographed team pennant, signed by
    11 players, including Artis Gilmore.............................. $50
San Antonio Spurs 1991-92 team autographed pennant.......... $65
San Diego Rockets NBA, gold on green felt $75
Utah Jazz 1991-92 team autographed pennant........................ $60
Washington Bullets 1986-87 autographed team pennant, signed by
    nine players, including Manute Bol and Jeff Malone $50
38th All-Star Game in Chicago, 1988.............................. $10
40th All-Star Game in Miami, 1990 .... $10
1994-95 NBA Finals pennants signed by Hakeem Olajuwon or
    Patrick Ewing $75
1985 autographed Boston Celtics mini banner, green and white, com-
    memorates the championships from 1957-84, signed by 10 players,
    including John Havlicek, Kevin McHale and Robert Parish $15
Charles Barkley autographed Phoenix Suns pennant $50
David Robinson 12x30 caricature pennant, autographed $40
James Worthy 12x30 caricature pennant, autographed............ $30

Hockey Pennants

Atlanta Flames red on white.. $45
Boston Bruins 1970s pennant with player names........................... $65
Boston Bruins 1980s pennant $5
Chicago Blackhawks 1960s pennant, red and white on black.... $65
Chicago Blackhawks 1970 Indian head, multi-colored on black $55
Chicago Blackhawks 1985-86 pennant $5

Detroit Red Wings 1969 pennant, white on red $45
Montreal Canadiens 1991-92 autographed team pennant
    (16 signatures) $80
Montreal Canadiens 1993-94 autographed team pennant......... $95
New York Rangers mid-1950s pennant, white on green, crossed
    hockey sticks and puck $100

1984-85 Washington Capitals pennant

Peter Mahovlich pennant

New York Rangers 1980s pennant $5
New York Rangers 1994-95 Stanley Cup Champions .... $15-$20
New York Islanders 1980s pennant $5
Philadelphia Flyers 1980s pennant, 12x30, lists players $30
Pittsburgh Penguins 1970s pennant, blue with a Penguins logo in a
    circle .... $40-$50

ABA Pennants

ABA pennants are some of the most colorful and desired in sports. The first-season issues and those of teams that failed early in the league's nine-year history can bring triple figures. However, in the last season of the ABA the pennants were mass-produced by one manufacturer, therefore pennants for defunct teams the-Baltimore Claws, San Diego Sails and Utah Stars-are not considered rare. The rarest and most commonly pursued ABA pennants:

1967-'68 Denver Rockets (ringsby logo) $100
1967-'68 Kentucky Colonels (green and white small size) $275
1967-'68 New Jersey Americans $300
1967-'68 New Orleans Buccaneers $300
1967-'68 Oakland Oaks $200
1968-'69 Miami Floridians $270
1968-'69 Denver Rockets (photo pennant)............................. $150
1968-'69 Oakland Oaks $200
1969-'70 Kentucky Colonels (green and white small size) $275
1969-'70 New Orleans Buccaneers $300
1969-'70 Pittsburgh Pipers.. $250
1969-'70 Washington Caps $250
1970-'71 Texas Chaparrals $200
1972-'73 San Diego Conquistadors $100
1973-'74 San Diego Conquistadors $100
1974-'75 Memphis Sounds $100

Football Pennants

Atlanta Falcons 1967 pennant... $25
Atlanta Falcons 1970s pennant $10
Baltimore Colts 1950s pennant .... $85-$135
Baltimore Colts 1980s pennant 12x30, blue with white letters and
    helmet... $10
Baltimore/Indy Colts 1983 autographed pennant with 45
    autographs, modern helmet design on blue felt $145
Buffalo Bills 1967 pennant, 12x30, blue/red/white.............. $35-$50
Buffalo Bills early 1980s white with updated logo................ $10-$20
Chicago Bears black with orange print and orange bear on it .$80-$100
Chicago Bears mid-1950s, runner with ball, orange on blue ...$80-$100
Chicago Bears mid-1960s, bear on dark blue .... $65-$85
Chicago Bears 1960s pennant, 12x30, shows a helmet ..... $30-$50
Chicago Bears Super Bowl XX Champs .... $15-$25
Chicago Cardinals 1950s pennant .... $70-$100
Cincinnati Bengals 1967 helmet, orange/black on white ..... $20-$40
Cincinnati Bengals 1981 AFC Champions, autographed by nine
    players, including Ken Anderson, Anthony Munoz $15
Cincinnati Bengals AFC Champions Super Bowl XVI Jan. 24, 1982$15
Cleveland Browns late-1940s Brownie tossing football, orange on
    white $150
Cleveland Browns late-1950s kicker, stadium, brown................ $85
Cleveland Browns mid-1960s pennant, player kicking the football
    over stadium, multi-colored on brown..................................... $75
Dallas Cowboys 1960s, player kicking football, white on blue $95

Dallas Cowboys 1960s.. $75
Dallas Cowboys 1970s.. $25
Dallas Cowboys Super Bowl XIII, Jan. 21, 1979, NFC Champs,
    Orange Bowl pictured.. $15-$25
Denver Broncos 1984 AFC West Champs $10
Denver Broncos Super Bowl XXI $10
Denver Broncos 1988 Super Bowl Champs $10
Denver Broncos 1993 team pennant, autographed $95
Detroit Lions early-1950s, runner with lion, gray on blue $85
Detroit Lions mid-1960s runner with lion, multi-colored on blue $65
Detroit Lions 1967 helmet pennant, silver on blue .... $20-$40
Green Bay Packers 1940s, gold/green with player running the ball $125
Green Bay Packers 1940s, player kicking the ball.................... $300
Green Bay Packers 1950s pennant, player running on state of
    Wisconsin, multi-colored on green $95
Green Bay Packers 1960s pennant, 12x30, shows helmet........ $50
Green Bay Packers 1967 helmet pennant, gold and white on green $40
Green Bay Packers Super Bowl II, gold on green $850
Houston Oilers early 1960s pennant................................. $90-$100
Kansas City Chiefs AFL helmet pennant $45
Kansas City Chiefs 1960s Indian in headdress, multi-colored on
    red.. $75
Kansas City Chiefs Super Bowl IV in New Orleans, AFL logo, gold
    on red.. $165
Los Angeles Rams 1940s pennant .... $100-$150

Chicago Bears pennant

1960s Cleveland Browns pennant

Los Angeles Rams 1960s ram's head in circle, white on blue ...$60-$85
Los Angeles Rams 1970s pennant, 12x30, white/blue/gold $20
Los Angeles Raiders Super Bowl XVII Champions....................$20
Los Angeles Raiders Super Bowl XVII Champions, 12x30, white with black letters $40
"Mean Joe" Greene 1981 football pennant, says "One for the Thumb in '81," cartoon shows him wearing four Super Bowl rings.............$25
Miami Dolphins early 1970s $40
Miami Dolphins World Champions 1972, white and teal on orange..$55
Miami Dolphins World Champions 1973 .... $50
Miami Dolphins Super Bowl VIII pennant $50
Minnesota Vikings early 1960s......................................$125-$150
Minnesota Vikings 1967 helmet, purple/yellow on white ..... $35-$50
Minnesota Vikings Super Bowl VIII pennant...................... $40-$50
Minnesota Vikings Super Bowl VIII phantom pennant......... $35-$50
Minnesota Vikings Super Bowl IX at New Orleans, NFC Champions ....$30-$45
Minnesota Vikings 1970s pennant, 12x30, shows helmet.......... $25
New England Patriots 1985 AFC Champs Super Bowl XX $12
New York Giants 1930s pennant, player kicking a ball, white on blue...$130-$150
New York Giants 1940s pennant, white on dark blue, runner with ball...$130-$150
New York Giants 1962 team picture pennant $145
New York Giants early-1960s, quarterback in Yankee Stadium, white/pink on blue... $65
New York Giants late 1970s pennant, quarterback throwing a football, red and blue on white $35
New York Giants 1987 Super Bowl XXI pennant, 12x30, with team photo $25
New York Giants Super Bowl XXI Champs .... $20-$30
New York Giants 1990-91 Super Bowl Champions, signed by 30 players, including Ottis Anderson, Phil Simms and Lawrence Taylor $225
New York Jets AFL logo series.......................................$100-$150
New York Jets AFL helmet ....$60-$75
New York Jets 1967 pennant, 12x30, green and white $75
New York Jets 1960s pennant, multi-colored runner on green felt...$85
New York Jets AFL helmet 1968 World Champs..................... $125
Oakland Raiders helmet 1967, silver/white on black.................. $50
Oakland Raiders 1970s pennant... $25
Oakland Raiders mid-1970s helmet pennant $25
Oakland Raiders Super Bowl XI Champions.................... $25-$40
Oakland Raiders Super Bowl XVII.................................. $20-$30

Oakland Raiders 1970s pennant, 12x30, black/silver/white....... $20
Philadelphia Eagles 1960s pennant................................... $40-$60
Philadelphia Eagles 1960 NFL Champions........................... $200
Philadelphia Eagles 1967 white helmet, green wings $55
Philadelphia Eagles 1967 pennant, 12x30, shows helmet $40
Philadelphia Eagles Super Bowl XV $10
Philadelphia Eagles Super Bowl XV pennant, 12x30, NFC Champions $20
Philadelphia Stars 1984 USFL Champs............................... $30
Pittsburgh Steelers 1950s gold on black .... $125-$150
Pittsburgh Steelers Super Bowl XIII pennant, black and gold with a team photo $30
Pittsburgh Steelers 1974 World Champions pennant, commemorates the team's Super Bowl victory......................................$55
Pittsburgh Steelers 1970s pennant, 12x30, gold/black/white..... $45
Pittsburgh Steelers World Champions 1974, white/black on gold....$30
Pittsburgh Steelers Super Bowl IX, New Orleans, Jan. 12, 1975, AFC Champs... $45
Pittsburgh Steelers Super Bowl X, Miami, Jan. 18, 1976, AFC Champs $35
Pittsburgh Steelers Super Bowl XIII Champs picture pennant ... $30
Pittsburgh Steelers Super Bowl XIV, Jan. 20, 1980, pictures the Rose Bowl $35
St. Louis Cardinals 1980s pennant, 12x30, red and white......... $30
San Diego Chargers mid-1960s pennant, AFL, but no AFL marking .... $80-$95
San Diego Chargers 1967 helmet pennant, lightning bolts on white helmet, on blue.. $35
San Diego Chargers 1970s pennant $15
San Francisco 49ers 1960s pennant, 12x30, shows a helmet, red/white/gold $40
San Francisco 49ers 1967 helmet, gold/white on red $35
San Francisco 49ers Super Bowl XXIII $10
San Francisco 49ers Super Bowl XXIII World Champions........ $15
Washington Redskins 1940s pennant.......................... $250-$300
Washington Redskins 1960s helmet pennant, yellow helmet/ maroon R $50
Washington Redskins 1960s Indian in white circle on maroon .. $95
Washington Redskins 1960s pennant, 12x30, helmet design with arrow, yellow and red $100
Washington Redskins 1970s pennant, 12x30, Indian head on helmet $30
Washington Redskins Super Bowl XVII .... $20-$30
Washington Redskins Super Bowl XVIII $15

Other Football Pennants

College pennants

Alabama 1963 Orange Bowl...$45-$65
Florida 1966 Sugar Bowl ....$40-$65
Illinois 1952 Rose Bowl ....$35-$50
Maryland 1950s pennant with tassles ....$30-$45
Michigan State 1966 Rose Bowl..$35-$50
Navy 1964 Cotton Bowl ....$50-$75
Notre Dame 1960s pennant ....$15-$30
Oklahoma 1972 Sugar Bowl ....$35-$45
Ole Miss. 1962 Cotton Bowl ....$40-$60
Penn State 1972 Cotton Bowl ....$30-$45
UCLA 1962 Rose Bowl...$35-$50

USFL pennants

Birmingham Stallions, Boston Breakers, Chicago Blitz, Denver Gold, Houston Gamblers, Jacksonville Bulls, L.A. Express, Memphis Showboats, New Jersey Generals, New Orleans Breakers, Oakland Invaders, Philadelphia Stars, Pittsburgh Maulers, San Antonio Gunslingers, Tampa Bay Bandits, Washington Federals ...$10-$20 each.
Baltimore Stars, Orlando Renegades .... $30-$50

World Football League pennants

Birmingham Vulcans, Charlotte Hornets, Chicago Wind, Jacksonville Express, Memphis Grizzlies, Portland Thunder, San Antonio Wings ....$20 each

Miscellaneous Pennants

All American Football Conference Pennants.................... $125-$175
MISL Soccer Pennants... $5-$10
NASL Soccer Pennants... $8-$15
WHA Pennants... $20-$45
1999 U.S.A. Women's World Cup Champions Pennant ...... $10-$15

Chapter 13

CEREAL BOXES

Collectible Of Champions

From Olympians Didrickson, Retton & Jenner to Jordan, Ruth & Payton, Wheaties Boxes Have Chronicled Sports History

By MICHAEL DACHS

What began by accident more than 75 years ago as a crispy whole wheat cereal flake with a catchy ad campaign has grown into one of America's most celebrated sports icons.

The popular cereal flake in the orange box was born in 1921 when a Minneapolis health clinician preparing a wheat bran mixture accidentally spilled some on a hot stove, creating tasty wheat flakes. The rest, as they say, is history.

Baseball and "The Breakfast of Champions"

Wheaties' association with sports first began in 1933 with the sponsorship of minor-league baseball broadcasts and eventually evolved into featuring athletes on the box.

Athlete testimonials were a key part of the "Breakfast of Champions" broadcast package. Some of the stars who endorsed Wheaties in the 1930s, '40s and '50s included Babe Ruth, Lou Gehrig, Joe DiMaggio, Jackie Robinson, Bob Feller, Stan Musial, Ted Williams, Yogi Berra and Mickey Mantle.

Of the 51 players selected for the 1939 Major League Baseball All-Star Game, 46 of them endorsed Wheaties at the time. More recently, athletes who have appeared on the front of a Wheaties box include Michael Jordan, Mark McGwire, Ken Griffey Jr., Tiger Woods, Joe Montana, Dale Earnhardt, Muhammad Ali and many past and present Olympians.

Did You Know?

New York Yankees slugger Lou Gehrig was the first athlete to appear on the Wheaties box, on the back of the package, in 1934. It wasn't until Olympian Bob Richards appeared on the front of the orange package in 1958 that the phenomenon of "being on the Wheaties box" really came into existence. Prior to 1958, athletes appeared solely on the back or side panels of the package.

Aviator Elinore Smith was the first female pictured on the back of the Wheaties box in 1934 and legendary golfer and Olympic gold medallist Babe Didrickson became the first female athlete to appear on the package when she was depicted on the back of the package in 1935.

In 1984, Olympic gold medalist Mary Lou Retton became the first female athlete to appear on the front of the Wheaties package. In case you're wondering, Michael Jordan has appeared on more Wheaties boxes than any other athlete – 18 times, all with the Chicago Bulls.

The 1987 World Series champion Minnesota Twins were the first team to be featured on the package, while the first non-orange Wheaties box (it was red and black) honored the 1992 NBA champion Chicago Bulls.

Collecting Today

Whether you're already a collector or simply looking to begin your collection today, this truly is the best time to buy.

In addition to the Wheaties boxes that are on your supermarket shelves right now, both the Internet and online auction sites available to collectors make it easier than ever to put together an impressive collection at an affordable price.

With more than 700 Wheaties boxes already produced since 1924, the question facing a new collector today is, "What should I collect?"

A good starting place would be to try and choose either a favorite athlete, sport or team to collect. You can collect home run hitters, first appearances of athletes on a box, regional boxes, team boxes, single-serving (1-ounce) boxes or anniversary boxes that commemorate a special event.

Any one of these collections can be started without spending a lot of money and if you cannot afford to buy boxes in mint condition, start out buying those boxes in the condition that you can afford.

Jared Bader, a collector from New York, collects Wheaties boxes which feature Hall of Famers.

"I can usually buy a box on eBay for as little as 30 percent of the guide price," he said. "There are boxes listed in the price guide for $100 in mint condition that have sold for as little as $15 due to the fact that there is a crease or tear somewhere on the box. Many times, this 'defect' is hardly visible and does not detract from the overall appearance of the box."

Another idea might be to collect factory flats. Factory flats are boxes which have not been formed and remain in the same condition as when they were printed.

Although these boxes generally command 10-20 percent more than formed boxes, many collectors are willing to pay the additional premium due to the fact that they are much harder to find.

Factory flats are not released to the public by General Mills and are usually sneaked out of the factory that they were printed in. Keep in mind that unformed boxes will take up more space, are harder to ship and are tougher to keep in mint condition.

For the collector with a little more money to spend, there are the always popular "phantom" boxes. A phantom box is a box that is printed by the factory, but is never released to the public.

The reason these boxes are printed in the first place is because General Mills cannot predict the outcome of which team is going to win a championship, so it prints boxes with both teams as champions, just in case.

The boxes that were produced for the losing team are supposed to be destroyed, but sometimes these phantom boxes – including the 1988 Denver Broncos Super Bowl Champions and 1988 Detroit Pistons NBA Champions boxes – find their way out of the factory and into the marketplace. Phantom boxes are priced in the $30-$100 range in mint condition.

When bidding on boxes on Internet auction sites, be very wary of sellers claiming that the boxes they are selling are "rare" or "limited editions."

With the exception of the boxes that are listed as "rare" or "hard to find" in the price guide, there are very few others that can also be categorized as such that have been produced since 1977.

To Open or Not To Open . . .

That is one of the most talked about topics among collectors with regard to whether or not the value of the box is diminished if opened.

The attitude of serious collectors is that the value of the box is determined by the condition of the box, not if it is full or empty. After all, the value is the box itself, not the cereal.

One of the reasons that collectors are leaning more and more toward removing the cereal is because it makes the boxes easier to store.

Once a box is flattened, it is almost one-sixth smaller than a formed box. Flat boxes can then be fit into mylar sleeves and be stored in much less space than a formed box would occupy.

Another reason to remove the cereal is the existence of bugs. Experts say there's no way to keep insect eggs out of your cereal and if you let boxes sit for long periods of time before you open them, you may discover live insects inside; what started out as an egg could develop into a worm, moth or some other flying insect.

The best way to avoid this problem is to empty the box or don't keep it in your collection much past the sell-by date printed on the bottom of the box.

Bader recalls winning a box from an auction site and receiving the box in the mail.

"When I opened the box (from 1992), it was infested with tiny bugs," he said. "I had to open it outside, throw away the cereal and spray the box with bug killer. From that day on, I remove all the contents of any box I purchase, whether the box is two weeks or two years old."

If you are going to keep your boxes full, here are some tips to follow.

1) If you are displaying or storing the box in its upright position, rotate the box every month to avoid the box bulging at the bottom. This bulge is caused by the cereal breaking down over time and settling at the bottom of the box. After an extended period of time, the cereal will start to settle at the bottom of the box and cause it to push out at the bottom, lessening the value of the box.

2) If possible, keep the box lying on its side as often as you can.

3) Avoid direct sunlight as this causes the color on the box to fade. If you want to display your boxes, use a case that will block out the harmful UV rays of the sun. There are inexpensive cases available to collectors that allow you to display your box by either hanging it on a wall or simply allowing it to stand upright in the case.

Regional Boxes

From time to time, General Mills will produce a Wheaties box for distribution only to a limited region of the country.

The region where the box is released is dependent upon the player featured on the box. Although years ago, this would have been a problem for collectors on opposite coasts, with today's online auctions and collectors' Web sites, it is fairly easy to obtain one for your collection.

Over the years, there have been numerous regional releases, including both teams and individuals being featured on the box.

As a collector, it is important to keep up with all the new regional issues that are produced. Often, collectors from two different regions will be completely unaware that a regional box has been produced.

If you are a collector in an area where a regional box has been released, it might be a good idea to pick up an extra box or two to use for future trading with other collectors who don't have access to them. Generally, these regional boxes are a little higher-priced than regular issues.

The Future

According to Gregory J. Zimprich of General Mills, "Collectors of Wheaties boxes should keep an eye out for some new boxes very soon. We usually start to choose who will appear on a Wheaties box 18 months before it is actually released. Of course, we can produce them faster if the situation warrants it."

As for now, start or keep adding any boxes that you think would add to the overall value of your collection.

Remember, collect boxes that you like, not boxes that you think will increase in value.

While Wheaties cereal boxes remain both the most popular and most collectible, there are still many other companies that also produce collectible cereal boxes. Athletes, movie tie-ins, Disney characters and other giveaways are all on your supermarket shelves right now waiting to be added to your collection.

Michael Dachs is a Wheaties box collector. He welcomes readers who have questions, comments or additions to contact him via e-mail at boxcollector1@aol.com.

CEREAL BOXES

Cheerios Baseball
1998 Marlins '97 WS Champs (HN) $8

Cheerios Canadian Hockey
1998 Brendan Shanahan (HHC) $15

Cheerios Racing
1998 Johnny Benson $7

General Mills Grand Slam Baseball
1998 McGwire/Thomas/Piazza $7

Kellogg's Chovcos
European
1996 M. Jordan Space Jam (Germany)... $30
1996 H. Olajuwon (Germany)............... $15
1997 M. Jordan Space Jam (Germany)... $30

Kellogg's Corn Flakes
Baseball
1970 Willie Mays $75
1983 San Diego Chicken...................... $50
1983 Mike Reilly (umpire).................... $50
1983 Fernando Valenzuela $40
1991 Hank Aaron $40
1991 Ernie Banks................................ $25
1991 Yogi Berra................................... $25
1991 Lou Brock $25
1991 Steve Carlton.............................. $25
1991 Bob Gibson $25
1991 Aaron/Berra/Mays/Spahn $30
1992 Mike Schmidt.............................. $30

1993 Roberto Clemente (Spanish) $35
1933 Nolan Ryan $20
1933 Nolan Ryan farewell $30
1994 Roberto Clemente batting........... $30
1994 Roberto Clemente bat (Spanish) $40

Kellogg's Corn Flakes
Basketball
1992 Larry Bird $30
1992 David Robinson........................... $25
1992 Bird/Malone/Mullin/Rob/Stockton
(2).. $20

Kellogg's Corn Flakes
Football
1983 Danny White $40

   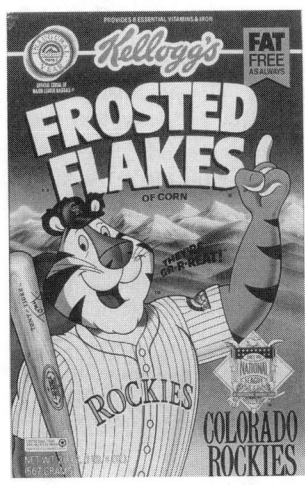

1995 J. Montana/D. Marino/D. Bledsoe Upper Deck cards (Spanish version) $25

Kellogg's Corn Flakes
Canadian Hockey
1992 Wendel Clark $20
1993 Montreal Canadiens $25
1996 Wendel Clark $15
1996 Gordie Howe.................................$20
1996 Mario Lemieux...............................$25
1996 Maurice "Rocket" Richard............$20
1996 Felix Potvin (Al)............................$20

Kellogg's Corn Flakes
Olympics
1992 Bonnie Blair speedskating...........$15
1992 Dan Jansen speedskating............$15
1994 Bonnie Blair speedskating...........$15
1996 D. Bailey track (Canada)...............$15
1996 D. Bailey (Canada w/metal) $20

Kellogg's Corn Flakes
Racing
1992 Richard Petty $30
1992 G. Sacks/H. Hyde $30
1992 Corn Flakes car #41 ....$30
1993 Terry Labonte holding helmet $30
1993 Corn Flakes Car #14 ....$30
1994 #5 car bursting through................$25
1994 #5 car with pit crew (18/24) $30
1994 Dale Earnhardt '93 Champ...........$40
1994 Terry Labonte eating cereal.........$25
1995 Terry Labonte/D. Waltrip $15
1995 #5 car at finish line $15
1995 "Corney" in uniform......................$8
1995 Dale Earnhardt '94 Champ $20
1995 D. Earnhardt 7-time champ (20) ..$20
1995 Terry Labonte w/Wilks trophy $15
1996 Terry Labonte Ironman $15
1996 Terry Labonte Ironman #5 car $15
1996 Terry Labonte/R. Petty.................$20
1996 Jeff Gordon '95 WC champ $25
1997 Terry Labonte Sam Bass art........$15
1997 Terry Labonte/Jeff Gordon...........$20
1997 Top-Four drivers $25
1997 Terry Labonte HC pack w/car $15
1998 Labonte/R. Byron $8
1998 NASCAR 50th Anniversary $5
1998 Terry Labonte car cut-out $8

Kellogg's Corn Pops
1993 Tom Seaver $20
1997 Penny Hardaway...........................$10
1997 Carlos Valdarama..........................$10

Kellogg's Corn Pops
Canadian Basketball
1997 Awesome Rookies.........................$15
1997 Defensive Dynamos $15
1997 Legendary Leaders $15
1997 Scoring Machines.........................$15

Kellogg's Corn Pops
Canadian Hockey
1996 Mario Lemieux..............................$20
1996 Maurice "Rocket" Richard...........$15

Kellogg's Frosted Flakes
Baseball
1991 Atlanta Braves NL Champs $30
1991 Braves WS (phantom) $75
1991 Twins WS Champs $35
1992 Blue Jays Champs (*Canada) $35
1992 Braves NL Champs $35
1992 St. Louis Cardinals $35
1993 Ken Griffey Jr. (20/25) $20
1993 Florida Marlins Inaugural.............$18
1993 Colorado Rockies Inaugural $18
1995 Carlos Baerga (Spanish)............$15
1995 Colorado Rockies (Spanish)........$15

Kellogg's Frosted Flakes
Basketball
1998 Grant Hill/Sheryl Swoopes $10

Kellogg's Frosted Flakes
Canadian Basketball
1994 Vancouver Grizzlies.....................$18
1994 Toronto Raptors...........................$18
1996 Hakeem Olajuwon $20
1996 Bryant Reeves.............................$15
1996 Damon Stoudamire $18

Kellogg's Frosted Flakes
Hockey
1992 JaromirJagr/Mario Lemieux.........$35
1933 Wayne Gretzky $40
1933 Montreal Canadiens $25
1933 L.A. Kings $35
1994 Brett Hull (Canada) $20
1994 Brett Hull w/Tony Tiger (Can.) $20
1994 N.Y. Rangers champs.................$30
1996 Brett Hull (Canada) $20
1997 Felix Potvin (Canada) $18

Kellogg's Frosted Flakes
Racing
1994 Tony Tiger in NASCAR uniform ... $10
1995 Bill Elliott.....................................$15
1995 Bill Elliott w/Tony the Tiger $10
1996 Dale Earnhardt w/Tony (15 oz.)... $15

1997 Terry Labonte w/Tony the Tiger... $12

Kellogg's Frosted Mini-Wheats
Baseball
1995 Reggie Jackson (20) $25

Kellogg's Frosted Mini-Wheats
Basketball
1992 Larry Bird $30
1992 Karl Malone................................ $25
1992 Chris Mullin $20
1992 David Robinson $20
1992 John Stockton $25
1995 Grant Hill ROY (20/24) $20
1995 Grant Hill dunking (16/19) $20
1996 Damon Stoudamire ROY (Can.).. $20

Kellogg's Frosted Mini-Wheats
Canadian Hockey
1996 Mario Lemieux $20
1996 Lanny McDonald $15

Kellogg's Frosted Mini-Wheats
Racing
1933 Jeff Gordon (Sam Bass art) $30
1994 Jeff Gordon $25
1995 Earnhardt/Gordon (red)............... $20
1995 Earnhardt/Gordon (org.)............. $20
1995 Earnhardt/Gordon (48) $20
1995 Jeff Gordon/#24 car at Indy........ $18
1995 Jeff Gordon Brickyard 400 .... $18
1996 Jeff Gordon '95 Champ (red) $20
1996 Jeff Gordon '95 Champ (org.) $20
1996 MBNA car................................... $15
1997 Top-Four drivers $20
1997 Jeff Gordon in helmet (19) $15
1997 Jeff Gordon in helmet (48) $20
1997 Terry Labonte/Jeff Gordon $18
1997 Dale Earnhardt in helmet $20
1998 Jeff Gordon '97 WC champ......... $15

Kellogg's Frosties
European
1996 M. Jordan Space Jam (Germany)...$30
1996 Hakeem Olajuwon (France) $15
1996 Hakeem Olajuwon (Germany)..... $15
1997 M. Jordan Space Jam (Germany) ...$30
1997 Scottie Pippen (France)............... $15

Kellogg's Fruit Loops
1983 Reggie Jackson/ Robin Yount/
Fernando Valenzuela $20

Kellogg's Honey Nut Loops
European
1996 M. Jordan Space Jam (Germany)...$30
1996 Hakeem Olajuwon (Germany)..... $15

Kellogg's Raisin Bran
Basketball
1992 Bird/Mal/Mull/Robinson/Stockton. $30
1992 Bird/Pippen/Hakeem college cards.$20
1992 David Robinson college card....... $20
1992 Scottie Pippen/David Robinson ... $20

Kellogg's Raisin Bran
Canadian Hockey
1996 Brett Hull.................................... $15
1996 Mario Lemieux............................ $20
1996 Lanny McDonald......................... $15
1997 Curtis Joseph $15
1997 Felix Potvin............................... $12

Kellogg's Raisin Bran
Racing
1993 Terry Labonte on back................ $40
1994 Bill Elliott/Joe Gibbs.................. $15
1996 Darrell/Michael Waltrip $15
1997 Top-Four drivers $20
1997 Dale/Ned Jarrett $15
1997 Terry Labonte/G. DeHart $15
1997 Dale Jarrett wearing helmet........ $15

Kellogg's Raisin Bran
Soccer
1996 A. Labs/T. Ramos $15

Kellogg's Rice Krispies
Basketball
1998 Grant Hill...................................$9

Kellogg's Special K
1991 Kristi Yamaguchi '91 WC $40
1991 Kristi Yamaguchi '92 GM $40
1996 Joanne Malar (Canada).............. $10
1996 Kurt Browning (Canada).............. $10
1997 Comets '97 WNBA champs......... $10

Kellogg's Sugar Pops
Canadian Hockey
1995 Mario Lemieux............................ $20

PLB Sports Promotions
1998 Doug Flutie (Red) $12
1999 Doug Flutie (Blue) $12
1999 Ed's Endzone O's $12

Post
Basketball
1994 Olajuwon, Ewing, Pippen, L. Johnson (Honeycomb)................................ $15
1995 Ewing/Mourning/Kemp (Honeycomb)................................ $15
1996 Olympic Dream Team (Honeycomb)................................ $20
1997 Penny Hardaway (FSW) $6
1997 Penny Hardaway (Honeycomb) $6
1998 Penny Hardaway (Waffle Crisp)..... $6
1998 Penny Hardaway (Golden Crisp) ... $6
1998 Penny Hardaway (Honey-Nut) $6

Post Alpha-Bits
Canadian Baseball
1994 Joe Carter.................................. $20

Post Alpha-Bits
Canadian Hockey
1982 Mike Bossy $35
1996 Brendan Shanahan $15
1997 Joe Sakic................................... $15
1998 Eric Lindros $20

Post 40% Bran Flakes
1960s Baseball cards on back.....$50-$100

Post Grape Nuts
1960s Baseball cards on back.....$50-$100

Post Grape Nut Flakes
Baseball
1959 Warren Spahn $45

Post Honeycomb
Baseball
1993 Barry Bonds, Ken Griffey Jr. $15
1994 Mattingly, Gonzalez, Bonds,Thomas, Olerud, Bonilla.............................. $20

Post Honeycomb
Canadian Hockey
1995 Tony Amonte $15
1995 Jason Arnott $15
1995 Ray Bourque $12
1995 Pavel Bure $12
1995 Chris Chelios $15
1995 Geoff Courtnall $12
1995 Russ Courtnall............................ $12
1995 Steve Duchesne $12
1995 Doug Gilmour $15
1995 Wayne Gretzky $25
1995 Eric Lindros $20
1995 Marty McSorley $12
1995 Kirk Muller $15
1995 Rob Niedermayer $12
1995 Felix Potvin $12
1995 Luc Robitaille $12
1995 Teemu Selanne $20
1996 Doug Gilmour $15
1996 Wayne Gretzky $20
1997 Curtis Joseph $15
1997 Paul Kariya $20
1997 Eric Lindros $20

Post Sugar Crisp
Baseball
1955 Ted Williams $50
1960s Baseball cards on back $50
1994 Mattingly/Gonzalez, Bonds, Thomas, Olerud, Bonilla.............................. $15

Post Raisin Bran
Baseball
1960s Baseball Cards on back.... $50-$100

Post Sugar Crisp
Canadian Baseball
1994 Joe Carter $20
1995 Devon White.............................. $15
1997 Moises Alou $15

Post Sugar Crisp
Canadian Hockey
1995 Martin Brodeur $15
1997 Chris Chelios $12
1995 Sergei Fedorov $20
1995 Theo Fleury $12
1995 Doug Gilmour $15
1995 Jarri Kurri $15
1995 Alexander Mogilny...................... $15
1995 Felix Potvin $12
1995 Joe Sakic................................... $15
1995 Alexei Yashin $15
1996 Wayne Gretzky (2)...................... $20
1997 Theo Fleury $12
1997 Eric Lindros $20

Post Toasties
Baseball
1960s Baseball cards on back .... $50-$100
Football
1960s Football cards on back .... $40-$80

Pro Stars
Canadian Hockey
1984 Wayne Gretzky $100
1985 Wayne Gretzky $100

1986 Wayne Gretzky........................... $75
1988 Wayne Gretzky........................... $60
1989 Wayne Gretzky........................... $50
1990 Wayne Gretzky (4)....................... $40
1991 Wayne Gretzky (3)....................... $30
1992 Wayne Gretzky............................ $20
1992 Wayne Gretzky............................ $25

Ralston
Cookie Crisp
1981 Jim Palmer $12
1984 Dale Murphy $10

Ralston
Donkey Kong
1983 Jim Palmer $12

Ralston
WWF Wrestling
1992 Hulk Hogan $15
1992 Legion of Doom $12
1992 Ultimate Warrior $12

Shreddies
Canadian Hockey
1996 Vincent Damphousse (GHS)....... $12
1997 Vincent Damphousse $12
1997 Doug Gilmour............................. $12
1997 Eric Lindros $20
1997 Eric Lindros (GHS) $20

General Mills
Wheaties
1935
Fancy Frame with Script Signature
Jack Armstrong $20
Wally Berger $20
Tommy Bridges $20
Mickey Cochrane $175
James "Rip" Collins $20
Dizzy Dean $55
Paul Dean $22
William Delaney $20
Jimmie Foxx $50
Frank Frisch $37
Lou Gehrig $225
Goose Goslin $30
Lefty Grove $45
Carl Hubbell $35
Travis Jackson $30
"Chuck" Klein $30
Gus Mancuso $20
"Pepper" Martin $20
Joe Medwick $35
Melvin Ott $50
Harold Schumacher $20
Al Simmons $30
"Jo Jo" White $20

1936
Fancy Frame with Printed Name and Data
Earl Averill....................................... $30
Mickey Cochrane $40
"Jimmie" Foxx $45
Lou Gehrig $225
Hank Greenberg................................ $40
"Gabby" Hartnett $30
Carl Hubbell $35
"Pepper" Martin, ... $17
Van L. Mungo $20
"Buck" Newsom $20
"Arky" Vaughan $30
Jimmy Wilson $20

1936
How to Play Winning Baseball
Lefty Gomez...................................... $35

Billy Herman $30
Luke Appling $35
Jimmie Foxx $45
Joe Medwick $35
Charlie Gehringer $35
Mel Ott $45
Odell Hale $20
Bill Dickey $50
"Lefty" Grove $50
Carl Hubbell $40
Earl Averill $35

1936
Thin Orange Border/Figures In Border
Curt Davis.................................... $20
Lou Gehrig.................................. $250
Charlie Gehringer $40
Lefty Grove $40
Rollie Hemsley $20
Billy Herman $30
Joe Medwick $30
Mel Ott.. $45
Schoolboy Rowe $20
Arky Vaughn $30
Joe Vosmik $20
Lon Warneke $20

1937
Color Series
Zeke Bonura $20
Tom Bridges $20
Harland Clift................................. $20
KiKi Cuyler $30
Joe DiMaggio $225
Robert Feller $75
Lefty Grove $50
Billy Herman $30
Carl Hubbell................................. $35
Buck Jordan................................. $20
"Pepper" Martin $20
Wally Moses $20
Van L. Mungo $20
Cecil Travis $20
Arky Vaughn $30

1937
How to Star In Baseball
Bill Dickey $50
Red Ruffing $30
Zeke Bonura $20
Charlie Gehringer $35
"Arky" Vaughn $20
Carl Hubbell................................. $35
John Lewis................................... $20
Heinie Manush $30
Lefty Grove $40
Billy Herman $30
Joe DiMaggio $225
Joe Medwick................................ $30

1937
Small Panels with Orange
Background Series
Zeke Bonura $40
Tom Bridges $40
Dolph Camilli $40
Frank Demaree $40
Joe DiMaggio $250
Billy Herman $70
Carl Hubbell................................. $75
Ernie Lombardi $55
"Pepper" Martin $40
Jo Jo Moore................................. $40
Van L. Mungo $40
Mel Ott.. $75
Raymond Radcliff $40

Cecil Travis $40
Harold Trosky $40
Vaughn, Arky $55

1937
Speckled Orange, White and Blue Series
Luke Appling................................ $30
Earl Averill $30
Joe DiMaggio $175
Robert Feller $75
Charles Gehringer $40
Lefty Grove $45
Carl Hubbell $45
Joe Medwick $35

1937
29 Series
"Zeke" Bonura $20
Cecil Travis $20
Frank Demaree $20
Jo Jo Moore $20
Ernie Lombardi $30
John "Pepper" Martin $25
Harold Trosky $20
Raymond Radcliff $20
Joe DiMaggio $225
Tom Bridges $20
Van L. Mungo $20
"Arky" Vaughn $30
Arnold Statz................................. $150
Fred Muller $150
Gene Lillard................................. $150

1938
Biggest Thrills In Baseball
Bob Feller $75
Cecil Travis $20
Joe Medwick $35
Gerald Walker $20
Carl Hubbell $35
Bob Johnson $20
Beau Bell $20
Ernie Lombardi $30
Lefty Grove $40
Lou Fette $20
Joe DiMaggio $250
Pinky Whitney $20
Dizzy Dean $55
Charlie Gehringer $40
Paul Waner $30
Dolf Camilli $20

1938
Dress Clothes or Civilian Series
Lou Fette $20
Jimmie Foxx $40
Charlie Gehringer $35
Lefty Grove $35
Hank Greenberg $35
Ernie Lombardi $30
Joe Medwick................................ $35
Lon Warneke $20

1938
Small Panels with Orange, Blue
and White Background
Zeke Bonura $40
Joe DiMaggio $250
Charley Gehringer $80
Hank Greenberg............................ $80
Lefty Grove $60
Carl Hubbell $60
John "Buddy" Lewis $40
Heinie Manush $60
Joe Medwick $60
Arky Vaughn $60

1939
100 Years of Baseball
Design of First Diamond..................... $20
Gets News of Nomination on Field....... $20
Crowd Boos First Baseball Glove........ $20
Curve Ball Just an Illusion................. $20
Fencer's Mask Is Pattern $20
Baseball Gets "All Dressed Up" $20
Modern Bludgeon Enters Game $20
"Casey at the Bat"......................... $20

1939
Personal Pointers Series
Ernie Lombardi $30
Johnny Allen................................. $20
Lefty Gomez................................. $35
Bill Lee $20
Jimmie Foxx $45
Joe Medwick $35
Hank Greenberg............................ $35
Mel Ott.. $50
Arky Vaughn................................. $30

1940
Champs of the U.S.A.
Bob Feller
Lynn Patrick
Charles "Red" Ruffing $50
Leo Durocher
Lynn Patrick
Charles "Red' Ruffing........................ $45
Joe DiMaggio
John Duge
Hank Greenberg.............................. $150
Joe DiMaggio
Mel Ott
Ellsworth Vines................................ $150
Bernie Bierman
Bill Dickey
Jimmie Foxx $40
Morris Arnovich
Capt. R. L. Baker
Earl "Dutch" Clark $20
"Matty" Bell
Ab Jenkins
Joe Medwick $20
Ralph Guldahl
John Mize
Davey O'Brien $20
Ralph Guldahl
Gabby Hartnett
Davey O'Brien $20
Bob Feller
John Mize
Rudy York..................................... $45
Joe Cronin
Hank Greenberg
Byron Nelson................................. $20
Ernie Lombardi
Jack Manders
George Myers $20
Bob Bartlett
Capt. R. C. Hanson
Terrell Jacobs $20
Lowell "Red" Dawson
Billy Herman
Adele Inge $20
Dolph Camilli
Antoinette Concello
Wallace Wade $20
Luke Appling
Stanley Hack
Hugh McManus $20

Felix Adler
Hal Trosky
Mabel Vinson................................. $20

1941
Champs of the U.S.A.
Felix Adler
Jimmie Foxx
Capt. R.G. Hanson $45
Bernie Bierman
Bob Feller
Jessie McLeod $45
Lowell "Red" Dawson
Hank Greenberg
J.W. Stoker $35
Antoinette Concello
Joe DiMaggio,
Byron Nelson.................................... $125
Capt. R. L. Baker
Frank "Buck" McCormick
Harold "Pee Wee" Reese..................... $45
Harry Danning
Barney McCosky
Buck Walters $20
William Robbins
Gene Sarazan
Gerald "Gee" Walker............................ $20
Joe "Flash" Gordon
Stan Hack
George Myers..................................... $20

1951
Bob Feller (Baseball) $100
John Lujack (Football) $60
George Mikan (Basketball) $100
Stan Musial (Baseball) $150
Sam Snead (Golfer).............................. $40
Ted Williams (Baseball) $150

1952
Larry "Yogi" Berra $40
Roy Campanella $40
Bob Feller.. $30
George Kell... $12
Ralph Kiner $20
Bob Lemon $20
Stan Musial $50
Phil Rizzuto $25
Elwin "Preacher" Roe $10
Ted Williams.. $75

Wheaties
Baseball
1964 Tom Tresh................................... $50
1985 Pete Rose (8 oz./24 oz.) R $40

1985 Pete Rose (12 oz./18 oz.) R $25
1986 Pete Rose (free poster) R $30
1987 Minnesota Twins WS_Champs R ...$15
1987 Minnesota Twins (w/autos) R $40
1989 Johnny Bench HOF R $35
1990 Jim Palmer HOF R $25
1990 Cincinnati Reds R $20
1991 Rod Carew (#'d to 1,000) R....... $200
1991 Twins WS Champ (.75 oz) R $100
1991 Twins WS Champs R.................. $30
1993 Lou Gehrig $12
1993 Willie Mays $12
1993 Babe Ruth $12
1995 Cal Ripken no O's logo R $25
1995 Cal Ripken w/O's logo $12
1995 Braves WS Champs R $12
1995 Indians AL Champs R $12
1996 Ken Griffey Jr. (HF) $10
1996 Griffey Jr. gold emb. (HF) $12
1996 Ken Griffey Jr. (no logo) (HF) $14
1996 Kirby Puckett R.......................... $14
1996 Braves NL Champs R.................. $12
1996 Cards Champs (phantom) $50
1996 Negro Leagues
(75th Anniversary) $10
1996 Yankees AL Champs R $10
1997 Jackie Robinson (All).................. $12
1997 Mariners '97 WD champs............ $15
1997 Cone/Maddix/Nomo $10
1997 Bonds/Griffey/Gwynn $10
1997 Piazza/Ripken/Sandberg............. $10
1997 Bonds/Griffey/C. Jones (HF) $12
1997 Griffey/Ripken/Thomas (CWR).... $10
1998 R. Clemens (Canada) (MFW) $10
1998 McGwire/Griffey/T. Martinez $12
1998 Ripken/Piazza/Alomar $12
1998 Thomas/McGwire/T. Martinez
(CWR) $12
1998 A. Rod/Maddux/Garciaparra (HF) ...$10
1998 Arizona Diamondbacks $12
1998 Mark McGwire/70HR $12
1998 Yankees WS Champs.................. $12
1998 Nolan Ryan Legend.................... $10
1998 Nolan Ryan Legend (CWR)......... $10
1998 Nolan Ryan Legend (HW) $10
1998 Ken Griffey Jr. (MVP)................. $10
1999 Joe Torre/Yankees WS $12
1999 Ken Griffey Jr. (Foot Locker)
(FW) R....................................... $12
1999 Ken Griffey Jr. (Trivia on back)
(FW) R....................................... $12

1999 Ken Griffey Jr. (1 oz.) (HFW)......... $8
1999Ken Griffey Jr. (vote for 10 best boxes)
(HFW) R...................................... $10
2000 Ken Griffey Jr. (Reds) R $12
2000 Ken Griffey Jr. (Reds) (HFW) $12
2000 Ken Griffey Jr. (Reds) (1 oz.)......... $8
2000 Ken Griffey Jr. (Sports Illustrated
for kids) (HFW) R $10
2001 Puckett/Winfield HOF R $12
2001 Cal Ripken Jr. (retirement) $10
2001 Barry Bonds (HR record) $15
2002 Hank Aaron (black history).......... $12
2002 Ozzie Smith (HOF).................... $12

Wheaties
Basketball
1988 LA Lakers (24 oz.) R $30
1988 LA Lakers (18 oz.) R $25
1988 Detroit Pistons (phantom) R........ $30
1989 Detroit Pistons R $45
1991 Chicago Bulls (.75 oz.) R $25
1991 Chicago Bulls (18) R $35
1992 Clyde Drexler R.......................... $35
1992 Chicago Bulls R.......................... $30
1992 Chicago Bulls (.75 oz.) R $25
1992 Dunk-A-Balls $30
1993 Larry Bird (.75 oz.) R.................. $40
1993 Larry Bird (18 oz.) R................... $14
1993 Chicago Bulls R.......................... $30
1994 Harlem Globetrotters R $12
1994 Harlem Globetrotters (Honey Gold).$15
1995 Boston Garden w/Auerbach, etc. R .$12
1996 Chicago Bulls R.......................... $20
1996 NCAA Final Four (HF 30) R $18
1998 Larry Bird Pacers R.................... $14
1998 Larry Bird Boston R.................... $14
1999 Larry Bird (giveaway) (1 oz.) R.... $20
2002 Kevin Garnett (back of box).......... $5

Wheaties
Boxing
1999 Muhammad Ali $12

Wheaties
Football
1984 Chris Spielman R $190
1986 Walter Payton com. (12).............. $45
1986 Walter Payton pointing FB (8) $45
1986 Walter Payton point FB (23/18/24) ..$45
1988 Steve Largent.............................. $70
1988 Redskins '88 champs R $25
1988 Broncos '88 champ (phantom) $30
1989 Bengals (phantom) R $75

1990 Boomer Esiason/Jim Kelly Pro Set .$20
1991 Joe Montana R $50
1991 Giants '90 champs R $25
1991 SEC Football R..........................$160
1992 Barry Sanders R..........................$35
1992 Redskins '91 champs R...............$30
1992 Cowboys R $20
1993 John Elway R..............................$35
1993 John Elway poster R....................$50
1993 Jim Kelly poster R.......................$45
1993 Warren Moon poster R $45
1993 Steve Young poster R $30
1993 Bills '92 champs R.......................$30
1993 Cowboys '92 champs R...............$15
1993 Steelers '92 champs R $40
1993 Vikings '92 champs R...................$35
1994 Jerry Rice R................................$15
1994 Cowboys '93 champs R...............$18
1994 NFL 75th Ann. (Silver) $12
1994 Quarterback Crunch....................$30
1995 Dan Marino.................................$12
1995 49ers '94 champs R....................$25
1995 Jacksonville Jaguars R................$14
1995 Carolina Panthers R....................$16
1995 Oakland Raiders R......................$20
1995 St. Louis Rams R $20
1995 Nebraska Nat'l Champs R $15
1995 Super Bowl 30th Anniversary $14
1996 Deion Sanders (HF) $10
1996 Deion Sanders (Sega offer) (HF) $10
1996 Steve Young (CW) $10
1996 QBs: Aikman/Elway/Marino.........$10
1996 RBs: Allen/Sanders/Thomas $10
1996 WRs: Brown/Reed/Rice...............$10
1996 49ers 50th Ann. R $15
1996 Starr/Bradshaw/Aikman SB 30th A. $18
1996 Cowboys '95 champs R...............$12
1996 Baltimore Ravens R.....................$10
1996 Steelers '95 AFC champs R $12
1996 SB XXX (three-pack) $30
1996 Neb. Nat'l Champs R...................$22
1996 Northwestern Wildcats R.............$12
1997 SB 30 Troy Aikman (HF)..............$12
1997 SB 30 Marcus Allen (Error) $35
1997 SB 30 Marcus Allen (Correct)......$12
1997 SB 30 Joe Namath $12
1997 SB 30 Roger Staubach................$12
1997 SB 30 Steve Young (CW) $12
1997 Franco Harris 25th Anniversary R...$10
1997 Packers NFC '96 champs $15

1997 Patriots AFC '96 champs R $14
1997 Marc & Nick Buoniconti R............$12
1997 Buoniconti (dinner giveaway) rare .$125
1997 Lambeau Field R.........................$15
1997 Tom Osborne: Nebraska $15
1997 Walter Payton $10
1997 Ronnie Lott (HFW) $12
1997 Roger Staubach $10
1997 Johnny Unitas.............................$10
1997 Mean Joe Greene (CWR) $12
1998 Broncos '97 champs....................$14
1998 Brett Favre 3-time MVP R $15
1998 M. Holmgren/V. Lombardi R $10
1998 Walter Payton Leg. $10
1998 Walter Payton Leg. (CWR)...........$10
1998 Walter Payton Leg. (HW)..............$10
1998 QBs (Favre, Elway, Young) $14
1999 Barry Sanders (all) $10
2000 St. Louis Rams R $12
2000 Walter Payton (18 oz.) $12
2000 Walter Payton (24 oz.) R $18
2000 QBs (Marino, Simms, Young) $10
2001 Baltimore Ravens R $10
2001 Jim Thorpe $10
2001 Cowboys Anniversary R (error) ...$20
2001 Redskins Anniversary R...............$16
2002 New England Patriots R $15

Wheaties
Golf
1996 Peter Jacobson R........................$15
1998 Tiger Woods (free golf balls) $10
1998 Tiger Woods (free golf balls) HF,
  CW $12
1998 Tiger Woods (swinging iron)........$10
1998 Tiger Woods CW $12
1998 Tiger Woods HF $12
1998 Tiger Woods (salesman's sample) $100
1999 Arnold Palmer (12 oz.) $15
1999 Arnold Palmer (18 oz.) $10
1999 Arnold Palmer (24 oz.) $20
1999 Tiger Woods (w/vitamin B) $10
1999 Tiger Woods (cancer banner)......$10
1999 Tiger Woods (cancer banner) CW ..$10
1999 Tiger Woods (36 oz. box) $14
2000 Tiger Woods CW $12
2000 Tiger Woods (1 oz. Sample)........$50
2000 Tiger Woods (Player of Year) $12
2000 Tiger Woods (3 Majors) $12
2000 Tiger Woods (Target) (all)............$12
2000 Tiger Woods (w/cd rom) $18

2001 Tiger Woods (Grand Slam) $10
2002 Tiger Woods (swinging into bowl of
  cereal CW) $14
2002 Tiger Woods (2 free issues of Golf
  Digest)..$12
2002 Tiger Woods (Double pack with Nike
  Golf balls $22

Wheaties
Hockey
1991 Pittsburgh Penguins Champs $30
1992 J. Jagr, M. Lemieux no logo R.....$30
1992 J. Jagr, W. Lemieux logo R........$100
1997 Legends 1980 Team USA $10
1998 Camp., Shan.(MFW Canada)......$15
1998 Canadian Womens Team............$15
1998 USA Women's Team $12
1998 Desja, Drolet (MFW Can.)...........$15
1998 Legends 1980 Team USA $10
2000 Minnesota Wild (1 oz.) $12

Wheaties
Figure/Speed Skating
1998 Kristi Yamaguchi HF...................$10
1998 Eric Heiden CW $10

Wheaties
Michael Jordan
1988 First Edition (MJ story, part 1)
  (12 oz./18 oz.) $90
1998 MJ story (part 2 college)
  (8 oz./12 oz./18 oz.) $30
1988 Pouring ($5 video rebate)
  (12 oz./18 oz. $25
1988 Eating cereal (12)........................$45
1989 Eating cereal (18) $30
1989 Cham. Trad. Cont. $45
1989 Green/post/video offer (18) $30
1989 Blue/post/video offer (18) $30
1989 Purple/post/video offer (18).........$30
1989 Story/video offer (8/12/18)...........$25
1989 Story part 2 (18)..........................$40
1990 Pouring cereal (12).......................$40
1990 Pouring cereal (18).......................$40
1990 Chan. Trad.Cont. (12)..................$20
1990 Blue w/poster; also 43A $30
1990 Green w/poster, also 43B............$30
1990 Purple w/poster, also 43C $30
1990 Free Poster.................................$25
1991 Single serve (1 oz.) $15
1991 Carrying bag $20
1991 Bag over shoulder $25

1991 Shoot hoops w/MJ......................$30
1991 Air Jordan Flight Club
   (12 oz./18 oz.) $60
1991 Pouring cereal (12 oz./18 oz./
   24 oz.) $35
1991 Picture yourself on box of
   Wheaties (12 oz./18 oz.) $30
1991 MJ pouring w/video offer $25
1991 Part 3: MJ plays for USA $45
1991 Bulls R $25
1991 Bulls R (3/4 oz.).........................$20
1992 Bulls (3/4 oz.) R.........................$50
1992 Bulls (1991 Champs) R $25
1992 Super single (1) $15
1992 Super single (1.5) $15
1992 Air Jordan (18)............................$25
1992 Eating cereal $20
1992 Cards Isiah Thomas (18) $30
1992 Cards: Jordan (18) $45
1992 Cards: L. Bird/D. Rodman (18) $35
1992 Cards: Scottie Pippen (18) $30
1992 Cards: Charles Barkley (18) $30
1992 Cards: Karl Malone (18) $30
1992 Cards: Patrick Ewing (18) $30
1992 Cards: David Robinson (18) $30
1993 Silver commemorative $15
1993 Silver com. Can. Bilingual...........$25
1993 Shoot Hoops w/game $14
1993 Playing golf (18) R $55
1994 Honey Gold (meet MJ) $50
1995 "He's Back" (18).........................$14
1995 Video game offer (HG 18) $20
1996 Bulls R $15
1996 Space Jam...................................$12
1996 Space Jam CW............................$14
1996 Space Jam HF............................$14
1997 Basketball offer...........................$10
1997 Basketball offer HF $12
1997 Basketball offer CW $12
1997 Basketball (yellow box) unconfirmed
   issue .... ----
1997 Redemption Basketball...............$40

Wheaties
Olympics
1976 Bruce Jenner $350
1980 Bruce Jenner $300
1984 Mary Lou Retton arms raised
   (1 oz.) $150
1984 Mary Lou Retton arms raise
   (12/18)...$150
1984 Mary Lou Retton on one foot (24) . $160
1986 Tom Dolan $8
1993 J. Faman Special Olmpics R $12
1994 H. McGee Special Olympics R $12
1995 M. Bedard mountain bike (Can.)..$15
1995 S. Galloway Special Olympics R.....$12
1995 Elvis Stoiko skating (Can.)...........$30
1996 Tom Dolan swimming $5
1995 T. Ferguson Spec. Oly. R $12
1996 Michael Johnson Track & field $12
1996 Dan O'Brien decathalon $10
1996 Dan O'Brien (error) $15
1996 Toffin/Stillings Spec. Oly. R..........$10
1996 Amy Van Dyken swimming $8

1996 Amy Van Dyken (error) $15
1996 USA Women's Gym. Team............$8
1996 100 Yrs. of Olympics $12
1997 J. Finzel Spec. Oly. R $7
1998 Michigan Spec. Olympics $7
1998 N.Y. Special Olympics $7
1998 Texas Special Olympics $7
1998 USA Women's Hockey $7
2000 Laura Wilkinson diving $10
2000 Stacy Dragila pole vault..............$10
2000 Brooke Bennett swimming...........$10
2002 Sarah Hughes (Sarah in bold).....$10
2002 Sarah Hughes (Hughes in bold) $125

Wheaties
Racing
1997 Dale Earnhardt (picture of car).... $20
1997 Dale Earnhardt (picture of Dale) $20
1997 Dale Earnhardt CW $25
1997 Dale Earnhardt HF $25
1998 A. Zanardi/J. Vasser $10
1998 Richard Petty Leg. $5
1998 Richard Petty Leg. (CWR)............$5
1998 Richard Petty Leg. (HW) $10
1999 Target Racing $12
2000 Target Racing R...........................$12
2000 Richard Petty Legends R $15
2000 Ned Jarrett Legends R $12
2000 Benny Parsons Legends R..........$12
2000 Cale Yarborough Legends R $12
2000 Bill Elliott.....................................$10
2000 Bill Elliott CW..............................$10
2000 Bill Elliott (w/car attached) HF $18
2001 Lee Petty $10
2001 David Pearson $8
2001 Bill Elliott.....................................$10

Wheaties
Soccer
1994 World Cup back 1A R...................$25
1994 World Cup back 1B R...................$25
1999 Brandi Chastain...........................$12
1999 Mia Hamm $12
1999 Kristine Lilly $12
1999 Briana Scurry $12
1999 Michelle Akers $12

Wheaties
Tennis
1987 Chris Evert (8 oz.) R...................$150
1987 Chris Evert (all others) R...........$120
1997 Arthur Ashe $12
2000 Pete Sampras..............................$15
2000 Althea Gibson..............................$10

Wheaties
Wrestling
2002 Carl Sanderson $15

Wheaties
Track & Field
1996 Boston Marathon 100th Ann. R... $12

Wheaties
Cycling
1999 Lance Armstrong.........................$10
1999 Lance Armstrong (w/cancer
   banner)..$12

Wheaties
75 Years of Champions
1999 L. Gehrig/W. Payton/C. Evert/etc. $12

Wheaties
1999 Reprints 75 Years of Champions
Lou Gehrig $10
Cal Ripken Jr.......................................$12
Jackie Robinson $10
Babe Ruth $10
Michael Jordan $18
John Elway $12
Walter Payton......................................$15
Tiger Woods $15
Mary Lou Retton $12
1980 US Hockey $10

Wheaties
Special Olympics
1993 Jeremy Faman R.........................$16
1994 H. McGee R $12
1995 Sherry Galloway R $14
1996 Stillings R $12
1996 Tammie Ferguson R....................$16
1997 Jennifer Finzel R $15
1998 Michigan Special Olympics R......$12
1998 New York Special Olympics R.....$10
1998 Texas Special Olympics R...........$12
1999 Tyron Floyd R $12
1999 New Jersey Special Olympics R.....$12
1999 Michigan Special Olympics R......$12

Wheaties
Anglers
1998 Angler of the Year (18 oz./36 oz.)....$10
1998 Angler of the Year HF, CW $12
1999 Angler of the Year........................$10
1999 Angler of the Year HF, CW $12

Wheaties
75 Years of Champions
1999 L. Gehrig/W. Payton/C. Evert/etc. ...$12

CANADIAN BOXES
Baseball
1998 Roger Clemens MFW.................. $15
Hockey
1998 Shanahan/Campbell (w/patch).... $15
1998 Shanahan/Campbell (w/puck) $12
1999 Shanahan.................................... $14
1998 Martin Brodeur $15
1998 Team Canada (woman)............... $25
1998 Desjardin/Drolet $15

Golf
1998 Tiger Woods $14
1998 Tiger Woods (1 oz. bags)............ $25
1998 Tiger Woods (swinging putter) $12

Other
1995 Myriam Bedard (biking)............... $30
1995 Elvis Stojko (skating)................... $15

Chapter 14

WRESTLING FIGURES & CARDS

This wrestling price guide contains issues of action figures and trading cards. All values listed in this guide are retail prices - the amount a dealer would sell the item for. Buy prices - the price a dealer would pay for an item - are less, ranging from about one-tenth the price listed for recent common items to perhaps one-half or more for high-value items. Values listed in this guide are intended to serve only as an aid in evaluating your collection and are not a solicitation to buy or sell on the part of the publisher or any other party. Remember actual market conditions are constantly changing, especially for current wrestlers whose in-ring performances during the course of the year can greatly affect the value of their items - both upward and downwards. Regional interest and other factors may cause the value of an item to vary from one part of the country to another.

The prices listed for the cards are for cards in mint condition. Mint cards are perfect cards. They have well centered borders with all corners sharp and square. The cards contain absolutely no creases, stains, edge nicks, surface marks, yellowing or fading, regardless of age.

The prices for action figures are for items still in their original packaging. Items not in their original packaging have a reduced value.

ACTION FIGURES

1985 REMCO AWA

SERIES 1 (2-PACKS)
Animal & Hawk	50.00
Baron Von Raschke & Rick Martel	50.00
Greg Gagne (white) & Jim Brunzell	70.00
Larry Zbyszko & Ric Flair	50.00
Stan Lane & Steve Keim	70.00

SERIES 2 (SETS)
Curt Hennig & Greg Gagne (black)	60.00
Bill Irwin & Scott Irwin	60.00
Buddy Roberts, Terry Gordy & Michael Hayes	80.00
Jimmy Garvin, Precious & Steve Regal	80.00
Paul Ellering, Hawk & Animal	70.00

GRUDGE SERIES
Abdullah the Butcher & Carlos Colon	90.00
Scott Hall & Jimmy Garvin	80.00
Nick Bockwinkel & Larry Zbyszko	80.00
Jerry Blackwell & Stan Hansen	90.00

SERIES 4 MAT MANIACS
Boris Zukoff	150.00
Buddy Rose	100.00
Doug Sommers	100.00
Marty Jannetty	100.00
Nord The Barbarian	150.00
Referee (brown hair)	100.00
Referee (grey hair)	100.00
Shawn Michaels	120.00
Shiek Adnan	180.00

MINI MASHERS
COMPLETE SET	30.00

Animal, Borris Zukov, Curt Hennig, Hawk, Larry Zbyszko, Marty Janetty, Nord The Barbarian, Ric Flair, Scott Hall, Stan Hansen, Shawn Michaels

THUMBSTERS
Animal & Ric Flair	20.00
Greg Gagne & Hawk	20.00
Rick Martel & Larry Zbyszko	20.00

1985-1989 LJN WWF
Adrian Adonis	50.00
Andre The Giant (long hair)	60.00
Andre The Giant (short hair)	60.00
Andre The Giant (strap)	150.00
Ax (of Demolition)	100.00
Bam Bam Bigelow	100.00
Big Bossman	100.00
Big John Studd	30.00
Billy Jack Haynes	60.00
Bobby The Brain Heenan	30.00
Bob Orton Jr.	40.00
Bruno Sammartino	50.00
Brutus Beefcake	50.00
Captain Lou Albano	35.00
Classy Freddy Blassie	30.00
Corpral Kirschner	25.00
Elizabeth	75.00
George The Animal Steele	30.00
Greg The Hammer Valentine	40.00
Hacksaw Jim Duggan	50.00
Haku	75.00
Hercules Hernandez	30.00
Hillbilly Jim	25.00
Honky Tonk Man	60.00
Hulk Hogan (yellow trunks)	50.00
Hulk Hogan (white shirt)	150.00
Hulk Hogan (red shirt)	150.00
Iron Sheik	30.00
Jake The Snake Roberts	75.00
Jesse Ventura	40.00
Jimmy Hart	30.00
Jimmy Superfly Snuka	60.00
Johnny Valiant	40.00
Junkyard Dog	40.00
Kamala	100.00
Ken Patera	50.00
King Harley Race	85.00
King Kong Bundy	50.00
Koko B. Ware	80.00
Magnificent Muraco	25.00
Mean Gene Okerlund	30.00

Mr. Fuji	30.00
Paul Orndorff	30.00
Nikolai Volkoff	25.00
One Man Gang	80.00
Outback Jack	40.00
Randy Savage	60.00
Ravishing Rick Rude	110.00
Rick Martel	125.00
Ricky The Dragon Steamboat	35.00
Rowdy Roddy Piper	35.00
SD Jones (Red Shirt)	30.00
SD Jones (Hawaiian Shirt)	30.00
Slick	30.00
Ted Arcidi	50.00
Ted Dibiase	50.00
Terry Funk	35.00
The Referee (Blue Shirt)	100.00
The Referee (White Shirt)	100.00
Tito Santana (Purple)	50.00
Ultimate Warrior	150.00
Vince McMahon	40.00
Warlord	120.00
Sgt. Slaughter (made by Hasbro for LJN)	100.00

TAG TEAMS
British Bulldogs	200.00
Davey Boy Smith	
Dynamite Kid	
Hart Foundation	300.00
Bret Hart	
Jim Neidhart	
Killer Bees	200.00
B. Brian Blair	
Jumpin' Jim Brunzell	
Strike Force	150.00
Rick Martel	
Tito Santana	

14-INCH
Hulk Hogan	50.00
Roddy Piper	75.00

BENDABLES
Andre The Giant	20.00

Big John Studd	20.00
Bobby The Brain Heenan	30.00
Brutus Beefcake	20.00
Captain Lou Albano	20.00
Corporal Kirchner	20.00
George The Animal Steele	20.00
Hillbilly Jim	20.00
Hulk Hogan	20.00
Iron Sheik	20.00
Jesse Ventura	20.00
Junkyard Dog	20.00
King Kong Bundy	20.00
Macho Man	20.00
Nikolai Volkoff	20.00
Paul Orndorff	20.00
Ricky Steamboat	20.00
Roddy Piper	20.00

1990 GALOOB WCW
Arn Anderson (White)	20.00
Barry Windham (Black)	20.00
Brian Pillman (Orange)	20.00
Butch Reed	30.00
Lex Luger (Blue)	20.00
Ric Flair (Blue)	20.00
Rick Steiner (Purple)	20.00
Ron Simmons	30.00
Scott Steiner (Yellow)	20.00
Sid Vicious (Black)	20.00
Sting (Blue)	20.00
Sting (Black)	20.00
Sting (Orange)	20.00
Tom Zenk	20.00

UK WCW
Arn Anderson (Red)	25.00
Barry Windham (Blue)	25.00
Big Josh	100.00
Brian Pillman (Blue)	25.00
Dustin Rhodes	100.00
El Gigante	75.00
Jimmy Garvin	60.00
Lex Luger (Green)	25.00

Lex Luger (Robe) ... 85.00
Michael Hayes ... 60.00
Ric Flair (Red) ... 25.00
Rick Steiner (Green) ... 30.00
Ron Simmons (Stripe) ... 60.00
Sid Vicious (Pink) ... 25.00
Scott Steiner (Pink) ... 25.00
Sting (Coat) ... 85.00

14-INCH

Lex Luger ... 100.00
Ric Flair ... 100.00
Sid Vicious ... 100.00
Sting.. ... 100.00

1990 JUSTOYS WCW

BENDIES

Arn Anderson ... 15.00
Barry Windham ... 15.00
Brian Pillman ... 15.00
Butch Reed ... 20.00
Lex Luger ... 15.00
Ric Flair ... 15.00
Rick Steiner ... 20.00
Ron Simmons ... 20.00
Scott Steiner ... 20.00
Sid Vicious ... 15.00
Sting.. ... 15.00
Tom Zenk ... 15.00

1990-1994 HASBRO WWF

SERIES 1

Akeem ... 100.00
Andre The Giant ... 150.00
Ax ... 50.00
Big Bossman (Sun Glasses) ... 25.00
Brutus Beefcake (Pink) ... 30.00
Hulk Hogan (Hulk Rules Shirt) ... 25.00
Jake The Snake Roberts ... 25.00
Macho Man (Orange) ... 30.00
Million Dollar Man ... 25.00
Rick Rude ... 50.00
Smash ... 30.00
Ultimate Warrior (Green) ... 30.00

SERIES 2

Dusty Rhodes ... 300.00
Hacksaw Duggan (No Shirt) ... 20.00
Honky Tonk Man ... 30.00
Hulk Hogan (Hulk Shirt) ... 25.00
Macho Man (King) ... 20.00
Million Dollar Man (G. Tux) ... 20.00
Roddy Piper ... 20.00
Superfly Jimmy Snuka ... 20.00
Ultimate Warrior (White) ... 50.00

SERIES 3

Big Bossman (No Sunglasses) ... 15.00
Brutus Beefcake (Zebra) ... 75.00
Earthquake ... 30.00
Greg Valentine ... 25.00
Hulk Hogan (Hulkster Rules) ... 20.00
Koko B. Ware ... 75.00
Macho Man (Macho Man On Trunks) ... 50.00
Mr. Perfect (Yellow) ... 50.00
Sgt. Slaughter ... 30.00
Texas Tornado ... 30.00
Typhoon ... 30.00
Ultimate Warrior ... 50.00

SERIES 4

Bret Hart (Black Top) ... 25.00
British Bulldog ... 30.00
Ricky Steamboat ... 20.00
Undertaker (Red Hair) ... 25.00

SERIES 5

Hulk Hogan (No Shirt) ... 20.00
I.R.S.. ... 20.00
Macho Man (Jacket) ... 30.00
Rick Martel ... 20.00
Skinner ... 20.00
Sid Justice ... 20.00
The Mountie ... 20.00
Virgil.. ... 20.00
Warlord ... 20.00

SERIES 6

Berzerker ... 20.00
El Matador ... 20.00
Jim Neidhart ... 20.00
Papa Shango ... 20.00
Repo Man ... 20.00
Ric Flair ... 20.00
Tatanka ... 20.00

SERIES 7 (YELLOW CARDS)

Crush (Yellow) ... 20.00
Kamala (Star) ... 20.00
Nailz ... 20.00
Owen Hart ... 20.00
Razor Ramon (Red) ... 20.00
Shawn Michaels (White) ... 20.00

SERIES 8 (RED CARDS)

Bam Bam Bigelow ... 15.00
Bret Hart (Pink Top) ... 15.00
Lex Luger ... 20.00
Mr. Perfect (Blue) ... 15.00
Undertaker (Brown Hair) ... 20.00
Yokozuna (Red) ... 20.00

SERIES 9 (PURPLE CARDS)

Doink The Clown ... 12.00
Hacksaw Duggan (Shirt) ... 12.00
Million Dollar Man ... 15.00
Rick Steiner ... 12.00
Scott Steiner ... 12.00
Tatanka (Re-release) ... 10.00

SERIES 10 (BLUE CARDS)

Butch #2 (Hat) (Brown) ... 10.00
Shawn Michaels (White Re-release) ... 20.00
Shawn Michaels (Black) ... 25.00

SERIES 11 (GREEN CARDS)

1-2-3 Kid ... 50.00
Adam Bomb ... 30.00
Bart Gunn ... 30.00
Billy Gunn ... 30.00
Crush (Purple) ... 30.00
Ludvig Borga ... 30.00
Yokozuna (White) ... 25.00

TAG TEAMS

Bushwhackers ... 20.00
Demolition ... 40.00
Legion of Doom ... 50.00
Nasty Boys ... 50.00
Rockers ... 20.00

MAIL AWAY FIGURES

Bret Hart ... 75.00
Hulk Hogan (Red Suit) ... 60.00
Undertaker ... 80.00

12-INCH TALKING FIGURES

Hulk Hogan ... 40.00
Ultimate Warrior ... 40.00

ROYAL RUMBLE MINI RING

With Hulk Hogan, Big Bossman, Jake Roberts, Sgt. Slaughter, Million Dollar Man ... 80.00

RR MINI 4-PACKS

Roddy Piper, Texas Tornado & Mr Perfect, Jim Duggan ... 20.00
LOD, Typhoon & Earthquake ... 20.00
Brutus Beefcake, Greg Valentine, Butch & Luke... ... 20.00

1994-1998 OLD SAN FRANCISCO TOY CO. WCW

SERIES 1

Brian Knobs (Black) ... 5.00
Hulk Hogan (Yellow) ... 5.00
Jerry Sags (Black) ... 5.00
Jimmy Hart (Yellow) ... 5.00
Johnny B. Badd (White) ... 5.00
Kevin Sullivan (Black) ... 5.00
Ric Flair (Dark Purple) ... 5.00
Sting (Blue) ... 5.00
Vader 5.00

SERIES 2

Hulk Hogan (Series 1 re-release) ... 5.00
Jimmy Hart (Red) ... 5.00
Johnny B. Badd (Silver) ... 5.00
Kevin Sullivan (Blue) ... 5.00
Macho Man (Yellow) ... 5.00
Ric Flair (Green) ... 5.00
Sting (Pink) ... 5.00
Sting (Green) ... 5.00
Vader (Series 1 re-release) ... 5.00

TAG TEAMS

Nasty Boys ... 10.00
Hulk Hogan (series 1 re-release) & Sting (Black) ... 10.00
Harlem Heat ... 10.00

SERIES 3

Alex Wright ... 5.00
Big Bubba Rogers ... 5.00
Booker T. (Black) ... 5.00
Craig Pittman ... 5.00
Hulk Hogan (Red) ... 5.00
Macho Man (Black) ... 5.00
Ric Flair (Red) ... 5.00
Stevie Ray ... 5.00
Sting 5.00
The Giant (Brown Hair) ... 5.00

NITRO (VIBRATING)

Chris Benoit ... 5.00
Hollywood Hogan ... 5.00
Kevin Nash (Black) ... 5.00
Kevin Sullivan ... 5.00
Lex Luger ... 5.00
Scott Hall (Black) ... 5.00
Sting.. ... 5.00
The Giant ... 5.00

TAG TEAMS & TWO PACKS

Sting & Lugar ... 30.00
Hall & Nash (Both Red) ... 30.00

NITRO (NON-VIBRATING)

Booker T. (Purple) ... 5.00
Brian Knobs (Yellow) ... 5.00
Hollywood Hogan (Beard)5.00
Jerry Sags (Yellow) ... 5.00
Kevin Sullivan (Red) ... 5.00
Macho Man (B/W) ... 5.00
Ric Flair (Light Purple) ... 5.00
Stevie Ray (Purple) ... 5.00
The Giant (Black Hair) ... 5.00

LATE RELEASE NITRO

Lex Luger ... 5.00
Sting (w/bat) ... 5.00
Sting 2 Pack (White & Red Face Paints) ... 10.00

FIGURES INC. EXCLUSIVE TAG TEAMS

Macho Man (Black & Silver) & Hollywood Hogan (No Beard) ... 15.00
Nasty Boys ... 15.00
Harlem Heat ... 15.00
Blue Bloods ... 15.00

WCW/NWO NEW STYLE HARD PLASTIC W/ MOVES

SERIES 1

Diamond Dallas Page ... 5.00
Kevin Nash ... 5.00
Raven (Plain Black Shirt) ... 5.00
Ric Flair ... 5.00
Sting (White) ... 5.00
The Giant ... 5.00

PPV MATCH-UPS

Hall vs. Luger ... 10.00
Hogan vs.Sting ... 10.00
Nash vs. The Giant ... 10.00
Nash vs. DDP ... 10.00

SERIES 2

Bret Hart (Wings On Chest) ... 5.00
Curt Hennig ... 5.00
Hulk Hogan ... 5.00
Lex Luger ... 5.00
Macho Man (White) ... 5.00
Scott Hall ... 5.00

SERIES 3

Bill Goldberg ... 5.00
Buff Bagwell ... 5.00
Chris Benoit ... 5.00
Rey Mysterio Jr. ... 5.00
Scott Steiner ... 5.00
Sting (Red) ... 5.00

K-MART EXCLUSIVE RING

w/ Sting with Jacket ... 30.00

RE-RELEASES

Raven (emblem on chest) ... 8.00
Bret Hart (Hitman on chest) ... 8.00
Macho Man (Red) ... 8.00

4-PACKS

Thunder Champions (w/belts)
Bill Goldberg, Bret Hart, Scott Hall & The Giant.. ... 25.00

FEARSOME FOURSOME

Ric Flair, Chris Benoit, Bill Goldberg & DDP 25.00

NWO HOLLYWOOD

Buff Bagwell, Scott Steiner, The Giant, & Hollywood Hogan ... 25.00

NWO WOLFPACK

Sting, Kevin Nash, Macho Man, & Lex Luger 25.00

4.5 INCH MINI-FIGURES

Goldberg ... 5.00
Hulk Hogan ... 5.00
Kevin Nash ... 5.00
Lex Luger ... 5.00
Macho Man ... 5.00
Ric Flair ... 5.00
Rick Steiner ... 5.00
Scott Hall ... 5.00
Scott Steiner ... 5.00
Sting.. ... 5.00
The Giant ... 5.00

12 INCH-FIGURES

Goldberg ... 15.00
Hollywood Hogan ... 15.00
Macho Man ... 15.00
Sting (White) ... 15.00
Sting (Red) ... 15.00

BELT BUCKLE 1/2 INCH FIGURES

Hogan & Sting ... 15.00
Nash & Hall vs. Nasty Boys ... 15.00

2-PACK (6" FIGURES)

Hollywood Hogan/Dennis Rodman ... 20.00

1994-present JUSTOYS WWF

BENDABLES

SERIES 1

Bret Hart (Purple) ... 8.00
Bret Hart (Pink) ... 20.00
Diesel ... 10.00
Doink The Clown ... 15.00
Lex Luger ... 15.00
Razor Ramon ... 10.00

SERIES 2

British Bulldog ... 4.00
1-2-3 Kid ... 4.00
Mable ... 4.00
Undertaker ... 6.00

SERIES 3

Ahmed Johnson ... 4.00
Goldust ... 4.00
Shawn Michaels ... 4.00
Yokozuna ... 4.00

SERIES 4

Marc Mero ... 4.00
Sid ... 4.00
Sunny ... 4.00
Vader. ... 4.00

SERIES 5

Faarooq ... 4.00
Mankind ... 4.00
Stone Cold Steve Austin ... 4.00
The Rock ... 6.00

SERIES 6

Animal ... 4.00
Hawk. ... 4.00
Hunter Hearst Hemsley ... 6.00
Undertaker 2 ... 4.00

SERIES 7

Crush. ... 4.00
Ken Shamrock ... 4.00
Owen Hart ... 4.00
Patriot ... 4.00

SERIES 8

Chyna ... 4.00
Jeff Jarrett ... 4.00
Kane.. ... 4.00
Taka... ... 4.00

SERIES 9

Brian Christopher ... 4.00
Cactus Jack ... 4.00
Sable. ... 4.00
X-Pac. ... 4.00

SERIES 10

Billy Gunn ... 4.00
Edge.. ... 4.00
Road Dogg ... 4.00
Steve Blackman ... 4.00

SERIES 11

Val Venis ... 4.00
Godfather ... 4.00
Vince McMahon ... 4.00
Al Snow ... 4.00

SERIES 12

Big Boss Man ... 4.00
Big Show ... 4.00
Mankind ... 4.00
Undertaker ... 4.00
Steve Austin ... 4.00

SERIES 13

D'Lo Brown	4.00
Bob Holly	4.00
Shane McMahon	4.00
Steve Austin	4.00
Droz ..	4.00

SERIES 14

Matt Hardy	4.00
Jeff Hardy	4.00
The Rock	4.00
Chris Jericho	4.00

POWER HOUSE BOX SET 7 FIGURES
(KB EXCLUSIVE)

Psycho Sid, Hunter Hearst Helmsly, Sunny, Ahmed Johnson, Paul Bearer, Goldust, Yokozuna .	20.00
Super Slam Ring w/ Paul Bearer	10.00

1996-present
JAKKS WWF/WWE
SERIES 1

Bret Hart	15.00
Diesel	45.00
Goldust	25.00
Razor Ramon	55.00
Shawn Michaels	20.00
Undertaker	20.00

SERIES 2

Bret Hart	8.00
Owen Hart	20.00
Shawn Michaels	8.00
Ultimate Warrior	30.00
Undertaker	8.00
Vader.	8.00

SERIES 3

Ahmed Johnson	6.00
Bret Hart	6.00
British Bulldog	6.00
Diesel	50.00
Goldust	10.00
Mankind	6.00
Shawn Michaels	6.00
Sid	6.00

SERIES 4

Faarooq	6.00
Hunter Hearst Hemsley	6.00
Jerry "The King" Lawler	6.00
Justin Hawk Bradshaw	6.00
Steve Austin	6.00
Vader.	6.00

SERIES 5

Flash Funk	6.00
Ken Shamrock	6.00
Savio Vega	6.00
Sid	6.00
Stone Cold Steve Austin	6.00
The Rock	6.00

SERIES 6

Hunter Hearst Hemsley	6.00
Jeff Jarrett	6.00
Marc Mero	6.00
Mark Henry	6.00
Owen Hart	6.00
Steve Blackman	6.00

SERIES 7

Edge ..	6.00
Steve Williams	6.00
Stone Cold Steve Austin	6.00
Val Venis	6.00
X-Pac	6.00
Undertaker	6.00

SERIES 8

Big Boss Man	5.00
Kane ..	4.00
Shawn Michaels	5.00
Ken Shamrock	5.00
Shane McMahon	5.00
The Rock	3.00

SERIES 9

Paul Wight (Big Show)	5.00
Bob Holly	4.00
Christian	4.00
Gangrel	7.00
Undertaker	3.00
Vince McMahon	5.00

RINGSIDE COLLECTION #1

Sable .	10.00
Sunny	10.00
The Referee	25.00
Vince McMahon	10.00

RINGSIDE COLLECTION #2

Honky Tonk Man	10.00
Jim Cornette	8.00
Jim Ross	8.00
Sgt. Slaughter	8.00
The Referee	12.00
Vince McMahon	12.00

SIGNATURE SERIES #1

Goldust	6.00
Hunter Hearst Hemsley	6.00
L.O.D. - Animal	6.00
L.O.D. - Hawk	6.00
Mankind	6.00
Stone Cold Steve Austin	6.00

SIGNATURE SERIES #2

B.A. Billy Gunn	6.00
Dude Love	6.00
Kane	6.00
Road Dogg	6.00
Shawn Michaels	6.00
Undertaker	6.00

SIGNATURE SERIES #3

Edge	6.00
Hunter Hearst Hemsley	6.00
Jacqueline	6.00
Stone Cold Steve Austin	8.00
The Rock	8.00
Undertaker	8.00

SIGNATURE SERIES 4

Steve Austin	4.00
Paul Wight	5.00
Ken Shamrock	5.00
Edge	5.00
X-Pac	5.00
The Rock	5.00

SIGNATURE SERIES 5

Al Snow	5.00
Steve Austin	4.00
Billy Gunn	5.00
Big Boss Man	5.00
Kane	5.00
Road Dogg	5.00

SIGNATURE SERIES 6

Steve Austin	4.00
Bob Holly	5.00
Triple H	5.00
Undertaker	4.00
Vince McMahon	5.00
Mankind	5.00

S.T.O.M.P - WAR ZONE

Ahmed Johnson	4.00
Brian Pillman	4.00
Crush .	4.00
Ken Shamrock	4.00
Stone Cold Steve Austin	4.00
Undertaker	4.00

S.T.O.M.P #2

Chyna	6.00
Mosh.	6.00
Owen Hart	6.00
The Rock	6.00
Thrasher	6.00
Stone Cold Steve Austin	6.00

S.T.O.M.P. #3

Animal	4.00
Hawk	4.00
Kane	4.00
Marc Mero	4.00
Sable	4.00
Undertaker	4.00

S.T.O.M.P #4 CAMO CARNAGE

Steve Austin	10.00
Chyna	10.00
Road Dogg	10.00
Billy Gunn	10.00
Triple H	10.00
X-Pac	10.00

S.T.O.M.P #4 CAMO CARNAGE
(WITHOUT GUNS)

Steve Austin	7.00
Chyna.	7.00
Road Dogg	7.00
Billy Gunn	7.00
Triple H	7.00
X-Pac	7.00

S.T.O.M.P SERIES 4 CAMO CARNAGE
SPECIAL ISSUE
(ELECTRONICS STORE EXCLUSIVE)

Steve Austin	10.00

(continued)

Chyna	10.00
Road Dogg	10.00
Billy Gunn	10.00
Triple H	10.00
X-Pac	10.00

BEST OF 1997 - SERIES 1

Ahmed Johnson	8.00
Bret Hart	8.00
British Bulldog	8.00
Owen Hart	8.00
Stone Cold Steve Austin	8.00
Undertaker	8.00

BEST OF 1997 - SERIES 2

Crush	6.00
Goldust	6.00
Hunter Hearst Hemsley	6.00
Ken Shamrock	6.00
Marc Mero	6.00
Shawn Michaels	6.00
The Rock	6.00
Undertaker	6.00

BEST OF 1998 - SERIES #1

Bradshaw	6.00
Brian Christopher	6.00
Chyna	6.00
Shawn Michaels	6.00
Stone Cold Steve Austin	6.00
Vader	6.00

BEST OF 1998 - SERIES #2

Dan Severn	6.00
Dude Love	6.00
Hunter Hearst Hemsley	6.00
Jeff Jarrett	6.00
Ken Shamrock	6.00
Mark Henry	6.00
Stone Cold Steve Austin	6.00
Undertaker	6.00

WRESTLEMANIA 14

Headbanger Mosh	6.00
Headbanger Thrasher	6.00
Hunter Hearst Hemsley	6.00
Shawn Michaels	6.00
Stone Cold Steve Austin	6.00
The Rock	6.00

SPECIAL EDITION #1

Ahmed Johnson	4.00
British Bulldog	4.00
Sunny	4.00
The Rock	4.00
Undertaker	4.00
Vader .	4.00
Yokozuna	4.00

SPECIAL EDITION #2

Faarooq	4.00
Goldust	4.00
Hunter Hearst Hemsley	4.00
Sable.	4.00
Savio Vega	4.00
Stone Cold Steve Austin	4.00
Yokozuna	4.00

SPECIAL EDITION #3

Animal	4.00
Dan Severn	4.00
Hawk.	4.00
Hunter Hearst Hemsley	4.00
Ken Shamrock	4.00
Marc Mero	4.00

SPECIAL EDITION #4

B.A. Billy Gunn	4.00
Chyna	4.00
Mankind	4.00
Road Dogg	4.00
Stone Cold Steve Austin	4.00
Undertaker	4.00

SPECIAL EDITION # 5
(KB TOYS EXCLUSIVE)

Al Snow	3.00
Ken Shamrock	3.00
Edge	3.00
X-Pac	3.00
Val Venis	3.00
Mark Henry	3.00

SLAMMERS #1

Bret Hart	5.00
Faarooq	5.00
Goldust	5.00
Mankind	5.00
Stone Cold Steve Austin	5.00
Undertaker	5.00

SLAMMERS #2

Brian Pillman	7.00
Dude Love	5.00
Kane	7.00
Patriot	7.00
Shawn Michaels	6.00
Taka	6.00

SHOTGUN SATURDAY NIGHT #1

Animal	6.00
Hawk	6.00
Henry Godwin	6.00
Pheneaus Godwin	6.00
Savio Vega	6.00
Stone Cold Steve Austin	6.00
The Rock	6.00
Undertaker	6.00

SHOTGUN SATURDAY NIGHT #2

Sable	6.00
Shawn Michaels	6.00
Jeff Jarrett	6.00
Kane	6.00
B.A. Billy Gunn	6.00
Road Dogg	6.00

LIVE WIRE #1

Chyna	6.00
Ken Shamrock	6.00
Mankind	6.00
Stone Cold Steve Austin	6.00
Undertaker	6.00
Vader.	6.00

LIVE WIRE #2

Marc Mero	6.00
Mark Henry	6.00
The Rock	6.00
Shawn Michaels	6.00
Val Venis	6.00
X-Pac.	6.00

DON'T TRUST ANYBODY #1

Chainz	6.00
Dude Love	6.00
8-Ball	6.00
Faarooq	6.00
Hunter Hearst Hemsley	6.00
Kane ..	6.00
Shawn Michaels	6.00
Vader.	6.00

DON'T TRUST ANYBODY #2

Al Snow	6.00
Blue Blazer	30.00
Edge	6.00
Jeff Jarrett	6.00
Steve Blackman	6.00
Undertaker	16.00

DON'T TRUST ANYBODY # 3

Godfather	5.00
Steve Austin	3.00
X-Pac.	4.00
Triple H	4.00
Christian	5.00
Ken Shamrock	5.00

FULLY LOADED #1

Al Snow	6.00
B.A. Billy Gunn	6.00
Hunter Hearst Hemsley	6.00
Kane ..	6.00
Road Dogg	6.00
The Rock	6.00

FULLY LOADED #2

Steve Austin	3.00
Road Dogg	3.00
The Rock	3.00
Test.	4.00
Shane McMahon	5.00
X-Pac.	5.00

BREAKDOWN

D 'Lo.	6.00
Droz.	6.00
Goldust	6.00
Mankind	6.00
Stone Cold Steve Austin	6.00
X-Pac.	6.00

MANAGER (2-PACKS)

Bob Backlund & The Sulton	10.00
Clarence Mason & Crush	10.00
Paul Bearer & Mankind	10.00
Sable & Marc Mero	10.00

TAG TEAMS

Headbangers	12.00
Legion Of Doom	12.00

New Blackjacks ... 12.00
The Godwins ... 12.00

2 TUFF #1

Chainz & 8 Ball ... 12.00
Goldust & Marlena ... 12.00
HHH & Chyna ... 12.00
Interrogator & Rekon ... 12.00

2 TUFF #2

B.A. Billy Gunn & Road Dogg ... 12.00
D 'Lo & Kama ... 12.00
Jackal & Kurgon ... 12.00
Jerry Lawler & Brian Christopher ... 12.00

2 TUFF #3

Hawk & Animal ... 12.00
Mankind & Kane ... 12.00
Rocky & Owen Hart ... 12.00
Undertaker & Steve Austin ... 12.00

2 TUFF #4

The Rock & Mankind ... 10.00
Billy Gunn & Val Venis ... 10.00
Undertaker & Kane ... 10.00
Steve Austin & Big Boss Man ... 10.00

2 TUFF #5

Steve Austin & The Rock ... 10.00
Debra & Jeff Jarrett ... 10.00
Viscera & Undertaker ... 10.00
Road Dogg & Billy Gunn ... 10.00

BEST OF 1998 TAG TEAMS

Hawk & Animal ... 12.00
Billy Gunn & Road Dogg ... 12.00
Mosh & Thrasher ... 12.00

2 PACKS

Bret Hart vs. Owen Hart ... 40.00
British Bulldog vs. Sid ... 12.00
HHH vs. Owen Hart ... 12.00
Ken Shamrock vs. Dan Severn ... 12.00
Luna vs. Sable ... 12.00
Mark Henry vs. Vader ... 12.00
Razor Ramon vs. Diesel ... 100.00
Road Dogg vs. Al Snow ... 12.00
Shawn Michaels vs. HHH ... 12.00
Shawn Michaels vs. Vader ... 12.00
Steve Blackman vs. Marc Mero ... 12.00
Stone Cold Steve Austin vs. Shawn Michaels ... 12.00
Stone Cold Steve Austin vs. Vince McMahon ... 12.00
Taka vs. Brian Christopher ... 12.00
Undertaker vs. Kane ... 12.00
X-Pac vs. Jeff Jarrett ... 12.00

SPECIAL COLLECTION TAG TEAMS

D Lo & Mark Henry ... 12.00
Mankind & Al Snow ... 12.00
Hawk & Animal ... 12.00

MULTI-PACKS

SURVIVOR SERIES

COMPLETE SET ... 60.00
Bret Hart, Shawn Michaels, Goldust, Ultimate Warrior

CHAMPIONSHIP BELT

COMPLETE SET ... 40.00
British Bulldog, Owen Hart, The Rock, Undertaker

KINGS OF THE IRON RUNGS

COMPLETE SET ... 40.00
Ahmed Johnson, Bret Hart, Referee, Stone Cold Steve Austin

BURIED ALIVE

COMPLETE SET ... 65.00
Mankind, Paul Bearer, The Executioner, Undertaker

RAW IS WAR

COMPLETE SET ... 30.00
Bret Hart, Sid, Sunny, Vince McMahon

TRIPLE THREAT

COMPLETE SET ... 35.00
Ahmed Johnson, Marc Mero, Yokozuna

NATION OF DOMINATION

COMPLETE SET ... 25.00
Clarence Mason, Crush, Faarooq, Savio Vega

WRESTLEMANIA 14

COMPLETE SET ... 30.00
Hunter Hearst Hemsley, Shawn Michaels, Stone Cold Steve Austin, Undertaker

WRESTLEMANIA (3-PACKS)

HHH, Shawn Michaels, & Thrasher ... 25.00
Steve Austin, Mosh & Undertaker ... 25.00

FACES OF FOLEY

COMPLETE SET ... 25.00
Cactus Jack, Dude Love, Mankind

ATTITUDE

COMPLETE SET ... 25.00
L.O.D. 2000, Shawn Michaels, Stone Cold Steve Austin

NO HOLDS BARRED

COMPLETE SET ... 25.00
Cactus Jack, Kane, Stone Cold Steve Austin

DEGENERATION - X

COMPLETE SET ... 25.00
Chyna, Billy Gunn, Hunter Hearst Hemsley, Road Dogg

BADD BLOOD

COMPLETE SET ... 40.00
Kane, Paul Bearer, Stone Cold Steve Austin, Undertaker

OFF THE MAT

COMPLETE SET ... 25.00
B.A. Billy Gunn, Road Dogg, Stone Cold Steve Austin, The Rock

SHOTGUN SATURDAY NIGHT

COMPLETE SET ... 25.00
Kane, Shawn Michaels, Stone Cold Steve Austin, The Rock

GO MENTAL

COMPLETE SET ... 25.00
Dude Love, Hunter Hearst Hemsley, Stone Cold Steve Austin, Undertaker

FULLY LOADED

COMPLETE SET ... 25.00
B.A. Billy Gunn, Road Dogg, Stone Cold Steve Austin, Undertaker

LEGENDS OF THE PAST & PRESENT

COMPLETE SET ... 25.00
Andre The Giant, Stone Cold Steve Austin, Undertaker

OVER THE EDGE

COMPLETE SET ... 25.00
Hunter Hearst Hemsley, Kane, Stone Cold Steve Austin, The Rock

JUDGEMENT DAY

COMPLETE SET ... 25.00
Stone Cold Steve Austin, Undertaker, Vince McMahon

SPECIAL COLLECTION

Steve Austin (3-pack) ... 25.00
Undertaker (3-pack) ... 25.00

BAD TO THE BONZ

Steve Austin (3-pack) ... 25.00

MISC. (6" FIGURES)

K-Mart Steve Austin (Gift Set #1) ... 15.00
K-Mart Steve Austin (Gift Set #2) ... 15.00
K-Mart The Rock (Gift Set #1) ... 15.00
KB Steve Austin (Give away) ... 15.00
Toy Fare Undertaker ... 20.00
Toy Fare Steve Austin ... 20.00
Whites Guide Sable ... 20.00
Whites Guide Undertaker ... 20.00
Jakks 1 in 40 Wrestlemania Contest Stone Cold Steve Austin ... 25.00

LEGENDS (7-INCH)

Andre The Giant ... 10.00
Cpt. Lou Albano ... 10.00
Classy Freddy Blassie ... 10.00
Jimmy Snuka ... 10.00

RIPPED & RUTHLESS #1 (7-INCH)

Goldust ... 10.00
Mankind ... 10.00
Stone Cold Steve Austin ... 10.00
Undertaker ... 10.00

RIPPED & RUTHLESS #2 (7-INCH)

Hunter Hearst Hemsley ... 10.00
Kane ... 10.00
Sable ... 10.00
Shawn Michaels ... 10.00

FANTASY WARFARE (7-INCH, 2-PACKS)

Mankind vs. Undertaker ... 15.00
Steve Austin vs. Andre ... 20.00

MINI FIGURES WRESTLEMANIA

COMPLETE SET ... 30.00
Bret Hart, Owen Hart, Sid, Shawn Michaels, Undertaker, Vader

RAW IS WAR

COMPLETE SET ... 25.00
Ahmed Johnson, Faarooq, Goldust, Hunter Hearst Hemsley, Mankind, Stone Cold Steve Austin

ROYAL RUMBLE

COMPLETE SET ... 25.00
Animal, British Bulldog, Hawk, Jerrry "The King" Lawler, Marc Mero, Paul Bearer

KING OF THE RING

COMPLETE SET ... 25.00
Brian Pillman, Mosh, Savio Vega, Sunny, Thrasher, The Rock

NO MERCY

COMPLETE SET ... 20.00
B.A. Billy Gunn, Hunter Hearst Hemsley, Mankind, Road Dogg, Stone Cold Steve Austin, Undertaker

SUDDEN THREAT

COMPLETE SET ... 20.00
Cactus Jack, Kane, Mosh, The Rock, Thrasher, Stone Cold Steve Austin

SUPER STUNNERS (ELECTRONICS STORE EXCLUSIVE)

Christian ... 12.00
Gangrel ... 12.00
Edge ... 12.00
Undertaker ... 12.00
Kane ... 12.00
Steve Austin ... 12.00

DEADLY GAMES

Edge ... 5.00
Triple H ... 4.00
Kurgann ... 4.00
Droz ... 5.00
Steve Austin ... 3.00
Road Dogg ... 3.00

ROAD RAGE

Godfather ... 7.00
The Rock ... 3.00
Gangrel ... 6.00
Hardcore Holly ... 4.00
Test ... 4.00
Al Snow ... 5.00

SUNDAY NIGHT HEAT

Billy Gunn ... 4.00
Road Dogg ... 3.00
Steve Austin ... 3.00
Undertaker ... 3.00
Sable ... 4.00
The Rock ... 3.00

BACKLASH SERIES 1 (KB TOYS EXCLUSIVE)

Steve Austin ... 3.00
Triple H ... 3.00
X-Pac ... 3.00
Road Dogg ... 3.00
Kane ... 3.00
Undertaker ... 3.00
The Rock ... 3.00
Big Boss Man ... 3.00
Shawn Michaels 3.00
Al Snow ... 3.00
Billy Gunn ... 3.00
Hardcore Holly ... 3.00
Edge ... 3.00

BACKLASH SERIES #2 (KB TOYS EXCLUSIVE)

Triple H ... 3.00
Hardcore Holly ... 3.00
X-Pac ... 3.00
Steve Austin ... 3.00
Undertaker ... 3.00
Test ... 3.00
Billy Gunn ... 3.00
Edge ... 3.00
The Rock ... 3.00

BACKLASH SERIES #3 (KB TOYS EXCLUSIVE)

Kane ... 3.00
Edge ... 3.00
Triple H ... 3.00
Billy Gunn ... 3.00
Undertaker ... 3.00
Steve Austin ... 3.00
The Rock ... 3.00
Big Boss Man ... 3.00
Test ... 3.00

BACKLASH SERIES #4 (KB TOYS EXCLUSIVE)

Edge ... 3.00
Billy Gunn ... 3.00
Triple H ... 3.00
Steve Austin ... 3.00
Kane ... 3.00
Undertaker ... 3.00
Big Boss Man ... 3.00
Test ... 3.00
The Rock ... 3.00

BACKLASH SERIES #5 (KB TOYS EXCLUSIVE)

Hardcore Holly3.00
The Rock ... 3.00
Undertaker ... 3.00
Test ... 3.00
Val Venis ... 3.00
X-Pac ... 3.00

RAW IS WAR

Steve Austin ... 3.00
Undertaker ... 3.00
Mankind ... 3.00
The Rock ... 3.00

SMACKDOWN (EACH FIGURE COMES WITH A MICROPHONE & A BELT)

Steve Austin ... 4.00
Undertaker ... 4.00
Big Show ... 4.00
The Rock ... 4.00

SMACKDOWN TITANTRON LIVE SERIES 1

Triple H ... 4.00
Gangrel ... 7.00
Shane McMahon ... 5.00
Edge ... 5.00
Billy Gunn ... 4.00

SMACKDOWN TITANTRON LIVE SERIES 2

Steve Austin ... 4.00
Road Dogg ... 4.00
Edge ... 5.00
Triple H ... 4.00
Mankind ... 5.00
Undertaker ... 4.00

TITANTRON LIVE SERIES 1

Steve Austin ... 4.00
Undertaker ... 4.00
Mankind ... 5.00
Road Dogg ... 4.00
The Rock ... 4.00
Kane ... 4.00

TITANTRON LIVE SERIES 2

Big Show ... 5.00
The Rock ... 4.00
X-Pac ... 5.00
Steve Austin ... 4.00
Ken Shamrock ... 5.00
Undertaker ... 4.00

TITANTRON LIVE SERIES 3

Chirs Jericho ... 5.00
Chyna ... 5.00
Big Boss Man ... 5.00
Steve Austin ... 4.00
The Rock ... 4.00
Test ... 5.00

TITANTRON LIVE SERIES 4 (*ALL FIGURES FROM THIS POINT ON HAVE REAL-SCAN TECHNOLOGY, UNLESS NOTED OTHERWISE***)**

The Rock ... 6.00
Cactus Jack ... 10.00
Big Show ... 6.00
Triple H ... 6.00
X-Pac ... 7.00
Road Dogg ... 6.00

TITANTRON LIVE SERIES 5

Kurt Angle ... 10.00
Steve Austin ... 5.00
Chris Jericho ... 5.00
The Rock ... 5.00
Undertaker ... 5.00
Test ... 5.00

TITANTRON LIVE SERIES 6

Big Show ... 5.00
Triple H ... 4.00
The Rock ... 4.00

Edge 5.00
Tazz 6.00
Jeff Hardy 6.00

TITANTRON LIVE SERIES 7

Undertaker 5.00
Stephanie McMahon 7.00
Kane.. .... 5.00
Chris Jericho 5.00
Kurt Angle 5.00
Triple H 4.00

TITANTRON LIVE SERIES 8

Buh Buh Ray Dudley 7.00
Rikishi 5.00
Road Dogg 4.00
The Rock 4.00
Matt Hardy 6.00
Jeff Hardy 7.00

TITANTRON LIVE SERIES 9

Chyna 5.00
Kurt Angle 5.00
Mick Foley 6.00
The Rock 4.00
Rikishi 5.00
Triple H 4.00

TITANTRON LIVE SERIES 10

Triple H 4.00
Kane.. .... 5.00
Rikishi 5.00
Matt Hardy 5.00
Billy Gunn 4.00
Steve Austin 4.00

TITANTRON LIVE SERIES 11

Kurt Angle 5.00
Steve Austin 4.00
Triple H 4.00
Jeff Hardy 6.00
Rikishi 5.00
Stephanie McMahon 7.00

TITANTRON LIVE SERIES 12

Undertaker 4.00
The Rock 4.00
Chris Jericho 5.00
Big Show 5.00
Steve Austin 4.00
Kurt Angle 5.00

TITANTRON LIVE SERIES 13

Undertaker 4.00
Triple H 4.00
The Rock 4.00
Lita 7.00
Steve Austin 4.00
Chris Jericho 5.00

RULERS OF THE RING SERIES 1

Al Snow 6.00
Edge.. .... 5.00
Ivory.. .... 6.00
Tazz... .... 6.00
Buh Buh Ray Dudley 7.00
D-Von Dudley 7.00

RULERS OF THE RING SERIES 2

Steve Blackman 5.00
Big Boss Man 5.00
Rikishi 5.00
Scotty 2 Hotty 8.00
Crash Holly 5.00
Grand Master Sexay 8.00

RULERS OF THE RING SERIES 3

Perry Saturn 13.00
Stephanie McMahon 8.00
Eddie Guerrero 10.00
Prince Albert 8.00
Raven 12.00
Steven Richards 10.00

RULERS OF THE RING SERIES 4

Bob Holly 5.00
Christian 5.00
Justin Credible 12.00
Molly Holly 12.00
Shane McMahon 10.00
William Regal 10.00

REBELLION SERIES 1

Chris Benoit 6.00
X-Pac 5.00
The Rock 4.00
Undertaker 4.00
Jeff Hardy 5.00
Chris Jericho 5.00

REBELLION SERIES 2

Kurt Angle 5.00
Chris Benoit 5.00
The Rock 4.00
Crash Holly 5.00
Undertaker 4.00
Chris Jericho 5.00

REBELLION SERIES 3

Steve Austin 4.00
Triple H 4.00
Jeff Hardy 6.00
D-Von Dudley 5.00
The Rock 4.00
Kurt Angle 5.00

REBELLION SERIES 4

Lita 7.00
Billy Gunn 5.00
Chris Benoit 5.00
X-Pac 5.00
Triple H 4.00
Edge 5.00

HOUSE OF PAIN

Tori 15.00
The Rock 4.00
Undertaker 4.00
Triple H 4.00
X-Pac 5.00
Steve Austin 4.00

NO WAY OUT SERIES 1 (WAL-MART EXCLUSIVE)

Chris Jericho 5.00
Grand Master Sexay 10.00
Kurt Angle 5.00
Scotty 2 Hotty 10.00
Steve Austin 4.00
The Rock 4.00

NO WAY OUT SERIES 2 (WAL-MART EXCLUSIVE)

Undertaker 4.00
Chris Jericho 5.00
Kurt Angle 5.00
Matt Hardy 5.00
Christian 5.00
Lita 7.00
Chris Benoit 5.00
Raven 10.00
Steve Austin 4.00

RINGSIDE CHAOS SERIES 1

Tazz.... .... 7.00
Steve Austin 4.00
Scotty 2 Hotty 7.00
Kurt Angle 5.00
The Rock 4.00
Undertaker 4.00

RINGSIDE CHAOS SERIES 2

Stephanie McMahon 7.00
The Rock 4.00
Steve Austin 4.00
Chris Jericho 5.00
Big Show 5.00
Kurt Angle 5.00

RINGSIDE CHAOS SERIES 3

Steve Austin 4.00
Eddie Gurrero 5.00
Kurt Angle 5.00
Triple H 4.00
Steve Blackman 6.00
The Rock 4.00

RAW HEAT SERIES 1 (ONLY THE FIRST SERIES WAS NOT REAL-SCAN)

Mankind 4.00
The Rock 4.00
Undertaker 4.00
Steve Austin 4.00

RAW HEAT SERIES 2

Undertaker 4.00
Triple H 4.00
The Rock 4.00
Chris Jericho 5.00

RAW HEAT SERIES 3

Matt Hardy 5.00
The Rock 4.00
Chris Jericho 5.00
Steve Austin 4.00

DOUBLE SLAM SERIES 1 (NOT REAL-SCAN)

Steve Austin & Shane McMahon 8.00
Kane & X-Pac 8.00
Vince McMahon & Undertaker 8.00
Edge & Christian 8.00

DOUBLE SLAM SERIES 2 (NOT REAL-SCAN)

Big Show & Steve Austin 8.00
The Rock & Billy Gunn 8.00
Undertaker & Kane 8.00
Triple H & X-Pac 8.00

DOUBLE SLAM SERIES 3 (NOT REAL-SCAN)

Mankind & Undertaker 8.00
Billy Gunn & Hardcore Holly 8.00
Big Show & Test 8.00
Steve Austin & Debra 9.00

DOUBLE SLAM SERIES 4

Chyna & Chris Jericho 10.00
Triple H & Billy Gunn 10.00
Matt Hardy & Jeff Hardy 25.00

DOUBLE SLAM SERIES 5

Triple H & The Rock 8.00
The Acolytes (Faarooq & Bradshaw) 25.00
Edge & Christian 15.00

FINISHING MOVES SERIES 1

Kurt Angle & Chris Jericho 10.00
Matt Hardy & Jeff Hardy 10.00
Triple H & The Rock 10.00

FINISHING MOVES SERIES 2

Rikish & Triple H 10.00
Undertaker & Kane 10.00
The Rock & Chris Jericho 10.00

FINISHING MOVES SERIES 3

Billy Gunn & Eddie Guerrero 10.00
Matt Hardy & Jeff Hardy 10.00
Chris Jericho & Chris Benoit 10.00

FINISHING MOVES SERIES 4

Lita & Buh Buh Ray Dudley 15.00
Edge & Kane 10.00
The Rock & Steve Austin 10.00

FAMOUS SCENES SERIES 1

Jeff Hardy & Matt Hardy 20.00
The Rock & Triple H 10.00
Mick Foley & Undertaker 20.00

FAMOUS SCENES SERIES 2

Chris Benoit & Chris Jericho 10.00
Triple H & Cactus Jack 25.00
Kurt Angle & Rikishi 10.00

FAMOUS SCENES SERIES 3

Steve Austin & Vince McMahon 10.00
The Rock & Triple H 10.00
The Dudley Boyz (Buh Buh Ray & D-Von) 12.00

FAMOUS SCENES SERIES 4

The Rock & Billy Gunn 10.00
Steve Austin & Undertaker 10.00
Lita & Test 12.00

RINGSIDE RIVALS SERIES 1

Bradshaw vs. Test 10.00
Steve Austin vs. The Rock 10.00
Vince McMahon Vs. Shane McMahon 10.00

RINGSIDE RIVALS SERIES 2

Edge vs. Christian 10.00
Kurt Angle vs. Undertaker 10.00
Triple H vs. Steve Austin 10.00
William Regal vs. Mick Foley 10.00
Matt Hardy vs. Buh Buh Ray Dudley 10.00
The Rock vs. Chris Jericho 10.00

RINGSIDE RIVALS SERIES 3

Edge vs. William Regal 10.00
Triple H vs. Kurt Angle 10.00
D-Von Dudley vs. Spike Dudley 15.00

RINGSIDE RIVALS SERIES 4

Vince McMahon vs. Ric Flair 10.00
Rob Van Dam vs. Test 10.00
Booker T vs. The Rock 10.00

RINGSIDE RIVALS SERIES 5

Undertaker vs. Hulk Hogan 15.00
Eddie Gurrero vs. Jeff Hardy 10.00
Triple H vs. Chris Jericho 10.00

RINGSIDE RIVALS SERIES 6

Edge vs. Kurt Angle 10.00
Test vs. Tajiri 10.00
Rob Van Dam vs. Booker T 10.00

FATAL 4-WAY SERIES 1

Lita 5.00
Edge 5.00
Jeff Hardy 5.00
Buh Buh Ray Dudley 5.00

FATAL 4-WAY SERIES 2

Steve Austin 5.00
Undertaker 5.00
Chris Jericho 5.00
Christian 5.00

FATAL 4-WAY SERIES 3 (REPAINTS OF FIGURES FROM THE FIRST TWO SERIES')

Chris Jericho 5.00
Jeff Hardy 5.00
Buh Buh Ray Dudley 5.00
Christian 5.00

R3 REAL REACTION SERIES 1

The Rock 4.00
Steve Austin 4.00
Matt Hardy 5.00
Chris Benoit 4.00
Chris Jericho 4.00
Kane 5.00

R3 REAL REACTION SERIES 2

The Rock 4.00
Steve Austin 4.00
Edge 5.00
Big Show 5.00
Undertaker 4.00
Jeff Hardy 6.00

R3 REAL REACTION SERIES 3

Kane.. .... 5.00
Undertaker 4.00
Big Show 5.00
Matt Hardy 6.00
Jeff Hardy 7.00
Steve Austin 4.00

R3 REAL REACTION SERIES 4

Triple H 4.00
Rikishi 5.00
Chuck Palumbo 5.00
Billy Gunn 5.00
Test.... .... 5.00
Kurt Angle 5.00

R3 REAL REACTION SERIES 5

Chris Benoit 4.00
Undertaker 4.00
Rob Van Dam 6.00
Kevin Nash 5.00
Jeff Hardy 6.00
Booker T 5.00

STUNT ACTION SUPERSTARS

Jeff Hardy 5.00
Triple H 4.00
X-Pac 5.00
Rikishi 5.00
Kurt Angle 5.00
Stephanie McMahon 5.00

STUNT ACTION SUPERSTARS 2

Undertaker 4.00
Lita 6.00
Dave Hebner (referee) 6.00
Matt Hardy 5.00
Triple H 4.00
The Rock 4.00

UNCHAINED FURY SERIES 1 (RELEASED ON BOTH RED & YELLOW CARDS, THE RED ARE THE HARDER TO FIND OF THE TWO)

Rob Van Dam (Red) 15.00
(Yellow) 10.00
Booker T (Red) 10.00
(Yellow) 7.00
Tajiri (Red) 10.00
(Yellow) 7.00
Hurricane Helms (Red) 10.00
(Yellow) 7.00
Lance Storm (Red) 10.00
(Yellow) 7.00
Ric Flair (Red) 10.00
(Yellow) 7.00

UNCHAINED FURY SERIES 1 (2 PACKS)

Booker T vs. Steve Austin 10.00
Rob Van Dam vs. Chris Jericho 12.00
Vince McMahon vs. Ric Flair 10.00

UNCHAINED FURY SERIES 2 (2 PACKS)

Kurt Angle vs. Edge 10.00
Chuck Palumbo & Billy Gunn (Red Tights) 10.00
Chuck Palumbo & Billy Gunn (Black Tights) 12.00
Diamond Dallas Page Vs. Christian 15.00

UNCHAINED FURY SERIES 3

Rob Van Dam 6.00
Booker T 5.00
Kurt Angle 5.00
Rhyno 10.00
Tajiri 5.00
Kevin Nash 5.00

N.W.O. SERIES 1

Hollywood Hogan (Jeans & N.W.O. Shirt) 15.00
Hollywood Hogan (Wrestling Tights) 15.00
Kevin Nash (Jeans & N.W.O. Shirt) 10.00
Kevin Nash (Wrestling Tights) 10.00
Scott Hall (Jeans & N.W.O. Shirt) 10.00
Scott Hall (Wrestling Tights) 10.00

N.W.O. SERIES 1 (2-PACKS)

Hollywood Hogan vs. The Rock 20.00
Steve Austin vs. Scott Hall 10.00
Kane Vs. Kevin Nash 10.00

TRASH TALKING CHAMPIONS

Kurt Angle 5.00
Chris Jericho 5.00

ROAD TO WRESTLEMANIA

Undertaker 4.00
D-Von Dudley 4.00
Chris Jericho 4.00
Jeff Hardy 4.00
Buh Buh Ray Dudley 4.00
Chris Benoit 4.00

WRESTLINGS MOST WANTED (2-PACKS)

Rob Van Dam & Hardcore Holly 10.00
Chris Jericho & Edge 10.00
Triple H & Chris Benoit 10.00

MATCH ENDERS

Lita 5.00
Undertaker 4.00
Triple H 4.00
Edge 4.00
Matt Hardy 4.00
Billy Gunn 4.00

FINAL COUNT SERIES 1

Billy Gunn & Edge 10.00
Matt Hardy & Lita 10.00
Steve Austin & Undertaker 10.00

FINAL COUNT SERIES 2

Billy Gunn & Triple H 10.00
The Rock & Chris Jericho 10.00
Steve Austin & Kane 10.00

FINAL COUNT SERIES 3

Billy Gunn & Jeff Hardy 10.00
Steve Austin & Chris Jericho 10.00
Buh Buh Ray Dudley & Rikishi 10.00

FINAL COUNT SERIES 4

Test & Christian 10.00
The Rock & Kurt Angle 10.00
Albert & Scotty 2 Hotty 10.00

FINAL COUNT SERIES 5

Trish Stratus & Jeff Hardy 20.00
Bradshaw & Undertaker 10.00
Rob Van Dam & Eddie Guerrero 10.00

FINAL COUNT SERIES 6

Hulk Hogan & Triple H 15.00
Chris Jericho & Chris Benoit 10.00
Chuck Palumbo & Billy Gunn 10.00

FINAL COUNT SERIES 7

Billy Kidman & Rey Mysterio 20.00
Jamie Noble & Hurricane Helms 10.00
Mark Henry & Batista 10.00

BACK TALKIN' CRUSHERS SERIES 1 (NOT REAL-SCAN)

Steve Austin 4.00
The Rock 4.00
Big Show 4.00
Undertaker 4.00

BACK TALKIN' CRUSHERS SERIES 2 (REAL-SCAN)

Steve Austin 4.00
Road Dogg 4.00
Mankind 5.00
The Rock 4.00

BACK TALKIN' CRUSHERS SERIES 3 (REAL-SCAN)

Triple H 4.00
Chris Jericho 5.00
Kurt Angle 5.00
The Rock 4.00
Steve Austin 4.00

BACK TALKIN' SLAMMERS SERIES 1

Triple H 4.00
The Rock 4.00
Steve Austin 4.00
Chris Jericho 5.00
Undertaker 4.00
Kurt Angle 5.00

BACK TALKIN' SLAMMERS SERIES 2

Chris Jericho 5.00
Triple H 4.00
Kurt Angle 5.00

ROLLIN' REBELS

Hollywood Hogan w/ motorcycle 15.00
Undertaker w/ Motorcycle 15.00

UNRELENTING

Booker T 5.00
Edge 5.00
Rob Van Dam 6.00
Chris Jericho 5.00
Jeff Hardy 6.00
Triple H 4.00

RAW DRAFT SERIES

#1 Undertaker 6.00
#2 Kevin Nash 6.00
#2 Scott Hall 7.00
#2 X-Pac 8.00
#3 Kane 6.00
#4 Rob Van Dam 10.00
#5 Booker T 8.00
#6 Big Show 6.00
#7 Buh Buh Ray Dudley 6.00
#8 Brock Lesnar (Figure Never Released)
#9 Willaim Regal 6.00
#10 Lita 8.00
#11 Bradshaw 6.00
#12 Steven Richards 10.00
#13 Matt Hardy 7.00
#14 Raven 15.00
#15 Jeff Hardy 8.00
#16 Mr. Perfect (figure Never released)
#17 Spike Dudley 20.00
#18 D'Lo Brown (Figure Never Released)
#19 Shawn Stasiak (Figure Never Released)
#20 Terri (Figure Never Released)

SMACKDOWN DRAFT SERIES

#1The Rock 6.00
#2 Kurt Angle 6.00
#3 Chris Benoit 6.00
#4 Hollywood Hogan 10.00
#5 Billy Gunn 6.00
#5 Chuck Palumbo 6.00
#6 Edge 6.00
#7 Rikishi 6.00
#8 D-Von Dudley 6.00
#9 Mark Henry (figure Never Released)
#10 Maven 10.00
#11 Billy Kidman (figure Never Released)
#12 Tajiri 7.00
#13 Chris Jericho 6.00
#14 Ivory 7.00
#15 Albert 6.00
#16 The Hurricane 7.00
#17 Al Snow 7.00
#18 Lance Storm 6.00
19 Diamond Dallas Page 15.00
#20 Torrie Wilson (figure Never Released)

RUTHLESS AGGRESSION SERIES 1

Rey Mysterio 20.00
Brock Lesner 20.00
Chavo Guerrero 10.00
Eric Bischoff 10.00
John Cena 10.00
Randy Orton 10.00

RUTHLESS AGGRESSION SERIES 2

Tommy Dreamer 10.00
Billy Kidman 10.00
Scott Steiner 10.00
Rico 10.00
Batista 10.00
Jamie Noble 10.00

WRESTLEMAINA X-SEVEN (FIGURES COME WITH GOLD PLATED BELTS)

Edge 7.00
Steve Austin 7.00
Kane 7.00
Chyna 7.00
Eddie Guerrero 7.00
Chris Jericho 7.00

WRESTLEMANIA X-8 (FIGURES COME WITH GOLD PLATED BELTS)

Rob Van Dam 10.00
Maven 10.00
Diamond Dallas Page 10.00
Triple H 6.00
Billy Gunn 8.00
Chuck Palumbo 8.00

SUMMER SLAM (FIGURES COME WITH GOLD PLATED BELTS)

Steve Austin 5.00
Edge 5.00
The Rock 5.00
Test 5.00
X-Pac 6.00

ROYAL RUMBLE

Earl Hebner (referee) 6.00
Tazz 6.00
Ric Flair 6.00
Triple H 4.00
William Regal 6.00
Chris Jericho 5.00

KING OF THE RING SERIES 1

Edge 6.00
Steve Austin 4.00
Kurt Angle 5.00
Matt Hardy 5.00
Jeff Hardy 5.00
D-Von Dudley 5.00

KING OF THE RING SERIES 2

Brock Lesner 25.00
Rob Van Dam 7.00
Chris Jericho 6.00
Test 6.00
X-Pac 6.00
Hardcore Holly 5.00

RAW 10TH ANNIVERSARY

Trish Stratus 15.00
Goldust 15.00
Jerry Lawler 15.00
Shawn Michaels 15.00
Undertaker 4.00
Triple H 4.00
Steve Austin 4.00
Jeff Hardy 10.00
Rob Van Dam 7.00
Shane McMahon 6.00
Kurt Angle 5.00
The Rock 4.00

SUPERSTARS UNCOVERED SERIES 1

The Rock 6.00
Hollywood Hogan 10.00
Triple H 6.00
Kurt Angle 6.00
Rob Van Dam 10.00
Undertaker 6.00

SUPERSTARS UNCOVERED SERIES 2

Rey Mysterio 20.00
Jeff Hardy 10.00
Matt Hardy 10.00
Rob Van Dam 10.00
Kane 8.00
Kurt Angle 8.00

FLEX' EMS SERIES 1

The Rock 5.00
Triple H 5.00
Chris Jericho 5.00
Hollywood Hogan 6.00
Kurt Angle 5.00
Edge 5.00

UNLIMITED SERIES 1

The Rock 8.00
Rob Van Dam 10.00
Chris Jericho 8.00
Hollywood Hogan 10.00
Kurt Angle 8.00
Edge 8.00

MATCH CHAMPS (K-MART EXCLUSIVE)

Triple H 8.00
Jeff Hardy 10.00
Booker T 8.00
Ric Flair 10.00
The Rock 8.00

RING LEADERS (WWESHOPZONE.COM EXCLUSIVE)

The Rock 10.00
Triple H 10.00
Hollywood Hogan 10.00
Undertaker 10.00
Chris Jericho 10.00

OFF THE ROPES (WAL-MART EXCLUSIVE)

Trish Stratus 15.00
Brock Lesnar 15.00
Hollywood Hogan 10.00
Triple H 4.00
Edge 5.00
Booker T 5.00

12" FEDERATION FIGHTERS SERIES 1

The Rock 15.00
Undertaker 15.00
Kane 15.00
Steve Austin 15.00
Steve Austin (Camo outfit) 20.00

12" FEDERATION FIGHTERS SERIES 2

Big Show 25.00
Undertaker 15.00
The Rock 15.00
Steve Austin 15.00

12" RINGSIDE REBELS (WITH REAL SCAN) SERIES 1

Undertaker 15.00
The Rock 15.00
Steve Austin 15.00

12" RINGSIDE REBELS (WITH REAL SCAN) SERIES 2

The Rock 15.00
Chris Jericho 15.00
Triple H 15.00

12" RINGSIDE REBELS (WITH REAL SCAN) SERIES 3

Booker T 15.00
Rob Van Dam 20.00
Triple H 15.00

12" RINGSIDE REBELS (WITH REAL SCAN) SERIES 4

Jeff Hardy 30.00
Hulk Hogan 30.00
The Rock 15.00

MULTI-PACKS

Brothers Of Destruction (Steve Austin, Undertaker, Kane) TRU Exclusive 25.00
Renegades (Raven, Steve Austin, Shane McMahon) K-Mart Exclusive 25.00
Leap of Faith (Matt Hardy, Jeff Hardy & Dave Hebner (referee)) Canadian Exclusive 30.00
Billion Dollar Trio (Triple H, Kurt Angle, Stephanie McMahon) K-Mart Exclusive 25.00
Wiseguyz (Triple H, Billy Gunn, Road Dogg, X-Pac) TRU exclusive 25.00
Picture Perfect (Edge & Christian) K-Mart Exclusive 25.00
Immortal Champions (The Rock, Triple H, Steve Austin) TRU Exclusive 20.00
Corporate Corruption (Steve Austin, Triple H, Vince McMahon) Ames Exclusive 25.00
A Cold Day In Dudleyville (The Rock, Buh Buh Ray Dudley, D-Von Dudley) TRU Exclusive 25.00
Get In the Groove (Scotty 2 Hotty (Red Outfit),Rikishi, Grand Master Sexay(white shirt) TRU Exclusive 25.00
Get In the Groove (Scotty 2 Hotty (Yellow Outfit), Rikishi, Grand Master Sexay (Blue Shirt) Mijires Exclusive 30.00
Back in The Ring (Steve Austin, Undertaker, Mick Foley) K-Mart Exclusive 25.00
Back in the Ring 2 (The Rock, Triple H, Rikishi) K-Mart exclusive 25.00
Smackdown Draft (Chris Jericho, Vince McMahon, The Rock Hulk Hogan) TRU exclusive 40.00
Raw Draft (Buh Buh Ray Dudley, Undertaker, Ric Flair, Steve Austin) TRU Exclusive 40.00
Triple Threat (Chirs Jericho, The Rock, Triple H) KB Exclusive 20.00

T.L.C. High Flyers (Jeff Hardy, Buh Buh Ray Dudley, Edge) Canadian Exclusive........ 30.00
Insurrection 10 Pack (Edge, Steve Austin, Jeff Hardy,Test, The Rock, Chirs Jericho,Buh Buh Ray Dudley, William Regal, Triple H, Kane) U.K. Exc.. 45.00
Wrestlemania X8 (Chris Jericho, Triple H, Stone Cold,Edge, The Rock, Undertaker) TRU Exclusive.. 40.00
Fueled By Fury (Ric Flair, Chris Jericho, Undertaker) Wal-Mart Exclusive........... 25.00
Hulk Still Rules (80's Hogan, Hollywood Hogan, and 2002 Hogan) K-Mart Exclusive.. 30.00
NWO Federation Poison (Kevin Nash, X-Pac, Scott Hall) K-Mart Exclusive................ 30.00
Razors Edge (Edge, Kurt Angle, Hulk Hogan) K-Mart Exclusive..................... 25.00
Brass Revenge (William Regal, Rob Van Dam, Edge) 25.00
Seek And Destroy (The Rock, Kane, Hulk Hogan) Wal-Mart Exclusive................... 25.00
Team Xtream (Matt Hardy, Lita, Jeff Hardy) K-Mart Exclusive 25.00
2 Xtream (Matt Hardy, Lita, Jeff Hardy) K-Mart Exclusive..................................... 30.00
Ramp Of Rage (Rob Van Dam, Jeff Hardy, Steve Austin, Undertaker (with Motorcycle) TRU Exclusive..................................... 45.00
World Championship Collection (Chris Jericho, Kurt Angle,The Rock, Triple H, Jeff Hardy, Steve Austin............................ 30.00
Ring Of Turmoil (Chris Jericho, Triple H & a Wrestling Ring) Ames Exclusive 25.00
Hardcore Action Ring (Jim Ross, Earl Hebner (referee) & a wrestling Ring) K-Mart Exclusive 30.00
Hardcore Action Ring w/Exclusive Mick Foley figure 15.00
TitanTron Live w/Vince McMahon figure. 10.00
Smackdown Entrance Ramp W/Big show figure (JC Pennys exc.) 20.00
Traxx West W/Al Snow figure (U.K. Exclusive)... 30.00

ECW (EXTREME CHAMPIONSHIP WRESTLING) SERIES 1

Sabu 10.00
Taz 10.00
Rob Van Dam 15.00
Justin Credible 10.00
Shane Douglas 10.00
Chris Candido...................................... 10.00

SERIES 2

Tommy Dreamer 10.00
Buh Buh Ray Dudley 10.00
D-Von Dudley 10.00
New Jack 10.00
Lance Storm 10.00

SERIES 3

Taz (Purple Tights) 10.00
Rob Van Dam (Black Tights) 15.00
Sabu (Orange tights..............................10.00
Justin Credible (Red Shirt)....................10.00
Tommy Dreamer (Yellow Shirt).............10.00
New Jack (Blue Shirt) 10.00

SERIES 4 CHAMPIONSHIP CLASHERS

Taz (purple Tights)10.00
Rob Van Dam (Black tights)..................15.00
Balls Mahoney 10.00
Rhino 10.00
Axl Rotten 10.00
Jerry Lynn...12.00
Raven. 12.00
Tajiri... ....10.00

SERIES 5 BASH OF THE BRAWLERS

Sabu 10.00
Justin Credible......................................10.00
Nova 10.00
Little Guido 10.00
Sandman...12.00
Steve Corino 10.00
Super Crazy 10.00
Mike Awesome......................................15.00

SERIES 6 THRILL ZONE

Rhino 10.00
Chris Candido 10.00
Lance Storm 10.00
Rob Van Dam 15.00
New Jack 10.00
Balls Mahoney 10.00
Tommy Dreamer 10.00
Raven 12.00
Rage War 2pack with Sabu (yellow tights) & Lance Storm (Blue Tights) 20.00
ECW Wrestling Ring with Exclusive Sabu (Silver Tights) And Rob Van Dam (Red Tights)..30.00

1997 PLAYMATES WWF

Undertaker 14".....................................25.00
Undertaker 9".......................................10.00
Sid 9". 10.00

RINGMASTERS

Bret Hart 8.00
Goldust 5.00
Shawn Michaels......................................5.00
Sid 5.00
Undertaker 5.00
Yokozuna 8.00

GRUDGE MATCH MINI FIGURES (2-PACKS)

Steve Austin/Bret Hart..........................15.00
Yokozuna/Ahmed Johnson....................15.00
Owen Hart/Shawn Michaels 15.00
Sid/Vader 15.00
Mankind/Undertaker 15.00
Savio Vega/Goldust...............................15.00

STRETCH'EMS

Bret Hart 10.00
Sid 10.00
Undertaker 10.00
Shawn Michaels....................................10.00

1999-PRESENT TOYBIZ WCW

SERIES 1

Bill Goldberg...6.00
Diamond Dallas Page..............................6.00
Hollywood Hogan 6.00
Kevin Nash..6.00
Lex Luger..6.00
Macho Man...6.00
Scott Hall 6.00
Sting.. ....6.00
The Giant 6.00

2-PACKS

Battle of the Giants
Kevin Nash vs. The Giant.......................20.00
Clash of the Champions
Sting vs. Hollywood Hogan....................25.00
Power & Beauty Macho Man & Miss Elizabeth 20.00

RING FIGHTERS

Booker T. 7.00
Bret Hart 7.00
Chris Benoit..7.00
Scott Steiner...7.00

BRUISERS

Bam Bam Bigelow...................................6.00
Billy Kidman..6.00
Stevie Ray...5.00
Diamond Dallas Page..............................6.00
Raven 7.00
Sting.. ....5.00
Rey Mysterio Jr. (Without Mask)...........10.00
Kevin Nash..5.00
Wrath. 5.00
Disco Inferno 5.00
Macho Man Randy Savage 5.00
Goldberg...7.00

SLAM 'N CRUNCH

Perry Saturn 25.00
Buff Bagwell..5.00
Goldberg...7.00
Konnan 6.00
Kevin Nash..5.00
Sting.. ....5.00

POWER SLAM SERIES 1

Dennis Rodman.....................................12.00
Hak 10.00
Sid Vicious..5.00
Hulk Hogan 7.00
Goldberg 7.00

POWER SLAM SERIES 2

Kanyon 20.00
Roddy Piper..7.00
Buff Bagwell..5.00
Kevin Nash 5.00
Sting.. ....5.00

THUNDERSLAM 2-PACKS

Sting & Bret Hart 8.00
Goldberg & Bam Bam Bigelow 10.00
Scott Hall & Kevin Nash...........................9.00

GRIP 'N FLIP SERIES 1

Dean Malenko & Chris Jericho 10.00
Goldberg & Hollywood Hogan 10.00
Diamond Dallas Page & Raven 10.00

GRIP 'N FLIP SERIES 2

Lex Lugar & Bret Hart 10.00
Sting & Buff Bagwell 10.00
Kevin Nash & Konnan 10.00
Rick Steiner & Scott Steiner..................10.00

RINGMASTERS

Lex Lugar 5.00
Chris Jericho 6.00
Bret Hart 5.00
Goldberg 5.00
Hollywood Hogan....................................6.00
Rick Steiner...5.00

SLAM FORCE

Sting.. ....10.00
Chris Benoit...11.00
Bret Hart..10.00
Kevin Nash 10.00
Goldberg 10.00
Hollywood Hogan..................................10.00

BASH AT THE BEACH

Diamond Dallas Page11.00
Lex Lugar 11.00
Goldberg 11.00
Sting.. ....11.00
Bret Hart..11.00

TNT

Vampiro...20.00
Jeff Jarrett...10.00
Scott Steiner..10.00
Goldberg 10.00

UNLEASHED

Shane Douglas 20.00
Billy Kidman 20.00
Vampiro...25.00
Billy Kidman 20.00

GROSS OUT WRESTLERS

Sting.. ....15.00
Sid Vicious 15.00
Goldberg 20.00

BEND N' FLEX

Sting 4.00
Scott Steiner..4.00
Scott Hall...4.00
Booker T..4.00
Goldberg 4.00
Kevin Nash 4.00
Bret Hart..4.00
Diamond Dallas Page 4.00

14" TUFF TALKIN' SERIES 1 (2-PACK)

Sting & Diamond Dallas Page 15.00
Goldberg & Kevin Nash 15.00

14" TUFF TALKIN' SERIES 2

Scott Steiner..10.00
Konnan..10.00
Macho Man Randy Savage 10.00
Buff Bagwell 10.00

WRESTLING CARDS

1982 WRESTLING ALL-STARS A

Complete Set (36):............................... 40.00

NM/M

1........ Andre The Giant 10.00
2........ Hulk Hogan 8.00
3........ Mil Mascaras.................................. .75
4........ Ted DiBiase 1.00
5........ The Junkyard Dog 1.00
6........ Dusty Rhodes 1.50
7........ Jack Brisco .... .50
8........ Harley Race.................................... .50
9........ Dory Funk Jr.................................... .50
10...... Terry Funk 1.50
11...... Nick Bockwinkel........................... 1.50
12...... Bob Backlund 1.25
13...... Bruno Sammartino........................ 2.00
14...... Pedro Morales................................. .50
15...... Don Muraco .... .50
16...... Bill Dundee..................................... .50
17...... Steve Olsonoskie............................ .50
18...... Tommy Rich.................................... .50
19 ......Angelo Mosca...................................50
20 ......Bruiser Brody.................................2.00
21 ......The Fabulous Moolah.......................50
22 ......Wahoo McDaniel...........................1.50
23 ......Billy Robinson...................................50
24 ......Ivan Koloff 50
25 ......Tony Atlas 50
26 ......Pat Patterson 1.00
27 ......Ric Flair..7.00
28 ......Ivan Putski...75
29 ......Dick Murdoch 1.00
30 ......The Crusher 1.00
31 ......Ken Patera 75
32 ......Ernie Ladd..50
33 ......Dick The Bruiser 1.00
34 ......Jerry Lawler....................................1.50
35 ......Cowboy Bill Watts..............................50
36 ......The Destroyer 50

1982 WRESTLING ALL-STARS B

Complete Set (36):................................30.00

NM/M

1 ....Rick Martel 2.00
2 ....Tony Garea 50
3 ....Bob Roop 50
4 ....Greg Gagne 1.00
5 ....Jim Brunzell.....................................1.00
6 ....Jay Strongbow 50
7 ....Kerry Von Erich 3.50
8 ........S.D. Jones 50
9 ....Brad Rheingans...................................50
10 ......Killer Kahn 50
11 ......Ricky Steamboat 2.00
12 ......Paul Orndorff...................................1.00
13 ......Tito Santana 1.00
14 ......Sergeant Slaughter 1.25
15 ......Verne Gagne 1.00
16 ......Bobby Heenan 1.25
17 ......Jerry Blackwell 50
18 ......Les Thornton 50
19 ......Adrian Adonis 50
20 ......Jesse Ventura 15.00
21...... Buck Zum Hofe................................ .50
22...... Jimmy Valiant .... .50
23...... Steve Keirn .... .50
24...... Ray Stevens .... .50
25...... The Iron Sheik............................... 1.50
26...... Mr. Wrestling II .... .50
27...... Col. Buck Robley.............................. .50
28...... Bobby Duncum .... .50
29...... Mike George .... .50
30...... Dino Bravo .... .50
31...... Baron Von Raschke 1.50
32...... Bobo Brazil .... .50
33...... Greg Valentine.................................. .75
34...... Joyce Grable .... .50
35...... Sweet Brown Sugar.......................... .50
36...... Dutch Mantell .... .50

1983 WRESTLING ALL-STARS

Complete Set (36): 30.00

NM/M

1........ "Superstar" Graham 1.75

22 Terry Taylor .40
23 Barry Windham .50
24 Johnny Weaver, J.J. Dillon .20
25 Tully Blanchard .50
26 Dick Murdoch .40
27 "Sweet" Stan Lane .20
28 Konga The Barbarian, Paul Jones .20
29 Linda Dallas, Misty Blue .20
30 The Road Warriors .75
31 "Sweet" Stan Lane, Sean Royal .20
32 Ricky Santana .40
33 Jimmy "Boogie" Woogie .20
34 Larry Zbyszko, Kendall Windham .40
35 Lex Luger 1.00
36 Shaska Whatley .20
37 Warlord .20
38 "Beautiful" Bobby Eaton .20
39 Dusty Rhodes .75
40 Paul Jones .20
41 Eddie "Hotstuff" Gilbert, Sting 1.00
42 "Wild" Butch Miller .20
43 Barry Windham, Arn Anderson .75
44 Michael Hayes .20
45 Larry Stephens .20
46 Black Bart .20
47 Gladiator 2 .20
48 Ric Flair, Sting 5.00
49 Ivan Koloff .20
50 Jamie West .20
51 Larry Zbyszko .60
52 Sean Royal, "Beautiful" Bobby Eaton .20
53 Arn Anderson, Lex Luger 1.00
54 Baby Doll .20
55 Tim Horner, Shaska Whatley .20
56 Jimmy Garvin, Tully Blanchard .50
57 Kendall Windham, Gladiator .20
58 Terry Taylor, Eddie "Hotstuff" Gilbert .50
59 Dick Murdoch .40
60 "Sweet" Stan Lane, Sean Royal .20
61 Magnum TA .50
62 Ricky Santana .40
63 "Crazy" Luke Williams .20
64 Robert "Bob" Gibson .20
65 Ronnie Garvin .20
66 Ivan Koloff .20
67 Larry Zbyszko, Kendall Windham .60
68 Ric Flair 5.00
69 Ricky Morton .20
70 Tommy Angel .20
71 "Sweet" Stan Lane, Sean Royal .20
72 Kendall Windham .20
73 Baby Doll .20
74 Barry Windham .50
75 Road Warrior "Hawk" .75
76 Mike Rotundo .20
77 Ron Simmons, Arn Anderson .60
78 J.J. Dillon .20
79 Shaska Whatley, Jimmy Valiant .20
80 Kat Lerouxz .20
81 Kendall Windham, Larry Zbyszko .40
82 Road Warrior "Animal" .75
83 Dick Murdoch/"Dr. Death" .20
84 Tully Blanchard .50
85 Konga The Barbarian .20
86 Robert "Bob" Gibson .20
87 Ricky Santana .40
88 Jimmy Valiant .20
89 Nikita Koloff, Ric Flair 5.00
90 Misty Blue, Linda Dallas .20
91 Kevin Sullivan .40
92 "Crazy" Luke Williams .20
93 Lex Luger, Arn Anderson 1.00
94 Big Bubba Rogers .20
95 Bobby Eaton .20
96 Paul Jones' Stable .20
97 "Wild" Butch Miller .20
98 Jimmy Garvin .20
99 Dusty Rhodes .75
100 Ivan Koloff .20
101 Larry Zbyszko .40
102 Sting 1.00
103 Baby Doll, Larry Zbyszko .40
104 Eddie "Hotstuff" Gilbert, Sting 1.00
105 Dusty Rhodes .75
106 Mighty Wilbur .20
107 Michael Hayes, Ric Flair 5.00
108 Tim Horner, Brad Armstrong .20
109 Terry Taylor .40
110 Dick Murdoch .40
111 Tully Blanchard .50
112 Ricky Santana, Warlord .40
113 Jimmy Valiant .20
114 Kevin Sullivan .40
115 Paul Jones .20
116 Lex Luger, Sting 1.00
117 Ivan Koloff .20
118 Larry Zbyszko, Barry Windham .50
119 Italian Stalion .20
120 Dusty Rhodes .75
121 Tim Horner, Chris Champion .20
122 Eddie "Hotstuff" Gilbert, Sting 1.00
123 Mighty Wilbur, Ivan Koloff .20
124 Barry Windham .50
125 Dick Murdoch, Nikita Koloff .40
126 Lex Luger 1.00
127 Nikita Koloff, Dusty Rhodes .75
128 Konga The Barbarian, Warlord, Ivan Koloff .20
129 Paul Jones .20
130 Arn Anderson, Barry Windham .75
131 Ivan Koloff .20
132 Baby Doll, Dusty Rhodes .75
133 Eddie "Hotstuff" Gilbert, Terry Taylor .40
134 Rocky King, Kendall Windham .20
135 Jimmy Garvin, Tully Blanchard .50
136 Lex Luger 1.00
137 Tim Horner, Gladiator .20
138 Kendall Windham .20
139 Magnum TA .40
140 Terry Taylor .40
141 Dick Murdoch, Steve Williams .40
142 Konga The Barbarian .20
143 Mad Dog Debbie .20
144 Steve Williams .20
145 Italian Stalion .20
146 Jimmy Valiant .20
147 Kevin Sullivan, Jimmy Garvin .40
148 Ronnie Garvin .20
149 Ricky Morton .20
150 Luke Williams .20
151 Paul Jones .20
152 Butch Miller .20
153 Warlord, Sting 1.00
154 Ricky Morton, Ric Flair 1.00
155 Black Bart .20
156 Gladiator 1, Gladiator 2 .20
157 Ivan Koloff .20
158 Larry Zbyszko, Baby Doll .40
159 Road Warrior "Hawk" .75
160 Bobby Eaton, Chris Champion .20
161 Paul Jones .20
162 Ric Flair, Michael "P.S." Hayes 5.00
163 "Crazy" Luke Williams .20
164 Dick Murdoch, Steve Williams .40
165 J.J. Dillon .20
166 Linda Dallas, Misty Blue .20
167 Mike Rotundo .20
168 Tommy Angel .20
169 Baby Doll .20
170 Road Warrior "Animal", Ivan Koloff .75
171 Mike Rotundo, Kevin Sullivan .40
172 Ronnie Garvin .20
173 Ron Simmons .20
174 Robert "Bob" Gibson .20
175 Four Horsemen 2.25
176 Pee Wee Anderson .20
177 Tony Schiavone .40
178 Tiger Conway .20
179 Nikita Koloff .20
180 Chris Champion .20
181 Kendall Windham .20
182 Paul Ellering, Paul Jones .20
183 Lex Luger 1.00
184 Johnny Ace .20
185 Jay Cougar .20
186 Missy Hyatt, Magnum TA .40
187 Precious .20
188 Kat Lerouxz, Misty Blue .20
189 Denny Brown, Nelson Royal .20
190 Johnny Weaver .20
191 Sting, Eddie "Hotstuff" Gilbert 1.00
192 Dick Murdoch .40
193 Ole Anderson .20
194 Sting 1.00
195 Konga The Barbarian .20
196 Road Warrior "Animal" .75
197 Michael "P.S." Hayes, Ric Flair 5.00
198 Paul "Number 1" Jones .20
199 Ricky Santana .40
200 Ronnie Garvin .20
201 Jimmy Valiant .20
202 Tully Blanchard .40
203 Shaska Whatley .20
204 Rock'N'Roll Express .40
205 Brad Armstrong .20
206 Misty Blue .20
207 Road Warriors .75
208 Larry Zbyszko .40
209 Bobby Eaton .20
210 Paul Jones, Warlord .20
211 Butch Miller .20
212 Lex Luger 1.00
213 Larry Stephens .20
214 Warlord, Sting 1.00
215 Steve "Dr. Death" Williams .20
216 Tommy Young .20
217 Nikita Koloff .20
218 George South .20
219 Dusty Rhodes, Ric Flair 5.00
220 Black Bart .20
221 Ivan Koloff .20
222 Barry Windham .40
223 Larry Zbyszko, Dusty Rhodes .75
224 Sean Royal .20
225 Kevin Sullivan, Jimmy Garvin .40
226 Eddie "Hotstuff" Gilbert .20
227 Ric Flair, Robert "Bob" Gibson 5.00
228 Eddie "Hotstuff" Gilbert .20
229 Rocky King, Nelson Royal .20
230 Mike Rotundo .20
231 Arn Anderson .75
232 Ron Simmons .20
233 Mighty Wilbur .20
234 Tony Schiavone .40
235 Skandor Akbar .20
236 Jimmy Garvin, Tully Blanchard .40
237 "Jive Tones" .20
238 Tim Horner .20
239 Arn Anderson .75
240 Ivan Koloff, Paul Jones .20
241 Paul Jones .20
242 Magnum TA, Arn Anderson .75
243 Kevin Sullivan, Mike Rotundo .40
244 Ricky Santana, Terry Taylor .40
245 Baby Doll .20
246 Eddie "Hotstuff" Gilbert, Ronnie Garvin .20
247 Steve "Dr. Death" Williams .20
248 Mike Rotundo, Jimmy Garvin .20
249 Mighty Wilbur .20
250 Kevin Sullivan, Jimmy Garvin .40
251 Dick Murdoch .40
252 Ronnie Garvin, Ric Flair 5.00
253 Trent Knight .20
254 Curtis Thompson .20
255 Mighty Wilbur .20
256 "Crazy" Luke Williams .20
257 Ricky Morton, Ric Flair .20
258 Missy Hyatt .20
259 Road Warrior "Animal" .75
260 Nelson Royal .20
261 Magnum TA .40
262 Road Warriors .75
263 Johnny Weaver .20
264 Precious .20
265 Robert "Bob" Gibson .20
266 Dick Murdoch .40
267 Arn Anderson .75
268 Ole Anderson .20
269 Konga The Barbarian .20
270 Ric Flair, Ronnie Garvin 5.00
271 Linda Dallas, Venus .20
272 Gene Ligon .20
273 Ricky Santana .40
274 Lex Luger, Nikita Koloff 1.00
275 Misty Blue, Linda Dallas .20
276 J.J. Dillon .20
277 David Isley .20
278 Teddy Long .20
279 Road Warriors .75
280 Kevin Sullivan .40
281 Road Warrior "Animal" .75
282 "Crazy" Luke Williams .20
283 Big Bubba Rogers .20
284 Jimmy Garvin .20
285 Denny Brown .20
286 Bobby Eaton .20
287 Robert "Bob" Gibson .20
288 Paul Jones .20
289 Butch Miller .20
290 Warlord, Road Warrior "Animal" .75
291 Tommy Young .20
292 Nikita Koloff .20
293 Black Bart .20
294 Gladiator 1 .20
295 Ivan Koloff .20
296 Ricky Nelson .20
297 Steve "Dr. Death" Williams .20
298 Rick Steiner 1.25
299 Larry Zbyszko .40
300 Sean Royal .20
301 Road Warriors .75
302 Baby Doll .20
303 J.J. Dillon, Lex Luger 1.00
304 Tim Horner .20
305 Paul Ellering .20
306 Lex Luger, Gladiator 1 1.00
307 J.J. Dillon .20
308 Midnight Express .60
309 The Sheepherders, Johnny Ace .20
310 Jimmy Garvin, Precious .20
311 Kat Lerouxz .20
312 "Gorgeous" Jimmy Garvin .20
313 Road Warriors .75
314 Ricky Morton .20
315 Konga The Barbarian .20
316 Linda Dallas .20
317 Sting, Eddie "Hotstuff" Gilbert 1.00
318 Italian Stalion .20
319 Ricky Santana .40
320 Jimmy Valiant .20
321 Shaska Whatley .20
322 Michael "P.S." Hayes .20
323 Misty Blue .20
324 Magnum TA .40
325 Venus .20
326 "Crazy" Luke Williams .20
327 Road Warrior "Animal" .75
328 Steve "Dr. Deatth" Williams .20
329 Bobby Eaton .20
330 Paul Jones .20
331 Butch Miller .20
332 Tully Blanchard .40
333 Warlord, Road Warriors .75
334 Ivan Koloff, Paul Jones .20
335 Jamie West .20
336 Larry Zbyszko, Dusty Rhodes .75
337 Lex Luger 1.00
338 Sean Royal .20
339 Four Horsemen 2.25
340 "Gorgeous" Jimmy Garvin, Michael "P.S." Hayes .20
341 Road Warriors, Paul Ellering .75
342 Comrade Olga .20
343 Magnum TA .40

1994 ACTION PACKED - WWF

Complete Set (42): 35.00

NM/M

1 Bam Bam Bigelow 1.75
2 I.R.S. .50
3 Doink The Clown .50
4 Diesel 5.00
5 Razor Ramon 4.00
6 Ludvig Borga .50
7 Shawn Michaels 3.50
8 Yokozuna .50
9 Head Shrinkers .50
10 Bushwackers .50
11 Bob Backlund .50
12 Undertaker 2.00
13 "Macho Man" Randy Savage 1.50
14 Adam Bomb .50
15 Bret "Hit Man" Hart 2.00
16 Luna .50
17 1-2-3 Kid 2.50
18 Owen Hart .75
19 Lex Luger 1.00
20 Bastion Booger .50
21 Quebecers .50
22 Marty Jannetty .50
23 Freddy Blassie .50
24 Steiner Brothers 1.00
25 Smoking Gunns .50
26 Andre The Giant 7.00
27 Paul Bearer .50
28 M.O.M. .50
29 Tatanka .50
30 Yokozuna .50
31 Diesel 5.00
32 Adam Bomb .50
33 Bastion Booger .50
34 Earthquake .50
35 Mabel .50
36 Ludvig Borga .50
37 Razor Ramon 4.00
38 Shawn Michaels 3.50
39 "Macho Man" Randy Savage 1.50
40 Bret "Hit Man" Hart 2.00
41 Steiner Brothers 1.00
42 Undertaker, Paul Bearer 2.00

1995 ACTION PACKED - WWF

Complete Set (42): 30.00

NM/M

1 Bret "Hit Man" Hart 1.25

2	Undertaker	1.50
3	Razor Ramon	3.00
4	Diesel	3.50
5	Heavenly Bodies	.50
6	Doink The Clown	.50
7	Lex Luger	.75
8	Alundra Blayze	.50
9	Yokozuna	.50
10	Bam Bam Bigelow	.75
11	British Bulldog	.75
12	Crush	.50
13	King Kong Bundy	.75
14	Nikolai Volkoff	.50
15	Tatanka	.50
16	Paul Bearer	.50
17	Head Shrinkers	.50
18	Duke The Dumpster	.50
19	Dink	.50
20	Bushwhackers	.50
21	Diesel	3.50
22	Mabel	.50
23	Smoking Gunns	.50
24	Undertaker	1.50
25	Shawn Michaels	3.00
26	Owen Hart	.75
27	Jim "The Anvil" Neidhart	.50
28	Mr. Fuji	.50
29	I.R.S.	.50
30	Luna	.50
31	Well Dunn	.50
32	Jerry Lawler	.75
33	Jeff Jarrett	.75
34	Mr. Bob Backlund	.50
35	Bull Nakano	.50
36	Ted DiBiase	.50
37	1-2-3 Kid	1.75
38	Shawn Michaels	3.00
39	Adam Bomb	.50
40	Bob "Spark Plugg" Holly	.50
41	Bret "Hit Man" Hart	1.25
42	Bam Bam Bigelow	.75

1995 CARDZ - WWF
Complete Set (100): 25.00
Common Card (1-100): .10

1998 DUOCARDS - WWF
Complete Set (72): 15.00

NM/M
1	Attitude	.10
2	Mr. Vince McMahon	.10
3	Commissioner Slaughter	.10
4	Mr. Pat Patterson	.10
5	Mr. Gerald Brisco	.10
6	Steve Austin	1.50
7	New Age Outlaws	.75
8	The Rock	1.00
9	D'Lo Brown	.10
10	Taka Michinoku	.10
11	Stone Cold Steve Austin	1.50
12	Undertaker	.75
13	Shawn Michaels	.75
14	Ken Shamrock	.40
15	The Rock	1.00
16	Triple H	.75
17	Kane	.60
18	Owen Hart	.40
19	Mankind	.60
20	Dude Love	.60
21	Cactus Jack	.60
22	Sable	1.00
23	X-Pac	.60
24	D'Lo Brown	.10
25	Mark Henry	.10
26	Bradshaw	.10
27	The Godfather	.10
28	Double J	.40
29	Dustin Runnels	.10
30	Marvelous Marc Mero	.10
31	Steve Blackman	.10
32	Al Snow & Head	.10
33	Taka Michinoku	.10
34	B.A. Billy Gunn	.60
35	Savio Vega	.10
36	Steve "Dr. Death" Williams	.10
37	Steve Regal	.10
38	Faarooq	.10
39	Scorpio	.10
40	Kurrgan	.10
41	Luna	.10
42	Dan "The Beast" Severn	.10
43	Golga	.10
44	Giant Silva	.10
45	Road Dog Jesse James	.60
46	Edge	.40
47	Darren "Droz" Drozdov	.10
48	Val Venis	.40
49	Papi Chulo	.10
50	Tiger Ali Singh	.10
51	D-Generation X	.75
52	The Nation	.40
53	Kaientai	.10
54	Kane, Mankind	.50
55	New Age Outlaws	.75
56	The Headbangers	.10
57	D.O.A.	.10
58	L.O.D. 2000	.10
59	Southern Justice	.10
60	Too Much	.10
61	Los Boricuas	.10
62	Paul Bearer	.10
63	Chyna	.10
64	Jackyl	.10
65	Jim Cornette	.10
66	Yamaguchi-san	.10
67	Jacqueline	.10
68	Paul Ellering	.10
69	Good ol'JR	.10
70	Jerry "The King" Lawler	.10
71	"Raw Is War"	.10
72	Checklist	.10

AUTOGRAPHS
Complete Set (13): 300.00
1	Steve Blackman	15.00
2	Chyna	30.00
3	B.A. Billy Gunn	30.00
4	Owen Hart	60.00
5	Hawk	20.00
6	Jacqueline	15.00
7	Road Dogg	30.00
8	Mankind	30.00
9	Paul Bearer	15.00
10	Redemption Card	40.00
11	Sable - Promo	60.00
12	Sable - Unsigned	20.00
13	The Rock	45.00

1998 TOPPS - WCW/NWO
Complete Set (72): 15.00

NM/M
1	Hollywood Hulk Hogan	1.50
2	Sting	.75
3	Kevin Nash	1.00
4	"Macho Man" Randy Savage	.50
5	Bret "Hit Man" Hart	.60
6	Lex Luger	.60
7	Giant	.75
8	Diamond Dallas Page	.60
9	Goldberg	1.00
10	Scott Hall	.50
11	Rick Steiner	.40
12	Scott Steiner	.40
13	Buff Bagwell	.60
14	Scott Norton	.10
15	Booker T	.10
16	"Rowdy" Roddy Piper	.40
17	Chris Benoit	.40
18	Raven	.40
19	Chris Jericho	.50
20	Rick Rude	.10
21	Konnan	.10
22	Saturn	.10
23	Sick Boy	.10
24	British Bulldog	.10
25	Juventud Guerrera	.10
26	Dean Malenko	.40
27	Eddy Guerrero	.40
28	Chavo Guerrero Jr.	.10
29	Ultimo Dragon	.10
30	Disco Inferno	.10
31	Wrath	.10
32	Rey Mysterio Jr.	.50
33	Psychosis	.40
34	Stevie Ray	.10
35	Jimmy Hart	.10
36	Steve McMichael	.10
37	Curt Hennig	.40
38	Meng	.10
39	Vincent	.10
40	Fit Finley	.10
41	Jay Leno	.10
42	Alex Wright	.10
43	Announcers	.10
44	Hugh Morrus	.10
45	Kaz Hayashi	.10
46	Kanyon	.10
47	The Disciple	.10
48	Jim "The Anvil" Neidhart	.10
49	Arn Anderson	.10
50	Eric Bischoff	.10
51	Ernest Miller	.10
52	Miss Elizabeth	.40
53	Gene Okerlund	.10
54	Ric Flair	.75
55	Brian Adams	.10
56	Lodi	.10
57	Riggs	.40
58	Frye	.10
59	Chae	.10
60	Kimberly	.10
61	Spice	.10
62	A.C. Jazz	.10
63	Tygress	.10
64	Whisper	.10
65	Hollywood Hulk Hogan	1.50
66	"Macho Man" Randy Savage	.50
67	"Rowdy" Roddy Piper	.40
68	Goldberg - Champion	1.00
69	Chris Jericho - Champion	.50
70	Bret "Hit Man" Hart - Champion	.60
71	Kidman - Champions	.10
72	Checklist	.10

AUTHENTIC SIGNATURES
Complete Set (37): 900.00
Arn Anderson	40.00
Chris Benoit	35.00
Disciple	25.00
Disco Inferno	25.00
Fit Finley	30.00
Frye	30.00
Giant	40.00
Juventud Guerrera	20.00
Eddy Guerrero	35.00
Jimmy Hart	20.00
Kaz Hayashi	20.00
Bobby Heenan	25.00
Hollywood Hulk Hogan	80.00
Chris Jericho	45.00
Kanyon	20.00
Kidman	25.00
Konnan	30.00
Lodi	20.00
Dean Malenko	30.00
Meng	25.00
Ernest Miller	20.00
Kevin Nash	100.00
Gene Okerlund	20.00
Diamond Dallas Page	60.00
Psychosis	25.00
Raven	40.00
Riggs	25.00
Saturn	20.00
Tony Schiavone	20.00
Sick Boy	20.00
Spice	30.00
Mike Tenay	20.00
Tygress	25.00
Vincent	25.00
Whisper	30.00
Wrath	20.00
Alex Wright	25.00

CHROME
Complete Set (10): 40.00
C1	Goldberg	7.00
C2	Diamond Dallas Page	5.00
C3	"Macho Man" Randy Savage	5.00
C4	Sting	5.00
C5	Hollywood Hulk Hogan	10.00
C6	Kevin Nash	10.00
C7	Konnan	3.00
C8	Bret "Hit Man" Hart	5.00
C9	Giant	5.00
C10	Lex Luger	5.00

RETAIL STICKERS
Complete Set (10): 8.00
S1	Goldberg	1.50
S2	Diamond Dallas Page	.75
S3	"Macho Man" Randy Savage	.75
S4	Sting	.75
S5	Hollywood Hulk Hogan	2.00
S6	Kevin Nash	2.00
S7	Konnan	.50
S8	Bret "Hit Man" Hart	.75
S9	Giant	.75
S10	Lex Luger	.75

1999 ARTBOX - WWF
Complete Set (40): 20.00

NM/M
1	Double-Chokeslam	.40
2	Stone-Cold Stunner	1.50
3	Kane's Chokeslam	.50
4	Kane's Tombstone	.50
5	Road Dogg Legdrop	.50
6	Corporate Elbow	1.00
7	Stone-Cold Stunner	1.50
8	Undertaker's Tombstone	.60
9	Undertaker vs. Mankind	.60
10	Tombstone on DX	.60
11	Double-Chokeslam	.40
12	Chokeslam	.40
13	Double-Tombstone	.60
14	Double-Suplex	.40
15	Double-Tombstone	.40
16	Kane's Suplex	.50
17	HHH Bodyslam	.60
18	NAO Doubleteam	.40
19	Two out of three	.40
20	The Pedigree	.60
21	Belly-to-Back Suplex	.40
22	Fireworks	.40
23	D-Gen-X Arrives!	.75
24	Rock sees stars	1.00
25	Smack Down	1.00
26	Rock drops HHH!	1.00
27	Rock Bodyslam	1.00
28	Clothesline	.40
29	Belt-Smash	.40
30	Rock Clotheslines HHH	.75
31	Backdrop	.40
32	Road Dogg Bodyslam	.40
33	Whoop-Ass 101	1.50
34	Austin vs. Mankind	1.50
35	McMahon	.40
36	Austin vs. Kane	1.50
37	Back Suplex	.40
38	The Rattlesnake	1.50
39	Teaching Old Dogs New Tricks!	.40
40	Stunner on Kane/Checklist	.75

1999 DUOCARDS - WWF WRESTLEMANIA LIVE!
Complete Set (54): 16.00

NM/M
1	WrestleMania	.40
2	WrestleMania 2	.10
3	WrestleMania 2	.75
4	WrestleMania 2	.10
5	WrestleMania III	1.25
6	WrestleMania III	.40
7	WrestleMania IV	1.25
8	WrestleMania V	1.00
9	WrestleMania VI	.40
10	WrestleMania VI	.40
11	WrestleMania VII	.75
12	WrestleMania VIII	.40
13	WrestleMania VIII	.75
14	WrestleMania IX	.10
15	WrestleMania IX	.10
16	WrestleMania X	.40
17	WrestleMania X	.10
18	WrestleMania XI	.40
19	WrestleMania XI	.10
20	WrestleMania XII	.50
21	WrestleMania XII	.10
22	WrestleMania 13	.50
23	WrestleMania 13	.40
24	WrestleMania XIV	.75
25	WrestleMania XIV	.40
26	Ken Shamrock	.40
27	Undertaker	.75
28	The Rock	1.00
29	Jeff Jarrett w/Debra	.60
30	The Brood	.40
31	New Age Outlaws	.60
32	Mankind	.75
33	Kane	.40
34	Goldust	.40
35	Stone Cold Steve Austin	1.50
36	Val Venis	.40
37	Sable	.75
38	Mr. McMahon	.40
39	Shane McMahon	.40
40	D'Lo Brown	.10
41	Mark Henry	.10
42	Owen Hart	.40
43	X-Pac	.60
44	Al Snow	.10
45	J.O.B. Squad	.10
46	Edge	.10
47	Gangrel	.10
48	Christian	.10
49	The Godfather	.40
50	Triple H	.75
51	Shawn Michaels	.75

52...... Chyna .40
53...... Attendance .10
54...... Checklist .10

1999 TOPPS - WCW/NWO
Complete Set (72): 15.00
NM/M
1...... Title Card/Checklist .10
2...... Bret "Hit Man" Hart .60
3...... Diamond Dallas Page .60
4...... Goldberg 1.00
5...... Rick Steiner .40
6...... Booker T .10
7...... Chris Jericho .50
8...... Saturn .10
9...... Bam Bam Bigelow .10
10...... Chavo Guerrero Jr. .10
11...... Disco Inferno .10
12...... Wrath .10
13...... Rey Mysterio Jr. .50
14...... Meng .10
15...... Super Calo .10
16...... Glacier .10
17...... Silver King .10
18...... Kaos .10
19...... Lenny Lane .10
20...... Norman Smiley .10
21...... Kidman .10
22...... Alex Wright .10
23...... Kanyon .10
24...... Raven .40
25...... Lodi .10
26...... Ernest Miller .10
27...... The Disciple .10
28...... Bobby Duncum Jr. .10
29...... Barry Windham .10
30...... Konnan .10
31...... Buff Bagwell .60
32...... Eric Bischoff .10
33...... Hollywood Hulk Hogan 1.50
34...... Scott Hall .50
35...... Horace Hogan .10
36...... Scott Steiner .40
37...... Stevie Ray .10
38...... Brian Adams .10
39...... Vincent .10
40...... Curt Hennig .40
41...... Randy "Macho Man" Savage .50
42...... Sting .75
43...... Kevin Nash 1.00
44...... Lex Luger .60
45...... Ric Flair .75
46...... Arn Anderson .10
47...... Dean Malenko .40
48...... Chris Benoit .40
49...... Steve McMichael .10
50...... Juventud Guerrera .10
51...... Eddy Guerrero .40
52...... Psychosis .40
53...... La Parka .10
54...... Damian .10
55...... Hector Garza .10
56...... Miss Elizabeth .40
57...... Kimberly .10
58...... Spice .10
59...... A.C. Jazz .10
60...... Tygress .10
61...... Whisper .10
62...... Chae .10
63...... Fyre .10
64...... Storm .10
65...... Goldberg Triumphant! 1.00
66...... The Venomous bite of Sting! .75
67...... Hogan for President 1.50
68...... Big Sexy 1.00
69...... Feel the Bang .60
70...... Larry Zbyszko, Bobby Heenan .10
71...... Doug Dellinger .10
72...... Sonny Onoo .10

AUTHENTIC SIGNATURES
Complete Set (37): 1000.00
A.C. Jazz 30.00
Brian Adams 30.00
Bam Bam Bigelow 40.00
Chae 30.00
Cyclope 20.00
Damian 20.00
El Dandy 20.00
Ms. Elizabeth 40.00
Hector Garza 25.00
Glacier 25.00
Goldberg 100.00
Chavo Guerrero Jr. 25.00
Scott Hall 75.00

Bret "Hit Man" Hart 80.00
Curt Hennig 35.00
Prince Iaukea 20.00
Silver King 20.00
Kenny Kaos 20.00
Kimberly 50.00
Lenny Lane 20.00
La Parka 35.00
Hugh Morrus 20.00
Jim "The Anvil" Neidhart 30.00
Scott Norton 35.00
Sonny Onoo 20.00
Nick Patrick 20.00
David Penzer 20.00
Charles Robinson 20.00
Randy "Macho Man" Savage 60.00
Billy Silverman 20.00
Norman Smiley 25.00
Rick Steiner 35.00
Sting 100.00
Storm 30.00
Super Calo 20.00
Ultimo Dragon 25.00
Larry Zbyszko 25.00

2001 FLEER WWF CHAMPIONSHIP CLASH
Complete Set (80) 15.00
Common Card: .10
NM/M
1...... The Rock 1.50
2...... K-Kwik .10
3...... Steve Blackman .10
4...... Eddie Guerrero .10
5...... Jerry Lynn .10
6...... Christian .60
7...... Kane .40
8...... Tazz .20
9...... Stone Cold Steve Austin 1.50
10...... Crash Holly .10
11...... Matt Hardy .40
12...... Undertaker 1.00
13...... Al Snow .10
14...... Tajiri .10
15...... Scotty Too Hotty .40
16...... Dean Malenko .10
17...... Raven .40
18...... Big Show .40
19...... Jeff Hardy .40
20...... Spike Dudley .60
21...... Chris Jericho .60
22...... Kurt Angle 1.00
23...... Test .10
24...... Chris Benoit .40
25...... William Regal .10
26...... Rikishi .60
27...... D-Von Dudley .60
28...... Mick Foley 1.00
29...... Triple H 1.00
30...... Albert .10
31...... Haku .10
32...... Perry Saturn .10
33...... "The One" Billy Gunn .20
34...... Hardcore Holly .10
35...... Shane McMahon .20
36...... Edge .60
37...... Rhyno .20
38...... Bubba Ray Dudley .60
39...... Justin Credible .10
40...... X-Pac .40
41...... The Rock 1.50
42...... K-Kwik .10
43...... Steve Blackman .10
44...... Eddie Guerrero .10
45...... Jerry Lynn .10
46...... Christian .60
47...... Kane .40
48...... Tazz .20
49...... Stone Cold Steve Austin 1.50
50...... Crash Holly .10
51...... Matt Hardy .40
52...... Undertaker 1.00
53...... Al Snow .10
54...... Tajiri .10
55...... Scotty Too Hotty .40
56...... Dean Malenko .10
57...... Raven .40
58...... Big Show .40
59...... Jeff Hardy .40
60...... Spike Dudley .60
61...... Chris Jericho .60
62...... Kurt Angle 1.00
63...... Test .10

64...... Chris Benoit .40
65...... William Regal .10
66...... Rikishi .60
67...... D-Von Dudley .60
68...... Mick Foley 1.00
69...... Triple H 1.00
70...... Albert .10
71...... Haku .10
72...... Perry Saturn .10
73...... "The One" Billy Gunn .20
74...... Hardcore Holly .10
75...... Shane McMahon .20
76...... Edge .60
77...... Rhyno .20
78...... Bubba Ray Dudley .60
79...... Justin Credible .10
80...... X-Pac .40

WWF FEMALES
Complete Set (10) 10.00
Common Card: 2.00
Inserted 1:4
WF1... Ivory 2.00
WF2... Tori 2.00
WF3... Lita 4.00
WF4... Molly Holly 2.00
WF5... Debra 3.00
WF6... Stephanie McMahon-Helmsley 2.00
WF7... Chyna 3.00
WF8... Teri 3.00
WF9... Jacqueline 2.00
WF10... Trish Stratus 4.00

PIECE OF THE CHAMPION
Complete Set (20): 375.00
Common Card: 20.00
Inserted 1:24
PC1.... The Rock 40.00
PC2.... Jeff Hardy 25.00
PC3.... Matt Hardy 25.00
PC4.... Chris Jericho 20.00
PC5.... Funaki 20.00
PC6.... Faarooq 20.00
PC7.... Essa Rios 20.00
PC8.... X-Pac 25.00
PC9.... Taka Michinoku 20.00
PC10... Kurt Angle 30.00
PC11... Scotty 2 Hotty 25.00
PC12... Spike Dudley 20.00
PC13... Steve Austin 40.00
PC14... Tajiri 20.00
PC15... Edge 25.00
PC16... Christian 25.00
PC17... Bradshaw 20.00
PC18... Jerry Lynn 20.00
PC19... Perry Saturn 20.00
PC20... Albert 20.00

DIVAS PRIVATE COLLECTION
Complete Set (10): 200.00
Common Card: 20.00
Inserted 1:30
DPC1 . Ivory 25.00
DPC2 . Tori 20.00
DPC3 . Lita 40.00
DPC4 . Molly Holly 30.00
DPC5 . Debra 25.00
DPC6 . Stephanie McMahon-Helmsley 25.00
DPC7 . Chyna 30.00
DPC8 . Terri 30.00
DPC9 . Jacqueline 20.00
DPC10 Trish Stratus 40.00

DIVAS PRIVATE SIGNING
Complete Set (10): 600.00
Common Card: 50.00
Inserted 1:120
DPS1 . Ivory 50.00
DPS2 . Tori 50.00
DPS3 . Lita 100.00
DPS4 . Molly Holly 60.00
DPS5 . Debra 75.00
DPS6 . Stephanie McMahon-Helmsley 60.00
DPS7 . Chyna 75.00
DPS8 . Terri 75.00
DPS9 . Jacqueline 50.00
DPS10 Trish Stratus 100.00

2001 FLEER WWF RAW IS WAR
Complete Set (100): 20.00
Common Card: .10
1...... Stone Cold Steve Austin 1.75
2...... Triple H 1.25
3...... Mick Foley 1.25
4...... Dean Malenko .10
5...... Chris Jericho .75

6...... Lita 1.25
7...... Buh Buh Ray Dudley .75
NM/M
8...... Jim Ross .10
9...... Bull Buchanan .10
10...... Kane .50
11...... Gerald Brisco .10
12...... The Goodfather .10
13...... Matt Hardy .50
14...... Rikishi .75
15...... Vince McMahon .50
16...... Ivory .10
17...... Trish Stratus 1.75
18...... Test .10
19...... Raven .10
20...... Albert .10
21...... Val Venis .10
22...... Tazz .10
23...... Chyna 1.25
24...... Molly Holly .25
25...... Christian .75
26...... Edge .75
27...... William Regal .10
28...... Crash Holly .10
29...... Jeff Hardy .50
30...... Kurt Angle 1.25
31...... K-Kwik .10
32...... Bradshaw .10
33...... Terri Runnels .75
34...... Hardcore Holly .10
35...... Grand Master Sexay .25
36...... Perry Saturn .10
37...... D-Von Dudley .75
38...... "The One" Billy Gunn .25
39...... The Rock 1.75
40...... Eddie Guerrero .10
41...... Steven Richards .10
42...... Pat Patterson .10
43...... Chris Benoit .50
44...... Big Show .50
45...... Faarooq .10
46...... Steve Blackman .10
47...... Undertaker 1.25
48...... Jacqueline .10
49...... Scotty 2 Hotty .25
50...... Chris Jericho .40
51...... Acolytes .10
52...... The One Billy Gunn vs. Val Venis .10
53...... Taka .10
54...... Triple H vs. The Rock .75
55...... Edge and Christian .40
56...... Big Show .25
57...... Hardy Boyz vs. Edge and Christian .25
58...... Deborah McMichaels .10
59...... Kurt Angle .60
60...... Kaientai .10
61...... Rock & Undertaker vs. Edge & Christian .40
62...... RTC .10
63...... Undertaker .60
64...... Billy Gunn w/Chyna .10
65...... Dudley Boyz vs. Edge and Christian .40
66...... Lita vs. Trish .75
67...... The Rock .75
68...... Stephanie McMahon-Helmsley .10
69...... The Dudley Boyz .40
70...... Triple H .60
71...... Stone Cold Steve Austin vs. Vinc McMahon .25
72...... Shane McMahon .10
73...... Radicalz w/Terri Runnels .10
74...... 2 Cool .10
75...... Mick Foley .60
76...... The Hardy Boyz .25
77...... Stone Cold Steve Austin .75
78...... Undertaker vs. Kane .25
79...... "Hardcore, Crash, and Molly Holly" .10
80...... William Regal .10
81...... Stone Cold Steve Austin vs. Triple H .60
82...... Vince McMahon .25
83...... RTC vs. Hardy Boyz .10
84...... Kane .25
85...... Rock vs. Undertaker .60
86...... Stone Cold Steve Austin v. William Regal .10
87...... Stone Cold Steve Austin vs. Chris Benoit .25
88...... Steve Austin vs. Rikishi and Angle .40
89...... Chris Jericho vs. The Rock .40
90...... Stone Cold Steve Austin vs. Kurt Angle .60
91...... Austin vs. Edge, Christian, Angle .40

RAW IS JERICHO

FEMME FATALE

TLC

FAMOUS NICKNAMES

WAR BOOTY

WAR BOOTY AUTOGRAPHS

2001 FLEER WWF ULTIMATE DIVA COLLECTION

THE BAD AND THE BEAUTIFUL

KISS & TELL

RING ACCESSORIES

MATCHING SET

SIGNED WITH A KISS

NATIONAL ASSETS

2001 FLEER WWF WRESTLEMANIA

48	Undertaker	1.25
49	Tiger Ali-Singh	.10
50	D'Lo Brown	.10
51	Kurt Angle	1.25
52	Stone Cold Steve Austin	1.75
53	Chaz	.10
54	Chris Jericho	.75
55	Jerry Lawler	.25
56	Mae Young	.10
57	Bradshaw	.10
58	Funaki	.10
59	Perry Saturn	.10
60	Val Venis	.25
61	Tori	.10
62	Debra	.25
63	Chyna	1.25
64	Ivory	.10
65	Jacqueline	.10
66	The Kat	.25
67	Lita	1.25
68	Trish Stratus	1.75
69	Molly Holly	.25
70	Terri	.75
71	Edge, Christian	.40
72	The Hardy Boyz	.25
73	The Dudley Boyz	.40
74	T&A	.10
75	Right to Censor	.25
76	The Radicals	.25
77	The Hollys	.10
78	K-Kwik, Road Dogg	.10
79	Low Down	.10
80	2 Cool	.25
81	"I Pity the Fool!"	.10
82	Hulkamania Runs Wild	.75
83	Rage in the Cage	.10
84	A New Attendance Record	.10
85	The Proud Chairman	.10
86	The Brain Awakens a Sleeping Giant	1.00
87	The Stars and Stripes Challenge	.50
88	"Don't Do It, Roddy!"	.10
89	When in Rome	.10
90	Megabucks vs. Megamaniacs	.50
91	"Good Friends, Better Enemies"	.10
92	Enter the Rattlesnake	.75
93	Dark Days Cometh	.50
94	The Rock & Rikishi - The Early Years	.75
95	Hardcore Highlight	.10
96	A Rough Night for Charlie Hustle	.10
97	The Stone Cold Age Begins	.75
98	Strike Two for the Hit King	.10
99	The Rattlesnake Reigns Supreme	.75
100	Tag Team Daredevils	.10

THE PEOPLE'S CHAMPION

Complete Set (15):		8.00
Common Card:		1.00
Inserted 1:2		
1	The People's Elbow	1.00
2	The Rock on the Mic	1.00
3	The People's Eyebrow	1.00
4	Blood From a Rock	1.00
5	Football Career	1.00
6	"The Rock, The Author"	1.00
7	The Great One	1.00
8	The Brahma Bull	1.00
9	Layeth the Smackdown	1.00
10	The Rock Bottom	1.00
11	Can You Smell What The Rock is Cooking?	1.00
12	Just Bring It Jabroni!	1.00
13	Five-Time WWF Champion	1.00
14	Millions...Millions...Of The Rock's Fans	1.00
15	Not Just a WWF Superstar	1.00

STONE COLD SAID SO

Complete Set (15):		5.00
Common Card:		.50
Inserted 1:2		
SC1	The Rock	2.00
SC2	Kurt Angle	1.50
SC3	Rikishi	1.00
SC4	Chris Benoit	.75
SC5	Chris Jericho	1.00
SC6	Triple H	1.50
SC7	Vince McMahon	.75
SC8	The Undertaker	1.50
SC9	Kane	.75
SC10	Stephanie McMahon-Helmsley	.50
SC11	X-Pac	.75
SC12	Mick Foley	1.50
SC13	Tazz	.50
SC14	Shane McMahon	.50

SC15	"The One" Billy Gunn	.50

SIGNATURE MOVES

Complete Set (15):		75.00
Common Card:		4.00
Inserted 1:24		
SM1	The Rock	15.00
SM2	Stone Cold Steve Austin	15.00
SM3	Kurt Angle	10.00
SM4	Triple H	10.00
SM5	Chris Jericho	8.00
SM6	Chris Benoit	5.00
SM7	The Undertaker	10.00
SM8	Kane	5.00
SM9	2 Cool	5.00
SM10	The Hardy Boyz	8.00
SM11	The Dudley Boyz	10.00
SM12	Tazz	5.00
SM13	Eddie Guerrero	4.00
SM14	"The One" Billy Gunn	4.00
SM15	Lita	10.00

FOREIGN OBJECTS

Complete Set (7):		275.00
Common Card:		30.00
Inserted 1:63		
FO1	The Rock	70.00
FO2	The Dudley Boyz	125.00
FO3	Stone Cold Steve Austin	35.00
FO4	Triple H	35.00
FO5	Chris Jericho	30.00
FO6	The Undertaker	30.00
FO7	Trish Stratus	60.00

LIP SERVICE

Complete Set (9):		2000.00
Common Card:		250.00
Production 50 Sets		
LS1	Molly Holly	250.00
LS2	Trish Stratus	500.00
LS3	The Kat	250.00
LS4	Lita	400.00
LS5	Chyna	350.00
LS6	Tori	250.00
LS7	Jacqueline	250.00
LS8	Ivory	250.00
LS9	Terri	300.00

2002 FLEER WWE ABSOLUTE DIVAS

Complete Set (1-100):		15.00
Common Card:		.10
Pack (8):		3.00
Wax Box (24):		75.00
		NM/M
1	Trish Stratus	1.25
2	Terri	.20
3	Ivory	.10
4	Lita	1.00
5	Jackie	.40
6	Stacy Keibler	1.25
7	Torrie Wilson	1.25
8	Jacqueline	.10
9	Molly	.10
10	Jazz	.10
11	Stephanie McMahon	1.00
12	Nidia	.10
13	Dawn Marie	.60
14	Victoria	.40
15	Linda	.20
16	Trish Stratus	1.25
17	Terri	.20
18	Ivory	.10
19	Lita	1.00
20	Jazz	.10
21	Stacy Keibler	1.25
22	Torrie Wilson	1.25
23	Jacqueline	.10
24	Molly	.10
25	Stephanie McMahon	1.00
26	Trish Stratus	1.25
27	Terri	.20
28	Ivory	.10
29	Lita	1.00
30	Jackie	.40
31	Stacy Keibler	1.25
32	Torrie Wilson	1.25
33	Jacqueline	.10
34	Molly	.10
35	Jazz	.10
36	Trish Stratus	1.25
37	Terri	.20
38	Ivory	.10
39	Lita	1.00
40	Stacy Keibler	1.25
41	Torrie Wilson	1.25
42	Jacqueline	.10
43	Molly	.10

44	Jazz	.10
45	Lita	1.00
46	Bubba Ray	.60
47	Jamie Noble	.20
48	Matt Hardy	.40
49	Brock Lesnar, Paul Hayman	.60
50	William Regal	.10
51	Triple H	1.00
52	Vince McMahon	.40
53	Booker T	.60
54	Tajiri	.20
55	Steven Richards	.10
56	Jericho	.60
57	D-Von Dudley	.60
58	Rob Van Dam	.60
59	The Rock	1.25
60	Ric Flair	1.00
61	Bradshaw	.10
62	Hulk Hogan	1.25
63	Hurricane	.10
64	Jeff Hardy	.40
65	Kurt Angle	1.00
66	Jazz	.10
67	Trish Stratus	1.25
68	Molly	.10
69	Lita	1.00
70	Stacy Keibler	1.25
71	Torrie Wilson	1.25
72	Trish Stratus	1.25
73	Jacqueline	.10
74	Ivory	.10
75	Trish Stratus	1.25
76	Lita	1.00
77	Terri	.20
78	Jacqueline	.10
79	Molly	.10
80	Dawn Marie	.60
81	Lita	1.00
82	Jacqueline	.10
83	Molly	.10
84	Stacy Keibler	1.25
85	Ivory	.10
86	Trish Stratus	1.25
87	Torrie Wilson	1.25
88	Terri	.10
89	Victoria	.40
90	Jazz	.10
91	Trish Stratus	1.25
92	Torrie Wilson	1.25
93	Ivory	.10
94	Lita	1.00
95	Dawn Marie	.60
96	Terri	.20
97	Linda	.20
98	Stacy Keibler	1.25
99	Molly	.10
100	Jackie	.40

MINI-POSTER

Complete Set (30):		10.00
Common Poster:		.10
1	Trish Stratus	1.25
2	Terri	.20
3	Ivory	.10
4	Lita	1.00
5	Jackie	.40
6	Stacy Keibler	1.25
7	Torrie Wilson	1.25
8	Jacqueline	.10
9	Molly	.10
10	Jazz	.10
11	Stephanie McMahon	1.00
12	Nidia	.10
13	Terri	.20
14	Jackie	.40
15	Stacy Keibler	1.25
16	Victoria	.40
17	Lita	1.00
18	Torrie Wilson	1.25
19	Dawn Marie	.60
20	Trish Stratus	1.25
21	Booker T	.60
22	Kurt Angle	1.00
23	Brock Lesnar	.60
24	Rob Van Dam	.60
25	Jeff Hardy	.40
26	Hulk Hogan	1.25
27	Triple H	1.00
28	Jericho	.60
29	Matt Hardy	.40
30	The Rock	1.25

INTER-ACTIONS

Complete Set (20):		15.00
Common Card:		.75
1IA	Swim Suit Competition	2.00

2IA	Terri wins the Hardcore Championship	.75
3IA	Six Person Intergender Match	1.50
4IA	Bra and Panties Paddle on a Pole Match	2.00
5IA	Mixed Tag Team Match	.75
6IA	Tag Team	2.00
7IA	Bikini Match	2.00
8IA	Table Match	.75
9IA	Intergender Tag Team Match	1.50
10IA	Tag Team Hardcore Women's Title Match	.75
11IA	Tag Team	.75
12IA	Judgement Day Match	1.50
13IA	Gravy Bowl Match	2.00
14IA	Tag Team Match	.75
15IA	Wrestlemania X8 Triple Threat	1.50
16IA	Tag Team	.75
17IA	Swim Suit Competition	2.00
18IA	Women's Title Match - KOTR	1.50
19IA	Bra and Panties Match (Women's Title)	2.00
20IA	Lingerie Match	2.00

COVER SHOTS

Complete Set (10):		15.00
Common Card:		.75
1CS	Ivory	.75
2CS	Jacqueline	.75
3CS	Lita	2.50
4CS	Dawn Marie	1.50
5CS	Stacy Keibler	4.00
6CS	Terri	1.00
7CS	Torrie Wilson	4.00
8CS	Trish Stratus	4.00
9CS	Stephanie McMahon	2.50
10CS	Torrie Wilson, Stacy Keibler	4.00

TROPICAL PLEASURES

Complete Set (10):		10.00
Common Card:		.75
1TP	Ivory	.75
2TP	Trish Stratus	4.00
3TP	Lita	2.50
4TP	Lita, Trish Stratus	3.00
5TP	Stacy Keibler	4.00
6TP	Terri	1.00
7TP	Torrie Wilson	4.00
8TP	Jacqueline	.75
9TP	Molly	.75
10TP	Victoria	1.00

LIP SERVICE

Stacy Keibler		225.00
Torrie Wilson		225.00
Dawn Marie		175.00
Jackie		150.00
Linda		125.00

SIGNED WITH A KISS

Stacy Keibler		350.00
Dawn Marie		250.00

DIVAS INK

Stacy Keibler		200.00
Torrie Wilson		200.00
Dawn Marie		80.00
Jackie		75.00
Linda		75.00

WARDROBE CLOSET

Lita		50.00
Molly		30.00
Nidia		25.00
Stacy Keibler t-shirt		60.00
Torrie Wilson shirt or pants		60.00
Trish Stratus top		60.00
Victoria		30.00

MATERIAL GIRL

Dawn Marie		50.00
Lita		50.00
Molly		30.00
Nidia		25.00
Stacy Keibler t-shirt & top		75.00
Torrie Wilson bikini		100.00
Trish Stratus top & ring mat		60.00
Victoria		30.00
Ivory		20.00
Jazz		15.00
Terri		40.00

2002 FLEER WWF ALL ACCESS

Complete Set:		20.00
Common Card:		.10
Wax Box:		70.00
		NM/M
1	Justin Credible	.10

2	Shane McMahon		.25
3	Tajiri		.25
4	Jerry Lynn		.10
5	Christian		.75
6	Haku		.10
7	Kurt Angle		1.25
8	Albert		.10
9	Chris Jericho		.75
10	Jeff Hardy		.50
11	Triple H		1.25
12	"The One" Billy Gunn		.25
13	Booker T		.75
14	Funaki		.10
15	Chris Benoit		.50
16	The Rock		1.75
17	Bradshaw		.10
18	Stephanie McMahon-Helmsley		.25
19	Crash Holly		.10
20	Rhyno		.25
21	Faarooq		.10
22	Al Snow		.10
23	Hardcore Holly		.10
24	Rikishi		.75
25	Rob Van Dam		.75
26	X-Pac		.50
27	D-Von Dudley		.75
28	Kane		.50
29	Spike Dudley		.10
30	William Regal		.10
31	Taka Michinoku		.10
32	Mick Foley		1.25
33	Undertaker		1.25
34	Edge		.75
35	Stone Cold Steve Austin		1.75
36	Jim Ross		.10
37	Bubba Ray Dudley		.75
38	Steve Blackman		.10
39	Test		.10
40	Molly		.25
41	Vince McMahon		.50
42	Stacy Keibler		.75
43	Torrie Wilson		.75
44	Perry Saturn		.10
45	Raven		.10
46	Scotty 2 Hotty		.50
47	Big Show		.50
48	Matt Hardy		.50
49	Tazz		.25
50	The Hurricane		.10
51	Kane		.50
52	Mick Foley		1.25
53	Lita		1.25
54	Justin Credible		.10
55	Big Show		.50
56	Chris Benoit		.50
57	Stone Cold Steve Austin		1.75
58	Edge		.75
59	Trish Stratus		1.75
60	Faarooq		.10
61	Linda McMahon		.10
62	Jeff Hardy		.50
63	Diamond Dallas Page		.75
64	The Hurricane		.10
65	Kurt Angle		1.25
66	Ric Flair		1.25
67	Undertaker		1.25
68	Tajiri		.25
69	Vince McMahon		.50
70	Chris Jericho		.75
71	Triple H		1.25
72	Tazz		.25
73	Rob Van Dam		.75
74	Sgt. Slaughter		.50
75	The Rock		1.75
76	Jim Ross		.10
77	Bradshaw		.10
78	Matt Hardy		.50
79	Perry Saturn		.10
80	X-Pac		.50
81	Maven		.10
82	Molly		.10
83	Big Show		.25
84	Edge		.50
85	Stone Cold Steve Austin		1.00
86	Vince McMahon		.25
87	Jeff Hardy		.25
88	Kane		.25
89	Lita		.75
90	Ivory		.10
91	Kurt Angle		.75
92	Triple H		.75
93	Rob Van Dam		.50
94	Trish Stratus		1.00
95	Nidia		.10
96	Matt Hardy		.25
97	Christian		.50
98	Mick Foley		.75
99	The Rock		1.00
100	Undertaker		.75

FAMOUS RIDES

Complete Set: 25.00
Common Card: 2.00
Inserted 1:6

1FR	Diamond Dallas Page's Pink Cadillac		2.00
2FR	Stone Cold's Truck		5.00
3FR	The Rock's Limo		5.00
4FR	D-Generation X's "Tank" Jeep		3.00
5FR	Stone Cold destroys Vince's 'Vette		3.00
6FR	Vince McMahon's Jet		2.00
7FR	Big Show's Purple Car		2.00
8FR	Kurt Angle's Scooter		4.00
9FR	Jeff Hardy's Motorcycle		3.00
10FR	Stone Cold's 18-Wheeler		5.00
11FR	D-Generation X's Bus		3.00
12FR	Al Snow's Lil' Racecar		2.00

MATCH MAKERS

Complete Set: 30.00
Common Card: 1.00
Inserted 1:6

1MM	Triple H, Stephanie		2.50
2MM	Kane, Undertaker		3.00
3MM	Debra, Stone Cold		2.50
4MM	Dudley Boys		3.00
5MM	The Rock, Mick Foley		4.00
6MM	Edge, Christian		3.00
7MM	Stephanie, Chris Jericho		2.00
8MM	Kurt Angle, Triple H		4.00
9MM	The Rock, Stone Cold		5.00
10MM	Kaientai		1.00
11MM	Chris Benoit, Chris Jericho		2.00
12MM	Stone Cold, Undertaker		4.00
13MM	Kurt Angle, The Rock		4.00
14MM	Matt Hardy, Lita, Jeff Hardy		3.00
15MM	Mr. McMahon, Stone Cold		3.00

PAY PER VIEW POSTERS

Inserted 1:24

1PPV	Backlash April 29, 2001 Chicago, IL		10.00
2PPV	Invasion July 22, 2001 Cleveland, OH		5.00
3PPV	Judgement Day May 20, 2001 Sacramento, CA		10.00
4PPV	No Mercy October 21, 2001 St. Louis, MO		10.00
5PPV	No Way Out February 25, 2001 Las Vegas, NV		10.00
6PPV	Summerslam August 19, 2001 San Jose, CA		15.00
7PPV	Unforgiven September 23, 2001 Pittsburgh, PA		15.00
8PPV	Vengeance December 9, 2001 San Diego, CA		10.00
9PPV	WrestleMania X-7 April 1, 2001 Houston, TX		15.00
10PPV	Survivor Series November 18, 2001 Greensboro, NC		10.00

ALL ACCESS MEMORABILIA

Complete Set: 600.00
Common Card: 25.00

D-Von Dudley	30.00
Funaki	25.00
The Hurricane	60.00
Jeff Hardy	40.00
Kane	60.00
Kurt Angle	80.00
Molly	30.00
Rob Van Dam	60.00
Stone Cold Steve Austin	60.00
The Rock	60.00
Triple H	50.00
Undertaker	80.00
Stacy Keibler	85.00
Tajiri	30.00
Torrie Wilson	100.00
Tazz	40.00
Scotty 2 Hotty	35.00

MATCH MAKERS MEMORABILIA

Complete Set: 425.00
Common Card: 50.00
Inserted 1:95

Kane, Undertaker	60.00
Dudley Boys	60.00
The Rock, Mick Foley	80.00
Edge, Christian	50.00
The Rock, Stone Cold	80.00
Stone Cold, Undertaker	80.00
Kurt Angle, The Rock	100.00

OFF THE MAT GRAPHS

Complete Set:1 ....300.00
Common Card: 100.00

The Hurricane	100.00
Lita	250.00
Trish Stratus	250.00
Jim Ross	100.00
Rob Van Dam	150.00
Maven	150.00
Stacy Keibler	300.00
Torrie Wilson	300.00

2002 FLEER WWF RAW VS. SMACKDOWN

Complete Set (1-90): 18.00
Common Card: 10
Pack (8): 3.00
Wax Box (24): 75.00

		NM/M
1	The Rock	1.50
2	Undertaker	1.00
3	Kurt Angle	1.00
4	Kevin Nash	1.00
5	Jim Ross	.10
6	X-Pac	.40
7	Chris Benoit	.40
8	Kane	.40
9	Hollywood Hulk Hogan	1.50
10	Rob Van Dam	.60
11	Billy Gunn	.20
12	Chuck Palumbo	.10
13	Booker T	.60
14	Edge	.60
15	Big Show	.40
16	Rikishi	.60
17	Bubba Ray Dudley	.60
18	D-Von Dudley	.60
19	Brock Lesnar	.60
20	Mark Henry	.10
21	William Regal	.10
22	Maven	.10
23	Lita	1.00
24	Billy Kidman	.10
25	Bradshaw	.10
26	Tajiri	.20
27	Steven Richards	.10
28	Chris Jericho	.60
29	Matt Hardy	.40
30	Ivory	.10
31	Raven	.10
32	Albert	.10
33	Jeff Hardy	.40
34	The Hurricane	.10
35	Jerry Lawler	.20
36	Al Snow	.10
37	D'Lo Brown	.10
38	DDP	.60
39	Shawn Stasiak	.10
40	Torrie Wilson	.60
41	Terri	.20
42	Scotty 2 Hotty	.40
43	Jacqueline	.10
44	Stacy Keibler	.60
45	Goldust	.10
46	Christian	.60
47	Trish Stratus	1.50
48	Test	.10
49	Justin Credible	.10
50	Faarooq	.10
51	Boss Man	.10
52	Tazz	.20
53	Tommy Dreamer	.10
54	Hardcore Holly	.10
55	Crash	.10
56	The Big Valbowski	.20
57	Mighty Molly	.20
58	Perry Saturn	.10
59	Spike Dudley	.10
60	Lance Storm	.10
61	Triple H	1.00
62	Vince McMahon	.40
63	Ric Flair	1.00
64	nWo	.40
65	Rico	.10
66	Debra	.20
67	Jazz	.10
68	Lita	1.00
69	Ivory	.10
70	Terri	.20
71	Torrie Wilson	.60
72	Jacqueline	.10
73	Stacy Keibler	.60
74	Trish Stratus	1.50
75	Molly Holly	.20
76	Rob Van Dam, Kurt Angle	.30
77	Big Show, Rikishi	.20
78	Undertaker, DDP	.30
79	Steve "Stone Cold" Austin, The Rock	.75
80	William Regal, Chris Jericho	.10
81	Bubba Ray Dudley, D-Von Dudley	.30
82	Trish Stratus, Torrie Wilson	.30
83	Stacy Keibler, Lita	.30
84	Ivory, Jacqueline	.10
85	Raven, Tajiri	.10
86	Brock Lesnar, The Rock	.30
87	Edge, Booker T	.30
88	Goldust, The Hurricane	.10
89	Bradshaw, Faarooq	.10
90	Kane, Hollywood Hulk Hogan	.20

CATCH PHRASES

Complete Set: 8.00

1CF	The Rock		2.00
2CF	Ric Flair		1.50
3CF	Kurt Angle		1.50
4CF	Steve "Stone Cold" Austin		2.00
5CF	Tazz		.50
6CF	Raven		.40
7CF	Trish Stratus		2.00
8CF	Triple H		1.50
9CF	The Big Valbowski		.50
10CF	Booker T		1.00
11CF	Chris Benoit		1.00
12CF	Hulk Hogan		2.00
13CF	Kevin Nash, Scott Hall, X-Pac		1.50
14CF	Jim Ross		.40
15CF	Chris Benoit		.75

EXPOSURE

Inserted 1:8

1X	Debra		1.00
2X	Ivory		.75
3X	Jacqueline		.75
4X	Jazz		.75
5X	Lita		1.75
6X	Molly Holly		.75
7X	Stacy Keibler		1.50
8X	Terri		1.00
9X	Torrie Wilson		1.50
10X	Trish Stratus		2.50

RAW CERTIFIED

Inserted 1:72

RC-KN	Kevin Nash/shirt	40.00
RC-RVD	Rob Van Dam/shirt	35.00
RC-WR	William Regal/shirt	25.00
RC-XP	X-Pac/shirt	25.00
RC-SD	Spike Dudley/shirt	20.00

SMACKDOWN AUTHENTIC

Inserted 1:36

SA-HH	Hollywood Hogan/shirt	75.00
SA-BG	Billy Gunn/headband	15.00
SA-CP	Chuck Palumbo/headband	15.00
SA-E	Edge/shirt	25.00
SA-U	Undertaker/shirt	30.00
SA-TH	Triple H/shirt	40.00
SA-DDP	DDP/pants	25.00

ULTIMATE EXPOSURE

Inserted 1:96

UX-D	Debra/ jacket	25.00
UX-L	Lita/bikini top	40.00
UX-MM	Molly Holly/purple swimsuit	25.00
UX-MM2	Molly Holly/white top	25.00
UX-SK	Stacy Keibler/shirt	60.00
UX-TW	Torrie Wilson/stockings	60.00

TRIPLE EXPOSURE

Inserted 1:1,200

T-TW-SK	Terri, Torrie Wilson, Stacy Keibler	225.00
L-D-MH	Lita, Debra, Molly Holly	125.00
MH-SK-D	Molly Holly, Stacy Keibler, Debra	180.00

PAY PER VIEW RELICS

Inserted 1:33

RVD-WR	Rob Van Dam, William Regal	25.00
KA-K	Kurt Angle, Kane	25.00
U-RF	Undertaker, Ric Flair	35.00
SC-SH	Stone Cold, Scott Hall	30.00
R-HH	Rock, Hollywood Hulk Hogan	40.00

WWF POP-UPS

Inserted 1:box

1PU	The Rock	15.00
2PU	Steve "Stone Cold" Austin	15.00

3PU ... Triple H		15.00
4PU ... Kurt Angle		12.00
5PU ... Trish Stratus		25.00
6PU ... Stacy Keibler		20.00
7PU ... Hollywood Hulk Hogan		15.00
8PU ... Chris Jericho		10.00
9PU ... Lita		20.00
10PU . Undertaker		12.00

2003 FLEER WWE ROYAL RUMBLE

Complete Set (1-90):	15.00
Common Card:	.10
Pack (8):	2.00
Wax Box (24):	50.00

NM/M

1	Big Show	.40
2	Booker T	.60
3	Bradshaw	.10
4	Brock Lesnar	.60
5	Bubba Ray Dudley	.60
6	Chris Nowinski	.10
7	John Cena	.10
8	D'Lo Brown	.10
9	Eddie Guerrero	.20
10	Goldust	.10
11	Jacqueline	.10
12	Jazz	.10
13	Jeff Hardy	.40
14	Randy Orton	.10
15	Kane	.40
16	Kevin Nash	1.00
17	Lita	1.00
18	Mark Henry	.10
19	Matt Hardy	.40
20	Molly	.20
21	Rob Van Dam	.60
22	Raven	.10
23	Shawn Michaels	1.50
24	Shawn Stasiak	.10
25	Spike Dudley	.10
26	Steven Richards	.10
27	Terri	.20
28	Ric Flair	1.00
29	William Regal	.10
30	X-Pac	.40
31	Al Snow	.10
32	Billy	.20
33	Billy Kidman	.20
34	Chris Benoit	.40
35	Christian	.60
36	Chuck	.10
37	D-Von	.60
38	Paul Heyman	.10
39	Edge	.60
40	Faarooq	.10
41	Funaki	.10
42	Chris Jericho	.60
43	Hollywood Hulk Hogan	1.50
44	The Hurricane	.10
45	Ivory	.10
46	Kurt Angle	1.00
47	Maven	.10
48	Nidia	.10
49	Rico	.10
50	The Rock	1.50
51	Tajiri	.20
52	Torrie Wilson	1.50
53	Triple H	1.00
54	Scotty 2 Hotty	.40
55	Stacy Keibler	1.50
56	Lance Storm	.10
57	Tazz	.20
58	Test	.10
59	Eric Bischoff	.10
60	Jackie	.10
61	Victoria	.10
62	Stephanie	.20
63	Vince McMahon	.40
64	Rikishi	.60
65	Jerry Lawler	.20
66	Jim Ross	.10
67	Deacon Batista	.10
68	Shane McMahon	.20
69	Albert	.10

70	Trish Stratus	1.50
71	Undertaker	1.00
72	Dawn Marie	.40
73	Chavo Guerrero	.10
74	Rey Mysterio	.10
75	Tommy Dreamer	.10
76	Eddie Guerrero	.20
77	Brock Lesnar	.60
78	Chris Benoit	.40
79	Triple H	1.00
80	Undertaker	1.00
81	The Rock	1.50
82	Jim Ross	.10
83	Jerry Lawler	.20
84	Ric Flair	1.00
85	Shawn Stasiak	.10
86	Kurt Angle	1.00
87	Shawn Michaels	1.50
88	Hollywood Hulk Hogan	1.50
89	Rob Van Dam	.60
90	Jeff Hardy, Matt Hardy, Lita	.60

GIMMICK MATCHES

Complete Set (10):	7.00
Common Card:	1.00
Inserted 1:4	

GM1	Triple H, Chris Jericho	1.50
GM2	Undertaker, Jeff Hardy	1.50
GM3	Rob Van Dam, Eddie Guerrero	1.00
GM4	Kurt Angle, Edge	1.50
GM5	Rob Van Dam, Jeff Hardy	1.00
GM6	Stacy Keibler, Trish Stratus	2.00
GM7	The Rock, Trish Stratus	2.00
GM8	Kurt Angle, Shane McMahon	1.50
GM9	Chris Jericho, Kane	1.00
GM10	Kurt Angle, Edge	1.50

DIVASTATING

Complete Set (15):	8.00
Common Card:	.50
Inserted 1:8	

D1	Ivory	.75
D2	Torrie Wilson	2.25
D3	Terri	1.25
D4	Stacy Keibler	2.25
D5	Trish Stratus	2.25
D6	Molly	.50
D7	Stephanie McMahon	1.25
D8	Jazz	.50
D9	Jacqueline	.50
D10	Lita	1.75
D11	Dawn Marie	1.50
D12	Nidia	.50
D13	Linda	.50
D14	Jackie	.50
D15	Victoria	.50

ROYAL RUMBLE RECAP

Complete Set (10):	35.00
Common Card:	2.00
Inserted 1:24	

RRR1	Kane	4.00
RRR2	Kane vs. Undertaker	6.00
RRR3	Triple H vs. Cactus Jack	6.00
RRR4	Vince McMahon	4.00
RRR5	Stone Cold	8.00
RRR6	Hollywood Hulk Hogan	8.00
RRR7	Ric Flair	5.00
RRR8	Rock vs. Mankind	8.00
RRR9	Shawn Michaels	8.00
RRR1	Mae Young	2.00

FACTIONS

Complete Set (5):	30.00
Common Card:	8.00
Inserted 1:120	

F1	Nation of Domination	12.00
F2	The Corporation	10.00
F3	Radicalz	8.00
F4	D-Generation X	15.00
F5	New World Order	12.00

DIVA STATING EVENT-USED

Complete Set (6):	225.00
Inserted 1:48	

1D	Ivory (undergarment)	40.00
2D	Torrie Wilson (skirt)	60.00

4D	Stacy Keibler (skirt)	60.00
5D	Trish Stratus (pants)	60.00
8D	Jazz	20.00
11D	Dawn Marie (dress)	40.00

FACTIONS EVENT-USED

Complete Set (4):	75.00
Common Card:	20.00
Inserted 1:48	

1F	Nation of Domination (Rock shirt)	25.00
2F	Corporation (X-Pac shirt)	20.00
4F	DX	30.00
5F	N W O (Shawn Michaels shirt)	30.00

GIMMICK MATCHES EVENT-USED

Common Card:	20.00
Inserted 1:36	

Triple H, Chris Jericho	30.00
The Undertaker, Jeff Hardy	25.00
Edge, Jeff Hardy	20.00
Stacy Keibler, Trish Stratus	30.00
The Rock, Trish Stratus	30.00
Chris Jericho, Edge	20.00

BASIC CARD EVENT-USED

Common Card:	20.00

4	Brock Lesnar (shirt)	40.00
23	Shawn Michaels (shirt)	50.00
34	Chris Benoit (ring skirt)	25.00
41	Funaki (shirt)	20.00
43	Hollywood Hulk Hogan (t-shirt)	60.00
47	Maven (t-shirt)	25.00
54	Scotty 2 Hotty (jeans)	20.00
57	Tazz (sweat pants)	20.00
74	Rey Mysterio (shirt)	25.00

DIVASTATING AUTOGRAPHS

Common Card:	100.00
Production: 100 sets	

D2	Torrie Wilson	150.00
D3	Terri	100.00
D4	Stacy Keibler	150.00
D10	Lita	150.00

2003 FLEER WWE WRESTLEMANIA XIX

Complete Set (1-90):	15.00
Common Card:	.10
Pack (5):	3.00
Wax Box (24):	55.00

NM/M

1	Scott Steiner	.60
2	Scotty 2 Hotty	.40
3	Albert	.10
4	Kurt Angle	1.00
5	Batista	.10
6	Chris Benoit	.40
7	Big Show	.40
8	Billy	.20
9	Eric Bischoff	.20
10	Bradshaw	.10
11	D'Lo Brown	.10
12	John Cena	.10
13	Christian	.60
14	Chuck	.10
15	Tommy Dreamer	.10
16	Bubba Ray Dudley	.60
17	Spike Dudley	.10
18	D-Von	.60
19	Edge	.60
20	Ron Simmons	.10
21	Ric Flair	1.00
22	Funaki	.10
23	Goldust	.20
24	Crash	.10
25	Eddy Guerrero	.20
26	Triple H	1.00
27	Jeff Hardy	.40
28	Matt Hardy	.40
29	Hollywood Hulk Hogan	1.50
30	The Hurricane	.10
31	Chris Jericho	.60
32	Kane	.40
33	Billy Kidman	.20
34	Jerry Lawler	.20
35	Brock Lesnar	.60
36	Mark Henry	.10

37	Maven	.10
38	The Godfather	.10
39	Johnny Stamboli	.10
40	Shawn Michaels	1.50
41	Rey Mysterio	.20
42	Kevin Nash	1.00
43	Chris Nowinski	.10
44	Randy Orton	.10
45	Raven	.10
46	William Regal	.10
47	Steven Richards	.10
48	Rico	.10
49	Rikishi	.60
50	The Rock	1.50
51	Jim Ross	.10
52	Al Snow	.10
53	Jamie Noble	.20
54	Lance Storm	.10
55	Booker T	.60
56	Tajiri	.20
57	Tazz	.20
58	Test	.10
59	Undertaker	1.00
60	Rob Van Dam	.60
61	Lilian Garcia	.10
62	Dawn Marie	.40
63	Trish Stratus	1.50
64	Jackie	.40
65	Victoria	.10
66	Stephanie	.20
67	Torrie Wilson	1.50
68	Stacy Keibler	1.50
69	Nidia	.10
70	Ivory	.10
71	Terri	.20
72	Jacqueline	.10
73	Jazz	.10
74	Lita	1.00
75	Molly	.20
76	Undertaker	1.00
77	Kane	.40
78	Hollywood Hulk Hogan	1.50
79	The Rock	1.50
80	Triple H	1.00
81	Kurt Angle	1.00
82	Chris Jericho	.60
83	Trish Stratus	1.50
84	Shawn Michaels	1.50
85	Ivory	.10
86	Lita	1.00
87	Jeff Hardy	.40
88	Ric Flair	1.00
89	Rikishi	.60
90	Stone Cold Steve Austin	1.50

DIVA LAS VEGAS

DLV-DM	Dawn Marie (# to 1,350)	30.00
DLV-TW	Torrie Wilson (# to 150)	125.00

MAT FINISH

MF-BL	Brock Lesnar	20.00
MF-E	Edge	10.00
MF-H	The Hurricane	12.00
MF-KA	Kurt Angle	12.00
MF-R	The Rock	20.00
MF-RVD	Rob Van Dam	15.00
MF-SCSA	Stone Cold Steve Austin	15.00
MF-T	Trish	20.00
MF-TH	Triple H	15.00
MF-U	Undertaker	15.00

TITLE SHOTS

TS-BL	Brock Lesnar	25.00
TS-K	Kane	25.00
TS-KA	Kurt Angle	25.00
TS-RVD	Rob Van Dam	25.00
TS-TH	Triple H	25.00
TS-U	Undertaker	25.00

WRESTLEMANIA FLASHBACK

WF-HH	Hollywood Hulk Hogan	40.00
WF-KA	Kurt Angle	20.00
WF-SCSA	Stone Cold Steve Austin	20.00
WF-TH	Triple H	30.00
WF-U	Undertaker	25.00

Chapter 15

MISCELLANEOUS

SPORTS GAMES

Generally, player- or team-related games are in greater demand than generic games, while board games are more valuable than card games. Game values are also determined in part by age (older is more valuable); company (Milton Bradley and Parker Bros. are two of the top); graphics/illustrations (those with higher quality of lithography and highly-detailed, colorful illustrations, especially on the box, are more valuable); box and board style (wooden boxes are more valuable than heavy cardboard; metal games are more valuable than cardboard ones); theme; the region in which the item is being sold; rarity; implements (game parts): and completeness (missing game cards or integral parts may drop a value by 50 percent). The American Game Collectors Association has archives of game instructions and can supply copies by contacting AGCA, 49 Brooks Ave., Lewiston, Maine 04240.

The game recognized as the first professional baseball game, The New Parlor Game of Baseball, was produced in 1869. Published by M.B. Sumner, the game included team rosters and lineup cards.

The first data-enhanced game based on player statistics appeared in 1950, when APBA Game Co. of Lancaster, Pa., created a dice and card game. The company produces new player game cards annually. The first game to be endorsed by a player—the Rube Walker & Harry Davis Baseball Game—was produced in 1905 by Champion Athletics. Since that time, several athletes have loaned their names to games—Hank Aaron, Bob Feller, Lou Gehrig, Walter Johnson, Mickey Mantle, Christy Mathewson, Willie Mays, Babe Ruth and Carl Yastrzemski, to name a few.

Generally, player- or team-related games are in greater demand than generic games. Condition is also a big factor in determining game values. Look for games that are in Very Good or Excellent condition—those that are not faded, water-stained, covered with soot or mildew, and have all the parts and instructions.

The best places to find games are at game conventions, collectibles shows, antique shops, flea markets, and through auction houses and hobby publications, such as Krause Publications' Toy Shop and Warman's Today's Collector publications. When buying sight-unseen through the mail, however, get a detailed description about condition and inquire if the seller has a return policy if the material is not satisfactory.

Many games are repairable, but that's best left to an archivist or other professional who can clean your game using special materials such as acid-free glue and paper. Rubber cement thinner can be used to remove price stickers or tape on the outside box covers on games that are taped shut. Mildew can be cleaned with a bathroom mildew remover and a damp sponge, but test a small area first.

Games should be kept out of extremely cold or hot temperatures and places with wide temperature fluctuations. Direct sunlight, spotlights and other bright lights should be avoided, too, to prevent fading. Damp areas can cause mildew buildup, so a dehumidifier is recommended. Also, although stacking is not suggested, if you are going to stack your games, do so by cross-stacking them, alternating them vertically and horizontally, so that the weight of the games on top do not crush those underneath.

Note: Because so few exist in that condition, games from 1844-1945 are virtually impossible to find in mint condition. Prices fluctuate, too, oftentimes based on auction fever, which tends to drive prices up. Remember, value is what someone is willing to pay, not necessarily the selling price.

SELECTED BASEBALL BOARD GAMES

ABC Baseball Game, 1910s .... $430-$715
Action Baseball, Pressman, 1965 .... $35-$75
Alexander's Baseball Game, 1930s .... $245-$400
All Pro Baseball, Ideal, 1950 .... $45-$110
All-Star Baseball Game, Whitman, 1935 .... $100-$165
All-Star Baseball, Cadaco-Ellis, 1959-60 .... $40-$90
All-Star Baseball Game, Cadaco-Ellis, 1962 .... $40-$50
All-Star Baseball, Cadaco, 1989 .... $12-$30
All-Star Electric Baseball & Football, Harett-Gilmar, 1955 .. $35-$90
All-Time Greats Baseball Game, Midwest Research,
    1971 .... $15-$35
Alpha Baseball Game, Redlich Mfg. Co., 1930s .... $110-$275
APBA Baseball Master Game, APBA, 1975 .... $35-$90
ASG Baseball, 3M, 1989 .... $12-$30

ASG Major League, Baseball, Gerney Games, 1973 ...... $55-$135
Atkins Real Baseball, Atkins & Co., 1915 .... $450-$750
Autograph Baseball Game, F. J. Raff, 1948 .... $110-$275
Auto-Play Baseball Game, Auto-Play Games Co.,
    1911 .... $425-$700
Aydelott's Parlor Baseball, Aydelott's Base Ball Card Co.,
    1910 .... $195-$325
Babe Ruth Baseball Game, 1933 .... $640-$1,075
Babe Ruth National Game of Baseball, Keiter-Fry Mfg. Co.,
    1929 .... $550-$910
Babe Ruth's Baseball Game, Milton Bradley, 1936 ... $200-$500
Babe Ruth's Official Baseball Game, Toy Town Corp.,
    1940s .... $430-$715
Ballplayer's Baseball Game, Jon Weber, 1955 .... $30-$75
Bambino, Johnson Store Equipment Co., 1933 .... $295-$490

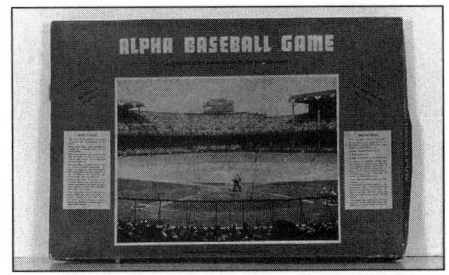  

Bambino Baseball Game, Mansfield-Zesiger Mfg. Co.,
1946...$145-$250
Base-Ball Game of 1886, McLoughlin Bros., 1886......$750-$1,300
Baseball, George Parker, 1885 ....$700-$1,000
Baseball, George B. Doan & Co., 1920 ....$70-$100
Baseball, J. Ottman Litho Co., 1915 ....$140-$200
Baseball Game, All-Fair, 1930................................$100-$125
Baseball, All-Fair, 1946..$30-$60
Baseball, Milton Bradley, 1940s.............................$35-$50
Baseball, Samuel Lowe Co., 1942..........................$15-$25
Baseball, Football & Checkers, Parker Bros., 1957.......$35-$90
Baseball & Checkers, Milton Bradley, 1910s ....$75-$150
Baseball Card All-Star Game, Captoys, 1987 ....$6-$15
Baseball Card Game, Ed-U-Cards, 1950s ....$20-$50
Baseball Challenge, Tri-Valley Games, 1980................$15-$35
Baseball Dominoes, Evans, 1910............................$250-$400
Baseball Game, Brinkman Engineering, 1925 ....$95-$135
Baseball Game, Corey Games, 1943.........................$70-$100
Baseball Game, Parker Bros., 1949 ....$10-$25
Baseball Game, Parker Bros.,1950 ....$10-$22
The Baseball Game, Horatio, 1988 ....$12-$30
Baseball Game & G-Man Target Game, Marks Bros.,
1940...$100-$165
Baseball's Greatest Moments, Ashburn, Ind., 1979 ....$5-$12
Baseballitis Card Game, Baseballitis Card Co., 1909.....$125-$205
Baseball Knapp Electro Game Set, Knapp, 1929......$125-$175
Baseball Mania The Board Game, Baseball Mania,
1993...$14-$30
Baseball Strategy, Avalon Hill, 1973 ....$10-$20
Baseball Wizard Game, Morehouse Mfg., 1916........$265-$450
Base Hit, Games Inc.,1944..$55-$90
Bases Full Hand Skill Game, 1930................................$45-$70
Batter-Rou Baseball Game, Memphis Plastic, 1950s....$100-$250
Batter-Up Card Game, Ed-U-Cards, 1949.....................$25-$60
Batter Up, M. Hopper, 1946.......................................$75-160
Bee Gee Baseball Dart Target, Bee Gee, 1935 ....$70-$115
Bible Baseball, Standard Publishing Co., 1950 ....$10-$25
Big League Baseball Card Game, Whitman Publishing,
1933...$35-$60
Big League Baseball Game, J. Chein & Co., 1930s ......$42-$60
Big League Baseball Game, A.E. Gustafson, 1938.....$85-$125
Big League Baseball, Saalfield, 1959.........................$55-$135
Big League Baseball Game, 3M Corp., 1966..............$55-$135
Big League Baseball, 3M Corp., 1971.........................$14-$30
Big Six: Christy Mathewson Indoor Baseball Game, Piroxloid
Products Corp., 1922...$775-$1,300
Big 6 Sports Games, Gardner & Co., 1950s ....$175-$450
Bob Feller's Big League Baseball, Saalfield Artcraft,
1950...$75-$250
Bobby Shantz's Baseball Game, Realistic Games,
1954...$80-$225
Boston Baseball Game, Boston Game Co., 1906 .....$495-$825
Boston Red Sox Game, Ed-U-Cards, 1964 ....$55-$135
Broadcast Baseball, J. Pressman & Co., 1938-40.......$70-$100
Carl Hubbell Mechanical Baseball, Gotham, 1950 ....$100-$300

Carl Yastrzemski's Action Baseball, Pressman, 1962 . $90-$195
Casey on the Mound, Kamm Games Inc., 1947........$190-$275
Challenge the Yankees, Hasbro, 1960s.......................$325-635
The Champion Game of Base Ball, Schultz, 1889...$4,100-$6,800
The Champion Base Ball Game, New York Game Co.,
1913...$140-$200
The Champion Game of Base Ball, Proctor Amusement Co.,
1890s...$60-$100
Championship Baseball, Championship Games Inc.,
1966...$10-$30
Championship Baseball, Milton Bradley, 1984 ....$18-$40
Championship Base Ball Parlor Game, Grebnelle Novelty Co.
1914..$1,050-$1,750
Charlie Brown's All-Star Baseball Game, Parker Bros.,
1965...$35-$90
Chicago Game Series Base Ball, George Doan Co.,
1890s...$1,175-$1,950
Classic Major League Baseball Classic green, 1987.....$115-$250
Classic Major League Baseball, Classic, yellow update,
1987...$18-$40
Classic Major League Baseball, Classic red, 1988 ....$7.50-$15
Classic Major League Baseball, Classic blue, 1988......$10-$20
Classic Major League Baseball, Classic, 1989..............$18-$40
Classic Major League Baseball, Classic travel orange,
1989...$10-$20
Classic Major League Baseball, Classic, 1989...........$7.50-$15
Classic Major League Baseball, Classic, 1990...........$7.50-$15
Classic Major League Baseball, Classic, 1990................$6-$13
Classic Major League Baseball, Classic 1990 ....$7.50-$15
Classic Major League Baseball, Classic, 1991................$6-$14
College Base Ball Game, Parker Bros., 1898............$350-$900
Computer Baseball, Epoch Playtime, 1966 ....$25-$65
Danny McFayden's Stove League Baseball Game, National
Games Co., 1927..$295-$490
Dennis The Menace Baseball Game, 1960...................$20-$70
The Diamond Game of Base Ball, McLoughlin Bros.,
1894..$1,275-$2,150
DiceBall, Ray-Fair Co., 1938 ....$90-$145
DiceBall, Intellijedx, 1993 ....$12-$25
The Dicex Baseball Game, Chester S. Howland, 1925...$195-$325
Double Game Board, Parker Bros., 1926 ....$165-$275
Double Header Baseball, Redlich Mfg. Co., 1935 .....$145-$250
Durgin's New BaseBall Game, Durgin & Palmer,
1885...$425-$700
Earl Gillespie Baseball Game, Wei-gill Inc., 1961 ....$25-$65
Ebbets Field Pro Baseball Game, Montminy Games, LLC,
1998...$10-$12
Egerton R. Williams Baseball Game, The Hatch Co.,
1886..$2,500-$5,000
Electric Baseball, Einson-Freeman Publishing Corp.,
1935...$35-$60
Electric Baseball, Jim Prentice, 1940s ....$55-$80
Electric Baseball, Jim Prentice, 1950s ....$30-$65
Electric Magnetic Baseball, 1900 ....$175-$295
Ethan Allen's All-Star Baseball, Cadaco Ltd., 1941.....$60-$150

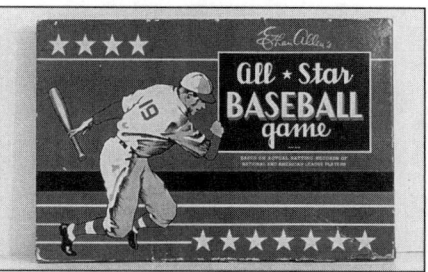
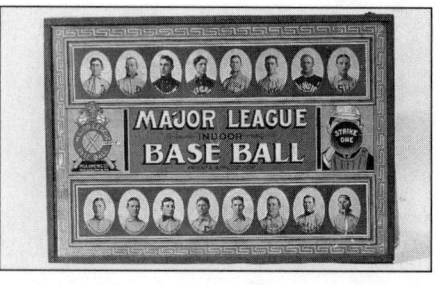

Ethan Allen's All-Star Baseball Game, Cadaco-Ellis, 1942 .... $60-$150

Ethan Allen's All-Star Baseball Game, Cadaco-Ellis, 1946 .... $28-$60

Ethan Allen's All-Star Baseball Game, Cadaco-Ellis, 1955 .... $22-$50

Extra Innings, J. Kavanaugh, 1975 .... $15-$35

Fan-I-Tis, C.W. Marsh, 1913 .... $110-$180

Follow The Stars Watts Indoor Baseball League, H. Allan Watts, 1922 .... $225-$375

Fortune Telling & Baseball Game, 1889 .... $85-$140

Game of Base Ball, J.H. Singer, 1888 .... $325-$550

Game of Baseball, Milton Bradley, 1910 .... $100-$150

Game of Baseball, Milton Bradley, 1925 .... $42-$60

Game of Baseball, Canada Games Co., 1925 .... $210-$300

Game of Batter Up, Fenner Game Co., 1908 .... $100-$165

George Brett's 9th-Inning Baseball Game, Brett Ball, 1981 .... $16-$40

Get The Balls Baseball Game, 1930 .... $20-$30

Gil Hodges Pennant Fever, Research Games, 1970 .... $65-$150

Golden Trivia Game, Western Pub., 1984 .... $6-$15

Gonfalon Scientific Baseball, General Specialties Corp., 1930 .... $110-$180

Goose Goslin's Scientific Baseball Game Wheeler Toy Co., 1935 .... $250-$400

Graham McNamee Radio Scoreboard World Series Baseball Game, Radio Sports Inc., 1937 .... $250-$400

Grand Slam, Sming Game Co.,1979 .... $14-$30

Graphic BaseBall, North Western, 1930s .... $165-$275

The Great American Baseball Game, William Dapping, 1906 .... $145-$250

The Great American Game, Frantz Toys, 1925 .... $110-$180

The Great American Game of Baseball, Pittsburgh Brewing Co., 1907 .... $145-$250

The Great American Game of Baseball, Hustler Toy Co., 1923 .... $105-$175

Great American Game of Pocket Baseball, Neddy Pocket Game Co., 1910 .... $140-$200

Great Mails Baseball Card Game, Walter Mails Baseball Game Co., 1919 .... $2,475-$4,100

Great Pennant Races, Great Pennant Races 1980 .... $14-$28

Grebnelle Championship Base Ball Parlor Game, Grebnelle Novelty Co., 1914 .... $150-$250

Hank Aaron Baseball Game, Ideal, 1973 .... $50-$125

Hank Aaron's Eye Ball Game, 1960s .... $85-$215

Hank Bauer's "Be A Manager," Bamo Enterprises, 1953 .... $75-$175

Hatfield's Parlor Base-Ball Game, Hatfield Co., 1914 ..... $140-$200

Hening's In-Door Game of Professional Baseball, Inventor's Co., 1889 .... $525-$875

Home Baseball Game, McLaughlin Bros., 1900 ..... $900-$1,700

Home Baseball Game, McLaughlin Bros., 1910 ..... $775-$1,100

Home Baseball Game, Rosebud Art. Co., 1936 .... $100-$150

Home Diamond The Great Baseball Game, Phillips Co., 1913 .... $175-$295

Home Plate, 1996, signed by Barry and Bobby Bonds $110

Home Run King, Selrite Products Inc., 1930s .... $275-$450

Home Run With Bases Loaded, T.V. Morrison, 1935..... $205-$350

Home Team Baseball Game, Ben Dickenson, 1917 ...... $140-$200

Home Team Baseball Game, Ben Dickenson/Selchow & Righter, 1918 .... $140-$200

Home Team Baseball Game, Selchow & Righter, 1957..... $35-$90

Home Team Baseball Game, Selchow & Righter, 1964..... $14-$30

Houston Astros Baseball Challenge Game Croque Ltd., 1980 .... $15-$35

In-Door Baseball, E. Bommer Foundation, 1926....... $100-$180

Inside Base Ball Game, Popular Games Co., 1913.. $300-$500

Jackie Robinson Baseball Game, Gotham Pressed Steel Corp., 1948 .... $425-$725

Jacmar Big League Electric Baseball, Jacmar, 1952 ..... $100-$250

JDK Baseball, JDK Baseball, 1982 .... $10-$25

Jim Thome's Pro Baseball Game, Montminy Games LLC, 1998 .... $10-$12

Joe "Ducky" Medwick's Big Leaguer Baseball Game, Johnson-Breier Co., 1939 .... $125-$200

Jose Canseco's Perfect Baseball Game, Perfect Game Co., 1991 .... $8-$20

Junior Baseball Game, Benjamin-Seller Mfg. Co., 1913 ... $100-$165

Kellogg's Baseball Game, Kellogg's, 1936 .... $21-$30

KSP Baseball, Koch Sports Products, 1983 .... $15-$35

Las Vegas Baseball, Samar Enterprises, 1987 .... $8-$20

Lawson's Patent Base Ball Playing Cards, T.H. Lawson & Co., 1884 .... $350-$700

League Parlor BaseBall, Bliss, 1880s .... $1,050-$1,750

League Parlor BaseBall, R. Bliss Mfg., 1889s........ $600-$1,000

Leslie's Base Ball Game, Perfection Novelty & Advertising Co., 1909 .... $145-$250

Lew Fonseca The Carrom BaseBall Game, Carrom Co., 1930s .... $525-$875

LF Baseball, Len Feder, 1980 .... $12-$30

Line Drive, Lord & Freber Inc., 1953 .... $60-$125

Little League Baseball Game, Standard Toycraft Inc., 1950s .... $25-$70

LongBall, Ashburn Industries, 1975 .... $30-$75

Look All-Star Baseball Game, Progressive Research, 1960 .... $35-$90

Lou Gehrig's Official Play Ball, Christy Walsh, 1930s .... $525-$875

Lucky 7th BaseBall Game, All-American Games Co., 1937 .... $55-$90

"Mac" Baseball Game, McDowell Mfg. Co., 1930s.... $145-$250

Main Street BaseBall, Main Street Toy Co., 1989......... $20-$55

Major League Ball, National Game Makers, 1921..... $325-$550

Major League Indoor Base Ball, Philadelphia Game Mfg. Co., 1913 .... $650-$1,000

The Major League BaseBall Game, 1910 .... $85-$145

Major Legue BaseBall, Negamco, 1959 .... $12-$25

Major League BaseBall Magnetic Dart Game, Pressman, 1958 .... $55-$135

 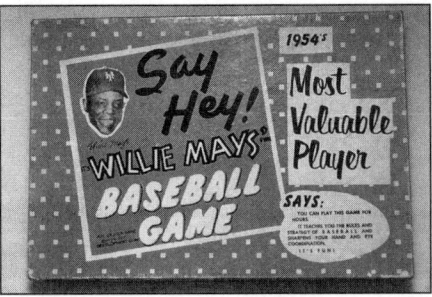 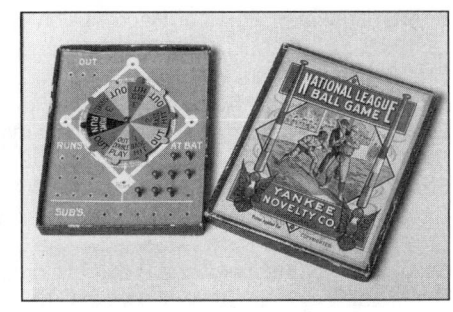

Major League Indoor BaseBall Game, Philadelphia Game Mfg. Co., 1912 .... $4,200-$6,000

Manage Your Own Team, Warren, 1950s.................... $55-$135

Mather's Parlor Base Ball Game, Mathers, 1908....... $350-$500

Mickey Mantle's Baseball Action Game, Kohner Bros., 1960s... $50-$175

Mickey Mantle's Big League Baseball, Gardner & Co., 1962 .... $125-$325

Mickey Mouse Baseball, Post Cereal, 1936 .... $55-$90

Monopoly: Boston Red Sox Collectors Edition, Parker Bros., 1999.. $20-$25

Monopoly: New York Yankees Collectors Edition, Parker Bros., 1999.. $20-$25

Montreal Expos Super Baseball, Super Sports Games, 1979 .... $7.50-$15

MVP Baseball The Sports Card Game, Ideal, 1989........ $8-$20

National American Base Ball Game, Parker Bros., 1910... $110-$180

The National Base Ball Game, National Baseball Playing, 1913.. $700-$1,200

The National Game of Base Ball, McLoughlin, 1901......$500-$875

The National Game, National Game Co., 1889 ......$875-$1,450

National League Ball Game, Yankee Novelty Co., 1890.. $350-$575

NBC Baseball Game of the Week, Hasbro, 1969............ $25-65

New Baseball Game, Clark & Martin, 1885................ $165-$275

The New Parlor Game Baseball, M.B. Summer, 1869... $7,000-$10,000

New York Recorder Newspaper Supplement Baseball Game, 1896.. $430-$715

Official Baseball Game, Milton Bradley, 1965.............. $175-450

Official Baseball Game, Milton Bradley, 1953........... $100-$250

Official Baseball Game, Milton Bradley, 1970.............. $55-$125

Official Denny McLain Magnetik Game, Gotham, 1968.. $115-$295

Official Dizzy and Daffy Dean Nok-Out Baseball Game, Nok-Out Manufacturing Co., 1930 .... $350-$575

Our National Ball Game, McGill & DeLany, 1887 ...... $425-$650

Our No. 7 Baseball Game Puzzle, Satisfactory Co., 1910.. $110-$180

Ozark Ike's Complete 3 Game Set, Builtrite, 1956 ...... $55-$135

Parlor Baseball, E.B. Pierce, 1878 .... $1,750-$2,900

Parlor Base Ball, American Parlor Base Ball Co., 1903.. $165-$250

Parlor BaseBall Game Chicago vs. Boston, 1880s .... $2,100-$3,000

Parker Bros. Baseball Game, Parker Bros., 1950 .... $45-$110

Pat Moran's Own Baseball Game, Smith, Kline & French, 1919.. $325-$550

Pee-Wee (Pee Wee Reese Marble Game), Pee Wee Enterprises, 1956 .... $175-$450

Peg Base Ball, Parker Bros., 1908 .... $105-$175

Pennant Chasers Baseball Game, Craig Hopkins, 1946....$25-$70

Pennant Drive, Accu-Stat Game Co., 1980 .... $8-$20

Pennant Puzzle, L.W. Harding, 1909......................... $250-$400

Pennant Winner Wolverine Supply & Manufacturing Co., 1939.. $175-$295

The Philadelphia Inquirer Baseball Game Philadelphia Inquirer, 1896.. $145-$250

Photo-Electric Baseball, Cadaco-Ellis, 1951 .... $55-$135

Pinch Hitter, J&S Corp., 1938.................................... $110-$180

Play Ball, National Game Co., 1920 .... $145-$250

Pocket Baseball, Toy Creations, 1940 .... $15-$25

Pocket Edition Major League Baseball Game, Anderson, 1943.. $85-$140

Polar Ball Baseball, Bowline Game Co., 1940............. $90-$145

Poosh-em-up Slugger, Bagatelle, North Western Products, 1946.. $30-$105

Popular Indoor Baseball Game, Egerton R. Williams, 1896.. $500-$850

Pro Baseball, 1940s .... $70-$115

Pro Baseball Card Game, Just Games, 1980s................. $6-$60

Pursue the Pennant, Pursue the Pennant, 1984 .... $25-$60

Psychic Base Ball Game, Psychic Baseball Corp., 1927. $60-$150

Psychic Base Ball Game, Parker Bros., 1935 .... $175-$295

Radio Baseball, Toy Creations, 1939 .... $50-$125

Real Action Baseball Games, Real-Action Games, 1966.. $20-$50

Real BaseBall Card Game, National Baseball, 1900..... $110-$275

Realistic Baseball Realistic Game & Toy Co., 1925 .. $205-$350

Red Barber's Big League Baseball Game, G&R Anthony Inc., 1950s.. $350-$900

Replay Series Baseball, Bond Sports Ent., 1983 .... $6-$15

Robin Roberts Sports Club Baseball Game, Dexter Wayne, 1960.. $100-$250

Roger Maris' Action Baseball, Pressman Toy Co., 1962.. $50-$175

Roll-O Junior Baseball Game, Roll-O Mfg., 1922...... $325-$550

Roulette Base Ball Game, W. Bartholomae, 1929..... $115-$195

Rube Bressler's Baseball Game, Ray B. Bressler, 1936.. $130-$215

Rube Waddell & Harry Davis Baseball Game, Inventors and Investors Corp., 1905 .... $875-$1,450

St. Louis Cardinals Baseball Card Game, Ed-U-Cards, 1964.. $35-$85

Sandlot Slugger, 1960s .... $35-$90

Say Hey! Willie Mays Baseball Game, Toy Development Co., 1954.. $200-$525

Scott's Baseball Card Game, Scott's BaseBall Cards, 1989.. $12-$30

Skor-It Bagatelle, Northwestern Products, 1930s ..... $145-$250

Slide Kelly! Baseball Game, B.E. Ruth Co. 1936 .... $70-$115

Slugger Baseball Game, Marks Bros., 1930 .... $110-$180

Snappet Catch Game with Harmon Killebrew, Killebrew Inc., 1960.. $55-$135

Spin Cycle Baseball, Pressman, 1965 .... $25-$65

Sporting News BaseBall, Mundo Games, 1986 .... $8-$20

Sport-O-Rama Pin-Bo, 1950s .... $35-$90

A Sports Illustrated Game Baseball, Time Inc., 1975.... $25-$65

Sports Illustrated Baseball, Sports Illustrated 1972 ...... $25-$65

Sports Illustrated Pennant Race Avalon Hill-Sports Illustrated, 1982 .... $7.50-$15
Star Baseball Game, W.P. Ulrich, 1941 .... $70-$115
Statis Pro Baseball, Avalon Hill, 1979 .... $17-$40
Strategy Manager Baseball, McGuffin-Ramsey, 1967 ... $20-$50
Strat-O-Matic Baseball, Strat-O-Matic, 1961 .... $100-$250
Strat-O-Matic Baseball, Strat-O-Matic, 1969 .... $10-$25
Strike-Like, Saxon Toy Corp., 1940's .... $55-$90
Strike-Out, All-Fair Inc., 1920s .... $175-$295
Strike 3 by Carl Hubbell, Tone Products Corp., 1946 ..... $275-$725
Superstar Baseball, Sports Illustrated, 1966 .... $30-$75
Superstar Baseball, Sports Illustrated-Time Inc., 1974 . $12-$25
Swat Baseball, Milton Bradley, 1948 .... $20-$50
Tiddle Flip Baseball, Modern Craft Ind., 1949 .... $20-$50
Time Travel Baseball, Time Travel, 1979 .... $8-$18
Tom Seaver Game Action Baseball, Pressman Toy Co., 1969 .... $50-$175
Toto The New Game BaseBall, Toto Sales Co., 1925 ... $55-$90
Triple Play, National Games Inc., 1930s .... $12-$20
Tru-Action Electric Baseball Game, Tudor, 1955 .... $25-$80
Ty Cobb's Own Game of Baseball, National Novelty Co., 1924 .... $350-$650
U-Bat-It, Schultz III Star Co., 1920s .... $70-$115
Ultimate Sports Trivia, Ram Games, 1992 .... $17-$35
Uncle Sam's Base Ball, J.C. Bell, 1890 .... $525-$875
Wachter's Parlor Base Ball, Wachter, 1888 .... $145-$250
Walter Johnson Base Ball Game, Walter Johnson Baseball Game, 1920s .... $125-$250
Walter Johnson Base Ball Game, Walter Johnson Baseball Game, 1930s .... $195-$325

Waner's Baseball Game, Waner's BaseBall Inc., 1939 .... $350-$575
Whirly Bird Play Catch, Game Innovation Industries, 1958 .... $20-$50
Whiz BaseBall, Electric Game Co., 1945 .... $42-$60
Wil-Croft Baseball, Wil-Croft, 1971 .... $10-$25
William's Popular Indoor Baseball, Hatch Co., 1889 ... $700-$1,175
Willie Mays Push Button Baseball, Eldon Champion, 1965 .... $175-$450
Willie Mays "Say Hey" Baseball, Centennial Games, 1958 .... $190-$450
Win A Card Trading Game, Milton Bradley, 1965 ...... $350-$900
Winko Baseball, Milton Bradley, 1945 .... $45-$70
Wiry Dan's Electric Baseball Game, Harrett-Gilmore, 1950 .... $15-$65
World's Championship Baseball, Champion Amusement Co., 1910 .... $175-$295
World's Championship Baseball Game, Beacon Hudson Co., 1930s .... $100-$150
World's Greatest Baseball Game, J. Woodlock, 1977 ... $30-$80
World Series Baseball Game, Radio Sports, 1940s .. $205-$350
World Series Big League Baseball Game, E.S. Lowe, 1945 .... $115-$150
World Series Parlor Baseball, Clifton E. Hooper, 1916 .... $150-$250
Yaz Action Baseball, unknown, 1962 .... $15-$20
"You're Out" Baseball Game, Corey Games, 1941 ...... $85-$140
Zimmer BaseBall Game, McLoughlin Bros., 1885 ... $1,300-$2,150

Football, Basketball, Hockey Games

Football games

ABC Monday Night Football, Aurora 1972 .... $8-$40
ABC Monday Night Football, Aurora,1973, Roger Staubach edition .... $10-$50
All-American Foot Ball Game, Parker Bros. 1925 ..... $100-$165
All-American Football Game, National Games, 1935 .... $35-$55
All-American Football, Cadaco, 1969 .... $35-$90
Alpha Football Game, Replica Mfg. Co. 1940s .... $75-$100
All-Star Electric Baseball and Football, Harrett-Gilmar, 1955 .... $35-$90
All-Star Football, Gardner & Co. 1950 .... $55-135
American Football Game Ace Leather Goods Co., 1930 .... $70-$115
American Football Game American News Co. 1930s ...... $60-$100
American Football Game, Intercollegiate Football Inc., 1935 .... $50-$75
America's Football,Trojan Games,1939 .... $55-$90
APBA Pro League Football, APBA 1964 .... $50-$75
APBA 1970s .... $35-$50
APBA 1980s .... $12-$30
Art Lewis Football Game Morgantown Game Co. 1955 .... $70-$175
Bart Starr Quarterback Game,1960s .... $175-$450
Baseball, Football & Checkers Parker Bros. 1957 .... $35-$90
The Benson Football Game, Benson, 1930s .... $85-$145
Big League Manager Football, BLM,1965 .... $20-$50
Big Payoff, Payoff Enterprises Co.,1984 .... $6-$15
Big Ten Football Game, Wheaties' Jack Armstrong Presents, 1936 .... $55
Big Time Colorado Football, B.J. Tall, 1983 .... $6-$15
Bo McMillan's Indoor Football, Indiana Game Co. 1939 .... $75
Booth's Pro Conference Football, Sher-Co., 1977 .... $10-$25
Bowl Bound!, Sports Illustrated,1973 .... $15-$40

Bowl Bound!, Avalon Hill-Sports Illustrated .... 1978 $7-$15
Boys Own Football Game, McLoughlin Bros., 1901 .... $325-$750
Challenge Football, Avalon Hill .... $10-$20
Chex Ches Football, Chex Ches Games 1971 .... $15-$40
College Football, Milton Bradley, 1945 .... $85-$125
Dan Kersteter's Classic Football, Big League Co. .... $10-$20
Electric Football, Electric Game Co.,1930s .... $55-$90
Elmer Layden's Scientific Football, Cadaco-Ellis, 1936 . $40-$80
F/11 Armchair Quarterback, James R. Hock, 1964 .... $10-$20
First Down, TGP Games,1970 .... $50-$125
Fobaga, American Football Co.,1942 .... $50-$75
Fooba-Roo Football Game, Memphis Plastic Ent., 1955 ... $25-$65
Football, J. Pressman & Co.,1940s .... $30-$45
Football, All-Fair, 1946 .... $55-$80
Football, Samuel Lowe, 1942, with baseball, basketball and hockey .... $50-$75
Football, Knapp Electro Game Set, Knapp Co.,1929 ..... $125-$205
Football, Wilder, 1930s .... $50-$80
Football, Parker Bros., 1898 .... $295-$495
Football-As-You-Like-It, Wayne W. Light, 1940 .... $85-$145
Football, Baseball & Checkers, Parker Bros., 1948 .... $15-$65
Football Fever, Hansen, 1985 .... $20-$50
Football Game, Parker Bros. 1910, Princeton vs. Yale $350
Football Strategy, Avalon Hill, 1962 .... $8-$45
Football Strategy, Avalon Hill, Sports Illustrated, 1972 .... $3-$15
Foto-Electric Football, Cadaco-Ellis, 1950 .... $50-$75
Frank Cavanaugh's American Football, F. Cavanaugh Assoc.,1955 .... $25-$60
Fut-Bal, The Fut-Bal Co., 1940s .... $35-$60
The Game of Football, George A. Childs, 1895 .... $350
The Game of Football, Parker Bros., 1892 .... $400
Game of Touchdown or Parlor Football Union, Mutual Life Insurance Premium, 1897 .... $125

 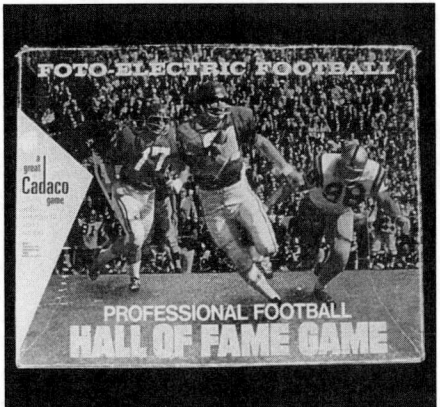 

Goal Line Stand, Game Shop Inc., 1980 .... $12-$30
Gregg Football Game, Albert A. Gregg, 1924 .... $175-$285
Half-Time Football, Lakeside, 1979 .... $5-$15
Hit That Line, The All-American Football Game, La Rue Sales,
    1930s .... $100-$165
Howard H. Jones, Collegiate Football Municipal Service,
    1932 .... $40-$100
Huddle All-American Football Game, 1931 .... $100-$165
Indoor Football, Underwood, 1919 .... $145-$250
Instant Replay, Parker Bros., 1987 .... $8-$20
Intercollegiate Football, Hustler-Frantz, 1923 .... $125-$245
Jerry Kramer's Instant Replay, Emd Enterprises, 1970 ...... $15-$40
Jimmy the Greek Oddsmaker Football, Aurora, 1974 .... $15-$35
Jim Prentice Electric Football, Electric Game Co., 1940 .... $50-$75
The Johnny Unitas Football Game, Play-Rite 1960 .... $125-$150
Johnny Unitas' Football, Pro Mentor, 1970 .... $25-$65
J.R. Quarterback Football, Built Rite, 1950s .... $30-$45
Kellogg's Football Game, Kellogg's Premium, 1936 ..... $25-$40
Knute Rockne Football, Radio Sports, 1940 .... $300
Linebacker Football, Linebacker Inc.,1990 .... $12-$30
Los Angeles Rams Football Game, Zondine Game Co.,
    1930s .... $175-$295
Monday Morning Quarterback, A.B. Zbinden 1963 .... $20-$50
NBC Pro Playoff, NBC-Hasbro, 1969$25- $65
The New Game, Touchdown, Hartford Mfg. Co.,1920 .... $100
NFL All-Pro Football, Ideal, 1967 .... $20-$50
NFL Armchair Quarterback Trade Wind Inc., 1986 .... $8-$20
NFL Franchise, Rohwood, 1982 .... $10-$25
NFL Game Plan, Tudor Games, 1980 .... $6-$15
NFL Play Action, Tudor, 1979 .... $7-$15
NFL Quarterback, Tudor, 1977 .... $14-$35
NFL Strategy, Tudor Games 1935 .... $45-$70
NFL Strategy ,Tudor, 1976... $5-$25
NFL Strategy, Tudor, 1986 .... $6-$15
Official Knute Rockne Football Game Radio Sports,
    1930 .... $250-$400
Official National Football League Quarterback, Toy Craft,
    1965 .... $50-$75
Official NFL Football Game, Ideal, 1968 .... $20-$50
Official Radio Football, Toy Creations, 1939................. $45-$75
Ot-O-Win Football, Ot-O-Win Toys and Games, 1920s...... $55-$90
Parlor Football Game, McLoughlin Bros., 1890s .... $525-$875
Paul Brown's Football Game,Trikilis, 1947................. $110-$275
Paydirt!, Sports Illustrated, 1973 .... $10-$25
Paydirt!, Avalon Hill, 1979... $10-$30
Pigskin, Parker Bros.,1940 .... $75-$100
    Parker Bros.,1956.. $30-$40
    Parker Bros.,1960.. $20-$30
Pigskin, Parker Bros., 1946, Tom Hamilton's Football .... $50-$75

Pigskin, Tom Hamilton's Football Game Parker Bros., 1934,
    stadium cover .... $75-$100
Play Football, Whitman, 1934....................................... $55-$90
Playoff Football, Crestline Mfg. Co.,1970s .... $20-$50
Pocket Football, Toy Creations, 1940 .... $35
Pocket Football, AMV Publishing..................................... $5-$10
Pro Bowl Live Action Football, Marx, 1960s .... $35-$95
Pro Coach Football, Mastermind Sports .... $30-$40
Pro Draft, Parker Bros.,1974 .... $15--$40
Pro Football, Milton Bradley, 1964.............................. $25-$35
Pro Football, 3M, 1964 .... $15-$20
Pro Football Franchise, Ron Wood., 1987 .... $10-$16
Pro Football, Strat-O-Matic,1968................................ $25-$35
    1960s cards... $15-$30
    1970s cards... $10-$20
    1980s cards... $6-$15
Pro-Foto-Football, Cadaco, 1977 .... $25-$60
Pro-Foto-Football, Cadaco, 1986 .... $8-$18
Pro Franchise Football, Rohrwood Inc. 1987 .... $10-$25
Pro Quarterback, Tod Lansing, 1964$20- $60
Pro Quarterback, Championship Games 1965 .... $75
Pro Replay Football, Pro Replay .... $15-$20
Quarterback, Littlefield Mfg. Co., 1914 .... $100-$165
Quarterback, Olympia Games, 1914................................... $50
Quarterback Football Game, Transogram 1969 .... $25-$65
Radio Football Game, Toy Creations, 1939................. $50-$125
Razzle Dazzle Football Game, Texantics Unlimited,
    1954.. $50-$125
Razz-O Dazz-O Six Man Football, Gruhn & Melton,
    1938.. $60-$100
Realistic Football, Match Play, 1976............................ $15-$35
Replay Pro Football, Replay Games$30- $45
Roll-O Football, Supply Sales Co., 1923 .... $35-$60
Rose Bowl Championship Football Game, E.S. Lowe Co.,
    1940s.. $40-$100
Rummy Football, Milton Bradley, 1944 .... $35-$60
Samsonite Football, Samsonite, 1969.......................... $20-$50
Scrimmage, SPI, 1973 .... $15-$35
Scrimmage, Scrimmage Inc.,1978 .... $5-$12
Sod Buster,D. Santee, 1980.. $10-$25
Sports Illustrated College Football, Time 1971 .... $8-$40
Sports Illustrated Pro Football, Time, 1970 .... $15-$40
Stars on Stripes Football Game, Stars & Stripes Games
    Co.,1941 .... $55-$90
Statis-Pro Football, Statis-Pro, 1970s.......................... $25-$65
Statis-Pro Football, Avalon Hill-Sports Illustrated............. $5-$15
Strat-O-Matic College Football Strat-O-Matic 1976....... $25-$60
Super Coach TV Football, Coleco, 1974 .... $25-$65
Tackle, Tackle Game Co., 1933 .... $75-$115

Tackle-Lite, Saxon Toy Corp.,1940s .... $50-$75
Talking Football, Mattel, 1971 .... $12-$30
Talking Monday Night Football, Mattel, 1977 .... $8-$20
T.H.E. Pro Football, T.H.E. Game Co. .... $15-$35
Thinking Man's Football, 3M, 1969 .... $15-$30
   3M, 1973 .... $10-$20
Thrilling Indoor Football Game Cronston Co. 1933 ..... $70-$115
Top Pro Football Quiz Game, Ed-U-Cards, 1970 .... $15-$40
Touchdown, Cadaco, 1937 .... $65-$110
Touchdown, Milton Bradley.,1930s$150- $250
Touchdown Football Game, Wilder Mfg. Co., 1920s.......$100-$165
21st Century Football, Kerger Co., 1930 .... $55-$90
Va-Lo Football Card Game, 1930s $125
Varsitee Football Playing Cards, Kerger Co. 1938............. $100
Varsity Football, PB, Kerger Co., 1925 .... $75
Varsity Football Game, Cadaco-Ellis, 1942 .... $45-$75
   Cadaco-Ellis, 1955 .... $25-$35
The VCR Quarterback Game, Interactive VCR Games,
   1986 .... $8-$20
Vince Lombardi's Game, Research Games Inc.,1970... $20-$75
Ward Cuff's Football Game, Continental Sales, 1938 ....$125-$200
Whiz Football, Electric Game Co., 1945 .... $50-$75
Wilder's Football Game, Wilder Mfg. Co., 1930s .... $50-$75
Wiry Dan's Electric Football Game, Harett-Gilmar, 1953....$25-$65
Yale Harvard Game, McLoughlin Bros., 1890...... $1,050-$1,775
Yale-Harvard Football Game, La Velle Mfg. Co., 1922 ...$200-$300
Yale and Princeton Football Game, McLoughlin Bros.,
   1895 .... $575-$950

Basketball games

APBA Pro Basketball, APBA .... $15-$35
All American Basketball, Corey Games 1941.............. $55-$135
All-Pro Basketball, Ideal, 1969 .... $15-$35
All Star Basketball, Gardner, 1950s........................... $55-$135
Basket, Cadaco-Ellis, 1938, blue box .... $50-$100
Basket, Cadaco-Ellis, 1962, red/yellow box.................. $35-$65
Basket, Cadaco-Ellis, 1969, photo cover...................... $25-$45
Basket, Cadaco-Ellis, 1973, photo cover...................... $25-$45
Basketball, Harlem Globetrotters Official Edition, Cadaco-Ellis,
   1970s...$45-$115
Basketball, Chaffee & Selchow, 1898.......................... $3,700
Basketball, Russell, 1929 .... $150-$350
Basketball, Samuel Lowe, 1942, with baseball, football,
   hockey... $50-$75
Basketball, A Game, 1903, celluloid ball, hoop $200
Basketball Card Game, Built-Rite Warren, 1940s .... $15-$25
Basketball Game, Warren Built-Rite, 1950s .... $20-$45
Basketball Strategy, Avalon Hill-Sports Illustrated .... $10-$25
Big League Basketball, Baumgarten & Co., 1920s ... $125-$200
Challenge Basketball All-Stars, Avalon Hill .... $10-$25
College Basketball, Cadaco-Ellis, 1954........................ $20-$55
Computer Basketball, Electric Data Controls Corp.,
   1969 ....$45-$115
Fastbreak Basketball, Mickey Games........................... $25-$45
Harlem Globetrotters Game, Milton Bradley, 1971 .... $30-$75
Home Court Basketball, Charlie Eckman Photo, 1954, Home
   Court..$145-$375
Junior Basketball Game, Rosebud Art Co. ....1930s$75
Let's Play Basketball, DMR, 1965 .... $10-$25
Mickey Mouse Basketball, Gardner, 1950s .... $55-$135
Negamco Basketball, Nemadji Game Co. 1975 .... $10-$25
Official Basketball Game, Toy Creations,1940 .... $55-$90

The Official Globetrotter Basketball, Meljak 1950s........ $50-$85
Official NBA Basketball Game, Gerney Games, 1970s..... $40-$75
Official Radio Basketball Game, Toy Creations, 1939........ $45-$75
Oscar Robertson's Pro Basketball Strategy Research Games,
   1964.. $70-$175
Play Basketball with Bob Cousy, National Games,
   1950s.. $115-$295
Quarter Bouncers, Coin Foul Shot Game Anderson &
   Association, 1993 .... $15-$35
Real-Life Basketball, Gamecraft, 1974 .... $10-$25
Samsonite Basketball, Samsonite, 1969 .... $15-$35
Sports Illustrated All Time All Star Basketball Sports Illustrated,
   1973... $20-$50
Sports Illustrated Pro Basketball, Avalon Hill, 1981 .... $7-$15
Star Basketball, Star Paper Products 1926 .... $125-$205
Swish, Jim Hawkers Games Mfg.,1948....................... $45-$115
Tak-Tiks, Midwest Products,1939 .... $15-$25
Top Pro Basketball Quiz Game Edu-Cards 1970 .... $15-$40
Top Ten College Basketball, Top Ten Game Co.,1980....... $10-$25
Tru-Action Electric Basketball, Tudor, 1961 .... $25-$75
Ultimate College Basketball, Ultimate Game Co. .... $35-$50
The VCR Basketball Game, Interactive VCR Games,
   1987... $6-$15

Hockey games

Blue Line Hockey, 3M, 1968 .... $25-$60
Box Hockey, Milton Bradley .... $35-$50
Face-Off, Con-Fro Game Co. .... $25-$35
Hoc-Key, Cadaco-Ellis, 1958 .... $15-$50
Ice Hockey, Milton Bradley, 1942 .... $25-$40
The Katzenjammer Kids Hockey, Jaymar, 1940s .... $40-$65
Lester Patrick's Official Hockey Game.......................... $55-$70
NHL All-Pro Hockey, Ideal, 1969 .... $10$25
NHL Strategy, Tudor, 1976.. $10-$50
National Pro Hockey, Sports Action, 1985.................... $15-$35
Nip and Tuck Hockey, Parker Bros., 1928.................. $115-$195
Nok-Hockey, Carrom, 1947 .... $20-$55
Official Hockey, Toy Creations, 1940 .... $50-$75
Play Hockey Fun with Popeye & Wimpy, Barnum Mfg.,
   1935.. $205-$350
Power Play Hockey, Romac Ind.,1970.......................... $30-$75
Slapshot, Avalon Hill, 1982.. $5-$12
Strat-O-Matic Hockey, Strat-O-Matic, 1978 .... $35-$85
Sure Shot Hockey, Ideal, 1970 .... $15-$40
Tit for Tat Indoor Hockey, Lemper Novelty Co., 1920s .... $45-$75
Top Hockey Game, Coren Game Co.,1943 .... $50-$75
The VCR Hockey Game, Interactive VCR Games, 1987..... $5-$12

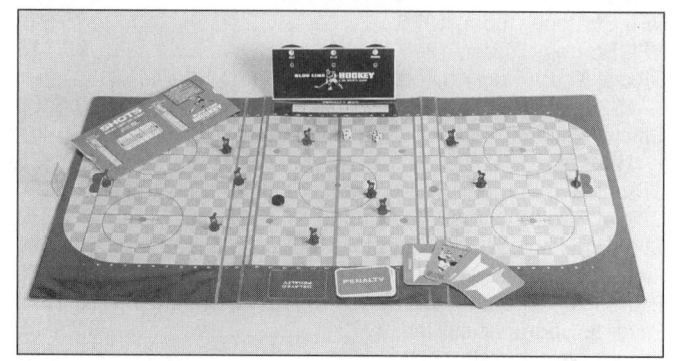

Sports Illustrated Posters

Sports posters have been around for quite some time, but the first foray into a standard line of posters geared toward consumers was launched by *Sports Illustrated (SI)* in 1968. It produced a number of baseball and football stars for mail order and limited store purchase. The era of sports poster was launched.

SI began to add other sports to their repertoire of posters including NHL Hockey and NBA Basketball in 1970. The posters were all sized at 24-by-36 inches with no border (termed "full bleed") and photos varying from action shots to standard poses. *SI* posters were printed on a thick paper stock that was durable, but lacked the photo quality that we now have today. The result was often grainy and at times, a poorly focused picture. *SI* began to change the poster stock in approximately 1973. It switched to a lighter, high gloss stock that increased the richness and clarity of the photo, but simultaneously weakened the durability. SI then abruptly stopped producing these posters in 1974-75.

Studio One, out of Holmes, PA, began to produce sports posters under the same name in 1975. It picked up on the new SI style and began running advertisements in the standard sports periodicals including *Baseball/Football Digest*, *SI*, *The Sporting News*, etc. But unlike *SI*, they were almost exclusively sold via mail order, thus making its product that much more scarce. This glossy, full bleed style of poster continued until 1977-78 when Studio One launched a new design utilizing a plain, white border. The white border poster became the standard design, superceding the full bleed style entirely. Studio One continued to produce this design exclusively until 1978-79, when, *SI* re-entered the sports poster market with the exact same white bordered design and all new photos.

Soon *SI* re-established market dominance and reduced Studio One posters to a competitive "also ran" until finally, the Studio One sports poster brand ended in approximately 1984. Conversely, *SI* posters began to penetrate sports stores, retail chains and even shoe giants like The Foot Locker, with large poster inventories and displays. This, coupled with the large mail order business, *SI* became the standard. It continued to produce the same white border style poster until 1987. 1988 ushered in a new style as well as a myriad of new competitors. The white border style sports poster had endured for over 12 years with few changes or variations.

1968-1972 Baseball

Aaron	$45
Agee, T	$50
Allen	$35
Alley	$30
Alou	$10
Alvis	$10
Andrews	$10
Aspromonte	$10
Banks	$15
Beckert	$20
Bell	$30
Bonds	$35
Boyer	$10
Brock	$15
Callison	$10
Campaneris	$10
Cardenas	$10
Carew	$15
Casanova	$10
Cepeda	$25
Clemente	$150
Conigliaro	$10
Cuellar	$10
Davis	$35
Davis, T	$15
Drysdale	$25
Epstein	$10
Ferrara	$10
Flood	$20
Freehan	$30
Fregosi	$10
Gibson	$15
Harelson	$15
Harrelson, K	$10
Holtzman	$10
Horlen	$10
Horton	$10
Howard	$25
Jackson, R	$175
John	$10
Jones, C	$60
Kaline	$40
Killebrew	$15
Koosman	$15
Let's Go Mets	$10
Lolich	$10
Lonborg	$10
Maloney	$10
Mantle	$175
Marichal	$25
Mays	$200
Mazeroski	$40
McCarver	$20
McCormack	$10
McCovey	$150
McDowell	$10
McLain	$20
Mincher (Angels)	$10
Mincher (Pilots)	$15
Monday	$10
Murcer	$40
Niekro	$60
Odom	$60
Oliva	$15
Parker	$25
Perez, T	$60
Petrocelli	$10
Powell, B	$150
Reichart	$10
Robinson, B	$150
Robinson, F	$150
Rose	$60
Santo	$25
Seaver	$200
Short	$10
Singer	$10
Smith	$10
Staub	$15
Stottlemyre	$15
Swoboda	$40
Tovar	$10
White	$20
Williams, W	$10
Williams, B	$25
Wilson	$10
Wynn	$10
Yastrzemski	$15

1973 Baseball
Sports Illustrated Posters

Bench	$60
Mays	$120
Seaver	$200

1974 Baseball
Sports Illustrated Posters

Aaron	$25
Clemente	$150
Gibson	$45
Jenkins	$225
Lolich	$15
Robinson, B	$150
Yaz	$15

1975 Baseball
Sports Illustrated Posters

Aaron (714)	$25
Allen	$25
Brock	$25
Jackson	$85
Jenkins (V2)	$250
Rose	$30
Santo	$30

1975 Baseball
Sports Illustrated Posters

Burroughs	$25
Busby	$35
Carlton	$60
Gross	$35
Hrabosky	$30
Madlock	$35
Medich	$45
Murcer	$55
Palmer	$60
Rudi	$60
Ryan	$140
Schmidt	$25
Seaver	$90
Simmons	$50
Sutton	$45
Torre	$50

1979 Baseball
Sports Illustrated Posters

Bench $15
Brett, G $35
Brett, G (V2) $35
Brett, K $40
Buckner $25
Burleson $15
Burroughs $25
Carew (Angels) $25
Carew (Twins) $35
Carlton $35
Carlton (V2) $35
Foster $25
Garvey (Dodgers) $15
Jackson (Yankees) $25
Luzinski $15
Maddox $30
Morgan $45
Murray $20
Nettles $15
Palmer $15
Parker $40
Parker (V2) $35
Perez $45
Randolph $15
Rice $10
Rose (Reds) $10
Rose (Phillies) $25
Ryan $100
Schmidt $15
Seaver $20
Seaver $30
Simmons $15
Sutter (Cubs) $10
Sutter (Cardinals) $30
Tanana $30
Templeton $35

1980 Baseball
Sports Illustrated Posters

Clark, J (Giants) $35
Clark, J (Cardinals) $25
Clark, J (Yankees) $40

1981 Baseball
Sports Illustrated Posters

Dent $30
Hernandez (Cardinals) $35
Hernandez (Mets) $20
Kemp (Tigers) $30
Kemp (Yankees) $35
Kingman $30
Mazzilli $30
Smalley (Yankees) $15
Smalley (Twins) $35
Stargell $25
Sundberg $15

1982 Baseball
Sports Illustrated Posters

Bell $25
Cerone $15
Charboneau $45
Horner $25
John $10
Lansford $35
Molitor $25
Murphy, D $20

1984 Baseball
Sports Illustrated Posters

Carter, G (Expos) $40
Carter, G (Mets) $20
Garvey (Padres) $20
Gibson $30
Guidry $35
Jackson (Angels) $10
Matthews, G $25
Murray (V2) $25
Porter $30
Remy $35
Rose (V2-Reds) $10
Sax $25
Wilson, W $20
Wison, M $25
Yount $40

1985 Baseball
Sports Illustrated Posters

BB Superstars $20
Fisk $40
Gooden $10
Gwynn $35
Kittle $35
Marshall, M $30
Mattingly $15
Morris $20
Oliver $30
Righetti $15
Ripken $35
Sandberg $35
Strawberry $15
Trammell $30
Winfield (Yankees) $10

1987 Baseball
Sports Illustrated Posters

Boggs $20
Clark, W $25
Clemens $30
Clemens (V2) $35
Cooper $45
Darling $15
Davis, E $10
Dawson $10
Gaetti $15
Henderson, R $15
Incavilia $10
Jackson, R (A's) $30
Joyner $15
McReynolds $25
Puckett $35
Scott $15
Smith, O $25
Snyder $15

1974 Football
Sports Illustrated Posters

Banasak $65
Greene $40
Harris $75
Lanier $85
Morris $125
Pastorini $75
Phipps $75
Reid $75
Unitas (Colts) $250
Unitas (Chargers) $300
Washington (SF) $125

Wilson $75

1979 Football
Sports Illustrated Posters

Alzado (Broncos) $20
Alzado (Browns) $65
Anderson, K $45
Anderson, K (V2) $25
Armstrong $35
Bartkowski $40
Bartkowski (V2) $40
Bradshaw $15
Bradshaw (V2) $45
Bradshaw (V3) $35
Campbell $35
Campbell (V2) $15
Casper $45
Dierdorf $15
Dorsett $35
Dorsett (V2) $20
Dorsett (V3) $45
Foreman $50
Fouts $20
Fouts (V2) $35
Griese $35
Griese (V2) $45
Grogan $15
Guy $35
Haden $40
Harris, F $10
Hart $40
Jaworski $60
Jones, B $25
Jones, B (V2) $35
Martie, H $50
McCutcheon $35
Morton $45
Payton $50
Payton (V2) $25
Payton (V3) $35
Payton (V4) $50
Pruitt, G $35
Stabler (Raiders) $75
Stabler (Oilers) $45
Staubach $45
Staubach (V2) $65
Walker $45
Wortman $25
Youngblood $45
Zorn $15
Zorn (V2) $25

1980 Football
Sports Illustrated Posters

Brazile $25
Burrough $45
Danielson $35
Francis, W $30
Galbreath $35
Ham $40
Hammond $40
Harper , R $25
Harris , C $40
Jefferson $45
Lambert $20
Manning $60
McKenzie $25
Pastorini $50
Riggins $100

Selmon $70
Theismann........................ $35
Theismann (V2) $40
Waters $45
White $40
Williams , D....................... $25
Youngblood $40

1982 Football
Sports Illustrated Posters
Anderson, OJ $25
Bleier $45
Ferragamo $65
Furness $25
Gradishar $35
Greene $15
Pruitt , M $40
Simms.............................. $30
Simms (V2) $25
Sipe $50

1984 Football
Sports Illustrated Posters
Abercrombie $30
Allen $25
Baumhower $45
Breunig, B......................... $35
Carpenter $25
Cefalo $30
Chandler........................... $40
Clark, D $25
Collingsworth $20
Cosbie $60
Donovan, P $50
Downs............................... $35
Duhe $35
Elway $50

Elway (V2) $45
Ferguson $55
Gastineau $40
Hipple $25
Johnson, B $60
Klecko $75
Kramer $25
Lyons $35
Martin, H $45
McMahon $20
McMahon (V2) $25
McNeil $35
Montana $50
Montana (V2) $45
Newsonme, T $40
NFL Superstars $30
Rogers, G $40
Salaam, A $35
Taylor, L $25
Todd $25
Watson $45
Winslow $40

1985 Football
Sports Illustrated Posters
Dickerson.......................... $35
Dickerson (Colts) $40
Eason (SBXX) $25
Grogan (SBXX) $25
Hogeboom $45
Largent $20
Lofton $45
Marino $50
Marino (V2) $45
McMahon, J (SBXX) $15
NFL Superstars $25

Payton (SBXX) $25
Sims $35
Singletary (SBXX) $25
Walker $35
Warner, C $25

1987 Football
Sports Illustrated Posters
Anderson, N $25
Bavaro $30
Bell $35
Christensen $20
Craig $35
Duper................................ $35
Esiason $35
Fencik $20
Flutie $35
Hampton $20
James, C $25
Kelly $35
Kosar $35
Krieg, D $25
Lipps $40
Lomax $20
Long $45
Malone, M $25
Manley $25
Mecklenburg $25
Morris, J $15
O'Brien $35
Schroeder $35
Singletary $20
Walker, H $35
White, D............................ $40

Studio One Posters

1976 Baseball
Studio One Posters
Bowa................................. $30
Brock $25
Burroughs......................... $25
Garvey.............................. $30
Gross $35
Hrabosky $30
Hunter............................... $75
Jackson $85
Lynn $30
Madlock $35
Morgan $60
Murcer $55
Palmer $60
Rose $30
Rudi $60
Ryan $140
Schmidt $25
Seaver $90
Stargell $35
Sutton $45
Torre $50

1977-1978 Baseball
78 NL All Stars................... $45
Bando $35
Baylor $40

Bell $60
Bench $60
Blyleven $60
Bowa $40
Brett $75
Brock $40
Busby................................ $40
Carlton $75
Cey $60
Fidrych.............................. $65
Fingers $75
Garvey $40
Grich $50
Gross $35
Hrabosky $35
Hunter $75
Jackson $40
Kingman $40
Kranepool $40
Lezcano $50
Luzinski $40
Lyle $40
Lynn $40
Madlock $45
Manning $75
Medich $40
Morgan $75

Munson.............................. $45
Palmer $75
Pro Baseball $40
Rose $40
Rudi $55
Ryan $175
Schmidt $40
Seaver $55
Singleton $40
Stargell $40
Sutton $40
Tanana.............................. $40
Tiant $40
Torre $45
Yazstremski $35
Yount................................ $50
Zisk.................................. $40

1977-1978 Baseball
Studio One Posters
Bailor, B............................ $35
Blue $40
Burroughs.......................... $35
Candelaria......................... $35
Carew (Twins) $45
Carew (Angels) $40
Cedeno $35

Clemente	$150
Concepcion	$50
Cowens	$35
DeCinces	$35
Dent	$35
Figueroa	$35
Fisk	$40
Foster	$45
Guidry	$50
Hisle	$35
Kemp	$35
Kuiper	$45
Lemon	$35
Nettles	$50
Parker	$35
Rice	$35
Rose (Phillies)	$25
Russell	$40
Simmons	$40
Sundberg	$35
Templeton	$40
Thompson J	$35
Valentine	$35
White, R	$35

1980 Baseball Studio One Posters

Bench	$40
Buckner	$35
Burleson	$35
Clark, J	$40
Jones, R	$30
Maddox	$35
Mazzilli	$35
Murray	$35
Randolph	$35
Rose	$30
Rose	$30
Sutter	$25

1981 Baseball Studio One Posters

Cerrone	$35
Horner	$35
Pinella	$40

1982 Baseball Studio One Posters

Valenzuela	$50

1984 Baseball Studio One Posters

BB College Stars	$40
Bell	$35
Carter, G	$40
Charboneau	$40
Gibson	$35
Hernandez	$35
Molitor	$35
Murphy, D	$35
Porter	$35
Sax	$35
Thomas, G	$40

1968-1973 Football Studio One Posters

Alworth	$250
Bakken	$15
Barney	$35
Biletnikoff	$85
Blanda	$50
Bradshaw	$150

Brockington	$125
Brodie	$60
Brown	$50
Bulaich	$50
Butkus	$100
Butkus (V2)	$150
Carter	$40
Coffey	$15
Cook	$35
Csonka	$125
Curtis	$40
Davidson	$75
Dawson	$150
Eller	$180
Farr	$40
Gabriel	$150
Gabriel (V2)	$100
Gabriel (Eagles)	$250
Garrett	$45
Garrett (Chargers)	$165
Grabowski	$15
Griese	$150
Griese (V2)	$90
Hadl	$110
Hawkins	$15
Hayes	$65
Jackson, R	$50
Johnson	$15
Jones	$75
Jurgensen	$75
Kapp	$125
Karras	$25
Kelly	$65
Kemp	$125
Lamonica	$175
Landry	$50
Lilly	$125
Little	$100
Lockhart	$100
Mackey	$15
Manning	$175
Matte	$45
Maynard	$100
Morton	$125
Namath	$125
Namath (V2)	$150
Nance	$100
Nelson	$50
Nitschke	$125
Nix	$15
Nobis	$45
Olsen	$100
Page	$100
Plunkett	$125
Reeves	$250
Russell	$15
Sayers	$45
Sellers	$35
Shaw	$35
Simpson	$200
Smith, J	$75
Snead	$35
Starr	$60
Staubach	$225
Taylor, C	$60
Taylor, O	$75
Warfield	$75

Washingon	$85
Webster	$40
Woodson	$15

1975 Football Studio One Posters

Anderson, D	$75
Bouniconti	$100
Farr	$50
Foreman	$75
Hill ,C	$75
Jackson, H	$125
Kilmer	$125
Kwalick	$50
Lane	$125
Lee	$75
Riggins	$175
Sanders	$50
Stabler	$125
Tucker	$50
Washington (SF)	$125
Yepremian	$45
Young	$50

1986 Football Studio One Posters

Anderson, K	$75
Armstrong	$65
Babich	$50
Bartkowski	$80
Berteisen	$75
Boryla	$75
Bryant, W	$75
Hadl	$100
Hanburger	$150
Hart	$50
Herron	$75
Hill, JD	$165
Hubbard	$150
Huff	$75
Little, L	$95
Mandich	$75
Metcalf	$75
Mitchell, L	$85
Pruitt	$50
Schreiber	$75
Woods	$50

1977-1978 Football Studio One Posters

Anderson , K	$75
Armstrong	$65
Babich	$50
Bartkowski	$80
Barzilauskas	$75
Bergey	$75
Biletnikoff	$90
Bradshaw	$90
Brown	$125
Caster	$95
Csonka	$125
Foreman	$75
Greene	$50
Griese	$100
Hampton	$125
Hanburger	$125
Harris, J	$115
Harris, F	$40
Hart	$45
Hill, JD	$165

Jackson, H	$125	Haden	$45	Guy	$40
Jackson, W	$125	Hammond	$50	Ham	$45
Jones, B	$45	Hart, J	$45	Harper, R	$25
Little	$95	Hart, T	$50	Harris, C	$40
Malone	$75	Houston	$75	Jefferson	$35
Mandich	$75	Jaworski	$90	Jones, B	$35
Manning	$150	Kilmer	$100	Lambert	$40
McCutcheon	$75	Landry	$50	Martin, H	$45
Metcalf	$75	Manning	$150	Selmon	$50
Mitchell	$85	McKenzie	$50	Theisman	$45
Page	$125	Moore, N	$65	Walker	$45
Pastorini	$75	Morton	$75	Waters	$40
Pruitt, G	$50	Moses	$75	White	$50
QB Montage	$65	Payton	$80		
Riggins	$180	Pearson	$55		
Simpson	$45	Pro Football	$45		
Stabler	$125	Rodgers	$75		
Staubach	$150	Tarkenton	$175		
Swann	$225	Thomas	$45		
Tarkenton	$200	Todd	$65		
Youngblood	$150	Van Pelt	$75		

1981 Football Studio One Posters

Faragamo	$50

1978-1979 Football Studio One Posters

1982 Football Studio One Posters

Barbaro	$45	Whitehurst	$55
Bell, R	$55	Williams, D	$45
Branch	$65	Woods	$45
Brazille	$35	Zorn	$40

Anderson, O	$30
Logan	$35
Wortman	$25

1980 Football Studio One Posters

1984 Football Studio One Posters

Cunningham	$35	Alzado	$65
D. Casper	$125	Armstrong	$35
Dobler	$85	Campbell	$40
Dorsett	$55	Danielson	$35
FB Superstars	$45	Dierdorf	$25
Ferguson	$75	Fouts	$35
Francis	$45	Francis, W	$25
Griffin	$75	Galbreath	$35
Grogan	$45	Gradishar	$40

Allen	$45
Clark, D	$35
Collingsworth	$35
Gastineau	$45
Gastineau (NS)	$35
Montana	$75
NFL College Stars	$50
Rogers, G	$45
Simms	$45
Winslow	$55

Costacos Brothers Posters

Founded in 1985 by brothers Tock and John Costacos, Seattle-based Costacos Sports grew rapidly to become the largest producer of creative licensed sports posters.

In 1994, Costacos entered into an agreement in which the company became the exclusive distributor for Nike posters. In 1996, Costacos was purchased by Indianapolis-based Day Dream, Inc., the world's largest poster and wall calendar company.

In 1997, Day Dream was purchased by Sidney, N.Y.-based AT-A-GLANCE Group, the world's largest manufacturer of time management products including desk calendars, student planners, three-ring binders, pocket portfolios and notebooks.

From the beginning, Costacos made an impact on the sports world with its innovative "fantasy" sports posters. Throughout the 1980s, superstar athletes would pose for some classic posters. Roger Clemens was "The Rocket," standing on the mound holding a smoking rocket-ball.

Costacos produces more than 200 new posters each year and has never kept a complete list of all the posters it has created since the mid-1980s.

In general, most poster prices in near mint condition do not fluctuate much and maintain their original suggested retail price on the current collectibles market.

Early Costacos Brothers Posters

Roger Clemens (The Rocket)	$6
Eric Davis (44 Magnum)	$5
Andre Dawson (The Hawk)	$5
McGwire/Canseco (Bash Brothers)	$8
Dave Winfield (Class)	$5
Cory Snyder (Gunsmoke)	$4
Frank Viola (Sweet Music)	$4
Barry Bonds (License to Thrill)	$5
Rickey Henderson (Lethal Weapon)	$6
Andy Van Slyke (Pirates Treasure)	$4
Ken Griffey Jr. (Kid Dynamite)	$10

Marketcom NFL Posters

1980

These white-bordered posters, measuring 5 1/2" by 8 1/2", feature 50 NFL stars. The player's name appears at the top of the card; Marketcom, the set's producer, is credited in the bottom lower right corner. A white facsimile autograph also appears on the card front. The back has the player's name at the top, and a card number on the bottom (Mini-Poster 1 of 50, etc.) Marketcom of St. Louis, sold the posters in packs of five.

	NM	EX	VG
Complete Set (50):	$225	$112	$67
Common Player:	.50	.25	.15
1 ..... Ottis Anderson	1	.50	.30
2 ..... Brian Sipe	.60	.30	.20
3 ..... L. McCutcheon	.60	.30	.20
4 ..... Ken Anderson	1.25	.60	.40
5 ..... Roland Harper	.50	.25	.15
6 ..... Chuck Foreman	.75	.40	.25
7 ..... Gary Danielson	.50	.25	.15
8 ..... Wallace Francis	.50	.25	.15
9 ..... John Jefferson	.75	.40	.25
10 ..... Charlie Waters	.75	.40	.25
11 ..... Jack Ham	1	.50	.30
12 ..... Jack Lambert	1.25	.60	.40
13 ..... Walter Payton	5	2.50	1.50
14 ..... Bert Jones	1	.50	.30
15 ..... Harvey Martin	.75	.40	.25
16 ..... Jim Hart	.60	.30	.20
17 ..... Craig Morton	.75	.40	.25
18 ..... Reggie McKenzie	.50	.25	.15
19 ..... Keith Wortman	.50	.25	.15
20 ..... Otis Armstrong	.75	.40	.25
21 ..... Steve Grogan	.75	.40	.25
22 ..... Jim Zorn	.75	.40	.25
23 ..... Bob Griese	2	1	.60
24 ..... Tony Dorsett	2	1	.60
25 ..... Wesley Walker	.75	.40	.25
26 ..... Dan Fouts	2	1	.60
27 ..... Dan Dierdorf	1	.50	.30

12 ..... Jack Lambert	1.25	.90	.50
13 ..... Walter Payton	5	3.75	2
14 ..... Bert Jones	1	.70	.40
15 ..... Harvey Martin	.75	.60	.30
16 ..... Jim Hart	.75	.60	.30
17 ..... Craig Morton	.75	.60	.30
18 ..... Reggie McKenzie	.50	.40	.20
19 ..... Keith Wortman	.50	.40	.20
20 ..... Joe Greene	1.50	1.25	.60
21 ..... Steve Grogan	.75	.60	.30
22 ..... Jim Zorn	.75	.60	.30
23 ..... Bob Griese	2	1.50	.80
24 ..... Tony Dorsett	2.50	2	1
25 ..... Wesley Walker	.75	.60	.30
26 ..... Dan Fouts	2	1.50	.80
27 ..... Dan Dierdorf	1	.70	.40
28 ..... Steve Bartkowski	.75	.60	.30
29 ..... Archie Manning	1	.70	.40
30 ..... Randy Gradishar	.75	.60	.30
31 ..... Randy White	1.25	.90	.50
32 ..... Joe Theismann	2	1.50	.80
33 ..... Tony Galbreath	.50	.40	.20
34 ..... Cliff Harris	.75	.60	.30
35 ..... Ray Guy	1	.70	.40
36 ..... Joe Ferguson	.75	.60	.30
37 ..... Ron Jaworski	.75	.60	.30
38 ..... Greg Pruitt	.75	.60	.30
39 ..... Ken Burrough	.60	.45	.25
40 ..... Robert Brazile	.50	.40	.20
41 ..... Pat Haden	1	.70	.40
42 ..... Ken Stabler	2	1.50	.80
43 ..... Lee Roy Selmon	.75	.60	.30
44 ..... Franco Harris	2	1.50	.80
45 ..... Jack Youngblood	1.25	.90	.50
46 ..... Terry Bradshaw	6	4.50	2.50
47 ..... Roger Staubach	6	4.50	2.50
48 ..... Earl Campbell	4	3	1.50
49 ..... Phil Simms	1.50	1.25	.60
50 ..... Delvin Williams	.50	.40	.20

1981

The 1981 Marketcom posters are the first set to include detailed information on the back of the poster. Along with biographical and statistical information for 1980 and the the player's career, a comprehensive summary of the player's accomplishments is provided. A poster number is also given. Each poster, measuring 5 1/2" by 8 1/2", has a full-color action photo of the player on the front, along with his facsimile signature. His name is listed in the upper left corner.

	NM	EX	VG
Complete set (50):	$32	$24	$13
Common player:	.50	.40	.20
1 ..... Ottis Anderson	.75	.60	.30
2 ..... Brian Sipe	.60	.45	.25
3 ..... Rocky Bleier	.75	.60	.30
4 ..... Ken Anderson	100	.70	.40
5 ..... Roland Harper	.50	.40	.20
6 ..... Steve Furness	.50	.40	.20
7 ..... Gary Danielson	.50	.40	.20
8 ..... Wallace Francis	.60	.45	.25
9 ..... John Jefferson	.60	.45	.25
10 ..... Charlie Waters	.75	.60	.30
11 ..... Jack Ham	.75	.60	.30

1982

These 50 mini posters from Marketcom are similar to design to the previous year's issue. Each poster is 5 1/2" by 8 1/2" and has a full-color action photo on the front, along with a facsimile signature in white letters. The backs are similar to the backs of the 1981 posters — they have a detailed career summary and biographical information, plus statistics for the player's career and 1981 season. In addition to a number, the back also says "St. Louis — Marketcom — Series C."

	NM	EX	VG
Complete Set (48):	$175	$100	$85
Common player:	2	1.50	.80
1 ..... Joe Ferguson	2.50	2	1
2 ..... Kellen Winslow	3	2.25	1.25
3 ..... Jim Hart	2.50	2	1
4 ..... Archie Manning	4	3	2.50
5 ..... Earl Campbell	15	11	6
6 ..... Wallace Francis	2	1.50	.80
7 ..... Randy Gradishar	2.50	2	1
8 ..... Ken Stabler	5	3.75	2
9 ..... Danny White	3	2.25	1.25
10 ..... Jack Ham	4	3	1.50
11 ..... Lawrence Taylor	20	15	8

12	Eric Hipple	2	1.50	.80
13	Ron Jaworski	2.50	2	1
14	George Rogers	2	1.50	.80
15	Jack Lambert	5	3.75	2
16	Randy White	5	3.75	2
17	Terry Bradshaw	15	11	6
18	Ray Guy	3	2.25	1.25
19	Rob Carpenter	2	1.50	.80
20	Reggie McKenzie	2	1.50	.80
21	Tony Dorsett	7.50	5.75	3
22	Wesley Walker	2.50	2	1
23	Tommy Kramer	2.50	2	1
24	Dwight Clark	3	2.25	1.25
25	Franco Harris	5	3.75	2
26	Craig Morton	2.50	2	1
27	Harvey Martin	2.50	2	1
28	Jim Zorn	2.50	2	1
29	Steve Bartkowski	2.50	2	1
30	Joe Theismann	5	3.75	2
31	Dan Dierdorf	3	2.25	1.25
32	Walter Payton	20	15	8
33	John Jefferson	2.50	2	1
34	Phil Simms	5	3.75	2
35	Lee Roy Selmon	2.50	2	1
36	Joe Montana	35	26	14
37	Robert Brazile	2	1.50	.80
38	Steve Grogan	2.50	2	1
39	Dave Logan	2	1.50	.80
40	Ken Anderson	4	3	1.50
41	Richard Todd	2.50	2	1
42	Jack Youngblood	3	2.25	1.25
43	Ottis Anderson	3	2.25	1.25
44	Brian Sipe	2.50	2	1
45	Mark Gastineau	2.50	2	1
46	Mike Pruitt	2	1.50	.80
47	Cris Collinsworth	2.50	2	1
48	Dan Fouts	5	3.75	2

Boxing Posters

Much of boxing's rich history is preserved on vintage boxing posters. For many, these posters are the only visual link to the past, as many early fights were not recorded on film. Understandably, collecting fight, and also film, posters has become extremely popular. Pre-1940s fight posters are desirable to collectors, but are scarce on the market. Additionally, these vintage posters in top condition usually command a significant price. The high cost and limited availability of vintage posters force most boxing collectors to begin their collection with posters issued during the 1940s and 1950s.

Heavyweight Bouts

Date	Opponents	Value
06/21/32	J. Sharkey vs. M. Schmeling	$12,500
09/24/35	J. Louis vs. M. Baer	$15,000
06/19/36	M. Schmeling vs. J. Louis	$30,000
06/22/38	J. Louis vs. M. Schmeling	$32,500
05/23/41	J. Louis vs. B. Baer	$10,000
06/18/41	J. Louis vs. B. Conn	$10,000
03/27/47	R. Robinson vs. B. Miller	$4,200
12/05/47	J. Louis vs. J. Walcott	$5,000
06/25/48	J. Louis vs. J. Walcott	$5,000
06/22/49	E. Charles vs. J. Walcott	$2,000
08/25/50	R. Robinson vs. J. Basora	$4,200
09/27/50	E. Charles vs. J. Louis	$5,000
03/07/51	E. Charles vs. J. Walcott	$2,000
06/10/51	R. Robinson vs. J. DeBruin	$3,000
07/18/51	J. Walcott vs. E. Charles	$2,000
10/26/51	R. Marciano vs. J. Louis	$22,500
06/05/52	J. Walcott vs. E. Charles	$2,000
09/23/52	R. Marciano vs. J. Walcott	$25,500
06/17/54	R. Marciano vs. E. Charles	$12,000
09/17/54	R. Marciano vs. E. Charles	$12,000
05/16/55	R. Marciano vs. D. Cockell	$11,000
07/22/55	R. Robinson vs. Castellani	$4,200
09/21/55	R. Marciano vs. A. Moore	$10,000
11/30/56	F. Patterson vs. A. Moore	$2,550
06/26/59	I. Johansson vs. F. Patterson	$1,100
06/20/60	F. Patterson vs. I. Johansson	$1,175
03/13/61	F. Patterson vs. I. Johansson	$1,175
07/09/62	R. Robinson vs. P. Moyer	$3,000
09/25/62	R. Robinson vs. T. Downes	$2,500
09/25/62	S. Liston vs. F. Patterson	$1,500
10/17/03	R. Robinson vs. D. Infantes	$3,000
11/15/62	C. Clay vs. A. Moore	$2,450
01/30/63	R. Robinsin vs. Dupas	$1,500
07/22/63	S. Liston vs.. F. Patterson	$1,525
02/25/64	C. Clay vs.. S. Liston	$15,000
05/25/65	M. Ali vs. S. Liston	$3,000
11/22/65	M. Ali vs. F. Patterson	$4,000
04/04/68	J. Frazier vs. B. Mathis	$800
11/28/70	J. Frazier vs. B. Foster	$900
03/08/71	J. Frazier vs. M. Ali	$3,500
09/20/72	M. Ali vs. F. Patterson	$3,500

11/21/72 ...... M. Ali vs. B. Foster $3,500	01/22/88 ...... M. Tyson vs. L. Holmes $50
01/22/73 ...... G. Foreman vs. J. Frazier $1,500	03/20/88 ...... M. Tyson vs. T. Tubbs $150
03/31/73 ...... K. Norton vs. M. Ali $3,000	06/27/88 ...... M. Tyson vs. M. Spinks $150
09/01/73 ...... G. Foreman vs. J. Roman $200	02/25/89 ...... M. Tyson vs. F. Bruno $200
09/10/73 ...... M. Ali vs. K. Norton $500	07/21/89 ...... M. Tyson vs. C. Williams $75
01/28/74 ...... M. Ali vs. J. Frazier $1,200	02/10/90 ...... B. Douglas vs. M. Tyson $200
03/26/74 ...... G. Foreman vs. K. Norton $1,200	10/25/90 ...... E. Holyfield vs. B. Douglas $45
10/30/74 ...... M. Ali vs. G. Foreman $5,000	03/18/91 ...... M. Tyson vs. R. Ruddock $45
09/30/75 ...... M. Ali vs. J. Frazier $4,000	04/19/91 ...... E. Holyfield vs.. G. Foreman $35
06/15/76 ...... G. Foreman vs. J. Frazier $500	06/28/91 ...... M. Tyson vs. R. Ruddock $75
09/28/76 ...... M. Ali vs. K. Norton $500	10/18/91 ...... R. Mercer vs. T. Morrison $35
09/29/77 ...... M. Ali vs. E. Shavers $600	11/23/91 ...... E. Holyfield vs. B. Cooper $75
02/15/78 ...... L. Spinks vs. M. Ali $1,500	02/07/92 ...... L. Holmes vs. R. Mercer $35
06/09/78 ...... L. Holmes vs. K. Norton $600	05/15/92 ...... M. Moorer vs. B. Cooper $35
09/15/78 ...... M. Ali vs. L. Spinks $800	06/19/92 ...... E. Holyfield vs. L. Holmes $10
10/02/80 ...... L. Holmes vs. M. Ali $800	07/18/92 ...... R. Bowe vs. P. Coetzer $30
06/12/81 ...... L. Holmes vs. L. Spinks $250	01/31/92 ...... L. Lewis vs. R. Ruddock $45
06/11/82 ...... L. Holmes vs. G. Cooney $50	10/31/92 ..... L. Lewis vs. R. Ruddock $45
05/20/83 ...... L. Holmes vs. T. Witherspoon $50	11/13/92 ...... R. Bowe vs. E. Holyfield $30
09/21/85 ...... M. Spinks vs. L. Holmes $75	02/06/93 ...... R. Bowe vs. M. Dokes $30
04/19/86 ...... M. Spinks vs. L. Holmes $35	06/07/93 ...... T Morrison vs. G. Foreman $15
11/22/86 ...... M. Tyson vs. T. Berbick $200	11/05/94 ...... G. Foreman vs. M. Moorer $100
03/07/87 ...... M.Tyson vs. Bonecrusher Smith $90	11/09/96 ...... M. Tyson vs. E. Holyfield $60
05/30/87 ...... M. Tyson vs. Pinklon Thomas $90	06/28/97 ..... E. Holyfield vs. M. Tyson $10
05/30/87 ...... T. Tucker vs. B. Douglas $200	03/14/99 ..... E Holyfield and L. Lewis (draw) $100
08/01/87 ...... M. Tyson vs. T. Tucker $75	04/21/01 ..... Rahman and L. Lewis (draw) $75
10/16/87 ...... M. Tyson vs. T. Biggs $35	

7-ELEVEN CUPS

These unnumbered white plastic cups feature color-line portraits of baseball, basketball and football players. In most cases, a facsimile signature appears below the portrait and above the player's name and team. In 1972-73, 7-Eleven convenience stores gave away, with the purchase of a soda or 14-ounce Slurpee crushed-ice drink, cups that feature portraits of Major League baseball players.

The 5 5/16-inch tall plastic cups are 3 1/4 in diameter at the top and 2 1/8 inches at the bottom. The player's full-color sketched picture is on one side of the cup above his name and the team name; on the opposite side, in between his team's logo and the 7-Eleven logo, is a brief biography.

The 1972 60-cup set includes 18 Hall of Famers. Twenty-one of the players were carried over to the 1973 set; all but seven (Dick Allen, Lou Brock, Cesar Cedeno, Ralph Garr, Willie Mays, Vada Pinson and Tom Seaver) were the same portraits. The

1973 cups differed little from the 1972 cups; the major change in format was that in 1972 the player's name and team name are flush left above his biography, while in 1973 they were centered.

The 80-cup 1973 series includes 20 old-time Hall of Famers, whose cups were the same format and styles as the current players' cups, except the portraits were done in gold rather than in color.

7-Eleven later produced full-color cups using reproduced photos. These, and the earlier cups, have not survived in quantity or quality, in part because too much dishwashing took its toll on them.

The backs include some basic biographical information and a handful of career highlights. A 7-Eleven logo is at the top, while a team helmet is at the bottom.

The cups are very susceptible to cracking, so don't put too much pressure on them, and keep them out of direct sunlight so they don't fade.

1972 7-Eleven Baseball Cups

Hank Aaron .... $25-$30	Bud Harrelson $6
Tommie Agee $4	Frank Howard $7
Rich Allen $6	Ron Hunt $4
Sal Bando $6	Reggie Jackson $35
Johnny Bench $25	Ferguson Jenkins $12
Steve Blass $5	Alex Johnson $6
Vida Blue $6	Deron Johnson $6
Lou Brock $20	Al Kaline $15
Norm Cash $6	Harmon Killebrew .... $15-$20
Cesar Cedeno $6	Mickey Lolich $6
Orlando Cepeda $10	Jim Lonborg $7
Roberto Clemente .... $35-$50	Juan Marichal .... $15-$25
Nate Colbert $7	Willie Mays $35
Willie Davis $7	Willie McCovey .... $15-$25
Ray Fosse .... $6-$7	Denny McLain $7
Ralph Garr $6	Dave McNally $4
Bob Gibson $15	Bill Melton $5
	Andy Messersmith $4

Bobby Murcer	$7-$12
Tony Oliva	$7-$10
Amos Otis	$4
Jim Palmer	$15-$20
Joe Pepitone	$7-$8
Jim Perry	$5
Lou Piniella	$7-$10
Vada Pinson	$8
Dave Roberts	$6
Brooks Robinson	$25-$30
Frank Robinson	$15-$20
Pete Rose	$25
George Scott	$5
Tom Seaver	$25
Sonny Siebert	$6
Reggie Smith	$6
Willie Stargell	$12-$20
Bill Stoneman	$5
Mel Stottlemyre	$7-$9
Joe Torre	$8
Maury Wills	$6
Don Wilson	$5
Rick Wise	$5
Wilbur Wood	$6
Carl Yastrzemski	$25

1973 7-Eleven Baseball Cups

Hank Aaron	$15
Dick Allen	$7-$8
Dusty Baker	$4-$6
Johnny Bench	$15
Yogi Berra	$10-$12
Larry Biittner	$6
Steve Blass	$4-$6
Lou Boudreau *	$6
Lou Brock	$5
Roy Campanella *	$15-$35
Bert Campaneris	$4-$6
Rod Carew	$9
Steve Carlton	$9
Cesar Cedeno	$4
Ty Cobb *	$15-$35
Nate Colbert	$4-$6
Willie Davis	$4
Bill Dickey *	$10
Bob Feller *	$10-$35
Carlton Fisk	$6-$8
Bill Freehan	$4-$7
Ralph Garr	$4-$6
Lou Gehrig *	$15-$65
Charlie Gehringer *	$10-$35
Bob Gibson	$10
Hank Greenberg *	$15-$35
Bobby Grich	$4-$8
Lefty Grove *	$6-$35

Toby Harrah	$6
Richie Hebner	$4
Ken Henderson	$4-$8
Carl Hubbell *	$6-$35
Jim Catfish Hunter	$7-$13
Reggie Jackson	$15-$20
Walter Johnson *	$10-$15
Don Kessinger	$4-$8
Leron Lee	$4-$6
Mickey Lolich	$4-$8
Sparky Lyle	$4
Greg Luzinski	$5
Mike Marshall	$4-$6
Mickey Mantle *	$25-$95
Carlos May	$4-$6
Lee May	$4-$6
John Mayberry	$4-$6
Willie Mays *	$20
John McGraw *	$10-$35
Joe Medwick *	$6-$35
Joe Morgan	$5-$12
Thurman Munson	$9-$25
Bobby Murcer	$8-$12
Stan Musial *	$15-$35
Gary Nolan	$4-$6
Tony Oliva	$8-$9
Al Oliver	$4-$6
Claude Osteen	$4-$6
Jim Palmer	$6
Gaylord Perry	$5-$12
Lou Piniella	$4
Vada Pinson	$4
Brooks Robinson	$15
Ellie Rodriguez	$4-$6
Joe Rudi	$4-$6
Red Ruffing *	$6-$12
Babe Ruth *	$25-$55
Nolan Ryan	$35-$45
Manny Sanguillen	$4-$6
Ron Santo	$9
Richie Scheinblum	$4
Tom Seaver	$25
Ted Simmons	$6
Reggie Smith	$4
Chris Speier	$4-$6
Don Sutton	$5-$12
Luis Tiant	$4
Pie Traynor *	$12-$35
Honus Wagner *	$20-$35
Billy Williams	$6-$10
Wilbur Wood	$4-$7
Carl Yastrzemski	$15-$20

• Old-time Hall of Famer

BASEBALL BOTTLE CAPS

1967-68 Coca-Cola Bottle Caps

These bottle caps were issued in 1967-68. Some of the players had changed teams from one year to the next, so some were dropped and others were added in 1968. The caps issued in 1967 are identified by an a; those issued in 1968 have a b. The caps were issued on bottles of Coke, Tab, Sprite, Fresca and some flavors of Fanta.

Although Coke caps are more common, there is no difference in price for the same player on different sodas. This was a national promotion, but only the All-Stars were issued across the country. Each major league team at the time was produced, except the St. Louis Cardinals. They were distributed in the local area of that team only, which makes completing a set of all 19 teams very difficult. The All-Stars are the most readily available, so a cap of the same player is generally more valuable from the regional set than the All-Star set. The numbering is on the inside of the cap. The system for the regional sets begins with an alphabetical designation sometimes corresponding to the team name (T for Tigers) and a number from 1-18. However, for the two cities which have two teams (New York and Los Angeles), the numbers go to 35. The All-Stars are numbered in one of two ways. The Major League All-Stars are numbered from 1-35 with no alphabetical designation; this set was pro-duced for those areas which did not have a major league city near by. The other set is divided between National (N19-N35) and American (A19-A35) League All-Stars. This set is a continuation of the regional sets. There were also eight game caps which could be sent in to Coca-Cola along with complete team sets for prizes, among which were the 1967 Dexter Press over-sized cards. The bottle caps are condition-sensitive because most were bent with a bottle opener and discarded.

Major League All-Stars

1. Richie Allen		$4
2. Pete Rose		$25
3. Brooks Robinson		$15
4. Marcelino Lopez		$1
5. Rusty Staub		$4
6. Ron Santo		$2.50
7. Jim Nash		$1
8. Jim Fregosi		$1.50
9. Paul Casanova		$1
10. Willie Mays		$35
11. Willie Stargell		$7
12. Tony Oliva		$2.50
13. Joe Pepitone		$1.50
14. Juan Marichal		$6
15. Jim Bunning		$2.50
16. Claude Osteen		$1
17. Carl Yastrzemski		$20
18. Harmon Killebrew		$8.50
19. Henry Aaron		$35
20. Joe Torre		$2.50
21. Ernie Banks		$15
22. Al Kaline		$15
23. Frank Robinson		$14
24. Max Alvis		$1
25. Elston Howard		$2.50
26. Gaylord Perry		$5
27. Bill Mazeroski		$2.50
28. Ron Swoboda		$1
29. Vada Pinson		$1.50
30. Joe Morgan		$7
31. Cleon Jones		$1
32. Willie Horton		$1
33. Leon Wagner		$1
34. George Scott		$1
35. Ed Charles		$1

National League All-Stars

N19. Henry Aaron		$35
N20. Jim Bunning		$2.50
N21. Joe Torre		$4
N22. Claude Osteen		$1
N23. Ron Santo		$2.50
N24. Joe Morgan		$7
N25. Richie Allen		$2.50
N26. Ron Swoboda		$1
N27. Ernie Banks		$15
N28. Bill Mazeroski		$6
N29. Willie Stargell		$7
N30. Pete Rose		$25
N31. Gaylord Perry		$5
N32. Rusty Staub		$4
N33. Vada Pinson		$1.50
N34. Juan Marichal		$6
N35. Cleon Jones		$1

American League All-Stars

A19. Al Kaline		$15
A20. Frank Howard		$2.50
A21. Brooks Robinson		$15
A22. George Scott		$1
A23. Willie Horton		$1
A24. Jim Fregosi		$1.50
A25. Ed Charles		$1
A26. Harmon Killebrew		$8.50
A27. Tony Oliva		$2.50
A28. Joe Pepitone		$1.50
A29. Elston Howard		$2.50
A30. Jim Nash		$1
A31. Marcelino Lopez		$1
A32. Frank Robinson		$14
A33. Leon Wagner		$1
A34. Max Alvis		$2
A35. Paul Casanova		$1

Atlanta Braves

B1a. Gary Geiger		$1.50
B1b. Cecil Upshaw		$1.50
B2a. Ty Cline		$1.50
B2b. Tito Francona		$1.50
B3. Henry Aaron		$45
B4a. Gene Oliver		$1.50
B4b. Pat Jarvis		$1.50
B5. Tony Cloninger		$1.50
B6a. Denis Menke		$1.50
B6b. Phil Niekro		$7.50
B7a. Denny LeMaster		$1.50
B7b. Felix Milan		$1.50
B8. Woody Woodward		$1.50
B9. Joe Torre		$3
B10. Ken Johnson		$1.50
B11a. Bob Bruce		$1.50
B11b. Marty Martinez		$1.50
B12. Felipe Alou		$1.50
B13. Clete Boyer		$1.50
B14a. Wade Blasingame		$1.50
B14b. Sonny Jackson		$1.50
B15a. Don Schwall		$1.50
B15b. Deron Johnson		$1.50
B16a. Dick Kelley		$1.50
B16b. Claude Raymond		$1.50
B17. Rico Carty		$2
B18. Mack Jones		$1.50

Baltimore Orioles

O1. Dave McNally		$2
O2a. Luis Aparicio		$5
O2b. Jim Hardin		$2
O3. Paul Blair		$2
O4. Frank Robinson		$18
O5a. Jim Palmer		$14
O5b. Bruce Howard		$2
O6a. Russ Snyder		$2
O6b. John O'Donoghue		$2
O7a. Stu Miller		$2
O7b. Dave May		$2
O8. Dave Johnson		$2
O9. Andy Etchebarren		$2

O10. Brooks Robinson $20
O11. John Powell $3
O12a. Sam Bowens $2
O12b. Pete Richert $2
O13. Curt Blefary $2
O14a. Ed Fisher $2
O14b. Mark Belanger $2
O15. Wally Bunker $2
O16a. Moe Drabowsky $2
O16b. Don Buford $3
O17. Larry Haney $2
O18. Tom Phoebus $2

Boston Red Sox
R1. Lee Stange $2
R2a. Carl Yastrzemski $25
R2b. Gary Waslewski $2
R3a. Don Demeter $2
R3b. Gary Bell $2
R4a. Jose Santiago $2
R4b. John Wyatt $2
R5. Darrell Brandon $2
R6. Joe Foy $2
R7a. Don McMahon $2
R7b. Ray Culp $2
R8. Dalton Jones $2
R9a. Mike Ryan $2
R9b. Gene Oliver $2
R10a. Bob Tillman $2
R10b. Jose Santiago $2
R11. Rico Petrocelli $3
R12. George Scott $2
R13a. George Smith $2
R13b. Mike Andrews $2
R14a. Dennis Bennett $2
R14b. Dick Ellsworth $2
R15a. Hank Fischer $2
R15b. Norm Siebern $2
R16. Jim Lonborg $3
R17a. Jose Tartabull $2
R17b. Jerry Adair $2
R18a. George Thomas $2
R18b. Elston Howard $3.50

California Angels
L19. Len Gabrielson $1.50
L20. Jackie Hernandez $1.50
L21. Paul Schaal $1.50
L22. Lou Burdette $1.50
L23. Jimmie Hall $1.50
L24. Fred Newman $1.50
L25. Don Mincher $1.50
L26. Bob Rodgers $1.50
L27. Jack Sanford $1.50
L28. Bobby Knoop $1.50
L29. Jose Cardenal $1.50
L30. Jim Fregosi $1.50
L31. George Brunet $1.50
L32. Marcelino Lopez $1.50
L33. Minnie Rojas $1.50
L34. Jay Johnstone $1.50
L35. Ed Kirkpatrick $1.50

Chicago Cubs
C1. Ferguson Jenkins $12
C2. Ernie Banks $20
C3. Glenn Beckert $3
C4. Bob Hendley $2
C5. John Boccabella $2
C6. Ron Campbell $2

C7. Ray Culp $2
C8. Adolfo Phillips $2
C9. Don Bryant $2
C10. Randy Hundley $3
C11. Ron Santo $5
C12. Lee Thomas $2
C13. Billy Williams $8.50
C14. Ken Holtzman $3
C15. Cal Koonce $2
C16. Curt Simmons $2
C17. George Altman $2
C18. Byron Browne $2

Chicago White Sox
L1. Gary Peters $1.50
L2. Jerry Adair $1.50
L3. Al Weiss $1.50
L4. Pete Ward $1.50
L5. Hoyt Wilhelm $6
L6. Don Buford $1.50
L7. John Buzhardt $1.50
L8. Wayne Causey $1.50
L9. Gerald McNertney $1.50
L10. Ron Hansen $1.50
L11. Tom McCraw $1.50
L12. Jim O'Toole $1.50
L13. Bill Skowron $1.50
L14. Joel Horlen $1.50
L15. Tommy John $4
L16. Bob Locker $1.50
L17. Ken Berry $1.50
L18. Tommie Agee $1.50

Cincinnati Reds
F1. Floyd Robinson $2
F2. Leo Cardenas $2
F3. Gordy Coleman $3
F4. Tommy Harper $2
F5. Tommy Helms $3
F6. Deron Johnson $2
F7. Jim Maloney $3
F8. Tony Perez $10
F9. Don Pavletich $2
F10. John Edwards $2
F11. Vada Pinson $2
F12. Chico Ruiz $2
F13. Pete Rose $25
F14. Billy McCool $2
F15. Joe Nuxhall $3
F16. Milt Pappas $2
F17. Art Shamsky $3
F18. Dick Simpson $2

Cleveland Indians
I1. Luis Tiant $5
I2. Max Alvis $3
I3. Larry Brown $2
I4a. Rocky Colavito $6
I4b. Tommy Harper $2
I5a. John O'Donoghue $2
I5b. Vern Fuller $2
I6a. Pedro Gonzalez $2
I6b. Jose Cardenal $2
I7a. Gary Bell $2
I7b. Dave Nelson $3
I8. Sonny Siebert $2
I9. Joe Azcue $3
I10. Lee Maye $2
I11. Chico Salmon $2
I12. Leon Wagner $2

I13a. Fred Whitfield $2
I13b. Eddie Fischer $2
I14. Jack Kralick $2
I14b. Stan Williams $2
I15. Sam McDowell $4
I16a. Dick Radatz $2
I16b. Steve Hargan $2
I17. Vic Davallio $3
I18a. Chuck Hinton $2
I18b. Duke Sims $2

Detroit Tigers

T1a. Larry Sherry $2
T1b. Ray Oliver $2
T2. Norm Cash $7
T3a. Jerry Lumpe $2
T3b. Mike Marshall $6
T4a. Dave Wickersham $2
T4b. Mickey Stanley $3
T5. Joe Sparma $2
T6. Dick McAuliffe $2
T7a. Fred Gladding $2
T7b. Gates Brown $2
T8. Jim Northrup $3
T9. Bill Freehan $4
T10. Earl Wilson $2
T11. Dick Tracewski $3
T12. Don Wert $2
T13a. Jake Wood $2
T13b. Dennis Ribant $2
T14. Mickey Lolich $7
T15a. Johnny Podres $2
T15b. Denny McLain $8
T16a. Bill Monbouquette $2
T16b. Ed Mathews $12
T17. Al Kaline $20
T18. Willie Horton $3

Houston Astros

H1. Dave Guisti $1.50
H2. Bob Aspromonte $1.50
H3. Ron Davis $1.50
H4a. Claude Raymond $1.50
H4b. Julio Gotay $1.50
H5a. Barry Latman $1.50
H5b. Fred Gladding $1.50
H6a. Chuck Harrison $1.50
H6b. Lee Thomas $1.50
H7a. Bill Heath $1.50
H7b. Wade Blasingame $1.50
H8a. Sonny Jackson $1.50
H8b. Denis Menke $1.50
H9. John Bateman $1.50
H10. Ron Brand $1.50
H11a. Aaron Pointer $1.50
H11b. Doug Rader $2
H12. Joe Morgan $9
H13. Rusty Staub $3
H14. Mike Cuellar $1.50
H15. Larry Dierker $1.50
H16a. Dick Farrell $1.50
H16b. Denny LeMaster $1.50
H17a. Jim Landis $1.50
H17b. Jim Wynn $3
H18a. Ed Mathews $12
H18b. Don Wilson $1.50

Kansas City Athletics

K1. Jim Nash $1.50
K2. Bert Campaneris $1.50

K3. Ed Charles $1.50
K4. Wes Stock $1.50
K5. John Odom $1.50
K6. Ozzie Chavarria $1.50
K7. Jack Aker $1.50
K8. Dick Green $1.50
K9. Phil Roof $1.50
K10. Rene Lachemann $1.50
K11. Mike Hershberger $1.50
K12. Joe Nossek $1.50
K13. Roger Repoz $1.50
K14. Chuck Dobson $1.50
K15. Jim Hunter $12
K16. Lew Krausse $1.50
K17. Danny Cater $1.50
K18. Jim Gosger $1.50

Los Angeles Dodgers

L1. Phil Regan $2
L2. Bob Bailey $3
L3. Ron Fairly $3
L4a. Joe Moeller $2
L4b. Jim Brewer $2
L5. Don Sutton $10
L6a. Ron Hunt $2
L6b. Tom Haller $2
L7a. Jim Brewer $3
L7b. Rocky Colavito $4
L8a. Lou Johnson $2
L8b. Jim Grant $2
L9a. John Roseboro $3
L9b. Jim Campanis $2
L10. Jeff Torborg $3
L11a. John Kennedy $2
L11b. Zoilo Versalles $2
L12. Jim Lefebvre $3
L13. Wes Parker $3
L14a. Bob Miller $2
L14b. Bill Singer $2
L15. Claude Osteen $3
L16a. Ron Perranoski $3
L16b. Len Gabrielson $2
L17. Willie Davis $2
L18. Al Ferrara $2

Minnesota Twins

M1a. Ron Kline $1.50
M1b. Rich Reese $1.50
M2. Bob Allison $1.50
M3a. Earl Battey $1.50
M3b. Ron Perranoski $1.50
M4a. Jim Merritt $1.50
M4b. John Roseboro $1.50
M5. Jim Perry $1.50
M6. Harmon Killebrew $10
M7. Dave Boswell $1.50
M8. Rich Rollins $1.50
M9. Jerry Zimmerman $1.50
M10. Al Worthington $1.50
M11. Cesar Tovar $1.50
M12a. Sandy Valdespino $1.50
M12b. Jim Merritt $1.50
M13a. Zoilo Versalles $1.50
M13b. Bob Miller $1.50
M14. Dean Chance $1.50
M15a. Jim Grant $1.50
M15b. Ted Uhlaender $1.50
M16. Jim Kaat $6
M17. Tony Oliva $4

M18a. Andy Kosco $2
M18b. Rod Carew $50

New York Mets

V19. Chuck Hiller $13
V20. Johnny Lewis $3
V21. Ed Kranepool $4
V22. Al Luplow $3
V23. Don Cardwell $3
V24. Cleon Jones $3
V25a. Bob Shaw $3
N7. Tom Seaver $50
V26. John Stephenson $3
V27. Ron Swoboda $3
V28. Ken Boyer $3
V29. Ed Bressoud $3
V30. Tommy Davis $3
V31. Roy McMillan $3
V32. Jack Fisher $3
V33. Tug McGraw $3
V34. Jerry Grote $4
V35. Jack Hamilton $3

New York Yankees

V1. Mel Stottlemyre $3.50
V2. Ruben Amaro $1.50
V3. Jake Gibbs $1.50
V4. Dooley Womack $1.50
V5. Fred Talbot $1.50
V6. Horace Clark $1.50
V7. Jim Bouton $3.50
V8. Mickey Mantle $75
V9. Elston Howard $5
V10. Hal Reniff $1.50
V11. Charley Smith $1.50
V12. Bobby Murcer $3.50
V13. Joe Pepitone $3
V14. Al Downing $1.50
V15. Steve Hamilton $1.50
V16. Fritz Peterson $1.50
V17. Tom Tresh $3
V18. Roy White $3

Philadelphia Phillies

P1. Richie Allen $5
P2. Bob Wine $1.50
P3. Johnny Briggs $1.50
P4. John Callison $2
P5. Doug Clemons $1.50
P6. Dick Groat $2
P7. Dick Ellsworth $1.50
P8. Phil Linz $1.50
P9. Clay Dalrymple $1.50
P10. Bob Uecker $12
P11. Cookie Rojas $2
P12. Tony Taylor $2
P13. Bill White $2
P14. Larry Jackson $1.50
P15. Chris Short $1.50
P16. Jim Bunning $5
P17. Tony Gonzalez $1.50
P18. Don Lock $1.50

Pittsburgh Pirates

E1. Al McBean $2
E2. Gene Alley $2
E3. Donn Clendenon $2
E4. Bob Veale $2
E5. Pete Mikkelsen $2
E6. Bill Mazeroski $9
E7. Steve Blass $4
E8. Manny Mota $2
E9. Jim Pagliaroni $2
E10. Jesse Gonder $2
E11. Jose Pagan $2
E12. Willie Stargell $9
E13. Maury Wills $4
E14. Roy Face $3
E15. Woodie Fryman $2
E16. Vernon Law $3
E17. Matty Alou $2
E18. Roberto Clemente $50

San Francisco Giants

G1. Bob Bolin $1.50
G2. Ollie Brown $1.50
G3. Jim Davenport $1.50
G4a. Tito Fuentes $1.50
G4b. Bob Barton $1.50
G5a. Norm Sieburn $1.50
G5b. Jack Hiatt $1.50
G6. Jim Hart $1.50
G7. Juan Marichal $7.50
G8. Hal Lanier $1.50
G9a. Tom Haller $1.50
G9b. Ron Hunt $1.50
G10a. Bob Barton $1.50
G10b. Ron Herbal $1.50
G11. Willie McCovey $10
G12. Mike McCormick $1.50
G13. Frank Linzy $1.50
G14. Ray Sadecki $1.50
G15. Gaylord Perry $6
G16. Lindy McDaniel $1.50
G17. Willie Mays $45
G18. Jesus Alou $1.50

Washington Senators

S1. Bob Humphreys $1.50
S2. Bernie Allen $1.50
S3. Ed Brinkman $1.50
S4. Pete Richert $1.50
S5. Camilio Pascual $2.00
S6. Frank Howard $3
S7. Casey Cox $1.50
S8. Jim King $1.50
S9. Paul Casanova $1.50
S10. Dick Lines $1.50
S11. Dick Nen $1.50
S12. Ken McMullen $1.50
S13. Bob Saverine $1.50
S14. Jim Hannan $1.50
S15. Darold Knowles $1.50
S16. Phil Ortega $1.50
S17. Ken Harrelson $1.50
S18. Fred Valentine $1.50

Commemorative Coca-Cola Bottles

Over the years, numerous baseball events have been commemorated on Coke. Various events have been covered including championships, All-Star games, new stadium openings, anniversaries of team foundings, new logos, old logos, inaugural seasons, attendance records, etc. Generally, bottles are issued regionally for professional, college and other amateur sporting events. Commemorative bottles have been produced in 6 1/2, 8, 10, 12, 16 and 32 oz. sizes.

The first 8 oz. sports commemorative was issued in 1991. According to Coca Cola, there are three basic guidelines when considering issuing a commemorative Coke bottle. First, it must commemorate a special event which has a potentially high level of interest. Next, issuance of the bottle would be expected to generate interest in the product in the geographic area of the event. Finally, it should be sought after by collectors as a keepsake to remember the event, team, or person. Subjects for commemorative bottles are limited to three general areas: 1. major national events or local events with a relatively large following, 2. Coca-Cola Collectors Club-related events, and 3. internal Coca-Cola Bottling Co. events such as anniversaries and retirements.

In order to be "collectible," bottles should be full, since the contents can be seen. This differs from collectible cans that may be opened (usually from the bottom) and emptied without losing value.

There are two versions of the Jackie Robinson bottle. The first was issued in Los Angeles and includes shades of blue, gold, red and white with a glossy finish. The second was issued in southern Michigan and includes blue and white only with a flat finish.

8 oz. Coca-Cola Bottles

Event	Year	Price
St. Louis Cardinals 100 Anniversary	1992	$8
Baltimore Orioles, MLB All-Star Game at Camden Yards	1993	6
Best of the Bay - Oakland A's (set of 6)	1993	4
Best of the Bay - S.F. Giants (set of 6)	1993	4
Colorado Rockies Inaugural Season	1993	6
Florida Marlins Inaugural Season	1993	6
San Diego Padres 25th Year	1993	10
Ballpark at Arlington	1994	4
Cincinnati Reds 5 World Championships	1994	5
Cincinnati Reds First Season Central Division	1994	3
Colorado Rockies MLB Attendance Record (D. Baylor sign.)	1994	3
Colorado Rockies MLB Attendance Record (McMorris sign.)	1994	3
Florida Marlins Second Season	1994	3
Johnny Mize - The Big Cat - Hall of Fame 1981	1994	50
Milwaukee Brewers 25th Anniversary	1994	3
Ty Cobb -The Georgia Peach	1994	125
All-Star Fan Fest (Baseball)	1994	3
Astrodome 30th Anniversary	1995	5
Cal Ripken Jr. Record-Breaking Year	1995	5
Cincinnati Reds Logo (1869) (1st of 5)	1995	3
Cincinnati Reds Logo (1907) (2nd of 5)	1995	3
Cincinnati Reds Logo (1911) (3rd of 5)	1995	3
Cincinnati Reds Logo (1939) (4th of 5)	1995	3
Cincinnati Reds Logo (1995) (5th of 5)	1995	3
Norwich Navigators Baseball	1995	3
Ty Cobb - Baseball's Best (1,008 bottles made)	1995	100
Atlanta Braves World Champs	1996	3
Cincinnati Reds Big Red Machine 20th Anniversary	1996	5
Jackie Robinson - 50th Anniversary (California version)	1997	3
Jackie Robinson - 50th Anniversary (Michigan version)	1997	3
John Smoltz - Cy Young Award Winner	1997	3
Reds (Cincinnati) Rally 25th Anniversary	1997	3
St. Louis Cardinals - Central Division Champs	1997	3
Texas Rangers - Western Division Champs	1997	3
Turner Field - Home of the Braves - Inaugural Season	1997	3
Zephyrs Field - Inaugural Season	1997	3
Florida Marlins - World Series Champs	1998	3
Roger Dean Stadium - Inaugural Season	1998	3
Yankee Stadium 75th Anniversary	1998	5

10 oz. Coca-Cola Bottles

Event	Year	Price
Baseball Winter Meetings - Hollywood, Fla.	1981	$125
Dizzy Dean Graduate League World Series	1982	15
St. Louis Cardinals - World Champions (Error)	1982	15
Birmingham Barons 1983 Southern League Baseball Champs	1983	5
Orioles - 1983 World Champions	1984	6
Johnston Coca-Cola Youth Baseball Classic	1985	10
Kansas City Royals - World Champions "Show Me Series"	1985	15
Ty Cobb - The Georgia Peach	1985	250
Johnston Coca-Cola Youth Baseball Classic	1985	10
Tyrus Raymond Cobb - Royston Lodge 52 Remembers Ty	1986	1,200
Johnston Coca-Cola Youth Baseball Classic	1988	10
Ty Cobb - First in the Hall of Fame	1989	175

Football Coke Caps

1964 Coca-Cola AFL All-Stars caps

These unnumbered caps, each measuring 1 1/8" in diameter, could be found under bottle caps of Coca Cola products (Coke, Tab, Fresca) in participating cities with AFL teams. The cap has a Coke logo and a football on the outside; the player's mug shot, name, position and number were included on the inside of the cap. A Cap Saver sheet was also issued; caps could be affixed to the sheet. Completed sheets could be turned in for prizes.

Complete set NM (44): $125.00
Common player: $3.00
1) Tom Addison (Boston Patriots)..... $3.00
2) Dalva Allen (Oakland Raiders) $3.00
3) Lance Alworth (San Diego
   Chargers) $19.00
4) Houston Antwine (Boston Patriots) $3.00
5) Fred Arbanas (Kansas City Chiefs)...$4.00
6) Tony Banfield (Houston Oilers)...... $3.00
7) Stew Barber (Buffalo Bills) $3.00
8) George Blair (San Diego Chargers)..$3.00
9) Mel Branch (Kansas City Chiefs) ... $3.00
10) Nick Buoniconti (Boston Patriots)..$10.00
11) Doug Cline (Houston Oilers) $3.00
12) Eldon Danenhauer (Denver
    Broncos)..................................... $3.00
13) Clem Daniels (Oakland Raiders). $4.00
14) Larry Eisenhauer (Boston Patriots).$3.00
15) Earl Faison (San Diego Chargers)..$3.00
16) Cookie Gilchrist (Buffalo Bills) ... $12.00
17) Fred Glick (Houston Oilers) $3.00
18) Larry Grantham (New York Jets) . $4.00
19) Ron Hall (Boston Patriots $3.00
20) Charlie Hennigan (Houston Oilers).$4.50
21) E.J. Holub (Kansas City Chiefs) .. $3.00
22) Ed Husmann (Houston Oilers) $3.00
23) Jack Kemp (Buffalo Bills)........... $35.00
24) Dave Kocourek (San Diego
    Chargers) $3.00
25) Keith Lincoln (San Diego Chargers)$5.00
26) Charley Long (Boston Patriots) ... $3.00
27) Paul Lowe (San Diego Chargers) $6.00
28) Archie Matsos (Oakland Raiders)$3.00
29) Jerry Mays (Kansas City Chiefs) . $4.00
30) Ron Mix (San Diego Chargers) ... $6.00
31) Tom Morrow (Oakland Raiders) .. $3.00
32) Billy Neighbors (Boston Patriots). $4.00
33) Jim Otto (Oakland Raiders)......... $8.00
34) Art Powell (Oakland Raiders) $4.00
35) Johnny Robinson (Kansas City
    Chiefs).. $6.00
36) Tobin Rote (San Diego Chargers)$4.50
37) Bob Schmidt (Houston Oilers)..... $3.00
38) Tom Sestak (Buffalo Bills) $3.00
39) Billy Shaw (Buffalo Bills).............. $5.00
40) Bob Talamini (Houston Oilers)..... $3.00
41) Lionel Taylor (Denver Broncos) ... $5.00
42) Jim Tyrer (Kansas City Chiefs) $4.00
43) Dick Westmoreland (San Diego
    Chargers) $3.00
44) Fred Williamson (Oakland Raiders) $5.00

1964 Coke NFL All-Stars caps

These unnumbered caps, each measuring 1 1/8" in diameter, could be found under bottle caps of Coca-Cola products (Coke, Tab, Fresca) in participating cities with NFL teams. The cap has a Coke logo and a football on the outside; the player's mug shot, name, position and number were included on the inside of the cap. A Cap Saver sheet was also issued; caps could be affixed to the sheet. Completed sheets could be turned in for prizes.

Complete set NM (44): $200.00
Common player: $3.00
1) Doug Atkins (Chicago Bears)........ $7.00
2) Terry Barr (Detroit Lions).............. $3.00
3) Jim Brown (Cleveland Browns) ... $30.00
4) Roger Brown (Detroit Lions).......... $3.00
5) Roosevelt Brown (New York Giants).$6.00
6) Timmy Brown (Philadelphia Eagles).$4.50
7) Bobby Joe Conrad (Chicago Bears) .$3.00
8) Willie Davis (Green Bay Packers) . $6.00
9) Bob DeMarco (St. Louis Cardinals) ..$3.00
10) Darrell Dess (New York Giants.... $3.00
11) Mike Ditka (Chicago Bears) $10.00
12) Bill Forester (Green Bay Packers)$3.00
13) Joe Fortunato (Chicago Bears) ... $3.00
14) Bill George (Chicago Bears) $7.00
15) Ken Gray (St. Louis Cardinals).... $3.00
16) Forrest Gregg (Green Bay Packers) $7.00
17) Roosevelt Grier (Los Angeles
    Rams).. $5.00
18) Henry Jordan (Green Bay Packers) $5.00
19) Jim Katcavage (New York Giants)$3.00
20) Jerry Kramer (Green Bay Packers).$6.00
21) Ron Kramer (Green Bay Packers) ..$3.00
22) Dick Lane (Detroit Lions)............. $7.00
23) Dick Lynch (New York Giants)..... $3.00
24) Gino Marchetti (Baltimore Colts) . $6.00
25) Tommy Mason (Minnesota Vikings)$3.00
26) Ed Meador (Los Angeles Rams) . $3.00
27) Bobby Mitchell (Washington
    Redskins) $6.00
28) Larry Morris (Chicago Bears) $3.00
29) Merlin Olsen (Los Angeles Rams)..$7.00
30) Jim Parker (Baltimore Colts) $6.00
31) Jim Patton (New York Giants) $3.00
32) Myron Pottios (Pittsburgh Steelers) $3.00
33) Jim Ringo (Green Bay Packers) .. $3.00
34) Dick Schafrath (Cleveland Browns) $3.00
35) Joe Schmidt (Chicago Bears) $6.00
36) Del Shofner (New York Giants) ... $5.00
37) Bob St. Clair (San Francisco 49ers)$6.00
38) Jim Taylor (Green Bay Packeis) .. $8.00
39) Roosevelt Grier (Chicago Bears) $3.00
40) Y.A. Tittle (New York Giants) $12.00
41) John Unitas (Baltimore Colts) ... $19.00
42) Larry Wilson (St. Louis Cardinals) ..$5.00
43) Willie Wood (Green Bay Packers)$5.00
44) Abe Woodson (San Francisco
    49ers) $3.00

In addition to the bottle caps made for All-Stars in 1964, Coca-Cola issued 35 unnumbered caps each for three teams - Cleveland, Detroit and San Diego - and 36 for Boston. Each cap, measuring 1 1/8" in diameter, has mug shot of the player underneath the cork on the inside of the cap. The caps, available in the respective teams' cities during the football seasonson, were available with Coke, Fresca and Tab products. They could be identified by the football on the outside of the cap. Collectors who completed an entire set on a special Cap Saver sheet could redeem them for a prize. The sheet also had a section for unnumbered caps for each of the 14 NFL teams — Baltimore Colts, Chicago Bears, Cleveland Browns, Dallas Cowboys, Detroit Lions, Green Bay Packers, Los Angeles Rams, Minnesota Vikings, New York Giants, Philadelphia Eagles, Pittsburgh Steelers, San Francisco 49ers, St. Louis Cardinals and Washington Redskins. They generally are about $4-$5 each, with a complete set at $50.

1964 Boston Patriots

Complete set NM (36): $120.00
Common player:............................... $3.00
1) Jon Morris $3.00
2) Don Webb $3.00
3) Charles Long $3.00
4) Tony Romeo.................................. $3.00
5) Bob Dee $3.00
6) Tom Addison $3.00
7) Bob Yates..................................... $3.00
8) Ron Hall $3.00
9) undetermined
10) Jack Rudolph $3.00
11) Don Oakes $3.00
12) Tom Yewcic $3.00
13) undetermined
14) undetermined
15) Larry Garron $4.00
16) Dave Watson............................... $3.00
17) Art Graham $4.00
18) Babe Parilli $6.00
19) Jim Hunt...................................... $3.00
20) Don McKinnon $3.00
21) Houston Antwine.......................... $4.00
22) Nick Buoniconti $8.00
23) undetermined
24) Gino Cappelletti $6.00
25) Chuck Shonta $3.00
26) Dick Felt $3.00
27) Mike Dukes $3.00
28) Larry Eisenhauer $3.00
29) Bob Schmidt................................ $3.00
30) undetermined
31) J.D. Garrett.................................. $3.00
32) Jim Whalen $3.00
33) Jim Nance $6.00
34) undetermined
35) Lonnie Fariner............................. $3.00
36) Boston Patriots Logo................... $3.00

1964 Cleveland Browns

Complete set NM (35): $120.00
Common player: $3.00
1) Walter Beach $3.00
2) Larry Benz $3.00
3) Johnny Brewer $3.00
4) Jim Brown................................ $30.00
5) John Brown $3.00
6) Monte Clark $3.00
7) Gary Collins $5.00
8) Vince Costello $3.00
9) Ross Fitchner $3.00
10) Galen Fiss $3.00
11) Bob Franklin $3.00
12) Bob Gain $3.00
13) Bill Glass $5.00
14) Ernie Green $4.00
15) Lou Groza $7.50
16) Gene Hickerson $3.00
17) Jim Houston $4.00
18) Tom Hutchinson....................... $3.00
19) Jim Kanicki $3.00
20) Mike Lucci $3.00
21) Dick Modzelewski $3.00
22) John Morrow........................... $3.00
23) Jim Ninowski $3.00
24) Frank Parker $3.00
25) Bernie Parrish $3.00
26) Frank Ryan $6.00
27) Charles Scales $3.00
28) Dick Schafrath $4.00
29) Roger Shoals $3.00
30) Jim Shorter............................ $3.00
31) Billy Truax $3.00
32) Paul Warfield $14.00
33) Ken Webb............................... $3.00
34) Paul Wiggin $3.00
35) John Wooten $3.00

1964 Detroit Lions

Complete set NM (35): $100.00
Common player: $3.00
1) Terry Barr $3.00
2) Carl Brettschneider $3.00
3) Roger Brown $3.00
4) Mike Bundra $3.00
5) Ernie Clark $3.00
6) Gail Cogdill $3.00
7) Larry Ferguson $3.00
8) Dennis Gaubatz $3.00
9) Jim Gibbons $3.00
10) John Gonzaga $3.00
11) John Gordy $3.00
12) Tom Hall $3.00
13) Alex Karras $10.00
14) Dick Lane $8.00
15) Dan LaRose $2.50
16) Yale Lary $7.00
17) Dick LeBeau $5.00
18) Dan Lewis $3.00
19) Garry Lowe $3.00
20) Bruce Maher........................... $3.00
21) Darris McCord $3.00
22) Max Messner $3.00
23) Earl Morrall $8.00
24) Nick Pietrosante $5.00
25) Milt Plum $5.00
26) Daryl Sanders $3.00
27) Joe Schmidt $8.00
28) Bob Sholtz............................. $3.00
29) J.D. Smith $3.00
30) Pat Studstill $5.00
31) Larry Vargo $3.00
32) Wayne Walker $3.00
33) Tom Watkins $3.00
34) Bob Whitlow $3.00
35) Sam Williams $3.00

1964 San Diego Chargers

Complete set NM (35): $120.00
Common player: $3.00
1) Chuck Allen $3.00
2) Lance Alworth $18.00
3) George Blair $3.00
4) Frank Buncom $4.00
5) Earl Faison $4.00
6) Ken Graham $3.00
7) George Gross $3.00
8) Sam Gruneisen $3.00
9) John Hadi $10.00
10) Dick Harris $3.00
11) Bob Jackson $3.00
12) Emil Karas $3.00
13) Dave Kocoure $3.00
14) Ernie Ladd $8.00
15) Bobby Lane $3.00
16) Keith Lincoln.......................... $6.00
17) Paul Lowe $6.00
18) Jacque MacKinnon..................... $3.00
19) Gerry McDougall $3.00
20). Charley McNeill $5.00
21) Bob Mitinger $3.00
22) Ron Mix $8.00
23) Don Norton $3.00
24) Ernie Park $3.00
25) Bob Petrich $3.00
26) Jerry Robinson $3.00
27) Don Rogers $3.00
28) Tobin Rote $6.00
29) Henry Schmidt $3.00
30) Pat Shea $3.00
31) Wait Sweeney $3.00
32) Jimmy Warren $3.00
33) Dick Westmoreland $3.00
34) Bud Whitehead $3.00
35) Ernie White $3.00

1965 Coca-Cola NFL All-Stars caps

These bottle caps, available in participating NFL cities, feature NFL All-Stars. The format and design are basically the same as Coke's prior issues, except these caps are numbered using a C prefix.

Complete set NM (34): $100.00
Common player: $3.00
C37 Sonny Jurgensen (Washington Redskins) $6.00
C38 Fran Tarkenton (Minnesota Vikings) $10.00
C39 Frank Ryan (Cleveland Browns) $3.00
C40 John Unitas (Baltimore Colts) .. $10.00
C41 Tommy Mason (Minnesota Vikings) $3.00
C42 Mel Renfro (Dallas Cowboys) $4.50
C43 Ed Meador (Los Angeles Rains) $3.00
C44 Paul Krause (Washington Redskins) $4.50
C45 Irv Cross (Philadelphia Eagles) . $3.00
C46 Bill Brown (Minnesota Vikings) .. $3.00
C47 Joe Fortunato (Chicago Bears) . $3.00
C48 Jim Taylor (Green Bay Packers) $6.00
C49 John Henry Johnson (Pittsburgh Steelers)............................ $6.00
C50 Pat Fischer (St. Louis Cardinals) $3.00
C51 Bobby Boyd (Baltimore Colts).... $3.00
C52 Terry Barr (Detroit Lions) $3.00
C53 Charley Taylor (Washington Redskins) $7.50
C54 Paul Warfield (Cleveland Browns) .$7.50
C55 Pete Retzlaff (Philadelphia Eagles) $3.00
C56 Maxie Baughan (Philadelphia Eagles) $3.00
C57 Matt Hazeltine (San Francisco 49ers) $3.00
C58 Ken Gray (St. Louis Cardinals) .. $3.00
C59 Ray Nitschke (Green Bay Packers) $6.00
C60 Myron Pottios (Pittsburgh Steelers) $3.00
C61 Charlie Krueger (San Francisco 49ers) $3.00
C62 Deacon Jones (Los Angeles Rams) $6.00
C63 Bob Lilly (Dallas Cowboys) $7.50
C64 Merlin Olsen (Los Angeles Rams) $6.00
C65 Jim Parker (Baltimore Colts) $6.00
C66 Roosevelt Brown (New York Giants) $6.00
C67 Jim Gibbons (Detroit Lions) $3.00
C68 Mike Ditka (Chicago Bears) $10.00
C69 Willie Davis (Green Bay Packers)..$6.00
C70 Aaron Thomas (New York Giants).$3.00

1965 Coca-Cola bottle caps

In 1965, Coca-Cola issued caps for five teams Buffalo (B), Detroit (C), New York Giants (G), New York Jets (J) and Washington Redskins (C). The caps follow the same format and concept as previous issues, but use letter prefixes for the numbers.

1965 Buffalo Bills

Complete set NM (35): $120.00
Common player: $3.00
B1 Ray Abbruzzese $3.00
B2 Joe Auer $3.00
B3 Stew Barber $3.00
B4 Glenn Bass $3.00
B5 Dave Behrman $3.00
B6 Al Bemiller............................. $3.00
B7 Butch Byrd $3.00
B8 Wray Carlton $5.00
B9 Hagood Clarke $3.00
B10 Jack Kemp $30.00
B11 Oliver Dobbins $3.00
B12 Elbert Dubenion $7.00
B13 Jim Dunaway $3.00
B14 Booker Edgerson $3.00
B15 George Flint........................... $3.00
B16 Pete Gogolak $6.00
B17 Dick Hudson $3.00
B18 Harry Jacobs $3.00
B19 Tom Keating $3.00
B20 Tom Day............................... $3.00
B21 Daryle Lamonica....................... $9.00
B22 Paul Maguire $5.00
B23 Roland McDole $3.00
B24 Dudley Meredith $3.00
B25 Joe O'Donnell $3.00
B26 Willie Ross $3.00
B27 Ed Rutkowski $3.00
B28 George Saimes $4.00
B29 Tom Sestak $3.00

B30 Billy Shaw.................................$6.00
B31 Bob Smith.................................$3.00
B32 Mike Stratton............................$6.00
B33 Gene Sykes..............................$3.00
B34 John Tracey..............................$3.00
B35 Ernie Warlick.............................$3.00

1965 Detroit Lions

Complete set NM (36): $100.00
Common player: $3.00
C1 Pat Studstill..............................$5.00
C2 Bob Whitlow................................$3.00
C3 Wayne Walker.............................$3.00
C4 Tom Watkins...............................$3.00
C5 Jim Simon..................................$3.00
C6 Sam Williams.............................$3.00
C7 Terry Barr..................................$3.00
C8 Jerry Rush.................................$3.00
C9 Roger Brown...............................$3.00
C10 Tom Nowatzke...........................$3.00
C11 Dick Lane.................................$8.00
C12 Dick Compton...........................$3.00
C13 Yale Lary.................................$8.00
C14 Dick Lebeau.............................$6.00
C15 Dan Lewis................................$3.00
C16 Wally Hilgenburg........................$3.00
C17 Bruce Maher.............................$3.00
C18 Darri s McCord..........................$3.00
C19 Hugh McInnis............................$3.00
C20 Ernie Clark...............................$3.00
C21 Gail Cogdill..............................$3.00
C22 Wayne Rasmussen......................$3.00
C23 Joe Don Looney........................$10.00
C24 Jim Gibbons..............................$3.00
C25 John Gonzaga............................$3.00
C26 John Gordy...............................$3.00
C27 Bobby Thompson........................$3.00
C28 J.D. Smith................................$3.00
C29 Earl Morrall..............................$5.00
C30 Alex Karras..............................$7.00
C31 Nick Pietrosante........................$5.00
C32 Milt Plum.................................$5.00
C33 Daryl Sanders...........................$3.00
C34 Joe Schmidt..............................$8.00
C35 Bob Scholtz..............................$3.00
C36 Team logo................................$3.00

1965 New York Giants

Complete set NM (35): $100.00
Common player: $3.00
G1 Joe Morrison..............................$3.00
G2 Dick Lynch.................................$3.00
G3 Andy Stynchula...........................$3.00
G4 Clarence Childs...........................$3.00
G5 Aaron Thomas.............................$3.00
G6 Mickey Walker.............................$3.00
G7 Bill Winter.................................$3.00
G8 Bookie Bolin...............................$3.00
G9 Tom Scott..................................$3.00
G10 John Lovetere............................$3.00
G11 Jim Patton................................$3.00
G12 Darrell Dess.............................$3.00
G13 Dick James..............................$3.00
G14 Jerry Hillebrand.........................$3.00
G15 Dick Pesonen............................$3.00
G16 Del Shofner..............................$6.00
G17 Erich Bames.............................$3.00
G18 Roosevelt Brown........................$8.00
G19 Greg Larson.............................$3.00
G20 Jim Katcavage...........................$4.00
G21 Frank Lasky..............................$3.00
G22 Lou Slaby.................................$3.00
G23 Jim Moran................................$3.00

G24 Roger Anderson.........................$3.00
G25 Steve Thurlow...........................$3.00
G26 Ernie Wheelwright......................$3.00
G27 Gary Wood................................$3.00
G28 Tony Dimidio.............................$3.00
G29 John Contoulis...........................$3.00
G30 Tucker Frederickson....................$6.00
G31 Bob Timberlake..........................$3.00
G32 Chuck Mercein...........................$3.00
G33 Ernie Koy.................................$3.00
G34 Tom Costello.............................$3.00
G35 Homer Jones.............................$3.00

1965 New York Jets

Complete set NM (35): $120.00
Common player: $3.00
J1 Don Maynard...............................$8.00
J2 George Sauer..............................$6.00
J3 Cosmo Iacavazzi..........................$3.00
J4 Jim O'Mahoncy.............................$3.00
J5 Matt Snell..................................$7.00
J6 Clyde Washington.........................$3.00
J7 Jim Turner..................................$5.00
J8 Mike Tailaferro............................$3.00
J9 Marshall Starks............................$3.00
J10 Mark Smolinski...........................$3.00
J11 Bob Schweickert.........................$3.00
J12 Paul Rochester...........................$3.00
J13 Sherman Plunkett........................$3.00
J14 Gerry Philbin.............................$5.00
J15 Pete Perreault............................$3.00
J16 Dainard Paulson.........................$3.00
J17 Joe Namath..............................$60.00
J18 Winston Hill..............................$3.00
19 Dee Mackey................................$3.00
J20 Curley Johnson...........................$3.00
J21 Mike Hudock..............................$3.00
J22 John Huarte...............................$6.00
J23 Gordy Holz................................$3.00
J24 Gene Heeler..............................$4.50
J25 Larry Grantham...........................$6.00
J26 Dan Ficca.................................$3.00
J27 Sam DeLuca...............................$3.00
J28 Bill Baird..................................$3.00
J29 Ralph Baker...............................$3.00
J30 Wahoo McDaniel.........................$8.00
J31 Jim Evans.................................$3.00
J32 Dave Herman.............................$4.00
J33 John Schmitt..............................$3.00
J34 Jim Harris.................................$3.00
J35 Bake Turner...............................$3.00

1965 Washington Redskins

Complete Set NM (36): $75.00
Common player: $3.00
C1 undetermined
C2 Fred Mazurek..............................$3.00
C3 Lonnie Sanders............................$3.00
C4 Jim Steffen................................$3.00
C5 John Nisby.................................$3.00
C6 George Izo.................................$6.00
C7 Vince Promuto.............................$3.00
C8 John Sample...............................$3.00
C9 Pat Richter.................................$3.00
C10 Preston Carpenter.......................$3.00
C11 Sam Huff..................................$8.00
C12 Pervis Atkins.............................$3.00
C13 Fred Barnett..............................$3.00
C14 undetermined
C15 Bill Anderson............................$3.00
C16 undetermined
C17 George Seals.............................$3.00
C18 undetermined

C19 undetermined
C20 undetermined
C21 John Paluck...............................$3.00
C22 Fran O'Brien..............................$3.00
C23 Joe Rutgens...............................$3.00
C24 Rod Breedlove............................$3.00
C25 undetermined
C26 Bob Jencks................................$3.00
C27 undetermined
C28 Sonny Jurgensen........................$10.00
C29 Bob Toneff.................................$3.00
C30 Charley Taylor............................$8.00
C31 Bob Shiner................................$3.00
C32 Bob Williams.............................$3.00
C33 undetermined
C34 Ron Snidow...............................$3.00
C35 Paul Krause...............................$7.00
C36 Team logo................................$3.00

1966 Coca-Cola
National NFL bottle caps

Complete set NM (70): $175.00
Common player: $2.50
1) Larry Wi lson...............................$5.00
2) Frank Ryan.................................$4.00
3) Norm Snead................................$3.00
4) Mel Renfro..................................$5.00
5) Timmy Brown...............................$3.00
6) Tucker Frederickson.......................$2.50
7) Jim Bakken.................................$2.50
8) Paul Krause.................................$5.00
9) Irv Cross....................................$3.00
10) Cornell Green.............................$2.50
11) Pat Fischer................................$2.50
12) Bob Hayes.................................$6.00
13) Charley Taylor............................$6.00
14) Pete Retzlaff.............................$2.50
15) Jim Ringo..................................$5.00
16) Maxie Baughan............................$3.00
17) Chuck Howley.............................$3.00
18) John Wooten...............................$2.50
19) Bob DeMarco...............................$2.50
20) Dale Meinert...............................$2.50
21) Gene Hickerson...........................$2.50
22) George Andrie.............................$2.50
23) Joe Rutgens................................$2.50
24) Bob Lilly...................................$8.00
25) Sam Silas..................................$2.50
26) Bob Brown.................................$3.00
27) Dick Schafrath............................$2.50
28) Roosevelt Brown..........................$5.00
29) Jim Houston...............................$2.50
30) Paul Wiggin................................$2.50
31) Gary Ballman..............................$2.50
32) Gary Collins...............................$3.00
33) Sonny Randle..............................$3.00
34) Charlie Johnson...........................$3.00
35) Cleveland Browns logo..................$2.50
36) Green Bay Packers logo.............$2.50
37) Herb Adderley.............................$5.00
38) Grady Alderman...........................$2.50
39) Doug Atkins................................$5.00
40) Bruce Bosley..............................$2.50
41) John Brodie................................$6.00
42) Roger Brown...............................$2.50
43) Bill Brown..................................$3.00
44) Dick Butkus................................$9.00
45) Lee Roy Caffey............................$2.50
46) John David Crow..........................$3.00
47) Willie Davis................................$5.00
48) Mike Ditka.................................$9.00
49) Joe Fortunato.............................$2.50

50) John Gordy $2.50
51) Deacon Jones $6.00
52) Alex Karras $6.00
53) Dick LeBeau $2.50
54) Jerry Logan $2.50
55) John Mackey $5.00
56) Ed Meador $2.50
57) Tommy McDonald $4.00
58) Merlin Olsen $5.00
59) Jimmy Orr $3.00
60) Jim Parker $5.00
61) Dave Parks $3.00
62) Walter Rock $2.50
63) Gale Sayers $11.00
64) Pat Studstill $2.50
65) Fran Tarkenton $9.00
66) Mick Tingelhoff $3.00
67) Bob Vogel $2.50
68) Wayne Walker $3.00
69) Ken Willard $3.00
70) Willie Wood $4.00

1966 Coca-Cola AFL/NFL All-Stars bottle caps

These caps, each measuring 1 1/8" in diameter, could be found under bottle caps of Coca-Cola products (Coke, Tab, Fresca) in participating cities with AFL or NFL teams. The cap has a Coke logo and a football on the outside; the player's mug shot, name, position, number and AFL or NFL were included on the inside of the cap. A Cap Saver sheet, indicating cap numbers, was also issued, caps could be affixed to the sheet. Completed sheets could be turned in for prizes.

1966 AFL Stars

Complete set NM (34): $125.00
Common player: $3.00
C37 Babe Parilli (Boston Patriots) $5.00
C38 Mike Stratton (Buffalo Bills) $5.00
C39 Jack Kemp (Buffalo Bills) $25.00
C40 Len Dawson (Kansas City Chiefs) $10.00
C41 Fred Arbanas (Kansas City Chiefs) $3.00
C42 Bobby Bell (Kansas City Chiefs) $7.00
C43 Willie Brown (Oakland Raiders) . $7.00
C44 Buck Buchanan (Kansas City Chiefs) $7.00
C45 Frank Buncom (San Diego Chargers) $3.00
C46 Nick Buoniconti (Boston Patriots) ..$7.00
C47 Gino Cappelletti (Boston Patriots) .$5.00
C48 Eldon Danenhauer (Denver Broncos) $3.00
C49 Clem Daniels (Oakland Raiders) $4.00
C50 Leslie Duncan (San Diego Chargers) $3.00
C51 Willie Frazier (Kansas City Chiefs) $3.00
C52 Cookie Gilchrist (Miami Dolphins) .$8.00
C53 Dave Grayson (Oakland Raiders)..$3.00
C54 John Hadl (San Diego Chargers) ..$6.00
C55 Wayne Hawkins (Oakland Raiders) $3.00
C56 Sherrill Headrick (K. C. Chiefs) .. $3.00
C57 Charlie Hennigan (Houston Oilers) $4.00
C58 E.J. Holub (Kansas City Chiefs) $3.00
C59 Curley Johnson (New York Jets)....$3.00
C60 Keith Lincoln (San Diego Chargers) $4.00
C61 Paul Lowe (San Diego Chargers) ..$5.00

C62 Don Maynard (New York Jets) ... $7.00
C63 Jon Morris (Boston Patriots) $3.00
C64 Joe Namath (New York Jets) ... $30.00
C65 Jim Otto (Oakland Raiders) $7.00
C66 Dainard Paulson (New York Jets) ..$3.00
C67 Art Powell (Oakland Raiders) $3.00
C68 Walt Sweeney (San Diego Chargers) $3.00
C69 Bob Talamini (Houston Oilers) ... $3.00
C70 Lance Alworth (San Diego Chargers, misspelled Alsworth) $12.00

1966 NFL Stars

Complete set NM (34): $100.00
Common player: $2.50
C37 Frank Ryan (Cleveland Browns) $4.00
C38 Timmy Brown (Philadelphia Eagles) $3.00
C39 Tucker Frederickson (New York Giants) $3.00
C40 Cornell Green (Dallas Cowboys) $3.00
C41 Bob Hayes (Dallas Cowboys) $6.00
C42 Charley Taylor (Washington Redskins) $6.00
C43 Pete Retzlaff (Philadelphia Eagles) $3.00
C44 Jim Ringo (Green Bay Packers) $5.00
C45 John Wooten (Cleveland Browns) .$2.50
C46 Dale Meinert (St. Louis Cardinals) $2.50
C47 Bob Lilly (Dallas Cowboys) $8.00
C48 Sam Silas (St. Louis Cardinals) . $2.50
C49 Roosevelt Brown (New York Giants) $5.00
C50 Gary Ballman (Pittsburgh Steelers) $3.00
C51 Gary Collins (Cleveland Browns)...$3.00
C52 Sonny Randle (St. Louis Cardinals) $3.00
C53 Charlie Johnson (St. Louis Cardinals) $3.00
C54 Herb Adderley (Green Bay Packers) $5.00
C55 Doug Atkins (Chicago Bears) $5.00
C56 Roger Brown (Detroit Lions) $3.00
C57 Dick Butkus (Chicago Bears)..... $9.00
C58 Willie Davis (Green Bay Packers)..$5.00
C59 Tommy McDonald (Los Angeles Rams) $3.00
C60 Alex Karras (Detroit Lions) $6.00
C61 John Mackey (Baltimore Colts) .. $5.00
C62 Ed Meador (Los Angeles Rams) $2.50
C63 Merlin Olsen (Los Angeles Rams).$3.00
C64 Dave Parks (San Francisco 49ers) $2.50
C65 Gale Sayers (Chicago Bears) .. $11.00
C66 Fran Tarkenton (Minnesota Vikings) $7.00
C67 Mick Tingelhoff (Minnesota Vikings) $2.50
C68 Ken Willard (San Francisco 49ers) $2.50
C69 Willie Wood (Green Bay Packers) .$4.00
C70 Bill Brown (Minnesota Vikings) .. $2.50

1966 Coca-Cola bottle caps

1966 Atlanta Falcons

Complete set NM (36): $75.00
Common player: $3.00
C1 Tommy Nobis $6.00
C2 Ernie Wheelright $3.00
C3 Lee Calland $3.00
C4 Chuck Sieminski $3.00
C5 Dennis Claridge $3.00
C6 Ralph Heck $3.00
C7 Alex Hawkins $4.00

C8 Dan Grimm $3.00
C9 Marion Rushing $3.00
C10 Bobbie Johnson....................... $3.00
C11 Bobby Franklin $3.00
C12 Bill McWatters......................... $3.00
C13 Billy Lothridge $3.00
C14 Billy Martin $3.00
C15 Tom Wilson $3.00
C16 Dennis Murphy $3.00
C17 Randy Johnson $4.00
C18 Guy Reese $3.00
C19 Frank Marchiewski $3.00
C20 Don Talbert $3.00
C21 Errol Linden $3.00
C22 Dan Lewis $3.00
C23 Ed Cook $3.00
C24 Hugh McInnis $3.00
C25 Frank Lasky $3.00
C26 Bob Jencks $3.00
C27 Bill Jobko $3.00
C28 Nick Rassas $3.00
C29 Rob Riggle $3.00
C30 Ken Reaves $3.00
C31 Bob Sanders $3.00
C32 Steve Sloan $4.00
C33 Ron Smith $3.00
C34 Bob Whitlow........................... $3.00
C35 Roger Anderson $3.00
C36 Falcons logo $3.00

1966 Baltimore Colts

Complete set NM (36): $100.00
Common player: $3.00
Cl Ted Davis $3.00
C2 Bobby Boyd $4.00
C3 Lenny Moore............................ $7.00
C4 Jackie Burkett $3.00
C5 Jimmy Orr $6.00
C6 Andy Stynchula......................... $3.00
C7 Mike Curtis $6.00
C8 Jerry Logan $3.00
C9 Steve Stonebreaker $3.00
C10 John Mackey........................... $8.00
C11 Dennis Gaubatz $3.00
C12 Don Shinnick $3.00
C13 Dick Szymanski $3.00
C14 Ordell Braase.......................... $3.00
C15 Len Lyles $3.00
C16 Rick Kestner $3.00
C17 Dan Sullivan $3.00
C18 Lou Michaels $3.00
C19 Gary Cuozzo $3.00
C20 Butch Wilson........................... $3.00
C21 Willie Richardson...................... $3.00
C22 Jim Welch. $3.00
C23 Tony Lorick............................. $3.00
C24 Billy Ray Smith........................ $3.00
C25 Fred Miller $3.00
C26 Tom Matte $5.00
C27 John Unitas............................ $16.00
C28 Glenn Ressler $3.00
C29 Alvin Haymond......................... $3.00
C30 Jim Parker.............................. $6.00
C31 Butch Allison $3.00
C32 Bob Vogel $3.00
C33 Jerry Hill $3.00
C34 Raymond Berry $8.00
C35 Sam Ball $3.00
C36 Colts logo $3.00

1966 Boston Patriots

Complete set NM (36) $120.00

Common player: $3.00
C1 Jon Morris $3.00
C2 Don Webb $3.00
C3 Charles Long $3.00
C4 Tony Romeo $3.00
C5 Bob Dee $3.00
C6 Tom Addison $3.00
C7 Tom Neville $3.00
C8 Ron Hall $3.00
C9 White Graves $3.00
C10 Ellis Johnson $3.00
C11 Don Oakes $3.00
C12 Tom Yewcic $3.00
C13 Tom Hennessey $3.00
C14 Jay Cunningham $3.00
C15 Larry Garron $3.00
C16 Justin Canale $3.00
C17 Art Graham $3.00
C18 Babe Parilli $3.00
C19 Jim Hunt $3.00
C20 Karl Singer $3.00
C21 Houston Antwine $3.00
C22 Nick Buoniconti $6.00
C23 John Huarte $5.00
C24 Gino Cappelletti $3.00
C25 Chuck Shonta $3.00
C26 Dick Felt $3.00
C27 Mike Dukes $3.00
C28 Larry Eisenhauer $3.00
C29 Jim Fraser $3.00
C30 Len St. Jean $3.00
C31 J.D. Garrett $3.00
C32 Jim Whalen $3.00
C33 Jim Nance $6.00
C34 Dick Arrington $3.00
C35 Lonnie Fanner $3.00
C36 Patriots logo $3.00

1966 Buffalo Bills
Complete set NM (36): $120.00
Common player: $3.00
B1 Bill Laskey $3.00
B2 Marty Schottenheimer $8.00
B3 Stew Barber $4.00
B4 Glenn Bass $3.00
B5 Remi Prudhomme $3.00
B6 Al Bemiller $3.00
B7 Butch Byrd $3.00
B8 Wray Carlton $4.00
B9 Hagood Clarke $3.00
B10 Jack Kemp $40.00
B11 Charley Warner $3.00
B12 Elbert Dubenion $6.00
B13 Jim Dunaway $3.00
B14 Booker Edgerson $3.00
B15 Paul Costa $3.00
B16 Henry Schmidt $3.00
B17 Dick Hudson $3.00
B18 Harry Jacobs $3.00
B19 Tom Janik $3.00
B20 Tom Day $3.00
B21 Daryle Lamonica $10.00
B22 Paul Maguire $6.00
B23 Roland McDole $3.00
B24 Dudley Merideth $3.00
B25 Joe O'Donnell $3.00
B26 Charley Ferguson $3.00
B27 Ed Rutkowski $3.00
B28 George Saimes $4.00
B29 Tom Sestak $3.00
B30 Billy Shaw $3.00
B31 Bob Smith $3.00

B32 Mike Stratton $3.00
B33 Gene Sykes $3.00
B34 John Tracey $3.00
B35 Ernie Warlick $3.00
B36 Bills logo $3.00

1966 Cleveland Browns
Complete set NM (36): $100.00
Common player: $3.00
C1 Jim Ninowski $3.00
C2 Leroy Kelly $8.00
C3 Lou Groza $8.00
C4 Gary Collins $4.00
C5 Bill Glass $3.00
C6 Dale Lindsey $3.00
C7 Galen Fiss $3.00
C8 Ross Fichtner $3.00
C9 John Wooten $3.00
C10 Clifton McNeil $3.00
C11 Paul Wiggin $3.00
C12 Gene Hickerson $3.00
C13 Ernie Green $3.00
C14 Mike Howell $3.00
C15 Dick Schafrath $3.00
C16 Sidney Williams $3.00
C17 Frank Ryan $6.00
C18 Bernie Parrish $3.00
C19 Vince Costello $3.00
C20 John Brown $3.00
C21 Monte Clark $3.00
C22 Walt Roberts $3.00
C23 Johnny Brewer $3.00
C24 Walter Beach $3.00
C25 Dick Modzelewski $3.00
C26 Gary Lane $3.00
C27 Jim Houston $3.00
C28 Milt Morin $3.00
C29 Erich Bames $3.00
C30 Tom Hutchinson $3.00
C31 John Morrow $3.00
C32 Jim Kanicki $3.00
C33 Paul Warfield $10.00
C34 Jim Garcia $3.00
C35 Walter Johnson $3.00
C36 Browns logo $3.00

1966 Dallas Cowboys
Complete set NM (36): $100.00
Common player: $3.00
C1 Mike Connelly $3.00
C2 Tony Liscio $3.00
C3 Jethro Pugh $6.00
C4 Larry Stephens $3.00
C5 Jim Colvin $3.00
C6 Malcolm Walker $3.00
C7 Danny Villanueva $3.00
C8 Frank Clarke $3.00
C9 Don Meredith $12.00
C10 George Andrie $3.00
C11 Mel Renfro $6.00
C12 Pettis Norman $3.00
C13 Buddy Dial $3.00
C14 Pete Gent $3.00
C15 Jerry Rhome $3.00
C16 Bob Hayes $6.00
C17 Mike Gaechter $3.00
C18 Joe Bob Isbell $3.00
C19 Harold Hays $3.00
C20 Craig Morton $6.00
C21 Jake Kupp $3.00
C22 Cornell Green. $3.00
C23 Dan Reeves $10.00
C24 Leon Donohue $3.00

C25 Dave Manders $3.00
C26 Warren Livingston $3.00
C27 Bob Lilly $8.00
C28 Chuck Howley $5.00
C29 Don Bishop $3.00
C30 Don Perkins $3.00
C31 Jim Boeke $3.00
C32 Dave Edwards $3.00
C33 Lee Roy Jordan $7.00
C34 Obert Logan $3.00
C35 Ralph Neely $3.00
C36 Cowboys logo $3.00

1966 Houston Oilers
Complete set NM (36): $120.00
Common player: $3.00
C1 Scott Appleton $3.00
C2 George Allen $3.00
C3 Don Floyd $3.00
C4 Ronnie Caveness $3.00
C5 Jim Norton $3.00
C6 Jackie Lee $3.00
C7 George Blanda $10.00
C8 Tony Banfield $3.00
C9 George Rice $3.00
C10 Charley Tolar $5.00
C11 Bobby Jancik $3.00
C12 Fred Glick $3.00
C13 Ode Burrell $3.00
C14 Wait Suggs $3.00
C15 Bob McLeod $3.00
C16 Johnny Baker $3.00
C17 Danny Bradshaw $3.00
C18 Gary Cutsinger $3.00
C19 Doug Cline $3.00
C20 Hoyle Granger $3.00
C21 Bob Talamini $3.00
C22 Don Trull $3.00
C23 Charlie Hennigan $5.00
C24 Sid Blanks. $3.00
C25 Pat Holmes $3.00
C26 John Frongilto $3.00
C27 John Whitehom $3.00
C28 George Kinney $3.00
C29 Charles Frazier $3.00
C30 Ernie Ladd $8.00
C31 W.K. Hicks $3.00
C32 Sonny Bishop $3.00
C33 Larry Elkins $3.00
C34 Glen Ray Hines $3.00
C35 Bobby Maples $3.00
C36 Oilers logo $3.00

1966 Kansas City Chiefs
Complete set NM (36): $120.00
Common player: $3.00
C1 E.J. Holub $4.00
C2 Al Reynolds $3.00
C3 Buck Buchanan $7.00
C4 Curt Metz $8.00
C5 David Hill $3.00
C6 Bobby Hunt $3.00
C7 Jerry Mays $5.00
C8 Joe Gilliam $3.00
C9 Wait Corey $3.00
C10 Solomon Brannan $3.00
C11 Aaron Brown $3.00
C12 Bert Coan $3.00
C13 Ed Budde $3.00
C14 Tommy Brooker $3.00
C15 Bobby Bell $8.00
C16 Smokey Stover $3.00
C17 Curtis McClinton $4.00

C18 Jerrel Wilson $5.00
C19 Ron Burton................................ $3.00
C20 Mike Garrett $10.00
C21 Jim Tyrer $4.00
C22 Johnny Robinson $6.00
C23 Bobby Ply $3.00
C24 Frank Pitts $3.00
C25 Ed Lothamer $3.00
C26 Sherrill Headrick $3.00
C27 Fred Williamson $6.00
C28 Chris Burford $3.00
C29 Willie Mitchell $3.00
C30 Otis Taylor $6.00
C31 Fred Arbanas $3.00
C32 Hatch Rosdahl $3.00
C33 Reg Carolan $3.00
C34 Len Dawson $12.00
C35 Pete Beathard $5.00
C36 Chiefs logo $3.00

1966 Los Angeles Rams

Complete set NM (36): $100.00
Common player: $3.00
C1 Tom Mack................................. $5.00
C2 Tom Moore $3.00
C3 Bill Munson $4.00
C4 Bill George $5.00
C5 Joe Carollo $3.00
C6 Dick Bass $5.00
C7 Ken Iman $3.00
C8 Charlie Cowam $4.00
C9 Terry Baker $3.00
C10 Don Chuy $3.00
C11 Jack Pardee $6.00
C12 Lamar Lundy $3.00
C13 Bill Anderson $3.00
C14 Roman Gabriel.......................... $7.00
C15 Roosevelt Grier $6.00
C16 Billy Truax $3.00
C17 Merlin Olsen $8.00
C18 Deacon Jones........................... $6.00
C19 Joe Scibelli $3.00
C20 Marlin McKeever $3.00
C21 Doug Woodlief $3.00
C22 Chuck Lamson $3.00
C23 Dan Currie $3.00
C24 Maxie Baughan $3.00
C25 Bruce Gossett $3.00
C26 Les Josephson.......................... $3.00
C27 Ed Meador $3.00
C28 Anthony Guillory $3.00
C29 Irv Cross $3.00
C30 Tommy McDonald $3.00
C31 Bucky Pope $3.00
C32 Jack Snow............................... $5.00
C33 Joe Wendryhoski $3.00
C34 Clancy Williams $3.00
C35 Ben Wilson $3.00
C36 Rams logo............................... $3.00

1966 New York Giants

Complete set NM (35): $100.00
Common player: $2.50
G1 Joe Morrison $3.00
G2 Dick Lynch $3.00
G3 Pete Case $2.50
G4 Clarence Childs $2.50
G5 Aaron Thomas $2.50
G6 Jim Carroll $2.50
G7 Henry Carr................................ $3.00
G8 Bookie Bolin $2.50
G9 Roosevelt Davis $2.50
G10 John Lovetere $2.50

G11 Jim Patton................................ $3.00
G12 Wendell Harris $2.50
G13 Roger LaLonde $2.50
G14 Jerry Hillebrand $2.50
G15 Carl Lockhart............................ $3.00
G16 Del Shofner $4.50
G17 Earl Morrall $5.00
G18 Roosevelt Brown........................ $5.00
G19 Greg Larson $2.50
G20 Jim Katcavage $3.00
G21 Smith Reed $2.50
G22 Lou Slaby................................ $2.50
G23 Jim Moran $2.50
G24 Bill Swain $2.50
G25 Steve Thurlow $2.50
G26 Olen Underwood $2.50
G27 Gary Wood $3.00
G28 Larry Vargo $3.00
G29 Jim Prestel.............................. $2.50
G30 Tucker Frederickson $3.00
G31 Bob Timberlake $3.00
G32 Chuck Mercein.......................... $3.00
G33 Ernie Koy $3.00
G34 Tom Costello $2.50
G35 Homer Jones $3.00

1966 New York Jets

Complete set NM (35) $120.00
Common player: $2.50
J1 Don Maynard $5.00
J2 George Sauer $3.00
J3 Paul Crane $2.50
J4 Jim Colclough $2.50
J5 Matt Snell $5.00
J6 Sherman Lewis $3.00
J7 Jim Turner................................ $3.00
J8 Mike Taliaferro $3.00
J9 Cornell Gordon $2.50
J10 Mark Smolinski $2.50
J11 Al Atkinson $3.00
J12 Paul Rochester $2.50
J13 Sherman Plunkett....................... $2.50
J14 Gerry Philbin $3.00
J15 Pete Lammons $3.00
J16 Dainard Paulson $2.50
J17 Joe Namath $25.00
J18 Winston Hill $2.50
J19 Dee Mackey $2.50
J20 Curley Johnson.......................... $2.50
J21 Verlon Biggs $3.00
J22 Bill Mathis $3.00
J23 Carl McAdams $2.50
J24 Bert Wilder............................... $2.50
J25 Larry Grantham $3.00
J26 Bill Yearby $2.50
J27 Sam DeLuca............................... $2.50
J28 Bill Baird $2.50
J29 Ralph Baker $2.50
J30 Ray Abruzzese $2.50
J31 Jim Hudson $2.50
J32 Dave Hennan $2.50
J33 John Schmitt.............................. $2.50
J34 Jim Harris $2.50
J35 Bake Turner $3.00

1966 Pittsburgh Steelers

Complete set NM (36): $100.00
Common player: $2.50
C1 John Baker................................ $2.50
C2 Mike Lind $3.00
C3 Ken Kortas $2.50
C4 Willie Daniel $2.50
C5 Roy Jefferson............................. $4.00

C6 Bob Hohn $2.50
C7 Dan James $2.50
C8 Gary Ballman $5.00
C9 Brady Keys $2.50
C10 Charley Bradshaw $3.00
C11 Jim Bradshaw........................... $2.50
C12 Jim Butler................................ $2.50
C13 Paul Martha $5.00
C14 Mike Clark............................... $2.50
C15 Ray Lemek $2.50
C16 Clarence Peaks $3.00
C17 Theron Sapp $3.00
C18 Ray Mansfield $2.50
C19 Chuck Hinton $2.50
C20 Bill Nelsen............................... $6.00
C21 Rod Breedlove $2.50
C22 Frank Lambert $2.50
C23 Ben McGee $2.50
C24 Myron Pottios $3.00
C25 John Campbell........................... $2.50
C26 Andy Russell............................. $5.00
C27 Mike Sandusky $2.50
C28 Bob Schmitz $2.50
C29 Riley Gunnels $2.50
C30 Clendon Thomas $3.00
C31 Tommy Wade............................. $2.50
C32 Dick Hoak $3.50
C33 Marv Woodson $2.50
C34 Bob Nichols $2.50
C35 John Henry Johnson $6.00
C36 Steelers logo............................. $2.50

1966 St. Louis Cardinals

Complete set NM (36): $100.00
Common player: $2.50
C1 Pat Fischer $3.00
C2 Sonny Randle $3.00
C3 Joe Childress $2.50
C4 Dave Meggysey, misspelled
    Meggyesy $5.00
C5 Joe Robb $2.50
C6 Jerry Stovall $3.00
C7 Ernie McMillan............................ $3.00
C8 Dale Meinert $2.50
C9 Irv Goode.................................. $2.50
C10 Bob DeMarco............................. $3.00
C11 Mal Hammack............................ $2.50
C12 Jim Bakken $5.00
C13 Bill Thomton............................. $2.50
C14 Buddy Humphrey........................ $2.50
C15 Bill Koman $2.50
C16 Larry Wilson $8.00
C17 Charles Walker $2.50
C18 Prentice Gautt............................ $5.00
C19 Charlie Johnson, misspelled
    Charley................................. $6.00
C20 Ken Gray.................................. $3.00
C21 Dave Simmons $3.00
C22 Sam Silas $2.50
C23 Larry Stallings............................ $3.00
C24 Don Brumm $2.50
C25 Bobby Joe Conrad $3.00
C26 Bill Triplett $2.50
C27 Luke Owens $2.50
C28 Jackie Smith.............................. $6.00
C29 Bob Reynolds $2.50
C30 Abe Woodson $3.00
C31 Jimmy Burson $2.50
C32 Willis Crenshaw $2.50
C33 Billy Gambrell $2.50
C34 Ray Ogden $2.50
C35 Herschel Turner $2.50

C36 Cardinals logo $2.50

1966 San Francisco 49ers

Complete set NM (36) $100.00
Common player: $2.50
C1 Bernie Casey $6.00
C2 Bruce Bosley $3.00
C3 Kermit Alexander $6.00
C4 John Brodie $10.00
C5 Dave Parks $3.00
C6 Len Rohde $2.50
C7 Walter Rock $2.50
C8 George Mira $5.00
C9 Karl Rubke $2.50
CIO Ken Willard $3.00
C11 John David Crow, misspelled
    Crowe $6.00
C12 George Donnelly $2.50
C13 Dave Wilcox $6.00
C14 Vern Burke $2.50
C15 Wayne Swinford $2.50
C16 Elbert Kimbrough $2.50
C17 Clark Miller $2.50
C18 Dave Kopay $3.00
C19 Joe Cerne $2.50
C20 Roland Lakes $2.50
C21 Charlie Krueger $3.00

C22 Billy Kilmer $7.00
C23 Jim Johnson $7.00
C24 Matt Hazeltine $2.50
C25 Mike Dowdle $2.50
C26 Jim Wilson $2.50
C27 Tommy Davis $3.00
C28 Jim Norton $2.50
C29 Jack Chapple $2.50
C30 Ed Beard $2.50
C31 John Thomas $2.50
C32 Monty Stickles $3.00
C33 Kay McFarland $3.00
C34 Gary Lewis $2.50
C35 Howard Mudd $2.50
C36 49ers logo $2.50

1971 Coca-Cola Green Bay Packer bottle caps

This 22-cap set, sponsored by Coca-Cola, features members of the Green Bay Packers. Each player's face is printed in black below his picture. The unnumbered caps, which measure approximately 1 1/8" in diameter, are listed alphabetically.

Complete set NM (22): $20.00
Common player: $1.00
1) Ken Bowman $1.00
2) John Brockington $2.50
3) Bob Brown $1.50
4) Fred Carr $1.50
5) Jim Carter $1.00
6) Carroll Dale $1.50
7) Ken Ellis $1.00
8) Gale Gillingham $1.50
9) Dave Hampton $1.50
10) Doug Hart $1.00
11) Jim Hill $1.00
12) Dick Himes $1.00
13) Scott Hunter $1.50
14) MacArthur Lane $2.50
15) Bill Lueck $1.00
16) Al Matthews $1.00
17) Rich McGeorge $1.00
18) Ray Nitschke $5.00
19) Francis Peay $1.00
20) Dave Robinson $1.50
21) Alden Roche $1.00
22) Bart Starr $7.50

Beer Nuts

Collectors Who Are Looking For A New Inexpensive Niche
May Want To Try Sports-Related Beer Cans

By Tom Hultman

Over the past few years, dealers, manufacturers and collectors have constantly been trying to find the next fad in the hobby. Since the mid-1990s, we've gone through POGs, Beanie Babies, Pokemon, jersey cards and bobbing heads.

There is another untapped sports collectible niche in the hobby that's about to have its top popped – sports-related beer cans.

Beer can collecting enjoyed its heyday in the mid-to-late 1970s and quickly faded away into oblivion.

Today, collectors may not have considered beer cans as a collectible. But with the recent influx of sports-related commemorative cans to a cooler near you, there are plenty from which to choose, many of them priced at less than $3.

Brewers like Anheuser-Busch, Coors, Heileman, Miller and Pittsburgh – the makers of Iron City Beer and the brewery that built the foundation for the sports commemorative cans – have produced cans honoring team and ex-player feats, along with tributes to major sporting events.

THE BEGINNINGS

Tracing the roots of the commemorative sports beer can phenomenon is not as clear-cut as one would think. According to beer can collector and checklister Bruce Remick of Springfield, Va., the first sports tribute can honored the Florida-Georgia Gator Bowl in Jacksonville, Fla., in 1963. The 16-ounce can, produced by Schlitz, is priced at $200-$300 today.

(Editor's note: The first beer cans with a sports theme – hunting, fishing, bowling, etc. – were produced in the 1950s. Brands like Pfeiffer, Meister Brau, Drewrys, Rainer and Schmidt had sports themes, but for this story we are not including those cans, as they featured general sports artwork and were not commemorative cans.)

Seven years later, in 1970, National produced two commemorative cans – A-1 Beer with the Phoenix Suns schedule and A-1 with the Phoenix Roadrunners schedule. Both featured bank tops (a slot in the top of the can) and didn't contain beer. Each is valued at $125-$150. In addition, Carling honored the 1969-70 Boston Bruins with a can that would set you back $30-$35 today.

That Bruins can lit a spark under Remick and led him down the road of beer can collecting.

"I started collecting cans in 1975," he said. "Before that I collected 12-ounce long-neck bottles when I traveled on business to different states. Someone gave me a Carling's Black Label Boston Bruins 1969-70 Stanley Cup can and it got me to looking in my local stores for other interesting beer cans and brands. I started buying different six-packs and soon had started a collection. I met others in the area who also collected and the bug has stayed with me ever since. But the main thing that has kept me going in the hobby was the great friendships I developed over the years."

Goldmine editor Greg Loescher of Iola, Wis., tailored his collection to focus on only sports-related beer cans. He began his quest in the early '80s and has now amassed 75.

"Sports-related cans are a lot more interesting than just the regular cans from the breweries," he said. "Many of them commemorate specific events, such as the Super Bowl; are for specific years, such as those with college football team schedules; or just have great artwork on them.

"I like the Big 10 football cans a lot, since I am a Badger/Midwest football fan and because they are cool looking."

A few commemorative sports beer cans hit the hobby between 19971-72, but the real explosion hit in 1973 when the Pittsburgh Brewing Co. struck a chord with sports fans and collectors with its Iron City "Pour It On Steelers" can that features the 1972 team's results and a 1973 schedule.

That can opened the floodgates for Pittsburgh Brewing, which is still producing commemorative cans today for the Steelers, Penguins and Pirates and its former players.

"Brewers overdid the commemorative can idea in the late-1970s to early 1980s, when it seemed like every other new can produced was an air-sealed, private 'novelty' issue made for collectors," Remick said. "Many believe this frustrated many new young collectors to the hobby.

"Today, the amount of commemorative or special cans is tolerable to most who still collect all the new cans. Just a few years ago, though, there was the beginning of a collector backlash or turnoff when Anheuser-Busch kept turning out annual 18-can series of golf hole cans on three varieties of Michelob. Too many near identical cans for collectors who like to display their cans on shelves. Plus the retail distribution left much to be desired."

A VERSATILE, INEXPENSIVE HOBBY

The beauty of the sports beer cans is they are very inexpensive. Besides the early Steelers cans, which sell for up to $12, and a few rare cans from other breweries, many of the sports cans can be picked up in the $1-$5 range, with many of them at less than $3.

Take a look on eBay and you'll notice a majority of the sports-related beer cans sell for $2-$5 (not including shipping) with many of them receiving less than five bids. Some of them finish without receiving a bid, which means you won't have much competition when bidding.

"Sports-related beer cans on eBay have been pretty quiet for the past year or so," Remick said. "The collector-to-collector market for common sports cans has pretty much dried up. Demand has been satisfied, but this is a good thing for anyone who wants to start a new collection of sports cans from scratch."

If you're not a computer whiz, check out rummage sales or flea markets. Chances are you'll come across a few sports-related beer cans at bargain-basement prices.

"I recently went to a rummage sale and was shocked when I found three Bears 70th season Old Style cans for a quarter and they were full," said Tuff Stuff basketball and football price guide analyst Dan Loken, who has been collecting cans for 25 years. "A person can get most any can from the last 30 years or so for under a buck if you look hard enough. Typically at flea markets/rummage sales a person can make a deal and get a box full for only pennies a can. Last year I picked up a box of close to 100 cans for $5."

Loescher agreed: "First of all, building a collection is very inexpensive at this time. Even the highest-priced can is less than $100, with most well under $5. So financially it isn't like trying to build a set of 1950s Bowman Baseball cards. Since so many of the post-steel-era cans have been recycled, however, finding those of the last 20 years might be somewhat hard. On the positive side, for now anyway, they won't cost much."

Remick, who has approximately 1,500 different U.S. sports-related beer cans in his collection, including some foreign cans which feature United States sports teams or players, said the great thing about collecting sports beer cans is there are no rules.

In other words, tailor your collection to serve your interests. If you're a college football fan, collect only those cans. According to our price guide, there are approximately 45 cans to complete the set. On top of that, if you choose not to collect the rare, expensive cans, most of the cans are easy to find, with the majority priced at $2-$3.

"I think the only way for a novice to enjoy the hobby today is to specialize, to keep the bulk manageable," Remick said. "Many collectors save only cans from their home state, from certain brands or breweries, cone top cans, and, of course, things like cans with sports themes.

"Within the sports category, some save only cans for a particular sport, or ignore those cans with sports they don't care about. If you're one of those who chooses to collect beer cans as an investment, there's money to me made, but usually not by the uninformed new collector. If you've got bucks to spend, time to wait and beer cans are your choice, then I would look for the scarce, old cans in top condition for my portfolio. Put them away for 10 to 15 years, cross your fingers, and hope the demand is still strong when you opt to sell. If it is, you will probably make a good profit."

Chuck Starrett of Sarasota, Fla., said sports-themed beer cans are some of the most popular collector cans in the hobby today.

"I'm sure they have helped introduce some collectors to the hobby," said Starrett, who specializes in pre-1970 cans from Michigan-based breweries. "There is always room for another sports can. There are quite a few around and most of them are very readily available and not very pricey. I packed my cans up and kept them until a few years ago. Like a lot of collectors today I got back into it because of eBay. I can now afford some of the cans I always wanted."

Among Remick's favorite cans is a set of 16-ounce Budweiser cans, one of which was made each year from 1979-93 for annual employee golf tournaments at the Kingsmill Golf Course in Williamsburg, Va.

"The cans were given to the participants and weren't sold," he said. "Many of the years are extrememly hard to locate and only a few collectors have been able to complete the full set."

Remick also is partial to oddball and error sports cans. For example, the 1997 16-ounce Coors can saluting the Baltimore Ravens' 1996 season was used only at the stadium but the cans were quickly pulled because of NFL trademark violations.

"Ninety-five percent of these cans that survive today were salvaged at the stadium by a couple collectors and all had been opened from the top by vendors," Remick said. "A few full ones later appeared on the market from people on the 'inside' and I was able to get one of those. I'll keep that one full."

Another "phantom" can that made its way into the hobby was the Miller Lite 16-ounce Super Bowl XXXII Green Bay Packers, Back-To-Back Super Bowl Champions can. The cans were produced before the game and served to the media and VIPs, anticipating a Packers' victory over Denver. Of course, Terrell Davis and John Elway put a kink into Miller's plans and the cans were pulled and destroyed quickly, but not before some squeaked their way into collectors' hands. If you can find this can today, expect to spend $30-$40 for it.

GETTING STARTED IN THE HOBBY

OK, so now your juices are starting to flow about cans. If you're ready to leap into the sports been can arena, what should you do?

"I would recommend you first decide what you'd like to collect and find a checklist/price guide that lists all the cans that would complete your specialty," said Remick, who contributed a large portion of our beer can checklist/price guide in this issue. "Take note of any expensive cans and be sure these won't frustrate your goal. Make sure you've got the space to display them. Anticipate changes in your collecting goals – might you decide

next year to include those neat soft drink sports cans that feature your favorite team/players to your collection?"

To keep up on the latest shows around the country, check out the Beer Can Collectors of America Web site (www.bcca.com) that lists show locations. When attending shows, make sure to mention to dealers what you're collecting and you'll probably be able to come away with a few cases of the common issues for $10 or less.

"eBay would be my second choice after you've been able to obtain most of the cheaper common cans elsewhere," Remick said. "Seldom will you find an eBay auction that contains an assortment containing only cans that you need. That means storing extras (that nobody wants) and shipping costs for small lots of common cans gets expensive after a while. eBay is a good place to watch for any of the more difficult cans you're looking for. There also are a few beer can dealers on the Web who sell all the recent new cans. Search them out, too, for the latest issues that aren't sold where you live."

Starrett said newcomers shouldn't feel out of place when they enter the beer can hobby.

"The people in the hobby will welcome you and bend over backwards to help get you going," Starrett said. "I display my cans on a special shelf made to fit the cans. Being from Michigan, I love the Red Wings and the new Molson 5-liter can commemorating the 2002 Stanley Cup Championship is my favorite right now."

Obviously with all of the new commemorative sports-related cans that have been produced recently it's tough to keep up with the news. The most important thing to do is make some contacts in the hobby and find some top-notch Web sites, including Spencer's Beer Can Korner at www.zianet.com/spencer, which features photos and information about the latest cans.

RESURGENCE IN THE HOBBY

After hitting the skids in the late-1970s, it seems like beer can collecting is making a comeback – albeit in a different way. Today, people are specializing their collection to focus on a certain theme.

"I think that the resurgence has been in the demand for scarce older cans in excellent original condition, many of which now command four-figure prices at auction and private sales," Remick said. "eBay has undoubtedly had a great influence here. The number of active beer can collectors seems to have stabilized over the past decade, with most collectors now choosing to specialize rather than attempt to acquire every beer can ever made."

Starrett gives credit to the Internet for giving beer can collecting a boost. "Many of today's collectors stumbled across beer can sites like mine, www.MIbeercans.com, using a search engine. It has also allowed collectors from around the country easy access to each other so they can buy, sell and trade cans."

Beer Can Collecting Tips

Open from the top or bottom?: Most can collectors do prefer cans opened from the bottom because a can seems choice and "unmolested" when sitting in a display with its pull tab intact.

Full or empty cans?: Empty. A full can that drops or falls from a shelf will usually dent or crimp, often ruining the can. With the pre-aluminum steel cans with the seam along the side, you can be sure that beer will find a way to seep out of that seam.

How to display them: Obviously, wall shelves are most often used to display beer can collections. All you need is a lot of empty wall space, preferably not in the living room. For a typical floor-to-ceiling arrangement, you could have 12 to 13 shelves, spaced to accomodate 16-ounce cans. A shelf 10-feet long could hold about 45 cans, or a total of up to 585 cans. This may help you decide how large a collection you will be able to display.

– Bruce Remick

Beer Can Price Guide

Editor's note: Bruce Remick contributed a majority of this price guide to Tuff Stuff. Even though he no longer writes a monthly sports beer can column on the Internet, his past columns still appear, as does his price guide. Check it out at www.zianet.com/spencer/sports.html.

Baseball
Anheuser Busch

Note: * The 12oz cans were produced and filled both in the United States and Japan. The U.S. export version has no Japanese characters in the bottom date code or on the lid.

Red Schoendienst Dedication of Schoendienst Field Germantown, Ill. (bank) ....(1977)..................$15-18
Budweiser, Century's Greatest Teams. 1927/1998 Yankees ....(1999)....................1-2
Budweiser, Century's Greatest Teams. 1927/1998 Yankees (Texas) ....(1999)....................2-3
Budweiser, Century's Greatest Teams. 1927/1998 Yankees (Chicago) ....(1999)....................2-3
Budweiser, Century's Greatest Teams. 1975 Cincinnati Reds ....(1999)....................1-2
Budweiser, Century's Greatest Teams. 1975 Cincinnati Reds (Texas) ....(1999)....................2-3
Budweiser, Century's Greatest Teams. 1975 Cincinnati Reds (Chicago) ....(1999)....................2-3
Budweiser, "Team of the Century". 1999 Yankees 16oz ....(1999)....................2-3
Budweiser, "Century's Greatest Team". 1999 Yankees 16oz ....(1999)....................2-3
Budweiser, Major League Baseball. Anaheim Angels (for Japan)* ....(1999)...........30-40
Budweiser, Major League Baseball. Anaheim Angels (for Japan) 16oz ....(1999)...........30-40
Budweiser, Major League Baseball. St Louis Cardinals (Japan)* ....(1999)...........30-40
Budweiser, Major League Baseball. St Louis Cardinals (Japan) 16oz ....(1999)...........30-40
Budweiser, Major League Baseball. Chicago Cubs (for Japan)* ....(1999)...........30-40
Budweiser, Major League Baseball. Chicago Cubs (for Japan) 16oz ....(1999)...........30-40
Budweiser, Major League Baseball. LA Dodgers (for Japan)* ....(1999)...........30-40
Budweiser, Major League Baseball. LA Dodgers (for Japan) 16oz ....(1999)...........30-40
Budweiser, Major League Baseball. New York Mets (for Japan)* ....(1999)...........40-50
Budweiser, Major League Baseball. New York Mets (for Japan) 16oz ....(1999)...........40-50
Budweiser, Major League Baseball. NY Yankees (for Japan)* ....(1999)...........30-40
Budweiser, Major League Baseball. NY Yankees (for Japan) 16oz ....(1999)...........30-40

Antilles
Home Run Malt Liquor, brewed in Puerto Rico for baseball fans 10oz ....(1969)..................50-60

Coors
Coors, Orioles 1991, "A Season to Remember" ..(1991).......................3-5
Coors, Colorado Rockies, salutes opening day, April 9, 1993........................(1993).......................2-3
Coors Light, Colorado Rockies, salutes opening day, April 9, 1993........................(1993).......................2-3
Coors Draft, Colorado Rockies, salutes opening day, April 9, 1993........................(1993).......................2-3
Coors Dry, Colorado Rockies, salutes opening day, April 9, 1993........................(1993).......................2-3
Coors Cutter, Colorado Rockies, salutes opening day, April 9, 1993........................(1993).......................2-3
Coors Light, 1996 Season, Pirates 110 Percent 16oz(1996)............2-3

Coors Light, The Beer that Takes you to the 1997 World Series (for Puerto Rico) 10oz ....(1997) 15-20
Coors, Safety Week. Rockies. Shows stadium, batter. Given to employees. (bank) 16oz ....(1997) 35-40
Coors, Safety Week. Rockies. Shows stadium, baseball. Given to employees. (bank) 16oz ....(1997) 40-45
Coors, "Big Bat" Series, Babe Ruth: The Called Shot ....(1998) 2-3
Coors, "Big Bat" Series, Roberto Clemente, The Last Hit ....(1998) 2-3
Coors, "Big Bat" Series, Kirk Gibson, The Injured Hero.....................................(1998) 2-3
Coors, "Big Bat" Series, Willie McCovey, 4-for-4 Debut ....(1998) 2-3
Coors, "Big Bat" Series, Carlton Fisk, "Go Fair!" ..(1998) 2-3
Coors, "Big Bat" Series, Ernie Banks, Down, Not Out ....(1998) 2-3
Coors Light, Pirates 1998 Season16oz ....(1998) 2-3
Coors Light, Coors Field, Field of Stars, July 7, 1998 16oz ....(1998) 3-5
Coors Light, salutes the 1998 World Series (for Puerto Rico) 10oz ....(1998) 15-20
Coors Light, Pittsburgh Pirates 1999. (sideways label format) 16oz..................................(1999) 2-3
Coors Light, salutes Tampa Bay Devil Rays 16oz (1999) 2-3
Coors Light, Catch Some Rays. Tampa Bay Devil Rays 16oz ....(2000) 2-3
Coors, "Nothing Beats an Original". Hank Aaron #44 16oz..................................(2001) 2-3

Fitger
Twins Lager Beer, implied association with Minnesota Twins.......................................(1969) 75-100

Genesee
Genny Light, salutes Rochester Red Wings Inaugural Season at Frontier Field ....(1997) 2-3
Genesee Light, salutes the Rochester Red Wings, 1997 Governor's Cup Champions...................................(1998) 2-3

Heileman
Old Style, Comiskey Park 1910-1990 16oz ..... (1990) 2-3
Old Style, Chicago's All Time Greatest #1. Ron Santo 16oz ....(1990) 2-3
Old Style, Chicago's All Time Greatest #2. Billy Williams 16oz ....(1990) 2-3
Old Style, Chicago's All Time Greatest #3. Fergie Jenkins 16oz ....(1990) 2-3
Old Style Light, Defending National Eastern Champs "Achieve Total CUB-osity" 16oz.....................(1990) 2-3
Old Style, Chicago Cubs Greatest Moments (lists six Cubs milestones) 16oz..................................(1991) 2-3
Old Style Light, Wrigley Great. Mom. (Billy Williams' 1,117th consecutive game) 16oz ....(1991) 2-3
Special Export, Minnesota Twins 1961-1991 A Family Tradition (green) 16oz..................................(1991) 2-3
Special Export Light, Minnesota Twins 1961-1991 A Family Tradition (blue) 16oz..................................(1991) 3-5
Export Light, salutes Minnesota baseball fans 16oz..................................(1992) 2-3
Special Export Beer, salutes Minnesota baseball fans 16oz..................................(1992) 2-3
Old Style, Wrigley Field, Home of Chicago Cubs 16oz..................................(1992) 2-3
Old Style Light, Wrigley Field, Home of Chicago Cubs 16oz..................................(1992) 2-3
Old Style, salutes Wrigley Field- The Ivy 16oz (1993) 2-3
Old Style Light, salutes Wrigley Field- The Ivy 16oz..................................(1993) 2-3
Old Style, salutes Wrigley Field- The Scoreboard 16oz..................................(1993) 2-3
Old Style Light, salutes Wrigley Field- The Lights 16oz..................................(1993) 2-3
Old Style, Wrigley Field 80th anniversary 16oz ....(1994).......................2-3

Old Style, 1945 NL Champ, Cubs 1945 home/away uniforms, season
   highlights 16oz .... (1995) 2-3
Old Style, Fan Can. Salutes baseball fans of America's Heartland.
   16oz .... (2000) 2-3
Old Style, "Ivy Can" Cubs logo with green ivy
   16oz .... (2001) 1-2
Old Style, "Ivy Can" 16oz .... (2002) 1-2

Hudepohl

Hudepohl, 1975 World Champion Cincinnati
   Reds .... (1976) 3-5
Hudepohl, 1976 World Champion Cincinnati
   Reds .... (1977) 2-3

Maier

Dodger Lager, introduced in LA, following Brooklyn Dodgers'
   move there "Contents" at bottom of label (gold metallic)
   (Flat) .... (1958) 60-80
"Contents" at bottom of label (light metallic)
   (Flat) .... (1958) 80-100
"Contents" at top of label (Flat) .... (1958) 60-80
"Contents" along seam (Flat) .... (1958) 60-80
"Contents" along seam (by Southern Brg) (Flat) .. (1958) 60-80
"Contents" at bottom/Zip Code at seam (Tab). (1969) 60-80

Miller

Lite, Los Angeles Dodgers 35 Years at Dodger Stadium
   16oz .... (1996) 10-12
Lite, 35 Years of Houston Astros Baseball. Astrodome 1965-1999, The
   Original 16oz .... (1999) 2-3
Lite, Nolan Ryan. The Ryan Express to Cooperstown
   16oz .... (1999) 2-3
Lite, Arizona Diamondbacks World Series Champions,
   16oz .... (2001) 3-4

Minnesota Brewing

Grain Belt, Ballpark Beer. "Vote Yes Saint Paul
   November 2" .... (1999) 2-3

National

National Bohemian, 1970 Orioles schedule (bank), given to adult fans
   at April 10, 1970 home opener .... (1970) 125-150
National Bohemian, 1991 Orioles- Memorial Stadium 1954-1991
   (#15- Land of Pleasant Living series) .... (1991) 2-3

Pete's Brewing Company (Strohs)

Pete's Wicked, Summer Brew. Shows baseball stadium
   scene .... (1996) 1-2

Pittsburgh

Iron City, Pirate Team Record (1887-1973) ...... (1974) 8-10
Iron City Draft, Pirate Team Record (1887-1973). (1974) 8-10
Iron City, Pirates in World Series .... (1974) 8-10
Iron City Draft, Pirates in World Series .... (1974) 8-10
Iron City, Pirates 1974 Home Schedule .... (1974) 8-10
Iron City Draft, Pirates 1974 Home Schedule .. (1974) 8-10
Iron City, Pirates 1974 TV Schedule .... (1974) 8-10
Iron City Draft, Pirates 1974 TV Schedule .... (1974) 8-10
Iron City, Pirates 1974 Roster- pitchers &
   catchers .... (1974) 8-10
Iron City Draft, Pirates 1974 Roster- pitchers &
   catchers .... (1974) 8-10
Iron City, Pirates 1974 Roster- infielders &
   outfielders .... (1974) 8-10
Iron City Draft, Pirates 1974 Roster- infielders &
   outfielders .... (1974) 8-10
Iron City, 1960 World Series .... (1974) 8-10
Iron City Draft, 1960 World Series .... (1974) 8-10
Iron City, 1971 World Series .... (1974) 8-10
Iron City Draft, 1971 World Series .... (1974) 8-10
Iron City, Baseball World Championships
   (1950-1973) .... (1974) 8-10
Iron City Draft, Baseball World Championships
   (1950-1973) .... (1974) 8-10
Iron City, Letter from Brewery President .... (1974) 8-10
Iron City Draft, Letter from Brewery President . (1974) 8-10
Iron City, salutes 1979 Champion Pirates .... (1980) 2-3
Iron City, Pirates- "Hardball 88 is waiting for you/You can't keep an Iron
   man down .... "(1988) 2-3
Iron City, Pirates- A Pittsburgh Tradition
   (period uniforms) .... (1990) 2-3

Iron City, Pirates- A Pittsburgh Tradition (period uniforms)
   16oz .... (1990) 3-5
Iron City, Pirates- "So close you can feel it"
   (ticket stubs) .... (1990) 2-3
Iron City, Pirates- "So close you can feel it"
   (ticket stubs) 16oz .... (1990) 3-5
Iron City, Pirates- National League Eastern Div
   Champions .... (1991) 2-3
Iron City, Pirates- National League Eastern Div
   Champions 16oz .... (1991) 3-5
Iron City, Pirates- Back-to-back Division
   Championships .... (1992) 2-3
Iron City, Pirates- Back-to-back Division
   Championships 16oz .... (1992) 3-5
Iron City, Roberto Clemente, #1 in a series of 4(1993) 2-3
Iron City, Roberto Clemente, #2 in a series of 4
   16oz .... (1993) 3-5
IC Light, Roberto Clemente, #3 in a series of 4(1993) 2-3
IC Light, Roberto Clemente, #4 in a series of 4
   16oz .... (1993) 3-5
Iron City, Pittsburgh's Greatest All-Stars, Bill Mazeroski,
   #1of 6 .... (1994) 2-3
Iron City, Pittsburgh's Greatest All-Stars, Bill Mazeroski,
   #2of 6 16oz .... (1994) 2-3
IC Light, Pittsburgh's Greatest All-Stars, R. Clemente,
   #3 of 6 .... (1994) 2-3
IC Light, Pittsburgh's Greatest All-Stars, R. Clemente
   #4 of 6 16oz .... (1994) 3-5
Iron City, Pittsburgh's Greatest All-Stars, Willie Stargell,
   #5 of 6 .... (1994) 2-3
Iron City, Pittsburgh's Greatest All-Stars, Willie Stargell, #6 of 6
   16oz .... (1994) 2-3
Iron City, A New Era of Pirate Baseball, Salutes Kevin McClatchy,
   new owner .... (1996) 1-2
Iron City, A New Era of Pirate Baseball, Salutes Kevin McClatchy,
   new owner 16oz .... (1996) 2-3
Iron City, Pittsburgh Pirates, pirate flag, ballplayer
   drawings .... (1997) 1-2
Iron City, Pittsburgh Pirates, pirate flag, ballplayer
   drawings 16oz .... (1997) 2-3
Iron City, IC and the Pirates- "What Baseball's All
   About .... "(1998) 1-2
Iron City, IC and the Pirates- "What Baseball's All
   About" 16oz .... (1998) 2-3
Iron City, Bill Mazeroski 2001 Hall of Famer. Photo, signature
   16oz .... (2001) 1-2

Rainier

Rainier Beer, Seattle Rainiers highlights (1938-1960)
   16oz .... (1994) 3-5

(Reynolds Aluminum)

Bob Feller- Richmond Braves Aluminum Can Night,
   July 23, 1980, Feller photo (bank) no mention of beer or
   brewery .... (1980) 12-15
Hank Aaron- Richmond Braves Aluminum Can Night, June 25,
   1981 Photo/autograph (bank) no mention of beer or
   brewery .... (1981) 25-30

Stevens Point

AF Base Brau, Appleton Foxes Beer, 1978
   (red/blue) .... (1978) 1-2
AF Base Brau, Appleton Foxes Beer, 1978
   (yellow/brown) .... (1978) 1-2
AF Base Brau, Appleton Foxes Beer, 1978
   (orange/green) .... (1978) 1-2
AF Base Brau, Appleton Foxes Beer, 1979
   (red/white/blue) .... (1979) 1-2
AF Base Brau, Appleton Foxes Beer, 1979
   (yellow/white/brown) .... (1979) 1-2
AF Base Brau, Appleton Foxes Beer, 1980 ..... (1980) 1-2
AF Base Brau, Appleton Foxes Beer, 1981 ..... (1981) 1-2

Stroh

Schaefer, Ebbets Field (Joe Black) .... (1995) 2-3
Schaefer, Forbes Field (Hal Smith) .... (1995) 2-3
Schaefer, League Park (Mel Harder) .... (1995) 2-3
Schaefer, Braves Field (Tommy Holmes) .... (1995) 2-3

Schaefer, Shibe Park (Bobby Schantz) .... (1995)........................2-3
Schaefer, Polo Grounds (Dusty Rhodes) .... (1995)........................2-3
Note: A limited number of player-autographed cans were inserted in 12/24 packs.

Valley Forge
Casey's Lager, Duke Snider #5 ....(1980)........................2-3
Casey's Lager, Richie Ashburn #8 ....(1980)........................2-3
Casey's Lager, Monte Irvin #19........................(1980)........................2-3
Casey's Lager, Whitey Ford #21 ....(1980)........................2-3
Note: 7 sets of 7 cans (49 total) were planned for the first year of Casey's Lager. Only 4 cans made it to market. Several display samples of the following three unreleased cans from the first set are reported to exist.
Casey's Lager, Ralph Branca (display sample) (1980)........................ –
Casey's Lager, Warren Spahn (display sample)...(1980)........................ –
Casey's Lager, Don Larson (display sample) ... (1980)........................ –

Yuengling
Yuengling Beer, salutes Allentown (Pa.) Patriots, 50 Years of Sports 1948-1998...(1998)........................2-3

Basketball

Anheuser Busch
Budweiser, US Forces, Okinawa. Shows two men playing hoops (sold in Okinawa) ....(1998).....................8-12
Budweiser, Century's Greatest Teams.1964-65 Boston
Celtics ....(1999)........................1-2
Budweiser, Century's Greatest Teams.1964-65 Boston Celtics
(Texas) ....(1999)........................2-3
Budweiser, Century's Greatest Teams.1964-65 Celtics
(Chicago logo) ....(1999)........................2-3
Budweiser, Century's Greatest Teams.1986 LA
Lakers ....(1999).......................1-2
Budweiser, Century's Greatest Teams.1986 LA Lakers
(Texas logo) ....(1999)........................2-3
Budweiser, Century's Greatest Teams.1986 LA Lakers
(Chicago logo) ....(1999)........................2-3

Coors
Coors, Magic Johnson. "Nothing Beats an Original"
16oz ....(2001)........................2-3

Heileman
Old Style Beer, Milwaukee Bucks schedule, 1982-83
(bank)...(1983)........................5-8
Old Style Beer, Milwaukee Bucks schedule, 1983-84
(bank)..(1984)........................5-8
Old Style Beer, Illinois State schedule, 1983-84
(bank)...(1984)...................12-15
Old Style Beer, "Coach Ray Meyer does it with Style"
(bank)..(1985)...................50-60
Old Style Beer, Old Dominion 1984-85 men's & women's basketball
schedule (bank) ....(1985)...................25-30
Old Style Beer, Univ. of Wisconsin basketball, hockey home schedules,
'93-94 16oz ....(1993)........................3-5
Colt .45 Malt Liquor, "Instant Winner" shoot basket for $1 million
16oz ....(1997)........................3-5

Lone Star
Lone Star Beer, San Antonio Spurs 1983-84 schedule (bank) sold only
at brewery store ....(1983)...................15-18
Lone Star Beer, San. Ant. Spurs 1984-85 schedule (bank) sold only at
brewery store ....(1984)...................30-40
Lone Star Beer, Fan Can. Salutes the Greatest Fans in the Nation
16oz ....(1999)........................2-3
Lone Star Beer, Fan Can. Salutes the Greatest Fans in the Nation
24oz ....(1999)....................... 2-3
Lone Star Light, Fan Can. Salutes the Greatest Fans in the Nation.
16oz ....(2000)........................2-3
Lone Star Light, Fan Can. Salutes the Greatest Fans in the Nation.
24oz ....(2000)........................2-3

Miller
Miller Genuine Draft, silhouettes of two basketball players
24oz ....(1998).....................8-10

National
A-1 Beer, 1969-70 Phoenix Suns schedule (bank)(1970)..........125-150
A-1 Beer, 1970-71 Phoenix Suns schedule (bank)(1971)..............50-75

A-1 Beer, 1971-72 Phoenix Suns schedule (bank)(1972) 30-40
A-1 Beer, 1972-73 Phoenix Suns schedule (bank)(1973) 25-30
A-1 Beer, 1973-74 Phoenix Suns schedule (bank)(1974) 15-20
A-1 Beer, 1974-75 Phoenix Suns schedule (bank)(1975) 12-15
Colt 45 Malt Liquor, 1973-74 Golden St. Warriors schedule
(bank) ....(1974) 15-18
Colt 45 Malt Liquor, 1975-76 Phoenix Suns schedule
(bank) ....(1976) 5-8
Colt 45 Malt Liquor, 1976-77 Phoenix suns schedule
(bank) ....(1976) 5-8
Tuborg Gold, 1977 Boston Celtics home schedule
(bank) ....(1977) 20-25
Tuborg Gold, 1977-78 Phoenix Suns home
schedule ....(1978) 3-5

Pearl
Pearl Light, 1983-84 Razorback SWC schedule(1984) 3-5

Pittsburgh
Iron City, NBA Champions (1947-1974)........... (1974) 8-10
Iron City Draft, NBA Champions (1947-1974) . (1974) 8-10

Football (Pro)

Anheuser Busch
Bud Light, Houston Texans Inaugural Season. (2002) ....$2-$3

Coors
Coors Light, salutes Baltimore Ravens 1996 season (used briefly
at Memorial Stadium. Cans withdrawn for NFL license violation)
16oz.. (1997) 10-15
Coors Light, 25th Anniversary- Franco's Immaculate Reception
16oz.. (1997) 2-3
Coors, "Pigskin can". textured to look like a
football .... (1998) 1-2
Coors, "Pigskin can". textured to look like a football
16oz.. (1998) 2-3
Coors, "Pigskin can". textured to look like a football
24oz.. (1998) 2-3
Coors, John Elway, The Mile High Legend 16oz ..(1999).................2-3
Coors, Joe Montana, The Road To Canton ..... (1999) 2-3
Coors, Joe Montana, The Road To Canton 24oz .(1999).................3-5
Coors Light, Joe Montana, The Road To Canton (1999) 2-3
Coors Light, Joe Montana, The Road To Canton
24oz.. (1999) 3-5
Coors, Grid Iron Warriors. Richard Dent.......... (2000) 1-2
Coors, Grid Iron Warriors. Hugh Green .... (2000) 1-2
Coors, Grid Iron Warriors. Jack Ham .... (2000) 1-2
Coors, Grid Iron Warriors. Deacon Jones .... (2000) 1-2
Coors, Grid Iron Warriors. Joe Klecko .... (2000) 1-2
Coors, Grid Iron Warriors. Ronnie Lott .... (2000) 1-2
Coors, Grid Iron Warriors. Karl Mecklenberg .. (2000) 1-2
Coors, Grid Iron Warriors. Charlie Waters .... (2000) 1-2
Coors, Barry Sanders. "Nothing Beats an Original"
16oz.. (2001) 2-3
Coors Light, Oakland Raiders 2001 AFC West Champs,
24oz.. (2002) 2-3
Coors Light, New England Patriots Super Bowl XXXVI Champs,
16oz.. (2002) 2-3

Crooked River
Stadium Lager, Cleveland Stadium. Shows Browns player
16oz.. (1999) 2-3

Evansville
Dog Pound Brew, 1993-94 (for Cleveland Browns
fans) .... (1993) 2-3
Dog Pound Brew, (no date) (for Cleveland Browns fans)
scarce .... (1994) 5-8
Steel Curtain Brew, 1993-94 (for Pittsburgh Steelers
fans) .... (1994) 2-3
Birds Brew, 1993-94 (for Philadelphia Eagles
fans) .... (1994) 2-3
Red White and Brew, (for new England Patriots
fans) .... (1994) 2-3
Whoomp! There It Is Brew, (for New Orleans Saints
fans) .... (1995) 2-3
Hog Brew, (for Redskins fans) like 1991 gold can, undated, #1 in
red .... (1995) 2-3

Florida

Dolphin Beer, design similar to Miami Dolphins' logo. Sold in S. Florida when Dolphins won AFC Championship..... (1985)........................3-5

Genesee

Genesee Beer, Pro football 1st Pro- William "Pudge" Heffelfinger..............................(1993)......................1-2

Heileman

Old Style, Chicago Bears 70 Seasons (1st in a series)
16oz ....(1989)........2-3
Old Style, Chicago's All-Time Greatest, Mike Ditka (2nd...)
16oz ....(1991)........2-3
Old Style Light, Chicago's All-Time Greatest, Mike Ditka (3rd...) 16oz..................................(1991)........2-3
Old Style, Chicago's All-Time Greatest, Dick Butkus (4th...) 16oz..................................(1991)........2-3
Old Style, Chicago's All-Time Greatest, Walter Payton (6th...) 16oz..................................(1991)........2-3
Old Style Light, Chicago's All-Time Gr'st, Walter Payton (7th...)
16oz ....(1991)........2-3
Old Style, Chicago's All-Time Greatest, Gale Sayers
16oz ....(1992)........2-3
Old Style Light, Chicago's All-Time Greatest, Gale Sayers
16oz ....(1992)........2-3
Old Style, "Crazylegs" Elroy Hirsch #40 16oz .. (1992)........2-3
Old Style, Fan Can. Salutes football fans of Chicagoland. Bears 2000 schedule 16oz.....................(2000)........2-3
Old Style, Chicago Beas Schedule ....(2002)........2-3

Huber

Head Hog Premium Beer, produced by Redskins "HOG", George Starke ....(1993)........2-3

Hudepohl

Hu-Dey, "Who dey think gonna beat dem Bengals?"...................................(1982)........2-3
Hu-Dey, 14K Premium. 1988 Bengals schedule ..(1988)........2-3
Hu-Dey, Bengals- AFC Champs, 1988-89 Super Bowl Edition ....(1989)........2-3

Jones

Hog Brew, 1991. Design similar to 1986 RWB Brewing issue (gold can)....................................(1991)........2-3
Hog Brew, 1992-93. Similar to 1991 issue (red can) ....(1992)........2-3

Latrobe

Rolling Rock, Heinz Field, Pittsburgh Steelers, Opening Season ....(2001)........2-3
Rolling Rock, Steelers 70 seasons.................(2002)........2-3

Miller

Lite, Official Beer of the Dallas Cowboys 16oz (1992)........2-3
Lite, Super Bowl XXVII, Sun, Jan 31, 1993, Pasadena, CA
16oz ....(1992)........2-3
Lite, 1993 Champions, Super Bowl XXVII, Dallas Cowboys
16oz ....(1993)........2-3
Lite, World Champions, Dallas Cowboys 16oz. (1993)........2-3
Lite, Super Bowl XXVIII, Sun, Jan 30, 1994, Atlanta, GA
16oz ....(1993)........2-3
Lite, Super Bowl XXIX, Joe Robbie Stadium, Jan 29, 1995
16oz ....(1995)........2-3
Lite, Super Bowl XXX, Sun Devil Stadium, Jan 28, 1996 ....(1995)........2-3
Lite, Super Bowl XXX, Sun Devil Stadium, Jan 28, 1996 16oz ....(1995)........2-3
Lite, Dallas Cowboys, Super Bowl XXX World Champs
16oz ....(1996)........2-3
Lite, Dallas Cowboys Five-Time Super Bowl Champs ....(1996)........2-3
Lite, Dallas Cowboys Five-Time Super Bowl Champs
16oz ....(1996)........2-3
Lite, Super Bowl XXXI, New Orleans Superdome, Jan 26, 1997 ....(1997)........2-3
Lite, Super Bowl XXXI, New Orleans Superdome, Jan 26, 1997
16oz ....(1997)........2-3
Lite, Green Bay Packers Super Bowl XXXI champions
16oz ....(1997)........3-5
Lite, Three Time Super Bowl Champions- Packers ....(1997)........2-3
Lite, New England Patriots 1996 AFC champions
16oz ....(1997)........3-5
Lite, Carolina Panthers, 1996 NFC West Champions ....(1997)........2-3
Lite, Tennessee Oilers Inaugural Season 24oz (1997)........3-5
Lite, Super Bowl XXXII, Qualcomm Stadium, Jan 25, 1998 ....(1997)........2-3
Lite, Super Bowl XXXII, Qualcomm Stadium, Jan 25, 1998 24oz...........................(1997)........3-5
Lite, Super Bowl XXXII, Green Bay Packers, Back to Back Super Bowl Champions. Limited Edition Championship can
16oz ....(1998)........30-40
Note: Miller brought these "new" cans to San Diego to serve the media, anticipating a Packers' win. The Broncos won. A few cans survived destruction and found their way to collectors.
Lite, Super Bowl XXXII Champions- Denver Broncos ....(1998)........2-3
Lite, Super Bowl XXXIII, Sunday, Jan 31, 1999, Miami, FL..................................(1998)........2-3
Lite, Congratulatory Beer. Back-to-Back Super Bowl Champions-Broncos. Super Bowl XXXIII. Blue panel at bottom........(1999)........2-3
Lite, Back-to-Back Champions-Broncos. Super Bowl XXXIII. Panel at top ....(1999)........2-3
Lite, Cleveland Browns. 1999 Commemorative collectors can...(1999)........2-3
Lite, Tennessee Titans 1999 Inaugural Season commemorative 24oz.......................................(1999)........2-3
Lite, Dallas Cowboys 40th Anniversary "True to Texas"
16oz ....(1999)........2-3
Lite, Baltimore Ravens. Super Bowl XXXV Champions ....(2001)........2-3

National

National Bohemian, "The Colt", shows helmeted colt holding football, jumping over goalpost. (assoc. with Baltimore Colts)
7oz..(1965)
  a. 3-piece steel tab, "The Colt" inside round "C" 20-25
  b. 3-piece steel tab, "The Colt inside squat "C" 15-20
  c. aluminum punch top 12-15
Note: All three varieties are difficult to find in top condition

O'Keefe (Canadian)

O'Keefe, Canadian Football League Grey Cup (1985) 3-4

Pittsburgh

Iron City, "Pour it on Steelers" 1972 results, 1973 schedule ....(1973)........10-12
Iron City, Defense! Defense! Defense! (helmets w/numbers)
16oz.......................................(1973)........10-12
Iron City, Pittsburgh Steeler Offense (facsimile autographs) ....(1973)........8-10
Iron City, Pittsburgh Steeler Defense (facsimile autographs) ....(1973)........8-10
Iron City, Super Bowl winners, 1967-1974....... (1974) 8-10
Iron City Draft, Super Bowl winners, 1967-1974(1974) 8-10
Iron City, Congratulations Super Steelers 1975, Pitt 16 - Minn 6 ....(1976)........3-5
Iron City, Steelers, 1975 Super Bowl Champs (team photo) ....(1976)........2-3
Iron City, Steelers, 1975 Super Bowl Champs (team photo)
16oz.......................................(1976)........5-8
Iron City, Steelers, 1976 Super Bowl Champs (team photo) ....(1977)........2-3
Iron City, Steelers, 1976 Super Bowl Champs (team photo)
16oz.......................................(1977)........3-5
Iron City, The 1976 Pittsburgh Steelers (team photo) ....(1977)........2-3
Iron City, Super Super Super Steelers ....(1980)........2-3
Iron City, The Team of the Decade- 1980 Pittsburgh Steelers (photo) ....(1980)........2-3
Iron City, Pittsburgh's Pride (team photo) ....(1981)........2-3
Iron City, Steelers 50 Seasons.....................(1982)........1-2
Iron City, The Pittsburgh Steelers, Chuck Noll and Art Rooney ....(1983)........1-2
Iron City, Super Steeler facsimile autographs .. (1984) 1-2
Iron City, Title Drive '85- Steelers ....(1985)........1-2
Iron City, Two Great Traditions, Steeler Autographs (1st Edition) ....(1986)........2-3

Iron City, Two Great Traditions, Steeler Autographs
(2nd Edition) .... (1986).....................2-3
Iron City, Two Great Traditions, Steeler Autographs
(2nd Edition) (error- used signatures from
3rd Edition can) .... (1986)...............20-25
Iron City, Two Great Traditions, Steeler Autographs
(3rd Edition) .... (1986).....................2-3
Iron City, Steeler Hall of Famers...................... (1987).....................2-3
Iron City, Jack Ham .... (1988).....................2-3
Iron City, Terry Bradshaw .... (1989).....................2-3
Iron City, Terry Bradshaw 16oz .... (1989).....................2-3
Iron City, Mel Blount .... (1989).....................2-3
Iron City, Mel Blount 16oz .... (1989).....................2-3
Iron City, Joe Greene, Hall of Famer .... (1990).....................2-3
Iron City, Joe Greene, Hall of Famer 16oz .... (1990).....................2-3
Iron City, Franco Harris, 1990 Hall of Famer .... (1990).....................2-3
Iron City, Franco Harris, 1990 Hall of Famer 16oz (1990).....................2-3
Iron City, Jack Lambert, Hall of Famer .... (1992).....................2-3
Iron City, Jack Lambert, Hall of Famer 16oz .... (1992).....................2-3
Iron City, Chuck Noll, Hall of Famer .... (1993).....................2-3
Iron City, Chuck Noll, Hall of Famer 16oz........ (1993).....................2-3
Iron City, salutes Myron Cope, voice of the
Steelers... (1994).....................2-3
Iron City, salutes Myron Cope, voice of the Steelers
16oz... (1994).....................2-3
Iron City, "It's a Blitzburgh Thing", '94 AFC Central Div
Champs .... (1995).....................1-2
Iron City, "It's a Blitzburgh Thing", '94 AFC Central Div
Champs 16oz.. (1995).....................2-3
Iron City, saluting Cleveland/Pittsburgh rivalry,
1950-1995 .... (1995).....................1-2
Iron City, saluting Cleve./Pittsburgh rivalry, 1950-95 -includes
Series Record 52-40 .... (1995).....................3-5
Iron City, saluting the Blitzburgh '95 AFC Champs,
Jan 28, 1996 .... (1996).....................1-2
Iron City, Super Iron Men, Andy Russell photo..... (1996).....................1-2
Iron City, Super Iron Men, Andy Russell photo
16oz... (1996).....................2-3
Iron City, Super Iron Men, Rocky Bleier photo . (1996).....................1-2
Iron City, Super Iron Men, Rocky Bleier photo
16oz... (1996).....................2-3
Iron City, Super Iron Men, Ray Mansfield photo(1996) 1-2
Iron City, Super Iron Men, Ray Mansfield photo
16oz... (1996).....................2-3
Iron City, "One For The Thumb- The Time Has Come"- Pittsburgh is Play-
off Bound-On The Road to New Orleans ...... (1997).....................1-2
IC Light, "One For The Thumb- The Time Has Come"- Pittsburgh is
Playoff Bound-On The Road to New Orleans
16oz... (1997).....................1-2
American, Buffalo's American Sports Legends,
Ed Rutkowski .... (1997).....................2-3
Iron City, Iron Mike (Webster), 1997 Hall of Famer- Webster
photo .... (1997).....................2-3
Iron City, Iron Mike (Webster), 1997 Hall of Famer- photo
16oz... (1997).....................2-3
Iron City, Steelers-Browns. "The Rivalry Rocks Again in
99 .... "(1998).....................2-3
Iron City, "Steel City Connection". Lists Bars that feature Iron
City.. (1998).....................1-2
Iron City, "Steel City Connection". Bars that feature Iron City
16oz... (1998).....................1-2

RWB, Perry, GA

Hog Brew, (for Washington Redskins fans) silver can(1986) 2-3

Football (College)

(Ball Canning)

Homecoming '82, Wm & Mary TRIBE vs Brown, Nov 6, 1982
(bank)... (1982)...............20-25

Coors

Coors Light, Colorado Buffalo Football, celebrating
100 years .... (1989)...............10-15
Coors Light, Federal Express Orange Bowl, Col vs Notre Dame
1990 .... (1989).....................3-5
Coors Light, Nebraska Huskers, Big 8 Champs 1990(1990) 3-5

Coors Light, salutes Colorado, "Mecca of College Football"
Colorado/Air Force Academy/
Colorado State .... (1991) 3-5
Coors Light, GMAC Bowl, Dec. 19, 2001........ (2001) 3-4

(Creative Products)

Bulldog Brew, "TO HELL WITH TECH- Brewed Between the Hedges on
AG. Hill" Georgia-Georgia Tech football novelty can
(unfilled)... (1962) 35-40
Yellow Jacket Brew, "TO HELL WITH GEORGIA- Brewed on the Flats
by Yellow Jackets" Georgia-Georgia Tech football novelty can
(unfilled)... (1962) 30-35

Duncan

Georgia Beer '84, 1984 football schedule (silver) (1984).......................3-5

Falstaff

Falstaff Beer, 1982 Iowa schedule.................. (1982) 2-3
Falstaff Beer, 1982 Nebraska schedule
(red helmet) .... (1982) 2-3
Falstaff Beer, 1982 Nebraska schedule
(white helmet) .... (1982) 2-3
Illini Beer, 1983 Illinois schedule
(Great Lakes Brewery) .... (1983) 2-3
Badger Beer, 1983 Edition. football schedule
(Great Lakes Brewery) .... (1983) 2-3

Great Lakes

World's Fair Beer, 3rd Edition. Orange. "In honor of Doug Atkins,
University of Tennessee 1950-52
All American . NFL Hall of Fame 1982" on narrow band around top
of can.. (1983) 2-3

Heileman

Old Style, 1983 Illinois State University schedule
(bank) .... (1983) 20-25
Old Style, 1983 Fighting Illini schedule (bank). (1983) 30-35
Old Style, 1983 Badger schedule (bank) .... (1983) 5-8

Jackson

Tiger Beer, celebrates LSU Tigers' undefeated 1958 season and
Sugar Bowl victory .... (1959) 80-100
Note: Don't confuse this original can with a later, high-quality, paper
label copy.

Pabst

Pabst, Go Badgers, Rose Bowl 1994, Wisconsin vs UCLA
16oz... (1993) 10-12
Note: Recalled from stores by brewery due to legal problems after
8,700 cases had been distributed)

Pearl

Pearl Light, 1975 Houston schedule*.............. (1975) 2-3
Pearl Light, 1975 Texas A&M schedule*.......... (1975) 2-3
Pearl Light, 1975 Texas schedule*................. (1975) 2-3
Note: * Very thin paint- difficult to find without scuff marks around top
and bottom of label)
Pearl Light, 1980 Razorback schedule .... (1980) 2-3
Pearl Light, 1982 Razorback schedule .... (1982) 2-3
Pearl Light, 1986 Razorback schedule .... (1986) 2-3
Country Club Malt Liquor, 1982 Georgia
schedule .... (1982) 3-5

Pickett

Hawkeye Beer, salutes University of Iowa football
team .... (1980) 2-3
Cyclone Beer, salutes Iowa State University football
team .... (1980) 2-3
Iowa Sports Premium Beer, includes mascots from various Iowa
colleges .... (1981) 3-4

Pittsburgh

Iron City, Mountaineers No. 1 (Mountaineer
running) .... (1972) 8-10
Iron City, Mountaineers (Mountaineer standing)(1974).....................3-5
Iron City, 1974 Penn State schedule .... (1974) 20-25
Iron City, Penn State Nittany Lions- Numero Uno(1974) 3-5
Iron City, 1974 Pitt schedule .... (1974) 80-100
Iron City, Pitt, National Championship Teams, #1 in
'80.. (1981) 1-2
Iron City, Pitt, National Championship Teams, 2nd Ed (no #1 in
'80) .... (1982) 3-5

Iron City, Pitt, Bicentennial 1987 "You're in for a game ...."(1987).....................1-2
Gambrinus, Ohio State Golden Highlights ...... (1975).......................3-5

Royal

Mizzou Brew, pictures Missouri mascot .... (1979).......................1-2
Mizzou Brew, Tiger Bowl "78 (Mizzou defeats LSU Tigers)...(1979).......................2-3
Mizzou Brew, Tigers vs Longhorns (matchups 1894-1979) ....(1979).......................2-3

Schlitz

Schlitz, Schlitz Men's Club of Tampa-- Florida vs Georgia, Gator Bowl, Jacksonville, Fla., Nov 9, 1963. (mug) a handful known. 16oz...(1963)...............200-300

United (Huber)

Illini Beer, 1984 schedule .... (1984).......................2-3

(No brewery listed)

Bulldog Brew, The Beer of Champions, 1980 Georgia football results (contained carbonated soft drink-not beer) ....(1981).....................10-12
East Rochester Bombers. "We are Number 1. You can bank on it!" For local football team. No beer or soft drink (bank)......(1995).......................8-10

Hockey

Anheuser Busch

Budweiser, 1990-91 Adirondack Red Wings schedule, MDA Night (air-sealed)..(1990)...................20-30
Budweiser, Century's Greatest Teams. 1972 Boston Bruins...(1999).......................1-2
Budweiser, Century's Greatest Teams. 1972 Boston Bruins (Texas) ....(1999).......................2-3
Budweiser, Century's Greatest Teams. 1972 Boston Bruins (Chicago) ....(1999).......................2-3
Budweiser, Century's Greatest Teams. 1973 NY Islanders ....(1999).......................1-2
Budweiser, Century's Greatest Teams. 1973 NY Islanders (Texas logo) ....(1999).......................2-3
Budweiser, Century's Greatest Teams. 1973 NY Islanders (Chicago) ....(1999).......................2-3

Carling

Black Label, Boston Bruins 1969-70 .... (1970)...................30-35
Black Label, Boston Bruins 1971-72 .... (1972)...................35-40

Coors

Coors Light, Penguins Silver Anniv (silver backgr'nd-red blade) 16oz...(1991).......................2-3
Coors Light, Penguins Silver Anniv (white backgr'nd-blue blade) 16oz...(1991).......................2-3
Coors Light, Pittsburgh Penguins 1993-94, "Cold Silver on Ice" 16oz...(1994).......................2-3
Coors Light, Penguins. "We're Back". 1994-95 Lock-out Season 16oz...(1995).......................2-3
Coors Light, Penguins 1995-96 season. "Kickin' Ice!" 16oz(1996) 2-3
Coors Light, Penguins Thirty Years of Hockey Excellence, 1967-1997 16oz..................................(1997).......................2-3
Coors Light, Pittsburgh Penguins, 1997-1998 16oz(1998).................2-3
Coors Light, Boston Bruins, 75th Year 16oz...... (1998).......................3-5
Coors Light, Penguins, "Thanks, Mario". Adrenaline on Ice 16oz...(2000).......................2-3
Coors, "Nothing Beats an Original". Gordie Howe #9 16oz...(2001).......................2-3

Genesee

Genesee, Rochester Americans, 1996 Calder Cup Champions.....................................(1997).......................2-3

Heileman

Old Style, salutes Chicago Blackhawks (white background) 16oz...(1991).......................2-3
Old Style Light, salutes Chicago Blackhawks (silver background) 16oz...(1991).......................2-3
Old Style, Chicago Blackhawks Highlights 16oz ..(1992).......................2-3
Special Export, salutes Minnesota North Stars 16oz...(1993).......................2-3
Special Export Light, salutes Minnesota North Stars 16oz...(1993).......................3-5
Old Style, salutes '92-'93 Chicago Blackhawks 16oz...(1993).......................2-3

Old Style Light, salutes '92-'93 Chicago Blackhawks 16oz...(1993) 2-3

Labatt's (CANADIAN)

Labatt's, Stanley Cup Crazy Series, 20-can series(2001)...................2 each

Miller

Lite, Detroit Red Wings, 1993-94 season 16oz (1993) 5-8
Miller Genuine Draft, Detroit Red Wings, 1993-94 season 16oz...(1993) 10-12
Miller Genuine Draft, Philadelphia Flyers, 1993-94 season 16oz...(1993) 2-3
Miller Genuine Draft, Boston Bruins, 1993-94 season 16oz...(1993) 2-3
Miller Genuine Draft, San Jose Sharks, 1993-94 season 16oz...(1993) 2-3
Lite, HockeyTown, '97 Champions (Detroit Red Wings) 16oz...(1997) 2-3
Lite, Detroit Red Wings, '98 Stanley Cup Champions 16oz...(1998) 2-3
Lite, Detroit Red Wings Stanley Cup Champions, 16oz...(2002) 2-3

Molson

Molson Canadian, Detroit Red Wings, 2002 Stanley Cup Champions, 5-liter .... (2002) 20-25

National

A-1 Premium Beer, Phoenix Roadrunners 1969-70 schedule (bank) .... (1970) 125-150
A-1 Premium Beer, Phoenix Roadrunners 1970-71 schedule (bank) .... (1971) 50-75
A-1 Premium Beer, Phoenix Roadrunners 1971-72 schedule (bank) .... (1972) 30-40
A-1 Premium Beer, Phoenix Roadrunners 1972-73 schedule (bank) .... (1973) 25-30

Pittsburgh

Iron City, Stanley Cup Champions (listing) ...... (1974) 8-10
Iron City Draft, Stanley Cup Champions (listing) ..(1974).................8-10
Iron City, Two great names on ice, Penguins and Iron City .... (1976) 2-3
Iron City, 1982 Pittsburgh Penguins (color team photo) .... (1982) 2-3
Iron City, Boys of Winter .... (1989) 3-5
Iron City, Boys of Winte 16oz............................ (1989) 2-3
Iron City, Penguins (player #90 in black uniform) ..(1990).......................2-3
Iron City, Penguins (player #90 in black uniform) 16oz...(1990) 2-3
Iron City, "Workin' on a Cold Iron" (goalie) ...... (1991) 2-3
Iron City, "Workin' on a Cold Iron" (goalie) 16oz(1991) 2-3
Iron City, salutes 1991 Stanley Cup Champions(1991) 2-3
Iron City, salutes 1991 Stanley Cup Champions 16oz...(1991) 2-3
IC Light, salutes back-to-back Stanley Cup championships .... (1992) 2-3
IC Light, salutes back-to-back Stanley Cup championships 16oz...(1992) 2-3
IC Light, salutes the back-to-back Stanley Cup champs "Go Pens, Go For the Hat Trick ...."(1993) 2-3
IC Light, "Go Pens" "Bring Back the Cup......."(1994) 2-3
IC Light, "Go Pens" "Bring Back the Cup" 16oz(1994) 2-3
IC Premium, Pittsburgh Penguins salute Russian Penguins 1993-94 inaugural season (in Russian, but sold in U.S.) .....(1994).......................2-3
IC Premium, Pittsburgh Penguins salute Russian Penguins (in English-first version exported to Russia) .... (1994) 12-15
IC Premium, The Russian Penguins (in English- second version exported to Russia) .... (1994) 8-10
IC Light, Wheeling Nailers, East Coast Hockey League .... (1996) 3-5
IC Light, Johnstown Chiefs, East Coast Hockey League 16oz...(1997) 3-5
IC Light, Pittsburgh Penguins 30th Anniversary Season .... (1997) 1-2
IC Light, "Mike's Language", salutes Pittsburgh Penguins' announcer, Mike Lang.. (1998) 1-2
IC Light, "Mike's Language", salutes Penguins' announcer, Mike Lang 16oz...(1998) 2-3
IC Light, "The Best on Ice" Pittsburgh Penguins 16oz...(1999) 2-3

Stroh

Stroh's, "salutes" Mario Lemieux, Hockey Hall of
Famer..(1998).....................2-3
Stroh's Light, "salutes" Mario Lemieux, Hockey Hall of
Famer..(1998).....................2-3
Stroh's, "honors" Mario Lemieux, Hockey Hall of
Famer..(1999).....................2-3
Stroh's, "honors" Mario Lemieux, Hockey Hall of Famer
16oz...(1999).....................2-3
Stroh's Light, "honors" Mario Lemieux, Hockey Hall of
Famer..(1999).....................2-3

Golf

Anheuser Busch

Michelob Golf Hole series cans..................(1994-97).....................1-3
John G. Oldani, 1947-78 retirement. Shows golfers on side
panel...(1978)..................8-10
Harry Johnson, 1945-83 retirement. Shows golfer on side
panel...(1983)....................5-8
Budweiser, Kingsmill Golf Club, Williamsburg, VA Jun 23, 1979,
16oz...(1979)..................80-90
Budweiser, Kingsmill Hole 5, Jun 21, 1980 16oz..(1980)..................80-90
Budweiser, Kingsmill Hole 17, Jun 20, 1981 16oz(1981)................60-70
Budweiser, Kingsmill Hole 8, Jun 19, 1982 16oz...(1982)................60-70
Budweiser, Kingsmill Hole 15, Jun 18, 1983 16oz (1983)................60-70
Budweiser, Kingsmill Hole 13, Jun 23, 1984 16oz (1984)................60-70
Budweiser, Kingsmill Hole 16, Jun 25, 1985 16oz (1985)................60-70
Budweiser, Kingsmill Plantation Course Hole 7, Jun 14, 1986
16oz...(1986)..................60-70
Budweiser, Kingsmill River Course Hole 3, Jun 20, 1987
16oz...(1987)..................80-90
Budweiser, Kingsmill River Course Hole 10, Jun 25, 1988
16oz...(1988)..................80-90
Budweiser, Kingsmill River Course Hole 9, Jun 24, 1989
16oz...(1989)..................80-90
Budweiser, Kingsmill River Course Hole 14, Jun 23, 1990
16oz...(1990)..................60-70
Budweiser, Kingsmill River Course Hole 11, May 25, 1991
16oz...(1991)..................60-70
Budweiser, Kingsmill River Course Hole 4, May 16, 1992
16oz...(1992)..................60-70
Budweiser, Kingsmill River Course Hole 7, May 8, 1993
16oz...(1993)..................60-70
Michelob, 1981 PGA Tour, Anheuser Busch Golf Classic Kingsmill Golf
Club, July 23-26, Williamsburg, VA.............(1981).....................5-8
Budweiser, 1981 PGA Tour, Anheuser Busch Golf Classic Kingsmill
Golf Club, July 23-26, Williamsburg, VA.....(1981).....................5-8
Michelob, 1982 PGA Tour, Anheuser Busch Golf Classic Kingsmill Golf
Club, July 22-25, Williamsburg, VA.............(1982).....................3-5
Budweiser, 1982 PGA Tour, Anheuser Busch Golf Classic Kingsmill
Golf Club, July 22-25, Williamsburg, VA.....(1982).....................3-5
Anheuser Busch Golf Classic, green shield with golf clubs
(air sealed)...(?).....................20-30
1984 Invitational Golf Outing, Metal Container Corp, Columbus, OH, June
30, 1984, Foxfire Golf Club, Lockbourne, Ohio, Incl. large Anheuser
Busch logo and drawing of golfer...................(1984)...............20-30
O'Doul's, Proud sponsor of the PGA Tour
(non-alcoholic)...(1995).....................1-2
O'Doul's, small PGA Tour logo, no golf background like 1995
can..(1996).....................1-2
O'Doul's Biere, like 1995 N-A can, but for sale in
Canada..(1996).....................2-3
O'Doul's, small PGA Tour logo, $5 Busch Gardens
rebate...(1996).....................2-3
O'Doul's, small PGA Tour logo, "Born-on Date"(1997).....................1-2
O'Doul's, small PGA Tour logo, "Now Richer &
Smoother"...(1999).....................1-2
O'Doul s Biere, for sale in Canada.................(1998).....................1-2
Michelob Light, Fairway to Heaven. "Titans of Rock meet the Giants of
Golf," on VH1...(1996).....................2-3
Michelob Light, Fairway to Heaven. Nov 16, 1996 on
VH1..(1996).....................2-3
Michelob Beer, 2-sided gold can with embossed golf ball
design...(2001).....................1-2
Michelob Light, 2-sided silver can with embossed golf ball
design...(2001).....................1-2

Coors

Coors Light, Phoenix Open, January 1991......(1991).....................2-3

Panther Brewing, Utica, NY

The Three Stooges Beer, shows the guys playing golf on back
panel...(1999).....................2-3

Pittsburgh

Iron City, Major Tournament Champions
1964-1974..(1975)..................8-10
Iron City Draft, Major Tournament Champions
1964-1974..(1975)..................8-10
Williams Country Club, Weirton, WV, Mighty Tin Can Invitational Golf
Tournament...(1981)..............10-15

Motor Sports

American National Can

BCCA CANvention 26 Indianapolis, shows checkered flag and race
car...(1996).....................3-5

Anheuser Busch

Busch NASCAR Race Track series cans... (1996-97).....................1-3
Busch, Busch Clash, Daytona Beach, Fla. 16th Anniversary
Commemorative can 16oz...........................(1994).....................2-3
Busch, Busch Clash, Daytona Beach, FL, 17th Anniversary
Commemorative can.....................................(1995).....................1-2
Busch, Busch Clash, Daytona Beach, FL, 17th Anniversary
Commemorative can 16oz...........................(1995).....................2-3
Budweiser, shows Budweiser/Kmart Indy car. (for Brazil) Chris Fittipaldi
signature ("Rio de Janeiro" on side panel) . (1996).....................5-8
Budweiser, shows Budweiser/Kmart Indy car. (for Argentina) Fittipaldi sig-
nature (fluted- "Santa Fe" on side panel)........(1997).....................5-8
Budweiser, shows Budweiser/Kmart Indy car. (for Paraguay) Fittipaldi sig-
nature (fluted- "Paraguay" on side panel)........(1997).....................5-8
Budweiser, shows Budweiser/Kmart Indy car. (for Japan)
16oz...(1996).....................5-8
Budweiser, US Forces Okinawa. Shows pit crew working on Budweiser
NASCAR car. (sold in Okinawa)................(1998)..................8-12
Budweiser, Century's Greatest Teams. 1986 Earnhardt Racing Team
(1999)..1-2
Budweiser, Century's Greatest Teams. 1986 Earnhardt Racing Team
(Texas logo)..(1999).....................2-3
Budweiser, Century's Greatest Teams. 1986 Earnhardt Racing Team
(Chicago logo)...(1999).....................2-3
Budweiser, Century's Greatest Teams. 1977 Yarborough Racing
Team..(1999).....................1-2
Budweiser, Century's Greatest Teams. 1977 Yarborough Racing Team
(Texas logo)..(1999).....................2-3
Budweiser, Century's Greatest Teams. 1977 Yarborough Racing Team
(Chicago logo)...(1999).....................2-3
Budweiser, 1999 Winston Cup Debut, Dale Earnhardt, Jr. Shows fac-
simile autograph and his Budweiser Car #8
16oz...(1999).....................2-3
Budweiser, 2000 Winston Cup Rookie Year. Color photo of Dale Earn-
hardt, Jr. & Daytona track 16oz.................(1999).....................2-3
Budweiser, 2000 Winston Cup Rookie Year. Number 8, Texas Motor
Speedway, Dale Earnhardt, Jr. signature. 16oz(2000).....................2-3
Budweiser, 2000 Winston Cup Rookie Year. Number 8, Texas Motor
Speedway, no signature. (sold in Virginia) 16oz(2000).....................3-5
Budweiser, 2000 Winston Cup Rookie Year. NH International Speed-
way, Dale Earnhardt, Jr. signature. 16oz ... (2000).....................2-3
Budweiser, 2000 Winston Cup. Team Work. Phoenix International
Raceway. Shows Dale Earnhardt, Jr. and crew.
16oz...(2000).....................2-3
Budweiser, Dale Earnhardt, Jr.'s NASCAR # 8 & Kenny Bernstein's
dragster. Proud supporter of the 2000 US Olympic Team
16oz...(2000).....................2-3
Budweiser, Dale Earnhardt Jr. 16oz...............(2002).....................1-2
Budweiser, Dale Earnhardt Jr. (Texas) 16 oz...(2002).....................2-3
Busch, Busch Champions....................................(2002).....................1-2
Busch, Busch Champions (Texas) 16oz..........(2002).....................2-3
Busch Light, Busch Champions 16oz..............(2002).....................1-2
Busch Light, Busch Champions (Texas).........(2002).....................2-3

Cold Spring

Raceways Beer, Knoxville, Iowa, August 8-11, 1979 19th Annual Super
Sprint National Championships..................(1979).....................2-3

Cook

Cook's 500 Ale, checkered flag, Indy car (cone top)(1953)............500-700

Cook's 500 Ale, checkered flag, Indy car
(flat top)..(1953)..............300-400

Coors

Coors, 1990 Camel Grand Prix, San Diego, CA(1990) 3-5
Coors, 1991 Camel Grand Prix, San Diego, CA(1991) 3-5
Coors, Official Beer of the Toyota Grand Prix, Long Beach,
CA 1990 ....(1990)......................3-5
Coors, Official Beer of the Toyota Grand Prix, Long Beach,
CA 1991 ....(1991)......................3-5
Coors, Official Beer of the Toyota Grand Prix, Long Beach,
CA 1992 ....(1992)......................3-5
Keystone, 1992 Winston Cup Series schedule (1992)......................2-3
Keystone Light, 1992 Winston Cup Series
schedule ....(1992)......................2-3
Keystone Dry, 1992 Winston Cup Series
schedule ....(1992)......................2-3
Keystone, 1993 Winston Cup Series schedule (1993)......................2-3
Keystone Light, 1993 Winston Cup Series
schedule ....(1993)......................2-3
Keystone Dry, 1993 Winston Cup Series
schedule ....(1993)......................2-3
Coors Light, 1995 Winston Cup schedule........(1995)......................2-3
Coors Light, Coors Light Racing, Winston Cup car #42
(K. Petty) ....(1995)......................2-3
Coors Light, Coors Light Racing, Winston Cup car #42
(K. Petty) 16oz ....(1995)......................3-5
Coors Light, Petty Facts, Fact #3501 ....(1996)......................2-3
Coors Light, Petty Facts, Fact #3502 ....(1996)......................2-3
Coors Light, Petty Facts, Fact #3505 ....(1996)......................2-3
Coors Light, Petty Facts, Fact #3509 ....(1996)......................2-3
Coors Light, Petty Facts, Fact #3513 ....(1996)......................2-3
Coors Light, Petty Facts, Fact #3514 ....(1996)......................2-3
Coors Light, 1996 NASCAR Schedule ....(1996)......................2-3
Coors Light, Texas Motor Speedway Inaugural Season, 1997
16oz ....(1997)......................3-5
Coors, 75th Motorcycle Race & Rally Week, Laconia, NH,
16oz ....(1998)......................3-5
Coors Light, Sterling Marlin's 1999 Coors Light NASCAR car
16oz ....(1999)......................2-3
Coors Light, Indy 500. Pep Boys Special Issue. Sold in Indiana
16oz ....(1999)......................3-5
Coors Light, Sturgis/Black Hills Rally 1999 16oz..(1999)......................3-5
Coors, Pikes Peak. Describes Pikes Peak Hill Climb race on side panel
(embossed) ....(1999)......................1-2
Coors, Pikes Peak. Describes Pikes Peak Hill Climb race on side panel
(smooth-3.2% alcohol) ....(1999)......................3-5
Coors Light, Racing 2000. Shows the 2000 NASCAR schedule
16oz ....(1999)......................2-3
Coors Light, 2000 Indy 500. Shows front of #91 IRL car
16oz ....(2000)......................2-3
Coors Light, Racing 2001. NASCAR Schedule
16oz ....(2001)......................2-3
Coors Light, 2001 Indy 500/IRL Northern Lights Series
16oz ....(2001)......................2-3
Coors Light, Kansas Speedway, 2001 Inaugural Season
16oz ....(2001)......................2-3
Coors Light, Sterling Marlin.......................(2002)......................2-3
Coors Light, Official Beer 86th Indianapolis 500
May 26, 2002 ....(2002)......................2-3
Coors Light, Kansas Speedway 2002 ....(2002)......................2-3

Falstaff

Indianapolis 500 Beer, 1984 First Edition........(1984)......................2-3

Jones

Stoney's Light, Racing Series #1 (checkered
flags) ....(1994)......................2-3
Stoney's Beer, Racing Series Collection. Sponsor of Stoney's Late
Model Div, Motordrome Speedway, Smithton,
PA ....(1995)......................2-3
Stoney's Light, Racing Series Collection. Sponsor of Stoney's Late
Model Div, Motordrome Speedway, Smithton,
PA ....(1995)......................2-3
Stoney's Light, Racing Series #3 Collection. Motordrome
Speedway ....(1996)......................2-3

Miller

Miller Genuine Draft, 76th Indianapolis 500, Miller #12 Indy car
16oz ....(1992)......................2-3

Miller Genuine Draft, 1992 MGD Indy Car Champ
16oz ....(1993)......................2-3
Miller Genuine Draft, Winston Cup car #2, MGD Thunderbird
16oz ....(1994)......................2-3
Miller Lite, back shows NASCAR car #2 with Lite logo on hood
16oz ....(1999)......................2-3
Miller Lite, Miller Brickyard 400 16oz ....(2002)......................2-3
Miller Genuine Draft, Rusty Wallace 16oz ....(2002)......................2-3

Specialty Brewing (Pabst)

Indiana's Best, shows Indy car ....(1996)......................2-3
Indiana's Best Light, shows stock car #18 ......(1996)......................2-3

Bowling

Florida

Big Strike Premium Beer, 1994, First Edition, American Bowling
Congress, celebrates 99th year, Mobile, AL, (1994) 2-3

Pabst

Pabst Blue Ribbon, American Bowling Congress Centennial,
1895-1995 ....(1995)......................2-3

Pittsburgh

Iron City, leading PBA averages, 1962-1973 ... (1974) 8-10
Iron City Draft, leading PBA averages, 1962-1973(1974)...............8-10

Soccer

Anheuser Busch

Budweiser, World Cup USA 94 ....(1994)......................1-2
Budweiser, World Cup USA 94 16oz ....(1994)......................2-3
Budweiser, World Cup USA 94 24oz ....(1994)......................3-5
Bud Light, World Cup USA 94 ....(1994)......................1-2
Bud Light, World Cup USA 94 16oz ....(1994)......................2-3
Bud Light, World Cup USA 94 24oz ....(1994)......................3-5
Bud Dry Draft, World Cup USA 94 ....(1994)......................1-2

Coors

Coors Light, shows soccer player in green shirt & red socks
24oz ....(2000)......................2-3
Coors, soccer player- kicking 24oz ....(2001)......................2-3
Coors Light, soccer player- kicking. "La bala de plata"
24oz ....(2001)......................2-3
Coors, soccer player- header. 24oz ....(2001)......................2-3
Coors Light, soccer player- header. "La bala de plata"
24oz ....(2001)......................2-3
Coors, soccer player- bicycle kick. 24oz ....(2001)......................2-3
Coors Light, soccer player- bicycle kick. "La bala de plata"
24oz ....(2001)......................2-3
Coors, soccer player- goalie save. 24oz ....(2001)......................2-3
Coors Light, soccer player- goalie save. "La bala de plata"
24oz...(2001)......................2-3

Miller

Miller Genuine Draft, action drawing of soccer player #9
16oz ....(1997)......................2-3
Miller Genuine Draft, shows two soccer players
24oz...(1998)......................2-3

Olympics

Anheuser Busch

Bud Olympic sports cans..........................(1996)......................1-3
Budweiser, "Proud sponsor, US Olympic Team" (1988) 2-3
Budweiser, "Proud sponsor, US Olympic Team"
16oz ....(1988)......................3-5
Bud Light, "Proud sponsor, US Olympic Team" (1988) 2-3
Busch, "Proud sponsor, US Olympic Team" ... (1988) 2-3
Busch, "Proud sponsor, US Olympic Team" 16oz(1988)......................3-5
Natural Light, "Proud sponsor, US Olympic Team"(1988)......................2-3
Bud Summer Games, 1992 Olympics sponsor (contained
water) ....(1992)......................2-3
Budweiser, Century's Greatest Teams. 1936 US Olympic men's track
and field team ....(1999)......................1-2
Budweiser, Century's Greatest Teams '36 US Olympic men's track, field
(Texas logo) ....(1999)......................2-3
Bud., Century's Greatest Teams. '36 US Olympic men's track, field
(Chicago logo) ....(1999)......................2-3
Budweiser, Century's Greatest Teams. 1980 US Olympic men's hockey
team ....(1999)......................1-2
Bud, Century's Greatest Teams. 1980 US Olympic men's hockey team
(Texas logo) ....(1999)......................2-3

Bud, Century's Greatest Teams. 1980 US Olympic men's hockey team
(Chicago logo) .... (1999)....................... 2-3
Busch, proud supporter of the 2000 US Olympic
Team .... (2000)...................... 1-2
Busch Light, proud supporter of the 2000 US Olympic
Team .... (2000)...................... 1-2

Bronco Industries
Winter Olympic Snow, XIII Olympic Winter Games, Lake Placid 1980.
Contains packet of "moisture" from Lake Placid
snow.. (1980)................... 8-10

Pabst
Pabst Blue Ribbon, promotes Beijing, China's 2008 Olympics
bid .... (2001).................. 20-25

Schlitz
Schlitz, "Official licensed beer of the 1980 Olympic Games" (aluminum)
Lake Placid 1980 and Moscow 1980 logos on side
panel .... (1980)...................... 3-5
Schlitz, "Official licensed beer of the 1980 Olympic Games" (steel)
Lake Placid 1980 and Moscow 1980 logos on side
panel .... (1980)...................... 3-5
Schlitz, "Official licensed beer of the 1980 Olympic Games" a run of
200,000 Olympic cans was printed with only the Lake Placid 1980
logo on side panel. Schlitz had second thoughts about leaving off
the Moscow 1980 logo and ordered the cans scrapped, but several
dozen were salvaged from the line by an employee who was also a
can collector. .... (1980).................. 20-25

Miscellaneous

American National Can Co.
BCCA CANvention 20, East Rutherford, NJ. Shows Giants Stadium
among features on map of New Jersey ...... (1990)..................... 2-3

Anheuser Busch
Budweiser, North Carolina State (shows mascot)
16oz .... (?).................. 15-20
Budweiser, East Carolina University Pirates (shows mascot)
16oz .... (?).................. 10-15
Budweiser, Florida State Seminoles (shows mascot) 16oz(1978) 15-20

Cold Spring
Sooner Extra Beer, (for Oklahoma sports fans) (1994) 2-3

Coors
Coors Light, New York City Marathon 16oz...... (1999)..................... 5-8
Coors Light, Three Rivers Stadium 1970-2001. Home of 6 World
Championships 16oz .... (2000)..................... 2-3
Coors Light, American Airlines Center, Dallas, TX
24oz .... (2001)..................... 2-3
Coors Light, XSS Xtreme Silver Summer. Promotes Xtreme
Games .... (2001)..................... 2-3

Great Lakes
Hoosier Dome, lists 1984 major fall sporting
events .... (1984)....................... 2-3

Miller
Miller High Life, Milwaukee County Stadium, 1953-2000
16oz.. (2000) 2-3

Pearl
VP Fair 1983, St. Louis' Fondest Memories. Mentions local teams:
Cardinals, Blues, Steamers, and Billikens.. (1983) 3-5

Pickett
Iowa Sports Beer, Hawkeyes-Cyclones-Panthers-Bulldogs,
1981-82 .... (1981) 2-3

Pittsburgh
Iron City, Three Rivers Stadium .... (1973) 5-8
Iron City, Civic Arena .... (1973) 5-8
Iron City, The Incline. Shows Three Rivers Stadium in
background.. (1973) 5-8
Iron City, Men of Iron and Steel-drawings of P'bgh sports figures
16oz... (1981) 3-5
Iron City, Civic Arena and Three Rivers Stadium..(1993)........................2-3
Iron City, The Pittsburgh Kid. Paul Spadafora, IBF Lightweight World
Champion 16oz .... (2000) 1-2
Iron City, tribute to 3 Pittsburgh sports stadiums ..(2000)....................... 1-2

Royal
Razorback Beer, shows University of Arkansas
mascot .... (1980) 2-3
Boilermaker Beer, Purdue University .... (1980) 2-3
Fighting Irish Beer, Notre Dame .... (1980) 2-3
Mizzou Brew Beer, Tiger Country, Missouri
(steel) .... (1980) 2-3
Mizzou Brew Beer, Tiger Country, Missouri
(aluminum) .... (1982) 3-5
Battlin' Bulldog Beer, Georgia (aluminum) .... (1982) 2-3
Fighting Wildcats Beer, Kentucky (aluminum) . (1983) 2-3

Schlitz
Schlitz, University of Illinois (shows mascot) 16oz(1969)....................20-25
Schlitz, University of Iowa (shows mascot) 16oz..(1969)....................20-25
Schlitz, Middlebury College Panthers (Vermont) (shows mascot)
16oz .... (1969) 75-100
Schlitz, NC State University (shows mascot)
16oz .... (1969) 40-50

Stroh
Schlitz Malt Liquor , "Instant Winner" Win trip to heavyweight
championship fight in Las Vegas with Larry Holmes
16oz.. (1997) 3-5
St. Ides Malt Liquor, The Sound and the Fury, Holyfield-Tyson II, May 3,
1997, MGM Grand, Las Vegas 24oz .... (1997) 3-5

Chapter 16
AUTOGRAPH ADVICE

Step Carefully

Whether you're collecting autographs or trading cards, a little knowledge can save you a lot of grief and money

By Rocky Landsverk

Collecting sports cards and autographs should be nothing but fun, and for decades, it was. Unfortunately, as sports collectibles became more valuable, they also became more difficult to collect because crooks joined collectors in looking for a profit.

So in the past decade or so, fake autographs have been a serious problem in the sports collectibles industry. And fake or counterfeit cards have been a serious problem for about 15 years.

In both cases, virtually every fake offers some telltale clues. Learning to look for these clues can help you avoid a lot of misery.

COLLECTING AUTOGRAPHS

Collecting the autograph of sports stars used to be a lot cheaper, but in many ways, it's gotten a lot easier as it's gotten more expensive. It used to be pretty difficult to find autographs of professional players. As they started charging money, however, it became available through mail order companies, and now of course the Internet makes it very easy to find sports autographs.

The Internet also makes it very easy to find fake autographs. It's so prevalent online today that for superstars like Michael Jordan, it's possible that 50-70

percent of autographs available through Internet auctions are fake.

"It's very easy to sell items online, and the anonymity makes people selling bad items feel a lot more safe than if they were selling them through a store," said Bert Lehman, autograph expert for *Sports Collectors Digest*.

Here's a pile of advice to keep in mind when you're collecting autographs, not only online but also at shows and through the mail.

• **Know what the athlete's autograph looks like.** This doesn't mean try to play "authenticator" yourself. There are experts who get paid a lot of money

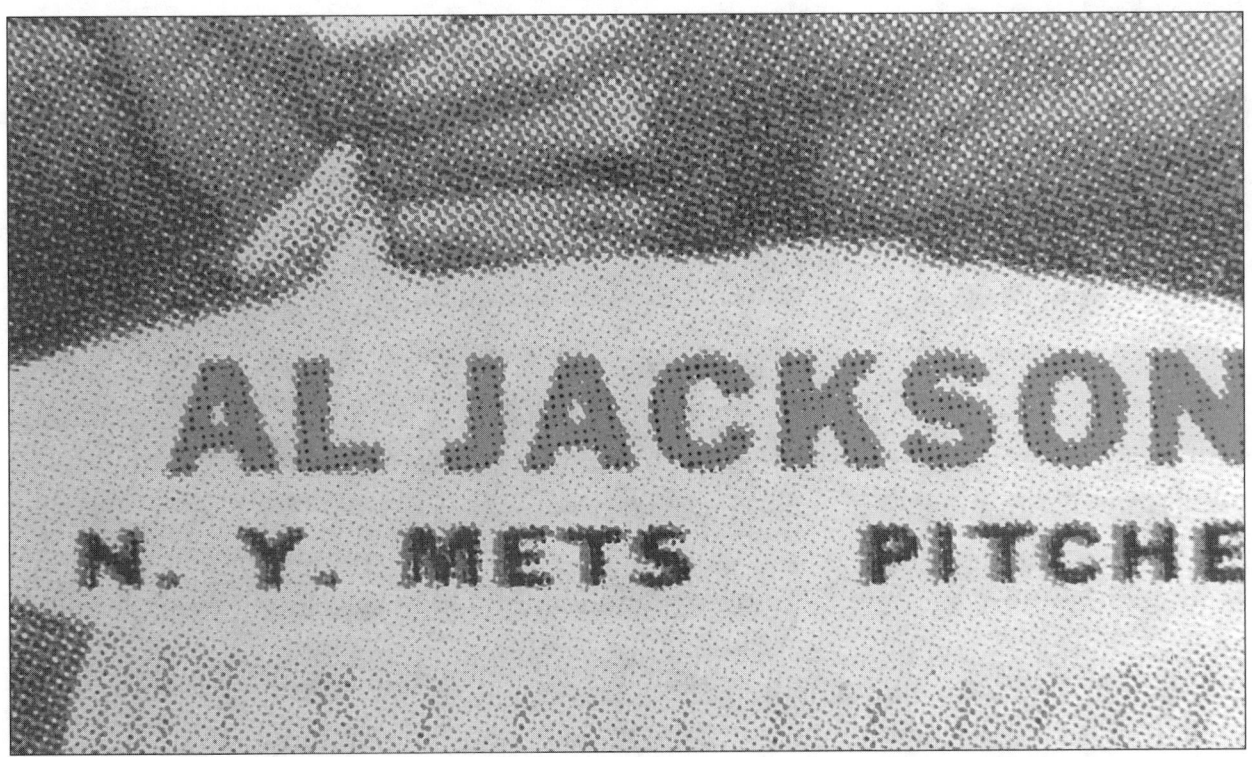

Here's what happens when people try to counterfeit trading cards-the result looks bumpy or full of dots, not smooth like a printing job should. It's a good idea to put a card under magnification before you buy it. A 5X magnifying glass should suffice.

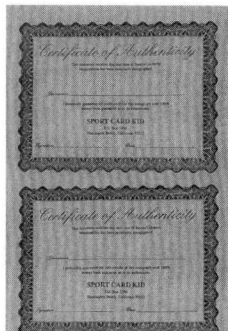

On this page are pictures of certificates of authenticity provided by the FBI in connection with its investigations into fake autographs. The FBI has determined that virtually all of the autographs associated with these COAs are fake because these COAs were created specifically to provide authenticity for fake autographs.

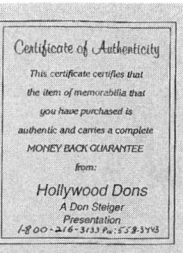

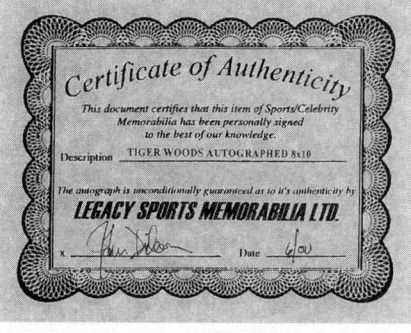

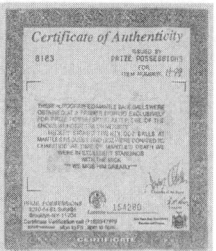

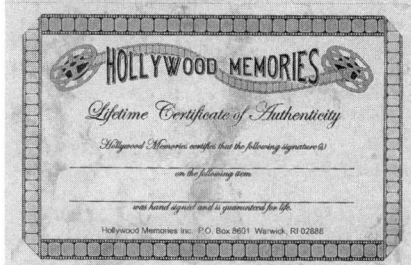

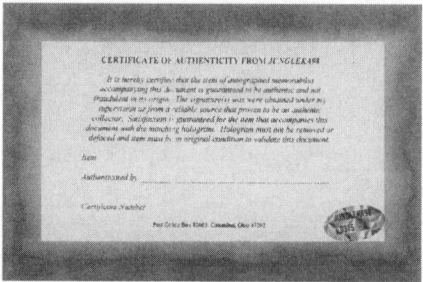

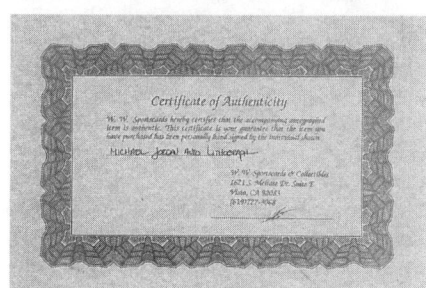

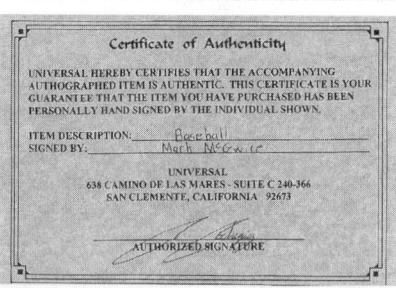

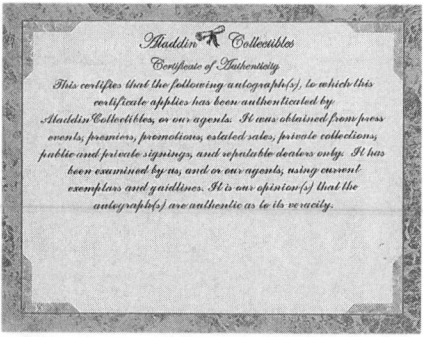

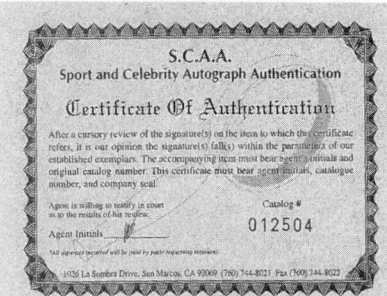

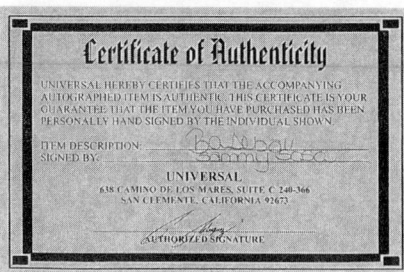

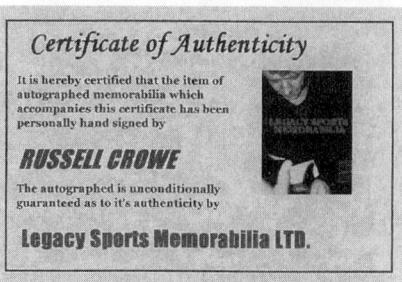

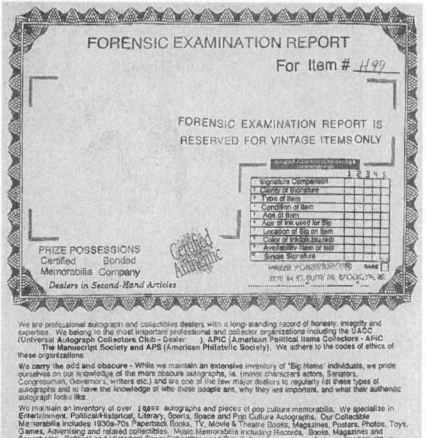

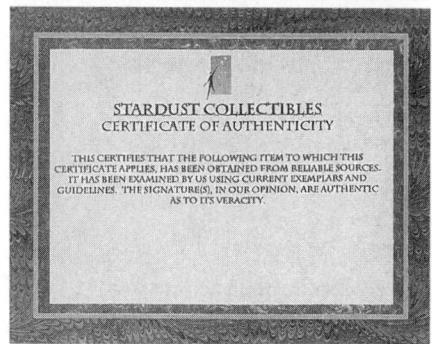

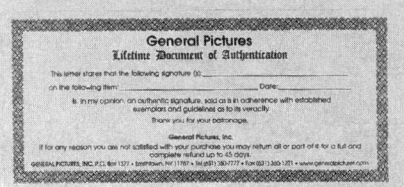

to be able to tell a well-executed forgery from a real autograph. This simply means you should have a general idea of what the athlete's autograph looks like before you spend a lot of money on it.

• **Know the company.** This is probably the most-important factor when buying an autograph. There are fewer than 10 companies that are well-known autograph producers, and you can learn about them in the pages of hobby magazines. You can start with the core companies that are part of Major League Baseball's authentication program: Upper Deck Authenticated, Steiner Sports, Tristar Productions, Mounted Memories/ Field of Dreams and allstarlineup.com. There are other companies that the industry knows to produce valid product, like Authentic Sports Investments, which counts Alex Rodriguez and Rafael Palmeiro among many exclusive autograph signers.

If you're not sure about the company, check out the sports memorabilia magazines and see if they advertise, and ask the local sports card dealer about them.

Above all, make sure you know the company's address and make sure they're still around. A lot of material sold online comes with "certificates of authenticity" from companies that don't exist and never did.

• **Be reasonable.** This means don't fall for something because it's cheap; don't let the great price convince you it's real because you really want it to be real. Superstars like Dan Marino and Joe Montana charge companies $50-$100 for their autograph. Their autographs can be found in small quantities more cheaply, but not in large quantities. If you see a stack of Marino signed 8-by-10 photos at a show for $20 apiece, where could they possibly be from?

• **Don't be fooled by fancy certificates of authenticity.** Related to the point above, COAs are as good as the company that backs them. A lot of fake material comes with a great-looking COA, as you see in some of the pictures in this article. Worry about the company backing the autograph, and get a COA from them, but don't be "wowed" by a certificate of authenticity.

• **Look for authentication programs.** Items that have holograms or other markings on them that were applied at the time of signing are the safest autographs you can buy, provided (as mentioned above) that the company that placed the hologram or mark on there is legitimate. The MLB authentication program is the model for the perfectly authenticated product. Deloitte & Touche, an accounting firm, sends a third-party (financially uninvolved) person to

Playing Authenticator

"Don't try this at home," but it is fun to pretend you're an expert and authenticate an autograph, after you've gotten a little experience. There are some things to look for when you're trying to determine the authenticity of an autograph.

1) Could the athlete have signed this item? Authenticators don't just look at the quality of the autograph. Actually, that's often last on their list of importance. First they determine if the item was produced during the player's lifetime. Arm yourself with a list of baseball presidents, for instance, if you're a baseball collector, because (for instance) Mickey Mantle signed very few Gene Budig balls (which came into use in 1995, the year Mantle died, and The Mick wasn't very healthy in 1995 and didn't sign often.)

2) Is the autograph shaky? Authenticators always use magnifiers and sometimes microscopes to check if the autograph looks like somebody was trying to "think" their way through the autograph. For instance, Mickey Mantle had a very smooth autograph, he wrote quickly and accurately. Often, forgers take their time in duplicating the autograph, and the result is blotches where the pen actually stopped, or quivers and unevenness. Below is a picture of a Mickey Mantle forgery, and you can see under magnification how shaky the autograph is.

Here is a fake Mickey Mantle autograph. As you can see below, it looks a little shaky or wavering upon magnification, and the telltale starts and stops of a forger are obvious. Few people — and Mantle wasn't one of them — hesitate while signing their own signature.

the signing to put the MLB hologram on the item. Other companies also use hologram systems. Holograms have become the standard of the industry.

COUNTERFEIT CARDS

Counterfeit trading cards are actually one area of the hobby that has been cleaned up significantly in the past 15-20 years. Before cards had fancy printing and gloss finishes and holograms, it was fairly easy to counterfeit cards. Giving credit where it's due, when Upper Deck brought in the hologram-on-every-card philosophy in 1989, it changed the way the hobby worked, and Upper Deck has never had a counterfeit card problem.

Plus today's cards are very expensive to print, so they aren't a target of counterfeiters. Add in the presence of grading companies – companies that put a grade on the quality of the card while also encasing it in plastic so it can't be damaged again – and

you have the elimination of many previous counterfeits from the marketplace.

However, all of this doesn't mean you don't have to be careful. Especially for cards like Mark McGwire or Michael Jordan rookie cards from the mid-1980s, and for virtually every set prior to that, you have to be careful. Here are some tips from the experts when you're collecting valuable trading cards that might have been counterfeited.

• **Watch for dot patterns and blurry images instead of smooth printing.** Most people don't know much about printing processes, but counterfeit cards are (fortunately) almost always identifiable by the dot patterns and blurry logos or pictures that result when a card is duplicated. The first time a card is produced, the ink goes smoothly onto the card. Except on outstanding counterfeits, when a card is counterfeited or reproduced using that original card as the printing tool, tiny dots show up all over the card, and they're almost always evident under magnification.

"A collector who's going to a show to purchase vintage cards or higher-priced cards should also carry a small magnifying glass," *Sports Collectors Digest* baseball card expert Joe Clemens said. "Most counterfeit cards do not hold up to 5- or 10-power magnification."

This can be especially evident in the small-type and small-logo areas, often on the back. They will often look horrible under magnification. Said Card Collecting Services grading expert Dennis Kaminer, "On many cards, the small trademarks on the back are so fuzzy you can't even see them. We had a Honus Wagner card come in, and when we blew it up, the dot matrix was obvious."

Another tell-tale pattern for fakes is that often cards have a picture inside a frame or border on the card. Many times this frame or border has a different-looking edge on it than the originals, for counterfeiting/printing reasons. "It can be too sharp, or it can be fuzzy, but in general, you can tell that the card doesn't look right," Kaminer said. "Really look the card over, because counterfeits almost never look right."

It will help if you have a known-good original to which you can compare the card you're thinking about buying.

• **If it sounds too good to be true ... it probably is.** "If it's a higher-priced card, beware if it's just too good of a deal," said Cliff May, president of Card Collector Services. "Sometimes a Michael Jordan $1,000 card will be for sale for $200. That should be an alert."

Keep in mind that many cards are priced well under book value nowadays, but not many rare and valuable cards are priced that cheaply.

Similarly, watch out of a card is just too perfect. For instance, old tobacco cards are very difficult (well, almost impossible) to find in great condition. If a dealer found a rare card in perfect condition, it would be placed into a prestigious auction, not sold to you. "Watch out for cards that are condition-sensitive as far as centering, but the centering on the card is too perfect," May said. "It's the same thing with perfectly sharp edges and corners on a card that's decades old."

• **Watch the quantities.** It's possible that a dealer has one or two of a given rare card and is selling them cheaply. If a dealer has dozens, then you want to watch out.

"If the person selling the cards has too many of them, that's a red flag," May said. "If it's a high-priced card and somebody has 10 of them, that should be an alert that something might be going on."

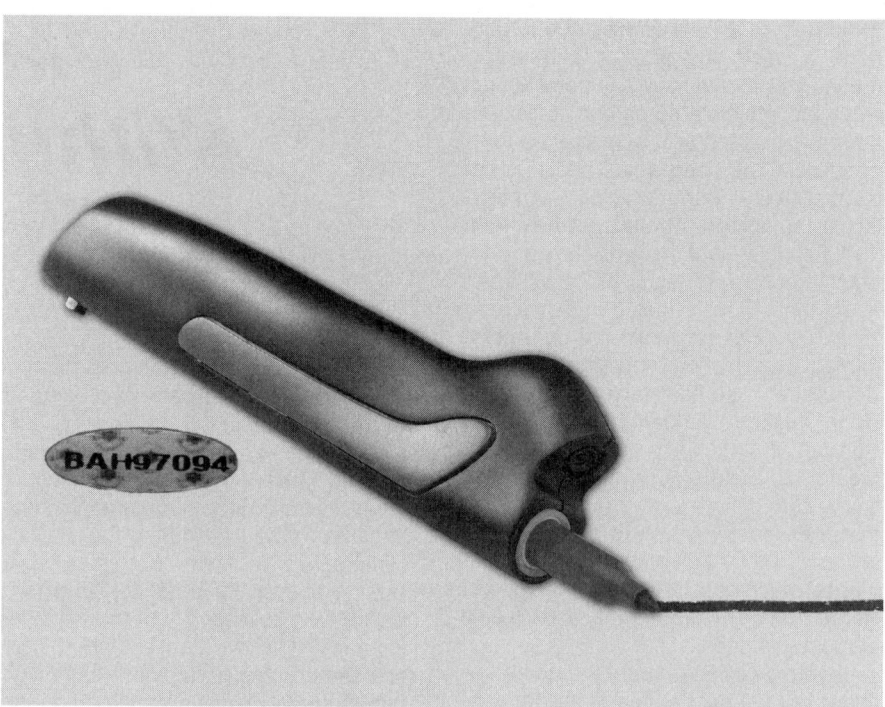

Upper Deck Authenticated is one of the leaders in authentication, having developed a five-step authentication process including a hologram (above left) and recently the PenCam (above right), a patented pen that takes actual video of an autograph being signed.

REMEMBER THIS...

FAKE AUTOGRAPHS

• Know the signature

• Know the company

• Authentication system, not COA.

FAKE CARDS

• Watch out for dot patterns or blurriness in small print areas.

• Watch out for stacks of the same rarecard available from one dealer.

• Know the grading company.

FAKE ANYTHING

• If it looks too good to be true, it probably is.

• **Don't believe all grading holders.** There are many start-up grading companies that are created just to deceive collectors. Their holders often have nothing but fakes in them. Make sure the grading company that has certified the card you're buying is a real company, and it helps if they have a track record in the industry. You'd be surprised how many of them don't exist when you try to track them down for a real phone number or address.

For much of this advice, beginning collectors will need to go to their local sports card dealer, or read collecting publications, or visit an online site for advice. How can a beginner tell that a card is too perfect?

Most likely that collector will need some help.

"Most of the publications will let you know about condition-sensitive cards, or us at Collectionmonster we'll let people know which cards to watch out for," because they're condition-sensitive, May said.

If you're a beginning collector and you're not sure if you're about to buy a counterfeit card, ask the seller to have the card authenticated before you buy it, promising to pay the cost if the card comes out OK.

(Rocky Landsverk has been an investigative reporter for Sports Collectors Digest for eight years).

Ruth's Signature Has Always Been Popular

By Ron Keurajian

As America entered the Roaring Twenties, it left behind economic hardship, the carnage of war, the horse and buggy and the dead ball era.

The once glistening stars of the Cobb era slowly faded into the backdrop of time. Tris Speaker, Honus Wagner, Wild Bill Donavan and the like were to step aside for a new type of player. Strategy was to give way to raw power. The stolen base was to give way to the home run.

Soon the sluggers were to dominate the game. Hack Wilson, Mel Ott, Jimmie Foxx and Lou Gehrig were the new stars of the grand old national pastime. But one man stood above all the rest. One man who could crush the ball like no other. His name was George Herman "Babe" Ruth.

Wherever Ruth traveled he was hounded by requests for his signature. Both child and adult alike clamored for a signature of the great Bambino. It was Ruth who made baseball autograph collecting what it is today.

Like Cobb, Ruth is a fairly common signature. Always an accommodating signer, Ruth penned his name on countless items. Value is derived from the need to possess a signature of the most beloved athlete of all time.

Ruth's handwriting was very bold and flashy. Large, thick, flowing strokes that border on the ostentatious. His handwriting is very fast, with large up-and-down strokes. See examples 1-3.

Ruth's signature developed through the 1920s. Early examples, circa 1920-1926, sometimes lack the large flowing signature most are used to seeing. Early Ruth examples are choppy and sometimes mistaken for "clubhouse signatures." See example 4.

Genuine Ruth signatures before 1920 are very rare and are typically limited to contracts and other such legal documents. Of the numerous Ruth signatures reputedly signed before 1920 that I have seen over the past 20 years, only two have been genuine.

By the late 1920s, Ruth's signature was well defined and varied little for the remainder of his life.

Ruth would sign just about anything. Ruth is common on baseballs, both single-signed and as part of a team. While hesitant to sign paper items, he often did. Signed photographs, album pages, government postcards and scorecards exist in quantities. Less common are bank deposit slips, currency and gum cards. Hall of Fame plaque cards are extremely rare and sell for several thousands of dollars. I have yet to see a genuine one.

Checks are plentiful and are typically signed "G.H. Ruth." However, in the last year of his life Ruth would sign checks jointly with his wife. This style of check is very rare and highly desirable because Ruth signed his name as "George Herman Ruth." Ruth rarely, if ever, signed non-legal documents with his real name.

A word of caution when it comes to Ruth and documents. Forged Ruth documents are common. There are two types. First are old blank documents generic in nature, typically sales and rent receipts containing a forged Ruth.

The second are fake bank checks. These were produced either on a computer or a small press. They are counter checks printed on dark green paper. The forgeries are poor. The thing to look for is the quality of the print. A genuine check or for that matter any bank document will have very high quality printing. The print on the fake checks are just a touch thicker and ever so slightly blurred. The print lacks the sharpness found on a genuine check.

Ruth is often perceived, incorrectly, as an over-stuffed kid with the intelligence to match. Letters by Ruth, both handwritten and typed, do exist but are uncommon. Handwritten letters border on the rare side. Content of Ruth letters is routine and rather boring. Ruth letters are usually limited to one page and utilize simple language. Letters are always gracious and offend no one.

Ruth's hand was always steady. A genuine Ruth signature exhibits no signs of shakiness. Even as the end of his life neared Ruth still signed with a strong hand. Examples signed just before his death are flowing and still exhibit that Ruth flash. For years I have seen postcard sized pictures with that famous Ruth batting pose. They contain a quirky signature and typically dated 1947 or 1948. The explanation often given for the odd looking signature is that Ruth was in ill health which affected his ability to write. I think the explanation for the odd looking signature is that they were signed by someone other than Ruth.

Forgeries of Ruth are very prevalent. In my opinion Ruth is a lot easier to forge than his counterpart Cobb. While no really good forgeries of Cobb exist in the market today, the same cannot be said for Ruth. There are some phenomenal Ruth forgeries out there. They are signed slowly but with a steady hand. I see these on balls, pictures and album pages, either alone or with Gehrig. Some are inscribed, some are not. While Cobb's writing style does not lend itself to a slow but steady appearance, Ruth's does.

"THE BABE"
Ruth autograph examples

1, 2, 3, 4, 5, 6, 7, 8

These Ruth forgeries have turned up over the past couple of years, leeched into the marketplace, and command some serious money. But while these fool the "experts" in the hobby, there is a simple little test to determine whether that Ruth you are about to purchase is genuine or a high-quality forgery. The test is not 100 percent, but its a fairly good indicator of genuineness.

The first tip off is the signatures are too neat, too perfect. Ruth signed in bold up-and-down strokes that correlated into a signature that is large, uneven, almost whimsical. The fake Ruths are level and lack the up-and-down strokes. What you need to do is focus on the bottom of the signature. The fake ones will be level as if written on a straight line.

Examples 5 and 7 illustrate this well. Sizes are enhanced to better illustrate the differences. What you are looking at are the bottom portions of well-executed Ruth forgeries. Examples 6 and 8 are genuine. Notice how the forged Ruths are level and exhibit no variation in height. The forgeries are signed in a methodical and calculated way. This is evidence of a slow and heavy hand. Now the genuine Ruth signatures bounce up-and-down. Heights vary and flowing loops are evident. When positioned right next to each other the differences are striking.

Sometimes the differences in height can be subtle but they are always present. The variation in height is typically much more prominent when Ruth penned his name to a baseball.

As good as these fake Ruths are, this simple test should expose the best of the Ruth forgeries. So next time you see a Ruth signature, take a good hard look. The genuine signature should have a nice bouncy feel to it.

A while back a gentleman approached me with one of these Ruth forgeries. With the greatest of confidence he guaranteed the genuineness of the Ruth. He said, "Authenticated by the top men in the autograph industry." "Yes," I said "but so were the Hitler diaries."

Cobb's Signature Is One Of The Most Coveted

By Ron Keurajian

Back in the summer of 1905 a young Georgian stepped off a rail car at the central train station in Detroit. He was there to finish out the season as a cheap substitute for Frank Navin's injury riddled Tigers. At that time no one could have guessed that he would spend the next 22 years in the Detroit outfield. No one could have guessed he would become one of the greatest players of all time. His name was Tyrus Raymond Cobb.

Cobb roared through the pages of baseball history, leaving behind terrified basemen, mythical numbers and a legend that today has translated into one of the sport's most coveted signatures.

Cobb is by no means a rare signature. There are literally tens of thousands of his signatures out there. Back in the early 1980s I spoke with Cobb's daughter, Beverly. She stated that the family released thousands of canceled bank checks in an effort to obtain donations for the Cobb Educational Foundation.

The value of Cobb lies not in rarity but in the insurmountable demand for his name. Contrary to popular belief, Cobb was a very willing signer, both in person and through the mail. Only when his health declined in the closing days of the 1950s did he stop replying to mail requests for his signature. And no, he did not rip off stamps from SASEs and use them for his own use!

Cobb wrote with an aggressive hand. His handwriting was rather flowing with large and thick curving strokes. Cobb's signature was bold and dominated whatever it was placed upon. In addition, his signature was very legible and almost always ended with a large paraph (flourish to discourage forgery).

To understand Cobb, or any other signature for that matter, one must look at the entire autograph. I am very leery of those who determine authenticity by examining each individual letter or slant. You know this person, he stands back and with the oratory skills of William Jennings Bryan exclaims, "the 'T' in Ty never touches the 'Y' and the 'C' is always connected to the 'O' and the first 'B' is always larger than the second 'B,'" and so on he rambles. At this point thank him for his time, hand him a dime for his services, and walk away. You have just talked to someone whose knowledge of handwriting analysis is a few bricks short of a chimney.

Cobb's signature remained relatively constant throughout his life. Early examples from the 1920s and 1930s are signed in a neat, eloquent hand. See example 1. As time went on, and Cobb became bombarded with requests for his signature, his hand became a bit more sloppy but still always legible. See examples.

In the late 1950s, Cobb's health began a downward spiral. Heart and kidney problems developed and cancer slowly infested his spine. Despite this, Cobb's handwriting remained flowing and smooth even through the early part 1960. Only very late in life, that being the last few months of his life, did his hand become unsteady. I see lots of Cobb "signatures" that were supposedly signed in the late 1950s with shakiness visible in the writing; these are fake and should be avoided.

Cobb had essentially two different ways of signing the 'T' in Ty. The first is the most common "mushroom cap" style seen in examples 1-5. On occasion he would sign with the less common "2" style. See example 6.

During his playing career he used the "2" style more than he did in retirement. But make no mistake, he would use this style throughout his life. Example 6 is from a letter dated 1959.

Cobb liked to sign in green fountain pen, exactly why I do not know or for that matter do not care. Some claim that Cobb only signed in green ink and that a Cobb signature in any other color must be fake. While Cobb's preferred color was green, he also signed in black, blue, pencil, ball-point and various other colors.

Unlike DiMaggio, Cobb really had no taboos when it came to signing. He would place his name on almost any medium. He really liked to sign photographs of himself, especially the portraits. The most common mediums Cobb can be found on are government postcards, album pages, checks, pictures, scorecards, letters and balls. Less common items are Hall of Fame plaque postcards and baseball cards.

Although he lacked any formal education, Cobb was a highly intelligent individual. Like his teammate Sam Crawford, Cobb loved to write letters. Most of the Cobb letters in existence today are handwritten. Typewritten letters are scarce. While handwritten letters of contemporaries like Honus Wagner and Cy Young are rare, Cobb letters are common. The contents of Cobb letters often mirrors a caustic personality and an unyielding sense of honor. Letters are gracious and extremely well written. Spelling errors are rare.

Over the years I have possessed about 20 of these letters. All were graced with wonderful content. Whether the true hit king was accusing the California government of being a "shakedown outfit" or baseball owners as "monopolistic animals," Cobb wrote with a sharp and cutting pen that rivals President John Adams.

In recent years many forged letters of Cobb have seeped into the marketplace. There are two types. The first are letters written on counterfeit personal letterhead (as discussed in a previous article). The second are letters written on genuine hotel stationary and are typically 5-by-7 inches or a little larger. They are usually written in either green ink or green pencil. They have surfaced over the past two to three years, so caution is warranted.

Cobb, along with Ruth, is one of the most forged names in the hobby. Forgers have gone to great lengths to create bogus Cobb material. Signed balls, bats, uniforms, and even fake checks have been produced.

Some years back someone decided to forge Cobb on old postcards. After many years, I still see these items offered. This was a wide scale attempt at forging Cobb. A brief description:

The postcards are the typical postcards one would find around the beginning of the 20th century. The front has a picture of some mundane subject on it, like a bridge, riverboat or a historical building. They contain a stamp and are postmarked between the years of 1907 and 1915. The postmarks are typically from larger cities like Chicago, Milwaukee, Cleveland, etc. On them are letters supposedly written by Cobb.

While not the mark of an expert forger, they are not bad.

A few things to look for. They are usually addressed to women, "Margaret," "Linda," etc. The contents of the letters vary in subject. Some contain profanity such as "God damned" or "God damnit." The letters are closed with a fluffy pleasantry like "With kind personal regards, sincerely yours, Ty Cobb." Under the Cobb signature is a handwritten date purportedly in Cobb's hand; it usually matches the date of the postmark.

Cobb has proved to be; an excellent investment and a highly prized signature. His is also one of the most commonly forged names in the sports autograph field. Care must be taken before purchasing a signature of the Georgia Peach.

KEEPING IT REAL
Example Cobb autographs

Wagner Signatures Are Tough

By Ron Keurajian

In the closing days of the 19th century, John Peter "Honus" Wagner sauntered into the world of baseball. It was the Gay Nineties and America was in the thick of the Gilded Age. The lumbering Wagner slammed out his first hit during the Presidency of William McKinley. He would play major league ball for 20 years and rack up numbers that rivaled Ty Cobb and Babe Ruth.

During the first part of the 20th century, Wagner was the anchor of a powerful Pittsburgh team. He was the greatest shortstop in the history of the game, he was the legendary Flying Dutchman.

Wagner was not what you would call the textbook definition of a ballplayer. Built like a Sherman tank, Old Honus appeared as graceful as a wooly mammoth. He was stocky, bowlegged, and had oversized limbs. But make no mistake, his swing was refined, his glove was solid, and his arm was nothing short of a cannon.

The legend of Honus Wagner has endured throughout the decades of American sport. He remains a giant among the early immortals of the game. His signature is one of the most sought after in the hobby.

The demand for Wagner's signature is great. The Dutchman is in the same class as Ty Cobb, Babe Ruth, Lou Gehrig and Christy Mathewson. Unfortunately, as with most deceased Hall of Famers, Wagner is a favorite of forgers. Most of the Wagner material offered for sale today is fake.

Wagner signatures are fairly plentiful. Throughout his long life he graciously granted requests for his autograph. Wagner was a willing signer both in person and through the mail. Like Cobb, the Dutchman went out of his way to sign for children. The legendary Pirates shortstop would sign well into the 1950s until illness forced him to stop.

Before one undertakes collecting signatures of the great Wagner — I offer this word of caution. Analyzing Wagner's hand is a nightmare. His handwriting went through many changes. He would change the way he signed on a mere whim. Signatures would slant back and forth. Some of his signatures are flowing while others appear choppy

The Dutchman had various ways of signing. The most common is J. Honus Wagner. But on occasion he would also sign as J. Hans Wagner and John H. Wagner.

Wagner's early hand is very flowing and has a certain artistic flare. Early signatures are very pleasing to the eye. Examples 1 through 4 illustrate this well. Example 3 is a good illustration of Wagner's variant writing style. Note how it slants slightly backwards. Why he did this I do not know, but it makes authentication difficult.

Wagner's hand remained strong until the mid to late 1940s. By the 1950s, Wagner entered the twilight of his life. The strength of his hand began to fade, writing became unsound. No longer was the signature flowing. Late signatures are very plain and exhibit a fair amount of shakiness (see Example 5).

Wagner's hand is fairly easy to copy. Though his signature is elegant, Wagner signed in a slower hand than most. His signature does not have a rapid appearance like that of Ed Barrow or Paul Waner. Consequently, there are some pretty good forgeries in the market today. Careful study is needed to separate the real from the fake. It goes without saying that it is easier to forge an old age Wagner signature.

Wagner can be found on a vast array of mediums. The most common are government postcards, album pages, index cards and checks. Anything else is scarce.

Government postcards are available as Wagner used to send them out to satisfy requests for his signature. Many a lucky collector received a signed penny postcard compliments of the Dutchman. Because of his love for government postcards, many are found addressed in Wagner's hand.

There are a lot of Wagner signed baseballs in the market today, but unfortunately most of them are fake. A genuine single-signed Wagner ball is a true rarity. In 20 some years of collecting I have seen fewer than 10 genuine single-signed Wagner baseballs.

Now the question arises: Does a signed Pirates team ball from Wagner's playing days exist? This is a question that has baffled mankind for centuries. Every once in a while a "signed" Pittsburgh Pirates ball from the teens will surface. They usually end up in auction and some poor soul gets stuck with a fake ball.

About a year ago, I had a collector call me in regard to just such a team ball. He told me he had just purchased, from an old estate, a 1909 Pittsburgh Pirates team-signed ball complete with Wagner, Fred Clarke, Vic Willis and the rest. He wanted my opinion as to whether it was genuine or not. Well, I told him it was fake. "But you haven't looked at it yet!" he responded. "I do not have to look at it," I replied.

Team-signed baseballs from Wagner's playing days very likely do not exist. If you run across one of these old team baseballs you should probably avoid it, you will save yourself a lot of grief and money.

Another Wagner item that everybody seems to want are signed black and white Hall of Fame plaque cards. These are exceedingly rare. I have never seen a genuine one.

Back in the early to mid-1980s, someone got a hold of a bunch of unsigned black-and-white plaques. Shortly thereafter there was a

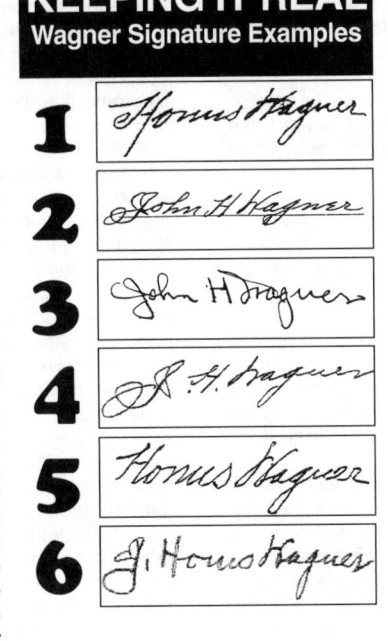

KEEPING IT REAL
Wagner Signature Examples

1. *Honus Wagner*
2. *John H Wagner*
3. *John H Wagner*
4. *J. H. Wagner*
5. *Honus Wagner*
6. *J. Honus Wagner*

flood of signed black-and-whites into the market. It seemed everybody had them. Unfortunately, the forgeries were pretty good and a lot of veteran collectors and dealers got stuck with them. Wagner was one so forged. Others included Tommy Connelly, Cy Young, Mickey Cochrane, Cobb, Connie Mack, Paul Waner, Eddie Collins, Tris Speaker, Nap Lajoie, Clark Griffith and a few others.

There were some phenomenal Zack Wheat forged plaques. These black-and-whites were well known in the hobby about a decade ago but it seems everybody has forgotten. They still turn up for sale and are floating around in quantities. Chances are if you have purchased a signed Wagner plaque in the past 15 years it came from this cache.

Wagner was a man of limited schooling, not uncommon for the era in which he grew up. Consequently, his writing skills were a bit lacking. Handwritten letters of Wagner usually contain misspelled words. His letters are composed utilizing simple sentences and generally avoid long words. Handwritten letters of Wagner are rare and highly desirable. Wagner liked to write letters while traveling, hence you will find letters penned on hotel stationary. Typewritten letters are a bit more common but still considered scarce.

Finally, there has been a good amount of controversy as to the scarcity of Wagner bank checks. When Wagner checks first hit the market they were touted as "very rare." Some have claimed that there are fewer than 50 checks in existence. At one time they were selling for $2,500 to $3,000 but have since fallen in price. Don't be fooled, there are hundreds upon hundreds, if not thousands, of Wagner checks in circulation. Today a Wagner check, free of cancellation marks, can be purchased for $600-$700.

Johnson's Signature Was Done With Steady Hand

By Ron Keurajian

In the summer of 1907, Walter Perry Johnson made his major league debut. "A string bean of a kid," Tiger's slugger Sam Crawford exclaimed. Washington manager "Rowdy Joe" Cantillon often referred to the young Johnson as the "Big Apple Knocker."

Johnson was the product of some loosely organized semipro league in Idaho, I think. Walter was a tall, gangly fellow, his arms were as long as African Pythons and had the power to fire a baseball through the sound barrier.

Most likely, Johnson was the fastest pitcher of all time, faster than Nolan Ryan, Lefty Grove, Tom Seaver or Bob Feller. When Ty Cobb faced Johnson for the first time he walked away in awe.

"Something of a blur flashed before my eyes," a stunned Cobb exclaimed. "As it passed it made a god awful sound....the ball hissed with danger," Cobb continued.

Johnson retired in 1927 with an incredible 416 victories and a .599 winning percentage. His 110 career shutouts and a dozen 20-win seasons were good enough for the inaugural class of the Hall of Fame. Johnson will forever be an immortal of the game of baseball.

Johnson's signature is very pleasing to the eye. He signed in a neat up-and-down hand. His signature is dominated by sharp angles and nice flowing lines. His hand is very legible and a pleasure to read. Johnson's signature remained relatively constant with very little variation (see examples 1-3). Occasionally, he would use a variant (see example 4), that lacked the more common flat top. Early examples from the early 1920s tend to be a bit more choppy. By the late 1920s Johnson's hand became refined and changed little for the remainder of his life.

Johnson is a favorite among forgers. The vast majority of Johnson material available today is spurious. Fortunately, his hand is rather difficult to copy, hence most Johnson fakes are poorly executed. There are no really good forgeries of Johnson in the market today, at least in large quantities. Most Johnson forgeries are crude and evidence shakiness as seen in example 5, and they are easy to identify by the labored appearance.

Example 6 is a well-executed forgery, and it has a nice flow and lacks any hesitation. This is a particularly good forgery and close examination is needed to spot the flaws. Fortunately, Johnson forgeries of this caliber are few and far between.

Johnson, a victim of cancer, died in 1946 at the relatively young age of 59. Since he never made it to old age, infirmity of hand is non-existent. If you run across a Johnson signature that appears slow and shaky, it should be considered suspect and avoided.

Common sense seems to be thrown out the window by so many collectors. I have met several collectors/dealers that have purchased fake Johnson material. Practically all of the forgeries exhibited signs of an unsteady hand. Now use your head: if Johnson died at a young age then why would one buy a Johnson "signature" that looks like it was signed with an elderly and infirm hand? If collectors would only stop and think just a little bit it would go a long way in combating forgery.

Johnson was an accommodating signer both in person and through the mail. Johnson's address was well known to collectors, thus he signed a lot of material through the mail. Demand for Johnson's signature was great, thus "The Big Train" is a rather common signature. He can be found on most mediums. Government postcards, album pages, bank checks and index cards exist in quantities. Less common are signed photographs, letters, and balls. Rare items include 8-by-10 photographs, Hall of Fame plaque cards and signed gum cards. In my years of collecting I have never seen a genuine signed Hall of Fame plaque or tobacco card. Every once in a while a "signed" T206 card will surface, unfortunately all the ones I have seen have been fake. Though a signed T-card is certainly possible.

Single-signed baseballs of Johnson border on the rare side though Johnson is more common than Honus Wagner, Tris Speaker or Nap Lajoie. Most single-signed balls are post-1930. Due to a long career that ended in 1927, Johnson is available on team-signed balls. Like Babe Ruth, Johnson liked to place his John Hancock on the sweet spot.

While not considered a prolific letter writer, Johnson letters are available. They are scarce but by no means rare. Content of Johnson letters mirrors a man of gentle character. His letters are gracious and rarely, if ever, harsh. Johnson letters are often penned on personal stationary that reads "Walter P. Johnson, Germantown, Md." His letters are well written and spelling errors are uncommon. Typewritten letters are a bit scarcer than handwritten letters.

In 1939 the Baseball Hall of Fame invited all the living inductees to Cooperstown for a weekend festival. It was a gathering to honor the immortals of the game. During the beginning of the festivities, the Hall of Fam-

ers assembled for a formal class portrait of sorts. There, the well-dressed Eddie Collins, Grover Alexander, and the rest (less one Mr. Cobb) posed in grand silence and left baseball with one of the most enduring images of all time.

Over the past few years this induction picture has turned up signed by all or some of the inductees. A common forgery of this picture is one bearing a fake Ruth signature with the inscription, "With some of my friends." In addition, I have seen many that were supposedly signed by Johnson. If you ever run across a signed 1939 Induction picture use extreme caution. Chances are near 100 percent that it is fake. In over 20 years of collecting I have seen hundreds of these "signed" pictures; and I have never seen a genuine one, not even one signed by George Sisler, who lived into the 1970s.

Johnson material has generally been a very good investment. The demand for Johnson material is very strong and will only continue to rise. Johnson signatures start out at $400-$500. Government postcards are highly desirable and sell for $750-$900. Signed 8-by-10 pictures are rare and will sell for a minimum of $2,000. Single-signed balls will run anywhere from $2,500-$3,500, with pristine examples selling for $5,000 and up. Checks have proven to be the one Johnson item that has failed to perform. They were released by the family in large quantities, no doubt more than a 1,000. Checks have actually fallen in price and can generally be purchased for $600 to $700, about $500 less than when they first entered the market a decade ago.

Handwritten letters have excellent eye appeal and sell for a minimum of $1,500, with good content letters selling nearly double that. Typewritten letters, while scarcer, are less desirable and sell for $900 to $1,000.

A signed tobacco card is extremely rare, while a genuine signed Hall of Fame plaque card is about as easy to find as the cure for cancer. A signed plaque card is worth a $1,000. Genuine signed equipment of any sort most likely does not exist.

KEEPING IT REAL
Find the good autograph(s)

1. *Walter Johnson*
2. *Walter Johnson*
3. *Walter Johnson*
4. *Walter Johnson*
5. *Walter Johnson*
6. *Walter Johnson*

Wilson Signed With Fluid, Bold Hand

By Ron Keurajian

Lewis Robert "Hack" Wilson was born on April 26, 1900. A product of Pennsylvania, Wilson grew up penniless but happy. Like most youths of his day Lewis had dreams of one day becoming a big league ball player.

As a young teen, Wilson worked many an odd job to put bread on the table. When Wilson turned 15 he embarked on a career as an iron worker, and it was here that Wilson would develop his bulky fireplug-like physique. It was also here that he would also develop a taste for whiskey.

To earn extra money, Wilson played for various semipro teams during these years and raw talent transformed itself into a graceful fielder and a powerful bat. In 1923, Wilson broke into the big leagues with John McGraw's New York Giants. He would spend 12 years in the Senior Circuit, slamming home runs and slamming booze. Wilson would retire in 1934 with four home run titles to his credit and would enter the Hall of Fame in 1980, 32 years after his death.

During the prime of his career, Wilson's popularity reached great heights and he was the idol of every red-blooded American boy. Due to his stature, Wilson was a coveted signature by fans of the day. He signed thousands upon thousands of signatures. Wilson's signature can be found on scorecards, album pages, and team-signed items. Only on premium items such as letters, Goudey gum cards and 8-by-10 photographs should Wilson be considered rare.

Wilson signed in an extremely fluid and bold hand. I consider Wilson's signature one of the finest in all of baseball. Despite the aggressive nature of Wilson's hand, his writing is extremely legible and very pleasing to the eye (examples 1 and 2). Example 1, which was penned in the early 1930s, is probably the finest Wilson signature I have run across.

Due to the wonderful bold and sharp strokes of Wilson's hand, his signature is very hard to forge. Well-executed forgeries are non-existent in the market today. Examples 3 and 4 are labored and rather unconvincing forgeries: note the slight hesitation in the strokes.

Wilson was not a prolific letter writer, hence letters are few and far between. Typed letters are rare, with handwritten ones even more so. In fact, I have never seen a genuine, full-page autographed letter signed. Short handwritten notes can be found on government postcards, but even so, Wilson government postcards are very scarce, if not rare.

Though signed 8-by-10 photographs of Wilson are rare, there are a fair amount of genuinely signed 5-by-7 photographs available in the market. These are typically sepia toned and picture Wilson in a finely tailored suit. It is an image that captures the long forgotten opulence of the Roaring Twenties.

Usually sporting a long inscription, these photos have excellent display value and are highly treasured.

Wilson can be found on signed team balls and team sheets of the Chicago Cubs and Brooklyn Dodgers, and to a lesser degree on the earlier Giants material. You would think that Wilson would be readily available on single-signed baseballs, but unfortunately he is not. Back in the old days, baseballs, to the young child, were an expensive thing to acquire, thus it was optimal to obtain many signatures on one ball. Single-signed baseballs were reserved for the select few superstars of the game like Ty Cobb and Babe Ruth, not for Hack Wilson.

Today, single-signed baseballs are extremely rare. In 20 years of collecting, I have only seen one. Now, on the other hand, if you want a forged Hack Wilson ball there are many to choose from, so caution is warranted.

About 10 years ago, some rather inept forger acquired a few old baseballs and placed forged Wilson signatures on the "sweet spot." These forgeries are of lesser quality. The signatures appear smaller and lack the large boldness of a genuine Wilson. In addition, the forgeries appear a bit shaky. Of note, all of these forged balls were signed in green ink. Every once in a while one of these spurious Wilson balls turns up, usually in a major auction house, complete with a certificate of authenticity from some nationally recognized dipstick handwriting expert. Just something to keep in mind when hunting for Wilson.

Back around 1984, a small cache of Wilson-signed bank checks was "unearthed" (I love that word). About 300 were found and released into the market. I remember in the summer of 1985 at the old Plymouth show, where a dealer walked into the show with about 40 to 50 of these checks. He was asking $100 apiece. While most collectors balked at the price, I talked him into selling me 10 for $750. I wish I still had them today. Most were quickly absorbed into the hobby and today reside in collections across the country. Every once in a while a Wilson check will surface and can be picked up for the right sum of cash. Wilson bank checks should be considered rare, albeit borderline.

As great as Hack Wilson was, he was an outcast among baseball's established class. Managers and owners alike despised his reckless use of alcohol and his live-for-

today lifestyle. He was considered a bad influence on teammates. During his prime, Wilson could slug down booze like no other. Doctors warned Wilson of the evils of whiskey, but their warnings fell on deaf ears. Wilson brushed aside any thought of cutting back on his drinking. When the 1940s rolled around Wilson's health began to fail, as years of drinking had taken its toll. By the spring of 1948, Wilson was dying and he could do nothing about it but stand by and watch. On Nov. 23, 1948, Wilson died. He was only 48 years old.

Since Wilson never reached old age, infirmity of hand does not exist. A genuine Wilson signature will exhibit no unsteadiness whatsoever. Any Wilson signature that appears labored should be considered a forgery and avoided.

KEEPING IT REAL

1 Hack Wilson

2 Hack Wilson

3 Hack Wilson

4 Hack Wilson

Demand for Wilson material is above average. For a price guide, I would assign the following values: a signature is worth $550, with a government postcard valued at $900 to $1,000. One should be able to obtain a typewritten letter for $1,250; the value of a handwritten letter is uncertain, but I would estimate a starting price of $3,500. Signed 8-by-10 photographs are highly treasured; expect to pay at least $2,500 for one. The aforementioned 5-by-7 signed photos (in civilian garb) are less desirable and can be had for $1,000 to $1,500. Signed Goudey gum cards are very rare and would probably sell for $2,500 to $3,000. A fairly nice single-signed ball should start at a minimum of $6,000. Canceled bank checks have excellent display value and can be purchased for $2,000 to $2,250. Signed baseball bats or equipment of any kind likely do not exist.

Wilson is one of those colorful characters that tumbled out of baseball lore from a time long since past. His signature is a welcome addition to any collection and will prove a fine investment in years to come.

Heilmann's Signature Worth Its Weight In Gold

By Ron Keurajian

The teen years of the 20th century brought forth some truly amazing things. Unfortunately, the Detroit Tigers weren't one of them. Gone were the pennant winning years of 1907, 1908, and 1909. Hughie Jennings' once-dominant Bengals settled peacefully into the twilight of mediocrity. The career of Wahoo Sam Crawford neared a dignified end and the one-time glorious pitching staff of Wild Bill Donovan, Ed Killian, Ed Willet and George Mullin was no more.

Though the Tigers would not see another pennant until the 1930s, all was not dark. The Detroit club could still claim a powerful array of batsmen, among the best of them was Harry Edwin Heilmann. Heilmann broke into the majors in 1914 and quickly established himself as a skilled batter. He was Cobb's most prized of students.

"Ole Slug" Heilmann retired from the game in 1931 with four batting crowns, a .403 season, and a stunning .342 lifetime average. To this very day he is considered one of the 10 greatest hitters of all time.

Demand for Heilmann's signature is very strong, and it is well worth it's weight in gold. Needless to say Harry Heilmann is highly desired by collectors.

Heilmann's handwriting is extremely neat and precise. The big looping "Hs" only enhance an already ornate signature (see examples 1 and 2). His hand exhibits fine right angles and is very legible.

Well into retirement, Heilmann remained close to the game. Throughout the 1940s Heilmann was a broadcaster for the Tigers. The great slugger would often be found wandering the hallowed halls of old Briggs Stadium signing autographs and chatting with fans. To this day my dad still refers to the current park as Briggs Stadium!

Consequently, Heilmann is most often found on album pages and scorecards, on anything else he is rare. I have never seen a genuine signed 8-by-10 picture or a signed gum card.

Heilmann is a commonly forged name. Fake Heilmann material can be found on a vast array of items. I have seen forged pictures, 1940 Play Ball cards, balls, bats, government postcards complete with postmarks, and gloves.

Due to the refined nature of his hand, Heilmann's signature is very difficult to forge. Most Heilmann forgeries are, at best, rudimentary. Example 3 is a good illustration of an amateurish attempt at a Heilmann forgery. Example 4 is a well-executed forgery. Fortunately, Heilmann forgeries of this caliber are not available in the market today.

'Round about 1949 Heilmann's health began to slide, and by late 1950 he was diagnosed with a fast spreading form of throat cancer. Within months he would die at his home in Southfield, Mich. It is said

that Cobb visited his old friend only days before he died. Cobb, who had feverishly worked to get Heilmann inducted into the Hall of Fame, left in tears. The year after he died Harry Heilmann finally found his way into Cooperstown.

Heilmann died at a relatively young age, he was only in his mid-50s, thus "shakiness of hand" does not exist. A genuine Heilmann is always steady and flowing. If you see a Heilmann that appears labored or wobbly avoid it.

Heilmann is available on several types of documents. In the early to mid-1980s his family released various signed documents. Checks, promissory notes and other bank documents exist, though they are considered rare.

Heilmann checks can be found with dates as early as 1925 through the mid-1940s. Most of the checks are drawn on the National Bank of Detroit at the Linwood & Clairmount branch. There are a handful of checks from 1944 and 1945 that are penned to former teammate and fellow Hall of Famer Heinie Manush, who endorsed on the back. The story is that Heilmann used to rent a house from Manush at $50 per month. These combination Heilmann/Manush checks are extremely rare and worth a hefty premium.

In addition to checks Heilmann can also be found on promissory notes. These are tougher to find than the checks and are very attractive. They are a little larger than checks and printed on white, document grade, paper. They are typically dated in the mid-1920s and signed "Harry E. Heilmann," and most of them have a large, circular, purple stamp through the signature.

Heilmann was a great broadcaster who mastered the English language with ease. Despite this he is not known as a prolific letter writer. Letters of Heilmann are very rare. Every once in a while a typed letter signed will surface, usually on radio station letterhead. Content is routine and rather boring. I have seen only four of these letters in 20 years of collecting. I have never seen a handwritten letter.

Single-signed baseballs of Heilmann are very rare. I have only seen three, maybe four genuine examples. All were signed on the side panel. I have never seen a genuine single-signed "sweet spot" Heilmann ball. Heilmann can be found on Detroit Tiger team balls from the late 1920s. Again, Heil-

mann signed these balls on the side panel as well.

As to a quick and easy price guide, I value Heilmann as follows: signature $350-$400: government postcards at $1,000. A nicely signed 8-by-10 picture would easily sell for $2,500. Single signed-baseballs are highly treasured and sell for $6,000 or more. Checks command $1,500 with the aforementioned Heilmann/Manush checks worth around $2,000. Typed letters are worth more than $1,000. The value of a handwritten letter is uncertain. Signed bats or other equipment are probably non-existent.

Now if you're playing on a team that can claim on its roster Cobb, Heilmann, and Crawford, you will tend to get overshadowed. Such was the case of Robert Hayes "Kentucky Bob" Veach. Veach was a great ballplayer with Hall of Fame

KEEPING IT REAL
Find the good autograph(s)

numbers. Veach batted over .300 10 out of 14 years and retired with a lifetime .311 average. Unfortunately, Father Time cruelly gave Veach the back of his hand and today the old Tiger great is mostly forgotten.

Genuine examples of Veach's signature are few and far between. Needless to say, he is a rare name indeed. I have only seen about half a dozen genuine examples of Kentucky Bob. All have been on album pages or government postcards. Veach's hand is flowing but more reckless than his counterpart Heilmann. Hence, Veach is an easier name to forge, and believe me there are several Veach forgeries in the market today. There are a few signed legal documents pertaining to Veach's business interests, but those are held in private hands and are not available for sale. Veach is a name that is on most advanced want lists and being often mentioned as a future Hall of Famer equals a highly valuable signature. Values for the most part are undetermined. An album page is worth between $500-$600. I have no idea what signed balls, pictures or letters are worth. I have in my possession a government postcard (see example 5); I recently turned down $1,250 for it.

The Detroit Tigers have produced some of the game's greatest stars. Heilmann and Veach are true legends of the game. Their signatures have proven to be a challenge to collect but well worth the effort. Both have proved to be fine investments and will enhance any signature library.

Don't Count Out Golf When Collecting Signatures

By Ron Keurajian

There is nothing quite like the game of golf. An ancient sport with its origins going back to the 1500s. A sport that demands the highest level of skill, concentration and strategy. The game of golf has given us some of the greatest names in the history of sports.

It seems like Ben Hogan, Bobby Jones and Walter Hagen will live on forever. But as the recent deaths of Sam Snead and Paul Runyan only prove that legend is only human. I guess time is the ocean in which we all must drown.

Round about 1925 the idea of the Masters was born. The dream became reality in 1934 when golf's biggest names gathered in the sleepy Southern town of Augusta, Ga. No one could have known back then just how big the Masters was to become. Today, the Masters is one of golf's six major tournaments and will continue as the most treasured of prizes.

Three of the early Masters winners are the focus of this article.

In 1934, Horton Smith won the inaugural Masters by beating Craig Wood. Smith would win it again in 1936 by outstroking fellow Hall of Famer Lighthorse Harry Cooper, 284 to 285. Smith was a master of precision, a man that possessed a wicked short game. During his prime he was one of the most feared golfers on the course. After retirement Smith became a golf instructor and later the president of the PGA. He remained close to the game until his death in 1963.

Horton Smith is a highly treasured signature. He is considered rare in all forms with the exception of signed album pages. Smith signed in a very graceful hand that borders on the feminine. His signature exhibits many curves and lacks sharp angles (see examples 1&2). Smith's hand is very neat and legible as evidenced by the lack of rapid motion. Consequently, his signature is one of the easier ones to forge. There are some very good forgeries of Smith in the market today. Since he died at the relatively young age of 55, shakiness of hand does not exist.

Smith is rare in most forms. There was simply very little demand for golf signatures before 1980. Now there are a few exceptions such as Hagen, Jones, Tommy Armour, and Francis Ouimet, but for the most part people just didn't collect golf material.

Most Smith material in the market today was likely signed at tournaments. Smith probably received only a scarce few autograph requests through the mail, this is evidenced by the lack of signed pictures, letters and government postcards. In my years of searching I have never found a genuine signed 8-by-10 picture.

Typed and handwritten letters are very rare and command good money. In the past year maybe 15 letters written by Smith to legendary golf photographer Alex J. Morrison surfaced but were quickly snapped up by collectors. Good luck in trying to find one. Signed golf balls likely do not exist. In general, a signed golf ball of any golfer that died before 1985 is likely forged.

The value of Smith material is, at present, unsettled. The fact of the matter is there is not much out there. Signatures are valued at $350 to $400. Typed letters sell for $600-$700, with handwritten letters approaching $1,000.

In 1935, the already established Gene Sarazen locked horns with famed long-ball hitter Craig Wood. When match play finished, both men were tied. Thanks to a phenomenal shot, Sarazen prevailed in the playoff, thus becoming the second Masters winner. Sarazen would win a total of seven Majors and earn a place as one of the all-time greats of the game.

Sarazen lived well into his nineties and was an avid signer his entire life. By no means can his be considered a rare name. Demand for Sarazen material is great and thus has driven prices higher in recent years.

Sarazen signed in a rather sloppy care free manner but his signature tends to be legible, though not that attractive. Sharp right up and down angles dominate his hand. His signature changed very little throughout his life (Example 3 is from 1934 and Example 4 is from 1991). Due to the carefree way in which he signed, forgeries of Sarazen tend to be well executed, and thus hard to spot. Up until the day he died his hand remained steady, shakiness of hand is nonexistent.

Sarazen is available in most forms, the one exception is handwritten letters. He willingly obliged requests both in person and through the mail. He remained a high profile figure in golf, thus collectors had easy access to "Squire" Sarazen.

At present Sarazen is affordable but not for long. Sarazen is valued as follows: A signature sells for around $25-$30, signed 8-by-10 pictures can be purchased between $75 and $100. Typed written letters sell for $100 while a nice handwritten letter will cost you anywhere from $200 to $400. Signed balls are available and generally sell for $100 to $125. A word of caution: most Sarazen signed golf balls are forged.

As the 1930s neared an end, golf's new rising star was a quiet gentle fellow named Henry G. Picard. Sporting finely woven knit sweaters, the stately Picard was always well dressed. Picard burst onto the scene winning the 1938 Masters by outpointing Ralph Guldahl by two strokes. A year later, Picard would capture the 1939 PGA Open, thus making him one of the chosen few double-major winners.

Picard retired from golf in the 1950s, but like most played the game until his death in the late 1990s. Being an early Masters champion makes Picard a highly treasured name. His hand changed very little throughout his life. Early examples tend to be a neat and clean (See example 5: this is one of the earliest known Picard signatures, circa 1935).

As Picard aged, his hand tended to become bolder and powerful (see example 6, circa 1990). In my opinion, Picard should be one of the easier names to forge, however all the forged Picards that I have seen have been poorly executed and stand out like a sore thumb. Picard lived well into his eighties, and his hand remained strong until the last year or so of his life. Late examples of Picard will exhibit a fair amount of shakiness and lack the bold flowing strokes.

Though he died only a few years ago, he is already considered a scarce name. Picard once told me that he received about five to10 requests for his signature per month, which correlates into very few examples.

A Picard signature is valued at $75, and signed 8-by-10 pictures run about $225. Handwritten letters are rare and sell for $300-$500, with typed letters at half that price. Signed golf balls of Picard are a rarity and easily sell for $350-$400. Picard is a tough name to acquire, but will prove to be a fine addition to any collection.

Golf signatures have exploded onto the market over the past few years and will only increase in popularity. Among the finest names to collect are those few men who can claim the title of "The Masters of Golf."

KEEPING IT REAL
Samples of golf autographs

1
2
3
4
5
6

Ben Hogan Signature Is Highly Sought After

By Ron Keurajian

It was the summer of 1946, the Second World War had just come to a long awaited close with America handing the Axis powers a crushing defeat. Normalcy returned to a nation, a nation hungry for sports.

1946 was a banner year for the game of golf. The dashing Lloyd Mangrum handily captured the U.S. Open. An unknown named Herman Keiser returned from Service just in time to win the Masters, and an upstart Yank named Sam Snead walked away with the title of British Open Champion.

Late that summer, golf's final major, the PGA Championship fell to a young slender built 34 year old. The bantam fellow outpointed long-ball hitter Edward Oliver to secure his first Major championship, there would be eight more, his name was Ben Hogan.

Hogan is a giant of American sport, as famous as Ty Cobb, Jack Dempsey, Babe Ruth, or Jim Thorpe. He is a titan among golfers and an immortal of the game.

Hogan is one of golf's most sought after signatures, but unfortunately, he is also the most commonly forged. Hogan has been a favorite among forgers, more so than Bobby Jones, Walter Hagen, Francis Ouimet, and Tommy Armour combined. There are two principal reasons (other than monetary gain) for this. First, is Hogan's rather slow and labored hand which lends itself to forgery. The second reason is the contemporary nature of Hogan material. Since Hogan died only a few years ago it is not necessary to find antique material or find ways to artificially age paper to place a forged Hogan on, in short it takes less effort to forge a Hogan than it would a Jones or Ouimet.

Hogan's hand went through a noticeable change during his lifetime. Early Hogan signatures exhibit a wonderfully smooth flow, with nice rounding curves and crisp right angles, (see example 1). His hand remained that way into the 1980s. As Hogan reached old age his hand became unsteady and the once smooth flow faded. As a result more recent Hogan signatures appear thicker, more labored, and slower, (See examples 2, 3, 4), it is this more recent signature that is most often copied by forgers.

Most Hogan material in the market today is fake. Hogan was a notoriously tough signer throughout his life, at least through the mail. For years collectors tried to obtain a coveted Hogan signature, but to no avail. Only in the early 1990s did he begin to honor mail requests, albeit erratically. For most collectors Hogan proved an elusive signer.

Hogan is by no means rare but certain signed items are considered scarce. Vintage Hogan material (that which was signed during his playing days) is typically limited to material that would have been signed at the tournaments such as album pages and programs. Vintage signed photographs are very tough and command good money.

Hogan was not a prolific letter writer, most Hogan letters deal with routine matters and lack sharp content. Handwritten letters are very scarce and border on the rare side, most of these letters date from 1950 to 1960. Typewritten letters are much more common and typically date from 1975 to his death. A word of caution about typewritten Hogan letters, while many are genuinely signed, many others contain a secretarial signature. The secretarial signatures have the rough outline of a Hogan signature but are easily detected as they are a bit crude.

Hogan's favorite medium to sign were 8-by-10 pictures, he would strategically place his signature as to give the picture maximum eye appeal. Hence, Hogan signed pictures have excellent display value and thus a good investment.

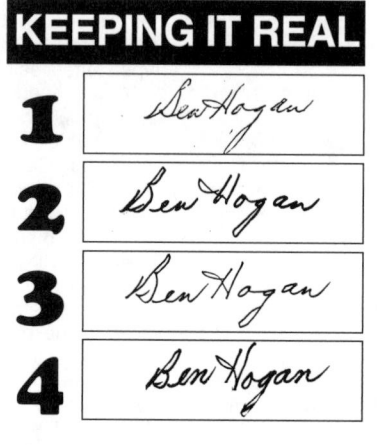

KEEPING IT REAL

1 *Ben Hogan*

2 *Ben Hogan*

3 *Ben Hogan*

4 *Ben Hogan*

Hogan is considered scarce to rare on multi-signed pictures. There are signed photographs of Hogan and Snead together, they are uncommon and in high demand, expect to pay $300 to $400 for one. The finest multi-signed Hogan picture known (at least to my knowledge) is one featuring Hogan walking down the fairway with fellow golf legends Cary Middlecoff, Byron Nelson, and Snead. There are but a handful of these pictures signed by all four, I would say under ten, they are truly in high demand. With a starting price of $1,000 they are a favorite among forgers.

Back in the early 1990s I had the opportunity to talk with Hogan. He was a very friendly fellow, a man that genuinely loved to speak of the game of yesteryear. Bantam Ben knew them all from the dapper Henry Picard to the calculating Max Faulkner and what stories he had.

During our conversation, Hogan stated that he never signed balls or equipment unless they were "Hogan" Brand products. This is an important statement given the popularity of signed golf balls. The demand for signed balls has skyrocketed in recent years. Collectors have been snapping up balls signed by the deceased Hall of Famers causing quite an increase in value.

I have seen hundreds of Hogan "signed" golf balls, most of them are forged. I have never seen a genuinely signed non-Hogan brand golf ball. The general rule is as follows: If you come across a Ben Hogan signature on a Non-Hogan brand ball, club etc... it should be considered suspect and avoided.

Permit me to deviate a bit on the subject of signed golf balls. This topic is one that really irritates me. Obtaining signatures on golf balls did not become fashionable until the late 1980s, and then only those players you could obtain at tournaments (i.e. Arnold Palmer, Ray Floyd, Gary Player, etc.). At that time, collectors were not getting balls signed by the old-timers.

I have seen "signed" balls of such greats as Denny Shute, Ralph Guldahl, Olin Dutra, and Bobby Locke. I have yet to see a real one. Signed golf balls of retired players who died before 1990 are, for all practical purposes, nonexistent. Extreme caution is needed when collecting signed golf balls. Sam Parks, Chick Harbert, Harry Cooper, Middlecoff, and Picard died but a mere few years ago, and signed balls of these individuals are very few and far between. Just something to keep in mind next time you get the opportunity to purchase a Bobby Jones signed golf ball.

Hogan has proven to be a fine investment and will continue so in the future. Demand for Hogan is tremendous. Hogan is available on most mediums and only the aforementioned handwritten letters are considered somewhat rare.

Value of Hogan is as follows: A signature is valued between $80 and $100. Signed 8-by-10 photographs sell for $200, with exceptional examples valued around $400. Signed golf balls are highly desirable, expect to pay a minimum of $250 for one. Typewritten letters sell for $150 to $200 while the more desirable handwritten letters sell at near $500. Over the past year or so, Hogan checks have entered the market, at first they were advertised as "rare" but as time passed it became apparent that Hogan checks exist in quantities. Initially they sold in the $500 range, today however you should be able to obtain one for $150 or so.

Chapter 17

OBTAINING AUTOGRAPHS

10 Things To Do When Obtaining Autographs Through The Mail

By: Bryan Petrulis

1) Always include a self addressed stamped envelope with your request. Do not leave it up to the player to place postage on it. It is you requesting the autograph so you should take every precaution to insure that your request gets back to you and makes it easier for the player to answer your request. You would not expect to pay the bill when someone asks you for a favor.

2) Always write a short letter asking the player for their autograph. Do not just stick cards in the envelope without a note hoping that the player knows what you want them to do with the cards. It is only polite to ask for something that you want. Players consider it rude that they do not get a note and might even keep your cards, thinking that is what you want them to do with those cards.

3) Always use the words please and thank you when asking for an autograph. It does not sound like a request when you do not say please, it sounds more like a command. Put yourself in their position. Would you like someone to say sign my card to you? Especially someone you do not know?

4) In your letter add something about the player that is unique to that particular player. It lets the player know that you care about him/her and are not just using them for an autograph and are an actual fan. Players love to reminisce about the past accomplishments and are really appreciative to hear from those who really seem to care about their career. Especially in today's game, where players see signing autographs like handing out money. It sounds a lot better to them when you make the letter more personal and not some cheap form letter sent to everyone.

5) Never send anything that you cannot afford to lose. Do not send one of a kind items in the mail to get autographed because it may get lost in the mail. It also may get damaged. Also, players may want to keep this special item and may not even ask your permission to keep it. You may never get it back. Also, some players do not even look at their mail, they just throw it away, so you would not want that 1985 World Series program signed by 45 of the 50 players to appear in that World Series to wind up in the trash heap. Players are also constantly on the move, getting traded or moving residences so your item also may get lost that way.

6) If you want an autograph signed with a particular type of pen, send it to that player. That player may not have that type of pen and he/she might sign it in what ever they have available. Some types of ink do not stick to a card or photo. I have had autographs come off the card on the envelope when the player sent it back to me. Some players like to sign in ball point pen but ball point does not show up on certain types of surfaces. What is the point of requesting and autograph that you can not see? Also, some team items may be signed in blue sharpie. To keep consistency you would want the item to be signed in blue and not black for instance. If you care what the autograph is going to look like send a pen.

7) Do not be greedy. Limit your request to between 3-5 cards or one 8x10 or one ball. Like I have mentioned before, players do not want to feel abused. Sometime players feel that you are in it for a profit if you want too many items to be signed. Especially bigger ticket items such as balls and 8x10's. Many feel one per person is enough.

8) If you are unsure if a player answers mail, send a letter with an index card asking them to check the box if they would sign the item you want signed if you send it to them. One box for yes and one for no on the index card. This also works if you want numerous items signed. This also falls under the category of a test letter to insure the player likes to sign and if the address that you are sending to is a good address. You might also want to have the player sign the index card to ensure it is him or her answering the mail and not someone who may have just opened the letter by mistake. This also works because many players have items that they will and will not sign. Some players will sign cards but not balls. Some will not sign cards but will sign 8x10's. You would not want to offend a player by simply sending them 50 cards to sign, not knowing if they will do it first.

9) If you can offer the player an item or two, a player is more apt to sign when there is something in it for them and they also appreciate the offer. Just put yourself it their position. Do you go to work just for the fun of it or do you get a pay check at the end of the week? We do not expect to give away our time and

effort without some sort of compensation. Sometimes offering a player a card or two is payment enough for that player. It is kind of a trade, a card for an autograph(s). Some players never collected their cards when they played so many of them are looking for some of the items that you are sending to them. It is better to offer than have them just keep your item without asking you. You might entice them to sign more for you.

10) Only send items for the player that you are writing to to sign. Many players get offended when you send them cards of a team-mate to get signed for you. They feel used and that your letter was not personal to them. If you want multiple players on the team write to each individually. It is also a bigger inconvenience to sign your stuff and bother another player to sign your stuff. Only send multiple requests to a single player if that player tells you to do so.

All of the above tips are designed to help you maximize you autograph success through the mail. In today's sports world, players are given every convenience and are leary of anyone they do not know requesting anything of them, especially autographs. Sports celebrities do not like the added responsibility of more work and sometimes stop signing autograph requests through the mail because it becomes a cumbersome task. The above tips help to alleviate some of the hassle that the player faces when answering autograph requests through the mail. Remember, sometimes your request is only one in several thousand that a player receives every season. So always put yourself in their position and ask yourself what would be acceptable to you? Good Luck!

10 Things To Do When
Obtaining Autographs In-Person

By: Ryan Semanko

Anytime an autograph collector ventures out to obtain signatures, they are taking a gamble that could pay rewarding dividends or be a waste of time. No matter who the player or the situation, there is always a chance the athlete will not oblige your request for an autograph. Fortunately there are countless ways to increase your chances of having success when chasing autographs. Here are 10 tips that will help build your autograph collection:

1) The number one tip that stands above anything else is to have common courtesy. Celebrities are humans just like anyone else, and thus, they want to be treated like every other person. Remember you are asking them for a favor; asking them to do something for you with little or no reward. You will get very few autographs by getting right in the player's face and begging them to sign, rather, players are much more likely to sign for a group of collectors that stand back and let them walk while politely asking for a signature. Saying please and thank you are the two most important things a collector can say.

2) Knowing what the players look like away from the field is a huge boost for anyone looking to add to their collection. The players get much more difficult to pick out when they are out of uniform and walking down the street. Very few players will ever let an autograph collector walk up to them and ask them who they are. Do research beforehand and study their faces and physical features, which can be found on the back of a card, on the Internet, or on television. Football and hockey players are usually the toughest players to recognize because they rarely are without a helmet when playing. Don't be afraid to guess and go up to a player if you are not 100% certain it is them. Remember, you will not succeed in autograph collecting if you stand back and are timid about going up to the celebrities.

3) Having the needed materials to obtain autographs is a key to anyone looking to add to their collection. One of the most important items a collector can have in hand is a pen for the celebrity to use when signing. Sharpies are the pen of choice for autograph collectors who obtain autographs on cards, 8x10 photos, or magazines. Any color sharpie will work, but blue and black are far and away the most popular with collectors. Silver or gold paint pens are great for getting pucks, jerseys, or any dark item signed. A ball-point ink pen is needed when obtaining autographs on baseballs. A sharpie signed on a baseball will not only look bad, but also eventually "bleed."

4) Along with having the correct pens, collectors must also bring something for the celebrity to sign. Some collectors like to get cards signed, some like 8x10 photos, and others like signed magazines. There are others who prefer to get three dimensional items such as balls, hats, gloves, bats, hockey sticks, pucks, jerseys, and helmets signed. It does not matter what type of item it is as long as you have something for the celebrity to sign, preferably something related to the player or his/her sport.

5) In the same category as the previous two tips, being prepared is a key aspect of collecting autographs. Not only being prepared with the correct materials, but also being prepared with information on the team or player from which you are getting autographs. I can't count the number of times I have seen a collector waiting for a team, and then a player walks by and they say, "I didn't know he was with them." Any serious collector checks the paper or Internet before they go for autographs to get a roster and see what players are currently with the team. In this day of free agency and professional athletes changing teams on a constant basis, it is vital to keep abreast of recent transactions. Before attempting to obtain autographs from a team, double check it's roster to see if any new players are with the team.

6) Knowing where is the best place to go to get autographs is another important component of a good autograph collector. Most experienced collectors know where to go to have the best chances of obtaining autographs. There are usually many entrances and exits to most team hotels and stadiums, so knowing where to position yourself is a must. It is fairly easy to spot where the top autograph spots are at these places because they usually are swarming with collectors. If it is your first time chasing autographs at a certain venue, get there a little early to scope the place out. Walk around the entire building and see where the possible entrances or exits are located, because there is nothing worse than being in the wrong spot and wasting your time.

7) Once you have obtained the signature from the desired celebrity, some collectors think their job is over as they quickly put their autograph away and leave. If you spent all this time and energy in attempting to obtain the autograph, isn't it just as important to make sure you take care of the signature? I have seen collectors get an autograph and carelessly throw it back in their bag with nothing to protect it. I usually bring a sleeve protector for any card or magazine I get signed so that the item does not get damaged. Another way I have seen collectors hurt their collection is by putting a signed item away before it dries. It usually takes about 10 seconds for a Sharpie to dry, but that can be longer depending on the weather. Paint pens take the longest to dry, so make sure to never put a signed paint pen item away without giving it a couple of minutes to dry completely.

8) One of the greatest resources for autograph collectors is the daily paper. Inside the paper you can find all the information about a certain team to help you prepare, but another resource are the advertisements. When a sports figure makes an autograph appearance at a store, it is usually advertised in the sports section. Finding these store signings by celebrities is a huge bonus because it is usually a fairly easy way to add some autographs to your collection. I've seen some store signings where the crowd is so sparse that you can get countless items signed. On the other hand, popular players usually draw a huge crowd; so remember to get there early.

9) Through the years of collecting autographs, I have seen hundreds of celebrities become angry when collectors ask for their signature. They are usually not mad because of when they were approached for their autograph, but rather where they were asked for their autograph. What upsets players more than anything when it comes to autographs is getting asked while they are eating at a restaurant. Very rarely will a player actually sign while eating and it usually upsets them, thus ruining your chances of getting a signature somewhere else. Following a celebrity into a restaurant or store also never helps and almost always upsets them even more. I have seen people follow Mark McGwire into a restaurant, and then wait outside until he was done eating. McGwire became furious that these collectors actually behaved in this manner. Needless to say, he did not sign anytime that day.

10) I started the tips list with the importance of common courtesy and I will end the list with something similar. The explosion of the Internet the last five years has given people an easy way to sell their autographs if so desired. Now anyone can get a signature, and one hour later have it selling on the Internet. This helps those who are attempting to purchase autographs, but it also has brought out a bad side of autograph collecting. Now more than ever before, more and more people are seeking signatures simply for the re-sale value. These dealers are in it only for profit, and that usually leads to greediness. Since they make a profit off every signature they obtain, the dealers are usually pushy and aggressive trying to get autographs. They also are the ones who usually go up to a player with multiple items looking to get all of them signed. Players know what they are doing with the autographs, which generally makes players negative toward signing.

Greediness is one of the worst aspects of autograph chasing, and it could potentially ruin an autograph experience. Hakeem Olajuwon once said he would sign one autograph for everyone after a team practice, but he never got to everyone because of a greedy collector who went up to him twice. Once Hakeem recognized the collector approaching him again for a signature, he walked away and said he was done signing. When you go for autographs, do not go up to a player with a handful of items, rather bring one or two items and you will receive much better results. It will only help everyone in the long run.

Top 10 Autograph Signers
By: Ryan Semanko

Contrary to what some people may say, for the most part, professional athletes are good about obliging their fans' requests for signatures. Yes, some people feel with the money today's athletes make, they should be signing every request. Just about every team has a player or two who may not be too fond of signing, but generally speaking most players will usually sign on a fairly consistent basis. Just as there are some players who do not sign very often, there are some who go above and beyond the call of duty. These are players that are virtually an automatic "yes" when asked for their autograph. I have compiled my top 10 list of best signers in professional sports. Some are specific players who are great about signing, while others on the list are groups that are all-stars with the pen. In no particular order, here are my top 10 signers in the sporting world:

1) NHL players-Yes, this is a large group to classify as good signers, but the fact is no other group in the major professional sports is as nice and generous to collectors as hockey players. It could be sub-zero temperatures outside, and the majority of members of most NHL teams would still stop and sign. Many NHL players are also willing to sign multiples when asked, which is something that is not quite as common with athletes from the other professional sports. Even the major stars are usually willing to accommodate autograph requests on a regular basis.

2) Another large group that deserves to be recognized for their signing habits are rookies, no matter what sport they play. When rookies first come into their respective leagues, they usually have not been pestered for their autograph all that much. Thus, it is somewhat fun for them to sign and interact with the fans. As their careers progress, that thrill seems to wear off for some players. Two NBA players are prime examples of this. Kobe Bryant and Kevin Garnett were great signers during their rookie season when they were young. Now because of the large demand, Bryant is tough to get while Garnett is one of the worst signers in sports.

3) A single person who surely deserves to be on the top 10 list is former boxing star Muhammad Ali. Try finding another person of his stature who is so good about signing and joking with fans. Ali is considered by many experts as one of the most influential people of the 20th century, so to be that cordial is really amazing. Just a couple of years ago, Ali was still signing through the mail free of charge. Since he has so many bodyguards, it is tough to get to him in person; but if you can, chances are good he will sign.

4) Another athlete who went above the call of duty for signing autographs is future Hall-of-Famer Cal Ripken Jr. It was well documented in the media how generous the former Orioles star was with fans, which was surely the case. For the last few years of his career, Ripken would not stay at the same hotel as his teammates simply to avoid the distraction with autograph seekers, but once he arrived at the stadium it was fair game. Before nearly every home and road game, Ripken would take 15 minutes or so to walk around the field and sign autographs. For his popularity, Ripken was an amazing signer who would constantly give to the fans.

5) As stated earlier, rookies are usually great about signing; and on the other end of the spectrum are retired players, who also deserve a spot in the top 10. Aside from the Hall-of-Famers who get constant attention from autograph fans, most former players are great about signing. If it's through the mail or in person, many retired players like the fact that someone remembers their playing days and are usually excited to sign or chat with you. I have seen numerous former players smile and laugh when you ask them for their signature since they assume that no one remembers when they played. Former Major League pitcher Bud Black is a great example. Black

always seems to enjoy signing autographs for those fans who have some of his old cards, and he will thank you for asking him for his autograph.

6) When you pick up the Monday paper each fall, very rarely will one ever find a story about an offensive lineman making the big play. They are a group of guys that do all the dirty work and get little publicity or headlines. Yet when it comes to signing, NFL offensive linemen are in a league of their own. Throughout my years of collecting autographs, I can count the number of times I have been turned down by an offensive lineman on one hand, while the number of skill players who say "no" would be triple digits. Offensive linemen are generally just like normal people. They usually lack the big ego that many of today's professional athletes possess. Hall-of-Famer Anthony Munoz is a prime example. He is regarded by many to be one of the greatest offensive linemen in the history of the NFL. Someone with his credentials should be a tough signature to obtain, but Munoz will always sign in person or through the mail, and he gives collectors a great looking signature.

7) How can a guy like Magic Johnson not be on the top 10 list since everytime you see Magic, he always has a big smile on his face. The former LA Laker star is one who enjoys himself no matter what he is doing. When it comes to signing autographs and interacting with the fans, few stars are much better than Magic. The NBA Hall-of-Famer constantly takes his valuable time to give back to fans and collectors. Just recently I saw Magic at a speaking engagement, and after the event, he gladly stood around signing autographs and posing for pictures for those who waited for him. During his playing days, Johnson was a fairly easy signature to obtain, even with his enormous popularity.

8) No matter what sport they are in, head coaches in professional sports are another group of fantastic signers. They are many times forgotten by collectors, but that is a mistake since nearly all of them are "A+" signers. Detroit Pistons head coach Larry Brown is a prime example of the generosity head coaches usually have. Brown will never turn down an autograph request, and when he is done signing, he asks if anyone has anything else to sign. How often do autograph collectors hear that? I have even seen him tell a group of

autograph hounds what time the team bus was leaving and when the players will likely be passing by. Many of the head coaches are like Brown in that they will go out of their way to sign for fans. Even the big name coaches like Joe Torre, Isiah Thomas, and Mike Holmgren are great with autograph requests. Next time you are chasing autographs, do not forget about the coaches on the team.

9) I have heard the saying a hundred times by collectors, "I wish I would have gotten (insert name) years ago when he was easy to get." That is a common phrase used by autograph collectors who are frustrated by certain athletes and their lack of signing. As most people know, these difficult signers were probably at one point easy to obtain. The problem is once they become stars and the demand for their signature becomes too large, so they cut back on signing. When these stars were in college, most collectors had very little interest in their signatures; but once they became stars in the pros, then everyone wanted them. College athletes are arguably the nicest group of players for autograph collectors. They will nearly always sign autographs at any time and any place. The problem is, very few people take advantage of their gracious attitude towards signing. Current NBA star, Glenn Robinson was a great signer while starring at Purdue, but now he is extremely difficult to obtain. Whether you attempt to get college athletes in person or through the mail, they are usually a great resource for collectors because of their fantastic signing habits.

10) No top 10 signing list would be complete without NBA rising star, Darius Miles. The 6-9 forward is a big part of the future for the Cleveland Cavaliers. Since coming into the league directly from high school in 2000, Miles has learned and improved to the point where he is today: on the brink of stardom. Even though he has yet to be an NBA all-star, Miles is already a Hall-of-Famer with autograph collectors. The quiet Miles never says a word when signing autographs, but the amount of time he spends signing is astonishing. I have seen him sign a dozen items for one collector at one time in the freezing weather, and I am still waiting for the time he actually turns down an autograph request. Hopefully the league's other young stars will learn from Miles about giving back to the fans.

Top 10 Toughest Autographs To Obtain

By: Ryan Semanko

Just like there are celebrities that go above and beyond to please the fans, there are also those who do very little if anything for autograph hunters. These would be the ones who constantly refuse to sign no matter what the situation is. Thankfully, this is a small percentage of the total number of sports figures. Much like the 10 best signers, there has to be a list of the 10 toughest signatures to obtain. In no particular order, here are the 10 most difficult signers in professional sports:

1) Why not start off with the leader of the pack when it comes to turning down autograph requests, NBA Hall-of-Famer, Bill Russell. The former Boston Celtic great is well known for his unfriendly ways with anyone asking for his signature. Even back in his playing days when autographs were not a big business, Russell would still not sign. Rumor has it, when teammates would ask him to sign a team ball, he would refuse to sign for some unknown reason. Russell is now benefiting from that unwillingness to sign in the past as he now makes occasional appearances at card shows and signs for an exorbitant fee. Yet, many are willing to pay the money for the basketball great because there are so few of his autographs on the market.

2) Five years ago, Tiger Woods was just emerging as a big-name golfer. Now he is arguably the most famous athlete on the planet. Five years ago, Woods was not only a generous signer in person, but also was great about answering his fan mail. Now, getting within ten feet of Woods is nearly impossible with the countless security guards he employs to keep fans and collectors away. It seems that Tiger is not a bad signer, but it is simply so hard to get near him that obtaining a signature is nearly impossible. The best chances of obtaining Woods are the practice days at golf courses, which take place a few days before the actual tournament. Chances of getting an autograph from Woods are very slim and that percentage keeps decreasing as he wins more events and becomes even more popular.

3) For the past few years, the New York Yankees have been the dominating team in baseball, with a roster which resembles an all-star team. With all the talent they have, the Yankees are a magnet for autograph seekers. Everywhere they go, they are surrounded by fans and collectors, and nearly everyone leaves without many autographs in hand. The endless supply of superstars are constantly turning down autograph requests from vir-

tually everyone who asks them. To make matters even worse, the Yankees employ a handful of full-time security employees who walk with the players whenever and wherever there is a possibility that fans might approach them. The security along with the bad signing habits of just about every Yankee make them a lock for a spot on the 10 toughest autographs list.

4) Speaking of superstars and their many bodyguards, how can we forget about Michael Jordan? One of the greatest players who ever played the game is easily one of the toughest autographs in all of sports. Jordan used to be reasonably good about signing in the late '80s, but that changed as he enjoyed unprecedented success on the court. Now, it is just about impossible to get Jordan to sign anything, so collectors are forced to buy his autograph from Upper Deck Authenticated, which is the only company with whom he does autograph business. In the past couple of years, I have seen Jordan on multiple occasions, and I have yet to see him sign one autograph. Even at charity appearances which he does every so often, Jordan still does not sign. In 2000, I was the only person outside a hotel following a banquet he attended. When he came out, he refused to sign my item. It has been said that Jordan is trying to limit the amount of his fake autographs on the market by not signing, so collectors know that only things from Upper Deck are legitimate. Whatever the case is, Jordan simply does not sign anymore.

5) For years hockey all-star Mark Messier has been causing headaches for autograph collectors who have to deal with one of the few tough signers in the NHL. Without a doubt, Messier is the worst signer in hockey, which is an honor he has had for quite some time. The future hall-of-famer is well known with collectors for his sneaky attempts to avoid being seen by collectors. Whenever he is near autograph hounds, Messier is always grumpy. If for some unknown reason he actually signs, collectors will be left with one of the ugliest looking signatures in all of sports.

6) Patrick Ewing, Alonzo Mourning, Allen Iverson, and David Wingate all have something in common. They all played their college basketball at Georgetown University for legendary coach John Thompson. Thompson was a great collegiate coach after his NBA playing career ended. One of his teammates while playing with the Celtics was center Bill Russell, who happens to be on this very same list. Russell and Thompson were good friends and Bill's attitudes about signing autographs rubbed off on Thompson, who is also very difficult to obtain. So once Thompson became a head coach, it seems he preached to his players to avoid signing autographs. That is why Ewing, Mourning, and Wingate are among the most difficult signatures to obtain in the NBA. While it is quite a challenge to get Iverson's autograph, it is still at least possible. The only good signing player that played for Thompson is all-star center Dikembe Mutombo, who normally takes time out on a regular basis to sign.

7) Two stars in baseball the past 20 years surely deserve spots on the most difficult list. Future hall-of-famers Eddie Murray and Rickey Henderson have been giving collectors a headache since they came into the league in the late '70s. Murray is

retired, but his views on signing have yet to change. In fact, I have seen him sign only one time in the countless opportunities I have had with him and that was at a charity banquet. Murray is always quiet when he is asked for his signature and many times for whatever reason, he responds to collectors asking for his signatures by saying, "No thank you." It makes no difference if it is at the ballpark, hotel, or some other venue, Murray will not sign for anyone.

8) Rickey Henderson has been labeled by former teammates and opponents as being somewhat of a strange individual. In fact, most of the people who come in contact with Henderson say he is a bit different. He has little interest in dealing with the fans, media, or autograph collectors, as he generally tries to avoid them all at any costs. The last time I saw Henderson sign in person was in the early 1990s when he was playing with the Oakland A's, and he stopped to sign for a small crowd. Henderson likes to keep to himself and share very little with the fans, which is why he deserves a spot on the 10 toughest autographs.

9) The Utah Jazz were a dominating force in the NBA's Western Conference for the entire 90s. While the team never won a championship, they were in the playoff hunt every year and came so close a couple of times. The Jazz have been led by future Hall-of-Famers, Karl Malone and John Stockton, who will be remembered as the greatest combo in the NBA. Both players are dominating on the court, and off the court they share much the same beliefs. Malone and Stockton like to keep their privacy, which means dealing with the fans is not a top priority. Malone used to be good about signing, but he has been nearly impossible the last five years. His former teammate is much tougher to obtain since Stockton has been refusing to sign items with his picture on it for 10 years. Stockton will not sign cards, photos, magazines, or anything that has his picture on the front. This leaves collectors trying to obtain a signature from him on something like a blank index card, and the number of times I have seen Stockton sign the last five years continues to be at zero. The bad attitude towards signing by the teams former stars has since rubbed off on other Jazz players who also have little interest in dealing with autograph fans.

10) Someone who needs to take a course in public relations is Minnesota Vikings wide receiver Randy Moss. The All-Pro wide-out who is one of the top offensive players in the game is known for his off the field actions that make any agent cringe. Moss has a long list of actions that has done nothing to help his popularity with the public. One of his many faults has been his lack of care for the fans, which would include autograph seekers. Moss just will not sign any autographs as I have been turned down by him dozens of times during his young NFL career. He will even refuse to sign for young kids who just want their football signed by him or to get a quick picture with the highlight reel receiver. At a team function where everyone was required to sign for 30 minutes, Moss did all he could to stall so that he would not have to sign as many autographs. Hopefully someone informs him soon about his mistakes and the effects it has on his image with the public.

MEMORABILIA AUCTION RESULTS

Note: Auction results accumulated over the past five years. 2003 results are in bold face.

Joe Jackson's "Black Betsy" bat	$577,610
Foursome with Tiger Woods, plus autos	425,000
Lou Gehrig's last glove	387,500
1948 "The Dugout" Rockwell original	345,000
1928 Cobb Philadelphia signed jersey	332,500
1937 Larry Kelley's Heisman Trophy	328,110
Del Webb's 1947-64 World Series rings	310,500
Lou Gehrig's road jersey	305,000
1930 Babe Ruth uniform	282,400
1925 Babe Ruth home jersey	**264,210**
1928 Cobb Philadelphia signed jersey	236,500
Pre-1912 Joe Jackson game-used, vault-marked bat	206,530
Lou Gehrig's road jersey	187,000
1979 Charles White's Heisman Trophy	184,000
1951 Roy Campanella MVP Award	**170,500**
1853 NY Knickerbockers trophy ball given to Chadwick	**161,992**
500 HR Club game-used bat set (17)	147,783
1931 Lefty Grove uniform	140,489
Joe Tinker Chicago Cubs uniform	132,105
1956 Don Larsen Perfect Game ball collection	120,750
1941 Ted Williams uniform	120,097
Ruth game-worn jersey	115,821
1963 Mickey Mantle home jersey	110,078
(23) Team Canada jerseys 2002 Olympics	109,177
1946 Ted Williams World Series uniform	107,000
1953 Roy Campanella MVP Award	**104,500**
1967 Pete Maravich sophomore LSU jersey	103,500
1920 Oversized Ruth photo with signature	103,269
1927 Ruth/Lou Gehrig signed photo	101,948
Muhammad Ali Ali/Frazier I trunks	99,445
Game-used Ruth bat	99,288
1955 Roy Campanella MVP Award	**99,000**
Babe Ruth white coach's glove	94,817
1907 Hans Wagner Tiffany Sterling Silver Loving Cup	**93,240**
Mickey Mantle game-worn jersey	90,563
1927-31 Ruth game-used notch bat	86,250
Gehrig road jersey	84,549
1969 Nolan Ryan Mets jersey	84,186
Tony Piet's Gallery of Greats original paintings (25)	**83,543**
1955 Sandy Koufax jersey	82,855
1920s Babe Ruth notched home run bat	82,599
Muhammad Ali fight-worn robe "Thrilla"	81,812
1957 Ted Williams home jersey	81,812
Ty Cobb game-used bat	79,810
1930s Gehrig cap	75,386
Alexander Cartwright family ball/letter	74,918
1924-28 Cobb game-used bat	**70,332**
1962 basketball from Wilt's 100-pt game	67,791
Wayne Gretzky's Rangers final game jersey	67,790
Original LeRoy Neiman Gretzky painting	67,790
T202 Hassan Mathewson ad. display	67,387
1940 Ted Williams flannel	66,312
19th century album with autographs/Chadwick	**66,000**
1916-20 Cobb game-used bat	64,100
1932 "Over The Fence" Ruth movie poster	64,100
1986 World Series "Mookie" ball	63,945
Bill Russell shirt	63,394
Michael Jordan uniform	63,250
T202 Mathewson Triple Folder ad display	62,540
1916 Ruth World Series award	62,618
Game-used Cobb mitt	62,301
Ruth single-signed ball	61,047
Henry Chadwick single-signed ball	61,047

2001 Barry Bonds 70th HR ball	60,375
Ruth's last bat (1935) from Wally Berger	59,662
Gehrig's passport	59,655
Collection of W600 Sporting Life Cabinets	59,562
1936 Gehrig's Sporting News MVP pocket watch	**59,551**
1887 Allen & Ginter store display ad poster	58,931
1961 Roger Maris home run ball	58,752
1861 Grand Match trophy baseball	58,139
1933 Rogers Hornsby game-worn jersey	58,131
1918 Jim Thorpe Giants game-used jersey	57,061
Duke Snider uniform	56,600
Pre-1921 Ruth game-used bat	56,026
DiMaggio San Francisco Seals bat	55,563
1957 Willie Mays game-worn jersey	54,232
1888 G76 Goodwin Old Judge Round Album poster	**52,854**
Rube Waddell letter	52,408
Ruth's last will and testament	51,971
1953 Ted Williams game-worn home flannel	51,859
1955 Mantle game-used World Series bat	51,519
1920s Ruth bat	50,931
1927 Ruth and Gehrig tour broadside	50,600
Jim Brown uniform	50,500
1997-98 Jordan game-worn uniform	**50,000**
1934 Gehrig Goudey advertising poster	49,223
1921-23 Gehrig game-used bat	49,223
1937 Carl Hubbell Giants game-worn jersey	48,048
Chesterfield ad with DiMaggio/Williams/Musial	48,019
George Foreman's champ. belt/Frazier	46,000
Mel Ott game-used bat	45,960
T202 Hassan Ty Cobb ad. display	45,920
1996 Dick Williams Yankees WS ring	45,540
Pete Rose 4,000th-hit ball, signed	45,335
1946 Mel Ott Giants game-used uniform	45,224
Ruth coach's uniform	45,224
N172 Old Judge uncut sheet/ad banner	44,824
Eddie Plank signed Federal League ball	44,820
1911 Addie Joss All-Star Game photo	44,748
Don Mattingly's Corvette	44,275
1963 Dodgers Koufax game-used jersey	44,000
1938 Ruth Brooklyn coach's jersey/pants	43,925
1922-25 Jackson game-used barnstorming bat	**43,679**
LeRoy Neiman original "Bartender"	43,679
Rookie era Red Faber White Sox uniform	**43,679**
1927 Ruth/Gehrig Tour photo	43,679
1956 Jackie Robinson's last game-used bat	43,679
1970 Stanley Cup winning Bobby Orr puck	43,670
1927 Ruth Sporting News ad display die-cut	43,614
1968-69 Bobby Orr game-used road jersey	42,871
1911 Rube Marquard jersey	42,577
1955 Brooklyn Dodgers Junior Gilliam World Series ring	**42,551**
Baseball Has Done It signed by Robinson to MLK	42,288
Basketball Maravich broke Robertson record	42,093
1957 Roy Campanella catcher's mitt	**41,800**
1956-57 Boston Celtics NBA trophy	41,700
1960 Clemente game-worn road vest	40,746
Jim Brown game-worn jersey	40,745
1956 Johnny Unitas Colts jersey	**40,700**
1920s Cobb H & B bat	40,675
1955 Mantle game-used All-Star bat	39,708
Round of golf with Tiger Woods	39,708
1910 Pres. Taft ball signed to Fred Clarke	39,708
1934 Dizzy Dean Cardinals road uniform	39,708
Ruth "Headin' Home" film	39,704
Homestead Grays team photo	39,704
1950 Stan Musial game-worn jersey	39,700

1920s Jimmie Foxx game-used bat	39,649
Lou Gehrig game-worn cap	39,100
1960s Lew Alcindor game-worn UCLA road	38,750
Joe DiMaggio game-used glove	38,706
1954 Jackie Robinson game-used bat	38,706
NBA's 50 Great Players signed litho	38,245
1920s-40s folk art bench w/ GU bats, signed balls	**38,073**
1965 Sandy Koufax game-worn home flannel	37,885
1930 Lou Gehrig game-used bat	37,065
1951 DiMaggio World Series ring	37,043
Elgin Baylor uniform	37,042
1959-60 Wilt Chamberlain Warriors rookie jersey	37,042
1967-2002 Full run of Super Bowl tickets	36,977
1998 Dick Williams Yanks WS ring	36,838
Pete Maravich NBA All-Star jersey	36,094
Rose 1975-76 World Series trophy	36,094
1893 Montreal AAA Stanley Cup ring, 1st Stanley Cup	**36,091**
1920s Cobb game-used bat	36,043
1952 Mikan All-Star game-used signed	35,431
Ferguson Jenkins Cy Young Award	35,250
1935 Ruth Boston Braves cap	**35,200**
1935 Ruth Boston Braves cap	35,187
1998 Yankees full-size salesman sample WS trophy	**35,187**
1960 Sandy Koufax home jersey	35,187
1977 Yankees World Series ring	35,187
1928 Howie Morenz Hart Trophy	35,165
Ruth-signed George Burke original photo	**35,100**
1954 Musial game-used jersey	34,788
1978 Yankees World Series ring	34,309
1950s Roy Campanella warmup jacket	**34,100**
1947 Joe DiMaggio game-worn jersey	34,100
1911 Addie Joss All-Star Game photo	34,100
1918 Ruth Red Sox contract	33,674
Wilt Chamberlain uniform	33,613
Joe Namath Jets uniform	33,300
Ernie Davis Heisman season Syracuse jersey	33,225
Signed Ruth store model bat	33,000
1964 Clay/Liston judges' scorecards	32,816
1912 L1 Leather collection of 11	32,816
1920s Ruth game-used H & B bat	32,816
1937 Rock-Ola World Series arcade game	32,816
1938 Dizzy Dean Chicago Cubs jersey	32,816
1909 Honus Wagner Colgan Chip ad display	32,816
1952 Musial Cardinals road jersey	32,816
1960s Gordie Howe Red Wings game-worn jersey	**32,810**
LeRoy Neiman original "Mickey Mantle"	32,766
Joe Namath jersey	32,535
1968 Nolan Ryan signed Mets jersey	32,186
1969 Tom Seaver Mets home jersey	32,186
1970s Joe Namath Jets jersey	**31,971**
Dan Marino Pittsburgh jersey	**31,971**
1968 Lance Alworth game-used Chargers jersey	**31,970**
1961 SI cover Arnold Palmer painting original	31,388
1927 original photograph of Ruth-Gehrig	**31,189**
1930 Rickenbacker Indy 500 trophy	30,166
DiMaggio San Francisco Seals contract	29,868
Joe Jackson game-used bat	29,833
1937 Carl Hubbell Giants game-used road jersey	**29,832**
1952 Satchel Paige All-Star bat	29,832
1922-24 Ruth Yankees contract	29,832
1937-38 Gehrig game-used bat	29,832
1917-21 H & B Ruth game-used bat	29,832
1975 Bobby Orr last Boston Bruins jersey	**29,827**
1957 Bill Russell warmup suit	29,827
1956 Bob Feller Indians jersey	29,827
1930s DiMaggio game-used bat	29,821
1955 All-Star game-used and signed Williams H & B	**29,786**
1970 Clemente game-used jersey	29,779
1941 Campanella East/West All-Star trophy	**29,700**
1929-30 Ruth game-used bat	**29,700**

1959 Sandy Koufax signed World Series bat	**29,534**
1920s Ruth game-used bat	29,534
1934 Tour of Japan signed team photograph	**29,486**
1920s Rogers Hornsby game-used bat	29,079
1941 Lefty Grove Red Sox road uniform	29,079
Charles Conlon's Cobb photo sliding, signed	29,079
Josh Gibson Winter League contract	29,065
1973 Henry Aaron's 701st HR bat	29,062
1930s DiMaggio game-used glove	28,882
1921-23 Ruth bat	28,600
1932 Ruth/Foxx signed original Wirephoto, PSA/DNA	**28,500**
1953 Warren Spahn signed Braves road jersey	28,353
Walter Payton jersey	28,328
1913 Boston Garter Cobb	28,318
1960 Bill Russell All-Star jersey/shorts	28,248
1971-72 Chamberlain game-worn home Lakers jersey	**28,242**
1971 Mays game-worn jersey	28,084
Mike Rozier's Heisman Trophy ring	28,083
Large Ruth photo signed to Larry Doyle	27,830
Jim Thorpe's Canton Bulldogs sweater	27,783
Marilyn Monroe's military jacket	27,782
1905 World Series last out ball, signed by McGraw	**27,500**
1958 Sandy Koufax jersey	27,500
1934-43 DiMaggio game-used bat	27,191
1933 Ruth Yankees contract	27,119
Magic Johnson Michigan State jersey	**27,118**
1934 Gehrig Yankees contract	27,115
1967 Orlando Cepeda MVP Award	**27,078**
Mathewson six-page handwritten letter	27,078
Ruth/Gehrig barnstorming photo, signed	27,078
1969 Mets Tug McGraw World Series shirt	27,072
Otto Graham Chapel Hill Navy Cloudbuster jersey	**27,068**
Gehrig game-used bat	26,940
Ott game-used bat	26,892
1996 Yankees World Series 25-inch trophy	26,844
1948-49 DiMaggio game-used H & B bat	**26,435**
1969-73 Chamberlain Lakers home jersey	26,435
1940 Mel Ott H & B game-used bat	**26,435**
1965 Paul Hornung NFL Championship ring	26,435
1981 Cal Ripken first MLB jersey	26,435
Guy Lafleur Conn Smyth Trophy	26,423
Ruth white mink coat	26,422
Y.A. Tittle jersey	26,410
1982 Cal Ripken game-worn rookie jersey	26,247
1920s Ruth game-used bat	26,021
1972 Muhammad Ali shoes	25,850
1910 Reach fielder's glove embossed tin sign	25,775
1887 Old Judge uncut sheet	25,530
1930s Newt Allen Kansas City Monarch jersey	25,530
1936 Diamond Stars uncut sheet	25,358
1964 Mickey Mantle game-used bat	25,300
1985 Pete Maravich Hall of Fame ring	25,300
1936 Joe DiMaggio rookie jacket	25,300
1995 Nebraska championship ring	**25,100**
1951 Robin Roberts Phillies road flannel	24,676
Walter Johnson 100th shutout ball	24,654
1910 Cobb Tobacco tin	24,654
NBA's 50 Great Players signed litho	24,653
Old Judge advertising poster	24,653
1934 Tour of Japan Earl Whitehill's album, signed	24,650
Mantle bat, game-used and signed	24,650
Gordie Howe game-used Red Wing jersey	24,650
1943-49 DiMaggio game-used bat	24,616
1952 Hank Bauer World Series ring	24,616
1984 Mark McGwire Olympic jersey	24,615
1920s Ruth game-used H & B bat	**24,608**
1950s Jackie Robinson game-worn jacket	24,360
1957 Campanella bronzed spikes from final game	**24,200**
1955 Don Hoak World Series ring	24,351
Babe Ruth and Lou Gehrig signed ball	24,200

1933 Negro League autographed ball, inc. Gibson 24,200
1967-68 Wilt Chamberlain 76ers home uniform 24,200
1932 Gehrig-signed photograph 24,107
1969 Aaron road flannel 24,079
1969 Aaron Atlanta signed home jersey......................... 24,032
1934 Gehrig Yankees contract 24,032
1937 Joe Louis championship belt 24,032
1912 St. Mary's yearbook with Ruth 24,032
Dr. James Naismith scrapbook 24,020
1976 Ali fight robe from Coopman bout 24,018
1972 Oakland A's World Series Trophy 24,018
1957 Bill Sharman's 1st NBA Championship ring 24,018
1927-31 Ruth bat.. 23,864
1968 Banks game-worn road jersey 23,830
1937 Rock-Ola World Series pinball machine 23,600
1927 Ruth and Gehrig signed original photo.................. 23,431
1934-35 H&B game-used bat 23,431
1930-66 Exhibit Supply Co. archives of original photos.. 23,431
Pee Wee Reese's personal Hall of Fame plaque 23,402
1986 Keith Hernandez Glove Glove Award 23,262
1903 World Series composite photo by Horner.............. 23,100
Jordan game-used jersey.. 23,050
2000 Lakers NBA Champ ring (front office).................... 22,660
1921 Ruth game-used bat... 22,412
1976 Mike Schmidt's Gold Glove 22,412
1973 Ted Williams game-used Rangers jersey 22,389
1950s Bob Pettit Hawks jersey 22,373
1969 Mets Ron Swoboda WS jersey 22,373
1942 Willie Pep featherweight championship belt 22,354
Charles Martin Conlon Ty Cobb photo 22,225
1939 Ruth handwritten letter 22,201
1934 Tour of Japan signed tour program, Ruth/Gehrig ... 22,152
1976-77 Munson glove signed by Yankees 22,152
Mickey Mantle game-used bat....................................... 22,145
1962 Eddie Mathews Braves road Tomahawk shirt............ 22,041
Steve Van Buren Philadelphia Eagles jersey 22,000
Johnny Unitas game-worn jersey 22,000
1928 Fro-Joy store display with Ruth 21,847
1970s Henry Aaron Atlanta jersey................................. 21,847
1991-92 Jordan game-used Bulls jersey......................... 21,847
1940-43 Carl Hubbell Giants home jersey...................... 21,847
1976-77 Lafleur Hart Trophy... 21,839
1973 Willie Mays game-worn uniform 21,835
1972 Bruins Cheever's Stanley Cup ring......................... 21,835
1967 MVP Award Orlando Cepeda 21,835
1907 Sol White *History of Colored Baseball* 21,656
1932 Olympics Eddie Tolan's items, inc. two gold medals ...21,647
1971 Chamberlain game-used road jersey 21,437
1908-65 Baseball Magazine complete run 21,437
1963 Bobby Richardson Gold Glove 21,429
1934 Gehrig Yankees contract 21,429
1954 Monte Irvin World Series ring 21,333
1967 Mays MacGregor game-used and signed glove 21,300
1932 Hack Wilson game-used bat.................................. 21,300
1953 Ted Williams game-used, signed bat...................... 21,300
1957 Aaron All-Star bat, signed 21,300
Original mutoscope with Ruth reel 21,300
1971 Manny Sanguillen World Series trophy 21,300
1972 Mercury Morris Super Bowl ring............................ 21,047
1977 Yanks WS trophy Mike Torrez................................ 21,040
1959 Mathews game-used road jersey 20,873
1975 Roger Staubach "Hail Mary" jersey 20,372
1996-97 Jordan game-worn uniform 20,436
Larry Bird Indiana State jersey................................... 20,373
Bob Cousy jersey... 20,372
John Havlicek jersey... 20,372
Pete Maravich Jazz jersey.. 20,338
1946 Ted Williams game-used bat 20,338
Howie Morenz' skates from final game........................... 20,336
Oakland A's 1974 World Series trophy (full size) 20,336

1889 John L. Sullivan silk and flag from Kilrain bout 20,295
Roger Staubach jersey... 20,240
Ruth-signed bat... 20,240
Ruth game-used bat.. 20,177
19th century proof set of baseball fans 19,861
1907 History of Colored Baseball by Sol White 19,861
Cal Ripken's last home run baseball............................ 19,861
1934-43 Mel Ott game-used bat.................................... 19,861
1962 Mantle game-worn jersey 19,851
1986 Bill Buckner's World Series glove 19,851
Vintage Joe DiMaggio bat, signed 19,850
1955 Dodgers Jake Pitler WS ring 19,800
Babe Ruth bat, signed... 19,800
1972 Larry Csonka Dolphins uniform 19,798
Ted Williams game-used bat 19,759
1998 Mark McGwire 20th home run ball 19,550
Gehrig Appreciation Day bowl....................................... 19,490
1984-85 Wayne Gretzky jersey 19,450
1920s Hornsby game-used bat...................................... 19,364
1952 Bob Feller signed Indians home jersey 19,364
Lou Gehrig photo, signed... 19,180
1968 Clemente game-used and signed bat 18,954
Jordan game-used and signed Wizards jersey 18,900
Gil Hodges' Gold Glove.. 18,851
1911 Addie Joss Day ball with Joe Jackson 18,828
1930 Indy 500 trophy, Billy Arnold's 18,752
Super Bowl XXVII trophy from Kenneth Gant................. 18,752
1991 Redskins Super Bowl ring...................................... 18,750
1917-21 Eddie Collins game-used bat............................ 18,725
Ruth/Gehrig autographed photo................................. 18,700
2001 Barry Bonds 1st home run bat 18,612
Ruth/Gehrig photo.. 18,528
1972 Muhammad Ali/Quarry fight-worn robe 18,522
1911 Addie Joss Day panorama 18,522
Cal Ripken rookie season jersey.................................... 18,520
Ruth and Gehrig signed ball... 18,520
Cy Young single-signed ball 18,520
1917 White Sox panoramic photo 18,498
1980 Wayne Gretzky Oilers jersey.................................. 18,250
1969 Mets Rod Gaspar jersey 18,090
1965-66 Mantle game-used H & B bat............................ 18,055
1973 Aaron's 701st home run bat 18,055
1991-92 Bulls NBA Champ Hodges ring.......................... 18,055
1965 Eddie Mathews game-worn Milwaukee jersey 18,047
Ruth and Gehrig signed ball 18,047
Photo signed by Gehrig and DiMaggio 18,045
Earle Combs game-used bat, signed by '27 Yankees.......... 17,898
1912 Joe Wood World Series medallion 17,608
1950 Mantle scouting questionnaire 17,590
1954 Brooklyn Dodgers yearbook original Mullin art 17,582
Turn-of-the-century baseball clock 17,582
1955 Brooklyn Dodgers World Series ring 17,477
Steve Carlton 4,000th strikeout uniform 17,455
Joe Montana game-worn jersey 17,437
1903 World Series game-used ball 17,050
1927 World Series panoramic photo 17,050
1912 Major League Base Ball table game 17,026
Baseball signed by last five .400 hitters 17,022
Cy Young's personal Hall of Fame plaque........................ 17,020
Marilyn Monroe signed ball w/inscription 16,837
Wilt Chamberlain Globetrotter warmup jacket 16,837
Ruth "Pride of the Yankees" uniform 16,837
Red Grange game-used helmet 16,837
1966 Mantle game-used and signed bat......................... 16,828
1931 Ruth game-used bat... 16,828
1971 Aaron game-worn home flannel 16,808
1909 Honus Wagner logo from his uniform 16,808
1976 Muhammad Ali fight-worn trunks............................ 16,808
Sullivan/Corbett program and ticket 16,808
Clemente game-used and signed bat 16,675

Yogi Berra game-used jersey and mask 16,626
1937 Ted Williams HR ball from San Diego Seals 16,583
1978 Bob Lemon's World Series ring **16,500**
1967 Packers Super Bowl II ring 16,413
1924 Jose Mendez Monarchs championship trophy 16,413
1964 Providence photo with Ruth 16,412
1943-49 Ted Williams game-used bat 16,413
1973-74 Jerry West game-worn road Lakers jersey **16,406**
1956 WS Rolex Hank Bauer 16,400
1946 Otto Graham Browns jersey 16,158
1986 Mets Darryl Strawberry WS trophy 16,136
1874 Boston Base Ball Club Cabinet card 16,002
1991-92 Messier signed, game-used Rangers jersey 15,855
1979 Montreal Guy Lafleur Stanley Cup ring 15,555
First Muhammad Ali/Liston fight ticket 15,548
1888 New York Giants large-format Cabinet photo **15,400**
1977 WS Jackson's 1st of 3 HR balls 15,306
1989 49ers Super Bowl ring/Tony Bennett 15,306
Catfish Hunter's Oakland A's World Series ring 15,297
1926-27 Dutch Reuther Yankees uniform 15,297
Honus Wagner personal floor safe **15,280**
1971 Gale Sayers Bears jersey 15,280
Frankie Frisch jersey 15,180
1953 Cards Slaughter game-worn jersey 15,128
1996 Jordan game-used Bulls uniform 15,100
1864 Resolutes Brooklyn carte de visite **15,094**
Henry Aaron game-used bat 15,073
Wayne Gretzky last game-used puck 14,999
2001 Bonds game-used jersey 14,999
1997 Ichiro Orix Blue Wave GW jersey 14,920
1930s Ruth trifold "Old Gold" display piece 14,920
1989 49ers Harry Sydney's Super Bowl ring 14,920
1903 World Series Boston full ticket 14,920
1907 History of Colored Baseball 14,920
1911 Philadelphia A's World Series press pin 14,920
1986 Buckner's World Series cleats 14,914
1991-92 Gretzky Kings jersey 14,913
1971 Pete Rose Reds road jersey 14,913
Ruth/Cobb and Tris Speaker signed ball 14,850
1978-79 Lafleur Stanley Cup Trophy 14,791
1986 Hornung Hall of Fame ring 14,578
1955-57 Aaron game-used bat 14,578
1919 Chick Gandil White Sox player's contract **14,548**
LeRoy Neiman original "Harmon Killebrew" 14,548
Reach tin advertising sign **14,548**
2001 Barry Bonds game-worn 552nd HR jersey 14,424
Clemente game-used bat 14,424
1972 Colts Unitas home jersey **14,300**
1909 Opening Day panorama 14,300
1996 Yankees WS ring 14,266
Ruth signed H & B store model bat **14,088**
1961-64 Roger Maris game-used bat 14,088
1921-31 Earle Combs game-used bat 14,088
LeRoy Neiman original "The Cut Man" 14,086
1986-87 Fleer Basketball unopened box **14,067**
1977-78 Pete Rose H & B milestone bat 14,067
1978 Dave Parker's Gold Glove 14,067
1931 WS photo with Ruth, Mack & McGraw 14,067
1955 Ted Williams All-Star Game cap 14,067
1950s Ted Williams game-used bat 14,067
1969 New York Mets 12-inch World Series trophy **14,041**
Barry Bonds pants, cap, wrist band HR No. 500 13,915
1920 "Headin' Home" Ruth 35-mm film 13,915
1920 Joe Jackson game-used bat 13,893
Mathewson Tuxedo advertising display 13,893
1969 Bill Russell All-Star uniform 13,891
1923 Ruth-signed 25th HR ball 13,753
Joe Sewell game-used bat 13,572
1981 Pete Rose Phillies 3,630-hit jersey 13,563
1930 Bill Arnold Indy 500 Rickenbacker Trophy **13,557**

1990 Ayrton Senna race-used suit **13,500**
1970 Billy Cunningham 76ers road jersey 13,452
1976 Aaron Brewers road jersey 13,447
1970s Ed Giacomin Rangers shirt 13,429
1951 Bowman Baseball set, 294 signed **13,400**
1978 Ernie Stautner's Cowboys Super Bowl ring 13,394
Eddie Mathews home run bat 13,359
1943-49 DiMaggio game-used bat 13,225
1915 Phillies World Series press pin 13,225
Ruth photo by George Burke, signed to Jimmy Reese 13,219
1934 Tour of Japan signed ball **13,200**
Bobby Orr game-worn skates 13,120
1948 Ted Williams game-used bat 13,112
1966 Clemente game-used, signed bat 13,112
Mike Schmidt's Home Run King crown 12,965
1907 Sol White History of Colored Baseball **12,887**
Lineup cards Game 6, 1975 WS 12,786
1919 Chicago Black Sox World Series press pin 12,641
Ruth's contract from "Babe Ruth Story" 12,641
1987 Jordan signed Bulls home jersey 12,629
Braves lineup card for 714th/715th HR games 12,368
1985 Payton game-used home Bears jersey **12,325**
John L. Sullivan White Sox Lifetime Pass 12,245
1950 Ted Williams game-used bat 12,236
1934 Goudey Canadian uncut sheet nr-mt 12,137
Josh Gibson oversized studio photo 12,806
1922-23 New York Giants sweater 12,788
1979 Munson Yankees road jersey 12,788
1934 Tour of Japan signed ball 12,788
1932 Crawfords photo w/Gibson & Paige 12,788
Ott game-used bat 12,650
1905 World Series program **12,650**
1922 Walter Johnson cap 12,547
1977 Walter Payton milestone jersey 12,326
Ruth and Cobb signed ball **12,203**
1934-43 Chuck Klein game-used H & B bat 12,052
1941-42 Williams H & B game-used rookie era bat **12,022**
1950s Willie Mays game-used H & B bat 12,022
1996 Yankees World Series front office ring **12,022**
1871 Mort Rodgers baseball photographic scorecard **12,022**
Polo Grounds figural sharis (2) 12,014
Lou Gehrig farewell photo, signed 12,014
1938 Gabby Hartnett Cubs home uniform 11,936
1995-96 Bulls NBA Champ ring (equip. guy) 11,936
1973 Ron Turcotte silks and pants, from Secretariat **11,909**
1980 Lake Placid Olympics silver hockey medal **11,909**
Jerry West uniform 11,904
1970 Johnny Bench jersey 11,764
1986 DiMaggio driver's license 11,750
1968 Bob Gibson Cardinals home jersey 11,641
1981 Steve Carlton Gold Glove 11,641
Maurice Richard "Leading Scorer" trophy 11,641
1907 WS panorama with Cobb at bat 11,625
Aaron McGregor game-worn glove 11,625
1911-15 Chick Gandil game-used Jackson 11,625
1961 Maris No. 51 home run bat 11,625
1989 Ken Griffey Jr. road jersey 11,625
Clemente game-worn cap 11,623
2000 Jordan game-used Wizards jersey 11,500
1912 Red Sox World Series award, Charles Hall **11,483**
Joe Namath game-used helmet 11,480
1907 Joe Jackson Victor Mills team photo 11,480
1950s Meadowlark Lemon Globetrotters shirt 11,388
1961 Paul Hornung's Packers team-signed football **11,364**
1938 Honus Wagner single-signed ball 11,364
1955 Nellie Fox White Sox home jersey **11,354**
Guy Lafleur's 500th goal puck 11,344
1938 Gehrig signed/inscribed photo 11,244
1923 Ruth-signed World Series photo 11,244
Jimmie Foxx game-used bat 11,211

1995-96 Gretzky game-worn Kings road jersey	11,208
Ruth/Gehrig signed NL Heydler ball	11,208
Ruth and Gehrig signed barnstorming photo	11,206
1960s Tommy Heinsohn Celtics jersey	11,206
1999 Yankees World Series trophy	11,206
1903 World Series game-used ball	11,205
1939 "Gehrig Day" signed letter	11,132
1918 Ruth bonus contract	11,208
Dale Earnhardt autographed helmet	11,205
Ebbets Field seats (2)	11,048
1967 Reggie Jackson game-worn jersey	11,000
1967 Killebrew home Twins jersey	10,928
1962 Roger Maris H & B All-Star game-used bat	**10,928**
Jackie Robinson Dodgers cap	10,928
Gehrig-signed Wire Photo	10,928
LeRoy Neiman original "Warren Spahn"	10,928
Inscribed Mathewson Won in the Ninth	10,922
1981 Al Campanis World Series trophy	**10,848**
2002 Sammy Sosa 499th HR game-worn jersey	**10,827**
1975 Pete Rose salesman sample WS ring	**10,793**
Jordan game-used and signed shoes	10,600
1966 Eddie Mathews Atlanta signed jersey	10,582
1942 Early Wynn Senators road jersey	10,582
High-grade Hartland Statue set with Batboy	**10,569**
1922-23 Vic Aldridge Cubs home jersey	**10,569**
1922 Mathewson signed check	10,569
1940s Homestead Grays game-used cap	**10,450**
1931 Heathcote Reds jersey	**10,450**
Sealed and unopened box of Heydler NL balls	**10,450**
Inscribed Ruth photo	10,350
1934 Ruth Tour of Japan autographed photo	**10,330**
1966 Billy Williams Cubs signed road jersey	10,330
1946 Jackie Robinson batting crown bowl	10,312
Thurman Munson's first contract	**10,278**
1999 Yankees World Series trophy	**10,221**
1950s Stan Musial game-used, signed bat	10,221
1930s Gehrig game-used bat	10,189
1914 Providence team photo with Ruth	10,189
1929 A's team-signed panoramic photo	10,187
1988 Jordan game-worn and signed jersey	10,185
Mike Piazza game-used catcher's mitt	10,102
Bobby Clarke game-worn jersey	10,102
2002 Luis Gonzalez spring training chewed gum	10,000
1932 U.S. Caramel President McKinley	10,000
Ruth single-signed ball, PSA/DNA auth.	10,000
1998 McGwire St. Louis "Stars" road jersey	9,935
Ruth game-used and autographed bat	9,935
1920s Eddie Collins game-used bat	9,935
1971 Manny Sanguillen World Series ring	9.935
Shaquille O'Neal Orlando rookie jersey	9,912
1948 Bob Lemon's Indians World Series ring	**9,900**
Campanella bronzed catcher's mitt award	**9,900**
Billy Martin's game-used glove	**9,895**
1915 Red Sox WS document with Ruth sig.	9,850
Veterans Stadium turf with Eagles logo	9,804
1986 Nolan Ryan Astros jersey	9,741
1887 World Series program	9,664
1970s Rose game-used bat	9,620
LeRoy Neiman original "Whitey Bimstein"	9,620
LeRoy Neiman original "Joe Namath"	9,620
1931 Joe Judge game-used jersey	9,611
1924-30 Hack Wilson game-used H & B bat	**9,607**
1994 Ken Griffey All-Star Game glove	9,607
1953 Brooklyn Dodgers signed Wirephoto, PSA/DNA	**9,600**
1986 Fleer Basketball (2) unopened boxes	9,600
1953 Milwaukee Braves Spahn home jersey	**9,570**
2000 Edgerrin James Colts game-used road	9,517
2203 UD Matsui Play Ball original art/signed	**9,500**
1986 Fleer Basketball unopened box	9,500
1933 Candian Goudey Gehrig, signed PSA/DNA	9,500

1995 Barry Bonds game-used Giants jersey	**9,499**
Gehrig photo from movie "Rawhide," signed	9,492
1969 Willie McCovey Giants jersey	**9,492**
1969 Honus Wagner's MLB 100th Anniversary Award	**9,488**
Oscar Charleston dual-endorsed check	9,391
1918 World Series program at Chicago	9,391
1920 Nemo Liebold White Sox uniform	**9,350**
Ruth/Gehrig/Left Gomez signed ball	**9,350**
Ruth payroll check	9,350
1919 World Series program	9,307
1958 Yogi Berra Yankees signed road jersey	**9,292**
1915 Phillies championship watch	9,292
Vintage poster with 4 of 5 initial HOF inductees	9,292
1929 Philadelphia A's signed photo album	9,262
1910 Boston Garter ad piece/Collins and Chase	9,262
1920s Cleveland WS team panorama	9,262
1998 McGwire game-used bat	9,262
1997 Barry Bonds game-used glove	**9,250**
Ruth game-used bat	9,200
Honus Wagner Tobacco label	**9,200**
Cal Ripken game-used jersey	9,200
1969 Mets WS ring Maury Allen	9,184
Cobb's personal effects given to Al Stump	9,183
1961-64 Mays H & B game-used bat	9,031
1970 Killebrew Twins signed road jersey	9,031
Mathewson personal check	9,026
1920s baseball slot machine	9,022
Michael Jordan shooting shirt	9,011
Ruth and Gehrig signed baseball	**9,000**
Elton Brand uniform (charity auction)	9,000
1889 Spalding American photo in Rome,	**8,947**
1994 Elway "Clock" game-used road jersey	8,896
Kansas City Chiefs Super Bowl ring	**8,895**
1987 Redskins Super Bowl ring	8,850
1976 Bob Lemon's Yankees AL Championship ring	**8,800**
Tin and cast iron peanut-warming machine	**8,800**
(10) balls signed by Mantle, DiMaggio, Williams	8,763
1918 Boston Red Sox World Series press pin	8,745
Emmitt Smith's last Cowboys TD signed jersey	**8,733**
1950s Stan Musial game-used, vault-marked bat	8,733
1921-22 Home Run Baker game-used bat	8,733
1994 Jordan game-used Birmingham Barons jersey	**8,700**
1961 Fleer Football unopened wax box Series II	8,700
1971 Fran Tarkenton Giants game-worn jersey	**8,632**
1889 Syracuse Stars photo w/Moses Walker	8,632
1973 Bill Walton game-worn UCLA home	8,625
Mathewson personal check	8,575
2002 Emmitt Smith game-used and signed home jersey	**8,536**
Emmitt Smith's game-used and signed Florida jersey	**8,536**
Reggie Jackson Oakland A's home vest	8,538
Bill Veeck's wooden leg	8,505
1960 Promotional Bobbin Head Bears, 131/2-inch	**8,500**
1952 Topps wax pack	**8,500**
2001 Bonds game-used HR No. 522 jersey	8,500
1893 Stanford-Cal program	**8,488**
1907 History of Colored Baseball, Sol White signed	8,456
1999 Yankees World Series trophy	8,447
Ruth, Aaron and Cobb signed ball	8,447
Ruth/Gehrig/Gomez signed ball, PSA/DNA authenticated	**8,400**
1993 Jeff Gordon race-used, signed firesuit	8,350
Kobe Bryant jersey	8,349
1998 Sammy Sosa's 50th home run ball	8,348
1971 Ali/Frazier I fight poster	8,291
Eddie Collins game-used bat	**8,250**
Bill Barber game-worn Flyers jersey	**8,250**
E-Z Gumball machine	**8,250**
1959 Fleer Life of Ted Williams set, signed	**8,250**
1923 telegram sent to Joe Jackson	**8,250**
1994 Troy Aikman game-used, signed jersey	8,250
1950s Williams Red Sox game-worn cap	**8,210**

1927 Bustin' Babes/Lous signed photo 8,210
1968 Harmon Killebrew Twins road jersey 8,210
1931 baseball autograph album (270) 8,151
1988 Magic Johnson game-worn Lakers jersey 8,134
1911 Mathewson Tuxedo Tobacco advertising sign 8,133
1919 Original "yard-long" photo of Black Sox/Decatur 8,119
1996 Alex Rodriguez game-worn, signed AS jersey 8,108
1994-95 Jordan game-worn Bulls jersey 8,100
1948 Leaf Baseball unopened wax box 8,056
1972 Bobby Hull game-worn Blackhawks jersey 8,000
1931 W517 Ruth, signed PSA/DNA 7,999
1871 Mort Rogers photographic scorecard 7,942
1930 Ruth signed payroll check 7,939
Fenway Park section (3-by-7 foot) of Green Monster 7,939
1953 Yankees WS ring salesman sample 7,938
1968 DiMaggio A's coach's road jersey, signed 7,938
1997 McGwire Oakland game-used jersey 7,938
1934 Cardinals World Series ring 7,938
1940 Seabiscuit race-worn horseshoe 7,900
1963 Harmon Killebrew game-worn, signed jersey 7,800
1908 Honus Wagner Elks Lodge gold watch fob 7,794
1930s Joe Jackson bat from barnstorming 7,787
1968-69 Emerson Boozer GU, signed road 7,780
Mark Messier's game-used skates 7,760
1999 Yankees World Series Trophy 7,760
Negro League flannel with 201 autographs 7,736
1914 Miracle Braves Les Mann jacket 7,700
1942 Satchel Paige broadside 7,679
1969 Leo Durocher Cubs home jersey 7,679
1999-00 O'Neal Lakers jersey 7,653
Emmitt Smith game-used and signed Florida jersey 7,589
1868 The Game of Base Ball by Chadwick 7,589
1907 Cubs World Series program 7,589
Satchel Pagie lifesize wax figure 7,589
Pre 1921 Honus Wagner model Louisville Slugger decal
  bat 7,500
Martin Luther King signed baseball 7,500
Connie Mack letters about Joe Jackson 7,464
1977 Yankees World Series ring (front office) 7,463
2001 Jordan Wizards game-used road jersey 7,458
1993 Jeff Gordon ROY racing suit 7,456
1911 Philadelphia A's panoramic photo 7,425
Jesse Owens college track jersey 7,407
1913 Boston Garter Frank Baker 7,395
1951 Casey Stengel game-used jersey 7,321
1961 Fleer Football unopened wax box Series I 7,299
2001 World Series Game Four second base 7,285
Walter Payton game-used and signed jersey 7,255
Ruth/Gehrig signed ball 7,250
1969-72 Clemente game-used bat 7,225
1989-90 Jordan Bulls game-worn jersey 7,225
1923 Four Horsemen & Rockne photo 7,216
1973 Nolan Ryan Angels home jersey, signed 7,216
1943-48 Ruth's last game-used bat 7,216
1952 Topps unopened wax pack 7,200
1950s Don Shula Colts jersey 7,200
1970 Topps Basketball unopened box 7,200
A.G. Spalding handwritten letter 7,150
Rogers Hornsby Wilson box and glove 7,046
Ruth/Gehrig signed ball 7,000
1959 Mickey Mantle game-used bat 7,000
1986-87 Fleer Basketball, two (2) unopened boxes 7,000
1920s Yankees sweater 6,981
1927 Yankees team photo 6,958
Yankees signed ball with DiMaggio and Marilyn Monroe .. 6,900
Ty Cobb's personal, custom-made golf club 6,899
1989-90 Jordan game-used shoes 6,899
1955 umpire's World Series ring 6,875
1948 Nat Fein Ruth photograph 6,875
1977 Tom Seaver Reds game-worn jersey 6,825

Cobb, Hornsby signed ball, 12 other HOFers 6,825
2000 Randy Moss game-used helmet 6,822
1890s Henley brand golf ball with "Union Jack" pattern... 6,800
1979 O-Pee-Chee Hockey wax box 6,800
1970 Rod Carew Twins jersey 6,785
1992 Roberto Alomar World Series Trophy 6,785
1909 Forbes Field turnstile 6,785
2001 Barry Bonds game-used Giants road jersey 6,780
1950s Bill Russell game-worn sneakers 6,778
1910 Kunte Rockne signed Notre Dame scrapbook 6,766
1919 Eddie Cicotte contract 6,750
1970s Ryan Angels signed road jersey 6,726
1993-94 Steve Yzerman game-used jersey 6,700
1990s Dan Marino game-used helmet 6,655
1987 Fleer Barry Bonds rookies (100) PSA 9 6,600
1992 Topps Traded Baseball 100-set case 6,600
1926 Honus Wagner National League season pass........... 6,587
1955 Joe Adcock Braves game-worn jersey 6,568
1949 Henrich Yankees signed home uniform 6,566
Mike Schmidt's 400th home run jersey 6,563
Brett Favre game-worn jersey 6,562
Tris Speaker single-signed ball 6,560
Wilt Chamberlain's retired 76ers jersey 6,500
Bill Bradley jersey 6,480
1997 Tiger Woods 8-by-10s photo set of (6) PRO 10s 6,437
1975 Walt Frazier Knicks game-worn jersey 6,412
1980-82 Ripken Louisville game-used bat 6,412
Dick Groat Hartland statue 6,401
1926-29 Pie Traynor game-used bat 6,393
1998 McGwire game-used home jersey 6,350
Clemente game-used bat 6,350
1908 Olympics gymnastics gold medal 6,346
Harmon Killebrew game-used glove 6,346
1936 DiMaggio handwritten letter 6,346
P. Lorrillard & Co. cabinet... 6,325
1930 Boston Bruins sweater 6,325
2001 Barry Bonds game-used and signed jersey 6,325
1972 Topps Baseball, two (2) wax boxes 6,300
1933 All-Star ball, signed by Ruth and 12 others, PSA/DNA ..6,299
1889 Harry Wright handwritten letter 6,271
1960s Clemente game-used bat 6,250
1943-48 Ernie Lombardi game-used bat................................ 6,204
Ruth-signed bat.. 6,160
Derek Jeter's first pro model game bat 6,123
1913 trophy of Cobb's given to Al Stump 6,090
1992 Pinnacle Mantle 30-card set, signed 6,111
1979-80 OPC Hockey wax box 6,100
1954 Bob Lemon game-used World Series bat 6,050
1911 Philadelphia A's pennant 6,050
Ruth/Gehrig signed ball, PSA/DNA 6,000
Ruth/Gehrig signed ball, PSA/DNA 6,000
1986 Fleer Basketball unopened box 6,000
Wilt Chamberlain's retired Kansas jersey 6,000
1969 Clemente game-used bat... 5,999
1995-96 Chicago Bulls team-signed basketball 5,983
Old Tom Morris signed St. Andrews studio portrait 5,983
1969 Stargell Pirates signed road jersey 5,970
Jesse Owens Olympic sweater vest 5,947
2002 Sosa 498th HR game-used bat 5,927
Complete Hartland Statue baseball set 5,910
1971 Gale Sayers game-worn jersey 5,900
1934 Gehrig original Wirephoto 5,900
1933 Goudey advertising poster 5,894
1947 Masters golf presentation album 5,833
1992 Ron Woodson 5,811
Babe Ruth signed photo 5,768
1984 Eric Dickerson Pro Bowl jersey 5,768
2000 All-Star Jeter game-issued jersey 5,768
1950 Campanella All-Star award plaque 5,750
1955 Dodgers/Yankees World Series pennant................. 5,750

1976 Reggie Jackson Orioles game-used jersey	5,750
1961 Yankees World Series ring, salesman sample	5,750
Eddie Gaedel signed index card	5,707
1952 Topps unopened wax pack, GAI 7	5,700
1952 Topps Mantle, signed	5,700
1937 Lou Gehrig autograph, GAI authenticated	5,600
1992 Topps Traded 100-set case	5,600
Mantle-signed photo with expletive	5,520
1901 Casey At The Bat first edition	5,500
1917 Comiskey season's pass booklet	5,500
1911 Philadelphia A's pennant	5,500
Brooks Robinson game-used glove	5,500
1914 Ed Walsh contract	5,500
1970 Topps Baseball unopened wax box	5,430
1977 Walter Payton game-used shoes	5,427
1998 Pedro Martinez All-Star jersey, signed	5,427
1945 DiMaggio signed insurance documents	5,423
1911 Addie Joss Day panoramic photo	5,420
1998 McGwire game-used road jersey	5,409
Pre 1965 Ernie Banks game-used bat	5,361
1964 Topps Baseball uncut sheets (2)	5,300
1913 Tris Speaker decal bat	5,300
1948 Baseball Mag. premium, Ruth-signed	5,299
Bobby Jones vintage, signed photograph	5,299
HOF signature collection (245)	5,299
1956 Mantle Rawlings signed ad/glove	5,299
2003 Upper Deck Ultimate Collection FB, four-case lot	5,265
1973-74 Gary Dornhoefer's Flyers Stanley Cup Trophy	5,244
Circa 1915 Red Sox team sweater	5,244
1954 Genco two-player basketball arcade game	5,199
1994 Don Mattingly Yankees jersey	5,182
1967 Brooks Robinson game-used bat	5,125
Sandy Koufax documents (8)	5,107
2003 Tennessee Titans Playoff Game "Experience"	5,100
2001 Donavan McNabb etopps cards (101)	5,000
1985 Barry Bonds minor-league game bat	5,000
1909 Honus Wagner cigar label	5,096
1912 Giants team-signed Cabinet photo	5,095
Mickey Cochrane Spalding Trophy/effects	5,052
1998 McGwire Rawlings game-used bat	5,032
Jim Mayfield orig. puzzle artwork of Kit Young	5,000
2001 Donruss Diamond King orig. art/Nolan Ryan	5,000
1952 Topps Baseball unopened wax pack	5,000
Set of original Hartland Baseball statues	4,995
Paul and Lloyd Wanter autographed photo	4,950
Max Carey game-used bat	4,950
Washington Redskins "spear" helmet	4,930
1933 Goudey Gehrig No. 160, signed PSA/DNA	4,900
Drew Bledsoe game-used and signed jersey	4,828
1980s Gretzky Edmonton game-worn helmet	4,817
1928 U.S. Open Amateur program, signed Hagen and Jones	4,767
Woods, Palmer and Nicklaus signed Masters display	4,767
1987-88 Edmonton Stanley Cup Trophy	4,767
1978-79 Montreal Stanley Cup Trophy	4,767
Jeremy Shockey game-used jersey	4,755
1917 Honus Wagner's "Wagner Day" pinback	4,689
Landry QBs Legacy artwork, signed by six	4,679
Jerry Rice game-used 49ers jersey	4,679
1960 Eagles championship game-used football	4,510
2001-02 McFarlane NFL Action Figures except 1 variant	4,500
1986-87 Fleer Basketball unopened box	4,450
Ruth-signed photo	4,431
1977 Jim Palmer Orioles home jersey	4,400
Set of original Hartland Baseball statues	4,245
2001-02 Vancouver Giants game-worn jerseys (21)	4,050
"Four Horsemen" autographed photograph	4,180
1991 Ayrton Senna race-used and signed gloves	4,175
2002 Ricky Williams game-used jersey	4,128

Ted Williams die-cut Wilson advertising sign	4,125
Shibe Park cornerstone	4,125
1908 Vardon, Braid, Taylor and Herd signed note	4,071
1947 Gil Hodges Dodgers contract	4,070
1979 Topps Hockey uncut sheet with Gretzky	4,051
UDA framed and signed 1-of-1 Jordan jersey	4,000
1973-75 Aaron game-used and signed bat	3,995
Babe Ruth on the links photograph	3,980
Kobe Bryant game-used Lakers jersey	3,969
1968 Olympics Mexico City torch	3,939
1972 Olympics Munich torch	3,939
1972 Topps Baseball wax box	3,900
D.B. Sweeney jersey from "Eight Men Out"	3,868
Philadelphia A's team-signed panoramic photo	3,850
Marshall Faulk San Diego State jersey	3,701
2001 Barry Bonds game-used SAM bat	3,700
Craig Morton game-used Cowboys helmet	3,698
2002 Ichiro game-used bat	3,650
1980s Nolan Ryan game-used warmup jacket	3,608
Barry Bonds game-used bat	3,606
Maris-signed photo	3,573
1952 Topps Baseball unopened wax pack	3,550
2002 Ichiro game-used and signed Mizuno bat	3,550
1986-87 Fleer Basketball wax box	3,500
1998 Roger Clemens game-used glove	3,500
1956 Topps Baseball five-cent unopened pack	3,500
1989 Ken Griffey Jr. game-used and autographed jersey	3,308
1908 Olympics gymnastics silver medal	3,255
1968 Topps Baseball uncut sheet with Ryan	3,250
Clinton Portis game-used jersey	3,197
1997-98 Jordan game-used sneakers	3,165
Willard Mullan original artwork of Roy Campanella	3,090
"Zimmer's" Base Ball Game variation	3,080
1979 Bob Lemon Yankees uniform	3,080
John Mackey Baltimore Colts game-used jersey	3,080
1908 Joe Tinker signed affidavit	3,080
1978 Topps Baseball three-box rack case	3,000
Aaron game-used bat	2,956
Roberto Clemente Bobbin' Head	2,745
UDA Kobe Bryant 1-of-1 basketball photo display	2,700
2001 Donruss Diamond King orig. art/Brett	2,700
NFL album signed by 521 players and coaches	2,552
Cal Ripken game-used and signed bat	2,463
Shaquille O'Neal Lakers warmup jacket	2,460
Cal Ripken batting helmet and cap	2,452
1954 Bob Lemon Indians stick pins	2,420
Pelle Lindberg game-used Flyers jersey	2,310
Fenway Park seat	2,310
Stanford Pottery Tigers man-face variation bank	2,265
Artis Gilmore game-used jersey	2,237
Barry Bonds home run baseball	2,040
Alfonsoa Soriano game-used bat	2,018
Briggs Stadium figural end seat	1,925
Bob Lemon's Hall of Fame plaque	1,870
Vladimir Guerrero game-used All-Star bat	1,834
Alex Rodriguez game-used and signed bat	1,808
Ruth autographed photo	1,760
Dempsey-Tunney "Long Count" fight program	1,760
Row of (2) Yankee Stadium seats	1,760
Luis Aparicio game-used bat	1,753
2001 Donruss Diamond King orig. art/Killebrew	1,700
Ken Griffey Jr. game-used bat	1,610
Early AFL Raiders Bobbin Head	1,565
Washington Redskins Kissing Pair Bobbin Head	1,500
Stanford Pottery Brooklyn Bum bank	1,500
1957 "Keep the Dodgers in Brooklyn" pin back	1,464
Detroit Lions Kail statue	1,251
2001 Donruss Diamond King orig. art/Reggie	1,000